Education Today

Issues, Policies & Practices

Education Today

Issues, Policies & Practices

Volume 1

Editor
Beryl Watnick, Ph.D.
Union Institute & University

SALEM PRESS
A Division of EBSCO Information Services, Inc.
Ipswich, Massachusetts

GREY HOUSE PUBLISHING

Publisher's Cataloging-In-Publication Data
(Prepared by The Donohue Group, Inc.)

Names: Watnick, Beryl, editor.
Title: Education today : issues, policies & practices / editor, Beryl Watnick, Ph.D.
Description: [First edition]. | Ipswich, Massachusetts : Salem Press, a division of EBSCO Information Services, Inc. ;
    Amenia, NY : Grey House Publishing, [2018] | Includes bibliographical references and index.
Identifiers: ISBN 9781682177129 (set) | ISBN 9781642650099 (v. 1) | ISBN 9781642650105 (v. 2) |
    ISBN 9781642650112 (v. 3)
Subjects: LCSH: Education--United States. | Education and state--United States. | Teaching--United States. |
    School management and organization--United States. | Educational technology--United States.
Classification: LCC LA210 .E38 2018 | DDC 370.973--dc23

CONTENTS

Volume 1

Volume 2

Volume 3

PUBLISHER'S NOTE

Education Today: Issues, Policies & Practices, is a new, three-volume set that includes 446 articles written by expert educators and education administrators. The articles are arranged in 25 sections, and cover a wide range of topics, starting with a historical look at education, and including sections on education theory, psychology, law, government, school safety, diversity, curriculum, counseling, teaching methods, technology in education, testing, alternative education, teacher education and international perspectives.

Each section includes 8 to 30 articles, each of which include the following sections:

- Overview – A brief paragraph that summarizes the topic and explains what the article will cover.
- Applications – Describes the various ways the topic translates from theory into the classroom.
- Viewpoints – Outlines the various views of the topic, controversial aspects, pros and cons, effectiveness and cautions.

- Further Insights – Details other related topics or theories that are not usually associated with the topic.
- Terms and Concepts – This list offers definitions of terms and concepts used in the article and also in the educational community.
- Bibliography – Complete citations of sources used to develop the article.
- Further Reading – A list of annotated books, articles, and web sites that will provide more information on the topic.

The set ends with a comprehensive list of Terms & Concepts and a detailed Subject Index. The content in this work has been developed with the advice of experts in a number of fields. Without the expertise of these individuals, this publication would not have been possible. A list of contributors follows the Introduction. Salem Press thanks everyone involved for their hard work and dedication.

INTRODUCTION

Education Today: Issues, Policies, and Practices is a compendium of articles that introduces students to the field of education. It is directed at students who are considering a career in teaching, those who are curious as to the purposes of education, as well as at the canon that has guided decision-making practices from early childhood through adult education. As a former public school teacher and administrator, as well as undergraduate college dean and doctoral faculty member, I consider this collection to be a comprehensive exploration into the landscape of education. The topics are vast in coverage and offer several sides of the debates that surface when stakeholders wrestle with key questions about schooling. Heated discourse is not uncommon when discussing the successes and failures of school reform efforts, the debt incurred by college students, the benefits of school uniforms, and weapons in schools, to name just a few.

This collection has been organized so that you, the reader, gain a broad view of the diverse range of influences that have shaped deliberate decision-making in education practice. The goal for this three-volume set is to stimulate your curiosity and encourage your deeper immersion into the issues, policies that are formulated, and practices that are instituted. Each article is followed by a dedicated selection of suggested readings that you can explore on your own to enrich a greater understanding of the topic. We want to not only stimulate your curiosity, but also encourage critical thinking.

Volume 1 offers a sweeping and interdisciplinary view of the philosophical, theoretical, and psychological underpinnings of educational practice. Its goal is to establish context for how the vision of schooling has evolved over decades, what we have learned through our reform efforts, what works and what needs to be changed.

Sections include *History of Education, Education Theory,* and *Education Law,* subjects that are woven throughout a traditional teacher education program for those who hope to teach. You will learn about the earliest roots of education and the reform movements that shaped modern education as well as past and current social justice concerns for women and minorities.

In addition to the attention paid to the past, there is abundant coverage of the latest findings in neuroscience, for example, *Education Psychology* introduces a selection of articles that share how educators are now applying what we have learned about the neuroplasticity of the human brain to praxis. How do we motivate students of all ages and keep them engaged in their studies? How do anxiety, sleep deprivation, and adolescent development influence learning? These questions are answered within this collection.

Those who study the field of education must gain a foundational understanding of how politics contribute to all reform efforts. The section on *Politics, Government, and Education* speaks to their influence on practice. Politics, government, and public policy are intricately connected and the sections within this volume shed light on how these play out in the educational arena. Almost all decisions that influence educational policy are rooted in politics and power is often the fulcrum for decisions being made. Our authors also provide windows into such topics as education and the economy, teachers' unions, school choice, and tuition-free college. You will learn more about these influences through your readings.

This first volume also shines a holistic light in its sections on *Public School* and *Higher Education.* Matters of pedagogy, curriculum, stakeholders, and communities are all addressed within these sections of Volume 1. Several articles explore how the rules of law dictate practice as well as share the intricacies of school administration. If you have never considered the complexity of school leadership, the articles in *School Administration and Policy* will enlighten you. The section on *School Safety* considers how educational communities can keep their students safe within, and outside, their brick and mortar facilities. School shootings are horrific occurrences and keeping students and personnel safe is of paramount importance. Social media has escalated awareness and concerns around issues such as bullying, hazing, and weapons in schools. Emotionally charged debates on zero tolerance policies, and the school to prison pipeline are also the focus of ongoing public discourse and are written about within the articles of this first volume.

Volume 2 narrows the lens on the realities of what takes place within the walls of our educational institutions. This volume opens with *Multicultural & Diversity Education.* This is followed by *Curriculum and Organization,* a section that presents multiple portraits of strategies, practices and purposes of curriculum design and delivery. "Education" and "curriculum" are not synonymous. "Education" occurs in the home, community, house of worship, and all other micro and macro systems that touch an individual's life. "Curriculum" is far more specific and concrete. As stated throughout Volume 1, curriculum is an outcome of politics and intentional decision-making. These are decisions made in consideration of the purpose and desired goals of education. Our contributing authors open portals to a wide range of curriculum frameworks starting from early childhood through college. The collection of topics includes home visiting, information technology literacy, advanced placement options, and student exchange programs, to name only a few.

As a former early childhood administrator and special educator, I hold dear the significance of, and responsiveness to, these populations. Among the sections in this volume is one dedicated to *Early Childhood* program options as well as many articles on *Special Education,* its theoretical frameworks, delivery models and types of disorders/disabilities. Although these sections are not all-inclusive, they focus on key areas of concern for parents, children, and their teachers.

Teaching Methods is the section that specifically speaks to the actual work involved in teaching, and authors share an expansive view of teacher practice from metacognition to reflective teaching. Students might not give much thought to how their teachers plan and deliver lessons. The art of teaching requires skills for solving engineering problems. Planning is an essential piece of the puzzle. Teachers need to decide on the content of a lesson, how to present it so that students will become fully engaged and find the material meaningful, what resources to use to support their content, and what assignment features will advance learning. They also need to enlighten their students to how individual lessons connect with each other so their learning becomes relevant to the larger context of the subject matter.

Guidance & Counseling, Physical Education, and *English for Speakers of Other Languages (ESOL)* are also included in their own sections with some depth. With the omnipotence of social media, increased dependence on technology, and the divergent demographics that now define our student populations, it seems important to gain an understanding for how schools are changing in response. Guidance and counseling services include the traditional responsibilities for academic interventions and course scheduling. But hurdles that students must now maneuver call for counselors to be accomplished in addressing issues of teen pregnancy, substance abuse, college placement, and gay, lesbian, bisexual, transgender matters. ESOL is another source for debate as we consider the best and most equitable strategies to meeting the needs of our language minorities. Another, sometimes overlooked, priority is the state of physical education in our schools. Far too many schools are witnessing the disappearance of PE from their schedules. Students spend more time sitting in front of computers or iPhones than they do in daily physical activity. We know that physical movement is critical to early learning, but it is also imperative for those students who need movement to attend to their other learning through the course of the day, or even discover physical prowess that might otherwise lay dormant. Articles in the *Physical Education* section also speak to the relationship between athletics and motivation, gender and school athletics, and character and moral development in sports.

Volume 3 starts with a section that answers the question: How do we prepare today's students for the skills needed in this 21st century? It has been written that today's students need to be able to: think critically so they can solve complex problems; collaborate with others; exhibit creativity; and master cultural and technological literacy. The articles in the section *Technology in Education* describe how technology has shaped, and continues to reshape, teaching practice across all age groups.

The collection of articles on *Testing and Evaluation* is particularly timely as testing has become a source of controversy for the past several years. As students, you might hold a unique perspective on how testing has impacted the path of your own education. High-stakes standardized testing has become a vigorously debated issue in school reform. The results of such testing not only impact the students, but the teachers and school administration as well. This section discusses specific types of tests, their wide-ranging purposes, and their impact on those who take and give them.

Additional sections direct your attention to alternative pathways for continuous learning. Their goal is to raise awareness of differences in curriculum and program options across all ages. You may already be familiar with some of the selected topics (such as *Teacher Education* and *Adult Education*) but you might be introduced to *International Perspectives* for the first time. The articles within this section reveal a range of global concerns such as gender disparities and poverty reduction strategies implemented throughout world regions. You will also be made aware of options for studying and/or teaching abroad. As our authors stress throughout these articles, it is crucial that our nation's students embrace a global mindset to better prepare them as the world becomes increasingly interconnected. The *Alternative Education* section sheds light on routes to educational pathways such as homeschooling, magnet schools, and blended learning. Less familiar alternatives are also covered, including military education, boarding schools, and agricultural education. *Extended Learning* has its own dedicated section of articles. This is a topic that many of you will have personally experienced. Extracurricular activities and community programs are two of the themes covered here. The section on

Service Learning is a subject that spans across all age groups. While the topic of civics education begins in the elementary schools, community service and volunteerism are encouraged throughout childhood and adulthood. This section explains in detail the variety of approaches to engaging student populations as contributing members to their communities.

As a self-proclaimed lifelong learner, I eagerly embraced the opportunity to work on this project. For those of you who envision a career in education, these volumes are essential to understanding the roots of educational practice and the forces that bring about change and equitable opportunities for all students. For those who are researching specific topics of interest, there is a wealth of resources to pull from within all three volumes. Although I left behind some of this information as I moved through my degree programs, I welcomed the chance to revisit all of it.

We each have a voice in how we envision social justice and excellence in education. All students, young and old, need to have their voices heard and valued. Only by knowing the past, and understanding the road we traveled to get to where we are today, can we plan for tomorrow.

Beryl Watnick, Ph.D.
January 25, 2018

CONTRIBUTORS

Angerame, Lisa
Arrington, Edith G.
Auerbach, Michael P.

Baker, Julie
Bartle, Sheila M.
Bennett, Carol
Berek, Daniel L.
Billings, Sabrina
Bouchard, Jennifer
Brown, Kirsty

Carter, Susanne
Carter-Smith, Karin
Chmiel, Marjee
Clapp, Marlene
Cohen, Ashley L.
Colona, Kyle
Connaughton, Ann
Conroy, Melissa
Conti, Holly
Cook, Kathryn
Coppus, Sally A.
Crothers, Katherine

DeMille, Ginny
Devenger, Nancy
Dewey, Joseph
Dicker, Joshua
Diorio, Gina L.
Donnelly, Matt

Eagleton, Maya B.

Fischer, Charles
Flynn, Simone I.
Frederick, Tom
Froiland, John Mark

Garda, Justin D.
Glenn, Hugh
Gould, Marie

Hahn, Allison
Hamilton, Eric
Hayden, Kellie
Haynes, Jerri
Hinkle Smith, Shelby L.

Holfester, Chris
Hornick-Lockard, Barbara

Kallio, Karen A.
Kretchmar, Jennifer

Link, Sharon
Loeser, John
Ludwig, Susan

Mance, Angelia
McFeeters, Belinda B.
McMahon, Maureen
Mercadal, Trudy
Merritt, R. D.
Myers, Sandra

Newton, Heather
Nicholas, Sinclair

Painter, Rebekah
Phillips, Kerri
Poradish, Christopher
Purdy, Elizabeth Rholetter

Rholetter, Wylene
Roberts, Jennifer Pilicy

Shkurkin, Ekaterina V. ("Katia")
Smith, Tricia
Solis, Kimberly
Stoica, Ioana
Suh, Rana

Tapper, Paul
Thomas, John E.
Thompson, Sherry
Tolbert-Bynum, Pamela

Vance, Noelle
Vejar, Cynthia

Weinstein, Norman
Wienclaw, Ruth A.

Zeng, Heather T.
Zimmer, Scott

Section 1: History of Education

Introduction

As students of the field of Education, an understanding of its historical underpinnings is crucial. Before one can begin to critically examine issues confronting American education today, an exploration into guiding philosophical conceptions for its purpose is central. We need to look back over time to understand the discourse on education as a tool to educate citizenry, to cultivate and nurture humanity, and/or prepare workers who can contribute to building the economy.

The following articles examine the history of education through an interdisciplinary lens. These authors share how conflicts, social and cultural issues, politics and legislation contour the landscape of education over time. These articles provide much needed context as we consider how best to prepare today's students for the 21st century skills of collaboration, communication, critical thinking, and creativity.

ARISTOTLE AND REALISM

Aristotle (384-322 BC) was a philosopher who greatly influenced educational philosophical thought for centuries. His search for truth led him to research many areas including metaphysics, ethics, rhetoric, logic, natural science, psychology and language (Gutek, 2009). His views on political and educational philosophy were mostly outlined in his works, Politics and Nicomachean Ethics. Out of Aristotle's political and educational philosophy evolved one of the oldest educational philosophies in Western culture, realism.

KEYWORDS: Aristotle; Character Development; Essentialism; Ethics; Golden Mean; Habits of Mind; Metaphysics; Realism; Syllogism; Universal Truth; Virtue

OVERVIEW

Aristotle (384-322 BC) was a philosopher who greatly influenced educational philosophical thought for centuries. His search for truth led him to research many areas including metaphysics, ethics, rhetoric, logic, natural science, psychology and language (Gutek, 2009). His father was a court physician to the royal family in the Greek colony of Stagira in Macedon. When he was 17, Aristotle became a pupil of Plato in his Athens' Academy, where he remained for 20 years. He left the Academy to tutor Alexander the Great, but eventually returned to Athens to found his own school called the Lyceum. In 335 BC, an anti-Macedonia reaction swept through Athens after the death of Alexander and Aristotle fled to Chaleis (where his mother was born) after he was indicted for impiety (Gruber, 1973). He died a year later. His views on political and educational philosophy were mostly outlined in his works, *Politics* and *Nicomachean Ethics*. Other great works include *Metaphysics, On Justice, On the Sciences, Political Theory* and *Art of Rhetoric*.

Gutek likens Aristotle to "a traditional college professor who connected his research with teaching." Aristotle would "do his research, reflect and digest his findings, then transmit his discoveries to his students in his lectures." Even though Aristotle was a student of Plato, Aristotle takes a different approach to the world of ideas than Plato did. For example, Plato believed that the only true reality is that within ideas. For Aristotle, reality or truth consists of matter; each piece of matter has universal and particular properties (Ozmon & Craver, 2008). To Aristotle, "the forms of things – those universal properties of objects – remain constant and never change but that particular components of objects do change." As an example of this concept, Ozmon and Craver relate the concept of an acorn. They explain that an acorn has the universal property of "*acornness,*" meaning that the form of a substance has certain universal properties or essences. The acorn may possess individual properties that are different from another acorn (i.e., perhaps the shell has been broken), but the idea of "acornness" will always be. Aristotle believes that there is design and order to the universe and there are universal properties to all that is; that things happen in an orderly fashion. As Ozmon and Craver point out, "The acorn follows its destiny to grow as an acorn." Such truths are tested by use of *syllogism,* the logical systematic form of ordering statements to prove their truths.

HUMAN NATURE

Aristotle believed that human nature involves two aspects—the irrational and the rational. Gruber explains that a person has no control over the irrational, as this concerns either fortune or luck. However, humans have control over that rational aspect of the soul, as the part that they control by reason is what is called *moral virtue.* Beauchamp (1982) defines *virtue* as "dispositions developed through the careful nurturing of one's capacities for living...to live well." *Moral virtues* are considered "universally praiseworthy features of human character that have been fixed by habituation." Those who possess moral virtue use their ability to determine what is right and then choose deliberately because it is right (Frankena, 1965). *Character* develops from moral virtue, as people develop habits that become well-established over time (Gruber). When people possess *excellent character,* they have settled into dispositions whereby "they want to act appropriately and do so without internal friction" (Urmson, 1988). However, not all people possess excellent character. There are those who possess, instead, a *strength of will.* A strength of will occurs when a person wants to "act improperly, but makes himself act properly," resulting in a good action.

Weakness of will occurs when "a person wants to act improperly, tries to make himself act properly, and fails." *Badness of character* occurs when a person wants "to act improperly, who thinks it is an excellent idea to do so, and does so without internal friction."

POLITICS & EDUCATION

According to Aristotle, the purpose of humans is to think; if they refuse to think through their free will, then humans "go against the design of the universe and the reason for [their] creations." To Aristotle, when humans go against their purpose, "they suffer the consequences of erroneous ideas, poor health, and an unhappy life" (Ozmon & Craver). Only through knowledge can they really understand their true destiny. Aristotle describes three types of knowledge:

- **Theoretical knowledge,** which is the highest form of knowledge in that its end in truth;
- **Practical knowledge,** which guides us in our political and social affairs, advising us about moral and ethical action;
- **Productive knowledge,** which shows us how to make things.

Endemic to Aristotle's aims of a liberal education is the idea that all education is under public control; education is universal and compulsory. The polity supports the goals of education, as outlined by Aristotle in the *Politics* (Taylor, 1955). These goals include: "producing people as will issue in acts tending to promote the happiness of the state; and, preparing the soul for the right enjoyment of leisure which becomes possible when practical needs have been satisfied" (Burnet, 1973). Ozmon and Craver state that "a reciprocal relationship always exists between the properly educated person and the properly educated citizen." To Aristotle, the major function of the state is to educate its citizens in the development of *right* habits. These right habits are thinking that becomes second nature (Gruber). Citizens are exposed to a liberal education, an education that tends toward making its recipient "a free man and not a slave in body or soul" (Taylor). The aims of educating also include promoting bodily health, developing character and enhancing the intellect with those subjects that exhibit useful knowledge as is indispensable to them (Burnet). This general education does not include a technical or professional training, as all

that is taught should contribute to "the formation of taste and character, serving to elevate and refine the mind" (Taylor).

VIEWS ON EDUCATION

Education provides a balance of the physical, the intellectual and character (Gruber). Children are taught useful things that are essential to their role in the state. By educating citizens in reading and writing, other subjects are opened up to them (Burnet). Educating citizens in bodily culture makes the body "strong and hardy, but also develops moral qualities of grace and courage" (Gruber). Children can also gain an appreciation of bodily beauty (Burnet).

Teaching art and music has direct influence on character development. Aristotle explains his stance on developing character in his seminal work called *Nicomachean Ethics. Ethics* is considered to contain "a systematic account of the principles by which ... [citizens'] conduct should be regulated" (Russell, 1945). The polity is responsible for educating citizens to become good persons by formulating good habits. Conduct begins with the soul, which is divided into two parts, the intellectual virtues and the moral virtues. All virtues "are means to an end, mainly happiness...an activity of the soul." Intellectual virtues result from teaching and moral virtues results from habit. Russell explains the idea that every virtue is a mean between two extremes. Aristotle provides the example of *courage*, a virtue that is at the mean of the continuum, with *cowardice* on one side of the continuum and *rashness* on the other.

Education leads people to develop habits that move them to good character. Students must submit to all suggestions from the teacher, suggestions that lead to the development of moral and intellectual character. The teacher (or the Master, as Aristotle calls him) must lead a disciplined life himself; through advancing this development, the teacher learns even more to enhance his own *happiness*. To Aristotle, happiness comes only from a well-balanced productive life. Gruber relates that the teacher directs "the unreflective energy of the young child so that the constructive powers are developed and the destructive are negated." Urmson states that children become "truthful, generous, fair, and the like by being told how to behave well and [are] encouraged to do so." By regulating the passions, habituation occurs. Teachers use their own reason to determine the method of training the youth, keeping in mind the balance of the intellect, the physical and character. As Urmson suggests, "With practice and repetition it becomes easier and easier [for children] to follow their counsel" to the point where they "come to enjoy doing things the right way, to want to do things the right way, and to be disturbed by doing thinks wrongly." Reason is the end result of education and teaches students to avoid excess and follow the Golden Mean (Gruber).

The Golden Mean "illustrates the notion of the soul as an entity to be kept in balance" (Ozmon & Craver). A good education leads to the Golden Mean and promotes "the harmony and balance of soul and body." According to Aristotle, there are practical rules for attaining the Golden Mean. People can achieve the mean by "keeping away from the extreme which is the more contrary to the mean, and by watching the direction in which they are most easily carried by their own natural tendencies"

Aristotle clearly defines the path to happiness through intellectual, physical and character development. He outlines the care of infants; that they should receive milk and space to walk. They should also be exposed to the cold, as the cold is "serviceable to health and preparation for military service" (Burnet). Early youth should be read stories that illustrate good character; they should not be exposed to indecent behaviors or foul language while during this formative stage. Other stages of education include that from the seventh year to puberty and from puberty to the 21st year. Aristotle states that any neglect by the state to educate their young is injurious to the state itself (Burnet). Education should be offered to every member of the state rather than just to the elite, as "public training is wanted in all things that are of public interest" (Burnet).

REALISM & ESSENTIALISM

Out of Aristotle's political and educational philosophy evolved one of the oldest educational philosophies in Western culture, *realism*. The major tenet of realism is the role of matter, that there are "actual sticks, stones and trees of the universe exist whether or not there is a human mind to perceive them" (Ozmon & Craver). According to Aristotle, ideas such as "the idea of a God or the idea of a tree, can exist without matter, but [that] no matter can exist without form." Realism maintains "that essential ideas and facts can best be learned only by a study of basic facts for the purpose of survival and the advancement of technology and science." Contemporary realist educators are called *essentialists* and place "a great emphasis on the practical side of education…[as well as] education for moral and character development." Essentialists advocate the Aristotelian approach that maintains "a proper understanding of the world…[through] an emphasis on critical reason aided by observation and experimentation."

Essentialism is a conservative educational philosophy that garners it roots from realism, as well as idealism. The tenets of essentialism can be directly traced to Aristotle's ordering of essential knowledge for the citizens of Athens. There are specific characteristics of essentialism, that:

- The first task is to teach basic knowledge…or basic tools that prepare students to function as members of a civilized society;
- Learning is hard work and requires discipline… and students need to focus their attention on the task at hand;
- The teacher is the locus of the classroom…as the teacher knows what the students need to know and is well acquainted with the logical order of the subject matter and the way it should be presented. (Knight, 1998).

In modern education, there are certain elements that promote the nature of realism and essentialism:

Character Education: The legacy of character education dates directly to Aristotle. He promoted the concept that children should be taught to behave virtuously (Noddings, 1995).

Competency-based Testing: Competency-based testing is an important aspect of the essentialist line of thought. The educational philosophy promotes a dependence on factual data to determine who has learned what knowledge. Competency testing has been "directed toward finding some way to gauge teacher effectiveness and students performance more efficiently, and many states already require students to pass competency tests before graduation" (Ozmon & Craver). The No Child Left Behind Act (2001) requires that both student and teacher knowledge bases be measured for competency.

Great Books: The study of Great Books, or books that contain knowledge that has been passed down "through the ages," is a curriculum that is organized around works of literature and philosophy that "still present fundamental knowledge about individual and social existence, human institutions, intellectual and moral endeavors and the natural order" (Ozmon & Craver).

Paideia Proposal: The Paideia Proposal is a curriculum design developed by Mortimer Adler that promotes the teaching of problem solving skills and core subjects that places a strong emphasis on ideas found in philosophy, literature and art. The Paideia group advanced two basic recommendations, "that schooling be a one-track system; and, that it be "general, non-specialized and nonvocational" (Ozmon & Craver).

Role of the teacher: The role of the essentialist teacher is "to present material in a systematic and organized way, [as students] use clearly defined criteria in making judgments about art, economics, politics and science" (Ozmon & Craver). Teachers teach what is essential for students to become productive citizens. Essentialist teachers consider whether particular activities are essential to the basic understanding of knowledge. They plan "the type of material [to be] presented; how it is organized; whether it suits the psychological makeup of the child; whether the delivery system is suitable; and whether or not it achieves the desired results."

Syllogism: Aristotle is concerned with truth; in order to test the truth of statements, he developed what is called a *syllogism*. The thought behind a syllogism is that people will "think more accurately by ordering statements about reality in a logical systematic form that correspond to the facts of the situation under study" (Ozmon and Craver). The seminal syllogism that illustrates this concept is:
All men are mortal.
Socrates is a man;
Therefore, Socrates is mortal.

REALIST REFORM MOVEMENTS

A resurgence of Realist educational philosophy that was promoted during the Age of Reason and again during the Enlightenment was revived under the direction of Admiral Hyman Rickover, at the time of the launching of the Russian satellite Sputnik in 1957. Rickover advocated an educational system that supported the essentials of education, with a focus on the technical and scientific in order to keep up with the race towards political superiority by the United States. A group of educators who formed the Council for Basic Education advocated a return to the teaching of the three R's—reading, writing and arithmetic. They stated that a general cultural malaise was sweeping the United States and that educators needed to focus on the essentials of education, under the guise of realism, whose roots directly related back to Aristotle's philosophy of educating youth (Ozmon & Craver).

Reformists Robert Hutchins and Mortimer Adler supported the study of universal truths that are inherent in the *Great Books,* or texts that passed on "the fundamental knowledge about individual and social existence, human institutions, intellectual and moral endeavors, and the nature order." Accordingly, Adler developed the *The Paideia Proposal* in 1982, a curriculum with a strong emphasis on truths found in philosophy, literature and art. He considered that there was a body of knowledge that "all students should encounter...and can best encounter through the Socratic methods of questions and answers" (Ozmon & Craver).

CRITICISM

Opponents of the realist movement of education state that realism (or essentialism) promotes "an elitist conception of education whereby only intelligent students are able to master the material with any real depth." However, Adler's *Paideia Problems and Possibilities,* his sequel to *The Paideia Proposal,* states that "his approach to learning was designed for all students, not just the college bound" (Ozmon & Craver).

Other critics of a Realist educational system argue that its exclusion of a multicultural understanding, no promotion of creativity, and a lack of focus on human relationships narrows education. Critics comment that realism focuses unduly on the facts and a promotion of ideas rather than on application, that there is "too much precision and order... that leads to mechanical approaches to education" (Ozmon & Craver). The realist system has also been criticized for its support of competency, accountability, and performance-based teaching methods that "can be measured in some form." However, essentialists believe that there is a strong need to "teach students the kinds of things that members of society need to know in order to survive" and that these things need to be measured in order to assure that what should be taught and learned are actually being comprehended.

TERMS & CONCEPTS

Ethics: Gruber defines ethics as "the study concerned with judgments of approval or disapproval, rightness or wrongness, goodness or badness, and virtue or vice."

Golden Mean: To Aristotle, the Golden Mean is considered to be the proper perspective, or a path between two extremes (Ozmon and Craver). He believed that the person who follows "a true purpose leads a rational life of moderation, avoiding extremes.". A thinking person looks for the mean to develop a life of moderation.

Habits of the Mind: Habits of the mind are aspects of conditioning oneself to act accordingly "to certain kinds of conduct and certain kinds of outcomes with certain feelings" (Robinson, 1995). Habits model what could be called *second nature*. By developing habits of the mind rather than rules of conduct, teachers are more concerned with "the kind of person one is rather than with every single act a person performs".

Metaphysics: Metaphysics is the study of the nature of ultimate reality, considering the question of what is genuinely real.

Universal Truth: Universal truth is truth that is absolute and is not dependent on different cultures.

Virtue: A virtue is "a disposition that is developed through the careful nurturing of one's capacities for living".

Tricia Smith

BIBLIOGRAPHY

Beauchamp, T. (1982). *Philosophical ethics.* New York: McGraw Hill.

Burnet, J. (1973). *Aristotle on education: Extracts from the Ethics and Politics.* Cambridge, MA: Cambridge UP.

Damian, R., & Robins, R. W. (2013). Aristotle's virtue or Dante's deadliest sin? The influence of authentic and hubristic pride on creative achievement. *Learning & Individual Differences, 26*156-160. Retrieved December 15, 2013, from EBSCO Online Database Education Research Complete.

Frankena, W. (1965). Toward a philosophy of moral education. In Carter, H. *Intellectual Foundations of American education.* (pp. 181-192). New York: Pitman Press.

Gruber, F. (1973). *Historical and contemporary philosophies of education.* New York: Thomas Y. Crowell.

Gutek, G. (2009). *New perspectives on philosophy and education.* Columbus, OH: Pearson.

Knight, G. (1998). *Issues and alternatives in educational philosophy.* Berrian Springs, MI: Andrews UP.

Lewis, P. (2012). In defence of Aristotle on character: Toward a synthesis of recent psychology, neuroscience and the thought of Michael Polanyi. *Journal of Moral Education, 41,* 155-170. Retrieved December 15, 2013, from EBSCO Online Database Education Research Complete

Noddings, N. (1995). *Philosophy of education.* New York: Harper Collins.

Ozmon, H., & Craver, S. (2008). *Philosophical foundations of education* (8th ed). Upper Saddle River, NJ: Pearson.

Robinson, T. (1995). *Aristotle in outline.* Indianapolis, IN: Hackett.

Russell, B. (1945). *A history of Western philosophy.* Hew York: Simon & Shuster.

Taylor, A. (1955). *Aristotle.* New York: Dover Press.

Urmson, B. (1988). *Aristotle's ethics.* New York: Basil Blackwell.

Walker, P. (2012). Teaching argument with Aristotle's common topics. *Kentucky English Bulletin, 61,* 14-18. Retrieved December 15, 2013, from EBSCO Online Database Education Research Complete.

SUGGESTED READING

Adler, M. (1997). *Aristotle for everybody.* New York: Touchstone.

– (1984). *The Paideia Program: An educational syllabus.* New York: Macmillan.

Aristotle. (1975). *The Nicomachean ethics of Aristotle* (D. Ross, Trans.). New York: Oxford UP.

– (1899). *Politics* (B. Jowett, Trans.). New York: Colonial Press.

Augusto, L. (2006). A little idealism is idealism enough: A study on idealism in Aristotle's epistemology. *Idealist Studies, 36,* 61-73.

Birondo, N. (2006). Moral realism without values. *Journal of Philosophical Research, 31,* 1-102.

Broadie, S. (1991). *Ethics with Aristotle.* New York: Oxford University Press.

Link, S. (2008). Essentialism and perennialism. *Essentialism and perennialism,* 1-11. Retrieved June 8, 2009, from EBSCO online database, Research Starters Education.

Null, J. (2007, April). William C. Bagley and the founding of essentialism. *Teachers College Record, 109,* 1013-1055.

Peterson, J. (2000). Conceptualism and truth. *Ratio, 13,* 234. Retrieved June 9, 2009, from EBSCO online database, Academic Search Complete.

Putnam, R. (2008). Why not moral realism? *International Journal of Philosophical Studies, 16,* 17-29. Retrieved June 8, 2009, from EBSCO online database, Academic Search Complete.

Reed, R., & Johnson, T. (2000). *Philosophical documents in education,* 2nd ed. New York: Longman.

Reeve, C.D.C. (1998). Aristotelian education. In Rorty, A. *Philosophies on education: historical perspectives.* (pp. 51-65). New York: Routledge.

– (1992). *Practices of reason: Aristotle's Nicomachean Ethics.* New York: Oxford UP.

Schollmeier, P. (1998). Aristotle and Aristotelians. *Social Theory and Practice, 24,* 133-151. Retrieved June 9, 2009, from EBSCO online database, Academic Search Complete.

Spangler, M. (1994). *Aristotle on teaching.* Lanham, MD: University Press of America.

Shtulman, A. (2008). The relation between essentialist beliefs and evolutionary reasoning. *Cognitive Science, 32,* 1049-1062.

Tabensky, P. (2007). Realistic idealism: An Aristotelian alternative to Machiavellian international relations. *Theoria: A Journal of Social and Political Theory,* 97-111. Retrieved June 8, 2009, from EBSCO online database, Academic Search Complete.

Verbeke, G. (1990). *Moral education in Aristotle.* Washington, DC: Catholic University of America Press.

EARLY ROOTS OF MODERN AMERICAN EDUCATION

The early roots of modern education stretch back to ancient Israel, where it was believed that education was a divine command, and to Greece and Rome, where learning was considered central to the formation of character and an essential motivator for responsible citizenship. During the middle ages, the clergy found itself preserving scholarship while also trying to spread Christianity. During the Renaissance, Greek humanist philosophy was rediscovered, and education began to be disassociated from the church. In colonial America, however, the Puritans continued to view education as a religious duty as they founded institutions like Harvard and Yale. As the country moved into the nineteenth century, however, economic prosperity began to shift education into the secular sphere as a way to increase prosperity and create equality among citizens. The Founding Fathers, influenced by the works of John Locke, furthered this secularization in the Declaration of Independence and the Constitution.

KEYWORDS: Colonies; Dark Ages; Education; Enlightenment; Humanists; In Loco Parentis; Middle Ages; New World; Protestantism; Renaissance

OVERVIEW

The Greek and Roman ideas about education, which were largely neglected in the West as the Dark Ages descended over Europe after the collapse of the Roman Empire in the 5th century, were rediscovered as the works of classical antiquity. Dutifully preserved in the Muslim world, they were reintroduced to Europe during the 13th and 14th centuries, paving the way for what came to be called the Renaissance. At that time, the largely secular educational ideas of Cicero and others were blended with the prevailing Christian piety and spread abroad by the dissemination of books and pamphlets written by English humanists such as Erasmus. Some evangelical Protestants, such as William Bradford, ventured to the New World in the seventeenth century, bringing Jewish ideas of education with them, and hoping that they would form a bulwark against the barbarism of the as-yet untamed American frontier.

The history of modern education stretches back to ancient times, and is comprised of many different cultural and intellectual influences, such as:

- The spiritual inheritance from the ancient Jews;
- The classical inheritance from Greece and Rome, which was never completely snuffed out in Europe after the collapse of the Roman Empire, but glowed ever more brightly as more and more texts reentered Europe from the Islamic world during the Renaissance, beginning in the 13th and 14 centuries A.D.;
- Over a millennium of Christian scholarship dating back to Justin Martyr in the 2nd century A.D., on through Augustine in the 5th century, Thomas Aquinas in the 13th century, and Erasmus in the 16th century;

- The social, political, cultural and economic realities to which the first European Americans had to adapt themselves as colonization began during the great Age of Exploration.

All of these influences came together to lay the groundwork for the educational system Americans know today.

ANCIENT EDUCATION CONCEPTS

Education, which one might loosely define as the effective transmission of important and useful information from one person to another, began before the invention of writing. We know this because the evolution of modern human beings from our hominid ancestors depended on the development of cooperation within social groups. As these social groups became more complex, and a division of labor became the norm, it became ever more important to share information and educate those of a new generation in the beliefs, stories, habits and - most importantly - the skills of the elders.

The ancient Jews, whose religion would become foundational to Western Civilization, believed in the presence of a personal god who gave commandments that his people should follow if they desired the greatest amount of joy in this life. The Jews, setting a precedent that was followed straight through the founding of the American colonies, established a link between education and religious duty (Shupak, 2003). According to the book of Deuteronomy, Jews were to become literate so that they could teach God's law to their children, thus retaining His favor. God tells the Jews, for example, to "Teach [my words] to your children, talking about them when you sit at home and when you walk along the road, when you lie down and when you get up" (Deut. 11:19, NIV). From the outset, the ancient Jews valued education as an act of worship, and this cultural value became an inheritance of Western Civilization through the spread of Christianity. It is also important to note the democratization of education in ancient Israel: all were to be educated in the ways of God.

EDUCATION IN ANCIENT GREECE & ROME

In the more secular civilizations of ancient Greece and Rome, where talk of the gods was more of a parlor game, education was also prized, but for quite different reasons than it was in ancient Israel. In Greece

the reasons were pragmatic: the male elite were to be educated so that they could rule their city-states and maintain proper order:

…[C]itizenship…was a degree to be attained to only after proper education… This not only made some form of education necessary, but confined educational advantages to male youths of proper birth. There was of course no purpose in educating any others….Education in Greece was essentially the education of the children of the ruling class to perpetuate the rule of that class (Cubberly, 2004).

This elitism moderated somewhat as city-states such as Athens become more prosperous and the club of citizens expanded, and teachers such as Socrates, Plato and Aristotle took on eager philosophy students and founded schools. The true contribution of the Greeks to modern education was their emphasis on – even their insistence that – education was important in creating involved citizens who would enjoy basic human freedoms of speech, the press and religion. Rather than placing an emphasis on education as a religious duty, it inverted the Jewish equation somewhat by making education the bulwark against oppressive ideologies imposed from without. The Greeks believed that only when free could a person become truly human, and they could only be free if they were educated to become citizens who would make contributions to lives beyond their own.

The Romans, living on the cusp of the Christian era, sought to expand upon Greek ideas. Cicero wrote that oratory, a lucrative skill prized by many Roman males, presupposed a broad liberal arts background. Concerned that Roman education was making men too intellectually myopic, he helped to articulate the idea that the goal of education was a well-rounded person with a thirst for knowledge that remained with him for life. According to Pascal (1984),

Education to the Romans had a broader context, going beyond the Greek arete, a concern for academic excellence, to a Ciceronian humanitas, education as a way to train not just through systematic instruction, but also as a means of achieving an understanding of human dignity and worthiness. The moral perspective, the stress on values was, according to Cicero, the mark of an educated man (Pascal).

For Cicero, the noble, mind-expanding and civilizing possibilities of education come through, and these concepts were readily adopted by leading

Americans of the Enlightenment such as Thomas Jefferson and Benjamin Franklin. Unlike the Jews, and later the Christians, the Romans and Greeks had little use for any education that indulged in supernatural speculations which would not help them live more virtuously in this life.

INFLUENCE OF EARLY CHRISTIANITY

From a far flung corner of the Roman Empire there emerged a new force: Christianity. The early Christians were initially a persecuted minority accused of atheism because they didn't worship the Roman gods. Soon well-read Christian converts like Justin the Martyr - and later Augustine of Hippo - claimed inheritance rights over the classical heritage from Greece and Rome, as well as the first books of the Bible, which they (somewhat disparagingly) referred to as the Old Testament. While it seems likely that Jesus himself and most of his early followers were barely literate, and Jesus left no writings of his own, as Christianity spread throughout the Roman Empire in the second and third centuries A.D., it began to win converts like wealthy Romans living in the cities. These educated Romans became, in time, educated Christians, thus helping to create an intellectual synthesis between Greek and Roman ideas on one hand, and Judeo-Christian ideas on the other. Cicero might have been right that education had moral and ethical ends, but those ends were redefined using Christian categories of sanctification, justification and salvation.

As the Roman legions withdrew from Europe and the Empire collapsed in the fifth century, Christian bishops, as de facto community leaders, found themselves in the curious role of preserving both the rule of law and some level of learning and scholarship, all the while trying to spread their message that a better world, both temporally and spiritually, was ahead. None of these tasks was easy, and the church was by no means entirely successful, but soon the greatest scholars of the age - the Alcuin of York, Venerable Bede, Anselm of Canterbury – were found in the monasteries that dotted Europe. In the Middle Ages, as Europe slowly began to recover politically, culturally, economically and even spiritually from the end of the Roman Empire, these and other church leaders began to found religious schools. The Jewish idea of education as worship was again in the ascendancy.

THE RENAISSANCE

As the Renaissance began in the 13th and 14th centuries, and the works of classical antiquity were reintroduced into Europe through trade with the Muslim world, many of the church intellectuals of the age, including Erasmus of Rotterdam, began to argue that a return to the humanism of Cicero and other ancients would be a useful corrective to the corruption and theological sloth they detected in the Roman Catholic Church hierarchy. Speaking about Erasmus, one scholar wrote:

His humanism is not limited in its functions to the field of education but tries to encompass the whole organism of human society, which it seeks to mold into a better and more harmonious shape (Caspari, 1947).

Others outside of leadership positions in the church, many inspired by reading ancient religious skeptics such Epicurus and Lucretius for the first time, deemphasized the role of religion and argued that education should have entirely secular means and ends. This sacred-secular fault line ran through pedagogical (and even political) debates during America's founding period, and it continues up through current debates over spending taxpayer money for religious school vouchers.

EDUCATION IN COLONIAL AMERICA

By the time the first permanent British settlement in America was established in the Jamestown in 1607, the European settlers were coming from a continent ravaged by decades of religious war between Catholics and Protestants, the disruption of centuries-old educational systems and great political upheaval. By learning lessons from the past, the American colonists hoped to prove that a new sort of society was possible and sustainable. On board the ship in 1630 that would take him and his fellows to the New World, John Winthrop, Puritan founder of the Massachusetts Bay Colony, wrote that the fledgling community would be a city upon a hill:

The eyes of all people are upon us. So that if we shall deal falsely with our God in this work we have undertaken, and so cause Him to withdraw His present help from us, we shall be made a story and a by-word through the world. We shall open the mouths of enemies to speak evil of the ways of God, and all professors for God's sake. We shall shame the faces of many of God's worthy servants, and cause their prayers to be turned into curses upon us till we be consumed out of the good land whither we are going (Winthrop, 1630).

Education in the colonies, from the outset, was placed in the hands of ministers, churches and church-affiliated organizations - not unlike the situation that prevailed in Europe during the Dark and Middle Ages. The Puritans (as well as the other Protestant and Catholic English colonists up and down the east coast of America) saw education as the primary responsibility of the nuclear family. Some of the wealthier immigrants brought books (even entire libraries) with them from England to use in education. The services of private tutors, particularly in the plantation culture of the Southern colonies, were secured to imbue upper class males with a sound understanding and appreciation of the Western heritage, with a special emphasis on the Bible. Wealthier Americans - those who wanted trained ministers in the family – also banded together to create institutions of higher learning such as Harvard (founded 1630) and Yale (founded 1701). Across all geographical regions of the colonies, those of the lower classes learned the basics and were apprenticed in a trade that, in all likelihood, was also the trade of their fathers and grandfathers (Morris, 1953).

EARLY EDUCATION LAWS

From a more practical standpoint, the Christian leaders of the American colonies took into account the need for education to supply a skilled and devout work force to help the colonies enter into a mutually beneficial economical relationship with England. Acting upon these impulses, in 1642 Massachusetts passed a law fining parents for neglecting the education of their children, and a 1647 law required all towns with more than 50 or more families to pay for a teacher of reading and writing. Those with at least 100 families were required to establish a Latin grammar school. All other New England states but Rhode Island had passed similar laws by 1689. By 1700, only several generations after the colonies were founded, the literacy rate for males across New England had climbed to a staggering 95 percent (Morris).

The trend toward universal education began in the British colonies almost from the outset. New England, governed by evangelical Protestants who believed that faith came by reading as much as by hearing, viewed education - particularly literacy – as being of eternal

significance. The Puritans believed that all humans were equally sinful - a democracy of depravity - and thus no child should be deprived of the chance to read and respond to the gospel's call to salvation. They also believed that as human beings understood more about the world, and indeed the universe itself, the more it would redound to the glory of God.

AMERICAN EDUCATION IN THE 18TH CENTURY

As the seventeenth century became the eighteenth, the colonists came to see themselves as having common interests, and they began to press for more and more concessions from England. Slowly and subtly, the strictly religious motivations for the American educational system were balanced with the more humanistic motivations that would have been familiar to the Greeks and Romans, such as patriotism, courage and virtue. Kessler (1992) notes that Alexis de Tocqueville saw just such a shift when he wrote "Democracy in America" in the 1830s:

De Tocqueville ... shows that most Americans of his day were more concerned with material comfort and prosperity than with any spiritual benefit attributable to faith. This shift in priorities can be seen in the lessons schoolchildren learned about wealth and property. Puritan public schools were Biblically oriented and, while Tocqueville doesn't say so explicitly, they probably taught that property was a gift from God to be used for His purposes . In Tocqueville's America, children learned that labor created property, that wealth was labor's just reward, and that property ownership entailed no moral obligations. Their first lesson in economic justice was not that theft is sinful, but that respect for the property of others is the best way to secure one's own possessions (Kessler).

Moreover, the Puritan philosophy of education was secularized and transformed by later generations of American educators into a tool for social progress and the reinforcement of American democratic ideals. Horace Mann, brother-in-law of Nathaniel Hawthorne and a man more than any other responsible for the creation of the American public education system, saw this clearly: "Education, then, beyond all other devices of human origin, is the great equalizer of the conditions of men, the balance-wheel of the social machinery" (Mann, 1848).

In one sense, the split between public and religious education that is still seen in America today has its roots in an ancient tension between the Jewish view that education is at heart a religious or missionary enterprise, and the Greek and Roman view that education's purpose is to create citizens prepared to work together for progress in a diverse world.

JOHN LOCKE, THE ENLIGHTENMENT & AMERICAN EDUCATION

The Enlightenment was an intellectual movement that began in Europe in the seventeenth century. Inspired by the scientific advances of Copernicus, Galileo and Newton, the thinkers of the Enlightenment believed that reason, secular values and science were the most reliable paths to knowledge about ourselves and the world. As the German philosopher Immanuel Kant put it, "Sapere aude! Dare to know! is therefore the slogan of the Enlightenment" (Kant, 1784).

Locke's influential book *The Reasonableness of Christianity*, as Delivered in the Scriptures (1695), shows Locke grasping for a common thread of moral agreement among warring Christian factions. A century later, Thomas Jefferson echoed those sentiments:

Reading, reflection and time have convinced me that the interests of society require the observation of those moral precepts only in which all religions agree (for all forbid us to steal, murder, plunder, or bear false witness), and that we should not intermeddle with the particular dogmas in which all religions differ, and which are totally unconnected with morality (Jefferson, 1809).

Locke argued that the young men of privilege should be educated to reason and become "young gentlemen," as well as that others should be taught the value and dignity of hard work. Locke's educational program for wealthy young boys included reading, writing, French and Latin.

Locke's ideas on education and representative government were brought to America by Benjamin Franklin in the 1740s and had an enormous influence on leading revolutionaries such as Washington, Jefferson and Madison. Americans drafting the Declaration of Independence and the Constitution were keen to ensure that there was a separation of church and state that would encourage liberty of conscience, political stability and, as one was so led, a personal piety. For many of the Founding Fathers, religion was a private matter that was not to be privileged in the educational system or in the marketplace of ideas.

Education in the American colonies was seen as the primary responsibility for the nuclear family, and this was declared so by statute. Eventually, as the colonies grew in size and complexity, and as religious ideals yielded to the economic and social realities in the New World and the forces of the Enlightenment, this responsibility shifted to schools acting *in loco parentis*. Later, those disenchanted with the secular turn of the public schools began to rely on private or religious schools to educate their children.

TERMS & CONCEPTS

Colonies: In the American context, the original thirteen British settlements in what would later be called the United States.

Dark Ages: The time in Europe between the collapse of the Roman Empire in the 5th century A.D. to approximately the 10th century A.D.

Enlightenment: An intellectual movement that began in Europe in the 17th century whose advocates believed that reason, secular values and science were the most reliable paths to knowledge about ourselves and the world.

Humanists: A group of European Christian thinkers in the late Middle Ages and the Renaissance who believed that Christian belief and practice could benefit from dialog with the writers of classical antiquity. Later humanism lost its Christian component.

In Loco Parentis: Latin for "in the place of a parent," typically applied to teachers and school officials.

Middle Ages: A period of time in Europe from approximately the 10th century to the 13th century, between the Dark Ages and the Renaissance, when the power of the Christian church was at its height.

New World: A term used to describe the continents of South and North America as they were discovered by Europeans beginning in the fifteenth century.

Protestantism: A branch of Christianity, started by Martin Luther in the 16th century, in which members can deny the need for any human mediators between God and the individual.

Renaissance: A period of time in Europe, beginning in the 13th century and extending for several centuries, during which there was a rebirth of knowledge derived from and inspired by rediscovered classical sources.

Matt Donnelly

BIBLIOGRAPHY

Caspari, F. (1947). Erasmus on the social functions of Christian humanism. *Journal of the History of Ideas, 8*pp. 78-106.

Cremin, L. A. (1970). *American education: The colonial experience, 1607-1783.* New York: Harper Torchbooks.

Cubberley, E. P. (2004). *The history of education.* Reprint, Whitefish, MT: Kessinger Publishing.

Jefferson, T. (1809). Letter to James Fishback. Cited in J.P. Foley, ed., *The Jefferson cyclopedia.* New York: Funk & Wagnalls, 1900, p. 593.

Kant, I. (1784). *An answer to the question, What is enlightenment?* Retrieved September 9, 2007, from the University of Pennsylvania http://www.english.upenn.edu

Kessler, S. (1992). Tocqueville's puritans: Christianity and the American founding. *The Journal of Politics, 54,* 776-792. Retrieved September 8, 2007 from EBSCO Online Database Academic Search Premier.

Mann, H. (1848). Report to the Massachusetts Board of Education. Reprinted in D. Ravitch, *The American reader.* (pp. 149-153). New York: Harper, 2000.

Mirel, J. (2011). Bridging the "widest street in the world" reflections on the history of teacher education. *American Educator, 35,* 6-12. Retrieved December 15, 2013, from EBSCO Online Database Education Research Complete.

Morris, R. B., ed. (1953). *Encyclopedia of American history.* New York: Harper & Brothers.

Pascal, N.R. (1984). The Legacy of Roman Education. *The Classical Journal, 79,* 351-355.

Prochner, L. (2011). 'Their little wooden bricks': A history of the material culture of kindergarten in the United States. *Paedagogica Historica, 47,* 355-375. Retrieved December 15, 2013, from EBSCO Online Database Education Research Complete.

Pulliam, J.D., and Van Patten, J.J. (2013). *The history and social foundations of American education.* Tenth edition, Upper Saddle River, NJ: Pearson.

Schneider, J. (2012). Socrates and the madness of method. *Phi Delta Kappan, 94,* 26-29. Retrieved December 15, 2013, from EBSCO Online Database Education Research Complete.

Shupak, N. (2003). Learning methods in ancient Israel. *Vetus Testamentum, 53,* 416-426. Retrieved September 8, 2007 from EBSCO Online Database Academic Search Premier.

Winthrop, J. (1630). *A model of Christian charity.* Retrieved September 8, 2007, from the University of Virginia http://religiousfreedom.lib.virginia.edu

SUGGESTED READING

Boone, R.J. (2006). *Education in the United States: Its history from the earliest settlements.* Reprint, Whitefish, MT: Kessinger Publishing.

Dejong, D.H. (1993). *Promises of the past: A history of Indian education in the United States.* Golden, CO: Fulcrum Publishing.

Dewey, J. (1916). *Democracy and education.* New York: Macmillan. Accessed September 9, 2007, from Worldwide School http://www.worldwideschool.org

Johnson, J. A., & Gollnick, D. M., eds. (2004). *Introduction to the foundations of American education.* Boston: Allyn & Bacon.

MacDonald, V-M, ed. (2004). *Latino education in the United States: A narrated history from 1513-2000.* New York: Palgrave Macmillan.

Nash, M. A. (2005). *Women's education in the United States, 1780-1840.* New York: Palgrave Macmillan.

Nock, A. J. (1932). *The theory of education in the United States.* New York: Harcourt, Brace and Company.

Rury, J. L. (2005). *Urban education in the United States: A historical reader.* New York: Palgrave Macmillan.

HISTORY OF PUBLIC EDUCATION IN THE U.S.

Public education in America in large part was the product of historical movements that swept the nation, including national incorporation, widespread urbanization, and modern industrialization. Public education began during the 17th century when the Massachusetts Bay Colony instituted compulsory education laws. The 19th century saw the establishment of specialized schools for the mentally and physically handicapped, the expansion of compulsory education laws, and the establishment of freemen's schools. As the country became increasingly industrialized, child labor laws were coupled with further compulsory education laws, and new educational theories were developed. During the 20th century, a number of court cases and legislative initiatives brought about the end of segregation, prohibited prayer in public schools, and improved educational opportunities for disabled and disadvantaged students.

KEYWORDS: Apprenticeship; Compulsory Education; Dame School; History of Education; Hornbooks; Public Education; Public Schools; Segregation

OVERVIEW

Public education in America has a history dating back nearly to the landing of the Pilgrims at Plymouth Rock in 1620. Although the first public school appeared well before both the Constitution and the Declaration of Independence, the small, independent public schools of centuries past bear little if any resemblance to the system of universal public education now in place in the United States. The factors which led to the inception, growth, and development of public education in America are numerous, and they include not only the pursuit of learning, but also, perhaps more importantly, the development of the nation's philosophy of who should teach and who should be taught.

Public education in America in large part was the product of historical movements that swept the nation, including national incorporation, widespread urbanization, and modern industrialization. In order to glean an accurate understanding of the history of America's educational system, each of these eras in our country's history must be studied in turn.

While these factors constitute a timeline in American educational history, they cannot be fully understood apart from a concurrent examination of the development of educational philosophy, the changing understanding of the purpose and aim of public education, and both the impetus for and impact of legislative decisions and judicial rulings affecting public education.

Therefore, a comprehensive portrayal of the myriad factors that constitute the development of American education requires an examination of 1) the philosophical roots of early-American education, 2) the growth and development of 19th Century public schooling within the newly-formed nation, 3) the impact of urbanization and the industrial revolution on the evolution of public school attendance in the latter half of the 19th Century and early 20th Century, and 4) the increased involvement of government in public education.

Colonial Era

EDUCATION IN PURITAN NEW ENGLAND

The first public school in America was established in 1635 in Boston, Massachusetts, in the home of Philemon Pormont. Attendance at the school was free and open to all children. Founded by New England Puritans, the school, called the Boston Latin School utilized religious instruction in the Bible as a launching pad for the study of Latin and Greek classics. It is important to note that, during the colonial

era, religion formed the basis for American life, and the local church or meetinghouse was the focal point of each community. To many people, the primary purpose of learning to read was to gain the ability to obtain religious instruction from the Bible.

The year following the opening of the Boston Latin School witnessed the establishment of America's first college, Harvard College, whose founding purpose was to train preachers. Hence, for those fortunate to attend, the college would be an extension of the religious instruction received in local schools.

In addition to local schools, during this period Dame Schools were popular. These schools were for young children ranging in age from 6-8, although often younger. Taught by women, often widows, Dame Schools usually met in the instructors' homes and focused on teaching reading skills rather than on mathematics and writing. Although titled a "school," it was not uncommon for Dame Schools also to function as early day care facilities for colonial children.

Apprenticeship programs were also primary sources of specialized education in colonial America, particularly among the poor. Through apprenticeships, young boys, and by the mid-17th Century girls as well, were paired with a skilled tradesman. The apprentice would spend several years working at his mentor's side, and upon completion of the apprenticeship, it was expected that the student would possess the requisite knowledge and ability to begin working on his own. Beyond teaching only the trade, however, mentors, or "Masters" were also expected to train their apprentices in matters of good moral behavior (Barger, 2004).

In these early American schools, a very common method of instruction was the hornbook. Dating as far back as fifteenth-century Europe, the hornbook was a small wooden paddle on which was mounted a sheet containing lessons. A piece of horn from oxen or sheep and later from materials such as leather or metal, covered the sheet to protect the lesson. Oftentimes, a hole would be placed in the horn handle, and this enabled pupils to fasten these early textbooks to their clothing or carry them around their necks. Standard studies contained on hornbooks included the alphabet, formations of vowels and consonants, and the Lord's Prayer.

In colonial America, education was deemed the responsibility of the family. Parents were ultimately responsible for the rearing and training of their children, and there was an absence of reliance upon government institutions or entities to provide quality education for the young. Nevertheless, in this early colonial world, one can identify the roots of today's compulsory education laws.

As early as 1642, Massachusetts passed a law that required that children be instructed in religious education as well as in the laws of the colony. Yet, the expressed onus for doing so fell not to the state or local communities, but rather to parents and apprenticeship masters. Negligence in either of these areas was punishable by fine. Furthermore, the law stated that parents and masters must "catechize" their children in the principles of religion, or if they were unable to do so themselves, that they must provide for it. The 1642 legislation also stipulated that if parents or masters failed to perform the duties outlined in the law, local authorities could remove the children and place them with masters who would properly instruct them. Although the Massachusetts Law of 1642 stopped well short of establishing a formal school system, its importance as the first piece of legislation to require schooling cannot be underestimated.

Soon after, the Massachusetts Law of 1647 required that every town comprised of 50 families or more hire a teacher for the purpose of instructing the town's children in reading and writing. Moreover, towns of 100 families or more were also required to have a Latin instructor in order to prepare students for entry into Harvard College. Although schooling was still considered a local family responsibility, at times the colonial government would fund payment for these teachers.

EDUCATION IN THE MIDDLE & SOUTHERN COLONIES

Education in the Middle Colonies differed slightly from that in New England. While schools in New England were primarily Puritan, schools in the Middle colonies were often developed by Mennonites or Quakers. It was German immigrant, teacher, and Mennonite Christopher Dock who, in 1710, penned the first book on pedagogy printed in America. Dock's work, *Schul-Ordnung,* or *School Management,* outlined a series of rewards and punishments aimed not at teacher dominance but at gaining student trust and affection (Sass & Ruth).

In the middle colonies, although the primary focus remained religious instruction for the formation of

moral character, schools also incorporated a level of practical instruction as well. Among those involved in the development of middle-colony schools was Benjamin Franklin who helped to establish the Academy of Philadelphia in 1751. This Academy later grew into the University of Pennsylvania (Penn in the eighteenth century).

In the southern colonies, too, public education was taking root. Even before the establishment of Roxbury and Harvard, Virginian Benjamin Syms passed away and bequeathed in his will a plot of 200 acres with clear instructions that it was to be used for the establishment of a free school. Another Virginia school soon followed, and by the close of the seventeenth century, public schools could be found in northern, middle, and southern colonies (Tyler, 1897).

EARLY NATIONAL LEGISLATION

As government took an increased interest in requiring and providing for the education of children, public schools continued to multiply. As the pivotal events leading up to the unification of the colonies into a nation occurred in the latter portion of the 18th Century, America witnessed additional landmark educational milestones. The two most significant of these were the Land Ordinance of 1785 and the Northwest Ordinance of 1787. Specifically applicable to the Western Territories, the Land Ordinance of 1785 allotted land in each western township for the establishment of a public school. Two years later, the Northwest Ordinance of 1787 provided that since religion, morality, and knowledge were prerequisite to good government, schools should be "encouraged."

Thus, by the time the Constitution became the law of the land, and before even the Bill of Rights had gained ratification, universal public education in America was well on the road to establishment.

Education in the New Nation

SPECIALIZED SCHOOLS

While public schooling was becoming more widespread, the implementation of government-mandated universal public education still lay well in the future. Nevertheless, significant developments in the 19th Century established a philosophical foundation and showed a practical application for compulsory education. Most significant of these was the establishment of specialized schools for the blind and deaf. The early half of the 19th Century saw the establishment of three such schools:

- The Connecticut Asylum at Hartford for the instruction of Deaf and Dumb Persons, founded in 1817 and the first permanent school for the deaf in America;
- The New England Asylum for the Blind, which became the nation's first school of its type when it opened in 1829;
- The New York State Asylum for Idiots, founded in 1851 and authorized by the New York State Legislature.

Such institutions segregated certain members of society for their schooling and led the way for the enactment of compulsory legislation, and many colonies pursued such legislation as a means of gaining statehood and, consequently, uniting with fellow-states to form a nation (Baker, 2004).

COMPULSORY EDUCATION LEGISLATION & THE NATIONAL TEACHER ASSOCIATION

In 1852, Massachusetts enacted the first compulsory education legislation in the nation. The act required that children ages 8 through 14 attend school for a minimum of three months out of the year, and of those three months, six weeks were required to be consecutive. Violation of this act was punishable by fine. Nevertheless, exceptions were made for certain children, including those who were deemed mentally or physically unable to attend.

Other states soon followed suit, and by 1885, sixteen states had passed compulsory attendance legislation. It would not be until 1918, however, that all states would have such educational requirements as part of their state law.

In addition to compulsory attendance legislation, the 1850s witnessed another educational milestone: the formation of the National Teachers Association in 1857. Founded by a small group of educators in Philadelphia, this group evolved into what is today known as the National Educators Association, the largest association of its kind in the world.

SEGREGATION

Yet, while the popularity of public education continued to rise during the 19th Century, the opportunity to attend was not equal for all, particularly in the southern states.

Throughout the 18th Century, while there were instances of integrated schools, most often in the Northern states, segregation between black and white was much more common. Yet, many slaves viewed illiteracy as a perpetrating factor of slavery; hence, many pursued education, often at great cost to themselves, as offenses such as the schooling of a slave could be met with severe punishment of both teacher and pupil. Nevertheless, African-Americans recognized the value of education to freedom, and in addition to learning individually, some established secret schools for the purpose of education (Dodge, 2006).

Following the Civil War, some freedmen sought to gain from the government a right to education. Even in many freedmen's schools, however, conditions were difficult, with lack of proper materials, crowded school rooms, and students who often themselves were under-clothed and under-fed. Nevertheless, the speed with which many African-Americans understood and mastered materials often came as a surprise to their instructors (Dodge).

Despite their new free standing, however, African Americans faced many obstacles in the road to gaining equal access to public education, and the end of the 19th Century witnessed the issuance of the famous United States Supreme Court decision in *Plessy v. Ferguson*. In this 1892 case, the Supreme Court upheld the constitutionality of Louisiana's "separate but equal" law. This ruling served as a basis for implementing and continuing the practice of segregated education.

Industrialization & Integration

EXTENDED COMPULSORY EDUCATION LAWS

While segregation between black and white remained intact for the next 58 years, national industrialization provided the impetus for integration of immigrant children into their new nation.

The turn of the 20th Century and the Industrial Revolution brought a marked increase in immigration. As parents went to work in cities and factories, children went to school in order to learn English and assimilate into their new culture. Despite the age of children, many families saw employment as more beneficial than education and preferred that their children work rather than study. This reality, coupled with the recognition of the negative effects of child labor and an uneducated populace, led to child labor laws and additional compulsory education laws. By 1918, compulsory education legislation existed in every state. By the following year, legislation providing funds for transporting students to school existed in every state as well.

CHANGING EDUCATIONAL THEORIES

The early decades of the 20th Century also witnessed significant development in philosophical thoughts related to education. American psychologist and educator G. Stanley Hall produced works investigating the relationship between adolescent development and education, and in 1916, American psychologist Lewis Terman announced what is today known as the Stanford-Binet Intelligence Test. This test helped lay the groundwork for standardized testing that it still used today.

In this same year, John Dewey published *Democracy and Education: An Introduction to the Philosophy of Education*. Dewey popularized the philosophy of experiential education, which encourages focusing more on a child's learning experience and less on the teacher's espousing a rigid formula for instruction.

Modern Legislation

THE NATIONAL DEFENSE EDUCATION ACT & THE ELEMENTARY & SECONDARY EDUCATION ACT

As new philosophies of education slowly overtook traditional ones, the role of the government in providing education also grew. In 1958, Congress passed the first comprehensive federal legislation regarding education. A reaction to the Cold War, the National Defense Education Act (NDEA) was born out of a necessity that the United States continue to have highly specialized technicians and engineers in order to compete with Soviet technology. In addition to funding loans for college, the NDEA provided support for improved mathematics and scientific instruction in elementary and secondary schools.

The following decade, Congress followed the NDEA with the ESAA, the Elementary and Secondary Education Act. While the NDEA focused on subject matter, the ESAA focused on social factors and sought to provide quality education to lower-income children. Despite increases in funding, however, the

measure has fallen short of complete fulfillment of its mission as many students from lower-income families continue to struggle educationally.

Brown v. Board of Education & Engel v. Vitale

The 1950s also saw the end of 58 years of legal segregation. On May 17, 1954, in the case of *Brown v. Board of Education*, the Supreme Court overturned its 1896 *Plessy v. Ferguson* decision, stating that separate educational facilities are by definition unequal. While discrimination in public schooling often continued, it no longer had the legal backing of the United States government, and *Brown v. Board of Education* paved the way for full educational equality for black and white Americans.

Perhaps the most significant 20th Century legal occurrence affecting education, however, came in 1962 with the Supreme Court ruling in *Engel v. Vitale*. In its decision, the Court held that prayer in public schools violated the Constitution. The following year, in *Abington v. Schempp*, the Court further ruled that official use of the Bible in public education was unconstitutional.

THE EDUCATION OF ALL HANDICAPPED CHILDREN ACT

By the latter half of the 20th Century, education was both universal and integrated, yet there remained individuals who still could not benefit from the public education system, namely, those who were physically handicapped or otherwise disabled. In 1975, Congress sought to change this with the passage of Public Law 94-142, the Education of All Handicapped Children Act. Not only did the act require that appropriate education be extended to handicapped children, but it also implemented a system of Individualized Education Plans (IEPs) whereby disabled students' educational needs are evaluated and, based on the evaluation, students receive individualized educational and other services aimed at helping them achieve specified goals.

THE U.S. DEPARTMENT OF EDUCATION & THE NO CHILD LEFT BEHIND ACT

In 1980, Congress officially established the U.S. Department of Education as a Cabinet agency. Although the Department of Education acknowledges that education remains primarily a responsibility of state and local government, increases in federal mandates on education have been met with resistance by some states even as they have been concurrently welcomed by many parents.

In 2001, the No Child Left Behind Act (NCLB) became the law of the land. The NCLB was a reauthorization of the ESAA and instituted requirements for both schools and teachers. Among these requirements are annual testing, statewide standards for measuring educational progress, publicized school report cards to inform parents of both school and teacher performances, penalties for schools who fail to achieve set standards in certain areas, and school choice options for parents whose children attend failing schools. While many parents welcomed the NCLB Act, many teachers viewed it as an underfunded mandate, setting requirements but providing no funding to achieve them. The National Education Association (NEA), the country's largest professional employee association, called for changes in the act to lessen penalties on schools and increase federal funding for initiatives.

The recession and global financial crisis that began in 2007 resulted in sustained and repeated budget cuts to public education, while NCLB mandated increased spending on programs and assessments. Federal funding decreased, but the primary source of school funding - property taxes - was greatly effected by the crash of real estate values nationwide. More than half the states instituted policy changes to allow greater flexibility for school districts to spend what monies they did receive, but year over year cuts required drastic reductions in staffing and programs (especially non-core subjects such as arts and music) and increased class sizes (Cavanagh, 2011). Meanwhile, schools struggled to raise standardized test scores and prevent flight to private schools or higher achieving public schools. Charter schools were met with parental enthusiasm, though performance of these alternative models was mixed, and per-student funding was lost to public schools with the exit of students attending charters. Advocates of charters, however, argued that the challenge of alternative models would force improvements at traditional schools (Maloney, Batdorff, May, & Terrell, 2013).

From the humble school in Philemon Pormont's Boston home to the present-day structure consisting of public school systems nationwide, education in American history boasts a long and vibrant heritage. As the effort continues to ensure that all children have equal access to quality education, public schooling in America will continue to play an integral part in our nation's future.

TERMS & CONCEPTS

Apprenticeship: The process of pairing a youth with a mentor or "Master" who is expert at a trade for the purpose of training the youth in the study of that trade as a lifetime career.

Compulsory Education: Education which is required by law.

Dame School: Type of school for young children popular in colonial and early America, usually taught by a woman, often a widow, and stressed reading over other subjects.

Hornbook: A small wooden paddle on which was mounted parchment containing lessons. The parchment was covered with horn. Colonial children utilized hornbooks to study materials such as the alphabet, letter formations, and the Lord's Prayer.

Public Education: Education required by the government and open to the public, funded by tax revenue.

Public Schools: Schools supported by funding from the public, usually via tax revenue, and providing free education for children.

Segregation: The act of separation based on race, class, or ethnicity; often used in reference to educational segregation between black and white students in the nineteenth and twentieth centuries.

Gina L. Diorio

BIBLIOGRAPHY

Baker, B. (2004). The functional liminality of the not-dead-yet-students, or, how public schooling became compulsory: a glancing history. *Rethinking History, 8,* 5-49. Retrieved January 27, 2007 from EBSCO Online Database Academic Search Premier.

Barger, R. (Ed.). (2004). *History of American education web project.* Retrieved January 27, 2007, from http://www.nd.edu

Cavanagh, S. (2011). Educators regroup in recession's aftermath. *Education Week, 30,* 6-10. Retrieved December 15, 2013, from EBSCO Online Database Education Research Complete.

ESEA: It's time for a change! NEA's positive agenda for the ESEA reauthorization. (2006). Retrieved January 7, 2007, from http://www.nea.org

Lauderdale, W. (1975). Moral intentions in the history of American education. *Theory Into Practice, 14,* 264. Retrieved January 27, 2007 from EBSCO Online Database Academic Search Premier.

Maloney, L., Batdorff, M., May, J., & Terrell, M. (2013). Education's fiscal cliff, real or perceived? public education funding during the economic downturn and the impact on public charter schools. *Journal of School Choice, 7,* 292-311. Retrieved December 15, 2013, from EBSCO Online Database Education Research Complete.

Massachusetts Bay School Law. (1642). Retrieved January 28, 2007, from http://personal.pitnet.net

Mirel, J. (2011). Bridging the "widest street in the world" reflections on the history of teacher education. *American Educator, 35,* 6-12. Retrieved December 15, 2013, from EBSCO Online Database Education Research Complete.

Penn in the eighteenth century: Academy of Philadelphia curriculum. Retrieved January, 27, 2007, from University of Pennsylvania Archives http://www.archives.upenn.edu

Pulliam, J.D., and Van Patten, J.J. (2013). *The history and social foundations of American education.* Tenth edition, Upper Saddle River, NJ: Pearson.

Sass, E. (Ed.) (2005). *American educational history: A hypertext timeline.* Retrieved January 27, 2006, from http://www.cloudnet.com

Schooling, education, and literacy in colonial America. (n.d.) Retrieved January 27, 2007, from http://alumni.cc.gettysburg.edu

T.E.C. (1973). Description of a dame or primary school in Boston about 1825. *Pediatrics, 51,* 475. Retrieved January 27, 2007 from EBSCO Online Database Academic Search Premier.

Tyler, L. (1897). Education in colonial Virginia. Part III: Free schools. *William and Mary College Quarterly Historical Magazine, 6,* 70-85. Retrieved November 27, 2007, from http://www.dinsdoc.com

United States Department of Education. Accessed January, 27, 2007, from http://www.ed.gov

Walsh, K. (2013). 21st-century teacher education. *Education Next, 13,* 18-24. Retrieved December 15, 2013, from EBSCO Online Database Education Research Complete.

SUGGESTED READING

Cox, W. Jr. (2000). The original meaning of the establishment clause and its application to education. *Regent University Law Review, 13,* 111-143. Retrieved January 28, 2007, from www.regent.edu

Derrick, M. G. (2001). Reflections on the history of gender bias and inequality in education. *Essays in Education, 1.*

De Young, A. (1987). The Status of American rural education research: An integrated review and commentary. *Review of Educational Research, 57,* 123-148. Retrieved January 28, 2007 from EBSCO Online Database Education Research Complete.

Henderson, C., Corner, J. P., Lagemann, E. C., Paige, R., Barber, B. R., Doyle, D. P., et al. (2004). Brown 50 years later. *American School Board Journal, 191,* 56-64. Retrieved January 28, 2007 from EBSCO Online Database Academic Search Premier.

Larson, E. (1998). *Summer for the gods: The Scopes trial and America's continuing debate over science and religion.* Cambridge, Massachusetts: Harvard University Press.

Pulliam, J., & Van Patten, J. (2007). *History of education in America* (9th ed.). Upper Saddle River, NJ: Prentice Hall.

JOHN LOCKE AND EDUCATION

This article examines why John Locke is considered one of the most influential philosophers in reshaping society from a system of monarchy and aristocracy to the modern concept of democracy and liberal capitalism. The article starts by giving a brief biography of Locke, including a concise description of the areas and issues that engaged Locke during his life. Next, it examines Locke's basic philosophy on reason, knowledge and critical thinking, and shows the relationship of this philosophy to his other seminal works. The paper briefly explains Locke's influence on Jefferson and the founding documents of America, as well as his continuing influence on American democracy. Finally, this article demonstrates the close correlation between Locke's thoughts on education and the way American education and pedagogy is perceived and practiced today.

KEYWORDS: Act/Belief Distinction; Blank Slate; Critical Thinking; Divine Right; Epistemology; Learner-Centered Education; Liberal Capitalism; Logical Fallacy; Rationalism; Social Sciences; Tabula Rasa

OVERVIEW

America's most important founding father, Thomas Jefferson, asserted that the three "greatest men that have ever lived" were Isaac Newton, Francis Bacon, and John Locke. Newton and Bacon were both central to developing modern science, but why did Jefferson believe John Locke was so important? Jefferson wrote that these three men "laid the foundation of those superstructures which have been raised in the Physical and Moral sciences," (Faulkner, 2008). Though the term "moral science" seems quite odd today, Jefferson is referring to what we would call the "social sciences" such as anthropology, sociology, psychology, political science, etc., though these fields of knowledge had not yet emerged as distinct disciplines in Jefferson's day. Now scholars and historians can clearly see the powerful influence of Locke's seminal works on all of these fields, and Jefferson seems to have astutely evaluated the historical importance of the three individuals who led the way to a new age of physical and social sciences.

The fact that Jefferson lists Locke as one of the most important men in human history also indicates that Locke highly influenced Jefferson as an intellectual, statesman, scientist, philosopher, U.S. President, and framer of America's most important document, the U.S. Constitution. Indeed, when we examine the works of John Locke, his importance on the development of human civilization in general becomes quite apparent. Locke contributed in many ways to the furtherance of modern society; he set the foundations for modern democracy, significantly contributed to many fields of knowledge, and also affected the way we perceive and practice education today. He modernized the meaning and method of education such that his basic principles are still the foundation of modern American education. To understand Locke's role in human history, and his influence on contemporary Western society, we must first briefly examine his life, the social institutions of his time, and the basic theories and tenets he forwarded. Once we consider these aspects, then it will become clear that Locke was, metaphorically, an intellectual bridge crossing from a previous period of human history to a new age of enlightenment and reason.

THE LIFE & TIMES OF JOHN LOCKE

In 1632, Locke was born in Somerset, England. He came from a prosperous family, and his father was a lawyer who owned a good deal of land. Through his father's influential contacts, Locke was accepted to one of the top English public schools of England,

Westminster School, where he was an excellent student. He received an Oxford University scholarship, where he earned a bachelor's degree in 1656, and in 1659 completed a master's degree. Locke stayed at Oxford, where he began teaching Greek in 1660, and later became a Rhetoric teacher. But Locke was not merely a teacher. He had a very broad interest in knowledge; for example, he was fascinated with developments in medicine, including the discovery that blood circulated throughout the human body. He decided to study medicine in his spare time, and eventually became a medical doctor, writing many treatises on the practice of medicine ("Fifty Major Economists," 2003). Locke was quite diverse in his intellectual pursuits, and he became a leading proponent on one side or another of many of the most important issues of his day. Locke also made important contributions in the theory of knowledge with his *An Essay Concerning Human Understanding*, and he contributed significantly to theories on education through his essay *Some Thoughts on Education*.

One of Locke's fundamental ideas was that humans are born with minds that are a "blank slate" (also known as "tabula rasa"). This means human development is highly influenced by environment, and that people fill their "blank slates" through life experiences that are reflected upon to gain knowledge (Henson, 2003). Gintis (2006) notes that this theory influenced the founders of modern sociology and anthropology, making Locke the original source of these new fields of knowledge. The "tabula rasa" concept also relates to Locke's theories on human reasoning. Locke believed all humans are capable of rationality and the ability to reason, and this led to his belief that individuals can and should collectively control the government. As Huyler writes, Locke proposed that civil society should be grounded in "a social contract signed by free and equal men rather than in a patriarchal theory that conferred divine-right grace on any sitting monarch" (1997).

Although the idea of each citizen voting and having power over government seems quite normal to us today, it is important to consider that during Locke's day, such a sociopolitical system did not exist. Many problems arose from societies being ruled by kings who believed God had bestowed upon them the divine right to rule over others, and religious institutions had a tendency to support this system by issuing that "divine right" to the king—as long as he supported the Church. As Huyler points out, "English-men feared and hoped to thwart ... the prospect of a monarch religiously responsive to the authority of a foreign Pope and puffed up by a pretentious divine-right doctrine." This system "threatened liberty in the political and the private sense" and it caused "intolerance, persecution, and conflict, as well as a dire disturbance to property and commercial freedom" (Huyler). In the historical and social context in which Locke developed his theories, the notion that citizens should control government seemed quite radical in his day. Through strong reasoning, Locke demonstrated the need and justification for "innate indefeasible, individual rights which limit the competence of the community and stand as bars to prevent interference with the liberty and property of private persons" (Huyler).

Thus, Thomas Jefferson had good reason to consider Locke one of the most important figures in human history, since Locke's philosophical treatises pushed feudalism and aristocracy aside to make intellectual space for individualism and the approaching age of commerce and industrialism. As Faulkner points out, "Bacon is best known for explaining the method of mastering nature; Locke, for explaining the political science of liberty."

REASON, DEMOCRACY & EDUCATION

Esperanza (2006) points out the philosophical transition, within Locke's mind, that caused his development to a more modern viewpoint. Esperanza writes that in his earlier writings, Locke concentrates more on theology and presents a viewpoint that seems more typical of seventeenth century thought. But then there is a psychological and philosophical shift wherein Locke begins developing a "strong inclination to empirical theories," and "began to show a deeper appreciation of the power of rational faculties and the role of sense-experience." Esperanza points out that this is why most scholars place Locke in the rationalist school of thought (Esperanza). Locke also states his firm belief that learning how to think, or exercising our ability to reason, is the most important thing any of us can achieve in our lives. In his essay *Some Thoughts Concerning Education*, Locke writes, "For when all is done, this [the ability to reason well], as the highest and most important faculty of our minds, deserves the greatest care and attention in cultivating it: the right improvement, and exercise of

our reason being the highest perfection that a man can attain to in this life."

Locke's belief in human reason is a key to the rest of his writing because this is the underlying system of thought that allows him to envision a differently organized society, and a new method of education as well. Locke's system of reasoning is what led him to propagate a modern democratic system based on individual rights, including human rights and property rights that complement and support today's global system of liberal capitalism. For Locke, reason is "the discursive faculty of the mind, which advances from things known to things unknown and argues from one thing to another in a definite and fixed order of propositions. It is this reason by means of which "mankind arrives at the knowledge of natural law" (Esperanza). Locke places sense perception at the center of this system of reasoning. For Locke, sense perception, which we can also interpret to mean experience, leads the way to knowledge. Esperanza observes that sense experience and reason, as the foundation of all knowledge, represents Locke's "most salient epistemological doctrine."

OPINION

However, Foley (1999) also brings up an important point about understanding Locke's epistemology. Foley argues that Locke's main concern is "not with how we acquire knowledge but rather with how we regulate opinion." Foley then observes that Locke defines knowledge such that it "requires certainty and, thus, is extremely scanty". On most topics or issues, all humans actually have are opinions, which is why Foley thinks Locke's epistemological philosophy is mostly concerned with how to best form one's own opinions (Foley). Thus, what are in effect critical thinking skills are at the center of Locke's thoughts on reason, knowledge, and rationalism. Citing Wolsterstorff, Foley outlines the fundamental principles that Locke espouses for best forming one's opinion. When examining these three principles, it seems clear that Locke is essentially giving advice on how to develop critical thinking skills:

- **Principle of evidence:** Base opinion on evidence, where evidence consists of what one knows;
- **Principle of appraisal:** Examine the evidence one has collected to determine its force, that is, appraise the probability of the proposition in question on that evidence;

■ **Principle of proportionality:** Adopt a level of confidence in the proposition that is proportioned to its probability on one's evidence (Foley).

Additionally, Locke warns us about the most common mistakes we make in forming our opinions; his advice on pitfalls in forming opinion is even more clearly related to the development of critical thinking skills:

■ False propositions are inculcated in us from youth as self-evident;

■ We become attached to familiar explanations and do not even consider alternatives;

■ Our opinions are motivated or influenced by our emotions rather than being the products of a disinterested concern for truth;

■ We give allegiance to authority (Foley).

Today we would call the above "opinion-forming" mistakes "logical fallacies," and these fallacies are a basic part of any course that teaches students how to develop critical thinking skills. Considering the attention Locke gives to avoiding shorted circuits in the critical thinking process, and the attention he gives to explaining the proper process, Locke does seem most concerned with helping others develop strong critical thinking skills.

Of course, beneath such a system of critical thinking is the premise that we are all capable of thinking independently and can arrive at our own sound opinion on any issue. Foley gives us a direct quote from Locke that clearly states that assumption: "Every man carries about him a touchstone if he will make use of it, to distinguish substantial gold from superficial glittering, truth from appearances ... [T]his touchstone ... is natural reason" (Foley). This quote inherently carries the foundation of modern democracy and liberal capitalism, as it focuses on the concept that every citizen possesses natural reason, can make rational decisions, and vote accordingly. Jefferson crafted the U.S. Constitution upon Locke's basic principle, that a government could be created that is "of, for, and by the people."

LOCKE'S INFLUENCE ON AMERICAN DEMOCRACY

When reading the U.S. Constitution, there seems a strong prevalence of reason at its foundation. It starts out with some basic propositions and moves forward from those propositions. Watson expresses this idea when he quotes a famous line from the second paragraph of the Declaration of Independence: "We hold these truths to be self-evident, that all men are created equal." As Watson observes, all literate citizens can read that line, use their own sense of reason and come to the rational conclusion that they agree with the premise. Even if society is constructed in opposition to that proposition, it nevertheless seems reasonable and fair that no individual should be born socially superior to another, and no individual should be uniquely chosen by God to rule over citizens without their consent. This is the foundation of modern society, and as Watson points out, "all liberal democratic forms of government recognize, if not explicitly then at least implicitly, the fundamental fact of human equality. Not to recognize such equality is to argue for another form of government, a non-liberal-democratic form" (Watson, 2006). Thus, Locke's philosophy strongly influenced the Declaration of Independence and Jefferson's ideas on government.

There are many other ways that Locke's ideas have infuenced and still influence America today. For example, Powers notes that Locke's ideas are still quite relevant in various legal decisions and precedences. A good example of this is Powers' observation that Locke is the underlying source of the act/belief distinction that Jefferson handed down to U.S. courts (Powers, 2007). The act/belief distinction is the idea that, in considering religious freedom, that freedom should only be limited if a religious act is against the good of society in general, and there is a reasonable civic law against some action in general. To oversimplify but get to the heart of this concept, we can see that human sacrifice as an act of religious freedom is nevertheless murder according to law, and will be punished as such. Locke expresses this concept in his writing, which Jefferson passed on to the U.S. judicial system. As Powers notes, "The rule Locke proposes is the same as that of the U.S. Supreme Court: 'those things that are prejudicial to the commonweal of a people in their ordinary use, and are therefore forbidden by laws, those things ought not to be permitted to churches in their sacred rites' (Powers). However, there are many situations where the legal line may blur, and it becomes quite uncertain as to whether religious freedoms should be restricted or not. This is why Powers argues that courts today should examine Locke's original principles on this subject when informing and forming their legal opinions and decisions.

LOCKE'S INFLUENCE ON EDUCATION

Locke wrote his ideas on education several centuries ago, but he still has a profound impact on how we practice education today in America. Henson argues that Locke is the original source of what we call today "experience-based education" and the contemporary concept of "experiential education." Henson made an analysis of learner-centered education literature, and came up with six basic principles that the literature outlines as the defining characteristics of leaner-centered education:

- Education should be experience based;
- Each individual learner's own unique qualities and disposition should be considered when planning experiences;
  - The learner's perceptions should shape the curriculum;
  - Learner's curiosity should be fed and nurtured;
  - Learning is best when it involves the emotions, and;
  - The learning environment should be free from fear (Henson).

Locke's essay, *Some Thoughts on Education*, powerfully and quite persuasively argues the case for adopting the above principles when educating students. Seventeenth century education had an entirely different approach, and that approach continued for a few more centuries, but eventually educators shifted their educational approach such that it matches the principles Locke outlines in his essay. In other words, the traditional approach of striking a student's hand with a ruler, for fumbling a rote memory line of text, has fallen out of use. If one reads Locke's essay on education, it becomes apparent that he is considering education from the point of view of the student rather than that of the teacher, which is the central principle of modern "learner-centered education." There are many examples in Locke's essay where we can see that leaner-centered approach underlying his advice to teachers.

The first proposition, that learning should be experience based, connects to a new way of perceiving and understanding education. Locke transformed learning itself from a more authoritarian system concentrated on memorizing and knowing information, to a more democratic system that concentrated on thinking about things and learning to reason. Locke places the ability to reason at the heart of his education philosophy:

It will perhaps be wonder'd, that I mention reasoning with children; and yet I cannot but think that the true way of dealing with them. They understand it as early as they do language; and, if I misobserve not, they love to be treated as rational creatures, sooner than is imagin'd" (Locke, 1693).

The next two principles that Henson outlines—that teachers should consider the unique disposition of each student, and that teachers should try to shape curricula according to the students' perceptions—are also important in Locke's educational principles. Locke writes that, "He therefore that is about children should well study their natures and aptitudes, and see by often trials what turn they easily take, and what becomes them" (Locke). As for allowing students to shape curricula, Locke has this principle in mind when he advises that teachers try to make the lesson and learning material:

…as much intelligible to him as suits the capacity of his age and knowledge. But confound not his understanding with explications or notions that are above it; or with the variety or number of things that are not to his present purpose. Mark what 'tis his mind aims at in the question, and not what words he expresses it in: and when you have informed and satisfied him in that, you shall see how his thoughts will enlarge themselves, and how by fit answers he may be led on farther than perhaps you could imagine (Locke).

The next principle, that of engaging the student's curiosity, can also be traced back to the educational principles of Locke. Locke writes that curiosity is "but an appetite for knowledge" and for that reason curiosity should be encouraged in students. Not only does Locke advise teachers to take advantage of the student's curiosity, but he also warns teachers to never discourage student questions, and never laugh at any question a student asks, but to always answer every question, and explain things well. Locke views curiosity as "the great instrument nature has provided to remove that ignorance they [students] were born with; and which, without this busy inquisitiveness, will make them dull and useless creatures (Locke). Locke's views on good teaching style are related to this idea. Locke believes that it is possible to actually make learning into fun, and he says as much in his essay:

I have always had a fancy that learning might be made a play and recreation to children: and that they

might be brought to desire to be taught, if it were pro-
posed to them as a thing of honour, credit, delight,
and recreation, or as a reward for doing something
else; and if they were never chided or corrected for the
neglect of it ... But then, as I said before, it must never
be imposed as a task, nor made a trouble to them.
There may be dice and play-things, with the letters on
them to teach children the alphabet by playing; and
twenty other ways may be found, suitable to their par-
ticular tempers, to make this kind of learning a sport
to them (Locke).

Henson's last two principles, that learning is best when it involves the emotions, and that the learning environment should be free from fear, also source back to Locke's essay. Locke writes that the teacher should be sensitive to what mood, emotion and state of mind a student is in before beginning a lesson, and that "a good disposition should be talk'd into them, before they be set upon any thing." Locke argues that if a teacher gets the student into a good frame of mind before teaching, then the student will learn and retain much more. Locke writes that, by getting the student into the right mood for learning, "a child will learn three times as much ... as he will with dou-ble the time and pains when he goes awkwardly or is dragg'd unwillingly to it." In the very next sentence of this same passage, Locke makes a comparison of his theory on education to the current practice of education in his day, and his discussion on that point covers the last principle, that of eliminating an envi-ronment of fear:

But no such thing is consider'd in the ordinary way
of education, nor can it well be. That rough discipline
of the rod is built upon other principles, has no attrac-
tion in it, regards not what humour children are in,
nor looks after favourable seasons of inclination. And
indeed it would be ridiculous, when compulsion and
blows have rais'd an aversion in the child to his task,
to expect he should freely of his own accord leave his
play, and with pleasure court the occasions of learn-
ing; whereas, were matters order'd right, learning any-
thing they should be taught might be made as much a
recreation to their play, as their play is to their learn-
ing (Locke).

CONCLUSION

Although the Locke's language is a bit archaic (he wrote his ideas over three hundred years ago), there is nevertheless a strong sense of modernity in his thoughts. His modern way of thinking is why he is arguably the broadest and strongest intellectual and philosophical bridge crossing from a seventeenth century system of authoritarian institutions over to the modern democratic systems of government and education that we use today. By serving as a bridge, Locke also significantly contributed to the establish-ment of the United States, by helping Jefferson build a framework founded on the concept of individual-ism. Locke would most likely be pleased were he to see how modern democracies function, and how today's public education has embraced his principles for creating independent critical thinkers who become responsible and intelligent citizens in control of their governments and other social institutions.

TERMS & CONCEPTS

Act/Belief Distinction: A legal concept that distin-guishes between the freedom to believe and the freedom to act. Freedom to believe is absolute, but the freedom to act based on belief is not. For example, this issue arose when the government prohibited polygamy. The U.S. Supreme Court made a sharp distinction between the freedom to believe and the freedom to act.

Blank Slate or Tabula Rasa: The concept that humans are born with minds that are like a "blank slate", wherein experience and contemplation fills in the blank slate. John Locke defined blank slate as a young mind not yet affected by experience.

Critical Thinking: The intellectually disciplined pro-cess of consciously analyzing and synthesizing information from observation, experience, reflec-tion, or reasoning, in order to form an opinion or take action. This system of thought is based on specific intellectual values such as fairness, accu-racy, consistency, relevance, evidence, and logical reasoning.

Divine Right: The doctrine that the right of a king to rule comes from God, and that kings are not answerable to the subjects of the kingdom but to God only. This doctrine originated in medieval Europe between the Church and secular rulers as to the origin of political power.

Epistemology: A branch of philosophy that is con-cerned with theories on knowledge. It is an analysis of the nature of knowledge as well as the limita-tions of knowledge. Epistemology tries to answer questions such as "What is knowledge?" and "How is knowledge acquired?"

Learner-Centered Education: A style and theory of teaching that puts the student at the center of the educational process. Leaner-Centered Education starts by examining and understanding the educational contexts from which a student comes. In learner-centered education, effective teaching is defined as teaching so as to make the student actively engaged and involved in the learning process.

Liberal Capitalism: An economic system wherein individuals and their rights to property and trade are promoted and protected, while government interference in the economic market is minimized.

Logical Fallacy: A mistake in the accepted and standard process of correct reasoning, or it may be an argument that uses bad reasoning. Fallacies were first pointed out and studied by Greek philosophers, but other philosophers such as John Locke, John Stuart Mill, and Jeremy Bentham also developed critical thinking theories that included pointing out logical fallacies.

Rationalism: A philosophical view that asserts reason is the primary source and test of knowledge. Rationalism is often placed in opposition to empiricism, the doctrine that all knowledge on matters of fact ultimately derives from sense experience. However, both philosophies are important for use in scientific inquiry and critical thinking, and John Locke seems to have espoused and used both types of inquiry.

Social Sciences: Scholarly or scientific disciplines that deal with the study of human society and of individual relationships in and to society. Examples of social sciences are sociology, psychology, anthropology, economics, political science, and history.

Sinclair Nicholas

BIBLIOGRAPHY

Esperanza, J. (2006). John Locke and the natural law: Yesterday and today: a critical analysis. *Excerpta et Dissertationibus in Philosophia;* 9-109. Retrieved May 30, 2009 from EBSCO Online Database Academic Search Complete.

Faulkner, R. (2008). Spreading progress: Jefferson's mix of science and liberty. *Good Society Journal;* 17: 26-32.

Retrieved June 1, 2009 from EBSCO Online Database Academic Search Complete.

Foley, R. (1999). Locke and the crisis of postmodern epistemology. *Midwest Studies in Philosophy;* 23, 1-20. Retrieved June 2, 2009 from EBSCO Online Database Academic Source Complete.

Gintis, H. (2006). Moral sense and material interests. *Social Research;* 73: 377-404. Retrieved June 3, 2009 from EBSCO Online Database Academic Search Complete.

Gregoriou, Z., & Papastephanou, M. (2013). The utopianism of John Locke's natural learning. *Ethics & Education, 8,* 18-30. Retrieved December 15, 2013, from EBSCO Online Database Education Research Complete.

Henson, K., (2003). Foundations for learner-centered education: A knowledge base. *Education;* 124: 5-16. Retrieved May 29, 2009 from EBSCO Online Database Academic Search Complete.

Huyler, J. (1997) Was Locke a liberal? *Independent Review;* 1: 523-543. Retrieved June 1, 2009 from EBSCO Online Database Academic Search Complete.

John Locke (1632-1704). (1999). *Fifty Major Economists;* 7-10. Retrieved June 1, 2009 from EBSCO Online Database Business Source Complete.

Locke, J. (1693). Some thoughts concerning education. *Modern History Sourcebook.* Retrieved May 28, 2009 from Fordham University.

McNulty, L. (2013). Lockean social epistemology. *Journal of Philosophy Of Education, 47,* 524-536. Retrieved December 15, 2013, from EBSCO Online Database Education Research Complete.

Platz, D., & Arellano, J. (2011). Time tested early childhood theories and practices. *Education, 132,* 54-63. Retrieved December 15, 2013, from EBSCO Online Database Education Research Complete.

Powers, T. (2007) The act/belief doctrine and the limits of Lockean religious liberty. *Perspectives on Political Science;* 36: 73-83. Retrieved May 28, 2009 from EBSCO Online Database Academic Search Complete.

Watson, B. (2006). Creed & culture in the American founding. *Intercollegiate Review;* 41: 32-39. Retrieved June 3, 2009 from EBSCO Online Database Academic Search Complete.

SUGGESTED READING

Bowden, G. (2008). Piety and property: Locke and the development of American protestantism. *Christian Scholar's Review;* 37, 273-287. Retrieved May 30, 2009 from EBSCO Online Database Academic Search Complete.

Carrig, J. (2001). Liberal impediments to liberal education: The assent to Locke. *Review of Politics;* 63, 41-76. Retrieved May 30, 2009 from EBSCO Online Database Academic Search Complete.

Crane, J. (2003). Locke's theory of classification. *British Journal for the History of Philosophy; 11*, 249-260. Retrieved June 2, 2009 from EBSCO Online Database Academic Source Complete.

Rudderman, R. and Godwin, K. (2000). Liberalism and parental control of education. *Review of Politics; 62*, 503-530. Retrieved May 30, 2009 from EBSCO Online Database Academic Search Complete.

MODERN EUROPEAN INFLUENCES ON AMERICAN EDUCATION

Beginning in the 17th century, as European powers colonized North America, they brought their ideas on education to the New World. After the colonial period, European ideas on education such as Herbartism (or New Education) began to find fertile soil in the United States, to be followed by the teachings of the truly transatlantic school of pedagogy called Progressive Education. In the 20th century, child-centered European views of education manifested in Montessori schools, as well as European-led theories of child cognitive development from Piaget and others, made lasting impacts on American teacher education and inspired movements such as unschooling and vocational education. For the past century, and continuing to the present, American and European pedagogues have engaged in an ongoing project of comparative educational research, strengthened by advances in technology, making today's educational influences between Europe and the United States truly bi-directional.

KEYWORDS: Cognitive Development; Comparative Education; International Education; Montessori Schools; New Education; Pedagogy; Progressive Education; Teacher Education; Unschooling; Vocational Education

OVERVIEW

During the colonial era, prominent American thinkers such as Cotton Mather, Benjamin Franklin and Thomas Jefferson carried on a lively, if at times contentious, exchange of ideas with leading thinkers in Europe. A theme that would continue throughout the 18th and 19th centuries was the American admiration for European culture on the one hand and their disdain for European social inequalities on the other. Americans like Jefferson put these inequalities down to anti-egalitarian proclivities within the European society, which he claimed were reinforced through the continent's education system.

While not following every European fashion, Americans sought to take the best ideas of the Old World and apply them in their circumstances in the New World. Beginning in the 19th century, Americans traveled to Europe to see European education firsthand:

After the end of the Napoleonic Wars, Americans were to be found increasingly traveling abroad, chiefly to Western Europe and particularly to Britain, France, and the German principalities. Benjamin Silliman, John Griscom, Calvin Stowe, Alexander Dallas Bache, William C. Woodbridge, and, of course, Horace Mann were among the first successful American students of international and comparative education (Fraser, 1968).

But to live in America, to promote its general welfare, one required a distinctly American education – even if that education retained some largely unspoken European influences. This national pride was evident everywhere, particularly after American independence. Thomas Jefferson put it well in a 1785 letter to an American correspondent living in Europe who sought his advice on the best European schools for Americans: "But why send an American youth to Europe for education? What are the objects of a useful American education?" (Wagoner, 1993)

American education began as a heavily modified form of the British system that was its colonial inheritance, but over time, as the nation grew in size and influence, ideas on education from mainland Europe also began to influence American intellectuals. After the Civil War, and for several generations, it became commonplace for American scholars to train for at least a year in German universities, where they absorbed current European ideas on topics including education. These leading German thinkers included Hegel (a great influence on John Dewey), Friedrich Froebel and Johann Herbart. Influential British thinkers on education included Herbert Spencer and his ideas about applied Social Darwinism.

Nonetheless, there never was an uncritical American acceptance of European ideas on education:

> *It should not be supposed, however, that Americans unanimously welcomed foreign ideas either imported by foreign commentators or brought back by returning American educators. William C. Woodbridge, an editor of one of America's first educational journals and an extensive traveler in Europe wryly noted that "we are aware that there is much sensitiveness in our country in regard to foreign improvements-and have received some hints of the danger of exciting it." Accordingly, some limitation must be placed on the efficacy, influence, and acceptance within America of "foreign" reports on its educational system (Fraser).*

EDUCATION COMES OF AGE

In the final decades of the 19th century, a movement called New Education took root in America as a reaction against entrenched methods of teaching history and other subjects. First developed in Germany by Johann Friedrich Herbart, supporters of New Education argued that students should be taught to think systematically and to ask questions, rather than memorize lists of facts. For example, supporters of New Education taught that the classroom syllabus should be organized around themes or units to get at common truths common across historical events. According to Herbart and the disciples of his New Education philosophy, education's grand purpose was delivering moral and ethical lessons.

American educator John Dewey (1859-1952) continued this thread in the early decades of the twentieth century with his emphasis on learning by doing. Dewey and other educators introduced a school of thought called Progressive Education, where importance was placed on tapping the life experience and cultural background of students in preparing and delivering lessons. They believed in the concept of learning by doing, and they stressed that students should be active, rather than passive, learners.

By the turn of the 20th century, Progressive Education had pervaded all aspects of society on both sides of the Atlantic, and pedagogic influences became largely bi-directional. "There is no doubt that the turn-of-the-century educational reform was an international phenomenon" (Biesta & Miedema, 1996).

Since that time there has been an increasingly fruitful dialogue between American and European educators, helped along in recent decades by the rise of a global communications network that includes email and the Internet. But one would do well to heed Foucault's remark that discussions about influence often tell one more about the individual making such connections than it does about the thinkers themselves.

This essay will focus on contributions to American education made by European thinkers who flourished in the 20th century. The thinkers discussed below contributed to the Zeitgeist, the spirit of the age, enriching the subject of education reform and helping to take pedagogy in new directions. The respective influences of European thinkers on American public education - direct or indirect - can be seen in the discussions and writings of their contemporaries, or sometimes even more clearly in retrospect.

ÉMILE DURKHEIM: WHAT THE STUDENT OWES SOCIETY

As a sociologist of education, the French sociologist Émile Durkheim (1858-1917) believed that education was important to the preservation of the social order because it helps individuals feel a part of something greater than themselves. This feeling, he said, is reinforced through learning about fellow countrymen who made the world a better place.

Durkheim has been criticized by educators in previous decades because of his belief that the role of education is to reinforce social roles. But his thinking that education should be tailored to the abilities and skills of individual students, therefore solidifying a division of labor in society, has been widely adopted, particularly in vocational education.

Durkheim's ideas also have some resonance in the context of today's American public schools, where some attribute relatively poor educational outcomes to a breakdown of order within the classroom. Given this assumption, Durkheim's views seem more relevant than ever. As two recent commentators on Durkheim's work note, "Today there is an increased concern for the teaching of basic morality in schools, as discipline continues to break down. The changes that are now occurring point, certainly indirectly, to the work of Durkeim" (Walford & Pickering, 1998).

JEAN PIAGET & LEV VYGOTSKY: STAGES OF STUDENT DEVELOPMENT

There is a large and growing body of literature in the field of educational psychology that seeks to apply the work of developmental psychologists to the interactions between teachers and students. In order to achieve a high level of professional success and satisfaction, experts generally agree that it is imperative for teachers to understand that the moral, intellectual, and emotional development of their students occurs in discrete stages.

Though they differ on important details, psychologists such as Jean Piaget (1896-1980) of Switzerland and Lev Vygotsky (1896-1934) of Russia stressed that students go through stages of cognitive, emotional, and moral development. Piaget, who began his career in biology, argued that what separates humans from non-human animals is what he called "abstract symbolic reasoning." He suggested, for example, that high school students should be encouraged to work in small groups and use alternative methods of learning because they have reached the third level of cognitive development he called Formal Operational Thinking. Students in elementary school, by contrast, are more literal thinkers who are less likely to think in abstract terms.

The work of European scholars such as Piaget and Vygotsky has played an increasingly prominent role in areas of education such as curriculum design and learning centers. Seymour Papert (1999), in an article for Time naming Piaget one of the most influential thinkers of the 20th century, summarized his pedagogical accomplishments:

Although not an educational reformer, he championed a way of thinking about children that provided the foundation for today's education-reform movements. It was a shift comparable to the displacement of stories of "noble savages" and "cannibals" by modern anthropology. One might say that Piaget was the first to take children's thinking seriously....

He has been revered by generations of teachers inspired by the belief that children are not empty vessels to be filled with knowledge (as traditional pedagogical theory had it) but active builders of knowledge - little scientists who are constantly creating and testing their own theories of the world (Papert).

MARIA MONTESSORI: CHILDREN AS NATURAL LEARNERS

A pioneer in early childhood education, the Italian educator Maria Montessori (1870-1952) believed that children were able to concentrate for long periods of time and preferred to have structured activities. She argued that children, as natural learners, could become responsible for their own surroundings and ultimately their own education. In such a situation children would be most likely to learn and thrive, albeit at their own pace.

Montessori said that there were "sensitive periods" during child development in which children were most easily taught educationally beneficial skills such as fine motor skills and pro-social behavior. Although her thinking on these "sensitive periods" was influenced by Dutch geneticist Hugo de Vries, it shares some affinity with the work of Piaget and Vygotsky. Unlike Piaget, however, her work focused primarily on education through the elementary school years.

Montessori opened her first Montessori school in Italy in 1907 and spread her educational philosophy across the globe. Her methods were popular in the United States in the early decades of the 20th century, but they were revived in 1960 when the American Montessori Society was founded. Now there are an estimated 5,000 Montessori schools in the United States alone, and their influence reaches into public and other private schools. A recent study in Science showed that when comparing students in Milwaukee who attended Montessori schools to those who attended public or other private schools, Montessori students more than held their own:

By the end of kindergarten, the Montessori children performed better on standardized tests of reading and math, engaged in more positive interaction on the playground, and showed more advanced social cognition and executive control. They also showed more concern for fairness and justice. At the end of elementary school, Montessori children wrote more creative essays with more complex sentence structures, selected more positive responses to social dilemmas, and reported feeling more of a sense of community at their school (Lillard & Else-Quest, 2006).

MARTIN BUBER: TEACHERS ARE MORE THAN CHEERLEADERS

Martin Buber's thinking on education stands as a counterweight to child-centered theories of learning, where the child's experience, and not his or her intellectual development, was most important. While the Austrian-Israeli Buber (1878-1965) was not one to praise authoritarian forms of teaching where students were emotionally (or even physically) abused, he was also wary of educational theories that left teachers without any authority in the classroom:

Buber, for his part, is unable to conceive of such a teacher in the role of an altogether uncommitted bystander. He cannot accept that aspect of the doctrine of the New Education which prohibits the teacher from making demands on the pupil, and limits the teacher's role to guiding the pupil to sources of information and to methods of approach only when the pupil is moved to request guidance. Buber believes that the teacher should adopt the role of critical guide and directing spirit. He argues that in no way can such an approach be regarded as coercive; although the teacher's role is founded on the principle of freedom, his function also expresses a point of view and an orientation (Cohen, 1979).

A.S. NEILL: IS SCHOOL A GOOD THING?

Writing between the two world wars, Buber's thinking on this subject echoed the work of A.S. Neill (1883-1973), a British educational theorist who founded the progressive Summerhill school in 1921. Neill understood Buber's work as a warning not to confuse freedom and permissiveness. For Neill, as for Buber, permissive education is the antithesis of an education in which a student is given a degree of freedom as he or she develops self-control. Without these limits, Buber argues, teachers abdicate their vital role as a "critical guide and directing spirit" for the young minds in their charge.

But Neill also took Buber's ideas in a new direction. Neill founded Summerhill School with the idea that student happiness required that they not be compelled to attend classes. Neill's 1960 book *Summerhill* helped spread his ideas to the United States, where they found a receptive audience within the Counterculture movement of the 1960s. Eventually Neill's ideas became the impetus for the "unschooling" movement, which holds that students learn best when they are taught outside of school by their parents. Many homeschooling families also subscribe to Neill's ideas.

JOHN DEWEY & TRANS-ATLANTIC EDUCATION REFORM

American John Dewey (1859-1952) is almost universally acknowledged as the intellectual father of what became known as the Progressive movement in education. Like Buber, however, Dewey expressed concern about the "one-sided emphasis ... upon pupils at the expense of subject matter" (Biesta & Miedema, 1996).

Dewey is a prototypical example of an intellectual in the late 19th and early 20th centuries, where the provenance of an idea - whether American or European or otherwise - was largely irrelevant. He was perhaps first in a line of American educators whose ideas, themselves influenced by European philosophy and psychology, were refined in an American context and then re-imported into Europe, where they exercised varying degrees of influence on leading pedagogues.

Although Dewey himself never visited Europe until he was nearly middle aged, the ideas of leading European intellectuals came down to him through his professors at university. The most prominent of these intellectuals, and the one that would have the most lasting influence on Dewey, was the German idealist philosopher Hegel. Though he later parted ways with Hegel on many issues, Dewey self-consciously embraced Hegel's belief in "the power exercised by the cultural environment in shaping ideas, beliefs, and intellectual attitudes of individuals" (Biesta & Miedema).

As an educational theorist, Dewey entered into a decades-long dialogue with the two prevailing educational orthodoxies of his age – Hegelianism and Herbartism, both European imports - and, in true Hegelian form, created a synthesis:

He criticized the Hegelians for their failure to connect the subject matter of the curriculum to the interests and activities of the child. Dewey argued that it is psychologically "impossible to call forth an activity without some interest" (Dewey 1972c).

But in the very same article Dewey also criticized the Herbartians, and other advocates of a strictly child-centered curriculum (most notably, representatives of the child study movement), for their failure to connect the interest and activities of the child to the subject matter of the curriculum. Here Dewey argued that "little can be accomplished by setting up interest as an end in itself" (Dewey). Dewey's idea that the ultimate problem of all education was "to co-ordinate the psychological and the social factors" (Dewey) (Biesta & Miedema).

Over the course of a life lived nearly to age 100, Dewey had the rare privilege for an academic of seeing some of his ideas on education come into practice. This happened not only in his native United States, but also in Russia and Turkey. The Russian example is perhaps most relevant to our discussion:

Since 1907, when Dewey's The School and Society was translated into Russian, his work had attracted a lot of attention, and a number of influential Russian educationalists such as Shatsky, his colleague Zelenko, Krupskaya, Lunacharsky, and Blonsky had been influenced by Dewey's ideas, especially, according to Passow, by his democratic model of the school and his ideas about the organization of the children's vital activities (Passow 1982; Rogatcheva 1993a). During the first two decennia, Dewey's views were brought into practice in the Moscow Settlement Program and in Shatsky's and Zelenko's summer colony, Bodraya Zhyzn (Rogatcheva; Dewey) (Biesta & Miedema).

Sometimes, though, it would seem that Dewey is given too much credit for influencing education in certain European countries. In Great Britain, for example, Dewey came under fire in recent decades by leading British politicians, including former Prime Minister John Major, and leading educational experts, including Anthony O'Hear, for his allegedly negative influence on the British educational system. This is curious, especially given a recent review by Brehony (1997) of discussions within British educational circles in the first decades of the 20th century, which shows that Dewey's influence was marginal, or at least unoriginal. "Much of what was identified with Dewey might equally have been derived from Froebel or Montessori or any other writer in the child-centred tradition."

Terms & Concepts

Cognitive Development: A term used to describe the progression in mental functioning as a child grows. Pioneering work on the process was done by the Swiss psychologist Jean Piaget and the Russian psychologist Lev Vygotsky in the first part of the 20th century.

Comparative Education: A branch of pedagogical studies in which educational systems and philosophies in different parts of the world are examined and compared.

International Education: A term used to describe education within a global context.

Montessori Schools: A series of schools set up to implement the pedagogical philosophy of Italian educator Maria Montessori.

New Education: A theory of education popularized by German Johann Herbart that taught that the classroom syllabus should be organized around themes or units to, for example, get at common truths common across historical events. For Herbart and the disciples of his New Education philosophy, education's grand purpose was delivering moral and ethical lessons.

Pedagogy: A term that refers broadly to the sweep of theories about educational beliefs and practices.

Progressive Education: A school of pedagogy where importance was placed on tapping the life experience and cultural background of students in preparing and delivering lessons.

Teacher Education: A term used to encompass the strategies, theories and philosophies taught to teachers both before and during their teaching career.

Unschooling: A philosophy of education that holds that children are best educated outside of a formal school setting.

Vocational Education: A form of high school education that emphasizes learning a trade so that a student is prepared to immediately enter the job market upon graduation.

Matt Donnelly

BIBLIOGRAPHY

Biesta, G. J. J., & Miedema, S. (1996). Dewey in Europe: A case study on the international dimensions of the turn-of-the-century educational reform. *American Journal of Education, 105*, 1-26.

Brehony, K.J. (1997). An 'undeniable' and 'disastrous' influence? Dewey and English education (1895-1939). *Oxford Review of Education, 23*, 427-445.

Cohen, A. (1979). Martin Buber and changes in modern education. *Oxford Review of Education, 5*, 81-103.

Donahoe, M., Cichucki, P., Coad-Bernard, S., Coe, B., & Scholtz, B. (2013). Best practices in Montessori secondary programs. *Montessori Life, 25*, 16-23. Retrieved December 15, 2013, from EBSCO Online Database Education Research Complete.

Fraser, S.E. (1968). Some foreign views of American education: The nineteenth century background. *Comparative Education Review, 12*, 300-309.

Lillard, A., and E. Else-Quest (2006). Evaluating Montessori education. *Science 313*, (5795), 1893-1894.

Papert, S. (1999, March 29). Jean Piaget. The Time 100: Most important people of the century. *Time.* Retrieved November 16, 2007 from: http://www.time.com

Rolstad, K., & Kesson, K. (2013). Unschooling, then and now. *Journal of Unschooling & Alternative Learning, 7*, 28-71. Retrieved December 15, 2013, from EBSCO Online Database Education Research Complete.

Veloso, L., & Estevinha, S. (2013). Differentiation versus homogenisation of education systems in Europe: Political aims and welfare regimes. *International Journal of Educational Research, 62187-198.* Retrieved December 15, 2013, from EBSCO Online Database Education Research Complete.

Wagoner, J.L, Jr. (1993). *"That knowledge most useful to us:" Thomas Jefferson's concept of "utility" in the education of republican citizens.* Paper presented at the Conference on Thomas Jefferson and the Education of a Citizen in the American Republic (Washington, DC, May 13-15, 1993). (ERIC Document Reproduction Service No. ED375052). Retrieved November 16, 2007 from EBSCO Online Education Research Database.

Walford, G., & Pickering, W.S.F. (1998). *Durkheim and modern education.* London: Routledge.

SUGGESTED READING

Berube, M.R. (1993). *American school reform: Progressive, equity and excellence movements, 1883-1993.* Westport, CT: Praeger.

DeVries, R. (n.d.). *Vygotsky, Piaget, and education: A reciprocal assimilation of theories and educational practices.* Cedar Falls, IA: Regents' Center for Early Developmental Education, University of Northern Iowa. Retrieved November 16, 2007, from the University of Northern Iowa http://www.uni.edu

McMurtrie, B. (2006). Europe's education chief seeks transatlantic cooperation. *Chronicle of Higher Education, 52,* A39-A39. Retrieved November 18, 2007 from EBSCO Online Database Academic Search Premier.

Silver, H. (1983). *Education as history: Interpreting nineteenth-and twentieth-century education.* London: Metheun.

CHAUTAUQUA MOVEMENT

The article presents an overview of the Chautauqua Movement which provided one of the foundations for adult education as we know it today. The movement began in 1874 with a summer assembly to train Sunday-school teachers at Chautauqua Lake, NY. The success of the first summer program indicated a greater demand for the Chautauqua's type of instruction. The article describes lessons from the Chautauqua movement that may be relevant for current adult and continuing education programs.

KEYWORDS: Adult Education; Book Club; Chautauqua Movement; Chautauqua Institution; Chautauqua Literary & Scientific Circle; Continuing Education Unit; Correspondence Course; Modern Chautauqua; University Extension Education

THE ROOTS OF ADULT EDUCATION

The Chautauqua movement began in 1874 with a summer assembly to train Sunday-school teachers at Chautauqua Lake, NY. Founded on the premise that adults of either sex are capable of learning, that intellectual opportunities should comprise of more than just formal education, and that adult education should examine current social issues, the movement symbolizes "one of the first attempts to deliver a national culture, as it brought its programs to rural and urban, east and west, north" and south areas of the U.S. The Chautauqua Literary and Scientific Circle was responsible for the first book club and correspondence course (Johnson, 2001). As radio and motion pictures began to provide alternative means for entertainment and teaching and were offered throughout the year, Chautauqua programs became less desirable. The last Chautauqua associated with the original concept was held in 1931. Renewed interest in Chautauqua-type events came about in the 1970s and continues throughout the U.S. today. The Chautauqua Institute, on the original N.Y. site, offers programming each summer for participants to benefit from the enjoyments of a scientifically, politically, and culturally rewarding summer break.

The Chautauqua Movement provided the foundation for "what we know today as adult education. Institutions such as libraries, museums, universities, arts programs, and university extension programs" have resulted from the movement. Many other aspects of 20th century American life, "such as theater, art and music appreciation were greatly influenced by the Chautauqua Movement" (Maxwell, 2000).

Chautauqua began when John Vincent, a Methodist minister, and Lewis Miller, a successful businessman, organized a summer training gathering for Sunday-school teachers at Chautauqua Lake, NY. The Chautauqua Sunday School Assembly, as it was called, took place during a time when religious camps and revival meetings were common. The founders, desiring their program to be different from these other gatherings, united daily study with healthful recreation at the Chautauqua site (where the Chautauqua Institution remains today).

The success of the first summer program in 1874 indicated a greater demand for the Chautauqua's type of instruction. The assembly underwent a transformation over the next several years. In 1876, the program was lengthened from two weeks to eight weeks and all denominations were invited to participate. Miller and Vincent recognized that the demand for education was not limited to Sunday school teachers and decided to extend its reach beyond the Chautauqua site (Howell & McGinn, 2006). Vincent's premise was that

- Mature men and women are able to learn;
- Educational opportunities should extend beyond formal schooling;
- Life is education;
- Adult education should examine current social issues (Scott, 1999, as cited in Howell & McGinn).

In 1878, the institution began to change to meet the needs of participants in every walk of life. The Chautauqua Literary and Scientific Circle (CLSC) was formed, beginning as a book club and correspondence course. The creation of the CLSC was the first major step in secularizing Chautauqua, moving the focus from providing religious instruction to teachers to providing a broader education to all who wanted (Howell & McGinn).

CREATING "CHAUTAUQUAS"

The creation of independent Chautauquas (also called "daughter" Chautauquas and later "tent" or "circuit" Chautauquas) "represents one of the first attempts to deliver a truly national culture, linking rural and urban, east and west, north and south" throughout the U.S. As a spin-off from the "mother"

Chautuaqua in NY, but without official affiliation, "towns organized local committees which took on the responsibilities for arranging the Chautauqua, from engaging talent to selling tickets and doing whatever else was necessary" (Johnson, 2001). A program typically extends for five to seven days and usually takes place in the town's largest auditorium or in a large tent. According to Johnson, "Morning sessions were usually devoted to Bible study. The remainder of the program consisted of lecturers, musical acts, debates, dramatic readers, bird callers, bell ringers, and–in the later years–radio and motion picture presentations" (Johnson).

Johnson continues to explain that early Chautauqua observers were fatigued, lonely men and women leading hard lives in rural America. For husbands and wives, the Chautauqua provided a great relief from their monotonous existence. The Chautauqua circuit not only ended isolation and built a culture for the country, but it also brought other enhancements to rural towns and small cities. The first benefit concerned education. "The short length of the assemblies prevented any kind of intensive education, but Chautauqua events stimulated its audiences to think. Chautauqua circuit organizers also cited an increase in community spirit and togetherness as another benefit. Most of the year, communities were divided into religious, political, and social groups, but at a Chautauqua these divisions were forgotten" since signatures of people from all creeds were needed to bring a Chautauqua to their community (Johnson).

INSTRUCTION AS ENTERTAINMENT

In the years after World War I, Chautauquas became increasingly focused on entertainment. The early 1920s brought radio and motion pictures as a competitive way of introducing a national culture to sections of the country that were extremely secluded. Most Chautauqua organizers recognized "that radio could more efficiently perform the same task as Chautauqua, namely the entertainment and instruction of millions simultaneously. Not only did radio provide a more convenient way for performers to reach an audience, audiences also found it more convenient to stay in the comfort of their homes to be entertained, safe from mosquitoes, hard benches, and rain. Radio audiences could also be part of events that Chautauqua could never bring them, events as diverse as presidential elections, inaugurals, and prize fights. Motion pictures, like radio programs, were increasingly available during the 1920s. Motion pictures shared with radio the advantage of convenience for both performers and audience" (Johnson).

Johnson ends by explaining that different sources of entertainment and education offered throughout the year make Chautauqua programs become slightly obsolete and "old-fashioned." The last Chautauqua associated with the original concept was held in 1931.

CONTINUING EDUCATION

Howell and McGinn explain that the Chautauqua movement pioneered the idea of extending learning opportunities to adults who had intellectual interest but could not attend formal universities, or those who wanted to continue learning beyond their formal schooling. Adult education programs continue to fulfill this need today. They suggest that adult educators can learn from Chautauqua's lessons, building future success on a foundation of tried-and-true principles. They discuss lessons for administrators of adult education programs in three areas:

- Financial management;
- Handling rewards;
- Responding to competition.

FINANCIAL MANAGEMENT

Since most adult educators also have administrative and financial responsibilities in addition to providing an educational program, it is important for them to have financial skills. One founder of Chautauqua admitted he did not have a talent for raising money, but the other founder not only brought his own money but also business know-how to ensure the financial and operational success of the original Chautauqua.

Initially, the founders acted as collection agents for Chautauqua assemblies, however they soon dispensed with collections in favor of a gate fee for all participants. While this decision solved an income concern, it also caused an expense since they had to build a fence around the property. The Chautauqua founders did not expect to become rich from their efforts and expended any profits upon facility improvements or program expansion.

Adult educators seem to share with their Chautauqua fathers a passion for learning and a willingness to sacrifice their own financial interests. Most adult education programs are nonprofit and are considered successful if the programs break even and cover costs. In these cases, excess financial reserves in one class may be used to subsidize a lower-enrolling but important course elsewhere.

Howell and McGinn suggest that the Chautauqua lesson for today's adult educators is that sound financial management is a necessity. If the skill set is not in either the responsible leader or among the leadership team it is only a matter of time until the program will meet its demise. Enough money allows adult education programs to perpetuate and in some cases leverage themselves so that they can expand to meet additional learner needs.

HANDLING REWARDS

Adult education administrators know about the importance of rewards in the learning experience of program participants. Some rewards are strictly defined by professional associations such as Continuing Education Units (CEUs), diplomas, and records of registration. Other administrators use small rewards such as cloth patches, T-shirts, lapel pins, trophies, or paper completion certificates (Howell & McGinn).

Chautauqua was "no different. Its reward system acknowledged participation, completion, and competency in an atmosphere of pomp and ceremony" (Howell & McGinn). The founders also realized that it was important that their rewards not be confused with the certificates and degrees associated with traditional institutions of higher learning. Although the Chautauqua Scientific Learning Circle (CSLC) diploma was radiant with thirty-one seals, it would not stand for much at Heidelberg, Oxford, or Harvard. The intent of Chautauqua's use of awards, as it is now in adult education, was to encourage, motivate, and sustain student learning.

This Chautauqua lesson, suggest Howell and McGinn, is that "adult educators should not overlook the importance of appropriate rewards and ceremony for their learners who reach certain milestones. [Administrators might] also benefit by analyzing their current reward system to see what additional rewards could help overcome learning obstacles" for some of their students.

RESPONDING TO COMPETITION

It is compliment to an adult education program when other institutions imitate the program, or when the associated university mainstreams the program. One of the most obvious Chautauquan imitations occurred when an entrepreneur combined the Chautauqua idea with the lyceum, an older American institution and came up with the traveling Chautauqua tent show. Even though the original Chautauqua founders did not sponsor these traveling tent shows, they were flattered by their popularity and the publicity that the use of their name had given the popular educational movement (Howell & McGinn).

Howell and McGinn describe a significant event associated with competition that resulted in the most important Chautauqua contribution to modern adult education. A Chautauqua-like imitation occurred just across the lake and was sponsored by the Baptist Church. While one of the Methodist founders was displeased that the rival institution was started across the lake, in plain view of the original, he had no objection to its existence, only to its location.

The founder's response to this competition was to hire one of the competitor's most promising educational luminaries, William Rainey Harper. After nearly ten years as an integral part of Chautauqua, Harper became president of the Rockefeller-financed and Baptist-affiliated University of Chicago. Harper's return to the Baptist-sponsored University of Chicago-an influential university that became a model for many other universities at the time-brought about the integration and legitimization of adult education programs as an official part of a traditional university.

This Chautauqua lesson, according to Howell and McGinn, is to "plan on successful adult education programs being imitated or taken over by the host university. The better the adult education program, the sooner it is adopted by others and the more widespread will be its effect."

MODERN CHAUTAUQUA

The 100th Anniversary celebration of the Chautauqua Movement in 1974 brought renewed interest in the Chautauqua Movement. Humanities Chautauquas, often referred to as the modern Chautauqua, began to develop throughout the U.S. However, "instead of presenting contemporary speakers, as did the historic circuit Chautauquas, these events are portrayals of historic persons in a first person setting. There are usually three to six scholars who portray characters linked to a central theme (Maxwell). Most Humanities Chautauquas are produced and sponsored by state humanities councils (Maxwell).

TYPES OF MODERN CHAUTAUQUA

For example, the Great Plains Chautauqua, originated by the Arts and Humanities Council of North Dakota in 1976, used a format that became a model for many other humanities councils. At this Chautauqua, "a scholar assumes the dress and character of a historic figure and delivers a monologue on stage in a large tent" (Maxwell). The scholar then answers questions from the audience from the character's perspective. In the final part of the event, the scholar puts aside the character and answers audience questions from a scholarly perspective (Maxwell). The event is usually begun with local musical entertainment.

History Alive, also known as School Chautauqua, is supported by grants from the National Endowment for the Humanities (NEH). "Children in many states have benefited from having "people from history" come into their schools to speak. Bringing a real person into contact with students enables them to have a better understanding of history and the people who shaped it."

Student Chautauquas, also known as "Junior Chautauquas," have become "a part of the curriculum of many schools across the nation in the past few years" (Maxwell). The children, on their own, study and research an individual from history and prepare a presentation to their peers by "becoming" the chosen character and producing a monologue to act out. Several of the humanities councils' Chautauquas sponsor auditions for the best of the Chautauqua students to broadcast at the start of their Chautauqua activities.

Senior Chautauqua "takes form in such programs as Elder hostel. The Southern Baptist Chautauqua, for example, provides bible study, crafts, and other special interest programs such as a golf tournament" (Maxwell).

Cyber Chautauquas, found on the Internet, provide access to online CEU credits for many professionals. Also online, browsers can download music, videos, movies, and skits at "virtual" Chautauquas.

Many current Chautauquan enthusiasts are unaware of the plethora of local and state events and only consider modern Chautauqua to be about the programs offered at the Chautauqua Institution. At the original Cautauqua site, several secular programs are offered each summer for Chautauquans to enjoy a scientifically, politically, and culturally stimulating vacation. Many of the visitors who return to Chautauqua year after year describe it as a renewal experience rather than a vacation. Each season, the Institution prepares a new program and promotes it through its website (http://www.ciweb.org/).

TERMS & CONCEPTS

Adult Education: This term defines the process of teaching adults in their work environment by allowing them to continue their education through outside colleges, universities, and secondary schools.

Book Club: This term refers to a group of people who meet to discuss a book or books that they have all chosen to read.

Chautauqua Movement: This describes the adult education movement in the United States that spread throughout rural America from the late 19th century until 1931; the movement brought entertainment and culture to communities with speakers, musicians, and entertainers.

Chautauqua Institution: Founded in 1874, the Chautauqua Institution is an education program for adults in Chautauqua, NY, on the site where the Chautauqua Movement began. The movement has continued, as a non-profit organization, for each summer since 1874, slowly broadening the length of each season and offering teachings that surround arts, education, religion and recreation.

Chautauqua Literary and Scientific Circle: This was begun as the first "book club" and "correspondence school" and was a major step in forming continuing education for adults in U.S. history.

Continuing Education Unit (CEU): This term refers to a unit of calculation that continuing education programs use to ensure that the individual maintains a professional license. CEO records offer proof of completion of requirements that were ordered by governmental licensing boards or certification groups.

Correspondence Course: This term refers to a course in print format offered by mail by an accrediting institution or agency; the modern form is distance learning available through Internet access.

Modern Chautauqua: This term refers to programs that have been organized in Chautauqua style since 1974, the 100th anniversary of the original movement.

University Extension Education: This term refers to courses offered at off-campus locations.

Sally A. Coppus

BIBLIOGRAPHY

Ferguson, N., & Burch, J. (2011). Religious camps: Common roots and new sprouts. *Camping Magazine, 84,* 48-53. Retrieved December 15, 2013, from EBSCO Online Database Education Research Complete.

Howell, S. & McGinn, A. (2006). The Chautauqua movement and its influence on adult education theory and practice. Retrieved December 10, 2007 from ERIC.

Imel, S. (2012). Civic engagement in the United States: Roots and branches. *New Directions for Adult & Continuing Education.* Retrieved December 15, 2013, from EBSCO Online Database Education Research Complete.

Johnson, R. (2001). Dancing mothers: The Chautauqua movement in twentieth-century American popular culture. *American Studies International 39,* 53. Retrieved December 10, 2007 from EBSCO online database, Academic Search Premier.

Maxwell, J. (2000). What is Chautauqua? In *The complete Chautauquan: A Guide to What 'Chautauqua' Means in America.* Retrieved December 10, 2007 from website http://members.aol.com

Scott, J., (2005). The Chautauqua vision of liberal education. *History of Education 34,* 41-59. Retrieved December 10, 2007 from EBSCO online database, Education Research Complete.

Sugarman, R. R. (2014). Music in the Chautauqua movement: from 1874 to the 1930s. Choice: Current Reviews For Academic Libraries, 51, 840. Retrieved December 15, 2013, from EBSCO Online Database Education Research Complete.

SUGGESTED READING

Bendiksen, M. (2007). The endless summers of Chautauqua. Reprinted from *New York Archives.* Retrieved December 10, 2007 from Chautauqua Institution, www.ciweb.org

Chatauqua Institution Website. (2008). Accessed December 10, 2007 http://www.ciweb.org

Ganiere, C., Howell. S., & Osguthorpe, R. (2007). Like produces like: John Heyl Vincent and his 19th century of character education [Electronic version]. *Journal of College & Character 8* . Retrieved December 10, 2007 from http://www.collegevalues.org

Maxwell, J. (2005). *The complete Chautauquan: A Chautauqua Collection.* Retrieved December 10, 2007 from website http://members.aol.com

EDUCATION OF WOMEN IN THE U.S.

Through the colonial years in America, the majority of women were illiterate and formal schooling for them was nonexistent. The first schools for girls were founded in the early 1800s. Many of the early women's academies became the first women's colleges or normal schools for teachers. The second half of the twentieth century brought new opportunities for young women as the baby boom generation flooded higher educational institutions. Fueled by the women's movement of the late 1960s, and backed by legislation, women realized historic educational and economic equity in the late twentieth century. Equity issues of the twenty-first century center on encouraging young women to take full advantage of opportunities, and social scientists continue to study gender differences.

KEYWORDS: Academies/Seminaries; Baby Boom; Beecher, Catherine; Civil Rights Act of 1964; Curricular Differentiation; Equal Educational Opportunities; Glass Ceiling; Normal schools; Title IX; Sanger, Margaret; Willard, Emma; Women's Educational Equity Act (WEEA)

OVERVIEW

Although women have traditionally not had the same opportunities for education and employment as men, it is too simplistic to paint them as victims of history. There is a rich legacy of women's education in the United States and it is at once a story of struggle and achievement. From the earliest years of the Republic, many promising opportunities arose for women. The majority of school teachers in America were women, and academies and women's colleges came to the fore through the nineteenth century. The women's rights movement, begun in the same century, began to raise awareness of the status of women and won for them the right to vote.

For decades, women were restricted from the getting the education required for entry into the professions, and in teaching, their pay differed significantly. In Maine, for example, in the 1840s, male teachers earned $15.40 a month, while women earned $4.80. The pattern was much the same in Ohio, where men received $15.42 to women's $8.73 (Matthews, 1976).

The colonial elite was interested in education for men to meet its needs for the "higher professions" of law, medicine, or religion, and their sons filled the elite eastern schools, but "by the time of the Revolutionary War, people were less homogeneous, and there was a commonly held belief that the democratic representative government would fail unless the state book a real responsibility in educating the children of all people" (Cheek, 2004). The Republic demanded a public education for social, economic, democratic, and national reasons.

From the signing of the Declaration of Independence and Constitution in the late eighteenth century, through most of the nineteenth century, the rights of citizens were never intended for women. Most public schools that were established were intended for boys and only a handful of colleges, public or private, were coeducational even by 1900 (Harwarth, Maline, & DeBra, n.d.). The first public high school opened in Boston in 1821 for boys only; a high school for girls did not open until 1857.

CHANGES IN THE NINETEENTH CENTURY

Early nineteenth-century lives were short, girls married young, and the time allotted for formal education in an agrarian society where families were big was very limited for both sexes. A high school education came to mean two years of post-elementary education for those between the ages of twelve and sixteen. As the nineteenth century progressed, private academies were joined by "common schools" and the public education propagated by education reformer Horace Mann spread. Female academies and seminaries opened, initially in private homes, between 1800 to 1875. "The seminaries in general... devoted themselves to providing religious training, home making skills and a degree of intellectual development for women" (Matthews).

Although they might be criticized for their limited vision of educating women, many of the early seminaries became women's colleges and the normal schools (colleges for teachers) that provided a foundation of states' higher education systems. By 1888, 63 percent of American teachers were women (Matthews). Emma Willard's seminary in Troy, New York, founded in 1822, emphasized preparing girls to become teachers, and her school became a model for teacher's programs ("Emma Hart Willard, 1787-1870," n.d.).

The first women's rights movement was inaugurated in 1848 with the primary objective of suffrage—obtaining the right of women to vote—which did not happen until 1920. Although it had little impact on education, it was symptomatic of cultural change at work and paralleled the impact of industrialization. By the turn of the twentieth century, the concept of the modern high school was forged, and girls were in the majority of the high school population, even though the total number of those enrolled in high school was very low (with only around 8 percent of the population enrolled) and fewer graduating. By the turn of the century, during the 1899–1900 school year, for example, a disproportionate number of the graduates were women vs. men. As the twentieth century progressed, the proportion was less marked and has, since World War II, approximately paralleled the percentage of the general population (National Center for Education Statistics, 2006).

Between 1840 and 1890, the public high school had emerged from the shadow of the private academy. While enrollments were still small by today's standards, by the 1870s and 1880s the number of public secondary schools was expanding (Mirel, 2006).

The history of education is inextricably tied to economic history. The decision to pursue education voluntarily involves economic considerations, and the ability for a society to provide education to its young people is an economic one as well. The opportunities for higher education, and even mandatory high school education, is a twentieth-century concept, and a post–World War II one at that.

THE EARLY TWENTIETH CENTURY

Through the turn of the century into the Depression era, "compulsory schooling requirements and child labor laws were typically weak or poorly enforced, … whether children attended school or worked for

wages was a decision that had to be made by individual families" (Tolnay & Bailey, 2006). Industrialization in the late nineteenth century drew massive immigration from Europe, and migration of blacks from the South to the urban North, called the Great Migration, changed literacy and educational demands from the nineteenth into the twentieth century. Young immigrant women filled the mills and factories. The inventions of electrical machinery, typewriters, sewing machines, etc. created a demand for new kinds of skills, and women were needed to participate in the workforce.

Tolnay and Bailey studied educational persistence of immigrant populations in 1920. They found that the economic pressures on families were so great "that immigrant children in nearly every group and in every city throughout the United States chose work when it was available over extended schooling prior to the 1930s. Blacks, conversely, appear to have placed a high value on education and sent their children to school at unusually high rates …" Their study also revealed that female blacks were disproportionately represented in the school population in 1920, possibly due to the lack of employment opportunities for them.

Educators and industrialists began to advocate for integrating training into the curriculum to suit job demands. In 1918, the National Education Association Curriculum and the Commission on the Reorganization of Secondary Education called for differentiated high school programs with tracks, defined as academic (college preparatory), vocational, commercial (secretarial), and general. Women flocked into the commercial curriculums as new opportunities for secretary or office worker were coming available (Mirel, 2006).

In 1930 an announcement appeared in *American School and University* stating, "For the first time in the history of the country, the number of boys and girls of high-school age who are in attendance upon our secondary schools has passed the 50-percent mark" ("Celebrating 70 years," p. 10). As the world sank into Depression during the 1930s and there were fewer jobs, particularly for young people, many turned to schooling. Attendance grew rapidly through the decade, until the beginning of United States participation in World War II, when more than seven million students aged 14 to 17 were in school (Mirel).

WORLD WAR II & BEYOND

By the end of 1941, the United States was embroiled in war. Young men went off to fight as mothers and daughters took their jobs in the factories and mills to keep the economy going and to fuel the war effort. Although most women deferred to the men when they returned and left their wartime jobs, what they did subsequently with their lives was not so predictable. Linda Eisenmann, in her 2002 study of postwar female citizens, found studies from the early 1950s that argued that women continued to constitute an important part of America's workforce. She also points to a national embarrassment during the Cold War when American women compared unfavorably to Soviet women who were very well represented in their ranks of scientists, engineers, and physicians that defies the image of 1950s housebound women (Eisenmann, 2002).

Eisenmann's thesis in "Educating the Female Citizen in a Post-War World: Competing Ideologies for American Women, 1945–1965" (2002) is that although it is generally thought that women followed the advice of social and political leaders and abandoned college and labor after the war, the numbers of women who stayed in the workforce and continued with their education grew steadily after the war. "By 1957, college had attracted one in every five U.S. women between ages 18–21" (Eisenmann).

The idealization of domestic life in the 1950s belied the festering social unrest that would soon reveal itself. Eisenmann believes that it was the tension of expectations versus the reality of the force of women in education and labor force that provoked the women's movement of the late 1960s. "Post-war women were caught between competing patriotic, economic, cultural, and psychological ideologies that sometimes recognized but never resolved the contradictions facing them as female citizens."

The subsequent decades put affordable higher education within reach of all who were capable, and gave rise to the women's movement that demanded new freedoms. The nation anticipated the major population influx in colleges in the 1960s and 1970s, and rushed to meet the expectation that higher education would be there for the huge population bubble of students who moved through the system. Between 1960 and 1970, college enrollment doubled, and by 1980 female enrollment exceed that of males (NCES).

The women's movement of the late 1960s into the 1970s helped force the doors open for major equity gains for women. The Civil Rights Act of 1965 had mandated equity for the sexes, and the amendments to it in the early 1970s, including Title IX, applied the law to education and specifically expanded the rights of women to participate in intercollegiate athletics. The Women's Equal Education Act legislated funds that supported efforts to achieve equity.

During this period, feminists and social scientists also began to study gender differences in earnest. A 1975 report on male-female achievement by the National Assessment of Educational Progress (NAEP) indicated that, at age nine, males and females perform at about the same level in all subjects but, "by age 13, girls have begun a decline in achievement which continues downward through age 17 and into adulthood" (Bornstein, 1979). Bornstein went on to point out how essential education is to women, particularly as so many end up finding themselves alone and self-supporting. The article, typical of its time period, pointed out how critical education is to every woman's economic survival.

Equity issues are not necessarily resolved today, and writers and social scientists continue to analyze opportunities for women and their place in society. Although women now outnumber men in colleges and most graduate programs, there is a continued concern about why they continue to lag behind in entering the sciences, engineering, and computer science. It is thought that this issue is not helped when an esteemed academic such as Harvard president Larry Summers commented that women lack the genetic gifts to achieve in the sciences (Pollitt, 2005). Summers later apologized, but not until after many women cried foul and he was loudly accused of sexism.

COLONIAL TIMES & THE EARLY REPUBLIC

Colonial women led hard lives. They married as teenagers and bore many children. There was little time for learning. It is estimated that 60 percent of Puritan women could not sign their names, while 11 percent of men were illiterate.

In 1667, the Farmington, Connecticut, town council opened a school for children to learn to read and write English. At the next town meeting, they rewrote their provision to state that only boys will attend the school. It was not until the end of the 1790s that girls went to town schools, and only at times when the school was not used for educating boys, and it was not until the early 1800s that they were attending year-round (Matthews).

THE REPUBLIC: 1820 TO 1870

Benjamin Rush, a signer of the Declaration of Independence and founder of Dickinson College, believed that women needed to have a broad utilitarian education because they had to serve as educators of their children, particularly their sons. He did believe, however, that women should learn English, bookkeeping, geography, and natural philosophy and de-emphasized the arts and French so as "to embellish the homes and societies of their husbands" (Matthews).

EMMA HART WILLARD

At the same time, new currents were at work in the country that offered new opportunities for women. Educational groundbreaker Emma Hart Willard (1787–1870) was about to open her female seminary in Troy, New York. Willard had opened the Middle Female Seminary in her home in 1814, from which she demonstrated the ability of her students to "master classical and scientific subjects, areas of study which were at the time largely considered appropriate only for young men" ("Emma Hart Willard").

Willard achieved international success and was invited by Governor DeWitt Clinton to start a school in New York. She opened the short-lived Waterford Academy in Waterford, New York, but then moved to Troy, where she opened a girl's preparatory school in 1822 that survives to this day as the Emma Willard School. Women's public high schools in Boston and New York opened five years after Willard opened her school, and Mary Lyon's Mount Holyoke Seminary in Massachusetts opened sixteen years later.

Female academies and seminaries had their heyday from 1800 to 1875; there were nearly 6,000 of them that enrolled 250,000 women by 1850 (Stevenson, 1995). They provided "religious training, home-making skills, and a degree of intellectual development for women" (Matthews). Catherine Beecher, who founded the Hartford Female Seminary in Connecticut, was one of the most renowned of seminary teachers. Attendees ranged in age from twelve to sixteen and studied a wide variety of subjects. The schools were criticized by some as frivolous, and completion rates were low, but they did produce some

teachers and were precursors of the normal schools that sprang up at the end of the century to educate teachers (Matthews).

THE WOMEN'S LIBERATION MOVEMENT

The sheer numbers of women moving through post–World War II society forced social and educational equality for young women. Likewise, postwar prosperity and the expansion of the middle class also allowed young people the opportunity and freedom to explore and pursue career alternatives and even extend the time before they would have to earn a living. Other factors came into play that also allowed women the freedom to pursue new directions on a par with men. One was the availability of the birth control pill in the late 1950s, that for the first time in history allowed a woman to be in control of her reproductive capabilities. Secondly, women also benefited from the civil rights and resultant women's liberation movement of the late 1960s, which secured for them the freedoms, mandated by legislation and precedents, to seek the education and careers of their choosing and capabilities.

Margaret Sanger was an angry young woman who had watched her mother suffer from the effects of poverty and the burden of mothering eleven children. She founded Planned Parenthood to keep other women from experiencing the same fate. Sanger, with the financial backing of Katherine McCormick, contracted with physician Gregory Pinks' laboratory to develop the first oral contraceptive. "The pill" was approved by the FDA in 1957. With control of their fertility, women could concentrate on other aspects of their lives, and "by 1990, 80 percent of all American women born since 1945 had tried [the pill]" (Leitzell, 2007).

The feminist movement of the late 1960s brought issues of gender inequity to the fore. Betty Freidan's book *The Feminine Mystique*, published in 1963, helped inaugurate the movement and gave the likes of Gloria Steinem, Bella Abzug, and legions of others the impetus to push for women's rights. The women were vocal and had to share the stage along with those demanding civil rights for blacks and others protesting the Vietnam War, but managed to help open the flood gates for young women of the 1970s and beyond to take advantage of new and potentially equal educational and employment opportunities.

CURRENT ISSUES IN WOMEN'S EDUCATION

In 1979, Rita Bornstein called the history of women in America "a sorry record of deprivation and oppression, guised in protection" (Bornstein). She points out that as late as 1945, most medical schools had quotas for women that were set around 5 percent, and although Oberlin was the first college to admit women along with men, the female students had to wash the men's clothes, clean their rooms, and serve them meals. Bornstein observed that, "Those women were not being prepared for careers, but to be more intelligent wives and mothers."

Few twenty-first-century feminists would take as cynical a tone as Bornstein. The lot of most American women today has of course improved, and those who partake of advanced education expect to enjoy equal employment, or at least equal economic opportunity. A study by Dr. Laura Perna of the University of Maryland shows that women reap more benefits from education than their male counterparts. Although men with college degrees average incomes comparable to men who have no postsecondary education, women who attain an associates, bachelor's, or advanced degree "average incomes that are 32, 45, and 81 percentage points higher than women with no secondary education" (Troumpoucis, 2004).

It has been pointed out that women have entered law and medicine because they are the most conspicuous routes into high paying, prestigious careers. Society, however, still struggles with gender equity in other fields. Teaching and nursing, for example, are still predominately female professions. Likewise, attracting women into science fields, computer science, and engineering continues to prove particularly challenging.

Sullivan (2007) quotes a National Science Foundation study that showed that at 16 percent, the number of college women majoring in engineering was down 20 percent from a decade earlier. This was despite the fact that high school girls take as many science courses as boys.

Sullivan cites research by Donna Ginther and Shulami Kahn, who found that when male scientists marry, they increase their chances of landing a tenure-track position, but when women do the same, their chances decrease. Further, having a child under the age of five lowers the probability further for women scientists by 8 percent (Sullivan). Sullivan also reports on efforts to recruit young people into engineering with a multimedia campaign that will change the stereotypes of engineering "as too nerdy, or that it's too difficult, or for boys only."

Some think the solution for women to overcome sexism and achieve their full potential lies in single-sex education. Baskin differs with this viewpoint. A graduate of all-female Mount Holyoke College, she says she attended the school for "the brainpower of the students and the caliber of the professors." She goes on to say that the school was "outstanding in spite of … [its] single-sex status…. Claiming otherwise only condescends to [its] highly capable students and reinforces the absurdity that succeeding in a co-ed world first demands steeling oneself in gender isolation…. It's the twenty-first century. I thought women were done sacrificing" (Baskin).

TERMS & CONCEPTS

Academies / Seminaries: Single-sex secondary schools were established in the nineteenth century and were called either "academies" or "seminaries." As the word "seminary" implies, religious education was part of the curriculum, typical of schools in the first half of the century.

Baby Boom: Baby boom is the term for the surge in population growth between 1946 and 1964. Baby boomers are children of the post–World War II era who crowded schools and colleges through the 1950s into the 1980s.

Beecher, Catherine, 1800–1878: Catherine Beecher founded the Hartford Female Seminary (Connecticut) and was one of a number of New England female educators who fought to improve education and educational opportunities for young women in the nineteenth century.

Civil Rights Act of 1964 & Title IX: The Civil Rights Act of 1964 ensures equal educational opportunity by outlawing segregation in education. Title VII of the act "prohibits discrimination by covered employers on the basis of race, color, religion, sex or national origin." The 1972 amendments to the act included educational institutions. Title IX was significant legislation for women students in that it ensured that they have the same opportunity for men to participate in athletics programs.

Curricular Differentiation: Based on a proposal by the NEA in 1918 that high schools be "comprehensive" and offer different curricula to meet different societal and economic needs, most urban high schools were employing curricular differentiation by 1920 by offering academic, vocational, general and commercial (secretarial) programs (Mirel).

Lyon, Mary, 1797–1849: Mary Lyon was the founder of Mount Holyoke Seminary in 1837, later to become Mount Holyoke College. She created a disciplined educational environment, which although unaffiliated, was Christian based, but emphasized the sciences, including chemistry, and other subjects that young women of the time were generally not taught.

Mann, Horace, 1796–1859: Horace Mann is sometimes called the "father of American education," who was the first secretary of the Massachusetts Board of Education. He promoted "common education" and opened fifty schools as well as establishing a mandatory six-month minimum school year. He later became president of Antioch College in Ohio.

Normal Schools: Normal schools were institutes of advanced learning whose primary objective was to train teachers. Early normal schools sprang from nineteenth-century academies for women and most today are integrated into states' systems of higher education. They were called "normal schools" because their curricular objective was to set teaching standards or norms. Some high schools also had a "normal curriculum," which trained young women to teach in the local elementary schools.

Willard, Emma, 1787–1870: New England educator Emma Willard is credited with opening the first U.S. academy for girls in Troy, New York in 1822. Originally called the Troy Female Seminary, and later named after her, the Emma Willard School is open to this day.

Women's Educational Equity Act (WEEA): Legislation enacted to help fund equity for women's education and support the tenets of Title IX of 1972. The WEEA was part of the Special Projects Act contained in the Education Amendments of 1974. Federal grants were appropriated for equity programs.

Barbara Hornick-Lockard

BIBLIOGRAPHY

Baskin, K. (2004). Singled out. *New Republic, 230,* 34. Retrieved November 27, 2007, from EBSCO online database, Academic Search Premier.

Bornstein, R. (1979). The education of women: Protection or liberation? *Educational Leadership, 36,* 331. Retrieved November 27, 2007, from EBSCO online database, Academic Search Premier.

Celebrating 70 years of excellence. (1997). *American School & University, 70,* 10. Retrieved November 27, 2007, from EBSCO online database, Academic Search Premier.

Coburn, C. (1991). Learning to serve: Education and change in the lives of rural domestics in the twentieth century. *Journal of Social History, 25,* 109. Retrieved November 27, 2007, from EBSCO online database, Academic Search Premier.

Cheek, K. (2004). The normal school. In R. Barger, *History of American Education Web Project.* Retrieved November 28, 2007 from http://www.nd.edu

Eisenmann, L. (2002). Educating the female citizen in a post-war world: Competing ideologies for American women, 1945–1965. *Educational Review, 54,* 133–141.

Emma Hart Willard, 1787–1870. (n.d.). *Women working, 1800–1930. Open Collections Program.* Harvard University Library. Retrieved November 29, 2007 from http://ocp.hul.harvard.edu

Examining women's status: Campus climate and gender equity. (2011). *ASHE Higher Education Report, 37,* 65–92. Retrieved December 20, 2013, from EBSCO online database, Academic Search Premier.

Harwarth, I., Maline, M., & DeBra, E. (n.d.). *Women's colleges in the United States: History, issues, and challenges.* Retrieved December 2, 2007 from Department of Education. http://www.ed.gov

Jefferson, T. (1997). The education of women. *Education of Women, 1,* 90. Retrieved November 27, 2007, from EBSCO online database, Academic Search Premier.

Klapper, M. (2002). 'A long and broad education': Jewish girls and the problem of education in America, 1860–1920. *Journal of American Ethnic History, 22,* 3. Retrieved November 27, 2007, from EBSCO online database, Academic Search Premier.

Leitzell, K. (2007). The passions behind the pill. *U.S. News & World Report, 143,* 68–69. Retrieved November 27, 2007, from EBSCO online database, Academic Search Premier.

Maher, F. A., & Tetreault, M. (2011). Long-term transformations: Excavating privilege and diversity in the academy. *Gender & Education, 23,* 281–297. Retrieved December 20, 2013, from EBSCO online database, Academic Search Premier.

Matthews, B. (1976). Women, education and history. *Theory Into Practice, 15,* 47–53. Retrieved November 27, 2007, from EBSCO online database, Academic Search Premier.

Michaels, W. (2006). Celebrating 125 Years of university women. *Diverse: Issues in Higher Education, 23,* 11.

Retrieved November 27, 2007, from EBSCO online database, Academic Search Premier.

Mirel, J. (2006). The traditional high school. *Education Next, 6*, 14–21. Retrieved December 2, 2007 from EBSCO online database, Education Research Complete.

Steinberg, A., Brooks, J., & Remtulla, T. (2003). Youth hate crimes: Identification, prevention, and intervention. *American Journal of Psychiatry, 160*, 979-989.

Stephan, W. G., & Finlay, K. A. (1999). The role of empathy in improving intergroup relations. *Journal on Social Issues, 55*, 729-744.

Stephan, W. G., & Stephan, C. W. (1995). *Improving intergroup relations*. Thousand Oaks: Sage.

Terenzini, P. T., Pascarella, E. T., & Blimling, G. S. (1996). Students' out-of-class experiences and their influence on learning and cognitive development: A literature review. *Journal of College Student Development, 40*, 610-623.

Umbach, P. D. & Kuh, G. D. (2003, May). *Student experiences with diversity at liberal arts colleges: Another claim for distinctiveness*. Paper presented at the 43rd Annual Association for Institutional Research Forum, Tampa, FL.

SUGGESTED READING

Hersch, J. (2015). How opting out among women with elite education contributes to social equality. *Indiana Journal of Law and Social Equality*, vol. 3, issue 2, viii-215.

Maslak, M. (2008). *The structure and agency of women's education*. Albany, N.Y.: State University of New York Press.

Monroe, D. (2015). *My unsentimental education*. Athens: University of Georgia Press

Ward, K. & Eddy, P. (2013). Women and academic leadership: Leaning out. *Chronicle of Higher Education*; n/a.

EDUCATION REFORM MOVEMENTS

The following article summarizes the major periods of reform in American education. Although each period of reform - the Common School Movement, the Progressive Reform Era, the Equity Movement, and the Standards-Based Reform movement - are all distinct from one another, educational reform in general shares some common characteristics. These common characteristics are discussed first, especially as they help explain the cyclical and persistent nature of reform.

KEYWORDS: Administrative progressivism; Child-centered progressivism; Committee of Ten; Common School Movement; Dewey, John; Equity Reform Movement; Intensification; Progressive Reform Movement; Restructuring; Standards-Based Reform Movement

OVERVIEW

Ironically, one of the most enduring characteristics of American education is the attempt to change it. In other words, educational *reform* has as long a history as education itself.

Historian Diane Ravitch (2000) writes, "it is impossible to find a period in the twentieth century in which education reformers, parents, and the citizenry were satisfied with the schools." While each period of reform has distinct characteristics, common elements and patterns have emerged as well.

Before reviewing the specific periods of reform, we'll first review educational reform in general in order to better understand its cyclical and persistent nature.

Researchers and historians argue that one of the main reasons educational reform has become cyclical in nature is because reformers themselves lack a historical perspective. Hunt (2005) writes, "unfortunately, education reforms have consistently been plagued by the reformers' lack of knowledge and appreciation of the history of education." New reforms are doomed to fail, he argues, because they ignore the collective wisdom of generations past. Although specific examples of reoccurring reform proposals are too numerous to cite, Warren (1990) offers career ladders as a prototype; late twentieth century proposals to reward teachers based on merit, he argues, ignore the lessons to be learned from the "various types of merit salary schedules that have been adopted and subsequently discarded in school districts across the country for more than a century."

Another reason education reform has persisted over the years is because educators, policymakers, and parents have very different views about education - its purpose, the people it's intended to serve, and the means by which they are best served. As Horn (2002) argues, even changes that appear superficial - such as incorporating accountability measures or implementing a new teaching strategy - are representative of deep ideological and philosophical differences.

Because different stakeholders have different ideas about the purpose of education, reform initiatives are often viewed as power struggles. "Educational reform is inherently political" and as power shifts from one group to another, educational practice and theory so follows (Horn).

Unfairly or not, schools are often viewed as a vehicle through which to cure social ills or respond to new social challenges. As a result, "educational reform is [never] solely about education" (Horn. Throughout history, schools have been shaped to assimilate immigrants, prepare students for the workforce, redistribute wealth, and help the United States compete in a global economy. Even the very first schools were designed as much to create a sense of national unity as they were to develop the nation's intellect. In sum, "typically, we have thought of schools as means to other ends" (Warren). It is no surprise, then, that as society and its needs have changed over the last century, schools continued to change as well.

Competing interests, unwillingness to learn from the past, and larger societal changes help explain why educational reform has been a significant part of the history of education in America, but the tendency for reform initiatives to fail lends insight as well. As old reforms die out with little substantial change, new reforms are offered in their place. Various explanations have been offered for reform failure, one of the most frequent being impatience on the part of reformers and the public - or, put differently, America's need for immediate gratification (Horn, 2002; Hunt, 2005). Reforms simply don't have enough time to come to fruition. Hunt also argues that many educational reforms fail because they address social problems that don't easily lend themselves to solutions offered by the scientific process.

Schools have arguably received an unfair amount of criticism, with criticism of failed reform efforts piled on top of criticism of the schools themselves. Pogrow (1996) and others have come to their defense, arguing that systemic reform is never easily achieved, and educational reform has been at least as successful as reform in other types of complex systems. In a similar vein, Paris (1995) suggests that reform fails because we ask too much of schools to begin with. He writes, "our constant crises may simply indicate that we have high and perhaps unrealistic expectations about what schools can and should do."

Given all that we expect, he continues, one shouldn't be surprised by our continual frustration.

PERIODS OF EDUCATIONAL REFORM

Educational historians classify reform movements in the United States differently. Some focus on reform in relation to curriculum development specifically, for example, while others analyze reform in relation to diversity and equity (Parkerson & Parkerson, 2001; Paris). Still others focus on the role of the government in relation to reform, looking at educational change through the lens of power and control (Horn). Nevertheless, many historians agree that educational reform in the United States can be defined according to four major periods of reform; as we progress through each, we'll touch upon specific issues such as curriculum and diversity, as well as the elements described above, such as competing ideologies and philosophies.

THE COMMON SCHOOL MOVEMENT

The Common School Movement took place in the early to mid nineteenth century, and although its impact varied somewhat from region to region, it is considered the first nationwide educational reform initiative (Warren). Prior to the Revolutionary War, colonists were participating in their own diverse educational initiatives. Even after the nation was formed, schooling varied tremendously based on community support and resources. By the early 1800s, Americans recognized the need for a more uniform educational system.

Although Americans were beginning to reach a consensus regarding the need for a common school, their motivations often differed. Some advocates argued that the formation of a common school was necessary to preserve the new republic. Thomas Jefferson wrote, for example, "universal education was 'necessary' in 'rendering the people...guardians of their own liberty'" (Parkerson & Parkerson, 2001). Similarly, others argued that education was necessary for responsible citizenship, particularly with respect to the vote. On the other hand, some common school advocates saw education not as protection against a tyrannical government, but as protection against the selfishness of man. They believed education would reduce crime, prevent 'anarchy of the masses' and create more peaceful communities (Parkerson & Parkerson).

The founders of the nation had lofty goals for the common school, and while the everyday American may have appreciated their vision, economic changes made the issue of public education most relevant for them. In the early nineteenth century, America became a market economy; while the changes presented great opportunity for advancement, they also presented equal opportunity for failure and loss of social, occupational, and economic status. As a result, individuals began looking to schools as an economic safety net, and also a potential vehicle for upward mobility (Parkerson & Parkerson).

Early Americans may have had the motivation for universal schooling before they had the means. As Warren writes, "with regard to education, the federal Constitution was silent, and no national agency or congressional committee existed to provide educational leadership." Amazingly, the reform initiative spread through informal networks, and created a surprising amount of consensus with regard to issues such as curriculum, teacher competency and preparation, school architecture, and measures of achievement. Of all the major periods of reform, perhaps the Common School Movement was most successful. By the mid to late 1800s most children in the north were attending school, while attendance in the south lagged only slightly. The movement was also important for establishing a link between education and citizenship, and for introducing the notion of inclusive education, available to all regardless of race, gender, religion, or social class (Warren).

THE PROGRESSIVE EDUCATION ERA

The Civil War and subsequent reconstruction spurred educational reform initiatives (Warren), but historians generally identify the early twentieth century as the next significant period of educational reform. Known as the Progressive Era, the years between 1880 and 1930 were characterized by widespread reform, not just in relation to education, but also with regard to labor, safety and health, and basic citizenship. Immigration, the growth of U.S. cities, and the shift from an agrarian-based society to an industrial one, all contributed to dramatic changes in American society, and as a result, the call for change.

In the wake of all these changes, policymakers and educators were debating the purpose of schooling. The Committee of Ten, sponsored by the National Education Association in 1893, represented what some refer to as the humanist viewpoint (Horn). They recommended a traditional liberal curriculum - instruction in the core subjects such as classics, mathematics, science, and history - for all students, regardless of whether the student intended to pursue higher education. One humanist referred to the core subjects as "windows of the soul" and argued that occupational decisions should be deferred until after graduation (Horn). Others however, and most especially businessmen and the politicians who represented them, believed students should be trained for their future occupation. They advocated a differentiated curriculum and vocational education.

By the early twentieth century, the humanists were losing ground. The National Education Association again convened a committee, but this committee was charged with developing a more relevant high school curriculum. As Horn argues, "this was the first time that school curriculum became the means through which nonacademic goals were to be attained." The committee proposed a curriculum based on "The Seven Cardinal Principles," which emphasized health, family relationships, citizenship, and vocation over academic instruction.

The debate described above was playing out simultaneously in a different arena - not only in the public school classroom, but the halls of the academy as well. John Dewey, arguably the most widely recognized educational philosopher and reformer of the twentieth century, advocated what has since become known as child-centered progressivism. Dewey believed the curriculum should be directed in part by the interests of the child, education should serve the whole child (e.g. her emotional, physical, moral, intellectual, and spiritual development), and that students learn by doing (Labaree, 2005). He also believed education could help eradicate social and racial inequity. At the same time, however, a second strand of progressivism - administrative progressivism - was gaining popularity through the work of Edward L. Thorndike. Based largely on principles of social efficiency and scientific management of schools, administrative progressivism led to practices such as tracking, achievement testing, bureaucratization of schools, and vocational education (Warren). As one historian argues, "one cannot understand the history of education in the United States ...unless one realizes that Edward L. Thorndike won and John Dewey lost" (Labaree).

Thorndike may have eventually won the war, but both 'sides' won many different battles along the way. A backlash against child-centered progressivism known as the Essentialist Movement emerged in the 1920s, calling for higher student expectations, more discipline, and more evaluation of achievement. In the 1930s, the Progressive Education Association declared victory with the publication of the Eight Year Study, proving that children educated in non-traditional environments did as well as, if not better, than their traditionally schooled counterparts on almost all academic measures (Feldman & Watson, 2003). By the beginning of WWII, reformers were calling for a Life Adjustment curriculum, once again advocating a non-academic agenda. Despite the many twists and turns of educational reform, the next significant call for change didn't occur until the late 1950s and 1960s.

THE EQUITY REFORM MOVEMENT

In 1957, the Russians beat Americans into space with the launching of the space satellite Sputnik; Americans interpreted this event as a sign of the nation's declining competitive edge, and as in times past, turned to the schools for a solution. Educators and policymakers criticized progressives for making students 'soft', and rallied for a back-to-basics movement, with an emphasis on science and math. While certainly a memorable event, Sputnik nevertheless didn't spawn a lengthy reform movement. Ravitch explains, "In 1963 and 1964, the post-Sputnik enthusiasm for academic improvement abruptly ended, replaced as the leading national topic by the 'urban crisis'." The 'urban crisis' was largely about providing equal educational opportunities for minority students, and so the reform emphasis shifted quickly from excellence to equity.

Momentum for the equity movement began to build with the 1954 Supreme Court decision, 'Brown v. Board of Education of Topeka.' In this landmark decision, the Court ruled that segregated schools - also known as "separate but equal" schooling for black and white children - were inherently discriminatory. The equity movement got another boost in 1964 with the passage of the Civil Rights Act; in addition to empowering minorities with voting and employment rights, the Civil Rights Act gave the government the power to withhold federal funds from schools who failed to comply with desegregation laws

(Horn). Finally, as another example of the expanding role of the federal government with regard to educational reform, the 1960s saw the passage of the Elementary and Secondary Education Act (ESEA). Part of President Johnson's larger "War on Poverty," ESEA attempted to eradicate social inequity for providing equal educational opportunity for minority and disadvantaged students; Head Start is one of the most widely recognized outgrowths of ESEA.

As with most reform initiatives, the efforts of the 1960s had its critics as well as its proponents. Those who argued against programs such as Head Start - also known as compensatory education programs - argued that they were modeled on a deficit view of minorities that regarded all differences - cultural, linguistic, cognitive, and behavioral - "as pathological conditions to be eliminated" (Pai, Adler, & Shadiow, 2006). Others claimed such programs simply didn't work. In 1996, James Coleman published a report - later known as the Coleman report - which stated student achievement was in no way related to the quality of academic facilities or curriculum. Compensatory education programs, therefore, couldn't correct student deficits. The report itself was then used to support divergent agendas; some saw it as evidence that differences in achievement were due to innate differences in intelligence, while others saw it as evidence that disadvantaged children needed access to the same *cultural capital* as white middle-class children. The latter argument was used to support busing programs, one of the many ways in which districts have attempted to integrate over the past several decades.

According to Ravitch, reformers' dissatisfaction with inequity in the school system resulted in "a rejection of virtually all manifestations of formal education...In the age of counterculture and the student revolution, the answer to most problems was freedom." Freedom manifested itself in practices such as the open classroom, increased electives, fewer curriculum requirements, pass-fail grades, and less discipline and teacher authority. Some went so far as the reject the notion of schooling altogether. The most renowned of such radicals was Ivan Illich; in his 1971 publication *Deschooling Society*, he argued that the very structure of schools crushed students' curiosity and independent thought. Although many of these educational innovations - in particular, the open classroom movement - gained popularity quickly, support waned almost as fast. By the late

1970s, excellence - not equity or freedom - was once again the keyword of educational reform.

THE STANDARDS-BASED REFORM MOVEMENT

The standards-based reform movement was ushered in by a watershed moment when, in 1983, President Reagan's National Commission on Excellence in Education issued a report titled 'A Nation at Risk.' Using rhetoric that quickly caught the attention of the public, the report warned of a "rising tide of mediocrity" and claimed America's security was at risk because of failing schools. Documenting declines in academic achievement as measured by standardized tests - not only in comparison to the performance of students in other industrialized nations, but compared to the performance of students in the United States in the 1950's - the report's authors advocated for a return to the basics, the creation of curriculum standards, the development of 'high-stakes testing', and increasing accountability for schools and teachers (Hayes).

Just as the efforts of previous reform eras fractured in different directions, the efforts of the 1980s lacked consensus as well. Horn differentiates between those who advocated restructuring versus those who advocated intensification. The former stressed teacher and parent empowerment, the involvement of the community in local schools, and a general rearrangement of power relationships. The latter, on the other hand, emphasized accountability, centralized authority and decision-making, and standardized curriculum. With recent initiatives like Goals 2000 and No Child Left Behind - both of which place heavy emphasis on standards and testing - most agree that "intensification has become the dominant reform philosophy" of the 1980s and 1990s (Horn).

Even though the latest reform movement has fractured in different directions, historians still argue that it is unparalleled in its scope and momentum (Murphy). "The level of concern and amount of energy being expended in thinking about public and secondary schooling are more intense now than at any other previous time in our history" (Sedlak, Wheeler, Pullin, & Cusick, as quoted in Murphy). The movement has been sustained longer than other movements in the past, has focused its attention on issues previously unaddressed, and has greater public support than has ever been previously shown.

According to some, the movement is already in its third wave of reform, and shows no sign of decline.

While the movement has been sustained longer than some movements in the past, whether or not it has been successful is a matter for debate. Critics argue that the move toward national standards and accountability has created a 'culture of sameness' that devalues diversity and creativity, depersonalizes education, and controls teachers (Horn). Others claim that the reforms of the last two decades have been too narrowly focused on the individual, and have failed to take into account the contextual nature of many of the problems facing education, such as institutionalized racism, poverty, and social class. On the other hand, proponents argue the reforms of the 1980s have been more successful than reforms of the past. "Available data support the contention that reforms, both individually and collectively, are connected to improvement in measures of student performance" (Murphy). This period of reform has been successful, they argue, because it was implemented within existing school structures, based on current research about the conditions that promote learning, and has the support of the public and school personnel.

Lunenburg (2013) is less sanguine about the claims of success and advocates for schools based on "core principles" that include individualized instruction and mastery of "essential" skills. Such programs are hard to implement in large, bureaucratic, standardized school settings with entrenched cultures. School choice became the rallying cry of the first decades of the twenty-first century, and many parents pulled their children from traditional schools and placed them in experimental charter schools. Unburdened with many of the regulations and mandates of regular public schools, charters developed programs that often yielded impressive results. Critics pointed out that charter school families tended to self-select for high achievement and the processes involved in applying and attending were discouraging to parents who did not have the time or inclination to pursue the option. Taylor, McGlynn, & Luter (2013) asserted that neighborhood conditions such as poverty and violence were frequently dismissed as obstacles to better school performance, and in fact charter schools attempting to meet the needs of these students were frequently unable to best the outcomes of established traditional school coping with the same issues. The long recession and foreclosure crisis resulted in repeated and sustained budget cuts to districts, which were then faced with meeting higher standards with fewer resources. In an effort to ease district budget constraints, many states allowed greater flexibility with how monies were spent. Further, schools sought partnerships with businesses and universities, tapping local and corporate resources to help save old programs or establish new ones.

CONCLUSION

Whether or not the standards-based reform movement is ultimately deemed successful, it is likely that another period of educational reform will soon follow. As history has proven, our schools have been asked to change in response to social and cultural changes, in response to shifts in power and ideology, and in response to new demands and needs. And they will undoubtedly be asked to change again. Those involved in the next stages of reform may do well to heed the advice of Warren: "there cannot be a reform without a past. And if we don't know where we have been with regard to educational improvement, and why we went there, we are left to chart our direction in the shallow waters of contemporary comparisons and current political moods."

TERMS & CONCEPTS

Administrative Progressivism: One of the two major strands of the progressive education movement of the early twentieth century. Most closely associated with the work of Edward L. Thorndike, advocates of this strand emphasized the role of the environment in teaching and learning, scientific management, social efficiency, and vocational education.

A Nation at Risk: Report published by President Reagan's National Commission on Excellence in Education in 1983. The report documented declines in student achievement as measured by standardized tests, and argued that the "rising tide of mediocrity" threatened the nation's security. The strong language used in the report generated public support for reform, and ushered in one of the most sustained reform efforts in the history of American education.

Child-centered Progressivism: One of the three strands of the progressive education movement of the early twentieth century. Most closely associated with the work of John Dewey and G. Stanley Hall, advocates of child-centered progressivism argued

that instruction should be tailored to the developmental stage and individual interests of the child.

Committee of Ten: Sponsored by the National Education Association in 1893, the Committee of Ten represented the views of progressive reformers known as humanists. The committee recommended a liberal arts education for all - weighted in favor of the core academic subjects - regardless of whether a student intended to pursue higher education or a vocation following high school graduation.

Coleman Report: Report published by James Coleman in 1965 that argued against the effectiveness of compensatory education programs. Evidence showed that student achievement was unrelated to curriculum and academic facilities, but rather was more closely associated with socioeconomic background.

Compensatory Education: Education programs of the equity reform movement of the 1960s and 1970s that attempted to eradicate social and racial inequities by providing disadvantaged children with equal educational opportunities. Such programs were criticized for not valuing different cultures and for being ineffective.

Dewey, John: One of the most prominent educational philosophers and reformers of the twentieth century whose name is most closely associated with the progressive education movement. Dewey argued that the curriculum should be based in part on the interests of each child, education should serve the whole child, and students learn best by doing. His ideas became known as child-centered progressivism.

Intensification: One philosophy of the education reform movement of the 1980s, advocating for a standardized curriculum, centralized authority, greater accountability, and less teacher autonomy. Intensification has become the dominant reform philosophy of the last two decades, overshadowing a competing philosophy known as restructuring.

Restructuring: One philosophy of the education reform movement of the 1980s, advocating for teacher and parent empowerment, community involvement in education, and less centralized power structure. Restructuring efforts have been overshadowed by a competing philosophy known as intensification.

Jennifer Kretchmar

BIBLIOGRAPHY

Feldman, D., & Watson, T. (2003). The eight-year study revisited: John Burroughs School, St. Louis, Missouri. *Educational Research Quarterly*, 27, 5-13. Retrieved April 2, 2007 from EBSCO online database, Education Research Complete.

Hayes, W. (2007). The progressive education movement: Is it still a factor in today's schools? Lanham, MD: Rowman and Littlefield Publishers, Inc.

Horn, R. A. (2002). Understanding educational reform: A reference handbook. Santa Barbara, CA: ABC-CLIO, Inc.

Hunt, T. (2005). Education reforms: Lessons from history. Phi Delta Kappa, 87, 8-89. Retrieved from EBSCO online database, Education Research Complete.

Knaak, W. C., & Knaak, J. T. (2013). Charter schools: Educational reform or failed initiative?. *Delta Kappa Gamma Bulletin, 79*, 45-53. Retrieved December 15, 2013, from EBSCO Online Database Education Research Complete.

Labaree, D. F. (2005). Progressivism, schools and schools of education: An American romance. *Pedagogica Historica*, 41, 275-288. Retrieved April 2, 2007 from http://search.ebscohost.com

Lunenburg, F. C. (2013). Why school reform efforts have failed: School reform needs to be based on a set of core principles. *National Forum of Educational Administration & Supervision Journal, 31*, 55-63. Retrieved December 15, 2013, from EBSCO Online Database Education Research Complete.

Murphy, J. (1990). The educational reform movement of the 1980s: A comprehensive analysis. In J. Murphy (Ed.), The educational reform movement of the 1980s (pp. 3-56). Berkeley, CA: McCutchan Publishing Corporation.

Pai, Y., Adler, S. A., & Shadiow, L. K. (2006). Cultural foundations of education. Upper Saddle River, NJ: Merrill Prentice Hall.

Paris, D. C. (1995). Ideology *and educational reform: Themes and theories in public education.* San Francisco, CA: Westview Press.

Parkerson, D. H., & Parkerson, J. (2001). *Transitions in American education: A social history of teaching.* New York, NY: Routledge.

Pogrow, S. (1996). Reforming the wannabe reformers. *Phi Delta Kappan*, 77, 656-663. Retrieved May 2, 2007 from EBSCO online database, Education Research Complete.

Ravitch, D. (2000). *Left back: A century of failed school reforms.* New York, NY: Simon & Schuster.

Taylor, H., McGlynn, L., & Luter, D. (2013). Neighborhoods matter: The role of universities in the school reform neighborhood development movement. *Peabody Journal of Education (0161956X), 88*, 541-563. Retrieved December 15, 2013, from EBSCO Online Database Education Research Complete.

Warren, D. (1990). Passage of Rites: On the history of educational reform in the United States. In J. Murphy (Ed.), The educational reform movement of the 1980s (pp. 57-82). Berkeley, CA: McCutchan Publishing Corporation.

SUGGESTED READING

Berube, M. R., & Berube, C. T. (2007). The end of school reform. New York, NY: Rowman & Littlefield Publishers, Inc.

Borman, K. M., & Greenman, N. P. (Eds.). (1994). Changing American education: Recapturing the past or inventing the future? Albany, NY: State University of New York Press.

Finn, C. E., & Rebarber, T. (Eds.). (1992). Education reform in the '90s. New York, NY: Macmillan Publishing Company.

Jossey-Bass reader on school reform. (2001). San Francisco, CA: Jossey-Bass, Inc.

Mondale, S. & Patton, S. (Eds.). (2001) *School: The story of American Public Education.* Boston, MA: Beacon Press.

MINORITIES AND EDUCATION IN AMERICA

This article describes the history of racial and language minorities in K–12 education in the United States. From almost the time they arrived in the United States, minorities such as African-Americans, Hispanics, and Asians have gone to extraordinary lengths in their efforts to seize a piece of the American Dream—some slaves, for example, risked their lives to attend illegal schools, and later free African Americans from the north gave of their time to educate emancipated slaves. Each minority group

has had a unique set of challenges to face: African-Americans had to overcome the bitter taste of slavery in order to succeed, and Hispanics and Asians faced language barriers and a sometimes subtle, sometimes overt form of racism to rise to become leaders in their communities. However, since the second half of the 20th century, many minority students have found themselves in under-performing or even failing schools as defined by the 2001 No Child Left Behind Act. Parents, community leaders and government officials have sought ways to enhance minority education, with some minority parents choosing public charter schools, and even homeschooling as ways to rediscover the quality minority schooling of the past. Indeed, decades of research have shown that socioeconomic factors are less important predictors of academic success than dedicated communities, challenging curriculum, dedicated principals and teachers, and involved parents.

KEYWORDS: Bilingual Education; Charter Schools; Failing Schools; No Child Left Behind Act of 2001 (NCLB); Public Schools; Racism; Slavery; Under-Performing Schools

OVERVIEW

One of the abiding myths in America is that it is a melting pot, a great cauldron into which one takes their racial and ethnic heritage, blends it with freedom and opportunity, and creates for themselves a new American persona. The United States has always been a nation of immigrants, and millions of new opportunity-seekers continue to arrive every year. In the 21st century, the United States is becoming more multicultural than ever before, and these trends are being reflected in minority student enrollment:

In 2007–2008, minorities constituted 42 percent of public school students in kindergarten through 12th grade, of which 16 percent were African American (National Center for Education Statistics, 2009). Between 1993–1994 and 2005–2006, the percentage of African American students in public schools increased from 16.5 to 17.2 percent while the percentage of Hispanic students increased from 12.7 percent to 19.8 percent of public school enrollment (Fry, 2007). By the fall of 2013, African American students represented 16 percent of the total enrollment at public schools, while Hispanic students represented 25 percent (National Center for Education Statistics).

Minority students can be divided into two groups: African American students, whose ancestors suffered from centuries of slavery but who also speak English, and others, such as Asians and Hispanics, who are both racial and linguistic minorities.

Government research indicates that while all these minority groups made educational gains in the past few decades, the rate of improvement was less than that enjoyed by white students. The end result is that while there are many individual exceptions to the rule, minority groups in the aggregate are falling further behind in terms of academic achievement. Those minorities who are showing the greatest academic progress appear largely to be those attending charter schools and home schools.

AFRICAN-AMERICANS IN THE SCHOOLS

Perhaps the most regrettable development in American history was the importation of African slaves beginning in the early 17th century. According to the 1860 census, the last conducted before the emancipation of slaves following the Civil War, there were nearly 4 million slaves in the United States, most of them of African ancestry (Historical Census Browser, 2004).

The institution of slavery was the opponent of education. Laws were passed in the South that made it against the law to teach a slave how to read. According to Erickson (1997), South Carolina adopted the first compulsory ignorance law in 1740. It was illegal for anyone to teach a slave to write, and a fine of one hundred pounds would be levied to anyone caught doing so.

"Eventually each [slave-owning] state had similar laws, nevertheless, some Blacks did achieve an education. That great Black orator and writer, Frederick Douglass, was taught to read and write by his Southern mistress. Some large Southern cities had "secret schools," and instances are known in which slaves and free Blacks attended school together, a highly dangerous practice" (Erickson).

One well-known slave, Henry Bibb, put it succinctly in 1850, "Slaves were not allowed books, pen, ink, nor paper, to improve their minds" (Bibb, 2006 [1850]). Even so, slaves in many major Southern cities, such as Charleston and Columbia, learned to read—those slaves on large, isolated plantations in the Deep South were the most isolated and stood the least chance of being educated. In the North, institutions such as the African Free School, founded in New York in 1787, produced leaders such as James McCune Smith, the first African American to earn a medical degree.

After the Civil War, when the 13th Amendment gave slaves their freedom, African American leaders in the South realized that the millions of newly emancipated slaves would not be able to take full advantage of their newfound freedom without educational opportunities. Within a context of political and economic oppression in the post-war South, African American educators made the best of an extremely difficult situation by creating a parallel universe of African American schools (Anderson, 1988). With help from philanthropists like Sears, Roebuck and Company President Julius Rosenwald, Union generals, and others, historically African American colleges and universities were created in the still-segregated South. African American educator Booker T. Washington, who was born in slavery, was pivotal in the movement that established over 5,000 primarily African American elementary and high schools across the South.

By the turn of the 20th century, African American primary and secondary schools were turning out national and community leaders. In Washington, D.C., Dunbar High School was one of many shining lights. African-American historian and economist Thomas Sowell notes that it succeeded against all odds:

"Back in 1899, when the schools of Washington, D.C. were racially segregated and discrimination was rampant, there were four academic high schools in the city—three white and one African American. When standardized tests were given that year, the black academic high school [Dunbar] scored higher than two of the three white academic high schools. Today, exactly a century later, even setting such a goal would be considered hopelessly utopian. Nor was this a fluke. That same high school was scoring at or above the national average on IQ tests during the 1930s and 1940s. Yet its physical plant was inadequate and its average class size was higher than that in the city's white high schools" (Sowell, n.d.).

AFRICAN AMERICAN EDUCATORS

From 1865 to 1954, during the time of legally segregated schools, there were many superb African American educators such as Alice Dunbar-Nelson, a high school teacher at the all-African American Howard High School in Wilmington, Delaware, who used her Master's degree from Cornell to instruct her high school English students in Chaucer, Milton, Shakespeare and Coleridge (Gibson, 1997). The quality of African American teachers in this period was nothing short of amazing, and they produced some of the most well-known leaders in U.S. history. Apart from Dunbar and Howard high schools, Booker T. Washington High School in racially-divided Atlanta produced Martin Luther King Jr., and Frederick Douglass High School in Baltimore produced Thurgood Marshall, the first African American justice of the U.S. Supreme Court.

ACHIEVEMENT AT ELEMENTARY LEVEL

On the elementary school level, there was not the gap between African American and white students that exists today. Indeed, some African American schools outperformed their white counterparts. For example, as African American economist Walter Williams notes:

African-American historian and economist Thomas Sowell compared] test scores for sixth-graders in Harlem schools with those in the predominantly white Lower East Side for April 1941 and December 1941. In paragraph and word meaning, Harlem students, compared to Lower East Side students, scored equally or higher. In 1947 and 1951, Harlem third-graders in paragraph and word meaning and arithmetic reasoning and computation scored about the same—in some cases slightly higher and in others slightly lower—than their Lower East Side counterparts (Williams, 2003).

"SEPARATE BUT EQUAL" EDUCATIONAL SYSTEM

Still, while African American high schools like Dunbar were sending graduates to Harvard by the 1920s, in the century between the end of the Civil War in 1865 and the beginning of the civil rights movement in the 1950s, African Americans were part of a system of "separate but equal schools"—whites would attend certain schools, and blacks would attend others. Most black schools achieved what they did despite overcrowding and inadequate resources—Dunbar itself had no school cafeteria for the first forty years of its existence. The 1896 U.S. Supreme Court decision *Plessy v. Ferguson* declared this "separate but equal" educational system to be constitutional, but that ruling was overturned in the 1954 Brown v. Board of Education decision (Thurgood Marshall won the case on behalf of the NAACP), a ruling that set off more than a half-century of attempts at school desegregation that continue today.

FUTURE OF AFRICAN AMERICAN
EDUCATORS & STUDENTS

Since Brown, the fortunes of African American students and teachers have turned somewhat sour.

Since the 1960s and 1970s there has been a steady exodus of white and middle-class African American families from urban centers, and now a full one-third of African Americans are middle-class suburbanites. This drain of students and resources left the poorest students—traditionally African American and now also Hispanic—behind in urban schools that have become pockmarked with violence, crime, and drug use. Making matters worse, local African American leaders have lost operational control of their community public schools to government education officials. Some former African American public school teachers, such as fourteen-year Chicago public schools veteran Marva Collins, left the public school system to found an inner-city school that would give African American students the opportunity for an education on par with that given to white students.

Given the sobering developments within public schools in urban areas, where African Americans still predominate, the gap between African American and white students has widened considerably since the middle of the twentieth century. By almost any objective measure, African American students perform at average levels lower than those of any racial group. Scholastic Achievement Test (SAT) scores for college–bound African Americans rose an average of 6 points for Verbal (though the number has returned to the 1986 level) and 16 points for Math from 1986 to 2006, but the scores are still below those of whites, Hispanics, and Asians (National Center for Education Statistics, 2011). There are some positive trends, however: Between 2000 and 2010, high school graduation rates for African Americans rose 13 percent to 62 percent (Strauss, 2013). In the 2011–12 school year, that number had increased to 69 percent (Adams, 2014).

Since the 1990s, many African American parents have become vocal supporters of school vouchers, government-funded payment coupons that can be used to pay most or all of the cost to send their children to public charter schools which tend to be safer than non-charter public schools and are widely believed to deliver a higher quality of education.

HISPANICS IN THE SCHOOLS

Hispanics are now the largest minority in the United States, having surpassed African Americans in 2002. They are also the fastest-growing minority group in public school, rising from 6 percent of

students in 1972 to 17 percent in 2000, 20 percent in 2008, and 25 percent in 2013 (Hoffman, Llargas & Snyder, 2003; National Center for Education Statistics 2009; 2016).

Many Hispanics speak either Spanish or Portuguese, with English as their second language, though more than half speak mainly English only at home (Llagas & Snyder). This language barrier has presented unique educational challenges to Hispanic students that African American students generally did not face. English as a Second Language (ESL) classes and bilingual education have attempted to ease the process of assimilation for new immigrants. During the 2013–14 school year, 4.5 million students, mostly Hispanic, were enrolled in ESL classes (National Center for Education Statistics, 2016).

A 2011 report by the President's Advisory Commission on Educational Excellence for Hispanic Americans summarized the challenges facing Hispanic students: "Latino students face persistent obstacles to educational attainment. Less than half of Latino children are enrolled in any early learning program. Only about half of all Latino students earn their high school diploma on time; those who do complete high school are only half as likely as their peers to be prepared for college. Just 13 percent of Latinos have a bachelor's degree, and only 4 percent have completed graduate or professional degree programs" (President's Advisory Commission on Educational Excellence for Hispanics, 2011).

Education experts and Hispanic community leaders are seeking ways to build on the educational progress being made by Hispanic students while seeking ways to increase early childhood program attendance and reduce the high school dropout rate. More research is also being done on the differences between foreign-born and native-born Hispanics, as well as the differences among immigrants from different Spanish- and Portuguese-speaking countries.

ASIANS IN THE SCHOOLS

The literature shows that Asian students, on average, do well in school. U.S. Department of Education data shows that Asians scored the highest of all racial/ethnic groups, including whites, in average Math SAT scores in 2013–14, and they scored second only to whites on the Critical Reading (or Verbal) part of the exam (National Center for Education Statistics, 2016).

Several studies compiled by Zhang and Carrasquillo (1995) reveal that there are some cultural reasons why Asian students have succeeded. Asian families "expect their children to do well academically, to obey authority figures, and to be aware of the sacrifices their parents have made for them and the need to fulfill obligations (Carrasquillo & London, 1993; Mordkowitz & Ginsburg, 1986). Mordkowitz and Ginsburg presented narrative support for a cultural explanation containing family socialization for high achievements. The students reported that their families underscored educational accomplishments, held high expectations for achievements, controlled the behavior of the students, and considered schooling very important (Sue & Okazaki, 1990)" (Zhang & Carrasquillo). Research also indicates that Asian students, among all racial groups, set the greatest expectations for themselves. Goyette & Xie (1999) write that all Asian groups have higher educational expectations than whites:

58.3% of white students expected to graduate from college, while all Asian groups reported higher percentages, ranging from 67.9% of Southeast Asians, to 84.8% for Japanese and Koreans, up to 95.7% of South Asian students who expected to graduate from college (Goyette & Xie).

Still, problems persist for Asian students. Statistics about Asian American success in school, such as the percentage of Asian American students enrolled in college or scoring high on the SAT, are misleading and mask those Asian American students who are not doing well. In fact, although it seldom makes news headlines, there is a serious problem of Asian American school failures (Siu, 1996).

The challenge for Asian leaders will be convincing political leaders that Asian students do face some of the same challenges faced by other racial and language minorities.

THE DECLINE IN MINORITY TEACHERS

There has been an appreciable decline in the number of minority public school teachers over the past several decades. This is happening even as the percentage of minority students attending public schools continues to set records. The trends are unmistakable:

According to the National Institute of Education Statistics (2009), more than 40 percent of students in today's public schools are minorities, and that

number is predicted to increase. Meanwhile, more than 80 percent of teachers in public schools were white in the 2011–12 school year (National Center for Education Statistics, 2015).

In addition, those teachers of color who do enter the profession are overwhelmingly female—male teachers are now only 24 percent of the profession (National Center for Education Statistics, 2015). MacPherson (2003) quotes then National Education Association President Reg Weaver's concerns that many young people come from fatherless homes, and that "when they're able to have access to a male teacher as a father figure, it certainly bodes well for them, and the same thing with minorities" (MacPherson).

Statistics show a precipitous decline in the percentage of African-American teachers in public schools. While 12.5 percent of public school teachers in 1974 were African American (Webb, 1986), that number fell to 6 percent in 2003 (MacPherson). The NEA adds that another 4 percent of public school teachers are other racial minorities. In New York City in 2006–2007, 71 percent of public school students were African-American or Hispanic, while 60 percent of their teachers were white (Chung, 2006). In the 2011–12 school year, 7 percent of teachers at public schools were African American and 4 percent were African American at (National Center for Education Statistics, 2015).

MINORITIES IN PRIVATE & HOME SCHOOLS

In the 2013–14 school year, 9 percent of K–12 students attending were African American, 6 percent were Asian, and 10 percent were Hispanic (Broughman & Swaim, 2016).

According to the latest figures from the U.S. Department of Education, private school students receive a superior academic education:

Students at grades 4, 8, and 12 in all categories had higher average scores in reading, mathematics, science, and writing than their counterparts in public schools. In addition, higher percentages of students performed at or above Proficient compared to those in public schools (Perie, Vanneman & Goldstein, 2005).

While data for homeschooling students is not as ample, the data that is available shows that homeschooling minority students perform on par with their white counterparts. According to a 1997 survey by the Home School Legal Defense Association, math and reading scores for minority home schooled children are virtually the same when compared to whites. In reading, both white and minority who are home schooled score at the 87th percentile. In math, they score in the 82nd percentile versus the 77th percentile (HSLDA, 1997).

BILINGUAL EDUCATION

Bilingual education in the United States involves teaching English language learners (ELLs) in both English and in the student's native language. Title VII of the federal Elementary and Secondary Education Act of 1968—commonly known as the Bilingual Education Act—required bilingual education in public schools, and the U.S. Supreme Court upheld the principle in Lau v. Nichols. However, the Bilingual Education Act has been superseded by the passage of the No Child Left Behind Act of 2001, which mandates yearly English-language tests for ELLs.

Bilingual education has caused controversy in the United States because of concerns that it undermines the role of English as the primary language in society and drives a socio-cultural wedge between English speakers and all others. Opponents of bilingual education prefer that non-native English-speaking students be placed instead in English language immersion programs to accelerate their learning (del Mazo, 2006). Supporters of bilingual education argue that students who first have a mastery of their native tongue will have a much easier time mastering English as a second language and thereafter learning in English (Krashen, 1999).

TERMS & CONCEPTS

Bilingual Education: The practice of educating non-English learners in their native tongue and in English.

Charter Schools: Public schools that retain local administrative control over matters such as teacher hiring and firing, salaries and curriculum

Failing Schools: Public schools that have shown over a period of years that they cannot enable the "proficiency of students in the basic four subjects of reading, writing, math, and science" (Anderson & Cotton, 2001).

No Child Left Behind Act of 2001 (NCLB): Legislation signed into law by President George W. Bush in 2001 that aimed to improve public education

in the United States. It was aimed especially at improving achievement for poor and minority children.

Public Schools: Publicly funded K-12 schools that retain a higher degree of state and federal oversight over hiring and other school policies and procedures.

Racism: An umbrella term from actions, words and attitudes that convey to a member of one race that they are considered inferior in talents and intellect.

Slavery: A practice of forcible servitude dating back to the earliest human civilizations. In the United States, slaves consisted mostly of those taken by slave traders from Africa and their descendants.

Under-Performing Schools: Public schools that have a mediocre, though not totally failing, track record in providing for the "proficiency of students in the basic four subjects of reading, writing, math, and science".

Matt Donnelly

BIBLIOGRAPHY

Adams, C. (2013). Advanced courses. *Education Week, 32*, 5. Retrieved November 15, 2014, from EBSCO Online Database Education Research Complete.

Adams, C. J. (2014). U.S. graduation rate rises—No matter how it's counted. *Education Week, 33*(30), 6. Retrieved January 21, 2016 from EBSCO Online Database Education Research Complete.

Anderson, P. L., & Cotton, C. S. (2001). Failing schools in Michigan: The surprising scale. *Michigan School District Review* (27 Feb 2001). Retrieved July 1, 2007, from the Anderson Economic Group. http://www.andersoneconomicgroup.com

Bibb, H. (1850/2006). Life and Adventures. In *Uncle Tom's Cabin & American Culture.* Charlottesville: University of Virginia. Retrieved June 30, 2007 from the University of Virginia Institute for Advanced Technology in the Humanities Electronic Text Center. http://www.iath.virginia.edu

Broughman, S. P. & Pugh, K.W. (2005). Characteristics of in the United States: Results from the 2001–2002 private school universe survey. *Education Statistics Quarterly, 6* . Retrieved July 1, 2007, from the U.S. Department of Education http://nces.ed.gov

Broughman, S. P., & Swaim, N. L. (2016). *Characteristics of in the United States: Results from the 2013–14 Private School Universe Survey.* National Center for Education Statistics. Retrieved December 20, 2016 from http://nces.ed.gov

Brown University. (2004). *Minority teacher recruitment, development, and retention.* Providence: Brown University. Retrieved July 1, 2007, from http://www.alliance.brown.edu

Chung, J. (2006, Sept 25). [New York] City's difficulty with recruiting minority teachers. *The Gothamist.* Retrieved July 1, 2007, from http://gothamist.com

del Mazo, P. (2006). The multicultural schoolbus: Is bilingual education driving our children, and our nation, towards failure? *2006 Education Law Consortium.* Retrieved July 1, 2007, from the Education Law Consortium http://www.educationlawconsortium.org

Erickson, R. (1997). The laws of ignorance designed to keep slaves (blacks) illiterate and powerless. *Education, 118,* 206. Retrieved June 30, 2007 from EBSCO Online Database Education Research Complete.

Fry, Richard. (2007, Aug 30). The changing racial and ethnic composition of U.S. public schools. *Pew Research Center.* Retrieved December 5, 2013 from http://www.pewhispanic.org

Gibson, J. Y. (1997). *Mighty oaks: Five black educators.* Retrieved June 30, 2007, from http://www.udel.edu

Goyette, K., & Xie, Y. (1999). Educational expectations of Asian American youths: Determinants and ethnic differences. *Sociology of Education, 72,* 22–36. Retrieved June 30, 2007 from EBSCO Online Database Education Research Complete.

Historical Census Browser. (2004). Retrieved June 30, 2007, from the University of Virginia Geospatial and Statistical Data Center http://fisher.lib.virginia.edu

Hoffman, L., & Sable, J. (2006). *Public elementary and secondary students, staff, schools, and school districts: School year 2003-04.* Retrieved June 29, 2007, from the U.S. Department of Education Institute of Education Sciences. http://nces.ed.gov

Hoffman, K., Llargas, C. & Snyder, T.D. (2003). *Status and trends in the education of Blacks.* Retrieved June 29, 2007, from the U.S. Department of Education Institute of Education Science http://nces.ed.gov

Home School Legal Defense Association (1997). *How do minorities fare in home education?* Retrieved June 30, 2007, from http://www.hslda.org

Jennings, J. (2013, Mar 28). Proportion of U.S. students is 10 percent and declining. *Huffington Post.* Retrieved December 5, 2013 from http://www.huffingtonpost.com

Krashen, S. D. (1999). *Bilingual education: Arguments for and (bogus) arguments against.* Retrieved July 1, 2007, from http://digital.georgetown.edu

Lakin, J. M. (2016). Universal screening and the representation of historically underrepresented minority students in gifted education. *Journal of Advanced Academics,* 27(2), 139–149. Retrieved December 20, 2016 from EBSCO Online Database Education Source.

Llagas, C. & Snyder, T. D. (2003). *Status and trends in the education of Hispanics.* Retrieved June 30, 2007, from the U.S. Department of Education National Center for Education Statistics http://nces.ed.gov

MacPherson, K. (2003, August 28). Study finds few male, minority teachers. *Pittsburgh Post-Gazette.* Retrieved July 1, 2007, from the Pittsburgh Post-Gazette http://www.postgazette.com

National Center for Education Statistics. (2006). *Characteristics of in the United States: Results from the 2003-2004 private school universe survey: Percentage distribution of students, by racial/ethnic background, and percentage minority students in , by selected characteristics: United States, 2001–02.* Retrieved June 29, 2007, from the U.S. Department of Education National Center for Education Statistics http://nces.ed.gov

National Center for Education Statistics. (2016). The condition of education: Racial/ethnic enrollment in public schools. *National Center for Education Statistics.* Retrieved January 21, 2016 from http://nces.ed.gov

National Center for Education Statistics. (2016). Fast Facts: English language learners. Retrieved December 20, 2016 from https://nces.ed.gov

National Center for Education Statistics. (2015). Fast Facts: Public and private school comparison. Retrieved December 20, 2016 from http://nces.ed.gov

National Center for Education Statistics. (2015). Fast facts: SAT scores. *National Center for Education Statistics.* Retrieved December 20, 2016 from https://nces.ed.gov

National Center for Education Statistics. (2015). Fast facts: Teacher trends. *National Center for Education Statistics.* Retrieved December 20, 2016 from http://nces.ed.gov

National Educational Association (2002). *Tomorrow's teachers. Help wanted: Minority teachers.* Retrieved July 1, 2007, from http://www.nea.org

Perie, M., Vanneman, A., & Goldstein, A. (2005). *Student achievement in : Results from NAEP 2000–2005.* Retrieved July 1, 2007, from the U.S. Department of Education Center for Education Statistics http://nces.ed.gov

Pippert, T. D., Essenburg, L. J., & Matchett, E. J. (2013). We've got minorities, yes we do: Visual representations of racial and ethnic diversity in college recruitment materials. *Journal of Marketing for Higher Education, 23,* 258–282. Retrieved November 15, 2014, from EBSCO Online Database Education Research Complete.

President's Advisory Commission on Educational Excellence for Hispanic Americans (2002). The road to a college diploma: The complex reality of raising educational achievement for Hispanics in the United States. In *The Interim Report of the President's Advisory Commission on Educational Excellence for Hispanic Americans.* Retrieved June 30, 2007, from http://www.yic.gov

President's Advisory Commission on Educational Excellence for Hispanics. (2011). Winning the future: Improving education for the Latino community. *White House.* Retrieved December 5, 2013 from http://www.whitehouse.gov

Siu, S-F. (1996). *Asian American students at risk: A literature review.* Retrieved June 29, 2007, from http://www.csos.jhu.edu

Strauss, V. (2013). U.S. high school graduation rate sees big minority gains. *Washington Post.* Retrieved December 5, 2013 from http://www.washingtonpost.com

Sowell, T. (n.d.). *Race, culture and equality.* Retrieved June 30, 2007, from http://www.tsowell.com

Williams, W. (2003). Black education. *Jewish World Review* (21 Jan. 2003). Retrieved June 30, 2007 from Jewish World Review. http://www.jewishworldreview.com

Zhang, S.Y., & Carrasquillo, A. L. (1995). Chinese parents' influence on academic performance. *New York State Association for Bilingual Education Journal, 10,* 46–53. Retrieved June 29, 2007, from The George Washington University Graduate School of Education and Human Development http://www.ncela.gwu.edu

SUGGESTED READING

Anderson, J. D. (1988). *The Education of Blacks in the South, 1860-1935.* Chapel Hill: University of North Carolina Press. Retrieved on June 30, 2007, from http://www.questia.com

Bower-Phipps, L., Homa, T. D., Albaladejo, C., Johnson, A. M., & Cruz, M. C. (2013). Connecting with the "other" side of us: A cooperative inquiry by self-identified minorities in a teacher preparation program. *Teacher Education Quarterly, 40,* 29–51. Retrieved November 15, 2014, from EBSCO Online Database Education Research Complete.

Frisby, C. L. (2015). Helping minority children in school psychology: Failures, challenges, and opportunities. *School Psychology Forum, 9*(2), 74–87. Retrieved January 21, 2016 from EBSCO Online Database Education Research Complete.

Fryer, Jr., R. G., & Levitt, S. D. (2006). The black-white test score gap through third grade. *American Law & Economics Review,* 8, 249–281. Retrieved July 2, 2007 from EBSCO Online Database Education Research Complete.

Fuligni, A. J. (1997). The academic achievement of adolescents from immigrant families: The roles of family background, attitudes, and behavior. *Child Development, 68,* 351–363. Retrieved June 30, 2007 from EBSCO Online Database Education Research Complete.

Gottfried, M. A., Conchas, G. Q., & Hinga, B. M. (Eds.). (2015). *Inequality, power and school success: Case studies on racial disparity and opportunity in education.* New York, NY: Routledge.

National Center for Education Statistics. (2007). The condition of education 2007 (NCES 2007-064), Table 23–1. Retrieved July 1, 2007 from the U.S. Department of Education National Center for Education Statistics. http://nces.ed.gov

Thernstrom, A.M. & Thernstrom, S. (2004). *No excuses: Closing the racial gap in learning.* New York: Simon & Schuster.

Ward, N. L., Strambler, M.J., & Linke, L. H. (2013). Increasing educational attainment among urban minority youth: A model of university, school, and community partnerships.

Journal of Negro Education, 82, 312–325. Retrieved December 5, 2013 from EBSCO online database, Education Research Complete. Retrieved December 5, 2013 from EBSCO online database, SocINDEX with Full Text.

HISTORY OF TEACHER EDUCATION

This article provides a historical overview of the field of teacher education. Teacher education refers to programs that help teachers develop quality and effective teaching and learning strategies to use in the classroom. The teacher education field began during the eighteenth century when Benjamin Franklin recognized the need to have quality, educated teachers who could train others to teach. Today, teacher education programs provide future teachers with a number of methods to use while teaching, including reflective teaching skills, tools to use while teaching in diverse settings, instruction on how to use the realistic approach, episteme & phronesis, use of computers & technology, training during early field experiences, tools to use when teaching disabled students, and enhanced focus on clinical experiences and training access during the five-year programs.

KEYWORDS: Accountability; No Child Left Behind (NCLB); Normal schools; Pedagogy; Teacher education; Teacher quality; Teacher preparation programs

OVERVIEW

Teacher education refers to programs that help teachers develop quality and effective teaching and learning strategies to use in the classroom (Hagger & McIntyre, 2000). The field of Teacher Education can generally be defined as a group of educational programs that prepare future teachers.

Research on teacher education shows that the profession involves more than just an understanding of teaching, but also an understanding of the process in which new teachers learn effective teaching techniques, and how they can be taught to do so. Hagger and McIntyre posit that initial teacher education can be understood best in terms of interactions among intelligent people in varying positions, who have their own agendas and have their own unique ways of pursuing them. The differences in ideas and understandings that new student teachers bring to the profession, the passion for their individual preconceptions, and how learning is influenced within teacher education programs all make up the body of research on teacher education today.

The teacher education field has a long history of development. The preparation of teachers in the Colonial and Revolutionary periods in the seventeenth and eighteenth century United States was very different. No high-school or college diploma was required during that time, so becoming a teacher involved obtaining approval from a local clergy member or board of trustees connected with a religious institution. As long as one could read, write, spell and was considered to have a positive moral character, he or she was deemed qualified to be a teacher (Ornstein & Levine, 2006).

Prior to the American Revolution in 1775, nine colonial colleges were charted, each existing to grant academic degrees. These institutions were: Harvard, Yale, Princeton, Penn, Columbia, Brown, Dartmouth, Cornell University, College of William & Mary and Rutgers University (Roche, 1986). Most teachers in these colleges were untrained women who were poorly paid, and others were ex-soldiers or indentured servants. Because individuals were struggling to make it on a new continent, they accepted whatever pay was offered (Parker, 1990).

In 1750, Benjamin Franklin recognized the need for quality, educated teachers who could train others to teach. He believed that future teachers could be educated in a Philadelphia academy that he helped establish, which had been modeled after some of the London academies in which he served as an apprentice. So, Franklin set out to make this plan come to fruition. Later, additional academies were created to educate future teachers by English Quakers, Baptists and other nonconformists, many of which were established because their sons had been barred from Oxford and Cambridge colleges which were controlled by the Church of England (Parker).

The academies, which offered applied subjects, operated as terminal secondary schools that appealed to many rising middle class Americans. Some of the academies were private for example, the early Zion Parnassus Academy (1785), located near Salisbury, NC. Others include a private academy in Concord, VT, Phillips Academy in Andover, MA, and seminaries in Plymouth, NH and Craftsbury, VT, all established by Congregational minister Samuel Read Hall (1795-1877), often referred to as a "teacher of teachers," (Parker). Hall created a number of instructor's manuals to use in the academies, which were later used by the normal schools as a textbook (Parker).

After 1827, the state of New York offered financial support to academies to prepare teachers, as most were private, multipurpose institutions, whose teacher education departments received little respect. Even the colleges had little respect for the teaching education programs in the academies, because most were liberal and believed that no professional training should take place at their institutions. Therefore, they offered no support toward preparing future teachers. Consequently, until the establishment of Normal Schools, teacher education had no real home (Parker).

Normal schools were established during the nineteenth century. They were two-year educational institutions that offered history and philosophy of education courses, methods of teaching, and practice teaching for those striving to become teachers. Many of these schools however, became four-year teacher education colleges by the end of the nineteenth century (Ornstein & Levine).

Enrollment in normal schools was initially slow. In 1839, enrollment in the first state-supported normal school consisted of only three female students. Student enrollment increased by 1840 however, with 26 students from ten states between Maine and California completing the teacher education programs by the end of the term. By 1875, enrollment had increased to over 23,000 in 70 state-supported normal schools throughout 25 states, including ten county-supported schools and ten city-supported normal schools. Courses on the history of education, teaching elementary school subjects, and the art of teaching made up the normal school curriculum. Each normal school included student teaching practice sites, also known as laboratory schools or practice schools (Parker).

When the public school systems began to form in the Midwest and western states in the late 1800s, growth in normal schools was significantly enhanced. Program duration for the normal schools began at one year, and later increased to three years once the schools became more secure (Parker). Normal schools received additional support in 1862, when the Morrill Act was established. It granted 30,000 acres worth of federal land grants to senators and representatives in the Congress in each state, and provided support to the teacher education profession. The land was used to establish college institutions focusing on engineering, agricultural education, liberal arts, as well as professional education (Andrews, 1918).

After 1900 the problems facing teacher education came to the forefront. Parker writes that low pay, part-year work (since schools were only open 3 to 7 months each year) and unfair hiring practices plagued the teacher education profession. Most teaching jobs went to relatives of school board members, and because it was so difficult to get a teaching position, few young people chose to spend time and money on teacher education in colleges or normal schools. This lack of interest in teacher education drove the efforts of the National Teachers Association, established in 1857 and reorganized in 1870 as the National Education Association (NEA). Its mission was to recruit teachers, promote teacher institutes, support normal schools and increase teacher salaries.

Though the NEA had the ability to advocate for various teacher issues, the teacher education profession faced other issues that were beyond its scope. For example, teacher quality and the guidelines required for certification/licensing was at issue. At this time, teacher certification was local and controlled by districts until individual states gained control. Because the need for teachers was so great, certification requirements were often low and often

overlooked, thereby resulting in poor teacher quality in many of the teacher education programs (Parker).

Historically, however, individual state education laws have governed teacher preparation programs in the United States, deeming that each state is responsible for the functions of public elementary and secondary education in their states. In addition, states are expected to play a significant role in licensing teachers. The rationale of state educator licensing programs is that parents need to send their children to school, and because they send their children to school, they have the right to expect that a reasonable amount of standard of care will be displayed while the school is in charge of their child. In addition, parents have the right to expect that teachers have the appropriate knowledge and skills necessary to provide their children with a quality education. Licenses protect educators from arbitrary dismissals based on the assertion that the teacher does not have the knowledge and skills needed for the task (Early, 1994).

Today, individual states must make necessary changes in their teacher education programs, and institutions must modify certification program requirements to maintain their historical role as arbitrator of educational quality (Bales, 2006). To date, all public school teachers in the United States are required to be certified by the state in their specific subject area or grade level. With the exception of alternative certification or temporary certification, a bachelor's degree or five years of college-level work is required to begin to teach (Ornstein & Levine; Kaye).

Decades ago, teachers could obtain teaching certificates that were good for life. Today certificates issued by the states are valid for three to five years, and require proof of positive evaluations or college coursework for renewal. The process of issuing teaching certifications is not without issue. Differences in requirements from state-to-state often lead to problems in teacher preparation programs. It becomes difficult to measure the preparedness of entering teachers because of the diversity of required arts and science semester hours. Across the nation, some programs require thirty hours and some require up to seventy-five hours. In addition, courses vary in content from program to program, making it difficult for states and institutions to guarantee that educators have studied the same concepts and have the same types of skills (Ornstein & Levine).

State mandates are also at issue for the teacher education profession. Though teacher education programs have traditionally been the responsibility of individual states, the United States Constitution affirms that one of its roles is to provide for the welfare of its citizens. With this obligation national policymakers issue state mandates to address student achievement and teacher quality, often during perceived educational crises. Examples include national policies and reauthorizations like the 1958 National Defense Education Act (NDEA), the 1963 ESEA (Elementary and Secondary Education Act), later referred to as No Child Left Behind (NCLB) in 2001, and the 1992 reauthorization of the Higher Education Act (HEA). Each mandate has been developed in an effort to push specific education reforms in each state (Royster & Chernay, 1981; Bales).

Teacher quality is one aspect of NCLB that is of great importance. The mandate requires all individuals who teach students to be "highly qualified" in the subject in which they teach. Highly qualified is defined as holding a state certification, at least an earned bachelor's degree, and successful completion of the basic skills and subject matter tests for their specific areas of interest. Some NCLB opponents feel this definition fails to include the quality of teaching in terms of content knowledge, and has caused many states to use paper-and-pencil tests as determinants of teacher quality. For example, in Washington State, the requirement for entering the teacher education program includes passing the basic skills test as well as the Praxis II, a timed paper-and-pencil exam of pedagogy and content knowledge (Selwyn, 2007).

REFLECTIVE TEACHING

Institutions have placed emphasis on producing "reflective" teachers who regularly observe and reflect on their teaching, then make the necessary adjustments to their teaching methods. This concept is also known as "expert decision-making," "higher-order self-reflection," and "inquiry-oriented teacher education" (Stewart, 1994; Yost, Sentner & Forlenz-Bailey, 2000; Risko, Vukelich & Roskos, 2002). Reflective teaching implies that teachers develop continuously so their training is an ongoing process (Korthagen & Kessels, 1999). Though teacher education programs vary from institution to institution, hundreds of programs have incorporated reflective teaching in their curriculums.

TEACHING IN DIVERSE SETTINGS

With the U.S. education system continuously becoming more and more diverse, it is necessary for future teachers to have some type of cultural competence training. Smith (1998), Claycomb (2000) and Holm & Horn (2003) suggest that many Teacher Education programs and teacher licensing programs require future teachers to prove that they understand why it is important to understand the backgrounds of diverse students. For example, the Praxis III, a teacher performance assessment, includes within its licensing agreement, that a candidate demonstrate a comprehensive understanding of the knowledge and experiences of students from different backgrounds.

REALISTIC APPROACH

Realistic mathematics education, also known as the Realistic Approach, assumes that students can and should develop their own mathematical notions based on practical experiences and/or problems. Because mathematics causes so many problems for so many children, finding ways to help children apply what they learn is necessary. The realistic approach for example, instructs the teacher to present an everyday problem to the child. He or she might encourage the child to attempt to solve the problem by using practical mathematics, inquiry and reflection, teamwork to help solve the problem, and hands-on activities. The idea is that the child acquires knowledge and skills through experience to use in a real-life dilemma (Korthagen & Kessels).

EPISTEME VS. PHRONESIS

Aristotle's concepts of episteme and phronesis are used to help explain confusion associated with the word "theory." Kessels and Korthagen posit that epistemic knowledge requires a teacher to offer general conceptions that apply to a variety of situations. This information is based on research and can be considered theory. Episteme strives to help individuals think in more broad terms, helping individuals know more about *many* situations. On the other hand, phronesis knowledge is situation-specific and should be applied on a case by case basis. This knowledge is more perceptual than conceptual, and focuses the attention of the individual on *specific* characteristics of the problem, and how one might perceive a particular situation. Phronesis is also considered to be a key element in the idea of theory development.

COMPUTER & TECHNOLOGY USE

Most teacher education programs today offer some type of training on computers and other technology. Coker and Wilson (1997), AACTE (2000) & Loschert (2003) suggests that 90% or more teacher education programs have some type of computer or technology laboratories, which include an extensive variety of activities. Future teachers are taught basic computer skills, introduced to elementary and secondary school hardware and software, and learn to use technology in their lesson design and delivery.

EARLY FIELD EXPERIENCE

During the early part of many teacher education programs, candidates are required to spend a great deal of time in elementary and secondary schools to help with their preparation. Classroom observation, teacher aide duties or similar field experiences at other schools are among the duties assigned. Most of these experiences relate significantly to pedagogical methods and educational psychology courses taught within the teacher education programs (Swanson, 1995; Berliner, 2000; Hove & Gill, 2003).

TEACHING DISABLED STUDENTS

Most teacher education programs require future teachers to interact with students with various disabilities. Because teachers often have special-needs students in their classes, this training helps prepare them for real-life experiences with disabled students. By law, disabled students must be included in regular classes as often as possible. Full inclusion of disabled students is the goal, regardless of the extent of the child's disability. For this reason, most teachers should expect to have responsibilities dealing with special needs of students (Strawderman & Lindsey, 1995; Littleton, 2000).

FIFTH-YEAR & FIVE-YEAR PROGRAMS

Several states and numerous institutions of higher learning incorporated fifth-year programs or extended teacher education programs through five years of training during the 1980s. In fifth-year programs, there are little to no professional-study courses involved during the first four years, and preparation for the teaching career is the focus of the fifth year. In five-year programs, candidates have an opportunity to experience professional preparation throughout the entire undergraduate term, with enhanced focus on clinical experiences and training (Darling-Hammond, 1998).

TEACHER EDUCATOR'S VIEW

Selwyn (2007) believes that potential teacher candidates who don't test well on the required exams by No Child Left Behind are being eliminated as a result of the increased emphasis on testing used to determine one's teaching abilities. This focus presents an image of teachers who cannot use their knowledge of the curriculum, students and human development to make good decisions.

Research findings have been inconclusive, however, in regard to whether teacher academic abilities explain how well they will perform in the classroom as teachers. Though there are over 600 tests used throughout the U.S. to measure candidates' content knowledge and basic skills, there are still no findings to suggest that these tests have the ability to predict who will be a good teacher (Cochran-Smith & Zeichner, 2005). There are many discrepancies about what the most effective teaching techniques are, so much so that it is impossible to quantify or test for what makes a good, quality teacher (Wilson & Youngs, 2005).

FUTURE EDUCATION RESEARCH & POLICYMAKING

Bales suggests that policymakers are not giving the teacher education field the opportunity to use its professional judgment in preparing future teachers. Instead, a "tug-of-war" between state and national authorities is present as these authorities feel that graduates of teacher education programs are not adequately prepared to address student achievement needs in the classrooms. The tug-of-war is over teacher licensing, recruitment, preparation and professional development policymaking, and has placed educators on the sideline in the war with little or no input.

As a result of the contention that in some populations student achievement levels are inadequate and are less likely to have fully prepared, licensed educators, various groups across the nation have advocated for a change in control and accountability. In turn, locus of control and accountability in U.S. policies on teacher education have changed over the last

20 years. For example, what used to be an incentive for the teacher education field is now a mandate, and what used to be local accountability systems are now state and national-level accountability systems. However, no one approach works for the entire field of teacher education. Throughout the United States educational system, the standards-based policy is present but only represents a single solution and does not account for the diversity found in individual schools, or consider the unequal opportunities to learn that exist in different school systems (Bales).

A second issue concerning state and national policymakers is the small body of knowledge available on teacher education research. Though some research exists on alternative certification programs in the U.S., policymakers believe that a strong research agenda including international teacher education research could provide the United States with other alternatives to use in teacher preparation programs (Bales).

Some research suggests that the most effective teachers are those who reflect on the interactions they have with their students, and in turn use the new information gained to guide their classroom curriculums. Policymakers wish to investigate how successful teachers have been in using this new knowledge in their teaching. Questions to ask are whether dispositions were present in candidates before entering a teaching preparation program, and can teaching preparation programs help cultivate a candidate's skills? Because U.S. teacher preparation programs are not without fault, policymakers believe these programs can learn from collaborations with international colleagues. Answers to these questions could support the need to change recruitment processes, licensing, and professional development policies (Bales, 2006).

Bales stresses that policymakers must give the teacher education field the opportunity to use its professional judgment in preparing future teachers. They must not ignore the input of teacher education professionals but rather include them in the decisions to identify the best methods and opportunities for students to learn.

TERMS & CONCEPTS

1862 Morrill Act: The first Morrill Act of 1862 granted 30,000 acres worth of federal land grants to senators and representatives in the Congress in each state to support higher education. This act gave institutions the ability to educate people in agriculture, home economics, mechanical arts, and other professions that were practical at the time, including teacher education programs.

Accountability: Accountability refers to the idea of holding teachers, administrators, and school board members responsible for the performance of students or for appropriate use of educational funds.

Locus of Control: Locus of control refers to an individual's generalized expectations concerning where control over subsequent events resides.

National Teachers Association: The National Teachers Association was an organization with interests in recruiting teachers, promoting teachers' institutes, supporting normal schools and increasing salaries in the early 1900s. Later became the National Education Association.

No Child Left Behind (NCLB): NCLB is a federal plan instituted in 2001 that called for schools to make annual gains in test scores on a pace to have all students meeting state-defined standards by the year 2014.

Normal Schools: Normal schools were two-year teacher education institutions established during the eighteenth century.

Pedagogy: Pedagogy is the art or science of being a teacher, generally refers to methods of instruction or a style of instruction.

Praxis Exam: The Praxis exam is a timed paper-and-pencil exam of pedagogy and content knowledge used to assess a teacher's performance. It is required to receive professional licensure for teacher certification and was created by the Educational Testing Service (ETS).

Standard of Care: The standard of care is the amount of caution required of an individual who is responsible for another.

Teacher Education: Teacher education refers programs that help teachers develop quality and effective teaching and learning strategies to use in the classroom.

Teacher Preparation Programs: Teacher preparation programs are courses of study that prepare candidates to become certified teachers within the K-12 school system. Programs offer candidates specific courses in general education, subject matter preparation, professional education, special seminars and colloquia, and other opportunities for practical field experiences.

Teacher Quality: Teacher quality refers to teaching ability. The law defines 'highly qualified' mostly in terms of content. According to the No Child Left Behind plan, to be highly qualified, teachers must be certified by the state, have at least a bachelor's degree, and pass basic skills and subject area tests.

Belinda B. McFeeters

BIBLIOGRAPHY

Andrews, B. (1918). The land grant of 1862 and the land-grant college. In A. C. Ornstein & D.U. Levine (Eds.), *Foundations of education.* (9th ed., p. 179). Boston, MA: Houghton Mifflin Company.

Aronson, B., & Anderson, A. (2013). Critical Teacher Education and the Politics of Teacher Accreditation: Are We Practicing What We Preach?. Journal For Critical Education Policy Studies (JCEPS), 11, 244-262. Retrieved December 15, 2013, from EBSCO Online Database Education Research Complete.

Bales, B. L. (2006). Teacher education policies in the United States: The accountability shift since 1980, *Teaching and Teacher Education, 22,* 395-407.

Berliner, D. C. (2000). A personal response to those who bash teacher education. In A.C. Ornstein & D.U. Levine (Eds.), *Foundations of education.* (9th ed., p. 14-15). Boston, MA: Houghton Mifflin Company.

Claycomb, C. (2000). High-quality urban school teachers. In A. C. Ornstein & D.U. Levine (Eds.), *Foundations of education.* (9th ed., p. 16). Boston, MA: Houghton Mifflin Company.

Cochran-Smith, M. (2005). The new teacher education: For better or for worse? *Educational Researcher, 34,* 3-17.

Cochran-Smith, M., & Zeichner, K. (2005). Executive summary: The report of the AERA panel on research and teacher education. In M. Cochran-Smith & K. Zeichner (Eds.), *Studying teacher education* (pp. 1-36). Mahwah, NJ: Lawrence Erlbaum.

Coker, D. R. & Wilson, M. (1997). Reconceptualizing the process of teacher preparation. In A. C. Ornstein & D.U. Levine (Eds.), *Foundations of education.* (9th ed., p. 179). Boston, MA: Houghton Mifflin Company.

Darling-Hammond, L. (1998). Teachers and teaching. In A. C. Ornstein & D.U. Levine (Eds.), *Foundations of education.* (9th ed., p. 15). Boston, MA: Houghton Mifflin Company.

Early, P. M. (1994). *Federal attention to teacher certification and licensure: Two policy case studies.* Unpublished doctoral dissertation, Virginia Polytechnic Institute and State University, Blacksburg, VA.

Hagger, H. & McIntyre (2000). What can research tell us about teacher education? *Oxford Review, 26 ,* 483-494.

Holm, L. & Horn, C. (2003). Priming schools of education for today's teachers. In A.C. Ornstein & D.U. Levine (Eds.), *Foundations of education.* (9th ed., p. 16). Boston, MA: Houghton Mifflin Company. Boston, MA: Houghton Mifflin Company.

Hove, A. & Gill, B. (2003). The Benedum Collaborative Model of teacher education. In A. C. Ornstein & D.U. Levine (Eds.), *Foundations of education.* (9th ed., p. 14-15). Boston, MA: Houghton Mifflin Company.

Kaye, E. A. (2003). Requirements for certification of teachers, counselors, librarians, and administrators of elementary and secondary schools. In A. C. Ornstein & D.U. Levine (Eds.), *Foundations of education.* (9th ed., p. 11). Boston, MA: Houghton Mifflin Company.

Kessels, J. P. A. M. & Korthagen, F. a. J. (1996). The relationship between theory and practice: Back to the classics. *Educational Researcher, 25,* 17-22.

Korthagen, F. A. & Kessels, J. P. (1999). Linking theory and practice: Changing the pedagogy of teacher education, *Educational Researcher, 28,* 4-17.

Littleton, D. (2000). Preparing teachers for hard-to-staff schools. In A. C. Ornstein & D.U. Levine (Eds.), *Foundations of education.* (9th ed., p. 15-16). Boston, MA: Houghton Mifflin Company.

Loschert, K. (2003). Are you ready? In A. C. Ornstein & D.U. Levine (Eds.), *Foundations of education.* (9th ed., p. 15). Boston, MA: Houghton Mifflin Company.

Mirel, J. (2011). Bridging the "widest street in the world" reflections on the history of teacher education. *American Educator, 35,* 6-12. Retrieved December 15, 2013, from EBSCO Online Database Education Research Complete.

Ornstein, A. C. & Levine, D. U. (2006). *Foundations of education.* Boston: Houghton Mifflin Company.

Parker, F. (1990). *Teacher education USA: Western Carolina University centennial in national perspective.* (ERIC Document Reproduction Service No. ED 360253)

Risko, V. J. Vukelich, C. & Roskos, K. (2000). Preparing teachers for reflective practice. In A. C. Ornstein & D.U. Levine (Eds.), *Foundations of education.* (9th ed., p. 15). Boston, MA: Houghton Mifflin Company.

Roche, J. (1986). *The colonial colleges in the war for American independence.* Millwood: Associated Faculty Press, Inc.

Royster, P. M. & Chernay, G. J. (1981). *Teacher education: The impact of federal policy.* Springfield: Banister Press.

Selwyn, D. (2007). Highly quantified teachers: NCLB and teacher education. (No Child Left Behind). *Journal of Teacher Education 58,* 124-137.

Smith, G. P. (1998). Common sense about uncommon knowledge. In A. C. Ornstein & D.U. Levine (Eds.), *Foundations of education.* (9th ed., p. 16). Boston, MA: Houghton Mifflin Company.

Stewart, D. K. (1994). Reflective teaching in preservice teacher education. In A.C. Ornstein & D.U. Levine

(Eds.), *Foundations of education.* (9th ed., p. 15). Boston, MA: Houghton Mifflin Company.

Strawderman, C. & Lindsey, P. (1995). Keeping up with the times. In A.C. Ornstein & D.U. Levine (Eds.), *Foundations of education.* (9th ed., p. 15-16). Boston, MA: Houghton Mifflin Company.

Swanson, J. (1995). Systemic reform in the professionalism of educators. In A.C. Ornstein & D.U. Levine (Eds.), *Foundations of education.* (9th ed., p. 14-15). Boston, MA: Houghton Mifflin Company.

Walsh, K. (2013). 21st-century teacher education. *Education Next, 13,* 18-24. Retrieved December 15, 2013, from EBSCO Online Database Education Research Complete.

Wilson, S., & Youngs, P. (2005). Research on accountability processes in teacher education. In M. Cochran-Smith & K. Zeichner (Eds.), *Studying teacher education.* (pp. 549-590). Mahwah, NJ: Lawrence Erlbaum.

Yost, D. S., Sentner, S. M. & Forlenza-Bailey, A. (2000). An examination of the construct of critical reflection. In A. C. Ornstein & D.U. Levine (Eds.), *Foundations of education.* (9th ed., p. 15). Boston, MA: Houghton Mifflin Company.

SUGGESTED READING

Allen, M. (2003). *Eight questions on teacher preparation: What does the research say?* Denver: Education Commission of the States.

Bales, B. (2002). Strange bedfellow? Title I funding, alternative certification programs, *and state teacher standards.*

In Paper presented at the American Association of Colleges for Teacher Education, New York City.

Cochran-Smith, M., & Lytle, S. L. (1999). Relationship of knowledge and practice: Teacher learning in communities. *Review of Research in Education, 24,* 249-306.

Cochran-Smith, M., & Zeichner, K. (2005). Executive summary: The report of the AERA panel on research and teacher education. In M. Cochran-Smith & K. Zeichner (Eds.), *Studying teacher education* (pp. 1-36). Mahwah, NJ: Lawrence Erlbaum.

Conant, J. B. (1964). *The education of American teachers.* New York: McGraw-Hill.

Hanushek, E. (2002). *Teacher quality.* In L. Izumi & W. Evers (Eds.), Teacher quality (pp. 1-12). Palo Alto, CA: Hoover Institution.

Hollins, E., & Torres Guzman, M. (2005). Research on preparing teachers for diverse populations. In M. Cochran-Smith & K. Zeichner (Eds.), *Studying teacher education* (pp. 477-548). Mahwah, NJ: Lawrence Erlbaum.

Murray, F. (1996). The *teacher educator's handbook: Building a knowledge base for the preparation of teachers.* San Francisco: Jossey-Bass.

Spillane, J. P. (1999). External reform initiatives and teachers' efforts to reconstruct their practice: The mediating role of teachers' zones of enactment, *Journal of Curriculum Studies 31,* 143-175.

Wilson, S., Floden, R. & Ferrini-Mundy, J. (2002). Teacher preparation research: An insiders' view from the outside, *Journal of Teacher Education 53,* 190-204.

WOMEN IN EDUCATION

This article provides a brief overview of some of the influential women in the history of education in the U.S. It discusses their selflessness, their passions for improving educational opportunities for others, as well as the significant contributions they made to the field of education and in related movements. Equity in the academy with regard to gender equality is also discussed.

KEYWORDS: Academy; Discrimination; Educational opportunity; Equity; Gender equality; Male privilege; Public education; Salary gap; Seminary; Women educators

OVERVIEW

Education has always been considered the ticket to upward mobility in the United States, promoting economic benefits such as higher earnings and increased national productivity, and noneconomic benefits like intellectual values, problem solving, and increased civic participation (Lewis, 2003). Historically, both men and women have desired these benefits. However, in many cases reaping the benefits has been more challenging for women than for men.

Women have historically been excluded from educational opportunities in the United States. During the colonial period, Americans dismissed the notion of women attaining an education and no significant education was offered to girls by the colonial schools. Some girls were taught to read, but they could not enroll in academies, colleges, or Latin grammar schools (Johnson, Musial, Hall, Gollnick, & Dupuis, 2004; Solomon, 1985). Despite the exclusivity, many women traveled the arduous road to pursue their education, open the doors for other women, and continued to make significant contributions to the education field.

MARGARETHE MEYER SCHURZ

Margarethe Meyer Schurz (1833-1876) is best known as the founder of the first American kindergarten. Born in Hamburg, Germany, to an affluent family, and educated in the arts and education, Schurz developed a passion for children and their kindergarten education (Johnson et al., 2004; Heuer, 1998).

When Schurz was a teenager, she was exposed to the teachings of Friedrich Froebel, German kindergarten founder and advocate. *Kindergarten* is a German term, literally translated as "children's garden." Margarethe Meyer Schurz became enthusiastic about the idea of a "garden for a crop called children." When she got married and moved to the United States, she brought the ideas and principles she learned from Froebel along with her (Heuer).

In 1856, Schurz and her husband settled in Watertown, Wisconsin, where she began to share Froebel's philosophy while caring for her daughter and four other children in her neighborhood. She taught them how to play games, sing songs, and perform in group activities that focused their energies and simultaneously prepped them for further schooling. Impressed with the results of Schurz's work, other parents asked her to work with their children as well. This led to the opening of the first kindergarten in the United States (Heuer).

Though small in its beginnings, with a total of five students, the idea spread quickly, due in part to speaking engagements her husband had been asked to give. Margarethe's husband, Carl Schurz, was a prominent activist and politician who was often called to do speaking engagements across the country. Margarethe traveled with him and used these opportunities to talk about the benefits of kindergartens. Soon, her work captured an audience, and kindergarten became a key component of American education. Kindergarten study was also accepted as a course of study for the preparation of elementary teachers (Heuer).

ELLA FLAGG YOUNG

Ella Flagg Young (1845-1918) was a female educator willing to tread new waters. A child of working-class parents, Young overcame a number of obstacles at an early age. She taught herself to read and write at age nine, and when she turned ten, her mother allowed her to attend school (Johnson et al.).

A born teacher, Ella Flagg Young took teacher education courses and found a public school teacher to help her create her own practicum opportunity to use in her own classroom upon graduation. After graduation, she worked in the Chicago public school system in various positions over 53 years. Her first role was to teach in a lower class Chicago high school as a math teacher. She then became the head of the practice-teaching classrooms, next a principal in Chicago's largest public school, and later the first female superintendent of the Chicago public schools (1909-1915), a major city school system. Flagg enjoyed many "firsts," as each of these achievements was considered extraordinary for a female during this time period (Johnson, et al.).

Young was passionate about improving democracy and education and wasn't afraid of a challenge. She was also the first female president of the male-dominated National Education Association (NEA) in 1910, a decade prior to suffrage for women (Johnson et al.). A true leader in education and women's suffrage, Ella Flagg Young is one to remember.

ANNE SULLIVAN MACY

Born in Feeding Hills, Massachusetts, to poor, illiterate Irish immigrants, Anne Sullivan Macy (1866-1936) is best known as Helen Keller's teacher and a strong educator and advocate for the American Foundation for the Blind (AFB). Her accomplishments however, are often overshadowed by Helen Keller's story (American Foundation for the Blind, 2007).

Anne Macy faced a number of challenges in her early years. She was known to have a bad temper, by age seven she was blind due to untreated trachoma, and she had no formal schooling during her adolescent years until age 14. In addition, Macy's mother was ill with tuberculosis and died when Anne was eight. To add to this, her father was an alcoholic who later abandoned her and her younger brother (American Foundation for the Blind, 2007).

According to the American Foundation for the Blind, Anne Macy's life changed significantly for the good in 1880 when she enrolled in the Perkins School for the Blind in Boston, Massachusetts. She quickly learned to read, write, and use the manual alphabet to communicate with a friend who was deaf and blind. Learning to use the manual alphabet was the key to the future success she enjoyed. While Macy was a student at Perkins, her sight improved significantly after several successful eye surgeries. In 1886 she completed her degree at Perkins and was the valedictorian of her class. Shortly thereafter, Macy met the family of Helen Keller and was asked to come to Tuscumbia, Alabama, to work with Helen, who was blind, deaf, and mute. Macy agreed and began her lifelong role as Helen Keller's teacher in 1887.

Anne Macy managed to connect with Helen Keller, who was then a rebellious and angry child. For thirteen years, Macy was Helen's educator. She used everything she had learned from the Perkins School for the Blind, and modified it to shape a smooth method of teaching for Helen. She taught Helen by signing words into Helen's hand, as a way to help her understand that everything had a name. In 1900, Helen Keller was admitted into Radcliffe College in Cambridge, Massachusetts, and Macy served as her interpreter for each class until graduation. Anne Macy took an initially unruly but bright child, and transformed her into an educated person. She did such an outstanding job that Mark Twain gave her the name "Miracle Worker" (American Foundation for the Blind).

Anne Sullivan Macy experienced great success with Helen Keller and began to receive public attention for her work. In various letters, she shared her success with the director of the Perkins School for the Blind, who later published them in the institution's annual reports. She also shared her work with Alexander Graham Bell, inventor of the telephone and also an educator of the deaf. Bell in turn publicized Macy's work through a New York newspaper and gained additional exposure (American Foundation for the Blind).

Because of their educational successes, many people wanted to meet Anne Sullivan Macy and Helen Keller. In 1888 for example, Macy went to Washington, D.C., along with Helen, her mother, and Alexander Bell, to meet with President Grover Cleveland to share what she they had learned (American Foundation for the Blind).

After Macy completed her assignment as Helen Keller's educator, she traveled throughout the United States with two friends, Helen and Polly Thomson, giving lectures about teaching the deaf and blind. In 1924, Anne Macy continued to work with Helen Keller as a partner, at the American Foundation for the Blind. For that year, the two served as advocates, counselors, and fundraisers for the foundation.

WOMEN IN THE ACADEMY

After World War II, women were encouraged to reduce their participation in the labor force and colleges, which had burgeoned during the war years. However, soon they began to return to the scene. By 1960, more women were working and studying in college than ever before (Eisenmann, 2002). However, prior to this time, women had been given few formal education opportunities, with unequal access to various fields of study (Johnson). They often experienced marginalization and were not considered serious students (Thelin, 2004). Despite significantly limited opportunities, some women chose to take a step toward improving education for women.

EMMA WILLARD

One woman who worked toward opening the doors for other women was Emma Willard (1787-1870). Willard was known as a pioneer and champion for the education of females during a period when very few educational opportunities existed for them. At this time, wealthy parents either hired private tutors or sent their daughters to a seminary for girls. Families with lower incomes taught their daughters to read and write at home, provided that another family member had the skills to do so (Johnson, Musial, Hall, Gollnick, & Dupuis).

Emma Willard was one of seventeen children born to a poor family. She was first taught by her father, a farmer and college-educated Revolutionary War captain. At fifteen, she attended the district schools and for a short period of time, she enrolled in a local academy. Eager to learn, Willard continued to seek education, including studying the mathematics and philosophy textbooks of her nephew, who attended Middlebury College at the time (Solomon).

Emma Willard realized the limitations of her educational background and was motivated to make other educational opportunities available to women. She was the first to publicly declare that advanced education for women should not depend solely on the individual and chance circumstances. Emma Willard's greatest accomplishment came in 1821, with the establishment of Troy Seminary, one of the first seminaries for women in Troy, New

York. With no endowment, the school opened to offer an educational program comparable to the boys' school. Owned and run by the Willard family for three generations, the school experienced great success for many years (Solomon; Johnson, et al.).

MARTHA CAREY THOMAS

Martha Carey Thomas, also known as M. Carey Thomas or Carey Thomas (1857-1935), was an educator and advocate for higher education for women. Like Emma Willard, she was known as a pioneer in women's education, and remembered for the roles she played at Bryn Mawr College, including serving as president of the institution (Lewis).

Thomas was born in Baltimore, Maryland, into a Quaker family and received her initial education in Quaker schools. Her father was a physician and her mother and aunt were very active in the Women's Christian Temperance Union (WCTU), a women's organization focused on eliminating the sale of alcohol in establishments (Lewis).

As a child, Martha was an avid reader with a strong will. With the influence of her mother and aunt, her interest in women's rights began early and enhanced her desire to attend Cornell University in the late 1800s. With her mother's support and despite the discouragement from her father (a trustee of the male-only Johns Hopkins University at the time) Martha enrolled in college at Cornell and earned a degree in 1877 (Lewis).

Additional education came in the form of formal tutoring. Because she was not allowed to take formal classes at John Hopkins, Martha was tutored privately. Again with reluctance, Martha's father allowed her to enroll at the University of Leipzig. She began to rethink her decision to attend the university when she was informed that the University of Leipzig would not award PhDs to women. In addition, classroom etiquette at the university was a problem for Martha. So that she did not distract male students, she was made to sit behind a screen during class time. Unwilling to deal with the discomforts at the University of Leipzig, Martha transferred to the University of Zurich and graduated summa cum laude, making her the first woman and foreigner at the institution to achieve these accomplishments (Lewis).

Martha Carey Thomas exhibited strong courage worthy of esteem. Lewis writes that after she graduated, she approached the trustees at Bryn Mawr, the new Quaker women's college, about becoming president of the institution. At the time, Thomas' father was a trustee there. She was appointed as dean and professor of English instead. These positions, however, entailed performing some presidential duties, so she was able to gain the experience after all.

When then president, James E. Rhoads, retired in 1894, Thomas sought the presidency again and narrowly won the vote as the president of Bryn Mawr. While there, Martha Carey Thomas insisted that education at Bryn Mawr was to be of a high standard, and demanded greatness from the students. She served as president until 1922 and as dean until 1908 (Lewis).

Other educational endeavors included working with Mary Gwinn, Mary Garrett, and other women in 1889 to ensure that women were admitted to the Johns Hopkins University Medical School on an equal basis. The group offered a large gift to the Medical School to guarantee that women would have an equal opportunity. In addition, Thomas kept a major interest in women's rights through her work with the National American Woman's Suffrage Association as well as other organizations. Her passion for education, equality, and peace places her as one of the most influential actors in women's education history (Lewis).

MARY MCLEOD BETHUNE

Mary McLeod Bethune (1875-1955) was one of the greatest African American educators and activists during the late 1800s and early 1900s, and is best known for fighting segregation of public venues and working toward equal opportunity in pay, hiring and education. Born in Mayesville, South Carolina, the 15th of 17 children, Bethune was the first family member not born into slavery. Along with picking cotton for wages, Bethune attended a Methodist mission school during her early years. Some reports indicate that when she came home from school, she taught her elder siblings what she had learned each day (Lewis; Johnson, et al.).

Mary McLeod Bethune received a scholarship to Scotia Seminary in North Carolina in 1888. She graduated in 1893 and enrolled in what is now Moody Bible Institute in Chicago, with the intent on doing missionary work in Africa. When informed that African Americans were not eligible for these assignments, she decided to become a teacher in the Presbyterian schools throughout Georgia and South Carolina (Lewis).

Bethune's major contributions began when she moved to Florida and found that schools were needed for the families of workers being brought in to do railway work. With a small number of students, she saw her first success in the opening of the Daytona Normal and Industrial Institute in 1904. As president of the school, Bethune raised all of the funds, ran the school, and taught the students with great success (Lewis). The Daytona Normal and Industrial Institute primarily focused on educating girls who had few options for obtaining an education. It began with an elementary focus and later added secondary courses including a focus on nursing. After adding nursing courses in 1911, Bethune also opened a hospital for African American students who could not use the whites-only hospital. This hospital later closed in 1931 (Lewis).

In the 1920s, as a result of Bethune's efforts, the school became affiliated with the Methodist Episcopal Church, and in 1923, it was merged with the Cookman Institute for men to become Bethune-Cookman College. With a focus on post-secondary courses, particularly teacher training, the school grew in number to 1,000 students. As a junior college, Bethune-Cookman won full accreditation in 1939 and became a four-year college in 1941 (Lewis).

Mary McLeod Bethune not only made contributions to education, but also became involved in political and civic issues. Lewis reports that Presidents Calvin Coolidge and Herbert Hoover chose her to serve on presidential commissions on child welfare, home building, and home ownership. She was later approached by President Franklin D. Roosevelt and First Lady Eleanor Roosevelt, with whom she became close friends. Bethune often consulted with President Roosevelt regarding minority affairs. In 1936, she played a major role in establishing the Federal Committee on Fair Employment Practice. This organization was designed to help eliminate discrimination and exclusion of African Americans by the defense industry (Lewis). Roosevelt appointed Bethune to serve in the administration of various New Deal programs. Among her work with youth nationwide, she was also the only African American in the administration responsible for disbursing funds.

This role included awarding scholarships to African American students (Lewis).

Though she continued to serve in political capacities, including serving as an advisor on interracial relations through President Harry S. Truman's administration, Bethune was a constant in the work of equal opportunity in hiring and education (Lewis). Her tenacity and persistence significantly impacted education as we know it today, particularly for African American women.

IS THERE EQUITY IN THE ACADEMY?

Over the years, women have progressed in the academy, but at a slow rate. In the 1980s and 90s, more and more full-time faculty members were women, representing 40 percent of those in the faculty ranks (Harvey, 2003). In addition, benefits improved with extended tenure-clocks for child-birth, adoption, and family illnesses. Child care centers were also opened at some institutions and employment services were offered for spouses and partners of new hires. In recent years, programs have been created to support women and remove barriers, allowing them to progress throughout the academic ranks and into upper-level administrative positions (cf. Center for the Education of Women, 2005).

Unfortunately, working women still face employment discrimination. Although laws such as the 1964 Civil Rights Act played a major role in reducing some acts of discrimination, racial exclusion and gender-typing continue to exist, although in a less blatant manner (Darity & Mason, 1998). The education literature seems to focus more on gender inequalities and salary gaps in higher education than in the public elementary and secondary schools. Over the years, women have become increasingly visible in higher education. According to the National Center for Education Statistics (NCES), in 2010 a majority of college degrees, undergraduate and graduate, were awarded to women: 57.4 percent of bachelor's degrees, 62.6 percent of master's degrees, and 53.3 percent of doctorates. However, in 2009, slightly less than half (47.1 percent) of the faculty in degree-granting institutions were women.

Much research has shown that historically, male privilege extends throughout academia, and adds challenges for those women who do work in higher education in various ways. For example, performance evaluations tainted by gender bias, strict tenure requirements and short tenure clocks favoring male faculty, minimal and ineffective mentoring and networking opportunities, competitive rather than collaborative work styles, and lack of support for pregnancies and family issues are obstacles that women have had to overcome in the academy (Basow, 1995; Bellas, 1992; Cohn, 2000; Gray, 1985; Handelsman et al., 2005; Jacobs, 1989a, 1989b, 2003; Kolodny, 2000; Long, 1990; Mason & Goulden, 2002; Nelson & Bridges, 1999; Orenstein, 1994, 2002; Park, 1996; Riger, Stokes, Raja, & Sullivan, 1997; Sadker & Sadker, 1994; Sorcinelli & Near, 1989; Yoder, 1985).

Salary gaps are at issue as well. Women generally earn on average, 86 cents per hour for every $1 a man earns across all fields (Johnson, et al.) "Wide pay gap is womens' biggest concern." Although there are more female faculty members at higher education institutions than ever before, they still steadily lag behind men in their earnings and the positions they hold. At every type of institution and at all ranks, uneven distributions of salary exist between men and women. Female full-time faculty continue to earn, on average, only 80 percent of what their male peers make in salary, and even at the full professorship level, women earn about 88 percent of what men make in the same position (Boulard, 2006). To say the least, women still have some way to go to experience true equity in the academy.

TERMS & CONCEPTS

1964 Civil Rights Act: The 1964 Civil Rights Act enforces the constitutional right to vote, to confer jurisdiction upon the district courts of the United States to provide injunctive relief against discrimination in public accommodations, to authorize the attorney General to institute suits to protect constitutional rights in public facilities and public education, to extend the Commission on Civil Rights, to prevent discrimination in federally assisted programs, to establish a Commission on Equal Employment Opportunity, and for other purposes.

Academy: The academy refers to a group of colleges and/or universities.

Employment Discrimination: Employment discrimination involves exclusion of specific individuals on the basis of race, sex, religion, national origin, physical disability, and age by employers. Discriminatory practices include bias in hiring, promotion, job assignment, termination, compensation, and various types of harassment.

Male Privilege: Male privilege refers to rights given only to men on the basis of their gender.

Normal Schools: Normal schools were two-year teacher education institutions established during the eighteenth century.

Public Schools: Public schools refer to elementary and high schools in the United States that provide free education to students of a community or district. These schools are supported by public funds.

Salary Gap: Salary gaps refer to unequal pay between individuals with the same qualifications performing the same job.

Seminary: A seminar is a specialized higher education institute which focuses on philosophy, theology and spirituality.

Teacher Education Courses: Teacher education courses are courses that help teachers develop quality, effective teaching and learning strategies to use in the classroom.

Belinda B. McFeeters

BIBLIOGRAPHY

American Foundation for the Blind. (2007). *Anne Sullivan Macy biography*. Retrieved May 11, 2007, from http://www.afb.org

Bach, R. L., & Perucci, C. C. (1984). Organizational influences on the sex composition of college and university faculty: A research note. *Sociology of Education, 57*, 193–198. Retrieved November 5, 2014, from EBSCO Online Database Education Research Complete.

Basow, S. A. (1995). Student evaluations of college professors: When gender matters. *Journal of Educational Psychology, 87*, 656–665. Retrieved November 5, 2014, from EBSCO Online Database Education Research Complete.

Bellas, M. L. (1992). The effects of marital status and wives' employment on the salaries of faculty men: The (house) wife bonus. *Gender & Society, 6*, 609–622. Retrieved November 5, 2014, from EBSCO Online Database SocINDEX with Full Text.

Boulard, G. (2006). Salary gap persists between women and men faculty, report finds. *Community College Week, 17*, 17. Retrieved November 5, 2014, from EBSCO Online Database Education Research Complete.

Center for the Education of Women. (2005). *Family-friendly policies in higher education: Where do we stand?* Retrieved May 8, 2007, from http://www.umich.edu

Cohn, S. (2000). *Race and gender discrimination at work.* Boulder: Westview.

Darity, W. A., Jr., & Mason, P. L. (1998). Evidence on discrimination in employment: Codes of color, codes of gender. *Journal of Economic Perspectives, 12,* 63–90. Retrieved November 5, 2014, from EBSCO Online Database Business Source Complete.

Eisenmann, L. (2002). Educating the female citizen in a post-war world: Competing ideologies for American women, 1945-1965. *Educational Review, 54,* 133–141. Retrieved November 5, 2014, from EBSCO Online Database Education Research Complete.

Examining women's status: Campus climate and gender equity. (2011). *ASHE Higher Education Report, 37,* 65–92. Retrieved December 20, 2013, from EBSCO Online Database Academic Search Premier.

Fiss, A. (2014). Cultivating parabolas in the parlor garden: Reconciling mathematics education and feminine ideals in nineteenth-century America. *Science & Education, 23,* 241–250. Retrieved November 5, 2014, from EBSCO Online Database Education Research Complete.

Glazer-Raymo, J. (1999). *Shattering the myths: Women in academe.* Baltimore: Johns Hopkins University Press.

Gray, M. W. (1985). The halls of ivy and the halls of justice: Resisting sex discrimination against faculty women. *Academe, 71,* 33–41.

Harvey, W. (2003). *Minorities in higher education, 20th annual status report, 2002-2003.* Washington, DC: American Council on Education.

Handelsman, J., Cantor, N., Carnes, M., Denton, D., Fine, E., Grosz, B., . . . Sheridan, J. (2005). More women in science. *Science, 309* (5738), 1190–1191. Retrieved November 5, 2014, from http://www.sciencemag.org

Heuer, M. (1998, April 20). Kindergarten's beginnings. *Howard Lake Herald & Winsted-Lester Prairie Journal.* Retrieved May 10, 2007, from http://www.herald-journal.com

Jacobs, J. A. (1989a). *Revolving doors: Sex segregation and women's careers.* Stanford, CT: Stanford University Press.

Jacobs, J. A. (1989b). Long-term trends in occupational segregation by sex. *American Journal of Sociology, 95,* 160–173. Retrieved November 5, 2014, from EBSCO Online Database SocINDEX with Full Text.

Jacobs, J. A. (2003). Detours on the road to equality: Women, work and higher education. *Contexts, 2,* 32–41.

Johnson, J. A., Musial, D., Hall, G. E., Gollnick, D. M., & Dupuis, V. L. (2004). *Introduction to the foundations of American education* (13th ed.). Boston: Allyn & Bacon.

Kolodny, A. (2000). Raising standards while lowering anxieties: Rethinking the promotion and tenure process. In S. Geok-Lim & M. Herrera-Sobek (Eds.), *Power, race, and gender in academe* (pp. 83–111). New York: Modern Language Association.

Konrad, A. M., & Pfeffer, J. (1991). Understanding the hiring of women and minorities in educational institutions. *Sociology of Education, 64,* 141–157. Retrieved November 5, 2014, from EBSCO Online Database SocINDEX with Full Text.

Kulis, S. (1997). Gender segregation among college and university employees. *Sociology of Education, 70,* 151–173. Retrieved November 5, 2014, from EBSCO Online Database SocINDEX with Full Text.

Lewis, A. C. (2003). U.S. graduates fall. *Education Digest, 68,* 70–71.

Lewis, J. J. (2007). *Mary McLeod Bethune: African American educator and activist.* Retrieved May 7, 2007, from http://womenshistory.about.com

Lomperis, A. M. T. (1990). Are women changing the nature of the academic profession? *Journal of Higher Education, 61,* 643–677. Retrieved November 5, 2014, from EBSCO Online Database Education Research Complete.

Long, J. S. (1990). The origins of sex differences in sciences. *Social Forces, 68,* 1297–1315. Retrieved November 5, 2014, from EBSCO Online Database Business Source Complete.

Mason, M. A., & Goulden, M. (2002). Do babies matter? The effect of family formation on the lifelong careers of academic men and women. *Academe, 88,* 21–27. Retrieved November 5, 2014, from EBSCO Online Database Education Research Complete.

National Center for Education Statistics. (2012a). *Fast facts: Degrees conferred by sex and race.* Retrieved December 23, 2013, from http://nces.ed.gov

National Center for Education Statistics. (2012b). *Employees in degree-granting institutions, by employment status, sex, control and level of institution, and primary occupation: Fall 2009* [Table]. Retrieved December 23, 2013, from http://nces.ed.gov

Nelson, R. L., & Bridges, W. P. (1999). *Legalizing gender inequality: Courts, markets, and unequal pay for women in America.* New York: Cambridge University Press.

Orenstein, P. (1994). *School girls: Young women, self-esteem, and the confidence gap.* New York: Doubleday.

Orenstein, P. (2002). Why science must adapt to women. *Discover, 23,* 58–63.

Riger, S., Stokes, J., Raja, S., & Sullivan, M. (1997). Measuring perceptions of the work environment for female faculty. *Review of Higher Education, 21,* 63–78. Retrieved November 5, 2014, from EBSCO Online Database Education Research Complete.

Roberts, B. E. (2007). Mary Somerville and the college she inspired. *British Heritage, 28,* 46–49. Retrieved May 8, 2007, from EBSCO Online Database Academic Search Premier.

Sadker, M., & Sadker, D. (1994). *Failing at fairness: How America's schools cheat girls.* New York: Maxwell Macmillan International.

Solomon, B. M. (1985). *In the company of educated women: A history of women and higher education in America.* Binghamton: Yale University Press.

Sorcinelli, M. D., & Near, J. P. (1989). Relations between work and life away from work among university faculty. *Journal of Higher Education, 60,* 59–81. Retrieved November 5, 2014, from EBSCO Online Database Education Research Complete.

Spillman, S. (2012). Institutional limits: Christine Ladd-Franklin, fellowships, and American women's academic careers, 1880–1920. *History of Education Quarterly, 52,* 196–221. Retrieved November 5, 2014, from EBSCO Online Database Education Research Complete.

Thelin, J. (2004). *A history of American higher education.* Baltimore: Johns Hopkins University Press.

Tolbert, P. S., & Oberfield, A. A. (1991). Sources of organizational demography: Faculty sex ratios in colleges and universities. *Sociology of Education, 64,* 305–315. Retrieved November 5, 2014, from EBSCO Online Database SocINDEX with Full Text.

Trower, C. A., & Chait, R. P. (2002, March–April). Faculty diversity: Too little for too long. *Harvard Magazine,* 33–37, 98. Retrieved November 5, 2014, from http://harvardmagazine.com

Valian, V. (1999). *Why so slow? The advancement of women.* Cambridge: MIT Press.

Wells, C. (2003). When tenure isn't enough. *Chronicle of Higher Education, 50,* C3. Retrieved November 5, 2014, from EBSCO Online Database Education Research Complete.

Wells, R. S., Seifert, T. A., Padgett, R. D., Park, S., & Umbach, P. D. (2011). Why do more women than men want to earn a four-year degree? Exploring the effects of gender, social origin, and social capital on educational expectations. *Journal of Higher Education, 82 ,* 1–32. Retrieved December 20, 2013, from EBSCO Online Database Education Research Complete.

Wide pay gap womens biggest concern on Suffrage Day. (2006, September 19). Human Rights Commission. Retrieved May 14, 2007, from http://www.hrc.co

Yoder, J. D. (1985). An academic woman as a token: A case study. *Journal of Social Issues, 41,* 61–72. Retrieved November 5, 2014, from EBSCO Online Database SocINDEX with Full Text.

SUGGESTED READING

Campbell, J. M. (1996). *The prairie schoolhouse.* Albuquerque: University of New Mexico Press.

Campella, G., Geismar, K., & Nicoleau, G. (1995). *Shifting histories: Transforming schools for social change.* Cambridge: Harvard Educational Publishing Group.

Edwards, J. (2002). *Women in American education, 1820–1955: The female force and educational reform.* Westport: Greenwood Press.

Eisenmann, L. (2006). *Higher education for women in post-war America, 1945-1965.* Baltimore, MD.: Johns Hopkins University Press.

Horowitz, H. L. (1999). *The power and passion of M. Carey Thomas.* Chicago: University of Illinois Press.

Maher, F. A., & Tetreault, M. (2011). Long-term transformations: Excavating privilege and diversity in the academy. *Gender & Education, 23,* 281–297. Retrieved December 20, 2013, from EBSCO Online Database Education Research Complete.

Marschke, R., Laursen, S., Nielsen, J. M., & Rankin, P. (2007). Demographic inertia revisited: An immodest proposal to achieve equitable gender representation among faculty in higher education. *Journal of Higher Education, 78,* 1–26. Retrieved May 1, 2007, from EBSCO Online Database Education Research Complete.

Saulnier, C. F., & Swigonski, M. (2006). As feminists in the academy… *Affilia: Journal of Women and Social Work, 21,* 361–364. Retrieved November 5, 2014, from EBSCO Online Database SocINDEX with Full Text.

Watts, R. (2013). Society, education and the state: Gender perspectives on an old debate. *Paedagogica Historica, 49,* 17–33. Retrieved November 5, 2014, from EBSCO Online Database Education Research Complete.

SOCIAL HISTORY OF AMERICAN EDUCATION

Throughout the birth, growth, and development of our nation's school system, social and cultural factors have contributed significantly to the process of American education. Throughout history there have been times during which great social change brought about equally great changes in education; likewise, there have been periods in which education changes have left indelible imprints upon society. This phe-nomenon is particularly true as education has come to be viewed as an institutional means by which knowledge and mores pertaining to the welfare of society are transmitted from teacher to pupil.

KEYWORDS: Common School; Dame School; Education Reform; Elementary and Secondary Education Act (ESEA); Industrialization; Mann,

Horace; National Association for the Advancement of Colored People (NAACP); National Organization for Women (NOW); No Child Left Behind Act (NCLB); Reconstruction; Segregation; Social History

OVERVIEW

On July 28, 1787, Benjamin Rush stood before visitors at the Young Ladies Academy of Philadelphia and addressed the crowd on the importance and manner of educating women in the new American Republic. A man esteemed as ahead of his time and, of his own admission, out of step with popular and fashionable habits of thinking, Rush decried then-current perceptions that relegated the value of women to the level of "personal charms and ornamental accomplishments" and praised instead the woman who was learned in matters of business, philosophy, history, and geography (Rush, 1787).

While domestic responsibilities were widely understood to comprise a core area of function for women, these did not preclude a liberal education and, indeed, Rush noted that they actually required it. For example, bookkeeping and accounting knowledge would be useful to a woman should her husband pass away and she be left to oversee his estate. Education in the philosophy and principles of liberty and government would enable women to raise well educated sons, and even such studies as astronomy and chemistry could prove useful to women.

Framed against the backdrop of early American cultural norms, Rush's remarks provide evidence that even in the early days of our nation's history, social perceptions and realities affected the process and practice of American education. From gender roles and racial discrimination to class inequities and demographic differences, social factors form an intricate part of the development of education in America, and education within American culture.

PERSPECTIVES ON SCHOOLS & SOCIETY

In *Education and Social Change: Themes in the History of American Education,* author John Rury asks the question, "Do schools change society, or does society change the schools?" (Rury, 2002). If education is a passive endeavor, then societal reforms and changes will eventually have an effect on education. If, however, education is an active pursuit, then its product of ideas and theories will, of necessity, affect society. According to Rury, the chain of influence leads both

ways. Throughout history there have been times during which great social change brought about equally great changes in education; likewise, there have been periods in which education changes have left indelible imprints upon society.

This phenomenon is particularly true as education has come to be viewed as an institutional means by which knowledge and mores pertaining to the welfare of society are transmitted from teacher to pupil. Rury writes that education "has contributed to economic growth and political change, and it has helped to forge a national identity from the country's rich variety of cultural and social groups." Conversely, education itself "has been influenced by changes in the economy, the political system, and other facets of the social structure" (Rury). As examples of ways in which society has changed schooling, Rury points to the impact of urbanization and industrialization upon school demographics and curricula. Inarguably, schools have often been a catalyst for social change; two examples of this being in the areas of women's education and African-American education.

Several years prior to Rury, Nasaw (1981) arrived at a similar conclusion regarding the interconnectivity of education changes and social reforms. Nasaw focuses on three periods of American history which he views as landmarks for American education: the pre-Civil War antebellum decades, which witnessed the reformation of "common schools;" the turn of the 20th Century, which saw the expansion of public education to "children of the plain people;" and the decades following World War II, during which education, and particularly higher education, witnessed the inclusion of sectors of society typically excluded as a result of race, class, and gender (Nasaw). Taking each in turn, Nasaw writes:

In each of these periods,' [sic] the quantitative expansion of the student population was matched by a qualitative transformation of the enlarged institutions. The common schools of the mid 1800s were charged with re-forming the moral character of the children of failed artisans and farmers from both sides of the Atlantic; the expanded high schools at the turn of the century with preparing their poor, working-class, and immigrant adolescents for future lives in city and factory; the "open-access" public institutions in the postwar period with moving their students off the unemployment lines and into lower-level white-collar and paraprofessional positions (Nasaw).

Prior to the appearance of the first public school in America, social norms in the New World dictated the delivery of education from one generation to the next. The Old World of England from which the colonists had emigrated had been characterized by rules of propriety and hierarchy, even within the family unit. English society placed high value upon authority and tradition, and this value affected the manner of English child-rearing.

Rury notes that in the New World, however, the colonists soon came to embrace a new societal order, void of many of the traditions and hierarchical structures of English society. As part of this new social order, Rury notes that parents did not so much "dictate" to their children as "educate" them (Rury). In colonial America, the primary avenue of education was found in the home, with young children learning the basics of reading and writing at the feet of their mothers.

Yet, even in the New World, distinct societies existed, and the cultural norms of each society affected the education of the youth. Geographically, for example, Rury notes that historians divide the colonies into three regions:

- The agricultural South, made up of Virginia, Maryland, Georgia, and the Carolinas;
- The diverse Middle Colonies, comprised of the Quaker colony of Pennsylvania, New Jersey, Delaware, and New York;
- The New England region, which spread north of the Middle Colonies.

Colonial & Revolutionary American Education

THE NEW ENGLAND COLONIES

The development of formal schooling occurred first in New England, and by far the New England colonies witnessed its greatest early development. The establishment of Dame schools in colonial New England allowed young children to be trained in religion and basic academic pursuits under the watchful eye of a schoolteacher. As New England Puritans believed firmly in the importance of learning to read Scripture, Dame schools were open to children regardless of sex. However, here is where equal access for young New England girls ended.

As children completed their time in Dame schools, gender and class differences began to affect their later education. Young boys had three choices for education following Dame school, and the option parents selected depended both upon vocational prospects and class standing. Sons whose parents were of a certain social standing and who aimed for their sons to attend college - and most likely enter the ministry or positions of civic leadership - were sent to Latin Grammar Schools to further their reading capabilities. Some families chose the monthly cost of apprenticeship and paired their sons with a craftsman to learn the skills of his trade. Finally, at no cost to the parents, a son could remain at home and be trained by his father in his occupation.

For girls, however, choices were much more limited. Since they were not permitted to attend the Latin Grammar Schools, they were also not expected to attend college or to enter positions of leadership in church or state. In earliest days, girls were also precluded from pursuing apprenticeships. But by the mid-seventeenth century, apprenticeships were being offered to poor girls as well, so they would be able to obtain some form of accommodation.

THE MIDDLE & SOUTHERN COLONIES

Schools were less plentiful in the Middle and Southern colonies. Rury attributes this to the link between religion and education. By virtue of their strongly religious culture, the New England colonies placed more emphasis on formal education. This did not mean that Middle and Southern colonies sustained an ill-educated culture, particularly when it came to literacy. Research indicates that formal schooling was but one avenue towards literacy in colonial America. For those colonists who boasted a certain level of wealth, private tutors represented another avenue, and Rury notes that in the South particularly, families of means often hired tutors to instruct their children in reading (Rury). While the importance of monetary standing for access to literacy education was not always a deciding factor, along with gender, it did prove indicative of who was educated and who was not.

The literacy statistics are interesting … but difficult to interpret. Not surprisingly, in all colonies literacy was highest for those with property and wealth, and it was considerably higher for men than it was for women. But literacy rates among the poor were highest in puritan New England, a fact that seems to support arguments for the importance of religion and schooling (Rury).

Moreover, much education in colonial America occurred informally and was provided by parents and through local churches (Rury).

AFRICAN AMERICAN EDUCATION

If schooling for white children in colonial America was less than guaranteed, for black children, and particularly slave children in the Southern colonies, it was actively discouraged. Many slave owners believed that educating slaves would increase the likelihood of rebellion, and Georgia and South Carolina went so far as to enact laws which criminalized teaching slaves to read and write. Nevertheless, missionaries attempted to combat this trend by setting up and administering schools for slaves. In addition, freed blacks and even some masters undertook to teach reading and writing to slaves. Black children from Northern and Middle colonies often fared better than their Southern counterparts, and in 1787, the New York Manumission Society established the New York African Free School to teach values and morals to the children of former slaves.

AFTER THE REVOLUTION

The American Revolution and creation of the new republic began a philosophical shift in the aim of education from training a child to become a moral adult to training the child to become an effective citizen. Although the formation of a national education system still lay years in the future, this change led to an increase in government interest in establishing a system of public education. Preparing young men to lead the new republic required that women be versed enough in literacy and principles of republican government to transmit this knowledge to their sons. Hence, the Revolution brought about the beginnings of a change in opinion regarding women's education, and this ideological change would become apparent in practice in the 19th Century.

NINETEENTH CENTURY: AGE OF INDUSTRIALIZATION

The 19th Century was an age of industrialization and urbanization in the new nation. Over the course of the century, manufacturing as a percentage of the gross national product grew from 5% to more than 50% (Rury). Moreover, the increase in factories coupled with the inflow of immigrants resulted in the burgeoning of American cities. With increased industrialization came an increased emphasis on education, and schooling began to take on a focus of preparing students to enter the workforce and become productive members of society. Nevertheless, this trend did not translate into equal educational experiences for all children, as poorer children of factory workers often served as child labor at the expense of attending school (Rury).

COMMON SCHOOLS

This century of change also saw the introduction of the nation's first public schools, or "common schools" as they were then termed. Originally begun as "charity schools" to provide an education for poorer children, public schools came to be under the purview of local board or government entities (Rury). While common schools found their most welcoming home in cities and urban centers in the early part of the century, in the rural countryside, education reform was slower to take hold. By the mid-19th Century the common school movement had taken hold, and the years 1830 through 1860 are now known as the "age of the common school" (Rury).

The common school found one of its greatest champions in education reform leader Horace Mann, and his efforts in pursuit of class and gender equality in education brought lasting effects. A social activist, Mann saw common schools as a mechanism for balancing social and economic inequalities between rich and poor. Possibly equating common schools with charity schools, the wealthy often elected to educate their children privately. Recognizing that the common school movement would not succeed without support from the wealthy, Mann set out to convince the well-to-do of the benefits of public schooling.

WOMEN'S EDUCATION

Mann became a staunch proponent of women's education. Yet, his advocacy for women stemmed from his belief that their nature lent itself to good teaching. Mann promoted the development of women as teachers more than advocated for their absolute equality with men in the educational setting. Nevertheless, the 19th Century represented a time of great advancement for women in American education. Rury notes that by the turn of the 20th Century, women had not only closed much of the educational gap between themselves and their male counterparts, their literacy rates actually exceeded those of men.

Moreover, by 1900, American high schools boasted more females than males (Rury). Noticeably, this trend was limited mostly to white women and, within this demographic, to women from the middle and upper social classes of society.

AFRICAN AMERICAN EDUCATION

The 19th Century also witnessed significant advancements in education for African-Americans. Particularly following the Civil War and emancipation, former slaves enthusiastically pursued schooling. In the post-Civil War years, the South witnessed the starting of thousands of schools, and by the end of the 1800's, more than two-thirds of the southern black population was literate (Rury). Their road was not an easy one, and deep-seated racism meant that schools were almost always segregated. Moreover, the collapse of Southern reconstruction meant the stagnation of many of the advances that had been made in the realm of African-American education, and not until well into the twentieth century would equal education for black Americans achieve full realization.

Twentieth Century: Age of Progressivism

JOHN DEWEY & PROGRESSIVE EDUCATION

The early 20th Century saw the continued acceleration in the rate of industrialization in America, and along with this came a significant development in educational philosophy. Credited to educational psychologist and reformer John Dewey, Progressive Education was broad in scope yet encompassed both a new emphasis on children's learning styles and relation to society and a focus on education as a whole as an important component of the larger economic order.

AFRICAN AMERICAN EDUCATION

Inequities persisted as well in African-American education. While there had been progress in the establishment of black elementary schools, the number of secondary schools for African-Americans remained quite limited. In addition, where black secondary schools did exist, the quality of education provided within them often lagged behind white schools, with the end result being that black students often did not have access to the training that was so necessary to compete economically within the nation's workforce.

By far one of the most pivotal events in the educational evolution of the 20th Century was the Second World War. Following President Truman's desegregation of the US Armed Forces soon after the war, the discrepancy between military desegregation and educational segregation became embarrassingly difficult to justify. In a bold move, the National Association for the Advancement of Colored People (NAACP) undertook a judicial challenge to the practice of racial segregation. In the 1954 landmark Supreme Court case of *Brown v. Board of Education* of Topeka, Kansas, the Court sided with the NAACP and ruled that educational segregation stood in violation of the United States Constitution. While altering public sentiment proved a much more lengthy process than issuing a judicial order, the *Brown* ruling set the wheels of change irreversibly in motion. Despite the Court's decision, however, racial integration in education was far from immediate, and segregation in practice persisted into the next decades. As a result, additional federal court decisions in the 1960's and 1970's provided legal requirements to reduce racial segregation.

THE ELEMENTARY & SECONDARY EDUCATION ACT

In the latter half of the 20th Century, class inequalities as they related to education also gained increased attention. As funding for public schooling remained largely local, wealthier areas by default were able to provide greater resources for their schools than poorer areas. In response, President Lyndon Johnson signed the Elementary and Secondary Education Act (ESEA) in 1965. Intended to help rectify funding inequalities, Title I of the ESEA provided for federal dollars to go to public education for children affected by poverty. The role of Title I funding for education continues today within the No Child Left Behind Act, the present-day version of ESEA.

WOMEN'S EDUCATION

Led by reformers such as Jane Addams, women gained a new level of equity during the progressive era; yet this was juxtaposed against the concurrent development of courses of study both stemming from and leading to traditional women's roles. For example, this period saw the development of home economics courses as well as vocational training in clerical duties, such as typing and stenography. While most schools were coeducational in attendance, there often existed internal gender segregation among the programs of study.

Concurrent with racial and economic developments in education in the latter half of the 1900's, women's issues also gained increased attention, and advocates of the feminist movement began to criticize curricula that perpetuated gender-based stereotypes. To address this issue, in 1967, the National Organization for Women (NOW) called for "equal and unsegregated education" to be realized in both academic and athletic school pursuits (Rury). Title IX of the Education Amendments of 1972 required that, in any programs supported by federal dollars, educational institutions not discriminate based on gender.

The significant 20th Century advances in race, gender, and class equity in education notwithstanding, deep-seated prejudices and traditions developed over centuries often take longer than decades to reverse. While the social development of education boasts great progress, it also holds promise for great future advancement. Indeed, the social history of American education is far from complete, and it remains for future generations to continue the story begun centuries ago.

TERMS & CONCEPTS

Common School: A nineteenth century public school. The term "common" was used to indicate, among other things, the provision of education to all students regardless of social class.

Dame School: Type of school for young children popular in colonial and early America. Taught by a woman who was often a widow and stressing reading over other subjects.

Elementary and Secondary Education Act (ESEA): Federal education legislation enacted in 1965; among other provisions, the Act provides funding for elementary and secondary education.

Industrialization: The process by which industry is created. In American history, the term often refers to the later years of the Industrial Revolution, c. 1850-1900.

National Association for the Advancement of Colored Persons (NAACP): The oldest civil rights organization in the United States; the NAACP's stated mission includes working for political, educational, social, and economic equal rights.

National Organization for Women (NOW): The largest feminist activist organization in the United States; NOW's stated purpose includes achieving equal rights for women.

No Child Left Behind Act (NCLB): Federal legislation reauthorizing several federal education programs for the purpose of improving educational standards and accountability and providing parents with additional options in school choice.

Reconstruction: The period from 1865-1877 during which the United States attempted to rebuild and reintegrate the former Confederate states back into the Union.

Segregation: The act of separation based on race, class, or ethnicity; often used in reference to educational segregation between black and white students in the 19th and 20th centuries.

Social History: The study of history within the light of social trends, reforms, and culture.

Gina L. Diorio

BIBLIOGRAPHY

Barger, R. (Ed.). (2004). *History of American education web project.* Retrieved April 7, 2007, from http://www.nd.edu

Bremner, R. (Ed.). (1970). Negro and Indian Children. *Children and youth in America: A documentary history.* 1. Cambridge, Massachusetts: Harvard University Press. Retrieved April 5, 2007, from http://www.h-net.org

Donato, R., & Hanson, J.S. (2012). Legally white, socially "Mexican" the politics of de jure and de facto school segregation in the American Southwest. *Harvard Educational Review, 82,* 202-225. Retrieved December 15, 2013, from EBSCO Online Database Education Research Complete.

Glenn, W.J. (2012). School resegregation: A synthesis of the evidence. *Educational Forum, 76,* 282-298. Retrieved December 15, 2013, from EBSCO Online Database Education Research Complete.

Nasaw, D. (1981). *Schooled to order: A social history of public schooling in the United States.* Oxford: Oxford University Press.

Rury, J. (2002). *Education and social change: Themes in the history of American education.* Mahwah, NJ: Lawrence Erlbaum Associates

Rush, B. (1787). Thoughts on female education. In N. Desmarais & J. McGovern (Eds.), *The essential documents of American history.* Retrieved April 03, 2007 from EBSCO Online Database Academic Search Premier.

Sass, E. (2007). *American educational history: A hypertext timeline.* Retrieved April 7, 2007, from http://www.cloud-net.com

Ward Randolph, A.L. (2012). "It is better to light a candle than to curse the darkness": Ethel Thompson Overby and democratic schooling in Richmond, Virginia, 1910–1958. *Educational Studies, 48,* 220-243. Retrieved December 15, 2013, from EBSCO Online Database Education Research Complete.

SUGGESTED READING

Altenbaugh, R. (2002). *The American people and their education: A social history* Upper Saddle River, NJ: Prentice Hall.

Labaree, D. (2005). Progressivism, schools and schools of education: An American romance. *Paedagogica Historica,* *41* (1/2), 275-288. Retrieved April 07, 2007 from EBSCO Online Database Academic Search Premier.

McClellan, B. & Reese, W. (1988). *The social history of American education.* Urbana, IL: University of Illinois Press.

Mirel, J. (2002). Civic education and changing definitions of American identity, 1900-1950. *Educational Review, 54,* 143-152. Retrieved April 07, 2007 from EBSCO Online Database Academic Search Premier.

Parkerson, D. & Parkerson, J. (2001). *Transitions in American education: A social history of teaching.* Oxford: Routledge Falmer.

Section 2: Education Theory

Introduction

Have you ever said that you had a "theory" about why something transpired in your life? By definition, a theory is "a plausible or scientifically acceptable general principle or body of principles offered to explain phenomena; a belief, policy, or procedure proposed or followed as the basis of action; an ideal or hypothetical set of facts, principles, or circumstances. (merriam-webster.com). This section shares several theories that have guided the evolving contours of education practice. Our articles begin with a discussion of Plato whose philosophy can be seen threaded through the works of present day educational scholars and concluding with a salient look at social justice in education.

PLATO AND EDUCATION

Plato (427-347 BC), an ancient Greek philosopher, is considered to be the father of educational philosophy. He founded the Academy in Athens in 387 BC and wrote a number of philosophical works including *The Republic*, which outlines Plato's utopian society and his thoughts about political and educational issues (Gutek, 2009). The keystone of the text promotes the classic tradition of reason, whereby education becomes the process of "perfecting those natural powers of intellect which all people have" (Wingo, 1965). Historically, Plato's tenets of philosophical thought are the tenets of perennialism, an educational philosophy based on idealism. Idealism is directly traced back to Plato, with concepts of the idealistic perspective influencing education today.

KEYWORDS: Antithesis; Dialectic; Idealism; Intrinsic Motivation; Mentoring; Paideia; Perennialism; Reason; Seminar; Thesis; Universal Truth

OVERVIEW

Plato (427-347 BC) is considered to be the father of educational philosophy. He founded the Academy in Athens in 387 BC and wrote a number of philosophical works including *The Republic*, which outlines Plato's utopian society and presents his thoughts about political and educational issues (Gutek). The keystone of the text promotes the classic tradition of reason within education whereby education becomes the process of "perfecting those natural powers of intellect which all people have" (Wingo). Plato was the student of Socrates (469 BC-399 BC), a Greek philosopher who emphasized *paideia*, education in the broadest sense, including "all that affects the formation of character and mind" (LoShan, 1998).

Plato's philosophy is a direct reaction to the state of flux of the Athenian culture during his time. Nash, Kazamias, and Perkinson (1965) point out that Plato lost faith in the existing forms of Athenian government and the foundations of its society. Sophists, a new group of traveling lecturers, promoted individualism rather than a communal culture, which led to a relativism that threatened to destroy the communal culture (Knight, 1998). Barrow (1976) suggests that their method was "to give public lectures for high fees, limiting education to the rich and excluding

the poor." To Plato, the Sophists were superficial instructors who lacked solid pedagogical techniques (Powers, 1996). Plato believed that citizens of Athens should follow an Absolute or universal truth, "the final and most ethical of all things and persons" (Knight). As Wingo explains, "To Plato, knowledge based on reason is regarded as superior to that based on sense experience."

Writing on Platonic and Socratic philosophies, respectively, as they influence present-day education, Kohan argues: "The former educates childhood to transform it into what it ought to be. The latter does not form childhood, but makes education childlike" (Kohan, 2013).

IDEALISM, PERENNIALISM & THE SEARCH FOR TRUTH

Historically, Plato's tenets of philosophical thought are the tenets of perennialism, an educational philosophy based on idealism. Idealism is directly traced back to Plato, with concepts of the idealistic perspective influencing education today. LoShan suggests that Platonic education can certainly serve as a model in any city at any time in history, as it is an ideal model "that any polity would do well to emulate as best it can, under the constraints of its history and circumstances." These specific concepts gleaned from Platonic philosophy include the idea that there is latent thought in all children. Platonic philosophy also proposes that the teacher can discover the process for acquiring this latent thought through the skillful method of asking probing questions to stimulate this recollection of ideas. Another tenet that directly relates back to the teachings of Plato is the idea that the teacher is the moral and cultural model of students. The beliefs of German philosopher Georg Hegel and American philosopher Ralph Waldo Emerson can be traced to Plato, as well as those of Augustine, Descartes, Berkeley, and Harris (Gutek; Ozmon & Craver, 2008).

Plato was a follower of Socratic education. This form of education encompasses the following points:

- Human beings should seek to live morally excellent lives;
- General education (today called *liberal arts education*) cultivates the knowledge every person needs as a human being;

- The kind of information that cultivates morally excellent persons…act according to reason;
- Concepts, the basis of true knowledge, exist within the mind and can be brought to consciousness [with] probing questions stimulat[ing] the learner to discover the truth…by bringing latent concepts to consciousness;
- Humans define themselves in terms of the criteria of universal truth;
- Socratic education involves mentoring (or modeling) (Gutek).

Plato believed that there is a world of perfect ideas that are "unchanging…universal and timeless concepts of truth, goodness, justice, and beauty" (Gutek). Perfect ideas are forms of the Good, which are considered the world of ideas at its highest point. The world of matter is "not to be trusted" (Ozmon & Craver). People are considered good and honorable when "their conduct conforms to the ideal and universal concepts of truth, goodness, and beauty" (Gutek). According to Ozmon and Craver, Plato argues that people should concern themselves primarily with the search for truth. Truth is "perfect and eternal, [and] cannot be found in the world of matter, which is imperfect and constantly changing."

The Allegory of the Cave

Plato's *Allegory of the Cave* provides an example of the concept that students must move beyond the world of matter to that of ideas. In the *Allegory of the Cave*, prisoners are chained in darkness in a cave. They see only shadows, which they take for reality. One prisoner is freed from his chains, advances up the steep slope and walks into the sunlight where he sees the true source of heat and light. He remembers his friends in the cave and returns to tell them of his discovery. They do not believe him and threaten his life.

According to Ozmon and Craver, people live in "a cave of shadows and illusions, chained to our ignorance and apathy." When one loosens his chains, he begins his education. Dialectic is the manner that carries one from the world of matter to that of the world of ideas. Dialectic (a critical discussion) moves participants from "mere opinion to true knowledge" (Ozmon & Craver). The good teacher leads the student as far as capable (Reed & Johnson, 2000).

To Plato, knowledge is not created, but discovered through education. Barrow relates that "education is the process of turning the mind in the right direction," specifically in the search for the truth. The essence of education is the nurturing of the student. Nettleship (1935) stresses that Plato sees the human soul as "emphatically and before all else something living, something which we can feed or starve, nourish or poison." Plato sees education as "the method for providing the natural and proper nurture of the souls."

Commenting on Platonic philosophy in present-day education, Ormell writes, "Anyone who aspires to philosophize about education (or anything else for that matter) needs to learn to 'stand back' from the all-too pressing and distracting detail and to try to see the situation 'as a whole.' The kind of cool perspective one can get from such standing back is the chief good which philosophy aims to provide" (2012).

The education of the average Greek gentleman is comprised of both mental and athletic methods. These methods begin at an early age; Plato believes that the young are plastic and malleable and that those who impact the young must take care in the handling and shaping of young minds and bodies. Nettleship states that a continued neglect of an education produces "aggravated results," wherein "the eye of the mind grows more and more unaccustomed to the vision of beauty and truth." Besides developing a knowledge base and the physical being of the young, Plato promotes a foundation of character education whereby the child is "to be bred in the belief that beings greater than himself have behaved in a certain way," and that his "natural impulse to imitate is thus to be utilized in forming his own character" (Nettleship).

Applications

Idealist Education Today

Elements of Platonic thought can be seen in today's classrooms under the guise of Idealism. The goal of Idealist education is to seek and to find Truth; a universal truth that is absolute. The purpose of Idealist education is to "expose students to the wisdom contained in the cultural heritage so that they can know, share in, and extend it through their own personal contributions" (Gutek). Schools are seen as institutions that are established to promote the society for "the primary purpose of developing students' spirituality or intellectuality." Schools are to provide a place where "the mind can *think* and *know* without being bothered by the transitory experience of everyday life." For the Idealist, the social function of the school is "to preserve the heritage and to pass on the knowledge of the past" (Knight).

The curriculum of today's Idealist educational institutions considers the lessons of the past in the shaping of what should be taught. Thus, schools should "preserve knowledge by transmitting the cultural heritage in a deliberate fashion by way of systematically ordered, sequential and cumulative curricula" (Gutek).

The Modern Idealist education promotes a liberal arts education, as opposed to an education specializing in technical skills. The liberal arts education presents a broader understanding of the world to students; students develop "habits of understanding, patience, tolerance, and hard work" (Ozmon and Craver). In general, a liberal (arts) education promotes:

- The teaching of ideas that are eternal, universal and unchanging and not dependent on or relative to changing times, situations, or circumstances [with] enduring truths and values encased in great works of literatures, arts, and music;
- The *classics*, constitut[ing] knowledge that is of most worth, form[ing] the core of the curriculum;
- Classics [that] capture something that touches people across ages;
- The study of philosophy, theology, history, and math;
- School curriculum designed to prepare students for adult life;
- Basic education (learning to read, write, calculate), as well as computer skills;
- Study of art and music;
- Civility (with respect for spirituality, learning and art) (Gutek).

The act of teaching also follows certain processes in the Idealist's classroom. The teacher is the "mature model of cultural values…in that he or she is the mature embodiment of the culture's highest values" (Gutek). The teacher is "the kind of person we want our children to become" (Ozmon & Craver). Also, he or she promotes the Socratic dialogue, "leading questions crucial to human concerns." While lecture is a part of the methodology of the Idealist teacher, lecture is viewed more as "a means of stimulating thought than as a mere conveyance of information."

As Plato promotes the thought that "true education occurs only within the individual self," the Idealist teacher promotes self-directed activity (Ozmon & Craver). The teacher provides the materials that are needed for influencing thought and it is the responsibility of the student to respond to the teacher through intrinsic motivation (Ozmon & Craver; Gutek).

VALUES, ETHICS & MORALS

Accordingly, values education is at the forefront of an Idealist teacher's classroom. Ethics are at the core of this classroom, ethics that are "contained within and transmitted by cultural heritage." Texts that are "bearers of the human moral tradition and represent the generalized ethical and cultural conscience of civilization" are the materials used in this philosophically-bound classroom (Gutek). Gutek further explains that "students should be exposed to and should examine critically the great works of art and literature that have endured through time…exposing students to valuable lessons."

Great Books are proposed as models of the human moral tradition. Books should be seen "not as literal renderings of events but as something that provides insight into ourselves and the universe (Ozmon & Craver). Great Books "carr[y] us to a higher point in our thinking…as vehicles for moving us not only into the world of ideas but also the realm of great ideas—the ideas that are of sustained value to us in understanding truth."

ELEMENTS OF IDEALIST EDUCATION

Additionally, there are other applications that are characteristic of an Idealist educational philosophy:

The *dialectic* is a critical discussion that advances one from mere opinion to true knowledge (Ozmon & Craver). Ozmon and Craver state that in the dialectic, "all thinking begins with a thesis, or point of view. An antithesis is established; through the anti-thesis (or the opposite point of view), one reexamines and defends the position." Dialectic is "a winnowing out process in which ideas are put into battle against each other, with the more substantial ideas enduring the fraying."

The *seminar* is an application of the Socratic Method. Fischer (2008) defines the seminar as a classroom format that encompasses the questioning of the Socratic Method. In this seminar format, students are "empowered to explore what they feel is important" in any discussion. They are taught "how to think, not what to think." An opening question starts the seminar; this question is generally open-ended and has no right answer. Types of seminar approaches include: Touchstones Seminars, Junior Great Books Seminars, Paideia Seminars, Harkness Table, Socratic Seminars, Socratic Circles, Literature Circles and the fishbowl method.

The Socratic Method is a methodology of "constantly asking questions in order to further investigate core issues and ideas" (Fischer). The term derived from methodologies presented in Plato's *Dialogues*, as Plato relates Socrates' inductive process that produced questions that resulted in deeper investigations of ideas and concepts (Copeland, 2005).

This method of questioning can be considered either teacher-directed or student-centered, depending upon the approach to how questions are asked and under what circumstances they are being asked. Teacher-directed dialogue results in the action of steering students in the direction of "pre-determined goal(s)" (Fischer). Questioning is not a "simple recall of facts that have been memorized in advance" (Gutek). The students are asked specific questions for which there are answers that the teacher has determined are correct answers. The teacher knows the answers prior to asking the questions. This method is an alternative to straight lecture and encourages rich dialogue (Fischer).

In the student-centered approach to the Socratic Method, the teacher becomes an equal participant in the discussion, rather than the teacher who holds all the answers. This approach to the Socratic Method "encourages students to do the work of thinking and analysis in a cooperative manner" (Fischer).

Schneider argues against some widely held notions about the Socratic Method, writing that it was not, in fact, passed down "from ancient Athens across continents and millennia" (2013). Instead, he contends, it was "re-created and reimagined by different groups of educators who were less concerned with establishing a consistent and specific meaning for the method than they were with using it to advance their own distinct agendas." Thus, while the Socratic method is commonly perceived as both identifiable and ancient, it is "in reality a vaguely defined and relatively modern pedagogical concept-a fact that should give pause to educators presuming to employ it," he argues.

VIEWPOINTS

Plato's influence on education today has been great. He set out to perfect a system of education that "epitomizes not only one current of thought during a crucial period of Greek life, but it also represents a dialogue between that period and the periods that preceded it" (Nash et al.). Characteristics of Plato's educational philosophy have weathered the ages and have become the backbone of Idealism in today's classroom. Proponents of current Idealist viewpoints see many benefits to what is promoted in today's idealist classroom, including the high cognitive level of education and its concern for safeguarding and promoting cultural literacy and learning. The thread of moral and character development in idealist classrooms is seen as having a strong influence on youth. Teachers are seen as revered leaders who are an integral part of the learning process, as they act as role models to be exemplified. Ozmon and Craver further promote Idealism as a "comprehensive, systematic holistic approach to education."

Those opposed to the idea of an Idealist education state that the goals of such an education are "too abstract and altruistic for today's society" (Gutek). While Idealism promotes intellectualism, some see this as a "detriment of the affective and physical side of the students … [and] leans toward elitism" (Ozmon and Craver). Idealism has also been perceived as promoting bookishness instead of making a connection with the material world. Ozmon and Craver point out that reading extensively "about goodness does not make a person good." An Idealist's "armchair knowledge" is more limiting "rather than insight[fullness] that comes from interaction with other people in the real world."

Detractors also perceive the Idealist perspective to be too conservative and too fundamental in its principles. As Ozmon and Craver suggest, "The idea that there is a finished universe waiting to be discovered has hindered progress in science and the creation of new ideas and processes." This approach may actually advance "conformity and subservience on the part of the learner."

TERMS & CONCEPTS

Antithesis: The antithesis is an opposing point of view to a thesis presented in an argument.

Forms: Forms are "the world of ideas that has the Good at its highest point"; the Good is considered to be the source of all true knowledge.

Intrinsic Motivation: Intrinsic motivation occurs when students are motivated to produce due to their own internal interest. There is "a positive attraction to a task" in which students express an interest.

Mentoring: Mentoring is "the close relationship between the teacher and the students to create within the student's character an ethical predisposition to discover and use truth to order and govern his life; also called *character building*".

Thesis: A thesis is a point of view in an argument.

Universal Truth: Universal truth is truth that is absolute and is not dependent on different cultures.

Tricia Smith

BIBLIOGRAPHY

Barrow, R. (1975). *Plato, utilitarianism and education.* London: Routledge and Kegan Paul.

Barrow, R. (1976). *Plato and education.* London: :Routledge and Kegan Paul.

Copeland, M. (2005). *Socratic circles: Fostering critical and creative thinking in middle and high school.* Portland, ME: Stenhouse.

Fischer, C. (2008). The Socratic method. *Research Starters Education.* Retrieved May 30, 2009. from EBSCO online database, Research Starters Education.

Gutek, G. (2009). *New perspectives on philosophy and education.* Columbus, Ohio: Pearson.

Knight, G. (1998). *Issues and alternatives in education philosophy.* Berrien Springs, MI: Andrews UP.

Kohan, W. (2013). Plato and Socrates: From an educator of childhood to a childlike educator? *Studies in Philosophy & Education, 32,* 313-325. Retrieved November 30, 2013, from EBSCO Online Database Education Research Complete.

LoShan, Z. (1998). Plato's council on education. In Rorty, A. (Ed.). *Philosophers on Education: New historical perspectives* (pp. 32-50). NY: Routledge.

Nash, P., Kazamias, A., & Perkinson, H. (1965). *The educated man: Studies in the history of educational thought.* NewYork: Jon Wiley.

Nettleship, R. (1935). *The theory of education in Plato's Republic.* Oxford, Oxford UP.

Ormell, C. (2012). The curiously personal enterprise of philosophy. *Prospero, 18,* 31-41. Retrieved November 30, 2013, from EBSCO Online Database Education Research Complete.

Ozmon, H., & Craver, S. (2008). *Philosophical foundations of education.* Upper Saddle River, NJ: Pearson.

Powers, E. (1996). *Educational philosophy: A history from the ancient world to modern America.* New York: Garland Publishing.

Reed, R., & Johnson, T. (2000). *Philosophical documents in education.* New York: Longman.

Schneider, J. (2013). Remembrance of things past: a history of the Socratic Method in the United States. *Curriculum Inquiry, 43,* 613-640. Retrieved November 30, 2013, from EBSCO Online Database Education Research Complete.

Wingo, G. (1965). *The philosophy of American education.* New York: DC Heath.

SUGGESTED READING

Adler, M. (1982). *The Paideia proposal.* New York: MacMillan.

Baggini, J. (2005, January 21). Plato vs. Aristotle: 2,300 years and we're still arguing about it. *Times Educational Supplement, 4618,* 6-7.

Baker, B. (2003). Plato's child and the limit-points of educational theories. *Studies in Philosophy and Education, 22,* 439-474. Retrieved May 30, 2009. from EBSCO online database, Academic Search Complete.

Barlow, D. (2009). The teacher's lounge. *Education Digest, 74,* 65-68. Retrieved May 30, 2009. from EBSCO online database, Academic Search Complete.

Billings, L. & Roberts, T. (2006). Planning, practice, and assessment in the seminar classroom. *High School Journal, 90,* 1-8. Retrieved May 30, 2009. from EBSCO online database, Academic Search Complete.

Biondi, C. (2008). Socratic teaching: Beyond The Paper Chase. *Teaching Philosophy, 31,* 119-140.

Cai, Z. (1999). In quest of harmony: Plato and Confucius on poetry. *Philosophy East and West, 49,* 317-339. Retrieved May 30, 2009. from EBSCO online database, Academic Search Complete.

Cordasco, F. (1991). Greek education. In Johnson, J., DuPuis, V., & Johansen, J. (Eds.). *Reflections on American education: Classical and contemporary readings* (pp. 12-126). Boston: Allyn and Bacon.

Daniels, H. (1994). *Literature circles: Voice and choice in the student-centered classroom.* York, ME: Stenhouse.

Ediger, M. (1997). Influence of ten leading educators on American education. *Education,118,* 267-276. Retrieved May 30, 2009. from EBSCO online database, Academic Search Complete.

Edmonds, C., & Edmonds, T. (1997). Educational idealism: One more reason to stress the perpetual. *Journal of Education for Business, 72,* 217-221. Retrieved May 30, 2009. from EBSCO online database, Academic Search Complete.

Greene, M. (1973). *Teacher as strangers: Educational philosophy for the modern age.* Belmont, CA: Wadsworth.

Hoddings, N. (1995). *Philosophy of education.* Boulder, CO: Westview Press.

Knox, H. (1980). Philosophers as educational reformers: The influence of idealism on British educational thought and practice [Book Review]. *British Journal of Educational*

Studies, 28, 241-242. Retrieved May 30, 2009. from EBSCO online database, Academic Search Complete.

Lankshear, C. (2005). Fragments of life before Foucault. *Educational Philosophy and Theory, 37,* 303-307. Retrieved May 30, 2009. from EBSCO online database, Academic Search Complete.

McFarland, A., & McDaniel, R. (2002). Would you hire Plato to teach Physical Education at your school? *Physical Educator, 59,* 1-10. Retrieved May 30, 2009. from EBSCO online database, Academic Search Complete.

Passmore, J. (1980). *The philosophy of teaching.* Cambridge, MA: Harvard University Press.

Perkinson, H. (1980). *Since Socrates: Studies in the history of Western educational thought.* New York: Longman.

Peters, R. (1978). *The philosophy of education.* Oxford: Oxford University Press.

Plato. (1974). *Plato's Republic.* Translation. Grube, G. Indianapolis, IN: Hackett.

Politis, V. (2001). Anti-realists interpretations of Plato: Paul Natorp. *International Journal of Philosophical Studies,* 9, 47-62. Retrieved May 30, 2009. from EBSCO online database, Academic Search Complete.

Rorty, A. (1998). The ruling history of education. In Rorty, A. (Ed.). *Philosophers on education: New historical perspectives* (pp. 1-13). NY: Routledge.

Scott, G. (2002). *Plato's Socrates as educator.* Albany, NY: State U. of NY Press.

Shim, S. (2008). A philosophical investigation of the role of teachers: A synthesis of Plato, Confucius, Buber, and Friere. *Teaching and Teacher Education, 24,* 515-535.

Smertenko, C. (1922). Platonism to the rescue. *Nation, 114*(2957), 290-293. Retrieved May 30, 2009. from EBSCO online database, Academic Search Complete.

Vandenberg, D. (2009). Critical thinking about truth in teaching: The epistemic ethos. *Educational Philosophy and Theory, 41,* 155-165. Retrieved May 30, 2009 from online database, Academic Search Complete.

Wilson, J. *Preface to the philosophy of education.* London: Routledge and Kegan Paul.

KARL MARX AND EDUCATION

This article is centered on Karl Marx's influence on educational theory. The article begins with a brief biography of Karl Marx, and then an examination of the basic beliefs that constitute a "Marxist" point of view. Next, the article explains how the works of Karl Marx politically and socially influenced the world. In terms of educational influence, we look at Marx's influence on one of America's most renowned educational theorists, John Dewey, and we also explore the ways in which educators are still applying Marx's ideas in courses and lessons today.

KEYWORDS: Bourgeoisie; Capitalism; Communism; Communist Manifesto; Dewey, John; Proletariat; Socialism; Soviet Union; Totalitarianism

OVERVIEW

At the end of the twentieth century, the British Broadcasting Corporation (BBC) issued a series of polls designed to allow the public to select the greatest historical figures over the last thousand years. In October of 1999, the BBC examined its public polls and discovered that England's choice for the "greatest thinker" of the millennium was Karl Marx. Surprisingly, Marx came in ahead of Einstein, Newton, and Darwin who were second, third and fourth ("Marx After Communism," 2002).

If we consider the amount of change each of these historical figures brought to society, then perhaps Marx's highest position makes sense. A German philosopher, Marx (1818-1883) contributed to radical changes in the world, and today is widely considered one of the most important political economists, historians, and philosophers in world history. His ideas are also considered to be the foundation of communism, though often his ideas and the practice of communism seem to greatly diverge. Nevertheless, his ideas have significantly influenced many areas of human activity, from political systems to pedagogical theory. Before examining Marx's influence on history, governments and education—including American education—we should first outline the most basic ideas that comprise the Marxist viewpoint.

MARX'S BASIC PRINCIPLES

Marx espoused four basic ideas from which most of his other ideas and arguments follow:

- Societies follow laws of motion simple and all-encompassing enough to make long-range prediction fruitful;
- These laws are exclusively economic in character: what shapes society, the only thing that shapes society, is the "material forces of production."

- These laws must invariably express themselves, until the end of history, as a bitter struggle of class against class;
- At the end of history, classes and the state (whose sole purpose is to represent the interests of the ruling class) must dissolve to yield a heaven on earth ("Marx After Communism").

As McLennan observes, Marx believed that his era (the late 1800's) was different from the previous periods of history in that, from the advent of industrialism, the wealthy upper class (the "bourgeoisie") had substantially intensified the divide between social classes. This division also therefore intensified the conflict between the bourgeoisie and the working class (the "proletariat"). From Marx's viewpoint, two distinct classes had grown out of the Industrial Revolution: the bourgeoisie owners of the means of production, and the proletarian wage laborers who worked in the means of production (McLennan, 1999). Viewing all of human history as one of class struggle is central to Marx's viewpoint, which is probably why Marx wrote as the very first line of *The Communist Manifesto,* "The history of all hitherto existing society is the history of class struggles." Marx believed the power of the working class would lead to a social and political upheaval.

Thus, Marx's central argument is that every society has been based on an antagonism between oppressing and oppressed classes, and that revolution was inevitable. Marx believed that "The proletarian movement is the self-conscious movement of the immense majority, in the interest of the immense majority," and he believed this new movement of the working class would globally end all class oppression. As Morgan (2005) points out, Marx believed this movement—leading to revolution—would also be a change in human consciousness, a change that would bring about changes in material existence as well as social life. Society would change to serve the enormous working class rather than serving the wealthy few. Morgan then observes that "this will have fundamental implications for intellectual life and consequently for education, for, as Marx puts it, 'The ruling ideas of each age have ever been the ideas of its ruling class'" (Morgan).

From an historical context, Marx viewed this social transformation as natural socioeconomic evolution: as industrialism and capitalism had replaced an age of agriculture and feudalism, so Marx believed that a new socioeconomic system of "socialism" would replace capitalism. This in turn would eventually create a classless society that represented mature "communism."

MARX'S HISTORICAL INFLUENCE

Although the Soviet Union and all other communist governments have regarded Karl Marx as the primary inspiration for their communist systems, it is an interesting question whether Marx would have approved of the totalitarian systems that grew out of the implementation of his theories. It is also an interesting question whether these same totalitarian systems would have evolved had Marx never been born. Perhaps these same totalitarian systems would have come into being by distorting the ideas of another historian, economist or philosopher. When declaring the winner of the above poll, the BBC announcer remarked that "although dictatorships throughout the 20th century have distorted [Marx's] original ideas, his work as a philosopher, social scientist, historian and a revolutionary is respected by academics today" ("Marx After Communism"). McLennan states this same idea when he notes that many "independent minded Marxists" believe that "the truths of Marxist theory and values can validly be separated from many of the ideological-political uses to which they have been put" (McLennan). Arendt's ideas resonate with McLennan's point when she argues that totalitarianism "could never have been foreseen or forethought, much less predicted or 'caused,' by any single man" (Arendt, 2002).

Clearly, Marx's most significant historical influence can be seen in communist nations, but Marx never writes about creating a totalitarian government. Rather, it seems likely that the harsh reality of totalitarianism mutated out of his idealism and naïve belief that a one-party socialist government of the proletariat would "wither away," leading to statelessness, so that people would live freely under no government at all. Marx believed that cooperation in society could best be achieved through a one-party system. However, he failed to recognize that, if this single party went astray or became corrupted through its sheer power over society, citizens would be left with no choice or means of replacing that political party with an opposing one. Thus, we should make a clear distinction between Marx as the socioeconomic analyst and Marx as the socioeconomic planner. His socioeconomic analysis is what to this day holds significance, while his idealistic plan for utopia has met clear failure. This is what Arendt means when she writes:

> *That Marx still looms so large in our present world is indeed the measure of his greatness. That he could prove of use to totalitarianism (though certainly he can never be said to have been its "cause") is a sign of the actual relevance of his thought, even though at the same time it is also the measure of his ultimate failure (Arendt).*

As the failures of the grand social experiments based on Marx's writing fade into history, the analytical side of his content is being re-assessed. Additionally, Marx as a writer has increasingly gained recognition. As McLennan points out, Marx as a *"writer, ironist and intellect"* has gained recognition perhaps even more than "Marx the revolutionary or theorist of capitalism". However, McLennan gives additional reasons for Marx's increasing recognition among academics. McLennan argues that "the winds of change have turned in the seminar rooms, and a new thirst for substantive commitment; for an end, or at least a supplement to, an intellectual diet of 'interminable self-critique.'" Additionally, McLennan points out that contemporary civilization supplies "warrant for the 'return' of Marx", and these factors also seem to be contributing to a new appreciation of the writings of Marx (McLennan).

Further Insights

MARX & DEWEY

Marx's approach to education can be seen in his resolution written in 1866 for the first Congress of the International Workingman's Association. Marx mentions three main elements of what he believed would create a sound educational system:

- Mental education;
- Bodily education;
- Technological training.

Though the resolution gives little clarification of the first two elements, it does further explain the idea of technological training. The resolution states that technological training will impart "the general principles of all processes of production, and, simultaneously, initiates the child and young person in the practical use and handling of the elementary instruments of all trades" (Small, 1984). Small argues that technological training was the most important part of Marx's view on education because it is "most directly linked with material production, but also as the part in which the theme of full human development appears most directly." Small concludes that technological training "is perhaps the most important element in the Marxian conception of education, as well as its most original contribution to later educational thought."

The educational approach of learning to produce things was promoted in the U.S. by one of America's most renowned educators, John Dewey. Karier and Hogan (1979) point out that, during the years Dewey published most of his writing on educational theory (1895 to 1925), America was rapidly developing into the modern market economy it is today. The authors observe that during the period that Dewey was becoming a prominent educational theorist, American monopolies were consolidating and "mass advertising and mass education were helping to shape the values and desires of a mass consumer-oriented society" (Karier & Hogan). Dewey was well aware of the theories of Marx because the newly formed Soviet Union was at that time intensively forwarding Marx's theories. Dewey had even traveled to the Soviet Union to examine its educational system. In fact, after analyzing the Soviet educational system, Dewey made the following observation:

> *I do not see how any honest educational reformer in western countries can deny that the greatest practical obstacle in the way of introducing into schools that connection with social life which he regards as desirable is the great part played by personal competition and desire for private profit in our economic life. This fact almost makes it necessary that in important respects school activities should be protected from social contacts and connections, instead of being organized to create them. The Russian educational situation is enough to convert one to the idea that only in a society based upon the cooperative principle can the ideals of educational reformers be adequately carried into operation (as cited in Karier & Hogan).*

Karier and Hogan argue that Marx and Dewey both believed that the capitalist system of private profit had a negative effect on social attempts to create a fair and compassionate social system. They echo Dewey's quote above when they argue that "unlike the Soviet schools, the American progressive schools could not be fully linked to the emerging economic social order without falling into the trap of enhancing and encouraging the private profit system." In any case, there is a clear similarity between Marx and Dewey because, as Harris points out, both Marx and Dewey believed that labor and production, through technological training, was important to incorporate in the general education process (Harris, 2006). Harris also observes that economic history was essential to Dewey's educational theory. Dewey writes that "Economic history deals with the activities, the career, and fortunes of the common man as does no other branch of history" (Harris). Thus, Marx was concerned with educating the "proletarian" in economic history and technological production, just as Dewey was concerned with educating the "common man" in these same areas.

The fundamental difference seems to be that Marx based his educational model upon the principle of class struggle, whereas Dewey did not believe class struggle was a productive viewpoint. Dewey seems to have placed his faith in science and social cooperation as the cure for the wrongs of capitalism. This is why, as Karier and Hogan point out, Dewey promoted a curriculum around occupations, but he intentionally avoided the topic of economic conflict or any other topic that he believed would create an awareness of class differences. Dewey believed that focusing on class differences leads to class conflict. Therefore, Dewey created an educational system that, in order to reshape the thinking of students, protected them from an unpleasant socioeconomic system based on greed, selfishness, profit, power, and class antagonisms (Karier & Hogan).

Once again there is a need to separate Marx as an analyst of social problems from Marx as a promoter of solutions. This is where Dewey seems to have made the separation. Though Dewey agrees with Marx's view of the social maladies that capitalism creates, Dewey was clearly against the Marxist principle of class struggle and the establishment of government-run economies. Rather than class war as the solution, Dewey chose science. This is quite clear when he writes:

> ...the rise of scientific method and of technology based upon it is the genuinely active force in producing the vast complex of changes the world is now undergoing, not the class struggle whose spirit and method are opposed to science (cited in Karier & Hogan).

Harris also observes that Dewey "logically opposed class struggle," and believed that any negative aspects of capitalism would be ameliorated through science and social cooperation. However, Harris comes to the conclusion that Dewey's solution is naïve. He writes, "the naivety of Dewey's views becomes apparent when we consider how undemocratic life has become in the modern capitalist world. Even exposing a problem will require struggle because there are people in positions of power who oppose it" (Harris). Thus, it seems Marx and Dewey understood and agreed upon the problems inherent within the capitalist economic model, but their differing solutions were both equally naïve.

Viewpoints

Teaching Marx in a Capitalistic Education System

A second important way that Marx has influenced education around the world is the way his ideas have affected teachers, who in turn affect students. Allman (1994) notes that some international educators have taken the works of Marx in order to argue that educators' claims of teaching in a "neutral" way is impossible. As Allman puts it, "If educators are not encouraging people to question (to see their reality as a problem), to challenge and to change their reality, then they must be enabling them to accept it, adapt to it and to engage in its reproduction ... therefore educators and every other cultural worker must make a political choice between domestication and liberation and in making that choice to be clear about whose interests they are serving" (Allman). From this point of view, educators either promote the status quo—meaning a consumer-based society where capitalism is praised—or educators challenge the economic model and point out the many problems that arise from our capitalist system.

Brosio is one such educator who shows students what a Marxist analysis of society is like. He also points out the effect of the economic system on American education in general. Brosio argues that educators should be aware of "the kindergarten through Grade 12 public school system's answerability to the capitalist imperative upon it," and he argues that our economic system, when giving assistance to public education, "demands thinly disguised vocational training for many students" (Brosio, 2003). Brosio also points out Allman's argument that "we [educators] must challenge the 'slippage of education into training and also the incorporation of education into the market paradigm'" (Brosio).

Allman points out that Marx—as well as educators who think the Marxian point of view possesses a validity that makes it worth teaching—are concerned that not teaching a critical socioeconomic viewpoint may ultimately support a system that is in need of change. Not teaching a viewpoint critical of capitalism promotes the system and prevents any change because the system is not questioned. This idea relates back to the argument that there is no such thing as teaching in a "neutral" way. Allman argues that teachers who use a Marxist point of view are essentially helping to develop "a critical (dialectical) perception of reality" in their students. Importantly, Allman argues that these educators are not teaching a Marxist viewpoint so as to indoctrinate students in a Marxist ideology. As Allman puts it, "their [educators'] role, however, is not to tell the people what to think but to enable them also to think critically" (Allman).

PITFALLS

Using Marxist viewpoints to criticize America's public education system presents some problems of which educators should be well aware. As Harris observes, presenting a critical view of our educational system creates opposition not only with our "existing educational traditions, but also with the opposition of those who are entrenched in command of the industrial machinery, and who realize that such an educational system if made general would threaten their ability to use others for their own ends" (Harris).

Additionally, Harris points out that teachers may create problems in their lives if they "explicitly link [Marxist] subject matter to the nature of capitalism." Harris avoided this problem when teaching a geography course because he intentionally kept Marx and his philosophy "in the background and focused on the nature of capitalism in relation to geographical themes." This approach allowed him to use Marxist viewpoints on capitalism without causing any political opposition among parents or the educational institution. However, Harris warns that using the ideas of Marx "may become an issue because of what one is teaching." He observes that educators who wish to use the ideas of Marx in the classroom fail to discuss the problem of what teachers should do if they do indeed face persecution or political opposition for presenting Marxian viewpoints.

McLennan argues that the entire profession of education may have experienced "proletarianization" since Marx observes how:

… professions which had previously enjoyed reverence and honour were being turned into routine forms of wage labour … this remains a convincing argument, and its theoretical force, one suspects, is being appreciated anew by academics as they helplessly witness the relentless commodification of knowledge and their own changing status within that process (McLennan).

Brosio makes a similar observation when he argues that the teaching profession "has been subsumed within the social relations of capitalist production," and that teachers with a critical view of capitalism "will realize that their work has become more controlled, supervised or managed and often deskilled or … de-intellectualized" (Brosio). He concludes that "dependence on the market in order to work—even for exploitative pay—becomes a matter of survival itself when the capitalist system becomes universal, or at least global" (Brosio).

Some contemporary educators would disagree with Dewey's belief that science and cooperation is the solution for eliminating the wrongs created by capitalism. As Harris points out:

To question the ossified school system, for instance, let alone the employer-employee relation, frequently requires a struggle even to be heard. A politics of exposing the various bureaucratic and ossified social structures for what they really are, and not what they pretend to be, involves a class struggle; Dewey, however, presented the problem as if it were one of everyone having a common interest in exposing problems. There are powerful people in social institutions who attempt to suppress the exposure of those problems. Progress does not result merely from technological development or the exposure of problems, but from the struggle to expose and address them outside the confines of capitalist society. Class struggle is the order of the day on several fronts (Harris).

Thus, some educators still recognize the importance of Marx's ideas in an educational setting, and they still use his ideas, both in the area of economic analysis as well as the area of social analysis. On the other hand, most contemporary educators who use the ideas of Marx also understand that there are plenty of flaws in the Marxian viewpoint. For example, McLennan points out that Marx's strict division of the bourgeoisie and the proletariat "has long seemed perverse and outmoded" because Marx "failed to foresee the decline of the classical proletariat and the corresponding growth of the middle class." The author also points out that Marx's prediction that the working class would increasingly become impoverished under a capitalist system, "ignores the general improvement of living standards across the capitalist world since he wrote" (McLennan). There are plenty of other areas where Marx was probably mistaken. However, this critical approach to Marx's ideas is exactly what education should be about; not the avoidance of Marxism as "evil communist ideology," but the presentation of Marx's ideas so as to question both our own capitalist system as well as Marx's ideas about that system.

TERMS & CONCEPTS

Bourgeoisie: A social classification describing a social class in capitalist economic systems. In Marxist vocabulary, the bourgeoisie is the wealthy class that owns the means for producing more wealth. Thus, factory owners are members of the bourgeoisie.

Capitalism: Refers to an economic system where industry and the means of production are privately owned and operated for profit, also referred to as "free enterprise" or a "liberal market economy". In capitalism, trade is done in an open or free market system.

Communism: Refers to an economic system and political ideology intended to create a society that has no social stratification based on wealth, and ultimately has no government at all. According to Marxist theory, communism is the state of society that follows socialism, a one-party government system intended to represent the proletariat.

Proletariat: A term Karl Marx used for the lower social class, the wage-labor working class. Marx called a member this class a "proletarian". The proletariat is also the class in capitalist societies which does not own the means of production. According to Marx, a proletarian's only means of living is to sell his or her labor power for a wage or salary.

Socialism: In the Marxist sense, is a form of economic organization in which the government controls and operates the national economy so that private ownership of factories does not exist. Socialism is aimed at creating common ownership of the means of production, and a Socialist society aims at giving equal access to all resources for all individuals. Karl Marx argued that a class struggle between the bourgeoisie and the proletariat would lead to a revolution that establishes socialism as a transitional stage from capitalism to communism.

Soviet Union: A socialist state that was officially established in 1922 and was strongly based on Marxist principles. The Soviet Union was a union of several Soviet republics such as Poland, Czechoslovakia, Hungary, and other surrounding states. The Soviet Union officially came to an end in 1991 after a revolution that centered in Moscow (the formal name is the Union of Soviet Socialist Republics—abbreviated USSR).

Totalitarianism: Refers to a form of government wherein a national government exercises absolute and centralized control over all aspects of a citizen's life. Under a totalitarian system, the individual is subordinated to the state, and any individuals or organizations that oppose the government are harshly suppressed.

The Communist Manifesto: The most primary book used to teach Marxist philosophy about communism. The book was first published in 1848, and is considered one of the most influential political manuscripts ever written. Karl Marx and Friedrich Engels authored the book, which presents a class struggle viewpoint on capitalist societies.

Sinclair Nicholas

BIBLIOGRAPHY

Allman, P. (1994). Paulo Freire's contributions to radical adult education. *Studies in the Education of Adults, 26,* 144-162. Retrieved July 15, 2009, from EBSCO online database Academic Search Complete.

Arendt, H. (2002). Karl Marx and the tradition of western political thought. *Social Research, 69,* 273-319. Retrieved July 14, 2009, from EBSCO online database Academic Search Complete.

Brosio, R. (2003). Critical education against global capitalism: Karl Marx and revolutionary critical education. *Educational Studies, 34,* 446-464. Retrieved July 15, 2009, from EBSCO online database Academic Search Complete.

Brosio, R. (2011). Marxist thought: Still primus inter pares for understanding and opposing the capitalist system. *Journal of Thought, 46*(1/2), 33-63. Retrieved December 15, 2013, from EBSCO Online Database Education Research Complete.

Gerrard, J. (2012). Tracing radical working-class education: praxis and historical representation. *History of Education, 41*, 537-558. Retrieved December 15, 2013, from EBSCO Online Database Education Research Complete.

Harris, F. (2006). Dewey's materialist philosophy of education: A resource for critical pedagogues? *European Legacy, 11*, 259-288. Retrieved July 16, 2009, from EBSCO online database Academic Search Complete.

Karier, C. & Hogan, D. (1979). Schooling, education and the structure of social reality. *Educational Studies, 10*, 245-277. Retrieved July 15, 2009, from EBSCO online database Academic Search Complete.

Marx after communism. (2002). *Economist, 365*(8304), 17-19. Retrieved July 14, 2009, from EBSCO online database Academic Search Complete.

McLennan, G. (1999). Re-canonizing Marx. *Cultural Studies, 13*, 555-576. Retrieved July 16, 2009, from EBSCO online database Academic Search Complete.

Morgan J. (2005). Marxism and moral education. *Journal of Moral Education, 34*, 391-398. Retrieved July 16, 2009, from EBSCO online database Academic Search Complete.

Skovsmose, O. (2011). Critique, generativity and imagination. *For the Learning of Mathematics, 31*, 19-23. Retrieved December 15, 2013, from EBSCO Online Database Education Research Complete.

Small, R. (1984). The concept of polytechnical education. *British Journal of Educational Studies, 32*, 27-44. Retrieved July 14, 2009, from EBSCO online database Academic Search Complete.

SUGGESTED READING

Hilmer, J. (2000). Two views about socialism: Why Karl Marx shunned an academic debate with Pierre-Joseph Proudhon. *Democracy & Nature: The International Journal of Inclusive Democracy, 6*, 85-93. Retrieved July 15, 2009, from EBSCO online database Academic Search Complete.

Morris, V. (1975). The way we work: Some notes on career education. *Journal of Career Education, 1*, 4-9. Retrieved July 14, 2009, from EBSCO online database Education Research Complete.

Sidorkin, A. (2004). In the event of learning: Alienation and participative thinking in education. *Educational Theory, 54*, 21-262. Retrieved July 15, 2009, from EBSCO online database Academic Search Complete.

Stromberg, R. (1977). The greening of Karl Marx. *National Review, 29*, 991. Retrieved July 15, 2009, from EBSCO online database Academic Search Complete.

PAULO FREIRE

Brazilian Paulo Freire (1921-1997) was known for his mass literacy campaigns for Latin American education. His approach to education was a critical reflection of his own practices as an adult educator as he examined authoritarian educational systems. In his many writings, Freire reflected upon the pedagogical activities that represented the political and historical milieu in the 1960's and 70's. He created a theory of education linked to issues of oppression and struggle and coined a term, "banking concept" of education (Jackson, 2007). Freire's most important text is Pedagogy of the Oppressed, a critical reflection of his own practices as an adult educator in Brazil.

KEYWORDS: Banking Concept; Consciousness-raising; Critical Theory; Domesticating Education; Dialogue; Freire, Paulo; Liberating Education; Liberation Pedagogy; Pedagogy of the Oppressed; Problem-posing Education; Praxis

OVERVIEW

Brazilian Paulo Freire (1921-1997) was known for his mass literacy campaigns for Latin American education. Philosophically, Freire was influenced by existentialism and Critical Theory (Gutek, 2009). As an intellectual as well as educator of adult learners, he developed a liberating conception of teaching and learning that is structural, purposeful and academically rigorous (Roberts, 1996). His approach to education was a critical reflection of his own practices as an adult educator, as he examined authoritarian educational systems. In his many writings, Freire reflected upon the pedagogical activities that represented the political and historical milieu of the 1960's and 70's. He created a theory of education linked to issues of oppression and struggle (Jackson).

Freire's most important text is *Pedagogy of the Oppressed*, a critical reflection of his own practices as an adult educator in Brazil. He worked with impoverished workers in Brazil, peasants who participated in Freire's cultural circles. Through Freire's methodologies, they realized an understanding about their culture and improved their literacy skills in just 40 days (Schugurensky, 1998). For Freire, learning "never takes place in a vacuum; learning always occurs in a social context, under specific political conditions" (Roberts). His works promoted a new view of teaching that moved the oppressed to better understand themselves in their world. To Freire, teaching becomes "a necessary interventional occupation, implying a commitment to a given ethical and political position, from which pedagogical principles and practices derive" (Roberts).

VIEWS OF SOCIETY & EDUCATION

To Freire, society is characterized by the relationship between power and domination over those who do not have power. Those in power, called the *oppressors*, exert power over those who are powerless, the *oppressed* (Mayo, 1993). Freire applied a dialectical analysis to what he considered to be *bourgeois education*. A bourgeois education supports certain characteristics of the interaction between teacher and learner. The teacher and learner are at "direct opposites, or in *dialectical contradiction*" (Allman, 1994, p. 8). The teacher possesses knowledge that the learner needs; the learner is subordinate and dependent on the teacher. This relationship is said to limit the learning and creative potential of both the teacher and the learner. Freire coined the term *banking education* to illustrate this point; teachers deposit the information and the learners acquire it (Allman, 1994). Freire proposes that this oppressive concept "perpetuates inequalities and injustices and stifles creativity" (Roberts). This form of education becomes an oppressive social function supported by the political entities that support education.

THE BANKING CONCEPT

Freire often criticized the version of mainstream education he found in most Latin American countries, which he termed "Banking Education." In the banking concept of education, the teacher controls the information that he or she deposits within the learner. Mayo defines the banking concept of education as "a top-to-bottom approach to knowledge transmission through which the teacher is the sole dispenser of knowledge and students are the passive recipients."

For example, the teacher may research a topic for his or her lecture, preparing the notes and organizing the presentation. The teacher chooses what the learner is to know and transmits this knowledge to the learner, with no active participation occurring on the part of the learner. The learner receives the information, without question or dialogue (Allman). As a passive learner, he or she may memorize the material and repeat it back to the teacher. In this manner, Freire believed that knowledge becomes "a gift to be bestowed by teachers upon voiceless, patient and ignorant students; knowledge becomes lifeless and static" (Roberts). This type of education dissuades critical thinking by the student and lead to domestication, which allows the further political oppression of citizens by an authoritative government.

McCarter (2013) views the "learned helplessness" of contemporary American high-school students as being very closely related to Freire's banking concept. He writes, "Instead of allowing their students to wallow in the complexity of the world in which we live, high school teachers must construct a static reality that can be memorized and then spewed out onto a multiple choice exam when test time comes." He likens this to Freire's banking concept of education (McCarter).

LIBERATING EDUCATION

Freire supported changing the approach to this teacher-learner relationship to a liberating education model. He conceived teaching and learning as two internally-related processes that occur within each person. To Freire, teachers must relinquish their authoritarian control over the learner and become part of the learning process. The learner joins together with the teacher "in a mutual process of teaching and learning" (Allman). Promoting Freire's problem-posing theory changes the dynamics of this relationship (Roberts). Within problem-posing education, learners begin "to understand their world in a depth hitherto unknown to them." Academic rigour is a characteristic of problem-posing education. Expectations are that teachers prepare themselves to be conversant in their content area of study, always learning more and more about the subject through their interaction with the material. Only through study can teachers prepare themselves to become facilitators of the process of learning (Roberts).

This can best be accomplished through dialogue. Dialogue is a problem-posing approach to effectively using questions to advance critical thinking. Dialogue is not random, but has a clear structure, generally supported through curriculum decisions reflected in a syllabus. Dialogue has a meaningful definitive focus that cohesively reflects the objectives of the lesson (Roberts) Critical thinking is required for dialogue to occur, and dialogue creates even further critical thinking. Dialogue becomes "a pivotal pedagogical process," as the teacher communicates and "re-learns" the material with the learner (Roberts). Both learners and teachers relate to one another in a horizontal, rather than hierarchical manner (in which the teacher controls the discussion) (Roberts). Instead of using the Socratic method to analyze Great Books, the focus of dialogue is on problem-posing.

In this critical theory, knowledge is not static and is viewed as transformational; learners scrutinize what they know and "constantly test its adequacy as a tool for illuminating…the real condition and informing our action" (Allman). Knowledge helps learners understand the characteristics of their lives; they constantly test and question their conditions. Knowledge can best be developed through this dialogue, where all participants "seek…to know, gather, reflect and pose problems."

The liberating teacher becomes a facilitator, whose responsibility is to furnish effective learning conditions in the classroom. The teacher gives "structure and direction to learning, while encouraging and enhancing academic rigor" (Roberts). The teacher does not indoctrinate the learner, but enables the learner to make discoveries and decisions on his or her own (Malcolm, 1999).

Kojima, Miwa, and Matsui (2013) wrote about the importance of problem-posing in mathematics education. Endeavoring to improve problem posing for novices, their study discussed an approach that supports learning from examples as a production task. They implemented a system that "presents examples of problem posing and supports learners in understanding the examples by having the learners reproduce them." The results demonstrated that "the learners successfully adapted the example when posing their own problems if they learned the example by the reproduction method" (Kojima et al.).

EDUCATION & POLITICS

Freire stated that education can never be neutral in its political stance. Teachers need not hide their political positions; however, they should not "coerce learners to accept [their] political position" (Roberts). To Freire, teaching can never be divorced from the "critical analysis of how society works," that "teachers must challenge learners to think critically about the social, political and historical realities within which they inhabit the world" (Jackson). No education "is neutral," education systems either "work to domesticate children or to liberate them" (Archer, 2007).

To Freire, the task of education in a democracy does not involve cultivating intellectual virtues. Instead, education helps people realize "the full range of untested feasibilities available to them as they yearn to complete themselves" and transform "the very society that has denied them the opportunity of participation" (Malcolm). Education gives learners choices to think critically and apply their thinking to liberate themselves and transform their reality (Crowther, 2005). Through learning, learners "make and remake themselves," as they take "responsibility for themselves as capable of knowing—of knowing that they know and knowing that they don't." (Jackson)

Applications

THE LIBERATING EDUCATOR

For Freire's pedagogy to succeed in contributing to social transformation, classroom teachers are encouraged to change their approach away from the Banking model. Simpson et al. (2006) outline the characteristics of teachers who exhibit Freirean professional attitudes, dispositions or behaviors. These educators:

- Demonstrate *humility*, which entails abandoning arrogance and cultivating self-confidence as well as the ability to listen to and learn from others;
- Use *common sense*, which demands rejecting authoritarian tendencies and employing experimental knowledge to work ethically, efficiently and effectively with others;
- Manifest *lovingness*, which involves uprooting negative attitudes and demonstrating concern for students, teaching, and colleagues as we cultivate a more humane and just society;
- Develop *courage*, which requires recognizing and overcoming our fears and taking risks, fighting myths, and choosing love;

- Exhibit *tolerance*, which includes opposing the intolerable and respecting those who are different from us as we work to create and sustain democratic classrooms and schools;
- Cultivate *decisiveness*, which involves breaking free from both arbitrariness and permissiveness and choosing from among our professional and personal options;
- Build *security*, which encompasses abandoning the insecurity of conformity and gaining professional competence, political clarity, and ethical integrity;
- Express *impatient patience*, which means discarding both sheer activism and passivism and reflectively pursuing the right and needs of students and faculty;
- Display *verbal parsimony*, which necessitates eliminating obstructed and uninhibited discourse and engaging in measured but passionate dialogue and advocacy;
- Pursue the *joy of living*, which calls for casting off the gloom of misfortune and oppression and fostering the joy of learning.

Critical thinking is encouraged in liberating education through problem-posing. Problem-posing is a dialogical strategy for enhancing critical thinking in a learner. Malcolm proposes that the method of problem-posing has several steps:

- Identify the problem, a problem that addresses an issue in learners' lives;
- Name the problem, as learners generate words for the problem;
- Codify the generative themes, describing and writing down the full ramifications of the problem;
- Engage critically with the problem, thoroughly analyzing the factors and the obstacles;
- Synthesize perceptions, perceiving obstacles differently but more equipped to transform them in new ways.

Study is the disciplined approach to understanding content. In a liberated classroom, study is a way of investigating content "through purposeful, structured, critical dialogue" (Roberts). Those who study must "muster [their] intellectual energies such that the learners transcend mere awareness and penetrate beneath the surface of the subject...under investigation."

VIEWPOINTS

While Paulo Freire was a prolific writer about his work in adult education theory, many critics had issues with specific elements of his writing. To some, Freire's writing is not accessible to the average reader, particularly in light of the fact that his theories are based on the development of adult learning. Schugurensky states that *Pedagogy of the Oppressed* is difficult to read, that it contains "pompous, snobbish, elitist, convoluted, arrogant, and metaphysical" and "sexist language" ("Some Problematic Areas"). Another criticism focuses on the prominent theme of oppression. Freire speaks extensively of class struggles, i.e., the oppression of peasants in Brazil. However, he clearly avoids race and gender issues in his work, as if oppression is only related to class struggles (Schugurensky).

To some critics, Freire's writing lacks the concrete methodology that could be used by teachers to teach adult education classes. Readers of his works have commented that they would have enjoyed 'how-to' methods for the ways in which he taught literacy to adult learners. None of his books give guidelines regarding how to read and write; his texts are far too theoretical to be useful as guides in teaching literacy (Schugurensky).

Nonetheless, education theorist Paulo Freire made an invaluable contribution to adult literacy development through his work in critical pedagogy. He raised the consciousness about education, "constructing a critical awareness of social, political and economic conditions and contradictions under which people live and work" (Gutek).

More recently, Webb (2012) has written that Freire was "the visionary instigator of utopian pedagogy." He cites the pedagogical necessity, recognized by Freire, of utopia "as process, orientation, and system." As such, "the role of the active utopian educator becomes one of unmasking reality, of illuminating the path toward humanization, of sharpening the curiosity, and radicalizing the hope of the educands, and, crucially, of directing their purposive action toward the realization of a utopian vision, system, and goal" (Webb).

While *Pedagogy of the Oppressed* (1972) was Freire's all-time best seller by an educationalist, other texts written by Freire include:

- Education for Critical Consciousness (1973);
- Cultural Action for Freedom (1972);
- Pedagogy in Process (1978);
- The Politics of Education (1985);

- Pedagogy of the City (1993);
- Pedagogy of Hope (1994);
- Letters to Christina (1996);
- Pedagogy of the Heart (1997);
- Pedagogy of Freedom (1998);
- Politics and Education (1998);
- Pedagogy of Indignation (2004).

TERMS & CONCEPTS

Consciousness-raising: Consciousness-raising is a theory that analyzes "control and power in institutions and schools and seeks to empower those who are marginalized in a capitalist society and economy".

Critical Theory: Critical theory is a philosophy that is "engaged in the great struggles and social movements of its times" (Noddings, 1995). Critical theorists analyze "the social conditions that underlie, accompany, and result from forms of domination".

Domesticating Education: Domesticating education is the banking concept of education that is characterized as a top-to-bottom approach to knowledge transmission. Domesticating education promotes authoritarian social relations and oppression.

Knowledge: From a Freirian position, knowledge is a means by which learners begin learning about themselves and their environment rather than as an end in itself. Knowledge helps learners understand the contradictions of their realities and becomes "the springboard for the creation of new knowledge or the deeper understanding of the world which [learners] need for developing a revolutionary praxis" in order to institute change.

Liberating Education: Liberating education is a learning process that respects people as "active and creative subjects rather than treating them as passive objects or receptacles".

Liberation Pedagogy: Liberation education is a concept of education developed by Paulo Freire that promotes education that "liberates people from oppression and guides them in their own self-empowerment".

Praxis: Praxis in a process whereby learners are "distanced from their world of everyday action in order to see it in a different, more critical, light with a view to transforming it".

Tricia Smith

BIBLIOGRAPHY

Allman, P. (1994). Paulo Freire's contributions to radical adult education. *Studies in the Education of Adults, 26,* 144-162. Retrieved June 24, 2009, from EBSCO online database, Academic Search Complete.

Archer, D. (2007). Education for liberation. *Adults Learning, 18,* 28-29. Retrieved June 23, 2009, from EBSCO online database, Academic Search Complete.

Crowther, J., & Martin, J. (2005). Twenty-first century Freire. *Adults Learning, 17,* 7-9. Retrieved June 26, 2009, from EBSCO online database, Academic Search Complete.

Gutek, G. (2009). *New perspectives on philosophy and education.* Upper Saddle River, NJ: Pearson.

Jackson, S. (2007). Freire re-viewed. *Educational Theory, 57,* 199-213. Retrieved June 23, 2009, from EBSCO online database, Academic Search Complete.

Kojima, K., Miwa, K., & Matsui, T. (2013). Supporting mathematical problem posing with a system for learning generation processes through examples. *International Journal of Artificial Intelligence in Education, 22,* 161-190. Retrieved December 1, 2013, from EBSCO Online Database Education Research Complete.

Malcolm, L. (1999). Mortimer Adler, Paulo Freire, and teaching theology in a democracy. *Teaching Theology and Religion, 2,* 77-89. Retrieved June 23, 2009, from EBSCO online database, Academic Search Complete.

Mayo, P. (1993). When does it work? Freire's pedagogy in context. *Studies in the Education of Adults, 25,* 11-31. Retrieved June 23, 2009, from EBSCO online database, Academic Search Complete.

McCarter, W. (2013). Education and learned helplessness. *Teaching American Literature, 6,* 69-72. Retrieved December 1, 2013, from EBSCO Online Database Education Research Complete.

Noddings, N. (1995). *Philosophy of education: Dimensions of philosophy series.* Boulder, CO: Westview.

Roberts, P. (1996). Structure, direction, and rigour in liberating education. *Oxford Review of Education, 22,* 295-307.

Schugurensky, D. (1998). The legacy of Paulo Freire: A critical review of his contributions. *Convergence, 31,* 17-29. Retrieved June 22, 2009, from EBSCO online database, Academic Search Complete.

Simpson, D., Boroda, G., Bucy, B., Burke, A., Doue, W., Faber, S., Fehr, M., Fryer, W., Gonzales, G., Harp-Woods, C., McMahan, S., Nesmith, S., Reynolds, S., Riegle, S., Romano, J., Willey, R., Wimberley, S., & Won, M. (2006). A teacher's indispensable qualities: A Freirean perspective. *Journal of Latinos and Education, 5,* pp. 163-165. Retrieved June 22, 2009, from EBSCO online database, Academic Search Complete.

Webb, D. (2012). Process, orientation, and system: the pedagogical operation of utopia in the work of Paulo Freire.

Educational Theory, 62, 593-608. Retrieved December 1, 2013, from EBSCO Online Database Education Research Complete.

SUGGESTED READING

Apple, M. (2003). Freire and the politics of race in education. *International Journal of Leadership in Education, 6,* 107-119. Retrieved June 23, 2009, from EBSCO online database, Academic Search Complete.

Apple, M., Gandin, L., & Hypolito, A. (2001). Paulo Freire. In, J. Palmer, ed. *Fifty modern thinkers on education.* London: Routledge.

Cho, D., & Lewis, T. (2005). Education and event: Thinking radical pedagogy in the era of standardization. *Simile, 5.* Retrieved June 26, 2009, from EBSCO online database, Academic Search Complete.

Freire, P. (1970). *Pedagogy of the oppressed.* M. Bergman Ramos, Trans. New York: Seaburg Press.

Freire, P. (1973). *Education for a critical consciousness.* New York: Seaburg Press.

Godotti, M. (1994). Trans by J. Milton. *Reading Paulo Freire: His life and work.* New York: State University of NY Press.

Hassett, M. (1994). Writing across the curriculum in the education classroom. *Contemporary Education, 65,* 104-109.

hooks, b. (1994). *Teaching to transgress: Education as the practice of freedom.* London: Routledge.

Knight, G. (1998). *Issues and alternatives in educational philosophy.* Berrian Springs, MI: Andrews University Press.

Lewis, T. (2009). Education in the realm of the senses: Understanding Paulo Freire's aesthetic unconscious through Jacques Ranciere. *Journal of Philosophy of Education, 43,* 285-299. Retrieved June 22, 2008, from EBSCO online database, Academic Search Complete.

Martin, J. (2008). Pedagogy of the alientated: Can Freirian teaching reach working-class Students? *Equity and Excellence in Education, 41,* 31-44. Retrieved June 22, 2009, from EBSCO online database, Academic Search Complete.

Mayo, P. (2007). Critical approaches to education in the work of Lorenzo Milani and Paulo Freire. *Studies in Philosophy and Education, 26,* pp. 525-544. Retrieved June 23, 2009, from EBSCO online database, Academic Search Complete.

McLaren, P., & Leonard, P. (1993). *Paulo Freire: A critical encounter.* London: Routledge.

Narayan, L. (2000). Freire and Gandhi. *International Social Work, 43,* 193-205. Retrieved June 24, 2009, from EBSCO online database, Academic Search Complete.

Otchet, A. (1997). Paulo Freire: Passionate to the end. *UNESCO Sources,,* 5. Retrieved June 23, 2009, from EBSCO online database, Academic Search Complete.

Powers, E. (1982). *Philosophy of education: Studies in philosophies, schooling and educationalPolicies.* Englewood Cliffs, NJ: Pearson.

Roberts, P. (2009). Education, death and awakening: Hesse, Freire, and the process of transformation. *International Journal of Lifelong Education, 26,* 57-69. Retrieved June 24, 2009, from EBSCO online database, Academic Search Complete.

Seals, G. (2006). Mechanisms of student participation: Theoretical description of a Freiren ideal. *Educational Studies, 39,* 282-295. Retrieved June 22, 2009, from EBSCO online database, Academic Search Complete.

Thomson, L. (2008). Revisiting teachers as learners. *Forum, 50,* 321-328.

Vandenberg, D. (1990). *Education as a human right: A theory of curriculum and pedagogy.* New York: Teachers College Press.

GAGNÉ'S CONDITIONS OF LEARNING

Gagné's theory of the conditions of learning—part learning theory, part theory of instructional design—underwent significant changes during the twenty years following its original publication. Largely behaviorist in orientation when first introduced in 1965, it became more cognitivist in orientation by its fourth printing in 1985. Gagné's theory was comprehensive, and included a taxonomy of learning outcomes, and an outline of the internal conditions necessary for learning (e.g. cognitive information processing stages), as well as an outline of the corresponding external conditions—or events of instruction—that best support learning. Gagné's contributions were unprecedented, and helped move the fields of education and psychology forward to their present states.

KEYWORDS: Attitudes; Cognitive Strategies; Conditions of Learning; Events of Instruction; Gagné, Robert; Intellectual Skills; Instructional Design; Motor Skills; Verbal Information

OVERVIEW

In a career that spanned over forty years, American psychologist Robert M. Gagné wrote numerous books and hundreds of articles about teaching and learning. The second half of the twentieth century was a volatile time in his field; psychology shifted from an almost exclusive focus on behavior to a nearly equally exclusive focus on cognition. Gagné's own work mirrored such shifts.

The name of Gagné's theory—the conditions of learning—is somewhat misleading. Although it does address the conditions of learning, the theory encompasses far more; in order to determine the optimal ingredients for learning, Gagné reasoned, one must first determine what is to be learned. He aimed to "identify the general types of human capabilities that are learned," and then give an account of "the conditions that govern the occurrence of learning and remembering" (Gagné, 1985). Thus his theory provides a taxonomy of outcomes as well as guidelines for instruction. Before we turn to the specifics of the theory, however, it is important to pause for several important points of emphasis.

Gagné began his career as the field of psychology poised itself for what many refer to as a paradigm shift. Largely behaviorist in orientation when Gagné himself was in school, psychology soon turned its attention to what was inside the "black box." Again, Gagné's student Tuckman (1996) reflects: "When you really think about it, you can see that he stood at the crossroads of psychology. He had been trained in [behaviorism], indeed had even developed a runway on which to test rats for his own dissertation, and was now drawn inextricably toward the light of what he called nonreproductive learning." Driscoll (2000) echoes this sentiment when she explains that "Gagné's conditions for learning has undergone development and revision for twenty or more years. With behaviorist roots, it now brings together a cognitive information-processing perspective on learning."

The shift from behaviorism to cognitivism brought with it another shift as well. Psychology moved away from its attempts to find the 'holy grail' of learning—a single theory that would explain all human learning—towards an understanding of the variety and complexity that personal growth entails. Gagné was one of the first to recognize the futility of "efforts to force-fit all learning into a single description" (Gredler. Gredler, in describing Gagné's approach, writes, "The human capacity for learning makes possible an almost infinite variety of behavioral patterns. Given this diversity, no one set of characteristics can account for such vivid activities as learning to define a word, to write an essay, or to lace a shoe. Therefore,

the task for learning theory is to identify a set of principles that accommodates both the complexity and variety of human learning."

Thus far, Gagné's theory has been described as a learning theory. And yet Gagné is considered to be one of the forefathers of instructional design; in other words, he is as much a practitioner of teaching as he is a theorist of learning. However, the distinction itself may be somewhat artificial and unnecessary. In 1969 Gagné wrote, "Much of the work designed to investigate the phenomena of human learning may be thought of as having its ultimate applicability in the design of effective conditions for instruction. In some general sense, it would be truly difficult to distinguish the psychology of instruction from the psychology of learning." What he noted, however, was that many theories of learning were difficult to apply in practice; much of his work was devoted to developing a theory that could be easily applied.

In the end, Gagné's ability to bridge the gap between learning theory and instruction may be one of his greatest and most remembered contributions. He began his career during World War II, helping the military train pilots for combat; from the beginning, the questions he asked about teaching and learning had real-world applications and consequences. As Gredler explains "prior learning theorists developed explanations of the learning process in the laboratory and extended the findings to the human situation." Robert Gagné, in contrast, began by observing the range of skills humans demonstrated in real life, and then determined the conditions that would best support the various types of skill development. In other words, Gagné moved educational research into the classroom and out of the laboratory. He and colleagues criticized laboratory research, noting that "the findings of many studies of human learning presently cannot be applied directly to instructional design for two major reasons: a) the conditions under which the learning is investigated…are often unrepresentative of conditions under which most human learning occurs; and b) the tasks set for the learner… appear to cover a range from the merely peculiar to the downright esoteric" (Gagné & Rohwer, 1969).

TAXONOMY OF LEARNING OUTCOMES
An introduction to Gagné's theory should perhaps start with an obvious question. How did Gagné define learning? First and foremost, Gagné differed from

developmental psychologists who attributed many changes in behavior to maturation or growth. For Gagné, learning itself was largely responsible for an individual's development (Gredler). Gagné also believed learning was cumulative and incremental; that is, an individual develops complex skills by building upon previously learned simple skills. Finally, Gagné believed learning resulted in a variety of different behaviors he called capabilities. The first step in his attempt to develop a comprehensive learning theory was to define all such capabilities.

Others before him had also attempted to catalog types of learning into different domains. Most notably, Benjamin Bloom and his colleagues developed a taxonomy of the cognitive domain, which others then followed with taxonomies of the affective and psychomotor domains (Driscoll). What made Gagné's taxonomy distinct, however, was that he was "the first to propose an integrated taxonomy of learning outcomes that included all three domains" (Driscoll). Three components of Gagné's taxonomy—verbal information, intellectual skills, and cognitive strategies—correspond to the cognitive domain, while attitudes and motor skills map to the affective and psychomotor domain, respectively. The following provides a brief description of each.

VERBAL INFORMATION

Gagné referred to verbal information as "one of the most familiar categories of learned capabilities." Consisting of names, facts, dates, and other organized knowledge, verbal information is also known as declarative knowledge. Being able to name Albany as the capital of New York, recite a poem, or identify the date WWII ended are all examples of verbal information. Because verbal information is more easily and naturally acquired than other types of capabilities, "it is not uncommon to hear disparaging statements about 'facts' or 'mere verbal knowledge' among teachers," Gagné noted. But verbal information is important, he argued, because, since we use facts in our everyday lives, it provides the foundation for other kinds of learning, and is "a vehicle for thought" (Gagné).

INTELLECTUAL SKILLS

When an individual interacts with her environment through the use of symbols, she is demonstrating intellectual skill. Most formal instruction, Gagné argues, addresses the development of intellectual

skill, the most typical type of which is the development of rule-governed behavior. Someone who is using a saw to cut a board is interacting directly with her environment, but the measurement she took before cutting the board required the manipulation of symbols (e.g., representing length in inches and centimeters) as well as the use of rules (e.g., subtraction of fractions). Gagné suggests four different subcategories of rules—concepts, discriminations, higher-order rules, and procedural rules.

COGNITIVE STRATEGIES

Cognitive strategies are defined as "skills by means of which learners regulate their own internal processes of attending, learning, remembering, and thinking" (Gagné). Many before Gagné—behaviorists and cognitivists alike—studied such processes, referring to them by various names like self-management behaviors and executive control processes. Today, psychologists most often refer to thinking about our own thinking as metacognition. Cognitive strategies typically vary by person, but Gagné believed some were better than others. He wrote, "The strategies that some people possess appear to be better than those of others…how to bring about improvement in cognitive strategies, so that every learner is 'working up to potential' is one of the challenging problems of education" (Gagné).

ATTITUDES

Part of the affective domain, attitudes are defined as "an internal state that influences (moderates) the choices of personal action made by an individual" (Gagné). Like other psychologists, Gagné defined attitudes in terms of three components parts—emotion, cognition, and behavior. Whereas others were most interested in the origin of attitudes, however, Gagné was most interested in how an attitude impacts behavior. "The internal states that influence these actions may well possess both intellectual and emotional aspects. However, it is their outcomes in human performance that provide the point of reference for our description of attitudes as learned dispositions" (Gagné). Attitudes can be learned, he suggested, from family members, from experiences of success and failure, or even as a result of a single experience.

MOTOR SKILLS

Motor skills correspond to the psychomotor domain, and were defined by Gagné as "the precise, smooth, and accurately timed execution of performances involving the use of muscles" (1988, as cited in Driscoll). Whereas other types of learning are not so easily distinguishable—a child sitting as his desk reading may be learning verbal information or developing intellectual skills—it is comparatively easy to identify a child performing motor skills. Practicing a sport technique is an obvious example of motor skills, but learning to write or play the piano requires motor skills as well. Gagné took pains to emphasize the equal importance of all types of learned capabilities; no single type was of greater or lesser value than any other (even though many educators believe cognitive skills are more important than affective or motor skills).

INTERNAL CONDITIONS OF LEARNING

In the prior section, we learned that Gagné understood learning to be cumulative; we also reviewed what he proposed were the five types of learning outcomes, or capabilities. An important element of Gagné's definition was left out—mainly, the part of the definition that answers the question, "How do humans learn?" According to Gagné, humans acquire capabilities as results of two factors—cognitive processing, or factors internal to the individual, and stimulation from the environment, or factors external to the individual. We'll review external conditions—or what Gagné referred to as the nine events of instruction—in the next section; now, we'll briefly review internal conditions of learning.

Internal conditions of learning should be understood similarly to the previously emphasized characteristics of learning; internal conditions are cumulative and of great variety and complexity. As Gagné noted, an individual doesn't approach a task with a blank slate, but rather builds upon knowledge and abilities she already possesses. "The child who is learning to tie shoelaces does not begin this learning 'from scratch' but already knows how to hold the laces, how to loop one over the other, how to tighten the loop, and so on. Previously learned capabilities make up the internal conditions necessary for learning" (Gagné). Second, Gagné recognized that different types of capabilities require different internal and external conditions for learning; "there are several varieties of performance types that imply different categories of learned capabilities. These varieties of performance may also be differentiated in terms

of the conditions for their learning" (Gagné). In other words, there is no single set of internal or external conditions that will facilitate all types of learning. The prerequisite knowledge one brings to learning how to swing a golf club, for example, is quite different from the internal conditions necessary to understand the law of gravity.

Gagné categorized the internal conditions of learning into nine phases, with each phase representing a sequential cognitive process that is a necessary component of learning. Gredler further categorized the nine phases into three separate stages: cognitive processes that facilitate preparation for learning, cognitive processes that facilitate actual acquisition and performance, and cognitive processes that facilitate the transfer of learning. The first stage involves attention, expectancy, and recall; the learner attends to a relevant stimulus, orients herself toward a particular learning goal, and retrieves relevant information from memory. In the second stage, selective perception, semantic encoding, retrieval and responding, and reinforcement constitute the "core phases of learning" (Gredler). In this phase, the learner recognizes a meaningful stimulus, stores it in long-term memory using a conceptual framework, retrieves the information from memory and executes a response, and receives feedback, either from self or others. In the final stage, learners develop cues to enhance later recall and generalize learning to new situations.

FURTHER INSIGHTS

As stated earlier, Gagné's ability to bridge the gap between theory and practice will be one of his enduring legacies. He wanted to better understand learning so that he could better design instruction. He knew that learning could occur in the absence of instruction, but he was interested in how to deliberately design instructional events to support learning. For Gagné, "an important characteristic of instruction is that external events occur in the context of the learner's internal control processes. Therefore, the external events do not produce learning; instead they can only support the learner's internal processing" (Gredler). As such, each of the nine events Gagné describes corresponds to one of the internal processes described above. The following is a brief introduction to each of the nine events of instruction; the corresponding internal condition is presented in parentheses.

The External Conditions of Learning: The Nine Events of Instruction

GAIN ATTENTION (ATTENDING)

Driscoll writes, "since learning cannot occur unless the learner is in some way orientated and receptive to incoming information, gaining attention is the obvious first event that must occur in instruction." How an instructor gains a student's attention depends on the type of task being learned; a gym teacher helping students develop motor skills might gain attention by demonstrating a cross-court backhand. A science teacher helping students gain intellectual skills might begin a lesson by asking a thought-provoking question.

INFORM THE LEARNER OF THE OBJECTIVE (EXPECTANCY)

The second event of instruction corresponds to the internal cognitive process of establishing expectations. Helping a student understand the goal of an activity will help them process relevant information and ignore information not related to the task at hand. If teachers don't provide explicit objectives, students will develop them on their own (Driscoll). Often times, however, the goal a student establishes is not the same one the teacher intended; a student may simply choose to complete a task, whereas a teacher may have hoped that the student would attend more to the process and skill development.

STIMULATE RECALL OF PRIOR LEARNING (RETRIEVAL)

For Gagné, learning is a process of developing increasingly complex skills by building upon a foundation of simpler skills. As a result, teachers must facilitate the recall of students' previous learning. In Gagné's earlier example, a teacher might have to remind a young child how to form a loop with a shoelace before proceeding with demonstrating the next step in the process of tying a shoelace.

PRESENT THE STIMULUS (SELECTIVE PERCEPTION)

Previous events help prepare students for learning. The presentation of the stimulus is the first of four events that will help the student acquire and/or perform a new skill. The presentation of the stimulus will depend on the type of skill being learned. If students are acquiring new verbal information, a teacher might present them with a new vocabulary list. If students are learning intellectual skills such as rules of grammar, a teacher might diagram sentences on the chalkboard.

PROVIDE LEARNER GUIDANCE (ENCODING)

Learner guidance facilitates the encoding of information in long-term memory. Helping students develop a meaningful framework for new information—by demonstrating how it relates to what they already know—will help them more easily retrieve it at a later time. The amount and type of guidance provided will depend on the age and ability of the learner, as well as the type of learning outcome desired.

ELICIT PERFORMANCE (RESPONDING)

The first five events are designed to ensure learning occurs. Learning must be inferred, however, from behavior. "Performance, then, enables the learners to confirm their learning—to themselves, their teachers, and others" (Driscoll). At this state, learners should be able to perform without penalty; in other words, performance at this stage gives students an opportunity to practice. Errors should be expected.

PROVIDE FEEDBACK (REINFORCEMENT)

Learners are oftentimes able to improve performance by self-correcting. Teachers, however, are also important sources of feedback. At this point, students are told whether their 'answers' are correct or incorrect; if incorrect, they are given information that will help them improve.

ASSESS PERFORMANCE (REINFORCEMENT)

Learning is not just a change in behavior, but a change in behavior that persists over time (Driscoll). Assessment at the end of a unit of instruction is one way to determine whether learning has occurred. Even though little guidance is provided during assessment, Gagné emphasized the importance of providing feedback at this stage of instruction as well.

ENHANCE RETENTION & TRANSFER (RETRIEVAL & GENERALIZATION)

Again, learning should persist over time. Students should also be able to apply what was learned in one situation to new situations they encounter that are similar, but not identical, to the original learning context. Helping students enhance transfer is not necessarily the last event of instruction; the facilitation of encoding may also be an event designed to help students recall and generalize. Nevertheless, Gagné suggested periodic reviews—at the end of a semester, or beginning of a new year—as a way to enhance retention of material previously learned.

APPLICATIONS

The academic literature offers ways in which Gagné's conditions of learning are being applied in the field of education. A Sri Lankan study was carried out to explore learner perceptions on the instructional design features of interactive multimedia (IMM), which was designed to support open and distance learners studying microbiology. The purpose of the IMM was "to explain the dynamic abstract concepts and processes of bacterial genetics that are hard to comprehend by referring to print course material." When developing the IMM package, emphasis was placed on the interface design, navigational design, and instructional design in particular. Instructional design was mainly based on Gagné's nine events of instruction, as well as Mayer's Cognitive Theory of Multimedia Learning on verbal and pictorial information. Evaluation "revealed many positive features to be incorporated into the design of IMM in providing better support for the learners." Findings of this study "throw light on designing effective learner-centered multimedia learning material" (Kulasekara, Jayatilleke, & Coomaraswamy, 2011).

Buscombe (2013) presents ways in which Gagné's instructional design model may be used to design lesson plans and teach procedural skills in small group settings. She uses the nine points described by Gagné to outline a "comprehensive lesson guide for teaching psychomotor skills" to medical students, using a surgical procedure as an example. Each of Gagné's instructional events is considered with specific activities for each, and with "the variety of activities delineated to meet diverse learning styles" (Buscombe).

In a research project by Mai, Tse-Kian, and Fui-Theng (2013) set in Malaysia, Gagné's nine instructional events were incorporated into the development of an interactive multimedia learning module that was embedded into a student-centered learning environment to enhance the knowledge transfer and the student learning process. Results showed that students "reported positive feedback in their attention to the content, their learning experiences, interaction, and with the presentation of the content, all of which provided strong support for the use of Gagné's nine instructional events as an instructional framework for the development of an interactive learning module within a student-centered learning environment" (Mai et al.).

VIEWPOINTS

Even though Gagné's theory has had a considerable influence in the field of education, and continues to be cited in educational journals and used in the classroom, it has not escaped criticism. Gagné's emphasis on using behavioral objectives (e.g. specifically defining what is to be learned before designing instruction), for example, has been received with mixed enthusiasm. Objectives have been criticized for being behaviorist in orientation, for being ineffective in improving learning, and for benefitting teachers more than students (Driscoll). Others suggest that his theory, although designed to be easily applied, is more useful for curriculum designers than actual classroom teachers (Gredler).

Apart from the specific criticisms of Gagné's theory, it is important to remember that it is just one of many approaches to understanding learning and teaching. Within the cognitive perspective alone, information-processing theorists, Gestalt psychologists, and motivational researchers have all put forth their own models of learning and development. Behaviorists, developmentalists, and constructivists, too, have all contributed to the conversation. Some theories conflict with Gagné's theory more than others, (e.g. constructivists question whether Gagné's events of instruction are compatible with the notion that students create their own knowledge); nonetheless, Gagné's mark on education is likely to endure.

TERMS & CONCEPTS

Attitudes: Gagné identified five different types of human capabilities, also known as outcomes of learning. Part of the affective domain, attitudes are defined as "internal state(s) that influence (moderate) the choices of personal action made by an individual".

Cognitive Strategies: Gagné identified five different types of human capabilities, also known as outcomes of learning. Cognitive strategies, more recently referred to as metacognition, are defined as "skills by means of which learners regulate their own internal processes of attending, learning, remembering, and thinking".

Conditions of Learning: According to Gagné, humans acquire capabilities as a result of two factors—cognitive processing, or factors internal to the individual, and stimulation from the environment, or factors external to the individual. He referred to these as the internal and external conditions of learning.

Events of Instruction: Gagné identified nine events of instruction, also referred to as the external conditions of learning. The nine events were designed to correspond to the internal cognitive processes of the leaner. The first three events prepare the student for learning. The following four events facilitate the actual acquisition of new skills, while the final two events foster retention and transfer.

Intellectual Skills: Gagné identified five different types of human capabilities, also known as outcomes of learning. Intellectual skills are skills that allow individuals to interact with their environment through the use of symbols. The most typical type of intellectual skill is rule-governed behavior.

Instructional Design: Gagné recognized that learning occurs naturally. Nevertheless, he was interested in learning that takes place in environments deliberately designed to support it—such as the classroom. The effort to create environments that support learning—based on knowledge about the learning process itself—is instructional design.

Motor Skills: Gagné identified five different types of human capabilities, also known as outcomes of learning. Motor skills correspond to the psychomotor domain, and were defined by Gagné as "the precise, smooth, and accurately timed execution of performances involving the use of muscles".

Verbal Information: Gagné identified five different types of human capabilities, also known as outcomes of learning. Gagné referred to verbal information as "one of the most familiar categories of learned capabilities," consisting mainly of names, facts, dates, and other organized knowledge.

Jennifer Kretchmar

BIBLIOGRAPHY

Buscombe, C. (2013). Using Gagné's theory to teach procedural skills. *Clinical Teacher, 10,* 302–307. Retrieved December 15, 2013, from EBSCO Online Database Education Research Complete.

Driscoll, M.P. (2000). *Psychology of learning for instruction.* Boston, MA: Allyn and Bacon.

Gagné, R.M. (1985). *The conditions of learning and theory of instruction.* New York, NY: CBS College Publishing.

Gredler, M.E. (2005). *Learning and instruction: Theory into practice.* Upper Saddle River, NJ: Pearson Education, Inc.

Gagné, R.M., & Rohwer, W.D. (1969). Instructional psychology. *Annual Review of Psychology, 20,* 381-418. Retrieved September 30, 2007, from EBSCO Online Database Academic Search Premier.

Kulasekara, G., Jayatilleke, B., & Coomaraswamy, U. (2011). Learner perceptions on instructional design of multimedia in learning abstract concepts in science at a distance. *Open Learning, 26,* 113–126. Retrieved December 15, 2013, from EBSCO Online Database Education Research Complete.

Mai, N., Tse-Kian, N., & Fui-Theng, L. (2011). Developing an interactive multimedia-mediated learning environment using Gagné's 9 events of instruction in a Malaysian classroom. *International Journal of Instructional Media, 38,* 379–389. Retrieved December 15, 2013, from EBSCO Online Database Education Research Complete.

Tuckman, B.W. (1996). My mentor: Robert M. Gagné. *Peabody Journal of Education, 71,* 3-11. Retrieved September 30, 2007, from EBSCO Online Database Academic Search Premier.

SUGGESTED READING

Gagné, R.M. (1980). Preparing the learner for new learning. *Theory into Practice, 19,* 6-9. Retrieved September 30, 2007, from EBSCO Online Database Academic Search Premier.

Gagné, R.M. (1975). *Essentials of learning for instruction.* Hinsdale, IL: The Dryden Press.

Gagné, R.M. (1974). *Principles of instructional design.* New York, NY: Holt, Rinehart, and Winston, Inc.

SEYMOUR PAPERT AND CONSTRUCTIONISM

This article is a summary of the theory of learning known as constructionism. Constructionism was developed by Seymour Papert in the 1980s, and while similar to Piaget's theory of learning known as constructivism, it differs in several significant ways. Both believe individuals learn by constructing knowledge, but Piaget emphasized internal processes, whereas Papert believes learning is facilitated by constructing actual artifacts or objects—whether a theory, a sandcastle, or a computer program—which can then be shared and discussed with others. Papert also values the concrete and emphasizes the social nature of learning, while Piaget valued the abstract and studied learning mostly as an independent activity. These differences are discussed in greater detail, as are Papert's thoughts on the art of teaching in relation to the art of learning. Applications of constructionism in the classroom are discussed, as is the influence of the theory in the educational and research community.

KEYWORDS: Bricolage; Constructionism; Constructivism; Education theory; Instructionism; Logo; Mathetics; Papert, Seymour; Piaget, Jean

OVERVIEW

On the surface, constructionism and constructivism have much in common. Both theories of learning share the belief that individuals make meaning. In other words, knowledge is constructed through experience and is not something that can simply be transmitted from one person to the next (Kafai & Resnick, 1996). Both theories were developed by colleagues—constructivism by Jean Piaget, constructionism by Seymour Papert, who studied with Piaget in Geneva, Switzerland in the 1950s. Despite the many similarities, however, the two theories differ in significant ways. Before we investigate these differences, and define constructionism in further detail, we must first qualify this exercise with words of wisdom from Papert himself.

Many of Papert's essays on constructionism, and specifically those with the aim of defining or summarizing the theory, begin in the same way—with Papert playfully arguing that it is impossible, and indeed antithetical, for him to tell the reader what constructionism is. To do so, he claims, would "transgress the basic tenet" of his entire theory. He explains, "if one eschews pipeline models of transmitting knowledge in talking among ourselves as well as in theorizing about classrooms, then one must expect that I will not be able to tell you my idea of constructionism. To do so is bound to trivialize it" (Papert, 1991). Rather, his intention is to "engage [the reader] in experiences" so that we construct our own idea of constructionism that is "in some sense" like his idea of constructionism. Whether the following summary attempts to engage or transmit, is perhaps for you (or Papert) to judge.

CONSTRUCTIONISM VS. CONSTRUCTIVISM

The first—and what is arguably the most substantial—difference between constructionism and constructivism should be characterized less as a point of conflict or disagreement and more as a shift in emphases. While both theories agree that individuals construct knowledge, Piaget focused more on mental constructions, Papert on constructions as they are manifested in objects 'in the world.' Papert calls such constructions public entities. As Kafai and Resnick explain, "constructionism suggests that learners are particularly likely to make new ideas when they are actively engaged in making some type of artifact—be it a robot, a poem, a sand castle, or a computer program—which they can reflect upon and share with others."

Papert further underscores the importance of this principle—learning-by-making—when he retells the story of how the idea for constructionism was born. While visiting a junior high school in Massachusetts in the early 1970s, he passed an art class on the way to the math class he was scheduled to observe. This particular art class was carving soap sculptures, and after several days of 'dropping in' and admiring their art, Papert was struck by the difference between what was happening in art class and what was happening in math class. As he writes, "An ambition was born: I wanted junior high school math class to be like that. I didn't know exactly what 'that' meant but I knew I wanted it. I didn't even know what to call the idea. For a long time it existed in my head as 'soap-sculpture math'" (Papert, 1991).

The second point of emphasis of constructionism follows logically from the first—a valuing of the concrete over the abstract. Papert is highly critical of schools and educators for what he calls a "perverse commitment to moving as quickly as possible from the concrete to the abstract" (Papert, 1993). He further argues that the almost singular focus on abstract-formal knowledge impedes the learning of many students, and even discriminates against some. His passion for this belief is best communicated again in his own words:

"This praise for the concrete is not to be confused with a strategy of using it as a stepping-stone to the abstract. That would leave the abstract ensconced as the ultimate form of knowing. I want to say something more controversial and subtle in helping to demote abstract thinking from being seen as 'the real stuff' of the working mind" (Papert, 1993).

Importantly, this point of emphasis again separates Papert from Piaget; Piaget valued the abstract and "emphasized how the average child...becomes detached from the world of concrete objects and increasingly able to internalize action and to mentally manipulate symbolic objects" (Ackerman, 1996). Piaget equated development and cognitive growth with the ability to think abstractly.

When one shifts the focus of learning from the abstract to the concrete, Papert argues, the process of learning itself changes as well. Rather than being guided by a pre-set plan, or formal rules of logic, a student is guided by his or her work as it proceeds (Papert, 1991). Furthermore, students seek to understand solutions to particular problems, without worrying about universals or generality. Papert, borrowing from the work of Levi-Strauss, uses the untranslatable French word "bricolage" to describe this process. "Bricolage is a metaphor for the ways of the old-fashioned traveling tinker, the jack-of-all trades who knocks on the door offering to fix whatever is broken. Faced with a job, the tinker rummages in his bag of assorted tools to find one that will fit the problem at hand and, if one tool does not work for the job, simply tries another without ever being upset in the slightest by the lack of generality" (Papert, 1993).

Constructionism turns conventional wisdom about intellect and learning on its head again with a shift in emphasis from the individual to the community. As Kafai and Resnick argue, "in the minds of many, Rodin's famous sculpture The Thinker provides the prototypical image of thinking: it shows a person, alone, in deep concentration." But constructionism—and more recently a wealth of other theories—bring more focus to the social aspect of learning. Indeed, Papert's emphasis on learning-by-making is important not only for the end-product itself, but because the product can be shared. It is the discussion, communication, critique with and by others about the product that is as important to the learning process as the making itself. Again, such emphasis distinguishes Papert from Piaget. According to Ackerman, Papert's knowledge is situational and relational. She argues that "such an emphasis on the processes by which people shape and sharpen their ideas in context provides a rich counterpoint to Piaget's stage theory."

The main principles of constructionism suggest some corollary themes Papert has introduced when discussing learning in general. First and foremost, all of these principles—learning-by-making, communicating with others, problem-solving in specific and concrete circumstances—require time. "Giving

yourself time," Papert (1996) exclaims "is an absurdly obvious principle." And yet, he believes, it is a principle that is blatantly violated by schools as they are currently structured. Because schools "chop time," students can't sit with a problem the way they might do in a more natural environment. Secondly, Papert argues that part of the learning process is talking about learning itself. Again, he suggests that schools, and culture in general, discourage such disclosure. He even goes so far as to argue "In most circles talking about what really goes on in our minds is blocked by taboos as firm as those that inhibited Victorians from expressing their sexual fantasies" (Papert, 1996).

Constructionism has, as of yet, little to say about teaching, per se, and indeed the omission is intentional. In fact, Papert situates constructionism in direct opposition to instructionism, arguing that the more opportunities students have to create their own meanings, the less attention educators will need to give to the act of teaching. He qualifies, "I do not mean to imply that constructionists see instruction as bad. That would be silly. But I do believe that changes in opportunities for construction would lead to improvements in learning more so than any new science about instruction itself" (Papert, 1991). Papert further questions the narrow-minded focus on methods of teaching when he rhetorically asks, "Why is there no word in English for the art of learning? Webster says that the word pedagogy means the art of teaching. What is missing is the parallel word for learning" (Papert, 1996). Papert introduces the word mathetics as a noun to indicate the art of learning; although co-opted by those who work with numbers, mathetics has Greek roots in two words that refer to learning in general. Mathmatikos meant 'disposed to learn' and manthanein was a verb meaning 'to learn.'

APPLICATIONS

Papert's lack of interest in teaching does not also mean he is uninterested in the application of constructionism to the classroom. On the contrary, Papert has dedicated his career to the practice of constructionism. For Papert, improving learning is about finding the tools that give students an opportunity to construct meaning. Much of his work has focused on the computer as one such tool, but constructionism is not limited to technological activities. As he explains, "The assertion that various constructionist learning situations…'work in one way' does not mean they are not very different. Indeed, in form they are very different, and intellectual work is needed to see what they have in common" (Papert, 1991).

LOGO

Papert's name is probably most often associated with Logo, a computer programming language, that has to date been used by "tens of millions of school children all over the world" (Kafai & Resnick). As Stager (1999) explains, "While reasonable people may differ about whether Papert is the Father of Logo, he can surely be considered its loving mentor." Logo was first developed by Papert and his MIT colleagues in the late 1960s, and is probably best known for its floor and screen turtles. The former is a robot attached to the computer, the latter a screen cursor with a retractable pen, both of which execute programming commands. The specifics of the programming language itself are less important, however, than the learning environment it creates. According to Papert, computers, and Logo in particular, have such enormous constructionist potential because they give students the opportunity to design (Resnick & Ocko, 1991). Design, as opposed to analysis, allows students to explore, to confront problems by seeking a workable solution rather than a right solution. Resnick & Ocko provide specific examples of students learning math and science through Logo, but suggest the materials and tools are necessary but not sufficient for learning through design. Students must also be in control of their learning experience, choose activities that are meaningful to them, and work collaboratively with their peers.

THINKING ABOUT & MAKING KNOTS

A more obscure application of constructionism in the classroom serves to underscore the point that constructionist activities come in a variety of forms, and not all are technology based. Strohecker (1991) used the activity of 'making knots' to demonstrate topology, a "branch of geometry concerned with properties of objects that are invariant when the object is distorted or deformed." Strohecker's classroom project demonstrated several core constructionist principles: allowing the activity to evolve and change in response to new ideas that developed mid-project; respecting student's individual approach and style to meaning making; learning by making objects to be shared and discussed; and a valuation of the

concrete over the abstract. The activity also demonstrates one of Papert's critiques of instructionism, mainly the "idea that the unique way to improve a student's knowledge about topic X is to teach about X" (Papert, 1993). By making knots, students learned about seemingly unrelated ideas.

CONSTRUCTIONISM THROUGH COLLABORATION

Kafai and Harel (1991) combine the use of a technological tool—instructional software design projects (ISDP)—while taking advantage of the ways in which children learn by teaching others. In their classroom, each fifth grader was charged with developing a computer program to teach fourth graders about fractions; upon completion of the project, the fifth graders then became programming consultants for the fourth graders, who themselves were charged with developing a program to teach third graders. Throughout the project, Kafai and Harel discovered two different types of collaboration, both equally important: one in which students actually work together on a specified project, the other—which they refer to as collaboration through the air—in which students simply exchange ideas and thoughts freely.

VIEWPOINTS

When Papert first developed constructionism, many of the ideas he proposed were unfamiliar. Educators typically thought of knowledge as something that could be transmitted from teacher to student, and not as something that is created by a student via her interaction with the world. Even if Papert—and others who were making similar claims at the time, like Piaget—were initially met with skepticism, some would argue their ideas have gained widespread acceptance today. "In the 1980s, many constructionist ideas were viewed as radical and out of the mainstream. But today, at educational research conferences, the idea that children actively construct new knowledge is taken almost as gospel..." (Kafai & Resnick).

Educators writing within constructionist circles don't just mention the success of Papert's theory as a sidebar, but go so far as to suggest that its own success is now its greatest challenge. Kafai and Resnick believe, for example, "in some ways, constructionist research is challenged by its success. The challenge is to continue to refine constructionist ideas, and to make sure that these ideas spread... ." Stager echoes such sentiments when he argues that constructionism has received "no serious criticism in academic circles." He continues, "People may disagree with a point or two in the books, but there has been no serious piece of scholarship arguing against [Papert's] ideas in Mindstorms."

But perhaps we might consider constructionism itself Papert's own 'public entity;' that is, it is the end result of his own process of 'learning-by-making.' These products, as we've learned, are meant to be shared, discussed, debated, and revised by other learners. It is then somewhat ironic, and perhaps unexpected, that the "most sinister attacks on Logo are acts of omission" (Stager). In other words, people aren't talking about it at all. Stager continues, "As a university teacher I receive countless textbooks on the theory, history and practice of educational computing.... The majority of these texts don't disagree with Logo research or the theories of Seymour Papert. They don't mention them at all."

The few voices who can be heard disagreeing with Papert offer criticisms that are logistical as opposed to theoretical in nature. Most teachers, Stager argues, criticize Logo or other constructionist activities because they take too much class time, they can't be easily evaluated, or they don't fit into a specific content domain. Stager believes, however, that "these are not criticisms of Logo as much as they are criticisms of school." Papert has also been criticized for his involvement in the marketplace; on the one side by those who disapprove of educators collaborating with companies whose objective it is to make money, and on the other side, by companies who believe Papert's products are "bad for business." "If kids construct their knowledge and express themselves in an environment designed to have 'no threshold and no ceiling', then you are not likely to buy lots of other software products" (Stager).

To suggest that constructionism is widely popular and free of criticism may be somewhat misleading. While constructionism per se may not have generated a lot of debate, it is clearly situated on one side of a divided camp, the two sides of which have been battling for centuries. Constructionism taps into larger epistemological questions about the nature of knowledge and knowing; since the times of Aristotle, Plato, and Descartes, philosophers have disagreed about whether truth is represented by an external

reality, independent of the knower, or whether it is something generated by the knower. The debate has never been resolved, and thus constructionism, to the degree it fuels this conversation, has as many detractors as it does proponents.

IN CONCLUSION

A summary of constructionism would be incomplete without mention of the ways it continues to evolve. As Kafai and Resnick explain, "constructionism is not a static set of ideas. Consistent with the theory we are writing about, we as researchers are continually reconstructing and elaborating what we mean by constructionism...." Recent trends in constructionism show a shift in emphasis toward ideas that, although part of the original theory, have been highlighted less than others. The role of community, for example, takes center stage in Kafai and Resnick's work titled "Constructionism in Practice: Designing, Thinking, and Learning in a Digital World." They also emphasize the importance of affect in learning, arguing that students are more likely to engage when working on "personally meaningful" activities and projects. Finally, those who continue to develop the theory stress the importance of diversity—diversity of learning styles and diversity of knowledge.

TERMS & CONCEPTS

Bricolage: An untranslatable French word Papert borrowed from the work of Levi-Strauss. In the constructionist framework, bricolage is a metaphor to represent a learner who, rather than following a pre-set plan, approaches a problem in context.

Constructionism: Constructionism is an outgrowth of constructivism. Constructionism emphasizes the situated, communal nature of learning, values the concrete, and holds that learning occurs best through the making of some shared entity—a poem, castle, or theory.

Constructivism: A theory of learning developed by Jean Piaget. Constructivism values the abstract, independent nature of learning. Most important, constructivism measures cognitive growth in terms of internal, mental structures.

Instructionism: For Papert, instructionism represents traditional teaching methods, the idea that knowledge can be transmitted from teacher to student. More generally, it is a term that represents that act of teaching itself. Papert believes student learning is a consequence of opportunities for construction, rather than a consequence of improved instruction. Rather than focus on the art of teaching, educators should focus on the art of learning.

Logo: A computer programming language developed by Papert and his MIT colleagues in the early 1960s. Best known for its turtle graphics, Logo has been used in classrooms across the world. Papert argues that it is not Logo itself, or computers in general, that are important, but the opportunities and environments they create for learning-by-making.

Mathetics: The term Papert uses to represent the art of learning. Mathetics, although it evokes ideas about what we now know as 'math', derives from two Greek terms which refer to learning in general. Mathmatikos meant 'disposed to learn' and manthanein was a verb meaning 'to learn.'

Jennifer Kretchmar

BIBLIOGRAPHY

Ackerman, E. (1996). Perspective-taking and object construction: Two keys to learning. In Y. Kafai and M. Resnick (Eds.), *Constructionism in practice: Designing, thinking, and learning in a digital world* (pp. 25-36). Mahwah, NJ: Lawrence Erlbaum Associates, Publishers.

Feurzeig, W., Papert, S. A., & Lawler, B. (2011). Programming-languages as a conceptual framework for teaching mathematics. *Interactive Learning Environments, 19,* 487-501. Retrieved December 15, 2013, from EBSCO Online Database Education Research Complete.

Kafai, Y., & Harel, I. (1991). Learning through design and teaching: Exploring social and collaborative aspects of constructionism. In I. Harel and S. Papert (Eds.), *Constructionism: Research reports and essays, 1985-1990* (pp. 85-110). Norwood, NJ: Ablex Publishing Company.

Papert, S. (1991). Situating Constructionism. In I. Harel and S. Papert (Eds.), *Constructionism: Research reports and essays, 1985-1990* (pp. 1-12). Norwood, NJ: Ablex Publishing Company.

Papert, S. (1993). *The children's machine: Rethinking School in the age of the computer.* New York, NY: Basic Books.

Papert, S. (1996). A word for learning. In Y. Kafai and M. Resnick (Eds.), *Constructionism in practice: Designing, thinking, and learning in a digital world* (pp. 9-24). Mahwah, NJ: Lawrence Erlbaum Associates, Publishers.

Papert, S. (n.d.) *Constructionism vs. Instructionism.* Retrieved June 18, 2007, from http://papert.org.

Resnick, M. (2012). Reviving Papert's dream. *Educational Technology, 52,* 42-46. Retrieved December 15, 2013, from EBSCO Online Database Education Research Complete.

Resnick, M., & Ocko, S. (1991). LEGO/Logo: Learning through and about design. In I. Harel and S. Papert (Eds.), *Constructionism: Research reports and essays, 1985-1990* (pp. 141-150). Norwood, NJ: Ablex Publishing Company.

Stager, G. S. (1999). *Never satisfied, only gratified: Perspectives on Papert.* Retrieved June 18, 2007, from http://stager.org.

Strohecker, C. (1991). Elucidating styles of thinking about topology through thinking about knots. In I. Harel and S. Papert (Eds.), *Constructionism: Research reports and essays, 1985-1990* (pp. 215-233). Norwood, NJ: Ablex Publishing Company.

Zhong-Zheng, L., Yuan-Bang, C., & Chen-Chung, L. (2013). A constructionism framework for designing game-like learning systems: Its effect on different learners. *British Journal of Educational Technology, 44,* 208-224. Retrieved December 15, 2013, from EBSCO Online Database Education Research Complete.

SUGGESTED READING

Ackerman, E. (n.d.). *Piaget's constructivism, Papert's constructionism: What's the difference.* Retrieved June 18, 2007, from http://learning.media.mit.edu.

Kafai, Y. (1996). Learning design by making games: Children's development of design strategies in the creation of a complex computational artifact. In Y. Kafai and M. Resnick (Eds.), *Constructionism in practice: Designing, thinking, and learning in a digital world* (pp. 71-96). Mahwah, NJ: Lawrence Erlbaum Associates, Publishers.

Papert, S. (1980). *Mindstorms. Children, computers, and powerful ideas.* New York, NY: Basic Books.

Papert, S., & Caperton, G. (1999, August). *Vision for Education: The Caperton-Papert Platform.* Paper presented at the 91st annual National Governor's Association meeting, St. Louis, Mo. Retrieved June 18, 2007, from http://papert.org.

POSTMODERNISM AND EDUCATION

This article provides an introduction to postmodernism. What began in the 1930s as an architectural movement has now influenced nearly every academic discipline in the humanities, from literary analysis to anthropology to education. Despite its far-reaching impact, postmodernism is difficult to define, largely because postmodernists themselves reject the idea that any phenomenon can be understood in just one way. Nonetheless, the following will attempt to introduce some of the core ideas of postmodernism, first by outlining its development in response to modernism, and then by looking at the work of several key postmodernist philosophers, including Lacan, Lyotard, Foucault, and Derrida. The impact of postmodernism on education, in terms of student-teacher relationships, research, and curriculum development is discussed. Finally, because postmodernism is one of the most widely contested recent developments in academia, some of its criticism is also presented.

KEYWORDS: Deconstruction; Derrida, Jacques; Discourse; Enlightenment; Foucault, Michel; Grand Narratives; Lacan, Jacques; Lyotard, Jean-Francois; Modernism; Performativity; Power; Relativism; Subjectivity

OVERVIEW

According to Clark (2006), "the reach of postmodernism on human thought has been extremely pervasive." What began in the early 1930s as an architectural movement has now touched nearly every academic discipline in the humanities, from literary analysis to anthropology to educational theory. In addition to its far-reaching impact, however, there are two other characteristics of the postmodern movement that deserve equal attention: its contentiousness and its inability to be clearly defined. Indeed, postmodernism has spawned disagreements within universities and academic departments that have no rivals in modern times. As Bloland (2005) explains, these disagreements often deteriorate into "bitter word warfare." It may seem surprising that a movement so pervasive and so contentious is also one that has yet to be clearly defined, as any attempt to provide a unitary definition would be antithetical to postmodernism itself.

A promising place to begin might be with a brief discussion of what postmodernism is certainly not. Usher and Edwards (1994) write, "In some ways it is easier to discern what it is against than what it is for." And what it is against, as its name suggests, is modernism. Modernity defines a period of time beginning with the Enlightenment in the late eighteenth century; modernism refers, in part, to the central organizing principles of the Enlightenment itself. These principles are typically delineated as: the centrality of reason, the belief in progress, access to truth,

individual agency, and faith in the scientific method (Bloland). And education as we know it, Usher and Edwards argue, is largely founded on these very same beliefs. "Historically, education can be seen as the vehicle by which…the Enlightenment ideals of critical reason, individual freedom, progress and benevolent change, are substantiated and realized." If postmodernism is against modernity, and education itself is modeled upon modern principles, one might wonder how postmodernism and education can be reconciled? What does education look like in a postmodern world?

Usher & Edwards further explain that, "certainly, [Postmodernism] is not a term that designates a systematic theory or comprehensive philosophy. Neither does it refer to a 'system' of ideas or concepts in the conventional sense, nor is it the name denoting a unified social or cultural movement" (Usher & Edwards). Postmodernism resists universal, all-encompassing, fixed understandings of phenomena and thus attempting to provide a singular or totalizing understanding of postmodernism is necessarily a contradiction. Indeed, the International Encyclopedia of Education (1994) says of postmodernism, "it may be better to see [it] as a complex intellectual map of late twentieth century thought and practice rather than any clear-cut philosophic, political, and/or aesthetic movement" (as cited in Barrow & Woods, 2006). But if postmodernism resists definition, it also said to resist seriousness (Usher & Edwards).

Many individuals have contributed to postmodern thought, but particular names appear in the literature more than others. The central tenets of this 'complex intellectual map' may be reviewed by looking at the contributions of key individuals—Lyotard, Derrida, Foucault, and Lacan—and begin with Lyotard, because in describing postmodernism as "incredulity toward metanarratives" (as cited in Blake, Smeyers, Smith, & Standish, 1998), he may shed the most light on the movement's resistance to definition.

THE DEMISE OF GRAND NARRATIVES
Lyotard was interested in language and made a distinction between 'the language games' of scientific knowledge and narrative knowledge; the former declaring itself the only legitimate language, the latter celebrating diversity, or rather "a form of tolerance toward other discourses" (Usher & Edwards).

Ironically, Lyotard argued, scientific knowledge relies on narrative knowledge to legitimate itself, even though it claims such narrative knowledge doesn't exist. The narrative knowledge science relies on to legitimate itself, what Lyotard calls grand or meta narratives, are ultimately two myths—that science leads to progress or the betterment of humanity, and that science contributes to uncovering the 'truth.' These grand narratives, however, have lost their ability to confer legitimacy as society has become skeptical, or rather, incredulous. What happens when grand narratives are abandoned? According to Lyotard, in the absence of universals and totalizing theories, small narratives take their place and small narratives—given the mere fact that they are innumerable, yet each legitimate in its own right—create room for multiplicity of meaning (Blake, et al.; Usher & Edwards).

Lyotard, in addition to coining the term "incredulity toward grand narratives,' is also credited with introducing the notion of performativity. Knowledge, rather than being judged according to its 'truth', he argued, is judged according to its efficiency or inefficiency, or performativity. As Usher explains, "Performativity is a critical feature of incredulity where the questions asked of knowledge become not just—is it true?—or does it contribute to human progress?—but what use is it?—and how will it enhance the performance of people and organizations?"

DECONSTRUCTION

If Lyotard is forever linked with the notion of 'incredulity' then Derrida is equally wedded, in the minds of many scholars, with the idea of deconstructing text. The first thing to understand is that 'text' refers to everything—or as Derrida himself once said, "there is nothing outside of text" (as cited in Hagen, 2005)—rather than simply words on a page, as is its traditional meaning. Therefore, text might refer to a theory of learning, rules of a game, a conversation, a film or a performance. Deconstruction, in Derrida's sense, is also more than its literal meaning, or the notion of 'taking apart.' As Parker (1997) argues, deconstruction is "a strategy," and one aimed specifically at unearthing contradiction and paradox. Deconstruction aims to turn the logic of a text upon itself, "showing that there is an inherent contradiction concealed at the rational heart of... any text," and that rationality itself is simply an attempt

to convince an audience of the truth of a text. Many argue that deconstruction is, as its name implies, destructive—breaking down text and revealing its 'folly' but leaving nothing in its place (Garrison, 2003). Others argue that deconstruction is also affirmative and that Derrida is clear about what he wants to affirm. For Derrida, deconstruction brings into focus what has been excluded from the text, or otherness. "Deconstruction urges recognition and respect for what is different, left out, or queer. It is [the] positive response to the 'other,' to those persons and situations different from the 'norm'" (Garrison).

MULTIPLE SUBJECTIVITIES

If postmodernism is about bringing multiplicity of meaning into the spotlight, and rejecting universals, then it is also about destabilizing the notion of 'self' and the recognition of multiple subjectivities. Lacan, who spent much of his academic career critiquing Freud's psychoanalysis, helped define the postmodern subject. Like Freud, Lacan agreed that subjectivity is largely determined by the unconscious and human desire. Unlike Freud, however, Lacan rejects the notion that desire can be explained by biology, or reduced to the idea of instincts or drives. Rather, desire is human, relational, constituted through language and unconscious. Because subjectivity is derived from desire, and desire is always social, Lacan's subject can no longer be viewed as a stable, centered, unitary whole. Rather, as Usher and Edwards explain, "If the self is always constructed through the way others see it, then it cannot be autonomous and coherent...any sense of selfhood is therefore continually shifting." Kilgore (2004) emphasizes the decentered subject in relation to the educational setting when she describes the postmodern learner as "always becoming, always in process, always situated in a context that also is always becoming."

POWER & KNOWLEDGE

Discussing key ideas of postmodernism in relation to a single scholar is somewhat arbitrary and an obvious oversimplification. Foucault, for example, talked about multiple subjectivities too, just as other scholars emphasized the relationship between knowledge and power. Nevertheless, Foucault's work is often cited when discussing power. First and foremost, Foucault emphasized that knowledge and power are intertwined, and necessarily so. He writes, "Knowledge and power are integrated with one another and there is no point in dreaming of a time when knowledge will cease to depend on power" (as cited in Usher & Edwards). Modernists, by contrast, believe that knowledge is separate from power, a claim Foucault argues simply reifies their own power and marginalizes other forms of knowledge. Secondly, Foucault was one of the first to suggest that power is not something possessed by individuals as is traditionally thought, but rather exists in cultural practices, institutions, systems of thought, or what he refers to as discourse (Usher & Edwards). As a result, power is not necessarily exerted physically or coercively, but rather operates more subtly, and is more pervasive. This type of power, what Foucault calls disciplinary power, is "targeted at the body of the person" who then becomes both disciplinarian and the disciplined. In other words, individuals both resist power, but also participate in their own oppression.

APPLICATIONS

Postmodernism presents ideas that are a bit difficult to reconcile with traditional ideas about education. If we are not rational, self-governing individuals, how can we conceptualize ourselves as students? If there are no longer universal truths, who decides what should be taught? If the scientific method has failed us, how do we conduct research?

STUDENT-TEACHER RELATIONSHIP

Given the postmodernist's emphasis on multiplicity of meaning and the relationship between knowledge and power, it might be of little surprise to learn that many take issue with traditional roles such as student and teacher. According to Kilgore, for example, moving toward a postmodern pedagogy involves "some degree of rejection of social positions like teacher and student, resulting in the emergence of a local, collective way of knowing and learning." Because postmodernists believe that the "transmissions of truth is a nostalgic dream" teachers are no longer imbued with the same authority as they are in traditional classrooms; Kilgore calls for 'the death of the teacher,' putting in its place a 'self-directed' learning environment where students are at the center of their own learning experience. But Kilgore also suggests redefining students as 'learners', in an attempt to value the multiplicity of roles and experiences they bring to the classroom,

all of which constitute their subjectivity as much if not more so than the role of student.

RESEARCH

Postmodernists reject the idea that truth is attainable through science and also reject the scientific method itself, all of which begs the question—how do postmodernists conduct research? Certainly, the way in which research is conducted differs, and the ends toward which postmodern research aims are different as well, but the result, postmodernists argue, is worthwhile nonetheless. First and foremost, the conceptualization of the researcher shifts from an objective outsider to an individual intricately involved with the study at hand. As Ramaekers (2006) argues, "The (re) introduction of the subjective, the (re)emphasizing of the researcher's investment, does not signify an abdication of truth and knowledge, but a fuller acknowledgement of human involvement in understanding the world." In addition, postmodernists no longer view the researcher as the authority on the research conducted; as Rolfe (2006) writes, "the authorial voice is no more privileged than the interpretations given to the text by its many and varied readers."

In addition to shifts in the role of the researcher, the end goal of research shifts as well. Postmodernists, rather than promising truth or final answers, instead aim to contribute to discussion and debate. Ramaekers explains, "In terms of educational research, the reliable answers that teachers and policymakers are (said to be) looking for are not (and cannot be) offered ready-to-hand by the educational researcher. Rather, what is offered is the possibility of dialogue." Rolfe, in a slightly different approach to the discussion of aims, argues that postmodernist researchers don't necessarily avoid making judgments, but simply rely on different criteria in order to make them. Rather than relying on validity or truth, in the traditional sense, to discern the quality of research findings, Rolfe argues educators need to rely on their own common sense and experience, what he calls prudence or practical wisdom. Based on the degree of experience, some educators will be better suited to make such judgments than others.

CURRICULUM

Postmodernism's impact on education is arguably the greatest with respect to curriculum. If knowledge itself has been fragmented, multiplied, and localized, and universal truths have been undermined, how do you decide what to teach? Parker, although perhaps representing an extreme view, writes simply, "as for curriculum, get rid of it." What he advocates in its place is a more personalized approach to learning, where students are more intimately connected to the subject matter. "Postmodern teachers will construct pedagogy out of local interests and concerns where worth and value is set within a narrative in which its players have a stake and a voice." By contrast, Parker argues that a national, standardized curriculum alienates children because they "recognize the humiliation of living as the distant effects of others' preferences." Reichenbach (1999) makes a similar argument for localizing curricula in the absence of universal criteria; agreement about curricular matters must still be reached, he explains, even though different groups may propose equally valid alternatives. Rather than expecting consensus about such matters to be reached nationally, however, educators should make such decisions on a much smaller scale. "The claims of the postmodern curricula become more modest: consensus becomes local."

VIEWPOINTS

The only thing one can say about postmodernism with any degree of certainty is what it is not; postmodernism developed in response to modernism—the belief in progress, access to truth, faith in the scientific method—and thus is in itself an argument against the modernist approach. Postmodernism is a contentious issue, and thus, it is perhaps time to turn the stage over to its critics. Giving voice to all of modernist's rebuttals would require far more time and space than we have here, but the following serve as a sample.

First and foremost, modernists take issue with the logic, or as they might argue—lack thereof—of postmodernists reasoning. As Barrow and Woods point out, if postmodernists are claiming that there is not truth, that we cannot know anything, how can this statement itself have any validity? "To get away with credit for perceiving correctly that there is no such thing as being correct would certainly be to have one's cake and eat it too." Secondly, modernists argue that indeed we can make claims about truth with respect to certain things. Barrows and Woods provide a simple example—the fact that nothing can be both a circle and a square—as evidence of truth. They write,

"Not only is it clearly the case that there must be some truths, it is also surely evident that to deny this involves a degree of insincerity and bad faith. For who does (who could) live their life on the genuine presumption that there is no such thing as truth? Our daily life is predicated on the assumption that some things are true and others not; that is why we generally catch the bus [on time], don't eat rat poison, and exercise. No philosopher who claims that he does not believe in truth is telling the truth."

Stated differently, modernist's belief in our ability to discern truth translates into a critique of postmodernism for its tendency to slip into relativism. If all truths are equally valid, how can we make judgments about anything? If 'anything goes' and we are unable to make distinctions between good and bad, truth and falsehood, how do we make decisions not just in education, but in life? Furthermore, the consequences of such thinking, modernists argue, can be catastrophic; postmodernism is not simply an academic debate taking place in the ivory tower, but is changing the practice of education itself. In the field of special education, for example, Polsgrove and Orcha (2004) write, "[postmodernism] is significantly affecting the course of educational programs for children with all types of disabilities. The atmosphere of uncertainty has fostered the general impression in the field that any intervention is acceptable without the need for documentation of effectiveness" (as cited in Kauffman & Sasso, 2006).

Finally, postmodernists accuse modernists of monopolizing truth claims, without reflecting upon or criticizing their own claims to truth. As Rapp (2003) argues however, the Western tradition is "dialectical at its core." That is, "it cannot be pinned down easily, because it is full of tensions, complexities, varieties of emphasis, and precarious balances which are always under scrutiny (and sometimes under sharp attack) from within the tradition itself." Thus, modernism is not as unified, reified, and normalized as postmodernists would claim, but rather is shifting itself, in response to its own internal contradictions and tensions. In addition, modernists take issue with postmodernist's conceptualization of the scientific method. As Bereiter (1994) argues, 'objectivity…is not an essential claim of science, but progress is." In other words, those adhering to the scientific method don't shy away from disagreement or alternative points of view, but they do believe such disagreements and viewpoints will lead to greater understanding. As Bereiter explains, "It is not necessary to believe that science is approaching some objective truth, but it is necessary to believe that today's knowledge is better than yesterday's."

TERMS & CONCEPTS

Deconstruction: A term largely associated with Derrida and used in reference to 'deconstruction of texts.' Texts, according to postmodernists, refer to everything—texts in the traditional sense, a performance, a film, a conversation. Deconstructing a text involves turning the logic of the text against itself, so that the inherent contradictions and paradoxes are uncovered. Some view deconstruction as merely destructive, but Derrida believed it was also affirmative in that it identifies and affirms 'the Other' excluded from the text.

Discourse: A term used by Foucault to help describe the location of power, as no longer being something possessed by people, but something expressed through our social practices and institutions. Discourses, then, are systems of thought that represent what can be said and who can say it. They operate behind the scenes, and while authorizing some 'voices,' exclude others.

Enlightenment: The period of history beginning in the eighteenth century, often identified as the beginning of modernism. It was during this time that reason, science, and rationality emerged as a challenge to the traditional authority of the Middle Ages, which was often based on superstition and irrationality.

Grand Narratives: One of the most well-known definitions of postmodernism is Lyotard's "incredulity toward grand narratives." He defined grand narratives as the 'myths' used to validate science—the belief in progress and the belief in our ability to access truth. Lyotard argues that these narratives have failed, and therefore our societies have become increasingly suspicious, or incredulous, of these them and other universal and totalizing claims.

Modernism: Postmodernism developed in reaction to modernism, a philosophical orientation that began with the Enlightenment in the eighteenth century. In general, modernists believe in centrality of reason, progress, access to truth, individual agency, and the scientific method.

Performativity: A term coined by Lyotard and offered as an alternative way to assess the merit of knowledge, rather than assessing it on its contribution to progress or its truth. Performativity essentially translates to efficiency; that is, knowledge is judged according to how efficient, effective, or useful it is.

Power: Postmodernists believe that power and knowledge are intertwined. Foucault's notion of power is one of the most often-cited; he suggested that power does not necessarily operate physically or coercively as it once did, but rather is more subtle and pervasive. People don't possess power, but rather power resides in our discourses—our institutions, our systems, our cultural practices, our bodies. People therefore participate in their own repression, but also resist.

Relativism: Often contrasted with objectivism, the notion of universal notions of truth. For relativists, all claims to truth are equally valid, and there are no criteria to judge the worth of one in relation to another. One of modernist's criticisms of postmodernism is that it advocates relativism.

Subjectivity: Subjectivity is a term that represents our thoughts about personhood. For modernists, subjectivity is defined as a unified whole; there is consistency to who we are, and we are self-governing individuals. For postmodernists, subjectivity is comprised of multiple selves, and always defined in relation to other people in our environment.

Jennifer Kretchmar

BIBLIOGRAPHY

Barrow, R., & Woods, R. (2006). An introduction to philosophy of education. New York, NY: Routledge.

Bereiter, C. (1994). Implications of postmodernism for science, or, science as progressive discourse. Educational Psychologist, 29, 3-12. Retrieved July 20, 2007, from EBSCO Online Database Education Research Complete.

Blake, N., Smeyers, P., Smith, R., & Standish, P. (1998). Thinking again: Education after postmodernism. Westport, CT: Bergin and Garvey.

Bloland, H. G. (2005). Whatever happened to postmodernism in higher education?: No requiem in the new millennium. The Journal of Higher Education, 76, 121-150. Retrieved July 14, 2007, from EBSCO Online Database Education Research Complete.

Clark, J. A. (2006). Michael Peters' Lyotardian account of postmodernism and education: Some epistemic problems and naturalistic solutions. Educational Philosophy and Theory, 38, 391-405. Retrieved July 14, 2007, from EBSCO Online Database Education Research Complete.

Gojkov, G. (2012). Postmodern pedagogy. *Journal Plus Education / Educatia Plus, 8*, 9-39. Retrieved December 15, 2013, from EBSCO Online Database Education Research Complete.

Hagen, K. L. (2005). The death of philosophy. Skeptic, 11, 18-21. Retrieved July 14, 2007, from EBSCO Online Database Academic Search Premier.

Juodaityte, A., & Šiauciuliene, R. (2012). Challenges of postmodernism for teacher training: Changing contexts of education and diversity of identities. *Teacher Education / Mokytoju Ugdymas, 19*, 158-171. Retrieved December 15, 2013, from EBSCO Online Database Education Research Complete.

Kauffman, J., & Sasso, G. (2006). Toward ending cultural and cognitive relativism in special education. Exceptionality, 14, 65-90. Retrieved July 20, 2007, from EBSCO Online Database Education Research Complete.

Kilgore, D. (2004). Toward a Postmodern Pedagogy. New Directions for Adult and Continuing Education, 104, 45-53. Retrieved July 14, 2007, from EBSCO Online Database Education Research Complete.

Parker, S. (1997). Reflective teaching in the postmodern world: A manifesto for education in postmodernity. Philadelphia, PA: Open University Press.

Ramaekers, S. (2006). No harm done: The implications for educational research of the rejection of truth. Journal of Philosophy of Education, 40, 241-257. Retrieved July 14, 2007, from EBSCO Online Database Education Research Complete.

Rapp, C. (2003). From pre-Socrates through postmodernism, western traditional dialectical at its core.

Humanitas, 16, 114-118. Retrieved July 14, 2007, from EBSCO Online Database Academic Search Premier.

Reichenbach, R. (1999). Postmodern knowledge, modern beliefs, and the curriculum. Educational Philosophy and Theory, 31, 237-243. Retrieved July 20, 2007, from EBSCO Online Database Education Research Complete.

Rolfe, G. (2006). Judgments without rules: Towards a postmodern ironist concept of research validity. Nursing Inquiry, 13, 7-15. Retrieved July 14, 2007, from EBSCO Online Database Academic Search Premier.

Usher, R. (2006). Lyotard's performance. Studies in Philosophy and Education, 25, 279-288. Retrieved July 14, 2007, from EBSCO Online Database Education Research Complete.

Segall, A. (2013). Revitalizing critical discourses in social education: Opportunities for a more complexified (un)knowing. *Theory & Research in Social Education, 41*, 476-493. Retrieved December 15, 2013, from EBSCO Online Database Education Research Complete.

Usher, R., & Edwards, R. (1994). Postmodernism and education. New York, NY: Routledge.

SUGGESTED READING

Ball, S. J. (Ed.). (1990). Foucault and education. New York, NY: Routledge.

Derrida, J. (1978). Writing and difference. trans. A. Bass. Chicago, IL: University of Chicago Press.

Lyotard, Jean-Francois.(1984) The Postmodern condition: a report on knowledge. Manchester: Manchester University Press.

Foucault, M. (1969). The Archaeology of knowledge. New York, NY: Routledge.

Foucault, M. (1975). Discipline and punish: The birth of the prison. New York, NY: Vintage Books.

AFFECTIVE DOMAIN

This article presents a summary of the affective learning domain. Historically, learning domains have been divided into three different categories: cognitive, affective, and psychomotor. Although the distinction is somewhat arbitrary, and behaviors typically include elements of all three, the division was made to facilitate the study of each independent of the others. Nevertheless, the affective domain has received far less attention in the research literature than the cognitive domain because it has been difficult to define and difficult to measure. In addition, Western culture has typically valued reason over emotion, and many teachers and parents believe values should be taught in the home, not in schools. Even if the affective domain as a single construct has received less research attention, however, its component parts—such as attitudes, values, and motivation—have become increasingly important to educators and researchers. This summary will review historical approaches to the affective domain—such as Krathwohl's taxonomy of the affective domain—as well as more recent research on motivation, values, and attitudes.

KEYWORDS: Affective Domain; Attitudes; Bloom, Benjamin; Cognitive Domain; Internalization; Motivation; Psychomotor Domain; Taxonomy; Values

OVERVIEW

As Kirk (2007) writes, "In the educational literature, nearly every author introduces their paper by stating that the affective domain is essential for learning, but it is the least studied, most often overlooked, the most nebulous and the hardest to evaluate of...[the three learning] domains." A quick glance at the literature proves this statement to be true. When Krathwohl, Bloom, and Masia (1964) introduced their taxonomy of the affective domain in 1964, for example, they began by describing the challenges they faced given the lack of clarity in the literature. More recently, others have introduced the affective domain by lamenting its inferior status relative to the cognitive domain, and its subsequent neglect in the classroom and in educational research (Bolin, Khramtsova, & Saarnia, 2005; Sonnier, 1982).

Researchers and educators have faced challenges in studying the affective domain and in striving to give it the legitimacy they feel it deserves. The affective domain is a multi-dimensional construct, and that while it may receive less attention as a construct studied in its entirety, a great deal of research attention has been given to its component parts. Motivation, attitudes, and values, for example, all fall under the affective domain, and educators have become increasingly interested in how each impacts the learning process. Before we begin to deconstruct it, however, we'll first define the affective domain, outline the challenges inherent in studying it, and uncover its historical roots.

LEARNING DOMAINS

Learning domains are typically organized into three categories: cognitive, affective, and psychomotor. Such a division is "as ancient as Greek philosophy, and philosophers and psychologists have repeatedly used similar tripartite organizations" (Krathwohl et al.). Nevertheless, many associate the division with the work of Benjamin Bloom and colleagues, who developed a taxonomy of educational objectives for the cognitive and affective domains in the 1950s and 1960s. Bloom and Krathwohl define the three domains as follows:

- **Cognitive:** The cognitive domain...includes those objectives which deal with the recall or recognition of knowledge and the development of intellectual abilities and skills (Bloom, 1954);
- **Psychomotor:** Objectives which emphasize some muscular or motor skill, some manipulation of material and objects, or some act which requires a neuromuscular co-ordination (Krathwohl et al.);
- **Affective:** [The affective domain] includes objectives which describe change in interest, attitudes, and values, and the development of appreciations and adequate adjustment (Bloom). We found a large number of such objectives in the literature expressed as interests, attitudes, appreciations, values, and emotional sets or biases (Krathwohl et al.).

TAXONOMIES & CATEGORIZATION

While taxonomies and categories help simplify complex phenomenon and arguably make them easier to study, they also misrepresent reality, to some degree. Or, as Krathwohl explains, "we should note that any classification scheme...does some violence to the phenomena as commonly observed in natural settings." In this instance, the misrepresentation results from creating an artificial where no such distinction in fact exists. In other words, most human behavior includes facets of each domain—cognitive, affective, and psychomotor—and cannot be reduced to one domain alone. As Ringness (1975) states, "It is probably obvious that attitudes and values have a cognitive as well as an affective component. That is, they are not simply composed of feeling for or against something, but include intellectualization as well." Learning about the history of racism, for example, is a cognitive activity that might result in a change in attitude, an element of the affective domain. Similarly, improving a student's motivation to study can create cognitive change.

A distinction that was meant to facilitate the study of each domain may in fact have hindered progress with respect to research in the affective domain in particular. Separating one from the other gave people an opportunity to understand each in isolation from the other, but also to *judge* each domain relative to the other. In a culture that has tended to value reason over emotion, it is of little surprise that the cognitive domain has outshined its "competitors." Indeed, Krathwohl et al. almost abandoned efforts to create a second taxonomy for affective objectives, given its poor reception in the education community. He writes, "few of the examiners at the college level were convinced that the development of the affective domain would make much difference in their work or that they would find great use for it, when completed" (Krathwohl et al.).

CULTURAL NORMS & CLASSROOMS

Even if emotion were valued to the same degree as reason, other cultural norms suggest the classroom is an inappropriate venue for teaching to the affective domain. Educators are comfortable evaluating students on achievement in intellectual matters, for example, but less comfortable evaluating students on their attitudes, values and motivation. As Krathwohl et al. writes, "teachers don't think it's appropriate to grade with respect to interests, attitude, and character development." And some parents tend to agree; Farley (2001) notes that many believe it's the responsibility of the home and community—not the schools—to teach values and develop appropriate attitudes. What Krathwohl calls the "public-private status of cognitive vs. affective behaviors" is deeply ingrained in our culture. "Achievement, competence, productivity, etc., are regarded as public matters. In contrast, one's beliefs, attitudes, values, and personality characteristics are more likely to be regarded as private matters" (Krathwohl et al.).

Despite that notion, however, an interest in incorporating the affective domain into classroom experiences and instruction does exist. Dunn and Stinson (2012), for example, wrote about a case for which drama pedagogy was used "to create a set of learning experiences designed specifically to simultaneously tap into both the cognitive and the affective domains." The work, the authors explain, sought to intentionally stimulate a broad "spectrum of emotions, from relief to resentment, fondness to frustration" (Dunn & Stinson).

Similarly, Kok-Siang, Chong Yong, and Shuhui (2013) reported on three school-based trial lessons in which students from two Singapore secondary schools were taught science concepts and skills "in the usual way," but with follow-up reflective activities requiring them to "draw from their learning experiences parallel scenarios in their daily lives," thereby addressing the affective domain. The students were taught chemistry topics, and at the end of each lesson, students were asked to discuss, reflect on, and respond to an everyday event or scenario that shared characteristics similar to the chemistry topic or skill they had just learned (Kok-Siang et al.).

DEFINING THE AFFECTIVE DOMAIN

Apart from the issues previously described, the most significant challenge faced by those studying the affective domain is one of definition—the affective domain has never been clearly defined. As Krathwohl et al. noted in 1964, "there was a lack of clarity in the statements of affective objectives that we found in the literature." More recently, in a report produced by the Department of Labor in the 1990s regarding the preparedness of students entering the workforce, "personal qualities" were emphasized, yet not clearly articulated. "An essential problem arises when attempts are made to implement the third area mentioned in [the report]: teaching personal qualities. This problem concerns failure of the report to define in a functional manner the nature of personal qualities. Specifically, a workable definition of the affective domain was not included" (McNabb & Mills, 1995). Assuming the domain itself were more clearly defined, educators and researchers would then need to reach consensus regarding which attitudes, or which values, should be taught. McNabb and Mills suggest this might be the most difficult task of all, since these are influenced by local cultures, parenting styles, and religious beliefs.

As one might suspect, given the lack of a clear definition, the affective domain has suffered from measurement issues as well. Krathwohl et al. found little information in the research literature about how to assess affect, and suggested it was not practiced in the classroom in any systematic fashion. Indeed, because attitudes and values are not directly observable in the way that changes in cognition are, assessing affect is difficult. Teachers and researchers must often rely on self-reports, which many worry are susceptible to response bias, with students intentionally portraying themselves more favorably (Dettmer, 2006).

While most agree that measuring affect is difficult, opinions diverge on whether measurement should be a goal at all. Farley (2001) argues, "we seem preoccupied with the observable, the measurable, the testable aspects of human behavior, while we ignore the significance of feeling, aspirations, hopes, fears, beliefs, values, and perceptions." He continues, "the humanities...have dehumanized themselves in order to specify bits and pieces of measurable substance and in the process have lost their unique potential for man." On the other hand, Krathwohl et al. believe "there must be some systematic method for appraising the extent to which students grow in the desired ways."

KRATHWOHL'S TAXONOMY OF THE AFFECTIVE DOMAIN

The idea for an educational taxonomy of the three learning domains was first discussed at an informal meeting of university examiners at the 1948 annual conference of the American Psychological Association. The group's original intention was to create a common framework of educational objectives that would facilitate the exchange of test items and materials among university examiners, and stimulate research on the relationship between education and evaluation. The taxonomy of educational objectives for the cognitive domain was completed in 1956, while the taxonomy of the affective domain followed in 1964. The group never completed a taxonomy for the psychomotor domain.

HIERARCHICAL ORGANIZATION OF THE COGNITIVE DOMAIN

Just as the taxonomy of objectives in the cognitive domain was organized hierarchically, Krathwohl et al. believed the taxonomy for the affective domain should be organized hierarchically as well. The principle they adopted to organize the hierarchy was the notion of internalization, a process whereby values and attitudes are acquired, first as a result of external influences, and gradually, as a result of internal ones. The continuum, as they describe it, is multidimensional, increasing in emotional intensity, the level of internal control, and the degree of conscious awareness. The levels of the taxonomy are introduced below.

Receiving (Attending): The lowest level of the taxonomy, separated into three sub-categories: awareness, willingness to receive, and controlled or selected attention. At this level, the student is sensitized to the existence of certain phenomena or stimuli. A teacher might help students become aware of various characteristics of art, for example, and assess his awareness by asking him to describe various paintings (Krathwohl et al.).

Responding: The second lowest level of the taxonomy, also separated into three subcategories: acquiescence in responding, willingness to respond, and satisfaction in response. A student at this level is doing more than merely noticing a phenomenon; Krathwohl et al. describe the student as "actively attending."

Valuing: The phenomenon a student attends to is perceived by her/him to have worth. "Behavior categorized at this level is sufficiently consistent and stable to have taken on the characteristics of a belief or an attitude" (Krathwohl et al.). The subcategories of this level of the domain are acceptance of a value, preference for a value, and commitment to a value.

Organization: As a student internalizes more values, he/she must develop a system to organize them and establish relationships among them. The building of a value system develops over time. Children make changes to their value system much more easily than adults.

Characterization by a Value or Value Complex: The final level of the taxonomy in which an individual's values are integrated in a life philosophy or worldview. The individual acts consistently with values, so much so that he/she is described as "being controlled by" his/her values. According to Krathwohl et al., "Realistically, formal education generally cannot reach this level, at least in our society...the maturity and personal integration required at this level are not attained until at least some years after the individual has completed his formal education." Someone who has attained the highest level of the affective taxonomy is typically also operating at the highest level of the cognitive domain.

INTERNALIZATION AND THE AFFECTIVE TAXONOMY

Given the significance of the concept of internalization to the affective taxonomy, it might be wise to end with the authors' own comments on the relationships between internalization and education in general, as distinct from training. As Krathwohl et al. points out, the taxonomy accounts for the development of conformity—those behaviors represented by the lower end of the taxonomy, externally motivated by authority figures, social mores, etc.—as well as the development of individuality—those behaviors represented by the upper end of the taxonomy, internally motivated and consistent with a personal life philosophy. The former behaviors are typically elicited through training, the latter, education. "Education demands inner direction and controls. [It] implies a progression from activities directed by others to self-direction and acceptance of one's unique characteristics. It implies learning to develop one's own talents, to become self-actualizing, and to be aware of the conflicts among one's values and within society" (Ringness).

FURTHER INSIGHTS

As mentioned previously, efforts to define and/or study the affective domain in its entirety have diminished significantly in the last few decades. Krathwohl's taxonomy was followed by Ringness' work titled "The Affective Domain in Education" but very little substantial work has addressed the entire domain since then. Instead, researchers have focused on its component parts—attitudes, motivation, and values, for example.

ATTITUDES

Attitudes are defined as systems or constructs composed of four interrelated components:

- Affective Responses;
- Cognitions;
- Behavioral Intentions;
- Behaviors.

Attitudes can be either positive or negative, and vary with regard to their intensity or amount (Miller, 2005). Most classroom activities—even those with a primarily cognitive focus—have an affective/attitudinal component. A lesson on the 19th Amendment and the Voting Rights Act of 1965, for example, teaches students U.S. history, but might also influence attitudes with respect to participation in democracy and/or the struggle of underrepresented groups (Miller). At other times, the affective domain may be the focus of instruction, as when educators conduct anti-drug campaigns. A number of different theories—ranging from cognitive dissonance theory to social judgment theory to functional theories—have been proposed to explain attitude formation and change. Fishbein and Ajzen (1975) developed one of the best known models to explain the relationship of attitudes to behavior.

MOTIVATION

Motivation is generally defined as an internal state that activates behavior and gives it direction toward a goal. As such, research on motivation has included a number of different facets, including goal setting, self-efficacy, attributions, self-regulation, and intrinsic and extrinsic factors (Wang, 2005). Researchers distinguish between performance and mastery goals,

for example, with success defined as either 'outperforming others' or 'developing new skills,' respectively (Wang). Educators typically attempt to facilitate mastery learning. Self-efficacy theory is based on the work of Bandura (1982). Defined as a self-judgment of one's ability to perform a task in a specific domain, self-efficacy has a significant impact on motivation. Attributions are the explanations an individual gives for success or failure. Weiner (1979) proposed that attributions have three characteristics—a locus of control, stability, and controllability. A student who attributes performance to luck, for example—an external, unstable, uncontrollable source—may be less motivated to put forth effort in future endeavors. Finally, researchers distinguish between intrinsic and extrinsic motivation; intrinsically motivated people invest time in activities without reward, because they find such activities rewarding in and of themselves. Extrinsic motivators engage in activities for the rewards themselves; grades, for example, are extrinsic motivators.

Regarding the relationship between intrinsic and external motivations, Cooper (2013) proposes a "hierarchy of wants, in which extrinsic motivations and goals are seen as attempts—albeit often unsuccessful ones—to reach the highest order, most intrinsic goals." His model also suggests that human beings are most likely to achieve a state of well-being when their goals are "synergistically related: determined both by the internal configuration of goals and external resources" (Cooper).

VALUES

Huitt (2004) defines values as "affectively-laden thoughts about objects, ideas, behavior, etc., that guide behavior, but do not necessarily require it." The act of valuing, he continues, is one of making judgments, expressing feeling, or adhering to a set of principles. According to Superka, Ahrens, and Hedstrom (1976), there are five basic approaches to values education (Huitt, 2004):

- Inculcation;
- Moral Development;
- Analysis;
- Values Clarification;
- Action Learning.

Inculcation occurs when students identify with culturally accepted norms and behaviors; the individual is viewed as a recipient, rather than an initiator of values. The moral development perspective proposes that moral thinking—especially with respect to concepts such as justice, equity, fairness, and dignity—develops in stages; the work of Lawrence Kohlberg (1984) is central to this perspective. The analysis approach emphasizes the role of reason and logic—as opposed to emotion and conscience—in the development of values. Those who advocate values clarification, based on the humanistic philosophy of Maslow (1970) and others, believe values arise from within the individual as he/she strives to self-actualize. Finally, the action learning approach, as its name implies, advocates combining feeling and acting. Students need opportunities to act on their values, which arise through interactions between individuals and society, rather than from one or the other alone.

VIEWPOINTS

If the impact of the affective domain on teaching and learning were measured in terms of the 'popularity' of Krathwohl's domain—arguably the most well-known conceptualization of the affective domain—one might conclude that it had no impact at all. As Nuhfer (2005) writes, "in comparison to Volume 1 [the taxonomy of the cognitive domain], the second is so rarely cited that application of the affective domain appears to suffer arrested development." In reality, however, the affective domain has had a tremendous impact, when redefined in terms of its component parts. As McNabb and Mills argue, "Defining 'affective' has become increasingly more complex. Early attempts, such as those made by Bloom…[provided]…a starting point; however, it represented a view much too broad." Educators may continue to argue about the importance of the affective domain relative to the cognitive one, and parents and teachers will undoubtedly continue to argue about *which* values and/or attitudes should be taught, but the proliferation of research on motivation, self-efficacy, attribution, and values education suggest that the affective domain has contributed significantly to what we know about teaching and learning.

TERMS & CONCEPTS

Affective Domain: Learning domains have historically been divided into three different types: cognitive, affective, and psychomotor. The affective domain includes objectives which describe change in interest, attitudes, and values, and

the development of appreciations and adequate adjustment (Bloom). We found a large number of such objectives in the literature expressed as interests, attitudes, appreciations, values, and emotional sets or biases.

Attitudes: Attitudes are defined as systems or constructs composed of four interrelated components: affective responses, cognitions, behavioral intentions, and behaviors. Attitudes can be either positive or negative, and vary with regard to their intensity or amount.

Cognitive Domain: Learning domains have historically been divided into three different categories: cognitive, affective, and psychomotor. The cognitive domain…includes those objectives which deal with the recall or recognition of knowledge and the development of intellectual abilities and skills.

Internalization: The construct used by Krathwohl et al. to order their hierarchy of the affective domain. Internalization refers to a process whereby values and attitudes are acquired first as a result of external influences, and gradually, as a result of internal ones.

Motivation: Motivation is generally defined as an internal state that activates behavior and gives it direction toward some goal. As such, research on motivation has included a number of different facets, including goal setting, self-efficacy, attributions, self-regulation, and intrinsic and extrinsic factors.

Psychomotor Domain: Learning domains have historically been divided into three different categories: cognitive, affective, and psychomotor. The psychomotor domain includes objectives which emphasize some muscular or motor skill, some manipulation of material and objects, or some act which requires a neuromuscular co-ordination.

Values: Huitt defines values as "affectively-laden thoughts about objects, ideas, behavior, etc, that guide behavior, but do not necessarily require it." The act of valuing, he continues, is one of making judgments, expressing feeling, or adhering to a set of principles. Values are typically believed to be 'taught' using one of five methods: inculcation, moral development, analysis, values clarification, and action learning.

Jennifer Kretchmar

BIBLIOGRAPHY

Bloom, B. S., Englelhart, M. D., Furst, E. J., Hill, W. H., & Krathwohl, D. R. (1954). *Taxonomy of educational objectives: The classification of educational goals. Handbook I: Cognitive Domain.* New York, NY: Longman, Inc.

Bolin, A. U., Khramtsova, I., & Saarnio, D. (2005). Using student journals to stimulate authentic learning: Balancing Bloom's cognitive and affective domains. *Teaching of Psychology, 32,* 154-159. Retrieved July 1, 2007, from EBSCO Online Database Education Research Complete.

Cooper, M. (2013). the intrinsic foundations of extrinsic motivations and goals: toward a unified humanistic theory of well-being and change. *Journal of Humanistic Psychology, 53,* 153–171. Retrieved December 17, 2013, from EBSCO Online Database Education Research Complete.

Dettmer, P. (2006). New blooms in established fields: Four domains of learning and doing. *Roeper Review, 28,* 70-78. Retrieved July 1, 2007, from EBSCO Online Database Education Research Complete.

Dunn, J., & Stinson, M. (2012). Learning through emotion: Moving the affective in from the margins. *International Journal of Early Childhood, 44,* 203–218. Retrieved December 20, 2013, from EBSCO Online Database Education Research Complete.

Ediger, M. (1993). The affective domain, science, and the middle school student. *Instructional Psychology, 20,* 314-318. Retrieved July 1, 2007, from EBSCO Online Database Education Research Complete.

Farley, J. (2001). Perceiving the student: Enriching the Social Studies through the Affective Domain. *Theory into Practice, 20,* 179-187. Retrieved July 1, 2007, from EBSCO Online Database Education Research Complete.

Griffin, K.G., & Nguyen, A.D. (2006). Are educators prepared to affect the affective domain? *National Forum of Teacher Education Journal Electronic, 16,* 3E. Retrieved July 1, 2007, from http://nationalforum.com.

Huitt, W. (2004). *Values.* Retrieved July 1, 2007, from Valdosta State University, http://chiron.valdosta.edu.

Kirk, K. (2007) *What is the affective domain anyway?* Retrieved July 1, 2007, from http://serc.carleton.edu.

Koballa, T. (2007). *Framework for the affective domain in science education.* Retrieved July 1, 2007, from http://serc.carleton.edu.

Krathwohl, D.R., Bloom, B.S., & Masia, B.B. (1964). *Taxonomy of educational objectives: The classification of educational goals. Handbook II: Affective Domain.* New York, NY: David McKay Company, Inc.

Kok Siang, T., Chong Yong, H., & Shuhui, T. (2013). Teaching school science within the cognitive and affective domains. *Asia-Pacific Forum on Science Learning & Teaching, 14,* 1–16. Retrieved December 20, 2013, from EBSCO Online Database Education Research Complete.

McNabb, J. G., & Mills, R. (1995). Tech prep and the development of personal qualities: Defining the affective domain. *Education, 115,* 589-592. Retrieved July 1, 2007, from EBSCO Online Database Education Research Complete.

Miller, M. (2005). Learning and teaching in the affective domain. In M. Orey (Ed.), *Emerging perspectives on learning, teaching, and technology.* Retrieved July 1, 2007, from http://coe.uga.edu.

Nuhfer, E.B. (2005). De Bon's red hat on Krathwohl's head: Irrational means to rational ends. *National Teaching and Learning Forum, 14,* 7-11.

Ringness, T.A., (1975). *The affective domain in education.* Boston, MA: Little, Brown and Company.

Sonnier, I. (1982). Holistic education: Teaching in the affective domain. *Education, 103,* 11-15. Retrieved July 1, 2007, from EBSCO Online Database Education Research Complete.

Wang, S. (2005). Motivation: A general overview of theories. In M. Orey (Ed.), *Emerging perspectives on learning, teaching, and technology.* Retrieved July 1, 2007, from http://projects.coe.uga.edu.

SUGGESTED READING

Adkins, S. (2004). Beneath the tip of the iceberg: Technology plumbs the affective domain. *TD, 58,* 28-33. Retrieved August 1, 2007, from EBSCO Online Database Education Research Complete.

Bandura, A. (1982). Self-efficacy mechanism in human agency. *American Psychologist, 37,* 122-147.

Fishbein, M., & Ajzen, I. (1975). *Belief, Attitude, Intention, and Behavior: An Introduction to Theory and Research.* Reading, MA: Addison-Wesley.

Green, Z.A. & Batool, S. (2017). Emotionalized learning experiences: Tapping into the affective domain. *Evaluation and Program Planning, 62,* 35-48.

Hyland, T. (2014). Mindfulness-based interventions and the affective domain of education. *Educational Studies,* 40 (3), 277-291.

Kohlberg, L. (1984). *The psychology of moral development.* San Francisco: Harper and Row.

Maslow (1970). *Toward a psychology of being.* Princeton, NJ: Viking Press.

Weiner, B. (1979). A theory of motivation for some classroom experiences. *Journal of Educational Psychology, 71,* 3-25.

ASSIMILATION THEORY

Assimilation theory, a cognitive learning theory developed by psychologist David Ausubel, holds that people learn best when they can link, or assimilate, new information with previous knowledge. In this way, learning becomes meaningful as learners construct their own understandings of new information, making it more likely that it will be retained. The six basic principles of assimilation theory are subsumption, superordinate learning, progressive differentiation, integrative reconciliation, obliterative subsumption, and advance organizers.

KEYWORDS: Advance Organizers; Assimilation Theory; Behaviorism; Cognitive Learning; Epistemology; Meaningful Learning; Reception Learning; Rote Learning; Social Learning Theory; Subsumption

OVERVIEW

ORIGINS IN BEHAVIORISM

The first theories on epistemology were classified as theories of behaviorism. Behaviorists, such as B. F. Skinner, believed that learning processes were researched most objectively when attention was given to stimuli and responses. Theories of behaviorism included claims that organisms are born as blank slates, that learning involves a change in behavior and is largely the result of environmental events (Barrett, 2003).

Cognitivism emerged in opposition to behaviorist ideas (Barrett). Early behaviorists would rather not include mental events in their learning theories due to the trouble of measuring them, but by the 1950s and 1960s, some psychologists began to turn away from this human learning approach (McGriff, 2001). The behaviorist perspective could not answer important questions such as why people attempt to organize what they learn or change the way the information is received. As a result, more cognitive research began to take place, and psychologists such as Edward Tolman and Jean Piaget laid the foundation for cognitive learning theories (McGriff).

COGNITIVE LEARNING

Edward Tolman further advanced the idea of cognitive learning, which referred to the development of learning from interacting with the environment and evaluating how the learner relates to it (McGriff). He came to his conclusions after performing an experiment on rats in a maze. Tolman periodically closed off portions of the maze, and the rats chose not to take the route that led to the closed path even though the other route was longer (McGriff). Cognitivism focuses on alterations in thought that are not directly observable (Barrett).

A Swiss psychologist, Jean Piaget, founded a research program that paved future viewpoints and theories of cognitive development. His cognitive theory sprang from his many years of keen observation. He determined that intellectual development appears in response to the child's relationship with the world around him or her. Throughout the child's development, according to Piaget, knowledge is invented and reinvented (McGriff). Piaget's theory "addressed children growing through a specific set of cognitive stages in which they develop increasingly sophisticated ways [of] handling the world of knowledge" (McInerney, 2005).

In Piaget's theory of development, assimilation and accommodation prove to be the most important cognitive processes responsible for progression through multiple stages (McGriff). Piaget often asserted that students of all kinds created the vast majority of their knowledge by way of their personal experiences and relationship to their surroundings. Piaget referred to this self-teaching as cognitive constructivism (McInerney). Cognitive constructivism acts as the foundation for which all other educational psychology research and theorizing builds upon, including the assimilation theory work of David Ausubel (McInerney). Ausubel's work in the context of instructional design is further explored in the 2011 book *The Instructional Design Knowledge Base: Theory, Research, and Practice* (Richey, Klein & Tracey; reviewed by Para, 2013).

Cognitive theories of learning deal directly with the mind as it relates to the reception, assimilation, storage, and recall of information. By understanding the mechanics of the learning process, cognitive theorists believe that they can recommend better teaching methods (McGriff). Most cognitive theorists agree on some basic principles of learning. General assumptions are that knowledge is organized and that each person is an active participant in their own learning. Learning also includes behavior differences in addition to the more subtle changes of mental association (Barrett). Cognitive theorists also believe that observations of behavior are necessary, and inferences can be made about mental processes based on observed behavior (Barrett). The implication is that people organize information as they receive it because new knowledge is easy to associate with already stored information (McInerney). As they grow or learn more, they are capable of more sophisticated thought (Barrett).

Since the mid-1970s, cognitive psychology has become one of the most dominant topics in educational research (McInerney). There have been amazing advances in the study of human learning and the nature of knowledge, many of which have sprung from the work of Tolman, Piaget, and Ausubel (Novak, 2003).

WHAT IS ASSIMILATION THEORY?

Ausubel developed his assimilation theory of learning in the 1960s. Influenced by Piaget, Ausubel's theory mainly concentrates on the acquisition and use of knowledge (McGriff). The theory focuses on the idea that learning, to be effective, must be meaningful (Novak). The belief is that each student needs to develop his or her own form of learning as it relates to key concepts and the relationship between different pieces of information (Novak).

Assimilation theory is applicable to reception learning, also known as expository learning. Reception learning is learning in which the concepts to be learned are presented explicitly to the learner (Novak, 1979). Concept introduction is the first step, and then an overview of information is presented (Andrews). Teachers who encourage reception learning execute carefully planned, methodical explication of meaningful information. Information is organized, explained, and connected to a bigger picture (McGriff). Students are then expected to process information and apply concepts (Andrews).

Under assimilation theory, it is believed that input, processing, storage, and \retrieval of all learned knowledge are at the core of every learning process and are universal for everyone (McGriff). Instructors remain the managers of the information but the learner is the one who carries out his or her own learning (McGriff). Teachers can only assist in learning by offering strategies and encouragement, but learning is a highly individualistic process that varies from person to person (Novak).

Meaningful learning is controlled by the learner and only takes place when new information is attributed to existing knowledge that the learner already possessed (McGriff). Reception learning provides the learner with the structure and motivation necessary to learn. Meaningful learning requires the learner to seek out relationships and incorporate the new learning into the knowledge base he or she already possesses (Novak). The learner then connects the two forms of information and joins them to create the newly attained knowledge (McGriff).

Learning can be extremely variable, comprising the most mundane repetition to complex and meaningful abstract thinking (Novak). Memorization and rote learning are used for information that is required but that a learner does not find meaningful (Novak). Memorization and rote learning are used because little prior knowledge is necessary to perform rote tasks, and it is easy for an instructor to conduct. Rote learning is most often used when a learner fails to try connecting his or her new knowledge to the old (Novak). Rote learning has negative consequences for creative problem-solving and attainment of organized knowledge, and rote learning often avoids the procedures, rules, and practices that are necessary for increasing the understanding and retention of new information (McGriff).

The process of assimilation is preferred because it is believed to strengthen the learner's knowledge structure (McGriff). If the learner's entire knowledge base is strengthened (like a muscle) the results are improved recall ability and an improved capacity to process more challenging information. Assimilation theory is thus named because it avers that new information is best acquired when the learner can assimilate it with or build off previous knowledge (Novak). Ausubel states that if he had to simplify educational philosophy the most important element influencing learning is "what the learner already knows. Ascertain this and teach him accordingly" (Ausubel, 1968). In one study, researchers looked at students with learning disabilities and examined whether "massive practice" in the form of repetitive and "spontaneous play" and involving what the children already knew, positively affected their cognitive development (Mahoney, 2013). Meaningful learning has three components:

- learner's relevant prior knowledge;
- meaningful material;
- learner's choice to use meaningful learning strategies (McGriff).

APPLICATIONS

The six basic principles of assimilation theory are:

- subsumption;
- superordinate learning;
- progressive differentiation;
- integrative reconciliation;
- obliterative subsumption;
- advance organizers.

SUBSUMPTION

In reception learning, existing concepts provide a base with which to link new information (McGriff). This is an interactive process between teacher and learner, and the process changes both the subsuming concept and the newly gained concepts for the learner.

- **Derivative subsumption** refers to the reference of a new concept that can be found in a concept that has been previously learned, stored, and retained (McGriff). If a learner already knows what a fish is and then learns about a specific type of fish, this new knowledge will be attached to the initial concept of fish, while at the same time avoiding any alteration to the original concept (McGriff);
- **Correlative subsumption** refers to learning that enriches a previous concept. Correlative subsumption requires a higher level of thinking than derivative subsumption. If a learner is introduced to new kind of fish that does not fit the accepted definition, like an eel, the learner has to receive the new information, then modify his or her concept of fish to include the possibility of no fins (McGriff).

SUPERORDINATE LEARNING

Superordinate learning refers to the process in which a more general and new concept relates to known examples of a concept (Novak). Superordinate learning occurs when new information is made up of many groups of "larger" information that were not initially thought of as being connected (McGriff). For example, a learner may already know about sharks, sting rays, and skates but later learns that these are all examples of fishes with a cartilage skeleton (McGriff). Again, the teacher needs to provide the exposition of concepts, but the learner must make the assimilation.

PROGRESSIVE DIFFERENTIATION

Progressive differentiation is a process of developing and refining existing cognitive structures (McGriff). When learning commences, the act of creating and

building upon subsuming concepts also takes place. Ausubel believes concept development is most effective with reception learning, when the simplest ideas are presented first and then elaborated, or differentiated, with more specific detail (McGriff). To carry out the fish example, this general concept can be expanded with concepts such as types of fish and the physical structure of a fish (McGriff). With rote learning, progressive differentiation is not possible because connections are not made.

INTEGRATIVE RECONCILIATION

Integrative reconciliation is a type of cognitive differentiation that connects links and new relationships between different concepts in the mind (McGriff). For instance, dolphins are animals that are quite similar to fish in many ways, but despite their fishlike appearance and their ocean habitat, they are mammals (McGriff). These complex concepts must be received and reconciled in the cognitive structure in order to be reconciled.

OBLITERATIVE SUBSUMPTION

Obliterative subsumption refers to learners sometimes forgetting what they learn (Lim, 1999). Ausubel argues that the amount of recall a learner can achieve depends on the degree of meaningfulness associated with the acquisition of information (McGriff). Rote learning has a high rate of obliterative subsumption. Reception learning can often be recalled much later because it is meaningful.

ADVANCE ORGANIZERS

Teachers can facilitate learning by better organizing information and presenting it in a way "so that new concepts are easily relatable to concepts already learned" (Ausubel). To assist with this aspect of reception learning, Ausubel "is credited with the learning theory of advanced organizers" (Ausubel). Advance organizers involve the use of general materials "that introduce new information and facilitate learning by providing an idea to which the new idea can be anchored" (Ausubel).

These organizers are "introduced in advance of learning itself, since the content of a given organizer is selected based on its appropriateness for explaining and integrating the new material" (Ausubel, 1963). Some devices include pictures, references to familiar stories, reviews of previously learned concepts, and video clips

(Ausubel). Ausubel emphasizes "that advance organizers are different from overviews and summaries, which simply emphasize key ideas and are presented at the same level of abstraction and generality as the rest of the material. Organizers act as a bridge between new learning material and existing related ideas" (Kearsley, 2007). Advanced organizers are an important element in successful reception of knowledge and a key aspect in Ausubel's assimilation theory.

VIEWPOINTS

Ausubel sets forth in his theory that it can only be applicable to reception or expository learning in educational environments (Kearsley). Ausubel favors reception learning, which is completed on one's own without outside aid or processes. This contrasts with a more recent emphasis on social learning and active student involvement (McGriff). Ausubel does agree that problem-solving skills must be taught, but asserts that a schools' primary responsibility is to deliver content. Teachers can engage learners by helping students search for relationships between new information and previously gained knowledge and by compensating successful connections with rewards (Novak).

Ausubel does not advocate "discovery learning, a process through which learners were expected to discover and construct their own understandings and knowledge from problems" (McInerney). Discovery learning requires students to make connections and recognize patterns before being introduced to concepts (Andrews, 1984). General introduction of concepts and disclosure of information is not provided until after student experiments or discoveries. Learning is less meaningful, according to Ausubel, because connections are made after application rather than during (Andrews). Ausubel also does not fully accept learner-centered instruction (McGriff). Rather, he embraces teaching methods that are more direct in nature, believing that it is the best way to absorb large bodies of content knowledge (McGriff).

Ausubel's assimilation theory suggests that learning is primarily in the hands of the learner, but he acknowledges that teachers can influence the student's decision to learn meaningfully by the way they organize and present information (Novak). He also stresses the importance of meaningful assessment methods as opposed to the traditional multiple-choice tests common in most schools and encourages rote learning over understanding

and retention (Novak). Meaningful learning, as Ausubel maintains, is defined as newly acquired knowledge that is capable of being attributed or related to previously acquired information. Meaningful learning, then, is often more easily gathered, stored, and applied (Ausubel). Karpicke and Grimaldi (2012) argue that the retrieval or gathering of information is key to understanding and to the promotion of learning. Because of these benefits, meaningful learning is an important tool for classroom instruction and the learning success of students.

CONCLUSION

There is a strong correlation between knowledge-based psychological research and learning processes. The knowledge and teaching methods exercised in classrooms should reflect the best research-based theories (McInerney). Some practices have had to evolve with changing times and technologies (McInerney). Other practices have become outdated or disregarded due to flawed research (McInerney). There has been an increased amount of validated research conducted on cognitive psychology. Research has focused on "the nature of effective skills and strategies, and whether they should be taught independent of or in conjunction with content" (McInerney). In addition, social learning theory and other theories like positive teaching and direct instruction all share an ever-present cognitive element that belies each process. As a result of cognitive theory research, many outlets have been receptive to the theory's application, improving the capture and organization of information and facilitating one's own ability to participate in their learning process (McGriff).

TERMS & CONCEPTS

Advance Organizers: Advance organizers involve the use of general materials that provide learners with new information and new ideas with which to anchor to other ideas.

Assimilation theory: The theory focuses on the idea that learning, to be effective, must be meaningful and that "each learner must construct his own understanding of key concepts and relationships".

Behaviorism: The predominant school of thought before cognitive learning that argued that "organisms are born blank slates and learning is largely the result of environmental events".

Cognitive Learning: Cognitive theories of learning deal with the mind's ability to accept, mold, and retain the information it receives.

Epistemology: The study of the nature of knowledge and learning.

Meaningful Learning: Meaningful learning refers to the belief that, for learning to be effective, each learner must create an individualized understanding of key ideas and the relationships between them.

Reception Learning: Reception learning is learning in which the concepts to be learned are presented explicitly to the learner. Reception learning requires carefully planned, methodical presentation of meaningful information.

Rote Learning: Rote learning is learning by routine and mechanical tasks, specifically memorization.

Social Learning Theory: "Social learning focuses on the learning that occurs within a social context. It considers how people learn from one another, encompassing such concepts as observational learning, imitation, and modeling".

Subsumption: Subsumption refers to the process of attaching new information with previously learned information.

Jennifer Bouchard

BIBLIOGRAPHY

Andrews, J. (1984). Discovery and expository learning compared: Their effects on independent and dependent students. *Journal of Educational Research, 78,* 80. October 28, 2007, from EBSCO Online Database Education Research Complete.

Ausubel, D. (1968). *Educational psychology: A cognitive view.* New York: Holt, Rinehart and Winston.

Ausubel, D. (2007). *Great ideas in education.* Retrieved October 21, 2007, from University of Florida College of Education, http://coe.ufl.edu.

Ausubel, D. (1963). *The psychology of meaningful verbal learning.* New York: Grune and Stratton.

Barrett, E. (2003). *Cognitive learning theory.* Retrieved October 18, 2007, from http://suedstudent.syr.edu.

Karpicke, J., & Grimaldi, P. (2012). Retrieval-based learning: A perspective for enhancing meaningful learning. *Educational Psychology Review, 24,* 401-418. Retrieved December 22, 2013, from EBSCO Online Database Education Research Complete.

Kearsley, G. (2007). *Exploring learning and instruction: Theory into practice database.* Retrieved October 22, 2007, from http://tip.psychology.org.

Lim, B. (1999). *Instructional design theories site.* Retrieved October 22, 2007, from Indiana University, http://indiana.edu.

McGriff, S. (2001). *ISD knowledge base/assimilation theory.* Retrieved October 18, 2007, from Pennsylvania State University, College of Education. http://personal.psu.edu.

McInerney, D. (2005). Educational psychology-theory, research and teaching: A 25-year retrospective. *Educational Psychology, 25,* 585-599. Retrieved October 21, 2007, from EBSCO Online Database Education Research Complete.

Mahoney, G. (2013). Assimilative practice and developmental intervention. *International Journal of Early Childhood Special Education, 5,* 45-65. Retrieved December 22, 2013, from EBSCO Online Database Education Research Complete.

Novak, J. (1998). *Learning, creating and using knowledge.* London: Lawrence Erlbaum.

Novak, J. (2003). The promise of new ideas and new technology for improving teaching and learning. *Cell Biology Education, 2,* 122-132. Retrieved October 18, 2007, from http://lifescied.org.

Para, S. (2013). Review of The Instructional Design Knowledge Base: Theory, Research, and Practice. *Journal of Applied Learning Technology, 3,* 49-51. Retrieved December 22, 2013, from EBSCO Online Database Education Research Complete.

SUGGESTED READING

Ausubel, D. (2000). *The acquisition and retention of knowledge: A cognitive view.* Dordrecht, The Netherlands: Kluwer.

Ausubel, D. (1977). *Theory and problems of adolescent development* (3rd ed.). New York: Grune and Stratton.

Bondy, J., Peguero, J., & Johnson, B. (2017). The children of immigrants' academic self-efficacy: The significance of gender, race, ethnicity, and segmented assimilation. *Education and Urban Society,* 49 (5), 486-517.

Novak, J. (1979). The reception learning paradigm. *Journal of Research in Science Teaching, 16,* 481-488. October 28, 2007, from EBSCO Online Database Education Research Complete.

ATTRIBUTION THEORY

Attribution theory is used to explain how people, who inherently work to organize and understand their life experiences, will attribute their successes and failures to four factors: ability, effort, task difficulty, and luck. Each of these factors has been analyzed using three characteristics (i.e., Locus of Control, Stability, and Controllability). Attribution Theory also draws from principles of Motivation Theory and Expectancy Theory to help explain how students' perceptions of their successes and failures impacts persistence and resiliency. This article also includes some best practice suggestions based on the tenets of attribution theory.

OVERVIEW

What makes a winner win? Is it all in one's attitude? Why do some people with apparent talents never seem to achieve as others predict? How can the interaction between a person's perceptions and the actual talents a person has be used to help each student reach full potential? These types of questions are often answered through the application of attribution theory. Attribution theory originated as a subsection of the theories of personality. Personality psychologists were working to describe what makes individuals unique by identifying the relatively unchanging aspects of people that make them unique individuals. However, there were many different approaches to the questions. Some psychologists focused on identifying and describing personality characteristics that define mental illness and poor social adjustment (i.e., abnormal psychology). Others chose to focus on identifying and describing the personality characteristics of people viewed as mentally healthy. They wanted to understand, and eventually be able to predict, why life events affect people in different ways. During this period of time, psychologists divided into two camps that differed on whether they believed one's inborn traits are integral in determining personality or whether the key factor is the environment in which one is reared (this argument has often been referred to as the continuing nature/ nurture debate). Almost everyone has come to a realization that there is most likely a mix of the two influences that work together to create uniqueness in individuals, although there is little agreement on how much

of each are contributing to that mix (Ridley, 2003). Attribution theory is one of the theories formulated using an assumption that both inborn traits and one's environment will be reflected in one's personality. It posits that people will inherently work to organize their observations as they try to make meaning of their experiences.

This organizing will necessitate the creation of categories into which the observations can be sorted. The categories will be created and labeled by each person and will be influenced by both personal temperament and life experiences (Weiner, Nierenberg, & Goldstein, 1976). For example, two students might attend the same campus party and, on telling their friends about their weekends, one might describe the party as fun and exciting while the other describes it as out of control and dangerous. The two students attended the same event but, based on their temperaments and past experiences, chose different categories in which to store their memories of the party.

As the theory of attribution was further refined and developed, researchers realized its impact on how people are motivated, moving the theory from ideas about what makes personalities unique to a theory of understanding how a student's self-perceptions intersect with all learning experiences (i.e., social learning theory). More recently, researchers have linked attribution theory to expectancy theory, which has helped them to better explain the role of persistence and resiliency in the learning process.

EXPLAINING BEHAVIOR

Attribution theory says that people will interpret their successes and failures in life in a way that relates to their existing thinking and behavior. It assumes that people try to figure out why they do what they do. The types of explanations people provide to explain their own behaviors can predict how persistent they will be when faced with a difficult task in the future (Weiner, 1985).

Research suggests a student's self-perceptions will strongly influence performance and expectations for success. Self-perceptions also influence the degree of effort a person will choose to put into a difficult or complex task. In most cases, a student will interpret his or her environment in such a way as to maintain homeostasis (i.e., a stable version of one's internalized self-image) (Festinger, 1957). For instance, if a person's self-perception is one of being a poor student, any success will be attributed to factors other than personal ability, whereas a person whose self-perception is one of being a good student will tend to attribute successes to ability (Maatt, Nurmi, & Stattin, 2007).

THE THREE ATTRIBUTES

Most theorists sort out explanations of success or failure using polarities of three attributes that can help define personality:

- Locus of control (Internal/External) - this indicates whether a person attributes successes and failures to personal characteristics and behaviors or external circumstances (Rotter, 1975);
- Stability (Stable/Changeable) - this indicates whether a person believes the causes of success or failure can be easily changed;
- Controllability (Controllable/Not Controllable) - this indicates whether a person believes the behavior or circumstance is something he or she has the power to personally alter or whether that person believes it is out of his/her control (Weiner et al., 1976).

Theorists believe future academic success can be predicted by listening to how a person describes her or his current successes and failures—combining the three attributes listed above with what the student expects to gain from the learning situation (Feather, 1988). These three attributes can be used to help define four constructs associated with learning situations:

- Ability;
- Effort;
- Task difficulty;
- Luck.

LOCUS OF CONTROL

Locus of control is best determined by finding who or what exercises the most control over the factors that lead to a learning outcome. If a student believes personal characteristics or behaviors are primarily affecting the outcome of a situation, the locus of control is internal. Some examples of internal control characteristics include attitude, intelligence, and ability. Some examples of internal control behaviors include class attendance, time spent studying, and quality of

effort put into studying. Hence, internal control factors can be defined as what the student is personally contributing to the learning experience.

If a student believes external factors are primarily affecting the outcome of a learning experience, the locus of control is external. If a student believes luck (good or bad) or classroom politics are primarily affecting the outcome of a learning experience, the locus of control is external. Some examples of statements that attribute the outcome to external control include: "good thing I brought my lucky rabbit's foot"; "the gods are against me"; and "the teacher doesn't like me." Additionally, if a student is completely unable to predict the outcome of a situation, it is considered a situation affected by external control (Rotter).

Locus of control is a very important variable in the attribution equation. Good students who believe luck is guiding their successes do not appear to gain confidence in their own abilities to initiate success. They may not acquire the sense of self-efficacy that is so very important in creating resiliency and persistence in difficult learning situations (Feather). Poor students who believe bad luck is guiding them are not motivated to work at getting a better grasp of the materials that need to be learned. On the converse, good students who attribute success solely to ability and do poorly on a test may have their faith in their abilities challenged, causing them to give up in despair. Research suggests students do better in future learning situations when they attribute poor performance to external controls and credit internal controls for their successes (Rotter).

STABILITY

The idea that ability, effort, task difficulty, and luck are either stable or changeable can be a bit confusing. Task difficulty and ability are identified as stable, however practice and study can increase skills (thereby decreasing task difficulty) because of an increase in ability. Students who are taught to rely on ability (which is an internal, stable factor)—and are also taught that ability can be changed with effort—will develop a healthy resilience that will help motivate them to learn and persist in the face of failure (Rotter). Luck is identified as changeable because general beliefs indicate luck changes at whim. Yet it is common knowledge that one can change one's own luck. It is detrimental for students to believe their success or failure lies purely in luck. These students will have low motivation to develop new learning strategies and will not be able to optimize the learning that can be gleaned from failures (Weiner et al., 1976).

Stability is best described as whether a student believes the causes of the learning outcome can be easily changed. People generally spend a lot of time thinking about past activities and outcomes. For example, if a student fails a major exam he or she may spend considerable time trying to determine what went wrong (this is sometimes referred to as the causative effect) (Darke & Freedman, 1997; Weiner et al., 1976). The student might decide the failure happened because of staying up all night on the Internet and not bothering to study. Or the student might attribute the poor test score to breaking up with a boyfriend/girlfriend just prior to the test. These types of causes are considered changeable because they are circumstances the student would be able to change if that student could convince the teacher to let him or her retest. On the converse, this student might attribute the test failure on an inability to grasp the subject contents despite best efforts at studying because the subject matter was too difficult for the student. Or the student may believe the test was highly subjective and the teacher did not like the student. These types of causes would be considered stable because they would be difficult or impossible to change in order to create success if the student could convince the teacher to give a second chance at the test. Regardless of how the student perceives the learning outcome, he/she is developing expectations for future learning experiences.

CONTROLLABILITY

Controllability indicates whether a person believes the behavior or circumstance can be personally altered should the person choose to alter it. Ability and task difficulty are generally perceived out of the student's purview of control. Luck is seen as partially in and partially out of the person's purview of control. Effort is primarily seen as an action controlled by the individual; however, in the face of failure, a teacher has great potential control a student's efforts.

Following the notion that good teaching will help children link ability to guided effort in the academic arena, some researchers have refined the word effort by renaming it strategic effort. They say a teacher can teach strategic effort by helping a student understand that failures are actually problem-solving situations

for which the student will need to strategize in order to succeed (Clifford, 1984).

EXPECTANCY THEORY

Expectancy theory suggests a student will use past experiences to forecast probabilities for success in a new learning experience. The perceived probability for success will contribute to the future behavior of the student (Mischel, Jeffrey, & Patterson, 1974; Weiner, 1991). If the probability for success is too high or too low, then the student will likely put little time or effort into studying.

Research by Weiner et al., strongly suggests expectancy of success is more closely correlated to stability than to locus of control, meaning that a student's belief that the factors can be changed to alter future outcomes is very important in creating the skill of persistence in students.

Expectancy theory was originated by Lewin (1938) as a theory of motivation. In 1957, Atkinson moved the theory neatly into achievement motivation theory by suggesting that expectancies for success, based on past experiences, drive an individual's future persistence and striving for success. Several psychologists have tested this theory in the real world and have expanded the definition set forth by Atkinson to create a clear, robust theory that provides a model of achievement choices relating to persistence and self-concept in children based on three constructs: expectancies for success, beliefs about ability or competence, and subjective task values (Feather; Wigfield, Tonks, & Eccles, 2004).

Expectancy is a very important piece of the attribution equation when trying to predict outcomes in learning situations. It describes how the previous experiences will contribute to determining how hard a student will be willing to work to master the material. When a student perceives two situations to be similar, outcome expectancies will tend to be generally the same. Experiences in other similar situations will influence what the student perceives as a potential outcome of the new situation, influencing the amount or quality of effort the student will be willing to contribute to the learning situation. The more similar the situation, the more specific will be the expectancies developed by the student. Also, the more experience the student has in similar learning situations, the stronger and more specific will be the expectancies of the student (Wigfield et al., 2004).

It is important to create learning situations in which students in younger grades can experience success. These students are developing expectancies that will be carried with them throughout their academic experience. Teachers can take care to create expectancies that align with what the children value in the school experience (e.g., belonging, love of learning, etc.) as they create a psychological atmosphere that will likely stay with the child for the duration of the K-12 experience. Positive early learning experiences that result in outcomes that are tied to a child's efforts and abilities will provide children the opportunity to develop perceptions and expectancies that will lead to academic success. If a child has developed an expectancy of failure (i.e., learned helplessness), it is important for teachers to take time and effort to alter the student's causal perceptions so that the child will be motivated to alter behaviors in or to create opportunities for future success (Weiner, 1991). It is equally important to create learning situations in which new college-age students can experience success and develop the skills needed to maintain resilience in difficult situations; this may come in handy during graduate school and during life in general.

APPLICATIONS

Effort does not mean asking the student to continue to try without providing the guidance and skills necessary to succeed. It involves devoting effective academic learning time to the task rather than just trying harder or spending more time doing what led to failure in the first place. Effective teachers provide guidance to their students, allowing the students to learn from failure while providing avenues in which the students can learn or improve the required skill set that can lead to success (Clifford). Telling a student who lacks the requisite ability to generally "try harder" or that the student did not "try hard enough" will only frustrate that student; he or she will think the teacher is accusing him or her of laziness when, in reality, that student may have worked very hard while lacking the requisite skills or study strategies to succeed. The situation will not motivate the student to succeed nor will it cultivate academic resilience in the student. It is important to understand that instructing a struggling student to generally try harder implies control for effort is in the student's purview when the guided effort provided by the teacher may be the only venue that will allow the student to succeed.

Additionally, allowing a student to fail repeatedly while making adequate efforts will discourage the student from making any serious efforts to succeed; the student will stop believing in his or her personal ability and will stop believing the failure is tied to lack of effort. Skilled teachers provide opportunities for success in between occasions of failure. This helps build resilience in students by helping establish a sense of personal ability in each student coupled with a knowledge that guided effort can lead to task mastery (Wigfield et al., 2004). Students with high ratings of self-esteem and high ratings of academic achievement tend to rate their successes as internal, stable, and uncontrollable while rating their failures as external, changeable, and controllable. Additionally, they tend to report an expectation for success (Weiner, 2000). Students who are high achievers are not reluctant to approach learning tasks. When faced with failure, they often conclude bad luck or a poor exam was the reason. However, it is fallacious to allow children to believe ability is the sole contributor to success or failure because they will often be intimidated by failure and quit prematurely, not realizing that a little practice or a little more effort would have resulted in task mastery. On the converse, low achievers do not even use success positively. They attribute their success to luck or some other external factor, avoiding the personal responsibility of bringing success to their assignments and thus divorcing themselves from the notion that they can succeed. Educators of young children can encourage success and lifelong learning commitments in students by helping them cultivate the belief that effort is personally initiated and will result in success. Children will acquire the skills needed to maintain persistence in challenging academic tasks if they can be taught to attribute their successes to effort and ability and their failures to lack of effort or bad luck (Feather).

IMPLEMENTING ATTRIBUTION THEORY IN THE CLASSROOM

How can teachers/professors construct a robust learning environment in which the students are motivated to succeed using the precepts of attribution theory? Here are a few ideas:

ACADEMIC DIVERSITY

K-12 teachers can diversify the learning experience by providing opportunities for students to enjoy successes relative to their own abilities. Successes optimally based on measures of each student's past performance will build confidence and a sense of self-efficacy in each student. Creating academic diversity can be a challenge—but it can be achieved. It might entail encouraging some students to complete a research paper describing democracy while other students are completing a research paper contextualizing Stalin's life, leadership, and eventual demise. It might include providing math problems at different levels of complexity for students of differing abilities. All students will need to work through achievable challenges (i.e., not too easy and not too hard) if they are to develop an internal locus of control for classroom success.

CONTINUED APPROVAL

Another important task that both teachers and professors can engage in to promote long-term resilience and self-efficacy is that of providing high levels of approval to encourage the development of an expectancy of achievement in each student. Provide encouragement and compliments when a student does well and attribute the student's success to internal control factors. When a student does poorly, identify some external factors that may have interfered with the student's ability to succeed, being careful to verbally identify the successes that may be interlaced with the poor performance (Lobel & Bempechat, 1993; Weiner, 1985).

Here is an example of the power of creating positive expectancies in a young student: A third grade student came bouncing out of the classroom to read to a parent volunteer. The volunteer remembered the child (from kindergarten) as one who had struggled with learning to read. She pulled out the lower-level readers as the boy sat down to read with her. The student smiled up at the volunteer and reminded her that she had volunteered in his class during kindergarten. Then he said, "I was the best reader in that class!" The volunteer smiled to herself and asked, "Wow, how did you know that?" The boy said, "My mom told me every day!" The subsequent reading session was a delight as the boy demonstrated his now excellent reading ability. Good educators (and parents) never underestimate the power of their words on students.

REGULATE CLASSROOM COMPETITION

Take care with how competition in the classroom is utilized. Classroom competitions tend to reinforce a sense of ability in high-ability students while diminishing a sense of ability in low-ability students. Competitions can lead to a sense of despair and lack of motivation in children who are constantly and publicly bested by their peers or it can be utilized in ways that alert students to what skills or knowledge sets they need to improve. Using general classroom competition sparely while encouraging students to improve their knowledge and skills based on their own performances can work to encourage students to strengthen their belief in internal controls for success while also allowing them to understand their own performances relative to the general class.

TERMS & CONCEPTS

Abnormal Psychology: The branch of psychology that studies the symptoms, causes, prevention, treatment, and complications of mental and emotional disorders (i.e., neuroses, psychoses, and developmental disabilities).

Construct: An abstract concept that has been made concrete by using testing or observable behaviors for the purposes of research (e.g., a psychologist may make intelligence concrete by measuring it via test scores, a student's class performance, or an assessment by a teacher).

Expectancy Theory: A commonly accepted theory that explains how people choose between alternative behaviors. Motivational force is believed to be the driving factor in decision making and the strength of that force can be calculated by multiplying expected outcome by performance expectations by value attached to the outcome. If any of the three variables is given a weight of zero, there will be no motivation to perform.

Homeostasis: A stable balance: equilibrium. A tendency to try to maintain balance between interdependent elements. People will work to balance personal beliefs with lived experiences, which may sometimes include ignoring or altering parts of the experiences that might create imbalance in the belief system.

Learned Helplessness: Individuals who are subject to negative experiences in which they believe they have no control over the outcome will eventually stop taking any action to avoid the adverse outcome. Students who expect to fail and believe control of the outcome is not in their hands will typically give up trying and passively suffer the adverse consequences.

Nature/Nurture Debate: Debates among members of the schools of psychology and philosophy over the relative importance of an individual's innate qualities (i.e., nature) versus personal experiences (i.e., nurture) in determining individual differences in how people behave. Studies grounded in genetic research suggest many key human traits should be, at least, partially attributed to innate qualities possessed by the individual.

Polarities: A term that, when defined, encompasses opposite direction or contrasted properties. For example, the opposite polarities included in the term "temperature" would be hot and cold.

Resiliency: The ability to keep going during very hard times without being overwhelmed or acting in dysfunctional or harmful ways.

Self-Efficacy: A person's beliefs regarding whether one has the power to create change with personal actions.

Sherry Thompson

BIBLIOGRAPHY

Abramson, L. Y., Seligman, M. E., & Teasdale, J. D. (1978). Learned helplessness in humans; Critique and reformulation. Journal of Abnormal Psychology, 87, 49-74.

Atkinson, J. W. (1957). Motivational determinants of risk-taking behavior. Psychological Review, 64, 359-372.

Bandura, A. (1994). Self-efficacy. In V. S. Ramachaudran (Ed.), Encyclopedia of Human Behavior 4, pp. 71-81. New York: Academic Press.

Carless, S., & Waterworth, R. (2012). The importance of ability and effort in recruiters' hirability decisions: An empirical examination of attribution theory. Australian Psychologist, 47, 232-237. Retrieved December 11, 2013, from EBSCO Online Database Education Research Complete.

Clifford, M. M. (1984). Thoughts on a theory of constructive failure. Educational Psychologist, 19, 108-120.

Darke P. R. & Freedman, J. L. (1997). The belief in good luck scale. Journal of Research in Personality, 31, 486-511.

Demetriou, C. (2011). The attribution theory of learning and advising students on academic probation. NACADA Journal, 31, 16-21. Retrieved December 11, 2013, from EBSCO Online Database Education Research Complete.

Feather, N. T. (1988). Added Values, valences, and course enrollment: Testing the role of personal values within an expectancy valence framework. Journal of Educational Psychology, 80, 381-391.

Festinger, L. (1957). A Theory of Cognitive Dissonance. Stanford, CA: Stanford University Press.

Lewin, K. (1938). The conceptual representation and measurement of psychological forces. Durham, NC: Duke University Press.

Lobel, T. E. & Bempechat, J. (1993). Children's need for approval and achievement motivation: An interactional approach. European Journal of Personality, 7, 37-46.

Maatt, S., Nurmi, J. & Stattin, H. (2007). Achievement orientations, school adjustment, and well-being: A longitudinal study. Journal of Research on Adolescence, 17, 789-812. Retrieved November 24, 2007, from EBSCO Online Database Education Research Complete.

Mischel, W., Jeffery, K. M., & Patterson, C. J. (1974). The layman's use of trait and behavioral information to predict behavior. Journal of Research in Personality, 8, 231-242.

Ridley, M. (2003) Nature Via Nurture: Genes, Experience, and What Makes us Human. Harper Collins.

Rotter, J. B. (1975). Some problems and misconceptions related to the construct of internal versus external control of reinforcement. Journal of Consulting and Clinical Psychology, 43, 56-67. Retrieved November 24, 2007, from EBSCO Online Database Education Research Complete.

Rotter, J. B. (1966). Generalized expectancies for internal versus external control of reinforcement. Psychological Monograph, 80, 1-28.

Webster's New World College Dictionary, 4th edition. (2001).

Weiner, B. (2000). Intrapersonal and interpersonal theories of motivation from an attributional perspective. Educational Psychology Review, 12, 1-14. Retrieved November 24, 2007, from EBSCO Online Database Education Research Complete.

Weiner, B. (1991). Metaphors in motivation and attribution. American Psychologist, 46, 921-930.

Weiner, B. (1985). An attributional theory of achievement motivation and emotion. Psychological Review, 92, 548-573.

Weiner, B. Nierenberg, R., & Goldstein, M. (1976), Social learning (locus of control) versus attributional (causal stability) interpretations of expectancy of success. Journal of Personality, 44, 52-48. Retrieved November 24, 2007, from EBSCO Online Database Education Research Complete.

Wigfield, A., Tonks, S. & Eccles, J. S. (2004). Expectancy - value theory in cross-cultural perspective. In D. McInerney & S. Van Etten (Eds.), Research on Sociocultural Influences on Motivation and Learning volume 4: Big Theories Revisited. Greenwich, CT: Information Age Press.

Wintle, W. D. (1965). The man who thinks he can. In H. Felleman (Ed.), Poems That Live Forever. New York, NY: Doubleday.

Yui-Chung Chan, J., Keegan, J. P., Ditchman, N., Gonzalez, R., Xi Zheng, L., & Fong, C. (2011). Stigmatizing attributions and vocational rehabilitation outcomes of people with disabilities. Rehabilitation Research, Policy & Education, 25 (3/4), 135-148. Retrieved December 11, 2013, from EBSCO Online Database Education Research Complete.

SUGGESTED READING

Borkowski, J. G., Schneider, W., & Pressley, M. (1989). The challenges of teaching good information processing to learning disabled students. International Journal of Disability, Development and Education, 36, 169-185.

Hsien, P. H. (2005). How college students explain their grades in a foreign language course: The interrelationship of attributions, self-efficacy, language learning, beliefs, and achievement. Dissertation Abstracts International Section A, 65 (10-A).

Jones, E. E., Kannouse, H. H., Kelley, R. E., Nisbett, S. V., & Weiner, B. (Eds.). (1972). Attribution: Perceiving the Causes of Behavior. Morristown, NJ: General Learning Press.

Peterson, S., & Schreiber, J. (2012). Personal and interpersonal motivation for group projects: Replications of an attributional analysis. Educational Psychology Review, 24, 287-311. Retrieved December 11, 2013, from EBSCO Online Database Education Research Complete.

Woodcock, S., & Vialle, W. (2011). Are we exacerbating students' learning disabilities? An investigation of preservice teachers' attributions of the educational outcomes of students with learning disabilities. Annals of Dyslexia, 61, 223-241. Retrieved December 11, 2013, from EBSCO Online Database Education Research Complete.

BEHAVIORISM

Behaviorists define learning as a change in behavior brought about by the environment; some deny the existence of internal mental events altogether, while others concede that mental events might exist, but that they cannot and should not be studied. Behaviorism spans decades, and many individuals have made significant contributions to its development. Two key individuals in the field, Ivan Pavlov and B. F. Skinner, developed classical and operant conditioning theories, which can be applied to education. While behaviorism contributed greatly to our understanding of human learning, most now believe it is insufficient for explaining more complex behavior. Thus, behaviorism has largely been supplanted by cognitive theories of learning, which focus on the very thing behaviorists were accused of ignoring—the mind.

KEYWORDS: Classical conditioning; Extinction; Operant conditioning; Pavlov, Ivan; Punishment; Reinforcement; Response; Shaping; Skinner, B.F.; Stimulus; Watson, John

OVERVIEW

Although many people associate behaviorism with the work of B. F. Skinner, it was John B. Watson who coined the term and who first introduced behaviorist principles into mainstream American psychology. Around the turn of the twentieth century, people began putting their faith in science as the way forward to a better future (Harzem, 2004). Watson shared in this optimism and suggested that psychology—like the natural sciences such as physics and biology—should become a science as well. In order to do so, he argued, psychologists should study only that which is observable and turn away from the study of consciousness and methodologies such as introspection. In a paper published in 1913 called "Psychology as the Behaviorist Views It," Watson wrote:

Psychology as the behaviorist views it is a purely objective experimental branch of natural science. Its theoretical goal is the prediction and control of behavior. Introspection forms no essential part of its methods. The behaviorist, in his efforts to get a unitary scheme of animal response, recognizes no dividing line between man and brute (as cited in Harzem).

The end of the story is well known. By denying the existence of mental events—Watson even denied the existence of the mind itself—behaviorists left themselves exposed to attack. And inevitably, the 1970s ushered in a new era of psychology—often called the cognitive revolution—whose subject of study was exactly that which the behaviorists had ignored—unobservable mental events, or what behaviorists refer to as 'the black box.' Behaviorism wasn't necessarily wrong in any fundamental sense, cognitive psychologists argued, but it was incapable of explaining complex human behavior. Thus, behaviorism was edged out of the spotlight, but its principles still hold sway, and its impact continues to be far-reaching. As Harzem wrote, "now behaviorism is like a cube of sugar dissolved in tea; it has no major, distinct existence but it is everywhere. It is an essential ingredient of scientific-psychological thought, whether psychologists wish it to be or not."

CLASSICAL CONDITIONING

Ivan Pavlov, a Russian physiologist, outlined one of the two major principles of learning that characterize behaviorism. His research was designed to uncover the neural mechanisms associated with digestion; while conducting his experiments, however, he noticed that his subjects, dogs, began salivating not just in response to the food, but also in response to other environmental cues, such as the lab attendants who brought the food. As Mazur (1994) writes, "Pavlov recognized the significance of this unexpected result, and he spent the rest of his life studying this phenomenon, which is now known as classical conditioning."

Pavlov began with what he called a neutral stimulus (NS)—in this particular case, a bell. When presented with the ringing of the bell, the dogs did, virtually, nothing. Pavlov then paired the ringing of the bell with the presentation of the food; he referred to the food as the unconditioned stimulus (UCS) because it elicited an unconditioned response (UCR), salivation. After several pairings of the bell and food, Pavlov then presented the ringing of the bell alone, at which time the dogs began salivating. The bell became a conditioned stimulus (CS), the salivation in response to the bell, a conditioned response (CR). This type of learning is also referred to as signal learning, because it is most effective when the conditioned stimulus is presented just before the unconditioned stimulus (Ormrod, 1990). It has been replicated in humans and animals alike with a variety of reflexive responses, such as blinking, galvanic skin response, taste-aversions, and drug tolerance.

Although the formula for classical conditioning is relatively simple, a number of corollary explanations of behavior evolved from it. Psychologists began to investigate how a conditioned response could be extinguished, why certain conditioned responses occurred in the presence of some stimuli and not others, and how classical conditioning could be applied in real-world settings.

EXTINCTION

Psychologists discovered that the passage of time has little effect on the strength of a conditioned response. That is, if a day, or week, or year passed before a dog were presented with the conditioned stimulus (the bell) again, the dog would still salivate at its sound (Mazur). What then, they wondered, would cause a subject to unlearn such a response? Through a process called extinction—the presentation of the conditioned stimulus without the unconditioned stimulus, or in this case, the bell without the food—the conditioned response gradually disappears.

SPONTANEOUS RECOVERY

The question then arises, is the dog whose conditioned response has been extinguished the same as a dog who was never conditioned in the first place? That is, is the association between the conditioned and unconditioned stimulus permanently erased through extinction? A phenomenon known as spontaneous recovery suggests the association remains intact, although weakened. Dogs who were conditioned on Day 1, for example, and extinguished on Day 2, displayed the conditioned response again on Day 3 even though the conditioned response had been fully extinguished on the previous day. Psychologists disagree about what causes spontaneous recovery, but the phenomenon itself has been well documented (Mazur).

RAPID REACQUISITION

Rapid reacquisition also suggests that the process of extinction does not return an organism to its preconditioned state. Dogs who learn to associate the ringing of the bell with the presentation of food, and whose conditioned response is then extinguished, will relearn the pairing of the two stimuli during a second phase of acquisition much more quickly than they learned it during the first phase.

STIMULUS GENERALIZATION

Organisms will sometimes display a conditioned response when presented with a stimulus that is similar to, but not exactly the same as, the original conditioned stimulus. Such a phenomenon is known as stimulus generalization. Pavlov's dogs, for example, might salivate at the sound of a second bell that rings at a different but similar frequency as the first bell.

STIMULUS DISCRIMINATION

On the other hand, organisms can be explicitly taught to discriminate between two stimuli. If Pavlov repeatedly paired a low-pitched bell with the presentation of the food, but did not pair a higher-pitched bell with the presentation of the food, the dogs would learn to salivate at the sound of the first but not the second.

HIGHER-ORDER CONDITIONING

In some cases, a stimulus that is never directly paired with the unconditioned stimulus can elicit the unconditioned response. For example, after dogs learned the association between the bell and food, Pavlov then began pairing the bell with a light flash, in the absence of the food. Dogs soon began salivating in response to the light flash alone, which they learned to associate with the bell, which they had previously learned to associate with food.

COUNTERCONDITIONING

Extinction is sometimes not a reliable way to extinguish conditioned responses (Ormrod). The rate at which extinction occurs is often unpredictable, and finding opportunities to present the conditioned stimulus without the unconditioned stimulus is often difficult. As a result, psychologists suggest that counterconditioning may be a more effective may to change behavior. In the classic case of Little Peter (Ormrod), a young boy somehow learned to be afraid of rabbits. By giving Peter candy at the same time he was in the presence of a rabbit, the conditioned response elicited by the candy—pleasure—began to replace the conditioned response elicited by the rabbit—fear. Since pleasure and fear are incompatible responses, Peter could not experience both at once; gradually, his fear of rabbits disappeared.

OPERANT CONDITIONING

Classical conditioning is just one of two theories of learning that characterize behaviorism. The second, known as operant conditioning, was developed by B. F. Skinner in the 1940s. Although both Pavlov and Skinner are considered behaviorists, they disagreed with one another. An editorial review of a talk given

by Skinner at the dinner of the Pavlovian Society in 1966, for example, states that "although very gracious, polite and deferential, Skinner implied that Pavlov was actually riding the wrong horse when he suggested that conditional reflexes could serve as a window to learned behavior. Skinner, of course, held to the unique power of the operant theory" (Skinner, 1996).

How does operant conditioning differ from classical conditioning? Simply defined, operant conditioning states that a response followed by a reinforcer is strengthened and therefore more likely to occur (Ormrod). The first distinction then addresses the order of presentation of the stimulus; in classical conditioning the reinforcing stimulus *precedes* the response and therefore is often called an antecedent stimulus, whereas in operant conditioning the reinforcing stimulus *follows* the response and is thus called a consequent stimulus. Second, classical conditioning emphasizes the association between two stimuli—the unconditioned and conditioned stimuli—whereas operant conditioning emphasizes the association between a stimulus and a behavior, or response. Finally, the response itself differs, in that the response elicited in classical conditioning is typically an involuntary response—such as salivation or an eye-blink—whereas the response exhibited in operant conditioning is a voluntary one. In other words, the organism has control over whether or not the behavior occurs, and the term "operant reflects the fact that the organism voluntarily operates on the environment" (Ormrod).

Operant conditioning typically is most effective when certain conditions are met: the reinforcement follows the response; the reinforcement occurs immediately after the response; and the reinforcement is contingent upon the response (Ormrod). This is not to say, however, that Skinner ignored what occurs before the response, or rather, the context in which it occurs. He argued, in fact, that a response typically occurs in the presence of a discriminative stimulus, such that the relationship between stimulus-response-reinforcement became a three-term contingency (Mazur). While these conditions provide the basic structure for operant conditioning, a number of corollary principles emerge, many of which have their counterparts in classical conditioning (Mazur). Extinction, spontaneous recovery, and generalization, for example, occur in operant conditioning just as they do in classical. The following provides a brief summary of a sampling of these corollary principles, as well as a review of different schedules of reinforcement.

FREE OPERANT LEVEL

In the operant conditioning paradigm, behaviors (responses) are voluntary. The frequency at which an organism displays a behavior even in the absence of a reinforcement is referred to as the free operant level. In other words, it is the baseline frequency of a behavior before it is reinforced.

EXTINCTION

In classical conditioning, extinction occurs by presenting the conditioned stimulus without the unconditioned stimulus. In operant conditioning, behavior is extinguished when a response is no longer followed by a reinforcer. A response that is not reinforced will decrease and then eventually return to its baseline rate. However, organisms sometimes exhibit spontaneous recovery of the extinguished response, even in the absence of reinforcement, just as they do in classical conditioning.

SHAPING

One of the central tenets of operant conditioning is that learning, or behavior change, occurs gradually. In order to explain the acquisition of more complex behavior, Skinner offered the notion of shaping. In shaping, or what is also known as successive approximations, the process begins by reinforcing the first behavior that in any way resembles the desired behavior; once the organism emits the first behavior with regularity, only behaviors that more closely resemble the desired behavior are reinforced, until finally, the desired behavior itself is being reinforced (Crain, 2000; Mazur).

SUPERSTITIOUS BEHAVIOR

When reinforcement is applied randomly, an organism will increase the behavior that occurs immediately beforehand. In an experiment with pigeons, Skinner presented reinforcement at regular intervals, regardless of the responses occurring at the time. Several hours later, each pigeon displayed a strange behavior they thought had been reinforced, such as thrusting the head into the corner of the cage or swinging their bodies back and forth (Ormrod). In other words, superstitious behavior occurs when

an organism thinks a response and reinforcement are related when in reality they are not.

TYPES OF REINFORCEMENT

Skinner makes distinctions between different types of reinforcement, describing some as primary—those that satisfy a biological need like food, water, and shelter—and others as secondary—because of their association with other reinforcers—such as money, grades, or recognition from one's peers. Reinforcement is also either positive or negative; positive reinforcement occurs when a stimulus is presented after a response occurs, thereby increasing the frequency of the response. Negative reinforcement, on the other hand, increases the frequency of the response through the removal of a stimulus, usually an aversive or unpleasant one.

PUNISHMENT

In contrast to negative reinforcement, which increases the response it follows, punishment is likely to decrease a response. There are two types of punishment—type I and type II. Type I involves the presentation of an aversive stimulus, whereas type II involves the removal of a pleasant stimulus.

SCHEDULES OF REINFORCEMENT

The consistency with which a reinforcement is applied impacts its effectiveness. A reinforcement might be applied continuously—for example, after each occurrence of the behavior—in which case learning takes place rapidly but is easier to extinguish. Reinforcement can also be applied intermittently, according to either ratio, interval, or differential schedules. Ratio schedules of reinforcement occur after a certain number of responses have been emitted, either a fixed amount or a variable amount of responses. Interval schedules of reinforcement occur when a response is emitted after a certain period of time has elapsed, either a fixed interval of time or a variable interval of time. Finally, a differential schedule of reinforcement is a combination of ratio and interval schedules—reinforcement occurs after a particular number of responses occur within a particular amount of time.

APPLICATIONS

Although the descriptions of classical and operant conditioning may seem abstract, both have many practical and concrete applications in real-world settings, and in the classroom as well. As Skinner himself wrote,

> An application to education was inevitable, but it has not been unopposed. The fact that much of the early work involved the behavior of lower animals such as rats and pigeons has often been held against it. But man is an animal, although an extraordinarily complex one, and shares many basic behavioral processes with other species.

Some of these applications, focusing more heavily on the work of Skinner and his theory of operant conditioning, are as follows:

CLASSROOM CLIMATE

As Ormrod argues, classical conditioning demonstrates the importance of creating a positive and comfortable learning environment. "When schoolwork, or a teacher, or even the school environment itself is associated with punishment, humiliation, failure, or frustration, school and its curriculum can become sources of excessive anxiety." Experiences of failure, while worthwhile and instructive, should be balanced, perhaps more heavily, by experiences of success.

A study published in 2011 examined the link between classroom emotional climate and student conduct, including as a mediator the role of teacher affiliation (that is, students' perceptions of their relationships with their teachers). The authors found a direct, positive relationship between classroom emotional climate and conduct that also was mediated by teacher affiliation. Effects were robust across grade level and student gender (Brackett, Reyes, Rivers, Elbertson, & Salovey, 2011).

Skinner too was concerned about the classroom environment; writing during a time when punishment was no longer in vogue, he nonetheless wrote "simply to abandon punishment and allow students to do as they please is to abandon the goals of education." Simply telling students about the long-term value of getting an education, or relying on innate curiosity, he argued, was futile; "all these measures fail because they do not give the student adequate reasons for studying and learning. Punishment gave him a reason, but if we are to avoid unwanted by-products, we must find non-punitive forms." Skinner's solution was to use positive reinforcement—to reward student's for studying and learning. The following are examples of non-punitive reinforcement in the classroom.

PROGRAMMED INSTRUCTION

Skinner believed that traditional education was ineffective largely because of the delay between response and reinforcement; a student might take a test on Monday, but not receive a grade—the reinforcement—until Friday. As a way to remedy the situation, Skinner developed programmed instruction, which evolved from the teaching machine and has now been applied to textbooks and computers. Regardless of its form, however, programmed instruction has several common elements: the material is presented in discrete units, students are active responders, students receive immediate feedback, and individual differences in learning rates are accounted for. The earliest teaching machines presented information in frames, with the first frame presenting a small unit of information, the second frame posing a question about the information on the first frame, and then presenting a second bit of information, and so on. With computers, programmed instruction or computer assisted instruction has become more complex, allowing for branching and more sophisticated display of information; it has been shown to be more effective in terms of student achievement and motivation than traditional teaching methods (Ormrod). This type of software-based instruction is now referred to as educational technology (Molenda, 2012).

BEHAVIOR MODIFICATION

Behavior modification is a powerful tool for shaping the behavior of both individuals and groups. While traditionally used to shape appropriate classroom behavior such as speaking out of turn or fighting with classmates, it can also be applied to behaviors that relate more directly to learning such as study habits or attention to task. Behavior modification plans typically include the following elements: defining the present and desired behaviors in measurable and observable terms; finding effective reinforcers; developing an intervention plan; measurement of the behavior before and during treatment; monitoring and making modifications to the treatment plan as necessary; and ultimately phasing out of the treatment (Ormrod). Behavior modification in groups is often implemented via group contingency plans; that is, the entire class has to perform the desired behavior—the identification of all fifty states, for example—for the reinforcement to occur. Token economies are also used with groups of students. When using token economies, a teacher selects several responses that will be reinforced—sitting quietly at one's desk, raising one's hand before speaking, etc. When a student exhibits such behavior, she is rewarded immediately with a token such as play money. At a later time, the tokens can be redeemed for various reinforcers, such as toys, snacks, or extra recess time.

In behavior modification based on classical conditioning, students can be thought of as blank slates that can be "molded towards a desired result through exposure to strategic stimuli" (Lineros & Hinojosa, 2012). Unconditioned behaviors such as desiring freedom or privacy can be used to create new conditioned behaviors such as listening attentively or changing seats (Lineros & Hinojosa).

BEHAVIORAL OBJECTIVES

The impact of behaviorism on the practice of teaching and learning is perhaps most evident with respect to the emphasis on goals and objectives. Behavioral objectives are specific statements about what behavior, which is both observable and measurable, that a student is to exhibit as a result of receiving instruction. As Skinner argued, "To say that a program is to 'impart knowledge', 'train rational powers', or 'make students creative' is not to identify the changes which are actually to be brought about. Something more specific is needed." Behavioral objectives, he argued, makes teaching more effective, straightforward, and rewarding. "When goals are properly specified, the teacher knows what he is to do and later, whether he has done it. Behavioral objectives remove much of the mystery from education."

VIEWPOINTS

Behaviorism, even as it was the preeminent theory of learning in psychology and education, also generated a great deal of controversy. While much of the criticism simply reflected differences of opinion about human learning, much of it also stemmed from misunderstandings and inaccuracies. As Wyatt (2005) argued, misrepresentations of Skinner and other behaviorists are frequent; he cited just one example of a "well-known author, writing in a well-known source" who mistakenly concludes that Skinner viewed all organisms as blank slates upon which the environment and experience would write. "How unfortunate it is that [the author] has evidently not read enough of Skinner to know that Skinner frequently wrote about the genetic contributions to

behavior" (Wyatt). Similarly, Crain corrected those who suggested that Skinner denied the existence of an internal world of thoughts and feelings. While some behaviorists certainly did make such proclamations—Watson to name just one—Skinner simply argued they had no place in scientific psychology.

Even if critics have exaggerated or misrepresented behaviorists with respect to their views on the 'black box'—unobservable mental events—it is also true that the 'black box' itself has increasingly become the subject of psychologists and educators' study. Even some behaviorists have acknowledged the role of internal events; neobehaviorists, for example, are sometimes referred to as S-O-R (stimulus-organism-response) theorists as opposed to S-R theorists, because of the role they attribute to the mind (Ormrod). Nevertheless, behaviorist theories of learning—whether neobehaviorist or not—have largely been supplanted by cognitive theories of learning. The contribution of behaviorism to our understanding of human learning is immense, but as cognitive theorists would argue, also incomplete.

TERMS AND CONCEPTS

Classical Conditioning: First introduced by Pavlov, classical conditioning is one of two learning paradigms that characterize behaviorism. In the classical conditioning model, an unconditioned stimulus (UCS) elicits an unconditioned response (UCR). A neutral stimulus is then paired the UCS; after repeated pairing with the UCS, the neutral stimulus becomes a conditioned stimulus (CS) which elicits a conditioned response. The conditioned response is similar to, although not exactly the same as, the unconditioned response. The most famous example of classical conditioning is the salivation of Pavlov's dogs at the sound of a bell which had been repeatedly paired with presentation of food.

Extinction: Both operant and classical conditioning suggest that previously reinforced behavior can be extinguished. In classical conditioning, extinction occurs when the conditioned stimulus is presented repeatedly in the absence of the unconditioned stimulus; in operant conditioning, extinction occurs when a response is no longer reinforced.

Operant Conditioning: First introduced by Skinner, operant conditioning if one of two learning paradigms that characterize behaviorism. According to the operant conditioning paradigm, responses that are reinforced will increase in frequency. Operant conditioning differs from classical conditioning in that the reinforcing stimulus occurs *after* the response, and the response itself is a voluntary one.

Reinforcement: In operant conditioning, reinforcers are presented after a response occurs and increase the frequency of the response. Reinforcers are either positive or negative; positive reinforcers involve the presentation of a *positive* stimulus after a behavior—for example, food or praise. Negative reinforcers involved the removal of an *aversive* stimulus following a behavior—such as a teacher's disapproving glare.

Punishment: Whereas reinforcers typically increase the frequency of a response, punishment descreases the responses it follows. Punishment occurs in two forms. Type I punishment involves the presentation of an aversive stimulus—such as a scolding—whereas type II involves the removal of a positive stimulus—such as taking away recess privileges.

Response: Behaviorism defines learning as a change in behavior; in both classical and operant conditioning, a behavior is typically referred to as a response. In classical conditioning, learning involves changes in involuntary responses; in operant conditioning learning involves changes in voluntary responses.

Shaping: In order to explain the acquisition of more complex human behaviors, behaviorists proposed the idea of shaping. In shaping, behaviors that become increasingly more like the desired behavior are reinforced gradually. The first behavior that is reinforced only slightly resembles the desired behavior; after the organism exhibits this behavior consistently, only behaviors that more closely resemble the desired behavior are reinforced, and so forth.

Stimulus: In both the classical and operant conditioning paradigms, behaviorists refer to environmental cues that result in behavior change as stimuli. In classical conditioning, the pairing of two stimuli—the conditioned and unconditioned stimuli—elicits a response. In operant conditioning, a reinforcing stimulus follows a response, and therefore increases its frequency.

Jennifer Kretchmar

BIBLIOGRAPHY

Brackett, M. A., Reyes, M., Rivers, S. E., Elbertson, N. A., & Salovey, P. (2011). Classroom emotional climate, teacher affiliation, and student conduct. *Journal of Classroom Interaction, 46,* 27–36. Retrieved from EBSCO Online Database Education Research Complete.

Crain, W. (2000). *Theories of development: Concepts and applications.* Upper Saddle River, NJ: Prentice Hall.

Harzem, P. (2004). Behaviorism for new psychology: What was wrong with behaviorism and what is wrong with it now. *Behavior and Philosophy, 32,* 5–12. Retrieved from EBSCO Online Database Academic Search Premier.

Lineros, J., & Hinojosa, M. (2012). Theories of learning and student development. *National Forum of Teacher Education Journal, 22,* 1–5. Retrieved from EBSCO Online Database Education Research Complete.

Mazur, J. (1994). *Learning and behavior* (3rd ed.). Englewood Cliffs, NJ: Prentice-Hall, Inc.

Molenda, M. (2012). Individualized instruction: A recurrent theme. *TechTrends: Linking Research & Practice to Improve Learning, 56,* 12–14. Retrieved from EBSCO Online Database Education Research Complete.

Ormrod, J. (1990). *Human Learning: Theories, principles, and educational applications.* Columbus, OH: Merrill Publishing Company.

Phelps, B. (2015). Behavioral perspectives on personality and self. *Psychological Record, 65*(3), 557–565. Retrieved from EBSCO Online Database Education Research Complete.

Skinner, B.F. (1996/1966). Some responses to the stimulus 'Pavlov'. *Integrative Physiological and Behavioral Science, 31,* 1–4. Retrieved from EBSCO Online Database Academic Search Premier.

Skinner, B. F. (1969). Contingency management in the classroom. *Education, 90,* 93–101. Retrieved from EBSCO Online Database Academic Search Premier.

Virues-Ortega, J., & Pear, J. (2015). A history of 'behavior' and 'mind': Use of behavioral and cognitive terms in the 20th century. *Psychological Record, 65*(1), 23–30. Retrieved from EBSCO Online Database Education Research Complete.

Wyatt, W. J. (2005). Misrepresentations of Skinner continue. *Behavioral Analysis Digest, 17,* 8. Retrieved from EBSCO Online Database Academic Search Premier.

SUGGESTED READING

Pigot-Upshall, T. (2017). How standardization and behaviorism foster inequality in public education: A comparative experience. *One World,* 4 (1), 11-19.

Skinner, B. F. (1948). *Walden Two.* New York, NY: Macmillan Publishers.

Skinner, B. F. (1985). Cognitive science and behaviorism. *British Journal of Psychology, 76*, 291–301. Retrieved from EBSCO Online Database Academic Search Premier.

Skinner, B. F. (1972). *Beyond freedom and dignity.* New York, NY: Bantam Vintage Publishers.

Staddon, John. (2014). *The new behaviorism.* 2nd ed. New York: Psychology Press.

Todd, J. T., & Morris, E. K. (Eds.). (1995). *Modern perspectives on B.F. Skinner and contemporary behaviorism.* Westport, CT: Greenwood Press.

Uttel, W. R. (2000). *The war between mentalism and behaviorism.* Mahwah, NJ: Lawrence Erlbaum Associates, Publishers.

COGNITIVE DISSONANCE THEORY

First proposed by Leon Festinger in the late 1950s, cognitive dissonance theory was a relatively simple and straightforward explanation of how human beings deal with inconsistency. The first empirical validation of the theory, however, inadvertently called into question one of the central tenets of behaviorism, the predominant paradigm in psychology at the time. Controversy ensued, and a flurry of research on dissonance soon followed. Several decades and thousands of publications later, cognitive dissonance has evolved into something quite different.

KEYWORDS: Attitudes; Aversive Consequences; Cognitions; Consonant Cognitions; Dissonance; Festinger, Leon; Foreseeable Consequences; Free Choice; Self-Affirmation Theory; Self-Consistency Theory; Self-Perception Theory

OVERVIEW

Cognitive dissonance theory was first proposed by Leon Festinger—a psychology professor at Stanford University—in the late 1950s. Part of the original appeal of the theory was its simplicity and parsimony; it seemed to provide a relatively straightforward and commonsense framework for explaining how human beings deal with inconsistency in thought and action. Very quickly, however, the theory stirred up a "proverbial hornet's nest of controversy" by unintentionally discrediting a central tenet of behaviorism, the predominant paradigm in psychology at the time (Cooper, 2007). The controversy, Cooper argues, propelled the theory forward; today, over one thousand studies have been published on cognitive dissonance theory, and the theory itself has evolved into something much different.

Further Insights

FESTINGER'S THEORY

What Festinger observed, and what became the central premise of his entire theory, was the simple fact that human beings like consistency. Furthermore, human beings strive to reduce inconsistency; that is, people are motivated to *do something* in order to eliminate the feelings of discomfort that result from what he called 'nonfitting relations among cognitions" (Festinger, 1957). Comparing dissonance to hunger, Festinger wrote, "cognitive dissonance can be seen as an antecedent condition which leads to activity oriented toward dissonance reduction just as hunger leads to activity oriented toward hunger reduction." He summarized his basic hypotheses as follows:

- The existence of dissonance, being psychologically uncomfortable, will motivate the person to try to reduce the dissonance and achieve consonance;

- When dissonance is present, in addition to trying to reduce it, the person will actively avoid situations and information which would likely increase the dissonance (Festinger).

COGNITIONS

Festinger's theory helped move the study of social psychology forward by introducing the concept of cognitions. Defined as "any knowledge, opinion, or belief about the environment, about oneself, or about one's behavior" (Festinger), cognitions allowed researchers to easily compare psychological phenomena—attitudes, behavior, opinions, and observations—which had previously been studied in isolation. When two cognitions are opposed to one another, or when "the obverse of one…would follow from the other," dissonance occurs. Festinger used the following as one example of dissonance; an individual may have a cognition representing a belief about smoking—it is bad for her health. This same person, however, continues to smoke. Thus, her cognition about her behavior is at odds with her cognition about her beliefs about smoking. As a result, the individual experiences dissonance.

MAGNITUDE OF DISSONANCE

Festinger introduced a second concept—the *magnitude* of dissonance—that further distinguished his theory from other 'inconsistency' theories. More specifically, he recognized that not all dissonance would be experienced equally. The magnitude of discomfort, he theorized, would depend on the importance of the cognitions (Festinger). A person who believes in animal rights, for example, but who fails to stop to help an injured animal might experience a great deal of dissonance; a person who eats a donut for breakfast, knowing that he is violating the diet he is unmotivated to maintain, might experience less. In addition to the importance of a particular set of cognitions, Festinger suggested magnitude could also be impacted by other relevant cognitions. If the person who ate a donut for breakfast, for example, ate only fruits and vegetables the day before, and also planned to exercise the day he consumed the donut, then these relevant consonant cognitions might help offset dissonance.

REDUCING DISSONANCE

The above example suggests one way in which dissonance might be reduced, but Festinger's original theory suggested several methods, some used more frequently than others. If dissonance occurs between knowledge about the environment and one's behavior, for example, an individual may change her behavior in order to reduce dissonance. If the donut eating exerciser planned to run outside, but a thunderstorm looms overhead, he might decide to run inside instead. Another way in which dissonance can be reduced is by changing one's environment. In many cases this is the most difficult way to reduce dissonance – the runner can hardly expect to stop the thunderstorm, for example—but this is sometimes a viable option in social environments as opposed to physical ones (Festinger). Dissonance can also be reduced by adding new cognitions that are consonant with the knowledge or behavior an individual

hopes to maintain; the dieter, for example, might seek out research which suggests a diet high in fat is good for one's health, and avoid all research which suggests otherwise. He might also reason that there are many worse things he could do for his health, such as smoking or drinking; such consonant cognitions help reduce the dissonance he experienced as a result of eating an unhealthy breakfast.

Relationship infidelity was studied as a dissonance-arousing behavior as well, and Foster and Misra (2013) found that perpetrators of infidelity respond in ways that reduce cognitive dissonance, such as through trivialization of the importance of the infidelity.

Just as changing the environment is often not a reasonable way in which to reduce dissonance, Festinger also recognized that behavior is often resistant to change. The behavior itself may be satisfying, or changing a particular behavior may result in pain or loss. As a result, the cognitions that most often change are the ones related to attitudes, beliefs, and opinions. As Cooper writes, "In general, it is difficult to change cognition about one's behavior. Therefore, when behavior is discrepant from attitudes, the dissonance caused thereby is usually reduced by changing one's attitude. The resistance to change of the behavioral cognition is what makes dissonance theory seem to be a theory of attitude change."

CONTEXT OF DISSONANCE

Finally, Festinger's original theory also addressed the context and/or environments in which dissonance might occur. Specifically, he suggested that dissonance occurs as the result of almost any decision a person might make in daily life. Decisions often involve making choices between two attractive alternatives, between two alternatives that have both pros and cons, or between multiple alternatives, so that regardless of the end result, "dissonance is an almost inevitable consequence of any decision" (Festinger). A person shopping for a car, for example, will recognize advantages and disadvantages to any choice she might make; one car may be more expensive, another uses less gas, a third might enhance her image. When faced with attractive alternatives, "the end result would be that having made the decision, and taken the consequent action, one would begin to alter the cognition so that alternatives which had previously been nearly equally attractive ceased to be so" (Festinger).

Although Festinger's theory addressed the dissonance that results from everyday decision-making, his theory is arguably best known for its explanation of dissonance resulting from forced compliance. When an individual is forced to behave publicly, or make a public proclamation, that runs counter to his or her privately held beliefs, dissonance will result. How will individuals resolve dissonance in such situations? Festinger hypothesized that it would depend on the magnitude of the dissonance, as well as the magnitude of the punishment (for noncompliance) or reward (for compliance), but that a change in attitude would likely occur. He explained, "the empirical question, of course, arises as to how one can identify and distinguish public compliance without private [attitude] change from instances where private opinion is also altered" (Festinger).

TESTING THE HYPOTHESIS

An empirical test of his hypothesis is exactly what Festinger, along with his colleague J. Merrill Carlsmith, pursued next. Students were asked to participate in an intentionally tedious and boring peg turning task, and believed they were being evaluated on their performance. After they had completed the task, they were told that they had been assigned to the control condition; if they had been in the experimental group, they would have been confronted by a confederate in the waiting room, who would have told them how much fun they were about to have turning pegs. The researcher then announced that his confederate had failed to show up yesterday, and asked the student if she would be willing to play the role. Half of the students were given $1 to play the confederate role, the other half twenty dollars. Almost all students agreed to play the role. They would now experience dissonance by saying something—the peg turning task was fun—that was counter to their experience—the peg turning task as they experienced it was dull and repetitious. After the students made their public proclamations, their attitudes toward the peg turning task were reassessed.

What exactly did Festinger and Carlsmith (1959) predict? And what were the results? According to Cooper, "Festinger and Carlsmith made a prediction that seemed less than obvious in terms of everyday wisdom but which followed logically from the theory of cognitive dissonance. They predicted that the speech given for a small amount of money would produce

more favorable attitudes toward the task than the speech given for the large amount of money." And indeed, this is exactly what they found. The large reward helped reduce the dissonance (by providing a consonant cognition), but those who received only $1 weren't able to explain away their inconsistency as easily. As a result, they reduced their dissonance by changing their attitude toward the task, so that it was more in line with the behavior they exhibited as a confederate. And herein is where the controversy arose; Festinger had just demonstrated that smaller rewards lead to greater change, which flew in the face of behaviorism, whose central tenet was that "organisms learn by reward and punishment. The greater the reward, the greater the learning" (Cooper).

EVOLUTION OF THE THEORY

Festinger never set out to challenge behavioral learning theory, and in fact, never directly addressed it when discussing his results. Nonetheless, upon publication of the above study, behaviorists set out to find alternative explanations for Festinger's findings. The challenges, Cooper argues, helped the theory evolve into what it has become today. The following section will briefly outline this evolution, drawing largely from Cooper's 50-year retrospective of the theory. The evolution can be categorized according to three major challenges and/or shifts:

- The search for mediating effects;
- Validation of dissonance as an experience not an inference;
- The introduction of the role of the self.

Viewpoints

THE SEARCH FOR MEDIATING EFFECTS

Rosenberg (1965, as cited in Cooper) launched the first counterattack on dissonance theory, arguing that the counterintuitive relationship between reward and attitude change demonstrated in Festinger's classic study resulted from subject-researcher interactions, rather than the relative drive to reduce dissonance. Specifically, Rosenberg hypothesized that students viewed the $20 reward as a bribe, especially because the amount of money was disproportionate to the nature of the task. Students then assumed the researcher was studying how they might react to a bribe, and therefore intentionally set out to prove "I can't be bought." Those who had been paid the larger amount, therefore, changed their attitudes less. Rosenberg needed to show that by eliminating what he called 'evaluation apprehension' students would be free to change their opinions in direct relation to the magnitude of the reward.

Rosenberg devised an experiment in which students were asked to write a counter-attitudinal essay for either a large or small amount of money. Students believed they were actually participating in two separate experiments; after writing the essay, they proceeded to the next experiment and were asked their opinions on a variety of issues, including the issue about which they had just written. As Cooper explains, Rosenberg "had the attitudes [assessed] by a completely different experimenter who was in a different room doing a different study. In this way, subjects would not feel that they were having their honesty and integrity assessed by the [original] experimenter and would not hold back their true opinion." The results supported Rosenberg's hypothesis: those given the larger reward for writing the counter-attitudinal essay changed their attitudes more than students given the smaller reward. Rosenberg had, or so it seemed, successfully discredited Festinger's theory.

THE FREE CHOICE FACTOR

Others, however, weren't quite so sure. Although Rosenberg had attempted to replicate Festinger's original study, changing only the manner in which post-experiment attitudes were assessed, he had inadvertently changed a second important variable. In Festinger's original study, students were given *a choice* about whether they wanted to play the confederate role. They could say yes or no, without consequence. In Rosenberg's study, however, students were not given a choice. They were told to write an essay they did not believe. Why might choice be an important variable relative to dissonance? Cooper explains "If I were *required* to write the essay, then that requirement serves as an important cognition consonant with my behavior. That cognition might have been powerful enough to eliminate all dissonance." In order to test this hypothesis, Linder, Cooper, and Jones (1967, as cited in Cooper) conducted an experiment, similar in design to the classic study, except that students were assigned two different conditions—low choice and high choice. They predicted only students in the high choice condition would experience dissonance, and only then would the magnitude of the reward

play a role in reduction of dissonance. The results supported their prediction, proving that "behavior that is at variance with attitudes causes dissonance, but only under conditions of high-decision freedom. In the absence of freedom, there is no dissonance" (Cooper, 2007).

Rosenberg's study, and Linder, et al's response, is an example of the way in which controversy and disagreement spurred the theory forward. As a result of the 'conversation' between theorists with opposing viewpoints, the role of an important caveat—the condition of free choice—was discovered. In the decades that followed, research would uncover a number of other important caveats, or what Cooper refers to as the "but only's." Dissonance occurs, *but only* under certain circumstances. In addition to the condition of free choice, research demonstrated that dissonance occurs, but only when people are committed to their behavior, only when the behavior leads to aversive consequences, and only when those consequences are foreseeable.

A NEW DISSONANCE THEORY EMERGES

A number of creative studies demonstrated these caveats. With respect to foreseeable consequences, for example, researchers asked students to write essays favoring an unwanted campus policy; half of the students were told their essays would be forwarded to the campus advisory committee, the other half were told their essays *might* be forwarded. After writing the essay, all students were then told that none of their essays would be forwarded. For those students who were told their essay might be forwarded, the good news eliminated their dissonance, and they demonstrated little attitude change in post assessments. For those who were told their essays would be forwarded, and for whom this outcome was not foreseeable, dissonance was not eliminated. "The unforeseeable nature of the good consequence did not allow these participants to be free of their dissonance and the need to change their attitudes" (Cooper).

The results of such studies were enough for Fazio and Cooper (1984, as cited in Cooper) to put forth an alternative theory altogether, rather than amend Festinger's original proposal with corollaries liked those described above. According to the new theory, "dissonance does not occur because of inconsistency per se, and attitude change is not in the service of restoring consistency. Rather, attitude change occurs to render the consequences of behavior non-aversive" (Cooper). In other words, dissonance results from our perceptions of unwanted and aversive consequences, not from inconsistency. It is important to note that such a theory represents a radical departure from Festinger's original theory. The new proposal, however, has generated some controversy of its own. Harmon-Jones (1999) writes, for example, "the present evidence convincingly demonstrates that dissonance effects can be generated by a cognitive discrepancy that does not produce aversive consequences. Indeed, the results suggest that the original version of the theory was abandoned prematurely" (Harmon-Jones).

VALIDATING DISSONANCE AS AN EXPERIENCE

Rosenberg's research precipitated a series of challenges and amendments to the original version of cognitive dissonance theory. So too did the work of Bem (Cooper). Citing the central tenets of his self-perception theory, Bem challenged the entire notion of cognitive dissonance, and argued that the results of Festinger's study could be explained more simply via the notion of inference. Just as we infer attitudes and opinions of other people from their behavior, so too do individuals infer their own attitudes and opinions from their own behavior. In other words, people don't always have direct access to their own thoughts, but rather scan their past behavior in order to infer their own beliefs. Thus, students in the original study would remember they had received twenty dollars to publicly express an opinion they didn't believe; the money would be enough to explain their behavior, thus requiring no change in attitude. Bem's theory was more parsimonious, in that it did not rely on internal states of arousal and the subsequent drive to reduce them. "It simply needed to invoke an inference process—the very same process that people use to infer the attitudes and characteristics of others" (Cooper).

Because Bem & Festinger explained the same results in different ways, it was initially difficult to determine which theory might provide the better explanation of the results. Zanna and Cooper (1974, as cited in Cooper) designed the first set of studies—called misattribution studies—to answer this question. Once again, the researchers replicated Festinger's classic study, except that one group of students was given a pill and told it would produce side-effects, such as arousal and tension, and others

were given a pill and told they would experience no side-effects. They then participated in the same attitude-discrepant experiment—duping their classmates into believing the peg-turning task would be fun—and were later assessed on their attitudes toward the task. Zanna and Cooper hypothesized that those who took the pill and believed it would produce arousal would experience little dissonance; they would simply attribute the unpleasant arousal to the pill, and therefore have no need to change their attitudes. Those who were not given an external stimulus upon which to misattribute their arousal would experience dissonance and change their attitudes. The results confirmed their hypotheses, providing support for Festinger's original notion that dissonance is *experienced*, not just inferred. (Cooper).

THE INTRODUCTION OF THE ROLE OF THE SELF

As the role of the self became increasingly prominent in social psychology, cognitive dissonance theory experienced yet another evolution. Self-affirmation theory and self-consistency theory have both been used to reexamine the phenomenon of cognitive dissonance. According to self-affirmation theory, "we are motivated to see ourselves as good and honest people and any evidence to the contrary will upset our equilibrium. People will distort their cognitions about themselves in the service of protecting their self-system" (Cooper). Importantly, self-affirmation theory proposes that threats to the self-system can be corrected in a variety of ways, not just by correcting the specific wrong. In a classic 1975 study of self-affirmation theory, Steele and colleagues (as cited in Cooper) showed that women whose sense of self was threatened—researchers told them their neighbors thought they were unhelpful—could restore their integrity by volunteering for a charity. Surprisingly however, women who were told they were bad drivers could also restore their sense of integrity/self by volunteering for a charity. "As Steele commented, it's the war, not the battle, that has to be won. If a specific, attitude-discrepant behavior threatens the self-system, the repair can be made at either the local or general level. If need be, the attitudes compromised by a particular behavior can be left intact, and the individual can find a way to bask in the glory of his or her other achievements" (Cooper).

Self-consistency theory shares many similarities with self-affirmation theory. Both say dissonance is significantly related to threats to the self-system and both believe most people generally have a healthy self-esteem. Self-consistency theory differs, however, in an important way; it suggests that people have *expectations* about how they should behave, and that when they fail to behave in line with expectations, inconsistency and dissonance results. If individuals with low self-esteem act in accordance with expectations (e.g., a person believes she isn't smart and acts accordingly), for example, then no dissonance will result. In the end, those with high self-esteem change their attitudes more than those with low self-esteem.

Self-affirmation theory, however, predicts the opposite. Because self-esteem acts as a global support system, if a student feels he has threatened his sense of self by lying to his classmate, he can look for other ways to affirm himself. Those with high esteem will find alternative ways quickly, experience less dissonance, and therefore, exhibit less attitude change.

Although the two theories appeared to contradict one another, Stone and Cooper (2001, as cited in Cooper) thought otherwise. They looked for ways in which the self plays a role in dissonance, and under what conditions it serves as a resource, an expectation, or both. They believed the missing piece of the puzzle could be found by analyzing the standards one uses to judge his or her behavior—recognizing that people typically use either normative standards, comparing themselves to a larger group, or personal standards, comparing themselves to their own standards. They discovered that when people rely on normative standards to evaluate their behavior, self-esteem does not play a role; when people rely on personal standards, however, self-esteem does matter. Although self-esteem plays a role when people rely on personal standards, Cooper concludes that individuals are more likely to use normative ones.

Conclusion

COGNITIVE DISSONANCE THEORY TODAY

Cognitive dissonance theory has traveled a long way since the late 1950s, but continues to evolve even to this day. In past research, "rarely has the person experiencing dissonance been conceived as a member of the group. Rather…virtually all dissonance research has focused on the individual acting alone (Cooper & Stone, 2000). In a laboratory test of group impact, Zanna and Sande (1987, as cited in Cooper & Stone) asked students to write counter-attitudinal essays, but asked some students to write a *group* essay, and others to write individual essays. Even though students in the group condition believed they had developed a more convincing essay, they experienced less dissonance, and therefore less attitude change, than those in the alone condition. "Apparently, the ability to diffuse responsibility to the rest of the group" mediated the experience of dissonance. Finally, researchers have also used dissonance theory to study social identity; recognizing that attitude change is not always a viable way to reduce dissonance when one's social identity is threatened, researchers have uncovered two alternative processes—increased hostility toward the out-group and repression. If a democrat makes a statement that threatens his identity as a liberal, for example, he may be unable to reduce dissonance by changing his political affiliation and becoming pro-republican. He must reduce the arousal, however, and does so by displacing it onto the already unattractive out-group; thus, he becomes even more hostile toward republicans. Alternatively, people may choose to repress behavior that threatens their identity; if the same democrat voted for Bush in the last election, he may choose to selectively forget how he voted in 2004, thereby eliminating dissonance that might result.

In its application to education, Pedder and Opfer (2013) studied patterns of cognitive dissonance and alignment between teachers' values and practices with regard to professional development, and made the discovery that only a minority of teachers are engaged learners. There is a "prevailing individualist approach to learning among the majority of teachers. And there are important between- and within-school differences in the mix of teachers' learning orientations." Consequently, the authors recommended "differentiated forms of support for promoting effective professional learning in schools" (Pedder & Opfer).

Walton (2011) studied and offered suggestions for applying cognitive dissonance to student instruction. He asked, "How might cognitive dissonance nurture, rather than constrain, meaningful reflection on alternative experiences, narratives, and social differences?" Among his conclusions were that critical educators should strive to help their students make personally relevant connections between new and previous learning experiences, and that educators might consider engaging students in critical conversations on topics and problems that are of particular importance to them, thus allowing more relevant and varied opportunities for disequilibrium to occur (Walton).

TERMS & CONCEPTS

Cognitions: Defined as "any knowledge, opinion, or belief about the environment, about oneself, or about one's behavior" (Festinger), cognitions allowed researchers to easily compare psychological phenomena—attitudes, behavior, opinions, and observations—which had previously been studied in isolation. According to the original theory, two inconsistent cognitions give rise to dissonance.

Consonant Cognitions: Festinger hypothesized that dissonance can be reduced in several ways—by changing one's behavior, by changing the environment, or by adding cognitions that are consistent with the belief or behavior one hopes to maintain. The latter are referred to as consonant cognitions.

Dissonance: Festinger defined dissonance as an uncomfortable psychological state resulting from inconsistency, or "non-fitting relations among cognitions." He compared dissonance to hunger, arguing that when either occurs, humans are motivated to reduce or eliminate such feelings.

Foreseeable Consequences: As research on dissonance progressed, investigators realized certain conditions were necessary for dissonance to occur. One such condition is the existence of foreseeable (and aversive) consequences. Only if an individual can foresee the negative consequences her 'inconsistent' actions might bring about, will dissonance occur.

Free Choice: As research on dissonance progressed, investigators realized certain conditions were necessary for dissonance to occur. One such condition is the existence of free choice. If individuals are forced to do or say something that contradicts their opinions or beliefs, the coercion itself eliminates dissonance.

Self-Affirmation Theory: In the latest evolution of dissonance research, investigators have become increasingly interested in the role of the self. Self-affirmation theory suggests that individuals like to see themselves as good and honest people; individuals are motivated to protect their self-system in the face of information that suggests otherwise. Importantly, self-affirmation theory proposes

that threats to the self-system can be corrected in a variety of ways, not just by correcting the specific wrong. Thus, global self-esteem helps protect the individual from dissonance.

Self-Consistency Theory: In the latest evolution of dissonance research, investigators have become increasingly interested in the role of the self. Self-consistency theory differs, however, in an important way; it suggests that people have *expectations* about how they should behave, and that when they fail to behave in line with expectations, inconsistency and dissonance results. Self-esteem helps buffer against dissonance, but only when people act according to expectations.

Self-Perception Theory: Self-perception theory provided one of the initial challenges to cognitive dissonance theory. Bem hypothesized that people were inferring their beliefs and opinions from past behavior, just as they infer the attitudes of others through observation. Only the process of inference, not the condition of arousal or uncomfortable psychological states, was needed to explain Festinger's data. Later research confirming physiological arousal validated Festinger's theory.

Jennifer Kretchmar

BIBLIOGRAPHY

Cooper, J., & Stone, J. (2000). Cognitive dissonance and the social group. In D. J. Terry & M.A. Hogg (Eds.), *Attitudes, behavior, and social context: The role of norms and group membership.* (pp. 227-244). Mahwah, New Jersey: Lawrence Erlbaum Associates, Publishers.

Cooper, J. (2007). *Cognitive dissonance: A fifty-year retrospective of a classic theory.* Thousand Oaks, California: Sage Publications.

Festinger, L. (1957). *A theory of cognitive dissonance.* Evanston, Illinois: Row, Peterson, and Company.

Foster, J.D., & Misra, T.A. (2013). It did not mean anything (about me): Cognitive dissonance theory and the cognitive and affective consequences of romantic infidelity. *Journal of Social & Personal Relationships, 30,* 835–857. Retrieved December 14, 2013, from EBSCO Online Database Education Research Complete.

Harmon-Jones, E. (1999). Toward an understanding of the motivation underlying dissonance effects: Is the production of aversive consequences necessary? In E. Harmon-Jones and J. Mills (Eds.), *Cognitive dissonance: Progress on a pivotal theory in social psychology.* (pp. 71-102). Washington, D.C.: American Psychological Association.

Pedder, D., & Opfer, V. (2013). Professional learning orientations: patterns of dissonance and alignment between teachers' values and practices. *Research Papers in Education, 28*, 539–570. Retrieved December 14, 2013, from EBSCO Online Database Education Research Complete.

Walton, J.D. (2011). Dissonance in the critical classroom: The role of social psychological processes in learner resistance. *College Student Journal, 45*, 769–785. Retrieved December 14, 2013, from EBSCO Online Database Education Research Complete.

SUGGESTED READING

Harmon-Jones, E., & Mills, J. (Eds.). (1999). *Cognitive dissonance: Progress on a pivotal theory in social psychology.* Washington, D.C.: American Psychological Association.

Mook, D. (2004). *Classic experiments in psychology.* Westport, CT: Greenwood Press.

Wicklund, R.A., & Brehm, J.W. (1976). *Perspectives on cognitive dissonance.* New York, NY: Lawrence Erlbaum Associates, Publishers.

COGNITIVE THEORIES

This article presents an overview of cognitive theories of learning. As a field, cognitive psychology gained popularity in the late twentieth century as educators and researchers became increasingly dissatisfied with behaviorism. Whereas behaviorists believed learning could be explained through manipulation of the environment alone, cognitive psychologists believed what was happening inside the mind was equally, if not more, important. Although the cognitive approach to learning has dominated the educational scene for the last several decades—and has been strengthened by advances in cognitive neuroscience—it is not without its critics. Constructivists, in particular, criticize cognitive psychologists for downplaying the interaction between the learner and the environment, and for ignoring socio-cultural, historical, and political influences on the construction of knowledge.

Centuries ago, philosophers grappled with the same questions psychologists and educators are asking today: How do we learn? What do we know? In philosophy, those who study the nature and origins of knowledge are called epistemologists, and from the beginning, epistemologists have had very different ideas about learning (Schunk, 2004). The rationalists believe that ideas are innate and people gain knowledge through reason and thought alone. Empiricists, on the other hand, believe that ideas cannot exist independently of our experience of the external world, and that knowledge arises through sensory impressions. Plato, Descartes, and Kant were rationalists, while Aristotle, Locke, and Hume subscribed to an empiricist point of view.

Modern theories of learning are grounded in philosophy, and while the distinctions between empiricism and rationalism have become blurred over time, advocates of behavioral and cognitive theories of learning can trace their origins, in large part, to one or the other (Schunk). Behaviorists tend to be empiricists, while cognitive theorists tend to be rationalists.

From the early part of the twentieth century until the mid-1970s, behaviorist theories of learning dominated the educational scene in the United States. Behaviorists believe that learning occurs as a result of external events—and while they acknowledge the existence of internal events such as thoughts, feelings, and beliefs—they argue that learning could be explained without them. For behaviorists, controlling the environment by arranging the appropriate stimuli, and then reinforcing the subsequent response, is more important than individual differences in learning styles, motivation, or the role of memory in learning. Even though many scientists laid the foundation for the behaviorist tradition—Thorndike, Pavlov, and Watson, to name a few—B. F. Skinner and his theory of operant conditioning are most often associated with behaviorism.

New theories often evolve because of perceived shortcomings in prevailing theories, and indeed, many educators and researchers became increasingly frustrated with behaviorism's inability to account for the complexity of human behavior and thought. The introduction of the computer—which gave psychologists a viable metaphor for studying the way humans process information—coupled with this frustration, paved the way for the cognitive revolution. While no single event marked the beginning of this revolution, the work of several individuals helped define the shift (Bruner, Schraw, & Ronning, 1999). In 1957, Noam

Chomsky repudiated Skinner's theory that language acquisition could be explained using the theory of operant conditioning; in 1956, G. A. Miller published an article describing the limits of our ability to process information; and in 1967, Ulrich Neisser published Cognitive Psychology, providing definition and structure for a growing field.

Early theories of cognition fell victim to some of the same pitfalls as behaviorist theories—mainly, the attempt to develop a single theory, or a single law, that would explain all human behavior and learning (Gredler, 1997). Once cognitive psychologists recognized the futility of this search, they began studying a multitude of different mental processes, including but not limited to memory, perception, attention, language development, motivation, and problem solving. Even though cognitive psychology addresses many different aspects of mental functioning, the field is held together by certain shared assumptions. The core assumptions outlined below are drawn from Bruning et al. (1999), Gredler, and Schunk.

- Cognitive theorists believe that what happens inside the mind—the mental processing of information—is an important part of learning;
- Cognitive theorists view humans as active learners; what students do with information once they receive it determines how much they learn;
- Cognitive theorists believe that student attitudes, motivation, and beliefs can impact the learning process;
- Cognitive theorists believe students can self-regulate their learning through awareness of their thinking and management of learning strategies;
- Cognitive theorists believe the meaningfulness of knowledge determines how well it can be applied in new situations;
- Cognitive theorists emphasize the importance of social interaction and context in the learning process.

FURTHER INSIGHTS

Gestalt Psychology: Gestalt psychology is one of the earliest theories of cognitive psychology. Founded by Germans Max Wertheimer, Kurt Koffka, and Wolfgang Kohler at the beginning of the twentieth century, gestalt psychology provided the first significant challenge to behaviorism. Concerned mainly with issues of perception, gestalt psychologists study the structure and organization that the mind imposes on sensory experience. Wertheimer recognized that our experience of sensory inputs is different from the inputs themselves—as when two blinking lights create the impression of motion—and concluded that humans are designed to experience meaningful wholes, and not just individual parts.

Gestalt psychologists also made contributions to learning and instruction. Their theory of insight learning posits that humans learn when they experience a state of cognitive disequilibrium, hypothesize possible solutions, and in a moment of insight, act on the appropriate solution. Wertheimer believed learning based on problem solving is much more effective than learning through memorization or rigid rules of logic (Hergenhahn & Olson, 1997).

Piaget: Jean Piaget began his academic career as a Swiss biologist in the early twentieth century, later applied biological principles to the study of intelligence, and became a world-wide authority in child development in the late 1960s. Like gestalt psychologists, Piaget believed that the human mind imposes structure and organization on experience. Unlike gestalt psychologists, however, Piaget did not believe these structures are innate, but rather develop as the individual matures (Hergenhahn & Olson). Piaget referred to these mental structures as schema. Information that matches existing schema, he argued, can be assimilated, but information that contradicts existing knowledge has to be accommodated. According to his theory, the process of accommodation results in intellectual growth. Piaget also defined four stages of mental development: sensor-motor, preoperational, concrete operations, and formal operations. Each stage identifies the intellectual abilities typically demonstrated by children of a particular age.

Because Piaget's theory is not a true theory of learning, nor easily translated into instructional practices, it was often misapplied when first introduced (Gredler). Since that time, however, it has significantly impacted educational practices. For example, Piaget was particularly interested in the development of operational thinking in science and math. He advised teachers to develop curricula by first identifying the intuitive beliefs held by their students, creating experiments that contradict their beliefs and result in cognitive dissonance, and then designing exercises that allow them to resolve the dissonance.

Gagné's Categories, Conditions & Phases of Learning:

Robert Gagné first became interested in learning and instruction while developing training programs for the military. He is credited with shifting research on learning from the laboratory to real-world settings, and with recognizing that learning is too complex and multifaceted to be explained by one single theory or principle (Gredler). As a result, he developed five different categories of learning: verbal information, intellectual skills, motor skills, attitudes, and cognitive strategies. Each is mutually exclusive, applicable to a variety of tasks, and requires different types of instruction (Gredler). Gagné believed learning results when the learner demonstrates internal readiness and progresses through a series of nine phases. The nine phases address issues of attention, memory storage and retrieval, development of meaningful frameworks, and application of learning to new situations.

While Gagné studied the mental processes involved in learning, he was equally interested in their application to the classroom. He believed the environment—the instructional environment in particular—can facilitate and support cognitive functioning. His principles of instructional design have been applied across of variety of subjects, the development of the elementary curriculum titled Science—A Process Approach being just one example. His model of instructional design includes fourteen separate steps that address, in broad terms, the identification of goals and objectives, the design of instructional events, and the evaluation of both the instruction and students' mastery of objectives (Gredler).

Bruner:

Jerome Bruner founded the Center for Cognitive Studies at Harvard in 1960. He is perhaps most well-known for his cognitive-development approach to curriculum design, the outcome of which was the "spiral curriculum." Bruner believed cognitive development occurs in three stages—enactive, iconic, and symbolic—and that curricula should be developed with the learner's stage in mind. Most important, instruction should be designed so mastery of skills at one stage

of development leads to development of more advanced skills. Bruner is also credited with defining discovery learning, or the acquisition of knowledge for oneself. He described discovery learning as a form of problem solving, emphasizing, however, that problem solving is a directed activity, and not something that happens by chance alone (Schunk).

Discovery learning is not appropriate for all learning situations (Schunk). For example, if students have little prior knowledge of a particular topic, discovery learning may be counterproductive. But discovery learning can be used across disciplines and age groups. A teacher might ask her third grade class to classify animals by examining their similarities and differences, rather than classifying the animals for them. An eleventh grade social studies class might learn about historical figures and events by engaging in role playing rather than watching a video. Assigning group projects in any content area with any age group is an example of having students discover their own knowledge (Schunk).

Information Processing Models:

Information processing models address how information is perceived, how it is understood and made meaningful, and how it is recalled at later points of time. Of all the cognitive approaches to learning, it is the one that relies most heavily on the computer metaphor. Those who approach cognition from this perspective believe learners process information in stages, and that the form of information in each stage differs from the form in other stages (Schunk).

A well-known information processing model—the two-store memory model—is discussed below.

According to this model, perception occurs in the sensory register. Once a stimulus is recognized as meaningful information, it is passed along to working memory, where it is held in our conscious awareness. Relevant information is retrieved from long-term memory and integrated with the new information within working memory. Finally, the integrated information is then stored in long-term memory.

In addition to describing the relationship between stages, information processing researchers have also done extensive research on what occurs within each stage. For example, some suggest information stored in long-term memory is stored in verbal form only, while others argue it can be stored in non-verbal (e.g., images, sounds, etc.) form as well (Gredler). In addition, research has shown that how individuals encode information while it resides in short-term memory impacts how well it will be remembered at a later point in time (Gredler).

Those who study cognition using information processing models have much to contribute to educational practices in the classroom, even if their research has been applied more slowly than some (Schunk). Recognizing that attention to information is an important first step in learning, those teaching elementary students should vary their presentations, use different materials, encourage student participation, and keep lessons short in an effort to maintain student focus (Schunk). High school students may have less difficulty maintaining focus; their teachers should employ strategies to help them make meaningful connections between new information and prior knowledge, as when an art teacher introduces a new unit by reviewing concepts of color, shape, and texture (Schunk).

Metacognition: Metacognition, traditionally defined as thinking about thinking, is a type of complex learning that had been ignored prior to the development of cognitive psychology. Beginning in the late 1970s, researchers began investigating the ways students manage their own learning through their awareness of their own thinking and their ability to apply appropriate learning strategies at the appropriate time (Gredler). Cognitive psychologists distinguish metacognition from subject-matter knowledge, and also identify differences in metacognitive abilities due to age and subject-matter familiarity.

Teachers can help students develop metacognitive skills by asking them to approach a learning task using a variety of different strategies and then asking them to reflect on the effectiveness of each strategy. For example, a teacher might give students a list of items to memorize, teach them different memorization strategies such as visualization, categorization, or the use of acronyms, and then ask them to explain why one technique worked better than another (Schunk).

Motivation: Motivation—the process of setting goals and working to achieve them—is closely related to learning. Motivated students employ different learning strategies, engage in self-directed activities more often, and make more meaningful connections between new and existing information (Schunk). Research on motivation has covered a wide range of topics including but not limited to perceptions of control, self-concept, conceptions of ability, values, and family influences. Research on motivation has many applications to the classroom, including but not limited to the role of teacher feedback, the use of social comparison, designing curricula with appropriate level challenges, and emphasizing the value of knowledge and learning.

VIEWPOINTS

Just as cognitive psychologists have criticized behavioral theories of learning for their inability to explain the complexity of human behavior, so too have cognitive theorists been criticized (Gredler; Schunk). Many researchers believe the computer metaphor is too simplistic, and that cognitive psychologists, while recognizing the importance of interaction and environment, are too focused on the individual learner and his or her mental processes. As a result, a school of thought known as constructivism developed late in the twentieth century. Constructivists emphasize the interplay between learner and situation, the active role the learner plays in the construction of knowledge, and the significance of social, cultural, and historical influences on the construction of disciplines of knowledge. Piaget, while largely a cognitive developmental psychologist, outlined several principles that contributed to the development of constructivism. Even Bruner, who founded the Center for Cognitive Studies, devoted the latter part of his career to the study of the impact of culture on education, criticizing cognitive psychologists for overlooking this critical dimension.

Despite this criticism, it is unlikely that growth in the field of cognitive psychology will slow any time soon. The computer may have been too simple a metaphor for human learning, but technology itself is helping us understand more about the functioning of the human brain. Cognitive neuroscientists are taking advantage of these technologies to study the brain, and as Kellogg (2003) argues, cognitive psychologists are providing them the theory and methods to structure their research. Using techniques such as positron emission tomography (PET), researchers are able to isolate the exact neural activity associated with the mental processes cognitive psychologists have been studying since the latter part of the twentieth century. How this new knowledge will be translated to learning and instruction remains to be seen.

TERMS & CONCEPTS

Behaviorism: A label applied to theories of learning that share the core belief that the environment determines learning. They agree that internal processes such as thought exist, but do not think they are necessary for explaining how humans gain knowledge.

Cognitive neuroscience: A close relative of cognitive psychology; uses technology to study the exact neural activity of the brain associated with particular cognitive functions.

Constructivism: A school of thought that developed as a result of the perceived shortcomings of cognitive theories of learning. Constructivism emphasizes the active role of the learning, the construction of knowledge, and the interaction between learning and environment. Constructivists also acknowledge historical and political influences in the construction of knowledge.

Discovery learning: A type of learning defined by Jerome Bruner in which the learner obtains knowledge for him or herself. Bruner viewed discovery learning as a form of problem solving, but argued that the conditions for problem solving have to be directed by the teacher and environment.

Empiricism: The philosophical belief that knowledge is gained through sensory experience; ideas are not innate and do not exist independently of sensory experience of the external world.

Gagné's categories, conditions, phases of learning: Gagné shifted educational research from the laboratory to real-world settings. He recognized that learning is too complex to be explained by a single theory. As a result, he identified different categories, conditions, and phases of learning.

Gestalt theory: One of the first theories to challenge behaviorism. Gestalt psychologists focus on issues of perception and argue that humans are designed to experience meaningful wholes.

Operant conditioning: Behavioral theory of learning developed by B. F. Skinner, which posits that the likelihood of a behavior occurring again is determined by the consequence that follows it.

Piaget, Jean: Jean Piaget authored a theory of cognitive development in which mental structures are referred to as schema. Information that confirms existing schema is assimilated, whereas information that conflicts with existing schema is accommodated. Accommodation results in cognitive growth. Piaget also outlined four stages of cognitive development.

Rationalism: The philosophical belief that knowledge arises through thought and reason alone; ideas are innate and exist independently of our sensory experience.

Jennifer Kretchmar

BIBLIOGRAPHY

Bruner, J. S. (1966). Toward a theory of instruction. Cambridge, MA: Harvard University Press.

Bruning, R.H., Schraw, G.J., & Ronning, R.R. (1999). Cognitive psychology and instruction (3rd ed.). New Jersey: Prentice Hall, Inc.

Gagné, R.M. (1985). The conditions of learning (4th ed.). New York: Holt, Rinehart, and Winston.

Gredler, M.E. (1997). Learning and instruction: Theory into practice (3rd ed.). New Jersey: Prentice Hall, Inc.

Hergenhahn, B.R., & Olson, M.H. (1997). An introduction to theories of learning (5th ed.) New Jersey: Prentice Hall, Inc.

Kellogg, R.T. (2003). Cognitive psychology (2nd ed.). Thousand Oaks, CA: Sage Publications, Ltd.

Mohammad, G., Ali, G., Zahra, Y., & Saeede, B. (2013). Cognitive strategies instruction: Attitudes toward learning and academic functioning in science. Bulgarian Journal of Science & Education Policy, 7 (1), 104-120. Retrieved December 3, 2013, from EBSCO Online Database Education Research Complete.

Pittman, J. (2013). From theory to assessment: A modern instructional course. Journal of Applied Learning Technology, 3 (2), 26-30. Retrieved December 3, 2013, from EBSCO Online Database Education Research Complete.

Schunk, D.H. (2004). Learning theories: An educational perspective (4th ed.). New Jersey: Prentice Hall, Inc.

Skinner, B.F. (1954). The science of learning and the art of teaching. Harvard Educational Review, 24(2), 86-97.

Swann, W. (2013). The impact of applied cognitive learning Theory on engagement with eLearning courseware.

Journal of Learning Design, 6 (1), 61-74. Retrieved December 3, 2013, from EBSCO Online Database Education Research Complete.

SUGGESTED READING

Balota, D.A., & Marsh, E.J. (Eds.). (2004). Cognitive psychology: Key readings. New York City, NY: Psychology Press.

Baars, B.J. (1986). The cognitive revolution in psychology. New York: Guilford.

Eysenck, M.W. (1993). Principles of cognitive psychology. Hove, United Kingdom: Lawrence Earlbaum Associates, Ltd.

Gardner, K. & Aleksejuniene, J. (2011). Power Point and learning theories: Reaching out to the millennials. *Transformative Dialogues: Teaching and Learning Journal*, 5 (1), 1-11.

Kohler, W. (1929). Gestalt psychology. New York: Horace Liveright.

Paas, F., & Sweller, J. (2012). An evolutionary upgrade of cognitive load theory: Using the human motor system and collaboration to support the learning of complex cognitive tasks. Educational Psychology Review, 24 (1), 27-45. Retrieved December 3, 2013, from EBSCO Online Database Education Research Complete.

Piaget, J., & Inhelder, B. (1969). The psychology of the child (H. Weaver, Trans). New York: Basic Books.

CONSTRUCTIVISM

The following article provides a summary of the theory of learning known as constructivism. Constructivism has received a great deal of recent attention in the educational literature, and as a result, has been defined in multiple ways. So many different definitions currently exist some scholars believe constructivism has been emptied of meaning altogether. The following will attempt to bring some clarity back to the theory by focusing on two different strands of constructivism; cognitive constructivism, as outlined in the work of Jean Piaget, and social constructivism, as outlined in the work of Lev Vygotsky. Implications for teaching are introduced, as well as an example of a constructivist classroom activity. The summary also introduces the larger epistemological debate surrounding constructivism.

KEYWORDS: Accommodation; Adaptation; Assimilation; Cognitive Constructivism; Disequilibrium; Objectivity; Piaget, Jean; Social Constructivism; Vygotsky, Lev; Zone of Proximal Development

OVERVIEW

In recent years, constructivism has become one of the most often cited theories of learning in the educational literature (Null, 2004). Its popularity has achieved such heights that it has been referred to by various scholars as fashionable, faddish, and even by some, as a religion (Prouix, 2006). The frequent discussion of constructivism isn't a problem per se, but it has created some confusion regarding its exact meaning. As Harlow, Cummings, and Aberasturi (2006) acknowledge, "constructivism has taken on as many different definitions as the number of people attempting to define it." As a result, they argue, it has also been "emptied of meaning." Others concur, suggesting that "the educational literature…is littered with [such] a range of definitions" that constructivism has become "almost…indefinable" (Null).

Perhaps more solid ground can be established by first recognizing the philosophical foundations of constructivism. Although a relatively recent development in education, the issues addressed are ones that have been debated for thousands of years. At the core, constructivism is about epistemology, a branch of philosophy that studies the nature of knowledge: what it is that we know, and how we know what we know. Although oversimplified, philosophers have generally fallen into two camps; those who believe knowledge is an approximation of an independent reality—a reality separate from the knower and representative of the ultimate Truth—and those who believe that knowledge is created by human minds. Constructivists fall in the second camp, arguing that knowledge is constructed by individuals through their experience, and is not necessarily representative of 'the real world.'

The notion of knowledge as a construction helps bring some clarity to this elusive concept, as does the recognition of one of its main pioneers. Although constructivism has roots in ancient philosophy, and its ideas have been extended by many modern day learning theorists, Piaget is most often credited with its development. As Prouix states, "Even if many other authors have contributed to numerous aspects of the theory in a tacit or indirect way (e.g., Dewey, Kant, Rousseau, Vico, etc.) the main pioneer of constructivism is without question Jean Piaget." The following summary, therefore, will focus largely on the work of Piaget. In addition, the theoretical work of Vygotsky will be introduced. Vygotsky's social constructivism is often contrasted with Piaget's cognitive constructivism, but the following will focus on the way in which these two strands are complementary.

PIAGET & COGNITIVE CONSTRUCTIVISM

In order to understand the significance of Piaget's contribution, we must first place it within the context of the epistemological debate referenced in the introduction. For the past several centuries, those who believe that knowledge is an approximation of an independent reality representative of the ultimate Truth have held sway in the philosophical courts. For equally as long, however, skeptics have argued that we cannot know the truth of our knowledge, because "we would need access to the world that does not involve our experiencing it" (von Glasersfeld, 1990, as cited in Prouix). Despite what von Glasersfeld calls "logically irrefutable arguments" on the part of the skeptics, they were always summarily dismissed by pointing to the achievements of human knowledge—in ancient times, the prediction of eclipses, for example, and in more recent times, the accomplishments of modern technology. "In the face of such successes," von Glasersfeld (2006) argues, "it would, indeed, be ridiculous to question the validity of knowledge."

What Piaget's theory does, however, is "make it possible to accept the skeptics' logical conclusion without diminishing the obvious value of knowledge" (von Glasersfeld, 1996). More specifically, Piaget introduced the concept of adaptation to epistemology. Having trained first as a biologist, Piaget studied the relationship between mollusks and their environment; the ability to adapt, he concluded, was simply the ability to survive in a given environment. Knowledge, then, is not important to the extent that it represents an external reality, but is important to the extent that it is *viable*. "Simply put, the notion of viability means that an action, operation, conceptual structure, or even a theory, is considered 'viable' as long as it is useful in accomplishing the task or in achieving a goal that one has set for oneself" (von Glasersfeld, 1998, as cited in Prouix). In other words, "truth" is what works.

The question of what knowledge is, from a constructivist perspective, has now been answered to some extent—it is *not* a representation of external reality or objective truth, but rather *is* 'truthful' to the extent it is viable and adaptive—but the exact mechanisms by which knowledge is constructed have not yet been explained. As Harlow et al. argue, those who overuse the term in the literature often ignore the 'how' of constructivism. In other words, educators often pay lip service to the idea that people make meaning, but fail to understand the processes by which this occurs. Even teachers with the best intentions sometimes forget that cognitive conflict, for example, is essential for new knowledge construction. We'll turn to Piaget's concepts of assimilation, accommodation, and disequilibrium for a better understanding of the underlying mechanisms.

According to Piaget, all learning is motivated by a desire to maintain a state of equilibrium (Prouix). When an individual is confronted by information or an experience that contradicts his or her prior knowledge, the learner is motivated to modify or adapt prior knowledge in order to return to equilibrium. Therefore, those things that cause disequilibrium—sometimes referred to a perturbations or cognitive conflicts—play a critical role in the learning process. "It is often through struggling to resolve the disequilibration caused by perturbations that one comes to a resolution that deepens and revises one's worldview" (Prouix). As Fosnot argues, in order to fully understand the concept of equilibration, one should understand its dynamic nature—"it is a dynamic 'dance'…of growth and change'." The dance occurs between two polar tendencies: our tendency to assimilate information and our tendency to accommodate information.

Assimilation occurs when new experiences or information 'fit' into our existing mental structures. Stated differently, "constructivism asserts that our previous experiences serve as the lenses through which we read the world" (Prouix). Therefore, assimilation is largely an unconscious process, one in which we make new experiences fit into what we already know. Accommodation, on the other hand, takes place in the face of perturbations. When new knowledge or experiences contradict what was previously known, the learner must modify her existing cognitive structures, the new knowledge/experience, or both. According to Prouix, "the learner tries to deliberately adapt—or accommodate—what is already known (previous knowledge) to a new experience that interrupts or contradicts established interpretations...." In general, the mind tends to assimilate; only when we have to accommodate does learning occur.

Although the basic structure of Piaget's theory of knowing has been put forth, it's worth noting a few other points of emphasis. First and foremost, for Piaget and other constructivists in general, learning is always an *active* process. Importantly however, 'active' implies both physical and *mental* activity; that is, active in the sense of creating new mental structures and not just active in the sense of physically moving one's body. As Prouix explains, "The word 'active' should then not be read in the literal sense because it has a broader meaning in constructivism. The idea that the learners have to be active does not imply that they have to construct a model physically with their hands, but instead that they develop their structures of knowledge—by reflecting, analyzing, questioning themselves, working on problems, and so on."

Secondly, Piaget's theory highlights the significant role of prior knowledge in the learning process, and the implications this has for teaching as well (Prouix). Students are not blank slates, and everything they experience in a classroom is interpreted in light of what they already know. As a result, teachers should recognize that learners possess knowledge already, and use that source of knowledge to build new understandings. Simply transmitting information to students, as traditional teachers do in a lecture-based classroom, does not acknowledge the learner as either active, or as an individual with pre-established cognitive structures.

As the two previous points imply, constructivists conceive of the classroom as learner-centered as opposed to teacher-centered. Learner-centered does not suggest, however, that students are free to create *any* meaning, to construct *any* knowledge. In other words, constructivists are often charged with promoting relativism, a charge they dismiss with reference to the concept of fit and viability. "Constructivism, with its concept of viability and 'fitting' does not imply that anything goes but merely that theories or explanations construed have to fit and be compatible with experiences lived" (Prouix). In other words, knowledge that is useful is 'more truthful' than knowledge that is not.

LEV VYGOTSKY & SOCIAL CONSTRUCTIVISM

Much of the current literature suggests that different strands of constructivism—mainly, cognitive constructivism as outlined by Piaget and social constructivism as outlined by Vygtosky—are at odds with one another (Cobb, 1996; Fosnot). "Thus there is currently a dispute over whether...learning is primarily a process of active cognitive reorganization or a process of enculturation into a community of practice" (Cobb). Others argue, however, that Piaget recognized the importance of social interaction in learning, even if he focused on it less than Vygotsky (Fosnot). Thus the two theories are complementary more than they are competitive, and learning should be understood as a cognitive *and* a social process, not either-or (Cobb).

Thus, although much of Vygotsky's work overlapped with Piaget's, he did in fact focus more heavily on the role of culture, language and social interaction in the construction of knowledge. Like Piaget, he believed learning to be developmental, but he made a distinction between what he viewed as the construction of spontaneous concepts (also known as pseudoconcepts) and the construction of scientific concepts (Fosnot). Spontaneous concepts, he believed, were developed by children during their everyday activities, in the course of everyday life; these pseudoconcepts were similar to those studied by Piaget. On the other hand, scientific concepts, he suggested, originate in more formal settings—like the classroom—and represent culturally-agreed upon concepts. On their own, children would be unlikely to develop scientific concepts, but with the help of adults and older children, they can master ideas and thought processes that extend their knowledge. The 'space' where children extend their current knowledge with adult assistance has become known as the Zone of Proximal Development.

Vygotsky is undoubtedly best known for the zone of proximal development, but two other concepts are also worthy of mention. Like Piaget, Vygotsky studied the language of preschoolers, but what Piaget concluded was 'egocentric' speech, Vygotsky concluded was social from the very beginning. He argued that inner speech was the mechanism by which "culturally prescribed forms of language and reasoning find their individualized realization" (as cited in Fosnot). Vygotsky also concluded that inner speech plays an important role in the development of spontaneous concepts, and in particular, the attempts by children to *communicate* the concept to others.

Finally, Vygotsky was most interested in the role of other people in the development and learning processes of children. He emphasized the cooperative nature of the learning task to such an extent, for example, that "he viewed tests or school tasks that only looked at the child's individual problem solving as inadequate, arguing instead that the progress in concept formation achieved by the child in cooperation with an adult was a much more viable way to look at the capabilities of learners" (Fosnot). He referred to cooperation as the dialogical nature of learning; others have since extended this idea through the notion of 'scaffolding.' Scaffolding is best exemplified by an infant/mother interaction, during which the mother at times imitates the baby, and other times, varies her response to further develop the child's response (Fosnot).

FURTHER INSIGHTS

One of the important distinctions theorists make about constructivism is that it is a theory of learning—and is even, at times, called a theory of knowing—and is *not* a theory of teaching. As a result, constructivism doesn't tell teachers what they should do, but rather provides a general framework within which they can work with students. As Prouix explains, "It is argued that constructivism brings a proscriptive discourse on teaching, one that sets boundaries in which to work, but does not prescribe teaching actions." von Glasersfeld elaborates, "It means that constructivism…cannot tell teachers very much about what they should do, but it can specify a number of things which they certainly should not do" (as cited in Prouix). Within the realm of what they should do, he further argues, the possibilities are limitless.

Therefore, providing a specific example of constructivist teaching in the classroom might be the best way to introduce its application to the classroom. Before we proceed with the example, however, it might be worthwhile to outline what Prouix refers to as "implications" for teaching (as opposed to directives), as well as some pitfalls to be avoided. For example, constructivist teaching does not suggest that teachers should stop explaining information; while teachers are encouraged to create disequilibrium, or perturbations, for their students, this should not occur at the expense of explanation and elaboration.

As Prouix argues, "constructivism is not saying that teachers should not explain, it only renders problematic the assumption that by 'telling' or explaining the learners will automatically understand." He further suggests that constructivism does not imply students are always right or that students will always learn on their own without guidance from teachers. Finally, he encourages teachers to acknowledge the importance of prior knowledge in the learning process, as well as the role of 'mistakes.' "Mistakes inform the learning process enormously and enable a better understanding of the domain…" Mistakes should not, he continues, be viewed as "humiliating blunders" never "to be repeated again" (Prouix).

Fosnot, in her edited book, "Constructivism: Theory, Perspectives, and Practice," devotes several chapters to examples of constructivist teaching in the classroom. The following example is taken from the chapter on constructivist perspectives in mathematics, and serves as a summary of what is outlined in greater detail by Schifter (1996). Schifter describes a lesson on measurement designed by a first-grade teacher; the teacher uses masking tape to outline the shape of a boat on the classroom floor, and asks her students how they would go about measuring it, in order to report its size to the King. After several days of allowing her students to search for answers, the class decided to report the measurement of the boat in terms of the length of Zeb's (a classmate) foot. The teacher describes:

On the third day of our exploration, I asked the children why they thought it was important to develop a standard form of measurement (or in words understandable to a first grader, measurement that would always be the same size) such as using only 'Zeb's foot' to measure everything. Through the discussions over the past several days, the children were able to internalize and verbalize the need or important for everyone to measure using the same instrument. They saw the confusion of using different hands, bodies, or feet because of the inconsistency of size" (Schifter).

The example highlights several characteristics of constructivist teaching. First and foremost, rather than telling the class exactly how to perform a task (e.g., measurement), the teacher poses it in the form of a problem and allows the class to come to its own solution. In other words, the teacher allowed the students to construct their own meanings. Secondly, the example highlights the importance of perturbations; the teacher's role wasn't necessarily to allay confusion, but even at times to further elicit it. In addition, the example demonstrates the role of social interaction in the learning process; the students made progress toward a solution by building upon each other's responses. And finally, the example emphasizes the role of prior knowledge in learning situations; students drew upon their previous experiences with 'measurement' and, in this case, modified their existing understandings in order to incorporate what they learned through this exercise.

VIEWPOINTS

As stated in the introduction, constructivism is a frequent topic of conversation in the educational literature, and has been defined in multiple ways. Limiting this summary to cognitive and social constructivism does not do justice to the many forms in which it exists. Von Glasersfeld, for example, while drawing heavily on the work of Piaget, has developed his own form of *radical* constructivism. Jerome Bruner (1990) has extended the work of Vygotsky and other social constructivists in focusing on the role of culture in learning. Similarly, this summary has only briefly touched upon the educational and philosophical foundations of constructivism; Null, for example, traces constructivist thought back to Rousseau and G. Stanley Hall. Others have emphasized the contribution of John Dewey.

Despite its popularity, there are many who oppose constructivism and its approach to teaching and learning. Constructivism, after all, addresses questions about knowledge and knowing that have been debated for over two thousand years; the debates are likely to continue. Alexander (2006), for example, discusses the "new skirmishes in the methodology wars," which have recently resurfaced after positivists and constructivists had supposedly agreed to 'peacefully coexist'." Although some (Alexander; Johnson, 2005) propose a middle ground, or what Alexander refers to as "a view from somewhere" that provides a place for both positivists and constructivists, it's likely that educators and philosophers will continue to have differences of opinion.

TERMS & CONCEPTS

Accommodation: According to Piaget's theory of knowing, humans attempt to maintain a state of equilibrium by either assimilating new information and experiences or accommodating them. Accommodation takes place when new information contradicts what was previously known, so that the learner must modify cognitive structures, modify the new information, or both.

Adaptation: Piaget transferred the concept of adaptation from his studies in biology to the studying of human learning. He defined adaptation as the ability to survive in one's environment; with regard to knowledge, he believed knowledge is 'true' to the extent that it's useful and adaptive, rather than the extent to which it mirrors an objective, independent reality.

Assimilation: According to Piaget's theory of knowing, humans attempt to maintain a state of equilibrium by either assimilating new information and experiences or accommodating them. Assimilation takes place when new information is consistent with what was previously known, so that it can be 'taken in' without modifying existing cognitive structures.

Cognitive Constructivism: Although there are many branches of constructivism, cognitive constructivism and social constructivism are considered two of the primary strands. Cognitive constructivism is based on the work of Piaget, and defines learning in terms of changes in cognitive structures. Although cognitive and social constructivism are often considered to be at odds, more recently scholars have recognized the ways in which they are complementary.

Disequilibrium: According to Piaget, learning is motivated by an individual's desire to maintain a state of equilibrium. Disequilibrium occurs when new information or experience conflicts with what was previously known, requiring the individual to modify or adapt in some way.

Scaffolding: An outgrowth of Vygotsky's social constructivism. Representative of the cooperative, dialogical nature of learning, scaffolding occurs in dyads. For example, when a mother imitates the gestures and sounds of an infant, but sometimes varies her response in order to elicit new responses from the child, she is engaged in scaffolding.

Social Constructivism: Although there are many branches of constructivism, cognitive constructivism and social constructivism are considered two of the primary strands. Social constructivism is based on the work of Vygotsky, and defines learning in terms of social interaction, language, and culture. Although cognitive and social constructivism are often considered to be at odds, more recently scholars have recognized the ways in which they are complementary.

Zone of Proximal Development: One of the primary concepts of Vygotsky's theory of social constructivism. According to Piaget, children are able to extend their current knowledge to a greater extent by working with adults and older children. The 'space' in which they are challenged to extend themselves has become known as the zone of proximal development.

Jennifer Kretchmar

BIBLIOGRAPHY

Alexander, H.A. (2006). A view from somewhere: Explaining the paradigms of educational research. *Journal of Philosophy of Education, 40,* 205–221. Retrieved June 10, 2007, from EBSCO Online Database Education Research Complete.

Al-Huneidi, A.M., & Schreurs, J. (2012). Constructivism based blended learning in higher education. *International Journal of Emerging Technologies in Learning, 7,* 4–9. Retrieved December 15, 2013, from EBSCO Online Database Education Research Complete.

Bächtold, M. (2013). What do students "construct" according to constructivism in science education?. *Research in Science Education, 43,* 2477–2496. Retrieved December 15, 2013, from EBSCO Online Database Education Research Complete.

Cardellini, L. (2006). The foundations of radical constructivism: An interview with Ernst von Glasersfeld. *Foundations of Chemistry, 8,* 177–187. Retrieved June 10, 2007, from EBSCO Online Database Academic Search Premier.

Cobb, P. (1996). Where is the mind? A coordination of sociocultural and cognitive constructivist perspectives. In C. T. Fosnot (Ed.), *Constructivism: Theory, perspectives, and practice.* New York, NY: Teachers College Press.

Elkind, D. (2005). Response to objectivism and education. *Educational Forum, 69,* 328–334. Retrieved June 10, 2007, from EBSCO Online Database Education Research Complete.

Ertmer, P.A., & Newby, T.J. (2013). Behaviorism, cognitivism, constructivism: Comparing critical features from an instructional design perspective. *Performance Improvement Quarterly, 26,* 43–71. Retrieved December 15, 2013, from EBSCO Online Database Education Research Complete.

Fostnot, C.T.. (1996). Constructivism: A psychological theory of learning. In C. T. Fosnot (Ed.), *Constructivism: Theory, perspectives, and practice.* New York, NY: Teachers College Press.

Harlow, S., Cummings, R., & Aberasturi, S. (2006). Karl Popper and Jean Piaget: A rationale for constructivism. *Educational Forum, 71,* 41–48. Retrieved June 10, 2007, from EBSCO Online Database Education Research Complete.

Johnson, M. (2005). Instructionism and constructivism: Reconciling two very good ideas. Retrieved June 10, 2007, from Education Resource Information Center, http://eric.ed.gov.

Moford, J. (2007). Perspectives constructivism: Implications for postsecondary music education and beyond. *Journal of Music Teacher Education, 16,* 75–83. Retrieved June 10, 2007, from EBSCO Online Database Education Research Complete.

Null, J. W. (2004). Is constructivism traditional? Historical and practical perspectives on a popular advocacy. *Educational Forum, 68,* 180–188. Retrieved June 10, 2007, from Education Resource Information Center, http://eric.ed.gov.

Prouix, J. (2006). Constructivism: A re-equilibration and clarification of concepts, and some potential implications for teaching and pedagogy. *Radical Pedagogy, 7,* 5. Retrieved June 10, 2007, from EBSCO Online Database Education Research Complete.

Schrader, D. E. (2015). Constructivism and learning in the age of social media: Changing minds and learning communities. *New Directions For Teaching & Learning, 2015*(144), 23–35. Retrieved January 6, 2016, from EBSCO Online Database Education Research Complete.

von Glasersfeld, E. (1996). Introduction: Aspects of constructivism. In C. T. Fosnot (Ed.), *Constructivism: Theory, perspectives, and practice.* New York, NY: Teachers College Press.

SUGGESTED READING

Brown, T.H. (2005). Beyond constructivism: Exploring future learning paradigms. *Education Today, 2,* 14–30. Retrieved June 10, 2007, from EBSCO Online Database Education Research Complete.

Bruner, J. (1990). *Acts of meaning.* Cambridge, MA: Harvard University Press. Meltzer, E. (2006). Constructivism and objectivism: Additional Questions. *Educational Forum, 70,* 200–201. Retrieved June 10, 2007, from EBSCO Online Database Education Research Complete.

Henson, K. T. (2015). *Curriculum planning: Integrating multiculturalism, constructivism, and education reform.* Long Grove, IL: Waveland Press.

Pass, S. (2004). *Parallel paths to constructivism: Jean Piaget and Lev Vygotsky.* Greenwich, CT: Information Age Publishing.

Flynn, P., Mesibov, D., Vermette, P., & Smith, R. (2004). *Applying standards-based constructivism: A two-step guide for motivating elementary students.* Larchmont, NY: Eye on Education, Inc.

Flynn, P., Mesibov, D., Vermette, P., & Smith, R. (2004). *Applying standards-based constructivism: A two-step guide for motivating middle and high school students.* Larchmont, NY: Eye on Education, Inc.

EPISTEMOLOGY

An overview of epistemology and knowledge, and incorporates a series of historical and current philosophers that have grappled with this concept throughout the centuries, such as Plato and Lehrer is presented. Additionally, an examination of the work conducted by world-renowned psychologists Jean Piaget and Sigmund Freud, who are often associated solely for their psychologically-driven contributions, is included with regard to their input on genetic epistemology, and epistemology as it relates to the "psychosexual stages of development." The second portion of this article is more applied, and relates theoretical epistemological tenets to educational and psychological settings. Differentiation between epistemology that focuses on process, content, and ethics is outlined, and concepts related to Aristotelian epistemology (i.e., that which is theoretical, qualitative, and performative) are broached. Albert Einstein's disillusionment with educational institutions and his thoughts on re-aligning academia so that it parallels creative ventures are discussed, followed by a short segue into a simplistic story-telling technique that serves as an epistemological device.

KEYWORDS: Aristotelian Epistemology; Epistemology; Equilibrium; Genetic Epistemology; Knowledge; Plato; Psychosexual Stages of Development; Reasoned True Belief

OVERVIEW
KNOWLEDGE & EPISTEMOLOGY
Epistemology, or the theory of knowledge (Hillerbrand, 1988), is a philosophical principle that has been investigated throughout the centuries by the world's greatest intellects, including Descartes, Durkheim, Bernard, Aristotle, and Plato. Plato classified knowledge (i.e., reasoned true belief) as the existence of three concepts: truth, belief, and evidence (Southerland, Sinatra & Matthews, 2001), and defined truth as that which reflects reality. Belief occurs when people grant authenticity toward such

a truth, and evidence is a person's ability to defend such a stance. To exemplify the interaction of this tertiary ideal, one might assume that Jane is interested in crossing a bridge and needs to determine the safety of such an activity, and relies on her knowledge base and ability to reason. Visually, Jane can see that the bridge is built out of steel and concrete, which coincide with the materials of bridges that she has previously crossed. Therefore, she *believes* that the bridge is safe, and this belief is grounded in reality, or *truth*. Also, Jane's sister Sally previously crossed the bridge and arrived safely on the other side. Sally is of similar height and stature to Jane, thus providing convincing *evidence* that the bridge is indeed safe. The decision-making process that allowed her to come to such a conclusion is based on the three-fold conception of knowledge set forth by Plato.

KEITH LEHRER
According to American philosopher Keith Lehrer (1990), knowledge can be depicted in terms of a person's proficiency in any given arena (e.g., "I know how to play the piano") as well as a means of indicating relationships (e.g., "I know Bob Smith"). Additionally, a person's knowledge is also representative of his or her established amount of accurate information. Information, in itself, is insufficient; if I look at my watch, which reads 3:00, I have acquired information regarding the time. However, unbeknownst to me, my watch broke several hours ago and therefore my acquisition of information is inadequate for the accurate possession of knowledge. The ability to decipher accurate information distinguishes human beings from other animals.

Moreover, Lehrer offers three conditions that serve as underpinnings for knowledge that resembles that which was proposed by Plato, including *truth, acceptance,* and *justification.* However, there are many inconsistencies that denote the obscurity of such a theory, and are therefore worthy of discussion. For example, a mother has a child that leaves for college, and is under the impression that the child is faring quite well. However, this *acceptance of truth* represents the mother's desire that her child is doing well, and is not based on a legitimate assessment. Thus, her willingness to consent to such a delusion is reinforced by the corresponding feelings of gratification that accompany her faulty belief. Therefore, one can infer that *acceptance* is not always based on *truth*.

Lehrer stipulates that "complete *justification*" surrounding what a person accepts is a necessary aspect of knowledge, as opposed to partial justification, in order to avoid making flawed assumptions. An example of partial justification is if Ann came to the determination that her husband would arrive home today at 12:00 noon from work, based on the fact that he always comes home at 12:00 noon for his lunch break. However, today, let us assume that her husband had an extended meeting, a flat tire, or was tempted to eat at a fancy restaurant in lieu of dining in with Ann. Hence her assumption, or partial judgment, defies that which is knowledge. Knowledge therefore, reflects complete justification of an accurate assessment on what one accepts as truth. This stance, as opposed to divergent opinions from philosophical predecessors who claim knowledge is a measurable and objective construct, assumes that although knowledge is based in accuracy, there is still a subjective air that affects its existence.

JEAN PIAGET

Piaget, one of the most eminent child psychologists of the 20th century, contributed greatly toward the understanding of child cognitions and is perhaps best known for highlighting the intellectual progress undertaken by the growing child. Incidentally, Piaget identified himself as neither a child psychologist, nor a genetic psychologist, but as a genetic epistemologist (Kitchner, 1986). According to Piaget, knowledge is the active relationship that people maintain with their surroundings. In other words, a young boy does not know how to tie his shoes because he passively observes his parents undertaking such a pursuit, but because he actively goes through the trial-and-error of crisscrossing the strands of lace that interweave his shoes. Moreover, Piaget felt that knowledge is reality-based, and that it is a limitless, never-ending process that continually evolves throughout the lives of human beings. He coined the term *orthogenesis* to refer to the fact that people intellectually strive for,

and advance toward an ideal of infinite wisdom, but that they never arrive at such a destination point. Therefore, the nature of knowledge lies in an intellectual quest that is categorized through the progression of various stages, as opposed to an actual state of intellectualism (Tsou, 2006).

Moreover, Piaget emphasized the inherent need of people forging a sense of harmony or adaptation with their environment. He coined the term "equilibrium" to describe the cognitive process that enables such a system. People achieve equilibrium through the process of assimilation, whereby they incorporate new experiences into pre-existing schemata and accommodation, or the process of changing schemata to make room for new information. Piaget felt that the ability for assimilation and accommodation, or finding equilibrium, was the hallmark of a highly intelligent person who successfully progressed through the stages of cognitive development at a rapid pace. Piaget felt that the feeling of disequilibrium essentially was a positive force, as it motivated people to seek equilibrium. Since humans are creatures of comfort, and therefore seek equilibrium when they are in the throes of duress, the process of cognitive growth is initiated with each unpleasant new encounter.

SIGMUND FREUD

Similarly, Sigmund Freud, the famous psychologist who pioneered many innovative theories, can also be linked with epistemological contributions. A prominent psychological Freudian concept is the creation of his stage theory that delineates human development, termed the "psychosexual stages of development" (Miller & Stine, 1951), through which each human travels. Each stage of this theory (e.g., oral, anal, phallic) designates an area of the body (e.g., mouth, anus, genitals) that becomes the physiological focal point. Based on parental methods during each stage the child can progress normally, become overly indulged, or become neglected, each of which manifest into specific adult characteristics. For example, during the oral phase, infants are dependent on their mother's milk; if they do not receive an adequate level of dietary consumption, the resultant adult is "stuck" at the oral stage, and possesses corresponding traits (e.g., overindulged: optimistic, gullible; neglected: pessimistic, suspicious). Perhaps the most controversial element of the psychosexual stages is the phallic stage, which Freud explains through the use of the Sophocles parable "Oedipus Rex," where people who are stuck in this stage are deemed as having an "Oedipal Complex." This stage is highly complex, and involves individuals who, in the process of identifying with their same-sex parent, begin to harbor feelings of lust and romantic love toward their opposite-sex parent. Abnormal resolution to this stage involves a variety of deviant personality and sex-related disorders (Phillips & Franco, 1954).

Although most psychologists and scholars consider Freud's "psychosexual stages of development" solely as an indicator for eventual adult behavior, Schermer (1999) offers piercing insight into the Oedipal stage of development as a barometer for epistemological development. Freud believed that infants innately bear primitive instinctual drives, but that their intellectual abilities parallel that of the John Locke's "tabula rasa," (Vogt, 1993) or blank slate theory. This suggests that people's experiences, observations, and in Freud's case, resolution with the psychosexual stages of development, coalesce into their eventual intellectual resources. Like Piaget, Freud believed that intelligence and life experience were one and the same. Also, when children rectify the Oedipal complex in a healthy manner, it imparts an intellectual symbolic framework that demarcates the roles of a proper family structure (i.e., the child does not mate with the parent). This intellectual framework persists throughout adulthood by providing a continual model that outlines appropriate human relations.

Although children overcome the obstacles present at each stage of psychosexual development, based on their combined internal qualities *and* the amount of parental involvement they receive, adults retroactively reconcile fixation at a stage (e.g., oral, anal, phallic) if they find themselves "stuck," based upon their intellectual prowess. Through the process of healing "stage fixation" they may find enlightenment through intellectual processes such as insight, acknowledgment, and disclosure, while ignorance and/or denial stifles such cognitive growth. Moreover, Freud emphasized the importance of unconscious realms as contributing largely to a person's life experiences, including their fears, ambitions, characteristics, and intellectual capabilities. Such unconscious realms are difficult to ascertain, as they unknowingly emerge through a person's behavior, through dreams, parapraxes (i.e., "Freudian slips"), and psychoanalysis.

Most people's unconscious motivations are hidden, and even though they are monumental indicators of intelligence, the analysis of such epistemological influences is often nebulous.

Applications

DEWEY, BAGLEY & SCHWAB

Null (2003) differentiates three educational epistemological paradigms based on three educational philosophers: John Dewey, William C. Bagley, and Joseph Schwab. According to Dewey, education is about process. Regardless of the actual subject pupils study, the act of learning inevitably instills a sense of problem-solving or "how to think" skills. In other words, it doesn't matter if students take "English Literature" or "Basket-weaving," because each subject requires a complex series of cognitive processes that supersede the actual content that is derived. Moreover, the knowledge that is derived when students perfect such a process transcends into different content areas. As such, the intellectual process involved with basket-weaving can be applied toward learning subsequent subjects, even those that are seemingly unrelated (e.g., Math, Science, etc.).

Bagley, on the other hand, focused on content as being the primary point of concern regarding knowledge transmission. He felt that schools place too much emphasis on the needs of the individual student, when in fact the individual student should hone disciplinary restraint and adhere to the educational principles set before him or her. Bagley asserted that, at the end of the educational experience students should depart with concrete knowledge, or content, that had been infused in them. A Math student, for example, who was learning about algebraic equations, should exit the course with the ability to solve problems related to such mathematical computations. Bagley, however, did not completely discount the process of learning and the application toward pertinent life realms. For example, if a group of geography students were lost in the wilderness it would be meaningful that they rely on the learned internal "compass" that they acquired in school by determining which direction was north, south, east, or west. Nevertheless, those same geography students should graduate from their geography studies with the ability to locate landmarks (e.g., the seven continents, the 50 states) on a map.

Finally, Schwab focused on the attainment of higher education, and how it relates to ethical and practical concerns. He felt that teachers-in-training should be equipped with real-life material, scenarios, and dilemmas to help define their educational pedagogy, as opposed to constructs that are more theoretical in nature. Null differentiates between the two in the following passage: "In contrast to 'How do children learn?' an example of a practical question would be: 'What should I *do* right now with *these* students in this classroom in *this* school district with *these* teachers as my colleagues and with *these* materials available to me at *this* time?'" The emphasis, therefore, is neither on process nor content in and of themselves, but on the practical application that is specific to any given educational situation. Additionally, Schwab suggested that engaging in real-life situations increases the probability that students would witness realistic, unethical dilemmas. This exposure would serve as a rehearsal before they segued into their professional domains, and would provide them with the ability to size-up appropriate and ethical responses in an extemporaneous way.

EPISTEMOLOGY & EDUCATION

In the middle of the 20th century, Haggard (1954) expressed concern surrounding the direction that the field of psychology was heading. In particular, he felt that the turn of the 20th century was an innovative era for the discipline, which was filled with dedicated theorists who were conducting fertile research on epistemological matters (e.g., James, Dewey, Thorndike). But by the 1950s, such voracity segued into repetitive complacency, and research focused on practical, technique-oriented issues. Decades later, Hillerbrand suggested that an epistemological model should be re-integrated into psychology graduate training programs, one that "addresses questions of how the psychology profession identifies, organizes, and communicates knowledge." In essence, this perspective suggests that without an understanding of the historical roots of knowledge, burgeoning psychologists are trained under vague or unfocused terms, yielding a profession that is riddled with ambiguity. As such, it would behoove the psychological community to emphasize Aristotelian epistemological tenets.

The Aristotelian tenets that Hillerbrand referenced were that rational knowledge could be categorized into three dimensions:

- Theoretical;
- Qualitative;
- Performative.

Theoretical knowledge is a set of generalizations that do not necessarily seek evolution into a practical set of procedures, and represents the adage "knowledge for the sake of knowledge." In the field of psychology, one presumes to understand mental ailments through the process of generalizations, as indicated by therapists who theorize their universal ability to recognize depressed clientele by their behavior or affect. Qualitative knowledge, on the other hand is the ability to recognize and revel in individuality. Although in psychology, therapists might *theoretically* recognize the similarities between depressed clientele, they should also recognize that each individual has a unique, individualized, or *qualitative* manifestation of such angst. Performative knowledge relates to the procedural guidelines that help guide people toward appropriate ways of acting. Psychologically speaking, performative knowledge might dictate how a person behaves clinically (e.g., the style in which a therapist asks questions).

Albert Einstein is most notably known for his renowned contributions toward the worlds of scientific and mathematic inquiry, and within the domain of physics created the "Theory of Relativity," for which he was eventually awarded the Nobel Prize. In addition to such scholarly contributions, Einstein was a pacifist, humanitarian, and also upheld very specific thoughts on knowledge, knowledge acquisition, and education. Einstein himself, struggled in school throughout his formative years, and received very negative feedback from his teachers based on his lack of conformity toward classroom ideology. Once he matured into a seasoned intellect and established scientist, Einstein reflected on educational standards, and expounded on ideals that he claimed would espouse educational veracity (Hayes, 2007).

In particular, Einstein felt that schools should channel creativity and be a boundless arena for innovation, mystery, and exploration. Dubious that schools were institutions that endorsed such ideals, Hayes relays comments about Einstein that "He remarked that education is what remains after one has forgotten what one has learned in school! He claimed that it was a miracle if children's curiosity survived their formal education, as it was driven out of them in the narrow pursuit of an imposed and pre-scribed curriculum." Einstein's scathing criticisms toward educational limitations are apparent. He felt that knowledge and logic provide a linear roadmap that enable people to sequentially proceed from one point to another. Ingenuity, on the other hand, super-sedes knowledge by tapping into unforeseen territory and forging new ground that is ground-breaking and contributory (i.e., "Imagination is more important than knowledge"). Einstein believed in perseverance, or the dedication to an intellectual pursuit, which is difficult to do in educational environments that typ-ically adhere to strict deadlines and promote time-liness order, which usurps the creative process that needs time, trial-and-error efforts, and boundless liberation.

One fairly simplistic epistemological implementa-tion that teachers can employ into the classroom is the tradition of story-telling. Based on a seminar con-ducted for nursing students, Bunkers (2006) reflects on the power of sharing personal narratives. Stories serve as an epistemological device because they uti-lize a straightforward and collective approach in which people can impart knowledge based on their personal struggles and triumphs, as well as a way of communicating cultural and world-related knowl-edge (Campbell, 1988). Storylines that are familiar offer a sense of validation and solidarity toward the human condition, while unfamiliar plots can reveal mysteries that relate to human endeavors and rela-tionships. Moreover, stories provide people with the-oretical knowledge that can initiate the reversal of maladaptive attitudes and behaviors.

CONCLUSION

Epistemology, or the theory of knowledge, is an age-old concept that is sophisticated and multi-dimensional. "What is knowledge" might appear to be a rudimentary question that necessitates a straight-forward and simplistic response. However, as this paper demonstrates, knowledge as an ideol-ogy has been examined and appraised from a variety of great thinkers ranging from Plato to Freud, all of whom investigated this issue from different angles and have therefore generated differing, sometimes

contradictory results. The implications of this article are quite expansive, and may differ drastically based on the individual background of the reader. One general inference surrounds the idea that knowledge is not concrete, nor is it stagnant, and thus should constantly be scrutinized based on new and innova-tive erudition, or cultural and historical norms that serve to expand its parameters. It would behoove educators, parents, and students to constantly dissect the theory of knowledge, and apply it to various con-textual, individualized, and philosophical accounts in attempt toward obtaining its elusive existence.

TERMS & CONCEPTS

Aristotelian Epistemology: According to Aristotle, knowledge can be categorized into three dimen-sions, including theoretical, qualitative, and per-formative.

Epistemology: A branch of philosophy that concen-trates on the theory of knowledge.

Equilibrium: According to Piaget, people strive to har-monize, or adapt to their environments through the process of equilibrium. People achieve equi-librium through the process of assimilation and accommodation.

Genetic Epistemology: A specific theory created by Piaget that focused on the study of knowledge in sequential stages.

Psychosexual Stages of Development: Freud created a controversial theory that delineated human development based on stages (e.g., oral, anal, phallic), each of which focused on a physiologi-cal part of the body. Parental involvement during each stage determines how a person progresses through each stage, and governs corresponding adult characteristics.

Reasoned True Belief: According to Plato, knowl-edge consists of three concepts: truth, belief, and evidence.

Cynthia Vejar

BIBLIOGRAPHY

Bunkers, S. S. (2006). What stories and fables can teach us. *Nursing Science Quarterly, 19*(2), 104-107. Retrieved December 15, 2007, from EBSCO online database, Academic Search Premier.

Campbell, J. (1988). *The power of myth*. USA: Apostrophe S Productions, Inc.

Haggard, E. A. (1954). The proper concern of educational psychologists. *The American Psychologist, 9,* 539-543.

Hayes, D. (2007). What Einstein can teach us about education. *Education 3-13, 35,* 143-152.

Hillerbrand, E. T. (1988). Aristotle and epistemology: Implications for professional psychological training. *Professional Psychology, 19,* 468-473.

Hsin-Kai, W., & Chia-Lien, W. (2011). Exploring the development of fifth graders' practical epistemologies and explanation skills in inquiry-based learning classrooms. *Research in Science Education, 41,* 319-340. Retrieved December 15, 2013, from EBSCO Online Database Education Research Complete.

Kitchner, R. F. (1986). *Piaget's theory of knowledge.* New Haven, London: Yale University Press.

Kotzee, B. (2013). Introduction: Education, social epistemology and virtue epistemology. *Journal of Philosophy of Education, 47,* 157-167. Retrieved December 15, 2013, from EBSCO Online Database Education Research Complete.

Lehrer, K. (1990). *Theory of Knowledge.* USA: Westview Press.

Macallister, J. (2012). Virtue epistemology and the philosophy of education. *Journal of Philosophy of Education, 46,* 251-270. Retrieved December 15, 2013, from EBSCO Online Database Education Research Complete.

Miller, D. R., & Stine, M. E. (1951). The prediction of social acceptance by means of psychoanalytic concepts. *Journal of Personality, 20,* 162-175. Retrieved December 15, 2007, from EBSCO online database, Academic Search Premier.

Null, J. W. (2003). Education and knowledge, not "standards and accountability": A critique of reform rhetoric through the ideas of Dewey, Bagley, and Schwab. *Educational Studies, 34,* 397-413. Retrieved December 15, 2007, from EBSCO online database, Academic Search Premier.

Phillips, L. & Franco, J. L. (1954). Developmental theory applied to normal and psychopathological perception. *Journal of Personality, 22,* 464-475. Retrieved December 15, 2007, from EBSCO online database, Academic Search Premier.

Schermer, V. L. (1999). To know a mind: Oedipus, Freud, and epistemology. *Psychoanalytic Studies, 1,* 191-211. Retrieved December 15, 2007, from EBSCO online database, Academic Search Premier.

Southerland, S. A., Sinatra, G. M., & Matthews, M. R. (2001). Belief, knowledge, and science education. *Educational Psychology Review, 13,* 325-351. Retrieved December 15, 2007, from EBSCO online database, Academic Search Premier.

Tsou, J. Y. (2006). Genetic epistemology and Piaget's philosophy of science. *Theory & Psychology, 16,* 203-224. Retrieved December 15, 2007, from EBSCO online database, Academic Search Premier.

Vogt, P. (1993). Seascape with fog: Metaphor in Locke's essay. *Journal of History of Ideas, 54,* 18-18. Retrieved December 15, 2007, from EBSCO online database, Academic Search Premier,

SUGGESTED READING

Feldman, R. (2002). *Epistemology.* USA: Prentice Hall.

Sosa, E. (2007). *A virtue epistemology: Apt belief and reflective knowledge.* USA: Oxford University Press.

Turri, J. (2013). *Epistemology: A Guide.* New York: John Wiley & Sons.

Williams, M. (2001). *Problems of knowledge: A critical introduction to epistemology.* USA: Oxford University Press.

EXISTENTIALISM

Existentialism is a philosophy whose popularity was greatest in the 20th century, particularly during and after World War II. Existentialist thought was introduced through literary works written by such masters as Sartre, Camus and Dostoevsky (Wingo, 1965). Danish philosopher Soren Kierkegaard insisted that one controls one's own life, that one has complete freedom "to choose and become what he wills himself to become." Jean-Paul Sartre stated that "the human project...is to create by free choice a life that is noble and beautiful self-construction" (Gutek, 2009). The founders of existentialism made little reference to education and the role of the teacher, the learner, the environment or the curriculum. However, much can be gleaned from the original words of existentialist thinkers that can apply to the state of an existentialist education.

KEYWORDS: Absurd Life; Anxiety; Authentic; Existential Moment; Existentialism; Kierkegaard; Knowledge; Pre-existential Period; Process of Learning

OVERVIEW
EXISTENCE PRECEDES ESSENCE
Existence precedes essence. We make ourselves, we create our essence; this expression encompasses the major theory behind the existentialist philosophy.

Its popularity was greatest in the 20th century, particularly during and after World War II. Existentialist thought was introduced through literary works written by such masters as Sartre, Camus and Dostoevsky (Wingo). Several existentialist philosophers have impacted the thinking that supports the tenets of this philosophy. Danish philosopher Soren Kierkegaard insisted that one controls one's own life, that one has complete freedom "to choose and become what he wills himself to become." Jean-Paul Sartre stated that "the human project...is to create by free choice a life that is noble and beautiful self-construction" (Gutek).

There is some question as to whether existentialism can really be called a philosophy because it lacks the systematic school of thought that other philosophies such as Idealism, Realism, or Pragmatism possess. However, there are common traits that encompass what many great thinkers perceive to be a philosophy that emphasizes the freedom of human beings (Noddings, 1995). Its major principle is that *existence precedes essence*. Thus, one's existence comes first, and then one defines him or herself through the choices he or she makes and the actions that evolve out of these choices. One is born and THEN he or she develops into who he or she will become as a person (Noddings). To existentialists, the world is

> ... *an indifferent phenomenon, which, while it may not be antagonistic to human purposes, is nonetheless devoid of personal meaning... in this world, each person is born, lives, chooses his or her course and creates the meaning of his or her own existence (Gutek).*

CONNECTING ELEMENTS OF EXISTENTIAL THOUGHT

Existentialism is best illustrated by the common elements of thought attributed to existentialist thinkers. One is the thought that we are *free* from all external elements. Although we have a past, this past does not factor into the present moment of our life. External elements are, or one's past life is, only important if one chooses to make them important (Noddings). Another connection is the concept of *responsibility*. While one is free to make one's own choices, each person is responsible for what choices he makes. As Noddings suggests, one cannot "give away [his or her] freedom" to outside agents such as "the state, to parents, to teachers, to weaknesses, to the past, and to environmental conditions."

Of importance to the existentialist is the common message that "every truth and every action implies a

human setting and a human subjectivity" (Noddings). While we know that there is a world full of reality, to the existentialist, this reality only becomes such when one is a basic part of it. Noddings states that "reality lies in [everyone's] experience and perception of the event rather than the isolated event." Noddings relates the example of the perception of two people listening to a speech:

> "... *two men may hear the same speech, the same words, the same voice. One man's reality may be that the speaker is a political demagogue, for the other man the reality is that the speaker is an awaited political savior.*"

According to existentialists, one must rely upon oneself and a relationship to those around him or her. One must possess a self-realization that one must relate to others, as he or she "lives out [his or her] life span in an adamant universe" (Noddings). One is "thrown into the universe in which there is no fixed course of action, nor final structure of meaning" (McLemee, 2003). Even though one is part of an adamant universe, one becomes the subject of his or her own life, a unique and idiosyncratic being. Noddings explains a basic concept of existentialism, that "people are not thrown into the world with a nature...only by planning, reflecting, choosing and acting, people can make themselves." To Greene (1973), a person only passes through life once and therefore must begin creating his or her own identity. In other words, people are born with no true identity or sense of self; they construct themselves over time. One can do this by taking "responsible action for the sake of wholeness, to correct lacks in concrete situations and thus alter themselves in the light of some projected ideal."

Knowledge is said "to be the way a [person] comes in touch with [his or her] world, puts questions to it, transforms its component parts into signs and tools, and translates [his or her] findings in words." This person uses this knowledge to make choices and determine future actions. Knowledge is used "to clarify and to open up a life" (Greene). Through knowledge, one builds a life day to day.

Rather than illustrating their messages through argumentation and persuasion, as other philosophies have done, existentialists use the venue of stories to propagate their message. They do this because they believe that "life is not the unfolding of a logical plan; one cannot argue from trustworthy premises what a life should be like or how it should be lived…meaning is created as we live our lives reflectively." Stories personify the reflective experience and provide accounts of "the human struggle for meaning" (Noddings). Characters generally face a life of "angst, anxiety and alienation in an absurd universe" (Gutek).

EXISTENTIALISM & EDUCATION

The founders of existentialism made little reference to education and the role of the teacher, the learner, the environment or the curriculum. The mission of existentialism "analyzes the basic character of human existence and calls the attention of [people] to their freedom" (Wingo). However, much can be gleaned from the original words of thinkers that apply to the state of an existentialist education, as education has come to be seen as "a foundation of human progress" (Park, 1968). Furthermore, a "careful" understanding of existentialism reveals "strong qualitative ties which provide a framework for understanding the roles individuals play, and how they struggle with those roles in educational institutions" (Duemer, 2012). A few modern philosophers, including Van Cleve Morris and George Kneller, have written extensively, applying existential thought to education.

In an existentialist school, individualism must be "the center of educational endeavor" (Knight, 1998). Van Cleve Morris (1968) sees education as a way "to awaken awareness in the learner," with the task of education falling chiefly on secondary schools at a time when schools provide "occasions and circumstances for the awakening and intensification of awareness" (Park). He says that prior to puberty (a time called the Pre-Existential Period), children are not really aware of the human condition or yet conscious of their personal identity and should learn the basics of education. After puberty, young adolescents experience their Existential Moment, when they become more aware of themselves in relation to the world (Gutek). To Morris, school should be concerned with developing "that integrity in [students] necessary to the task of making personal choices of action, and taking personal responsibility for these choices, whether the culture smiles or frowns."

School policy that supports the existentialist philosophy focuses on the individual student, as teachers enter the "private world" of the student. The *here and now* life experiences are more important than the messages from the past. Teachers encourage personal

responsibility and show students respect and belief in their potential, always keeping in mind that the students should be themselves (Sungur, 2002). They do not teach problem-solving, a popular methodology espoused by other philosophies such as pragmatism. Problem-solving is "too linked to universal reason," and to an existentialist teacher, "problem-solving is acceptable only if the problem originates in the life of the [student] who has to appropriate the solution" (Kneller, 1968).

Formal values training is not part of the existential curriculum. People are not born with values, or the propensity to be good. Each is free to become whatever he or she wants to become. Knight states that an individual can make choices that are harmful to others, but they can also make ethical choices. One has "the great potential of bettering, worsening, or even destroying human existence." To existentialists, "living the responsible life includes acting upon one's decision to be true or authentic to his or herself." Teachers should help develop competencies in free choice by using strategies in the Ethical Method, providing sources that prompt discussion about perennial issues that challenge people throughout their lives (Power, 1982).

Teachers are faced with a dilemma when they teach; they are confronted with questions that are value-based. They have to determine what is the right thing to teach, when to teach it, and when to leave a student alone to his or her devices. Existentialist thinker Soren Kierkegaard asserted that the main duty of teaching is to be a learner who actively shares views with the student, thus facilitating personal and social transformation. This learning relationship "furnishes a model of conviction for all who can see, a context for trust and the way of establishing a mutual vision" (Walters, 2008).

Pointing to an additional dilemma, Kline and Knight Abowitz, in an essay on the dehumanization of school educators, cite "Teaching Philosophy in Europe and North America," a paper from United Nations Educational Scientific and Cultural Organization that argues that "efficiency and effectiveness are the main considerations in the values of education." The authors write of teachers being "conscious beings and existing"; however, a "culturally constructed burden" molds their professional choices and actions (Kline & Knight Abowitz, 2013).

Humanities are a major part of an existentialist education. Humanities provide the insight into life's major dilemmas, providing both the positive and negative perspectives that illustrate people making choices (Knight). The fundamentals of traditional education should be studied as well, as they are a "foundation of creative effort and individual ability to understand oneself." Other subject areas may be included for study, as long as they have meaning for the individual.

Noddings, writing of the lack of existentialist principles in present-day secondary-school liberal arts education, argues that what "passes for the liberal arts in high school—the specific disciplines of English, mathematics, history, and the sciences—are little more than preparation for further study in those narrowly defined subjects. Not only do they make few connections to existential themes, they make almost no connection to one another" (Noddings). She continues, "Rather than setting up the liberal arts as a separate program to be studied in preference to something less desirable, I would like *to draw* on the liberal arts to enrich everything we teach."

Philosophers who have shaped the tenets of existentialism are: Soren Kierkegaard, Friedrich Nietzsche, Martin Heidegger, and Jean-Paul Sartre.

Applications

EXISTENTIALIST METHODS & PRINCIPLES IN THE CLASSROOM

Modern followers of existentialism in education offer methods and principles that can be adapted in the contemporary classroom.

Ethical Method: The Ethical Method is any method that promotes facilitating the way to choose and the habit of choosing. Teachers facilitate situations whereby students "grapple with urgent perennial issues," asking such questions as: "How can self-interest be accommodated to the general welfare?" The purpose of providing method in making choices is that when faced with the need to make choices, "persons will have the courage, the social stamina and the personal vigor to do so" (Power).

Existentialist Learning Principles: Pine (1974) states that there are certain principles of learning that existentialists support:

- The learner's beginning point in creating values and learning is the setting of goals, as the learner is a free and responsible agent;

- Learning is an experience which occurs inside the learner and is activated by the learner, with the *process of learning* primarily controlled by the learner and not the teacher;
- Learning is the discovery of the personal meaning and relevance of ideas, with the learner deciding what is meaningful and what must be discovered;
- Learning occurs from the consequence of experience, authentic experience;
- Learning is emotional as well as intellectual, in that the state of the whole person impacts learning;
- Learning is a valuing experience, with the student sharing that which he or she values most;
- Teaching is learning, with the teacher becoming part of the process of learning as he or she learns from the learning.

Existentialist Teaching Principles: Existentialists believe that there is "a special facilitative human relationship between the student and the teacher" (Pine). An existentialist teacher will design a teaching approach to increase the student's freedom, to discover meaning for his or her life and to improve his or her encounters along the way. Pine states that teachers who follow the existential philosophy may follow these principles:

- They teach with an existentialist attitude in mind rather than through technique; they strive to know the student's reality and to see as the student sees;
- They view students as subjects, not objects; they do not rely on diagnosing or evaluating per established standards and norms.

Facilitative Learning: Pine also outlines certain conditions that facilitate learning within an existentialist classroom. Learning is facilitated in an atmosphere which:

- Encourages people to be active;
- Promotes and facilitates the individual's discovery of the personal;
- meanings of ideas;
- Emphasizes the uniquely personal and subjective nature of learning;
- Encourages openness of self rather than concealment of self;
- Supports difference as good and desirable;

- Recognizes people's rights to make mistakes;
- Encourages trust in people as well as to trust themselves;
- Creates teachers who become learners and resource people rather than transmitters of knowledge.

VIEWPOINTS

There are those thinkers who do not consider existentialism to be a philosophy at all. Up to the inception of this thought process, philosophical views have been well-developed systematic bodies of thought that support arguments and conclusions that are based on argument. Opponents see existentialism as an approach, more than a philosophy (Wingo), more of "an inclination rather than a systematic school of thought" (Gutek). Existentialists see life as "too varied, complex, confused and unpredictable to be arranged in neatly structured philosophical categories."

While existentialism may be viewed as a philosophy of thought, there are those who are not impressed with this stream of thinking. While existentialism supports growth of one's own being, opponents of this philosophy make continued reference to existentialism as "a pessimistic negative philosophy...a source of nihilistic gloom...a meaninglessness that provokes anxiety" (Solomon, 2007). However, existentialists view their philosophy as an "important stream of American life and thought... that supports individualism and insistence on self-reliance." Existentialism is said to be more interested in "the affective side of man, his capacity to love, to appreciate, and to respond emotionally to the world about him" (Morris).

Those who live the existentialist life may consider any other philosophical approach to be "propaganda served to a captive audience" (Knight). Education under any other philosophical view prepares students for "consumerism or makes them into cogs in the machinery of industrial technology and modern bureaucracy." To existentialists, much of education "stifles and destroys individuality and creativity."

Existentialism promotes individual possibilities as limitless, as "no absolute limit can be set with respect to either human accomplishment or aspiration" (Power). However, while this may be a lofty goal for existentialists, there is just not enough time for one to accomplish everything one chooses. When making choices, students must be focused in their approach to study. Power points out that "immature, untutored

students need some help to realize personal genius, whatever it may be." Curriculum should be used as "a means to develop hidden talent and not allow it to enslave students."

There are certain trends that reduce personal choice and self-direction and interfere with an existential approach to life. Gutek states that educational systems have the potential to impede personal authenticity and depersonalize the teaching/learning experience. Today's focus on standardized testing encourages teachers to teach to the test; "uniformity becomes the norm and uniqueness and difference" is seen as abnormal, thus, "authenticity becomes limited."

TERMS & CONCEPTS

Absurd Life: Existentialism has coined the term *absurd life*, meaning that one begins life without a prior destined path (*a priori*), that life is empty before one gives meaning to it. Noddings provides an example of this: "If we feel ourselves bored or discouraged, asking daily "Is this all there is? ... it is up to us either to accept the emptiness of life or to fill it with meaning through our choices and action."

Anxiety: Existentialist literature often reflects anxiety within its characters, as they face "existences that are temporary and that will disappear; living with this knowledge is a source of anxiety".

Authentic: To be *authentic* means to "choose a course of action and then complete it".

Existential Moment: The Existential Moment occurs when young people become "conscious of their presence as a self in the world." This generally occurs around the time of puberty and is characterized by "an awareness of one's presence in the world, insight into one's own consciousness and responsibility for one's conduct".

Knowledge: Knowledge, to an existentialist, is "intuitive." Knowledge "originates in and is composed of what exists in the individual consciousness and feelings as a result of [one's] own eyes and the projects one adopts in the course of [one's] life" (Kneller). Knowledge is only valued if it has value for the individual.

Pre-existential Period: This term, coined by Van Cleve Morris, reflects the period in a child's life prior to puberty when the child is not "really aware of his or her human condition, not yet conscious of his or her personal identity or destiny".

During this period, students should learn basics, subject matter and problem-solving skills.

Process of Learning: Under the existentialist philosophy, learning occurs when the student is involved and personal meaning occurs. Pine states that the learning process "has to do with something which happens in the unique world of the learner." This process is controlled by the learner and not the teacher. If the student feels involved and can make personal meaning with the subject, then the student will learn; if not, "it will be shut out from [his or] field of perception."

Tricia Smith

BIBLIOGRAPHY

Barash, D. (2001). America's essence: What would Sartre say? *Chronicle of Higher Education, 47*, 45. Retrieved June 20, 2009, from EBSCO online database, Academic Search Complete.

Duemer, L.S. (2012). Existentialism as a framework for qualitative research: understanding freedom and choice in educational organizations. *Journal of Philosophy & History of Education, 62* 171-179. Retrieved November 29, 2013, from EBSCO online database Education Research Complete.

Gutek, G. (2009). *New perspectives on philosophy and education.* Columbus, OH: Pearson.

Greene, M. (1973). *Teacher as stranger: Educational philosophy for modern age.* Belmont, CA: Wadsworth.

Kneller, G. (1968). Existentialism and education. In J. Park (Ed.), *Selected readings in the philosophy of education* (pp. 324-238). London, England: Macmillan.

Kline, K., & Knight Abowitz, K. (2013). Moving out of the cellar: a new (?) existentialism for a future without teachers. *Critical Questions in Education, 4*, 156-167. Retrieved November 29, 2013, from EBSCO online database Education Research Complete.

Knight, G. (1998). *Issues and alternatives in educational philosophy.* Berrien Springs, MI: Andrews University Press.

McLemee, C. (2003). Sartre redux. *Chronicle of Higher Education, 50*, A10-A13.Retrieved June 22, 2009, from EBSCO online database, Academic Search Complete.

Morris, V. C. (1968). An overview: Existentialism and education. In J. Park (Ed.), *Selected readings in the philosophy of education* (pp. 303-315). London, England: Macmillan.

Noddings, N. (1995). *Philosophy of education: Dimensions of philosophy series.* Boulder, CO: Westview.

Noddings, N. (2011). Renewing a declining tradition. *Philosophy of Education Yearbook*, 49-51. Retrieved November 29, 2013, from EBSCO online database Education Research Complete.

Park, J. (Ed). (1968). *Selected readings in the philosophy of education.* London, England: MacMillan.

Pine, G. (1974). Existential teaching and learning. *Education, 95*, 18-25. Retrieved June 20, 2009, from EBSCO online database, Academic Search Complete.

Power, E. (1982). *Philosophy of education: Studies in philosophies, schooling, and education policies.* Englewood Cliffs, NJ: Prentice Hall.

Solomon, R. (2007). Pessimism vs. existentialism. *Chronicle of Higher Education, 53*, B5. Retrieved June 20, 2009, from EBSCO online database, Academic Search Complete.

Sungur, N. (2002). A study of the development of the existential educational administration inventory. *Educational Science, 2*, 295-298. Retrieved June 20, 2009, from EBSCO online database, Academic Search Complete.

Walters, D. (2008). Existential being as transformative learning. *Pastoral Care in Education, 26*, 111-118. Retrieved June 22, 2009, from EBSCO online database Academic Search Complete.

Wingo, M. (1965). *The philosophy of American education.* New York, NY: D.C. Heath.

SUGGESTED READING

Aspden, P. (1993, September 10). The greatest of thinkers, the smallest of men? *Times Higher Education Supplement,* (1088), 15.

Camus, A. (1942). *The myth of Sisyphus.* Paris: Gallimard.

Carroll, J. (2007). Existentialism's call to action [Letter]. *Chronicle of Higher Education, 53*, B14. Retrieved June 20, 2009, from EBSCO online database Academic Search Complete.

Ediger, M. (1992). Philosophy of education and the mathematics curriculum. *Journal of Instructional Psychology, 19*, 236-241. Retrieved June 20, 2009, from EBSCO online database Academic Search Complete.

Feldman, A. (2007). Teachers, responsibility and action research. *Educational Action Research, 15*, 239-252. Retrieved June 20, 2009, from EBSCO online database Academic Search Complete.

Heslep, R. (2002). Haugeland's new existentialism [Book Review]. *Studies in Philosophy and Education, 21*, 505-516. Retrieved June 22, 2009, from EBSCO online database Academic Search Complete.

Ozmon, H., & Craver, S. (2008). *Philosophical foundations of education.* Upper Saddle River, NJ: Pearson.

Sartre, J.-P. (1947). *Existentialism.* Trans. B. Frechtman. New York: Philosophical Library.

Vandenberg, D. (2001). Identity politics, existentialism and Harry Broudy's educational theory. *Educational Philosophy & Theory, 33*(3/4), 365-380. Retrieved June 20, 2009, from EBSCO online database Academic Search Complete.

PRAGMATISM

Pragmatism is a philosophy of personal experience that encourages people "to seek out the processes and do the things that work best to help us achieve desirable ends" (Ozmon & Craver, 2008). The roots of pragmatism are traced as far back as the classical period, where the Academic Sceptics rejected the idea that there was an absolute truth that could be achieved (Rescher, 2000). The name pragmatism (the Greek word for work) was coined by Charles Peirce in the 1870's. In education, pragmatism has evolved into "a multi-faceted movement aimed at changing school practice" (Englund, 2000). To pragmatists, the direction of formal education is to develop a progressive pattern of growth and learning. Pragmatism is basically about the experiential, as opposed to gaining truth through ideas. Instead of relating to the abstract, people relate to the concrete; an empiricism that has a physical character (Moore, 1961). Famous pragmatists include Francis Bacon, John Locke, Jean-Jacques Rousseau, Charles Darwin, Charles Peirce, William James, and John Dewey.

KEYWORDS: Complete Act of Thought; Dewey, John; Empiricism; Growth; Pragmatism; Progressivism; Problem-solving; Social Intelligence

OVERVIEW
TRUTH, REALITY & THE SELF
Pragmatism is a philosophy that encourages people "to seek out the processes and do the things that work best to help them achieve desirable ends" (Ozmon & Craver). The roots of pragmatism are traced as far back as the classical period, where the Academic Sceptics rejected the idea that there was an absolute truth that could be achieved (Rescher). The name *pragmatism* (the Greek word for work) was coined by Charles Peirce in the 1870's. To Peirce, "truth simply is," as "all understanding must itself be the product of doing; whatever we know is the product of inquiry, an activity of ours" (Rescher). William James continued the evolution of pragmatic thought (1842-1910). To James, "truth pivots on the successful guidance of experience." Both saw truth to be grounded in experience.

John Dewey systemized and grounded his pragmatism in the social. Truth is not static, but it is "what gets endorsed and accepted in the community" (Rescher).

Truth is validated through social acceptance and custom; when truths "no longer satisfy social needs, other…truths are found to replace them." Inherent in the framework of pragmatism is that ideas are true insofar as they are useful in a specific situation, "what works today in one case may not work tomorrow in another case" (Younkins, 2009v). There is no reality that is constant or absolute; reality occurs when people interact with their environment, shaping it to their wills. People are "free to choose their own way of thinking and to create whatever reality they want to embrace" (Younkins). In other words, ideas evolve from experience in relation to a particular problem, rather than "as a mere mental construct" (Ozmon & Craver).

Pragmatism is a philosophy of personal experience. Shusterman (1997) explains that the self is "an individual, …a changing creation." To Dewey, every self produces actions but is also the product of its acts and choices; no person is "a fixed, ready-made, finished self." One's aim is to continually grow, with growth as "the highest moral ideal." Life is growth itself and that "growth is not something done to the young, but instead is something they do" (Thayer, 1968). Children experience social and intellectual growth; growth cannot be imposed upon them.

Growth expands one's thinking. The main goal of thought is to reconstruct a situation in order to solve a problem. Younkins states that truth cannot be known in advance of action. One must first act and then think; only then can reality be determined. To Thayer, pragmatists define the process of thinking (the activity of inquiry) as "a process having certain phases occurring within certain limits." Thinking "starts as a perplexed, troubled or confused situation at the beginning, and becomes cleared up, unified, resolved situation at the end." This scientific thinking is orderly and coherent and when applied "to the problems of life [is] designed to bring about a better life for all" (Ozmon & Craver).

PRAGMATISM IN DEMOCRACY & EDUCATION
One of democracy's most compatible philosophies is pragmatism (Minnich, 1999). The democratic ideal is considered to infiltrate every aspect of life (Younkins). When speaking in terms of educating for democracy, the role of education is not to transfer one image of American identity, but "to foster mutual

respect among the diverse cultures and peoples that make up the American people" (Ryan, 1996). People experience personal development to achieve and this benefits democracy. Only "enlightened individuals can operate a thinking democracy." People become enlightened through education, as education is "a key requisite for a workable democracy" (Rescher). To pragmatists, a progressive education equals a progressive society equals democracy (Marcell, 1974).

In education, the pragmatist philosophy has evolved into "a multi-faceted movement aimed at changing school practice" (Englund). Until the 20th century, education had largely been considered a preparatory process for life in which the students learned what teachers wanted them to learn in order to become educated (Marcell, 1974). For pragmatists, the direction of formal education is to develop a progressive pattern of growth and learning. Growth becomes an ongoing self-corrective educative process in which the students are provided the dynamics to expand their capacity to grow and learn. They acquire "the habit of learning; they learn to learn" (Marcell). The process of learning itself becomes its own end. Hence, people become life-long learners of their own lives: "As long as life continues, education continues" (Thayer).

Applications

PRAGMATISM IN SCHOOLS

Progressive schools who base their education on the philosophy of pragmatism teach their students "how to know and how continually to grow in their capacity of knowing" (Marcell). These schools produce students who constantly strive "to acquire new knowledge and who progressively seek newer and deeper meaning to that knowledge." Through education, the culture is transmitted (Ozmon & Craver). Progressivists foster a social consciousness that develops thinking, as children "serve and adapt to others" (Younkins). Through exposure to a social environment, children can examine natural human processes and develop their own thinking processes. Education is that process which "renews people so they can face problems encountered through their interaction with the environment" (Ozmon & Craver).

To pragmatists, teaching "abstract, general principles and eternal …truth is beyond a child's understanding and a barrier to the authentic growth and development of the child" (Younkins). Moore explains

that the most valuable and effective learning takes place when children follow the development of a process "from its initial problematic condition to its final resolution, through actively participating in the situation through personal inquiry and investigation." Students go from passive to active participants in their learning process when their "native curiosity and intelligence… are exercised through [experiential] activities."

While character education is not proposed by pragmatists, a sense of duty is a prevalent theme within this philosophy. Self-realization is one's duty; one has a fundamental obligation to make the most of opportunity by realizing oneself as fully as possible. One has what Rescher calls "a generic duty" to use one's reason "to capitalize its potential for the good" for the world at large as well as for oneself. When opportunity to realize one's own potential is wasted, one is "being less than he/she can be and thus fails in that most fundamental of all duties, the ontological obligation to make the most of one's opportunities for the good."

There are many ways in which people can flourish:

- Thriving in the pursuit of happiness;
- Using one's intelligence as a guide;
- Enjoying the good things of life;
- Developing [some of] one's productive talents and abilities;
- Making some constructive contribution to the world's work;
- Fostering the good potential of others;
- Achieving and diffusing happiness;
- Taking heed for the interest of others (Rescher).

OTHER KEY CONCEPTS OF PRAGMATISM
Growth

To pragmatists, the major aim of education is growth. To assure growth, education should do the following:

- Be experimental in nature;
- Assist in social renewal;
- Promote a humane spirit in people;
- Desire to find new answers to current economic, political and social problems;
- Promote individual and social institutions (Ozmon and Craver).

Curriculum

Pragmatists "reject separating knowledge from experience or fragmenting or compartmentalizing knowledge" (Ozmon & Craver). They include cross-disciplinary approaches to the curriculum.

Problem-solving

Dewey promoted a process of genuine thought which he called his Complete Act of Thought. In a problem situation, each problem is viewed as "unique and can be dealt with experimentally by investigating the probable consequences of acting in particular ways" (Ozmon & Craver). To Dewey, the thinking process is of utmost importance. In his work, *How We Think*, he outlines five stages to the problem-solving method, whereby the problem-solver identifies:

- A *felt difficulty* that occurs because of a conflict in one's experiences or a hitch or block to ongoing experience;
- Its *location and definition*, establishing the limits or characteristics of the problem in precise terms;
- *Suggestions* of possible solutions, formulating a wide range of hypotheses;
- *Development of reasoning* of the bearings of the suggestions, such as reflecting on the possible outcomes of acting on these suggestions—in short, mulling things over;
- *Further observation and experiment*, leading to its acceptance or rejection, as well as testing hypotheses to see whether they yielded the desired results (1997 [1910]).

The role of the teacher

The pragmatist teacher encourages active participation in a classroom that discourages routine. In theory, students have an inherent desire to learn, and it is up to the teacher to capture this motivation to enhance learning. The teacher must establish a proper learning community "in order to stimulate the desired intellectual and emotional growth" (Ozmon & Craver). The teacher must also know the subject matter, and must be

> ... *an exceptionally-competent person who possesses a depth and breadth of knowledge, understands current conditions that affect the lives of students, knows how to organize and invest student investigation, understands psychological development and learning theory, provides supportive environment in which students can learn, and possesses refined understanding of school and community resources.*

Teaching methodologies

There are many approaches that teachers use to promote the tenets of pragmatism. Methods should be "experiential, flexible, open-ended, and oriented toward growth of the individual's capacity to think and to participate intelligently in social life" (Ozmon & Craver). To pragmatists, all knowledge is related in some way. They encourage problem-solving that takes place in the practical setting of the classroom. Pragmatist teachers serve as resources, or guides, to the learning process. Their role is to arouse student interests and to help launch new projects that are process-based.

Viewpoints

SOME CRITICISM OF PRAGMATISM

Opponents of pragmatism state that pragmatism is too indefinite; that there are many competing pragmatic philosophies that lack unity. Each pragmatic thinker brings an altered approach to pragmatism (Rescher). While pragmatists see varied approaches as a positive philosophical perspective, opponents see the approach as being too relative and as a situational rejection of values that have been tried and true over time (Ozmon & Craver).

Pragmatism proposes that people's innate characters drive them to learn and that by ignoring their characters they are not reaching their full potential. To opponents of pragmatism, this perspective conceals "the class nature" of this philosophy; that those who don't learn for learning's sake must subsequently become laborers (Wells, 1971).

In a pragmatist approach to teaching, the teacher's role is to get in touch with their students' natural impulses and instincts and then utilize this understanding about their students to organize activities that promote habits of learning. For teachers, the start of activity must come from the child. However, opponents state that "the sole function of the teacher should be to supply stimuli and materials which allow for expression" (Wells). Hence, the teacher must play a more active role in the classroom as the teacher realizes students' abilities through the activity process. To pragmatists, the end interest of the children is that starting point of activities and this must be discovered prior to the activity.

Additionally, pragmatist opponents state that pragmatist philosophy develops children who are not particularly knowledgeable. While they may be exposed to certain rich experiences, they lack the background or knowledge that frames experiences. With what opponents see as a watered-down curriculum, students are exposed to a curriculum that provides little depth and exposure to basic knowledge (Ozmon & Craver).

TERMS & CONCEPTS

Complete Act of Thought: The Complete Act of Thought is John Dewey's concept of thinking that is based on the scientific methodological process that follows certain logical steps. These steps include realizing that one is in a problematic situation; defining it as such; researching the problem; developing a hypothesis to solve it; and choosing and acting on that particular hypothesis.

Empiricism: Empiricism is the theory that there is no source of knowledge outside of experience itself.

Growth: In pragmatism, growth is what Dewey sees as his sole end of education. Growth means "to have more experience, more problems, more resolutions to problems, and a greater network of social relationships that makes life more effective, meaningful, and satisfying".

Social Intelligence: Social intelligence is defined as "the process by which individuals create meaning through their association and participation in a community based on sharing experiences".

Tricia Smith

BIBLIOGRAPHY

Bruce, B. C., & Bloch, N. (2013). Pragmatism and community inquiry: A case study of community-based learning. *Education & Culture, 29*, 27-45. Retrieved December 15, 2013, from EBSCO Online Database Education Research Complete.

Dewey, J. (1916). *Democracy and education.* New York: Macmillan.

Dewey, J. (1997 [1910]). *How we think.* Mineola, NH: Dover.

Englund, T. (2000, March). Rethinking democracy and education: Towards an education of deliberative citizens. *Journal of Curriculum Studies, 32*, 305-313. Retrieved June 12, 2009, from EBSCO online database, Education Research Complete.

Gutek, G. (2009). *New perspectives on philosophy and education.* Columbus, OH: Pearson.

Hammond, M. (2013). The contribution of pragmatism to understanding educational action research: Value and consequences. *Educational Action Research, 21*, 603-618.

Retrieved December 15, 2013, from EBSCO Online Database Education Research Complete.

Marcell, D. *Progress and pragmatism: James, Dewey, Beard, and the American idea of Progress.* Westport, CT: Greenwood Press.

Minnich, E. (1999). Experiential education. *Liberal Education, 85*, 6-14. Retrieved June 15, 2009, from EBSCO online database, Education Research Complete.

Moore, E. (1961). *American pragmatism: Peirce, James and Dewey.* New York: NY: Columbia P.

Ozmon, H., & Craver, S. (2008). *Philosophical foundations of education.* Columbus, OH: Pearson.

Pugh, K.J. (2011). Transformative experience: An integrative construct in the spirit of Deweyan pragmatism. *Educational Psychologist, 46*, 107-121. Retrieved December 15, 2013, from EBSCO Online Database Education Research Complete.

Rescher, N. (2000). *Realistic pragmatism: An introduction to pragmatic philosophy.* Albany, NY: State of U Press.

Rosiek, J. (2013). Pragmatism and post-qualitative futures. *International Journal of Qualitative Studies in Education (QSE), 26*, 692-705. Retrieved December 15, 2013, from EBSCO Online Database Education Research Complete.

Ryan, A. (1996). Pragmatism, social identity, patriotism, and self-criticism. *Social Research, 63*, 1041-1064. Retrieved June 17, 2009, from EBSCO online database, Academic Search Complete.

Shusterman, R. (1997). *Practicing philosophy: Pragmatism and the philosophical life.* New York, NY: Routledge.

Thayer, H. (1968). *Meaning and action: A critical history of pragmatism.* New York, NY: Bobbs-Merrill.

Wells, H. (1971). *Pragmatism: Philosophy of imperialism.* Freeport, NY: Books for Libraries P.

Younkins, E. (n.d.). Dewey's pragmatism and the decline of education. Retrieved from Rebirth of Reason, http://rebirthofreason.com.

SUGGESTED READING

Baldacchino, J. (2008). 'The Power to Develop Dispositions': Revisiting John Dewey's deomocratic claims for education [Book Review]. *Journal of Philosophy of Education, 42*, 149-163. Retrieved June 14, 2009, from EBSCO online database, Education Research Complete.

Bauerlein, M. (1997). *The pragmatic mind: Exploration in the psychology of belief.* Durham, NC: Duke University Press.

Biesta, G. (1994). Pragmatism as a pedagogy of communicative action. *Studies in Philosophy & Education, 13* (3/4), 273-291.

Colapietro, V. (2007). Aligning Deweyan pragmatism and Emersonian perfectionism: Reimagining growth and educating grownups. *Journal of Philosophy of Education, 41*, 459-469. Retrieved June 15, 2009, from EBSCO online database, Education Research Complete.

Dewey, J. (1958). *Experience and education*. New York: Dover.

Guelzo, A. (2009, May 25). Is there an American mind? *National Review*, 61, pp. 44-48. Retrieved June 17, 2009, from EBSCO online database, Academic Search Complete.

Henry, S. (2005). A different approach to teaching multiculturalism: Pragmatism as a pedagogy and problem-solving tool. *Teachers College Record, 107*, 1060-1078. Retrieved June 18, 2009, from EBSCO online database, Academic Search Complete.

Kaag, J. (2009). Pragmatism and the lessons of experience. *Daedalus, 138*, pp. 63-72.

Lehmann-Rommel, R. (2000). The renewal of Dewey: Trends in the nineties. *Studies in Philosophy and education,19* (½), pp. 187-218. Retrieved June 18, 2009, from EBSCO online database, Academic Search Complete.

McCarthy, C. (2000). Dewey pragmatism and the quest for true belief. *Educational Theory, 50*, 213-217. Retrieved June 17, 2009, from EBSCO online database, Academic Search Complete.

Menand, L. (1997). *Pragmatism*. New York, NY: Vintage Books.

Neiman, A. (1996). Rorty's Dewey: Pragmatism, education and the public sphere. *Studies in Philosophy and Education, 15*(½), 121-130.

Rucker, D. (1969). *The Chicago pragmatists*. Minneapolis, MN: U of Minnesota Press.

Saito, N. (2006). Philosophy as education and education as philosophy: Democracy and education from Dewey to Cavell. *Journal of Philosophy of Education, 40*, 345-356. Retrieved June 18, 2009, from EBSCO online database, Academic Search Complete.

Scheffler, I. (1974). *Four pragmatists*. New York, NY: Humanities Press.

Schneider, S., & Garrison, J. (2008). Deweyan reflections on knowledge-producing schools. *Teachers College Record, 110*, 2204-2223.

Seigfried, C. (1996). *Reweaving the social fabric: Pragmatism and feminism*. Chicago, IL: U of Chicago Press.

Sund, P., & Wickman, P. (2008). Teachers' objects of responsibility: Something to care about in education for sustainable development. *Environmental Education Research, 14*, pp. 145-163.

Thigpen, C. (1994). Meiklejohn and Maritain: Two views on the end of progressive education. *Teachers College Record, 96*, 87-103.

Vandenberg, D. (2009). Critical thinking about truth in teaching: The epistemic ethos. *Educational Philosophy and Theory, 41*, 155-165.

Vanderstraeten, R, & Biesta, G. (2006). How is education possible? Pragmatism, communication and the social organization of education. *British Journal of Educational Studies, 54*, 160-714. Retrieved June 16, 2009, from EBSCO online database, Education Research Complete.

Weber, E. (2008). Dewey and Rawls on Education. *Human Studies, 31*, pp. 361-382.

Westbrook, R. (1991). *John Dewey and American democracy*. Ithaca, NY: Cornell.

THEORY OF MIND

An overview of Theory of Mind and its role and impact on student learning in public school education environments is presented. Also presented is a brief look at the current research pertaining to Theory of Mind and its relationship to children and their developmental processes. Further analyzed are ways social skills are impacted by Theory of Mind in accordance with age related behavioral processes. This article discusses implications for classrooms and applications are described that include roles and impact on certain groups including students, teachers, and administrators. Solutions are offered to help professionals develop the most effective programs through consistent, research based methodologies and philosophies.

KEYWORDS: Emotion Understanding; False Belief; Prefrontal Cortex; Self Awareness; Theory of Mind (ToM)

OVERVIEW

Theory of Mind (ToM) is the term given to "the human ability to infer the intentions of others and to understand that their actions are guided by beliefs about the world" (Mizrahi, Korostil, Starkstein, Zipursky & Shitij, 2007). Theory of Mind can also be described as "the ability to understand and reason about [a child's] own and others' mental states (such as understanding that the mind can misrepresent reality)" (Birch & Bernstein, 2007, p. 99). According to McHugh, Barnes-Holmes, Barnes-Holmes, Stewart, & Dymond (2007), an individual's "knowledge of informational states in the self and others develops across five levels originating from simple visual perspective taking to understanding true and false beliefs."

The first three levels of Theory of Mind consist of

- Simple visual perspective taking,
- Complex visual perspective taking;

- Applying information based on the principle of seeing leads to knowing.

Levels 4 and 5 of this framework "consist of the development of understanding true and false beliefs. According to this model, the skills of perspective-taking are believed to be essential prerequisites for the development of true and false beliefs" (McHugh et al.). The study of the Theory of Mind is a relatively new area of brain research. Findings from these studies are leading educators to better understanding developmental processes of children in new and expanded ways. This paper seeks to outline research, practice, and implications for educational professionals and psychologists seeking to better understand how brain development impacts student thinking and behavior.

THEORY OF MIND IN YOUNG CHILDREN

One of the findings from research is that Theory of Mind is age related and developmentally related. This holds multiple meanings in terms of educational and social planning. In particular, several studies have been conducted with three-year-old children. One such study involved showing a child a closed candy box and asking the child to determine what was inside the box. Typically, three-year-old children state the answer as "candy." However, after the researcher opened the box to reveal pencils and then closed the box again and asked the child what he or she thought was inside the box before it was opened, the child answered, "pencils" (Wellman, Cross, & Watson, 2001). Typically, when adults ask preschool aged children to state facts and later ask them if they have known these facts for a long time or just learned them today, children will insist that they have known these facts all along and that their friend will also know (Taylor, Esbensen, & Bennett, 1994). These are important findings from Theory of Mind research that relate specifically to hindsight.

HINDSIGHT BIAS

Conclusions have been proposed that support children's Theory of Mind relationship to hindsight bias in adults as shared core components of a similarly occurring phenomenon (Bernstein, Erdfelder, Meltzoff, Peria & Loftus, 2011). This core component consists of a tendency to be biased by one's current knowledge when attempting to remember or make sense of a more naïve cognitive state. In order to more fully understand hindsight bias a more developmental approach should be able to provide a unified understanding of the nature of hindsight bias (Birch & Bernstein). Researchers studying Theory of Mind need to understand that the research and theoretical framework constructing this new knowledge is potentially explosive in impacting both the fields of education and psychology in brain research and child learning. It could be argued that Theory of Mind is one of the key theories on the forefront of unlocking how to teach and socialize in accordance with developmental milestones based on the notion of when children can begin to integrate interpersonal perspective-taking within their social and learning framework.

Theorists argue that hindsight bias bears a striking resemblance and connection to Theory of Mind and the types of errors that young children make in Theory of Mind reasoning. These errors demonstrate that young children who are taught new information are unable to recall which information they have known longer, information they learned moments before, or information they have known for a long time (Taylor et al.). Moreover, these deficits spill over into their judgments regarding the knowledge of other people. For example, it has been demonstrated that preschool children tend to behave as if seeing a small uninformative part of an object is sufficient for someone else to know the object's identity (Taylor, 1988) regardless of the age or identity of the person with whom they are sharing joint attention. In order to help children develop Theory of Mind, lessons could be constructed in the classroom using quadrants of pictures or art. Children could then be asked to determine the full object based on their model of perception. Misperceptions and myths could then be dispelled using this lesson framework. This lesson could be utilized at various ages to facilitate perception development for older students as well as younger students.

From an educational perspective, it should be noted that Theory of Mind changes as children age. Generally, four-and-five-year-olds tend to perform much better on Theory of Mind tasks. With age, research suggests that children improve in their ability to better understand sources of knowledge

(Gopnik & Graf, 1988; Roberts & Blades, 2000), about what others are likely to know based on limited information (Taylor; Taylor et al.), and regarding their own and other's false beliefs (Wellman et al.). However, in other studies of Theory of Mind task correlations were established between children's Theory of Mind and adult's Hindsight bias. Birch and Bloom demonstrated that when sensitive measures are used, adults can also experience difficulty reasoning about false beliefs. During investigations that sought to determine this connection, findings reported that outcome knowledge can compromise an adult's ability to reason about their own false beliefs and internal assumptions (Birch & Bernstein, 2007). Wimmer and Perner similarly determined that younger children could not complete Theory of Mind tasks successfully because they were unable to reconcile the conflict between reality and their own knowledge of the truth (Wellman et al.).Other studies have demonstrated an even more cogent relationship between age and developmental stages.

THE ROLE OF DECEPTION

According to other Theory of Mind research, in order to successfully complete many Theory of Mind tasks, children must reach a developmental stage termed as Level 5. Evidence of this can be found from research that has been done to better understand deception.

"Deception involves understanding other minds, because it requires a person to make someone else believe that something is true when in fact it is false" (McHugh et al.). From a Theory of Mind construct, deception involves the deliberate planning and communication of a false belief to another. In typically developing children, deception can occur successfully in a child that is about six-years-old (Marvin, Greenberg, & Mossler, 1976). In order to deceive, Theory of Mind researchers delve further into the complex cognitive abilities that produce deception. Theorists posture that deception requires a myriad of complex intra-personal perspective taking. First, to deceive, a child must be able to take the perspective of another individual to determine what the other person will believe from the information provided. Second, the child must be able to reason within the framework of "if-then relation" controlling the transfer of information.

Third, the child must be able to transfer information in accordance with a "relation of distinction" (McHugh et al.). Again, this research indicates that very young children are impaired in their ability to take the perspectives of others. The inability to possess a well-developed Theory of Mind poses several negative impacts for children and adults.

THEORY OF MIND & SOCIAL SKILLS

In terms of social society, Theory of Mind plays an essential role. An individual with a well-developed Theory of Mind should be able to think about, make intelligent inferences, and accurately infer another person's mind set and emotions. This person would be good at speculating what another person might be thinking and would have a greater awareness of other people's thoughts, feelings, and potential motives. Research has suggested that Theory of Mind can be considered as a module within the human mind dedicated solely to reading the intent and mind set of other persons (Abbas, 2006). In terms of children, Theory of Mind activities must be researched and applied in a classroom setting in order to support children in developing a Theory of Mind. However, for some children and adults, Theory of Mind deficits impact empathy and social connectivity.

For example, children with high functioning autism or Asperger Syndrome seem to lack Theory of Mind altogether and possess "mindblindness." Baron-Cohen has argued that these two disorders manifest an imbalance between two types of intelligence and that individuals with these disorders lack an ability to understand people while possessing an overdeveloped ability to understand systems, movement, and mechanical thinking. More interestingly, one theory suggests that the reason males tend to be diagnosed at a greater rate than females is because of the female's natural inclination to possess higher degrees of empathy (DeSoto, Bumgarner, Close, & Geary, 2007). Individuals possessing Theory of Mind deficits are unable to infer emotional states and may have difficulties contributing to diverse human behaviors like empathy, forethought, and social intelligence (Geary, 2004; Humphrey, 1976). For both children and adults with Theory of Mind deficits understanding and Social Skills Training should be considered.

Applications

STUDENTS

For students, Theory of Mind plays a potentially important role in their social relationships with others and in their interpersonal assumptions and intra-personal perspective taking. In children's relationships with one another, Theory of Mind seems to be one of the key factors in helping children form bonds with one another and in developing empathic, socially intelligent relationships. In a classroom setting, Theory of Mind could be a potential explanation for children's behavior. Further study needs to investigate Theory of Mind in terms of physiological and psychological relevance.

Additionally, Theory of Mind deficits serve as predictors of children's social interactions and internal assumptions. Deficits in Theory of Mind or "mindblindness" typically preclude social inadequacies and should be studied further to determine relatedness not only to autism disorders but also mental health disturbances, deceit, and other social disturbances that interfere with success in a classroom setting. For students with these deficits, Social Skills Training should be offered that specifically addresses and names Theory of Mind, Theory of Mind deficits, internal assumptions, and intra-personal perspective taking as indicators for both educational and therapeutic intervention aimed at improved social awareness (Stichter, O'Connor, Herzog, Lierheimer & McGhee, 2012).

In children identified with an autism disorder or other social deficits, Theory of Mind holds one of the essential components for understanding how current brain research impacts learning and student success. This study goes beyond providing a framework of generalized developmental milestones and links a physiological component for helping researchers understanding the "how" and "why" resulting in specific behaviors.

TEACHERS

Theory of Mind study clearly extends beyond a simple outline of human behavior presented in most undergraduate educational psychology classes. Instead, Theory of Mind research presents some of the most recent and relevant psychological study aimed at better understanding the human brain. In order to teach children at their level, we cannot forget Piaget or Vygotsky and their contributions to helping educators understand developmental milestones, but we must recognize the current research and relevant contributions of present day psychologists and researchers in helping us unleash the potential of the human mind and the physiological connective tissue that underscores psychological development.

For teachers to better understand how to teach students and help them form positive social relationships with their peers, teachers need to have some background knowledge about Theory of Mind and information about how Theory of Mind brain research impacts how and when students learn. Teachers must teach in accordance with each individualized physiological and psychological composition of each child. Theory of Mind research potentially supports the need for differentiated instruction and meeting each child in accordance with their developmental progress (Pavarini, Hollanda Souza & Hawk, 2013). The investigations that have been conducted to support these findings clearly demonstrate ways that educators can enfold these concepts into rethinking their instruction. However, before teachers can begin to practice these "radical" new ways of thinking, teachers need to understand their own internal assumptions and intra-personal perspective taking. From the research, it has been concluded that adults and hindsight deficits connect similarly to Theory of Mind deficits in children. Educators may experience some of these same deficits in their own thinking and may not recognize it. If educators are to model strategies for overcoming Theory of Mind deficits, educators must examine their own mental models to transform their thought patterns.

Instructionally, limited research on Theory of Mind has been conducted to better hone the skills for better preparing students to understand the perspectives of others. However, literature circles, group and individual reading activities integrating these kinds of exercises would allow students to practice perspective taking, role plays, and invite them to wrestle with their potential false beliefs (Comer Kidd & Castano, 2013). For younger students, picture readers or picture books without words that allow children to analyze the facial expressions of characters in the book should allow teachers a window into their student's thinking regarding perspective taking. Finally, teachers need to be keenly observant of their students at various ages to determine if students are able to engage in perspective taking in social and academic situations. Teachers are on the front lines of observing children and facilitating interventions if interventions are required.

ADMINISTRATORS

Administrators serve as key instruments in creating change in educational cultures, and principals are considered as the instructional leaders in schools. Within this framework, many administrators may not be familiar with present research, unless they have been exposed to information that supports a different way of thinking and the research itself. Much of the Theory of Mind research rests in studies pertaining to autism. For educators and researchers, autism is only one lens for the research in this area. The implications for this research are substantial and should be continued to be researched for updated, present, and relevant findings. Administrators should also be aware that they play a key role in facilitating access to the most present educational research that supports student learning. If administrators do not have the time or the ability to function as an instructional leader, professional development specialists or academic coaches could also serve in this role.

Administrators should also note that leadership today is a formative and an ongoing process of facilitating change and transformation. The educator's job has been designed to foster the developmental and educational needs of children. The administrator's job is to foster the developmental and educational needs of adults they serve in educational settings. These are important mandates for all educational professionals to look at our times and the amounts of information being gathered pertaining to the dramatic physiological constructs of learning. This decade alone has produced an onslaught of new ideas and different ways of thinking supported by research. These are new lenses for looking at ourselves and our practices. Administrators play a crucial role in leading staffs to research and renewed thinking.

Issues

OVERCOMING BARRIERS TO UNDERSTANDING THEORY OF MIND

Theory of Mind has been most presently regarded as a lens for understanding social deficits experienced by individuals with special needs, particularly those impacted by autism disorders. However, after reviewing the research and literature pertaining to Theory of Mind and Theory of Mind deficits, the relevance of Theory of Mind and its connection to schizophrenia and psychotic disorders (Mizrahi et al.), child deception (McHugh et al.), physiological and hormonal predeterminants (DeSoto et al.), self-awareness and perspective-taking (Howlin, Baron-Cohen & Hadwin, 1999) deeply impact present thought in terms of educational and social implications in a public education classroom environment. While once only a narrow field of research, Theory of Mind research has become an extremely broad field, encompassing multiple components of mental-state reasoning within both normal and atypical development. Presently, much of the Theory of Mind research includes representations of conscious awareness of beliefs, desires, intentions, including deception, and knowledge. Based on children's conceptions of what others know or do not know is the primary lens for researching Theory of Mind (Thompson & Thornton, 2007).

One of the barriers to understanding Theory of Mind is that most practitioners only understand the relevance of Theory of Mind and its relationship to atypical social development. However, based on present research, Theory of Mind is deeply relevant in broader academic and social arenas. As an undergraduate student, Theory of Mind might only be "covered" in a surface overview, or it may not be taught at all. To better understand Theory of Mind and to engage students in the most recent, brain research and child developmental processes, these theories should be introduced in educational psychology courses at the university level if this has not occurred.

The last critical barrier to overcome to better understand Theory of Mind is that researchers should shift their focus to academic applications. Theory of Mind has largely been conducted in theoretical arenas. Now it is time to apply the research in academic settings with meaningful curriculum that encompasses the brain research and developmental processes. Students need to be engaged in practices that allow them to think in terms of intra-perspective taking, because Theory of Mind holds the key for helping students socially connect. Since the classroom is both a socially and academically rich environment, Theory of Mind research could dramatically improve social and academic relationships especially with instruction specifically geared toward constructing new ways of thinking and acting.

CONCLUSION

Theory of Mind is a relatively new area of brain research that has amazing potential for creating new ways of thinking about the connection between social and academic relationships. This area of research possesses unique properties with vast potential in helping educators better understand how to work with all children and especially those expressing difficulties showing empathy or social connectivity. This area of study also fits nicely with internal assumption making practices by both children and adults. Most notably, the Theory of Mind research while once limited to evaluating individuals with incapacities for intrapersonal perspective taking can now be extended to all children in helping them develop emotional understanding, dispel false beliefs, improve social cognition and social relationships, and examine their own assumptions. Armed with some knowledge about Theory of Mind, teachers should be able to evaluate students to better understand their internal assumption making processes and teach them new ways of thinking. Especially useful for this kind of work is collaboration with peers and opportunities to discuss internal assumptions in a guided methodology that allows all children the opportunity to share their thoughts and assumptions in a safe environment. The goal in this work is to create a "system of diversity" that makes school a safe and nurturing place both academically and socially.

TERMS & CONCEPTS

Emotion Understanding: Emotion Understanding has been described as a developmental milestone when children begin to set aside their own ultimately inappropriate emotion to attribute a false emotion to a given situation. An example is that despite receiving a disappointing gift a child will exhibit happiness.

False Belief: Mastery of false belief has been described as the first clear evidence that children realize their beliefs are mental representations and not direct reflections of reality.

Prefrontal Cortex: The Prefrontal Cortex is the part of the brain that research has demonstrated impacts theory of mind tasks, the ability to understand deception, and intra-personal perspective taking.

Self-Awareness: The developmental stage when children are aware of and able to articulate their own psychological state.

Theory of Mind (ToM): Theory of Mind can best be described as an individual's ability to think about, make intelligent inferences about, and accurately assess another individual's mind set and emotions.

Sharon Link

BIBLIOGRAPHY

Abbas, J. H. (2006). Modularity hypothesis: Presentation and analysis. *Disarat: Human and Social Science, 32,* 200-212.

Bernstein, D. M., Erdfelder, E., Meltzoff, A. N., Peria, W., & Loftus, G. R. (2011). Hindsight bias from 3 to 95 years of age. *Journal of Experimental Psychology. Learning, Memory & Cognition, 37,* 378-391. Retrieved on December 10, 2013, from EBSCO Online Database Education Research Complete.

Birch, S., & Bernstein, D. (2007). What can children tell us about hindsight bias: A fundamental constraint on perspective taking? *Social Cognition, 25,* 98-113. Retrieved December 30, 2007, from EBSCO Online Database Academic Search Premier.

Birch, S. A. J., & Bloom, P. (2007). The curse of knowledge in reasoning about false beliefs. *Psychological Science.* Manuscript in press.

Comer Kidd, D., & Castano, E. (2013). Reading literary fiction improves theory of mind. *Science, 342*(6156), 377-380. Retrieved on December 10, 2013, from EBSCO Online Database Education Research Complete.

DeSoto, M. C., Bumgarner, J., Close, A., & Geary, D. (2007). Investigating the role of hormones in theory of mind. *North American Journal of Psychology, 9,* 535-544. Retrieved December 30, 2007, from EBSCO Online Database Academic Search Premier.

Geary, D. C. (2004). *The origin of the mind: Evolution of brain, cognition, and general intelligence.* American Psychological Association, Washington D.C.

Gopnik, A., & Graf, P. (1988). Knowing how you know: Young children's ability to identify and remember the sources of their beliefs. *Child Development, 59,* 1366-1371. Retrieved December 30, 2007, from EBSCO Online Database Academic Search Premier.

Roberts, K. P., & Blades, M. (2000). *Children's source monitoring.* Mahwah, NJ: Erlbaum.

Howlin, P., Baron-Cohen, S., & Hadwin, J. (1999). *Teaching children with autism to mind-read. A practical guide.* Chichester, England: Wiley.

Humphrey, N. K. (1976). The social function of intellect. In P.P.G. Bateson & R.A. Hinde (Eds.), *Growing points in ethology* (pp. 303-317). New York: Cambridge University Press.

Marvin, R. S., Greenberg, M. T., & Mossler, D. G. (1976). The early development of conceptual perspective taking: Distinguishing among multiple perspectives. *Child Development, 47,* 511-514. Retrieved December 30, 2007, from EBSCO Online Database Academic Search Premier.

McHugh, L., Barnes-Holmes, Y., Barnes-Holmes, D., Stewart, I., & Dymond, S. (2007). Deictic relational complexity and the development of deception, *The Psychological Record, 57,* 517-531. Retrieved December 30, 2007, from EBSCO Online Database, Academic Search Premier.

Mizrahi, R., Korostil, M., Starkstein, R., Zipursky, R., Shitij, K. (2007). The effect of antipsychotic treatment of theory of mind. *Psychological Medicine, 37,* 595-601.

Pavarini, G., Hollanda Souza, D., & Hawk, C. (2013). Parental practices and theory of mind development. *Journal of Child & Family Studies, 22,* 844-853. Retrieved on December 10, 2013, from EBSCO Online Database Education Research Complete.

Stichter, J., O'Connor, K., Herzog, M., Lierheimer, K., & McGhee, S. (2012). Social competence intervention for elementary students with Aspergers Syndrome and high functioning autism. *Journal of Autism & Developmental Disorders, 42,* 354-366. Retrieved on December 10, 2013, from EBSCO Online Database Education Research Complete.

Taylor, M. (1988). Conceptual perspective taking: Children's ability to distinguish what they know from what they see. *Child Development, 59,* 703-718. Retrieved December 30, 2007, from EBSCO Online Database Academic Search Premier.

Taylor, M., Cartwright, B. S., & Bowden, T. (1991). Perspective taking and theory of mind: Do children predict interpretive diversity as a function of differences in observers' knowledge? *Child Development, 62,* 1334 - 1351. Retrieved December 30, 2007, from EBSCO Online Database Academic Search Premier.

Taylor, M., Esbensen, B. M., & Bennett, R. T. (1994). Children's understanding of knowledge acquisition: The tendency for children to report that they have always known what they have just learned. *Child Development, 65,* 1581-1604.

Thompson, B., & Thornton, B. (2007). Exploring mental-state reasoning as a social-cognitive mechanism for social loafing in children. *The Journal of Social Psychology, 147,* 159-174. Retrieved December 30, 2007, from EBSCO Online Database, Academic Search Premier.

Wellman, H. M., Cross, D., & Watson, J. (2001). Meta-analysis of theory of mind development: The truth about false belief. *Child Development, 72,* 655-684. Retrieved December 30, 2007, from EBSCO Online Database Academic Search Premier.

SUGGESTED READING

Baron-Cohen, S. (1995). *Mindblindness: An essay on autism and theory of mind.* MIT Press/Bradford Books.

Baron-Cohen, S., Tager-Flusberg, H., & Cohen, D. (2000). *Understanding other minds: Perspectives from developmental cognitive neuroscience.* 2nd ed. Oxford: Oxford University Press.

DeAngelo, G. & McCannon, B. (2017). Theory of Mind predicts cooperative behavior. *Economics Letters,* 155, 1.

Dunn, J. (1988). *The beginnings of social understanding.* Cambridge, MA: Harvard University Press.

Wellman, H. M. (1990). *The child's theory of mind.* Cambridge, MA: MIT Press.

SOCIAL LEARNING THEORY

Most often associated with the work of Albert Bandura, social learning theory incorporates principles of both behaviorism and cognitive theories of learning. In its simplest form, social learning theory explains how people learn by observing the behavior of others. Bandura suggests that this process has four component parts: attention, retention, motor reproduction and motivation. Environmental and cognitive factors can influence the process as well. The theory has many practical applications for understanding behavior in the classroom, and in society more generally. However, despite its far-reaching impact, social learning theory is not without its critics.

KEYWORDS: Behaviorism; Cognition Theory; Modeling; Operant Conditioning; Reciprocal Determinism; Self-Efficacy; Self-Regulation; Vicarious Reinforcement

OVERVIEW

Social learning theory is often characterized as a stepping stone between two diametrically opposed theories of learning (Ormrod, 1990). By defining human learning as a function of both the environment and mental processes, social learning theory blended behaviorism—the dominant theory of learning in the 1950s and 1960s—and cognitive theories of learning, which gained prominence in the 1970s and have remained popular into the twenty-first century. Although many individuals contributed to the development of social learning theory, Albert Bandura, a Stanford professor whose career spans more than 60 years, is most often recognized as its creator. The following summary will outline Bandura's work, showing that what began as a blending of behaviorism and cognition, has shifted more heavily toward the latter, following the lead of larger trends in psychology and education (Ormrod).

History

Bandura's shift toward a more cognitive orientation, however, began very late in his career. When he first started as a professor at Stanford in 1953, behaviorism was in its heyday. In many ways, then, social learning theory developed in reaction to behaviorism, or to what Bandura perceived as its limitations in explaining human learning. Bandura observed, for example, that human learning occurred much more rapidly than behaviorists had proposed. Whereas behaviorists suggested that learning occurs gradually—through trial and error and with the aid of reinforcement—Bandura believed learning could take place all at once, without any practice or reinforcement whatsoever, simply by observing other people (Crain, 2000). Bandura also wanted to leave room for individual agency, and found behaviorists' emphasis on the role of the environment limiting (Bandura, 1977). Emphasizing certain factors, like the environment, to the exclusion of others, like cognition, led to what he called "a truncated image of the human potential" (Bandura).

Operant Conditioning

More specifically, Bandura didn't believe observational learning—that is, learning that occurs by observing a model exhibit a particular behavior, and then imitating that behavior oneself—could be explained by operant conditioning, the mechanism behaviorists suggest explains most changes in behavior. According to the operant conditioning paradigm, voluntary behaviors exhibited by either an animal or a human are modified by the consequences that follow; reinforcement

increases the frequency of a behavior, whereas punishment decreases the frequency. The voluntary behavior, or response, typically occurs in the presence of a discriminative stimulus, and the consequence, either reinforcement or punishment—immediately follows. According to behaviorists, observational learning fits neatly into this paradigm (Mazur, 1994); the behavior to be imitated (the model) serves as the discriminative stimulus, and the imitation of the behavior is the response itself. Whereas a rat might learn to press a lever in the presence of a red light, and is then rewarded with food, for example, a young boy might imitate the behavior of his father, when in his father's presence, and receive a reward, such as verbal praise.

Examples of operant conditioning in the classroom, write Lineros and Hinojosa (2012), might include the instructor's granting a higher grade for quality writing and a lower one for the inverse. Or, the authors write, the instructor's "consistently smiling [at] and asking easier questions of the left side of a classroom. As the left side contributes to class discussion, the positive instructor reinforcement tends to push students towards that side" (Lineros & Hinojosa).

Lineros and Hinojosa add that instructors can also inadvertently create these behaviors through subconscious positive and negative reinforcement. "This can insidiously harm diversity as instructors unknowingly reward through positive body language or speech tone those who mirror their espoused beliefs," they write.

Why did Bandura feel operant conditioning was an insufficient theory for explaining observational learning? Why did he feel it was an adequate model for explaining some types of behavior, and not others? Bandura's criticisms were threefold (Ormrod). Because operant conditioning suggests a behavior must be emitted first, and then shaped by the subsequent reinforcement or punishment, Bandura wondered how it could explain behaviors that are emitted correctly the first time. As Ormrod writes, "The learning of an entirely novel response—responses that an individual has seen but never previously emitted in any form—is difficult to explain from a Skinnerian perspective." Secondly, according to behaviorists, the discriminative stimulus, response, and reinforcement occur immediately after one another; Bandura pointed out, however, that imitation of behavior and subsequent reinforcement is often delayed. Such delayed imitation suggests that learning occurs at the time the discriminative stimulus—in this case, at the time the individual observes the model—and importantly, occurs even in absence of reinforcement. Thus, unlike behaviorists, Bandura didn't believe reinforcement was a necessary component of learning. He also demonstrated that learning and behavior are distinct from one another. Finally, Bandura pointed out that people often imitate behavior for which they are never reinforced; simply watching other people reinforced for their behaviors is often enough incentive for an individual to exhibit the behavior herself. Again, operant conditioning falls short in explaining this phenomenon, too.

Principles of Social Learning Theory

Given the limitations of behaviorism, and operant conditioning more specifically, Bandura's theory of social learning (which he first called a theory of observational learning) began to take shape. Before delving into the specific mechanisms through which people learn by observing others, the key elements of social learning theory, as discussed by Ormrod, are outlined below.

- People can learn by observing the behavior of others, as well as from the consequences of those behaviors;
- Learning and performance are not necessarily the same thing; people can learn behaviors at the time they observe them, but not perform them until a later time, or not at all;
- Reinforcement plays a role in learning, although is not a necessary component of the learning process;
- Cognitive processes play a role in learning. As Crain elaborates, "When new behavior is acquired through observation alone, the learning appears to be cognitive. Thus, Bandura, unlike Skinner, believes that learning theory must include internal cognitive variables."

Bandura identifies four components to observational learning:

- Attention;
- Retention;
- Motor reproduction;
- Motivation/Reinforcement.

Bandura writes, "people cannot learn much by observation unless they attend to, and perceive accurately, the significant features of the modeled behavior" (p. 24). Secondly, the observer must remember what was observed. Thus, the behavior observed must be retained, and this occurs, Bandura argues, by using two different symbolic systems: by representing the behavior in image form, as a visual picture, or by representing it in verbal form, as a series of instructions. If a child is learning how to play tennis, for example, she may retain an image of her instructor demonstrating the proper forehand technique, and she might also retain a series of instructions, such as "I step forward with my left foot, turning my body perpendicular to..." Next, as the previous example suggests, one must be able to replicate the behavior. In other words, the individual must have the motor reproduction skills to enact the behavior she observed. If the tennis student doesn't have the strength to swing a racquet, she might not be able to reproduce the behavior. The final component of observational learning is motivation; people do not imitate all the behavior they learn but rather must be motivated to do so. Two points deserve emphasis; again, the distinction between learning and performance—people don't perform all behaviors they have learned, only those they are motivated to perform. And secondly, expectation of reward can be as motivating as the reward itself. Bandura writes, "Reinforcement does play a role in observational learning, but mainly as an antecedent rather than a consequent influence. Anticipation of reinforcement is one of several factors that can influence what is observed and what goes unnoticed." It also influences what is performed, and what is not.

Models

Why do some people pay attention to certain models and not others? Why do people imitate the same behavior differently? These are the questions Bandura attempted to answer in identifying some of the variables that influence the modeling process. Characteristics of the model, for example, determine to some extent whether or not they will be imitated (Ormrod). Models who are more similar to the person observing the behavior are more likely to be imitated, thus girls tend to imitate others of their same gender, and boys, vice versa. Models who are highly visible and competent—perceived to have power and prestige—are also more likely to be imitated. Movie stars and athletes, as a result, often find their behavior and appearance imitated. Finally, when the model's behavior is relevant to the observer, the model is more likely to be imitated (Ormrod). Characteristics of the observer can also influence the process; younger children tend to imitate others more often, as do those who are more uncertain of their own behavior (Mazur).

The characteristics of models and learners certainly affect the modeling process, but the consequences to both the model and learner play an equally important role. As the following discussion suggests, reinforcement is both an environmental and cognitive variable. Consider the following ways in which the environment reinforces modeling. An observer might be reinforced directly by the model she is imitating, as when the tennis instructor praises the student for demonstrating proper technique in swinging a forehand. Alternatively, an observer might be reinforced by a third party. The girls' teammates, for example, might reward her improved skills by asking her to play with them more often. The modeled behavior itself might be rewarding; if the young student gets more tennis balls across the net, and wins more points, for example, she will continue to model the behavior of her instructor. And finally, the instructor might be rewarded, which could be reinforcing for the observer as well. As Ormrod explains, "if a model is reinforced for a response, chances are greater that the observer will also show an increase in that response, a phenomenon known as vicarious reinforcement."

To some degree, vicarious reinforcement is effective because people's behavior is influenced by expectations. If an individual observes a model being rewarded for a certain behavior, they could reasonably expect to be rewarded for similar behavior. Expectation is a cognitive process, and as described earlier, illustrates the major difference between operant conditioning and Bandura's theory. "In operant conditioning, reinforcement influences the learning of the behavior it follows. In social learning, on the other hand, an expectation of reinforcement influences the learning of a behavior it precedes." Similarly, people must first be aware of response-reinforcement contingencies in order for them to influence future behavior (Ormrod); awareness, like expectations, is a cognitive function. Finally, Bandura has placed increasing emphasis on the role of self-regulation of behavior. As people learn which behaviors are appropriate and which are not through both direct and vicarious reinforcement and

punishment they begin to develop and internalize standards of their own. By developing such standards, individuals become self-reinforcing, and rely less on external rewards and punishments. As Bandura writes, "the development of self-reactive functions thus gives humans a capacity for self-direction."

Reciprocal Determinism

Before turning to the many ways in which social learning theory has been applied in the classroom, and toward understanding human development more generally, it is apropos to conclude with Bandura's notion of reciprocal determinism. Bandura introduced the notion of reciprocal determinism to represent the interaction of environment, person, and behavior. Importantly, Bandura conceptualized these interactions as two-way interactions. Thus, the environment might influence a person's behavior, for example, but behavior can also change the environment. Modeling itself—an environmental factor—influences both the person (e.g. her expectations) and her behavior (e.g., what she chooses to perform). In sum, each factor is capable of influencing the other two factors, as well as being influenced by them in return. Through the notion of reciprocal determinism, Bandura was able to meld together both behaviorist and cognitive principles.

APPLICATIONS

As Crain explains, "On a broader level, one of Bandura's primary, if sometimes implicit, concerns has been the socialization process—the process by which societies induce their members to behave in socially acceptable ways." Similarly, Bandura was equally as interested in personality development as he was the learning process (Mazur). He wanted to know why some people become aggressive, others peaceful, for example. Or why some were introverted, others more outgoing. According to Bandura, personality differences could be explained by learning experiences as well as heredity. As a result, the applications of his theory are far-reaching, and while relevant to learning that takes place in the classroom, they extend far beyond these boundaries.

Aggression

What became known as the "bobo doll study" (Bandura) is arguably one of the most famous studies conducted under the guise of social learning theory.

Through it, Bandura demonstrated that aggression could be learned by observing aggressive behavior in others (as cited in Mazur). This study also underscored the distinction between acquisition and performance of new behaviors. In this experiment, children watched a short film of an adult acting aggressively—punching, kicking, shouting, etc.—toward a large, inflatable rubber doll. The children were then assigned to three groups—the first group saw the model rewarded for his aggressive behavior, the second group saw the model punished, and the third group saw the model receive no consequences. When the children were then given an opportunity to play with a similar doll, the children who saw the model rewarded or the model who received no consequences exhibited the most aggressive behavior, while the children who saw the model punished exhibited the least. That the latter group showed the least aggressive behavior demonstrated the principle of vicarious punishment. In a second phase of the study, the same children were told they would be rewarded if they exhibited the behavior of the model; all the children were able to imitate the aggressive behavior, suggesting that all had originally learned the behavior, but not all had demonstrated it (depending on which type of consequence they observed).

As a result of the "Bobo doll study" and other similar studies, educators and parents became concerned about the influence of television and media. If children learned aggression by observing it in others firsthand, could they also learn it by watching TV characters, cartoon or otherwise? Bandura, Ross, and Ross (1963) believed the answer was 'yes' (as cited in Ormrod). They demonstrated that children who observed aggressive behavior by an adult or a cartoon character in a film exhibited just as much aggression as those who had witnessed the live model. As Ormrod concludes, "even cartoons that display violent behaviors, including such classics as 'Tom and Jerry' and 'Roadrunner,' may not be as harmless as they appear." Others have criticized such conclusions, however, arguing that such studies show correlation between aggression and watching violent TV, but do not prove causation (Mazur).

Achievement Motivation

Just as modeling can sometimes result in negative behaviors, modeling can also be used to help children develop positive ones. Bandura and Kupers (1964) conducted an experiment to determine if modeling could help explain self-discipline and achievement motivation (as cited in Mazur). In the first phase of the experiment, children observed adults playing a bowling game. Some children observed adults reward themselves after scoring 20 points, while some observed adults rewarding themselves after scoring just 10 points. When they were then given an opportunity to play the game themselves, the children selected the same criteria for rewarding themselves as they had observed in the adults. As Mazur concludes, "this study showed that children can learn to apply either strict or lenient standards of self-discipline by observing a model."

Pro-Social Behavior

In a similar vein, others have conducted experiments to determine if modeling can help children develop pro-social behaviors, such as sharing, helping, cooperation, and altruism. Crain describes one such experiment conducted by Rushton (1975) in which children observed an adult donate some of his winnings to a charity after playing a bowling game. Children who witnessed the altruistic model—compared to a control group who did not see the model—donated their winnings to charity to a far greater extent when given an opportunity to play the same game. Importantly, when observed 2 months later, those who had observed the generous behavior were still more generous themselves. As Crain concludes, "Evidently, even a relatively brief exposure to a generous model exerts a fairly permanent effect on children's sharing." Crain reviews studies that suggest pro-social behavior is learned best by observation, rather than by command. Children who are told to 'share,' for example, are much more influenced by what the adult actually does than what the model says to do. In other words, 'practicing what you preach' will help children learn.

Moral Development

Bandura believed that people's judgments about good and bad are largely learned by observing other people (Mazur). In order to prove his hypothesis, he replicated a moral reasoning task first developed by Piaget. Children were told a series of stories, in some of which the protagonist had good intentions but caused a great deal of damage, and in some of which the protagonist had poor intentions, but caused little damage. In one such story, for example, a young boy accidentally broke several cups as he entered the kitchen in response to his mother's call; his intentions were good—he obeyed his mother—but the amount of damage was large. By contrast, another young boy broke just one cup, but did so while climbing on the counter to reach the cookie jar when his mom looked the other way. Typically, children judge whether or not an act is 'bad' by the consequences, not the intention. Bandura, however, was able to show that after observing an adult model make the opposite judgment (regardless of the direction of the child's initial judgment), children's own judgments easily shifted. Such changes were maintained over time, and applied in new situations. Bandura concluded that moral reasoning was learned through observation, and was not the result of maturational development that occurred in fixed stages, as Piaget had suggested (Crain).

Elimination of Phobias

Just as modeling can be used to encourage positive behaviors, it can also be used to eliminate unwanted behaviors. As a result, modeling has had a significant impact in the field of behavior therapy. Bandura, Grusec and Menlove (1967) demonstrated, for example, that children's fear of dogs could be eliminated by observing other children interacting positively with dogs, regardless of whether the model was rewarded for such behavior or not (as cited in Mazur). Others have used modeling to counteract hyperactivity in children in the classroom environment. By modeling self-instructive behavior, teachers were able to eliminate the careless performance caused by a student's lack of attention and erratic behavior (Mazur).

VIEWPOINTS
The Behaviorist Response

Bandura's social learning theory generated a significant amount of healthy academic debate among psychologists and educators. When he first proposed his theory, not everyone agreed with its principles and some even argued it was an unnecessary addition to learning theory. Behaviorists, for example, continued to insist that observational learning can be explained by operant conditioning, or what they refer to in the

case of modeling as generalized operant conditioning. Novel responses, they argue, are nothing more than variations of previously emitted responses that were reinforced in the past. That is, reinforcement can generalize to an entire of class of responses, strengthening not just a single behavior, but similar behaviors as well. Behaviorists also claim they have recognized the distinction between performance and learning since the Tolman and Honzik (1930) experiment (as cited in Mazur); some have even "concluded that reinforcement is not essential for learning but it is essential for the performance of learned behaviors."

The Developmentalist Response

In addition to behaviorists, developmental psychologists also took Bandura's ideas to task. As Crain writes, "among the developmentalists, it has been the Piagetians who have become most embroiled in debates with Bandura." In fact, "Bandura and his colleagues conducted some classic studies that were designed to demonstrate the superiority of their theory [over Piaget's]" (Crain). Their disagreements were twofold. Piagetians believe children learn due to intrinsic interest in novel events; Bandura believes children learn in order to obtain reinforcements, and that intrinsic interest doesn't develop until after children surpass their own achievement standards (Crain). Furthermore, he argues, if children were motivated to learn in the presence of novel events, they would be learning all the time, which he observes, is not the case. Nevertheless, some believe Bandura's own studies contradict his findings, for children in the Bobo doll experiment displayed what appear to be intrinsically satisfying behaviors, in the absence of rewards (Crain).

Secondly, Bandura dismisses Piaget's notion that children develop according to fixed and invariant stages. Piaget believed, for example, that children could not learn the concept of conservation until a particular age, due to maturational deficits. Social learning theorists have attempted to show, however, that cognitive skills can be learned through modeling. Rosenthal and Zimmerman (1972, 1978) demonstrated that four- and five-year-old children who observed an adult perform the conservation task correctly improved their own performance. These children were younger than children who typically master this task, and their learning generalized to other types of conservation tasks and across time.

Self-Efficacy

Despite the criticisms, it is perhaps the evolution in Bandura's own thinking that has resulted in significant changes to his theories over time. Increasingly cognitive in focus, Bandura's later theories place less emphasis on the role of modeling and more on what he calls self-efficacy—beliefs and judgments about our abilities (Crain). Self-efficacy, he believes, has a significant impact on motivation, such that an individual will work hard when she believes she is good at a task, such as math, even in the face of obstacles, but will put forth less effort and be more likely to give up when she doubts her abilities. Studies have demonstrated that students who believe they are good at a subject will perform better than those who don't, even when actual ability levels are equal (Collins, 1982, as cited in Crain). Although people might overestimate their abilities, Bandura believes "optimistic self-efficacy is beneficial," especially in life that often presents "disappointments, setbacks, impediments, and inequities" (Crain).

Arslan (2013) found "significant relationships between students' opinions about sources of self-efficacy related to learning and performance and their gender, academic achievement, socioeconomic status, grade level, and learning style." He offers these recommendations for educators, among others, based on his study: Mastery experiences and vicarious experiences are effective for boys and girls, so should be used to increase self-efficacy of both; mastery experiences and vicarious experiences are effective for both high and low achievers, so should be used to increase self-efficacy of both; and mastery experience and social persuasion are effective for medium achievers.

Corkett, Hatt, and Benevides (2011) examined the relationship between teacher self-efficacy, student self-efficacy, and student ability. Their findings were that teachers' perceptions of the students' self-efficacy was significantly correlated with students' abilities; however, "student literacy self-efficacy was not correlated with their literacy ability. Additionally, there was no correlation between the teachers' perception of the students' literacy self-efficacy and the students' literacy self-efficacy." Furthermore, the teachers' self-efficacy was significantly correlated with their perception of the students' self-efficacy (Corkett et al.). Karwowski, Gralewski, and Szumski

(2015) found that the expectations of teachers had a significant impact on students' creative self-efficacy, and more so among female than male students, suggesting that many interwoven factors, such as gender, have a major role in shaping self-belief.

Along with his interest in self-efficacy, Bandura put forth equal effort in studying human agency, or our ability to control our personal destinies (Bandura). Social learning theory has also expanded beyond the concepts originally introduced by Bandura. Significantly, the idea has been investigated through the field of neuroscience, with several studies suggesting physiological pathways for social learning. The brain cells known as mirror neurons have in particular been identified as a potential important factor in the learning process, including the social type. However, such research remains highly experimental.

TERMS & CONCEPTS

Behaviorism: Social learning theory developed in reaction to behaviorism, or its perceived limitations in explaining human learning. According to behaviorists, learning is the equivalent of a change in behavior, and is determined by factors in the environment. Behaviorists do not recognize unobservable mental processes. Social learning theory incorporated both behaviorists and cognitivist principles.

Cognition Theory: Cognitive theorists believe that what happens inside the mind—the mental processing of information—is an important part of learning. Humans are active learners; what students do with information once they receive it determines how much they learn.

Modeling: Social learning theory explains how individuals learn by observing others, or, more specifically, by modeling the behavior of others. There are four components to the modeling process: attention, retention, motor reproduction, and motivation. Many factors impact the modeling process, including both characteristics of the model and learner.

Operant Conditioning: The mechanism by which learning occurs according to behaviorist principles. In operant condition, an animal or person elicits a response in the presence of a discriminative stimulus. The response is immediately followed by reinforcement. Behaviorists believe operant conditioning can explain learning by observation, whereas Bandura believes such explanations fall short.

Reciprocal Determinism: Reciprocal determinism represents the idea that behavior, person, and environment are all interdependent. The environment might impact behavior, for example, through the presence of reinforcement. A person's behavior might influence her future expectations. Reciprocal determinism helps emphasize the important role both cognitive and environmental variables play in the learning process.

Self-Efficacy: A person's beliefs or judgments about their abilities. Bandura's most recent work has focused on self-efficacy and the notion of individual agency, or the ability to direct one's personal destiny. A person's self-efficacy has been shown to significantly impact motivation and performance.

Self-Regulation: As children learn which behaviors are appropriate, and which are not, through both direct and vicarious reinforcement and punishment—they begin to develop and internalize standards of their own. By developing such standards, individuals become self-reinforcing, and rely less on external rewards and punishments.

Vicarious Reinforcement: If a model is reinforced for a particular behavior, there is a greater likelihood the observer will imitate that behavior herself. This phenomenon—known as vicarious reinforcement—demonstrates that watching another person rewarded for a behavior can be as powerful as direct reinforcement—having one's own behavior rewarded. Vicarious reinforcement was first demonstrated in Bandura's classic "Bobo doll" study. The same principles apply to vicarious punishment.

Jennifer Kretchmar

BIBLIOGRAPHY

Arslan, A. (2013). Investigation of relationship between sources of self-efficacy beliefs of secondary school students and some variables beliefs of secondary school students and some variables. *Educational Sciences: Theory & Practice, 13*, 1983–1993.

Bandura, A. (1977). *Social learning theory.* Englewood Cliffs, NJ: Prentice-Hall, Inc.

Bandura, A. (1997). Self-efficacy. *Harvard Mental Health Letter, 13*, 4–7. Retrieved July 24, 2007, from EBSCO Online Database Academic Search Premier.

Bandura, A. (2001). Social cognitive theory: An agentic perspective. *Annual Review of Psychology, 52*, 1–26. Retrieved July 24, 2007, from EBSCO Online Database Academic Search Premier.

Corkett, J., Hatt, B., & Benevides, T. (2011). Student and teacher self-efficacy and the connection to reading and writing. *Canadian Journal of Education, 34*, 65–98. Retrieved December 12, 2013, from EBSCO Online Database Education Research Complete.

Crain, W. (2000). *Theories of development: Concepts and applications.* Upper Saddle River, NJ: Prentice Hall.

Karwowski, M., Gralewski, J., & Szumski, G. (2015). Teachers' effect on students' creative self-beliefs is moderated by students' gender. *Learning & Individual Differences, 44*, 1–8. Retrieved January 8, 2016, from EBSCO Online Database Education Research Complete.

Lineros, J., & Hinojosa, M. (2012). Theories of learning and student development. *National Forum of Teacher Education Journal, 22*, 1–5. Retrieved December 12, 2013, from EBSCO Online Database Education Research Complete.

Mazur, J. (1994). *Learning and behavior* (3rd ed.). Englewood Cliffs, NJ: Prentice-Hall, Inc.

Miller, B. b., & Morris, R. G. (2016). Virtual peer effects in social learning theory. *Crime & Delinquency, 62*(12), 1543–1569. Retrieved December 8, 2016, from EBSCO Online Database Education Source.

Ormrod, J. (1990). *Human Learning: Theories, principles, and educational applications.* Columbus, OH: Merrill Publishing Company.

Webster, C. A., Buchan, H., Perreault, M., Doan, R., Doutis, P., & Weaver, R. G. (2015). An exploratory study of elementary classroom teachers' physical activity promotion from a social learning perspective. *Journal of Teaching in Physical Education, 34*(3), 474–495. Retrieved January 8, 2016, from EBSCO Online Database Education Research Complete.

SUGGESTED READING

Bandura, A. (1997). *Self-efficacy: The exercise of control.* New York: W. H. Freeman.

Bandura, A. (1986). *Social foundations of thought and action: A social cognitive theory.* Englewood Cliffs, NJ: Prentice-Hall.

Bandura, A. (1973). *Aggression: A social learning analysis.* Englewood Cliffs, NJ: Prentice-Hall.

Durlak, J. A. (2015). *Handbook of social and emotional learning: research and practice.* New York, NY: Guilford Press.

Kostelnik, M. J. (2015). *Guiding children's social development and learning: Theory and skills.* Stamford, CT: Cengage Learning.

EXPERIENTIAL LEARNING

This article presents an overview of the concept of experiential learning, an umbrella term that has encompassed a diverse body of educational theories and practices which share a common core of key principles. Although theories about experiential learning can be found in ancient Greek and Chinese philosophy, the term assumed great public prominence in the 1960s with an intense public interest in alternative schools based upon student-centered curriculum and instruction. Experiential learning, since the 1960s, has been generally understood as a systematic approach to applied learning catalyzed by students extracting from various experiences, within and beyond the classroom, meaningful methods promoting lifelong learning.

KEYWORDS: Affective Learning; Applied Learning; Continuity of Experience; HOT (Higher-Order Thinking); Inquiry Method; Learner-Centered; LOT (Lower-Order Thinking); Progressive Education; Scaffolding; Service Education; Socially Constructed; Tacit Knowledge; Virtual Reality; Zone of Proximal Development

OVERVIEW
HISTORICAL RELEVANCE
Educators are in general agreement that the term "experiential learning" began with John Dewey's 1938 book, "Experience and Education," a concise distillation from lectures given late in Dewey's career as a philosopher of education. It is notable how often this single text is quoted by both proponents and opponents of experiential education nearly seven decades after its publication. Central to Dewey's understanding of experiential learning are a handful of key principles. These include the importance of offering students quality learning experiences since "experience and education cannot be directly equated to each other" (Dewey). Dewey defines a quality learning experience as one that moves a student forward progressively to learn more and more about a worthwhile subject of inquiry. For Dewey, any educational experience can either distort or block a student's curiosity, or enhance a student's intellectual energy so that he or she wants to advance. Sound experiential learning encourages what Dewey labels "the continuity of experience," meaning that

a student's curiosity is constantly fueled by engaging learning experiences so that a student wants to stretch beyond known boundaries. In terms of Vygotsky's theory of the "zone of proximal development," experiential learning offers students a painless way to stretch their intellectual horizons because they are encouraged to take their experiences as seriously as any assigned textbook or classroom lecture (Vygotsky, 1986).

IMPORTANCE OF INTERACTION
The other key principle underscored in Dewey's book is the importance of interaction in promoting the value of experiential learning. Learning in Dewey's world is primarily socially-constructed, meaning that learning is an intellectual and emotional energy generated from the quality of interactions between students, and between students and teachers. This view contrasts with a traditionally held view of learning in which knowledge is mined from the repositories of texts and class lectures offered to individual students under a teacher's authoritarian guidance. The acquisition of knowledge in terms of Dewey's theory is an active, questing process, an act of community construction from the building materials that established texts and lectures provide (Dewey).

CONTROVERSIAL OUTLOOKS
Controversy has always surrounded these cornerstones of Dewey's definition of "experiential learning" for a variety of reasons. In terms of assessment of student achievement, how can teachers and administrators quantify what is essentially the quality of student learning experiences? Since so much of the history of twentieth century American education has been marked by reliance upon quantitative scoring of academic achievement through standardized testing, there has been a bypassing of the development of reliable and commonly accepted assessment tools to evaluate the educational value of quality, experientially-based learning experiences. These assessment issues have also presented complex challenges since experiential learning programs often utilize sites other than schools. For example, in service learning, students often learn how to practice problem-solving skills in environments with marginalized populations in need of social services, or in

environmentally degraded areas in need of restoration. These "learning by doing" programs that are based on the premise that the classroom is the world raise the question of who functions as an evaluating teacher of student learning, and how such potentially life-altering learning experiences can be accurately assigned a grade.

EVALUATION TOOLS

Although Dewey left the assessment issues surrounding experiential learning largely unanswered, proponents of experiential learning over the decades since Dewey's work have developed a number of evaluation tools including student generated portfolios and journals containing evidence of student academic achievement, as well as a variety of oral, written, and computer-based learning projects summarizing student learning from experience. Advocates of experiential learning often acknowledge that achievements realized by students through this approach often resist simple assessment. How can an educator quickly and accurately assess such achievements as independent thinking, flexible and creative thinking, and self-motivation to become a lifelong learner? Could a "one size fits all" standard be developed to assess students in such slippery and complex categories? The results of students undergoing learning from experience are not as subject to instant assessment simply because such learning plants potentialities in students. These potential bits of knowledge might not be manifest in an obvious way for months or years, unlike the achievement of students selecting the right answer to a multiple choice question on an exam based on a textbook reading assignment.

To offer another form of experiential learning as an example of the difficulty of assessment, the last half century in education has witnessed a large number of outdoor environmentally-centered learning programs. These range from after-school activities that entail cleaning up an environmentally polluted site to Outward Bound programs emphasizing survival skills in a cross-disciplinary fashion. Students and educators bring a variety of different assumptions to these programs, depending on cultural background and years of experience in urban or rural settings. A program in New York State in the 1970s that offered the experience

for inner-city New York City teenagers of learning a variety of survival skills in a mountainous wilderness area was strongly criticized by a number of students and their parents for not adequately preparing students for a learning experience so alien to their previous experiences. This could serve as a reminder that proper timing, setting and preparation are crucial if experiential learning is to be achieved and retained by students. If a student is not properly prepared in knowing how to encounter a fresh learning experience, and able to integrate it seamlessly with previous learning experiences, then many of the potential advantages of experiential learning will be lost.

As Dewey's proponents and opponents often admit, Dewey loaded the word "experience" with thick layers of connotative (and occasionally vague) meaning. For example, in some of his writings, Dewey insists that students need to have learning experiences that carry much of the tradition of the accumulated wisdom of Western civilization. It has been debated whether such an idealized view of tradition-laden personal experience is realistically commonly found among most students. Further, students might not always be conscious of whether a learning experience is immediately interconnected to the Western canon of thought. Even more challenging is to be aware of whether the learner has thoroughly extracted all that could or should be learned from an experience. Thus, the need exists for teaching students how to comprehensively work with the multiple, and often paradoxically conflicting meanings attached to any learning experience. Learning how to interpret experience wisely calls for students highly motivated to get to the essence, the essential gist of what a life experience means, and that might be heavily dependent upon an intellectual and emotional maturity many students need to cultivate.

THE "REAL WORLD" PROBLEM-SOLVING GROUP PROJECT METHOD

The most common technique used by educators embracing experiential learning methodologies is the "real world" problem-solving group project. With the rapid advance of computers in classroom, "real world" learning can also be used to refer to sophisticated computer simulations of objective reality created for educational purposes. These computer generated simulations of objective reality are called "virtual reality," and these immersive models of reality are increasingly described in the research literature of experiential learning as integral to experiential learning. Problem-solving education clearly predates John Dewey's theories of education by thousands of years. The ancient Greek word "praxis," found in ancient philosophical tracts denotes acting and following an action with critical reflection in order to learn. Connected to this understanding of the learner's need to transition from action to reflection is associated with the educational term "scaffolding," donating a temporary support mechanism built into lessons that is progressively withdrawn to help students gradually gain confidence in their capacity to actively teach themselves. Transitioning from a learning experience to critical reflections upon the meaning of that experience and then application is a characteristic of what educators today call "HOT" (higher-order thinking.). This refers to the capacity for analysis, synthesis, and evaluation by students. Opposite to this would be "LOT" (lower-order thinking). This refers to recall and comprehension of factual information. Current educational research indicates how a number of experiential learning strategies, including role-playing, outdoor education, and service education, can significantly positively affect higher-order thinking. Its impact on lower-order thinking appears to be not significantly different than that found with students involved with traditional learning methods.

THE DAVID A. KOLB THEORY

Yet another spin off from the ancient Greek sense of praxis is the theory of experiential learning proposed by David A. Kolb (1985). Kolb described experiential learning as a four-part cycle that most often begins with students having a concrete experience. They then practice observation and reflection upon the concrete experience in order to comprehend the nature of their experience. They form abstract concepts that enable a single experience to be transferable to numerous other life situations, and then they test their understanding in a variety of life situations to see if their abstract concept functions in the real world.

Applications

TYPICAL CLASSROOM SETTING

One possible generalization about classrooms where experiential learning is taking place is that there will be more sound stemming from interactions among students, and between students and the materials they are using to learn with (e.g., computers, craft materials, Camcorders) than in a traditional classroom where the sound of a teacher's voice might likely dominate. While an educator promoting experiential learning might, at appropriate moments, call a halt to such busy and noisy group activity to give a mini-lecture or read a section from a textbook, visible student activity marks a classroom where experiential learning is routinely practiced.

PROGRAMS

Paradoxically, the typical classroom where experiential learning is practiced might not be a traditional classroom within a school building. In one of the best known innovative experiential learning programs at the high school level, Eliot Wigginton and the Foxfire Fund encouraged students to research the lives of people living traditional lifestyles in the Appalachian Mountains by actually traveling with his students to remote locales. Students tape recorded life stories and compiled oral histories into a nationally bestselling set of books. This was called the "Foxfire Project," and it has spawned a variety of experiential learning programs in various high schools across the country (The Foxfire Fund, 1982). Another experiential learning high school program situated outside of conventional classrooms is the Presidential Classroom, which enables high school students internationally to meet and learn from public officials about the making of public policy.

VIRTUAL LEARNING

Yet another type of classroom increasingly used for experiential learning is not a physical space but a place in a technologically-mediated realm popularly known as "cyberspace" or "virtual reality." Through the Internet, students in real time internationally can engage in active problem-solving projects through text messaging and video conferencing. While online education does not necessarily mean that experiential learning is occurring—traditional lectures can be delivered over a computer monitor or iPod during which students assume a passive or disinterested stance—innovative Experiential Education is increasingly being developed that requires more activity from students than occasional mouse-clicking on a screen icon. Several business education programs are experimenting with using online classes to simulate stock market and investment corporation activities that students can play roles within (Dolan & Stevens, 2006; Haytko, 2006).

Typical Classroom Assignments Supporting Experiential Education

PORTFOLIO

A portfolio of individual and/or small student group work has often been used both for purposes of integrated subject matter and facilitating educator assessment of student learning. These can assume the form of scrapbooks, yearbooks, or print products supplemented by audio and/or videotapes. Implicit in the portfolio format is an educator's belief in the pedagogical value of having in concrete, often narrative, form a tangible record of what students have extracted from their learning experiences. Such a portfolio is also a crucial tool in enhancing the emotional maturity of students since students can learn to take pride in an accumulated, tangible record of their experiential learning. A portfolio is an open-ended exercise in affective as well as cognitive education since the portfolio engages not merely the intellectual voice of the student but also offers a space for visual expression that often carries emotional weight.

ROLE—PLAYING

Role-playing is another common strategy in experiential learning since it enables students to "try on" various perspectives other than their habitual ones. Role-playing strategies have included students acting the roles of mythological and folkloric characters in spontaneously improvised classroom skits and role-playing past or contemporary political or artistic figures caught in crucial conflict situations. A key figure for educators working to teach students how to improvise roles in the classroom is Viola Spolin, author of several books on teaching improvisation as a learning tool for students of all ages. A number of professional health science and social service programs, both undergraduate and graduate, have extensively used role-playing in order to help future helping professionals learn what it feels like to be a client in severe need of help (Edwards, 2003).

"BARE-BONES" NARRATIVE

A particularly popular form of experiential learning in language arts and social studies programs involve the teacher introducing a "bare bones" narrative about a key historic or artistic figure—and then having students, individually or in small groups, "flesh out" the rest of the story through research and imaginatively informed speculation in order to complete an accurate and imaginatively fashioned, realized story. This assignment often leads to a discussion of how any famous person or event can be interpreted through a variety of interpretations, depending on one's political and cultural assumptions.

THE INQUIRY METHOD

A common characteristic of all classroom assignments guided by experiential learning is a temporary de-emphasis on absolute teacher intellectual authority and an evolving sense of student intellectual authority. This is furthered by teachers refusing to immediately answer all student queries and instead offering tools for students to discover answers for themselves through independent inquiry. The "inquiry method" is essentially a method actualized through teachers asking increasingly demanding questions of students while providing fewer immediate answers to those questions, done in a manner to motivate students to explore intensely their own key questions. This might be a contemporary version of the ancient "Socratic Method" in that educator questioning is the "fuel in the engine" that propels students forward in their thinking. The largest difference between the two approaches might come from the extraordinary plenitude of print and electronic resources modern students can draw upon compared to the heavy dependence ancient Greek students had upon their own sensory experience solely.

Viewpoints

TEACHER'S AUTHORITY VS. STUDENT AUTHORITY

Decades of controversy surrounding experiential learning can be distilled into a few recurrent themes. Perhaps the key theme involves tensions between teacher authority and student authority.

If an educator's primary role is to transmit with unrelenting authority culturally-acceptable subject matter to students whose role is to absorb this content unquestioningly and demonstrate mastery of this knowledge through standardized testing, then experiential learning has little to no relevance to classroom practice. On the other hand, if an educator's chief role is to provide the tools for students to transform themselves into lifelong, independent learners who assess truths in subjects through their own authoritative analysis of feelings and thoughts, then experiential learning has a legitimate place in classrooms.

Complicating this conflict of views is nothing less than the rationale for public education held by different individuals and groups. In the companion book to a public television series on the story of American public education, editors Sarah Mondale and Sarah H. Patton (2001) offer a spectrum of representative and often clashes views by respected liberal and conservative authorities on this issue. If public education is first and foremost the educating of future generations of workers, then the place of experiential learning might be limited to problem-solving simulations drawn from current job types. In fact, as Mondale and Patton indicate, those who assume that public education should be solely worker preparation see experiential learning as having led American education downhill (Mondale & Patton). If public education is believed to prepare future workers—but also to prepare students for an active role as citizens in a democratic society—then experiential learning might expand far beyond job-centered exercises. American public education at the start of the 21st century seems to reflect chiefly a school-to-workplace orientation, with high-stakes testing based upon the content of rigidly defined subject categories. This tilt might easily change, as it often has throughout American history as liberal or conservative politicians at the Federal and State levels prevail, a fact noted by historian Larry Cuban in the PBS series. The politically conservative position that public schools need a "Back to Basics" approach implies little to no involvement with forms of experiential learning since that educational approach only surfaced as a viable option in the public schools a little over a half-century ago and never emphasized a nostalgia for 19th century curricular content or teaching methodologies. On the other hand, the politically liberal idea that education should be as wholly student-centered as possible implies that public education has no responsibility to uphold the traditional political and economic values of the past. It also can create contradictions between parents who believe public school curricula should be largely shaped by young energy—but who usually insist on the primacy of absolute adult authority when it comes to task organization and forms of learning in the home.

IN CONCLUSION—THE NEED FOR BETTER TOOLS

Both friends and foes of experiential learning might agree about the need for better, more precise and more comprehensive tools to assess student learning. While portfolio assessment of student work has been presented as an alternative to high-stakes yearly testing, many teachers of all educational philosophies report that assessing student portfolios is intensively time-consuming. No educator has invented a reliable and straightforward rubric to measure the worth of a huge range of types of student learning experiences. And since experiential learning often leads to gains in tacit knowledge—that informal, unconscious, non-book-centered form of learning often achieved outside schools—our ability to test for gains in tacit knowledge is still in a primitive state. There is a huge difference in testing to determine a student's retention of a fact, say a date in history of a significant event, and whether a student has grasped the importance of thinking critically before offering an uninvited or unpopular opinion in an arena of heated community controversy. Some of what can be called categorized as "tacit knowledge" might fit under the umbrella term of "character education," or more simply be labeled common sense, the practically applied knowledge of how to get along successfully in the world.

TERMS & CONCEPTS

Affective Learning: Learning that deals largely with the emotions and psychological outlook of students. It has been labeled by the psychologist Daniel Goleman (1997) as "emotional intelligence."

Applied Learning: Any form of learning immediately put into the context of a real world, practical problem-solving context. It is often applied when analyzing vocational education programs.

Continuity of Experience: A concept offered by John Dewey that implies that a student's learning experiences should optimally be generative of increasingly more educative experiences.

Higher Order Thinking: Thinking skills reflecting a movement away from general knowledge skills to skills like synthesis, analysis, comprehension, application, and evaluation.

Inquiry Method: A methodology valuing the generation of student questions about a topic in ever-widening circles of levels of inquiry sparking student research.

Learner-Centered: A concept first clearly outlined in the writings of John Dewey who declared "the child is the curriculum," meaning that every child has unique learning needs demanding a variety of teaching methodologies.

Lower Order Thinking: Thinking skills reflects general knowledge skills like simple recall and recitation of remembered text.

Progressive Education: Progressive Education is a term, used to describe ideas and pedagogy that aim to make schools more effective agents of a democratic society. experiential learning has long been held in high esteem by educators in this movement, many of whom cite John Dewey's writings as encouraging experiential pedagogy.

Scaffolding: A temporary learning aid to help students gain confidence in their capacity to independently learn.

Service Education: This is a form of learning through student volunteer activity beyond the school coordinated with critical reflection upon the meaning of volunteer experiences.

Socially Constructed: A sociological and political term used by a variety of social scientists that proposed that knowledge is not so much a unique individual achievement as an achievement communally

Tacit Knowledge: A philosophical and educational concept categorizing knowledge that is practical and derived from experiences outside of formal schooling.

Virtual Reality: A computer-mediated parallel universe used for education, training, and education purposes in which objective social reality is shout-out so that an individual's entire sensory experience is electronically evoked.

Zone of Proximal Development: A concept proposed by the modern Russian educational psychologist Lev Vygotsky that suggests that there are crucial moments in a child's development when he or she can most effectively cognitively stretch to attain a new level of thinking, bridging the gap between current and future achievement actualized in a community context.

Norman Weinstein

BIBLIOGRAPHY

Chickering, A. A. (1977). *Experience and learning: An introduction to experiential learning.* New Rochelle, NY: Change Magazine Press.

Dewey, J. (1938). *Experience & education.* NY: Collier Books.

Dolan, R. C., Stevens, J. L. (2006). Business conditions and economic analysis: An experiential learning program for economics students. *Journal of Economic Education, 37,* 395-405. Retrieved June 14, 2007, from EBSCO Online Database Education Research Complete.

Edwards, C. (2003). Reality-play–experiential learning in social work training. *Social Work Education, 22,* 363. Retrieved June 14, 2007, from EBSCO Online Database Education Research Complete.

Foxfire Fund Inc. (1982). Gillespie, P. (ed.). *Foxfire 7.* NY: Anchor Books.

Goleman, D. (1997). *Emotional Intelligence: Why It Can Matter More than I.Q.* NY: Bantam Books.

Hansen, G. (2012). When students design learning landscapes: designing for experiential learning through experiential learning. *NACTA Journal, 56,* 30-35. Retrieved December 15, 2013, from EBSCO Online Database Education Research Complete.

Haytko, D. L. (2006). The price is right: An experiential pricing concepts game. *Marketing Education Review, 16,* 1-4. Retrieved June 14, 2007, from EBSCO Online Database Education Research Complete.

Keenan, D. S. (2013). Experiential learning and outcome-based education: A bridge too far within the current education and training paradigm. *Journal of Applied Learning Technology, 3,* 13-19. Retrieved December 15, 2013, from EBSCO Online Database Education Research Complete.

Kolb, D. A. (1985). *Experiential learning: Experience as the source of learning and development.* NY: Prentice-Hall.

Lien, A. D., & Hakim, S. M. (2013). Two approaches, one course: An experience in experiential learning. *Journal of Prevention & Intervention in the Community, 41,* 128-135. Retrieved December 15, 2013, from EBSCO Online Database Education Research Complete.

Maclean, J. S., & White, B. J. (2013). Assessing rigor in experiential education: A working model from Partners in the Parks. *Journal of the National Collegiate Honors Council, 14,* 101-108. Retrieved December 15, 2013, from EBSCO Online Database Education Research Complete.

Mondale, S. & Bernard, S., eds., (2001) *School: the story of American education.* Boston: Beacon Press.

Spolin, V. (1986). *Theater games for the classroom: A teacher's handbook.* Evanston, IL: Northwestern University Press.

Vygotsky, L. (1986). *Thought and language—revised edition.* Cambridge: MA: The MIT Press.

SUGGESTED READING

Baker, A. C., Jensen, P. J., & Kolb, D., (2005). Conversation as learning experience. *Management Learning,* 36, 411-427. Retrieved August 2, 2007, from EBSCO Online Database Education Research Complete.

Breunig, M. (2005). Turning experiential education and critical pedagogy into praxis. *Journal of Experiential Education,* 28, 106-122. Retrieved June 14, 2007, from EBSCO Online Database Educational Research Complete.

Cornu, A. L. (2005). Building on Jarvis: Towards a holistic model of the processes of experimental learning. *Studies in the Education of Adults,* 37, 166-181. Retrieved June 14, 2007, from EBSCO Online Database Education Research Complete.

Levine, M. (2007). The essential cognitive backpack. *Educational Leadership,* 64, 16-22. Retrieved June 14, 2007, from EBSCO Online Database Education Research Complete.

Rogers, A. (2006). Learning from experience. *Adults Learning,* 18, 30-31. Retrieved June 14, 2007, from EBSCO Online Database Education Research Complete.

TRANSFORMATIVE LEARNING

Transformative learning is the learning that takes place as a person forms and reforms meaning. This article provides an overview of the transformative learning theory developed by Jack Mezirow. The article provides an overview of Mezirow's theory and why it is appropriate for adult education. The article describes transformative learning theory in detail and discusses best practices for educators. Also covered are critical views of transformative learning theory.

KEYWORDS: Adult Education; Autonomous Thinking; Constructivism; Experiential Learning; Frames of Reference; Habits of Mind; Point of View; Transformative Learning

OVERVIEW

WHAT IS TRANSFORMATIVE LEARNING?

According to Jack Mezirow, the founder of transformative learning theory, a defining condition of the human experience is that we have to make meaning of our lives (Mezirow, 1997). Transformative learning is the learning that takes place as a person forms and reforms this meaning. It has become a hot topic in adult education due to its involvement more than classroom learning and connects learning to the learner's own life (Florida State University, 2002). Mezirow believes that in today's world people must learn to make their own interpretations as opposed to listening to and acting on the beliefs and explanations of others. The goal of adult education is to facilitate this understanding rather than to provide it. The goal of transformative learning is to develop "autonomous thinking" (Mezirow).

Mezirow developed the theory of transformative learning in the 1970s (Florida State University). Mezirow's theory focuses on the individual as a reflective learner. Transformative learning requires the acquisition of information that upsets prior knowledge and triggers a changing of ideas and perceptions (Davis, 2006). The principles of constructivist learning are important to transformative learning because knowledge and meaning are a direct result of experience (Stansberry & Kymes, 2007). Constructivism states that meaning is constructed from a person's existing knowledge base and perception of the world.

Transformative learning occurs when a person encounters an event or situation that is inconsistent with his or her existing perspective (Stansberry & Kymes). Transformational learning experiences cause the learner to become critical of his or her beliefs and how they affect the way the learner makes sense of the world (Stansberry & Kymes).

FURTHER INSIGHTS

Children commonly acquire the knowledge structures necessary to think autonomously. This includes the ability to recognize cause-effect relationships, make analogies and generalizations, recognize and control emotions, develop empathy, and think abstractly (Mezirow). In addition, adolescents learn to hypothesize and reflect on what they read, see, and hear. The primary goal for adult education is to strengthen and build on this foundation in order to assist the learner to become more critical in assessing one's own beliefs, values, and judgments of others (Mezirow). This awareness will allow adult learners to become more responsible and better equipped to work with others to solve problems and modify previously held beliefs (Mezirow).

Mezirow maintains that transformative education is extremely different than the types of education appropriate for children (Davis). Acquiring new information is just one aspect of the adult education process (Davis). Adults, throughout their lives, develop a body of associations, concepts, values, and feelings based on their experiences. These are frames of reference, the mental collection of assumptions that are responsible for how people comprehend their experiences and define their worlds (Mezirow). Once a person's frames of reference are set, it is extremely difficult to accept those that do not fit our preconceptions (Mezirow). Learning can only be meaningful when new information is integrated with existing frames of reference (Davis).

Older adults, in particular, write Lawton and La Porte (2013) of transformative learning in community art classes for seniors, have "a wealth of knowledge and experience, a broad range of interests and cognitive abilities, and a unique vantage point: the wisdom acquired with age. The reinterpreting of past experiences and understanding them in a new way may provide meaningful creative inspiration. Transformative experiences can occur for adults across cultures and generations through activities such as storytelling, social interaction, and collaborative artmaking."

HABITS OF MIND, POINT OF VIEW

A frame of reference includes cognitive and emotional components and consists of two divisions: habits of mind and a point of view (Mezirow). Habits of mind are abstract but habitual ways of thinking. This may be based on culture, education, socio-economics, or psychological factors (Mezirow). An example of a habit of mind is ethnocentrism, the tendency to view others outside one's own group as inferior. As a result of this habit of mind, people have mixed feelings, attitudes and may pass judgments on specific individuals or groups such as homosexuals, minorities, or the

poor (Mezirow). Point of view is the perspective from which something is viewed and considered. "Habits of mind are more durable than points of view as points of view are continually changing" (Mezirow).

CRITICAL SELF-REFLECTION

"Transformative learning involves critical self-reflection of deeply held assumptions" (Davis). The theory of transformative learning applies to adults engaged in a variety of learning environments. Mezirow explains that it requires the learner to "interpret past experiences from a new set of expectations about the future, thus giving new meaning perspectives to those experiences" (cited in Davis, "Promoting Transformation"). Transformation occurs upon the completion of a series of 10 stages the individual must go through (Stansberry & Kymes). This shift in perspective can be gradual or sudden, as the individual moves through the stages and experiences a cognitive restructuring of experience and action (Stansberry & Kymes). The learner then begins the process of changing expectations to a more comprehensive perspective.

Mezirow believed that transformative learning takes place through experience, reflection, and discourse (Stansberry & Kymes). The process can be disruptive and uncomfortable as the learner is forced into seeing the world differently than previously accepted (Davis). Transformative learning is considered to have taken place once learners make choices or takes action based on the new understandings (Stansberry & Kymes).

THE 10 STAGES OF TRANSFORMATIVE LEARNING

Mezirow developed several stages that people experience on the way to transformation. According to Mezirow, these phases are required in order for a true transformation to take place (Merriam & Caffarella, 1999):

- Experiencing a disconcerting dilemma;
- Performing an examination of self;
- Critically assessing assumptions;
- Recognizing that others share similar experiences;
- Exploring options for action;
- Building self-confidence;
- Forming a plan of action;
- Acquiring skills and information for implementation;
- Practicing a new plan and roles;
- Reintegrating into society with new perspective.

"After identifying their problem or challenge, people often enter a phase where they reflect critically on this challenge. During this process, people often can no longer accept their old ways of thinking and thus they are compelled to change" (Lieb, 1991). Finally, the learner must take action and do something in reaction to this change. This process could take a long time, and people sometimes reflect on beliefs and ideas for years before they are ready to accept new beliefs and enact change (Merriam & Caffarella).

PROCESSES OF TRANSFORMATIVE LEARNING

There are four processes or approaches to transformative learning:

- **Elaborate on an existing point of view:** In this process, a learner seeks to support an initial bias and expand the range of that point of view (Mezirow). This process does not constitute an actual transformation, as it does not require the learner to change point of view; it merely asks the learner to broaden his or her definition of something;
- **Establish new points of view:** The learner encounters a new situation and creates new meaning to accommodate the situation (Mezirow). Again, this process does not require the learner to alter an existing point of view. This process gives the opportunity to add a new point of view on something that was previously unfamiliar;
- **Transform a point of view:** Based on an experience that results in a critical reflection of the learner's misconceptions, a learner may be forced to alter their existing point of view. If this experience or similar experiences occurs repeatedly, a transformation of the learner's habits of mind make take place (Mezirow);
- **Transform a habit of mind:** These types of transformations are rare as such dramatic changes in perception that shake existing frames of reference do not occur often, but when they do the learner becomes critically reflective of a generalized bias (Mezirow).

REFLECTION

Reflection is a key action in the transformation process. Mezirow distinguishes among three kinds of reflection:

- **Content Reflection:** Learners ponder and evaluate the content of a problem;

- **Process Reflection:** Process reflection involves a rational contemplation of strategies that could solve the problem;
- **Premise Reflection:** Learners question the importance of the problem and question the assumptions underlying the problem Premise reflection can lead to transformative learning.

BEST PRACTICES FOR TRANSFORMATIVE LEARNING

According to Mezirow, transformative learning takes place through communicative learning, discourse and critical reflection. Communicative learning involves at least two people trying to comprehend the meaning of an interpretation or justify for a belief (Mezirow). Ideally, communicative learning involves reaching a consensus. It is essential for learners to become critically reflective of the assumptions underlying intentions, beliefs, and feelings (Mezirow). Discourse is a dialogue devoted to discussing competing interpretations. Critical discourse evaluates evidence, analyzes arguments, and examines differing points of view (Mezirow). People learn together through discourse by analyzing similar experiences to come to a common understanding (Mezirow). Critical reflection is where frames of reference begin to change. A learner can become critically reflective of the assumptions and interpretations upon which he or she bases his or her beliefs and habits of mind (Mezirow). Such self-reflection can lead to significant personal transformations.

In addition to the three strategies, the following is a list of suggestions to help make transformative learning more successful:

- Establish and support "hot groups." Thomas Kelley and Jonathan Littman, in their book *The Art of Innovation* define hot groups as a collaboration of diverse but compatible people in pursuit of similar goals (cited in Davis). Such collaboration often generates a discourse and an energy that encourages reflection and can bring about transformation;
- Acknowledge that resistance and adverse ideas can be useful accessories in personal development (Davis). Richard Daft, a Vanderbilt University professor states, "Only the ideas you disagree with have the power to change you" (cited in Davis). Divergent opinions and creative ideas help to stimulate the phases of transformative learning. Educators who abuse dialogue over conflicting ideas can develop an environment that discourages transformative learning (Davis);

- Fail your way to success. "Management experts Warren Bennis and Robert Thomas aver that most people learn more from their mistakes than from their accomplishments" (cited in Davis). Great discoveries often happen when rational thought ends and human imagination begins. "Failures and mistakes should become the catalyst for change rather than regression" (Davis).

Viewpoints

CRITICS OF TRANSFORMATIVE LEARNING

Many people have criticized Mezirow's ideas (Cranton, 1996). Some of them feel that the phases of transformation are rather artificial and that transformation can happen instantly without critical reflection (Cranton). Many agree with Mezirow that "critical reflection is important to transformative learning, but some studies find critical reflection overemphasized rational process and overlooks the role of feelings and emotions. Studies have shown that learners who experienced a transformation responded to the initiating dilemma without reevaluating their assumptions or beliefs" (Taylor, 2001). Instead of engaging in critical reflection, most learners trusted their assumptions and projected critique at the situation rather than the self (Taylor).

Morrice (2013) argues the importance of context for transformative learning. She draws on empirical research with refugees and considers the processes of "transforming experience and learning" that accompany transition to life in a different culture. Morrice argues for the importance of social context and non-formal learning, and suggests that models and theories based on transformative learning that *ignore* context provide "only a partial and distorted picture of the learning and identity processes at work" for the particular group of immigrants she studied (Morrice).

Adult learning is different from elementary and adolescent learning because it is voluntary, self-directed, and experiential (Baumgartner, 2007). Transformative learning theory is somewhat self-directed, but it is not problem based, experiential and often impractical (Baumgartner). Some critics argue that Mezirow's theory focuses too much on individuals (Cranton). They assert that true change requires the collaboration of society and cannot happen in an individual apart from society (Cranton). On the flip side, sometimes teachers can trigger critical reflection but need to tread lightly

when it comes to how they go about it. Teachers cannot pre-plan transformative learning experiences nor can they force critical reflection (Cranton). Since adult education operates on a more voluntary basis, the learners may or may not choose to push their limits and challenge their own habits of mind (Ettling, 2006). This creates a problem when a theory cannot be effectively implemented into educational practice.

Kucukaydin and Cranton (2013) take some issue with what they describe as the "subjective" nature of transformative learning. "Knowledge about transformative learning has been constructed by a community of scholars working to explain how adults experience a deep shift in perspective that leads them to better justified and more open frames of reference," they write. "Knowledge about transformative learning is practical in nature, and as such, it is subjective. If we accept this, then the validity of knowledge about transformative learning needs to be based on critical meaning-making through discourse" (Kucukaydin & Cranton).

Ethical issues can actually arise for an educator who approaches instruction from the perspective of transformative learning (Ettling). As early as 1985, Paulo Freire addressed the question of the ethics of transformative education. He asserted that the educator never has the right to impose his or her position on the learner (cited in Ettling). At the same time, an educator should never be unresponsive to social questions (Ettling). Implementing transformative learning theory requires a constant examination of an educator's methods and regular evaluation of student results as the point of view and habits of mind of the teacher are unavoidably present in the classroom (Ettling).

Mezirow's view requires educators to recognize the web of connectedness between the world and the learner. Transformation should be viewed more as a set of emerging patterns than a process to be taught and followed (Ettling). Another complication with this is that there exists little information on how to effectively apply transformative learning theory in the classroom. Thus, both the teacher and the student are works in progress (Ettling). This brings us back to the question of whether or not educators have the right to impose situations which ask learners to reevaluate their basic assumptions about the world.

The bottom line is that educators need to be vigilant in setting objectives that encourage autonomous thinking, discourse and critical reflection. Education should center on the learner and include group discourse, reflective thought and interactive problem solving. (Mezirow). Instruction that reflects life experience is designed to encourage evaluation and, if necessary, transformation, but it is up to the learner to have the necessary reflective judgment. Learning takes place through discovery as long as the student is willing to discover (Mezirow).

Conclusion

Mezirow believed that adult education is all about challenging our perceptions and previous learnings. By doing so the learner will be free from his or her imprecise concepts of the world (Cranton). In the fast paced society that is the 21st century, the ability to adapt to changing environments is essential and growing more important by the minute (Mezirow). Experts acknowledge that training resources should be directed toward creating a future workforce that can be critically reflective, collaborate with others and adapt to changing conditions (Mezirow).

"The educator's responsibility is to help learners reach their objectives in such a way that they will function as more autonomous, socially responsible thinkers" (Mezirow). Reflection of outside assumptions is fundamental to effective problem solving, but critical reflection of the learner's own assumptions is the key to transforming frames of reference, and this is the key to learning for adapting to change (Mezirow).

Terms & Concepts

Adult Education: refers to the act and practice of teaching adults in the classroom, the workplace and other venues.

Autonomous Thinking: Autonomous thinking refers to thinking that is developed independently without outside influence. It is the ultimate goal of transformative learning.

Constructivism: Constructivism is a learning theory based on Jean Piaget's belief that meaning is constructed from a person's existing knowledge base and his/her perception of the world.

Experiential Learning: Experiential learning refers to learning that is derived from previous knowledge or experience.

Frames of Reference: This term refers to the mental collection of assumptions that are responsible for how they comprehend their experiences and define their worlds.

Habits of Mind: Habits of mind refer abstract but habitual ways of thinking. This may be based on culture, education, socio-economics, or psychological factors.

Point of View: Point of view refers to the perspective from which something is viewed and considered.

Transformative Learning: Transformative learning involves the gathering of information that disrupts prior knowledge and triggers a reshaping of ideas and perceptions.

Jennifer Bouchard

Bibliography

Baumgartner, L. (2007). Understanding and promoting transformative learning (2nd ed.). *Adult Education Quarterly, 57,* 264-266. Retrieved November 21, 2007, from EBSCO online database, Education Research Complete.

Cranton, P. (1996). *Professional development as transformative learning.* San Francisco: Jossey-Bass, 75-117.

Davis, S. (2006). Influencing transformative learning for leaders. *School Administrator, 63,* 10-16. Retrieved November 21, 2007, from EBSCO online database Education Research Complete.

Dirkx, J. (2006, Spring). Engaging emotions in adult learning: a Jungian perspective on emotion and transformative learning. *New Directions for Adult & Continuing Education,* 109. 15-26. Retrieved November 21, 2007, from EBSCO online database Education Research Complete.

Ettling, D. (2006, Spring). Ethical demands of transformative learning. *New Directions for Adult & Continuing Education,* 109, 59-67. Retrieved November 21, 2007, from EBSCO online database Education Research Complete.

Kucukaydin, I., & Cranton, P. (2013). Critically questioning the discourse of transformative learning theory. *Adult Education Quarterly, 63.,* 43–56. Retrieved December 19, 2013, from EBSCO Online Database Education Research Complete.

Lawton, P., & La Porte, A.M. (2013). Beyond traditional art education: Transformative lifelong learning in community-based settings with older adults. *Studies in Art Education, 54,* 310–320. Retrieved December 19, 2013, from EBSCO Online Database Education Research Complete.

Merriam, S. & Caffarella, R. (1999). *Learning in adulthood: A comprehensive guide, 2nd Ed.* San Francisco: Jossey-Bass.

Mezirow, J. (1997, Summer). Transformative learning: Theory to practice. *New Directions for Adult & Continuing*

Education, 74, 5. Retrieved November 19, 2007, from EBSCO online database Education Research Complete.

Morrice, L. (2013). Learning and refugees: Recognizing the darker side of transformative learning. *Adult Education Quarterly, 63,* 251–271. Retrieved December 19, 2013, from EBSCO Online Database Education Research Complete.

Stansberry, S., & Kymes, A. (2007). Transformative learning through Teaching With Technology electronic portfolios. *Journal of Adolescent & Adult Literacy, 50,* 488-496. Retrieved November 21, 2007, from EBSCO online database Education Research Complete.

Taylor, E. (2001). Transformative learning theory: a neurobiological perspective of the role of emotions and unconscious ways of knowing. *International Journal of Lifelong Education, 20,* 218-236. Retrieved November 19, 2007, from EBSCO online database Education Research Complete.

SUGGESTED READING

Burk, A. (2006, Spring). Do the write thing. *New Directions for Adult & Continuing Education,* 109, 79-89. Retrieved November 21, 2007, from EBSCO online database Education Research Complete.

King, K. (2005). *Bringing transformative learning to Life.* Malabar, FL: Krieger Publishing.

Mezirow, J. (1991). *Transformative dimensions of adult learning.* San Francisco: Jossey-Bass.

Davis-Manigaulte, J., Yorks, L., & Kasl, E. (2006, Spring). Expressive ways of knowing and transformative learning. *New Directions for Adult & Continuing Education,* 109, 27-36. Retrieved November 21, 2007, from EBSCO online database Education Research Complete.

MULTIPLE INTELLIGENCES

Multiple intelligence is a theory developed by Howard Gardner and first published in his 1983 book "Frames of Mind." This theory views human intelligence as a complex web of abilities that are evident in one's products and preferences for learning. Gardner developed his theory after careful review in various fields that study the values and the potential of mankind. Though Gardner is a psychologist, his theory has been embraced by many educators as an explanation for the many ways their students learn and achieve. They are accordingly adapting classroom instruction so that students can demonstrate their strengths and improve upon their weaknesses.

KEYWORDS: Bodily-Kinesthetic Intelligence; Existential Intelligence; Intelligence Profile; Interpersonal Intelligence; Linguistic Intelligence; Logical-Mathematical Intelligence; Multiple Entry Points; Musical Intelligence; Naturalistic Intelligence; Spatial Intelligence

OVERVIEW

Multiple Intelligences (MI) theory is based on the belief that human beings possess a complex set of abilities beyond what is measured through traditional Intelligence Quotient (IQ). The theory was developed by Howard Gardner in 1983 not as an educational model but as a way to explain the way the mind works. Supporters of the theory believe that intelligence, as it is traditionally defined, does not take into consideration the wide range of abilities human beings use to solve problems. Though the theory has been criticized for having its basis in intuition rather than empirical evidence, Gardner and his supporters argue otherwise. According to Chen (2004) the theory is grounded in comprehensive review of studies in biology, neuropsychology, developmental psychology, and cultural anthropology.

The theory appeals to educators because it articulates what they experience on a daily basis; that students learn and succeed in different ways and have an individual profile of strengths and weaknesses that can be exploited to deliver effective instruction (Moran, Kornhaber, & Gardner, 2006). Key to the application of multiple intelligence theory in the classroom is the intentional use of multiple entry points into instruction and providing students with various ways to show what they have learned.

MI is often confused with the notion of learning styles, which became popular in the 1950's. However, learning styles refers to personality characteristics or preferences that are evident in the process of learning. Intelligence refers to the ability to solve a problem, perform a skill, or deliver a service (Shearer, 2004). Multiple intelligences theory differs from learning styles theory in that both the ability to learn and apply new material in various individualized ways is considered in multiple intelligences theory.

GARDNER'S SEVEN INTELLIGENCES

Originally, Gardner defined seven key intelligences:

- Linguistic;
- Logical-mathematical;
- Musical;
- Bodily-kinesthetic;
- Spatial;
- Interpersonal;
- Intrapersonal.

The first two are those that are traditionally valued in schools. Linguistic intelligence refers to the ability to use words and language and to use language as a means of thinking and learning. Those with a high level of linguistic intelligence may succeed at careers such as writing, teaching, and law. Logical-mathematical intelligence refers to the ability to discern patterns, think logically, and perform mathematical operations. This intelligence is typically associated with mathematical and scientific thinking.

Three of the intelligences are associated with the arts. Musical intelligence involves the ability to express and feel ideas and feelings musically. It includes the ability to recognize and produce a variety of rhythms, tones, and pitches. Bodily-kinesthetic intelligence refers to the ability to use one's body to solve problems and the ability to organize oneself in space, such as in dance. Such learners typically are most comfortable with a hands-on approach rather than lectures. Spatial intelligence is the ability to visualize and use space. Such people are often artistically inclined.

The final two intelligences are described by Gardner (2000) as personal intelligences. They are associated with one's relationship with oneself and others. Interpersonal intelligence is the ability to discern the feelings, desires, and motivations of other people. Counselors, salespeople, and leaders require a strong interpersonal intelligence. Intrapersonal intelligence refers to the understanding of one's self. They are successful with subjects such as philosophy and learn best when given opportunities for careful reflection.

OTHER INTELLIGENCES

In 2000 Gardner described two additional intelligences: naturalistic and existential. People with a high level of naturalistic intelligence have a high level of sensitivity to the natural world and their place within it. They are typically successful with growing and caring for plants and animals. Existential intelligence refers to the understanding of life's profound and universal questions, such as the meaning of life and death. The last two intelligences were not as well accepted as the first seven. Other intelligences suggested by Gardner are moral and spiritual.

INTELLIGENCE INTEGRATION

Advocates of multiple intelligences claim that every person has all types of intelligence to some degree, and, if given the appropriate environment, can develop their weaker areas to a level of competency. Each type of intelligence functions and interacts within each person in different ways, and the interaction is essential to completing various tasks. For example, to cook a meal, one must use linguistic intelligence to read the cookbook, logical-mathematical to measure the correct portions, and bodily-kinestetic intelligence to mix to the desired consistency.

Gardner did not intend the theory to be used to categorize people. He wanted multiple intelligences to be a way of disaggregating people, showing ways in which they differ from one another, and not a way of putting labels on them (Gardner). According to Gardner's research, there are greater variations within groups of people than there is between groups of people.

APPLICATIONS

Proponents of this theory argue that more children would learn successfully and with efficiency if a wide variety of methodologies, activities, and assessments were used. Contrary to the MI way of teaching is the traditional skill based curriculum in which all students learn the same thing in the same way and the same measures are used to evaluate their competency with the material. MI teaching requires that students be given a variety of ways to show their understanding of a concept, and the emphasis is on application and ownership of information rather than on rote memorization.

A study of English-language learners in Malaysia supports intelligence integration. Findings from this study suggest that in a learning environment where multiple intelligences may not be actively used, there is a tendency to have "weak and negative correlation between multiple intelligences and English language achievement" (Pour-Mohammadi, Zainol Abidin, & Yang Ahmad, 2012).

INTELLIGENCE PROFILES

Central to the application of MI theory is the concept of the profile of intelligences. An individual's profile is the combination of strengths or weaknesses among and between the different types of intelligences. This orientation eliminates the delineation between high, medium, and low achieving children, as all areas in which a child may achieve are considered and valued. Instead of looking at a child as simply capable or not capable of learning, the profile of intelligences takes into consideration how a child learns best and what sorts of products children may create that reflect their learning. Educational researcher Michael Rettig (2005) has found that this approach is successful from the earliest years of schooling and applies to teaching children of various abilities, including those with cognitive and physical disabilities. The MI approach to intelligence requires the educator to ask "not how smart a child is, but how they are smart" (Rettig).

Most people, according to Gardner and his colleagues, have jagged profiles. This refers to a profile in which a student processes some types of information better than other types. Students with "laser" profiles have a wide variety in their profile with strength in one or two types of intelligence. Other areas may be weak by comparison. These students can follow a clear path dictated by their intelligence that leads to success in a particular field. Those with "searchlight" profiles have less pronounced differences between their intelligences, and such students will have a greater challenge in choosing a suitable career (Moran et al.).

ASSESSING INTELLIGENCES

There exists no single tool that assesses a child's intelligences and offers a profile of results. Armstrong (1994) maintains that discerning someone's intelligence profile requires careful professional judgment, observation and time. Though packaged assessments may be enticing, an intelligence profile is a complex reflection of an individual's learning strengths, weaknesses, and production capacity and cannot be defined without context. "If anyone should tell you that they have a computer scored test that in 15

minutes can provide a bar graph showing the eight peaks and valleys of each student in your class or school, I suggest you be quite skeptical" (Armstrong). Armstrong suggests that the best tool for determining a child's intelligence profile is observation.

Children begin to show what Gardner refers to as proclivities or preferences early in life that offer educators insights into what their intelligence profile is like. These inclinations are usually formed by the time the child begins school and their preferences for certain activities and ways of learning may offer insight into what their particular proclivities are. A child with a high level of musical intelligence may enjoy singing and tapping his feet, a spatially intelligent child may enjoy drawing and playing with logos, while an interpersonally intelligent child may be a natural leader. It is important to keep in mind that most children are intelligent in more than one area (Armstrong).

In addition to looking at what a child enjoys in determining their intelligence profile, Armstrong advises looking at the ways in which a child misbehaves. The kinesthetic student may be fidgeting, the linguistic student may be talking out, and the spatial student may be doodling. This misbehavior may indicate how a child needs to be taught. Using MI as a theoretical base for instruction may reduce behavior problems in class, as children become engaged in the subject matter in ways that they can be most effective as learners. Keeping detailed anecdotal records and notes over time about a student's behavior and preferences may ultimately yield insight into their intelligence profile. Other sources such as school records, work samples, past teachers, and parents can all provide information that is valuable in determining how a child will best learn.

MULTIPLE ENTRY POINTS

Multiple entry points are key to MI instruction and refer to the variety of ways teachers provide students with access to the material that students are expected to learn. A teacher who provides multiple entry points to instruction does not rely on a single method or activity to deliver instruction. Rather, he or she uses various ways to transmit information to learners. A teacher may employ art, movement, and various media into their delivery. Wares (2013), for example, illustrates how MI instruction via multiple entry points can be applied in mathematics classrooms in the context of an origami project.

This approach ensures that children with strengths in the various types of intelligences will be able to access the material in a way that most makes sense to them (Gardner).

VARIED ASSESSMENT TOOLS

The use of varied assessment tools refers to the way teachers create situations in which children can show their understanding of the material. In this way, children can show what they have learned in ways that best mirror their abilities (Ozdemir, Guneysu & Tekkya, 2006). A teacher might present children with a menu of choices for assessment to include choices like dramatic renditions, dance, or drawing.

Children with high levels of spatial intelligence learn best when instruction is delivered through art or images such as multimedia, pictures or photographs. It is often a good assessment to have them draw their ideas or develop models that illustrate their understanding of a concept. They also benefit from graphic organizers or diagrams that illustrate visually the main themes or ideas of a lesson.

Heidari and Khorasaniha (2013) found a "significant positive correlation" between visual (spatial) intelligence and reading proficiency. They concluded that MI should be "highly considered" by educators as they develop strategies for reading instruction.

Kinesthetic learners do well with a variety of manipulatives and hands on activities. Such students benefit from a variety of tools as they integrate ideas into their knowledge base. As they apply the tools provided, they can best show what they have learned.

Children who are strong in intrapersonal intelligence are generally motivated from within and can be given work in which various stages need to be checked before moving on to the next. Intrapersonal learners can facilitate discussions between students and conduct interviews or seek information from those with real life experiences on a topic.

Students with a strong naturalistic intelligence learn best when activities are connected to the natural world. Outdoor activities and classification and connections to the environment help these children make connections with learning objectives. By observing and considering how classroom objectives interact with the natural world, these students can learn in a way that makes sense to them. Assessment activities may include observation

and classification with an emphasis on relationships within and between things in the environment.

Music is a way of connecting knowledge to feelings. Students with a high level of musical intelligence learn well through sound. This intelligence is closely related to logical mathematical intelligence because of the attributes of music that relate to pattern and progression.

Teachers who subscribe to MI theory often find that they can develop cooperative learning experiences and projects in which children with various abilities can participate and excel (Moran et al.). A class publication can provide rich opportunities for children to be experts in their areas of strength. A linguistic child can write articles, a spatial learner can participate in laying out the articles and submit drawings and photographs. A student with a high level of interpersonal intelligence can conduct interviews and solicit subscriptions. A logical-mathematical child can work on calculating costs and number of copies needed to print. A kinesthetic student would be successful delivering the paper and working with a musically inclined learner to develop advertising commercials. Changes in roles over time can help students develop the intelligences that are not their natural strong points.

Students with a high level of logical mathematical intelligence can follow the logical progression of traditional lessons with ease, as their minds are primed to connect to ratio and regularity with a linear argument and presentation. These students also perform calculations easily and can be assessed in a logical and linear format, as this mode of assessment reflects their natural way of assimilating and organizing information.

It is important to note that most occupations require facility in more than one area of intelligence. A teacher must be linguistic, interpersonal, intrapersonal, and logical-mathematical within a single day. A firefighter must possess high levels of spatial intelligence to understand the path of fire within a building and develop plans for rescue. They must have kinesthetic intelligence to execute their plans and linguistic intelligence to communicate to their fellow firefighters. Accountants must be logical-mathematical and interpersonal to be successful. Students should understand the range of abilities required in daily living so that they realize that all types of abilities are valuable and necessary to function in society (Gardner).

Viewpoints

EVALUATING GARDNER'S RESEARCH

It is difficult for scholars and scientists to evaluate Gardner's theory because measures have not been developed for the various intelligences (Chen). Gardner prefers to evaluate intelligence by products such as work samples and efficiency in problem solving rather than tests. His definition of intelligence is oriented toward products and occupations that are valued by societies around the world and across cultures as well as the biological potential to produce valued products and solve problems.

Central to MI theory are the brain systems involved in each of the different intelligences. Gardner studied the outcomes of brain injured patients and savants and used such cases to support the role of brain structures in intelligence. These patients had suffered traumatic breakdown in one or more physical areas of the brain and still maintained areas of competence in one or more of the intelligences. For example, a savant that was unable to speak could still produce music stunning in its clarity while a brain injured patient that had lost memory could still speak and solve problems verbally (Shearer).

Gardner's definition of intelligence has sparked some conflict and calls the traditional definition of intelligence into question. Is intelligence a quantifiable characteristic an individual possesses, like body weight? This notion of intelligence as quantifiable is at the root of well-known intelligence tests, such as the Stanford-Binet, which yields a numerical score. These types of popular tests consider primarily the two types of intelligence upon which the Western educational system is based: linguistic and logical mathematical.

MULTIPLE INTELLIGENCES IN THE CLASSROOM

Many educators rejoice over MI theory and the promise they believe it holds for their students. The promise of MI theory in practice is that no longer will students who are strong in the linguistic and logical mathematical intelligences be classified as successful while students with strengths in other areas seen as failures. Rather, all students will be seen as successful in a variety of areas and in different ways.

Adoption of the MI perspective requires that teachers be open to new ways of thinking and learning. They must learn to deliver instruction in new ways that may be different from what they experienced as students or from what they learned in their pre-service programs. They must regularly incorporate ways of assessment that promote the various intelligences and let students show what they have learned and how it is meaningful to them. In addition to allowing students to use their preferred intelligences as routes for learning and assessment, teachers must also consider ways in which they can help their students strengthen the intelligences that are areas of relative weakness for them.

MULTIPLE INTELLIGENCES & STANDARDIZED TESTING

Other changes in education that have been informed by MI theory are the more focused consideration of the individual learner, teachers and students looking at a few topics with an eye toward understanding rather than rote memorization, and an emphasis on thought processes and the manipulation of ideas (McMahon, Rose, & Parks, 2004). In general, these changes have occurred alongside an increased emphasis on standardized testing and school funding that is contingent upon quantifiable successes, such as test scores.

As so many states and school divisions continue to revise and entrench their high stakes testing orienting curriculums, it remains to be seen how and if MI theory will play a role in this highly politicized drama. After nearly a quarter of a century of scholarship and research in the area of Multiple Intelligences since Gardner's groundbreaking 1983 book, it appears that MI theory has a wide intuitive appeal and utility among educators even though the issues of validity regarding the theory have not been satisfactorily addressed.

TERMS & CONCEPTS

Bodily-Kinesthetic Intelligence: The ability to coordinate physical movements to understand and express ideas.

Existential Intelligence: Understanding of life's major issues and questions.

Intelligence Profile: A web of an individual's strengths and weaknesses in the various areas of intelligence.

Interpersonal Intelligence: The ability to understand other's feeling and motivations.

Intrapersonal Intelligence: The ability to understand one's self.

Linguistic Intelligence: The ability to use words and language, both spoken and written.

Logical-Mathematical Intelligence: The ability to use mathematical operations and discern logical progressions.

Multiple Entry Points: An instructor uses multiple entry points to present information so that students with different intelligence profiles can best learn.

Musical Intelligence: The ability to interpret pitch, harmony and rhythm.

Naturalistic Intelligence: The ability to understand and interact with the natural world on its terms.

Spatial Intelligence: The ability to orient ideas and objects in three dimensional space.

Holly Conti

BIBLIOGRAPHY

Armstrong, T. (1994). *Multiple intelligences in the classroom.* Alexandria: Association for Supervision and Curriculum Development.

Association for Supervision and Curriculum Development. (2007). *Education Topics: Multiple Intelligences.* Retrieved July 23, 2007, from www.ascd.org.

Brody, N. (1999). What is intelligence? *International Review of Psychiatry, 11,* 19-25. Retrieved July 10, 2007, from EBSCO Online Database Academic Search Premier.

Campbell, B. (1991). *Multiple intelligences in the classroom.* Retrieved June 26, 2007, from http://context.org.

Chen, J., (2004). The theory of multiple intelligences: Is it a scientific theory? *Teachers College Record, 106,* 17-23.

Chipongian, L. (2000). *Multiple intelligences in the classroom.* Retrieved July 1, 2007 from http:// brainconnection. com.

Gardner, H. (1983). *Frames of mind: The theory of multiple intelligences.* New York: Basic.

Gardner, Howard. (2000). *Intelligence reframed: Multiple intelligences for the 21st century.* New York: Basic. Gardner, H. (2003). *Multiple intelligences after 20 years.* Paper presented at the American Educational Research Association, April 21, 2003. Retrieved July 4, 2007, from http:// pzweb.harvard.edu.

Gardner, H. (2006). *Multiple Intelligences: New Horizons.* New York: Basic Books.

Gardner, H. (2007). *Five minds for the future.* Boston: Harvard Business School Publishing.

Heidari, F., & Khorasaniha, N. (2013). Delving into the relationship between LOC, MI, and reading proficiency. *Journal of Language Teaching & Research, 4,* 89–96.

Retrieved December 11, 2013, from EBSCO Online Database Education Research Complete.

Loori, A. (2005). Multiple intelligences: A comparative study between the preferences of males and females. *Social Behavior and Personality: An International Journal, 33,* 77-88. Retrieved July 10, 2007, from EBSCO Online Database Academic Search Premier.

McMahon, S., Rose, D., & Parks, M.,(2004). Multiple intelligences and reading achievement: An examination of the Teele Inventory of Multiple Intelligences. *Journal of Experimental Education, 73,* 41-52. Retrieved July 10, 2007, from EBSCO Online Database Education Research Complete.

Moran, S., Kornhaber, M., & Gardner, H (2006). Orchestrating multiple intelligences. *Educational Leadership, 64,* 23-27. Retrieved July 10, 2007, from EBSCO Online Database Education Research Complete.

Odzemir, P., Guneysu, S., & Tekkaya, C. (2006). Enhancing learning through multiple intelligences. *Journal of Biological Education, 40,* 75-78. Retrieved July 10, 2007, from EBSCO Online Database Education Research Complete.

Pour-Mohammadi, M., Zainol Abidin, M., & Yang Ahmad, K. (2012). The relationship between students' strengths in multiple intelligences and their achievement in learning English language. *Journal of Language Teaching & Research, 3,* 677–686. Retrieved December 11, 2013, from EBSCO Online Database Education Research Complete.

Rettig, M. (2005). Using the multiple intelligences to enhance instruction for young children and young children with disabilities. *Early childhood education, 32,* 255-259. Retrieved July 10, 2007, from EBSCO Online Database Education Research Complete.

Shepard, J. (2004). Multiple ways of knowing: Fostering resiliency through opportunities for participating in learning. *Reclaiming Children and Youth, 12,* 210-216. Retrieved July 10, 2007, from EBSCO Online Database Education Research Complete.

Shearer, B. (2004). Multiple intelligences theory after 20 years. *Teachers College Record, 106,* 2-16. Retrieved July 10, 2007, from EBSCO Online Database Education Research Complete.

Strasser, J. & Seplocha, H. (2005). How can university professors help their students understand issues of diversity through interpersonal and intrapersonal intelligences?. *Multicultural Education, 12,* 20-24. Retrieved July 10, 2007, from EBSCO Online Database Education Research Complete.

Wares, A. (2013). An application of the theory of multiple intelligences in mathematics classrooms in the context of origami. *International Journal of Mathematical Education in Science & Technology, 44,* 122–131. Retrieved

December 11, 2013, from EBSCO Online Database Education Research Complete.

SUGGESTED READING

Campbell, B. (1994). *The multiple intelligences handbook: Lesson plans & more.* Standwood: Campbell & Assoc.

Educational Broadcasting Corporation. (2004). *Workshop: Tapping into multiple intelligences.* Retrieved July 23, 2007, from http://www.thirteen.org/edonline/concept-2class/mi/index.html

Gardner, H. (1993). *Multiple Intelligences: The Theory in Practice.* New York: Basic.

Celebrating Multiple Intelligences. St. Louis: New City School.

Tamilselvi, B. & Geetha, D. (2015). Efficacy in teaching through "Multiple Intelligence" instructional strategies. *Journal on School Educational Technology.* 11 (2). 1-10.

LEARNING STYLES

Learning styles is an umbrella term that covers a highly diverse and controversial body of educational theories and practices. The term represents a generally accepted belief among the majority of educators that students differ widely in their ways of learning, demonstrating preferences in the way they process classroom experiences, and that pedagogical practices should be designed with an awareness of marked differences among students in how they learn. The term first surfaced widely in educational literature during the 1960s when it was strongly linked to a widespread interest in experiential learning. While that link is still prevalent in the literature and classroom practices of the 21st century, the concept of learning styles has recently assumed new importance since U.S. schools are increasingly dealing with reconciling differences in how students learn with the intellectual rigors and emotional pressures of repeated, high-stakes, standardized student testing.

KEYWORDS: Constructivism; Instructional Design; Learning-Style Inventory; Multiple Intelligences; Myers-Briggs Type Indicator; Psychological Types; Stylistic Flexibility; Tacit Knowledge; Visual, Auditory, Kinesthetic (VAK)

OVERVIEW

While the term "learning styles" has only gained popularity in educational circles during the past half-century, it is an ancient concern. Evidence of an interest in learning styles can be found in the centuries-old scripture and interpretative theological texts of Judaism, Christianity, Islam, and Buddhism. For example, during the Jewish holiday of Passover, parents are instructed to educate their children about the holiday's meaning by assuming one line of questioning for the children they perceive as intellectually mature and another for children with less intellectual sophistication. The Letters of Paul in the New Testament and the message of Muhammad in the Koran both emphasize the need to tailor the essential spiritual message to vastly different learners. Buddhist scripture suggests that the transmission of spiritual knowledge must take into account the emotional intelligence as well as the intellectual intelligence of individuals and often suggests using paradoxical, oxymoronic verbal narratives as a way to appeal to the emotional and tacit knowledge of people who might think of themselves as purely intellectual, book-centered learners.

The term learning styles represents a generally accepted belief among the majority of educators that students differ widely in their ways of learning, demonstrating preferences in the way they process classroom experiences, and that pedagogical practices should be designed with an awareness of marked differences among students in how they learn. Who knows exactly what kind of learning experience catalyzes change in a learner? What types of environments and teaching strategies are most potent for what kinds of intelligences? Do classrooms contain learners with a myriad of diverse learning styles—or hold a myriad of diverse personalities who learn differently because of deep-seated personality differences?

INFLUENCE OF MODERN PSYCHOLOGY.

Contemporary interest among educators in learning styles developed at the same time as the genesis of theories of psychology in the late 19th century in Europe and the U.S. If the mysterious and often invisible mechanisms of human learning could be successfully researched so that the mechanisms of learning could be clearly visible, early psychologists believed, then teaching could become a science. Teachers would no longer have to guess how best to instruct a child if that child's personality or mental capacities, as measured by a standardized IQ test, could become transparent to the teacher. However, this dream of a perfect marriage between psychological knowledge and best pedagogical practice has never actualized. Part of the difficulty in the late 19th century, and a continuing problem in the 21st century, is the absence of any one widely accepted theory of human psychology that comprehensively accounts for learning. While psychologists practicing behaviorism might see learning style only in terms of a student's visible behaviors, psychologists practicing Jungian psychology might view learning styles in terms of multiple invisible forces impacting a learner's personality.

ADVANCES IN NEUROLOGICAL SCIENCE.

Advances in medical imaging and understanding of the neurological biochemistry of the human brain finds the interface between psychological theories and teaching more complex. Since medical science currently possesses the technological tools (CAT scans, for example) needed to view some of the brain's neural processes biochemically as learning tasks are given to experimental subjects, more knowledge has been secured about how different areas of the brain in different individuals engage with various learning tasks. This research is still in the early stages so few definitive findings are established that can be practically used by educators. Inaccurate simplifications of the differences between the brain hemispheres reported in the popular media have led some ill-informed educators into thinking their students are either "left-brained" or "right-brained." The cover of a best-selling book for parents with children diagnosed with ADD, *Right-Brained Children in a Left-Brained World: Unlocking the Potential of Your ADD Child* by Jeffrey Freed and Laura Parsons features a blurb that reads: "You can win over teachers and principals to the right-brained approach the ADD child thrives on" (Freed & Parsons, 1998).

APPLICATIONS
Multiple Intelligences

Perhaps the single greatest impact of any theory about learning styles in the 20th century comes from Harvard educator Howard Gardner's theory of multiple intelligences. First encapsulated in his book *Frames of Mind: The Theory of Multiple Intelligences* (1983), this theory argues that there are eight kinds

of intelligence, and individuals learn best by using their strengths in one or more of them:

- Linguistic;
- Logical-mathematical;
- Musical;
- Spatial;
- Bodily-kinesthetic;
- Interpersonal;
- Intrapersonal;
- Naturalist-ecological.

Gardner theorized that learners can excel or need remediation in these eight categories of intelligence. This promotes the study and use of a variety of classroom practices by teachers to meet a rich variety of different learning styles, which run counter to the "one size fits all" type of teacher lesson plan based on the assumption that all learners are cognitively alike and possess an identical learning style.

The virtues of Gardner's theory in making teaching a stimulating intellectual adventure in pedagogical experimentation can also be also a practical shortcoming in actual daily classroom practice. It is a daunting enough challenge to teach a standardized curriculum to thirty different students at once. If a teacher is face-to-face with thirty different students with thirty different learning styles, it can invite despair over the impossibility of ever reaching all students successfully. Yet another challenge involves the assessment of student work. Should a student who shows evidence of above average linguistic intelligence and below-average mathematical intelligence be tested and graded in the same fashion as a student manifesting the opposite balance of talents?

One practical way to apply a facet of Gardner's theory that many teachers have found attractive involves engaging whatever sensory channels are most available in their students. While the overwhelming majority of students in the U.S. depend primarily upon their sense of sight for learning, a significant minority learn primarily through hearing, and a small minority by touch, or taste. This has led some educators to design curricula emphasizing a blending of visual, auditory, and kinesthetic (VAK) stimuli for students. Particularly in the elementary school grades, various teaching strategies have evolved in language arts curricula to accommodate different student learning styles to accommodate a range of learning styles marked by different sensory priorities.

Sternberg's Triarchic Theory

A theory similar to Gardner's theory of multiple intelligences was developed by the psychologist Robert Sternberg. Sternberg divides the eight types of intelligence identified by Gardner into three types: analytic intelligence, creative intelligence, and practical or successful intelligence. In place of the phrase Gardner and other educators favor, "learning styles," Sternberg refers to "thinking styles," but the terms have been used interchangeably by many educators and psychologists since no learning of any style occurs without prior thinking. Like Gardner, Sternberg believes that students demonstrate different styles of learning in ways that bypass the assumptions about learning held by most U.S. school administrators. Sternberg is particularly critical of standardized testing as a method to test anything more than a limited number of memory-related and problem-solving skills. Of particular interest to Sternberg is how students can obtain "street smarts" as opposed to "school smarts," his re-framing of the theory of tacit knowledge found in *The Tacit Dimension* (1966) by Michael Polanyi. Polanyi believes that humans know more than they tell of what they know since we often learn through informal experiences we rarely see as actual lessons. Since it is a commonplace assumption of modern psychologists and philosophers that no two individuals experience daily life in the identical way that would imply that each of us learns from our unique life experiences in different styles.

Constructivism

How significant attentiveness is when dealing with differences in learning styles among students varies among educators, depending upon their philosophy of education. If the purpose of education is seen essentially as preparation for economic livelihood and traditional family and citizenship roles and responsibilities, then differences in learning styles might be seen as a relatively insignificant issue. All students would profit from being seen as a homogenous group needing to attain the same educational goals at the same pace through the same methods. If the purpose of education is seen as preparing students to create a world fundamentally different than the one they inherit from their parents, then differences in learning styles would become a central concern. This philosophy of education, commonly identified with

a philosophy called constructivism, would emphasize the primacy of highly individualized learning programs designed in synchronization with self-initiated student behaviors that might call for educators to try very different methods to suit different student learning inquiries within in the same class.

Mvududu and Thiel-Burgess (2012) stress the relevance of constructivism in the 21st century this way: "Constructivism represents one of the big ideas in education. Its implications for how teachers teach and learn to teach are enormous. If our efforts in reforming education for all students are to succeed, we must focus on students. To date, a focus on student-centered learning may well be the most important contribution of constructivism."

Psychological Typing

Two other major contributions to theories regarding learning styles have been presented by Carl Jung and David Kolb. The psychologist Carl Jung emphasized that individuals across all cultures can be classified as types. These psychological types demarcated those who live and learn largely within the bounds of their sense of a deeply unique interior identity, a type he categorized as "introverts." Those who largely live and are acutely aware of the impact that people and their environments have on their socialization and learning he labeled as "extroverts." Few psychological theories of personality types have ever achieved widespread popularity among educators with the exception of this theory, and that was related to how Jung's personality theory could be practically applied to students if one accepted the accuracy of a personality test based upon Jung's categories. That test, the Myers-Briggs Type Indicator (MBTI) is an easy-to-administer 93 item questionnaire that draws its design from Jung's book *Psychological Types* (1971).

The questionnaire can serve as a tool in discovering different learning styles through posing all persons as habitually moving between four sets of dichotomies. The first, as mentioned earlier, is extraversion and introversion. Then Jung distinguishes between "sensing" types, those relying heavily upon sensory experiences daily, and "intuitive" types, those who rely heavily on hunches when discerning the meaning of experience. Yet another pair of opposed characteristics are illustrated by those who are "thinking" types, meaning that their favorite way of processing experience is cerebral and marked by rational analysis as opposed to those who are "feeling" types, who rely upon wellspring of emotion to interpret experience. Finally, Jung establishes a continuum between the "judging" types, those who come quickly to value judgments about experiences as opposed to the "perceiving" types, those who try to let their experiences speak for themselves without rushing to judgment. The MBTI does not result in some students showing more aptitude for one or the other polarity within these four dichotomies. Rather it establishes preference patterns that help establish a psychological type.

Part of the test's enormous popularity among educators might be related to the fact that the qualitative categories central to the test, extraversion and introversion, seem to be reformulations of the ancient folk belief that some children are predisposed to be "social butterflies" while others appear born to be loners. If these are indeed stable psychological types, educators can then easily discern these two types in class and plan accordingly. Since it is also a qualitative test profiling personality, it is acceptable to educators who might resent any quantitative student test to evaluate learning styles, since purely quantitative psychological testing is objected to by many teachers as a dehumanizing act reducing students to mere numbers.

An adult-education study investigated the relationship of learning-strategy preference to personality type. Learning-strategy preference was identified with the Assessing The Learning Strategies of AdultS (ATLAS), and personality type was measured with the MBTI. The findings indicated that "while overall personality type is not related to learning strategy preference, three of the four indicators of personality type show a relationship to learning strategy preference" (Conti & McNeil, 2011). As a result of these findings, the authors conclude that while stereotypes cannot be made to link approaches to learning with overall personality types, certain personality traits "can be indicators of how one might be approaching learning tasks."

Educator David A. Kolb created the Learning-Style Inventory (LSI) that is as intensely rooted in the theories of John Dewey as the MBTI is rooted in Jung's theories. Kolb posits two ranges of learning styles to be measured in students. He notes that

some learners are extremely engaged and active experimenters while others are more inwardly reflective and non-participatory observers. Some learners move quickly into forming abstract, symbolic concepts from their experiences while others interpret their experience in more concrete and literal terms. The LSI, like the MBTI, indicates a pattern of learner preferences.

VIEWPOINTS

Few educators, not to mention parents, will unequivocally claim that any two children learn a lesson in exactly the same way. Yet this commonplace view has not been converted remotely into a generally accepted way to assess learner differences in order to better tailor teaching strategies to meet individual student types and needs. The fact that over seven dozen very different competing theories of learning style are present in the intellectual marketplace for educators to sort among indicates the extreme lack of consensus.

The Traditional Approach

Another school of thought among educators invested in traditional pedagogical approaches holds that while differences in learning styles will always be a fact in any group of students, these differences in learning style are not as significant as the content of curriculum packaged into universally engaging lesson plans and a traditional, classics-based curriculum. Within schools based upon the "Classical Christian" philosophy of education, in the U.S., such thinking is often based upon the premise that teaching the classics of Western civilization can be so intrinsically stimulating to students of various learning styles that all types of learners will engage with the assigned subject matter if offered in an age-appropriate manner. As Douglas Wilson (1997) suggests, all students should learn grammar by rote in early childhood, and dialectics and rhetoric through class discussions and written assignments in their teen years. Further, some educators in this camp believe that stylistic flexibility should be encouraged among all children at the same time rather than individualizing lessons to the unique learning style of every student. Christian classical educator Stuart Fowler (1997) suggested the need for avoiding "the risk of treating students as learning style types rather than uniquely individual learners whose learning styles will never wholly fit any type."

High-Stakes Testing

Another issue for educators involves judging the utility of sensitizing themselves to differences in learning styles during an era of intensive, routine, high-stakes standardized testing. While this test-centered atmosphere might drive teachers deeper into discovering how to design lessons for different kinds of learners, some would say that preparing all students for such rigorous universal academic testing takes away the prep time that is needed to tailor lessons individually to learners displaying different learning styles. Overcrowding in urban classrooms is also believed to make alternative evaluations of student learning styles and achievement more difficult.

Cultural Learning Styles

Another controversy surrounding the way students learn involves cultural differences among children attending the same school. What is categorized as a particular learning style by a teacher with an Anglo-American, Protestant, Caucasian, middle-class background might be viewed by a student from an Hispanic or Philippine heritage as simply "the way things are done." For example, the haptic sense, the sense of touch, is often an integral part of the learning style of children raised in African and Asian families cohered by highly traditional folkways. However, the sense of touch has never been a dominant avenue of instruction for children in American public schools. Ackerman (1990) offers significant evidence as to how learners from various cultures take for granted that the sensory channels from which they most prefer to learn are universal, when that is not the case.

The Learning Process

Differing viewpoints about learning styles are also connected to differing definitions of the learning process and when that process begins and ends. For example, John Dewey defined learning as solving real world problems within the context of a community of learning facing the same acknowledged problem. By way of contrast, Cardinal Newman, a significant figure in Catholic education who also influenced secular education, saw learning as the inculcation of a moral and religious sensibility synthesized with the presentation of issues involving analytic reasoning. In Dewey's model, learning is achieved when a learner can demonstrate agility with problem-solving tools to better the world. For Newman, learning is an act of devoted attentiveness to worldly and otherworldly challenges through which a learner develops a character embodying moral sensibility. When talking about styles of learning, an educator with Dewey's philosophy will focus upon a learner's preferences for solving worldly problems while successfully navigating the interpersonal world of a school.

An educator favoring Newman's concept of learning will focus upon the learner's potential to contact the wellsprings of faith and reason within their innate personality for the sake of redeeming religiously all of creation. This dichotomy suggests that learning styles can be seen as preferences, aptitudes, or even manifestations of innate character. Depending on cultural context, an unusual learning style manifested by a non-conforming child might be interpreted as a symptom of madness induced by supernatural forces.

Instructional Design

One practical way to work with learners that might well unite opposing educational camps entails highly flexible instructional design. Instructional design refers to how the content of a lesson is offered in terms of sequencing, quantities of data given within what schedules, and the means of delivery (actual classroom lecture and/or discussion, virtual on-line networks, etc.). Inspiring educators of all persuasions have long taught students that there are many possible routes to attaining a correct answer or authoring a convincing, well-organized expository essay. As educational software grows in sophistication, it might be possible to envision programs that can quickly adapt in real time to variations in style of learning. Prototypes of such software are being developed for training purposes by the U.S. Army based upon "fuzzy logic," meaning that a computer develops a profile of a user's learning style through remembering recent keyboard and mouse activity and will gradually alter the usually programmed array of learning tasks to tailor the program objectives to the user's style of learning.

Demski (2012) wrote that "by marrying the principles of personalized learning with the tools of technology, some educators believe that they have a chance to create the kind of customized learning environment that can finally break schools out of the Industrial-age model of education to bring about true 21st-century school reform." She cites the following four "key" technological elements as being important to reaching that goal: a well-implemented 1-to-1 laptop initiative, learning-management systems, access to online remedial coursework, and open access to search tools (Demski).

Whatever one's belief regarding learning styles, there is no question that education has never been a simple matter of delivering knowledge into identical minds. As long as learners continue to not be simple receptacles of educator wisdom, questions pertaining to how the minds of different students engage differently with the same task will continue to challenge educators.

Criticisms

In addition to the lack of consensus among proponents of the learning styles concept, there also exists significant controversy over whether the idea is useful at all. Increasingly, arguments from neuroscientists and other researchers claim that efforts to match alleged student learning styles with certain types of instruction show no impact on learning outcomes. Willingham, Hughes, and Dobolyi (2015) found that despite public conceptions, there is little scientific evidence to support the efficacy of any theory of learning styles. Several studies have noted that all measurements of learning styles are flawed and that such models are too variable to provide any useful data. Others have suggested that exposing students to narrowed ideas about how they learn could in fact limit their openness to learning and prevent them from thinking in new ways.

TERMS & CONCEPTS

Constructivism: An educational theory based upon the concept that learners actively construct meaning for themselves through the activity of synthesizing sensory impressions and thoughts into concepts that are regularly tested experientially for validity.

Instructional Design: A form of educational research and practical application concerned with the possible forms of how academic content can be optimally presented to learners verbally and through other means.

Learning-Style Inventory: An instrument created by the educational psychologist David A. Kolb intended to measure differences between learners favoring the abstract presentation of subject matter and learners favoring more concrete and literal presentations of subjects.

Multiple Intelligences: A theory created by educational psychologist Howard Gardner marked by eight categories of human intelligence: linguistic, logical-mathematical, musical, spatial, bodily-kinesthetic, interpersonal, intrapersonal, and naturalist-ecological.

Myers-Briggs Type Indicator: An instrument to indicate personality types delineated as archetypal in the theory developed by psychologist Carl Jung. It consists of a questionnaire offering insights into the learning preferences of sixteen different archetypal personalities and was developed by Katharine Cook Briggs and Isabel Briggs Myers.

Psychological Types: A theory advocated by psychologist Carl Jung claiming that all individuals across time and cultures can be known psychologically through an analysis of personality types that they are often unconscious of in daily life.

Stylistic Flexibility: The ability of learners to "shift gears" and transition among various ways of thinking and learning, a notion the ancient Greeks described as "polytropos," being of many minds having many mental tools at one's disposal to solve different kinds of challenges.

Tacit Knowledge: A philosophical and educational concept categorizing knowledge that is practical and derived from experiences outside of formal schooling.

Visual, Auditory, Kinesthetic (VAK): A type of learning where the senses of vision, hearing, and touch play particularly key roles.

Norman Weinstein

BIBLIOGRAPHY

Ackerman, D. (1990). *A natural history of the senses.* NY: Vintage Books.

Claxton, C. S. & Murrell, P. H. (1987). *Learning styles: Implications for improving educational practice.* Washington, DC: Association for the Study of Higher Education.

Conti, G.J., & McNeil, R.C. (2011). Learning strategy preference and personality type: Are they related? *MPAEA Journal of Adult Education, 40,* 1–8. Retrieved December

11, 2013, from EBSCO Online Database Educational Research Complete.

Demski, J. (2012). This time it's personal. *T H E Journal, 39,* 32–36. Retrieved December 11, 2013, from EBSCO Online Database Educational Research Complete.

Dunn, R. & Griggs, S. A. (1988), *Learning styles: Quiet revolution in American secondary schools.* Reston, VA: National Association of Secondary School Principals.

Freed, J. & Parsons, L. (1998). *Right-brained children in a left-brained world: Unlocking the potential of your ADD child.* NY: Simon & Schuster.

Gardner, H. (1983). *Frames of mind: The theory of Multiple Intelligences.* NY: Basic Books.

Jung, C. (1971). *Psychological types (collected works of C.G. Jung, volume 6).* Translated by Gerhard Adler and R.F.C. Hull. Princeton, NJ: Princeton University Press.

Kavale, K.A. & Forness, S.R. (1987). Substance over style: assessing the efficacy of modality testing and teaching. *Exceptional Child, 56,* 228–239.

Kolb, D. A. (1985). *Experiential learning: Experience as the source of learning and development.* NY: Prentice-Hall.

Lambert, I. & Mitchell, S., (eds). (1997). *The crumbling walls of certainty: Towards a Christian critique of postmodernity and education.* Herefordshire, UK: Graceway Ltd.

Mvududu, N., & Thiel-Burgess, J. (2012). Constructivism in practice: The case for English language learners. *International Journal of Education, 4,* 108–118. Retrieved December 11, 2013, from EBSCO Online Database Educational Research Complete.

Polanyi, M. (1966). *The tacit dimension.* Garden City, NY: Doubleday Books.

Schank, R. (2001). *Designing world-class e-learning: How IBM, GE, Harvard Business School, and Columbia University are succeeding in e-learning.* NY: McGraw-Hill.

Schenck, J. (2015). Evolving Kolb: Experiential education in the age of neuroscience. *Journal of Experiential Education, 38*(1), 73–95. Retrieved December 14, 2016, from EBSCO Online Database Education Source.

Sims, R. R. & Sims, S. (1995). *The importance of learning styles: Understanding the implications for learning, course design, and education.* Westport, CT: Greenwood Press.

Sternberg, R. J. (1997). *Thinking styles.* Cambridge, U.K.: Cambridge University Press.

Willingham, D. T., Hughes, E. M., & Dobolyi, D. G. (2015). The scientific status of learning styles theories. *Teaching of Psychology, 42*(3), 266–271. Retrieved January 6, 2016, from EBSCO Online Database Education Research Complete.

Wilson, D. (1997). *Recovering the lost tools of learning: An approach to distinctive Christian education.* Wheaton, Illinois: Crossway Books.

SUGGESTED READING

Anderson, M. (2016). *Learning to choose, choosing to learn: The key to student motivation and achievement.* Alexandria, VA: ASCD.

Denig, S. J. (2004). Multiple intelligences and learning styles: Two complimentary dimensions. *Teachers College Record, 106,* 96–111. Retrieved July 29, 2007, from EBSCO Online Database Educational Research Complete.

Franklin, S. (2006). VAKing out learning styles-why the notion of 'learning styles' is unhelpful to teachers. *Education 3-13, 34,* 81–87. Retrieved July 29, 2007, from EBSCO Online Database Educational Research Complete.

Jones, C., Reichard, C., & Mokhtari, K. (2003). Are students' learning styles discipline specific? *Community College Journal of Research & Practice, 27,* 363–376. Retrieved July 29, 2007, from EBSCO Online Database Educational Research Complete.

Kaminska, P.M. (2014). *Learning Styles in Second Language Education.* United Kingdom: Cambridge Scholars Publishing.

Newton, P. (2015). The Learning Styles myth is thriving in higher education. *Frontiers in Psychology.* 6.

Pritchard, Alan. (2014). *Ways of learning: Learning theories and learning styles in the classroom.* New York, NY: Routledge.

Zhang, L. & Sternberg, R. J. (2005). A threefold model of intellectual styles. *Educational Psychology Review, 17,* 1–53. Retrieved July 29, 2007, from EBSCO Online Database Educational Research Complete.

TAXONOMY OF EDUCATIONAL OBJECTIVES—THE COGNITIVE DOMAIN

The following article is a summary of Bloom's Taxonomy of Educational Objectives. The Taxonomy was developed in the late 1940s by a group of university examiners—one of whom was Benjamin Bloom of the University of Chicago—for the purpose of facilitating the sharing of test materials. Although developed for a select audience, the Taxonomy became a worldwide phenomenon and was soon part of the everyday vocabulary of educators worldwide. The Taxonomy itself is a hierarchy of behaviorally defined educational outcomes; the six objectives are knowledge, comprehension, application, analysis, synthesis, and evaluation. Despite its popularity, there are many who argue the Taxonomy is philosophically and empirically unsound. Still others suggest it hasn't made a substantial impact on what teachers do in the classroom.

KEYWORDS: Analysis; Affective domain; Application; Cognitive domain; Comprehension; Evaluation; Knowledge; Objectives; Synthesis; Taxonomy

OVERVIEW

As one historian observes, descriptions of Bloom's taxonomy of educational objectives (Taxonomy) usually begin with superlatives (Kreitzer & Madaus, 1994). "Only the tersest, driest, or most academic writing concerning the Taxonomy fails to include a comment about its tremendous impact, utility, fame, publicity, or influence." Indeed, forty years after its original publication, "The Taxonomy of Educational Objectives" has sold more than one million copies and has been translated into more than twenty different languages. It is discussed in nearly every education textbook and has become one of the most frequently cited sources in educational research (Bloom, 1994).

Many point out that frequent reference to a piece of work is an insufficient standard by which to measure its impact as an effective tool (Sosniak, 1994). In other words, although the Taxonomy has become part of the vocabulary of educators, it may be a less central component of their practice. With regard to curriculum development, for example, Sosniak (1994) argues the Taxonomy has become a mere footnote. But a discussion of how the Taxonomy might fall short is premature without first understanding what it was intended to do. As Kreitzer and Madaus explain, "The authors of the Taxonomy made remarkably modest claims about it."

The idea for an educational taxonomy was first discussed at an informal meeting of university examiners at the 1948 annual conference of the American Psychological Association. The group's original intention was to create a common framework of educational objectives that would facilitate the exchange of test items and materials among university examiners, and stimulate research on the relationship between education and evaluation. The Taxonomy was intended to be "a small volume" for a select audience, but instead turned into a "basic reference for all educators worldwide" (Bloom). The phenomenal popularity of the Taxonomy can only be explained, Bloom himself argues, "by the fact that it filled a void; it met a previously unmet need for basic, fundamental planning in education. For the first time, educators were able to evaluate the learning of students systematically."

In addition, larger cultural shifts, and changing ideas about the purpose of schooling, helped create an environment receptive to the development of clearly defined educational outcomes (Airasian, 1994). In the 1960s, President Johnson declared a war on poverty, a significant part of which was the investment of federal funds into educational programs for students from disadvantaged backgrounds. Along with the funding, however, came an increased emphasis on accountability, "with each program having to be evaluated in terms of students' achievement of the program's objectives" (Airasian). Federally funded programs such as Head Start also signaled a seismic shift in beliefs about teaching and learning, from the notion that students were limited by innate ability to the idea that it is the environment that affects learning most. "Once the notion that most students could learn was accepted, emphasis in testing shifted away from sorting individuals and toward finding ways to enhance and certify student learning" (Airasian). Objectives gave educators a tool to demonstrate student learning and the effectiveness of federally funded programs.

Although the Taxonomy has become known as "Bloom's Taxonomy," Benjamin Bloom—then an examiner at the University of Chicago—was just one of many who contributed to the project. As he himself explains, "the development of the Handbook was truly a group project. It was the direct outgrowth of the thinking of more than thirty persons who attended the various meetings at which the idea of a taxonomy was discussed" (Bloom). Even after the Taxonomy was complete, the group printed a preliminary edition of 1,000 copies and distributed it to professors, teachers, and administrators; their feedback was included in the final version.

The authors of the Taxonomy approached the task of defining and classifying educational outcomes in much the same way that biologists classified living things into the categories phylum, class, order, family, genus, and species (Bloom). Bloom also likened the process to "the development of a plan for classifying books in a library" (Bloom). The group made it clear that *what* they intended to classify was the change produced in an individual as a result of participating in an educational experience. In Bloom's own words, "What we are classifying is the intended behavior of students—the ways in which individuals are to act, think, or feel as a result of participating in some unit of instruction." The outcomes, they believed, reflected changes in behavior that could be observed across different content areas, so that "a single set of classifications should be applicable in all...instances" (Anderson & Sosniak, 1994). The group aimed to develop taxonomies in three different domains—the cognitive, affective, and psychomotor domains—but only completed the first two. What follows is a description of the Taxonomy of educational objectives of the cognitive domain.

DESCRIPTION OF THE TAXONOMY

The Taxonomy was developed with several guiding principles in mind, the first of which is reflected in the intention to classify educational objectives as changes in *behavior*. The authors noticed that teachers spoke about learning in 'nebulous terms', referring to student outcomes as 'understanding', 'comprehension' and 'grasping the core or essence' of something. They wanted to give teachers a tool to speak about outcomes with greater precision, and thus proposed that "virtually all educational objectives...have their counterparts in student behavior" (Bloom).

Although the authors recognized that by defining learning in behavioral terms they were making a value judgment, they strove for impartiality and objectivity to the greatest extent possible. They believed the classification should be "a purely descriptive scheme in which every type of educational goal can be represented in a relatively neutral fashion" (Bloom). In other words, the Taxonomy was not intended to suggest that certain outcomes were better than others, or exclude certain types of outcomes from the Taxonomy altogether.

As the group began to brainstorm lists of educational objectives, they quickly realized that complex behaviors included simpler behaviors. In order to incorporate this relationship into the Taxonomy, they organized their educational objectives as a hierarchy. "Thus, our classifications may be said to be in the form

where behaviors of type A form one class, behaviors of type AB form another class, while behaviors of type ABC form still another class" (Bloom). The educational process, they concluded, was one of building upon simpler behaviors to form more complex behaviors.

The following six categories form the hierarchy of Bloom's Taxonomy:

- Knowledge;
- Comprehension;
- Application;
- Analysis;
- Synthesis;
- Evaluation.

Before defining each category in greater detail, a fourth guiding principle should be brought to light. Specifically, Bloom and the authors made a distinction between *knowledge* and the other five objectives of the Taxonomy—which they referred to collectively as *skills and abilities*. They regarded knowledge—the remembering of information—as a necessary but not sufficient outcome of learning. In other words, knowledge is a prerequisite for other types of outcomes, and not the sole aim of education. "What is needed is some evidence that students can do something with their knowledge, that is, that they can apply the information to new situations and problems" (Anderson & Sosniak). Given the rapidly changing culture of the 20th century, they argued, skills and abilities would help students adapt to new situations more readily than the mere acquisition of information.

The Six Objectives

KNOWLEDGE

The first educational objective—knowledge—is defined as "those behaviors and test situations which emphasize remembering, either by recognition or recall, of ideas, material, or phenomena. The behavior expected of a student in the recall situation is very similar to the behavior he was expected to have during the original learning situation" (Bloom). The authors then make a distinction between concrete types of knowledge and more abstract forms of knowledge, which they organize into three separate categories: knowledge of specifics, knowledge of ways and means of dealing with specifics, and knowledge of universals and abstractions in a field. Remembering the exact date of an event is an example of knowledge of specifics, understanding how culture has changed over time is an example of knowledge of ways and means of dealing with specifics, and familiarity with theoretical approaches to education is an example of knowledge of universals and abstractions in a field.

COMPREHENSION

Comprehension, what the authors argue is the largest class of the five skills and abilities, occupies the second rung of the hierarchy. Although the largest, it is also perhaps the least intuitive, since most think of comprehension either in terms of reading comprehension or as complete understanding of a message. Instead, the authors of the Taxonomy define it as "those objectives, behaviors, or responses which represent an understanding of the literal message contained in a communication" (Bloom). Understanding of the literal message is communicated in three ways—the ability to *translate* the original communication into other terms, the ability to *interpret* what was said (e.g., understanding the relative importance or interrelationships between ideas expressed), and the ability to *extrapolate* the information by making inferences or judgments.

APPLICATION

Application is relative to comprehension; it requires the skills and abilities of lower classifications, but goes beyond them as well. A student who applies a principle when prompted to do so demonstrates comprehension, but a student who applies a principle in a new situation in which a solution has not been specified is demonstrating application. In other words, application is about transfer of training. The authors argue that developing good problem solving skills, as opposed to learning how to apply specific facts in specific situations, encourages transfer. Being able to discuss current events in relation to principles of civil liberties and civil rights is an example of application.

ANALYSIS

Analysis, requiring even more complex skills than those required in comprehension and application, "emphasizes the breakdown of the material into its constituent parts and the detection of the relationships of the parts and of the way they are organized" (Bloom). When teachers ask students to identify

supporting statements and conclusions, for example, or to distinguish fact from opinion, they are asking students to engage in analysis. They further organize this objective into analysis of elements, analysis of relationships, and analysis of organizational principles. The ability to identify a hypothesis is an example of analysis of elements, the ability to detect logical errors in an argument is an example of analysis of relationships, and the ability to infer an author's point of view an example of analysis of organizational principles.

SYNTHESIS

The fifth level of the hierarchy is defined as "the putting together of elements and parts so as to form a whole. This is a process of working with elements, parts, etc., and combining them in such a way as to constitute a pattern or structure not clearly there before" (Bloom). The authors identify synthesis as the educational objective most closely related to creativity, and further delineate it according to three different *products* of synthesis: a unique communication, a plan or proposed set of operations, or a set of abstract relations. The ability to speak extemporaneously is an illustration of the first product. The ability to develop a lesson plan for an instructional unit is example of the second product, while the ability to develop a theory of learning is an example of the third.

EVALUATION

Evaluation sits at the top of the hierarchy because the authors believe it includes behaviors defined in each of the other five categories. In addition to those behaviors, however, it also includes an element of judgment. "Evaluation is defined as the making of judgments about the value, for some purpose, of ideas, works, solutions, methods, material, etc." (Bloom). Even though evaluation is last in the Taxonomy, the authors argue that it shouldn't be viewed as the last step in thinking; "It is quite possible that the evaluative process will in some cases be the prelude to the acquisition of new knowledge" (Bloom). Bloom distinguishes between judgments made in terms of internal evidence—as when a student evaluates whether an author's ideas flow logically from one to the other—or in terms of external criteria—such as when a student evaluates a piece of artwork according to external standards of that style or period of art.

FURTHER INSIGHTS

As Bloom himself recognized, "a final criterion is that the taxonomy must be accepted and used by the workers in the field if it is to be regarded as a useful and effective tool. Whether or not it meets this criterion can be determined only after a sufficient amount of time has elapsed" (Bloom). One of the more immediate applications was made by teachers, who quickly recognized that as much as 90% of their instructional time was spent teaching to the lowest level of the Taxonomy, "with very little time spent on the higher mental processes that would enable students to apply their knowledge creatively" (Bloom). Given the test of time however, the Taxonomy might not fare so well. Although widely *known*, it may be less widely *used*. The following discusses the impact of the Taxonomy on testing, curriculum development, research, and teacher education.

According to Airasian, "objectives per se have been very influential in the testing and evaluation movement over the past quarter century, but not objectives stated in the form advocated in the Taxonomy." The authors of the Taxonomy intended for their objectives to be tailored to the needs of local teachers and administrators; therefore, the objectives themselves, what Airasian calls *behavioral* objectives, were specific and concrete, but broad enough that they still required teachers to further specify them for their own uses. Since that time, testing has become more centralized and standardized; as a result, the "external testing programs [have] served to reduce the incentive for and reliance on locally stated educational objectives" (Airasian).

As stated earlier, the original intention of the Taxonomy was to facilitate the exchange of test materials among university examiners. What it was intended to do beyond this is less clear. Sosniak argues that its attention to curriculum development was merely an afterthought, and one without much substance. She writes, "the Taxonomy was developed first; attention to curriculum was inserted later." Although the language was changed, it was changed "without considerable rethinking or rewriting of the volume" (Sosniak). As a result, the Taxonomy has not informed the practice of curriculum development to the extent its popularity suggests. In addition, Sosniak speculates, the trend toward increased specificity

and detail in educational objectives has made it burdensome for teachers to incorporate them into lesson plans. Finally, disagreement about the nature of objectives—specifically, whether behavioral-based objectives represent all kinds of learning—limited their use in the classroom.

Moreover, the way the educational community talks about student learning goals has changed over time (Marken & Morrison, 2013). "The same forces that have moved the field away from the term *behavioral objectives* may also be moving the field away from *instructional objectives*," the authors write. "If there has been a shift over the last several decades from a focus on training and instruction to a focus on education and learning, then it is perhaps not surprising to see a reduction in the terms *instructional* and *behavioral objectives* and a rise in the use of *educational* and *learning objectives*" (Marken & Morrison).

Anderson (1994) corroborates the limited impact of the Taxonomy on teachers, despite the heavy emphasis teacher education programs place on the use of the Taxonomy in the classroom. Thus, even though teachers learn how to use the Taxonomy to plan lessons, prepare tests, ask questions, and assign classroom tasks, research suggests teachers no longer rely on the Taxonomy once they begin teaching on their own. Studies show most teachers develop lesson plans in terms of what they want students to do (e.g., activities) as opposed to what they want students to learn (e.g. outcomes) (Anderson). In addition, teachers continue to focus their instruction and evaluation on lower-order thinking; a recent review of over 9,000 test items revealed that over 80% were written at the lowest level of the Taxonomy.

Marzano (2013), in an effort to support the application of the Taxonomy to instructor lesson-planning, published five recommendations for educators seeking to clearly delineate what they want students to learn and know. They are: 1) Create an internally consistent system; 2) Start with objectives that focus on a single unit of instruction; 3) Break the objective into a learning progression; 4) Use the learning progression to establish daily targets; and 5) Translate daily targets into student-friendly language (Marzano).

Although limited in terms of its impact in the classroom, the Taxonomy has made tremendous contributions to educational research (Anderson, 1994). With regard to teaching methods, for example, significant empirical evidence has been found to support the notion that methods utilizing one-way communication (e.g., lecture) help students achieve lower-order objectives, while methods requiring two-way communication (e.g., group activities) foster higher-order objectives (Anderson). Similarly, research has shown that real-world experiences facilitate the attainment of higher-order objectives to a greater extent than classroom activities. Within the classroom, descriptive studies reveal that teacher questioning focuses on lower-order objectives, with only 20% of questions actually requiring students to think (Anderson). This finding is consistent across age, subject matter and ability level.

VIEWPOINTS

While some may quibble about whether the Taxonomy is a useful tool for classroom teachers, others take issue with the Taxonomy itself. The following section will briefly outline some of the philosophical and empirical arguments against the guiding principles and content of the Taxonomy, and end with a word about how the Taxonomy has evolved in response to such criticism.

Furst (1994) summarizes the arguments of many of the critics, taking aim first at the author's claim of impartiality and neutrality. A taxonomy of educational objectives that excludes any and all objectives that cannot be behaviorally specified, he argues, is inherently partial. Secondly, he outlines philosophical arguments against the separation of content from process. Referencing the philosophy of Wittgenstein, who insisted on the study of particulars as opposed to the development of general categories, Furst stresses the artificiality of such a separation. The process of remembering, for example, cannot be separated from the remembering of some *thing* (Sockett, as cited in Furst). The separation of the cognitive domain from the affective domain has also garnered critical attention, for parceling out "the world of knowledge from the world of values" (Furst).

In addition to philosophical criticisms of the Taxonomy, others have taken issue with the hierarchical relationship between the objectives. As Bloom explained, the structure of the taxonomy should reflect 'real' relationships, thus researchers should expect to find empirical validation in support of such structure. Kreitzer & Madaus summarize two types of empirical investigations—those that investigate the reliability of classifications of test items according to taxonomic level and those that investigate the

cumulative/hierarchical nature of the taxonomy. In sum, studies show reliability varies according to the level of training, and that despite increasingly sophisticated statistical techniques, no one has been able to validate the hierarchical structure. At the same time, "no one has been able to demonstrate that [the structure] does not exist" (Kreitzer & Madaus). In the end, Kreizter & Madaus suggest that empirical validation may be unnecessary, especially given that the Taxonomy—validated or not—helped educators "make sense of their world."

A discussion of Bloom's Taxonomy wouldn't be complete without mention of the ways in which it continues to evolve. Just as it has been translated into multiple languages, the Taxonomy has been shaped and reshaped by educators in response to criticisms and the changing educational environment. Anderson and Krathwohl, two of the contributing authors to the original Taxonomy, have developed a revised Taxonomy; the new Taxonomy further delineates knowledge as factual, conceptual, procedural, and metacognitive, partially in response to criticisms of the separation of process from content. (Weisburg [2012] offers reviews of online resources for the revised Taxonomy for those seeking additional information.) In the end, it is the adaptability and evolution of the Taxonomy that may be the greatest measure of its contribution to teaching and learning, rather than the impact of the Taxonomy as it was conceived over fifty years ago.

TERMS & CONCEPTS

Analysis: The fourth level of the Taxonomy, defined as breaking information down into its separate elements, and revealing the relationships among them.

Application: The third level of the Taxonomy, defined in terms of the transfer of learning, so that abstractions and principles learned in one situation can then be applied to new problems in new situations.

Comprehension: The second level of the Taxonomy, defined as the understanding of a literal message, and the ability to translate it, interpret it, and extrapolate from it.

Evaluation: The highest level of the Taxonomy of educational objectives; it incorporates behaviors from the five lower levels, but also includes notions of judgment. Judgments can me made relative to internal considerations (e.g., of a piece of work) or relative to external criteria.

Knowledge: The lowest level of the Taxonomy of educational objectives. Defined as the remembering of information, it is a prerequisite for advancement to higher levels. Knowledge is further categorized from the more concrete to the more abstract.

Objectives: The authors of the Taxonomy define objectives as the intended outcomes of participation in an educational activity. Objectives are defined in *behavioral* terms, so that they represent observable changes as a result of an educational experience.

Synthesis: Synthesis is the fifth level of the Taxonomy and the one authors believe is most closely related to creativity. They define it as the putting together of different elements to form a whole or structure not evident from viewing the elements separately.

Taxonomy: Taxonomy is a system of classification in which the relationships among the items in the taxonomy are not arbitrary, but rather reflect 'real' relationships in the natural world. For example, the ordering of objectives from knowledge to evaluation corresponds to the increasing level of complexity of the objectives.

Jennifer Kretchmar

BIBLIOGRAPHY

Airasian, P. (1994). The impact of the Taxonomy on testing and evaluation. In L.W. Anderson & L.A. Sosniak (Eds.), *Bloom's Taxonomy: A forty-year retrospective* (pp. 1-8). Chicago, IL: The University of Chicago Press.

Anderson, L.W. (1994). Research on teaching and teacher education. In L.W. Anderson & L.A. Sosniak (Eds.), *Bloom's Taxonomy: A forty-year retrospective* (pp. 1-8). Chicago, IL: The University of Chicago Press.

Bloom, B.S., Englehart, M.D., Furst, E.J., Hill, W.H., & Krathwohl, D.R. (1954). Taxonomy *of educational objectives: The classification of educational goals. Handbook I: Cognitive Domain.* New York, NY: Longman, Inc.

Bloom, B. S. (1994). Reflections on the development and use of the Taxonomy. In L.W. Anderson & L.A. Sosniak (Eds.), *Bloom's Taxonomy: A forty-year retrospective* (pp. 1-8). Chicago, IL: The University of Chicago Press.

Furst, E.J. (1994). Bloom's Taxonomy: Philosophical and educational issues. In L.W. Anderson & L.A. Sosniak (Eds.), *Bloom's Taxonomy: A forty-year retrospective* (pp. 28-40). Chicago, IL: The University of Chicago Press.

Krathwohl, D.R. (2002). A revision of Bloom's Taxonomy: An overview. *Theory into Practice,,* 212-218. Retrieved May 22, 2007, from EBSCO online database Education Research Complete.

Kreitzer, A.E., & Madaus, G.F. (1994). Empirical investigations of the hierarchical structure of the taxonomy. In L.W. Anderson & L.A. Sosniak (Eds.), *Bloom's Taxonomy: A forty-year retrospective* (pp. 28-40). Chicago, IL: The University of Chicago Press.

Marken, J., & Morrison, G. (2013). Objectives over time: a look at four decades of objectives in the educational research literature. *Contemporary Educational Technology, 4,* 1–14. Retrieved from EBSCO online database Education Research Complete, December 7, 2013.

Marzano, R.J. (2013). Targets, objectives, standards: How do they fit? *Educational Leadership, 70,* 82–83. Retrieved from EBSCO online database Education Research Complete, December 7, 2013.

Rohwer, W.D., & Sloane, K. (1994). Psychological perspectives. In L.W. Anderson & L.A. Sosniak (Eds.), *Bloom's Taxonomy: A forty-year retrospective* (pp. 41-63). Chicago, IL: The University of Chicago Press.

Sosniak, L.A. (1994). The Taxonomy, curriculum, and their relations. In L.W. Anderson & L.A. Sosniak (Eds.), *Bloom's Taxonomy: A forty-year retrospective* (pp. 41-63). Chicago, IL: The University of Chicago Press.

Weisburg, H.K. (2012). Knowledge in bloom. *School Librarian's Workshop, 33,* 19. Retrieved from EBSCO online database Education Research Complete, December 7, 2013.

SUGGESTED READING

Anderson, L.W., & Krathwohl, D.R. (Eds.). (2001). A taxonomy for learning, teaching, and assessing: A revision of Bloom's taxonomy of educational objectives. New York, NY: Addison Wesley Longman, Inc.

Bissell, A.N., & Lemons, P.P. (2006). A new method for assessing critical thinking in the classroom. *Bioscience,* 56, 66-72. Retrieved May 22, 2007, from EBSCO online database Academic Search Premier.

Lord, R., & Baviskar, S. (2007). Moving students from information recitation to information understanding: Exploring Bloom's Taxonomy in creating science questions. *Journal of College Science Teaching,* 36, 40-44. Retrieved May 22, 2007, from EBSCO online database Education Research Complete.

Krathwohl, D.R., Bloom, B.S., & Masia, B.B. (1964). *Taxonomy of educational objectives: The classification of educational goals. Handbook II: Affective Domain.* New York, NY: David McKay Company, Inc.

Marzono, R.J., & Kendall, J.S. (2007). *The new taxonomy of educational objectives.* Thousand Oaks, CA: Corwin Press.

Roberts, J.L., & Inman, T.F. (2007). *Strategies for differentiating instruction: Best practices in the classroom.* Waco, TX: Prufrock Press, Inc.

EDUCATIONAL ANTHROPOLOGY

The following article summarizes the academic discipline known as educational anthropology. Although the field was institutionalized and professionalized in the 1960s, it has roots in the broader discipline of anthropology, and thus dates back to the nineteenth and early twentieth century. Once the field solidified in the late twentieth century, practitioners distinguished their field from others by declaring their primary focus of study the transmission of culture through education, both formal and otherwise. In addition to bringing more awareness to the role culture plays in education, anthropologists also made significant contributions to the social sciences through innovations in methodology. Anthropologists are credited with the ethnographic approach to research, emphasizing the importance of 'the other' through comparative methods, and finding the 'unfamiliar and exotic' in the study of familiar cultures, even one's own.

KEYWORDS: Comparative method; Culture; Cultural pluralism; Cultural therapy; Cultural transmission; Educational anthropology; Ethnography; Mead, Margaret; Spindler, George; Spindler, Louise; Educational Theory; Educational Anthropology

OVERVIEW
HISTORY OF EDUCATIONAL ANTHROPOLOGY

"Educational Anthropology or anthropology of education, (either one sounds awkward) has as long a history as anthropology itself" (Spindler, 1987). This quote provides a fitting introduction to the field of anthropology and education. George Spindler, one of the modern-day founders of the discipline, organized a conference in 1954 that became a pivotal moment in the institutionalization of the field, but even as he argues himself, the roots of the discipline run much deeper. The quote is playful, too, in recognizing that along with the formalization of the field came the formalization of a name that is difficult to say.

That the roots of the discipline run deep is demonstrated most aptly by the contribution of one of the most recognizable anthropologists of the early twentieth century. Margaret Mead, who earned notoriety in 1928 with the publication of "Coming of Age in Samoa," gave a great deal of attention to the concepts of teaching and learning. Indeed, she

once categorized cultures according to whether they are 'learning cultures' or 'teaching cultures,' defining the former as "small, homogenous group(s) that show little concern for transmitting culture because there is virtually no danger of anyone going astray" and the latter as those cultures in which it is necessary for "those who know to inform and direct those who do not know" (Wolcott, 1987).

Of course, Mead was just one of many anthropologists making contributions to our understanding of education in the early twentieth century. Indeed, Eddy (1987) refers to the period between 1925 and 1954 as "The Formative Years" and notes that a bibliography of studies that addressed formalized education and enculturation reads like a "Who's Who of American and British founders of modern anthropology." In addition to the people who were studying education and anthropology during this time, the Formative Years were notable for other reasons as well. Much of the funding for studies in anthropology came from private sources, such as the Rockefeller Foundation and Carnegie Corporation, and anthropology was viewed largely as an applied science. In 1941, the U.S. Government contracted with anthropologists to study the 'educational problems' of Native Americans; the work of other anthropologists contributed significantly to the 1954 Supreme Court ruling *Brown v. Board of Education of Topeka* that ended segregation. And abroad, anthropologists studied the problems of education in Africa, although it wasn't until mid-century that practitioners "recognized the need to adapt education to individual and community needs rather than to transfer Western educational practices wholesale" (as quoted in Eddy).

While the contributions of anthropologists to educational issues during the first half of the twentieth century were impressive, as Margaret Mead stated at the 1954 Stanford Conference, they were largely "dependent upon personalities rather than any on-going institutionalized process of any sort" (Eddy). The conference would later come to signify the institutionalization and specialization of educational anthropology, although the conference itself was not the direct cause. Indeed, higher education enrollment growth following World War II, along with a tremendous increase in public funding (and a simultaneous shift away from private funding), led to a focus on the development of the profession within the academy. Curriculum development needs of the 1950s and 1960s, and the recognition of the failure of schools to meet the needs of the urban poor and urban minorities, gave anthropologists an opportunity to formalize their contribution to education in specific ways. The formalization and specialization process culminated in 1970, with the development of the Council on Anthropology and Education (CAE). As Eddy argues, the organizing principles of the CAE reflect "remarkable continuity" between educational anthropology's past and future. The principles, listed below, provide insight into a definition of the field:

- Anthropology, as a discipline, is concerned with cross-cultural and comparative studies;
- American society is a multi-cultural society and an important subject of inquiry in its own right;
- Anthropology has contributions to make to the study of child development and learning, in all the various ways and environments in which they occur;
- Ethnography is an effective tool for studying learning and teaching systems, and the results of ethnographic studies can contribute to educational policy;
- And, education today takes place within context of large cultural, social, political, economic, and technological change.

WHAT IS EDUCATIONAL ANTHROPOLOGY?

As educational anthropology became a more formalized and specialized discipline, those who studied it felt it was important to distinguish it from other disciplines. Recognizing that "learning fell more or less in the province of the psychologists and social structure in the province of sociologists and social anthropologists, we felt that cultural transmission would be a natural [focus] for anthropological applications to education" (Spindler). Pai, Adler, and Shadow (2006) similarly place the emphasis on culture, arguing that educators have not "always been clear and precise about the myriad ways that cultural factors influence the process of schooling, teaching, and learning." Our lack of awareness, they claim, has led to "unsound educational policies, ineffective school practices, and unfair assessment of learners."

Culture Defined: Because anthropology of education is about culture, and specifically the ways in which culture is transmitted, it's important to begin with a definition of culture itself. As with most subjects of study, scholars debate the exact meaning of culture, but agree with the following basic definition.

"Culture is most commonly viewed as that pattern of knowledge, skills, behaviors, attitudes, and beliefs, as well as material artifacts, produced by a human society and transmitted from one generation to the next" (Pai et al.).

Pai et al. further describe culture as goal-oriented and as a system of norms and controls designed to govern behavior. They emphasize the process of symboling,—or the bestowing of meaning upon objects and actions—as a critical in the development of culture, explaining that it is the process by which, for example, "an ordinary cow becomes a sacred cow and plain water becomes holy water." Finally, culture is pervasive and impacts nearly every aspect of human life. Studies suggest that our experience of pain is shaped by the language available to us to describe it, and that even something as simple as our perception of colors and shapes is not just a physiological response, but depends on the categories available to us to understand them (Pai et al.).

The above definition perhaps begs the question, "How does the individual relate to the larger culture?" As described, it might seem that any single person is determined by the norms of the larger group, but anthropologists are quick to qualify their definition with the acknowledgement that "every person's interpretation of his or her culture is idiosyncratic and cultural knowledge varies from person to person, depending on age, sex, status, and individual experience" (Spindler). Furthermore, anthropologists liken culture to a map; in the same way a map is an abstract representation of a territory and not the territory itself, culture is an abstract representation that provides only a general understanding of a group of people (Pai et al.). Implicit norms and the processes through which individuals relate to one another may tell us as much about a group of people as the explicitly stated norms.

SCHOOLS AND THE TRANSMISSION OF CULTURE—A BRIEF HISTORY

Scholars argue about the purpose of schools—specifically, whether they are intended to reproduce societies, transform societies, or some combination of both. Stated differently, the question is also whether schools provide equal opportunity for all, or whether they maintain class structure, limiting opportunity for certain groups of people. While the question may still be open for debate, what is undeniable is that the history of schooling in America tells a story of the transmission of the dominant culture, even when the rhetoric surrounding schooling suggested otherwise. The following is a brief summary of what Pai et al. describe in greater detail in their chapter titled "Schooling as Americanization: 1600-1970s."

Puritan Perspective (1647-1870): Schools during this time period were viewed as a primary mechanism of Americanization. They were intended to enculturate students who belonged to the white, Anglo-Saxon, Protestant (WASP) community and acculturate those from a different heritage (Pai et al.). The puritan school was intolerant and hostile toward diversity, and helped establish a single, dominant culture.

Keeping America American (1870-1920s): This period was characterized by massive immigration to the United States; most of the immigrants were from southern and eastern Europe, or Asia, and were not English-speaking, Anglo-Saxon or Protestant. Rather than embrace an increasingly diverse society, educators viewed schools as a way to assimilate the newcomers. Immigrants were expected to divest themselves of their own culture, and as they did so, educators argued, prejudice and discrimination would disappear.

The Melting Pot Ideal (1920s—1965): Educational rhetoric during this period took a more liberal tone, arguing that a common society should be created from its diverse elements—a new synthesized culture that was not any single element but rather a 'melting pot' of diverse influences. "In reality, what happened…was that all varieties of ethnicities were melted into one pot, but the brew turned out to be Anglo-Saxon again" (Pai et al.). As the century progressed, increasing attention was paid to achievement and excellence in schools—largely as a result of the perception that American students were falling behind when compared to their international counterparts—but little attention was paid to cultural diversity.

The Great Society & Beyond: Educational policy during the 1960s and 1970s attempted to address social and economic inequality by giving everyone—especially urban, poor, minorities—equal access to education. Compensatory education programs such as Head Start, for example, were designed to give students the necessary skills to succeed. Critics argued, however, that such programs were modeled on a deficit view of minorities.

Cultural Pluralism: Pai et al. argue that education in the United States has moved from one of cultural imperialism to one in which diversity is now more highly valued. If the twentieth century was about Americanization, they argue, the twenty-first century is about cultural pluralism. Cultural pluralism, a term first coined by Harvard-educated philosopher Horace Kallen in 1915, is "an ideal that seeks to establish and encourage not only cultural diversity but also a basis of unity from which the United States can become a cohesive society enriched by shared, widely divergent, ethnic experiences" (Pai et al.).

It's important at this point to make a distinction between cultural pluralism and cultural relativism. Pluralists do not argue that all cultures are equal, in particular equally functional, or that all cultures should be practiced regardless of the consequences to the larger society. They recognize that there are objective standards by which cultural practices can and should be judged. Pai et al. provide several examples of cultural practices that are functional to greater or lesser degrees. In other words, because a cultural practice exists does not necessarily imply it is the best way of meeting the need it was designed to meet.

HOW IS EDUCATIONAL ANTHROPOLOGY STUDIED AND APPLIED?

Ethnography: The introduction of ethnography to the social sciences was so significant a contribution that anthropology and ethnography have become nearly synonymous. So much so, in fact, that, practitioners lament the fact that it overshadows other contributions each field of study can make. Wolcott wrote:

"In the 1970s, 'things ethnographic' definitely caught the educator eye. Wide interest in ethnography provides us with an unusual opportunity to demonstrate that anthropology has more to offer to the field of education than simply a 'fieldwork' approach to research. Perhaps anthropology can serve as a reminder to educational researchers that their preoccupation with method borders on making method an end in itself. Anthropological concern has never been with method per se. Its focus is in making sense of the lived-in world."

The popularity of ethnography surpassed the practice itself, as practitioners doing any kind of qualitative research began calling it ethnography. George and Louise Spindler (1987), pioneers in educational anthropology, argued that it "shouldn't be called ethnography unless it [was]" and set out to correct the misunderstandings by providing clear guidelines for its practice. The following is a brief summary of what they describe in their chapter titled "Teaching and Learning How to Do the Ethnography of Education" (Spindler).

According to Spindler and Spindler, "the most important requirements for an ethnographic approach, as we see it, is that behavior in situations must be explained from the native's point of view, and both the behavior and explanation must be recorded as carefully and systematically as possible..." More specifically, they outline ten criteria for 'good ethnography,' which are:

- Observations are contextualized;
- Hypotheses emerge *in situ*, as the study goes on in the selected setting;
- Observation is prolonged and repetitive;
- The native view of reality is inferred through observation and other forms of inquiry;
- Ethnographers elicit socio-cultural knowledge from informant-participants;
- Tools such as instruments, codes, schedules, and questionnaires, are generated *in suti*, as the study goes on in the selected setting;
- Ethnographers adopt a comparative approach, and recognize cultural variation;
- Ethnographers recognize that some sociocultural knowledge will be implicit and tacit;
- Ethnographers do not predetermine responses from natives by the kinds of questions asked but rather cultural knowledge must emerge in natural form;

- And, ethnographers should use all and any tools that will enable them to collect more live data.

Spindler and Spindler conclude playfully by arguing that ethnographers must be 'pesky people,' willing to suffer resentment and rejection in the field, and willing to persist in the face of informants who are unwilling to share personal information. They also caution against the pitfalls of inference, arguing that true ethnographies are those that offer observations first and foremost, and inference only minimally. Inference, they argue, should come at a later stage in the research process, when doing ethnographic interpretation.

Importance of the Other: Another significant contribution of anthropology to social science methodology is the comparative method, or the introduction and emphasis on 'the other.' Anthropologists argue that by studying different cultures you not only learn about the other culture itself, but gain a new perspective on your own culture as well. As Spindler argues, "We felt then and we feel now that the comparative stance is essential to an anthropological position. We have lost sight of this in recent time and most articles published as educational anthropology are published as though they were dealing with only one culture."

Making the familiar exotic: Just as the comparative stance is essential to anthropological methodology, so too is it sometimes necessary to study one's own culture. As anthropologists acknowledge, this can sometimes be more difficult than studying 'the other,' so comfortable and familiar is one's own culture. Margaret Mead is remembered for once quipping that if a fish became an anthropologist, the last thing it would discover would be water (Spindler). And Spindler argues that making "the exotic and different familiar enough to be perceived and communicated..." may be the central problem for the field researcher."

Indeed, in many ways this was Spindler's challenge as a young anthropologist conducting a 1951 classroom study of teacher Roger Harker, a case that in many ways helped define his career and the field. After spending weeks studying the Menominee Indians, Spindler found little to 'observe' in the typical American classroom. What he discovered in the end, however, was nearly as startling as his inability to first see it, for he was able to prove that Roger Harker, hailed for his teaching ability, was teaching to only sixty-percent of the children in his classroom, and virtually ignoring the others.

This young man, with the best of intentions, was…informing Anglo middle-class children that they were capable, had bright futures, were socially acceptable, and were worth a lot of trouble. He was also informing lower-class and non-Anglo children that they were less capable, less socially acceptable, less worth the trouble. He was defeating his own declared educational goals (Spindler).

Cultural Therapy: The 'Roger Harker' study was important to Spindler, not only for shaping his career, but for highlighting teachers' need for cultural therapy. Loosely defined, cultural therapy is "a process of bringing one's own culture, in its manifold forms—assumptions, goals, values, beliefs, and communicative modes—to a level of awareness that permits one to perceive it as a potential bias in social interaction…" (Spindler). In the case of Roger Harker, Spindler demonstrated to the teacher how his narrow, upper-middle class, white Protestant background impacted his interactions with students who didn't share his culture. In the process of bringing Harker's culture to his awareness, he also helped Harker understand cultures different from his own.

EDUCATIONAL ANTHROPOLOGY IN THE FUTURE

As America becomes an increasingly diverse country, and as the boundaries between countries become more permeable in the twenty-first century global economy, educational anthropology has more to offer than ever before. According to Census projections, Hispanics will comprise 18% of the U.S. population in 2025, while African Americans and whites will comprise 13% and 62% respectively (Pai et al.). Already, nearly 40% of school-age children live in low-income families, while 17% live below the poverty level.

In such a diverse society, then, giving teachers the capacity to recognize and value cultural differences will be imperative. What is at stake, some argue, is nothing less than the human dignity. "The culture to which one belongs [is] the root of the individual's identity…To reject a person's cultural heritage is to do psychological and moral violence to the dignity and worth of that individual." (Pai et al.).

TERMS & CONCEPTS

Acculturation: The process whereby children in school learn a culture that is new and different—the dominant culture—from the culture they practice at home. A minority student living in urban America, for example, being taught by a white, middle-class teacher is learning a white, middle-class culture.

Comparative Method: An approach to research that emphasizes the role of 'the other'—not only in an attempt to better understand 'the other' but also in an attempt to enhance understanding of one's self or own culture. Educational anthropologists often study the educational systems of other cultures, partly to bring insight to the educational systems of their own culture.

Compensatory education: The belief that disadvantaged, poor, and minority students can succeed if given access to the same kinds of experiences that enabled middle-class, white children to succeed. Programs such as Head Start were predicated on the compensatory model of education, but critics argue such programs denigrated minority culture while upholding white, middle-class values.

Culture: The pattern of knowledge, skills, behaviors, attitudes, and beliefs, as well as material artifacts, produced by a human society and transmitted from one generation to the next.

Cultural pluralism: An ideal that seeks to establish and encourage cultural diversity. Cultural pluralism also advocates building a cohesive society that is strengthened by shared, widely divergent, ethnic experiences.

Cultural therapy: A process of bringing one's own culture to a level of awareness that permits one to perceive it as a potential bias in social interaction. Although therapy is often synonymous with psychology, Spindler suggests that it is a teacher's culture that impacts her interactions with students more so than her personality.

Cultural transmission: Educational anthropologists distinguish their discipline from psychology and sociology by declaring the 'transmission of culture' through education—both formal and otherwise—as their main focus of study. Although many disagree, schools are often viewed as the primary vehicle through which a society transfers cultural knowledge to the next generation.

Deficit view: When members of a minority culture are perceived to be lacking because they don't practice the dominant culture. The dominant culture is viewed as the 'right' or 'normal' culture, and all minority cultures as 'sick' or 'wrong.'

Enculturation: The process whereby children in school learn their own culture. Students who belong to the dominant culture are said to be 'enculturated,' while those who belong to minority cultures are said to be 'acculturated.'

Ethnography: Qualitative methodology first introduced by anthropologists in which the researcher becomes a participant-observer in the culture he/she is trying to understand. Ethnographers believe behavior must be understood from the natives' point of view.

Jennifer Kretchmar

BIBLIOGRAPHY

Demerath, P. (2012). Toward common ground: The uses of educational anthropology in multicultural education. *International Journal of Multicultural Education, 14,* 1-21. Retrieved December 15, 2013, from EBSCO Online Database Education Research Complete.

Eddy, E.M. (1987). Theory, research, and application in educational anthropology. In G.D. Spindler (Ed.), *Education and cultural process: Anthropological approaches* (pp. 5-25). Prospect Heights, IL: Waveland Press, Inc.

Ló Pez, F. A., Heilig, J., & Schram, J. (2013). A story within a story: Culturally responsive schooling and American Indian and Alaska Native achievement in the National Indian Education Study. *American Journal of Education, 119,* 513-538. Retrieved December 15, 2013, from EBSCO Online Database Education Research Complete.

Pai, Y., Adler, S.A., & Shadiow, L.K. (2006). Cultural foundations of education. Upper Saddle River, NJ: Merrill Prentice Hall.

Spindler, G.D. (1987). Preview. In G.D. Spindler (Ed.), *Education and cultural process: Anthropological approaches* (pp. 2-4). Prospect Heights, IL: Waveland Press, Inc.

Spindler, G.D. (Ed.). (2000). *Fifty years of anthropology and education: 1950-2000.* Mahwah, NJ: Lawrence Earlbaum Associates, Publishers.

Weis, L., & Fine, M. (2013). A methodological response from the field to Douglas Foley: Critical bifocality and class cultural productions in anthropology and education. *Anthropology & Education Quarterly, 44,* 222-233. Retrieved December 15, 2013, from EBSCO Online Database Education Research Complete.

Wolcott, H.F. (1987). The anthropology of learning. In G.D. Spindler (Ed.), *Education and cultural process: Anthropological approaches* (pp. 5-25). Prospect Heights, IL: Waveland Press, Inc.

SUGGESTED READING

Cherneff, J.B.R., & Hochwalk, E. (Eds.). (2006). Visionary Observers: Anthropological inquiry and education. Lincoln, NE: University of Nebraska Press.

Kneller, G.F. (1965). Educational Anthropology: An introduction. New York, NY: John Wiley & Sons, Inc.

Kohlman, M. J. (2013). Evangelizing eugenics: A brief historiography of popular and formal American eugenics education (1908-1948). *Alberta Journal of Educational Research, 58,* 657-690. Retrieved December 15, 2013, from EBSCO Online Database Education Research Complete.

Orellana, M.F. (2017). Solidarity, transculturality, Educational Anthropology and (the modest goal of) transforming the world. *Anthropology and Education Quarterly,* 48 (3); 210-220.

Spindler, G. D. (2000). The four careers of George and Louise Spindler: 1948-2000. *Annual Review of Anthropology, 29,* 25-50. Retrieved April 24, 2007, from EBSCO online database Academic Search Complete.

Spindler, G. D. (1988). Doing the ethnography of schooling. Prospect Heights, IL: Waveland Press, Inc.

Spindler, G.D., & Spindler, L. (1983). Anthropologists view American culture. *Annual Review of Anthropology, 12,* 49-78. Retrieved April 24, 2007, from EBSCO online database Academic Search Complete.

Vasudevan, L. (2014). More than playgrounds: Locating the lingering traces of Educational Anthropology. *Anthropology and Education Quarterly;* 45 (3); 235-240.

SOCIOLOGY OF EDUCATION

This article presents an overview of the sociology of education. Unlike many academic disciplines, the sociology of education is a relatively new field of study. Despite its short history, however, it is a rich and diverse field. Educational sociologists study a variety of topics, using a variety of theoretical approaches and methodologies. Unlike educational psychologists who study the relationship between learning and an individual student's mental processes (e.g., memory, attention, and perception), educational sociologists are interested in the relationship between learning and variables outside the individual's control—such as family background, race, access to resources, and social class. They also study education as a social institution, and its relationship to other institutions and society in general. The following will highlight some of the theoretical, methodological, and topical contributions of the field.

KEYWORDS: Conflict Theory; Durkheim, Emile; Interaction Theory; Positivism; Postmodernism; Sociology; Structural-Functionalism; Qualitative Methodologies

OVERVIEW

Unlike many academic disciplines, the sociology of education is a relatively new field of study. Although it is an outgrowth of sociology, whose origins date to the turn of the 20th century, sociologists didn't begin systematically studying educational institutions until the 1950s. Prior to that time, sociological studies in education were few in number, were largely based on anecdotal evidence and value judgments, and avoided the more controversial aspects of teaching and learning (Ballantine, 1997; Boocock, 1985).

In general, sociology is the study of people in groups, or more specifically, the study of human societies and social interaction. Sociologists sometimes describe their field as the study of social structures and institutions, and the *processes* that bring the structures and institutions alive (Ballantine). Education and schools are but one institution of society; others include family, religion, politics, economics, and health. The sociology of education should also be distinguished from the psychology of education, which focuses on the mental processes—such as memory, perception, and cognitive stages of development—that affect learning. Whereas psychologists study achievement in relation to the individual, sociologists study achievement in relation to the larger social environment.

Even though the sociology of education emerged more recently than some academic disciplines, it has grown exponentially in the last several decades. As a field, the diversity of theoretical perspectives, levels of analyses, and questions asked make it impossible to singularly define it. As one sociologist explains, "any attempt to encompass or sum up the sociology of education within a single framework is fraught with difficulties. Indeed, there is no single, unified or stable discipline or intellectual project to which we can refer" (Ball, 2004). Nevertheless, the following will attempt to summarize the discipline by outlining its theoretical and methodological history, and by taking a brief look at some of its core topics of study.

Applications: Theoretical & Methodological Approaches

STRUCTURAL-FUNCTIONALISM

As a theoretical perspective, structural-functionalism is known by many different names which include functionalism, consensus theory, and equilibrium theory (Ballantine). Functionalists approach the sociology of education from a macro level, arguing that society and its institutions are made up of interdependent parts, all of which function together to create a whole. They often use the body as a metaphor, suggesting that schools contribute to the healthy functioning of society in much the same way as the heart, for example, contributes to the healthy functioning of the body.

Emile Durkheim, a professor of pedagogy in early 20th century France, was not only one of the earliest proponents of functionalism, he is also considered the "father of sociology," and one of the first to study education from a sociological perspective. Durkheim studied many aspects of society—including but not limited to religion, crime, and suicide—but his contributions to the sociology of teaching and learning are documented in his works *Moral Education, The Evolution of Educational Thought,* and *Education and Sociology.*

One of the questions Durkheim spent much of his lifetime studying was the way in which societies maintain and reproduce themselves. As a functionalist, he believed schools served a critical role in perpetuating a society. He wrote, "Education is the influence exercised by adult generations on those that are not yet ready for social life. Its object is to arouse and to develop in the child a certain number of physical, intellectual and moral states which are demanded of him by...the political society" (as quoted in Ballantine). He also recognized that schools would differ across time and place, in relation to the larger society in which they were embedded.

Critics of Durkheim and of functionalists more generally, argue that functionalism fails to take into account conflict and instability. It may explain how some societies maintain the status quo, but it doesn't adequately represent reality to the extent that groups of people often have different agendas and goals, and subscribe to different ideologies. Ballantine suggests "that the dominant theoretical approach of structural-functionalism has not been capable of moving the field ahead because of its status quo orientation in a society faced with constant change."

Michael Apple (2013), on the other hand, wrote that "one of the things that sets [educational sociologist] Stephen Ball apart from many others is his insistence that both structural and post structural theories and analyses are necessary for 'bearing witness' and for an adequate critical understanding of educational realities" (Apple). Apple then demonstrates how Ball "creatively employs both sets of traditions."

CONFLICT THEORY

As its name suggests, conflict theory assumes a much less stable view of society than structural-functionalism. Based largely on the writings of Karl Marx and Max Weber, conflict theorists suggest that a society is largely defined by two groups—those who have a larger share of the resources, often referred to as 'the haves,' and those who have few resources, often referred to as the 'have nots.' Societies are generally unstable because the 'have nots' compete with the 'haves' to gain more resources; change is inevitable and happens quickly.

One of the predominant issues studied by present-day conflict theorists is class structure, and the role education plays in its perpetuation. Schools are often thought to be vehicles for upward social mobility, but according to conflict theorists, "education in fact serves to reproduce inequalities based on power, income, and social status" (Ballantine). Bowles and Gintis (1976), and more recently Apple and Giroux (1994), suggest that capitalists control access to educational resources, thereby reproducing existing class structures. But conflict theorists recognize the possibility of change, and the individual's ability to fight the system. Willis' (1979) classic study of working-class boys in England was one of the first to document the ways in which students resist the dominant power structure.

INTERACTION THEORIES

While structuralists and conflict theorists understand society and education very differently, both have been criticized for ignoring what happens in schools on a micro-level—in terms of the person-to-person interactions between students and teachers, for example, and in terms of *what* (content) is taught and *how* (method) it is taught. As a result, interaction theorists have adopted a more social-psychological approach to education, studying individuals in interaction with one another, recognizing that they bring shared norms to the interaction, as well as individual differences based on social class, race, gender, and experience.

Some of the questions that interactionists have introduced to the field include the impact of teacher expectations on student achievement, the relationship of socio-economic status to achievement, and the way in which a student's understanding and experience of education is a function of her cultural and ethnic background.

Labeling Theory—the idea that labels can lead to self-fulfilling prophecies, as when a teacher calls a student dumb and he acts in such a way as to confirm the label—and Exchange Theory—the notion that there are rewards and costs in every interaction—are two offshoots of interaction theories (Ballantine).

STANDPOINT THEORIES

Before discussing the theoretical approach of what are sometimes called 'standpoint theories' (Ball), it is important to make a note about methodology. Although methodology and theory are not necessarily determined by one another, Ball shows how shifts in the way education is studied (method) can lead to shifts in theory and content as well. While positivism—the notion that the social sciences can be studied in much the same way as the natural sciences, using empirical, objectivity-seeking, quantitative analysis—brought legitimacy to the developing field of sociology of education in the 1950s, it was the rejection of positivism in the 1970s and 80s that opened to the door to standpoint theories. In a critique of the positivists, qualitative methodologists argue "No theorizing, however ingenious, and no observance of scientific protocol, however meticulous, are substitutes for developing a familiarity with what is actually going on in the sphere of life under study" (as quoted in Ball).

Standpoint theorists—defined as those who had previously been marginalized in the research process for reasons such as gender, race, disability, or sexuality—were the first to turn a critical eye toward the field of sociology itself (Ball). Feminist sociologists, for example, recognized the absence of women practicing sociology, and criticized the field for the absence of attention given to gender as a viable research topic. Feminists were also critical of positivist methodologies, and instead brought attention to the researcher's subjectivity as well as the subjectivity of those being researched. As one example of standpoint theorists, feminists theorists have researched gender stereotyping in schools, the reproduction of masculine and feminine identities, and the role of patriarchy in women's oppression. Early feminist theories, however, were criticized for failing to acknowledge the diversity of women's experience. "'Woman', it is argued, frequently stands for white, middle-class, heterosexual females" (Ball).

POSTMODERN THEORY

Postmodernism is a theoretical approach that has left few academic disciplines untouched, and more than other theoretical approaches has created a great deal of controversy. Ball writes, "the postmodern or linguistic turn can be seen, in typical paradoxical fashion, both as an invigoration of, and threat to, the sociology of education, or rather to modernist social science generally." In general, postmodernists believe that all ideas are socially and politically situated, and thus reject narratives or explanations that claim

dominance over other narratives. They also question one of the foundations of Western thought—the notion of progress and growth through knowledge—and thereby question one of the foundations of the sociology of education, which has always considered itself a redemptive discipline (Ball). As the field moves forward, Apple and other sociologists are calling for an integration of the disparate theoretical approaches, by 'simultaneously thinking about the specificity of different practices and the forms of articulated unity they constitute' (as quoted in Ball).

TOPICS OF STUDY

Educational Sociologists not only study education from a variety of theoretical and methodological angles, they also ask a wide range of questions. The following section will highlight some of the core topics—social class, race, and gender—but is in no way meant to be a comprehensive representation of the field. The questions below demonstrate the diversity of topics addressed, and begin to reveal the breadth of the field:

- What is the relationship between academic achievement and social class?
- What functions do schools serve?
- Why do girls take fewer math and science courses than boys?
- Are achievement tests biased against students of different ethnicities?
- Is ability grouping an effective teaching practice?
- Who should decide what is taught?

SOCIAL CLASS

Many believe that schools are vehicles of social mobility, and that earning an education can help a student move from a lower social class to a higher one. Educational sociologists have challenged this notion repeatedly, but the classic 1979 study by Jencks is one of the most often cited. In his conclusion, Jencks writes "The evidence suggests that equalizing educational opportunity would do very little to make adults more equal" (as quoted in Ballantine). Jencks argued that family background and attitudes toward education were more significant determinants of achievement than the school itself.

Even with equal educational opportunity, Jencks showed that a more egalitarian society was not likely to result. Others have shown that the social structure is perpetuated because equal opportunity itself is rare. For example, the common practice of tracking or grouping students according to ability, often disadvantages students of a particular race or socioeconomic status. Studies have also shown that student experience in different tracks is significantly different, with greater disruptions in lower-track classrooms, and therefore different student motivations and self-concepts. "Of the three major ways in which reproduction theorists argue that classes are reproduced (public versus private schooling, socioeconomic class composition of school communities, and ability grouping of students), research shows tracking to be the most important mechanism in the reproduction process (Ballantine).

Houtte, Demanet, and Stevens (2013) studied teachers' perceptions and expectations for tracked students. Analyzing data for 6,545 students in 46 Flemish secondary schools with self-reported student measures and teacher evaluations of students, the study showed that teachers perceive lower track students as less able and less diligent because of those students' social and cognitive characteristics and anti-school behavior. Accounting for the latter, the authors wrote, teachers even evaluate lower track students as putting forth slightly more effort.

Educational sociologists are not only interested in what happens in formal learning environments, such as schools, but also recognize the importance of learning that occurs informally, in everyday life situations. Indeed, as Jencks (1979) discovered, variables outside school—such as family background -influence a student's chance of success as much, if not more than what occurs within the school. Research in this area has documented the relationship between student achievement and the social class of the family, parenting styles, number and birth order of children, parental involvement in education, and parental aspirations for children. Bourdieu (1970) coined the term 'cultural capital' to represent the knowledge and skills parents pass onto children—knowledge and skills which give students power and status.

GENDER

The study of gender in education—in many disciplines, in fact—was largely absent until the feminist theorists brought it to the fore in the 1970s and 80s.

Many believed, and continue to believe, that the educational system serves men and women equally, and that "if women want to get ahead, all they have to do is work hard like anyone else who 'makes it' in society" (Ballantine). Educational sociologists have called this belief into question.

Many sociologists focus on the ways in which boys and girls are socialized into sex-appropriate roles. By investigating children's toys, textbooks, and gender-stereotypes, sociologists demonstrate the many ways in which boys and girls, but especially girls, are limited by the roles ascribed to them. Recent studies of textbooks, for example, shows that math problems are often accompanied by pictures of girls cooking, sewing, shopping, or jumping rope; such images send important messages to girls about appropriate behavior. Other studies have shown that teachers give more attention to boys and that girls become increasingly silent in the classroom as they move through adolescence (Ballantine).

One of the most persistent questions in the study of gender in education is between boys and girls in math and science. Part of the answer, sociologists argue, is that "girls have been systematically tracked toward traditional, sex-segregated jobs, and away from the areas of study that lead to high-paying jobs in science, technology, and engineering" (as quoted in Ballantine). While girls' participation in math and science has increased into the early 2000s, differences in participation and achievement persist. Researchers have investigated teacher and parental expectations, attributional styles, and developmental pressures faced by girls—in terms of physical maturation and accompanying social pressures—as partial explanations for the persistent patterns.

Stromquist (2013) examined federal gender-equity legislation Title IX and found only "modest efforts to enforce the law, raising doubts about the commitment of the state to transform the social relations of gender" (Stromquist). The United States government's framing of gender equality "exclusively in terms of non-discriminatory practices falls short of fostering changes in gender mentalities and identities in U.S. educational institutions—an outcome reflected in the persistent gender clustering of fields of study at the university level," the author argued.

RACE

The Coleman Report, a milestone study in the sociology of education published in 1966, was the first study to look at the opportunities and achievement of minority students compared to white students. Known for its sample—which included 5 percent of all schools and over half a million students—as well as its results, the study concluded that minority students scored lower on achievement tests than white students, most students attended segregated schools, the socio-economic status of the school and family impacted students' achievement levels while curriculum and facilities made little difference, and white students had greater access to educational resources than minority students (Ballantine). The results of Coleman's study have largely been replicated over the years, the mounting evidence used to support desegregation policies.

The impact of desegregation—on communities, student achievement, and race relations—has been the subject of numerous studies in the social sciences. In general, studies have found that minority student self-concept and self-esteem suffers in integrated school settings, but that academic achievement typically improves. Thus, "black students in desegregated schools, especially males, have a higher likelihood of attending college and completing more years of schooling than those from segregated schools" (Ballantine). Attempts at desegregation have led to an unforeseen phenomenon known as 'white flight'—the departure of white, middle-class families from cities to avoid school integration. School districts and courts have responded to racial imbalances differently and desegregation—first mandated by the Supreme Court in 1954 in the case *Brown v. Board of Education*—remains an unfulfilled mission.

As the demographic make-up of the United States changes—in particular, as the Hispanic population becomes the predominant minority—attention will shift to the educational experience of different sub-populations. Already, a great deal of research attention has been given to the topic of bi-lingual education, and whether it's best to instruct students in their native language or English. Some believe learning English early is necessary for later school success, while others argue that requiring students to learn English makes it more difficult for them to learn in general, in addition to devaluing their culture (Ballantine).

CONCLUSION

According to Torres and Mitchell (1998), the developing field of the sociology of education can be defined by two emerging trends: the introduction of methodologies that vary significantly from empiricism and positivism, and the dichotomy between modernism and postmodernism. As the field moves forward, some predict integrated analyses of race, class, and gender will become more prominent, as scholars attempt to negotiate the careful balance between 'grand narratives' and the multiplicity of experience, power, and knowledge. Torres and Mitchell conclude:

"Indeed, what the new scholarship of class, race, and gender...tells us is that oppression, domination, and discrimination in schools and societies have not disappeared or gone away. If anything, oppression, discrimination, and domination have increased...What this scholarship for social empowerment also tells us is that there is still enough democratic energy and utopian optimism to figure out that, in the long haul, fighting for a system of public education of good quality is a good fight for the good life of children and, by implication, for all of society."

TERMS & CONCEPTS

Conflict Theory: A theoretical approach to the study of sociology based largely on the writings of Max Weber and Karl Marx. Conflict theorists believe societies are comprised of two groups—the 'haves' and the 'have nots'—who are in a constant state of struggle against one another. Change is inevitable and happens quickly.

Durkheim, Emile: Known as 'the father of sociology,' Durkheim was a turn-of-the-century professor of pedagogy in France. He was one of the first to apply sociology to the study of education, and was largely interested in understanding how societies perpetuate themselves.

Interaction Theory: A theoretical approach to the study of sociology that focuses on micro-level interactions between individuals or groups of people. As a social-psychological approach, interactionists believe people are guided by social norms, but also recognize individual differences based on race, class, gender, and experience.

Positivism: An empirical, quantitative approach to the study of the social sciences modeled after the methodological approach used in the natural sciences. Positivism helped educational sociology gain respect as a discipline in the 1950s, but has been challenged more recently by qualitative, postmodern methodologies.

Postmodernism: A theoretical movement that argues all ideas are socially and politically situated. Postmodernists question the purpose of research itself, especially in relation to notions of progress and improvement. Postmodernism has created rifts in academia; how the conflicts will be resolved remains to be seen.

Sociology: Sociology is the study of people in groups, or more specifically, the study of human societies and social interaction. Sociologists study the structures of society—such as family, religion, education, and the economy—and the processes that bring the structures alive.

Structural-Functionalism: One of the earliest theoretical approaches to the study of sociology developed, in large part, by Emile Durkheim. Functionalists believe society is comprised of different parts, all of which work together to create an integrated whole. Functionalists helped explain how societies are perpetuated, but the theory fell short in accommodating notions of conflict and change.

Qualitative Research: A methodological approach distinguished from positivism, or quantitative methodologies. Largely an outgrowth of the development of feminist theories, qualitative methodologies question the assumption of objectivity, and believe the subjectivity of the individual(s) conducting the research, as well as those being researched, should be acknowledged. Qualitative methodologists believe researchers should spend time immersed in the environment they are trying to understand.

Jennifer Kretchmar

BIBLIOGRAPHY

Apple, M. (1996). Power, meaning, and identity: Critical sociology of education in the United States. *British Journal of Sociology of Education, 17*, 125-44. Retrieved April 13, 2007, from EBSCO Online Database Academic Search Premier.

Apple, M. (1993). Official knowledge. New York, NY: Routledge.

Apple, M.W. (2013). Between traditions: Stephen Ball and the critical sociology of education. *London Review of Education, 11*, 206–217. Retrieved December 8, 2013, from EBSCO Online Database Education Research Complete.

Ball, S. J. (Ed.). (2004). The RoutledgeFalmer reader in sociology of education. London, England: RoutledgeFalmer.

Ballantine, J.H. (1997). The sociology of education: A systematic analysis. Upper Saddle River, NJ: Prentice Hall, Inc.

Boocock, S.S. (Ed.). (1985). Sociology of education: An introduction. Lanham, MD: University Press of America, Inc.

Bourdieu, P., and Passerson, J.C. (1977). Reproduction in education, society, and culture. Beverly Hills, CA: Sage Publications.

Bowles, S., & Gintis, H. (1976). Schooling in capitalist American: Education and contradictions of economic life. New York, NY: Basic Books.

Demain, J. (Ed.). (2001). Sociology of education today. New York City, NY: Palgrave Publishers.

Giroux, H. A. (1994). Educational reform and the politics of teacher empowerment. In J. Kretovics & E. J. Nussel (Eds.), Transforming Urban Education. Boston, MA: Allyn and Bacon.

Houtte, M., Demanet, J., & Stevens, P. (2013). Curriculum tracking and teacher evaluations of individual students: selection, adjustment or labeling? *Social Psychology of Education, 16*, 329-352. Retrieved December 8, 2013, from EBSCO Online Database Education Research Complete.

Stromquist, N.P. (2013). Education policies for gender equity: Probing into state responses. *Education Policy Analysis Archives, 21*, 1-28. Retrieved December 8, 2013, from EBSCO Online Database Education Research Complete.

Torres, C. A., & Mitchell, T. R. (Eds.). (1998). Sociology of education: Emerging perspectives. Albany, NY: State University of New York Press.

Willis, P. (1979). Learning to labor: How working class kids get working class jobs. Hampshire, England: Saxon House.

SUGGESTED READING

Apple, M. (2006). How class works in education. *Educational Policy, 20*, 455-462.

Bills, D.B. (2004). The sociology of education and work. Malden, MA: Blackwell Publishing.

Dillabough, J. (2003). Gender, education, and society: The limits and possibilities of feminist reproduction theory. Sociology of Education, 76, 376-379. Retrieved April 13, 2007, from EBSCO Online Database Education Research Complete.

Lingard, B., Taylor, S., & Rawolle, S. (2005). Bourdieu and the study of educational policy: An introduction. Journal of Educational Policy, 20, 663-669. Retrieved April 13, 2007, from EBSCO Online Database Education Research Complete.

Bowles, S., & Gintis, H. (2003). Schooling in capitalist American twenty-five years later. Sociological Forum, 18, 343-349. Retrieved April 13, 2007, from EBSCO Online Database Academic Search Premier.

Viadero, D. (2006). Race report's influence felt 40 years later. Education Week, 25, 1-24. Retrieved April 13, 2007, from EBSCO Online Database Education Research Complete.

Wong, K., & Nicotera, A.C. (2004). Brown v. Board of Education and the Coleman Report: Social science research and the debate on educational equity. Peabody Journal of Education, 79, 122-135. Retrieved April 13, 2007, from EBSCO Online Database Education Research Complete.

SOCIAL CHANGE EDUCATION

This essay begins with orienting the reader to Social Change Education (SCE), defining the theory in terms of design and utility, and tracking how it has evolved as an effective means of augmenting communication and action for the oppressed. The reader is offered a comparison of the SCE design to the hegemonic "classic" model of education. Orientation to the growing popularity of social change education with examples of local, historical and more global applications is underscored by examples of SCE in practice, and its relative success in one global health care initiative. This essay advocates for SCE; a contrasting view is recognized but is not fully explored within the scope of this document. The literature review and analysis is intriguing and readers will likely look for further examples of the model's utility.

KEYWORDS: Authoritarianism; Capitalism; Consciousness; Globalization; Hegemony; Marginalized; Oppressed; Popular Education; Social Change Education; Social Justice

OVERVIEW

We live in a global society; electronic communication happens in the blink of an eye. Realistically, electronic interconnectedness can limit important face to face engagement. Email, cell phones, and the Internet are but a few reasons why electronic communication is outpacing valuable interpersonal interaction. As a society, we've become less invested in relationships and more invested in information-sharing, enhanced by the very facility of our instant electronic connections. Because of our busy lives, too often we shelter up in our homes at night and listen passively to headlines delivered to our living room. News headlines are real, but most don't really seem to impact our day to day living. Many forget to question the veracity of what we are told by the media; seldom do we forcefully question the rhetoric of those in power. We are told what to buy in our capitalist society; sometimes this power is so insidious we are not even aware of its impact. We hear about war and terrorism, and we assume our government is doing the right thing for all concerned. The politicians vying for presidential nominations are honest, we hope; or are they sponsored by the rich and powerful, colluding to keep us in our ignorance?

In our conscience, we know there are injustices for which we should take ownership: The environment is deteriorating; crime holds communities in fear; fuel prices are becoming prohibitive; countries threaten ours, and we live in fear of terrorism or natural disaster. Making positive change requires that we become agents for social change. Social change education has evolved over the years in response to exploitation and alienation of the lower classes. Social change speaks for the downtrodden or marginalized; it addresses unjust conditions under which groups of people suffer economically, socially, or politically. It is of no surprise that the wealthy, the capitalists and the politicians are presumed averse to the SCE movement. It is primarily through control and intellectual supremacy that the lower classes may be quieted.

HOW DOES SOCIAL CHANGE HAPPEN?

Social Change Education (SCE) is not the answer to the world's injustices, but it does provide a proven framework through which the weaker, poorer, less educated, and exploited can speak and be heard. SCE doesn't look like a college course. There are no books or exams in the classic sense, no podium from which a professor lectures. In SCE, the instructors are the students and the students the instructors. The opposite of authoritarianism and intolerance, SCE builds success through the self-reflection of its participants; it encourages and builds reflexive, not rigid responses to change. Bringing people together who are like-minded, with a common mission and goals to challenge existing power arrangements, can turn a single railroad car into a proverbial speeding locomotive.

WHAT IS SOCIAL CHANGE EDUCATION (SCE)?

Every organization, every community has a unique culture, no matter the size or construct. All of us have experienced the flavor of a workplace, a religious organization or an academic institution; and many of us have been challenged to understand the way decisions are made or why events sometimes happen to us rather than with us. When groups are not involved in the decision-making process, unrest, mistrust, and perceived (or real) oppression occurs. These inherent problems, common to any group with designated leaders and followers, can be mitigated by using SCE.

SCE

SCE is not a new philosophy; its essential principles for success date back decades. The reader will understand more by reviewing the summary below:

The key underpinnings to SCE include:

- Jointly involving people to draw in their history and experience, broadening perspective and providing a much more robust learning experience than a classic didactic lecture model;
- Getting people invested and excited when group learning is facilitated well—and everyone is guaranteed a voice;
- Allowing members to feel ownership in decisions. SCE is not about having information pushed to the learner from a leader. SCE does not promote a leader that limits input from all constituents, intentionally or unintentionally.

SCE (POPULAR EDUCATION) DEFINED

Social Change Education has developed over time in response to exploitation and social alienation of affected groups. The oppressed, a term which should be considered broadly, refers to those not of the elite class (even the middle class, for example)—but of those who must learn to examine their responsibility to make change and speak for themselves. Knowledge of social change is not inherent, especially for ordinary people, oppressed or disadvantaged; it is a learned skill that requires facilitative leadership. Many people live under the hand of hegemony, and it is only when they become aware of opportunities for successful change that they can begin to coalesce their local experience and wisdom to change their oppressive circumstances. SCE is a threat to the dominant class in any hierarchal setting; keeping the oppressed in a status quo limits their very desire to challenge. The oppressed class, like a captive, cannot see 'outside the box' and often becomes afraid to voice resistance.

A three year collaborative called Globalizing Civil Society from the inside Out (GCS), from the Center for Justice, Tolerance and Community of the University of California, Santa Cruz, and the Inter-American Forum of the Collins Center for Public Policy in Miami Florida, is quoted below:

> "Popular Education {synonymous with SCE} has a rich history in social justice struggles around the world, and is being used today by grassroots organizations as a leadership development tool that builds critical consciousness, as an organizational methodology, and even as a philosophy of life. Grassroots organizations, looking to unpack the abstract concepts that oftentimes muddle the public's understanding of global economy, have devoted themselves to popular education as a means to communicating the issues and the connections to their membership base." ("Globalizing civil society," 2005)

SCE appears to have made some inroads to teacher education as well. In a qualitative practitioner-research case study, four university faculty members attempted to "disrupt the hegemonic domestication of candidates enrolled in an undergraduate teacher education program (Ritchie, Cone, Sohyun, & Bullock, 2013)." During the semester right before their student teaching, 16 candidates at a large public university in the southeastern U.S. enrolled in four content methods courses. Taught by Ritchie, Cone, Sohyun, and Bullock themselves, the curriculum of these courses "emphasized social justice dimensions of teaching rather than just focusing on skills and strategies." Drawing from the multiple data sources, the authors found both possibilities and limitations of teacher education for social change and argued that greater resources are needed for teacher education to effect true social change (Ritchie et al.).

Barriers to Social Change

APATHY & MARGINALIZATION

A sense of discomfort lurks in the minds of many Americans. Here in our freedom and wealth, too few proactively contribute to broad social initiatives for improvement. The reality is that many of us try to assuage our culpability, convinced that we're only one person; manipulated by unnamed powerful, wealthy people controlling our world and its resources. We complain, we point fingers and we blame the 'leadership.' We are like lemmings, distancing ourselves from engaging in improvements for the many, focusing on our own concerns, usually our own small circle of influence. Yet before we chastise ourselves too harshly, most can admit that we have the intelligence and the heart to make a change, but most of the time we just don't know where to start.

Further, imagine those living in poverty, uneducated, whose lot in life is worse than many of us can even imagine. These are the people whose oppressed status pushes them even further from having a voice. They grow up understanding that their social position causes them to be weaker, less valued; they do not fight and rather accept the status quo. The oppressed remain oppressed. But there is good news: Today there are fire-starters, change agents who value and encourage SCE, to leverage the peoples' voice, to help them become coordinated, thoughtful and strong. They focus their work on engaging and attracting stakeholders to improve representation for all constituents who believe in an important cause, whatever it may be. Social change can occur in our local sphere of influence, or broadly across societies; anywhere that oppression can occur and change is needed.

Historical Perspective—Understanding Change at Different Levels

INDIVIDUAL EXPERIENCE

Have you ever shown up for work Monday morning and found the memo in your inbox from 'the administration.' It announces a new improved mission and supporting goals, yet this is the first you've heard of it. Do you feel like you missed the planning meetings; question whether you were you left out intentionally? Do you think, 'Where did this come from and why wasn't I allowed some input; after all, we workers {students, educators, key constituents) are the ones who know what goes on around here aren't we?' This scenario plays out over and over every day in businesses, schools, and government. Disallowing people sufficient input to important issues gives them the feeling they are being controlled by hierarchy. They simply do not feel valued, no matter the decision-makers' intent. What is lacking is the richness captured when broad brainstorming and reflective discussions capture others' experiences—these are the supporting structures for robust improvement. It must be clear to the reader that certainly not every decision can or should involve group input; further discussion follows which clarifies this point.

GOVERNMENTAL APPLICATION

Lift yourself to a 50,000-foot view and look down at the swirling firestorm surrounding the 2008 presidential primary elections. It's surprising in this era of technological advancement, high-powered information systems, and national databases, that we still practice an archaic and inexact means of tallying our citizens' votes. When government recognized that through globalization and cyber fraud, voting outcomes could be manipulated, their reflex response was to mandate that every voter produce official identification before exercising their vote. On the surface, this reaction sounds reasonable. Yet, research shows that citizens from lower socioeconomic classes are less likely to vote than are those who enjoy greater financial success. This same lower class is also far less likely to possess personal identification documents; hence the new mandates effectively impose a barrier to their input on the future leadership of their country. Some are convinced that this is a subversive means to limit the vote—architecture for control developed by the global elite—the ones with sufficient political and financial strength to marginalize the lower class. Perceived by many as top-down decision-making that should be more integrated, SCE could provide such a model.

HISTORY REPEATS ITSELF

Now, turn your imagination back to the Middle Ages. Scene: Ancient Rome. Patricians were the dominant class whose prosperity led to strength and power. This power was tightly protected by its stakeholders; strategies of the leaders focused on battling infiltration from outside groups and the continual marginalization of lower class citizens. Suppression of a weaker class was the norm then, as it has continued to be throughout the world's history. Lack of financial independence resulted in loss of a political voice for the minority classes in ancient Rome. Historians point to obvious racial differences as a hallmark distinguishing Roman Patriarchs from weaker, poorer classes. Upon the poor, rights to freedom and property were overtaken; civil liberties were squelched; and the powerful led on comfortably in their society of hegemony. Status quo was comfortable for those with the means to keep it so.

Application

CASE STUDY: HIV IN WOMEN

The HIV epidemic, particularly in women, sparked a research effort to identify the determinants of risk and their relation to the victim's cultural, social and empowerment capacity. The study highlighted in the article examined the efficacy of varied strategies for decreasing HIV infection. Historically, classic educational tools proved limited in their efficacy to decrease infection and transmission. In support of SCE, the study analyzed and compared prior efforts to educate an afflicted female population, to those introduced by the SCE initiative. Not surprisingly the SCE effort presented robust evidence of substantially greater efficacy credited to the Social Education model. A snapshot of the results is below; the reader will recognize classic features of SCE at work. What is particularly notable is the strength of this study and its findings, quantitatively supported by the research data.

"With growing concerns about the limitations of models that focus on proximal, individual determinants of behavior and that do not include community

capacity to define and address their health concerns, Woman to Woman was developed as an intervention for high-risk women to move from individualistic and information-drive notions of AIDS education to a multidimensional socioecological model of community empowerment and community mobilization. The majority of knowledge questions regarding HIV transmission and prevention methods in the aggregated population showed statistically significant changes between the pretest and posttest. For certain questions where the participants already had an understanding of the virus, there was a ceiling effect and therefore no significant change. Although the time from pretest to posttest (close to 1 month) was likely insufficient to predict behavior change, two items were significant in the direction of positive change: 'In the last month, when you had sex, was a condom/latex barrier used? (mean change from 2.97 to 3.17) and 'In the last month have you had unprotected sex? (mean change from .67 to .62, a reduction in risk; $p=0.41$)'" (Romero et al., 2006).

DISCOURSE

So why the remarkable contrast between outcomes with SCE and the hegemonic model of education, and why does it work when it works? Experts question the quality and efficacy of the hegemonic means of disseminating education. The literature reflects concerns about the *No Child Left Behind* legislation in public schools today, under the classic model of teaching. Questions arise as to whether teachers are teaching to assure that students pass their tests, or whether they focus on teaching, engaging and helping students learn to be socially responsive via a rich and robust model—which just might develop a new generation of socially responsible thinkers.

A quote from author Larry Olds follows from his draft memoir on SCE. The reader will notice his comparison of the hegemonic model of teaching in the classroom to other industries where information and understanding are the foundation to their very livelihood. "Stripped to its essence, the hegemonic model is a four-step process." Educators are to:

- Determine vision, goals, competencies, objectives;
- Select activities, resources, methods;
- Carry out activities;
- Evaluate/assess in terms the goals, competencies and objectives.

This is also the essence of most strategic planning models as well as most organizational development models. It now seems to permeate all spheres of social endeavor" (Olds, n.d.).

Mr. Olds continues in support of the SCE model, "My basic principles for popular education in the classroom—the tasks in a transformative model-again interlocking and overlapping (Olds):

- Helping people name their world, tell the stories of their experience, speak and find their voice at the educational event;
- Using tools of social analysis that help people connect their experience to a broader understanding of that experience, to an understanding of the historical, political and other social connections;
- Using the arts, music, theater, dance and other such creative modes as a different kind of voice and way of knowing in the process of naming, understanding, and transforming our world;
- Advocating a people/community-centered versus a banking approach to knowledge-in other words, a participant-centered process of knowledge creation rather than a podium-centered process of knowledge distribution."

Furthermore, effective SCE may result from different approaches. Chang (2013) studied and compared the similarities and differences between popular education forms in two regions: Highlander education in the Appalachian Mountains in the United States and study circles in Sweden. The findings were that, influenced by the folk schools' education "connecting to the social, political and economic problems of life," Highlander education and Swedish study circles "dealt with the problems of life in education, but took different directions due to their different social and political contexts. Influenced by the radical philosophy of adult education, Highlander education attempted to achieve social and economic justice through social liberation in local communities; based on humanistic education philosophy, Swedish study circles pursued social democracy mainly through individual development" (Chang).

The Sport for Development and Peace movement (SDP), concentrated mainly in Australia and nearby regions, uses athletics as a context to provide young people with social, personal, and health education (Spaaij & Jeanes, 2013). Spaaij and Jeanes believe that "Freirean pedagogy" (SCE guided by the writings of educator and philosopher Paulo Freire) could be better utilized within SDP education, and they outline some of the practical implications of doing so. They argue for the need for flexibility in SDP curriculum development and the importance of ensuring that this is grounded within a local context (Spaaij & Jeanes).

CONCLUSION

This high-level insight to SCE has provided an overview and a comparison of the hegemonic teaching versus SCE model; it offers a compelling argument supporting SCE. The one research study cited worked with small numbers but successfully elicited statistically significant findings in primary efficacy of SCE in a population of HIV-infected women. The essay portrays SCE as an intriguing paradigm shift from the popular means by which groups interact and move to action. The opportunities for lifting up the oppressed and the voiceless are boundless when considered locally or globally in the context of SCE. Oppressed populations have benefited from SCE implementation, as have successful industries; it is predictive that with more success and exposure, SCE could be the new model for the 21st century.

TERMS & CONCEPTS

Hegemony: Leadership or dominance of one group over another.

Marginalization: Trends in group or culture in which individuals tend to be excluded as a result of their perceived standing in the society.

Oppression: The experience of being kept suppressed by injustice or power.

Quantitative Research: Objective research which reports and relies on statistical analysis of the variables and results.

Social Change Education: A model of continuous group collaboration and dialogue that encourages a common group to share their collective knowledge to make changes for improvement in society. Commonly a facilitator knowledgeable in the model is employed.

Social Justice: A shared belief that every individual and group is entitled to fair and equal rights regardless of educational, financial or political standing.

Suppression: The experience of being kept suppressed by injustice or power.

Nancy Devenger

BIBLIOGRAPHY

Chang, B. (2013). Education for social change: Highlander education in the Appalachian Mountains and study circles in Sweden. *International Journal of Lifelong Education, 32,* 705–723. Retrieved December 18, 2013, from EBSCO Online Database Education Research Complete.

Dela Torre, E. (2007). How to make education for all. *Adults Learning, 19,* 18-20. Retrieved January 30, 2008, from EBSCO Online Database Academic Search Premier.

Globalizing civil society from the inside out. (2005). Center for Justice, Tolerance, and Community at University of California, Santa Cruz and the Inter-American Forum at the Collins Center for Public Policy in Miami, Florida. Retrieved January 30, 2008, from http://cjtc.ucsc.edu.

Loftin, C. (2007). Unacceptable mannerisms: Gender anxieties, homosexual activism, and swish in the United States, 1945-1965. *Journal of Social History, 40,* 577-596. Retrieved January 30, 2008, from EBSCO Online Database Academic Search Premier.

Olds, L. (n.d.). Journey book section four: Popular education in the college classroom. In *The making of a popular educator.* Minneapolis MN: Larry Olds. http://popednews.org.

Ritchie, S., Cone, N., Sohyun, A., & Bullock, P. (2013). Teacher education for social change: Transforming a content methods course block. Current Issues in Comparative Education, 15, 63–83. Retrieved December 18, 2013, from EBSCO Online Database Education Research Complete.

Romero, L., Wallerstein, N., Lucero, J., Fredine, H., Keefe, J., & O'Connell, J. (2006). Woman to woman: Coming together for positive change–using empowerment and popular education to prevent HIV in women. *AIDS Education & Prevention, 18,* 390-405. Retrieved January 30, 2008, from EBSCO Online Database Academic Search Premier.

Spaaij, R., & Jeanes, R. (2013). Education for social change? A Freirean critique of sport for development and peace. *Physical Education & Sport Pedagogy, 18,* 442–457. Retrieved December 18, 2013, from EBSCO Online Database Education Research Complete.

SUGGESTED READING

Brown, T. (2006). Organizing for the future: Labour's renewal strategies, popular education and radical history. *Studies in Continuing Education, 28,* 33–48. Retrieved January 26, 2008, from EBSCO Online Database Academic Search Premier.

Choules, K. (2007). Social change education: Context matters. *Adult Education Quarterly, 57,* 159-176. Retrieved January 26, 2008, from EBSCO Online Database Academic Search Premier.

Seas, K. (2006). Enthymematic rhetoric and student resistance to critical pedagogies. *Rhetoric Review, 25,* 427-443. Retrieved January 26, 2008, from EBSCO Online Database Academic Search Premier.

Tappan, M. (2006). Reframing internalized oppression and internalized domination: From the psychological to the sociocultural. *Teachers College Record, 108,* 2115-2144. Retrieved January 26, 2008, from EBSCO Online Database Academic Search Premier.

SOCIAL DEVELOPMENT MODEL

The social development model (SDM) is a theory of human behavior that is used to explain the origins and development of delinquent behavior during childhood and adolescence. By taking into account risk factors as well as protective influences, the SDM predicts whether children will develop prosocial or antisocial behavioral patterns as they age. The SDM is used by criminologists, child psychologists, and educators in order to identify and provide early intervention for children likely to develop antisocial dispositions. Researchers frequently use the SDM in order to carry out studies on adolescent drug and alcohol use, violence, and delinquent behavior. Recently, a number of studies have proven the applicability of the SDM to all children and adolescents in the United States, despite differences in ethnicity or gender.

KEYWORDS: Antisocial; Juvenile Delinquency; Prosocial; Protective Influence; Risk Factor; Social Development Model (SDM); Socializing Unit; Socioeconomic Status

OVERVIEW

The Social Development Model (SDM) is a theory of human behavior that is used to explain the origins and development of delinquent behavior during childhood and adolescence. By taking into account risk factors as well as protective influences, the SDM predicts whether children will develop prosocial or antisocial behavioral patterns as they age. The SDM hypothesizes that children adopt the beliefs and behavioral patterns of the social unit—such as family, peers, or neighborhood—to which they are most firmly bonded. If the social unit has prosocial attitudes, then the child adopts a prosocial orientation; if the social unit is antisocial, then the child often manifests problem behavior (Catalano, Kosterman, Hawkins, Newcomb, & Abbott, 1996).

The SDM is used by criminologists, child psychologists, and educators in order to identify and provide early intervention for children likely to develop antisocial dispositions. Researchers frequently use the SDM in order to carry out studies on adolescent drug and alcohol use, violence, and delinquent behavior. Several long-term studies that were undertaken during the 1980's and early 1990's have demonstrated the effectiveness of the SDM as a tool for improving children's adoption of prosocial beliefs and behaviors (Kosterman, Hawkins, Spoth, Haggerty & Zhu, 1997; O'Donnell, Michalak & Ames, 1997).

A long-running debate over the applicability of the SDM model to all children and adolescents in the United States across ethnic, gender, and regional differences has been settled in recent years. Numerous studies addressing this issue have provided evidence that the SDM can indeed be applied generally to all youths (Choi, Harachi, Gilmore, & Catalano, 2005; Fleming, Catalano, Oxford, & Harachi et al., 2002).

Applications

WHY THE SOCIAL DEVELOPMENT MODEL IS USEFUL

There are many reasons why the social development model was initially developed, and why it continues to be such a useful tool for reducing the incidence of childhood behavioral problems, juvenile delinquency, and violent crimes committed by young adults.

CHILDHOOD VIOLENCE & ADULT VIOLENCE

First, children who begin to use violence in childhood are at a high risk for committing serious violent offenses as adults. This risk diminishes when children first begin to use violence at later ages. For example, one study found 45% of children who took part in violent activities before they were 11 years

of age had committed violent criminal offenses by the time they were in their early 20s. Among those children who had begun to use violence when they were between 11 and 12 years of age, only 25% had committed violent criminal offenses by the time they reached their early 20s. An even smaller percentage of children who began to use violence when they were between the ages of 13 and 17 had committed violent criminal offenses by their early 20s (Herrenkohl, Huang, Kosterman, Hawkins, Catalano, & Smith, 2001). Most young adults who commit serious criminal offenses begin to offend at around the age of 10, with their offenses escalating in seriousness gradually until the youths are approximately 17 years of age, at which time peak involvement in delinquent activities usually occurs (Ayers, Williams, Hawkins, Peterson, Catalano, & Abbott, 1999). All of this means that the sooner educational professionals can identify and treat violent or antisocial tendencies in young children, the more effective they will be at lowering the violent crime rate.

CONCURRENT BEHAVIORS

Secondly, most children who commit delinquent behaviors tend to commit more than one. A child or young person who engages in truancy, for example, is likely to engage in vandalism or substance abuse as well. Moreover, such children are at a higher risk for developing school-related problems (Choi et al.). These facts indicate that the most effective way to deal with children who have behavior problems, as well as with juvenile delinquents, is to target not individual activities, but general antisocial attitudes and behaviors. The SDM allows educational professionals to do this because it traces the roots of the antisocial tendencies that manifest in various delinquent activities.

CHRONIC OFFENDERS

Third, reducing crime rates among young people means targeting chronic, not isolated offenders. Studies have shown that more than 50% of adolescents living in the United States today participate in antisocial behaviors such as delinquency, violence, substance use and abuse, and risky sexual activity (Choi et al.). Furthermore, most young people take part in a delinquent activity at least once during their adolescence. The average youth's participation in problem behaviors is infrequent and is of short duration, and accordingly accounts for only a small fraction of criminal offenses committed by juveniles. In contrast, more than 50% of all juvenile offenses, and almost all serious, violent crimes, are committed by a tiny minority of young people—between 5 and 10%. Accordingly, efforts to reduce juvenile crime rates should aim to target this 5-10% of youth who become chronic offenders. The SDM is so useful in this respect because it offers the possibility of predicting which youths are at risk of becoming chronic offenders before they even commit their first criminal offense. Valuable prevention and intervention resources could then be used to prevent these particular children from beginning to participate in delinquent activities, or to prevent them from escalating their involvement in these activities if they have already begun to participate in them (Ayers et al.).

ENVIRONMENTAL INFLUENCES

Finally, location and age both affect the likelihood that youth will manifest antisocial behaviors. While many problem behaviors, such as substance use, are universal problems among adolescents, affecting rural, urban, and suburban adolescents at a relatively constant rate, there are certain risk factors for these behaviors that are directly related to location (Kosterman et al.; O'Donnell et al.). Sites of urban poverty, for example, usually feature low neighborhood attachment and community disorganization, both of which put children living in such areas at risk for developing antisocial attitudes and behaviors (O'Donnell et al.). In terms of age, evidence shows that children are particularly vulnerable to initiating or escalating their involvement in problem behaviors during transitional periods, such as the switch from home or pre-school to elementary school, elementary school to middle school, and middle school to high school (Kosterman et al.; Ayers et al.). The SDM addresses these points by predicting how anti-social community influences will affect youths coming from different types of family backgrounds, and at what transitional period points at-risk youth are likely to begin manifesting or escalating their involvement in problem behaviors.

HOW THE SOCIAL DEVELOPMENT MODEL WORKS

The social development model represents a synthesis of the most widely substantiated elements of three different theories used in the field of criminology to explain the etiology of antisocial behavior. It uses elements from control theory to identify factors that cause the development of antisocial behavior; elements from social learning theory to find factors that either encourage or put an end to antisocial behavior; and elements from differential association theory to identify the numerous separate paths that lead to either prosocial or antisocial behavior (Catalano et al.).

RISK & PROTECTIVE FACTORS

In predicting prosocial and antisocial behavior, the SDM takes into account both risk factors and protective factors. Risk and protective factors can be biological, psychological, or social. Social risk factors occur in various areas of social experience, such as within the family unit, at school, within peer groups, or within a community (Catalano et al.). Socioeconomic status, age, ethnicity and gender all help to determine the types of risk and protective factors to which a child or adolescent will be exposed (Choi et al.). Risk factors increase the probability that a child will become delinquent, while protective factors explain why some children who are at high risk for becoming delinquent fail to do so. Protective factors thus protect high-risk children from risk factors, or lessen the effects of exposure to these factors (Catalano et al.).

SOCIALIZATION

As its name suggests, the social development model is concerned with socializing processes. According to the SDM:

> "Children are socialized through processes involving four constructs: (a) perceived opportunities for involvement in activities and interactions with others, (b) the degree of involvement and interaction, (c) the skills to participate in these involvements and interactions, and (d) the reinforcement they perceive as forthcoming from performance in activities and interactions" (cited in Catalano et al.).

These constructs are ordered casually, meaning that the more opportunities a child perceives for social interactions, the more social interactions that child will participate in. This increase in social interactions causes the child to develop more social skills, which in turn allows the child to perceive more positive reinforcement for participating socially (Fleming et al.).

When the socializing processes occur on a consistent basis, a social bond involving attachment and commitment forms between the child being socialized and the person or group by whom he or she is being socialized, or the socializing unit. Once this bond has formed and been reinforced, it begins to exhibit an influence on the child's future behavior, in that the bond the child feels will cause him or her to conform to the norms of the socializing unit. This is because deviant behavior, if exposed, could threaten the strength of the social bond. The child will thus behave in the way that the socializing unit behaves, and believe the same things that the socializing unit believes. Or, at a minimum, the child will have a disincentive to behave in different ways or believe different things (Catalano et al.).

Socializing processes occur during four distinct developmental periods: the period during which a child stays at home or attends a preschool; elementary school; middle school; and high school (Catalano et al.). The dominant socializing unit to which a child becomes bonded does not remain constant throughout these periods. Rather, the family unit dominates socialization during the home and elementary school periods, with school beginning to play a stronger role during the latter. During elementary school, peers and neighborhood influences begin to make an impact until they increasingly dominate socializing processes throughout middle and high school (Fleming et al.).

PROSOCIAL & ANTISOCIAL PATHS

The socializing process eventually results in the child learning either prosocial or antisocial behavioral patterns. A socializing process that culminates in prosocial behavioral patterns develops along the following path: a child perceives opportunities for prosocial interactions; the child participates in prosocial interactions, and understands that he or she is positively rewarded for his or her participation; child develops emotional, cognitive, and behavioral skills that allow him or her to earn, perceive and experience positive reinforcement. The prosocial path and the skills that it leads to thus culminate in a prosocial disposition. A child who has experienced such a socialization process will have internalized society's standards for normal behavior, and will believe in the rightness of society's laws and rules. The child will grow into a law-abiding citizen, whose beliefs inhibit him or her from participating in anti-social behavior (Catalano et al.).

The SDM predicts that the path to antisocial behavior has three elements: a child perceives a reward for antisocial behavior; the child becomes bonded to persons, groups, or institutions that participate in antisocial behavior; the child develops beliefs in antisocial values. The more the child has bonded to antisocial units, the more committed the child becomes to antisocial behaviors and values. In direct contrast to the child with a prosocial orientation, the child with an antisocial orientation internalizes and normalizes a standard of behavior that is antisocial. The child often knows that this standard varies from society's normative rules of conduct, and rationalizes this difference by thinking of the antisocial standard as either an alternative to society's rules or as a code that supersedes society's rules (Catalano et al.).

Of course, a child may experience elements from both of these paths. The elements from the first, prosocial path become protective factors, while the elements from the second, antisocial path become risk factors. When protective factors outweigh risk factors, the child will have a prosocial orientation, and when the risk factors outweigh protective factors, the child will have an antisocial orientation.

STUDIES THAT HAVE USED THE SOCIAL DEVELOPMENT MODEL

The social development model is a theory of human behavior, and is used by criminologists and child psychologists as a theoretical foundation upon which to carry out research studies. In order to apply the abstract concepts of the SDM to study participants, researchers gather data from participants about the social processes with which the SDM is concerned. Usually, they do this by asking participants questions or by interviewing a third party, such as a teacher, about the participants. Once this data is collected, researchers use a plethora of statistical models and equations in order to analyze it and draw conclusions.

Most researchers working with the SDM use it to predict the emergence of problem behavior in children in elementary school, middle school, and high school. Data is collected during one developmental period and is used to predict behavior in the next period. For example, researchers looking to predict which children will begin to exhibit behavioral problems during elementary school will look for prosocial and antisocial interactions during the home/preschool period (Catalano et al.). This approach is especially effective since research has shown that youths frequently begin to exhibit problem behavior during the transitions between the four developmental periods (Ayers et al.).

The long-term nature of the predictions made by the SDM necessitate that the researchers using it have access to the same group of study participants for long periods of time—most often a decade or more. Thus, these researchers usually complete longitudinal studies, which follow a group of children's development from the preschool or elementary school years all the way through high school.

Below, three studies utilizing the SDM are summarized. One of these studies uses the SDM to explain the etiology of violent behavior in adolescents, while the other two use the SDM as a tool for creating intervention and prevention programs aimed at reducing problem behavior in children and adolescents. The summaries below pay special attention to how the studies apply the abstract theory contained in the SDM to real student populations.

USING THE SDM TO EXPLAIN THE ORIGINS & DEVELOPMENT OF VIOLENT BEHAVIOR

A study published in 2001 entitled "A comparison of social development processes leading to violent behavior in late adolescence for childhood initiators and adolescent initiators of violence" used the SDM to explain the differences between social processes that lead children who begin to use violence in childhood to continue to do so in adolescence, and the social processes that lead nonviolent children to begin to use violence during adolescence. This distinction is important because, as discussed previously, children who initiate violence during childhood rather than during adolescence are more likely to commit violent crimes as adults. In order to carry out this study, researchers utilized data gathered from a longitudinal study entitled The Seattle Social Development Project (SSDP), which monitored a group of children living in low-income, violence-prone school districts in Seattle from the time the children entered the fifth grade in 1985

through the time the youth were 18 years of age, in 1993 (Herrenkohl et al.).

In order to construct etiologies of violent behavior beginning in childhood and adolescence, the researchers devised questions correlating with each of the SDM's four constructs, and which applied these constructs to the various social domains of home, peers, school and community. To measure opportunities for prosocial interaction, for example, researchers asked students if they knew where to join community clubs, knew how to participate in extracurricular activities, if they had nice neighborhood playgrounds to visit, and if they participated in family decision making, amongst other questions. To gauge opportunities for antisocial interaction, researchers asked whether students had been invited to join gangs, whether they had siblings or peers who used drugs, and whether their parents set firm rules of conduct at home. To measure prosocial and antisocial bonding, researchers asked whether students liked their teachers, classes, and school and whether they wanted to emulate their parents, or whether students wanted to emulate antisocial friends who used drugs or broke the law (Herrenkohl et al.).

Various statistical methods were then used to translate the answers of these questions into data, which showed all prosocial and antisocial forces affecting the social development of the children in the study. Analysis of this data allowed researchers to conclude that there were no significant differences between the etiology of violent behavior initiated in childhood and the etiology of violent behavior initiated during adolescence. This means that even though childhood initiators of violence are more likely to commit violent crimes as adults than adolescent initiators of violence, there is no appreciable difference in the factors that lead these two groups to commit violence during adolescence. This conclusion led the researchers to suggest that prevention and intervention programs should be made available to adolescents as well as to younger children (Herrenkohl et al.).

USING THE SDM TO DEVELOP EFFECTIVE PREVENTION & INTERVENTION PROGRAMS

Two other studies, both published in 1997, focus on how the SDM can be used as a tool to create programs that effectively prevent students from engaging in anti-social behavior, or encourage students already engaged in such behavior to instead engage in prosocial behavior. The first study, entitled "Effects of a preventive parent-training intervention on observed family interactions: Proximal outcomes from preparing for the drug free years," investigates the extent to which parents can be trained to create a stronger, more pro-social bond between themselves and their children, and by doing so prevent their children from using substances during adolescence (Kosterman et al.). The second study, entitled "Inner-city youths helping children after-school programs to promote bonding and reduce risk" investigated how after-school mentoring programs might help to build prosocial bonds between adolescents, the children they mentored, the children's school, and their community, and in doing so reduce the strength of antisocial bonds between these children and adolescents and various peer and neighborhood forces (O'Donnell et al.).

The first study tested the efficacy of Preparing for the Drug Free Years (PDFY), a parenting curriculum based on the theories of the SDM. The study used participants in two low-income school districts in the midwest. Parents who participated in the study attended five workshops that focused on raising awareness about adolescent substance abuse; teaching parents how to communicate positively with their children and to set explicit rules about their children's behavior; teaching parents and their children skills with which to resist peer pressure; teaching parents how to manage conflict within the family in such a way as to reduce the frequency of negative interactions with their children; teaching parents to strengthen prosocial family bonding by creating opportunities for prosocial interaction and by rewarding children for participating in such interaction (Kosterman et al.).

Prior to completing the series of workshops, the parents were measured for their skills in conducting proactive communication, their tendency to participate in negative interactions with their children, and for the overall quality of the relationship they had with their children. Then, after they completed the workshop, parents were measured in these areas again. Researchers found that compared to a control group that did not participate in the workshops, the parents who did participate had significantly improved the prosocial quality of the interactions they had with their children. The authors of the study hypothesized that this increase in prosocial bonding to the family unit should help to prevent adolescent substance abuse. This hypothesis, however, went untested (Kosterman et al.).

The second study examined The Collaborative Afterschool Prevention Program, which was designed as a result of the 1992 findings of The Task Force on Youth Development and Community Programs. The after-school program used adolescents residing in inner-city neighborhoods as mentors for elementary school children also living in these neighborhoods. The program had the double aim of preventing the children from becoming involved in problem behaviors as adolescents by bonding them to prosocial units; and discouraging the adolescents from engaging in antisocial behavior by providing them with an opportunity for prosocial interaction. The mentors and children participated in various types of prosocial activities together, such as sports, field trips, arts and crafts, and community projects. The mentors rewarded the children for prosocial interactions and encouraged them to be open about their emotions and feelings.

Evidence from interviews conducted at the completion of the after-school program suggested that the adolescents and children were less likely to take part in antisocial behavior as a result of their involvement in the after-school program. As a result, the authors recommended that similar after-school programs based on the SDM theory should be instituted in other high-risk communities (O'Donnell et al.).

VIEWPOINTS

Until recently, many researchers felt that there was not enough conclusive evidence proving that the social development model can be applied to different gender, ethnic, and income groups and achieve standard results (Fleming et al.) One reason that this question of the generalizability of the SDM remained unsettled for so long is that early studies of the efficacy of the SDM were performed using populations that were overwhelmingly Caucasian, or whose race was unspecified (Choi et al.). Two recent studies seem to have settled this question by proving that the SDM predicts behavior for African American, Asian Pacific

Islander, multi-racial, and other non-Caucasian youth just as well as it does for American Caucasian youth. (Choi et al.; Fleming et al.).

TERMS & CONCEPTS

Antisocial: Used to describe beliefs, actions, and patterns of behavior that violate legal codes, including those relative to age. Includes violent as well as nonviolent crimes, as well as the use of illegal drugs and the abuse of legal ones.

Juvenile Delinquency: Criminal acts committed by juveniles, or youth under 18 years of age. Common types of juvenile delinquency include vandalism, violence, illegal drug use, and theft.

Prosocial: Used to describe beliefs, actions, and patterns of behavior that accord with legal codes and normative social values.

Protective Influence: Prosocial bonds that explain why some children who are at high risk for becoming delinquent fail to do so. Protect high-risk children from risk factors, or lessen the effects of exposure to these factors.

Risk Factor: A factor that increases the probability that a child will develop problematic patterns of behavior. Common risk factors include low socioeconomic status, living in a high-crime neighborhood, and having an older sibling who exhibits problem behavior.

Social Development Model (SDM): A theory of human behavior that is used to explain the origins and development of delinquent behavior during childhood and adolescence.

Socializing Unit: Any person, party, or institution that gives a child opportunities and rewards for social interaction, and thus forms a bond with the child. Common socializing units include parents, peers, community, and school.

Socioeconomic Status: A family's social and economic status, based on family income, educational levels, occupation, and social standing in the community.

Ashley L. Cohen

BIBLIOGRAPHY

Ayers, C. D., Williams, J. H., Hawkins, D. J., Peterson, P., Catalano, R., & Abbott, R. (1999). Assessing correlates of onset, escalation, de-escalation, and desistance of delinquent behavior. *Journal of Quantitative Criminology, 15,* 277-306. Retrieved April 12, 2007, from EBSCO Online Database Academic Search Premier.

Catalano, R., Kosterman, R., Hawkins, J. D., Newcomb, M. & Abbott, R. (1996). Modeling the etiology of adolescent substance use: A test of the social development model. *Journal of Drug Issues, 26,* 429-455. Retrieved April 12, 2007, from EBSCO Online Database Academic Search Premier.

Choi, Y., Harachi, T., Gilmore, M, & Catalano, R. (2005). Applicability of the social development model to urban ethnic minority youth: Examining the relationship between external constraints, family socialization, and problem behaviors. *Journal of Research on Adolescence, 15,* 505-534. Retrieved April 12, 2007, from EBSCO Online Database Academic Search Premier.

Chui, W., & Chan, H. (2012). An empirical investigation of social bonds and juvenile delinquency in Hong Kong. *Child & Youth Care Forum, 41,* 371-386. Retrieved December 15, 2013, from EBSCO Online Database Education Research Complete.

Fleming, C., Catalano, R., Oxford, M., & Harachi, T. (2002). A test of the generalizability of the social development model across gender and income groups with longitudinal data from the elementary school development period. *Journal of Quantitative Criminology, 18,* 423-439. Retrieved April 12, 2007, from EBSCO Online Database Academic Search Premier.

Herrenkohl, T., Huang, B., Kosterman, R., Hawkins, D. J., Catalano, R. F., & Smith, B. H. (2001). A comparison of social development processes leading to violent behavior in late adolescence for childhood initiators and adolescent initiators of violence. *Journal of Research in Crime & Delinquency, 38,* 45-63. Retrieved April 12, 2007, from EBSCO Online Database Academic Search Premier.

Kosterman, R., Hawkins, D. J., Spoth, R., Haggerty, K., & Zhu, K. (1997). Effects of a preventive parent-training intervention on observed family interactions: Proximal outcomes from preparing for the drug free years. *Journal of Community Psychology, 25,* 337-352. Retrieved April 12, 2007, from EBSCO Online Database Academic Search Premier.

Maguire, E. R., Wells, W., & Katz, C. M. (2011). Measuring community risk and protective factors for adolescent problem behaviors: Evidence from a developing nation. *Journal of Research in Crime & Delinquency, 48,* 594-620. Retrieved December 15, 2013, from EBSCO Online Database Education Research Complete.

O'Donnell, J., Michalak, E., & Ames, E. (1997). Inner-city youths helping children after-school programs to promote bonding and reduce risk. *Social Work in Education, 19*, 231-241. Retrieved April 12, 2007, from EBSCO Online Database Academic Search Premier.

Sullivan, C. J., & Hirschfield, P. (2011). Problem behavior in the middle school years: An assessment of the social development model. *Journal of Research in Crime & Delinquency, 48*, 566-593. Retrieved December 15, 2013, from EBSCO Online Database Education Research Complete.

SUGGESTED READING

Bishop, A., Hill, K., Gilman, A., Howell, J., Catalano, R. & Hawkins, J. (2017). Developmental pathways of youth gang membership: A structural test of the social development model. *Journal of Crime and Justice*, 4 (3), 275-296.

Catalano, R., Fleming, C., Haggerty, K., Abbott, R., Cortes, R., & Park, J. (2005). Mediator effects in the social development model: An examination of constituent theories. *Criminal Behaviour & Mental Health, 15*, 221-235. Retrieved April 12, 2007, from EBSCO Online Database Academic Search Premier.

Hartwell, S. (2000). Juvenile delinquency and the social development model: The retrospective accounts of homeless substance abusers. *Criminal Justice Policy Review, 11*, 217-233. Retrieved April 12, 2007, from EBSCO Online Database Academic Search Premier.

Kosterman, R., Hawkins, D. J., Guo, J., Catalano, R., & Abbott, R. (2000). The dynamics of alcohol and marijuana initiation: Patterns and predictors of first use in adolescence. *American Journal of Public Health, 90*, 360-366. Retrieved April 12, 2007, from EBSCO Online Database Academic Search Premier.

SOCIAL JUSTICE IN EDUCATION

This article provides a summary of social justice in education, with an overview of definition and theory, practical applications, and contesting viewpoints. While social justice is an idea with roots in ancient Greek philosophy, as a more formalized area of study within education, it is a much more recent development. Given the field's evolving nature, little theoretical consensus exists; the significant influence of postmodernism has only encouraged fragmented viewpoints and multiplicity of perspective. Nonetheless, the practice of social justice, and particularly its practice in the classroom, is a growing trend. Educators are designing curricula and activities specifically with the aim of eliminating forms of oppression such as racism, classism, and sexism. Such efforts have not been undertaken without controversy; many believe that the classroom isn't the appropriate environment for what are sometimes perceived as political agendas. Such debate taps into larger disagreements about the fundamental purpose of schooling.

KEYWORDS: Ableism; Associative Justice; Classism; Distributive Justice; Heterosexism; Oppression; Postmodernism; Racism; Recognitional Justice; Sexism

OVERVIEW

Social justice has a long history; almost as soon as human societies were formed, philosophers began thinking about how individual and collective needs could be met simultaneously (Griffiths, 1998). They sketched out the defining characteristics of a just society, and developed arguments for just behavior on the part of individuals. Even more recently in modern American education, policymakers have addressed issues of social justice. Gender equity and desegregation, for example, are about distribution of resources; at their core, they are efforts to achieve good for the individuals in a society, and good for the society itself.

Social justice in education, as a more formal and organized area of study, is a relatively recent development. Even those who are at the forefront of the movement concede that it has yet to solidify as a field of study (Merchant & Shoho, 2006). Differences of opinion about what social justice is, and how it can best be achieved, for example, contribute to instability and discontinuity. As Merchant and Shoho argue, "Theory building involving social justice in education has been scant. Unless a coherent body of scholarly work can produce an empirically validated model for social justice, the likely outcome is fragmentation...."

For many scholars contributing to research in social justice, fragmentation is exactly the point. Postmodern theorists, with their emphasis on plurality and fragmented subjectivity, argue that the "way forward" is to "develop a continuously revisable framework in place of the timeless universalism of current ones" (Griffiths). Similarly, Bogtoch argues "there can be no fixed or predictable meanings of social justice;" they must be "continuously reinvented and critiqued, again and again."

This emerging field faces external challenges as well. Social justice scholars have often found themselves in the center of the larger academic debate between conservatives and liberals. As Kohl (1999) explains, the tradition of social justice in education is not a neutral one; "there is an agenda manifested in one way or another…." For those anchored on the other end of the political spectrum, the agenda is the problem. David Horowitz, a prominent spokesperson for the conservative right, is dedicated to fighting what he perceives to be the liberal bias in the classroom. He argues, "Becoming a college professor is not a way to change the world. If you want to change the world, you go into politics…you don't go into the classroom" (Salas, 2006).

Difference and disagreement may go hand-in-hand with the study and practice of social justice, but surprising unity emerges among social justice scholars with regard to the identification and definition of injustice. Although any one researcher may focus on one or more of the forms of oppression in varying degrees, they generally agree that each merits attention. Forms of oppression include, but are not limited to, racism, classism, heterosexism, ableism, sexism, and anti-Semitism (Adams, Bell, & Griffin, 1997). Each describes a general form of oppression, but the *experience* of oppression, as it plays out in our day-to-day lives, scholars argue, may vary from person to person.

FURTHER INSIGHTS

Before we turn to a brief discussion of the ways in which social justice educators have attempted to fight some of these injustices in the classroom, we'll return first to issues of theory and definition. Later, we'll revisit the arguments of conservative critics, and discuss some scholars' attempts to find a middle ground.

DEFINITION & THEORY

While the term social justice is a relatively new one as applied to education, the underlying concepts it represents are not. Educators have been discussing equal opportunity and equality for centuries, which

begs the question, is the new terminology necessary? According to Griffiths, "the discourses of equality [and educational opportunity] in schools are becoming unhelpful." Because 'equal opportunity' was co-opted by "both the right and left to argue for different versions of…values," she argues, the terminology of the 1960s and 1970s is no longer able to support their agenda.

Use of the term 'social justice,' Griffiths argues, is the way forward, but in order to understand its potential contribution, we must first look back to ancient Greece in 400 BC. Plato and Aristotle were the first to offer a definition as "the good of the community which respects the good of the individuals within it" and to some degree, present-day definitions still reflect this philosophical foundation (Griffiths). Aristotle also suggested that social justice could not be imposed upon a community by its leaders but rather had to be agreed upon by its individual members in order to be effective. Modern day theorists emphasize self-determination too, as when Adams et al. write, "we do not believe that domination can be ended through coercive tactics, and agree with Kreisberg (1992) in a 'power with' vs. 'power over' paradigm for enacting social justice goals." More recently, Rawls (1972) has highlighted Aristotle's notion of distributive justice. As summarized by Griffiths, Rawls defines social justice as "a way of assigning rights and duties, and distributing the benefits and burdens of social co-operation." In other words, justice is more than just the following of rules.

While Griffiths relies heavily on philosophical foundations in defining social justice, she nevertheless suggests that theoretical advancement depends on scholars' willingness to move beyond a "framework of individualism" toward postmodernism. The notion of individual rights and merit, she argues, are difficult to apply to social justice issues in education; not only does the notion of 'individual' imply a rational, choosing adult being (as distinct from a typical school-age child), but merit is difficult to define, and may not be relevant in decisions about allocation of educational resources. Griffiths believes postmodern theories which emphasize plurality and multiplicity of experience and perspective, as opposed to the notion of 'the universal citizen,' offer more promise for social justice theory and practice in the future.

Perhaps heeding Griffith's advice, Gewirtz (2006) draws upon principles of postmodernism in her proposal for a contextualized analysis of social justice in education. She writes that "it is not possible to resolve the question of what counts as justice in education at a purely abstract level, and that what counts as justice can only be properly understood within specific contexts of interpretation and enactment" (Gewirtz). Because justice is multi-dimensional, mediated by competing interests, and dependent on the perspective of the person(s) seeking it, it can never exist in a 'pure' form apart from its practice.

Gewirtz's analysis of social justice is significant not only for its emphasis on context, but also for further 'flushing out' a working definition of social justice. Building upon the work of Iris Young, Gewirtz partitions social justice into three components—distributive, recognitional, and associative justice. Distributive justice, as previously defined, refers to the distribution of goods and resources. Recognitional justice is defined as respect and recognition for a person's culture and way of life; to experience the absence of it, Young writes, "is to experience how the dominant meanings of a society render the particular perspective of one's own group invisible" (as quoted in Gewirtz). Finally, associative justice is most closely aligned with the concept of democracy; that is, each individual should have the opportunity to participate fully in the decisions that affect his or her life.

Other theories of social justice in education show a similar shift in emphasis from distribution of resources to notions of self-determination and individual agency. Walker (2006) proposes a "capability-based" theory of social justice based on the work of Amartya Sen (1992), arguing that economic growth should not be the key measure of the quality of a person's life. According to Sen, "in the capability-based assessment of justice, individual claims are not to be assessed in terms of the resources or primary goods the persons respectively hold, but by the freedoms they actually enjoy to choose the lives that they have reason to value" (as quoted in Walker). Therefore, this approach draws heavily on the concept of freedom, and in particular, the freedom to choose what one wants to be and do.

Recent theories of social justice are shifting away from distributive definitions of justice in a second way as well. Distribution of resources and goods implies an end state; while scholars acknowledge that social justice is indeed a goal, many are emphasizing the need to think of it as a process as well (Adams et al.). According to Enslin (2006), for example, "justice is relational rather than static, and is concerned with action and process." And in Griffiths' book titled "Action for Social Justice in Education," she too honors social justice as a process and defines it as a verb (Elijah, 2003). Griffiths' thesis is twofold: she attempts to understand how we can honor diversity and difference within a single humanity, and how we can take *action*, through education, to create a "more humane, just world which will benefit individuals and society" (Elijah).

SOCIAL JUSTICE PRACTICE IN THE CLASSROOM

Griffiths' (2003) definition provides a logical segue into a brief discussion of the ways in which social justice is practiced through education. As mentioned, many critics disagree with the 'activist' stance taken by social justice educators; for them, teachers should transmit knowledge and information, and do little more. For social justice educators, efforts to achieve change are a critical component of their professional identities. As Shaull (1988) argues, "there is no such thing as a neutral educational process" (as quoted in Shapiro & Purpel, 2005). In other words, education either maintains the status quo, or prepares young people to think critically about their world and participate in its transformation. Social justice educators attempt to do the latter.

The social justice movement began in the 1960s and 1970s with a focus on issues surrounding social class, but as Griffiths explains, issues of class were soon overtaken by issues of race and gender. More recently, the field has expanded once again to include social justice concerns surrounding sexuality, disability, and religion. Adams et al., editors of "Teaching for Diversity and Social Justice," provide the most comprehensive resource for social justice practice in the classroom. Their guidelines for practice are organized around the notion of eliminating oppression; what follows are examples of their suggestions for classroom activities and curriculum development geared toward the elimination of sexism, racism, ableism, and heterosexism.

SEXISM

Botkin, Jones, & Kachwaha (2007) define sexism as "a system of advantages that serves to privilege men, subordinate women, denigrate women-identified values and practices, enforce male dominance and control, and reinforce forms of masculinity that are dehumanizing and damaging to men." They further argue that binary conceptions of gender are too simplistic to capture the complexity of identity, that sexism is closely connected to other forms of oppression such as heterosexism, and that sexism operates through power, dominance, violence, and control.

Their curriculum is designed to help students understand sexism and the toll it exacts on both men and women. They offer over 12 hours of classroom activities—including but not limited to—exercises designed to reveal the socially-constructed nature of gender roles, the normalcy of violence in our lives, and the institutionalized and interpersonal forms of power that perpetuate sexism. In one activity, for example, students are asked to identify rules of behavior for men and women, the ways in which they were taught those rules, the advantages and disadvantages of the rules, and the consequences for ignoring them.

RACISM

Adams et al. define racism as "a system of advantage based on race and supported by institutional structures, policies, and practices that create and sustain benefits for the dominant white group, and structure discrimination, oppression, and disadvantage for people from target racial groups." Although many Americans—and especially white Americans—believe racism no longer exists, Adams et al. point to segregated schools and neighborhoods, pay inequities, and stereotypes as a few of the ways in which it has persisted.

Their curriculum is designed to increase awareness of racism, help students understand the ways in which they are socialized into a system of white privilege, and empower them to work for racial equality and social justice. Some of the discussions are centered around the history of racism in the United States, white privilege and unearned advantage, institutional racism, and power. In one activity designed to demonstrate the different ways and degrees to which individuals experience racism, students are asked to physically place themselves along a continuum between the two anchors—"true for me" and "not true for me"—as the teacher reads of series of statements. Examples of the statements include: "You

have had a racist or ethnically derogatory statement made to you" and "you worry about discrimination in your community." Students then explain their response to the rest of the class.

Loftin (2011) writes that totally eradicating pervasive discrimination, racism, and prejudice in public schools will not occur until we "recognize the root of those ills and stop ignoring the role that race occupies in building our institutions." He argues that "consciously and explicitly assuming the democratic privilege of students can serve as a vehicle for eradicating white complicity with regard to institutionalized and socialized racism" (Loftin).

ABLEISM

The disability rights movement has become a more organized and cohesive movement in the last 30-40 years. Ableism is one of the more complex forms of oppression to address, given the wide range of disabilities people experience, but the movement has been unified in "rejecting the notion that being disabled is an inherently negative experience or in any way descriptive of something broken or abnormal" (Adams et. al.). Disability advocates argue that becoming disabled is both a loss and gain, that living with a disability is simply another interesting and meaningful way to live, and that people experience oppression and discrimination not because of the disability itself, but because of other people's beliefs and prejudices.

In designing a curriculum and classroom activities to combat ableism, Griffin, Peters, and Smith avoided those activities that, while well-intentioned, might perpetuate the notion that a disability is a deficiency. For example, asking students to "live" with a disability for a day inadvertently reinforces the idea that a disability is an individual deficiency, rather than focusing on disability in the larger context of oppression as institutional, cultural, and societal phenomenon. Indeed, token efforts at addressing the topic of disability generally do manifest as so-called "disability awareness days" and tend to include such "disability simulations," which have been "long condemned by disability rights activists as promoting cultural attitudes that are ableist in nature" (Lalvani & Broderick, 2013). Instead, Griffin et al. ask students to identify how socialization might have influenced their beliefs about disability, educate students on different types of disabilities, and emphasize the socially-constructed nature of disability. Students are given opportunities to interact with individuals with disabilities in a question and answer format, and participate in group activities such as creating a vision for an inclusive and accessible society.

HETEROSEXISM

Until the 1970s, homosexuality was viewed as a pathology, and was even given an official classification by the American Psychiatric Association as a 'psychological disorder.' Although a great deal of progress has been made since that time, many people still view the acceptance of gay, lesbian, bisexual, and transgender (GLBT) people as an indication of the moral decay of society. Social justice educators continue their advocacy on behalf of GLBT individuals by combating heterosexism, "the system of advantage afforded to heterosexuals in institutional practices and policies and cultural norms that assume heterosexuality as the only natural sexual identity and expression" (Griffin, Derrico, Harro, & Schiff, 2007).

Gorski, Davis, and Reiter (2013) wrote that heterosexism and homophobia are pervasive in U.S. educational institutions. Their study found that GLBT concerns are often "invisible in multicultural teacher education coursework in the United States" and that, when these concerns are covered, they generally are addressed in "decontextualized ways that mask heteronormativity" (Gorski et al.).

Griffin et al. advise teachers to disclose their own sexuality when teaching about heterosexism, and—while respecting religious beliefs—steer students away from religious and moral debates, which tend to be unproductive. The goal of their curriculum is not to change beliefs, necessarily, but to help people understand how heterosexism hurts and limits people of all sexual orientations. They ask students to research historical perspectives of same-sex relationships, share stories about their own gender and sexuality development, and consider ways in which heterosexism is institutionalized in the workplace, home, legal system, health care system, and schools.

VIEWPOINTS

Because social justice is such a contested issue, it's worthwhile to take a closer look at the controversy surrounding it. Even social justice scholars acknowledge

that the field is marked by disagreement as much as it is by sameness of opinion. Griffiths writes, "At our own period of history, there is as little agreement on what justice consists in, as there is on moral judgments, or on judgments of rationality." Brown (2002) makes the same point when he refers to disagreements regarding social justice as "an ideological quagmire."

Dudley (2005) brings a variety of perspectives to bear on social justice issues. What becomes apparent is that opinions vary not only on how to address social justice issues, but on whether or not such issues exist in the first place. For example, contributing author Horowitz argues against the very notion that African Americans are oppressed in American society. More African Americans are incarcerated, he argues, because more African Americans are committing crimes, a statistic the liberal left ignores in citing institutional racism as the cause. Others acknowledge racism as a characteristic of American life, but disagree on whether programs such as affirmative action should be used to combat it. Some believe affirmative action programs have had a positive impact on society, increasing opportunities for African Americans without unfairly disadvantaging non-minorities. Others, however, ascribe to an individualist model of society, and believe it's unjust to "penalize the children of a given race for wrongs perpetrated by their remote ancestors" (Dudley).

Others have tried to find a middle ground. Poplin and Rivera (2005) describe the evolution of a teacher education program from one focused solely on social justice, to one that acknowledged the importance of opposing ideologies. They write, "though we continue to support the teaching of [social justice] ideologies in teacher education, we find them unbalanced without equal attention to the contesting ideologies and unproductive without an equal emphasis on accountability for achievement gains of traditionally marginalized students." Even standardized tests, they argue, with a long history of working against poor and minority students, can in the future work in favor of these same students. Whether or not any individual agrees with a particular practice or point of view is less important, Poplin and Rivera suggest, than exposing them to the alternate view in the first place. "It is one thing for a university program to build its vision around a particular set of ideologies (a valid choice); it is another to allow teacher candidates [to be] uninformed of alternative ones."

In the end, the only course of action may be an agreement to disagree, as long as each side has the freedom to express its views. Ironically, both conservatives and liberals believe their freedom of expression is being compromised by the other, particularly in the classroom. Lukianoff (2007), for example, writing in the *Chronicle of Higher Education,* criticizes Columbia Teacher's College for making "a commitment to social justice" a requirement for graduation. He argues "vague, subjective, and politicized evaluation standards are dangerous. They invite administrators and faculty members to substitute their own opinions and political beliefs in place of evaluating students' skills as teachers." Apart from the issue of graduation requirements, those on the conservative end of the spectrum believe the classroom has become a hostile place for even expressing non-liberal ideas (Salas). Liberals also believe academic freedom is being compromised, but believe the conservative right is responsible. Giroux (2006) writes, "higher education in the United States is currently being targeted by a diverse number of right-wing forces who…have waged a focused campaign to undermine the principle of academic freedom." They have done so, he argues, "ironically, by adopting a vocabulary of individual rights, academic freedom, balance, and tolerance."

TERMS & CONCEPTS

Ableism: Also referred to as disability oppression, ableism refers to a system of advantage that creates and sustains benefits for the dominant able-bodied group, while creating disadvantage for people with disabilities.

Associative Justice: One of three forms of social justice outlined by Gewirtz, associative justice is most closely aligned with the concept of democracy; that is, each individual should have the opportunity to participate fully in the decisions that affect his or her life.

Distributive Justice: One of three forms of social justice outlined by Gewirtz, and also the form most closely aligned with Rawls' classic definition, distributive justice refers to the distribution of resources and goods—the benefits of social cooperation—as well as the distribution of burdens and duties.

Heterosexism: A system of advantage or privilege afforded to heterosexuals in institutional practices and policies and cultural norms that assume heterosexuality as the only natural sexual identity and expression.

Oppression: A system that maintains advantage and disadvantage based on social group memberships and operates, intentionally and unintentionally, on individual, institutional, and cultural levels (Adams, et al.). Oppression is pervasive and hierarchical, and is experienced differently by individuals based on multiple memberships in different social groups.

Postmodernism: Postmodernism emerged in a variety of fields—architecture, art, music, film, and sociology—as a reaction against and critique of modernity. Postmodernists celebrate multiplicity of perspective, fragmentation, and subjectivity as opposed to the notion of grand narratives or overarching theories.

Racism: a system of advantage based on race and supported by institutional structures, policies, and practices that create and sustain benefits for the dominant white group, and structure discrimination, oppression, and disadvantage for people from target racial groups.

Recognitional Justice: One of three forms of social justice outlined by Gewirtz, recognitional justice is defined as respect and recognition for a person's culture and way of life.

Sexism: A system of advantages that serves to privilege men, subordinate women, denigrate women-identified values and practices, enforce male dominance and control, and reinforce forms of masculinity that are dehumanizing and damaging to men.

Jennifer Kretchmar

BIBLIOGRAPHY

Adams, M., Bell, L. E., & Griffin, P. (Eds.). (2007). Teaching for diversity and social justice. New York, NY: Routledge.

Adams, M., Blumenfeld, W. J., & Castaneda, R., & Hackman, H.W., & Peters, M. L., & Zuniga, X. (Eds.). (2000). Readings for diversity and social justice: An anthology on racism, anti-Semitism, sexism, heterosexism, ableism, and classism. New York, NY: Routledge.

Bogtoch, I. (2000). Educational leadership and social justice: Theory into practice. Paper presented at the Annual Meeting of the University Council for Educational Administration. Retrieved May 7, 2007, from Education Resource Information Center.

Botkins, S., Jones, J., & Kachwaha, T. (2007). Sexism curriculum design. In Adams, M., Bell, L. E., & Griffin, P. (Eds.). *Teaching for diversity and social justice* (pp. 195-218). New York, NY: Routledge.

Brown, C. (2002). A principle in search of a practice: On developing guidelines / standards to evaluate social justice. Paper presented at American Education Research Association. Retrieved May 7, 2007, from Education Resource Information Center http:// eric.ed.gov.

Dudley, W. (Ed.). (2005). Social justice: Opposing viewpoints. New York, NY: Greenhaven Press.

Elijah, R. (2003). Action for social justice in education. *Encounter*, 19, 54-56. Retrieved May 6, 2007, from EBSCO online database Academic Search Premier.

Gewirtz, S. (2006). Towards a contextualized analysis of social justice in education. *Educational Philosophy and Theory*, 38, 69-81. Retrieved May 6, 2007, from EBSCO online database Education Research Complete.

Giroux, H. A. (2006). Academic freedom under fire: The case for critical pedagogy. *College Literature*, 33, 1-42. Retrieved May 6, 2007, from EBSCO online database Education Research Complete.

Gorski, P.C., Davis, S.N., & Reiter, A. (2013). An examination of the (in)visibility of sexual orientation, heterosexism, homophobia, and other LGBTQ concerns in U.S. multicultural teacher education coursework. *Journal of LGBTQ Youth, 10*, 224–248. Retrieved December 8, 2013, from EBSCO online database Education Research Complete.

Griffin, P., D'errico, K., Harro, B., & Schiff, T. (2007). Heterosexism curriculum design. In Adams, M., Bell, L. E., & Griffin, P. (Eds.). *Teaching for diversity and social justice* (pp. 195-218). New York, NY: Routledge.

Griffin, P., Peters, M., & Smith, R. (2007). Ableism curriculum design. In Adams, M., Bell, L. E., & Griffin, P. (Eds.). *Teaching for diversity and social justice* (pp. 195-218). New York, NY: Routledge.

Griffiths, M. (1998). Towards a theoretical framework for understanding social justice in educational practice. *Educational Philosophy and Theory*, 30, 175-192. Retrieved May 6, 2007, from EBSCO online database Education Research Complete.

Kohl, H. (1999). Social justice and leadership in education: Commentary. International Journal of Leadership in Education, 2, 307-311. Retrieved May 11, 2007, from EBSCO online database Education Research Complete.

Lalvani, P., & Broderick, A.A. (2013). Institutionalized ableism and the misguided "Disability Awareness Day": Transformative pedagogies for teacher education. *Equity & Excellence in Education, 46,* 468-483. Retrieved December 8, 2013, from EBSCO online database Education Research Complete.

Loftin, T.P. (2011). Guarding against complicity: Educating for democratic privilege. *Journal of Philosophy & History of Education, 61,* 207-215. Retrieved December 8, 2013, from EBSCO online database Education Research Complete.

Lukianoff, G. (2007). Social justice and political orthodoxy. *Chronicle of Higher Education*, 53, B8-B8. Retrieved May 6, 2007, from EBSCO online database Education Research Complete.

Marshall, C., & Oliva, M. (2006). Building the capacities of social justice leaders. In C. Marshall & M. Oliva (Eds.), *Leadership for social justice: Making revolutions in education* (pp. 1-15). New York, NY: Pearson Press.

Merchant, B. M., & Shoho, A. R. (2006). Bridge people: Civic and educational leaders for social justice. In C. Marshall & M. Oliva (Eds.), *Leadership for social justice: Making revolutions in education* (pp. 85-109). New York, NY: Pearson Press.

Poplin, M., & Rivera, J. (2005). Merging social justice and accountability: Educating qualified and effective teachers. *Theory into Practice*, 44, 27-37. Retrieved May 6 from EBSCO online database Education Research Complete.

Salas, A. (2006). Academic freedom: Under siege from claims of liberal bias. *Education Digest*, 72, 55-59. Retrieved May 6, 2007, from EBSCO online database Education Research Complete.

Shapiro, H. S., & Purpel, D. E. (Eds.). (2005). Critical social issues in American education: Democracy and meaning in a globalizing world. Mahwah, NJ: Lawrence Erlbaum Associates, Publishers.

Walker, M. (2006). Towards a capability-based theory of social justice for education policy-making. Journal of Education Policy, 21, 163-185. Retrieved May 6, 2007, from EBSCO online database Education Research Complete.

SUGGESTED READING

Enslin, P. (2006). Democracy, social justice and education: Feminist strategies in a globalizing world. *Educational Philosophy and Theory, 38*, 57-67. Retrieved May 6, 2007, from EBSCO online database Education Research Complete.

Harrell-Levy, M., Kerpelman, J., & Henry, D.J. (2016). Practices of exemplary transformative teachers, as perceived by students transformed by an urban high school social justice course. *Urban Review, 48*, 73-100.

Sikes, P., & Rizvi, F. (Eds.). (1997). Researching race and social justice in education: Essays in honour of Barry Troyna. London, England: Trentham Books Limited.

Spring, J. (2016) (8th Ed.) *Deculturalization and the struggle for equality.* New York: Routledge.

Strouse, J. H. (1997). Exploring themes of social justice: Readings in social foundations. Upper Saddle River, NJ: Merrill Prentice Hall.

Section 3: Education Psychology

Introduction

Each of us has our own story to share about our schooling experiences. The following Educational Psychology articles illuminate the empirical research into the relationships of cognition and learning, individual differences in how we learn, what motivates us as learners and what educational practitioners can do to nurture student understanding.

This section opens with scientific findings on the architecture of the human brain and how experience contributes to the shaping of the brain's physiology. Contributing authors move on to explore a myriad of theories that shed light on how schools deeply touch the lives of those who walk through their doors.

COGNITIVE NEUROSCIENCE

The basic question of interest to cognitive neuro-scientists—what is the relationship between mind and brain—is described; the development of the field is then put into historical context by reviewing how others—ancient philosophers and behavioral psychologists, for example—have either addressed or ignored the relationship between the mind and brain. Cognitive neuroscience has relied on new technologies as well as the insights from a variety of different fields; the importance of collaboration and different types of methodologies are explored. Finally, the implications of cognitive neuroscience research for education and learning are explored.

KEYWORDS: Brain; Cognitive Psychology; Functional Magnetic Resonance Imaging (fMRI); Information Processing Theory; Lesion Studies; Mind; Network Theory

OVERVIEW

As an academic discipline, cognitive neuroscience is in its infancy; the term itself was coined in 1970, and the Cognitive Neuroscience Society didn't hold its inaugural meeting until 1994 (Bly & Rumelhart, 1999). Lack of maturity, however, does not necessarily imply lack of productivity. Cognitive neuroscience has been a remarkably fertile field in an especially limited amount of time. "Biologist E.O. Wilson even referred to the recent period of scientific fecundity within cognitive neuroscience as the occurrence of a rare 'heroic period' of science—comparable to 'the heroic periods of molecular biology, plate tectonics in geology, and the modern synthesis of evolutionary biology'" (Ilardi & Feldman, 2001). Cognitive neuroscience is perhaps heroic not only for its fecundity, but also for exploring what many refer to as the final frontier.

What exactly is this final frontier, the subject of study of the cognitive neuroscientist? The obvious answer for many might be 'the brain'—while correct, such an answer would be incomplete and misleading. Cognitive neuroscientists don't study an object such as the brain, per se, but rather a relationship—more specifically, the relationship between the brain *and* mind. Gazzaniga (2000) defines it this way: "at the core, the cognitive neuroscientist wants to understand how the brain enables the mind." Bly and

Rumelhart provide a similar definition: "the goal of cognitive neuroscience is to understand how brain function gives rise to mental abilities such as memory, reasoning, vision, or movement." The focus on the *relationship* is what distinguishes cognitive neuroscientists from cognitive scientists; cognitive scientists also study mental processes such as memory, but they do so by focusing on the function independent of 'the organ which gives rise to the function' (Bly & Rumelhart). In other words, cognitive neuroscientists integrate physical (neural) and functional levels of analysis.

Gazzaniga describes exploration in this final frontier as 'a very tricky business'; indeed, it's difficult to ignore the significant challenges facing those who study the brain and its relation to our cognitive faculties. But there is also something *uniquely* challenging about this field of study. As Smith (2002) explains, "the mind and its expression in consciousness is at the same time the subject of our study and the means by which we carry on that discussion. I believe that this makes our attempt at understanding the mind both uniquely challenging and extraordinarily interesting to all of us." In other words, we are using our mind to investigate itself, making it both the object and subject of study.

DEVELOPMENT OF THE FIELD

Cognitive neuroscience might be a relatively new field, but one of the questions cognitive neuroscientists are trying to answer—what is the nature of the mind and the nature of consciousness—is one that philosophers have been grappling with for centuries. Smith argues, however, that the tools available to the philosopher—mainly introspection and logic—significantly limited their ability to answer such questions. "The classic tools of the philosopher have been the mainstay of the study of human nature, but contribute little to our understanding of the material world around us, including our physical selves. One result has been a dualistic approach to our study of ourselves, with cognition separated from anatomy and physiology by a philosophical wall." Only by embracing science—empiricism and observation as opposed to introspection and logic—have we gained insights into the mind.

Behaviorism

Not all science has contributed to our understanding of consciousness equally. A substantial portion of the twentieth century was dominated by a theoretical orientation known as behaviorism. Behaviorists relied on observation, defining all learning as changes in observable behavior. In addition to relying on the observable, however, many behaviorists denied the existence of the mind altogether, or argued the futility of attempting to study it. Watson, often cited as the father of the behaviorist movement, wrote "the reader will find no discussion of consciousness and no reference to such terms as sensation, perception, attention, and will..." (as quoted in Smith). For many years, the mind and brain were virtually ignored, causing many to wonder "can a serious student again undertake a serious study of consciousness after nearly half a century hiatus produced by the embracing of behaviorism?" (Smith).

Cognitive Psychology

The answer, of course, is 'yes' and the academic discipline that gave the serious student the opportunity to study the mind again was cognitive psychology. With renewed vigor, cognitive psychologist focused their energy on the black box—the very thing behaviorists ignored—and began studying cognitive functions such as memory, attention, and language development. Even though cognitive psychologists didn't study function in relation to physiology directly, they did embrace models that suggested how the mind and brain might work. Many cognitivists adopted an information processing model, for example, theorizing that the brain worked in much the same way as a computer. Even as neuroscientists entered the scene, the computer remained a viable model, with some suggesting that the individual neuron of the brain mimicked the digital communication of artificial intelligence systems.

Network Theory

Ultimately, however, as researchers began to understand more about the structure of the brain, both the computer metaphor and the reductionist focus on the individual neuron became unsatisfactory ways to explore the mind and brain. The computer metaphor assumed human thought was logical and linear, an assumption that would prove to be false.

And "individual neurons didn't provide a reasonable model of complex behavior and thought" (Smith). Instead, scientists began developing a more sophisticated understanding of the brain, investigating neurons as clusters of cells as opposed to single entities, and recognizing that communication between neurons and clusters of neurons was bi-directional and multi-layered. The model that now guides most cognitive neuroscience research is referred to as 'network theory' (Smith).

Cognitive neuroscientists, and the field more generally, didn't evolve in isolation. In fact, Martin & Rumelhart (1999) describe it as "inherently multi-disciplinary" and Gazzaniga explains that the pioneers of the field were "fed by the instinct that people in various camps needed to be talking to one another." Smith suggests that cognitive neuroscience rests equally on the contributions of three fields—artificial intelligence, cognitive psychology, and neuroscience. Others may define the players more broadly, with even greater emphasis on the collaborative nature of the field. "In cognitive neuroscience, we consider data collected by researchers studying behavior, cognition, neurophysiology, neuroanatomy, and computation, and each new finding provides additional fodder for theories of brain function. Theory building thus becomes a process of trying to fit together a wide variety of different types of information into a more complex, integrated whole" (Bly & Rumelhart).

Methodology

Prior to the last several decades, researchers didn't have direct access to the healthy brains of living people. The earliest studies of the relationship between the brain and cognitive function relied on observations of individuals who had suffered brain damage; loss of function was documented, and then correlated with the damaged areas of the brain upon subsequent postmortem investigation. Patient case studies such as these have been utilized since the 19th century (Chatterjee, 2005). One of the more recent well-known case studies of this sort is the study of a patient referred to as H.M.; after undergoing brain surgery as a last resort effort to eliminate seizures, H.M. suffered severe memory loss. Because doctors knew the specific areas of the brain damaged by surgery, they learned a lot of its relationship to cognitive functions such as language and memory.

IMAGING TECHNIQUES

While useful, case studies of brain-damaged individuals—also referred to as lesion studies—did not give researchers information about the healthy brain in relation to cognition and learning. Not until imaging techniques were developed did scientists get a glimpse inside the brains of 'normal-functioning' individuals while they were performing mental and physical tasks. Some of the more common imaging techniques include positron emission tomography (PET scans), electroencephalography (EEG), and functional magnetic resonance imaging (fMRI). Whereas EEG measures the electrical activity of neurons in the brain, both PET scans and fMRI measure increased blood flow. As a result, different imaging techniques are used for different purposes—only the later help identify the specific location associated with a particular mental event.

Even if fMRI helped researchers identify the part of the brain associated with a particular mental or physical event, they didn't always know what increased activity or blood flow actually meant. "Because fMRI is non-invasive it is ideal for monitoring the brain activity of a person conducting mental or physical tasks. But it has previously been a 'black box', because a change in neuron activity, indicated by greater blood flow, could mean one of several things" (Logothetis, Pauls, Augath, Trinath, & Oeltermann, 2001). More specifically, researchers weren't sure if the increased blood flow showed "the input to or the output from nerve cells, or something else entirely" (Logothetis et al.). Recent research suggests the fMRI signal is most closely associated with input to nerve cells, a finding many think makes intuitive sense. Receiving a signal requires more energy than sending a signal, and the energy comes in the form of glucose which is carried by the blood. Even as fMRI has given us more insight into the specific location and processes associated with particular cognitive functions, mysteries still remain. Scientists have observed, for example, that the brain receives more energy—in the form of blood—than it often needs; the reason for it is unknown.

IMAGING VS. LESION STUDIES

Given the insights into the brain and cognitive function we have gained as a result of imaging technology, it is perhaps of little surprise that this methodology has grown in popularity. In 2005, for example, the bulk of research submitted to the Cognitive Neuroscience Society used imaging and electrophysiological methodologies; by comparison, only 16% used patient-based case studies (Chatterjee). Not all agree, however, that imaging studies are superior to case-based lesion studies. In fact, only lesion studies have the possibility of establishing a causal relationship between structure and function. "Functional imaging by necessity provides correlational data" (Chatterjee). Which causes many to wonder, according to Chatterjee, "despite the greater 'in-principle' inferential strength of lesion than functional imaging studies, why in practice do they have less impact on the field?" (Chatterjee).

Researchers cite sociological and practical considerations, as opposed to considerations based on scientific merit, as the reason for the imbalance between imaging and lesion studies. Novelty, for example, plays a role—people generally believe new technology is good technology—as does accessibility to data. It's often difficult to gain access to clinical patients. In the end, however, both methodologies are important. "The strengths and weaknesses of lesion and imaging studies are complementary. The point is not to bemoan the impact of imaging studies on cognitive neuroscience as much as to ask how the impact of lesion studies might be enhanced."

Applications

EDUCATIONAL IMPLICATIONS

The most obvious potential application of cognitive neuroscience research is, arguably, in the field of education and learning. Indeed, much has been written in the recent educational psychology literature about how teachers should evaluate and apply what scientists learn about the brain and cognition. Surprisingly perhaps, many urge great caution, suggesting that findings in cognitive neuroscience need to be validated further before educators begin to use them. Bruer (1997, as cited in Stanovich, 1998) describes the direct leap from cognitive neuroscience to education as "a bridge too far." Wittrock (1998) concurs, writing "Useful implications about important applied problems do not follow directly from one individual study…in neuroscience or any other field. It is a long way from research by Gauss and Maxwell to the telephone, telegraph, and the computer. Perhaps it is less of a long way from Thorndike's neural bonds…to classroom teaching, but it is still a long way."

Caution is urged because caution has not always been exercised. One of the most infamous examples of inappropriately applied research occurred in the late twentieth century, when information about the different hemispheres of the brain became a teaching fad. As Stanovich explains "[Educators] have no desire to spawn another round of the left-brain-right-brain nonsense that has inundated education through workshops, inservices, and the trade publications of non-academic publishers." Others urge caution by emphasizing the bi-directionality of neuroscience and cognitive psychology; information about the neural basis of learning disabilities, for example, is dependent upon understanding the psychological and behavior characteristics of such individuals (Stanovich).

Although many advise educators to exercise caution, they are advising them with equal urgency to familiarize themselves with cognitive neuroscience research. The rationale for such a recommendation is twofold. First and foremost, cognitive neuroscience has something to tell us about teaching and learning. In contrast to many school reforms, often based on politics and social and cultural issues, cognitive neuroscience provides an evidence-based approach to school change (Geake & Cooper, 2003). Secondly, becoming well-versed in how the brain works will help empower teachers, and re-establish the respect many feel is lacking. "A good reason for educationists to embrace cognitive neuroscience is the hope that such an endeavor might stem the increasing marginalization of teachers as pedagogues" (Geake & Cooper). The social status of doctors improved in the last century as they adopted evidence-based practice; so too, Geake and Cooper argue, will the social status of teachers.

MEMORY & LEARNING

Geake and Cooper define adaptive plasticity as the brain's capacity "to change at a neurophysiological level in response to changes in the cognitive environment." Citing a model proposed by Donald Hebb (1949), Geake and Cooper suggest that the signal between neurons—or synaptic functioning—strengthens as a result of repetition and practice, resulting in "permanent physiological change." As a result, they suggest that "the most important implication for education is that Hebb's model strongly supports what teachers have long known: that repetition

is necessary for effective learning." The model also puts forth an explanation to account for difficulty of correcting erroneous learning; any learning that gets repeated, whether correct or not, is strengthened and thus more resistant to change. Naïve science beliefs of children and adults may result from this process.

DECISION-MAKING & EMOTION

In both psychology and economics, decision-making was long thought to be a rational, cognitive process in which an individual weighs the costs and benefits of a particular course of action (Naqvi, Shiv, & Bechara, 2006). More recently, however, researchers' observations of individuals in high-risk and high-uncertainty decision-making situations demonstrated that people often rely on biases and emotions in choosing an appropriate course of action. Recent neuroscience research has confirmed these observations, demonstrating that both the ventromedial prefrontal cortex (vmPFC) and amygdala play important, but different, roles in decision-making. Those with damage to the vmPFC, for example, have difficulty anticipating the emotional impact of future rewards and punishments, while those with damage to the amygdala have difficulty registering the emotional impact of rewards and punishments as they are occurring. Both deficits make it more difficult for such individuals to use information about rewards and punishments when choosing behaviors in the future. Cognitive neuroscientists have extended this research to examine the role of emotion in different types of decisions. Activation in the vmPFC is greater when making moral decisions that impact others; "these findings suggest that moral decisions, compared to nonmoral decisions, engage emotions, especially when one is required to consider the consequences of one's actions for another's well-being" (Naqvi et al.).

AGING & CULTURE

Park and Gutchess' (2006) research on aging and culture provides a good example of how findings in cognitive neuroscience are used in conjunction with current knowledge about cognitive function. Behavioral data suggests decreases in efficiency in basic cognitive processes—short and long term memory, speed of processing, etc—as a result of the aging process. Researchers have assumed that deficits in functioning were mirrored by similar changes in brain circuitry—loss of volume of neurons, and less activation between neurons. Imaging research has shown that while the aging brain does demonstrate loss of volume in particular regions, it is able to compensate for such changes in other ways, rearranging circuitry so that it utilizes more parts of the brain, and both hemispheres rather than just one. "Advances in neuroimaging have been largely responsible for views suggesting that the brain has residual plasticity" (Park & Gutchess).

In addition to aging, Park and Gutchess were also interested in the impact of culture on brain structure; they hypothesized that differences in cultural norms—East Asians' tendency to focus on relationships and group function in contrast to Westerners' tendency to focus on the individual—might translate into different neural connections. More specifically, East Asians have been found to interpret stimuli more holistically, focusing on context, while Westerners focus more on the object itself, and less on the context or background. Park and Gutchess found that young East Asians and Westerners had equally developed circuitry for responding to both object and background information, but that as individuals aged, the circuitry corresponding to the behavior *not* valued by their culture became less active. In other words, "the data...suggest that after a lifetime of culturally biased information processing the neural circuitry for looking at scenes may be sculpted in a culturally biased way" (Park & Gutchess).

CONCLUSION

Few would argue against the utility of the field of cognitive neuroscience. Disagreements won't arise over whether or not furthering our understanding of the brain is a worthwhile endeavor, but rather, as we have seen, over the methods and potential implications of such research: does cognitive neuroscience confirm or invalidate previous theories of cognitive functioning? What methods should be used to best answer our questions about brain structure and function? How and when should cognitive neuroscience research be applied in the classroom, and in larger world settings? As we move forward, the answers to these questions may shift. In the meantime, perhaps the one thing most can agree upon is the need to move forward itself. "Cognitive neuroscience is...a field of scientific inquiry that has more to do than has been done" (Gazzaniga).

TERMS & CONCEPTS

Brain: Cognitive neuroscientists are interesting in studying the relationship between our physical selves—specifically, our brain—and the cognitive and mental abilities it gives rise to—collectively known as 'the mind.' The relationship between mind and brain is the subject of study, rather than the brain itself.

Cognitive Psychology: Cognitive psychologists are distinct from cognitive neuroscientists in that they study cognitive function, independent of its physical origins in the brain. Cognitive neuroscientists, however, rely heavily on research conducted by cognitive psychologists (among others), as knowledge about function informs knowledge about structure.

Functional Magnetic Resonance Imaging (fMRI): Functional Magnetic Resonance Imaging is a newly developed technique that allows researchers to observe a 'normal' healthy brain as it performs a cognitive or motor task. Previously, researchers had to rely on information from patients who suffered brain damage, by correlating observed function with post-mortem investigations of brain structure. Functional Magnetic Resonance Imaging measures increased blood flow to active parts of the brain.

Information Processing Theory: Information processing theory is an example of a model put forth by cognitive psychologists to explain the way humans select, attend to, and remember information. Advances in cognitive neuropsychology help confirm or disconfirm previous understandings of cognitive function; recent evidence seems to suggest that our brains are less linear in the processing of information than we previously thought. Rather, we seem to process data in neural clusters that are multi-layered and communicate bi-directionally; researchers refer to this new model as the network theory.

Lesion Studies: Lesion studies were the first available method for studying the brain in relation to cognitive function. Individuals who suffered brain damage were observed; their cognitive deficits were then understood in relation to the changed structure of their brains, investigated post-mortem. Despite advances in technology, lesion studies are still an important methodology, allowing investigators to make more causal connections that other methodologies allow.

Mind: Cognitive neuroscientists are interesting in studying the relationship between our physical selves—specifically, our brain—and the cognitive and mental abilities it gives rise to—collectively known as 'the mind.' In the past, philosophers have attempted to study the brain using the only methods available to them—introspection and logic. Many argue such methods have yielded little insight, and suggest that furthering our knowledge of the brain holds great promise.

Jennifer Kretchmar

BIBLIOGRAPHY

Battro, A.M., Calero, C.I., Goldin, A.P., Holper, L., Pezzatti, L., Shalóm, D.E., & Sigman, M. (2013). The cognitive neuroscience of the teacher-student interaction. *Mind, Brain & Education, 7*, 177-181. Retrieved December 15, 2013, from EBSCO Online Database Education Research Complete.

Berninger, V.W., & Corina, D. (1998). Making cognitive neuroscience educationally relevant: Creating bidirectional collaborations between educational psychology and cognitive neuroscience. *Educational Psychology Review, 10*, 343-354. Retrieved November 1, 2007, from EBSCO Online Database Academic Search Premier.

Bly, B.M., & Rumelhart, D.E. (Eds.). (1999). *Cognitive science.* New York, NY: Academic Press.

Cartwright, K.B. (2012). Insights from cognitive neuroscience: The importance of executive function for early reading development and education. *Early Education & Development, 23*, 24-36. Retrieved December 15, 2013, from EBSCO Online Database Education Research Complete.

Chatterjee, A. (2005). A madness to the methods of cognitive neuroscience? *Journal of Cognitive Neuroscience, 17*, 847-849. Retrieved November 1, 2007, from EBSCO Online Database Academic Search Premier.

Gazzaniga, M.S. (2000). *Cognitive neuroscience: A reader.* Malden, MA: Blackwell Publishers, Inc.

Geake, J., & Cooper, P. (2003). Cognitive neuroscience: Implications for education? *Westminster Studies in Education, 26*, 7-20. Retrieved November 1, 2007, from EBSCO Online Database Academic Search Premier.

Ilardi, S.S., & Feldman, D. (2001). Cognitive neuroscience and the progress of psychological science: Once more with feeling (and other mental constructs). *Journal of Clinical Psychology, 57*, 1113-1117. Retrieved November 1, 2007, from EBSCO Online Database Academic Search Premier.

Kroeger, L.A., Brown, R., & O'Brien, B.A. (2012). Connecting neuroscience, cognitive, and educational theories and research to practice: A review of mathematics intervention programs. *Early Education & Development, 23*, 37-58. Retrieved December 15, 2013, from EBSCO Online Database Education Research Complete.

Naqvi, N., Shiv, B., & Bechara, A. (2006). The role of emotion in decision making: A cognitive neuroscience perspective. *Current Directions in Psychological Science, 15*, 260-264. Retrieved November 1, 2007, from EBSCO Online Database Academic Search Premier.

Logothetis, N.K., Pauls, J., Angath, M., Trinath, T., & Oeltermann, A. (2001). A neurophysiological investigation of the basis of the fMRI signal. *Nature, 412*, 150-157. Retrieved November 8, 2007, from http://nature.com.

Park, D., & Gutchess, A. (2006). The cognitive neuroscience of aging and culture. *Current Directions in Psychological Science, 15*, 105-108. Retrieved November 1, 2007, from EBSCO Online Database Academic Search Premier.

Schunk, D.H. (1998). An educational psychologist's perspective on cognitive neuroscience. *Educational Psychology Review, 10*, 411-417. Retrieved November 1, 2007, from EBSCO Online Database Academic Search Premier.

Smith, R.H. (2002). *Cognitive neuroscience: A functionalist perspective.* New York, NY: University Press of America, Inc.

Stanovich, K. (1999). Cognitive neuroscience and educational psychology: What season is it? *Issues in Education, 10*, 419-426. Retrieved November 1, 2007, from EBSCO Online Database Academic Search Premier.

Wittrock, M.C. (1998). Comment on 'The educational relevance of research in cognitive neuroscience.' *Educational Psychology Review, 10*, 427-429. Retrieved November 1, 2007, from EBSCO Online Database Academic Search Premier.

SUGGESTED READING

Banich, M.T. (2004). *Cognitive neuroscience and neuropsychology* (2nd ed.). New York, NY: Houghton Mifflin Company.

Easton, A., & Emery, N.J. (Eds.). (2005). *Cognitive neuroscience of social behavior.* New York, NY: Psychology Press.

Gazzaniga, M.S. & Ivry, R. (2013) (4th Ed.). *Cognitive Neuroscience: The Biology of the Mind.* N.Y.: W.W. Norton & Company.

Johnson, M. H. (1997). *Developmental cognitive neuroscience: An introduction.* Cambridge, MA: Blackwell Publishers, Inc.

Lane, R.D., & Nadel, L. (Eds.) (2000). *Cognitive neuroscience of emotion.* New York, NY: Oxford University Press.

Ward, J. (2015). (3rd Ed.) *The Student's Guide to Cognitive Neuroscience.* N.Y.: Psychology Press.

BRAIN-BASED LEARNING

The old notion that brains are fixed, with learning potential already wired in the brain, is being replaced with the theory that the brain is flexible. This article presents information on the concept of Brain-Based Learning. Recent technological advances have allowed researchers to identify actual physical changes in the brain when learning occurs. This research has come to be known as brain-based learning, or neuroplasticity. Understanding what is happening in the brain during the learning process can help educators to tailor classroom instruction to facilitate increased learning.

OVERVIEW

Since the late twentieth century, learning has most often been studied using a social cognition frame. This frame has three specific dynamics—environmental factors, behavioral factors, and personal perceptions—which have been believed to interrelate with each other in ways that create the context in which learning takes place.

Although social cognition theory has been instrumental in describing the social construction of knowledge and the very individualized task of learning, it does not seem to go far enough in examining the role of the personal perception dynamic. Learning is not just about the perceptions and attentiveness of each person: it is also affected by physiological changes in the person. The majority of this physiological activity is happening in the brain—learning actually creates physical changes to the brain. Technological gains have allowed scientists to examine the changes that occur in the brain during the learning process and to speculate on improved methods of teaching (Zull, 2004).

PHYSIOLOGICAL ACTIVITY IN THE BRAIN

Technology has provided the means for researchers to learn what is happening in the brain during the learning process and supports the theories that:

- When a person practices something, the neurons in the related area of the brain fire more frequently and dendrite growth increases—in fact the dendrites may grow enough to begin to interconnect (creating new potential paths for cognitive connections);

- When a person is learning, synapses work to organize neurons into a cohesive network that draws in some of the more isolated neurons—the networks are the physical equivalent of knowledge;
- Changes in the synaptic connections occur when learning is taking place;
- Synaptic activity is greatly enhanced when the brain is flooded with emotion chemicals (i.e., adrenalin, dopamine, and serotonin);
- Exposure to new experiences and complex thinking actually increases synaptic connections and density between neurons in specific parts of the brain and also increases dendrite growth and connections within the brain (Draganski, 2004; Healy, 1990; Trachtenburg, 2002; Zull).

These findings lead to the conclusion that learning may be enhanced through practice and by engaging emotion into the process.

Technology has also allowed researchers to refute the notions that the brain is hard-wired for learning and that learning ability decelerates with age (Schwartz & Begley, 2002). It also calls for a reconsideration of how teaching translates into a learning experience for both adults and children in classrooms. An examination of these new advances in neuron-scientific research opens the door for creating new, more effective types of learning experiences in the classroom.

NEW HYPOTHESES

The old notion that brains are fixed, with learning potential already wired in the brain, is being replaced with the theory that the brain is flexible. It is always rewiring itself and will continue to do so as long as there is new information for it to accumulate and store.

However, how educators approach learning (and therefore teaching) needs to be critically analyzed in light of the new findings in the area of neuroscience. Caine and Caine (1990) formulated a list of what has been learned from research on brain-based learning. This list includes the following hypotheses: the brain is a complex adaptive system that builds upon what already exists.

Complex adaptive systems are able to recognize and organize patterns from a given set of complex examples (Leshno, Moller, & Ein-Dor, 2003). The brain will assimilate new knowledge based upon what it has already stored. What a person will learn is moderated by the already existing bank of knowledge possessed by that person and the level of complexity in the learning situation. The brain is not able to make neural connections if the paths do not already exist (Caine & Caine; Zull).

People who describe themselves as working from intuition (or a gut-feeling) are often reacting to subtle physiological changes of which they are largely unaware. In these cases, the paths existed and learning has occurred that alters a person's behavior although the person has yet to find the ability to articulate that which has been learned. (Schwartz & Begley).

The brain is social. This idea is often referred to as the social brain hypothesis. It suggests that, via evolution, humans developed larger, more complex brains (primarily in the neocortex—which constitutes five-sixths of the human brain—and in the limbic system) and this development is attributed to the complex relationships humans created by living in bonded social groups. The complexities present in successfully navigating such complex social groups required a new need for the development of language (both written and spoken), logical thinking skills, and the ability to plan for the future. These are all social skills that are known to develop in the neocortex. Additionally, people living in social groups are relying on basic memory, emotion charged memories linked to both attachment and tradition, expression of emotions, and love (i.e., a sense of belonging). These are all social skills that are known to develop in the limbic system. Some social group indices that correlate positively with brain size include:

- Social group size;
- The frequency of social play;
- The frequency of tactical deception (Caine & Caine; Dunbar, 2003; Lewis, 2001).

This refutes the long-standing theory that larger human brains were the direct result of early humans learning to craft tools and strategies needed to develop individual hunting skills to survive.

The search for meaning is innate and that search occurs through patterning. Emotions are critical to patterning.

A review of how human brains function suggests the brain is hard-wired to make meaning of one's external environment. This can be understood using the Triune model, which describes the brain in three layers. The most primitive layer lies buried in the more recently evolved portions of the brain. First, the reptilian complex is the most primitive portion of the brain. It is comprised of the brain stem and the cerebellum. These portions of the brain are responsible for the automatic body functions that work to maintain homeostasis in the body such as balance, digestion, circulation, sleep regulation, breathing, and the fight or flight response to danger. These maintenance activities are primarily performed without conscious control or sensation. It is this area of the brain that encourages territorial and dominant behaviors that were once meant to increase one's chances for survival.

The limbic system links emotion with behavior and promotes interpersonal attachments. It is comprised of the amygdala, which works to associate events with emotion, and the hippocampus, which works to create long-term memory and memory recall. The hippocampus uses special nerve networks of neurons and dendrite paths to enhance memory storage from both lived experiences and academic studying. When the brain is flooded with emotion hormones, memory recall (and, thus, learning) is enhanced by the interaction of the hippocampus and the amygdala.

The cerebrum contains all of the centers that receive and interpret external information; it is covered with the neocortex. It also analyzes incoming information, invokes logic and reasoning, and experiences the emotions created in concert with the amygdala. These three layers interact with each other with two-way communication as the brain seeks to create meaning to one's experiences. The functions of the three areas of the brain are automatic and cannot be switched off. The only change one can impose is that of altering the focus of how meaning is being made (Caine & Caine; Freudenrich, 1997; MacLean, 1997).

The brain has a natural proclivity for identifying patterns as it strives for meaning making. As new experiences are processed, the existing neuronal paths will be utilized and expanded to accommodate complexity and identify information that can be stored and retrieved along similar paths. The brain is constantly comparing information to determine how similar or dissimilar new information is in comparison to what has already been learned. It is difficult for the brain to store and retrieve information that is not related, or contextualized, to already existing knowledge. Again, the flooding of emotion facilitates the identification and storage of knowledge as the brain works to identify patterns. Emotions related to expectancy, biases, humor, self-efficacy, self-esteem, and social bonding facilitate the learning process as emotion and thought are physically entwined via the brain's inherent functions (Caine & Caine; Eichenbaum, 1997; Zull).

There are at least two ways of organizing memory: rote memorization and experiential learning. Factual learning will be enhanced if the student is engaged in making connections between the factual information and lived experience.

Cognitive science acknowledges at least two major forms of memory that are navigated by separate and distinct pathways in the brain. The brain retains and stores factual knowledge (such as what a student learns in a traditional school setting where lecture and memorization are the primary teaching methods) in the neocortex. Knowledge gained from lectures and rote memorization will result in a learning structure that is fairly inflexible when one seeks to transfer that knowledge to a different topic.

The functioning of the hippocampus is critical to the organization and storage of knowledge gained through lived experiences. The interaction of the hippocampus and the amygdale, coupled with the additional interplay with the cerebrum (in which higher thinking skills reside), result in strong memory-based learning that is contextualized and firmly attached to one's life experiences. Research indicates the acquisition of factual knowledge in a school setting is actually facilitated when the brain uses experiential knowledge to process and recognize patterns within factual information. In other words, academic learning that is contextualized with experiential learning creates a more flexible knowledge structure that allows for better quality integrative thinking and simple transfer to different topics (Eichenbaum).

Complex learning is enhanced by challenge and inhibited by threat.

As discussed above, the brain uses emotion to facilitate learning and to create the neural connections to enable fact retrieval. Higher thinking skills, located in the cerebrum, are facilitated by processes residing in the limbic system when a person is challenged in a learning situation. Emotions generated from struggling to acquire new skills and knowledge will aid the brain in meaning making, the effective creation of memories, and motivation for future learning success if the learning environment is perceived to be safe and supportive. Teaching that is punctuated with threats of failure, punishment, or social humiliation will engage the processes residing in the reptilian complex, resulting in an automatic fight or flight response that will inhibit the functions of the hippocampus and halt effective learning.

Every brain simultaneously perceives and creates parts and wholes and learns from that on which attention is focused while simultaneously learning from what is contained in its "peripheral attention."

The brain continuously processes information from its external environment. It adds upon its knowledge gleaned from a lesson being presented in the classroom while it simultaneously takes in actions and reactions of the teacher and other students, the physical environment of the classroom (e.g., what posters on the wall say, teacher attitude toward the subject and the class members, background noise, cleanliness of the environment, etc.). It compiles new knowledge in ways that allows it to check for the most efficient ways to store it while also comparing the new knowledge to what is already known—sometimes integrating old knowledge with new knowledge while sometimes rearranging old knowledge to accommodate new knowledge. It breaks knowledge into smaller pieces to accommodate learning while simultaneously combining it in ways that will provide context and meaning in sometimes surprising and exciting ways. As it performs these mental gymnastics, it will continuously change its own wiring and neural networks— this is what is meant by plasticity of the brain and the developing networks are the physical equivalent of knowledge (Draganski et al.; Zull).

Every brain is uniquely organized.

All learning entails the gathering of information, making meaning from what has been gathered, creating new ideas and knowledge from these meanings, and testing the knowledge via physical or mental activities (Kolb, 1984). Although brain functions and changes work the same in every person, each brain is organized in a unique manner. Some students will learn more easily if mathematics is incorporated into a lesson while others will learn more easily if the language arts are used. All learning depends on the prior connected knowledge each student brings to the classroom (i.e., wiring of the brain) and the student's current physical state (e.g., wakeful, threatened, respected, drugged, etc.).

Different students will connect with different teaching methods, some responding to demonstrations, others to complex explanations, and others to simple explanations as they work to understand the course materials. Some educators, when finding their students seem to be struggling with a curriculum topic, will employ the help of students who have newly mastered the material to re-teach the material. A learner who has recently mastered the material is able to remember where the learning was difficult and may create teaching methods that better help connect the material to the students' life experience (Zull).

APPLICATIONS

Although the neurosciences are relatively new, they tend to confirm what good teachers have always known intuitively while helping to articulate why good teaching practices actually work. There are many ways to incorporate brain-based learning in the classroom structure.

Educators have known for many years that students who find intrinsic rewards in a learning situation are more motivated in the long term. Current research has also borne this out. Students who are challenged by the curricular material and find their rewards in the mastery of a difficult topic (as opposed to being rewarded with extrinsic rewards) will experience feelings such as frustration, challenge, mastery, pride, happiness, (and perhaps relief). These emotions will cause the emotional flooding necessary to ensure enhanced synaptic activity and, as a result, enhanced learning. Educators need to ensure course topics create a challenge for the students and should provide the mental space (i.e., adequate time paired with appropriate assistance) in which each student can struggle to master the course material. Educators should take care not to provide an excess of explanations or extrinsic rewards, which may lessen the students' motivation to learn while detracting from the learning experience itself.

Educators should ensure the classroom is a safe place in which errors can be made as learning occurs. Although there is great benefit from the release of emotion chemicals, an excessive flood of negative emotions (e.g., abject frustration, despair, etc.) will not result in enhanced learning. Threat includes engaging in or allowing social humiliation of students in the classroom. Classroom structures need to create spaces in which struggles over challenges can occur; however, the educator needs be available to provide assistance as needed and create learning situations in which students can make non-fatal mistakes. It is the rare child who can learn to ride a bike without falling off a few times. Brain-based learning suggests a similar approach for classroom instruction. Learning should be approached in a way that:

- Allows the student to learn by doing rather than via lecture;
- Provides the hand on the seat of the bike (i.e., guidance) as the lesson begins;
- Keeps the guidance of the hand to a minimum (e.g., perceived independence, practice in a safe environment, and a sense of mastery);
- Creates opportunities for practice rather than punishment in the face of failure (allowing the necessary neural connections while providing the teacher feedback that can be used as clues to furthering the lesson);
- Facilitating the production of emotion chemicals to enhance the learning experience.

TERMS & CONCEPTS

Adrenaline: Also known as epinephrine. This hormone is released from the adrenal gland into the bloodstream when a person perceives danger or threats. When it reaches the liver, it stimulates the release of glucose for rapid energy. Abrupt increases can work to shut down functioning of the hippocampus, inhibiting the ability to learn.

Amygdala: An almond-shaped mass of gray matter located in the middle of the brain (anterior temporal lobe) that is connected to the hippocampus, and plays a role in emotionally-laden memories (Schwartz & Begley).

Axon: Each neuron has only one axon (and may have several dendrites). This long, thick fiber carries outgoing messages to the dendrites of target cells.

Correlate/Correlation: A statistical tool used to test the strength of a relationship between two variables. It does not prove that one variable causes another; it only indicates the presence and magnitude of existing relationships.

Dendrites: These hair-like strands are fairly thick where they emerge from the cell body and branch out in hundreds of directions, becoming thinner and wispier with each division. Their chief function in life is to carry incoming electrochemical messages from other neurons to the cell to which they belong. Each neuron usually has many, many dendrites.

Dopamine: A powerful and common neurotransmitter primarily involved in producing a positive mood or feeling. Secreted by neurons in several brain areas.

Hippocampus: The area of the brain essential for memory and learning. Half of it is situated in the left half of the brain and half of it is situated in the right half of the brain. All memories must be registered in the hippocampus before being stored in the brain.

Neocortex: Also known as the cerebral cortex. The gray matter that covers the outer surface area of the brain. Gray matter most usually contains the cell bodies of the neurons. The neocortex contains two specialized regions: one for voluntary movement and one for processing sensory information.

Neurons: The grayish or reddish cells of the brain that are the fundamental functional unit of the nervous system.

Self-Efficacy: One's personal belief regarding one's level of capability and ability to influence situational outcomes.

Serotonin: A common neurotransmitter most responsible for promoting relaxation, regulating mood, and inducing sleep. Antidepressants (like Prozac) usually suppress the absorption of serotonin, alerting the body to increase its serotonin production.

Synapse: The actual gap in which a reaction will occur between the axon of one neuron and the dendrites of another neuron cell when they are communicating information back and forth.

Sherry Thompson

BIBLIOGRAPHY

Caine, R. N. & Caine, G. (1990). Making Connections: Teaching and the Human Brain. Nashville, TN: Incentive Publications.

Draganski, B., Gaser, C., Busch, V., Schuicrer, G., Bogdahn, U., & May, A. (2004). Neuroplasticity: Changes in grey matter induced by training. Nature, 427(6972), 311-312. Retrieved October 31, 2007, from EBSCO online database, Academic Search Premier.

Dunbar, R. I. M. (2003). The social brain: Mind, language, and society in evolutionary perspective. Annual Review of Anthropology, 32, 163-181. Retrieved October 31, 2007, from EBSCO online database, Academic Search Premier.

Eichenbaum, H. (1997). How does the brain organize memories? Science, 277(5324), 330-333. Retrieved October 28, 2006, from EBSCO online database, Academic Search Premier.

Freeman, G. G., & Wash, P. D. (2013). You can lead students to the classroom, and you can make them think: Ten brain-based strategies for college teaching and learning success. Journal on Excellence in College Teaching, 24, 99-120. Retrieved December 10, 2013, from EBSCO Online Database Education Research Complete.

Freudenrich, C. C. How Your Brain Works. Retrieved October 17, 2007, from http://health.howstuffworks.com.

Healy, J. M. (1990). Endangered Minds: Why Our Children Don't Think. New York, NY: Simon & Schuster.

Keppel, G. & Wickens, T. D. (2004). Design and Analysis (4th ed.). Upper Saddle River, N.J.: Prentice Hall.

Kolb, D. A. (1984). Experiential Learning. Englewood Cliffs, NJ: Prentice-Hall.

Leshno, M., Moller, D., Ein-Dor, P. (2003). Neural nets in group decision process. International Journal of Game Theory, 31, 447-478.

Lewis, K. P. (2000). A comparative study of primate play behavior: Implications for the study of cognition. Folia Primatologica, 71, 417-421.

MacLean, P. D. (1997). The brain and subjective experience: Question of multilevel role of resonance. Journal of Mind and Behavior, 18, 247-267.

Moghaddam, A., & Araghi, S. (2013). Brain-based aspects of cognitive learning approaches in second language learning. English Language Teaching, 6, 55-61. Retrieved December 10, 2013, from EBSCO Online Database Education Research Complete.

Pajares, F. (2002). Overview of social cognitive theory and of self-efficacy. Retrieved June 5, 2007, from http://des.emory.edu.

Schwartz, J. M. & Begley, S. (2002). The Mind and the Brain. New York, NY: Regan Books.

Trachtenberg, J. T., Chen, B. E., Knott, G. W., Feng, G., Sanes, J.R., Welker, E. et al. (2002). Long term in vivo imaging of experience-dependent synaptic plasticity in adult cortex. Nature, 420(6917), 788-795. Retrieved October 30, 2007, from EBSCO online database, Academic Search Premier.

Webster's New World College Dictionary, 4th edition. (2001).

Zakrajsek, T. D., & Doyle, T. (2013). Teaching for brain-based learning: A message from the guest editors. Journal on Excellence in College Teaching, 24, 1-6. Retrieved December 10, 2013, from EBSCO Online Database Education Research Complete.

Zull, J. E. (2004). The art of changing the brain. Educational Leadership, 62, 68-72. Retrieved October 17, 2007, from EBSCO online database, Academic Search Premier.

SUGGESTED READING

Caine, R. N. & Caine, G. (1990). Understanding a brain-based approach to learning and teaching. Educational Leadership, 48, 66-70. Retrieved November 2, 2007, from EBSCO online database, Academic Search Premier.

Goleman, D. (1997). Emotional Intelligence. New York, NY: Bantam.

Healy, J. M. (1990). Endangered Minds: Why Our Children Don't Think. New York, NY: Simon & Schuster.

Moffett, N., & Fleisher, S. C. (2013). Matching the neurobiology of learning to teaching principles. Journal on Excellence in College Teaching, 24, 121-151. Retrieved December 10, 2013, from EBSCO Online Database Education Research Complete.

Pete, B. M., Fogarty, R. J. (2003). Twelve brain principles that make the difference. Thousand Oaks, CA: Corwin Press.

Samur, Y., & Duman, B. (2011). How an awareness of the biology of learning may have an effect on performance. Education as Change, 15, 257-270. Retrieved December 10, 2013, from EBSCO Online Database Education Research Complete.

COGNITIVE DEVELOPMENT

The term cognitive development describes the way in which individuals learn about and perceive themselves and their environment. The pioneering theorist of the field was Jean Piaget, who contributed stage independent and stage dependent, but other theorists have built upon his work with theories like information-processing, social cognition, and sociocultural perspectives. Biological and cultural factors can also affect cognitive development across the lifespan. Educators can apply these theories to the classroom as they work with both young and adult learners to develop higher-order thinking.

KEYWORDS: Cognitive Development; Concrete Operational Stage; Emerging Adulthood; Formal Operational Stage; Information-Processing; Operations; Piaget, Jean; Post-formal Thought; Preoperational Stage; Schemata; Sensorimotor Stage; Socio-cultural; Social Cognition; Sociocultural Approaches to Cognitive Development; Structures; Theory of Mind

OVERVIEW

At the heart of the study of cognitive development are the questions: "What do we know?" and "How did we come to know it?" Answering these questions involves examination of the multiple processes that influence mental and intellectual functioning across the lifespan. In that regard, it is of interest to explore aspects of cognitive development such as cognition, which entails thinking and perception, language, memory, and attention as they pertain to individuals from infancy and throughout adulthood.

The investigation of cognitive development begins with the seminal work of Jean Piaget. It then addresses other theories and recent work in cognitive development such as sociocultural approaches and theory of mind. Some applications of cognitive development theories are discussed in relation to moral development and classroom strategies. Issues of culture and life-stage are also explored in relation to cognitive development.

PIAGET ON COGNITIVE DEVELOPMENT

Jean Piaget was a Swiss scholar who, though untrained in psychology, made a tremendous impact on the field—particularly in the areas of cognitive, developmental, and educational psychology. Among his many contributions, Piaget posited theories on cognitive development that were stage-independent and stage-dependent. At the heart of his theories of cognitive development was the understanding that knowledge could be innate, learned, or developed through a self-regulated process (Egan, 1982). Piaget's stage-independent theory presents a number of concepts integral to understanding the process of cognitive development detailed in his stage-dependent theory.

STAGE-INDEPENDENT THEORY

Schemata, structures, equilibration, and operations are the constructs of interest in Piaget's stage-independent theory on cognitive development (Muuss, 1996). A schema is a cognitive representation of concepts or behaviors that have meaning in people's everyday lives. Schemata, or more than one schema, are adapted repeatedly over the lifespan due to maturation and experience. Structures arise as schemata become more complex and organized in relationship to one another. Cognitive development proceeds as individuals engage with structures in their environment and mature as a result of these experiences. Aiding this process is what Piaget referred to as equilibration.

Equilibration is characterized by dual practices of assimilation and accommodation. When an individual encounters unfamiliar information in their environment they must address the disruption to their equilibrium that results by making accommodations to existing structures. Adapting to new information by integrating it into current structures is assimilation. The actions taken in the equilibration process, and many other processes, are what Piaget termed operations. Operations are extensions of schemata and structures and are integral to Piaget's stage-dependent theory of cognitive development.

STAGE-DEPENDENT THEORY: THE FOUR STAGES OF COGNITIVE DEVELOPMENT

As Muuss details, according to Piaget, the four broad stages of cognitive development are the:

- Sensorimotor;
- Preoperational;
- Concrete operational;
- Formal operational stages.

The time frame for the stages ranges from birth through adolescence with stages ordered sequentially. From birth through the age of two years, the sensorimotor stage sees children move from reflex actions to intentional movement. Children also become aware of object permanence and begin to use schemata to explore new situations. In the preoperational stage, children from age two to seven years see their language skills grow and learn based on how things appear to them at a surface level. Children in this stage remain egocentric for the most part but do begin to internalize representations.

The concrete operational stage involves children age seven to eleven years who develop abilities such as classifying objects and seeing how such objects relate to one another. Conservation is probably the hallmark of the concrete operational stage and it entails the recognition that manipulating an object in different ways does not change its properties. The most well-known example of the principle of conservation is recognizing that pouring all of the water from a short, wide glass into a tall, thin glass does not increase the amount of water.

The final stage in Piaget's stage-theory of cognitive development is the formal operations stage. This stage is thought to begin at adolescence and entails abstract and logical thought. It also involves youth being able to reflect about what they are thinking (also known as metacognition), create theories on various topics, and explore the relationship between reality and possibility (Muuss). Piaget suggested that formal operations might be experienced by adolescents in diverse ways based on their unique abilities, proclivities, and skills.

Other Perspectives on Cognitive Development

INFORMATION-PROCESSING

The information-processing approach to cognitive development focuses on how individuals respond to stimuli in their environment. Integral aspects of this theory are:

- Attention;
- Memory;
- Processing speed (Arnett, 2004).

Information-processing can occur consciously or unconsciously and involves individuals creating and acting upon cognitive representations of stimuli (David, Miclea, & Opre, 2004). At any given time there are myriad stimuli at play in the environment. When individuals encounter these stimuli they must make decisions as to what they will pay attention to in that moment; this information will then exist at the sensory memory level.

Processing information using perceptual and learning skills helps transition it into either short-term or long-term memory. Information stays in short-term memory for brief periods of time while it can be stored for retrieval at any time in long-term memory. Processing speed refers to the length of time it takes an individual to attend to stimuli, work with information in their memory, and then offer a response of some sort. The components of the information—processing approach-attention, memory, and processing speed—operate in continuous and concurrent ways. As individuals mature, they are able to attend to more than one stimulus at a time, hold more information in their short- and long-term memory, and process information more quickly and more accurately (Arnett; David et al.).

SOCIAL COGNITION

Albert Bandura is a social psychologist whose contributions to the field of psychology span across decades and topics. His perspective on cognitive development is one that emphasizes social learning or social cognition. By social cognition, Bandura meant the process by which individuals think about and subsequently act within the social environment (Grusec, 1992). Social cognition relates to how people—from childhood through adulthood—regulate, reflect upon, and reinforce their behavior as they interact in the world at large (Muuss). Another integral concept in social cognition is self-efficacy, or an individual's belief in their ability to exert control on their environment (Bandura, 1993).

Cognitive, motivational, affective, and selection processes exert influence in social cognition. Selection relates to what individuals attend to and engage with in their environment. Affective states, such as anxiety or depression, are what Bandura refers to as "emotional mediators" and they can impact all facets of social learning particularly self-efficacy. Motivational processes include the attributions made, expectations held, and goals set by individuals (Bandura). Of relevance to the motivational process is vicarious reinforcement, or the impact that the observation of others' behavior and the response to that behavior has on an individual's thoughts and actions (Muuss). Forethought, or the ability to think into the future in regard to goals and expectations, is a salient cognitive process in the realm of social cognition (Bandura).

SOCIOCULTURAL APPROACHES

Lev Vygotsky was a Russian psychologist whose work from the early part of the twentieth century has grown in impact in the late twentieth and early twenty-first century (Arnett). For Vygotsky, development was "the transformation of socially shared activities into internalized processes" (John-Steiner & Mahn, 1996). History and language are examples of the "socially shared activities" Vygotsky believed were internalized by individuals as they lived and acted within particular cultural contexts.

Vygotsky's constructs of scaffolding and the zone of proximal development have been major contributions in the area of cognitive development (Arnett). The zone of proximal development is "each person's range of potential for learning" (McInerney, 2006). When individuals are in the zone of proximal development they are at the upper range of their ability and skill and need assistance from others to achieve a goal or complete a task. Scaffolding occurs when individuals are provided more assistance as they first encounter a challenging task and less assistance as they develop mastery in the area. It is important to be aware of an individual's zone of proximal development when using scaffolding techniques in order to provide the appropriate amount and type of assistance and maximize learning potential.

Rogoff and Chavajay (1995) build upon Vygotsky's framework in their cross-cultural exploration of cognitive development. They found that some aspects of Western theories of cognitive development did not hold the same meaning in non-Western cultures. Rogoff and Chavajay describe Piaget's acknowledgment that the formal operation stage of his theory of cognitive development was likely to vary across cultures. This cultural variance is supported in a collection of studies on cognitive development (Keller, 2011). Rogoff and Chavajay further assert that learning is both structured by and comprised of sociocultural activities grounded in specific contexts. In that regard, the indicators of cognitive development, and the meaning ascribed to them, are influenced by the social and historical factors at play in any given environment.

NEW VANTAGE POINTS ON COGNITIVE DEVELOPMENT

The notion of theory of mind has gained prominence since the late twentieth century. In theory of mind, individuals are seen as "intentional agents" (Carlson, Mandell, & Williams, 2004) who seek to understand themselves and the world through mental representations. Researchers have used false-belief, appearance-reality, and visual perspective-taking tasks to assess the mental states that comprise theory of mind (Flavell, 2000). Much of the research in theory of mind focuses on infants and young children in order to ascertain at what age various components of theory of mind develop (Rakoczy, 2012). In his review of theory of mind research, Flavell notes that a developing theory of mind is characterized in infancy by the ability to discriminate stimuli, such as faces, and an awareness of how people relate to objects, also known as "aboutness." He describes beliefs, desires, pretense, and thinking as mental states in theory of mind that develop after age one through early childhood.

Carlson et al. have posited that theory of mind is related to another burgeoning area of interest within the field of cognitive development—executive functioning. Zelazo, Carter, Reznick, and Frye (1997) define executive function as the process by which individuals recognize a problem exists, determine and implement steps to solve the problem, and assess how successful those steps have been. In other words, Zelazo et al. assert that executive function consists of four components:

- Representation;
- Planning;
- Execution;
- Evaluation.

Results of their review of a body of research on executive function illustrate that between two and five years of age all aspects of executive function grow in a variety of ways such that children come to exert more control in problem-solving.

Applications

PIAGET'S THEORY OF COGNITIVE DEVELOPMENT

Educators have implemented strategies or programming in their classrooms based on aspects of Piaget's theory of cognitive development. For instance, Moran (1991) implemented classroom strategies to promote post-formal thought, or ways of thinking that emphasize the relative nature of knowledge, with adult learners. He delineated the following steps:

- Choose a topic in an area familiar to the learner;
- Have a facilitator create a dilemma to be solved in that topic area and then provide information that promotes post-formal thinking;
- Require learners to gather and present information on the dilemma and later receive critique from peers or the facilitator;
- Support the learner's integration of critiques into the resolution they came up with for the dilemma.

Another prime example of an application of Piaget's theories is Lawrence Kohlberg's cognitive-developmental theory of morality. Kohlberg posits three levels (consisting of two stages at each level) of moral development: the pre-conventional level, or the view that events or behaviors are good or bad based on feedback received or the power of those enforcing the rules; the conventional level, or maintenance of the moral status quo; and the post-conventional level, or a self-definition of morality based on external or internal principles. The post-conventional level is also referred to as the autonomous or principled level.

Kohlberg asserted that aspects of Piaget's theory of development shape moral development. He cited the ability to perform concrete and formal operations as related to skills in moral reasoning. Kohlberg posited that individuals in the concrete operational stage of cognitive development were usually at the pre-conventional level of moral development. As people progressed in formal operational thought, Kohlberg believed they would move through the conventional level of morality and potentially into the post-conventional level (though he did not believe more than 10 percent of adults at the formal operational stage of cognitive development would attain a post-conventional level of morality).

Along with the theoretical work of Kohlberg and other scholars, a good deal of research was conducted based on Piaget's ideas. Whereas some results supported many aspects of Piaget's theory, results of other studies led to revision of aspects of Piaget's work by Piaget himself and theorists that came to be known as neo-Piagetians. In time, perspectives from other theorists in the area of cognitive development garnered their share of attention.

Gauvain (2005) asserts that fruitful information may be gleaned from investigations of the relationship between biological factors and social context in cognitive development. The following sections examine neuroscientific and then cultural and contextual perspectives in understanding cognitive development.

NEUROSCIENCE AND COGNITIVE DEVELOPMENT

Nelson, Moulson, and Richmond (2006) discuss the role of neuroscience in cognitive development. They reference neuron-imaging, such as *fMRI*, and neuron-physiological techniques, for example, event-related potentials (ERP), as providing insight into how regions of the brain function and relate to aspects of cognition (such as face recognition by infants and the development of distinct types of memory). Nelson et al. posit that cognitive development is influenced by sensitive periods of development and argue for long-term studies that will further elucidate the relationship between cognition and activities in the neural system. The role of neuroscience in cognitive development is an intriguing area of study that will undoubtedly garner more attention from researchers (Kelly, 2011).

Culture and context also play important roles in understanding cognitive development. Since definitions of adolescence or adulthood are culturally situated, new conceptions of adolescence or adulthood or changes in functioning during these periods of life bring about unique views on cognitive development. Burgeoning research in the area of emerging adulthood as well as increased attention to older adulthood are prime examples.

COGNITIVE DEVELOPMENT AND EMERGING ADULTHOOD

Arnett posits that the period between eighteen and the mid-twenties no longer fits into the traditional view of adulthood, nor is it a part of adolescence. He refers to this time of life as emerging adulthood and has devoted more than a decade of work to providing information about this developmental period. According to Arnett, emerging adulthood is characterized by exploring identity and possibilities, feelings of instability and being in-between, and being focused on the self.

Labouvie-Vief (2006) discusses the development of mature thought among emerging adults. Labouvie-Vief asserts that when emergent adults participate in contexts where they are challenged to think in more complicated ways, be it through education or social interactions, a movement to a more mature level of thought, beyond Piaget's formal operational thought and Kohlberg's post-conventional level of morality takes place. Arnett contends that pragmatism and reflective judgment, or the evaluation of the soundness of a line of reasoning, are examples of the mature thought patterns, or post-formal thought that develop during emerging adulthood.

COGNITIVE DEVELOPMENT IN ADULTHOOD

Salthouse (1998, 2011) states that while many aspects of cognitive functioning are maintained through adulthood, functioning in the areas that involve fluidity in cognition can decrease with age. He maintains that a consensus has not been reached on the reason for declines in aspects of cognitive functioning for older adults. Changes in information processing, such as longer processing speed, or deterioration of some physiological functioning, for example, eyesight, have been viewed as plausible explanations.

Happé, Winner, and Brownell (1998) detail the results of their study of the experience of wisdom for older adults. Theory of mind abilities for older adults was commensurate with, and at times more advanced than, the level of theory of mind displayed by their younger counterparts in the study. Abilities that tapped into memory skills were worse for older adults than for younger participants.

CONCLUSION

From the foundation laid by Piaget through newer perspectives such as theory of mind, understanding cognitive development requires an approach that examines multiple dimensions of cognition from diverse individuals across the lifespan—from birth through older adulthood. New insights about cognitive development are likely to be discovered as researchers work to understand more about the many social, contextual, and biological factors that can impact individuals as they participate in their environments.

TERMS AND CONCEPTS

Concrete Operational Stage: The concrete operational stage is the third out of four sequential steps in Piaget's stage-dependent theory of cognitive development. Children in this stage are between 7 to 11 years of age. The concrete operational stage is characterized by the achievement of conservation.

Emerging Adulthood: Emerging adulthood occurs when individuals are between 18 and approximately 30 years of age and is distinct from adolescence and adulthood. The development of aspects of post-formal thought, such as pragmatism, takes place during emerging adulthood.

Formal Operational Stage: The formal operational stage is the fourth and final step in Piaget's stage-dependent theory of cognitive development.

This stage begins in adolescence and is characterized by abstract and logical thought.

Information-Processing: The information-processing approach to cognitive development addresses how individuals interpret and respond to stimuli in their environment. Attention, memory, and processing speed are key aspects of information-processing.

Operations: Operations are extensions of schemata and structures in Piaget's stage-independent theory of cognitive development.

Piaget: Jean Piaget was a Swiss researcher whose theories of cognitive development included constructs such as schemata and equilibration as well as a stage-dependent theory that focused on cognition from birth through adolescence.

Postformal Thought: Post-formal thought is conceptualized as the next stage of cognitive development after Piaget's formal operational stage. It is seen as developing in emerging adulthood and includes reflective judgment.

Preoperational Stage: The preoperational stage is the second of four sequential steps in Piaget's stage-dependent theory of cognitive development. Children in this stage are between 2 to 7 years of age. The preoperational stage is characterized by increasing language skills and egocentrism.

Schemata: Schemata are cognitive representations of concepts and behavior. They are adapted over time due to maturation and experience.

Sensorimotor Stage: The sensori-motor stage is the first of four sequential steps in Piaget's stage-dependent theory of cognitive development. Children in this stage are between birth and 2 years of age. The sensori-motor stage is characterized by children's movement from reflex to intent and the awareness of object permanence.

Social Cognition: Social cognition theory asserts that cognitive development takes place as people think about and act on the social environment. Self-regulation and self-efficacy are examples of key social cognition constructs.

Sociocultural Approaches to Cognitive Development: Socio-cultural approaches to cognitive development focus on learning as it shaped by social and cultural factors in individuals' environments. Vygotsky's work on the internalization of shared social activities being integral to learning is an example of a socio-cultural approach to cognitive development.

Structures: Structures are more complex schemata organized in relationship with one another.

Theory of Mind: Theory of mind is the notion that individuals are active participants in understanding self and the world through awareness of and attention to their and others' mental states and representations.

Edith G. Arrington

BIBLIOGRAPHY

Alderson-Day, B., & Fernyhough, C. (2015). Inner speech: Development, cognitive functions, phenomenology, and neurobiology. *Psychological Bulletin, 141*(5), 931–965. Retrieved from EBSCO Online Database Education Research Complete.

Amerian, M., & Mehri, E. (2015). Transcendence of cognitive development: The incorporation of task-based instruction into the transfer tasks of dynamic assessment. *Journal of Language Teach and Research, 6*(6), 1311–1319. Retrieved from EBSCO Online Database Education Research Complete.

Arnett, J. J. (2004). *Adolescence and emerging adulthood: A cultural approach* (Second Edition). Upper Saddle River, NJ: Prentice Hall.

Bandura, A. (1993). Perceived self-efficacy in cognitive development and functioning. *Educational Psychologist, 28*, 117–148. Retrieved from EBSCO Online Database Academic Search Premier.

Carlson, S. M., Mandell, D. J., & Williams, L. (2004). Executive function and theory of mind: Stability and prediction from ages 2 to 3. *Developmental Psychology, 40*, 1105–1122.

David, D., Miclea, M., & Opre, A. (2004). The information-processing approach to the human mind: Basics and beyond. *Journal of Clinical Psychology, 60*, 353–368. Retrieved from EBSCO Online Database Academic Search Premier.

Egan, K. (1982). What does Piaget's theory describe? *Teachers College Record, 84*, 453–476. Retrieved from EBSCO Online Database Education Research Complete.

Flavell, J. (1999). Cognitive development: Children's knowledge about the mind. *Annual Review of Psychology, 50*, 21–45. Retrieved from EBSCO Online Database Academic Search Premier.

Flavell, J. (2000). Development of children's knowledge about the mental world. *International Journal of Behavioral Development, 24*, 15–23. Retrieved from EBSCO Online Database Education Research Complete.

Gauvain, M. (2005). With eyes to the future: A brief history of cognitive development. In L. Arnett Jensen & R. Larson (Eds.), *New Directions for Child and Adolescent Development, Vol. 1: Developmental Horizons.* (pp. 119–126).

San Francisco: Sage. Retrieved from EBSCO Online Database Academic Search Premier.

Grusec, J. E. (1992). Social learning theory and developmental psychology: The legacies of Robert Sears and Albert Bandura. *Developmental Psychology, 28,* 776–786.

Happé, F. G. E., Winner, E., & Brownell, H. (1998) The getting of wisdom: Theory of mind in old age. *Developmental Psychology, 34,* 358–362.

John-Steiner, V., & Mahn, H. (1996). Sociocultural approaches to learning and development: A Vygotskian framework. *Educational Psychologist, 31* (3/4), 191–206. Retrieved from EBSCO Online Database Education Research Complete.

Keller, H. (2011). Culture and cognition: Developmental perspectives. *Journal of Cognitive Education & Psychology, 10,* 3–8. Retrieved from EBSCO Online Database Education Research Complete.

Kelly, A. E. (2011). Can cognitive neuroscience ground a science of learning? *Educational Philosophy & Theory, 43,* 17–23. Retrieved from EBSCO Online Database Education Research Complete.

Kohlberg, L. (1999a). Definition of moral stages. In R. E. Muuss & H. D. Porton (Eds.) Adolescent behavior and society: A book of readings (Fifth Edition) (pp. 223). New York: McGraw-Hill. (Reprinted from *The Journal of Philosophy,* 1973).

Kohlberg, L. (1999b). The cognitive-developmental approach to moral education. In R. E. Muuss & H. D. Porton (Eds.) Adolescent behavior and society: A book of readings (Fifth Edition) (pp. 222, 224–233). New York: McGraw-Hill. (Reprinted from *Phi Delta Kappan, 56,* pp. 670–677, 1975).

Labouvie-Vief, G. (2006). Emerging structures of adult thought. In J. J. Arnett & J. L. Tanner (Eds). *Emerging adults in America: Coming of age in the 21st century.* (pp. 59–84). Washington, DC: American Psychological Association.

McInerney, D. (2005). Educational psychology - Theory, research, and teaching: A 25-year retrospective. *Educational Psychology, 25,* 585–599. Retrieved from EBSCO Online Database Education Research Complete.

Moran, J. (1991, Winter). Promoting cognitive development through adult education. *Education, 112,* 186–194. Retrieved from EBSCO Online Database Academic Search Premier.

Muuss, R. E. (1996). *Theories of Adolescence: Sixth Edition.* New York: McGraw-Hill.

Nelson, C., Moulson, M., & Richmond, J. (2006, September). How does neuroscience inform the study of cognitive development? *Human Development, 49,* 260–272. Retrieved from EBSCO Online Database Academic Search Premier.

Piaget, J. (1999). Intellectual evolution from adolescence to adulthood. In R. E. Muuss & H. D. Porton (Eds.) Adolescent behavior and society: A book of readings (Fifth Edition) (pp. 66–73). New York: McGraw-Hill. (Reprinted from *Human Development,* 15, pp. 1–12, 1972.)

Rakoczy, H. (2012). Do infants have a theory of mind? *British Journal of Developmental Psychology, 30,* 59–74. Retrieved on from EBSCO Online Database Education Research Complete.

Rogoff, B., & Chavajay, P. (1995). What's become of research on the cultural basis of cognitive development? *American Psychologist, 50,* 859–877.

Salthouse, T. A. (1998). Cognitive and information-processing perspectives on aging. In I. H. Nordhus, G. R. VandenBos, S. Berg, & P. Fromholt (Eds). *Clinical geropsychology.* (pp. 49-59). Washington, DC: American Psychological Association. Retrieved from PsycBOOKS database.

Salthouse, T. A. (2011). Neuroanatomical substrates of age-related cognitive decline. *Psychological Bulletin, 137,* 753–784. Retrieved from EBSCO Online Database Education Research Complete.

Zelazo, P. D., Carter, A., Resnick, J. S., & Frye, D. (1997). Early development of executive function: A problem-solving framework. *Review of General Psychology, 1,* 198–226.

SUGGESTED READING

Baker, C. (2016). African American and Hispanic fathers' work characteristics and preschool children's cognitive development. *Journal of Family Issues,* 37 (11), 1514-1534.

Bandura, A. (2001). Social cognitive theory: An agentic perspective. *Annual Review of Psychology, 52,* 1–26. Retrieved from EBSCO Online Database Business Source Complete)

Byers, P. (2016) Knowledge claims in cognitive development research: Problems and alternatives. *New Ideas in Psychology,* 43, 16-27.

Healy, J. (2004). Your child's growing mind: Brain development and learning from birth to adolescence. N.Y.: Broadway Books.

Kozulin, A. (1999). Sociocultural contexts of cognitive theory. *Human Development, 42,* 78–82. Retrieved from EBSCO Online Database Education Research Complete.

McGonigle-Chalmers, M. (2015). *Understanding cognitive development.* Los Angeles: Sage.

Steiner, H., & Carr, M. (2003). Cognitive development in gifted children: Toward a more precise understanding of emerging differences in intelligence. *Educational Psychology Review, 15,* 215–246. Retrieved from EBSCO Online Database Education Research Complete.

Ulset, V., Vitaro, F., Bendgen, M., Bekkus, M., & Borge, M. (2017). Time spent outdoors during preschool: Links with children's cognitive and behavioral development. *Journal of Environmental Psychology, 52,* 69-80.

Wellman, H., & Gelman, S. (1992). Cognitive development: Foundational theories of core domains. *Annual Review of Psychology, 43,* 337–375. Retrieved from EBSCO Online Database Academic Search Premier.

SOCIAL COGNITION

Social Cognition theory has broadened our knowledge of the role people play in their own learning experiences. This article follows the evolution of the theory of Social Cognition by examining concepts such as human agency, symbolic learning, self-reflection, reinforcements, and reciprocal determinism. It also discusses the importance of the concepts, self-efficacy and self-regulation, to the theory. The theory of Social Cognition, when coupled with works of theorists like Lev Vygotsky, work to explain how reality is socially constructed and that all learning occurs within the frame of this constructed reality.

KEYWORDS: Cognition; Collaborative Learning; Introspection; Mediated Learning; Reciprocal Determinism; Scaffolding; Self-Efficacy; Self-Reflection; Self-Regulation; Vicarious Learning

OVERVIEW

Mary needs to teach her son, Rick, to turn his homework in to his teacher. Rick loves to build model cars at home. Mary talks to his teacher and they devise a plan. Each day that Rick turns in his homework, the teacher will give him a piece of a model car that Rick has been dying to build. What is the behavior Rick is supposed to learn? How might the above scenario be teaching Rick to learn the desired behavior? Does the rewarding of a new behavior guarantee success? Are there any other factors that might determine whether this learning experience is successful?

Theories of learning have been shaped by two primary theories, Behaviorism and Social Cognition. In order to understand the underpinnings of Social Cognition, one must first have a general understanding of Behaviorism.

Defining Learning

Early researcher's defined learning as the observable changes resulting from rewards or punishments directed at shaping a new behavior (Pajares, 2002). This school of thought was called Behaviorism because direct, observable reinforcements were used to induce the learning experience and the learner's observable behavior was the only accepted measure of learning success. Behaviorists believed that people were fairly passive in the learning experience; learning could be induced by simply providing appropriate reinforcements for a desired new behavior. According to Behaviorists, practicing (reinforced with immediate rewards) is what leads to learned behavior. Behaviorism became a popular practice for teachers and parents who wanted to teach children new ways to behave. However, some psychologists believed that what was going on inside the learner's head was an important factor in the learning equation. Albert Bandura was one of those psychologists. He believed that "a psychology without introspection cannot aspire to explain the complexities of human functioning" (Pajares).

Social Cognition Theory

In the mid-1960s Bandura developed a theory of Social Learning, based on the works of Piaget, which eventually evolved into the theory of Social Cognition. He believed that what a person thinks (i.e., cognates) about happenings in the environment needs to be considered as a factor in the complex experience called learning (Bandura, 1994). Social Cognition theory has broadened knowledge of the role people play in their own learning experiences. Key to this theory is the idea that cognitive processes, not reinforced practice, guides a learner's behaviors (Hartman, 1996). It includes concepts of human agency and symbolic learning while pointing out that the mental state of the learner impacts potential learning.

Social Cognition theory is grounded in the notion of human agency, meaning learners are "contributors to their life circumstances, not just products of them" (Bandura). It is important to note that the individual identity that provides the foundation for human agency has been socially constructed—no individual develops in isolation (Bandura). A learner may use introspection (i.e., self-reflection) to decide how a new experience fits with current knowledge and to determine whether to attach value to the new knowledge. The learner may facilitate or resist learning a new behavior by planning alternative strategies to the learning experience. These strategies could shorten the time needed to learn a new behavior or may thwart any attempts at teaching new behaviors. Most importantly, each learner must be capable of symbolic learning.

Symbolic Learning

Symbolic learning is a complicated process requiring memory, attention to social prompts, and meaning making on the part of the learner. Learners acquire 'memory codes' of all they see and hear. These memory codes aid in scripting future behavior. Information regarding appropriate models for behavior can be conveyed by social prompts, consequences of particular behaviors, or the conveyance of information that is meant to alter current patterns of behavior (Hartman). However, learning potential is affected by the degree of attention the learner pays to the modeling. The perceptions and current mental state of the learner impact potential learning. Degree of attention will be affected by:

- The relevance and credibility of the model from the perspective of the observer;
- The prestige of the model;
- The level of satisfaction currently experienced by the observer in the modeled area;
- The level of self-esteem of the observer (Hartman).

Social Cognition theorists did not abandon the Behaviorist belief in the importance of reinforcements but, using the notions of symbolic learning and social modeling, built upon the definition to include consideration for instances of indirect reinforcement that may result in the learning of new behaviors. They include:

- Direct Reinforcement;
- Vicarious Reinforcement;
- Self-reinforcement.

Direct Reinforcement is the same type of reinforcement described by Behaviorists. Learners are given immediate feedback for behavior in the form of rewards or punishments. Vicarious Reinforcement

occurs when the learner observes the actions of another person and notes the consequences that person receives for those behaviors. The learner will remember whether the observed actions resulted in desirable consequences and will store that information for future use. Self-reinforcement occurs when the learner experiences feelings regarding whether personal performance is meeting established personal standards (Hartman; McInerney, 2005).

Reciprocal Determinism Model

Later works in Social Cognition focused on the development of the multidimensional constructs for the Reciprocal Determinism model. This model describes how three dynamics interact with each other during the learning process. The triadic interplay among one's behavior, the environment, and personal characteristics affects the learning process (Bandura). The environment sets a cultural stage that frames the learning experience. The environment is created via the use of artifacts in which the individual has imbued meaning. The structures of family, school, neighborhood, and religious affiliations have worked to describe the world to the learner and have set limits and expectations for the learner's future (Bandura, Cole & Wertsch, 1985). The behaviors of the learner will also impact the learning process; whether the learner is attentive, persistent, skilled, self-disciplined, etc. will impact what can be learned and how difficult the material to be learned may be. Additionally, the learning process is affected by the learner's personal characteristics. The intelligence, emotional state, level of self-efficacy, and thinking habits will interact with the other two dynamics to determine the quality of the learning process. According to Pajares, each of the three dynamics interacts with each other to create the context in which learning takes place (see Figure 1).

The interrelation of these three dynamics illustrates how a learner's cognitive processes create an individualized version of what is valued and can be expected based on one's observations of the environment. These expectations and values work to inform the behaviors of the learner and to impose a structure on how the learner will act. The consequences of the resultant behavior will, in turn, inform and alter both the environment and subsequent behaviors (Pajares). In other words, "people create social systems, and these systems, in turn, organize and influence peoples' lives" (Bandura). Concepts of self-regulation and self-efficacy are integral factors in the theory of Social Cognition.

Personal Standards for Behavior

Each learner develops a set of personal standards for behavior by utilizing cognitive ability to self-observe, self-judge, and self-evaluate. These personal standards become internalized and are used by the learner to self-regulate (i.e., make choices, create action plans, and construct and adhere to appropriate courses of action). The learner's success at attaining self-regulation and in incorporating a sense of accomplishment into one's perceptions of oneself helps to create a sense of self-efficacy. Self-efficacy (i.e., one's confidence in one's ability to control outcomes) informs the choices people make, levels of persistence, and the courses of action they are willing to pursue (Bryan, Glynn & Kittleson, 2011). It is a powerful influence that often creates a self-fulfilling prophecy of success or failure for the learner. A person with a low level of self-efficacy may shy away from challenging tasks, give up quickly when faced with failure or setbacks, set lower goals and aspirations, dwell on personal attributes that may contribute to lack of success, and experience higher incidences of stress, social isolation, and depression. A person with a high level of self-efficacy will most likely set high goals and aspirations, view setbacks or failures as surmountable by personal skills improvement and perseverance, examine task processes that may contribute to a lack of success, enjoy greater social success, and experience significantly lower levels of stress and depression (Bandura; Pajares; Komarraju & Nadler, 2013).

Self-efficacy is constructed from both social and individual feedback. A learner's evaluation of personal self-efficacy appears to be derived, in part, from past performance, vicarious learning, social feedback, and one's physiological state. It is fluid; it can be altered by situational factors such as socioeconomic status, educational structures, family structures, and economic conditions (Bandura). However, it does not always have a basis in reality; a person with a record of low performance may have a high level of self-efficacy. This superficially high level of self-efficacy may aid the person in attaining future success (Pajares). Dr. Bandura's research found

that the level of self-efficacy is a robust predictor of behaviors leading to future success and is independent from actual ability (Bandura & Locke, 2003). Given two students of equal ability, the student with the higher level of self-efficacy will be more successful (Pajares). People's actions and levels of motivation are based more on what they believe they can do than on what is objectively true (Bandura. Hence, a person's behavior is better predicted by beliefs about his or her capabilities than by what they are actually judged as capable of accomplishing.

The tenets of Social Cognition support the philosophy that reality is socially constructed. Research suggests that, because social learning is socially situated in the learner's culture, it would be difficult to argue that psychological concepts such as individual success are not socially constructed (Bandura). Indeed, all classroom performance appears to be socially negotiated based upon opportunities made available and constraints imposed upon each student (Rosenholtz & Rosenholtz, 1981).

Model by Dr. Lev Vygotsky

Complementary to the theory of Social Cognition were the works of Dr. Lev Vygotsky. In contrast to Piagetian theory that children construct knowledge through their actions, he emphasized that learning occurs individually, yet always within societal constructs; that learners are constantly using an interaction between their personal meaning-making activities and their social environment to construct meaning (Cole & Wertsch). Based on his conclusions, he worked to develop curriculum activities that would enhance classroom learning. Among these ideas were scaffolding, mediated learning, and collaborative learning as they are used in American schools today (McInerney) to support learning in the social context. Dr. Vygotsky's research strongly supports the position that learning is an accumulation of experiences of the individual within a social culture that has been shaped and defined by prior generations (Cole & Wertsch). Thus, each person's range of potential for learning and opportunities for success are limited by the social culture in which the learning occurs and is largely controlled by the classroom teacher (McInerney). This theorizing has led to further work in understanding how both teaching and learning are impacted via cultural constructivism.

Emphasis of Cultural Constructivism

Cultural constructivism emphasizes the wider social, cultural, and historical contexts of learning. It explores the reciprocal interaction of these contexts to construct shared knowledge and emphasizes the importance of language, artifacts, and heritage in the construction of meaning (Cole & Wertsch). This position has become the basis for calls for social justice within the learning environment—Constructivism asserts that all knowledge is individually constructed, equally valid, and should be honored as such (von Glaserfield, 1995 as cited in McInerney). It asserts that current scholastic and societal structures limit what is accepted as knowledge and it challenges the notion that Eurocentric perspectives are the only acceptable forms of knowledge. It also challenges the principle that knowledge is fixed and immutable while arguing that homogeneous teaching in a classroom filled with ethnically diverse students actually serves to lower the levels of self-efficacy for children of color (McInerney).

FURTHER INSIGHTS

Self-Efficacy

Self-efficacy is an important concept within the American educational system. Self-efficacy is the belief that one has the power to take actions which will produce desired effects (Bandura & Locke). High levels of self-efficacy can create capable, confident graduates who are able to succeed in meeting their life goals, or it can support teachers faced with difficult work situations.

Educators at all educational levels affect the self-efficacy of their students. Teachers and professors who conscientiously provide support to students are helping them to develop competencies, self-efficacy and enabling beliefs that will aid them in successfully attaining their future goals (Bandura). Teachers who utilize classroom differentiation and multidimensional instruction allow students a wider variety of opportunities in which they can experience mastery (Rosenholtz & Rosenholtz). The No Child Left Behind Act of 2001 (in the K-12 system) combined with a push toward testing and accountability in the higher education system did not recognize the importance of consciously cultivating high levels of self-efficacy in students and the success of the act was disputed (Liebtag, 2013). Additionally,

teachers often neglect to acknowledge differing perspectives and abilities of students from diverse ethnic backgrounds, as well as differences based on gender. These situations may leave students at risk of future failure because their educational experiences did not provide adequate supports toward the attainment of self-efficacy. Enhanced self-efficacy may provide teachers the resilience needed to continue to work with difficult students or classroom situations. It could increase over-all morale at the schools as teachers find themselves less stressed or socially isolated. Teachers with high levels of self-efficacy would also be more willing to examine processes and personal skills when faced with failures or setbacks. Teacher efficacy, school/classroom efficacy, and collective efficacy are the topics most commonly discussed in today's practitioner journals (McInerney).

Reciprocal Determinism

Teachers and professors can examine how Reciprocal Determinism is playing out in their classrooms and consider changes to any of the three categories. They may elect to correct self-beliefs or personal thinking habits, improve their self-regulatory classroom practices, or alter existing structures within the school that appear to be undermining student successes.

Social Modeling

Social modeling, in the form of mentoring programs, can be used to bridge the gap between high school and college for students who come from low income homes. Students can learn what college attendance looks like, can be encouraged to envision themselves living and succeeding in the higher education environment, and can participate in experiences that could increase their levels of self-efficacy and their sense of human agency.

Motivation

The theory of Social Cognition has greatly informed theories of motivation during the past two decades. Unfortunately, the majority of this theory has not been incorporated into daily classroom instruction. Despite considerable research suggesting a Social Cognition frame would greatly enhance learning and motivation in the classroom, the current American public school structure has not successfully incorporated the following practices into the classroom:

- Emphasis should be on master goals rather than performance goals;
- Students should be encouraged to be active participants in their learning;
- Feelings of personal worth should be purposefully cultivated in the classroom as they are directly related to learning and achievement;
- Effective learning and motivation starts with self-determination and the presence of choices for students;
- Students should be carefully taught that effort and skills attribute to success and failure—rather than causes such as luck;
- Expectations for achievement and the valuing of success must be carefully cultivated in the classroom as it is closely correlated to academic success.

These suggestions do not intersect well with traditional ways of teaching. School curriculum and teacher training have been traditionally grounded in teacher-driven learning with assessment emphasizing performance goals. Schools need to be reinvented if they are to become places of success for all students (McInerney).

ISSUES

Social Cognitive theory was a prominent school of thought in the 1980s. Research and discussions regarding the positive effects of modeling was at the forefront of pedagogical theory. However, the precepts introduced in Social Cognition have been difficult to implement in American public schools, given current classroom structure and the policy foci of their governing bodies. Public policy such as No Child Left Behind creates curriculum requirements that do not leave adequate time to focus on the psychological well-being of most students. Studies suggest that leaving these needs unmet does not support the student in attaining future success. The purpose and goals of education need to be further discussed by educational leaders and policy-makers to determine how instructional formats could be revised to support all students in acquiring knowledge and skills while also gaining a high level of self-efficacy.

TERMS & CONCEPTS

Cognition: The thinking processes involved in the acquisition, organization and use of information.

Collaborative Learning: A teaching strategy wherein the teacher groups or pairs students to work together for the purpose of achieving an academic goal.

Introspection: A self-reflective process in which people explore their own cognitions and beliefs as they try to make sense of their personal behaviors.

Mediated Learning: The teacher, or another adult, inserts herself between the learner and the instructional material with intent of assisting the student in extracting information from the instructional material and aiding the student in making connections between the material and other content areas.

Reciprocal Determinism: The view that the environment, personal behavior, and personal factors of cognition and self-efficacy are interrelated in the learning process.

Scaffolding: A teaching strategy in which the teacher provides close attention and lots of feedback and assistance to a learner at the beginning of a learning event and then slowly backs off; allowing the learner more freedom as levels of mastery and self-efficacy rise.

Self-Efficacy: A person's beliefs regarding whether one has the power to create change with personal actions.

Self-Reflection: The metacognitive ability to reflect upon oneself and the adequacy of one's thoughts and actions.

Self-Regulation: Exercise of influence over one's own motivation, thought processes, emotional states, and patterns of behavior.

Vicarious Learning: People are capable of learning a new behavior by observing the actions of other people and the consequences of those actions.

Sherry Thompson

BIBLIOGRAPHY

Bandura, A. (1994). Self-efficacy. In V. S. Ramachaudran (Ed.), Encyclopedia of Human Behavior (Vol. 4, pp. 71-81). New York: Academic Press.

Bandura A. (2006). Toward a Psychology of Human Agency. Perspectives on Psychological Science, 1, 164-180.

Bandura, A. & Locke, E. A. (2003). Negative self-efficacy and goal effects revisited. Journal of Applied Psychology, 88, 87-99.

Bryan, R. R., Glynn, S. M., & Kittleson, J. M. (2011). Motivation, achievement, and advanced placement intent of high school students learning science. Science Education, 95, 1049-1065. Retrieved on December 11, 2013, from EBSCO Online Database Education Research Complete.

Cole, M. & Wertsch, J. V. (1985). Beyond the individual-social antimony in discussions of Piaget and Vygotsky. Retrieved June 5, 2007, from http://massey.ac.nz.

Gokhale, A. A. (1995). Collaborative learning enhances critical thinking. Journal of Technology Education, 7.

Hartman, H. (1996). Social Learning Theory. Retrieved June 20, 2007, from http://candor.admin.ccny.cuny.edu.

Komarraju, M., & Nadler, D. (2013). Self-efficacy and academic achievement: Why do implicit beliefs, goals, and effort regulation matter?. Learning & Individual Differences, 2567-72. Retrieved on December 11, 2013, from EBSCO Online Database Education Research Complete.

Kozulen, A. & Presseisen, B. Z. (1995). Mediated learning experience and psychological tools: Vygotsky's and Feuerstein's perspectives in a study of student learning. Educational Psychologist, 30, 67-75.

Liebtag, E. (2013). Moving forward with Common Core State Standards implementation: Possibilities and potential problems. Journal of Curriculum & Instruction, 7, 56-70. Retrieved on December 11, 2013, from EBSCO Online Database Education Research Complete.

McInerney, D. M. (2005). Educational psychology—theory, research, and teaching: A 25-year retrospective. Educational Psychology, 25, 585-599.

Pajares, F. (2002). Overview of social cognitive theory and of self-efficacy. Retrieved June 5, 2007, from from EBSCO Online Database Education Research Complete.

Rosenholtz, S.J. & Rosenholtz, S.H. (1981). Classroom organization and the perception of ability. Sociology of Education, 54, 132-140.

SUGGESTED READING

Bassi, M., Steca, P., Fave, A. D., & Caprara, G. V. (2007). Academic self-efficacy beliefs and quality of experience in learning. Journal of Youth & Adolesence, 36, 301-312.

Nadge, A. (2002, September). From research to reality: Enhancing learning and psycho-social development. Pastoral Care in Education, 20, 3-11.

Nasato, S.R. (2014). Advances in Social Cognition Research. N.Y.; Nova Science Publishers.

Pajares, F. (2003). Self-efficacy beliefs, motivation, and achievement in writing: A review of the literature. Reading and Writing Quarterly, 19, 139-158.

Yost, D. S. (2006). Reflection and self-efficacy: Enhancing the retention of qualified teachers from a teacher education perspective. Teacher Education Quarterly, 33, 59-76.

SOCIO-EMOTIONAL DEVELOPMENT

Children's socio-emotional development is central to how well they attach to their primary caregivers, adapt in educational and community settings, and integrate within society. Disruptions in socio-emotional development typically lead to many of the deeply challenging and problematic behaviors that teachers often experience in classrooms. Possessing an understanding of socio-emotional development and related attributes is one of the most crucial factors in determining how students adapt in schools, form peer relationships, and develop self-confidence, relationship skills, self-management, and emotional competencies required for successful participation in group learning (Thompson, 2002).

KEYWORDS: Attachment Theory; Behavior; Children; Family Systems Theory; Public Schools; Resilience; Socio-Emotional Development; Teaching Pyramid

OVERVIEW

Children's socio-emotional development is central to how well they attach to their primary caregivers, adapt in educational and community settings, and integrate within society. Disruptions in socio-emotional development typically lead to many of the deeply challenging and problematic behaviors that teachers often experience in classrooms. Possessing an understanding of socio-emotional development and related attributes is one of the most crucial factors in determining how students adapt in schools, form peer relationships, and develop self-confidence, relationship skills, self-management, and emotional competencies required for successful participation in group learning (Thompson).

Socio-emotional competence has been described as "cooperative and pro-social behavior, instigation and continuation of peer friendships and adult relationships, appropriate management of aggression and conflict, development of a sense of mastery and self-worth and emotional regulation and reactivity" (Aviles, Anderson, & Davila, 2006). Young children between the ages of 0 to 3 depend on their relationships with adults to teach them about themselves and the world in which they live. Thompson and Happold (2002) noted that "child-adult relationships have a more significant impact on a child's learning than educational toys or pre-school curricula" (Aviles et al.). Parents play an important role in securing an appropriate and healthy environment for their children (NIMH, 2000) and in fostering their socio-emotional development (Dumont & Paquette, 2013; Hurd, Varner & Rowley, 2013). Kingston, Tough & Whitfield (2012) found that maternal distress can lead to poor socio-emotional development in children. Research also suggests that environments that are abusive, difficult and intimidating place young children at risk of impairments in their social-emotional development (Aviles et al.). Four main potential risk factors that risk a child's socio-emotional competence include:

- Early childhood trauma;
- Family discord and volatility;
- Participation in the child welfare system;
- Neighborhood peril and inadequate means (Barbarin, 2000).

With the multiple risk factors experienced in today's urban environments, particularly, daily trauma is a risk factor that cannot be avoided.

FAMILY SYSTEMS & ATTACHMENT
Central to educator understanding regarding potential risk factors and school difficulties, educational professionals should develop a rudimentary understanding of family systems theory and attachment. Psychologists have reported that many of the roles we play in our families and the attachments that we make are integrally related to how we behave in other environments. Briefly, family systems are characterized by

- Wholeness and order, although this order could be dysfunctional;
- Hierarchical structures;
- Adaptive self-organization (Cox & Paley, 2003).

Sroufe & Waters (1977) described attachment as "an organizational construct that integrated development in the domains of affect, cognition, and behavior during infancy and served as a foundation for social and emotional development during infancy" (as reported in Vaughn, 2005).

Contrasted with bonding, the attachment experience is not limited to the first weeks or months of life, but rather it is a gradual and interactive process in the child's responses and feelings toward the child's caregiver (Mercer, 2006). While there are multiple aspects of the attachment experience, disrupted attachment occurs when the primary caregiver's relationship to the child is characterized by risk factors. Teachers may not understand how or why the child's behaviors are problematic, but many theorists suggest a correlation between disrupted attachment and impaired socio-emotional development that later manifests in a school environment.

These correlations become more obvious as children progress through stages of development (such as those that Piaget described) and they face risk factors impairing appropriate socio-emotional developmental processes. These risk factors can impair socio-emotional development and progress can be deeply impacted. One potential way they could be affected is with difficulties in reading and probable difficulties in writing creatively (Barr, 2001). Unknown by many educators, exposure to early childhood trauma, violence in either the home or community environments, or abuse or neglect directly interferes with a child's socio-emotional development and as a result children may suffer from intellectual, cognitive, and academic impairments (Huth-Bocks, Levendosky, & Semel, 2001). These impairments should be considered as a potential for academic problems, social problems with peers, and other impaired attachment behaviors. Other inappropriate behaviors such as expressing unusual directness, requiring inappropriately close adult proximity, or insecurity might be indicators of complicated attachment relationships (Vaughn). Typically, normal attachment reflects the "operation of a secure base relationship" and directly relates to age-appropriate adaptation. Attachment is deeply evocative of how children will behave in school and with other adults.

APPLICATIONS
PROMOTING SOCIO-EMOTIONAL DEVELOPMENT
THE TEACHING PYRAMID
One method of promoting socio-emotional development is the teaching pyramid. The teaching pyramid

is a three-tiered model of classroom strategies that promote socio-emotional development for all children while specifically supporting and addressing the needs of children that are "at-risk for or who have challenging behaviors" (Fox, Dunlap, Hemmeter, Joseph, & Strain, 2003). The model was designed to be implemented by educational professionals with support from mental health professionals and is supported by two primary assumptions:

- That there is a strong relationship between children's socio-emotional development, communication skills, and problematic behavior;
- That in order to address the needs of these problematic behaviors all of the professionals working to alleviate these behaviors need a range of strategies (Hemmeter, Ostrosky, & Fox, 2006).

Behavioral strategies are aimed at four levels of practice with the first two purposed toward improving relationships and designing supportive environments. These are considered "universal" approaches and benefit everyone. The next two are aimed at teaching social and emotional compensatory strategies with the "targeted" level directed at providing intensive, individualized instruction. Within these constructs, specific characteristics utilized in promotion and prevention practices include:

- Evaluating physical settings where children spend the majority of their time;
- Providing predictable schedules, routines, transitions, activity type, size, length, and expectations;
- Behavioral demands;
- Teacher behaviors (Hemmeter et al.).

The basic implication attributed to implementing the teaching pyramid is that most problem behaviors exhibited by children are most likely to be found and alleviated by examining and modifying adult responses to problem behaviors. In other words, adults must examine their own assumptions and make flexible changes to accommodate the needs of their students. Positive adult relationships with students are central to providing support to students.

CULTURAL INFLUENCES

Another contribution to behavioral integration and modification are the individual and culturally based assumptions and beliefs experienced by adults working with children of specific backgrounds who behave in seemingly inappropriate ways. Professionals may have pre-set notions and assumptions about certain groups and populations. These beliefs may directly affect socio-emotional development expectations. In outlining specific attributes of the teaching pyramid, Vaughn expressed a high level of importance in constructing collaborative relationships with parents and families in order to promote healthy relationships, foster different perspectives, and offer the possibility of expanding viewpoints. These diverse perspectives were reported as deeply helpful in cultivating dialogue to implement a "multi-tiered approach to supporting young children's social-emotional competence and decreasing the incidence of challenging behavior." All of these constructs lead to developing and fostering a "system of diversity" for classrooms in chaos.

RESILIENCE

Walsh (1998) defined resilience in families as the "capacity to rebound from adversity, strengthened and more resourceful." According to Walsh, "Highly resilient people reached out for help when needed, turning to kin, social, and religious support systems, as well as helping professionals." For children experiencing socio-emotional developmental impairments, resilience is an "ongoing dynamic process rather than a static characteristic of children and adolescents" and prevention programs that promote resilience especially for youth in peril should be "long term and geared toward assisting high-risk youth across successive periods of development" (Cicchetti & Rogosch, 2002).

Benard (1993) suggested that resiliency could be described "as the ability to bounce back successfully despite exposure to severe risks." O'Connell-Higgins (1994) stated that unlike the term "survivor," resiliency emphasized that potential subjects were able to 'snap back' in order to complete the important developmental tasks that confront them as they grow. Resilience suggests that people do more than merely get through difficult emotional experiences, hanging on to inner equilibrium by a thread.

Tusaie and Dyer (2004) wrote that "individuals who do experience disruption from stress but then use personal strengths to grow stronger and function above the norm are considered resilient." Resilience is "not static," but is instead a cluster of processes that enable individuals to adapt to risks that are unavoidable in life that include increased self-esteem and self-efficacy.

"The impact of stressors involved with these risks accumulated over time and posed risks to the health and mental health of everyone" (Heldring, 2004).

O'Connell-Higgins argued that resilience, like growth itself, was a developmental phenomenon propelled by vision and stamina that evolves over time. She further indicated that adult individuals who commonly possessed characteristics of resilience often shared a variety of common traits. They were often above average to superior intelligence and possess exceptional talents, which include highly developed creativity and other inner resources. Adult individuals possessing resilience commonly have obtained higher economic levels than their family of origin and demonstrate high levels of ego development; have sustained close, empathically attuned relationships in childhood, adolescence, and adulthood. Interestingly, resilient individuals often have psychologically compromised siblings and maintain strong political and social activism. These indicators directly impact strategies for developing best programs for individuals with impaired socio-emotional development. These traits should be evaluated and taught to students as a direct instruction for how to integrate a new conceptual framework to make adaptations within the socio-emotional developmental construct.

STUDENTS

Based on research collected from multiple sources, the impacts of socio-emotional development on success in childhood are broad and not only affect children, but parents, teachers, and peers. For students, early indicators of problem behaviors include: temperamental difficulties, aggression, language difficulties, and non-compliance (Stormont, 2002). Interventions for students should target the child's ability to express their emotions appropriately, "regulate their emotions, solve common problems, build positive relationships with their peers and adults in their environment, and engage and persist in challenging tasks" (Hemmeter et al.). In order for children to be adequately prepared to cope with societal and community functions, coping behaviors must be nurtured. Bullying, non-compliance, inappropriate anger, and aggressive behavior are symptoms of socio-emotional developmental impairments. Additionally, children may not know how to express ways of sharing their experiences or feelings

meaningfully with adults. Adults must offer strategies to help children construct these conversations.

TEACHERS

Early education teachers often feel unprepared to handle challenging behaviors effectively (Buscemi, Bennett, Thomas, & Deluca, 1995; Hemmeter et al.). It is for this reason that teachers need to understand how socio-emotional development impacts school settings (Aviles et al.). Additionally, teachers of adolescents must understand the behavioral manifestations of ways specific behaviors are presented and the connection to potential abuse. All teachers should be vigilant in their observations and realize that outbursts or other negative behaviors may be significantly connected to underlying home issues the child is potentially attempting to hide. Also prevalent and of significant concern is in disciplining the child by suspending the student from school. Researchers have indicated multiple ways that this form of discipline further exacerbated the child's difficulties in school, because this caused more missed assignments and other difficulties in negotiating multiple aspects of the school environment.

While the role of attachment begins between the parent and child, teachers play a central role in providing a secure relationship with children in a classroom environment. A child's future development and ability to operate within various social and physical environments depends significantly on attachment (Vaughn). Teachers should be aware of different behavior management programs that can be enlisted to initiate positive changes. The Teaching Pyramid is an example of a program that teachers can utilize to help students with difficulties. To learn more about other programs, teachers and paraprofessionals that work directly with troubled children "should be given professional development to gain knowledge of socio-emotional needs of children and tools for best recognizing these needs" (Aviles et al.). Teachers have a responsibility to understand the broad scope of services that schools provide in helping children to be successful in multiple ways. From this framework, teachers should develop a substantial understanding of critical roles within the school environment. These roles are often not provided within educational programs, and roles are often confused with titles.

COUNSELORS & PSYCHOLOGISTS

For example, while the role of the school counselor sounds like a true mental health role, often the school counselor's role varies in terms of practice, especially between elementary schools and secondary schools. For example, within the elementary school, counselors sometimes provide conflict resolution, administer character education classes, and provide administrative support for discipline issues. At the secondary level, school counselors typically provide services that have more to do with scheduling classes than in providing mental health support services. Although this role and the amount of time spent on tasks depends on how individual schools and school districts define these roles.

School psychologists also have a confusing role both at the elementary and secondary levels. While it seems that school psychologists have a direct responsibility in providing mental health type services, teachers should understand that school psychologists typically administer the bulk of special education testing in a given educational environment. The work of the school psychologist usually drives the special education department at a given school. The school psychologist might share a small portion of overlapping responsibilities with the school counselor, but many times the roles of these professionals are confusing, because they both sound more like they are heavily tied to mental health services. It is very important for teachers to understand multiple behavior modification strategies and interventions for socio-emotional developmental impairments. Teachers are encouraged to ask questions and seek answers in educational environments where they are hired. Teachers should also note that most times they will be expected to seek understanding rather than having all of the roles explained by the professionals engaging these roles.

ADMINISTRATORS

Administrators play a key role in providing support to the educational team, acting as a resource as needed and facilitating much of the behavior management programs in given schools. Within these constructs, administrators should understand the statistical aspects of behavioral issues in educational environments and serve as both a consultant and professional development leader for the educational team.

Another role that administrators play is in providing professional development trainers to teach teachers and other educational staff in ways that can help children with socio-emotional developmental impacts.

Issues

OVERCOMING BARRIERS TO SOCIO-EMOTIONAL DEVELOPMENT

Multiple barriers exist that hinder socio-emotional development. The first barrier is related to family systems structures. Secure attachment begins at home and is based on nurturing emotionally sensitive relationships between children and their caregivers. When these relationships lack a secure attachment, children have the potential for barriers to appropriate socio-emotional development. One way to overcome this potential barrier is for parents to attend parenting classes. Parenting classes are typically designed to ensure that parents have the knowledge and skills needed to provide the nurturing, positive care that promotes "healthy development" (Powell, Dunlap, & Fox, 2006).

Another significant barrier to promoting socio-emotional development is a shortage of school personnel directly funded to deliver mental health services and focus their efforts directly on the socio-emotional development of children. Much of these limitations are due to a lack of federal and state funds. Teacher education programs should more strongly emphasize the role of socio-emotional development and its part in producing healthy and resilient students (Avila et al.).

CONCLUSION

This article purposed to improve understanding of the importance of socio-emotional development and its relevance in school settings. Several elements of the socio-emotional developmental process were presented in order to provide a brief overview into the multiple aspects of socio-emotional developmental process. These aspects included the roles of attachment, family systems theory, resilience, and potential training for schools to utilize designed to help children develop socially and emotionally.

The main difficulty for educators in understanding children's socio-emotional development is in not understanding attachment barriers the child may have experienced earlier in life. These attachment barriers are predictors for academic and behavioral impairments in the classroom environment. Teachers are often the beneficiaries of problem behaviors, which were likely formed within the home environment. Another significant conclusion is in understanding that children having difficulties in school often have parents with similar difficulties. Some parents have a negative attitude regarding school. These assumptions then are projected onto their own children and impact the child's socio-emotional development and academic progress. Teachers need to be aware of these issues and approach parent relationships gently and positively.

TERMS & CONCEPTS

Attachment Theory: An organizational construct that integrates development in the domains of affect, cognition, and behavior during infancy and serves as a foundation for social and emotional development during infancy.

Family Systems Theory: Family systems are characterized by (a) wholeness and order, although this order could be dysfunctional; (b) hierarchical structures, and (c) adaptive self-organization. These structures operate within the framework of the family organization characterized by an open, living system, open to adaptation or challenges

Resilience: Resilience is characterized by the capacity to rebound from adversity, strengthened and more resourceful.

Socio-Emotional Development: Social emotional development can be viewed as the intertwined and interdependent foundational relationship that fosters healthy attachment, appropriate socialization in multiple environments, and success in school and other cultures.

Teaching Pyramid: The Teaching Pyramid is a model for promoting young children's social-emotional development while addressing challenging behavior and its link to critical outcomes for children, families, and other childhood programs.

Sharon Link

BIBLIOGRAPHY

Aviles, A. M., Anderson, T. R., Davila, E. R. (2006). Child and adolescent social-emotional development Within the Context of School. *Child & Adolescent Mental Health,* *11,* 32-39. Retrieved October 25, 2007, from EBSCO Online Database Academic Search Premier.

Barbarin, O. A. (2002). The view from research: Culture and ethnicity in social, emotional, and academic development. *The Kauffman Early Education Exchange, 1,* 45-61.

Barr, R. (2001). Research on the teaching of reading. In V. Richardson (Ed.), *Handbook of research on teaching* (4th Ed.). Washington DC: American Educational Research Association.

Benard, B. (1993). Fostering resiliency in kids. *Educational Leadership, 51,* 44-48. Retrieved October 25, 2007, from EBSCO Online Database Education Research Complete.

Buscemi, L., Bennett, T., Thomas, D., & Deluca, D. A. (1995). Head Start: Challenges and training needs. *Journal of Early Intervention, 20,* 1-13.

Cicchetti, D., & Rogosch, F. (2002). A developmental psychopathology perspective on adolescence. *Journal of Consulting and Clinical Psychology, 34,* 541-565.

Cox, M. J. & Paley, B., (2003). Understanding families as systems. *Current Directions in Psychological Science, 12,* 193-197. Retrieved October 25, 2007, from EBSCO Online Database Academic Search Premier.

Dumont, C., & Paquette, D. (2013). What about the child's tie to the father? A new insight into fathering, father–child attachment, children's socio-emotional development and the activation relationship theory. Early Child Development & Care, 183(3/4), 430-446. Retrieved on December 26, 2013, from EBSCO Online Database Education Research Complete.

Fox, L., Dunlap, G., & Cushing, L. (2002). Early intervention, positive behavior support, and transition to school. *Journal of Emotional and Behavior Disorders, 10,* 149-157. Retrieved October 25, 2007, from EBSCO Online Database Education Research Complete.

Fox, L., Dunlap, G., Hemmeter, M. L., Joseph, G., & Strain, P. (2003). The teaching pyramid: A model for supporting social competence and preventing challenging behavior in young children. *Young Children, 58,* 48-53. Retrieved October 25, 2007, from EBSCO Online Database Education Research Complete.

Heldring, M. (2004). Talking to the public about terrorism: Promoting health and resilience. *Families, Systems & Health, 22,* 67-71.

Hemmeter, M. L., Corso, R., Cheatham, G. (2006). *Issues in addressing challenging behaviors in young children: A national survey of early childhood educators.* Manuscript in preparation.

Hemmeter, M. L., Ostrosky, M., & Fox, L. (2006). Social and emotional foundations for early learning. *School Psychology Review, 35,* 583-601. Retrieved October 25, 2007, from EBSCO Online Database Academic Search Premier.

Hurd, N., Varner, F., & Rowley, S. (2013). Involved-vigilant parenting and socio-emotional well-being among black youth: The moderating influence of natural mentoring relationships. *Journal of Youth & Adolescence, 42*, 1583-1595. Retrieved on December 26, 2013, from EBSCO Online Database Education Research Complete.

Huth-Bocks, A.C., Levendosky, A. A., & Semel, M.A. (2001). The direct and indirect effects of domestic violence on young children's intellectual functioning. *Journal of Family Violence, 16*, 269-290.

Kaiser, B., & Raminsky, J. S. (2003). *Challenging behavior in young children: Understanding, preventing, and responding effectively.* Boston: Allyn & Bacon.

Kingston, D., Tough, S., & Whitfield, H. (2012). Prenatal and postpartum maternal psychological distress and infant development: A systematic review. *Child Psychiatry & Human Development, 43*, 683-714. Retrieved on December 26, 2013, from EBSCO Online Database Education Research Complete.

Lawry, J., Danko, C., & Strain, P. (1999). Examining the role of the classroom environment in the prevention of problem behaviors. In S. Sandall & M. Ostrosky. (Eds.), *Young exceptional children: Practical ideas for addressing challenging behaviors* (pp. 49-62). Longmont, CO: Sopris West; Denver, CO: Division for Early Childhood (DEC).

Mercer, J.(2006). The many stages of attachment. *Scholastic Parent & Child, 13*, 50 -51. Retrieved October 25, 2007, from EBSCO Online Database Academic Search Premier.

National Institute for Mental Health (NIMH) (2000). *A good beginning: Sending America's children to school with the social and emotional competence they need to succeed.* Bethesda, MD: The Child Mental Health Foundation and Agencies Network. (ERIC Document Reproduction Service No. ED445810). Retrieved December 14, 2007, from EBSCO Online Education Research Database.

Neilson, S. L., Olive, M. L., Donovan, A., & McEvoy, M. (1999). Challenging behaviors in your classroom? Don't react, teach instead. *Young Exceptional Children, 2*, 2-10.

O'Connell-Higgins, G. (1994). *Resilient adults: Overcoming a cruel past.* San Francisco: John Wiley & Sons.

Powell, D., Dunlap, G., Fox, L. (2006). Prevention and intervention for the challenging behaviors of toddlers and preschoolers. *Infants & Young Children: An Interdisciplinary Journal of Special Care Practices, 19*, 25-35. Retrieved October 25, 2007, from EBSCO Online Database Academic Search Premier.

Sainato, D. M., & Carta, J. J. (1992). Classroom influences on the development of social competence in young children with disabilities. In S. L. Odom, S. R. McConnell, & M. A. McEvoy (Eds.), *Social competence of young children with disabilities: Issues and strategies for intervention* (pp. 93 -109). Baltimore: Brookes.

Sandall, S., Schwartz, I., Joseph, G., Chou, H., Horn, E. M., Lieber, J., et al. (2002). *Building blocks for teaching preschoolers with special needs.* Baltimore: Brookes.

Squires, J. (2002). The importance of early identification of social and emotional difficulties in preschool children. Retrieved December 14, 2007, from University of Oregon, Center for International Rehabilitation, http://asq.uoregon.edu.

Stormont, M. (2002). Externalizing behavior problems in young children: Contributing factors and early intervention. *Psychology in the Schools, 39*, 127-138. Retrieved October 25, 2007, from EBSCO Online Database Education Research Complete.

Strain, P., & Hemmeter, M. L. (1999). Keys to being successful. In S. Sandall & M. Ostrosky (Eds.), *Young exceptional children: Practical ideas for addressing challenging behaviors* (pp. 17-28). Longmont, CO: Sopris West; Denver, CO; Division for Early Childhood (DEC).

Thompson, R., & Happold, C. (2002). The roots of school readiness in social and emotional development. *The Kauffman Early Education Exchange, 1*, 8-29.

Tusaie, K. & Dyer, J. (2004). Resilience: A historical review of the construct. *Holistic Nursing Practice, 18*, 3-10.

Vaughn, B. E. (2005). Discovering pattern in developing lives: Reflections on the Minnesota study of risk and adaptation from birth to adulthood. *Attachment & Human Development, 7*, 369-380. Retrieved October 25, 2007, from EBSCO Online Database Academic Search Premier.

Walsh, F. (1998). *Strengthening family resilience.* New York: The Guilford Press.

Suggested Reading

Bowlby, J. (1988). *A secure base: Parent-child attachment and healthy human development.* London: Perseus Book Group.

Cowan, C. P., & Cowan, P. A. (2000). *When partners become parents: The big life change for couples.* Mahwah, NJ: Erlbaum.

Galinsky, E. (2010). *Mind in the making: The seven essential life skills every child needs.* N.Y.: Harper Collins.

Karr-Morse, R. & Wiley, M. (2013). *Ghosts from the nursery: Tracing the roots of violence.* N.Y.: The Atlantic Monthly Press.

Lombardi, J. (2003). *Time to care: Redesigning childcare to promote education, support families, and build communities.* Philadelphia: Temple University Press.

Tabors, P. O. (1997). *One child, two languages: A guide for preschool educators of children learning English as a second language.* Newton, MA: Butterworth-Heinemann.

PYRAMID MODEL

The Pyramid Model for Supporting Social Emotional Competence in Infants and Young Children, commonly called the pyramid model, was created by the Center on Social Emotional Foundations of Early Learning, which is housed at Vanderbilt University. The purpose of the pyramid model is to provide a framework for early childhood educators, care providers, and parents of infants and young children, based on research and evidence based practices, so that they can support the development of the children in their care, especially those with developmental issues.

KEYWORDS: Inclusion; Intervention; Response to Intervention: Universal Promotion

OVERVIEW

The pyramid model is used because it provides a simple, graphical representation of the theoretical approach used by early childhood professionals to identify and meet the needs of the children in their care, particularly those with developmental delays or those who have been identified as being at risk for developmental delays. The pyramid has four layers. The bottom two layers fit within the category of universal promotion, meaning that they describe elements of care that are needed by all children with or at risk of developmental delay. The third layer is in the category of secondary promotion, and the fourth, topmost layer is in the category of tertiary promotion. As one moves up the pyramid, the elements described become more and more specific to the needs of children with more severe developmental issues. Part of the inspiration for the pyramid model was the public health model, which divides activities into promotion, prevention, and intervention (Snyder et al., 2013).

The bottom layer is the first part of the universal promotion category, and is meant to symbolize nurturing and responsive relationships. These are important for all young children, because when children are very young, the relationships they have to their parents, teachers, and caregivers form a kind of nest which shelters them and gives them a space in which they can grow and develop. When this space is not present or not reliable, then children may be reluctant to explore their world or develop new skills through discovery, because they will feel unsafe taking such risks.

The second layer, also included within universal promotion, represents the need for a supportive environment of high quality. This level of the pyramid serves as a reminder to parents and caregivers that young children need safe and predictable routines that provide adequate stimulation and opportunity for exploration, and it instructs early childhood educators as to the need for their classrooms to be inclusive and diverse, to be physically safe yet exciting places to discover, and for there to be a variety of activities that encourage children to engage with one another and with their learning environment (Reddy, 2011).

The third layer of the pyramid, which is also the category of secondary promotion, represents the fact that all children need time and modeling as they learn how to regulate and express their own emotions. Doing this requires that children begin to develop social skills to help them manage their interactions with other people, and these social skills are also advanced through practice and modeling. While all children need guidance from their teachers and caregivers to develop socially and emotionally, it is common at this stage for some children to need more intense assistance than others. As these children are identified, early childhood professionals can work with parents to develop strategies tailored to the individual needs of each child.

The fourth layer, or top of the pyramid, is the category of tertiary intervention. Children whose developmental needs have not been met by the lower levels of the pyramid will receive more intense combinations of skill development and problem solving training in an effort to resolve the issues that are preventing them from progressing further. This often involves the use of what is known as positive behavior support. A team of professionals work with the parents or caregivers to create a behavior support plan. The behavior support plan is designed to identify challenging behaviors and the stimuli that are triggering them, and to then provide alternative behaviors to replace the challenging ones, while also trying to avoid triggers (Hyson, 2014).

FURTHER INSIGHTS

The best way of making sure that an early childhood program's staff are properly performing the appropriate duties according to the pyramid model is to use one of two available assessment tools. Deciding which test to use in a particular early childhood setting depends upon the age of the children being assisted in the program (Cook, 2015). For children who are newborn up until the age of two, the appropriate test to use is called the Teaching Pyramid Infant Toddler Observation Scale. For children who are older than two but still young enough for preschool, the assessment that is proper to use is called the Teaching Pyramid Observation Tool.

These tests are administered by an observer periodically, and the observer indicates whether the early childhood education staff are performing the tasks specified in the pyramid model in the appropriate manner and with the necessary frequency. It is the responsibility of the facility's administration to make sure that these tests are performed at consistent intervals and that the results are then analyzed to determine if staff are performing adequately.

If areas needing improvement are identified, then the administration will usually arrange for additional staff training to address the skills that staff need to work on (Shavinina, 2013). This training should ideally be performed by experienced instructors, but in some cases, it can also be conducted by other teachers at the facility acting as mentors to the newer instructors.

The pyramid model demands the collection of a large amount of data, and it requires early childhood staff to study and analyze that data so they can determine whether or not the interventions being performed under the model are producing the results that they are intended to. This is necessary because the pyramid model is evidence based. Administrators at facilities using the pyramid model must be well versed in two classes of data: fidelity data and outcomes data. Fidelity data is used to determine whether the staff at the facility is adhering to the pyramid model (Snyder et al.), while outcomes data is used to determine whether the interventions specified under the pyramid model are producing tangible benefits for the children who are being cared for at the facility.

VIEWPOINTS

One of the most challenging aspects of implementing the pyramid model is having access to a well-trained, effective workforce to implement its recommendations. In fact, the availability of such a workforce is often included in illustrations of the pyramid model, as a foundation block upon which the pyramid rests. The reason that it is problematic to find an adequate workforce is that teaching, child care, and particularly the education and care of infants and very young children, remain some of the poorest paid professions in the entire economy.

Social scientists largely agree that this is due primarily to the fact that education and any field related to children are still considered to be "women's work," and compensation for women in almost every type of work still lags far behind the pay that men receive (Fox & Hemmeter, 2011). Becoming a qualified teacher of young children requires many years of education, with the most skilled early childhood specialists requiring at least one master's degree, yet early childhood educators can expect to earn tens of thousands of dollars less per year than people in other fields with the same number of years of preparation. Many of those who enter the profession have fewer qualifications and often have fewer expectations regarding the demands of the job. Thus, the first hurdle to be overcome when implementing the pyramid model is often that of bringing together and talented workforce (Gartrell, 2014).

Just as important as an engaged and well-trained workforce is having administrators at the early childhood facility who understand how important the pyramid model is and how crucial it is for them to perform their roles appropriately. If the administration is not on board with the pyramid model, then it is likely that the model will not be able to serve children and their families as effectively as it might. The act of making sure that an early childhood program's use of appropriate intervention modalities remains faithful to the ideals specified in the pyramid model is referred to in the literature of education as "intervention fidelity," because it requires the program personnel to not only understand what they should be doing but to also do it consistently.

Most early childhood professionals agree that the process of fully implementing the pyramid model at a site requires at least two years. This is because the

275

administrator of the site must train staff, establish policies that support the pyramid model and make sure these are written down and accessible. The administration must also work with parents to explain the pyramid model to them and to guide them as they learn what their role in the pyramid model will be; this can be especially challenging for families who are at risk or otherwise dealing with poverty, unemployment, addiction, or some combination of these challenges (Ostrosky, Sandall, & Council for Exceptional Children, 2013).

All of this work is made that much harder by staff turnover at the facility. Because of the relatively low pay received by early childhood educators, many staff do not stay long in one position, but transfer to other centers where they can earn more or have better prospects for advancing into an administrative role (Bredekamp, 2014). Each time this happens, the center administrator must go through a hiring process and hope to locate a replacement familiar with the pyramid model, then train that person and guide them until they are accustomed to their new role. This often becomes a continuous process, with a few new teachers always on board and learning to fit in, a few veteran teachers acting as their mentors and trainers, and a few "short timers" who are preparing to leave, either to retire or to work elsewhere (Hemmeter, Fox, & Snyder, 2013).

Terms & Concepts

Inclusion: Inclusion is an educational philosophy that emphasizes the importance of including children with disabilities, such as social and emotional control difficulties, in the regular classroom. Proponents of inclusion feel that having students of varying ability levels in the same group prevents those children with disabilities from feeling stigmatized, and helps the other children understand that differences in ability are normal.

Intervention: Within the context of education, an intervention is a response by a teacher or a school to an issue being experienced by a student. If a student is experiencing difficulty with reading, for example, the teacher might try to provide extra tutoring to that student, as a form of intervention. If the tutoring proved ineffective, then the teacher might explore additional interventions, such as having the child tested to determine if some type of learning disability is interfering with

the student's reading ability. A crucial component of interventions is that they must be measurable so that it can be determined whether they accomplished the purpose they were designed for.

Response to Intervention: Response to Intervention is an educational and developmental approach that tries to help students succeed regardless of their ability or disability, by conducting various forms of screening on all students in order to identify those with learning challenges that might require some form of outside assistance. Students so identified can then be approached with interventions designed to address their particular learning difficulties.

Universal Promotion: Universal promotion is an idea used to describe the bottom layer of the pyramid model. It refers to the fact that young children in early childhood settings and at home who are at risk for developmental delays all need certain basic elements of care to be in place, regardless of any variations in the children's developmental progress. Some of these elements include the presence of caregivers who can respond to the child's needs in a timely and caring way, encouraging children to explore and develop new skills, and a stable and consistent environment in which to develop.

Scott Zimmer, JD

Bibliography

Bredekamp, S. (2014). Effective practices in early childhood education: Building a foundation. Boston, MA: Pearson.

Cook, R. E. (2015). Adapting early childhood curricula for children with special needs + enhanced pearson etext... access card. S.l.: Prentice Hall.

Fox, L., & Hemmeter, M. L. (2011). Coaching early educators to implement effective practices: Using the pyramid model to promote social-emotional development. Zero to Three (J), 32(2), 18–24. Retrieved January 12, 2016, from EBSCO Online Database Education Research Complete.

Gartrell, D. (2014). Guidance approach for the encouraging classroom. Belmont: Wadsworth.

Hemmeter, M. L., Fox, L., & Snyder, P. (2013). Teaching pyramid observation tool (TPOT) for preschool classrooms manual. Baltimore, MD: Paul H. Brookes.

Hemmeter, M. L., Hardy, J. K., Schnitz, A. G., Adams, J. M., & Kinder, K. A. (2015). Effects of training and coaching with performance feedback on teachers' use of pyramid model practices. Topics in Early Childhood Special Education, 35(3), 144–156. Retrieved January 12, 2016, from EBSCO Online Database Education Research Complete.

Hyson, M. (2014). The early years matter: Education, care, and the well-being of children, birth to 8. New York, NY: Teachers College.

Ostrosky, M., Sandall, S. R., & Council for Exceptional Children. (2013). Addressing young children's challenging behaviors. Los Angeles, CA: Division for Early Childhood of the Council for Exceptional Children.

Reddy, L. A. (2011). Group play interventions for children: Strategies for teaching prosocial skills. Washington, DC: American Psychological Association.

Shavinina, L. V. (2013). The Routledge international handbook of innovation education. Abingdon, Oxon: Routledge.

Snyder, P. A., Hemmeter, M. L., Fox, L., Bishop, C. C., & Miller, M. D. (2013). Developing and gathering psychometric evidence for a fidelity instrument: The teaching pyramid observation tool—pilot version. Journal of Early Intervention, 35(2), 150–172. Retrieved January 12, 2016, from EBSCO Online Database Education Research Complete.

SUGGESTED READING

Artman-Meeker, K., Hemmeter, M. L., & Snyder, P. (2014). Effects of distance coaching on teachers' use of pyramid model practices. Infants & Young Children: An Interdisciplinary Journal of Early Childhood Intervention, 27(4), 325–344. Retrieved January 12, 2016, from EBSCO Online Database Education Research Complete.

Branson, D., & Demchak, M. (2011). Toddler teachers' use of teaching pyramid practices. Topics in Early Childhood Special Education, 30(4), 196–208. Retrieved January 12, 2016, from EBSCO Online Database Education Research Complete.

Fox, L., Carta, J., Strain, P. S., Dunlap, G., & Hemmeter, M. L. (2010). Response to intervention and the pyramid model. Infants & Young Children: An Interdisciplinary Journal of Early Childhood Intervention, 23(1), 3–13. Retrieved January 12, 2016, from EBSCO Online Database Education Research Complete.

Hurley, J. J., Saini, S., Warren, R. A., & Carberry, A. J. (2013). Use of the pyramid model for supporting preschool refugees. Early Child Development & Care, 183(1), 75–91. Retrieved January 12, 2016, from EBSCO Online Database Education Research Complete.

ADOLESCENT DEVELOPMENT

One of the most important factors of quality middle schools, according to experts, is responsiveness to the findings of developmental psychology regarding the emotional and intellectual development of students as they operate with peer groups. Current thinking about adolescent self-esteem, self-concept and identity formation stems from work such as that of Freud, Piaget, Erikson, and recently, Fitzgerald's description of adolescence as an existentialist crisis of varying proportions. Adolescence takes place within multiple contexts, and experts are agreed that adults who display authenticity in dealing with adolescents stand the best chance of guiding or mentoring them along the path to an intellectually, emotionally and physically healthy adulthood.

KEYWORDS: Adolescence; Authenticity; Concrete Operational Thinking; Developmental Psychology; Developmental Responsiveness; Ego; Existentialism; Formal Operational Thinking; Id; Identity Formation; Multiple Contexts; Peer Groups; Role Confusion; Self-Concept; Self-Esteem; Stages of Development; Superego

OVERVIEW

According to the National Forum to Accelerate Middle-Grades Reform, there are three main criteria for a quality middle school in the United States. The middle school must be:

- Academically excellent—they challenge all of their students to use their minds well;
- Developmentally responsive—they are sensitive to the unique developmental challenges of early adolescence and respectful of students' needs and interests;
- Socially equitable, democratic, and fair—they provide every student with high-quality teachers, resources, learning opportunities, and supports and make positive options available to all students (Lipsitz & West, 2006).

While the first and second criteria might seem like common sense, the second criterion—developmental responsiveness—is perhaps less obvious. The Forum defines *developmental responsiveness* in this context as a school that "provides access to comprehensive services that foster healthy physical,

social, emotional, and intellectual development...
and develops alliances with families to support the
well-being of students" (Lipsitz & West).

In order for middle schools and even high schools
to deliver on the promise of a higher quality education for all students, parents, teachers and administrators need to develop a better understanding of
adolescent development and its possible implications
for pedagogy.

ADOLESCENT DEVELOPMENT'S MANY INFLUENCES

Adolescent development takes place within many
contents, only one of which is school or the classroom. This "multiple contexts" view allows developmental psychologists, parents and educators to look
at adolescent development in the broadest possible
sense and help address the many different ways adolescents can be influenced. Youngblade and Theokas
(2006) offer insight as to how adolescents can be
guided in their behavior:

More broadly, working from the perspective of
developmental systems theory and contextual psychology, researchers theorize that behaviors arise
from the dynamic, bidirectional interaction between
a person and multiple levels of his or her ecology
(e.g., Bronfenbrenner & Morris, 2006; Lerner, 2006;
Magnusson & Stattin, 2006; Petraitis, Flay, & Miller,
1995). Youth will thrive when there is a goodness of
fit between individual developmental needs and contextual resources (Chess & Thomas, 1999; Lerner,
Dowling, & Anderson, 2003). In addition, researchers in the field of developmental psychopathology
suggest that multiple contextual factors influence
both competent and risky developmental trajectories (e.g., Cicchetti & Aber, 1998; Cummings, Davies,
& Campbell, 2000; Masten & Curtis, 2000; Sroufe,
1997) (Youngblade & Theokas).

Thinking about and characterizing adolescent
behavior goes back at least to the ancient Greeks.
Among the Greeks we hear echoes of sentiments that
would be repeated throughout history by those who
observe, parent or teach adolescents. Socrates (470
BC-399 BC), for example, said young people are
"inclined to contradict parents and tyrannize their
teachers," while Aristotle (384 BC-322 BC) wrote,
"youth are heated by Nature as drunken men by
wine" (cited in Dahl, n.d.).

Since the end of the 19th century, researchers have
learned much more about adolescent development

by applying scientific tools and methods, and pedagogues have been sought to apply those insights to
areas such as curriculum development, rewards and
punishments, and classroom management. This article offers a history of research on adolescent development, some key figures in the discussion and a
discussion of how it bears upon education.

G. STANLEY HALL: ADOLESCENCE AS A "NEW BIRTH"

In 1904, G. Stanley Hall (1844-1924) published
Adolescence, a seminal treatise on child psychology,
with an emphasis on adolescent biology—such as
was known in the days before DNA and brain scans.
Evoking biblical imagery, he described adolescence
as a "new birth" in which, following the metaphor,
the old child dies, only to be reborn as a new man or
woman. But as with any birthing process, the event is
not without its share of trauma, and certainly there
can be emotional complications that may persist to
adulthood.

Dahl and Hariri (2005) describe Hall's approach
to the study of adolescent development:

One overarching principle evident throughout Hall's work-and an issue of increasing salience
today-is the importance of a multidisciplinary framework for understanding adolescence. Hall drew from
many different areas of investigation and observation.
The title of his book, Adolescence, Its Psychology and
its Relations to Physiology, Anthropology, Sociology,
Sex, Crime, Religion, and Education, speaks to
this diverse range of interests. Hall sought to integrate understanding across multiple disciplines. He
focused attention on the role of physical growth,
the biologic changes of puberty, brain development,
genetic influences, sleep and biological rhythms,
physical health, social transitions, religious, educational, and cultural influences.

SIGMUND FREUD: ADOLESCENCE AS AN INNER STRUGGLE

Sigmund Freud (1856-1939) viewed adolescence
as a time of inner turmoil. It is during adolescence
that, after a time of pre-adolescence Freud called
the "latency" period, the superego (the conscience)
formed during childhood collides head on with
the id (a primitive drive for food, comfort, shelter)
that first manifested itself in infancy. Whereas the id
and the ego (the sense of self) gradually came into

balance within the child as he or she approached adolescence, the tug-of-war between the libertine id and the puritanical superego leads to inner stress and turmoil within the adolescent.

ERIK ERIKSON: ADOLESCENCE AS A SEARCH FOR SELF

While eschewing some of Freud's more overt sexualizing of the process of child development, Erik Erikson (1902-1994) accepted Freud's view that human development occurs in discrete psychosocial stages marked by social or cultural changes. However, Erikson viewed ages 12-18 as the stage characterized by the struggle for identity in the face of role confusion. The main objective of the adolescent, then, is to create a sense of self-identity by weeding through and then synthesizing all the information he or she had acquired during childhood. Well-adjusted adults are those who successfully worked through this integration process as adolescents (Fitzgerald, 2005).

JEAN PIAGET: ADOLESCENCE AS THE ENTRYWAY TO ABSTRACT REASONING

Jean Piaget (1896-1980) also accepted the idea of stages of development, but he held that the stages were marked by advances in the child's mode of thinking. Piaget understood adolescence as the period of time, beginning at age 12, when a child moves from Concrete Operational Thinking (where a child can think logically) to Formal Operational thinking (where a child reasons abstractly).

BILL FITZGERALD: ADOLESCENCE, ANGST & ENNUI

Most recently, Fitzgerald (2005) has shown that adolescent's quest for meaning has much in common with the existentialist philosophy popularized by Kierkegaard, Nietzsche and Sartre. He argues that all the core themes of existentialism—most importantly the idea that humans are left largely on their own to make their own sense (or non-sense) of the universe—are played out in the lives of adolescents for the first time, and their ramifications are perhaps felt the most keenly.

It is commonly agreed that adolescence is a time filled with conflicts. A number of these conflicts closely resemble existential issues. Among these are an increase in freedom, choice, responsibility, and awareness of isolation. In addition, there is a search for meaning which may result in increased anxiety and a sense of personal emptiness (Damon, Menon, & Bronk, 2003; Frankl, 1984; Fry, 1998; Hacker, 1994; Weems, Costa, Dehon, & Berman, 2004; Yalom, 1980) (Fitzgerald, 2005).

ADOLESCENT DEVELOPMENT TODAY

Summarizing current thinking on adolescent development, Youngblade and Theokas note that researchers are now taking a more positive view of adolescent development. As such, they are laying more emphasis on ways to enhance adolescent development, rather than looking at the ways in which healthy development can become sidetracked:

More recently, however, researchers and policy makers have begun to embrace the notion that optimal youth development owes not simply to a reduction in negative behavior but the growth of strengths and competencies that will prepare youth for the future. Healthy development embodies happiness and a sense of purpose and meaningful relationships that leads to youth being engaged and contributing to their families, schools, communities, and society (Youngblade & Theokas).

In Great Transitions: Preparing Adolescents for A New Century, a report of the Carnegie Council on Adolescent Development at the Carnegie Foundation of New York, parents, educators and all concerned about the health and welfare of adolescents are urged to band together to help adolescents make a successful transition to adulthood. According to the Council, adolescents growing up in today's Western world must:

- Master social skills, including the ability to manage conflict peacefully;
- Cultivate the inquiring and problem-solving habits of mind for lifelong learning;
- Acquire the technical and analytic capabilities to participate in a world-class economy;
- Become ethical persons;
- Learn the requirements of responsible citizenship;
- Respect diversity in our pluralistic society (Carnegie Council on Adolescent Development, 1995).

Adolescence is a pivotal time in a person's life when he or she experiences a perfect storm of biological, psychological and emotional waves that, once they recede, will have washed the young person onto the shores of adulthood.

Further Insights

ADOLESCENT BIOLOGY

The most obvious changes that take place in adolescence are biological. Both boys and girls travel through puberty, a time when each becomes sexually mature. Typically girls tend to mature a year and a half earlier than boys, which leads to what one might term a maturity gap—this gap shows itself most often in the behavior of middle school boys and how they relate to girls the same age. Researchers have found that boys who mature faster tend to reap benefits in athletics and the social status that success at sports brings. Girls who mature faster, on the other hand, are more likely to find themselves socially at odds with slower-maturing girls, and this can put the faster-maturing girls on a path to depression and eating disorders. Slower-maturing boys who are often less skilled at sports and other forms of physical activity sometimes face ridicule and other forms of social stigma from their peers (Wigfield, Lutz & Wagner, 2005).

Educators and school counselors should pay close attention to the changes that the onset of puberty bring into the lives of adolescents, and how boys and girls tend to view sexual maturity in quite opposite ways.

ADOLESCENT PSYCHOLOGY

One of the most noteworthy psychological changes in adolescents is that they move from what Piaget called Concrete Operational thinkers to Formal Operational, or abstract, thinkers. This involves more reflection on their actions and pondering of hypothetical situations. Paradoxically, the prefrontal cortex, the part of the brain responsible for higher mental functioning, matures during adolescence, yet it is also during adolescence that many boys and girls engage in risky behavior, such unprotected sex or the use of drugs or alcohol (Wigfield et al.).

While this paradox has yet to be resolved, neurobiologists using fMRI (functional magnetic resonance imaging) techniques have detected quite considerable synaptic rewiring, increased levels of neurotransmitters, and hormonal changes, which may be the cause of the mood swings that affect many young people. There is also evidence linking hormones to "puberty-specific increases in sensation seeking-with its relevance to a wide range of risk behaviors emerging in adolescence (Martin et al., 2002; Dahl, 2004)" (Dahl & Hariri).

The current state of research would seem to indicate that this group is beginning to be able to think through more complex life decisions and, through practice, to understand that their actions can have either positive or negative consequences. For teachers and anyone else working with adolescents, the task at hand is to help guide and mentor adolescents through the vagaries of ethical and moral decision-making, without in the process alienating them. What remains to be determined by science, perhaps, is why students with such rapidly maturing brain function, particularly in the prefontal cortex, nonetheless resort at times to a high level of irrational or even self-destructive behavior.

HOW ADOLESCENTS VIEW THEMSELVES

During adolescence, young people begin to step outside themselves and look at themselves as actors in life's grand drama. This development is summarized under three headings: self-concept, self-esteem and identity formation. According to Wigfield et al.,

- Self-concept is the individuals' beliefs about and evaluations of their characteristics, roles, abilities, and relationships;
- Self-esteem is the individual's sense of his or her overall worth or value as a person;
- Identity is a term broader than either self-concept or self-esteem, referring to individuals' general sense of themselves and their psychological reality that includes many different beliefs and attitudes about the self.

They explain,

Identity formation involves the successful negotiation of a variety of activities and relationships during adolescence, including school achievement, social relations with others, and development of career interests and choices, along with a great deal of exploration of different activities and roles (Harter, 1999) (Wigfield et al.).

Of interest to educators is the research finding that self-esteem is often at its lowest point for adolescents when they make the transition from elementary school to middle school, and then from middle school to high school. This suggests that careful efforts should be made to help adolescents ease this transition, thus helping them boost their self-esteem.

ADOLESCENT DISCONNECT FROM SCHOOL

Children entering adolescence tend to think less of their academic abilities than students in elementary school. This attitude, if left unchecked, can result in lower effort in school, on the principle that it makes little sense to try if failure is inevitable. As a result, students reaching adolescence tend to be less motivated to do well in school than they had been several years earlier. There are some students who continue to have a drive to succeed in school without any external motivators, but this group seems to be the exception.

For parents and educators witnessing such a disconnection in the adolescent, it becomes especially important to encourage the young person and remind him or her, using techniques such as those from cognitive behavioral therapy, that they are in charge of how well they do (or do not do) in school. Adolescents may also respond well to incentives for good academic performance—whether those incentives are tangible or intangible. Other adolescents do well in learning situations where some friendly competition is involved.

ADOLESCENTS & PEER RELATIONSHIPS

The transition from elementary school to middle school can be traumatic when the adolescent's circle of friends, constructed throughout his or her early school years, becomes split up in middle school. Further, as adolescents develop a more refined sense of self, they may feel that they've "outgrown" some of their previous friends and may seek access to different peer groups.

Contrary to conventional wisdom, say Wigfield et al., peer groups appear to be self-selected by adolescents to reinforce certain aspects of the adolescent's personality, or even a certain skill or interest that they feel best about:

Although pressure from peers to engage in misconduct does increase during adolescence, many researchers disagree with the simplistic view that peer groups mostly have a bad influence on adolescents (Brown, 2004). Brown reviewed studies showing that it is poor parenting that sometimes leads children to get in with a "bad" peer group, rather than the peer group pulling the child into difficulties (Wigfield et al.).

Both conventional wisdom and decades of research highlight the importance of peer groups in adolescent development. Those who have an interest in the education of adolescents will look at students involved in negative peer groups and seek to help them find alternative routes for validation.

One important area where adolescence shows its ugly side is bullying. Research indicates that bullying is most common at precisely this junction between childhood and adulthood that occurs in middle school—it is less prevalent in elementary and high school. While some children compensate for feelings of low self-esteem, anger and resentment by inflicting verbal and/or physical violence on their peers, others, particularly those who are perceived to be physically weak or "nerdy," are often the victims of bullies. In the wake of school shootings in the 1990s and 2000s, in which bullied students exacted revenge through mass murder, this area of adolescent psychology has become important to politicians, educators and parents.

As young people mature into adults, they come to question or reassess the lessons they learned from influential adults in their lives, especially their parents and teachers. As part of the entirely normal process of making the wisdom of the species their own, adolescents sometimes cross the line and question authority in an inappropriate manner. This inappropriate form of questioning may manifest itself in many different forms, such as disrupting the teacher's lesson with under-the-breath comments, asking irrelevant questions or displaying a lack of desire to study certain subjects.

Because they have to stand before a classroom of adolescents with varying degrees of respect for authority, teachers should work to establish their credibility by showing the relevance of the subject material to the lives of their students. Equally important is that the teacher show his or her care and concern for adolescents—what some have called authenticity.

TERMS & CONCEPTS

Adolescence: A period of time for a young person, beginning between ages 10-12, when he or she experiences profound biological, emotional and intellectual changes.

Authenticity: In the context o adolescence, a term used to describe genuine interest and affection shown by a teacher for his or her students.

Concrete Operational Thinking: A term coined by the Swiss psychologist Jean Piaget to describe the ability of a pre-adolescent to think logically.

Developmental Psychology: A field of psychology devoted to the study of human development and the application of its findings.

Developmental Responsiveness: A term used to describe the ability of school teachers and administrators to adjust their expectations of adolescents to take into account the best thinking on adolescent development.

Ego: A term coined by the psychologist Sigmund Freud to describe the child's sense of self.

Existentialism: A school of philosophy, as well as a more general philosophical stance, that stresses the need for the individual, acting alone, to make sense of his or her place in the cosmos.

Formal Operational Thinking: A term coined by the Swiss psychologist Jean Piaget to describe the ability of a adolescent to employ abstract reasoning.

Id: A term coined by the psychologist Sigmund Freud to describe the fundamental human desire for primitive drive for necessities of life such as food, comfort and shelter.

Identity Formation: The "individuals' general sense of themselves and their psychological reality that includes many different beliefs and attitudes about the self" (Wigfield, Lutz & Wagner, 2005)

Multiple Contexts: A term, within the context of adolescent psychology, that emphasizes the many influences—internal and external—that mold the mind of the adolescent.

Peer Groups: Associations of like-minded students who each validate the other's intellectual and/or emotional needs.

Role Confusion: As discussed by psychologist Erik Erikson, the adolescent's sense that he or she is no longer feels comfortable in the role of the child, yet is not prepared to take on the role of an adult.

Self-concept: The "individuals' beliefs about and evaluations of their characteristics, roles, abilities, and relationships".

Self-esteem: The "the individual's sense of his or her overall worth or value as a person".

Stages of Development: The view, popularized by Piaget, Freud, Erikson and others, that all human beings progress through discrete stages of emotional, intellectual and physical development on the journey from birth to death.

Superego: A term coined by the psychologist Sigmund Freud to describe the individual conscience.

Matt Donnelly

BIBLIOGRAPHY

Benko, S.L. (2012). Scaffolding: An ongoing process to support adolescent writing development. *Journal of Adolescent & Adult Literacy, 56,* 291-300. Retrieved December 15, 2013, from EBSCO Online Database Education Research Complete.

Carnegie Council on Adolescent Development, Carnegie Corporation of New York. (1995). Great transitions: Preparing adolescents for a new century. Washington, DC: Retrieved September 1, 2007, from http://carnegie.org.

Dahl, R. (n.d.). *Adolescent brain development: A framework for understanding unique vulnerabilities and opportunities.* Pittsburgh: University of Pittsburgh Medical Center. Retrieved December 1, 2007, from the Wisconsin Council on Children & Families, http://wccf.org.

Dahl, R., & A. Hariri (2005). Lessons from G. Stanley Hall: Connecting new research in biological sciences to the study of adolescent development. *Journal of Research on Adolescence (Blackwell Publishing Limited), 15,* 367-382. Retrieved December 1, 2007, from EBSCO online database Academic Search Premier.

Fitton, V., Ahmedani, B., Harold, R., & Shifflet, E. (2013). The role of technology on young adolescent development: Implications for policy, research and practice. *Child & Adolescent Social Work Journal, 30,* 399-413. Retrieved December 15, 2013, from EBSCO Online Database Education Research Complete.

Fitzgerald, B. (2005). An existential view of adolescent development. *Adolescence, 40,* 793-799. Retrieved December 1, 2007, from EBSCO online database Academic Search Premier.

Pinquart, M., & Silbereisen, R. (2005). Understanding social change in conducting research on adolescence. *Journal of Research on Adolescence (Blackwell Publishing Limited), 15,* 395-405. Retrieved December 1, 2007, from EBSCO online database Academic Search Premier.

Lipsitz, J. & West, T. (2006). What makes a good school? Identifying excellent middle schools. *Phi Delta Kappan, 88.* 57-66. Retrieved December 1, 2007, from EBSCO online database, Academic Search Premier.

Watson, S., & Gable, R. (2013). Cognitive development of adolescents at risk or with learning and/or emotional problems: Implications for teachers. *Intervention in School & Clinic, 49,* 108-112. Retrieved December 15, 2013, from EBSCO Online Database Education Research Complete.

Wigfield, A., Lutz, S. & Wagner, A. (2005). Early adolescent development across the middle school years: Implications for school counselors. *Professional School Counseling, 9,* 112-119. Retrieved December 1, 2007, from EBSCO online database Academic Search Premier.

Wiley, R.E., & Berman, S.L. (2013). Adolescent identity development and distress in a clinical sample. *Journal of Clinical Psychology, 69,* 1299-1304. Retrieved December 15, 2013, from EBSCO Online Database Education Research Complete.

Youngblade, L., & Theokas, C. (2006). The multiple contexts of youth development: Implications for theory, research, and practice. *Applied Developmental Science, 10,* 58-60. Retrieved December 1, 2007, from EBSCO online database Academic Search Premier.

SUGGESTED READING

Beal, C., Grable, L. & Robertson, A. (2001). *Curriculum integration: Adolescent development.* North Carolina State Humanities Extension/Publications, North Carolina State College of Education, North Carolina State University. Retrieved December 2, 2007, from North Carolina State University, http://ncsu.edu.

Child and adolescent development research and teacher education: Evidence-based pedagogy, policy, and practice – Summary of roundtable meetings: December 1-2, 2005 and March 20-21, 2006 (2007). Washington, DC: National Institute of Child Health and Human Development and the National Institutes of Health, U.S. Department of Health and Human Services, and the National Association for the Accreditation of Teacher Education. Retrieved November 30, 2007, from the *National Council for Accreditation of Teacher Education,* http://ncate.org.

Fredricks, J., & Eccles, J. (2006). Extracurricular involvement and adolescent adjustment: Impact of duration, number of activities, and breadth of participation. *Applied Developmental Science, 10,* 132-146. Retrieved December 1, 2007, from EBSCO online database Academic Search Premier.

Gilligan, C. (1987, May). Adolescent development reconsidered. *10th Annual Konopka Lecture.* University of Minnesota, Twin Cities. Retrieved December 1, 2007, from the University of Minnesota, Twin Cities, http://konopka.umn.edu.

Jackson, S. (2006). *Handbook of adolescent development.* New York and London: Psychology Press.

Meece, J., & Daniels, D. H. (2007). *Child and adolescent development for educators,* 3rd ed. New York: McGraw-Hill Humanities/Social Sciences/Languages.

Pipher, M. (1994). *Reviving Ophelia: Saving the selves of adolescent girls.* New York: G.P. Putnam's Sons.

Poirier, R., Colarusso, E., Bischoff, A. & Robertson, E. (2007). Exploring adolescent development through the use of popular non-fiction novels. *Teaching and Teacher Education 23,* pp. 1345-1349.

Rice, F. P., & Dolgin, K. D. (2007). *The adolescent: Development, relationships, and culture,* 12th ed. Boston: Allyn & Bacon.

The Teenage Brain: A work in progress (2007, November 29). NIH Publication No. 01-4929. Washington, DC: National Institute of Mental Health, National Institutes of Health. Retrieved November 30, 2007, from the National Institute of Mental Health, http://nimh.nih.gov.

ADDRESSING STUDENT SLEEP DEPRIVATION

Proper sleep is critical to healthy development and lifestyles. Inadequate sleep has been associated with problems ranging from poor academic performance and risk taking behavior, to increased risk of health problems such as obesity. While sleep is essential to all people of all ages, it is especially critical for children and adolescents. For this reason, parents, health officials, academics, and policy makers are invested in determining why some adolescents get too little sleep, the effects of sleep deprivation, and ways to encourage better sleep hygiene among adolescents. Solutions to these problems range from later school start times, lessening homework loads, and reducing student screen time.

KEYWORDS: Depression; Insomnia; Obesity; Sleep Deprivation; Somatic Health; Psychosocial Health; Sleep Hygiene; Short Sleep; Screen Time

OVERVIEW

Doctors and researchers have produced a large body of literature documenting the changes to sleep patterns that occur when children enter adolescence. These changes are often the result of later bedtimes as well as inadequate sleep once an adolescent goes to bed. Among the sleep hygiene problems that have been studied are insomnia and daytime sleepiness. Additionally, longer term studies have linked somatic and psychosocial health problems, low academic performance and risk taking behavior with not achieving enough sleep (Sochat, Cohen-Zion & Tzischinsky, 2013). These problems affect students during their school years and additionally produce a habit of poor sleep that can continue to affect students long after graduation.

Sleep deprivation can be understood in several different conditions. Insomnia describes the inability to fall asleep or stay asleep for the desired period of time. This can occur if a student is overly stressed and stays up all night worrying about an upcoming exam or family situation. Bright lights, an undesirable temperature, loud noises, or distracting entertainment media can also make it difficult for students to fall asleep when they desire to do so. Insomnia can also be caused by medical conditions such as asthma, which makes it difficult for the student to breathe well throughout the evening, and joint pain, which makes it difficult for students to comfortably lay in a bed (Ford, Cunningham, Giles & Croft, 2015). Insomnia has been linked to overall poor health, whereas adequate sleep is commonly associated with a positive health status.

Sleep deprivation is defined by the National Sleep Foundation as any time that an individual fails to get enough sleep, which for adolescents is between eight and ten hours each night. While some students can function well on less than the prescribed eight and ten hours each night, few students can function on less than six hours each night (Meldrum, 2014). A student who is consistently sleep deprived, has a limited ability to learn, listen, concentrate, and critically think. Sleep deprived students may even forget information that they have previously acquired. Additionally, sleep deprived students are more prone to poor health decisions such as eating too much or eating unhealthy foods. Sleep deprived students are also more likely to engage in risk taking behaviors, including the use of psychoactive substances such as nicotine and marijuana. Additionally, a connection has been made between sleep deprivation and driving while intoxicated.

The majority of adolescents experience fewer than nine hours of sleep on school nights and sleep for longer periods of time on the weekend. Although they may catch up on missed sleep over the weekend, doing so results in different bed and awakening times on the weekend and school nights. These changes result in a disruptive sleep cycle and an inadequate number of sleep hours, both of which can have dramatic effects on their physical and mental health (Noland, Price, Dake & Telljohann, 2009). Because of their disruptive sleep schedules, students may be extremely tired, moody, lacking motivation, and have difficulty concentrating when school begins again on Monday morning.

FURTHER INSIGHTS

Studies have linked adolescent sleep deprivation to many factors including stress, sleep apnea, caffeine consumption, alcohol consumption, exercise, afterschool jobs, homework, sports, poor time management, and school start times. While there are a variety of causes, many are directly linked to activities that result in students going to bed later and waking earlier than medically desirable.

Among the most immediate effects of student sleep deprivation are poor school attendance, late arrival at school, sleeping in class, low alertness, poor concentration, and poor grades. For example, one study proved that students earning a C or below tended to go to bed significantly later and received an average of three fewer hours of sleep per week than those earning B's or higher (Sochat et al.). Students who have not slept enough are also prone to anger, impulsivity, and depression. While teachers and administrators must address these effects, researchers and policy makers stress the need to also address the long-term, underlying reasons why students are sleep deprived.

Many schools have chosen to follow the example of Minneapolis Public Schools and adapt their starting times to accommodate adolescent sleep schedules. Other schools have chosen to address other issues such as too much homework, afterschool activities, and student stress. All of these changes are driven by the debilitating effects of sleep deprivation among students.

One commonly proposed reason for student sleep deprivation is that their schools begin too early. The common solution to this cause is changing the start time and academic work load for middle and high school students. It is argued that because adolescents commonly go to bed after 11:00 p.m., it is impossible for them to achieve six, let alone eight hours of sleep each night if their school day begins at 7:30 a.m.. While some students choose to stay up late, many are required to stay up later than desired to complete large amounts of homework. Minnesota Public Schools changed their start time to 8:40 a.m. resulting in marked improvements in student performance (Noland et al.). Yet, the National Sleep Foundation suggests that high schools not begin before 9:00 a.m. to ensure that students are learning at the time in which they are most likely to be awake and engaged in the classroom. At least seventy public school districts in the United States have changed their start times in accordance with these recommendations (Owens, Drobnich, Baylor & Lewin, 2014). An additional number of schools have made small changes to their start times, or maintained traditional start times of 9:00 a.m. for elementary, middle, and high schools.

VIEWPOINTS

Beyond changing school start times, it is recommended that students learn the fundamentals of healthy sleep. This education can occur in biology, health, and social studies classes in lessons that address questions of quality sleep and the effects of sleep on humans to encourage students to both understand and practice quality sleep hygiene. For students who are experiencing sleep difficulty, especially gifted students, it is suggested that teachers and parents teach meditation or relaxation techniques that will allow students to unwind at the end of the day and address fears before bed (Lamont, 2012). Students are then able to go to bed and go to sleep at a desirable time.

REDUCING SCREEN TIME

A second large cause of adolescent sleep deprivation is the use of "screens" such as television, computer, and cell phones. The suggestion is that by limiting "screen time" before bed, students will be able to achieve sleep faster and maintain better sleep hygiene (Sochat et al.). A National Sleep Foundation survey found that 95 percent of Americans use technology within the last hour before they go to sleep. While adolescents might intend to use a screen for only a short time and then go to sleep, they often lose track of time and stay up much later than intended. Having a television in the bedroom, or access to a cell phone while in bed has a significant effect on student inability to go to sleep at the desired time (Wethington, Pan & Sherry, 2013). In addition to losing track of time, blue light emitted by a television, computer, and cell phone screens decreases the production of melatonin that is necessary for a healthy sleep cycle. This means that even after a student goes to sleep, they may not have a full sleep cycle and therefore wake up groggy and/or moody. The solution to these problems is relatively simple, students should be taught to not use screens before bed and should never take their screens, such as cell phones, to bed with them.

All of the solutions to student sleep deprivation aim at establishing a habit of healthy "sleep hygiene," which is defined as a combination of regular bedtimes, limited napping during the day, and restricted access to caffeine, nicotine, and alcohol. Additionally, healthy sleep hygiene requires a favorable sleep environment that is free from disruptions and distractions, such as watching television, eating, working on schoolwork, or using screens such as laptops and cell phones. These habits, if established while students are in school, will set a foundation for lifelong healthy sleep.

HEALTH RISKS

Students lacking healthy sleep hygiene are at risk for academic failings as well as serious and long-term effects on student health, including increased risk of obesity, depression, and the establishment of unhealthy risk-taking habits and behaviors. Long-term effects of student sleep deprivation include high risk of obesity. One study followed 800 children from 3rd to 6th grade and showed that sleep deprivation significantly increased the risk of obesity. In this study, each additional hour of sleep decreased the chance of obesity by 40 percent. (Sochat et al.) These risks occur because inadequate sleep commonly results in greater calorie intake. Students desire more calories because they are missing leptin, a hormone produced when sleeping and critical to reducing hunger and cravings for sweets, starches, and salty snacks (Noland et al.).

Additionally, sleep deprivation causes lower energy levels, resulting in decreased interest in exercise and lower calorie expenditures when exercising. Childhood obesity has received significant attention from public health officials and policy makers. For example, Michelle Obama's Lets Move! campaign encourages children and adolescents to get more exercise and therefore decrease obesity. Improved sleep hygiene is critical to the success of these programs so that students are awake and energetic when they participate in exercise programs.

MOOD DISORDERS

Beyond obesity, sleep deprivation may result in mental and/or emotional dysfunctions including depression and low self-esteem. Both inability to sleep and oversleeping are signs of clinical depression. While sleep deprivation does not directly cause depression, getting too little sleep can make depression worse. The relationship between sleep and depression is explained by the role of sleep as a tool to release tension and restore a strong mental state of mind. Without enough sleep, students are prone to fatigue, moodiness, and depression.

RISK BEHAVIORS

Even among students who are not depressed, a lack of sleep has been linked to the inability or decreased ability to control emotions, including anger, sadness, and fear. Additionally, researchers indicate that there is a direct link between insomnia and risk taking behaviors such as smoking, delinquency, driving when sleep deprived, and/or drinking and driving (Catrett & Gaultney, 2009). It might seem easy to prevent some of these problems by simply prohibiting students from driving at night when they are at the greatest risk of being sleep deprived. However, many students drive because they are participating in after-school sports, clubs, or employment. For many students, driving is not a choice, but a necessity to complete all of their required and desired activities.

AFTERSCHOOL WORK LOADS

Even if they do not drive at night, participating in afterschool activities and employment has a significant effect on sleep duration. Researchers focusing on Quebec high school students have recommended that educators specifically focus on the ways that afterschool work is affecting students, with special emphasis on girls who are combining work and study (Laberge, Ledoux, Aucliar & Gaudreault, 2014). While both boys and girls may be engaged in afterschool work, girls are more likely to be expected to also do chores at home. Some of these girls may become so sleep-deprived that they will begin to fall behind in one or all of their activities. While many towns and cities regulate the times that students may work, they do not have the power to regulate housework and chores, resulting in an unknown but suspected effect on student sleep.

In addition to work, chores, and homework, educators need to pay attention to the hours when sporting events, practices, and clubs end in the evening to ensure that students, especially those driving, have the opportunity to drive home safely. If the school day begins at 7:30 a.m., this means that school activities must conclude by 7:30 p.m. to ensure that students have twelve hours to eat, sleep, and complete homework before returning to school again the next day. These changes might have a significant effect on the culture of afterschool sports, artistic events such as plays or musicals, and tutoring for standardized tests. However, not changing student work load and school start times may have long-term effect on student sleep hygiene and health.

TERMS & CONCEPTS

Depression: Feeling sad, hopeless, or unimportant. Depression has effects on student feelings, critical thinking skills, and behavior and can lead to emotional and/or physical problems.

Insomnia: A sleep disorder that causes difficulty falling asleep or staying asleep. Insomnia can be caused by stress, illness, a poor sleep environment, medication or travel.

Obesity: Weight that is higher than desirable for the student's height and age, characterized by the excessive storage of fat on the body.

Sleep Deprivation: When an individual achieves less than the medically recommended amount of sleep. For adolescents this is between eight and ten hours each night

Somatic Health: Physical health, referring to the body.

Psychosocial Health: Mental, emotional, social, and spiritual health, all of which are necessary to a strong mental state.

Sleep Hygiene: Practice of achieving and maintaining quality nighttime sleep and daytime awakening on a regular basis.

Short Sleep: Sleeping for less than six hours each night. For "natural short sleepers" this is enough to maintain quality sleep hygiene, but for many students this is a sign of sleep deprivation.

Screen Time: Time spent using or occupied by a computer, television, or cellular phone. The American Association of Pediatrics recommends that children and teenagers should not use electronic media for entertainment for more than two hours each day.

Sleep Environment: The place where a student sleeps, when assessing a sleep environment it is necessary to pay attention to external stimuli such as loud noises, strong smells, uncomfortable temperatures, bright lights, and uncomfortable beds.

Allison Hahn, PhD

BIBLIOGRAPHY

Auclair, J., Gaudreault, M., Laberge, L., & Ledoux, É. (2014). Determinants of sleep duration among high school students in part-time employment. Mind, Brain & Education, 8(4), 220–226. Retrieved January 12, 2016, from EBSCO Online Database Education Research Complete.

Catrett, C. D., & Gaultney, J. F. (2009). Possible insomnia predicts some risky behaviors among adolescents when controlling for depressive symptoms. Journal of Genetic Psychology, 170(4), 287–309. Retrieved December 30, 2015, from EBSCO Academic Search Complete with Full Text.

Ford, E. S., Cunningham, T. J., Giles, W. H., & Croft, J. B. (2015). Trends in insomnia and excessive daytime sleepiness among US adults from 2002 to 2012. Sleep Medicine, 16(3), 372–378. Retrieved January 3, 2016, from EBSCO Academic Search Complete with Full Text.

Laberge, L., Ledoux, É., Auclair, J., & Gaudreault, M. (2014). Determinants of sleep duration among high school students in part-time employment. Mind, Brain, and Education, 8(4), 220–226. Retrieved December 30, 2015, from EBSCO Academic Search Complete with Full Text.

Lamont, R. T. (2012). The fears and anxieties of gifted learners: Tips for parents and educators. Gifted Child Today, 35(4), 271–276. Retrieved December 30, 2015, from EBSCO Academic Search Complete with Full Text.

Meldrum, R. C., & Restivo, E. (2014). The behavioral and health consequences of sleep deprivation in high school students: Relative deprivation matters. Preventative Medicine, 6(3), 24–28. Retrieved December 30, 2015, from EBSCO Academic Search Complete with Full Text.

Noland, H., Price, J. H., Dake, J., & Telljohann, S. K. (2009). Adolescents' sleep behaviors and perceptions of sleep. Journal of School Health, 79(5), 224–230. Retrieved January 12, 2016, from EBSCO Online Database Education Research Complete.

Owens, J., Drobnich, D., Baylor, A., & Lewin, D. (2014). School start time change: An in-depth examination of school districts in the United States. Mind, Brain, and Education, 8(4), 182–213. Retrieved December 30, 2015, from EBSCO Academic Search Complete with Full Text.

Shochat, T., Cohen-Zion, M., & Tzischinsky, O. (2014). Functional consequences of inadequate sleep in adolescents: A systematic review. Sleep Medicine Reviews, 18, 75–87.

Wells, P., & Baggish, R. (2013). For students, yes—sleep is mission critical. Independent School, 72(2), 5. Retrieved January 12, 2016, from EBSCO Online Database Education Research Complete.

Wethington, H., Pan, L., & Sherry, B. (2013). The association of screen time, television in the bedroom, and obesity among school-aged youth: 2007 National Survey of Children's Health. Journal of School Health, 83(8), 573–581. Retrieved December 30, 2015, from EBSCO Academic Search Complete with Full Text.

SUGGESTED READING

Fite, P. J., Becker, S. P., Rubens, S. L., & Cheatham-Johnson, R. (2015). Anxiety symptoms account for the link between reactive aggression and sleep problems among Latino adolescents. Child & Youth Care Forum, 44(3), 343–354. Retrieved December 30, 2015, from EBSCO Academic Search Complete with Full Text.

Keller, P. S., Smith, O. A., Gilbert, L. R., Bi, S., Haak, E. A., & Buckhalt, J. A. (2015). Earlier school start times as a risk factor for poor school performance: An examination of public elementary schools in the commonwealth of Kentucky. Journal of Educational Psychology, 107(1), 236–245. Retrieved December 30, 2015, from EBSCO Academic Search Complete with Full Text.

Vigo, D. E., Simonelli, G., Tuñón, I., Pérez Chada, D., Cardinali, D. P., & Golombek, D. (2014). School characteristics, child work, and other daily activities as sleep deficit predictors in adolescents from households with unsatisfied basic needs. Mind, Brain, and Education, 8(4), 175–181. Retrieved December 30, 2015, from EBSCO Academic Search Complete with Full Text.

DEVELOPMENTAL PSYCHOLOGY

The roots of developmental psychology stem from the early part of the 20th Century in the seminal work of B.F. Skinner, Jean Piaget, and Erik Erikson, who promulgated theories of behaviorism, constructivism, and psychosocial development, respectively. The latter half of the century saw the rise of constructivism, which compares learning and brain function to the inner workings of computers. The most recent develop-ments in learning theory are multiple intelligences, a theory that attempts to explain the ways in which different individuals learn; and neurophilosophy, which tries to unite neuroscience and previously held theories on learning and brain function.

KEYWORDS: Behaviorism; Cognitive Science; Computationalism; Constructivism; Developmental

Psychology; Learning Theory; Multiple Intelligences; Neurophilosophy; Neuroscience; Psychosocial Development; Social-Pragmatic Theory

OVERVIEW

Developmental psychology is the branch of psychology that studies the intellectual, social and emotional development of preschool and school-aged children. During the earliest years of life, the human brain sees explosive growth and development. Scientists estimate that during this time, a baby's brain consumes 60 % of the body's total energy, compared with an adult brain that on average uses only between 20% and 25% (Brunton, 2007). Research has shown that memory begins not long after birth and matures significantly by the age of six. The development of sight, hearing, and other senses reaches its peak at three months, and at four months babies start distinguishing between the faces of loved ones and strangers ("Inside a Baby's Brain," 2005).

Much has been learned in recent years about brain development during this stage. Babies, it seems, are much more aware of and influenced by their surroundings than was once thought. And the mechanical ways in which the brain processes information—along with how the mind learns—can have a tremendous bearing on a child's intellectual, emotional, and social outcomes. Undoubtedly, understanding brain function and learning can only help adults teach children better. The purpose of this article is to explore the evolution of learning theory and of cognitive science (as an extension of learning theory) since the beginning of the 20th Century. It defines constructivism, behaviorism, psychosocial development and multiple intelligences simply as learning theories, whereas computationalism is (in addition to being a learning theory) an offshoot of cognitive science, as it also examines the inner workings of the brain.

BEHAVIORISM

The roots of behaviorism can be traced back to the beginning of the 20th Century and the close of the Industrial Revolution. Behaviorism was a widely held learning theory for more than a half century, until cognitive science emerged after 1950 (Bush, 2006). While behaviorism concerns itself mainly with changes in an organism's outward behavior as a result of learning, cognitive science tries to "look under the hood" to understand what occurs in the brain during the learning process.

A Harvard-trained psychologist, Burrhus Frederic (B.F.) Skinner (1904-1990) is the figure most associated with behaviorism (Bush). By experimenting with pigeons, Skinner developed his theories on "operant conditioning." Operant conditioning differed from Ivan Pavlov's work in "classical conditioning," which showed that an existing behavior can be changed by associating it with a new stimulus. Studies done by Skinner revealed that through operant conditioning, a desired behavior can be reached by rewarding partial steps toward that behavior (WGBH, 1998). For example, Skinner got pigeons to turn a complete circle in a chosen direction by giving them food rewards every time they turned even partially in that direction. In time, the birds associated the rewards with turning that way and learned to turn completely around before receiving any reward. Skinner extrapolated that humans could be taught complicated tasks in this way. Many computer programs today that enable people to teach themselves use Skinner's reward-for-desired-behavior models (WGBH).

Unlike most learning theorists who would emerge later, Skinner was uninterested in the psyche and the inner workings of the brain. He was a strict behaviorist: He concerned himself only with how behavior is shaped from without (WGBH). It was because of this rigidity that he would find his ideas supplanted by new ones. The years following 1950 saw the gradual emergence of cognitive science, which was born of a growing frustration over behaviorism, which concerned itself only with observable phenomena. An increasing amount of research was being done on language and on how the brain processes information (Bush).

CONSTRUCTIVISM

It is widely believed that the single greatest contributor to 20th century learning theory was Jean Piaget. A Swiss psychologist born in 1896, Piaget began experimenting on his own children in the 1920s. His studies eventually led him to believe that babies less than nine months old have no comprehension of how the world around them functions. Piaget is best known for his "constructivist" theories, which maintain that children must construct concepts of how the world around them works from experience. He discovered, for example, that nine-month-olds cannot grasp "object permanence," the idea that objects and people continue to exist when they are not in view. It is only through accumulated experience that babies come to understand that things and people continue to exist, even when they leave the room (Brunton).

Piaget broke the mind's inner learning processes into four components: schemata, assimilation, accommodation, and equilibrium. Schemata are cognitive processes and thought structures used by a child's brain to conceptualize and categorize incoming stimuli, enabling him either to generalize about or make distinctions between particular events. At first, a child tries to assimilate new stimuli into existing schemata. Assimilation is the cognitive process by which a child integrates new stimuli into present schemata, which may expand as a result (Clark, 2005).

When entering stimuli do not match pre-existing concepts, disequilibrium occurs. The mind then tries to accommodate the stimuli and return to equilibrium (Harlow, 2006). Accommodation is when a child's existing schemata change as a result of the assimilation of new stimuli, either by being modified or further developed. When stimuli do not match any existing schemata, new concepts and cognitive processes are invented to assimilate similar stimuli in the future (Clark). This is the manner in which the environment enters through all of the five senses and is reconstructed as knowledge in the brain, or, as Piaget himself said, "For me, it's quite the contrary of a copy of the world: it's a reconstitution of reality by the concepts of the subject who, progressively and with all kinds of experimental probes, approaches the object without ever attaining it in itself" (cited in Harlow).

Piaget asserted that children pass through four major cognitive developmental stages:

- Sensorimotor: occurs between infancy and 2 years of age. Children acquire knowledge that leads to grasping object permanence and to goal-directed behaviors;
- Preoperational: children, ages 2 to 7 years, show an increasing ability to represent objects in their world using symbols—such as words and numbers—images, and gestures;
- Concrete operational: between 7 and 11, children learn to put objects in logical order—by size, shape, color—and show beginning mastery of not only measurement, but also of time and quantity. During the concrete operational phase, children also use other mental operations, such as object

classification and conservation (the understanding that a thing remains essentially the same, even when small changes are made to its appearance or form);
- Formal operational: after age 11, children enter an open-ended phase, during which they begin using logic and abstract thinking and can form new knowledge using information already known. The mind in this stage learns to contemplate what is possible, instead of staying fixed on what already exists (Meece & Defrates-Densch, 2002).

Piaget's findings and conclusions were widely embraced for decades, but since the 1980s critics have begun to doubt some of his theories. They question whether constructivism really explains how children learn and how their minds develop. Some are confused by the term "schemata" and how it relates to what is actually going on in the physical brain.

Some question Piaget's research methods and whether his four stages of cognitive development can be applied universally. Others are skeptical about equilibration and whether it really explains how the mind develops. Still, Piaget's work has largely stood the test of time, as it reveals a great deal about how children of different ages think (Meece & Defrates-Densch).

Constructivist theories would dominate education and psychology until the mid-1980s, when they began to be supplanted by new ideas. Research done by psychologists and scientists produced new information leading to the belief that infants are born already possessing knowledge of their world. These "nativist" theories also maintain that babies arrive with basic tools for learning language and arithmetic (Brunton).

PSYCHOSOCIAL DEVELOPMENT

Erik Erikson was born in Frankfurt, Germany, in 1902. His mother was Danish, and he never knew his biological father. Erikson was cared for lovingly by his mother and a stepfather, but the desire to know more about his real father never left him. It is possible that it was this gap in his own childhood memories that drove Erikson to study children and author his theories of "psychosocial development" ("Erik Erikson," 2001). Though Erikson would never find his real father, the search helped him become a key figure in the study of developmental psychology.

In the early 1920s, Erikson enrolled at the Vienna Psychoanalytic Institute where he studied Sigmund

Freud's theories on human behavior. Eventually he would break from Freud, believing not that biological instinct drives humans (a Freudian tenet), but that social interaction drives us ("Erik Erikson"). In 1933, Erikson immigrated to America and joined the faculty of Harvard Medical School. While also working as a private practitioner of child psychoanalysis, he began developing his own theories. Humans endure eight stages of development, he believed, the first of these occurring during childhood. During each stage, we must resolve a set of inner conflicts arising from demands placed on us as children by our parents and by society. As these conflicts are resolved (or left unresolved), we go to the next stage ("Erik Erikson").

- Stage one, "trust versus mistrust:" by the time children are one year old, they must learn to trust their environments. When parents and caregivers are loving and nurturing, children learn this trust and feel safe and accepted;
- Stage two, "autonomy versus shame and doubt:" between the ages of 18 months and three years, children want to test their independence and explore the world. When adults fail to indulge this desire—while continuing to meet needs for love and nurturing—they can instead instill feelings of doubt and shame;
- Stage three, "initiative versus guilt:" from ages 3 to 6 years, children have achieved considerable language mastery and are overflowing with questions, anxious to acquire new skills and eager to socialize with other children and resolve inner conflicts, especially through play. They depend on adults for feelings of safety and acceptance. If this desire to communicate and connect with the world around them is ignored or overlooked, children can act out aggression by lashing out physically or verbally.

If conflicts from these first three phases are not met and resolved during childhood, they can—as can challenges from later stages—recur in later life and hamper the individual's development ("Erik Erikson").

APPLICATIONS

This section discusses theories that have risen in the last 20 years. Though behaviorism, constructivism, and psychosocial development, still influence the fields of psychology and education, the

following theories are more the center of current study. Multiple intelligences theory is a learning theory that proposes new and unique ideas as to how the human mind solves problems. Connectionism and neurophilosophy draw parallels between brain function and how computers process information and try to close the schism that has long existed between past philosophies of learning and brain function, and neuroscience.

MULTIPLE INTELLIGENCES

In 1983, cognitive psychologist Howard Gardner introduced his theory of multiple intelligences (Wehrheim, 2006). Gardner believes that intelligence tests are too limited in scope to assess human intelligence for three reasons: One, they engage a range of cognitive abilities that is too narrow. Two, they require individuals to express answers to problems in notation or language. Three, human problem solving really occurs, not in one area of general intelligence, but within a number of different areas, or intelligences (Kornhaber, 1999).

Most tasks, jobs and careers draw on more than one of the eight intelligences. Likewise, different people carry strengths and weaknesses in each of the eight categories in different combinations (Moran, Kornhaber, & Gardner, 2006). So, teachers might teach more effectively if they take into account the different learning styles and intelligences of different children and crafted lessons with these things in mind. The eight intelligences are: bodily kinesthetic, interpersonal, intrapersonal, linguistic, logical-mathematical, musical, naturalist, and spatial (Kornhaber).

Bodily-Kinesthetic: Able to coordinate physical movement; expressive with body, athletic.

Interpersonal: Understands and interfaces well with others, could excel in sales or politics.

Intrapersonal: Skilled in understanding one's own nature (feelings, thoughts, desires.); could go into business for oneself or write with a preference for autobiographical, experiential subjects.

Linguistic: Understands spoken and written language well; articulate, poetic.

Logical-Mathematical: Grasps numerical symbols and mathematical functions and logic.

Musical: Grasps musical concepts such as melody, harmony, rhythm; may be gifted in composing music.

Naturalistic: Gifted in identifying and categorizing creatures and things found in nature.

Spatial: Skilled in manipulating three-dimensional space; perhaps suited to being an architect. (Moran, Kornhaber, & Gardner, 2006)

To this list Gardner adds a ninth "half-intelligence," one that is important to human reasoning, but does not meet all of his criteria for being an intelligence. (Wehrheim) "Existential intelligence" is used to contemplate concepts and questions that may lie beyond human understanding, such as philosophical issues regarding the existence of God and the meaning of life (Moran et al.).

Gardner's theory is thought-provoking and, if applied correctly, could make teaching much more effective and learning much easier for challenged and gifted children alike. As innovative as it is, his work stands on the shoulders of theories dating back to the turn of the 20th century, when behavior offered the only clues to how children learn. Today, the field of developmental psychology draws from the rich and diverse theories of scientists who have analyzed not only human behavior—but also computers and cognitive science—to link learning to the inner workings of the brain.

Teachers who understand their students' strengths within these intelligences are in a position to tailor their teaching to them and understand why these students struggle with certain teaching approaches. For example, to help pupils who are strong in the area of linguistic intelligence, teachers need to use language to which they can relate and is clear and understandable. Students with musical intelligence are often found to have this intelligence at an early age and should be nurtured with classes in music analysis. Those possessing mathematical-logical intelligence begin by ordering objects, such as marbles. In time, they are able to do computations in their heads and eventually excel in following long chains of deduction and reasoning. These pupils can become model students, as they are able to follow the logic and sequencing of lesson plans in most subjects, and should be nurtured and encouraged in math and math-related subjects (Nolen, 2003).

According to Nolen, teachers can reinforce the strengths of children with spatial intelligence by teaching them using pictures, diagrams, overheads, films and photographs, as well as asking them to draw their ideas. Activities like chess—that use a spatial, strategic logic—appeal to these students. Bodily-kinesthetic pupils are very skilled with their hands and are able to manipulate objects and perform precise movements. Such students—who can become surgeons, sculptors, athletes, dancers—are able to express different emotions through movement. Teaching of these children can be done through physical movement, the use of manipulatives, and by getting them to use their hands in some way.

Individuals possessing interpersonal intelligence frequently become politicians, religious figures, teachers, therapists or counselors. Activities in which children work together draw on their natural abilities. Children with intrapersonal intelligence need to be praised a lot in class and thrive on activities that call upon their imaginations. Long-term projects that develop in stages and progress with teacher approval are good, as they call upon these students to conceptualize ideas and then execute them, step by step. Students with naturalistic intelligence are adept at sorting and classifying plants, animals, insects. These students thrive when taught in an outdoor environment or when given activities that entail observing nature, collecting plant and insect specimens, or monitoring environmental changes. In planning effective lessons, teachers should try to accommodate all of the different styles to reach all of the learning styles within a single classroom (Nolen).

NEUROSCIENCE

Neuroscience, or "brain science," draws from neurology, psychology, physiology and other disciplines. Among the contributions made by neuroscience are brain imaging techniques that allow scientists to observe the brain as it performs different cognitive functions. Brain imaging, or "neuroimaging" has enabled scientists to study brain as it performs speech, reading, math, and language functioning. And it has made it possible for scientists to study how drugs—such as Ritalin—can enhance cognitive and academic performance (Goswami, 2004).

Cognitive neuroscience has already found ways to study how teaching affects the brain. Recent research may eventually help identify certain special educational needs early, and show how different kinds of curricula and teaching techniques affect brain function. Already neuroscience can assess how teaching affects children with dyslexia and other special needs and, in time, it very likely will offer insights into how to tailor teaching to fit the different learning styles of different students (Goswani).

Neuroscience has also helped dispel certain myths about how human beings learn. It has been found that the concept of "left brain" versus "right brain" learning is unfounded. Despite the claim of some philosophers, scientists and teachers, that certain learning (of language, e.g.) is done by the hemispheres of the brain and that teaching should be done to one or the other hemisphere has not been supported by neuroimaging. Both hemispheres work together equally in all cognition. Neuroscientists are still in the process of identifying these and other myths about how people learn. While some scientists believe that neuroscience is still too young to guide education in any meaningful way, others maintain that findings already made have laid adequate groundwork for beginning to answer some questions about how education impacts brain function (Goswani).

CONNECTIONISM & NEUROPHILOSOPHY

Another cognitive science, connectionism, compares computers and the brain, but uses the brain, *not* the computer, as its starting point. Further, it points to the anatomy of the brain to offer a more scientific explanation of assimilation and accommodation, facets of Piagetian constructivism thought by some critics to be incomplete or too abstract (Clark).

Connectionists try to explain cognitive processes without separating them from the mechanical functioning of the brain. A number of theories and research agendas are being developed within connectionism. One of these, neurophilosophy (Clark), combines neuroscience and philosophy of mind functioning into one academic discipline. Until the 1980s, neuroscientists and philosophers had remained in their separate camps, ignorant of, and, at times, even hostile towards one another (Kalinka, 2005). But in 1986, Patricia S. Churchland, a philosophy professor at the University of California, published "Neurophilosophy: Toward a Unified Science of the Mind/Brain," a book arguing for the confluence and co-evolution of the fields of neuroscience, philosophy and psychology. According to Churchland, "many philosophers used to dismiss the relevance of neuroscience on grounds that what mattered was the 'software, not the hardware,' [but] increasingly, philosophers have come to recognize that understanding how the brain works is essential to understanding

the mind." (Churchland, n.d.) Churchland—who is credited for coining the term, neurophilosophy—and other neurosphilosophers are studying consciousness, the self, free will, learning, and other older philosophical issues, using knowledge brought forth by neuroscience (Churchland).

This increased focus on the inner workings of the brain has brought to the fore much information about how it develops in young children. Children enter the world already possessing most of the brain cells they will require. These cells are isolated but over time develop synapses, which bridge them, making communication and information sharing possible. During the earliest years of life, the brain overproduces synapses, but it compensates later by eliminating ones it does not need. Also during the earliest years, it begins producing myelin, a nerve coating it will manufacture until middle age. Myelin insulates nerves and increases the rate of information transfer through the synapses. In time, it allows the brain to multitask ("Inside a Baby's Brain").

At six months, babies recognize the basic sounds of most languages—a skill that peaks around eight months, but is lost at one year when most children begin learning a single language. The ability to form mental images develops dramatically after eight months and allows children to picture objects and people when they are not present. At this time, separation anxiety can be observed in babies when a parent leaves the room. Higher reasoning develops more gradually. Its growth—which increases a child's emotional control—reaches zenith after the first year of life and continues into the teenage years ("Inside a Baby's Brain").

Though much is known about how infants' brains develop in the earliest years, much remains to be discovered about how learning actually occurs within the physical brain. Neuroscience is working to determine how learning disabilities can be discovered and diagnosed early and how different teaching methods and strategies are received by the mind. Neurophilosophy hopes to close the gap between neuroscience and philosophy. And multiple intelligences theory seeks to explain the different ways in which people learn and how they can be taught more effectively.

VIEWPOINTS

Since the 1970s, researchers in the field of developmental psychology have tried to determine how young children learn new words from conversation. What exactly does a child take from either hearing others talk or from his own initial attempts to converse that helps him build a lexicon? Studies done within the last 20 years have given rise to two new theories.

The first, social-pragmatic theory, states that children learn word meanings by inferring or otherwise determining the subject of a speaker's focus and the intentions and reasons for communicating. Through participation in regular, routine verbal interactions with adults, children learn to infer subject and intention more quickly and acquire new words more rapidly. An important implication of social-pragmatic theory for teachers is that children learn language more effectively when styles of adult-guided verbal interaction are consistent. In this way, they can understand what is being said without necessarily being familiar with the words spoken and can in time learn new words at their own pace (Hoff & Naigles, 2002).

A second theory revolves around the "data-providing" elements of speech and says that children are able to amass vocabulary simply by hearing words and sentence structures contained in everyday conversation. In time, a child recognizes familiar sentence structures and familiar words, and uses context to determine the meanings of any unknown words spoken (Hoff & Naigles). Adults who are in constant contact with early language learners can help them acquire language by using familiar phrases and vocabulary, while inserting newer vocabulary and using it frequently and repetitively.

However, Hoff & Naigles point out that these two theories do not sit in opposition to one another. Rather, research has shown that children rely on multiple sources for building vocabulary and that their style of building both lexical and syntactical skills is an integrated one. The dynamics of such theories continue to keep the field of developmental psychology intriguing and ever-changing.

TERMS & CONCEPTS

Behaviorism: Learning theory advocated by B.F. Skinner that concerns itself solely with changes in external behavior in an organism that results from learning

Cognitive Science: A science that draws on psychology, computer science, philosophy and linguistics, to study how the brain functions and performs mental tasks

Computationism: A cognitive science that uses computers as the basis for analyzing the functions of the human brain.

Constructivism: A set of theories based on the premise that children "construct" concepts of their environments through experience

Developmental Psychology: The branch of psychology that studies the intellectual, social, and emotional development of children

Multiple Intelligences: Introduced in the 1980s by Howard Gardner, a theory that says humans solve problems not with one central intelligence, but instead using a combination of eight basic intelligences

Neurophilosophy: Theory introduced in 1986 that combines neuroscience and philosophy of mind functioning into one academic discipline

Neuroscience: Scientific study of that brain that draws from neurology, psychology, physiology and other disciplines

Psychosocial Development: A learning theory developed by psychoanalyst Erik Erikson that states that humans go through eight main developmental stages and must resolve unique inner conflicts during each before moving to the next stage

Social-Pragmatic Theory: A recent proposal stating that children learn new words by inferring the subject on which the speaker is focused and on his intention

John E. Thomas

BIBLIOGRAPHY

Arnst, C. (2003, August 21). I can't remember. *Business Week, 12*, 115-136. Retrieved February 10, 2007, from http://businessweek.com.

Brunton, M. (2007, Jan. 29). What do babies know? *Time, 169*, 94-95. Retrieved February 1, 2007, from EBSCO Online Database Academic Search Premier.

Bush, G. (2006). Learning about learning: From theories to trends. *Teacher Librarian, 34*, 14-18. Retrieved February 10, 2007, from EBSCO Online Database Academic Search Premier.

Churchland, P. S. (n.d.). *Patricia Smith Churchland*. Retrieved February 26, 2007, from http://philosophy-faculty.ucsd.edu.

Clark, J. (2005). Explaining learning: From analysis to paralysis to hippocampus. *Educational Philosophy & Theory, 37*, 667-687. Retrieved February 2, 2007, from EBSCO Online Database Academic Search Premier.

Erik Erikson. (2001). *Early Childhood Today, 15,* 49. Retrieved February 7, 2007, from EBSCO Online Database Academic Search Premier.

Gayles, J.G., & Molenaar, P.M. (2013). The utility of person-specific analyses for investigating developmental processes: An analytic primer on studying the individual. *International Journal of Behavioral Development, 37,* 549-562. Retrieved December 15, 2013, from EBSCO Online Database Education Research Complete.

Goswami, Usha. (2004). Neuroscience, education and special education. *British Journal of Special Education, 31,* 175-183. Retrieved February 28, 2007, from EBSCO Online Database Academic Search Premier.

Harlow, S., Cummings, R., & Aberasturi, S. M. (2006). Karl Popper and Jean Piaget: A rationale for constructivism. *Educational Forum, 71,* 41-48. Retrieved February 1, 2007, from EBSCO Online Database Education Research Complete.

Hoff, E. & Naigles, L. (2002). How children use input to acquire a lexicon. *Child Development, 73,* 418. Retrieved March 6, 2007, from EBSCO Online Database Academic Search Premier.

Inside a Baby's Brain. (2005, Aug. 15). *Newsweek, 146,* 36-37. Retrieved February 5, 2007, from EBSCO Online Database Academic Search Premier.

Jordan, N.C., Hansen, N., Fuchs, L.S., Siegler, R.S., Gersten, R., & Micklos, D. (2013). Developmental predictors of fraction concepts and procedures. *Journal of Experimental Child Psychology, 116,* 45-58. Retrieved December 15, 2013, from EBSCO Online Database Education Research Complete.

Kalinka, E. (2005). Neuroethics: A philosophical challenge. *American Journal of Bioethics, 5,* 31-33. Retrieved February 24, 2007, from EBSCO Online Database Academic Search Premier.

Kornhaber, M. (1999). Enhancing equity in gifted education: A framework for examining assessments drawing on the theory of multiple intelligences. *High Ability Studies, 10,* 143. Retrieved February 9, 2007, from EBSCO Online Database Academic Search Premier.

Laursen, B., & Hartl, A.C. (2013). Understanding loneliness during adolescence: Developmental changes that increase the risk of perceived social isolation. *Journal of Adolescence, 36,* 1261-1268. Retrieved December 15, 2013, from EBSCO Online Database Education Research Complete.

Meece, J. & Defrates-Densch, N. (2002). *Child & Adolescent Development for Educators* (2nd ed.). Burr Ridge, IL: McGraw-Hill College.

Moran, S., Kornhaber, M., & Gardner, H. (2006). Orchestrating multiple intelligences. *Educational Leadership, 64,* 22-27, 6. Retrieved February 5, 2007, from EBSCO Online Database Academic Search

Nolen, J. L. (2003). Multiple intelligences in the classroom. *Education, 124,* 115-119. Retrieved February 27, 2007, from EBSCO Online Database Academic Search Premier.

Wehrheim, C. A. (2006). Current research in learning: the brain, intelligences, bullying. *Clergy Journal, 82,* 9-10. Retrieved February 9, 2007, from EBSCO Online Database Academic Search Premier.

WGBH Educational Foundation. (1998). B. F. Skinner. *A Science Odyssey: People and Discoveries.* Retrieved February 11, 2007, from http://pbs.org.

SUGGESTED READING

Hansen, C. C., & Zambo, D. (2005). Piaget, meet Lilly: Understanding child development through picture book characters. *Early Childhood Education Journal, 33,* 39-45. Retrieved February 2, 2007, from EBSCO Online Database Academic Search Premier.

McInerney, D. M. (2005) Educational psychology—theory, research, and teaching: A 25-year retrospective. *Educational Psychology, 25,* 585-599. Retrieved February 6, 2007, from EBSCO Online Database Academic Search Premier.

Maker, J. & Mi-Soon, L. (2006). The discover curriculum model: Nurturing and enhancing creativity in all children. *KEDI Journal of Educational Policy, 3,* 99-121. Retrieved February 11, 2007, from EBSCO Online Database Education Research Complete.

PERSONALITY THEORIES

Personality theories are rooted in the field of psychology. Personality theory is rich in complexity and variety. The classical approaches to personality theory are psychoanalytic theory as developed by Sigmund Freud, Alfred Adler, and Carl Jung; trait theory as developed by Gordon Allport, Abraham Maslow, and Raymond Cattell, and the Big Five approach; behavioral theory as developed by John B. Watson, B. F. Skinner, and Ivan Pavlov; and social cognition as developed by Albert Bandura, George Kelly, and Norman S. Endler and David Magnusson.

KEYWORDS: Architectonic; Behaviorist Theory; Defense Mechanisms; Denial; Factor Analysis;

Hedonist; Humanism; Humanist Psychology; Idiographic Approach; Individuation; Nomothetic Approach; Personality Theory; Personality Traits; Projection; Psychoanalytic; Rationalization; Reaction Formation; Repression; Social Cognition; Sublimation; Tabula Rasa; Thematic Apperception Test; Trait

OVERVIEW

"Oh, don't worry about him, he just isn't himself today."

What is the self? How does one use personality to come to understand a person? Can personality theory be used to predict what a person will do? How do we come to even know what a personality is? Researchers have developed theories describing what contributes to the personality, yet many of the theorists disagree with each other.

To discuss theories of personality, one must first consider what the words personality and theory mean. A theory is generally a model created to describe, explain, understand, or predict (and some say to control) a phenomenon or concept of life. The concept of personality is abstract and refers to how the habits, thought processes, motivations, defense mechanisms, and emotional states are woven together to form a view of a person. So, in a simplistic sense, theories of personality are models created to help describe, understand, predict, or control the habits, thought processes, motivations, coping mechanisms, and emotional states of a person. Some personality theorists take an ideographic approach; meaning they attempt to delineate differences in people by trying to establish what is unique or different to a specific person. Other theorists take a nomothetic approach, meaning they try to identify commonalities in individuals and then measure how much or how little each person possesses of the common characteristics. A change in approach will often add to the depth of knowledge regarding a theory—or it can work to refute the conclusions that have been drawn about that theory.

ROOTS IN PSYCHOLOGY

Most theories of personality were based on hypotheses created by psychologists who were working with patients in need of some type of therapy (Fakouri & Hafner, 1984). The cycle of theory building necessitates the use of experimentation to create support for hypotheses. Hence, specific types of therapies and research methods have been tied to the various theories. This is why many people will refer to theories of personality as the primary architectonic of all psychology topics.

The various approaches to studying the personality were led by psychologists who are familiar names to students of psychology and counseling. One of the best known of all personality theorists was Sigmund Freud. He and his followers believed the secrets to personality could only be unlocked by an awareness of consciousness brought about by psychoanalysis. Gordon Allport developed the trait approach: a theory that relies on classifying personal dispositions to describe one's personality. He believed a personality is comprised of dispositions and behaviors that may be inborn, conveyed by society, or developed by circumstance. For Allport and his followers, personality is based partly on who one is, partly on with whom one lives, and partly on which needs are being met. The behaviorists B. F. Skinner and John B. Watson theorized personality could best be described through rational, scientific observation of actual, observed behaviors. Albert Bandura started out as a behaviorist but set the foundations for theories of social cognition when he noted that personality tends to be an interactive construct: a person's world affects behavior and a person's behavior affects that person's world and a person's perceptions of the world is affecting both.

The Psychoanalytic and Neo-analytic Approaches

Sigmund Freud

"Who I am is determined by the interaction of my id, ego, and superego. Only through guided introspections will I be capable of really getting in touch with who I am."

Sigmund Freud assumed people are pulled by conflicting hedonistic desires to avoid pain while pursuing pleasure. He developed a well-known structural model to describe how people mediate their internal conflicts arising from their desire for an object and their concomitant need to do the right thing. He explained how a healthy superego works like a parent, balancing the needs of a person's drive to pursue events that give pleasure (the id) and a person's self-reflection that is reality-based and constantly working to keep the person responsible and societally acceptable (the ego) (Seward, 1938). He also articulated a number of defense mechanisms people use to cope with disappointment and feelings of inadequacy; namely:

- Repression;
- Projection;
- Displacement;
- Rationalization;
- Reaction Formation;
- Denial;
- Sublimation (Boeree, 2006; Myers, 2006).

Many students are fascinated by Freud's use of an underlying sexual nature to delineate the psychosexual developmental stages of human personalities. The oral stage (infancy) is associated with childhood behaviors of nursing and being weaned. If this stage does not go well, Freud hypothesized the child would grow up to be orally fixated (e.g., verbal, overweight, a chronic gum chewer, etc.). The anal stage (toddlerhood) is associated with toilet training and control. If this stage does not go well, the child is thought to grow up to be stingy, compulsively neat, or very messy. The phallic stage (describing Freud's Oedipus and Electra complexes) alleges children must fall in love with their opposite-sex parent on their journey to sexual individuation. Once in love, the child will mimic the activities and adopt the values of the same-sex parent in an attempt to steal away the love of the opposite-sex parent. If this stage does not go well, Freud assumed that the child would grow up minus the traditional gender values. The latency stage is the short period in which a pre-adolescents' sexuality is thought to hibernate for a time, and, lastly, the genital stage in which the now mature person can seek out adult love relationships (Garcia, 1995; Myers).

Freud believed there was therapeutic value in exploring one's unconscious, internal conflicts if a person was to really get in touch with the true personality. He developed a therapeutic technique called psychotherapy to aid patients in reaching into the depths of their subconscious. It entailed out-loud reflections of the patient guided by introspective questions posed by the psychotherapist and included exercises such as free association, dream interpretation, projective tests (e.g., the Thematic Apperception Test), and hypnosis (Myers). If you have ever had a slip of the tongue, Freud would encourage you to examine that slip for its underlying message, theorizing that your subconscious was trying to tell you something.

ALFRED ADLER

Two of Freud's followers, Alfred Adler and Carl Jung, later added to Freud's theories and models, sometimes challenging the foundations of his theory. Adler was best known for his works on inferiority and birth order. Adler's theory begins with the notion that all people are born with feelings of inferiority that must be overcome. He posited that the inferiority complex is based on personal weaknesses and that each person must learn how to compensate for these weaknesses by building upon other personal strengths, eventually overcoming some of the feelings of inferiority to emerge with a healthy personality (or, conversely, the person will become clinically neurotic). It is at this juncture that Adler disagreed with Freud's theory; he posited that fear, not sex, is really the driving force behind psychological development (Bagby, 1923; Vaughan, 1927). He also conducted research showing how one's birth order has a direct effect on the development of personality. His resultant theory of psychosocial dynamics suggests that children growing up in the same home are often going through vastly different experiences based on their location within the family unit—and these experiences have a direct effect on personality (Fakouri & Hafner).

CARL JUNG

Jung was a contemporary of Freud's and was considered to be his theoretical heir. However, Jung's work began to diverge sharply from Freud's as Jung developed his theory that the psyche is comprised of three specific layers:

- **The Self:** The seat of the consciousness of self as well as the persona presented to the outside world;
- **The Personal Unconscious:** This layer is filled with attitudes that the Self has chosen to ignore (i.e., the shadow) and the counter-self-image (i.e., anima/animus) carried by each person, which are often projected onto someone else as they are too painful to be accepted;
- **The Collective Unconsciousness:** The archetypal stories and myths by which one creates values and ethics based on the experiences of earlier generations.

He believed the Self to be the center of personality while Freud's concept of the ego was only the seat of consciousness (Aldridge & Horns-Marsh, 1991).

Jung is best known for his typology of personality describing how various orientations (e.g., introversion or extroversion) and four stylistic preferences of each person (i.e., sensing, thinking, intuiting, and feeling) work to shape how each person perceives and interacts with the environment. The Myer-Briggs Type Indicator is a currently popular test based on Jung's theory of personality (Boeree).

THE TRAIT APPROACH

"I wonder who I am? I think I will take a test and see what it can tell me. I am starting to suspect that who I believe I am is often based on the situation I find myself in."

Trait theorists believed it would better to develop theories of personality based on stable patterns of behavior a person exhibits over time and across a variety of situations. They relied on self-report, developing personality inventories (such as the 16 Personality Factor test, Minnesota Multiphasic Personality Inventory, California Personality Inventory, etc.) to aid in describing the construct, personality.

GORDON ALLPORT

Gordon Allport is often identified as the father of trait theory (and one of the original founders of humanist psychology). His theory postulates that each person's personality is composed of several different trait subsystems. The most notable of the subsystems are:

- **Individual:** Traits unique to a person;
- **Common:** Traits held in common by many people (most likely based on community mores);
- **Cardinal:** A trait that is unchangeable and dominates the overall personality and behavior of the person (not everyone develops one of these);
- **Central:** The dispositions that are used to describe a person (e.g., happy, depressed, sweet, bitter, dumb, smart, etc.);
- **Secondary:** Traits that create a consistency but do not define the core personality of the person (e.g., she loves shoes, she has a hard time adapting to change, she is passionate about gymnastics).

Each person is a unique mix of different trait subsystems. Allport later changed the word trait to the phrase personal disposition, in an attempt to clarify

what he was measuring—the unique characteristics of a person (Boeree).

Allport is not as well known as other personality theorists, yet his theory tends to be the one behind many of the personality tests available today in popular magazines by readers curious about themselves and taken by students in the public K-12 system to help them identify appropriate career tracks based on interests. Allport's trait theory created the foundation for research conducted by other researchers such as Maslow and Cattell. Factor analysis was also used to create the currently popular taxonomy called the Big Five structure.

ABRAHAM MASLOW AND RAYMOND CATELL

Abraham Maslow is best noted for his theory creating a hierarchical order of needs (and is also noted as one of the original founders of humanist psychological thought). He postulated that people will always be interested in their most immediate needs, taking actions that they hope will lead to the fulfillment of those needs. Needs are divided into two types: deficit (the person is seeking something that is required for survival, such as shelter, safety, a sense of belonging, or self-esteem) and growth (the person is moving forward in efforts toward self-actualization, knowledge, and understanding) (Maslow, 1943). His works became seminal to studies on motivation theory.

Raymond Cattell, taking the work of Allport one step further, took a nomothetic approach. He concluded that all traits are either surface traits (the traits people observe to draw conclusions regarding one's personality) or source traits (the underlying traits that are responsible for the manifestation of the surface traits). He constructed 171 bipolar scales to describe personality using a trait list developed by Allport (Goldberg, 1990). Some of the primary source traits are temperament, innate motivations, socially constructed motivations, and attitude.

He created the 16 Personality Factor test, introducing a statistical procedure called factor analysis into the study of personality. He noted that research observations can be gathered from self-reports, from information gathered about a person's life, or from results of an actual experiment; and that the information gleaned from each type of information may conflict. Cattell noted that aspects of a personality are based on states (the temporary, changeable characteristics of a person based on the existing culture or environment) as well as traits (the relatively permanent personal disposition of the person) (Hamaker, Nesselroade, & Molenaar, 2007).

Several researchers found that, by applying factor analysis methodology to lists of adjectives describing people, one typically finds five significant factors—the Big Five—which allow researchers to simplify the study of personality theory. These five factors cluster the adjectives under five categories:

- Extroversion;
- Agreeableness;
- Conscientiousness;
- Neuroticism;
- Openness to experience.

Each category is a scale variable (meaning each factor has many highly interrelated adjectives built into the variable). Although the research can be easily replicated using only one-word adjectives, researchers have not yet had similar success when working to fit many-word phrases from personality inventories on the same frame. If this simplification holds up under research scrutiny, personality theorists may be able to learn more about personalities and how they are molded or affected by the five factors (Goldberg).

THE BEHAVIORAL APPROACH

"To determine who I am, I only need to objectively observe my quantifiable actions and behaviors. Problem is, I can't really see myself!"

Psychologists such as J. B. Watson and B. F. Skinner disagreed with the psychoanalytic and trait researchers. They strongly believed one did not need to fuss with the mental processes and structures to create a theory of personality. That which manifests as personality could be defined as a collection of response tendencies that a person uses when faced with specific stimulus situations. Each person is born a "tabula rasa" (blank slate) and responses are learned through life experience. Thus, it is the environment that shapes, molds, and defines one's personality. And that personality is easily observed; motives, thoughts, and introspection are not relevant to the discussion. The behaviorists began promoting observational research and were always careful to describe a behavior without attributing any intent behind it.

J. B. WATSON

Watson drew his working hypotheses from his studies of animals. He is known for stating that, if he could be

given twelve infants, he could apply his behavior-based training techniques to produce different types of adults from those infants. He did not believe that what a person thought or felt was germane to how personality is developed. Drawing from his own work and Ivan Palov's experiments in classical conditioning he defined and studied conditioned reflexes and noted that people, like animals, could be taught to provide reflexive responses to artificial stimuli. Pavlov had noted a phenomenon he referred to as classical conditioning based on an experience he had with dogs he kept in his lab to pursue various experiments. The dogs were fed every day when the five o'clock bell sounded. Pavlov noticed the dogs (who had previously salivated at the sight of their food) began salivating when the bell rang. He quit providing food when the bell rang and noted the dogs continued to salivate at the sound of the bell. His theory of classical conditioning goes like this: to create a specific response (e.g., salivation), first pair the naturally triggering event with a neutral event (e.g., food and a bell, respectively). The subject will begin to mentally pair both events with the desired response. After the response has been reinforced several times, remove the natural event and the desired response will continue to present itself any time the artificial event is initiated (Myers). Watson believed that personality is created in a similar manner.

Watson tested Pavlov's theory of classical conditioning in humans by experimenting with a boy who has come to be known as Albert (an 11-month-old boy who was being raised in a hospital environment). Watson exposed Albert to a variety of objects including a white rat, various masks, a rabbit, a dog, etc. Albert did not show fear at the sight of any of the objects. Next, Albert was allowed to interact with each of the objects yet every time the white rat was presented to him (i.e., the artificial, or conditioned, stimulus) a loud noise was generated (natural, or unconditioned, stimulus) which startled Albert and made him cry and fuss. After the white rat and the loud noise had been paired several times, the experimenters again brought the white rat to Albert without creating the loud noise. Albert continued to begin crying at the sight of the white rat. Thus, Albert effectively demonstrated how fear had become the response to the white rat even after the two stimuli were uncoupled (Watson & Raynor, 2000).

B. F. SKINNER

Taking the idea of conditioning a step further, Skinner used related experiments to develop his theory of operant conditioning. Skinner is best known for his studies in which he taught rats to push a bar to obtain food. Hungry rats were placed in a box that contained a lever. The rat would run around the cage in search of food and never find any. Eventually the rat would bump against the lever and be rewarded with a pellet (the reinforcer). In time, the rat would learn through a series of consistent reinforcers that, if he were hungry, he needed to push the bar to obtain his food. Skinner's theory suggests people are similarly conditioned to behave in specific ways in anticipation of reinforcers (the consequences the behavior brought about in the past). In other words, people have been conditioned to provide responses to specific stimuli. The composite of their resultant behavior is what we can observe and use to scientifically describe behavior (and, hence, personality). Operant conditioning is also seen as a wonderful way to control behavior and, thus, the development of personality. Reinforcements are powerful and can be both negative (punishment) and positive (reward) (Boeree; Myers).

The Social Cognition Approach

ALBERT BANDURA

Albert Bandura, who had been working with theories of behaviorism, came to the conclusion that the environment initiates behaviors and, conversely, behaviors work to shape the environment. He also introduced the notion that a person will create a mental image to indirectly determine what might constitute success. This is the point at which he broke ranks with the behaviorists to become the father of the cognitive school of thought (Bandura, 2006).

The importance of social cognition on personality comes into focus when examining how a person groups and classifies life experiences—the characteristic way a person chooses to perceive life experiences (i.e., personal constructs) is the manifestation of personality (e.g., pessimistic vs. optimistic view of life). This is why different people will present differing perceptions of the same event. Constructs become the lens through which one views life and predicts the outcomes of events and are composed of polar opposites (e.g., smart-stupid, kind-cruel, ugly-beautiful, etc.). A personality change is most likely to come about when one alters the perception of these constructs—the altered view will alter the interactions

with the environment because of the concomitant changes in behavior (Kelly, 1955). Endler and Magnusson (1976) built upon Kelly's work to develop and test an interactional model of personality. Their research results suggest psychodynamic and trait theories were constrained in their ability to create robust models of personality because they failed to account for the interaction of the causal factors located in situation dynamics.

The Biological Approach

HANS EYSENCK

Psychologist Hans Eysenck began researching the genetic determinates of personality in the 1950s. By the 1970s, the field of behavioral genetics became increasingly prominent, with researchers working to differentiate the genetic and environmental influences on various personality traits. Eysenck held that genetics are the primary factor in determining an individual's personality traits, with environmental influences having only a secondary effect. He proposed a hierarchical model of personality traits, in which a few genetically determined traits give rise to a larger array of secondary personality traits. For example, Eysenck proposed that introverted individuals are genetically predisposed to having higher levels of physiological arousal, causing them to develop shyness as a personality trait. Long-term studies of temperament have found that people's temperaments are fairly stable from infancy to adolescence, although environmental factors and trauma can have a significant impact on an individual's temperament. With the advent of electroencephalography (EEG), positron emission tomography (PET), and functional magnetic resonance imaging (fMRI) technologies, as well as vast improvements in the scientific understanding of the human genome, researchers in the twenty-first century are exploring the biological, neurological, and genetic factors of personality more in depth.

TERMS AND CONCEPTS

Architectonic: The overall structure and design used in the scientific systematization of knowledge.

Defense Mechanisms: Strategies used by the ego to safeguard one against inappropriate or unwanted thoughts and impulses.

Denial: Threatening events or facts are psychologically blocked by one's refusing to recognize or believe them.

Factor Analysis: A form of multivariate analysis which groups a large number of variables into factors (or clusters of similar variables) that can be used to create a more succinct explanation of the interrelations among the variables or objects.

Hedonist: A doctrine or philosophy that the seeking of pleasure is the sole or chief good in life—seek pleasure and avoid pain.

Humanist Psychology: A school of thought that developed in reaction to behaviorism and psychoanalytic branches of psychology. It took a more holistic view of what constitutes the personality and follows five basic tenets: humans cannot be reduced to components; humans are uniquely human (as differentiated from animals); human consciousness includes an awareness of oneself in the context of others' perceptions; humans have choices and are also subject to imposed responsibilities; and humans are intentional and engage in meaning making activities, value clarification, and creative thinking.

Idiographic Approach: People have unique personality structures and the cardinal traits are most important in understanding the personality.

Individuation: The act of recognizing oneself as separate and individual from others—most usually referring to children creating a self identity which is separate from that of mother or father.

Nomothetic Approach: People's unique personalities can be understood as them having relatively greater or lesser amounts of traits that are present in all people to some degree.

Projection: Attributes (or blames) one's personal feelings, thoughts, or intentions on others.

Rationalization: Coping with disappointment or anxiety by explaining it away with reasonable (though dishonest) explanations or justifications.

Reaction Formation: A conscious decision to engage in an exaggerated response or activity to block the original forbidden impulse.

Repression: Prevents thoughts that create discomfort and anxiety from entering the consciousness.

Sublimation: Inappropriate impulses or thoughts are diverted into advantageous activities that benefit the person.

Tabula Rasa: The idea that each person is born without any innate or pre-existing mental content.

Thematic Apperception Test: A projective test of personality comprised of 31 picture cards which are shown to the subject one at a time. The subject then tells a story about what is happening in the picture. The test administrator uses those stories to identify dominant themes, drives, emotions, complexes, sentiments, and conflicts in the subject's life.

Trait: Concrete, easily recognized consistencies in a person's behaviors.

Sherry Thompson

BIBLIOGRAPHY

Agnes, M. E. (Ed.). (2001). *Webster's new world college dictionary* (4th ed.). Webster's New World.

Aldridge, J. & Horns-Marsh, V. (1991). Contributions and applications of analytical psychology to education and child development. *Journal of Instructional Psychology, 18,* 151. Retrieved from EBSCO Online Database Academic Search Premier.

Bagby, E. (1923). The inferiority reaction. *The Journal of Abnormal Psychology and Social Psychology, 18,* 269–273.

Bandura A. (2006). Toward a psychology of human agency. *Perspectives on Psychological Science, 1,* 164–180.

Boeree, G. C. (2006). *Personality theories.* Retrieved from http://webspace.ship.edu.

Bugental, J. (1965). *The search for authenticity: An existential-analytic approach to psychotherapy.* New York, NY: Holt, Rinehart, & Winston.

Endler, N. S. & Magnusson, D. (1976). Toward an interactional psychology of personality. *Psychological Bulletin, 83,* 956–974.

Fakouri, E. B. & Hafner J. H. (1984). Early recollections of first borns. *Journal of Clinical Psychology, 40,* 209–213.

Garcia, J. L. (1995). Freud's psychosexual stage conception: a developmental metaphor for counselors. *Journal of Counseling & Development, 73,* 498–502.

Goldberg, L. R. (1990). An alternative "description of personality": The big-five factor structure. *Journal of Personality and Social Psychology, 59,* 1216-1229.

Hamaker, E. L., Nesselroade, J. R., & Molenaar, C. M. (2007). The integrated trait-state model. *Journal of Research in Personality, 41,* 295-315.

Hessels, C., van den Hanenberg, D., de Castro, B., & van Aken, M.G. (2014). Relationships: Empirical contribution: Understanding personality pathology in adolescents: The five factor model of personality and social information processing. *Journal of Personality Disorders, 28*, 121–142. Retrieved from EBSCO Online Database Education Research Complete.

Kelly, G. A. (1955). *The psychology of personal constructs.* New York, NY: Norton.

Maslow, A. H. (1943). A theory of human motivation. *Psychological Review, 50*, 370–396.

Myers, D. (2006). *Psychology* (8th ed.). London, UK: Worth Publishers.

Phelps, B. (2015). Behavioral perspectives on personality and self. *Psychological Record, 65*(3), 557–565. Retrieved from EBSCO Online Database Education Research Complete.

Seward, G. H. (1939). Dialectic in the psychology of motivation. *Psychological Review, 46*, 46–61.

Vaughan, W. F. (1927). The psychology of Alfred Adler. *The Journal of Abnormal and Social Psychology, 21*, 358–371.

Watson, J. B. & Raynor, R. (2000). Conditioned emotional reactions. *American Psychologist, 35*, 313–317 [Reprinted].

Yeager, D. S., Miu, A. S., Powers, J., & Dweck, C. S. (2013). Implicit theories of personality and attributions of hostile intent: A meta-analysis, an experiment, and a longitudinal intervention. *Child Development, 84*, 1651-1667. Retrieved from EBSCO Online Database Education Research Complete.

Yeager, D., Trzesniewski, K. H., & Dweck, C. S. (2013). An implicit theories of personality intervention reduces adolescent aggression in response to victimization and exclusion. *Child Development, 84*, 970–988. Retrieved from EBSCO Online Database Education Research Complete.

SUGGESTED READING

Bandura, A. (1976). *Social learning theory.* Upper Saddle River, NJ: Prentice Hall.

Bandura, A. (1985). *Social foundations of thought and action: A social cognitive theory.* Upper Saddle River, NJ: Prentice Hall. Dolnick, E. (1997). *Madness on the couch: Blaming the victim in the heyday of psychoanalysis.* New York, NY: Simon & Schuster.

Frankl, V. (2000). *Man's search for meaning.* Boston, MA: Beacon Press.

Freberg, L. A. (2015). *Discovering behavioral neuroscience: An introduction to biological psychology.* 3rd ed. Boston, MA: Cengage Learning.

Haan, N. (1965). Coping and defense mechanisms related to personality inventories. *Journal of Consulting Psychology, 29*, 373–378.

Harris, B. Whatever happened to Little Albert? *American Psychologist, 34*, 151-160.

SELF-DETERMINATION THEORY

Self-determination theory is a theory of motivation which posits that humans continually and actively seek challenges and new experiences to develop and master. Within education, the theory considers that students are motivated to achieve different objectives. When a behavior is self-determined, the individual determines that the locus of control is internal to the self, whereas when the behavior is controlled, the locus of control is external to self. The important distinction between the internal or external determinants is not in whether the behaviors are motivated or intentional, but in their internal regulatory processes and how the internal regulatory processes drive external behaviors (Deci, Vallerand, Pelletier, & Ryan, 1991).

KEYWORDS: Autonomy; Competence; Extrinsic Motivation; Goals; Intrinsic Motivation; Learner-Centered; Locus of Control; Self-Determination Theory

OVERVIEW

Self-determination theory is a theory of motivation which posits that humans continually and actively seek challenges and new experiences to develop and master. Within education, the theory considers that students are motivated to achieve different objectives. Unlike other motivational theories, self-determination theory offers the "distinction that falls within the class of behaviors that are intentional or motivated. These motivated actions are self-determined to the extent that they are endorsed by one's sense of self" (Deci et al.). When a behavior is self-determined, the individual determines that the locus of control is internal to self, whereas when the behavior is controlled, the locus of control is external to self. The important distinction between the internal or external determinants is not in whether the behaviors are motivated or intentional, but in their internal regulatory processes and how the internal regulatory processes drive external behaviors. The qualities of the components of the behaviors are vastly different and need to be understood in order to promote self-determination in a classroom environment (Deci et al.).

The Building Blocks of Self-Determination

INTRINSIC MOTIVATION

The most self-determined type of behavior is intrinsic motivation. These behaviors are induced for their own sake, and are linked to feelings of pleasure, interest and satisfaction derived directly from participation in the behavior. Individuals that are intrinsically motivated engage in behaviors because of internal feelings of satisfaction derived from the behavior. While engaging in these behaviors, humans are self-regulated, interested in the activity, choosing to engage in the activity, and function without the aid of external rewards or constraints (Deci & Ryan, 1985). Thus, intrinsic behaviors are initiated because the individual chooses to engage in the activity according to their own wishes. When a child chooses a specific book to read and reads it just for the sake of enjoyment, this exemplifies intrinsic motivation.

EXTRINSIC MOTIVATION

Extrinsic behaviors are "instrumental in nature. They are not performed out of interest, but rather because they are believed to be instrumental" in producing a desired outcome. While research previously has indicated that extrinsic motivation is not a building block of self-determination, recent research has suggested that "these behavioral types differ in the extent to which they represent self-determined" behaviors in contrast to a more controlled response and furthermore, when paired with intrinsic motivators extrinsic motivators may not inhibit motivation (Wormington, Corpus & Anderson, 2012). The determining factor that makes these behaviors more self-determined rather than extrinsic is the factor of internalization (Deci et al.).

Internalization is a proactive process through which individuals transform their regulatory processes into internal processes (Schafer, 1968). In self-determination processes, internalization is viewed as a motivated process. Self-determination theorists report that they believe that (a) people are innately induced to internalize and integrate within themselves "the regulation of uninteresting activities

that are useful for effective functioning in the social world" and (b) that the extent to which the process of internalization and integration proceeds effectively is a "function of the social context." The four types of extrinsic motivation that can be integrated within the interpersonal framework include:

- External;
- Introjected;
- Identified;
- Integrated regulation (Deci et al.).

External Regulation

External regulation behaviors are "performed because of an external contingency, and are considered the loci of initiation and regulation. External regulation represents the "least self-determined form of extrinsic motivation". External regulation behaviors are typically induced by the offer of reward or punishment. An individual displaying external regulation is an individual that might study just because they know they will be rewarded for doing well (Deci et al.).

Introjected Regulation

Introjected regulation is a second type of extrinsic motivation in which individuals bow to internal pressure. These pursuits are either based on the pursuits of "self-aggrandizement and (contingent) self-worth or in the avoidance of feelings of guilt and shame." Introjected regulation is a behavior that is "partially internalized and is within the person, but the individual has not accepted" the behavior as emanating from self. In short, the behaviors caused by introjected regulation are not derived from the person's sense of self and can be described as behaviors that are pressured or coerced. An example of this kind of behavior is an example of a student who studies before playing outside because they would feel guilty about not working first and playing later (Vansteenkiste, Lens & Deci, 2006).

Identified Regulation

Identification is "the process of identifying with the value of an activity and accepting regulation of the activity as one's own" (Vansteenkiste et al.). When individuals value the personal relevance of an activity and willingly engage in the activity, then this represents a more significant form of internalization than other types of externalization. While behaviors resulting from identification are still extrinsic in nature, identified regulation occurs because of one's own volition, which approximates intrinsic motivation. In this way, identification behavior integrates the two types of motivation into a composite behavior. An individual executing identification behavior may study a given subject despite personal difficulty or dislike; for example, because the student knows the subject is integral in fulfilling a self-selected goal (Vansteenkiste et al.). While the student may express personal distaste for a specific area like statistics, the student realizes and understands the importance of the course of study in helping them achieve their goal.

Integrated Regulation

In the case of integrated regulation, the behavior is fully integrated within the individual's sense of self. These identifications are combined with the individual's other sense of their values, needs, and identities. A student might have one view of self-interpretation as a good student and the other as a good athlete. While these two self-identities may seem conflicting and cause internal tensions for the student, the two can become integrated and dwell harmoniously within the person and with the students' sense of self. When this internal harmony is realized then the integrated processes are completely self-willed and mainly occur in adult stages of development. Integrated regulation appears to be very similar to intrinsic motivation, because both integrated regulation and intrinsic motivation cause willing behaviors, develop creativity, and foster understanding. However, intrinsic motivation is different than integrated regulation even though they seem similar in many ways (Deci et al.).

Applications

MOTIVATION IN A PUBLIC SCHOOL SETTING

In a public school setting, self-determination, or "student-directed learning" involves teaching students multiple strategies that allow them to regulate and direct their own behavior (Agran, King-Sears, Wehmeyer, & Copeland, 2003). Student directed educational strategies are aimed at teaching students to set appropriate goals for themselves, self-monitor their own performances, identify solutions to present or future problems, verbally direct their own behaviors, reinforce their own behaviors, and evaluate their own performances (Agran, Hong, & Blankenship, 2007). These are general strategies and outcomes that can be utilized to create a student directed learning environment.

Research has suggested that teachers utilize a multitude of teaching strategies to create student-directed and learner-centered environments (Hsu & Malkin, 2011). In learner-centered classrooms, teachers are attentive to issues surrounding children's "cognitive and metacognitive development, the affective and motivational dimensions of instruction, the developmental and social aspects of learning, and individual differences in learning strategies that are in part, associated with children's cultural and social backgrounds" (Daniels & Perry, 2003). In learner centered classrooms, teachers provide several teaching practices that are motivational. Strategies that are used are numerous and include:

- Motivating students by providing a range of instructional activities relevant to children's lives and differentiated according to an individual's developmental needs;
- Frequently interacting with students to monitor development and progress and providing help as needed;
- Creating positive relationships with children to address socio-emotional and developmental needs.

Within this framework, the most important element of these learner centered strategies is the children's perceptions of teacher strategies that they determine to be motivational.

In one interview, children of elementary school age indicated several strategies that promoted motivation in a learning environment. Children reported the desire to be known as a "unique person and learner." Children also desired to be known as an individual and felt secure afterward. Eventually, as students matured, they reported feeling less reliant on teachers and more reliant on peers. Children reported the need to "participate in interesting learning activities." Children expressed boredom with too many repetitive activities. Another factor children indicated was they "want to make their own choices...sometimes." They reported feeling most empowered when they could make their own educational choices. Children also indicated the need to "work with classmates" and reported the desire to work collaboratively with their peers. All of these factors indicated that children's perceptions of learner centered educational environments promoted student motivation, self-perceived competence, and achievement (Daniels & Perry). The perceptions of children regarding their own learning hold several implications for how learning centered strategies can be applied in educational settings.

STUDENTS

Rewards such as prizes and money have long been used to motivate students to promote success in school. However, research conducted thirty years ago demonstrated that students who participated in activities and received rewards tended to lose interest in and the willingness to work on the activity in the absence of rewards. Other research seeking to outline primary differences between internalization and intrinsic rewards, demonstrated that rewards for work consistently indicates that these behaviors seek to control behavior at an operational level, but also these behaviors "undermine intrinsic motivation for interesting tasks and impeded internalization of regulations for uninteresting tasks" (Deci et al.). Other "external events designed to motivate or control people including deadlines and competition were similarly determined to decrease intrinsic motivation" (Deci et al.). All of these behaviors elicit external controls on behaviors. When an individual's sense of autonomy is diminished, intrinsic motivation is decreased.

In response to students' behaviors, teachers will also become more controlling over students that act fidgety and inattentive during a lesson. Based on this observation, students that appear to be more motivated and autonomous in school may elicit a greater amount of respect and support derived from the behavior of the student and the teacher's assumptions regarding these indicators (Deci et al.). In response to this research, it can be concluded that the most effective internalization and self-determined form of regulation will occur in students if

- Children are able to understand the value and application of a given activity;
- Are provided choices regarding the activity;
- If their feelings and perspectives are acknowledged (Grolnick & Ryan, 1989).

This research further implies that teachers have a deep responsibility for promoting these classroom structures.

TEACHERS

Deci, Schwartz, et al. (1981) reasoned that some teachers were more supportive of student autonomy, while other teachers were more oriented toward controlling their students and their behaviors. Results from their study indicated that students in classrooms of teachers who supported student autonomy were more likely to demonstrate intrinsic motivation, academic competence, and self-esteem than students learning in classrooms of controlling teachers (Deci et al.). Other studies have demonstrated that students in classrooms with supportive teachers were more likely to:

- Stay in school (Vallerand, Fortier, & Guay, 1997);
- Experience enhanced creativity (Koestner, Ryan, Bernieri, & Holt, 1984);
- Develop a preference for optimal challenge (Shapira, 1976), and greater conceptual understanding (Benware & Deci, 1984, Grolnick & Ryan);
- Develop more positive emotionality (Patrick, Skinner, & Connell, 1993);
- Possess higher academic intrinsic motivation (Deci et al.);
- Produce better academic performance (Boggiano, Flink, Shields, Seelbach, & Barrett, 1993);
- Higher academic achievement (Flink, Boggiano, Main, Barrett & Katz, 1992).

These are strong indicators of the role of the teacher in providing academic structures that empower and motivate students' success.

Teachers can very easily fall into academic structures that disempower students and cause them to rely too heavily on the teacher for support and learning. From an observed standpoint, students that rely too heavily on their teachers for support are less apt to thrive in academic environments when teachers stylistically do not provide systematic control over all aspects of the learning environment. In other words, teachers that provide their students with an autonomous classroom setting are able to nurture more active learning from their students and promote student potential (Wright, 2011). This statement is supported by other research that demonstrated that a teacher's supportive style that respected and valued students, rather than neglected or frustrated them, nurtured high interest, motivation, and achievement (Goodenow, 1993; Midgley, Feldlaufer, & Eccles, 1989; Ryan & Grolnick).

ADMINISTRATORS

Deci et al. indicated that when teachers feel pressured or controlled by their superiors regarding student outcomes, they were more likely to control their students. In studies conducted to determine the impact of teachers under pressure in contrast to less control, evidence indicated "that when teachers were more controlling of students, students performed less well in problem-solving activities, both during instruction" (Deci et al., 1991) and subsequent to the instruction. Pressure from administrators to ensure student controls directly related to the autonomy and support provided by teachers to students (Deci et al.). Central to these administrative controls, other controls included mandates made by "government agencies, parent groups, and other forces outside of the school system also produced a negative impact on students' self-determination, conceptual learning, and personal adjustment." Maehr (1991) determined that classroom practices are dictated in large part by school policies. Administrators certainly should be aware of their role in creating a school environment that nurtures the child's frame of reference. Specific supports for self-determination includes offering some choices, minimizing harsh controls, acknowledging feelings, and making information available for decision making and for performing target tasks.

PROMOTING SELF DETERMINATION IN CHILDREN

Professional development that supports teachers in better understanding learning through a child's lens is vital to enabling educational professionals to structure learning environments that are child centered. The relationships between administrators, parents, and teachers are also central to understanding the needs of the child. It is recommended practice in the learner-centered educational environment that "talking with children's parents can often fill in the gaps concerning children's learning interests and experiences outside school" (Daniels & Perry). Furthermore, collecting background information and knowledge about individual children is "necessary" for providing meaningful and appropriately challenging activities that will enable children to

be the most successful in their academic endeavors. These opportunities factor heavily in creating and honoring a "system of diversity" and enable differentiated learning for individual student needs while supporting teachers in diverse educational environments. Utilizing these strategies and understanding the needs of the child are the first indicators of educational environments designed to promote self-determination in children (Daniels & Perry).

CONCLUSION

Teachers must understand self-determination theory and use ways of teaching students that are intrinsically motivating to prosper academic success for children. Schools have changed dramatically over the last thirty years in the way discipline is approached and in how relationships among students, teachers, administrators, and parents are structured.

For new teachers entering an educational setting, unfamiliar with the curricula mandates of a given school and the students, offering students choices about their learning, building relationships with parents, and supporting students to develop a deep understanding of themselves as learners are central to gaining insight into the framework of the learner-centered classroom. To learn new curricula in a given grade level takes approximately one year to explore. When teachers realize the choices within given curricula and allow students the opportunity to co-explore, it simply creates less work for the new teacher, because this system allows the students a good share of the responsibility for their own learning.

New teachers are often caught up in creating much of their own curriculum, comprehension questions, and paper-and-pencil activities that could be alleviated by giving students more choices. To further ensure classroom successes, new teachers need to communicate their goals with others, including parents. After all, when students are placed in charge of much of their own learning the responsibility for success becomes shared and places more accountability on all parties, in turn easing teachers from carrying the whole burden for students' success.

TERMS & CONCEPTS

Autonomy: Autonomy in a learning environment can be described as possessing the independent ability to make an academic choice and act on that choice.

Competence: Competence in a learning environment can be described as doing an activity well or to a required standard.

Extrinsic Motivation: Extrinsic motivation can be ascribed to behaviors that are performed out to avoid risk or seek reward. Behaviors that occur as a result of extrinsic motivation are not performed because of an individual's deep interest, but are performed because they are believed to be instrumental in producing a desired outcome.

Intrinsic Motivation: Intrinsic motivation can be described ascribed to behaviors that are performed because of the internal desire and regulation of the individual performing the behavior. These are behaviors that elicit joy and pleasure to the individual without external regulators promoting the behavior.

Self-Determination Theory: A theory of motivation which posits that humans continually and actively seek challenges and new experiences to and develop and master. Within education, the theory considers that students are motivated to achieve different objectives.

Sharon Link

BIBLIOGRAPHY

Agran, M., King-Sears, M., Wehmeyer, M., & Copeland, S. (2003). *Teacher's guide to inclusive practice: Student-directed learning.* Baltimore, MD: Paul H. Brookes.

Agran, M., Hong, S., & Blankenship, K. (2007). Promoting the self-determination of students with visual impairments: Reducing the gap between knowledge and practice. *Journal of Visual Impairment & Blindness, 101,* 453=464. Retrieved November 7, 2007, from EBSCO Online Database Academic Search Premier.

Amabile, T. M., Dejong, W., & Lepper, M. R. (1976). Effects of externally imposed deadlines on subsequent intrinsic motivation. *Journal of Personality and Social Psychology, 34,* 915-922.

Benware, C., & Deci, E. L. (1984). The quality of learning with an active versus passive motivational set. *American Educational Research Journal, 21,* 755-765.

Boggiano, A. K., Flink, C., Shields, A., Seelbach, A., & Barrett, M. (1993). Use of techniques promoting students' self-determination: Effects on students' analytic problem-solving skills. *Motivation and Emotion, 17,* 319-336.

Daniels, D., & Perry, K. (2003), "Learner-centered" according to children. *Theory into Practice, 42,* 102-108.

Retrieved November 7, 2007, from EBSCO Online Database Academic Search Premier.

Deci, E. L., Betley, G., Kahle, J., Abrams, L., & Porac, J. (1981). When trying to win: Competition and intrinsic motivation. *Personality and Social Psychology Bulletin, 7,* 79-83.

Deci, E. L., Nezlek, J., & Sheinman, L. (1981). Characteristics of the rewarder and intrinsic motivation of the rewardee. *Journal of Personality and Social Psychology, 40,* 1-10.

Deci, E. L. & Ryan, R. M. (1985). The General Causality Orientations Scale: Self-determination in personality. *Journal or Research in Personality, 19,* 109-134.

Deci, E. L. & Ryan, R. M. (1991). A motivation approach to self: Integration in personality. In R. Dienstbier (Ed.), *Nebraska Symposium on Motivation: Vol. 38. Perspectives on motivation* (pp. 237-288). Lincoln: University of Nebraska Press.

Deci, E. L., & Ryan, R. M. (2000). Self-determination theory and the facilitation of intrinsic motivation, social development, and well-being. *American Psychologist, 55,* 68-78.

Deci, E. L., & Ryan, R. M. (2002). Overview of self-determination theory: An organismic dialectical perspective. In E. L. Deci & R. M. Ryan (Eds.), *Handbook on self-determination research* (pp. 3-33), Rochester, NY: University of Rochester Press.

Deci, E. L., Schwartz, A., Sheinman, L., & Ryan, R. M. (1981). An instrument to assess adults' orientations toward control versus autonomy with children: Reflections on intrinsic motivation and perceived competence. *Journal of Educational Psychology, 73,* 642-650.

Deci, E. L., Spiegel, N. H., Ryan, R. M., Koestner, R., & Kauffman, M. (1982). Effects of performance standards on teaching styles: Behavior of controlling teachers. *Journal of Educational Psychology, 74,* 852-859.

Deci, E. L., Vallerand, R. J., Pellitier, L. G., & Ryan, R. M. (1991). Motivation and education: The self-determination perspective. *Educational Psychology, 26,* 325-346. Retrieved November 7, 2007, from EBSCO Online Database Academic Search Premier.

Flink, C., Boggiano, A. K., Main, D. S., Barrett, M., & Katz, P. A. (1992). Children's achievement-related behaviors: The role of extrinsic and intrinsic motivational orientations. In A. K. Boggiano & T. S. Pittman (Eds.), *Achievement and motivation: A socio-developmental perspective* (pp. 189-214). New York: Cambridge University Press.

Goodenow, C. (1993). Classroom belonging among early adolescent students: Relationships to motivation and achievement. *Journal of Early Adolescence, 13,* 21-43.

Grolnick, W. S., & Ryan, R. M. (1987). Autonomy in children's learning: An experimental and individual difference investigation. *Journal of Personality and Social Psychology, 52*, 890-898.

Grolnick, W. S., & Ryan, R. M. (1989). Parent styles associated with children's self-regulation and competence in school. *Journal of Educational Psychology, 81*, 143-154.

Hsu, A., & Malkin, F. (2011). Shifting the focus from teaching to learning: Rethinking the role of the teacher educator. *Contemporary Issues in Education Research, 4*, 43-50. Retrieved on December 12, 2013, from EBSCO Online Database Education Research Complete.

Koestner, R., Ryan, R. M., Bernieri, F., & Holt, K. (1984). Setting limits on children's behavior: The differential effects of controlling versus informational styles on intrinsic motivation and creativity. *Journal of Personality, 52*, 233-248.

Maehr, M. L. (1991). *Changing the schools: A word to school leaders about enhancing student investment in learning.* Paper presented at the annual conference of the American Educational Research Association, Chicago.

Midgley, C., Feldlaufer, H., & Eccles, J. S. (1989). Student/teacher relations and attitudes toward mathematics before and after the transition to junior high school. *Child Development, 60*, 981-992. Retrieved November 7, 2007, from EBSCO Online Database Academic Search Premier.

Mossholder, K. W. (1980). Effects of externally mediated goal setting on intrinsic motivation: A laboratory experiment. *Journal of Applied Psychology, 65*, 202-210.

Patrick, B. C., Skinner, E. A., & Connell, J. P. (1993). What motivates children's behavior and emotion? Joint effects of perceived control and autonomy in the academic domain. *Journal of Personality and Social Psychology, 65*, 781-791.

Ryan, R. M., & Grolnick, W. S. (1986). Origins and pawns in the classroom: Self-report and projective assessments of individual differences in children's perceptions. *Journal of Personality and Social Psychology, 50*, 550-558.

Schafer, R. (1968). *Aspects of internalization.* New York: International Universities Press.

Vallerand, R. J., Fortier, M. S. & Guay, F. (1997). Self-determination and persistence in a real-life setting: Toward a motivational model of high-school dropout. *Journal of Personality and Social Psychology, 72*, 1161-1176.

Vallerand, R. J., Gauvin, L. L., & Halliwell, W. R. (1986). Negative effects of competition on children's intrinsic motivation. *Journal of Social Psychology, 126*, 649-657.

Vallerand, R. J., Hamel, M., & Daoust, H. (1991). *Cooperation and competition: A test of their relative effects on intrinsic motivation.* Unpublished manuscript, University of Quebec at Montreal, Montreal Canada.

Vansteenkiste, M., Lens, W., & Deci, E. (2006). Intrinsic versus extrinsic goal contents in self-determination theory: Another look at the quality of academic motivation. *Educational Psychology, 4*, 19-31. Retrieved November 7, 2007, from EBSCO Online Database Academic Search Premier.

Wormington, S. V., Corpus, J., & Anderson, K. G. (2012). A person-centered investigation of academic motivation and its correlates in high school. *Learning & Individual Differences, 22*, 429-438. Retrieved on December 12, 2013, from EBSCO Online Database Education Research Complete.

Wright, G. (2011). Student-centered learning in higher education. *International Journal of Teaching & Learning in Higher Education, 23*, 92-97. Retrieved on December 12, 2013, from EBSCO Online Database Education Research Complete.

SUGGESTED READING

Atkinson, J. W., & Feather, N. T. (1966). *A theory of achievement motivation.*

Atkinson, J. W., & Feather, N. T. (1966). *A theory of achievement motivation.* New York: Wiley. Deci, E. L., & Ryan, R. M. (1985). *Intrinsic motivation and self-determination in human behavior.* New York: Plenum.

Emery, A., Heath, N., & Rogers, M. (2017). Parents' role in adolescent self-injury: An application of self-determination theory. *School Psychology Quarterly, 32* (2), 199-211.

Fromm, E. (1976). *To have to be?* New York: Continuum.

Kasser, T. (2002). *The high price of materialism.* London: MIT Press.

Shogren, K., Villareal, M., Lang, K., & Seo, H. (2017). Mediating role of self-determination constructs in explaining the relationship between school factors and post school outcomes. *Exceptional Children, 83* (2), 165- 180.

Vroom, V. H. (1964). *Work and motivation.* New York: Wiley.

MOTIVATION

As a topic of interest for well over a century, motivation has been studied from multiple angles, including from physiological, instinctual, behavioral, psychoanalytical, and humanistic perspectives. As the field of psychology has become more cognitive in its orientation, however, so has research on motivation. The cognitive theories of motivation include: intrinsic motivation, goal theory, achievement motivation, attribution theory, and social cognitive theory. Their impact on achievement and learning will be discussed as well.

OVERVIEW

Educators and psychologists have been studying motivation for well over a century. As a result, it has been investigated from nearly every angle: physiological, behavioral, instinctual, psychoanalytical, and humanistic. In the last several decades, however, the field of psychology has become more cognitive in its orientation and so too has research on motivation. Learning theorists have begun to realize that motivation, like other mental processes such as attention, perception, and memory, is an important ingredient in the learning process and can help to explain both academic success and failure (Clinkenbeard, 2012). Thus, cognitive theorists define motivation as "the process whereby goal-directed activity is instigated and sustained" (Pintrich & Schunk, 2002; Schunk, 1996). Even though motivation is defined as a cognitive construct, it is nonetheless something that must be inferred from behavior. Because researchers cannot directly measure motivation, cognitivists use behavioral indicators—such as persistence, task choice, and self-reports—to better understand why people are motivated to act as they do.

Although the way motivation works is only partially understood, many researchers have attempted to implement systems to control motivation to improve achievement in settings such as school and the workplace. Many such efforts draw on the various models developed within psychology and education studies, but others rely on flawed conceptions of scientific research or introduce unsubstantiated claims. Many companies rely on theories and techniques developed by motivation researchers in order to improve employee motivation or to conceptualize organizational structure and activity. Teachers also use motivation theories in efforts to stimulate learning among students. Limited research has even been conducted on the use of drugs to affect elements of brain chemistry that may be linked to motivation; these methods are highly experimental and unproven, however.

SIGMUND FREUD'S THEORY

Freud developed a complex and intricate theory of personality, as well as a revolutionary method of therapy known as psychoanalysis. Although he did not use the same terminology, his concept of trieb (a German word meaning moving force), is similar in meaning to motivation (Pintrich & Schunk). More specifically, Freud viewed motivation as psychic energy,

part of a larger system of energy within an individual that he believed was closed; energy might change its form, but it never changes in amount. When a need develops, Freud proposed that energy was directed toward behaviors that satisfy a need; need reduction is pleasurable, he argued, because the build-up of energy is unpleasant. Although many times energy is aimed toward reducing a particular need, Freud also believed it was often repressed. Repressed energy does not disappear, however, but rather manifests itself in other ways. In this view, sexual energy might result in overeating, for example.

The idea that individuals sometimes do not have access to thoughts that are influencing their behavior is arguably one of Freud's most significant contributions to our understanding of motivation and is mirrored in current theories regarding implicit motives (Pintrich & Schunk). However, Freud elevated unconscious forces to unreasonable heights, many argue, and therefore disregarded the impact of cognitions and the environment; people do have conscious goals and values, the attainment of which is sometimes altered by forces beyond their control (Pintrich & Schunk).

DRIVE THEORY

Clark Hull, who became a well-known American psychologist in the early twentieth century for his work on hypnosis, became even better known for his contribution to drive theory. Approaching the question of motivation from a physiological perspective, Hull believed behavior was comprised of two elements: the actual performance, and the variables that determine performance (Beck, 2000). He identified these determining variables as habit strength—the strength of the association between a stimulus and response—and drive, or "the motivational construct energizing and prompting organisms into action" (Schunk). Hull argued that drive results primarily from physiological deficits; if an organism is hungry, drive will activate the organism to behave in ways to reduce the hunger. When the deficit is eliminated, drive subsides. Because much of human behavior is not directly related to survival needs, Hull introduced the notion of secondary reinforcers. Money, for example, is a secondary reinforcer because it allows individuals to buy shelter and food. Thus, secondary reinforcers, by being paired with reinforcers that satisfy primary physiological needs, influence behavior.

Even though Hull had tried to broaden his theory by introducing secondary reinforcement, many still felt it fell short, especially with regard to explaining human behavior (Schunk). As Schunk argues, there are many times people will ignore a primary need—such as hunger—to attain a valued goal, such as winning a race or studying for an exam. In addition, people often strive for long-term goals over a period of months or years; drive theory adds little insight to this type of behavior.

CONDITIONING THEORIES

In the early twentieth century—and largely in reaction to Freud's emphasis on the unconscious and unobservable—behaviorism came into prominence. Behaviorists explained all learning in terms of observable events: stimuli in the environment and the responses those stimuli elicited. Many behaviorists denied the existence of so-called mental events altogether; those who did not nevertheless suggested they could not and should not be studied. Thus, motivation is understood in terms of probability and frequency of behavior, not as a cognitive construct. Many theories explained human learning from a behaviorist point of view, but two theories in particular, classical conditioning theory and operant conditioning theory, became the hallmark theories.

CLASSICAL CONDITIONING

Classical conditioning, first discovered by Russian physiologist Ivan Pavlov, occurs when a previously neutral stimulus, upon being paired with an unconditioned stimulus, elicits a response. In the classic study, for example, Pavlov noticed that dogs salivated in the presence of food. Food served as an unconditioned stimulus that elicited an unconditioned response, salivation. When Pavlov then paired the sound of a bell (a neutral stimulus) with the presentation of the food, dogs soon learned to salivate in response to the bell alone. The bell then became a conditioned stimulus, the salivation in the presence of the bell a conditioned response. Schunk explains, "this is a passive view of motivation... because the motivational properties of the unconditioned stimulus are transmitted to the conditioned stimulus" (Schunk). In other words, it is assumed to be an automatic process.

OPERANT CONDITIONING

Operant conditioning also explains motivation in terms of relationships between stimuli and response. Proposed by B. F. Skinner, who is known as the father of behaviorism, operant conditioning explains behavior in terms of an antecedent stimulus, the behavior itself, and the consequences of behavior. The consequence—either positive or negative—determines the future likelihood the behavior will be exhibited again; a positive consequence increases the frequency of behavior, a negative consequence decreases the frequency of a behavior. According to Skinner, "operant conditioning requires no new principles to account for motivation. Motivated behavior is increased... by effective contingencies of reinforcement" (cited in Pintrich & Schunk).

Reinforcements do influence behavior. According to cognitive psychologists, however, it is a person's beliefs or expectations about the reinforcements that influence behavior as much, if not more so, than the reinforcements themselves. By ignoring these cognitive processes, such as expectation, beliefs, and memory, behaviorists "offer an incomplete account of human motivation" (Schunk).

HUMANISTIC THEORY

Abraham Maslow developed a humanistic theory of motivation; like many theorists before him, Maslow defined motivated behavior in relation to needs. Unlike drive theories, however, Maslow identified needs other than physiological or biological ones. He classified needs into a hierarchy of five categories:

- Physiological;
- Safety;
- Belongingness;
- Esteem;
- Self-actualization (Schunk).

According to Maslow, individuals must satisfy lower-order needs first, before attending to higher-order needs. For example, a person is unlikely to worry about achievement or recognition from others, which are classified as esteem needs, if they cannot meet their physiological needs for food and water. Maslow was most interested in the highest level of the hierarchy, or self-actualization needs, defined as "ongoing actualization of potentials, capacities and talents, and fulfillment of mission" (Maslow, 1968, as cited in Schunk). He believed self-actualization could be achieved in a variety of ways—one person might become self-actualized through athletic achievement, for example, another through parenting—but that only 1 percent of the population ever achieved it completely.

While many of Maslow's principles apply to our understanding of motivation in general, his theory has been difficult to validate empirically; research on self-actualization in particular, has yielded mixed results (Schunk). In addition, operational definitions of deficiencies of needs have remained elusive; what one person experiences as a deficiency of belongingness needs, another may experience as an overabundance of love and connectedness.

COGNITIVE THEORIES OF MOTIVATION

The following section will highlight some of the prominent cognitive theories of motivation, including:

- Intrinsic motivation;
- Goal theory;
- Achievement motivation;
- Attribution theory;
- Social cognitive theory of motivation.

Each theory has its own specific emphasis—some emphasize goal setting whereas others emphasize perceptions of control—but they are similar in their emphasis on cognitive processes.

INTRINSIC MOTIVATION

Intrinsic motivation is defined as motivation to engage in an activity for its own sake (Pintrich & Schunk). It is often contrasted with extrinsic motivation, or motivation to engage in an activity as a means to an end (to earn a reward for example, or the recognition of others). With respect to learning, educators have long suspected that those who are intrinsically motivated are more likely to put forth greater effort, and more likely to achieve (Froiland, Oros, Smith & Hirchert, 2012).

One of the more recent theories of intrinsic motivation is known as flow, or the psychology of optimal experience. Csikszentmihalyi (1990) did not intend to develop a theory of motivation or learning when he first started investigating flow; he simply want to understand "how people felt when they most enjoyed themselves, and why." What he discovered is that enjoyment is experienced by people in essentially the same way and that an enjoyable experience is, at its core, one that will help a person grow. The universal elements

of enjoyment—the sum of which Csikszentmihalyi termed "flow"—include loss of self-consciousness, intense concentration, an increased sense of control, and a transformed sense of time. The activities themselves are typically ones that have clear goals and provide immediate feedback, and in which the challenge is met with an equal amount of skill. Finally, he argued, flow is maintained only when individuals seek increasingly higher levels of challenge that they then meet with increasingly higher levels of skill. In sum, "the flow experience acts as a magnet for learning" (Csikszentmihalyi, 1997).

Csikszentmihalyi's work follows a long line of research into intrinsic motivation. One of the earliest perspectives was proposed by White (1959, as cited in Schunk), who referred to intrinsic motivation as effectance motivation. Defined as an "inherent need to feel competent and interact effectively with the environment" (Puntrich & Schunk), White believed effectance motivation was a global construct that affected all activities equally; he focused primarily on the ways in which successful interaction with one's environment spurred development, and on its adaptive and evolutionary value. Harter (1981, as cited in Pintrich & Schunk) expanded White's original conceptualization, focusing on motivation in relation to both success and failure, and in relation to specific activities. Harter believes that an individual's perceived level of competence in a particular activity determines, in part, his or her level of motivation. Research using Hart's model has revealed that intrinsic motivation drops as children age; many suggested the drop might be fueled by an increase in extrinsic motivation, but no such evidence has been found. Thus, extrinsic and intrinsic motivation seem to operate independently of one another, such that an increase in one does not necessarily suggest a decrease in the other (Pintrich & Schunk).

GOAL ORIENTATION THEORY

Goal theory, as its name suggests, addresses the way in which different types of goals influence achievement. Research has uncovered two distinct types of goals, and although they have been given different labels across various studies, they are conceptually similar (Pintrich & Schunk). Referred to as performance and learning goals—or simultaneously as task-focused and ability-focused, ego-involved and task-involved, or performance goals and mastery goals—they share many similarities with the notions of intrinsic and extrinsic motivation. Whereas extrinsic and intrinsic motivation are considered more trait-like, however, goal orientation is more context-dependent and situation-specific.

The type of goal a student adopts has an impact on both his subsequent behavior and the learning process itself. Those who choose mastery or learning goals tend to concentrate on learning strategies and processes that help them improve their skills. The focus is on developing skills, accomplishing something challenging, and learning according to self-standards of improvement (Pintrich & Schunk). By contrast, those who adopt performance goals focus more on task completion, and less on the processes used to complete the task. Such students are more likely to be competitive, comparing their performance to others rather than to self-standards (Li, Solmon, Lee, Purvis, & Chu, 2007). Research has generally shown that students who adopt process or mastery goals achieve at higher levels than those who adopt performance goals, regardless of the frequency of feedback from instructors (Schunk). The type of feedback a student receives, however, can impact which type of goal a student chooses; feedback about qualitative aspects of a skill, rather than outcomes-based feedback, helps students become more task and mastery oriented as opposed to performance or ego oriented (Li et al.).

ACHIEVEMENT MOTIVATION

Achievement motivation refers to a person's motivation to perform difficult tasks to the best of their ability (Schunk). Theories of achievement motivation are also known as expectancy-value theories of motivation because they suggest that behavior can be explained in relation to two variables: how much an individual values a particular outcome, and their expectation (e.g. likelihood) of attaining that outcome as a result of their behavior. As the first theory of achievement motivation, Atkinson's (1978, as cited in Schunk) expectancy-value theory helped shift motivation research away from behaviorist S-R models, toward an understanding of the role of perceptions and beliefs.

Later expectancy-value theories have incorporated a number of other cognitive and environmental variables into explanatory models of achievement motivation. Eccles' (1983, as cited in Schunk) model,

for example, incorporated the impact of cultural factors and past performance, as well as goals and perceptions of ability. More specifically, Eccles proposed that expectations of success are influenced by task-specific self-concepts, or an individual's perceptions of ability or competence in a specific domain. An individual might have a favorable self-concept with regard to English, but a less favorable self-concept with regard to math. Similarly, an individual's interpretation of her past performance might affect her future expectations of success; if she thinks she performed well as a result of luck, for example, she might not expect future success. Finally, Eccles recognized that the value of an outcome—or the answer to the question "Why should I engage in this task?"—could also be impacted by cognitive and environmental variables. A person might choose to engage in a particular task, for example, because they find it intrinsically rewarding, or because it is valued by the culture in which he or she lives.

ATTRIBUTION THEORY

Attributions are the explanations people give for causes of behavior. Early attribution research focused on locus of control; Rotter (1966, as cited in Schunk) suggested that people either believe outcomes are unrelated to behavior (an external locus of control) or that outcomes are dependent on behavior (an internal locus of control). Perceptions of control are believed to affect achievement, such that students who believe they have control over outcomes are more likely to engage in academic tasks. Similarly, Heider (1958, as cited in Schunk) suggested that people typically do not know what causes behavior; his naïve analysis of action theory suggested people attribute causes to internal factors and external factors, and that expectations of success were dependent on the interaction between the two.

Weiner (1971, as cited in Schunk) developed an attribution model that built upon the work of Rotter and Heider. He suggested that when students attempt to explain their successes and failures in academic settings, they typically attribute them to one of four causes: ability, effort, task difficulty, and luck. These attributions exist along three different dimensions: external vs. internal, stable vs. unstable, and controllable vs. uncontrollable. Effort, for example, is internal but unstable; it varies across different tasks. It is also controllable, such that a person can choose to put forth greater or less effort. The stability dimension is believed to affect expectations of success; those who attribute success to stable causes such as effort and ability are more likely to expect future success. The locus of control dimension influences affect; students who attribute failure to external causes, for example, are less likely to feel shame than if they attributed failure to lack of ability. Some research suggests attributions may vary by gender and ethnicity—some studies have found girls are more likely to attribute failure to internal causes and success to external causes, for example—but the results have been inconsistent and inconclusive to date (Espinoza, Quezada, Rincones, Strobach & Gutiérrez, 2012). Nevertheless, attribution theory has far-reaching applications; it has been used to study everything from success in a foreign language classroom (Gobel and Mort, 2007) to romantic jealousy in dating relationships (Bauerle, Amirkhan, & Hupka, 2002).

SOCIAL COGNITIVE THEORY

The social cognitive theory of motivation was developed by Albert Bandura and emphasizes the importance of goals and expectations in learning (Schunk). Bandura proposed that people set goals and then self-evaluate their progress toward those goals. The goals people choose to set are influenced by expectations of success and self-efficacy beliefs. Self-efficacy, or judgments of one's capability, can either lower or raise one's expectations for success, and therefore cause people to set more easily or less easily attainable goals (Bryan, Glynn & Kittleson, 2011). An important element of Bandura's theory is the influence of models, or social comparison. People often observe others—others who are similar to themselves—in order to make predictions about their own performance. If they observe someone succeed at a task, the observer's self-efficacy may rise, and they may be more motivated to attempt the task themselves. If a person observes someone fail, they may believe they too are less likely to attain a similar outcome or goal.

A number of different factors can influence an individual's efficacy as she engages in a learning task. Not all experiences of failure and success are the same, for example. An individual who earns a low grade on one math exam, after having received fifteen perfect scores in a row, may experience little change in efficacy. Task difficulty also impacts how a student feels about her ability. If she succeeds in

something that required little effort, her efficacy might not change; if she succeeds in something that requires great effort, however, she may develop more confidence in her abilities. Finally, the source of feedback a student receives influences performance. Self-efficacy is more likely to be enhanced if a teacher tells a student she is capable than if she receives the same feedback from a fellow student. Schunk suggests there are a number of ways teachers can design classroom activities to improve efficacy, by focusing on goal setting, performance feedback, rewards, and instructional presentation, to name just a few.

TERMS & CONCEPTS

Attributions: Attributions are the explanations people give for their behavior and the behavior of others. Attributions exist along three dimensions: internal and external, stable and unstable, and controllable and uncontrollable. The attributions people typically use in achievement settings are ability, effort, task difficulty, and luck.

Conditioning Theories: Behaviorists defined motivation in terms of the frequency and rate of observable behaviors. Conditioning theories of motivation—classical and operant conditioning, for example—explain motivation in terms of the relationship between stimuli and responses; motivation is not explained as a cognitive or mental event.

Drives: Early theories explained motivation largely in terms of physiological deficits. When an organism or human experienced a need such as hunger, drive serves as the motivational construct that prompts the organism to act in such a way to reduce the need—in this case, to find food.

Expectancy-Value Theories: Also, known as achievement motivation, expectancy-value theories suggest that motivation is a result of how likely a person thinks she is to attain a particular outcome, and how highly she values it. More recent expectancy-value theories believe other cognitive variables—such as goals and perceptions of ability—also impact motivation.

Extrinsic Motivation: Extrinsic motivation is motivation to engage in an activity as a means to an end. Grades and money are examples of extrinsic motivators. By contrast, those who are intrinsically motivated find activities enjoyable as ends in themselves.

Flow: Flow is a theory of intrinsic motivation. Individuals who attain flow experience loss of self-consciousness, intense concentration, an increased sense of control, and a transformed sense of time. Activities that foster flow are typically ones that have clear goals and provide immediate feedback, and in which the challenge is met with an equal amount of skill. In order to maintain flow, individuals must seek increasingly higher levels of challenge.

Intrinsic Motivation: Intrinsic motivation is defined as motivation to engage in an activity for its own sake. It is often contrasted with extrinsic motivation, or motivation to engage in an activity as a means to an end—to earn a reward for example, or the recognition of others.

Learning Goals: Goal orientation theory suggests that the type of goal a student adopts impacts behavior and motivation. Those who choose mastery or learning goals tend to concentrate on learning strategies and processes that help them improve their skills. The focus is accomplishing something challenging, and learning according to self-standards of improvement. Students who adopt mastery or learning goals tend to achieve at higher levels than those who adopt performance or outcome goals.

Performance Goals: Goal orientation theory suggests that the type of goal a student adopts impacts behavior and motivation. Those who adopt performance goals focus on task completion, as opposed to the processes used to complete the task. Such students are more likely to be competitive, comparing their performance to others rather than to self-standards. Research has generally shown that students who adopt process or mastery goals achieve at higher levels than those adopt performance goals.

Self-Actualization: Maslow's humanistic theory of motivation established a hierarchy of needs, the highest level of which was self-actualization. Self-actualized people use their talents and capabilities to fulfill their potential; people can become self-actualized by pursuing a variety of activities, but very few people ever attain it.

Self-Efficacy: Self-efficacy is a judgment about one's ability. Self-efficacy varies according to activity, such that a person might have high self-efficacy in English, but low self-efficacy in mathematics.

Its impacts the goals people set for themselves, as well as the amount of effort they put forth to obtain them.

Jennifer Kretchmar

BIBLIOGRAPHY

Bauerle, S. Y., Amirkhan, J. H., & Hupka, R. B. (2002). An attribution theory analysis of romantic jealousy. *Motivation and Emotion, 26,* 297-319. Retrieved September 26, 2007, from EBSCO Online Database Academic Search Premier.

Beck, R. C. (2000). *Motivation: Theories and principles.* Upper Saddle River, New Jersey: Prentice Hall.

Borders, A., Earlywine, M., & Huey, S. (2004). Predicting problem behaviors with multiple expectancies: Expanding expectancy-value theory. *Adolescence, 39,* 539-550. Retrieved September 26, 2007, from EBSCO Online Database Academic Search Premier.

Bryan, R. R., Glynn, S. M., & Kittleson, J. M. (2011). Motivation, achievement, and advanced placement intent of high school students learning science. *Science Education, 95,* 1049-1065. Retrieved on December 4, 2013, from EBSCO Online Database Education Research Complete.

Clinkenbeard, P. R. (2012). Motivation and gifted students: Implications of theory and research. *Psychology in the Schools, 49,* 622-630. Retrieved on December 4, 2013, from EBSCO Online Database Education Research Complete.

Csikszentmihalyi, M. (1990). *Flow: The psychology of optimal experience.* New York, NY: Harper Perennial Publishing.

Espinoza, P., Quezada, S., Rincones, R., Strobach, E. E., & Gutiérrez, M. (2012). Attributional bias instrument (ABI): Validation of a measure to assess ability and effort explanations for math performance. *Social Psychology of Education, 15,* 533-554. Retrieved on December 4, 2013, from EBSCO Online Database Education Research Complete.

Froiland, J., Oros, E., Smith, L., & Hirchert, T. (2012). Intrinsic motivation to learn: The nexus between psychological health and academic success. *Contemporary School Psychology, 16* 91-100. Retrieved on December 4, 2013, from EBSCO Online Database Education Research Complete.

Gobel, P., & Setsuko, M. (2007). Success and failure in the EFL classroom: Exploring students' attributional beliefs in language learning. *EUROSLA Yearbook, 7,* 149-169. Retrieved September 26, 2007, from EBSCO Online Database Education Research Complete.

Hui-ju, L. (2015). Learner autonomy: The role of motivation in foreign language learning. *Journal of Language*

Teaching & Research, 6(6), 1165–1174. Retrieved January 8, 2016, from EBSCO Online Database Education Research Complete.

Li, W., Solmon, M.A., Lee, A.M., Purvis, G., & Chu, H. (2007). Examining the relationship between students' implicit theories of ability, goal orientations, and the preferred type of augmented feedback. *Journal of Sport Behavior, 30,* 280-291. Retrieved September 26, 2007, from EBSCO Online Database Academic Search Premier.

Na Wei. (2016). An investigation of motivation in children's foreign language learning process–A case study on the basis of needs analysis. *Theory and Practice in Language Studies, 6*(7), 1413-1419. Retrieved December 29, 2016, from EBSCO online database Education Source.

Pintrich, P.R., & Schunk, D. H. (2002). *Motivation in education: Theory, research, and applications.* Columbus, OH: Merrill Prentice Hall.

Schunk, D.H. (1996). *Learning theories: An educational perspective.* Columbus, OH: Merrill Prentice Hall.

Speirs Neumeister, K. L., Fletcher, K. L., & Burney, V. H. (2015). *Perfectionism and achievement motivation in high-ability students. Journal for the Education of the Gifted, 38*(3), 215–232. Retrieved January 8, 2016, from EBSCO Online Database Education Research Complete.

SUGGESTED READING

Barry, N.H. (2007). Motivating the reluctant student. *American Music Teacher, 56,* 23-27. Retrieved September 26, 2007, from EBSCO Online Database Academic Search Premier.

Oyserman, Daphna. (2015). *Pathways to success through identity-based motivation.* New York, NY: Oxford University Press.

Schunk, D.H., & Zimmerman, B.J. (Eds.). (1994). *Self-regulation of learning and performance: Issues and educational applications.* Hillsdale, NJ: Lawrence Erlbaum Associates, Publishers.

Stipek, D. J. (1993). *Motivation to learn: From theory to practice.* Boston, MA: Allyn and Bacon.

Studer, B., & Knecht, S. *Motivation: Theory, neurobiology, and applications.* Amsterdam: Academic Press.

Wadsworth, L.M., Husman, J., Duggan, M.A., & Pennington, M.N. (2007). Online mathematics achievement: Effects of learning strategies and self-efficacy. *Journal of Developmental Education, 30,* 6-14. Retrieved September 26, 2007, from EBSCO Online Database Academic Search Premier.

HUMANISM

Humanist philosophies, under different names, have developed in many cultures worldwide over thousands of years. This article discusses the history and basic tenets of humanism as an educational movement. The philosophies of prominent humanists, including Abraham Maslow, Carl Rogers, and John Dewey, are discussed. Instructional strategies based upon humanistic principles are described. Counter philosophies are briefly outlined.

KEYWORDS: Affecive; Behaviorism; Cooperative Learning; Learner-Centered; Open Classroom; Paradigm; Progressive Education; Self-Actualization; Self-Directed learning

OVERVIEW

Humanism is "a philosophy of life inspired by humanity and guided by reason" (Institute for Humanist Studies, n.d.). Humanism "provides the basis for a fulfilling and ethical life without religion." Humanist philosophies, under different names, have developed in many cultures worldwide over thousands of years.

Humanism as a paradigm, philosophy, or pedagogical approach developed in the 1960s in reaction to the psychoanalysis and behaviorism that dominated psychological thought in the first half of the twentieth century. Humanism soon became known as the third force in psychology, leading to the birth of the Journal of Humanistic Psychology in 1961, the formation of the Association of Humanistic Psychology in 1963, and recognition of humanistic psychology as a field by the American Psychological Association in 1971. There are two primary branches of humanism: secular and religious (Huitt, 2000). Secular humanists believe that individuals have everything they need to grow and develop to their fullest potential. In contrast, religious humanists believe that religion plays an important role in human development.

In the educational realm, humanism gained popularity as an alternative to the overly mechanistic approaches to learning and teaching that dominated schools at the time, as well as many cognitive theories of learning and motivation that failed to recognize the importance of student affect in learning (McInerney,

2005). Most learning theories focus on what learning is and how it takes place, focusing on limited aspects of learning such as acquisition, management, and formation of knowledge (Zhou, 2007). These theories neglect the "relevance of learning to the learner as a holistic experience of personal growth" (Zhou). Humanism, in contrast, "is the only learning theory that emphasizes the reciprocal relationship between learning and the learner and the reciprocal relationship between individual actualization and social transformation that make learning a unique human experience.".

Humanism views education as a method of fulfilling human potential based upon individuals' needs and interests ("Humanism," 2007). The humanistic approach emphasizes human freedom, dignity, and potential. It is based on the belief that "human beings are capable of making significant personal choices within the constraints imposed by heredity, personal history, and environment" (Elias & Merriam, 1980). Humanist principles are grounded in the following major assumptions:

- Human nature is inherently good;
- Individuals are free and autonomous, thus they are capable of making major personal choices;
- Human potential for growth and development is virtually unlimited;
- Self-concept plays an important role in growth and development;
- Individuals have an urge toward self-actualization;
- Reality is defined by each person;
- Individuals have responsibility to both themselves and to others (Elias & Merriam).

ROGERS & MASLOW

These principles provided the foundation for major developments in psychology and education (Hiemstra & Brockett, 1994). The most well-known psychologists contributing to this new paradigm were Abraham Maslow and Carl Rogers. Maslow (1970) believed "the process of education should lead to the discovery of identity and understanding of self as a whole person." He developed a motivation theory based on human needs, and his five-level Hierarchy of Human Needs includes physiological/ biological needs, safety, belonging and love, need for esteem, and self-actualization. Only when lower, more basic order needs are satisfied are individuals capable of attending to higher order needs. Conversely, if the things that satisfy lower order needs disappear,

individuals are no longer concerned with higher order needs. For example, children who have witnessed a violent act such as a school shooting and consequently fear for their safety are incapable of learning until they are assured they are safe.

Carl Rogers (1961) developed the concept of "client-centered therapy" designed to help clients develop greater-self-direction. Humanistic education is based on similar ideas. Patterson (1973) believed "the purpose of education is to develop self-actualizing persons." Valett (1977) defined the purpose of humanistic education as the development of "individuals who will be able to live joyous, humane, and meaningful lives."

HUMANISTIC EDUCATION

Humanistic education seeks to provide a foundation for personal growth and development that allows individuals to learn throughout their lives in a self-directed way (DeCarvalho, 1991). In humanism, learning is student-centered and personalized (Ediger, 2006). Education of the whole child is emphasized, and learning is considered a "personal growth experience" (Lamm, 1972). Testing may measure specific learning but humanists believe there are many other ways to evaluate learning (Ediger). Multiple intelligences (Gardner, 1991) are recognized and celebrated. Because of their diverse skills, talents, abilities, all students should not be held accountable to the same standards.

Maslow's Hierarchy of Needs

The major goals of humanistic education are to:

- Accept the learner's needs and purposes and create educational experiences and programs for the development of the learner's unique potential;
- Facilitate the learner's self-actualization and feelings of personal adequacy;
- Foster the acquisition of basic skills and competencies (e.g., academic, personal, interpersonal, communicative, and economic) for living in a multicultural society;
- Personalize educational decisions and practices;
- Recognize the importance of human feelings, values, and perceptions in the educational process;
- Develop a learning climate that is challenging, understanding, supportive, exciting, and free from threat;
- Develop in learners a genuine concern and respect for the worth of others and skill in resolving conflicts (Tomei, 2004).

Gage and Berliner (1991) define five basic objectives of the humanistic view of education:

- Promote positive self-direction and independence;
- Develop the ability to take responsibility for what is learned;
- Develop creativity;
- Curiosity;
- An interest in the arts.

These objectives were developed based upon the following principles (Gage & Berliner):

- Students will learn best what they want and need to know;
- Knowing how to learn is more important than acquiring a lot of knowledge;
- Self-evaluation is the only meaningful evaluation of a student's work;
- Feelings are as important as facts;
- Students learn best in a non-threatening environment.

From a humanistic perspective, teachers strive to make learning more responsive to students' affective (emotions, feelings, values, and attitudes) needs. The focus of teaching is on meeting both the affective and cognitive needs of students to promote their self-actualization in a cooperative, supportive environment ("Humanism"). Thus, teaching is more than presenting subject matter in an organized way; it also involves helping students "derive personal meaning from the information" so they are motivated to learn (Tomei). An integrated curriculum, with a strong emphasis on the arts, is generally advocated by humanists (Ediger).

There are a variety of ways teachers can implement a humanist approach in their teaching (Huitt). Some of these include:

- Allow students to have a choice in the selection of tasks and activities whenever possible;
- Help students learn to set realistic goals;
- Allow students to participate in group work, especially cooperative learning, in order to develop social and affective skills;
- Act as a facilitator for group discussions when appropriate;
- Act a role model for the attitudes, beliefs, and habits you wish to foster in your students, always striving to become a better individual.

Although humanism has met with varying degrees of acceptance, Combs' (1978) rationale for the need for humanistic education has continued to hold relevance:

- Problems facing humans are changing daily. We have created a very complex and interdependent society. Our primary problems are "no longer physical but human ones." In order to prepare students who will be capable of solving current and future problems related to the environment, overpopulation, war, etc. will require an educational system that has a "humanistic orientation."
- The future cannot be predicted. The "information explosion and extraordinary rate of change in modern society" have made it impossible to predict what people will need to know in the future. "New goals for education must be holistic and human. Prime goals must be the development of intelligent behavior, the production of self-propelled, autonomous, creative, problem solving, humane, and caring citizens" (Combs);
- A broader definition of personality to include "mental states and processes" as well as behavior;
- A broader concept of learning that includes not only the conveyance of new knowledge but the personal meaning of information for the individual;
- The importance of the self-concept as a vital part of the learning process.

PIONEERS OF HUMANISM

Abraham Maslow and Carl Rogers were instrumental in the development of humanistic thought. Their contributions are summarized here.

MASLOW'S HIERARCHY OF NEEDS

Maslow's Hierarchy of Needs has direct application to student learning (Tomei; Ediger). For instance, children who are hungry, sleepy, fearful of their safety, have low self-esteem, and/or have untreated health concerns cannot be expected to learn in the classroom.

Definitions of each level and illustrative educational examples are outlined in the following chart. It should be noted that the hierarchy is dynamic and each level does not exist in isolation. Needs change continually and are based on situations. Behaviors may also cross several levels.

SELF-DIRECTED LEARNING

Carl Rogers believed children have a natural desire to learn. He advocated a child-centered curriculum in which children could explore freely to satisfy their academic needs without fear of threat or criticism. He believed in students being self-directed learners through development of self-reliance and independence (Ediger). Rogers believed that schools should provide opportunities for students to select and pursue their own educational interests in order to become lifelong learners, and that teachers should serve primarily as facilitators of learning who share the responsibility of learning with their students (Tomei). He viewed humanistic teachers as both guides and models, providing students with resources to enable them to learn.

PROGRESSIVE EDUCATION

Another well-known humanist was John Dewey, considered the father of the progressive education movement in the United States (Field, 2007). He believed that education should be student-centered, emphasize the student instead of the subject matter, encourage curiosity, and approach the learning process as equally important to what is being learned. Dewey viewed schools as a microcosm of society and felt they should prepare students to become active, cooperative members of society. He believed that self-directed learning is the best way to prepare students for the "demands of responsible membership within the democratic community."

Applications

COOPERATIVE LEARNING

Cooperative learning is a teaching and learning strategy whereby students work together in small teams on assigned projects (Education Broadcasting Corporation, 2004). Students are evaluated both individually and as a group. For cooperative learning to be effective, five elements must be present (Tomei):

- Positive interdependence. Students must share common goals, assign tasks, share resources and information, assume responsibility for different roles, and be rewarded based on group performance;
- Face-to-face interaction. Students must discuss tasks, decide how to approach assignments, and problem solve together. "The importance of helping others is stressed."

- Individual accountability. "Each student must develop a sense of personal responsibility to the group."
- Collaborative skills. Students need to be taught the necessary skills to work together cooperatively;
- Group processing. Students need to discuss and evaluate their progress and learn how to maintain good working relations among team members.

The Open Classroom

The Open Classroom movement as a humanistic approach to elementary education teaching evolved during the late 1960s and early 1970s (Tomei). Open classrooms include seven basic components:

- Provisions for learning. Students work with a diverse range of materials. They move about and talk freely in the classroom. Students are not grouped according to ability;
- Humaneness, respect, warmth. Use of student-made materials. Teachers deal with behavior problems by communicating with the student without involving the group;
- Diagnosis of learning events. Students correct their own work while teachers observe and ask questions;
- Individualized instruction. Students have no textbooks or workbooks;
- Individualized evaluation. Teachers take notes and assess students individually. Formal testing is minimal;
- Professional growth. Teachers work with other educators to offer a range of diverse learning opportunities;
- Assumptions about students. The environment is "warm and accepting" while involving students closely in all aspects of learning.

Research on open education indicates it is effective in improving cooperation, creativity, achievement motivation, and independence, but traditional classrooms are more effective on measures of academic achievement (Tomei).

Role of Technology

Technology has become an integral part of the learning process for students of the twenty-first century (Zhou). In keeping with humanistic educational philosophy, technology has the capability of providing opportunities for "self-directed, self-motivated, and self-evaluated" learning experiences. It is a powerful tool that can be used "to facilitate and advance a person's freedom to learn." In addition to individual learning, technology also provides a collaborative environment that connects online communities of learners worldwide and promotes social interaction.

A HUMANISTIC APPROACH TO TEACHING READING

In contrast to a state-mandated reading curriculum, humanistic education emphasizes a developmental program in which students sequence their own learning (Ediger). As an example, students have input in selecting a book to read as a group. Under teacher guidance and supervision, the group discusses what they have read. In addition to discussing facts, concepts, and generalizations based upon what they have comprehended, the students engage in critical thinking, creative thinking, and problem solving. Each student uses his/her individual talents in the creation of a group evaluative project. Each student may also develop an individual portfolio containing a representative sampling of work that documents his/her individual reading achievement. According to Gunning (2000), a rationalization for a humanistic approach to reading instruction includes:

- Motivation for learning to read and reading to learn comes from within the individual student;
- Student interest is a powerful factor in student reading and learning. Giving students a choice increases interest;
- Purpose for reading comes from within the student;
- Sequence of learning comes from within the student;
- Reading achievement and goals come from the student (Gunning).

SECOND LANGUAGE LEARNING

Second language learning for non-native speakers has been greatly influenced by humanism (Lei, 2007). Second language teaching is learner-centered, in which it is assumed that students learn best when they are treated as individuals with specific needs. Second language teachers create a supportive psychological atmosphere to minimize anxiety and enhance personal security. Both affective and cognitive activities work together to educate the whole student.

Viewpoints

CRITICISMS OF HUMANISM

Fundamentalists on the religious right criticize humanism for being in conflict with religious principles. In The Christian's Response to Humanism, Bert Thompson states: "If there ever existed a formula guaranteed to provide a sin-sick life on this Earth, and a home in hell in the life to come, humanism is it." Thompson asserts that humanism is not just a system of thought that places a high importance on humankind. Far more than that, humanism is a very subtle, disarming, and sophisticated way of saying "atheism."

In Education and New Age Humanism, Russ Wise (1995) expresses his concern that:

"Humanism is the dominant view among leading educators in the U.S. They set the trends of modern education, develop the curriculum, dispense federal monies, and advise government officials on educational needs. In short, they hold the future in their hands. As Christian taxpayers we are paying for the overthrow of our own position."

Although humanism emphasizes the "here and now," not all humanists deny the autonomy and existence of a god and believe that educators can maintain their religious beliefs while engaging in humanistic education practices (Hiemstra & Brockett).

A second criticism of humanism is that it is a self-centered approach to life. Humanists counter this argument with the assertion that individuals find self-actualization, in part, by focusing on problems outside of themselves.

Behaviorist B.F. Skinner argued that less teacher control of student learning, as practiced by humanistic educators, does not imply more student control (Tomei). Skinner felt that less teacher control would result in other conditions controlling student learning and that teachers needed to understand the behavioral process to facilitate learning. Behaviorists also maintain that an emphasis on students' affect is not sufficient for effective instruction, and that placing a higher value on affect than cognition goals may be harmful for both affective and cognitive development. Cognitivists criticize humanistic education for what they perceive is an "absence of clear direction or purpose in the classroom–direction that provides the structure for knowledge to be constructed," thus preventing mastery of basic skills (Tomei).

TERMS & CONCEPTS

Affective: Affective relates to the experience of feeling or emotion in learning.

Behaviorism: Behaviorism is a philosophy of psychology based on the proposition that all behavior be described scientifically without recourse either to internal physiological events or to hypothetical constructs such as the mind.

Cooperative Learning: Cooperative learning is an instructional method in which students work together in groups to support individual as well as group learning.

Learner-Centered: Learner-centered is a "perspective that couples a focus on individual learners (their heredity, experiences, perspectives, backgrounds, talents, interests, capacities, and needs) with a focus on learning (the best available knowledge about learning and how it occurs and about teaching practices that are most effective in promoting the highest levels of motivation, learning, and achievement for all learners). This dual focus then informs and drives educational decision making".

Open Classroom: An open classroom is a student-centered classroom design format that was popular in the United States in 1970s. Some schools were built without walls between classrooms.

Paradigm: Paradigm refers to "an example that serves as a pattern or model for something, especially one that forms the basis of a methodology or theory".

Progressive Education: Progressive education is an educational movement based on the philosophy of John Dewey that was a reaction to formalism. This educational approach focuses on "democratic ideals, creative and purposeful activity, receptivity to student needs, and interaction with the community".

Self-Actualization: Self-actualization refers to Maslow's last level of psychological development achieved when all basic and meta needs are fulfilled and the "actualization" of the full personal potential is realized.

Self-Directed Learning: Self-directed learning is "a process in which students take the initiative to diagnose their learning needs, formulate learning goals, identify resources for learning, select and implement learning strategies, and evaluate learning outcomes. The role of the instructor shifts from being the 'sage on the stage' to the 'guide on the side' in a self-directed learning environment".

Susanne Carter

BIBLIOGRAPHY

Alterator, S., & Deed, C. (2013). Teacher adaptation to open learning spaces. Issues in Educational Research, 23, 315-330. Retrieved December 9, 2013, from EBSCO Online Database Education Research Complete.

Brady-Amoon, P. (2011). Humanism, feminism, and multiculturalism: Essential elements of social justice in counseling, education, and advocacy. Journal of Humanistic Counseling, 50, 135-148. Retrieved December 9, 2013, from EBSCO Online Database Education Research Complete.

Combs, A. (1978). Humanism, education, and the future. Educational Leadership, 35300-303. Retrieved November 5, 2007, from EBSCO online database, Education Research Complete.

DeCarvalho, R. (1991). The humanistic paradigm in education. The Humanistic Psychologist, 19, 88-104.

Ediger, M. (2001). Motivating pupils to learn in mathematics. (ERIC Document Reproduction Service No. ED 449038).

Ediger, M. (2002). What makes a good reading curriculum? (ERIC Document Reproduction Service No. ED 464314).

Ediger, M. (2006). Present-day philosophies of education. Journal of Instructional Psychology, 33, 179-182.

Education Broadcasting Corporation. (2004). What are cooperative and collaborative learning? Retrieved November 3, 2007, from http://thirteen.org.

Elias, J. L., & Merriam, S. (1980). Philosophical foundations of adult education. Malabar, FL: Krieger.

Field, R. (2007). John Dewey. Internet Encyclopedia of Philosophy. Retrieved November 5, 2007, from http://iep.utm.edu.

Gage, N., & Berliner, D. (1991). Educational psychology (5th ed.). Boston: Houghton, Mifflin.

Gardner, H. (1991). Multiple intelligences: Theory into practice. New York: Basic Books.

Gunning, T. (2000). Creating literacy instruction for all children. Boston, Allyn and Bacon.

Humanism. (2007). Learning-Theories.com. Retrieved November 3, 2007, from http://learning-theories.com.

Institute for Humanist Studies. (n.d.). Humanism in brief. Retrieved November 5, 2007, from Institute for Humanist Studies, http://humaniststudies.org.

Kurtz, P. (2000). Humanist manifesto 2000: A call for a new planetary humanism. Amherst, New York: Prometheus Books.

Lamm, Z. (1972). The structure of knowledge in the radical concept of education. In D. E. Purpel & M. Belanger (Eds.) Curriculum and the cultural revolution: A book of essays and readings. Berkeley, CA: McCutchan.

Lei, Q. (2007). EFL teachers' factors and students' affect. US-China Education Review, 4, 60-67.

Maslow, A. H. (1970). Motivation and personality (2nd ed.). New York: Harper & Row.

McCombs, B. L., & Whisler, J. S. (1997). The learner-centered classroom and school: Strategies for increasing student motivation and achievement. San Francisco: Jossey-Bass.

McInerney, Dennis M. (2005). Educational psychology Theory, Research, and Teaching: A 25-year retrospective'. Educational Psychology, 25:6, 585-599.

Northeast Texas Consortium. (n.d.). Self-directed learning. Retrieved November 5, 2007, from Northeast Texas Consortium, http://netnet.org.

Paradigm. (n.d.). Encarta World Dictionary. Retrieved November 5, 2007, from http://encarta.msn.com.

Patterson, C. H. (1973). Humanistic education. Englewood Cliffs, NJ: Prentice-Hall.

Porwancher, A. (2011). Humanism's sisyphean task: curricular reform at Brown University during the Second World War. History of Education, 40, 481-499. Retrieved December 9, 2013, from EBSCO Online Database Education Research Complete.

Progressive Education. (n.d.) Thesaurus. Retrieved November 5, 2007, from Education Resources Information Center Website, http://eric.ed.gov.

Rogers, C. R. (1961). On becoming a person. Boston: Houghton-Mifflin.

Thompson, B. (n.d.). The Christian's response to humanism. Montgomery, AL: Apologetics Press.

Tomei, L. (2004). An examination of humanism: The psychology of the individual student. Learning theories: A primer exercise. Retrieved November 3, 2007, from http://academics.mu.edu.

Valett, R. E. (1977). Humanistic education: Developing the total person. St. Louis: C.V. Mosby.

Wise, R. (1995). Education and New Age humanism. Retrieved November 5, 2007, from Probe Ministries, http://probe.org.

Zhou, L. (2007). Supporting humanistic learning experiences through learning with technology. International Journal of Learning, 13, 131-136. Retrieved November 5, 2007, from EBSCO online database, Education Research Complete.

SUGGESTED READING

Herrick, J. (2005). Humanism: An introduction. New York: Prometheus Books.

Martinez, M. R., & Mcgrath, D. (2013). How can schools develop self-directed learners?. Phi Delta Kappan, 95, 23-27. Retrieved December 9, 2013, from EBSCO Online Database Education Research Complete.

Maslow, A. H. (1970). Motivation and personality (2nd ed). New York: Harper & Row.

Rogers, C., & Freiberg, H. J. (1994). Freedom to learn (3rd ed.). New York: Macmillan.

Shehadeh, A. (2012). Learner-centered instruction in the ELT classroom: What, why and how?. Perspectives (TESOL Arabia), 19, 5-12. Retrieved December 9, 2013, from EBSCO Online Database Education Research Complete.

INTELLIGENCE SCALES

Intelligence scales are used to measure intelligence. Intelligence scales and tests which are individually administered include the Stanford-Binet Intelligence Scale and the Wechsler Intelligence Scale for Children. Intelligence tests in educational settings are typically administered by a school psychologist or other trained examiner. Intelligence tests are widely used in the assessment of learning disabilities for special-education services and in the identification of gifted students. Statistical analyses are commonly conducted to analyze and evaluate intelligence-test scores. Intelligence tests have advantages in that they are highly regarded by both educational researchers and school personnel. Research has demonstrated the benefits of cross-battery intelligence- test assessment to measure and compare theory-based cognitive factors.

OVERVIEW

Standardized intelligence scales are tests used as assessment instruments to measure the intelligence of individuals. Although there are group intelligence tests, this article will be concerned primarily with individually administered measures of intelligence. The most widely used and educationally applied intelligence scales are the Stanford-Binet Intelligence Scale and the Wechsler Intelligence Scale for Children.

Generally speaking, an individual's intelligence is dependent on general mental abilities involved in processes such as learning, using language, reasoning, classifying, making calculations, and adjusting to novel situations. Intelligence is related to an individual's performance on intelligence tests that include items requiring various tasks—verbal, mathematical, perceptual, and problem-solving, for example. The performance of individuals on intelligence tests is compared with others of the same age group and/or level of ability. Thus, intelligence quotients (IQs) are based on an individual's norm group (Gage & Berliner, 1988; Weber, 1991).

The mean intelligence scale or intelligence test IQ score is defined as 100. IQs above 130 are generally considered as superior. Scores between IQ 85 and 115 are considered to be within the average range of intelligence (Lewis & Doorlag, 1987). Scores between IQ 70 and 85 are considered low average. IQ measures can be thought of as tests of mental age. High scores on intelligence tests mean that children are developing more rapidly than their age-mates. The environment in which a child develops is critical in enhancing intelligence, particularly fluid intelligence. Environmental and emotional factors during childhood and adolescence can cause IQ scores to vary moderately (Kirk & Gallagher, 1989; Lewis & Doorlag; Piaget, 1981; Roid, Shaughnessy, & Greathouse, 2005).

HISTORY

In 1905, the French educator Alfred Binet (1857-1911) and Theophile, or Théodore, Simon (1873-1961) developed tests to use in classifying students for entrance and appropriate grade placement in a new nationwide French public school system. Binet and Simon sought to develop the most diverse tests possible to determine the frequency of success of students as a function of age. The original Binet-Simon Scale of Intelligence consisted of 30 subtests of age-graded items—questions to answer, problems to solve, and tasks to perform—which children of different ages should be able to do. These tests were the precursors of all later intelligence tests (Piaget; Weber).

The Binet-Simon Scale

Based on the Binet-Simon Scale of Intelligence, a child who can answer questions that average nine-year-olds can answer are assigned a mental age (MA), of nine (Weber). The child's MA, as measured by the intelligence test, is then compared to his or her actual chronological age (CA). The German psychologist William Stern concluded that simple comparisons between MA and CA are insensitive to degrees. Stern advocated using a ratio of MA to CA to measure intelligence. However, in Stern's historic formula, he multiplied the initial quotient by 100 in order to eliminate the decimal point. Thus, Stern's formula for this intelligence quotient (IQ) is: $MA \div CA \times 100 = IQ$. Examples of the calculation of three different intelligence quotients is shown in Table 1. In Case 1 of Table 1, where a child's CA exceeds his or her mental age, the child is classified as "slow" and is assigned to a lower grade level. In Case 2 where a child's MA equals his or her chronological age, the resulting IQ is 100, the mean IQ level. In Case 3 where a child's MA exceeds his CA, the child is classified as "bright" and is resultantly assigned to a higher grade level (Weber).

The Stanford-Binet Scale

In 1916, Lewis Terman (1877-1956), a Stanford University psychologist, revised the original Binet-Simon Scale of Intelligence. The revised Binet-Simon Scale, titled the Stanford-Binet Intelligence Scale, was restandardized on new populations of children and published by the Houghton Mifflin Company. Terman was also well known for his work with gifted children. In 1920, he began a longitudinal study that was to continue for more than 50 years in which he followed over 1500 gifted children into maturity and old age (Dallmann, Rouch, Char, & DeBoer, 1982; Kirk & Gallagher; Weber).

The Stanford-Binet Intelligence Scale is the traditional intelligence scale and cognitive intelligence test battery. It is perhaps the best known of the individually administered measures of intelligence, and is more suitable for testing children than late adolescents and adults (Borg & Gall, 1989).

There are newer versions of the Stanford-Binet that are linked to older, previous editions, including the original version. There are full-scale or complete cognitive batteries of the regular Stanford-Binet and abbreviated batteries (Glutting, 1989). A well-known earlier edition of the instruments representing the third revision is the Stanford-Binet Form L-M version published in 1960, comprised of two scales serving different purposes. Unfortunately, the Stanford-Binet Form L-M has less power to measure IQs at the high end of intelligence and has norms that discriminated against gifted students (Silverman & Kearney, 1992). The fifth edition of the Stanford-Binet Intelligence Scale, or SB5, was introduced in 2003.

The Stanford-Binet can be administered in long-form or full-scale, or in short-form via any of a number of subtests that represent designated areas such as:

- Verbal Reasoning;
- Abstract-Value Reasoning;
- Quantitative Reasoning;
- Short-Term Memory (Weber).

The Stanford-Binet measures of intelligence quotients or IQs yield standard-age, full-scale/long-form, test-composite or total-composite scores and short-form area scores. The Verbal Reasoning Subtest, for example, provides a verbal IQ score.

The Wechsler Scales

The individual intelligence tests that are most often administered are the Wechsler tests, originally dubbed the Wechsler-Bellevue Intelligence Scales, which were developed by David Wechsler, and were published by the Psychological Corporation of San Antonio, Texas (Dallmann et al.; Weber).

The Wechsler Intelligence Scale has also published a number of versions. The Wechsler Intelligence Scale for Children-Revised (WISC-R) is administered to school-age children. It is a "downward extension" of the Wechsler Adult Intelligence Scale or WAIS and is appropriate for use in testing children between the ages of 5 and 17 (Borg & Gall; Lewis & Doorlag; Weber). The fourth version of the scale, or WISC-IV, was introduced in 2003. The Wechsler Intelligence Scale for Children-Fourth Edition maintains many of the features of prior editions (Mayes & Calhoun, 2007).

Another version of the Wechsler that was published for younger children was the Wechsler Preschool and Primary Scale of Intelligence, or WPPSI. It was designed to test children between the ages of 4 and 6 and a half (Borg & Gall; Field, 1987). The Wechsler Adult Intelligence Scale-Revised or WAIS-R is administered to individuals over age 16 and is suitable for use in testing late adolescents and adults (Borg & Gall; Weber). There are also editions that are published in languages other than English (e.g., Japanese, Spanish, French, and Hebrew).

The Wechsler can be implemented in full-scale/full-form and also in abbreviated or split-half short forms making use of various individual subtests of interest. The Wechsler scale has two subscales: a verbal scale and a performance scale. Each edition of the Wechsler has a somewhat variant number of verbal and performance subtests. The verbal subscale includes questions and tasks that involve information, arithmetic, vocabulary, comprehension, similarities, and "digit span." The Digit Span subtest is a measure of short-term memory. The verbal subtests require students to listen to questions and to reply orally. The performance scale is made up of visual-motor tasks and includes several subtest short forms. The subtests are:

- Coding or Mazes;
- Picture Completion;
- Picture Arrangement;
- Object Assembly;
- Block Design (Axelrod & Paolo, 1998; Comninel & Bordieri, 2001; Lewis & Doorlag; Lynn et al., 2005; Nicholson & Alcorn, 1993; Weber; Wyver & Markham, 1998).

The Wechsler scales have achieved increasing prominence in the field of intelligence testing due in part to the fact that they yield a number of useful subscores in addition to an overall IQ score. WISC-R yields total-test scores called full-scale IQ (FSIQ) scores, which are comprehensive measures of intelligence, and two other global scores—a Verbal IQ (VIQ) and a Performance IQ (PIQ) (Borg & Gall; Lewis & Doorlag). The VIQ is calculated by adding the scaled scores of all of the verbal subtests except Digit Span. The PIQ is obtained from five of the performance subtest scale scores (Nicholson & Alcorn).

The WISC-R also yields factor-based scores on four different indices:

- Verbal Comprehension Index or VCI;
- Perceptual Organization Index or POI;
- Freedom from Distractibility Index or FDI;
- Processing Speed Index or PSI (Calhoun & Mayes, 2005).

In addition, a test of memory impairment yields the Wechsler Memory Scale Memory Quotient (WMS MQ) (Prifitera & Barley, 1985).

Other Intelligence Scales

There are a variety of other intelligence scales that are sometimes used in intelligence testing. These include:

- The Kaufman Brief Intelligence Test or K-BIT;
- The Leiter International Performance Scale and the Leiter International Performance Scale-Revised;
- The Merrill Palmer Developmental Scale-Revised;
- The Fagan Test of Infant Intelligence or FTII;
- The Bayley Scales of Infant Development.

APPLICATIONS

Administration

Standardized intelligence scale instruments require special training for their administration and interpretation. The tests are typically administered individually by a school psychologist or other trained examiner. The examiner is usually involved in the selection of tests that are administered and in the general approach for administration. The experience level of the examiner in the facilitation of tests is important in avoiding examiner and administration errors. The use of the same examiner can minimize the factor of errors arising from administration, possible bias, and/or influence. Some intelligence tests have advantages and disadvantages in the relative ease or difficulty of accurate administration (Avant, 1987; Dallmann et al.).

Administration may involve a full battery or a short-form procedure. Any of a number of subtests can be administered as a screening device when complete administration is not feasible (Haynes, 1985).

Because the performance of students may be influenced by the conditions of administration, the tests may be administered more than once. Students may suffer the effects of anxiety or have problems with seating or other physical arrangements in a first administration that make a second administration necessary. An examinee's scores from different administrations, previous and current, can be compared.

Measurement

The measurement of an individual school-aged child's intelligence provides information about his or her overall or global intellectual ability and the specific factors of intelligence. The measurement of the child's higher or lower levels of cognition include his or her relative cognitive ability, cognitive skills and sub-skills, cognitive processes and capacities, cognitive development and functioning, and cognitive strengths and weaknesses. In order to measure the child's intelligence, the various specific aptitudes or abilities contributing to his or her total behavior must be measured (Lewis & Doorlag; Nicholson & Alcorn; Roid et al.).

G Factor Intelligence

Measurements of intelligence emphasize g factor intelligence. The g factor is the most general and relevant cognitive ability and is one of the most important predictors of academic achievement. It has also been found to relate to a variety of other socially relevant behavioral outcomes (Juan-Espinosa, Cuevas, Escorial, & Garcia, 2006; Robinson, 1992).

The measurement of intelligence involves the measurement of constructs—psychological characteristics or variables such as verbal functioning and reasoning, visual-spatial processing, and memory processing. Intellectual ability is positively correlated with an individual's speed of mentally processing information. This proposition, as a theory of intelligence, has strong supportive evidence and underlies most tests of mental abilities (Osterlind, 1998). Among other types of exercises used in intelligence testing and measurement are inductive reasoning tasks. Inductive reasoning can be defined as the ability to apply specific experiences to general rules. Inductive reasoning problems are commonly expressed as analogies (Osterlind).

Determining Intellectual Performance

Intelligence assessment can be used to determine the factors influencing the intellectual performance, development, and capabilities of students. Schoolchildren's performance can be compared with the use of recent norms so as to identify the typical intellectual performance of high achievement-level students and the intellectual performance of low achievement-level students.

Relative performance in general or global areas of intelligence is recognized by the variation in full-scale IQ points and in significantly lower or higher FSIQs. Children's performance varies on the dichotomous constructs of verbal abilities and performance abilities as measured by the Wechsler Intelligence Scales. This can be recognized by the variation in verbal IQ points and lower or higher verbal IQ scores.

Performance areas of intelligence, as measured by performance scales, reveal differences in performance IQ and relative lower or higher IQ points (Kaufman, 1994).

The fact that there is comparability from one age to another permits performance to be compared across multiple age levels, from children to adolescents and adults. Children's mental performance also varies at different ages. There is a range in ability levels (e.g., II through V) of students demonstrated in IQ tests and IQs.

There are gender performance differences exhibited in IQs. Males are consistently more variable than females in areas such as spatial visualization, quantitative reasoning, spelling, and general knowledge. Using the Wechsler Intelligence Scales, these cognitive gender differences decrease for adolescents but not for adults (Feingold, 1992; Feingold, 1993; Lynn et al.).

Identification of Gifted and Learning Disabled Children

Intelligence testing is used for the selection and placement of students in various educational programs. Binet invented his metrical scale of intelligence with a view to determining the degree of advancement or degree of disability. Intelligence is assessed by advancement or disability according to the mean statistical age for correct solutions (Piaget).

Intelligence testing has also been commonly used to identify gifted children. In the past, many programs for the gifted relied almost exclusively on norm-referenced tests of intelligence for the assessment of students. Early definitions of giftedness were based on IQ scores above a certain designated point—115, 130, 140, et cetera—on the Stanford-Binet Intelligence Scale. However, both the Stanford-Binet and the WISC-R are used for the identification of academically talented students (Kirk & Gallagher; Lewis & Doorlag; Robinson).

Intelligence tests are widely used in the assessment of learning disabilities for special education services. The scales are used as diagnostic tests to screen, identify, select, and place children in school programs and settings especially at the early-childhood and preschool levels. Among the types of special education students assessed by intelligence tests include individuals who are experiencing cognitive delays and have informational-processing deficits, those with cognitive and learning disabilities, the intellectually disabled, those with developmental disorders such as attention deficit/hyperactivity disorder (ADHD), children with serious mental and emotional disorders, and behaviorally disturbed children. Most states generally require students to achieve an IQ score in the low average range, that is, 70 to 85, to qualify for special education services for the learning disabled. Below-average intellectual performance is a criterion for intellectual disability (Avant; Comninel & Bordieri; Field; Flynn, 1985; Gussin & Javorsky, 1995; Lewis & Doorlag; Roid et al.; Ross-Kidder, 2000; Shah & Holmes, 1985; Silverstein, 1984; Zimet & Adler, 1990). Intelligence testing can also be used to assess preschool children with autism and high-functioning autism (Bolte & Proustka, 2004; Delmolino, 2006; Minshew, Turner, & Goldstein, 2005).

The intellectual functioning of visually- and hearing-impaired students can be assessed using adapted, modified, and/or specially designed measures. Most of the individuals referred for testing are eligible for modifications and/or accommodations. An adaptation of the Stanford-Binet Intelligence Scale, the Perkins-Binet Intelligence Scale, is designed to be used with visually-impaired individuals aged 2 to 22. The latter adaptation has two forms: one for those with usable vision and another for those with nonusable vision. The verbal section of the WISC-R has also been used to assess schoolchildren with visual impairments (James, 1984; Lewis & Doorlag; Ross-Kidder; Wyver & Markham).

Statistical Analysis of Intelligence Scores

Statistics has wide application and multifaceted uses with regard to the analysis of intelligence test scores. Sources of measurement error in intelligence testing include scoring, time sampling, and content sampling. The magnitude of errors is explored with standard deviation of scores and standard errors of estimate and measurement (Hanna, 1981).

The collection of validity and reliability information is essential in establishing the efficacy of intelligence measures. Test-retest reliability and alternate-form reliability are types of reliability often used in intelligence testing. The Stanford-Binet Intelligence Scales have proved their usefulness in educational research and practice because of the considerable amount of evidence that has been collected regarding its validity and reliability (Borg & Gall).

Comparisons and correlations are made among different intelligence scale instruments, versions, and forms. Correlation coefficients between full scales/full protocols and short/subtest forms can be positive or negative, consistently low or high, significant or non-significant. The quality of means, analyses of variances and covariances, comparability of different scales, degree of parallelism of scales, similarities and variabilities across scales, and subtests based on test and subtest scores are analyzed (Evans, 1985; Quereshi & Ostrowski, 1985).

VIEWPOINTS

Advantages

Intelligence tests are highly regarded by both educational researchers and school personnel. They provide a relatively rapid and convenient estimation of an individual's general level of intelligence. Intelligence tests are efficacious in predicting school achievement because they measure the aspects of intelligence required for success in school learning. They also serve as a vital diagnostic tool for children in special education. High-quality intelligence tests can produce objective measures of cognitive abilities, capacities, and functioning that are valid, reliable, and replicable (Borg & Gall; Piaget; Roid et al.).

Disadvantages

Intelligence scales and IQ tests have limitations and drawbacks. They are expensive to use and can be administered and interpreted only by special personnel (Lewis & Doorlag; Piaget).

Many feel that society places too much weight on intelligence, versus other factors such as motivation and perseverance that are important to education. Intelligence tests are not able to assess vital abilities and dimensions such as creativity, leadership potential, and specific talents. Many assessment professionals focus on full-scale global scores and do not explore the whole-score intelligence profile (Lewis & Doorlag; Roid et al.).

There is no uniformity or standardization of practices with regard to how states and school districts use IQ scores. For example, as relates to eligibility for services for gifted students, IQ scores of 115 may qualify in one state or school district whereas a score of 130, 140, or higher may be required in another. The ultimate uses of test scores are dictated by legislation and regulation rather than clinical exploration (Lewis & Doorlag; Roid et al.).

Intelligence tests have long been criticized because they involve knowledge of language, and results may not fully reflect the real abilities of children with language problems or for whom English is a second language. Intelligence tests have also been charged with being biased, favoring middle- and upper-class students and discriminating against those who are learning disabled or come from minority cultures (Dallmann et al.; Lewis & Doorlag).

Research

Research has explored the relationship between intelligence tests, made correlations of intelligence scales with other measures, and examined the possibility of substitution of one instrument for another in studies.

Cross-Battery Assessment

A good example of the value of drawing on research findings from past studies is examining the related theory associated with the development of what has come to be known as the Cattell-Horn-Carroll or CHC model of intelligence (Roid et al.). The theory of fluid and crystallized intelligence was developed by Raymond Cattell (1943). Cattell's theory was expanded and detailed to include other factors by John Horn (1985). The hierarchical nature of cognitive factors and the prominence of the fluid and crystallized factors of intelligence was verified by John Carroll (1993). The end result of this evolutionary theory development was the Cattell-Horn-Carroll model, which increased the validity of intelligence test interpretation by permitting comparisons to be made across many batteries (Roid et al.). Because the subtests of major intelligence batteries are normed separately, subtests from different batteries can be administered to develop results that provide a very thorough intelligence assessment of an individual. Thus, this research has cumulatively shown the benefits of "cross-battery assessment"—using individual subtests across batteries to measure and compare theory-based cognitive factors (Flanagan & Ortiz, 2001; McGrew & Flanagan, 1998; Roid et al.).

The CHC model and related theory have established the multifaceted nature of intelligence (Roid et al.). The Stanford-Binet V, for example, has a hierarchical theoretical model consisting of the g or general factor and five additional cognitive factors:

- Fluid reasoning;
- Knowledge or crystallized ability;
- Quantitative reasoning;
- Visual-spatial ability;
- Working memory (Roid et al.).

Ability vs. Age Levels

Another gravitation that has evolved in intelligence testing is that of basing the level of difficulty of items on ability levels or functional levels versus the original use of age levels. Stanford-Binet has traditionally had ability levels built in since 1916 (Roid et al.). This practice allows an individual's general level of intellectual functioning to be initially identified and then the remainder of the intelligence test is custom-tailored to that person's ability level. Additionally, Roid et al. have found that ability levels provide greater precision and reliability in measures of intelligence within a shorter time period.

TERMS & CONCEPTS

Chronological Age (CA): An individual's actual numerical age in years since birth; a term used in calculating IQ.

Constructs: A psychological characteristic or variable such as verbal reasoning or memory processing that is measured in intelligence testing.

G Factor: Also general factor; a common factor in all tests of mental ability; the most global cognitive ability and one of the most important predictors of academic achievement.

Intelligence Profiles: Representations of individuals' intelligence(s) made up of their subtest scores across one or more intelligence test batteries used to compare characteristic cognitive abilities, common cognitive factors, prototypes, typical and atypical patterns, similarities and dissimilarities, and strengths and weaknesses.

Intelligence Quotients (IQ): Ratios of mental age (MA) to chronological age (CA) and calculated by the formula $IQ = MA \div CA \times 100$.

Intelligence Scale: An intelligence test instrument that is used to measure intelligence.

Mental Age (MA): The age of most individuals who display a particular level of performance; a term used in calculating IQ.

Norm Group: A group of individuals against which an individual's test performance is compared.

Norm-Referenced Test: Tests in which comparisons can be made between a student and other students who form a norm group.

Short Forms: Subtests that are used as assessment instruments in only certain designated areas to measure specific constructs such as verbal reasoning or quantitative reasoning.

Standard Error of Measurement: A statistical and psychometric quantity that tells how much a test score would be expected to vary if a very large number of repeated measurements were made with the same instrument.

Subtests: Short forms of full-scale tests or of a test battery that represent an assessment in only certain designated areas to measure constructs such as verbal reasoning or quantitative reasoning.

Test Battery: A group of several tests that are comparable, the results of which are used individually, in combination, and/or totally.

Test-Retest Reliability: A measure of reliability that is obtained by administering the same test again after a short time interval and by correlating the two sets of scores.

R. D. Merritt

BIBLIOGRAPHY

Avant, A. H. (1987). An examination of the relationship between the WISC-R and K-ABC for selection of students for special education programs. Washington, DC: Education Resources Information Center (ERIC Document Reproduction Service No. ED291785).

Axelrod, B. N., & Paolo, A. M. (1998). Utility of the WAIS-R seven-subtest short form as applied to the standardization sample. Psychological Assessment, 10, 33-37.

Bergeron, R., & Floyd, R. G. (2013). Individual part score profiles of children with intellectual disability: A descriptive analysis across three intelligence tests. School Psychology Review, 42, 22-38. Retrieved December 5, 2013, from EBSCO Online Database Education Research Complete.

Bolte, S., & Poustka, F. (2004). Comparing the intelligence profiles of savant and nonsavant individuals with autistic disorder. Intelligence, 32, 121-131.

Borg, W. R., & Gall, M. D. (1989). Educational research: An introduction. New York, NY: Longman.

Calhoun, S. L., & Mayes, S. D. (2005). Processing speed in children with clinical disorders. Psychology in the Schools, 42, 333-343. Retrieved October 5, 2007, from EBSCO Online Database Education Research Complete.

Carroll, J. B. (1993). Human cognitive abilities. New York, NY: Cambridge University Press.

Cattell, R. B. (1943). The measurement of human intelligence. Psychological Bulletin, 40, 153-193.

Comninel, M. E., & Bordieri, J. E. (2001). Estimating WISC-III scores for special education students using the Dumont-Faro Short Form. Psychology in the Schools, 38, 11-16. Retrieved October 5, 2007, from EBSCO Online Database Education Research Complete.

Dallmann, M., Rouch, R. L., Char, L. Y. C., & DeBoer, J. J. (1982). The teaching of reading. New York, NY: Holt, Rinehart and Winston.

Delmolino, L. M. (2006). Brief report: Use of DQ for estimating cognitive ability in young children with autism. Journal of Autism and Developmental Disorders, 36, 959-963. Retrieved October 5, 2007, from EBSCO Online Database Education Research Complete.

Dubovoy, S. C. (1996). The personal intelligences: Linking Gardner to Montessori. NAMTA Journal, 21, 64-78.

Eisenstein, N., & Engelhart, C. I. (1997). Comparison of the K-BIT with short forms of the WAIS-R in a neuropsychological population. Psychological Assessment, 9, 57-62.

Evans, P. G. (1985). Accuracy of the Satz-Mogel procedure in estimating WAIS-R IQs that are in the normal range. Journal of Clinical Psychology, 41, 100-103. Retrieved October 5, 2007, from EBSCO Online Database Education Research Complete.

Feingold, A. (1992). Sex differences in variability in intellectual abilities: A new look at an old controversy. Review of Educational Research, 62, 61-84.

Feingold, A. (1993). Cognitive gender differences: A developmental perspective. Sex Roles: A Journal of Research, 29, 91-112. Retrieved October 5, 2007, from EBSCO Online Database Education Research Complete.

Field, M. (1987). Relation of language-delayed preschoolers' Leiter scores to later IQ. Journal of Clinical Child Psychology, 16, 111-115.

Flanagan, D. P., & Ortiz, S. O. (2001). Essentials of cross-battery assessment. New York, NY: Wiley.

Flanagan, R. (1995). The utility of the Kaufman assessment battery for children (K-ABC) and the Wechsler intelligence scales for linguistically different children: Clinical considerations. Psychology in the Schools, 32, 5-11. Retrieved October 5, 2007, from EBSCO Online Database Education Research Complete.

Flynn, J. R. (1985). Wechsler Intelligence Tests: Do we really have a criterion of mental retardation? American Journal of Mental Deficiency, 90, 236-244.

Gage, N. L., & Berliner, D. C. (1988). Educational psychology. Boston, MA: Houghton Mifflin Company.

Glutting, J. J. (1989). Introduction to the structure and application of the Stanford-Binet intelligence scale-fourth edition. Journal of School Psychology, 27, 69-80.

Gussin, B., & Javorsky, J. (1995). The utility of the WISC-III Freedom from distractibility in the diagnosis of youth with attention deficit hyperactivity disorder in a psychiatric sample. Diagnostique, 21, 29-42.

Hanna, G. S. (1981). Estimating major sources of measurement error in individual intelligence scales: Taking our heads out of the sand. Journal of School Psychology, 19, 370-376.

Haynes, J. P. (1985). Comparative validity of two WAIS-R short forms with clients of low IQ. Journal of Clinical Psychology, 41, 282-284. Retrieved October 5, 2007, from EBSCO Online Database Education Research Complete.

Horn, J. L. (1985). Remodeling old models of intelligence. In B. B. Wolman (Ed.), Handbook of intelligence (pp. 267-300). New York, NY: Wiley.

James, R. P. (1984). A correlational analysis between the Raven's Matrices and WISC-R performance scales. Volta Review, 86, 336-341.

Juan-Espinosa, M., Cuevas, L., Escorial, S., & Garcia, L. F. (2006). Testing the indifferentiation hypothesis during childhood, adolescence and adulthood. Journal of Genetic Psychology, 167, 5-15. Retrieved October 5, 2007, from EBSCO Online Database Academic Search Premier.

Karmel, L. J., & Karmel, M. O. (1978). Measurement and evaluation in the schools. New York, NY: Macmillan Publishing Co., Inc.

Kaufman, A. S. (1994). A reply to Macmann and Barnett: Lessons from the blind men and the elephant. School Psychology Quarterly, 9, 199-207.

Kirk, S. A., & Gallagher, J. J. (1989). Educating exceptional children. Boston,

Kirk, S. A., & Gallagher, J. J. (1989). Educating exceptional children. Boston, MA: Houghton Mifflin Company.

Lewis, R. B., & Doorlag, D. H. (1987). Teaching special students in the mainstream. Columbus, OH: Merrill Publishing Company.

Lynn, R., Raine, A., Venables, P. H., Mednick, S. A., & Irving, P. (2005). Sex differences of the WISC-R in Mauritius. Intelligence, 33, 527-533.

Mayes, S. D., & Calhoun, S. L. (2007). Wechsler intelligence scale for children- third- and fourth-edition: Predictors of academic achievement in children with attention-deficit/ hyperactivity disorder. School Psychology Quarterly, 22, 234-249.

McGrew, K. S., & Flanagan, D. P. (1998). The intelligence test desk reference (ITDR): Gf-Gc cross battery assessment. Boston, MA: Allyn & Bacon.

Merchán-Naranjo, J., Mayoral, M., Rapado-Castro, M., Llorente, C., Boada, L., Arango, C., & Parellada, M. (2012). Estimation of the intelligence quotient using

Wechsler Intelligence Scales in children and adolescents with Asperger syndrome. Journal of Autism & Developmental Disorders, 42, 116-122. Retrieved December 5, 2013, from EBSCO Online Database Education Research Complete.

Minshew, N. J., Turner, C. A., & Goldstein, G. (2005). The application of short forms of the Wechsler intelligence scales in adults and children with high functioning autism. Journal of Autism and Developmental Disorders, 35, 45-52. Retrieved October 5, 2007, from EBSCO Online Database Academic Search Premier.

Mishra, S. P. (1982). Intelligence test performance as affected by anxiety and test administration procedures. Journal of Clinical Psychology, 38, 825-829.

Moran, S., Kornhaber, M., & Gardner, H. (2006). Orchestrating multiple intelligences. Educational Leadership, 64, 22-27. Retrieved October 5, 2007, from EBSCO Online Database Education Research Complete.

Nicholson, C. L., & Alcorn, C. L. 91993). Interpretation of the WISC-III and its subtests. Washington, DC: Education Resources Information Center (ERIC Document Reproduction Service No. ED 367 668).

Osterlind, S. J. (1998). Constructing test items: Multiple-choice, constructed-response, performance and other formats. Boston, MA: Kluwer Academic Publishers.

Piaget, J. (1981). The psychology of intelligence. Totowa, NJ: Littlefield, Adams & Co.

Prifitera, A., & Barley, W. P. (1985). Cautions in interpretations of comparisons between the WAIS-R and the Wechsler Memory Scale. Journal of Consulting and Clinical Psychology, 53, 564-565.

Quereshi, M. Y., & Ostrowski, M. J. (1985). The comparability of three Wechsler adult intelligence scales in a college sample. Journal of Clinical Psychology, 41, 397-407.

Robinson, N. M. (1992). Stanford-Binet IV, of course!: Time marches on. Roeper Review, 15, 32-34.

Roid, G. H., Shaughnessy, M. F., & Greathouse, D. (2005). An interview with Gale Roid about the Stanford-Binet 5. North American Journal of Psychology, 7, Retrieved October 5, 2007, from EBSCO Online Database Academic Search Premier.

Ross-Kidder, K. (2000). Gender differences in psychometric profiles of adults with learning disabilities. Washington, DC: Education Resources Information Center (ERIC Document Reproduction Service No. ED445423).

Shah, A., & Holmes, N. (1985). The use of the Leiter international performance scale with autistic children: Brief report. Journal of Autism and Developmental Disorders, 15, 195-203.

Silverman, L. K., & Kearney, K. (1992). The case for the Stanford-Binet L-M as a supplemental test. Roeper Review, 15, 34-37.

Silverstein, A. B. (1984). Standard errors for short forms of Wechsler's intelligence scales with deviant subjects. Journal of Consulting and Clinical Psychology, 52, 913-914.

Tasbihsazan, R., Nettelbeck, T., & Kirby, N. (2003). Predictive validity of the Fagan test of infant intelligence. British Journal of Developmental Psychology, 21, 585-597.

Tylenda, B., & Brogan, D. T. (2011). More than numbers: Intelligence testing with the intellectually disabled. Brown University Child & Adolescent Behavior Letter, 27, 1-6. Retrieved December 5, 2013, from EBSCO Online Database Education Research Complete.

Vialle, W. (1994). Profiles of intelligence. Australian Journal of Early Childhood, 19, 30-34.

Weber, A. L. (1991). Introduction to psychology. New York, NY: Harper Collins Publishers.

Wilson, M. S., & Reschly, D. J. (1996). Assessment in school psychology training and practice. School Psychology Review, 25, 9-23.

Wyver, S. R., & Markham, R. 91998). Do children with visual impairments demonstrate superior short-term memory, memory strategies and metamemory? Journal of Visual Impairment & Blindness, 92, 799-811.

Zimet, S. G., & Adler, S. S. (1990). Methodological and clinical issues in studies of the performance of emotionally disturbed children and adolescents on abbreviated forms of the WISC-R: A review. Journal of School Psychology, 28, 133-146.

SUGGESTED READING

Boake, C. (2002). From the Binet-Simon to the Wechsler-Bellevue: Tracing the history of intelligence testing. Journal of Clinical & Experimental Neuropsychology, 24, 383-405. Retrieved October 5, 2007, from EBSCO Online Database Academic Search Premier.

Cheramie, G. M., Stafford, M. E., Boysen, C., Moore, J., & Prade, C. (2012). Relationship between the Wechsler Adult Intelligence Scale - Fourth Edition (WAIS-IV) and Woodcock-Johnson-III Normative Update (NU): Tests of Cognitive Abilities (WJ-III COG). Journal of Education & Human Development, 5, 1-9. Retrieved December 5, 2013, from EBSCO Online Database Education Research Complete.

Kubinger, K. D. (1998). Psychological assessment of high-ability: Worldwide-used Wechsler's intelligence scales and their psychometric shortcomings. High Ability Studies, 9, 237-251. Retrieved October 5, 2007, from EBSCO Online Database Academic Search Premier.

Minton, B. A., & Pratt, S. (2006). Identification discrepancies. Roeper Review, 28, 232-236. Retrieved October 5, 2007, from EBSCO Online Database Academic Search Premier.

Mleko, A. L., & Burns, T. G. (2005). Test review. Applied Neuropsychology, 12, 179-180. Retrieved October 5, 2007, from EBSCO Online Database Academic Search Premier.

Yam, P. (1998). Intelligence considered. Scientific American Presents, 6-11. Retrieved October 5, 2007, from EBSCO Online Database Academic Search Premier.

Zettergren, P. (2003). School adjustment in adolescence for previously rejected, average and popular children. British Journal of Educational Psychology, 73, 207-221. Retrieved October 5, 2007, from EBSCO Online Database Academic Search Premier.

ABSTRACT THINKING SKILLS

Abstract thinking skills develop over the course of a child's early developmental years and throughout adolescence. Development of these cognitive skills is largely dependent on stage of growth and on various biological processes including myelination, which increases the speed at which an individual can process information. Researchers have developed the information processing model to describe the actions of the brain when human beings think. This model helps us explain how human beings achieve higher cognitive abilities. Abstract thinking skills are developed in various ways, in and out of the classroom.

KEYWORDS: Abstraction; Adolescence; Developmental Psychology; Information Processing Model; Metacognition; Myelination; Strategies; Symbols

OVERVIEW

The skills and individual needs to excel in today's workplace have changed dramatically since the advent of our modern education system. Our economy has become increasingly global, more technologically advanced, and the competencies individuals display in order to work in the majority of fields today reflect these changes. Today's economy largely requires a college education, and a skill set that includes being able to think abstractly.

Historically, how children learn and what they are able to do has been shaped largely by the work of two noteworthy researchers: Jean Piaget and Lev Vygotsky. The work of both theorists continue to be applied to educational methods today. Piaget and Vygotsky were concerned with the development of higher cognition and social behavior in human beings. Piaget described intelligence as the process by which an individual could adapt to its environment using two processes—assimilation and accommodation, and identified four stages of cognitive development that occurred from infancy throughout adulthood. In each stage, certain behaviors and capabilities were noted, from object permanence in infancy to the ability to use symbols to represent abstract concepts in and throughout adulthood (Huitt & Hummel, 2003).

Vygotsky believed that interactions with others shape human beings in their behavior and ability to think and learn. He believed that social interaction with others was critical to learning, and that all higher quality learning actually occurs as a result of these relationships. Furthermore, Vygotsky's theory also purported that there are certain cognitions that can only occur in a specific time frame of an individual's life—the *zone of proximal development*—and what and how much an individual learns depends upon interactions with those around them. His theory argued that the guidance of an adult or peers could teach an individual much more than they could learn on their own (Wertsch, 1985).

The theories of Piaget and Vygotsky were influential to other educational researchers and psychologists, including John Dewey and Jerome Bruner. However, we are still learning about the most successful ways to develop and encourage abstract thinking skills in an educational setting. While these early theories very much shaped how we view the development of thinking and learning today, more recent research has shed light on the development of abstract thinking. While Piaget was focused largely on stages of development, and saw these stages as separate and related to a child's age, current research has focused largely on the information processing theory, which akins the human brain to a computer that manages information by storing knowledge, and getting to that knowledge by utilizing a range of strategies. Thinking occurs as human beings store and retrieve information. The information processing model sees development of thought as a more fluid model, rather than progress occurring in stages of development as Piaget described it.

Abstract thinking is the ability to take concrete experiences and knowledge and apply them to other ideas and problems. It is an essential skill in problem solving, and experts agree that all substantial and noteworthy learning involves abstract thinking (Poole, Miller, & Church, 2005). Developing abstract thinking skills is imperative for children, and development takes place throughout their education, well into adulthood.

Educational psychology is closely linked to developmental and cognitive psychology. Research from all of these fields helps us explain how abstract thinking skills develop in individuals, and how these skills can be encouraged in a school setting. One of the most critical areas in which abstract thinking skills can and should be developed is in the classroom. Teachers and schools can use various strategies and instructional methods to encourage students to think abstractly.

The development of abstract thinking skills has become an important part of instructional techniques in schools largely due to a shift in the requirements necessary to compete in the current and future global economy. As technology advances, it becomes imperative that individuals have the skills to solve problems and that are becoming increasingly complex.

STAGES OF HUMAN DEVELOPMENT & COGNITIVE FUNCTION

Developing abstract thinking skills goes hand in hand with human development, the conditions in which individuals develop, and by whom they are surrounded. The development of abstract thinking skills starts when children are very young, and the adults who surround children can help them develop these proficiencies as they grow older; especially once a child enters formal schooling (Poole et al.). There are four stages of development that are recognized as critical periods in which cognitive function develops:

- Prenatal;
- Infancy;
- Middle Childhood;
- Adolescence.

During prenatal development, the first major stage, growth is impacted by the quality of prenatal care. A mother's actions such as drinking excessive alcohol or smoking, or poor nutrition can have a negative impact on the development of the fetus, and can have adverse effects on cognitive development (Pressley & McCormick, 2007). Additionally, external factors like a mother's exposure to a stressful environment during pregnancy can negatively impact a child's development (Henrichs et al., 2011).

During infancy, the brain grows larger, and a variety of abilities including language and social skills develop. Between two and five years of age, the years where most children enter school, brain growth is continuing; simultaneously, myelination of the cells in the nervous system is occurring. As a result of increased myelination, children are able to process information at faster speeds as they grow older (Pressley & McCormick, 2007). Around the age of two, a significant transformation occurs in that children are able to abstract concepts from their environment to other objects or experiences (Poole et al.). Language, social, and thinking skills continue to increase, and the development during these years can be largely impacted by the adults present in the child's life (Pressley & McCormick).

Most children in the United States enter elementary school around the age of five or six, and finish elementary school between the ages of twelve and thirteen. These developmental years are often referred to as "middle childhood" years. During this period children continue to develop language skills, and begin to gain knowledge and develop problem solving techniques that will have a large impact in their success in school, and thus on their ability to think abstractly. This is also the stage of development in which children cultivate a sense of whether they are successful or not in various areas of their schooling (Pressley & McCormick).

Adolescence usually begins at about twelve years of age, and continues into the late teens. The human brain reaches the adult weight and size by the age of sixteen, on average, but the brain continues to change and mature in various ways. Strategies for various cognitive skills, such as memory, continue to progress, as well as social interaction skills (Pressley & McCormick).

Classroom instructors and professionals in the field of education should be aware of these developmental periods. What students are cognitively capable of depends partly upon their developmental status. For a five-year old, abstract thinking may involve being able to use a certain toy as a symbol for another object in dramatic play, while a senior in high school may apply learned math skills to solve a problem in physics.

APPLICATIONS

Early models of thought and cognition primarily described the development of thinking skills in stages. Piaget's model focused on four stages that were descriptive of various ages throughout early childhood and adolescence. Each stage listed milestones, and the final stage, formal operations, culminated in an ability to use symbols logically and relate these symbols to abstract concepts. Piaget suggested that in each stage, a child should be challenged with tasks that would scaffold them to the next stage—consistently stimulating their minds to make the leap to the next level of complexity (Huitt & Hummel).

INFORMATION PROCESSING THEORY

Recent research has brought to light another model of how thinking skills develop—the information processing theory. The information processing theory likens the human mind to a computer—that human beings have short-and long-term memory "storage." When items in this storage are activated and applied to the present situation or problem, thinking occurs. From this perspective, the development of thinking skills, including the ability to think abstractly, is advanced through the progress of what an individual knows and what they can remember (Pressley & McCormick). Short- and long-term memory and knowledge develop as children grow. Between the ages of three and sixteen, children increase their abilities in storing items in their short-term memory (Pressley & McCormick). Increasing the memory capacity and knowledge that a child retains contributes significantly to how adept they will become at solving problems effectively, a hallmark of abstract thinking (Bjorklund, 2000).

DEVELOPING ABSTRACT SKILLS

The importance of mastering basic operations during the early years of elementary school is not to be taken lightly. Activities such as counting and simple mathematical skills, knowing the alphabet, and learning how to read, are imperative to building abstract thinking skills. Parents and teachers can

also help develop abstract thinking by helping children remember events and facts—repetition can be a powerful tool.

Teachers who work with children in infancy or early elementary years are working with individuals with rapidly developing brains. Teaching throughout the daily established routines is important at this age. Children are rapidly compiling knowledge about the world surrounding them, and during the early years of schooling should be encouraged to explore various textures, colors, and objects, as well as their functions. By the time a child reaches the age of one, he or she will begin to understand how everyday objects have use, and begin to build a knowledge base of uses and characteristics that certain objects have (Poole et al.).

By ages three and four, children are able to begin to abstract numbers—they understand that anything can be counted, and apply counting skills. Children at this age also become adept at using one object as a symbol for another; for example, during play, children may use a stick or a piece of fruit as a "phone" to "call" a friend in another "location." All of these types of actions are important to developing abstract thinking skills. Being able to identify and use symbols especially is an important skill in abstraction.

BUILDING KNOWLEDGE

Additionally, experience is very important in building a knowledge base. For example, a child may learn numbers at a young age; when they begin applying these numbers to other things in their lives, they are beginning to think abstractly. Three-and four-year olds are old enough to describe their experiences, and connect these incidents to the rest of the world around them. When teaching younger children, it is important to engage them in a variety of activities in which they can apply and practice skills they have learned in school (Rigolon & Alloway, 2011). The breadth of experience helps students apply their knowledge and learned skills to a range of topics. Introducing children to a variety of encounters and fields of study through field trips, stories, and other activities helps them build their knowledge base and apply their knowledge, which will cultivate their ability to think abstractly (Poole et al.).

USING STRATEGIES

Effectively learning and using strategies in school can help increase the thinking skills of youth and adolescents throughout their education. In addition to building knowledge and experiences, strategy use is another important facet of the information processing model. Strategies are complex activities used to accomplish a certain goal. Strategizing is often used interchangeably with problem solving, but the true process of solving problems is more complex than being able to answer a math problem or an analogy. In order to achieve higher cognitive skills such as abstract reasoning, an individual must be able to identify the problem, solve it, and then reflect upon how one solved it or did not solve it. The process requires a great deal of self-awareness and metacognition, or being aware of one's own thought processes. To use strategies effectively, a student must first have a base of knowledge on how to solve a problem or address the issue (Pressley & McCormick).

Teaching strategies to individuals in the classroom is not an easy task, and many adults do not use effective strategies themselves, especially because strategies get more complex as students advance in school (Bjorklund). Teaching strategies is more complex than memorization or teaching a single skill. Strategies help students apply the knowledge they have learned, or take the knowledge from the problem they have solved and transfer it to another situation. While some students learn and apply strategies on their own, it is important that teachers teach their students various strategies and how to apply them.

Learning to use strategies is often difficult for students. However, teachers can increase the rate at which students will actually apply strategies to the problems they are trying to solve. Research has shown that students will use strategies when they understand how they will help them achieve their goals, and when a student is aware of their own thinking patterns when using strategies (Askell-Williams, Lawson & Skrzypiec, 2012). Increasing metacognition (the awareness of the thought process) in students, and increasing their aptitude in this skill also has been shown to help students use strategies (Pressley & McCormick).

Teaching professionals can help students learn how to think abstractly by introducing new knowledge, teaching skills to solve various problems, and encouraging students to use these strategies in other areas. Developing abstract thinking skills is largely based around being able to solve problems and apply these solutions to other problems. The road to being able to think abstractly comes through solving

problems throughout one's life, starting in infancy. These skills can be applied to all disciplines; furthermore, they are important skills that will help individuals meet further and ever more complex challenges.

The information processing theory helps explain how human beings think, and how we develop higher cognitive aptitude. Problem solving can run the gamut from figuring out how to retrieve a fallen toy to using statistical analysis to play poker to applying themes from a certain literary period from one novel to the next. By understanding the theory behind cognitive development, teachers can help develop these skills through various age-appropriate classroom methods.

Applying Abstract Thinking Skills in the Classroom

MATHEMATICS

Teaching mathematics requires a great deal of abstract thinking. Particularly, learning and understanding algebra represents a shift towards advanced reasoning skills. However, many students have trouble making this leap. Research supports that beginning to hone abstract thinking skills early in a child's academic career, specifically when learning arithmetic and simple functions, which build the foundation for algebra, can help students make this shift. The two critical elements that help build these skills are helping kids understand explicitly what they understand implicitly, and supporting the professional development of teachers who teach mathematics (Carpenter, Levi, & Farnsworth, 2000).

Researchers have found that students understand many fundamental characteristics of numbers and how to manipulate them. However, students are often not told explicitly the rules in which these characteristics apply, and thus may become unsure how to apply these properties to other problems, or even oversimplify the parameters that guide their knowledge of a certain skill. When this type of knowledge is unequivocally explained rather than simply inferred or left to the student to deduce, understanding and being able to perform algebraic functions become much more logical for students, and will assist them in applying these higher order thinking skills to more complex problems (Carpenter et al.).

The quality of teaching is imperative to good learning. From what researchers know about teaching algebra, we understand that when math skills build on each other, and students clearly understand the operations they are performing and why they are performing them, the leap to algebra is more straightforward. Classroom instruction to build algebraic skills can begin as early as first or second grade, with teachers discussing with students the rules and theories behind numbers and their operations. However, in order for these discussions to occur, and for children to gain this knowledge, schools need to support development for teachers in how to properly teach what they know, and transfer the knowledge effectively to their students at various levels of their development (Carpenter et al.).

READING

Learning to read can be a difficult task. Reading involves abstraction from the very first steps; from learning to read for content, to reading for various themes or abstract ideas. Many colleges and universities now require incoming freshman to take a course in knowing how to read and write effectively. These classes often work to increase abstract thinking skills through various methodologies.

Teaching abstract thinking skills through reading involves a number of applications. First, students need to be taught to read "actively." When an individual employs active reading, he or she may be looking to accomplish a number of things. First, reading for factual content—the who, what, when, where, why, and how of the piece. However, the individual is also looking for certain concepts or generalizations, main ideas, or trying to apply these concepts, generalizations, and main ideas to other works (Ediger, 2003). Teachers can help guide students in various ways, such as using specific questioning techniques, helping students compare and contrast the information they are reading to other works, and encouraging students to be aware of their thought processes while reading and deciphering new information.

CONCLUSION

Abstract thinking skills elevate an individual's ability to solve problems through a variety of methods—mental imagery, using and interpreting symbols, and creating and executing a plan (Perry, 2004). These thinking skills are cultivated throughout a child's life, and parents and teachers can help encourage abstract thinking skills through various methods that are age level appropriate. Abstract thinking does not develop automatically. While some students begin the steps to abstract thinking—using and applying strategies or reading for main ideas and themes—on their own, the guidance of a teacher or influence of peers is critical.

Developing these cognitive skills is a long process built on previously learned skills. Supporting and encouraging children to move to the next level is critical to their success. Repetition is extremely important in developing abstract thinking skills. When children are young, they must establish steps of knowledge that will allow them to further their cognitive development. Learning to count sets children up to learn how to add, then multiply, and then solve algebraic problems. Furthermore, during the child's developmental years, children learn to think responsively to the environment around them. Many researchers believe that exposure to a variety of environments, opinions, and experiences will help children and adolescents develop abstract thinking skills (Perry).

Teachers can help students develop skills through methods such as using manipulatives in teaching so that students can build representations and models of the concepts they are being taught. When discussing various topics, classifying things into groups according to similar or different characteristics will assist students in categorizing and arranging their thoughts and knowledge. Finally, questioning is at the root of abstract thinking. Students should be taught to question: Why or why not? What if? So what? Teachers should help guide students seeking answers to these questions (Bjorklund).

Cultivating abstract thinking skills is important for success in the majority of fields, including the sciences and the technology sector, which have become critical factors in our new brain-based economy. These skills can be taught and nurtured through classroom instructional techniques, and at home. However, it requires a high level of commitment and expertise from teachers, administrators, and families.

TERMS & CONCEPTS

Abstraction: Abstraction is the ability to apply knowledge or experience about one topic or task to another.

Adolescence: Adolescence is a stage of development that occurs prior to adulthood.

Developmental Psychology: Developmental psychology is a branch of psychology that researches psychological conditions in human beings at different ages. The branch is closely related to a variety of fields, including education, as well as social and cognitive psychology.

Information Processing Model: The information processing model was describes a theory of how human beings think—by storing and retrieving information.

Metacognition: Metacognition means to think about one's thoughts, or to be aware of one's thinking process. The practice has been shown to increase abstract thinking skills.

Myelination: Myelination is biological process that occurs in our cells as we learn to process information more quickly.

Strategies: Strategies are techniques that help students learn and apply knowledge to various situations or tasks in order to solve problems.

Symbols: Symbols are an object that represents another object. Being able to recognize and apply symbols is indicative of abstract thought.

Rana Suh

BIBLIOGRAPHY

Askell-Williams, H., Lawson, M., & Skrzypiec, G. (2012). Scaffolding cognitive and metacognitive strategy instruction in regular class lessons. *Instructional Science, 40*, 413-443. Retrieved on December 7, 2013, from EBSCO Online Database Education Research Complete.

Bjorklund, D.F. (2000). *Children's thinking: Developmental function and individual differences (3rd Ed.).* Belmont, CA: Wadsworth/Thomson Learning.

Carpenter, T., Levi, L., & Farnsworth, V. (2000). *Building a foundation for learning algebra in the elementary grades.* Washington, D.C: Office of Educational Research and Improvement. (ERIC Document Reproduction Service No. ED 499015). Retrieved November 26, 2007, from Educational Resources Information Center, http://eric.ed.gov.

Cléments, D. & Sarama, J. (2004). Think big! How to use math to build your child's abstract- thinking skills. *Scholastic Parent &Child, 11*, 36-46. Retrieved November 26, 2007, from EBSCO Online Database, Academic Search Premier.

Ediger, M. (2003). *Patterns of thinking in reading.* (ERIC Document Reproduction Service No. ED 478765). Retrieved November 26, 2007, from Educational Resources Information Center, http://eric.ed.gov.

Henrichs, J., Schenk, J.J., Kok, R., Ftitache, B., Schmidt, H.G., Hofman, A., & Tiemeier, H. (2011). Parental family stress during pregnancy and cognitive functioning in early childhood: The Generation R study. *Early Childhood Research Quarterly, 26*, 332-343. Retrieved on December 7, 2013, from EBSCO Online Database Education Research Complete.

Huitt, W., & Hummel, J. (2003). Piaget's theory of cognitive development. *Educational Psychology Interactive.* Valdosta, GA: Valdosta State University. Retrieved November 26, 2007, from http://chiron.valdosta.edu.

Perry, B.D. (2004). What's going on in there? What happens in the brain as abstract thinking develops. *Scholastic Parent & Child, 11*, 36-46.

Poole, C., Miller, S.A., & Church, E.B. (2005). *Early Childhood Today,19*, 45-47. Retrieved November 26, 2007, from EBSCO Online Database, Academic Search Premier.

Pressley, M., & McCormick, C.B. (2007). *Child and adolescent development for educators.* New York, NY: Guilford Press.

Rigolon, A., & Alloway, M. (2011). Children and their development as the starting point: A new way to think about the design of elementary schools. *Educational & Child Psychology, 28*, 64-76. Retrieved on December 7, 2013, from EBSCO Online Database Education Research Complete.

Wertsch, J.V. (1985). Cultural, Communication, and Cognition: Vygotskian Perspectives. Cambridge University Press.

SUGGESTED READING

Alexnder, J.M., Schwanenflugel, P.J.& Carr, M.(1995). Development of metacognition in gifted children: Directions for future research. *Developmental Review, 15*, 1-37.

Dewey, J. (1997). *How we think.* New York: Dover Publications.

Piaget, J. (1972). *The psychology of the child.* New York: Basic Books.

Renner, J., Stafford, D., Lawson, A., McKinnon, J., Friot, E., & Kellogg, D. (1976).

Renner, J., Stafford, D., Lawson, A., McKinnon, J., Friot, E., & Kellogg, D. (1976). *Research, teaching, and learning with the Piaget model.* Norman, OK: University of Oklahoma Press.

Stillings, N, Feinstein, M., Garfield, J., Rissland, E., Rosenbaum, D., Weisler, S., & Baker-Ward, L. (1987). *Cognitive science: An introduction.* Cambridge, MA: MIT Press.

Vygotsky, L., & Vygotsky, S. (1980). *Mind in society : The development of higher psychological processes.* Cambridge: Harvard University Press.

PSYCHOLINGUISTICS

Psycholinguistics focuses on the skills and processes involved in the perception and expression of language. This article first describes levels of language representation, for example, semantics and grammar. It then delves into various language competencies, such as reading and speech that comprise language acquisition and production. Applications of psycholinguistics are also reviewed in the current article along with topics of interest in the field of psycholinguistics such as bilingualism.

KEYWORDS: Discourse; Grammar; Language Acquisition; Language Production; Language Skills; Morphology; Phonology; Psycholinguistics; Psychology; Semantics; Syntax

OVERVIEW

Psycholinguistics is more than just the psychology of language. More specifically, it has been defined as "the study of human language processing, involving a range of abilities, from cognition to sensorimotor activity, that are recruited to the service of a complex set of communicative functions" (Garman, 2000). Psycholinguistics is concerned with how individuals communicate through symbols, or semiotics, via a number of language skills.

In detailing the components and processes involved in learning a language, Widdowson (2000) asserted that individuals must first gain an awareness of the various meanings within a language and then learn how to enact these meanings when using the language. Language can be spoken and written and involves production and reception. Therefore, language skills, or competencies, include speaking, writing, listening, and reading. Language ability entails how individuals put language skills to use.

Psycholinguistics deals with the reception, storage or representation, and production of words (Baker, Croot, McLeod, & Paul, 2001). How individuals receive, or perceive, words and then produce them is a type of language process. The perception of words is initiated when individuals encounter an input signal. The words produced are output signals. Psycholinguistics attends to the processes that take place in the period between input and output signals. Understanding psycholinguistics requires investigation of the multiple components and psychological aspects of the various language processes that comprise language development, including language reception, or acquisition, and language production.

COMPONENTS OF LANGUAGE DEVELOPMENT

In their work, Baker et al. discussed the important construct of underlying representations or how words exist, or are represented, in an individual's mind. Representations are stored in input and output lexicons. Gernsbacher and Kaschak (2003) detailed "sub-word-level processing, word processing, sentence-level processing, discourse processing, and issues of… neural architecture…" as processes and components related to language representations and skills.

Sub-word-level and word processing appear to be the building blocks of language and its development. Grammar is a pertinent construct in language development because it is through knowledge of grammar that individuals are able to construct and understand language through sentences. Clifton (2000) defined grammar as including syntax, morphology, and phonology. According to Clifton, syntax is the relationship between various components of a sentence; morphology refers to how words are composed and relate to other words and phrases; and phonology is the configuration of sounds that comprise a language. Phonemes are the most basic units of sound and can be combined to form phonetic units (Kuhl, 2004). Representation at the phonetic, phonemic, lexical-phonological, and semantic levels influences recognition and comprehension of words (Martin, 2003).

Semantics, or the meaning conveyed by language processes at the word (or lexical), sentence, and discourse levels (Sanford, 2000), is another integral construct in language development. Miller (1999) emphasized the import of knowing what a word means and the contexts in which the word will be used in his discussion of semantics. Aspects of semantics reviewed by Miller include logical, linguistic, sentential, and lexical semantics. Logical semantics refers to a theory on the arrangements of meanings found in a language. Linguistic semantics is the description of meanings for a language while sentential semantics focuses on what statements mean. Lexical semantics refers to the manner in which words that have individual meanings combine within a sentence to create another meaning. Finally, discourse, as defined by Singer (2000), is the logical arrangement of sentences in written or spoken format.

In regard to the neural architectural aspect of language development, Gernsbacher and Kaschak provided an overview of research on neuroimaging, including positron emissions tomography (PET) and functional magnetic resonance imaging (fMRI), and language processing. In these studies, individuals were monitored while completing tasks or responding to stimuli, such as semantic judgments and word generation, so that areas of the brain involved with the tasks and stimuli could be ascertained. Once words began to be processed, orthographic, or symbolic, representations of words were found to give way to phonological level processing. Pertinent results from Gernsbacher and Kaschak's review are included in the language acquisition and language production sections below.

LANGUAGE ACQUISITION

Processing word representations in the input lexicon is part of language acquisition, or reception. With regard to lexicons, Miller asserted that closed-class and open-class words comprise the English lexicon. How the format and meaning of words interrelate create the framework for a lexicon. For closed-class words, such as pronouns and conjunctions, the functional role is in grammar. Open-class words are more numerous than closed-class words with meaning created by their relationships with other open-class words. Incorporated in language acquisition then are the language competencies of listening, or comprehension, and reading of words in a lexicon.

Bates, Devescovi, and Wulfeck (2001), review an investigation of language acquisition for children across multiple nations that addressed the genesis of word-level processing for language. Results indicated that children begin to understand words at between 8 to 10 months and start producing words between 11 to 13 months. By two years of age, children may be able to produce upwards of 500 words. The rate at which words are produced between initial word production and two years of age varies greatly across language. Grammar development also differs across languages and has been posited to be connected to vocabulary growth as well.

According to Ziegler and Goswami (2000), reading involves comprehension of written speech to ascertain meaning. Reading incorporates connecting

visual symbols to sound. Phonological recoding takes words at the lexical level and maps them onto the sound levels. This process requires phonological awareness. Discrepancies in phonological awareness may lead to a language disorder such as dyslexia.

Brown (2005) investigated how children learn words and grammar. Of interest to Brown was children's engagement with the social environment as an influence of children's word and grammar learning. Dale (2004) explored the role of negative feedback children receive in regard to word learning and early grammar usage. Both word learning and early grammar usage relate to word-and sentence-level language processing. Dale stated that overextension occurs when children use one word for several others, such as apple for other fruit such as orange and pear. Social responses to overextension are a form of feedback that lends to the word learning process for youth with caregiver responses to children's language also shaping grammar development.

In a similar vein, Bates et al. investigated psycholinguistic concepts such as cue costs and cue validity from a cross-linguistic perspective. Cue costs are how much processing is required to use various formats of language while cue validity is the information garnered from different aspects of language. Cue costs and cue validity may differ in relevancy and reliability based on language. For example, in English cue validity is often ascertained by the context in which words are situated. As individuals use concepts such as cue costs and receive feedback from others to refine their language acquisition and comprehension, language competencies develop and are enacted through language production.

LANGUAGE PRODUCTION

Language production entails language competencies such as speech and writing. As Martin (2003) reviews, language production models usually begin at a nonlinguistic level of representation. Lexical-semantic levels of representation follow and involve words in relation to one another, an example being noun and verb association. Syntactic representation is the next level and entails how words relate to one another in order to convey various functions. Lexical-phonological representation leads to phonetic representation of words. Throughout the process individuals maintain words in their working memory.

One manifestation of language production is writing. Negro and Chanquoy (2005) define the process of writing as requiring the ability to plan, translate, and revise words across various levels of representation. Another aspect of language production is speech production. Speech production incorporates information at phonological, semantic, grammatical, orthographic (or spelling), and motoric levels (Baker et al.). Chang, Dell, and Bock (2006) explored the role of syntax in the process by which individuals acquire and produce speech. Syntax is composed of categories, functions and rules. For individuals to produce speech, Chang et al. suggest that they predict words based on what has been presented so far syntactically.

Diehl, Lotto, and Holt (2004) also address theories about speech perception. Speech perception research has addressed the relationship between acoustic signals and aspects of language processing. At its base level, speech perception is the way in which individuals interpret sounds as part of language. Speech perception emphasizes articulatory, along with acoustic or auditory, events. Articulatory events are gestures or vocal tract utterances that individuals perceive in the environment that provide information as to their surroundings.

NEURAL ARCHITECTURE OF PSYCHOLINGUISTICS

Neuroimaging studies provide insight about the relationship between brain functioning and language development. In terms of language acquisition, according to Gernsbacher and Kaschak's review, initiation of speech processing occurred in both left and right regions of the temporal lobe, specifically in the superior temporal gyrus. Additionally, word processing intersected at the auditory and visual level in many instances.

A central role of activity does exist in the frontal regions of the brain for several levels of representation in the language production process (Martin). Gernsbacher and Kaschak also note that the left frontal regions of the brain are related to phonological and semantic processing and likely the retrieval and production of word formation. Semantic processing also occurs in other areas of the frontal region of the brain (e.g., middle and anterior frontal regions) and temporal regions. Temporal regions of the brain are also involved in word retrieval and production and limited phonological processing. Sentence processing takes place in Wernicke's and Broca's areas and temporal and frontal regions of the brain. Discourse processing appears centered in the right hemisphere.

APPLICATIONS

Psycholinguistics has been applied to areas as diverse as forensics and education. In regard to educational applications of psycholinguistics, Baker et. al (2001) stated that some strands of psycholinguistic research address "the way in which children process speech and language at a cognitive or psychological level and thus aim to formulate hypotheses about the psychological processes or components that may be impaired." For example, Mackie and Dockrell (2004) focused on students with and without a language learning disorder (LLD) in order to understand how writing competencies may vary in expression due to impairments in language skills. Students with an LLD in the oral language arena had difficulty in some aspects of written language expression.

Other educational applications of psycholinguistics include Hall's (1995) description of a game, a modification of "Hangman," that integrated components of psycholinguistics, such as semantic, syntactic, and graphophonic cues, in the development of reading skills and abilities. Additionally, Widdowson described task-based learning as a method of teaching language within a psycholinguistic framework so that individuals develop and refine language abilities and ultimately, communicate more effectively.

Issues

LANGUAGE DISORDERS

Relevant contemporary issues of interest in psycholinguistics include language disorders and bilingualism. Language disorders can be conceptualized as developmental language disorders or acquired language disorders (Garman). Acquired language disorders often arise from brain injuries. Other language disorders can be attributed to learning disabilities or specific language impairments (SLIs). Tijms, Hoeks, Paulussen-Hoogeboom, and Smolenaars (2003) defined developmental dyslexia as a disorder involving phonological processing that impacts reading and spelling. Specifically, individuals with dyslexia find it difficult to represent words phonologically in their mental lexicon.

Conti-Ramsden, Botting, and Faragher (2001) delineated the relationship between shortcomings with verbal memory, language processing, and specific language impairments (SLIs). Nonword repetition and sentence recall were psycholinguistic markers most accurate in identifying youth with SLIs. Martin detailed how damages to Broca's and Wernicke's areas of the brain impact language. In terms of damage to Broca's area, language production was impaired whereas the ability to understand language was affected by damage to Wernicke's area.

BILINGUALISM

Bilingualism refers to an individual's aptitude in use of at least two languages (Baker). Second-language acquisition (SLA) is a term that refers to an individual's progression towards becoming bilingual (Hakuta, 2000). SLA may occur during childhood or adulthood. Regardless of the timing of its occurrence, SLA, or becoming bilingual, involves the use of similar language processes as those that occur during first, or native, language learning. Research has indicated that individuals may have disparate level of skill across the various competencies that comprise language acquisition and production in their first- (L1) and second-languages (L2) (Sandoval & Durán, 1998). Another phenomenon of interest in regard to bilingual individuals is code-switching. In code-switching, a bilingual person improvises with language skills and competencies in their L1 and L2 languages by using both languages while communicating with others (Hakuta). Psycholinguistics is interested in the meaning code-switching has in the communication process for bilingual individuals.

CONCLUSIONS

Psycholinguistics is an area of study that aims to explicate the varied ways in which individuals comprehend and use language. Language acquisition and production occur across multiple levels of representation-from word-level to discourse processing. Neuroimaging provides insight into how regions of the brain relate to competencies used and expressed in language development. Psycholinguistics has been applied in educational arenas and in other areas such as forensics. Language disorders and bilingualism are issues of interest in psycholinguistics and illustrate how language competencies may be expressed and experienced based on language impairment or knowledge of more than one language. Psycholinguistics offers a viable and valuable perspective by which to understand human communication and development through language.

TERMS & CONCEPTS

Discourse: Discourse is the spoken or written combination of sentences such that there is a logical representation of meaning.

Grammar: Grammar includes syntax, morphology, and phonology and is the mechanism by which sentences are constructed.

Language Acquisition: Language acquisition is the process by which individuals perceive and receive language. Language skills comprising language acquisition are listening and reading.

Language Production: Language production is the process by which individuals put language into use. Language skills comprising language production are speech and writing.

Language Skills: Language skills are competencies that reflect various language processes. Language skills are used in the acquisition and production of language and can be written or spoken. Language skills include reading, writing, listening, and speech.

Morphology: Morphology is the nature of the composition of words and their relationship to other words in a sentence.

Phonology: Phonology is the nature of the sound of words; it includes phonemes, the smallest units of sounds, and larger phonetic units.

Psycholinguistics: Psycholinguistics is the study of language processes and skills used by individuals to produce and acquire language.

Semantics: Semantics refers to the meaning conveyed at the word, sentence, or discourse level of language processing.

Syntax: Syntax is the aspect of grammar that refers to the characteristics, functions, and relationships of words within a sentence.

Edith Arrington

BIBLIOGRAPHY

Baker, E., Croot, K., McLeod, S., & Paul, R. (2001). Psycholinguistic models of speech development and their application to clinical practice. *Journal of Speech, Language & Hearing Research, 44,* 685-702. Retrieved October 25, 2007, from EBSCO Online Database Education Research Complete.

Baker, C. (2000). Bilingualism. In M. Byram (Ed.), *Routledge Encyclopedia of Language Teaching & Learning* (pp. 82-84). London: Routledge. Retrieved November 12, 2007, from EBSCO Online Database Education Research Complete.

Bates, E., Devescovi, A., & Wulfeck, B. (2001). Psycholinguistics: A cross-language perspective. *Annual Review of Psychology, 52,* 369-396. Retrieved October 25, 2007, from EBSCO Online Database Business Source Complete.

Brown, P. (2005). What does it mean to learn the meaning of words? *Journal of the Learning Sciences, 14,* 293-300. Retrieved October 26, 2007, from EBSCO Online Database Education Research Complete

Chang, F., Dell, G. S., & Bock, K. (2006). Becoming Syntactic. *Psychological Review, 113,* 234-272.

Clifton Jr., C. (2000). Psycholinguistics: Syntax and grammar. In A. E. Kazdin (Ed), *Encyclopedia of psychology, Vol. 6* (pp. 364-367). Washington, DC, US: Oxford University Press.

Conti-Ramsden, G., Botting, N., & Faragher, B. (2001). Psycholinguistic Markers for Specific Language Impairment (SLI). *Journal of Child Psychology & Psychiatry & Allied Disciplines, 42,* 741-748. Retrieved October 25, 2007, from EBSCO Online Database Education Research Complete.

Dale, R. (2004). Cognitive and behavioral approaches to language acquisition: Conceptual and empirical intersections. *Behavior Analyst Today, 5,* 336-358. Retrieved October 25, 2007, from EBSCO Online Database Academic Search Premier.

Diehl, R., Lotto, A., & Holt, L. (2004). Speech perception. *Annual Review of Psychology, 55,* 149-179. Retrieved November 6, 2007, from EBSCO Online Database Academic Search Premier.

Garman, M. (2000). Psycholinguistics: An overview. In A. E. Kazdin (Ed.), *Encyclopedia of psychology, Vol. 6* (pp. 361-364). Washington, DC, US: Oxford University Press.

Gernsbacher, M., & Kaschak, M. (2003). Neuroimaging studies of language production and comprehension. *Annual Review of Psychology, 54,* 91-114. Retrieved November 6, 2007, from EBSCO Online Database Academic Search Premier.

Gibbs, R.W. (2013). The real complexities of psycholinguistic research on metaphor. *Language Sciences,* 4045-52. Retrieved December 15, 2013, from EBSCO Online Database Education Research Complete.

Hakuta, K. (2000). Bilingualism. In A. E. Kazdin (Ed.), *Encyclopedia of psychology, Vol. 6* (pp. 410-414). Washington, DC, US: Oxford University Press.

Hall, A. (1995). Sentencing: The psycholinguistic guessing game. *Reading Teacher, 49,* 76- 77. Retrieved October 25, 2007, from EBSCO Online Database Education Research Complete.

Kuhl, P. K. (2004) Early language acquisition: cracking the speech code. *Nature Reviews Neuroscience, 5,* 831-843. Retrieved November 13, 2007, from http://ling.umd.edu.

Mackie, C., & Dockrell, J. (2004). The nature of written language deficits in children with SLI. *Journal of Speech, Language & Hearing Research, 47,* 1469-1483. Retrieved November 15, 2007, from EBSCO Online Database Education Research Complete.

Martin, R. (2003). Language processing: Functional organization and neuroanatomical basis. *Annual Review of Psychology, 54,* 55-89. Retrieved November 6, 2007, from EBSCO Online Database Academic Search Premier.

Miller, G. (1999). On knowing a word. *Annual Review of Psychology, 50,* 1-19. Retrieved November 6, 2007, from EBSCO Online Database Academic Search Premier.

Negro, I., & Chanquoy, L. (2005). The effect of psycholinguistic research on the teaching of writing. *L1-Educational Studies in Language & Literature, 5,* 105-111. Retrieved October 25, 2007, from EBSCO Online Database Education Research Complete.

Roberts, L. (2012). Psycholinguistic techniques and resources in second language acquisition research. *Second Language Research, 28,* 113-127. Retrieved December 15, 2013, from EBSCO Online Database Education Research Complete.

Sandoval, J., & Durán, R. P. (1998). Language. In J. H. Sandoval, C. Frisby, K. F. Geisinger, J. D. Scheuneman, J. R. Grenier, & J. Ramos (Eds.), *Test interpretation and diversity: Achieving equity in assessment* (pp. 181-211). Washington, DC: American Psychological Association.

Sanford, A. J. (2000). Psycholinguistics: Semantics. In A. E. Kazdin (Ed.), *Encyclopedia of psychology, Vol. 6* (pp. 367-369). Washington, DC, US: Oxford University Press.

Singer, M. (2000). Psycholinguistics: Discourse comprehension. In A. E. Kazdin (Ed.), *Encyclopedia of psychology, Vol. 6* (pp. 369-372). Washington, DC, US: Oxford University Press.

Smith, S. S., & Shuy, R. W. (2002). Forensic psycholinguistics: Using language analysis for identifying and assessing offenders. *Law Enforcement Bulletin, 71,* 16-21.

Tijms, J., Hoeks, J., Paulussen-Hoogeboom, M., & Smolenaars, A. (2003). Long-term effects of a psycholinguistic treatment for dyslexia. *Journal of Research in Reading, 26,* 121-140. Retrieved October 25, 2007, from EBSCO Online Database Education Research Complete.

Van Moere, A. (2012). A psycholinguistic approach to oral language assessment. *Language Testing, 29,* 325-344. Retrieved December 15, 2013, from EBSCO Online Database Education Research Complete.

Widdowson, H. (2000). Skills and knowledge in language learning. In M. Byram (Ed.), *Routledge Encyclopedia of Language Teaching & Learning* (pp. 548-553). London: Routledge. Retrieved October 25, 2007, from EBSCO Online Database Education Research Complete.

Ziegler, J. C., & Goswami, U. (2000). Reading acquisition, developmental dyslexia, and skilled reading across languages: A psycholinguistic grain size theory. *Psychological Bulletin, 131*, 3-29.

SUGGESTED READING

Lorch, M. (2000). Disorders of language. In M. Byram (Ed.), *Routledge Encyclopedia of Language Teaching & Learning* (pp. 182-183). London: Routledge. Retrieved November 12, 2007, from EBSCO Online Database Education Research Complete.

McKoon, G., & Ratcliff, R. (1998). Memory-based language processing: Psycholinguistic research in the 1990s. *Annual Review of Psychology, 49*, 25-42. Retrieved November 6, 2007, from EBSCO Online Database Academic Search Premier.

Pennebaker, J., Mehl, M., & Niederhoffer, K. (2003). Psychological aspects of natural language use: Our words, our selves. *Annual Review of Psychology, 54*, 547-577. Retrieved November 6, 2007, from EBSCO Online Database Academic Search Premier.

Traxler, M. & Gernsbacher, M. (2006) (2nd Ed.). Handbook of Psycholinguistics. San Diego, CA.; Elsevier Inc.

INSTRUCTIONAL DESIGN

The concept of Instructional Design was adopted as a means of organizing learning and providing objective-based methodologies for conveying knowledge. Instructional Design Theories and Models are still changing over time, as educational philosophies and current trends in modern education evolve. This article presents an overview of the concept of Instructional Design (ID) in American education, and provides further insights into specific aspects of Instructional Design such as the Behaviorist, Programmed Instruction, Constructivist and Direct Instruction approaches which are still used in some form today. Instructional Systems Design is used in technological, computer and industrial learning for training in the rapidly changing environments of the modern information age.

KEYWORDS: ADDIE Model; Behaviorism; Bloom's Taxonomy; Classical Conditioning; Constructivism; Dick and Carey Model; Instructional Design; Instructional Systems Design; Instructional Delivery System; Learning Models; Learning Objectives; Mastery Learning; Nine Events of Instruction; Operant Conditioning; Programmed Instruction; Reinforcement; Task analysis

OVERVIEW

Instructional Design can be defined as the systematic development of instructional specifications using learning theory to ensure the quality of instruction. It includes the analysis of learning needs and objectives and the development of a delivery system including instructional materials and activities to meet those objectives. Evaluation of all instruction and learner activities is central to the theory. Its main foundation is that of an objective-oriented model for managing the instructional process, which is rooted in theories that specify how high-quality instruction should be performed. A successful learning situation is one in which behavior goals are reached through mastery of a series of small steps or tasks which represent a larger objective. Each step or task is clearly defined and outcomes and activities are continually assessed to evaluate efficiency.

Instructional Design theory has evolved over many decades and consists of several different models which can be applied to many types of learning situations. As a discipline, Instructional Design developed slowly from the time of Plato and Socrates to the philosophers of the 17th and 18th centuries. By the turn of the 20th century, the concepts of learning theory and educational psychology were beginning to take form in modern thought. The turmoil of the first half of the 20th century brought political and social changes which in turn encouraged new ways to look at the purpose and functions of our education system. By the 1950's, educational theories abounded, and Instructional Design was quickly adapted to many theories and models.

Theories that were used to approach Instructional Design were originally conceived in the military. During World War II, personnel had to be trained quickly and efficiently to perform their duties. Military researchers developed training films and corresponding programs to get the troops ready. The development of this task-oriented method of instructional technology spurred further research into the formulation of theoretical models of learning (Leigh, n.d.).

INFLUENCE OF BEHAVIORISM

The developers of early Instructional Design models were associated with the Behaviorist school of learning theory. Behaviorism looked at learning as a stimulus, response, and reinforcement process (S-R-R), first outlined by Ivan Pavlov's Classical Conditioning theory, and continued by B. F. Skinner. Such reactive behavior was documented in animals and adapted to human learning situations, positing that all behavior is explained by external events. The influence of Behaviorism on learning led to a form of Instructional Design that incorporated immediate feedback and reinforcement with drill and practice procedures and programmed instruction that allowed the learner to repeat tasks that were not performed correctly until they were mastered. Behavioral outcomes were directly connected to instruction systems.

The 1950's in America were characterized by a huge economic boom which followed World War II. The launch of the Soviet satellite Sputnik triggered an education panic in the U.S., prompting politicians and educators to send large amounts of Federal money to research on education, especially concentrating on studies in cognition and instruction. In Universities around the country, theoretical models of learning were being developed by educational theorists and psychologists such as B. F. Skinner and Benjamin Bloom. Skinner's work in Operant Conditioning and Stimulus-Response-Reinforcement theory ultimately led to what is considered a first incarnation of Instructional Design, called Programmed Instruction (PI). PI emphasized formulating behavioral objectives, breaking down instructional content into smaller units and rewarding correct responses early and often. Benjamin Bloom's 1956 taxonomy of educational objectives (Bloom's Taxonomy) and theory of mastery learning formed the basis of a standardized design process introduced by Robert Glaser in 1962. Glaser's model linked learner analysis to the design and development of instruction. His 'instructional systems' assessed students' entry-level behavior to determine the extent to which they would learn needed objectives. This not only tested the learners, but tested the learning system as well.

Also in 1962, Robert Mager developed the idea of Learning or Behavioral Objectives. His central concept was that training needs should be analyzed and the learning goals (objectives) of the program be defined. Each objective should then be broken down into smaller tasks. Each behavioral objective should have three criteria: Behavior, Condition and Standard. In 1965 Robert Gagné introduced the Nine Events of Instruction, a series of distinct steps necessary for learning to occur. Gagné also introduced the concept of task analysis, previously used in military training, which broke each task to be mastered down to its most basic components, or subtasks. The theories of both of these scholars are still used today in modern Instructional Design systems.

INSTRUCTIONAL DESIGN IN THE SCHOOLS & BEYOND

During the 1960's and 1970's, Instructional Design in one form or another was widely adopted in the public schools as the most effective teaching process available. Robert Morgan and Leslie Briggs conducted several studies which demonstrated that an instructionally designed course could yield up to a 2:1 increase over conventionally designed courses in terms of achievement, reduction in variance, and reduction of time-to-completion. This was four times greater than that of a control group which received no training. New teachers were extensively trained in Instructional Design, primarily with the Behaviorist approach.

Instructional Design models flourished in the 1970's and into the 1980's, with many researchers contributing to the field, such as Robert Branson and W. Dick and L. Carey. With the onset of the Information Age, many organizations established formal education and training departments to educate employees in the rapidly developing uses of computers and technology. Instructional Design programs proved effective and efficient in introducing employees to new technological methods and concepts and training them to perform the new skills needed.

Instructional Systems Design (ISD), as the field is now sometimes called, has become a significant tool in the computer and technology training fields, as well as in computer-aided education in the schools. It has also been adopted in one form or another in corporate training programs for technical and other employees. Today, the ADDIE Model of Instructional Systems Design is widely used in all forms of instruction, particularly web-based and on-line computer instruction. Second to ADDIE is the Dick and Carey Model of Instructional Design, although it has recently been criticized as rigid.

Since the 1990's, the models have moved away from the Behaviorist approach and adopted a Constructivist approach to creating learning environments with less formal structure and facilitated by teachers. These are based on the theory of Constructivism, which differs vastly from Behaviorism in that it holds that knowledge is internal and tested by the individual in reality. Instructional Design models in today's school classroom are vastly different from their behavioral roots, but still valuable tools for effective teaching.

FURTHER INSIGHTS

The following relevant concepts have influenced and shaped Instructional Design in the Twentieth century, including their applications in Education today:

- Stimulus-Response theory;
- Behaviorism;
- Programmed instruction;
- Operant Conditioning;
- Constructivism;
- John Dewey and Pragmatism;
- Direct Instruction and DISTAR;
- Madeline Hunter and Theory into Practice;
- Computer-Assisted learning.

STIMULUS-RESPONSE THEORY

Stimulus-Response theory is the premise that stimuli exist that directly cause unconditioned, or instinctive physiological and behavioral responses in humans and animals. Ivan Pavlov first studied this phenomenon in 1927, which led to his model of Classical Conditioning. Pavlov demonstrated that stimulus and response could be controlled, or conditioned, to manipulate the responses into changed behaviors. His most famous experiment involved the association of food (unconditioned stimulus) to the salivation response (unconditioned response) of a dog. When paired with the sound of a bell (conditioned stimulus), the sight of the food causes the dog to salivate. However, after conditioning, the dog learns to salivate only at the sound of the bell (conditioned response), with no food present. Pavlov's Classical Conditioning theory, based on stimulus-response, was ultimately embraced by the Behaviorist school of learning psychology, and modified by B. F. Skinner's theory of Operant Conditioning, in which post-response consequences were introduced to provide additional motivation for positive behavioral outcomes.

BEHAVIORISM

Behaviorism is a school of psychology which holds that all behavior of all organisms is caused directly by responses to our environment. First introduced by John Watson and B.F. Skinner, Behaviorism has been widely studied and incorporated into educational learning theory. The doctrine of Behaviorism holds that psychology is the science of behavior, and not of the mind, and that behavior is explained exclusively by external, observable events. This movement ran in direct opposition to Sigmund Freud's school of Psychoanalysis, which was gaining popularity simultaneously. In the classroom, behavioral teaching is the arrangement of consequences and reinforcement by which students learn. Through Operant Conditioning, punishment will deter poor learning results and reinforcement will encourage positive ones. Today, Skinnerian Behaviorism is generally considered radical. Instructional Design incorporates behavioral objectives in its models, which encourage the mastery of tasks and learning. For example, an evaluation portion of the learning activity that is executed with letter grades is a form of stimulus-response-reinforcement. A good letter grade (A) is positive reinforcement. A poor letter grade (F) is punishment.

PROGRAMMED INSTRUCTION

First popularized by B.F. Skinner in the 1950's, Programmed Instruction is a teaching method that provides students with small, manageable and precisely defined increments of learning followed by positive reinforcement for mastery. Programmed Instruction is considered the first phase of several developments that led to Instructional Design. Today, Programmed Instruction is still used in computer-aided classrooms and is generally broken down into two types. Linear Programmed Instruction guides the student through a set sequence of tasks and students do not advance to the next step until the current step is successfully completed. Branched Programmed Instruction allows the student to choose different paths to the correct outcome, and assumes that the learning process can be different for different learners. Both styles offer frequent and immediate feedback and reinforcement. While Programmed Instruction is still used in schools today for some types of learning, it is primarily found in industrial settings and in the armed forces, where training large numbers of personnel for specific tasks is required.

While many educators agree that Programmed Instruction and the Behaviorist approach to Instructional Design can serve as valuable supplement to other teaching methods, others have criticized the approach as not providing enough learning synthesis for problem-solving in other environmental situations. Norma Feshback and J. W. Eshleman are two critics of the theory. They have written that Programmed Instruction does not account for individual differences in students and does not apply well to higher-level material. Feshback believes that Programmed Instruction may be more appropriate for a specific group of students at a specific level, but not for general groups. Eshleman points out that Programmed Instruction does not introduce students to new material after the initial task, and its rigid sequencing is not appropriate for all learning contexts.

OPERANT CONDITIONING

Also, known as Behavior Modification, Operant Conditioning uses systems of consequences to modify behavior. It was first studied by Edward Thorndike in the 1920's; he theorized that positive behavior was ingrained over time by successful outcomes. In other words, organisms could learn to use only the behavior that produced a rewarding outcome and discard behaviors that did not. Later, B. F. Skinner, a Behaviorist, expanded the model and constructed a more detailed theory. The central concepts of his theory of Operant Conditioning are reinforcement, punishment and extinction. Reinforcement is a consequence that causes a behavior to occur more frequently, while punishment is a consequence that causes a behavior to occur less frequently. Extinction is the lack of either consequence after a response, rendering the response inconsequential. This will eventually also lead to a reduction in the occurrence of the inconsequential behavior. Operant Conditioning is incorporated in Instructional Design by the use of positive reinforcement for the mastery of tasks and objectives.

CONSTRUCTIVISM

Constructivism is attributed to the work of philosopher and developmental psychologist Jean Piaget, who pioneered the cognitive learning theory. The constructivist theory holds that knowledge is constructed internally within the individual, and we continually construct new knowledge through experience. In the classroom, the constructivist theory is usually employed with less formal structure in the planning of lessons and teachers take the role of facilitators who guide students to their own conclusions. Students discover knowledge through a journey of interaction and experience through the learning process. Rather than the step-by-step systematic approach to learning inherent in Behaviorism, Constructivists believe that learning is ultimately social and cognitive, and Constructivism in schools fosters peer learning in a culturally and socially relevant environment. Today, most Instructional Systems Design models use a Constructivist approach.

JOHN DEWEY & PRAGMATISM

While Programmed Instruction and behaviorist approaches to Instructional Design were prominent in the mid-twentieth century, another view was making its way into education theory. John Dewey was a philosopher and educational reformer, and had died before learning theory became an educational discipline. Dewey was a leader in the school of Pragmatism, and believed that education should not be the mere teaching of facts but an interactive process which should require critical thinking skills to bring knowledge into a student's life. He argued that traditional reinforcement and programming in instruction did not lead to deep learning. He promoted "learning by doing" and pioneered several efforts at school reform toward the Progressive education movement in the 1930's, which ultimately failed. While popular, few of Dewey's philosophies were ever adopted into mainstream Instructional Design. However, in the latter part of the 20th century many of his theories have been revisited by new reformers in the field.

DIRECT INSTRUCTION & DISTAR

One of the most widely used yet controversial Instructional Design models in recent years is the Direct Instruction model. Siegfried Engelmann and Wesley C. Becker developed the model to provide systematic instruction for disadvantaged elementary school children. DISTAR (Direct Instruction System for Teaching Arithmetic and Reading) programs were implemented around the country in underperforming schools. While Direct Instruction is considered a comprehensive model of school reform in the 1980's and 90's, it has been highly controversial among educational theorists regarding its efficacy. Humanists have questioned the return of DI to a rote-style, teacher-directed model which discourages social growth and inquiry. However, recent long-term studies (such as Project Follow Through) have shown that lower-socioeconomic groups taught by a DI model have been shown performance improvement. Still, many educators feel that DI should only be used in limited situations (or not at all) and not as a primary method.

MADELINE HUNTER & THEORY INTO PRACTICE

Perhaps no one more than Madeline Hunter found problems in traditional Instructional Design theory. An educator and prolific writer, Hunter recognized foremost that most Instructional Design theory and models did not spell out in plain language specific methods that teachers could implement in the real life classroom. Hunter followed a Direct Instruction model and developed the Theory into Practice teaching model. She demonstrated with specific examples how a teacher should incorporate objectives and goals into everyday lesson plans. Her Seven Components of Teaching are still taught to and used by classroom teachers today.

COMPUTER-ASSISTED LEARNING

With the increase in new media, especially the explosion of the Internet, computer-assisted learning has become widely adopted in schools. Instructional Design for computer-aided education has also evolved quickly. Originally, computer enhanced programs employed a basic Behaviorism-based approach with heavy emphasis on Programmed Instruction. Today, like in most classrooms, a Constructivist approach has become the norm. One of the leading educational theorists in the computer-aided learning field is Seymour Papert. Known as the father of Artificial Intelligence, Papert has developed a learning approach called Constructionism, an offshoot of Constructivism. He was one of the first to bring information technology to the classroom. His Logo computer language and MIT Media Lab are at the forefront of developing instruction for computer learning.

TERMS & CONCEPTS

ADDIE Model: An early (1975) Instructional Systems Design model adopted by the armed forces and is still widely used in the industrial and technology fields today. ADDIE stands for Analysis, Design, Development, Implementation and Evaluation.

Behaviorism: A school of thought in psychology which holds that all behavior can be studied and explained scientifically through observable actions and responses. Internal thoughts and feelings are not considered as they cannot be seen.

Bloom's Taxonomy: A classification of educational objectives developed by Benjamin Bloom. Knowledge is categorized into three domains: the Affective, the Cognitive, and the Psychomotor. Within each domain occur different levels of learning, from simple recall to higher critical skills. Also called the Taxonomy of Educational Objectives.

Classical Conditioning: The process of manipulating stimuli to condition behavioral responses.

Constructivism: A school of thought in psychology which holds that knowledge is constructed internally within the individual, and we continually construct new knowledge through experience.

Dick and Carey Model: An ISD model similar to ADDIE but more complex in orientation. While still used today, it has been criticized by some as too cumbersome for the average design process.

Instructional Design: the systematic development of instructional specifications using learning theory to ensure the quality of instruction.

Learning Objectives: A clearly defined goal or set of goals to be reached and mastered in a learning activity.

Mastery Learning: An Instructional Design method in which students are provided a specific series of tasks and do not advance to the next task until the first is mastered.

Model of Learning: A theoretical outline for instruction which follows a learning theory.

Nine Events of Instruction: A model developed by Robert M. Gagné which proposed that nine conditions had to occur for successful learning. They are: Gain attention, Inform learner of objective, Stimulate recall of prior learning, Present stimulus material, Provide learner guidance, Elicit performance, Provide feedback, Assess performance and Enhance retention transfer.

Operant Conditioning: The process of modifying behavior through reinforcement—rewarding positive or punishing negative responses.

Programmed Instruction: A method of instruction which adopts the behaviorist theory of learning.

Reinforcement: The encouragement of a desired behavior or response with positive feedback or reward, in order to increase the frequency of the desired behavior.

Task Analysis: The process of breaking down a task into its fundamental components to understand how the task should be learned and performed.

Karen A. Kallio

BIBLIOGRAPHY

Cates, W.M. (1993). Instructional technology: The design debate. *Clearing House, 66.* Retrieved October 20, 2006, from EBSCO online database, Education Research Complete.

Chevalier, R.D. (2011). When did ADDIE become addie? *Performance Improvement, 50,* 10-14. Retrieved December 15, 2013, from EBSCO Online Database Education Research Complete.

Christie, N.V. (2012). An interpersonal skills learning taxonomy for program evaluation instructors. *Journal of Public Affairs Education, 18,* 739-756. Retrieved December 15, 2013, from EBSCO Online Database Education Research Complete.

Graham, G. (2005). Behaviorism. *Stanford encyclopedia of philosophy.* Retrieved October 19, 2006 from http://plato.stanford.edu.

Luebke, S., & Lorié, J. (2013). Use of Bloom's Taxonomy in developing reading comprehension specifications. *Journal of Applied Testing Technology, 14,* 1-27. Retrieved December 15, 2013, from EBSCO Online Database Education Research Complete.

Leigh, D. (n.d.). A brief history of instructional design. Retrieved October 18, 2006, from Performance Improvement Global Network, http://pignc-ispi.com.

McNeil, S. (2006). A hypertext history of instructional design. Retrieved October 18, 2006, from University of Houston College of Education, http://coe.uh.edu.

Pascopella, A. (2005). Catalyst for change. *District Administration 41.* Retrieved October 20, 2006, from EBSCO online database, Education Research Complete.

Ryder, M. (n.d.). Instructional design models. *Instructional technology connections.* Retrieved October 18, 2006, from University of Colorado at Denver, http://carbon.cudenver.edu.

Shibley, I., Amaral, K.E., Shank, J.D., & Shibley, L.R. (2011). Designing a blended course: Using ADDIE to guide instructional design. *Journal of College Science Teaching, 40,* 80-85. Retrieved December 15, 2013, from EBSCO Online Database Education Research Complete.

Spector, J. M. (2001). Philosophical implications for the design of instruction. *Instructional Science, 29* (4/5), 381-402. Retrieved October 20, 2006, from EBSCO online database, Education Research Complete.

Programmed instruction. (n.d.). *WikEd.* Retrieved October 18, 2006, from University of Illinois, Urbana-Champaign, http://wik.ed.uiuc.edu.

Wiburg, K. M. (n.d.) An historical perspective on instructional design: Is it time to exchange Skinner's teaching machine for Dewey's toolbox? Retrieved October 19, 2006, from http://internettime.com.

SUGGESTED READING

Bloom, Benjamin. (1956). *The taxonomy of educational objectives.* Addison-Wesley.

Dewey, John. (1959). *Dewey on education: Selections from the child and the curriculum.* Teacher's College Press.

Gagné, Robert M. (1965). *The conditions of learning.* Holt, Rinehart and Winston.

Gagné, Robert M., Leslie Briggs and Walter W. Wager. (1992) *Principles of instructional design.* 4th ed. Harcourt Brace Jovanovich College Publishers, 1992.

Skinner, B.F. (1954). *Behavior of organisms.* Acton, MA: Copley. Thorndike, E. (1966). *Human learning.* (New impression edition) MIT Press.

TOKEN ECONOMY

A token economy is a type of behavioral modification method used in an array of health and education settings. The token economy aims to shape behavior by rewarding individuals that meet target behaviors with reinforcers that they can use to obtain some type of reward. Standard components of a token economy are target behaviors, reinforcers, and rewards. Response costs and backup reinforcers are also aspects of the token economy. An example of a modification to the token economy is the level system. Concerns related to implementation of a token economy include generalizability and response maintenance.

KEYWORDS: Backup Reinforcer; Contingent Reinforcement; Level System; Natural Contingencies; Non-Contingent Reinforcement; Reinforcer; Response Cost; Response Maintenance; Reward; Self-Reinforcement; Targeted Behavior; Token Economy

OVERVIEW

Within the educational and mental health arenas, token economies are just one of several forms of behavioral methods used to decrease or increase certain types of behavior (Filcheck, McNeil, Greco, & Bernard, 2004). Liberman (2000) dated the 1960s as the time period in which token economies were created and first implemented. Montrose Wolf has been credited with developing the initial idea and terminology for a token economy in the early 1960s (Risley, 1997). It has been argued that the concept of a token economy arose well before the 1960s; Rodriguez, Montesinos, and Preciado (2005) asserted that the history of the token economy can be traced to work described in a textbook from the middle of the 19th century.

No matter the date of origin of the token economy, it is widely accepted that a token economy entails the distribution of tokens after the display of behavior deemed appropriate, (targeted behavior) where tokens can later be used to claim various items for redemption (Zlomke, & Zlomke, 2003). Rodriguez et al. more specifically define a token economy as, "a reinforcement system in which the occurrence of appropriate behavior (or the absence of problem behavior) produces secondary reinforcement in the form of tokens (e.g., poker chips) that can periodically be exchanged for other reinforcers (e.g., food, toys, free time)." Liberman noted that prompts and reinforcers were used to shape behavior in this reinforcement system and that a token economy became the designation for the system because of the ease of using tokens as reinforcers.

Key to token economy efficacy is rewarding tokens soon after the target behavior has been observed and as often as the behavior takes place (Kazdin, 2000). Positive attributes of token economies include a set structure that lends to consistent reinforcement of specific behaviors, reinforcers that can be generalized across context, and the ease of using tokens in terms of distribution and attainment (Tarbox, Ghezzi, & Wilson, 2006). Kazdin described the use of positive reinforcement to promote positive behavior and reduce inappropriate behavior as the goal of token economy.

Tokens, backup reinforcers, or rewards, and the rules regarding rewards comprise the foundation of the token economy. In defining the components of the token economy, Kazdin made the analogy that tokens, or reinforcers, are income while a backup reinforcer would be an expenditure. Behaviors that earn tokens would be work and as individuals obtain tokens they would amass savings. Another aspect of a token economy is response cost. A token economy with response cost refers to an intervention where reinforcers are taken away if individuals participating in the intervention display inappropriate behaviors (LeBlanc, Hagopian, & Maglieri, 2000).

APPLICATIONS

The token economy has been implemented in a number of formats and across various contexts. Much of the research that has focused on the token economy can be divided into investigations of single subjects, classrooms, and health settings. An example of single subject research on the token economy comes from Zlomke and Zlomke. The researchers conducted an investigation of the impact of a joint token economy and self-monitoring intervention for an adolescent. Teachers engaged in a point system with the student throughout the day. The student had been trained in self-monitoring and for a portion of the study the student participated in a point system and self-monitoring. Targeted behaviors were seen significantly less frequently when baseline was compared to the period when the point system was implemented. Behaviors further decreased when self-monitoring took place. Although classroom behavior was impacted by the token economy and self-monitoring, home behaviors did not change.

AT THE CLASSROOM LEVEL

Kazdin explored the impact of a token economy in six elementary school classrooms. Students in classrooms that received contingent reinforcement, or the receipt of reinforcers when target behaviors were demonstrated, evidenced significantly more appropriate behavior after the intervention was implemented. Generalizability of behaviors was more evident for students in contingent reinforcement groups as compared to students who received non-contingent reinforcement, or reinforcement that was not based on the display of targeted behaviors.

Swain and McLaughlin (1998) referred to the token economy as a token-reinforcement program during their study of middle school students in special education. Math accuracy was the target behavior of interest. Students were awarded points for a number of behaviors and response costs for other behaviors were also implemented. A bonus contingency, or the opportunity for students to earn additional points if they achieved a certain score on the assessment of math accuracy, was another aspect of the study. Math accuracy was higher during the bonus contingency portion of the token-reinforcement as compared to the baseline period.

Token economies have also been implemented at the college and university level. For instance, Boniecki and Moore (2003) used a token economy in a college classroom in order to increase student participation. Students received a token after participating during class. Tokens were then to be used for extra credit by students. Compared to a baseline period before the initiation of the token economy, significantly more students participated in class, as evidenced by the number of students responding to questions posed during class. Participation declined after the token economy intervention ended. Hodge and Nelson (1991) also employed a differential reinforcement intervention during a university level course. The purpose of their study was to promote class participation for those students who did not participate often and decrease participation for the few students who tended to dominate class participation. After the intervention was conducted, the instructor deemed classroom participation was more evenly distributed across students.

OTHER EDUCATIONAL APPLICATIONS

Lazarus (1990) detailed the aspects of a cooperative home-school token economy. In a cooperative home-school token economy, students who display targeted behaviors in either the home or school setting have an opportunity to accumulate tokens or points. A "Point Balance Passbook" is given to each student who brings the passbook home for review by parents and also uses it at school with teachers. The cooperative home-school token economy promoted communication between parent and child as well as parent and teacher. Parents also played a role in developing the program and received training on token economies.

HEALTH SETTINGS

Health settings, such as psychiatric hospitals or hospitals in general, are settings in which the token economy has been consistently put into practice for quite some time. Inpatient psychiatric units are an example of a setting where token economies have been utilized to promote a functional environment and reduce negative behavior such as violence (LePage, DelBen, Pollard, McGhee, VanHorn, Murphy, et al., 2003). LePage and colleagues studied a psychiatric unit over time where periods before and after token economy implementation were examined. Injuries, between patients and toward staff, were significantly reduced during the token economy intervention.

In an investigation of patients in a psychiatric hospital by Bedell and Archer (1980), comparisons were made between token economies that were either peer managed, staff managed, or used a non-contingent reinforcement schedule. Individuals in the

peer managed and staff managed token economy programs earned higher amounts of tokens than did participants in the non-contingent reinforcement group. In another study described by Bedell and Archer in the same article, a group performance incentive group and standard individual incentive group were compared. In the group performance incentive group, some of the points individuals could earn were due to how many points earned by the group of patients with which they were aligned. No statistically significant differences were found between the incentive groups in regard to how many points participants earned. Similar amounts of points were earned in both studies reviewed in the article.

The Behavioral Rehabilitation and Interpersonal Treatment Environment, or BRITE program, is another example of a token economy implemented in a psychiatric hospital (Bellus, Vergo, Kost, Stewart, & Barkstrom, 1999). As part of the BRITE program, a token economy with a response cost and level system component was put in place to affect changes in assaults and self-injuries in the hospital. Self-injury and assaults for BRITE participants were significantly lower after two years of operation of BRITE as compared with levels of self-injury and assaults in traditional wards in the psychiatric hospital.

Other health issues addressed with the token economy have been substance use and eating disorders. Vouchers have been used to promote targeted behavior such as abstinence from cocaine use for individuals with cocaine dependence (Higgins, Roll, Wong, Tidey, & Dantona, 1999). In the intervention conducted by Higgins and colleagues, individuals participating in interventions where vouchers were contingent upon abstinence from substance use were significantly more likely to remain abstinent than those who received vouchers in a noncontingent manner. Another population with whom token economies have been used were individuals with anorexia nervosa (AN) (Okamoto, Yamashita, Nagoshi, Masui, Wada, Kashima, et al., 2002). In one study, activity restriction therapy and token economy were integrated (TET) and then compared to two other forms of behavior therapy to promote weight gain. Therapy that integrated a token economy showed an increase in body mass index for study participants. Individuals that received TET showed greater gains in BMI than one of the other forms of therapy and somewhat fewer gains than the form of therapy that showed the greatest overall gains.

Modification of the Token Economy

LEVEL SYSTEMS

Level systems are modifications of a token economy and posited to be effective and relevant strategies for educating students with emotional and behavioral disorders (EBD) (Farrell, Smith, & Brownell, 1998). Level systems have been, "designed to be an organizational framework based on token economies within which a teacher can shape desired student behaviors by systematically applying behavioral principles (Farrell et al.)."

Steps, or levels, comprise the foundation for a level system. A step within a level system is composed of a set of rules and reinforcers such that when students follow the rules they are able to obtain reinforcers and move to the next step within the system (Farrell, Smith, & Brownell, 1998). In a level system a multi-tiered chart is constructed so that one level is a starting point and levels above and below represent students' engagement in appropriate or inappropriate behavior, respectively (Filcheck et al.). Rewards are delegated several times throughout the day by the teacher based on how students have moved up or down the levels.

In an investigation of teachers of students with EBD, a solid majority of teachers (71%) used level systems (Farrell et al.). An example of a level system used with EBD students is the system used by The Turning Point Program-a program that works with school-age youth whose emotional and behavioral challenges led them to be educated outside of regular education classrooms (Havill, 2004).

Havill described the level system process in The Turning Point Program by noting that students complete a note sheet about their behavior every day. Staff participate in a level review with the student to evaluate on what level the staff and student believe the student should be placed. In The Turning Point Program, five levels-A, B, C, D, and OOPS-comprise the system such that the lowest level is D with levels ascending to the A level. The fifth, or OOPS, level represents when a student is "out of program status."

Filcheck and colleagues described the implementation of a whole-class token economy, or level system, intervention with preschool children. A whole-class intervention was chosen due to its capacity to save time and money when implemented and its avoidance of focusing on individual children. Comparisons were made to a parent-training method of behavior management. Filcheck and colleagues found there were less frequent displays of inappropriate behavior by preschool students participating in the whole-class token economy intervention. Additional reduction of inappropriate behavior was seen when other behavior management skill techniques were integrated with the level system.

IN COMBINATION WITH OTHER STRATEGIES

Along with modifications to the token economy, such as the level system, token economies can be one of several components in an intervention. For example, Musser, Bray, Kehle, and Jenson (2001) depicted an intervention with students with serious emotional disturbance (SED) in which the token economy was implemented along with other intervention strategies such as precision requests and antecedent strategies. The multicomponent intervention reduced displays of inappropriate behavior. Another example of research on a token economy modification incorporated differential reinforcement of alternative behavior (DRA) as a type of reinforcement-based intervention. DRA was used concurrently with a token economy to address childhood feeding disorders (Kahng, Boscoe, & Byrne, 2003). If the study participant accepted the food presented to them, a reinforcer was given to them. This type of reinforcer was a differential positive reinforcement of alternative behavior. If the participant obtained enough tokens mealtime could be curtailed; this was a differential negative reinforcement of alternative behavior. Food acceptance increased over the course of the investigation for the study participant.

ISSUES

There are a number of pertinent issues in regard to the token economy. Attending to treatment integrity is integral to the efficacy of the token economy as it is implemented and to obtaining sound information from a program evaluation (Kazdin). More research on the token economy helps to promote treatment integrity, yet researchers have noted that studies focused on the token economy have been seen less frequently in the current research landscape (Swain & McLaughlin, 1998) and a recent meta-analysis suggests that the efficacy of the token economy is not supported by research (Maggin, Chafouleas, Goddard & Johnson, 2011).

Another area to consider in regard to token economies is that despite the success of the token economy across a number of contexts, some treatment gains are not sustained in individuals when left their particular settings (Liberman). In this regard, response maintenance, or sustaining changes brought about through the intervention after a token economy has been ended, is the area of concern. Novak and Hammond (1983) denoted self-reinforcement and natural contingencies as strategies to promote response maintenance. Self-reinforcement involves individuals giving tokens, or reinforcers, to themselves when they meet a set of criteria. Natural contingencies are the reinforcers that exist within an environment that individuals can be trained to recognize and use to shape behavior.

Kazdin had several suggestions for how to increase response maintenance and transfer after a token economy has concluded. Examples of his suggestions were slow withdrawal of the token economy, enacting reinforcers across different contexts, or using ordinary reinforcers existing in the environment instead of tokens. A study by Novak and Hammond served to illustrate some aspects of Kazdin's suggestions on response maintenance. A fourth grade classroom was split into four groups and a token economy was implemented. Students were randomly assigned into one of four groups:

- Self-reinforcement;
- Natural contingencies;
- A combination of self-reinforcement and natural contingencies;
- Token reinforcement.

All groups saw more completions of reading problems after the various treatments were implemented as compared to baseline levels. The combination treatment group was the sole group that showed response maintenance after reinforcers were removed.

Other concerns about the token economy are notions that the token economy does not focus on the individual and can be abusive (LePage et al.). For instance, Kazdin noted the concern about the possibility of coercion and what can be considered a reinforcer in light of patient rights. Johnson (1999) argued that reinforcement theory is both the foundation for point systems and misplaced as a means to modify behavior in residential treatment. She asserted that natural contingencies are more effective in behavior change and less bound to the power struggles and punitive aspect she perceived in point and level systems. Kazdin has noted that tokens are not the only reinforcers that have an impact on shaping behavior; praise and feedback can successfully influence behavior also, as can the implementation of self-management programs (Shogren, Lang, Machalicek, Rispoli & O'Reilly, 2011).

Other factors found to impact the use of token economies included difficulties of training staff to use the token economy, the applicability of a token economy in less structured contexts than inpatient hospitals, and finding natural reinforcers outside of the hospital setting (Liberman). Training staff in implementing a token economy has been promoted through the use of tactile prompts such as a pager whereby staff are reminded to monitor the classroom for events such as target behavior to reinforce (Petscher & Bailey, 2006). Research has also shown the effectiveness of a token economy administered by peers rather than teachers or other authority figures (Alstot, 2012). Educational applications of the token economy have extended the reach of token economies outside of hospitals and broadened the types of reinforcers found to be effective.

CONCLUSIONS

Since its popular inception, the token economy has played an integral role in behavior modification across a number of settings most notably in the education and health arenas. The idea that reinforcing individuals for their behavior with rewards can promote or reduce any number of target behaviors has been accepted and implemented by many people in schools, hospitals, and other environments. There have been concerns about the generalizability and implementation of the token economy and the manner in which behavior change occurs in a token economy. Research into the token economy has been more infrequent in recent years. Despite concerns about the token economy and reduced attention to the token economy in terms of research, valuable lessons have been learned about behavior and change from work on the token economy over the years. The lessons learned about the token economy have benefited many individuals across age ranges and contexts.

TERMS & CONCEPTS

Backup Reinforcer: A backup reinforcer is the actual reward an individual receives as part of a token economy. An individual would accumulate a certain number of tokens, or reinforcers, as part of a token economy and exchange them for backup reinforcers such as free time in a classroom setting.

Contingent Reinforcement: Contingent reinforcement refers to the receipt of reinforcers when target behaviors are demonstrated.

Cooperative Home-School Token Economy: A cooperative home-school token economy refers to a token economy that is extended between the home and school contexts. Students are able to earn tokens or points at home and in school.

Level System: A level system is a modification of a token economy such that an individual is situated at a starting point on a chart and can move up or down levels, or steps, based on behavior they exhibit. Rewards are distributed based on points individuals accumulate during specified intervals of time.

Natural Contingencies: Natural contingencies are reinforcers that exist within an environment that individuals can be trained to recognize and use to shape behavior.

Non-contingent Reinforcement: Non-contingent reinforcement is reinforcement individuals receive that is not based on the display of targeted behaviors.

Reinforcer: A reinforcer is what individuals receive in a token economy when they exhibit target behavior. Tokens are prime examples of reinforcers used in a token economy. Points are also frequently used as reinforcers in a token economy.

Response Cost: Response cost occurs when reinforcers are taken away from an individual for displaying inappropriate behavior.

Response Maintenance: Response maintenance refers to sustaining changes brought about through a token economy after the intervention has been ended.

Reward: A reward in a token economy is what individuals exchange the tokens or points they receive for displaying the target behavior in the token economy. Rewards are also referred to as backup reinforcers.

Self-reinforcement: Self-reinforcement refers to individuals giving tokens, or reinforcers, to themselves when they meet a set of criteria.

Token Economy: A token economy is a form of behavior modification where a reinforcer is distributed when an individual meets a target behavior. Reinforcers are then used to obtain rewards.

Edith Arrington

BIBLIOGRAPHY

Alstot, A. E. (2012). The effects of peer-administered token reinforcement on jump rope behaviors of elementary physical education students. *Journal of Teaching in Physical Education, 31,* 261-278. Retrieved on December 17, 2013, from EBSCO Online Database Education Research Complete.

Bedell, J., & Archer, R. (1980). Peer managed token economies: Evaluation and description. *Journal of Clinical Psychology, 36,* 716-722. Retrieved November 25, 2007, from EBSCO Online Database Academic Search Premier.

Bellus, S., Vergo, J., Kost, P., Stewart, D., & Barkstrom, S. (1999). Behavioral rehabilitation and the reduction of aggressive and self-injurious behaviors with cognitively impaired, chronic psychiatric inpatients. *Psychiatric Quarterly, 70,* 27-37. Retrieved November 26, 2007, from EBSCO Online Database Academic Search Premier.

Boniecki, K., & Moore, S. (2003). Breaking the silence: using a token economy to reinforce classroom participation. *Teaching of Psychology, 30,* 224-227. Retrieved October 25, 2007, from EBSCO Online Database Education Research Complete.

Farrell, D., Smith, S., & Brownell, M. (1998). Teacher perceptions of level system effectiveness on the behavior of students with emotional or behavioral disorders. *Journal of Special Education, 32,* 89-98. Retrieved December 2, 2007, from EBSCO Online Database Education Research Complete.

Filcheck, H., McNeil, C., Greco, L., & Bernard, R. (2004). Using a whole-class token economy and coaching of teacher skills in a preschool classroom to manage disruptive behavior. *Psychology in the Schools, 41,* 351-361. Retrieved October 25, 2007, from EBSCO Online Database Education Research Complete.

Havill, L. (2004). Levels of involvement: the power of choice in a middle school level system. *Reclaiming Children & Youth, 13,* 155-161. Retrieved December 2, 2007, from EBSCO Online Database Education Research Complete.

Higgins, S. T., Roll, J. M., Wong, C. J., Tidey, J. W., & Dantona, R. (1999). Clinic and laboratory studies on the use of incentives to decrease cocaine and other substance use. In S. T. Higgins, & K. Silverman (Eds). *Motivating behavior change among illicit-drug abusers: Research on contingency management interventions.* (pp. 35-56). Washington, DC, US: American Psychological Association.

Hodge, G., & Nelson, N. (1991). Demonstrating differential reinforcement by shaping classroom participation. *Teaching of Psychology, 18,* 239-241. Retrieved November 26, 2007, from EBSCO online database, Education Research Complete.

Johnson, M. (1999). Managing perceptions: a new paradigm for residential group care. *Child & Youth Care*

Forum, 28, 165-179. Retrieved December 2, 2007, from EBSCO online database, Academic Search Premier.

Kahng, S., Boscoe, J. H., & Byrne, S. (2003). The use of an escape contingency and a token economy to increase food acceptance. *Journal of Applied Behavior Analysis, 36,* 349-353. Retrieved November 26, 2007. from http://pubmedcentral.nih.gov.

Kazdin, A. E. (2000). Token economy. In A. E. Kazdin (Ed). *Encyclopedia of psychology,* Vol. 8. (pp. 90-92). Washington, DC, US: Oxford University Press.

Kazdin, A. E. (1982). The token economy: A decade later. *Journal of Applied Behavior Analysis, 15,* 431-445. Retrieved November 26, 2007. from http://pubmed-central.nih.gov.

Lazarus, B. (1990). A cooperative home-school token economy. *Preventing School Failure, 34,* 37-40. Retrieved November 25, 2007, from EBSCO Online Database Academic Search Premier,

LeBlanc, L., Hagopian, L., & Maglieri, K. (2000). Use of a token economy to eliminate excessive inappropriate social behavior in an adult with developmental disabilities. *Behavioral Interventions, 15,* 135-143. Retrieved October 25, 2007, from EBSCO Online Database Academic Search Premier.

LePage, J., DelBen, K., Pollard, S., McGhee, M., VanHorn, L., Murphy, J., et al. (2003). Reducing assaults on an acute psychiatric unit using a token economy: a 2-year follow- up. *Behavioral Interventions, 18,* 179-190. Retrieved October 25, 2007, from EBSCO Online Database Academic Search Premier.

Liberman, R. (2000). The token economy. *American Journal of Psychiatry, 157,* 1398. Retrieved November 25, 2007, from http://ajp.psychiatryonline.org.

Maggin, D. M., Chafouleas, S. M., Goddard, K. M., & Johnson, A. H. (2011). A systematic evaluation of token economies as a classroom management tool for students with challenging behavior. *Journal of School Psychology, 49,* 529-554. Retrieved on December 17, 2013, from EBSCO Online Database Education Research Complete.

Musser, E., Bray, M., Kehle, T., & Jenson, W. (2001). Reducing disruptive behaviors in students with serious emotional disturbance. *School Psychology Review, 30,* 294-304. Retrieved October 25, 2007, from EBSCO Online Database Academic Search Premier.

Novak, G., & Hammond, J. (1983). Self-reinforcement and descriptive praise in maintaining token economy reading performance. *Journal of Educational Research, 76,* 186-189. Retrieved November 13, 2007, from EBSCO Online Database Education Research Complete.

Okamoto, A., Yamashita, T., Nagoshi, Y., Masui, Y., Wada, Y., Kashima, A., et al. (2002). A behavior therapy program combined with liquid nutrition designed for anorexia nervosa. *Psychiatry & Clinical Neurosciences, 56,* 515-520.

Retrieved November 25, 2007, from EBSCO Online Database from Academic Search Premier.

Petscher, E. S., & Bailey, J. S. (2006). Effects of training, prompting, and self-monitoring on staff behavior in a classroom for students with disabilities. *Journal of Applied Behavior Analysis, 39,* 215-226. Retrieved November 26, 2007, from http://pubmedcentral.nih.gov.

Risley, T. R. (1997). Montrose M. Wolf: The origin of the dimensions of applied behavior analysis. *Journal of Applied Behavior Analysis, 30,* 377-381. Retrieved December 1, 2007, from http://pubmedcentral.nih.gov.

Rodriguez, J. O., Montesinos, L., & Preciado, J. (2005). A 19th century predecessor of the token economy. *Journal of Applied Behavior Analysis, 38,* 427. Retrieved December 1, 2007, from http://pubmedcentral.nih.gov.

Shogren, K. A., Lang, R., Machalicek, W., Rispoli, M. J., & O'Reilly, M. (2011). Self- versus teacher management of behavior for elementary school students with Asperger Syndrome: Impact on classroom behavior. *Journal of Positive Behavior Interventions, 13,* 87-96. Retrieved on December 17, 2013, from EBSCO Online Database Education Research Complete.

Swain, J., & McLaughlin, T. (1998). The effects of bonus contingencies in a classwide token program on math accuracy with middle-school students with behavioral disorders. *Behavioral Interventions, 13,* 11-19. Retrieved November 26, 2007, from EBSCO Online Database Academic Search Premier.

Tarbox, R., Ghezzi, P., & Wilson, G. (2006). The effects of token reinforcement on attending in a young child with autism. *Behavioral Interventions, 21,* 155-164. Retrieved October 25, 2007, from EBSCO Online Database Academic Search Premier.

Tiano, J. D., Fortson, B. L., McNeil, C. B., & Humphreys, L. A. (2005). Managing classroom behavior of head start children using response cost and token economy procedures. *Journal of Early and Intensive Behavior Intervention, 2,* 28-39. Retrieved December 2, 2007 from http://behavior-analyst-today.com.

Zlomke, K., & Zlomke, L. (2003). Token economy plus self - monitoring to reduce disruptive classroom behaviors. *Behavior Analyst Today, 4,* 177-182. Retrieved October 25, 2007, from EBSCO Online Database Academic Search Premier.

SUGGESTED READING

Cruz, L., & Cullinan, D. (2001). Awarding points, using levels to help children improve behavior. *Teaching Exceptional Children, 33,* 16-23. Retrieved December 2, 2007, from EBSCO Online Database Education Research Complete.

Didden, R., De Moor, J., & Bruyns, W. (1997). Effectiveness of DRO tokens in decreasing disruptive behavior in the classroom with five multiply handicapped children. *Behavioral Interventions, 12,* 65-75. Retrieved November 26, 2007, from EBSCO Online Database Academic Search Premier.

Filcheck, H. & McNeill, C.B., (2004). The use of token economies in preschool classrooms: Practical and philosophical concerns. *Journal of Early and Intensive Behavior Intervention,* 1 (1), 94-104.

Sran, S. & Borerro, J. (2010). Assessing the value of choice in a token system. *Journal of Applied Behavior Analysis,* 4 (3), 553-557.

Tiano, J., Fortson, B., & McNeill, C. (2005). Managing classroom behavior of Head Start children using response cost and token economy procedures. *Journal of Early and Intensive Behavior Intervention,* 2 (1), 28-39.

Truchlicka, M., McLaughlin, T., & Swain, J. (1998). Effects of token reinforcement and response cost on the accuracy of spelling performance with middle-school special education students with behavior disorders. *Behavioral Interventions, 13,* 1-10. Retrieved November 13, 2007, from EBSCO online database, Academic Search Premier.

MATHEMATICS ANXIETY

Math anxiety is the feeling of nervousness and apprehension toward math problems, classes, or exams. It generally begins when a child is in fourth grade and escalates throughout high school. Math anxiety is not just a psychological problem as it can cause students to discontinue taking math classes beyond high school requirements, limiting their choices with regard to college or career opportunities. Teachers and parents have been shown to influence math anxiety, and both can assist in easing the psychological and physical symptoms children experience. Practice with various math problems, having no time limit for exams, and being encouraged through errors have been shown to ease math anxiety.

KEYWORDS: Math Anxiety; Mathematics; Phobia; Psychology; Short-Term Memory; Working Memory

OVERVIEW

Math anxiety is the feeling of worry, frustration, agitation, and a fear of failure with regard to taking a math class, completing math problems, and/or taking a math exam. Being anxious about math can begin when a child is in fourth grade and generally increases when students are in middle and high school. Some studies have focused on students as young as first grade experiencing math anxiety (Harari, Vukovic, & Bailey, 2013). In addition to past experiences with math, teachers and parents can influence the anxiety a child feels when presented with math problems. A person suffering from math anxiety usually experiences the physical signs of having a phobia or anxiousness: increased heart rate, stomach discomfort, sweating, trembling, and weakness within the body. Anyone who has experienced extreme discomfort being in a crowded elevator (claustrophobia) or looking out a window on the top floor of a building (vertigo) can relate to the sense of panic when a math test is placed in front of a person suffering from math anxiety.

Math anxiety is so pervasive that it has been researched for over fifty years. According to Bower (2001), math anxiety has been shown to actually "disrupt mental processes needed for doing arithmetic and drag down math competence." Other kinds of anxiety or phobias can inhibit a person's activities; for example, a person suffering from claustrophobia may take several flights of stairs rather than getting on an elevator, and a person experiencing acrophobia can choose not to go to the top of the Empire State Building. However, math-anxious people suffer from an actual dysfunction in brain activity; more specifically, working memory is affected. Working memory allows people "to retain a limited amount of information while working on a task—and block out distractions and irrelevant information" (Cavanagh, 2007a). Furthermore, Gardner (1983) asserts that "the most central and least replaceable feature of the mathematician's gift is the ability to handle skillfully long chains of reasoning" (Gardner). If the capability to work with long strings of numbers is affected due to math anxiety, solving such problems can be impossible.

HOW DOES MATH ANXIETY AFFECT CHILDREN?

Unfortunately, when faced with a math problem that he or she does not understand, the child suffering from math anxiety becomes filled with negativism and focuses on that, distracting him- or herself from attempting to work through the problem. Furthermore, this distraction can start a negative cycle in which the same child rushes though the problem and makes a mistake because he or she is not focusing on the problem itself. The mistake then reinforces the negativism and increases the need to rush through homework or an exam ("Math Anxiety," 2007). And unlike the people who avoid the situations that make them anxious, a student does not have the option of avoiding math during the school day—or afterward, for that matter, when faced with assigned homework.

Ashcraft and Kirk (2001) note that there are specific types of math problems that tend to give students the most anxiety. Those problems are the ones that deal with large numbers and require several steps such as carrying and borrowing numbers and long division—tasks that require working memory. Amanda McMahon, a ten-year-old fifth grader, was working on algebra in her elementary class. She identified confusion as a feeling she got when working on her assignments because "letters divided by other letters are somehow supposed to equal a different set of letters multiplied by other letters" (personal communication, October 24, 2007). At the end of the school year, McMahon would take a comprehensive New York State standardized exam in mathematics in addition to culminating math exams required by her school district. Her view of math was not a positive one.

POTENTIAL CONSEQUENCES

Such a negative view could be very costly. The issue with students such as McMahon—those who complete their homework and pass tests but fear doing either—is not simply a psychological concern; it is a lifetime concern. Students who feel anxious when faced with math problems or who perform poorly on math exams tend to stop taking math classes beyond the point at which they are required. By not taking higher-level classes, students greatly limit their options regarding higher education and employment possibilities. While it is commonly believed that boys outperform girls on math achievement, there is evidence that whenever such a divide is noted, the divide is not permanent. Woolfolk (1998) points out that the difference in gender and math performance can "decrease substantially or disappear altogether when the actual number of previous math courses taken by each student is considered" (Fennema & Sherman, 1977; Oakes, 1990; Pallas & Alexander, 1983, as cited in Woolfolk). The more classes a student takes, the more familiar with the material he or she will become,

and the more comfortable manipulating math problems he or she will be. However, when faced with the option of feeling frustrated and anxious much of the time, it is easy to see why boys and girls cease taking math classes rather than adding to their frustration with additional courses in their not so favorite subject.

When looking toward higher education, a lack of math experience can cause the need for non-credit bearing courses in college, in addition to the required math courses for any specific field. This adds to tuition bills and the time it takes to complete a degree, and, when in conjunction with math anxiety, can cause psychological problems as well. Karin Killough, Director of the Learning Center at the State University of New York College at Plattsburgh, noted that in the 2006-2007 academic year, her tutors accumulated 10,000 contact hours assisting students in various subjects. Math courses, including statistics and calculus, totaled almost one quarter of those contacts (personal communication, October 24, 2007).

Sarah Taylor, a math tutor in the Learning Center, indicated that when having to break down the number of contacts she had with students who had trouble with math problems versus those with math anxiety, the breakdown differed depending on the time of the semester. During mid-terms and final exams, more than three-quarters of the students she assisted had anxiety issues; on the other hand, during the less stressful times of the semester, almost the same amount came to her for assistance with math problems. Taylor, a math and accounting major, attributed this discrepancy to the high stakes of exams and students' lack of confidence in their math ability when those stakes are higher (personal communication, October 24, 2007). When a final grade is at stake, it is likely that college students who experience math anxiety will not continue taking math courses beyond what is required of them.

Applications

TEACHER'S ROLE

It is important that teachers understand when the introduction to mathematics takes place in the life of a child. According to Gardner, introduction to the concept of math begins when infants first learn "the world of objects. For it is in confronting objects, in ordering and reordering them, and in assessing their quantity, that the young child gains his or her initial and most fundamental knowledge about the logical-mathematical realm. From this preliminary point, logical-mathematical intelligence rapidly becomes remote from the world of material objects. The individual becomes more able to appreciate the actions that one can perform upon objects. Over the course of development, one proceeds from objects to statements, from actions to the relations among actions, from the realm of the sensorimotor to the realm of pure abstraction—ultimately, to the heights of logic and science" (Gardner).

Math anxiety develops shortly after children enter the world of structured education. If left on their own, Gardner asserts, children will manipulate objects and utilize them in a way that best fits their needs. Once they enter into a school system, however, fitting their needs loses priority to goals, objectives, and standardized tests outside their control. Furthermore, there is research that points to teachers being the possible culprits of the math anxiety their students experience. In a study conducted by Jackson and Leffingwell (1999), the researchers identified several teacher behaviors that cause math anxiety in students:

- Being hostile;
- Exhibiting gender bias;
- Having an uncaring attitude;
- Expressing anger;
- Having unrealistic expectations;
- Embarrassing students in front of their peers (as cited in Furner & Duffy, 2002).

In addition, Oberlin (1982) found that teaching techniques such as "assigning the same work for everyone, teaching the textbook problem by problem, and insisting on only one correct way to complete a problem" can increase a student's anxiousness (as cited in Furner & Duffy). Furthermore, Woolfolk notes that "some elementary school teachers spend more academic time with boys in math and with girls in reading. In one study, high school geometry teachers directed most of their questions to boys, even though the girls asked questions and volunteered answers more often." It is plausible to expect that if teachers have positive attitudes, treat students respectfully and individually, and treat girls and boys as if both genders have the same potential for success in math, the instance of math anxiety would decline. Researchers have also indicated that the use of breathing exercises before exams may greatly impact math anxiety in students. This may be a possible area for teachers or other school staff to explore (Brunyé et al., 2013).

EFFECT ON SUCCESSFUL MATH STUDENTS

In the article "Overcoming Math Anxiety," it is noted that even students showing success with math can have math anxiety to the degree that it impairs their short-term memory. This information is in contrast to historical research citing that math anxiety only occurs in students who are weak in math. It also proves that students need to be treated as though math anxiety could be a concern regardless of their performance. In addition, the article states that "a lack of role models in mathematics and the sciences—along with stereotypical assumptions that Blacks, Hispanics, and women are poor math students—can negatively impact those groups' math performance. Furthermore, work with learning-disabled students suggests that students' language processing skills should not be overlooked when it comes to beating math anxiety. Students who lack the grammar skills necessary to grasp the meaning of mathematical word problems may be more intimidated than students who can process the language and interpret the logic of such problems. Mathematics professors have discovered that working in groups is an effective way to combat—and conquer—fear of math. Engaging in group problem solving with peer role models can show students that there may be alternate ways to express and solve a problem and provide much-needed support to those who may have become culturally conditioned to believe that math is too difficult a subject for them" ("Overcoming Math Anxiety").

WHAT TEACHERS CAN DO

There are several things teachers can do to decrease their students' anxiety with math. For instance, providing the names and histories of role models who have been successful in math can help students think beyond their own classrooms. More specifically, discussing past mathematicians who were women or minorities can show children that anyone can be successful in the subject. Also, showing students that wrong answers can be helpful to figuring out a correct answer is also advantageous in helping students ease their anxiety. Finally, abstraction and mathematical terms are a problem for many students. Seeing a problem through real life situations with familiar words or pictures can make problems of money, time, size, and distance easier to understand. Problems that require computation outside of any real life context are difficult to appreciate when compared to how much allowance a student will have remaining after purchasing a book and a video game. Identifying how many miles it is to Grandma's house and figuring out the fastest way to travel there is much more meaningful than addition or division with numbers produced from a text book (Ruffins, 2007).

ROLE OF PARENTS

Parents have a greater effect on a child's propensity toward math anxiety than teachers do. Vukovic, Roberts, and Green (2013) found that when parents are involved with and supportive of math work at home, math anxiety was reduced for those students. Scarpello (2007) points out that "students' grades in math were higher when students perceived that their parents were encouraging their effort in math." Parents also have a stronger influence than teachers when it comes to the classes students choose and the career choices they make (Scarpello). For example, if a parent shrugs off a child's belief that he or she simply can't "do math" by not encouraging the child to try harder or to take a different class, the desire to continue with math classes will not exist, and the child's options for the future will be limited.

Scarpello notes that limited options are not always seen negatively in the minds of students: "Some students choose [career and technical education] CTE as a consequence of many years of unsuccessful academic classroom experience, which has persuaded them not to aspire to college. To many CTE students, the learning environment of career and technical classes is more comfortable than the typical academic classroom. These students may not like academic subjects, may have performed poorly in them, and may have developed self-perceptions that they should avoid occupations that require college" (Scarpello).

In addition, Tsui and Mazzocco (2007) conducted a study and found that "three measures were positively correlated with math anxiety: concern over mistakes, doubts about actions, and parental criticism" (Tsui & Mazzocco). Parents are the first role models children have. It should be clear, then, that the influence parents have regarding a child's education would have both positive and negative effects for the child. For example, if parents have expectations that are too high, children can develop math anxiety to the point that they see every error as reinforcement that they are failures when it comes to math: "I tried, but I still couldn't do it. I'm a loser." On the flip-side, a low expectation from a parent may make a child

feel that he or she is unable to be part of the world of math and that it is okay to avoid it completely as a result: "I just can't do it, and I don't like it anyway. I guess I won't bother with any more classes." Both ideals can have detrimental effects for children.

OVERCOMING MATH ANXIETY

Students can learn to overcome math anxiety. First, it is important for all children to know that mathematicians come in all shapes, sizes, and colors. Furthermore, boys are not necessarily better at math than girls. Oftentimes, boys are simply encouraged more. Second, effective teaching strategies must be used in math classes. Students need to practice math problems even when they understand what they are doing, and teachers have to offer students the opportunity to experience taking math tests in timed situations when there are no stakes involved. Taking only final exams or standardized tests in timed situations will increase anxiety levels regardless of a student's ability in math. Practicing how to be prepared for and how to react in light of a timed exam can help students make progress toward lowering their math anxiety. Also, teachers need to know at what levels their students fall throughout the classroom. Teaching all students the same material at the same pace leaves the weaker, slower students behind once the teacher moves on. In addition, teachers can group students together to complete math problems. This takes the individual pressure off students and helps to assure students that they are not alone in misunderstanding specific problems. Finally, teachers also need to communicate with parents, and both need to offer encouragement as much as possible when their students/children are working on math assignments and planning their academic futures.

VIEWPOINTS

In 1992, high school science teacher Lou D'Amore gave his ninth-graders a ten-question math test originally created by William Elwood Hume in 1932 for third-grade students (Cornwall, 1999). Most of D'Amore's ninth-graders failed the ten-question exam, while "only 25% obtained perfect scores" (Standing, 2006). In 2006, Standing administered the same test to seventy-five undergraduate students at a liberal arts college. In addition to the math test, the students were given a questionnaire in which they had to "rate their liking for math, the math teaching in high school, computers, and general science," as well as "their natural math ability and math anxiety." They were given no time limit to complete the D'Amore test. Twenty-five of the seventy-five students obtained perfect scores on the test, with the overall mean of the exam being a score of 8.71 out of ten. The "scores increased with self-rated math ability... and decreased with self-rated math anxiety.... They were also correlated with the subject's own prediction of the score s/he would achieve." Fifty out of seventy-five undergraduate students got at least one question incorrect on a mathematics exam created for third graders. To note the concern created by this and the D'Amore study, the test questions created by Hume were published on the *Reader's Digest Canada* website:

- Subtract these numbers: 9,864 − 5,947;
- Multiply: 92 × 34;
- Add the following: $126.30 + $265.12 + $196.40;
- An airplane travels 360 kilometers in three hours. How far does it go in one hour?
- If a pie is cut into sixths, how many pieces would there be?
- William bought six oranges at 5 cents each and had 15 cents left over. How much had he at first?
- Jane had $2.75. Mary had 95 cents more than Jane. How much did Jane and Mary have together?
- A boy bought a bicycle for $21.50. He sold it for $23.75. Did he gain or lose and by how much?
- Mary's mother bought a hat for $2.85. What was her change from $5?
- There are 36 children in one room and 33 in the other room in Tom's school. How much will it cost to buy a crayon at 7 cents each for each child? ("Are You Concerned," 1999).

These questions were administered in untimed testing situations. In several cases, the problems cannot be solved in just one step and, therefore, require working memory. For the third graders taking the test, they were showing what they had learned in their class up to that point. For the ninth graders, however, they had something to prove, and therefore, the stakes were higher for their answers being correct. The same can be said for the college students. That more than half of the seventy-five test-takers got at least one question wrong could be the result of many variables, including hurrying through the exam or feeling the pressure of needing to pass a test created for third-graders. It is difficult to speculate, but as Bracey (1996) notes, the United States ranks fourteenth out of fifteen countries when it comes to math skills (as cited in Standing). This may be because problems like those in the D'Amore test cannot be answered without the use of working memory, which is affected by anxiety-provoking math testing situations.

Burns (1998) identified that two thirds of adults in the United States "fear and loathe" math (as cited in Furner & Duffy). While the general public may view math anxiety as the result of students' simply not understanding the math they are learning, research shows that self-doubt about math ability can cause anxious tendencies (Cavanagh, 2007a). If college students make mistakes on problems of addition, the testing environment and the students' preconceived notions regarding their ability in math have to be taken into account, and experience with math at an early age must be considered a factor.

If teachers can promote math in a positive way, encouraging students to ask questions and applauding them for trying even when mistakes are made, students will be less likely to see themselves as not being able to "do math." And they will be less likely to fear the prospect of taking additional math classes. Educators do not hold the key, however; parents do. Parents need to be as positive as possible about math as well. Instead of declining to help their kids with math homework (possibly because they themselves do not know how to do it), parents need to learn the solutions right alongside their children to prove that it can be done. In addition, parents need to support their children (especially their daughters) by impressing upon them that math is just one more subject to be learned, not one that is more difficult.

TERMS & CONCEPTS

Math Anxiety: Math anxiety is the feeling of nervousness and apprehension toward math problems, classes, or exams.

Phobia: An irrational fear of an activity or objects (flying, snakes, heights) that causes the behavioral changes required to avoid the activity or object.

Short-Term Memory: The part of a person's memory that retains information for a short period of time.

Working Memory: The part of a person's memory that allows for several activities at one time, like solving a math problem that requires numerous steps.

Maureen McMahon

BIBLIOGRAPHY

Are you concerned about the way our children are being taught math? (1999). *Reader's Digest Canada*. Retrieved October 22, 2007, from http://readersdigest.ca.

Ashcraft, M. A., & Kirk, E. P. (2001). The relationships among working memory, math anxiety, and performance. *Journal of Experimental Psychology: General, 130*, 224–237. Retrieved October 9, 2014, from EBSCO Online Database PsycINFO.

Bower, B. (2001). Math fears subtract from memory, learning. *Science News, 159*, 405. Retrieved October 9, 2014, from EBSCO Online Database Education Research Complete.

Bracey, G. W. (1996). The sixth Bracey report on the condition of public education. *Phi Delta Kappan, 78*, 127–138. Retrieved December 12, 2007, from EBSCO Online Database Academic Search Complete.

Brunyé, T. T., Mahoney, C. R., Giles, G. E., Rapp, D. N., Taylor, H. A., & Kanarek, R. B. (2013). Learning to relax: Evaluating four brief interventions for overcoming the negative emotions accompanying math anxiety. *Learning & Individual Differences, 27*, 1–7. Retrieved December 26, 2013, from EBSCO Online Database Education Research Complete.

Burns, M. (1998). *Math: Facing an American phobia.* Sausalito, CA: Math Solutions Publications.

Cavanagh, S. (2007a). 'Math anxiety' confuses the equation for students. *Education Week, 26*, 12. Retrieved October 22, 2007, from EBSCO Online Database Education Research Complete.

Cavanagh, S. (2007b). Understanding 'math anxiety'. *Teacher Magazine Online.* Retrieved October 23, 2007, from http://teachermagazine.org.

Cornwall, C. (1999, Feb.). Why Johnny can't add. *Reader's Digest, 154*, 38–43.

Fennema, E., & Sherman, J. (1977). Sex-related differences in mathematics achievement, spatial visualization and affective factors. *American Educational Research Journal, 14*, 51–71.

Furner, J. M., & Duffy, M. L. (2002, Nov.) Equity for all students in the new millennium: Disabling math anxiety. *Intervention in School & Clinic, 38*, 67–75. Retrieved October 25, 2007, from EBSCO Online Database Academic Search Premier.

Gardner, H. (1983). *Frames of mind: The theory of multiple intelligences.* New York: Basic Books.

Harari, R. R., Vukovic, R. K., & Bailey, S. P. (2013). Mathematics anxiety in young children: An exploratory study. *Journal of Experimental Education, 81*, 538–555. Retrieved December 26, 2013, from EBSCO Online Database Education Research Complete.

Hume, W. E. (1932). *The opportunity plan: Arithmetic, senior third class.* Toronto: Thomas Nelson & Sons.

Jackson, C. D., & Leffingwell, R. J. (1999). The role of instructors in creating math anxiety in students from kindergarten through college. *Mathematics Teacher, 92*, 583–586. Retrieved October 9, 2014, from EBSCO Online Database Education Research Complete.

Math anxiety. (2007). *Gifted Child Today, 30*, 9. Retrieved October 22, 2007, from EBSCO Online Database Education Research Complete.

Oakes, J. (1990). Opportunities, achievement, and choice: Women and minority students in science and mathematics. *Review of Research in Education, 16*, 153–222.

Oberlin, L. (1982). How to teach children to hate mathematics. *School Science and Mathematics, 82*, 261.

Overcoming math anxiety. (2007). *Journal of Developmental Education, 30*, 40–41. Retrieved October 22, 2007, from EBSCO Online Database Educational Research Complete.

Pallas, A. M., & Alexander, K. (1983). Sex differences in quantitative SAT performance: New evidence on the differential coursework hypothesis. *American Educational Research Journal, 20*, 165–182. Retrieved October 9, 2014, from EBSCO Online Database Education Research Complete.

Ruffins, P. (2007). A real fear. *Diverse: Issues in Higher Education, 24*, 17–19. Retrieved October 9, 2014, from EBSCO Online Database Education Research Complete.

Scarpello, G. (2007). Helping students get past math anxiety. *Techniques: Connecting Education & Careers, 82*, 34–35. Retrieved October 22, 2007, from EBSCO Online Database Education Research Complete.

Standing, L. G. (2006). Why Johnny still can't add: Predictors of university students' performance on an elementary arithmetic test. *Social Behavior & Personality: An International Journal, 34*, 151–159. Retrieved October 22, 2007, from EBSCO Online Database Academic Research Premier.

Tatar, E. (2012). The relationship between mathematics anxiety and learning styles of high school students. *New Educational Review, 28*, 94–101. Retrieved October 10, 2014, from EBSCO Online Database Education Research Complete.

Tempel, T., & Neumann, R. (2014). Stereotype threat, test anxiety, and mathematics performance. *Social Psychology of Education, 17*, 491–501. Retrieved October 10, 2014, from EBSCO Online Database Education Research Complete.

Tsui, J. M., & Mazzocco, M. M. M. (2007). Effects of math anxiety and perfectionism on timed versus untimed math testing in mathematically gifted sixth graders. *Roeper Review, 29*, 132–139. Retrieved October 21, 2007, from EBSCO Online Database Education Research Complete.

Vukovic, R. K., Roberts, S. O., & Green Wright, L. (2013). From parental involvement to children's mathematical performance: The role of mathematics anxiety. *Early Education & Development, 24*, 446–467. Retrieved December 26, 2013, from EBSCO Online Database Education Research Complete.

Woolfolk, A. E. (1998). *Educational psychology* (7th ed.). Boston, MA: Allyn and Bacon.

SUGGESTED READING

Dreger, R. M., & Aiken, L. R. (1957). The identification of number anxiety in a college population. *Journal of Educational Psychology, 48*, 344–351. Retrieved October 9, 2014, from EBSCO Online Database PsycARTICLES.

Dreyden, J., & Gallagher, S. A. (1989). The effects of time and direction changes on the SAT performance of academically talented adolescents. *Journal for the Education of the Gifted, 12*, 187–204.

Frost, R. O., & DiBartolo, R. M. (2002). Perfectionism, anxiety, and obsessive-compulsive disorder. In G. L. Fleet & P. L. Hewitt (Eds.), *Perfectionism: Theory, research and treatment* (pp. 341–372). Washington DC: American Psychological Association.

Frost, R. O., & Marten, P. A. (1990). Perfectionism and evaluative threat. *Cognitive Therapy and Research, 14*, 559–572.

Frost, R. O., Marten, P. A., Lahart, C., & Rosenblate, R. (1990). The dimensions of perfectionism. *Cognitive Therapy and Research, 14*, 449–468.

Gregor, A. (2005). Examination anxiety: Live with it, control it or make it work for you? *School Psychology International, 26*, 617–635. Retrieved October 22, 2007, from EBSCO Online Database Education Research Complete.

Hillyer, K. (1988). Problems of gifted children. *Journal of the Association for Study of Perception, 21* (1/2), 10–26. Retrieved October 9, 2014, from EBSCO Online Database PsycINFO.

Kellogg, J. S., Hopko, D. R., & Ashcraft, M. H. (1999). The effects of time pressure on arithmetic performance. *Journal of Anxiety Disorders, 13*, 591–600.

Lupkowski, A. E., & Schumacker, R. E. (1991). Mathematics anxiety among talented students. *Journal of Youth and Adolescence, 20*, 563–572.

Miyake, A. (2001). Individual differences in working memory: Introduction to the special section. *Journal of Experimental Psychology: General, 130*, 163–168. Retrieved October 9, 2014, from EBSCO Online Database PsycARTICLES.

National Council of Teachers of Mathematics. (2000). *Principles and standards for school mathematics.* Reston, VA: Author.

Parker, W. D. (1997). An empirical typology of perfectionism in academically talented children. *American Educational Research Journal, 34*, 545–562. Retrieved October 9, 2014, from EBSCO Online Database Education Research Complete.

Parker, W. D., & Adkins, K. K. (1995). Perfectionism and the gifted. *Roeper Review, 17*, 173–176. Retrieved December 12, 2007, from EBSCO Online Database Education Research Complete.

Parker, W. D., & Mills, C. J. (1996). The incidence of perfectionism in gifted students. *Gifted Child Quarterly, 40*, 194–199. Retrieved October 9, 2014, from EBSCO Online Database Education Research Complete.

Parker, W. D., & Stumpf, H. (1995). An examination of the Multidimensional Perfectionism Scale with a sample of academically talented children. *Journal of Psychoeducational Assessment, 13*, 372–383.

Richardson, F. C., & Suinn, R. M. (1972). The mathematics anxiety rating scale: Psychometric data. *Journal of Counseling Psychology, 19*, 551–554. Retrieved October 9, 2014, from EBSCO Online Database PsycARTICLES.

Rosenthal, T. L. (1980). Modeling approaches to test anxiety and related performance problems. In I. G. Sarason (Ed.), *Test anxiety: Theory, research and applications* (pp. 245–270). Hillsdale, NJ: Erlbaum.

Schmidt, W. H. (1998). Changing mathematics in the U.S.: Policy implications from the third international mathematics and science study. Presented at the 76th annual meeting of the National Council of Teachers of Mathematics, Washington, DC.

Suinn, R. M., Edie, C. A., Nicoletti, J., & Spinelli, P. R. (1972). The MARS, a measure of mathematics anxiety: Psychometric data. *Journal of Clinical Psychology, 28*, 373–375. Retrieved October 9, 2014, from EBSCO Online Database Education Research Complete.

Suinn, R. M., Taylor, S., & Edwards, R. W. (1988). Suinn mathematics anxiety rating scale for elementary school students (MARS-E): Psychometric and normative data. *Educational and Psychological Measurement, 48*, 979–986.

Taylor, B., & Fraser, B. (2013). Relationships between learning environment and mathematics anxiety. *Learning Environments Research, 16*, 297–313. Retrieved October 9, 2014, from EBSCO Online Database Education Research Complete.

Zeidner, M. (1998). *Test anxiety: The state of the art.* New York: Plenum Press.

AFFECTIVE VARIABLE

The Affective Variable is a learning motivation aspect which is part of the affective domain. Affect refers to the emotions, attitudes, feelings and beliefs that condition behavior. In language learning, the affective variable refers to how emotions, attitudes, etc. impact learners' second language acquisition. A primary affective variable is motivation. Research has found that when students are motivated, they are more likely to be successful. Motivation has been conceptualized many ways, and several theories have been posited to explain what motivates students. Other affective factors have also been identified. There are many ways teachers can use their knowledge of the affective variable to help students in the classroom.

KEYWORDS: Affective Filter Hypothesis; Affective Variable; Attribution Theory; Autonomous Motivation; Community Language Learning; Expectations and Values-Related Theory; Extrinsic Motivation; Goal-Related Theory; Instrumental Orientations; Integrative Attitude; Intrinsic Motivation; Learning Strategies; Motivation; Second Language (L2); Self-Determination Theory

OVERVIEW

Language learning is a complex process that is influenced by multiple factors. One of the most important factors is the affective variable. Affect refers to the emotions, attitudes, feelings and beliefs that can condition behaviors (Arnold & Brown, 1999).

Affect and cognition are closely-integrated in the learning process. Some argue that affect precedes and motivates both cognition and behavior (Cuddy, Fiske & Glicke, 2007). That is, one's emotions, feelings and attitudes influence one's perceptions of an event; thereby determining what one thinks about and does before, during and after the event. Neurobiologists have shown that affect has an important impact on memory. Strong emotions can interfere with one's working memory, thereby interfering with the learning process. At the same time, affect can reshape long-term memory (Stevick, 1999).

AFFECT & MOTIVATION

Due to its importance in learning, much research has been done to uncover the exact nature of affect and how it can be used to promote achievement. One of the most researched affective factors is motivation. Studies have consistently shown that motivated students are likely to be more successful in learning a second language (Masgoret & Gardner, 2003). In general, this is because students in a classroom that stimulates positive emotions are likely to enjoy the learning experience and will gain the attitude that learning in the context is desirable. Thus, they will be motivated to try hard and gain greater achievement. On the other hand, students in an environment that stimulates negative emotions will dislike the experience and gain the attitude that learning is undesirable. They will lack motivation, put little effort into their work, and have lower achievement.

But what causes motivation? Why are some students more motivated than others? Are there different types of motivation?

INTEGRATIVE & INSTRUMENTAL ORIENTATIONS

Motivation has been conceptualized in various ways. Dörnyei (2003) provides a historical overview of motivation research in second language acquisition, and his timeline is generally followed here. He begins with the work of Lambert and Gardner (1972), who identified two types of attitudes that contribute to one's motivation to learn a second language (L2). These are integrative and instrumental:

- An integrative orientation refers to an individual's desire to associate with members of the culture who speak the target language. This theory states that learners who want to be more like the people who speak the target language are going to be more willing to adopt the behaviors and language style of the new culture. Therefore, they will quickly learn the language;
- Instrumental orientation refers to the practical reasons that an individual learns a language, such as to get a better job.

Dörnyei points out that Lambert and Gardner were working in the multicultural Canadian context composed of two distinct language communities comprised respectively of French and English speakers. In this context, they found integrativeness to be a "primary" (Dörnyei) force for aiding or interfering with intercultural communication. However, not all L2 situations involve two communities coming into contact. In fact, many students learn a language as a foreign language in their own language environments (e.g., Chinese students learning English in China). Dörnyei highlights other researchers who suggest that the concept of integrativeness might not have to refer to an actual integration of an individual into a community, but could generally refer to an individual's developing self-concept. In this instance, the term would refer to an ideal-self with attributes of the L2 (Dörnyei & Csizer, 2002 as cited in Dörnyei).

SELF-DETERMINATION & MOTIVATION

While Lambert and Gardner worked from a social psychology perspective, subsequent advances in cognitive psychology greatly influenced motivation studies. One of the most important cognitive theories dealing with affect is Deci and Ryan's (1995) Self-determination Theory (SDT). SDT categorizes an individual's motivation according to whether, and to what extent, the individual freely chooses the goal to be accomplished. In this theory, there are two general types of motivation: extrinsic and intrinsic.

- Extrinsic motivation is that which is inspired by factors that exist outside of the individual such as rewards and punishments;
- Intrinsic motivation refers to an individual's internal desires and needs to do well and to accomplish one's goals.

Extrinsic and intrinsic motivation represent opposite poles along a continuum of self-determination. Several sub-types of motivation are identified along the continuum, particularly related to extrinsic motivating factors. In these subtypes, it is recognized that even if motivation is extrinsic, an individual can agree with the goal. The greater the degree of agreement and acceptance of the motivating factor, the greater self-determination the individual will feel. For instance, studying English to gain a promotion is considered an extrinsic motivation. If the individual is forced to apply for the promotion, he or she is not likely to perceive the move to study English as one that is freely chosen. However, if the individual believes that the promotion is going to benefit him or her and is one that is desirable, then studying English is likely to lead to a greater sense of freedom and self-determination (Noels, 2003).

Noels, Pelletier, Clément & Vallerand (2003) have been instrumental in applying SDT to L2 acquisition. In their research, they have found that when students perceive greater freedom of choice in the classroom and hold perceptions of themselves as competent, they are more likely to report more self-determined forms of motivation. Students who report higher levels of internalized motivation also report being more comfortable and persevering in their L2 learning. On the other hand, when students feel less freedom of choice and/or low levels of competence, they are less intrinsically motivated. These researchers suggest that this and similar research could mean that autonomy-supportive environments encourage intrinsic motivation and thus should result in higher levels of achievement.

However, some researchers have questioned the validity of SDT in cultural contexts where collectivism and conformity is valued over independence and individuality. Some have posited that SDT may be less relevant to students from Asian cultures (Vansteenkiste, Zhou, Lens, & Soenens 2005). To test whether this is the case, numerous studies have been done on autonomous motivation, which is defined as a combination of intrinsic motivation and an internalized kind of extrinsic motivation in which the learner believes that the behavior needed to achieve a goal is personally valuable. Though more research is likely to be done on this question, in two studies investigating the relationship between autonomous motivation and Chinese students, both studies found that autonomous study motivation positively predicts adaptable learning attitudes, academic success and personal well-being. In contrast, controlled motivation, or motivation that is regulated by external factors or ones that are only partially-internalized, was associated with higher drop-out rates, maladaptive learning attitudes and ill-being. Moreover, parents who used autonomy supportive styles had children with more adaptive learning styles and higher well-being (Vansteenkiste et al.).

GOAL-RELATED THEORY

Goal-related Theory is an important cognitive theory stating that the kinds of goals that learners set for themselves impact motivation. Challenging and specific goals are more likely to lead to high levels of motivation as are goals that are set by the learners rather than by an external source. Goals affect attitudes and motivation by

- Focusing the learner's attention on activities and behavior which are goal-relevant;
- Assisting the learner in evaluating the success of effort;
- Assisting the learner in gauging the intensity of effort needed;
- Encouraging persistent effort;
- Encouraging learners to draw up short term and long-term plans in a more systematic way in order;
- To achieve the goal (Macaro, 2003).

ATTRIBUTION THEORY

A third cognitive theory that has been used in motivation studies is Attribution Theory. Weiner (1992) argues that the reasons to which an individual attributes past successes and failures influence one's current and future motivation. If one believes failure has been due to lack of ability, then one is less likely to pursue similar activities in the future. On the other hand, if failure is attributed to an inappropriate use of learning strategies or lack of effort, then one may be more likely to try again (Arnold & Brown; Dörnyei). Attribution Theory is related to the Expectations and Values-related Theory. This theory holds that our perceptions of our expectations for success and the value we place on the tasks we attempt to accomplish influences motivation. Within this theory, expectations for success are developed based on a learner's attributions of past successes, their feelings of self-efficacy (or sense of what they think they can realistically do) and their self-worth (Macaro).

NEUROBIOLOGICAL RESEARCH

Two final areas of motivation studies come from neurobiological research and what Dörnyei calls the "situated conception" of motivation. Schumann (1999) describes a stimulus-appraisal-response system where an individual's brain evaluates a stimulus based on five dimensions. These evaluations then form the basis of individual motivation. The "situated conception" refers to studies that examine the impact of the classroom context on motivation. Researchers working within this paradigm examine how the course design, the teacher and the classroom group dynamics influence student motivation.

OTHER AFFECTIVE FACTORS

While motivation is well-researched, it is but one of many affective factors. Other affective factors that are frequently said to influence learning are:

- Anxiety;
- Inhibitions;
- Extroverted vs. Introverted Personalities;
- Self-Esteem;
- Learning Styles (Arnold & Brown).

In Walqui's (2000) list of contextual factors that influence achievement in the classroom, some of those related to affect include:

- The language attitudes of the learner;
- The learner's peer group;
- The school;
- The neighborhood;
- Society at large.

Examples of attitudes that might have an affective impact include whether L2 acquisition is viewed as an act that replaces a first language or as the acquisition of an additional language; whether different dialects are acceptable in the classroom and whether the language and the culture of those who share it have status in the society. Additionally, Walqui lists individual and classroom factors that include peer pressure (e.g., is it perceived to be acceptable to learn the language?), presence of role models, level of home support, diverse needs and goals, learning styles, and the nature of classroom interactions.

Each of the above factors has been discussed in the literature and is generally assumed to have an impact on language learning. However, the exact impact of any individual factor is difficult to assess. This is because it is not easy to isolate many of these factors from larger social and/or educational contexts, and from other related factors. Therefore, while from a common-sense perspective, one might be able to easily articulate why someone who is anxious about his or her ability to learn a language or who has low self-esteem would find it more difficult to achieve in the classroom, the research is less definite about their actual impact. For instance, in a study of 88 first-year-university French students that attempted to determine the role of personality variables in second language acquisition (SLA) and to integrate these variables into Gardner's socio-educational model, Lalonde & Gardner (1984) found a general lack of relationship between personality variables and French achievement or language aptitude, even though the study found that some personality variables did correlate with motivation, which has been generally shown to directly affect achievement.

Interestingly, some research suggests that increased language achievement can sometimes become a negative affective factor. In a study that examined the relationship between immigrants' linguistic acculturation, socioeconomic status, perceived discrimination, social support networks, general health and psychological well-being, Jasinskaja-Lahti and Liebkind (2007) found that linguistic acculturation was directly and negatively related to psychological well-being. That is, as immigrants gained a better control of the language, they were less happy. The reasons for this are unclear. The authors suggest that as immigrants become acculturated they may lose contact with their first language primary support groups, or their language abilities allow them to better perceive discrimination against them and begin to internalize negative attitudes and stereotypes. Whatever the reason, the negative relationship between linguistic acculturation and well-being raises interesting questions about the reciprocal relationship between affect and achievement.

Applications

INCREASING MOTIVATION IN THE CLASSROOM

In the classroom, teachers concerned with the affective variable want to know how to create a positive learning environment that encourages intrinsic motivation. They also want to know how to overcome the effects of negative factors that exist within and outside the classroom. Both teachers and researchers have offered guidelines for increasing motivation. Macaro cites two studies that resulted in suggestions for teachers who want to increase motivation. The first list from a study by Dörnyei and Csizer resulted from a survey of 200 practicing teachers. They are:

- Set a personal example with your own behavior;
- Create a pleasant and relaxed atmosphere in the classroom;
- Present the tasks properly;
- Develop a good relationship with the learners;
- Increase the learner's linguistic self-confidence;
- Make the language classes interesting;

- Promote learner autonomy;
- Personalize the learning process;
- Increase the learners' goal-orientedness;
- Familiarize the learners with the target language culture (cited in Macaro).

The second list springs from a study by Williams & Burden:

- Recognize the complexity of motivation;
- Be aware of both initiating and sustaining motivation;
- Discuss with learners why they are carrying out activities;
- Involve learners in making decisions related to learning the language;
- Involve learners in setting language-learning goals;
- Recognize people as individuals;
- Build up individual's beliefs in themselves;
- Develop internal beliefs;
- Help move towards a mastery-oriented style;
- Enhance intrinsic motivation;
- Build up a supportive learning environment;
- Give feedback that is informational (cited in Macaro).

While these suggestions sound good considering some of the theories of motivation that have been discussed above, Macaro expresses concern that there is nothing language specific about these procedures.

There is nothing on the issue of use of the target language or the exclusion of the L1. There is nothing on progression with respect to the difficulty of the content itself. There is very little mention of the relationship between the individual's cultural identity and the culture of the target country or countries. There is no mention of the dominance of English as an international language and the effects of this on both learners of English as an L2 and on English (L1) learners of languages other than English.

LEARNING STRATEGIES

Considering this dearth, he cautions that the answer for teachers who want to spur language learning motivation cannot only be found in generic motivations for motivating learners. He points to the teaching of learning strategies as one potentially effective way that teachers can encourage and sustain student motivation. Learning strategies are the actions that students can use to learn new information. There are multiple learning strategies. Some of these are specific to reading, listening, speaking and writing. For instance, in reading, students may learn strategies to help them discover the meaning of words in contexts such as looking for synonyms and definitions in the sentences near the unknown word. Macaro hypothesizes that research will find that when students effectively use strategies, they experience success in language learning and this success will in turn lead them to be more motivated to pursue their studies.

Although he says there are few studies to test this hypothesis, he points to Goal Theory and theories of self-determination as a basis for his ideas. He says that evidence shows that one of the reasons for students' poor attitudes toward language learning is that they find it difficult. Since Goal Theory suggests that non-challenging goals are not motivating, he states that instead of making classes easier, teachers should provide challenging goals and teach students the strategies they can use to achieve them. In terms of self-efficacy, he says that teaching students to use strategies promotes independence and learner autonomy. When students choose from a selection of strategies and evaluate them for effectiveness, they feel empowered and in control of their language learning processes, which thereby increases motivation (Macaro).

AFFECTIVE FILTER HYPOTHESIS

In addition to advice to generally spur motivation, teachers also have access to a few specific language methodologies that have affect as a primary component of the method. Krashen & Terrell's (1983) Natural Approach is formulated around five hypotheses, one of which is the Affective Filter Hypothesis. This states that a learner's emotional state can act as a filter that impedes or blocks input of language acquisition. Community Language Learning is a method that aims to relieve the anxiety that students feel when they learn a new language by using counseling techniques (Kerper, 2002).

In conclusion, the affective variable encompasses a broad range of factors related to emotions, attitudes, beliefs and feelings. It is an important variable because the impact of affective factors on student achievement is believed to be substantial. Thus, teachers should consider affect when planning their classroom activities.

TERMS & CONCEPTS

Affective Filter Hypothesis: States that emotions can act as a filter that blocks language acquisition.

Attribution Theory: States that the reasons learners attribute for their past successes and failures influences their future motivation and behavior.

Autonomous Motivation: Describes a highly internalized and intrinsic motivation.

Community Language Learning: A method of L2 teaching that uses counseling techniques to reduce learner anxiety.

Expectations and Values-Related Theory: States that the degree of success an individual expects to have and the value that he or she places on one's activities influences motivation.

Extrinsic Motivation: Refers to motivation that is inspired by factors external to the learner such as getting a reward or avoiding a punishment.

Goal-Related Theory: States that learners are more motivated when they freely choose goals that are challenging and that are close to being accomplished.

Instrumental Orientations: Refer to learner attitudes that language learning is done for practical reasons such as getting a better job.

Integrative Attitude: Refers to an individual's desire to associate with, and become more like, members of the culture who speak the target language.

Intrinsic Motivation: is motivation that is caused by a learner's internal desire to do well.

Learning Strategies: Are actions that a learner takes to improve learning. There are many learning strategies specific to many learning activities such as reading or listening.

Self-Determination Theory: States that learners are more motivated when they are able to freely choose the goals that they set out to accomplish.

Noelle Vance

BIBLIOGRAPHY

Arnold, J., & Brown, H. D. (1999). A map of the terrain. In J. Arnold (Ed.), *Affect in language learning* (pp. 1-24). UK: Cambridge University Press.

Bell, S., & McCallum, R. (2012). Do foreign language learning, cognitive, and affective variables differ as a function of exceptionality status and gender? *International Education, 42,* 85-105. Retrieved December 15, 2013, from EBSCO Online Database Education Research Complete.

Cuddy, A., Fiske, S., & Glick, P. (2007). The BIAS Map: Behaviors from intergroup affect and stereotypes. *Journal of Personality, 92,* 631-648.

Deci, E. L., & Ryan, R. M. (1985). (Eds.). *Intrinsic motivation and self-determination in human behavior.* New York: Plenum.

Dörnyei, Z. (2003). Attitudes, orientations, and motivations in language learning: advances in theory, research and applications. In A. Cumming (Series Ed.) & Z. Dörnyei (Vol. Ed.), *Language Learning: Attitudes, orientations, and motivations in language learning.* (Vol. 53, Supplement 1). (pp. 3-32). The Best of Language Learning Series. Ann Arbor, MI: Blackwell Publishing.

Gardner, R.C., & Lambert, W. (1972). *Attitudes and motivation in second language learning.* Rowley, MA: Newbury House.

Jasinskaja-Lahti, E., & Liebkind, K. (2007). A structural model of acculturation and well-being among immigrants from the former USSR in Finland. *European Psychologist, 12*80-92.

Kerper, J. (2002). Second language teaching methods. Retrieved Oct. 2, 2007, from http://coe.sdsu.edu.

Kondo-Brown, K. (2013). Changes in affective profiles of postsecondary students in lower-level foreign language classes. *Foreign Language Annals, 46,* 122-136. Retrieved December 15, 2013, from EBSCO Online Database Education Research Complete.

Krashen, S. D., & Terrell, T. D. (1983). *The natural approach: Language acquisition in the classroom.* Hayward, CA: Alemany Press.

Lalonde, R. N., & Gardner, R. C. (1984). Investigating a causal model of second language acquisition: where does personality fit? *Canadian Journal of Behavioral Science, 16,* 224-237.

Lindsey, E. W., & Colwell, M. J. (2013). Pretend and physical play: Links to preschoolers' affective social competence. *Merrill-Palmer Quarterly, 59,* 330-360. Retrieved December 15, 2013, from EBSCO Online Database Education Research Complete.

Macaro, E. (2003). *Teaching and learning a second language: A review of recent research.* New York: Continuum.

Masgoret, A. M., & Gardner, R. C. (2003). Attitudes, motivation, and second language learning: A meta-analysis of studies conducted by Gardner and associates. In A. Cumming (Series Ed.) & Z. Dörnyei (Vol. Ed.), *Language learning: Attitudes, orientations, and motivations in language learning.* (Vol. 53, Supplement 1). (pp. 167-210). The Best of Language Learning Series. Ann Arbor, MI: Blackwell Publishing.

Noels, K. (2002). Learning Spanish as a second language: learners' orientations and perceptions of their teachers' communication style. In A. Cumming (Series Ed.) & Z. Dörnyei (Vol. Ed.), *Language learning: Attitudes, orientations, and motivations in language learning.* (Vol. 53, Supplement 1). (pp. 97-136) The Best of Language Learning Series. Ann Arbor, MI: Blackwell Publishing.

Noels, K., Pelletier, L.G., Clément, R., & Vallerand, R.J. (2002). Why are you learning a second language? Motivational orientations and Self-determination Theory. In A. Cumming (Series Ed.) & Z. Dörnyei (Vol. Ed.), *Language Learning: Attitudes, orientations, and motivations in language learning.* (Vol. 53, Supplement 1). (pp. 33-63). The Best of Language Learning Series. Ann Arbor, MI: Blackwell Publishing.

Schumann, J. (1999). A neurobiological perspective on affect and methodology in second language learning. In J. Arnold (Ed.), *Affect in language learning* (pp. 28-42). UK: Cambridge University Press.

Stevick, E. (1999). Affect in learning and memory: From alchemy to chemistry. In J. Arnold (Ed.), *Affect in language learning* (pp. 43-57). UK: Cambridge University Press.

Vansteenkiste, M., Zhou, M., Lens, W., & Soenens, B. (2005). Experiences of autonomy and control among Chinese learners: Vitalizing or immobilizing? *Journal of Educational Psychology, 92,* 631-648.

Walqui, A. (2000). *Contextual factors in second language acquisition.* Washington, D.C.: Center for Applied Linguistics. (ERIC Document Reproduction Service No. ED444381) Retrieved October 17, 2007, from EBSCO Online Education Research Complete Database.

Weiner, B. (1992). *Human Motivation: Metaphors, Theories and Research.* Newbury Park, CA: Sage.

SUGGESTED READING

Arnold, J. (Ed.). (1999). *Affect in language learning.* UK: Cambridge University Press.

Cumming, A. (Series Ed.) & Dörnyei, Z. (Vol. Ed.), *Language learning: Attitudes, orientations, and motivations in language learning* (Vol. 53, Supplement 1). The Best of Language Learning Series. Ann Arbor, MI: Blackwell Publishing.

Dörnyei, Z. & Kormos, J. (2000). The role of individual and social variables on oral task performance. *Language Teaching Research.* 4(3).

Tae-II, Pae. (2013). Effects of skill-based L2 anxieties on learners; affective variables and their factorial similarity across gender. *English Teaching.* 68(4).

Vansteenkiste, M., Zhou, M., Lens, W., & Soenens, B. (2005). Experiences of autonomy and control among Chinese learners: vitalizing or immobilizing? *Journal of Educational Psychology, 92,* 631-648.

SECTION 4: EDUCATION AND THE LAW

Introduction

As a democracy, the laws of the land provide the framework for our system of public and private education. Constitutional principles direct practice in the design and delivery of a free and appropriate education for all students.

This section focuses on the law's reach and influence on education and all of its stakeholders. Articles cover a broad range of legal issues that impact the freedoms and rights of all those who attend and work in our schools. Our authors also shed light on the debates that make many of the legal decisions cause for controversy and discourse.

EQUAL EDUCATIONAL OPPORTUNITY

The promise of racially integrated public schools, mandated by the Brown v. Board of Education decision of the Supreme Court in 1954 and the Civil Rights Act of 1964, spawned decades of civil rights activism and court-ordered desegregation plans. By the mid-1980s, significant racial integration had been achieved across the U.S.; however, demographic data indicate that since then the public schools have become less integrated over the last fifteen years resulting in "resegregation." Minority students are less likely to attend school with white students than in the past and a larger percentage of the school-aged population is poor. In an effort to retain and ensure integrated schools, districts have developed their own voluntary plans; however, the Supreme Court decision in June 2007 that struck down plans in Seattle, Washington and Louisville, Kentucky are forcing schools across the country to re-evaluate their efforts. Similar rulings are expected over the next several decades from a more conservative Supreme Court. School districts are looking for alternative criterions for school assignment other than race. Some school districts have successfully used socioeconomic status as a factor to integrate their schools and are offering families new educational options.

KEYWORDS: Amicus Curiae; Brown v. Board of Education; Charter Schools; Civil Rights; Desegregation / Segregation / Resegregation; Equal Protection Clause; Equal Educational Opportunity; Fourteenth Amendment of the U.S. Constitution; Integration; Magnet Schools; Resegregation; Strict Scrutiny; Unitary Status; Vouchers

OVERVIEW

This article discusses equal opportunity in education in the United States. One of the most contentious and seemingly irresolvable problems in American public education is the provision of equal educational opportunity. Racial integration of the public schools, once a primary strategy of achieving racial equality in our society, has been diminished over the last decade as school district desegregation plans are being challenged in the courts. This paper covers some of these cases, including the Supreme Court decision in June 2007 that struck down two school districts' voluntary

desegregation plans and how school districts are now re-evaluating their programs and seeking new ways to achieve diversity. Some districts are attempting to integrate students of different socioeconomic rather than racial backgrounds. Others are using non-coercive offerings such as vouchers and charter or magnet schools to appeal to students and parents seeking alternative means to a quality education.

THE LEGAL HISTORY OF EQUAL EDUCATIONAL OPPORTUNITY

The legal basis for all of the equal education litigation is the equal protection clause of the *14th Amendment*. This clause dictates that the laws of a state, not the Federal government, must treat an individual in the same manner as others in similar conditions and circumstances. "The equal protection clause is not intended to provide "equality" among individuals or classes but only "equal application" of the laws. The result, therefore, of a law is not relevant so long as there is no discrimination in its application. By denying states the ability to discriminate, the equal protection clause of the Constitution is crucial to the protection of civil rights" (Legal Information Institute, 2007).

The Supreme Court decision of *Brown v. Board of Education* of 1954 is recognized as the seminal case that opened the door to racial desegregation in schools. Volumes have been written about this important case that promised integration and equal educational opportunities, and ushered in a thirty year period of subsequent legislation, federal court decisions, and civil unrest. For the most part, the fallout of school integration occurred during the 1960s and 1970s after passage of the *Civil Rights Act* of 1965. On the whole, integration goals were achieved. Ironically, a little noticed accomplishment was that the South, long the most resistant and most segregated region, "… remained for a third of a century the nation's most integrated" (Orfield, 2007, p. 14).

Support for forced integration began waning during the 1980s. Court orders for desegregation plans expired, and, for the most part, school district integration strategies became voluntary. Orfield notes that "five of the last seven Presidents actively opposed urban desegregation and the last significant federal aid for desegregation was repealed 26 years ago in 1981." The past ten years have seen a new era of court decisions, a tremendous influx of Hispanics into the school system, and major societal shifts including the fruition of the white flight to the suburbs.

BROWN V. THE BOARD OF EDUCATION & THE CIVIL RIGHTS ACT OF 1964

A series of Supreme Court decisions and legislation drove the integration of U.S. public schools for thirty years beginning with *Oliver L. Brown et.al. v. the Board of Education of Topeka (KS) et.al.* The 1954 landmark U.S. Supreme Court decision disallowed racial segregation of schools, and in 1955, after a second hearing, the Court ordered desegregation to proceed with "all deliberate speed."

It was not, however, until after the passage of the *Civil Rights Act* of 1964 that aggressive desegregation and integration began to occur throughout the country. The law prohibited discrimination in public places, and outlawed discrimination in employment and education. Now, the executive branch of the federal government was empowered to enforce integration.

SUBSEQUENT RULINGS

In the thirty years after *Brown,* there was a stream of significant Supreme Court cases that advanced desegregation in the nation's schools. In order to meet racial integration goals, students in some areas had to be bused from their neighborhoods to more distant schools in their districts. The *Swann v. Charlotte-Mecklenberg Board of Education* decision of 1971 ruled that busing was constitutional.

Norwood v. Harrison (1973) ruled that States could not avoid the mandates of Brown by providing financial aid to private schools that discriminate based on race. This was followed by *Keyes v. School District No. 1. Denver, Colorado* which said that schools outside of the South which engaged in actual practice (*de facto*) segregation were as subject to the mandates of *Brown* as the schools in the South that were segregated by law (*de jure*).

The issues started to become more ambiguous in the mid-1970s as the courts began to draw lines defining how far civil rights actions could go. *Milliken v. Bradley* (1974) was significant in that it said that federal courts could impost inter-district desegregation remedies on a city and its suburbs without proving that school district boundaries were drawn with the intention to discriminate. The decision emphasized local control of schools and essentially exempted suburbs from participating in integration.

Although the case pertained to higher education, *Bakke v. Regents* of *the University of California* impacted affirmative action planning across all strata of education and employment. The ruling held that setting racial quotas is unconstitutional, but did not rule out race-based admissions completely. It provoked a debate about setting goals for diversity in education that was not resolved until the Supreme Court ruled in 2003 (*Gratz v. Bollinger* and *Grutter v. Bollinger*) that limited race-based admission may be justified.

Supreme Court decisions made in the early 1990s marked the demise of court-ordered desegregation plans. In the *Board of Education of Oklahoma City v. Dowell* (1991), a divided Supreme Court determined "that school official needed only to establish that they were operating with the Equal Protection Clause and that it was 'unlikely [they] would return to [their] former ways." (Daniel, 2005).

Freeman v. Pitts (1992) followed on this trend when a Georgia school system sought final release "from judicial supervision of its desegregation efforts." The Court ruled that release from judicial rulings can be incremental; i.e., a school district can be released from the portions of its plan that have been met and must be held to the remaining criteria until "unitary status" is achieved. (Daniel).

The last case in this sequence was *Missouri v. Jenkins* (1995) which pertained to local control of the schools. The Supreme Court ruled as unconstitutional prescribed remedies set by a federal district court that were deemed to go beyond its power. This and the three previous cases all mark the period of the disappearance of court-ordered desegregation plans. They made it evident that the plans were meant as temporary fixes to resolve a problem; once school districts were found "unitary," judicial oversight would end.

PARENTS INVOLVED IN COMMUNITY SCHOOLS V. SEATTLE SCHOOL DISTRICT

Parents Involved in Community Schools v. Seattle School District (2007) is a turning point in Supreme Court decisions. The ruling overturned lower court decisions that upheld the voluntary desegregation plans of the Louisville (Jefferson County), Kentucky and Seattle, Washington school districts. The impact of the decision remains to be seen, but experts recommend using other variables than race to achieve diversity in schools.

Jefferson County Public Schools (Louisville, Kentucky) operated an integrated school system as a result of a 1975 Federal court decree. When released from the decree twenty-five years later, the school district decided to continue to ensure integration by using its own voluntary integration guidelines, which were written in 2000 ("Is the Jefferson County Plan," 2007, p. 9). These guidelines specified that each elementary school was to be at least fifteen-percent and no more than fifty-percent black. As a result of this policy, the Jefferson County school district had one the most racially balanced school systems in the U.S.

In Louisville, a white mother brought suit against the school district, claiming that, because of this policy, her son was unable to attend the elementary school closest to their home, which, she said, violated her son's rights under the Equal Protection Clause of the Fourteenth Amendment. The case was decided in the Federal District Court for the Western District of Kentucky in 2004 by Judge John G. Heyburn, who ruled that the Jefferson County Board of Education plan was constitutional. He was guided in his opinion by the recently decided Supreme Court cases of *Grutter v. Bollinger* and *Gratz v. Bollinger* (2003) which upheld "race-conscious admissions policies at the University of Michigan Law School and University of Michigan, College of Literature, Science and the Arts" ("Is the Jefferson"). The judge's decision drew on strict scrutiny standard that has typically been applied by the Supreme Court in discrimination cases, which holds that "racial classifications must further a compelling governmental interest and must be narrowly tailored to meet that interest" ("Is the Jefferson").

The situation in Seattle was similar to that in Louisville. Complainants in *Parents Involved in Community Schools vs. Seattle Schools* sued the school district, believing that their children were not accepted into their first choice high schools because they were white. The Seattle schools had never been charged with court-ordered segregation and the district's integration guidelines were wholly voluntary. They were adopted in 1998 to prevent "segregation that was caused by the self-segregation in housing patterns in the area" (Bullock, 2006).

Numerous amicus curiae ("friends of the court") briefs were submitted to the Supreme Court including one from Solicitor General Paul D. Clément, who urged the Justices to rule with the belief "... that true use of racial classification to achieve a desired racial balance in public schools is as unconstitutional as racial segregation" (Bullock). The Court concurred with a 5-4 majority that overturned the ruling of the lower courts, and in the view of many, ignored fifty years of judicial precedent. Writing for the *New York Times*, in reaction to the decision, Jeffrey Rosen predicted that the central premise of Brown, "that integrated public schools are the most important institution in a pluralistic society," would "not survive the 21st century."

The outcome of the 2007 Seattle case clearly diverged from the University of Michigan Law School decision, which was settled a few short years before in 2003. Sandra Day O'Connor, who cast the swing vote in *Grutter v. Bollinger* and *Gratz v. Bollinger* for a 5-4 majority, was influenced by the many amicus curiae briefs that urged the value of racial diversity. However, her written argument that voiced her general opposition to affirmative action plans was one more segue to the court's shift to more restrictive decisions.

THE FUTURE OF EQUAL EDUCATIONAL OPPORTUNITY

Clearly, the desegregation plans mandated by *Brown v. Board of Education* and the *Civil Rights Act* of 1965 are no longer practical. School administrators and civil rights leaders are now embarking on what Arthur Coleman and Scott Palmer titled their article in the *Chronicle of Higher Education*, "A More Circuitous Path to Racial Diversity." Coleman and Parker argued that educators must accommodate "the hostility of... [the] four most 'conservative' justices to race-conscious policies ..." However, the authors did note that there may be promise in Justice Kennedy's dissenting statement that the "decision today should not prevent school districts from continuing the important work of bringing together students of different racial, ethnic, and economic backgrounds" (Coleman, 2007).

The recent decision was not surprising to those who have followed integration trends and perhaps least of all to administrators in the Seattle and Jefferson County school districts. The Seattle school district anticipated the decision and had suspended their program for the five years during which the case was moving through the courts. A *New York Times* article reported that "school officials cast the ruling as more victory than defeat, saying it would provide guidance for their efforts to promote racial diversity" (Lewin, 2007). Mandatory racial desegregation may no longer be feasible, the article continued, but the Supreme Court did recognize in its decision the benefits of diverse schools. Consequentially, it is probable "… that the decision will lead more districts to consider income as a race-neutral means of achieving school diversity" as is already done in a number of school districts throughout the country (Lewin).

Further Insights

EDUCATION & RACIAL EQUITY DATA

The most comprehensive current study on racial balance in the schools is available from the UCLA Civil Rights project, an organization that analyzes data, and publishes and asserts recommendations related to civil rights and equal opportunities. Their report written by Gary Orfield and Chungmei Lee, "Historic Reversals, Accelerating Resegregation, and the Need for New Integration Strategies," was released in August 2007. The work is full of data from the National Center for Education Statistics (NCES), an office of the U. S. Department of Education, which they interpret to show the reversal in segregation.

Briefly, their analysis indicates that more students of all races are attending schools with a larger percentage of poor students; that whites are the most segregated of all the races and Asians the least; and that Latinos are the most segregated of the minority groups with "increasing patterns of triple segregation - ethnicity, poverty, and linguistic isolation" (p. 32).

RESEGREGATION

Integration and desegregation, the buzz-words of the 1950s and 1960s, are now replaced by a new one: "Resegregation," which is increasingly used by politicians, civil rights leaders, and researchers to describe a resurgence of racially imbalanced schools. The data indicate that, since the 1980s, students have become increasingly racially isolated. A *New York Times* study in 2000, "The Lost Promise of School Integration," by Jeffrey Rosen, presented compelling data that showed that between 1989 and 1997, there was a measurable

decline, state by state, in the "likelihood that a black student will have classmates who are white …[and] the percentage of a typical black student's classmates [who] are likely to be white."

Gary Orfield & Chungmei Lee further documented the trend in their August 2007 report. The scholars reported that the " … country's rapidly growing population of Latino and black students is more segregated than they have been since the 1960s and we are going backward faster in the areas where integration was most far-reaching." (p. 4)

The issue of educational inequality is at heart a socioeconomic one. Those in the lowest economic strata are predominately minorities who tend to live in poor communities where resources are limited. Likewise, many urban centers have are predominately inhabited by minorities, where there are fewer whites to make integration a commonsense possibility. A lack of fulfillment of basic needs gets in the way of learning and even though "a given student who is poor has the same potential as any other student … concentrating poor students together can overwhelm teachers, given the multitude of problems poor students often bring into the classroom … hunger, exposure to violence, or substandard housing" (Feldman, 2005).

ALTERNATIVE DESEGREGATION STRATEGIES IN SELECTED U.S. SCHOOLS

Although the prospects for school integration look bleak, school districts have been experimenting with alternative strategies, many based on socioeconomic status, rather than racial categories. Some have found new ways to attract an integrated student body. Situations vary from city to city, and state to state, so strategies that are effective in one locale may not be suitable for another.

The Wake County school district, which includes Raleigh, North Carolina and its suburbs, is one of the most successfully integrated districts in the country. A point in its favor is that the school district is a county-run system, which makes it easier to integrate urban and suburban areas. Wake County's population is also growing fast and is becoming increasingly diverse.

The district has tried to cap the proportion of low-income students in each of the county's 143 schools at 40 percent (Glater). Wake County has also opened several magnet schools that have met with a great deal of success and attracted national attention. The Washington Gifted and Talented Magnet Elementary School in Raleigh, North Carolina draws applicants from all racial groups and socioeconomic classes, even though it is adjacent to a poor neighborhood. Almost 95% of its nearly 600 students test at or above grade level, "even though 32% of its students receive free and reduce-price lunches" (Hardy).

Not all school districts have been so successful in using magnet schools to achieve diversity. Rosen calls Kansas City's strategy a "field-of-dreams" theory; i.e., if you improve the schools, white students will come. They "... spent nearly $200 million to build a state-of-the-art magnet school. The white students failed to materialize" (Rosen). Likewise, a study of Miami-Dade, Florida magnet schools showed a decline in diversity after the district was released from its desegregation order (Davis).

St. Louis, one of the most segregated cities in the country, used an inter district transfer program for a number of years. Over 10,000 city students transferred to the suburban schools at state expense, and 1,000 suburban students attended school in the city. City schools did not improve, but many city students have reportedly done well at the suburban schools (Hardy). St. Louis' program ended in a 2009 without having established significant long-term desegregation. In 2013, the majority of Louisiana's public school districts were still under federal oversight, and a plan to issue vouchers to public school students to be applied to private school tuition was met with resistance from the Department of Justice (Federal Oversight Backed, 2013).

San Francisco is unique in that around a third of its school-age population is of Chinese heritage. The city has also lost many middle class families because of the high cost of raising children there. Rather than using race as a factor in placing students, the school district initiated a desegregation plan in 2002-03 based on socioeconomic diversity. "Students apply to the school they want to attend, and the district uses a 'diversity index' for assignment when the school is oversubscribed" (Glater, 2007). The formula has reportedly worked to some extent, but racial integration within the San Francisco schools is far from complete.

Charlotte-Mecklenburg, North Carolina's largest school district has also tried an economic integration plan but has had problems administering it. On the other hand, Cambridge, Massachusetts, a smaller district, has been using socioeconomic status to assign students to its 12 elementary schools since 2002. Students there showed marked progress in reading proficiency (Glater).

VIEWPOINTS

After release of the decision in the case of "*Parents Involved in Community Schools v. Seattle School District,*" some civil rights leaders and politicians proclaimed the death of racial integration. Some saw it as the end of fifty years of progress in desegregation. On the other hand, others are more optimistic as they realize the need to continue the struggle to ensure equal educational opportunities for all students. Many civil rights leaders, recognizing the trends and the conservative climate, recommend making the best of the alternative educational options that are offered.

Many magnet schools or charter schools, however controversial, are demonstrating higher levels of achievement, and are attractive to families of all racial and socioeconomic strata. A 1998 survey conducted by the Public Agenda, showed that 82 percent of the black parents "said that raising academic standards was more important than achieving more diversity and integration" (Rosen). The academic performance of charter-management organizations-consisting of three or more charter schools-is not better than non-CMO charters. According to a Stanford University Center for Research on Education Outcomes (CREDO) study, charters affiliated with management organizations (CMOs) tend to deliver greater academic gains among poor and minority students than traditional public schools, though performance is predicated on strong, well run programs that are effective beginning in their first year (Cavanagh, 2013).

Because housing patterns tend to be segregated, integrating the schools is complicated, and may be near impossible. "Many of the nation's largest urban districts now have so few white students that any large-scale effort at racial balance would be impractical" (Lewin). Assigning students on the basis of income rather than race may be practical, but, as has been shown in San Francisco, may not be fully successful. Richard Kahlenberg, a senior fellow at the Century Foundation still encourages school districts to pursue it: "not only do you get a fair amount of racial integration that's legally bullet-proof, but the research shows that for individual students, it's more closely aligned with achievement, with higher test scores, than racial integration." (Lewin).

Nebraska State Senator Ernie Chambers received some national attention in 2006 for his proposal to rezone the Omaha, Nebraska schools into three districts along racial lines. Surprisingly this was coming from a 69-year-old African-American, who himself had attended segregated schools. He told the *American School Board Journal* that "… you can have single-race schools and still have a quality education. Don't try to make schools do what society won't. Since we'll always have segregated neighborhoods, we'll have segregated schools." He believes that the public schools have never been integrated. Times have changed. "I'm not interested in segregation or integration. I'm interested in quality education" ("Five Questions," 2006).

TERMS & CONCEPTS

Amicus Curiae: Literally means "friends of the court" and refers to parties that are invited by a court to speak to the issue of litigation, usually by submitting briefs, in which they may have an interest, but are not directly involved.

Charter Schools: Publicly funded schools that are freed of some of some restrictions of other public schools in exchange for other forms of accountability. Charter schools are intended to provide educational alternatives. In some cities, most notably New York City, admission is highly competitive as families flee underperforming schools.

Equal Protection Clause: The Equal Protection clause is the last clause of the first section of the *Fourteenth Amendment* of the *U.S. Constitution*. It states that "… All persons born or naturalized in the United States, and subject to the jurisdiction thereof, are citizens of the United States and of the state wherein they reside. No state shall make or enforce any law which shall abridge the privileges or immunities of citizens of the United States; nor shall any state deprive any person of life, liberty, or property, without due process of law; *nor deny to any person within its jurisdiction the equal protection of the laws."*

In other words, Federal law prohibits states from denying any person within its jurisdiction the equal protection of law. A violation would occur, for example, if a state prohibited an individual from entering into an employment contract because he or she was a member of a particular race.

Magnet Schools: Schools that are administered within a public school system, exist outside of zoned school boundaries, and generally provide more direct funding for students. Magnet schools sprang up in the 1980s and 1990s as a way to attract students to voluntarily attend a school, without busing or other coerced integration, and thus increase the diversity of the school. A magnet school frequently offers alternative modes of instruction and specialized programs, and most foster high levels of parental involvement.

Resegregation: Describes the trend of de facto desegregation in U.S. schools.

Strict Scrutiny: The principal used by the Supreme Court in reviewing civil rights cases, first used in "… *Korematsu v. United States* (1944), where it found all racial classifications to be immediately suspect" and subject to "the most rigid scrutiny

Unitary Status: "Unitary status," or "unity," describe the achievement of the racial integration goals that are part of a court-ordered desegregation plan.

Vouchers: Direct financial support for parents who wish to have more choice in where to educate their children. Parents may choose to educate their children in private schools or a public school of their choice.

Barbara Hornick-Lockard

BIBLIOGRAPHY

Bell, D. (2007). Desegregation's demise. *Chronicle of Higher Education, 53*, B11-54. Retrieved September 20, 2007, from EBSCO Online Database Academic Search Premier.

Bernstein, M. (2007). Our kids need a diversity lesson. Will the court allow it? *School Administrator, 64*, 55. Retrieved September 20, 2007, from EBSCO Online Database Education Research Complete.

Bullock, L. (2006, August 31). Bush administration turns its back on school integration. *New York Amsterdam News, 97*, 33-41. Retrieved September 20, 2007, from EBSCO Online Database Academic Search Premier.

Cavanagh, S. (2013). Charters' success or failure set early. *Education Week, 32*, 12-13. Retrieved December 15, 2013, from EBSCO Online Database Education Research Complete.

Coleman, A. L. & Palmer, S. R. (2007, July 13). A more circuitous path to racial diversity. *Chronicle of Higher Education, 53*, p. B10-53. Retrieved September 20, 2007, from EBSCO Online Database Academic Search Premier.

Daniel, P. (2005, January). The not so strange path of desegregation in America's public schools. *Negro Educational Review, 56*, 57-66. Retrieved September 20, 2007, from EBSCO online database, Academic Search Premier.

Davis, M. (2007). Magnet schools and diversity. *Education Week, 26*, 9. Retrieved September 20, 2007, from EBSCO Online Database Academic Search Premier.

Federal oversight backed for Lousiana voucher plan. (2013). *Education Week, 33*, 5. Retrieved December 15, 2013, from EBSCO Online Database Education Research Complete.

Feldman, J. (2005). Integrated public education is still worth fighting for. *Human Rights: Journal of the Section of Individual Rights & Responsibilities, 32*, 13-14. Retrieved September 20, 2007, from EBSCO Online Database Academic Search Premier.

Five questions...for Ernie Chambers on the Omaha controversy. (2006). *American School Board Journal, 193*, 11. Retrieved September 20, 2007, from EBSCO Online Database Academic Search Premier.

Glater, J. D. & Finder, A. (2007, July 15). Diversity plans based on income leave some schools segregated. *New York Times*, 24.

Hardy, L. (2006, September). Separate our students by race and income to meet NCLB? *Education Digest, 72*, 12-20. Retrieved September 20, 2007, from EBSCO Online Database Academic Search Premier.

Huang, J. (2013). Intergenerational transmission of educational attainment: The role of household assets. *Economics of Education Review, 33*112-123. Retrieved December 15, 2013, from EBSCO Online Database Education Research Complete.

Is the Jefferson County Public Schools' desegregation plan unconstitutional? (2007). *Supreme Court Debates, 10*, 2-3. Retrieved September 20, 2007, from EBSCO Online Database Academic Search Premier.

Legal Information Institute. Cornell University Law School. (2007). *Equal protection*. Retrieved September 24, 2007, from www.law.cornell.edu.

Lewin, T. (2007, June 29). Across U.S., a new look at school integration efforts. *New York Times*, A25-A25. Retrieved September 20, 2007, from EBSCO Online Database Academic Search Premier.

McDermott, K.A., & Nygreen, K. (2013). Educational new paternalism: Human capital, cultural capital, and the politics of equal opportunity. *Peabody Journal of Education (0161956X), 88*, 84-97. Retrieved December 15, 2013, from EBSCO Online Database Education Research Complete.

Orfield, G. & Lee, C. (2007 August). *Historic reversals, accelerating resegregation, and the need for new integration strategies*. A report of the Civil Rights Project / Proyecto Dechechos Civiles. Los Angeles, California: UCLA. Retrieved September 22, 2007, from www.civilrightsproject.ucla.edu.

Resegregation now. (2007, June 29). [Editorial]. *New York Times*, A28.

Roberts Rules. (2007). *New Republic, 237*, 1-4. Retrieved September 20, 2007, from EBSCO Online Database Academic Search Premier.

Rosen, J. (2000, April 2). Bus stop: the lost promise of school integration. *New York Times*, 1.

Russo, C. (2002). An American perspective on equal educational opportunities. *Education & the Law, 14* (1/2), 25-32. Retrieved September 20, 2007, from EBSCO Online Database Academic Search Premier.

Supreme Court delivers setback to Brown v. Board progress. (2007). *NEA Today, 26*, 15. Retrieved September 20, 2007, from EBSCO Online Database Academic Search Premier.

Trotter A. (2006). Diverse views offered on Supreme Court race cases. *Education Week, 26*, 31-33. Retrieved September 20, 2007, from EBSCO Online Database Academic Search Premier.

Williams, S.M. (2013). Micropolitics and rural school consolidation: The quest for equal educational opportunity in Webster Parish. *Peabody Journal of Education (0161956X), 88*, 127-138. Retrieved December 15, 2013, from EBSCO Online Database Education Research Complete.

SUGGESTED READING

Barnes, A. (2005). The conundrum of segregation's ending: the educational choices. *Marquette Law Review, 89*, 33-51. Retrieved September 20, 2007, from EBSCO Online Database Academic Search Premier.

Bell, Derrick. (2004). *Silent covenants: Brown v. Board of Education and the unfulfilled hopes for racial reform*. Oxford, NY: Oxford University Press.

Charne, I. (2005). The Milwaukee cases. *Marquette Law Review, 89*, 83-85. Retrieved September 20, 2007, from EBSCO Online Database Academic Search Premier.

Frankenberg, E. & Orfield, G. eds. (2007). *Lessons in integration: realizing the promise of racial diversity in American schools*. Charlottesville: University of Virginia Press.

Mead, J. & Green, P.C. (2012). *Chartering equity: Using charter school legislation and policy to advance equal educational opportunity*. National Education Policy Center.

Ogletree, C. & Robinson, K.J. (2015). *The enduring legacy of "Rodriguez": Creating new pathways to equal educational opportunity*. Cambridge, MA.: Harvard Education Press.

Tatum, B. D. (2007). *Can we talk about race: And other conversations in an era of school resegregation*. Boston: Beacon Press.

UCLA. Civil Rights Project. *Looking to the future: Voluntary K-12 school integration*. Retrieved September 20, 2007, from www.civilrightsproject.ucla.edu.

U. S. Supreme Court. *Parents involved in Community Schools v. Seattle School District* no. 1. et al. Washington, DC: Government Printing Office. Retrieved September 20, 2007, from www.supremecourtus.gov.

Wang, H. (2016). Equalizing educational opportunity: In defense of bilingual education – a California perspective. *CATESOL* Journal, 28 (2), 105-120.

Wraga, W. (2006). The Heightened significance of Brown v. Board of Education in our time. *Phi Delta Kappan, 87,* 425-428. Retrieved September 20, 2007, from EBSCO Online Database Academic Search Premier.

SCHOOL DESEGREGATION

Segregation is the act of separating racial, ethnic, or gender groups by designating certain public spaces—such as schools or buses—for the use of one racial, ethnic, or gender group alone. Integration is the act of equally incorporating different racial, ethnic, and gender groups in public spaces. In the United States, the discussion of integration has often centered on racial integration in schools. *Brown v. Board of Education* and the Civil Rights Act of 1964 made major strides against de jure segregation, though in many districts de facto segregation still continues. In recent years, research has actually shown an increase in de facto segregation.

KEYWORDS: Brown v. Board of Education; De Facto Segregation; De Jure Segregation; Desegregation; Integration; Plessy vs. Ferguson; Re-segregation; Segregation

OVERVIEW

Segregation is the act of separating racial, ethnic, or gender groups by designating certain public spaces—such as schools or buses—for the use of one racial, ethnic, or gender group alone. Integration is the act of equally incorporating different racial, ethnic, and gender groups in public spaces. While there are many spheres in which segregation and integration can occur, this article will focus on racial segregation and integration in American public schools.

The fight against discrimination and segregation began in the South. While discrimination in the North manifested itself in school closures and under-funding, its southern counterpart was more flagrant, with Jim Crow laws preventing whites and blacks from sharing public resources like schools and buses. Jim Crow laws were an elaborate system of customs and laws in the post-Reconstruction South meant to separate blacks and whites in daily life.

Plessy v. Ferguson

Plessy v. Ferguson (1896) was the first significant legal case in which an African American challenged Jim Crow laws. Homer Plessy was a black man who was arrested under these laws for sitting in the white section of a Louisiana train. Plessy asserted that being forbidden to sit with white passengers was a violation of his Thirteenth Amendment rights and especially his Fourteenth Amendment rights, which call for equal protection of all citizens under the law (Robertson, 2006).

The court ruled against Plessy, saying

… laws permitting, and even requiring, their separation, in places where they are liable to be brought into contact, do not necessarily imply the inferiority of either race to the other, and have been generally, if not universally, recognized as within the competency of the state legislatures in the exercise of their police power. The most common instance of this is connected with the establishment of separate schools for white and colored children, which have been held to be a valid exercise of the legislative power even by courts of States where the political rights of the colored race have been longest and most earnestly enforced (as cited in Robertson, 2006).

The "separate but equal" doctrine set forth in *Plessy v. Ferguson* was not challenged in the court again until 1951 with *Brown vs. Board of Education.*

Brown v. Board of Education, Topeka, Kansas

Brown v. Board of Education was a legal suit filed against the Topeka school board by Oliver Brown on behalf of his daughter, Linda, who, instead of attending the elementary school in her neighborhood, was bussed 21 blocks away from her home to attend an African-American elementary school. Brown lost initially; the judge ruled that white and "colored" schools were essentially equal in their offerings to children, so no child was suffering discrimination (McGrane, 2004).

But Brown persisted, and the case became the heart of a cluster of suits that would eventually rise to the Supreme Court. A number of black parents from other states—Delaware, Kansas, South Carolina, Virginia, Washington, D.C.—joined him in suing for their children to attend white schools. And like Brown, they too were initially denied the right by a judge who cited the "separate but equal" doctrine first delineated in the landmark civil rights case, *Plessy v. Ferguson* (McGrane).

The National Association for the Advancement of Colored People (NAACP) soon became involved in the *Brown* suit, assigning to the case its legal director of 15 years, Thurgood Marshall. He began by attacking segregation in post-graduate schools before working down to secondary and elementary education. In 1954, the Supreme Court handed down its unanimous decision. "In the field of education," wrote Justice Earl Warren, "the doctrine of 'separate but equal' has no place. Separate educational facilities are inherently unequal" (as cited in McGrane).

The *Brown* decision was directed at ending *de jure*, or lawfully imposed, segregation—not *de facto*, or "in practice" segregation. The *Brown* ruling affected southern schools more than northern schools, as most southern schools were practicing *de jure* segregation. Most northern states, however, were practicing *de facto* segregation—a more subtle form created by the choices of individuals and communities about matters like where they will live, shop, work, or go to school (Chapman, 2005).

Swann v. Charlotte-Mecklenburg

Though the ruling did end *de jure* segregation, it did not end it immediately. There was confusion and debate after the ruling as to how individual school systems should go about complying with the new law. In 1970 the Supreme Court handed down the *Swann v. Charlotte-Mecklenburg Board of Education* decision, a busing and integration plan for Charlotte-Mecklenburg, North Carolina, that would eventually be adopted across the country (Armor, 2006). Though the Swann ruling helped solve the problem in the south, it took another decision, *Keyes v. Denver School District No. 1,* to achieve comprehensive desegregation in the north.

ECONOMIC FACTORS

By the time of *Swann,* African-American parents in northern cities were already deeply embattled with their own school boards over *de facto* segregation. The 1950's and 60s were prosperous times for big cities and the populations living in them. Job growth in urban factories and warehouses drew many African-Americans into the cities. With the increase in wealth, urban schools were able to acquire better teachers and more resources, making them considerably superior to rural schools. In some cases, urban African-American schools even outperformed similar white schools (Chapman).

But the late 1960s saw a precipitous decline in industry and many urban economies. Factories and plants were downsized, hurting cities with predominantly working class populations. Workers holding only high school diplomas or vocational degrees were increasingly unemployed. As urban economies declined, cities allotted less money to their schools. One way school boards dealt with shrinking budgets was by closing schools in minority neighborhoods while reducing funding to the remaining schools in those neighborhoods, causing overcrowding and diminishing the quality of education for minority students. The combination of the deterioration of the schools and rise of the civil rights movement led the first black parents in northern cities to challenge their school districts in court (Chapman).

But because *de facto* segregation was more difficult to prove in court, parents in many cities—like Detroit, Boston, Chicago, Milwaukee, Kansas City, Oklahoma City, St. Louis—would be in litigation for nearly thirty years (Chapman). One major step in bringing equal opportunity education to both northern and southern schools was the passage of the 1964 Civil Rights Act.

THE 1964 CIVIL RIGHTS ACT

In 1963, nine years after the Supreme Court ruled in favor of *Brown,* President John F. Kennedy set forth a civil rights bill that would end de jure segregation in public schools and public spaces and protect the rights of African American voters. Kennedy would not live to see passage of the bill, but his successor, President Lyndon B. Johnson, signed it into law in a nationally televised ceremony on July 2, 1964. The act allowed the attorney general to sue for the desegregation of colleges and public schools. It banned segregation in public gathering places such as parks and museums run by state and local governments and made it unlawful for federally assisted programs to discriminate against race, color, and national origin. The act also gave more protection to the rights of minority voters and forbade employers from discriminating against workers and job candidates (Fonte, 1997).

RESEGREGATION

Despite the progress made in the 60s and 70s, some experts say integration suffered a setback in the 80s. Two studies have revealed that resegregation is occurring in some school districts; one looked at schools nationwide ("New Study," 2001) while the second looked a resegregation in in districts formerly under a court order to desegregate, once that court order was lifted (Reardon, Grewal, Kalogrides, & Greenberg, 2012).

The first study, done by the Civil Rights Project at Harvard University, examined schools nationwide during the 1998-99 year. The study found that in southern states the percentage of black students in predominantly white schools declined steadily between 1988 and 1998—though the level of segregation in these states is still less than what it was at the end of the 60s (28 percentage points less in 1999 than in 1969) ("New Study," 2001).

While findings concerning students of color were telling, the most startling data pertained to Hispanic pupils, who were more likely to attend minority schools than black students (Zehr, 2001). The segregation of Latinos—whose population in this country between 1970 and 1999 swelled by 245%—increased 13.5% between 1970 and 1999 ("New Study"). During the 1998-99 school year, 70.2% of African-American students attended schools with mostly minority students, up from 66% in 1991-92, and up from 63% in 1980-81. But the number of Hispanics attending predominantly minority schools was even higher: 76% in 1998-99 and 73% in 1991-92. These figures constitute what Gary Orfield, co-director of the Harvard study, referred to as resegregation. "Segregation is actually increasing," Orfield was quoted as saying, in "Ignoring that reality leads to adoption of education policies that punish people who haven't had equal educational opportunities... it's a direct threat to the future of a multiracial society" (as cited in Zehr).

INCREASE IN PUBLIC SCHOOL SEGREGATION

White students, it was found, were most commonly separated away from other ethnic groups. Most attended public schools where at least 80% of the enrollment was Caucasian ("New Study"). While segregation in public schools increased during the 90s, it was even more prevalent in private schools. Between 1997 and 1998, 78% of American private school students were white, while most black students attended schools that were only 34% white. At the same time, 64% of public school students were white, and most African-American students attended schools that were 33% white. In addition, white students who attended private schools were more racially isolated than white students who attend public schools. Forty-seven percent of whites attended public schools that were between 90% and 100% Caucasian, while 64% of Caucasian private school students attended schools where whites made up between 90% and 100% of the student body ("Private Schools," 2002).

Poverty was also found to be associated with symptoms of educational inequality such as poor test performance. Most Hispanic and African-American students were found to attend schools with more than twice as many disadvantaged students as normally attend schools with Caucasian students ("New Study").

The Harvard study concluded that whites have become the most isolated of all the races. Orfield expressed concern for African-American students, as the average black student attends schools where 55% of students are black—and for Latino students, who attend schools where 53% of the students are Hispanic. These schools, argued Orfield, are almost always inferior to white-majority schools in "every dimension" (as cited in Zehr).

A more recent study (Reardon et al.) by researchers from Stanford University looked at resegregation in 483 school districts that had been under a court-supervised desegregation order in 1990; the authors believe their study included all districts with at least 2,000 students that were under a court-supervised desegregation order as of 1990, including 96 non-Southern school districts. The Stanford study found that when districts are released from desegregation orders, they tend to become desegregated, with the greatest resegregation occurring in the elementary school grades. Resegregation was also associated with the size of the school districts (more resegregation in larger districts), in districts with large numbers of African American students, and in districts with a high degree of residential segregation.

One possible reason for resegregation is the change in the nation's political climate that began in the 1980's, as the social science research on which *Brown* relied came under fire, along with conflicting data produced in research done after *Brown*. When hearings were held by a House of Representatives subcommittee to examine how desegregation and busing initiatives might have positive effects, the hearings didn't yield conclusions about long-term effects of desegregation, but they determined which studies and data were reliable. Not surprisingly, judges at both the federal and district levels became less inclined to rule in favor of segregation cases in the 90s (Chapman).

Resegregation, writes Orfield, can be blamed partly on the federal judicial system, which has lagged in its commitment to *Brown*. But the public must also shoulder some responsibility. Many families choose to live in neighborhoods full of people of their own skin color. The 1960s saw the beginnings of "white flight," a movement in which many whites left the cities for suburbia (Zehr).

CHARTER SCHOOLS

Charter schools, i.e., publicly-funded schools exempt from certain local regulations, have become increasing common in the United States. According to the National Center for Education Statistics, In the 2010-2011 school year, 41 states and the District Columbia had passed legislation allowing the creation of charter schools. Growth of charter schools has been rapid: in 2011 1.8 million students were enrolled in 5,300 charter schools, a marked increase from the 0.3 million students enrolled in charter schools in 1999. Despite this dramatic increase, however, only 2.5% of public school students attend charter schools, with five states accounting for most of the enrollment: California, Florida, Texas, Arizona, and Michigan (Frankenberg & Siegel-Hawley, 2011).

Although charter schools are not allowed to discriminate on the basis of race or ethnicity, some researchers believe that charter schools in practice are increasing segregation. Frankenberg and Siegel-Hawley found that charter schools tend to increase segregation of African American students (nationally, 70% of African American charter school students

attend a racially isolated school, defined as a school whose student body is at least 90% drawn from under-represented minority groups; this is double the percentage of African American students overall who attend racially isolated schools. Half of Latino charter school students also attend racially isolated schools, while data from some states in the South and Midwest suggest that charter schools are allowing White students to attend schools with primarily or entirely White enrollment (white flight) rather than attending more integrated non-charter public schools.

RECENT COURT DECISIONS

In June 2007, the U.S. Supreme Court handed down two rulings concerning *de facto* school segregation. *Parents Involved in Community Schools v. Seattle School District No. 1* and *Meredith v. Jefferson County Public Schools*. In *Parents*, the Seattle School District was sued by a parents' group for using race as a major factor in deciding which students would be granted entrance into the city's most popular, and oversubscribed, high schools. In *Meredith*, Jefferson County Public Schools were sued by a parent for using race as a major determinant when assigning children to elementary schools and ruling on transfer requests. Both plaintiffs contended that the school districts violated the Equal Protection clause of the Fourteenth Amendment.

Though the policies were meant to uphold the districts' commitments to diversity, the Supreme Court ruled that using racial classifications as a "tie-breaker" for admission was not directed toward a "compelling government interest," since student body diversity is constituted of other factors than race alone (e.g., gender, family income, religion, life experiences, etc.). The Court further found that the districts' policies were not sufficiently "narrowly tailored" to promote diversity since:

- They only distinguished between white and non-white or black and non-black students;
- The districts had failed to identify the level of diversity needed to obtain the educational benefits diversity is claimed to confer, relying instead on the districts' overall racial composition as a guide.

The court ruled in favor of the plaintiffs, with Chief Justice John Roberts succinctly concluding his opinion, writing, "The way to stop discrimination on the basis of race is to stop discriminating on the basis of race" ("Parents Involved," 2007).

Although the Supreme Court ruling in *Parents Involved in Community Schools v. Seattle School District No.1* and *Meredith v. Jefferson County Public Schools* meant that school districts could no longer use race-based lotteries, or more explicit race-based selection methods, to achieve racial balance in magnet schools (public schools organized around a theme and drawing students from a wide geographic area), some large school districts, such as those in Los Angeles, Chicago, and Baltimore County, continue to operate a number of magnet schools to promote diversity and excellence within the school system (Fleming, 2012). Consideration of factors such as economic background is allowed in student selection and placement, and these factors can indirectly help increase racial diversity within schools. For instance, Chicago sorts applicants to competitive schools based on characteristics of their home census tract, such as family income and percent of families owning their own home, with students competing only with others within their tract. The Wake County School District in North Carolina also uses economic rather than racial factors in their attempts to increase diversity, and has enjoyed some success, as affluent families are voluntarily enrolling their children in the county's public schools. However, the county's success may not be replicable in other districts; the county has always been somewhat affluent, and its plethora of magnet schools—not its home schools—have proved to be the strongest attraction ("Still Separate," 2007).

Further Insights

RECOMMENDATIONS OF THE HARVARD CIVIL RIGHTS PROJECT

Researchers involved in the Harvard Civil Rights Project study made numerous recommendations on how to promote integration and improve conditions in minority schools. Included in these recommendations was the development of an exchange program for teachers in urban and suburban schools, as well as training programs for instructors on running multi-ethnic classrooms ("New Study"). Researchers called for the study and reform of current educational and housing practices in the interest of arresting resegregation. In addition, the study urged the development of a system allowing students to transfer between districts with relative ease (Zehr).

The researchers also suggested expanding the federal government's magnet school program, but adding certain desegregation provisions. Recommendations were also made for the creation of "two-way" bilingual schools, wherein students with Spanish as a first language and students with English as a first language attend classes together to become fluent in both languages (Zehr). The study called for an increase in the number of professionals qualified to teach desegregation and race relations at the state education department levels. Finally, it called for surveys to be done of schools practicing interracial education in order to document merits of the practice ("New Study").

Other experts have made suggestions for improving conditions at minority schools. John H. Jackson, director of education for the NAACP, recommends reducing class sizes and supplying city schools with highly qualified instructors (Zehr).

PROMOTING INTEGRATION THROUGH TEACHING

Much can also be done by teachers. A number of college and high school courses address segregation and integration, often as part of a larger subject such as the history of public education, U.S. history, or African-American history. Some schools have broadened the term "integration" to embrace not only individuals of different races, ethnicities, and religions, but also of different sexual orientations.

The following are examples of elementary and secondary level teaching being done to promote integration:

- Through a cooperative project with the Benton Harbor Public Library in Michigan, elementary students from 90% black Benton Harbor public schools met weekly with mostly white children from nearby Bridgman. The children painted self-portraits of one another in a highly successful project that taught interracial awareness (Knuth, 2002);

- High school students in a course about the third world were asked to write "initial impression" essays on photographs from India. Next, the instructor led a discussion about the pictures, the students' first impressions of them, and the possible societal, personal, and cultural roots of their opinions. The exercise was designed to make students more aware of the difference between sensitive first impressions and stereotypes (Lintner, 2005);

- The Southern Poverty Law Center's web project recommends a number of tolerance and racial awareness projects for all grades. One, called "Mix It Up!" asks students to not sit with their usual friends during one lunch period, but instead sit with a different group of students. In another project, lower-grade children (grades 1-3) make illustrated books about the meaning of friendship and the qualities of a good friend. Afterward, the teacher leads a discussion about how it feels to be new in class, how people feel when they meet someone who speaks with an unusual accent or whose appearance is quite different, and how to be friends with someone who has different interests or a different family background ("A New Friend," n.d.).

VIEWPOINTS

Many experts agree with the conclusions drawn from the Harvard Civil Rights Study, but some differ with Orfield on the causes of resegregation. Christine H. Rossell, professor of political science at Boston University writes, "We are in complete agreement that there is something wrong with a society in which people of one color live in one place, and people of another color live in another place" (as cited in Zehr). But, she argues, origins of the problem can be traced back to principles of desegregation espoused by Orfield. Initial plans to end segregation—such as busing—led to white flight and caused many white parents to enroll their children in predominantly white schools that were not busing blacks. Rossell also argues that the study failed to point out that the lower birthrate among whites leads in part to a decrease in the ratio of white to minority students (Zehr).

THE ACHIEVEMENT GAP

While *Brown* was widely lauded as the end to a long period of institutionalized racism and discrimination, it also has its critics. Some say it did little to improve the nagging "achievement gap" suffered by African-American students, who continue to lag behind Caucasian students in test scores and overall academic performance. But this disparity, says Armor, is detectable in African-American children as early as age 3 (as early as it can be detected), two years before the children even enter school. Studies have shown, Armor continues, that the achievement gap is determined overwhelmingly by influences at home. What

factors count much more towards a child's cognitive development than race are:
- Parents' IQ;
- Cognitive stimulation/instruction (usually by parents but could be others);
- Emotional support/nurturance;
- Parents' educational attainment;
- Family income and poverty status;
- Family structure: marital status, number of parents;
- Mother's age when child born;
- Number of siblings;
- Child's nutrition (including breast feeding);
- Child's birth weight (Armor).

Concern over the achievement gap has led to increased educational funding and massive early intervention initiatives. Since 1965 the federal program Head Start has served 23 million preschool-aged, academically at-risk children from disadvantaged families (Shipley & Oborn, 1996). In 2001, President George W. Bush launched No Child Left Behind (NCLB), a policy demanding that all students meet specific proficiency standards by 2014. Though test scores in many schools have improved, Armor cautions that it is still too early to know if NCLB will be a success. Strategies developed for the program seem to be increasing achievement levels ("NCLB is Working," n.d.).

TERMS & CONCEPTS

Brown v. Board of Education: A 1954 Supreme Court ruling that ended sanctioned segregation in public schools.

De Facto Segregation: A practice prevalent in the northern states that segregated students through policy and funding choices made by individual school districts and communities.

De Jure Segregation: A practice prevalent in the southern states in which people of different races were kept separate by law.

Desegregation: A push to end segregation and racially integrate public schools that began in the 50s.

Integration: Incorporating people of different races and ethnicities into society as equals.

Plessy v. Ferguson: An 1896 court ruling that said keeping children of different races in different schools was neither unfair nor a violation of their Constitutional rights.

Resegregation: A recent trend in which white students and minority students are becoming more and more isolated in schools, indicating a possible resurgence of segregation.

Segregation: The act of separating groups of people by race or ethnicity and forbidding their interaction in public gathering places.

Karen Kallio

BIBLIOGRAPHY

A New Friend. Retrieved April 14, 2007, from the Southern Poverty Law Center web project, http://tolerance.org.

Armor, D.J. (2006). Brown and black-white achievement. *Academic Questions, 19,* 40-46. Retrieved March 17, 2007, from EBSCO Online Database Academic Search Premier.

Chapman, T. (2005). Peddling backwards: Reflections of Plessy and Brown in the Rockford public schools de jure desegregation efforts. *Race, Ethnicity & Education, 8,* 29-44. Retrieved March 14, 2007, from EBSCO Online Database Academic Search Premier.

Fleming, N. (2012, May). Magnets adjust to new climate of school choice. *Education Week, 31,* p. 1Đ2, 17. Retrieved December 22, 2013, from EBSCO Online Database Education Research Complete.

Fonte, J. (1997). The tragedy of civil rights. *Society, 34,* 64-76. Retrieved April 14, 2007, from EBSCO Online Database Academic Search Premier.

Frankenberg, E., & Siegel-Hawley, G. (2011, Jan.). Choice without equity: Charter school segregation and the need for Civil Rights standards. *Education Digest, 76,* p. 44Đ47. Retrieved December 22, 2013, from EBSCO Online Database Education Research Complete.

Glenn, W. J. (2012). School resegregation: A synthesis of the evidence. *Educational Forum, 76,* p. 282Đ298. Retrieved December 22, 2013, from EBSCO Online Database Education Research Complete.

Knuth, A. (2002). Drawing connections. *NEA Today, 48,* 50-53. Retrieved April 13, 2007, from EBSCO Online Database Academic Search Premier.

Lintner, T. (2005). A world of difference: Teaching tolerance through photographs in elementary school. *Social Studies, 96,* 34-37. Retrieved April 13, 2007, from EBSCO Online Database Academic Search Premier.

McGrane, M. (2004). Brown v. board of education: "Separate but equal" has no place in our society. *Florida Bar Journal, 78,* 8. Retrieved April 12, 2007, from EBSCO Online Database Academic Search Premier.

New study finds school segregation on the rise. (2001). *Techniques: Connecting Education and Careers, 76,* 13-15. Retrieved March 15, 2007, from EBSCO Online Database Academic Search Premier.

No Child Left Behind: an overview. Retrieved April 15, 2007, from the U.S. Department of Education, http://ed.gov.

No Child Left Behind is working. Retrieved April 15, 2007, from the U.S. Department of Education, http://ed.gov.

Parents involved in community schools v. Seattle school district No. 1 et al. (2007). Supreme Court opinion syllabus. Retrieved July 7, 2007, from http://supremecourtus.gov.

Reardon, S. F., Grewal, E. T., Kalogrides, D., and Greenberg, E. (2012). The end of court-ordered school desegregation and the resegregation of American public schools. *Journal of Policy Analysis & Analysis, 31,* p. 876Đ904. Retrieved December 22, 2013, from EBSCO Online Database Education Research Complete.

Private schools are more segregated, study finds (2002). *School Law News, 30,* 4. Retrieved April 11, 2007, from EBSCO Online Database Education Research Complete.

Robertson, J. E. (2006). Foreword: "Separate but equal" in prison: Johnson v. California and common sense racism. *The Journal of Criminal Law & Criminology, 96,* 795-848. Retrieved April 14, 2007, from EBSCO Online Database Academic Search Premier.

Shipley, G. L., & Oborn, C. S. (1996). *A review of four preschool programs: Four preschool models that work.* Annual Meeting of the Mid-Western Educational Research Association. (ERIC Document Reproduction Service No. ED401034).

Still separate after all these years. (2007). *Economist, 383* (8526), 31-32. Retrieved July 7, 2007, from EBSCO Online Database Academic Search Premier.

Ways to teach tolerance. (2005). *NEA Today, 24,* 54. Retrieved April 14, 2007, from EBSCO Online Database Academic Search Premier.

Zehr, M.A. (2001). Schools grew more segregated in 1990s, report says. *Education Week, 20,* 16-17. Retrieved April 13, 2007, from EBSCO Online Database Academic Search Premier.

SUGGESTED READING

Clotfelter, C.T. (2004) Private schools, segregation, and the southern states. *Peabody Journal of Education, 79,* 74-97. Retrieved April 12, 2007, from EBSCO Online Database Academic Search Premier.

Foner, E. & Kennedy, R. (2004, May 3) Brown at 50. *Nation, 278,* 15-17. Retrieved April 12, 2007, from EBSCO Online Database Academic Search Premier.

Jankov, P. & Caref, C. (2017). Segregation and inequality in Chicago public schools, transformed and intensified under corporate education reform. Education Policy Analysis Archives, 25 (56).

Orfield, G., Ee., J., & Frankenberg, E. (2016). *Brown at 62: School segregation by race, poverty, and state.* Los Angeles, CA.: University of Southern California Civil Rights Project.

Orfield, G. & Lee, C. (2004). *Brown at 50: King's Dream or Plessy's Nightmare.* Cambridge, MA: Harvard Civil Rights Project. Boston.

Rowe, E. & Lubienski, C. (2017). Shopping for schools or shopping for peers: Public schools and catchment area segregation. *Journal of Education Policy,* 32 (3), 340-356.

Warkentien, S. (2016). Trajectories of exposure to racial school segregation and the transition to college. *Society for Research on Educational Effectiveness.*

EVOLUTION VS. CREATION

This article discusses the legal issues surrounding the teaching of creationism and evolution in public school science classrooms in the United States. Since the early 20th century, parents, teachers, and politicians have often been embroiled in contentious debates regarding freedom of religion as applied to the role of religious interpretations of science in the public school science curriculum. Religious fundamentalists view evolution as both unscientific and amoral and advocate its replacement with a faith-based account of the origin of man. Others accept that evolution is fundamental to science and therefore important for students to study. The courts have consistently ruled that creationism and, later, Intelligent Design are not science and therefore do not belong in the public school science classroom.

KEYWORDS: Creationism; Darwinism; Evolution; Intelligent Design (ID); Freedom of Religion; Religious Fundamentalists; Scopes Trial; Separation of Church & State

Overview

HISTORY

Encompassing science, religion, philosophy, and especially politics, the debate between creationism and evolution in the United States has been anything but boring. The legal controversy has spilled over into America's public school science classrooms a number of times-first in the Scopes Trial of 1925 to *Kitzmiller v. Dover Area School District* (2005) and ongoing debate among the members of the Texas Board of Education about the inclusion of both debate of evolutionary theories and information regarding Intelligent Design.

The traditional battle lines in the creation/evolution debate have been clear enough. On one side are creationists, those who believe that God created the entire universe less than 10,000 years ago. On the other side are evolutionists, many of them professional scientists, who believe that the universe has unfolded over billions of years through an unguided, natural process, called evolution. Evolutionists in America are often known as Darwinists, after the British naturalist Charles Darwin (1809-1882), who proposed in *The Origin of Species* (1859) that all life on earth evolved through evolution by natural selection-an unguided process that "selects" as the fittest those individuals that leave the most offspring.

Most would agree that the real sparks fly when the contemporary creation/evolution debate in the United States moves into the realm of biology, particularly the area of human origins. Creationists, who interpret the Bible's book of Genesis literally, believe that human beings are the special, divine creation of an almighty God, and therefore fundamentally distinct from all other creatures on earth. Evolutionists believe that humans are big-brained mammals who not only share a common ancestor with chimpanzees, but are related organically to all other life forms on the planet.

In the early 1990s, a group of creationists who supported the scientifically determined age of the universe diverged from traditional creationism and founded a movement called Intelligent Design (ID). Supporters of Intelligent Design have been less dogmatic than old-line creationists about the nature of the Designer, but they agree with creationists that human beings are not the end product of a solely naturalistic process of evolution.

The debate between creation and evolution takes place within a fiercely religious cultural context. The United States has always been a religious nation. Polls consistently indicate that over 90 percent of the American people believe in God, including a 2011 Gallup poll in which 92 percent answered yes to the question "Do you believe in God?" (Newport, 2011).

Church attendance in America is high compared to other industrialized nations. Though America does not have an established church, there is a widespread belief that the preservation of religion-in whatever form it takes-is essential to the continued health of the country.

From the founding of the United States through the nineteenth century, most education was provided by parents and churches. Beginning with the Puritans, many Americans accepted the statement in the Old Testament that parents were to be the primary educators of their children. The idea was that parents would instill the moral and ethical values necessary for the happiness of the individual and the health of the nation. However, with the industrial revolution of the 19th century requiring more men and women to join the workforce, the education of Americans was increasingly left to public schools and state boards of education.

However, this did not imply that parents and pastors wanted their children to be taught in an amoral environment. For example, in early twentieth-century Tennessee-which would take center stage in America's first major nationwide creation/evolution debate-the influential evangelical Christian churches grew increasingly supportive of public schools because they viewed them as a bulwark against creeping secularism (Israel, 2004).

In practice, however, the symbiotic relationship between parents, churches, and public schools was more an ideal than reality. First, the long-established doctrine of the separation of church and state, which was implicit in the First Amendment and then articulated by Founding Fathers Thomas Jefferson and James Madison, required that public schools not become proxy churches. Impartiality was the intent, and teaching any one religiously based viewpoint was suspect, if not unconstitutional. Second, even though a viewpoint was held by a majority of parents and pastors did not necessarily mean that it represented a scholarly consensus on the topic. While some parents and pastors were college-educated, many were not, and those who did attend school often had little more than a few years of formal schooling. Along these same lines, there was a growing sentiment among American intellectuals that majority rule was a clear and present danger to the civil liberties of those with minority political and religious viewpoints. In the

view of many educated Americans, these minorities should enjoy full and equal protection under the law (Larson, 1997).

Given these factors, perhaps it was not very surprising that in some regions of the country, particularly in the South and the Midwest, the educational authorities ran afoul of public opinion. With tension growing between majority rule and individual rights, the teaching of evolution became a flash point. Beginning in the early twentieth century, there were numerous attempts made by anti-evolutionists (later known as creationists) to ban the teaching of evolution in public schools. Under pressure from these constituents, state legislatures in 15 states were considering bans on the teaching of evolution by 1925.

Some creationists opposed evolution on scientific grounds, charging that it was more theory than fact, while others insisted that evolution-often called Darwinism-undermined the authority of the Bible, thus putting the nation's moral health in peril. For this latter group, it was time to get back to religious fundamentals, and an influential book series by that title ("The Fundamentals," 1910-1915) gave the world a new term: fundamentalism. In addition to Roman Catholicism, socialism, and higher biblical criticism, the authors of "The Fundamentals" included Darwinism as a menace to all that was good and holy (Numbers, 2006).

This anti-Darwinian sentiment was made even stronger by the events of World War I. Americans struggled to make sense of the fact that Germany, the most scientifically and intellectually advanced nation in the world, could draw the world into a global conflict. The answer given in popular books such as Vernon Kellogg's "Headquarters Nights" (1917) and Benjamin Kidd's "Science of Power" (1918) was that German militarism was directly linked to the German leadership's support of Darwinism. For many religious Americans who had lost sons and fathers on the killing fields of Europe, this was proof enough that the scourge of Darwinism must not be exported to the United States.

PROMINENT COURT CASES

Soon the battle over creationism and evolution in the public schools became a subject for litigation. In 1925, the state legislature in Tennessee passed the Butler Act, a law banning the teaching of evolution in the state's public schools. The pertinent section of the Act forbade the teaching of "any theory that denies the story of the Divine Creation of man as taught in the Bible, and to teach instead that man has descended from a lower order of animals."

The American Civil Liberties Union (ACLU), which had been founded in 1920 to defend the civil rights of minorities, took up the case of Dayton, Tennessee, football coach John T. Scopes, who was charged with violating the Butler Act by teaching Darwinism on the day he was a substitute high school biology teacher. The ACLU recruited famed defense attorney Clarence Darrow to defend Scopes and challenge the law. Darrow was opposed in the courtroom by three-time Democratic presidential candidate William Jennings Bryan, a well-known orator who supported the right of the majority to mandate what public schools taught. Bryan had pushed for the passage of the Butler Act because he believed that Darwinism led to immorality by sanctioning the domination of the strong over the weak (Larson).

Scopes v. Tennessee-or the "Scopes Monkey Trial," as it has become known to history-was an instant media sensation. Broadcast live to the nation on radio, the trial brought to the surface many of the central themes of American democracy-majority rule, minority rights, separation of church and state, and concern for the moral fiber of the nation. In the end, Scopes was found guilty of violating the Butler Act, a misdemeanor, and was fined $100. The Butler Act was not repealed until 1967, but Scopes was hired again the next year.

In the 1930s the creationists shifted their focus from state education boards and had substantial success in influencing local school boards to either ban or water down the teaching of evolution in various school districts. Public school teachers who taught evolution ran the risk of breaking the law and losing their jobs. The problem of intellectual freedom became more and more acute, and for about forty years many Southern states banned the teaching of evolution.

After World War II, the legal winds began to shift. First, in 1947, the U.S. Supreme Court ruled in the case of Everson v. Board of Education that the Establishment Clause of the First Amendment, through the Equal Protection Clause of the Fourteenth Amendment, applied to states as well as the federal government. One implication of

this decision was that the federal government now had legal jurisdiction in creation/evolution cases. Second, in 1953, President Dwight Eisenhower appointed Earl Warren as the Chief Justice of the U.S. Supreme Court, thereby ushering in an era of federal judicial activism in which many of the provisions of the Bill of Rights were applied to the states.

The only substantial creation/evolution case decided by the Warren court was Epperson v. Arkansas in 1968. At issue was the constitutionality of a 1928 law passed by the Arkansas legislature to ban the teaching of evolution in the state's public schools. Little Rock high school teacher Susan Epperson asked the state courts for a ruling on the legality of the law, and the case was appealed all the way to the U.S. Supreme Court. Speaking for the majority of the court, Supreme Court Justice Abe Fortas ruled, "The law's effort was confined to an attempt to blot out a particular theory because of its supposed conflict with the Biblical account, literally read. Plainly, the law is contrary to the mandate of the First, and in violation of the Fourteenth Amendment to the Constitution" (cited in NCSE, 2005).

In the wake of Epperson, creationists suffered an unbroken series of losses in state and federal courts throughout the 1970s and 1980s. In 1972, United States District Court for the Southern District of Texas, Houston ruled in Wright v. Houston Independent School District that mandating the teaching of evolution does not violate the Establishment Clause or students' freedom or religion. Anticipating a later U.S. Supreme Court decision, in 1975 the U.S. Sixth Circuit Court of Appeals ruled in Daniel v. Waters that giving "equal time" to the teaching of evolution and creationism in the public school classroom violated the Establishment Clause. In 1977, in *Hendren v. Campbell*, an Indiana state superior court used similar reasoning to rule that a young-earth creationist textbook could not be used in the state's public schools.

After the Epperson decision, Arkansas legislators adjusted state law so that creationism would be taught alongside evolution. Despite the ruling in *Daniel v. Waters* that "equal time" measures were unconstitutional, the state persisted. In *McLean v. Arkansas* (1982), Judge William Overton of the U.S. District Court for the Eastern District of Arkansas struck down the law (NCSE).

The U.S. Supreme Court didn't weigh in on the constitutionality of "equal time" laws until five years later. In *Edwards v. Aguillard* (1987), the nation's highest court struck down a Louisiana law that required "alternative theories" of creation to be taught alongside evolution. Echoing a line of reasoning going back to Everson, the justices declared that the law did violate the Establishment Clause (NCSE).

Even though they struck down "equal time" laws, the Supreme Court left one possible loophole for creationists: the justices ruled in Aguillard that only "scientific theories" of origins could be taught in public schools. In an attempt to fit through the legal loophole, some creationists who supported an old earth theory banded together under the banner of Intelligent Design (ID). Led by a coterie of intellectuals with doctoral degrees in the arts and sciences, ID advocates argued that their brand of creationism could pass muster as a legitimate scientific theory, on par with Darwinian evolution. Prominent ID leaders such as law professor Philip Johnson, mathematician William Dembski, and biochemist Michael Behe began arguing that the structures of living organisms, to say nothing of the universe itself, could not have arisen through a slow, step-by-step process of evolution. There must, they argued, be a designer-though not necessarily the God of the Bible-behind the development of life.

The issue came to a head in 2004 when the school board in Dover, Pennsylvania voted that 9th grade biology students must be read a statement about ID. The school board and its supporters argued that the Aguillard "loophole" meant the reference to ID was constitutional. Some parents brought suit against the school board, and in December 2005 - a month after all the anti-evolution members of the school board were voted out of office - federal judge John E. Jones ruled in *Kitzmiller v. Dover Area School District* that ID was not science and therefore was not entitled to inclusion in the public school science curriculum. "In making this determination," Jones wrote, "we have addressed the seminal question of whether ID is science. We have concluded that it is not, and moreover that ID cannot uncouple itself from its creationist, and thus religious, antecedents" (Jones, 2005; NCSE)

Creationists have also suffered legal defeats in the area of science textbook disclaimers. They lost *Selman v. Cobb County School District*, a case brought in 2002 by six parents in Cobb County, Georgia, who sued to have a sticker on public school science textbooks removed. The sticker read: "This textbook contains material on evolution. Evolution is a theory, not a fact, regarding the origin of living things. This material should be approached with an open mind, studied carefully, and critically considered." In December 2006, after four years of legal wrangling, the Cobb County school board reached a legal settlement with the ACLU in which the stickers would be removed in exchange for the parents halting all litigation against the board. Other states, such as Alabama, continue to place similar stickers on their public school science textbooks. In 2008, Florida revised its science textbook standards to endorse the teaching of evolution. In 2009, the Texas Board of Education voted overwhelmingly that Intelligent Design must be taught alongside evolution, but in 2013, the board reversed its course, adopting "mainstream" curriculum, deciding not to include the theory of Intelligent Design in its science textbooks (Forsyth, 2013).

In the immediate aftermath of the Dover verdict William Dembski, a leading supporter of ID, pledged that he and other supporters of ID will not let the teaching of evolution in public schools go unchallenged:

… The [Dover] ruling is not a Waterloo for the intelligent design side. Certainly, it will put a damper on school boards interested in promoting intelligent design. But this is not a Supreme Court decision. Nor is it likely this decision will be appealed since the Dover school board that caused all the trouble was voted out and replaced this November [2005]. Thus we can expect agitation for ID and against evolution to continue. School boards and state legislators may tread more cautiously, but tread on evolution they will - the culture war demands it! (Dembski, 2006, Para. 3)

Dembski infers that the status of ID within public school science classrooms will be decided by a future U.S. Supreme Court decision. Meanwhile, in many private religious schools across the United States, the teaching of ID or creationism continues unchallenged.

Further Insights

CREATIONISM

Within the context of the creation/evolution debate, creationists are those who believe that the world was created by a Supreme Being, whom they typically equate with the God of the Bible. Young-earth creationists, who take the early chapters of the book of Genesis literally, believe that the entire universe, including the earth, is between 6,000-10,000 years old. They dispute the scientific evidence, coming from many disciplines, that the universe is 13-15 billion years old. Old-earth creationists interpret Genesis more metaphorically, with each "day" in Genesis 1 representing an indefinite period of time, and thus they agree with scientists about the age of the universe. Both young-earth and old-earth creationists accept what they describe as microevolution, or changes within a given biological species (a Biblical kind), but they reject macroevolution, which they typically describe as one species evolving into two separate species that cannot interbreed (Ruse, 2003; Numbers). While Christian creationists predominate in the United States, it is important to note that many Muslims also describe themselves as creationists, though these views have not yet influenced the creation/evolution debate in America.

INTELLIGENT DESIGN

Intelligent design is the theory that some aspects of the natural world are too complex to have resulted from evolutionary processes alone. Supporters aim to steer a middle course between creationism (the belief that evolution is entirely false) and materialism (the belief that the supernatural does not exist). Biochemist Michael Behe, in his influential book "Darwin's Black Box" (1996), argued that the creation of various "molecular machines" (such as the bacterial flagellum) require the infusion of intelligent information. Hearkening back to design arguments found in the writings of Cicero, Thomas Aquinas, and William Paley, supporters of ID argue that some of the complex features of the world are presumptive evidence of intelligent design, which they contrast with the unplanned design of evolution through natural selection. Some ID supporters are practicing Christians who believe the God of the Bible designed certain features of the natural world, while others are agnostic about the identity of the designer. The theory of ID is almost universally opposed by the scientific community-Darwinists such as philosopher of science Michael Ruse call it "creationism lite" (Ruse), and a statement from the American Association for the Advancement of Science said "the lack of scientific warrant for so-called 'intelligent design theory'

makes it improper to include as a part of science education" (AAAS 2002). Young-earth creationists also oppose ID, pointing out that ID supporters tend to be too open-minded about certain aspects of Darwinian evolution, including natural selection and descent with modification. Indeed, Behe and other leading supporters of ID have publicly admitted that Darwin's theory of common descent is at least partially correct (Behe). Arguments for and against the teaching of ID received a thorough hearing in *Kitzmiller v. Dover Area School District* (2005).

MICROEVOLUTION / MACROEVOLUTION

Many of the creation/evolution debates have been portrayed as creationists on one side and evolutionists on the other. In point of fact, all creationists accept microevolution, or what they describe as variation within a kind, a reference to the term used repeatedly in Genesis 1. While there is no agreement among biblical scholars on how kind should be defined, most creationists define it as a biological species, though some expand the meaning to include a genus or a family. All creationists agree, however, that the definition of microevolution cannot be stretched to the point where humans and chimpanzees share a common ancestor. 16th century German Protestant Reformer Martin Luther found microevolution to be a powerful argument for the existence of God:

'Tis a good argument, and has often moved me much, where [Cicero] proves there is a God, in that living creatures, beasts, and mankind engender their own likeness. A cow always produces a cow; a horse, a horse, etc. Therefore it follows that some being exists which rules everything (Luther, n.d.).

through entirely natural processes, is opposed by all creationists, many of them describing it as tantamount to materialism or atheism. On the other hand, some of the leading supporters of ID accept Darwinian concepts such as common descent and natural selection, but argue that they needed to be "supplemented" by intelligent intervention.

Viewpoints

"TEACH THE CONTROVERSY"

After a series of stinging legal rebukes from state and federal courts in the 1970s and 1980s, creationists searched for new ways to gain access to public school science classrooms. They hit upon the slogan "teach the controversy" to argue that there was a real debate within the scientific community regarding the validity of evolution, and therefore that students should be exposed to the arguments on both sides. Upon learning of this new approach, prominent scientists and leading scientific organizations challenged the premise that there were any serious scientific contenders to evolution. While readily admitting that a vigorous debate is taking place regarding the mechanisms of evolution and their relative importance in the evolutionary process, none disagree with the fundamental Darwinian conclusion that all life on earth can be traced back to one common ancestor. In the twenty-first century, and most notably in *Kitzmiller v. Dover Area School District*, courts have generally agreed with the scientific community that there is no controversy in science about whether evolution happened.

WORLD RELIGIONS ON CREATION / EVOLUTION

Historically, only the Abrahamic religions of Judaism, Christianity, and Islam have had internal debates regarding creation and evolution. This is because all three accept the Old Testament's account of a God who created and sustains the universe. Since the Scientific Revolution of the 16th and 17th centuries, many Jews, Christians, and Muslims have interpreted the Genesis creation account as metaphor or myth, but some members of each religion continue to take the account more literally, thus earning the name fundamentalists or creationists. In recent decades many Jewish and Christian sects have spoken out against creationism and ID, thereby allying themselves with the mainstream scientific community. Other major world religions, such as Hinduism or Buddhism, have creation myths without a single creator God, and thus they can much more easily accommodate Darwinian evolution.

SCIENCE & RELIGION

The dialog between science and religion has been a recurring theme in Western culture, but as this article shows, it has taken on a distinct hue in the United States. Charles Bleckmann surveyed 120 years of reporting on the debate as it appeared in Science, the leading American scientific journal, and he detected several patterns:

Scientists often believed that religious opposition to evolution was declining only to find resurgence. Critics of evolution have failed, or refused, to understand either the basic facts or the intellectual underpinnings of evolution. Scientists have consistently called for better education of the public as the solution; however, there is little evidence that education, as it has been practiced, has helped. (A reviewer of this manuscript suggested that there is little evidence that education has actually been tried.) Literalist, fundamentalist religious leaders have initiated attacks on science; however, reconciliations of religion and science have resulted in the modification of theology, not science (Bleckmann, 2006).

Not all will agree with Bleckmann's assessment, and it is indeed the case that religious belief continues to flourish across the United States. Through the patronage of billion-dollar philanthropic foundations such as the Templeton Foundation, it seems certain that the dialog between science and religion, two of the most important cultural forces in America, will continue for the foreseeable future.

TERMS & CONCEPTS

Creationism: In its broadest sense, the belief that the universe was created by a Supreme Being; in common usage, the belief that all life on earth is not descended from a common ancestor.

Darwinism: Often used interchangeably with evolution, it refers to the specific views of British naturalist Charles Darwin (1809-1882) regarding the mechanisms of evolution, specifically concepts such as descent with modification, natural selection, and sexual selection.

Equal Protection Clause: A clause in the Fourteenth Amendment to the U.S. Constitution that states "No state shall ... deny to any person within its jurisdiction the equal protection of the laws."

Establishment Clause: A clause in the First Amendment to the U.S. Constitution that states "Congress shall make no law respecting an establishment of religion, or prohibiting the free exercise thereof."

Evolution: In common usage, the belief that the present state of the universe, including life on earth, emerged through a gradual process of change that took place over billions of years. Creationists often distinguish between microevolution and macroevolution, though most scientists charge that the distinction is largely artificial.

Freedom of Religion: The right of the individual to practice (or not practice) any form of religious expression as he or she sees fit, free from government interference.

Intelligent Design (ID): The belief that at least some aspects of nature show evidence of intelligent, often supernatural, design.

Kind: A term used in the book of Genesis in the Bible to describe the way in which God created life on earth. Biblical scholars are uncertain of the meaning in the original Hebrew.

Separation of Church and State: The American democratic view that religion and government operate in two separate spheres and should not interfere with each other.

Matt Donnelly

BIBLIOGRAPHY

American Association for the Advancement of Science (AAAS). (2002). *AAAS board resolution on intelligent design theory.* Retrieved April 1, 2007 from the American Association for the Advancement of Science, http://aaas.org.

Baker, J. O. (2013). Acceptance of evolution and support for teaching creationism in public schools: The conditional impact of educational attainment. *Journal for the Scientific Study of Religion, 52,* 216–228. Retrieved October 13, 2014 from EBSCO online database Academic Search Complete.

Barnes, R., & Church, R. (2013). Proponents of creationism but not proponents of evolution frame the origins debate in terms of proof. *Science & Education, 22,* 577–603. Retrieved October 13, 2014 from EBSCO online database Education Research Complete.

Braiker, B. (30 March 2007). God's numbers. *Newsweek Online.* Retrieved April 10, 2007 from MSNBC/Newsweek, http://msnbc.msn.com.

Behe, M. (1996). Darwin under the microscope. *The New York Times.* Section A. Page 25. Retrieved April 1, 2007 from Access Research Network, http://arn.org.

Bleckmann, C. A. (2006). Evolution and creationism in Science: 1880-2000. *Bioscience, 56,* pp. 151-158. Retrieved March 31, 2007, from EBSCO online database Academic Search Premier.

Brigandt, I. (2012). Roger S. Taylor and Michel Ferrari (eds): Epistemology and science education: Understanding the evolution vs. intelligent design controversy. *Science & Education, 21,* 579–582. Retrieved December 4, 2013, from EBSCO online database, Education Research Complete.

Dembksi, W. (2006). Life after Dover. *Science & Theology News.* Retrieved March 31, 2007 from Science & Theology News (via Google), http://72.14.253.104/search?q=cache:MjWN0pex-H8J:www.stnews.org.

Forsyth, J. (2011, July 22). Texas education board sticks to teaching of evolution. *Reuters.* Retrieved December 4, 2013, from http://reuters.com.

Israel, C.A. (2004). *Before Scopes: Evangelicalism, education, and evolution in Tennessee, 1870- 1925.* Athens: University of Georgia Press.

Jones, J. E. (2005). Kitzmiller v. Dover Area School District. *U.S. District Court for the Middle District of Pennsylvania.* Retrieved March 31, 2007, from U.S. District Court for the Middle District of PA, http://pamd.uscourts.gov.

Larson, E. J. (1997). *Summer for the gods: The Scopes trial and America's continuing debate over science and religion.* New York: Basic Books.

Luther, M. (n.d.). The table-talk of Martin Luther. Trans. William Hazlitt. *Philadelphia: The Lutheran Publication Society.* Retrieved April 1, 2007, from the Christian Classics Ethereal Library, http://ccel.org.

National Center for Science Education (NCSE). (2005). Evolution education and the law: Legal issues, lawsuits, documents, trial materials, and updates. *National Center for Science Education.* Retrieved April 1, 2007, from the National Center for Science Education, http://www2.ncseweb.org.

Newport, F. (2011, June 3). More than 9 in 10 Americans continue to believe in god. *Gallup.* Retrieved December 4, 2013, from http://gallup.com.

Numbers, R. (2006). *The creationists: From scientific creationism to intelligent design.* Expanded Ed. Cambridge, Ma. and London: Harvard University Press.

Ruse, M. (2003). Creationism. Stanford Encyclopedia of Philosophy. Retrieved March 31, 2006, from *Stanford Encyclopedia of Philosophy,* http://plato.stanford.edu.

———— (2006). Keep intelligent design out of science classes. *Beliefnet.* Retrieved April 1, 2007, from Beliefnet, http://beliefnet.com.

Werth, A. J. (2013). An evolutionary focus improves students' understanding of all biology. *Reports of the National Center for Science Education, 33,* 3–20. Retrieved October 13, 2014, from EBSCO online database Academic Search Complete.

SUGGESTED READING

Barbour, I. (1997). *Religion and science: Historical and contemporary issues.* San Francisco: Harper San Francisco.

Behe, M (1996). *Darwin's black box.* New York: Free Press.

God vs Darwin: The war between evolution and creationism in the classroom. (2011). *Reports of the National Center for Science Education, 31,* 9. Retrieved December 4, 2013, from EBSCO online database, Education Research Complete.

Hewlett, M. and T. Peters (2006). Evolution in our schools: What should we teach? *Dialog: A Journal of Theology.*

Vol. 45, 106-109. Retrieved March 31, 2007, from EBSCO online database Academic Search Premier.

Justice, B. (2005). *The war that wasn't: Religious conflict and compromise in the common schools of New York State, 1865-1900*. Albany: State University of New York Press.

Lac, A., Heimovich, V., & Himelfarb, I. (2010). Predicting position on teaching creationism (instead of evolution) in public schools. *The Journal of Educational Research*, 103 (4), 253-261.

Larson, E.J. (2003). *Trial & error: The American controversy over creation & evolution*. Third Edition. New York: Oxford University Press.

National Academy of Sciences (1999). *Science and creationism: A view from the National Academy of Sciences*. Second edition. Washington, D.C.: National Academies Press. Retrieved March 31, 2007 from the National Academy of Sciences, http://books.nap.edu.

Numbers, R. (5 Nov 1982). Creationism in 20th-century America. *Science, 218*: 538-544. Retrieved March 31, 2007 from the Virginia Tech History Department, http://history.vt.edu.

Pennock, R. (1998). *Tower of Babel: Scientific evidence and the new creationism*. Cambridge, Mass.: M.I.T. Press.

Pigliucci, M. (2005). Science and fundamentalism: A strategy on how to deal with anti-science fundamentalism. *EMBO reports 6*, 1106-1109. Retrieved March 31, 2007, from the European Molecular Biology Organization, http://nature.com.

Ruse, M., ed. (1988). *But is it science? The philosophical question in the creation/evolution controversy*. Buffalo, N.Y.: Prometheus.

_____ (2005). *The creation-evolution struggle*. Cambridge, Ma. and London: Harvard University Press.

Sober, E. (March 2007). What is wrong with intelligent design? *Quarterly Review of Biology, vol. 82*, 3-8. Retrieved March 31, 2007 from http://philosophy.wisc.edu.

Whitcomb, J.C. & H.R. Morris (1961). *The Genesis flood: The biblical record and its scientific implications*. Philadelphia: Presbyterian and Reformed Publishing Company.

SCHOOL PRAYER

School prayer has remained a subject of national debate in the United States throughout the 20th Century. *Engel v. Vitale* ushered in an era in which school prayer was effectively forbidden; however, with the passage of the Equal Access Act in 1984, some forms of school prayer were again sanctioned. The Department of Education now issues a guide to help school administrators practically apply congressional laws and Supreme Court decisions concerning school prayer. An international perspective shows that current U.S. policy towards school prayer is relatively unique, as most developed countries disallow prayer in public schools.

KEYWORDS: Constitutionally Protected Prayer; Equal Access Act; Establishment Clause; First Amendment; Fourteenth Amendment; Freedom of Religion; Freedom of Speech; Free Exercise Clause; Moment of Silence; Prayer in School; Separation of Church and State

OVERVIEW

For much of the 20th Century and into the 21st, school prayer has been the focal point of an ongoing debate about the role of religion in American society. The question of the legality of prayer in public schools brings together a number of important concepts in American government and legal theory. Opponents and proponents of school prayer couch their arguments in such major constitutional issues as the separation of church and state, the right to free speech, the right to free exercise of religion, and the respective powers of local, state, and national governments. Since hearing its first case on the issue in 1962, the United States Supreme Court has handed down at least one decision dealing with school prayer in each successive decade. All of this makes school prayer an enduring and highly significant topic in the fields of education and law.

School prayer is a practical as well as a theoretical point of contention. Besides understanding and navigating the legal dimensions of this issue, school officials must also take into consideration local public opinion and community needs in order to formulate district policy. The United States educational system, rooted as it is in local and state educational agencies, necessitates that each individual school administrator decide how to apply Supreme Court rulings and national laws concerning religion in public schools. The Clinton and George W. Bush administrations have both released guides intended to help local districts accomplish this task.

The debate over school prayer shows no signs of ending in the near future. However, several principles have been established with as much consensus as can be expected. An understanding of these, as well as of the history of prayer in public schools and the constitutional points crucial to the debate, will provide a solid foundation for further inquiry into any aspect of this multifaceted subject.

HISTORY

Until the early 20th Century, prayer was an accepted aspect of public education. Throughout the 18th and 19th centuries, America remained a de facto Christian nation, and public school curriculum reflected this fact. The contemporary, mainstream debate about prayer in public schools actually began in 1948, when the Supreme Court handed down its first decision on the issue of religion in public schools, ruling in *Illinois ex. rel. McCollum v Board of Education* that it is unconstitutional to conduct religious education within public school buildings ("Keeping the Faith," 2000). This decision formed a basis for later decisions on school prayer. Since then, there have been two distinct periods in the history of school prayer. During the first, which lasted from approximately 1962-1984, school prayer was virtually excised from public schools. The public debate about school prayer during this period focused on the Establishment Clause of the First Amendment and the principle of separation of church and state. The second period in the history of school prayer began in 1984 and continues into the present. This period has witnessed a limited return of prayer in public schools, with public debate about the issue emphasizing the First Amendment rights to freedom of speech, expression, and religion.

Engel v. Vitale

The watershed moment that inaugurated the first of these periods came in 1962, when the Supreme Court handed down its most important decision regarding prayers in public schools to date. In *Engel v. Vitale* the Court ruled a non-denominational prayer used in New York public schools unconstitutional because it violated the doctrine of the separation of church and state. In 1963, all voluntary prayer and Bible readings were banned as well ("Keeping the Faith").

For the next 20 years, religion virtually disappeared from public schools. Not only were prayers and Bible readings absolutely abolished, but discussion of religion was also excised from textbooks and curriculum. Students were directed not to speak

about religion in the classroom; in other words, to "leave their religion at the schoolhouse door" (Haynes, 2006). Most administrators preferred to err on the side of caution. Rather than make potentially controversial decisions concerning contexts in which school prayer might be legal, administrators applied a zero-tolerance policy to school prayer. They interpreted the far from conclusive Supreme Court decisions as leaving no place at all for religion or prayer in public schools (Walsh, 2003).

THE EQUAL ACCESS ACT

All of this changed in 1984, when Congress passed the Equal Access Act, which opened the second distinct period in the history of prayer in public schools. This piece of legislation was designed to correct the widely held perception that religious speech was prohibited in public schools (Balk, 2001). The Equal Access Act mandated that all students and student groups be given equal access to school facilities. It also prohibited discrimination based on the content of student speech. The most important ramifications of this act were on school clubs. The law states that if a school allows its students to form any school clubs, then it must sanction the formation of all school clubs, even if a club's focus is religious in nature. Student groups were granted a level of autonomy by this legislation, as schools could no longer sponsor, participate in, direct, or otherwise control the activities of student groups (Balk).

One effect of the Equal Access Act was to reintroduce prayer, in certain very specific contexts, back into public schools. Students now had the articulated legal right to form religious groups, including prayer groups and Bible study groups. So, long as these groups were formed and run by students, they could engage in prayer within public school facilities, albeit not during instruction time.

Following the passage of the Equal Access Act, the debate over school prayer shifted. While in earlier decades the debate addressed one's freedom *from* a state established religion, new discussions about school prayer emphasized the student's right *to* freedom of speech and religious expression (Haynes). Previously, the Establishment Clause of the First Amendment had been used to argue that school prayer violated the prohibition against the establishment of state religion. Now, the First Amendment's Free Exercise clause was being used to argue that a ban on school prayer violated a student's right to the free exercise of religion, free speech, and free expression. Once it was clear that some speech about religion was allowed in public schools if it was initiated by students, advocates of school prayer began attempting to reintroduce prayer to non-curricular school events, such as graduation ceremonies and sports competitions. The Supreme Court also bolstered school prayer supporters when, in 1985, it issued unofficial guidelines on how legislation calling for a moment-of-silence during the school day should be crafted in order to be constitutional (Davis, 2003). Since then, many state legislatures have passed moment-of-silence legislation, which effectively allots time during the school day for students to say a silent prayer or engage in some other form of thoughtful reflection.

FURTHER RULINGS

The Supreme Court has ruled on the legality of prayer at various extra-curricular school functions. In 1992, in *Lee v Weisman,* the Court declared prayer at graduation ceremonies to be unconstitutional. In this particular case, the prayer recited was not student-initiated, but part of a speech given by a religious leader chosen by school administrators as a graduation speaker. Thus, rather than prohibit all prayer at extra-curricular events, this ruling prohibited only prayer sponsored or endorsed by school authorities (Balk). In 2000, the Supreme Court similarly ruled in *Santa Fe Independent School District v Doe* that student-led prayers before school football games were unconstitutional. These prayers were being delivered via the school's P.A. system, and so constituted public, not private speech. In addition, the Santa Fe school in question was too involved with this student led process—it assisted with a vote that was part of the process for picking a prayer leader and passed policy related to the prayer at a school board meeting (Speich, 2001). According to the Supreme Court, all this meant that these student-led prayers were really encouraged and sponsored by the school (Balk). The question of the legality of student religious speech delivered independently (with total school neutrality) before an audience was not settled (Haynes).

SCHOOL PRAYER TODAY

Even though the Supreme Court struck down these two attempts to expand school prayer, the legal climate of the past decade has nonetheless been a warm one for proponents of prayer in public schools. Throughout the George W. Bush era, the U.S. Department of Education has vigorously maintained that it is the responsibility of school administrators to protect students' right to free religious speech in school. Critics of this policy have even charged the administration with "pushing the envelope" on the school prayer issue and capitulating to religious conservatives (Walsh). In order to ensure that students' religious rights were being protected, the No Child Left Behind Act of 2001 (NCLB) required the Department of Education to issue a booklet of guidelines on "constitutionally protected prayer" in United States public schools (U.S. Department of Education, 2003). Moreover, as a condition of receiving Elementary and Secondary Education Act (ESEA) funds, each local educational agency had to certify to its state educational agencies that none of its policies would impede students' right to constitutionally protected prayer as set forth in the booklet of guidelines (U.S. Department of Education). The guidelines set forth in the booklet have themselves garnered criticism for issuing strict rules on points that had not yet been settled by the Supreme Court. For example, the guidelines affirmed the legality of "student-initiated" religious speech at public events such as graduation ceremonies, while the Supreme Court had yet to do so ("School Prayer Guide Gets Mixed Reviews," 2003).

Despite the Bush administration's guidelines about constitutionally protected student prayer, all indications showed that state-sponsored school prayer in United States public schools is a thing of the past. In May 2006, Senator Robert Byrd of West Virginia introduced, for the eighth time in 44 years, a Constitutional amendment that would guarantee students the right to pray in school if they wished to (Davis).

Applications

THE CONSTITUTIONAL BASIS FOR SCHOOL PRAYER DEBATES

The question of the legality of school prayer hinges on two amendments in the United States Constitution: the First Amendment and the Fourteenth. The First Amendment is comprised of two main clauses, known as the establishment clause and the free-exercise clause. The establishment clause refers to the injunction that "Congress shall make no law respecting the establishment of religion," while the free exercise clause refers to the next pronouncement that it shall not make laws "prohibiting the free exercise, thereof" (U.S. Government Printing Office, 2002). In the debate over school prayer, the establishment clause is most often invoked by the opponents of school prayer, who argue that prayer in public schools is tantamount to the establishment of state religion. Proponents of school prayer use the free exercise clause to argue that prohibiting prayer in school interferes with students' free exercise of—and free speech about—religion (Haynes).

The Fourteenth Amendment is also key to this debate because it states that state and local governments, including agencies such as public schools, are bound by the First Amendment. In their official capacities, school administrators, teachers, and staff are all representatives of the State. Thus, a superintendent's approval of guided prayer before sporting events would be equivalent to State-sponsored prayer, which would violate the principle of separation of church and state. Similarly, prayer at school board meetings is illegal because the school board is a representative of the state.

Despite the complexity of these constitutional issues, the Supreme Court's various rulings show a basic consensus on how the First Amendment impacts school prayer. According to the United States Department of Education, "the First Amendment forbids religious activity that is sponsored by the government but protects religious activity that is initiated by private individuals" in school (U.S. Department of Education). School officials, representing the state, should be neither hostile, nor partial to school prayers or other religious expressions, but should maintain a stance of neutrality (U.S. Department of Education)

PRACTICAL GUIDELINES ON SCHOOL PRAYER
As the Education Department's "Guidance on Constitutionally Protected Prayer in Public Elementary and Secondary Schools" suggests, school administrators often need guidance on how to pragmatically apply congressional laws and Supreme Court decisions to the day to day administration of their schools. Accordingly, the guidebook lists a

number of practices that are either legal or illegal according to Supreme Court rulings.

School officials cannot legally do any of the following:
- Lead classes in prayer or devotional Bible readings;
- Attempt to persuade/compel students to participate in any religious activities, such as prayer;
- Decide to include prayer in a school-sponsored event, such as a graduation ceremony or an athletic event;
- Participate in religious activities while in an official capacity;
- Encourage or discourage students from praying during a moment of silence if their school observes this practice during the school day (U.S Department of Education, 2003).

The Education Department guidebook also specifies practices in which students have a legal right to partake at school. School officials were obligated by the No Child Left Behind Act (2001) to ensure that:
- Students have the constitutional right to free speech at school, which includes the right to pray amongst themselves so long as they are not disrupting classroom instruction;
- Students can make religious remarks in front of a public audience so long as the school maintains a neutral stance towards student speakers and the content of their speech;
- Students may engage in religious activities such as praying, reading the Bible, saying grace, etc. when not receiving classroom instruction (during recess, lunch hour, or any other free period);
- Students may or may not pray during a moment of silence if their school observes this practice during the school day;
- Students may be dismissed from class in order to pursue a religious obligation;
- Students may express their religious beliefs in classroom work or homework, and such work must be neutrally evaluated according to academic standards;
- Student speakers (so long as they are chosen neutrally, meaning not on a basis that either favors or disfavors religious expression) are entitled to express religious statements at public school assemblies, including graduation ceremonies (U.S. Department of Education).

POLLS & SURVEYS

Because school prayer is a contentious issue in the United States, it is frequently the subject of public opinion polls. One poll administered by the Gallup Organization in 2005 shows significant public support for some form of prayer in public schools. Seventy-six percent of those adults polled said they favored a Constitutional amendment allowing voluntary prayer in public schools. Twenty-three percent were opposed to such an amendment (A Prayerful Nation, 2006). School-aged participants also favored school prayer. Fifty-eight percent of 13-17 year olds thought that a non-denominational spoken prayer should be allowed, and 44% thought that a prayer that specifically mentions Jesus Christ should be allowed. The vast majority of this group, eighty-four percent, were in favor of a moment of silence that would allow students to pray if they wanted to (Bowman, 2006).

INTERNATIONAL PERSPECTIVES

On a global level, the school prayer issue shows the United States to be relatively unique amongst developed nations in its relationship to school prayer. While school prayer remains a contentious legal issue in America, abroad it is not: "Even countries that have not maintained a strict separation of church and state have, by and large, tended to eschew state-sponsored school prayer" (Walsh). Of 72 countries with unified prayer-policies that were polled by the A.C.L.U of Southern California, only 11 have state-sanctioned prayers in public school. Of these 11 nations, most have relatively homogenous populations in terms of religion (cited in Walsh). Thus, countries that have a state-sponsored religion are the most likely to endorse prayer in state run, public schools. Those countries with populations that are heterogeneous in terms of religion—similar to the United States—by and large have decided against allowing even a non-denominational state sponsored school prayer in public schools.

TERMS & CONCEPTS

Constitutionally Protected Prayer: As outlined by the U.S. Department of Education in its booklet, Guidance on Constitutionally Protected Prayer in Public Elementary and Secondary Schools, the religious expression that students have a Constitutional right to freely engage in at school.

Equal Access Act: Congressional legislation passed in 1984, it mandates that all student groups be given equal access to school facilities. It paved the way for reintroducing prayer into public schools by guaranteeing students the right to form school prayer groups if they have the right to form other types of school clubs.

Establishment Clause: The clause in the first amendment that prohibits Congress from making any law respecting the establishment of religion.

First Amendment: Part of the Bill of Rights, it prohibits Congress from establishing state religion, and it grants citizens the rights to freedom of speech, free exercise of religion, freedom of the press, freedom to assemble peaceably, and freedom to petition the government to redress grievances.

Fourteenth Amendment: Ratified in 1868, one of its clauses states that state and local governments, including government agencies, are bound by the First Amendment.

Freedom of Religion: As guaranteed in the Free Exercise clause of the First Amendment, citizens of the United States have the right to freely exercise any and all religions.

Freedom of Speech: As guaranteed in the First Amendment, all United States Citizens possess the right to express themselves without interference or constraint from the government.

Free Exercise Clause: The clause in the First amendment that guarantees citizens the free exercise of any religion.

Moment-of-Silence: An officially recognized span of time -usually from thirty seconds to one minute—during which students may or may not engage in silent prayer or reflection.

Prayer in School: A controversial issue in the United States, state sponsored prayer in school has been ruled illegal by the United States Supreme Court. However, student-initiated prayer in school is legal in certain contexts. According to the No Child Left Behind Act, a student's right to constitutionally protected prayer in school must be protected as a pre-condition for receiving federal funds.

Separation of Church and State: One of the cardinal principles of America's secular democracy, it refers to the political doctrine of keeping government and religious institutions autonomous and independent from one another.

Ashley L. Cohen

BIBLIOGRAPHY

Balk, H. (2001). Chandler v. James: A student's right of prayer in public schools. *BYU Journal of Public Law, 15*, 243-262. Retrieved March 13, 2007, from EBSCO Online Database Education Research Complete.

Bowman, K. (Ed.). (2006). A prayerful nation. *American Enterprise, 17*, 54-55. Retrieved March 13, 2007, from EBSCO Online Database Education Research Complete.

Davis, D. (2003). Moments of silence in America's public schools: Constitutional and ethical considerations. *Journal of Church & State, 45*, 429-442. Retrieved March 14, 2007, from EBSCO Online Database Educational Research Complete.

Davis, M. (2006, May 10). Sen. Byrd introduces prayer amendment. *Education Week, 25*, 26. Retrieved March 14, 2007, from EBSCO Online Database Education Research Complete.

Fox, R. A., Buchanan, N. K., Eckes, S. E., & Basford, L. E. (2012). The line between cultural education and religious education: Do ethnocentric niche charter schools have a prayer?. *Review of Research in Education, 36*, 282-305. Retrieved November 15, 2014, from EBSCO Online Database Education Research Complete.

Haynes, C. (2006). From battleground to common ground. *School Administrator, 63*, 10-15. Retrieved March 13, 2007, from EBSCO Online Database Education Research Complete.

Jones, N.R. (2012). Of prayer, public schools and the constitution. *Church & State, 65*, 24-25. Retrieved December 15, 2013, from EBSCO Online Database Education Research Complete.

Keeping the faith. (2000, September 29). *Current Events (Teacher's Edition), 100*, 1-2. Retrieved March 13, 2007, from EBSCO Online Database Education Research Complete.

Lunenburg, F.C. (2011). Church-state relations in public schools: Religious influences and accommodations. *FOCUS on Colleges, Universities & Schools, 6*, 1-4. Retrieved December 15, 2013, from EBSCO Online Database Education Research Complete.

School prayer guide gets mixed reviews. (2003, March 8). *Christian Century, 120*, 16. Retrieved March 14, 2007, from EBSCO Online Database Education Research Complete.

Speich, J. (2001). Santa Fe Independent School District v. Doe: Mapping the future of student-led, student-initiated prayer in public schools. *Albany Law Review, 65*, 271-314. Retrieved on March 14, 2007, from EBSCO Online Database Education Research Complete.

Supreme court decisions. (2012). *Journal of Law & Education, 41*, 363-375. Retrieved November 15, 2014, from EBSCO Online Database Education Research Complete.

U.S. Department of Education. (2003). *Guidance on constitutionally protected prayer in public elementary and secondary schools*. Washington, D.C. Retrieved March 13, 2007, from http://ed.gov.

U.S. Government Printing Office. (n.d.) *Constitution of the United States of America, analysis and interpretation* (2002 ed.). Retrieved March 14, 2007, from http://gpoaccess.gov.

Walsh, M. (1995, May 31). Most nations eschew prayers in public schools, report says. *Education Week, 14*, 9. Retrieved March 13, 2007, from EBSCO Online Database Education Research Complete.

Walsh, M. (2003, February 19). Critics say agency 'pushing the envelope' with school prayer guide. *Education Week, 22*, 25. Retrieved March 13, 2007, from EBSCO Online Database Education Research Complete.

Warnick, B.R. (2012). Student rights to religious expression and the special characteristics of schools. *Educational Theory, 62*, 59-74. Retrieved December 15, 2013, from EBSCO Online Database Education Research Complete.

SUGGESTED READING

Alley, R. (1994). *School prayer: The Court, the Congress, and the First Amendment* Buffalo, NY: Prometheus Books.

Covaleskie, J. F. (2012). The first amendment goes to school. *Journal of Philosophy & History of Education, 62*17-28. Retrieved November 15, 2014, from EBSCO Online Database Education Research Complete.

Garnett, R. (2005). Bush v. Holmes: School vouchers, religious freedom, and state constitutions. *Education & the Law, 17*, 173-183. Retrieved March 14, 2007, from EBSCO Online Database Education Research Complete.

Primary and secondary education. (2005). *Journal of Law & Education, 34*, 295-313. Retrieved March 14, 2007, from EBSCO Online Database Education Research Complete.

Shotwell, T. (2004). Mandatory prayer in public schools: The British Virgin Islands school system. *Negro Educational Review, 55*, 197-208. Retrieved March 13, 2007, from EBSCO Online Database Education Research Complete.

Studying the question of Bible study. (2006). *Magna's Campus Legal Monthly, 21*, 4-6. Retrieved March 14, 2007, from EBSCO Online Database Education Research Complete.

FREEDOM OF RELIGION AND PUBLIC EDUCATION

As the founding fathers were writing the Constitution, they believed that government needed to be secular in order to keep the peace between religious factions, and they went to great lengths to create a state without any religious aspirations. In accordance with this goal, as public education was spread through the nation, a law was passed to prohibit the use of public funds to support sectarian schools. Rather than teach religion, it became the task of schools to create good Americans. Over the course of the 20th century, a number of Supreme Court cases refined the relationship between public education and religious freedom. The public debate over this relationship continues today.

KEYWORDS: Common School; Democracy; Horace Mann; Proselytize; Public Education; Religion; Sectarian; Secular; Secularism; Secular Humanism; Separation of Church and State; Supreme Court

Overview

FREEDOM OF RELIGION

Freedom of religion is the right to worship as one pleases, the right to choose (or not choose) a religion without fear of reprisal from government. As democracy spreads across the world, many evolving countries are incorporating this right into their government's foundation. Davis (2006) recognizes that, "the number of democracies worldwide has more than tripled (to 120) in the last 30 years... most democracies today are "liberal" democracies, which means that fundamental rights or liberties of the citizens are built into the legal structure of the regime" (Davis). With the spread of democracy around the world, freedom of religion is becoming a basic human right.

The principle of freedom of religion is not new. Some of the first written evidence mankind has of this ideal appears on the Cyrus Cylinder, dated to around 539 BC. Cyrus, King of the Persian Kingdom, liberated Babylon from Nabonidus, by walking into the city and taking it. He wrote, "I took great care to peacefully (protect) the city of Babylon and its cult places. (And) as for the citizens of Babylon, whom Nabonidus had made subservient in a manner totally unsuited to them against the will of the gods, I released them from their weariness and loosened their burden" (Chavalas, 2006). As Cyrus was taking over the famed city, he did so with toleration of its inhabitants and their holy places. This was done in order to keep peace with the citizens of Babylon.

American founding fathers in the 18th century addressed freedom of religion in the First Amendment of the Constitution. Within the outline for a new government, placing Freedom of Religion first showed how important the founding fathers knew this idea to be. The First Amendment says, in part:

"Congress shall make no law respecting an establishment of religion, or prohibiting the free exercise thereof..."

THE CONSTITUTION WITHOUT RELIGION

Religion played a central role in early American settlers' lives. By the time the Constitution was being written, there were many different Christian sects already well established in the new world. Some colonists came to American for religious freedom, but many more came for commercial opportunities and to establish profitable plantations and businesses for their benefactors back in England and continued to adhere to their own versions of Christianity.

As Jefferson, Madison, Hamilton et al. were writing the Constitution, they knew they could not get the widely varying sects in each colony to agree on which doctrine was the most proper and suited to govern all the inhabitants of the country. Forming a government based on one religion would be divisive at a time when the founders were trying to unite a nation together, so they solidly rejected the idea of a Christian state. They sought instead to create laws providing that the property and health of citizens not be hindered by fraud or violence and left religion out of it. They saw government as needing to be non-secular in order to keep the peace and they went to great lengths to create a state without any religious aspirations. The new government "would not serve the glory of God; it would merely preside over a commercial republic, an individualistic and competitive

America preoccupied with private rights and personal autonomy" (Kramnic & Moore, 1996).

EDUCATION IN EARLY AMERICA

Prior to the establishment of the United States, the Constitution and the federal government, education in Colonial America was designed to create and sustain a Christian civilization. In the 1640s, Massachusetts and Virginia passed laws that required children receive some education. Massachusetts fared better than Virginia in this endeavor, as the Puritans placed a strong emphasis on learning. For more than 100 years, beginning around 1690, most school learning was done using the New England Primer, a textbook created by the Puritans, whose "great theme was God and our relationship to Him" (Nord, 1995). The main purpose to sending children to school during this time was to learn their parents' and community's religious doctrine.

Before the Civil War, schoolbooks accepted Christian accounts of the world almost certainly. Slowly, the movement for tax supported "common schools" began. Common schools were non-sectarian in design and begun for a variety of reasons. "Some scholars see the movement as a natural extension of democracy and liberalism..." (Nord). It was an effort to create skilled workers in order to ensure America's economic status worldwide, or possibly to "accept the common values of order and discipline within a society" (Nord). Public common schools were supported by tax dollars and educating children became mandatory in America.

Although they professed to be, common schools were not entirely without religion. Horace Mann, a Protestant, propagated the idea of a common school education stressing only those convictions upon which 'men of goodwill' agreed. The Bible was to speak for itself without any of the nuances in Christianity that caused division along sectarian lines. At first, many Protestants protested this schooling idea. They felt their religion should be a central part of the education process. However, they began to rally around the idea as more Roman Catholics immigrated to America. Opinion shifted to be that children are better off in a school where the Bible is not interpreted than being educated by or under strict guidance of a Roman Catholic priest. Catholics revolted against this idea and created a huge parochial system of education, which still exists today.

Then, because tax dollars supported common schools, Catholics argued for tax dollars to support their schools as well.

In 1875, Congress fell only a few votes shy of passing a constitutional amendment prohibiting the use of all public funds for sectarian education. Congress did, however, pass a law in 1876 stating all new member-states must provide means for creating public schools free from sectarian control. During this period, "many states adopted constitutional amendments prohibiting the use of state funds for sectarian schools" (Nord).

EDUCATION WITHOUT RELIGION

The largest motivational factor for outlawing sectarian schools, according to constitutional scholar Douglas Laycock, was "trace(ed back) not to any careful deliberations about constitutional principles of the proper relations of church and state. Rather it traces to vigorous 19th century anti-Catholicism and nativ(e) reaction to Catholic immigration" (as cited in Nord). In order to keep the peace, educators at the time came to the same conclusion the founding fathers had: eliminate what is discordant. Take religion out of everyday classrooms and find another central purpose for educating youth. Rather than teach religion, it became the task of schools to create good Americans.

Schools began espousing ideas about America and Americanism rather than religion. Textbooks presented America as being the most prosperous, successful country in the world. This idea became more important as the country was flooded with immigrants. Public schools became "cultural factories of Americanization, transforming the raw material of foreign cultures into good American citizens" (Nord). During this time, America's economy continued to grow and the middle class took more opportunity to shape and develop what was taught in schools. A major reason high school became popular was that businesses required a better-trained work force. In 1917, Congress passed the Smith-Hughes Act, the first act encouraging and funding vocational education.

FIRST SUPREME COURT CASES

During the ensuing years, the Supreme Court viewed its role in public education as furthering the Jeffersonian principle of creating a "wall" between church and state. A host of Court decisions, laid out bit by bit, erected this wall high in the middle part of the 20th century. There were several cases within a 30 year span that helped build up this idea.

In 1940, *Minersville School District v. Gobitis* presented a case in which two young students were expelled from school for not participating in the Pledge of Allegiance. As Jehovah's Witnesses, they were forbidden by their religion to do so. The Court extended the opinion that the state can overrule individual freedoms of religion, stating, "The mere possession of religious convictions which contradict the relevant concerns of a political society does not relieve the citizen from the discharge of political responsibilities" (*Minersville School District v. Gobitis*). In essence, duty to the state comes before one's religious convictions. Seven years later in *Everson v. Board of Education*, Everson, a taxpayer, thought it inappropriate to use public funds to bus students to parochial schools. The Court agreed, with only one judge dissenting. The very next year, the McCollum v. Board of Education ruling denied release time during the school day for on-campus religious instruction.

In the case of *Engel v. Vitale*, the court ruled that "state officials may not compose an official state prayer and require that it be recited in the public schools of the State at the beginning of each school day - even if the prayer is denominationally neutral and pupils who wish to do so may remain silent or be excused from the room while the prayer is being recited" (*Engle v. Vitale*, 1962). The Court saw the act of praying in school equivalent to establishing religious beliefs therein. Because school attendance is compulsory, sponsoring prayer in school becomes, essentially, proselytizing to students.

Although the wall between education and religion had been firmly put into place by the Constitution, the Supreme Court was careful not to say that religion is not worth studying. In 1963, in *School District of Abington Township v. Schemp* the Court opinion read, "...one's education is not complete without a study of comparative religion or the history of religion and its relationship to the advancement of civilization. It certainly may be said that the Bible is worthy of study for its literary and historic qualities." In this specific case, however, the high court failed to allow the continuation of Bible readings during school time, going on to say, "In the relationship between man and religion, the State is firmly committed to a position of neutrality" (*Abington Township v. Schemp*).

Further Insights

IS NEUTRAL REALLY NEUTRAL?

The secularization of public schools has been determined by some on the religious right to be "suppression not only of the teaching of religion, but also of religiously grounded moral values" (Blum, 1987). Blum also believes that this suppression "teach(es) that these (moral) values are false, or at least irrelevant to man's affairs." This particular theory assumes that values can only be taught within the context of religious training and teaching. Dr. Paul Vitz, a professor of psychology at NYU, took an empirical look at textbooks given to students in public schools to determine what, if any, values are taught in American classrooms. He found that religious values were being left out of textbooks, "16 of 22 textbooks contain no reference to God, Christianity or Judaism" (as cited in Blum). Blum calls the omission of religion censorship, saying censorship occurs most often in those courses that are most important - on both intellectual and imaginative levels - in shaping the moral values of the students.

The argument continues that without religion in the classroom, students are led to believe it is an unimportant part of daily life:

When we teach our children that religion is to be omitted from their education, we destroy the very foundations of our moral values... (Blum).

Boller (1987) noted that, ultra-fundamentalists reject the possibility that secular institutions can uphold moral values...any values that fail to conform to its own values are dubbed 'immoral.' They condemn the public schools for not teaching their specific religious doctrines or promoting their political interpretations of the world (Boller).

When the Vitz study came out during the Reagan Administration, religious fundamentalists thought they found their proof that the educational system was devoid of morals and values. But upon further study of the source, scholars such as Doerr have found "his work sloppy, and Vitz himself has an axe to grind; he dislikes public education in principle and favors tax support of sectarian private schools" (Doerr, 1987).

The practice of teaching that man can solve problems on his own, through math, science and literature and without God, has been compared to proselytizing "secular humanism" as a religion. In March,

1987, Judge Brevard Hand of Alabama ruled that 44 textbooks should be banned from schools because, by omitting reference to religion, they were in fact teaching secular humanism, thereby giving preference to that religion over others. A federal appeals court later overturned this judgment.

CONTINUING THE DEBATE TODAY

School systems land in court over religion every day. In the case of *Skoros v. City of New York* (2007), the City school system allowed Christmas trees, menorahs, Santa Claus decorations and Islamic star and crescent symbols within the school, but not the crèche, which displays the newborn Jesus. This case involves Andrea Skoros, a Roman Catholic who sued because "to (not) allow crèches while permitting Jewish and Islamic religious symbols "conveyed the impermissible message of disapproval of Christianity" and violated the First Amendment's prohibition against a government establishment of religion, as well as her family's free-exercise-of-religion right" (Walsh, 2007). A federal district court and the U.S. Court of Appeals upheld the school system's argument as having a "valid secular purpose" because their school "policy barred any display of deities, and that it did not allow religious displays for Jewish holidays such as Rosh Hashanah and Yom Kippur that had not attained secular significance" (Walsh).

The reasoning for the school district is that, "Because a significant number of New York City schoolchildren or their parents are immigrants, sometimes from countries that place little value on either diversity or tolerance, city schools play a particularly important role in teaching these essential elements of pluralism to future generations of Americans," according to the opinion of Judge Reena Raggi for a 2-1 majority of the (New York) 2nd Circuit court. "The fact that they do so ... through cheerful multicultural holiday displays rather than formal textbook assignments does not diminish the importance of the lesson, much less call into question its actual secular purpose" (cited in Walsh). In other words, it's the job of schools to create Americans, knowledgeable of customs and tolerant of each other's differences. It's not the job of the schools to place deities of any religion into the schools.

Doerr argues that, "teaching about religion and promoting ethical or moral values are two different things and pose different sets of problems for educators" (Doerr). Public schools teach honesty, fairness, decency, good citizenship and integrity every day. These are moral values, and yet they have nothing to do with religion. The decision the public schools face is the difference between teaching about religion and not teaching religious doctrine. Until now, educators and textbook publishers were not willing to take a chance on the distinction and have left religion out of the curriculum,

But rather than being the result of some dark conspiracy against or hostility toward religion, the slighting of religion in public schools stems from a justifiable fear on the part of educators and textbook publishers of handling a very controversial issue, from lack of a real demand for academic study of religion, and from simple lack of agreement as to precisely what should be taught (Doerr).

Viewpoints

THE PATH FORWARD

...(W)hat's at stake is the future of public education in this country - the kind of education we want to have. Do we want to have education with sectarian strife - split and fragmented schools in which teachers and administrators can't present a wide diversity of ideas, where the pluralism of American culture can't come together and be exposed? (Crane, 1987).

It would be hard to present a fair and balanced view about religion, without proselytizing various doctrines, in a classroom setting.

Are churches ready to have students learn about religion and how religion has shaped the world? Historically, religion is responsible for millions of deaths around the world, from the beginning of time right up to today. It is also responsible for scientific facts taking an inordinate amount of time to be allowed into mainstream thought. The Catholic Church placed Galileo under house arrest for the last 8 years of his life because he dared to say the earth revolved around the sun and not the other way around. In modern times, Christian groups are vehemently opposed to stem cell research. Should classes

...describe a few religious holidays, list a few religious 'heroes,' and say a few pleasant things about the Pilgrims, the Quaker abolitionists, Martin Luther King Jr., Mother Teresa, Thomas Paine, Annie Besant, Avicenna, and Gandhi? Or do we also teach about the Inquisition, religious wars, persecutions and pogroms, heresy trials, terrorism, and the fact that, for every Christian abolitionist, there were many more who used the Bible to justify slavery? Do we present static pictures of a few of the "mainstream" religions, or do we also acquaint students with religious dissent, freethought, humanism, and religious liberalism? (Doerr).

Coming together to agree upon what is taught would be very difficult. In light of this, it is perfectly understandable that textbooks and educators stay away from religion in the classroom.

If it is still the goal of schools to create good citizens able to vote and perpetuate democracy in America, a question we as a society face is whether educational facilities are doing a disservice to students by not incorporating religion into classrooms. However, "(v)ery few teachers are adequately or properly trained to teach appropriately about religion. There are no standards for teacher certification." There aren't any textbooks "on the market that (are) adequately balanced, objective, and neutral" (Doerr). And yet, in present times, voters are asked to weigh in on stem-cell research, abortion, euthanasia, and same-sex marriage. Coincidentally, these topics are highly controversial on a religious level, as morally right or wrong. If schools are not taking part in teaching about religion, are they truly preparing students to make educated decisions that will shape the way our country, our natural resources, our sciences and our society continue?

Although it strayed from the curriculum, religion is a topic that has never strayed too far from the peoples' conscience. Religion may have a place in the education of America's youth. "However, constitutional requirements of objective presentation within a secular curriculum must be rigorously honored" (Branch, 2007, p. 1473). It remains for teachers and school administrations to address the best ways to inculcate religion into America's classrooms without alienating anyone within them.

TERMS & CONCEPTS

Common School: Term coined by Horace Mann, indicating a school that serves individuals of all faiths, regardless of religion, and without religious doctrine.

Proselytize: To induce one to convert to another's way of thinking or religion.

Sectarian: Relating to a particular sect or religious belief.

Secular: Separate from religion.

Separation of Church and State: Concept that government and religious organizations remain free from each other in all dealings.

Jennifer Pilicy Roberts

BIBLIOGRAPHY

Allen, B. (2006). *Moral minority: Our skeptical founding fathers.* Chicago: Ivan R. Dee Publisher.

Blum, V. C. (1987). Secularism in public schools. In *Religion and politics: Issues in religious liberty.* Hudson: Gary E. McCuen Publications, Inc.

Boller, D. (1982). Liberty and justice for some: defending a free society from the radicalright's holy war on democracy. In *Religion and politics: Issues in religious liberty.* Hudson: Gary E. McCuen Publications, Inc.

Branch, C. E. (2007). Unexcused absence: Why public schools in religiously plural society must save a seat for religion in the curriculum. *Emory Law Journal. 56,* 1431-1474. Retrieved September 29, 2007, from EBSCO Online Database Academic Search Premier.

Chavalas, M. (Ed). (2006). *Translation: The ancient near east.* Retrieved September 14, 2007, from British Museum: Cyrus Cylinder, http://britishmuseum.org.

Crane, D. (1987). CNN "Take Two." In *Religion and politics: Issues in religious liberty.* Hudson: Gary E. McCuen Publications, Inc.

Davis, D. H. (2006). *The evolution of religious liberty as a universal human right.* Retrieved September 14, 2007, from US Department of State: Democracy Dialogues: Freedom of Religion, http://usinfo.state.gov.

Doerr, E. (1987). Religion in public education. In *Religion and politics: Issues in religious liberty.* Hudson: Gary E. McCuen Publications, Inc.

Doerr, E. (1996). Teaching about religion in public schools. *Humanist, 56,* 42-43. Retrieved September 16, 2007, from EBSCO Online Database Academic Search Premier.

Engel v. Vitale. (1962). Retrieved September 22, 2001, from FindLaw, http://caselaw.lp.findlaw.com.

1st Cir. rebuffs Establishment Clause challenge to N.H.'s pledge law. (2011). *School Law News (LRP Publications), 39,* 7. Retrieved December 15, 2013, from EBSCO Online Database Education Research Complete.

Fusarelli, B.C., & Eaton, L.E. (2011). A day of silence, a day of truth, and a lawsuit. *Journal of Cases in Educational Leadership, 14,* 35-48. Retrieved December 15, 2013, from EBSCO Online Database Education Research Complete.

Kramnick, I. & Moore, L. R. (1996). *The Godless constitution: The case against religious correction.* New York: W. W. Norton & Company.

Minersville School District v. Gobitis (1940). Retrieved September 21, 2007, from FindLaw, http://caselaw.lp.findlaw.com.

Nord, W. A. (1995). *Religion and American education: Rethinking a national dilemma.* Chapel Hill: The University of North Carolina Press.

School District of Abington Township v. Schempp. (1963). Retrieved September 19, 2007 from FindLaw, http://caselaw.lp.findlaw.com.

Walsh, M. (2007). Justices decline appeal on holiday school display. *Education Week, 26,* 23. Retrieved September 17, 2007, from EBSCO Online Database Academic Search Premier.

SUGGESTED READING

Glenn, C. L. (1987). Curriculum in public schools: Can compromise be reached?" In *Religion and politics: Issues in religious liberty.* Hudson: Gary E. McCuen Publications, Inc.

Heinrich, J. (2015). The devil is in the details: In America can you really say "God" in school? *Educational Review, 67* (1), 64-78.

Hitchcock, J. (2004). *The Supreme Court and religion in American life, vol 1: Odyssey of the religion clauses.* Princeton, N.J.: Princeton University Press.

Justice, B. (2015). Originalist case against vouchers: The First Amendment, religion and public education. *Stanford Law & Policy Review, 26* (2), 437-484.

Nord, W. A. (1995). Religion and American education: Rethinking a national dilemma. Chapel Hill: The University of North Carolina Press.

Saperstein, D. & Bergstrom, C. (1987). Banning books isn't the answer. In *Religion and politics: Issues in religious liberty.* Hudson: Gary E. McCuen Publications, Inc.

Wang, C. (2013). Fostering critical religious thinking in multicultural education for teacher education. *Journal of Beliefs & Values: Studies in Religion & Education, 34,* 152-164. Retrieved December 15, 2013, from EBSCO Online Database Education Research Complete.

FREEDOM OF EXPRESSION AND PUBLIC EDUCATION

This article focuses on freedom of expression and public education. The boundaries and limits of students' rights to free expression in public schools are discussed. This article describes the relationship between freedom of expression in schools, the First Amendment, and the United States Supreme Court. Areas of inquiry include symbolic dress, free speech, and religious expression. The issues associated with government regulation and oversight of religious expression in public schools are addressed.

KEYWORDS: American Civil Liberties Union; Bill of Rights; Equal Access Act; Establishment Clause; First Amendment; Free Exercise Clause; Free Speech; Freedom of Expression; Libel; Public Education; Religious Expression; Slander; Supreme Court; Symbolic Clothing; Symbolic Dress; Symbolic Speech

OVERVIEW

In the United States, freedom of expression is guaranteed and protected by the First Amendment of the United States Constitution. The First Amendment, part of the Bill of Rights, prohibits the national government from limiting freedom of expression. The First Amendment states that the government and "Congress shall make no law respecting an establishment of religion, or prohibiting the free exercise thereof; or abridging the freedom of speech, or of the press; or the right of the people peaceably to assemble, and to petition the government for a redress of grievances." Freedom of expression refers to a person's right to say or publish what he or she believes and comes with societal and legal parameters. For example, the U.S. Supreme Court has named numerous instances of impermissible speech. Throughout the twentieth century, the Supreme Court ruled on conflict surrounding issues related to freedom of expression, such as free speech, free press, obscenity, libel, slander, symbolic speech, and commercial speech, and, as a result, has defined the parameters of free speech acceptable in society and in public schools.

The U.S. democratic process invites and facilitates questioning and challenging the rights and liberties described in the U.S. Constitution and the Bill of Rights. The U.S. Constitution and the Bill of Rights are living documents subject to ongoing reinterpretation. New environments and scenarios arise that require constitutional interpretation. Public education is a prime location of constitutional challenge and interpretation. Public institutions are held accountable for abiding by and promoting the laws of the nation. Public education and public schools are subject to the laws as specified in the U.S. Constitution. The public school system, in the twentieth century, has become a location of constitutional challenge and interpretation. The U.S. public education system, a relatively new and still evolving public program, is often in tension with constitutional law. Throughout the twentieth century, the Supreme Court has both upheld the rights of administrators to censor students' rights for free expression and the rights of students themselves. The corresponding tension is a ubiquitous part of American society. The current socio-political climate creates students who know their rights and administrators charged with protecting the safety of diverse students and communities.

Students and teachers have significantly different experiences of and protections of freedom of expression in public schools. Students' rights to freedom of expression is, for the most part, protected and guaranteed in public schools. Exceptions to student freedom of expression rights do occur. U.S. courts have found that school officials can censor student expression only when student speech is a substantial disruption of school activities or is determined to be vulgar, profane, or offensive. In contrast to the student experience, teachers, as employees, have their freedom of expression severely curtailed in the public school setting. U.S. courts have ruled that teachers may not introduce personal opinion or belief into their teaching. The First Amendment does not protect teacher speech in a public school setting (Simpson, 2007).

The following section provides an overview of the relationship between freedom of expression, the Bill of Rights, and the United States Supreme Court. This section serves as the foundation for later discussion of the connection between students' rights to free expression and public education. Areas of inquiry include symbolic dress, free speech, and religious expression. The issues associated with religious expression in the public schools, particularly the *Presidential Guidelines on Religion in the Schools,* are addressed.

FREEDOM OF EXPRESSION, THE BILL OF RIGHTS & THE U.S. SUPREME COURT

The Bill of Rights, which makes up the first ten amendments to the U.S. Constitution, was added to the U.S. Constitution in 1791. The Bill of Rights, which includes 10 Constitutional amendments from 1791, three post-Civil War amendments, and the Nineteenth Amendment from 1920, protects individual rights. The framers of the Bill of Rights, notably James Madison and Thomas Jefferson, were influenced by the Age of Enlightenment. The First Amendment illustrates the framers' high opinion of reason, truth, inquiry, liberty, and questioning of authority. The First Amendment concerns and protects freedom of speech, association, assembly, press, and religion.

First Amendment stakeholders, including policymakers, students, teachers, religious groups, and legal groups, have taken their challenges on freedom of expression issues, such as prayer, dress, and student publications, to the U.S. Supreme Court. The Constitution and the Supreme Court allow for and encourage Americans to test and establish the social and legal parameters of freedom of expression. The U.S. system of government includes two forces: Majority rule through elected representatives and limitation of power to insure individual rights. First Amendment cases are often brought by legal rights organizations such as the American Civil Liberties Union (ACLU). The American Civil Liberties Union, and other legal defense organizations, believes that freedom of expression requires constant legal vigilance and protection. The American Civil Liberties Union, established in 1920, is a legal organization dedicated to protecting civil liberties such as first amendment rights, equal protection under the law, right to due process, and right to privacy.

Numerous First Amendment cases have been heard in the U.S. Supreme Court. These cases have created the law of the land. The history of the U.S. Supreme Court's protection of First Amendment rights is relatively short. In Abrams v. U.S. (1919), the Supreme Court ruled that speech acts could only be punished if the speech act presented a clear and present danger of imminent harm. Throughout the twentieth century, the Supreme Court heard freedom of expression cases. The Supreme Court has ruled that free speech protections include nonverbal expressions. Constitutionally protected symbolic speech includes works of art, t-shirt slogans, political buttons, music lyrics, and theatrical performances ("Freedom of Expression," 1997).

The Supreme Court has also passed ruling on unprotected expression. The Supreme Court has found that government may place time, place, and manner restrictions on speech as long as the restrictions are reasonable. Examples include permits for public meeting or demonstrations. Limited exceptions to First Amendment protection were decided in the following cases. In *Chaplinsky v. New Hampshire* (1942), the Supreme Court ruled that the First Amendment does not protect fighting words intended to inflict injury or incite an immediate breach of the peace. In *New York Times Co. v. Sullivan* (1964), the Supreme Court held that defamatory falsehoods about public officials may be punished if the offended official can prove the falsehoods were published with malice. In *Miller v. California* (1973), the Supreme Court established three conditions that must be present if a work is to be deemed officially and legally obscene ("Freedom of Expression," 1997). The conditions include the following:

- The work must appeal to the average person's prurient interest in sex;
- The work must depict sexual conduct in a patently offensive way as defined by effected community;
- The work, taken as a whole, must be considered to lack serious significant literary, artistic, political, or scientific value.

Applications

STUDENTS' RIGHTS & PUBLIC EDUCATION

The U.S. Constitution does not guarantee the right to public education. Historically, public education has been the domain of individual state governments. In the second half of the twentieth century, control of public education began to switch from the state to the federal government. Areas of federal control include funding, administration, and standards. Public education in the United States, which began on a large scale in the twentieth century, is in constant tension and negotiation with the freedom of expression rights and liberties guaranteed in the Bill of Rights.

CIVIL RIGHTS ACT

The modern period of American public education, which began in the 1920s, is characterized by the rise of the testing movement, the development of adult education, the growth of progressive education, the influence of civil rights on education, the spread of federal aid to public schools, and the adoption of academic

standards. Students' civil rights and civil liberties were expanded and clarified in the Civil Rights Act of 1964. The Civil Rights Act has the following goals:

- To enforce the constitutional right to vote; to confer jurisdiction upon the district courts of the United States to provide injunctive relief against discrimination in public accommodations;
- To authorize the Attorney General to institute suits to protect constitutional rights in public facilities and public education; to empower the Commission on Civil Rights;
- To prevent discrimination in federally assisted programs;
- To establish a Commission on Equal Employment Opportunity.

DEPARTMENT OF EDUCATION

The U.S. Department of Education was established in 1980 under the Department of Education Organization Act. Prior to the Department of Education Organization Act, the Department of Education and the Department of Health and Human Services were united in one agency called the Department of Health, Education, and Welfare. The U.S. Department of Education oversees funding and education law. Today, public education is decentralized and the domain of both state and federal governments. Throughout the public education system, there is a tension between the interests of public school administrators and the individual constitutional rights of students for free expression. This tension in the public school environment and relationships is part of a larger tension between law, liberties, belief, and expression found in American democratic society (Martinson, 2000).

PREMISES OF STUDENT EXPRESSION

Civil liberties scholar Thomas Emerson argued that freedom of expression rests on four basic premises:

- The freedom of expression must ensure student self-fulfillment;
- The freedom of expression must aid the student in discovering the truth;
- The freedom of expression must aid the student to participate in decision making;
- The freedom of expression must strike a balance between stability and change.

Policymakers and school administrators have incorporated Emerson's views on free expression

(Martinson). Ultimately, public schools can control student expression in instances when the student's expression relates to pedagogical concern. Public schools cannot suppress legitimate and constitutionally protected student expression or extend control beyond the school environment (Marczely, 1992). Perceptions of student rights have changed over the last century. Student rights have been influenced by school curriculum, increased instruction regarding student rights, the civil rights movement, and courts' decisions on student rights (Ratliff, 1978). Court decisions on student rights, described below, have centered on symbolic clothing in schools, student speech, and religion in schools.

SYMBOLIC CLOTHING

Students often wear clothing or style symbolic of their political, social, or religious identity. Examples include the jilbab, political t-shirts, and Rastafarian dreadlocks (Gereluk, 2006). Are students wearing controversial clothing and styles, with politics, religion, sex, drugs, and guns content and messages, protected under the First Amendment? The U.S. Supreme Court has heard numerous cases about symbolic clothing in the public schools. In 1969, the U.S. Supreme Court heard the Tinker v. Des Moines Independent Community School District case. This case involved a situation in which a small group of students were suspended in 1965 for wearing black armbands to school to protest the United States' military action in Vietnam. The students and their supporters argued that public school administrators had violated their First Amendment rights with the suspension punishment. This case produced a landmark ruling. The U.S. Supreme Court ruled that students and teachers do not shed their constitutional rights to freedom of speech or expression at the schoolhouse gate. The U.S. Supreme Court found that schools could only censor student speech when school officials can show that student speech poses a substantial interference with the educational process. From then on, symbolic dress worn to school for political reasons became an expression protected by the First Amendment (Bowman, 2003). Numerous appeals to the Supreme Court have been made based on the Tinker ruling. For example, in 2006, the Harper v. Poway Unified School District appeal to the Supreme Court concerned the disciplining of two students who went to school wearing T-shirts with messages critical of gays (Trotter, 2006).

STUDENT SPEECH

In many instances throughout the twentieth century, students have been punished for public representation and endorsement of controversial messages at school-sponsored parades, on school grounds, and in school publications. Some students and their supporters have chosen to appeal their punishments to local and national courts. While the Supreme Court found in favor of student rights to wear symbolic clothing in 1960, the Supreme Court ruled in favor of school administrators in two landmark student speech cases in the 1980s. In 1986, the U.S. Supreme Court heard the *Bethel School District No. 403 v. Fraser* case and found that schools could censor and punish students for lewd, indecent, or offensive speech. The Supreme Court argued that public school students' First Amendment rights are not equal to those of adult citizens. In 1988, the Supreme Court heard the *Hazelwood School District v. Kuhlmeier* case and concluded that the free speech rule, as specified in the Tinker case, need not apply to school-sponsored activities. The Supreme Court found that student speech that is inconsistent with a basic educational mission may be censored (Bowman). Ultimately, U.S. courts have found that school officials can censor student expression only when student speech is a substantial disruption of school activities or is vulgar, profane, or plainly offensive (Simpson).

The Supreme Court's 1988 *Hazelwood School District v. Kuhlmeier* ruling has had a significant effect on all subsequent student speech cases and student publications in general. The Hazelwood ruling has changed the scope and focus of student journalism. Students and administrators know that censorship of student expression in school newspapers and yearbooks is constitutional so long as the speech is pedagogically relevant. The response of states to the Hazelwood ruling has been extreme. In response to the Hazelwood ruling, four states, including Arkansas, Colorado, Iowa, and Kansas, enacted state freedom of expression laws covering high school journalists. Massachusetts amended its freedom of expression law. Scholars and educators continue to look out for a Hazelwood effect on student speech. The perception remains among some educators that Hazelwood has had a major negative impact on freedom of the high school press (Paxton & Dickson, 2000).

401

FREEDOM OF RELIGION

The First Amendment includes two clauses related to religious expression: The establishment clause and the free exercise clause. The establishment clause prohibits the establishment of a nationally sanctioned religion. The free exercise clause protects rights of free speech and expression (Baylis-Heerschop, 2006). Local, state, and federal courts have heard numerous cases concerning student religious rights. For example, does the First Amendment protect a student's right to read a Bible story in class? In 1962, the U.S. Supreme Court heard *Engel v. Vitale* and ruled that the New York Regent's prayer violates the First Amendment. The State of New York was prohibited from requiring that an official state prayer be recited at the beginning of each school day. In 1985, the U.S. Supreme Court heard the *Wallace v. Jaffree* case and found that Alabama's authorization of silent prayer and teacher-led voluntary prayer violated the First Amendment. In 2000, the U.S. Supreme Court heard the *Santa Fe School District v. Doe* case and found that the district's authorization of student prayer before football games violated the First Amendment (Sass, 2007).

Issues

GOVERNMENT OVERSIGHT & REGULATION OF RELIGION IN THE PUBLIC SCHOOLS

Public schools and religious students and families have been in tension since the 1962 ruling in *Engel v. Vitale* that prohibited organized prayer in public schools. To support the public school system's efforts to abide by constitutional law, the U.S. Secretary of Education distributed a document entitled the *Presidential Guidelines for Religious Expression in Public Schools* (1995). The Secretary of Education stated that the purpose of the presidential guidelines was to end the confusion over religious expression in the nation's public schools. School administrators use these federal guidelines to direct their responses to religious expression in the schools.

THE EQUAL ACCESS ACT

The presidential guidelines are informed by and based on the Equal Access Act. The Equal Access Act, which passed in 1984, ensures that student religious activities are afforded the same access to public school facilities as student secular activities. The Equal Access Act states that schools are required to

treat all of their student-led non-curriculum clubs, including religious groups, equally. Student religious groups at public secondary schools have the same right of access to school facilities as all other comparable student groups. The Act protects prayer and worship during lunch-time and recess and guarantees equal access to means of publicizing meetings such as the announcement system, school periodicals, and bulletin board space (Riley, 1998). The guidelines cover the following topics:

- Student prayer and religious discussion: The guidelines state that students have the same right to engage in individual or group prayer and religious discussion during the school day as they do to engage in other comparable activity;
- Graduation prayer and baccalaureates: The guidelines state that school officials may not mandate or organize prayer at graduation nor organize religious baccalaureate ceremonies;
- Official neutrality regarding religious activity: The guidelines state that teachers and school administrators are representatives of the state and are prohibited by the establishment clause from soliciting or encouraging religious activity and from participating in religious activity with students;
- Teaching about religion: The guidelines state that public schools may not provide religious instruction but they may teach about religion. Examples of permissible religious studies include the history of religion, comparative religion, the Bible-as-literature, and the role of religion in the history of the United States;
- Student assignments: The guidelines state that students may express their beliefs about religion in the form of homework, artwork, and other written and oral assignments free of religious discrimination;
- Religious literature: The guidelines state that students have a right to distribute religious literature to their schoolmates on the same terms as they are permitted to distribute other literature that is unrelated to school curriculum or activities;
- Religious excusals: The guidelines state that schools enjoy discretion to excuse individual students from lessons that are objectionable to the student or the students' parents on religious grounds;
- Released time: The guidelines state that schools have the discretion to dismiss students to off-premises religious instruction;

- Teaching values: The guidelines state that schools may play an active role with respect to teaching civic values and virtue and the moral code that holds the community together;
- Student garb: The guidelines state that schools enjoy substantial discretion in adopting policies relating to student dress and school uniforms (Riley).

The *Presidential Guidelines on Religion in the Public Schools* were updated in 2001. Religious groups continue to lobby the federal government for more opportunities for prayer and religion in the schools. Negotiating constitutionally protected prayer in public schools is an ongoing process. Due to the contentious issue of religious expression in the public schools, Section 9524 of the Elementary and Secondary Education Act (ESEA) of 1965, requires the Secretary of Education to issue guidance on constitutionally protected prayer in public elementary and secondary schools. Education law requires local school districts to certify in writing to their state educational agency (SEA) that the local district has no policy that prevents constitutionally protected prayer in public schools as described in the presidential guidelines. Ultimately, the relationship between religion and public school is governed by the Constitution but overseen and mediated by the U.S. Department of Education.

CONCLUSION

While the First Amendment prohibits Congress from making laws that inhibit freedom of expression, speech, and religion, the population, as a whole, does not share all the same values. Constitutional challenge and tension arise when stakeholders hold competing values. The process of defending the First Amendment rights of students in the public schools is an ongoing process undertaken by legal organizations, families, and students themselves. At the beginning of the 21st century, defending freedom of speech and expression in the public schools is growing increasingly important and difficult as a result of technology, knowledge-sharing, globalization, and heightened student violence (Martinson).

TERMS & CONCEPTS

American Civil Liberties Union: A legal organization, established in 1920, dedicated to protecting civil liberties such as first amendment rights, equal protection under the law, right to due process, and right to privacy.

Bill of Rights: The first ten amendments to the U.S. Constitution.

Equal Access Act: An act, passed in 1984, which ensures that student religious activities are accorded the same access to public school facilities as are student secular activities.

Establishment Clause: The portion of the First Amendment that reads, "Congress shall make no law respecting an establishment of religion."

First Amendment: An amendment to the Constitution that states that the government and Congress shall make no law respecting an establishment of religion, or prohibiting the free exercise thereof; or abridging the freedom of speech, or of the press; or the right of the people peaceably to assemble, and to petition the government for a redress of grievances.

Free Exercise Clause: First Amendment provision that prohibits the government from interfering with the practice of religion.

Freedom of Expression: A person's right to say or publish what he or she believes.

Libel: The publication of false statements with the potential to damage someone's reputation.

Slander: Spoken defamation of someone's reputation.

Supreme Court: The highest federal court in the United States.

Symbolic Clothing: Clothing that represents political, social, or religious identity.

Symbolic Speech: A form of nonverbal communication.

Simone I. Flynn

BIBLIOGRAPHY

Bowman, D. (2003). Principals walk fine line on free speech. *Education Week, 22,* 1. Retrieved November 2, 2007, from EBSCO Online Database Education Research Complete.

Baylis-Heerschop, C. (2006). Prayer and the bible in schools. History of American education web project. Retrieved November 2, 2007, from http://ux1.eiu.edu.

Corngold, J. (2006). A paradigm of an intractable dilemma. *Philosophy of Education Yearbook,* 115-118. Retrieved November 2, 2007, from EBSCO Online Database Education Research Complete.

District wields inappropriate editorial control over newspaper. (2012). *Pro Principal (LRP Publications), 7,* 7-8. Retrieved December 15, 2013, from EBSCO Online Database Education Research Complete.

Elementary and secondary education. (2013). *Journal of Law & Education, 42,* 713-729. Retrieved December 15, 2013, from EBSCO Online Database Education Research Complete.

Freedom of expression. (1997). ACLU Position Paper. American Civil Liberties Union. Retrieved November 2, 2007, from http://aclu.org.

Gereluk, D. (2006). Why can't I wear this?! Banning symbolic clothing in schools. *Philosophy of Education Society Yearbook,* 106-114. Retrieved November 2, 2007, from EBSCO Online Database Education Research Complete.

Guidance on constitutionally protected prayer in public elementary and secondary schools. (2003). U.S. Department of Education. Retrieved November 2, 2007, from http://ed.gov.

Lunenburg, F.C. (2011). Do constitutional rights to freedom of speech, press, and assembly extend to students in school?. *FOCUS on Colleges, Universities & Schools, 6,* 1-5. Retrieved December 15, 2013, from EBSCO Online Database Education Research Complete.

Martinson, D. (2000). A school responds to controversial student speech: Serious questions in light of Columbine. *Clearing House, 73,* 145. Retrieved November 2, 2007, from EBSCO Online Database Education Research Complete.

Paxton, M. & Dickson, T. (2000). State free expression laws and scholastic press censorship. *Journalism & Mass Communication Educator, 55,* 50-60.

Ratliff, R. (1978). Schools, courts, and student's freedom of expression. *Educational Leadership, 35,* 634. Retrieved November 2, 2007, from EBSCO Online Database Education Research Complete.

Riley, R. (1998). Secretary of Education's statement on religious expression. U.S. Department of Education. Retrieved November 2, 2007, from http://ed.gov/Speeches/08-1995/religion.html

Sass, E. (2007). American educational history: a hypertext timeline. Retrieved November 2, 2007, from http://cloudnet.com,

Schools have legal right to bar Bible stories. (1999). *School Law News, 27,* 1-2. Retrieved November 2, 2007, from EBSCO Online Database Education Research Complete.

Simpson, M. (2007). What's disruptive? *NEA Today, 25,* 23-23. Retrieved November 2, 2007, from EBSCO Online Database Education Research Complete.

Student freedom in the wake of Hazelwood and Bethel. (1992). *The Clearing House, 65,* 269-273.

3d Circuit rules for student in Internet free speech case. (2011). *School Law News (LRP Publications), 39,* 6. Retrieved December 15, 2013, from EBSCO Online Database Education Research Complete.

Trotter, A. (2006). Student speech on the docket? *Education Week, 26,* 23-23. Retrieved November 2, 2007, from EBSCO Online Database Education Research Complete.

SUGGESTED READING

Butler, C. (2012). *Child rights: The movement, international law, and opposition.* West Lafayette, Ind.: Purdue University Press.

Holding, R. (2007). Speaking up for themselves. *Time, 169,* 65-67. Retrieved November 2, 2007, from EBSCO Online Database Education Research Complete.

Kohl, H. (1991). The politically correct bypass: multiculturalism and the public schools. *Social Policy, 22,* 33-40. Retrieved November 2, 2007, from EBSCO Online Database Education Research Complete.

Samuels, C. (2006). Guidelines urge a dialogue on gay issues in schools. *Education Week, 25,* 5-14. Retrieved November 2, 2007, from EBSCO Online Database Education Research Complete.

Waggoner, C. (2012). The impact of symbolic speech in public schools: A selective case analysis from Tinker to Zamecnik. *Ethics and Critical Thinking Journal. 2,* 1-17.

PARENTAL RIGHTS AND PUBLIC EDUCATION

Parental rights advocates believe parents should have authority to determine what, when, where, and how information is taught to children in schools. School rights advocates argue that education cannot be tailored to meet every parent's individual instructions and goals. State governments are responsible for ensuring that the educational needs of children are met, but in recent years, the federal government has become influential in shaping school standards. Many lawsuits involving parental rights in public schools have been decided by American courts. The complexity of the issue poses a continual challenge for families, schools districts, and the nation's legal system.

KEYWORDS: Advocate; Curriculum; Due Process; First Amendment; Fourteenth Amendment; Parent Rights; Psychotropic drugs; Referendum; Right; School Rights

OVERVIEW

The American public school system is responsible for creating safe learning environments in which children can expand their knowledge and skills. Approximately 50.1 million students attend public schools each day; they come from a variety of religious, cultural, educational, and economic backgrounds. Most adults agree on the importance of providing children with quality instruction designed to produce well-informed, contributing members of society. However, establishing consensus on what knowledge is, how knowledge should be communicated, and who is entitled to receive knowledge has been debated in the United States for centuries.

Parental rights advocates insist that the authority to determine educational parameters should lie in the hands of parents, citing amendments in the United States Constitution and 20th century Supreme Court rulings. School rights advocates contend that the uniqueness of the American public school environment necessitates that such power be reserved for teachers and school administrators.

HISTORICAL PERSPECTIVE

Since Horace Mann created the nation's first public school system in Massachusetts in the 1800s, American society has undergone significant changes. People in the United States have witnessed realities of war, immigration, and an expanding global economy. They have seen advances in transportation, technology, and communication. They have challenged attitudes on religion, sexuality, and politics. Changes in the ways people live, work, and think have affected American communities, businesses, governments, and families. They have also affected the American public school system.

SUPREME COURT CASES

The United States Constitution does not directly address the concept of public schooling, so each state is responsible for establishing an educational system for its citizens and resolving education-related problems. Yet, on several occasions, disagreements about parental rights in schools have demanded federal intervention: Do parents have the power to dictate which learning materials are presented to students? Can parents refuse to send children to public schools? Should parents be required to send children to public schools for a set number of years? These questions have ultimately been addressed by the United States Supreme Court. Three prominent cases present examples of Federal intervention in resolving parental rights issues:

MEYER V. STATE OF NEBRASKA

Following World War I, a school district in Nebraska was sued after a teacher offered German language instruction to students at Zion Parochial School. Nebraska law prohibited the teaching of foreign languages in public and private schools, and the Nebraska Supreme Court ruled in favor of the state. The case was appealed to the United States Supreme Court and in *Meyer v. State of Nebraska* (1923), the lower court's ruling was overturned. The Court ruled that forbidding schools to teach languages other than English violated citizens' due process protections guaranteed by the Fourteenth Amendment (*Meyer v. State of Nebraska*). In the decision written by Associate Justice James Clark McReynolds, the court showed support for parental rights in schools by emphasizing parents' constitutional liberties "to marry, to establish a home and bring up children" (*Meyer v. State of Nebraska*).

PIERCE V. SOCIETY OF SISTERS

In 1922, voters in the state of Oregon passed a referendum requiring all children in the state between the ages of 8 and 16 to attend public schools. Two private schools, the Hill Military Academy and the Society of Sisters of the Holy Names of Jesus and Mary, sued the state. They claimed that their First Amendment and Fourteenth Amendment rights had been violated. An Oregon District Court ruled in favor of the referendum, and the ruling was appealed to the United States Supreme Court. In *Pierce v. Society of Sisters* (1925), the Supreme Court ruled in favor of private schools, stating that the Oregon referendum interfered "with the liberty of parents and guardians to direct the upbringing and education of children" (*Pierce v. Society of Sisters*). According to the Court, parents must comply with compulsory attendance laws, but they maintain the right to choose between public and private school options (Russo, 2005).

WISCONSIN V. YODER

In the early 1970s, an Amish community in the state of Wisconsin refused to send their children to school after the students had graduated from the eighth grade. Wisconsin law required all students to attend school until age 16. The Amish viewed the state's law as a direct threat to their religion and cultural way of life. In *Wisconsin v. Yoder*, the Supreme Court ruled in favor of Amish parents, declaring that the state's compulsory attendance law conflicted with protections afforded by the First Amendment (*Wisconsin v. Yoder*, 1972). In the opinion of the Court, "a state's interest in universal education...is not totally free from a balancing process when it impinges on fundamental rights...and the traditional interest of parents with respect to the religious upbringing of their children...." (*Wisconsin v. Yoder*).

THE PARENTAL RIGHTS & RESPONSIBILITIES ACT

Reading, writing, math, and science remained the core of curriculum in most public schools throughout the 20th century, but changing needs of society led to changes in classrooms, too. Schools added courses in health education, sexuality, and cultural diversity. They began requiring immunizations as prerequisites for enrollment. They created student questionnaires on topics like suicide attempts, preferred sexual orientation, and typical home environments. Schools viewed the changes in curricula, medical requirements, and surveys as vital to their educational missions.

Some parents became concerned with the increasing influence and power schools had assumed. In 1993, the Parental Rights and Responsibilities Act (PRRA), was sent to Congress as legislation to limit government's involvement in children's lives, especially within the boundaries of the public school system. The bill found sponsors in 28 states (Billitteri, 1996), and its advocates claimed the legislation was needed to empower parents against the established educational bureaucracy (Billitteri).

Professional and governmental organizations, such as the National Education Association and the American Civil Liberties Union, opposed PRRA. Affording greater legal power to parents, the groups argued, would undermine the nation's public education system, lead to exorbitant legal bills incurred fighting parent-instigated court battles, and result in a lessening of child-protection standards in schools

(Billitteri). Passage of the bill, they warned, would limit schools' abilities to teach sex education courses, select library books, and offer pregnancy and drug counseling to teenagers (Billitteri). The Parental Rights and Responsibilities Act failed to pass.

Yet, the impetus that initiated PRRA did not dissipate with the bill's failure to become law. In a nationwide telephone survey conducted by International Communications Research in 1999, 52% of adults felt that schools had strayed too far from teaching the basic subject materials ("Americans willing," 1999). Many respondents wanted expanded legal control over curriculum, discipline, and values that their children were exposed to in public schools. Some parents argued it was not the job of teachers to offer curriculum instruction on subjects such as homosexuality or contraception. Others did not want schools to dictate what medications children should be required to take. A few believed school-sponsored questionnaires were too intrusive on children's privacy.

NO CHILD LEFT BEHIND ACT OF 2001

In 2001, Congress passed federal legislation, called the No Child Left Behind Act (NCLB), designed to connect federal funding with measurable improvements in public school standards. Among other things, the law required:

- Each public school teacher be certified or licensed and demonstrate mastery of relevant subject matter;
- Each student be tested in math and reading (and later science) in grades 3-8 and at least once in high school; and that;
- Parents be allowed to enroll children in an alternative school if their assigned one was identified as needing improvement ("Four Pillars," 2001).

Some parental rights advocates viewed NCLB as a positive step to ensuring parents' abilities to provide quality education to children. They believed public schools would be more accountable to taxpayers and that children would benefit from increased educational options (White, n.d.). Other parental rights advocates viewed NCLB as a negative interference by the federal government into local control of schools. They complained that programs and restrictions imposed by NCLB were not adequately funded and that standardized tests (used to measure schools' successes and failures) were unreliable (McKenzie, 2003). Both sides agreed that reforms were needed if

NCLB was to continue to shape school goals through federal funding.

In 2012 President Barack Obama began issuing waivers to states that freed them from the requirements of NCLB as long as they demonstrated that they would raise educational standards and improve accountability. By 2013 thirty-two states and the District of Columbia had been given waivers.

ONGOING ISSUES

Attempts to balance rights of parents with needs of schools continue to cause conflicts in America's public school system. The following four issues, in particular, pose significant challenges.

CURRICULUM

American courts typically rule in favor of schools when parents sue for control of school districts' curriculum choices:

- In California, a federal court ruled that a public school could require seventh-grade students to participate in a course about Islam in spite of objections from parents ("Time to restore," 2007);
- A judge in Texas ruled that schools do not have to reschedule classes to conform to an individual child's schedule (Simpson, 2003);
- A Connecticut court ruled that parents could not demand that children be excused from mandatory health education lessons (Simpson).

SEX EDUCATION

One of the most challenging curriculum questions debated, however, concerns sex education. A 2003 poll conducted by National Public Radio (NPR), the Kaiser Family Foundation, and Harvard's Kennedy School of Government found that most Americans believed basic courses on sex education should be taught in public schools ("Sex education," 2003), but lacked consensus on exactly what such education should include.

Historically, sex education programs in schools were aimed at preventing teenage pregnancy and sexually transmitted diseases. The 2003 NPR poll discovered, however, that 15 percent of adults wanted schools to limit lessons on sexuality to abstinence without providing information on contraception usage. Forty-six percent believed that teaching abstinence was best, but wanted schools to include lessons on contraceptives. Interestingly, respondents'

definitions of the word "abstinence" varied widely: some applied it to mean intercourse and oral sex, while others defined it to include kissing and intimate touching. Federal money was made available to schools willing to offer abstinence programs; thirty percent of school principals reported that their schools complied in order to receive the funds ("Sex education,").

By 2010, under President Barack Obama, the government had begun dedicating federal funding to comprehensive sex education. The administration eliminated funding for two-thirds of abstinence programs and added $190 million for new evidence-based programs. Additional funds for comprehensive and progressive programs were granted throughout 2011 and 2012. Sex education also had a place in the Patient Protection and Affordable Care Act, which included a program (the Personal Responsibility Education Program, or PREP) for personal responsibility to reduce the risk of unintended pregnancy. Among other topics, PREP teaches adolescents about how both abstinence and contraception prevent pregnancy and sexually transmitted infections.

When asked questions pertaining to homosexuality, respondents to the 2003 NPR survey were more decisive. Fifty-two percent at the time agreed schools should acknowledge and define homosexuality, but only 8% wanted it deliberately presented as an acceptable lifestyle ("Sex education,"). By 2013, nine states required an inclusive discussion of sexual orientation in sex education and American tolerance toward homosexuality had increased, with over 60 percent of people believing that gay people should be accepted in society.

MEDICAL REQUIREMENTS

Public schools have assumed a greater role in the physical and mental health of students in recent decades, and parental rights advocates have challenged schools' authority to do so.

ON-SITE HEALTHCARE

In the 1990s, the number of school-based medical clinics rose substantially, from about 200 at the beginning of the decade to 1,135 at the end (Green, 2001). The clinics were created to combat rising occurrences of HIV/AIDS, to provide contraceptives, to conduct pregnancy testing, and to offer treatments for sexually transmitted diseases. Parents were often unaware of services and medical referrals provided to students by the clinics (Green). Bauer notes, for example, a situation in which two sisters in Stephens County, Georgia, (ages 14 and 15) were transported to a birth control clinic by a public school employee without their parents' consent or knowledge; the children received birth control pills, pelvic examinations, and underwent AIDS testing (Bauer, 1997).

MEDICATIONS

In 2013 it was estimated that approximately 6.4 million children from age four to seventeen in the United States have been diagnosed with Attention Deficit Hyperactivity Disorder (ADHD). To maintain discipline in classrooms and ensure effective learning environments for all students, many schools have insisted that students suffering from the disorder take psychotropic drugs to alleviate symptoms prior to attending classes. Some parents believe schools should not have the power to require medications as prerequisites for access to public education, but attempts to pass federal legislation aimed at ending the practice have been unsuccessful ("Time to restore," 2007).

In the summer of 2006, the Centers for Disease Control and Prevention recommended that all girls be vaccinated against Human Papilloma Virus (HPV) starting at age 12. The immunization prevents a virus that is transmitted through sexual intercourse that can cause cervical cancer. Social conservatives and parental rights advocates across the nation opposed the forced immunization. By 2013 there were two HPV vaccines on the market and they are recommended for both girls and boys. Many states have legislation requiring HPV vaccinations and education.

STUDENT SURVEYS

A volunteer mental health counselor at Mesquite Elementary School in San Francisco, California sent a letter to parents informing them that students would be given a survey about early childhood experiences and asking for parental consent. The permission form did not note there would be questions of a sexual nature on the survey. The survey was administered to students at the school, ages seven to ten. In *Fields v. Palmdale School Dist.* (2005), a circuit court ruled in favor of the school, stating that while parents could determine the forum for a child's education

(Davis, 2006), parents did not have exclusive rights to provide sexual information to children and could not dictate public school curriculum (Trotter, 2006).

In *C.N. v. Ridgewood Board of Education* (2005), a New Jersey circuit court also ruled in favor of schools concerning surveys. Middle and high school students had been given a survey concerning their exposure to alcohol and drug use, sexual activity, and violence (Davis, 2006). The court ruled that school officials had not violated privacy rights of students or parents by administering a voluntary, anonymous survey on personal behaviors and relationships (Russo).

DRESS CODES

Nearly one in four public elementary schools, and one in eight public middle and high schools, in the United States have clothing policies (as cited in Motsinger, 2007), many requiring students to wear uniforms. By 2010, 10 percent of high schools required student uniforms. In *Canady v. Bossier Parish School Board* (1998), a circuit court ruled that a school had the right to require students to wear uniforms if its policy was designed to promote education and not as censorship on students' freedom of expression (*Canady v. Bossier Parish School Board*, 2001).

Yet, some parents continued to insist that school uniform rules violated First Amendment rights (Mitchell, 2003). Laura and Scott Bell sued the Anderson, Indiana school district over its policy that students wear black, navy or khaki pants or skirts and solid-color shirts with collars. The Bells claimed that in addition to violating their children's constitutional rights of free expression, the school's policy also denied them access to free education since purchasing the special clothing would cost their family more than $600 (Motsinger, 2007).

According to David Hudson, a First Amendment scholar at the First Amendment Center in Nashville, Tennessee, most lawsuits against school uniforms fail because courts view dress codes as a way to promote school learning environments and not as a direct attack on freedoms of expression (as cited in Motsinger). However, courts sometimes contradict one another in their rulings. The 9th U.S. Circuit Court ruled that a public school could ban a child from wearing an anti-homosexual T-shirt; the 2nd U.S. Circuit Court ruled that a public school could not ban a student from wearing an anti-government one ("Time to restore,").

CONCLUSION

The issue of parental rights in schools continues to challenge those invested in the education of American children. Parental rights advocates believe decisions involving children should be made by parents, and they cite the United States Constitution and past Supreme Court rulings as the legal basis for their position. They want parents to have control over what information is conveyed to children, when and where information is given, and how information is provided. School rights advocates argue that the unique environment of the public school necessitates that authority to determine what is in children's best interests be given to teachers and school administrators. They claim they cannot logistically, or financially, tailor each child's education to parents' individual instructions and goals.

Throughout the past century, United States courts have ruled on issues concerning parental rights in schools. The Supreme Court has ruled in favor of parental rights in cases involving foreign language instruction and compulsory education requirements. Lower courts have typically ruled in favor of schools concerning control over educational curriculums, school medical mandates, student privacy issues, and dress code policies.

TERMS & CONCEPTS

Advocate: To favor; to maintain a cause.

Curriculum: Courses offered by a school, or a program of courses mandated at the governmental level and required for study in the public schools.

Due Process: A legal requirement that protects an individual from unfair or unreasonable treatment as a result of enacted laws; formal legal proceedings based on established rules and principles.

First Amendment: "Congress shall make no law respecting an establishment of religion, or prohibiting the free exercise thereof; or abridging the freedom of speech, or of the press; or the right of the people peaceably to assemble...."

Fourteenth Amendment (Section 1): "...nor shall any State deprive any person of life, liberty, or property, without due process of law; nor deny to any person within its jurisdiction the equal protection of the laws."

Psychotropic Drugs: Medications that act on the mind, usually given to children with ADHD.

Referendum: A legislative measure or proposal submitted for popular vote.

Right: A claim of power, entitlement, or privilege.

Julie Baker

BIBLIOGRAPHY

Americans willing to pay for improving schools. (1999). Retrieved August 10, 2007, from http://npr.org.

Announcing proposed federal legislation to protect families: The parents' rights and responsibilities act of 2007. (2007). American Coalition for Fathers and Children. Retrieved on August 11, 2007, from http://fafny.org.

Attention deficit hyperactivity disorder (ADHD). (2007). Retrieved November 4, 2014, from http://nimh.nih.gov.

Bauer, G. L. (1997). Parental rights are fundamental. *Headway, 9,* 7. Retrieved August 8, 2007, from EBSCO Online Database Academic Search Premier.

Billitteri, T. J. (1996). Are new laws needed to empower parents? *The CQ Researcher, 6,* 937–960.

Canady v. Bossier Parish School Board, 240 F.3d 437 (5th Cir., 2001). Retrieved August 14, 2007, from http://firstamendmentschools.org.

Davis, E. (2006). Unjustly usurping the parental right: *Fields v. Palmdale School District,* 427 F.3d 1197 (9th Cir. 2005). *Harvard Journal of Law & Public Policy, 29,* 1133–1144. Retrieved August 8, 2007, from EBSCO Online Database Academic Search Premier.

Emerson, J. (2011). "Who's in a family?": Parental rights and tolerance-promoting curriculum in early elementary education. *Journal Of Law & Education, 40,* 701–710. Retrieved December 11, 2013, from EBSCO Online Database Education Research Complete.

Fege, A. F. (2013). Missing in action. *Education Week, 33,* 27. Retrieved November 4, 2014, from EBSCO Online Database Education Research Complete.

Four pillars of NCLB. (2001). Retrieved August 12, 2007, from http://ed.gov.

Green, T. L. (2001, March/April). Not in my school. *Family Voice.* Retrieved September 20, 2007, from http://cwfa.org.

Konheim-Kalkstein, Y. L. (2006). A uniform look. *American School Board Journal, 193,* 25–27. Retrieved November 4, 2014, from EBSCO Online Database Academic Search Complete.

Lavoie, D. (2007, February 16). Schools ask court to dismiss suit over homosexuality discussions. *Philadelphia Gay News, 31,* 15.

McKenzie, J. (2003). *Gambling with the children.* Retrieved August 12, 2007, from http://nochildleft.com.

Meyer v. State of Nebraska, 262 U.S. 390 (1923). Retrieved November 4, 2014, from http://law.cornell.edu.

Myers, R. S. (2011). Same-sex marriage, education, and parental rights. *Brigham Young University Education & Law Journal, 2*, 303–322. Retrieved December 11, 2013, from EBSCO Online Database Education Research Complete.

Motsinger, C. (2007, August 6). Ironing out policies on school uniforms. *USA Today*, p. 3A.

Pierce v. Society of Sisters, 268 U.S. 510 (1925). Retrieved November 4, 2014, from http://law.cornell.edu.

Price, J. H. (2006, April 30). Parents sue school over gay storybook. *The Washington Times*, p. A2.

Robelen, E. W. (2012). N.H. parents gain leverage to challenge curricula. *Education Week, 31*, 6. Retrieved November 4, 2014, from EBSCO Online Database Education Research Complete.

Russo, C. (2005). Conflicts over directing the education of children: Who controls, parents or school officials? *Journal of Education, 186*, 27. Retrieved August 8, 2007, from EBSCO Online Database Academic Search Premier.

Sex education in America: An NPR/Kaiser/Kennedy School Poll. (2003). Retrieved August 10, 2007, from http://npr.org.

Simpson, M. D. (2003). Judges reject 'parental rights.' *NEA Today, 22*, 20. Retrieved August 8, 2007, from EBSCO Online Database Academic Search Premier.

Time to restore parental rights. (2007, March 18). *Chattanooga Times Free Press*, p. B9.

Trotter, A. (2006). Justices decline to hear parental-rights appeal. *Education Week, 26*, 20. Retrieved August 8, 2007, from EBSCO Online Database Academic Search Premier.

Westman, J. C. (2012). A parenthood pledge as the prerequisite for parental rights. *Brown University Child & Adolescent Behavior Letter, 28*, 8. Retrieved December 11, 2013, from EBSCO Online Database Education Research Complete.

Weyrich, P. M. (2007, February 22). *Public schools: Parental rights in jeopardy.* Retrieved August 8, 2007, from http://web.renewamerica.us.

White, D. (n.d.). *Pros & cons of the No Child Left Behind Act.* Retrieved August 12, 2007, from http://usliberals.about.com.

Wilson, B. (2007, February 5). *States consider requiring HPV vaccine for girls.* Retrieved August 10, 2007, from http://npr.org.

Wisconsin v. Yoder, 406 U.S. 205 (1972). Retrieved November 4, 2014, from http://law.cornell.edu.

SUGGESTED READING

Darden, E. C. (2013). Does safety conflict with parental rights?. *Phi Delta Kappan, 94*, 68–69. Retrieved December 11, 2013, from EBSCO Online Database Education Research Complete.

Holtzman, M. (2013). GLBT parents' rights during custody decision making: The influence of doctrine, statute, and societal factors in the United States. *Journal of GLBT Family Studies, 9*, 364–392. Retrieved December 11, 2013, from EBSCO Online Database Education Research Complete.

Kertscher, T. (2006, May 16). The survey says what? Sexual-orientation questions cause stir at Port high school. *Milwaukee Journal Sentinel*, pp. 1A, 8A.

Maddox, N. T. (2012). Silencing students' cell phones beyond the schoolhouse gate: Do public schools' cell phone confiscation and retention policies violate parents' due process rights? *Journal of Law & Education, 41*, 261–269. Retrieved November 4, 2014, from EBSCO Online Database Education Research Complete.

Mitchell, H. W. & Knechtle, J. C. (2003). Uniforms in public schools and the first amendment: A constitutional analysis. *Journal of Negro Education, 72*, 487. Retrieved August 13, 2007, from EBSCO Online Database Academic Search Premier.

Morgan, K. L. (1997). *Real choice, real freedom.* Lanham, MD: University Press of America.

Peters, S. F. (2003). *The Yoder case.* Lawrence, KS: University Press of Kansas.

Simpson, M. D. (2002). ESEA extends federal reach in schools. *NEA Today 20*, 20. Retrieved August 13, 2007, from EBSCO Online Database Academic Search Premier.

Viteriti, J. P. (1999). *Choosing equality: School choice, the constitution, and civil society.* Washington, DC: Brookings Institution Press.

STUDENT RIGHTS IN THE PUBLIC SCHOOLS

The First and Fourth Amendments have had an increasing relevance on student rights in American public schools. The First Amendment is often drawn into debates on the protections and limitations of students' freedoms of speech and expression in library book selections, school publications and presentations, and clothing options. The Fourth Amendment is often cited in cases of students' privacy rights as imposed by search and seizure practices, uses of technology, and changes in federal legislation. Discussion and difficulties continue as families, school districts, and the U.S. legal system seek to balance student rights with the needs of public schools.

KEYWORDS: Due Process; First Amendment; Fourteenth Amendment, Section 1; Fourth Amendment; In Loco Parentis; Probable Cause; Reasonable Suspicion; Search; Search Warrant; Seizure

OVERVIEW

The definition of student rights in American public schools– and the extent to which that definition may legally be applied– has undergone significant changes in the past fifty years. Prior to the 1970s, the role of schoolteachers and administrators was viewed by courts as *in loco parentis,* in place of the parents. School district officials were legally empowered to determine what constituted acceptable forms of speech, expression, and privacy for students entrusted to their care. Students were expected to conform to schools' policies just as they would to parental rules.

In the 1969 case of *Tinker v. Des Moines Independent Community School District,* however, the Supreme Court declared that students did not lose their constitutional rights upon entering a public school facility. The judgment was a direct challenge to the traditional definition of *in loco parentis.* In subsequent decades, the American legal system, school districts, and families have struggled to define the exact extent to which constitutional rights apply to students. Debates between those interested in providing safe and effective learning environments and those demanding students' rights to certain freedoms and protections resulted in an unprecedented number of legal battles. The most debated issues centered on interpretations of the First Amendment and the Fourth Amendment to the United States Constitution.

STUDENT RIGHTS & THE FIRST AMENDMENT

The First Amendment states:

"Congress shall make no law respecting an establishment of religion, or prohibiting the free exercise thereof; or abridging the freedom of speech, or of the press; or the right of the people peaceably to assemble...."

The amendment protects the rights of citizens to speak, write, assemble, and worship without fear of government censure. But what if the demands for freedom of speech are made by children in a public school setting?

In the 1960s, several students in Des Moines, Iowa wore black armbands to school in protest of the Vietnam War. School officials forced them to remove the bands, and a lawsuit was filed claiming that the students' First Amendment rights to freedom of speech and expression had been violated. Heder (1999) explains that in *Tinker v. Des Moines Independent Community School District* (1969), the United States Supreme Court acknowledged the necessity for schools to maintain order and control of students' conduct, but ruled in favor of the students by declaring that children did not lose their constitutional rights when they attended school. The ruling protected the rights of the Des Moines students to political freedom of expression, but it also served as a foundation for future constitutional debates involving a variety of issues surrounding other modes of expression like school library books, publications, assembly speeches and clothing choices.

LIBRARY BOOKS

The Court viewed the Des Moines students' armbands as reflections of individuals' opinions and ruled in favor of protecting such forms of expression. In another legal case, argued thirteen years later, the Supreme Court again ruled in favor of students' First Amendment rights by protecting their access to controversial books in school libraries. In *Island Trees School District Board of Education v. Pico* (1982), students sued the Island Trees Union Free School District in New York after school board members refused to permit several books, which it described as "anti-American, anti-Christian, anti-Sem[i]tic, and just plain filthy" (*Island Trees School District Board of Education v. Pico,* 1982, para. 1), to be placed on school library shelves for students to check out. The Supreme Court ruled that the school board could not ban library books based on its own political opinions, religious preferences, or nationalism (*Island Trees School District Board of Education v. Pico*). More recently, in *Counts v. Cedarville School District,* an Arkansas district court ruled that requiring students to obtain parental permission prior to checking particular books out of school libraries (in this case, books in the Harry Potter series) infringed on students' First Amendment rights to free speech and press (DeMitchell & Carney, 2005).

STUDENT PUBLICATIONS

Does the First Amendment's protection of free speech and press also give students the right to publish, in school-sponsored forums, opinions that school officials perceive as controversial or offensive? In *Hazelwood School District v. Kuhlmeier* (1988), the Supreme Court said no.

In 1983, a school principal in St. Louis County, Missouri removed from a high school newspaper two stories which described students' personal experiences with pregnancy and divorce. In *Hazelwood School District v. Kuhlmeier*, the Supreme Court ruled that students' First Amendment rights were not violated by the actions of the school since the newspaper was not a forum for public expression. The paper's contents, declared the Court, were subject to reasonable censorship by school officials (*Hazelwood School District v. Kuhlmeier*, 1988).

OFFENSIVE LANGUAGE & FREE SPEECH RIGHTS

The Supreme Court also ruled on pivotal cases involving students' freedom of expression in speeches given on school property and on banners displayed off school property.

In *Bethel School District No. 403 v. Fraser* (1986), the Court was asked to decide if a student's First Amendment rights had been violated when he was suspended from school for using obscene words and sexual metaphors during a speech given at a school assembly. The Supreme Court ruled that the student's rights had not been violated and declared that his language was inappropriate and detrimental to the school's educational mission (*Bethel School District No. 403 v. Fraser*).

In *Morse v. Frederick* (2007), the Supreme Court was asked to decide if a student's First Amendment rights had been violated when he was suspended for unfurling a 14-foot banner that read "Bong Hits For Jesus" while participating in a school activity. The Court narrowly ruled in favor of the school, noting that the banner's message was inappropriate for a student in spite of the fact that it was displayed on a public sidewalk and not on school property (*Morse v. Frederick*).

CLOTHING

Nearly one in four public elementary schools and one in eight public middle and high schools in the United States have policies limiting students' clothing choices (Motsinger, 2007). In lawsuits contesting the policies, courts generally rule in favor of schools.

Many large school districts argue that dress codes, including school uniform policies, are vital to prohibiting students' physical expressions of gang membership or hate-group messages. In *Jeglin v. San Jacinto Unified School District* (1993), for example, a school's dress code, which prohibited clothing with sports team insignias because gang members often bullied and intimidated students who wore them, was challenged. The court ruled in favor of the school's policy, declaring that the regulations were designed to promote student safety (LaMorte, 1999).

In another case, a student was suspended for wearing sagging pants in violation of a school's dress code policy. The student sued the school district, claiming that his First Amendment rights to freedom of expression and his Fourteenth Amendment rights to due process had been violated. Attorneys for the school argued that the dress code was needed since the act of wearing such pants was a physical symbol of gang membership. In *Bivens v. Albuquerque Public Schools* (1997), the court ruled in favor of the school (*Bivens v. Albuquerque Public Schools*). According to David Hudson, a First Amendment scholar at the First Amendment Center in Nashville, Tennessee, most dress code lawsuits fail because courts view schools' clothing policies as a method to promote learning environments and not as a direct attack on freedoms of expression (as cited in Motsinger).

But the issue of school dress codes continues to draw both strong support and strong opposition throughout the country. Laura and Scott Bell, for example, recently sued the Anderson, Indiana school district over its policy requiring students to wear black, navy or khaki pants or skirts and solid-color shirts with collars. The Bells claimed that, in addition to violating their children's constitutional rights of free expression, the school's policy also denied them access to free education since purchasing the special clothing would cost their family more than $600 (Motsinger).

Charles Haynes, of the First Amendment Center, promotes ending dress-code policies altogether in American public schools for three reasons:

- Limiting students' clothing choices conflicts with America's tradition of free choice;
- Conflicts over dress codes increase the number of lawsuits in the nation's already burdened court system;
- Uniformity limits expressions of diversity (Carroll, 2005).

Stephen Daniels of the North Carolina Family Policy Council points out, however, that in spite of any public opposition, a majority of school principals will continue to enforce dress codes because they perceive them as having positive influence on school discipline, safety, and overall student learning goals (Carroll).

STUDENT RIGHTS & THE FOURTH AMENDMENT

The Fourth Amendment states:

"The right of the people to be secure in their persons, houses, papers, and effects, against unreasonable searches and seizures, shall not be violated, and no Warrants shall issue, but upon probable cause, supported by Oath or affirmation, and particularly describing the place to be searched, and the persons or things to be seized."

The Fourth Amendment protects rights of ordinary citizens to privacy, but defining the extent to which it applies in a public school setting has resulted in numerous lawsuits and government legislation. Springer (2002) uses the legal case of *Owasso Independent School District v. Falvo* (2001) as a simple example of school-related privacy confrontations. An Oklahoma mother claimed that her children's rights to privacy were violated when a teacher required them and their classmates to exchange papers for peer grading. The Supreme Court heard the case and ruled that although students may have been embarrassed by peer access to individual grades on assignments, the use of a paper-exchange grading process in classrooms did not violate their rights of privacy (Springer).

Other student privacy issues considered by judges and government officials have included the legality of searches and seizures, surveillance systems, and access to academic records.

SEARCH & SEIZURE

In 1980, a teacher at Piscataway High School in Middlesex County, New Jersey discovered two 14-year-old girls smoking in a school restroom and took them to the vice principal's office. One girl refused to confess to smoking, and the vice principal searched inside her purse. He found a package of cigarettes, cigarette-rolling papers, some marijuana, a pipe, empty plastic bags, a large amount of money, a list of students who owed money to the girl, and letters suggesting she was dealing marijuana. The girl, known as "T.L.O." in court documents, confessed to police that she had sold drugs at school, and charges were filed against her (*New Jersey v. T.L.O.*, 1985).

In court hearings, T.L.O.'s attorney argued that the vice principal's actions had violated the girl's Fourth Amendment rights against unreasonable search and seizure because the vice principal had not obtained a search warrant prior to looking through her purse (*New Jersey v. T.L.O.*). In the landmark case, the Supreme Court ruled in favor of the New Jersey school and declared:

- Students have less privacy rights than ordinary citizens;
- School officials do not need to obtain warrants prior to conducting searches;
- Searches are acceptable if school officials use methods that are not excessively intrusive for the age and sex of students involved (*New Jersey v. T.L.O.*).

In *Vernonia School District v. Acton* (1995), the Supreme Court expanding its ruling on the issue of searches and seizures in public schools. Authorities at Vernonia School District in Oregon, acting on an informer's tip that student athletes were involved in the school's drug problem, conducted random urinalysis testing on all students who were participating in its athletic programs. One student refused to submit to the test, and he was not allowed to join the school's football team. The student and his parents filed a lawsuit against the school district, claiming violation of his Fourth Amendment rights due to unreasonable search. The Supreme Court ruled that in circumstances when drug use by student athletes potentially affects school safety, random drug testing is justified (*Vernonia School District v. Acton*). In 2002, the Court ruled to permit random drug testing of all public school students who participate in all extracurricular activities (*Board of Education v. Earls*, 2002).

Searches and seizures in schools have been used to promote safety and deter misbehavior, but their legality and necessity continue to be debated. Torres and Chen (2006) argue that courts have not sufficiently defined what constitutes a reasonable suspicion, who can conduct searches, or the extent to which invasion into students' privacy is legal. Political science professors Joe Blankenau and Mark Leeper contend that random school searches are not only ineffective, but teach children that a school's need for authority is more important than a student's right to privacy (cited in Carroll).

SURVEILLANCE

In the 1990s, some public schools in the United States installed video surveillance cameras in their buildings and on buses to aid in tracking students' movements and behaviors. Decisions to use monitoring devices were prompted by increases in school violence, expanded criminal activities on school campuses, and a number of sensationalized school shootings. By the year 2000, according to statistics compiled by the United States Department of Education, nearly 15% of public schools relied on surveillance equipment to enhance their safety strategies (US Department of Education, 2003).

Innovations in technology led to the expansion of surveillance use in public schools throughout the early years of the 21st century. Tewksbury Memorial High School in Massachusetts, for example, installed video cameras that were linked to monitors mounted at the town's local police station and inside its police cruisers ("Caught on Camera," 2002). Other school districts invested in computer software programs designed to send parents up-to-the-minute information via e-mail if a child was absent from class or misbehaved during school hours (Pascopella, 2002).

ACCESS TO ACADEMIC RECORDS

For three decades, the Family Educational Rights and Privacy Act of 1974 (FERPA) gave parents and students the right to privacy in matters concerning academic records. Under FERPA regulations, any school that received federal monies could not release information about a student's grades or educational progress to third parties without the permission of the student or the student's parents (Carroll).

Following the terrorist attacks on the United States in September, 2001, the federal government created the "Uniting and Strengthening America by Providing Appropriate Tools Required to Intercept and Obstruct Terrorism Act" (USA PATRIOT Act). The Act altered the primary rule of FERPA by allowing the nation's Attorney General, or his assistant, to obtain court orders giving access to academic records without informing students (Carroll).

VIEWPOINTS

Some argue that courts have not done enough to protect student rights guaranteed in the United States Constitution. Journalism professor David L. Martinson promotes expansion of students' freedoms of speech and expression, claiming that such freedoms give students outlets for tensions and frustrations (Carroll). Heder believes the tendency of courts to favor schools in privacy-related lawsuits will lead to more frequent searches of students' property, increase the presence of police-liaison officers in school hallways, and broaden the use of metal detectors in school entrances. Such limitations on student rights, Nancy Murray of the American Civil Liberties Union fears, will make American public schools resemble prison facilities (cited in "Caught on Camera").

Others argue the courts have not done enough to protect schools' rights to implement policies and actions for ensuring safety. Author David L. Stader, for example, argues that the First Amendment should not give students unlimited power to conduct "verbal, written, or symbolic expression that is obscene, intimidating, or threatening" to the mission of public schools (as cited in Carroll). Concern about schools' rights even prompted the United States House of Representatives to consider legislation, called the Student and Teacher Safety Act of 2006, aimed at limiting students' freedoms on school property. The bill did not become law, but it would have allowed school officials to conduct random searches of any public school student as long as the searches were done to ensure classrooms, school buildings, school property, and students "remain[ed] free from the threat of all weapons, dangerous materials, or illegal narcotics" (Student and Teacher Safety Act).

Student rights advocates continue to insist that freedoms and protections guaranteed in the United States Constitution should be preserved for students. School officials argue that restrictions must be imposed on students' rights in order to ensure conditions of safety and optimal learning. Determining the legal boundaries of First Amendment and Fourth Amendment applications to issues of student rights in public schools continues to challenge the nation's families, school districts, and legal system.

TERMS & CONCEPTS

Due Process: a legal requirement that protects an individual from unfair or unreasonable treatment as a result of enacted laws; formal legal proceedings based on established rules and principles.

First Amendment: "Congress shall make no law respecting an establishment of religion, or prohibiting the free exercise thereof; or abridging the freedom of speech, or of the press; or the right of the people peaceably to assemble...."

Fourteenth Amendment, Section 1: "...nor shall any State deprive any person of life, liberty, or property, without due process of law; nor deny to any person within its jurisdiction the equal protection of the laws."

Fourth Amendment: "The right of the people to be secure in their persons, houses, papers, and effects, against unreasonable searches and seizures, shall not be violated, and no Warrants shall issue, but upon probable cause, supported by Oath or affirmation, and particularly describing the place to be searched, and the persons or things to be seized."

In Loco Parentis: in place of the parent; in the role of a parent with respect to the care, supervision, and discipline of a child.

Probable Cause: based on facts and circumstances that would lead a reasonable person to believe a law is being, or has been, violated.

Reasonable Suspicion: a reasonable belief based on circumstances or information, but without proof, that something wrong or illegal has occurred.

Search: the examination of a person's home, car, or other personal space, or person, in an attempt to find something that is illegal or stolen or that provides some evidence of that person's guilt of some criminal act.

Search Warrant: a written order, signed by a judge, which directs an official to look for stolen goods or unlawful possessions and bring them to court for use in criminal prosecution.

Seizure: when a person or property is forcefully taken away by legal process.

Julie Baker

BIBLIOGRAPHY

Bethel School District No. 403 v. Fraser, 478 U.S. 675 (1986). Retrieved August 24, 2007, from http://oyez.org.

Bivens v. Albuquerque Public Schools, 131 F.3d 151 (10th Cir., 1997). Retrieved August 17, 2007, from http://openjurist.org.

Board of Education v. Earls, 536 U.S. 822 (2002). Retrieved July 30, 2007, from http://oyez.org.

Carey, J. (2014). A student's right to remain silent. *Journal of Law & Education, 43,* 575–580. Retrieved October 10, 2014, from EBSCO Online Database Education Research Complete.

Carroll, J. (2005). *Students' rights: Opposing viewpoints.* Farmington Hills, MI: Greenhaven Press.

Caught on camera. (2002). *Current Events, 101,* 3. Retrieved October 10, 2014, from EBSCO Online Database Academic Search Complete.

DeMitchell, T. A., & Carney, J. J. (2005). Harry Potter and the public school library. *Phi Delta Kappan, 87,* 159–165. Retrieved September 21, 2007, from EBSCO Online Database Education Research Complete.

Epley, B. (2013). Educators' personal liability for violating student rights. *Kappa Delta Pi Record, 49,* 126–130. Retrieved December 15, 2013, from EBSCO Online Database Education Research Complete.

Hazelwood School District v. Kuhlmeier, 484 U.S. 260 (1988). Retrieved August 17, 2007, from http://oyez.org.

Heder, B. O. (1999). The development of search and seizure law in public schools. *Brigham Young University Education & Law Journal, 99,* 71–118. Retrieved July 30, 2007, from EBSCO Online Database Education Research Complete.

Island Trees School District Board of Education v. Pico, 457 U.S. 853 (1982). Retrieved August 17, 2007, from http://oyez.org.

LaMorte, M. W. (1999). *School law: Cases and concepts.* Boston: Allyn and Bacon.

Lunenburg, F. C. (2011). Do constitutional rights to freedom of speech, press, and assembly extend to students in school? *FOCUS on Colleges, Universities & Schools, 6.* Retrieved December 15, 2013, from EBSCO Online Database Education Research Complete.

Morse v. Frederick, 551 U.S. 393 (2007). Retrieved August 16, 2007, from http://oyez.org.

Motsinger, C. (2007, August 6). Ironing out policies on school uniforms. *USA Today.* Retrieved August 24, 2007, from EBSCO Online Database Regional Business News Plus.

New Jersey v. T.L.O, 469 U.S. 325 (1985). Retrieved July 30, 2007, from http://oyez.org.

Pascopella, A. (2002). The spy who loved me: Software that can track a student's every move. *District Administration, 38,* 22–28. Retrieved August 14, 2007, from EBSCO Online Database Education Research Complete.

Springer, A. D. (2002). Do students have a right to privacy? *Academe, 88,* 70. Retrieved August 14, 2007, from EBSCO Online Database Academic Search Premier.

Spung, A. (2011). From backpacks to Blackberries: (Re)examining New Jersey V.T.L.O. in the age of the cell phone. *Emory Law Journal, 61,* 111–159. Retrieved December 15, 2013, from EBSCO Online Database Education Research Complete.

Student and Teacher Safety Act of 2006, H.R. 5295, 109th Cong. (2006). Retrieved August 24, 2007, from https://govtrack.us.

Time to restore parental rights. (2007, March 18). *Chattanooga Times Free Press*, p. B9.

Torres, M. S., Jr. (2012). Differentiated jurisprudence? Examining students' Fourth Amendment court decisions by region of country. *Journal of School Leadership, 22*, 1087–1108. Retrieved October 10, 2014, from EBSCO Online Database Education Research Complete.

Torres, M. S., Jr., & Chen, Y. (2006). Assessing Columbine's impact on students' Fourth Amendment case outcomes: Implication for administrative discretion and decision making. *NASSP Bulletin, 90*, 185–206. Retrieved July 30, 2007, from EBSCO Online Database Education Research Complete.

United States. Department of Education. National Center for Education Statistics. (2003). *A brief profile of America's public schools* (NCES 2003-418). Washington, DC: US Government Printing Office. Retrieved August 24, 2007, from http://nces.ed.gov.

Vernonia School District v. Acton, 515 U.S. 646 (1995). Retrieved July 30, 2007, from http://oyez.org.

Warnick, B. R. (2012). Student rights to religious expression and the special characteristics of schools. *Educational Theory, 62*, 59–74. Retrieved December 15, 2013, from EBSCO Online Database Education Research Complete.

SUGGESTED READING

Buckley, P. (2014). Subjects, citizens, or civic learners? Judicial conceptions of childhood and the speech rights of American public school students. *Childhood, 21*, 226–241. Retrieved October 10, 2014, from EBSCO Online Database Education Research Complete.

Finn, K., & Willert, J. (2006). Alcohol and drugs in schools: Teachers' reactions to the problem. *Phi Delta Kappan, 88*, 37–40. Retrieved July 30, 2007, from EBSCO Online Database Education Research Complete.

Hoff, D. L., & Mitchell, S. N. (2007). Should our students pay to play extracurricular activities? *Education Digest, 72*, 27–34. Retrieved August 14, 2007, from EBSCO Online Database Education Research Complete.

Pierce West, S. (2016). They've got eyes in the sky: How the Family Educational Rights and Privacy Act governs body camera use in public schools. *American University Law Review*, 65 (6), 1533-1567.

Rathbone, C. H. (2005). A learner's bill of rights. *Phi Delta Kappan, 86*, 471–473. Retrieved August 14, 2007, from EBSCO Online Database Education Research Complete.

Reutter, E. E. (1975). *The courts and student conduct.* Topeka, KS: National Organization on Legal Problems of Education.

Silverman, F. (2004, Nov.). Student suits. *District Administration*. Retrieved August 14, 2007, from http://districtadministration.com.

Essay by Julie Baker, M.Ed. Julie Baker is an adjunct professor of writing at Daniel Webster College and Southern New Hampshire University. She earned an M.Ed from the Lynch School of Education at Boston College and is the author of several history-related books for young adult readers.

UNDOCUMENTED IMMIGRANT STUDENTS

This article presents an illustration of the positive and negative impacts on school systems that children of undocumented immigrants present as unwitting components (and, sometimes, victims) of the complex issue of immigration. Second, this article attempts to separate the politics of the issue from the welfare of the students, assessing the advantages, disadvantages, and performance of children of undocumented immigrants while enrolled in public schools. Within this framework, the reader gains an interesting perspective on an important if underreported part of the enormous and extremely complex issue of immigration in the twenty-first-century United States.

KEYWORDS: English as a Second Language; No Child Left Behind; Plyler v. Doe; Public School; Student Performance; Undocumented Immigrant

OVERVIEW

Countless world events and trends have caused significant increases in emigration and immigration throughout the world. War, civil conflict, natural disasters, poverty, famines, and (innocuously enough) the opportunity for better jobs have sent countless individuals and their families in search of a new life in a neighboring or distant nation.

At the turn of the twentieth century, the United States, a nation founded by immigrants, found itself in a conflicted policy situation. On one hand, a steady influx of German, Irish, and southern European immigrants filled previously vacant factory jobs, fueling a fragile pre-Depression American economy. On the other hand, the increase in foreign workers (and their families) was seen as a threat to legal residents' way of life. The policy response from legislators was to create quotas on immigration. In 1921, Congress passed the Emergency Quota Act, severely curtailing the number of immigrants allowed into the country each year. Three years later, deeming the 1921 law too lenient, Congress passed the Immigration Act of 1924. Nearly 500,000 immigrants were denied entry into the US each year thereafter, although 150,000 to 200,000 northern and western European aliens continued to enter the country at the same time.

Although repeated attempts have been made throughout modern U.S. history to curtail immigration and, in particular, illegal immigration, the number of those who seek to experience the American dream by leaving their home countries continues to rise. According to the Center for Immigration Studies, there were about 40 million immigrants in the country in 2010, and an estimated 28 percent of those (over 11 million) were here illegally (Camarota, 2012).

With millions of undocumented immigrants, it comes as no surprise that this issue has become such a sensitive and yet salient one for nearly every facet of the American political economy. Reforming current immigration laws to govern those illegal migrants who are already in the country, as well as stemming the tide of those who seek to cross U.S. borders, remains just as pivotal in the twenty-first century among political aspirants as it was nearly a hundred years ago.

Of course, it is difficult to estimate exactly how many individuals are in this nation illegally. The Pew Hispanic Center puts the number of illegal immigrants in the United States in 2010 at about 11.2 million (after peaking at 12.2 million in 2007). Of that figure, approximately 1 million were children under the age of 18 (Passel & Cohn, 2011).

What does this high number of school-aged illegal immigrants mean for the American public school system? This question has been a focal point for education researchers, as well as a politically charged issue among pro- and anti-immigration activists. This paper takes a critical look at the issue and presents an illustration of the positive and negative impacts on school systems and public funds that children

of undocumented immigrants present as unwitting components (and, sometimes, victims) of the complex issue of immigration. Second, this paper attempts to separate the politics of the issue from the welfare of the students, assessing the advantages, disadvantages, and performance of children of undocumented immigrants while enrolled in public schools. Within this framework, the reader gains an interesting perspective on an important if underreported part of the enormous and extremely complex issue of immigration in the twenty-first-century United States.

Applications

THE MANY FACES OF PUBLIC SCHOOL

In 1975, the Texas Legislature modified its education laws in reaction to the influx of illegal immigrants into the state. The new laws allowed the state to withhold funding for local school districts that allowed the children of illegal immigrants to attend public education institutions. They also authorized local districts to deny enrollment for the children of people who were not "legally admitted" into the country. A class action suit was summarily filed on behalf of a group of Mexican students who claimed that under the 14th Amendment, they were entitled to equal protections and services under the law, and that the Texas laws were unconstitutional.

When the case, *Plyler v. Doe*, reached the US Supreme Court in 1981, the plaintiffs' case was validated, albeit by a narrow majority, and a tremendously polarizing issue was borne: allowing illegal aliens (and their children) the right to attend US public schools. Writing for the majority, Justice William Brennan stated that regardless of an immigrant's legal status, he or she should receive protections and public services as long as they are in the nation:

"Appellants argue at the outset that undocumented aliens, because of their immigration status, are not 'persons within the jurisdiction' of the State of Texas, and that they therefore have no right to the equal protection of Texas law. We reject this argument. Whatever his status under the immigration laws, an alien is surely a 'person' in any ordinary sense of that term" (Cornell University Law School, 2007).

Although the Supreme Court's decision cemented the rights and protections owed to all residents of the

United States (whether here legally or illegally), the backlash that occurred thereafter is one that continues to divide the American public decades later.

BEHIND THE BACKLASH

There are two main elements at play in explaining the public's push against allowing the children of illegal immigrants access to public services and, in particular, public schooling. The first of these factors is the belief that illegal immigrants, as the term suggests, are breaking the law by entering without documentation and drawing state benefits without contributing to the system. In 2003, the state of Oregon considered passage of a law that allows the children of illegal immigrants to pay in-state tuition for state colleges if they graduate from an Oregon high school, a bill that would mirror similar laws in California, Washington, and several other states. Opposition was fierce, as is the case nationwide. A representative for one anti-illegal immigrant group summarized the opposition: Jim Ludwick, president of Oregonians for Immigration Reform, said of the measure, "This is a slap in the face to everyone who believes in the rule of law. No matter what you do for these people, it's not enough, they want more. The sky's the limit" ("More in-state tuition," 2003). Whether or not Mr. Ludwick's stance is entirely accurate is debatable, as undocumented immigrants cannot receive Medicaid, welfare, or food stamps; although they do frequently use hospital emergency rooms, they do pay sales and payroll taxes, and one in three pays income taxes (Mallaby, 2007). Regardless, however, the perception espoused by a growing percentage of the population that the government must halt benefits for undocumented immigrants remains a driving force behind opposition to allowing their children access to public schools.

The second factor is one that is not necessarily relevant to the educational needs of children. The fear of Americans losing jobs to immigrants, an issue that is centuries old, remains salient among workers. In 2007, legislative efforts to extend an exemption to the seasonal foreign worker laws (known as H-2B visas), one that allows foreign workers to return to the same job in the following year without applying for a new visa, fell short of expectations. The biggest opposition to this exemption came not from xenophobic attitudes (although such sentiments almost certainly existed as well) but from those who fear losing jobs.

This position is unfounded, as the H-2B visa program requires that employers exhaust all recruitment resources for local residents before they look abroad for seasonal assistance. Interestingly, this fact plays out in industries in which "undocumented" workers are employed (allegedly unbeknownst to the employers) in great numbers versus more homogenous workplaces. One pundit has suggested that those who angrily denounce the presence of illegal aliens in the workforce as detrimental to the American worker do not work in the same areas in which foreign employees operate (Thredgold, 2006). Nevertheless, the perception that foreign workers will take American jobs, which remains a major political issue on both sides of the aisle, plays into the US population's attitudes concerning the children of illegal aliens.

A COST-BENEFIT ANALYSIS?

Because they are denied federal services such as welfare and food stamps, and because their immigration status cannot be questioned for enrollment in public schools, it is difficult to accurately gauge how many children in the public school system are in fact from families of illegal immigrants. Still, rough estimates can assist in painting a picture of the number as well as performance of the children of undocumented immigrants in schools. The Bell Policy Center, for example, estimated in 2006 that there are about 29,000 undocumented children aged 5 to 17 living in Colorado. If the average state funding per pupil is nearly $6,200 and each of these school-aged children were enrolled in the public system, the Center determined, then Colorado paid approximately $176 million to educate undocumented children (Jones & Baker, 2006).

Thanks to *Plyler v. Doe,* children of undocumented immigrants have the ability to enroll in public schools. This fact also means that school administrations are therefore not "deputized" as enforcers of immigration laws. This freedom means that backgrounds are not investigated and, unless a child makes his or her status known to the administration voluntarily, there is no way to truly determine the size of this demographic *and* there is no way to fully assess the performance of these children within the system. In light of the status of their parents, who are statistically likely to have poverty-level incomes, speak limited or no English, and are not likely to have advanced educational backgrounds, these children may have certain disadvantages that may hinder their progress. Still, without the ability to identify individuals within this demographic, any accurate illustration of their performance is at best limited.

In a rural Texas community, the fact that children of illegal immigrants go unidentified recently caused a nightmarish scene at its 4,000-student school district. After a morning immigration raid at a meat-packing plant, school personnel became aware of the arrests only because of the hundreds of federal agents and vehicles that clogged the roads of this small town as they proceeded to the plant. The school superintendent, who suspected a federal raid, knew with absolute certainty that the incident would have repercussions at the schools. If undocumented immigrants were the target of the raid, he said, many of the students in the system would go home to find their parents missing (Lafee, 2007).

Fortunately, the "No Child Left Behind" (NCLB) law, passed in 2001, renders this issue moot. Creating standards that push for yearly progress meant that state and local school systems had to implement programs for students to meet those standards, regardless of the child's status, or else face intervention or loss of funding. The law also requires that fully qualified teachers must also effectively engage parents, regardless of whether they are proficient in English or not (Urban Institute, 2007).

The facts that schools are not the tools of enforcement of immigration policy and that NCLB does not discriminate among demographics in its quest to improve student performance leave systems with a simple directive: Educate all of the children within the system. As the president of one Texas town's school board succinctly states, "No matter who the child is, if they show up at our [school] door and want to be educated, we are going to offer them an education" (Karlin, 2007).

MAKING THE GRADE

With the nation's highest constitutional interpreter having weighed in on the contentious issue of immigration and public schools, the focus now turns to how to educate newcomers in such a way that federal standards are met. Environmental factors at home, such as poverty, limited parental education, and other related elements must be addressed by means outside of the school (if governmental intervention or assistance can occur at all). Within the school walls, however, an obstacle for the children of undocumented immigrants may both be removed and at the same time serve as a target area for observation of immigrant educational performance.

As stated earlier, non-English-speaking children are already handicapped in English-only school environments. While in the US, students do not have to declare their immigration status at any time in school, a Canadian study revealed immigrant performance improvements as students seek help in English as a second language (ESL) programs as well as their status as children of legal or undocumented immigrants. The National Longitudinal Survey of Children and Youth (NLSCY), performed over three survey years in the late 1990s, revealed school performance of native Canadian children (who, it is assumed, speak English and/or French), children of immigrants who speak English and/or French, and children whose parents do not speak English or French. The survey revealed a very important result: that young children whose parents do not speak English or French are placed at a significant disadvantage in grammar and vocabulary lessons when compared to natives or children whose immigrant parents speak English or French. However, as the three sets of children advanced in age, that differential was significantly narrowed, especially in math and reading testing. The conclusions to be drawn are that, as children of non-native-speaking languages are initially immersed in an Anglophone or Francophone setting, they are likely to experience a major handicap in performance. However, as they get older within the same school system, they develop just as well as their native peers (Worswick, 2004). Although the NLSCY survey does not differentiate between legal and non-legal immigrants, logic dictates that the children of undocumented immigrants, while initially at a major disadvantage upon entering the system, can in fact flourish and succeed with the proper guidance and tutelage.

CONCLUSION

As the truism suggests, those who do not learn from history are likely to repeat it. Throughout American history, there have been instances in which immigrants' arrivals in this country were not welcome to some. From the mid-1880s to the early twentieth century through the present, not all Americans espoused the tenets inscribed at the base of the Statue of Liberty: "Give me your tired, your poor, your huddled masses yearning to breathe free." The concept of the melting pot, as well as one of the best-known Latin phrases among Americans, *E pluribus unum* ("From many, one") is more of a novelty than a creed, convenient except when one's way of life is seemingly threatened.

The fact that there exists a large population of undocumented immigrants in this nation causes some unease among native residents and legal immigrants alike. The notion that these illegals could be using local, state, and federal services at the expense of already strapped budgets, however accurate or inaccurate in truth, only exacerbates these anti-immigration sentiments.

It is these conceptions that give rise to drawing a proverbial line in the sand when it comes to allowing children of illegal immigrants (most of whom were mere babies when they arrived or were born in this country after their parents arrived) entry to public schools. Of course, these anti-immigrant attitudes are not the norm among all Americans. When Texan legislators embraced public opinions that illegal aliens (and their children) should not be allowed to use public school resources, passing laws that deny illegals admittance to public schools, the American way of life pushed back. *Plyler v. Doe* was not an act of activism but a clear definition of legal rights and responsibilities. First, the Supreme Court ruled, children of illegal aliens should receive the same protections and resources afforded to any other resident. Second, whether or not a child is the offspring of illegal immigrants is irrelevant—school administrations are not the enforcers of immigration policy, and therefore cannot investigate or deny a student based on his or her parents' legal status (this responsibility rests on the shoulders of law enforcement officials and the government that funds them).

Unfortunately, the children of undocumented immigrants continue to be caught in the middle of the multifarious "war" on illegal immigration in this country. The Texas raid described earlier in this paper was part of a multi-state crackdown on one company—several other school districts were also impacted by those arrests, as thousands of undocumented workers employed at these plants had children in local schools, and although they could not (nor would not) question children's immigration status, administrators knew without a doubt that their school district contained such youths and that

there would be repercussions for the student body. Still, teachers and administrators remain steadfast in their commitment to not enforcing federal immigration laws, but to ensuring that each child, regardless of his or her background, receives the best education possible.

With legal matters now behind them, thanks to *Plyler* and the subsequent dedication of educators and school administrators, these school-aged children must now focus, as they should, on their studies. So, how are the children of undocumented immigrants doing once they enroll in school? While it is difficult to gauge performance of this segment of the student body (due to the fact that the children's family's legal status is not always evident), one can determine the capabilities of non-English-speakers in comparison to natives and English-speaking immigrants. Within this paradigm, it is a fair hypothesis that the children of undocumented immigrants, having come from homes that are at or near the poverty level with little household education, are at a severe disadvantage that is worsened by an inability to speak English. However, although this "handicap" is evident particularly among young students, those who remain in the system during their school years eventually perform just as well as those who speak English and native residents.

Adding to the good news for these youths is the fact that, regardless of the disadvantages they have, the children of undocumented immigrants are not just welcome in public schools—those who teach them have a federally-mandated obligation to ensure their success. Of course, educators who acknowledge the Supreme Court's decision in *Plyler* understand that their job is to teach the entire student body to the best of their ability, regardless of the legal status of their parents.

TERMS & CONCEPTS

English as a Second Language: Privately or publicly funded course teaching English language skills to individuals of all ages.

No Child Left Behind: 2001 law introduced by President George W. Bush, setting standards for student performance that are tied to federal funding and incentives.

Plyler v. Doe: Landmark 1982 Supreme Court decision in which access to public school systems by children of illegal immigrants was granted.

Public School: Educational institution supported by federal, state, and local funds and presenting students with a government-approved curriculum.

Student Performance: System by which student achievement and progress is monitored and gauged, using test scores, grades, and other quantifiable methods.

Undocumented (or Illegal) Immigrant: Individual who enters a country without a required visa, identification, or other form of authorization.

Michael P. Auerbach

BIBLIOGRAPHY

Camarota, S. A. (2012). *Immigrants in the United States, 2010: A profile of America's foreign-born population.* Center for Immigration Studies. Retrieved December 30, 2013, from http://cis.org.

Cornell University Law School Legal Information Institute. (2007). Supreme Court collection. Retrieved November 6, 2007, from http://law.cornell.edu.

Enriquez, L. E. (2011). "Because we feel the pressure and we also feel the support": Examining the educational success of undocumented immigrant Latina/o students. *Harvard Educational Review, 81,* 476–499. Retrieved December 30, 2013, from EBSCO Online Database Education Research Complete.

Galindo, R. (2012). Undocumented & unafraid: The DREAM Act 5 and the public disclosure of undocumented status as a political act. *Urban Review, 44,* 589–611. Retrieved December 30, 2013, from EBSCO Online Database Education Research Complete.

Jewell, M. (2012). What your undocumented-immigrant students want you to know about them. *Education Week, 31,* 29. Retrieved December 30, 2013, from EBSCO Online Database Education Research Complete.

Jones, R., & Baker, R. (2006, June 30). Costs of federally mandated services to undocumented immigrants in Colorado. *Bell Policy Center Issue Brief Number 4.* Retrieved November 7, 2007, from http://thebell.org.

Karlin, S. (2007). The invisible class. *American School Board Journal, 194,* 24–27. Retrieved November 7, 2007, from EBSCO Online Database Academic Search Complete.

Lafee, S. (2007). Fighting for immigrant children's rights. *School Administrator, 64,* 10–16. Retrieved November 8, 2007, from EBSCO Online Database Education Research Complete.

Mallaby, S. (2007, April 30). Lazy, job-stealing immigrants? *Washington Post.* Retrieved November 7, 2007, from http://cfr.org.

More in-state tuition for illegal immigrants. (2003, May 22). CNN.com. Retrieved November 6, 2007, from http://cnn.com.

Passel, J. S., & Cohn, D. (2011). *Unauthorized immigrant population: National and state trends, 2010.* Pew Hispanic Center. Retrieved December 30, 2013, from http://pewhispanic.org.

Sutton, L. C., & Stewart, T. J. (2013). State challenges to Plyler v. Doe: Undocumented immigrant students and public school access. *Educational Considerations, 40,* 23–25. Retrieved December 30, 2013, from EBSCO Online Database Education Research Complete.

Thredgold, J. (2006). Thoughts on immigration. *Enterprise/Salt Lake City, 36,* 9–10.

Urban Institute. (2007). Immigration studies. Retrieved November 6, 2007, from http://urban.org.

Worswick, C. (2004). Adaptation and inequality: Children of immigrants in Canadian schools. *Canadian Journal of Economics, 37,* 53–77. Retrieved November 7, 2007, from EBSCO Online Database Business Source Complete.

SUGGESTED READING

Crawford, E.R., & Fishman-Weaver, K. (2016). Proximity and policy: Negotiating safe spaces between immigration policy and school practice. *International Journal of Qualitative Studies in Education, 29* (3), 273-296.

Illegal, but useful. (2007). *Economist, 385*(8553), 39. Retrieved November 8, 2007, from EBSCO Online Database Academic Search Complete.

Kim, E., & Díaz., J. (2013). Undocumented students and higher education. *ASHE Higher Education Report, 38,* 77–90. Retrieved December 30, 2013, from EBSCO Online Database Education Research Complete.

Padron, E. J. (2006). Beyond debate. *Hispanic, 19,* 14. Retrieved November 8, 2007, from EBSCO Online Database Business Source Complete.

Rodriguez, S. (2017). "People hide. But I'm here. I count." Examining undocumented youth identity formation in an urban community school. *Educational Studies, 53* (5), 468-491.

Sneed, M., & Civin, J. (2007). Questioning immigration status when students enroll. *School Administrator, 64,* 12. Retrieved November 8, 2007, from EBSCO Online Database Education Research Complete.

Sutton, L. & Stewart, T. (2013). State challenges to "Plyer vs Doe". Undocumented immigrant students and public school access. *Educational Considerations,* 40 (3), 23-25.

Zarate, M.E. & Burciaga, R. (2010). Latinos and college access: Trends and future directions. *Journal of College Admissions,* 209, 24-29.

Zehr, Mary Ann. (2007, June 6). Amid immigration debate, settled ground. *Education Week, 26,* 1–13. Retrieved November 8, 2007, from EBSCO Online Database Education Research Complete.

TITLE IX

Title IX of the Educational Amendments to the 1964 Civil Rights Act was signed into law in 1972. It bans any educational institution that receives federal funds from discriminating on the basis of sex, and applies to all academic and extra-curricular programs. Title IX has been praised as the chief factor behind the advances made in gender equity in education over the past three decades. In addition, the significant advances of women in higher education and in the workplace since the 1970s have been attributed by some to Title IX. Despite all this, Title IX is most well known for the impact it has had on intercollegiate athletics. The scale of women's collegiate athletic programs has increased exponentially during the past four decades, principally as a result of Title IX.

KEYWORDS: College Athletics; Educational Institution; Equal Rights; Federal School Funding; Gender Equity; Nonrevenue Sports; Revenue Sports; School Sports; Sex-Based Discrimination; Three-Part Test; US Department of Education's Office for Civil Rights

OVERVIEW

Title IX has been called "the most controversial topic in college sports," and its legacy has likewise been called "a legacy of debate" (Suggs, 2002). A component of the 1972 Educational Amendments to the 1964 Civil Rights Act, Title IX was designed to end discrimination on the basis of sex in education, just as Title IV of the original 1964 Civil Rights Act had been designed to end discrimination on the basis of race. While many claims have been made about the exact impact Title IX has had on gender equity in education, one result of Title IX is overwhelmingly clear: it began, and continues to fuel, a vigorous debate about funding for, participation in, and the purpose of intercollegiate athletics.

After the passage of Title IX, educational institutions accepted and applied the legislation to their academic programs without any resistance or debate (Suggs). Most college and secondary school athletic programs, however, virtually ignored Title IX until a series of Supreme Court decisions during the 1990s made it clear that lack of compliance left schools vulnerable to lawsuits with monetary-damage claims. Partly as a result of this threat of prosecution,

educational institutions increased their efforts to comply with Title IX's athletic provisions throughout the 1990s (Anderson, Cheslock, & Ehrenberg, 2006). These efforts persist, albeit not without continued controversy.

Over the first four decades of its existence, Title IX has garnered many vocal supporters and critics. The supporters praise Title IX for expanding women's educational opportunities and changing American culture's expectations of what women can achieve. The critics charge Title IX with discriminating against men, as efforts to comply with the legislation have led some institutions to eliminate men's teams in less widely popular sports such as wrestling and swimming. Despite these accusations, Title IX is legislation with which all educational institutions must comply.

History

THE POLITICAL CLIMATE SURROUNDING TITLE IX

During the late 1960s and the 1970s, the women's movement, what many refer to as the second wave of feminism, succeeded in focusing national attention on the sex-based inequalities that hampered American women's lives. One of the most deleterious of these inequalities was the earning gap between men and women. Although women had, by this time, become a vital part of the American workforce, female wage earners were rarely paid as much as their male peers. Women's organizations and advocacy groups asserted that this earnings gap could be traced back to sex-based inequalities in education. Women filed class action lawsuits against colleges, universities, and the US federal government, alleging that these institutions discriminated against women. All this encouraged Congress to focus on sexual discrimination in education and hold hearings on the subject in the summer of 1970 (U.S. Department of Justice, 2001).

This was the political climate out of which Title IX was born. Hoping to build on the momentum gained by the special hearings a year before, Representative Edith Green made an unsuccessful attempt to add a ban on sex-based discrimination to the 1971 Education Amendments. The next year, in an attempt to derail the renewal of the 1964 Civil Rights Act, conservative Southern congressmen added gender to the categories protected against discrimination. They hoped that the idea of equal opportunities for women would be distasteful enough to prevent the passage of the entire bill (Suggs). To their chagrin, the legislation was passed and Title IX became law.

TITLE IX & ATHLETICS

Title IX prohibits any educational institution receiving federal funds from discriminating in any activity or program on the basis of sex. In all academic and extra-curricular fields except athletics, Title IX was adopted and applied with little or no controversy (Suggs). In contrast, decades passed before Title IX was effectively enforced in the field of athletics. When Title IX became law in 1972, most colleges simply did not have varsity sports teams for women. According to the National Collegiate Athletic Association (NCAA), while approximately 170,000 men participated in college sports programs in 1972, just under 30,000 women also participated (Suggs). In the first few years after Title IX was passed, it was unclear what, if anything, colleges and universities would be required to do to remedy this situation. The first interpretation of how Title IX applies to intercollegiate athletics was not issued until 1975, with a delayed compliance date of 1978. These initial instructions were generally felt to be too vague, so a more comprehensive plan was issued by the US Department of Education's Office for Civil Rights in 1979 (Anderson et al.).

ENFORCING TITLE IX

Although the 1979 plan included a three-part test to prove compliance with the portion of Title IX dealing with athletics, the test was ignored throughout most of the 1980s. The Carter, Reagan, and George H. W. Bush administrations put a low priority on enforcing Title IX, and as a result, educational programs felt no real need to comply with the law (Anderson et al.). When, in 1984, the Supreme Court ruled that Title IX was only applicable to the specific programs that directly received federal aid, athletic programs became legally exempt from compliance (Suggs). This situation lasted until 1988, when Congress, over-riding a veto by President Reagan, enacted the Civil Rights Restoration Act. This law restored the broad interpretation of Title IX, in which Title IX applied to all programs or activities at institutions that received federal funds, whether or not a program was a direct recipient of these funds (U.S. Department of Justice).

Efforts on the part of collegiate athletic programs to enforce Title IX increased throughout the 1990s for several reasons. The US Department of Education's Office for Civil Rights is responsible for enforcing Title IX, and does so on a complaint-driven basis (Barnett, 2003). Until students started reporting discrimination, and doing so in such a way that threatened more than just inconvenience for educational institutions, Title IX would not be enforced. This process of upping the stakes of Title IX compliance began in 1992 when the Supreme Court ruled in *Franklin v. Gwinnett County Public Schools* that the plaintiff in a Title IX lawsuit was entitled to monetary damages as long as the discrimination was intentional. In 1996, *Cohen v. Brown University* contributed to the increasing wariness on the part of colleges and universities of Title IX lawsuits. In this case, the Supreme Court held that Brown University was obliged to "adhere to strict criteria for demonstrating gender equity in intercollegiate athletics" (Anderson, et al.). This decision was particularly startling because Brown already had more women's sports teams than any other university besides Harvard. The decision convinced schools that until they were in strict compliance with Title IX, they would be vulnerable to lawsuits. Another factor that helped plaintiffs in such lawsuits was the Equity in Athletics Disclosure Act, which Congress passed in 1994. This law mandated that institutions give free access to data about their men's and women's athletics programs. Access to this data helped the federal government more easily gauge compliance with Title IX. Finally, unlike its predecessors, the Clinton administration made enforcing Title IX a priority (Anderson et al.).

Currently, educational institutions are generally committed to enforcing Title IX in their educational programs. Compliance, however, is not always easy. Much controversy has been caused in recent years by schools who have decided to eliminate men's sports teams, especially wrestling teams, in order to attain compliance with Title IX.

Applications

CONTENT OF TITLE IX

According to the US Department of Education, Title IX "is designed to eliminate (with certain exceptions) discrimination on the basis of sex in any education program or activity receiving federal financial assistance" (Office for Civil Rights, 1980). This essentially means that institutions must provide students with academic and extra-curricular opportunities on a "gender-neutral basis" (Anderson et al.). While Title IX is most well-known in relation to college athletics, the legislation is applicable to myriad other aspects of education. The text of Title IX specifies the law as being applicable to admission, recruitment, housing, facilities (such as locker rooms), access to course offerings, access to schools operated by local educational agencies (LEAs), counseling, financial assistance, employment assistance to students, health insurance benefits, athletics, textbooks and curricular materials, and marital/parental status. In regard to this last category, Title IX has made it illegal for high schools to prevent a pregnant teenager from finishing her degree (U.S. Department of Education, Office for Civil Rights). Title IX additionally prohibits sexual harassment and requires, "as a condition of receipt of federal financial assistance [that] if a recipient is aware, or should be aware, of sexual harassment, it must take reasonable steps to eliminate the harassment, prevent its recurrence and, where appropriate, remedy the effects" (U.S. Department of Education, Office for Civil Rights). Only educational institutions that are operated by an entity controlled by a religious organization whose religious tenets are inconsistent with Title IX are exempted from enforcing the legislation's various provisions (U.S. Department of Education, Office for Civil Rights).

What Is Sex-Based Discrimination?

Title IX prohibits three distinct types of sex-based discrimination: disparate treatment, disparate impact, and retaliation. The U.S. Department of Justice defines disparate treatment as "actions that treat similarly situated persons differently on the basis of a prohibited classification," such as sex. Disparate impact "focuses on the result of the action taken, rather than the intent." Disparate impact applies to a policy that seems to be sex-neutral but that has the result of discriminating on the basis of sex. For example, a successful lawsuit brought against the National Merit Scholarship program claimed that by relying solely on SAT scores in determining scholarship eligibility, the program discriminated against female applicants. Title IX's prohibition of retaliation is designed

to protect people who file Title IX complaints as well as the people who investigate these complaints from retaliation by the accused. In short, it is intended to "preserve the integrity and effectiveness of the enforcement process itself."

Title IX & College Athletics

Title IX is most well known for its provisions related to college athletic programs. Title IX specifically requires schools to provide men's and women's sports programs with equal "benefits and services." This includes "scholarships, travel expenses, practice and competitive facilities, equipment and supplies, scheduling and practice times, and number and compensation of coaches and locker rooms" (Burnett). The legislation also contains more opaque compliance criteria. For this reason, the U.S. Department of Education has issued very specific guidelines about what schools must do in order to be in compliance with Title IX.

The Three-Prong Test

These guidelines include what was originally referred to as the three-part test (U.S. Department of Education, Office for Civil Rights) but today is known as the "three-prong test." The three-prong test has become the primary measure used in lawsuits to gauge institutional compliance with Title IX (Anderson et al.). According to the Office for Civil Rights, an institution is judged to be in compliance if it meets any one of three parts of the following test:

- "the percent of male and female athletes is substantially proportionate to the percent of male and female students enrolled at the school; or,
- "the school has a history and continuing practice of expanding participation opportunities for the underrepresented sex; or,
- "the school is fully and effectively accommodating the interests and abilities of the underrepresented sex" (Dept. of Education, 2005).

The most effective way to prove compliance with the three-prong test has long been considered to be the first criteria: ensuring that the ratio of men to women who participate in the sports programs is proportionate to the ratio of men to women enrolled in the college or university. As long as a college has the same proportion of female athletes as it does female students, it can claim "substantial proportionality" and be safe from potential lawsuit (Suggs, 2002). Recently, more schools have begun to explore test three, often using surveys to prove that they are accommodating female students' interests and abilities. As a result, the US Department of Education's Office for Civil Rights in 2005 offered new guidelines on how to properly compose and administer such a survey.

Viewpoints

IMPACT OF TITLE IX: THE FIRST 25 YEARS

Significant disagreement exists as to the exact impact Title IX has had on education, American culture, and college sports. The Department of Education has credited Title IX with many of the advancements women have made in education and in the workplace (U.S. Department of Education, Office for Civil Rights, 1997). In a press release celebrating the 25th anniversary of Title IX, it refers to women's advancements in these fields as "the great untold story of success that resulted from the passage of Title IX" (U.S. Department of Education, Office for Civil Rights). The report goes on to cite a number of statistics as evidence of this claim:

- "In 1994, 63 percent of female high school graduates aged 16-24 were enrolled in college, up 20 percentage points from 43 percent in 1973."
- "In 1994, 27 percent of both men and women had earned a bachelor's degree. In 1971, 18 percent of young women and 26 percent of young men had completed four or more years of college."
- "In 1994, women received 38 percent of medical degrees. When Title IX was enacted in 1972, only 9 percent of medical degrees went to women."
- "In 1994 women earned 38 percent of dental degrees, whereas in 1972 they earned only 1 percent of them."
- "In 1994 women accounted for 43 percent of law degrees, up from 7 percent in 1972."
- "In 1993-94, 44 percent of all doctoral degrees awarded to U.S. citizens went to women, up from only 25 percent in 1977" (U.S. Department of Education, Office for Civil Rights).

The report also includes statistics on women's involvement in college athletics, the area in which Title IX is considered to have had the biggest impact:

- "Today [in 1997], more than 100,000 women participate in intercollegiate athletics–a fourfold increase since 1971."

- "In 1995, women comprised 37 percent of college student athletes, compared to 15 percent in 1972."
- "In 1996, 2.4 million high school girls represented 39 percent of all high school athletes, compared to only 300,000 or 7.5 percent in 1971. This represents an eightfold increase" (U.S. Department of Education, Office for Civil Rights).

Since 1997, the percentage of women involved in high school and college athletics has only increased (Suggs; Anderson et al.).

TITLE IX AT 40

Despite many the myths and misconceptions that still surrounding Title XI, quite a lot has changed in women's participation in athletics over the past forty years. For example,

- "The number of young women who played high school sports was just under 300,000 in the early 1970s. By 2011, the figure was over 3 million "(Kane, 2012; Ladda, 2012);
- "Prior to Title IX, sports scholarships for women were unheard of. By 2012, almost 43 percent of all college athletes who received scholarships were women" (Kane);
- "Of the gold medals won by the American team during the 2012 Olympic Games in London, England, 66 percent were won by women "(Kane).

THE DEBATE OVER TITLE IX

As is evidenced by the above statistics, most commentators on the debate over Title IX, and especially Title IX's supporters, tout the legislation as causing a sea of change in American culture's attitude towards women. The most common debate about Title IX is not over whether the legislation has been effective, but over whether its gains have been worth the cost. Namely, have male students and men's athletic programs suffered as a result of Title IX?

MEN'S ATHLETICS

Critics of Title IX charge that it has "spawned resentment and confusion" and led to a state of affairs where there is "serious discrimination going on against men" (Darden, 2007; Suggs). These critics are angered by the decision of many universities to achieve Title IX compliance by cutting men's nonrevenue sports. If a school cannot afford to achieve "substantial proportionality" by boosting the number of its women's sports teams, then it may find the funds to do so by eliminating some men's teams. For many schools this has meant cutting less popular sports such as wrestling and tennis. Many college athletic coaches claim that this approach is especially illogical because there are simply more men on campus interested in playing sports. These coaches find that while they have to recruit women on campus to fill spots on some women's teams, they have to turn campus men away from walk-on spots on men's teams (Suggs).

Supporters of Title IX disagree (Suggs) and point out that the same athletic departments that cut men's wrestling and tennis teams spend an enormous portion of their budget on revenue-generating sports such as men's football and basketball. According to Fagan and Cyphers (2012), Division 1-A schools spent 59 percent of their athletic budget for men's sports on football (59 percent) and basketball (19 percent) in the 2009–2010 school year. When non-revenue generating men's sports such as wrestling or tennis are cut, it is usually not to fund women's programs but rather to put more money into the already successful revenue-generating sports programs such as football. Rutgers University, for example, cut the men's tennis program in 2006, which had a budget of $175,000. The university spent that same amount in 2006 housing football players in hotel rooms the night before six home games (National Women's Law Center, 2012).

CHANGING ATHLETIC MODELS
This debate over Title IX has sparked a larger debate over the nature of college athletic programs. Many intercollegiate athletics programs are run on a "commercial model," whereby schools invest in the most lucrative sports, namely football, and hope to generate revenue by doing so (Porto, 2005). Supporters of Title IX suggest that educational institutions' sports programs should instead follow a "participation model," whereby athletics are valued not according to their commercial worth, but as a rewarding part of a liberal arts education. In a participation model, the principal beneficiaries of college athletics are not fans, television stations, colleges, or athletic departments, but student athletes.

At this point in time, male athletes and men's sports coaches continue to file lawsuits challenging the application of Title IX to intercollegiate athletics.

Despite the anger generated over the elimination of men's sports teams, all indications show that college athletic departments will have to continue to make Title IX compliance a top priority when allocating resources and balancing budgets. Although future lawsuits might slightly alter protocols for complying with Title IX, the general spirit of the legislation with its absolute insistence on gender equity will almost certainly remain unchanged.

TERMS & CONCEPTS
Educational Institution: A local educational agency (LEA), meaning a school district that supervises public elementary and secondary schools; a preschool; a private elementary or secondary school; any institute of undergraduate or graduate higher education; or any institute of professional or vocational education.

Gender Equity: The equal and fair assignment of resources, opportunities, and decision-making responsibilities to both men and women.

Nonrevenue Sports: Often referred to as Olympic sports, this group includes swimming, wrestling, and men's gymnastics, among others. These sports do not typically generate revenue at the college level.

Revenue Sports: Collegiate level sports such as football and basketball, which sometimes (but not always) generate revenue through ticket sales or participation in major tournaments.

Sex-Based Discrimination: Situation in which the sex of an individual either directly or indirectly results in their receiving unequal treatment, all other factors being equal.

Three-Part Test: Devised by the U.S. Department of Education's Office for Civil Rights, it is the primary means used to gauge institutional compliance with Title IX's athletic provisions.

US Department of Education's Office for Civil Rights: The mission of this government office is to ensure that all citizens are given equal access to education. This office assists those who face discrimination in education by resolving discrimination complaints and by attempting to prevent discrimination. The Office does this in part by helping institutions to reach voluntary compliance with all civil rights laws.

Ashley L. Cohen

BIBLIOGRAPHY

Anderson, D., Cheslock, J., & Ehrenberg, R. (2006) Gender equity in intercollegiate athletics: Determinants of Title IX compliance. *Journal of Higher Education, 77*, 225-250. Retrieved March 16, 2007, from EBSCO Online Database Education Research Complete.

Burnett, S. (2003, June 9). Revolution number IX. *Community College Week, 15*, 6-9. Retrieved March 16, 2007, from EBSCO Online Database Education Research Complete.

Darden, E. (2007). Even out the playing field. *American School Board Journal, 194*, 41-42. Retrieved March 16, 2007, from EBSCO Online Database Education Research Complete.

Fagan, K., & Cyphers, L. (2012, April 29). Five myths about Title IXZ. *ESPN W*. Retrieved December 12, 2013, from http://espn.go.com.

Kane, Mary Jo. (2012, September). Title IX at 40: Examining mysteries, myths, and misinformation surrounding the historic federal law.*Fortieth Anniversary of Title IX: Status of Girls' and Women's Sports Participation, 13*, 2–9. Retrieved December 12, 2013, from https://presidentschallenge.org.

Ladda, Shawn. (2012, September). Examining Title IX at 40: Historical development, legal implications, and governance structures. *Fortieth Anniversary of Title IX: Status of Girls' and Women's Sports Participation, 13*, 10–20. Retrieved December 12, 2013, from https://presidentschallenge.org.

McAndrews, P. J. (2012). Keeping Score: How universities can comply with Title IX without eliminating men's collegiate athletic programs. *Brigham Young University Education & Law Journal,*, 111–140. Retrieved December 13, 2013, from EBSCO Online Database Education Research Complete.

National Women's Law Center. (2012, January 30). Debunking the myths about Title IX and athletics. *Title IX Fact Sheet*. Retrieved December 12, 2013, from http://nwlc.org.

Pieronek, C. F. (2012). The 2010 "dear colleague" letter on Title IX compliance for college athletic programs: Pointing the way to proportionality... again. *Journal of College & University Law, 38*, 277–318. Retrieved December 13, 2013, from EBSCO Online Database Education Research Complete.

Porto, B. (2005). Changing the game plan: A participation model of college sports. *Phi Kappa Phi Forum, 85*, 28-31. Retrieved March 16, 2007, from EBSCO Online Database Education Research Complete.

Stromquist, N. P. (2013). Education policies for gender equity: Probing into state responses. *Education Policy Analysis Archives, 21*, 1–28. Retrieved December 13, 2013, from EBSCO Online Database Education Research Complete.

Suggs, W. (2002, June 21). Title IX at 30. *Chronicle of Higher Education, 48*, A38-41. Retrieved March 16, 2007, from EBSCO Online Database Education Research Complete.

U.S. Department of Education. (1997). *Title IX: 25 years of progress*. Washington, D.C. Retrieved March 16, 2007, from http://ed.gov.

U.S. Department of Education, Office for Civil Rights. (1980). *Title IX regulations*. Washington, D.C. Retrieved March 16, 2007, from http://usdoj.gov.

U.S. Department of Education, Office for Civil Rights. (2005). *Additional clarification of intercollegiate athletic policy: Three-part test - Part three*. Washington, D.C. Retrieved March 16, 2007, from http://ed.gov.

U.S. Department of Justice. (2001). *Title IX legal manual*. Washington, D.C. Retrieved March 16, 2007, from http://usdoj.gov.

SUGGESTED READING

Anderson, D. & Cheslock, J. (2004, May). Institutional strategies to achieve gender equity in intercollegiate athletics: Does Title IX harm male athletes? *American Economic Review, 94*, 307-311. Retrieved March 16, 2007, from EBSCO Online Database Education Research Complete.

Gender equity in college sports. (2007). *The Chronicle of Higher Education*. Washington, D.C. Retrieved March 17, 2007, from http://chronicle.com.

Hardy, L. (2012). The legacy of Title IX. *American School Board Journal, 199*, 12–15. Retrieved December 13, 2013, from EBSCO Online Database Education Research Complete.

Hogshead-Makar, N. (2003). The ongoing battle over Title IX. *USA Today Magazine, 132*(2698), p. 64-66. Retrieved March 16, 2007, from EBSCO Online Database Education Research Complete.

Pickett, M., Dawkins, M. P., & Braddock, J. (2012). Race and gender equity in sports: Have white and African American females benefited equally from Title IX?. *American Behavioral Scientist, 56*, 1581–1603. Retrieved December 13, 2013, from EBSCO Online Database Education Research Complete.

U.S. Department of Education, Office for Civil Rights. (2004). *Sex discrimination*. Retrieved March 17, 2007, from http://ed.gov.

INCLUSIVE EDUCATION LAWS

Inclusive education for students with disabilities is designed to ensure that all children receive a proper education in an environment that is not restricted. The major laws governing inclusive education are the Education for All Handicapped Children Act and the Individuals with Disabilities Education Act. Since the original acts were passed, subsequent court cases have revolved around the exact definition of "least restrictive environment." Research has shown that inclusive education can improve academic achievement among disabled students, as well as foster more positive social interaction among disabled and non-disabled students. However, inclusion can deprive disabled students of specialized instruction, and, in some cases, disrupt the learning of non-disabled students.

KEYWORDS: Continuum of Alternative Placements; Education for All Handicapped Children Act; Inclusion; Individualized Education Plan (IEP); Individuals with Disabilities Education Act (IDEA); Least Restrictive Environment; Mainstreaming; Related Services; Supplementary Aids and Services; Students with Disabilities

OVERVIEW

In 1975, Congress passed the Education for All Handicapped Children Act. The law came about, in part, after a report found that over 60% of the country's disabled students were not receiving an appropriate education, and some research indicated that millions of children were constantly being excluded from school, or were not getting a proper education that could help, not hinder, their disabilities (Yell, 1998; Irmsher, 1995, as cited in McCarty, 2006). The law's intent was to make sure that students with disabilities would be taught with other children who did not have disabilities (Kluth, Villa & Thousand, 2002, as cited in McCarty). In 1991, the Education for All Handicapped Children Act was renamed the Individuals with Disabilities Education Act (Irmsher, as cited in McCarty). Along with the renaming of the act, certain learning disabilities were reclassified, and autism and traumatic brain injury were added (McCarty).

The Individuals with Disabilities Education Act (IDEA) requires that students with disabilities be taught in the "least restrictive environment" possible with students who are not disabled (Lipton, 1994, as cited in McCarty) and that schools must take steps to ensure the comfort of children with disabilities in the regular classroom. These steps could include giving supplementary aids and changing the curriculum of the general education class (Yell). The updated Act also mandates that "various alternative placement options are required also by the regulations of the Act in order to assure that each student with disabilities receives an education which is appropriate for his/her individual need" (Wigle, Wilcox & Manges, 1994, as cited in McCarty). Another part of the act says that "special classes, separate schooling, or other removal of handicapped children from the regular education environment occur only when the nature or severity of the disability is such that education in regular classes with the use of supplementary aids and services cannot be achieved satisfactorily" (Yell; McCarty).

THE LEAST RESTRICTIVE ENVIRONMENT MANDATE

The Individuals with Disabilities Education Act requires schools to educate students with disabilities in the least restrictive environment possible, which means they should be educated as closely as possible with students who do not have disabilities. Thus, students with disabilities have a right to be educated in a regular education classroom with their peers. The second part states that students do not have to be educated in a regular classroom with their non-disabled peers if they cannot be satisfactorily educated. This means that if students with disabilities cannot receive an education in a regular classroom that meets their particular needs, they may move to a different educational setting where they can receive an appropriate education. With respect to least restrictive environments, a general education classroom is considered to be the least restrictive and any educational setting that affords students with disabilities little contact with their non-disabled classmates is considered to be more restrictive (Yell). The less an educational setting for students with disabilities mirrors a general education environment, the more restrictive the environment is considered to be (Gorn, 1997, as cited in Yell).

A least restrictive environment is considered to be any setting that is limited in its educational restraining for the student, which allows them to grow, learn, and succeed in an educational setting. It is up to each student's individualized education program (IEP) team or a group consisting of parents, educators, and others who are involved with students with disabilities to determine what constitutes a least restrictive environment for each disabled student (McCarty).

INTERPRETING THE LAW

With the laws that helped establish inclusive education came court cases that specify what should be the proper implementation of inclusive education, but there is still no clear-cut language in court decisions that states how this should be done. This lack of clarity results in schools, school districts, and states interpreting the language of the law, which results in interpretations that match their particular view on inclusive education and the degree to which their students with disabilities are immersed in a regular general education classroom (McCarty). Issues and interpretations are further complicated by the fact that people both inside and outside of the education field often talk about "least restrictive environment," "inclusion," and "mainstreaming" as if they mean the same things when, in actuality, they cannot be used interchangeably (Douvanis & Hulsey, 2002, as cited in McCarty).

The concept of educating students in a least restrictive environment developed in the 1970s from the Education for All Handicapped Children Act, and has since become a requirement in all schools (Bateman & Bateman, 2002). Inclusion refers to having students with disabilities in a general education classroom with non-disabled students, and "implies that students with disabilities will be taught outside a regular education classroom only when all available instructional methods have been utilized and failed to meet their needs" (Bateman & Bateman, as cited in McCarty). Full inclusion refers to placing children with disabilities in a regular education classroom every day (McCarty. Students with disabilities in an inclusive setting still receive direct support from special educators (Hines, 2001). Inclusion is different from mainstreaming because "students are part of only the general education classroom and do not belong to any other specialized education setting based on their disability" (Halvorsen & Neary, 2001, as cited in Hines).

Mainstreaming is used to refer to when students with disabilities are "in a special education classroom setting for most of the day and then go into a general education classroom for parts of the school day" when the general education class is working on activities where it is believed that the disabled student will excel (McCarty).

THE CONTINUUM OF ALTERNATIVE PLACEMENTS

To make sure that schools provide a range of educational opportunities for students with disabilities with respect to differing levels of least restrictive environment, the Individuals with Disabilities Education Act requires school districts to have a continuum of alternative placements. Continuum of placements can include being taught in regular classes and schools as well as special classes and schools. Education in homes, hospitals or institutions is also included (Bateman & Bateman). The purpose of having a continuum of alternative placements is to enable the schools to select from a number of options when determining a student's placement so that they are not either completely included or completely excluded from participating with their non-disabled peers. Having a choice helps ensure that students with disabilities will not be educated in environments that are more restrictive than necessary. If a student's individualized education program (IEP) planning team believes that placing the student in the regular classroom is not appropriate for the student, then the student can be moved along the continuum of placements that exist until the team matches the student with an educational setting that provides the least amount of separation from the non-disabled students. While inclusion is not specifically required by the Individuals with Disabilities Education Act, it does state that the primary consideration in determining the least restrictive environment for students with disabilities must be done in conjunction with each student's individual needs (Yell).

Further Insights

COURT CASES AFFECTING INCLUSION

Several lawsuits have resulted in U.S. Court of Appeals decisions that affect the way schools and school districts interpret the Individuals with Disabilities Education Act. The crux of inclusive education law deals with providing a least restrictive environment.

The challenge is what constitutes a least restrictive setting for each student and how that decision is made. The laws are vague enough that schools, school districts, and parents may interpret them differently, which is when lawsuits may occur.

Daniel R.R. v. State Board of Education

In 1989, the first case, *Daniel R.R. v. State Board of Education,* was decided by the U.S. Court of Appeals for the 5th Circuit. The standard set by this court dictates that when a court reviews a case about least restrictive environment it must determine if the school has complied with the mainstreaming requirement of the Individuals with Disabilities Education Act. This means that courts should determine whether education in a regular classroom using supplementary aids and services will provide an appropriate education for the student. If it has been decided that it cannot, and the school plans to take the student out of the regular classroom, then is the student being mainstreamed to an appropriate degree? According to the Court, there are three factors to consider in determining whether education in a regular classroom is appropriate for a student and is in compliance with the least restrictive environment component of the Individuals with Disabilities Education Act (Yell):

- Whether the student will benefit educationally by being placed in a general classroom environment. In this case, the benefit may be defined as either academic benefit or nonacademic (social) benefit;
- The student's overall educational experience in being placed in a mainstream environment. This requires schools to look at the benefits that can be derived from a mainstream education versus those that can be derived from a special education setting. Although some interpret this to mean that schools must attempt to mainstream the student (Julnes, 1994, as cited in Yell), the Court of Appeals stated that mainstreaming may not be good for the student because regular classroom instruction may not meet the student's needs even if supplementary aids and services are provided;
- The effect the student has on the education of the other students in the classroom, which may be detrimental to the other students in the classroom if the student demonstrates disruptive behavior or if the student places undue burden on the instructors (Yell).

If it is determined that the school does not really try to keep the student in the general classroom, then the school has not satisfied the first part of the test. If the student's individualized education program (IEP) team decides whether or not the student can do well in a general education classroom, then the court tries to determine if the student is mainstreamed to the highest degree possible, and the school must afford the student as much exposure to non-disabled students as possible. In *Daniel R.R.,* the Court decided that the student should be mainstreamed when appropriate, during lunch, recess, and in nonacademic classes. According to this U.S. Court of Appeals, schools that meet both components of the *Daniel R.R.* test have complied with the Individuals with Disabilities Education Act (Yell).

Sacramento City School District v. Rachel H.

In 1994, the U.S. Court of Appeals for the 9th Circuit in *Sacramento City School District v. Rachel H.* came up with another standard for reviewing least restrictive environment cases. According to this decision, when reviewing least restrictive environment cases, courts must look at:

- The educational benefits of a general education classroom with supplementary aids and services as compared with the educational benefits of a special classroom;
- The nonacademic benefits of having interaction with non-disabled students;
- The effect the student's presence in the general education classroom has on the instructor's ability to teach and other students' ability to learn;
- The cost of mainstreaming the student (Yell).

Hartmann v. Loudoun County

A few years later in 1997, the U.S. Court of Appeals for the 4th Circuit added a different interpretation in its ruling on *Hartmann v. Loudoun County.* It stated that the least restrictive environment requirement of the Individuals with Disabilities Education Act was a preference for inclusion and not a federal mandate. With that in mind, it developed a slightly different test for courts to use when determining whether or not a school district has met its obligations under the Individuals with Disabilities Education Act. The court gave three scenarios in which a school district does not have to place a student with disabilities in a general education classroom with non-disabled students. They determined that:

- Mainstreaming is not absolutely necessary if a student with disabilities is not expected to receive any benefits from being in a general education classroom with non-disabled students;

- Mainstreaming is not required if any marginal benefit that may be attained by being in a general education classroom would be drastically outweighed by enhancements that may be attained in a separate instructional setting;

- Mainstreaming is not required if the student poses a threat to the peace of the general education classroom (Yell).

Viewpoints

ADVANTAGES OF INCLUSION
There can be benefits for both non-disabled students and students with disabilities when the latter are included in the general education classroom. Some research has shown that students with disabilities who are included in a regular classroom setting seem to do better both academically and socially than those students with disabilities who are not in an inclusive setting (Irmsher, n.d., as cited in McCarty). Students with disabilities who are integrated into the regular classroom are able to meet their non-disabled peers and develop friendships with them. These relationships can also provide students with disabilities role models for correct behavior. Non-disabled students can also benefit by having students with disabilities in the classroom with them because their presence can give non-disabled students a better understanding of people with disabilities (McCarty). Inclusion may also lead to non-disabled students acquiring greater acceptance of students with disabilities and to come to understand that all disabilities are not necessarily obvious. Inclusion may also help promote better understanding of the similarities between students with disabilities and non-disabled students (Kochhar, West & Taymans, 2000, as cited in Hines).

Inclusion can help facilitate better social behavior for students with disabilities through generally higher expectations in a general education classroom. Inclusion can also promote higher achievement or achievement at least as high as what comes from a learning environment that is less inclusive. It can also offer students with disabilities a larger support system by promoting social interaction with non-disabled students. In addition, inclusion can improve the ability of students and instructors to adapt to different instructional and student learning styles (Kochhar, West & Taymans, as cited in Hines).

There can also be academic benefits for non-disabled students. Having students with disabilities in the regular classroom may mean that there is additional professional staff in the classroom, which may allow for smaller group and individualized instruction for everyone; and they may also assist in developing academic adaptations for other students who have not been classified as having disabilities (Hines, as cited in McCarty). Students without disabilities in an inclusive setting also learn that students with disabilities are a portion of the whole community and can still contribute in many ways to society (McCarty).

DISADVANTAGES OF INCLUSION
There can also be disadvantages to inclusive programming. For some students, full inclusion is not the best placement, since most general education classrooms do not provide individualized instruction and not all services can be provided to students in a regular classroom setting (Bateman & Bateman). Some advocates feel that students with disabilities should be completely included in a regular classroom even if they are disruptive to the other students; however, this is probably the largest disadvantage of inclusive education. If a student is so disruptive that the instructor cannot teach and the other students are distracted, then such inclusion is not good for all the students because they are not learning as much as they should.

Another possible disadvantage to students with disabilities relates to the special services they may not receive if they are integrated into a regular classroom, such as occupational therapy, speech therapy, and adapted physical education. Students with disabilities who have been fully integrated may also be taught by instructors who do not have extensive training in special education, like those working in more non-inclusive settings will have. Additionally, if students are fully integrated, they could lose one-on-one, more specialized instruction that they need to understand some subject areas, which means they will undoubtedly struggle more in their weaker subjects than they would if they were in a less inclusive setting (McCarty).

These divergent opinions are one reason why having laws regarding inclusive education are necessary (McCarty). The disagreements parents, schools, and school districts have over the Individuals with Disabilities Education Act tend to be over the "matter of full inclusion of the student in a general education classroom, and most court cases have ruled in favor of students over school districts" (Kluth et al., as cited in McCarty).

As seen in the court cases and other information presented in this paper, laws that govern inclusion for students with disabilities are subject to interpretation because there really are no clear-cut guidelines. For example, the school and instructor may find a student's behavior very disruptive and detrimental to the class, and the student's parents may not; and how one school interprets disruptive behavior may be entirely different from how a neighboring school does. Providing services for students with disabilities will continue to be debated, since the laws can be interpreted in different ways. As new court decisions are handed down and laws are updated, how inclusion is determined may change. For now, schools and districts should be consistent in their interpretation of the Individuals with Disabilities Education Act and act in good faith to try to avoid having to defend against legal action while still affording students with disabilities the best education they possibly can.

TERMS & CONCEPTS

Continuum of Alternative Placements: The continuum of alternative placements is mandated by the Individuals with Disabilities Education Act, and means that schools must provide a range of educational opportunities for students with disabilities with respect to differing levels of least restrictive environment.

Education for All Handicapped Children Act: The Education for All Handicapped Children Act was enacted in 1975 and required every public school that received federal money should give equal education and access to that education to students with disabilities. The schools must assess the children, develop teaching plans, and include parental influences to create a learning atmosphere that closely resembles that of non-disabled children.

Individualized Education Program (IEP): An individualized education program is a specific description of the goals, evaluation techniques, behavioral management plan, and behavior of each student who needs special education services.

Individuals with Disabilities Education Act (IDEA): The Individuals with Disabilities Education Act, formerly the Education for All Handicapped Children Act, requires all states receiving federal funds for education to provide students with disabilities the option to receive a proper public education that can meet the child's individual needs and equip them with the skills needed for future job opportunities and independent living.

Least Restrictive Environment: Least restrictive environment is a legal principle requiring students with disabilities to be educated as closely as possible with students without disabilities.

Mainstreaming: The practice of teaching students with disabilities in regular classrooms with non-disabled students when the general education class is working on activities where it is believed that the disabled student will excel.

Supplementary Aids and Services: Supplementary aids and services are accommodations that students with disabilities may receive outside of a regular general classroom, such as occupational therapy, speech therapy, one-on-one instruction, and recording equipment.

Sandra Myers

BIBLIOGRAPHY

Bateman, D. & Bateman, C. (2002). What does a principal need to know about inclusion? Retrieved September 29, 2007, from Education Resources Information Center, http://eric.ed.gov.

Hines, R. (2001). Inclusion in middle schools. Retrieved September 29, 2007, from Education Resources Information Center, http://eric.ed.gov.

Israel, M., Maynard, K., & Williamson, P. (2013). Promoting Literacy- Embedded, Authentic STEM Instruction for Students With Disabilities and Other Struggling Learners. Teaching Exceptional Children, 45, 18-25. Retrieved December 15, 2013, from EBSCO Online Database Education Research Complete.

McCarty, K. (2006). Full inclusion: The benefits and disadvantages of inclusive schooling. Retrieved September 29, 2007, from Education Resources Information Center, http://eric.ed.gov.

Minarik, D.W., & Lintner, T. (2011). The push for inclusive classrooms and the impact on social studies design and delivery. *Social Studies Review, 50*, 52-55. Retrieved

December 15, 2013, from EBSCO Online Database Education Research Complete.

Yell, M. (1998). The legal basis of inclusion. *Educational Leadership*, 56, 70. Retrieved September 29, 2007, from EBSCO online database, Academic Search Premier.

SUGGESTED READING

Bartlett, L., Etscheidt, S. & Weisenstein, G. (2006). *Special Education Law and Practice in Public Schools.* Upper Saddle River, NJ: Prentice Hall.

Mandlawitz, M. (2006). *What Every Teacher Should Know About IDEA 2004 Laws & Regulations.* Boston, MA: Allyn & Bacon.

Nind, M., Simmons, K., Sheehy, K., & Rix. J. (2014). *Ethics and Research in Inclusive Education: Values into Practice.* Hoboken, N.J.: Routledge.

Osborne, A. & Russo, C. (2006). *Special Education and the Law: A Guide for Practitioners.* Thousand Oaks, CA: Corwin Press.

Wright, P. & Wright, P. (2005). *IDEA 2004.* Hartfield, VA: Harbor House Law Press, Inc.

ACADEMIC FREEDOM

The topic of academic freedom on public college and university campuses has garnered national media attention and stirred passionate arguments from educators, students, and third party interests alike. This article explores the historical development of the philosophy of academic freedom and discusses its evolution from a teacher-centered to a teacher-student inclusive principle. It examines current divergent viewpoints regarding the definition and scope of academic freedom as it pertains to teachers' rights and students' rights and studies the political overtones that have come to characterize the nature of the academic freedom debate. Furthermore, the article discusses certain efforts that have been made to protect academic freedom on college and university campuses.

KEYWORDS: Academic Bill of Rights; Academic Freedom; American Association of University Professors; Bias; Diversity; Freedom of Speech; Lehrfreiheit; Lernfreiheit; Students' Rights; Students for Academic Freedom; Tenure

OVERVIEW

The concept of academic freedom on American college and university campuses is a principle fiercely guarded by educators and administrators alike. In recent years, many perceived and actual violations of this autonomy of thought and idea have met with vocal resistance, strong criticism, and, often, national media attention. Furthermore, particularly since the events of September 11, legislative and judicial intervention in academic freedom cases has increased the profile of many such cases and increased the debate surrounding the meaning and limits of what is and is not acceptable speech and action on American campuses and university classrooms.

Traditionally, academic freedom has been understood to apply to what is taught in the classroom, but educators and administrators do not hold the monopoly on academic freedom rights. Increasingly, students are asserting that these rights belong equally to them. The entrance of students into the arena of debate has not only challenged the traditional meaning of academic freedom but has also brought to the forefront of national attention the question of balancing freedom with responsibility while ensuring that the classroom remains a vibrant forum for the exchange and exploration of ideas and philosophies.

HISTORY

Belief in academic freedom as a necessary bulwark to a quality educational experience is not unique to the United States. In fact, the roots of such freedom extend as far back in history as the ancient Greeks. The great philosopher Socrates raised the ire of Athenian leaders by encouraging young people to ask questions in pursuit of truth. So great was the outcry against this ideological exploration that Socrates found himself on trial, accused of corrupting the youth. Convicted and sentenced to execution, Socrates nevertheless refused to succumb to the pressures of the state, maintaining until death his belief in the necessity of unfettered inquiry to the discovery of truth. Socrates' student Plato soon took up the cause of his mentor and established the Academy as a place of open discourse and learning in the pursuit of truth. Unlike his predecessor, Plato's work did not earn him a sentence of death, and one might say that his endeavor marked the first victory for academic freedom. To Socrates and Plato, academic freedom was not an end in and of itself. Rather, it was a means to an end: namely, the discovery of truth.

In medieval times, academic freedom and the pursuit of truth found a welcoming home on the first university campuses in Europe. Crabtree (2002) holds that this stemmed from a general adherence among academics and society as a whole to the Christian worldview, which taught that pursuit of truth was not merely a hobby or interest but rather a God-given calling. Thus "[a]cademic freedom was rooted in the belief that academics were carrying out a mission that transcended the authority of any man or human institution to countermand" (Crabtree, 2002). As a result, secular and religious authorities allowed universities to operate with significant amounts of intellectual autonomy.

Fellman's work (2003), however, qualifies this assertion. He notes that, until the late 16th century, while universities were often institutionally independent, instructors were nevertheless subject to strict limitations placed upon them both by internal and external authorities. With the 1575 founding of the university at Leiden, Germany, however, he notes that the philosophy of academic freedom found fertile ground in which to take root.

With the advent of the Enlightenment and the spread of philosophical liberalism, the concept of academic freedom as an open mechanism for the exchange of ideas grew in popularity and acceptance. Fellman notes, "[T]he rise of political, religious, and economic liberalism … [gave way to] a logical transition from the competition of the marketplace to the competition of ideas" (Fellman, 2005).

Like their medieval predecessors, American universities have staked their claim to academic freedom in the foundation of religious calling. Most early universities in the New World were religious in nature and identified their purpose as the preparation of individuals for Christian work. In keeping with this calling, universities understood academic freedom to mean the ability to function autonomously and to pursue truth apart from the interference of outside governmental entities and dictates.

Further Insights

ACADEMIC FREEDOM IN 20TH CENTURY AMERICA
Following the American Civil War, the general understanding of academic freedom changed. Crabtree

credits this to the increased adherence among intellectuals to secularist philosophies. Education became more a means of preparation for societal contributions than training for religious endeavors, and academics found themselves entering more and more into the public arena of political discourse. As a result, academic freedom in America came to mean the ability of individual professors to state their opinions and speak their ideas in the classroom without fear of retribution. As educational philosophy has come to focus on students' learning experiences as well as educators' teaching practices, however, the definition of academic freedom has expanded to encompass the right of students to learn.

THE 1915 DECLARATION OF PRINCIPLES
In 1915, the American Association of University Professors (AAUP), under its president John Dewey, and the AAUP Committee on Academic Freedom and Academic Tenure, adopted a General Declaration of Principles, today commonly known as the 1915 Declaration of Principles. The Declaration identified the meaning of academic freedom as stemming from the German principle of *Lehrfreiheit* and *Lernfreiheit*, the former being the freedom of the teacher to teach and the latter referring to the freedom or right of the student to learn. The Declaration held that academic freedom consisted of three elements:

- "freedom of inquiry and research;
- "freedom of teaching within the university or college;
- "freedom of extramural utterance and action" (AAUP's 1915 Declaration of principles).

Echoing the post-Civil War shift in popular understanding of the purpose of education from religious training to societal preparation, the Declaration outlined the three functions of academic institutions:

- "To promote inquiry and advance the sum of human knowledge;
- "To provide general instruction to the students;
- "To develop experts for various branches of the public service" (AAUP's 1915 Declaration of Principles).

The Declaration concluded that this function was only possible in an atmosphere of academic freedom. However, such freedom was not deemed to be the ability to say what one pleases with no regard for the opinions or others or to discount the beliefs of others through intimation or open hostility. Highlighted in the Declaration was a specific admonition that rights and responsibilities are inseparable, and, while teachers should not be required to hide their opinions, neither should they attempt to suppress or discredit the viewpoints of others. According to the Declaration, the professor must "above all, remember that his business is not to provide his students with ready-made conclusions, but to train them to think for themselves, and to provide them access to those materials which they need if they are to think intelligently" (AAUP's 1915 Declaration of Principles).

THE 1940 STATEMENT OF PRINCIPLES ON ACADEMIC FREEDOM & TENURE

Twenty-five years later, in 1940, the American Association of University Professors and the Association of American Colleges (AAC), now the Association of American Colleges and Universities, produced the 1940 Statement of Principles on Academic Freedom and Tenure. This statement followed a series of joint conference meetings begun in 1934 and was similar in perspective to the 1915 Declaration. The purpose of the 1940 Statement was "to promote public understanding and support of academic freedom and tenure and agreement upon procedures to ensure them in colleges and universities" (American Association of University Professors, 1940).

The Statement described the purpose of education as promotion of the common good rather than the advancement of the interests of any individual person or institution. Furthermore, the Statement noted that such an advancement of the common good "depends upon the free search for truth and its free exposition" (American Association of University Professors). Consistent with earlier understandings of academic freedom, the 1940 Statement approached the principle primarily from the perspective of instructors rather than from the viewpoint of students. Nevertheless, in promoting academic freedom for teachers, the Statement held that such freedom would safeguard both the instructors' rights and the students' rights. As outlined in the Statement, academic freedom consisted of three main principles:

- "Teachers are entitled to full freedom in research and in publication of the results, subject to adequate performance of their other academic duties;

- "Teachers are entitled to freedom in the classroom in discussing their subject, but they should be careful not to introduce into their teaching controversial matter which has no relation to their subject;

- "College and university teachers are citizens, members of a learned profession, and officers of an educational institution. When they speak or write as citizens, they should be free from institutional censorship or discipline, but their special position in the community imposes special obligations. As scholars and educational officers, they should remember that the public may judge their profession and their institution by their utterances. Hence, they should at all times be accurate, should exercise appropriate restraint, should show respect for the opinions of others, and should make every effort to indicate that they are not speaking for the institution" (AAUP).

KEYISHIAN V. BOARD OF REGENTS

In 1967, the United States Supreme Court provided an endorsement of academic freedom in the case of *Keyishian v. Board of Regents*, 385 U.S. 589 (1967). The plaintiffs in this case consisted of both faculty and non-faculty employees of the State University of New York. The faculty employees claimed that their employment had been unjustly terminated by the university due to their refusal to abide by requirements that they assert they were not members of the Communist party, and the non-faculty employees claimed unjust termination based on their refusal to swear under oath that they had never advocated or identified with a group that had ever advocated the forceful overthrow of the government.

In this landmark case, the Court identified academic freedom as a Constitutional right found in the First Amendment. The Court stated in its opinion: "Our Nation is deeply committed to safeguarding academic freedom, which is of transcendent value to all of us and not merely to the teachers concerned. That freedom is therefore a special concern of the First Amendment, which does not tolerate laws that cast a pall of orthodoxy over the classroom" (*Keyishian v. Board of Regents*).

In light of this interpretation, the AAUP and the AAC reconvened in 1969 to evaluate the 1940 Statement and recommend any revisions or changes. The result of this conference was a presentation of the 1970 Interpretations on the 1940 Statement. The

Interpretations confirmed that the Statement should not be understood to discourage controversy of opinion but that it should rather be a caution that professors not introduce into the classroom materials unrelated to the subject matter at hand. While additional revisions have been made to the Statement since 1979, the core philosophical components remain the foundation among American colleges and universities for understanding and interpreting the principle and practice of academic freedom.

VIEWPOINTS

The existence of a formal document defining such freedom and outlining its purpose has not, however, served to alleviate the debate, discussion, and disagreement surrounding the legitimate parameters of academic freedom and the point at which many believe a professor's right to teach impinges upon a student's right to learn. Moreover, as in 1915, political factors weigh heavily in the debate, and opposing arguments are most often categorized not in academic terms but rather by the partisan labels of right-wing versus left-wing.

STUDENTS FOR ACADEMIC FREEDOM & THE ACADEMIC BILL OF RIGHTS

On one side of the issue are groups such as Students for Academic Freedom (SAF), who believe that liberal bias among professors has become so prevalent on college campuses that students are no longer able to obtain a fair and objective education. Founded by conservative leader David Horowitz, SAF operates as a watchdog, chronicling cases of reported abuse of power by university professors. SAF agrees with the premise of AAUP's 1915 Declaration but holds that many public universities and university professors today do not abide by the principles contained in the document.

According to Horowitz (2006), not only are faculty at most universities politically and philosophically biased and overly partisan, but course selections and allowable classroom debate also reflect only one side of any issue. Furthermore, groups such as SAF hold that students whose political or religious viewpoints differ from those of professors are often publicly disparaged. Such complaints of violation of academic freedom extend beyond the classroom, sometimes to student groups granted funding by universities, and SAF seeks to chronicle cases in which conservative or religious groups or speakers are not afforded the same university resources as liberal organizations or speakers.

In an effort to counter his perceived liberal bias among university professors and institutions of higher learning, Horowitz authored the Academic Bill of Rights, which outlines eight principles of academic freedom intended to protect both teachers and students against undue ideological influence and pressure from governmental or other sources or partisan interests. Among the principles are the provision that students be graded solely on their academic abilities and performance and not on their religious or political beliefs, that professors not utilize the platform of the classroom to advance their own political, religious, non-religious, or ideological viewpoints, that university funds be allocated to groups and speakers that reflect the diversity and pluralism of the students, and that universities themselves remain neutral with regard to ideological, political, or religious disputes arising as a result of faculty or other professional research.

Horowitz's Academic Bill of Rights has garnered significant state and national attention by academics and legislators alike, yet on the other side of the academic freedom debate stand those who believe that the Bill is nothing more than a restriction of freedom masquerading as a defense of the same. Ivie (2005) takes particular aim at Horowitz's methodology and conclusions, holding that his assertion of liberal bias on college campuses is "unwarranted" and a result of a "so-called study" which consisted of "a skewed sample, shoddy data collection, slanted statistics, and presumptive attributions of cause" (Ivie). Ivie holds that efforts by SAF and similar organizations to label universities as politically and religiously biased are, in reality, thinly veiled attempts to promote a conservative, right-wing agenda and relegate universities to a position of self-defense.

Similarly, Minnich (2006) claims that the conservative movement to secure academic freedom is, in reality, "organized pressure" to teach a certain political or religious ideology. Rather than protecting freedom, Minnich argues, this movement restricts such freedom by encouraging "spying" in the classroom and "monitoring" classroom discussion. The American Association of University Professors agrees. In a statement on the Academic Bill of Rights, the AAUP held that the Bill is "improper and dangerous" and actually threatens the very academic freedom it purports to defend (AAUP Statement on Academic Bill of Rights, 2003). By recommending guidelines for diversity in the representation of political viewpoints among faculty, for example, the Bill, according to AAUP, belies the practice of institutional neutrality which it claims to support.

ACADEMIC FREEDOM AFTER 9/11

While the conservative versus liberal debate in academia has been present for some time, the events of September 11, 2001, and the subsequent U.S. War on Terror brought the issue to the center of the national stage. Professors on several university campuses who have spoken out in critique of the war or in perceived sympathy to the perpetrators of the 9/11 attacks have found themselves under fire from students and outside organizations for their remarks, while students taking positions opposite to these and other professors have, likewise, found their viewpoints ridiculed or discounted. This reality has brought increased attention to the questions of what is and what is not appropriate classroom discussion and when does academic freedom cross the line to partisan bias.

According to Greg Lukianoff, president of the Foundation for Individual Rights in Education (FIRE), current cases of reported abuse on college campuses are similar to cases that appeared 10 and 20 years ago, yet the heightened sensitivity aroused by 9/11 has resulted in added attention being drawn by these cases. As national attention has focused increasingly on the prospect of balancing liberty with security in a post-9/11 world, public interest in the political activities and opinions of university faculty and their relationship to student freedom has grown (Gravois, 2006).

STUDENTS' ACADEMIC FREEDOM

Taking neither the extreme left or extreme right positions, some believe that while academic freedom remains alive and well for institutions of higher learning and for students, the same freedom for university professors is weakening. According to Gary Pavela, director of judicial programs at the University of Maryland, College Park, students have become more aware of their right to academic freedom, and institutions are enjoying judicial support for their autonomy. Pavela points to the 2003 Supreme Court decisions in *Gratz* and *Grutter* in which the Court upheld the rights of institutions to exercise judgment in certain educational matters. At the same time, however, Pavela expresses concern that grassroots and legislative movements to support academic freedom for students may come at the expense of a certain degree of

freedom for faculty (cited in "Balancing student and faculty academic freedom," 2005).

CONCLUSION

In the arena of public debate, the competition between the liberal and conservative interpretations of academic freedom offers few signs of reprieve and leaves educators, administrators, legislators, and students alike searching for ways to balance opposing interests while maintaining the vigor of academic exploration that is vital to intellectual pursuit. As Bollinger (2005) notes, the climate of freedom on today's campuses requires a "renewed understanding" of four basic principles of academic freedom. He asserts that the position of professor carries with it the concurrent responsibility to nurture students' scholastic endeavors while acting with sensitivity towards divergent viewpoints. He calls for a balanced approach in which professors are free to state their opinions but not to portray their opinions as holding greater merit than all others, yet maintains that professors must exercise caution when entering the political realm and must clearly distinguish between their actions as professors and their activities as private citizens. Finally, he urges that preservation of academic freedom remain the responsibility of universities and professors and not that of outside groups, politicians, or the media.

As students, professors, educational institutions, and outside groups seek to advance their respective causes, the debate over the proper practice of academic freedom will undoubtedly continue. Despite differences of opinion in practice, the principle of academic freedom is central to sincere intellectual exploration, and, in the melting pot of ideas that form today's universities, presentation of divergent viewpoints allows students to challenge themselves intellectually while pursuing the truth that is the aim of all education.

TERMS & CONCEPTS

Academic Bill of Rights: A document written by David Horowitz and distributed by Students for Academic Freedom which outlines eight principles for achieving an educational environment free of bias.

Academic Freedom: The right of a teacher or professor to perform research and state their beliefs without fear of professional retribution. The term has also come to apply to the right of students to learn without fear of having their beliefs discounted.

American Association of University Professors: An organization of professors and academics whose mission is to advance academic freedom, set standards for Higher Education, and work towards using Higher Education for the common good.

Diversity: As it pertains to academic freedom, a variety of viewpoints represented by students and professors with differing opinions.

Lehrfreiheit: The right of teachers to teach.

Lernfreiheit: The right of students to learn, particularly as it relates to the right of students to choose their own course of study.

Students' Rights: The right of students to pursue learning and express opinions in the classroom without fear of bias or disparagement from faculty or administration.

Students for Academic Freedom: An organization whose goal is to end political bias on university campuses and return to campuses the objective pursuit of knowledge.

Tenure: The state of holding a position permanently without contract renewals.

Gina L. Diorio

BIBLIOGRAPHY

AAUP's 1915 declaration of principles. (1915). Retrieved March 5, 2007, from http://cms.studentsforacademicfreedom.org.

American Association of University Professors. (1940). *1940 Statement of principles on academic freedom and tenure.* Retrieved March 5, 2007, from www.aaup.org.

American Association of University Professors. (2003). Statement on Academic Bill of Rights. Retrieved March 6, 2007, from www.aaup.org.

Balancing student and faculty academic freedom. (2005). *National On-Campus Report, 33,* 1-6. Retrieved March 06, 2007, from EBSCO Online Database Academic Search Premier.

Bollinger, L. (2005, Apr.). The value and responsibilities of academic freedom. *Chronicle of Higher Education, 51,* B20-B20. Retrieved March 06, 2007, from EBSCO Online Database Academic Search Premier.

Crabtree, D. (2002). *Academic freedom.* Retrieved March 5, 2007, from www.mckenziestudycenter.org.

Fellman, D. (2003). Academic freedom. In P. P. Weiner (Ed.) *Dictionary of the history of ideas* (pp.10-17). Retrieved March 5, 2007, from http://etext.virginia.edu.

Gravois, J. (2006). Despite post-9/11 fears, groups that protect academic freedom remain strong. *Chronicle of Higher Education, 53,* A12-A12. Retrieved March 06, 2007, from EBSCO Online Database Academic Search Premier.

Horowitz, D. (2006). *Academic bill of rights.* Retrieved March 6, 2007, from http://cms.studentsforacademicfreedom.org.

Horowitz, D. (2006). *Mission and strategy.* Retrieved March 6, 2007, from http://cms.studentsforacademicfreedom.org.

Ivie, R. (2005). A presumption of academic freedom. *Review of Education, Pedagogy & Cultural Studies, 27,* 53-85. Retrieved March 06, 2007, from EBSCO Online Database Academic Search Premier.

Keyishian v. Board of Regents, 385 U.S. 589 (1967). Retrieved March 5, 2007, from http://caselaw.lp.findlaw.com.

Minnich, E. (2006). Between impartiality and bias. *Change, 38,* 16-23. Retrieved March 06, 2007, from EBSCO Online Database Academic Search Premier.

SUGGESTED READING

Benjamin, E. (2006). Reflections on academic boycotts. *Academe, 92,* 80-83. Retrieved March 06, 2007, from EBSCO Online Database Academic Search Premier.

Gibbs, P. (2013). Role virtue ethics and academic ethics: A consideration of academic freedom. *International Journal of Educational Management, 27,* 720-729. Retrieved December 15, 2013, from EBSCO Online Database Education Research Complete.

Lee, D., & Garrett, J. (2005). Academic freedom in the middle and secondary school classroom. *Clearing House, 78,* 267-268. Retrieved March 06, 2007, from EBSCO Online Database Academic Search Premier.

Lipka, S. (2007). Campus speech codes said to violate rights. *Chronicle of Higher Education, 53,* A32-A32. Retrieved March 06, 2007, from EBSCO Online Database Academic Search Premier.

Macfarlane, B. (2012). Re-framing student academic freedom: A capability perspective. *Higher Education, 63,* 719-732. Retrieved December 15, 2013, from EBSCO Online Database Education Research Complete.

Ren, K., & Li, J. (2013). Academic freedom and university autonomy: A Higher Education policy perspective. *Higher Education Policy, 26,* 507-522. Retrieved December 15, 2013, from EBSCO Online Database Education Research Complete.

Salas, A. (2006). Academic freedom: Under siege from claims of liberal bias. *Education Digest, 72,* 55-59. Retrieved March 06, 2007, from EBSCO Online Database Academic Search Premier.

Swanger, D. (2005, Dec.). Academic freedom: If it ain't broke.... *Community College Week, 18,* 4-5. Retrieved March 06, 2007, from EBSCO Online Database Academic Search Premier.

Out of School Faculty Behavior

At the beginning of the 21st century, public school faculty are facing scrutiny and accountability for their behavior in and out of school. In their professional roles, faculty are faced with ethical issues, increased student needs, increased student violence, new technology, new teaching standards, and battles over teachers' rights. Different laws and mores govern faculty behavior in and out of school. Faculty at all levels, including elementary, secondary, and higher education, are held to different work standards and personal standards by parents, teachers, unions, school boards, and the society at large. Out of school, faculty speech is protected under the First Amendment. Out of school, the teacher-student relationship limits and curtails faculty behavior as it is related to students. In school, faculty are subject to the rules and laws that govern employee-employer relationships as well as the standards and laws that direct teacher student relationships.

Keywords: American Civil Liberties Union; Bill of Rights; Blogs; Boundary Violations; Ethics; Faculty; Fiduciary Relationship; First Amendment; Freedom of Expression; Mentors; Public Schools; School Districts; Supreme Court; Teacher Student Relationships

Overview

At the beginning of the twenty first century, faculty face scrutiny and accountability for their behavior in and out of school. In their professional roles, faculty are faced with ethical issues, increased student needs, increased student violence, new technology, new teaching standards, and battles over teachers' rights. Different laws and mores govern faculty behavior in and out of school. Faculty at all levels, including elementary, secondary, and higher education, are held to different work standards and personal standards by parents, teachers' unions, school boards, and the society at large. Out of school, faculty speech is protected under the First Amendment. Out of school, the teacher student relationship limits and curtails faculty behavior as it is related to students. In school, faculty are subject to the rules and laws that govern employee-employer relationships as well as the standards and laws that direct teacher student relationships.

This article provides an examination of the issue of faculty behavior out of school. It addresses the question of whether or not teachers have the right to free speech outside of school as well as the liberties guaranteed teachers outside of school and the curtailment of some teacher student relationships and behaviors. The following sections discuss teachers' First Amendment rights. The relationship between faculty behavior, district policies, and federal education law are also discussed. The line between professional and personal faculty behavior and teacher student relationships is addressed and the role of faculty as mentor is examined.

Faculty Rights & the First Amendment

Inside and outside of the school environment, faculty enjoy different First Amendment protections. In school, faculty are subject to the desires, wills, commands, and perspectives of their employers. Inside the school environment, the personal opinions of faculty are not protected as free speech. Outside of the school environment, the First Amendment protects the personal opinions of faculty. In the United States, freedom of expression is guaranteed and protected by the First Amendment of the Bill of Rights. The First Amendment of the Bill of Rights prohibits the national government from limiting freedom of expression. It states that the government and Congress shall make no law respecting an establishment of religion, or prohibiting the free exercise thereof; or abridging the freedom of speech, or of the press; or the right of the people peaceably to assemble, and to petition the government for a redress of grievances. Freedom of expression refers to a person's right to say or publish what he or she believes. Freedom of expression comes with societal and legal parameters. For example, the U.S. Supreme Court has defined numerous instances of impermissible speech. Throughout the twentieth century, the Supreme Court, the highest federal court in the United States, ruled on conflicts surrounding issues related to freedom of expression, such as free speech, free press, obscenity, libel, slander, symbolic speech, and commercial speech. Supreme Court rulings have defined the parameters of free speech that are acceptable in our society.

THE AMERICAN CIVIL LIBERTIES UNION

The American Civil Liberties Union (ACLU) protects the free speech rights of public school teachers. The American Civil Liberties Union, established in 1920, is a legal organization dedicated to protecting civil liberties such as First Amendment rights, equal protection under the law, right to due process, and right to privacy. The American Civil Liberties Union, and other legal organizations, believes that freedom of expression requires constant legal vigilance and protection. The American Civil Liberties Union publishes information about the free speech rights of teachers as related to speech outside of school, speech inside the classroom, teachers' clothing, classroom or office decoration, bulletin boards, on-campus conversations with colleagues, and on-campus demonstrations or meetings open to the public. According to the American Civil Liberties Union, the First Amendment protects teacher speech outside of the school environment. The American Civil Liberties Union promotes information about the law to inform teacher and school district behavior and relations. The American Civil Liberties Union shares the following information about teachers' rights with the general public:

- Teachers do not forfeit the right to comment publicly on matters of public importance simply because they accept a public school teaching position;
- Teachers cannot be fired or disciplined for statements about matters of public importance unless it can be demonstrated that the teacher's speech created a substantial adverse impact on school functioning;
- A teacher's off-campus statements regarding the war or participation in an off-campus political demonstration are not acceptable bases for job discipline or termination.

APPLICABLE COURT CASES

The Constitution provides little protection for teachers who express their beliefs in the classroom. Two court cases illustrate the different free speech protections afforded teachers inside and outside the classroom. In 2003, the *Mayer v. Monroe County Community School Corporation* court case found that public employees, including primary and secondary school teachers, do not have a constitutional right to share their own beliefs and opinions when speaking as employees. The court case was brought by a teacher, Deborah Mayer, whose contract was not renewed after telling her students, "I honk for peace," during a discussion of war protests and the war in Iraq. The court case followed a January 2003 ruling by the Seventh U.S. Circuit Court of Appeals that declared a teacher's speech to be a commodity that he or she sells to an employer in exchange for a salary (Egelko, 2007).

In contrast, a 2006 court case between a substitute teacher, Jeffrey Herman, represented by the American Civil Liberties Union of Massachusetts, and the Boston Teachers Union illustrates the free speech rights of teachers outside of school. In this case, the teacher Jeffrey Herman was put on a do not employ list by a school headmaster after the headmaster heard the teacher testify at a City Council hearing against the spending of one million dollars on Junior Reserve Officer Training Corps (JROTC) programs in the Boston public schools. The parties involved settled the case out of court. The attorneys at the American Civil Liberties Union of Massachusetts issued a statement explaining that teachers, out of school, are entitled to political opinions like other members of society.

The current socio-political climate creates students and teachers who know their rights and administrators charged with protecting the safety of a diverse student body. The U.S. democratic process invites and facilitates the process of questioning and challenging constitutional rights and liberties. As society and culture develop, new environments and scenarios arise in public institutions that require constitutional interpretation. Educational institutions, as a cornerstone of society, require constitutional review, oversight, and interpretation. The interpretation of the Constitution is an ongoing process. The public education system has become a location of Constitutional challenge and interpretation. The U.S. education system, a relatively new and still evolving public institution, is often in tension with public mores and Constitutional law.

Applications

TEACHER STUDENT RELATIONSHIPS

While the speech of teachers is constitutionally protected out of school, teacher student relationships out of school are not protected, allowed, or encouraged by families, school districts, and the law. Incidents of teacher student fraternization and sexual relationships have received publicity over the past decade. Scholars and law enforcement professionals debate whether or not the high profile cases represent a rising trend in teacher student boundary violations. The teaching profession, over the past twenty years, has undergone increased professionalization. Examples of the change in professional standards include the move from state certification to state licensure, more rigorous post baccalaureate certification exams for prospective teachers, and rigorous continuing education requirements for employed teachers. The No Child Left Behind Act (2001) put a focus on teacher competency, certification, and continued education. While the focus on teaching standards has risen, there has been little focus on standardizing professional conduct. While other human service professions, including medicine, psychology, and law, have developed professionally recognized and enforceable codes of ethics, teaching has not.

THE NATIONAL EDUCATION ASSOCIATION CODE OF ETHICS

In 1975, the National Education Association (NEA) created a code of ethics for the teaching profession. The National Education Association code of ethics of the education profession (1975) includes a statement of commitment to the student and to the profession of teaching. The code states that the educator will make the following commitments:

- The educator shall not unreasonably restrain the student from independent action in the pursuit of learning;
- The educator shall not unreasonably deny the student's access to varying points of view; the educator shall not deliberately suppress or distort subject matter relevant to the student's progress;
- The educator shall make reasonable effort to protect the student from conditions harmful to learning or to health and safety;
- The educator shall not intentionally expose the student to embarrassment or disparagement;
- The educator shall not, on the basis of race, color, creed, sex, national origin, marital status, political or religious beliefs, family, social or cultural background, or sexual orientation, unfairly exclude any student from participation in any program or rant any advantage to any student;
- The educator shall not use professional relationships with students for private advantage;
- The educator shall not disclose information about students obtained in the course of professional service unless disclosure serves a compelling professional purpose or is required by law.

The National Education Association guidelines are vague and not enforceable by law. High profile cases of teacher student relationships have received wide-spread publicity. Criminal misconduct by teachers, in the area of relationships with students, has not resulted in professional and enforceable ethical and behavioral standards. While there is an implicit moral code for teachers in America, no professional code of ethics for teachers yet exists. Teacher student boundary violations are a serious occurrence (Barrett & Headley, 2006). Teachers and students are involved in a fiduciary relationship. Fiduciary relationship refers to a special relationship in which one person accepts the trust and confidence of another to act in the latter's best interest. Fiduciary relationships differ from consensual relationships between peers or adults. Relationships between teachers and students are always fundamentally asymmetric in nature. The student teacher relationship has distinctive issues with power, ethics, and boundaries. There are five main types of power including reward, coercive, legitimate, referent, and expert. Teachers enjoy or experience all five types of power (Plaut, 1993).

TEACHERS AS MENTORS

Teachers often serve as mentors to their students. The mentoring relationship is multifaceted and includes multiple roles: Teacher, sponsor, guide, exemplar, counselor, believer, and evaluator.

- **Teacher:** The mentor's role is to enhance the student's skills and intellectual development;
- **Sponsor:** The mentor uses his or her influence to facilitate the student's entry and advancement into a chosen field or domain;
- **Guide:** The mentor welcomes the student into a new knowledge domain or field;
- **Exemplar:** The mentor serves as one whom the student can emulate;
- **Counselor:** The mentor's role in times of student stress is to serve as counselor and empathic listener;
- **Believer:** The mentor's role is to facilitate the student's academic, personal, and professional development;
- **Evaluator:** The mentor evaluates the student's performance.

Mentor relationships are complicated by the following factors: Parent-peer balance, mutuality, and social interaction.

- Parent-peer balance refers to the mentor's primary function as a transitional figure. The mentor represents a combination of parent and peer;
- Mutuality in the mentor peer relationship refers to the student and mentor's desire to see their success as reflecting on one another;
- Social interaction acknowledges that student mentor relationships serve a number of important functions. The functions include the following: Enhance the teaching and learning relationship; help acquaint the student with a new field or domain of knowledge; and help contribute to the personal development of the student.

BOUNDARIES

Teachers and mentors are required to establish boundaries with their students. Boundaries refer to a spectrum of activities that have the potential to exploit the dependency of a student in a number of ways. Boundaries are the limits of a fiduciary relationship. Appropriate boundaries are not restricted to sexual contact. Boundaries are required to limit the development of dual relationships between teachers and students. Dual relationship can confuse roles for the student. Boundary violations, which refer to relationships outside the professional relationship, may compromise the integrity and effectiveness of the student-teacher relationship. Boundary violations between teachers and students have academic consequences for students. Some students who have become sexually involved with their mentors may change or abandon the educational programs or may be dismissed from the academic program. In addition, boundary violations have the potential of personal harm to the student if there is a student history of poor self-esteem, dependency, or victimization (Plaut).

Teachers and students are engaged in social roles. Social roles have inherent expectations about how a person in a particular role is to behave as well as the rights and obligations which pertain to that role. Role conflicts arise when the expectations attached to one role call for behavior which is incompatible with that of another role. Student teacher boundary violations occur most often when dual role relationships exist. A dual role relationship exists when an individual simultaneously or sequentially participates in two role categories (Gottlieb, 1993).

The prevention of teacher student boundary violations requires vigilance and self-awareness on the part of teachers. Teachers must pay attention to the following issues: Risk factors, transference issues for student, predatory sexism, and psychological vulnerabilities. Ultimately, there exist constant risk factors inherent in the professional or institutional setting itself-a closed system (Plaut). State boards of education and school districts issue guidelines to faculty for managing teacher student relationships in and out of school. For example, the Pennsylvania State Education Association promotes the following strategies for teacher-student relationships in an effort to avoid liability:

- **Maintain personal space:** Teachers cannot permit students to invade their personal space. Teachers cannot allow students to touch them, stroke their hair or hang on them to gain attention;
- **Avoid double entendres:** Teachers must be extremely careful when choosing their words. Students may report teacher remarks to their parents or administrators in ways that distort the context in which they were intended;
- **Do not discuss sexually explicit topics:** Teachers cannot afford to be drawn into conversations regarding sexually explicit topics, song lyrics, jokes or movies. Teachers should always discourage and try to stop such conversations in their presence;
- **Do not be alone with students:** Teachers should avoid being alone with a student in an enclosed space where teachers will not be observed by another adult. Examples of unacceptable situations include after-school detention, keeping a student in from recess, make-up tests, and tutoring are all examples of potentially risky situations;
- **Do not become friends with students:** Teachers should always maintain the line which lets students know that they are the teacher. If this line becomes blurred, students may become too comfortable with the teacher. This comfort can lead the student to make romantic overtures toward the teacher;
- **Do not socialize with students:** Teachers must be careful not to socialize with students outside of school. If teachers are seen in public with a student, people may assume an inappropriate relationship exists.

Primary, secondary, and higher education faculty are subject to different laws and standards. The following colleges have policies against consensual sexual relations between professors and students: William and Mary, Tufts, Indiana, Harvard and Radcliff, Amherst, Oberlin, Stanford, Yale, Duke, the University of Virginia, Ohio Wesleyan, the University of Iowa, College of William and Mary, University of Michigan, University of California, and Ohio Northern University. These colleges and universities all consider faculty student romantic relationships to be an ethics violation but vary in the formality and severity of their rules and regulations on student faculty relationships. The rationale for college bans on student teacher relations is based on the imbalance of power between teachers and students (Oliviero, 1994). The imbalance of power between teachers and students is less in higher education settings but still does exist. Teacher student boundary crossings and violations are more common in higher education than in primary and secondary school settings. As a result, colleges and universities are increasingly creating rules and guidelines for faculty student social interactions.

CONCLUSION

In the final analysis, faculty behavior, as it relates to student relationships, is subject to the same laws inside and outside of the school environment. In contrast, out of school faculty speech is not subject to the same education laws as in school faculty speech. Outside of the school environment, faculty speech is, for the most part, protected by the First Amendment. Possible exceptions to out of school faculty free speech protections are arising from new communication technologies. New communication technologies, such as email, instant messaging, and blogging, blur the lines that once demarcated out of school and in school faculty behavior. Blogs refer to online personal journals with frequent posts of links and content. Are faculty who choose to keep personal blogs on which to write about their work environments protected under the First Amendment protections that shelter other off campus teacher speech? School boards and school districts have broad statutes about professional and unprofessional conduct. For example, the California Education Code discusses and allows dismissal of teachers on the grounds of immoral or unprofessional conduct. This statute could be used to limit and curtail First Amendment speech rights with regard to blogging. Ultimately, the U.S. Supreme Court, school districts, society at large, and faculty themselves will mediate the parameters of out of school faculty behavior.

TERMS & CONCEPTS

American Civil Liberties Union: A legal organization, established in 1920, dedicated to protecting civil liberties such as first amendment rights, equal protection under the law, right to due process, and right to privacy.

Bill of Rights: The first ten amendments to the U.S. Constitution.

Blogs: Online personal journals with frequent posts of links and content.

Boundary Violations: Relationships outside the professional relationship.

Ethics: A perception and determination of right and wrong.

Faculty: Members of the teaching profession.

Fiduciary Relationship: A special relationship in which one person accepts the trust and confidence of another to act in the latter's best interest.

First Amendment: An amendment to the Constitution that states that the government and Congress shall make no law respecting an establishment of religion, or prohibiting the free exercise thereof; or abridging the freedom of speech, or of the press; or the right of the people peaceably to assemble, and to petition the government for a redress of grievances.

Freedom of Expression: A person's right to say or publish what he or she believes.

Mentor: A teacher who serves as a counselor and role model.

Public Schools: The elementary or secondary school system in the United States supported by public funds.

Supreme Court: The highest federal court in the United States.

Simone I. Flynn

BIBLIOGRAPHY

ACLU and Teachers Union Settle Free Speech Lawsuit Against City of Boston. (2007).The American Civil Liberties Union. Retrieved November 14, 2007, from http://aclu.org.

Barrett, D., Headley, K., Stovall, B., & Witte, J. (2006). Teachers' perceptions of the frequency and seriousness of violations of ethical standards. *Journal of Psychology, 140*, 421-433. Retrieved November 14, 2007, from EBSCO Online Database Academic Search Premier.

Belch, H. (2011). Teachers Beware! The Dark Side of Social Networking. *Learning & Leading With Technology, 39*, 15-19. Retrieved December 15, 2013, from EBSCO Online Database Education Research Complete.

Code of Ethics of the Education Profession. (1975). The National Education Association. Retrieved November 14, 2007, from http://nea.org.

Eckes, S.E. (2013). Strippers, beer, and bachelorette parties: Regulating teachers' out-of-school conduct. *Principal Leadership, 14*, 8-10. Retrieved December 15, 2013, from EBSCO Online Database Education Research Complete.

Egelko, B. (2007). Supreme Court denies hearing for fired 'honk for peace' teacher. *The San Francisco Chronichle*, A-7. Retrieved November 14, 2007, from http://sfgate.com.

Free speech rights of public school teachers. (2003). The American Civil Liberties Union. Retrieved November 14, 2007, from http://aclu-wa.org.

Gottlieb, M. (1993). Avoiding exploitive dual relationships: A decision-making model. *Psychotherapy, 30*, 41-48.

Henshaw, C. (2004). Boundary issues between faculty and students in associate degree nursing programs. Seattle University Press, 145.

Johnston, P. 2005. I walk the line. *Chronicle of Higher Education, 51*, C1-C4. Retrieved November 14, 2007, from EBSCO Online Database Academic Search Premier.

Oliveiro, T. (1994). (E)strange(d) bedfellows: Thoughts on the bans against faculty-student sexual relations and how they can hurt us. *Radical Teacher, 45*, 9.

Owen, P., & Zwahr-Castro, J. (2007). Boundary issues in academia: Student perceptions of faculty-student boundary crossings. *Ethics & Behavior, 17*, 117-129.

Plaut, M. (1992). Boundary issues in teacher-student relationships. *The Journal of Sex and Marital Therapy, 19*, 210-219.

Sex and schools: By the numbers. (2013). *Phi Delta Kappan, 94*, 32-33. Retrieved December 15, 2013, from EBSCO Online Database Education Research Complete.

Shipley, G. (2011). Cyber misconduct: Discipline and the law. *Leadership, 41*, 14-16. Retrieved December 15, 2013, from EBSCO Online Database Education Research Complete.

Staying out of trouble: Teacher-student relationships. Pennsylvania State Education Association. Retrieved November 14, 2007, from http://heyteach.org.

Young, V. (2012). Not guilty, but not fit. *School Administrator, 69*, 9. Retrieved December 15, 2013, from EBSCO Online Database Education Research Complete.

SUGGESTED READING

Blackburn, R., & Lindquist, J. (1971). Faculty behavior in the legislative process: Professorial attitudes vs. behavior concerning inclusion of students in academic decision-making. *Sociology of Education, 44*, 398-421. Retrieved November 14, 2007, from EBSCO Online Database Academic Search Premier.

Morgan, B., & Korschgen, A. (2001). The ethics of faculty behavior: Students' and professors' views. *College Student Journal, 35*, 418. Retrieved November 14, 2007, from EBSCO Online Database Academic Search Premier.

Stratton, R., Myers, S., & King, R. (1994). Faculty behavior, grades, and student evaluations. *Journal of Economic Education, 25*, 5-15. Retrieved November 14, 2007, from EBSCO Online Database Education Research Complete.

SEXUAL MISCONDUCT IN THE SCHOOLS

Court cases help shape educational misconduct policy and news grabbing headlines bring public attention to this educational problem. The most notorious type is sexual misconduct of teachers with students. Sexual misconduct occurs about equally among male and female teachers. Ultimately, this behavior seriously hurts children. This article presents an overview of sexual misconduct in school, with viewpoints on how to prevent such educator misconduct and how to track and fire the individuals who commit the crimes.

KEYWORDS: Disciplinary Action; Grooming; Liable; No Child Left Behind Act of 2001 (NCLB); Sexual Misconduct; Staff or Educator Misconduct; Statute of Limitations; Title IX of the Education Amendments of 1972

OVERVIEW

Educator misconduct covers a variety of offenses. The most publicized type in the media and the High Court system are ones where school employees make poor judgments in their relationships with their students and sexual misconduct occurs. Public school educators can include but are not limited to administrators, counselors, secretaries, teachers, substitute teachers, teacher's aides, coaches, custodians, security guards, bus drivers, cafeteria workers, volunteers or others who may encounter a student in a school-based setting (Sutton, 2004).

EXAMPLES OF MISCONDUCT IN THE MEDIA

- In 1997, Alaskan teachers had disciplinary action taken for the following types of misconduct: sexual misconduct; conviction of theft; theft of Ritalin from student supplies and use of fraudulent transcript (Green, 1998);
- In 1997, a Pennsylvania teacher surrendered his license because he was showing pornographic movies and giving alcohol to eighth and ninth graders (Zemel, 1999);
- In 2007, 167 Ohio bus drivers were found to have (DUI) Driving Under the Influence or other drug related license suspensions (Marshall, 2007);
- The tight-knit Pennsylvania State University community was shaken by the 2011 child sexual abuse scandal involving Gerald "Jerry" Sandusky, the university football team's former defensive coordinator. In 2012, Sandusky was convicted of forty-five out of forty-eight counts of sexual abuse involving ten underage boys over a fifteen-year period. Sandusky had met the boys through Second Mile, a charity that he and his wife had founded in 1972 (Chappell, 2012; Gladwell, 2012);
- In 2013, a California elementary school teacher was sentenced to twenty-five years in prison for lewd conduct against 23 Los Angeles school children at Miramonte Elementary School (Winton & Ceasar, 2013).

TYPES OF SEXUAL MISCONDUCT

In Educator Sexual Misconduct: A Synthesis of Existing Literature, Carol Shakeshaft (2004) defines sexual misconduct as behavior by an educator that is directed at a student and intended to sexually arouse or titillate the educator or the child. The behaviors are "physical, verbal, or visual. Examples include touching breasts or genitals of students; oral, anal, and vaginal penetration; showing students pictures of a sexual nature; and sexually related conversations, jokes, or questions directed at students" (Shakeshaft).

Goorian (1999) describes two types of sexual misconduct recognized by the law:

Quid pro quo (this for that) occurs when a school employee explicitly or implicitly grants a student a favor in exchange for sexual gratification. The employee may, as a condition for a student's participation in an educational activity or in return for an educational decision, request that the student submit to unwelcome sexual advances, grant sexual favors, or agree to engage in other verbal, nonverbal, or physical conduct of a sexual nature. Hostile environment means unwanted and unwelcome verbal or physical contact of a sexual nature that is sufficiently severe, persistent, or pervasive to limit a student's ability to participate in or benefit from an educational program or activity (Goorian).

Goorian also explains that sexual misconduct behavior can be classified in three levels that include contact and non-contact behavior:

- Level I includes non-contact behavior such as exhibitionism and sharing sexual photos. Contact behavior includes fondling, touching, kissing, and sexual hugging;
- Level II is non-contact actions that include sexual comments, taunting, and asking about sexual activity;
- Level III is contact behavior that includes all types of sexual or genital contact (Goorian).

LEGITIMATE NONSEXUAL TOUCHING

The U.S. Department of Education's Office of Civil Rights (OCR) offers examples of legitimate nonsexual touching: a coach hugs a student who makes a goal or a kindergarten teacher hugs a student who skinned a knee. However, repeated hugs under inappropriate circumstances can make for a hostile environment (Goorian).

TEACHERS WHO ABUSE

Studies have shown that almost 43 percent of all educator sex offenders are women. Because claims involving female misconduct may be underreported, this number may be low (Sutton). The idea that a woman could sexually assault a young man would have been dismissed a decade ago; however, if a person in a position of trust or authority has consensual or nonconsensual sex with a student before he or she is 18, it is a crime. Psychological profiles show female teachers who are involved in sexual misconduct with students are generally socially immature rather than sexually deviant (Driedger, 2003).

While teachers and coaches tend to be under media scrutiny most often, sexual misconduct exists in all educator categories. Music teachers or coaches often spend one-on-one time with individual students, and as a result they are more likely to sexually abuse. Between 1995 and 2003, 25 percent of the educators in Texas who were coaches or music teachers were disciplined for sexual infractions involving students. Washington state teachers who coach were "three times more likely to be investigated by the state for sexual misconduct than non-coaching teachers" (Shakeshaft).

How Sexual Abusers Manipulate

Students are taught to trust their instructors and leaders, but sexual abusers in schools manipulate students into sexual contact by lying, controlling and exercising their authority over them. Often predators victimize students who are vulnerable or marginalized and often needy for attention. These marginal students are also more likely to be unaccepted as plausible and trustworthy complainants. In elementary schools, the abuser is often a favorite teacher and is often professionally accomplished. Successful educators are most likely to connect quickly and easily with children. At the later levels of education, namely middle and high schools, abusers are not necessarily always wonderful educators. Initially, the acts are more often open opportunities, a result of poor choices or a misguided sense of authority (Shakeshaft).

Most abuse occurs with "grooming" and enticement. Abusers try to spend additional time with students, and they may send invites to non-education based activities like trips, movies, and parties that occur during after-school hours. Abusers may also buy students gifts, tell sexual jokes, and tease them sexually. This form of verbal abuse is a method of "grooming" victims. As such joking continues without being reprimanded, abusers may advance their intimate play by touching and making other sexual advances that probably will not be reported (Goorian).

Offenders work hard at maintaining secrecy and silence. Many children have been abused by others, or they fear punishment. Some children do not realize that they are being abused. However, they may be able to understand the inappropriate relationship as shameful, unwanted, wrong, or frightening. Oftentimes, children will assume that such behavior is "love," as this is what is explained to them by their abusers. Offenders use intimidation, exploitation of power and manipulation of child's affection to keep the misconduct a secret (Shakeshaft).

Further Insights

The Law

The No Child Left Behind Act of 2001 (NCLB) was an amendment to the Section 5414 mandate of the Elementary and Secondary Education Act of 1965 (ESEA) that called for a deeper exploration into the issue of sexual misconduct in school systems. This mandate required the U.S. Department of Education to administer a literature review study of sexual abuse in U.S. schools. This review is called Educator Sexual Misconduct: A Synthesis of Existing Literature (Shakeshaft).

In addition, court cases help shape and define education policy on employee misconduct in public schools. Title IX of the Education Amendments of 1972 is used by many victims who were sexually abused by educators to plead their cases. Though this amendment avoids dealing directly with educator sexual harassment, it restricts all forms of sex discrimination in any organization that collects federal money (Sutton). Stein (2000) explains the relationship of Title IX.

According to the US Department of Education Office for Civil Rights' guidelines, schools are required by the Title IX regulations to adopt and publish grievance procedures providing for prompt and equitable resolution of all sex discrimination complaints, including complaints of sexual harassment. Students should be notified of the procedures which should be written in language appropriate to the age of the school's students. Without a widely understood grievance procedure in place, a school (or school district) is held liable regardless of whether or not sexual harassment has occurred. (Stein).

In the 1992 court case Franklin v. Gwinnett County Public Schools, Christine Franklin sued for $6 million in a civil suit against her school district. Franklin claimed that she was continually sexually harassed beginning the fall of 1986. Originally, the Title IX statutes did not authorize damages as a way to solve the problem legally. But, they allowed back pay and prospective relief for school employees. The lower courts figured that since she was not an employee at the time of the harassment, she could not receive monetary damages. However, in a summary judgment, the Supreme Court decided to enforce Title IX legally by authorizing a damages remedy (Sutton).

In 2010, childhood sexual abuse survivor and child advocate Erin Merryn began urging legislators in Illinois to pass laws requiring school districts to add age-appropriate child sexual abuse education to elementary school curricula, and educate teachers, administrators, and parents about abuse prevention. Illinois was the first state to pass what became known as Erin's Law on February 14, 2011. Other states have since passed similar legislation (Erin's Law, 2012).

SCHOOL DISTRICTS MAY BE LIABLE FOR TEACHER'S MISCONDUCT

In 1998, the court case *Gebser v. Lago Vista Independent School District* involved a student in the eighth-grade and a high school teacher who maintained a sexual relationship for over a year. The student asked for damages for sexual harassment, insisting that the school district and offending teacher had infringed upon her rights as stated under Title IX. The student claimed the teacher acted as the school district's agent, as he was employed by the school district, making the district liable. The student also faulted the school district on the grounds that it had never warned or educated instructors, students, and parents about the realities and dangers of sexual harassment (Sutton).

In the end, The Supreme Court supported the lower courts, concluding that damages could not be recovered because school officials with power to correct the teacher misconduct did not have knowledge of the misconduct. Therefore, the district could not be held liable by the student. The Supreme Court also held that the district did not constitute deliberate indifference because of lack of a grievance procedure (Sutton).

However, in *Doe v. Warren Consolidated Schools* (2003), a federal district court in Michigan ruled that the school district could be held liable for teacher sexual harassment under both Section 1983 and Title IX because school administrators knew of a teacher's long history of sexual misconduct with female students. The district failed to remove him from

having contact with students. The court ruled that the district could be held liable for sexual misconduct because the district knew the employee's sexual misconduct history and did not take steps to try to prevent contact with the students" (Sutton).

SEXUAL MISCONDUCT CASES IN THE MEDIA

In State of *Florida v. Beth Friedman* (1999), a 42-year-old Broward County public school teacher was under suspicion of having sexual relations with a 15-year-old student. Though Friedman confessed to her involvement and the jury acquitted her of statutory rape, she was convicted of contributing to the delinquency of a minor because she had given the student drugs and alcohol (Sutton).

One of the most known cases, *Washington State v. Letourneau* (2000), involved a Seattle elementary school teacher, Mary Kay Letourneau. Married with four children, Letourneau began a sexual relationship with her sixth-grade student, Vili Fualaau in 1996. She was arrested in 1997. Letourneau was pregnant with their child and was sentenced to six months in jail. Letourneau was found 30 days after her release by authorities with Fualaau in a parked car after no contact with her former student was ordered. She was arrested for having sex with a minor, and served seven and a half years in prison (Sutton).

In 2013, Cristina Preston, a former special education teacher at Veterans Memorial Middle School in Columbus, Georgia, was convicted of aggravated child molestation, child molestation, statutory rape, and sexual assault of person in custody and sentenced to 25 years in prison. Preston, who was forty-five years old at the time of her conviction, was accused of starting a sexual affair in 2011 with a male student who was thirteen years old at the time (Chitwood, 2013).

PENALTIES FOR MISCONDUCT

Public school employees can receive penalties of censure and reprimand, fines (up to $10,000 for each violation), suspension from job and/or probationary terms may be imposed on licenses. On severe cases of misconduct, employees may have licenses revoked, loss of job or position, or even jail time ("Professional Misconduct," 2004).

KEEPING TRACK OF MISCONDUCT

If misconduct has been committed, most states have a complaint process. Complaints can be filed with state education departments. Complaints will be followed up by the department, and if substantial evidence is found, disciplinary action will be pursued ("Professional Misconduct"). As Sutton says, "all states require some form of criminal background checks as part of the screening process for certifying or hiring teacher candidates" (Sutton). The Washington State Supreme Court ruled in 1990 in "*Brouillet v. Cowles Publishing Co.* that records of teacher sexual misconduct shall be open to public inspection and that revealing them does not violate teacher privacy" (O'Hagan & Willmsen, 2003).

If the complaint of misconduct is made at the school or district level, the school district's policy regarding misconduct should be handled for reporting, grievance, and investigation procedures. Reacting quickly may shield the school district from legal liability. School districts could even incur civil damages from the Department of Education or individual citizens under the Title IX law if the district fails to acknowledge implications of sexual misconduct, or fails to create its own sexual misconduct policies (Goorian).

Most school districts require that employees report to their superintendent once they have been "charged by summons, warrant, indictment or information with the commission of a felony; a misdemeanor involving: sexual assault; obscenity and related offenses, drugs; physical or sexual abuse or neglect of a child; public drunkenness; driving under the influence of alcohol or drugs; reckless driving; or disturbing the peace" (Newport News Public Schools, 2007).

The National Association of State Directors of Teacher Education and Licensing keeps a national database of actions on teacher licenses; however, it is available only for members. Only Ohio, Texas, Vermont and Florida offer online versions. Texas and Ohio's data bases are intended primarily for administrators to use in the hiring of new teachers. Most states collect such information and make it available through an open-records request (Honawar, 2007).

Viewpoints

PROBLEMS WITH THE MISCONDUCT REPORTING SYSTEM

According to the Sarasota Herald-Tribune, there are hundreds of Florida teachers still in the classroom although they have molested, physically attacked, or harassed students at previous jobs. The article revealed that when schools find a teacher to be involved in misconduct, they will quietly allow them to resign instead of firing them. Many teachers are able to find a new job and some repeat the same misconduct in another school (as cited in Marshall).

In 1990, a New York teacher of special education "was convicted of selling $7,000 worth of cocaine and was sent to prison. But, it took was another two years before the New York City Board of Education finally fired the teacher after a year-long hearing that cost $185,000. New York spends on average nearly $200,000 and 476 days on each teacher dismissal hearing (Weele, 1994). According to a New York State Education Department report obtained by Gannett's Journal News, in 2011, the teacher dismissal hearing process took an average of 632 days for a guilty decision, 1,070 days for a not-guilty decision, and 287 days for settlements (Matthews, 2012). Some point to the teacher unions as the problem of ridding the system of bad teachers. The Chicago Teacher's Union attorneys argue "that a union's job is to protect its members" (Weele). It does not hire the incompetent teachers and administrators have to follow due-process procedures.

C. Edward Lawrence, author of the Marginal Teacher and How to Handle Staff Misconduct, does not agree with the advocates who want everything public when an allegation is made: the accusation, the investigation, findings and how the matter was or will be resolved. He believes that during an internal disciplinary action that teacher privacy must be respected. If everything is made public, reputations will be destroyed (as cited in Lemberg, 2004).

PREVENTING EDUCATOR SEXUAL MISCONDUCT

Teachers and administrators need to: "take rumors, whispers, and oblique complaints, particularly from students, seriously. Because socializing with students may be an appropriate means of establishing rapport, it is important to have district-wide policies in place that ensure prompt, professional investigation of complaints and incidents to determine their merit" (Goorian).

Another problem is that sometimes teachers are asked to quietly resign or give up a license due to misconduct. These teachers are never disciplined and are able to teach in other school districts. Or, a principal will write a false letter of recommendation to "help" the teacher leave the district (Zemel).

Researchers who have studied teacher sexual misconduct offer some ideas or recommendations to keep abusive teachers out of the classroom:

- There should be no statute of limitations on charges from children in abuse cases;
- Schools should be given access to registry of child abuse reports and a list of sex offenders;
- Teacher applications should require disclosure of any prior dismissals, arrests, or outstanding warrants;
- When teachers file for certification or when they apply for a job, both federal and state fingerprint checks should be completed;
- School officials must write accurate recommendations. It should be a violation if principals write a false letter of recommendation to rid the school of a bad teacher;
- Lawsuits should be easier for victims to file;
- Educator misconduct should be included in introductory college courses, and student teachers should have better educator misconduct training;
- All school districts should write rules against educator sexual misconduct and inappropriate educator-student relationships, including those between staff and students that may be consensual. The behavior of the misconduct needs to be clear and concise within the policy so no ambiguity can be detected;
- Educators should be trained to discern the signs of educator sexual misconduct;
- Educator sexual misconduct information should be stored in a centralized place, and a case coordinator should be assigned;
- Both the child protection and law enforcement agencies should be told of allegations (Shakeshaft).

CONCLUSIONS

Clearly, educator sexual misconduct is a problem in our public schools, and children's lives and wellbeing are at stake. Misconduct ranges from watching inappropriate movies with students to sexually abusing a student. The sexual misconduct charges make news headlines and schools scramble to make policies that are ultimately shaped by the court system. Sexual abusers exist in schools, and they must be stopped by fellow educators, parents and administrators. Public schools can work harder to prevent misconduct by following the recommendations of experts in the field and by making and following policies on educator misconduct.

However, when investigations ensue, it is important that they are quick and thorough. Opening everything to the media, such as the accusation, the investigation, the findings and how the matter was or will be resolved can have disastrous repercussions if the educator is found to be innocent. Teachers who harm or commit misconduct should be disciplined, but innocent teachers should be protected from being charged and labeled.

Teaching is a tough but rewarding profession. The vast majority of educators are professional, kind and caring. Districts need to make and follow policies for the protection of all involved and to keep sexual misconduct from occurring in schools.

TERMS & CONCEPTS

Disciplinary Action: A disciplinary action can be taken when educator misconduct occurs, and the investigation proves that the misconduct was committed. It can include censure (a formal reprimand that is an expression of strong disapproval or harsh criticism), and suspension (postponement of sentence: a delay in the carrying out of a sentence or the making of a decision or judgment), probationary terms (under terms not final or fully worked out or agreed upon), and/or licenses revoked (educator license is taken away).

Grooming: Grooming is usually a deliberate action that is intended to befriend and establish an emotional attachment and coercion over a student. This results in the lowering of a child's inhibitions, making it easier for his or her sexual abuse.

Liable: Liable is the state of being responsible or obligated. Therefore, a person or organization can be liable for negligence, carrying out an act that they were contracted to do, or for commission of a crime. When the responsibility or obligation is not met to the expected standard, a lawsuit can result, leading to potential criminal prosecution.

No Child Left Behind Act of 2001 (NCLB): This federal act by Congress amended the mandate in Section 5414 of the Elementary and Secondary Education Act of 1965 (ESEA), directing that the issue of sexual misconduct be explored.

Sexual Misconduct: Sexual misconduct is any inappropriate behavior by an educator or school staff member that is aimed toward a student or minor.

Usually, the behavior is used as a means to sexually arouse either the educator or the child. The behaviors can be physical, verbal, or visual.

Staff or Educator Misconduct: Staff or educator misconduct is wrongful educator behavior, inappropriate acts, deliberate wrongful acts or omission

Statute of Limitations: A statute of limitation is the time period that legal action can be taken.

Title IX of the Education Amendments of 1972: This amendment does not directly deal with educator sexual misconduct or pedophilia. However, it bans any discrimination on the basis of sex in any organization that receives federal money.

Kellie Hayden

BIBLIOGRAPHY

Chappell, B. (2012, June 21). *Penn State abuse scandal: A guide and timeline.* Retrieved December 12, 2013, from http://npr.org.

Chitwood, T. (2013, June 4). Update: Former middle school teacher gets 25 years in prison for sex with student. *Columbus Ledger-Inquirer.* Retrieved December 12, 2013, from

http://ledger-enquirer.com.

Driedger, S. (2003). The teacher's lesson. *Maclean's, 116,* 56. Retrieved September 11, 2007, from EBSCO Online Database Academic Search Premier.

Erin's Law. (2012). *Our work.* Retrieved December 12, 2013, from http://erinslaw.org.

Gladwell, M. (2012). In plain view. *New Yorker, 88,* 84–90. Retrieved December 12, 2013, from EBSCO Online Database Academic Search Complete.

Goorian, B. (1999). *Sexual misconduct by school employees* (ERIC No. ED436816). Retrieved September 15, 2007, from http://files.eric.ed.gov.

Green, S. (1998). *Alaska State Professional Teaching Practices Commission (PTPC): Annual report, fiscal year 1997* (ERIC No. ED423231). Retrieved September 12, 2007, from http://files.eric.ed.gov.

Honawar, V., & Holovach, R. (2007). Online databases of misdeeds by teachers raising concerns. *Education Week, 27,* 6. Retrieved September 15, 2007, from EBSCO Online Database Education Research Complete.

Lemberg, J. (2004). Forbidden fruit: Bad apples. *News Media & the Law, 28,* 11–13. Retrieved September 12, 2007, from EBSCO Online Database Academic Search Premier.

Marshall, J. (2007). Education reporting reveals shocking stories. *Quill, 95,* 43. Retrieved September 12, 2007, from EBSCO Online Database Academic Search Premier.

Matthews, C. (2012, April 22). What it costs to fire a teacher: State, schools spend millions on cases that take years. *Journal News.* Retrieved December 12, 2013, from http://lohud.com.

Newport News Public Schools. (2003). *NNPS policies & procedures manual.* Retrieved September 26, 2007, from http://boarddocs.com.

O'Hagan, M., & Willmsen, C. (2003, December 14). Union, district joined forces to block records. *The Seattle Times.* Retrieved September 13, 2007, from http://seattletimes.nwsource.com.

Professional misconduct enforcement. (2004, November 1). Retrieved September 17, 2007, from http://op.nysed.gov.

Sex and schools: By the numbers. (2013). *Phi Delta Kappan, 94,* 32–33. Retrieved December 12, 2013, from EBSCO Online Database Education Research Complete.

Shakeshaft, C. (2004). *Educator sexual misconduct: A synthesis of existing literature.* Retrieved September 17, 2007, from http://ed.gov.

Shakeshaft, C. (2013). Know the warning signs of educator sexual misconduct. *Phi Delta Kappan, 94,* 8–13. Retrieved December 12, 2013, from EBSCO Online Database Education Research Complete.

Spitalli, S. J. (2012). An epidemic of shame. *American School Board Journal, 199,* 26–27. Retrieved November 5, 2014, from EBSCO Online Database Education Research Complete.

Stein, N. (2000). *Sexual harassment in schools.* Retrieved September 26, 2007, from https://mainweb-v.musc.edu.

Sutton, L. C. (2004). Educator sexual misconduct: New trends and liability. *School Business Affairs, 70,* 6–8. Retrieved September 15, 2007, from http://asbointl.org.

Weele, M. (1994). Why it's too hard to fire bad teachers. *Washington Monthly, 26,* 12. Retrieved September 11, 2007, from EBSCO Online Database Academic Search Premier.

Winton, R., & Ceasar, S. (2013, November 15). Miramonte teacher sentenced to 25 years in prison for lewd conduct. *Los Angeles Times.* Retrieved December 12, 2013, from http://articles.latimes.com.

Young, V. W. (2012). Not guilty, but not fit. *School Administrator, 69,* 9. Retrieved November 5, 2014, from EBSCO Online Database Education Research Complete.

Zemel, J. E. (1999, November 2). Dirty secrets: More than 'a wink' needed to stop abuse. *Pittsburgh Post-Gazette.* Retrieved September 16, 2007, from http://postgazette.com.

SUGGESTED READING

Involve stakeholders in revamping sexual misconduct policy. (2012). *Student Affairs Today, 15,* 3. Retrieved December 12, 2013, from EBSCO Online Database Education Research Complete.

Jehlen, A. (2007). NEA defends educators against unfair accusations on the job. *NEA Today, 26,* 28–33. Retrieved October 15, 2007, from EBSCO Online Database Education Research Complete.

Johansson, S. (2013). Coach-athlete sexual relationships: If no means no does yes mean yes? *Sport, Education & Society, 18,* 678–693. Retrieved December 12, 2013, from EBSCO Online Database Education Research Complete.

Lawrence, C. E. (2005). *The marginal teacher: A step-by-step guide to fair procedures for identification and dismissal* (3rd ed.). Thousand Oaks, CA: Corwin Press.

Lawrence, C. E., & Vachon, M. K. (2003). *How to handle staff misconduct: A practical guide for school principals and supervisors* (2nd ed.). Thousand Oaks, CA: Corwin Press.

Surface, J. L., Stader, D. L., & Armenta, A. D. (2014). Educator sexual misconduct and nondisclosure agreements: Policy guidance from Missouri's Amy Hestir Student Protection Act. *Clearing House, 87,* 130–133. Retrieved November 5, 2014, from EBSCO Online Database Education Research Complete.

SCHOOL SAFETY LEGISLATION

This article examines laws designed to keep students safe while on school grounds and at school-sponsored events. It focuses on laws at both the national and state level that regulate possession of firearms or other weapons, bullying and anti-bullying legislation and their impacts, and on emergency preparedness for students, teachers, and staff. The article also deals with major influences on legal trends that have served to motivate legislators to pass new laws in response to events and parental and community pressure to make schools safer.

KEYWORDS: Alternative schools; Anti-bullying measures; Bullying; Gun-Free School Acts; Individuals with Disabilities Education Act (IDEA); No Child Left Behind Act; Safe and Drug Free Schools and Communities Act; Safe School Initiative; School safety; Zero tolerance

OVERVIEW

Since the late twentieth century, the safety of children and youth during school hours has been of increasing concern to legislators at all levels. "School safety" encompasses such factors as ensuring that school facilities and equipment meet all safety standards and that all maintenance is performed according to strict schedules. School safety also involves providing students with clean air, providing safe playground equipment, monitoring vehicles to make sure that no small children have been left inside, removing hazards that may cause accidents, blocking unauthorized access to school buildings, and protecting athletes from heat stress during hot summer months. Additionally, school safety entails participating in regular emergency drills that teach teachers, staff, and students how to deal with crisis situations.

Since 1999 and the school shooting at Columbine High School in Littleton, Colorado, in which twelve students and one teacher were killed and another twenty-one injured, much of the focus has been on keeping weapons off of school grounds. Protecting students from being bullied by others is also considered a major priority because of high profile cases in which bullied students have committed suicide because they felt they could no longer face constant harassment by others. Experts on school safety contend that all schools should establish comprehensive school security reviews (Dunlap, 2013) in order to keep a check on all aspects of school safety. Legislators have passed laws designed to prohibit the presence of weapons on school grounds, ensure that school officials are prepared to deal with any crisis that does occur, and establish anti-bullying regulations that protect students from harassment or physical abuse by other students.

School violence first became an issue of national importance in the United States in the 1970s. Between December 1974 and May 2000, at least thirty-seven incidents of targeted school violence were reported (Dunlap). In the 1980s, the Reagan administration declared war on drugs, and Congress passed the Anti-Drug Abuse Act, which contained the Drug-Free Schools and Communication Act that required all schools to ban alcohol and drugs on school grounds.

In 1982, the Association for Middle Level Association (AMLA) began publishing its landmark series This We Believe: Keys to Educating Young Adolescents, which has served as a policy guide for lawmakers, educators, and organizations involved in defining the educational experience for middle-school students.

American schoolchildren have long participated in emergency preparedness drills. The postwar years and the dominance of Cold War politics led to "duck and cover" exercises in which students were taught how to react to the dropping of nuclear weapons. Schools, particularly those in the most vulnerable areas, added emergency drills for dealing with fires, tornadoes, or earthquakes. The prevalence of school shootings has led many schools to add drills in reacting to armed intruders within schools. In 2013, the need for increased emergency preparedness was made even clearer when two elementary schools in Oklahoma were destroyed by tornadoes that came without warning, killing seven children.

APPLICATIONS

Legislators first began mandating zero tolerance for bringing weapons onto school property or engaging in violent, threatening, or disruptive behavior in the 1980s. By 1989, California, New York, and Kentucky had passed innovative zero tolerance legislation. By the 1990s, approximately 90 percent of American schools had instituted similar policies. In 1990, President George H. W. Bush's administration sponsored the Gun-Free School Zones Act with the intention of keeping guns off of school property. The Supreme Court refused to accept the congressional assertion of its right to regulate under the interstate commerce clause and held in *United States v. Lopez* (514 U.S. 549) in 1995 that the law was unconstitutional. Congress responded by passing the Gun-Free School Act of 1995 requiring all schools receiving federal funding to comply with the ban on weapons at schools and mandating expulsions for a period of one year as punishment for bringing guns onto school property.

Over time, the concept of zero tolerance on school grounds was broadened to encompass engaging in such acts as fighting, using alcohol or drugs, participating in gang activity, possessing over-the-counter medications, sexual harassment, threats, and vandalism (Koch, 2000). Throughout the United States, schools enacted stricter zero tolerance policies after the shooting at Columbine High. They also enhanced school safety through such actions as installing metal detectors designed to detect weapons and prevent their being brought onto school properties. Some schools began requiring students to wear uniforms in order to level out obvious socioeconomic differences that have been identified with bullying behaviors and prevent gang members from flaunting their affiliations. Other schools hired police officers to act as deterrents for school violence and to be on hand if a crisis did occur.

Pressured by the administration of George W. Bush, Congress passed the No Child Left Behind Act in 2001, reauthorizing the Elementary and Secondary School Education Act. The law was designed to fix problems that had been plaguing U.S. schools for decades. Section 4121 threw the considerable weight of the federal government into dealing with the use of illegal drugs and violence in schools and promoting safety and discipline. Districts were required to identify schools that had persistently been considered dangerous.

In 2002, Congress passed the Safe School Initiative in which the Secret Service and the Department of Education worked together to create threat assessments for schools and oversee the establishment of the Safe and Drug-Free Schools Program. In 2007, legislatures in several states passed legislation concerning the implementation of school safety policies. Some states tightened policies, but others were more concerned with fairness in implementation. North Carolina began mandating notification of parents or guardians of suspended or expelled students. Louisiana implemented strict penalties for students carrying firearms on buses or at school-related activities. Kansas required all schools to establish anti-bullying policies and train teachers and staff to deal with incidents of bullying. Rhode Island gave school districts additional leeway in handling cases covered by zero-tolerance laws.

Although the Supreme Court had held in 1969 in *Tinker v. Des Moines* (393 U.S. 503) that students did not leave their First Amendment rights at the door of schoolhouses, the Court decided in *Morse v. Frederick* (551 U.S. 393, 2007) that educators did not violate First Amendment rights of students when they punished them for appearing to advocate the use of drugs at school-related activities. In 2008, a national coalition made up of educators, civil rights activists, law enforcement, and youth advocates formed the National Safe Schools Partnership to lobby legislators for anti- bullying legislation because the problem of bullying had become so prevalent. That same year, gun control advocates placed considerable pressure on the Virginia legislature to tighten rules that allowed buyers to purchase firearms at gun shows without a background check. Support for gun control was particularly strong in the state because of the attack on the Virginia Tech campus on April 16 of the previous year in which thirty-two were killed and seventeen wounded. The gun lobby proved too strong, however, and the law was not changed. The National Rifle Association also managed to kill a federal bill introduced in the Senate by Frank R. Lautenberg (D-NJ) and Jack Reed (D-RI) requiring background checks when guns were purchased at gun shows.

In 2010, AMLA's This We Believe identified bullying as a major threat to the safety of middle-school children and called for anti- bullying legislation designed to assist schools in creating safe environments for vulnerable students. By that time, forty-three states had passed anti-bullying legislation, which defined bullying, set up procedures for reporting and investigating incidences of bullying, and established punishment for those convicted of bullying behavior. Research on bullying suggests that bullying, which may involve either physical or emotional abuse, or both, is most likely to begin in late elementary school and continue throughout the middle-school years (Kueny & Zirkel, 2012).

Since the late twentieth century, cyberbullies have used intimidating e-mails and social media sites to carry out bullying campaigns. While bullying has been considered a major priority in the field of school safety for decades, the issue became more urgent following the suicide of Massachusetts teenager Phoebe Prince, who had emigrated from Ireland only months before. Six teenagers faced criminal charges for bullying her to the point of suicide. After pleading guilty, they were sentenced to either probation or community service. Prince's death motivated Massachusetts and other states to enact anti-bullying laws.

Using data from the 2013 School Crime Supplement to the National Crime Victimization Survey, the National Center for Educational Statistics estimates that approximately 21.5 percent of students aged 12 to 18 have been bullied (National Center for Education Statistics, 2015). The most common forms of bullying include insults or being made fun of (13.6 percent) and becoming the subject of rumors (13.2 percent). Around 6 percent were shoved, tripped, or spit upon, and more than 2 percent were forced to do things they did not want to do by bullies (National Center for Education Statistics). Kueny and Zirkel identify four actors commonly found in bullying scenarios: the dominant, impulsive bully who is often angry and easily frustrated; the victim who tends to be isolated from others and may be insecure; the bully-victim who becomes a bully after being victimized by others; and the bystander who knows that the bullying is occurring but does nothing to stop it.

School safety continues to be a major priority for both national and state legislators. Title IV of the Twenty-first Century Schools Act, better known as the Safe and Drug Free Schools and Communities Act, sets up a grants program to help states keep violence out of the schools and promotes bans on drugs, alcohol, and tobacco on school grounds. The law also encourages the establishment of safe passage areas to make traveling to and from school safer through monitoring by law enforcement and community patrols.

ISSUES

By the mid-1990s, it had become obvious that zero tolerance policies were too all inclusive, and legislators began recognizing the need for schools to have some leeway when awarding punishments. Even those who support school safety legislation are sometimes critical of the fact that punishments too often target racial and ethnic minorities. Other criticisms focus on the issue of mandating zero tolerance for special needs students who may act disruptive because of medical or development issues. The Individuals with Disabilities Education Act (IDEA) of 1990 requires schools to place special needs students who are expelled in alternative schools. Alternative schools were first established in the United States in the early 1970s to deal with students who had been expelled from regular schools because they were perceived of as disruptive. They were also used to meet the needs of students with major medical or psychological problems that could not be dealt with in regular classrooms. As the numbers of students suspended or expelled for school safety violations increased, the number of students attending alternative schools rose accordingly. Research on alternative schools has revealed that students assigned to alternate schools are more likely than others to return to regular classes once suspensions are completed and are less likely to become involved with gangs (Koch).

One oft-repeated complaint concerning school safety legislation is that legislators have gone so far in banning weapons or potentially violent behavior from schools that school administrators have ended up punishing students for behavior that is in no way threatening to either the student involved or to others. Incidents such as a six-year-old boy in York, Pennsylvania, being suspended for bringing nail clippers to school, a second-grader being suspended in Columbus, Ohio, for drawing a picture of a gun and aiming it at students after it was cut out, a sixth-grader suspended for bringing a knife to school in a lunch bag for the purpose of cutting an orange, a 12-year-old being handcuffed after splashing classmates when walking through a puddle, and a 15-year-old Utah girl being suspended for dying her hair auburn have been labeled as absurd.

By 2015, all fifty states, the District of Columbia, and Puerto Rico had enacted legislation designed to control bullying and make schools safer. Most of those laws followed the guidelines established by the U.S. Department of Education that included such elements as a statement of purpose, the scope of the regulation, the conduct that was prohibited, teacher and staff training, preventative measures, and monitoring and reporting. While most anti-bullying legislation tends to be enacted at the state level, students may be protected from bullying and harassment by Title IV of the Civil Rights Act of 1964, which prohibits any discrimination that is motivated by race, color, or national origin. Subsequent laws and legal interpretations have included protection from discrimination based on religion, gender, disability, and sexual orientation. Proposed federal legislation such as the Safe Schools Improvement Act and the Student Non- Discrimination Act failed to garner sufficient support for passage.

Despite national attention and the passage of anti-bullying legislation, bullying continues to be a major cause of teen suicides and accounts for large numbers of school absences every day. Critics of existing anti-bullying legislation insist that schools are often more interested in preventing bullying than in dealing with bullying once it occurs. Some observers suggest that anti-bullying laws punish youth for being mean-spirited even though it is a natural part of growing up. Others suggest that bullies are criminals who should be prosecuted to the fullest extent of the law. Legislators in Utah have gone so far as to make it a criminal offense for school employees to fail to report bullying. Laws in Delaware, Florida, Georgia, and Utah allow state governments to withhold funds for school districts that do not comply with anti-bullying legislation.

Considerable attention has been paid to arming teachers and staff. Both Kansas and South Dakota have passed laws permitting teachers with permits to carry concealed weapons to carry arms while at school. In 2014, the Georgia legislature passed the Safe Carry Protection Act, popularly known as the "guns everywhere bill" that allows guns to be carried in school zones, churches, bars, government buildings, and designated areas of airports with some restrictions. Bills allowing teachers to be armed were defeated in Mississippi and Wyoming. A Florida bill requiring police notification any time the zero tolerance policy was violated was also defeated. In New York, the legislature passed a law that increased penalties for bringing guns onto school grounds and improved emergency planning training.

On December 14, 2012, events proved that even the youngest children are not safe from violence when twenty children and six adults were gunned down at Sandy Hook Elementary School in Newtown, Connecticut. Most of the victims were first graders. The public outcry led to new demands by both gun control advocates and Second Amendment advocates. Suggestions for making schools safe from violence included placing armed police or security officers in all schools and tightening existing school security measures (Shah & Ujifusa, 2013). Other proposals involved video surveillance, panic alarms, access-control systems, closing off side entrances, increased safety drills, and requiring identification badges for students, staff, and visitors. Schools created task forces to study school safety, and new safety laws were passed to improve facility safety. In West Virginia, for instance, the School Building Authority began requiring shatterproof glass in all school windows. In Joplin, Missouri, Irving Elementary School was built with one safety room for students, teachers, and staff, and another for members of the community.

TERMS & CONCEPTS

Alternative schools: Schools designed to educate students that have been removed from regular classrooms because of medical, psychological, or behavioral issues in a non-traditional environment.

Anti-bullying measures: Laws and regulations designed to fight bullying in schools. Measures range from training teachers and staff to identify and react to bullying to turning violent bullies over to criminal justice officials.

Bullying: Actions designed to harass or intimidate others through sustained patterns of physical or emotional abuse.

Gun-Free School Acts: National legislation that used first the Interstate Commerce Clause and then the power of federal funding to force schools to institute bans on weapons on or near school grounds.

Individuals with Disabilities Education Act (IDEA): Act passed by Congress in 1990 that deals with the rights of disabled students to an education and requires the placement of disabled students who are expelled in alternative schools.

No Child Left Behind Act: Comprehensive legislation designed to protect the right of all children to receive an education. It contains a provision that requires districts to identify schools with records of persistent violence.

Safe and Drug Free Schools and Communities Act: Twenty-first century legislation that promotes school safety through violence prevention programs and federal bans on alcohol, tobacco, and drugs on school grounds.

Safe School Initiative: Federal legislation passed in 2002 that was designed to ensure the physical safety of students while at school by prohibiting weapons and drugs on school grounds.

School safety: Concept that encompasses the physical and emotional environment of schools and extends to protecting students from bullying and violent acts by others.

Zero tolerance: Policy that requires schools to enact mandatory punishment for students engaging in acts that are perceived as violent, threatening, or disruptive.

Elizabeth Rholetter Purdy

BIBLIOGRAPHY

Dunlap, E. S. (Ed.). (2013). *The comprehensive handbook of school safety*. Boca Raton, FL: CRC Press/Taylor Francis.

Kenney, M. (2013). Seeking safer schools. *American School and University, 84*(10), 18–24. Retrieved December 19, 2014, from EBSCO online database Education Research Complete.

Kueny, M. and Zirkel, P. (2012). An analysis of school anti-bullying laws in the United States. *Middle School Journal, 43*(4), 22–31. Retrieved December 19, 2014, from EBSCO online database Education Research Complete.

National Center for Education Statistics. (2015, April). *Student reports of bullying and cyber-bullying: Results from the 2013 school crime supplement to the national crime victimization survey. National Center for Education Statistics.* Retrieved December 19, 2016, from https://nces.ed.gov.

Russo, C. J. (2016). Update on school searches. *School Business Affairs, 82*(11), 33–35. Retrieved December 19, 2016, from EBSCO Online Database Education Source.

Schargel, F. (2014). *Creating safe schools: A guide for school leaders, teachers, counselors, and parents.* Hoboken, NJ: Taylor and Francis.

Shah, N., & Ujifusa, A. (2013). Safety legislation: A tally by state. *Education Week, 32*(29). Retrieved March 22, 2015, from EBSCO Online Database Education Research Complete.

This we believe: Keys to educating young adolescents. (2010). Waterville, OH: Association for Middle Level Education.

Vaillancourt, K., & Rossen, E. (2012). Navigating school safety law and policy. *Communique, 41*(4), 1–23. Retrieved December 19, 2014, from EBSCO online database Education Research Complete.

Harpur, P., & Suzor, N. (2014). The paradigm shift in realizing the right to read: How e-book libraries are enabling in the university sector. Disability & Society, 29(10), 1658-1671. Retrieved March 22, 2015, from EBSCO Online Database SocINDEX with Full Text.

Martinez-Estrada, P. D., & Conaway, R. N. (2012). EBooks: The next step in educational innovation. Business Communication Quarterly, 75(2), 125-135. Retrieved March 23, 2015, from EBSCO Online Database Business Source Complete.

Murphy, D., Walker, R., & Webb, G. (2013). Online learning and teaching with technology: Case studies, experience and practice. Hoboken, NJ: Taylor and Francis.

Pacansky-Brock, M., & Ko, S. S. (2013). Best practices for teaching with emerging technologies. New York, NY: Routledge.

Rieders, W. (2011). ATG special report—looking beyond e textbooks and tapping into the personal learning experience. Against the Grain, 23(3), 42-44. Retrieved March 22, 2015, from EBSCO Online Database Education Research Complete.

Spring, J. H. (2012). Education networks: Power, wealth, cyberspace, and the digital mind. New York, NY: Routledge.

Sunghee, S. (2014). E-book usability in educational technology classes: Teachers and teacher candidates' perception toward e-book for teaching and learning. International Journal of Distance Education Technologies, 12(3), 62-74. Retrieved March 22, 2015, from EBSCO Online Database Business Source Complete.

Zucker, T. A., Moody, A. K., & McKenna, M. C. (2009). The effects of electronic books on pre-kindergarten-to-grade 5 students' literacy and language outcomes: A research synthesis. Journal of Educational Computing Research, 40(1), 47-87. Retrieved March 22, 2015, from EBSCO Online Database Education Research Complete.

SUGGESTED READING

Conaway, J. (2014). Public and school safety: Risk assessment, perceptions and management. *Safety and Risk in Society* (series), N.Y.: Nova Science Publishers.

Glockman, W.T. (2009). *School Crime, Safety, and Threats.* N.Y.: Nova Science Publishers.

Sabia, J. & Bass, B. (2017). Do anti-bullying laws works? New evidence on school safety and youth violence. *Journal of Population Economics*, 30 (2), 473-502.

Zang, A., Wang, K., Zhang, J., & Oudekerk, B. (2017). Indicators of school crime and safety: 2016 NCES 2017-064/NCJ 250650. *National Center for Education Statistics.*

SEARCH AND SEIZURE IN THE PUBLIC SCHOOLS

Courts recognize the role of the United States Constitution's Fourth Amendment in protecting ordinary citizens against unreasonable government searches imposed upon themselves, their homes, private papers and personal property. Defining the extent to which the Amendment applies to privacy rights of public school students, however, continues to pose a legal dilemma. Public schools provide education to millions of children each day in learning environments that are increasingly influenced by the availability of drugs and weapons. The need to limit criminal behaviors and illegal materials on school grounds, often compels officials to order searches of students' lockers, clothing, purses, and automobiles; they require students to submit to random drug tests and examination by drug-sniffing dogs. While the legal system has defined some boundaries regarding searches and seizures in public schools, debate on the issue continues to challenge educators, students and courts of law.

KEYWORDS: Confiscate; Due Process; Fourteenth Amendment; Fourth Amendment; In Loco Parentis; Informer; Intrusive Searches; Probable Cause; Reasonable Suspicion; Search; Search Warrant; Seizure

OVERVIEW

The Fourth Amendment to the U.S. Constitution protects citizens against unreasonable governmental searches and seizures on persons, houses, papers, and private property. The Amendment requires government authorities to have probable cause before conducting search and seizure on a place, person, or thing. This Amendment protects the rights of ordinary citizens to privacy.

In the last half of the 20th century, the extent of the Fourth Amendment's protections when applied to students in public schools began to be challenged. Were students "ordinary citizens" under the definitions of Constitutional law? Were they entitled to privacy and protection from unreasonable searches and seizures while on school grounds? Were schoolteachers and administrators under legal obligation, equal to police officers and other government authorities, to show probable cause and obtain warrants prior to searching students and students' belongings?

The pursuit of answers gained momentum following several Supreme Court rulings concerning students' rights to free speech, free expression, and access to free education. In *Tinker v. Des Moines Independent Community School District* (1969), the Court recognized school officials' need to maintain order and control of pupils' conduct, but determined that students did not lose their constitutional rights upon entering a public school facility (Heder, 1999). The ruling protected the rights of Des Moines students to wear black armbands in protest of the Vietnam War, but it also served as a foundation for future Fourth Amendment decisions involving nation-wide search and seizure practices in schools.

Another factor that influenced the legal definition of students' rights to privacy under the Fourth Amendment, was increased availability of illegal drugs and weapons in the United States. In nationwide studies conducted in the 1990s, students admitted bringing approximately 135,000 guns into schools each day; twenty percent of high schoolers reported carrying some type of weapon to school at least once a month (Mitchell, 1998). A 2005 survey of teenagers and parents, conducted by The National Center on Addiction and Substance Abuse, found 62% of high school students and 28% of middle school students attended schools where drugs were used, kept, or sold; the numbers represented a 47% and 41% increase, respectively, over the previous three years. As dangers associated with illegal materials on school grounds multiplied, so did the frequency and invasiveness of school-authorized searches and seizures (as cited in Finn & Willert, 2006).

Further Insights

LOWER-COURT RULINGS

If a principal suspects weapons are located in a student's locker, does he have the legal right to look inside? If a teacher asks a student to remove his jacket and empty his pockets, is he acting in the capacity of "substitute parent" or representative of the United States government? Are metal detectors, drug-sniffing dogs and strip searches appropriate in school settings?

Until the middle of the 20th century, the answers to such questions were rarely debated. The role of schoolteachers and administrators was generally viewed by courts and families as 'in loco parentis,' – in place of the parents. Searches and seizures conducted on public school students and their belongings were not considered a violation of Fourth Amendment rights. Just as parents can enter their child's bedroom and look through drawers and closets for particular objects, it was acceptable for public school teachers and administrators to search through students' lockers, purses, and pockets.

According to Heder, the concept of search and seizure as a legal issue in public schools was nonexistent prior to the 1960s. For most of the 20th century, he notes, education-related court battles traditionally revolved around issues of educational quality, roles of parents, and compulsory laws for school attendance.

In the latter half of the century, however, young people's access to drugs and guns prompted school officials to rely on extensive searches of students to uncover suspected criminal behaviors and illegal materials. Continuing to operate under the conventional definition of in loco parentis, schools rejected students' claims of constitutionally-protected privacy, arguing that maintenance of school safety took precedence. In the late 1970s, students appealed to the

nation's courts for clarification and support of their Fourth Amendment rights.

The following court cases describe a few search and seizure lawsuits filed by students and parents against schools in the late 1970s and early 1980s. The cases outline some of the challenges lower courts encountered in defining the application of terms like "government" and "unreasonable" in regard to public school environments. The cases also give historical perspective to the difficulties associated with balancing students' needs for privacy with school officials' duties to maintain safe learning opportunities.

Bellnier v. Lund

In 1977, a teacher in New York learned that three dollars had been stolen from a student's coat pocket and ordered a strip search of all students in the classroom. Students were taken to the school's restrooms, ordered to strip down to their undergarments, and then their clothing was searched by a group of teachers and school officials. Students were allowed to return to their classroom when the search failed to locate the stolen money. A second search was conducted on the students' books, desks, and coats. Again, the missing money was not found. In a lawsuit filed against the school, a district court ruled in *Bellnier v. Lund* that although the teacher likely had a reasonable suspicion that someone in the classroom had taken the money, the teacher did not have sufficient facts to substantiate the intrusiveness of the search to which students were subjected. The court ruled that specific and reliable information must be available prior to an invasive search of a particular student or students by school officials (Essex, 2003).

Horton v. Goose Creek Independent School District

In 1978, officials at Goose Creek Independent School District in Louisiana were concerned with the increasing numbers of drug and alcohol problems they were encountering among students. In an effort to combat the trouble, school officials hired a company that specialized in drug-sniffing dogs to conduct an unannounced inspection of the students' lockers, book bags, cars, and clothes. The dogs were taken into the schools while classes were in session and sniff-searched the students and their belongings. If a dog signaled that a bag or locker had an illegal substance, the particular student was ordered to submit the article for search. If the dog signaled that a student was in possession of an illegal substance, the student was taken to the school's office and searched (*Horton v. Goose Creek*).

Several students sued the school district claiming the searches violated their Fourth Amendment rights to protection from unreasonable searches and seizures, as well as their Fourteenth Amendment rights which guaranteed they would not be deprived of property or freedom without due process. The students claimed that searches by drug-sniffing dogs were upsetting and embarrassing; one student detailed her fear of dogs and the negative effect the event had on her ability to succeed on an important examination that day.

The case, *Horton v. Goose Creek Independent School District* (1982), was initially decided in favor of the school. But upon appeal, the Fifth Circuit Court of Appeals split its decision into two separate rulings. The court decided that dogs could sniff students' lockers and cars without violating Fourth Amendment rights since such an action was not considered a "search" under the definition of the law. Dogs could not sniff students, however, since the physical act of dogs' noses touching them would intrude on privacy. The court further ruled that using dogs to sniff every student in the district was unreasonable because each child was not individually under suspicion of carrying drugs or alcohol (*Horton v. Goose Creek*).

SUPREME COURT RULINGS

Over the course of several decades, lower courts created legal boundaries for searches and seizures in U.S. public schools, but their rulings were inconsistent. Courts in one region of the country often contradicted those in others. District courts' decisions were frequently overturned by appeals courts. In 1985, a case concerning search and seizure in public schools finally came before the United States Supreme Court. The Court's decision on the important case provided schools and families with much-needed clarification and cohesion on the volatile issue.

New Jersey v. T.L.O.

The first United States Supreme Court case concerning Fourth Amendment law in schools, and the one most often cited, was *New Jersey v. T.L.O.* (1985). The case involved events at Piscataway High School

in Middlesex County, New Jersey in 1980. A teacher discovered two 14-year-old girls smoking in a school restroom and took the girls to the vice principal's office. One girl admitted to smoking, but the other one refused to confess. The vice principal looked through the uncooperative girl's purse and found a package of cigarettes and cigarette-rolling papers. He then conducted a more thorough search of the purse and confiscated a small amount of marijuana, a pipe, empty plastic bags, a large amount of money, a list of students who owed the girl money, and letters which suggested she was dealing marijuana. The girl's mother was notified, and the evidence was turned over to police. The girl, known as "T.L.O." in court documents, confessed to police that she had sold drugs at school and charges were filed against her (*New Jersey v. T.L.O.*).

In court hearings, T.L.O.'s attorney argued that the vice principal's actions had violated the girl's Fourth Amendment rights against unreasonable search and seizure since the vice principal had not obtained a search warrant prior to looking through her purse. The attorney further insisted that T.L.O. was entitled to rights equal those enjoyed by ordinary citizens suspected of illegal activity or criminal intent: probable cause or a warrant must exist before a search could be administered (*New Jersey v. T.L.O.*).

The Supreme Court ruled in favor of the New Jersey school; however, it also established legal parameters for defining students' privacy rights in relation to school-authorized searches and seizures. According to the Court:

- Special needs of schools justify less privacy entitlement to students than those extended to private citizens;
- The role of school officials extends beyond that of *in loco parentis*: school officials are considered representatives of the government when conducting searches and seizures;
- Because schools have special needs, school officials are not required to obtain probable cause or warrants prior to searching students; existence of a reasonable suspicion is enough to initiate a search;
- Searches are acceptable when schools adopt reasonable methods related to the objectives of the search and when those methods are not excessively intrusive for the age and sex of the student and the nature of the infraction (*New Jersey v. T.L.O.*).

Vernonia v. Acton & Board of Education v. Earls

In *Vernonia v. Acton* (1995), the Supreme Court expanding its ruling on searches and seizures in public schools. Authorities at Vernonia School District in Oregon, acting on an informer's tip that student athletes were involved in the school's troubling drug problem, conducted random urinalysis testing on all students who were participating in its athletic programs. One student refused to submit to the test and was denied the ability to join the school's football team. The student and his parents filed a lawsuit against the school district, claiming violation of his Fourth Amendment rights due to unreasonable search. The Supreme Court ruled that in circumstances when drug use by student athletes potentially affects school safety, random drug testing is justified (*Vernonia Sch. Dist. v. Acton*). In 2002, in *Board of Education v. Earls,* the Court ruled to permit random drug testing of all public school students who participate in all extracurricular activities (*Board of Education v. Earls*).

VIEWPOINTS

Over the years, American courts have ruled on cases involving searches and seizures in public schools, sometimes favoring students' privacy rights and sometimes favoring school officials' safety policies. The courts' decisions have been widely debated and criticized.

Some argue that courts have not done enough to protect rights guaranteed in the Fourth Amendment. Lynch (2006) fears that recent rulings not only lessen privacy rights of students, but also threaten privacy rights for all American citizens. He predicts that court decisions favoring schools in cases involving searches and seizures will result in youngsters growing to adulthood with few expectations of privacy from government (Lynch).

Heder agrees and notes the courts' willingness to uphold searches of students' property, the presence of armed, police-liaison officers in school hallways, and the use of metal detectors in school entrances. An example of Heder's concern is found in a lawsuit filed against the Unified School District of Los Angeles, California in 1998. The school district had a written policy allowing school officials to conduct daily random searches on pupils with hand-held metal detectors. One morning, an assistant principal searched students who entered his school building at least 30 minutes late for classes. His metal detector found a knife hidden on a girl named Latasha. In *People v. Latasha W.* (1998), the California Court of Appeals ruled that the search was conducted within legal boundaries (*People v. Latasha W.*).

Others argue that the courts have not sufficiently empowered school officials with enough legal tools to ensure safe school facilities. In September 2006, the United States House of Representatives passed the Student and Teacher Safety Act to reinforce the ability of public school districts to search students if the searches were conducted by full-time teachers or school officials. The legislation, which did not become law, stated that school officials "acting on any reasonable suspicion based on professional experience and judgment," could conduct a search of any public school student, if the search was conducted to ensure that classrooms, school buildings, school property, and students "remain free from the threat of all weapons, dangerous materials, or illegal narcotics" (United States Congress, 2006, section 3B). Prior to the legislation's consideration, however, the American Civil Liberties Union (ACLU) warned legislators that the language of the Act was too broad and would allow school officials to conduct random, school-wide searches without any individualized suspicion of specific students breaking laws or school rules.

Other critics oppose general search and seizure policies in public schools altogether. Torres and Chen (2006) argue that courts have not sufficiently defined what constitutes a reasonable suspicion, who can conduct searches, or the extent to which invasion into students' privacy (if any) is legal. Both Fredrickson and McCurdy (2006), of the ACLU, insist that educators would be more effective in securing children's safety by focusing on suspicious behaviors of specific individuals instead of inflicting mass search techniques on large groups.

CURRENT CASES & FUTURE DEBATES

On November 5, 2003, armed police officers in SWAT team uniforms entered Stratford High School in Goose Creek, South Carolina, with authorization from the school's principal, and forced 150 teenagers to the floor and against walls as a drug-sniffing dog searched their book bags ("Landmark settlement," 2006).

On February 18, 2004, students at Mumford High School in Detroit, Michigan were lined up against the school's walls as police conducted physical pat-downs on each and inspected all pockets, purses, and book bags. Students were then taken to the school auditorium, where they were held for more than an hour and a half as police searched the rest of the building for guns and drugs ("ACLU challenges," 2007).

On March 17, 2004, a student at Nazareth High School in Nazareth, Pennsylvania was caught with a cell phone on school property during school hours; students were allowed to carry cell phones, but using them was a violation of school policy. After seizing the phone, a teacher and an assistant principal called nine students listed on its directory to determine if other students were also violating school policy. The teacher and assistant principal then accessed the phone's text messages, listened to its stored voice mails, and held a conversation on the phone with the student's brother without identifying themselves (*Klump v. Nazareth Area Sch. Dist.*, 2006).

Each of these events resulted in lawsuits claiming students' Fourth Amendment rights had been violated by searches and seizures in public schools. Public school districts across the nation serve the educational needs of nearly 50 million schoolchildren each day. Educators struggle to find ways to provide safe, effective learning environments for children while respecting each student's constitutional rights to privacy. Yet, the cases described above, and similar ones throughout the United States, suggest that debates on searches and seizures in public schools will continue to pose challenges for families, school districts, police departments, and the U.S. court system for years to come.

TERMS & CONCEPTS

Confiscate: to seize; to take possession by force or by legal process.

Due Process: a legal requirement that protects an individual from unfair or unreasonable treatment as a result of enacted laws; formal legal proceedings based on established rules and principles.

Fourteenth Amendment, Section 1: "...nor shall any State deprive any person of life, liberty, or property, without due process of law; nor deny to any person within its jurisdiction the equal protection of the laws."

Fourth Amendment: "The right of the people to be secure in their persons, houses, papers, and effects, against unreasonable searches and seizures, shall not be violated, and no Warrants shall issue, but upon probable cause, supported by Oath or affirmation, and particularly describing the place to be searched, and the persons or things to be seized."

In Loco Parentis: in place of the parent; in the role of a parent with respect to the care, supervision, and discipline of a child.

Intrusive Searches: a search that is not welcomed or invited; one that is highly personal in nature, such as a strip search.

Probable Cause: based on facts and circumstances that would lead a reasonable person to believe a law is being, or has been, violated.

Reasonable Suspicion: a reasonable belief based on circumstances or information, but without proof, that something wrong or illegal has occurred.

Search: the examination of a person's home, car, or other personal space, or person, in an attempt to find something that is illegal or stolen or that provides some evidence of that person's guilt of some criminal act.

Search Warrant: a written order, signed by a judge, which directs an official to look for stolen goods or unlawful possessions and bring them to court for use in criminal prosecution.

Seizure: when a person or property is forcefully taken away by legal process.

Julie Baker

BIBLIOGRAPHY

ACLU. (2004). *ACLU challenges Detroit police over mass searches of public school students.* Retrieved July 23, 2007, from http://aclu.org.

ACLU. (2006). *Landmark settlement reached in notorious school drug raid caught on tape.* Retrieved July 23, 2007, from http://aclu.org.

Across the nation: Districts. (1995). *Education Week, 15,* 4. Retrieved July 30, 2007, from EBSCO Online Databases Education Research Complete.

Board of Education of Independent School Dist. No. 92 of Pottawatomie Cty v. Earls, 536 U.S. 822 (2002). Retrieved July 30, 2007, from http://law.cornell.edu.

Essex, N. (2002). *School law and the public schools: A practical guide for school leaders* (2nd ed.). Boston: Allyn and Bacon.

Essex, N. (2003). Intrusive searches can prove troublesome for public school officials. *The Clearing House, 76,* 195-7. Retrieved July 20, 2007, from EBSCO Online Database Education Research Complete.

Essex, N. (2006). The legal toll of drug sweeps in hallways. *School Administrator, 63*, 46. Retrieved July 20, 2007, from EBSCO Online Database Education Research Complete.

Finn, K. & Willert, J. (2006). Alcohol and drugs in schools: Teachers' reactions to the problem. *Phi Delta Kappan, 88*, 37-40. Retrieved July 30, 2007, from EBSCO Online Database Education Research Complete.

Foldesy, G. (1991). The legal implications of canine searches. *The Clearing House, 65*, 26. Retrieved July 20, 2007, from EBSCO Online Database Education Research Complete.

Fredrickson, C. & McCurdy, J. (2006). *Oppose H.R. 5295, the Student Teacher Safety Act of 2006*. ACLU Letter to the House of Representatives. Retrieved on July 23, 2007, from http://aclu.org.

Heder, B. O. (1999). The development of search and seizure law in public schools. *Brigham Young University Education & Law Journal, Winter 99*, 71. Retrieved July 30, 2007, from EBSCO Online Database Education Research Complete.

Hoover, L. A. (2007). Getting schooled in the Fourth Amendment. *The FBI LawEnforcement Bulletin, 76*, 22-32. Retrieved July 20, 2007, from EBSCO Online Database Academic Search Premier.

Horton v. Goose Creek Independent School District. (1999). Great American Court Cases. Retrieved September 21, 2007, from http://law.jrank.org.

H.R. 5295–109th Congress (2006). *Student and Teacher Safety Act of 2006*. Retrieved July 23, 2007, from http://govtrack.us.

Klump v. Nazareth Area School District, 425 F. Supp. 2d 622, (E.D. Pa., 2006).Retrieved July 30, 2007, from http://paed.uscourts.gov.

Lynch, M. (2006). Mere platitudes: The "domino effect" of school-search cases on the Fourth Amendment rights of every American. Iowa Law Review, *91*, 781.

Mitchell, J. C. (1998). An alternative approach to the Fourth Amendment in public schools: Balancing students' rights with school safety. *Brigham Young University Law Review, 1998*, 1207-1241. Retrieved July 30, 2007, from EBSCO Online Database Academic Search Premier.

New Jersey v. T.L.O., 469 U.S. 325 (1985). Retrieved July 30, 2007, from http://law.cornell.edu.

People v. Latasha W., 70 Cal. Rptr. 2d 886 (Cal. Ct. App. 1998). Retrieved 30 July, 2007, from http://courtinfo.ca.gov.

Principal violates Fourth Amendment in seizure, search of high school student. (2011). *ERS e-Bulletin, 38*, 10. Retrieved December 15, 2013, from EBSCO Online Database Education Research Complete.

Sharp increase in drugs in schools. (2005). *The Brown University Digest of Addiction Theory & Application, Supplement 10, 24* (S10), 1-2.Retrieved July 30, 2007, from EBSCO Online Database Academic Search Premier.

SRO's scare tactics during seizure of pupil could lead to 4th Amend. liability. (2013). *School Law Briefings, 17*, 8-9. Retrieved December 15, 2013, from EBSCO Online Database Education Research Complete.

Student and Teacher Safety Act of 2006. Section 3B. (2006). Washington, DC: U.S. Government Printing Office. Retrieved August 24, 2007, from http://govtrack.us.

Torres, M., Brady, K. P., & Stefkovlch, J. A. (2011). Student strip searches: The legal and ethical implications of Safford Unified School District v. Redding for school leaders. *Journal of School Leadership, 21*, 42-63. Retrieved December 15, 2013, from EBSCO Online Database Education Research Complete.

Torres, M., & Chen, Y. (2006). Assessing Columbine's impact on students' Fourth Amendment case outcomes: Implication for administrative discretion and decision making. *NASSP Bulletin 90*, 185-206. Retrieved July 30, 2007, from EBSCO Online Database Education Research Complete.

Vernonia Sch. Dist. 471 v. Acton, 515 U.S. 646 (1995). Retrieved 30 July, 2007, from http://law.cornell.edu.

Suggested Reading

Alexander, K. & Alexander, M. (2004). *American public school law*. Boston: Wadsworth Publishing.

Baker, J. (2014). Search & seizure in the public schools. School Safety and Policy Procedures. *Gale Virtual Reference Library*, 75-80.

Persico, D. (1998). *New Jersey v. T.L.O: Searches in schools*. Berkeley Height, NJ: Enslow Press.

Torres, M., Brady, K., & Stefkovich, J. (2011). Student strip searches: The legal and ethical implications of Safford Unified School District v. Redding for school leaders. *Journal of School Leadership*, 21 (1), 42-63.

Dispensing Birth Control in Public Schools

This article focuses on the controversial practice of dispensing birth control in public schools. Minors' constitutional right to contraception is described. This article explores the way in which the federal government frames teen pregnancy as a public problem with a public policy solution. The differences in state laws governing the practice of dispensing birth control in public schools are described. The history, funding, and scope of school-based health centers is explored. The debate over promoting the Title

V abstinence education program versus dispensing birth control in public schools is included.

KEYWORDS: Abstinence; American Civil Liberties Union; Birth Control; Comprehensive Sex Education; Public Policy; Public Problems; Public Problem Solving; Public Schools; School-Based Health Centers; Supreme Court; Values

OVERVIEW

Adolescents are a population at high risk for pregnancy and sexually transmitted disease. The Guttmacher Institute, a reproductive health advocacy group, reported that in 2008, there were nearly 750,000 pregnancies among women younger than 20 in the United States. The pregnancy rate among women aged 15 to 19 was nearly 68 pregnancies per 1,000 women—a decline of 42 percent from its high of nearly 117 in 1990 (Kost & Henshaw, 2012). Researchers associate the decline with teenagers' decision to delay sex and an increase in contraceptive use. Despite declining teen pregnancy rates, the United States still has one of the highest teen pregnancy rates among major industrialized nations. In addition to the high risk and likelihood of pregnancy resulting from sex between teenagers, sexually transmitted diseases are common. In 2003, the American Civil Liberties Union reported that approximately half of all new HIV/AIDS infections in the United States occur in teenagers. In the United States, three million teenagers contract a sexually transmitted disease annually. Possible consequences of sexually transmitted diseases include infertility, infection, and death. Legal and medical advocates argue that limiting students' access to contraceptives puts students at risk for disease and pregnancy.

Society debates the role that public schools should play in dispensing birth control to students. Health and sex education became common in public schools in the 1960s. School-based health clinics began to appear in public schools in the 1970s. Pregnancy and sexually transmitted diseases among teens became recognized as a public problem in the 1970s. The first school-based comprehensive health clinics, which included family planning services, were established in St. Paul, Minnesota, in 1972. Schools began teaching and advocating abstinence decades before discussing and promoting contraception. While state, federal, and church-funded abstinence education programs

continue, numerous public schools now dispense contraceptives to sexually active teens. Supporters of the practice of dispensing birth control in the public schools cite studies that illustrate how schools that dispense or prescribe birth control lower their student pregnancy rates significantly. Opponents of the practice of dispensing birth control in the public schools argue that providing birth control to students promotes promiscuity (Ruby, 1986).

In the United States, federal and state governments approach teen pregnancy as a public problem with a public policy solution. When teen pregnancy is recognized as a public problem, birth control becomes official public policy. Government-funded contraceptive programs, in schools, community clinics, and throughout society, provide and promote contraception to avoid unwanted pregnancy and to lower the risk of contracting sexually transmitted diseases. A limited number of school-based health centers dispense birth control, such as condoms, oral contraceptives, patches, and emergency contraceptives, to students. Despite the relationship between dispensing birth control in the public schools and lowered teen pregnancy rates, significant religious, legal, and moral opposition remains against this practice.

The following section provides an overview of minors' constitutional right to contraception. This section serves as a foundation for later discussion of the way in which the federal government frames teen pregnancy as a public problem with a public policy solution. The differences in state laws governing the practice of dispensing birth control in public schools are described. The history, funding, and scope of school-based health centers is explored. The debate over promoting abstinence versus dispensing birth control in public schools is included.

MINORS' CONSTITUTIONAL RIGHT TO CONTRACEPTION

The U.S. Supreme Court has ruled that minors do not need to get permission from parents to attain contraceptives. In 1977, the court heard *Carey v. Population Services International.* In this case, the Supreme Court overturned a New York law that forbade the sale of nonprescription contraceptives to adolescents under 16. The Supreme Court found that both minors and adults have a right to privacy in situations that affect procreation.

In 1983, a U.S. District Court heard *Planned Parenthood Association of Utah v. Matheson.* In this decision, the U.S. District Court overturned a Utah statute that required parents or guardians to be notified before contraceptives could be dispensed to a minor. The District Court found that the Utah law was unconstitutional in that it infringed on the right of a minor to decide whether to bear children. Minors and adults alike have a constitutionally protected right to determine whether they want to have a child or use contraceptives. Ultimately, the federal government protects the constitutional rights of minors and does not require minors to attain parental consent and notification for contraceptive services. Title X and Medicaid, the two major sources of federal family planning funds in the country, provide contraceptive services to all teens in these programs without parental permission or notification.

TEEN PREGNANCY AS A PUBLIC PROBLEM

Teen pregnancy is a religious, ethical, social, and economic problem for stakeholders in society. The financial and social costs of teen pregnancy affect everyone in society. As a result, the federal government treats teen pregnancy as a public problem with a public policy solution. Public problems, such as teen pregnancy, are characterized as undesirable conditions that impinge on a society. All undesirable conditions within society do not become classified as public problems. Citizens and their elected officials establish their public problem agendas based on their levels of tolerance for specific adverse conditions. Theoreticians use decision or choice theory, which studies how real or ideal decision-makers make decisions and how optimal decisions can be reached, to explain how public problems are solved in ideal circumstances. In reality, historical, social, and economic variables make many public problems difficult to solve if not intractable. Declining teen pregnancy rates suggest that teen pregnancy is not an intractable public problem.

The U.S. government addresses public problems, such as teen pregnancy and teen parents, through multiple means and strategies. In government, public administrators and politicians are responsible for solving many types of public problems. A common, generally applied problem-solving or decision-making model includes the following steps:

- Determine whether a problem exists;
- State decisional objectives, alleviations, or solutions;
- Identify the decision apparatus and possible action options;

- Specify alternatives;
- State recommendations;
- Ascertain ways to implement recommendations.

Public problems may be routine, out-of-the-ordinary, small-scale, or large-scale. Teen pregnancy is a large-scale public problem that occurs in each geographic sector of the nation. Systematic decision-making processes may or may not be used in their entirety to solve or alleviate the public problem. Factors influencing the formal adoption and use or a problem-solving process or model include agency or department regulations, personal preference of public administrator, and the variables of the public problem at hand (Hy & Mathews, 1978).

While teen pregnancy rates are declining, the public problem of teen pregnancy still requires multiple types and categories of problem-solving techniques. Problem solving strategies are often situation or condition-specific requiring carefully selected problem-solving strategies and techniques such as the multiple criteria decision making model (MCDM), consensus or group decision making, ethical decision-making, and finance-based or budget-maximizing decision making. The federal government's problem-solving process involves activities such as intergovernmental collaboration, public budgeting, public policy, public education, and regulation (Andranovich, 1995). Important trends in public problem solving include increased community participation in government decision-making and collaborative public decision-making (Irvin, 2004). The political economy of public problems, and closely related public policy, is a long-established area of study and interest. The federal government uses economic tools of analyses to determine the economic effects of public problems and their solutions. The economic problem of teen pregnancy, possibly more than any other factor, drives the federal government to promote contraceptive and abstinence programs and policies in public institutions such as schools.

STATE LAWS & BIRTH CONTROL IN PUBLIC SCHOOLS

State and federal governments work cooperatively on education and health policy for minors. States differ significantly in their laws and guidelines for sex education, health services, and contraceptives in the public schools. As of 2013, according to the

Guttmacher Institute, twenty-one states and the District of Columbia explicitly allowed all minors to receive contraceptive services, and twenty-five states allowed it in limited circumstances ("Minors' access," 2013). The following are examples of state actions to dispense birth control in the public schools as a means to address the problem of teen pregnancy:

- **Minnesota:** In 1972, Minnesota became the first state to have school-based comprehensive health clinics which included family planning services. In Minneapolis, Minnesota, many high school students can access free contraception directly from clinics at their schools. Prior to 1998, high school students received birth control vouchers that they could redeem for free at community health clinics. The Minneapolis Department of Health and Family Support found that the majority of students did not use the vouchers. In 1998, school-based health clinics, which operate under the assumption that making contraceptives more accessible does not lead to increased sexual activity among adolescents who were not already sexually active, started dispersing birth control directly to students (Ham, 2003);

- **Maryland:** In the 1970s, Maryland passed a law that allows a minor confidential access to contraception. School clinics in Maryland have been distributing contraceptives on a limited basis since 1988. In 1992, Baltimore public health officials decided to offer Norplant to public school students. The controversial decision was made to address the high rate of teen pregnancy. Baltimore has one of the highest teen-age pregnancy rates in the nation. In Baltimore, one in ten young women, from 15 to 17 years old, gave birth in 1990 (Lewin, 1992);

- **New York:** In 1986, the New York State Health Department provided funding for eight school-based health clinics. These eight clinics joined the 71 other school-based clinics that were opened in schools around the country in the early 1980s. Two of the eight New York City school-based clinics dispensed birth control to students. The school board allowed the schools to dispense birth control because they recognized that family planning was a part of comprehensive health care. The schools' decision to dispense birth control to students was challenged by the New York Catholic Diocese, United Parents Organization, and African People's Christian Organization. In 1985, the New York City Board of Education banned the distribution of contraceptives at high school health clinics in the city citing the fear of increased promiscuity among students (Ruby). In 2011, however, a pilot program was launched to distribute morning-after pills and other contraceptives to students in selected schools; parents were given the choice to opt out of having contraceptives made available to their children, but only 1 to 2 percent did so (Hartocollis, 2012);

- **Washington:** In 1993, Planned Parenthood, in cooperation with the school board, put condom-dispensing machines in Seattle public high schools;

- **California:** In 2005, Santa Rosa City Board of Education passed a plan to dispense low- to no-cost contraceptives. The Elsie Allen High School clinic was authorized by the school board to prescribe and distribute the contraceptives to students from the entire school district. The school district continues to face strong opposition from religious organizations such as the Eagle Forum of California. The Eagle Forum, a pro-family advocacy organization founded in 1972, is demanding that the Santa Rosa City Board of Education to stop dispensing birth control and teach abstinence education;

- **Maine:** In 2007, the Portland school board, in cooperation with the Portland Division of Public Health, approved a plan to allow middle-school students to obtain prescription birth control medications without parental notification. The Portland school board is creating independently operated health care centers at middle schools and high schools that provide services such as immunizations, physical checkups, birth-control medications, and counseling for sexually transmitted diseases. The district's three middle schools, which teach kids from 11 to 13 years old, had 17 reported pregnancies among students since 2003. The district saw a need for contraceptives in the school body;

- **Virginia:** In 2010, the Alexandria school district installed an adolescent health center in T. C. Williams High School with a full-time primary care physician and nurse practitioner; previously, the clinic, which dispenses contraceptives in addition to other health services, had been three blocks down the street. The year before the move, there were 50 pregnancies in the school; the year after the move, there were 35, and the number was set to continue to decline in the 2011–12 school year (Welsh, 2012).

Ultimately, state stakeholders, including state governments, school boards, communities, parents, and students, debate whether or not dispensing birth control at public schools promotes sexual activity. These interested stakeholders use their values and mores to determine whether or not contraceptives should be dispensed in their schools.

Applications

SCHOOL-BASED HEALTH CENTERS

School-based health centers began appearing in public schools in the 1970s. School-based health centers, found in urban, suburban, and rural locations across the country, are generally dedicated to reducing teen pregnancy, incidents of sexually transmitted diseases, and overall student health. In poor or rural locations, school-based health centers may provide primary or preventive medical care for some students. There is debate throughout the United States about the scope of care that school-based health centers should provide their students. Sexually active teenagers may have family planning and contraceptive needs. Who is responsible for helping teens meet those needs? Some states and school boards limit the ability of school-based health centers to distribute contraceptives on school grounds. Some school-based health centers are independent operations and some are sponsored by larger health agencies such as a hospital, medical school, health department, or school system.

Funding sources for school-based health centers include state, federal, and private sectors. Federal money for school-based health centers comes mainly from the maternal and child health block grant program. In some instances, school-based health centers may seek third-party reimbursement from Medicaid. States provide competitive block grants to clinics and school districts as well as funding Maternal and Child Health Block Grant under Title V of the Social Security Act. States have also allocated tobacco taxes to fund school-based health clinics. Increased state funding has been a major factor in the development of school-based health centers over the course of the

past decade (Whitman, 1987). Private sources of student health funding come from foundations such as the Robert Wood Johnson Foundation. The foundation created a national grant program, called Making the Grade, to assist states in raising the finances necessary to grow their school-based health centers.

The funding sources of school-based health centers significantly influence a clinic's ability to dispense birth control. For example, in 2007, the Mathis, Texas, school district opened the first school-based health clinic in the coastal bend. The clinic's funding was tied to limitations. The grant that the clinic receives prohibits the clinic from offering family planning services.

School-based health centers usually have a multidisciplinary staff including nurse practitioners, physicians, and mental health providers. School-based health centers provide a selection of the following types of services: treatment for chronic and acute illnesses; prescription services; lab tests; sports physicals and general health assessments; vision and hearing screenings; and mental health services. Reproductive health services may include pregnancy testing, HIV/AIDS counseling, sexual transmitted disease testing and treatment, contraceptive counseling, gynecological examinations, pap smears, sexual orientation counseling, contraceptive dispensing, and prenatal care.

Despite the fact that the practice, in some areas, of dispensing birth control in school-based health clinics is decades old, significant opposition and controversy remains. In 1994, a report by the U.S. General Accounting Office (GAO) found that the controversy regarding school-based family planning services limited and hindered the capability of school-based health centers to meet some important health needs. In 2000, approximately 75 percent of school-based health centers, located in middle or high schools, were stripped of the ability to dispense contraceptives. Stakeholders recognize that any increased willingness to allow birth control in the public schools may be related to HIV/AIDS. The prevalence and danger of the HIV/AIDS virus convinced numerous parents and school communities that students needed to be able to protect themselves with readily-available contraceptives. Hundreds of student clinics opened in high schools in the 1980s. The Roman Catholic Church, and numerous other religious groups and sects, condemned these clinics and the practice of dispensing birth control to students (Whitman).

In 1999, the National Assembly on School-Based Health Care (NASBHC) reported that the number of school-based health clinics across the country had grown to 1,135 (Dallard, 2000). Since then, the number of school-based health centers has grown over the following decade to approximately 1,700. The Center for Health and Health Care in School reported that the number of school-based health centers across the country grew from 607 in 1994 to 1,498 in 2002. As of 2002, school-based health centers were located in forty-three states as well as the District of Columbia. The top ten states with the most school-based health centers are New York, California, Arizona, Florida, Connecticut, Massachusetts, Texas, Maryland, Louisiana, and Michigan.

Issues

PROMOTING ABSTINENCE VERSUS DISPENSING BIRTH CONTROL IN PUBLIC SCHOOLS

Sex education, in some form, is almost universal in U.S. public schools. Schools vary in the scope and content of their sex instruction. Topics of instruction include abstinence, sexually transmitted diseases, birth control, and gaining access to sexually transmitted disease and contraceptive services (Landry, 2003). School districts and communities debate abstinence-only versus comprehensive approaches to sex education. Comprehensive sex education refers to instruction, provided in partnership with parents and teachers, which gives correct, comprehensive, and age appropriate information on human sexuality. It includes risk reduction strategies such as abstinence, contraceptives, and sexually transmitted disease protection. Comprehensive sex education works in concert with other educational programs to promote the steady development of important personal and interpersonal skills (Constantine, 2007).

While the type and scope of sex education provided in the schools would seem a community choice based on values and mores, sex education curriculum and policy is increasingly tied to school funding. The "no sex outside of marriage" policies of public schools in the United States are largely a result of the federal Title V abstinence education program (Lippman, 2000). In 1996, President Bill Clinton's welfare reform package included nationally instituted abstinence-only programs. The Title V abstinence education program was a central part of the original 1996 welfare reform act officially called the Personal Responsibility and Work Opportunity Reconciliation Act (PRWORA). Title V distributes money to states that adhere to certain requirements such as prohibiting teachers from discussing contraceptive methods and requiring all public school teachers to say that sex is only socially acceptable within marriage.

Despite the control that the Title V abstinence program exerts on sex education in public schools across the country, the federal government does provide funds for all types of sex education and contraception. According to the Heritage Foundation, contraceptive programs are currently supported federally through eight different programs: Medicaid; Temporary Assistance for Needy Families; Title X Family Planning; Indian Health Service funding; the Division of Adolescent School Health of the Centers for Disease Control and Prevention; the Social Services Block Grant; the Community Coalition Partnership Program for the Prevention of Teen Pregnancy; and the Preventive Health and Health Services Block Grant.

CONCLUSION

In the final analysis, the United States is only one of many industrialized countries debating the role of public schools in student health and family planning. In November 1999, France became the first country to permit public school nurses to dispense post-coital contraception pills. The French Council of State overturned the decision in June 2000. Despite the constitutional right of minors in the United States to make their own family planning decisions in private, stakeholders continue to debate how and when minors should have access to contraceptives.

TERMS & CONCEPTS

Abstinence: Refraining from sexual intercourse.

Birth Control: Any method used to prevent pregnancy.

Comprehensive Sex Education: Instruction, provided in partnership with parents and teachers, which gives correct, comprehensive, and age appropriate information on human sexuality. It includes risk reduction strategies such as abstinence, contraceptives, and sexually transmitted disease protection.

Public Policy: The basic policy or set of policies that serve as the foundation for public laws.

Public Problems: Undesirable conditions that impinge on a society.

Public Problem Solving: The approaches and strategies that citizens and their elected representatives undertake to solve or alleviate public problems.

Public Schools: The elementary or secondary school system in the United States supported by public funds.

School-Based Health Centers: Clinics in schools dedicated to reducing teen pregnancy, incidents of sexually transmitted diseases, and overall student health.

Values: Personally and culturally specific moral judgments.

Simone I. Flynn

BIBLIOGRAPHY

Andranovich, G. (1995). Achieving consensus in public decision making: Applying interest-based problem solving to the challenges of intergovernmental collaboration. *Journal of Applied Behavioral Science, 31,* 429-446.

Brindis, C., Starbuck-Morales, S., Wole, A., & McCarter, V. (1994). Characteristics associated with contraceptive use among adolescent females in school-based family planning programs. *Family Planning Perspectives, 26,* 160. Retrieved November 26, 2007, from EBSCO Online Database Academic Search Premier.

Conlin, M. (2004, September 13). Birth control of a nation. *Business Week.* Retrieved November 26, 2007, from EBSCO Online Database Business Source Complete.

Constantine, N., Jerman, P., & Huang, A. (2007). California parents' preferences and beliefs regarding school-based sex education policy. *Perspectives on Sexual and Reproductive Health, 39,* 167-176.

Dallard, C. (2000). School-based health centers and the birth control debate. *The Guttmacher Report on Public Policy, 3.* Retrieved November 26, 2007, from www.guttmacher.org.

Darroch, J., Landry, D., & Singh, S. (2000). Changing emphases in sexuality education in U.S. public secondary schools, 1988-1999. *Family Planning Perspectives, 32,* 204-265. Retrieved November 26, 2007, from EBSCO Online Database Academic Search Premier.

Dryfoos, J. (1985). A time for new thinking about teenage pregnancy. *American Journal of Public Health, 75,* 13-14. Retrieved November 26, 2007, from EBSCO Online Database Business Source Complete.

Facts on sex education in the United States. (2006). Guttmacher Institute. Retrieved November 26, 2007, from www.guttmacher.org.

Haley, T., Puskar, K., Terhorst, L., Terry, M., & Charron-Prochownik, D. (2013). Condom use among sexually active rural high school adolescents personal, environmental, and behavioral predictors. *Journal Of School Nursing (Sage Publications Inc.), 29,* 212–224. Retrieved October 3, 2014, from EBSCO Online Database Education Resource Complete.

Ham, B. (2003). *School clinics best way to get birth to students.* Center for the Advancement of Health. Retrieved November 26, 2007, from http://hbns.org.

Hoyman, H. (1969). Should birth control be taught? *Education Digest, 35,* 28-30.

Hartocollis, A. (2012, September 23). More access to contraceptives in city schools. *New York Times.* Retrieved December 17, 2013 from www.nytimes.com.

Hy, R., & Mathews, W. (1978). Decision making practices of public service administrators. *Public Personnel Management, 7,* 148. Retrieved November 26, 2007, from EBSCO Online Database Business Source Complete.

Irvin, R., & Stansbury, J. (2004). Citizen participation in decision making: Is it worth the effort? *Public Administration Review, 64,* 55-65. Retrieved November 26, 2007, from EBSCO Online Database Business Source Complete.

Jones, R. K., Biddlecom, A. E., Hebert, L., & Mellor, R. (2011). Teens reflect on their sources of contraceptive information. *Journal of Adolescent Research, 26,* 423-446. Retrieved December 17, 2013, from EBSCO Online Database Education Research Complete.

Koo, H., Dunteman, G., George, C., Green, Y., & Vincent, M. (1994). Reducing adolescent pregnancy through a school- and community-based intervention: Denmark, South Carolina, revisited. *Family Planning Perspectives, 26,* 206-217. Retrieved November 26, 2007, from EBSCO Online Database Academic Search Premier.

Kost, K., & Henshaw, S. (2012). *U.S. teenage pregnancies, births and abortions, 2008: National trends by age, race and ethnicity.* Retrieved December 17, 2013, from the Guttmacher Institute, www.guttmacher.org.

Landry, D., Singh, S., & Darroch, J. (2000). Sexuality education in fifth and sixth grades in U.S. public schools. *Family Planning Perspectives, 32,* 212-219. Retrieved November 26, 2007, from EBSCO Online Database Academic Search Premier.

Lewin, T. (1992, December 4). Baltimore school clinics to offer birth control by surgical implant. *New York Times.* Retrieved November 26, 2007, from http://query.nytimes.com.

Minors' access to contraceptive services. (2013). *State policies in brief*. Guttmacher Institute. Retrieved December 17, 2013, from www.guttmacher.org.

State survey of school-based health center initiatives. (2002). Center for Health and Health Care in Schools. Retrieved November 26, 2007, from http://healthinschools.org.

Welsh, P. (2012, April 3). Column: Schools dispensing birth control. *USA Today*. Retrieved December 17, 2013 from: http://usatoday30.usatoday.com.

Whitman, D. (1987). Student clinics: A sexy issue. *U.S. News & World Report, 103*, 12.

Widman, L., Choukas-Bradley, S., Helms, S. W., Golin, C. E. & Prinstein, M. J. (2014). Sexual communication between early adolescents and their dating partners, parents, and best friends. *Journal of Sex Research. 51*, 731–741. Retrieved October 3, 2014, from EBSCO Online Database SocINDEX with Full Text.

SUGGESTED READING

Benda, B., & Corwyn, R. (1999, June). Abstinence and birth control among rural adolescents in impoverished families: A test of theoretical discriminators. *Child & Adolescent Social Work Journal, 16*, 191-214. Retrieved November 26, 2007, from EBSCO Online Database Education Research Complete.

Haley, T., Puskar, K., Terhorst, L., Terry, M., & Charron-Prochownik, D. (2013). Condom use among sexually active rural high school adolescents: Personal, environmental, and behavioral predictors. *Journal of School Nursing, 29*, 212-224. Retrieved December 17, 2013, from EBSCO Online Database Education Research Complete.

Hansen, H., Stroh, G., & Whitaker, K. (1978). School achievement: Risk factor in teenage pregnancies? *American Journal of Public Health, 68*, 753-759. Retrieved November 26, 2007, from EBSCO Online Database Business Source Complete.

Joyce, T. (1988). The social and economic correlates of pregnancy resolution among adolescents in New York City, by race and ethnicity: A multivariate analysis. *American Journal of Public Health, 78*, 626-631. Retrieved November 26, 2007, from EBSCO Online Database Business Source Complete.

Perry, R. W., Braun, R. A., Cantu, M., Dudovitz, R. N., Sheoran, B., & Chung, P. J. (2014). Associations among text messaging, academic performance, and sexual behaviors of adolescents. *Journal Of School Health, 84*, 33–39. Retrieved October 3, 2014, from EBSCO Online Database Education Resource Complete.

RACE, CLASS, AND SCHOOL DISCIPLINE

School discipline exerts a notable impact on students and school operations. It is a crucial element in order to maintain class control, enable learning, and encourage harmony and the safety of students and school staff. In the United States, there is ongoing controversy as to the role that discipline should play in public schools, and its implementation. Mandatory methods such as exclusionary and zero tolerance policies, have created lively debate among school administrators, parents, teachers, policymakers, and advocates. Many argue that these methods have been shown to disproportionately and unjustly target minority students of color, while others support these methods positing they are necessary and effective.

KEYWORDS: Deterrence; Disability; Discipline; Exclusionary; Just; Tolerance; Zero Tolerance

OVERVIEW

Modern school discipline aims to manage student behavior, gain student compliance, and establish parameters that will allow the development of self-control. With these goals in sight, educators and administrators establish discipline methods that promote obedience to rules and regulations. In general, school discipline seeks to act as deterrence for truancy, insubordination, and other forms of disorderly behavior. Exclusionary discipline methods such as suspension have proven successful with students if they are viewed as just and fair. Nevertheless, research shows that when students deem punishment as unjust, the rates for non-compliance, truancy, and dropping out increase. Therefore, punishment methods are effective deterrents when they are applied within a framework of consistency, transparency, and a coherent discipline plan. When applied arbitrarily, too frequently or unfairly, it increases negative results (Skiba & Rausch, 2006).

Research has shown that exclusionary measures such as school suspension are harmful to students—particularly those in marginal situations. Exclusionary practices increase educational inequalities. In fact, a look at suspension rates shows bias along gender, race, and disability lines. Nevertheless, over 3.45 million students are suspended yearly from school for disciplinary problems (Losen, 2014).

The United States has one of the highest rates of incarceration worldwide, disproportionate to its level of crime and population. Moreover, its prison system is overwhelmingly filled with young people of color, many of whom end there through the phenomenon known as the "school-to-prison pipeline." Harsh and punitive disciplinary measures that disproportionately target minority students are viewed by many of these as arbitrary and unjust. Already marginalized, their self-regard and educational opportunities are further diminished by practices that, as experts posit, increasingly resemble those of the criminal justice system, such as relying on police authorities (Weissman, 2015).

FURTHER INSIGHTS

The social inequalities that prevail in American society are reflected in the public school system. For example, between 2009 and 2011, fourth and eighth grade African American students—on average—scored significantly lower than white and Asian students. Moreover, statistics reflect that minority students are punished more frequently and harshly than non-minority students (The National Center for Educational Statistics, 2011). These policies and practices violate the educational rights of children, according to many scholars, and also violate notions of fairness and justice (Reyes, 2006). Consequently, students realize they are victims of injustice and lose faith in the system. Shedding light on these punitive policies is important so that school administrators and educators may fully comprehend the effects of zero tolerance policies on the most vulnerable students and develop more effective and inclusive student-centered disciplinary policies and strategies.

Case studies reflect the disparities in disciplinary practices in public schools. In one study, African Americans composed about 21 percent of the school population, but received removal suspensions up to three times that number. The juvenile justice system reflects this imbalance: African American minors enter the juvenile system at rates disproportionate to their numbers in the general population. Studies have shown that up to 50 percent of African Americans aged ten to seventeen were referred for delinquency, even though they account for only 22 percent. The situation became glaring enough that

the U.S. Attorney General and the Secretary of the U.S. Department of Education co-wrote a letter urgently calling for an end to racial disparities in school disciplinary practices to end (Walker, 2014).

This inequality has a historic trajectory. Since *Brown v. Board of Education* (1954), minority students have been suspended more frequently, for similar offenses, than white students. By the 1970s, African Americans were suspended at twice the rate of white students in some states. The higher rate of punishment for minority students is a nationwide pattern. In fact, African American students are not only suspended, but also referred to administration office at a higher rate, at all school levels (Skiba & Rausch; Walker).

This disparity increased after the implementation of zero tolerance policies in the 1980s. Zero tolerance policies were worsened by the War on Drugs and the Columbine school shooting of 1999. These policies appropriately aim at deterring drug and weapons infractions, by imposing suspensions, expulsions, and other mandatory sanctions for clear-cut violations. However, data shows that rather than applying mandatory sanctions solely to drug or weapons infractions, zero tolerance developed a set of ambiguously defined rules and policies applied to behavior that poses no security threat, such as disrespect and disorderly conduct (Walker).

In fact, suspension rates for minority students have increased since the inception of the twenty-first century. Besides racial minorities, low income students and students with disabilities are often targeted. Students with disabilities tend to be racial minorities, and are suspended at thrice the level of students without disabilities. This is exacerbated along gender lines, with the numbers of African American females punished at even higher rates than any other racial minority group (Walker).

These practices not only set children up for failure, they also steer them into the school-to-prison-pipeline, according to experts. Experts also see a greater shift of school discipline strategies toward law enforcement procedures. These include a greater reliance on practices such as arrest and detention, often by officers unfamiliar in dealing with children and youth. These scenarios often lead to violations in due process, as several prominently broadcast cases of police violence against unruly minority adolescents have evidenced. In short, zero tolerance policies were developed with the best intentions, but results run contrary to best practices. They worsen racial inequality and failure-to-graduate rates, criminalize student behavior, and ignore the needs of special education and low-income children (Reyes, 2006). In this manner, they contribute to institutionalized racism and diminished opportunities for minority children and youth.

DISCOURSE

There are many educational discipline ideologies and strategies, and people feel strongly about them. In the U.S. public school system, a preference exists for exclusionary methods that are considered appropriate for serious offenses, usually related to drugs, weapons, or physical injury. It is understood that exclusionary methods, such as suspension, must be applied fairly, judiciously and as a last resort. Upon considering when and how to apply exclusionary discipline, educators and administrators must balance and safeguard both the rights of the sanctioned student and the welfare of the school population. Ideally, punishment must be effective and serve as deterrence for others, as well as a learning experience for the suspended student. Punishment should always align with notions of fairness and justice and be based on evidence and coherent standards.

Ideal approaches to school discipline include teachable moments; for example, those that model self-discipline for students to emulate. Effective sanctions can deter or correct problematic behaviors, or remove those students whose misbehavior is too serious for basic school discipline. In order for punishment to be effective, it is important to establish some fundamental strategies that are clear and coherent to all students. These strategies should also be considered reasonable and sustainable by the school community at large.

Many experts have tried to develop strategies in order to implement school discipline in a way that fosters equality and democracy and improves the public school community. Legal and education scholar Brenda L. T. Walker (2014) recommends that educators, policymakers, and other education experts engage in group study and critical discussion of issues related to people of color. Participants should deconstruct available data related to disciplinary actions such as suspension and expulsion, by running them across race and gender lines, in order

to more accurately illuminate the extent to which minorities are disproportionately overrepresented along lines of disciplinary practices.

Other strategies include:
1. Peace-oriented workshops
   These should use narratives that counter violent activity in urban or underserved communities. Group interaction and work should lead to peaceful resolutions.
2. Studying equality legislation
   All stakeholders should be familiar with *Brown v. Board of Education*, as well as due process rights as guaranteed in the fourteenth Amendment. School personnel, parents and even students should understand students' rights to equality and to fair due process.
3. Foster a culturally affirming school climate
   That is, schools should work towards an environment that welcomes and respects all cultural backgrounds.
4. Analyze disciplinary policies through a critical framework
   Policies should define clearly and specifically what school infractions are punishable under its policies. School authorities and students must abide by what is delineated and documented in its policy. Therefore, infractions and sanctions related to school safety, for example, should be spelled out clearly.

Educators can also foster a more inclusive, democratic environment in the classroom without sacrificing class control and discipline. The National Forum of Educational Administration (2015) offers a detailed guideline for teachers, which begins by recommending educators engage in self-evaluation. Students usually carry the burden of blame in teacher-student disciplinary problems. However, there are different ways of achieving results than seeking to place the blame on somebody. In order to practice self-evaluation that leads to best practices and positive results, the forum presented a list of suggestions, which include the following.

■ Organize and routinize. When teachers spend too much time looking for supplies and other things, it invites unruly behavior. Time management and organization allow teachers and students to focus efficiently on the teaching and learning process;

■ Clarity. Instructions and assignments should be as detailed as possible. Note the difference between

"Now you may review for a while" and "During the next 10 minutes see how many of the gas law problems you can complete. They are found on page X of your book."

- Naturalness. In other words, a teacher should be herself or himself, rather than present a persona she or he believes would be more pleasing. Students can figure out dishonesty;

- Acting age appropriate. Students do not expect teachers to be peers. Instead they expect their teachers to behave like mature adults and to offer guidance. In an effort to be popular with students, teachers can create or exacerbate disciplinary problems;

- Fairness and consistency. Students become confused when teachers accept some types of behavior one day and punish it another. Consistency implies fairness; that is, teachers should not show favoritism. This is especially important in ethnically diverse classrooms. Perceptions of favoritism or discrimination invite or worsen disciplinary problems;

- Avoid arguments. Teachers must be firm and fair but not become involved in prolonged arguments with a student or group of students. For example, it is often better to handle something privately and quietly, such as changing disruptive students from one place to another, instead of engaging in verbal confrontations with a student in front of the class, or else, sending a student to the office for disruption;

- Avoid temper tantrums. A teacher must model maturity, self-discipline and emotional maturity. This does not occur if a teacher yells or breaks down;

- Values. Learn the school policy and uphold it. Some teachers may develop their own set of values or standards and end up taking rigid stands on issues that are not important in the long run. Upholding a school policy allows the teacher to let school administrators enforce it when necessary;

- Do not threaten. Students should be informed of behavioral standards and expectations. When students are aware of expectations, it is not necessary to make threats when an infraction occurs. If the infraction calls for a specific sanction, the teacher must sanction. It is not necessary to enter into arguments or threats. It is also not recommended to continuously postpone action or repeatedly threaten a student with sanctions the next time he or she violates the rules;

- Do not humiliate students. Sometimes a teacher must engage in sanctioning a student. Actions or statements that offend or humiliate a student, however, are counterproductive. Addressing students in public to comment on their speech patterns, attire, ethnic background, or other personal elements can cause disruptive behavior if a student feels publicly shamed. It is also important to understand, in a culturally diverse population, that some words carry different meanings to different people;

- Give students responsibility if appropriate. If students are mature or prepared enough to manage some class projects or endeavors, give them responsibility. This makes them feel respected and engaged in classroom work.

Effective teachers are not born that way. They learn from their errors and grow. In order to do so, they constantly reflect upon and re-evaluate their teaching methods and practices, including their effect on class discipline. For example, effective teachers are organized, actively learn about and implement educational best practices, and avoid an environment of teacher versus students. The practices delineated above are steps in the right direction towards creating a sense of fairness and mutual respect among students, teachers and school administration.

Studies show that on the issue of deterrence, consistency in disciplinary methods work better than ambiguity and harshness. Exclusionary sanctions tend to be unproductive when students believe these are inconsistent, unfair or when applied to students with emotional disabilities or behavioral problems. In general, removing students from school tends to make students feel alienated from the school community. Removing students from underserved communities from school causes them to be further excluded, barring them from access to other opportunities.

On the other hand, abundant research studies have shown that in schools in which students are well informed about disciplinary rules and perceive these as just and fair, there is significantly less unruliness, insubordination, and truancy. Transparency and information are appropriate steps towards making students feel involved in the disciplinary process, and fosters the development of trust, respect for the system, self-discipline, a democratic environment, and functional schools.

TERMS & CONCEPTS

Deterrence: To use the threat of sanctions or punishment as a way to deter people from breaking the rules.

Disability: A term that encompasses a series of impairments and limitations, which may be physical, emotional, or mental.

Discipline: The control of behavior by requiring obedience to rules and orders. It often is linked to the threat of punishment for infractions of the rules.

Exclusionary: Behaviors or policies that exclude others.

Just: A concept that refers to that which is correct and fair.

Tolerance: The capacity to accept behaviors, habits, and beliefs different from one's own.

Zero Tolerance: Policies aimed at deterring drug and weapons infractions by imposing suspensions, expulsions, and other mandatory sanctions for clear-cut violations.

Trudy Mercadal, PhD

BIBLIOGRAPHY

Bireda, M. R. (2002). Eliminating racial profiling in school discipline: Cultures in conflict. Lanham, MD: Rowman & Littlefield Education.

Greene, R. W. (2014). Lost at school: Why our kids with behavioral challenges are falling through the cracks and how we can help them. New York, NY: Scribner.

Hanna, J. L. (1988). Disruptive school behavior: Class, race and culture. Teaneck, NJ: Holmes and Meier.

Losen, D. J. (2014). Closing the school discipline gap: Equitable remedies for excessive exclusion. New York, NY: Teachers College Press.

Milner, H. R., & Howard, T. (2015). Rac(e)ing to class: Confronting poverty and race in schools and classrooms. Cambridge, MA: Harvard Education Press.

National Center for Education Statistics. (2011). Condition of education 2011. Washington, DC: U.S. Department of Education NCES.

National Forum of Educational Administration and Supervision. (2015). How teachers can avoid contributing to discipline problems in schools: Could I be part of the problem? National Forum of Educational Administration and Supervision Journal, 38(2), 64–70. Retrieved December 3, 2015, from EBSCO Education Research Complete.

Reyes, A. H. (2006). Discipline, achievement, and race: is zero tolerance the answer? New York, NY: Rowman & Littlefield Education.

Skiba, R. J., & Rausch, M. K. (2006). Zero tolerance, suspension and expulsion: Questions of equity and effectiveness. In C. M. Evertson and C.S. Weinstein (Eds.), Handbook of Classroom Management: Research, Practice, and Contemporary Issues (pp. 1063–1092). Mahwah, NJ: Erlbaum.

Walker, B. L. T. (2014). Suspended animation: A legal perspective of school discipline and African American learners in the shadows of Brown. Journal of Negro Education, 83(3), 338–351. Retrieved December 3, 2015, from EBSCO Education Research Complete

Weissman, M. (2015). Prelude to prison: student perspectives on school suspension. Syracuse, NY: Syracuse University Press.

SUGGESTED READING

Hines-Datri, D. (2015). When police intervene: Race, gender and discipline of black male students at an urban high school. Journal of Cases in Educational Leadership, 18(2), 122–133. Retrieved December 3, 2015, from EBSCO Education Research Complete.

Mayworm, A. M., & Sharkey, J. D. (2014). Ethical considerations in a three-tiered approach to school discipline, policy and practice. Psychology in the Schools, 51(7), 603–794. Retrieved December 3, 2015, from EBSCO Education Research Complete.

Singleton, G. E. (2014). Courageous conversations about race: A field guide for achieving equity in schools. Thousand Oaks, CA: Corwin.

Triplett, N. P., Allen, A., & Lewis, C. W. (2014). Zero tolerance, school shootings, and the post-Brown quest for equity in discipline policy: An examination of how urban minorities are punished for white suburban violence. Journal of Negro Education, 83(3), 352–370. Retrieved December 3, 2015, from EBSCO Education Research Complete.

NO CHILD LEFT BEHIND ACT OF 2001

The No Child Left Behind Act (NCLB) of 2001 developed out of the Elementary and Secondary Education Act of 1965, as well as the recommendations made by the National Commission on Education Excellence during the 1980s. Today, it forms the basis for current United States educational policy. Through its focus on standards, accountability, and parental options, it seeks to provide a quality education for all students and to close the between low-income and minority students and their peers. The law has been hotly debated, with its proponents citing higher test scores and improved urban schools; while critics claim that federal funds are not sufficient to support the law, and that the law encourages an overly narrow curriculum.

KEYWORDS ; Achievement Testing; Adequate Yearly Progress (AYP); Charter School; Highly Qualified Teacher; Local Education Agency (LEA); No Child Left Behind (NCLB); School Vouchers; Supplemental Educational Services (SES); Title I

OVERVIEW

The No Child Left Behind Act (NCLB) has been called "the most sweeping federal education legislation in our nation's history" (McReynolds, 2006). Since President George W. Bush signed the Act into law on January 8, 2002, opinions have not lacked regarding its benefits, drawbacks, and overall viability in bringing about long-term improvements in public education. Intended to close the learning gap between advantaged and disadvantaged students, between wealthy and non-wealthy students, and between minority and non-minority students (McReynolds), NCLB has elicited both praise and complaint from educators and legislators alike. Mathis (2005) notes that while there is general agreement regarding the overall aim of the legislation—ensuring the education of every child—there is widespread disagreement surrounding the implementation of the legislation—what will be the cost, who will fund it, and how the goal should be accomplished.

While consensus on these issues will not be reached instantly, an understanding of the history of NCLB, its main provisions, and the chief praises and criticisms directed towards it will provide a basis from which to formulate sound opinions and from which to work towards the goal of quality education for all students.

HISTORY

According to the National Conference of State Legislatures (NCSL), the history of the No Child Left Behind Act can be traced back over four decades to the Elementary and Secondary Education Act

(ESEA) of 1965 (History of the Federal Role in Education). The ESEA, signed by President Lyndon Johnson as part of his "War on Poverty," appropriated approximately $2 million for the advancement and improvement of educational opportunities for the underprivileged within the states. NCSL reports that for the next 10 years, federal investment into education grew by nearly 200 percent. Yet, a declining economy from 1975 to 1980 took its toll on federal education spending, and during this five-year period, federal investment in education rose by only 2 percent.

McReynolds also traces the roots of NCLB philosophy back several decades, but she goes even further and cites the 1957 launching of Sputnik as a foundational element in the American educational attitude that produced NCLB. According to McReynolds, the launch of Sputnik marked a significant turning point in American educational policy as it underscored a need for American children to be able to compete globally in the areas of math and science. As a result, the federal government began to take a more active interest in the education of American children in these subject areas.

The expansion of the federal government's role in education came to a near halt, however, with the swearing in of President Ronald Reagan in 1980 (History of the Federal Role in Education). According to the NCSL, during the first five years of President Reagan's administration, federal funding for education fell by 21 percent. As a result of his philosophy of smaller government and local educational control, Reagan believed that the federal role in education should decrease, and, as the NCSL indicates, he petitioned for the abolition of the U.S. Department of Education.

Still, Reagan left his mark on public education through the National Commission on Education Excellence (NCEE). Convened by Reagan and then Secretary of Education Terrell Bell, the Commission was charged with examining the state of education in the United States. The culmination of the Commission's work came in the form of the 1983 report, "A Nation at Risk: The Imperative for Educational Reform" (History of the Federal Role in Education). Included in the report's specific scope of analysis were the following:

- "Assessing the quality of teaching and learning in our nation's public and, colleges, and universities;

- "Comparing American schools and colleges with those of other advanced nations;
- "Studying the relationship between college admissions requirements and student achievement in high school;
- "Identifying educational programs which result in notable student success in college;
- "Assessing the degree to which major social and educational changes in the last quarter century have affected student achievement;
- "Defining problems which must be faced and overcome if we are successfully to pursue the course of excellence in education" (A Nation at Risk, 1983).

In light of its findings in these areas, the commission reported that there was an "urgent need for improvement, both immediate and long term" (A Nation at Risk). To address this need, the NCEE offered recommendations in five areas: content, standards and expectations, time, teaching, and leadership and fiscal support. The commission recommended establishing core curriculum standards but left the primary responsibility for establishing these standards to the states (History of the Federal Role in Education). Likewise, the primary responsibility for financing educational improvements also went to state and local officials (A Nation at Risk).

According to NCLS, President Reagan's entrusting standards development to the states led states to begin to develop standards of achievement for different grade levels, and by 1990, almost 40 percent of high school graduates had achieved the goals set forth in core curriculum standards (History of the Federal Role in Education). The NCEE's research, analysis, and recommendations spurred the growth of standards-based accountability that, consequently, played a significant role in the development of NCLB (History of the Federal Role in Education).

President Reagan's successors, Presidents George H.W. Bush and Bill Clinton held a more active view of the federal government's role in education. President Bush's National Education Summit, convened in 1989, produced America 2000, a progressive educational agenda that established six goals to be reached by the year 2000. These goals ranged from school safety to academic achievement. Following in Bush's steps, President Clinton transformed America 2000 into Goals 2000. Among its initiatives, Goals 2000 created the National Education Standards

and Improvement Council, which held the authority to accept or reject state-generated content standards (History of the Federal Role in Education). While many saw this as an unwelcome growth in federal involvement in education, others applauded the increased focus on accountability. Eventually, the Council was done away with, but, as the NCSL reports, the federal role in accountability continued.

In 1994, President Clinton signed the Improving America's Schools Act (IASA), which was, in essence, a revision and reauthorization of President Johnson's 1965 Elementary and Secondary Education Act (ESEA). Coming full circle nearly 30 years after its original appearance, IASA required states to develop and implement content standards and mechanisms for measuring the achievement of the same (History of the Federal Role in Education).

Applications

POLICY & PILLARS

All of these leading factors from 1957 through 2000 point to the fact that NCLB did not develop in a vacuum. Less than one week after taking office in 2001, President George W. Bush introduced the No Child Left Behind Act, which he described as "the cornerstone of ... [his] administration" (Executive Summary of NCLB, 2004). NCLB was an outgrowth both of President Bush's support for public education and his belief that "too many of our neediest children are being left behind" (Executive Summary of NCLB, 2005). NCLB was intended to close the gap existing in America's educational system as a result of economic and social factors and to ensure that, when it comes to receiving a quality education, no child is left behind.

As adopted in 2001, NCLB was a reauthorization of ESEA and consisted of four main components: stronger accountability for results, more freedom for states and communities, proven education methods, and more choices for parents (Four Pillars of NCLB, 2004).

STRONGER ACCOUNTABILITY FOR RESULTS

NCLB set the goal to have all students perform at or above grade level in math and reading by the year 2014. NCLB's accountability measures require that states and school districts provide annual report cards to parents and communities to show progress in the schools and the state. If schools fall short of making adequate yearly progress (AYP), as evidenced in part by the achievement of students, NCLB requires that the schools provide supplemental educational services to students. These services may include tutoring and after-school programs. After five years, if a school is determined still to be failing to achieve standards in progress, the school may be forced to undergo major changes, such as restructuring, state takeover, conversion into a charter school, or dissolution (Four Pillars of NCLB, 2004; Jennings and Rentner, 2006).

NCLB Waivers

MORE FREEDOM FOR STATES AND COMMUNITIES
The U.S. Department of Education indicates that NCLB provides states and school districts with "unprecedented flexibility" in the use of federal education funds (Four Pillars of NCLB, 2004). One major facet of this flexibility is the allowance for states and local education agencies (LEA) to transfer up to 50 percent of federal funding received under certain grant programs to fill a qualified need of the state's choice. The allowable grant programs are Teacher Quality State Grants, Educational Technology, Innovative Programs, and Safe and Drug-Free Schools. LEAs may use funding from these programs for needs such as personnel hiring, salary raises, professional development or to their Title I programs (Executive Summary of NCLB, 2004).

The flexibility provision also allows up to seven states to consolidate federal grant funds to be used for any educational purpose allowed under ESEA. One requirement of this consolidation is that the states involved must form up to 10 local performance agreements with LEAs to allow them similar levels of flexibility in consolidating funds (Executive Summary of NCLB).

PROVEN EDUCATION METHODS
Under NCLB, federal funding is allocated to programs that have a proven level of effectiveness in producing positive results in educational achievement. By relying on scientific research and evaluation, NCLB seeks to direct federal dollars to those programs that can show objective improvements and progress. To ensure accuracy in scientific research, NCLB seeks to move research methodology to a "medical model," in which a random population

sample is taken, a control group is established, and research is performed based on this sampling (Questions and Answers on No Child Left Behind: Doing What Works, 2003).

MORE CHOICES FOR PARENTS
Perhaps one of the most often-mentioned, and widely debated, provisions of NCLB is the increase in choices for parents. This provision encompasses three situations:

- Parents of children in low-performing schools that have failed for two consecutive years to meet state established standards have the option of transferring their children to a better public or charter school within the same school district. In these instances, the district remains responsible for providing transportation for the students to the new schools and may use Title I funds if necessary;
- Children from low-income families who attend a school that for three years or more has failed to meet state standards qualify to receive supplemental educational services, including tutoring, after-school assistance, and summer school;
- Parents whose children attend a school that is dangerous and/or who have been the victims of violent crime while in school are permitted to transfer their children to a safer school within the same school district (Four Pillars of NCLB).

ADDITIONAL PROVISIONS
In addition to these four pillars, NCLB also included additional provisions applying to reading, teacher qualification, and English language instruction (Executive Summary of NCLB). Regarding reading, President Bush set a specific goal of ensuring that every child can read by the end of third grade: The Reading First initiative. In support of this initiative, NCLB called for an increase in federal funding for scientifically based reading instruction programs. In addition, the Reading First initiative made available grants and other awards to states and LEAs for the purpose of enhancing reading and language arts development.

To attain its goal of having a highly qualified teacher in every classroom, NCLB created the Improving Teacher Quality State Grants program, which allows states and LEAs to determine the most effective means of achieving the goal of having highly qualified teachers. In exchange for this allowance, however, NCLB requires local education agencies to provide evidence that they are making progress towards full realization of providing highly-qualified teachers in the classrooms (Executive Summary of NCLB). Finally, to assist states and school districts in educating students for whom English is not the primary language, NCLB established a new formula grant program to assist states in educating English language learning students while concurrently helping them to excel academically (Executive Summary of NCLB).

VIEWPOINTS

Since its passage in 2001, debate surrounding the goals, methods, and overall effectiveness of NCLB have not ceased. The law's reauthorization process provided a new platform for discussion of the successes, failures, and recommendations for improvement of NCLB. As the national conversation grew, many within the Administration and Department of Education are touting the great educational advancements resulting from NCLB, while others in government and education alike express concern over what they see as subjective measures of accountability and shortages in federal funding for NCLB.

EFFECTS OF NCLB

In examining the impact of NCLB, the Center on Education Policy (CEP) reached four main conclusions:

- NCLB has caused a change in teaching and learning;
- A majority of states and school districts report an increase in scores on state tests;
- The number of schools identified as needing improvement under NCLB has remained fairly steady, despite predictions that the number would increase significantly. Moreover, rates of participation in tutoring and utilization of school choice options remain low;
- The greatest benefits of NCLB are evident in urban school districts (From the Capital to the Classroom: Year 4 of the No Child Left Behind Act, 2006).

While these conclusions appear generally positive at first glance, Jennings and Rentner (2006), respectively the president and director of national programs at CEP, provide an additional look at 10 major

effects of NCLB on public schools. The following is a short summary of several of their key findings:

While state test scores are rising, it is unclear whether the actual academic gains are as great as the scores seem to indicate. Under NCLB, states have flexibility in establishing their testing programs and methods. As a result, states utilize various means of testing, and the results may, at times, indicate that more students are performing according to standards than is actually the case. Jennings and Rentner support this assertion by noting that, while some national studies concur with states' reports of rising achievement, others do not.

Due to NCLB accountability standards, schools are spending more time on math and reading and often less time on other core subjects. Math and reading are the two subjects for which NCLB mandates testing. As a result, many schools have shifted energies and resources to ensure adequate progress and achievement in this area, and, oftentimes, this has come at the expense of teaching in other areas. For example, Jennings and Rentner report that more than 70 percent of school districts have indicated that their elementary schools are spending less time than before on non-math and non-reading subjects, and the subject that has borne the greatest brunt of these cutbacks is Social Studies.

Schools are increasingly focusing on joining curriculum with instruction and are relying, at least to some extent, on test data to guide instruction. This change is most apparent in schools that have failed to meet adequate yearly progress for two years. To escape major restructuring or even dissolution that may come after five years of underachievement, these schools are looking to how they may change or improve their teaching methods, increase professional development opportunities for teachers, and provide supplemental instruction to low-performing students.

LOW-PERFORMING SCHOOLS ARE RECEIVING "MAKEOVERS" RATHER THAN COMPLETE RESTRUCTURING

Under NCLB, schools that have underperformed for five consecutive years are subject to restructuring. Jennings and Rentner report that, rather than experiencing state takeovers, transition into a public charter school, or complete dissolution as some anticipated, these schools are receiving a "makeover," which often involves enhancements in the areas of curriculum, staffing, and leadership. Furthermore, they indicate that, although only approximately 3 percent of schools required restructuring in 2005–2006, as time passes and more schools fail to make AYP, this 3 percent figure is likely to increase.

Students are taking more tests. Jennings and Rentner note that NCLB has resulted in students taking more tests than before. Whereas in 2002, fewer than half of the states issued yearly reading and math tests for students in grades 3–8, by 2006 the percentage had risen to 100. Moreover, beginning in the 2007–2008 school year, testing requirements under NCLB will extend to science, thus further increasing the number of tests students must take.

Schools are increasingly aware of achievement levels among subgroups of students. Due to NCLB's requirement that schools address not only overall academic achievement but also academic achievement among subgroups of students—including students with disabilities, students from low-income families, racial or ethnic minorities, and students learning English—schools are devoting additional time and resources to ensuring the educational progress of these identified groups. This factor, however, has not been without problems and has been a cause for concern among educators and state officials. Many question the requirement regarding administering state tests to disabled students and those learning English. For the mentally disabled, educators argue that certain state tests may be inappropriate, while for those learning English, educators question the value of administering English and language tests. Jennings and Rentner indicate that while the US Department of Education has made certain changes in these areas, many officials and educators believe more changes are needed.

States and school districts are taking more active roles in education but often without necessary federal funding. NCLB resulted in increased requirements for states and local school districts. Among these are ensuring teacher quality, testing to standards, and assisting schools in need. Where requirements are not lacking, however, funding and resources often are, and Jennings and Rentner report that in 2005, thirty-six of the fifty states

indicated insufficient staff to fulfill NCLB requirements. Moreover, 80 percent of school districts indicated two consecutive years of insufficient funds to carry out NCLB mandates.

Criticism

FEDERAL FUNDING CRITICISM

Less glowing in his analysis of the flaws of NCLB, Del Stover (2007) cites adequate yearly progress (AYP) formulas and federal funding as among the most "divisive" and "crucial" issues affecting the reauthorization of NCLB. According to Stover, almost one-third of schools may be failing to meet AYP standards, and this percentage is likely to rise as NCLB's 2014 deadline for reading and math proficiency approaches. If good schools increasingly fail to meet AYP, Stover indicates, the net effect of these failures may be the loss of credibility of the NCLB legislation. Furthermore, according to Stover, NCLB has been underfunded in the amount of $31.45 billion. Whereas Congress authorized $91.25 billion in 2001 for public education and NCLB implementation, only $59.8 billion was actually provided.

Stover is not alone in his criticism of federal funding shortages for NCLB. The National Education Association (ESEA: It's Time for a Change!) argues that federal funding falls far short of meeting the requirements set forth in NCLB. Yet, at the same time, the Department of Education and other federal administration officials often indicate that NCLB is fully-funded (Mathis).

Mathis explains this discrepancy and examines the different perspectives on "fully funded" that are often utilized in public rhetoric, either to support the assertion that NCLB is fully funded or to deny the same. Among these are the "relative" approach, which looks at funding as an overall percentage of federal appropriation dollars, the "authorization level" approach, which compares actual appropriation levels of funding with authorization levels, and the "money left on the table" approach, which points to states' retaining unspent federal education dollars. While Mathis examines these, and three additional approaches, in much greater depth, the notable feature of his work is that it highlights the semantic tactics utilized both by NCLB supporters and critics in arguing either for or against the reality of full-funding for NCLB.

METHODOLOGICAL CRITICISMS

While funding and AYP rank high on the list of criticisms of NCLB, they do not complete the list. Educational organizations such as the National Education Association (NEA) also find fault with other NCLB provisions. Among the NEA's specific concerns with NCLB are the following:

- "It imposes invalid one-size-fits-all measures on students, failing to recognize that different children learn in different ways and with different timelines;
- "Its vision of accountability focuses more on punishing children and schools than on giving them the support they need to improve;
- "It favors privatization, rather than teacher-led, family-oriented solutions" (ESEA: It's Time for a Change!).

FEDERAL CRITICISMS

Criticism of NCLB is not limited to outside organizations, and despite the fact that much of the praise of NCLB comes from the federal administration, so, too, does some of the critique. In "Building on Results: A Blueprint for Strengthening the No Child Left Behind Act" (2007), U.S. Secretary of Education Margaret Spellings reviews five years under NCLB, notes significant accomplishments, and presents recommendations for improvement. Spellings points to specific advances in reading and math scores among younger students and a closing of the gap in reading and math between African-American and Hispanic nine-year-olds and their white counterparts. At the same time, however, Spellings notes a continual underperformance among late middle and high school students, to the point at which reading scores and math scores among certain students have actually fallen.

Spellings recommends addressing these concerns while not straying from the NCLB's core components. Specifically, Spellings recommends greater efforts to close the, better curricula to prepare middle and high-school students to enter postsecondary education or the labor force, flexibility for states to restructure low-performing schools, and options for families (Building on Results, 2007).

While few would dispute the laudable aims of the No Child Left Behind Act, many question the effectiveness of the. As educators, administrators, and federal, state, and local officials work to improve the performance of our nation's schools and students, debate will continue regarding the best way to ensure that, when it comes to education, no child is left behind.

OBAMA ADMINISTRATION BLUEPRINT FOR REVISING ESEA

In March 2010, President Obama released A Blueprint for Reform: The Reauthorization of the Elementary and Secondary Education Act (US Department of Education, 2010), which was a revamping of the NCLB law and called for overall changes in the ways in which schools and school districts are judged to be succeeding or failing. The Blueprint also called for the elimination of the NCLB 2014 deadline for academic proficiency. Rather than referring to the Blueprint as a targeting reform of NCLB, the Obama administration described the Blueprint as building "on the significant reforms already made in response to the American Recovery and Reinvestment Act of 2009" (USDE). In essence, the Blueprint was a move from the criteria-referenced, proficiency-based system of the NCLB law to a norm-referenced, improvement-centered system. The Blueprint focused on four areas of revision:

- "Improving teach and administrative effectiveness;
- "Providing information to families to help them evaluate and improve their child's school;
- "Implementing college- and career-ready standards in schools;
- "Targeting the country's lowest-performing schools first by providing intensive support and effective interventions.

NCLB WAIVERS

In August 2011, President Obama ordered Secretary of Education Arne Duncan to continue with plans to offer options to states facing hardship due to proficiency standards of NCLB and their 2014 deadline. As a result, in September 2011, Obama established a formal and approved process by which states could apply for flexibility from some provisions. Known as waivers, states would be allowed avoid some of the requirements of NCLB without penalty. By February 2012, ten states had been granted waivers on the condition that they "raise standards, improve accountability, and undertake essential reforms to improve teacher effectiveness" (CNN, 2012). As of December 2013, forty-two states, the District of Columbia, and eight California CORE (California Office to Reform

Education) districts had been granted waivers by the Department of Education. In order to be granted waivers, a state must agree to and have a plan in place to put into operation the tenants of the President's Blueprint for Reform of 2010.

TERMS & CONCEPTS

Achievement Testing: The difference between the standardized test performance of low-income and minority students and their peers.

Adequate Yearly Progress (AYP): The minimum progress that states, school districts, and schools must show on the way to achieving full compliance with state academic standards.

Charter School: A publicly funded school that operates independently of the mainstream public school system and is overseen by educators, parents, community leaders, and others.

Highly Qualified Teacher: A state-certified teacher who has a college degree and has demonstrated skillful competency in his or her subject matter.

Local Education Agency (LEA): A public authority, such as a school board, within a state that exercises administrative oversight over public schools within its jurisdiction.

No Child Left Behind (NCLB): Federal legislation reauthorizing the Elementary and Secondary Education Act for the purpose of improving educational standards and accountability and providing parents with additional options in school choice.

Supplemental Educational Services (SES): Additional education services provided to low-income students who have attended a school that has been underperforming for two years. These services may include tutoring, summer school, and/or other academic help.

Title I: The first section of ESEA. Title I is the portion of NCLB that supports programs intended to assist the most disadvantaged students. Title I funds are distributed to states which, in turn, distribute them to school districts based on the number of low-income children in each district.

Gina L. Diorio

BIBLIOGRAPHY

CNN. (2012, February 10). Ten states freed from some 'No Child Left Behind' requirements. Retrieved December 21, 2013, from http://cnn.com.

Coats, L. T., & Xu, J. (2013). No Child Left Behind and outreach to families and communities: The perspectives of exemplary African-American science teachers. *Research Papers in Education, 28,* 609–627. Retrieved December 20, 2013, from EBSCO Online Database Education Research Complete.

ESEA: It's time for a change!. (n.d.) Retrieved February 23, 2007, from National Education Association, http://nea.org.

Executive summary of NCLB. (2004). Retrieved February 23, 2007, from http://ed.gov.

Four pillars of NCLB. (2004). Retrieved February 23, 2007, from http://ed.gov.

From the capital to the classroom: Year 4 of the No Child Left Behind Act. (2006). Retrieved February 23, 2007, from Center on Education Policy, http://cep-dc.org.

History of the federal role in education. (n.d.) Retrieved February 23, 2007, from National Conference of State Legislators, http://ncsl.org.

Jennings, J., & Rentner, D. (2006). Ten big effects of the No Child Left Behind Act on public schools. Phi Delta Kappan, 88, 110-113. Retrieved February 21, 2007, from EBSCO Online Database Academic Search Premier.

Kaufman, A., & Blewett, E. (2012). When good enough is no longer good enough: How the high stakes nature of the No Child Left Behind Act supplanted the Rowley definition of a free appropriate public education. *Journal of Law & Education, 41,* 5–23. Retrieved December 20, 2013, from EBSCO Online Database Education Research Complete.

Klein, A., & Superville, D. R. (2014). States mixed on new waiver flexibility for teacher evaluations. *Education Week, 34,* 17. Retrieved October 8, 2014, from EBSCO Online Database Education Research Complete.

Labaree, D. F. (2014). Let's measure what no one teaches: PISA, NCLB, and the shrinking aims of education. *Teachers College Record, 116,* 1–14. Retrieved October 8, 2014, from EBSCO Online Database Education Research Complete.

Mathis, W. (2005). The cost of implementing the federal No Child Left Behind Act: Different assumptions, different answers. PJE. Peabody Journal of Education, 80, 90-119. Retrieved February 21, 2007, from EBSCO Online Database Academic Search Premier.

McReynolds, K. (2006). The No Child Left Behind Act raises growing concerns. Encounter, 19, 33-36. Retrieved February 21, 2007, from EBSCO Online Database Academic Search Premier.

A nation at risk. (1983). National Commission on Excellence in Education. Retrieved February 23, 2007, from http://ed.gov.

NEA's positive agenda for the ESEA reauthorization. (2006). Retrieved February 23, 2007, from http://nea.org.

Polikoff, M. S. (2012). Instructional alignment under No Child Left Behind. *American Journal of Education, 118,* 341–368. Retrieved December 20, 2013, from EBSCO Online Database Education Research Complete.

Questions and answers on No Child Left Behind - Doing what works. (2003). Retrieved

February 23, 2007, from http://ed.gov.

Smith, E. (2005). Raising standards in American schools: The case of No Child Left Behind. Journal of Education Policy, 20, 507-524. Retrieved February 21, 2007, from EBSCO Online Database Academic Search Premier.

Stover, D. (2007). NCLB–Act II. American School Board Journal, 194, 20-23. Retrieved February 21, 2007, from EBSCO Online Database Academic Search Premier.

US Department of Education. (2007). Building on results: A blueprint for strengthening the No Child Left Behind Act. Retrieved February 21, 2007, from http://ed.gov.

US Department of Eduction. (2010). A blueprint for reform: The reauthorization of the Elementary and Secondary Education Act. Retrieved December 21, 2013, from http://www2.ed.gov.

SUGGESTED READING

Farstrup, A. (2007). Five years of NCLB: Where do we go from here? Reading Today, 24, 20-20. Retrieved February 23, 2007, from EBSCO Online Database Academic Search Premier.

Hoff, D. (2007). Bush offers 'blueprint' for NCLB. Education Week, 26, 1-25. Retrieved February 21,

2007, from EBSCO Online Database Academic Search Premier.

Hoff, D., & Cavanagh, S. (2007). Bush plan would heighten NCLB focus on high school. Education Week, 26, 1-21. Retrieved February 23, 2007, from EBSCO Online Database Academic Search Premier.

Klein, A. (2007). School board members hit D.C. to weigh in on NCLB. Education Week, 26, 19-20. Retrieved February 23, 2007, from EBSCO Online Database Academic Search Premier.

Koyama, J. P. (2012). Making failure matter: Enacting No Child Left Behind's standards, accountabilities, and classifications. *Educational Policy, 26,* 870–891. Retrieved December 20, 2013, from EBSCO Online Database Education Research Complete.

Koyama, J. P. (2013). Global scare tactics and the call for US schools to be held accountable. *American Journal of Education, 120,* 77–99. Retrieved October 8, 2014, from EBSCO Online Database Education Research Complete.

Kyung Eun, J. (2011). Thinking inside the box: Interrogating No Child Left Behind and Race to the Top. *KEDI Journal of Educational Policy, 8,* 99–121. Retrieved December 20, 2013, from EBSCO Online Database Academic Search Complete.

Woestehoff, J. & Neill, M. (2007). Chicago school reform: Lessons for the nation. Retrieved February 23, 2007, from http://fairtest.org.

EVERY STUDENT SUCCEEDS ACT (ESSA)

The *Every Student Succeeds Act of 2016 (ESSA)* is a twenty-first century continuation of the 1965 *Elementary and Secondary Education Act* (ESEA). It succeeds the 2001 *No Child Left Behind Act,* which succeeded the *Improving America's Schools Act* of 1994, which succeeded the *Education Consolidation and Improvement Act* of 1981. ("educationLaws.com," 2012, p. 2) Each of these acts increased federal involvement in education, while attempting to bridge the poverty gap in America.

OVERVIEW
HISTORICAL PERSPECTIVE
The Constitution of the United States gives the states of the union the responsibility of providing for the education of its citizens. As a result, there has historically been very little federal involvement in education. As a further result, there was very little uniformity of education throughout the nation. Schools within one state were markedly better than schools in another state. Even schools within a state were often unequal; they were frequently unequal based upon racial and economic divisions.

In 1965, the federal government, in combination with President Lyndon Johnson's *Great Society* program, passed the Elementary and Secondary Education Act (ESEA). This act served two purposes. First, it provided a medium for addressing the inequalities within public education which was ascertained, in part, to lead to economic inequalities within the general society, and secondly, it sought to level the playing grounds within the newly mandated desegregation of schools throughout the nation.

With the passing of that act, the separation between federal and state responsibilities for education lessened. With federal monies came federal guidelines;

with federal guidelines came an increase in the role of the federal government in the public education realm; with an increase of federal intervention came a dependence of the state on federal dollars.

Since 1965, the Elementary and Secondary Education Act has been renewed every five years. In some years, it has become known by slightly different titles. Some of these titles are listed below. It is important to be aware of the history of this act in order to understand the influence and the rationale behind the most current version of this bill which is entitled the *Every Student Succeeds Act (ESSA)*.

Elementary and Secondary Education Act of 1965
Education Consolidation and Improvement Act of 1981
Improving America's Schools Act of 1994
No Child Left Behind Act of 2001
Every Student Succeeds Act of 2015 (educationlaws.com, p. 1-2)

No Child Left Behind (NCLB)

It is difficult to discuss *the Every Student Succeeds* Act without making reference to its predecessor version of the bill. Indeed, a background into the 15-year period before ESSA is essential to complete understanding.

No Child Left Behind, the predecessor to *ESSA,* introduced accountability into K-12 education. It required states to create and measure student achievement in each of its schools and school districts. It further required that that schools measure academic achievement within various traditionally underperforming sub-populations in the K-12 environment. It mandated that changes occur within schools and school districts. It prescribed interventions for schools that did not meet new standards. In doing so, it expanded federal involvement within K-12 education.

The stated goal of *No Child Left Behind* was that all children in America would be reading and applying mathematical applications on grade level by the year 2014. This included all subgroups within schools. Subgroups included students with disabilities, students who in the previous school year scored within the lowest twenty-five percent of the school population, Speakers of Second languages who had been American schooled for at least two years, African-Americans, Hispanics, Asians, and American Indians/Indigenous Populations. Schools had to meet standards for sub-populations with a sample size exceeding ten.

Proponents of *NCLB* argued that this approach to education raised academic standards, addressed inequities within underperforming subgroups of the population, and introduced accountability into public education. They stressed that previous attempts by the federal government to improve education were mostly failures because of the lack of accountability for stakeholders. They purported that holding states, school districts, schools, principals, and teachers accountable for results within schools would lead to educational reform. (Darrow, 2016) They hypothesized that action research would result in positive change.

Critics of *NCLB* argued that the goal of achieving one hundred percent mastery of standards was impossible. In addition, they argued that the cost of creating, norm setting, and implementing assessment systems was prohibitive. They argued that the time spent within classrooms addressing tested outcomes left time for little else in the school day. Critics claimed that one test (or a battery of several tests) could not adequately measure the effects of classroom instruction, and they insisted that this intrusion of the federal government into education was in contradiction to the separation of education from the federal government to the states as penned by our founding fathers. (Darrow).

For all of its positives during its fifteen year run as the educational mantra of its time, it became increasingly evident that NCLB would not achieve its original goals. Its emphasis on testing, action research, and accountability, however, left a lasting impact on the field of education. Yet, as Thomas and Brady (2005) were able to point out early in the experiment, "the increased federal role in public education has pointed out serious limitations in understanding how to best address the educational challenges faced by traditionally disadvantaged children." A "one size fits all" approach could not be identified to address the "complex issues involved in serving disadvantaged children" (Thomas & Brady).

Every Student Succeeds Act

By the second term of the Obama administration, it was evident that a change from *No Child Left Behind* was needed. The goals of the original legislation (100% of children in America would be reading on grade level by 2014) were recognized by both political parties as impossible. Failing to achieve legislative reform within his first term, Obama "began granting flexibility to States regarding specific requirements of NCLB in exchange for rigorous and comprehensive State-developed plans designed to close achievement gaps, for increased equity, for improvements in the quality of instruction, and for increased outcomes for all students. ("Congressional Digest," 2017) These exceptions to NCLB implementation led to a watering down of the original legislation. It was in the interest of both political parties to investigate a bipartisan reform of NCLB.

On December 10, 2015, President Obama signed the Every Student Succeeds Act. ESSA received overwhelming support in both the Senate (85 to 12) and the House of Representatives (359 to 64). ("Congressional Digest") This was a quite unusual bipartisan action within the congress of its day.

This revision to NCLB offered some interesting changes. The most important are listed below.

- ESSA involves a changing of the federal role in public education. While keeping the testing and accountability measures of NCLB, it "gives states greater authority to determine the specifics of what is measured and how those measures are used in school accountability." (Martin, 2016);

- Admitting that all students are not college bound, ESSA has goals addressed to both college and career. ESSA requires that a college and a career curriculum be made available to all students. It requires high school counseling in both areas (Darrow);

- ESSA requires states to address academic achievement inequities, but it allows states to determine their own measuring devices as long as they include multiple measures and that a majority of the weight be on academic indicators. (Darrow);

- States are encouraged to be creative in identifying the needs of underperforming schools. They are given permission to use federal monies to investigate new ways to improve academic achievement, as long as the intervention is research based. (Ujifusa, 2016);

- States are encouraged to preserve annual assessments as an informing mechanism that does not overshadow teaching and learning (Sharp, 2016);

- Access to quality preschool educational programs is stressed (Sharp);

- ESSA places "a focus on providing a 'well rounded' education for all students" (Neel, 2017). This includes subjects beyond the core of reading, writing, science, and mathematics. It specifically addresses the arts;

- ESSA requires states to develop plans to address bullying and harassment (Darrow);

- The bill places a cap on the number of exceptional education students who are allowed to take alternate testing. This insures that only the most seriously impaired students are exempt from academic testing (Darrow);

- While still requiring states to employ "highly qualified" employees, the bill permits each state to define the term "highly qualified." It also urges states to reward highly successful educators with monetary incentives.

The Every Student Succeeds Act of 2015 reiterated accountability in the public education field. It continued to require grade level testing, reporting by subgroups, and school-by-school/ district-by-district accountability. However, it "gives states greater authority to determine the specifics of what is measured and how those measures are used in school accountability." (Martin)

ESSA recognized the importance of federal funding for the nation's schools. It admitted that education was still the most recognized pathway out of poverty. The war on poverty would still be fought within the nation's schools. Yet in doing this, it admitted that educational reform was the responsibility of each individual state. The fuel for reform was best handled as close to the action as possible.

TRUMP ADMINISTRATION AND ESSA

As this article is being written in October of 2017, there are still many questions as to the new administration's response to ESSA.

At this point, we can simply respond with the following quote from U.S. Secretary of Education Betsy DeVos to the chief State school officers on March 13, 2017:

"My philosophy is simple: I trust parents, I trust teachers, and I trust local school leaders to do what's right for the children they serve. ESSA was passed with broad bipartisan support to move power away from Washington, D.C., and into the hands of those who are closest to serving our Nation's students.

States, along with local educators and parents, are on the frontlines of ensuring every child has access to a quality education. The plans each State develops ... will promote innovation, flexibility, and accountability to ensure every child has a chance to learn and to succeed." (Congressional Digest).

FEDERAL BUDGET FOR ESSA

The United States government allocates a significant part of its budget to K-12 public education. These dollars provide supplemental services for school programs, employee training, interventions, community learning centers, magnet schools, charter schools, early childhood education, and educational support for the disadvantaged.

Funding in this act comes in the way of titles, or chapters, or, even better, line items of the grant. The information below gives some insight into the type of services provided through federal education dollars.

Title I of the Act provides federal funding to improve basic programs in schools operated by the state and local educational agencies.

Title II of the Act provides federal funding for preparing, training and recruiting high-quality teachers, principals, and other school leaders.

Title III funds language instruction for English learners and immigrant students.

Title IV provides funding student support and academic assistance, for community learning centers, for expanding opportunity through charter schools, for magnet school assistance, and for family engagement in education programs.

Title V strengthens state innovation and local flexibility.

Title VI provides assistance for Indian, Native Hawaiian, and Alaska Native education.

Title VII provides impact aid in relation to the purchase of federal real property, payments for eligible federally connected children, and policies relating to children residing on Indian lands.

Title VIII includes general provisions in the areas of consolidation of funds, prohibitions, and state control over standards.

Title IX provides provisions to guarantee gender equity, funding for the homeless, study of graduation rates, student home access to digital learning resources, rights to being educated by highly qualified educators, and federal early childhood education programs (www.congress.gov).

CONCLUSION

When the founding fathers decided that the education of its citizens would be the responsibility of the states instead of the federal government, they made a fundamental decision. It was as fundamental as was the decision to form executive, legislative, and judicial branches of the federal government. Giving education to the states insured that the federal government would not use education as a force for its own power.

At the time that this decision was made, there was not a mandatory attendance public school system. That didn't arrive until the middle of the nineteenth century. Yet the founding fathers recognized the power of education. They wanted to guarantee that any federal government did not usurp this institution as a means of expanding its own power.

As the middle of the twentieth century arrived, Lyndon Johnson and his Great Society program realized that America had problems. While the nation was indeed a melting pot and the American dream was real, the country had continued to be a country of the haves and the have-nots. Poverty and bigotry existed. White collar and blue collar workers existed in different worlds. Unemployment was isolated into immigrant and ethnic pockets. Society needed a revival. Recognizing that poverty and education were intertwined, the Great Society program challenged the long standing lack of federal involvement in education.

The Elementary and Secondary Education Act of 1965 signaled the first federal intervention into public education. Throughout the years, enormous amounts of money have been funneled to the states to assist with education. Known by different names throughout the years, this initial educational funding act has been reauthorized by Congress every year since 1965. While not always perfect, this federal intervention into public education has been relatively successful. Poverty still exists, yet a means out of poverty has been created. Racial issues still exist, yet much progress has been made. Education has been recognized as the great equalizer.

The latest version of this bill *Every Student Succeeds,* in many ways, is a reaction to the previous version of the bill. The previous bill *No Child Left Behind* introduced accountability into the public education sector. It introduced high stakes testing and transparency. It focused education upon desired outcomes and applications. Yet, in doing so, *No Child Left Behind* signaled a step up in federal control over education. With its manifests and sanctions, this version of the education bill introduced a higher degree of federal involvement. To some, it was almost meddling; to others, it was an impetus towards real change and reform.

The *Every Student Succeeds Act* reasserts the rights of the States to control education. It places the responsibility of providing a highly effective education for every child rightfully upon each state's government. It keeps the high standards, testing, and accountability of the previous decades. It continues the necessary monies from the federal government with the intent of improving educational equity and improving the economic state of Americans. Yet it moves the important functions of public education to the state and local authorities. Through research, training, and accountability, education across the nation can be improved. Every student can succeed; every school can be successful; and our nation can be a better place for each of its citizens.

TERMS & CONCEPTS

Elementary and Secondary Education Act of 1965: A law passed by the US government in 1965 that provided federal funds to support education. This was the first major undertaking by the federal government into education. Its purpose was to promote economic and racial equity.

No Child Left Behind (2001): A 2001 reauthorization of the Elementary and Secondary Education Act of 1965. This version of the law introduced assessment and accountability as requirements for federal funding. It included specific provisions for reporting data by state, district, and school. It broke down data into specified subgroups.

Accountability: Accountability implies responsibility for action. With the 2001 *No Child Left Behind* reauthorization, educational institutions were held responsible for the test results of students. Institutions not meeting established benchmarks were subject to sanctions.

Academic achievement inequities: Research has indicated discrepancies in academic achievement within certain groups of people. This discrepancy has been known as the achievement gap. The achievement gap has been noted in relation to economics, immigrant status, racial status, and language proficiency, as well as other subgroups.

Students with Disabilities: Students with disabilities refer to PK-12 children who have been diagnosed with a physical, mental, or cognitive challenge. It is synonymous with the previous term of "exception student education."

Second Language Learners: A second language learner in the US is an individual whose native language is a language other than English. Second language strategies are used to assist these children in learning English.

Subgroups: After 2001, educational assessment was required to be reported by various subgroups. Reporting subgroups included students with disabilities, students scoring in the lowest 25% during the previous assessment, African Americans, Hispanics, Asians, and American Indian/Indigenous populations. Schools needed to report on any of these subgroups that were represented by a minimum of ten students within the school.

Tom Frederick

REFERENCES

Cong. Rec. 1 (2015, 10/10/2015).

Darrow, A. (2016, October, 2016). The Every Student Succeeds Act (ESSA). *General Music Today, 30*(1), 41-44. https://doi.org.

Elementary and Secondary Education Act. (2012). Retrieved from http://scribd.com.

Every Student Succeeds Act: Federal Elementary and Secondary Education Policy. (2017). Retrieved from www.CongressionalDigest.com.

Martin, M. (2016). School Accountability Systems and the Every Student Succeeds Act. Retrieved from http://eric.ed.gov.

Neel, M. (2017, March, 2017). The Every Student Succeeds Act (ESSA) and What It Means for Music and Arts Education. *Choral Director, 14*(2), 8-10.

Sharp, L. A. (2016, Sum, 2016). ESEA Reauthorization: An Overview of the Every Student Succeeds Act. *Texas Journal of Literary Education, 4*(1), 9-13. Retrieved from http://eric.ed.gov.

Thomas, J. Y., & Brady, K. P. (2005). The Elementary and Secondary Education Act at 40: Equity. Accountability, and the Evolving Federal Role in Public Education. In *Review of Research in Education* (29 ed., Ch. 3). New York: Amer Educational Research Assn.

Ujifusa, A. (2016, Sept. 28, 2016). Loosening the Reins on Federal Improvement Aid: The Every Student Succeeds Act Has State and Local Officials Looking for Creative

Ways to Use Federal Funds to Boost School Performance. *Education Week*, *36*(06), 35. https://doi.org.

What is the Elementary and Secondary Education Act of 1965? (2012). Retrieved from http://scribd.com.

SUGGESTED READINGS

Brennan, Jan. (2017). ESSA: Mapping Opportunities for Civic Education. Education Trends. *Education Commission of the States*. 2017 10 pp.

Darrow, A. (2016). The Every Child Succeeds Act. *General Music Today*. 30(1), 41-44.

Johns, S. K. & Kachel, D.E. (2017). ESSA. *Teacher Librarian*. 44 (4), 8-11.

Jones, D.; Khalil, Dixon, D., & Davis, R. (2017). Teacher advocates respond to ESSA: "Support the good parts - resist the bad parts." *Peabody Journal of Education* 92 (4), 445-465.

Klein, A.& Ujifusa, A. (2017). First wave of ESSA plans gives early look at state priorities. *Education Week*. 36(28) 16-19.

Superville, D. R. (2017). Hard listening as states seek public's voice in ESSA. *Education Week*. 36 (16), 10-13.

FEAR OF LITIGATION

Many school districts and teachers believe that they are constantly under attack by circumstances that are beyond their control. In addition to providing a safe learning environment for students of a community, many educational professionals are being threatened with litigation. Preventative law can be a proactive approach toward eliminating litigation in school districts. Also, parent involvement in local school districts can encourage positive relationships between parents, students, teachers and principals.

KEYWORDS: Educational Law; First Amendment; Litigation; Weedsport Central School District; No Child Left Behind Act; Parent; Public Schools; Preventive Law; Standardized Tests; Wisniewski, Aaron

OVERVIEW

Many school districts and teachers believe that they are constantly under attack by circumstances that are beyond their control. In addition to providing a safe learning environment for students of a community, many educational professionals are being threatened with litigation. Over the years, there have been many cases focusing on issues such as sex, racial discrimination, and freedom of speech.

Harris Interactive Market Research (2004) was contracted on behalf of Common Good to conduct a survey on litigation in public schools. The organization was charged with exploring how regulations, due process and lawsuits affect the way that public school principals and teachers perform their jobs. Some of the specific areas that they were asked to target include:

- Overall job satisfaction among teachers and principals;
- Their concerns and awareness of possible legal challenges;
- How legal anxiety affects their attitudes toward their jobs;
- How legal anxiety impacts their teaching and managing;
- Possible solutions to improve the overall quality of education while reducing the potential influence of legal overload in education (p. 4).

The firm contacted 500 K-12 public school teachers and 301 K-12 public school principals between September 18 and October 6, 2003. The researchers spoke to the participants via the telephone and interviewed each person for about 15 minutes. After the researchers conducted the first set of interviews, they reviewed the data and realized that additional questions were raised regarding the degree to which fear of legal challenge is an issue for educators and how much this concern affects their attitudes and behaviors as educators.

As a result, the decision was made to follow-up by re-interviewing all of the respondents by asking them a subset of questions from the original survey in order to gain a better understanding of the educators' views. Two hundred and thirty teachers and 167 principals were successfully re-interviewed. The second set of interviews occurred between October 24 and November 2, 2003. The data for the teachers were weighted by age, gender, education, race and ethnicity, region and urbanicity in order to ascertain that their proportions were representative of the population. Data for principals were weighted by type of school, gender, race and region.

Significant findings from the study were as follows:

ATTITUDES & CONCERNS TOWARD THE CURRENT ENVIRONMENT

- Most educators agreed that the current legal climate has resulted in a phenomenon that could be considered "defensive teaching."
- While educators are generally satisfied with their jobs, more than half were concerned about the risks of legal challenges. Such concerns have increased over the years;
- Consistent with their overall level of concern about legal challenge, the findings show that for significant proportions of teachers and principals, concern about legal challenge is the same or greater than their concern about compliance with the No Child Left Behind Act and results on standardized tests;
- A majority of the educators are somewhat worried that a decision they make will be challenged legally;
- This concern and fear about legal challenges has caused a majority of the educators to engage in a variety of protective behaviors.

EXPERIENCE WITH OR KNOWLEDGE OF LAWSUITS OR LEGAL CHALLENGES

- While the majority of educators have never been sued personally, significant minorities of teachers and principals know other educators who have been sued by students or parents. While this may not be widespread, principals are more vulnerable to these situations than teachers.

IMPACT OF THE CURRENT ENVIRONMENT

- The potential for increased legal challenges and legal mandates have hurt many educators' ability to do their jobs;
- Consistent with the previous findings, majorities of teachers and principals believe fewer laws; rules and legal mandates would help them and would improve the quality of education and discipline;
- Fear of legal challenge has affected the willingness of many educators to perform a variety of activities.

REASONS FOR AN INCREASED LEGAL ENVIRONMENT & POSSIBLE SOLUTIONS

- Educators unanimously agreed that a bureaucratic mindset was a main reason for an increased legal environment. Many also felt that distrust of teachers was a major contributing factor;

- However, some aspects of education as a profession appear to need attention, especially as they relate to retaining good professionals;
- There is strong support for a variety of solutions, many of which would shift the balance of power back into the hands of educators rather than having the law loom over every decision made and action taken. Reducing the potential to legally challenge daily management decisions, and replacing lawsuits or legal hearings with oversight by a school-based committee, are viewed as possibly being helpful in improving the quality of education.

CONTEXT FOR EXAMINING THE CURRENT ENVIRONMENT

- Despite their concerns over the threat of legal challenges, educators have high levels of job satisfaction and believe they are providing quality education;
- Since starting in education, many teachers and principals believe their ability to provide a quality education or maintain order in the classroom has worsened or remained the same;
- Teachers and principals perceive that students and parents view them as legitimate authority figures. They also think that students have at least some knowledge of their potential legal rights and are willing to exercise these rights;
- When it comes to the administration of discipline in schools, teachers and principals have different views about the degrees of fairness and strictness. Principals, perhaps because they have a larger role in shaping the discipline policy in a school, have more positive views than teachers of how discipline is administered in their schools.

COURT CASES INVOLVING PUBLIC SCHOOLS

Are these concerns valid, and does the public school system have to worry about potential lawsuits? Yes, the concerns are valid. The number of lawsuits filed against teachers and school districts is on the rise. For example, let's consider the court case, Weedsport Central School District v. Wisniewski.

WEEDSPORT CENTRAL SCHOOL DISTRICT V. WISNIEWSKI

Ardia (2007) provided background information on how this court case started. Aaron Wisniewski was an eighth grader in the Weedsport Central School District.

He sent an instant message to a group of his friends, and the message included a "buddy icon" that Aaron had designed. The icon was a picture of a pistol firing at a man's head with the words, "Kill, Mr. VanderMolen." Mr. VanderMolen was one of Aaron's teachers.

For three weeks, Aaron used the icon on his avatar as he corresponded with 15 of his friends. He never sent the instant messages during school hours or to school staff. However, a classmate saw Aaron's IM avatar and sent of copy of it to Mr. VanderMolen When the teacher saw the icon, he became distressed and contacted the principal. The principal informed the superintendent and the police (Carvin, 2007). When the school district became aware of the icon, school officials suspended Aaron for five days. However, the time was extended to a full semester once there was a Superintendent's hearing. In addition to the suspension, the school ruled that Aaron could not participate in extracurricular activities during this period of time (Ardia).

Aaron and his parents sued the school district and superintendent in a federal court in New York on the grounds that they had violated Aaron's first amendment rights. According to the parents, no actual threat was intended and the suspension violated his free speech rights, especially since the action in question took place off campus (Carvin). The district court granted the school district's motion for a summary judgment, in which it was ruled that the icon constituted a true threat. Therefore, the icon was not protected by the first amendment (Ardia).

The 2nd Circuit affirmed this ruling when it was appealed. The 2nd U.S. Circuit Court of Appeals stated that "even if sending the message could be seen as an expression of opinion, it still crossed the boundary of protected speech and constituted student conduct that posed a reasonably foreseeable risk that the icon would come to the attention of school authorities and disrupt the work of the school" (Hamblett, 2007). The circuit referred to *Tinker v. Des Moines Independent Community School District* as a case that set precedence for this type of ruling (Hamblett; Carvin).

Application

PREVENTIVE LAW

Based on recent trends, it appears that litigation is on the rise in educational institutions.

Research has indicated that most cases can be tied to decisions boards have made. For example, Hazard

(1978) believes that the role of the school boards in policy making has changed. It appears that when parents and local groups do not like the decisions made by the board, they see it as an opportunity to pursue litigation. Hazard formulated several propositions about outside influences on board policy making:

- Little is known about the way board decisions are influenced by court decisions;
- Court decisions on policy issues may be more dramatic than other determinants, but whether they are more effective is not clear;
- The impact of court-made policy on the schooling process is largely unknown;
- Court decisions are more powerful determinants of educational policy than any action of local control or school board autonomy;
- How can the school system minimize the risk of costly lawsuits, such as the one mentioned above, from happening? Hawkins (1987) believes that this can be done through preventive law. He believes that this type of law is needed due to:
- Changing elements in educational law that make it difficult to understand and administer complex regulations;
- Educators making decisions contrary to their own personal value systems;
- Disagreements resulting from individuals who do not follow the rules;
- The problem of enforcing rules;
- A significant increase in litigation and a need for an alternative process for handling conflict (p. 9).

Preventive law is based on the assumption that "the greater the use of preventive law strategies, the less the need for conflict resolution through litigation" (Hawkins, 1985). As a result, the concept of preventive law should assist school districts with minimizing court cases as well as improve the probability of a ruling in favor of the district when disputes go to litigation.

Viewpoint

PARENT INVOLVEMENT

When there is a problem, it is typical of human behavior to place the blame on others. As one looks to the school system, there is a tendency to place its failure at the hands of a variety of stakeholders. "Parents, children, educators and service providers often blame each other while the children are caught in the middle" (Lawson,

Briar-Lawson & Miami University, 1997). However, this vicious cycle must be broken. Communities must come together to decide what is best for the child. Otherwise, there is potential for the United States to lose its economic power as the result of an uneducated and under prepared working population.

Many communities across the country have been supportive of initiatives that form a partnership between schools, parents and students. In an effort to increase participation from all three constituencies, policy guidelines have been developed to assist in the implementation of potential programs and opportunities for these three groups to come together.

Griffith (1998) conducted a study, which focused on the examination of the features of a school's physical and social environment that may be associated with different levels of parent involvement. He believed that his results would provide the reasons or motivational bases for parent involvement, which could be the first step in developing interventions that would increase parent involvement. His findings were categorized into two levels - individual and school. The results were as follows:

INDIVIDUAL LEVEL

- Hispanic, African American and Asian American parents reported less participation in school activities than did white parents;
- Lower socioeconomic standing was associated with lower parent participation in school activities;
- Parents of children enrolled in special education and English as a Second Language (ESOL) reported less involvement whereas parents of students enrolled in the gifted and talented programs reported more involvement;
- Parents of second grade children and those who had multiple children attending public schools were more involved; whereas, parents of fifth and sixth graders were less involved;
- Parents who perceived their school as safe, as empowering parents and as having a positive climate reported higher participation in school activities.

SCHOOL LEVEL

- The composition of the student population was related to parent involvement;
- Schools having lower parent involvement had greater student turnover, both students new to the district and to the school;

- Schools with lower involvement had greater percentages of students living in poverty households and greater percentages of children who were African American, Asian American, and Hispanic;
- Schools having more parent involvement had parents who perceived the school as empowering them and not informing them of their children's education;
- Schools perceived by parents as lacking safety, quality instruction, and student recognition had more parent involvement (Griffith).

"Governing boards and administrators must deal with conflict and bring about acceptable solutions" (Hawkins). The coalition between teachers, principals, parents and students may be a way to minimize the effects and anxiety of litigation in the public schools across the country. By coming together and communicating, each constituency will have the opportunities to express their concerns as well as some of the potential problems that could occur in the school districts. It is only through open communication and trust that the public school systems can minimize the risk of costly litigations and get back to the business of what they were hired to do - provide a conducive learning environment that allows children to be educated.

CONCLUSION

Many school districts and teachers believe that they are constantly under attack by circumstances that are beyond their control. In addition to providing a safe learning environment for students of a community, many education professionals are being threatened with litigation. Over the years, there have been many cases focusing on issues such as sex, racial discrimination, and freedom of speech.

Harris Interactive Market Research (2004) was contracted on behalf of Common Good to conduct a survey on litigation in public schools. The organization was charged with exploring how regulations, due process and lawsuits affect the way that public school principals and teachers perform their jobs.

How can the school system minimize the risk of costly lawsuits, such as the one mentioned above, from happening? Hawkins believes that this can be done through preventive law. He believes that this type of law is needed due to:

- Changing elements in educational law that make it difficult to understand and administer complex regulations;

- Educators making decisions contrary to their own personal value systems;
- Disagreements resulting from individuals who do not follow the rules;
- The problem of enforcing rules;
- A significant increase in litigation and a need for an alternative process for handling conflict (p. 9).

When there is a problem, it is typical of human behavior to place the blame on others. As one looks to the school system, there is a tendency to place its failure at the hands of a variety of stakeholders. "Parents, children, educators and service providers often blame each other while the children are caught in the middle" (Lawson et al.). However, this vicious cycle must be broken. Communities must come together to decide what is best for the child. Otherwise, there is potential for the United States to lose its economic power as the result of an uneducated and under prepared working population.

The coalition between teachers, principals, parents and students may be a way to minimize the effects and anxiety of litigation in the public schools across the country. By coming together and communicating, each constituency will have the opportunities to express their concerns as well as some of the potential problems that could occur in the school districts. It is only through open communication and trust that the public school systems can minimize the risk of costly litigations and get back to the business of what they were hired to do - provide a conducive learning environment that allows children to be educated.

TERMS & CONCEPTS

Aaron Wisniewski: Eighth grade student at Weedsport Middle School in the Weedsport Central School District, who was suspended for creating an icon negatively depicting a teacher.

Educational Law: The area of law relating to schools; deals mainly with schools, school systems and school boards charged with educating our children.

First Amendment: An amendment to the Constitution of the United States guaranteeing the right of free expression; includes freedom of assembly, freedom of the press, freedom of religion and freedom of speech.

Litigation: A legal proceeding in a court; a judicial contest to determine and enforce legal rights.

Weedsport Central School District: School district in the state of New York, which was involved in litigation with a student by the name of Aaron Wisniewski.

No Child Left Behind Act: A federal law to improve education for all children.

Parent: A natural or adoptive parent of a child; a guardian, but not the state if the child is a ward of the state; or a foster parent if the natural parents' authority to make educational decisions on the child's behalf has been extinguished and the foster parent has an ongoing, long-term parental relationship with the child and is willing to make the educational decisions required of parents.

Public Schools: An elementary or secondary school in the United States supported by public funds and providing free education for children of a community or district.

Preventive Law: The voluntary revision of school district policies and procedures to lessen or obviate potential litigation.

Standardized Tests: A test administered and scored in a standard manner. The tests are designed in such a way that the "questions, conditions for administering, scoring procedures, and interpretations are consistent" and are "administered and scored in a predetermined, standard manner."

Marie Gould

BIBLIOGRAPHY

Ardia, D. (2007, October 23). Weedsport Central School Distinct V. Wisniewski. Retrieved November 29, 2007, from http://citmedialaw.org.

Carvin, A. (2007, July 10). Court rules against student suspended over threatening instant messaging avatar. Retrieved November 29, 2007, from http://pbs.org.

Griffith, J. (1998). The relation of school structure and social environment to parent involvement in elementary schools. *The Elementary School Journal, 99,* 53-80.

Hamblett, M. (2007, July 6). 2nd Circuit upholds student's suspension for instant messaging violent image. *New York Law Journal.*

Harris Interactive Market Research (2004, March 10). Evaluating attitudes toward the threat of legal challenges in public schools.

Hawkins, H. (1986). Preventive law: Strategies for avoidance of litigation in public schools. UCEA monograph series.

Hazard, W. (1978). *Education and the law,* 2nd edition. New York: The Free Press.

Holben, D., & Zirkel, P.A. (2011). Empirical trends in teacher tort liability for student fights. *Journal of Law & Education, 40*, 151-169. Retrieved December 15, 2013, from EBSCO Online Database Education Research Complete.

Holben, D., Zlrkel, P.A., & Caskie, G.L. (2009). Teacher fear of litigation for disciplinary actions. *Journal of School Leadership, 19*, 559-585. Retrieved December 15, 2013, from EBSCO Online Database Education Research Complete.

Lawson, H., Briar-Lawson, K., & Miami University (1997, January 1). Connecting the dots: Progress toward the integration of school reform, school-linked services, parent involvement and community schools. (ERIC Document Reproduction Service No. ED409696).

Zirkel, P.A. (2013). Public school student and suicidal behaviors: A fatal combination?. *Journal of Law & Education, 42*, 633-652. Retrieved December 15, 2013, from EBSCO Online Database Education Research Complete.

SUGGESTED READING

Bushweller, K. (2003). Threat of legal action worries educators. *Education Week, 23*, 11. Retrieved December 3, 2007, from EBSCO Online Database Academic Search Complete.

Gross misconduct is a difficult claim to prove. (2002). *ERISA Litigation Alert, 8*, 6-7. Retrieved December 3, 2007, from EBSCO Online Database Academic Search Complete.

Toglia, T. V. (2007). How does the family rights and privacy act affect you?

Education Digest, 73, 61-65. Retrieved December 3, 2007, from EBSCO Online Database Academic Search Complete.

Zimmerman, S., Kramer, K., & Trowbridge, M.J. (2013). Overcoming legal liability concerns for school-based physical activity promotion. *American Journal of Public Health, 103*, 1962-1968. Retrieved December 15, 2013, from EBSCO Online Database Education Research Complete.

Essay by Marie Gould. Marie Gould is an Associate Professor and the Faculty Chair of the Business Administration Department at Peirce College in Philadelphia, Pennsylvania. She teaches in the areas of management, entrepreneurship, and international business. Although Ms. Gould has spent her career in both academia and corporate, she enjoys helping people learn new things - whether it's by teaching, developing or mentoring.

Section 5: Politics, Government & Education

Introduction

Politics and Government are ubiquitous partners in the shaping of our education system. Competing debates and political climate spawn decisions that impact all aspects of how we disseminate knowledge, structure our schools, fund education, and care for the diverse needs of our student populations. Special interest groups, community organizations, and political parties often reflect conflicting agendas and power plays that directly impact all stakeholders.

These disparate viewpoints can be seen in the following collection of articles. Our authors survey a wide range of concerns that have inspired legislative action and directly touch the lives of most of our populace.

EDUCATION AND THE ECONOMY

The majority of education and economy experts believe that their fields are intrinsically linked. That is, a stable economy depends on a skilled, educated populace, and quality education institutions depend on funding and support from individuals living in a prospering economy. A survey of the history of education and the economy shows the close link between an educational institution and its surrounding community. Speculations on the future of the nation's economy and its education institutions are also reviewed as are comparisons between the U.S. and other nations. Education will prepare students for employment in the "new economy," however failure to prepare may have devastating consequences. Some alternative viewpoints argue that government entities may actually be fostering poor quality education systems for their own economic gains.

KEYWORDS: Digital Divide; Economic Development; Human Resources; Market Economy; New Economy; No Child Left Behind (NCLB); Public School; Standardized Test; Workforce

OVERVIEW

For those who live in the United States, education is seemingly a free commodity for persons age five to eighteen. Much like the water that comes from the taps, bridges that connect two separate land masses, or the paved roads that enable transportation, public education is something people take for granted and assume will always be there. Despite its nature, education is not free. Citizens pay for administrators and teachers' salaries, classrooms and school halls, computers and textbooks, and other components of their schools through taxes. In this way, the previous generation funds the education of the current one, which is usually monitored or controlled by politics, public opinion, and voting (Glomm & Ravikumar, 1992).

HISTORICAL PERSPECTIVES

After World War II, the United States, working with such international organizations as the United Nations, sought to build its education systems in order to create and secure solid, prospering economies for its citizenry. The United States, like most other developed nations, began funding public

education institutions grades K-12 and requiring all persons of a certain age to attend these institutions. Such efforts enabled more advancement among the socioeconomic classes and gave everyone, regardless of their income, a chance to better their position in life. K-12 education provides better income and employment opportunities for the individual and also fosters a solid economic environment for communities and the country overall. Decidedly, high priority was given to economic development and funding education was seen as key (Resnik, 2006).

In the 1960s, economists of education started seeing publicly funded education as an investment or a commodity much the same way one would invest in the open market. Economists such as Friedrich Edding began measuring public education in terms of return on investment, costs, human capital, and residual factors (Resnik). Economists such as Adam Smith, John Stuart Mill, Alfred Marshall, and others closely tied education to capital. Neoclassical economist Marshall believed education was a national investment and said that "public education unleashed reserves of talent latent in the population." Seeking to correlate numbers and data to education and the economy, Theodore Schultz and Gary S. Becker developed the theory of human capital which built quantitative indicators of human resource development. Using these tools, economists were able to determine that high quality human capital was closely linked to strong economic development. In other words, talented, skilled, educated people built and sustained robust economies.

PUBLIC VERSUS PRIVATE EDUCATION

Though the federal government partially provides funding to all public schools, K-12 public education is largely funded by its own district and state. As such, the wealth of a school district usually mirrors the wealth of its surroundings. In this way, affluent neighborhoods tend to fund schools with superior facilities such as modern computer, library, and science labs. These districts typically can pay better wages to teachers thereby attracting educators with more experience and better reputations. Districts in financially strapped communities may lack the resources to provide such funding for their schools. As a result these schools are more likely to lack such modern facilities and are less likely to be able to recruit and retain quality teachers. Teacher to student ratio tends to be higher in poorly funded schools, which has been shown to negatively impact student learning (Glomm & Ravikumar).

Conversely, private schools do not rely on public funding and are therefore dependent on the donations of parents, relatives, or community leaders to operate. It is a long-held belief by many in the U.S. that private schools offer better educational opportunities when compared to their public school counterparts. In a 1992 study Glomm & Ravikumar compared the two domains and found that in fact private education is typically superior to public education, provided that the income of those who support the private school continues to remain high. Private schools can often afford current technologies and resources and often can afford to pay higher salaries in order to recruit better educators. This evidence shows the reciprocal relationship between quality education and a strong economy. In other words, those have funds and who are the beneficiaries of a thriving economy can pay for quality education that will in turn foster its continued economic prosperity. For better or worse, public education does serve to lessen the impact of income differential for the individual student. In other words, all students within the same public school district, regardless of their individual family income, are able to achieve the same goals.

STATE BY STATE DIFFERENCES

Since public schools both at the K-12 level and at the college level are so heavily dependent on the state for funding and support, it should surprise no one that each state differs vastly in regard to such spending. Along these lines, the state's legislature and other elected government officials play a significant role in allocating funds to public schools. In giving a speech to state legislators, David Wyss, Standard & Poor's chief economist, said, "States with the highest percentage of college graduates boast the highest personal incomes and lowest unemployment rates" (Weinberg et al., 2005). While such messages may reinforce the importance of education, state legislatures often have many valuable public entities and groups competing for the same limited budget. Considering these factors as well as political

influences, legislators are often pushed to cut spending in one or more areas. Because quality public schools are so closely linked with their surrounding economies, many legislatures recognize the importance of making sure their schools receive adequate funding. Yet because the payoff for an educational investment is not seen immediately, public school funding is sometimes reduced due to more pressing concerns (Weinberg et al.).

LOOKING FORWARD

In the post-World War II era, the United States thrived and prospered; the country was an economic powerhouse that seemed unstoppable in terms of growth and sustainability. In the early 1990s, a shift occurred where Asian countries such as Japan, South Korea, Thailand, and others saw huge development that outshined U.S. and European growth. People then started making comparisons between the U.S. and Asian nations and the stark contrasts between educational attainments began to gain attention. Where the U.S. once dominated, its education systems were now lukewarm. With economic security more dependent on a skilled, educated labor force than ever before, what kind of picture is being painted of the nation's future? Since having a strong economy depends on having an educated, capable workforce, many are concerned that the standard of living may actually worsen. Hanushek (2002), a senior fellow at the progressive Hoover Institution, says, "The evidence suggests that the American K–12 education system is falling behind those of other developed nations. As a result, it is unclear whether we will be able to count on the education system to fuel future U.S. economic growth." Of particular concern are U.S. students' test scores in areas of mathematics and science, which show to be average or even below average when compared to other countries. Since these skills are of the utmost importance in the 21st century economy, Hanushek suggests that the U.S. may have to partially rely on an international workforce to fill such high-skill jobs if its K-12 schools do not take drastic steps to reform and improve student learning (Hanushek).

According to the National Center for Education Statistics, results from the 2012 Program for International Student Assessment (PISA), American students continue to perform academically below students of other industrialized nations. On the 2012 PISA, U.S. 15-year-olds scored below 27 other countries/education systems, with only 9% of U.S. students performing at the highest level of proficiency; by way of comparison, the OECD (Organisation for Economic Co-operation and Development), 55 percent of students from Shanghai scored at the highest level, as did 13 percent of students from all OECD countries combined. The average mathematics score for American students was 481, below the OECD average of 494, and below that of students in 29 other systems. In science, only 7% of U.S. students scored at the highest level of proficiency, not statistically different from the OECD average of 8%, but below that of 17 other countries. The average science score for U.S. students was 497, also not statistically different from the OECD average of 501, but below that of students in 22 other systems, including Shanghai, whose students received the highest average score of 580. In reign, 8% of U.S. students scored at the highest proficiency level, not statistically different from the OECD average, but below students in 14 education systems, including the highest scorer Shanghai (25%). The average score for U.S. students was 498, not statistically different from the OECD average of 496, but below 19 education systems, including the highest scorer, Shanghai.

EDUCATION FOR THE NEW ECONOMY

In preparing for the "new economy," which is based on globalization, service sector growth, and technological innovation, Hall (2007) sought to discover which states or regions were best prepared to educate, train, and retain a workforce capable of thriving in this new market. In order to maintain or bolster a state's economy, the local government needs to ensure that educated, skilled graduates will stay in the area and not take their skills to another state. Therefore, states need to attract new economy businesses such as information-based industries, rather than rely on manufacturing and other "old economy" staples. In order to grow, states need to work with education and business sectors to implement innovative solutions to solve these problems of the new economy. Hall argues, "The most important human resources for innovation (new economy development) are experienced scientists and engineers, as well as individuals who are training to become scientists and engineers." In his study, he concludes that a

state's ability to find innovative ways to educate these workers and attract businesses to employ them will yield long-term economic prosperity. States such as New York, California, and Massachusetts that have large populations with solid governmental, educational, and economic systems in place are better prepared for the new economy than states that are sparsely populated with fragmented infrastructures. To prosper, these states will need to embrace innovation to find ways to grow in the new economy or they are likely to stagnate (Hall).

In this new economy, those with in-demand skills or talent will be heavily recruited and paid top dollar salaries while others will work low-wage, repetitive jobs that offer little growth or security. College-educated persons will typically see the results of their efforts pay off as more of them will earn higher paying jobs. Though most jobs will offer little in terms of employer security when compared to generations past, educated workers are more equipped and capable of changing jobs or even careers over the course of a lifetime. On the other side of the coin, the future looks bleak for blue collar, low-skill, poorly educated individuals whose jobs are being outsourced, replaced by immigrants who will accept low wages, or by technological innovations (Roth, 2007).

THE DIGITAL DIVIDE

To better prepare students to be successful in the new economy, teaching students how to use computers has become a core of any contemporary K-12 education institution. With the focus of tomorrow's future shaped around information technology, students attending schools equipped with current technologies have a marked advantage over those who do not. The term "digital divide" is often used to refer to the gap between those with information technology skills and those without them. Closing this disparity is a goal for educators and also for those in business who know a vital economy depends on a tech-savvy workforce. The digital divide often reflects socioeconomic divides in society. However, many people who use computers see the digital divide as a choice, believing that age and an unwillingness to learn account for it more than wealth or accessibility (Clark, Demont-Heinrich, & Webber, 2004). As such, they felt that neither schools nor the government was necessarily responsible for providing people with computer instruction or access. According to Clark, et al., many who did not use or have access to computers said they felt using computers was a luxury and not something needed in today's society. Few thought the government should fund programs that would enable low-income families to own computers, even when they acknowledged that having computers would give them educational advantages. In this way, those without computers typically did not fully grasp their importance, particularly when it referred to their future employment opportunities or potential salaries.

EXAMPLES FROM PRESCHOOL

Sustainable economic development has been linked to education programs at all levels from pre-kindergarten to high school and from technical training to postdoctoral studies. In efforts to improve the overall capabilities and skills of its state's workforce, a Washington-based Committee for Economic Development sought to review the relationships between certain education programs and economic growth. In a report, the Committee found that individuals who attended pre-K education programs had better chances of attaining and keeping quality, high-paying jobs than those who did not. As a result, committee members sought to find ways to better fund these programs as well as give students greater access to them (Hurst, 2004). However, critics such as Krista Kafer of the state's Heritage Foundation argued that no hard evidence could be found that directly linked pre-K education to success in high school, college, and career. She concluded that any connections were coincidental. In this example, business leaders and others showed reluctance in funding pre-K programs until long-term positive results could be more conclusive (Hurst).

During the 1960's, the High/Scope Perry Preschool Study began to follow a large group of students from preschool through adulthood and study life outcomes. The High/Scope Perry Preschool Study is convincing of the importance of pre-K education. The study compared two groups of low-income, African-Americans at different phases of life. Fifteen of the individuals attended a pre-K education program and the other fifteen did not. When comparing the two groups at ages 11, 14, 15, 19, 27, and 40, the results overwhelmingly showed better outcomes for those individuals who attended pre-K. Specifically, the individuals who attended pre-K had better high

school and college graduation rates, were more likely to hold steady jobs, were more likely to own their own home, were more likely to avoid the criminal justice system, and were less likely to need social services than those who did not. This study shows how states and community organizations can receive exponential benefit in the long-run by investing in such pre-K programs for low-income families. The study also suggests that from an economic vantage point, the local, state, and federal governments can save thousands of dollars in long-term, adult care programs by investing in pre-K (Manning & Patterson, 2006).

PUBLICLY FUNDED HIGHER EDUCATION

Despite the problems with today's K-12 public education schools, U.S. institutions of higher education remain world renown in attracting large numbers of international students. According to the *Digest of Education Statistics* produced by the National Center for Education Statistics, in 2009-2010, total expenditures for degree-granting institutions in the U.S. totaled over $281 million, with average per-student expenditures of $35,679 for students at 4-year institutions and $11,902 for students at 2-year institutions. State by state comparisons show a stark contrast in per state spending, tuition rates, and private donations. Morgan, Kickham, & LaPlant (2001) argue that state funding for higher education works closely along with supply and demand economic principles. If enrollment dictates that an institution needs to grow, then the state may consider increasing funding to that institution, particularly if its programs are closely tied with need in the local area. This supply and demand also can affect tuition pricing, causing the cost of in-demand programs to rise in some circumstances. More often than not, state funding mimics the funding by the federal government. That is, when the federal government gives a solid amount to one state's public universities, that state feels more secure and will follow suit.

The wealth of the state or even of the university community affects how much state funding goes to higher education institutions. Affluent communities expect and demand more out of their universities and colleges; they demand good facilities, topnotch faculty, and cutting edge programs. Understanding how such an investment benefits its economy, states follow the example of their wealthier residents and pour money into the universities. Conversely, states

495

that are struggling to keep afloat may not make funding of higher education a priority, which will negatively impact their community over the long run. In this way, the link between education and wealth cannot be denied (Morgan et al.).

Viewpoints

THE QUASI-PRIVATIZATION OF PUBLIC EDUCATION

In recent years, one way of attempting to improve the quality of public education in grades K-12 has been through "quasi privatization" and use of standardized testing. In 2001, President George W. Bush passed the No Child Left Behind (NCLB) legislation that gave the state and federal government the power to base school funding on the performance of its students. Schools whose students performed poorly on standardized tests could lose their funding and actually be forced to close their doors or become private enterprises (Leistyna, 2007). Numerous corporations such as Edison Schools/Newton Learning Corporation, Educational Testing Service's ETS K-12, Advantage Learning Systems, Measured Progress, Data Recognition, Questar Educational Services, Kaplan, Princeton Review, BP, AT&T, Tribune, McGraw-Hill, IBM, and Dupont – and the politicians who accept donations from them – are turning huge profits by forcing schools to purchase testing and related materials. By closely following the money trail, one can see that funds go from taxpayers to the government, to schools, and then to publishing or educational companies.

TEACHING TO THE TEST

Though in one form or another standardized testing has been used for years, it is now used so extensively with NCLB that "teaching to the test" has become the norm. Since the schools depend on their students' achievement of passing test scores in order to get funding, they now spend money to buy test-prep materials. Leistyna argues that rather than spending the money on student learning, money is being spent on acquiring these publications and other educational services. Pedagogy has been replaced by mnemonics and strategizing to better ensure that students will pass standardized testing. Moreover, in affluent school districts, parents can pay for costly private tutoring sessions and expensive prep books that "guarantee" success. Since the

passage of NCLB, public schools administer nearly 50 million tests each year at a cost of about $400 to $700 million (Leistyna). Private tutoring company Educate Inc., which owns Sylvan Learning Centers, has seen its profits increase 250 percent. From public schools in affluent suburban communities to those in impoverished inner-city neighborhoods, there seems to be virtually no consensus from teachers and administrators on how, if at all, NCLB and its standardized testing is improving learning for students (Leistyna).

ANOTHER VIEW OF NCLB

In a highly controversial opinion, some have suggested that NCLB was intentionally designed to fail. In this way, schools that failed to meet NCLB accountability standards would close their doors thereby forcing students to attend private or charter schools. Money from the private schools would then go into the pockets of educational service corporations and the politicians who accept donations from such companies (Leistyna). Bill Bennett, former Secretary of Education under the Reagan administration, gave evidence to this type of thinking in a discussion with Intel director Reed Hundt. When Hundt asked Bennett if he would help him get legislation passed to help fund Internet capabilities in all classrooms and libraries in the country, an effort extending from a bill passed from the Clinton administration, Bennett replied,

> *"That he would not help, because he did not want public schools to obtain new funding, new capability, new tools for success. He wanted them to fail so that they could be replaced with vouchers, charter schools, religious schools, and other forms of private education"* (as cited in Leistyna).

THE COMMON CORE STATE STANDARDS (CCSS)

Another attempt to improve performance by American students nationwide is creation of the Common Core State Standards (CCSS), a set of standards developed in 2010 by the National Governors Association Center for Best Practices and the Council of Chief State School Officers, in consultation with education researchers, parents, teachers, and school administrators. The goals of the CCSS include establishing high goals and expectations for education across the country, and fostering state cooperation in developing educational materials and assessments. The federal government played no role in developing the CCSS, and state adoption of the CCCS is voluntary; however, as of December 2013, forty-five states and the District of Columbia have adopted the CCSS. Although implementation of the CCSS is still in progress (the first assessments will be performed in the 2014-2015 school year), some see it as an admirable attempt to raise the quality of education across the U.S., while others see it as a means of reducing local control and imposing national standards that may not be appropriate to a local school system. In addition, because American school systems are funded primarily at the local and state levels, the imposition of standards without increased funding is seen by some as essentially courting or ensure failure for students in poorly-funding school systems.

TERMS & CONCEPTS

Digital Divide: Slang term for the gap between those who have and use computers and those who do not. It also refers to people who are computer literate and those who are not.

Economic Development: The economic development of a community is related to jobs and income, as well as standard of living, including factors such as human development, education, health, and environmental sustainability.

Human Resources: Related to economics, the term human resources is the study of how people allocate scarce resources to produce various commodities and the distribution of those commodities for consumption.

Market Economy: A market economy, as the one in the U.S., is an economy in which most production, distribution, and exchange is controlled by private individuals and corporations rather than by the government; a capitalistic system in which the government involvement in the market is minimal.

New Economy: The new economy, a term that was first coined in the 1990s, involves industry sectors producing computers and related goods and services such as e-commerce. It is characterized by an accelerated rate of productivity, innovative ideas, and new ways of doing business.

No Child Left Behind Act of 2001 (NCLB): Initiated by President George W. Bush in 2001, the NCLB education reform plan incorporates four different principles: a stronger liability for improved results,

expanded flexibility and local control, broadened options for parents, and an emphasis on methods of instruction that have worked in the past.

Public School: Public school is largely defined as a tax-supported elementary or high school open to anyone. In the U.S., public schools are operated by state and local governments.

Standardized Test: A test administered in accordance with explicit directions for uniform administration. It compares the performance of every individual subject with a norm or criterion.

Lisa Angerame

BIBLIOGRAPHY

Cavanagh, Sean. (2012, Jan.). Complex policy options abound amid international comparisons. *Education Week 31*, p. 6-10. Retrieved December 27, 2013, from EBSCO Online Database Education Research Complete.

Clark, L.S., Demont-Heinrich, C., & Webber, S. A. (2004). Ethnographic interviews on the digital divide. *New Media & Society, 6,* 529-547.

Digital divide. (n.d.). Webster's New Millennium Dictionary of English, Preview Edition. Retrieved August 9, 2007, from http://dictionary.reference.com.

Glomm, G. & Ravikumar, B. (1992). Public versus private investment in human capital: Endogenous growth and income inequality. *The Journal of Political Economy, 100,* 818-834. Retrieved August 6, 2007, from EBSCO Online Database Business Source Premier.

Hall, J. L. (2007). Informing state economic development policy in the new economy: A theoretical foundation and empirical examination of state innovation in the United States. *Public Administration Review, 67,* 630-646. Retrieved August 6, 2007, from EBSCO Online Database Business Source Premier.

Hanushek, E. (2002). The seeds of growth. *Education Next, 2,* 10-17. Retrieved August 6, 2007, from http://media.hoover.org.

Hoffman, T. (2005, October 4). The candid Bennett. *eSchool News: Ed-Tech Insider.* Retrieved August 6, 2007, from http://eschoolnews.com.

Human resources. (2005). The Columbia Encyclopedia, Sixth Edition. Retrieved August 6, 2007, from http://bartleby.com.

Hurst, M. D. (2004, Nov. 3). Groups link preschool education, economic growth. *Education Week, 24,* 8. Retrieved August 6, 2007, from EBSCO Online Database Education Research Complete.

Lee, J., and Reeves, T. Impact of NCLB high-stakes school accountability, capacity, and resources: State NAEP 1990-2009 reading and math achievement gaps and trends.

(2012, June). *Educational Evaluation & Policy Analysis 34,* p. 209-231. Retrieved December 27, 2013, from EBSCO Online Database Education Research Complete.

Leistyna, P. (2007). Corporate testing: Standards, profits, and the demise of the public sphere.

Teacher Education Quarterly, 34, 59-84. Retrieved August 8, 2007, from EBSCO Online Database Education Research Complete.

Manning, M. & Patterson, J. (2006). Lifetime effects: The high/scope Perry preschool study through age 40. *Childhood Education, 83,* 121.

Market economy. (2002). The New Dictionary of Cultural Literacy, Third Edition. Retrieved August 8, 2007, from http://bartleby.com.

Morgan, D. R., Kickham, K., & LaPlant, J.T. (2001). State support for higher education: A political economy approach. *Policy Studies Journal, 29,* 359-372. Retrieved August 8, 2007, from EBSCO Online Database Business Source Premier.

New economy. (n.d.). Online Glossary of Research Economics. Retrieved August 8, 2007, from http://econterms.com.

Public school. (n.d.). The Columbia Encyclopedia, Sixth Edition. Retrieved August 8, 2007, from http://bartleby.com.

Resnik, J. (2006). International organizations, the "education-economic growth" black box, and the development of world education culture. *Comparative Education Review, 50,* 173-195, 309. Retrieved August 8, 2007, from EBSCO Online Database Education Research Complete.

Ribeiro, R. & Warner, M. (n.d.). Economic development. *Measuring the Regional Importance of Early Care and Education: The Cornell Methodology Guide.* Retrieved August 9, 2007, from http://government.cce.cornell.edu.

Schleicher, A. (2011, Oct.). Is the sky the limit to education improvement? *Phi Delta Kappan 93,* p. 8-62. Retrieved December 27, 2013, from EBSCO Online Database Education Research Complete.

Department of education, state of Indiana. (2005). *Standardized test.* Retrieved August 6, 2007, from http://doe.state.in.us.

United States Department of Education. (2003, August 23). *Fact sheet on the major provisions of the conference report to* H.R. 1. Retrieved August 8, 2007, from http://ed.gov.

Weinberg, S., Eckl, C., Perez, A., Ramsdell, M., Bell, J., & King, M. (2005). Solving big problems: A different perspective: Advice from four national experts on addressing the critical problems in the economy, homeland security, education and health care. *State Legislatures, 31,* 18. Retrieved August 7, 2007, from EBSCO Online Database Academic Search Premier.

SUGGESTED READING

Checchi, D. (2006). *The economics of education: Human capital, family background and inequality.* Cambridge, England: Cambridge University Press.

Gilmore, A. & Comunian, R. (2016). Beyond the campus: Higher education, cultural policy, and the creative economy. *International Journal of Cultural Policy.* 22 (1).

Miles, J. (2014). Focus on the children, help the economy: The importance of including

financial education in Kansas graduation requirements. *Kansas Journal of Law and Public Policy.* 24 (1), 136-155.

Schweke, W. (2004). *Smart money: Education and economic development.* Washington, DC: Economic Policy Institute.

Walberg, H.J. & Bast, J. L. (2004). *Education and capitalism: How overcoming our fear of markets and economics can improve America's schools.* Stanford, CA: Hoover Institution Press.

PUBLIC EDUCATION FINANCE

Public education institutions are funded primarily by the state and local governments, with some money coming from the federal level. The systems set in place to ensure adequate funding are complicated and as a result, many schools do not receive the funding they should. Low income students particularly do not receive the funding that is earmarked for their use. States vary in how they fund wealthy as well as impoverished education institutions, and some measures are being taken to ensure greater equity. Higher education funding differs greatly from primary and secondary school funding and higher education tuition costs have been on the rise. Some controversy also surrounds the funding of charter schools.

KEYWORDS: Charter School; Equitable Funding; Low Income; Per-Pupil Spending; Public Education; Revenues; Tax & Expenditure Limitation; Title I; Wealth Neutrality

OVERVIEW

Public schools in the United States receive the bulk of their funding from taxpayer dollars. Specifically, local and state governments supported by taxpayers provide funding for schools within their community districts. As is typically the case, wealthy communities are able to provide ample funding for neighborhood schools enabling these institutions to recruit and retain quality teachers, to maintain facilities and equipment and to buy the latest computers and library resources. Not surprisingly, students at these schools tend to receive a better education and are more likely to graduate and attend college. Cash-strapped communities typically struggle to provide adequate funding for their schools, which causes an assortment of problems such as dilapidated facilities, lack of quality teachers, and outdated computer equipment and library resources. Along these lines, students at such schools are more likely to drop out and less likely to attend college (Wood & Theobald, 2003).

SYSTEMS USED FOR FUNDING SCHOOLS

The funding of public schools has been and continues to be a complicated matter. Increasing per-pupil spending has historically been seen to be the solution for improving student performance. Yet, as U.S. student performance continues to lag behind that of other nations and stagnate, many have wondered if this solution is effective. In many ways, school funding and operations have changed little in the past fifty years. Though advances in information technology have affected almost every aspect of society from commerce and the economy to communications and transportation, education systems (including what students learn) has changed little (Hess, 2007).

Whether public education financing is sufficient, and whether it is applied equally to all school districts and all students, has been a cause of many lawsuits and much public debate in the U.S. Determining how much money states spend on public education, how much goes to each student, and what programs are funded at the cost of others remains decidedly elusive. Complicated formulas and equations are used to determine the funding of programs. To further obscure the matter, political, economic, and social factors heavily influence funding though ideally the numbers and statistical analyses should alone determine appropriate financing. However, it is not uncommon for one area or program to receive financing because it has been deemed as "in-need" by a politically motivated administrator even though the numbers do not support such a claim. Overfunding one area at the expense of another area, particularly when that area truly lacks sufficient financing, hurts the overall school and its students (Hoffman & Hayden, 2007).

BUSINESSES & PUBLIC EDUCATION FUNDING

It seems as though everywhere a business leader, board member, or politician has a formula for improving the performance of the nation's schools. The relationship between the business sector and the public education sector is tumultuous. The education system is wary of big business financing education reform programs, often mistrusting their intentions. Yet schools readily accept donations from businesses in the form of monetary donations, training, computers, and equipment (Hess).

Education leaders' primary concern about businesses providing equipment to public schools has to do with separation between private and public funding. If schools have an established curriculum to teach, its content could be too heavily influenced by a business. Alfie Kohn, author and expert on school finance, says:

> There may be some sort of shadowy business conspiracy at work to turn schools into factories, but this seems unlikely if only because no such conspiracy is necessary to produce the desired results.... To an extraordinary degree, business's wish becomes education's command (as cited in Hess).

Rather than serving the public good, Kohn and others believe that businesses' investments in education serve their own purpose. In this way, businesses want an educated workforce that will support their enterprises, but they are often less concerned with pedagogy or providing a quality education to all students.

Supporting of the greater good, community, corporate citizenship, or securing the future are some reasons given by business executives for supporting educational endeavors. Businesses give $2.5 billion each year to public education, which is still quite small when compared to total spending. Moreover, some businesses support educational endeavors through mentoring programs or other service related programs other than monetary support (Hess).

COMPETITION FOR EDUCATION FUNDING

In 1983, a report was published by the National Commission on Excellence in Education that called attention to the gaps and shortcomings in the U.S. public education system. The report, titled *A Nation at Risk*, caused schools across the nation to increase their per-pupil spending, to raise their level of accountability, to increase their district equity while reducing disparity, and to improve student achievement for all (Murray, 2007). Though the states' commitment to public education spending increased at that time, it has remained relatively stable since then. Though education counts for about one quarter of the average state's spending budget, it has had to compete against other costly projects such as Medicare and other social services used primarily by senior citizens. According to Murray, as the baby-boomer generation continues to age and depend more and more on such social services, it will compete heavily for financing earmarked for education. As the elderly population will not directly benefit from education programs, they are less likely to vote for education spending (Murray).

Though most education spending comes from state and local governments, the federal government's role in this spending has increased in recent years with the passage of the No Child Left Behind Act of 2001 (NCLB). The Act has forced states to spend more money on teacher preparation programs, student assessments, and training programs. If schools fail to perform according to NCLB's standards, they risk losing their federal funding. In this way, many have argued that NCLB forces schools to spend money on overhead, assessment, and other costs rather than student learning (Murray).

Various waivers for aspects of the NCLB standards have been offered by the federal government at different times. For instance, in 2011, President Barak Obama announced that states could have waivers on two major requirements of NCLB (the gains students are expected to make annually in math and reading, the requirement that by 2014 almost all students must score as proficient in both subjects). However, in order to be eligible for this waiver, states would have to accept several other requirements, including a teacher evaluation system based on test scores, which would impose additional costs on the school districts and which some districts perceive as interfering with their rights to make decisions regarding education in their district. However, according to the U.S. Department of Education, as of December, 2013, 42 states, the District of Columbia, and Puerto Rico have been granted waivers on some NCLB requirements, with an additional three states having proposals for NCLB waivers under review.

EXAMPLES OF SPENDING BY STATE

According to the National Center for Education Statistics, in 2010, states spent an average of $10,636 per pupil for public elementary and secondary schools; in inflation-adjusted dollars, average per-pupil spending has increased gradually over the years, from $7,967 in 1995, $8,849 in 2000, $9,768 in 2005, and $10,611 in 2009. However, per-pupil spending varies widely between states: in 2010, the District of Columbia spent the most ($20,910), followed by New York state ($18,167), and Idaho spent the least ($7,100).

Each state's government makes efforts to appropriate funds equally to all of their school districts using "per pupil" revenues. Such systems attempt to make sure that each student is allocated a certain number of funds regardless of their local school district. However, because of politics and other factors, equitable funding is not always realized. In forty-three states, lawsuits have been filed alleging that funds have been misappropriated (Wood & Theobald). Typically, more conservative-leaning states give the local governments more control and decision-making power. Such entities are less concerned with across the board equity in terms of providing funding for all students regardless of their neighborhood's revenue generating capacity. More liberal-leaning states give the local authorities less control and are more concerned with equity and with allocating per pupil funding in a way that is more democratic.

SCHOOL FUNDING FOR THE WEALTHY, POOR

Because each state manages its own financing for public schools, one can examine different states in order to get a glimpse of how such affairs are handled. For better or worse, the wealth of a student's immediate neighborhood is typically a good predictor of the quality of his or her public school education. Wealthy neighborhoods tend to adequately fund their schools, while poorer communities often must put their money into other programs, leaving schools under funded. To obtain greater equality across the nation and across each state, lawsuits have been filed in attempts to force the states to provide more adequate funding regardless of district or property wealth. Martin Feldstein and others have argued for "wealth neutrality" among school districts where a state-local matching-grant scheme brings about greater equity between wealthy and poor school districts. In this way, education for wealthy communities would cost more and education for poorer communities would cost less. He argues that by each community paying within the range of what they can afford, the wealth-education disparity would greatly diminish. The state would attempt to match the equivalent of property taxes from wealthy districts and provide this funding to poorer ones (as cited in Black, Lewis, & Link, 1979). Though grant-matching proposals may sound appealing to many, the state of Delaware has tested such a plan, yielding mixed results. All things being equal, Feldstein's theory for providing greater equality for schools across a state proved much more complicated in actuality than in theory (Black et al.).

FUNDING INTENDED FOR LOW-INCOME STUDENTS OFTEN MISUSED

Under President Lyndon B. Johnson in 1965, anti-poverty legislation was passed in order to help the poor escape cycles of poverty and improve their quality of life. Title 1 funding, part of this new legislation, was established to better finance impoverished K-12 schools and thereby enhancing their educational quality. When the act was established, the hope was that in a generation or so, low-income students could attain similar levels of quality education as their higher income counterparts. However, this vision has never been fully realized due to intentional or unintentional misappropriation of funds. For better accountability, a clause was added to Title 1 stating that "school districts must equalize educational services purchased with state and local funds" before dipping into the barrel of Title 1 (Rosa, Miller, & Hill, 2005). This stipulation sought to better ensure that funding was used for schools in need rather than for "general use," a frequent cause of past mishandling. Another stipulation forbade districts from subtracting state and local funds as Title I funds became available. This was commonly referred to "supplement, not supplant" and served as a reminder that the Title 1 funding was designed to add to existing funds rather than replace them. Regardless of school administrators' intentions, mishandling of Title 1 funding is commonplace. Because public school financing is so complicated, multi-layered, and open to interpretation, it is easy to accidentally or purposely over or under fund. According to Rosa et al.:

District budgeting practices systematically favor schools with the fewest educational challenges, to the detriment of those with the most. In some cases, arcane district funds-allocation practices can actually funnel Title I funds to schools in the wealthiest communities.

For instance, experienced, better quality teachers and their higher salaries often go to wealthier school districts as low income, large population schools cannot afford them. When comparing five sizable Texas school districts and eliminating categorical spending (special education or English as a Second Language programs, for instance) the results showed how wealthier schools received more Title 1 money in terms of per pupil spending. According to Rosa et al.:

In four of the five districts, schools with the greatest need (that is, those with the highest concentrations of students from low-income families) receive considerably less money from the school district's non-categorical or basic resources. They range from $296 less per student in Fort Worth to $472 less per student in Houston.

Administrators, board members, teachers, parents and others are often unaware that low-income students actually receive less funding and that this disparity is in part created by the complicated funding system of the nation's public schools. Because they are often in the dark about this disparity, they are not able to take steps to find solutions to repair the problems.

PUBLIC FUNDING FOR HIGHER EDUCATION

Similar to the role they play for public primary and secondary educational institutions, the states are responsible for higher education funding at a ratio of four to one over federal dollars. Since the late 1970s, state funding for higher education has decreased. According to the National Center for Education Statistics, comparing 2010-11 with 2005-2006, tuition and fees constituted a larger proportion of funding for public higher education (19 percent) in the later period, as compared to the earlier period (17 percent), while the percent of funding from public sources decreased over the same period from 48 percent to 46 percent. While many factors have caused this lack of financing, the passage of the Tax and Expenditure Limitation (TEL) bill may be partially to blame. The bill puts limits on the growth of state revenue when compared to growth of personal income (Archibald & Feldman, 2006). Higher education institutions must compete with funding for Medicare, correctional facilities, transportation, health services, and other priorities in order to receive their share of state dollars. Depending on opinions of voters, their political leanings, and what they see as a priority, higher education funding is oftentimes not given top precedence (p. 629). However, a study by Archibald & Feldman found that when overall state revenue was up, spending for health services, corrections, and higher education increased equally. Politics also plays a significant role as liberal states tend to budget to spend more on higher education than more conservative states.

The cost of tuition is closely linked to how much taxpayer dollars fund public universities and colleges. With less money from the state going to institutions of higher education, some colleges have had to increase their tuition rates, which makes a college education more formidable for high achieving, low income students. Scholarships, grants, and more friendly financial aid programs have been implemented in some states to overcome such barriers. Despite such efforts, research has shown that high tuition costs prevent fewer low-income individuals from applying to state universities, which reduces overall accessibility. This is counter intentional because state institutions historically have given greater opportunity for those of low income. Archibald & Feldman argue, "Low tuition for all creates a broad base of political support for spending on higher education, and it keeps the price down for low-income students." When state universities raise their tuition too much when compared to inflation, it negatively affects education quality because it reduces diversity and the pool of qualified applicants. University leaders today continually struggle to generate sufficient revenues to keep their institutions afloat while maintaining quality standards. In many ways such institutions are forced to act as private enterprises, listing one tuition cost for the general public but offering discounted rates for students of special circumstances (Archibald & Feldman).

EXAMPLES IN THE STATE OF CALIFORNIA
Once a leader in student learning, California's current public K-12 education system represents one of the most fragmented and disjointed systems in the nation. Recognizing its numerous failures, groups from both political parties have come together in order to figure out how to turn around the system for both the short and long term, by commissioning a large group of studies by top researchers. According to the reports, summarized by Jacobson (2007), one of the problems has been that money would be spent in one area or another but little if anything was done to oversee its specific use. Furthermore, no one made assessments to determine if throwing money at a problem did anything to solve it. In this way, ineffective practices continued with little monitoring or examination (Jacobson). Another issue was that resources were distributed in such an unequal fashion that students in near identical types of school districts might receive very different levels of funding. A summary of the conclusions of one report says:

> Spending formulas are tied to arcane and complicated criteria established in the 1970s and are combined with a confusing mix of categorical programs that do not systematically address differences in needs across districts or allow districts and schools to spend resources in a way that help students achieve their goals.

While the reports highlight in detail the many quandaries of California's current school financing system—poor-performing school districts' inability to retain quality teachers, for example—solutions to the problems remained more elusive and convoluted. Different political and educational leaders continue to argue about how best to go about repairing and even overhauling the state's educational financing system.

PUBLIC FUNDING & CHARTER SCHOOLS
From the time when charter schools were first launched, their existence has been the source of much debate and controversy. Those in favor of the institutions have argued that charter schools have made it possible for low-income and minority students to obtain a quality education, something that traditional public schools have been failing to do. Those against charter schools contend that the institutions have an agenda and do not provide an orthodox, sound education to the majority. Much of the disagreement regarding charter schools stems from the fact that they are publicly funded yet have mission statements, visions, or specific educational goals rather than broad educational purposes. Charter schools have also been controversial because they

have engendered a new type of segregation where students of a particular ethnic group or of a certain political or religious persuasion attend their own schools. Though charter schools have an open door policy, as is required by publicly funded institutions, their mission statements tend to dictate the population of students who attend their institutions. Moreover, teachers and administrators at charter schools are given much leeway in regard to the curriculum that is taught, which has drawn both praise and criticism (Community Dividend, 2006).

In Colorado, much controversy was generated over a bill proposal that would have given more than half of state funding to charter schools. While charter school representatives and advocates said that the move was to make up for years of inadequate funding, others contend that taxpayer dollars should not be used for agenda-driven learning institutions (Albanese, 2002).

The state of California has Charter Management Organizations (CMO) to manage its High Tech High charter schools which also serve as teacher training institutions. Financially supported by the Bill & Melinda Gates Foundation, High Tech High emphasizes hands-on learning that is technology driven. While many have pointed to its successes, administrators concede that the program probably could not sustain itself or work without the private support it receives. Publicly funded dollars simply would not be enough to sustain these schools (Robelen, 2007). This evidence supports the argument that because charter schools have such specific education goals, they cannot truly be successful when supported only by the state.

In the Los Angeles unified school district, charter schools have filed lawsuits against the state alleging inadequate funding and lack of access to charter schools for those of low income. Because facilities typically need to be built for charter schools, states are partially responsible for covering these costs. States in turn argue that funding of new facilities for charter institutions is not feasible given other, more pressing costs. Given over crowded conditions in the district's existing schools, which often need add-on facilities, public schools argue that the charter schools' requests for more space is "unreasonable." However, state law stipulates that somehow, both charter and standard public schools must share the limited funding that is available (Miners, 2007).

TERMS & CONCEPTS

Charter School: A charter school is a publicly funded school that, in accordance with an enabling state statute, has been granted a charter exempting it from selected state or local rules and regulations. It is typically governed by a group or organization under a contract with the state (http://nces.ed.gov).

Equitable Funding: Equitable refers to just, impartial and unbiased position. In education it is used to determine how funding is allocated equally to all students regardless of income.

Low Income: Students are considered low income when the annual income of the household is less than 80 percent of the area's median income, taking into consideration the size of the family. Low income is often used to determine Title 1 and other types of funding.

Per-Pupil Spending: The amount of money that is spent on each student via public funding; it is also the amount of money used to compare spending from one state to the next or one district to the next.

Revenues: Revenue is the income of a government from taxation, excise duties, customs, or other sources, appropriated to the payment of the public expenses (http://reference.com).

Tax & Expenditure Limitation: A Tax and Expenditure Limitation (TEL) restricts the annual growth in state government spending. Most TELs limit the government expenditure to the combined rates of population growth and inflation.

Title I: Formerly known as Chapter 1, Title 1 is part of the federal Elementary and Secondary Education Act of 1965. Its mission is to close the achievement gap between low-income and other students and allocate additional resources to states to provide remedial education for low-income students. The 1994 reauthorization of Title I shifted the program's emphasis to helping all disadvantaged children meet state academic standards. In return, school districts and states must meet accountability requirements for raising student performance (http://naeyc.org).

Wealth Neutrality: Within the realm of education, wealth neutrality means that no relationship should exist between the education of children and their wealth or family wealth.

Lisa Angerame

BIBLIOGRAPHY

Albanese, E. (2002). Colorado house approves charter school funding bill. *Bond Buyer, 339* (31538). Retrieved August 22, 2007, from EBSCO Online Database Business Source Premier.

Archibald, R. B. & Feldman, D. H. (2006). State higher education spending and the tax revolt. *Chronicle of Higher Education, 77*, 618-644. Retrieved August, 2007, from EBSCO Online Database Business Source Complete.

Black, D. E., Lewis, K. A., & Link, C. R. (1979). Wealth neutrality and the demand for education. *National Tax Journal, 32*, 157-164. Retrieved August, 2007, from EBSCO Online Database Business Source Complete.

Charter School. (2007). *National Assessment of Educational Progress.* Retrieved August 21, 2007, from http://nces.ed.gov.

Community Dividend. (2006). Charter school basics. *Fedgazette,*, 2. Retrieved August 21, 2007, from EBSCO Online Database Business Source Premier.

Fahy, C. (2011). Education Funding in Massachusetts: The Effects of Aid Modifications on Vertical and Horizontal Equity. *Journal of Education Finance 36*, p. 217-243. Retrieved December 27, 2013, from EBSCO Online Database Education Research Complete.

Hess, F. M. (2007). How business can fix K-12 education. *American: A Magazine of Ideas, 1*, 78-85. Retrieved August 17, 2007, from EBSCO Online Database Business Source Complete.

Hoffman, J. L. & Hayden, F. G. (2007). Using the social fabric matrix to analyze institutional rules relative to adequacy in education funding. *Journal of Economic Issues, 41*, 359-367. Retrieved August 17, 2007, from EBSCO Online Database Business Source Complete.

Jacobson, L. (2007). California's schooling is 'broken'. *Education Week, 26*, 1-20. Retrieved August 17, 2007, from EBSCO Online Database Education Resource Complete.

Miners, Z. (2007). L.A. unified and charter schools butt heads. *District Administration, 43*, 20. Retrieved August 21, 2007, from EBSCO Online Database Academic Search Premier.

Murray, S. E., Rueben, K. & Rosenberg, C. (2007). State education spending: Current pressures and future trends. *National Tax Journal, 40*, 325-345. Retrieved August 17, 2007, from Business Source

National School Boards Association, (2007). Public schools spend nearly $500 billion to educate kids. *American School Board Journal, 194*, 8. Retrieved August 14, 2007, from EBSCO Online Database Education Research Complete.

Revenue. (n.d.). *The American Heritage Dictionary of the English Language,* Fourth Edition. Retrieved August 21, 2007, from http://reference.com.

Edition. Retrieved August 21, 2007, from http://reference.com.

Robelen, E. W. (2007). Learning where they teach. *Education Week, 26*, 29-31. Retrieved August 21, 2007, from EBSCO Online Database Academic Search Premier.

Roza, M., Miller, L., & Hill, P. (2005). *Strengthening Title I to help high-poverty schools: How Title I funds fit into district allocation patterns.* Seattle, Washington: Center on Reinventing Public Education, Daniel J. Evans School of Public Affairs, University of Washington. (ERIC Document Reproduction Service No. ED485895).

Stover, D. (2013, April). Hidden Inequities. *American School Board Journal 200*, p. 10-13. Retrieved December 27, 2013, from EBSCO Online Database Education Research Complete.

Title 1 (n.d.). National Association for the Education of Young Children. Retrieved August 14, 2007, from http://naeyc.org.

Wood, B. D. & Theobald, N. A. (2003). Political responsiveness and equity in public education finance. *The Journal of Politics, 65*, 718–738. Retrieved August 14, 2007, from EBSCO Online Database Business Source Complete.

Wong, K.K. The design of the Rhode Island school funding formula: Developing new strategies of equity and accountability. *Peabody Journal of Education*, p. 37-47. Retrieved December 27, 2013, from EBSCO Online Database Education Research Complete.

FT.-Wright, S. (2013). Two steps forward, one step back: The Kentucky Education Reform Act a generation later. *Journal of Law & Education 42*, p. 567-573. Retrieved December 27, 2013, from EBSCO Online Database Education Research Complete.

SUGGESTED READING

Evers, W. M., Clopton, P., Hirsch, E. D., Lindseth, A. A., & Hanushek, E. A. (Ed.). (2006). *Courting failure: how school finance lawsuits exploit judges' good intentions and harm our children* Stanford, CA: Education Next Books.

McCluskey, N. P. (2007). *Feds in the Classroom: How big government corrupts, cripples, and compromises American education.* Lanham, MD: Rowman & Littlefield Publishers.

West, M. R. & Peterson, P. E. (Eds.). (2007). *School money trials: The legal pursuit of educational adequacy.* Washington, DC: Brookings Institution Press.

EQUALIZATION AID

Equalization aid, a term often used synonymously with state aid, refers to general use financial assistance that is available to public school districts in the United States. The use of such funding is considered non-restrictive and can be used for a broad range of purposes to be determined by the district (Wisconsin Department of Public Instruction, 2006). How much equalization aid is awarded to each school district is determined by complicated formulas that vary in each state. At its simplest level, the calculation of equalization aid considers factors such as student enrollment, school assessed value, and levels of poverty when measured or compared against target spending levels and target property tax rates. Though each state may use a different formula to precisely calculate aid, this measuring tool provides a general understanding of how such aid is determined.

KEYWORDS: Adequacy; Average Daily Attendance (ADA); Brown v. Board of Education; Elementary and Secondary Education Act (ESEA); Equalization Aid; Per-Pupil Spending; Revenues; Segregation; Serrano v. Priest; Unification Clause; Vouchers

OVERVIEW

Equalization aid, a term often used synonymously with state aid, refers to general use financial assistance that is available to public school districts in the United States. The use of such funding is considered non-restrictive and can be used for a broad range of purposes to be determined by the district (Wisconsin Department of Public Instruction, 2006). How much equalization aid is awarded to each school district is determined by complicated formulas that vary in each state. At its simplest level, the calculation of equalization aid considers factors such as student enrollment, school assessed value, and levels of poverty when measured or compared against target spending levels and target property tax rates. Basically, equalization aid is determined according to the following formula: "the aid per pupil equals target spending per pupil minus what the school district can raise on its own" ("State Aid to Local Schools," n.d.). Though each state may use a different formula to precisely calculate aid, this measuring tool provides a general understanding of how such aid is determined.

HISTORICAL PERSPECTIVES

As a nation that prides itself on democratic values, justice, and prosperity, the U.S. has always seen education as a way for the poor or oppressed to better their prospects and raise their positions in life. Equalization aid is based on this philosophy. By financing low-income schools and increasing per-pupil expenditures, those students have equal chances of succeeding or prospering as those in wealthier communities. One government policy that supports such thinking is the 1994 reauthorization of the Elementary and Secondary Education Act (ESEA), originally known as Title 1 funding. To better support and assist schools that serve primarily low-income students, the ESEA enables school districts to use revised, more flexible calculations in determining federal, state, and local funding. Research has shown that low-income students can succeed and do well in school but may need more resources to achieve such academic goals. This shift in policy enables teachers, administrators, and other school officials to have greater flexibility in deciding what works for their particular school population. This method of school management has been shown to be more effective than the federal government's dictating local policies (United States Department of Education. Policy Studies Association, 1998). In receiving such government funding, each school district must show how it is using the money in a responsible, deliberate, and purposeful manner. In other words, schools must show a plan for how they will distribute such state aid funding and then show how these funds were actually distributed.

EQUALIZING WEALTH DISPARITIES

In the United States, all young people between the ages of 5 and 18 have the inalienable right to a quality education provided by the government. It is largely each state's responsibility to finance and support the educational endeavors of the population of those who reside within its borders. Local financing of school districts has proven to be problematic as wealthy communities who pay higher property taxes can pay for good, quality elementary and secondary schools while more impoverished neighborhoods struggle to adequately finance their schools. To make financing more equal, the states have come up with various polices and formulas to better ensure that students in low-income communities can receive a quality education (Payne, 2005). Some states have voluntarily developed programs to provide aid to these low-income schools while others have had their hands forced to action through legislation. For most states, however, determining which schools get aid and how much they should receive remains a contentious issue influenced by politics, wealth, community mores, and population makeup. Some states, such as Kentucky, have had success with finance reform programs. Recognizing a need for real change, Kentucky reformed its local governance, curriculum, school finance, and more. By pairing these changes with providing additional resources to its low-income students, the state saw a significant increase of the academic performance of its low income, traditionally underserved minority population.

EXAMPLES OF HOW EQUALIZATION AID WORKS IN DIFFERENT STATES

States are largely responsible for funding their own public schools, which includes being responsible for ensuring that funds are distributed in an even-handed fashion. Title 1 and other legislative acts state that per-pupil spending must be similar regardless of a school district's wealth. Equalization aid helps to ensure that low-income students in impoverished communities receive comparable funding so that they may receive a quality education.

STATE OF CALIFORNIA

In the state of California, the 1971 *Serrano v. Priest* state court case ruled that school district funding could not be solely based on income from property taxes as this was inherently unequal and unconstitutional. In other words, all students, regardless of their family income, had the right to receive quality education provided by the state. In order to determine equal distribution of funds, Lee (1998) states that "wealth-related differences in school funding must be reduced within a 'band' of equality extending $100 per pupil above and below the state average in per pupil spending." In other words, no more than a plus or minus $100 disparity when compared to the standard should exist between per pupil expenditure regardless of familial income.

Since *Serrano v. Priest*, various legislations have been passed to ensure general purpose funds are

distributed accordingly and fairly. In 1983, the revenue limit, cost of living adjustment and equalization aid policies were revised to provide districts of the same category the same dollar amounts per average daily attendance (ADA). This approach was modified to allow low-performing school districts to receive more equalization aid. The amount received largely depended on how much funding was needed to bring its revenue limit to the average amount in its slated category. Moreover, aid was significantly affected by student attendance; something that previously was not a consideration. Equalizing the funding for all the school districts within the state itself has proven a difficult endeavor due to the cost of applying such equalization policies and determining what specifically constitutes "adequate equalization." Lee argues that using a sliding scale for calculating cost of living adjustment (COLA) may be the most efficient and effective way for determining equalization aid allotment, so that low-revenue school districts receive sufficient levels of funding (Lee).

WASHINGTON & OREGON

In efforts to ensure that every student within its state received a quality education, Oregon established its Quality Education Model (QEM). The QEM is the standard for which Oregon's elementary, middle school, and high school students receive funding. It also determines how much funding low income schools should receive. One issue the state faces is a significant rural population that comprises about one third of the state's geography. Due to transportation costs, smaller pupil-teacher ratios, telecommunications costs, spotty infrastructure, and related expenditures, it is an accepted fact that such per pupil spending is higher than for students of larger populated urban areas. As such, these factors must be considered when allocating state aid to low income rural communities to ensure such students receive similar resources as available to those in urban areas (Hill, 2001).

In Washington, a 1987 levy equalization aid measure was passed to limit the contribution of revenue generated from property taxes. In general, schools with lower than average valuation per pupil are slated to receive equalization aid (Plecki, 1998). In 1997, about 66 percent of school districts were eligible for this equalization aid. Since such measures were put in place, analysis shows that overall school districts have improved their equitability or aid distribution (p. 10). Due to modifications of the levy equalization aid bill, districts are allowed to collect more and more funding from local revenue sources, typically property taxes. Such a trend threatens to negatively affect the equalization of school district funding as a whole.

ILLINOIS

In Chicago, Illinois, wealth disparities among communities largely reflect wealth disparities among school districts despite efforts in state aid that have tried to correct this gap. For instance, Rondout School District, the wealthiest school district in the state, generated $26,356 per pupil from property tax revenue. The Ford Heights School District, one of the state's poorest, generated $5,548 per pupil from its property tax revenue even though its property tax rate is over five times more than the Rondout district (Lowenstein, 2005). Wealthy neighborhoods with high real estate value can have lower tax rates because they attract prospering businesses, creating jobs for members of the community. Such neighborhoods can support affluent school districts, thereby providing a quality education to those in their community. Conversely, areas such as Ford Heights must make up for lack of business revenue by increasing property taxes, thereby discouraging new businesses from setting up in the area. Funds in a mostly empty pot must go to support already fledging schools that struggle to meet minimum standards of performance. To put it another way, Lowenstein says, "Since the districts with the lowest tax rates were home to properties six times more valuable than the districts with the highest tax rates, they generated more local revenue. In all, local sources in districts with the lowest tax rates generated nearly $11,752 per pupil, while local sources in districts with the highest tax rates generated nearly $5,783 per pupil" (Lowenstein). Though such school districts do receive equitable aid, it does not compare to the tax revenue received by schools in wealthy neighborhoods.

EQUALIZATION AID & SCHOOL VOUCHERS

The birth of school vouchers came about as a way for states to financially enable some students in low-income communities with poor performing school districts to attend school in a higher performing school district. Vouchers serve as a guarantee of compensation from the state for a student's educational expenses for attending a "school of their choice" outside their own residential school district. Voucher programs have shown to be somewhat controversial as it is an issue of concern whether public funds or aid should be used to finance private (sometimes religious) education programs. It has also been argued that such voucher programs violate the "uniformity clauses" in constitutions that state school learning from one public school to the next should be relatively the same. In the state of Florida for instance, the *Bush v. Holmes* case argued that state voucher programs were unconstitutional in that they violated this uniformity clause. In other words, since it cannot be verified that the schools of choice have a similar curriculum to public schools, the state cannot ask the public to finance this non-uniform educational experience (Dycus, 2006). Finally, it was decided that such voucher programs would hurt public schools by taking away their slated funding and funneling elsewhere. In other words, aid marked to go toward a low-income school may actually indirectly end up going toward a private school as a result of the voucher program.

EQUAL OPPORTUNITY IN EDUCATION

Generally speaking, school administrators, legislators, state officials, and the voting public support equalization aid or state aid and see it as a way to enable low-income communities to better educate their youth. Conventional thinking states that better educated students are more likely to get higher paying jobs, strengthen their communities, and better provide for their own children. The notion of equal opportunity for all is a widely supported American value referenced in the U.S. Constitution. The notorious Brown v. Board of Education case in 1954 stipulated clearly that segregating schools by race was unconstitutional because such a system failed the litmus test of "equal opportunity." Fifty years after the historic Supreme Court case, some scholars believe that Southern states have maintained *de facto* segregation policies as a way to work around Brown (Baker & Green, 2005).

DETERMINING NEED

While legislation in the 1950s focused on equalization regardless of race or income, legislation in the 1980s until present day has focused on the notion of adequacy. In theory, adequacy is more concerned with students from all school districts in a state achieving the same established performance goals than it is with ensuring that each school district receives the same amount of funding to meet those same performance goals. Under this new shift in policy, schools that need more financing to meet adequacy standards should get it (Baker & Green). Undoubtedly, some low-income school districts have benefited from this new way of determining need; however, other scholars claim it has benefited school districts with a predominantly white, middle-class population. For instance, in an economically disadvantaged school district with a large immigrant population, the school may receive more state funding so that it can serve its sizable population of limited-English-proficiency students. In wealthier communities, a school may receive aid so that it can fund its advanced placement or gifted programs or continue to pay expected higher salaries for teachers. What constitutes as a need varies greatly from one community to the next.

DE FACTO SEGREGATION IN FUNDING

Moreover, loopholes in the law have enabled Southern states and others to follow pre-Brown segregationists funding policies that separate by wealth or family income thereby indirectly separating students by race. Since most legislation focused on desegregation by law rather than *de facto* segregation, many pre-Brown funding policies remained in place. In addition, because state aid was largely viewed as a positive development for low-income and minority populations, its limits were not often scrutinized by legislators, civil rights advocates, and policy makers. According to Baker and Green, "School finance litigation is often depicted both as a means of moving beyond race as the salient issue in education reform and as an effective way to achieve educational equity." This assumption often meant that actual disparities in state aid and policies that supported pre-Brown segregation were unnoticed.

When looking at historically segregated Alabama for instance, state aid is allocated according to teacher units required per grade level and class size. Costs are assigned in relation to the education and experience of instructors in a given district (Baker & Green). Baker and Green's case study revealed that experienced teachers who held master's degrees were more likely to teach in school districts that were predominantly white while teachers with less experience

and without master's degrees were more likely to teach in predominantly black schools. Following the state's aid allocation policy, those schools with the better teachers continued to receive more funds to support their teachers while those with the less experienced teachers continued to receive less funding. This teacher-unit aid allocation method illustrates how some states have used aid to maintain segregationist values and better assist white schools rather than low-income black schools (Baker & Green).

TERMS & CONCEPTS

Adequacy: In the realm of education, the term adequacy refers to an approach to school funding that considers the amount of funding schools should receive based on a cost estimate of achieving the state's educational goals (http://edsource.org).

Average Daily Attendance (ADA): Average daily attendance refers to the total number of days of student attendance divided by the total number of days in the regular school year. The state of California, for instance, uses ADA calculations to determine the school district's funding, whether it be general-purpose or state aid (http://edsource.org).

Brown v. Board of Education: This landmark case, one of the most significant in U.S. history in improving race relations, stated that segregating schools by race, or separate but equal, was unconstitutional. The 1954 case broke down the legalities of racial segregation in School systems and public establishments.

Elementary and Secondary Education Act (ESEA): The Elementary and Secondary Education Act, enacted in 1965 as part of the War on Poverty, is a federal law pertaining to K-12 education. The No Child Left Behind Act (NCLB) is ESEA's most recent reauthorization, which supports the education of the country's poorest children.

Equalization Aid: Often used interchangeably with state aid, equalization aid refers to funds allocated by the state in order to bring attention to inequalities and increase the funding level of school districts by lowering the revenue limits toward the state average. Such aid is typically calculated on size and type of school district.

Per-Pupil Spending: The amount of money that is spent on each student via public funding; it is also the amount of money used to compare spending from one state to the next or one district to the next.

Revenues: Revenue is the income of a government from taxation, excise duties, customs, or other sources, appropriated to the payment of the public expenses (http://reference.com).

Segregation: In the United States, segregation is the practice of separating people of different races or ethnicities away from the dominant race. Segregation can be by law, (*de jure* segregation), or in fact (*De facto* segregation). De jure segregation has been prohibited in the United States since the mid-1960s. Segregation in fact occurs when social practice, political acts, economic circumstances, or public policy result in segregation even though no laws are in place to sanction the separation. *De facto* segregation continues despite state and federal civil rights laws to discourage it.

Serrano v. Priest: A 1960s-1970s California court case that challenged the inequities created by using property taxes as the principal source of revenue for public schools. The case ruled that wide wealth discrepancies in school funding because of local wealth differences represented a denial of equal opportunity (http://edsource.org).

Unification Clause: The unification clause states that public school districts within a state must offer a similar curriculum covering largely the same or similar lesson plans. The term is often used to talk about the differences between public and, which are often given the freedom to offer differing curriculums.

Vouchers: A payment from the state that guarantees all or part of a student's education expenses for any school or college of the recipient's choice. Vouchers are sought when a student resides in a low-income, poor-performing school district.

Lisa Angerame

BIBLIOGRAPHY

Adequacy. (2004). *A Glossary of School Finance Terms.* Retrieved September 2, 2007, from http://edsource.org.

Average daily attendance. (2004). *A Glossary of School Finance Terms.* Retrieved September 2, 2007, from http://edsource.org.

Baker, B. D. & Green, C. P. (2005). Tricks of the trade: State legislative actions in school finance policy that perpetuate racial disparities in the post-Brown era. *The American Journal of Education, 111,* 372-413. Retrieved August 28, 2007, from ProQuest Database.

Brown v. Board of Education. (2004, April). *Brown vs. the Board of Education - About the Case.* Retrieved September 9, 2007, from http://brownvboard.org.

Fahy, C. A. (2012). Fiscal capacity measurement and equity in local contributions to schools: The effects of education finance reform in Massachusetts. *Journal of Education Finance, 37,* 317-346. Retrieved December 15, 2013, from EBSCO Online Database Education Research Complete.

Dycus, J. (2006). Lost opportunity: Bush v. Holmes and the application of state constitutional uniformity clauses to school vouch schemes. *Journal of Law and Education, 35,* 415-459. Retrieved August 28, 2007, from EBSCO Online Database Education Research Complete.

Hill, J. (2001). *The Oregon quality education model applied to schools characterized by low student enrollment, sparse distribution of students, and remote settings with findings relating to equity of services.* Washington, DC: U.S. Government Printing Office. Retrieved August 28, 2007, from (ERIC Document Reproduction Service No. ED456009). Retrieved October 18, 2007, from EBSCO Online Education Research Database.

Lee, J. (1999). *Equalizing school district funding: Option for a sliding scale COLA. A Legislative Analyst's Office Report.* Washington, DC: U.S. Government Printing Office. (ERIC Document Reproduction Service No. ED438592). Retrieved August 28, 2007, from EBSCO Online Education Research Database.

Lowenstein, J. K. (2006). Never-ending cycle: Illinois' reliance on property taxes as the major source of school funding has major consequences for communities throughout the state. *The Chicago Reporter, 35,* 16-20.

New study finds inequities in state education funding formulas. (2012). *District Administration, 48,* 14. Retrieved December 15, 2013, from EBSCO Online Database Education Research Complete.

Payne, A. A. (2005). Helping children left behind: State aid and the pursuit of educational equity. *National Tax Journal, 58,* 843- 846. Retrieved August 28, 2007, from EBSCO Online Database Education Research Complete.

Plecki, M. L. (1998). *School finance in Washington state 1997-98: Emerging equity concerns.* Washington, DC: U.S. Government Printing Office. (ERIC Document Reproduction Service No. ED426447). Retrieved August 28, 2007, from EBSCO Online Education Research Database.

Revenue. (n.d.). *The American Heritage Dictionary of the English Language,* Fourth Edition. Retrieved August 21, 2007, from http://reference.com.

Segregation. (n.d.). *Encarta Online Encyclopedia,.* Retrieved August 21, 2007, from (http://encarta.msn.com/encnet/refpages/RefArticle.aspx?refid=761580651&para=20)

Serrano v. Priest. (2004, August). *A Glossary of School Finance Terms.* Retrieved September 2, 2007, from http://edsource.org.

State Aid to Local Schools. (n.d.). *A simple version of the school aid formula.* Retrieved August 27, 2007, from http://agecon.purdue.edu.

United States Department of Education. Policy Studies Association. (1998). *Implementing school-wide programs. Volume I. An idea book on planning.* Washington, DC: U.S. Government Printing Office. (ERIC Document Reproduction Service No. ED423615). Retrieved August 28, 2007, from EBSCO Online Education Research Database.

Wisconsin Department of Public Instruction. (2006). *Equalization aid - Section F of basic facts.* Retrieved August 27, 2007, from http://dpi.state.wi.us.

SUGGESTED READING

Driscoll, L.G. & Salmon, R.G. (2008). How increased state equalization aid resulted in greater disparities: An unexpected consequence for the Commonwealth of Virginia. *Journal of Education Finance.* 33 (3), 238-261.

Reed, R.J., Hurd, B. (2016). A value beyond money? Assessing the impact of equity scholarships: From access to success. *Studies in Higher Education.* 4 (7), 1236-1250.

Roy, J. (2011). Impact of school finance reform on resource equalization and academic performance: Evidence from Michigan. Education Finance and Policy. 6 (2), 137-167.

Sracic, P. A. (2006). *San Antonio V. Rodriguez and the pursuit of equal education: The debate over discrimination and school funding (landmark law cases and American society).* Lawrence, KS: University Press of Kansas.

West, M. R. & Peterson, P. E. (Eds.). (2007). *School money trials: The legal pursuit of educational adequacy.* Washington, DC: Brookings Institution Press.

Yinger, J. (2004). *Helping children left behind: state aid and the pursuit of educational equity.* Cambridge, MA: The MIT Press.

IDENTITY POLITICS IN EDUCATION

This article takes a closer look at identity politics in the educational arena. Reviewing two major social issues, homosexuality and illegal immigration, as a backdrop, the reader gleans a better understanding of the conditions that give rise to school-based activism on behalf of those who lack a voice.

KEYWORDS: GLBT; Identity Politics; Illegal Immigrant; In-state Tuition; Plyer v. Doe; Public School

OVERVIEW

THE SNCC: AN EXAMPLE OF IDENTITY POLITICS

In 1960, an organization formed that would make an indelible mark on American society. In the face of a segregated South, the nation already had several prominent anti-segregation and civil rights organizations. Among them were the National Association for the Advancement of Colored People (NAACP), which had scored a major litigation victory with the Supreme Court ruling on Brown v. Board of Education, and the Southern Christian Leadership Conference (SCLC), which was led by Dr. Martin Luther King, Jr. and formed after Rosa Parks' historic act of civil disobedience. However, whereas the NAACP's preferred venue was the courtroom and the SCLC was adept at high-profile protests, another group worked on a much broader scale. The Student Nonviolent Coordinating Committee (SNCC) targeted multiple communities in multiple states at one time, organizing protests, fostering black electoral races and even generating international attention to the issues facing southern America. In only its first few years, the SNCC had grown into an extensive, formidable nationwide network. Former President Jimmy Carter once cited the difference between the SNCC and SCLC's tactics and rate of success. "If you wanted to scare white people in southwest Georgia, Martin Luther King and the Southern Christian Leadership Conference wouldn't do it," he said. "All you had to say is one word: SNCC" (Bond, 2000).

What is one of the most interesting points about the SNCC's success are the organization's origins. The group was not founded by prominent civil rights activists, politicians or celebrities. Rather, the SNCC's foundation occurred shortly after a series of sit-in protests conducted by students enrolled in North Carolina and Tennessee. Theirs was a single-minded purpose—to highlight the injustices of segregation not by legal means or grand protest venues, but at their local stores and restaurants and finding roots in their schools. For too long, the SNCC's founders professed, the laws of segregation kept down people of color, creating two unequal playing fields and thus preventing any real social growth. The SNCC was founded inside academic walls—a dynamic example of what is known as "identity politics."

Identity politics was hardly a new concept in 1960. The academic arena, after all, gave air to countless social issues across the globe, including slavery, religious freedom, class disparity and women's suffrage. Academia and identity politics seem closely linked, likely due to the fact that school is not an environment in which people are told how to think—they are simply encouraged to think for themselves.

This paper takes a closer look at identity politics in the educational arena. Reviewing two major social issues, homosexuality and illegal immigration, as a backdrop, the reader gleans a better understanding of the conditions that give rise to school-based activism on behalf of those who lack a voice.

IDENTITY

Wherever there has been "somebody" in society, there is always "somebody else," an individual or group who operates at a higher, lower or equal sociological level. The fundamental goal of "diversity" movements is to create an environment in which each of these "somebodies," regardless of race, economic status, gender, ethnicity, creed or orientation, coexist on an equal plane.

Unfortunately, however, such a "perfect world" environment is extremely rare, for humanity has a tendency to organize its social systems in hierarchical fashion. In some cases, majority rules—groups who outnumber others hold the higher positions in society. In others, socio-economics is a major factor—those who are more financially solvent hold more clout than those with little money. Even those who rest on the same plane but who represent different groupings often hold fast as a single segment of the population rather than mix in with others on that plane. Humanity, one can argue, is not necessarily a "melting pot," but rather a "tossed salad."

The basic theme of "diversity," that different samplings of the population live and work together with mutual respect, can still be achieved in this environment. A CEO of a major multinational corporation and a pizza delivery person may operate on a different economic plane, for example, but both play an important role as part of a larger body politic and economy. It is when the CEO uses his or her social standing or income bracket to prevent the pizza delivery person from moving upward that marginalization and conflict arise. Prejudice, racism, ethnocentrism and chauvinism are all factors that isolate other groups and, if economic and/or political power is held by those who espouse these attitudes, interclass conflict can be created.

COHESION

Given the multitude of social groupings that exist on varying economic class levels in each country, it comes as no surprise that, rather than "blend in," most of these individual groups hold on to their identity. A study in Great Britain analyzed the aftermath of ethnic and racial violence in that country's northern regions. Investigators in that situation recommended afterward not that the Caribbean and Asian combatants in those incidents find a way to integrate under the Union Jack. Rather, they concluded, it was necessary for them to find a way to coexist. What was once a policy of "integration" transformed into a new way of unifying ethnicities: cohesion (Shukra, 2004).

In academia, the notion of cohesion rather than integration seems prevalent as well. Educational institutions, which are microcosms of any society, seem to naturally compartmentalize much as the rest of the culture does. And, as is the case in overall human society, it is when power is exerted to isolate, marginalize or intimidate lower-class or minority groups that conflict occurs. In some ways, as was the case in the South, the degree to which differentiation occurs necessitates a strong response from the marginalized group—some act through litigation, others demonstrate civil disobedience and protests. In other situations, however, the exertion and/or acceptance of identity may be manifest more subtly in the form of awareness campaigns and educational programming.

It should be no surprise, therefore, that identity politics, which can be defined as political activity that is used to advance disenfranchised groups and highlights the experiences of these segments of the population, is so closely linked to the world of academia (Hayes, 2007). After all, these institutions, as stated earlier, are themselves microcosms of the "tossed salad" of society, yet also contain the will to appreciate the diversity this motif creates. In doing so, academics will likely develop an interest in highlighting the plight of disadvantaged social groups.

COMING OUT IN A SCHOLASTIC SETTING

Among the most salient of social issues facing the United States today is the increased call for tolerance toward gay, lesbian, bisexual and transgender (LGBTQ) individuals. The work toward equality is of ongoing concern. LGBTQ youths face their own challenges regarding their identity and perception among their peers and adults in their lives. In early 2007, for example, one student's written call for tolerance of homosexuals not only echoed the rest of the nation's divided attitudes on the subject of being gay in 21st century America; it set off a political firestorm over the right to free speech and freedom of the press.

The incident in question was an op-ed piece written by a sophomore student at a Midwestern high school. She opined that for one to accept his or her homosexual orientation (and allow others to know about it) must be challenging in society. The teacher who oversaw the student paper in which the story was run was immediately warned by the school principal not to allow "contentious" materials to appear in the publication. Not long after the story was printed, the teacher was suspended. The students who served on the paper's staff came quickly to her defense—a few months later, the teacher was reinstated, only after a lawsuit was threatened and after she agreed that she would not advise another student paper in that district (Garcia, 2007).

As the diverse populations of school systems are often microcosms of society, it only follows suit that anti-discrimination laws that apply in the United States are applicable within school walls. Since schools are part of our nation (perhaps the most critical of society's components), one would assume that there be no question about applying the myriad of anti-discrimination laws in educational institutions. Then again, the notion that "all men are created equal" was conveniently modified to exclude certain racial groups until the mid-20th century. Similarly, the idea that gay, lesbian, bisexual and transgender students should be treated equally by their peers and certainly by administrative personnel also seems a given in this modern era, and yet such discrimination persists. In New Jersey, where anti-discrimination laws are in place to protect gay men and women in the workplace, their enforcement in the public school system was not a foregone conclusion. A lawsuit that went before the state Supreme Court in 2007 alleged that LGBTQ students were not being protected under these laws. That Court agreed with the plaintiffs, asserting that more needed to be done to protect gay students as is the case in places of business (Kelley, 2007).

THE ROLE OF THE CHURCH

Even one of the most conservative institutions, the Catholic church, has had to accept homosexuality as part of student life. Despite decades of speaking out against the "sin" of the gay lifestyle, the church, which operates countless educational institutions throughout the world, has had to acknowledge that just as there are heterosexual students exploring their sexual orientations as part of adolescent development, there are also gay and lesbian students coming to grips with their own orientations. The Church has therefore placed itself (due to its willingness to accept any student willing to learn) in a difficult position, cautioning against homosexual activity but insisting that students be given equal protection under the laws of the United States. American Catholic leaders have taken a significant step to distance themselves from the Vatican's more conservative ways. The election of Pope Francis in 2013, however, brought a slightly more sympathetic perspective to the Catholic Church. The pope indicated that he believed homosexual people should be treated with respect and that their spiritual needs should be met. In the United States, bishops argue, gay students are prevalent and should be given equal treatment:

> Educationally, homosexuality cannot and ought not to be skirted or ignored. The topic must be faced in all objectivity by the pupil and the educator when the case presents itself. First and foremost, we support modeling and teaching respect for every human person, regardless of sexual orientation (Maher, 2007).

In this case, the major issue of equal rights for gay, lesbian, bisexual and transgender students was addressed not by political leaders or even the Judiciary—rather, it is being addressed by institutions of faith, removing limitations on the growth and development of gay youth.

THE NEW KID ON THE BLOCK

In late 2007, the Governor of the State of New York, Elliot Spitzer introduced a measure that would allow illegal immigrants to obtain legal US driver's licenses. When faced with an overwhelming 70 percent voter disapproval of the measure, Spitzer abandoned his bill. However, he said, his effort to pass this bill was part of a larger plan to document previously undocumented aliens living in his state. The federal government, he said, had "lost control" on immigration policies in this country, and states were therefore left to deal with the consequences in their own individual ways (Associated Press, 2007).

Indeed, the "battle" to protect the borders of the United States from illegal immigrant infiltration, particularly in this era of high demand for tight security, has created a firestorm of calls for hard-line immigration reform. Federal law explicitly states that illegal immigrants cannot receive most forms of assistance (such as welfare, Social Security and food stamps). However, the notion (however valid or invalid) that an undocumented alien could be receiving some benefit that is normally reserved for a legal resident has added fuel to an already volatile political issue.

EDUCATION & ILLEGAL IMMIGRANTS

In education, the question of whether the children of undocumented immigrants (or the immigrants themselves) should be allowed to enroll in public schools was actually answered by the U.S. Supreme Court. In 1982, that august body ruled that US public schools have a responsibility to teach all children who wish to learn, and that their immigration status was irrelevant. *Plyer v. Doe*, as the case was named, became a landmark in an ongoing, highly charged political debate over immigrant rights.

Still, with pro- and anti-immigration camps continuing to lock horns over this issue, the hard and fast ruling in Plyer, which has been consistently upheld in the two decades that followed, hardly answered the question of the rights of certain students. While that decision empowered and protected children from discrimination within public schools, the battle rages on over other education-based rights and privileges.

IN-STATE TUITION

One such arena is that of in-state tuition for state colleges and universities. Public colleges and universities commonly offer tuition at far lower rates for state residents than those who come from other states. However, when undocumented residents take advantage of such benefits (although they did not proceed through the public school system of that state), the perception is that they are enjoying the same lower tuition costs that legal residents of the state do, and that they are given a significant advantage over out-of-state, legal American students. As of 2013, fifteen states offer tuition benefits to undocumented immigrants, although all fifty states have at some point considered such a change to the law.

On one side of the issue, proponents argue that the high number of public school dropouts, particularly among children of illegal immigrants, represents a drain on a state's workforce development. If students enter a state's higher public education system, they are likely to receive better training and contribute more to the economy. Opponents, however, counter that public colleges and universities already lose revenues when they offer in-state tuition to residents, and this loss is offset by out-of-state residents' tuition. Adding undocumented immigrants to the rolls will increase that loss during a time when state budgets are extremely austere (National Conference of State Legislatures, 2007).

The question of whether undocumented immigrants and their families are eligible to receive public educations in the United States has been answered. However, as the hot-button issue of illegal immigration rages on, and relevant reforms to the current laws are being offered and debated, immigrant students who have been empowered by Plyer remain in the center of a political crossfire.

CONCLUSIONS

In 1998, a young Mexican immigrant and her family moved to Omaha, Nebraska in the hopes of pursuing the American dream. She became an American citizen a short time later, but still teaches the importance of the family's Mexican heritage to her children. In fact, she has had a hard time doing what this country's mythical heritage has promoted—joining into the "melting pot" in the vein suggested by that iconic Latin phrase: E Pluribus Unum ("from many, one"). Rather, she resists giving up her cultural identity, saying, "When my skin turns white and my hair turns blonde, then I'll be an American" (Branigin, 1998).

Indeed, modern American society more resembles a "tossed salad" than a melting pot. For those who reside in this country, which is comprised people of all races, creeds, ethnicities and sexual orientations, identity is one of the most critical components of their way of life. In just the last century of this nation's modern history, however, there have been trends and attitudes in which not all of these sects are considered worthy of equal treatment under the law and within the framework of the Constitution.

In many ways, the plight of homosexuals, bisexuals and transsexuals is reflective of a similar struggle by black men and women in America through the 1960s. There is still a large contingent of individuals who, based on an interpretation of religious texts or simply reflective of discomfort from different lifestyles, view non-heterosexual orientations as "deviant" and therefore worthy of discrimination.

Immigrants, both legal and illegal, have also found themselves the target of discrimination in modern American society. Perhaps exacerbated by the horrific events of September 11, 2001, resident Americans have become increasingly viewed as detrimental to the budgets of federal, state and local governmental institutions and, to some, risky to the security of this nation.

While LGBTQ Americans and immigrants are, according to constitutional interpretation and in most state and federal laws, afforded the same basic rights and privileges as other American citizens, in reality, there are situations in which inequities and discrimination exist without intervention. These groups' identities continue to be marginalized, placed beneath other social groups on an arbitrarily-created hierarchical scheme.

Interestingly, quite often, the "battleground" in which an effort to address these inequities takes place is in a microcosm of society: Public schools. While they should be protected, so-called minority groups remain marginalized as part of a wider political issue. In the case of the plight of gay students, the idea of exploring a young person's burgeoning sexual orientation is abhorrent to some, and as a result, many choose to repress their identities. The children of illegal immigrants also keep their status a secret out of fear of reprisal from the so-called "majority."

Identity politics in the American educational system remains a salient issue, worthy of continued study. A time-honored tradition established in the US Constitution maintains, in no uncertain terms, that no individual shall be denied his or her basic human rights. Schools, as evident by the fact that *Plyer v. Doe* has yet to be challenged, are simple places of learning, not subject to the political forces that have polarized the American public on these issues. As many scholars, educators and even politicians themselves state, schools should not deny any student of his or

her right to an equitable education. The battle over such issues must therefore be waged elsewhere as individual students, regardless of their social identity, continue to develop their minds in the classroom.

TERMS & CONCEPTS

LGBT: Lesbian, gay, bisexual and transsexual.

Identity Politics: Political activity that is used to advance disenfranchised groups and highlights the experiences of these segments of the population.

Illegal Immigrant: Individual who enters a country without the required visa, identification or other form of authorization.

In-state Tuition: Discounted state college tuition rate based on state residency.

Plyer v. Doe: Landmark 1982 Supreme Court decision in which access to public school systems by children of illegal immigrants was granted.

Public School: Educational institution supported by federal, state and locally-generated funds and presenting students with a government-approved curriculum.

Michael P. Auerbach

BIBLIOGRAPHY

Águila, J. R. (2013). The politics of immigration and national identity. Aztlan, 38, 125–130. Retrieved December 10, 2013, from EBSCO Online Database Education Research Complete.

Associated Press. (2007, November 14). Spitzer to drop immigrant N.Y. license plan. Retrieved November 14, 2007, from msnbc.com.

Bond, J. (2000). SNCC: What we did—Student Nonviolent Coordinating Committee. Monthly Review, 52. Retrieved November 12, 2007, from http://findarticles.com.

Branigin, W. (1998, May 25). Immigrants shunning idea of assimilation. Washington Post Online Edition, A1. Retrieved November 14, 2007, from http://washingtonpost.com.

Garcia, M. (2007, June 19). Better seen and not heard? The Advocate, 987, 34-36.

Hayes, C. (2007, November 2). Identity politics. Stanford encyclopedia of philosophy. Retrieved November 12, 2007, from http://plato.stanford.edu.

Kelley, T. (2007, February 22). Court rules that schools in New Jersey must take steps to stop harassment of gay students. New York Times, 156 (53863), B5.

Maher, M. (2007). Gay and lesbian students in Catholic high schools: A qualitative study of alumni narratives.

Catholic Education: A Journal of Inquiry and Practice, 10, 449-472. Retrieved November 13, 2007, from EBSCO Online Database Education Research Complete.

National Conference of State Legislatures. (2007). College tuition and undocumented immigrants. Retrieved November 14, 2007, from http://ncsl.org.

Russell, A. (2007). In-state vs. out-of-state tuition. Diverse: Issues in Higher Education, 24, 18. Retrieved November 14, 2007, from EBSCO Online Database Education Research Complete.

Sherman, R., & Ibarra, H. (2013). Being here, but not here. Phi Delta Kappan, 94, 39–41. Retrieved December 10, 2013, from EBSCO Online Database Education Research Complete.

Shukra, K., Back, L., Keith, M., Khan, A. & Solomos, J. (2004). Race, social cohesion and the changing politics of citizenship. London Review of Education, 2, 187-195. Retrieved November 12, 2007, from EBSCO Online Database Education Research Complete.

Svirsky, M., & Mor-Sommerfeld, A. (2012). Interculturalism and the pendulum of identity. Intercultural Education, 23, 513–525. Retrieved December 10, 2013, from EBSCO Online Database Education Research Complete.

SUGGESTED READING

Addison, N. (2007). Identity politics and the queering of art education. International Journal of Art and Design Education, 26, 10-20. Retrieved November 14, 2007, from EBSCO Online Database Education Research Complete.

Jones, P. (2006). Toleration, recognition and identity. Journal of Political Philosophy, 14, 123-143. Retrieved November 14, 2007, from EBSCO Online Database Academic Search Complete.

Mains, S. (2000). An anatomy of race and immigration politics in California. Social and Cultural Geography, 1, 143-154. Retrieved November 14, 2007, from EBSCO Online Database Academic Search Complete.

McCowan, T. (2012). Human rights within education: Assessing the justifications. Cambridge Journal Of Education, 42, 67–81. Retrieved December 10, 2013, from EBSCO Online Database Education Research Complete.

Szkudlarek, T. (2011). Semiotics of identity: Politics and education. Studies In Philosophy & Education, 30, 113–25. Retrieved December 10, 2013, from EBSCO Online Database Education Research Complete.

CULTURAL CAPITAL & U.S. EDUCATION

Cultural capital refers to the knowledge or skills a group of people possesses that can be attributed to what they learn from their family, culture, and those around them rather than through formal education. Middle-class, white cultural capital dominates and serves as a normative role throughout all levels of U.S. society, including education. Those who possess these values tend to be more successful than those who do not. Thus, cultural capital plays in all levels of education, including elementary school, high school, and higher education. Furthermore, the cultural capital of different racial and ethnic groups may affect their success in an academic environment. Lastly, masculinity, and the cultural capital placed on it, may impose conflicting views on students.

KEYWORDS: Assimilation; Cultural Capital; Dual Socializations; Habitus; Legitimate; Outcast; Privilege; Selective Flight; Social Status; White Flight

OVERVIEW

Education is typically thought of as a school or classroom setting with an instructor teaching a lesson to a group of students. Yet learning in non-formal, less institutionalized terms begins at home, where children acquire the social practices of their parents, family members, and those who surround them. While parents may teach their children to count or say the alphabet in order to prepare them for school, parents also teach them manners, customs, and appropriate behaviors. It is in this way that children begin to develop their mores, personalities, and characteristics. Loosely defined, cultural capital refers to this intangible knowledge that we learn from the people who surround us. Most often this knowledge includes how one's family or culture views school and formal educational institutions. Silva (2006) defines cultural capital as "an appropriate form of investment that can secure a return, in the form of an accumulating asset bearing on social position."

HISTORICAL PERSPECTIVES

Cultural Capital Theory (CCT), first articulated by Pierre Bourdieu and his associate Jean-Claude Passeron in France in the 1960s, looks at the relationship between one's cultural resources and his or her learning outcomes (Barone, 2006). The term "habitus" is sometimes used in conjunction with the term cultural capital as a way of very specifically defining individual cultural behaviors or developments. In the 1930s, Norbert Elias used habitus in a social context to discuss daily practices of individuals, groups, and societies as well as the totality and lasting impact of these learned habits. In other words, these habits become so deeply ingrained or associated with a certain group that they become second nature (the English translation of the term, habitus) (King, 2005). CCT argues that in contemporary societies, each social class strives to maintain a certain rooted cultural identity. Such an identity maintains its resiliency over time and strongly influences how people perceive "the educational system, the labor market, leisure time, and the political arena" (Barone). For instance, how a young person's culture or social class feels about education, whether it is highly or minimally valued, strongly affects that person's attitude toward learning and their performance in a school setting. In this way, Barone states that,

> Cultural capital is considered the main determinant of a school's success. Students' performance is not evaluated according to (class) neutral standards. On the contrary, pedagogical practices and assessment procedures are related, to a significant extent, to the culture of the upper class.

CCT argues that these entrenched cultural habits, rather than monetary resources, can largely explain why the affluent continue to attend prestigious schools and obtain high-paying jobs while the working class continue to attain minimal education levels and earn low-wage jobs. However, many academics and sociologists argue against this theory, pointing out that cultural identities are in a state of continuous flux rather than in a state of stagnation. Moreover, they argue that human capital or economic means more heavily influences cultural capital and education achievement (Barone).

WHAT CULTURAL CAPITAL CAN BUY

Different stratagems of society value different activities, possessions, abilities, or lifestyles. Silva writes that, according to Bourdieu, it is the rich who decide which cultural values are legitimate and which ones are common. Art, theater, opera, and cuisine are cultivated by the affluent; the mainstream bourgeoisie mimic the rich and invest their resources in developing high tastes, luxury goods, and a pretentious

attitude. The poor, according to Bourdieu, make little distinction between life's necessities and cultural desires interweaving the two areas (cited in Silva). Whether it is due to economic necessities or cultural values, the poor or working class are less likely than the others to invest in education. Working class individuals who do strike out on their own to obtain an education with the goal of bettering their situation in life often express feelings of loneliness or of not fitting in with their college-going peers. Moreover, some admit to feeling shunned or spurned by those in their local community and even by family members who see their actions as a putdown. Though many sociologists recognize the validity of some of Bourdieu's observations, they argue that some of his arguments and conclusions are too simple. Not only are class structures more porous than his theories contend, but also individualism and other factors influence cultural tastes, educational pursuits, and occupational goals.

RACE & CULTURAL CAPITAL

Since the history books are written by the predominantly white, rich, and powerful class, they have had the privilege of deciding which type of capital culture has value. By ignoring or disregarding the cultural capital of minorities, the power-holders have been able to discount the cultural capital of others. In the school setting, for instance, minority children are taught to embrace the cultural capital of white, mainstream society. In this way, children learn to hold the mainstream culture in higher esteem than their own, which is viewed as somehow inferior (Yosso, 2005). Students of color who lack knowledge of mainstream, white cultural capital are viewed as socially deficient though this same attitude is not applied to mainstream whites who are unfamiliar with the cultural capital of different minority groups. Minority students are pitied or looked down on for lacking this knowledge and it is assumed they must embrace white cultural capital if they are to be successful in educational endeavors. Yosso argues, "In education, Bourdieu's work has often been called upon to explain why Students of Color do not succeed at the same rate as Whites. According to Bourdieu, cultural capital refers to an accumulation of cultural knowledge, skills and abilities possessed and inherited by privileged groups in society." Of course, students of color do bring their own set of skills and knowledge to school and society at large but because white, middle-class society does not value these skill sets, they dismiss them, often taking the position that such populations simply lack knowledge.

EXAMPLES FROM ELEMENTARY SCHOOL

Even among the youngest of students, the importance of cultural capital can be seen in the classroom. Minority, low-income students are at a disadvantage in the classroom even at this level. Parents who are uneducated tend to be less involved in their children's schools, often lacking the knowledge or cultural capital that tells educated parents to get more involved. Uneducated parents often focus less on their children's homework, extracurricular activities, parent-teacher conferences, and other activities, because they do not recognize their importance (Jung-Sook & Bowen, 2006). In addition, minority parents tend not to associate with other parents at their children's school, so there are fewer networking and out-of-school socialization opportunities. Uneducated parents may feel that since they did not take school seriously they are not entitled to push their children in school. In this way, they may feel that they do not have the competence or skills to help their children with their homework or school projects. Since this group tends to have lower expectations of their children's performance at school, they do not as closely monitor their children's TV or play time when compared to time for homework or reading. The cultural capital of middle-class families encourages parents to structure their children's free time to include school-related activities as well as recreation.

EXAMPLES FROM THE HIGH SCHOOL LEVEL: STUDENTS CHASING CULTURAL CAPITAL IN LOS ANGELES

In Los Angeles, middle-class families go to great lengths to gain cultural capital. More so than many other large cities, sought-after destinations are dispersed across the vast sprawling county rather than located in one or two cultural hubs. Pair this fact with the city's notoriously congested freeways, and it is not uncommon for Los Angeles residents to commute an hour here and forty minutes there in order to reach their target destination. For many middle-class Los Angeles families, Montgomery (2006) says, "Children reside in one neighborhood, attend schools in another area, and play in parks distant from their homes. For

these children and their parents, the 'daily round' of activities that infuse places with meaning and value span segregated residential areas."

A city known for its diverse population, it is not uncommon for minority parents with some means to send their children to a magnet, charter, or private school with a predominantly white population on the other end of town. Though such parents may lament having to go to such lengths to provide better educational opportunities for their children, for the cultural capital gained, many feel it is worth the price. More than school, parents of means aim to have their children socialize and play in structured, culturally beneficial manners. While low-income youth have few options but to hang out in neighborhood community centers, parks, or on the corner, those with means have more options and choose to exercise them. Instead of spending time with others in the same, lower-positioned class, those who are able choose to attend organized and more cultured social events to give their children greater chances of upward social mobility. This type of socialization often involves minority youth associating themselves with white or more mainstreamed peers. Many African American middle-class young people adopt and develop "dual socializations": one for mainstreaming into society and one for keeping a sense of their urban roots.

SELECTIVE FLIGHT

In cities such as Chicago, Detroit, and Philadelphia, the term 'white flight' referred to white affluent populations migrating in droves to the suburbs, geographically distancing themselves from urban neighborhoods. In Los Angeles the term "selective flight" better fits. Selective flight may be applied to a Hispanic or African American family who resides in a neighborhood of people of their own race for reasons of comfort or familiarity, but who urge their children to socialize in distant, more affluent communities for the benefits such socialization may provide. Such parents may begin to actively put up barriers or hindrances to prevent their children from hanging around in the neighborhood, such as scheduling activities that take place in the other side of town (Montgomery). The term selective flight can also be applied to affluent white families who send their children to exclusive private schools because too many low-income minority students are being bused in or somehow transferred in to their otherwise middle-class, affluent, localized public school.

EXAMPLES OF CULTURAL CAPITAL IN IMMIGRANT COMMUNITIES

The United States has long been a nation of immigrants whereby new arrivals and their children, over time, develop the language, skills, and cultural norms of their new homeland. Though each immigrant's story varies, the typical immigrant story begins with the parents or new arrivals taking on hard, labor-intensive, low-skill jobs in order to give better educational and employment opportunities to their children (Perreira, Harris, & Lee, 2006). However, when the children of immigrants do not complete high school, thereby failing to reach contemporary standards of educational attainment, this population can end up almost as disadvantaged as their immigrant parents. Many theories of immigration assimilation exist. Some argue that the cultural differences between immigrant groups and native populations diminish over time. Others argue that over time, an immigrant's roots become even more significant, heavily influencing attitudes toward education such as completing high school or attending college.

Looking closely at high school drop-out rates between immigrant and native student populations, the ethnic-racial makeup of the immigrant group in question must be considered. For instance, Asian immigrants are far less likely to drop out of high school than Hispanic immigrants. First generation immigrants do typically attain higher educational goals than their parents, but the trend then stagnates. For many Hispanic immigrants, whether or not they work has a significant effect on whether they drop out or graduate from school. The values (or cultural capital) placed on work may therefore be a factor in achieving educational goals. Surprisingly, analyzing Asian immigrant students, those of disadvantaged economic means are *less* likely than their wealthier counterparts to drop out of school. This trend indicates that this group's cultural capital places a high value on education (Perreira et al.).

CULTURAL CAPITAL & HIGHER EDUCATION

Though much has been done through federal policy and legislation to make higher education more accessible for low-income, minority, and other historically underrepresented populations, these groups still face many barriers to obtaining a college education. In 2001, the National Center for Education Statistics found that "hundreds of thousands of low-income, college-prepared students are left behind each year, unable to go to four-year colleges because they cannot afford to attend" (John, 2006). Research in the fields of sociology and education has shown that parents' education levels and occupations have a significant impact on the educational attainments of their children. That is, students are more likely to attend college if their parents are college educated. Such a background gives the student greater exposure to the higher education experience and career opportunities, thus giving them greater cultural capital. Moreover, students whose parents lack a college education have many misunderstandings about how to pay for college. Minority, low-income students may assume that they cannot afford college or have great misconceptions on how financial aid, government grants, scholarships, and loans for college work. Because they do not have this cultural capital, they often lack the resources or know-how to obtain accurate information about financing a college education. Some minority students such as Latinos put a strong emphasis on values such as work, location, and family. These students want to make sure the college is near home so they could still reside with their families and work nearby. Their set of values makes choosing a community college a more popular option.

Viewpoints

WHEN CULTURAL CAPITAL BOTH DEFIES & COMPLIES WITH TRADITIONAL NORMS

Klein (2005) asks what happens in society when a particular trait both earns and loses cultural capital in mainstream society. Looking at masculinity and its ever-changing role, one sees how macho attitudes, competitiveness, and violence is both rewarded and spurned in contemporary American high schools. Males who outwardly display high levels of masculinity, strength, dominance, and toughness gain high cultural capital within the strata of high school hierarchy. Males who lack these characteristics and instead display weakness, indecisiveness, frailty, and more feminine traits tend to be less popular. These students receive less social rewards and less clout than their more masculine peers. As a result, some males from this group will become outcasts, isolating themselves from the more popular groups, who may mock or tease them. These outcasts may adopt what they see as hyper or idealized masculine values and turn to violence to directly or indirectly increase their clout or cultural capital. Ironically, these ostracized males adopt the hyper-masculine behaviors that once eluded them. Klein says, "boys who have difficulty acquiring traditional masculinity status may act out against conventional masculinity role models—jocks and preps—using typical masculinity signifiers (i.e., violence) to demonstrate an alternative and more accessible form of masculinity."

The outcasts who commit school shootings have later expressed feelings of deep resentment toward athletes and others with highly ranked cultural capital. These males take idealized masculinity in the form of extreme violence in order to seek their revenge. While school shootings resulting in death are met with outrage, other acts of violence acted out by overly aggressive males, such as on the football field, are met with social affirmation. Through the media and athletics, society demonstrates an ambivalent view of violence and overly macho attitudes. Serious violent offenders are penalized by the criminal justice system, while aggressive, hard-edged behavior is rewarded in sports and other social situations. As a result, some young men see any kind of violence as a way to increase or maintain their status.

TERMS & CONCEPTS

Assimilation: Assimilation refers to the process by which immigrants of different ethnicities and cultures acquire the social and psychological characteristics of a mainstream group.

Cultural Capital: Cultural capital refers to family background and commitment to education that contributes to an individual's or group's position in society and achievement in education. It questions what constitutes valued knowledge in contemporary society, suggesting that powerful groups determine what counts. Following this concept, some students (for example, those advantaged by higher social status) are more able to acquire knowledge because of cultural advantages they bring to education based on class, race, or gender (http://learnnc.org).

Dual Socializations: Dual socialization (also called "biculturalism") occurs when minority students become acquainted with two different cultural behaviors so that they can be successful in different cultural environments. For instance, an African American youth may adopt and demonstrate one set of behaviors and characteristics while attending a predominantly white school and demonstrate more culturally specific characteristics while at home around other African Americans.

Habitus: Somewhat difficult to define, habitus refers to the cumulative habits, behaviors, ideals, values, and tastes a group develops. Overtime, habitus becomes second nature or assumed traits of a particular group.

Legitimate: In regard to cultural capital, the term legitimate is used to refer to cultural activities or interests that are deemed of high value by upper-class society. For instance, fine art is regarded as legitimate culture because it is represented in established institutions such as museums.

Outcast: An outcast is someone who is shunned by society, either through official or unofficial channels. In an educational setting, an outcast may be a student who lacks cultural capital and does not belong to popular groups.

Privilege: Privilege is a special advantage, right, or benefit granted to or enjoyed by an individual or class.

Selective Flight: Selective flight occurs when a racial or ethnic group selectively associates with similar or dissimilar racial groups depending on the situation or circumstance.

Social Status: Social status is the honor or prestige attached to one's position in society. It is influenced by one's profession, occupation, family name, wealth, and other factors.

White Flight: The term white flight refers to the relocation of middle-class whites from neighborhoods undergoing racial integration.

Lisa Angerame

BIBLIOGRAPHY

Barone, C. (2006). Cultural capital, ambition and the explanation of inequalities in learning outcomes: A comparative analysis. *Sociology, 40*, 1039–1058.

Hale, J. E. (1986). *Black children: Their roots, culture, and learning styles.* Baltimore: Johns Hopkins University Press.

John, E. P. (2006). Contending with financial inequality: Rethinking the contributions of qualitative research to the policy discourse on college access. *American Behavioral Scientist, 49,* 1604–1620.

Jung-Sook, L., & Bowen, N. K. (2006). Parent involvement, cultural capital, and the achievement gap among elementary school children. *American Educational Research Journal, 43,* 193–218.

King, A. (2005). Structure and agency. In A. Harrington (ed.), *Modern social theory: An introduction.* (pp. 215–232). Oxford, UK: Oxford University Press.

Klein, J. (2006). Cultural capital and high school bullies: How social inequality impacts school violence. *Men and Masculinities, 9,* 53–75.

Montgomery, A. F. (2006). Living in each other's pockets: The navigation of social distances by middle class families in Los Angeles. *City & Community, 5,* 424–450. Retrieved September 16, 2007, from EBSCO Online Database Academic Search Premier.

Paino, M., & Renzulli, L. A. (2013). Digital dimension of cultural capital: The (in)visible advantages for students who exhibit computer skills. *Sociology of Education, 86,* 124–138. Retrieved December 18, 2013, from EBSCO Online Database Education Research Complete.

Perreira, K. M., Harris, M. K., & Lee, D. (2006). Making it in America: High school completion by immigrant and native youth. *Demography, 43,* 511–533.

Silva, E. B. (2006). Homologies of social space and elective affinities: Researching cultural capital. *Sociology, 40,* 1171–1189.

Sommerfeld, A. K., & Bowen, P. (2013). Fostering social and cultural capital in urban youth: A programmatic approach to promoting college success. *Journal of Education, 193,* 47–55. Retrieved December 18, 2013, from EBSCO Online Database Education Research Complete.

Stephan, J. L. (2013). Social capital and the college enrollment process: How can a school program make a difference? *Teachers College Record, 115,* 1–39. Retrieved December 18, 2013, from EBSCO Online Database Education Research Complete.

Yosso, T. (2005). Whose culture has capital? A critical race theory discussion of community cultural wealth. *Race, Ethnicity & Education, 8,* 69–91. Retrieved September 21, 2007, from EBSCO Online Database Education Research Complete.

SUGGESTED READING

Björk, L. G., Lewis, W. D., Browne-Ferrigno, T., & Donkor, A. (2012). Building social, human, and cultural capital through parental involvement. *Journal of School Public Relations, 33,* 237–256. Retrieved December 18, 2013, from EBSCO Online Database Education Research Complete.

Bourdieu, P. (1987). *Distinction: A social critique of the judgement of taste.* Cambridge, MA: Harvard University Press.

Dixon-Román, E. J. (2013). The forms of capital and the developed achievement of black males. *Urban Education, 48,* 828–862. Retrieved December 18, 2013, from EBSCO Online Database Education Research Complete.

Jerelyne, C. W. (2006). *The Brackenridge colored school: A legacy of empowerment through agency and cultural capital inside an African American community.* Bloomington, IN: AuthorHouse.

Jun, X., & Hampden-Thompson, G. (2012). Cultural reproduction, cultural mobility, cultural resources, or trivial effect? A comparative approach to cultural capital and educational performance. *Comparative Education Review, 56,* 98–124. Retrieved December 18, 2013, from EBSCO Online Database Education Research Complete.

Vogel, T. (2004). *Rewriting white: Race, class, and cultural capital in nineteenth-century America.* Piscataway, NJ: Rutgers University Press.

MERITOCRACY

This article presents a discussion of meritocracy in U.S. higher education. Meritocracy is a system in which those who possess coveted talents, abilities, or superior intellectual capabilities attain high level, prestigious executive positions while those lacking these abilities are slated to the lower to middle ranks of society. Many experts argue that achievement based education is fundamental to a prospering democracy, while others argue that meritocracy only creates a new elitism leaving those without means or ability to remain dispossessed. An unequal playing field—the historical presence of racism, biases, and socioeconomic factors—prevent a true meritocracy from coming to fruition. Controversial policies such as affirmative action have attempted to overcome such limitations with some success. As long as nepotism, cronyism, and privilege prominently exist in many higher education institutions, true meritocracy remains decidedly elusive. This article provides an overview of meritocracy, gives contemporary examples of its use, and discusses some highly controversial or opposing views on the subject.

KEYWORDS: Affirmative action; Egalitarianism; Elitism; Equal Opportunity; Nepotism; Privilege; Situational Ethics; Social status; Standardized testing; SAT

OVERVIEW

In an educational context, meritocracy is defined as an institutionalized system in which advancement is based on talents, skills, and abilities rather than on tenure, seniority, nepotism, or other similar factors. Egalitarian by its very nature, a meritocracy ideally enables any qualified individual who demonstrates high intellect or ability to rise to a leadership or executive-level position regardless of his or her background, race, socioeconomic status, or gender. However unintended, meritocracy in practice creates its own stratified hierarchical system in which gifted, highly talented, or otherwise intellectually superior individuals form their own class excluding average or below-average performing individuals. In other words, instead of chasms that separate those born with birth rights from those born with no birth right, a meritocratic system separates those who demonstrate superior intellectual performance from those who do not (Horowitz, 2006).

HISTORICAL PERSPECTIVES

Starting in the mid-1940s in London, England, Michael Young, commonly referred to as the father of meritocracy in the realm of education, exposed the value of meritocracy and helped to create a public education system based on merit rather than birth order. His book *The Rise of Meritocracy* and published articles such as "Let Us Face the Future" helped to revolutionize the public education system and enable children of a range of backgrounds to attend school when they would not have been able to under the traditional system. This new way of thinking about education coincided nicely with post-World War II England, where an emerging economy demanded a greater number of skilled workers to rebuild and sustain a hard-hit but recovering nation (Horowitz).

In the short-run, a public school system based on meritocracy did seem to produce a larger educated populace where a greater number of individuals could obtain skilled positions for which they received commensurate wages. Over time, merit based advancement rather than elitist entitlement became the norm in most post-World War II, Western-thinking nations. It continues to be the norm even today. However, Young and his contemporaries who originally postulated the benefits of meritocracy largely failed to foresee its long-term effects: creating a "haves-versus have-nots" pecking order based on aptitude equal to the stratified aristocratic system of yester year (Horowitz, 2006).

STANDARDS & MEASUREMENT

Creating a hierarchical system based on merit also meant that an error-resistant measurement tool needed to be devised in order to properly determine a student's intellectual capacity. Thus, came the advent and use of standardized testing to determine a student's general intelligence, areas of strengths and weaknesses, and potential to achieve. Envisioned by Henry Chauncey in 1948, standardized testing sought to accurately measure the cerebral abilities of students and to then properly place them along a stratified range from the lowest achievers up to the highest ones (Tellez, 2001). Students who tested at the uppermost echelon would be slated to attend prestigious universities, which would in turn prepare them for a prominent career earning commensurate pay. Those who fell in the mid ranges on the scale would be led to a trade or low-level college career where they would learn skills appropriate for low-to middle-class lifestyles. Those individuals who performed at the lowest levels would largely be prevented from attending any type of higher education institution and could, at best, hope to eke out a living as a laborer or service worker (Tellez).

Standardized testing soon became synonymous with the SATs (Scholastic Aptitude Tests) that for decades have been the biggest determiner for acceptance into higher education institutions. In the late 1960s and early 1970s, use of SAT scores to determine college admissions occurred almost without question. Later on, voices of SAT critics started to increase in volume and number as more and more people such as professors, college graduates, teachers, social activists, and intellectuals began discussing the limits and ramifications of the SATs. Leaders of the African American community argued that SATs were geared toward middle-class white students while professors and intellectuals argued that SATs gave no weight to talents such as creativity, leadership, and other non-measurable abilities of importance. Moreover, the great emphasis placed on scoring well on the SATs led to a "teaching to the test" practice in which students memorized by rote various facts and figures but were unable to use critical thinking and problem solving skills to gain a deeper understanding of concepts (Tellez).

The history of meritocracy in education is rich with innate conflict. From a benevolent viewpoint, one sees well intentioned education leaders like Chauncey, Young, and their contemporaries such as William Turnbull who sought to create a more democratic system. This fair-handed system, they envisioned, would mean that anyone, regardless of their wealth or background, could get ahead. The days of the wealthy entitled few and the poor uneducated many, they argued, would soon be a thing of the past. Their assumption was that merit trumped birthright each and every time. Such a system, they felt, would raise the standard of living for those on the bottom giving them unprecedented opportunities. And while it is true that many from low income, previously underrepresented communities benefited under the new system, these policy and education leaders failed to understand that meritocracy would create its own anti-utopia caste system leaving many still disenfranchised (Tellez).

MERITOCRACY: THEORY VS. REALITY

Meritocracy in both the secondary and post-secondary education systems largely reflects the socioeconomic consciousness of white middle-class ethos. A system structured on merits and abilities has become so normalized that it is rarely scrutinized or examined; it is usually taken for granted. College students from affluent, privileged backgrounds tend not to recognize their advantages over others, believing wholeheartedly in the virtues of a pure meritocratic system that some say in reality does not exist (Applebaum, 2005). These students adopt a liberal position that emphasizes individual achievement and embraces antiracist attitudes. However ideological these views may sound, they often result in these students having little or no empathy or understanding of real racial and socioeconomic barriers that may prevent others from accomplishing their goals.

The color-blind framework makes it more likely that white students will see the opportunity structure as open and institutions as impartial.... Such students often end up explaining inequality by either blaming the individual or his/her subordinate group and its cultural characteristics for the resultant lower economic and academic achievement (Applebaum).

Under the guise of meritocracy, middle-class students can pretend real socioeconomic impediments do not exist making them hardened to those who cannot prosper or better themselves. Furthermore, such thinking distances these students from the role they themselves may play in the larger institutional and societal structures that are bias or class-specific (Applebaum).

EXAMPLES FROM THE HIGH SCHOOL LEVEL

From coast to coast, primary and secondary public schools in the United States function using a meritocratic system. More commonly known as tracking, advanced placement, remedial courses, gifted, or other such terms, students are ranked, filed, and set to attend classes with similarly performing students. Starting at the primary grade levels, students are tested and put into tracks depending on test outcomes. More often than not, students remain, sometimes until graduation, in the same track with the same peer groups. Tracks are more porous today, so that a student testing high in English but average in math will be tracked accordingly. Previously "smart kids" were tracked high in all subject areas regardless of individual subject performance. To increase the chances of success for some minorities and those in low-income population segments, sometimes students are tracked up or "detracked." In other words, below-average performing students may be placed in a higher track to level the playing field and bolster their achievement chances (Yonezawa & Jones, 2006).

In interviews with a variety of students at large school districts representing a diverse urban population, Yonezawa & Jones learned that many students found the system of tracking to be "unfair." Students were largely unaware of the purpose of tracking or how they were placed. The study found that "students were often incorrect when asked to identify their track and usually could not accurately assess whether or not they had been detracked" (Yonezawa & Jones. Many students felt that high-track or advanced students got the better teachers, thus enabling them to be more successful, while those in the lower tracks got the "bad" teachers. Many felt that it was very difficult to move into a better track and that using test scores for track placement was innately unjust. Some students spoke out against tracking saying, "Just because you're taking the regular class, [you] shouldn't get less of an education." Others in advanced placement tracks "believed their inherent intelligence and motivation warranted greater access to good teachers and rigorous curriculum." These examples show how a meritocracy functions in a typical high school setting today and what students think of tracking, a common tool of measurement used for such a system.

EXAMPLES AT THE COLLEGE LEVEL: THE ROLE OF AFFIRMATIVE ACTION

In most higher education systems in the United States today, the practice of meritocracy is the norm. With the exclusion of a dozen or so elite institutions, students are accepted into colleges and universities based on their abilities, measured by standardized tests such as the SATs, rather than by name, cronyism, or family wealth. While using achievement to determine college admission sounds fair on the surface, it is much more complicated underneath. Because inequalities in higher education reflect those of society at large, new government policies were initiated with the goal of trouncing racial, gender, ethnic, and other biases and creating equal opportunity for college admissions. A term first coined in the 1960s, affirmative action policies were created in order to "overcome the effects of past societal discrimination by allocating resources to members of specific groups, such as minorities and women" (Affirmative Action, n.d.). In the realm of higher education, this meant that a certain number of minority students, often referred to as a quota, would be admitted to the school to increase diversity, to give underprivileged students a chance at improving their position in life, and to attempt to correct past wrongs. These students would often fall short of meeting admission requirements such as having high grades or SAT scores.

Since affirmative action was first initiated, its practice has been highly contentious. The U.S. Supreme Court case, *Regents of the University of California v. Bakke*, in 1978, which allowed race to be a determining factor in college admissions, illustrates its divisiveness. Centering on all-American values such as meritocracy, equality, justice, and the right to better one's self, the arguments for and against the implementation of affirmative action are diverse and plentiful (Kim, 2005). Those against the policy often speak of a backlash in which qualified white applicants are rejected in order to allow non-qualifying minority students to attend colleges and universities. Minority leaders and some academics argue that these policies have, as intended, granted students from underprivileged segments access to education opportunities

and that these students have been successful in this context. Others argue that such policy benefits no one and only creates a system in which minorities appear to improve their status when no real advancement occurs. These individuals question the spirit of affirmative action, arguing the policy never intended to improve the status of minorities but only make it appear as such.

AFFIRMATIVE ACTION & ITS BACKLASH

In today's higher education environment, affirmative action policies tend to be more voluntary due to a shift in the public's consciousness. More and more, people question the value of affirmative action, who it benefits, and whether it is still needed. Underlying these questions is the growing sentiment that college acceptance based on merit outweighs admission based on race, ethnicity, or gender. In 1995, in a move that reflected a change of thinking of the population, the California Board of Regents banned race- and ethnicity-based admission and financial aid policies at its public colleges and universities (Kim). "Special consideration" could be used when determining admission of persons who have overcome serious social, economic, or other barriers; however, race alone could not be the criteria for deciding admission. Though the change in policy sought to eradicate preferential treatment and bolster the use of merit when determining college admission, in reality the policy merely recast who the beneficiaries of preferential treatment would be. Meritocracy purists would likely argue against any type of non-merit-based preferential treatment—whether based on race or "extraordinary circumstances." The water is further muddied when one questions why preferential treatment based on race is disallowed while preferential treatment based on socioeconomic circumstances is permissible. Kim asks, "What, one might ask, makes categories such as race, national origin, religion, and sex artificial preferences, if class and social disadvantages are viewed as promoting the value of individual rights?" In other words, why is one type of preferential treatment acceptable while another is not?

WEALTH CLOSELY LINKED TO HIGHER EDUCATION

Not only does the system of meritocracy create its own hierarchy under the guise of egalitarianism, few can deny that the old structure based on nepotism, wealth, or status still exists. In other words, students' wealth still heavily influences whether and where they attend college. For students with comparable grades and test scores, rich and upper-middle-class students are far more likely to be admitted to a good college than students of low income. In other words, despite meritocratic or progressive attitudes toward aptitude and actual achievement, wealth rather than merit is still more closely correlated with higher education. Regardless of aptitude, the estimated chances for obtaining a bachelor's degree by age twenty-four are: one in two for a family with $90,000 annual income; one in four for a family with $61,000-$90,000 annual income; one in ten for a family with $35,000-$61,000 annual income; and one in seventeen for a family whose income is less than $35,000 annually (Douthat, 2005). Meritocracy is lacking most notably at the Ivy League schools where diversity goals are often usurped by funding needs. Higher education institutions need the wealth that upper-middle-class and rich students can provide for both the short-term and the long-term, such as that provided by alumni giving and establishment of foundations. University presidents and their constituents feel that their universities would lose prestige by enrolling a greater number of low income and minority students, which would dissuade wealthier students from attending their institutions (Douthat). The cycle of wealth and poverty thus continues as better-educated individuals attain higher paying jobs and live in neighborhoods with quality schools while those without an education attain low-paying jobs, live in low-performing school districts, and do not attend college because of lack of finances or abilities.

Some elite institutions such as the University of Virginia are making policy changes to foster real change and enable talented but underprivileged students to attend their institution. In 2004, the University announced that "for families with incomes below 150 percent of the poverty line, it would eliminate need-based loans and would instead offer grants" (Douthat). The University is also seeking ways to cap student debt and more actively seek funding through grants. Proponents for meritocracy hope that the University of Virginia's move may start a trend among its constituents; the results of that remain to be seen.

VIEWPOINTS

The system of meritocracy has its supporters and critics. Some closely align it with democratic values and others blame it for the current gap between the rich and poor.

WHITE PRIVILEGE AS A FORM OF AFFIRMATIVE ACTION

Coleman (2003) turns the notion of equal opportunity or affirmative action on its head and postulates that whites and the white privileged class actually benefit more from affirmative action than minorities ever have. He argues that whites have long benefited from a type of affirmative action where they got accepted into colleges based on their race (or whiteness) rather than on their capabilities. To the majority of whites, accepting current affirmative action policy means relinquishing their long held white privilege, something from which many whites seem unaware they have even benefited. In other words, whites do not protest when a white person gets accepted into a college because of their race, name, wealth, or other non-merit factors (Coleman). However, they do argue for the value of merits only when the situation applies to African-Americans and other minorities. Blacks' and whites' opinions differ vastly when asked about preferential treatment and affirmative action. "Seventy eight percent of whites believe that it is 'very likely' or 'somewhat likely' that less qualified blacks get admitted to colleges or universities over more qualified whites, yet sixty two percent of blacks believe that this is 'not likely'" (Coleman). These numbers reveal a stark contrast of how the two races see the realities of affirmative action policies.

SITUATIONAL ETHICS & MERIT

At Harvard University and other elite institutions, nepotism and wealth often still trump merit when looking at first-year university admittance records. In the 1980s, a group of Asian-Americans filed a complaint in a federal courtroom against Harvard because they were denied admission even though they had higher test scores than white privileged students. In a highly controversial case, the court agreed with Harvard that holding highly sought-after admission spots for "legacy candidates was justifiable as this practice was part of Harvard's diversity initiative" (Klein, 2005). Cases such as this give weight to the notion that support of admission determined by merit is situationally based (Klein).

TERMS & CONCEPTS

Affirmative Action: Policies created in order to overcome the effects of past societal discrimination by allocating resources to members of specific groups, such as minorities and women.

Egalitarianism: Egalitarianism affirms, promotes, or characterizes the belief in equal political, economic, social, and civil rights for all people.

Equal Opportunity: Equal opportunity is the goal of giving all persons an equal chance to an education and employment, and to protect their civil rights, regardless of their race, religious beliefs, or gender.

Nepotism: Nepotism is favoritism granted to relatives or close friends, without regard to their merit. It is also defined as patronage bestowed or favoritism shown on the basis of family relationship, as in business and politics.

Privilege: Privilege is a special advantage, immunity, permission, right, or benefit granted to or enjoyed by an individual, class, or caste.

Situational Ethics: Situational ethics is a theory concerned with the consequences of an action. In the case of situation ethics, the ends can justify the means.

Lisa Angerame

BIBLIOGRAPHY

Affirmative Action. (n.d.). *Columbia Electronic Encyclopedia.* Retrieved July 25, 2007, from http:// reference.com.

Applebaum, B. (2005). In the name of morality: Moral responsibility, whiteness and social justice education. *Journal of Moral Education, 34*, 277-290. Retrieved July 24, 2007, from EBSCO Online Database Education Research Complete.

Coleman, M. G. (2003). African American popular wisdom versus the qualification question: Is affirmative action merit-based? *Western Journal of Black Studies, 27*, 35-44. Retrieved July 24, 2007, from EBSCO Online Database Education Research Complete.

Douthat, R. (2005). Does meritocracy work? Not if society and colleges keep failing to distinguish between wealth and merit. *The Atlantic Monthly, 296*, 120-126. Retrieved July 24, 2007, from EBSCO Online Database Education Research Complete.

Egalitarian. (n.d.). *The American Heritage Dictionary of the English Language,* Fourth Edition. Retrieved July 29, 2007, from http://dictionary.reference.com.

Equal opportunity. (n.d.). *The American Heritage New Dictionary of Cultural Literacy,* Third Edition. Retrieved July 29, 2007, from http://dictionary.reference.com.

Horowitz, I. L. (2006). The moral economy of meritocracy. *Modern Age, 48*, 281-286. Retrieved July 24, 2007, from EBSCO Online Database Academic Search Premier.

Kim, J. K. (2005). From Bakke to Grutter: Rearticulating diversity and affirmative action in higher education. *Multicultural Perspectives, 7*, 12-19. Retrieved July 24, 2007, from EBSCO Online Database Education Research Complete.

Klein, J. M. (2005). Merit's demerits. *Chronicle of Higher Education, 52*, B12-B13. Retrieved July 25, 2007, from EBSCO Online Database Education Research Complete.

Liu, A. (2011). Unraveling the myth of meritocracy within the context of US higher education. *Higher Education, 62*, 383-397. Retrieved December 15, 2013, from EBSCO Online Database Education Research Complete.

Nahai, R. N. (2013). Is meritocracy fair? A qualitative case study of admissions at the University of Oxford. *Oxford Review of Education, 39*, 681-701. Retrieved December 15, 2013, from EBSCO Online Database Education Research Complete.

Nepotism. (n.d.). *The American Heritage New Dictionary of Cultural Literacy,* Third Edition. Retrieved July 29, 2007, from http://dictionary.reference.com.

Privilege. (n.d.). *The American Heritage Dictionary of the English Language,* Fourth Edition. Retrieved July 29, 2007, from http://dictionary.reference.com

Tellez, K. (2001). 'The Big Men': A journalist's look at the Scholastic Aptitude Test. *Journal of Curriculum Studies, 33*, 247-260. Retrieved July 23, 2007, from EBSCO Online Database Education Research Complete.

Wiley, S., Deaux, K., & Hageiskamp, C. (2012). Born in the USA: How Immigrant Generation Shapes Meritocracy and Its Relation to Ethnic Identity and Collective Action. Cultural Diversity & Ethnic Minority Psychology, 18, 171-180.Retrieved December 15, 2013, from EBSCO Online Database Education Research Complete.

Yonezawa, S. & Jones, M. (2006). Students perspectives on tracking and detracking. *Theory Into Practice, 45*, 15-23. Retrieved July 23, 2007, from EBSCO Online Database Education Research Complete.

SUGGESTED READING

Herrnstein, R. J. & Murray, C. (1996). *The bell curve: Intelligence and class structure in American life.* New York: Free Press.

Lemann, N. (2000). *The big test: The secret history of the American meritocracy.* New York: Farrar, Straus and Giroux.

Mijs, J. (2016). The unfulfillable promise of meritocracy: Three lessons and their implications for justice in education. *Social Justice Research.* 29 (1), 14-34.

McNamee, S. J. (2004). *The meritocracy myth.* Lanham, Md: Rowman & Littlefield.

Soares, J. (2017). Meritocracy dismissed. *Ethnic and Racial Studies.* 40 (13), 2300-2307.

White, J.W., Ali-Kahn, C., & Zoellner, B. (2017). Deconstructing meritocracy in the college classroom. *College Teaching.* 65 (3), 115-129.

Young, M. (1994). *The rise of the meritocracy* (classics in organization and management series). Piscataway, NJ: Transaction Publications.

TEACHER'S UNIONS—PAST AND PRESENT

Modern teachers' unions grew out of the labor movement of the 1930s, but were not legitimized until the 1960s when they expanded dramatically and won the right for their members to bargain collectively in many states. The two major teachers' unions are the National Education Association (NEA) and the American Federation of Teachers (AFT). Early in their histories, the unions' emphasis was on improving compensation and working conditions for their members, but they have transitioned to become much more active politically and have a forceful lobby for public educational policy. Despite issues and setbacks such as losing members to small unions and non-affiliated teachers organizations, membership in the unions continues to grow overall.

KEYWORDS: AFL-CIO; Association of American Educators (AAE); American Federation of Teachers (AFT); Collective Bargaining; National Education Association (NEA); National Labor Relations Act; No Child Left Behind Act (NCLB); Political Action Committee; Public Employees; Shanker, Albert; Taft-Hartley Labor Act; Unions

OVERVIEW

In her 1982 article, "Teachers are Organized, But to What End?" educational activist and teacher Susan Ohanian was critical of the motivations of teacher unions. They appeared to her at the time to be less interested in teachers than in public relations and setting a political agenda (Ohanian, 1982). Whether the unions have sufficient interest in the concerns of their members may still be argued today, but there is no doubt that the two major national unions, the National Education Association (NEA) and the American Federation of Teachers (AFT) carry as much political clout as they ever have.

The National Education Association (NEA) was founded in 1856 as the National Teachers' Association. Modern teachers' unions, however, are little more than forty years old. Their membership did not expand significantly until the early 1960s, a time of social ferment of all kinds. The movement was spurred by the actions of the United Federation of Teachers in New York City. Among the activists was Al Shanker, who came to personify the teacher's

union movement. He was involved as early as the 1950s in fighting for teachers' rights, bringing collective bargaining to New York in the 1960s. Later, as President of the American Federation of Teachers, he transitioned the national organization into a powerful lobby for educational policy by the time of his death in 1997.

"Ironically, it was the fear of Mr. Shanker that helped push the National Education Association toward collective bargaining, thus spreading teacher unionism around the country" (Kerchner, Weeres, & Koppich, 1997). At the time that Ohanian's article appeared, the report, "A Nation at Risk" by the National Commission on Excellence in Education (1983) criticized public education for permitting a "rising tide of mediocrity." Shanker used the opportunity to remold the union away from their labor union model to one more concerned with strengthening education. Shanker "… realized that teachers couldn't be strong when education was weak" (Kerchner et al.).

The teachers' unions of the 1960s were modeled on the steel and auto workers' unions that were validated in the 1930s with passage of the Norris-LaGuardia Act of 1932 and the Wagner Act of 1935. Norris-LaGuardia ensured that employees could join unions without employer interference and a few years later, the Wagner Act, also known as the National Labor Relations Act (NLRA), protected union members from retribution by anti-union employers. Later, the Taft-Hartley Act (1947) modified the Wagner Act and reined in unions by outlawing requiring employees to join a union and requiring advanced notice of a strike.

COLLECTIVE BARGAINING FOR STATE EMPLOYEES

These laws, of course, applied to the private sector, not to public employees. It was not until 1962 when President Kennedy signed an Executive Order (10988) that collective bargaining rights were granted to Federal employees. State employees, however, were excluded because each state was viewed as a separate political entity, not subject to Federal legislation but Kennedy's action gave impetus to state employees to organize (Wright & Gunderson, 2004). Wisconsin was the first state to grant collective bargaining rights to public employees.

Although a majority of states allow public employees to organize and conduct collective bargaining, many have "no strike" restrictions. A strike would impede delivery of essential public services, such as providing education to students or fighting fires. Northern and Midwestern states, with their history of labor union and industrialization, have been most receptive to teachers' unions and collective bargaining.

THE NEA & AFT

The National Education Association is the largest teachers' union. In its report to the Department of Labor for 2005-2006, it listed its membership at 2.76 million including teachers, support professionals, students, and retirees. Critics charge that the organization is too top-heavy with a national staff of more than 600 employees, more than half of whom earn over $100,000 a year. Total disbursements for the NEA were reported at $344 million (U.S. Department of Labor, 2007).

The U.S. Department of Labor website posted the American Federation of Teacher's report for 2006-2007 in September 2007. The AFT evolved historically from working class immigrant roots and is affiliated with the AFL-CIO. It reported 832,000 members and reports disbursing nearly $200 million. A large proportion of the AFT's membership is located in urban areas, in contrast to the much larger NEA whose membership is spread throughout the country (U.S. Department of Labor). Because of the AFT's concentration in the cities it has had more visibility over the years than the NEA due to its easier access to the ears of the national media. Attempts have been made for the two unions to merge since their common objectives generally outweigh their differences. They do share a formal partnership and frequently join to support specific legislative actions.

Although teachers' unions are the only labor organizations that have shown measurable growth in the last decade, they still face membership challenges. At the 2004 annual convention of the NEA, membership and revenue were at the top of the agenda and the organization inaugurated new strategies to expand membership (Golden, 2004). The AFT also recently initiated strategies to foster commitment to membership after years of inaction ("AFT Organizing," 2006). Newer, younger teachers are particularly a hard sell because they do not have the historical perspective of the purpose of unions and do not necessarily appreciate the significance of union membership. They also are less willing to pay rising membership fees, which vary from state to state, but may exceed $600 a year, which include local, state and national dues.

RECENT CORRUPTION

The image of the union has not been helped by several recent corruption cases in which leaders of two major local affiliates of the AFT were charged with embezzlement. Union members were demoralized when the head of the United Teachers of Dade County (UTD—Miami, Florida) and the Washington Teachers Union (WTU-Washington, DC) were jailed for embezzling union funds. The President of WTU admitted to siphoning more than $4.6 million from 1995 to 2002. Five months later, the president of the Miami local was indicted after an audit revealed that he had taken $3.5 million over a decade. Officers of the national organization acted fast to remedy the situations but could not escape pointed criticism for their lack of oversight. The damage at the local level was devastating, and neither union has fully recovered (Blair, 2004).

As in all occupations, the preoccupation of those in the teaching rank and file is with their daily duties in their assigned classrooms. They pay their dues to their union, participate as required, and rightfully go about their important assignment of educating children. When asked about her reaction to the Washington Teachers Union scandal, prekindergarten teacher Tanya Copeland said that restoring union trust there was going to be a long process and commented that, "I'm not a political person—I'm a productive person. Teaching and learning come first" (cited in Blair).

Teachers' unions, like other unions and powerful professional organizations, also protect their own, and may even defend "bad teachers." Elementary school principal Michael Jazzar (2006) writes of his frustration with the unions and desire to work with poor teachers to further their ends. He says that "the unions undermine their verbal commitment to having a qualified teacher in every classroom by their opposition to the disciplining or dismissal of weak teachers and to providing merit pay or bonuses for outstanding teachers" (Jazzar). Critics accuse unions of standing in the way of progress and needed educational reforms. At the same time,

"... many leading unionists agree that their future is not in bread, butter, and classroom size bargaining but in their ability to improve the quality of education and the status of teaching as a profession" (Meyer, 2005).

THE UNIONS' POLITICAL ACTIVITY

The teachers' unions' involvement in politics and educational legislation has been contentious and at times divisive. The union rights struggle is an on-going win-some, lose-some proposition. In June 2007 the Supreme Court in *Davenport v. Washington Education Association* (WEA) issued a decision that was viewed to have some impact on union political activity. It upheld a 1992 Washington State statute prohibiting unions from using nonmembers' agency fees to make political contributions (Levinson, 2007). Although viewed as a win for nonmembers, the decision is unlikely to have widespread impact, especially since in the end it had to do as much with how they collected the fees rather than what they did with them.

A win for the unions came during the same month as the Supreme Court decision, June 2007, when the Missouri Supreme Court restored collective bargaining rights to that state's public employees and teachers. The case was viewed as a victory by members of the states' NEA affiliate (Honawar, 2007).

ALTERNATIVES TO UNION MEMBERSHIP

Teachers' unions often espouse liberal causes. The NEA involves itself in supporting controversial issues such as gay rights, gun control and reparations for slavery (NEA, 2007). Both major unions encourage their members to be politically active and to lobby their state and federal officials.

What if a teacher does not agree with its union's stance on a political or social issue? An individual member can do little. A union represents teachers in collective bargaining and personnel issues, but dues are also sent to the state and national organizations. In many states there are no alternatives to union membership. If a teacher does not want to pay dues, they are still required to pay the union's agency fees for services.

In states without collective bargaining laws, teachers may join non-union professional organizations. In fact, not all of the nation's teachers belong to the NEA or AFT. There are also over 800,000 non-affiliated teachers in the country, and others are members of smaller local or regional unions. Non-union teachers' groups with at least 250,000 members in 18 states offer "... lower state dues and no required fee that goes to a national organization," as well as "... a less-confrontational attitude toward school boards and fewer social pronouncements" (Golden).

However, an umbrella organization for non-union teachers' groups, the Association of American Educators (AAE), is increasingly visible nationally. Along with the NEA and AFT, they have a Washington, DC central office, but they state pointedly that they do "not spend any of our members' dues on partisan politics, nor do we support or oppose controversial agendas unrelated to education" (Association of American Educators, 2007).

Even though the AAE vows not to enter into politics or controversy, their affiliates do not necessarily follow the lead. Funding for teachers' non-union groups is reportedly coming from conservative foundations including the John M. Olin Foundation and Walton Family Foundation (Walt-Mart). "... Nonunion associations are becoming political too ... whether they intend to or not, according to Director Doug Rogers of the 100,000 member Association of Texas Professional Educators," (cited in Golden). Ironically, politics and teachers' organizations seem to be inseparable whether the lobbying is directed from the Washington offices of the big unions or through financial support from conservative foundations. Golden says that the groups are mirroring the origins of the NEA before it transitioned into a union in the 1960s. Like the NEA, the non-union associations provide liability insurance and other benefits and a modicum of teacher training, and they lobby state legislatures for more education spending.

REAUTHORIZING NCLB

The NEA's political action committee (PAC) gave $1.8 million to candidates for federal office for the 2006 election campaigns of which Democrats received 89 percent (Caruso, 2007). After the elections of 2006 swung Democrats into power in Congress, NEA and AFT officials could rightfully be optimistic that their recommendations for revisions to the No Child Left Behind Act of 2001 (NCLB), scheduled for reauthorization in 2007, would be supported.

The unions' websites prominently display their agendas for revamping the act. The NEA advocates going beyond tests to measure learning and school performance; wants to reduce class sizes; and wants to increase the number of highly qualified teachers in schools (NEA). The AFT wants to "get NCLB right" and has four areas of focus including:

- Changing the adequate yearly progress formula (AYP) to distinguish between effective and ineffective schools;
- Better implementing the highly qualified teacher requirements;
- Improving schools and student services;
- Appropriating more funding to education to support the NCLB mandates (AFT).

On the last point, the NEA, AFT and Democratic leaders clearly agree. Each has criticized the Bush administration for not putting additional funding behind the mandates of NCLB, but Caruso warns that the unions are expecting too much of the politicians and they may be bound for disappointment if they think they are going to get an ambitious overhaul of NCLB. She reports that it is unlikely that the Act will be reauthorized until 2009, after the Presidential elections.

MERIT PAY

Teachers' unions are on record as resisting merit pay programs. The concept has also been rejected by many teachers who don't want to be seen as competing against one another. The NEA states that the Democratic Presidential candidates are opposed to merit pay; however, Congressional leaders are considering it as part of the NCLB reauthorization (NEA). The AFT stance is less adamant in opposing merit pay if it is given in restricted ways, but finds it acceptable if it raises the quality of teaching (Dillon, 2007).

Dillon reported on a successful program in Minnesota that was funded with $86 million dollars and with the cooperation of the teacher's unions. The Minnesota plan is very specific in that it rewards teachers who work with mentors and then receive bonuses after raising student achievement. Denver voters also recently approved a new pay system that rewards teachers for their skills and achievements (Dillon).

The U.S. Department of Education awarded 18 grants in 2007 worth $38 million and $42 million November to eighteen states for providing financial incentives to teachers, so although limited, schools are feeding what Dillon says is a "consensus ... that rewarding teachers with bonuses or raises for student achievement ... can energize veteran teachers and attract bright rookies to the profession."

VIEWPOINTS

Although teachers' unions were modeled on the industrial American labor unions and their reason for being was to improve work conditions and compensation, the difference between them has always been professional identity. Labor unions began as grassroots movements to ensure rights and improve working conditions for uneducated, and in most cases, unskilled workers. Teachers, of course, have academic training and degrees and, as a consequence, involvement of professional teachers in a union still is contradictory to some. On the other hand, there are those who question whether teaching is a profession. Paradoxically, because their members are credentialed, the teachers' unions are further legitimized.

Although their reports to the U.S. Department of Labor clearly indicate that NEA and AFT officials are well compensated, they are also generally highly qualified. Many of them moved into the union positions because they were recognized as outstanding teachers and leaders. The presidents of the NEA and AFT should know whereof they speak as each experienced years of teaching in the classroom before they found their calling as union administrators.

Industrial labor unions have declined in the United States, but teachers' unions continue to evolve of their on accord and as they venture farther from their models. Although the teacher's unions remain strong, they are continually scrutinized and threatened with membership loss. As the teachers' union movement matured, organizations that centered solely on the concerns of the teachers was limiting. Without a strong educational system, unions saw that they could not be successful; the two are intrinsic to one another.

Questions are raised by both supporters and critics about the teachers' union's place in 21st century American education. Does an organized teacher workforce advance or hinder student success? Does it have any impact at all? Union advocates point to a scholarly research study by Steelman, Powell and Carini (2000), who asked the question "Do Teacher Unions Hinder Educational Performance?" They studied state SAT and ACT scores and did find a correlation that teachers' unions correlate positively with the test results. The authors claim that their inquiry began from an unbiased viewpoint, but they found such a strong and consistent relationship "across so many permutations of analysis should give pause to those who characterize teacher unions as adversaries of educational success and accountability" (Steelman et al.). The results are not definitive; the authors called for more empirical studies.

TERMS & CONCEPTS

AFL-CIO: The American Federation of Teachers is an affiliate of the AFL-CIO (The American Federation of Labor-Congress of Industrial Organizations) along with fifty-four other unions representing over ten million members. The organization promotes the union movement and endorses improvement of work conditions and compensation for its affiliated membership.

Association of American Educators (AAE): The Association of American Educators is the largest national, non-union, professional teacher association. It serves as an alternative to the large teacher's unions and has a central office in Washington, D.C.

American Federation of Teachers (AFT): The American Federation of Teacher, the United States' second largest union of educators, traces its origins to 1916 and is closely aligned with the labor movement as an affiliate of the AFL-CIO.

Collective Bargaining: The practice where a group of workers or professionals (teachers) select a single organization to represent them in contract negotiations with employers.

National Education Association (NEA): The National Education Association (NEA) is the largest teachers' union in the United States and has as its motto, *"great public schools for every child."*

National Labor Relations Act: Also known as the Wagner Act of 1935, the National Labor Relations Act protects employees who choose to organize and "to bargain collectively through representatives of their own choosing, and to engage in concerted activities for the purpose of collective bargaining or other mutual aid and protection." The law also provides for the National Labor Relations Board that enforces union member rights.

No Child Left Behind Act of 2001 (NCLB): No Child Left Behind Act—Federal legislation enacted in 2001 that is due for renewal in 2007. A primary goal of the Act is to close educational achievement gaps and to bring underperforming schools up to higher, acceptable standards. This includes the requirement that every child should be taught by a highly qualified teacher.

Political Action Committee: A political action committee or PAC is a private group that is organized to elect or defeat federal political candidates or legislation. The NEA and AFT PACs are among the most influential and wealthiest. All PACs are regulated by the Federal Election Commission and are restricted by the amounts of money they may distribute or contribute to individual politicians.

Public Employees: A public employee works for a tax-supported entity such as school or government agency as opposed to a private entity. Employment laws for public employees of state or local governments or school districts are set by the states and may vary.

Shanker, Albert: Albert Shanker personified the teachers' union movement. Born in 1928 in New York City, he became active in New York City teachers' employment issues in the 1950s and was instrumental in the modern union with collective bargaining in the 1960s. When he died in 1997, he was President of the American Federation of Teachers, a position in which he had served for 25 years.

Taft-Hartley Labor Act: The Taft-Hartley amendment to the National Labor Relations Act of 1935 was passed in 1947 over a veto by President Truman. The legislation dampened the unions' power by not requiring employees to join a union and requiring notice of a strike. It also specified that union officials take an oath that they were not members of the Communist Party.

Barbara Hornick-Lockard

BIBLIOGRAPHY

AFT organizing agenda stresses growth and member activism. (2006). *American Teacher, 90,* 10.

American Federation of Teachers (AFT). Retrieved October 7, 2007, from http://aft.org.

Association of American Educators (AAE). (2007). *About us.* Retrieved October 12, 2007, from http://aaeteachers.org.

Blair, J. (2004). State of the unions. *Education Week, 23,* 30-33. Retrieved October 7, 2007, from EBSCO Online Database Academic Search Premier.

Caruso, L. (2007). Teacher tensions. *National Journal, 39,* 27-28.

Dellinger, J., Osorio, I. & Hybner, J. (2007). Teachers unions fighting for universal preschool. *Human Events, 63,* 17-20. Retrieved October 7, 2007, from EBSCO Online Database Academic Search Premier.

Dillon, S. (2007, June 18). Long reviled, merit pay gains among teachers. *New York Times,* A1, A14.

Drevitch, G. (2006). Merit pay: good for teachers? *Instructor, 115,* 21-23. Retrieved October 7, 2007, from EBSCO Online Database Academic Search Premier.

Golden, D. (2004, July 28). Nonunion teacher groups cost NEA membership and clout. *Wall Street Journal—Eastern Edition,* A1-A6.

Honawar, V. (2007). Missouri's high court rules for union rights. *Education Week, 26,* 17. Retrieved October 7, 2007, from EBSCO Online Database Academic Search Premier.

Jazzar, M. (2006). Leading a unionized elementary school. *Principal, 85,* 70. Retrieved October 7, 2007, from EBSCO Online Database Education Research Complete.

Keller, B., & Honawar, V. (2006). Union filings give in-depth look at spending patterns. *Education Week, 25,* 7. Retrieved October 7, 2007, from EBSCO

Kerchner, C. T., Weeres, J. G. & Koppich, J. E. (1997). Teacher unions: a key to school reform. *Christian Science Monitor, 89,* 19. Retrieved October 7, 2007, from EBSCO Online Database Academic Search Premier.

Kirkpatrick, David. W., Hawley, W. D. & Jones, D. R. (2003). Teacher unions. In J. W. Guthrie (Ed.), *Encyclopedia of Education* (2nd ed.) (Vol. 7). New York: Macmillan Reference USA.

Levinson, R. B. (2007). Restrictive ruling on agency fees. *Academe, 93,* 9.

Long-anticipated NEA lawsuit challenges NCLB funding. (2005). *What works in teaching and learning, 37,* 2.

Meyer, H-D. (2005). Trade, profession, or entrepreneurs? The market faithful raise important questions about the future of teacher unions. *American Journal of Education, 112,* 138-143. Retrieved October 7, 2007, from EBSCO Online Database Education Research Complete.

National Education Association (NEA). (2007). Retrieved October 7, 2007, from http://nea.org.

National Education Association (NEA). (2007). *Democrats running for President reject using test scores to pay teachers.* Retrieved October 12, 2007, from http://nea.org.

Ohanian, S. (1982). Teachers are organized, but to what end? *Learning, 11,* 88-90.

Steelman, L. C., Powell, B., & Carini, R. M. (2000). Do teacher unions hinder educational performance? Lessons learned from state SAT And ACT scores. *Harvard Educational Review, 70,* 437-467.

The new generation (2006). *American Teacher, 90,* 13-15.

Tierney, M. (2004). Turn the Paige? *District Administration, 40,* 19.

U.S. Department of Labor, Office of Labor-Management Standards. (2007).

Retrieved October 12, 2007, from http://dol.gov/esa/olms_org.htm

U. S. National Archives & Records Administration. (1935). *National Labor Relations Act.* Retrieved October 12, 2007, from http://ourdocuments.gov.

Wilson, T. (2005). *Institute of Public Affairs Review, 57,* 34-35. Retrieved October 7, 2007, from EBSCO Online Database Academic Search Premier.

Wright, C. & Gundersen, D. E. (2004). Unions and teachers; differences in the state of the nation. *ALSB Journal of Employment and Labor Law, 10,* 1-12.

SUGGESTED READINGS

Brimelow, P. (2003). *The worm in the apple; how teacher unions are destroying American education.* New York: Harper Collins.

Casey, L. (2007). The quest for professional voice. *American Educator, 31,* 20-47.

Diegmueller K. (2002). Unions labor to shape education policy. *Education Week, 22.* Retrieved October 7, 2007, from EBSCO Online Database Academic Search Premier.

Keller, B. (2007). NEA wants role in school improvement agenda; track record, friends, foes, and union's own affiliates could derail undertaking. *Education Week, 26,* 1-24. Retrieved October 7, 2007, from EBSCO Online Database Academic Search Premier.

Keller, B., Sack, J. & Hoff, D. (2005). Union, state wages frontal attack on NCLB. *Education Week, 24,* 1-18. Retrieved October 7, 2007, from EBSCO Online Database Academic Search Premier.

Meier, D. (2004). On unions and education. *Dissent, 51,* 51-55. Retrieved October 7, 2007, from EBSCO Online Database Academic Search Premier.

National Commission on Excellence in Higher Education. (1983). *A nation at risk.* Retrieved October 12, 2007, from http://ed.gov/pubs/NatAtRisk/risk.html

Ravitch, D. (2006/2007). Why teacher unions are good for teachers and the public. *American Educator, 30,* 6-8.

COLLECTIVE BARGAINING AND TEACHERS' UNIONS

The process of collective bargaining is fundamental to the union movement. Teachers' unions in all but five states may use collective bargaining to negotiate for higher wages, improved work conditions and other terms of employment that are determined by state statutes. Negotiations are by their nature adversarial, but bargaining teams can use proven strategies to achieve mutual gains. There has been a call for reform of the collective bargaining process, and the Bush administration, backed by the No Child Left Behind Act of 2001 (NCLB), has asserted pressure to include achievement goals in bargaining agreements, merit pay and more flexibility to transfer teachers. Unions have resisted and so far NCLB has had little impact at the negotiating table, but there have been other indirect changes outside of it. Union leaders contend that collective bargaining has in the long run improved student achievement.

KEYWORDS: American Federation of Teachers (AFT); Arbitration; Collaborative Bargaining (or Negotiating); Collective Bargaining; Fact Finding; Good Faith/Bad Faith Negotiating; Lockout; Mediation; Myers-Briggs Type Indicator (MBTI): National Council for Teacher Quality (NCTQ); National Education Association (NEA);National Labor Relations Act (NLRA) Wagner Act of 1935: No Child Left Behind Act (NCLB); Public Employee; Professional Unionism; Right-to-Work States; Strike; Unfair Labor Practice; Union Security

OVERVIEW

Although each has roots going back as far as the mid-nineteenth century, the two largest unions in the United States, the National Education Association (NEA) and the American Federation of Teachers (AFT), did not flourish until the early 1960s. Until that time, public employee unions were restricted and did not have the right to bargain collectively. After President Kennedy issued Executive Order 10988 in 1962 that granted federal employees the right, many states followed suit and enacted legislation that allowed their public employees, including teachers, to organize.

The teachers' unions were modeled on the industrial labor unions that won their rights to organize in the 1930s. The early days of the labor movement were contentious and even violent, and industrial employers had the upper hand. Passage of the Norris-LaGuardia

Act of 1932 and the National Labor Relations Act (NLRA) of 1935 ensured that labor unions and their members were protected and their First Amendment constitutional right to peaceable assembly was assured.

By the early twenty-first century, the power of industrial unions had waned and employees in public sector unions outnumbered those in the private; 35.9 percent of public employees belonged to unions in 2012 while only 6.6 percent of private employees did (U.S. Bureau of Labor Statistics, 2013). In 2010-11, the nation's two largest teachers' unions boasted a combined membership of 4.6 million (Winkler, Scull & Zeehandelaar, 2012).

The desire for a fair wage and improved working conditions are two issues that spawned the labor unions for both industrial workers and public sector employees including teachers and government workers. Consequently, in the 1960s, state laws were written that defined negotiable topics for public employees and laid out the often complex processes for forming, joining, and operating a union.

Negotiable issues vary from state to state but almost always include salaries and benefits, but other items such as evaluation and grievance procedures, job assignments, and education-related issues such as academic freedom and student discipline. Local units of the larger national and state union organizations are responsible for bargaining with local school districts, although some states, such as Oregon and Rhode Island (McComb, 2000; "Report Submitted," 2004), have explored state-wide negotiations.

Although membership in the large unions is not growing so rapidly and they have been challenged by non-union organizations, they are still a force. In June of 2007, the Missouri Supreme Court ruled that public employees in that state had the right to engage in collective bargaining, which overturned 60 years of legal precedent (Honawar, 2007a). On the other hand, as of 2009, twenty-three states had right-to-work statutes to counteract what is known as union security (U.S. Bureau of Labor Statistics). Teachers in those states are not compelled to join a union.

HOW COLLECTIVE BARGAINING WORKS

Collective bargaining is practiced when a group of employees with like interests join together and elect a single organization to represent them in contract negotiations with their employer. Negotiators work toward completing collective bargaining agreements, which are "complex and often lengthy written contracts that are legally binding on both management and the union(s) representing its employees" (Lunenberg, 2000).

Teachers may not be the only employees in a school district who are organized. Support staff, maintenance, and even administrators may belong. However, depending on state laws and local history, they may be members of the same or separate units. It is usually in the best interests of both unions and school districts to have a minimal number of bargaining units, but only those who share a "community of interests" as defined by state statutes may come together in a specific unit. Many states have a public employee relations board (PERB) that oversees the regulations (Imber, 2004).

When it is time to negotiate a contract, each side selects its representatives to serve on a negotiating team. Negotiating parties are required to negotiate in good faith. An unwillingness of either party to bargain over an item that is mandatory by state law is considered negotiating in bad faith and a violation or "unfair labor practice." Teachers' union and school district representatives meet until a contract is negotiated for whatever period of time they determine. Negotiations take place in face-to-face meetings, and the parties exchange proposals and counterproposals. If an agreement cannot be reached, the parties are at an impasse and further procedures are followed until there is resolution. The sequence of alternative methods to reach resolution is mediation, fact finding, and arbitration (Lunenberg).

CIRCUMSTANCES FOR STRIKE

A strike may be called when an impasse cannot be resolved and union members refuse to report to work. A lockout is the opposite of a strike; the employer does not provide work and shuts down the schools. Only a dozen states allow strikes (National Council on Teacher Quality, 2013), and there are conditions before one may be called, such as giving prior notice. Major strikes such as the September 10-18, 2012, teacher strike in the Chicago Public Schools can include tens of thousands of teachers and may address wide-ranging issues from health benefits to hiring and firing of teachers to curriculum oversight

(Ashack, 2013). Strikes are increasingly rare and are outlawed in most of the country's major cities; however, even though strikes are illegal, that does not mean that a union will not initiate one.

After decades of experience, most of the nation's teachers unions and school districts have developed techniques and processes to improve the collective bargaining process and to avoid impasse and strikes, which are costly to all parties, not least of all to students.

Collective bargaining originated as an adversarial process, but increasingly professional educators and administrators who must negotiate a contract have been trained to defuse it and turn it into a positive for both sides.

COLLABORATIVE BARGAINING

Collaborative bargaining has been used for quite some time as a strategy to lessen the stress of collective bargaining (Liontos, 1987). Also known as "win-win" bargaining, collaborative bargaining encourages problem solving between the parties and frequently uses joint committees that meet during the contract period instead of waiting until a contract expires and they meet at the negotiating table. The term "professional unionism" describes the processes that unions and schools have used to move the adversarial negotiating processes into expectations by both sides for mutual gains. It is a system that "connects teacher participation in educational decisions to taking responsibility for outcomes" (Lunenberg).

PRINCIPAL-CENTERED NEGOTIATIONS

The school principal is regarded as having the pivotal role in promoting professional unionism and encourages a proactive approach to dealing with human resources and other negotiable issues. The negotiated contract has a day-to-day impact as well as long-term effect on the activities of a school, and as front-line administrator, the principal is there to respond to the issues as they arise (Lunenberg).

Bennett and Gray (2007) advocate principal-centered negotiations. Their experience in California suggests that principals should be on negotiating teams and charged as advocates for quality educational services, which are often lost when "fiscal considerations become the primary focus of negotiations" (Bennett & Gray). They argue that school districts spend more time on financial preparation for negotiations than on academic concerns and recommend that the schools become more proactive by making a link between the union's salary demands to student achievement. "Collective bargaining contracts must support and encourage the delivery of high-quality educational services for students and not impede or harm the delivery of those services" (Bennett & Gray).

Advocating that site administrators be at the center of collective bargaining is further justified by Hewitt's (2007) research. He used Myers and Briggs Type Indicators (MBTI) to understand teachers' personalities and the school environment that they inhabit. Based on his analysis, the teacher populations exceeded the general population as predominately Sensory Judging (SJ) individuals (49%), who are tagged as givers, have a strong sense of duty, and meet their obligations, and secondly as Intuitive Feeling (NF) individuals (26%), who are sensitive, care for other human beings, and allow emotions to rule their judgment. He then offered specific recommendations for district officials for communicating effectively with teachers of these types. These personality types respond to "ongoing communication, personal contact and recognition of the valuable individuals making up our teaching staffs [and] are the most important factors in successful collective bargaining" (Hewitt). Who better to understand this than the school principal?

EFFECTS OF FEDERAL LEGISLATION ON UNION NEGOTIATIONS

The No Child Left Behind Act (NCLB) has been a factor in all major educational policy decisions and actions in the U.S. since President George W. Bush signed it into law in 2002. The act mandates that schools meet improvement standards and that all children must be taught by a highly qualified teacher. Schools have struggled to meet the mandates, and teachers' unions have fought them, even bringing suits against the Department of Education.

There were early concerns that the provisions of NCLB might override collective bargaining agreements. Unions were wary that school districts would use NCLB compliance to undercut bargaining (Keller, 2006). Among the most provocative provisions of NCLB to teachers and unions was that if a school were found "in need of improvement" for at least four years, it might trigger disbanding an entire school staff and thereby run afoul of contract provisions offering job protection on the basis of seniority.

The NCLB does contain the provision that nothing in the law "shall be construed to alter the terms of collective bargaining agreements" (cited in Keller). Despite this, there were continued concerns among the union members that the door would be opened to negotiate around NCLB requirements in subsequent contracts. There were fears that the Bush administration would push to have unions relinquish some "seniority privileges, pensions, and performance pay" (Keller). However, the Department of Education backed off, and it was acknowledged that collective bargaining and the unions had won the day.

By 2011, it had become apparent that NCLB was not working as intended, and waivers were made available for states that promised to set and meet achievable alternative benchmarks for progress in underperforming schools ("No Child Left Behind," 2011). The Obama administration changed the focus to its Race to the Top program, established in December 2009, in which states compete for funds based on student achievement. Much as NCLB did before it, Race to the Top measures achievement via student performance on standardized tests and ties it to teacher evaluations (Heitin & Cavanagh, 2011). Consequently, test-based accountability and teacher assessment have become hot-button subjects in teacher contract negotiations. Further, in early 2011, over a dozen states passed laws changing or restricting collective bargaining by teachers' unions, tenure policies, hiring and firing practices, and evaluations.

STATE STATUTES & REGULATIONS

Each state government regulates rights for its public employees and employers, including teachers and school districts. Each has also enacted statutes that cover the rights to organize (or not) and collective bargaining. A collective agreement is enforceable under state law.

As an example, under its labor laws, New York State has a specific Labor Relations Law, article 20. The law establishes an employment relations board and defines the rights of employees and unfair labor practices.

Section 703 reads:

Employees shall have the right of self-organization, to form, join, or assist labor organizations, to bargain collectively through representatives of their own choosing, and to engage in concerted activities, for the purpose of collective bargaining or other mutual aid or protection, free from interference, restraint, or coercion of employers, but nothing contained in this article shall be interpreted to prohibit employees from exercising the right to confer with their employer at any time, provided that during such conference there is no attempt by the employer, directly or indirectly, to interfere with, restrain or coerce employees in the exercise of the rights guaranteed by this section (New York State Labor Relations Act, 1937).

The Labor Relations Law is followed by article 20-A, the Labor and Management Improper Practices Act, which was directed at union personnel and administration who abuse the system and fail to meet fiduciary obligations.

TEACHERS' CONTRACTS

Most teachers' contracts cover a period of two or three years and are lengthy documents. An example is the Denver School District's for the time period from September 1, 2005 to August 31, 2008 (National Council for Teacher Quality). The contract was typically lengthy, running 134 pages. The Denver team employed "interest-based bargaining" in achieving the agreement, which they expected to "contribute to the joint ownership, enforcement and commitment of the resulting Agreement" ("Agreement," 2005). It established committees to promote a collaborative approach to student achievement, instruction and educational reform, and a Task Force on School and District Climate. It also delineated a grievance procedure and includes procedures for handling assaults on teachers and by teachers. As expected, the contract also details salary, benefits, extra duty compensation, and leave policies.

Fuller and Mitchell (2006) use the Milwaukee Public Schools' 232-page contract from 1997, which had 2,000 supporting documents, to illustrate what is wrong with collective bargaining. They view the contract as a complicated guide for a school district that is steeped in "an endless debate about what is and is not allowed in the daily governance of the school system and the creation of an environment where interests of students are routinely subordinates to those of adult teachers."

There are those, however, who would argue that a detailed, presumably unambiguous, clearly written contract serves as an operating guide for teachers and administrators, and the length is not necessarily an indicator of bureaucracy. Fuller and Mitchell (2006) argue that the public should have greater awareness of the collective bargaining process, but do not recommend eliminating it.

Viewpoints

What impact does a unionized faculty and collective bargaining have on students and the educational system? Data can be found to support both sides of the issue. Some see teachers' unions and school boards as having the most entrenched and archaic procedures in the public sector, while others see that collective bargaining has been good for schools and that the best interest of students has been served.

The pressure for higher standards and accountability has forced both unions and administrators to rethink their approach to collective bargaining agreements. Superintendents in some school districts point to contracts as restricting improvements. Hess (2005) worries that "teacher contracts usurp managerial authority, stifle creative staffing, and protect ineffective educators." Those who defend unions claim that collective bargaining can be a tool to improve teacher quality and professionalism.

In his study, Hess looked at how collective bargaining affects improvement and reform in twenty school districts. He found that negotiations in the twenty school districts were generally quiet affairs and prompted little publicity. He also discovered that contracts were less restrictive than school district administrators perceived and their language was more ambiguous than expected. He advises that most school administrators are less assertive about exercising management prerogatives than the language in their contracts allows.

Hess and West (2006) indict collective bargaining agreements calling them "a harmful anachronism in today's K-12 education system, where effective teachers are demanding to be treated as respected professionals and forward thinking leaders are working to transform schools into nimble organizations focused on student learning."

The paper reiterates Hess's argument that school officials should not be afraid to spotlight and work to correct ambiguities in union contracts. Hess and West also advocate tracking student progress and tying it to teacher pay and professional development. Choice and competition are additional keywords that they use to advocate for creating more charter schools.

Kerchner and Koppich (2007) approach the issue from a different perspective. They agree that the labor union model is in need of some revision but think that it should be retained, and recommend drafting a new labor law that includes student achievement goals. They believe that professional unionism has waned and should be renewed as teachers are willing and capable to take on more responsibility for improving performance, more so than is commonly thought. Education, and the process that distributes money and authority, they say, "needs to attach private interests to the larger public good of student achievement."

TERMS & CONCEPTS

American Federation of Teachers (AFT): The United States' second largest union of educators traces its origins to 1916 and is closely aligned with the labor movement as an affiliate of the AFL-CIO, the congress of labor unions. Most of its locals are in urban areas.

Arbitration: Usually the last step in the process when negotiators are at impasse and all other alternatives for resolution have failed. The arbitrator chooses one proposal or the other. "Binding arbitration" means that the decision is final and parties must accept it.

Collaborative Bargaining (or Negotiating): Involves techniques to deal with issues as they arise rather than waiting for them to be presented at the negotiating table. Schools frequently have committees that meet as problems surface, and the negotiators are trained to use cooperative processes and to expect mutual gains by both unions and administrators. Collaborative bargaining is synonymous with win-win negotiating.

Collective Bargaining: A process where a group of employees with like interests join together and elect a single organization (union) to represent them in contract negotiations with their employer.

Fact Finding: Using a group or committee to report on facts that are presented to both parties who are at an impasse in negotiations. Their "recommendations are generally made public, which places additional pressure on the parties to come to agreement".

Good Faith/Bad Faith Negotiating: Union and administrative representatives are expected to join the negotiating table and bargain in good faith, i.e., they subscribe to following the state laws and procedures for negotiating. Negotiating in bad faith is an unwillingness to negotiate in violation with state law or proscribed procedures.

Lockout: Also called a shutout, rarely employed in education, occurs when the employer shuts down the organization so that the union members cannot work. It is the opposite of a strike.

Mediation: The process where a neutral party meets with negotiators who are at impasse and helps them work their way to compromise.

Myers-Briggs Type Indicator (MBTI): A popular and widely used personality-assessment tool. The test has been used for since the early 1940s and "both critics and supporters say that [it] endures because it does a good job of pointing up differences between people, offers individuals a revealing glimpse of themselves and is a valuable asset in team-building, improving communication and resolving personality-based conflict" (Shuit, 2003). It is used for personal and interpersonal understanding, organizational development, and career planning.

National Council for Teacher Quality (NCTQ): An independent organization that receives no federal funds but is privately funded by a number of foundations, including the Bill and Melinda Gates Foundation. Their website includes a large database of collective bargaining agreements, board policies, and teacher handbooks from the fifty largest school districts.

National Education Association (NEA): The largest teachers' union in the United States and has as its motto, prominent on its website: "Great public schools for every child."

National Labor Relations Act (NLRA) Wagner Act of 1935: The act protects employees who choose to organize and "to bargain collectively through representatives of their own choosing, and to engage in concerted activities for the purpose of collective bargaining or other mutual aid and protection." The law also provides for the

National Labor Relations Board that enforces union member rights.

No Child Left Behind Act (NCLB): Federal legislation enacted in 2001. A primary goal of the act is to close educational achievement gaps and to bring underperforming schools up to higher, acceptable standards. This includes the requirement that every child should be taught by a highly qualified teacher. By 2011, waivers were available for all states, provided that they could set and meet achievable benchmarks for progress.

Public Employee: An employee who works for a public or tax-supported entity, such as school or government agency, as opposed to a private entity, usually a business or professional office that is owned by individuals or shareholders. Employment laws for public employees of state or local governments or school districts are set by the states and may vary.

Professional Unionism: A phrase used to describe the movement away from adversarial relationships and the mutual belief of union and management that negotiating can be a "win-win" process. Fred. C. Lunenburg cites Charles Kerchner's comparison of industrial versus professional unionism in his article on union-management relations: industrial unionism emphasizes separation of labor and management, adversarial relationship, and protects teachers; professional unionism emphasizes collaboration, the strength of the whole, and protection of teaching.

Right-to-Work States: States that have passed laws that ensure that unions cannot make being a member a requirement of employment either before or after hiring an employee.

Strike: Refusal to work. Strikes have historically been the most visible tactic of labor unions to achieve their goals in attempt to bring management to its knees. Teachers unions have held strikes when they have met impasse with their school districts, but it is not an effective public relations strategy as a teacher strike is viewed as denying school children their rights to receive a public school education. It is illegal for teachers to strike in most states, and although the law has not always stopped them, strikes have become increasingly rare in both public education and industry.

Unfair Labor Practice: May occur when an employer does not meet its obligation to the employee and violates labor law.

Union Security: Describes provisions in a contract that help ensure the survival of a union; i.e., requiring all employees to be members of the union and pay dues.

Barbara Hornick-Lockard

BIBLIOGRAPHY

Agreement and partnership between School District No. 1 in the City and County of Denver, State of Colorado and Denver Classroom Teachers Association. (2005). Retrieved October 22, 2007, from http://nctq.org.

Ashack, E. A. (2013). Profiles of significant collective bargaining disputes of 2012. Monthly Labor Review, 136, 50-53. Retrieved December 17, 2013, from EBSCO online database Education Research Complete.

Bennett, R., & Gray, J. (2007). Principal-centered negotiations. Leadership, 36, 22-24. Retrieved October 20, 2007, from EBSCO Online Database Academic Search Premier.

Department of Administration, State of Rhode Island. (2004). Cost/benefit analysis of a statewide teacher contract; report submitted to the General Assembly. Providence, Rhode Island: Department of Administration. Retrieved October 21, 2007, from http://budget.ri.gov.

Fuller, H., & Mitchell, G. (2006). A culture of complaint. Education Next, 6, 18-22.

Heitin, L., & Cavanagh, S. (2011). Legislatures approve tougher teacher policies. Education Week, 30, 26-36. Retrieved December 17, 2013, from EBSCO online database Education Research Complete.

Hess, F. (2005). Reform at the table. American School Board Journal, 192, 32-35. Retrieved October 16, 2007, from EBSCO Online Database Academic Search Premier. <

Hess, F., & West, M. (2006). A better bargain: Overhauling teacher collective bargaining for the 21st century. Retrieved October 22, 2007, from Harvard University, Program on Education Policy and Governance, http://ksg.harvard.edu.

Hewitt, P. (2007). Bargaining within the school culture. Leadership, 36, 26-30. Retrieved October 16, 2007, from EBSCO Online Database Academic Search Premier.

Honawar, V. (2007a). Missouri's high court rules for union rights. Education Week, 26, 17. Retrieved October 7, 2007, from EBSCO Online Database Academic Search Premier.

Honawar, V. (2007b). Online teacher-contract database launched. Education Week, 26, 5-13. Retrieved October 16, 2007, from EBSCO Online Database Academic Search Premier.

Imber, M., & van Gell, T. (2004). A teacher's guide to education law (3rd ed). Mahwah, NJ: Lawrence Erlbaum Associates.

Keller, B. (2006). Report: NCLB law hasn't superseded contracts. Education Week, 25, 8-9. Retrieved October 16, 2007, from EBSCO Online Database Academic Search Premier.

Kerchner, C., & Koppich, J. (2007). Negotiating what matters most: Collective bargaining and student achievement. American Journal of Education, 113, 349-366.

Lionitos, D. (1987). Collaborative bargaining in education. ERIC Digest Series, 20. Retrieved December 15, 2007, from http://ericdigests.org.

Lunenburg, F. C. (1996). Union-management relations and school reform. Clearing House, 70, 67. Retrieved October 16, 2007, from EBSCO Online Database Academic Search Premier.

Lunenburg, F. C. (2000). Collective bargaining in the public schools; issues, tactics, and new strategies. Huntsville, TX: Sam Houston State University. (ERIC Document Reproduction Service No. ED452587). Retrieved December 15, 2007, from EBSCO Online Education Research Database.

McComb, J. (2000 March). Statewide collective bargaining for teachers. Issue brief. Salem, OR: Legislative Policy, Research, and Committee Services. Retrieved October 21, 2007, from http://leg.state.or.us.

National Council for Teacher Quality. (n.d.). Teacher rules, roles and rights; search for districts. Retrieved October 18, 2007, from http://nctq.org.

National Council for Teacher Quality. (2013). State influence. Retrieved December 17, 2013, from, http://nctq.org.

New York State Labor Relations Act. (1937). Article 20. Retrieved October 21, 2007, from FindLaw, http://caselaw.lp.findlaw.com.

New York State Labor Relations Act. (1937). Article 20-A, Labor and Management Improper Practices Act. Retrieved October 21, 2007, from FindLaw, http://caselaw.lp.findlaw.com.

No child left behind. (2011, September 19). Education Week. Retrieved December 17, 2013, from, http://edweek.org.

Paige, M. (2013). Applying the "paradox" theory: A law and policy analysis of collective bargaining rights and teacher evaluation reform from selected states. Brigham Young University Education & Law Journal, 21-43. Retrieved December 17, 2013, from EBSCO online database Education Research Complete.

Shuit, D. (2003). At 60, Myers-Briggs is still sorting out and identifying people's types. Workforce Management, 82, 72-74. Retrieved October 21, 2007, from EBSCO Online Database Academic Search Premier.

Strike threat may prompt new regulations in Chicago. (2007). American School Board Journal, 194, 9. Retrieved October 21, 2007, from EBSCO Online Database Academic Search Premier.

Tucker, M. (2012). A different role for teachers unions?. Education Digest, 77, 4-10. Retrieved December 17, 2013, from EBSCO online database Education Research Complete.

U.S. Bureau of Labor Statistics. (2013, January 23). Union members-2012. Retrieved December 17, 2013, from United States Department of Labor, http://dol.gov.

U.S. Bureau of Labor Statistics. (2009). State right-to-work laws and constitutional amendments in effect as of January 1, 2009, with year of passage. Retrieved December 17, 2013, from Wage and Hour Division, United States Department of Labor, http://dol.gov.

Winkler, A. M., Scull, J., & Zeehandelaar, D. (2012, October). How strong are U.S. teacher unions? A state-by-state comparison. Washington, DC: Thomas B. Fordham Institute. Retrieved December 17, 2013, from http://edexcellence.net.

SUGGESTED READING

Casey, L. (2007). The quest for professional voice. American Educator, 31, 20-47.

Cohen-Vogel, L., & Osborne-Lampkin, L. (2007). Allocating quality: Collective bargaining agreements and administrative discretion over teacher assignment. Educational Administration Quarterly, 43, 433-461.

Hannaway, J., & Rotherham, A. (Eds.). (2006). Collective bargaining in education; Negotiating change in today's schools. Cambridge, MA: Harvard University Press.

Maciejewski, J. (2007). Broadening collective bargaining. District Administration, 43, 34-39. Retrieved October 16, 2007, from EBSCO Online Database Academic Search Premier.

Wise, A. E., & Usdan, M. D. (2013). The teaching profession at the crossroads. Educational Leadership, 71, 30-34. Retrieved December 17, 2013, from EBSCO online database Education Research Complete.

Wright, C., & Gundersen, D. E. (2004). Unions and teachers: Differences in the state of the nation. ALSB Journal of Employment and Labor Law, 10, 1-12.

MINORITY TEACHER SHORTAGES

The school-aged population and the demand for teachers have increased steadily over the last decade in the U.S., but minorities are disproportionately underrepresented in the teaching profession. Many college-educated minorities have not been encouraged to consider teaching as a career and have chosen to work in other, higher paying fields. Many who do join the profession do not want to work in low income schools where most minority students are. More individuals, including minorities, are qualifying as teachers through alternative teacher certification rather through the traditional teachers' colleges. Teacher testing has also been a roadblock for minorities, who have a failure rate higher than whites causing critics to charge that some tests are racially and/or culturally biased. Hispanics make up the largest minority group in the U.S., but they and African Americans, Asians, and Native Americans are all underrepresented in the teaching profession. There are many initiatives to increase the number of minority educators. Professional organizations and local, state and federal governments support recruitment campaigns and offer scholarships and mentoring strategies.

KEYWORDS: Alternative Teacher Certification; Brown v. Board of Education; Mentoring; Minority Serving Institutions (MSI); National Association for Multicultural Education (NAME): National Education Association (NEA); Reciprocal Journaling; Reflective Thought; Stereotype Threat

OVERVIEW

In 1954, the year of Brown v. Board of Education, many US schools were segregated and most black students had black teachers. In fact, at that time, most college-educated African Americans were teachers and approximately 82,000 of them were responsible for the education of two million black public school students. By 1964, when the Civil Rights Act was passed, there were 38,000 fewer black educators nationwide (Torres, 2004). Ironically, black teachers were lost in the desegregation struggle as integrated schools held fewer slots for them.

The Civil Rights legislation of the 1960s and subsequent affirmative action programs through the 1970s and 1980s did open a greater range of professions to minorities, who took advantage of new educational opportunities. Glass ceilings were broken as careers were launched in unprecedented numbers in all the professions.

Still, after decades, minorities are underrepresented in many professional fields, and no more visibly so than in the ranks of elementary and secondary public educators, where 80% of the teachers are white, even though 41% of the students in U.S. elementary and secondary public schools are of color.

A PLEA FOR MINORITY TEACHERS

In 1989, Bob Chase, then President of the NEA (National Education Association), directed a plea to the black community that espoused the need for more than token representation of minority teachers in America's schools and reported on efforts to recruit minorities into the profession in keeping with the tenet of affirmative action, righting wrongs of the past, but not granting preferential treatment. He said that competence must be the defining criterion for hiring any teacher, and that excellence and diversity are not mutually exclusive.

SOME IMPORTANT STATISTICS

In 1993-94 the school-aged population was 67 percent white with 33 percent minorities; in 2003, the white school-aged population shrank to 58.3 percent and minority students had swelled to 41.7 percent of the school-aged population (National Center for Education Statistics, 2007a).

Whites constituted 87% of the elementary and secondary school teacher population in 1993-94 and 83.3% in 2003-04. Although the black student population lost some share in the ten-year period from 16.6 percent to 16 percent, the percentage change of black teachers from 7.2 percent to 7.8 percent is marginal and still far from falling into the same proportion as the student percentage. Hispanics realized greater teacher gains from 4.2 percent (1993) to 6.2 percent (2003), but this is not at all in proportion to the sizable growth in student percentages of 12.1 percent to 18.6 percent, respectively (National Center for Education Statistics, 2007b).

According to a 2013 report by the National Center for Education Statistics, in 2011/12, there were a total 3,850,100 teachers for elementary and secondary schools. Of these, 82.7 percent were white; 7.5 percent were of Hispanic origin; 6.4 percent were African American, 1.8 percent were Asian American; 0.1 percent were Native Hawaiian/Pacific Islander American, 0.4 percent were American Indian/Alaskan Natives, and 1.0 percent were two or more races. The 2013 NCES report did not specify whether teachers were full-time, part-time, or both.

Job prospects look good today for all qualified teachers. With a teacher shortage in many regions, the ongoing retirements of Baby Boom generation teachers, and the projected continued growth of school-age populations through the century, the well-prepared teacher is an in-demand commodity. With such opportunity, why aren't there more minority teachers?

RECRUITMENT OR RACISM?

The NEA and other professional organizations, state departments of education and school districts have initiated recruitment campaigns and have offered scholarships and funding incentives to recruit minorities into the teaching fold, but have realized only modest success. Kitty Kelly Epstein (2005) asks in her scholarly study and social critique of the problem, if the reason is due to a problem of recruitment or a problem of racism. As with most social issues, there is no single factor why, and very few of the reasons are backed with research data.

PERCEPTIONS OF STATUS

June Gordon, Professor at University of California, Santa Cruz, claims she has some of the answers that emerged from extensive interviews with black professionals and teachers of color. Her overwhelming conclusion is that students of color are discouraged from entering teaching by their family and teachers. "Over one half of the teachers interviewed claimed that the negative image and low status of teachers were among the main reasons students of color are not entering the field of teaching" (Gordon, 1997). This is amplified the longer the community has contact with mainstream society (Gordon). In other words, the dominant (white) culture believes that teaching is a low status career, so the minority culture believes it all the more.

Furthermore, Gordon found irony in that the majority of her black teacher interviewees weren't more confident in their careers, even though most were seasoned professionals who were at the top

of their earning power and most owned their own homes. Consequently, most assumed that today's prospective student wouldn't be happy in a career of teaching because of opportunities in other professions, where they could make more money and have advancement opportunities.

Although most of her interviewee teachers thought that teachers of color could be more effective with like students, most admitted that they were at a loss what to do with low-income and troubled kids. Most saw themselves as middle class even though they might have grown up in poverty themselves. Surprisingly, reluctance to teach in low-income black schools was a socioeconomic decision (Gordon).

LACK OF TEACHER RETENTION

There are other societal factors at work against increasing the pool of minority teachers. It is clear that there is much more mobility in all of the professions and it is acknowledged that today's young people do and will change jobs more frequently than previous generations. A study, "Quality Counts 2000," reported that young teachers who leave the profession early are often the brightest. It found that the majority of those who stayed were those whose test scores fell into the lower test score percentile (Duarte, 2000). This is not encouraging if schools are going to meet today's accountability standards.

Torres, Santos, Peck, & Cortes (2004) of The Education Alliance at Brown University issued a comprehensive review of research relating to "Minority Teacher Recruitment, Development, and Retention" in 2004. The authors asked five research questions about minority decisions to enter teaching through the retention of employed minority teachers. They uncovered numerous studies and data that pointed to the advantages of a racially diverse teacher workforce and suggested further avenues of research. Besides the reasons for underrepresentation of minority teachers previous discussed, they added inadequate academic preparation, unsupportive working conditions, and lack of cultural and social support (Torres et al.).

A 2011 article by Richard M. Ingersoll and Henry May cited data from 2004-05, the year they said had the highest minority teacher attrition rate in the two-decade period they studied. According to the data, 47,600 minority teachers entered teaching in the 2003 and 2004 school year but about 56,000 minority teachers or 20 percent left teaching by the beginning of the following school year. Of these, about 30,000 teachers left to pursue another job or career or due to dissatisfaction with their teaching job.

TEACHING AS A SECOND CAREER

A more promising trend for the teaching profession is that is that second-career older workers are becoming educators. Some see it as an opportunity to leave a less fulfilling job and move into a career where they can make a difference. Maturity and life experience can have a tremendous impact on the ability to handle difficult teaching jobs and to guide young lives. Many of these career-changers are entering teaching through alternative teacher certification programs rather than working their way through the traditional college program educational curriculum.

DO MINORITY TEACHERS MAKE A DIFFERENCE?

Another obvious question that must be asked is if minority teachers are scarce, and minority individuals choose not to enter the professions, does it really matter? That is, does it really make a difference if a student is taught by someone of his or her own race? After all, in a diverse society with integrated schools, should this question even be asked? The widely accepted answer is that it indeed does make a difference, particularly to students in those schools where self-esteem and family income are low. Many believe that students growing up in low income minority communities, role models, particularly male, are sorely needed for students of color.

In an attempt to test these beliefs, Thomas Dee, Professor at Skidmore College and an affiliate of the National Bureau of Economic Research, conducted an extensive and elaborate analysis of grade school students, black and white, though four years of schools (K-3) in Tennessee. His investigation "effectively compared the performance of students assigned to teachers of the same race with the performance of students who were assigned to teachers of a different race but who were in the same grade and who entered the experiment in the same school and year" (Dee, 2004). He concluded that black students who had a black teacher for a year had statistically significant higher test scores both in math and reading; interestingly, the results were almost as significant for white students who had a white teacher.

Dee recognized that there are a variety of factors at work that would explain why race could matter.

He believes that teacher and student racial relationships in a classroom might also be affected by what is known as "stereotype threat." Researchers at Stanford University, Claude M. Steele and Joshua Aronson, tested students and found that if they believed a stereotype about their racial group, they would conform to the stereotype; i.e., when told that their verbal exam was a lab problem unrelated to ability black students performed as well as their white peers, but when told that it was a diagnostic of ability they under-performed (cited in Dee). Dee also recognized that there may be unintended biases in teachers' behaviors. Certain studies suggest that teachers may be more generous of time with those of like race.

STATISTICS: TEACHER SHORTAGES AMONG ALL US MINORITIES

There are also teacher shortages within nearly every non-white minority category, including Hispanic, American Indian/Alaskan, Asian American, and Pacific Islander.

The statistics clearly indicate that Hispanics constitute the fastest growing ethnic group in the country. Recruitment of Hispanics is complicated by the issue of language and more significantly, by the exponential growth in the populations. U.S. school districts and state departments of education, particularly in the border states, cannot keep up with the growth in the student population, let alone hope to find enough qualified teachers of the same ethnic heritage and who have bilingual language skills.

Other ethnic groups are much smaller, but have similar difficulty recruiting teachers. It has long been recognized that American Indian students who stay on their reservations and who are taught by local teachers are much more successful. The struggle to provide quality education to American Indian students has a long and difficult history that is well documented. The US Department of Education provides various initiatives to encourage American Indian teachers, including Indian Education Professional Development funds to support full state certification for Native American education students ("Indian Education," 2004).

Gordon focused one of her studies on Asian Americans. She quizzed young Asian Americans why they were reluctant to become educators in the United States when teaching careers were so positively perceived in their ancestral countries. They responded that they were encouraged to enter higher status and higher income fields, but she also found that they felt inadequate to teach, perceiving that teaching required near perfection, and that they would only feel comfortable within their own nationality zones, pointing out that Asian cultures—Chinese, Indian, Japanese and others—are not the same (cited in Bracey, 2001).

Recruiting Initiatives

There are impressive numbers of initiatives to increase diversity in the teaching ranks. One of the most comprehensive was a collaboration of major national education associations who met in a summit in 2004 and produced the report, "Assessment of Diversity in America's Teaching Force: A Call to Action." The post-No Child Left Behind Act (NCLB) conference recognized that diversity must be brought into the equation if quality standards are to be achieved. They specifically recommend increasing research on "culturally responsive teaching," eliminating obstacles to potential teachers of color, making resources equitable and directing resources to recruiting and preparing more teachers of color.

A highly publicized example of private funding is that offered by Tom Joyner, nationally syndicated radio host and celebrity whose foundation, in collaboration with the NEA, has provided over $55 million to certify minority teachers. Scholarships are provided through historically black colleges with the goal of encouraging minority education students to complete their certification and teach in a public school with large minority student populations (National Education Association, 2006).

Minority-serving institutions (MSIs), primarily located in the South, are the largest source of teachers of color. These schools grant nearly half of the degrees in education earned by African Americans and Latinos and 12 percent by American Indians. The US Department of Education has consistently targeted funds to MSIs to encourage professional diversity. So desperate to correct underrepresentation on their faculties, California school districts are known to recruit out-of-state at these colleges in an effort to draw newly minted, qualified teachers (Becker, 2002).

SUPPORTING TEACHER DIVERSITY

State education departments are responsible for meeting federal standards, setting state standards,

and licensing teachers to ensure high quality, but at the same time they are often the primary agents for increasing diversity within educator ranks. Most of the funding is not granted directly to students or teachers, but is channeled through the states' colleges and universities. A cross section of state funding initiatives include:

- Connecticut: Minority Teacher Incentive Grant—candidates must be nominated by college/university dean gives scholarships while in an education program and grants funds to pay off school loans while working as a teacher;
- Florida: Florida Fund for Minority Teachers—"provides scholarships to eligible students interested in pursuing teaching careers in Florida, assists prospective teachers with job placement and career development, and serves as an information resource for students, employers and educators."
- Illinois: Minority Teachers of Illinois (MTI) Scholarship Program—for minority students preparing to be preschool, elementary, or secondary teachers; $5,000 annual awards;
- New York: Teacher Opportunity Corp—offers competitive grants to supports teacher preparation programs and has as its primary goal to increase the participation rate of historically underrepresented and economically disadvantaged individuals in teaching."
- North Carolina: The Public School Forum—offers a state-legislated teaching fellows program that has as one of is stated goals to recruit African American and American Indian students to teaching. Promising high school graduates are identified and are given grants through their undergraduate education in exchange for promising to teach in the North Carolina schools. Recruits have been 20 percent minorities and 30 percent males.

STRATEGIES FOR DEVELOPING & RETAINING MINORITY TEACHERS

Torres et al. authors of the Brown University study, included "unsupportive working conditions" and "lack of cultural and social support groups" as additional reasons why minorities continue to be underrepresented in the schools (Torres). Recruiting minority teachers is one step, but developing and retaining them is another. Good school districts work to support mentoring, professional development and help teachers avoid burnout.

Antoinette Ellison and Michael Jazzar (2007) recommend that African American teachers be retained by also employing reflection and reciprocal journaling with mentoring. As experienced teachers retire or leave the profession, they take with them years of skills and knowledge that is lost. Mentoring is advocated as a very constructive way for one seasoned teacher to help a less experienced teacher improve instruction skills. They also advocate reflective thinking as a means for teachers to evaluate their actions and to not place blame on students or the school. They use thinking skills to make adjustments to classroom techniques to be more effective rather than making excuses or blaming others for their lack of success. The authors suggest reciprocal journaling, a fifteen-minute-a-day session of having new teachers record their thoughts, keeping in mind that a mentor will read the entries. The writing serves as a vehicle for further conversation and as a way for the new teachers to process what they have accomplished and where they are headed.

Viewpoints

TESTING

In August, 2007, more than half of all black and Hispanic applicants for teaching jobs in the state of Massachusetts failed the state licensing test, compared to less than 25 percent of the white applicants. This has jolted the Massachusetts state education system to launch a state task force to investigate the problem. A Cambridge lawyer is said to be planning a class action lawsuit against the state as minority applicants point to specific test questions that they claim are biased ("More than Half," 2007).

The scenario in Massachusetts was consistent with the trend around the country where African Americans and other minorities had lower pass rates on state teacher exams than white prospective teachers. There have also been a number of highly publicized cases where courts have heard arguments that the tests are culturally biased. As the Federal government demands accountability, state departments of education and many local school districts struggle to strike a balance between having to test and license educators in an equitable manner and raising the quality of education for all students.

There are some positive signs, however, that minority teachers are excelling. Increasing numbers

of African Americans, Hispanics, and American Indians, are earning certification from the National Board for Professional Teaching Standards. In 2007, only 55,000 teachers held this certification, an increasingly prestigious recognition that also results in financial bonuses for those who achieve it. In 2013, 106,000 teachers held the certification (National Board for Professional Teaching Standards, 2013). The organization also actively offers support programs for certified teachers to go out and mentor other promising teachers in high-need school districts (Keller, 2007).

TERMS & CONCEPTS

Alternative Teacher Certification: Refers to alternatives to the traditional, college-based teacher education programs for certifying teachers. All states require that teachers be licensed and have approved various routes to certification. There are currently nearly 500 alternative certification programs nationwide, most of which were developed since 2000. Critics argue that alternative teacher certification programs are not adequate, particularly since they don't include as much practical training as traditional routes, but some research indicates otherwise.

Brown v. Board of Education: Oliver L. Brown et. al. v. the Board of Education of Topeka (KS) et al. The 1954 landmark US Supreme Court decision that disallowed racial segregation of schools and other public facilities.

Mentoring: Mentoring is the process where experienced teachers are paired with inexperienced teachers with whom they share their knowledge and offer guidance.

Minority Serving Institutions (MSI): Colleges around the country that include historically black colleges and universities (HBCUs), Hispanic serving institutions (HSIs), and tribal colleges and universities (TCUs).

National Association for Multicultural Education (NAME): A national organization of education professionals who advocate for educational equality and social justice.

National Education Association (NEA): The largest union of teachers and educational professionals with 3.2 million members.

No Child Left Behind Act of 2001 (NCLB): Federal legislation enacted in 2001 that was due for reauthorization, an update, in 2007. As of 2013, the legislation remains as it was since its last update in 2002. A primary goal of the act is to close educational achievement gaps and to bring underperforming schools up to higher, acceptable standards. The legislation gives students more rights to transfer to better schools. Advocates point to success with improvements of standardized test scores and reforms in school districts; critics say that the act creates further inequities, particularly with testing, and does not back mandates with financial support for educational improvements.

Reciprocal Journaling: An individual records short daily journal entries, logging thoughts about successes and problems to be read later by a mentor for discussion.

Reflective Thought: Reflective thought or reflective inquiry skills are techniques used to make decisions based on evidence rather than on assumptions or perceptions.

Stereotype Threat: The fear that one will conform to the stereotype of the group with which one identifies; i.e., if a female student or African American student believes the stereotype that girls / African Americans are not good at math, she or he may not perform well on math tests, particularly for a male/white teacher.

Barbara Hornick-Lockard

BIBLIOGRAPHY

Becker, A. (n.d.). Districts look past state for talent. California: Center for the Future of Teaching and Learning. Retrieved September 15, 2007, from http://cftl.org.

Bracey, G. (2001). Why so few Asian American teachers? Phi Delta Kappan, 83, 14. Retrieved September 7, 2007, from EBSCO Online Database Academic Search Premier.

Clark, E., & Flores, B. (2002). Narrowing the pipeline for ethnic minority teachers: standards and high-stakes testing. Multicultural Perspectives, 4, 15-20. Retrieved September 7, 2007, from EBSCO Online Database Academic Search Premier.

Dee, Thomas S. (2004). The race connection: are teachers more effective with student who share their ethnicity? Education Next, 2. Hoover Institution. Retrieved September 8, 2007, from http://ww.hoover.org.

Duarte, A. (2000). Wanted: 2 million teachers, especially minorities. Education Digest, 66, 19. Retrieved September 7, 2007, from EBSCO Online Database Academic Search Premier.

Ellison, A. & Jazzar, M. (2007). Retaining African American teachers through mentoring, reflection, and reciprocal journaling. Connexions. Retrieved September 15, 2007, from http://cnx.org.

Epstein, K. (2005). The whitening of the American teaching force: a problem of recruitment or a problem of racism? Social Justice, 32, 89-102. Retrieved September 8, 2007, from EBSCO Online Database Academic Search Premier.

Gordon, J. (2002). The color of teaching revisited. Multicultural Perspectives, 4, 3-7. Retrieved September 7, 2007, from EBSCO Online Database Academic Search Premier.

Gordon, J. A. (1997). Teachers of color speak to issues of respect and image. Urban Review, 29, 41-66. Retrieved September 15, 2007, from EBSCO Online Database Education Research Complete.

Gursky, D. (2002) Recruiting minority teachers; programs aim to balance quality and diversity in preparing teachers. American Teacher. Retrieved September 10, 2007, from http://aft.org.

Haberman, M. (1989). More minority teachers. Phi Delta Kappan, 70, 771-776.

Holloway, J. (2002). Mentoring for diversity. Educational Leadership, 59, 88. Retrieved September 7, 2007, from EBSCO Online Database Academic Search Premier.

Honawar, V. (2007). Alternative-certification programs multiply. Education Week, 26, 16-16. Retrieved September 8, 2007, from EBSCO Online Database Academic Search Premier.

Indian Education Professional Development (2004). Education Grants Alert (Aspen Publishers Inc, 14, 3-4. Retrieved September 15, 2007, from EBSCO Online Database Education Research Complete.

Ingersoll, R. M., & May, H. (2011). The minority teacher shortage: Fact or fable? Phi Delta Kappan, 93, 62-65. Retrieved December 17, 2013, from EBSCO Online Database Education Resource Complete.

Keller, B. (2007). More minority teachers earn national certification. Education Week, 26, 14. Retrieved September 8, 2007, from EBSCO Online Database Academic Search Premier.

More than half of minority teacher applicants fail test. (2007, August 19). The Boston Globe. Retrieved September 7, 2007, from http://boston.com.

National Board for Professional Teaching Standards (2013). Nation's corps of accomplished teachers grows as global stakes rise for America's students. Retrieved December 17, 2013, from http://nbpts.org/newsroom.

National Center for Education Statistics. (2007). Context of elementary and secondary education, Tables 33-1a-33-1c. Washington, DC: Government Printing

Office. Retrieved September 13, 2007, from http:// nces.ed.gov.

National Center for Education Statistics. (2007). Participation in education, Table 5-1. Washington, DC: Government Printing Office. Retrieved September 13, 2007, from http://nces.ed.gov.

National Center for Education Statistics (2011). Table 94. Public elementary and secondary enrollment, student race/ethnicity, schools, school size, and pupil/ teacher ratios, by type of locale: 2008-09 and 2009-10. Retrieved on December 9, 2013, from http://nces.ed.gov.

National Center for Education Statistics (2013). Characteristics of Public and Private Elementary and Secondary School Teachers in the United States: Results from the 2011Ð12 Schools and Staffing Survey. Retrieved on December 9, 2013, from http://nces. ed.gov.

National Education Association. (2002-06). The Tom Joyner Foundation and the National Education Association are helping to make a difference; full teacher certification makes a difference for all children. Retrieved September 15, 2007, from http:// nea.org.

Shure, J. (2001). Minority teachers are few and far between. Techniques: Connecting Education & Careers, 76, 32. Retrieved September 7, 2007, from EBSCO Online Database Academic Search Premier.

Szecsi, T., & Spillman, C. (2012). Unheard voices of minority teacher candidates in a teacher education program. Multicultural Education, 19, 24-29. Retrieved December 17, 2013, from EBSCO Online Database Education Resource Complete.

Torres, J. A., Santos, J., Peck, N. L., & Cortes, L. (2004). Minority teacher recruitment, development and retention. Providence, RI: Education Alliance at Brown University, Northeast and Island Regional Educational Laboratory. Retrieved September 15, 2007, from http://alliance.brown.edu.

Villegas, A., Strom, K., & Lucas T. (2012). Closing the racial/ ethnic gap between students of color and their teachers: An elusive goal. Equity & Excellence in Education, 45, 283-301. Retrieved December 17, 2013, from EBSCO Online Database Education Resource Complete.

SUGGESTED READING

Brown, J., & Borman, K. (2005). Highly qualified minority teachers: do high-stakes teacher tests weed out those we need most? International Journal of Educational Policy, Research & Practice, 6, 105-137. Retrieved September 8, 2007, from EBSCO Online Database Education Research Complete.

Ford, D., & Grantham, T. (1997). The recruitment and retention of minority teachers in gifted education. Roeper Review, 19, 213. Retrieved September 7, 2007, from EBSCO Online Database Academic Search Premier.

Gay, G. (2004). The paradoxical aftermath of Brown. Multicultural Perspectives, 6, 12-17. Retrieved September 7, 2007, from EBSCO Online Database Academic Search Premier.

Gordon, J. A. (2000). The color of teaching. London, NY: Routledge, Falmer.

Haberman, H. (1999). Increasing the number of high-quality African American teachers in urban schools. Journal of Instructional Psychology, 26, 208. Retrieved September 7, 2007, from EBSCO Online Database Academic Search Premier.

Jacobs, J. (2006). Supervision for social justice: supporting critical reflection. Teacher Education Quarterly, 33, 23-39. Retrieved September 8, 2007, from EBSCO Online Database Education Research Complete.

Oguntoyinbo, L. (2013). System breakdown. Diverse: Issues in Higher Education, 30, 16-17. Retrieved December 17, 2013, from EBSCO Online Database Education Resource Complete.

Quiocho, A., & Rios, F. (2000). The power of their presence: minority group Teachers and Schooling. Review of Educational Research, 70, 485.

Schmitz, S. A., Nourse, S. W., & Ross, M. E. (2012). Increasing teacher diversity: Growing your own through partnerships. Education, 133, 181-187.

Simmons, C. (2002). Each one, teach many. Black Enterprise, 32, 48. Retrieved September 7, 2007, from EBSCO Online Database Academic Search Premier.

Steele, C. M. and Aronson, J. (1995). Stereotype threat and the intellectual test performance of African Americans. Journal of Personality and Social Psychology, 69, 797-811.

Villegas, A., & Lucas, T. (2004). Diversifying the Teacher Workforce: A Retrospective and Prospective Analysis. Yearbook of the National Society for the Study of Education, 103, 70-104.

Watras, J. (2006). Teacher tests, equal opportunity, and the foundations of education. Educational Studies, 39, 124-134. Retrieved September 8, 2007, from EBSCO Online Database Academic Search Premier.

U.S. EDUCATIONAL INDICATORS

Public education remains a central issue for American society. Federal, state, and local governments, charged with the responsibility of ensuring that public school students succeed in their coursework, have endeavored to establish benchmarks by which they may monitor student progress. These indicators focus on several areas: quality of student life, student backgrounds, teacher qualifications, and, of course, student performance. This paper takes an in-depth look at each of these indicators and how they are used to both paint an accurate illustration of the state of public schools and prompt change where needed.

KEYWORDS: Demographics; Educational Indicators; Education Reform; K-12; Standardized Testing

OVERVIEW

In the late eighteenth century, American public schools were a dreadful sight. Students only attended classes for a few weeks during the winter months, due to the cold. Their teachers were untrained and inexperienced, and the facilities were substandard at best. In Massachusetts, one man (who himself came from a childhood of poverty and school disrepair) took it upon himself to improve public schools. Horace Mann, the State Senate President, became exasperated with school conditions and resigned his post in order to head a new state Board of Education to address the issues affecting those institutions. Mann's efforts included extending the school year, providing adequate teacher training, supplying students with the proper books and working to renovate and improve school structures. In essence, Mann was establishing a series of educational indicators by which school improvements could transpire (PBS Roundtable, 2001).

Mann's crusading ways on behalf of the Massachusetts public school system served as an inspiration for other school systems to take similar steps. Since that early phase in the history of American public schools, Mann's work continues as a work in progress. There remain countless school buildings in states of disrepair, issues concerning adequately trained staff, classroom size and an overall desire to improve upon the way Americans educate their children using taxpayer dollars.

The twenty-first century is an era in which the most complex technologies in human history are central elements in virtually any of life's activities; a strong educational background is paramount for an individual's success. Modern society demands advanced training not only in these technologies, but in the most basic skills as well. Among these capabilities are writing, reading, analysis, and computation. Each of these basic proficiencies are developed and honed not just at a secondary school level, but at every level prior to and beyond the high school years.

Of course, one's education is not just useful for his or her own personal development. In fact, an educated population is essential to a local, regional, and national economy as well. A trained, well-schooled workforce is both a powerful attribute for existing employers and an enticing incentive for relocating companies. In short, an educated workforce in no small part contributes to the establishment of a competitive, successful economy.

It comes as no surprise, therefore, that political leaders consider education a top issue, one that is always salient and can never be overemphasized. In the hotly contested presidential election of 2000, at center stage was the fact that voters felt that the nation's educational system was treated with a sort of laissez-faire approach—that fundamentally, American public schools were sound and that any problems they experienced would eventually be corrected with minimal government intervention. Some observers believe that this attitude was a major factor in propelling George W. Bush into the White House during that crucial election, as his call for attention to failing public schools echoed the views of Horace Mann, whereas Democrats, who had enjoyed the presidency for two terms prior, seemed ineffectual at addressing the issues facing American schools (Winston, 2008).

Indeed, public education remains a central issue for American society. Federal, state, and local governments, charged with the responsibility of ensuring that public school students succeed in their coursework, have endeavored to establish benchmarks by which they may monitor student progress. These indicators focus on several areas: quality of student life, student backgrounds, teacher qualifications, and, of course, student performance. This paper takes an in-depth look at each of these indicators and how they are used to both paint an accurate illustration of the state of public schools and prompt change where needed.

QUALITY OF STUDENT LIFE

As was the case with Horace Mann in the eighteenth century, the first place leaders look when attempting to assess school performance is the institution itself. First, enduring stories from across the country of antiquated schools with asbestos in the walls, bacteria-laden ventilation systems, broken heat and air-conditioning systems, leaking roofs, and poor lighting stimulate loud calls to action not only by parents of enrolled students but from political leaders and others as well. Indeed, the physical state of public education institutions is just as important an indicator of a system's performance as the student bodies within their walls.

FACILITY CONDITIONS

In 2000, the General Accounting Office (GAO) released the results of a study that estimated that as much as $112 billion was needed to fully repair deteriorating public schools. This figure was twice as much as the GAO estimated was needed only five years prior. That impressive number was even called into question by the National Education Association, which more than doubled the GAO's estimate to $254 billion. Adding to this issue is the fact that district leaders, municipal and even state governments would likely never be able to raise and distribute the funds their school systems need to avoid posing health risks and otherwise dampening student performance (Agron, 2000).

CLASSROOM SIZE

The quality of student life as an important factor to take into consideration is by no means localized entirely to repairs to the building, either. How many students are in each classroom is also an important indicator for determining public school performance. In the last few years, studies of a variety of public school systems took a critical look at the effects of programs designed to reduce classroom size. Although the systems in question were very different in composition and geography, the results were very similar. Most of these analyses reported that reduced classroom size-oriented efforts led to greater parental involvement, helped reduce instances of misbehavior and violence and fostered a renewed pleasure in classroom learning among students, all of which lead to improved student performance (Myers, 2000).

FINANCIAL & POLITICAL IMPLICATIONS

The fact that the physical state of schools and the number of students in a classroom are considered critical indicators of a school system's overall performance gives rise to political focus on each of these issues. As mentioned earlier, federal government estimates reveal hundreds of billions of dollars would be needed to meet the needs of the multitude of deteriorating schools. While the figures themselves are subject to debate, there is no doubt that leaky pipes, poor ventilation and lighting, the presence of asbestos, and other problems are perceived to weigh heavily on the minds of those who track school performance, even if the means to solve the problems (namely costs) are elusive.

The same point can be raised on classroom size. Clearly, to address the concern of overcrowded classrooms, money must be spent to hire more teachers. The issue is indeed a salient one, and the policy response is clear: more teachers and classroom space is necessary to address a growing student population. However, while the solution is clear, the size of its cost is unanticipated and likely cannot be implemented without gobbling up budgets at the same time (Moore, 2006).

Without a doubt, the comfort a student feels while in school is an important factor in his or her academic development. It is no surprise that analysts consider the physical state of the building and classroom size as significant indicators for gauging the performance of a school system. Unfortunately, the daunting financial implications involved in correcting issues as they surface tend to result in the problem persisting.

STUDENT DEMOGRAPHICS

Along with the study of the physical conditions of the schools in question, another important indicator focuses on the personal characteristics of the students who attend those schools. Indeed, student demographics are a critical arena to analyze when assessing system performance, as these features can help policymakers and others assess how programs and curricula impact student development. They can also help those same groups follow money streams to ensure that budget appropriations are in fact cost-effective.

ACCEPTING DIVERSITY

Demographics are extensive and diverse in nature. This area includes ethnicity, race, gender, economic background, special needs or handicap, religion, and sexual orientation. Such information is used not to segregate students based on differences; rather, it is used to understand how each of these demographics react to uniform school policies and lesson plans. School systems whose student populations include large numbers of wealthy and poor children may find value in assessing this demographic to determine the price of books, meals, and other goods and services. Similarly, systems in urban areas with large numbers of Spanish-, Creole-, Vietnamese- or African-speaking students may want to determine the scope and expense of bilingual or English immersion programs based on demographic data. Even special education programs designed to assist those with behavioral conditions, physical handicaps, or developmental challenges rely on information that reflects the number of students in need of specific assistance in order to qualify for state and federal aid.

The point of using student demographics as an indicator of school performance is fairly straightforward. If administrations wish to ensure that each student is able to understand curricula, acquire strong marks, graduate during his or her senior year of high school, and, ultimately, become a contributing part of the economy, they must be willing to fully appreciate the diverse populations walking through school hallways.

For example, a recent study of urban schools focused on the transition of boys from middle school into high school. The goal of the study was to assess student performance as affected by ethnic and racial perceptions during these school years. The result of the study was that young people, particularly African American boys, who felt isolated due to what the authors called "ethnic incongruence" during their middle school years developed a sense of withdrawal of interest in continuing their education when they entered high school. In fact, they became concerned about their own academic performance when they left middle school and entered the far more complex and diverse world of high school (Benner & Graham, 2007).

DIVERSE CLASSROOMS

Student demographics may also help administrations appreciate the best possible format by which teachers may lead diverse classes. In many situations, a teacher who leads a class by him- or herself may prove effectual in delivering lessons to diverse classrooms. However, there may be conditions, such as those found in classrooms that include children with physical, developmental, or emotional handicaps, or even those in which English is not the primary language spoken, in which a teacher may need help. Team teaching, in these cases, may prove better at helping students by creating more opportunities for one-on-one or small group treatment (Carpenter, 2007).

Sensitivities toward notions of racial or ethnic profiling and/or discrimination remain on the minds of those who are witness to the use of social demographics as an indicator of educational performance. Nevertheless, there is little doubt that in many capacities, careful use of this key indicator may help policymakers better understand how budget dollars are best spent to ensure a positive response.

TEACHER QUALIFICATIONS

Another important element to assess in the analysis of a school system is one that likely generates the most controversy. Ideally, any teacher working in a given school system is fully conversant in subject matter and, overall, well-qualified to work with students. Arguably, instances to the contrary are few and far between. Of course, in the never-ending and often fiercely political environment of education reform, those who present the lessons and issue the grades are often viewed as potentially part of the problem when a problem exists.

In many states, the aptitude of teachers is just as important an indicator of educational performance as student scoring. In Arkansas, a program designed as an incentive to teachers to facilitate strong student performance, the Awarding Excellence in Achievement program, offers bonuses to teachers based on student gains on state examinations as well as in assessments by principals and their teaching peers ("State board sets performance-pay rules," 2007).

The notion of the educator (and, in fact, the other members of the faculty and school administration) as central to positive student performance is illustrative of his or her role as a bellwether for gauging that aptitude. A Harvard University study of school performance in high-poverty areas suggests the role of educators is critical to the improvement of test scores and grades in low-income students:

> *"Schools should be run by school principals who know how to recruit and support effective teachers and provide them with the tools to do this work. Schools should attract and support experienced, skilled teachers committed to working together over an extended period to continuously improve instruction. School staff should monitor the learning of every student, intervene at the first sign that a student is not making good progress toward mastering critical skills, and provide alternatives when conventional pedagogies are not effective"* (Murnane, 2007).

Education reform, one of the most pressing domestic issues in the United States today, is as complex as it is challenging. Although the issue of teacher qualifications is sensitive and highly politically charged, there can be no doubt that in addition to the role of parents, teachers and their peers play an important part as well. The skills and professional qualifications of teachers are therefore a useful area to assess when studying school performance.

STUDENT TESTING

The most potent response to issues with student performance has been in student testing. Like assessments of teacher qualification, the testing of students as an indicator of how school systems succeed (or fail) is a politically charged issue, although useful in many ways. Proponents of this long-used gauge assert that those who do not believe in testing in this manner are attempting to hide the shortcomings of the system. Former US Secretary of Education Rodney Paige summarizes this point: "Anyone who opposes annual testing is an apologist for a broken system of education that dismisses certain children and classes of children as unteachable" (Samuelsen, 2001).

CONTROVERSY OVER TESTING

Testing does have strong merits. Standardized assessments of students in mathematics, writing, and other basic skills have their place, particularly for educators and administrators who hope to better comprehend the capabilities of their students. Such tests may help reveal shortcomings in curricula, such as a lack of focus on algebra or grammar. Standardized testing, which has been in use in the United States for decades (on every level of the K–12 progression), has helped evaluate student familiarity with basic skills and subjects to ensure that when an individual moves to the higher grade, he or she has the tools necessary for success.

What makes student testing such a controversial issue is a perceived emphasis by state and federal agencies on test scores as the sole indicator of a student's academic capabilities. There is considerable opposition, particularly among teachers, to emphasizing the bulk of curricula on helping develop the capability not to master certain subject areas but rather to master them to the point of passing a standardized test. To some, it is best to leave assessment to the teachers themselves, as these are the individuals on whose shoulders student achievement falls. Others believe that preparing students for passing state and federal performance tests takes away from other forms of learning (Stiggins, 2007).

Still, even though there are issues to be resolved in the format and practice of standardized testing, there remains a viable use of this measure for assessing student performance in school systems. As is the case with quizzes, midterm exams, and finals, standardized test scores can provide strong evidence of the areas in which improvement can be made and, if employed properly, can even help students progress through each critical grade level in a way that is satisfactory for political leaders, educators, administrators, and parents.

CONCLUSIONS

Virtually every advanced society on the planet believes that the education of young people is the highest priority in terms of policymaking. After all, an educated individual contributes more to society in any form of employment, contributing to the economy instead of drawing from it, and perhaps even helping that society to forge a new path to the future.

It comes as no surprise, therefore, that political leaders in particular have taken a strong interest in ensuring that students be afforded every possible resource and that they derive the maximum benefit from those resources. Those who fail in school, they argue, become less of a contributor and less useful to the economy. If school systems show signs that they are not reaching students, leaders look for reasons for those shortcomings. In short, they look for a series of indicators that may suggest why systems are not performing in the manner society demands.

This paper has outlined a few of the key indicators used in the assessment US educational system. They center on a number of areas—quality of student life, social demographics, teacher qualifications, and, of course, the academic capabilities of the students themselves.

First, the conditions of the schools themselves provide an important series of clues about the state of a learning institution. If ventilation or lighting is poor, or there are environmental conditions that can influence a student's health and concentration, an accounting of this key indicator will likely provide an illustration of the issue at hand. Similarly, if classroom conditions are prohibitive to student growth (e.g., classes are overcrowded, thereby hindering one-on-one attention), academic development may also be placed at risk.

There is also considerable importance placed on demographics as a key indicator for educational assessment. As this paper has demonstrated, how students interact with diverse groups of varying ethnicity, race, creed, or orientation can affect development and, with relevant and tangible data available, serves as a vital tool for studying student performance.

Naturally, the study of trends in educational development and student performance cannot be discussed without also paying attention to the qualifications of those who work with these young people. While political posturing and confrontational rhetoric sometimes apply a somewhat negative connotation to this component of education, there can be little doubt that a qualified teacher who remains dedicated to the development of his or her students is an integral component of the educational system. Their qualifications as a member of a system's faculty are therefore an important indicator of systemic performance.

Finally, there remains a place in educational performance assessment for student testing. Like teacher qualifications, this indicator is not without controversy, particularly when the value of the test and the application of collected data are called into question. Testing can yield important clues, however, of the areas of study that are either strong or deficient. In use for over 50 years, and likely to continue being used for years to come, standardized tests represent a culmination of the work that goes into a public school education by the school system, the teachers, administrations, and, above all else, the students themselves.

TERMS & CONCEPTS

Demographics: Social groupings based on ethnicity, race, gender, economic status, and orientation.

Educational Indicators: Key elements in the assessment of performance in school systems.

Education Reform: Political and social movement to revise and update the public school system.

K–12: Basic grade-level track in US public school system - Kindergarten through 12th grade.

Standardized Testing: Examinations issued by federal, state, and local agencies to assess student performance in varying subject areas.

Michael P. Auerbach

BIBLIOGRAPHY

Agron, J. (2000). Building support. *American School and University, 72,* 12. Retrieved November 30, 2007, from EBSCO Online Database Education Research Complete.

Benner, A. D. (2007). Navigating the transition to multi-ethnic urban high schools. *Journal of Research on Adolescence, 17,* 207–220.

Carpenter, D., Crawford, L., & Walden, R. (2007). Testing the efficacy of team teaching. *Learning Environments Research, 10,* 53–65.

Harney, J. O. (2011). Trends & indicators 2011: College readiness. *New England Journal of Higher Education, 1.* Retrieved December 30, 2013, from EBSCO Online Database Education Research Complete.

Hightower, A. M. (2013). States show spotty progress across swath of education gauges. *Education Week, 32,* 42–44. Retrieved December 30, 2013, from EBSCO Online Database Education Research Complete.

Moore, D. (2006). The politics of education reform. *School Planning and Management, 45,* 10.

Murnane, R. J. (2007). Improving the education of children living in poverty. *Future of Children, 17,* 161–182. Retrieved December 1, 2007, from EBSCO Online Database Education Research Complete.

Myers, D. (2000). Studies say classroom size matters. *Las Vegas Business Press, 17.*

PBS Roundtable, Inc. (2001). School: The story of American public education. Retrieved November 28, 2007, from http://pbs.org.

Samuelsen, S. (2001, December). Student testing: The stakes are rising. *National Conference of State Legislatures Magazine.* Retrieved December 2, 2007, from http://ncsl.org.

State board sets performance-pay rules. (2007). *Education Daily, 40,* 6.

Stiggins, R. (2007). Five assessment myths and their consequences. *Education Week, 27,* 28–29. Retrieved December 3, 2007, from EBSCO Online Database Education Research Complete.

Supovitz, J., Foley, E., & Mishook, J. (2012). In search of leading indicators in education. *Education Policy Analysis Archives, 20,* 1–22. Retrieved December 30, 2013, from EBSCO Online Database Education Research Complete.

Winston, D. (2008). The right Republican strategy. *Education Next, 8.* Retrieved November 29, 2007, from http://hoover.org.

SUGGESTED READING

Bryant, A. L. (2007). Straight talk on graduation rates. *District Administration, 43,* 78. Retrieved December 4, 2007, from EBSCO Online Database Education Research Complete.

Carey, K. (2007). Truth without action: The myth of higher-education accountability. *Change, 39,* 24–29. Retrieved December 4, 2007, from EBSCO Online Database Education Research Complete.

Mahoney, J. (2006). How value-added assessment helps improve schools. *Edge: The Latest Information for the Education Practitioner, 1,* 3–18. Retrieved December 3, 2007, from EBSCO Online Database Education Research Complete.

Wolfe, F. (2013). U.S. highest in per-student spending in OECD nations. *Education Daily, 46,* 1–2. Retrieved December 30, 2013, from EBSCO Online Database Education Research Complete.

Zuckerman, M. (2003). A hard look at what works. *US News and World Report, 135,* 83–84. Retrieved December 3, 2007, from EBSCO Online Database Academic Search Premier.

BUSING

Although schools in a few areas of the country had been occasionally busing children to distant schools to resolve overcrowding problems on an as-needed basis, on May 17, 1954, the U.S. Supreme Court made segregation illegal. With their ruling in *Brown v. Board of Education Topeka,* the Court outlawed the practice of segregating students based on race, creed, color, or national origin in public elementary and secondary schools in the United States (Bryant, 1993). Busing was chosen as the method to desegregate schools. School bus transportation takes students from the city or neighborhood in which they live to suburbs, from the suburbs into the city, or even from their home county to another county.

KEYWORDS: Brown *v.* Board of Education; Busing; Civil Rights; Contained Unit Plan; De Facto Segregation; Desegregation; Magnet Schools; Plessy *v.* Ferguson; Public Schools; Segregation; Swann *v.* Charlotte-Mecklenburg Board of Education

OVERVIEW

Prior to 1954, public schools in the United States were almost completely segregated. Throughout the country and especially in the South, there were "black schools" and "white schools" with each school almost always comprised exclusively of students of one race. The prevailing wisdom at that time was generally based on interpretation of the 1896 *Plessy v. Ferguson* Supreme Court decision—that the races were "separate but equal." Indeed, since blacks and whites seemed to have the same types of educational facilities, adequate teachers, and a curriculum for each subject area and grade level, it was assumed both racial groups of young students were getting the same type of equal education (*Brown v. Board of Education,* 1954).

One reason for the separation of racial groups in the U.S. during this time was the work migration of clusters of unemployed minority people after the Second World War. Blacks who had been living in the rural south now moved west to fill jobs in the defense industry. This industry and others aggressively looked for workers and even provided transportation to California to get the men west quickly and efficiently. Shipyards were eager to get the additional employees, almost all of them black men, and the schools in those areas became segregated simply by the influx of minority families to a particular area (Green, 2006). At the same time, many school districts in cities in the North had long functioned with largely black or largely white student bodies. This pronounced segregation was not necessarily purposeful; but rather a result of economics, available housing, or other situations ("Controversy in Congress," 1974).

THE BROWN DECISION

Although schools in a few areas of the country had been occasionally busing children to distant schools to resolve overcrowding problems on an as-needed basis, on May 17, 1954, the U.S. Supreme Court made segregation illegal. With their ruling in *Brown v. Board of Education Topeka,* the Court outlawed the practice of segregating students based on race, creed, color, or national origin in public elementary and secondary schools in the United States (Bryant). In his *Brown* opinion, Chief Justice Earl Warren asserted that segregating school students is actually harmful to black children. Warren also implied that those classrooms that have only black students are inferior to those with a mix of races and that academics for both groups of students can improve when there is a mixture of races (cited in Richer, 1998).

Even when the actual building and other parts of a school may seem to be equal, Chief Justice Warren argued that the segregation of racial groups in the public schools of a state denies some groups the equal protection of the laws guaranteed by the Constitution. The "separate but equal" doctrine which came from the *Plessy v. Ferguson* case was deemed to not apply to the area of education (*Brown v. Board of Education*). With this landmark case began the desegregation of American public schools, mandated by law.

THE SOLUTION

Busing was chosen as the method to desegregate schools. School bus transportation takes students from the city or neighborhood in which they live to suburbs, from the suburbs into the city, or even from their home county to another county. Physically moving the students in this way is sometimes thought of as the best solution to even out the ratio of black and white children in certain schools and areas. The Supreme Court ordered this forced desegregation practice in cases in the late 1950s until the 1970s ("Controversy in Congress").

In the early 1950s, Greensburgh, New York bused white children from then-overcrowded white schools to a black school with just half its capacity filled. This move was more practical than anything else, and

wasn't strictly to desegregate the schools, although this ended up being one of its results (Ozmun, 1972).

To comply with the Supreme Court, Massachusetts passed the Racial Imbalance Act in 1965 which aimed to abolish racial inequity in schools in that state. A school is said to be racially disproportionate when over fifty percent of its students are minority students. The Racial Imbalance Act forced school committees to create a plan to balance those schools in their area for which there was not a fair balance of school students (Richer). In most cases, the solution to the desegregation of schools meant forced busing, and in 1968 the courts ruled that schools could not be "white" or "black," but simply "schools."

Some states were still formulating plans for how they would achieve desegregation in their schools. However, Supreme Court Justice William Brennan issued the decision that ordered all schools be integrated immediately. Other judges followed his lead and ordered mandatory forced busing for racial balance and equality (Richer). The word "desegregation" was often used instead of "forced busing" during this time, mainly because it tended to have more of a positive connotation (Brudnoy, 1975).

RESPONDING TO BUSING

The idea of busing generated plenty of opposition from the start. Following the *Brown* decision, the courts were determined to create a system where all racial groups were represented in equal proportions in the country's schools and classrooms (Green). The Supreme Court's busing decision began a culture shift throughout the country. Up to this time, all racially segregated schools were not necessarily viewed in a negative light. Teachers and administrators in the inner-city schools were often seen as the leaders in their communities and the public school building itself was often the center hub of the neighborhood. Desegregation seemed likely to threaten this delicate neighborhood balance and challenge the power of the black communities (Zimmerman, 2006).

In general, many white parents feared busing and they worried most about the type of school to which their child would be bused. Many affluent whites feared that their children would be forced to attend an inferior school with mediocre academic standards, substandard school buildings and equipment, possible racial problems, and an atmosphere less welcoming than their neighborhood school. Less-privileged white parents may not have had the same fears for their children and may have reasoned that the schools weren't that much different from their own (Kelley, 1974). Still, parents of both black and white students protested loudly, violence often ensued, and in many neighborhoods there was complete opposition to moving students from their schools as parents, teachers, administrators, and students attempted to stop the plan to bus children from their neighborhood schools and bus other children into those desks (Zimmerman).

THE CONTAINED UNIT

Soon after the *Brown* decision, St. Louis, Missouri began the process of desegregating its schools to comply with the Supreme Court mandate. In 1955, black children in some overcrowded schools in that city were bused to white schools that actually had empty classrooms and plenty of room. True integration wasn't realized though, as black students attended classes with the black students they were bused into the school with - a process known as the contained unit plan. This accommodated method of desegregation was in effect for a few years with increasing opposition from civil rights leaders who asserted that this type of busing wasn't really desegregation at all and wasn't what the Court had in mind (Ozmun).

In Illinois, the Supreme Court was asked to rule in a similar case, *McNeese v. Board of Education* (1963) where racial segregation within a school was taking place. Minority students there were bused to formerly all-white schools but were required to use school entrances and exits that were separate and apart from the white students. They could only attend classes that were expressly for the black students and these were held in a particular part of the school. The Supreme Court did not issue a ruling in the *McNeese* case because it was decided that the petitioners had not taken the case to the appropriate state-level court first, but mention of this case serves to show what was going on in the schools during that time, as cities and school districts fought desegregation even when appearing to comply (Schwartz, 1986).

SERIOUS EFFORTS

Baltimore began busing soon after the 1954 Brown decision. Even though as many as 2,000 students were transported to other schools to help relieve the overcrowding in the black-majority ones, the continuing flood of new students to Baltimore urban areas made it difficult to resolve the city's overcrowding problems. In addition, as black students were bused into white schools, many white students left for private schools. It wasn't until nine years later that the Baltimore school system was finally able to desegregate their schools. They eliminated geographical school boundaries and bought enough buses to transport about 5,000 students to racially desegregated schools. This solution worked to eliminate the all-white and all-black public schools in the Baltimore city area (Ozmun).

Other areas of the country, particularly the South, experienced their own difficulties as they attempted to abide by the Supreme Court's orders. School districts found that it was difficult to implement a way to alter decades of customs and realizing this predicament, the Supreme Court did not demand a timetable be followed. Instead, the Court permitted school systems to forge their own agenda for desegregation (Bryant). The result was that in the years after the 1954 Supreme Court ruling, scant progress was achieved to eradicate segregation in schools in those areas where there were two functioning school systems still sustained by state law (Ozmun).

DODGING THE COURT

North Carolina, for example, used semantics to ignore the ruling. Under North Carolina Judge John Parker's interpretation, to comply with the Supreme Court's *Brown* ruling, the government could not deny any child the right to attend a public school. He reasoned that since all North Carolina schools were open to all children, white or black, they were already in compliance with the law (Schwartz). Many people found Judge Parker's interpretation to be shrewd and asserted that he was actually taking advantage of some areas of the Supreme Court's *Brown* decision that may not have been addressed clearly. Since the Judge was aggressive in making his distinctions about what the Supreme Court actually ruled, his ideas were reluctantly accepted and adopted in school districts in that state for ten years without the state being confronted about it (Garrow, 2004). Schools there remained segregated.

At the same time in an attempt to dodge forced desegregation and busing in their area, many whites in Virginia hastily created private schools exclusively for white students. As white students exited the public schools there, they were instrumental in closing the entire public school system rather than be forced to integrate. Although most school districts reopened after a 1959 action on the part of Virginia's General Assembly, this was not true in one area of Virginia. In Prince Edward County, school district officials and the newly formed Prince Edward Foundation helped parents and white students by quickly creating private schools for whites only so they would not be educated with black children in formerly all-black public schools. The difference was that even after the 1959 judgment, Prince Edward County public schools did not reopen and the new schools, collectively called Prince Edward Academy, became a symbol of white protest to school integration. The black children of this county suffered badly. From 1959 until 1963, black students in Prince Edward County had no schools at all to attend until their own public schools could be opened again. During the five years the schools were being created and staffed anew, little or no provision was made to educate the black students. Although some churches taught groups of black children, and other children worked with relatives or by groups formed for this purpose, black students living in Prince Edward County missed years of schooling (Virginia Historical Society, 2004).

SWANN V. CHARLOTTE-MECKLENBURG BOARD OF EDUCATION (1971)

Although some cities believed busing to be against the law and were dragging their feet about complying, the Supreme Court disagreed. In 1971 a Supreme Court decision in the well-known case of *Swann v. Charlotte-Mecklenburg Board of Education* said that busing children from their own neighborhoods was one way to achieve school desegregation and it was, in fact, constitutional. In the ensuing twenty years following the *Swann* decision, many court-supervised school desegregation busing plans were implemented. With this decision, Chief Justice Warren Burger noted that in this and similar cases conflict continued to occur in those states with a policy of segregating students based on their race (Ozmun).

With this decision, the Supreme Court said that schools have a duty to get students ready for the world by having a ratio of white and minority students in their schools that mimicked that of the school district and the country as a whole. Those schools that

were unable to achieve that racial balance on their own would be subject to mandates decided by the court (Ozmun).

The *Swann* decision in North Carolina was reversed in 2001. A federal appeals court ruled that since Charlotte, North Carolina does not purposefully segregate their students by race, its busing program is not necessary ("30 years later," 2001).

By 1972, almost half of Americans polled said that they believed that segregation of black and white students in our country's schools was morally wrong, while at the same time three-quarters of the group sampled said that they opposed forced busing as a way to desegregate those schools (Ozmun). By 1976 in California, approximately 40,000 students in fourth through eighth grades were being bused, some for as long as two to four hours round-trip in an attempt to make schools more racially balanced (Mawdsley, 1987).

In the meantime, in Richmond, Virginia the District Court had ruled that schools within that city were inferior to those in the surrounding areas. Richmond city schools were in serious disrepair, had violence and drug problems, and despite busing mandates, were attended by a majority of black students. Judge Robert R. Merhige, Jr. began an avalanche of protest when he decided that the counties of Henrico and Chesterfield (both of which had housed independent school districts since 1871) be merged with the city of Richmond to create a single united education system (Ozmun, 1972). Judge Merhige's decision, although generally well received by the black community, caused the white community to threaten the judge's life and that of his family (White). His decision meant that many black students would be bused to previously all-white schools in the now-unified school districts. Merhige's order was eventually reversed when it was determined that the judge did not have the power to order that school districts be consolidated into one (Ozmun).

CONCLUSIONS

There are many reasons busing has not worked as well as many had originally hoped. Some minority students may have still been in classes with only other minority students and without any of the white students the desegregation plan was supposed to bring together. A mix of higher-achieving students in their peer group is the favored scheme for optimum student benefit (Harris, 2006).

Many people today can still vividly recall the busing headlines of the 1970s. As it turns out, busing as a solution to school racial imbalance failed and one of its main goals, improving the academic performance of students, was not reached (Jacoby, 1999). While plenty of progress has been made in many parts of our country's education system in the decades since the *Brown v Board of Education* Supreme Court decision was handed down, there are still thousands of schools within the United States that are segregated by race ("Report Explores Racial Consequences," 2007).

"While busing obviously has the ability to desegregate schools, the practice has continued to be extremely unpopular and has been largely abandoned in current times" (Harris). Many school systems around the country have attempted other types of desegregation approaches, with magnet schools being the most popular (Harris). Many school districts have used a combination of methods to keep student populations balanced and the skew of races diverse. Aside from magnet schools, these include building new schools where needed and taking advantage of technology by studying demographic information to adjust school plans, to include teacher hiring and grade assignments (Richer).

NEW RE-SEGREGATION

Through their research, the Civil Rights Project at Harvard University has found that schools in some areas are actually re-segregating now that legal barriers are no longer in place. It is feared that this practice will weaken the thriving magnet schools in many areas as additional schools which are segregated by income and/or race are created (The Civil Rights Project, 2006).

For example, in 2012 the school system in Boston, Massachusetts, still heavily relied on busing to transport 64 percent of students out of their neighborhoods to different schools; most of these students are minorities with white children accounting for 13 percent of public school students and Latino and black students accounting for 42 and 35 percent, respectively. This means that students who live on the same street often attend different schools-schools that are determined by a race-blind computerized algorithm. One of the many criticisms of the system, aside from its high cost, is that it also limits aspects of community in regard to things like public safety and citizen

relations. Overall in the United States during the 2009–2010 school year 80 percent of Latino students and 74 percent of black students attended schools where more than half of the students were minorities; over 40 percent of these students went to schools where minorities made up 90–100 percent of the population.

Our country's racial imbalance has not gone away and still shows up in our classrooms; the academic achievement disparity between white and minority students is still present. An evaluation of math and reading scores from students in about half the states came to the conclusion that at each grade level and in both math and reading, students enrolled in those schools in poorer economic areas improved less than those students in more economically advantaged areas (Ogletree, 2007). Harvard sociologist David J. Armor's research on the effect of busing in the cities of Boston, Massachusetts; Ann Arbor, Michigan; Riverside, California; New Haven, Connecticut; Hartford, Connecticut; and White Plains, New York concluded that there was no measurable improvement for students in important academic or social skills among those studied (Ozmun). "Contrary to popular belief, the average black child and average white child live in school districts that spend almost exactly the same per pupil" (Jacoby).

TERMS & CONCEPTS

Brown v. Board of Education Topeka: *Brown v. Board of Education Topeka* was a landmark 1954 Supreme Court decision. In the *Brown* case, black parents in a Topeka, Kansas neighborhood were unable to enroll their children in a neighborhood school since it was an all-white school. Instead they were told their children needed to attend an all-black school outside the neighborhood. The Supreme Court ruled this unconstitutional and the Court's decision is widely accepted at the beginning of busing and school desegregation.

Busing: Busing means transporting children to school outside their neighborhood, usually as a way of achieving racial balance.

Civil Rights: Civil rights are the legal protections of the rights of the people of a country. In the United States, these rights include the equal treatment of all citizens.

Contained Unit Plan: A contained unit plan is one in which all students arriving at a particular school on the same bus will attend classes together and without other students.

Desegregation: Desegregation means eliminating segregation -isolation by race.

Magnet School: A magnet school is a public school that offers a specialized curriculum.

Plessy v. Ferguson: *Plessy v. Ferguson* is a 1896 Supreme Court decision saying that separate facilities for blacks and whites were constitutional as long as they were equal. This decision was overturned in 1954 with the *Brown v. Board of Education* Supreme Court decision.

Segregation: Segregation is the practice of isolating people by race.

Susan Ludwig

BIBLIOGRAPHY

30 years later, busing ends in Charlotte. (2001). *Curriculum Review, 41*, 2. Retrieved September 28, 2007, from EBSCO Online Database Education Research Complete.

Brown v. Board of Education, 347 U.S. 483. (1954). Retrieved September 30, 2007, from the National Center for Public Policy Research http://nationalcenter.org.

Brudnoy, D. (1975). Busing for the sake of busing. *National Review, 27*, 282-299. Retrieved September 30, 2007, from EBSCO Online Database Education Research Complete.

Bryant, S. Q. (1973). *Why I do not like bussing.* New York: Vantage Press.

Controversy in Congress over school busing. (1974). *Congressional Digest, 53*, 99. Retrieved September 28, 2007, from EBSCO Online Database Education Research Complete.

Danns, D. (2011). Northern desegregation: A tale of two cities. *History Of Education Quarterly, 51*, 77–104. Retrieved December 5, 2013, from EBSCO Online Database Education Research Complete.

Garrow, D. (2004). Why *Brown* still matters. *The Nation, 278*, 45-50. Retrieved October 1, 2007, from The Nation, http://thenation.com.

Green, M. (2006). From classroom to courtroom. *American Educational History Journal, 33*, 27-33. Retrieved September 28, 2007, from EBSCO Online Database Education Research Complete.

Harris, D. (2006). *Lost learning, forgotten promises: A national analysis of school racial segregation, student achievement, and "school choice" plans.* Washington, D. C.: Center for American Progress. Retrieved September 30, 2007, from American Progress http://americanprogress.org.

Hock, J. (2013). Bulldozers, busing, and boycotts: Urban renewal and the integrationist project. *Journal Of Urban History, 39*, 433–453. Retrieved December 5, 2013, from EBSCO Online Database Education Research Complete.

Jacoby, T. (1999, July 21). Beyond busing. *Wall Street Journal.* Retrieved September 28, 2007, from the Manhattan Institute, http://manhattan-institute.org.

Kelley, J. (1974). The politics of school busing. *Public Opinion Quarterly, 38*, 23-39. Retrieved September 28, 2007, from EBSCO Online Database Education Research Complete.

Klarman, M. J. (2013). The supreme court of racial injustice. *Chronicle Of Higher Education, 59*, B11–B13. Retrieved December 5, 2013, from EBSCO Online Database Education Research Complete.

Mawdsley, R. (1987). *Legal Aspects of Pupil Transportation.* Topeka: National Organization on Legal Problems of Education.

Ogletree, Jr. C. (2007). The demise of Brown vs. Board of Education? Creating a blueprint to achieving racial justice in the 21st century. *Crisis, 114*, 1-7. Retrieved September 28, 2007, from EBSCO Online Database Education Research Complete.

Ozmun, H. (1972). *Busing: A moral issue.* Bloomington, Indiana: Phi Delta Kappa Educational Foundation.

Report explores racial consequences of segregation. (2007). *American School Board Journal, 194*, 7. Retrieved September 28, 2007, from EBSCO Online Database Education Research Complete.

Richer, M. (1998). Busing's Boston massacre. *Policy Review.* Retrieved September 28, 2007, from the Hoover Institution, http://hoover.org.

Schwartz, B. (1986). *Swann's Way.* New York: Oxford Press.

The Civil Rights Project. (2006). *Response to U. S. Supreme Court decision about voluntary school integration.* Retrieved October 2, 2007, from Civil Rights Project http://civil-rightsproject.ucla.edu.

Virginia Historical Society. (2004). The closing of Prince Edward County's schools. *The Civil Rights Movement in Virginia.* Retrieved September 30, 2007, from http://vahistorical.org.

White, A. (1972, January 24). A judge under siege. *Time.* Retrieved October 1, 2007, from Time Inc., http://time.com.

Zimmerman, L. M. (2006). Reflections on Brown. *American Educational History Journal, 3*89-96. Retrieved September 28, 2007, from EBSCO Online Database Education Research Complete.

SUGGESTED READING

Bifulco, R., Buerger, C., & Cobb, C. (2012). Intergroup relations in integrated schools: A glimpse inside interdistrict magnet schools. *Education Policy Analysis Archives, 20*, 1–27. Retrieved December 5, 2013, from EBSCO Online Database Education Research Complete.

Dimond, P. R. (2005). *Beyond busing: Reflections on urban segregation, the courts, and equal opportunity.* Ann Arbor: University of Michigan Press.

Eaton, S. (2001). *The other Boston busing story: What's won and lost across the boundary line.* New Haven: Yale University Press.

Formisano, R. (2003). *Boston against busing: Race, class, and ethnicity in the 1960s and 1970s.* Chapel Hill: University of North Carolina Press.

Gaillard, F. (2006). *The dream long deferred: The landmark struggle for desegregation in Charlotte, North Carolina.* Chapel Hill: University of North Carolina Press

Rubin, L. (1973). *Busing and backlash: White against White in an urban school district.* Berkeley: University of California Press.

Sugrue, T. J. (2012). Northern lights: The black freedom struggle outside the south. *OAH Magazine Of History, 26,* 9–15. Retrieved December 5, 2013, from EBSCO Online Database Education Research Complete.

OVERCROWDING IN SCHOOLS

Overcrowding occurs when a school facility enrolls more students than it was designed to accommodate. Most schools identified as overcrowded are in areas where the school-age populations are growing fast, particularly in California, Florida, Texas, and Las Vegas, Nevada. Overcrowded schools are also a chronic issue in our largest urban areas—New York, Chicago, and Los Angeles—as immigrant populations continue to grow and more public education options are made available. Charter schools and educational accountability dictated by the No Child Left Behind Act allow families to transfer students from inadequate schools to those with more successful educational programs causing imbalances within school districts. Some claim that school overcrowding would not be a serious issue if immigration were restricted in addition to a crackdown on illegal aliens. The long-term solution to overcrowding is to build new facilities and upgrade old ones. Taxpayers funded a construction boom that reportedly improved the situation around the country and proposed legislation at the federal level could help, but overcrowded schools may never fully be eliminated in a mobile society.

KEYWORDS: Charter Schools; Class Size; Density; Critically Overcrowded School Program (COS); Overcrowded/Crowded/Overenrolled; Qualifying Zone Academy Bond (QZAB); Teacher-Student Ratio (TSR)

OVERVIEW

Overcrowding in public schools has been a challenge throughout the history of American education as school districts have had to adjust to meet the needs of growing or shifting demographics. A 1963 *Education Digest* article, written when the peak of the Baby Boom generation was moving through elementary school, reported that there was a shortage of 121,200 classrooms in the United States with half of those needing to be replaced and the other half to be built to relieve overcrowding ("Classroom Shortage," 1963). The issue resurfaced in the late 1990s and has continued since then, as the school-age population has bubbled once again and high-growth areas of the country have struggled to meet the demands.

Overcrowding in schools is a significant problem in areas of the western and southern United States, which continue to experience rapid population growth with an influx of immigrant populations and from mobile Americans seeking jobs and warmer climates. The stress of overcrowded schools has been most disproportionate in our most populous state, California, which has tackled the problem with expansive initiatives, but many other states including Florida, North Carolina, and Texas are also struggling to cope. Las Vegas, Nevada, one of the fastest growing cities in the country, on average, opened a new school each month between 1994 and 2003 to deal with a fifty percent increase in the school-age population (Zehr, 2006).

Major urban school districts throughout the country are also experiencing school-aged population growth. New York City, always a melting pot, has experienced a boom in its school-age minority and immigrant populations, but new educational options such as charter schools and the legislated accountability of the No Child Left Behind Act, Race to the Top, and Common Core State Standards have required juggling acts of school administrators as parents move their children from poorly performing schools to those with successful track records or more desirable programs.

For example, the A. Phillip Randolph Campus High School in Harlem, a model amidst failing schools, experienced major overcrowding at the start of the 2004–5 school year as many new students enrolled to take advantage of its success (Watson, 2004). Most other major cities, including Los Angeles, Chicago, Atlanta, and Houston, can point to similar situations as they have struggled to meet the consequences of higher standards.

CROWDING, OVERCROWDING & OVERENROLLED

When does a crowded school become an over-crowded one? Is there a difference? Probably not. Many would argue that any number of students that exceed the planned capacity of a classroom or a school building impact the quality of instruction and learning because of the stresses that it places on access to teachers and services, not to mention additional wear and tear on the facilities.

The National Center for Education Statistics (NCES) at the U.S. Department of Education conducted surveys of public school principals in 1999 and 2005 that quantified the extent of the problem nationally. Overenrolled, synonymous with crowded and overcrowded, is the term used in the study to define what occurs when the number of students enrolled in a school facility is larger than the number of students it is designed to accommodate, statistically defined as more than 5 percent of the capacity of a school building (National Center, 2000; 2007).

The good news is that data from the second survey from fall 2005 indicated that progress was made over the five-year period in addressing over enrollment at many schools. Principals in 1999 reported that 14% of their schools were overcrowded by 6–25% of capacity; the 2005 figures are improved with 10% overcrowded by 6–25%. However, 8% of the schools were overcrowded by more than 25%, unchanged over the five-year period. Another plus was that 40% of the principals in the 2005 survey indicated that they "anticipated that the overcrowding would be substantially reduced or eliminated within the next 3 years" (National Center, 2005).

A SAMPLING OF SOLUTIONS

Although the data indicated some improvement, overcrowding is a real, day-to-day crisis in a significant number of school districts and the expedient overrides the long-term solutions. Most of the decisions on dealing with overcrowding are not dictated by national or state laws or standards but are decided at the local level. School boards and their administrators, down to principals and teachers, must deal with the fallout of over enrollment when they encounter it—often unexpectedly on the first day of class. When there are no seats for some students, principals look to what free space they have. Cafeterias, libraries, gymnasiums, and closets and other common spaces are pressed into service.

Budget-pressed school officials, caught in the push and pull of local politics, are often forced to find ways to pack more students into inadequate buildings. In New York, the teachers' union and parents claimed that the A. Philip Randolph Campus High School was overenrolled when it had 1,900 students, but school officials asserted that it could accommodate 100 more. The well-respected principal, with his track record of success, was confident that all would be well (Watson).

Although officials in some school districts squeeze pupils into crowded classrooms, the state of Florida has a found a way to penalize school districts that do so. Palm Beach County school district faced fines for over enrollment in four of its schools in violation of the state's class-reduction law, which capped class sizes scaled to grade levels ("Palm School," 2006).

The Florida class size law was approved by voters in 2002. Caps for grades were: K to 3, no more than 18 students per teacher; grades 4 to 8, cap of 22 students per teacher; grades 9 to 12, cap of 25 per teacher. It was reported that although the enrollment did not increase overall in the fall of 2006 in the Palm Beach County schools, "some faced a space crunch because campuses need more classrooms to comply with the law" ("Palm School").

Other creative short-term solutions that are used to diminish overcrowding are:
- Staggered scheduling;
- More lunch periods during a day;
- Different start times during the school day;
- Variable start dates during the school year.

Online learning (also called distance learning) has also been considered in a number of districts. None of these, however, get to the heart of the problem.

The most popular interim solution to providing classroom space is to bring in portable buildings. Mobile buildings can provide more than adequate instructional space and are frequently used on a permanent basis by school districts to house special functions or programs. They are air-conditioned, which is not the case for many school buildings in northern climates. The 2005 NCES survey reported that 78% of those principals with overcrowded schools had used temporary portable classrooms, 44% had increased class sizes, and some (5%) had to resort to using off-site instructional facilities.

Long-Term Solutions

Regardless of whether a school must be expanded or remodeled or constructed, the long-term solution to overcrowding takes time. Planning and funding of new facilities often gets bogged down in local politics and issues can be debated for years. Money is always an issue as construction is costly and local taxpayers generally must pay all or part of the bill, usually by issuing bonds or raising taxes, and often with little help from state coffers.

During the late 1990s, a prosperous economic time, voters approved many construction bonds in districts across the country. They did this in response to hearing a decade of public complaints from many quarters about the poor condition of many American schools. The criticism was backed by a 1995 study for Congress by the General Accounting Office in 1995 that said that $112 billion was needed nationally to bring schools up to code.

Even though the national economy slumped in the early 2000s, the approved funds were still there for a construction boom, which carried into the decade with record expenditures on construction and renovation projects. Joetta Sack reported in an *Education Week* article that "... beginning in 2002 and for the first time construction of new schools sharply outpaced renovations or additions to existing facility, reversing a long standing trend" (Sack, 2004).

Although the country-wide investment in renovation and new construction of schools has shown signs of relieving overcrowding (with the exception of periods of economic stress such as the Great Recession of 2007–9), it is argued that progress is slow in low-income and minority school districts where overcrowding is most severe.

BEST released a study in 2006 that analyzed the disparities and advocates for the federal government and states to provide aid to poorer schools and school districts. The report asserted that over $600 billion was spent on school construction between 1995 and 2005, an impressive figure, but also stated that "the least affluent school districts made the lowest investment ($4,800 per student), while the most affluent districts made the highest investment ($9,361 per student)" (Filardo, Vincent, Sung, & Stein, 2006).

Population Growth

The bubble in the school-age population that began in the late 1990s has been attributed in part to what is termed the "Baby Boom echo," which refers to the children who entered school through the first decade in this century. They are "... direct descendants of the Baby-Boom Echo—the expanding birth rate begun in 1977 when millions of young adults born between 1948 and 1975 began to have children themselves..." (U.S. Department of Education, 1999).

Census projections indicate that the school-age population will grow steadily to mid-century and reflect a declining percentage share of white student populations, an unchanging percentage of African Americans, and a strikingly disproportionate percentage increase in Hispanic/Latino students.

Even more striking is an analysis of the immigrant school-age populations. The Center for Immigration Studies' data show that "... by itself Mexican immigration accounted for more than a third of the national increase in the size of the school-age population since the early 1980s" and a quarter of the schoolchildren in California have Mexican immigrant mothers. Children of immigrant mothers from all countries account for 43 percent of all of California's school-age population (Center for Immigrant Studies, 2001).

Although the birth rate of US citizens has been in decline, the school-age population has swelled with immigrant children. It has also been pointed out that Hispanic families have on average more children than white families (CIS, 2001).

Federal, State & Local Initiatives

Funding for schools from federal sources is rarely granted directly to school districts and legislation specifically to alleviate overcrowding needs has been slow to materialize. However, as part of the Federal Tax Relief Act of 1997, the federal government began offering some indirect support for repairs and renovation (not new construction) through the tax code and the Qualified Zone Academy Bond (QZAB) program. The program helps qualifying districts (generally low income) cover the interest on construction bonds. QZAB has saved local taxpayers billions.

In 2002, the California legislature approved the Critically Over-crowded Schools (COS) facility program, which made it easier for overenrolled schools to speed up the process to receive funding for construction. The program was backed with the allocation of billions of dollars of additional state funds over subsequent years. Other programs provide funding for construction of new classrooms to reduce school site pupil density and to replace portable classrooms with permanent construction (California Department of Education, 2006; 2007).

Although the bill need not pass through Congress, Representative Dennis Kucinich (D-Ohio) introduced a measure in in August 2007 to "fund capital projects of state and local governments," which included plans for an allocation of billions for school infrastructure (U.S. Fed News, 2007).

New school construction also boomed in Los Angeles with local support and the help of state funding. The Los Angeles school district opened 13 new schools in 2006 and 150 new schools were anticipated by 2012 ("L.A. Continues," 2007).

In 2014, New York governor Andrew Cuomo signed a bill into law that requires the School Construction Authority (SCA) to use population data in conjunction with five-year educational facilities capital plans when determining new school construction, including additions, across the state.

In the summer of 2014 Congressman Jared Huffman (D-California) proposed the Investing for Tomorrow's Schools Act of 2014 to improve financing for school construction and repair, among other school-related upgrades. The bill calls for schools to utilized green construction, and the bill is supported by several national and state organizations, including the American Federation of teachers (AFT), the National Education Association (NEA), and Rebuild America's Schools.

Additionally, by 2015, several schools had begun to transition to year-round schooling as a more cost-effective means of dealing with the issue of overcrowding. According to the National Center for Education Statistics, the number of public year-round schools had increased by 26 percent from the 2006–7 school year to the 2011–12 school year. Proponents of this method argue that multitrack systems implemented in year-round schooling allows the school to stagger vacations and provide education for a larger amount of students without having to increase the physical capacity of the building (Will, 2014).

Many other states have been addressing overcrowding with planning and significant allocations of construction funding. For example:

- The North Carolina legislature was presented with a comprehensive study on construction funding in early 2007. The report specified that local school districts would require nearly $10 billion for new facilities and repairs and proposed issuance of bonds and increases in sales taxes upon voter approval (North Carolina House, 2007);
- New Mexico Governor Bill Richardson made education a priority. His state provided $90 billion during 2007 for school construction and the citizens of Albuquerque agreed to a tax increase to pay for the city's new schools (Zehr);
- In 1997, Ohio formed the Ohio School Facilities Commission with the charge to help "school districts fund, plan, design, and build or renovate schools." The agency has fulfilled a 12-year plan, "Rebuilding Ohio's Schools," for completion in 2012. In August 2007, the commission targeted a new category as part of their building replacement funding program—"overcrowded" schools (Ohio School Facilities Commission, 2007).

VIEWPOINTS

Since the late 1990s, there have been many positive signs of improvement in the condition of overcrowded schools, with much new construction. Taxpayers have been forthcoming in approving funding, often including self-imposed tax increases (except for periods of recession), while state legislatures have often been creative in offering support, sometimes focused on the neediest districts. There are even hopes that Congress will include schools in the push to revitalize the American infrastructure.

There are those who argue, however, that all of this would be unnecessary and overcrowding would not exist if the country were to restrict immigration and crack down on illegal immigrants. Billions would not have to be laid out by taxpayers to support new or non-citizens, critics say. The numbers do confirm the huge stress that immigrants, particularly Mexicans, have placed on the system.

The *National Review* argued that the there is no shortage of teachers and classrooms, but there is

"… a 'longage' of immigrant students, and students who are the children of immigrants. It cited the statistic that births in California increased by 204,000 between 1970 and 1994, but the births to native-born American women fell by 9,000 ("Another Schools Crisis," 1996). In the same article, then New York mayor Rudolph Giuliani was quoted as saying that it would be wrong to "blame" immigrations and to do so would "… feed a national agenda which says that immigrant children should be thrown out of school" ("Another Schools Crisis").

TERMS & CONCEPTS

Charter Schools: Publicly funded schools that are freed of some of some restrictions of other public schools in exchange for other forms of accountability. Charter schools are intended to provide educational alternatives. In New York City there is competition and overcrowding in some successful charter schools as families flee underperforming schools.

Class Size: Smaller class size promotes a better learning environment, a belief that is increasingly supported with research findings. Caps on class size are left to local school districts and in the case of Florida, voter approved.

Class Density: The physical space allotted per student and teacher in a classroom.

Critically Overcrowded School Program (COS): A major initiative in California to ease the process for getting construction and remodeling funds to beleaguered, overcrowded school districts with overcrowded schools.

Overcrowded/Crowded/Overenrolled: Synonyms for the same problem—with more students than a classroom or facility were designed to accommodate.

Qualifying Zone Academy Bond (QZAB): Federal grants to qualifying school districts that relieve the district of paying interest on bonds used to pay for school expansions and renovations.

Teacher-Student Ratio (TSR): Also called pupil-teacher ratio; one way to identify an overcrowded school. There is no national standard. Acceptable teacher student ratios may vary depending on student needs within a classroom (special needs, second language, etc.) or grade level (lower grades—higher ratio).

Barbara Hornick-Lockard

BIBLIOGRAPHY

Agron, J. (2007). Federal funding redux. *American School and University.* Retrieved September 5, 2007, from http://asumag.com.

Another schools crisis. (1996). *National Review, 48,* 14–16. Retrieved August 31, 2007, from EBSCO Online Database Academic Search Premier.

Classroom shortage. (1963). *Education Digest, 28,* 60.

Construction spending at record highs, but disparities remain. (2006). *American School Board Journal, 193,* 6–7. Retrieved August 31, 2007, from EBSCO Online Database Academic Search Premier.

Dessoff, A. (2006). NCLB'S purity. *District Administration, 42,* 43–46. Retrieved September 6, 2007, from EBSCO Online Database Academic Search Premier.

Fan, F. A. (2012). Class size: Effects on students' academic achievements and some remedial measures. *Research in Education, 87,* 95–98. Retrieved December 19, 2013, from EBSCO Online Database Education Research Complete.

Filardo, M., Vincent, J., Sung, P., & Stein, T. (2006). Growth and disparity: a decade of U.S. public school construction. Retrieved September 5, 2007, from Building Educational Success Together, http://edfacilities.org.

Gardner, L., & Blumenstyk, G. (2012). For golden state's public colleges, no silver bullet. *Chronicle of Higher Education, 58,* 40. Retrieved November 15, 2014, from EBSCO Online Database Education Research Complete.

L.A. continues school expansion. (2007). *School Construction News, 10,* 10.

Lighthall, C. (2012). Easing overcrowded high schools with limited capital funds. *Educational Facility Planner, 46,* 35–38. Retrieved November 15, 2014, from EBSCO Online Database Education Research Complete.

National Center for Education Statistics. Institute of Education Sciences. (2007). *Public school principals report on their school facilities: fall 2005; statistical analysis report.* (NCES 2007-007). Washington, D.C: US Government Printing Office. Retrieved August 31, 2007, from http://nces.ed.gov.

National Center for Education Statistics. Office of Educational Research and Improvement. (2000, June). *Condition of America's public school facilities: 1999. (NCES 22000032).* Washington, DC: US Government Printing Office. Retrieved August 31, 2007, from http://nces.ed.gov.

North Carolina House Select Committee on Public School Construction Funding. (2007). *Report to the 2007 General Assembly of North Carolina. Raleigh, North Carolina.* Retrieved September 5, 2007, from http://ncga.state.nc.us.

Ohio School Facilities Commission. Retrieved September 5, 2007, from http://osfc.state.oh.us.

Overcrowded schools. (2007). *California Department of Education.* Retrieved September 5, 2007 from http://cde.ca.gov.

Palm School District to challenge financial penalty for overcrowding. (2006, November 16). *South Florida Sun-Sentinel.*

Qualified Zone Academy Bond Program (QZAB). Retrieved September 5, 2007, from http://qzab.org.

Ross, R. (2002). School choice where none exists. *Education Week, 22*, 37.

Sack, J. L. (2004). School construction defies fiscal doldrums. *Education Week, 23*, 1. Retrieved August 31, 2007, from EBSCO Online Database Academic Search Premier.

Samuels, C. A. (2012). Study: L.A. building boom led to gains for young students. *Education Week, 32*, 5. Retrieved December 19, 2013, from EBSCO Online Database Education Research Complete.

School-age population. (2001). *Center for Immigrant Studies.* Retrieved September 5, 2007, from http://cis.org.

SFP: Critically overcrowded school facilities program. (2006). *California Department of General Services.* Retrieved September 5, 2007, from http://opsc.dgs.ca.gov.

US General Accounting Office. (1995). *School facilities; Condition of America's schools. Report to Congressional requestors.* Washington, DC: Government Printing Office. Retrieved September 5, 2007, from http://gao.gov.

US Government Printing Office. (2007). *H. R. 3400. A bill to fund capital projects of state and local government, and other purposes.* Washington, DC: Government Printing Office. Retrieved September 5, 2007, from http://frwebgate.access.gpo.gov.

Watson, J. (2004). Where shall they go? *New York Amsterdam News, 95*, 1–32. Retrieved August 31, 2007, from EBSCO Online Database Academic Search Premier.

Weissbourd, R., & Dodge, T. (2012). Senseless extravagance, shocking gaps. *Educational Leadership, 69*, 74–78. Retrieved December 19, 2013, from EBSCO Online Database Education Research Complete.

West, S. S. (2016). Overcrowding in K-12 STEM classrooms and labs. *Technology & Engineering Teacher, 76*(4), 38–39. Retrieved December 19, 2016, from EBSCO Online Database Education Source.

Will, M. (2014). Popularity grows anew for year-round schools. *Education Week, 34*(7), 6. Retrieved January 6, 2016, from EBSCO Online Database Education Research Complete.

Zehr, M. (2006). Boom or bust? *Teacher Magazine, 17*, 22–23. Retrieved August 31, 2007, from EBSCO Online Database Education Research Complete.

Zehr, M. (2007, January 24). New Mexico governor pushing a wide array of ideas for education. *Education Week, 26*, 28. Retrieved August 31, 2007, from EBSCO Online Database Academic Search Premier.

SUGGESTED READING

Dessoff, A. (2011). Is year-round schooling on track?. *District Administration, 47*, 34–45. Retrieved December 19, 2013, from EBSCO Online Database Education Research Complete.

The end of the real world. (2012). *TES: Times Educational Supplement, (4977)*, 49. Retrieved November 15, 2014, from EBSCO Online Database Education Research Complete.

Focusing on transportation—For school staff. (2015). *School Business Affairs, 81*(6), 34. Retrieved January 6, 2016, from EBSCO Online Database Education Research Complete.

Herzenhorn, D., & Gootman, E. (2005, February 15). Gates fund prods city on big schools. *New York Times,* pp. B1–B6.

Long, C. D. There Is a There There. *Planning for Higher Education, 44*(3), 61–85. Retrieved December 19, 2016, from EBSCO Online Database Education Source.

Qiu, M., Hewitt, J., & Brett, C. (2012). Online class size, note reading, note writing and collaborative discourse. *International Journal of Computer-Supported Collaborative Learning, 7*, 423–442. Retrieved December 19, 2013, from EBSCO Online Database Education Research Complete.

Stellitano, C. (2004). Construction in the fast lane. *School Planning & Management, 43*, 31–38.

Stevenson, K. (2001). School physical environment and structure; their relationship to student outcomes. *School Business Affairs, 67*, 40–42, 44.

Tanner, C. K. (2000 Dec). The classroom; size versus density. *School Business Affairs, 66*, 21–23.

Viadero, D. (2004, June 16). Personal touches. *Education Week, 23*, 39-41. Retrieved August 31, 2007, from EBSCO Online Database Academic Search Premier.

US Department of Education. (2000). *Growing pains: the challenge of overcrowded schools is here to stay; a back to school special report on the baby boom echo.* Washington, DC: US Government Printing Office. Retrieved September 4, 2007, from http://ed.gov.

Wadsworth, D., & Remaley, M. H. (2007). What families want. *Educational Leadership, 64*, 23–27. Retrieved August 31, 2007, from EBSCO Online Database Academic Search Premier.

ENGLISH-ONLY MOVEMENT

Language is a strong tool that has been used in the past to socialize immigrant populations to American culture. After the Civil Rights movement, school law and policy began to support the use of native languages in the public school setting. However, when a large influx of immigrants was coupled with large budget cuts to educational programs, many states began to legislate English-only policies. Educators working under English-only policies can avail themselves of several alternatives to teach immigrant students.

KEYWORDS: Bilingual Education Act (BEA); Class Action; Colonization; Constitutional Entitlement; Cultural Identity; Elementary and Secondary Education Act (ESEA); English as a Second Language (ESL); English Language; English-only Movement; English-only Education; Limited English Proficiency; Multicultural Education; Rulemaking; State Initiatives

OVERVIEW

The second-grade classroom is deeply engrossed in learning. The teacher has asked the students to add letters to the word, *ice*, to create new words. Students are providing letters as the teacher helps them to learn spelling and vocabulary: *nice, rice, lice*, etc. Carlos is vigorously waving his arm, begging for the teacher to call on him. The teacher smiles and asks Carlos for his letters.

> *"P and r. The word will be price!" exclaims Carlos.*
> *"Yes! And can you use the word in a sentence Carlos?"*

"Oh, yes!" exclaims Carlos using his thick Spanish accent. "If your parents give you a dollar you can try to get a price from the price machine!"

As the teacher provides a gentle correction, the classroom atmosphere changes. The children, mostly Latino, cannot differentiate the sounds between "price" and "prize" and the teacher, speaking only English as mandated by law, struggles to explain the difference between the two words; how they sound and what they mean confuses the children. The learning moment quickly ends and the children who speak English as their second language largely disconnect from the lesson.

Would the lesson continue to be compelling and engaging if the teacher could have provided the Spanish words for "price" and "prize," quickly described (in Spanish if necessary) the hard *s* sound as how one differentiates the words, and then moved on? Would more effective learning have occurred for her students? The teacher works in one of the twenty-seven states that have declared English as the official language (Crawford, 2012) and her school's policies preclude her from finding out if mixing Spanish and English in the classroom would be a more effective teaching technique for her students (80 percent of whom are Latinos).

There is a large controversy in America regarding how to properly educate immigrant children in the public school arena. There appear to be two major questions driving this controversy:

- As the majority of the states have formally recognized English as the official language of America, how should children who speak English as a second language be allowed to utilize their homeland language in the public schoolhouse;
- How should immigrant children be taught the English language?

ENGLISH AS THE OFFICIAL LANGUAGE OF AMERICA

Past generations were taught that America is a "melting pot." The people who immigrated to the United States were eager to take on its customs, ideologies, and language as they sought opportunities and advancement within American society (Citrin, Reingold, Walters, & Green, 1990). In the 1960s, civil rights issues challenged the notion of a national melting pot. People began to wonder how diverse people were supposed to take on a singularized identity without losing large portions of their cultural identities. People of color began to rebel against what they believed to be the colonization of minority populations in the United States. Many people of color began to fight to create public spaces in which they could cultivate and carry on their culture (or the culture of their ancestors). Language was identified as one of the areas in which they sought change. They claimed a constitutional entitlement to language rights and began to insist on public information being available in their native language (often, but not always, Spanish). For approximately a decade, the English speaking majority appeared to be amenable to the changes; laws, regulations, and judicial decisions appeared sympathetic to the language rights cause.

THE BILINGUAL EDUCATION ACT & LAU V. NICHOLS.

In 1968, the Bilingual Education Act was enacted. The Bilingual Education Act (BEA) is Title VII of the Elementary and Secondary in 2001 and renamed again in 2010 by President Obama as A Blueprint and Secondary Education. BEA was the first federal recognition of the differentiated needs of children with limited English speaking ability. It provided federal funds to offer bilingual education and to develop classes promoting an appreciation of culture and ancestral language for students from low-income families who were non-English or limited English speakers. However, it did not explicitly require students to be taught in their native language in school. The monies were disbursed via competitive grants and could be used for:

- Teacher training, development, and dissemination of educational materials;
- Projects that promoted meaningful parental involvement;
- Resources for educational programs (Stewner -Manzanares, 1988).

Its objective was to support children who spoke a predominant language other than English in becoming fully literate in English while preserving an appreciation for their cultural identities.

The 1974 amendment to the BEA Although the original BEA went far in recognizing the needs of bilingual students, it remained a bit ambiguous as to how to create equal educational opportunities. Additionally, program participation was voluntary; the program was inconsistent in the provision of services for limited English speaking students. Lau v. Nichols was a class action suit alleging the San Francisco school district was denying equal educational opportunity to its Chinese students because of their limited English proficiency. The lower courts ruled for the school district, but in 1974 the Supreme Court overturned that decision. The Court wrote that, just as "separate but equal" does not constitute educational equality (*Brown v. Board of Education*,1954) providing students of vastly differing language abilities the same facilities, textbooks, teachers, and curricula did not automatically provide equality of educational opportunity (Crawford; *Lau v. Nichols*, 1974). This decision appeared to influence the BEA amendment.

Hence, the 1974 amendment to the BEA specified that educational instruction was to be provided in both English and the native language of the student to prepare the student to eventually succeed in mainstream classrooms. The low-income rule was eliminated, giving all students of limited English proficiency a chance to participate. Time-limited funding was provided to allow school districts the opportunity to research, staff and develop the new programs. A national clearinghouse was established to collect and disseminate information regarding bilingual education (Stewner-Manzanares).

THE LAU REMEDIES

The Department of Health, Education, and Welfare prepared a set of guidelines (known as the Lau Remedies) to provide guidance in the development of educational plans that would remedy civil rights violations. The Lau Remedies specifically provided for native language instruction, and the population to be served was expanded to include any student population that had twenty or more students speaking the same language as their primary language, *regardless of proficiency and income*. Racial segregation was strictly prohibited, which created more complexity in providing meaningful services without creating isolation of the students from their English speaking peers (Stewner-Manzanares).

Soon after the 1974 reauthorization, social and economic pressures began to create public resistance to the bilingual programs. The United States was experiencing a recession; federal and local funds were being cut as a result. The public became aware that the expenses of the bilingual programs (coupled with large budget cuts) were limiting educational opportunities for the other students in their schools. Additionally, the public began to object to the use of federal funds to promote language maintenance among non-English speaking students.

NEW AMENDMENTS

The amendments made to the BEA in 1978 reflected these growing public concerns. They expanded the scope of service to include all students of limited English proficiency and mandated that programs were to be utilized as transitional vehicles in which the goal was to move the students to regular classroom instruction as quickly as possible. Any programs designed to maintain native language were prohibited, and the amendment clearly required that native language only be used in ways that were necessary to assist the students in becoming proficient in English. Accountability issues were addressed by funding an evaluative piece that would measure the effectiveness of the BEA programs.

REMOVAL OF THE LAU REMEDIES

Another lawsuit in 1979, *Northwest Arctic v. Department of Health Education and Welfare*, created the need for the rules set forth in the Lau Remedies (and all future proposed regulations) to be subject to the laws of rulemaking. After a long year of public comment, debate, and argument (and an effort by Congress to stop implementation by claiming educational instruction in any language other than English was inappropriate), the Lau Remedy regulations were withdrawn (Stewner-Manzanares). The subsequent two decades experienced a decline in funding and support for bilingual education programs and dissension regarding how to most appropriately educate children who are not proficient in English.

A NATIONAL CLASSROOM IDENTITY?

Similar to a period between 1910 and 1920, the 1990s experienced a wave of immigration that appeared to threaten the homogeneity inherent in American culture, and people in the majority began to worry about the loss of a unifying national identity. The opinions of the masses began to be voiced via state initiatives, which clearly stated their desire for English to be the official language of the United States (Citrin et al.). Having noted undercurrents of division and suspicion when students spoke a language other than English in class, some teachers started to create and promote English-only policies in their classrooms. They have argued that these rules are implemented to maintain classroom control, to ensure safety of all students, and help to prevent bullying in a foreign language. These rules have been upheld by school administration (Zehr, 2007). Proponents of civil rights continue to remind the public how past actions to punish students for speaking their native language in school had been denounced as discriminatory and abusive. They often remind the public of the Navajo Indians' contribution to America's success in World War II. Their native language, the same language for which they had been prohibited from using in school, was used to transmit coded, undecipherable messages (Reyhner, 2001).

There have been many discussions about what feelings and sentiments motivate the movement to make English the official language. Some researchers believe the driving force is a "pervasive public desire to reaffirm an attachment to a traditional image of Americanism that now seems vulnerable" (Citrin et al.). Regardless of the conflicts of attitudes and opinions, school administration must identify the most effective means of educating non-English speaking children in the public school system.

HOW SHOULD IMMIGRANT CHILDREN LEARN ENGLISH?

There are several schools of thought regarding how English can be taught to immigrant children. However, the bulk of the theories fall into one of the following categories:

- Transitional;
- Native Language;
- Immersion;
- Two-Way Bilingual.

TRANSITIONAL BILINGUAL METHOD

The transitional bilingual school of thought places children in classes in which their native language is used to teach core curriculum, while the children are also being taught English (Berriz, 2006). This program asserts that children cannot learn in mainstream classrooms until they have mastered English. Children are transitioned into English speaking classrooms once they become functionally literate in English. There is some debate surrounding how long it should take children to become literate when participating in a program of this type. Most research states it will take three to seven years. However, most school policies only allow for one year because the 2001 No Child Left Behind Act mandates accountability in the requirement to demonstrate that non-English speaking children are progressing in English fluency as demonstrated by their inclusion in mainstream classes. Some argue this is why schools often limit the time allowed in transitional bilingual programs to one year, rather than extending them to meet the needs of each individual student (Berriz). It is often seen as divisive; immigrant children are placed in sheltered classes within a school that encourages the use of their native language, isolates them from students who would model appropriate English usage, and creates a separate culture that can be difficult to bridge in later years.

One of the benefits to a program of this type is that immigrant parents can still help their children with homework, which provides an opportunity for parents to connect to the educational system in a meaningful way. English-only supporters note that most teachers hired to teach a transitional bilingual program are not fluent English speakers and often choose to teach only in their primary language. As a result, the students never become proficient in English even though they are still placed in mainstream classrooms after a specified period of time.

NATIVE LANGUAGE METHOD

The native language philosophy is often used to prepare under-educated children for eventual participation in some type of transitional or bilingual program. Many immigrant children have taken a circuitous route to America and have not had the opportunity to enjoy regular school attendance. They may have missed portions of their formal schooling due to multiple moves made by the families as they try to locate employment and affordable housing. When they enter the American public school system, it is a return to a school environment in which they are already behind academically when compared to their same-age peers. The children often lack grade-appropriate knowledge in English, Math, Science, and a variety of other subjects. These students must work to catch up scholastically while learning English and trying to adapt to a new country and culture. Some researchers suggest it may be expecting too much of these children when they are asked to catch up using a foreign language (English). They have found that students who are not proficient in English language rarely participate in mainstream classes, stunting their ability to master the new language (Rubenstein-Avila, 2006).

Programs based on the native language precepts provide enrichment in subject matter knowledge in the native language in an effort to help the student acquire the basic knowledge needed to succeed in school at grade level. Some resistors of the English-only educational movement claim a student's literacy in a different language can become a solid bridge to English literacy. A student who already excels in utilizing literary skills, such as skimming and contextual clues, when reading in any language will be more successful in shifting those skills when learning a second language (Rubenstein-Avila). At least one study

has suggested that students allowed to read a book in their native language and then discuss the content in class in English will help the students to better comprehend the text while integrating their knowledge with their new language (Moll & Dias, 1987). So, the argument goes, continue teaching the children in their primary language until they have learned these skills and then facilitate the shifting of good reading practices to the learning of English.

IMMERSION

Using immersion, students are enrolled in mainstream classrooms on their first day of school and are expected to learn the language as they master the coursework. The students are provided enrichment classes one or more periods a day in which they are taught the English language. Each teacher is expected (yet sometimes ill-prepared) to accommodate the language needs of the student by altering lesson plans and modifying text so that non-English speaking children are provided the opportunity to learn the curriculum. Non-English textbooks are not allowed; the children are tested for achievement utilizing English only tests.

Research in California (after the passage of Proposition 227, which mandates English-only instruction in public schools) shows that limited-English students who are placed in immersion programs from the start show huge gains in their English speaking abilities when compared to children who participated in bilingual programs for the same period of time (Salinas, 2006). In 2003, 10 percent of English learners scored in the proficient or advanced categories. That number rose to 20 percent by 2009. Similarly, the English proficiency test given to non-English speaking students showed that test takers who scored in the early advanced or advanced categories rose from 25 percent in 2001 (when the test was first administered) to 39 percent in 2009 (MacDonald, 2009).

Proponents of English-only instruction is that it costs less to administer and is more effective in teaching English to students; therefore, it is the best way to educate immigrant children. However, opponents counter with a meta-analysis conducted using four studies that suggests bilingual instruction is most successful (Rolstad, Mahoney, & Glass, 2005). They believe bilingual education is the only way to create a welcome school environment that is respectful and can effectively teach children the contents of the curriculum (Berriz). They view the act of mainstreaming children into the regular school program, while providing English language enrichment as a separate class or program, as "unwelcoming and disempowering" and claim that academic achievement will suffer because of the program configuration (Berriz). They sagely note the irony that students are required to be proficient in two languages to graduate from high school while, at the same time, students already proficient in an alternative language are discouraged from using it in the classroom.

The two-way bilingual program forms classes comprised of both English speaking students and students who speak another language (usually Spanish) as their primary language. All students are instructed in both English and the other language and students support each other in proper use and pronunciation.

AUTHOR'S VIEWPOINT

This author observed a class of thirty first-grade students as part of a reading research project. Although we lived in a very white, homogeneous school district, the children in this classroom were predominantly Latino. The teacher taught in English; the children appeared to be able to understand and follow her instructions. The children were allowed to play in a general area once they had completed their deskwork. A group of five Latina children were chatting amicably in Spanish while playing with some plastic farm animals. A shy, blonde girl sidled up to the group and watched them play and chat. The Latina girls scooted around to make room for the white girl and easily switched their chatter from Spanish to English and the cooperative play continued.

A white female student attends the junior high school in the same area. While discussing diversity, the student joined the conversation to assert the Mexican kids at her school are "mean." When probed for more information the girl described how the kids at her school speak perfect English in class yet "pretend" they don't understand English when they are in the halls. She asserted the Mexican kids spoke only Spanish in the halls as a way to exclude the white kids from their social groups. She noted an incident in which a white girl had worked to become friends with the Mexican girls only to be beaten up after school. These older students are most likely siblings and neighbors of the children in the elementary school class.

CONCLUSION

Language can be used to include or exclude others in society. As children grow up in our current American culture, they note the tensions that arise between people from diverse backgrounds. They learn how to use language to include others as a gesture of acceptance and openness; they also learn how to exclude others by being subjected to incidents of exclusion themselves. When legislation unilaterally dictates how newly immigrated children are to be taught in the public school system (while ignoring the different abilities and knowledge of those children), they rob the individual schools of the ability to ensure all students are being taught in a welcoming, safe environment. Principals and teachers lose the ability to meet the diverse needs of their students; some of whom may be best served by placing them in mainstream English speaking classes and some of whom may be best served in a course that allows them to master curriculum material in a familiar language.

When segregated schools are created within schools to deliver instruction in languages other than English, all students are divested of an opportunity to become acquainted with different cultures; students often begin to harbor prejudices against other students who are viewed as "the other." There are a variety of means to introduce non-English speaking students into this American society via its school system. Tailoring programs to meet the needs of each student (whether the student needs to learn to speak English quickly or speak another language for a few years) could help to create opportunities for academic rigor for all students while helping everyone learn how to redesign the melting pot in a manner that encourages an inclusive, welcoming society in the long term.

TERMS & CONCEPTS

Class Action: A lawsuit brought by one or more plaintiffs on behalf of themselves and a larger group of others who have the same grounds for action.

Colonization: A theory that people with cultures differing from the majority culture are oppressed and used to the benefit of the major culture. The oppression takes place as the minority groups are stripped of their languages, stories, and pasts.

Constitutional Entitlement: A right to benefits or privilege guaranteed to the people covered by the Constitution.

Cultural Identity: Cultural identity is the feeling of belongingness/identification to a group or culture. In American society the minority cultures are generally learned by children at home and the dominant one at school. The dominant culture generally has more prestige in the society than the minority ones.

Elementary and Secondary Education Act (ESEA): The federal law that funds the basic public school programs such as Title I and Title VII. It is currently known as the No Child Left Behind Act and is reauthorized every six years.

Limited English Proficiency: Students with sufficient difficulty speaking, reading, writing, or understanding the English language to deny them the opportunity to succeed in classrooms where the language of instruction is English (Public Law 95-561)

Rulemaking: Rulemaking is the process used by an administrative agency to formulate, amend, or repeal a rule or regulation. Congress usually enacts ambiguous laws expecting that public administrators will create policies and rules based on interpretations of the laws. The process ensures a specific period of time is allowed for public comment before the rule will be enacted.

State Initiative: A movement most often initiated by a private citizen or interest group to put a specific issue up for a vote. If the initiator gathers enough signatures in support of putting the issue to a vote, it will appear on the ballot in the next state general election.

Sherry Thompson

BIBLIOGRAPHY

Ballester, E. (2012). Child L2 English acquisition of subject properties in an immersion bilingual context. *Second Language Research, 28,* 217–241. Retrieved December 20, 2013, from EBSCO Online Database Education Research Complete.

Berriz, B.R. (2006). Unz got your tongue; What have we lost with the English-only mandates?. *Radical Teacher, 75,* 10-15. Retrieved September 1, 2007, from EBSCO Online Database Education Research Complete.

Brown v. Board of Education, 347 U.S. 483 (E.D. 1954)

Crawford, J. (2000). *At war with diversity: U.S. language policy in an age of anxiety.* Buffalo, NY: Multilingual Matters.

Crawford, J. (2012). Language legislation in the USA. Retrieved December 21, 2013, from http://language-policy.net.

Crawford, J. (1994). *Revisiting the* Lau *Decision - 20 Years After.* Paper presented at the National Commemorative Symposium Held in San Francisco, California. Oakland, Calif.: ARC Associates, 1996.

Lau v. Nichols, 414 U.S. 563 (E.D. 1974)

MacDonald, Heather. (2009). The bilingual ban that worked. *City Journal, 19.* Retrieved December 21, 2013, from http://city-journal.org.

Menken, K. (2013). Restrictive language education policies and emergent bilingual youth: A perfect storm with imperfect outcomes. *Theory Into Practice, 52,* 160–168. Retrieved December 20, 2013, from EBSCO Online Database Education Research Complete.

Orelus, P. W. (2011). Linguistic apartheid and the English-only movement. *Encounter, 24,* 15–22.Retrieved December 20, 2013, from EBSCO Online Database Education Research Complete.

Reyhner, J. (2001). Cultural survival vs. forced assimilation: the renewed war on diversity. *Cultural Survival Quarterly, 25.*

Rolstad, K., Mahoney, K.S., & Glass, G.V. (2005). Weighing the evidence: A meta-analysis of bilingual education in Arizona. *Bilingual Research Journal, 29,* 43-67.

Rubenstein-Avila, E. (2006). Connecting with Latino learners. *Educational Leadership, 63,* 38-43. Retrieved August 11, 2007, from EBSCO Online Database Education Research Complete.

Salinas, R. A. (2006). All children can learn...to speak English. *National Forum of Educational Administration and Supervision Journal, 23,* 20-24. Retrieved September 1, 2007, from EBSCO Online Database Education Research Complete.

Stewner-Manzanares, G. (1988). The Bilingual Education Act: Twenty years later. *New Focus, 6.*

Webster's New World College Dictionary, 4th edition. (2001).

Zehr, M.A. (2003). Classroom ban on Spanish protested. *Education Week, 23.* Retrieved on August 11, 2007, from EBSCO Online Database Education Research Complete.

SUGGESTED READING

Barbosa, A. (2013). Bilingual education in the United States: Possible moral transition toward global citizenship. *Educacao E Pesquisa, 39,* 673–688. Retrieved December 20, 2013, from EBSCO Online Database Education Research Complete.

Barker, V. & Giles, H. (2002). Who supports the English-only movement? Evidence for misconceptions about Latino group vitality. *Journal of Multilingual and Multicultural Development, 23,* 353-370.

Burns, M. (2007). A community divided. *Quill, 95,* 20-25.

Dowling, J. A., Ellison, C. G., & Leal, D. L. (2012). Who doesn't value English? Debunking myths about Mexican immigrants' attitudes toward the English language*. *Social Science Quarterly (Wiley-Blackwell), 93*, 356–378. Retrieved December 20, 2013, from EBSCO Online Database Education Research Complete.

Hunter, S. H. (1996). *The Unbreakable Code.* Flagstaff, AZ: Rising Moon.

Garcia, C. & Bass, L. E. (2007). American identity and attitudes toward English language policy initiatives. *Journal of Sociology & Social Welfare, 34*, 63-82.

Rodriguez, R. (1983). *Hunger of memory: The education of Richard Rodriguez.* New York: Bantam.

SCHOOL CHOICE

School choice is the effort of some public school supporters to encourage educational reform through competition within public schools themselves, as well as between public schools and private schools, Christian schools or parochial schools. School choice is also seen as a way to enable lower-class and middle-class parents to withdraw their children from failing public schools. As an exercise in free market education, school choice is bound up with the notion that the best schools will receive parental support, while the poorly performing schools will be easier to identify and reform. In one sense, the idea of letting parents choose a school for the children is noncontroversial, yet when school choice is defined as the use of public funds—through school vouchers—to pay for students to attend private schools, Christian schools or parochial schools, heated disputes arise. The school voucher program in the United States began in Milwaukee in 1990 and has since spread to other U.S. cities. Experts are divided over whether school choice actually delivers the improved educational outcomes touted by its supporters.

KEYWORDS: Christian School; Educational Reform; Free Market Education; Parochial School; Private School; Public School; School Choice; School Vouchers

OVERVIEW

School choice, the notion that parents should be able to send their children to any public or private school of their choosing, or educate them at home, is not a new idea, even in the United States (West, 1996), though it has received increased attention since the middle of the twentieth century.

Private schools, even religious schools, generally are not controversial, having been a fixture on the American educational landscape since the founding of the country. According to Broughman, Swaim,

and Burke, one in ten K–12 students in the United States attends a private school (Broughman & Swaim, 2006; Burke, 2009). According to the biennial Private School Universe Survey (PSS) conducted by the National Center for Education Statistics at the U.S. Department of Education, 30,861 private schools enrolled 4.5 million students in 2011–2012. Among members of the 111th Congress (2009–2010), 36 percent of Representatives and 44 percent of Senators sent their children to private schools. Thirty-five percent of members of the Congressional Black Caucus and 31 percent of Congressional Hispanic Caucus members sent their children to private school. (Burke).

School choice operates in several different ways, depending on the state and the public school district. At heart, according to supporters, school choice is an attempt to separate the excellent public schools from the public schools badly in need of reform. According to Dodenhoff (2007), school choice "assume[s] the existence of a sizeable core of good schools from which parents can choose, and on which parents can believe that their time and effort are not being wasted."

SCHOOL CHOICE OPTIONS

How does school choice play out in practice? First, in most states students have the option to attend a public charter school. Charter schools are a form of public school authorized by a governing body, such as a local school board, state department of education, nonprofit organization, or (in several states) a for-profit corporation. They are chartered for a period of time, with renewals based on performance. Charter schools are distinct from traditional public schools in two respects: they are free of many of the bureaucratic entanglements, and they tend to use more innovative educational techniques. Put another way, charter schools are left free to experiment in exchange for greater accountability.

Unlike private schools, charter schools are public schools supported by taxpayers, and they are not wholly free of oversight by local school boards and state and federal education agencies. Supporters refer to them as "public schools of choice" (WestEd, 2000) because it gives lower-income parents the option to send their children to charter schools instead of traditional public schools. Like wealthier parents who choose to send their children to private schools, parents without those financial resources have a choice about where their children will be educated. Another important difference is that charter schools do not charge tuition. Finally, charter schools are distinctive in that they seek to defend and improve public education, and do not challenge its legitimacy or efficacy.

Students attending charter schools might be bused, at taxpayer expense, to that school. Parents can also take advantage of busing to have their children attend another public school in a different neighborhood or even a different city. Busing has been used to send children of color into predominately white suburban schools, sometimes—as was the case in Boston in the 1970s—provoking racial tension.

SCHOOL VOUCHERS

Students exercising school choice might be given the option to attend a private or religious school, at least partially at the expense of taxpayers, through a voucher. This form of school choice has become the focus of considerable controversy since the 1980s.

School choice becomes especially contentious when taxpayer dollars are involved. In a seminal 1955 essay, economist Milton Friedman proposes that parents be given same-as-cash government vouchers to help them defray the costs of sending their children to the school of their choice. The idea was first proposed by Thomas Paine in *The Rights of Man* in 1791 (Salisbury, 2003), but Friedman (1955) brought the idea to a wider American audience:

"Governments could require a minimum level of education which they could finance by giving parents vouchers redeemable for a specified maximum sum per child per year if spent on "approved" educational services. Parents would then be free to spend this sum and any additional sum on purchasing educational services from an "approved" institution of their own choice. The educational services could be rendered by

private enterprises operated for profit, or by non-profit institutions of various kinds. The role of the government would be limited to assuring that the schools met certain minimum standards such as the inclusion of a minimum common content in their programs, much as it now inspects restaurants to assure that they maintain minimum sanitary standards" (Friedman).

As a free market economist in the tradition of Adam Smith and Friedrich Hayek, Friedman believed that vouchers would empower parents, force failing public schools to improve, and generally better the quality of K–12 education across the country. Friedman puts it this way:

"Let the subsidy be made available to parents regardless where they send their children—provided only that it be to schools that satisfy specified minimum standards—and a wide variety of schools will spring up to meet the demand. Parents could express their views about schools directly, by withdrawing their children from one school and sending them to another, to a much greater extent than is now possible" (Friedman).

Friedman went on to win the Nobel Prize in economics in 1976, and his thinking on school vouchers inspired several generations of economists, politicians, and parents to look at vouchers as a way to improve America's languishing public school system. For many parents, teachers, and politicians, supporting school choice has become tantamount to supporting school vouchers.

CHANGING TIMES IN PUBLIC SCHOOLS

It took several decades before the idea of school vouchers became widely known to the general public. But by the 1970s, change was in the air. There was a growing consensus that the top-down, overly bureaucratic public school system was struggling to deliver the educational outcomes demanded by politicians, parents, and teachers. This was documented in *A Nation at Risk*, the sobering 1983 U.S. government report on public education. There was also the sense that one-size-fits-all education was out of sync with accumulating evidence that suggested smaller class sizes and greater community involvement in schools are crucial to producing students ready to take on the challenges of a burgeoning knowledge-based economy. Moreover, many Americans were alarmed at the disparities in the education provided to poor and lower-income students, many of whom were children of color.

Justified or not, there has since the late twentieth century been a concern that some public schools, particularly in urban areas, are failing the students they serve. Through a combination of violence, teacher apathy, and low expectations on the part of school administrators, the poor and minority students who make up the majority of the student body in many urban schools are being shortchanged. Many critics argue that parents with children stuck in underperforming schools should be offered a government voucher to help them pay the cost of a private school education. Then, given competition from private schools, failing public schools either will be forced to improve or will save taxpayer dollars by shutting their doors.

VOUCHERS: FROM THEORY TO PRACTICE

Friedman's idea of school vouchers held the promise of not only improving the quality of the nation's public schools, but also of providing poor and inner-city parents an alternative to sending their children to crime-ridden and drug-infested inner-city schools.

President Ronald Reagan, who appointed Milton Friedman to his Economic Policy Advisory Board in 1981, trumpeted the idea of school vouchers in the 1980s as a free market approach to resolving what many conservatives and liberals alike felt was a crisis in American public education. Vouchers also earned the support of Reagan's successor, George H. W. Bush. By 1990, halfway through Bush's term, the city of Milwaukee had begun the nation's first educational voucher program. Other school districts have followed Milwaukee's example.

But there continue to be some concerns about vouchers. According to Chick (2007),

- "Some middle class parents who currently are paying private school tuition without government assistance argue that vouchers are another form of welfare that places an additional tax burden on working families."
- "From the perspective of public school teacher unions and pressure groups such as the National Education Association, vouchers are nothing more than a scheme to undermine public education in the United States by funneling money and the best students to private schools."
- "From the perspective of some private schools themselves—especially those operated by religious

organizations and churches—vouchers are an attempt to entangle private schools in government red tape and thereby hamper their educational effectiveness."
- "Some others argue that providing public money to private schools—many of which have a religious basis—is a violation of the Constitutional principle of the separation of church and state, and therefore is prohibited."
- "More pragmatic critics argue that, even if one were to concede their legality, vouchers don't deliver the intended result of helping poor and minority students improve academically" (Chick).

LEGAL ISSUES

Cleveland's school voucher plan was challenged in the mid-1990s on the grounds that it violated the Establishment Clause of the First Amendment, which forbids government endorsement of religion. This was because the vast majority of publicly funded vouchers were used to pay tuition at Catholic schools in and around the city. The case was appealed all the way up to the U.S. Supreme Court. In *Zelman v. Simmons-Harris*, an important ruling in 2002, the Court ruled 5–4 that the Cleveland voucher program did not violate the First Amendment because the overriding purpose of the voucher program was secular. It remains unclear whether the Court's ruling applies with equal force to all existing or proposed voucher programs. In 2006, a Florida State Supreme Court banned a statewide voucher program, and in 2013 the Louisiana Supreme Court struck down the state's method for funding the voucher program stating that the per-pupil allocation of funds must be used for public school students.

VOUCHER SUPPORT

Despite these and other legal wrangling, there have been many supporters of vouchers, including those minority parents whose children are, in their view, forced to attend poor quality schools. Many of these parents argue that vouchers will help address the implicit racism in a public educational system that lets middle class white families choose better schools while not allowing poor families of color the same privilege. They also note that many of the fiercest critics of vouchers in the U.S. Congress—both African American and white—send their own children to private schools (cf. Burke). Friedman touched upon these themes in an interview shortly before his death in 2006:

> *"As to the benefits of universal vouchers, empowering parents would generate a competitive education market, which would lead to a burst of innovation and improvement, as competition has done in so many other areas. There's nothing that would do so much to avoid the danger of a two-tiered society, of a class-based society. And there's nothing that would do so much to ensure a skilled and educated work force"* (as cited in Gillespie, 2005).

Other supporters of vouchers argue that the success of school vouchers depends on how many regulatory strings are attached. While not arguing for or against vouchers, one researcher compared the methods of funding education in five countries, including the United States, and concluded "it is not the source of funding that is important; it is whether the funding carries political restrictions on the decision-making powers of the private schools that matters" (Toma, 1996).

Viewpoints

WHY DO PARENTS CHOOSE PRIVATE SCHOOLS?

Despite the popular conception that parents choose private schools merely for academic reputation, there are various reasons why parents choose private school over public school for their children.

A 2001 study from Brown University looked at reasons why parents in Brown's immediate vicinity of Providence, Rhode Island, were choosing private schools. When the researchers talked to private school parents, they identified a wide variety of reasons.

The researchers found that 43 percent of private school parents had students who had previously attended public schools. When asked what, if anything, would lead them to put their children back in public schools, the leading responses were smaller class sizes, school safety, better trained teachers, and more attention given to their children. When private school parents were given a list of four hypothetical public school improvements, "[t]he most popular change was programs for gifted students (named by 58 percent of parents), followed by reading programs (48 percent), after school programs (42 percent),

and new computers and Internet access (25 percent)" (West).

HOW PUBLIC SCHOOL CHOICE WORKS

School choice presupposes a core of quality public schools worth fighting for. School choice, when applied to public schools, involves a complex matrix of government funding and government regulation. The goal of public policymakers is to strike the appropriate balance so that public schools benefit from needed reforms and innovations while also remaining accountable for a set of minimum academic standards.

As the National Working Commission on Choice in K–12 Education indicates, public schools with the greatest amount of spending and the lowest degree of regulations tend to produce the best results. The hope and expectation of school choice advocates is that increased competition will lead to a proliferation of quality public schools that can compete effectively with their charter school, private school, and religious school counterparts.

DOES SCHOOL CHOICE MAKE A DIFFERENCE TO CHILDREN & COMMUNITIES?

The debate over school choice is not simply about dollars and cents. Rather, it goes beyond money to more fundamental questions: Do most parents make informed choices about where to send their children to school? Does school choice help improve the quality of life in communities across the country? Taking the first question about informed parental choices, a 2007 study of the school voucher program in Milwaukee found the following:

- "it is estimated that just under 35 percent of [Milwaukee Public Schools] MPS parents actively choose a school for their child, rather than simply opting for the default neighborhood school."
- "about 45 percent of parents who actively choose a school for their child are estimated to do so after considering at least two schools."
- "64.8% of two-choice parents [considered] academic factors when choosing a school" (Dodenhoff).

Only one in ten Milwaukee Public School parents fit into all three categories, leading some critics of school choice to conclude that school choice in such cases is more imagined than real. How, then, is this situation an improvement over states and school districts that do not allow school choice? Dodenhoff suggests that this lack of parental involvement is taking the pressure off public schools in need of reform:

"When it comes to public school choice, the estimates presented above indicate that few parents are sufficiently invested in the choice process to create the kind of serious pressure on individual schools that would result in necessary, dramatic improvements" (Dodenhoff).

In terms of community development, a 2007 report noted that school choice in Milwaukee since 1990 had led to $126 million in school building and improvement projects, many in economically distressed areas of the city (School Choice Wisconsin, 2007). Similar results have been found elsewhere.

Another interesting aspect of school choice is the argument that it might even have environmental benefits in controlling suburban sprawl:

"The standard formulation is that sprawl harms urban school systems by draining middle-class students and their tax-paying families. But any parent will tell you that urban schools also promote sprawl by driving away families who can afford to leave. Michael E. Lewyn, a visiting professor of law at George Washington University, has observed that we give urban parents three choices: They can send their kids to the lousy and possibly dangerous public schools in the city. They can ante up the exorbitant tuition for private school, assuming their kids can get in. Or they can move to the best suburb they can afford, where decent public schools are available to anyone with the price of a house" (Akst, 2005).

"Ignoring the chain of causality between bad schools and [suburban] sprawl leads environmentalists to overlook the simplest and potentially most powerful anti-sprawl measure available, which is to let urban parents choose their kids' schools—even if those schools aren't in the city or aren't even public" (Akst).

TERMS & CONCEPTS

Christian School: Often operated by Christian religious organizations or various Protestant Christian denominations, these schools tend to emphasize conservative social values and a biblical world view in addition to academic excellence.

Educational Reform: An umbrella term used to describe various efforts to improve educational outcomes for schoolchildren.

Free Market Education: The idea that loosening government regulation of education will lead to an educational system that delivers results superior to those of a government-run public school system. Many free market reformers support vouchers as a means to this end.

Parochial School: Private schools operated by the Catholic Church that stress the moral and ethical development of the child along with their intellectual development. They were started in the 1840s in response to what Catholics perceived to be the Protestant nature of the American public school system, but they now accept students of any religious background.

Private School: A type of school that does not admit all students who apply, is not funded by taxpayers, and operates with a minimal amount of state or federal regulation and oversight.

Public School: A type of school funded by public funds collected through taxes. Public schools are legally obligated to accept all students seeking an education. Some public schools serve students in their community, while others serve students from a wider geographical region.

School Choice: The notion that parents should be able to send their children to any public or private school of their choosing, or educate them at home.

School Vouchers: Taxpayer-funded credit slips that parents can use the same as cash to pay for all or part of the tuition and fees at a private school of their choice.

Matt Donnelly

BIBLIOGRAPHY

Akst, D. (2005, October 6). Choose you can use: School choice could be an answer to sprawl. Grist. [Online version]. Retrieved November 7, 2007, from http://grist.org.

Beal, H., & Hendry, P. (2012). The ironies of school choice: Empowering parents and reconceptualizing public education. *American Journal of Education, 118*, 521–550. Retrieved December 5, 2013, from EBSCO Online Database Education Research Complete.

Broughman, S. & Swaim, N. (2013). *Characteristics of private schools in the United States: Results from the 2011–2012 Private School Universe Survey.* U.S. Department of Education, Institute of Education Sciences. Retrieved November 15, 2014, from the National Center for Education Statistics, http://nces.ed.gov.

Burke, L. (2009). *How many members of the 111th Congress practice private school choice*. Retrieved November 14, 2014, from http://heritage.org.

Center for Education Reform (2005). Nine lies about school choice: Proving the critics wrong. Retrieved November 4, 2007, from the *Center for Education Reform*, http://edreform.com.

Chick, K. (2007, June 22). Voucher students don't star. *Washington Times*, (DC).

Coulson, A. J. (2011). Do vouchers and tax credits increase private school regulation? A statistical analysis. *Journal of School Choice, 5*, 224–251. Retrieved December 5, 2013, from EBSCO Online Database Education Research Complete.

Dexter, E. G. (1906). *A history of education in the United States*. New York: Macmillan.

Dodenhoff, D. (2007). Fixing the Milwaukee public schools: The limits of parent-driven reform. *Wisconsin Policy Research Institute*. Retrieved November 7, 2007, from the Wisconsin Policy Research Institute, http://wpri.org.

Feinberg, E. (2007). How members of Congress practice private school choice. Backgrounder #2066, 1-7. Retrieved September 22, 2007, from the Heritage Foundation, http://heritage.org.

Friedman, M. (1955). The role of government in education. [Electronic version]. In R. A. Solo (Ed.), *Economics and the public interest*. Piscataway, NJ: Rutgers University Press. Retrieved November 4, 2007, from http://school-choices.org.

Gillespie, N. (2005). The father of modern school reform. Reason.[Online version]. Retrieved November 4, 2007, from *Reason Magazine*, http://reason.com.

Khazem, J. H., & Khazem, H. A. (2014). The role of accelerated learning in the school choice debate. *International Journal of Education Research, 9*, 26–42. Retrieved November 15, 2014, from EBSCo Online Database Education Research Complete.

Linkow, T. (2011). Disconnected reform: The proliferation of school choice options in U.S. school districts. *Journal of School Choice, 5*, 414–443. Retrieved December 5, 2013, from EBSCO Online Database Education Research Complete.

National Center for Education Statistics. (2006). Private School Universe Survey. Retrieved November 4, 2007, from *U.S Department of Education*, http://nces.ed.gov.

National Commission on Excellence in Education. (1983). A nation at risk: The imperative for educational reform. Washington, DC: U.S. Government Printing Office. Retrieved November 4, 2007, from http://ed.gov.

National Working Commission on Choice in K-12 Education. (2003). School choice: Doing it the right way. Retrieved November 5, 2007, from *Brown Center on Educational Policy*, Brookings Institution, http://brookings.edu.

Prothero, A. (2015). When choice doesn't feel like a choice. *Education Week, 35*(1), 14–17. Retrieved January 15, 2016, from EBSCO Online Database Education Research Complete.

Salisbury, D.F. (2003). What does a voucher buy? A closer look at the cost of private schools. Policy Analysis, No. 486. Retrieved November 5, 2007, from the *Cato Institute*, http://cato.org.

School Choice Wisconsin (2007). School choice and community renewal. Retrieved November 7, 2007, from *School Choice Wisconsin*, http://schoolchoiceinfo.org.

Toma, E. (1996). Public funding and private schooling across countries. *Journal of Law & Economics, 39*, 121–148. Retrieved September 23, 2007, from EBSCO Online Database Business Source Premier.

Tooley, J. (2002). The changing role of government in education. Encyclopaedia of Education. Retrieved November 4, 2007, from E.G. West Centre, School of Education, University of Newcastle, http://ncl.ac.uk.

U.S. Department of Education. (2004). Innovations in education: Successful charter schools. Washington, DC: U.S. Department of Education Office of Innovation and Improvement. Retrieved October 27, 2007, from the *U.S. Department of Education*, http://uscharterschools.org.

West, D. M. (2001, September). Why Providence parents send their children to private schools, and what would bring them back. Providence, RI: Taubman Center for Public Policy, Brown University. Retrieved September 21, 2007, from *Brown University*, http://brown.edu.

West, E.G. (1996, July 1). The spread of education before compulsion: Britain and America in the nineteenth century. The Freeman. Retrieved November 4, 2007, from the *Independent Institute*, http://uscharterschools.org.

SUGGESTED READING

Abernathy, S.F. (2005). *School choice and the future of American democracy*. Ann Arbor: University of Michigan Press.

Cato Institute. (n.d.). Education and child policy: School choice. Retrieved November 4, 2007, from the *Cato Institute*, http://cato.org.

Ehrcke, T. (2015). Is school choice undermining public education? *Our Schools / Our Selves, 25*(1), 107–122. Retrieved January 15, 2016, from EBSCO Online Database Education Research Complete.

Enlow, R.C., & Ealy, L.T. (Eds.). (2006). *Liberty & learning: Milton Friedman's voucher idea at fifty*. Washington, DC: Cato Institute.

McGinn, K. C., & Ben-Porath, S. (2014). Parental engagement through school choice: Some reasons for caution. *Theory & Research in Education, 12*, 172–192. Retrieved November 15, 2014, from EBSCO Online Database Education Research Complete.

Villavicencio, A. (2013). "It's our best choice right now": Exploring how charter school parents choose. *Education Policy Analysis Archives, 21*, 1–19. Retrieved December 5, 2013, from EBSCO Online Database Education Research Complete.

Yongmei, N., & Arsen, D. (2011). School choice participation rates: Which districts are pressured? *Education Policy Analysis Archives, 19*, 1–26. Retrieved December 5, 2013, from EBSCO Online Database Education Research Complete.

SCHOOL VOUCHERS

Many people see private school vouchers as a solution to the problem of underperforming schools in the United States. Allowing those who are unhappy with their public school the opportunity to enroll in a more favorable private school is often cited as a way for students to be happy and reach academic expectations, for public schools to benefit from competition, and for an equal education to be had by all who desire it. Controversy about their legality abounds, and the reality is that there is no uniform voucher system in the country and there is no one state with a model program for others to follow.

KEYWORDS: A Nation at Risk; Certified Teacher; Curriculum; Education Reform; Florida Opportunity Scholarship Program; Friedman, Milton; Jencks, Christopher; Low Income; Polarized; Private School; Public School; School; School Choice; Selective Admission; Teacher's Union; Under-Performing Schools; Voucher

OVERVIEW

In general terms, vouchers are tuition coupons parents can redeem to send their child to the public or private school of their choice. By giving the flexibility of choice to parents, all children are able to attend the school that may best serve their needs. The voucher idea has been around for over fifty years, but are presently only in a few U.S. states and on a limited basis (Jacobsen, 2004). Controversy about their legality abounds, and the reality is that there is no uniform voucher system in the country and there is no one state with a model program for others to follow.

At first glance, the rationale behind school vouchers seems simple enough. Under this system, the government will permit parents to send their children to any school they want—public or private—and provides grants in the form of coupons to make this possible. The establishment of a voucher system attempts to free public schools from holding a monopoly on education since with this system, parents who don't like a particular school can send their children elsewhere (Jencks, 1972). According to proponents, the voucher system could ultimately improve all schools and encourage innovation and high standards of excellence.

Those in agreement with the voucher system claim these grants could effectively overhaul the education system by generating needed competition for U.S. public schools. Ideally, disadvantaged students would benefit from getting out of some of the worst schools in the country and would enjoy higher academic achievement and enhanced social opportunities. Naysayers argue that public schools don't need the competition—they are already doing a fine job and need all the financial support they can get. By handing students vouchers to leave public schools, they say, both resources and children would flow out (Moe, 2001).

HISTORY

Most will agree that parents with the financial means already have the right of school choice by virtue of where they live, or that they can send their children to a particular private school (Garnett & Pearsall, 2005). Vouchers are seen as a way to help those parents and children for whom school choice is desired but is not a financial option.

MILTON FRIEDMAN

In the 1950s, noted economist Milton Friedman argued in favor of the idea of education vouchers. He reasoned that public schools were a government-run monopoly and whether they performed well or not, were still provided with students and resources. This system gave schools little incentive to improve or innovate, and Friedman claimed that this was a reason the education system was stagnant and mediocre. He suggested that a voucher system would allow the government to provide subsidies but not operate as a supplier to a monopoly (cited in Moe).

Friedman believed that vouchers enabling any student to go to private schools if they choose to would help improve education for all. However, he acknowledged that these types of programs could still segregate students by race and income, so his innovative education ideas did not get much support. Although his original views about school choice were published in the 1950s, Friedman restated them forty years later when he said that the solution to the education system's problems is to privatize it (cited in Weil, 2002).

CHRISTOPHER JENCKS

In the 1970s, Harvard academic Christopher Jencks suggested a regulated voucher system, where all children in a particular area would qualify for vouchers of a certain value, but children of low-income families would be entitled to larger vouchers. Jencks further proposed that private schools be required to accept the voucher as full tuition payment. Students with vouchers of a higher value would be more attractive to private schools, which would probably conclude that even if remediation were needed for those lower-performing voucher students, the schools would still find themselves ahead (Moe).

Jencks's ideas were shot down by teachers' unions and other education groups. Just one pilot program, in Alum Rock, California, was started in the 1970s, bearing only a vague resemblance to Jencks's original idea. The program ended after three years.

THE POLITICS OF VOUCHERS

By the end of the 1970s, there was still no serious talk of or support for vouchers as a way to improve the country's education system. At that time, reliance on the private sector and markets to improve schools was being thought of as a positive idea, but until Ronald Reagan was elected president in 1980, there was little support or even serious talk of school vouchers. Reagan spoke of choice and competition as important ways of improving the education system, and he actively lobbied for school vouchers. President Reagan's proposed legislation was not supported by

Congress, but in 1983, *A Nation at Risk* was published. This report about the country's education system issued the warning that U.S. schools were in crisis and immediate reforms were necessary to attempt to improve their performance. Since this study was published, presidents and governors have attempted to be dubbed the "education president" or the "education governor" as a way to affirm their commitment to improving the education system (Moe).

In the beginning of the 1990s, Republican President George H. W. Bush proposed $1,000 vouchers for children whose families' income was below the national average. Although the legislation did not pass the Democratic Congress, it did gain the attention of the media and the public. Since teachers' unions helped elect Bill Clinton president in 1992, he was compelled to oppose the voucher system, but in the 1996 election campaign, Republican Bob Dole proposed vouchers for low-income families. The issue became polarized, with George W. Bush favoring vouchers for those in underperforming schools in the 2000 campaign, and Democrat Al Gore opposing vouchers of any kind (Moe).

In the aftermath of Hurricane Katrina in 2005, President George W. Bush attempted to create a voucher program for affected students in Louisiana to enroll in the school of their choice. This effort was defeated by Congress, with some dissenters saying Bush's idea was more political opportunism at a time of tragedy than a way for students to get the best education possible ("After Katrina," 2005).

Since 2005, there has been little talk of vouchers on a national level. In those states that do have some type of voucher system in place, the types of school choice plans and public opinion can vary greatly. In a study conducted by a national research firm, it was found that when asked about their feelings for school vouchers, 11 percent of the respondents thought school vouchers were a good idea and would ultimately solve the country's education deficiencies; 67 percent of respondents thought vouchers were a good idea but wouldn't solve the nation's education problems, and 17 percent of the respondents said vouchers were not a good idea and would actually make our country's education problems worse (Weil).

VOUCHER PROGRAMS TODAY

As of 2013, voucher programs could be found in twelve states and the District of Columbia ("School voucher laws," 2013). School voucher programs in Cleveland, Ohio; Milwaukee, Wisconsin; and Washington, D.C., all target low-income students in underperforming schools. Milwaukee's city-wide voucher program is intended for the very poor. Opponents argue that those served by this system are typically not those who pay taxes and the middle- and upper-middle-class taxpayers are subsidizing the education for the poor. As with all voucher systems, parents are actually being taxed twice whether they use it or not: first when they are funding public education for all and again when they are paying for vouchers to move children from public to private schools. The voucher program is not open to everyone in Milwaukee who may qualify—no more than 15 percent of a school district's students are eligible to receive the voucher to attend a private school.

There is a smorgasbord of variations on the school voucher program in other areas of the country; for example, a statewide voucher program in Ohio is open to those students enrolled in failing schools. Arizona has a voucher program specifically for children in foster care, and both Maine and Vermont offer vouchers for those students in rural towns without their own public schools. In 1999, both Maine and Vermont courts ruled that religious schools could not participate in the states' voucher programs (Larson, 2002). Utah's voucher program provides funding to every public school student who wishes to attend a private school. Georgia offered a voucher program for special education students for the first time in 2007, and Florida's McKay Scholarship program provides vouchers for students with disabilities ("School voucher laws," 2013).

THE FLORIDA OPPORTUNITY SCHOLARSHIP PROGRAM

The country's first statewide voucher program was started in Florida in 1999 in response to a high school on-time graduation rate of less than 60 percent. Dubbed the Florida Opportunity Scholarship Program, the voucher program was not limited to low-income families and permitted students in failing public schools (those schools receiving a letter grade of "F," based on student performance, for two years in any four-year period) throughout Florida to attend a private or high-performing school. As it was originally written, the statute would have used tax money to pay tuition for private schools to those students requesting it (Davis, 2006).

The original program was successfully overturned in Florida courts with the argument that it diverted tax dollars into private systems in competition with public schools. The courts said that public schools are in the business of educating Florida's children and state funds should not be undermining this goal. In addition, private schools should not be considered on a par with public schools, since they often don't require teachers to be certified, while public schools have stringent systems of regulation designed to keep standards high. It was also noted that the curriculum in Florida public schools is set by the state's board of education, while often private schools use a curriculum adopted by some other nonpublic school curriculum development area (Davis). The Florida Opportunity Scholarship Program is still in operation, with students attending failing public schools given the option to attend another public school of their choosing ("Opportunity Scholarship Program," n.d.).

PROPONENTS OF VOUCHERS

Generally, those in favor of school vouchers tend to argue that education must be available to all children regardless of their race, their culture, their first language, or their particular special needs. Social mobility is not guaranteed for the less privileged in this country and the voucher system is one way to close this gap. Proponents say that often public schools are not able to provide an education to all students. One point often mentioned is that public school teachers in some areas enroll their own children in private schools—seeming to admit that their public schools are not good enough for them. Those in favor of vouchers often say that all parents who desire it should be able to send their children to private schools if they believe they are superior to the public schools in their area (Weil).

African American children often endure low-quality public schools, and their parents tend to embrace the idea of school vouchers. Many parents have attempted to improve the schools in their neighborhoods but have been frustrated by seemingly unresponsive administrators. The prevailing wisdom tends to be that the public schools need to be improved, but right now each child needs to be educated (Malveaux, 2003). Private, independent schools are often seen as a solution because they are more effective than public schools. They have a clear sense of their mission and are not constrained by politics and bureaucracy (Gill, 2001). Without a system like vouchers, proponents believe, school reform will likely never come to bright but low-income students enrolled in failing schools. Vouchers and private schools could pave the way for success for these students (Magnusson, 2003).

The U.S. education system cost taxpayers over $600 billion for the 2009–2010 school year. Aside from educating students, the system provides teachers, administrators, and a host of others with employment. Most proponents of the voucher system agree that the education system would not be harmed by the program. Although public schools would lose some students and resources to private schools, this would provide public schools needed incentive to compete and therefore improve (Moe). With vouchers, private schools would actually be in a position to compete with public schools, as they would get the same amount of public money per pupil as the public schools. It can be argued that the quality of public school education would be improved by removing it from its present status as a near-monopoly of the education system and subjecting it to the competition of the free market (Havighurst).

OPPONENTS OF VOUCHERS
Those against the voucher system say that vouchers threaten our country's public education system. Vouchers permit and even encourage students and resources to go to the private sector, and as students and funding leave the public schools, this ultimately means lost jobs, less money to spend on programs, and a smaller public school system. Teachers unions would suffer too, as the decline in teachers would mean less dues and less power to be influential in education decisions and legislation (Moe).

The drain of children and resources to the private sector could make it more difficult for public school performance to improve, especially in poorer areas. As the most motivated and more socially advantaged students and parents leave these underperforming schools for what they perceive to be a better opportunity, they would also take their demands for school improvements with them, leaving others—usually the less aggressive parents—to push for change and to participate in school affairs (Moe).

Some opponents allege that parents are too ignorant to make intelligent choices among schools for their children (Jencks, 1972). Indeed, not all parents

may consider moving their children from their present public school for quality educational reasons. Instead, some may decide to have their children leave their public school because the students' peers have chosen to leave, or because of the private school's proximity to their home. Some children may not have transportation to private schools, so refrain from considering them, and racial problems that already exist in public schools would likely get worse (Moe).

There are many other subsets of students for whom vouchers just won't work. These include students who may want a voucher but for a variety of reasons are unable to get one; those students who are happy with their present public school and don't want to leave, but can detect its weakening by the diverted funds and students; students who experience specific program cutbacks because needed funds have gone to vouchers; and students for whom private schools are not convenient or even available or otherwise don't meet their needs (Weil).

ARE PRIVATE SCHOOLS REALLY SUPERIOR?
Opponents also mention that private schools can be inferior in their own way. Since they are usually not covered by achievement assessment testing laws and lack standards and accountability, private schools may not be seeing the same types of results public schools are expected to. Since private schools are not compelled to take all students who apply for admission, they may exercise selective admission and choose to only accept students of a certain academic level (Weil). Even with the possible influx of students, a study of private schools found they would not plan to grow under vouchers and would likely continue to limit the number of students they chose to admit (Shires, 1994). Private schools are often are not able to adequately educate those students who are enrolled in special education programs or those for which English is a second language (Jacobsen). Even typically-abled students can be closed out of private schools: Most of these schools don't have free lunch programs, for example, and many don't have adequate busing systems (Weil). The reality is that many students end up being left behind in public schools which now have less funding because of the decrease of students (Jacobsen).

It should be noted that most private schools are affiliated with a church or a particular religion; in fact, nationwide over three-quarters of the private schools in operation are religious schools, and about 85 percent of students enrolled in a private school are attending this type of private school (Weil). Many opponents of the voucher system believe using vouchers to fund a religious-affiliated private school violates the separation of church and state. They say that religion should be kept out of education that is paid for by the taxpayer (Moe).

CONCLUSION

There is no consensus as to whether vouchers are a viable way to improve education in the United States. Although they may offer a solution to some students' dissatisfaction with the public school they are zoned to attend, studies conducted thus far indicate the system ultimately doesn't improve academic results.

Research has shown that there is not a direct correlation between student academic achievement and vouchers for academic choice. A study of the Cleveland voucher program found that participating students did not show higher test-score gains than students who did not use vouchers. The voucher students were found to perform slightly worse in math achievement (Robelen, 2006). A study of the Washington, D.C., program made public in June 2007 concluded that there were no significant academic differences between students who attended public schools and those who used a voucher to attend a private school (Collins, 2007).

Despite the lack of correlation between student performance and private schools, there are other reasons private schools may not be the answer. Unlike public schools, private ones operate as a business. As such, they can relocate and even abandon their students as they see fit. Public schools must be available and accessible to all students all the time and do not operate for a profit but for a human bottom line, the benefit of students. They cannot relocate. The improvement therefore needs to come from within their walls.

TERMS & CONCEPTS

A Nation at Risk: A Nation at Risk is a 1983 report published by the U.S. Department of Education's National Committee on Excellence in Education. The report is generally cited as the originator of education reform efforts in the United States.

Certified Teacher: A certified teacher is one who has completed an approved teacher education program.

Curriculum: Curriculum is the courses of study offered by a particular school or educational institution.

Low Income: Low income generally means a household income below a particular percentage of the federal poverty level.

Polarized: Polarized means to divide among sharply opposing sides, such as political parties.

Selective Admission: Selective admission means that a potential student must meet certain criteria, usually academic, to be considered for admission to a particular school.

Teachers' Union: A teachers' union is an organization of teachers and other educators who work together to promote quality education, good working and learning conditions, and fair labor practices for all members.

Underperforming School: An underperforming school is that does not meet the educational expectations on state and national assessments in core subjects areas as outlined by the local, state, or national guidelines.

Susan Ludwig

BIBLIOGRAPHY

After Katrina, Bush pushes school vouchers. (2005, October 18). *Christian Century, 122,* 14. Retrieved September 24, 2007, from EBSCO Online Database Education Research Complete.

Butcher, J. (2013). School choice marches forward. *Education Next, 13,* 20-27. Retrieved December 13, 2013, from EBSCO Online Database Education Research Complete.

Carr, S. (2012, August 21). School vouchers make comeback amid concerns about quality. *NBC news* Retrieved December 13, 2013, from http://usnews.nbcnews.com.

Chakrabarti, R. (2013). Vouchers, public school response, and the role of incentives: Evidence from Florida. *Economic Inquiry, 51,* 500-526. Retrieved December 13, 2013, from EBSCO Online Database Education Research Complete.

Collins, C. (2000). School choice and charter schools. *Independent Schools, 59,* 40. Retrieved September 24, 2007, from EBSCO Online Database Education Research Complete.

Davis, W. N. (2006). Vouchers tested. *ABA Journal, 92,* 16-17. Retrieved September 24, 2007, from EBSCO Online Database Education Research Complete.

Garnett, R., & Pearsall, C. S. (2005). Bush v. Holmes: School vouchers, religious freedom, and state constitutions.

Education & the Law, 17, 173-183. Retrieved September 24, 2007, from EBSCO Online Database Education Research Complete.

Gill, B. P. (2001). *Rhetoric versus reality and what we need to know about vouchers and charter schools.* Santa Monica, CA: Rand Publishing.

Larson, L. (2002). *School Vouchers.* Retrieved September 25, 2007, from the Minnesota House of Representatives Research Department, http://house.leg.state.mn.us.

Havighurst, R. (1972) The unknown good: Education vouchers. In J. A. Mecklenburger & R. W. Hostrop (Eds.), *Education vouchers: From theory to Alum Rock.* Homewood, IL: ETC Publications.

Jacobson, E. (2004). The voucher argument [reprint]. *Voting in the 2004 elections.* Retrieved September 24, 2007, from the New England Literacy Resource Center, http://nelrc.org.

Jencks, C. (1972). Giving parents money for schooling: Education vouchers. In J. A. Mecklenburger & R. W. Hostrop (Eds.), *Education vouchers: From theory to Alum Rock.* Homewood, IL: ETC Publications.

Magnusson, P. (2003). The split over school vouchers. *Business Week, 3853,* 125-126. Retrieved September 24, 2007, from EBSCO Online Database Academic Search Premier.

Malveaux, J. (2003). School vouchers: A wedge issue for African Americans? *Black Issues in Higher Education, 20,* 31. Retrieved September 24, 2007, from EBSCO Online Database Education Research Complete.

McEwan, P. J. (2004). The potential impact of vouchers. *Peabody Journal of Education, 79,* 57-80. Retrieved September 24, 2007, from EBSCO Online Database Education Research Complete.

Moe, T. M. (2001). *Schools, Vouchers, and the American Public.* Washington, DC: Brookings Institution Press.

Opportunity Scholarship Program. (n.d.). *Florida school choice.* Florida Department of Education. Retrieved December 13, 2013 from http://floridaschoolchoice.org.

Robelen, E. W. (2006). No test score edge found for Cleveland voucher students. *Education Week, 22,* 18. Retrieved September 24, 2007, from EBSCO Online Database Education Research Complete.

School voucher laws: State-by-state comparison. (2013). *National Conference of State Legislatures.* Retrieved December 13, 2013, from http://ncsl.org.

Shires, M. (1994). *The effects of the California voucher initiative on public expenditures.* Santa Monica, CA: Rand Publishing.

Sutton, L. C., & King, R. A. (2013). Financial crisis not wasted: Shift in state power and voucher expansion. *Journal of Education Finance, 38,* 283-303. Retrieved December 13, 2013, from EBSCO Online Database Education Research Complete.

Weil, D. (2002). *School vouchers and privatization: A reference handbook.* Santa Barbara, CA: ABC-CLIO.

Wolf, P. J., Kisida, B., Gutmann, B., Puma, M., Eissa, N., & Rizzo, L. (2013). School vouchers and student outcomes: Experimental evidence from Washington, DC. *Journal of Policy Analysis & Management, 32,* 246-270. Retrieved December 13, 2013, from EBSCO Online Database Education Research Complete.

SUGGESTED READING

Filer, R. K., & Munich, D. (2013). Responses of private and public schools to voucher funding. *Economics of Education Review, 34,* 269-285. Retrieved December 13, 2013, from EBSCO Online Database Education Research Complete.

Howell, W. (2006). *The education gap: Vouchers and urban schools.* Washington, DC: Brookings Institution Press.

Kahlenberg, R. (Ed.). (2003). *Public school choice vs. private school vouchers.* Washington, DC: Century Foundation Press.

National Council on Excellence in Education. (1983). *A nation at risk.* Washington DC: USA Research.

Van Dunk, E., & Dickman, A. (2004). *School choice and the question of accountability: The Milwaukee experience.* New Haven, CT: Yale University Press.

Zirkel, P. A. (2012). Is vouchering the way to vouch for special education? *Journal of Law & Education, 41,* 649-650. Retrieved December 13, 2013, from EBSCO Online Database Education Research Complete.

SPELLINGS REPORT

The 2006 publication of the controversial report of the Spellings Commission on the Future of Higher Education has sparked a national dialogue about the state of postsecondary education in the United States. The report places higher education in crisis and calls for a number of radical reforms in the areas of accessibility, accountability, affordability and quality. While most constituents agree that some change would improve the establishment, not all concur that a crisis exists or that radical reform is necessary for its survival. In the year since its publication, a number of important changes have been introduced while others are being considered for adoption. The impact of the report on the higher education community will be discussed.

KEYWORDS: Accountability; Accreditation; Financial Aid; Higher Education; Institutional Effectiveness; Negotiated Rulemaking; Spellings Commission; Spellings Report; United States Department of Education (USDOE)

OVERVIEW

In 2005, U.S. Secretary of Education Margaret Spellings established a 19-member commission to "consider how best to improve our system of higher education to ensure that our graduates are well prepared to meet our future workforce needs and are able to participate fully in the changing economy" (US Department of Education, 2006). One year later, the commission submitted its report and published *A Test of Leadership: Charting the Future of U.S. Higher Education: A Report of the Commission Appointed by Secretary of Education Margaret Spellings* (2006). The Spellings commission examined four key areas of higher education:

- Access;
- Affordability;
- Quality;
- Accountability.

They concluded with six strong recommendations for reform directed at colleges and universities, accrediting agencies, governing boards, policymakers, elementary and secondary schools, the business community, parents and students (USDOE).

For the purposes of the report, the commission defined higher education as inclusive of:

"... *all public and private education that is available after high school, from trade schools, online professional training institutions and technical colleges to community colleges, traditional four-year colleges and universities, and graduate and professional programs" (USDOE).*

Among its goals were the continuation of a world-class educational system that recognizes and adapts to changes in demographics, technology, and globalization, accessibility of higher education to all Americans throughout their lives, efficiency and cost-effectiveness within and among institutions and graduates with workplace skills adequate to a rapidly changing economy (USDOE).

FINDINGS

The report strongly criticizes the current state of U.S. higher education and has stirred a great deal of debate among educators, administrators and policymakers. A recent article quotes the report as saying,

"*Castigating American higher education as complacent, the report claims the U.S. educational system is risk-averse, self-satisfied, and unduly expensive. Like railroads and steel manufacturers, the report warns, the education industry must adapt or risk being left behind by educational systems in other countries*" (*"Spellings report spells"*).

The Commission asserts that higher education is not simply a means for social mobility and holds that "everyone needs a postsecondary education" (USDOE). Moreover, the Spellings Commission blames higher education for the lack of continuity between secondary and postsecondary education, which often results in inadequate preparation for college and poor retention of those who do attempt college level work (USDOE).

Further, the commission found that,

"*Many students who earn degrees have not actually mastered the reading, writing and thinking skills we expect of college graduates [as] over the past decade, literacy among college graduates has actually declined*" (*USDOE*).

The consequences of these and other compounding problems, such as a lack of accountability in higher education and a confusing and inadequate system for disbursing financial aid, impact all Americans. However, they "are most severe for students from low-income families and for racial and ethnic minorities" (USDOE).

Finally, the report states that the changing demographics of current college students have not yet been recognized. Americans tend to believe undergraduates are:

"... *18-to-22 years old with a recently acquired high school diploma attending classes at a four-year institution*" (*USDOE*). In reality, "*of the nation's nearly 14 million undergraduates, more than four in ten attend two-year community colleges. Nearly one-third are older than 24 years old. Forty percent are enrolled part-time*" (*USDOE*).

Some of these conditions remain true today. For instance, A 2011 report from the National Center for Public Policy and Higher Education, *Affordability and Transfer: Critical to Increasing Baccalaureate Degrees* notes that in many states the majority of students in higher education are enrolled in 2-year institutions, but that difficulties in transferring credits stand in the way of these students earning a bachelor's degree. The same report notes that African American, Hispanic, and American Indian/Alaska Native students are disproportionately likely to enroll in 2-year institutions in many states, so that inadequate recognition of their needs makes it more difficult for these students to complete their education.

While a number of other studies have been published in the past decade, the Spellings Commission findings differ in significant ways (Basken, 2007). The Commission does not suggest that additional funding is necessary; nor does it suggest that shifts in academic priorities are required. "The Spellings panel proposed a direct challenge to some deeply cherished and longstanding ways in which colleges operate, calling on higher education to shed some of its mystery and fundamentally prove the value it delivers" (Basken). To accomplish that change, the commission called upon institutions to measure and publish student learning outcomes including developing standardized tests, administering them and compiling data, including total student costs and college completion rates. This kept the Commission from granting its unanimous approval of the report. According to Basken, "one member, David Ward, president of the American Council on Education, withheld his vote, saying he could not be sure how Congress might translate his colleagues' language into legislation."

The commission shed light on issues surrounding accessibility, affordability and accountability. Ward believes that "so far the political responses have left the ball in our court. If the efforts currently underway continue and institutions adopt them, I believe we will avoid costly, complex and misguided federal policy solutions" (Ward, 2007).

ACCESSIBILITY

Among its findings, the Spellings Commission reports that access to higher education remains limited for many Americans, especially those in low-income classes, racial and ethnic minority groups and underserved and nontraditional groups. The commission stresses that this is a critical issue as these populations will comprise a large portion of the workforce in coming years (USDOE). The report states,

"Access to higher education in the United States is unduly limited by the complex interplay of inadequate preparation, lack of information about college opportunities, and persistent financial barriers" (USDOE).

The higher education community recognizes obstacles related to access and diversity and has made these issues a priority; the Commission's report has focused increased attention on an already critical concern. Efforts are underway to actively address such issues. According to Andrew Ward, president of the American Council for Education (ACE),

"ACE joined with Lumina Foundation for Education and the Advertising Council to develop the KnowHOw2Go public access campaign, which is using national advertising to expose millions of first-generation and low-income middle school students to important information regarding college preparation and financial aid."

Furthermore, ACE, State higher Education Executive Officers (SHEEO), and the National Association of System Heads (NASH) are working with Achieve on its American Diploma Project Network, a project which targets making the high school diploma a true indicator of preparedness for college (Ward).

COST & AFFORDABILITY

The Commission found that issues surrounding cost and affordability posed persistent and significant barriers for Americans seeking postsecondary education. Describing the system as "dysfunctional," the commission describes rapidly declining state subsidies and rising tuition costs at a time when the cost per student is increasing faster than inflation or family income (USDOE). The Commission asserts, "colleges and universities have few incentives to contain costs because prestige is often measured by resources, and managers who hold down spending risk losing their academic reputations" (USDOE). Reeves (2007) supports the Commission's findings and states,

"Many observers have become alarmed by the ever-escalating price of a college degree. A study released in

2006 by the National Center for Public Policy and Higher Education gave 43 states the grade of "F" for affordability."

FINANCIAL AID

The Commission found that major reform is needed to ensure that students who are in need of financial assistance for postsecondary education are able to access it,

> *"The entire financial aid system—including federal, state, institutional, an private programs—is confusing, complex, inefficient, duplicative, and frequently does not direct aid to students who truly need it" (USDOE).*

They further found that need-based aid was not rising commensurately with tuition increases, leaving a gap that many students are unable to bridge. Among the major issues listed were the number of federal programs available, the complexity of the Free Application for Federal Student Aid (FAFSA) forms, the timing of the award notifications, the unmet needs of low-income families and concerns about the amount of debt with which students graduate (USDOE).

One clear effect of the report has been a renewed interest in need-based student aid (Ward),

> *"In his FY2008 budget, President Bush called for significant cuts in subsidies paid to banks in the federal student loan program, with the savings being used to finance large increases in Pell Grants provided to low-income students" (Ward).*

In September 2007, Congress, with broad bipartisan backing, approved the largest increase in federal student aid since the GI Bill in 1944 (Basken). While this legislation was somewhat different from what the President suggested, it is apparent that the Spellings Commission addressed this issue and policy makers are responding with programs that will assist low-income students, institutions, and the nation (Ward).

The Spellings panel was not the only force pressing for a change that would make college more affordable for families and more responsive to the needs of the U.S. economy (Basken). In 2006, Democrats who had been urging a substantial increase in federal student aid took control of Congress and subsequently approved large increases to the federal student aid programs. According to Basken,

> *"The department's own Advisory Committee on Student Financial Assistance, in a September 2006 report...warned that between 1.4-million and 2.4-million potential U.S. college graduates would fail to enroll or to complete their classes because of financial obstacles" (Basken).*

In August, 2013, President Barak Obama announced an initiative to address these issues by create a rating system for colleges that would take into account measures such as affordability, proportion of low-income students enrolled, student indebtedness, and graduation rates. The ratings would be tied to federal student financial aid and the proposed plan which would begin in the 2015 school year, is intended to make college more affordable and help students and their families select colleges that produce graduates with a manageable amount of student debt.

LEARNING

The Commission found that though international rankings have placed the U.S. twelfth in higher education attainment and sixteenth in high school graduation rates, there is still little movement towards increasing learning outcomes and economic value in higher education (USDOE),

> *"Several national studies highlight shortcomings in the quality of U.S. higher education as measured by literacy, rising time to degree, and disturbing racial and ethnic gaps in student achievement...." (USDOE).*

Reeves asserts, "There is strong evidence suggesting that academic standards have dropped, that anti-intellectualism is rampant, that leftist partisanship reigns, and that degrees signify little." Citing a number of studies published in the past decade, Reeves concludes, "evidence of an intellectual decline in higher education has been accumulating for years."

While the Modern Language Association (MLA) (2006) supports the validity of many of the claims in the commission's report, it states,

> *"The report ignores the humanities' role in training workers for the new global knowledge economy and their ability to help citizens think more imaginatively, feel greater sympathy with others, and make sounder moral judgments."*

The commission discusses the need for employees who are able to solve problems, write and think critically; these skills are most often taught in humanities courses. The report offers no support for humanities; however, it focuses on the need for continued expansion in technical and scientific fields. "By the Spellings report's own logic, then, and even by its rather narrowly utilitarian standards, the humanities deserve strong support and 'increased federal investment.'" (MLA).

ACCOUNTABILITY

Accountability, also known as institutional effectiveness, has been at issue in higher education for some time. While it is accepted that institutions must be responsible to stakeholders, plans for how to collect and report data tend to be individualized and compartmentalized. The commission found that this was a critical issue and states "there is inadequate transparency and accountability for measuring institutional performance, which is more and more necessary to maintaining public trust in higher education" (USDOE). Financial health and adequate resources are no longer enough of a measure. Further, despite increasing attention paid to student learning outcomes by institutions and accreditation agencies, parents and students still have no means through which to compare data across programs or institutions (USDOE).

According to Ward, subsequent to the publication of the Commission's report,

> "The Department of Education launched a controversial effort—through an administrative process known as "negotiated rulemaking"—to rewrite the federal regulations it uses to oversee accrediting agencies. The outcome, whether intended or not, would have led to the federalization of accreditation."

Simultaneously, the Department attempted an expansion of its regulatory control of the National Advisory Committee on Institutional Quality and Integrity, which approves accrediting agencies (Ward).

Congress intervened soon after the negotiated rulemaking session closed, and both the House and the Senate Appropriations committees prohibited the department from issuing new regulations without new legislative authority (Ward).

> "Faced with overwhelming Congressional pressure and great concern within the higher education community, the secretary announced that she would not issue new regulations on accreditation [until it had been considered as a part of the reauthorization of the Higher Education Act]" (Ward).

The report is critical of the accreditation process because of its strong emphasis on resources, process and governance and its lack of attention to student learning outcomes. Calling for more transparency, the report asserts that accreditation should focus on "results and quality rather than dictating, for example, process, inputs, and governance which perpetuates current models and impedes innovation" (USDOE). The American Association of University Professors (AAUP) counters,

> "This characterization ignores both the changes in the accreditation process that have already been underway for two decades and the historical foundations that produced the higher education system so highly prized both here at home and abroad" (AAUP, 2006).

The higher education community seems to have responded to the call for greater accountability. Ward states, "these efforts avoided a one-size-fits-all, federally mandated solution and stressed the need to be sensitive to the rich diversity of institutional missions." Almost concurrent with the publication of the Spellings report came an open letter published collectively by several higher educational organizations, *Addressing the Challenges Facing American Undergraduate Education*, which discussed many of the same issues as that of the commission and outlined several accountability initiatives ("Addressing the Challenges," 2006). One of these is the Voluntary System of Accountability set forth by the American Association of State Colleges and Universities (AASCU) and the National Association of State Universities and Land-Grant Colleges (NASULGC):

The proposed system would include, for those colleges and universities that choose to participate, reporting scores on student engagement measures using one of three standardized measures of student learning. Leaders at AASCU and NASULGC hope dozens of institutions will begin using the system once it is approved by their boards (Ward).

The Association of American Universities (AAU) and the National Association of Independent Colleges and Universities (NAICU) have also announced voluntary accountability efforts. In Spring 2008, the 60 U.S. members of AAU will start providing information about undergraduate student performance to the public. It will also offer cost estimators that will provide more accurate information about the net cost students will pay to study at a specific institution. (Ward). The University and College Accountability Network developed by NAICU will give private colleges a framework with which to describe and present data on student learning outcomes in a way appropriate to institution mission and campus need (Ward). This framework "will not include any test-based data. [NAICU] contends that the missions of private colleges are too varied and too complex to be captured by any broad-based tests" (Basken).

INNOVATION

The commission found that higher education has failed to take advantage of "important innovations that would increase institutional capacity, effectiveness and productivity" and that "government and institutional policies created during a different era are impeding the expansion of models designed to meet the nation's workforce needs" (USDOE). While much scholarly research has been done on best practices in teaching and learning, those results are not often translated into practice at either the K-12 or postsecondary level. Failure to take advantage of new technology, adherence to traditional semester calendars, barriers to accepting transfer credits and concerns about accreditation and funding are all viewed as impediments to innovation (USDOE).

CRITICISM

The commission's report sparked a great deal of controversy within the higher education community. Basken states,

> "It overlooked major problems such as the conflict-of-interest scandal that subsequently enveloped both college financial-aid offices and the student-loan industry. It had no student representation. It contained no significant international comparisons."

The commission's recommendation of a centralized national database that could pose a risk to student privacy and security and there are concerns that the commission's recommendations for student learning outcomes could lead to the adoption of a single instrument or test through which to compare one institution of higher education with all others (Quevedo, 2007).

David Ward, president of the American Council on Education, and the only commission member who did not sign or endorse the final report asserts,

> "The recommendations as a whole...fail to recognize the diversity of missions within higher education and the need to be cautious about policies and standards based on a one-size-fits-all approach."

The American Association of University Professors' (AAUP) Committee on Government Relations (2006) described the report as "seriously flawed" in its insistence that higher education was in "crisis" and faulted the report for its limited mention of faculty.

According to the American Federation of Teachers (AFT) (2006),

> "The recommendations miss the boat by not attending to two of the most significant issues in higher education-the academic staffing crisis and the decline in funding by the states."

The commissioned failed to discuss the increasing reliance on part-time and adjunct faculty in higher education and the impact of that on content and quality. It also did not mention the recent decline in state support for higher education.

The AAUP asserts that,

> "What emerges from the report is a vision of higher education as a marketplace that should increasingly rely on uniform standards to measure outcomes and technological means to provide training in skills necessary for global economic competition. The process and quality of the educational experience, so central to the formation of a love of learning, civic virtues and social capital, are marginalized to the point of irrelevance."

CONCLUSION

The findings of the Spelling's commission place the higher education community at a critical juncture wherein numerous changes must be made to ensure that it meets the needs of both the American people and the global economy. While some of the reforms suggested were already being considered, others are still being debated. "Such epochal aspirations motivate many government commissions. One year later, however, there is accumulating evidence that the vision in this case might, at least in some key aspects, actually be realized" (Basken).

TERMS & CONCEPTS

Accountability: Accountability in higher education refers to the institution's responsibility to provide the high quality programs and services within the context of its stated mission to its students and its willingness to report related outcomes to all stakeholders.

Accreditation: Accreditation is the non-governmental process through which peer review and self-study ensure that federally funded educational institutions and programs in the United States are operating at a basic level of quality.

Financial Aid: Financial Aid refers to the numerous federal grant and loan programs administered by the Office of Federal Student Aid, which is a department within the USDOE. Its core mission is to ensure that all eligible individuals benefit from federal financial assistance-grants, loans and work-study programs-for education beyond high school.

Higher Education: Higher Education includes all public and private education that is available after high school, from trade schools, online professional training institutions and technical colleges to community colleges, traditional four-year colleges and universities, and graduate and professional programs.

Institutional Effectiveness: Institutional effectiveness is an information-based decision-making model wherein the data gathered through organizational learning activities is used for quality improvement. Specifically, it refers to the ongoing process through which an organization measures its performance against its stated mission and goals for the purposes of evaluation and improvement.

Negotiated Rulemaking: Negotiated rulemaking is a process that brings together representatives of various interest groups and a federal agency to negotiate the text of a proposed rule. The goal of a negotiated rulemaking proceeding is for the committee to reach consensus on the text of a proposed rule.

United States Department of Education (USDOE): The United States Department of Education was created in 1980 through a merger of several offices. Its mission is to promote student achievement and preparation for global competitiveness by fostering educational excellence and ensuring equal access.

Karin Carter-Smith

BIBLIOGRAPHY

Addressing the challenges facing American undergraduate education. (2006). Retrieved December 3, 2007, from http://aetl.umd.edu.

American Association of University Professors. (2006). AAUP statement on Spellings commission report. Retrieved December 3, 2007, from http://aaup.org.

American Federation of Teachers. (2006). Spellings commission report gets an 'incomplete' from AFT. Retrieved December 3, 2007, from http://aft.org.

Basken, P. (2007). A year later, Spellings report still makes ripples. *Chronicle of Higher Education, 54,* A1—A22. Retrieved December 3, 2007, from EBSCO online database Education Research Complete.

Liu, O.L. (2011, Sept.). Outcomes assessment in higher education: Challenges and future research in the context of voluntary system of accountability. *Educational Measurement: Issues & Practice 30,* p. 2-9. Retrieved December 27, 2013, from EBSCO Online Database Education Research Complete.

Hillman, N.W. (2013, Nov./Dec.). Economic diversity in elite higher education: Do no-loan programs impact Pell enrollments? *Journal of Higher Education 84,* following p. 806-831. Retrieved December 27, 2013, from EBSCO Online Database Education Research Complete.

Kim, J. (2012, March). Exploring the relationship between state financial aid policy and postsecondary enrollment choices: A focus on income and race differences. *Research in Higher Education 53,* p. 123-151. Retrieved December 27, 2013, from EBSCO Online Database Education Research Complete.

Spellings report spells out future for higher education. (2006). *BizEd 5,* 10. Retrieved December 3, 2007, from EBSCO online database Academic Search Premier:

Modern Language Association. (2007). Comments on the Spellings commission report from the executive council of the modern language association of America. Retrieved December 3, 2007, from http://mla.org.

Quevedo, S. (2007). Spellings report targets higher education. *The ASHA Leader Online. 12,* 1. Retrieved December 3, 2007, from, http://asha.org.

Reeves, T. C. (2006). The Spellings report: An inadequate fix. *Academic Questions. 20,* 56—60. Retrieved December 3, 2007, from EBSCO online database Academic Search Premier.

Suspitsyna, R. (2012, Jan./Feb.). Higher education for economic advancement and engaged citizenship: An analysis of the U.S. Department of Education discourse. *Journal of Higher Education 83*, p. 49-72. Retrieved December 27, 2013, from EBSCO Online Database Education Research Complete.

United States Department of Education. (2006). *A Test of Leadership: Charting the Future of U.S. Higher Education.* Washington DC. Retrieved December 3, 2007, from http://ed.gov.

Ward, D. (2007). One year after the Spellings commission: Did it make a difference? *Presidency. 10*, 5-6. Retrieved December 3, 2007, from EBSCO online database Education Research Complete.

SUGGESTED READING

Association of American Colleges and Universities. (2006). Statement on Spellings commission report. Retrieved December 3, 2007, from, http://aacu.org.

Huot, B. (2007). OPINION: Consistently inconsistent: business and the Spellings commission report on higher education. *College English. 69*, 512-525. Retrieved December 3, 2007, from EBSCO online database Academic Search Premier.

Padro, F. (2007). The key implications of the 2006 Spellings commission report: Higher education is a "knowledge industry" rather than a place of learning? *International Journal of Learning 14*, 97-104. Retrieved December 3, 2007, from EBSCO online database Education Research Complete.

Venezia, A., Kirst, M. & Anotonio, A. (2003). Betraying the college dream: How disconnected K-12 and postsecondary education systems undermine student aspirations. Retrieved December 3, 2007, from Stanford University, http://stanford.edu.

Zemsky, R. (2007). Lower college costs and improved student learning: Real answers missing from the Spellings Commission Report. *About Campus, 12*, 2 -7. Retrieved December 3, 2007, from EBSCO online database Academic Search Premier:

TEACHER TENURE

Academic tenure differs in scope for teachers employed in public K–12 schools and teachers at colleges and universities. Among K–12 teachers, tenure prevents schools from dismissing teachers without cause or due process. In higher education, tenure is meant to ensure professors' academic freedom. Over the years, discussion has begun to focus on the possibility of tenure reform. Advocates of reform argue that tenure makes it too difficult and costly to dismiss underperforming K–12 teachers; among college professors, it is alleged that,in reality, tenure does not allow professors academic freedom and that tenure evaluations discriminate against women and minorities.

KEYWORDS: Academic Freedom, Academic Research, Cause, De facto Tenure, Due Process, Faculty Governance, Public Realm/Private Realm Theory, Tenure

OVERVIEW

Tenure is a guarantee that a teacher will not be parted from a job without at least due process. At a casual glance it appears to be a simple topic, yet it is actually quite complex. Tenure rules are different for teachers in public K–12 systems and those who are professors teaching in the higher education system.

However, both tenure systems are grounded in rights protected under the 1st and 14th amendments of the Bill of Rights. The 1st amendment asserts the right to free speech and the 14th amendment creates the rules of due process that protect a teacher/professor within academia.

In order to understand tenure in public K–12 schools and institutions of higher education, how it is attained, protections it provides, and impacts it may have on institutional structures must be explored.

TENURE IN THE PUBLIC SCHOOLS SYSTEM

For a public school teacher in the American K–12 system, tenure can be fairly defined as the right to due process (Jordan, 2005) and is most usually attained in the third year of teaching. Tenure reviews generally consist of an assessment of a teacher's effectiveness based on:

- A personal assessment of performance;
- Results of a supervisory classroom observation
- Comments provided by parents of children from the teacher's classroom.

In many states, classroom test scores have begun to be factored into the review equation (Bernstein, 2006). Once the assessments are complete, the teacher is given a formal performance review and taken off of probationary status. At that point, contracts move from an annual renewal to one encompassing a period of time (typically up to five years). Tenure does not confer a guarantee of lifetime employment or even a choice of schools in which the teacher will work (Christie, 1997).

A tenured teacher cannot be released from an employment contract without cause and without due process. This means a teacher must have done something that violated the rules and policies of the school system (cause) and must be afforded certain protections, steps, and appeals in the firing process (due process). Typically, a teacher must have been formally notified that there is a problem and given help to fix the problem: these efforts at remediation must be well documented. Performance reviews must be balanced, listing instances of sub-par performance as well as instances of satisfactory performance. The teacher must be allowed a hearing that is fair and timely; allowing the teacher a chance to challenge charges and allegations of poor performance. Academic freedom is not really a component of the K–12 mission because there are not requirements to generate new knowledge in the form of research (Desmond, 2003).

There is a lot of controversy regarding the impact tenure has on the public school system. Some educators believe the tenure system does not allow a fair evaluation of a teacher, especially if classroom test performance is to be factored into the equation. Others believe the tenure system, coupled with a strong teacher's union, makes it virtually impossible to dismiss a teacher who is underperforming. Criticisms of the systems for granting tenure has led some school systems to reform rather than abolish the way teachers are evaluated for tenure: for instance, for the 2011–12 school year, New York City introduced a framework for evaluation of teachers, to be used citywide, focusing on three areas: impact on student learning, instructional practice, and professional contributions. Within each category, a teacher is graded on a four-point scale (ineffective, developing, effective, and highly effective). The framework also includes guidelines for the type of evidence that may be used in the tenure evaluation, including student achievement, classroom observation, annual reviews, and feedback from students, parents, and colleagues.

Teachers in the majority of districts in North Carolina became increasingly frustrated after a 2013 budget measure determined that tenure in the state would be phased out by 2018, to be replaced by limited contracts. By the following year, attempts were made to remedy the imminent loss of tenure by instituting a pay mandate requiring districts to offer one quarter of their teachers four-year contracts with a pay raise. However, by that time some counties had begun to sue the state to overturn the law, and in 2015, the North Carolina Court of Appeals ruled the law unconstitutional. In 2014, a landmark case in California, *Vergara v. California*, deemed five provisions of the California Education Code to be unconstitutional; the ruling will ostensibly make it easier to dismiss or deny tenure to underperforming teachers. In this case, the defendants had specifically argued that the tenure statutes had disproportionately negative impacts on poor and minority students. The outcome of this case directly sparked lawsuits in the state of New York, which argued that the state's statutes valued career length over job performance in consideration for tenure.

TENURE IN THE HIGHER EDUCATION SYSTEM

The concept of tenure was established in higher education by the American Association of University Professors in 1915. It was meant to ensure academic freedom (i.e., "the freedom to teach, conduct research, and perform other duties without fear of job loss or censure" [Williams & Ceci, 2007]) and to shore up the practice of faculty governance (Bok, 1982). Higher education in America is predicated on three pillars: Academic Freedom, Tenure, and Faculty Governance. Professors need the ability to push students to examine their personal beliefs, making them hold the beliefs more strongly or adjust their beliefs to accommodate new knowledge without the fear of being fired for creating these challenges. Education is meant to be a free exchange of ideas resulting in robust debate and potential disagreement within a nurturing environment (Desmond).

The meaning of tenure in the higher education arena is a bit different from that of the public school system. First, the freedom to conduct research is added to the notion of the freedom to teach. Second, the career-long commitment is a permanent, life-long commitment to the professor for as long as the professor chooses to teach or conduct research. Third, the time it takes to become tenured is long (typically seven years or longer) and is predicated on an apprenticeship model in which the professor is promoted through the ranks from Assistant Professor, to Associate Professor, to Professor via a series of scheduled performance reviews (Desmond).

Procedurally, a professor on the tenure-track receives yearly reviews with extensive, formal reviews in at least the third and seventh years (and, most usually, the fifth year). The formal reviews include external reviewers and are critical junctures in which the faculty member may receive a one-year notice of intent to dismiss (AAUP, 1940; Hofstadter & Metzger, 1956). If the faculty member is retained, the formal reviews explicate what needs to be done to obtain a positive review during the next formal review period. The seventh year review is the actual opportunity to become a fully tenured professor. The assistant professor presents the review committee with a file containing evidence of exemplary research, teaching, and service activities. The file wends its way through a carefully prescribed review process with a yes or no decision rendered at each step. The university president makes the final decision (based on the entire review process) and is the only one who can grant tenure (Desmond).

According to the American Association of University Professors, "The primary purpose of tenure is to add knowledge to the common good and not to further the interest of either the individual professor or the institution as a whole. The common good depends upon the free search for truth and its free exposition." Tenure works to protect academic freedoms that allow professors to speak to controversial matters, pursue and research politically unpopular topics, and report unethical practices of their peers (Williams & Ceci). Tenured professors have earned the right to test new ideas, many of which will fail. Their tenure status allows them the protection needed to risk failure minus the threat of punishment (Desmond). Additionally, tenure is credited with helping to attract talented faculty members, raise graduation rates, and protect the speech and writings of contrarians (Bowen, 2007).

However, tenure does impose some restraints on an institution's ability to manage effectively. Administration often struggles to manage annual budgets that are based on available state funding and student enrollment rates while disregarding the expenses incurred in retaining commitments to tenured professors. This can create potential

financial burdens during years of fiscal stress (Honan & Teferra, 2001). Also, tenured professors who are viewed as incompetent or negligent are still entitled to their jobs and there are no built-in incentives to motivate exceptional performance once tenure has been attained (Desmond).

Tenure is often promoted as the only secure protection for academic freedom in teaching, research, and service. Tenure systems are most common in four-year public institutions, according to the 2015 *Digest of Education Statistics* published by the National Center for Education Statistics. In 2013–14, 74.6 percent of public four-year institutions had tenure systems, with the tenure system nearly universal (99.6 percent) in doctoral institutions; however, a tenure system was less common in two-year institutions (58.9 percent). Among not-for-profit four-year institutions, 61.8 percent had tenure systems, and among not-for-profit two-year institutions, 12.5 percent had tenure systems. Tenure systems were rare in for-profit institutions, with only 1.2 percent reporting having a tenure system.

Despite the presence of a tenure system in most four-year institutions, universities are increasingly hiring faculty members on an adjunct or contingent basis, so that they are not on the tenure track and, in many cases, are hired on a per-class or per-semester basis. According to the annual faculty salary report by the American Association of University Professors (AAUP), released in 2015, only 20.35 percent of instructional faculty are full-time tenured and tenure track (Barnshaw & Dunietz, 2015).

Questions have been raised as to whether tenure actually provides the claimed protections and rights in the changing academic environments in both the public K–12 and higher education systems.

CALLS FOR CHANGE TO THE K-12 TENURE SYSTEM

There has been a movement to increase the time required for public school teachers to attain tenure (Bernstein; Jordan). Some arguments are grounded in concepts assuming most teachers are competent; some are grounded in concepts assuming bad teachers are able to use current tenure rules to usurp any efforts to remove them from their positions.

Politics have created a trend that requires teachers to be evaluated with an increased focus on student test scores. Some people believe it is unfair to the teacher and the community to place so much weight on test scores when the teacher has only two to three years of data available when the tenure review comes due. Therefore, many administrators and political leaders have suggested extending the probationary period to five or six years (Bernstein).

However, many other educational leaders wonder whether good teachers can be recruited and retained if they are required to navigate their school's bureaucracy devoid of procedural rights for the suggested five-year period (Jordan). As states move toward lengthening the time to tenure for public school teachers concerns regarding the ability of new teachers to implement new ideas and innovations into the education system have risen to the forefront (Jordan). Opponents of the movement contend the existing state laws already allow for the firing of teachers who show gross incompetence or misconduct. They posit that behind every bad teacher that has successfully resisted being fired is a cadre of bungling school administrators (Jordan).

Other leaders and community members are calling for change in the tenure system because of perceived negative impacts of the system. Some of these arguments outlined by Reeder (2005) are:

- Tenure, combined with a historical administrative reluctance to give substantive negative evaluations or to remediate underperforming teachers, detracts from meaningful accountability. In fact, data from an investigative report of the Illinois school system indicate tenure has evolved into near total job protection that mocks the goal of accountability;

- Due Process procedures diminish a school board's ability to dismiss poor teachers; it is often left to the discretion of a hearing officer. This process can take years and cost over Due Process procedures diminish a school board's ability to dismiss poor teachers; it is often left to the discretion of a hearing officer. This process can take years and cost over $100,000 per incident;

- "It isn't tenure itself that makes it hard to fire a teacher. It is the vigorous defense provided by teacher unions" (Kerchner, as cited in Reeder). Teachers' unions often create additional procedural hurdles that work to leave underperforming teachers in place. The hurdles may include elaborate systems of evaluating every public school teacher in the state coupled with a remediation program to coach underperforming teachers. If all of the procedures are not scrupulously followed

prior to a dismissal, the teacher may remain in place. Dismissed cases most often hinge on questions of whether forms were completed correctly rather than whether the teacher was actually doing a good job at teaching (Reeder).

Each of these circumstances may result in the retention of underperforming teachers. However, even successful firings are costly and time consuming if the teacher decides to fight the action. Take, for example, the firing of Cecil Roth in the state of Illinois. He was employed by the Geneseo School District for twenty years and received positive evaluations up until the last year, despite student recollections that he was the worst teacher in the Geneseo public schools (this is common according to attorneys who handle terminations for school districts). School district efforts to document his poor performance were crafted in highly diplomatic language devoid of descriptions of Mr. Roth's actual behaviors (e.g., "We have no evidence to suggest Mr. Roth has done anything to promote or contribute to a positive school climate and rather isolates himself from staff and students"). Five years after his firing was upheld in court, Mr. Roth continued to file frivolous motions and actions to sue his former employer. The school district retained an attorney to answer each of his filings and Mr. Roth was cited for contempt of court several times. One judge described Roth's efforts this way, "Roth is engaging in litigation terrorism. He is attempting to hijack the court system and use litigation before the court to advance his own personal agenda and call attention to himself and his cause..." (Reeder).

TRENDS IN HIGHER EDUCATION: INADEQUATE NUMBERS OF TENURED FACULTY

Many colleges and universities appear to be trying to remain competitive by investing their money in the accoutrements that attract more students (e.g., new recreational facilities, renovated sports fields, updated dorms, etc.). This leaves less money to recruit tenured faculty and often results in the hiring of non-tenured faculty to conduct the bulk of the teaching. The quality of instruction may be diminished by the lack of experienced, tenured professors who are available to provide cohesiveness within the curriculum. Many of the non-tenured faculty members do not have the luxury of offices, professional development opportunities, or paid time for office hours. They are often absent from campus during non-teaching hours because they are busy teaching at other colleges or universities. Their students do not have the opportunity to informally contact the professor and engage in discourse as they seek to master scholarship and exercise their own freedom in inquiry. Faculty governance is also weakened when the majority of teachers are not tenured and, thus, ineligible to participate in campus governance (ARUP, 2003; Shih, 2003).

The question, then, becomes, "What good is tenure if no one is receiving it?"

Viewpoints

DO WE NEED TENURE REFORM?

Tenure reform has been considered in higher education. Proponents of reform contend that tenure, coupled with the advancement structure, creates strong incentives for hard work during the first years of a professor's academic career and poor incentives forever after (Levitt, 2007). They also contend that the tenure process rarely protects scholars who are conducting politically unpopular research and classroom lectures (since, they contend, these activities rarely occur). However, it protects tenured scholars who underperform or produce low-quality work (Williams & Ceci). Additionally, research suggests that tenure is not liberating professors in their speech and research because the institutional structure provides a more powerful force in stymieing these freedoms for anyone who is not a full professor. Junior faculty competing for tenure are most likely to simply work to please the ruling senior faculty (Williams & Ceci).

Opponents of tenure reform are concerned with how academia would be restructured minus tenure rights. The absence of tenure would erode the other two pillars—faculty governance and academic freedom. How would universities and colleges successfully hire and recruit if senior faculty members (who are committed to faculty governance) could now fire each other? The academic structure functions as an organized anarchy (Baldridge, Curtis, Ecker, & Riley, 1977) wherein faculty governance functions would most likely evolve into a more hierarchical system with a boss. An established boss would most likely begin to chip away at academic freedom as internal and external pressures to avoid specific topics may be applied (Mankiw, 2007).

A less cited, though perhaps more persuasive argument than the one of faculty governance, is that tenure helps to preserve academic standards. At all but the few institutions with exceptionally large endowments, administrations are largely motivated to increase the number of students at the institution. This motivation, left unchecked, would result in ever-declining admissions requirements and ever-rising grade inflation. A faculty that is tenured and that does not share directly in the profits of the institution is motivated less by maintaining enrollment numbers than by maintaining its academic reputation among its peers. Thus, tenure protects academic rigor from competitive forces that would erode that rigor in favor of attracting and retaining greater numbers of students.

TENURE NEEDS TO BE CHANGED TO REMOVE PRIVILEGE FOR MALES

Historically white males have been in a privileged position when it comes to attaining tenure. This can be mostly attributed to the steady presence of upper-middle-class white men in the higher-education realm from its inception. The requirements of tenure were constructed and shaped by negotiations between these men and their employers, and men are reluctant to acknowledge that institutional structures provide them advantage (Marshall, 1998; Thornton, 2004). Women, people of color, and people from lower socioeconomic classes have only recently become an employed presence in higher-education institutions (Sadker & Sadker, 1984).

Despite the stronger presence of women (in particular) in academia for the past thirty years, tenure requirements have not appeared to evolve in ways which make the academy equitably accessible to men and women. Literature and research suggest advancement discriminations within the workplace are often subtle and based on the division of labor described in private sphere/public sphere theory and have worked to create double standards for advancement in academia (Hartsock, 1983; Thompson, 2007). Female professors who are working to attain tenure are often struggling to balance their desire for tenure with their desire to have children. Studies show that having a baby enhances a man's, and stymies a woman's, tenure opportunities (Armenti, 2004). At issue is whether the tenure process is a structural roadblock to increasing the percentage of women choosing to become professors (van Anders, 2004).

Additionally, female and minority faculty are quite likely to agree that tenure is an outmoded concept and an 'old boys' club.' Tenure evaluations are often conducted in secret sessions by committees that keep no minutes. Tenure committees often provide no details to the tenure candidate on the reasons why tenure was denied. Such secrecy makes it easy for one or a few faculty members to sabotage a tenure case for a tenure candidate they dislike.

TERMS & CONCEPTS

Academic Freedom: The freedom of faculty to teach (and conduct research in institutions of higher education) relative to one's subject area "without undue interference and fear from inside and outside institutions".

Academic Research: Ongoing research and related publication that must be conducted by all faculty in higher education, and upon which tenure decisions are made.

Cause: Sufficient reason.

De facto Tenure: To all intents and purposes the teacher is considered to have tenure although tenure has not been formally granted.

Due Process: The principle that the government must respect all of a person's legal rights when the government deprives a person of life, liberty, or property. This principle applies to teachers who are being deprived of employment in the public system.

Faculty Governance: The system whereby the faculty run the university or college.

Public Realm/Private Realm Theory: The theory describing how work in the private realm (i.e., most usually the unpaid work of women as volunteers and mothers) is not valued as equally as work in the private realm (i.e., the paid work of men and women in the workplace).

Tenure: The employment commitment made between an institution and the teacher. Tenure confers rights to due process (Desmond). Tenure is said to preserve academic freedom for both the faculty members and the institution.

Sherry Thompson

BIBLIOGRAPHY

Armenti, C. (2004). May babies and posttenure babies: Maternal decisions of women professors. *The Review of Higher Education, 27*, 211–231.

Baker, B. D., Oluwole, J. O., & Green, P. C. (2013). The legal consequences of mandating high stakes decisions based on low quality information: Teacher evaluation in the race-to-the-top era. *Education Policy Analysis Archives, 21* (4/5), 1–16. Retrieved December 27, 2013, from EBSCO Online Database Education Research Complete.

Baldridge, V. J., Curtis, D. V., Ecker, G. P., & Riley, G. L. (1977). Alternative models of governance in higher education. In G. L. Riley and V. J. Baldridge (Eds.), *Governing Academic Organizations.* Berkeley, CA: McCutchan Publishing Corporation.

Barnshaw, J., & Dunietz, S. (2015). Busting the myths. *Academe, 101*(2), 4–84. Retrieved January 4, 2016, from EBSCO Online Database Education Research Complete.

Bernstein, M. F. (2006). Delaying teacher tenure for education's good. *School Administrator, 63*, 51. Retrieved July 15, 2007, from EBSCO Online Database Education Research Complete.

Bok, D. (1982). *Beyond the ivory tower: The responsibilities of the modern university.* Cambridge, MA: Harvard University Press.

Bowen, R. W. (2007). An uncertain future for tenure as we know it. *The Chronicle Review, 53*, B21.

Christie, K. (1997). Teacher tenure. *NASBE Policy Update, 5*, 1.

Contingent appointments and the academic profession. (2003). *Academe, 89*, 59–72. Retrieved January 4, 2016, from EBSCO Online Database Education Research Complete.

Desmond, T. (2003). The tenure trek. *Continuum, 12*, 1–7.

Dimaria, F. (2012). Tenure and America's community colleges. *Education Digest, 78*, 44–47. Retrieved October 16, 2014, from EBSCO online database Education Research Complete.

Eagan, M. K., Jr., Jaeger, A. J., & Grantham, A. (2015). Supporting the academic majority: Policies and practices related to part-time faculty's job satisfaction. *Journal of Higher Education, 86*(3), 448–483. Retrieved December 27, 2016, from EBSCO online database Education Source.

Hartsock, N. C. M. (1983). The feminist standpoint: Developing the ground for a specifically feminist historical materialism. In S. Harding and M. B. Hintikka (Eds.), *Discovering reality: Feminist perspectives on epistemology, metaphysics, methodology, and philosophy of science.* Dordrecht, Holland: D. Reidel Publishing.

Herbert, A., & Tienar, J. (2013). *Studies in Higher Education, 38,* 157–173. Retrieved December 27, 2013, from EBSCO Online Database Education Research Complete.

Hofstadter, R., & Metzger, W. P. (1956). *The development of academic freedom in the United States.* New York, NY: Columbia University Press.

Honan, J. P. & Teferra, D. (2001). The US academic profession: Key policy changes. *Higher Education, 41* (1/2), 183–203. Retrieved July 15, 2007, from EBSCO Online Database Academic Search Premier.

Jordan, S. (2005). Changing the rules on teacher tenure PROP. 74: Is this education reform? This plan will drive away teachers. *San Francisco Chronicle.* Retrieved July 15, 2007, from http://sfgate.com.

Kezar, A. (2012). Spanning the great divide between tenure-track and non-tenure-track faculty. *Change, 44,* 6–13. Retrieved December 27, 2013, from EBSCO Online Resource Education Research Complete.

Levitt, S. D. (2007). Editorial Comment. *The Chronicle Review, 53,* B4.

Mankiw, N. G. (2007). Editorial Comment. *The Chronicle Review, 53,* B4.

Marshall, C. (1998). Critical feminist policy analysis: Toward demanding and disrupting policy analyses. (ERIC Document Reproduction Service No. ED428022).

Premeaux, S. R. (2012). Tenure Perspectives: Tenured Versus Nontenured Tenure-Track Faculty. *Journal of Education for Business, 87,* 121–27. Retrieved October 16, 2014, from EBSCO online database, Education Research Complete.

Reeder, S. (2005). Cost to fire a tenured teacher? More than $219,000. *The Hidden Costs of Tenure.* Retrieved from http://thehiddencostsoftenure.com.

Robertson, M. (2015). Blaming teacher tenure is not the answer. *Journal of Law & Education, 44*(3), 463–471. Retrieved January 4, 2016, from EBSCO Online Database Education Research Complete.

Sadker, M., & Sadker, D. (1994). *Failing at fairness: How America's schools cheat girls.* New York, NY: Charles Scribner's Sons.

Sawchuk, S. (2014). N.C. districts sour on state's anti-tenure law. *Education Week, 33*(29), 1–17. Retrieved January 4, 2016, from EBSCO Online Database Education Research Complete.

Shih, E. (2003). Transient professors: How important is tenure? *The Yale Herald,* 36.

Thompson, S. A. (2007). *Should I stay or should I go? An examination of faculty satisfaction and intent to leave.* Unpublished doctoral dissertation, University of Utah, Salt Lake City.

Thornton, S. (2004). Where—not when—should you have a baby? *The Chronicle of Higher Education, 51,* B–12. Retrieved July 31, 2007, from EBSCO Online Database Academic Search Premier.

Van Anders, S. (2004). Why the academic pipeline leaks: Fewer men than women perceive barriers to becoming professors. *Sex Roles, 51* (9/10), 511–521.

Williams, W. M., & Ceci, S. J. (2007). Does tenure really work? *The Chronicle Review, 53,* B16.

SUGGESTED READING

Acker, S., & Armenti, C. (2004). Sleepless in academia. *Gender and Education, 16,* 3–24. Retrieved July 31, 2007, from EBSCO Online Database Education Research Complete.

Caplan, P. (1993). *Lifting a ton of feathers: A woman's guide to surviving in the academic world.* Toronto: University of Toronto Press.

Herreid, C. F., Prud'homme-Généreux, A., Schiller, N. A., Herreid, K. F., & Wright, C. (2015). A peek behind the curtain of tenure and promotion. *Journal of College Science Teaching, 45*(1), 61–65.

Hochschild, A. R., & Machung, A. (1990). *The second shift.* New York, NY: Quill Books.

Lawrence, J. H., Celis, S., & Ott, M. (2014). Is the tenure process fair? What faculty think. *Journal of Higher Education, 85,* 155–88. Retrieved October 16, 2014, from EBSCO online database, Education Research Complete.

Ross, C. G. (2015). Toward a new consensus for tenure in the twenty-first century. *Academe, 101*(3), 14–21. Retrieved January 4, 2016, from EBSCO Online Database Education Research Complete.

Valian, V. (1998). *Why so slow? The advancement of women.* Cambridge, MA: MIT Press.

TUITION-FREE COLLEGE

This article focuses on how areas across the country have implemented tuition-free college programs. One of the best kept secrets is a list of those institutions that offer free tuition for attending their colleges and universities. The criteria are different, but all have the same focus. The article provides a list of schools that offer free tuition and discusses the stipulations that may apply. In addition, there is a review of a study that was conducted on tuition waivers for older adult students.

KEYWORDS: Associates Degree; Grade Point Average (GPA); Higher Education; Loan Forgiveness; No Child Left Behind Act; Peace Corps; Public Service; Teach for America

OVERVIEW

Education is seen as the tool to expand one's chances of earning more money. But, the cost of earning a degree has skyrocketed and "students from middle-class and working-class families have been forced to borrow huge sums of money, in recent years to pay for college, often saddling them with hefty loan payments long after graduation" (Schworm & Wertheimer, 2007). Part of the American dream was not to be debt-ridden. According to Porter (2002):

> The escalating cost of higher education is causing many to question the value of continuing education beyond high school. Many wonder whether the high cost of tuition, the opportunity cost of choosing college over full-time employment, and the accumulation of thousands of dollars of debt, is in the long run, worth the investment.

There is a way to have the best of both worlds. Students do not have to forgo their dreams if they can tap into a source that is seldom used. There are colleges that will offer tuition for free, especially if you meet the required criteria. Before a student gives up, it may benefit him/her to search the internet to see if he/she qualifies for any of these programs.

FREE TUITION

"Going to college tuition free is an increasingly attractive option for students who don't want to begin their working lives owing money on loans" (Brandon, 2006). One of the best kept secrets is a list of those institutions that offer free tuition for attending their colleges and universities. The criteria are different, but all have the same focus; attracting students to their campuses. Some of these programs include:

TUITION FREE WITH A STIPULATION

Koshzow (n.d.) provided a list of schools that provide free tuition with a stipulation. Some of the schools on the list were:

- Berea College in Berea, Kentucky; mandatory work study programs;
- College of the Ozarks in Point Lookout, Missouri; mandatory work study and chapel requirements;

- Cooper Union in New York, New York; programs are focused on architecture, art and engineering focused;
- Curtis Institute of Music in Philadelphia, Pennsylvania; only for those focused on music careers and studies;
- Deep Springs College in Deep Springs, California; all-male, liberal arts college in the desert;
- F.W. Olin College of Engineering in Needham, Massachusetts; only for those focused on studying engineering;
- U.S. Military Academy in West Point, New York; five-year service requirement after graduation.

TUITION FREE FOR STAYING HOME

Brandon provided a list of schools that offer free tuition to high school graduates if they elect to attend a college in their community. This approach is an effort to help build a high-quality homegrown workforce. Some of the programs include:

- **The Kalamazoo Promise:** Graduates of public high schools in Kalamazoo, Michigan can receive a scholarship that pays tuition for up to four years at any Michigan public university or community college if they make regular progress toward a degree or certification, maintain a 2.0 grade point average (GPA), and take a minimum of 12 credit hours per semester. The tuition benefit is graduated based on time spent in the Kalamazoo public schools, with students who attended grades k-12 getting 100 percent of their tuition paid. Students must have been enrolled in the school district for at least four years to qualify;
- **Oklahoma Higher Learning Access Program:** Oklahoma residents with a family income of less than $50,000 at the time of enrollment who maintain a 2.5 high school GPA and take a set of required college-preparatory courses may receive free tuition at Oklahoma public institutions and partial tuition at Oklahoma private schools if they maintain a 1.7 GPA for their first 30 credit hours and a 2.0 GPA after that;
- **Garrett County Commissioners Scholarship Program:** One may qualify for this program if they have been a resident of Garrett County, Maryland for two or more years and graduated from a Garrett County high school as well as enroll full time at Garrett College and maintain a 2.0 GPA. This scholarship program will awarded the difference

between the other forms of aid for which the students qualify and the full cost of tuition;

- **Educate and Grow Scholarship:** This program is for high school graduates of any Kingsport, Tennessee, city or Sullivan County high school whose parents have been residents for at least one year. These graduates may receive two years' free tuition to Northeast State Community College if they maintain a 2.0 GPA and work towards an associate's degree;
- **J. F. Drake State Technical College:** This college located in Huntsville, Alabama offers free summer-session tuition to recent high school graduates of Madison, Jackson, Bedford, Franklin, Giles, Lawrence, Lincoln, Marion, Marshall, and Moore counties who have at least a 2.5 high school GPA;
- **The Newton Promise:** In a program recently approved by voters and expected to begin in 2007, all students who graduate from a Newton, Iowa high school, reside in the district, and have been students there for four or more years will receive college tuition funding for four years at an Iowa university, two years at an Iowa community college, or an equivalent amount to apply toward tuition at a private college in Iowa. The amount of funding depends on a student's years of residency in the Newton district and attendance at its public schools (Brandon).

PROPOSALS

Although it has been stated that many are concerned about the cost of higher education, there still is a desire to make sure that certain constituents have the opportunity to earn a college education. Two of those areas surround gifted students and students who are actively involved in public service. Two public officials have stepped up to the plate and offered their opinions on how special interest groups can earn a free education.

GOVERNOR BILL RICHARDSON (NEW MEXICO)

Governor Richardson is a 2008 Democratic presidential candidate, and has been making pledges in the event he becomes president. One of his proposals is to offer two years of loan forgiveness to pay for students' tuition costs at public universities in exchange for one year of public service (Loring, 2007). Positions that would be eligible for the "loan payment for service program" would include the Peace

Corps, AmeriCorps, Teach for America, firefighters, police officers, public interest attorneys who earned less than $45,000 per year; National Health Service Corps, and teachers and medical professionals in underserved areas. In addition, his plan would discard the No Child Left Behind Act and offer incentives for colleges to keep their costs down. Although the proposed plan has received support, there are those who have some concerns.

- **Strengths of the Plan:** Encourages students to give back to the community by devoting time to public services; reignites the spotlight on public service careers; raises awareness and candidates for public leadership; and rewards young people who decide to pursue a career in public service;
- **Concerns about the Plan:** Only available to students attending public universities; discrepancy in how to define what types of careers would be considered public service; and the costs of administering such a program.

GOVERNOR MCGREEVEY (NEW JERSEY)

When Jim McGreevey was the governor of New Jersey, he proposed that the state offer free tuition at any of the state's 19-community colleges to the top 20 percent of graduating high school seniors. Based on his estimates, there would be approximately 9,000 students eligible for this program (University Business, 2004). This program would cost approximately $6 million dollars during the first year. However, there are three significant benefits.

- First, the State is making an effort to woo the top students in its high schools to continue their education in the same state;
- Secondly, the program provides an opportunity for the brightest students in the state to continue their education regardless of financial circumstances;
- Finally, the proposed increase to the cap for capital improvements would allow the community colleges to free up their funds for other projects.

OLDER ADULT STUDENTS

Many colleges and universities had established policies that offered older adult students free or reduced tuition by the early 1970s. These policies were created in response to the decrease in the number of traditional age students, which created a need to attract nontraditional students; and the increased public interest in improving the life style of older persons. The purpose for offering free tuition was to eliminate the financial barriers and encourage older individuals in fixed income and lower socio-economic groups to further their education. When these policies were first established, institutions saw an increase in the number of older adult students. However, the increase was not consistent over the years. Also, during this same period of time, there were economic changes. As a result of the increasing demand for existing educational funds, many thought it appropriate to examine the free or reduced tuition policies and determine:

- To what extent are policies increasing access to learning activities?
- Are these policies benefiting persons from lower-socio-economic groups?
- Are these policies covering the type of courses through which persons can find assistance in meeting their diverse learning needs?
- Is the source of funding for these policies a factor in determining the extent to which an institution will publicize their availability? (Butcher, 1980).

Butcher conducted a study that sought to answer the questions listed above. The study was limited to two-year community, junior, and technical colleges. The purpose of the study was to examine the existence of state-wide policies regulating these institutions, as well as policies established by individual institutions in states without these policies. The study also explored whether or not these policies covered the types of courses taken by the majority of older adult students or benefited/limited lifelong learning opportunities.

A letter and questionnaire was mailed to state administrators of community colleges in all fifty states. The letter requested the following information:

- Existence of a state-wide policy of free or reduced tuition for older adult students, the provisions of such a policy, and a copy of each legislative act or board policy;
- Enrollment figures for the past three years or an indication of the enrollment trend if this information was not available;
- The extent of state funding for credit and noncredit courses, the extent of funding for tuition waivers, and other sources of funding available at the state level for noncredit community education courses.

In addition, there were interviews conducted with a number of state administrators of community colleges to better understand:

- The complexities of funding credit and noncredit courses in certain states;
- The methods of approving noncredit courses in which the majority of seniors register;
- The ways the study might determine the strength of a state's commitment to the older adult student.

A sample of 146 institutions having policies of tuition waivers for older adult students were mailed letters and questionnaires. These were addressed to the director of continuing education or community services. Forty six state administrators of community colleges returned their surveys. The remaining four states were contacted via a telephone call. The interviewers were able to confirm that these states did not have statewide policies. One hundred and eleven of the community colleges responded to the survey, of which 62 were located in urban areas and 49 were rural areas.

The findings of the study can be broken down into four categories, which are indicated below:

STATE-WIDE POLICIES WAIVING TUITION FOR OLDER ADULT STUDENTS

- State-wide policies affecting community, junior, and technical colleges existed in 22 of the 50 states;
- Seven states had policies established by state boards of education;
- Two states had policies waiving tuition for the four-year institutions in a state, but not for the two-year community or junior colleges;
- Policies usually waived tuition for credit courses only. Some state acts or board policies specifically restrict tuition waivers to credit courses;
- Many policies do not specify the type of course qualifying under the provisions of the policy, but it is felt that they relate to credit rather than to self-sustaining noncredit courses;
- Some state policies waive tuition, but prohibit institutions from including these waivers in the computation for state funding;
- Some states had policies with space availability restrictions;
- States that waive tuition for credit and noncredit courses and indicate that they will fund both types of courses have made a positive commitment to aid the older student.

ENROLLMENT DATA FOR OLDER ADULT STUDENTS

- There was an increase in enrollment, especially among older students. Many of these students took courses on a part-time basis;
- The majority of the seniors enrolled in noncredit courses in the continuing education or community service section of community colleges;
- Sixty-eight of the institutions reported an increase in enrollment, and noted that they believe that tuition waivers were an important factor affecting this trend.

NONCREDIT COMMUNITY EDUCATION DIVISION OF A COMMUNITY COLLEGE IS USUALLY RESPONSIBLE FOR COORDINATING & ADMINISTERING SENIOR PROGRAMS

- The majority of the senior programs are run from the continuing education or community service division of the college;
- In certain states where tuition waivers only cover credit courses, many classes were packaged to conform to the guidelines for credit courses.

FUNDING CREDIT & NONCREDIT COMMUNITY EDUCATION PROGRAMS

- State administrators listed other sources of funding available at the state level for senior programs;
- California had no tuition in state supported schools for credit courses. After Proposition 13, the legislature eliminated funding for noncredit courses except for a few specific categories;
- North Carolina had one of the most progressive tuition waiver policies, along with Maryland. Both funded both credit and approved noncredit courses.

CONCLUSION

"Going to college tuition free is an increasingly attractive option for students who don't want to begin their working lives owing money on loans" (Brandon). One of the best kept secrets is a list of those institutions that offer free tuition for attending their colleges and universities. The criteria are different, but all have the same focus; attracting students to their campuses.

Although it has been stated that many are concerned about the cost of higher education, there still is a desire to make sure that certain constituents have the opportunity to earn a college education. Two of those areas surround gifted students and students who are actively involved in public service. Two public officials have stepped up to the plate and offered their opinions on how special interest groups can earn a free education.

Many colleges and universities had established policies that offered older adult students free or reduced tuition by the early 1970s. These policies were created in response to the decrease in the number of traditional age students, which created a need to attract nontraditional students; and the increased public interest in improving the life style of older persons. The purpose for offering free tuition was to eliminate the financial barriers and encourage older individuals on fixed income and lower socio-economic groups to further their education. When these policies were first established, institutions saw an increase in the number of older adult students. However, the increase was not consistent over the years. Also, during this same period of time, there were economic changes.

Butcher conducted a study that sought to answer the questions listed above. The study was limited to two-year community, junior, and technical colleges. The purpose of the study was to examine the existence of state-wide policies regulating these institutions, as well as policies established by individual institutions in states without these policies.

TERMS & CONCEPTS

Associates Degree: An academic degree conferred by a two-year college, sometimes known as a junior college.

Grade Point Average (GPA): The average numerical grade earned, calculated by dividing the grade points earned by the number of credits attempted.

Higher Education: Education beyond the secondary level.

Loan Forgiveness: The cancellation of part or all of an educational loan by the federal government.

No Child Left Behind Act: A federal law to improve education for all children.

Peace Corps: A federal government organization, set up in 1961, that trains and sends American volunteers abroad to work with people of developing countries on projects for technological, agricultural, and educational improvement (peacecorpsonline.org).

Public Service: Employment within a governmental system, and performed for the benefit of the public, such as within the civil service or a non-profit organization.

Teach for America: A non-profit organization whose mission is to end educational inequity by enlisting the nation's most promising future leaders (teachforamerica.org).

Marie Gould

BIBLIOGRAPHY

$30M spent in 6 Years on Kalamazoo scholarships. (2011). *Community College Week, 24,* 13. Retrieved December 15, 2013, from EBSCO Online Database Education Research Complete.

Brandon, E. (2006, April 8). Go to college tuition free. *U.S. News & World Report.* Retrieved November 29, 2007, from http://usnews.com.

Butcher, L., & American Association of Community and Junior Colleges (1980, March 1). Free and reduced tuition policies for older adult students at two-year community, junior, and technical colleges. (ERIC Document Reproduction Service No. ED184645).

Davis, R.J., Nagle, B., Richards, D.R., & Awokoya, J.T. (2013). The impact of the Gates Millennium Scholars Program on college choice for high-achieving, low-income African American students. *Journal of Negro Education, 82,* 226-242. Retrieved December 15, 2013, from EBSCO Online Database Education Research Complete. .

Hillman, N. W. (2013). Economic Diversity in Elite Higher Education: Do No-Loan Programs Impact Pell Enrollments?. Journal Of Higher Education, 84, 806-831. Retrieved December 15, 2013, from EBSCO Online Database Education Research Complete.

Kollman, M., & Beck, L. (2013). Free CTE college tuition and certification funding: KS SB155 at work. *Techniques:*

Connecting Education & Careers, 88, 38-42. Retrieved December 15, 2013, from EBSCO Online Database Education Research Complete.

Koshzow, C. (n.d.). Tuition-free colleges - How to go to college for free. Retrieved November 29, 2007, from http://collegelife.about.com.

Loring, N. (2007, November 8). Something to serve for. Retrieved November 29, 2007, from http://media.www.dailyorange.com.

Plan would make tuition free at Ore. colleges. (2013). *Community College Week, 25,* 5. Retrieved December 15, 2013, from EBSCO Online Database Education Research Complete.

Porter, K. (2002). The value of a college degree. Retrieved November 29, 2007, from http://ericdigests.org.

Schworm, P., & Wertheimer, L. (2007, November 11). Defraying the high cost of a degree. Retrieved November 29, 2007, from http://boston.com.

University Business. (2004, August). New Jersey gives students a free ride: Top grads are offered free tuition in community college system. Retrieved November 29, 2007, from http://findarticles.com.

SUGGESTED READING

Basken, P. (2007). Thompson's plans for higher education remain largely a mystery. *Chronicle of Higher Education, 54,* 21. Retrieved December 3, 2007, from EBSCO Online Database Education Research Complete.

K.F. (2006). Mass. merit aid fails to increase access. *Chronicle of Higher Education, 52,* A29. Retrieved December 3, 2007, from EBSCO Online Database Education Research Complete.

Two colleges in twin cities offering free tuition to inner-city students. (2006). *Diverse: Issues in Higher Education, 22,* 15. Retrieved December 3, 2007, from EBSCO Online Database Education Research Complete.

SECTION 6: SCHOOL ADMINISTRATION & POLICY

Introduction

In today's times, educational leaders require a far more complex and sophisticated skill set than was needed twenty years ago. The challenges confronting our schools and communities require leaders who are self-reflective and committed to social justice. Educational politics and organizational complexities call for navigators who can diagnose, innovate, implement, motivate and inspire change and reform that works. Pendulums swing and diverse interest groups assume positions of power. Therefore, leaders must also be skilled communicators, negotiators, and capable of political savvy.

The following articles examine the dimensions and scope of responsibilities that accompany each rung of the leadership hierarchy. The reader will gain insight into the complexities of leadership from leading a school's student government to leading an entire school district.

BECOMING A PUBLIC SCHOOL ADMINISTRATOR

Public school administrators' responsibilities have greatly increased since the passage of the No Child Left Behind Act. Besides the coordination of a school or school district's day to day operations, administrators are now responsible for providing instruction leadership that will raise students' academic achievement levels to meet annual yearly progress goals. Besides the formal training gained from a school leadership program, new administrators should also make use of induction programs, mentoring opportunities, and professional support groups as they settle into their positions. These practical supports can connect theory to practice and help new administrators navigate the challenges of managing a school or district.

KEYWORDS: Adequate Yearly Progress; Induction; Mentoring; No Child Left Behind Act of 2001 (NCLB); Principals; Professional Development; Reflection; School Leadership Programs; School Superintendents

OVERVIEW

A school principal's job is more complex than ever before (Archer, 2004; Institute for Educational Leadership [IEL], 2000, as cited by Grubb & Flessa, 2006). Besides their traditional duties of hiring and firing instructors, coordinating bus schedules, dealing with parents, disciplining students, overseeing the cafeteria, and supervising special education and other special programs (Grubb & Flessa), they are now also expected to provide instructional leadership (Cotton, in press; Leithwood, Louis, Anderson & Wahlstrom, 2004; Stein & Nelson, 2003; Tillman, 2005, as cited in Grubb & Flessa). Additionally, some principals are also expected to develop support services for low-income students (National Research Council, 2003, as cited in Grubb & Flessa). Every school has its own history, environment, and unique employees. Therefore, new principals need to be able to quickly assimilate into their new workplaces, manage an incredible workload, and learn their schools' unique protocols. If they are former teachers, new principals may also find it rather disconcerting to transition from a peer relationship with teachers into a supervisory relationship (Lashway, 2003a).

Principals' responsibilities have greatly increased with the 2001 passage of the The No Child Left Behind Act. The act mandates that states set annual measurable objectives "based on the percentage of students performing at or above proficiency. These standards are used to determine if schools, districts, and states make annual yearly progress" (Linn, 2005). If the percentage of students passing state tests is insufficient, schools have not made adequate yearly progress. "Sanctions are imposed on schools not meeting their annual yearly progress two years in a row, and the consequences are increasingly severe for schools not meeting targets for third, fourth, and fifth years in a row" (Linn). Students may be transferred to other schools, staff may be replaced, the state may take over the school, and federal funding may be withdrawn (Linn). States and the federal government put accountability for achieving No Child Left Behind Act mandates at the school level (Lashway, 2003b), putting enormous pressure on school principals to meet annual yearly progress levels.

In the past, students who majored in leadership administration programs have typically earned their degree, obtained a job, and only then received occasional professional development. That has changed in recent years with stakeholders realizing the importance of providing professional development opportunities on an ongoing basis. Another way new principals are being transitioned into their job is through participation in an induction period during which they receive mentoring and other structured support (Malone, 2001, as cited by Lashway, 2003b). Although professional development and induction had been primarily sponsored by local school districts, more and more states are supporting these types of programs by requiring principals to obtain additional certification that can include mentoring, reflection, and portfolio development (Lashway, 2003b).

SCHOOL LEADERSHIP PROGRAMS
According from the most recent statistics from the National Center for Education Statistics, most school principals have at least a master's degree, although there is a great deal of variation between the public and private sectors. According to the National Center for Education Statistics findings from 2015-2016,

2.3 % of all public school principals hold a bachelor's degree, 61.3% hold a master's degree, 26.6 % hold an education specialist certificate or professional diploma, and 9.9 % hold a doctorate or first professional degree.

With the nation currently enmeshed in such a high-stakes environment, principals are facing a high degree of pressure to perform. New principals are faced with challenges not addressed in their schooling, and principals who have been in the profession for many years may not have the skills now required of them. Nevertheless, principals are charged with delivering student success, and expectation that may require them to undergo additional training. One study found that 69% of school principals and 80% of school superintendents felt that school leadership programs do not accurately reflect the reality of managing a school or school district (Farkas et al., 2001, as cited in Lashway, 2003b). Over 85% of both school principals and superintendents think that revamping leadership programs would help improve leadership, but no research has been conducted on the subject of improving leadership programs (Lashway, 2003b). A 2001 survey of 450 principal certification programs found that only 6% of the programs reviewed the personal qualities most desired in today's principals, and only 40% listed teaching experience as an entrance requirement (Creighton & Jones, 2001, as cited in Lashway, 2003b).

CHOOSING A PROGRAM

For prospective principals and school district administrators trying to select a school leadership program, several factors should be considered to assess a program's suitability. Some of these factors hinge on whether or not:

- The purpose of the program is explicitly stated and relevant to the prospective student's needs;
- The curriculum mirrors the program's stated purpose and is rigorous in nature;
- The curriculum effectively balances theory with practical experience;
- The faculty includes professional instructors as well as practitioners still working in the field;
- The admissions criteria are rigorous and relevant;
- The program is fully accredited and practices continual self-assessment (Assam, 2005).

RESEARCH & CRITICISMS

In 2005, a four-year study was released that focused on the outcomes of students who participated in school leadership programs in the United States to determine if these graduates would be adequately prepared for the challenging situations in which they would find themselves. The report, Educating School Leaders, which was part of the Education Schools Project, followed national surveys of alumni, deans, faculty, and principals, including 28 detailed case studies (Assam). Assessing each program's core curriculum, admissions policy, instructor quality, practical training opportunities, and self-evaluation efforts, the study found that only one school demonstrated its ability to effectively train new administrators (Assam). Accordingly, these six components of school leadership programs need to be re-assessed (Assam):

- **Core Curriculum.** The core curriculum in most programs is comprised of abstract survey courses that are not integrated with actual leadership practices professionals encounter once employed;
- **Admissions.** School leadership programs tend to admit almost anyone who applies, and applicant's standardized test scores are among the lowest of all students pursuing any kind of graduate degree. The researchers believe this is because many of the students attending these programs have no interest in working in school administration: they just want to earn graduate credits to improve their instructor's salary. Because their leadership programs are so lucrative, schools accommodate these students by making the programs easy to complete;
- **Instructor Quality.** Programs either have too many part-time instructors from the field who are not up to date on best practices and current research, or else they have too many full-time professors who have little current field experience. Additionally, many faculty members have never worked as a school administrator, which severely limits their understanding of the workplace their graduates will encounter upon employment;
- **Practical Training.** Programs tend to lack meaningful internships or field instruction;
- **Evaluation.** Programs tend not to follow up on graduate outcomes, such as whether or not

graduates become successful administrators, or contribute to higher student achievement in the schools they lead.

The study found that, for the most part, leadership programs should be redesigned in order to better align curriculum with the expectations placed upon educational leaders.

REDESIGNING SCHOOL LEADERSHIP PROGRAMS

While experts generally advise that higher education curriculum be updated to meet today's more rigorous expectations of school administrators, how this should be done is widely debated. Both academic study and practical experience have benefits and limitations. Academic study can provide a solid foundational knowledge of the field, but the profession encompasses so much more than academic theories. Practical experience can be an effective way to give students a taste of the field as it really exists, but this method only teaches students what is, not what could be (Daresh, 2002, as cited in Lashway, 2003b). Therefore, a good balance between the two is most beneficial to students.

School districts can support leadership development programs by working with local colleges and universities to develop curriculum, and to create internships in the schools so that students can attain a practical understanding of the field. School districts can also encourage their professional staff to serve as mentors and to even teach part-time in the program (Lashway, 2003b).

Support for New Administrators

INDUCTION

Induction programs can be very helpful for new administrators. A good program can keep new administrators focused on the big picture while still helping them deal with more immediate needs. Since the majority of new principals are most concerned with learning what they need to know to get through their first year, an effective induction program will help them be more reflective as they learn and work. Induction should consist of more than just mentoring. School districts can employ a number of different strategies including portfolios, professional development plans, study groups,

focus groups, workshops, visits to other schools, and retreats (Peterson, 2001, as cited in Lashway, 2003a). This means that induction should be continuous and combine a number of strategies to facilitate reflection (Lashway, 2003a).

MENTORING

Mentoring can be an effective tool to acclimate new administrators. Good mentors are empathetic and experienced. They can coach new administrators in technical skills; help them understand the politics of their positions; and provide new, fresh perspectives on administrative duties (Lashway, 2003a). However, the mentoring process can go awry if a mentor becomes controlling or tries to mold the new administrator into a mirror image of him or herself. Additionally, mentors who have a limited perspective and are unable to provide much help (Crow and Mathews, 1998, as cited in Lashway, 2003a). Good, effective mentors provide instructional support by keeping new administrators focused on learning issues, and also by providing models of successful, proven practices. They can also provide administrative and managerial support not only by giving practical advice, but also by helping the new administrator set priorities, and asking appropriate questions to encourage deeper thought and reflection. Good mentors can also provide emotional support during stressful times (Dukess, 2001, as cited in Lashway, 2003a).

SUPPORT GROUPS

School districts can set up special programs for administrators, including support groups comprised of principals working in similar circumstances such rural schools, large schools, or schools with high percentages of low-income, minority, or at-risk students. Grouped together, these professionals can share their concerns and challenges with one another and work together to generate solutions. School districts can also actively encourage their principals to visit each other's schools to observe their operations and practices. While visiting each school, principals can review the school's goals and objectives, examine their test data, and discuss instructor performance. Then they can visit each classroom to observe how other schools' instructors teach and interact with students. Each visit can end with an evaluation meeting (Lashway, 2002).

Other Support Resources

School districts that serve more rural areas, have difficulty finding appropriate personnel, or do not have the funds to develop comprehensive induction programs can partner with other school districts and states to create a more regional type of induction program. Professional associations, too, have a variety of professional development resources available. Some may require a fee; others can be attained at no cost. National and regional associations may provide many workshops, skills assessments, and training opportunities that can be helpful (Lashway, 2003a). Resources are also available online in the form of web casts and online reference libraries.

Further Insights

With the complexities, time constraints, and workloads accompanying administrative positions—and the repercussions that can occur if schools are not making adequate yearly progress—it is understandable that there is a high turnover in the profession and a shortage of instructors interested in becoming a principal (Gilman & Lanman-Givens, 2001, as cited in Grubb & Flessa). With all the duties that require immediate attention, it can be difficult for principals to address instructional issues, which also need attention if a school is to meet No Child Left Behind Act adequate yearly progress requirements.

Multiple Principals

Although the majority of schools have continued to use the model of dividing tasks between a principal and vice principal, some schools have begun the practice of employing more than one principal. Having more than one principal can allow principals to spend more time on instruction and the development of student services. It can also provide an opportunity for principals to have more meaningful contact with instructors and parents (Grubb & Flessa).

Dividing Tasks

School have adopted many different approaches to employing a multiple principal model (Grubb & Flessa):

- In some cases, principals share responsibilities and do not divide the school into separately run sections. Each principal is responsible for particular duties, such as instructional issues, teacher observations, or student services and after-school programs. For duties that require more cohesiveness, such as hiring, instructor evaluations, and staff meeting, the two are jointly responsible;

- Other schools may divide the principals' responsibilities along grade lines, so that, for example, one manages kindergarten through fourth grade, and the other manages fifth grade through eighth grade. With this kind of separation of grades, certain duties are divided: only one principal would be in charge of professional development for the entire school, only one would handle external communications, etc;

- In larger schools, more than two principals may be employed with different principals responsible for certain grades and another principal responsible for organizational issues such as finances, representing the school to the public, and the overall organization of the school. But even in cases of multiple principals, all of them would be involved in hiring, developing the curriculum, and determining the direction of the school.

The difference between the multiple principals model and the principal and assistant principal model is the degrees of authority. With the multiple principals model, the principals share decision-making power, whereas in the principal and assistant principal model, only the principal has this authority. When employing the multiple principal model, it is important for the school to remain as one entity, rather than turn into separate schools occupying the same building or buildings. To help retain cohesiveness, schools should meet as a whole, and all committees should include people from every part of the school (Grubb & Flessa).

Benefits & Challenges

There can be many advantages to having more than one principal. Someone is always on site who can make decisions, which can be even more important to year-round schools. Having more than one principal also makes it easier for teachers and parents to access a principal and get their needs met in a timely manner. Multiple principals should also be able to accomplish more. And if one principal resigns, continuity can still be preserved in the institution, making employees less uneasy as about the changes a new principal may bring. There may be some confusion among instructors, students, and parents about each principal's responsibilities, but, if the separation of duties is clearly spelled out, the confusion should be minimal and quickly overcome. Some people may try to play one principal off another, but his can be prevented if the principals have recognized the potential danger, have a good working relationship, and communicate extensively and effectively with each other (Grubb & Flessa).

CONCLUSION

New principals encounter many situations that were probably not addressed in their education, and principals with many years directing schools may not have some of the skills that are now required of them. With the potential ramifications of not meeting No Child Left Behind Act mandates of adequate yearly progress, most school districts and states no longer assume that an advanced degree denotes a candidate's readiness to become a principal or school superintendent. School districts and states now see the importance of providing ongoing professional development and assistance programs for their administrators to help meet state and federal standards for student achievement.

Principals need to be more flexible than ever and have sound backgrounds in instruction. The former is especially true if they work with a school that employs more than one principal. School administration can be a thankless job with many challenges and expectations. To compound the challenge of locating and retaining quality school administrators, salary considerations may be preventing others from entering the profession or transitioning from a teaching position into an administrative position. The Educational Research Service tracks salaries and wages for 33 different public school positions. While overall administrators have earned more than instructors, it was found that at the elementary school level, the difference in pay can be as little as 4% (Archer, 2002). Considering that most instructors work 10 months out of the year while administrators work 12 months, that many administrators often work well beyond regular working hours, and that administrators are placed under so much pressure to meet state and federal mandates for student accountability, it is more likely

than not that administrators are not interested in a salary increase. It takes a special person with a strong vision and a sound background in instructional theory, as well as the support of the school district and state to be successful in today's high-stakes environment.

TERMS & CONCEPTS

Adequate Yearly Progress: Part of the No Child Left Behind Act, adequate yearly progress refers to annual measurable objectives based on the percentage of students performing at or above proficiency.

Induction: Induction is a comprehensive, ongoing program intended to help new administrators transition into their positions by providing them with both instructional and administrative guidance.

Mentoring: Mentoring describes a relationship in which a more experienced person, the mentor, guides, instructs, encourages, and corrects a less experienced person.

No Child Left Behind Act of 2001 (NCLB): The No Child Left Behind Act of 2001 is the latest reauthorization and a major overhaul of the Elementary and Secondary Education Act of 1965, the major federal law regarding K-12 education.

Professional Development: Professional development refers to training that helps professionals stay current with changing technology and practices in a field.

Reflection: Reflection is the process of deriving meaning and knowledge from an experience and consciously connecting this experience to areas of one's life, such as work.

Sandra Myers

BIBLIOGRAPHY

Archer, J. (2002). Survey finds little pay advantage for principals. *Education Week, 21,* 5. Retrieved October 6, 2007, from EBSCO Online Database Academic Search Premier.

Ash, R. C., Hodge, P. H., & Connell, P. H. (2013). The recruitment and selection of principals who increase student learning. *Education, 134,* 94-100. Retrieved December 15, 2013, from EBSCO Online Database Education Research Complete.

Assam, A. (2005). The unprepared administrator. *Educational Leadership, 62,* 88-89. Retrieved October 6,

2007, from EBSCO Online Database Academic Search Premier.

DeAngelis, K. J., & O'Connor, N. (2012). Examining the pipeline into educational administration: An analysis of applications and job offers. *Educational Administration Quarterly, 48*, 468-505. Retrieved December 15, 2013, from EBSCO Online Database Education Research Complete.

Eddins, B., Kirk, J., Hooten, D., & Russell, B. (2013). Utilization of 360-degree feedback in program assessment: Data support for improvement of principal preparation. *National Forum Of Educational Administration & Supervision Journal, 31*, 5-19. Retrieved December 15, 2013, from EBSCO Online Database Education Research Complete. e

Grubb, W. & Flessa, J. (2006). "A job too big for one": Multiple principals and other nontraditional approaches to school leadership. *Educational Administration Quarterly, 42*, 518-530. Retrieved October 6, 2007, from EBSCO Online Database Academic Search Premier.

Lashway, L. (2002). *Developing instructional leaders.* Washington, D.C.: Office of Education Research and Improvement. (ERIC Document Reproduction Service No. ED466023). Retrieved October 6, 2007, from EBSCO Online Education Research Database.

Lashway, L. (2003a). *Inducting school leaders.* Washington, D.C.: Office of Education Research and Improvement. (ERIC Document Reproduction Service No. ED479074). Retrieved October 6, 2007, from EBSCO Online Education Research Database.

Lashway, L. (2003b). *Transforming principal preparation.* Washington, D.C.: Office of Education Research and Improvement. (ERIC Document Reproduction Service No. ED473360). Retrieved October 6, 2007, from EBSCO Online Education Research Database.

Linn, R. (2005). Issues in the design of accountability systems. *Yearbook of the National Society for the Study of Education, 104*, 79-98. Retrieved May 2, 2007, from EBSCO Online Database Education Research Complete.

National Center for Education Statistics (1996). *Schools and staffing in the United States: A statistical profile, 1993-94.* Retrieved October 6, 2007, from http://nces.ed.gov.

National Center for Education Statistics (2017). *Characteristics of Public Elementary and Secondary School Principals in the United States: Results from the 2015-16 National Teacher and Principal Survey.* Retrieved September 21, 2017, from https://nces.ed.gov.

SUGGESTED READING

Boris-Schacter, S. & Langer, S. (2006). *Balanced leadership: How effective principals manage their work.* New York, NY: Teachers College Press.

Dimmock, C. & Walker, A. (2005). *Educational leadership: Culture and diversity.* Thousand Oaks, CA: Sage Publications.

Kowalski, T. (2007). *Case studies on educational administration.* Boston, MA: Allyn & Bacon.

Lunenburg, F. & Ornstein, A. (2007). *Educational administration: Concepts and practices.* Florence, KY: Wadsworth Publishing.

Marshall, C. & Gerstl-Pepin, C. (2005). *Re-Framing Educational Politics for Social Justice.* Boston, MA.: Pearson.

Marzano, R., Waters, T. & McNulty, B. (2005). *School leadership that works: From research to results.* Alexandria, VA: Association for Supervision & Curriculum Development.

Wagner. T., Kegan, R., Lahey, L., Lemons, R., Garnier, J., Helsing, D., Howell, A., & Thurber Rasmussen, H. (2006). *Change Leadership: A Practical Guide to Transforming our Schools.* San Francisco, CA.: Jossey Bass.

CENTRALIZED ADMINISTRATION

There are two types of public school governance: centralized and decentralized. This article will examine both models of governance through a historical lens as well as discuss the philosophical underpinnings, implications and alternative viewpoints for each model.

KEYWORDS: A Nation at Risk (1983); Ancillary Structures; Centralized Administration; The Civil Rights Act of 1964; Decentralized Administration; Governance; Localized Administration; The National Defense Education Act (NDEA)

OVERVIEW

There are two types of public school governance: centralized and decentralized. A centralized school administration is one that is managed by the government, while a decentralized administration has the public managing all aspects of its governance. A centralized administration is generally seen as negative by educators because the power to make change is not in the hands of the people most affected by that change. The public only gets to control change in a decentralized school administration. The United States has seen many variances of both systems since the early 1900's and there is still a debate as to which method of governance is the most effective, as determined by student performance.

Successful administration of a public school requires many things. While expert supervision, credentialed teachers, strong financial standing, and parental support are essential to running an effective school system, a dependable method of governance is even more essential. Whereas a centralized administration may be the most successful for one district, a decentralized or localized administration may be what is most productive for another. For others, still a trial of one as reform for another may be what is needed. In any event, it is important to understand who takes on what responsibility within a school district based on his or her position within that district. It is also important to understand the history of education governance before trying to establish a standard of administration.

In the greater scheme of school governance, there are two basic philosophies. The first is known as a decentralized school administration. In this case, the public will authorize, fund, and operate the schools within the district (not including parochial schools—which require tuition—or charter or magnet schools, which are independently owned). This system is generally managed by a board of educators elected by the public. State and local funds support the district, and a district manager, generally a superintendent oversees the day-to-day operations of the district. The second philosophy is one that establishes public authorization, public funding, but independently operated schools; charter schools and magnet schools fall into this category of centralized administrative schools. The difference here is not the size of the supervising body (a board of education versus an established owner or corporation); it is the power behind that body: the public versus the government. A district administration is considered centralized when the government manages it. Decentralization occurs when the public takes control over a district's supervision.

THE DECENTRALIZED SCHOOL DISTRICT

A centralized district will not have a board of education; if it does, the board does not have the decision making power of either the superintendent or a supervisor to which the superintendent and board report. In a decentralized administration,

the school board (with each member being elected by the community) establishes policies, makes personnel decisions, and supervises all members of the district, including the superintendent. The superintendent, in turn, manages each separate school, with the schools' principals reporting directly to the superintendent; he or she then reports to the board. A centralized district, on the other hand, has a supervising entity—sometimes a business owner, a corporation, or some form of government—in the role of the board of education. The superintendent (if there is one) oversees each school and reports directly to the entity in charge. Whereas the public elects a board of education and votes on policy creation in the decentralized structure, the public has little say in the administration on a centralized structure. With a great deal of effort and commitment, a district may choose to change the way its administration is run, although moving from a decentralized administration to that of a centralized form of governance is generally easier than the public gaining control over a government-run system.

HISTORY OF EDUCATION GOVERNANCE

Historically, community members have pushed for governance at the local level, the assumption being that such localized management would mean that the public has a voice in the way its schools are run. At the beginning of the twentieth century, however, school districts were forced to move from decentralized, community-managed systems to those funded and supervised by state governments. A series of changes brought about this new centralized administration, but the primary force was depressed and recessed economic times. When localized education cost more than the public could afford in taxes, schools needed financial assistance to stay afloat. Thus, they agreed to let the state step in, which it did, taking control over education away from the local communities. As a result, parents lost control to professionals, generally superintendents; local schools lost power to centralized office administration; and districts lost jurisdiction to the state.

In addition to these changes, other changes occurred as well over the next fifty years. Sociologist Wayland Sloan describes these other changes as "ancillary structures" because they were neither mandated nor incorporated into a formalized construction of public education (as cited in Raywid, 1980).

Furthermore, being ancillary also made them free from public control. For example, the production and marketing of textbooks put publishers at the forefront of consumerism. Also, the creation of standardized exams, the establishment of accrediting associations, and the increased value of teacher education—more trends out of the control of local communities—made pulling district governance away from state hands a challenging endeavor (Raywid).

In addition, the government also made it difficult to take back local control over education. The National Defense Education Act (NDEA) of 1958 provided financial aid to schools agreeing to enhance various academic and social sectors of education. Areas like math, science, languages, technical instruction, geography, English as a second language, and guidance counseling were slated for advancement under this act of Congress. In addition, the Civil Rights Act of 1964 influenced districts by threatening to withhold federal funding to school districts engaging in racial, religious, or ethnic discrimination. These legislative creations have been positive for educators and the students they serve, but they are still requirements passed down from the federal level that assure compliance through intimidation. While few people would encourage schools to abandon the teaching of math or science, and even fewer people would advance a racist school structure, these acts of the legislature have made it financially harmful to do so.

According to Dennis Doyle (1993), in the 1990s school districts had taken back what control they lost, and while the United States' system of education may have its difficulties, it can tout that it is:

"… democratic, egalitarian, and meritocratic. It is robust, dynamic, and resilient. It is responsive—at least to fads of the moment—and it is well financed, by any measure. It is radically decentralized, at least by world standards, and each component of the education system, from humble rural school districts to great research universities, stands on its own bottom" (as cited in Schultz, 1994).

The United States is continuously compared to other industrialized nations because as countries with the power to succeed, we should be all successfully educated individuals. However, with freedom comes choice, and many people choose to be fair educators, okay administrators, and average students. What is

average in America, though, is considered poor—and offers no competition—to other countries. "If an unfriendly foreign power had attempted to impose on America the mediocre educational performance that exists today, we might well have viewed it as an act of war. As it stands, we have allowed this to happen to ourselves," so says the National Commission on Excellence in Education's report, A Nation at Risk (1983). When the power to make critical decisions about something as defining as education is in the hands of the "people," that power can be used or misused depending on the desire of those people including the dismissal of this policy or that teacher or education as a whole, in the case of the students Doyle references above.

Applications

IMPLICATIONS OF DECENTRALIZED ADMINISTRATION

One of the problems with decentralized administration is that there is no absolute proof of its success (Olson, 1997). School boards (as well as constituents) believe that the people working most closely with students—the teachers—have the best information and are therefore the most qualified regarding how to offer effective education to their audience. Unfortunately, the only way to determine if decision-making systems have been effectively changed via decentralization is through student performance, which is best detected through test scores.

It is difficult to know what is going to work when it comes to improving the standard of education within a community. It is reasonable to think that the current administration is not successful and to propose change; that change, however, can only manifest itself in one way. And, for community members with so much at stake, letting go of control is difficult and often risky.

IMPLICATIONS OF CENTRALIZED ADMINISTRATION

What is wrong with privatized control over a public school system? Bennett (1992) believes nothing. It can be a positive measure for districts as it can cause schools to fight for student enrollment, increasing performance among teachers and students and encouraging the public's ability to choose. In the centralized system of education, teachers, administrators, and the staff of a school remain employed by the public, but are managed by a private entity, either a person, a corporation, or some form of government.

Bennett identifies a "utilities model"—a form of management successful in energy and telephone companies as well as for the postal service (Bennett). For-profit competition is a driving force in the United States; shouldn't people be able to own their own schools like they own their own fast-food franchises? Giving members of the public school community the opportunity to focus only on education—rather than on governance—should yield stronger academic programs, teachers who can pursue professional development opportunities because they know the information will be used, and students who do not have to worry about the principal looking over their teachers' shoulders.

Bennett points out something very important to note: accountability. When people are held accountable, they tend to prove their worth. In public school systems run by community members, that worth can be more subjective than in school systems that are actually marketing students. For example, a new restaurant offering the same food as the restaurant down the street has to give consumers an additional reason to eat its food or it will risk going out of business. Parents can look toward the accountability factor to help them choose what's best for their children: a school system that offers students more effective teachers (because they chose to apply there), advanced technology (because they are not reliant on public funding only), or a supervisor who trusts his/ her administration (because s/he hand-picked its members from a lengthy list of qualified individuals), for example.

In this scenario, centralized education does not look so bad. It offers students and parents options, and, in many instances, quality teachers and staff members, and it offers the community a different look at school management structures. Finally, it offers students the ability to succeed. If they do not, they can always go back to the public school system they left, and the centralized system will falter on its own due to the lack of achievement expected from it.

VIEWPOINTS

One of the concerns of a school board made up of community members is that members of the community have friends within the community; these friends have children in the school district, are vying

for employment positions in the district, and who pay taxes to the district. With friends on the board, it may be difficult not to call in a favor when a child is about to be suspended, or a job is about to be appointed, or taxes are going to be increased. These types of favors have been asked of Don McAdams, professor and director of the Center for Reform of School Systems at the University of Houston and member of the Education Commission of the States' National Commission on Governing America's Schools (McAdams & Urbanski, 1999). According to McAdams and Urbanski:

> "… most board members will acknowledge that they are frequently asked by constituents or vendors to influence a personnel or contract decision, and maybe sometimes have tried to do so. At the same time, many board members are frustrated by their lack of power to fundamentally change schools. My own view, the view of a school board member, is that the commission's report provides an exciting opportunity for boards to make the two changes that will most improve the performance of the schools they serve: Govern more, and manage less" (McAdams & Urbanski).

In the article "Governing Well" (1999), McAdams and Urbanski, both members of the National Commission on Governing America's Schools, detail the commission's description of possible scenarios regarding public school governance. The commission proposed two management systems, which are discussed by the authors.

The first scenario seeks to establish "publicly authorized, publicly funded, and publicly operated schools. The traditional, one-size-fits-all school system becomes a diversified and high-performance system of schools" (McAdams & Urbanski). In this system, schools—not school boards—are given the power to make decisions. Students and their parents get more choice within the schools, and schools get to decide their own budgets, hire staff members, determine class size, and choose which outside resources to purchase from vendors. Schools receive funding per student, as they are public institutions, and are held to greater accountability because parents can choose to send their children elsewhere if increased academic performance is not noted (McAdams & Urbanski).

The second scenario puts together community members, school districts, and private organizations, much like charter or magnet schools, to run an entire system of schools. These schools are "publicly authorized, publicly funded, and independently operated" (McAdams & Urbanski). These schools weigh governance authority in a different manner than the traditional example from the first scenario. In this second scenario, school boards delegate specific operations to the superintendent and principals, who work directly with the state's department of education and whoever else regulates education standards. So, a board of education, in this scenario, cannot manipulate decisions about the hiring or firing of a teacher, as the superintendents evaluate the performance of the students, the employees, and the schools (McAdams & Urbanski).

It is clear that the Commission has student success at the forefront of its proposal. While there are many different views about how that achievement is to be evaluated, the Commission does agree on several things. For example, nobody is suggesting that public schools should cease to exist. School governance needs to be strengthened; student achievement is not only the proof of that strength but it is also the only means by which district administration should be accountable. In addition, schools should have the power to decide how they are to operate—on an individual level. Finally, schools have responsibility to publicize enough information about their overall performance, including that of their faculty and students, so as to provide the public with the opportunity to choose which school is right for them.

DISCUSSION

We are a diverse nation, one that is threatened by a growing disparity between the rich and the poor, minorities and privileged white Americans, and those with full access to technology and those who are isolated from it. Any governance change must ameliorate these inequities as well as address academic excellence. Excellence without equity is not excellence, it is privilege. Our goal should not be to help some to opt out; rather, it must be to help all children gain access to good schools and a good education (McAdams & Urbanski).

Noting the bottom line of these authors, it is easy to see why the administration of a school district is a concern to community members. It is also easy to see how complicated a process of governance public school administration is. A common ground can only be found if the common goal of student achievement

is always the objective. In many of the examples noted (and, in all likelihood, even more that are not noted), however, the concern has been who is in control rather than how they are controlling.

TERMS & CONCEPTS

A Nation at Risk (1983): A report often noted as the root of education reform efforts after its publication by the U.S. Department of Education's National Commission on Excellence in Education.

Ancillary Structures: Constructs that have not been mandated or incorporated into formal structures of public education but do impact it, such as textbook marketing or teacher education.

Centralized Administration: Moving power from many to few; removing power from the local level to one of more authority, higher up (e.g., shifting the hiring power for individual schools from their principals to the superintendent of the school district).

The Civil Rights Act of 1964: Created a system that withholds federal aid to any school district practicing discrimination (racial, religious, or ethnic).

Decentralized Administration: Shifting power from the top to the bottom; removing power from a higher authority and dividing it among constituents of a lower rank (e.g., superintendent relinquishing hiring power to individual school principals).

Governance: The system of government within an institution or organization.

Localized Administration: Decentralizing administration and granting its authority to local subjects (e.g., making those on a local school board in charge of hiring teachers rather than a centralized superintendent making the decision). The National Association for the Advancement of Colored People (NAACP): The most influential civil rights organizations in the United States, established in 1909.

The National Defense Education Act (NDEA): This 1958 law provided financial support to schools in math, science, and foreign languages and rejected the idea that federal aid should (and would) take the form of per-student grants to each state.

Maureen McMahon

BIBLIOGRAPHY

Bartlett, S. (2007, November 22). Class-size concerns spur series of community forums. Press Republican 114, p. A3.

Bennett, D. (1992). Will public/ private control reinvent school system governance? Education Digest, 58, 30. Retrieved November 18, 2007, from EBSCO online database, Education Research Complete.

Currie-Knight, K. (2012). Education, decentralization, and the knowledge problem: A Hayekian case for decentralized education. Philosophical Studies in Education, 43 117-127. Retrieved December 19, 2013, from EBSCO Online Database Education Research Complete.

Geruson, G. J., Healey, C. L., Sabatino, A., Ryan, D., & Haney, R. (2013). School boards and effective Catholic school governance: Selected presentations from the 2012 Catholic Higher Education Collaborative Conference. Catholic Education: A Journal of Inquiry & Practice, 17, 186-223. Retrieved December 19, 2013, from EBSCO Online Database Education Research Complete.

Hendrie, C. (1999). No easy answers. Education Week, 19, 36. Retrieved November 18, 2007, from EBSCO online database, Education Research Complete

McAdams, D. & Urbanski, A. (1999). Governing well. Education Week, 19, 44. Retrieved November 18, 2007, from EBSCO online database, Education Research Complete.

Millard, E. (2011). Going the distance. University Business, 14, 34-39. Retrieved December 19, 2013, from EBSCO Online Database Education Research Complete.

National Commission on Excellence in Education. (1983). A nation at risk: The imperative for educational reform. Washington, DC: U.S. Government Printing Office. Retrieved November 28, 2007, from http://ed.gov.

Olson, L. (1997). Shaking things up. Education Week, 17, 29. Retrieved November 18, 2007, from EBSCO online database, Education Research Complete.

Raywid, M. A. (1980). Restoring school efficacy by giving parents a choice. Educational Leadership, 38, 134. Retrieved November 18, 2007, from EBSCO online database, Education Research Complete.

Schultz, F. (Ed.) (1994) Education 94/95: Annual Editions. Dushkin Publishing Group, Inc.: Connecticut.

SUGGESTED READING

Albanese, E. (2004, Jun). Federal judge refuses to halt Arkansas school mergers. Bond Buyer, 348 (31902), 29. Retrieved November, 28 from EBSCO online database, Business Source Premier.

Colwell, B. (2007). School governance. Yearbook of Education Law, 43-64. Retrieved November 28, 2007, from EBSCO online database, Education Research Complete.

Gann, N. & Sutcliffe, J. (2007). Gold-dust governors. Times Educational Supplement, 4741, 28. Retrieved November 28, 2007, from EBSCO online database, Academic Search Premier.

Gross, S., & Shapiro, J. (2013). The New DEEL (Democratic Ethical Educational Leadership) and the work of reclaiming a progressive alternative in educational administration from preK-20. International Journal of Progressive Education, 9, 1-21. Retrieved December 19, 2013, from EBSCO Online Database Education Research Complete.

Many governors 'ill-equipped to cope', claims new report. (2007). Education, 14637073, 1. Retrieved November 28, 2007, from EBSCO online database, Academic Search Premier.

Moss, G. (1991). Restructuring public schools for internal democratic governance: A circular approach. School Organization, 11, 71. Retrieved November 28, 2007, from EBSCO online database, Academic Search Premier.

Moorer, T. D. (2007). Working group formed on mayoral control and school governance. New York Amsterdam News, 98, 3. Retrieved November 28, 2007, from EBSCO online database, Academic Search Premier.

Shatkin, G. & Gershberg, A. (2007). Empowering parents and building communities. Urban Education, 42, 582-615. Retrieved November 28, 2007, from EBSCO online database, Education Research Complete.

State prepares to return control to Jersey City, Newark boards. (2007). Education Week, 26, 6. Retrieved November 28, 2007, from EBSCO online database, Academic Search Premier.

DECISION-MAKING STRUCTURES AND PROCESSES

This article discusses decision-making structures and processes in the U.S. Public School systems. Decision-making structures model a variety of approaches in the educational system. Many schools use a model of site-based decision-making or school-based management.

These structures often involve numerous stakeholders in differing levels of authority. The process varies in each system and often between each campus. Identified and explained are different structures and processes for the campus decision-making model.

KEYWORDS: Community; Continuous learner; Decentralization; Decision-making; Participation in decision-making; School-based management; Stakeholders

OVERVIEW

It is imperative that a school has an effective decision-making structure and process to be able to provide a quality educational experience for the community's students. Decision-making methods are developed and determined through the collaboration of the school's administration, board, community leaders, and parental involvement. Thus, the approach varies, contingent on the needs and preferences of the school personnel and community.

Leadership strategies differ primarily in the role of the leader in relation to employees/teachers, parents, students, and the community. The leader can function as an authoritarian, develop teamwork, or engage all levels of personnel in the process. There are various names for these leadership strategies such as hierarchical, transformational, facilitative, instructional, visionary, contributory, site-based management, or shared decision-making.

Essentially the decision-making structures range from top-down to ground-based approaches. These two basic models function from opposite ends of a decision-making spectrum. One is a passive model where faculty and staff wait to be told the policy change, where improvement is needed, or how and what to do about it. The other is collaborative with the staff and faculty, allowing them to be more active in evaluating their own situation, clarifying the circumstances, and suggesting initiatives (Morehead, 2003).

FIVE STRUCTURES IN DECISION-MAKING

The decision-making process is often organized by the administrator around five different structures, all with different levels of centralized authority.

The fifth structure is a top-down, centralized approach which can be referred to as the Hierarchical decision-making structure. This structure involves a unilateral decision which has the administrator making the decision without consulting or involving faculty in the decision (Hoy & Tarter, 1993). This leadership strategy usually consists of a senior

management team, often including the superintendent, and/or assistant superintendent(s), and several principals. This can result in school policy being made by the head of school and a few senior members of staff thus contradicting the hypothesis that everyone can contribute. This structure has the head and a small fixed team identifying and discussing an area for change. The senior management team either presents their deliberations at a full staff meeting for further discussion or directly instructs staff to implement their action plan.

The fourth structure is recognized as an Individual Advisory. Here the administrator consults individually with pertinent faculty having expertise to assist in the decision. The administrator then makes a decision which may or may not reflect their opinions (Hoy & Tarter).

The third possible structure is the Group Advisory in which the administrator solicits opinions of the entire group, discusses the implications of group suggestions, and then makes a decision which may or may not reflect the group's desires (Hoy & Tarter).

The second structure is the Group Decision involving participants in the decision-making and a group decision using parliamentary procedures. All members share equally as they evaluate; attempting consensus although a decision is usually made by the majority (Hoy & Tarter).

The first structure is a Group Consensus involving participants in the decision-making process. In this process, all group members share equally as they generate and evaluate a decision with a complete consensus required before a decision can be made (Hoy & Tarter).

APPLICATIONS

The successful application of these decision-making structures is conditional on the decision situation (Hoy & Tarter). Structures one and two reflect the ground-based approach (which can be referred to as the contributory model) or a decentralized form of organization. It is task-orientated and has the head and those closest to the situation explore the problem together. In this scenario no one has imperatives about their sphere of work drawn up without input. A feeling of ownership of the decisions made and consequently, a vested interest in putting those decisions into practice generates a contributory atmosphere. It also means that everyone may be involved at some stage as each committee may have a different membership and includes those most affected.

SCHOOL-BASED MANAGEMENT

Many names are used to identify the ground-based, decentralized model of School-based Management (SBM) including: "site-based management, school-site autonomy, school-site management, school-centered management, decentralized management, school-based budgeting, site-based decision-making, participation in decision-making (PDM), responsible autonomy, school-lump sum budgeting, shared governance, the autonomous school concept, school-based curriculum development, and administrative decentralization" (Clune & Whilte, 1988 as cited in Rodriguez & Slate, 2005b). The ground-based/ decentralized model or school-based management (SBM) has many different forms but the basic concept is that each school campus sets its own policies, controls its own budget, and choices are made by groups or committees of school and community representatives. These decisions or policies are not to conflict with district or board policies thus the extent of the power of SBM varies between districts and campuses (Cuban, 2007).

Public attention has spotlighted academic results, higher standards for students and teachers, and SBM which includes teacher participation, parent participation, and community participation in school decision making. Under these initiatives, all stakeholders including teachers, staff, parents, and community members have opportunities to become empowered through SBM committees (Bauch & Goldring, 1998).

SBM attempts "to raise the level of involvement of stakeholders in the governance and management of schools" (Robertson, Wohlstetter, & Mohrman, 1995). The involvement of diverse stakeholders is thought to provide a number of benefits to the school by allowing "the school to craft its own decisions, making the best possible use of the resources available to the local unit. SBM also provides a greater range of individual participation in the decision-making process, facilitating a richer base for decision-making and one that should provide empowerment for implementation" (Brown & Cooper, 2000). Empowering those with the most investment at the local campus should provide the ability to affect how the school is performing.

SBM should additionally enhance school performance and, thus student achievement.

PROCESS OF SBM

The SBM process requires: "a clear purpose and a long-term commitment by the superintendent and the school board. SBM effectiveness requires control over a large portion of the school budget and the district office's investing in training so those involved understand their roles and options. Without these pieces, SBM can become an empty and time-consuming process of writing strategic plans. Through SBM comes joint ownership for school outcomes to stakeholders, but such ownership necessitates technical know-how and determination not present in some school communities. The right balance between district direction and school flexibility takes time and patience" (Cuban, The Right Balance). Emphasis is on collaborative school governance, although there is greatly varied implementation from campus to campus (Rodriguez & Slate, 2005a). The campus or school district will be challenged through this process to become a learning organization in the course of understanding the past, using research, managing the change process, and taking action for improvement.

Generally, the three domains of SBM are: budgeting, curriculum, and personnel. Goals and organizational structure are developed to direct the functionality of the committees (Rodriquez & Slate, 2005b). The overall vision and direction of the institution are formulated and defined by the school board while SBM is often used in developing the school improvement plan and operational issues.

Budgeting occurs when a lump sum of money is allocated to the campus allowing SBM to decide how the money will be dispersed thus creating greater flexibility regarding how the campus money is spent and where they purchase (Rodriquez & Slate, 2005b). Selecting curriculum which meets the objectives set by board and district administration is placed with SBM committees to determine instructional materials including the selection of textbooks, learning activities, and supplemental instructional materials (Rodriquez & Slate, 2005b). The hiring of staff and faculty moves from the central office to the school campus where committees may interview and make final decisions which are then sent back to the central office.

SBM DECISION-MAKERS

The central premise of SBM is a delegation of decision-making members from the central office of a school system to the school level to the stakeholders at the school campus level through the creation of formal structures of committees (Rodriguez & Slate, 2005a; 2005b). SBM basic committee make-up includes stakeholders such as teachers, parents, and administrators, additionally some committees may include community and business representatives (Rodriguez & Slate, 2005a).

The superintendent's and the principal's job in SBM is to facilitate rather than dictate. The superintendent's job also includes the traditional role of supervising and monitoring schools as well as reporting to the school board regarding school activities and performance. SBM must be tied to authentic reform "in how educators interact with one another and in how they teach their students" as well as "augmented by organizational conditions that encourage interactions among stakeholders, and far reaching curricular and instructional reforms that can guide those interactions" (Latham, 1998). When the central office is on the same reform page as an SBM committee, district administrators can locate and provide resources and services that no SBM committee alone could acquire easily or in sufficient supply (Cuban).

A major component of SBM is faculty involvement in shared decision-making, which occurs by placing faculty members on committees. However, Hoy and Tarter note that always involving faculty members may be as unthinking as never involving them. Participation using the right strategy and linked to the right situation can improve the quality of decisions and promote cooperation of faculty and administration (Hoy & Tarter). This creates an environment where faculty feel valued and are enabled to contribute to the development of the school, which in turn promotes job satisfaction and development of a long-term commitment to their schools (Morehead). Expanding involvement to all staff members encourages genuine participation in school decision-making that can be difficult at times. Often one's own long held personal theories are extensively modified through the effective operation of this process (Morehead).

A faculty member's involvement on a committee should consider the following questions:

- Is there a personal stake in the decision outcome?
- Do I have expertise to contribute to the decision?

The decision-making involvement process is the degree to which administrators give teachers the authority to make decisions and their actual participation in the process (Hoy & Tarter).

The principal considers the most effective strategy for collaborative decision-making by matching personnel with the appropriate situation. The principal judges the following administrative roles for collaborative decision-making (Hoy & Tarter):

- "The principal is an integrator when bringing teachers together for consensus decision making. Here the task is to reconcile divergent opinions and positions;
- The principal as parliamentarian facilitates open communication by protecting the opinions of the minority and leads teachers through a democratic process to a group decision;
- The principal as educator reduces resistance to change by explaining and discussing with teachers the opportunities and constraints of the decisional issues;
- The principal as consultant solicits advice from teacher-experts. The quality of decisions is improved as the principal guides the generation of relevant information;
- The principal as director makes unilateral decisions in those instances where the teachers have no expertise or personal stake. Here the goal is efficiency" (Hoy & Tarter).

Faculty empowerment through SBM also considers the role of parents in participatory decision-making creating a communal school environment that values democratic discourse. Dominant themes in school restructuring have been parent participation and teacher empowerment in school decision-making (Bauch & Goldring).

Within schools is a professional culture which parents may be reluctant to violate. SBM creates opportunities for parental involvement in campus-wide or school-wide decisions. There has been little evidence that professional-client relationships have been significantly altered (Bauch & Goldring). Some states have legislated SBM including parental involvement. This has transferred some authority to parents and the community holding teachers and principals more accountable for what goes on in the schools (Bauch & Goldring). SBM and other types of school improvement plans involve parents in governance matters creating a balanced power relationship as teachers and parents work together effectively (Bauch & Goldring,).

FURTHER INSIGHTS

Policies on shared decision-making are determined by the superintendent and school board using the following suggested guidelines (Boehlje, 1995):

1. "Maintain public accountability.
2. Develop trust based on collegiality, collaboration, and consensus.

   Participants of SBM must trust that the administration and board value their work and views even when asked to adjust a decision.
3. Establish the scope of authority of decision teams. The focus of shared decision-making teams should be on developing and implementing a plan for student learning within the parameters of the district's goals.
4. Determine the membership of the shared decision-making teams.

   Team members may include faculty, students, parents, business, or community representatives reflecting diversity in cultural, ethnic, and economic areas."

As shared decision-making is established through carefully crafted policies, trust and confidence is fostered. The effectiveness of the shared decision-making approach lies with the policies' accountability provisions. According to Fowler (2000) when involved in adopting a new policy, three key questions should be answered in the affirmative:

- "Do we have good reasons for adopting a new policy?" (Fowler). The motives for new policy need to be determined;
- "Is this policy appropriate for our school or district?" (Fowler);
- "Does the policy have sufficient support with the key stakeholders?" (Fowler).

Members of an SBM committee should plan for decisions, communication, and implementation.

Faculty members involved in extensive participation in the decision-making process should expect involvement in the process as early and as long as possible. Extensive collaboration is maximized when teachers or other administrators are brought into the process as early as possible to share in the definition, the elaboration of the problem, and are then involved in each succeeding step of the cycle (Hoy & Tarter).

Teacher knowledge and skill base must broaden and deepen as compared to the traditional teacher role. The knowledge and skill of the teacher are expanded in areas as a continuous learner, an expert to collaboration, in teaching and learning, in the knowledge and skills of community, in the change process, and in moral purpose (Fullan, 1995).

VIEWPOINTS

School decision-making initiatives that include SBM have expectations that there are strong-minded adults who know and care for our children, who have opinions, believe in our youth, and the future of this country (Meier, 1999). However, there is concern that an overemphasis on teachers in decision-making could lead to a corresponding weakening of the heart of the teaching, meaning qualities such as 'caring' and 'compassion' (Bauch & Goldring). A loss of the heart of teaching might thus diminish school improvement.

Public education is a public good, which benefits the whole society. Superintendents and administrators work for the community who directly supports public education by taxes paid, therefore, they are "responsible to, and should be accountable to, all the taxpayers–not just the parents" (Spillane & Regnier, 1998). The creation of a balance of power that encourages the interests and understandings of stakeholders who care the most for the children and know them the best encompasses the whole community. Our future is to create schools that are "more personal, more compelling, and more attractive than the internet or TV—schools where youngsters can always find interesting and powerful adults. To create such schools, we must increase, not decrease, local decision-making powers while we limit the size and bureaucracy of our schools" (Meier).

As a final point, are we to make schools better by turning decisions over to those closest to the schools? Do we make schools better through superintendents who centralize district decision making? Either/or thinking by school board members, superintendents, faculty, parents or the community comes and goes with many educational fads. School improvement lies neither in centralized leadership nor school-based management to make a marked difference in school operations or student outcomes, as is historically evidenced (Cuban).

TERMS & CONCEPTS

Change Process: Transformation through understanding and managing models of system change.

Community: Relations and understanding between parents, business, social agencies, and organizations including local and state, with regard to schools.

Continuous Learner: A professional constantly engaged in self-improvement through the intellectual and emotional habits of critical reflection and action.

Decentralization: A form of organization that identifies school-based management in that the power and the decisions that are made by the superintendent and school board are shared with those who are closest to the students: teachers, the principal, parents, citizens, and students.

Learning Organization: An organization learning and growing from the past, through research, in understanding and applying change, and measuring improvement.

School-based Management (SBM): A process in which a measure of formal authority in decision-making at the district level is distributed to the campus level. Also called Site-based Management.

Stakeholders: Any individual, group, or organization who has a vested interest whether financial, social, or otherwise in the educational organization. Anyone in a community may have something at stake, including students, parents, alumni, parent organizations, businesses, community organizations, school personnel, local and state policymakers, ethnic and cultural organizations, neighborhood organizations, service groups and religious organizations.

Paul Tapper

BIBLIOGRAPHY

Bauch, P., & Goldring, E. (1998). Parent—teacher participation in the context of school governance. *Peabody Journal of Education, 73*, 15-35. Retrieved Wednesday, March 21, 2007, from EBSCO Online database Education Research Complete.

Boehlje, B. W. (1995). Share the decision-making. *Education Digest*, 60, 12. Retrieved March 31, 2007, EBSCO Online database Education Research Complete.

Brown, B. R., & Cooper, G. R. (2000). *School-based management: How effective is it?* National Association of Secondary School Principals. NASSP Bulletin, 84, 77-85.

Cuban, L. (2007). No more magical thinking: Leading from top or bottom. School Administrator, 64, 6. Retrieved March 21, 2007, EBSCO Online database Education Research Complete.

David, J. (1995). The who, what, and why of site-based management. *Educational Leadership, 53*, 4-9. Retrieved Tuesday, April 10, 2007, from EBSCO Online database Education Research Complete.

Fowler, F. C. (2000). *Policy studies for education leaders.* Upper Saddle River, NJ: Prentice-Hall.

Fullan, M. (1995). The school as a learning organization: Distant dreams. *Theory Into Practice, 34*, 230. Retrieved Tuesday, April 10, 2007, from EBSCO Online database Education Research Complete.

Hoy, W. K & Tarter, C. J. (1993). A normative theory of participative decision making in schools. *Journal of Educational Administration, 31*, 4-20.

Jianping, S., Cooley, V. E., Reeves, P., Burt, W. L., Ryan, L., Rainey, J., & Wenhui, Y. (2010). Using data for decision-making: Perspectives from 16 principals in Michigan, USA. *International Review of Education/ Internationale Zeitschrift Für Erziehungswissenschaft, 56*, 435-456. Retrieved December 15, 2013, from EBSCO Online Database Education Research Complete.

Latham, A. (1998). Site-based management: Is it working?. *Educational Leadership, 55*, 85-86. Retrieved Tuesday, April 10, 2007, from EBSCO Online database Education Research Complete.

Lawler, E. S., de Young, C. A., & Hagman, H. L. (1941). Budgeting in public schools. *Review of Educational Research, 11*, 172-177. Retrieved December 15, 2013, from EBSCO Online Database Education Research Complete.

Mayer, A., Donaldson, M. L., LeChasseur, K., Welton, A. D., & Cobb, C. D. (2013). Negotiating site-based management and expanded teacher decision making: A case study of six urban schools. *Educational Administration Quarterly, 49*, 695-731. Retrieved December 15, 2013, from EBSCO Online Database Education Research Complete.

Meier, D. (1999). The company they keep. *The American School Board Journal*, 186, 25. Retrieve March 21, 2007, from Database: H.W. Wilson—EDUC.

Morehead, G. (2003). Getting the climate right. *Education Review, 16*, 86-90. Retrieved Wednesday, March 21, 2007, from the Education Research Complete database.

Spillane, R. R., & Regnier, P. (1998). *The superintendent of the future: Strategy and action for achieving academic excellence.* Gaithersburg, MD: Aspen Publishers.

Rodriguez, T. A. & Slate, J. R. (2005a, Fall). Site-Based Management: A Review of the Literature Part I: Past and Present Status [computer file]. *Essays in Education,* 15, 171-185. Retrieved March 24, 2007, from http://usca.edu.

Rodriguez, T. A. & Slate, J. R. (2005b, Fall). Site-Based Management: A Review of the Literature Part II: Past and Present Status [computer file]. *Essays in Education,* 15, 186-212. Retrieved March 24, 2007, from http://usca.edu.

SUGGESTED READING

Beck, L., & Murphy, J. (1998). Site-Based Management and School Success: Untangling the Variables. *School Effectiveness & School Improvement, 9,* 358-385. Retrieved from EBSCO Online database Education Research Complete.

Enderlin-Lampe, S. (1997). Shared decision making in schools: Effect on teaching efficacy. *Education, 118,* 150.

Retrieved from EBSCO Online database Education Research Complete.

Holloway, J. (2000). The Promise and Pitfalls of Site-Based Management. *Educational Leadership, 57,* 81-82.

MacPherson, R. J. S. (1996). *Educative accountability: Theory, practice, policy and research in educational administration.* Tarrytown, NY: Elsevier Science.

Oakley, D., Watkins, S., & Sheng, B. (2017). Illinois public school superintendents: Influencing state-level education legislation and policy making in Illinois. *AASA Journal of Scholarship & Practice.* 14 (1), 4-18.

Sergiovanni, T. J., Kelleher, P., McCarthy, M., & Wirt, F. (2003). *Educational governance and administration (5th Ed.).* Boston: Allyn and Bacon.

Shakeel, M.D. & DeAngelis, C. (2017). Who is more free? A comparison of the decision-making of private and public school principals. *A Journal of School Choice.* 11 (3), 442-457.

Wohlstetter, P., & Smyer, R. (1994). Models of high-performance schools. In S. A. Mohrman, P. Wohlstetter, & Associates (eds.). *School-Based Management Organizing for High Performance* (ed. by). San Francisco: Jossey-Bass.

SCHOOL SUPERINTENDENCY

The school superintendent occupies a highly public position as he or she oversees the management and development of a community's schools. The job is often fraught with controversy. The superintendent must balance the interests of teachers, administrators, parents, and community groups all while seeking to serve the students' best interests. To be successful, a superintendent must effectively communicate his vision, foster positive relationships between stakeholders, and, when necessary, be willing to exercise his or her authority to resolve conflicts. Before accepting a superintendency, candidates should carefully research a district's political climate to ensure a good fit between him or herself and the district.

KEYWORDS: American Association of School Administrators (AASA); Central-Office Position; Participatory Management; Public Education; Public Schools; School Board; Superintendent; Superintendency

OVERVIEW

Approximately 14,000 school districts make up our nation's public education system (Richard, 2000).

While many people may unintentionally take ubiquitous access to public schools for granted, the truth is that it is the local school district leadership that enables schools to function as they do. Serving as the primary face of this leadership is the District Superintendent.

Our school superintendencies are occupied by experienced and accomplished men and women. While most enjoy their work, few will argue that the job isn't demanding. School superintendents must be leaders, communicators, mediators, decision makers, and supporters. The job holds unique challenges that, for many, make it more of a vocation than an occupation.

Educational consultant and 1990 National Superintendent of the Year Don Draayer offers a unique parsing of the word "super-in-tend-ent" to arrive at the essence of what it means to be one (Draayer, 2006). A superintendent, he writes, is responsible for "tending" the school district. He or she "watches over, guards and responds to the needs of those within his or her charge: early childhood, K-12 and adult learners, co-workers, community and society at large" (Draayer).

A superintendent is also responsible for the district's "intending." Beyond tending to the day to day needs of the district, the superintendent must:

> ... set forth goals, strike direction and achieve purposes. Status quo goes out the window. Homeostasis is found not in what was or is, but what shall be. Leadership, action and change form centerpieces of the job description. Boldness, risk and opportunity come together intentionally when this fuller measure of the superintendent's job is properly understood (Draayer).

Finally, superintendency, in exceeding the demands of most other jobs, is more of a vocation than an occupation. Draayer notes that "[a]ccepting the title of school superintendent requires a willingness to apply both the mind and heartfelt values to the cause of education with a level of devotion and direction that clearly goes beyond the ordinary. Accountability is tied to the highest standards" (Draayer).

Despite the "super" nature of the superintendency, White (2007) observes that the superintendency is only as strong as the level of support which it receives from the school district. White suggests that while superintendents must lead their respective districts, they must also remain aware that "the key leaders are the teachers and the principals who supervise them" (White, 2007).

QUALIFICATIONS

The qualities a superintendent needs to be successful vary from district to district. Every district has its own difficulties and political situations which require different skills and experiences from its superintendent. When choosing a superintendent, school boards tend to look most closely at the candidate's academic qualifications, administrative experience, community relationships, and personal qualities (Glass 1993).

The majority of superintendents hold doctorate degrees, usually in education administration; most other superintendents hold masters' degrees. However, some studies indicate that education administration programs often do not sufficiently prepare students for the challenges they will face as administrators (Glass; Jacobon, 2005). Programs tend to emphasize theory over practice, resulting in graduates who have not had the opportunity to test what they have learned in the real world of education.

Rather than their academic credentials, superintendents usually cite their experiences serving in other administrative positions as the best preparation for a superintendent position. In a 1991 study of superintendents whom their peers identified as exemplary, most had followed a career path from teacher to principal to central office to a superintendency. Sixty-three percent of these exemplary superintendents had spent five or fewer years teaching, and 68.5% began their first administrative position before they reached the age of thirty (Glass). Administrative positions help aspiring superintendents gain a better understanding of school board operations and the relationship between boards or committees and superintendents, as well as how to manage financial resources and build support among stakeholders (Hord et al., 1993).

Another major consideration is how well a superintendent understands and relates to the district in which he or she is serving. Meeting a community's educational needs requires the support of a variety of groups including school board members, principals, teachers, students, and parents. Often, these groups have conflicting interests. A superintendent must maintain strong relationships with all of these stakeholders in order to effectively mediate between them for the good of the district.

Finally, a superintendent must demonstrate certain personal qualities which inspire trust and confidence within the district. School boards often ask that candidates have good judgment, personality, poise, intelligence, a sense of humor, good physical and mental health and an open mind (Hord et al). Superintendents are highly visible figures in their communities, and can quickly attract criticism for actual or perceived mistakes. They must have the strength of character to work with districts through the pressures attending their jobs.

DISTRICT VISION & GOALS

School boards and superintendents should also have similar visions for their districts. Some school boards are more or less satisfied with their community's schools and only need the superintendent to maintain their performance. Other boards might desire specific improvements like raising test scores;

they need someone who will work with them to develop the district, but not fundamentally change it. Another board may have come to a point where its members believe deep, systemic change is needed. Their superintendent must be willing to provide and implement a deep, comprehensive vision that will radically change how the district functions. Though school boards and superintendents may disagree on the specifics of how plans should be executed, to maintain a good working relationship, it is crucial that they share similar visions of the district's future (Hord et al.).

At its core, the superintendency is a position both of leadership and accountability and of support and personnel development. A successful superintendent has "the ability to bring out the best leadership qualities in colleagues, parents and students and engender in them the same kind of passion for the district's vision and goals" (White). In and of itself, however, this can often prove a daunting task. Board members, administrators and teachers can sometimes be less than enthusiastic about implementing changes or improvements proposed by the superintendent. Such a lack of support, White notes, can be a source of tension which not only delays the implementation of program improvements but can also cause relational roadblocks between the superintendent and the school board.

COMMUNICATION

Because so many stakeholders are involved in the future of a school district, White emphasizes that communication is vital. He writes, "Communication is the essential tool for building the case for change and creating the mandate for destroying the status quo. It is the key to neutralizing or defeating the common attitude of 'this reform, too, shall pass'" (White). One of the best ways to create an environment conducive to success is for the superintendent to nurture relationships with school boards, administrators, and teachers in order to effectively delegate tasks and leadership.

The superintendent must also be sure that his vision is clearly communicated to teachers and administrators—people who work most closely with students. In the end, it will be these people who see out the day to day implementation of the superintendent's vision. White recommends "comprehensive recruitment, effective staff development, and clearly

defined and supported expectations." However, it is the superintendent who ultimately bears the praise or the blame for success or failure. "[T]he superintendent," White writes, "is always responsible for what happens in the school district" (White).

BY THE NUMBERS: GENDER IN THE SUPERINTENDENCY

While the demographics of many professions have changed over time to better reflect national or even regional demographics, school superintendencies have in many ways remained demographically static. This is particularly visible in the percentages of women and minorities who fill—or perhaps more accurately, who do not fill—these leadership roles in public education.

According to the American Association of School Administrators (AASA), the years 2001-2010 will witness a superintendent job-opening rate of 1,000 per year (Richard). AASA expects that this will be due to a higher-than-average rate of retiring superintendents. These openings may provide much-needed opportunities for women and minorities to move into positions in which they are underrepresented. Richard notes that, although the percentage of female superintendents doubled from 1992 to 2000—growing from 6.6% to 13.2%—in 2000, 86.6% of superintendents were male. In addition, while minority superintendents had also seen an increase in percentage, it was limited at best. As of 2000, minorities still held only 5.1% of the nation's superintendencies.

Grogan and Brunner (2005) deconstruct the demographics of the superintendency to arrive at some surprising and puzzling conclusions. They compared a nationwide survey of women superintendents and women in central-office positions commissioned by AASA with the findings of "The 2000 AASA Study of the Superintendency." The following statistics reflect Grogan and Brunner's findings, which show both differences and similarities between male and female superintendents:

- 70% of superintendents are 55 years of age or younger, and this percentage holds true both for men and for women. As of 2003, women held the leadership of 18% of the nation's 13,728 school districts;
- 47% of women earned their highest degrees within the past decade. For men, this number lags

behind at 36%, and over 40% of men earned their highest degree at least 15 or more years ago;

- 58% of female superintendents hold undergraduate degrees in education as compared to 24% of male superintendents;
- Female superintendents as a whole have more years of classroom experience than their male counterparts, while almost 40% of men had spent five years or fewer in the classroom prior to moving into an administrative position (Grogan & Brunner).

This extra experience in education may play a role in the future advancement of female administrators and superintendents. Though in the past superintendents have tended to have strong backgrounds in administration, candidates with backgrounds in curriculum and instruction are becoming more and more attractive to school boards. A degree in education and solid classroom experience demonstrate that a candidate understands these fields both theoretically and practically. Candidates with experience in elementary education may have a particular advantage, since they will likely be more familiar with the fundamentals of math and literacy. They will also be more likely to have experience working with parents, since parents tend to be most involved in their children's education at the elementary school level (Grogan & Brunner).

Interestingly, the path to the top also differed in some aspects for men and for women. Half of women superintendents indicated that they moved from being a teacher to a principal to a central-office position, and then to being a superintendent; yet some moved directly from principal to superintendent, and still others moved directly from teaching to central-office to superintendent. Men, on the other hand, were less likely to bypass the position of principal on their journey to superintendent.

The study indicated that the majority of superintendents enjoy their positions, but even here a marked difference exists between men and women. While 74% of women responded that they would choose the same occupation if they were able to make the choice again, only 67% of men said the same.

The high rate of positive response to this question among women is particularly interesting since superintendency is known to place a high degree of stress on family life. Their survey found that 30% of female respondents indicated that they had waited until their children were a bit older before deciding to move forward in pursuing a superintendency. One the other hand, 35% of women superintendents raised children under the age of 20 while at the same time serving in the superintendent position. Of these, 32% raised children who were 15 years old or younger.

At the same time, however, the women surveyed indicated that marriage was often a casualty of their jobs. Of the 13% who were divorced, many indicated that the divorce was a result of the job demands of the superintendency. Conversely, married female superintendents cited support from their spouses as an important factor in their success and ability to handle both the demands of the job and their family responsibilities.

By the Numbers: Race in the Superintendency

When Grogan and Brunner turned to racial considerations, the numbers are also telling. Of greatest note, perhaps, is the lack of correspondence between race ratios in the overall population and race ratios in the superintendency. AASA's 2000 study showed that 8% of respondents indicated that they were superintendents of color, and only 1% of women in the Grogran/Brunner study identified themselves as Latina. Yet, this statistic is not reflective of the American population as a whole.

Grogan and Brunner further explain:

African-American women do not obtain superintendencies as quickly as their white counterparts: 56 percent of African-American women were hired within the first year of actively seeking a superintendency compared with more than 70 percent of white aspirants. Moreover, 25 percent of African-American women report waiting five or more years to obtain a superintendency compared to only 8 percent of white women and 9 percent of white men (Grogan & Brunner).

Their study also revealed that school boards which have a high degree of diversity among their members are more likely than non-diverse boards to hire minority superintendents.

Hidden Truths of the Superintendency

Former superintendent Terry Furin (2004) tells of the morning he learned that a friend and fellow superintendent had committed suicide. A mere two months prior to this, Furin relates that another of his superintendent colleagues had been sentenced to prison for theft and forgery. Two years later, still another superintendent committed suicide amid hearings regarding "alleged misdeeds" (Furin).

What is perhaps most disturbing about these tragedies is that, as Furin writes, they are not isolated. Rather, he notes, many superintendents experience similar serious problems. Seeking to uncover the root cause, Furin asks, "Was it a question of not knowing the relevant laws or district policies? Doubtful. Did these individuals lack personal ethics? Not the ones I have in mind. Did they recklessly jeopardize their careers, families and lives for comparatively few extra dollars? Hard to believe" (Furin). What, then, does he conclude? Simply this: "Sometimes something breaks down in the twilight zone between leadership theory and practice. The certainties of leadership theory so nobly taught and learned in graduate school simply do not ring true with the demands of the real world—at least not for some" (Furin).

THEORY & PRACTICE IN PARTICIPATORY MANAGEMENT

This "twilight zone," Furin writes, is created by the dichotomy between the belief that superintendents should foster a climate of "participatory management" and the expectation that superintendents act with authority when making decisions. In participatory management, decisions are made by those affected by the decisions. A superintendent who works in this model seeks contributory participation from teachers, administrators, parents, and other people with a stake in the district's schools. The theory is that such synergistic participation leads the participants to a greater understanding one another, bettering the group as a whole (Furin).

When put into practice, however, Furin notes that reality often does not bear out theory. While the democratic process of transformational leadership may sound appealing, in truth, the very participating members of such a process—administrators, teachers, parents, etc.—often want a decisive leader who will stand up and make difficult decisions. As Furin writes, stakeholders "want the top school official to be a person who can show muscle. Be tough. Be every place at once. Make quick decisions. Make all decisions" (Furin).

Thus, superintendents find themselves in positions in which they must determine when to act alone and when to draw upon input from others. This position, Furin writes, leads them into "a twilight zone where they experience a disconnect between what they have been taught and what is expected. And they enter it alone" (Furin). The result of these conflicting expectations can be a situation in which superintendents develop what Furin refers to as a "personality cult of self." If superintendents become isolated, they may take undue possession of their vocation, transforming every aspect of their job into a vital part of their ego—"'my' vision, 'my' curriculum, 'my' teachers, 'my' building, 'my' test, 'my' lunch menu, 'my' bus schedule" (Furin). Such isolation leads to tragedy, as attested to by the three scenarios described above.

Superintendents must strike a balance between negotiating compromises between conflicting interests, and exercising their authority. Barbara A. Vonvillas, a Rhode Island superintendent, recommends that administrators always try to reach a consensus among stakeholders before stepping in to resolve a conflict. If a consensus is not forthcoming, however, she writes that the decision should be based on disinterested research and principles which affirm the best interests of the students (Vonvillas, 2007).

SCHOOL DISTRICT CLIMATE & POLITICS

Before stepping into a superintendent position, candidates should also thoroughly research the professional and political climate of a district to determine if it will be a good fit for them. The most important factors in evaluating a superintendency are relationships and organizational results (Sternberg et al., 2002). Because relationships are so important when leading a school district, candidates need to evaluate how well stakeholders relate to one another and the superintendent; candidates should also assess how effective the district is in communicating and implementing its initiatives.

Sternberg suggests reviewing the school board voting history to see how often its members agree, and if it has a record of supporting the superintendent's decisions, initiatives, and recommendations. When interviewing with the board and other stakeholders, ask about their goals and objectives. Pay attention not just to their responses, but to how they interact with one another. Do some people or groups undercut others, or do they generally support one another? Ask, too, about their relationships with the previous superintendent. Pay attention to how they respond to you, as well. Do some people or groups appear hostile or indifferent, or are they all equally committed to considering your candidacy? (Sternberg et al.).

Public information can be revealing. What are the district's racial and family income statistics? Are families moving into the district or moving away? What are students' test scores, what percentage are on a free lunch program? The yellow pages are a good source for finding out what sort of businesses are supported by the population (Sternberg et al.).

Candidates should also speak with people inside the district to who are involved in education, but not politically or personally committed. Secretaries, journalists, newspaper editors, coaches, and parents can all be helpful. Ask what they believe the district's objectives to be and how well it accomplishes them. Ask if there have been any major staff changes and, if so, why. One superintendent even suggests contacting a realtor to look at houses in order to casually talk with homeowners about what they think of the school district (Sternberg et al.).

While there is no foolproof way to avoid obstacles on the way to the superintendency or to avoid challenges once in the position, understanding the demands of the job while recognizing the great opportunities inherent in the position may help current and future superintendents place in perspective the stresses and rewards of the position. As the number of superintendent openings grows nationwide, qualified men and women of diverse experiences and ethnicities will no doubt rise to the challenge of filling these leadership positions in our nation's public school system.

TERMS & CONCEPTS

American Association of School Administrators (AASA): A professional organization senior-level administrators and chief executive officers representing school districts across the country, whose stated mission is "to support and develop effective school system leaders who are dedicated to the highest quality public education for all children."

Central-Office Position: A position in the office that serves as the administrative center of a school district.

Cult of Self: A psychological state created when a person takes excessive control of his or her leadership position. Following an authoritarian leadership model rather than a democratic model, these people become isolated and out of touch with the people they are meant to be leading.

Participatory Management: A management model in which decisions are at least partially made by those affected by the decision. Such synergistic participation is supposed to enable participants to learn from each other, benefiting the group as a whole.

Public Education: Education required by the government and open to the public.

Public Schools: Schools supported by funding from the public, usually via tax revenue, which provide free education for children.

School Board or Committee: The governing body in charge of overseeing local public schools.

Superintendent: As pertaining to schools, the individual who holds supervisory and executive oversight and authority within a school district. The superintendent is often responsible for personnel hiring, firing, and development, budget preparation, and implementation of school policies and procedures.

Superintendency: The office of superintendent; the act of superintending.

Karen A. Kallio

BIBLIOGRAPHY

Draayer, D. (2006). What does the title 'super-in-tend-ent' mean to you? *School Administrator 63*48. Retrieved April 27, 2007, from EBSCO Online Database Education Research Complete.

Furin, T. (2004). Tragedy at the top. *School Administrator, 61,* 16-19. Retrieved April 23, 2007, from EBSCO Online Database Education Research Complete

Graves, B. (2011). Stretched superintendents. (cover story). *School Administrator, 68,* 12-19. Retrieved December 15, 2013, from EBSCO Online Database Education Research Complete.

Grissom, J. A., & Andersen, S. (2012). Why superintendents turn over. *American Educational Research Journal, 49,* 1146-1180. Retrieved December 15, 2013, from EBSCO Online Database Education Research Complete.

Grogan, M., & Brunner, C. (2005). Women leading systems. *School Administrator, 62,* 46-50. Retrieved April 23, 2007, from EBSCO Online Database Education Research Complete.

Jacobson, J. (2005). The Ed.D.—Who needs it? *Chronicle of Higher Education, 52*, A20—A24. Retrieved August 16, 2007, from EBSCO Online Database Academic Search Complete.

Richard, A. (2000). Studies cite lack of diversity in top positions. *Education Week, 19*, 3. Retrieved April 23, 2007, from EBSCO Online Database Academic Search Premier.

Sternberg, R., Friedman, R., & Harrison, P. (2002). The new job: Tailored fit or misfits? *School Administrator, 59*, 6. Retrieved April 23, 2007, from EBSCO Online Database Education Research Complete.

Superintendent frustrations grow, but intangible rewards remain high. (2012). *District Administration, 48*, 63-64. Retrieved December 15, 2013, from EBSCO Online Database Education Research Complete.

Vonvillas, B. (2007) You can't please everyone. *School Administrator, 64*, 54-55. Retrieved August 16, 2007, from EBSCO Online Database Education Research Complete.

White, E. (2007). The primacy of the superintendent. *School Administrator, 64*, 58-58. Retrieved April 23, 2007, from EBSCO Online Database Education Research Complete.

Glass, T. (1993). Exemplary superintendents: Do they fit the model? In *Selecting, Preparing and Developing the School District Superintendent* (pp. 57—70). Bristol, PA: The Falmer Press, Taylor & Francis Inc. (ERIC Document Reproduction Service No. ED393215). Retrieved August 16, 2007, from EBSCO Online Education Research Database.

Hord, S. & Estes, N. Superintendent selection and success. In *Selecting, Preparing and Developing the School District Superintendent* (pp. 57—70). Bristol, PA: The Falmer Press, Taylor & Francis Inc. (ERIC Document Reproduction Service No. ED393215). Retrieved August 16, 2007, from EBSCO Online Education Research Database.

SUGGESTED READING

Beem, K. (2007). Superintendent mentoring the state way. *School Administrator, 64*, 10-18. Retrieved April 28, 2007, from EBSCO Online Database Education Research Complete.

Brunner, C. (2000). Seeking representation: Supporting black female graduate students who aspire to the superintendency. *Urban Education, 35*, 532. Retrieved April 28, 2007, from EBSCO Online Database Academic Search Premier.

Christie, K. (2002). Leadership: A message for state legislatures. *Phi Delta Kappan, 83*, 345. Retrieved, April 23, 2007, from EBSCO Online Database Academic Search Premier.

Dana, J., & Bourisaw, D. (2006). Overlooked leaders. *American School Board Journal, 193*, 27-30. Retrieved April 23, 2007, from EBSCO Online Database Academic Search Premier.

Kowalski, T., McCord, R.S., Peterson, G., Young, P. & Ellerson, N. (2011) *The American School Superintendent: 2010 Decennial Study.* The American Association of School Administrators.

Raymond, J. (2007). Lonely at the top. *School Administrator, 64*, 61-61. Retrieved April 28, 2007, from EBSCO Online Database Education Research Complete.

SCHOOL BOARDS AND COMMITTEES

America's public schools operate under the governance of nearly 15,000 school boards. While often garnering limited public attention and interest, school boards perform a vital function in the administration and oversight of local public schools, though the specific agenda of a board can vary with individual districts' needs. In most cases, board members are elected; however, voter turnout tends to be low when elections do not coincide with federal, state, or municipal elections. Setting up effective committees is a key part of running a successful school board.

KEYWORDS: Committeemen; Consolidated Elections; Public Education; School Board; School Districts; Selectmen; Special Elections; Standing Committee

OVERVIEW

The United States' system of public schooling is rooted in a long tradition of local control and directional independence. Rather than operate under the direct control of the central federal government, the nation's nearly 15,000 school systems and districts each maintain a certain degree of autonomy and independence in their administration and function. Hess (2002) notes that this methodology of "[l]ay governance of public education is a uniquely American institution, with roots in the locally controlled schools of the New England colonies and in the common school movement of the mid-19th century" (Hess).

As autonomy breeds variety, precisely due to the local, lay nature of school governance, arriving at general conclusions regarding the makeup, nature, and function of school boards is often difficult. Further complicating the issue are the numerous committees and subcommittees which populate the organizational chart of America's school boards. If understanding of school boards as a whole is lacking, understanding of school board committees is even more so. Yet, an examination of research that has been conducted into these bodies that direct the education of America's youth will reveal certain trends and truths that will greatly enhance one's understanding and appreciation of the more than 95,000 men and women who govern America's school boards.

How is the average school board defined? Assigning quantitative values to factors such as median size, demographic distribution, or gender makeup may provide an outline of school board bodies, but it hardly fills in the lines to paint a full picture. Frederick Hess endeavors to dig deeper than the surface characteristics of boards and board members to uncover the true essence of America's school boards. In doing so, Hess poses several questions which guide his exploration of the nature of school boards. Among these are the following (Hess):

- How are board members selected for office?
- How competitive are board elections?
- What kinds of people serve on school boards
- How demanding is school board service?

To these questions, it will be helpful also to add the following:

- What is the basic function of a school board?
- How are boards organizationally structured?
- What are the various types of committee assignments within boards?

According to Allen and Plank (2005), the purpose of school boards is to "set the policy agenda for public schools." In "The Purpose of School Boards" (1982), the National School Boards Association (NSBA) expands upon this broad definition by exploring the history and development of school boards.

History

COLONIAL SCHOOLS

As early as the 1620 *Mayflower Compact,* the philosophy of local and lay control of education is strongly visible. In colonial America, an expectation that government would assume the responsibility of educating children was virtually unheard of. If a community were intent upon offering localized public education, it remained for average citizens and local leaders to take up the reins and establish a local school. As history indicates, this is precisely how early American education unfolded.

In colonial New England, Dame schools for boys and girls, grammar schools for boys, and Latin schools all developed under the oversight and administration of local leaders. As the new nation would model over a century later, elected representation formed the backbone for school administration. The NSBA notes that, in the earliest days of public schooling, town officials, also known as selectmen, held the responsibility of administering public schools. As time progressed, however, education administration became a delegated task, falling to committees the members of which were named by the town officials.

In colonial days, school committeemen were responsible for finding a location to hold classes and locating a qualified adult—namely, one who could read and write—to become schoolmaster. In addition, once a schoolmaster and location were selected, committeemen were charged with providing food and shelter for the former and maintaining the upkeep of the latter. Aside from the logistical concerns of administering a public school, colonial committeemen also maintained oversight of students' academic progress. This was done in part through visitations to the school. According to the NSBA, committeemen would visit the school during session several times per year to observe classroom activity.

After the advent of textbooks in the mid-1700s, committeemen also oversaw textbook selection and even petitioned the town to fund their purchase. From the 1600s through to the beginning of larger-scale organization of public schools in the 1800s, school boards constituted the governing bodies that directed and oversaw nearly every organizational aspect of local public schools. In brief, school boards performed the tasks of "administration, supervision, testing, personnel, evaluation, textbook adoption, plant maintenance, and community relations—all in embryo stages; and all without administrative help" ("The Purpose of School Boards").

20TH CENTURY SCHOOL BOARDS

As the U.S. population both increased in number and migrated in direction, school boards proliferated. According to the National School Boards Association, however, such expansion eventually took a toll on function as school boards soon became numerous enough to hinder their own effectiveness. For example, as smaller towns and villages grew into larger cities, the addition of new schools resulted in the addition of new school boards, and at one point, the cities of Chicago, Buffalo, and Detroit each had twelve or more school boards operating within their respective districts ("The Purpose of School Boards").

Rather than advancing public education, such duplication of organizational responsibility soon clarified the need to combine boards in order better to serve the learning population. The consolidation of school boards that followed laid the foundation for the structure of public school boards as they exist today. In this structure, each town or city generally maintains one school board, and all schools within the locality operate under the jurisdiction of one superintendent, who is subject to the authority of the school board.

Within this broad framework, then, what is the profile of the average school board? In an effort to create an accurate picture of today's school board, Hess undertook a comprehensive survey of school board members in 2,000 school districts.

Rural v. Small School Boards

Regarding school boards in general, a distinct difference exists between larger, urban school boards and their smaller, more rural counterparts. In school districts serving student populations of 25,000 or greater, for example, Hess writes, "[b]oards are relatively political bodies, with more costly campaigns, more attentive interest groups, more politically oriented candidates, and more hotly contested elections." He notes, however, that these larger boards represent only 2% of the nation's school boards. Contrasted with this, school boards in smaller areas "tend to be relatively apolitical bodies that attract little attention and feature inexpensive, often uncontested campaigns" (Hess).

The concerns faced by school boards vary in relation to their relative size. Whereas school boards in larger areas must often deal constantly with issues of violent crime, school boards in less populated areas are usually less occupied with handling such a threat. Despite their differences, however, both large-and small-district school boards share the same commitment to advancing academic achievement for the students they serve. Moreover, Hess notes, that across population demographics, "[b]oard members nationwide … contribute considerable time to school leadership, and two-thirds of them receive no pay for their work" (Hess).

Moreover, in larger districts, candidates and the general public alike must contend with outside factors in the form of special interest groups, lobbying organizations, and, at times, political parties that seek to influence the outcome of school board elections. While these pressures are not by necessity absent in smaller school districts, their presence is less pronounced than in small districts' larger counterparts.

SCHOOL BOARD ELECTIONS

How, then, do these public servants, many of whom are elected volunteers, come to earn the title of school board member? While a position on a small percentage of school boards in America is by appointment, the vast majority of school board members step into their roles through public election. As indicated, the level of contest in these elections is often reflective of the size of the school district. Likewise, the costs of school board elections vary according to similar data. Hess writes that while most candidates for school board will spend less than $1,000 during the course of their campaign, in larger districts, approximately two-fifths of school board elections carry a price tag of $5,000 or greater.

Despite the recognized importance of school boards to the operation of a town's or district's public school, voter turnout at school board elections remains disappointingly low. Allen and Plank examine this issue and its relation to the timing of board elections by studying school elections in four Michigan districts. Two of the districts held consolidated elections, meaning that the school board elections were concurrent with general municipal elections in November, and the remaining two districts held special elections, meaning that the school board elections took place in June separately from municipal elections. Allen and Plank concluded that school board elections held in November drew decidedly larger turnout than those held in June. In fact, voter turnout was as much as three times higher or more in November elections than in June elections. While in one sample June election, only 4% of voters in the two districts participated, 13% of voters in the two November election districts turned out (Allen & Plank). This finding corresponds with Hess's conclusion that "[s]chool board election turnout is substantially higher when board elections are held at the same time as elections for state, federal, or general municipal offices" (Hess).

THE WORK OF THE SCHOOL BOARD MEMBER

For those candidates who have successfully passed the milestone of election day, school board service holds challenges and opportunities uniquely its own. From time investment to policy considerations, the duties of board members are varied and broad. Through his research, Hess learned that the average school board meets approximately 23 times per year; yet, this time commitment alone represents merely one-third of the total time invested by board members. Indeed, members report spending an average of 25 hours per month on board business. Yet, like other aspects of board service, the factor of time investment varies depending upon the size of the school district (Hess).

For example, some board members serving larger school districts devote as many as 20 hours per week, or 80 hours per month, to their board service, while most members representing smaller districts spend fewer than 7 hours per week occupied with board business (Hess). When one takes into consideration that for most board members, education is not their profession, the time commitment assumes a new level of importance and notice. Indeed, like the committeemen of colonial days, today's school board members are often interested and concerned citizens who choose to enter into public service for the advancement of education. Among respondents to Hess's study, only 13% of board members reported a professional background in education. Contrasted with this, 45% percent stated their background as professional or business, and over 25% were homemakers or retirees. Interestingly, these percentages varied between larger and smaller school districts, with larger districts boasting a higher rate of educators than smaller districts (Hess).

BENEFITS OF STANDING COMMITTEES

Diversity of backgrounds notwithstanding, once members take their seat on the school board, their focus is the same: providing a high-quality education for their district's students. While the accomplishment of this goal may often be complex and always requires determination, it forms the basis for school board activity. In Governance by Committee, Doug Eadie indicates that governing committees are vital to the successful operation of a school board. According to Eadie, "standing committees are one of the preeminent keys to doing the kind of high-impact governing work that makes a significant difference in district affairs" (Eadie, 2005). Eadie highlights the three important benefits of organizing school boards based around standing committees:

IN-DEPTH ATTENTION

The scope and nature of a school board's responsibility is often so great that board meetings do not provide adequate time for members to address in-depth the many important issues at hand. Committees, however, are able to give to the issues the attention that the full board cannot, thus relieving the full board of time-consuming work while at the same time providing more targeted focus to each issue. The net result of this system is that the board as a whole is able to accomplish more than it could without the assistance of its internal committees.

EXPERTISE & OWNERSHIP

Eadie notes that participation on standing committees increases board members' sense of "ownership" of their position and the issues within their purview. He writes, "Dig[ging] into governing matters in detail builds board members' expertise where it really matters—in the meat of governing work. This … builds feelings of ownership among board members, consequently fueling their commitment to governing" (Eadie).

Holliday (2003) echoes this point in addressing the importance of effective communication between the school district and the public, and he encourages districts to utilize the school board, among other resources, as a tool for communications. He writes that school boards should appoint at least one advisory committee per year to focus on a specific issue. In becoming experts on this issue, committee members will be able to provide accurate information to district communicators, and they, in turn, can convey this information to the public at large.

CONTINUOUS IMPROVEMENT

A final benefit of governance by committee is the overall betterment of board functions and service as a result of the work and dedication of standing committee members. As a case in point, Eadie describes a committee whose mission is community relations and how this committee initiated the development of a speakers' bureau to schedule school board members to address local community groups.

Eadie writes that, at base, each school board should include the following standing committees with their corresponding responsibilities:

- **Governance or Executive Committee:** Comprised of the superintendent, standing committee chairs, and board president; responsible for directing the agenda of the board;
- **Planning Committee:** Responsible for budgetary and operational planning and recommendations;
- **Performance-Monitoring Committee:** Responsible for documenting academic and financial performance within the district and recommending appropriate changes or improvements;
- **External Affairs Committee:** Responsible for establishing and maintaining relationships between the district and the public at large.

While Eadie recommends specific committees, he also cautions against forming committees that do not correspond to the overall mission and governing responsibilities of the school board. For example, committees created to address secondary education might appear to be valid formations. In reality, however, they do little to further a school board's core function and in the end, as Eadie writes, "are more like technical advisory bodies than governing vehicles" (Eadie).

ESTABLISHING SCHOOL BOARD COMMITTEES

To avoid this mistake and to capitalize on the benefits of adopting a structure of standing committees, Eadie offers four guidelines for establishing school board committees:

- "To avoid stretching board members too thin, every member should serve on one and only one standing committee—with the exception of committee chairs, who also serve on the governance or executive committee;
- "Standing committees should be the only path to the full board agenda for recommended action items and informational reports. This will give committees real teeth and keep them from being mere discussion groups;
- "Standing committees do not take any formal action on behalf of the whole board; these committees are always advisory in nature;
- "Standing committee chairs and members should be rotated regularly—both to expose board members to the full range of governing work and to prevent an unhealthy degree of 'functional ownership'" (Eadie).

Few would dispute that no two districts identically mirror each other. Indeed, growing as they did from the local independence of colonial America, today's locally controlled school boards reflect the spirit of early American education. Yet, with their diversity and the invaluable functions they perform, school boards and committees make possible the system of public education that today flourishes across the country. From small rural towns to large urban centers, the vital service of school board members remains a keystone in our country's system of public education.

TERMS & CONCEPTS

Committeemen: In colonial America, men appointed by town officials to a committee responsible for the oversight of local schools.

Consolidated Elections: School elections held in November, concurrently with federal, state, and municipal elections.

Public Education: Education provided by the government and funded through tax revenue.

School Board: The governing body of a school district. School board members are usually elected, although in limited instances they are appointed.

Selectmen: Another word for town official or member of the board of officers of a town; the term applies to New England towns.

Special Elections: School board elections held separate from federal, state, and municipal elections. Special elections are often held in Spring.

Standing Committee: A permanent committee that is continually operational as long as the overall governing body is in session.

Gina L. Diorio

BIBLIOGRAPHY

Allen, A. & Plank, D. (2005). School board election structure and democratic representation. *Educational Policy, 19*, 510-527. Retrieved March 27, 2007, from http://epx.sagepub.com.

Blumsack, K., & McCabe, T. (2013). 7 practices of highly effective board members. *American School Board Journal, 200*, 21-25. Retrieved December 15, 2013, from EBSCO Online Database Education Research Complete.

Dawson, L. J., & Quinn, R. (2013). 4 questions for school boards. *American School Board Journal, 200*, 26-29. Retrieved December 15, 2013, from EBSCO Online Database Education Research Complete.

Eadie, D. (2006). Governance by Committee. *American School Board Journal, 193*, 24-26. Retrieved March 26, 2007, from EBSCO Online Database Academic Search Premier.

Hess, F. (2002). School boards at the dawn of the 21st century: Conditions and challenges of district governance. National School Boards Association. Retrieved March 27, 2007, from http://nsba.org.

Holliday, A. E. (2003). Communicating on a peanuts budget. *School Administrator, 60*, 33. Retrieved March 27, 2007, from EBSCO Online Database Education Research Complete.

Johnson, P. A. (2012). School board governance: The times they are a-changin'. *Journal of Cases in Educational Leadership, 15*, 83-102. Retrieved December 15, 2013, from EBSCO Online Database Education Research Complete.

National School Boards Association. (1982). The purpose of school boards. In *Becoming a better board member: A guide to effective school board service*. Retrieved March 27, 2007, from http://aasb.org.

SUGGESTED READING

Beaudoin, N. (2006). Giving stakeholders a voice. *Educational Leadership, 63*, 74-75. Retrieved March 26, 2007, from EBSCO Online Database Academic Search Premier.

Colson, H. (2006). The board's role development. *Independent School, 66*, 70-80. Retrieved March 27, 2007, from EBSCO Online Database Academic Search Premier.

DeKuyper, M. (2006). The well-run board. *Independent School, 66*, 58-68. Retrieved March 27, 2007, from EBSCO Online Database Academic Search Premier.

Eadie, D. (2007). From information to action. *American School Board Journal, 194*, 64-65. Retrieved March 26, 2007, from EBSCO Online Database Academic Search Premier.

Ford, M. & Ihrke, D. (2017). Are we on the same page? Determinants of school board member understanding of group accountability perceptions. *Public Organization Review.* 17 (3), 451- 479.

Frankel, M. T., & Schechtman, J. L. (2006). How to pick good trustees. *Independent School, 66*, 38-47. Retrieved March 26, 2007, from EBSCO Online Database Academic Search Premier.

Lister, G. (2007). 7 tips for effective boardsmanship. *American School Board Journal, 194*, 44-45. Retrieved March 27, 2007, from EBSCO Online Database Academic Search Premier.

Plough, B. (2014). School board governance and student achievement: School board members' perceptions of their behaviors and beliefs. *Educational Leadership and Administration: Teaching and Program Development.* 25, 41-53.

Rooney, J. (2005). No failure to communicate. *Educational Leadership, 62*, 90-91. Retrieved March 27, 2007, from EBSCO Online Database Academic Search Premier.

EDUCATION LEADERSHIP POLICY

This article examines the role of educational leadership in the broad context of U.S. educational history so as to understand what events, studies, commissions, recommendations and policies have affected the role of school leaders in elementary and secondary public education. The article examines the past and present educational models, and in particular, explores the essential differences between authoritarian and democratic educational models. It then applies these models to current U.S. public education policy to inspect the position of the United States' current public educational model.

KEYWORDS: Authoritarian Education Model; Charter Schools; Democratic Education Model; Educational Leadership; Education Voucher; Elementary and Secondary Education Act (ESEA); No Child Left Behind Act of 2001 (NCLB); School Leadership

OVERVIEW

Educational leadership within the U.S. public educational system has constantly adapted to new circumstances that American society has imposed upon it. The political and public expectations imposed upon today's educational leaders, the objectives that current leaders establish as priorities, their educational philosophies and styles of management, and even their daily routines as school leaders have changed during the course of American history. The impact of these changes cannot be adequately understood without first examining—at least briefly and generally—the history of American public education. An overview of the larger socio-economic and historical events that affected past public educational philosophy and policy is essential if we are to clearly understand the future role of U.S. educational leadership. Additionally, examining past public education problems and issues helps explain educational leadership's current crossroads, thus giving us a better picture of an emerging new role; such analysis can assist politicians, educators, institutions and citizens in helping to formulate the correct legislation, programs and policies for shaping effective educational leadership for this millennium.

Summarizing Education Leadership History

One of the most significant periods in America's system of secondary education occurred from the late 1800s to the early 1900s. Before this period, the government was not overly concerned with developing well-envisioned educational policies, so there was not yet a comprehensive national system for ensuring educational standards. However, this lack of standardized policy was not necessarily a failing of the federal government since there were far fewer colleges, and one-room country schoolhouses were not in dire need of comprehensive educational policies for guidance. In an age of settlers and the Homestead Act, learning basic reading, writing, and arithmetic were an adequate set of objectives.

But the need for defining specific educational public policy increased as American society outgrew its settlement period; the nation was transformed by railroads and telegraphs spanning the entire country, and by the rigorous industrialism that arose and consequently placed new burdens on the nation's public schools. Thus, it is not surprising that after the American Civil War had ended, as rural populations and European immigrants flooded into the burgeoning cities, the federal government initiated its first earnest attempt at formulating a comprehensive policy to guide public education. In 1893, the Committee on Secondary School Studies—often referred to as the

"Committee of Ten"—gathered to analyze the status quo of U.S. public education; the committee issued the "Report of the Committee of Ten on Secondary Studies," which outlined its proposal for standardizing secondary education. This seminal report established the U.S. public high school curricula, and set the age levels at which students should begin their courses of study. It also established the weekly number of hours—as well as the specific number of years—that students should spend on the standardized curricula (Passow, 1975).

After the Committee of Ten, other committees and organizations, such as the "Carnegie Unit" or the Commission on the Reorganization of Secondary Education, continued to shape and develop the U.S. public educational system. This period from the late 1800s until the beginning of World War II represents the most significant phase wherein the unique character of America's educational system was formed. The U.S. educational system made some significant departures from the European system, departures that, in many ways, are what made American high schools distinctly American. For example, foreign languages were drastically lowered in priority, while vocational training received much more emphasis (Passow). These recommendations and reports of the 1930s are what led to a long period of marginalized foreign language study, while vocational "shop classes" became part of every high school's educational program. However, for this period of American history, such prioritizations were perhaps effective and logical: in a nation of booming industrialism, students did well to learn the skills of making furniture and overhauling car engines—whereas studying foreign languages, at that time, held much less practical advantage. Students passing through such a system were well-prepared for a long phase of American history that historians consider a time of "nation-building."

However, when this era had ended after the Great Depression and World War II the nation entered a period wherein technology became a top priority. In 1957, the Soviet Union launched the first man-made object to orbit the Earth. Americans were bewildered, and understandably concerned, about falling behind technologically. The U.S. government decided that it was time to re-examine the public educational system. As Weaver points out about the Sputnik launch, "President Eisenhower challenged

Americans to strengthen math and science education, and the educational system answered the call" (Weaver, 2007). Part of answering that call was the National Defense Education Act of 1958, which earmarked government funds for strengthening those particular areas of education that had originally been de-emphasized: sciences, math, and foreign languages (Passow).

Approximately a decade later, America found itself once again in need of examining its public education system; the cultural revolution of the 1960s had much to do with this particular re-examination. The student uprisings and sit-ins against conservative, authoritarian leadership—within government and educational institutions alike—raised obvious and important questions: Why are so many intelligent students resisting formal education? And what was causing a "generation gap" that seemed more like a generation chasm? Such questions, provoked by the enormous social upheaval of that period, caused educational leaders to initiate new analyses of the public educational system. In the early 1970s, several national studies got under way. Three of these studies, sponsored by governmental departments such as the National Commission on the Reform of Secondary Education, were concentrated upon developing an accurate picture of the state of America's secondary educational system. The findings of these studies had very few positive or optimistic statements; in fact, one of the studies, published by the United States Office of Education (USOE) concluded that, "We have succeeded in producing a youth society housed in an overburdened institution excessively isolated from the reality of the community and the world" (Passow). The other reports, issued by educational conferences and symposia, were concentrated on developing recommendations that might cure America's ailing educational system.

Identifying the Problems

A feature that had been prevalent in the public educational system since the outset—although ignored until the launching of the 1970s studies—was the authoritarian style of leadership entrenched within the nation's educational system. The study of the 1970s finally grappled with this problem. One of the 1970s reports advised that administrative leadership should "focus on strategies for using an information rich environment rather than maintaining the role and philosophy of serving a role that is information-dispensing" (Passow). Harber says about the authoritarian educational model, "With this form of school organization, came a view of knowledge as factual and certain, and of there being one true answer to questions. It was the purpose of schools to transmit these 'true facts' to their students" (Harber 1997). Harber also says that authoritarianism "is a model that stems from the introduction of mass schooling at the end of the nineteenth century, when a key purpose of the spread of formal education was to socialize young people into the routinized and subordinate norms and behaviors required of workers in large-scale bureaucratic organizations such as factories and offices" (Harber).

Although the studies and reports issued in the 1970s make no specific mention of an "authoritarian model," the reports do express the same fundamental viewpoint as Harber about where educational leaders should take the educational system—and some of the reports acknowledge, at least implicitly, that an authoritarian model is prevalent. The United States Office of Education (USOE) report says that "student participation in school management has been kept at a safe distance... more out of the constraints inherent in the management of large institutions than in real philosophic hostility to democratic concepts" (Passow), which indicates the panel's awareness of an authoritarian leadership model in public education, though the passage blames the problem on organizational size rather than an intentional (or perhaps unconscious) authoritarian philosophy. It should also be noted that the panels of the day were quite aware of the bureaucratic unwieldiness of the public education system, and made recommendations for relieving that as well (Passow).

Many of the recommendations from the panels of the 1970s are also quite progressive and inherently point to a need for transitioning educational leadership from its authoritarian model into what Harber calls the "democratic educational model." For example, the USOE panel advises that a comprehensive education should be focused on five main areas that, when considered collectively, seem concentrated on enlightening the student as an individual; as a participating citizen as opposed to an obedient and well-trained subject. The five areas of emphasis are: personal values, citizenship, the arts, the humanities, and career education. Three of these five areas are traditionally the domains of liberal education; as for the other two, the panel advises that career education should be "moved out of the high school," and education for citizenship should be "community-centered" (Passow). Thus, the 1970s studies make recommendations that guide public education leaders to open more to the outside world and allow teachers and students to collaborate in decision-making, which are the signposts of a democratic education model.

Other recommendations from the studies and reports of the 1970s also guided public education toward a democratic model. For example, the National Commission on the Reform of Secondary Education (the Kettering Commission report) lists such priorities as removing sexism and racism from textbooks through state legislation, focusing on basic international literacy, promoting equal opportunities and recognition of female students, and cultivating a "global education" that is concerned with "scientific, ecological and economic issues that affect everyone." Also in keeping with the collaborative nature of democracy, the USOE report "urges creation of programs which would be designated *participatory education*" (Passow).

In 1965, President Lyndon B. Johnson signed the Elementary and Secondary Education Act (ESEA), which was designed to help children from low-income families to have equal opportunities in education. In 1970, President Nixon gave his "Special Message to the Congress on Educational Reform," and in this speech indicated the direction that the U.S. government would take public education. Nixon said, "For years the fear of 'national standards' has been one of the bugaboos of education" and he declared that the National Institute of Education would develop methods of measuring school performance and what he called "educational output," a term that pushed the idea of education into becoming more of a measurable product, or what others have come to view as a market commodity, as we shall see. Aside from measuring performance, Nixon also set out another prime directive. In that same message to Congress, Nixon said, "From these considerations we derive another new concept: *accountability*" (Nixon, 1970). The thrust of the U.S. educational system under the 2001 No Child Left Behind Act (NCLB), with its emphasis on standardized testing and its stress on the "accountability" of educators, could be considered a reinstatement of Nixon's earlier education policy.

The policy drastically reshaped education in the US before attracting widespread criticism from virtually all points on the political spectrum.

Making an Assessment

NCLB provided the comprehensive reauthorization of the Elementary and Secondary Education Act of 1965, and this is where educational policy remained until the 2015 signing of the Every Student Succeeds Act (ESSA) by President Barack Obama. Over time, educational leadership has slowly been taken from the leadership of local administration and has been nationalized. School leadership today—if it is to consist of local educators—must satisfy the regulations, programs, and standardized testing that the federal government has imposed, and only then can public school administrators attempt to lead their schools toward their own visions of public education.

David Kirp identifies the 1970s as the turning point in what he calls a rise of market-driven thinking in higher education. In a 2004 interview, he says that the "relatively no-strings attached federal funding policies dry up," and there is a shift in outlook, so that higher education begins moving toward a market-driven philosophy (Kirp, 2004). Luis Baez makes a similar observation about the 1970s when he compares the No Child Left Behind (NCLB) Act to its legislative predecessor, the ESEA. Baez says that President Johnson's legislation "did not create situations where the federal government was specifically directing pedagogy ... they [education leaders] were doing a lot of remedial stuff, taking kids out of classrooms and providing them with services," and he notes that the NCLB caused bilingual education to suffer because the federal government created so many impediments that removed school leaders' flexibility which the ESEA had initially provided, (Capellaro, 2004).

Apple (2007) notes that the No Child Left Behind Act redefined "accountability" as something "reducible to scores on standardized achievement," so that NCLB took the position that "only that which is measurable is important," and this caused what Apple refers to as an "audit culture." Apple also notes this trend of viewing education as a market commodity or consumer product: "Indeed, the movement toward marketization and 'choice' requires the production of standardized data based on standardized processes and 'products' so that comparisons can be made and so that 'consumers' have relevant information to make choices on a market."

Along with this process of commercializing education into a product, there has been a significant diminishment of local control, according to Apple (and Baez, quoted above); the process has also been accompanied by a militarization of schools and the larger society (Apple). Apple—and other authors whom Apple quotes—insist that this market approach to education, as though public education should be treated as a commodity and forced into the language of buying and selling, does damage to public education even as it removes the authority of public educators; it forces relationships into a "market model" that makes students the "customers" of teachers. Apple believes that public education should be safeguarded from this.

Harber writes that democratic governments are "more concerned with questions of access, funding and examination results rather than values and goals." And this holds true for the United States. Instead of pursuing the slow, difficult path of significantly reforming the educational model of public education, the U.S. government has increasingly pursued an authoritarian model, evidenced by its enforcement of standardized testing and the punishment of schools that do not meet government criteria. This forces the public education system to continue in its outdated "information-dispensing" role. According to Harber, standardized exams—increasingly structured as multiple choice tests that offer one true answer to relatively uncomplicated questions—prevent public education leaders from transforming their local institutions into a more democratic model of education.

When answering whether educational leaders are still practicing an authoritarian model of education (with an additional "market" approach added into this), the answer becomes complicated: Their main partner, the federal government, highly encourages educational leaders to obey its policies, which standardize education and view it as a commodity; this policy pushes an authoritarian model of leadership from the top down; but, in spite of this, many educational leaders, even as they have been authoritatively burdened with additional bureaucratic responsibilities, are working hard to find innovative methods for creating a more democratic model of leadership;

in doing so, they are following the forgotten recommendations of the government's neglected 1970s advisory panels, and are doing their best to work around the federal government's mandates so as to lead their schools with personal visions and beliefs about education.

Creating New Studies

Some leaders of public education have found it necessary to begin funding their own studies so as to create an informed plan for significantly shaping public education in their local institutions. A 2000 study commissioned by the National Association of Secondary School Principals, *Secondary Schools in a New Millennium: Demographic Certainties, Social Realities*, gave educational leaders some important facts to consider as they attempt to innovate their profession on their own. The study is revealing: The school-age population is set to change radically. Hispanics and Asians will account for more than 60 percent of the US population growth by 2025, which will significantly alter the school-age population. A large percentage of students will enter US secondary schools speaking a language other than English (Tirozzi, 2004). In response, scholars and administrators alike have examined potential methods of increasing the number of minority principles and other educational leaders, calling for greater diversity in such positions in order to better reflect and serve the increasingly diverse student population.

Another study, done by the Educational Research Service (ERS) for the National Association of Elementary School Principals and the National Association of Secondary School Principals, indicates that there is already a shortage of principals in general. According to the study, "About half of the surveyed districts reported a shortage of qualified candidates for the principal positions they had attempted to fill. This shortage was present among all types of schools (rural, urban, suburban) and among all levels of vacancies (elementary, junior high/middle, and high school)" (Tirozzi).

The study's most frequently listed hindrance to attracting public school principals is that, for the job requirements, the compensation was too low. The job stress and time-demanding work that come with a principal position were also cited as reasons that the job is not attractive. Other comments from the respondents included: "Societal problems (e.g., [student] poverty, lack of family support) make it difficult [for students] to focus on instruction; testing/accountability pressures are too great; the job is viewed as less satisfying than it had been previously; inadequate funding is available for schools." Tirozzi sums up the situation by saying, "The principals of tomorrow's schools must be instructional leaders who possess the requisite skills, capacities, and commitment to lead the accountability parade, not follow it" (Tirozzi).

VIEWPOINTS
Trying Out Innovations

Some educational leaders are trying to take their schools toward a more democratic model on their own. One such innovation has helped a few fortunate principals to ease the time demands of overseeing school building operations in order to dedicate much more time fulfilling the more important role of being a school leader. In one example, the 4,500-student Talbot County, Maryland system created the position of "school manager" to tend to the practical operations of schools—handling building maintenance, arranging field trips, overseeing cafeteria operations, scheduling buses before and after school—so that the county's public school principals could concentrate on being true educational leaders.

The principals in Talbot County could now concentrate on raising student performance. They also could now spend much more time observing teachers and students in classrooms, which aids them in showing teachers new methods of teaching, and gives them the time to plan professional development activities for the district's teachers. Kelly Griffith, who had been a principal in Talbot County for thirteen years, said of the system, "It really has given me more of a hands-on approach to being an instructional leader" (cited in Archer, 2004).

Other districts have tried other innovations to make the administrative burden lighter. The Mansfield, Massachusetts, public schools have had two principals in each elementary school. In California, the Long Beach Unified district uses pairs of "co-principals" at its high schools.

But these are just a few principals whose daily tasks are highly concentrated on being an educational leader. Surveys show that many of America's 84,000 public school principals are still performing thoroughly

administrative roles—but a myriad of commissioned studies consistently indicate that principals should be serving a different role. A research summary by Mid-Continent Research for Education and Learning (McREL) analyzed seventy studies and identified the most important aspects to a principal's job; those aspects largely have their foundations in the democratic educational model: "fostering shared beliefs, monitoring the effectiveness of school practices, and involving teachers in implementing policy" (Archer).

There is little disagreement among educational professionals that administrator preparation in the United States also needs an overhaul. Marc S. Tucker, the president of the National Center on Education and the Economy, a Washington-based policy group that runs a training program for principals, confirmed this need: "The quality of leadership and management training in our schools of education is, on the whole, terrible" (cited in Archer). However, unless the public educational system itself is first transformed, there isn't much need for quality educational leadership training. As Archer notes, "principals can't change their schools if they're not allowed to, and many building leaders say they're not" (Archer). Indicating the truth of this, a 2001 Public Agenda poll showed that only 30 percent of the nation's principals agreed that "the system helps you get things done." In contrast, 48 percent said they had to "work around" the system to accomplish their goals. The goals of progressive educational leaders who promote a democratic model of leadership continue to be countered by the more authoritarian aims of the government's policies; a conflict in educational leadership likely to last even into the next century.

TERMS & CONCEPTS

Authoritarian Education Model: An educational philosophy wherein students have little control or power over school curriculum or organization, and are largely seen as recipients of knowledge and instructions.

Charter Schools: Elementary or secondary schools that are publicly funded but are exempted from some of the rules, regulations, and statutes that apply to other public schools, in order to offer alternative education options which fulfill areas otherwise unaddressed by the public schools in the region.

Democratic Education Model: An educational philosophy that argues "for students to question, to be involved critically in their learning, to debate the social, economic and political context of education and to have control over their own learning through participation in educational decision-making structures".

Educational Leadership: Achieving common educational goals through the effective management of teachers, students, and parents within a school system.

Education Voucher: Also called "school choice," a certificate with which parents can pay to educate their children at a neighboring school of their choice, sometimes in another district, rather than in the local public school.

Elementary and Secondary Education Act (ESEA): A United States federal statute enacted in 1965 to fund primary and secondary education. The act mandates that the funds are authorized for educators' professional development, instructional materials, and resources to support educational programs, and promote parental involvement. The act has been reauthorized every five years since its enactment.

No Child Left Behind Act of 2001 (NCLB): A United States federal educational reform law (a reauthorization of the ESEA) that emphasized mandatory standardized tests in public schools and a voucher system that allowed money for student education to be paid to private schools, including religious schools.

School Leadership: The process of carrying out educational policies by collaborating with teachers, pupils, and parents in a school district or building. This term replaced an older term, *educational administration,* in the United States.

Standardized testing: A testing procedure that tests knowledge of a content area in a way that designs test questions, the scoring procedures and interpretations of responses so that the answers are uniform and consistent. The method generally does not allow for multiple responses to be correct, and is most often represented by multiple choice or true-false testing so that results are computer scored.

Sinclair Nicholas

BIBLIOGRAPHY

Apple, M. W. (2007). Ideological success, educational failure? *Journal of Teacher Education, 58,* 108–116. Retrieved March 19, 2007, from EBSCO online database Education Research Complete.

Archer, J. (2004) Tackling an impossible job. *Education Week, 24,* S1–S7 eLibrary. Retrieved March 13, 2007, from EBSCO online database Education Research Complete.

Ball, S. J. (2011). A new research agenda for educational leadership and policy. *Management in Education, 25,* 50–52. Retrieved December 11, 2013, from EBSCO online database Education Research Complete.

Birnbaum, M., & Weddington, T. (2012). Media review: American higher education, leadership, and policy: Critical issues and the public good. *Journal of Student Affairs Research & Practice, 49,* 237–239. Retrieved December 11, 2013, from EBSCO online database Education Research Complete.

Capellaro, C. (2004). Brown, Latinos and equality. *Rethinking Schools, 18.* Retrieved March 26, 2007, from http://rethinkingschools.org.

Chitpin, S. (2014). Principals and the professional learning community: Learning to mobilize knowledge. *International Journal of Educational Management, 28,* 215–229. Retrieved December 2, 2014, from EBSCO Online Database Education Source.

Davies, P. M., Popescu, A., & Gunter, H. M. (2011). Critical approaches to education policy and leadership. *Management in Education, 25,* 47–49. Retrieved December 11, 2013, from EBSCO online database Education Research Complete.

Diem, S., & Young, M. D. (2015). Considering critical turns in research on educational leadership and policy. *International Journal of Educational Management, 29*(7), 838–850. Retrieved January 8, 2016, from EBSCO Online Database Education Research Complete.

Farrell, C. C., & Marsh, J. A. (2016). Metrics matter. *Educational Administration Quarterly, 52*(3), 423–462. Retrieved December 7, 2016, from EBSCO Online Database Education Source.

Harber, C. (1997). International developments and the rise of education for democracy. *Compare: A Journal of Comparative Education, 27* 179–191. Retrieved February 18, 2007, from EBSCO online database Education Research Complete.

Hatcher, R. (2014). Local authorities and the school system: The new authority-wide partnerships. *Educational Management Administration & Leadership, 42,* 355–371. Retrieved December 2, 2014, from EBSCO Online Database Education Research Complete.

Hoff, D. (2005). Movement afoot to reframe finance-adequacy suits. *Education Week, 25,* 25–34. Retrieved

February 19, 2007, from EBSCO online database Academic Search Premier.

Jackson, K. (2012). Influence matters: The link between principal and teacher influence over school policy and teacher turnover. *Journal of School Leadership, 22,* 875–901. Retrieved December 2, 2014, from EBSCO Online Database Education Abstracts (H.W. Wilson).

Kirp, D. (2004). The administrator interview: David Kirp. *Administrator, 23,* 1–7. Retrieved March 26, 2007, from EBSCO online database Education Research Complete.

Kodrzycki, Y. K. (2002, October). Education in the 21st century: Meeting the challenges of a changing world. *New England Economic Review,* 3–19. Retrieved March 13, 2007, from EBSCO online database Academic Search Premier.

Nixon, Richard M. (1970, March 3). Special message to the Congress on education reform. *American Presidency Project.* Retrieved March 17, 2007, from http://presidency.ucsb.edu.

Passow, A. H. (1975, Dec.). Once again: Reforming public education. *Teachers College Record, 77,* 161–187. Retrieved February 15, 2007, from EBSCO online database Education Research Complete.

Tirozzi, G. (2001, Feb.). The artistry of leadership: The evolving role of the secondary school principal. *Phi Delta Kappa, 82* 434–439. Retrieved March 13, 2007, from EBSCO online database Education Research Complete.

Weaver, R. (2007). Maintaining our edge. *NEA Today, 25,* 7. Retrieved February 18, 2007, from EBSCO online database Education Research Complete.

SUGGESTED READING

Bottery, M. (2016). *Educational leadership for a more sustainable world.* New York, NY: Bloomsbury Academic.

Foley, R. (2001). Professional development needs of secondary school principals of collaborative-based service delivery models. *High School Journal, 85,* 10–22. Retrieved February 19, 2007, from EBSCO online database Education Research Complete.

Kipling, K., & Ferren, A. (2000) Closing the gaps: A leadership challenge. *Liberal Education, 86,* 28–36. Retrieved March 13, 2007, from EBSCO online database Education Research Complete.

Lewis, A. (2005). Washington scene. *Education Digest, 70,* 68–71. Retrieved March 13, 2007, from EBSCO online database Education Research Complete.

Post, M. (2013). Education leadership and policy. *Reading Today, 31,* 4. Retrieved October 8, 2014, from EBSCO Online Database Education Source.

Starnes, B. A. (2006). Even when repeated, lies about public education are STILL lies. *Education Digest, 72,*13–17. Retrieved February 18, 2007, from EBSCO online database Academic Search Premier.

Starr, K. (2015). *Education game changers: Leadership and the consequence of policy paradox.* New York, NY: Rowman & Littlefield.

Tienken, C. (2012). Neoliberalism, social darwinism, and consumerism masquerading as school reform. *Interchange, 43,* 295–316. Retrieved December 11, 2013, from EBSCO online database Education Research Complete.

SCHOOL LEADERSHIP

This article explores the challenges facing today's school leaders and various ways in which schools are trying to address the increased responsibilities of the principal. Primarily, the article focuses on the changing scope of the role of the school principal especially with regard to instructional leadership and leadership for learning. Furthermore, distributing leadership among capable teachers is discussed as a strategy to not only help alleviate the pressures on school leaders, but also to create sustainable leadership opportunities and to broaden the scope of responsibility and decision making within a school. Lastly, the co-principal model is addressed as yet another strategy to spread leadership responsibilities and to work toward ideal conditions for school improvement.

KEYWORDS: Co-Principal Model; Distributed Leadership; Edison Whole-School Reform Model; Instructional Leadership; Learning Leader; School Principal

OVERVIEW
EXPECTATIONS OF SCHOOL LEADERS

Eckman indicates that the work of the school principal has transformed since the late twentieth century to include increasingly more complex demands. In particular, principals are required to:

- Be instructional leaders;
- Close the achievement gap;
- Respond to accountability measures in laws such as No Child Left.

Behind (NCLB) and initiatives such as Common Core State Standards,

- Meet the needs of students with disabilities;
- Report to state and federal agencies;
- Provide support to parents in need;
- Respond to increased demands for home-school communication;
- Maintain safe school environments;
- Ensure all students achieve on standardized tests;
- Act as change agents;
- Provide visionary leadership in schools desperately in need of new directions (Eckman).

Among the myriad of expectations of today's school leaders, the new generation of principals needs to create the conditions necessary for professional learning communities to flourish. They need to act as lead learners and set the tone within the organization that all community members continue to learn best practices and continue to work to meet the needs of all students. They must develop the skills necessary to collect and use data from a variety of sources to respond to accountability measures set forth in performance standards and help inform decisions related to school improvement (King). They must fully understand the scope and sequence of NCLB, Race to the Top, Common Core, and other federal and state education reforms, and must prove their ability to meet the standards and expectations set forth by the law. They must have the communication and interpersonal skills necessary to interact with all constituents of a school community including parents, students, teachers, central administrators, and community members. Furthermore, they must be able to create safe school environments and respond to issues particularly related to rising security concerns in the wake of various incidents of school violence.

King asserts that today's school leaders are expected to realize many of these goals with relative ease, quickly and without becoming overwhelmed. King further illuminates that schools continue to serve increasingly diverse student populations and principals are expected to respond to constantly changing environments with fewer resources, less people, and in many cases less funds available to address these needs. Often, principals are unable to meet these demands as well as personal obligations, thus contributing to low job satisfaction and a relatively low average for the number of years that one principal leads a given school (Eckman).

Traditionally, school administration is hierarchical in nature. One individual serves in the role of school leader while the rest of the faculty and staff consist of teachers, administrative support, etc. The problem inherent in this model is that all of the leadership responsibility is placed on one individual. Few schools have branched out to embrace new models of school leadership. With increasing demands, less resources, and fewer people willing to take on the significant challenges faced by school leaders, many researchers and educators ask the question—is one individual truly able to successfully lead a school? Or do schools need to find ways to distribute leadership or develop innovative strategies to respond to the increasing demands, such as developing a co-principal model? Rutherford suggests that as schools become too complex for one individual to lead, it is time for new organizational and leadership structures to meet these complex demands.

LEADERSHIP FOR DIFFERENT CONTEXTS

King discusses the fact that leadership depends greatly on the actual needs of the school community. Every school faces different demands and different expectations, from teachers to parents and from state to federal governments. No two schools serve the same student population or have the same demographics when comparing socioeconomic status, race, academic needs, family needs, etc. Every school is unique; therefore, every school leader faces a unique set of challenges and must be equipped with the knowledge and skills necessary to provide the type of leadership required to lead a school toward overall improvement.

For example, a school may have large numbers of students with particularly low achievement scores when compared to standards (King). In such a school, the leader(s) may focus on collecting and analyzing data regarding student achievement to develop possible solutions to help increase overall student performance. In another school, academic achievement may not be the main focus, but rather improved instructional practice may be necessary to help teachers grow professionally. In this case, leadership may focus on increased opportunities for professional growth through workshops, seminars, study groups, additional faculty positions such as reading and/or math coaches, etc. (King). In yet another school, significant teacher turnover may pose a problem as the organization is unable to grow due to consistent loss of faculty members. Leadership in this context may focus on ways to retain teachers or to increase job satisfaction in order to sustain growth and reward individuals for excelling in the field.

While every school almost always faces the same general challenges at one time or another, each school responds to these challenges in a different way depending on the school community served. The priorities that different school leaders set are largely a function of the school community and climate in which they operate. Regardless of environmental context, however, all schools aim to provide the best possible education for all students so that they are able to achieve optimal learning outcomes.

INSTRUCTIONAL & LEARNING LEADERS

King indicates that the focus of school leaders has shifted since the late twentieth century to include an increased emphasis on instructional leadership. She also highlights the fact that the role of the school principal has further transformed to encompass professional development, data-driven decision making, and accountability. When principals act as instructional leaders, they focus primarily on everything related to teaching and learning. In essence, an instructional leader is the lead learner of a school in that he or she models a passion for professional development and enhancement of instructional strategies and methodologies. An instructional leader creates an organizational structure that largely supports the type of inquiry and growth necessary for instructional improvement. He or she sets the tone for lifelong learning and creates the conditions necessary for teachers to enhance their craft.

Effective instructional leaders are visible throughout the school day. The office door is always open and their presence is felt throughout the school. Effective instructional leaders are people-oriented and have the strong interaction skills necessary to work with a variety of individuals. They do not allow themselves to become isolated or secluded (Niece, 1993, as cited in Whitaker, 1997). Whitaker asserts that principals never have a strong sense of a school and its culture unless they immerse themselves in the educational environment by visiting classrooms, working with students, eating lunch with students and faculty, etc. When actively participating in school culture, leaders need to ensure there is a meaning and purpose behind their involvement and that others understand the principal's role as an instructional leader.

Furthermore, effective instructional leaders work with other school leaders to develop strong relationships and provide advice when necessary. Whitaker indicates that strong instructional leaders have a support group of colleagues outside their school to provide the type of support needed to make effective decisions and analyze ideas with peers. Moreover, Niece (cited in Whitaker) found that successful instructional leaders are trained by administrative practitioners who act as mentors for them and guide them through the learning process.

Smith and Andrews (1989; cited in Whitaker) identify four characteristics of successful instructional leaders:

- First, effective instructional leaders are resource providers. They must know the strengths and weaknesses of each teacher and be willing and able to provide the type of resources necessary to help each teacher grow;
- Second, effective instructional leaders are strong instructional resources. They are able to identify strong teaching and provide the type of feedback necessary to encourage and enhance improved pedagogy;
- Third, effective instructional leaders are strong communicators. In every mode of communication, they convey the core beliefs of the school and focus solely on optimal learning outcomes;
- Finally, they are visible and present in every school occurrence (Smith & Andrews; cited in Whitaker).

Dufour (2002) challenges the traditional definition of an instructional leader and instead suggests that educators think of the principal as a "learning leader." He indicates that principals become "learning leaders" when they shift their focus from helping individual teachers improve instruction to helping teams of teachers create the conditions necessary for students to achieve intended learning outcomes.

Therefore, principals become "learning leaders" when they shift from an emphasis on teaching to one on learning. Dufour asserts that a "learning leader" puts student and adult learning at the center of everything that he/she does throughout the school.

King further emphasizes the renewed definition of the principal as a "learning leader." She asserts that principals and superintendents are learning leaders whey they actively participate in ongoing, collaborative learning experiences to improve teaching and learning. They recognize their own need to grow professionally and become involved as active adult learners in activities such as study groups, examinations of student work, and other professional growth opportunities (King).

DISTRIBUTED LEADERSHIP

King indicates that today's educational leaders spend a large amount of their time working to develop leadership capacity in other school community members in order to distribute leadership and develop a strong sense of shared decision-making among all constituents. By distributing leadership, principals send the message that decisions related to the school reside with the whole community as opposed to one individual and thereby create a strong sense of community and ownership of school related decisions. Furthermore, Lambert (1998; cited in King) highlights that when leadership is distributed, the principal also sends the message to faculty that everyone has the potential and the capacity to work as a leader. In doing so, principals also work to cultivate young and aspiring leaders.

Traditionally, schools are not organized in such a way as to promote teachers for meeting objectives or excelling in their jobs. Teaching, in general, lacks a "career ladder" structure and therefore, teachers do not have many opportunities to get involved in a leadership capacity unless principals find unique ways to create such positions. Sallis (1996) highlights that schools are traditionally organized in such a way that all of the power and authority rests in the hands of one or two administrators. This is often the reason why, in some schools, a division is created between school administrators and faculty that hinders developing the conditions necessary for a shared vision and a strong sense of community. Katzenmeyer and Moller (2001) assert that schools will be unable to meet the needs of students unless teachers begin to

assume some of the roles that are traditionally considered the responsibilities of the principal.

When school leaders distribute leadership capacity among teachers it does not necessarily imply that the entire faculty controls decisions related to the school. Rather, principals create leadership positions that allow capable and willing teachers to work in a more focused leadership capacity. For example, a few teachers in one school may have expertise in a particular area of the curriculum or in a specific instructional methodology and may take on the role of a curriculum coach or may facilitate study group discussions, etc. Alternatively, a school leader may choose a few teachers to work collaboratively on a shared decision making team comprised of teachers, administrators, and parents or may encourage a few teachers to lead certain school organizations. A school leader can distribute leadership in a variety of ways and can set the tone that leadership resides with many, not one.

EDISON WHOLE-SCHOOL REFORM MODEL

Rutherford discusses one specific model of distributed school leadership: the Edison Whole-School Reform model. The central belief behind this reform movement is the idea that by distributing leadership and management of a school among a variety of stakeholders, the school will be more likely to succeed and meet intended student learning and achievement outcomes (Edison Schools, 2003; cited in Rutherford). In order to distribute leadership effectively in this model, the entire organization must be restructured to create the positions necessary to meet the various objectives and goals set forth by the school.

A hallmark of this particular distributed leadership model is that concerns and judgments flow upward from teachers as opposed to downward from the top administrators. Teachers feel empowered and have ownership of the decision making process as they are included in the process (Rutherford). This particular model serves to increase the overall sum of leadership capabilities within a school and to create the conditions necessary for teachers to influence each other and help improve overall instructional practice (Rutherford).

Wang and Manning (2000; cited in Rutherford) indicate that by distributing leadership among a group of stakeholders, schools become much more resilient organizations simply because improvement can be sustained and developed further, regardless of personnel changes. Traditionally, when the school leader retires or moves on from the organization, the vision is also retired as a new leader emerges and takes the school on a different journey. When leadership is distributed throughout the school and decision making rests in the hands of many as opposed to one, then, if one leader retires or leaves the school the vision is sustainable and the organization's strategic goals and objectives remain intact.

Co-Principal Model

The co-principal model is yet another way to effectively distribute leadership and create the type of ideal working conditions necessary to maximize school improvement. Eckman points out that the co-principal model is not a new idea. In fact, the model was first proposed in the 1970s. However, not many school districts have adopted the model (most likely because of budget issues). Eckman further highlights that due to the small number of schools working with the model, little research exists regarding the benefits and disadvantages of the model. Regardless, the co-principal model holds quite a bit of potential as an alternative to the traditional hierarchy of school administration.

School leaders who work in schools that embrace the co-principal model point to its many advantages as reasons for high levels of job satisfaction. Co-principals indicate that working in a team provides the conditions necessary for them to share ideas, problem solve, discuss situations with a trusted colleague, etc. Furthermore, they are able to distribute their time more evenly among teachers and invest more energy into helping teachers help students achieve learning outcomes. Eckman further illuminates that the co-principal model offers more opportunities for women to take on leadership roles, as the low representation of women in high school principalships has been a problem for many years. By dividing the job responsibilities equally between two individuals, the principalship becomes much more manageable, principals are better able to balance personal and professional demands, and teachers and students are better able to achieve desired learning outcomes.

Although the co-principal model seems like an ideal solution to ease the increasing demands of school leaders, principals who work in such relationships do indicate some of the disadvantages inherent in the model. For example, whenever two people are in a leadership position, sometimes it proves very difficult to share power and decision making responsibilities (Eckman). Furthermore, issues related to miscommunication, lack of trust, different perspectives, and different relationships with students, teachers, and parents all contribute to some of the interpersonal difficulties faced by people who participate in the co-principal model (Eckman). However, if the right match is found and the support is available to encourage and enhance the working relationship, co-principals have great potential to be dynamic school leaders.

Conclusion

Due to the increasing demands facing school leaders in today's society, many educators believe the job is too complex and too overwhelming for just one individual. As the role of the principal continues to move toward increased focus on instructional leadership, the position continues to grow beyond the scope of the capabilities of one individual. In order to effectively meet increasing demands, principals have begun to distribute leadership among faculty members to increase leadership capacity and to broaden the scope of responsibility. Furthermore, models such as the Edison Whole School Reform model and the co-principal model are increasing in popularity as schools begin to realize organizational changes are necessary in school administrations to effectively meet the increased expectations of the twenty-first century.

Terms & Concepts

Accountability: The responsibility for the quality education of public school students, as measured by achievement testing and other federal and state education reforms. School leaders are held to standards of accountability for their schools.

Co-Principal Model: The co-principal model is one way to effectively distribute leadership and create the type of ideal working conditions necessary to maximize school improvement by sharing the leadership responsibilities between two or more individuals.

Distributed Leadership: Today's educational leaders spend a large amount of their time working to develop leadership capacity in other school community members in order to distribute leadership and develop a strong sense of shared decision-making among all constituents.

Edison Whole-School Reform Model: The central belief behind this particular reform movement is the idea that by distributing leadership and management of a school among a variety of stakeholders, the school will be more likely to succeed and meet intended student learning and achievement outcomes.

Instructional Leadership: When principals act as instructional leaders, they focus primarily on everything related to teaching and learning. In essence, an instructional leader is the lead learner of a school as he/she models a passion for professional development and enhancement of instructional strategies and methodologies.

Learning Leader: Principals become "learning leaders" when they shift their focus from helping individual teachers improve instruction to helping teams of teachers create the conditions necessary for students to achieve intended learning outcomes. Therefore, principals become "learning leaders" when they shift from an emphasis on teaching to one on learning.

John Loeser

BIBLIOGRAPHY

Calik, T., Sezgin, F., Kavgaci, H., & Kilinc, A. (2012). Examination of relationships between instructional leadership of school principals and self-efficacy of teachers and collective teacher efficacy. *Educational Sciences: Theory & Practice, 12*, 2498–2504. Retrieved December 9, 2013, from EBSCO Online Database Education Research Complete.

Dufour, R. (2002). The learning-centered principal. *Educational Leadership, 59*, 12. Retrieved July 19, 2007, from EBSCO Online Database Education Research Complete.

Eckman, E. (2006). Co-principals: Characteristics of dual leadership teams. *Leadership & Policy in Schools, 5*, 89–107. Retrieved July 19, 2007, from EBSCO Online Database Education Research Complete.

Goff, P., Mavrogordato, M., & Goldring, E. (2012). Instructional leadership in charter schools: Is there an organizational effect or are leadership practices the result of faculty characteristics and preferences?. *Leadership & Policy in Schools, 11*, 1–25. Retrieved December 9, 2013, from EBSCO Online Database Education Research Complete.

Katzenmeyer, M., & Moller, G. (2001). *Awakening the sleeping giant: Helping teachers develop as leaders* (2nd ed.) Thousand Oaks, CA: Corwin Press.

King, D. (2002). The changing shape of leadership. *Educational Leadership, 59*, 61. Retrieved July 19, 2007, from EBSCO Online Database Education Research Complete.

Knaus, C. (2014). Seeing what they want to see: Racism and leadership development in urban schools. *Urban Review, 46*, 420–444. Retrieved November 3, 2014, from EBSCO online database Education Research Complete.

Lambert, L. (1998). *Building leadership capacity in schools.* Alexandria, VA: Association for Supervision and Curriculum Development (ASCD).

Letizia, A. (2014). Radical servant leadership: A new practice of public education leadership in the post-industrial age. *Journal for Critical Education Policy Studies (JCEPS), 12*, 175–199. Retrieved November 3, 2014, from EBSCO online database Education Research Complete.

Niece, R. (1993). The principal as instructional leader: Past influences and current resources. *NASSP Bulletin, 77*, 12–18.

Rutherford, C. (2006). Teacher leadership and organizational structure. *Journal of Educational Change, 7* (1/2), 59–76. Retrieved July 19, 2007, from EBSCO Online Database Education Research Complete.

Sallis, E. (1996). *Total quality management in education* (2nd ed.). London: Kogan Page Ltd.

Smith W. & Andrews, R. (1989). *Instructional leadership: How principals make a difference.* Alexandria, VA: Association for Supervision and Curriculum Development (ASCD).

Wallin, D., & Newton, P. (2013). Instructional leadership of the rural teaching principal: Double the trouble or twice the fun?. *International Studies in Educational Administration (Commonwealth Council For Educational Administration & Management (CCEAM)), 41*, 19–31. Retrieved December 9, 2013, from EBSCO Online Database Education Research Complete.

Wang, M. C., & Manning, J. (2000). *Turning around low performing schools: The case of the Washington DC schools.* Philadelphia, PA: Temple University.

Whitaker, B. (1997). Instructional leadership and principal visibility. *Clearing House, 70*, 155. Retrieved July 19, 2007, from EBSCO Online Database Education Research Complete.

SUGGESTED READING

Ackerman, R., & Mackenzie, S. (2006). Uncovering teacher leadership. *Educational Leadership, 63*, 66–70. Retrieved July 19, 2007, from EBSCO Online Database Education Research Complete.

Brown, P. (2006). Preparing principals for today's demands. *Phi Delta Kappan, 87,* 525–526. Retrieved July 19, 2007, from EBSCO Online Database Education Research Complete.

Copland, M. A. (2001). The myth of the superprincipal. *Phi Delta Kappan, 82,* 528–533.

Drago-Severson, E., & Pinto, K. (2006). School leadership for reducing teacher isolation: Drawing from the well of human resources, *9,* 129–155. Retrieved July 19, 2007, from EBSCO Online Database Education Research Complete.

Edison Schools. (2007). *Edison Schools, 2007.* Retrieved July 19, 2007, from http://edisonschools.com.

Elmore, R. (1995). Structural reform and educational practice. *Educational Researcher, 24,* 23–26.

Elmore, R. (2002). Hard questions about practice. *Educational Leadership, 59,* 22–25. Retrieved August 1, 2007, from EBSCO Online Database Education Research Complete.

Fulmer, C. (2006). Becoming instructional leaders: Lessons learned from instructional leadership work samples. *Educational Leadership & Administration, 18,* 109–129.

Retrieved July 19, 2007, from EBSCO Online Database Education Research Complete.

Hallinger, P., & McCary, C. E. (1990). Developing the strategic thinking of instructional leaders. *Elementary School Journal, 91,* 89. Retrieved July 19, 2007, from EBSCO Online Database Education Research Complete.

McCray, C. & Beachum, F. (2014). *School Leadership in a Diverse Society: Helping Schools Prepare All Students for Success.* Charlotte, NC.: Information Age Publishing.

Pilch, B. & Quinn, T. (2011). *School Leadership: Case Studies Solving School Problems.* Lanham, MD.: Rowman & Littlefield Education.

Stewart, V. (2013). School leadership around the world. *Educational Leadership, 70,* 48–54. Retrieved December 9, 2013, from EBSCO Online Database Education Research Complete.

Stone-Johnson, C. (2014). Responsible leadership. *Educational Administration Quarterly, 50,* 645–674. Retrieved November 3, 2014, from EBSCO online database Education Research Complete.

Wallace Foundation (2011). *The school principal as leader: Guiding schools to better teaching and learning.* New York, NY: The Wallace Foundation.

PUBLIC SCHOOL ACCOUNTABILITY

Accountability in K-12 education is a concept through which student outcomes are assessed and reported to stakeholders. At its core, accountability centers on how well schools deliver services in terms of students' academic achievement of a set of curricular standards; however, accountability is currently equated most heavily with teacher quality and student performance on basic skills assessments under the guidelines set forth by The No Child Left Behind Act of 2001 (NCLB). This article defines accountability, discusses the historical context of curricular goals and assessment and then focuses upon NCLB, standardized testing and teacher performance.

KEYWORDS: Accountability; Adequate Yearly Progress; Confidence Intervals; Instructional Sensitivity; N-Size; No Child Left Behind Act of 2001 (NCLB); Socioeconomic Status; Standards-based Reform

OVERVIEW

Accountability in education refers to a local educational agency's (LEA) responsibility to meet the expectations of its stakeholders. Districts as well as individual schools are required to meet the goals set forth by the state and federal governments. According to Finn (2007), while it may be one of the most commonly used words in contemporary American education, its definition is, at best, nebulous; he describes four strategies through which accountability can be defined and achieved.

THE COMPLIANCE INTERPRETATION

A compliance interpretation of accountability is the most traditional, hierarchical and bureaucratic of those outlined by Finn. Working within the existing system, this model involves adopting standards and measuring progress against them, managing available resources and their distribution and quality control. It is a top-down framework in which "participants in the enterprise are chiefly accountable for...obeying instructions and managing inputs and processes" (Finn). LEAs are chiefly accountable to themselves and to the government agencies that set forth the standards and administer funding.

PROFESSIONAL NORMS & EXPERTISE

The professional norms and expertise definition, or professional accountability model, is characterized by putting faith in the expertise of professionals and professional groups such as noted researchers, accrediting agencies and professional organizations (Finn). Although there are elements of accountability to standards-based compliance and the policies set forth by elected bodies, and while some attention is given to serving clients, this framework holds LEAs to the "creeds, gurus, and belief structures of the educational profession" (Finn). The highest standards of professionalism rather than standards-based assessment or client satisfaction are the basis for this definition of accountability (Finn).

CONSUMERISM

The third model includes a definition of compliance that centers on consumerism and makes LEAs answerable to their clients through "market dynamics" (Finn). Private and charter schools respond to this type of accountability on a regular basis as they risk losing enrollment and revenue if they are not responsive to client needs. Some of these principles have filtered into public education with the various manifestations of public school choice, virtual and magnet schools and voucher systems (Finn). "It remains, however, the most controversial of these four strategies, for it's the only one that employs a flexible definition of public education [which] allows tax-generated monies to flow into schools not directly controlled by governmental bodies" (Finn).

STANDARDS-BASED REFORM

Finally, the most widely accepted definition of accountability in education today involves standards-based reform, especially in light of the policy-making decisions of elected bodies and the current goals set forth by The No Child Left Behind Act of 2001 (NCLB). The model is a hierarchical, externally-imposed framework for change wherein standards for achievement for children are set, testing is done to measure that achievement and consequences for both children and practitioners are imposed if standards are not met (Finn). Within standards-based reform, it is most often an outside non-educational agency or political body that establishes the standards for the individual entities (e.g., the children, the teachers, the school, the school district, the state, etc.) to achieve and that determines how that achievement will be measured (Finn). Rewards for meetings goals and sanctions for under-achievement are then dispensed at the discretion of that same outside agency.

Of the four strategies, standards-based reform is the most directly related to academic achievement, in part because the older compliance and professional accountability models failed to focus sufficiently on student outcomes (Finn). Insofar as the accountability model that is most likely to result in effective educational and increased student achievement in public schools, standards-based reform has begun to emerge as the best practice despite the difficulty in implementation (Finn). According to Finn, "there's plenty of evidence that private schools do a pretty good job both of producing relatively high-achieving students and of satisfying their clients. There's mixed evidence with respect to charter schools, most of which are still new."

The current and most widely accepted view of accountability in public education centers on the attainment of benchmarks in the areas of reading and mathematics. Seen as the most critical areas for student achievement and success by the legislative bodies that impose the standards, states and school districts strive to meet these goals, often to the exclusion of other curricular areas. This focus upon basic skills, however, is relatively new as historically, the goals of public education were significantly broader (Rothstein & Jacobsen, 2007).

BACKGROUND

The creation of public education system in the United States was a primary concern for the founding fathers, who believed that education was fundamental to creating an informed citizenry, which could make sound political decisions and continue the growth of the democracy that was being designed (Rothstein & Jacobsen). Benjamin Franklin emphasized physical education equally with intellectual development and believed that history should be used as a springboard for the teaching of morality, ethics, reading, speaking and writing (Rothstein & Jacobsen). In his initial state of the union address, George Washington instructed the Congress to encourage schools to teach students the values of citizenship, especially where it concerned the protection of their rights, and to be aware of the difference between oppression and rightful authority (Rothstein & Jacobsen).

The concept of diversity in education is not a recent development and dates back to both Washington and Thomas Jefferson. "Washington also urged a public education system that could foster a sense of national identity when students from diverse backgrounds learned together under the same educational roof" (Rothstein & Jacobsen). Jefferson spent a great deal of time structuring the public education system in Virginia in large part due to his believe that the most reliable means through which to prevent a return to tyranny was education. According to Rothstein and Jacobsen, Jefferson's goals for a comprehensive educational system were:

> To give every citizen the information he needs for the transaction of his own business; To enable him to calculate for himself, and to express and preserve his ideas, his contracts and account, in writing; To improve, by reading, his morals and faculties; To understand his duties to his neighbors and country, and to discharge with competence the functions confided to him by either; To know his rights; To exercise with order and justice those he retains; and to choose with discretion the fiduciary of those he delegates; and to notice their conduct with diligence, with candor, and judgment; And, in general, to observe with intelligence and faithfulness all the social relations under which he shall be placed.

Clearly, students' moral, ethical and political development was as important to Franklin, Washington and Jefferson as was their achievement in reading, writing and mathematics.

The nineteenth century marked a continuation and expansion of the comprehensive view of public education. Horace Mann, the first superintendent of the Massachusetts Educators, also advocated a balanced set of educational goals that stressed the importance of political awareness in the clear context of democratic values, as well as other curricular areas such as vocal music, environmental awareness, public health policy, physical education and ethics (Rothstein & Jacobsen). Mann advocated an accountability system within education that judged not only students' achievement but also students' commitment to and excitement about continued learning (Rothstein & Jacobsen).

The tradition continued into the twentieth century, when, in 1918, a committee commissioned by the federal government to review secondary education issued its report demanding a "balanced approach to education, urging schools to take responsibility for physical activity and health, academic skills, responsible family behavior and morality, vocational preparation, appreciation of the arts and training for democratic civic participation" (Rothstein & Jacobsen). In the aftermath of the turmoil of the early part of the twentieth century and the time preceding the Second World War, the American Association of School Administrators joined with the National Education Association to convene an Education Policies Commission, which in turn "set forth 'four great groups of objectives' for public education: self-realization, human relationships, economic efficiency and civic responsibility" (Rothstein & Jacobsen). The commission's 1938 report was reflective of the world and national climate and emphasized math and literacy skills as important components of education (Rothstein & Jacobsen). The report also stressed other areas for development, specifically outlining the importance of "developing students' morality, justice and fair dealings, honesty, truthfulness, maintenance of group understandings, proper respect for authority, tolerance and respect for others, habits of cooperation, and work habits such as industry and self-control, along with endurance and physical strength" (Rothstein & Jacobsen).

No Child Left Behind (NCLB)

It is interesting to note, then, that at the beginning of the twenty-first century, and amidst new national and world crisis, the legislature enacted the No Child Left Behind Act of 2001 (Public Law 107-110), which makes states accountable only for test scores in areas of basic academic skills and discounts the historic balanced list of outcomes generated throughout national history (Rothstein & Jacobsen). Rothstein and Jacobsen notes:

> "... at various times throughout American history some goals have been emphasized more than others, there always has existed a consensus around a broad set of goals, a consensus that stands in stark contrast to the philosophy of No Child Left Behind."

In January 2002, No Child Left Behind (NCLB) was signed into law and became the most recent and comprehensive attempt at standards-based education reform. The law reauthorized many programs aimed specifically at improving the performance of elementary and secondary schools by increasing the accountability for states, school districts and schools. It also empowered parents with more options for school choice and increased focus on literacy skills for children. The law did not set national standards for assessment or achievement; rather it charged individual states with those tasks. States relying on federal funding for education have had to comply with the requirements of NCLB. The central goal of NCLB is for students to be proficient, according to reported test scores, in the areas of reading and mathematics by the end of the 2013-14 school year (Hoff, 2007). Students are tested in the areas of reading and mathematics in grades 3, 8 and once in high school. By then end of the 2007-2008 school year, students will also be tested in the area of science once in grades 3-5, once in grades 6-8 and once in grades 10-11 (NCLB, 2002).

The framework upon which NCLB is structured relies heavily on the idea that testing is central to having teachers teach and students learn (Levenson, 2007). Thus, there progress toward setting, meeting and assessing academic goals has been made while the curriculum has continually been narrowed so that students are able to achieve on the standardized tests. Teachers are teaching to the tests, and students are learning only what is being tested (Levenson). Levenson argues that while some blame resistance to change for the continued lack of improved performance in American schools, "others are beginning to argue it is unrealistic for educators to assume total responsibility for overcoming the significant effects on children of poverty, homelessness and poor health."

APPLICATIONS

Within the framework of standards-based reform under NCLB, teachers are held accountable for the performance of their students. According to Ingersoll (2007), "Since the seminal Nation at Risk report in 1983, a seemingly endless stream of studies, commissions, and national reports have targeted low teacher quality as one of the central problems facing schools."

TEACHER PERFORMANCE

One perception is that schools do not hold teachers accountable for instruction or for meeting curricular

goals; it suggests that teachers are not doing their jobs within their individual classrooms (Ingersoll). The result, according to this viewpoint, is that there is poor performance on standardized tests and low achievement among students. At the heart of this perception is the belief that poor teachers are the result of poor teacher preparation programs, a poor knowledge base, a lack of commitment to and engagement with the profession and a general lack of effort and ability (Ingersoll). Those who support this perception believe an increase in the centralized control of school would hold teachers more accountable and "advocate standardized curriculums, teacher licensing examinations, merit-pay programs, and explicit performance standards coupled with more rigorous teacher and school evaluations. Many of these accountability mechanisms have been put in place with the implementation of No Child Left Behind" (Ingersoll).

While accountability in schools is important and teacher performance is a primary concern, it often obfuscates the ways that school management and organization contribute to the problems that exist (Ingersoll). School districts and schools themselves are highly centralized organizations; principals and school boards make the key decisions in schools that shape the instructional program including curricular decisions and textbook choice. Teachers do not. According to Ingersoll:

Teachers often have little input in decisions concerned with their course schedules and class sizes, the office and classroom space they will use, and the use of school discretionary funds for classroom materials. On average, teachers have limited control over which courses they are assigned to teach and which students will be enrolled in their courses. In addition, teachers generally have little input into school-wide behavioral and disciplinary policies and rarely have the authority to have disruptive students removed from their classrooms, even temporarily. Likewise, teachers often have little say about what kind of ability grouping their school uses or about student placement in those groups. They typically have little influence over decisions concerning whether to promote particular students or hold them back. They usually have little input into hiring, firing, and budgetary decisions; the means and criteria by which they or the school administrators are evaluated; and the content of their own on-the-job development and in-service training programs (Ingersoll).

One of the distinguishing characteristics of professionalization of an occupation is the degree of power and control that practitioners have in the making of workplace decisions (Friedson, 1986, as cited in Ingersoll). Professional employees usually enjoy a degree of freedom, control and autonomy in their professional practice, and they are usually able to approach senior management about issues that arise (Ingersoll). They have an impact on the development and character of their profession in ways that those in other occupations not classified as professions do not. Teachers, however, do not have power and control over key decisions commensurate with their professional status and preparation. According to Ingersoll:

As a result, teaching is an occupation beset by tension and imbalance between responsibilities and power. On the one hand, the work of teaching...is both important and complex. But on the other hand, those entrusted with the training of this next generation are not entrusted with much control over many of the key decisions concerned with this crucial work.

He argues that accountability without the power to make crucial decisions is both unfair and harmful (Ingersoll).

Under the current system of teacher accountability, teachers focus too much instructional attention on test preparation thereby depriving students of the broader elements of the curriculum not assessed on the accountability tests (Popham, 2007). Further, under pressure from governing bodies, schools and teachers are forced to interpret results to demonstrate achievement even when students are not attaining requisite knowledge rather than addressing issues of effective instruction and remediation (Popham). Levenson (2007), recognizes the drawbacks of the accountability system currently in place and suggests instead:

"a standards-based world of shared responsibility for student learning...[so that] if some part of this necessary context for all students reaching mastery is missing, educators, community leaders and advocates need to figure out together how to put it into place."

STANDARDIZED TESTING

Test scores remain central to the current system of accountability in K-12 education. Thus, large-scale,

standardized assessment tools have become increasingly important for states and schools. Scores on these assessments influence legislators and policy makers and impact everything from funding to instructional methods (Popham). "The premise underlying the use of these accountability tests is that students' test scores will indicate the quality of instruction those students have received" (Popham).

Those in favor of standards-based reform rely heavily on these tests and believe that teachers who know that their performance will be evaluated based upon the test scores of their students will be more effective and that those in authority will be able to intervene where test results indicate that inadequate instruction is being offered (Popham). Unfortunately, few tests in use are able to measure the effect of instruction on students' test scores; they are instructionally insensitive and therefore only able to measure whether or not students know the answers to the questions posited. According to Popham: "A test's instructional sensitivity represents the degree to which students' performances on that test accurately reflect the quality of the instruction that was provided specifically to promote students' mastery of whatever is being assessed.

INSTRUCTIONALLY SENSITIVE TESTING

A test that was instructionally sensitive could distinguish between effective and inadequate instruction and would allow interpreters to relate higher test scores to effective instruction in meaningful ways (Popham). The socioeconomic status (SES) of the student population is believed to have more influence than instructional quality on most accountability tests currently in use. "That is, such instructionally insensitive accountability tests tend to measure the SES composition of a school's student body rather than the effectiveness with which the school's students have been taught," (Popham).

Instructionally sensitive assessment is a major factor in the creation of valid accountability program; however, there are a number of factors that impact it. The first is that states tend to publish comprehensive curricular goals that cannot all be met. Hence, individual teachers or departments are left to determine which goals take precedence for their students, and they may not be the same as those being assessed in that year (Popham). Secondly, without a clear understanding of the skills and knowledge that will be assessed, it is difficult for teachers to prepare students for testing. Additionally, there must be a sufficient number of items on the test to allow evaluators and interpreters to determine if each goal has been achieved. According to Popham, this is crucial, as "If teachers can't tell which parts of their instruction are working and which parts aren't, they'll be unable to improve ineffectual instructional segments for future students." Finally, items on the test must be judged to be sensitive to instruction by reviewers (Popham).

Instructionally sensitive evaluation instruments are an important factor given the current K-12 accountability focuses on student outcomes in terms of instruction.

VIEWPOINTS

A number of issues have arisen in the five years since the enactment of NCLB, and it is currently scheduled for reauthorization with significant revisions proposed (Levenson; Hoff; Miller, 2007). The current administration advocates minimal changes to the existing legislation; however, current reporting systems exclude millions of children from the law's accountability system (Miller). Currently, the law allows schools to use large N-sizes, or numbers of children that must belong to a subgroup, in order to be included in its reports of adequate yearly progress (AYP) (Miller). Because schools can have N-sizes of up to 200, a subgroup of 199 would not be included in the school's disaggregated AYP. According to Miller:

"The damage from this loophole is enormous. Last year, in an exhaustive investigation, the Associated Press found that nearly 2 million students nationwide are simply left out of disaggregated AYP calculations, including an estimated 15 percent of minority students nationwide."

Another issue impacting a true measure of improvement is that the current law allows states to use wide statistical ranges, or confidence intervals, in the reporting of student performance in the areas of reading and math (Miller). Miller explains:

"Looking at one state, the [Congressional Research Service] found that the number of schools that did not meet their AYP targets increased by nearly 8 percent because the state used a confidence interval of 99 instead of 95."

He asserts that as many as half the states are using confidence intervals of 99, making a real assessment of school performance and academic achievement difficult (Miller).

Allowing such wide variances for reporting progress weakens the accountability system that the legislation put in place. Miller suggests a number of reforms, among them allowing states to assess school performance using indicators in addition to reading and math examinations. He (Miller) states:

"If we keep a strong focus on student progress in reading and math, but also allow additional indicators to play a role, we can have a richer, better understanding of what's really happening inside our schools."

The draft legislation reauthorizing NCLB demonstrates plans to revise the system of accountability by continuing to assess students' academic progress in reading and mathematics in grades 3 and 8 and then once again in high school, and testing them in science once in elementary school, once in middle school and once in high school by the end of the 2007-2008 academic year, but it also adds other indicators to give a more comprehensive look at achievement. Those indicators could include scores on states' tests in subjects other than reading and math, as well as on graduation and college-enrollment rates. (Hoff). The new version would also allow states to use growth models to track progress toward NCLB's goal that all students should score as proficient in math and reading by the end of the 2013-14 academic year (Hoff).

TERMS & CONCEPTS

Accountability: Within the context of K-12 education, accountability refers to the process through which states, LEA's and schools report their progress, at predetermined intervals, toward meeting short and long-term performance and improvement goals to their stakeholders and to the federal government.

Adequate Yearly Progress: Adequate Yearly Progress is a component of NCLB's accountability system and is based upon a set of performance goals that every school, LEA, and state must achieve within specified time frames in order to meet the 100% proficiency goal established by NCLB.

Confidence Intervals: A confidence interval is a statistical term used to indicate the reliability of an estimate; a result with a small confidence interval is considered more reliable than a result with a large confidence interval.

N-size: N-size is a statistical term used to describe the number within a sample group.

No Child Left Behind Act of 2001 (NCLB): A reauthorization of the Elementary and Secondary Education Act of 1965, which served at the primary federal law governing K-12 education. Among the goals of NCLB are to improve student achievement, to close achievement gaps and to educate all students to 100 percent proficiency by 2014.

Instructional Sensitivity: Instructional sensitivity refers to the degree to the quality of instruction offered to promote the learning of the material in preparation for and to be assessed on a test is reflected in the students' performance on the test.

Socioeconomic Status (SES): Socioeconomic status (SES) is based upon family income, parental education level(s), parental occupation(s), and social status within the community and is considered a factor that impacts academic achievement in children.

Standards-Based Reform: Standards-based reform involves the establishment of clear, measurable standards for all school children. In support of meeting those standards, resources are allocated, curriculum is designed and revised, assessments are designed, administered and interpreted and professional development activities are offered.

Karin Carter-Smith

BIBLIOGRAPHY

Finn, C. (2007). Real accountability in k-12 education: The marriage of Ted and Alice. Retrieved December 2, 2007, from http://media.hoover.org.

Ingersoll, R. (2007). Short on power, long on responsibility. *Educational Leadership 65*, 20- 25. Retrieved December 2, 2007, from EBSCO online database Education Research Complete.

Jacobsen, R., Saultz, A., & Snyder, J.W. (2013). When accountability strategies collide: Do policy changes that raise accountability standards also erode public satisfaction?. *Educational Policy, 27*, 360-389.Retrieved December 15, 2013, from EBSCO Online Database Education Research Complete.

Levenson, M. (2007). A standards base and three new R's. *School Administrator. 64*, 32-35. Retrieved December 2, 2007, from EBSCO online database Education Research Complete.

Smith, J. (1983). Quantitative versus qualitative research: An attempt to clarify the issue. *Educational Researcher, 12*, 6 -13.

Vivar, C., McQueen, A., Whyte, D., & Armayor, N. (2007). Getting started with qualitative research: Developing a research proposal. *Nurse Researcher, 14*, 60-73. Retrieved December 7, 2007, from EBSCO online database, Academic Search Premier.

Yilmaz, K. (2013). Comparison of quantitative and qualitative research traditions: Epistemological, theoretical, and methodological differences. *European Journal of Education, 48*, 311-325. Retrieved December 15, 2013, from EBSCO Online Database Education Research Complete.

SUGGESTED READING

Ashworth, P. (1997). The variety of qualitative research nonpositivist approaches. *Nurse Education Today,17*, 219-224.

Barbour, R., & Barbour, M. (2003, May). Evaluating and synthesizing qualitative research: The need to develop a distinctive approach. *Journal of Evaluation in Clinical Practice, 9*, 179-186. Retrieved December 7, 2007, from EBSCO online database, Academic Search Premier.

Brannen, J. (Ed.). (1992). *Mixing methods: Qualitative and quantitative research.* Aldershot: Avebury.

Bruns, B., Filmer, D., & Patrinos, H. (2011). *Making Schools Work: New Evidence on Accountability Reforms.* Washington, D.C. World Bank.

Collins, R. (1984). Statistics versus words. In R. Collins (Ed.), *Sociological Theory* (pp. 329-362). San Francisco, CA: Jossey-Bass.

Devers, K., & Frankel, R. (2000, July). Study design in qualitative research -2: Sampling and data collection strategies. *Education for Health, 13*, 263-271. Retrieved December 7, 2007, from EBSCO online database, Academic Search Premier.

Duffy, J. (2005, Dec.). Critically appraising quantitative research. *Nursing and Health Sciences, 7*, 281-283. Retrieved December 7, 2007, from EBSCO online database, Academic Search Premier.

Elmore, P., & Woehlke, B. (1998). Statistical methods employed in *American Educational Researcher* and *Review of Educational Research* from 1978 to 1987. *Educational Researcher, 17*, 19-20.

Escue, C. (2012). Adequate yearly progress as a means of funding public elementary and secondary education for impoverished students: Florida funding. *Journal of Education Finance. 37* (4), 347-373.

Foley, G. & Nelson, S. (2011). The impact of annual yearly progress on middle school principals job satisfaction. *National Forum of Educational Administration & Supervision Journal. 28* (2), 27-50.

Fossey, E., Harvey, C., McDermott, F., & Davidson, L. (2002, December). Understanding and evaluating qualitative research. *Australian and New Zealand Journal of Psychiatry, 36,* 717-732. Retrieved December 7, 2007, from EBSCO online database, Academic Search Premier.

Greene, J., Caracelli, V., & Graham, W. (1989). Toward a conceptual framework for mixed-methodevaluation designs. *Educational Evaluation and Policy Analysis, 11,* 235-274. Guba, E., & Lincoln, Y. (1981). *Effective evaluation.* San Francisco, CA: Jossey-Bass.

Johnson, R., & Onwuegbuzie, A. (2004). Mixed methods research: A research paradigm whosetime has come. *Educational Researcher, 33,* 14-26.

Johnson, R., & Waterfield, J. (2004). Making words count: The value of qualitative research. *Physiotherapy Research International, 9,* 121-131. Retrieved December 7, 2007, from EBSCO online database, Academic Search Premier.

Koch, T., & Harrington, A. (1998). Reconceptualizing rigor: The case for reflexivity. *Journal of Advanced Nursing, 28,* 882-890.

Lund, T. (2005, April). The qualitative-quantitative distinction: Some comments. *Scandinavian Journal of EducationalResearch, 49,* 115-132. Retrieved December 7, 2007, from EBSCO online database, Academic Search Premier.

National Research Council. (2011). *A Plan for Evaluating the District of Columbia's Public Schools: From Impressions to Evidence.* Washington, D.C.: National Academies Press.

Onwuegbuzie, A. (2002). Positivists, post-positivists, post-structuralists, and post- modernists: Why can't we all get along? Towards a framework for unifying research paradigms. *Education, 122,* 518-530.

Onwuegbuzie, A. (2003). Effect sizes in qualitative research: A prolegomenon. *Quality And Quantity: International Journal of Methodology, 37,* 393-409.

Onwuegbuzie, A., & Daniel, L. (2002). A framework for reporting and interpreting internal consistency reliability estimates. *Measurement and Evaluation in Counseling and Development, 35,* 89-103.

Rolfe, G. (2006, February). Validity, trustworthiness and rigour: Quality and the idea of qualitative research. *Journal of Advanced Nursing, 53,* 304-310. Retrieved December 7, 2007, from EBSCO online database, Academic Search Premier.

Rossman, G., & Wilson, B. (1985). Numbers and words: Combining quantitative and qualitative methods in a single large-scale evaluation study. *Education Review, 9,* 627-643.

Tashakkori, A., & Teddlie, C. (1998). *Mixed methodology: Combining quantitative and qualitative approaches.* Thousand Oaks: CA: Sage.

Westerman, M. (2006). What counts as "good" quantitative research and what can we say about when to use quantitative and/or qualitative methods? *New Ideas in Psychology, 24,(3),* 263-274.

SCHOOL IMPROVEMENT PLANS (SIP)

Since the 2001 No Child Left Behind (NCLB) legislation was passed into law, school improvement plans are formally defined in the United States. No Child Left Behind is a policy that seeks to ensure that schools are educating students effectively. It attempts to measure this by using standardized tests and by setting annual progress goals for each school. If a school's standardized test scores do not meet the annual progress goals for two years in a row, then under the requirements of NCLB, that school must, within three months, prepare a school improvement plan.

KEYWORDS: Disaggregated Data; Academic Status; No Child Left Behind (NCLB); Professional Development; Scientifically Based Research; Scientifically Based Research; State Education Agency

OVERVIEW

The No Child Left Behind legislation that shaped the landscape of American education for over a decade has often been the subject of controversy, with critics stating that it focused too much on setting goals and giving tests, and not enough on reinventing instruction and funding schools. One of the core premises underlying NCLB was that schools that were not functioning well only needed to have a plan to follow. For this reason, NCLB established standards for schools to meet, and set annual goals for each school to reach on the way to meeting the standards. Many educators complained that the annual goals which were set were often unrealistic given a particular school's challenges, but the fact remained that schools either met the goals or they didn't. Those that did not meet their annual goals for two years in a row were placed on "academic status," meaning that they were under a heightened level of scrutiny and had to demonstrate how they would improve their performance. One of the requirements of schools in academic status was to create a school improvement plan (SIP), describing the steps that the school would take to improve instructional effectiveness and help students perform better (Tirozzi, 2013).

The purpose of requiring schools to create an (SIP) is to give all stakeholders—administrators, teachers, students, parents, school board members—a framework with which to define what the problems are and what some potential solutions might be. Like any framework, the SIP must contain certain elements to be considered complete (Walker, Cheney & Horner, 2012). Among the required elements of the SIP are:

- Provisions for teacher mentoring;
- Descriptions of how parental involvement in the school improvement process will be incentivized;
- Explicit discussion of the problems with academic achievement that were the main cause of the school failing to meet its annual progress goals;
- Strategies based on scientific research that will improve the school's standardized test scores on reading and math (these are the main subjects of interest in NCLB);
- Establish a time line of objectives that will enable the school to meet its objectives, as well as defining which constituency (local education agencies, state education agencies, administration, etc.) will be responsible for each specific part of the SIP.

At first blush, the purpose of school improvement plans seems straightforward enough: defining a roadmap for improving a school that has gradually found itself off course. As often happens, however, unexpected difficulties can arise when it comes time to work with the school staff, students, and parents. This is because the changes embodied in an SIP are more than just abstract ideas written into a report and then filed away in a binder and forgotten. Changes in curriculum and instructional practices can be huge disruptions to the routines teachers have established over many years, even decades. Getting teachers to understand the need to change what they are doing can be an uphill battle because some teachers take the attitude that if change is necessary then it must be because the teachers are doing something wrong. In other words, the teachers, when told about the need for an SIP, may become personally offended.

When teachers believe they are being blamed for student underperformance, they may react as if the school's failure to meet annual progress goals is a personal failure on their part. They can become extremely defensive, feeling that they are being attacked and their professional qualifications called into question (Hirsh & Foster, 2013). For this reason, the creation and implementation of an SIP can be an extremely difficult test of the school administration's leadership abilities.

The principal or the principal's designees must very carefully educate the entire school community about which areas of performance the school is strong at, and which ones are weaker and need to be improved as part of the SIP. Ideally, prior to approaching the entire school community about these issues, the school leadership will have private consultations with those teachers whose subjects have been identified as underperforming. This way, these teachers will be less likely to feel blindsided by a school-wide announcement that could be interpreted as pointing the finger at them, and they will be able to brainstorm with the school leaders about different strategies that could be incorporated into the SIP (Carter, 2013). When the school-wide announcement is made, these teachers will feel that they are part of the solution to the school's problems, instead of feeling that they are being accused of being the problem. Overall, the most important thing school leaders can do when developing an SIP is to find ways to get everyone working together toward a common goal, namely the need to raise the school's performance up to the level required by the annual progress goals. If the leadership can make this happen and sustain it, then it is less likely that the various members of the school community will fall back into old behaviors or begin pointing fingers at one another to find someone to blame for the state of the school (Lick, Clauset & Murphy, 2013).

One strategy frequently included in school improvement plans, in part because of its effectiveness and in part due to its low cost, is that of teachers at the school observing one another during the course of instruction. The theory behind this approach is that it can help teachers trust the school improvement process more because they are learning from colleagues whom they know instead of learning from strangers. This process is successful in schools where faculty are on good terms; in schools where there are difficult personal relationships among colleagues, classroom observation can be challenging or even counterproductive (Feeney, Moravcik & Nolte, 2013). Many teachers also report that it can be very challenging to even schedule such classroom observations, since all teachers at a school tend to teach all day long, so the only way one teacher can go observe another is by obtaining a substitute, which directly impacts instruction in the observing teacher's own classroom.

Another frequently implemented strategy used in SIPs is the professional learning community (PLC). Establishing a PLC means providing time for teachers at a school to regularly meet together, discuss their curricula and problems, and work together to come up with ideas about new teaching methods to try out. PLCs are sometimes viewed by teachers as an imposition at first, but in most cases these attitudes change as the SIP progresses and teachers come to understand that the PLC means they no longer need to feel isolated as they try to figure out how to help their students learn (Tanner, 2014).

VIEWPOINTS

Throughout the years that NCLB has been in effect, there has been debate about whether the legislation is designed to help students acquire a better grasp of the curriculum or to help them simply perform better on standardized tests (Dimmock, 2012). One of the positive results achieved by the use of SIPs is that it has the power to help teachers truly incorporate the academic standards into their day to day instruction, so that over time students learn the course content appropriate for their grade level and not simply the best strategies to use when taking standardized tests. Teachers who have been through the process of developing and implementing an SIP frequently comment that as worthwhile as their teacher preparation courses in college were, nothing has prepared them for the classroom like their regular participation in their PLC. This is because the PLC work they do is tied directly to their real work in the classroom.

Feedback such as this is often cited by supporters of SIP and of NCLB, as evidence of their success (Kowalski, 2012). They key to this success, they say, lies in the fact that bringing school accountability down to the level of the local school system is the best way of personalizing the problems that exist in the American education system in a way that state and national data simply cannot. SIPs are a way of getting a community to recommit to making its school successful by drawing attention to the challenges the school faces and then asking for the help of every group in the community to overcome those challenges.

NCLB presses school systems to produce disaggregated data so that it is possible to drill down all the way to the student level in order to discover what areas of instruction are working and which need support. SIPs are actually another means by which school reform champions can drill down to discover the problems confronting their local school system. When a state reports that its reading scores for the year are down 10 percent, parents do not have to be satisfied with that basic level of detail. If their local schools are subsequently identified as underperforming within this larger, statewide trend, then the specific problems being experienced at those schools will be revealed and analyzed, and will have solutions proposed, debated, and implemented. Most would agree that this is a much more effective response than simply lamenting the decline in scores (Tomal, 2015).

TERMS & CONCEPTS

Disaggregated Data: Disaggregated data is data that can be broken down into subgroupings and categories; it is the opposite of aggregated data, which lumps together data from many different groups. In the past, schools kept mostly aggregated data, which made it impossible to tell if the school was educating all students effectively. For example, if a school only recorded the average grade point average for all students in the school, this would hide the fact that (hypothetically) grade point averages for a particular minority group were a full point lower than for students from the dominant culture. To prevent schools from being able to hide situations like this, NCLB and other legislation has required schools to keep disaggregated data as well as aggregate data.

Academic Status: A NCLB implemented probationary status indicating a school has not met its annual goals for two years; as a result it must prepare an SIP.

No Child Left Behind (NCLB): Legislation passed into law in 2001 and signed by President George W. Bush. NCLB relied heavily on defining educational standards, creating progress goals for schools based on those standards, and using standardized tests to assess whether or not schools were meeting the goals that had been set for them. Schools unable to meet the annual progress goals for two years in a row were required to formulate an SIP outlining how the school would bring its performance up to expectations.

Professional Development: Professional development activities in the field of education are different forms of teacher training, which are required of teachers on an ongoing basis during their careers. They are usually opportunities for teachers to learn about new curricula, new teaching methods and projects, and to network with other educators for professional support. SIPs usually must include some provisions for professional development, on the theory that part of the reason for the school's unsatisfactory performance may be that the school's teachers need a refresher course in how to engage students with the material.

Scientifically Based Research: To help schools avoid being taken in by unsubstantiated products and curricula, SIPs are required to base themselves on scientifically based research. Thus, if a school wants to include a new package of math tutoring software as part of its SIP, there needs to be scientifically based research showing that the software produces a tangible benefit when students use it as it was designed.

State Education Agency: A state education agency is the state level counterpart to a local education agency; usually this means that the state education agency is the state's department of education. Just as is the case with LEAs, when a school is required to develop an SIP, there are specific requirements that the state education agency must perform.

Scott Zimmer, JD

BIBLIOGRAPHY

Caputo, A., & Rastelli, V. (2014). School improvement plans and student achievement: Preliminary evidence from the quality and merit project in Italy. Improving Schools, 17(1), 72–98. Retrieved January 12, 2016, from EBSCO Online Database Education Research Complete.

Carter, H. M. (2013). Creating effective community partnerships for school improvement: A guide for school leaders. New York, NY: Routledge, Taylor & Francis Group.

Dimmock, C. A. J. (2012). Leadership, capacity building and school improvement: Concepts, themes and impact. London, UK: Routledge.

Feeney, S., Moravcik, E., & Nolte, S. (2013). Who am I in the lives of children?: An introduction to early childhood education. Boston, MA: Pearson.

Hirsh, S., & Foster, A. (2013). A school board guide to leading successful schools: Focusing on learning. Thousand Oaks, CA: Corwin.

Huber, D. J., & Conway, J. M. (2015). The effect of school improvement planning on student achievement. Planning & Changing, 46(1/2), 56–70. Retrieved January 12, 2016, from EBSCO Online Database Education Research Complete.

Kowalski, T. J. (2012). Case studies on educational administration. Upper Saddle River, NJ: Pearson.

Lick, D. W., Clauset, K. H., & Murphy, C. U. (2013). Schools can change: A step-by-step change creation system for building innovative schools and increasing student learning. Thousand Oaks, CA: Corwin Press.

Tanner, J. (2014). The pitfalls of reform: Its incompatibility with actual improvement. Lanham, MD: R&L Education.

Tirozzi, G. N. (2013). Stop the school bus: Getting education reform back on track. San Francisco, CA: Jossey-Bass.

Tomal, D. R. (2015). Supervision and evaluation for learning and growth: Strategies for teacher and school leader improvement. London, UK: Rowman & Littlefield.

Van Der Voort, G., & Wood, L. (2014). Assisting school management teams to construct their school improvement plans: an action learning approach. South African Journal of Education, 34(3), 1–7. Retrieved January 12, 2016, from EBSCO Online Database Education Research Complete.

Walker, B. A., Cheney, D., & Horner, R. H. (2012). The SAPR-PBIS manual: A team-based approach to implementing effective school-wide positive behavior interventions and supports. Baltimore, MD: Paul H. Brookes.

SUGGESTED READING

Babbage, K. J. (2012). Reform doesn't work: Grassroots efforts can provide answers to school improvement. Lanham, MD: Rowman & Littlefield Publishers.

Bauer, S. C., & Brazer, S. D. (2012). Using research to lead school improvement: Turning evidence into action. Thousand Oaks, CA: Sage.

Duke, D. L. (2013). Are we pushing for greatness?. Phi Delta Kappan, 94(5), 45–49. Retrieved January 12, 2016, from EBSCO Online Database Education Research Complete.

Isernhagen, J. C. (2012). A portrait of administrator, teacher, and parent perceptions of Title I school improvement plans. Journal of At-Risk Issues, 17(1), 1–7. Retrieved January 12, 2016, from EBSCO Online Database Education Research Complete.

Sparks, S. O. (2013). School improvement: A citywide effort in Syracuse. Education Digest, 79(4), 16–21. Retrieved January 12, 2016, from EBSCO Online Database Education Research Complete.

School Accreditation

Accreditation is the process through which a school's services and operations are reviewed by an accrediting agency to determine if the school meets the minimum standards necessary to provide a quality education. There are six private, nonprofit regional accreditation agencies that accredit over 19,000 high schools and 9,000 other schools throughout the nation (Portner, 1997). To qualify for accreditation, schools must conduct a self-study, receive a visit from an accreditation committee, and follow any recommendations the committee makes toward improving its educational programming. Since most colleges prefer to accept students from accredited high schools, accreditation is valuable to students as well as instructors, administrators, school districts, and tax payers.

KEYWORDS: Accreditation; Accreditation Agency; Curriculum; Fees; Focus Visit; No Child Left Behind Act of 2001 (NCLB); Self-Study; Standards

OVERVIEW

Although public education falls under some federal agencies, such as the U.S. Department of Education, there is no centralized governance of the nation's schools. In recent years, state and local governments have increased supervision over education, especially with the passage of the No Child Left Behind Act, but schools still have considerable autonomy. For more than a century, educators have seen the need to measure school programs against agreed-upon standards of excellence by awarding accredited status to schools. Six regional accrediting associations provide programs and services to monitor school performance and improvement efforts. These associations serve anywhere from 2 to 19 states. Accreditation agencies aim to maximize student learning by relaying best practices about student learning and support of learning to the schools they serve (New England Association of Schools and Colleges, n.d.[a]).

APPLICATIONS

The accreditation process begins with a school applying for accreditation and paying all required fees. Guided by standards outlined by the accreditation agency, the school must then conduct a self-study of its programs, a process which can take up to a year to complete. These standards are research-based practices and concepts designed to guide schools in every facet of education, including the academic, civic, and social development of their students. They are periodically reviewed and adjusted in order to stay abreast of current best practices. In recent years, keeping up with best practices has shifted the standards' focus from administration and toward teaching and learning (Manzo, 2000).

The school then receives a site visit from an accreditation committee which evaluates the school on the goals and standards described in the school's self-study. A typical accreditation visit will include interviews with instructors about their curricula, staff members asked about their dropout statistics and other information, an inspection of all facilities, and making sure that the equipment in the labs is all updated and in working order. The committee completes a report on "the quality and comprehensiveness of the school's self-study, offers recommendations for further study and implementation, and assesses the extent to which standards are met" (Northwest Association of Accredited Schools, 2007). The school uses this report to establish goals and begin implementing processes to reach these goals.

A school that is awarded accreditation has met the standards outlined in the self-study, "and is willing to maintain [the standards] and improve its educational programming by implementing the recommendations of the evaluation team" (NEASC, n.d.[a]). Schools may be accredited from anywhere between five and ten years, but a interim site visit or report may be required to document the school's progress toward meeting the accreditation recommendations. The year before accreditation is due to expire, the school begins the accreditation process again with another self-study (Northwest Association of Accredited Schools).

ACCREDITATION AGENCIES & FEES

There are six private, nonprofit regional accreditation agencies that accredit over 19,000 high schools and 9,000 other schools throughout the nation (Portner). Almost all have been in existence since the late 1800s and early 1900s.

- **The Middle States Association of Colleges and Schools (MSACS)** serves five states: Delaware, Maryland, New Jersey, New York, and Pennsylvania plus the District of Columbia (*Middle States Association*, 2006). It accredits over 60% of the high schools that it serves (Portner);

- **The New England Association of Schools and Colleges (NEASC),** founded in 1885, is the nation's oldest regional accrediting association, and serves six states: Connecticut, Maine, Massachusetts, New Hampshire, Rhode Island, and Vermont (NEASC, n.d.[b]). It accredits over 75% of the high schools in the states it serves (Portner);

- **The North Central Association of Schools and Colleges (NCASC)** serves the most states of any regional accreditation agency: Arkansas, Arizona, Colorado, Iowa, Illinois, Indiana, Kansas, Michigan, Minnesota, Missouri, North Dakota, Nebraska, New Mexico, Ohio, Oklahoma, South Dakota, West Virginia, Wisconsin, and Wyoming (Portner; *North Central Association of Schools*, 2007). It accredits about 50% of the high schools in states that it serves (Portner);

- **The Northwest Association of Accredited Schools (NAAS)** serves seven states: Alaska, Idaho, Montana, Nevada, Oregon, Utah, and Washington (NAAS, 2005). It accredits over 90% of the high schools in states that it serves (Portner);

- **The Southern Association of Colleges and Schools (SACS)** serves 11 states: Alabama, Florida, Georgia, Kentucky, Louisiana, Mississippi, North Carolina, South Carolina, Tennessee, Texas, and Virginia (*Southern Association of Colleges*, 2006). It accredits over 90% of the high schools in the states it serves (Portner);

- **The Western Association of Schools and Colleges (WASC),** founded in 1962 serves only two states: California and Hawaii (Portner; *Western Association of Schools*, n.d.). It accredits about 95% of the high schools in the states it serves (Portner).

There are annual dues for accreditation. The fee schedules vary with each agency: some charge a flat fee, some base fees on the size of the school, and still others base fees on the type of school (i.e. elementary, middle, high, all-inclusive K-12, etc.) The lowest annual fee is currently $200 (NAAS, 2006), and the highest is currently over $1,000 (NEASC, n.d.[c]).

Other fees may also be associated with accreditation. In addition to membership fees, schools may be charged self-study fees based on the number of committee members involved, initial visit fees, application fees, revisit fees, rescheduling fees, revisiting fees for schools that require a focus visit, and appeals fees (WASC Fee Schedule, 2007).

STANDARDS OF ACCREDITATION

Accreditation agencies develop standards for accreditation that serve as benchmarks for accreditation decisions. As part of a school's self-study, school personnel, students, and the community address each standard by describing how well the school meets it and, if it does not, how it plans to do so in the future. Each accreditation agency may have slightly different standards, but they are all developed to reflect the "minimum requirements that have been substantiated by research, direct observation, or the judgment of experienced educators as basic requirements for a satisfactory program of education" (NAAS). All agencies cover the basics of curriculum, instruction, assessment, resources, and support services; however, some may focus more on physical plant and facilities, resources, and instruction, while others may highlight continuous improvement, communications and relationships, or instruction, governance, and mission.

Self-studies may also vary slightly. In general, the self-study lists a standard, such as "the school's mission statement describes the essence of what the school as a community of learners is seeking to achieve," followed by a series of expectations that support the standard, like "the school's mission statement represents the school community's fundamental values and beliefs about students learning" (NAAS). However, these components may be broken down differently. One agency may limit itself to three or four standards and use multiple expectations within each standard, and another may use nine or ten standards without any smaller, supporting expectations.

Depending on the agency, schools may respond to expectations and/or standards through a multiple choice format, an open response format, or a combination of the two. NAAS, for example, asks schools to respond to the expectations by choosing an answer from among "substantially met," "partially met," and "not presently met." For any expectation that is not "substantially met," the school must explain why it isn't being met, and how it plans to meet the expectation in the future.

Examples of different standards and questions from the Northwest Association of Accredited Schools are noted below:

Teaching and Learning Standard—Mission, Beliefs, and Expectations for Student Learning

... i.e., the school's mission statement and expectations for student learning are developed by the school community and approved and supported by professional staff, the school board, and other school-wide governing organizations.

Teaching and Learning Standard—Curriculum

... i.e., "the curriculum is aligned with the school-wide academic expectations and ensures that all students have sufficient opportunity to achieve each of those expectations."

Teaching and Learning Standard—Instruction

... i.e., "Instructional strategies are consistent with the school's mission statement and expectations for student learning."

Teaching and Learning Standard—Assessment

... i.e., "Teachers base classroom assessment of student learning on school-wide and course-specific indicators."

Support Standard—School Services

... i.e., "the school allocates resources, programs, and services so that all students have an equal opportunity to achieve the school's expectations for student learning."

Support Standard—Facilities and Finance

... i.e., "the physical plant and facilities meet all applicable federal and state laws and are in compliance with local fire, health, and safety regulations."

School Improvement Standard—Culture of Continual Improvement

... i.e., "the school has developed and implemented a comprehensive school improvement plan that is reviewed and revised on an ongoing basis" (NAAS).

Reports & Recommendations

Schools usually receive the visiting committee's written report with recommendations within a month of their visit. The classification of the visit can vary depending on the accrediting agency. The NAAS, for example, divides its classification system into four categories: approved, advised, warned, and dropped. A school is considered 'approved' when it meets the standards, or will have to make only minor improvements to meet standards. A school is "'advised' when it fails to identify or is in the process of addressing standards that are 'not presently met'" (NAAS). A school is classified as 'warned' if the school is failing to meet a number of standards, or has continued to miss standards after receiving an 'advised' classification. Schools are normally 'advised' first before being 'warned' to give them an opportunity to meet the standards. A school is 'dropped' and loses its accreditation if, after being 'warned' twice in succession, it still fails to meet standards the school has two consecutive 'warned' classifications and still has not met standards. Rescinding accreditation is ultimately at NAAS's discretion, however.

The Value of Accreditation

Accreditation carries value for students, administrators, instructors, districts, school board members, and taxpayers. Since they are the recipients of a school's educational programming, students are the group most affected by accreditation. If a student has to change schools, his or her credits are more likely to be accepted by the new school if the previous school was accredited; and because accreditation testifies to the quality of a student's education, colleges prefer accepting students from accredited schools.

Accreditation can also be valuable to both school administrators and instructors as it provides them with the opportunity to work toward educational improvement. The self-study process can give these groups a better understanding of their roles within the overall operations of the school, and can help clarify their individual purposes (NASC, n.d.[a]). By giving instructors and administrators the opportunity to analyze present teaching and learning conditions, the self-study process provides direction for the planning and implementation of any needed improvements.

Similarly, accreditation provides school districts with a plan for school review and improvement that they can use to stay in compliance with local, state, and federal mandates. The standards also provide districts with a basis on which they can make comparisons of the consistency of all the schools in the district. These comparisons can help with the school district's mission and with the coordination of curriculum across the district's schools.

Since school board members are responsible for the quality of a schools' educational programming, accreditation can help ensure that their educational policies and plans are sound. The self-study also provides an opportunity for school board members to gain a detailed knowledge about a school's operations.

Taxpayers can also find value in accreditation as it assures them that their schools are using tax money to support rigorous academic standards and meaningful programs. Accreditation can impact property values as well, since communities with accredited schools are more likely to attract new families than those without accredited schools, and parents may choose to move away from a community in which the schools have lost their accreditations (NEASC, n.d.[a]).

LOSING ACCREDITATION

Fewer than 3% of all the schools lose their accreditation each year. However, before a school loses its accreditation, it is first placed on probation and given an opportunity to develop a plan to fix its deficiencies (Portner). Trying to meet an accreditation agency's standards can be expensive. Schools may be in fine standing until an agency updates its standards. In 2002, for example, SACS updated its standards to increase the number of library books a middle school must have on hand for its students from 1,500 to 2,000. Middle schools with more than 1,500 students were likewise required to increase their holdings from 10,000 books to 15,000. One Florida school district with 38 middle schools had to come up with an extra $800,000 to purchase the books required to retain its accreditation (Ishizuka, 2003). Similarly, in 2004 a Massachusetts high school put itself at risk for losing its accreditation when budget cuts forced it to reassign its media specialist as a social studies teacher. It had to prove to the NEASC that the loss of the position didn't deprive students of "adequate library services" (McCaffrey, 2004).

Increasingly, schools that do not receive accreditation may decide to take legal action. Although postsecondary schools often go to court when faced with the loss of accreditation, according to the six regional accrediting agencies, legal action was unheard of in secondary education until 1997 when a group of Hartford, Connecticut parents and district leaders filed a lawsuit against the NEASC and won a state court injunction to temporarily block NEASC from rescinding Hartford Public High School's accreditation. To give some idea of just how important accreditation can be, the mere possibility of the school losing its accreditation prompted the state to take over the entire school district. The district replaced the superintendent and the entire board of trustees, "put a mechanism in place for monitoring district leaders, and replaced much of the administration [at the high school]" (Viadero, 1997).

CONCLUSION

Although schools are not required to maintain accreditation, losing accredited status can affect a school's prestige and cause it to lose students. "Since more than 85% of colleges and universities nationwide prefer to accept applicants from accredited schools," students who have choice will prefer to attend accredited schools (McCaffrey). Elementary and secondary schools that seek and maintain accreditation demonstrate their desire and ability to uphold high academic standards and continuous improvement.

TERMS & CONCEPTS

Accreditation: Accreditation is the process through which a school's services and operations are reviewed by an accrediting agency to determine if the school meets the minimum standards necessary to provide a quality education.

Curriculum: Curriculum is the entire body of courses taught to students.

Focus Visit: A focus visit is a second visit from an accrediting team to specifically determine if the recommendations from the original site visit have been addressed.

No Child Left Behind Act of 2001: The No Child Left Behind Act of 2001 is the latest reauthorization and a major overhaul of the Elementary and Secondary Education Act of 1965, the major federal law regarding K-12 education.

Self-Study: A self-study is a guided self-assessment a school completes in preparation for accreditation. The self-study describes the accreditation agency's standards and helps schools determine if they meet these standards or, if not, what they will do to meet the standards.

Standards: Standards are established criteria for institutional quality that must be addressed in a self-study.

Sandra Myers

BIBLIOGRAPHY

Accrediting Commission for Schools. (2007). *WASC fee schedule 2007-2008.* Retrieved November 10, 2007, from http://acswasc.org.

Cram, H.G. (2011). De-mystifying accreditation: What are the basics?. *International Educator, 26,* 11. Retrieved December 15, 2013, from EBSCO Online Database Education Research Complete.

Hoffman, E. (2013). Ratings, quality, and accreditation: Policy implications for educational communications and technology programs in a digital age. *Techtrends: Linking Research & Practice To Improve Learning, 57,* 47-54. Retrieved December 15, 2013, from EBSCO Online Database Education Research Complete.

Ishizuka, K. (2003). Broward schools try to keep accreditation. *School Library Journal, 49,* 22. Retrieved October 16, 2007, from EBSCO Online Database Academic Search Premier.

Manzo, K. (2000). Secondary accreditation to target academics. *Education Week, 19,* 3. Retrieved October 16, 2007, from EBSCO Online Database Academic Search Premier.

McCaffrey, M. (2004). MA high school accreditation at risk. *School Library Journal, 50,* 22. Retrieved October 16, 2007, from EBSCO Online Database Academic Search Premier.

Middle States Association of Schools and Colleges. (2006). *About us.* Retrieved November 10, 2007, from http://css-msa.org.

New England Association of Schools and Colleges. (n.d.[a]). *The meaning and value of accreditation.* Retrieved November 10, 2007, from http://neasc.org.

New England Association of Schools and Colleges. (n.d.[b]). *About NEASC.* Retrieved November 10, 2007, from http://neasc.org.

New England Association of Schools and Colleges. (n.d.[c]). *Commission on Public Elementary and Middle Schools.* Retrieved November 10, 2007, from http://neasc.org.

North Central Association of Schools and Colleges. (2007). *North Central Association of Schools and Colleges.* Retrieved November 10, 2007, from http://ncacasi.org.

Northwest Association of Accredited Schools. (2007). *Annual report and standards for the Northwest Association of Accredited Schools.* Retrieved November 10, 2007, from http://boisestate.edu.

Northwest Association of Accredited Schools. (2006). *Policies and procedures* (2006 Ed.) Retrieved November 10, 2007, from http://boisestate.edu.

Northwest Association of Accredited Schools. (2005). *Northwest Association of Accredited Schools.* Retrieved November 10, 2007, from http://boisestate.edu.

Portner, J. (1997). Once status symbol for schools, accreditation becomes rote drill. *Education Week, 16,* 1. Retrieved October 16, 2007, from EBSCO Online Database Academic Search Premier.

Southern Association of Colleges and Schools. (2006). *Southern Association of Colleges and Schools.* Retrieved November 10, 2007, from http://sacs.org.

Viadero, D. (1997). Hartford high school retains accreditation, gets probation instead. *Education Week, 17,* 6. Retrieved October 16, 2007, from EBSCO Online Database Academic Search Premier.

WASC International Accreditation. (2011). *International Educator, 25,* 11.Retrieved December 15, 2013, from EBSCO Online Database Education Research Complete.

Western Association of Schools and Colleges. (n.d.). *Western Association of Schools and Colleges.* Retrieved November 10, 2007, from http://wascweb.org.

SUGGESTED READING

Bernhardt, V. (2001). *The school portfolio tool kit: A planning, implementation, and evaluation guide for continuous school improvement.* Larchmont, NY: Eye on Education.

Flanders. (1997). *Educational improvement through school accreditation and peer review*. Evanston, IL: Northwestern University.

National Study of School Evaluation (2004). *Accreditation for quality school systems: A practitioner's guide*. Schaumburg, IL: National Study of School Evaluation.

Simmons, E. (1976). *The emerging trend towards elementary school accreditation*. Cambridge, MA: Harvard University.

Southern Association of Colleges and Schools (2004). *Accreditation and school improvement: The handbook for the next generation*. Decatur, GA: Southern Association of Colleges and Schools Council on Accreditation and School Improvement.

SCHOOL-BASED MANAGEMENT

School-based management (SBM) is a policy used in public schools to decentralize decision-making power. In this strategy, management decisions move from a larger, more centralized authority such as the school district, to smaller units that are closely adjacent to the school, such as teachers, parents, and administrators. Currently, the data on the relationship between school-based management and increasing students' learning is mixed, with uncertain conclusions. Nevertheless, the policy is growing and stakeholders including teachers, administrators, and community members are supportive of the concept.

KEYWORDS: Administrative Decentralization; Autonomous School Concept; Decentralization; Participatory Decision-Making; Restructuring; School Autonomy; School-Based Governance; School Empowerment; Shared Governance

OVERVIEW

School-based management (SBM) is a policy used in public schools to decentralize decision-making power. In this strategy, management decisions move from a larger, more centralized authority such as the school district, to smaller units that are closely adjacent to the school, such as teachers, parents, and administrators. Historically, public schools in the United States have been run by both the centralized power of state and district control, as well as smaller entities such as community school boards or parents (Darling-Hammond, 1988). While there have been many predecessors to school-based management as we know it today in American schools, the strategy became more defined out of the 1980s school reform movement. While there are many similarities between this policy and previous attempts at decentralization, school-based management is much more complex and requires more of an overhaul of organization at both the district and individual school levels than previous concepts of decentralization (Cotton, 1992).

In school-based management, the roles of different groups in and around a school may change drastically. The district and state lend more discretion in certain areas directly to the school, while still finding ways to support their endeavors. Principals tend to become facilitators rather than decision makers. Teachers, community members, and students may be called upon for input. It is important to understand that school based management is more than a change in the way schools work. It fundamentally alters traditional roles, while shifting responsibilities and authority (Cotton).

The logic behind school-based management originally lies in research from the business world. Studies found that when the decision-making process was restructured to include all levels of employees, worker satisfaction increased. Researchers found the process especially appropriate for work places that were evolving, fast paced, and required individuals to work together (Banicky, Rodney & Foss, 2000). The proliferation of school-based management in schools has increased rapidly across the United States and internationally in recent years.

Throughout the late 1980s, school based management was often seen as a political reform to shift power from central entities to those within the school community. Supporters hoped that the policy would engender a sense of community within those who were closest to the school, driving improvement and creating a sense of cooperation and ownership. Implementing the strategy of school-based management was the end goal in driving change when the policy first gained popularity. Today however, in the climate of accountability, SBM has increasingly come under question regarding how it affects student achievement (Briggs & Wohlstetter, 2003).

Proponents of school-based management today see it as a strategy to improve many aspects of schools. The topics for discussion as decentralization occurs may include budgeting, curriculum and instruction, and plans for student discipline (Oswald, 1995). Stakeholders that may be affected include administrators, teachers, parents, students, community members, school boards, and state and district offices. The core ideals behind this approach are rooted in the belief that school decisions should be made by those who are the closest to the impact of those decisions. Consequently, school-based management brings all of these stakeholders together in a more cooperative approach to solve problems and improve schools (Banicky et al.).

Because school-based management requires extensive changes, it is a challenging management strategy to implement, and requires the cooperation between various entities (Banicky et al.).

Applications

STUDENTS

Under school-based management, students, especially older students, may participate in the decision making process for their individual school. Students may serve on committees discussing topics from discipline to curriculum or data collection. When this method is employed, student satisfaction with schools has been shown to increase (Oswald). However, the statistics regarding student achievement and outcomes remains unclear.

Multiple studies have attempted to measure the effect of school-based management on student achievement. Outcomes have generally been very mixed, with no persistent link found between implementation of SBM and gains in academic achievement, attendance rates, or disciplinary issues (Oswald).

Increasing student achievement was not necessarily a primary goal of the original school-based management models. Rather than aiming to enhance student performance, school-based management was employed to shift the balance of decision-making power from centralized authority to individual schools (Banicky et al.). Oswald states that some schools who implement SBM do not make instruction their top priority. Thus, it is perhaps not surprising

that research has not found a persistent relationship that school-based management positively or negatively affects student learning.

While school-based management may not contribute directly to increased student achievement, several outcomes from successful implementation have the potential to improve grades and test scores of students. Drury and Levin (1994) found the following improvements: better use of time and resources, more involvement from the community, and improvements in curriculum. They also noted increased professionalism among teachers in the schools. However, the research as it stands today does not indicate school-based management largely affects student achievement.

TEACHERS

Teachers in schools have a variety of roles. In school-based management, these roles shift more towards working in teams with others. School-based management systems have focused on changing a variety of aspects in the management of a school, related or not to classroom practice. In some models, schools focus on classroom-based changes. In others, more administrative matters are addressed. Cotton concludes that research shows teachers want to be involved in decision-making regarding what to teach and how to teach it in their schools. However, school-based management systems that do not address these issues have often produced negative reactions from teachers. Nir (2002) conducted a longitudinal study in which he measured how school-based management implementation affects different areas of teacher work. He found that teachers felt the policy and implementation had both negative and positive aspects. Nir indicated that freedom in the classroom coupled with satisfactory rewards were imperative for teacher satisfaction and commitment in implementing a school-based management model. Without these elements, teacher commitment to their school and their students may actually wane. The topics which school-based management address are an important ingredient or barrier to success in the eyes of teachers.

While teachers are most interested in changes in curriculum and instruction, this is the sphere in which district and state policymakers are often least willing to give up control (Banicky et al.). However, this area may be the one that stands to gain the most from school-based management. Studies conducted examining the relationship between teacher participation in decision-making and student outcomes indicate that the two are positively correlated—when teachers are more involved in decision-making, students tend to perform better (Banicky et al.).

ADMINISTRATORS

School principals and other administrators may see their job descriptions undergo enormous changes under school-based management. A school principal, in particular, often plays a crucial role in the implementation's success. In school-based management, the role of the school principal changes from supervisor and manager to facilitator. The job function becomes much more collaborative and involves increased interaction with staff, students and the community (Banicky et al.). Gaul, Underwood, and Fortune (1994) found that while school administrator's work hours increased during and after implementation of school-based management, administrators were most likely to embrace the new system.

DISTRICT & STATE

School based management does not lower the importance of a centralized form of governance. Decisions being made at the school level need support from the district to be successful (Banicky et al.). Working closely with schools and the constituents to assist them in making this transition is imperative. The district must make decisions on where it is more helpful to decentralize power, and what components are important to keep at a centralized level.

ISSUES

It is important to consider how the desired outcomes of school-based management have changed as we enter the twenty-first century in the history of American education. With current emphasis on accountability, closing the achievement gap, and achieving equitable educational opportunities for all, strategies such as school-based management are especially important to consider carefully before implementing in a school.

No management strategy should be considered without contemplating its effect on student learning. The earlier days in which decentralization and shared

decision-making were the final goals of school-based management have given way to a larger question of whether or not school-based management affects student learning.

While the documented benefits of school-based management on specific players involved are inconclusive, there have been some studies that conclude school-based management has positive effects (Briggs & Wohlstetter). There needs to be further research conducted questioning whether school based management can increase student achievement by creating an environment that positively affects learning. However, it is widely agreed upon that highly qualified and committed teachers, coupled with a focused and challenging curriculum, are necessary ingredients for increasing student achievement. School-based management may be a worthy strategy for achieving these two goals, thereby increasing student achievement.

Empowering and engaging highly qualified teachers into the decision making process may help improve student outcomes. Centralized government officials who support decentralization see school-based management as an enabler—school officials will be better equipped to make decisions that supply the direct needs of their students (Wohlstetter & Mohrman, 1994). Studies of schools who have implemented school-based management have found that it can lead to teacher empowerment when the decisions teachers are making are directly linked to learning and curriculum (Marks & Louis, 1999). Other studies suggest a link between school-based management and other indicators of "a strong professional community" (Briggs & Wohlstetter). These indicators include increased collaboration, a greater focus on professional development, and increased awareness of accountability. Schools who are thinking of implementing school-based management should consider whether it would help teachers teach students. Highly qualified teachers are a significant indicator of student achievement, and schools should weigh carefully how much this type of management can contribute to that goal.

It is also important to consider the areas of control given the individual school. The breadth and scope of issues school-based management may address is enormous. Different schools may want to target different areas to implement this strategy. For example, a school that has a number of highly qualified teachers, and can create a community through school-based management where those teachers are empowered to make decisions regarding curriculum and instruction in the classroom, may work to give teachers increased control over classroom practices. Schools who are having trouble recruiting or retaining high quality teachers, or who do not have a high percentage of experienced teachers may choose to focus their school-based management strategy on giving teachers more professional development opportunities regarding classroom instruction and student learning, helping them make informed decisions about how best to reach their students in the classroom. Each of these scenarios can use school-based management, but the way in which the strategy is focused follows the issue of what is needed to improve student outcomes.

Research in recent years focused on the link between school-based management and new classroom practices related to the policy. Studies have found that when school-based management gives teachers more direct power to improve their classroom outcomes, the impact was twofold: teachers improved their teaching, and students learned more (Briggs & Wohlstetter). School-based management, when used in a way that directly addresses the issue of raising student achievement, may help students perform better. However, more research is needed to substantiate the specific features of school-based management that assist in this endeavor.

As with any new endeavor in schools, the strengths and weaknesses already present should be taken into account before any action is taken. In the example of teachers, a school with teachers who have one set of skills may approach school-based management differently than a school with teachers who are of a different background or skill level. The focus of the strategy is different, although the implementation can still use input from many different groups attached to the school.

ACHIEVEMENT GAP

The achievement gap and serving underserved students is one of the largest issues that American education faces today. Can school based management help schools achieve equitable education? Jenkins et al. (1994) studied the effects of school-based

management on low performing students. The researchers found that while teachers appreciated and encouraged the change process, student outcomes were not affected in achievement or behavior. However, more research, especially longitudinal research, is needed on this topic. Again, previous elements of the individual school are important to consider before implementing school-based management. The population of students that are served by the school will impact if and how the policy is amenable to the situation.

There seem to be several key elements deemed as ingredients to success while implementing a school-based management strategy geared towards improving student achievement. First, it should concretely concentrate on improving teaching and learning, synchronized with high performance standards for students and teachers. Studies of school-based management have found connecting the restructuring process to higher performance goals was more likely to be accepted by teachers and administrators, as well as parents and other community members (Briggs & Wohlstetter). This aspect of change represents a significant difference in the way school-based management was approached in its early years.

Rather than focusing on procedural aspects, the power to change and improve classroom practices, instruction methods, and the delivery of curriculum are key ingredients to successful school-based management strategy (Cotton). This requires states and districts to allow those who are closest to the school control and direct issues of curriculum and instruction. However, these entities should still guide individual schools in ensuring that their changes will meet up to state and national standards. If the focus of change is on how to improve student achievement, teachers will likely take more interest, and the gains will be more than if the issue is not central to the reform.

PROFESSIONAL DEVELOPMENT

As previously discussed, decentralization represents an enormous change in the workplace. The structure of a school and the roles of those individuals in and around it are transformed. One of the greatest opportunities that arise out of this policy is to focus and increase professional development opportunities (Cotton). Studies have found school-based management succeeds when a larger proportion of teachers and administrators participate in professional development opportunities. Professional development must be meaningfully connected to classroom (Briggs & Wohlstetter). Development focus includes topics such as team-building and group problem-solving.

Relationship building and increased communication are also essential to using school-based management to increase student learning and improve outcomes (Briggs & Wohlstetter). Involving a variety of groups within the school and community in the implementation process is important. Having formal and informal channels of communication for these parties is also imperative, as many more players are involved in the discussion and decision making process. Additionally, access to information will help participants make informed decisions, as will a clear mission statement (Banicky et al.).

School-based management requires increased time and energy on the part of many participants in and close to the school. Rewarding participation, through monetary or non-monetary means, plays an important role in successful implementation of school-based management. Schools that have successfully implemented school-based management have found rewards were used frequently for specific milestones or contributions. In struggling school based management schools, however, rewards were often scarce of vague (Briggs & Wohlstetter).

ORGANIZATION OF POWER

School-based management implementation gives schools a large number of possibilities regarding what decision-making power may be brought down to the school level, and what remains centralized. Deciding the scope of power is important. Decentralizing power does not mean that all decisions are now made at the school level. It may be more beneficial to have greater power in one area than mediocre impact on several areas (Banicky et al.). For example, schools may decide that they want to make more decisions on instruction methods, but do not want to change or discuss procedures for student discipline, depending on their larger goals.

As with any new implementation, time is an important factor. School based management is a complex endeavor, requiring alignment of resources

and parties involved. Real change often takes years. Expecting results quickly is neither feasible nor realistic. Thus, three to five years should be allotted for school-based management to be implemented, take effect, and show outcomes (Banicky et al.).

As a concept, school-based management may seem simple—localize and place power in the hands of those who best know the school. However, implementing the actual policy has a wide range of issues and permutations to consider. In previous educational eras the larger purpose was the decentralization of school governance, aiming to bring school decision-making processes closer to those who it actually affected. Today, policy officials have increasingly shifted to focus on improving student outcomes (Briggs & Wohlstetter). With this change, school-based management has evolved to become part of a widespread reform strategy for schools rather than a stand-alone restructuring.

CONCLUSIONS

Currently, the data on the relationship between school-based management and increasing students' learning is mixed, with uncertain conclusions. Nevertheless, the policy is growing and stakeholders including teachers, administrators, and community members are supportive of the concept. However, its widespread support can likely be less attributed to having a quantifiable impact on student learning; more likely, many stakeholders prefer decentralized and local control of a school rather than management decisions that come from an unseen and far off entity such as a central school district governance.

School-based management, in the context of today's education landscape, is not simply another method of decentralization. Rather, it is a strategy and process by which all stakeholders work together to increase and galvanize the learning process for students. However, the method is multi-faceted, and requires an increased workload and specific training over a long period. School-based management may require some infrastructure before the implementation can begin. These include but are not limited to the capacity of teachers and administrators in the schools, the support of community members, the foundation and reinforcement provided from the district or state level,

and the students who are being served in the particular school (Fullan & Watson, 2000).

As school-based management becomes more
prevalent, researchers will need to study if the policy
can help schools positively impact student achievement. Furthermore, it will be necessary to compare
successful implementations to unsuccessful ones
so that components and practices that lead to student success are further identified. Armed with this
knowledge, schools can then begin making changes
to achieve their goals, based on sound research and
knowledge.

TERMS & CONCEPTS

Administrative Decentralization: Administrative
decentralization refers to bringing school management matters closer to the school, rather than keeping them centralized, i.e. at the school district level.

Autonomous School Concept: Autonomous school
concept describes the concept of an individual
school having more power over decisions regarding the individual school.

Decentralization: Decentralization is the redistribu-
tion of power from a central authority, to more
local or regional authority.

Participatory Decision-Making: Participatory decision-making is a decision-making process marked
by the participation of a diverse group of individuals in schools.

Restructuring: Restructuring refers to the process of
changing elements of the school.

School Autonomy: School autonomy describes a
school that is free from some or all centralized
decision-making.

School-Based Governance: School-based governance
is another term for school-based management,
marked by decentralization of certain decisions to
the individual school.

School Empowerment: School empowerment is giving official authority to make decisions to local
and individual schools.

Shared Governance: Shared governance refers to
the cooperation between individual schools and
more centralized authorities in making decisions
regarding school practices.

Rana Suh

BIBLIOGRAPHY

Banicky, L., Rodney, M., & Foss, H. K. (2000). *The prom-
ises and problems of school-based management.* Dover, DE:
University of Delaware Research and Development
Center.

Briggs, K. L., & Wohlstetter, P. Key elements of a successful
school-based management strategy. *School Effectiveness
and School Improvement, 14,* 351-372.

Bush, T. (2013). Autonomy and Accountability: Twin
Dimensions of the Reform Agenda. Educational
Management Administration & Leadership, 41, 697-
700. Retrieved December 15, 2013, from EBSCO Online
Database Education Research Complete.

Cotton, K. (1992). *School-based Management.* Retrieved
July 20, 2007, from Northwest Regional Educational
Laboratory, http://nwrel.org.

Darling-Hammond, L. (1988). Accountability and teacher
professionalism. *American Educator, 12,* 38-43.

David, J. L. (1989). Synthesis of research on school-
based management. *Educational Leadership, 46,* 45-53.
Retrieved July 20, 2007, from EBSCO Online Database
Education Research Complete.

David, J. L. (1996). The who, what, and why of site-based
management. *Educational Leadership, 53,* 4-9. Retrieved
July 20, 2007, from EBSCO Online Database Education
Research Complete.

Drury, D., & Levin, D. (1994). *School-based management:
The changing locus of control in American public education.*
U.S. Department of Education: Office of Educational
Research and Improvement.

Fullan, M., & Watson, N. (2000). School-based management: Reconceptualizing to improve learning outcomes. *School Effectiveness and School Improvement, 11,*
453-474. Retrieved July 20, 2007, from EBSCO Online
Database Education Research Complete.

Gaul, T. H., Underwood, K. E., & Fortune, J. C. (1994).
Reform at the grass roots. *The American School Board
Journal, 181,* 35-40.

Grimes, S. (2012). School-based model for struggling readers. *Reading Today, 29,* 34. Retrieved December 15, 2013,
from EBSCO Online Database Education Research
Complete.

Honig, M. I., & Rainey, L. R. (2012). Autonomy and school
improvement: What do we know and where do we go
from here?. *Educational Policy, 26,* 465-495. Retrieved
December 15, 2013, from EBSCO Online Database
Education Research Complete.

Jenkins, J. R., Ronk, J., Schrag, J. A., Rude, G. G.,
Stowitschek, C. (1994). Effects of using school-based
participatory decision making to improve services for
low-performing students. *The Elementary School Journal,
94,* 357-372.

Marks, H. M., & Louis, K. S. (1999). Teacher empowerment and the capacity for organizational learning. *Educational Administration Quarterly, 35*, 707-750. Retrieved July 20, 2007, from EBSCO Online Database Education Research Complete.

Nir, A. E. (2002). School-based management and its effect on teacher commitment. *International Journal of Leadership in Education, 5*, 323-341. Retrieved July 20, 2007, from EBSCO Online Database Education Research Complete.

Oswald, L. (1995). *School-based management.* Retrieved July 20, 2007, from Clearinghouse on Education Policy and Management, http://eric.uoregon.edu.

Wohlstetter, P., & Mohrman, S. A. (1994). *School-based management: promise and process.* New Brunswick, NJ: The Consortium for Policy Research in Education. Retrieved July 20, 2007, from Department of Education, http://ed.gov.

Wohlstetter, P., Van Kirk, A. N., Robertson, P. J., Mohrman, S. A. (1997). *Organizing for successful school-based management.* Alexandria, VA: Association for Supervision and Curriculum Development (ERIC Document Reproduction Service No. ED 413655).

SUGGESTED READING

Brown, D. J. (1990). *Decentralization and school-based management.* London: The Falmer Press, 1990.

Cabardo, J. (2016). Levels of participation of the school stakeholders to the different school-initiated activities and the implementation of school-based management. *Journal of Inquiry and Action in Education.* 8 (1), 81-94.

Castagno, A. & Hausman, C. (2017). The tensions between shared governance and advancing educational equity. *Urban Review: Issues and Ideas in Public Education.* 49 (1), 96-111.

Chion-Kenney, L. (1994). *Site-based management and decision-making: Problems and solutions.* Arlington, VA: American Association of School Administrators.

Clune, W. H., & White, P. A. (1988). *School-based management: Institutional variation, implementation, and issues for further research.* New Brunswick, NJ: Rutgers University, Eagleton Institute of Politics, Center for Policy Research in Education.

Dee, J.R., Henkin, A.B., & Pell, S.W.J. (2002). Support for innovation in site-based-managed schools: Developing a climate for change. *Educational Research Quarterly, 25*, 36-50. Retrieved July 20, 2007, from EBSCO Online Database Education Research Complete.

Milligan, C. (2015). School centered evidence based accountability. *Universal Journal of Educational Research.* 3 (7), 460-462.

Murphy, J. F., & Beck, L. G. (1995). *School-Based Management as School Reform: Taking Stock.* Thousand Oaks, CA: Corwin Press.

Race, R. (2002). Teacher professionalism or deprofessionalisation? The consequences of school-based management on domestic and international contexts. *British Educational Research Journal, 28*, 4590-463. Retrieved July 20, 2007, from EBSCO Online Database Education Research Complete.

STUDENT GOVERNMENTS

Student Governments are present today in the majority of K-12 schools and throughout Higher Education. Student governments are usually extracurricular activities available to students within schools. They present opportunities for student leadership and are one possible facet of school-based management. Student governments are responsible for certain components of school organization and governance. Their forms and responsibilities may be different at various grade levels. Students who participate in student government tend to have higher GPAs and fewer unexcused absences, and tend to be more informed about politics.

KEYWORDS: Extracurricular Activity; Leadership Skills; Leadership Studies; Organizational Activities; Policy-Making; School-Based Management; Social Activities; Students' Association; Student Council; Student Leadership

OVERVIEW

A student government is a group within a school that is responsible for certain facets of school organization and governance. Usually categorized as an extracurricular activity, student governments are run primarily by students. Their functions are different from school to school; for example, they may act as a liaison between school administrations and students, representing the student body views regarding institutional, local, or national issues. Or, they may oversee specific activities such as fundraising or student clubs. Faculty, staff, and community members may also participate in student governments, in various capacities, depending on the educational institution. Student governments in the United States are common at all school levels today—elementary, middle, and high school, as well as at colleges and universities. The roles they play in the schools and their communities are diverse—some have large budgets and great power in their learning communities; others are smaller and hold modest sway over school policymaking.

STUDENT GOVERNANCE IN PUBLIC SCHOOLS

Student participation in governance of their educational institution has a long and diverse history. In K-12 education there are a variety of examples throughout educational history in which students have been involved in school management. Vineyard and Poole (1930) note that at Plato's Academy, pupils elected students for certain school tasks every ten days. Other European schools decreed that students be allowed to participate in school governance side by side with the administration. Structures included senates made up of representatives elected by students in 16th century Germany, schools that assigned "monitors" (an older student as an assistant teacher) in 18th century India, and assemblies that were chosen each month in 18th century America. Monitorial schools also found their way to America, and became a tool to teach students how to handle affairs that would prepare them for life after school (McGown, 1944).

The goals behind student participation in school governance today vary widely. In the United States, K-12 participation in student government is often used as a tool for civic training—helping students understand the process of democracy, rather than giving students actual power to influence policy. Goals also include teaching teamwork and participation, as well as the ideals of a democratic state (Vineyard & Poole, 1930).

STUDENT GOVERNANCE IN HIGHER EDUCATION

Student governance in Higher Education began as university learning expanded. Universities in their early days were very loosely organized—interested students traveled to those individuals who were willing to teach them. By the 13th century, the numbers of students and teachers had increased so dramatically that improved guidelines and management was necessary, and began within the institutions (McGown). The convening of student nations at universities in Bologna beginning in the 12th century, which brought together students from similar regions, is one of the earliest examples of student governance. These nations elected representatives who helped run the day-to-day activities of the school (McGown).

In the history of American Higher Education, the first institution known to encourage student participation was the College of William & Mary, in the late 18th century. The students elected representatives to a council who handled discipline issues. Other examples of student governments were established at Oberlin College, founded in 1833, which not only gained recognition for admitting all students, regardless of race, but also allowed significant participation from students regarding management issues (McGown). Other forms of student organization and governance in Higher Education were organized by students due to dissatisfaction with characteristics of life within college institutions. For example, the concept of fraternities sprouted from poor living conditions, literary clubs sprung from the lack of library resources, and athletic teams formed of students seeking a respite from the heavy emphasis on classroom learning (Hodgekinson, 1971, as cited by Miller & Nadler, 2006). These organizations were also precursors to student governments as we know them today.

In the 1900s, student governments began playing a larger role in the social aspects of colleges and universities, and by the 1960s students at many institutions were demanding increased student participation regarding the decision-making process at schools across the country (Hodgekinson, as cited by Miller & Nadler). After World War II, the rapid growth of colleges and universities in the United States fueled the expansion of student governments to help operate these schools (Mackey III, 2006). The highly politicized atmosphere of the 1960s led to increased demand for student involvement (Miller & Nadler). In the 1970s however, interest in student governments diminished, and many disappeared (Mackey III). Since the 1970s student governments have become prevalent again in all levels and types of education.

663

STUDENT GOVERNMENTS TODAY

Today, student governments are present in nearly all schools across the country, in K-12 public schools, private schools and in Higher Education. Factors that increased the number of student governments include the rise of local, state, and national organizations that supported student governance, the growth of extracurricular activities, and the emphasis on teaching leadership in schools (McGown). There are many parallels to be found between the American government and student councils. Many have a written Constitution and bylaws, outlining the rights and responsibilities of all parties involved. Members of student governments are often elected by their peers, and election procedures may include debates, speeches, and various ceremonies. Minutes are taken during meetings, and reported to peers, administrators, and/or other bodies that the council may represent or work with (McGown).

GENERAL ORGANIZATIONAL STRUCTURE

There are many permutations of student government organization—it is unlikely there are two student governments in the entire country that are the same. Student governments may differ in the number of people involved, the types of responsibilities and tasks that they are responsible for, and the configuration of the organization (McGown).

TITLES & OFFICES

Titles and offices organize student governments internally. Possible offices or titles include president, vice-president, secretary, treasurer, and representatives. Individuals involved may also include leaders from various clubs, living quarters, or homerooms. All of these individuals will have specified roles depending on the responsibilities of the student government:

- The president and vice-president are most often responsible for planning meetings and running them in an efficient manner while delegating duties;
- The secretary will record minutes, attend to correspondence needed, and create documents;
- The treasurer is responsible for overseeing any financial activities of the student governments or the groups that the student government manages and oversees. For example, in many colleges, student governments are responsible for distributing money from student activities budgets to various clubs and organizations. The treasurer acts as the point person for all of these discussions and transactions;
- Other officers may represent the interests of their homeroom, club, or housemates.

A student government may be made up of officers through election or appointment. When student government officers are elected, they may be elected at the beginning of a year for that year, or at the end of the year, to be inaugurated the following year. Schools may also hold elections twice, to account for the cyclical nature of education institutions (McGown).

The structure of a student government will depend upon the school and its needs. In K-12 student governments often elect representatives from homerooms or classrooms, or by grade. In a more complex institution, such as a large university, there may be many other representatives from clubs, sports teams, or fraternities and sororities. The organization of a student council may be very simple to very complex. They may involve only a few students, or hundreds of students. Student governments may be directly overseen by faculty or administration, or may be largely unsupervised. These distinctions are different from school to school and grade level to grade level (McGown).

RESPONSIBILITIES

The responsibilities afforded to student governments can vary from informal to very specific. Informal councils are marked by limited authority and a lack of power to determine policy. Other councils may be extremely detailed in their duties (McGown). For example, the management of student social events, as well as managing and organizing clubs may fall under the jurisdiction of a student government. A student government with these duties would need many members with specific tasks, and a variety of specific policies to deal with the myriad of situations that could surface. In a case study of schools in the United States, Wittes, Chesler, and Crowfoot (1975) found high schools had many different ways of incorporating student governments into their communities. Some schools involved students heavily in decision making; others did not. The scope of responsibility of student governments can include:

- Managing clubs and student organizations;
- Fundraising;

- Social activities planning;
- Student discipline;
- Settling disputes;
- As a forum for discussion of changes within the school.

COLLEGE & UNIVERSITY STUDENT GOVERNMENT

The organizational structure of student governments in Higher Education institutions often have characteristics similar to that of the United States government, other nation's governments, or roles similar to what one might find in a corporation or business.

STUDENT GOVERNMENT & THE ADMINISTRATION

There are over 4,000 college and universities in the United States today. The students, faculty, and administrations at these institutions are enormously diverse, as are the student governments. Unlike most K-12 student governments, many student-governing bodies at colleges and universities hold a great deal of responsibility, and will often act as the student liaison between students and administrators and other school leaders. Many school administrations count on the student government to manage certain aspects of life on campus, and seek opinion from student councils when making important policy decisions. When specific problems or issues arise, the school administration may gather a special council that includes students. The responsibilities of student governments in Higher Education institutions today may include, but are not limited to:

- Representing the ideas and beliefs of the student body while acting as a liaison between students and teachers and administrators;
- Distributing money to various student organizations from a budget;
- Organizing and sponsoring social and entertainment activities;
- Acting as the governing body for student organizations (Love & Miller, 2003; Miller & Nadler).

ELECTIONS

The process by which students are elected or designated to serve on student governments differs from institution to institution. Often, elections occur on campus in which the student body may vote on they deem best to represent their interests. Campaigning is common, at all levels, but procedures may differ school to school.

CHANGING STUDENT POPULATIONS

Another important role of many student governments today includes representing changing student bodies. Today, many college campuses house increasingly diverse student bodies whose requirements and views adjust with each new generation of students. Student governments often bridge the gap and school administrations often look to these councils to represent these changes (Miller & Nadler). Schools may even have several student governments within the institution. For example, universities may have a separate student government for undergraduates and graduate students.

PUBLIC SCHOOL STUDENT GOVERNMENT

The majority of elementary, middle, and high schools across the country have some form of student government. These governing bodies are often loosely modeled after the American system of government. More senior positions are usually reserved for older students, and younger students may act as class representatives. For example, in an elementary school, a sixth-grader may serve as President, a fifth-grader as vice-president, and fourth-graders as Secretary and Treasurer. These officers will be elected by the entire school, while Representatives will be elected from each classroom. Middle and high school governments may feature a set of officers from each grade level. An adult—most often a teacher or faculty member at that school, may oversee a student government in K-12 schools (McGown).

VIEWPOINTS

Researchers do not necessarily agree upon the benefits of participation in school government for students and educational institutions. The evolution of student governments and their roles in schools has been a long process. Today, allegations are often heard that student governments have many flaws: they do not represent the student body, they have no real power, and that elections have degenerated into a popularity contest more than an exercise in democracy (Mackey; Miller & Nadler). While there may be some truth to these accusations, there are also several studies that link participation in student government to certain benefits. School governments are usually classified as a student activity. Marsh (1988) conducted a study in which he studied post-secondary outcomes related to having participated in student activities in high school. Academic factors such as academic achievement and college attendance were measured. The study concluded that students benefited from participation depending on the particular activity, but involvement in too many activities was detrimental. Specifically, participation in student government was consistently linked positively to later outcomes.

BENEFITS FOR PUBLIC SCHOOL STUDENTS

In 1992, 96.5% of public high school seniors recruited for a study reported that they had access to student government as an activity (O'Brien & Rollefson, 1995). Furthermore, the difference in availability between less affluent and more affluent public schools was insignificant. Niemi & Chapman (1998) used the factors of attendance, academic achievement, and whether the student expected to attend college as markers for successful school participation. They found that students who participated in school activities had lower rates of unexcused absences and skipped classes, higher GPAs, scored higher on standardized exams, and expected to earn at least a bachelor's degree at a higher rate than their peers who did not participate in school activities.

Student government may also act as a venue in which to educate students about the ideals and practices of democracy, as well as teach values and practices regarding leadership and cooperation. Characteristics of civic development include "political knowledge, attention to politics, political participation skills, political efficacy, and tolerance of diversity" (Niemi & Chapman). A study researching the civic development of high school students found that students who participated in student government "tend to be more knowledgeable about politics, more confident in their participation skills, more confident that they understand politics, and more tolerant of public libraries carrying controversial books" (Niemi & Chapman) compared to students who did not participate in student government, even after controlling for a variety of factors.

The effect of participation in extracurricular activities has also been linked to lower rates of alcohol and drug use. Results from a study surveying over 5,600 students, grades 5 through 12, suggest that students who participate in school activities were less likely to use drugs, tobacco, or alcohol than their peers who did not participate in extracurricular activities (Cooley, Nelson, & Thompson, 1992).

BENEFITS AT THE COLLEGE LEVEL

Student governments at the Higher Education level often hold much more power and responsibility than at the K-12 level, and at many institutions have become largely accepted by administrations and faculty as an important body to cooperate with in shaping school policy (Miller & Nadler). However, there has been little concrete evidence that participating in student governments is effective at teaching participation and citizenship (Bray, 2006). While research results seem promising, and implies a positive link between participation in student government and high achievement, we cannot be sure whether the strong positive correlation is due to the activity (in this case, student government) actually improving student outcomes, or whether students who would have done well regardless are choosing to participate more often in the student governments.

BUILDING LEADERSHIP SKILLS

Many student governments are not necessarily run effectively, nor do they have actual power. However, students may benefit from teaching leadership development through the practices of student government. Leadership development is a developing field that focuses on building management skills through a variety of activities, as a central part of the curriculum (Mangan, 2002, as cited by Langdon, 2005). Shoenberg (1992, as cited in Langdon) challenges various educational institutions to involve students in governance of a school, regardless of how much actual power the student government holds. Burns (1978, as cited in Langdon) argued that the United States is in the midst of a leadership crisis—not enough individuals have the proficiency to manage others. Participation in student governments may be a positive tool for teaching leadership skills.

GENDER & CULTURE

Participation in student government does appear to differ across race and gender lines. Davila and Mora (2007) conducted a study measuring civic engagement among high school students, using the measures of involvement in community service or student government. They found that females tend to have higher participation rates than males, and that Asians had the highest participation rates, with Hispanics the least involved. Given what we know about the achievement gap between students of different backgrounds in the United States, this information could have important policy implications for schools that serve a diverse population of students. More research is necessary on the impact of participation in student government on students of various backgrounds.

CONCLUSION

Student governments are prevalent at all levels of education today. Langdon (2005) challenges schools to empower these organizations, and argues that there are ways to create more effective school governments if the group is lacking in motivation or influence. Cohen (1998, as cited by Langdon) suggests forming associations statewide to petition to decision-making bodies such as administrators or school boards to give students of all ages a voice in school policy making. Shoenberg (as cited by Langdon) argues that encouraging student involvement is crucial to developing leadership skills.

The concrete benefits of student governments are uncertain; however, there are many ways in which a student government is important and useful to an institution. Some teach students leadership skills and demonstrate the processes of a government—elections, campaigns, and debate. Others are crucial to monitoring and responding to generational changes in student bodies and their needs. For example, students who attend an institution that has a large commuter or parent population have very different needs from a residential four-year college that serves mostly 18-24 year old traditional students. Student governments can be involved heavily in policy-making; others have minimal sway over these issues. The essential features of successful school governments are to ensure students have support from administration and staff, that their goals and missions are clear, and that roles and cooperation between governing parties are clearly defined. Research shows that participation in student government is highly correlated with a number of desirable outcomes. While correlation is not causation, student governments can be a useful tool for teaching and reaching students in different ways, while empowering students to think about and take part in important discussions.

TERMS & CONCEPTS

Extracurricular Activity: Extracurricular activities are activity that is not required by the school, such as sports teams or clubs.

Leadership Studies: Leadership studies is a course of study that helps students build management skills through activities directly built into the curriculum.

Policy-Making: Policy-making is the process by which schools make decisions; may be influenced by outside forces, such as school district offices, and/or inside forces, such as administrators, faculty, and students.

School-Based Management: School-based management is a form of school management that decentralizes certain duties and responsibilities to those closest to the school.

Social Activities: Social activities are events or activities that take place outside of the classroom that allow students to socialize with peers, such as concerts, socials, or speakers.

Students' Association: Students' association is another term used for student government. The student government at a school may be called the Students' Association.

Student Council: Student council is another term used for student government. The student government at a school may be called the Student Council.

Student Leadership: Student leadership occurs when student manage or run an activity or organization in a school. Examples may include activities in the classroom such as debate, or extracurricular activities such as captaining a sports team, or serving as student body president.

Rana Suh

BIBLIOGRAPHY

American Council on Education. (1994). The student personnel point of view. In A.L. Rentz (Ed.), *Student affairs: A profession's heritage* (pp. 66-77). Lanham, MD: University Press of America (Original work published in 1937).

Brasof, M. (2011). Student input improves behavior, fosters leadership. *Phi Delta Kappan, 93*, 20-24. Retrieved December 15, 2013, from EBSCO Online Database Education Research Complete.

Bray, N.J. (2006). Effects and Assessment of Student Involvement in Campus. In M.T. Miller & D.P. Nadler (Ed.), *Student Governance And Institutional Policy: Formation And Implementation* (pp. 19-32). Charlotte, NC: Information Age Publishing.

Burns, J.M. (1978). *Leadership.* New York: Harper & Row.

Cohen, A.M. (1998). *The shaping of American Higher Education: Emergence and growth on the contemporary system.* San Francisco: Josey-Bass.

Cooley, V., Henriksen, L., Nelson, C., & Thompson, J. (1995). A study to determine the effect of extracurricular participation on student alcohol and drug use in secondary schools. *Journal of Alcohol and Drug Education, 40*, 71-87. Retrieved August 10, 2007, from EBSCO Online Database Academic Search Premier.

Davila, A., & Mora, M.T. (2007). *Do gender and ethnicity affect civic engagement and academic progress.* CIRCLE Working Paper #53. Center for Information and Research on Civic Learning and Engagement. Retrieved September 21, 2007, from www.civicyouth.org.

Hodgkinson, H.L. (1971). *Institutions in transition: A profile of change in Higher Education.* New York: McGraw-Hill Book Company.

Kuh, G.D., Schuh, J.H., & Witt, E.J. (1991). *Involving colleges: Successful approaches to fostering student learning and development outside the classroom.* San Francisco: Josey-Bass.

Langdon, E.A. (2005). Student governance and leadership. In R.L. Ackerman (Ed.), *Student freedom revisited: Contemporary issues & perspectives* (pp. 138-149). Washington, D.C.: NASPA-Student Affairs Administrators in Higher Education.

Levine, A., & Cureton, J.S. (1998). *When hope and fear collide: A portrait of today's college student.* San Francisco: Josey-Bass.

Love, R., & Miller, M. (2003). Increasing student participation in self governance: A comparison of graduate and undergraduate student perceptions. *College Student Journal, 37*, 532-534. Retrieved August 24, 2007, from EBSCO Online Database Academic Search Premier.

McGown, H.C. (1944). *The student council.* New York: McGraw-Hill Book Company, Inc.

Mackey, R. (2006). The role of a typical student government. In M.T. Miller & D.P. Nadler (Eds.), *Student Governance And Institutional Policy: Formation And Implementation* (pp. 62-68). Charlotte, NC: Information Age Publishing.

Mangan, K. (2002). Leading the way in leadership. *The Chronicle of Higher Education, 48*, A10-A12. Retrieved August 10, 2007, from EBSCO Online Database Academic Search Premier.

Marsh, H.W. (1988). *Extracurricular activities: A beneficial extension of the traditional curriculum or a subversion of academic goals.* (ERIC Document Reproduction Service No. ED 301578). Retrieved August 10, 2007, from EBSCO Online Education Research Database.

Miles, J. M. (2011). Reflections of student government association leaders: Implications for advisors. *College Student Journal, 45*, 324-332. Retrieved December 15, 2013, from EBSCO Online Database Education Research Complete.

Miller, M. T., & Nadler, D. P. Student involvement in governance: Rationale, problems, and opportunities. In M. T. Miller & D. P. Nadler (Eds.), *Student Governance and Institutional Policy: Formation and Implementation* (pp. 9-18). Charlotte, NC: Information Age Publishing.

Niemi, R. G., & Chapman, C. (1998). *The civic development of 9th through 12th grade students in the United States: 1996.* Washington, DC: National Center for Education Statistics.

O'Brien, E., & Rollefson, M. (1995). *Extracurricular participation and student engagement.* Washington, D.C.: National Center for Education Statistics.

Shelly, B. (2011). Bonding, bridging, and boundary breaking: The civic lessons of high school student activities. *Journal of Political Science Education, 7*, 295-311. Retrieved December 15, 2013, from EBSCO Online Database Education Research Complete.

Smith, J. (1951). *Student councils for our times: Principles & practices.* NY: Teachers College, Columbia University.

Vineyard, A. M., & Poole, C. F. (1930). *Student participation in school government.* NY: A.S. Barnes and Company Incorporated, 1930.

Wittes, G., Chesler, J., & Crowfoot, D. (1975). *Student power: Practice & promise.* New York: Citation Press, 1975.

SUGGESTED READING

Cuyjet, M. J., & Terrell, M. C. (1994). *Developing Students Government Leadership: New Directions in Student Services.* San Francisco: Jossey-Bass.

Morrell, S. A. & Morrell, R. C. (1986). Learning through student activities. In P.S. Breivik (Ed.), *Managing Programs for Learning Outside the Classroom: New Directions for Higher Education* (pp. 77-87). San Francisco: Jossey-Bass.

Roberts, D. C. & Ullom, C. (1989). Student leadership program model. *NASPA Journal, 27*, 67-70.

Rudolph, F. (1962). *American college and university: A history.* New York: Alfred A. Knopf.

Vaars, J. (2005). *Student Government and Class Activities: Leaders of Tomorrow (Cocurricular Activities Their Values and Benefits) (Library Binding).* Broomall, PA: Mason Crest Publishers.

INSTRUCTIONAL LEADERSHIP

Instructional leadership is a leadership policy primarily used by school principals. The policy shifts principals' focus from day-to-day school administration to the improvement of curriculum and classroom instructional practices. While the principal retains a pivotal role in the policy's current form, leadership responsibilities are also disseminated among teachers, school administrators, and district and state supervisors. Studies have shown the policy to be effective when it is fully supported by principals, teachers, and administrators. Principals can improve its probability for success by creating a climate of collaboration among the involved parties, preparing themselves through practical study, offering teachers and administrators professional development opportunities, and becoming adept at data collection and analysis.

KEYWORDS: Autonomous Climate; Curriculum; Data Driven Reform; High-Stakes Testing; Instruction; Leadership; Principal; Professional Development; School Improvement; School Management; Student Outcomes; Teaching

OVERVIEW

Instructional leadership is a policy implemented by schools which redefines the roles of the various parties involved in a school, especially principals and administrators, towards the end of improving curriculum and instruction. Prior to the 1980s, the roles of school principals and administrators in the United States and other developed countries focused on administrative duties such as evaluating teachers and managing school budgets, schedules, and facilities. Today, however, principals and administrators are increasingly involved in classroom practices and teaching. In these new roles as "learning leaders" they are responsible for planning curriculum, observing classrooms, and teaching classroom instructors educational methods and philosophies (Lashway, 2002). The National Association of Elementary School Principals (2001, as cited by Lashway, 2002) builds the concept of instructional leadership around the goal of transforming schools into communities in which continuous learning is a central part of everyone's job function, including school leaders.

The concept of instructional leadership first became popular in the United States in the 1980s as researchers concluded from various studies that the principals who lead the most effective schools were primarily focused on curriculum and instruction rather than on other administrative matters (Hallinger, 2005). In the 1990s, as the concept of school-based management made its way into mainstream practice, instructional leadership took a backseat in school leadership discussions (Lashway). Recently though, in the current climate of standards-based learning, high stakes accountability, and relentless attention to improving educational opportunities for underserved students, instructional leadership has made its way back to the forefront of education policy (Lashway). Today, a school principal's main responsibility is not performing the day-to-day tasks related to school administration, but accounting for student achievement (Zepeda).

Research has proven that principal leadership can indeed affect student outcomes (Zepeda). However, instructional leadership today is very different from the form it took during the 1980s. When it was first introduced, the policy cast the principal as a singular, heroic, and charismatic leader brought in to direct, control, and revitalizes the school (Lashway). However, Elmore (2000) points out that such natural leaders are few and far between. Today, the responsibility for implementing successful instructional leadership now falls on a variety of parties within the school system. Administrators, policy-making bodies, and teachers are all as significant and involved and as the principal (Lashway).

While principals are responsible for successfully adapting the instructional leadership model to improve their schools, policymakers, superintendents, researchers, and teachers also all have specific roles in implementing instructional leadership (Elmore). The principal must work with administrators and others outside of the school to develop the best strategies for school improvement as well as work with instructors inside the school to raise student achievement. Teachers are then responsible for implementing these strategies in the classroom to realize improved learning outcomes. These roles are all interdependent; each group has an impact on the overall success of the reform.

Applications

THE PRINCIPAL'S ROLE

Principals who employ instructional leadership as a strategy for improving student learning attend more closely to classroom practices than other matters related to school administration. While principals are still not directly responsible for teaching students, their roles as instructional leaders are pivotal in influencing student outcomes (Zepeda).

Principals who are transitioning into instructional leadership must develop a number of competencies for the transition to produce successful outcomes. Elmore isolates several that are important instructional leaders. First, instructional leaders must direct their actions towards improving teaching, and in turn, improving student outcomes. This requires instructional leaders to be up to date on instructional methods and model what they expect of their teachers. Instructional leadership also demands that a culture of collective learning be established and valued within the school. To affect this culture, the principle must again be a model to the teachers.

Another major aspect of leadership is teaching others to lead (Elmore). Instructional leaders provide teachers with the tools they need become leaders themselves. This development of leadership can strengthen the organization of a school. In this way, a principal can directly affect classroom practices and align them with the school's mission of improvement (Zepeda).

Instructional leaders support teachers in curriculum development and provide opportunities for teachers to shape the cultures of their schools (Zepeda). Barth (2001a) calls for teachers to contribute to a number of aspects of running a school including developing curriculum, choosing materials, evaluating performance, building the budget, and setting policy and practices for hiring, promotion, and retention.

Research has also shown that the most tangible improvement in student outcomes is made by placing highly qualified teachers in the classroom (Zepeda). The instructors at any school bring to the institution a broad range of experiences and competencies.

Principals who are instructional leaders must recognize and support these competencies while also providing professional development opportunities for those who need greater support in improving classroom practices (Zepeda). Instructional leaders may mentor teachers towards becoming leaders, establish times when teachers can directly contribute to important school conversations, and develop a school culture in which teachers feel invested in one another and the school (Zepeda). Principals must recognize a variety of teacher needs.

THE DISTRICT'S ROLE

Instructional leaders must be supported by the districts in which they work. In the current era of standards based reform, school districts have a responsibility to ensure that their students are learning. Districts can support principals and teachers by providing professional development opportunities that target instructional leadership issues (Lashway). Furthermore, they must carefully negotiate any barriers their policies may pose to instructional leaders. These barriers are further discussed in the Viewpoints section below.

THE TEACHERS' ROLE

With the advent of instructional leadership, teacher leadership has evolved to become as much of a factor for success as principal leadership. Frost and Durrant (2002, as cited by Zepeda) conclude that leadership development in teachers is fundamental to improving schools.

As a school's principal and administrators develop teachers' leadership skills, teachers may be called upon to perform a variety of tasks which may change their roles within the school. Teachers in public schools are often isolated in their classrooms; they may feel a clear delineation between their classroom and the rest of the school. With the implementation of instructional leadership, teachers may be called upon to contribute to school functions like choosing instructional materials, writing curriculum, deciding school policies and hiring practices, and analyzing and evaluating budgets (Zepeda).

Imperative to the success of this new role is the acceptance of new teaching practices and a new school culture. Instructional leaders will usually observe classroom practices more often and increase their overall presence in classrooms. In this sense, the principal becomes less of a supervisor and more of a mentor. For instructional leadership to be successful, it is crucial for teachers and principals to accept and embrace these changes, form strong relationships in which teachers are not afraid of failure, and constantly work towards learning and implementing better teaching practices (Zepeda).

Viewpoints

Instructional leadership is one of the most empirically supported policies recognized by the education community. Studies on instructional leadership and its effectiveness abound, extolling the policy's impact on student learning and the health of the overall institution. When implementation is successful, students are successful. However, some barriers to success and conditional requirements need to be taken into account.

THE AUTONOMY GAP

As we have seen, the breadth of leadership involved in instructional improvement is quite wide. A wide range of duties must be performed and supported by parties both inside and outside the school. As instructional leadership requires the support of many parties, when these parties do not fulfill their roles and requirements are not met, the policy may not be successful.

A successful instructional leader must be supported by district and states supervisors as well as by teachers and administrators within the school. In a study of thirty-three elementary school principals, Adamowski, Therriault, & Cavanna (2007) define the "autonomy gap" as "the difference between the amount of authority that district school principals think they need in order to be effective leaders and the amount they actually have." Their research found several barriers to effective instructional leadership which result from various policies that are beyond principals' control. Many of these barriers exist in the area of hiring practices and policies which can limit principals' freedom to choose staff for their schools.

When principals' autonomy is limited by outside policymakers, the transition to instructional leadership becomes much more difficult. Instructional leadership requires the principal to promote student achievement through teacher learning by leading curriculum development and instructional practices. However, curriculum and instruction are the areas over which district and state policymakers often most hesitate to relinquish control (Banicky, Rodney, & Foss, 2000). Though research proves that instructional leadership can improve educational outcomes for students, principals may not have enough power to make the necessary changes to curriculum and instruction.

Glanz, Shulman, & Sullivan (2007) conducted a study surveying instructional leadership in several New York City public schools. They found that a centralized education system posed significant barriers to instructional leadership. Management that comes directly from within a school is much more effective at improving student learning. They also found that when instructional leadership practices which stressed collaboration and improved instruction from teachers were instituted, students achieved at higher rates, including students whose first language was not English.

Fullan (2001, as cited by Michael & Young, 2005) also found that school reform was most likely to be successful if decision making power was decentralized to schools, rather than mandated from a peripheral source. Michael & Young conducted a study to pinpoint characteristics of "inspired" schools—schools that are effective, resilient, and promote a community of learning. Their research suggests that these "inspired" schools, because of their shared mission, were better equipped to address problems and issues facing schools today. These schools shared many characteristics, including a belief in lifelong learning which is central to the practice of instructional leadership.

ACADEMIC TRAINING

The impact of instructional leadership may also be directly correlated to the academic training of the principals implementing the policy. Byrd, Slater, and Brooks (2006) conducted research analyzing the effectiveness of principals according to their academic degrees. They found that student outcomes were significantly related to whether a school's principal held a Ph.D. or an Ed.D. Principals who completed Ed.D. programs, which tend to be oriented towards practice, were more successful at improving student achievement than those who completed Ph.D. programs, which tend to focus on research over practice.

TEACHER SUPERVISION

Teacher supervision poses additional challenges to instructional leaders. Hallinger notes that school principals often have less subject knowledge than teachers, especially at the high school level. Furthermore, the classroom has long been a space in which teachers and students can work without outside interference. Often, a feature of instructional leadership is increased principal presence in the classroom as he or she observes and mentors teachers. However, Hallinger notes that there is no empirical evidence to indicate that principals spend more time on classroom instruction today than they did twenty-five years ago. This finding is suggestive of a barrier between teachers and principals, even as the concept of instructional leadership has gained ground as an important policy change in schools.

NORMATIVE & AUTONOMOUS CLIMATES

In addition to the individual participants and a principal's preparation, other issues impact the success of instructional leadership. Rosenholtz (1986, as cited by Elmore) argues that schools which are not committed to a concrete set of goals are unlikely to be effective in improving student learning. She draws the distinction between collaborative versus autonomous climates. In the former, characteristics include a focus on teamwork, relationship building, and a culture of continuous improvement and learning for all. These schools are led by principals who concentrate on improving teachers' skills so that they may in turn positively impact student learning. All the players are united by a set of common goals. In the latter type of climate, however, goals are not only ambiguous, but unarticulated. The emphasis is placed on the individual rather on the group as it works together towards a collective goal. Isolation is common, and the principals' main role is not centered on curriculum and instruction practices but rather on school administration.

To create a climate in which all individuals within the school support and are supported by instructional leadership, it is crucial for all the involved parties to buy into the school's goals and culture. Hallinger builds on Rosenholtz's findings. He describes three core functions that are imperative to successful instructional leadership: delineating the school's mission, coordinating the school's curriculum and instructional practices, and creating a positive environment focused on continuous improvement.

PROFESSIONAL DEVELOPMENT

The professional development of leaders and teachers is also crucial. Instructional leadership today denotes changes in everyone's roles (Timperley, 2005). Using the case study of a school seeking to employ instructional leadership, Timperley argues that providing professional development opportunities related to instructional leadership skills within the school is more effective than offering outside professional development opportunities. By providing these opportunities within school teachers are able to adapt new perspectives and skills to the context of their environment.

DATA COLLECTION & ANALYSIS

In today's world of educational accountability, schools are required to demonstrate either proficiency or improvement. Instructional leaders, therefore, must be proficient in data collection and analysis (Zepeda). Schools may use a number of methods to collect data and monitor progress including surveys, standardized testing, and focus groups (Zepeda).

Instructional leaders can utilize data collection and analysis in a variety of ways. First, they can pinpoint areas in which their schools are strong, and areas which need improvement. This way, the conclusions they draw are not unsupported—they are backed by the numbers (Zepeda). Instructional leaders may also use data to monitor progress. As the various facets of the reforms associated with instructional leadership are implemented, it is important to monitor progress to determine whether or not the reforms are helping the school (Zepeda, 2004). Enough time must be allotted for the reforms to be implemented, however, as schools may take time to produce tangible results (Banicky et al.).

Togneri (2003) writes that districts and schools can improve data collection in three ways. First, they should focus on the process rather than the data. For example, if the data shows negative outcomes, districts will be more successful if they push leaders to accept the data and think of solutions to the problems it presents instead of placing blame. Second, when districts help leaders collect and analyze data, the analysis should identify positive and negative trends and be useful to leaders as they determine courses of improvement. Finally, if data is provided from a source outside the district, principals and teachers should be trained to analyze the data and use it as a basis for improvement.

CONCLUSION

The primary player in instructional leadership is the principal. However, the days are over in which principals are expected to act alone. The demands placed on schools today are too broad for an individual to single-handedly improve a school. Today, principals' endeavors to improve curriculum and instruction are supported by districts, administrators, and teachers. Of course, the most important aspect of instructional leadership is whether the principal can teach instructors effectively, and thus impact the learning of students.

Elmore describes the high expectations often placed on principals:

Reading the literature on the principalship can be overwhelming, because it suggests that principals should embody all the traits and skills that remedy all the defects of the schools in which they work. They should be in close touch with their communities, inside and outside the school; they should, above all, be masters of human relations, attending to all the conflicts and disagreements that might arise among students, among teachers, and among anyone else who chooses to create conflict in the school; they should be both respectful of the authority of district administrators and crafty at deflecting administrative intrusions that disrupt the autonomy of teachers; they should keep an orderly school; and so on.

In short, school principals are expected to possess nearly super-human capabilities. Rosenholtz (as cited by Elmore) found that principal collegiality with teachers had no significant effect on school performance directly, but that when collegiality was connected to goals set by the school, there was an impact on the school's performance. In the era of standards based reform, leadership should be refocused to make the improvement of student outcomes its central goal. If the leadership has this goal, and can diffuse it to other parties involved in the school, student outcomes may improve (Elmore).

The research on instructional leadership has provided proof of the policy's many positive outcomes. However, one area that needs further study is the effect of instructional leadership at different grade levels. While there is a wealth of research on the effects instructional leadership at elementary schools, the findings have not necessarily been applied to secondary schools whose sizes, natures, and politics are far more complex (Hallinger).

When implementing instruction leadership, many barriers can arise. Some are rooted in the educational bureaucracy, others include teacher hesitancy, a lack of professional development opportunities, and principals' proficiency with data collection and analysis. These obstacles must be addressed carefully to improve educational outcomes for students. However, there is no doubt that changing the role of the principal to focus more directly on improving teacher competency can greatly improve student outcomes.

TERMS & CONCEPTS

Autonomous Climate: A school culture in which goals are ambiguous or unarticulated, individuals rather than groups are emphasized, and principals and other administrations are not heavily involved in curriculum or instruction.

Curriculum: Is the body of knowledge schools teach to students.

Data Driven Reform: The use of data collection and analysis to make informed decisions about school reform and improvement.

High-Stakes Testing: A testing program that has important consequences for teachers, students, or administration at a school, primarily the possible loss of funding.

Instruction: The teaching methods employed in a classroom.

Principal: The leader of a school. The position's specific responsibilities may vary across schools, but the primary role is to act as a bridge between the district and the individual school.

Professional Development: The building of professionals' knowledge and competencies. In the educational and development field, this may be done through courses of study, travel, research, internships, or sabbaticals.

School Management: The way in which schools are organized and supervised. Management may come from an outside source, such as the school district, or an internal source, such as the principal or other administrators.

Student Outcomes: The competencies displayed by students through a variety of measurement tools intended to assess whether students have successfully learned material.

Rana Suh

BIBLIOGRAPHY

Adamowki, S., Therriault, S.B., & Cavanna, A.P. (2007). *The autonomy gap: barriers to effective school leadership.* Washington, D.C.: American Institutes for Research & Thomas B. Fordham Institute.

Banicky, L., Rodney, M., & Foss, H.K. (2000). *The Promises and problems of school-based management.* Dover, DE: University of Delaware Research and Development Center.

Barth, R.S. (2001a). Teacher leader. *Phi Delta Kappan, 82,* 443-449.

Blink, R.J. (2007). *Data-driven instructional leadership.* Larchmont, NY: Eye on Education.

Brazer, S., & Bauer, S. C. (2013). Preparing instructional leaders: A model. *Educational Administration Quarterly, 49,* 645-684. Retrieved December 15, 2013, from EBSCO Online Database Education Research Complete.

Byrd, J.K., Slater, R.O., & Brooks, J. (2006). *Educational administration quality and the impact on student achievement.* (ERIC Document Reproduction Service No. ED 493288). Retrieved September 1, 2007, from EBSCO Online Education Resources Database.

Elmore, R.F. (2000) *Building a new structure for school leadership.* Washington, D.C.: The Albert Shanker Institute. Retrieved September 17, 2007, from http://shankerinstitute.org.

Flanz, J., Shulman, V., Sullivan, S. (2007). *Impact of instructional supervision on supervision and student achievement: Can we make the connection?* (ERIC Document Reproduction Service No. ED496124).

Frost, D., & Durrant, J. (2002). *Instructional leadership for school improvement.* New York: Eye on Education.

Fullan, M. (1991). *The new meaning of educational change* (3rd ed). New York, NY: Teachers College Press.

Hallinger, P. (2005). Instructional leadership and the school principal: A passing fancy that refuses to fade away. *Leadership and Policy in Schools, 4,* 221-239. Retrieved September 17, 2007, from EBSCO Online Database Education Research Complete.

Lashway, L. (2002). *Developing instructional leaders. ERIC digest.* University of Oregon: Clearinghouse on Educational Management. (ERIC Document Reproduction Service No. ED466023).

Michael, C.N., & Young, N.D. (2005). *Seeking meaningful school reform: Characteristics of inspired schools.* (ERIC Document Reproduction Service No. ED 490677). Retrieved September 1, 2007, from EBSCO Online Education Research Database.

National Association of Elementary School Principals. (2001). *Leading learning communities: Standards for what principals should know and be able to do.* Alexandria, VA: Author.

Neumerski, C. M. (2013). Rethinking instructional leadership, a review: What do we know about principal, teacher, and coach instructional leadership, and where should we go from here?. *Educational Administration Quarterly, 49,* 310-347. Retrieved December 15, 2013, from EBSCO Online Database Education Research Complete.

Rosenholtz, S. J. (1986). Organizational conditions of teacher learning. *Teaching and Teacher Education, 2,* 91-104.

Supovitz, J.A., & Poglinco, S.M. (2001). *Instructional leadership in a standards-based reform.* Philadelphia, PA: Consortium for Policy Research in Education.

Timperley, H.S. (2005). Instructional leadership challenges: The case of using student achievement information for instructional improvement. *Leadership and Public Policy in Schools, 4,* 3-22.

Togneri, W. (2003). *Beyond islands of excellence: What districts can do to improve instruction and achievement in all schools—A leadership brief.* Washington, D.C.: Learning First Alliance. (ERIC Document Reproduction Service No. ED 475875).

Wallin, D., & Newton, P. (2013). Instructional leadership of the rural teaching principal: Double the trouble or twice the fun?. *International Studies in Educational Administration (Commonwealth Council for Educational Administration & Management (CCEAM)), 41,* 19-31. Retrieved December 15, 2013, from EBSCO Online Database Education Research Complete.

Zepeda, S.J. (2004). *Instructional leadership for school improvement.* Larchmont, NY: Eye on Education.

SUGGESTED READING

Barth, R. (1990). *Improving schools from within.* San Francisco: Josey-Bass.

Blase, J. & Blase, J. (2000). Effective instructional leadership: Teachers' perspectives on how principals promote teaching and learning in schools. *Journal of Educational Administration, 38,* 130-141.

Chase, G. & Kane, M. (1983). *The principal as instructional leader: How much more time before we act?* Denver, CO: Education Commission of the States.

Hassenpflug, A. (2013). How to improve Instructional leadership: High school principal selection process versus evaluation process. *A Journal of Educational Strategies, Issues, and Ideas.* 86 (3), 90-92.

Jamentz, K. (2002). *Isolation is the enemy of improvement: Instructional leadership to support standards-based practice.* San Francisco: WestED.

Spillane, J., Halverson, R. & Diamond, J. (2000). *Toward a theory of leadership practice: A distributed perspective.* Evanston, IL: Institute for Policy Research.

Sapulding, D. & Smith. G. (2012). *Instructional Coaches and the Instructional Leadership Team: A Guide to School Building Improvement.* Thousand Oaks, CA.: Corwin Press.

Weiner, J. (2016). Under my thumb: Principals' difficulty releasing decision-making to their instructional leadership team. *Journal of School Leadership.* 26(2), 334.

Zepeda, S. (2004). *Instructional Leadership for School Improvement.* Larchmont, N.Y.: Routledge.

HIGHLY QUALIFIED TEACHERS

The U.S. Department of Education has mandated that all teachers of core academic subjects in the classroom be "highly qualified." Through the No Child Left Behind Act (NCLB), there are three essential criteria for a teacher to be deemed highly qualified: attaining a bachelor's degree or higher in the subject that the teacher teaches; obtaining full state teacher certification; and demonstrating knowledge in the subject(s) taught (U.S. Department of Education, 2006). According to the U.S. Department of Education (2006), the highly qualified teacher (HQT) is one of the most important factors in student achievement. Berry, Hoke and Hirsch (2004) state, "Consensus is growing among school reformers that teaches are the most important school-related determinant of student achievement."

KEYWORDS: Bias; Core Academic Subjects; Demonstration of Competency; Elementary and Secondary Act of 1965; High, Objective, Uniform State Standard of Evaluation (HOUSSE); Highly qualified teachers; No Child Left Behind Act of 2001 (NCLB); Out-of-Field Teaching; Retention; State Requirements; TEACH Act; Title II

OVERVIEW

The U.S. Department of Education has mandated that all teachers of core academic subjects in the classroom be "highly qualified." Core academic subjects are English, reading or language arts, mathematics, science, foreign languages, civics and government, economics, arts, history, and geography. Through the No Child Left Behind Act (NCLB), there are three essential criteria for a teacher to be deemed highly qualified:

- Attaining a bachelor's degree or higher in the subject that the teacher teaches;

- Obtaining full state teacher certification;
- Demonstrating knowledge in the subject(s) taught (U.S. Department of Education).

Berry et al. state that requiring highly qualified teachers in every classroom "offers unprecedented ways to reshape teacher preparation in ways that finally produce the gains in student achievement that reformers have long sought."

In 2001, the Senate and House of Representatives were charged with the reauthorization of the Elementary and Secondary Education Act of 1965. The reauthorization of this act was called the No Child Left Behind Act, keeping intact basic principles of the original act, with the addition of new regulations that identify districts and schools per state that are most in need of highly qualified teachers in Pre-K through university (Kysilka, 2003). The act was amended in 2002, to assure that "all children have a fair, equal and significant opportunity to obtain a high-quality education" (U.S. Department of Education). The TEACH Act, or Teacher Excellence for All Children Act was proposed by the U.S. Representatives George Miller (D-California) and Howard McKeon (R-California) and added provisions to the current Title II of the NCLB law. Title II is specifically directed to teacher-quality issues. TEACH Act provides bonuses up to $12,500 for outstanding highly qualified teachers who transfer to high-poverty and low-achieving schools and work for a minimum of four years. The act also provides similar incentives for principals who transfer, as well. Under this act, master teachers can supplement their salaries by up to $10,000 a year if they agree to mentor new teachers (Hoff, Keller, Zehr, & Klein, 2007).

According to the U.S. Department of Education, a highly qualified teacher (HQT) is one of the most important factors in student achievement. Berry et al. state, "Consensus is growing among school reformers that teachers are the most important school-related determinant of student achievement." Teacher quality results from teaching experience; the quality of the preparation programs; the type of certification; coursework taken in preparation for the profession; and the test scores of the teacher (Thompson & Smith, 2004-2005).

THE 6-POINT PLAN

The U.S. Department of Education monitors each state to determine if it is meeting its goals of providing highly qualified teachers in all subject-matter classrooms, including classrooms in under-performing schools and high-poverty communities (U.S. Department of Education). States must publicly report what they are doing to improve teacher quality (Berry et al.). For those states that did not meet or show a good-faith effort of providing highly qualified teachers in every core classroom by the academic year 2006-2007, the U.S. Department of Education provided a Six-Point Protocol for a Successful Plan to meet the guidelines. The Plan includes:

- A thorough analysis of the data identifying teachers that do not meet the HQT requirements;
- Steps local districts will take to help teachers quickly attain HQT status;
- Technical assistance, programs, and resources that can be offered to achieve these goals;
- Actions that states will face if they do not attain goals;
- Alternative methods for teachers to attain HQT status;
- Steps to ensure that minority students and students from low-income families are not disproportionately taught by inexperienced or unqualified teachers (U.S. Department of Education).

FUNDING

Funds are available for those states that are in the process of meeting HQT status. These funds are as follows:

- The President's 2007 Budget, to help states meet their teacher quality requirements;
- Title I Funding, for school districts that are required to use five percent of their Title I funds for HQT progress;

- Teacher Incentive Fund, providing financial incentives to teachers for improved achievement in high-poverty schools;
- Loan Forgiveness, for up to $17,500 loan forgiveness for highly qualified math and science teachers who choose to serve low-income schools (U.S. Department of Education).

MEETING HIGHLY QUALIFIED STATUS

The U.S. Department of Education has provided areas of flexibility for those teachers applying for highly qualified teacher status. For example, The HOUSSE (High, Objective, Uniform State Standard of Evaluation) for current teachers provides for certain provisions for experienced teachers to demonstrate subject-matter competency that recognizes experience, expertise, and professional training garnered over their professional lives. They are not required to get a degree in every subject they teach to demonstrate competency. Middle school teachers also are provided by flexible rulings, as the state may approve rigorous content-area assessments to determine if a middle school teacher should be awarded HQT status. Under these flexible rulings, states may develop teacher tests for subjects and levels of knowledge needed for effective instruction. Additionally, special education teachers are not required to demonstrate content area competency if they are not providing direct instruction in core academic areas (Department of Education).

To provide further opportunities to meet HQT status, the U.S. Department of Education has expanded its areas of flexibility to include rulings for rural teachers, science teachers, and current multi-subject teachers. Rural teachers who are highly qualified in one subject area will have three years to become highly qualified in any additional subjects they teach. Science teachers can demonstrate that they are highly qualified in either a general science or in individual fields of science (such as physics, biology or chemistry). Additionally, the U.S. Department of Education also provides flexibility in allowing states to evaluate current, multi-subject teachers to demonstrate through one process that they are highly qualified in each subject area (U.S. Department of Education).

The NCLB is not without controversy. Thompson and Smith cite a 1996 report by The National Commission on Teaching and America's Future which outlines the concern that teachers need more than content knowledge to be highly qualified; in fact, the report contends that teachers need a blend of pedagogy and content to be successful teachers. Teacher candidates can be highly effective if they "develop practices that accommodate student diversity, develop the habits of reflective practitioners and gain a fuller understanding of the teacher's changing roles" (Thompson & Smith). Berry et al. state that all teachers should be required to know how students learn and how to manage that learning. Teachers can do this best as they learn "to manage classrooms; develop standards-based lessons; assess student work fairly and appropriately; work with special needs students and ELL; and use technology to bring curriculum to life for the many students who lack motivation."

Many teachers never reach the highly qualified status, as they leave the profession before they achieve this status. Retention rates for new teachers reveal that many of them will quit within five years. Scherer (2005) outlines ways to retain new teachers. Scherer suggests that individual schools must create a positive teaching culture, providing strong leadership, professional development, good facilities, and resources in order to retain novice teachers. Providing this collegial atmosphere improves working conditions, resulting in improved retention of teachers so that they can achieve the highly qualified teacher status required of all states. School systems can also hire highly effective teachers if they prepare in certain ways, by hiring early before other systems and providing adequate teacher compensation.

Ingersoll (2005) states, "Few educational problems have received more attention than has the failure to ensure that the nation's classrooms are staffed by highly qualified teachers." Despite the controversy surrounding the No Child Left Behind Act, statistics show that states are indeed making the effort to improve student learning by providing all children with highly qualified teachers.

Applications

PARAPROFESSIONAL REQUIREMENTS

Paraprofessionals are required to meet the highly qualified mantra of the NCLB Act, for those who were hired after January 2002. They must have "two years of Higher Education, an associate's degree, or meet rigorous standards in reading and math" (Kysilka).

SPECIAL EDUCATION REQUIREMENTS

Special Education teachers must meet requirements for highly qualified teachers by becoming certified in Special Education or passing their state's special education licensure exams. They must hold a bachelor's degree and demonstrate knowledge of each subject for which they are the primary teachers; they are allowed extra time to meet content area standards in a second subject ("Special Education," 2004).

VARIANCE BY STATE

The number of highly qualified teachers within content classrooms varies significantly from state to state, as states work to achieve NCLB requirements. Reports from 2004 reveal that those states with the highest number of highly qualified teachers within the content classrooms are: Wisconsin, Idaho, Arkansas, Connecticut, Minnesota, Indiana, Massachusetts, Utah, Michigan, Pennsylvania, Kentucky and Wyoming. Alaska held the lowest number of highly qualified teachers in 2004 ("Special Education").

COMPONENTS NECESSARY FOR PROVIDING STRONG HUMAN RESOURCES IN THE WORLD MARKETPLACE

Jusuf (2002) outlines components for "producing human resources with high quality," that provides a global perspective. Gleaned from the 2003 California Master Plan for Education, Jusuf states that these components should be provided to all students enrolled in public schools throughout the world:

- Qualified and inspiring teachers in the classroom;
- A rigorous curriculum that will prepare all students for success in post-secondary education, work and society;
- Current textbooks, technology and instructional materials aligned with learning expectations;
- Adequate learning support services;
- Qualified school or campus administrators to create an educational culture that is inviting and safe and that places a high value on student achievement and teaching excellence;
- A physical learning environment that is safe, well-equipped and well-maintained (Jusuf).

BENEFITS OF MINORITY TEACHERS

Brown and Borman (2005) suggest that the benefits of supplying minority teachers in low-income, low-performing schools outweighs benefits of those teachers who are considered highly qualified but are not minority teachers. The benefits are:

- Minority teachers from non-dominant cultures understand how to help students construct the bridge that links both world views as they are also participants in both worlds;
- They possess mainstream cultural norms that diverse students need to be successful (autonomy, self-reliance and individualism);
- They know about immigrant and indigenous groups and accept students who are a part of these groups;
- They provide students with role models who possess the same linguistic features as their students and may allow their students to use their home language in the classroom.

VOCATIONAL EDUCATION TEACHERS
Vocational Education teachers are not content area teachers and are not bound by the NCLB Highly Qualified Teacher regulations. However, if a Vocational Education teacher teaches a course (such as applied physics) that counts toward core academic courses, then that teacher is held to the HQT standards ("Vocational Education Teachers," 2003).

Viewpoints

ALTERNATIVE ROUTES
Alternative routes to Highly Qualified Teacher status are controversial in that a teacher who is making adequate progress toward full certification or are novice teachers are considered in the same category as the HQT. According to Berry et al., teachers during this progression period should be determined as *minimally qualified* instead of *highly qualified.*

OUT-OF-FIELD TEACHING
Out-of-field teaching occurs due to teacher shortages or the number of teachers available in any given subject area. Ingersoll suggests that out-of-field teaching is a detriment to providing highly qualified teachers in the classroom. When teachers teach out-of-field, they are assigned "to teach subjects that do not match their training or education." As Ingersoll states, highly qualified teachers who teach out of their field of expertise can quickly become "highly unqualified

teachers if they are assigned to teach subjects for which they have little background or preparation."

LINK BETWEEN TEACHER EXCELLENCE & STUDENT ACHIEVEMENT
Perkins-Gough (2002) suggest that teacher excellence and student achievement are inherently linked. The U.S. Department of Education's report "Meeting the Highly Qualified Teachers Challenge" (2003) outlines this link:

- Teachers' verbal and cognitive skill levels are important determinants in student success, particularly at the elementary school level;
- Subject-matter background has a positive effect on student performance. If teachers major in the subject they teach, they have better results than out-of-field teachers;
- Teachers who spend more time on developing pedagogy (resulting in Education degrees) are less likely to impact student performance than those who spend more time studying content;
- Students enrolled in schools of education are less accomplished than other university students, as education students have not been exposed to the intellectual rigor of content degree programs (U.S. Department of Education).

IMPORTANCE OF TRAINING IN PEDAGOGY
The Educational Testing Service states that developing pedagogical skills and social abilities is more important than content area knowledge in developing strong teachers (Perkins-Gough). The ETS suggests that highly qualified teachers possess:

- Skills in designing learning experiences that inspire and interest children;
- Enthusiasm for the job;
- A caring attitude to students;
- A thorough understanding of the subject;
- Several years of experience as a classroom teacher;
- An advanced degree from a good school of education;
- Involvement with parents.

TEACHER DEFICIT PERSPECTIVE
Ingersoll states that the problem of under-qualified teachers is largely one of perceived shortcomings in the teachers themselves. These include weaknesses in

preparation, lack of knowledge, lack of motivation, or weak pedagogical abilities. Rather than looking at teacher deficits, school systems should review their own contributing factors in responding to these criticisms. They should consider problems with working conditions, recruitment and retention. Ingersoll contends that the real problem is in the low stature and social standing that the teaching profession must face in today's society.

BIAS IN TEACHER TESTING

Brown and Borman assert that the non-traditional teacher is discriminated against through bias in teacher testing. Bias in testing can stem from a number of sources:

- The cultural content embedded in any given test;
- The linguistic demands inherent in any given test;
- Lack of representation within norm samples for individuals with diverse backgrounds in any given test;
- A belief that language reduced tests alone are sufficient to overcome bias and communication barriers.

TERMS & CONCEPTS

Bias: Hambleton and Rogers (1995) define bias as "the presence of some characteristics of an item that results in differential performance for individuals of the same ability but from different ethnic, sex, cultural or religious groups."

State Requirements: The No Child Left Behind Act requires states to:

- measure the extent to which all students have highly qualified teachers, particularly minority and disadvantaged students;
- adopt goals and plans to ensure all teachers are highly qualified;
- publicly report plans and progress in meeting teacher quality goals (U.S. Department of Education).

Demonstration of Competency: Middle and high school teachers must prove that they know the subject they teach with:

- a major in the subject they teach;
- credits equivalent to a major in the subject;
- passing a state-developed test in the content area;

- HOUSSE for current teachers only;
- an advanced certification from the state; or,
- a graduate degree (U.S. Department of Education).

High, Objective, Uniform State Standard of Evaluation (HOUSSE): For current teachers, states are permitted to develop additional ways to demonstrate subject-matter competency and meet HQT requirements. Competency can be awarded through a combination of teaching experience, professional development and knowledge of the subject area through a period of time.

Collegial Atmosphere: A collegial atmosphere exists in a school when the school invites novice teachers to ask questions, suggest new ideas, and allow observations of teachers whose work they respect.

Out-of-Field Teaching: Out-of-field teaching occurs when teachers are assigned to teach subjects that do not match their training or education. Out-of-field teaching occurs due to teacher shortages or the number of teachers available in any given subject area.

Retention Rates: Retention rates are the percentages of teachers who stay within the teaching profession of leave their position for another career. Retention rates for new teachers reveal that many of them will quit within five years.

Tricia Smith

BIBLIOGRAPHY

Berry, B., Hoke, M., & Hirsch, E. (2004). The search for highly qualified teachers. *Phi Delta Kappan, 85*684-689. Retrieved November 21, 2007, from EBSCO online database, Academic Search Premier.

Brown, J., & Borman, K. (2005). Highly qualified minority teachers: Do high-stakes teacher tests weed out those we need most? *Internet Journal of Educational Policy, Research and Practice, 6,* 105-137. Retrieved November 21, 2007, from EBSCO online database, Education Research Complete.

Chin, E., & Wong, P. (2013). Preparing teachers: Highly qualified to do what? Editors' introduction. *Education Policy Analysis Archives, 21,* 1-5. Retrieved December 15, 2013, from EBSCO Online Database Education Research Complete.

Gujarati, J. (2012). A comprehensive induction system: A key to the retention of highly qualified teachers. *Educational Forum, 76,* 218-223. Retrieved December 15, 2013, from EBSCO Online Database Education Research Complete.

Hambleton, R., & Rogers, J. (1995). *Item Bias Review* (Report No. 19951001). East Lansing, MI. (ERIC Document Reproduction Service).

Hoff, D., Keller, B., Zehr, M., & Klein, A. (2007). Draft retains quality rules for teachers (Cover Story). *Education Week, 27,* 1-23. Retrieved November 21, 2007, from EBSCO online database, Academic Search Premier.

Ingersoll, R. (2003). *Out-of-field teaching and the limits of teacher policy.* Seattle, WA: Center for the Study of Teaching Policy.

Ingersoll, R. (2005). The problem of unqualified teachers: A sociological perspective. *Sociology of Education, 78,* (2) 175-178. Retrieved November 21, 2007, from EBSCO online database Academic Search Premier.

Jusuf, H. (2005, January). Improving Teacher quality: A keyword for improving education facing global challenges. *Turkish On-Line Journal of Education Technology, 4,* 33-37. Retrieved November 21, 2007, from EBSCO Education Research Complete.

Kysilka, M. (2003). No Child Left Behind. *Curriculum and Teaching Dialogue, 5,* 99-104. Retrieved November 21, 2007, from EBSCO online database, Academic Search Premier.

Karelitz, T. M., Fields, E., Levy, A., Martinez-Gudapakkam, A., & Jablonski, E. (2011). No teacher left unqualified: How teachers and principals respond to the highly qualified mandate. *Science Educator, 20,* 1-11. Retrieved December 15, 2013, from EBSCO Online Database Education Research Complete.

Perkins-Gough, D. (2002). Teacher quality. *Educational Leadership, 60,* 85. Retrieved November 21, 2007, from EBSCO online database, Academic Search Premier.

Scherer, M. (2005). The right new teachers. *Educational Leadership, 62,* 7. Retrieved November 21, 2007, from EBSCO online database, Academic Search Premier.

Special education: 'Highly Qualified' teachers needed. (2004). *Education Week, 24,* 51. Retrieved November 21, 2007, from EBSCO online database, Academic Search Premier.

Thompson, S., & Smith, D. (2004 /2005). Creating highly qualified teachers for urban schools. *Professional Educator, 27* (1/2), 73-88. Retrieved November 21, 2007, from EBSCO online database, Academic Search Premier.

U.S. Department of Education, Office of Policy Planning and Innovation. (2003). *Meeting the Highly Qualified Teachers Challenge: The Secretary's Annual Report on Teacher Quality.* Retrieved November 21, 2007, from http://ed.gov.

U.S. Department of Education. (2006, August). *Highly Qualified Teachers for Every Child.* Retrieved November 21, 2007, from http://ed.gov.

U.S. Department of Education. (2002, January 8). No Child Left Behind Act of 2001. Public Law 107-110, ncbe.gwu.edu.

Voc ed teachers dodge 'highly qualified' rule. (2002). *Vocational Training Newsletter, 33,* 1-3. Retrieved November 21, 2007, from EBSCO online database, Education Research Complete.

SUGGESTED READING

Berry, B. (2004, March). Recruiting and retaining "Highly Qualified Teachers" for hard to staff schools. *NASSP Bulletin, 88,* 5-27. Retrieved November 21, 2007, from EBSCO online database, Academic Search Premier.

Clément, M. (2009). Hiring highly qualified teachers begins with quality interviews. *Phi Delta Kappan.* 91(2), 22-24.

Darling-Hammond, L., & Berry, B. (2006, November). Highly qualified teachers for all. *Educational Leadership, 64,* 14-20. Retrieved November 21, 2007, from EBSCO online database, Academic Search Premier.

Envadia. (2007, July). Recruitment and retention of highly qualified teachers. *District Administration, 43,* 64-54. Retrieved November 21, 2007, from EBSCO online database, Academic Search Premier.

Keller, B. (2005, December 14). Actual measure of highly qualified teachers just beginning to come to light across nation. *Education Week, 25.* Retrieved November 21, 2007, from EBSCO online database, Academic Search Premier.

Minority Teacher Act (1991). ORS 342.433 to 342.449.

The National Committee on Teaching and America's Future. (1996, September). *What matter's most: Teaching for America's future: Summary report.* New York: Authors.

Number of 'highly qualified' teachers varies by state. (2004, January). *Techniques: Connecting Education and Careers, 57.* Retrieved November 21, 2007, from EBSCO online database, Academic Search Premier.

Ortiz, S., & Ochoa, H. (2005). Intellectual assessment: A nondiscriminatory interpretive approach. In D. Flanagan & P. Harrison (Eds.). *Contemporary Intellectual Assessment, 2nd ed.* (pp. 234-250). NY: Guilford.

Park, S.J. (2013). Do highly qualified teachers use more effective instructional practices than other teachers: The mediating effect of instructional practices. Society for Research on Educational Effectiveness. 13 pp.

Robinson, H. (2011). Highly qualified teacher status and the reading achievement of students with disabilities. *American Secondary Education.* 39 (3), 42-66.

Safier, K. (2007). Improving teacher quality in Ohio: The limitations of the highly qualified teacher provision of the NCLB Act of 2001. *Journal of Law and Education,* *36,* 65-87. Retrieved November 2, 2007, from EBSCO online database, Education Research Complete.

Then and now: Developing highly qualified teachers. (2007, Summer). *Delta Kappa Gamma Bulletin, 73,* 26-30.

Retrieved November 21, 2007, from EBSCO online database, Academic Search Premier.

Toppo, G. (2007, February 14). What makes a teacher 'effective'? *USA Today.*

Valdes, R., & Figueroa, R. (1994). *Bilingualism and testing: A special case of bias.* Norwood, NJ: Ablex.

PERFORMANCE-BASED SALARIES

Performance-based salaries are a reform option for improving teacher accountability in U.S. public schools. Parents and government officials want teachers to be held accountable for their effectiveness, and different pay scenarios have been created both in the United States and in other developed countries to create systems of accountability. Whether or not performance-based pay incentives result in increased student performance has not been proven. Debate continues over how, if performance-based salaries were implemented, teachers' performances ought to be assessed, and how to award salaries.

KEYWORDS: Average Income; Global Economy; Gross Salary; Median Income; Merit Pay; Modernization; No Child Left Behind Act of 2001 (NCLB); Performance-Based Pay

OVERVIEW

School district administrators work tirelessly to balance their budgets. While state and federal governments pay per student enrollment dollars toward those budgets, teacher salaries and pensions take a large percentage of those resources. While the general public may disagree, teachers are not paid higher salaries when compared to employees in other professions. Parents and government officials want teachers to be held accountable for their effectiveness, and different pay scenarios have been created both in the United States and in other developed countries to create systems of accountability. Whether or not performance-based pay incentives result in increased student performance has not been proven.

For many, becoming a teacher is a dream; it is an employment opportunity in which they can practice an education philosophy they have established while positively influencing the lives of children. For others, however, it is an employment opportunity that offers a decent wage, health benefits, a pension, and summers off. For those who are of the less dedicated bunch, employment research may be necessary before a final determination is made regarding a life's work. Studies show that dollar for dollar, teachers do not make as much as professionals in other positions, nor do they (necessarily) focus all of their time on the subject of study they regard so highly.

Teachers begin learning their craft in college, for the most part. In addition, many of those teachers graduate and find positions teaching while earning advanced degrees or specialized certifications. They teach and study their field and earn a wage respective of their education and experience. In some districts in the United States, however, teachers are earning a wage depending on their students' academic achievements. Performance-based pay structures have been offered in other nations and are becoming popular in the U.S. for the equity they claim to offer regarding teacher pay, though the idea still creates some controversy.

Historically, teacher salary has been an issue among tax-payers. Taxes increase as district budgets compensate for raises, lost state funding, and lower student enrollments. For those on the outside, a work day that lasts from 7:30 a.m. to 3:30 p.m., Monday to Friday, and an employment year that only lasts 180-190 days can seem excessively light. On the other hand, helping students develop into academically and morally sound individuals is a large task. Each state has its own specific formula for determining district budgets, and teacher salaries and pensions are factored into that formula.

There is nothing universal within the U.S. regarding how much a teacher should earn because state and local funding varies from district to district within and among states. As a result, budget disparity makes it unfair to create a blanket wage for everyone with the same credentials. One thing that does tend to be universal is the way teacher salaries are misinterpreted and misrepresented. $45,000 per year for someone who works less than half of it seems like a pretty good buck. When seriously considered, though, much more than dollars needs to be examined. Bracey (2007) responds to a paper by Greene and Winters (2007) summarizing the pay of public school teachers in the United States for the 2005 year. Greene and Winters break down a comparison between teachers, economists, and architects, and Bracey criticizes them for not reporting accurate information based on the statistics provided by the Bureau of Labor Statistics' National Compensation Survey (NCS).

How do We Measure Teacher Salary?

Bracey's biggest complaint is that the respective salaries are interpreted by the hour, and teacher salaries do appear to be greater when compared to that of other professions in that light. The rate of pay for each of the three professions is broken down hourly, showing teachers earning an estimated $34.06, architects $30.22, and economists $33.85. When calculated by hours worked per year, however, the figures flip, with architects earning $65,108, economists $72,810, and teachers $46,995. Greene and Winters claim that teachers are paid better than most other professionals based on their hourly salary; their claim is not clearly substantiated, and Bracey points out their reporting limitations (Bracey).

In addition, the original data used by Greene and Winters came from an analysis of over sixteen professions broken down into the following "skill criteria": "knowledge needed, supervision received, guidelines applied, complexity, scope and effect, personal contacts, purpose of contacts, physical demands, work environment, and supervisory duties. When these researchers compared teachers' salaries to 16 other occupations that had similar total numbers on the criteria, teachers trailed all but one, the clergy. They trailed architects by $275 a week" (Bracey).

Leaving the Profession

A teacher new to the profession does not begin a career expecting it to end within a few years. However, those who left the profession in 2004-2005 outnumbered the teachers who moved to different schools (or from the public to the private sector) in the same year. That statistic shows the highest rate of teachers leaving their profession since data started being

collected through a survey from the National Center for Education Statistics in 1988-1989 (as cited in Bracey). Furthermore, teachers with less than three years or more than twenty on the job, those younger than thirty or older than fifty, and those making less than $30,000 or more than $40,000 were more likely to be the ones who leave (as cited in Bracey). Finally, teachers working in both public and private schools cited similar reasons for leaving their schools: dissatisfaction with working conditions and administrative support. While public school teachers changed schools, private school teachers were more likely to leave the profession entirely and change careers (as cited in Bracey).

The Case in New York...

Something to note with this data is that the private sector generally requires less credentials for their teachers; according to the National Center for Education Statistics (2013), during the 2011–12 school year, 56.7 percent of full-time private school teachers had only a bachelor's degree or less, compared to 44.5 percent of full-time public school teachers. In New York State, a teacher working in public schools has three years following the acquisition of a bachelor's degree in which to earn a master's degree. Many candidates work provisionally while gaining that second degree, and teachers are required to maintain professional development standards in the way of recertification after receiving teaching permanency. In contrast, many private schools require no education past the bachelor's degree level. It may be that once teachers in the private sector leave their schools, they have limited options within the teaching profession, and that is the reason they change careers. The private sector in New York State also pays a wage considerably less than that of the public sector. On average, public school teachers' salaries in New York State are the highest in the nation.

That being the case, teachers in the New York City public schools tend to fare worse than their counterparts in nearby counties. For the 2012–13 school year, the median salary for public school teachers (as calculated by district) started at $69,901 in the Bronx, Manhattan, and Brooklyn and ranged as high as $72,990 (Bronx), $75,092 (Manhattan), and $75,796 (Brooklyn), compared to a statewide median salary of $75,279. Salaries in Queens and Staten Island hovered around or slightly above the median. Meanwhile, median salaries in nearby Suffolk, Nassau, and Westchester Counties ranged from $73,249 to $112,870, $89,096 to $132,249, and $71,668 to $137,017, respectively (Empire Center for Public Policy, 2014).

... AND ELSEWHERE

Between 2001–2 and 2011–12, average (mean) teacher salaries throughout the United States declined 2.8 percent when adjusted for inflation. Colorado, Florida, Georgia, Illinois, Indiana, Michigan, North Carolina, South Carolina, Virginia, and Washington State all saw declines of 5 percent of more, with North Carolina having the largest decrease (15.7 percent). Average salaries for the 2011–12 school year ranged from $38,804 in South Dakota to $73,398 in New York State. In one year, from 2010–11 to 2011–12, average salaries declined 0.1 percent nationwide (not adjusted for inflation), with Illinois seeing the largest decrease, of 10.7 percent (National Education Association, 2013).

ALTERNATIVE PAY SCENARIOS

Enticing, developing, and maintaining effective teachers is a concern not just for the United States but for other industrial countries as well, especially in the fields of computer science, math, foreign languages, and science. As such, salary alternatives have been explored within the region and abroad. In some areas of the United Kingdom, for example, higher education costs are forgiven for teachers who work in specific areas and remain in the position for at least ten years. In addition, "[c]ountries such as Austria, Denmark, Finland, and Scotland are offering fewer benefits but higher pay for teachers–more comparable with salaries in other professions–in the early years of their careers" (Jacobson, 2006). Furthermore, areas in Singapore that show a shortage of teachers in specific subject areas and for students with disabilities have started offering teachers supplements to their salaries for changing fields or student populations (Jacobson).

Former attempts to restructure teacher pay offer little with which to push restructuring forward. For example, "[d]uring the 1980s, states experimented with merit-pay plans that tied teachers' salaries, in part, to evaluations of their performance, and with career ladders that paid some teachers more for taking on extra roles and responsibilities. But teachers often complained that the evaluations were too subjective, and that the limited pots of money available for such programs encouraged unhealthy competition between colleagues. And when tight budget times came, such initiatives were often the first to go" (Olson, 2007).

Something to consider here is that in most professions, the employee has little to say with regard to how s/he is evaluated or what taking on additional responsibilities should cost an employer; those decisions are made by someone else.

PERFORMANCE-BASED SALARIES

In addition to incentives created to lure teachers to the profession, some districts are changing the way teachers earn their paychecks once on the job. Paying teachers based on their performance is a strategy that districts in the United States and abroad are discovering might benefit both students and teachers. However, paying teachers according to their performance poses many challenges, such as how that performance is assessed. While that assessment tends to be objective, it depends on student achievement, which may be impacted by variables other than how a teacher does his or her job. Also, performance based pay can focus on individuals or teams of teachers, such as all of the teachers in a grade or those working on a specific project. And districts can offer incentives other than those tied with a monetary value. For example, in a team-teaching situation, the team may receive a reduction in classes in order to prepare their students for a project or exam. Teachers may also receive promotions or public recognition for their efforts in lieu of or in addition to a financial reward, which may be a onetime remuneration or an ongoing salary increase (Lavy, 2007).

INCREASING TEACHER EFFECTIVENESS WITH PERFORMANCE-BASED PAY

In a global economy, when countries compete with each other for interest in oil, consumer goods, and employment opportunities, the education sector becomes universally significant. Those in the teaching profession lie at the heart of that significance, and as such, industrialized nations want to heighten teacher performance whenever possible. Increasing teacher effectiveness, presumably, should revolve around compensating teachers for that increase (Lavy). In order to do that, one teacher needs to prove to the public (as well as administrators) that he or she goes above and beyond what the next teacher does, therefore requiring additional compensation for what he or she offers students. The motivation would be to earn additional pay, improve student performance, and be recognized for skills that are considered valuable to the profession. Furthermore, a district that offers performance based pay will attract the teacher who is motivated by the incentive, with the result being an improvement in student performance and retention and possibly increased enrollment for the district as a whole.

Performance-based pay can also lend itself to a district's sweeping itself of mediocrity with regard to its teachers. The teachers who tend to be less productive (those who show to earn a paycheck yet find no reward in going above and beyond the minimum requirements) will find motivation within the performance-based pay structure as well. The minimalists will find themselves earning less than their more motivated peers, lacking the same opportunities for advancement, and receiving less recognition from their district administration. In addition, these minimalists may also find themselves without a job if what they instill in their students is a minimalist approach to academics. The goal is to improve student performance; if teachers cannot do that within this payment structure, they will be held accountable by losing their positions.

IMPLICATIONS FOR PERFORMANCE-BASED PAY

An additional concern for districts is the possibility that they might not be responsible for the performance goals or oversight of accountability of their teachers. A draft bill presented by the House Education and Labor Committee in 2007 encouraged districts to make attempts at paying teachers based on their performance (i.e., based on student test scores) as a measure to ensure the reauthorization of the No Child Left Behind Act of 2001. The two largest teachers' unions, the National Education Association (NEA) and the American Federation of Teachers (AFT), are strongly opposed to federal interference regarding how school districts should pay teachers (Olson). Whether districts choose to keep teacher salaries weighted on a traditional scale (i.e., based on education and experience) or offer performance -based incentives is currently up to each district. If every school district had the same budget, the same student population, and the same teacher credential requirements, the overarching

standards of the proposed bill might be plausible, especially when evidence of teacher performance is based entirely on standardized test scores. The reality of public education in the United States, however, suggests that each district needs control over how teachers will be evaluated and on what basis they are compensated for their efforts.

One of the concerns about performance-based pay is that when it is not teams who are rewarded but individuals, and other individuals are not rewarded, competition among teachers and the havoc the competition could wreak on professional relationships can cause schools to become divided, with the payment structure backfiring on student performance. Additionally, within a performance-based pay structure, someone has to be assessing the performance. Making principals or other administrators take on that burden creates an additional stress of resources for districts. For example, if the principal is now spending all of his or her time monitoring teachers, who is putting parents' minds at ease, working with school boards, or planning for next year's budget? Also, putting administrators in the position of offering financial gain, a promotion, or job security to a teacher gives the district more power than it has traditionally had (Lavy).

Additional concerns about performance-based pay involve a more personal aspect of education delivery. The teachers who teach because they feel a sense of internal satisfaction with the profession may find that having to prove themselves on a daily basis takes away from that satisfaction. "This threat is particularly real for teachers, who, as a group, exhibit strong intrinsic motivation flowing from the value they place on interacting with children and seeing them succeed" (Lavy). Finally, if the goal is to improve student performance, it may seem appropriate for teachers to focus their time on students they believe have the potential to improve, making the strongest and the weakest students less warranting of the teachers' attention (Murnane & Cohen, 1986, as cited in Lavy). Neither federal nor local governments want that as a result of any salary incentive.

CONCLUSION

Teachers earn their degrees and enter into a profession in which (it seems) their performance is always in question. If students are not achieving academically, it must be the fault of the teacher, even though several factors play a role in a student's success. If teachers are easy to blame they should be just as easy to praise when student test scores improve and retention rates increase. Offering teachers incentives to raise standards is a motivating enticement, but it is also a way for district administrators to keep a watchful eye on their teachers, which may be counterproductive, as it is not a scenario most new teachers consider when entering the field. Generally speaking, teachers should *want* to help their students improve academically. The pay, health benefits, time off, and pension can only go so far if a person is not internally satisfied with the profession he or she walks into each day. Performance-based pay is an option for school districts, but it is also a means to an end that can cause undesired results in schools.

TERMS & CONCEPTS

Average Income: The income determined by adding together all salaries and dividing the total by the number of incomes within the group.

Gross Salary: Income earned in total, before taxes, health benefits, retirement, or other benefits have been deducted.

Median Income: The income mid-point based on a group of salaries (A+B+C+D = B.5).

Merit Pay: Salary based on teaching effectiveness for specific outcomes: the highest increase in standardized test scores over a period of time, for example.

Modernization: Making standards (i.e., teaching credentials, expectations, etc.) in agreement with current beliefs.

No Child Left Behind Act of 2001 (NCLB): Legislation enacted to ensure that all students (regardless of ethnicity, socioeconomic status, or disability) have access to instructional approaches that have been proven to be successful.

Performance-Based Pay: Salary based on student achievement, improvement, and dropout rates— the results of teaching effectiveness.

Maureen McMahon

BIBLIOGRAPHY

2007 city facts: Education. (2007). *Crain's New York Business, 23,* 14. Retrieved November 11, 2007, from EBSCO Online Database Regional Business News.

Albanese, E. (2006, December 12). Colo.'s Jeffco district uses taxable debt for pensions. *Bond Buyer,* p. 35. Retrieved November 14, 2007, from EBSCO Online Database Business Source Premier.

Barbieri, R. (2012). Merit pay? *Independent School, 72,* 50–57. Retrieved December 15, 2013, from EBSCO Online Database Education Research Complete.

Bracey, G. W. (2007). Get rich: Be a teacher. *Phi Delta Kappan, 88,* 634–635. Retrieved November 11, 2007, from EBSCO Online Database Education Research Complete.

The compensation question. (2012). *Education Next, 12,* 68–78. Retrieved December 15, 2013, from EBSCO Online Database Education Research Complete.

Empire Center for Public Policy. (2014, January 27). *Public school teacher salaries, 2012–13.* Retrieved October 27, 2014, from http://seethroughny.net.

Fehr, E., & Goette, L. (2007). Do workers work more if wages are high? Evidence from a randomized field experiment. *American Economic Review, 97,* 298–317. Retrieved October 10, 2014, from EBSCO Online Database Public Affairs Index.

Greene, J. P., & Winters, M. A. (2007). *How much are public school teachers paid?* (Civic Report No. 50). New York: Manhattan Institute. Retrieved October 10, 2014, from http://files.eric.ed.gov.

Honawar, V. (2007). AFT survey finds pay for teachers is falling behind. *Education Week, 26,* 8. Retrieved November 11, 2007, from EBSCO Online Database Education Research Complete.

Jacobson, L. (2006) Teacher-pay alternatives may be found in other nations. *Education Week, 26,* 9. Retrieved November 13, 2007, from EBSCO Online Database Education Research Complete.

Klein, A. (2007). Iowa teachers to get historic pay increase. *Education Week, 26,* 22. Retrieved November 11, 2007, from EBSCO Online Database Education Research Complete.

Lauen, D. (2013). Jumping at the chance: The effects of accountability incentives on student achievement. *Journal of Research on Educational Effectiveness, 6,* 93–113. Retrieved December 15, 2013, from EBSCO Online Database Education Research Complete.

Lavy, V. (2007). Using performance-based pay to improve the quality of teachers. *Future of Children, 17,* 87–109. Retrieved November 11, 2007, from EBSCO Online Database Education Research Complete.

Levin, B. (2011). Eight reasons merit pay for teachers is a bad idea. *Our Schools / Our Selves, 21,* 131–137. Retrieved December 15, 2013, from EBSCO Online Database Education Research Complete.

Murnane, R., & Cohen, D. K. (1986). Merit pay and the evaluation problem: Why most merit pay plans fail and a few survive. *Harvard Educational Review, 56*, 1–17. Retrieved October 10, 2014, from EBSCO Online Database Education Research Complete.

National Center for Education Statistics. (2013, May). *Digest of Education Statistics: Advance release of selected 2013 digest tables.* Retrieved October 27, 2014, from http://nces.ed.gov.

National Education Association. (2013). *Ranking of the states 2012 and estimates of school statistics 2013.* Retrieved October 27, 2014, from http://nea.org.

Olson, L. (2007). Teacher-pay experiments mounting amid debate. *Education Week, 27*, 1+. Retrieved November 11, 2007, from EBSCO Online Database Education Research Complete.

Samuels, C. A. (2007). Teacher pay, pensions among issues in W.Va. *Education Week, 26*, 24. Retrieved November 11, 2007, from EBSCO Online Database Education Research Complete.

Woessmann, L. (2011). Cross-country evidence on teacher performance pay. *Economics of Education Review, 30*, 404–418. Retrieved December 15, 2013, from EBSCO Online Database Education Research Complete.

SUGGESTED READING

Clough, S. (2007, October 3). Placing pay raises inside state aid formula hurts Oklahoma school budgets. *Journal Record Legislative Report.* Retrieved October 10, 2014, from EBSCO Online Database Regional Business News Plus.

Fetler, M. (1999). High school staff characteristics and mathematics test results. *Education Policy Analysis Archives, 7.* Retrieved October 10, 2014, from http://epaa.asu.edu.

Barth, P. (Ed.). (2000). Honor in the boxcar: Equalizing teacher quality [Special issue]. *Thinking K–16, 14.* Retrieved October 10, 2014, from http://files.eric.ed.gov.

Increase in K-12 teacher pay luring community college professors. (2006). *Community College Week, 18*, 25. Retrieved November 13, 2007, from EBSCO Online Database Education Research Complete.

Inwood, D. (2014). Performance-related pay and why it is changing the dynamics of teaching. *Education Journal, 209*, 15. Retrieved October 27, 2014, from EBSCO Online Database Education Research Complete.

Lavy, V. (2007). Using performance based pay to improve the quality of teachers. *The Future of Children.* 17(1), 87-109.

Monk, D. H. (1994). Subject area preparation of secondary mathematics and science teachers and student achievement. *Economics of Education Review, 13*, 125–145.

Murnane, R. J., & Phillips, B. R. (1981). Learning by doing, vintage, and selection: Three pieces of the puzzle relating teaching experience and teaching performance. *Economics of Education Review, 1*, 453–465.

Sanders, W. L., & Rivers, J. C. (1996). *Cumulative and residual effects of teachers on future student academic achievement.* Knoxville, TN: University of Tennessee Value-Added Research and Assessment Center.

Scottish pay agreement 'yet to have effect on pupils.' (2007). *Education, 252*, 3. Retrieved November 13, 2007, from EBSCO Online Database Education Research Complete.

Strauss, R. P., & Sawyer, E. A. (1986). Some new evidence on teacher and student competencies. *Economics of Education Review, 5*, 41–48. Retrieved October 10, 2014, from EBSCO Online Database EconLit.

STAFF PERFORMANCE EVALUATIONS

Evaluations generally take two different forms: formative evaluation or summative evaluation. Many policy-makers and researchers call for evaluation not only to hold teachers and administrators responsible for teaching students, but also to provide professional development opportunities, increase leadership capabilities, and improve teacher quality. Performance evaluations may include the following procedures: observation, portfolio assessment, and assessment centers. Successful evaluation procedures can have a large impact on improving schools, as well as addressing issues such as teacher retention and professional isolation.

KEYWORDS: Assessment; Assessment Centers; Formative Evaluation; Observation; Portfolio; Professional Development; Reliability; Summative Evaluation; Teacher Quality

OVERVIEW

Teachers and administrators are faced with the task of educating individuals to aptly prepare them to thrive in today's economy. Staff performance evaluations have been instituted in a large majority of schools across the country to assess school staff in this undertaking, from teachers to administrators. Evaluating staff in a school is often a daunting process, as there are many people to assess, as well as a variety of methods to from which to choose. Schools are also often highly stressful environments, with teachers and administrators having minimal amounts of time. Furthermore, working in schools is often an isolated profession, in which supervision can be met with suspicion or nervousness.

The methods and policies for staff performance evaluations vary widely from school to school. Aspects of the school that influence performance evaluations include the school district, the size of the school, and the school culture. In the past teachers were often evaluated and supervised solely to ensure that they met standards, rather than to facilitate their growth as professionals (Sullivan & Glanz, 2004). However, today educational experts largely call for evaluation procedures for school staff to focus on constructive criticism and improving the skills of educators and school administrators, in addition to holding them accountable for student learning (Nolin, Rowand, & Farris, 1994).

EVALUATION GOALS

Evaluation must be reliable, effective, and efficient in order to achieve its goals. Reliable results are consistent—similar tests give similar results. A survey by the National Center for Education Statistics (Nolin et al.) found that the majority of educational administrators and teachers agree that evaluations can help them improve educational excellence. However, evaluations must be conducted carefully to meet these goals. The survey also found that performance evaluation processes are firmly established in schools across the country, that most teachers are evaluated by their principal, and the chief method of teacher evaluation is through classroom observation. Survey results report that teachers are supportive of evaluations when they aim to improve teaching skills rather than using the results to fire teachers or determine pay scales (Nolin et al.).

Staff performance evaluations face complicated questions regarding various elements. They include: what the staff should be evaluated for, who should evaluate them, and what the outcome of the evaluation should be. Researchers largely agree that the goals of evaluation today are twofold: accountability and professional development (Anderson, 1989). However, these goals are often difficult to reach due to various factors in schools.

WHO & WHAT IS EVALUATED?

The fundamental question for staff evaluation is *what* schools need to evaluate to ensure they are gathering enough information to judge a teacher or supervisor (Darling-Hammond, 1983). The broad range of possible evaluation aspects include subtle areas such as a teacher's rapport with students and the social responsibility displayed by an individual, as well as concrete features including test scores, lesson plans, and teaching methods. Experts largely recognize that there are two types of evaluations that differ in their goals: formative evaluations are used to improve skills, while summative evaluations are used to make decisions regarding school personnel. Many evaluation methods used by schools and districts are characterized by both forms of evaluation.

Historically, teachers were supervised largely by local authorities, and schools functioned as individual entities over which the teacher had a large amount of autonomy. As schools and districts became more organized in the face of a changing economy and world-wide competition, teachers were supervised by superintendents and then supervisors in schools, usually by the administration. While the initial focus on performance evaluation centered on teachers, recently there has been considerable attention on administrators as well. Research on principal evaluations is still scarce; however, the research on school organization suggests that the quality of leadership in schools has a significant impact on student learning and success, leading to educational experts calling for performance evaluations for principals (Connecticut Principals' Academy, 1990).

In the early 1970s, very few states across the country required evaluation for principals, or had a set procedure. Nearly twenty years later, that number had grown to include most states (Peters, 1988, cited by Anderson). While teacher evaluations have a fairly long history, performance evaluations for administrators only became popular during the school reform movement in the 1980s (Connecticut Principals' Academy). By the late 1980s, when research validated that principals have a key impact on the performance of teachers and students, as well as the culture of a school, school districts began to mandate, research, and implement formal performance evaluation procedures for principals

(Anderson). Peterson believes that evaluation for administrators, especially principals, is important for a number of reasons. Evaluation procedures can help open lines of communication, facilitates the process of goal setting, and encourages principals to improve their leadership skills.

Applications

EVALUATION PHASES

Too often districts and schools do not plan well enough for effective evaluation procedures that meet the diverse needs of a school. Schools need to be held accountable for their teaching and outcomes, while concurrently providing opportunities for staff members to improve their professional skills (Anderson). In order to achieve these goals, evaluation plans should have three phases:

- Planning for the evaluation;
- Collecting the information necessary;
- Using the information collected (Bolton, 1980).

Planning, allows schools and districts to address important aspects of the environment, school mission, and philosophy that will shape how and why a school or district will evaluate its staff members. It is important that this first phase involves a wide breadth of people—from the top district officials to the teachers in the individual schools, and everyone in between—for input. During this phase, the expectations and goals and objectives of the evaluation procedures will be set (Anderson).

Collecting data is the second phase of effective evaluation procedures. The methods of data collection are varied, and may include strategies such as observation, assessments, or other evidence such as collecting test scores of the students in the school. A school may engage in only one method of collecting data, or they may decide to use a variety of methods in their evaluation process (Anderson).

In the final phase of evaluation, supervisors analyze the data and make decisions based on the information. Depending on the type of data available, as well as the goals of the evaluation, the third phase may include resolutions such as awarding merit pay, firing or hiring of employees, or giving certain feedback to the evaluated individuals (Anderson).

FORMATIVE EVALUATION

Formative evaluation helps staff members evaluate and improve their teaching or leadership skills, improving their work performance. This type of evaluation requires that the relationship between evaluator and evaluatee is ongoing. In this type of assessment, the role of the evaluator is closer to that of a counselor, guiding the staff member and consistently providing feedback and assistance. The process can be extensive, even lasting many years, depending on the goals of the evaluation (Barrett, 1986; Anderson).

The goal of formative evaluation is to improve skills in some aspect of the job and provide the guidance, support, and feedback that will help the individual succeed. The larger focus is to improve the school and the education system, rather than singularly judge the performance of an individual.

SUMMATIVE EVALUATION

Summative evaluations are used primarily to judge a staff member—the teacher or administrator—and come to some sort of conclusion. The process is familiar, resulting in a decision based on the competencies of the individual. Unlike formative evaluation, summative evaluation may not require any sort of relationship between the staff member and the evaluator, and the evaluation process is often brief and focused (Barrett; Anderson).

Summative evaluations are used to make various decisions such as promotion or demotion, pay raises or bonuses, and other decisions important to the school. The process of summative evaluation is focused on how the individual performs in his or her daily tasks, rather than improving performance; there is an end result to the evaluation procedure.

EVALUATING THE TEACHER

Teacher quality is one of the foremost indicators of student success (Darling-Hammond). Thus, the most basic reason for evaluating teachers is to ensure that students are learning and that a school is successfully meeting its goals. Today, more than ever before, teachers are being charged with the responsibility of educating tomorrow's workforce, and the public demands accountability from their educators. Teacher performance evaluations are seen as a critical element in school accountability and improvement today (Glickman, Gordon, & Ross-Gordon, 2004; Patty, 2007).

Early on in American education, teachers were supervised and evaluated because the profession was seen as needing close inspection. Today, the focus has shifted: the literature and research largely focuses on using evaluation in order to help teachers develop their professional skills, enabling them to improve their methods and reach their instructional goals (Sullivan & Glanz). Today, teachers are most often evaluated by their principals or other administrators in the school, and methods can vary widely from the familiar classroom observation to walk-throughs or action research.

OBSERVATION

The most basic form of evaluation is classroom observation, in which a teacher prepares a lesson, and their supervisor sits in to view them. Observation can have various facets, and can be a tool for formative or summative evaluation. Many individuals will likely associate observation with discomfort and feelings of having to prove themselves—receiving a "grade" as a teacher (Marshall, 2005; Dudney, 2002). There are methods of observation, however, that can be a used for formative evaluations as well. For example, when a teacher and supervisor engage in pre- and post-observation discussions regarding the teacher's goals, strengths, and weaknesses, the process is less about a decision on a score or ranking and more about the goal of improvement. This latter procedure of observation, in which teachers are heavily involved in the process, is based on a clinical supervision model, developed in the 1960s under the idea that teachers should employ the practice of goal-setting (Aseltine, Faryniarz, & Rigazio-DiGilio, 2006; Sullivan & Glanz).

ACTION RESEARCH

Many schools also employ evaluation tactics such as action research. Here, colleagues in a school work together to study conditions within their school and make improvements in teaching based on their research (Glickman et al.).

WALK-THROUGHS

In walk-throughs, groups of teachers visit other teachers' classrooms to gain an idea of their teaching methods and theories on learning (Sullivan & Glanz). Schools may further engage in tactics such as teacher mentoring programs or coaching programs in which more experienced teachers help less experienced teachers improve their instructional methods and reach their goals.

Evaluating teachers can be a complex process. A school must think about balancing development opportunities for teachers with ensuring that teachers are performing up to standards. Schools may choose to employ various types of evaluation, depending on needs and goals. Many types of evaluation used today allow teachers to be supervised by individuals other than their principals. This helps principals empower other teachers as leaders, as well as to foster group development and teamwork in a traditionally isolated profession.

EVALUATING THE PRINCIPAL

The abilities of a principal in a school have a large impact on the success of that school in fostering student learning and improving student outcomes (Peterson). In an era in which research has confirmed lasting inequities in education, especially among minority and/or low income families, the competencies of leaders is especially important to student learning and the success of a school. While principal evaluation has a shorter history than evaluating teachers, recent research points to the importance of evaluating principals. However, the research is still sparse. Much of the evaluation procedures for principals is based on leadership research in other organizations, rather than on actual educational leaders (Green, 2004).

Just as a variety of people can be involved in the evaluation of teachers, different groups can also be involved in principal or other administrator evaluation. Principals may be evaluated by the district their school resides in or the teachers of the school they lead. For example, confidential staff surveys in which the school's teachers rate the principal on various aspects of the job (such as leadership capabilities or relationship building skills) may be used to give school districts information on their principals, and provide feedback to the principal based on the survey results (Anderson). Today, the two most common forms of principal evaluation are

- Rating scales;
- Management by objectives (Green).

RATING SCALE

A rating scale evaluation involves a form that a school district creates based on its needs. The form lists a variety of objectives, the principal is made aware of the expectations, and the form will be completed by the principal's supervisor. The results are discussed between the two after the evaluation. The items on the list may vary from district to district. While the rating scale process is easy to manage and implement, many principals do not report that it actually helps to improve their performance as leaders of a school (Green).

MANAGEMENT BY OBJECTIVES

Management by objectives, the second most common form of principal evaluation, involves setting goals, establishing incentives, and then discussing the progress on these goals with a supervisor after the proper time period has passed. There are advantages and disadvantages to this approach. While it involves principals in the process of evaluation, and helps them improve their skills, it also has the potential to lead to an increased focus on reaching short-term goals rather than the bigger picture (Green).

OTHER METHODS

Other evaluation practices for principals include
- 360 degree evaluation;
- Assessment centers;
- Portfolios.

In the first principals are evaluated by a number of those who work with them. For example, evaluators may include teachers, other principals, and the district supervisors. Assessment centers use simulations to "test" principals on certain matters associated with their work. Portfolios may contain self-reflections, plans for professional development, and evidence of leadership collected by the principal (Green).

While the research on principal evaluation is scarce, we do know that principals prefer to be involved in the evaluation processes, in development and participation. Studies show that principals often prefer hybrids of various methods, rather than a single assessment tool (Green).

Research on principal evaluation is not as abundant or transparent. However, it is apparent that effective principals are crucial to student learning. It is further evident that today's principals are tasked with an incredible undertaking: running the day to day operations of a school, supporting a large number of teachers, answering to parents and the community, as well as their supervisors—the school district.

VIEWPOINTS

Working and teaching in a school is traditionally a highly stressful occupation, associated with elevated levels of isolation and depersonalization, often leading to burnout (Hastings & Bham, 2003). Education professionals who leave their school or the profession often cite that their school had a clear hierarchy, they felt underappreciated from their superiors, or expectations were not clear (Bryne, 1998; Friedman, 1991). Research has found that while strategies such as salary increases may help promote teaching as a profession, the most effective tool to combat high attrition levels in education is to implement strategies that improve the conditions in which teachers work—the culture of the school, and giving individuals input on various decisions (Friedman & Farber, 1992).

Education is one of the best predictors of success that we have. Today's economy relies on a well-educated work force. Individuals who receive an education not only earn more over a lifetime, but also live longer, have better health, rely on social and welfare programs at a lower rate, and are less likely to end up in jail (Geske & Cohn, 1998). The inequities that are largely present in education can be addressed by employing proficient professionals in our schools. Teacher quality is the foremost indicator of how much students learn, and whether they will have positive experiences in school. School leadership is also crucial to improving educational outcomes for students.

Evaluation of the staff in schools is one method by which to address these issues. While school professionals must certainly be held accountable for whether students are learning, the other aspect of evaluation, professional development, is one that often goes overlooked. One of the foremost questions regarding performance evaluations in schools is whether the two branches—formative and summative—are complementary. Many researchers argue that it is important that districts and schools use both approaches in order to improve schools and hold them accountable. Summative evaluations are essential for providing meaningful evidence that schools are doing what they are supposed to do. On the other hand, formative evaluations enhance the experience of teaching and ensure that schools and districts are putting their resources into improvement, guiding teachers and administrators rather than letting them flounder (Anderson).

Effective evaluation takes time and effort. Evaluation not only reveals the skills and leadership capabilities of school professionals; it can promote their expertise, develop leadership, and further career goals. The research on evaluating teachers shows that principals are the central individuals in establishing effective evaluation processes based on a culture of mutual respect and collaboration for teachers in schools (Glanz, Shulman, & Sullivan, 2007). However, evaluation is no easy task for principals. Many are too busy with other areas of running the school to effectively evaluate teachers over the course of a school year. Formative evaluation especially takes a large amount of time and effort, over the course of a longer period. If the teachers in the school are inexperienced, the task falls even more heavily on school administration rather than other teachers to provide feedback and professional development opportunities to teachers.

Green reasons that it is important that school evaluations are clear and involve the parties they are supervising. For example, principals should know what the expectations for their job entail, and how they will be evaluated on them. They should also be involved in planning the evaluation—setting goals and discussing how to reach them. The same should be true for teachers. Teachers need to have a voice in how evaluations take place, and their role in them. Evaluation should also address local needs, and requires a commitment of time and resources from a number of parties. Once committed, these resources should be used efficiently (Barrett). In the most effective schools, evaluations can help improve teaching methods, leadership skills, the school culture, and in turn positively impact student learning. Often effective evaluation procedures will help address other issues such as isolation and a lack of understanding of expectations that battle the attrition issue for teachers and principals. Evaluation is not an easy task; organizations struggle with it constantly. However, evaluation is a valuable investment for schools, and results in exceptional returns for school professionals and their students.

TERMS & CONCEPTS

Assessment Centers: Assessment centers use simulations to test principals on every day aspects of their job.

Formative Evaluation: Formative evaluation is a type of evaluation that is used to help teachers and administrators improve the skills important to their position.

Observation: Observation is a type of evaluation in which teachers are observed by supervisors. This type of observation can be formative or summative.

Portfolio: Portfolios are used in evaluations to help individuals self-reflect, set goals, and provide proof of their accomplishments.

Professional Development: Professional development refers to activities that improve various skills or continue the education of an individual within a school. Opportunities may include classes, lectures, or trainings.

Reliability: Reliable results from evaluation are consistent—if similar tests are given to similar individuals, you get the same results each time.

Summative Evaluation: Summative evaluation is used to make a decision regarding school professionals.

Teacher Quality: Teacher quality is one of the best predictors of student achievement. Evaluation today is often aimed at improving teachers' skills.

Rana Suh

BIBLIOGRAPHY

Anderson, M.E. (1989). Evaluating principals: Strategies to assess and enhance their performance. *OSSC Bulletin, 32.*

Aseltine, J.M., Faryniarz, J.O., & Rigazio-DiGilio, A.J. (2006). *Supervision for learning.* Alexandria, VA: Association of Supervision and Curriculum Development.

Barrett, J. (1986). *The evaluation of teachers.* Washington, DC: ERIC Clearinghouse on Teacher Education. (ERIC Document Reproduction Service No. ED278657). Retrieved October 30, 2007, from EBSCO Online Education Research Database.

Benedict, A.E., Thomas, R.A., Kimerling, J., & Leko, C. (2013). Trends in teacher evaluation. *Teaching Exceptional Children, 45,* 60-68. Retrieved December 15, 2013, from EBSCO Online Database Education Research Complete.

Bolton, D.L. (1980). *Evaluating administrative personnel in school systems.* New York: Teachers College Press.

Connecticut Principals' Academy. (1990). *A Guide to the Process of Evaluating School Principals. Monograph No. 2.* East Lyme, CT: Author (ERIC Document Reproduction Service No. ED 319141). Retrieved October 30, 2007, from EBSCO Online Education Research Database.

Darling-Hammond, L. (1998). *Investing in quality teaching: State-level strategies 1999.* Education Commission of the States.

Darling-Hammond, L., Wise, A.E., & Pease, S.R. (1983). Teacher evaluation in the organizational context: A review of the literature. *Review of Educational Research, 53,* 285-328.

Darling-Hammond, L., Amrein-Beardsley, A., Haertel, E., & Rothstein, J. (2012). Evaluating teacher evaluation. *Phi Delta Kappan, 93,* 8-15. Retrieved December 15, 2013, from EBSCO Online Database Education Research Complete.

Dudney, G.M. (2002). *Facilitating teacher development through supervisory class observations.* Washington, DC: U.S. Department of Education, Office of Educational Research and Improvement. (ERIC Document Reproduction Service No. ED 469715). Retrieved October 9, 2007, from EBSCO Online Education Research Database.

Friedman, I.A., & Farber, B.A. (1992). Professional self-concept as a predictor of teacher burnout. *Journal of Education Research, 86,* 28-35.

Geske, T.G. and E. Cohn (1998). Why is a high school diploma no longer enough?: The economic and social benefits of higher education. In: R. Fossey & M. Bateman (Eds.), *Condemning students to debt, College loans and public policy.* New York: Teachers College Press.

Glickman, C.D., Gordon, S.P., & Ross-Gordon, J.M. (2004). *SuperVision and instructional leadership, brief edition.* Upper Saddle River, NJ: Allyn & Bacon.

Green, J.E. (2004). *Evaluating principals: Issues and practices.* Bloomington, IN: Phi Delta Kappa Educational Foundation.

Hastings, R.P., & Bham, M.S. (2003). The relationship between student behaviour patterns and teacher burnout. *School Psychology International, 24,* 115-127.

Mangiante, E. (2011). Teachers matter: Measures of teacher effectiveness in low-income minority schools. *Educational Assessment, Evaluation & Accountability, 23,* 41-63. Retrieved December 15, 2013, from EBSCO Online Database Education Research Complete.

Marshall, K. (2005). It's time to rethink teacher supervision and evaluation. *Phi Delta Kappan, 86,* 727-735. Retrieved October 9, 2007, from EBSCO Online Database Academic Search Premier.

Nolin, M.J., Rowand, C., & Farris, E. (1994). *Public elementary teachers' views on teacher performance evaluations.* Washington, DC: National Center for Education Statistics.

Patty (2007). New study highlights role of principal. *International Educator, 21,* 28-28. Retrieved October 9, 2007, from EBSCO Online Database Education Research Complete.

Paige, M. (2013). Applying the "paradox" theory: A law and policy analysis of collective bargaining rights and teacher evaluation reform from selected states. *Brigham Young University Education & Law Journal,,* 21-43. Retrieved December 15, 2013, from EBSCO Online Database Education Research Complete.

Peters, S. (1988). *State-mandated principal evaluation: A report on current practice.* Paper presented at the Annual Meeting of the American Educational Research Association, New Orleans, Louisiana.

Peterson, D. (1991). *Evaluating principals.* Eugene, OR: ERIC Clearinghouse on Educational Management. (ERIC Document Reproduction Service No. ED 3300064). Retrieved October 30, 2007, from EBSCO Online Education Research Database.

Sullivan, S., & Glanz, J. (2004). *Supervision that improves teaching: Strategies and techniques.* Thousand Oaks, CA: Corwin Press.

SUGGESTED READING

Bell, C.R. (1996). *Managers as mentors: Building partnerships for learning.* San Francisco: Berrett-Koehler Publishers.

Brown, G., & Irby, B.J. (1997). *The Principal Portfolio.* Thousand Oaks, CA: Corwin Press.

Marshall, K. (2005). It's time to rethink teacher supervision and evaluation. *Phi Delta Kappan.* 727-735.

Pfeiffer. Millman, J. & Darling-Hammond, L. (1990). *The new handbook of teacher evaluation: Assessing elementary and secondary school teachers.* Newbury Park, CA: Sage Publications.

Piro, J., Weimers, R. & Shutt, T. (2011). Using student achievement data in teacher and principal evaluations. *International Journal of Educational Leadership Preparation.* 6(4).

Razik, T.A., & Swanson, A.D. *Fundamental concepts of educational leadership and management.* Englewood Cliffs, NJ: Prentice-Hall.

Slaughter, C.H. (1989). *Good principals, good schools: A guide to evaluating school leadership.* Holmes Beach, FL: Learning Publications, Inc.

Viles, J. & Bondi, J. (2004) *Supervision: A guide to practice* (6th ed.). Upper Saddle River, NJ: Merrill Prentice Hall.

TEACHER SUPERVISING

The supervision of teachers has been a consistent expectation in schools across the country. The methods used and the goals achieved through supervision vary widely, including increasing teacher quality and autonomy, and improving professional development and school culture. Methods used by administrators in supervising teachers include observation, action research, walk-throughs, and various group development approaches. Effective supervision has the power to improve student outcomes, as well as improve other issues such as teacher retention and reducing teacher burnout.

KEYWORDS: Action Research; Clinical Supervision; Observation; Group Development; Instructional Leadership; Professional Development; Supervision; Teacher Autonomy; Teacher Quality; Teacher Supervision; Walk Through

OVERVIEW

The methods and policies used by administrators supervising teachers in schools vary widely, from the reasons why teachers are supervised, to the methods and policies that are used for supervision. The most basic reason for teacher supervising is to ensure the success of a school. School success criteria in the United States are not universally agreed upon; individual schools and districts define success in different ways, and engage in various methods to achieve their goals (Glickman, Gordon, & Ross-Gordon, 2004).

In the early history of American education, supervision of teachers was mostly performed by local authorities, and teachers often had a large amount of autonomy over their schools. In the late 19th century, schools became much more organized due to a call for education to meet the demands of a newly industrialized nation. By the end of the 19th century, one role of the superintendent encompassed teacher supervision. At this time, those who were in the teaching profession were largely seen as unskilled and needing someone to watch over them to ensure they did not fail (Sullivan & Glanz).

At the beginning of the 20th century, schools began to employ the use of individuals they called "special supervisors" to assist teachers in their lessons and subjects. A "general supervisor," the precursor to today's assistant principal or vice-principal, performed administrative duties and also helped evaluate teachers by collecting data during supervisory tasks (Sullivan & Glanz).

GOALS FOR TEACHER SUPERVISION

The goals of supervising teachers have changed. Today's educational goals largely revolve around the improvement of teaching in order to improve student outcomes. The research and literature on teacher supervision today largely focuses on how to help teachers develop professionally, as well as solve problems and issues in the classroom and the school. Educational success in the United States today is increasingly measured through high-stakes testing, and students are expected to be on par with certain standards. Researchers largely agree that teacher quality is the foremost indicator of student success, regardless of other barriers (Darling-Hammond, 1998). Therefore, improving the quality of teaching is one of the foremost steps to help students from all backgrounds succeed. Furthermore, teacher accountability is seen as increasingly important, especially for schools that are failing to meet requirements for improvement. Schools may have differing mission statements or methods; however, teacher supervision occurs throughout most schools and teachers have some accountability in carrying out the learning goals of the institution, while also improving their skills as instructors.

Successful and valuable supervision today is usually charged with the task of helping teachers increase their effectiveness in instruction, and ensuring that all teachers are aligned in their instructional methods in meeting the school's goals, rather than finding fault. Research has shown that effective supervision in schools is crucial to other elements contributing to learning, including professional development, classroom management, and curriculum and instruction, and that effective supervision of teachers can help raise the academic outcomes of a school (Glickman et al.; Patty, 2007).

Teacher supervision today can be very simple or very complex. Supervision can be carried out directly through the administration, with the principal or assistant principal doing much of the direct supervising, or more indirectly, through approaches such as mentoring or action research, in which other, usually more experienced teachers may be involved in the supervision of newer teachers. Schools may also use hybrids of these techniques—using both direct and indirect supervision techniques. Policies on supervision of teachers may come from a more centralized authority, such as the school district or superintendent, or be left up to individual schools and their administrators.

Teacher supervising methods are diverse and dependent upon the school needs and school culture. Individual supervision includes methods such as observation and individual conferences with teachers. Other approaches include walk-throughs, mentoring and peer coaching programs, and action research.

OBSERVATION

Dudney (2002) describes a model of teacher supervision in American schools that is perhaps most familiar to the: the principal sits in the back of the classroom while a lesson is going on; the teacher has prepared a lesson beforehand; the principal provides a write up, perhaps makes some suggestions, and moves on to the next teacher.

Teaching has been traditionally an isolated career choice. Often the only observations or feedback that teachers receive are annual or bi-annual observations from their principals. These visits are usually announced, but at their simplest form, there is no pre-discussion and very little or no face-to-face follow up. These types of interactions have often produced atmospheres in schools in which observations are met with trepidation, discomfort, and ambiguity (Marshall, 2005; Dudney). However, while teacher observation is often seen as the most antiquated form of teacher supervising, and in some schools and districts still carries the stigma as a method of supervision that is constantly searching for mistakes that the teacher is making (Dudney), there are methods of observation that can be powerful tools for improving instruction, and empowering teachers

to become actively engaged in their own learning process (Sullivan & Glanz).

ISSUES WITH OBSERVATION

There are many issues with using teacher observation as a form of supervision, especially if the goal is to provide teachers with concrete, useful feedback and create a culture of assessment and improvement. Principals can often only evaluate a tiny percentage of a teacher's classes per year, and these small subsets of evaluations often carry little weight. Furthermore, when teachers know they are being evaluated, they may prepare an elaborate lesson, or feel uncomfortable about the evaluation, giving the evaluator little insight into the true strengths and weaknesses of that teacher because the lesson observed is uncharacteristic. This is especially true if the teacher is uncertain about the expectations during the observation, or in their work (Marshall).

A TOOL TO IMPROVE INSTRUCTION

However, observing teachers can also be a powerful tool for improving instruction. Teaching is a difficult skill that can be constantly refined. Observation from a supervisor can be beneficial to teachers and a school in many ways. Perhaps the most important factor is ensuring that a teacher does not see class observation as an opportunity to unfairly criticize or find mistakes. Rather, in an ideal situation, the teacher and supervisor will become partners in improvement through constructive criticism, goal-setting, and support. This approach may be more difficult than it sounds, because not all teachers may buy into or believe in the goals of the observation. Teachers who are resistant to the method, or find it hard to reveal their opinions to a supervisor may have had negative experiences with supervision in the past (Glickman et al.).

A COMPREHENSIVE APPROACH

Dudney encourages an approach to observation in which the teacher and supervisor engage in pre-observation discussions, conferring to determine the focus of the evaluation, and the methods by which information will be collected. During the evaluation, the supervisor will collect the data, focusing on the previously discussed and agreed upon focus. Afterwards, the teacher and supervisor meet and discuss the observation, the supervisor provides feedback, and together they set goals for further evaluations.

This method of evaluation is certainly more time-intensive and difficult than simply filling out a form with no face-to-face interaction; however, the rewards of this type of observation can be much more beneficial. Observation may be most helpful to newer teachers with less experience, as it provides an opportunity for self-reflection and critique in the most crucial years of their development as a beginner teacher.

CLINICAL SUPERVISION

The type of observation that Dudney describes falls under the umbrella of clinical supervision, developed in the 1960s on the basis that teachers should set goals and be assessed on these goals using various methods (Aseltine, Faryniarz, & Rigazio-DiGilio, 2006; Sullivan & Glanz). Successful clinical supervision is dependent upon several factors: it is goal oriented and intent upon improving both the individual teachers and the school; there must be a high degree of mutual trust between the teachers and observers, as well as a commitment to carrying out the mission of the school; the observers must have a high degree of expertise in teaching and learning methods in order to provide feedback (Sullivan & Glanz).

INDIVIDUAL CONFERENCES

Conferences entail sitting down with a supervisor, usually a principal or an assistant principal, and discussing issues of personal professional development, as well as classroom issues. Meetings are usually held one-on-one and it is important to note that, much like clinical supervision, trust must be established between the teacher and supervisor for the conferences to be fruitful—that they are helping teachers solve problems and develop better teaching and classroom practices (Garubo & Rothstein, 1998).

Conferences must be carefully planned by both parties involved: how often they will meet, what the goals are, and what the role of the supervisor will be. For more novice teachers, supervisors may take a larger lead in making suggestions or giving options. In another conferencing relationship, in which the teacher is more experienced, the supervisor may simply act as a sounding board or guide to help the teacher in certain issues. Practiced and competent supervisors will assist their teachers in

answering the questions that improve their teaching—their motivations, strengths, weaknesses—as well as the requisite needs of their students (Garubo & Rothstein).

Individual conferences with teachers on a regular basis can go a long way in another realm of school issues—the isolation that is so prevalent in schools. Through these conversations and goal-setting meetings, teachers will not feel detached and alone in dealing with their problems and triumphs in the classroom.

WALK-THROUGHS

Walk-throughs are a type of supervisory tool that is more indirect than observations or conferences. The walk-through helps reduce the isolation of teachers in the classroom, displays and discusses what they are doing well, and what they can improve on. The requirements of successfully implementing walk-throughs as a supervision method are similar to that of clinical supervision—mutual trust, a culture of collaboration, and an understood mission (Sullivan & Glanz).

There are many models of walk-throughs; however, there are characteristics that they share. Walk-throughs often occur on a professional development day in which students are absent from the building. On the designated day, teachers visit assigned classrooms, review student work, and look for proof that students are learning according to the school's mission. Teachers may view student portfolios, lesson plans, or other aspects of the classroom. Afterwards, teachers meet and discuss the observations, and some sort of observation is given back to the principal or administration (Sullivan & Glanz).

This method has several goals and benefits. One of the primary goals is to reduce isolation of teachers that is so prevalent in many schools. Another is a professional development opportunity—learning from teachers around them, and relating what one individual is doing to another in the same building. If successful, the walk-through can provide validation, constructive criticism, valuable new ideas, as well a sense of connection to other teachers and administrators in the institution. Walk-throughs may also occur during class time, in which teachers are observed by other groups of teachers, or teachers take over each others' classes to learn or teach various methods (Sullivan & Glanz).

GROUP DEVELOPMENT

One of the most underrated tasks of a supervisor is fostering leadership ability in others. Researchers often call for increased autonomy and leadership opportunities for teachers. These leadership tasks often come up the most when teachers work in groups. Improving group dynamics is a crucial task in supervision of teachers, especially in many models of instruction today that stress teamwork and collaboration. An effective supervisor must be able to foster group activity, while dealing with conflicts that are sure to arise.

Supervisors may use various tasks to foster group development:

- They may create teams of teachers within schools to address various issues such as curriculum and instruction or other school issues such as disciplinary procedures (Glickman et al.);
- Teachers may supervise other teachers in teams;
- Mentoring or peer coaching programs may be instituted (Sullivan & Glanz).

ACTION RESEARCH

Action Research is a practice in which colleagues in a school study the conditions within their institution in order to make improvements in teaching and learning (Glickman et al.). The concept stems from the ideas of Kurt Lewin, a social scientist who believed that research should not be conducted in the vacuum of a laboratory, but should focus on reflection on actions, and whether these actions improve the quality of life (Lewin, 1948). The theory is applied to education by asking teachers and administrators to evaluate and reflect on teaching and learning in the classroom.

Action research allows the supervisor to empower teachers to improve the school. It requires the supervisor to engage at various levels—from the beginning teacher to the teacher who is already an established leader, and choose an appropriate strategy for improving the school, while enhancing leadership skills in others (Glickman et al.).

The tasks of action research vary and include selecting a focus area, designing a plan, carrying out that plan, and evaluation. The process often takes a significant period of time, and may result in considerable changes in the school. The role of the supervisor in action research is to provide teachers with enough information and guidance so that they are successful. This may include a variety of tasks: convincing some teachers that this is the right course of action, providing instruments to gather and analyze data, and providing the time and resources to teachers when they run into issues or problems they need to solve (Glickman et al.).

ISSUES

Glickman et al. call successful supervision the "glue of a successful school"—a practice that has enormous potential to improve teacher instruction, and consequently student achievement, throughout an entire institution. However, it is not an easy task to bridge the gap between simply supervising teachers and using supervision techniques to meet goals such as improving student outcomes, or improving individual teaching skills.

SUPERVISION & LEADERSHIP

Supervision that achieves these goals requires the supervisor to have a wide breadth of knowledge about teaching and how to improve teaching, interpersonal skills, the ability to steer a group towards a common goal, and the skills to develop leadership in others. Patty reported on a study of principals which found that in addition to effective teachers, principals who were less bogged down in the daily administrative tasks of running a school and were more concerned with and involved in improving classroom practices could positively impact student achievement. Schools with leaders who were open to change, and made teacher improvement their first priority, led schools in which students were achieving at high rates.

Glanz, Shulman, & Sullivan (2007), in a case study which was part of a three-part study of supervision and leadership, found that principals are central to establishing a culture of empowering teachers and cultivating an ethos of collaboration. A principal who is dealing with the breadth of individual personalities and competency levels of various teachers may need different supervision styles based on the individual they are supervising. Glickman et al. write of a variety of approaches and techniques based on the goals the supervisor is attempting to accomplish and the individual teachers' competency levels. The researchers stress the importance of moving towards teacher autonomy and leadership; however, they recognize that certain situations and individuals require more decisive supervision than others.

IMPROVING STUDENT OUTCOMES

The research suggests that effective teacher supervision can directly improve student outcomes. In a case study of three schools—urban, rural, and suburban—Aseltine et al. found that using the classroom data garnered from supervising teachers and applying that data to promote learning opportunities for teachers universally raised student test scores, aligned professional development, and increased the capacity for decision making and intervention for teachers on behalf of their students.

However, Marshall reminds us that supervision often fails to achieve this goal. Reasons include that principals are often too busy to effectively evaluate teachers and that evaluations often do not focus on student learning. Today there is greater pressure than ever, especially in public schools, to improve student achievement or face consequences. Schools face penalties, which do not create a situation for improving learning opportunities for teachers; rather, the supervision process may be fraught with nervousness and covering flaws rather than fixing them.

TIME CONSTRAINTS

Today's principals, the primary supervisors in public schools, often have a Herculean task in simply running the day to day operations of a school. Supervision takes a large amount of time when the supervisor performs cursory evaluations; in-depth supervision and support takes even more time and effort, even when supervisors delegate these tasks to others in the school. The hurdles that supervisors face in schools and from the outside are often barriers to effective supervision. Principals may be bogged down by other responsibilities that take up much of their time. Many unions have kept teacher supervision from becoming a part of teacher's evaluation (Aseltine et al.); furthermore, the culture and conditions of a school play a large role in how effective supervision of teachers can be at raising student achievement and professionally developing teachers to become more effective classroom instructors.

The goals of teacher supervision are varied. However, in the most effective schools, school leaders use supervision to improve teaching methods, and in turn further foster student learning. Effective supervision may have other benefits that improve schools, including higher teacher retention, more focused professional development, and a better understood school culture because supervision techniques can often help alleviate symptoms such as isolation and lack of understanding regarding a teacher's role and responsibility, which lead to high attrition rates and burnout (Gold, 1984). Supervising teachers effectively can have a direct impact on the success of a child's education.

TERMS & CONCEPTS

Action Research: Action research is a type of supervision in schools in which members of the institution study the conditions within the school in order to make improvements to teaching and learning.

Clinical Supervision: Clinical Supervision is a type of supervision in which teachers set goals and are assessed on these goals through observation by and discussion with their supervisor.

Group Development: Group development includes tasks such as mentoring or peer coaching, in which teachers often supervise each other, or work in groups to improve teaching and learning.

Instructional Leadership: Instructional leadership is a type of leadership practiced by principals in which they are more involved in classroom practices and improving teaching in the classroom.

Observation: Observation is the most familiar type of teacher supervision in schools, where supervisors sit in and observe classes taught by teachers, and then give feedback in one way or another.

Professional Development: Professional development refers to activities that improve various skills or continue the education of an individual within a school. Opportunities may include classes, lectures, or trainings.

Teacher Autonomy: Teacher autonomy occurs when teachers reach a level of expertise that grants them more independence or self-sufficiency in classroom matters. Many researchers argue that increasing teacher autonomy should be a goal of administrators who supervise teachers.

Teacher Supervision: Teacher Supervision refers to a variety of methods supervisors use to ensure teachers are measuring up the standards set by the school or district. Teacher supervision may also be used to improve teaching methods and student outcomes.

Walk-Through: Walk-through is a method of supervision in which groups of teachers visit assigned classrooms, review student work, and meet to discuss observations.

Rana Suh

BIBLIOGRAPHY

Aseltine, J. M., Faryniarz, J. O., & Rigazio-DiGilio, A. J. (2006). *Supervision for learning.* Alexandria, VA: Association of Supervision and Curriculum Development.

Bullock, S. (2012). Creating a space for the development of professional knowledge: A self-study of supervising teacher candidates during practicum placements. *Studying Teacher Education: Journal of Self-Study of Teacher Education Practices, 8,* 143–156. Retrieved December 15, 2013, from EBSCO Online Database Education Research Complete.

Darling-Hammond, L. (1998). *Investing in quality teaching: State-level strategies 1999.* Denver, CO: Education Commission of the States.

Dudney, G. M. (2002). *Facilitating teacher development through supervisory class observations.* Washington, DC: U.S. Department of Education, Office of Educational Research and Improvement. (ERIC Document Reproduction Service No. ED469715). Retrieved October 9, 2007, from EBSCO Online Education Research Database.

Garubo, R. C., & Rothstein, S. W. (1998). *Supportive supervision in schools.* Westport, CT: Greenwood Publishing Group, Inc.

Glanz, J., Shulman, V., & Sullivan, S. (2007). *Impact of instructional supervision on student achievement: Can we make the connection?* Chicago, IL: Annual Meeting of the American Educational Research Association (AERA). (ERIC Document Reproduction Service No. ED496124). Retrieved October 9, 2007, from EBSCO Online Education Research Database.

Glickman, C. D., Gordon, S. P., & Ross-Gordon, J. M. (2004). *SuperVision and instructional leadership, brief edition.* Upper Saddle River, NJ: Allyn & Bacon.

Gold, Y. (1984). Burnout: A major problem for the teaching profession. *Education, 104,* 271–275. Retrieved September 15, 2007, from EBSCO Online Database Academic Search Premier.

Hine, G. C., & Lavery, S. D. (2014). Action research: Informing professional practice within schools. *Issues in Educational Research, 24,* 162–173. Retrieved November 3, 2014, from EBSCO online database Education Research Complete.

Kalule, L., & Bouchamma, Y. (2013). Supervisors' perception of instructional supervision. *International Studies In Educational Administration (Commonwealth Council For Educational Administration & Management (CCEAM)), 41,* 89–104. Retrieved November 3, 2014, from EBSCO online database Education Research Complete.

Lewin, K. (1948). *Resolving social conflicts.* New York, NY: Harper and Brothers.

Marshall, K. (2005). It's time to rethink teacher supervision and evaluation. *Phi Delta Kappan, 86,* 727–735. Retrieved October 9, 2007, from EBSCO Online Database Academic Search Premier.

Moss, C. M., & Brookhart, S. M. (2013). A new view of walk-throughs. *Educational Leadership, 70,* 42–45. Retrieved December 15, 2013, from EBSCO Online Database Education Research Complete.

Patty, A. (2007). New study highlights role of principal. *International Educator, 21,* 28. Retrieved October 9, 2007, from EBSCO Online Database Education Research Complete.

Range, B., Scherz, S., Holt, C., & Young, S. (2011). Supervision and evaluation: The Wyoming perspective. *Educational Assessment, Evaluation & Accountability, 23,* 243–265. Retrieved December 15, 2013, from EBSCO Online Database Education Research Complete.

Rooney, J. (2005). Teacher supervision: If it ain't working… *Educational Leadership, 63,* 88–89. Retrieved October 9, 2007, from EBSCO Online Database Academic Search Premier.

Sullivan, S., & Glanz, J. (2004). *Supervision that improves teaching: Strategies and techniques.* Thousand Oaks, CA: Corwin Press.

SUGGESTED READING

Acheson, K., & Damien, G. M. (1997). *Techniques in the clinical supervision of teachers* (4th ed.). New York, NY: Longman.

Bell, C. R. (1996). *Managers as mentors: Building partnerships for learning.* San Francisco, CA: Pfeiffer.

Fantozzi, V. B. (2013). "Oh God, she is looking at every little thing I am doing!" student teachers' constructions of the observation experience. *Current Issues in Education, 16,* 1–13. Retrieved November 3, 2014, from EBSCO online database Education Research Complete.

Firestond, W. A., & Riehl, C. (Eds). (2005). *A new agenda for research in educational leadership.* New York, NY: Macmillan.

Hesselbein, F., Goldsmith, M., & Bechard, R. (1996). *The leader of the future: New visions, strategies, and practices for the next era.* San Francisco, CA: Pfeiffer.

Ingersoll, R. (2003). *Who controls teachers' work: Power and accountability in America's schools.* Cambridge, MA: Harvard University Press.

Viles, J., & Bondi, J. (2004) *Supervision: A guide to practice* (6th ed.). Upper Saddle River, NJ: Merrill Prentice Hall.

CLASSROOM AUTONOMY

It has been contended that professional autonomy enhances efficiency because employees are given more decision-making power over their own activities (Luthans, 1992, as cited in Gawlik, 2007). Educational organizations have moved toward granting more teacher autonomy since the 1960s, giving instructors more control over their curriculum (Tamir, 1986, as cited in Gawlik). A more decentralized management of schools has meant that instructors have been more involved in a school's decision-making processes and management than in the past. However, while some instructors embrace teacher autonomy and want the freedom that comes along with it, other instructors may view their own autonomy as a way for principals and administrators to avoid doing what they are paid to do (Frase & Sorenson, 1992, as cited in Pearson & Moomaw, 2006).

KEYWORDS: Centralized Management; Classroom Autonomy; Curriculum; High-Stakes Testing; Job Satisfaction; Motivation; No Child Left Behind Act of 2001; Standardized Testing; Standards-Based Curriculum; School-Based Management; Teacher Autonomy

OVERVIEW

Autonomy is an abstract concept. By definition, it generally means individual freedoms or rights. For public school instructors, it can have a variety of meanings and there can be a range of degrees of teacher autonomy; the highest degree being complete freedom and the lowest degree being absolutely no freedom. Classroom autonomy can refer to instructors having control over specific aspects of their work life such as scheduling, the curriculum, textbooks used in class, and instructional planning.

Just as instructors can have autonomy, so can schools. An autonomous school is one that governs itself; defines its own goals, develops its own programs and plans to achieve its goals (Carlos & Amsler, 1993, as cited in Gawlik). An autonomous school has complete control over personnel, including who to hire, who to let go, and how much to pay (Briggs & Wohlstetter, 1999, as cited in Gawlik). These schools also have sole discretion over professional development opportunities, curriculum and instruction, how

funds are allocated, and how instructors will teach (Gawlik). Autonomous schools also have complete control over the students they serve (Horn & Miron, 2000, as cited in Gawlik), which effectively rules out public school as being completely autonomous. Autonomous schools are generally private schools, as government funding demands government oversight and regulation.

Between 1983 and 1985 there were still many regulations established by states, and more than 700 statutes were enacted by state legislators. These laws effectively took away a lot of authority that traditionally belonged to instructors, principals, school districts, and parents by regulating instructors and schools, which affects classroom autonomy (Futrell, n.d., as cited in Hicks & DeWalt). The next movement of education reform brought about efforts for instructors, principals, superintendents, school boards, parents, and business and community leaders to work collaboratively to improve their schools and students' education (Hicks & DeWalt).

It has been contended that professional autonomy enhances efficiency because employees are given more decision-making power over their own activities (Luthans, as cited in Gawlik). Educational organizations have moved toward granting more teacher autonomy since the 1960s, giving instructors more control over their curriculum (Tamir, as cited in Gawlik). A more decentralized management of schools has meant that instructors have been more involved in a school's decision-making processes and management than in the past. Therefore, teachers are now participating in issues that were once solely a principal or administrator's responsibility, such as budgeting, resource allocation, and finance (Gawlik). However, while some instructors embrace teacher autonomy and want the freedom that comes along with it, other instructors may view their own autonomy as a way for principals and administrators to avoid doing what they are paid to do (Frase & Sorenson, as cited in Pearson & Moomaw).

PERCEPTIONS OF AUTONOMY: PRINCIPALS & TEACHERS

Perception can also play a role in determining teacher autonomy in schools. Hicks and DeWalt present a recent survey of elementary school teachers and principals that looked at the differences in teacher and principal perceptions when it comes to teacher autonomy in the classroom. When it came to teacher involvement in determining the curriculum at their schools, 62 percent of teachers and almost 94 percent of principals felt that teacher were involved in curriculum decisions. Every principal that responded to the survey and 86 percent of the elementary teachers felt that instructors were sometimes to almost always involved in deciding on other instructional materials. A little over 61 percent of the teachers surveyed felt that they were seldom or almost never involved in setting student promotion and retention policies whereas almost 73 percent of principals felt that they were sometimes to almost always involved in setting the policies (Hicks & DeWalt).

Another area where the teachers and principals disagreed was in setting standards for student behavior. Every principal surveyed and only 58 percent of the teachers felt that they were involved in setting these standards. Principals and instructors also differed in their opinions on setting school and school district goals. Almost 91 percent of principals felt that teachers were sometimes to almost always involved in goal setting while only 45 percent of teachers felt that they were involved in the process (Hicks & DeWalt).

Perceptions of the degree of classroom autonomy attained are also related to factors within each instructor's work environment but not factors such as academic ability, quality of prior training, and years of experience (Pearson & Hall, 1993, as cited in Pearson & Moomaw). One area where high school instructors seem to have a great deal of autonomy in their classrooms nationwide is with respect to grades. According to a 1997 College Board survey of high schools, almost 85 percent of those schools surveyed reported that instructors could award any distribution of grades they chose to base on student performance. While 85 percent of the high schools surveyed allowed their instructors complete autonomy over grades and grading, only 6.6 percent required their instructors to follow general guidelines and 3.5 percent required their instructors to follow strict guidelines regarding grade distribution (Boston, 2003).

There have been many documented studies that indicate that what constitutes teacher autonomy has changed a lot over the years and continues to change, especially with the passage of the No Child Left

Behind Act and increased use of standardized tests. An older concept of teacher autonomy was based on independence through isolation and alienation. A more recent concept views teacher autonomy as being based on collaborative decision making and the freedom to make professional choices concerning what services are given to students (Willner, 1990, as cited in Pearson & Moomaw). While government mandates seem to be firmly in place, instructors are becoming more involved in the general administration of the school itself. Many instructors feel that they are qualified to be involved in the instructional process because they have expertise in specialized fields, that they have the right to coordinate how learning occurs in their classrooms, and that they formulate their own personalized rules in their classrooms (Pearson & Moomaw).

EFFECTS OF NO CHILD LEFT BEHIND

School districts determine how much classroom autonomy instructors have based on how specific they are about the curriculum. Instructors will have less autonomy the more specific the curriculum is. If there are no curriculum mandates, then instructors will have total autonomy and can teach whatever they want. If a district has adopted very specific curriculum standards that note what is to be taught, how it should be taught, and when it should be taught, then teachers have little autonomy over curriculum. In the past, most school districts have allowed extensive autonomy in the classroom. However, since the No Child Left Behind Act and the era of high-stakes testing, more districts have found it necessary to implement curriculum restrictions because of the ramifications if schools and districts do not meet the new mandates. With curriculum requirements being implemented to make sure all competencies are addressed in the classroom, teachers find themselves with less control over what happens in their own classrooms. Those districts that are reluctant to infringe on teacher autonomy in the classroom and yet still want to make sure all the standards are met may make sure that instructors know what will be covered on the high-stakes tests and leave the how and when the material will be taught up to each instructor's discretion (Squires, 2004).

Teacher authority and autonomy can be diminished by a standards-based curriculum and the focus on high-stakes testing performance. Standards-based education makes instructors accountable for making sure their students meet specified standards. These standards are now often predicated on student performance on high-stakes tests. Now, student performance on such tests can have negative impact on students, instructors, schools, and school districts if adequate yearly progress has not been made (Tutwiler, 2005). Proponents of the No Child Left Behind Act have noted that high-stakes test results provide instructors with invaluable information about how well their students are doing so that they can adjust their teaching accordingly. Thus, they still have classroom autonomy (Seaton, Dell'Angelo, Spencer & Youngblood, 2007).

In the advent of high-stakes testing, instructors often take the brunt of criticism if their students do not perform well on standardized tests. Those who oppose such high-stakes testing note that it causes a loss of teacher autonomy and creativity-and even threatens their status as professionals-because they need to be concerned about test scores and focus instruction on meeting those test competencies. High-stakes testing is also considered a threat to teacher autonomy because school districts can mandate approaches to teaching, such as declaring that phonics must be the approach instructors use to try to improve students' reading ability. This further diminishes teacher autonomy because instructors cannot choose which methods they want to use in the classroom (Tutwiler).

DECENTRALIZED MANAGEMENT & TEACHER AUTONOMY

School processes and activities can be divided into two separate entities:

- **School wide,** which consist of administrative activities such as management, planning, budget, and resource allocation;
- **Classroom,** which consist of teaching and educational activities (Barr and Dreeben, 1983; Lortie 1969, 1975, as cited in Ingersoll, 1996).

To determine how centralized or decentralized a school is can be judged by how much autonomy teachers have over educational matters in their classrooms. Instructors who have high levels of autonomy over issues of classroom instruction are considered to be more decentralized (Firestone 1985; Meyer & Scott, 1983, as cited in Ingersoll). Schools that give instructors a greater say and more influence in school-wide decisions and policy matters are also more decentralized than those that do not (Ingersoll).

Research over the past 20 years has shown that authority has been shifting from individual schools to a more centralized model (Allington, 2002a, 2002b; Berliner, 1997; Hoffman, 2000, as cited in Moloney, 2006). This shift has brought about external control over the education process and limited teacher autonomy in the classroom (Allington, 2002b, as cited in Moloney), by focusing on identifying teaching programs instead of promoting effecting classroom techniques (Duffy & Hoffman, 1999, as cited in Moloney). This has brought about the contention that these authorities have focused on developing a "teacher-proof" curriculum (Allington, 2002b; Shannon, 2000, as cited in Moloney), which takes away teacher autonomy in the classroom (Allington, 2002b, as cited in Moloney).

Proponents of giving instructors more influence and increase in teacher autonomy note that instructors will make better informed decisions about educational issues than district or state officials because they are in the classroom. It is also noted that decisions coming from the top to those in the field generally fail because they do not have the support of those who are responsible for implementing the decisions (Ingersoll & Alsalam, n.d., as cited in Pearson & Moomaw). In a survey completed by the National Center for Education Statistics, a nationally representative sample of instructors was asked to determine their influence on classroom and school-wide issues. Instructors who responded to the survey indicated that they felt their influence was pretty much limited to classroom issues like textbook adoption and teaching strategies (Shen, 1998, as cited in Pearson & Moomaw). However, collaborative autonomy in schools can be seen where instructors work with the school's administration to make decisions about curriculum, instruction, and scheduling (Willner, as cited in Pearson & Moomaw).

TEACHER ACCOUNTABILITY

There are some who believe that if instructors are to be empowered and viewed as professionals then they need to have the freedom to do what they deem appropriate for their students and not be required to abide by other dictates (Pearson & Moomaw). If teachers are to be held accountable, they should have a great deal of autonomy. It is not fair to impose accountability without autonomy, just as it is not a good idea to give teachers too much autonomy over decisions for which they will not be held accountable (Gawlik). However, with the passage of the No Child Left Behind Act, specific expectations have been stated and need to be achieved in order to avoid the ramifications of not meeting adequate yearly progress. It is up to school administrators and districts to work with instructors to ensure that the balance of teacher autonomy and government mandates with respect to student achievement can work together in the classroom.

Viewpoints

CLASSROOM AUTONOMY AS A LEGAL RIGHT

For the most part, classroom autonomy is not considered a valid legal defense for teachers who have been dismissed. With few exceptions, the courts side with the school boards as long as their decisions are not attained by any way that implies inappropriate motives on the board's part. Interpretation of court cases regarding public school curricula is on the school board's side, which means that an instructor usually does not have the right to use classroom materials that the school board finds objectionable or inappropriate; and that continued use of material that has been considered objectionable or inappropriate could result in the instructor being dismissed based on continued insubordination. This was noted in the Supreme Court case *Board of Education, Island Trees v. Pico*. This particular court decision also included language that indicated boards of education should have formal procedures in place for solving curriculum conflicts and any challenge to a teacher's decisions in the classroom (Sacken, 1989).

Local school boards can also implement an approval process for deciding if classroom materials are appropriate and can be used in the classroom, which also severely limits teacher autonomy. This can be interpreted to mean that instructors may have autonomy over curriculum in their classrooms as long as there are not official, comprehensive policies or procedures instituted by their school boards or states. Depending on legal interpretation and the comprehensiveness of school board policies, teachers may still have substantial autonomy in their classrooms. However, with most court cases being decided in favor of the school board, classroom autonomy appears to be more of a privilege than a legal right (Sacken).

CLASSROOM AUTONOMY & TEACHER MOTIVATION/ JOB SATISFACTION

Classroom autonomy is one common element that shows up when exploring instructors' thoughts on teacher motivation, job satisfaction, stress levels, instructor burnout, professionalism, and teacher empowerment (Brunetti, 2001; Kim & Loadman, 1994; Klecker & Loadman, 1996; Ulriksen, 1996, as cited in Pearson & Moomaw). Many researchers have found that instructors need to have autonomy for increased motivation and job satisfaction and lower stress levels and job burnout (Erpelding, 1999; Jones, 2000; Wilson, 1993, as cited in Pearson & Moomaw). Teacher autonomy also appears to be a key variable when education reform policies are debated (Pearson & Moomaw). While teacher autonomy has been "a common link that appears when examining teacher motivation, job satisfaction, stress (burnout), professionalism, and empowerment," there are very few studies that specifically address teacher autonomy because autonomy can be difficult to separate from other factors (Pearson & Hall, as cited in Pearson & Moomaw).

In looking at what motivates instructors both intrinsically and extrinsically, intrinsic motivations included a desire to help their students achieve, wanting to make a difference in society, and having a feeling of satisfaction when their students learn. Extrinsic motivations included the pay received, non-monetary fringe benefits, and recognition of good performance (Ashbaugh, 1982; DeJesus, 1991; Dinham & Scott, 1996; Farrar, 1981; Firestone & Pennell, 1993; Picard, 1986; Porter, 1993; Swanson & Koonce, 1986, as cited in Pearson & Moomaw). In a 1981 study, the National Institute of Education found that overall intrinsic rewards were a better motivating factor for instructors than extrinsic rewards. Three major intrinsic reasons why instructors decide to quit teaching are:

- The need for personal growth;
- A desire for a philosophy of education;
- A lack of respect and recognition of their efforts in the classroom (Brown, 1996, as cited in Pearson & Moomaw).

Five main intrinsic reasons why instructors decide to remain in the teaching profession are:

- A love of learning;
- Their love for children;
- Resilience;
- Collegiality;
- Reflectivity (Sarafoglu, 1997, as cited in Pearson & Moomaw).

With teacher autonomy being one component of teacher motivation (Khmelkov, 2000; Losos, 2000; White, 1992, as cited in Pearson & Moomaw), analyses of instructor job satisfaction and dissatisfaction have been undertaken. Studies have shown that the degree of teacher autonomy perceived by instructors is an indication of their job satisfaction level (National Center for Education Statistics, n.d.; Charters, 1976; Franklin, 1988; Gnecco, 1983; Hall, Villeme & Phillippy, 1989; Pearson & Hall, as cited in Pearson & Moomaw). One report on job satisfaction noted administrative "support and leadership, good student behavior, positive school climate, and teacher autonomy as working conditions that are most associated with teacher satisfaction" (Perie & Baker, 1997, as cited in Pearson & Moomaw. Other researchers have found that a lack of autonomy is related to tension, frustration, and anxiety among instructors (Bacharach, Bauer & Conley, 1986; Blase & Matthews, 1984; Cedoline, 1982; Dinham & Scott, 1996; Dworkin, Haney, Dworkin & Telschow, 1990; Evers, 1987; Lortie; Natale, 1993; Woods, 1989; Yee, 1991, as cited in Pearson & Moomaw).

TERMS & CONCEPTS

Classroom Autonomy: Classroom autonomy can include instructors having control over specific aspects of their work life with respect to scheduling, curriculum, textbooks adoption, and instructional planning.

Curriculum: Curriculum refers to the entire body of courses taught to students.

High-Stakes Testing: High-stakes testing is the use of test scores to make decisions that have important consequences for individuals, schools, school districts, and/or states and can include high school graduation, promotion to the next grade, resource allocation, and instructor retention.

No Child Left Behind Act of 2001 (NCLB): The No Child Left Behind Act of 2001 is the latest reauthorization and a major overhaul of the Elementary and Secondary Education Act of 1965, the major federal law regarding K-12 education.

Standardized Testing: Standardized testing is the use of a test that is administered and scored in a uniform manner, and the tests are designed in such a way that the questions and interpretations are consistent.

Standards-Based Curriculum: Standards-based curriculum sets academic standards for what students should learn and be able to do with clear, measurable outcomes for students.

Sandra Myers

BIBLIOGRAPHY

Boston, C. (2003). *High school report cards.* Retrieved October 11, 2007, from Education Resources Information Center, http://eric.ed.gov.

Dierking, R.C., & Fox, R.F. (2013). "Changing the way I teach": Building teacher knowledge, confidence, and autonomy. *Journal of Teacher Education, 64,* 129-144. Retrieved December 15, 2013, from EBSCO Online Database Education Research Complete.

Gawlik, M. (2007). Beyond the charter schoolhouse door. *Education & Urban Society, 39,* 524-553. Retrieved October 11, 2007, from EBSCO Online Database Academic Search Premier.

Hicks, G. & DeWalt, C. (2006). *Teacher empowerment in the decision making process.* Retrieved October 11, 2007, from Education Resources Information Center, http://eric.ed.gov.

Ingersoll, R. (1996). Teachers' decision-making power and school conflict. *Sociology of Education, 69,* 159-176. Retrieved October 11, 2007, from EBSCO Online Database Education Research Complete.

Moloney, K. (2006). Teaching to the test. *International Journal of Learning, 13,* Research Complete.

Ostovar-Namaghi, S. (2012). Constraints on language teacher autonomy: A grounded theory. *TESL Reporter, 44,* 37-55. Retrieved December 15, 2013, from EBSCO Online Database Education Research Complete.

Pearson, L. & Moomaw, W. (2006). Continuing validation of the teaching autonomy scale. *Journal of Educational Research, 100,* 44-51. Retrieved October 30, 2007, from EBSCO Online Database Academic Search Premier.

Robertson, L., & Jones, M. (2013). Chinese and US middle-school science teachers' autonomy, motivation, and instructional practices. *International Journal of Science Education, 35,* 1454-1489. Retrieved December 15, 2013, from EBSCO Online Database Education Research Complete.

Sacken, D. (1989). Rethinking academic freedom in the public schools: The matter of pedagogical methods. *Teachers College Record, 91*, 235-255. Retrieved October 11, 2007, from EBSCO Online Database Education Research Complete.

Seaton, G., Dell'Angelo, T., Spencer, M. & Youngblood, J. (2007). Moving beyond the dichotomy: Meeting the needs of urban students through contextually relevant education practices. *Teacher Education Quarterly, 34*, 163-183. Retrieved October 11, 2007, from EBSCO Online Database Education Research Complete.

Squires, D. (2004). *Aligning and balancing the standards-based curriculum.* Thousand Oaks, CA: Corwin Press.

Tutwiler, S. (2005). *Teachers as collaborative partners: Working with diverse families and communities.* New York, NY: Routledge.

SUGGESTED READING

Blase, J. & Blase, R. (2000). *Empowering teachers: What successful principals do.* Thousand Oaks, CA: Corwin Press.

Ingersoll, R. (2003). *Who controls teachers' work? Power and accountability in America's schools.* Cambridge, MA: Harvard University Press.

Sparks, D. & Malkus, N. (2015). Public school teacher autonomy in the classroom across school years 2003-04, 2007-08 and 2011-12. *National Center for Education Statistics, 23* pp.

Vangrieen, K. (2017). Teacher autonomy and collaboration: A paradox? Conceptualizing and measuring teachers' autonomy and collaborative attitude. *Teaching and Teacher Education, 67, 302-315.*

Westheimer, J. (1998). *Among school teachers: Community, autonomy, and ideology in teachers' work.* New York, NY: Teachers College Press.

SCHOOL CULTURE AND SCHOOL REFORM EFFORTS

School culture is defined differently, but it generally refers to the values, practices, and actions of any particular school community, including the students, teachers, administrators, and related stakeholders, such as parents. School culture came to be defined as an essential contributing factor in school reform efforts, as it explains differences in the success in implementing some types of reforms across schools, and in enhancing student performance. It can enhance reform or be a barrier to change, depending on the nature of the culture of the school, and how thoroughly cultural issues have been considered in the reform and implementation processes.

KEYWORDS: Administrators; Anthropology; Collegiality; Cultural Capital; Education Reform; Leadership; Professionalization of Teaching; School-Based Management; School Culture; School Reform; Social Capital; Stakeholders

OVERVIEW

WHAT IS SCHOOL CULTURE?

School culture is defined differently, but it generally refers to the values, practices, and actions of any particular school community, including the students, teachers, administrators, and related stakeholders, such as parents. The extent to which any one of those groups is involved in determining or contributing to

school culture is likely to vary from school to school, but all are involved. School culture can be viewed as either negative or positive; the former meaning it is a barrier to positive change and the latter meaning it either contributes to increased productivity on the part of participants (teachers and students especially) and /or contributes to increased satisfaction on the part of participants. In essence, school culture moves away from short-term targeted issues such as test scores and achievement, and is instead about the people in and around the school; the ways in which they relate to one another, group expectations about the way things are done, and the ultimate outcomes of their actions.

School culture came to be defined as an essential contributing factor in school reform efforts, as it explains differences in the success in implementing some types of reforms across schools, and in enhancing student performance. It can enhance reform or be a barrier to change, depending on the nature of the culture of the school, and how thoroughly cultural issues have been considered in the reform and implementation processes.

The Center for Improving School Culture (2007) lists several more-specific definitions of school culture, reflecting some variations among theorists on the subject. School culture, broadly defined, encompasses everything that happens within and relating to the school, and the attitudes and responses of everyone within the greater school community to those events.

A Model for School Reform

At a more theoretical level, the concept of school culture as described by Deal and Petersen (1990) is seen as a model to approaching school change, from among five possible model options, including:

- A human resources model, which focuses on the competencies and needs of educators;
- A structural model, focusing on how schools are structured and operate;
- A political model, based on the relationships of powerful stakeholders in the school community;
- A free market model, emphasizing school choice and free market principles;
- A school culture model, and anthropology-based model that considers a holistic view of the school including all stakeholders (Deal & Peterson).

Any one of the above school culture models encompasses elements of all the other models as well; making it greater than the sum of the parts.

Like any culture, Deal and Peterson suggest the culture of a school is "the character of a school as it reflects deep patterns of values, beliefs and traditions that have been formed over the course of its history." That character is then revealed or disseminated among community participants through "symbolic language and expressive action."

WHY IS SCHOOL CULTURE IMPORTANT?

Deal and Peterson note that "institutions work best when people are committed to certain commonly held values and are bonded to one another" (p. 9). To the extent that the school community can experience that commonality and bonding, it is thought that the performance of its members can be improved. If teachers, staff, students, administrators, and parents are striving towards common ideals and the rituals, daily actions, and rhetoric of the school community reflects that striving, then the school is regarded as having a "positive" culture, which is considered likely to enhance performance and overall satisfaction of its stakeholders.

Deal and Peterson suggest that productivity, which might be defined in terms of student achievement, student learning, teacher satisfaction, or in some other way, is related to certain elements of strong institutional culture. In schools, they specify that a positive culture involves:

- Strong values;
- An emphasis on basic skills for all students;
- High expectations for all students;
- Strong leadership;
- Shared beliefs throughout the school;
- Good role models;
- An atmosphere that is orderly, while not oppressive.

According to Boyd (2007), other elements that enhance cultural internalizing are:

- Common language;
- Criteria for inclusion and exclusion: clear boundaries;
- Ideology;
- Power and status structure;
- Rewards and punishments;
- Rules for understanding relationships.

These positive elements, they state, can lead to better outcomes, such as:

- Improved test scores;
- Improved morale of teachers;
- Reduced staff turnover;
- Community satisfaction with the program.

However, Deal & Peterson note that in order to see such improvements, in addition to a strong school culture, "instructional curricular and economic systems must run smoothly."

Fullan (1999), however, who has written extensively on leadership and change, recommends assessing improvement in terms of how well educational leaders have been groomed, prepared and encouraged to continue and sustain the process of improvement, and to prepare other leaders.

HISTORY OF THE SCHOOL CULTURE CONCEPT

School culture came to be studied in depth during discussion of education reform in what became known as the second wave of reform policy-in which teachers began to be viewed as critical participants in the reform process.

Bates (2006) describes the history of educational reform theory throughout the 20th century, indicating that theories moved from a bureaucratic, leadership-focused model, to a more inclusive model, with a greater focus on culture than authoritarianism. He writes, "It is this dialogue between institutional and personal authority, the battle between bureaucracy and culture, which has characterized the debate over the nature, purpose and effectiveness of leadership in education for the past century." He goes on to describe the school as a "nexus" for cultural struggle both within the school community and reflecting the larger community within which the school operates, and cautions that improvement in schools can only occur if the interconnecting relationships among all participants, communities, and inter-related cultures, are considered in the context of all the others, and a climate of continual learning is understood throughout.

Deal and Peterson concur that it is essential to understand both the school *and* the local community culture, and how they interact. And they emphasize the challenges in addressing school cultural reforms. Any kind of culture, they report, is "deeply rooted" by nature, and thus must be considered carefully, and respected for its strengths, before introducing elements of change.

Bates describes schools as operating under two distinct pressures: the pressure of market forces, and economic pressure to improve, against the pressure of existing school cultures that may be resistant to change. He recommends, therefore, a comprehensive understanding of the forces acting upon schools and their stakeholders.

AN ANTHROPOLOGICAL PERSPECTIVE

Bates argues that Fullan and Deal and Peterson brought many ideas about leadership and executive or corporate culture into the realm of education, but suggests that an even deeper, more anthropological understanding of the meaning of culture is necessary to truly understand how school culture can lead to change. He notes also that while school culture can certainly be influenced by its leaders and staff, it cannot be controlled by them, and that an anthropological perspective of culture is more all-encompassing, much more complex and interrelated with other factors, and more about understanding than control. He references the work of Bowles and Gintis, and Bourdieu, relating school culture to national culture, and issues of race, class, social capital, and cultural capital. Fullan's work also emphasizes the

importance of context, and levels of context (including state, district, community) in understanding and implementing reform in schools.

Various theorists (and failed reform efforts along the way) suggested that reform imposed from above may be less successful than reform implemented by teachers themselves. Subsequent investigations into school culture, and the possibility of changing an individual school's culture, began to be explored.

OTHER MODELS OF SCHOOL REFORM

Hess (1991) describes three models of school improvement:

- Technical transfer, in which the knowledge of researchers and academics is passed along to schools;
- Professionalization, which emphasizes teacher knowledge and power;
- Client empowerment, in which parents and the community take on the authority to change schools, as in Chicago's school-based management programs.

Several useful sources defining culture and why it is important to consider school culture when considering school reform, are cited and described by Boyd. She reports that, among staff, professional collaboration, affiliative or collegial relationships and feelings of efficacy and self-determination are essential to developing a "learning community," in which both students and staff are committed to a process of continuous learning and improvement. Fullan agrees that "collaborative schools or "professional learning communities" are essential for success" in reforming schools.

Muijs, Harris, Chapman, Stoll, & Russ (2004) report that a number of other factors are also implicated in successful reform, including a blame-free atmosphere allowing constructive criticism; coherent policies and rules; collaboration among staff and other members of the community; and high expectations for all students.

Kelleher and Levinson (2004) report that "for culture to change in a school or school district, teachers, principals and other staff must relate to each other in different ways and actually do something differently." This is challenging, but the payoff is high, as "cultural change in work activities is deep and lasting. It requires time and team building, often through recruiting people who have a shared vision and dedication to implement it." Kelleher and Levinson report that it seems easier to build a culture of shared decision-making than one of shared accountability. Some administrators, they note, are breaking large urban schools into smaller school communities, but they emphasize that this will likely only succeed if the same principles are applied to culture changes as in large schools.

HOW CAN SCHOOL CULTURE IMPROVE?

Peterson and Deal report that by introducing new rituals, symbols, language and action, culture within a school *can* be changed although change may be gradual, and may differ from school to school.

Wagner (2005) summarizes various studies of culture-based reform and concludes that the following factors must also be in place for reform of school culture to be effective:

- The culture must be assessed; and participants must feel they have efficacy and self-determination around the reform process;
- Analysis of the needs of the school must occur;
- Only a few areas should be targeted for improvement at a time; not all change can occur at once;
- The process should be closely monitored and adjusted if not successful.

THE ROLE OF ADMINISTRATORS

Early models of reform (technical transfer) ascribed authority to academics, principals, and other administrators, as the arbiters of good management policy. In this model, those authority figures were given the role of assessing what reforms were needed, disseminating information as necessary, and implementing reforms.

Challenges arose as teachers resisted the imposition of rules from above, and school cultures often proved immutable. Muijs et al. report that distributed demographic forms of leadership, rather than a single leader, have been found to be most successful in encouraging reform. This led to the development of more teacher-based models of change.

THE ROLE OF TEACHERS

Professionalization of teaching became a rallying point in school reform, and teachers began to be perceived as being at least as essential to the change process as leaders, administrators, and other authority figures in the education process. Muijs et al. summarize findings on the effectiveness of creating "learning communities" among teachers in a school, and reflect that such communities can lead to longer-term sustained change than merely addressing single-target goals such as raising test scores. They may also reduce teacher turnover in low-performing schools, as teachers feel empowered and able to positively influence school culture and outcomes.

To become effectively engaged in the reform process, however, teachers must feel that their efforts are effective, that the intervention is effective, that they are involved in a learning community (with their peers), and that they are supported in their efforts by the school community (Muijs et al.). Continuous professional development-linked to school and embedded in the workplace is also essential for success.

Throughout the literature, collegiality (meaning teachers working together and sharing knowledge) and clear communication are mentioned as essential elements for teacher engagement in the reform process.

THE ROLE OF STUDENTS

Students *can* benefit from the change process, and may also be influential regarding successful implementation or failure. Wagner recommends that students (and parents) be informed about the reform process, be familiar with the expectations and goals of the school, and be invited to participate to enhance prospects of reform.

Boyd reports that "Just as the perceptions, attitudes, beliefs, and values of teachers impact change efforts, student beliefs and attitudes influence school improvement. Students must believe that they are respected as persons and that they are tied to the school." She notes that alienation and boredom can be reasons for student resistance, and that some students experience conflict between their school and home cultures, which can impede engagement in school culture and activities. If their efforts are recognized, however, and they feel that they have some impact on school culture and outcomes, they are more likely to engage in school processes.

Bissett, Markham, and Aveyard (2007) studied 25,000 students across the UK, and concluded that a positive school culture can reduce student drug and alcohol use. That, in turn, may contribute to better outcomes for students in those schools.

Peer culture is also a critical element in accepting change, or internalizing school culture as well, says Boyd. In addition, staff attention to student engagement in culture is essential. If students feel that the school's culture supports them, they are more likely to support and enhance that culture themselves.

THE ROLE OF PARENTS & THE COMMUNITY

Parents are also inherently involved in a school's culture, although the degree of their involvement may be influenced by the school, class and race issues, or other contextual variables. Boyd reports that school culture often reflects aspects of local culture, and schools must focus on the community outside the school as well as inside it when considering reforms.

Parents are considered to be essential to the change process in the more inclusive models of change, but not as critical in others. Muijs et al. describe varying involvement levels of parents in low-income schools in detail, reporting that some low-income schools attempt to reduce parent involvement as it can be considered detrimental to the effectiveness of the school. Schools in higher-income areas report positive effects of increased parental involvement. They conclude that although parents are inevitably involved, effective reform may require that parents be involved in culture change or reform somewhat later in the process in some schools than others, depending on the context of the community.

The rest of the community, including taxpayers and school board members, is also inherently involved in school culture. Boyd summarizes other authors who suggest that schools must be responsive to the community, and that those communities may or may not support reform efforts, and thereby have some influence. Like other aspects of cultural change, involving the community can be successful if it is inclusive, informative, and collegial as possible.

CONCLUSION

School culture is now widely accepted as a necessary element to consider when attempting to implement educational reforms. Although clear data on the impact of cultural change are difficult to find, some evidence shows that culture *can* be effectively changed, most often through a gradual and inclusive process, and can lead to improved outcomes in terms of student achievement, student behavior, staff turnover, staff satisfaction, leadership training, and school coherence.

Change is likely to be most successful if all stakeholders are informed about the change process and share a united vision of what the end results will be. Many theorists believe that early involvement of stakeholders at all levels can increase engagement in the process, while others suggest that some stakeholders (e.g., parents) may be brought in later in the process for maximum success. Continued engagement of all stakeholders in the process, with ongoing collaboration and communication, will help to develop the traditions, actions, language, and stories necessary to maintain the reformed culture. These help to maintain awareness of the actions necessary to maintain positive changes. If those positive actions are enhanced by rewards or incentives for participation, a school can maintain interest in, and support for, reforms as the process continues.

TERMS & CONCEPTS

Administrators: Here, administrators include school principals, vice principals, superintendents, and others who have policy-making and supervisory roles within an educational system.

Anthropology: Anthropology is the study of humans and humanity, and emphasizes long-term, immersed, ethnographic study with attention to context.

Collegiality: Collegiality refers to the inclusion of teachers in decision-making processes regarding school reforms.

Cultural Capital: Cultural capital is a term meaning any knowledge, education, or skill that gives one a higher status in society.

Educational Reform: Educational reform refers to the process of attempting to improve the educational process and/or administration of schools.

School-Based Management: School-based management is a reform concept focusing on the management of schools by parents, teachers, and other local stakeholders, rather than managed from above by other authorities.

Social Capital: Social capital refers to any resources gained from participation in particular social groups, such as neighborhoods, schools, communities.

Professionalization of Teaching: Professionalization of teaching refers to the idea that teachers, as a group, should be respected for their professional expertise just as doctors, lawyers, and other professionals; and that they should have a decisive role in determining and directing school outcomes, based on their knowledge and experience (rather than being directed by administrators, academics, or policy-makers.

Kirsty Brown

BIBLIOGRAPHY

Bates, R. (2006). Culture and leadership in educational administration: A historical study of what was and what might have been. *Journal of Educational Administration & History, 38,* 155-168. Retrieved October 30, 2007, from EBSCO Online Database Education Research Complete.

Bisset, S., Markham, W.A. & Aveyard, P. (2007). School culture as an influencing factor on youth substance use. *Journal of Epidemiology & Community Health, 61,* 485-490. Retrieved October 29, 2007, from EBSCO Online Database Academic Search Premier.

Boyd, V. (2007). *School context: Bridge or barrier to change?* Retrieved October 31, 2007, from Southwest Educational Development Laboratory, http://sedl.org.

Center for improving school culture. (2007). Retrieved October 31, 2007, from http://schoolculture.net.

Deal, T. E., & Peterson, K. D. (1990). *The principal's role in shaping school culture.* Office of Educational Research and Improvement, Washington, DC. Retrieved October 29, 2007, from http://eric.ed.gov.

Fullan, M. (1999.) *Change Forces: The Sequel.* Philadelphia, PA: Falmer Press.

Gomez, M., Marcoulides, G. A., & Heck, R. H. (2012). Examining culture and performance at different middle school level structures. *International Journal of Educational Management, 26,* 205-222. Retrieved December 15, 2013, from EBSCO Online Database Education Research Complete.

Hess, A. (1991.) *Chicago and Britain: Experiments in empowering parents.* (ERIC Document Reproduction Service No. ED334644).

Kelleher, P., & Levenson, M.R. (2004.) Can school culture change? *School Administrator, 61.* Retrieved October 31, 2007, from EBSCO Online Database Education Research Complete.

Lippy, D., & Zamora, E. (2012). Implementing effective professional learning communities with consistency at the middle school level. *National Forum of Educational Administration & Supervision Journal, 29,* 51-72. Retrieved

December 15, 2013, from EBSCO Online Database Education Research Complete.

Mujis, D. Harris, A., Chapman, C., Stoll, L., & Russ, J. (2004). Improving schools in socioeconomically disadvantaged areas - a review of research evidence. *School Effectiveness and School Improvement, 15,* 149-175. Retrieved October 31, 2007, from EBSCO Online Database Academic Search Premier.

Roberson, S. (2011). Defying the default culture and creating a culture of possibility. *Education, 131,* 885-904. Retrieved December 15, 2013, from EBSCO Online Database Education Research Complete.

Wagner, C. (2004/2005). Leadership for an improved school culture. *Kentucky School Leader.* Retrieved October 29, 2007, from Center for Improving School Culture, http://schoolculture.net.

SUGGESTED READING

Bower, H. & Parsons, E. (2016). Teacher identity and reform: Intersections within school culture. *The Urban Review.* 48(5), 743.

Brown, K. (2014). School culture & school reform efforts. In: *School Systems & Administration.,* p 55-60.

Fullan, M.G. (1991). *The new meaning of educational change* (2nd ed.). New York: Teachers College Press.

Fullan et al. (2000.) *The Jossey-Bass reader on educational leadership.* San Francisco, CA: Jossey-Bass Publishers, 2000.

Guidera, I.A. (2014). Principals Implementing Growth Mindset Norms: Insights on School Culture Reform. UCLA Education, http://escholarship.org.

Gruenert, S.& Whitaker, T. (2015) School Culture Rewired: How to Define, Assess and Transform It. ASCD.

Johnston, J.A., Bickel, W.E., & Wallace, Jr., R.C. (1990). Building and sustaining change in the culture of secondary schools. *Educational Leadership, 47,* 46-48. Retrieved October 31, 2007, from EBSCO Online Database Education Research Complete.

Krueger, J. P. & Parish, R. (1982). We're making the same mistakes: Myth and legend in school improvement. *Planning and Changing, 13,* 131-140.

Patterson, J.L., Purkey, S.C., & Parker, J.V. (1986). *Productive school systems for a nonrational world.* Alexandria, VA: Association for Supervision and Curriculum Development.

Sarason, S.B. (1996). *Revisiting the Culture of the school and the problem of change* (2nd ed.). Boston, MA: Allyn & Bacon.

Sarason, S.B. (1990). *The predictable failure of educational reform - Can we change course before it's too late?* San Francisco: Jossey Bass.

Sergiovanni, T.J. & Corbally, J.E. (1984). *Leadership and organizational culture.* Chicago, IL: University of Illinois Press.

SCHOOL CLIMATE

Components of school climate include leadership, quality of instruction, expectations, communication, and safety. School climate is critical to student success, and a demoralized or unsafe school climate degrades the ability of students to learn. To promote a positive school climate, schools need to place an emphasis on the positive psychological development of students, administrators, and staff. Intrinsic motivation to learn, positive school engagement, positive expectations, and gratitude are particularly important strengths for educators and parents to promote.

KEYWORDS: Authoritative; Autonomy Supportive Communication; Behavioral Engagement; Intrinsic Motivation to Learn; Positive Psychology; Response to Intervention (RtI); Self-Determination Theory

OVERVIEW

School climate entails the psychosocial environment that students and staff experience as they participate in daily life within the school building. School climate is important because a positive school climate can promote the mental health and academic success of students. On the other hand, a negative school climate can contribute to the development of boredom, apathy, anxiety, lowered attendance, and lower achievement. Some notions of school climate include the extent to which parents feel welcomed at school and trust staff; however, these signs of a healthy parent-school relationship are often studied separately from school climate (Froiland & Davison, 2014). School climate is influenced by a number of adult related factors, such as principal leadership, teacher communication style in the classroom, teacher stress, parental support of student's intrinsic motivation to learn and do homework at home, pressure from the school board and government to improve test scores, and the percentage of staff turnover each year.

Although adults play a crucial role in creating the school climate, students also have contributed in significant ways. For example, students are more likely to feel like they belong at school when they have satisfying social relationships with peers (Cemalcilar, 2010), even when accounting for the effects of relationships with adults, perceived levels of school violence, and the physical environment. The physical environment, e.g., clean restrooms, aesthetically pleasing buildings, ample space and ergonomically appropriate fixtures and furnishings for students so they don't feel crowded or uncomfortable (Cemalcilar), can facilitate a positive school climate, but positive psychological factors are necessary to create a strongly positive school climate. Peers also affect each other's motivation to learn, whether positively or negatively. Namely, if a student's good friends love learning, they are more likely to develop a stronger love for learning.

Berg & Cornell (2015) found that when students are authoritative (rather than controlling or passive), students are less aggressive and teachers experience less stress. Likewise, numerous studies have found that when teachers are controlling, students become less intrinsically motivated to learn and exhibit lower levels of classroom behavioral engagement (Froiland, 2014). Lower intrinsic motivation to learn and lower classroom engagement, in turn, lead to lower levels of achievement (Froiland, Mayor & Herlevi, 2015; Froiland & Oros, 2014). Furthermore, lower levels of intrinsic motivation to learn also put students at risk for anxiety and depression (Froiland, 2011), the feeling that they do not belong at school, and dropping out (Froiland, 2014).

APPLICATIONS

A large prevention program, Caring School Community, has been successful at reducing drug abuse, increasing intrinsic motivation to learn, and increasing the sense of school belonging by employing principles from self-determination theory (e.g., helping teachers to be autonomy supportive). The Caring School Community program also includes activities that build stronger relationships between students in different grade levels (Battistich, Solomon, Kim, Watson & Schaps, 1995). However, programs that focus on parental autonomy support and parent involvement (Froiland, 2014) should also be implemented, because parents play a crucial role in promoting student's intrinsic motivation to learn, classroom engagement, and expectations for succeeding in school and college (Froiland, Peterson & Davison, 2013). Each of these factors also promotes achievement, which predicts further engagement, attendance, and completion of high school (Froiland

& Leavitt, 2013). Furthermore, teachers are also influenced by students, rather than only vice versa (Froiland, 2014). Namely, when students come to school with lower levels of intrinsic motivation, they show signs of disinterest and apathy, which leads many teachers to respond, albeit ineffectively, with more controlling styles of teaching (e.g., making more demands, focusing students on tangible rewards, using harsher language, and showing less affection). Subsequently, students show even lower intrinsic motivation to learn, which leads to a negative spiral (Skinner & Belmont, 1993). Therefore, parents can contribute to school climate indirectly, by promoting a strong love for learning at home (Froiland, 2015).

School climate can feel like a nebulous term, but if school-wide preventive interventions are to be successfully implemented, it is important to measure the effects of those interventions. Furthermore, measures need to be utilized that help identify the strengths and weaknesses of a school, in terms of school climate, so that school psychologists, school administrators, and other members of school-wide teams know what aspects of climate require improvement. One measure that shows promise is the School Mental Health Capacity Instrument, which can be used to examine overall mental health capacity, as well as the following subscales: Prevention and Promotion, Early Recognition and Referral, and Intervention (Feigenburg, Watts & Buckner, 2010).

The Prevention and Promotion subscale seems especially useful, as it examines the extent to which schools support the development of resilience, identify students' strengths, and intentionally promote psychosocial health. However, there are many other aspects of school climate that one can assess and consider for potential interventions, such as the average level of happiness of teachers, administrators, support staff, and students. If the average level of happiness is not as high as one would like, there are numerous science-based interventions that promote the happiness of both students and adults, such as the gratitude journal, setting intrinsic life goals, mindfulness, practicing novel acts of kindness and sharing positive events (Froiland, 2014).

In order to strongly enhance school climate, it may be necessary to make sure that the intervention program is comprehensive, rather than focusing solely on students. For example, both teachers and students can benefit from employing the gratitude journal, but it is more common for schools to have only students write in them. Teachers could model engagement with the gratitude journal for their students by writing in theirs, whenever students are required to do so. Furthermore, this could help the teachers become happier and less likely to experience burnout and turnover. When implementing such a program, it is important to remember that schools are often pressured by the government to increase achievement scores. Thus, a savvy consultant or interventionist will find ways to help the school integrate Positive Psychology with learning. For example, teachers and students can both record their gratitude journals during literacy instruction, rather than trying to add gratitude journals to an already busy day (Froiland, Peterson & Smith, 2012).

Another important consideration for improving school climate in the United States is Response to Intervention (RtI). RtI involves three tiers. Tier 1 involves universal prevention programs to promote psychological health as well as high quality instruction, whereas tier 2 focuses on students at risk for academic and psychological disorders, and tier 3 focuses on those who are greatly struggling (Froiland, 2011b). School psychologists, consultants, school social workers, and others interested in helping a school enhance school climate, could speak the language of most schools by referring to a school climate intervention within tier 1 of the RtI framework. Within RtI a key emphasis is progress monitoring, which entails repeated measurement of response to science-based interventions. In fact, progress is often graphed so that one can see how the intervention or prevention program has an effect or not over time. Taking on the challenge of enhancing school climate is no easy task, so it would often be helpful to build team momentum by celebrating small victories, which are more likely to be noticed through rigorous ongoing data collection and graphing of results.

VIEWPOINTS

School climate is a rather ubiquitous term and significantly enhancing school climate in a school that is struggling requires a comprehensive approach. As mentioned before, it is not enough to focus solely on teacher-student relationships or even teacher and student well-being. Principals and other school administrators often exert a large influence on school climate. Helping them to improve may require the help of an appropriately trained psychological or organizational consultant. In some cases, helping principals and other school administrators to overcome controlling styles will help increase the engagement and happiness of both teachers and students. In other cases, principals, deans, athletic directors, and assistant principals may need to learn and master servant leadership skills, because teachers are more likely to be inspired by an administrator that demonstrates their passion for helping the school to improve, rather than interacting with staff in a hands-off way.

It is also important to recognize that peers influence each other and often come to school with social goals as well academic ones. Therefore, a wise school climate interventionist will evaluate and intervene (as indicated) in order to help students develop stronger positive relationships and spread prosocial values, such as treating others well, refraining from gossip, and a love for learning.

Another factor that may affect school climate requires thinking outside the walls of the school and outside of the homes of the students. Neighborhoods affect the development of children and youth, as well as the expectations and achievements that take place in schools (Froiland, Powell, Diamond & Son, 2013). For example, neighborhoods with signs of socioeconomic well-being and safety (e.g., many residents with a college education or beyond, a high percentage of occupied homes, and few residents below the poverty line) create conditions in which parents are more likely to encourage each other to get highly engaged with literacy at home and at school (Froiland et al., 2013). Furthermore, neighborhoods (including relatively impoverished neighborhoods) with greater social cohesiveness are more likely to have less crime and more support of healthy student development (Froiland, Powell & Diamond, 2014).

TERMS & CONCEPTS

Authoritative: Stemming from the parenting literature, it describes a style of interacting with children that entails high levels of warmth and sensitivity, accompanied by high levels of structure (e.g., clear expectations for children's behavior; Baumrind, 1991). Teachers can also interact with students in an authoritative way.

Autonomy Supportive Communication: Autonomy supportive communication involves helping children see the beauty in learning, explaining how

they could use what they learn to eventually help others, or pointing to the intriguing aspects of learning.

Behavioral Engagement: Paying attention in class, asking thoughtful questions, and otherwise carrying oneself in a way that indicates rich participation.

Intrinsic Motivation to Learn: Finding learning and studying interesting and enjoyable, or otherwise finding learning to be purposeful and related to psychological needs. For example, a high school student may enjoy learning chemistry because she views is as preparation for becoming a scientist that will help people through her research.

Positive Psychology: The science of developing happiness, engagement, and other positive psychological indicators. Positive Psychology is in stark contrast to traditional emphases on diagnosis of disorder and special education placement in schools.

Response to Intervention (RtI): An approach to helping children thrive that involves three levels of support: 1) school-wide prevention services that all students receive, such as all staff and students practicing the gratitude journal; 2) interventions for smaller groups of students designed to help students at risk for greater psychological or academic difficulty; and 3) Intense individualized psychological and academic interventions for students who do not improve enough in the context of high quality prevention and group interventions.

Self-Determination Theory: Deci and Ryan's well-supported theory that all people have a need for feeling connected to others, expressing their unique identity, and developing competence in various domains of life (Deci, Vallerland, Pelletier & Ryan, 1991). When these needs are met, students and teachers are much more likely to enjoy school, be highly engaged with school, and be happy.

John Mark Froiland, PhD

BIBLIOGRAPHY

Battistich, V., Solomon, D., Kim, D., Watson, M., & Schaps, E. (1995). Schools as communities, poverty levels of student populations, and students' attitudes, motives, and performance: A multilevel analysis. American Educational Research Journal, 32, 627–658.

Baumrind, D. (1991). The influence of parenting style on adolescent competence and substance use. Journal of Early Adolescence, 11 (1), 56–95.

Berg, J. K., & Cornell, D. (November 2, 2015). Authoritative school climate, aggression toward teachers, and teacher distress in middle school. School Psychology Quarterly. Retrieved January 12, 2016, from http://psycnet.apa.org.

Cemalcilar, Z. (2010). Schools as socialisation contexts: Understanding the impact of school climate factors on students' sense of school belonging. Applied Psychology, 59(2), 243–272. Retrieved January 12, 2016, from EBSCO Online Database Education Research Complete.

Deci, E. L., Vallerand, R. J., Pelletier, L. G., & Ryan, R. M. (1991). Motivation and education: The self-determination perspective. Educational Psychologist, 26(3/4), 325–346. Retrieved January 12, 2016, from EBSCO Online Database Education Research Complete.

Feigenburg, L. F., Watts, C. L., & Buckner, J. C. (2010). The school mental health capacity instrument: Development of an assessment and consultation tool. School Mental Health, 2, 142–154.

Froiland, J. M. (2011). Parental autonomy support and student learning goals: A preliminary examination of an intrinsic motivation intervention. Child and Youth Care Forum, 40, 135–149. Retrieved January 12, 2016, from EBSCO Online Database Education Research Complete.

Froiland, J. M. (2011). Response to intervention as a vehicle for powerful mental health interventions in the schools. Contemporary School Psychology, 15, 35–42. Retrieved January 12, 2016, from EBSCO Online Database Education Research Complete.

Froiland, J. M. (2014). Inspired childhood: Parents raising motivated, happy, and successful students from preschool to college. Seattle, WA: Amazon.

Froiland, J. M. (2015). Parents' weekly descriptions of autonomy supportive communication: Promoting children's motivation to learn and positive emotions. Journal of Child and Family Studies, 24, 117–226. Retrieved January 12, 2016, from EBSCO Online Database Education Research Complete.

Froiland, J. M., & Davison, M. L. (2014). Parental expectations and school relationships as contributors to adolescents' positive outcomes. Social Psychology of Education, 17, 1–17.

Froiland, J. M., & Leavitt, R. (2013). Racial inequality: High school dropout rates. In J. Ainsworth (Ed.), Sociology of Education: An A-to-Z Guide (pp. 636–637). Thousand Oaks, CA: Sage Publications. Retrieved January 1, 2016, from http://knowledge.sagepub.com.

Froiland, J. M., Mayor, P., & Herlevi, M. (2015). Motives emanating from personality associated with achievement in a Finnish senior high school: Physical activity, curiosity, and family motives. School Psychology International, 36(2), 207–221. Retrieved January 12, 2016, from EBSCO Online Database Education Research Complete.

Froiland, J. M., & Oros, E. (2014). Intrinsic motivation, perceived competence and classroom engagement as longitudinal predictors of adolescent reading achievement. Educational Psychology, 34, 119–132. Retrieved January 12, 2016, from EBSCO Online Database Education Research Complete.

Froiland, J. M., Peterson, A., & Davison, M. L. (2013). The long-term effects of early parent involvement and parent expectation in the USA. School Psychology International, 34, 33–50. Retrieved January 12, 2016, from EBSCO Online Database Education Research Complete.

Froiland, J. M., Powell, D. R., & Diamond, K. E. (2014). Relations among neighborhood social networks, home literacy environments, and children's expressive vocabulary in suburban at-risk families. School Psychology International, 35(4), 429–444. Retrieved January 12, 2016, from EBSCO Online Database Education Research Complete.

Froiland, J. M., Powell, D. R., Diamond, K. E., & Son, S.-H. (2013). Neighborhood socioeconomic well-being, home literacy, and early literacy skills of at-risk preschoolers. Psychology in the Schools, 50, 755–769.

Froiland, J. M., Smith, L., & Peterson, A. (2012). How children can be happier and more intrinsically motivated while receiving their compulsory education. In A. Columbus (Ed.), Advances in Psychology Research, Vol. 87 (pp. 85–112). Hauppauge, NY: Nova Science.

Skinner, E. A., & Belmont, M. J. (1993). Motivation in the classroom: Reciprocal effects of teacher behavior and student engagement across the school year. Journal of Educational Psychology, 85, 571–581.

SUGGESTED READING

Eyal, O., & Roth, G. (2011). Principals' leadership and teachers' motivation: Self-determination theory analysis. Journal of Educational Administration, 49(3), 256–275.

Lazowski, R. A., & Hulleman, C. S. (December 1, 2015). Motivation interventions in education: A Meta-analytic review. Review of Educational Research. Retrieved January 1, 2016 from http://rer.sagepub.com.

Lindstrom Johnson, S., Pas, E. & Bradshaw, C.P. (2016). Understanding the association between school climate and future orientation. Journal of Youth and Adolescence. 45(8), 1575-1586.

Malone, M. Cornell, D., & Shukla, K. (2017). Association of grade configuration with school climate for 7th and 8th grade students. *School Psychology Quarterly.* 32(3), 350-366.

Mitchell, M. M., Bradshaw, C. P., & Leaf, P. J. (2010). Student and teacher perceptions of school climate: A multilevel exploration of patterns of discrepancy.

Journal of School Health, 80(6), 271–279. Retrieved January 12, 2016, from EBSCO Online Database Education Research Complete.

Zullig, K. J., Koopman, T. M., Patton, J. M., & Ubbes, V. A. (2010). School climate: Historical review, instrument development, and school assessment. Journal of Psychoeducational Assessment, 28(2), 139–152.

"SICK" SCHOOL BUILDINGS

The pollution and toxic problems of public school buildings can make students and school staff sick. Information about the causes of sick building syndrome and mold are also included in this article, as well as information on building-related illness and how it differs from sick building syndrome, environmental conditions and problems, and indoor air quality. The estimated number of schools that have air quality and environmental issues and the cost to remediate these issues are also included.

KEYWORDS: Asbestos School Hazard Abatement Act of 1984; Building Related Illness; Education Infrastructure Act of 1994; Environmental Conditions; Indoor Air Quality; Mold; Public Schools; Remediation; Sick Building Syndrome

OVERVIEW

Sick building syndrome describes a situation in which a building's occupants have health and comfort issues that seem to be linked to the amount of time they spend in the building. Usually, no specific illness or cause is identified. Sick building syndrome can occur throughout a building, in an area of a building, or localized in only one room of a building. Some indicators of a sick building include occupants' complaining of symptoms such as:

- Headaches;
- Eye, nose, or throat irritations;
- Persistent cough;
- Dizziness;
- Nausea;
- Fatigue;
- Difficulty concentrating.

The cause of the symptoms is not known, and most of the people complaining of the symptoms find relief after they leave the building.

"Building-related illness" is a term used when symptoms of a diagnosed illness are due to airborne building contaminants. Building-related illness can be detected when occupants begin complaining of conditions such as:

- Coughing;
- Chest tightness;
- Fever; or,
- Chills and muscle aches.

The symptoms can be clinically defined and have an identifiable cause, and the people complaining of the symptoms may require prolonged recovery times after they leave the building (United States Environmental Protection Agency, 1991).

According to a report by the National Center for Education Statistics (Alexander & Lewis, 2014), during the 2012–13 school year, the average age of U.S. public school buildings was forty-four years, and 18 percent of schools had not been substantially renovated since 1978 or before. This can be troublesome because many older schools have not received proper preventive maintenance over the years, which can lead to sick buildings and poor indoor air quality.

However, these problems are not limited to only older school buildings. New buildings can have issues with mold, air quality, and other environmental problems. Sometimes it can be something simple. One new school had students and staff getting sick shortly after the school opened; all complained of allergy-like symptoms. It was determined that dust left over from the construction was the culprit, creating the air quality issues. With new construction, however, schools and districts have a chance of recouping all the costs associated with cleanup by using legal means to recover the money from the builders or others associated with the construction and completion of the project (Buchanan, 2007).

According to the NCES report (Alexander & Lewis), 30 percent of the nation's public schools had permanent (as opposed to portable) buildings in which the quality of the air ventilation/filtration system was rated fair or poor (rather than "excellent" or "good"). Heating systems and air-conditioning systems were also in fair or poor condition in 30 percent of schools, and 53 percent of schools reported needing to spend an average of $4.5 million each on repairs, renovations, and modernizations in order to be in good overall condition. In addition, a 2013 report by the U.S. Green Building Council's Center for Green Schools estimated that $271 billion was needed simply to repair or upgrade facilities for them to be deemed in "good repair," while twice that amount would be necessary over the next ten years to both repair and "modernize facilities to meet current health, safety and educational standards" (Filardo et al., 2013). In its last review of the state of US public school facilities, the US Government Accountability Office (GAO, previously the General Accounting Office) stated that "about half the schools reported at least one unsatisfactory environmental condition, such as poor ventilation or heating or lighting problems" (United States General Accounting Office, 1996).

There are schools in adequate and inadequate condition in every state and type of community. However, certain subgroups, including central cities, the western part of the nation, large schools, schools with at least 50 percent minority students, and schools with at least 70 percent poor students, tend to have more building problems than other schools (United States General Accounting Office).

CAUSES OF SICK BUILDING SYNDROME

Many elements can contribute to a sick building. They can act in combination with each other and may also be reinforced by other complaints about the building's temperature, humidity, or lighting. According to the EPA, the following have been shown to cause or contribute to sick building syndrome (US Environmental Protection Agency):

- **Inadequate ventilation.** During the energy crisis of the 1970s, building ventilation codes were changed to reduce the outdoor air ventilation rates. The rate reduction of outdoor air ventilation was later found to be insufficient to retain health

and provide comfortable amenities for residents. Poor ventilation can result when a building's heating, ventilation, and air conditioning systems do not work well enough to move air freely throughout the rooms and floors;

- **Indoor chemical contaminants.** Most indoor air pollution is the result of what is inside the building. Items that are capable of emitting pollutants and causing health issues include adhesives, carpeting, upholstery, wood products, copy machines, pesticides, and cleaning products. Improperly vented kerosene heaters, gas space heaters, and gas stoves can also contribute to poor air quality and a sick building;

- **Outdoor chemical contaminants.** Outdoor pollutants, such as motor vehicle exhaust and emissions, can enter a building by way of air intake vents, windows, and other openings that have been placed in poor locations throughout the building. Pollutants from plumbing vents and bathroom and kitchen exhausts can also enter the building the same way;

- **Biological contaminants.** Bacteria, mold, pollen, and viruses are biological contaminants and can easily multiply in any water that has been sitting stagnant in ducts, humidifiers, drain pans, ceiling tiles, carpeting, and insulation. Biological contaminants can also include insect and avian excrement;

- **Radon and asbestos.** Radon and asbestos are not associated with either sick building syndrome or building-related illness because they tend to cause long-term diseases that occur years after the person has been exposed, rather than acute or immediate health problems (US Environmental Protection Agency).

THE PROBLEM WITH MOLD

Mold is the most common environmental problem for schools (Buchanan, 2007). There have been cases where mold has made it necessary for schools to close forever, districts to start the school year late, and high-school students to take classes in middle schools or be bused to other high schools. Mold has been the cause for at least a dozen schools closing for days or weeks, and three schools have been forced to close permanently. Mold can be an expensive problem too. Instructors have filed lawsuits over illnesses that are associated with mold, such as asthma, shortness of breath, and loss of memory. Mold has cost districts millions of dollars to clean up the problem (Stricherz, 2001).

Since mold can grow practically anywhere there is moisture and oxygen, it is necessary to pay attention to ceiling tiles, carpeting, wood, drywall, and any porous surface. Many times the problem can be traced back to inferior construction materials, poor ventilation, and a lack of proper maintenance that allows leaks to go unattended or be inappropriately repaired. For example, not replacing ceiling tiles that have become wet provides a breeding ground for molds that will then become airborne (Stricherz).

High Cost of Cleanup

Mold cleanup can be expensive, and its remediation can wreak havoc on the school and district as they try to deal with the problem. One school district had to delay the opening of the school year when mold was found on an elementary school's roof and in 20 classrooms. Instructors had been complaining of watery eyes, backaches, and bronchitis. Once the problem was discovered, time was needed to figure out how to clean it up and what to do with the students. The students ended up being transferred to three other schools. The school district spent nearly $2 million on cleanup and associated legal fees, and the school was closed for eight months. Another district closed a school permanently due to mold. The principal and some instructors had complained for fifteen years about headaches and asthma, but nothing had been done until it was too late. The school district ended up having to rent two buildings and pay $100,000 every three months in rent, a major expense that could not have been anticipated when determining the year's budget (Stricherz).

Found in Old & New Buildings

Even new buildings can have mold issues. Students and staff at a new elementary school began complaining of upper respiratory problems soon after the building opened. In November, not too far into the first year of the school, the building was shut down and did not reopen until September of the following year. The cost to remediate the mold problem was $2 million because they had to basically gut the building. It cost the district another $1 million to bus

the students to other schools (Colgan, 2003). Mold issues in buildings can also end up costing taxpayers. A school in Vermont became overrun with mold of all types after a wet summer and improper maintenance. The cleanup cost more than $4.7 million, which has translated into an increase in property taxes to help pay for the cleanup effort ("A Growing Problem," 2007; Parent, 2007).

Abundance of Litigation

Mold can also result in lawsuits being filed by parents, instructors, and school staff if they feel their school districts have failed to prevent the illness they believe they contracted because of the building. In one case, instructors filed a $6 million lawsuit against their district (Stricherz). Instructors and students sued the builder of their new school after complaining of asthma and other respiratory problems that could have been prompted by mold exposure in schools. A subsequent investigation discovered that slightly wet walls, along with other damp occurrences, were not corrected, which resulted in mold in various places in the building that had to be reconstructed. They ended up agreeing to a $650,000 settlement from the builder ("Wis. Students, Teachers Agree to Settle," 2006).

A district that had already spent more than $28 million on mold remediation and repair work additionally faced lawsuits from instructors, students, and the school's contracted employees over the mold. Instructors had complained about having health-related problems for more than ten years before the mold was found growing behind the walls, in the ceiling tiles, in the cabinets, and in the kitchen, which led to the school being closed from March until August of the following year. A judge ruled that the instructors could not sue the district for damages because their claims should fall under workers' compensation. However, students and the school's contracted workers not covered by the insurance were allowed to continue with the lawsuit against the district (Colgan, 2003).

Applying the Law

Indoor air quality has resulted in legal action and arbitration, with court decisions changing what is considered an acceptable response when a school receives indoor air quality complaints from school staff and/or students. Acceptable indoor air quality is now legally defined, according to Hays (2000), as a "reasonable standard of care," which makes indoor air quality more than a building issue in terms of regulations, standards, and codes; now it is also a health and safety issue. Schools should keep solid documentation of all their actions in terms of following sound engineering and building principles; but since most indoor air quality litigation is based on negative health effects, schools need to make sure they document all actions proving standard of care (Hays).

In the past, when students or staff began a claim against a school and tried to recover damages, they had to demonstrate that the school had a legal obligation to protect them from harm. Many court decisions agreed that a school does have a duty to protect its staff and students from harm and provide a "reasonable standard of care," meaning what a "knowledgeable" person would do under similar conditions. Claimants then had to demonstrate that the school failed to provide a reasonable standard of care, which constitutes negligence. The reporting of symptoms is often considered enough to demonstrate that the school did not provide a reasonable standard of care. The final step was that claimants needed to prove a cause-and-effect relationship, meaning that they needed to prove a specific contaminant was the cause of their health problems. This was almost impossible to do, so very few claimants won. The term "sick building syndrome" came about, which is now used to identify a situation where no cause could be determined. With that in mind, school and district administrators are encouraged not to use the term "sick building syndrome" in any documentation or they could eliminate the need for the claimant to establish causation (Hays).

FURTHER INSIGHTS

Asthma is the top chronic disease that causes student absenteeism, leading to an estimated 14.4 million missed school days in 2008 alone (Meng, Babey, & Wolstein, 2012). When students are ill, they can miss class, which can easily affect their academic performance. In addition, when students do not feel well, it can be difficult for them to concentrate and learn (Buchanan).

MAINTAINING THE BUILDINGS

It has been determined that well-maintained and periodically renovated buildings can have a life expectancy similar to that of a brand new building. Many understand that any learning environment has the potential to affect the education students will receive in it. Decent facilities contribute to a high-quality learning environment. A court has defined decent facilities as being structurally safe, having a clean and healthy water supply, having proper sewage disposal, and being in good repair, among other things. However, many schools are considered to be in poor condition and in need of several major repairs due to leaking roofs, poor plumbing, or bad heating, ventilation, or cooling systems (United States General Accounting Office). According to the NCES report, at least 17 percent of public schools with permanent buildings and 28 percent of public schools with portable buildings rated at least one of eight environmental factors—artificial lighting, natural lighting, heating, air conditioning, ventilation, indoor air quality, water quality, and acoustics or noise control—as "unsatisfactory" or "very unsatisfactory," with the most common complaints being air-conditioning and ventilation quality (permanent buildings) and natural lighting (portable buildings). In general, rural schools and city schools had the highest rates of environmental problems, while suburban schools had the lowest (Alexander & Lewis). The nation's oldest schools need the most attention, but many of them do not have plans for improvement, as funding issues are the main obstacle to making the needed repairs (Dunne, 2001).

FUNDING BUILDING MAINTENANCE

Federal programs do provide some money to help schools and districts meet new federal guidelines, but these programs often do not offset all the costs involved with the new mandates. For example, the aid given for asbestos management under the Asbestos School Hazard Abatement Act of 1984 failed to cover all the costs associated with its mandates. For a three-year period, the Environmental Protection Agency gathered requests for funds totaling $599 million, but they only awarded $157 million to about a third of the districts that qualified. Congress then passed the Education Infrastructure Act of 1994 and appropriated $100 million for grants to fix, renovate, or construct schools. But those funds were destroyed the following year, and the funds were never distributed (United States General Accounting Office).

At the time the GAO performed its survey, of the 60 percent of schools that were considered to be in decent condition except for at least one feature in need of repair, most needed multiple features repaired, such as walls, roofs, floors, windows, plumbing, heating, air conditioning, and ventilation. When it came to the environmental factors of lighting, heating, ventilation, indoor air quality, noise control, energy efficiency, and building security, 13 percent of schools reported five or more unsatisfactory conditions. The GAO estimated that at least 25 million students attended schools that had at least one substandard environmental condition (United States General Accounting Office).

REMEDIATION REQUIREMENTS
Schools and districts tend to have difficulty with environmental and indoor air quality challenges. When budgets are tight, as they are for most schools and districts, it is easy to put off preventive maintenance. Most have learned from litigation and professional journals that they need to replace wet and stained ceiling tiles and not simply paint over them. They also need to make sure their maintenance personnel not only fix and report any potential issues but also determine what caused the wetness and created the issues in the first place so that they can be fixed (Buchanan).

KEEPING SCHOOLS HEALTHY
There are also some things that schools can do to help reduce environmental and air quality threats:

- Schools should implement an indoor air quality program. The U.S. Environmental Protection Agency provides schools with a plan to help improve air quality in school buildings;
- Schools should watch the use of pesticides on school property and try to use them as little as possible. If at all possible, application of pesticides should be done when students and staff are not in school or on the grounds;
- Schools should also try to paint and apply any flooring finishes after school hours when no one is around because most of these products create fumes that can cause health issues. Also, the building should be properly and well ventilated during and after any painting or refinishing;
- Schools should be sure to fix any water leaks as soon as they are noticed to try to avoid possible

mold problems. In addition, moldy ceiling tiles and carpets should be thrown away and replaced immediately;
- Schools should do periodic walk-through inspections to look for any signs of potential problems. Signs can include musty odors, dirty carpets, leaky water pipes, and water damage. Any problems noted should be quickly taken care of to reduce risk of further damage;
- Schools should practice preventive maintenance, which is the most effective way to avoid problems in the first place. Preventive maintenance includes servicing heating and air conditioning units on a regularly scheduled basis;
- Schools should make sure that buses and cars are not allowed to idle near any school buildings because carbon monoxide fumes can quickly accumulate inside a building. School doors and windows should be closed when students are arriving and leaving (Environmental Protection Agency, n.d., as cited in Buchanan).

Parents can also help by monitoring their children for signs of sick building syndrome. Signs include sneezing, coughing, wheezing, runny nose, itchy eyes, headaches, and general fatigue. If their child exhibits these symptoms at school, parents need to go to a doctor and try to rule out other factors, then work with school personnel to make sure a proper evaluation of the room is completed (Environmental Protection Agency, n.d., as cited in Buchanan).

Currently, the federal government does not require air monitoring in schools. However individual states or localities may institute their own monitoring requirements. Schools have an obligation to provide a healthy environment for both their students and all school personnel. There are things that can be done to help keep environmental and air quality issues from cropping up and costing hundreds of thousands or millions of dollars to remediate. Therefore, it is important that school personnel and districts are vigilant and proactive so they are not cleaning up a huge mess later and defending themselves against lawsuits.

TERMS & CONCEPTS
Asbestos School Hazard Abatement Act of 1984: The Asbestos School Hazard Abatement Act of 1984 handed out loans and grants to public and private

schools that needed financial aid in order to rectify asbestos problems. It was funded until 1993.

Building Related Illness: Building related illness defines the symptoms experienced of a diagnosed illness that are directly relatable to airborne building pollutants.

Education Infrastructure Act of 1994: The Education Infrastructure Act of 1994 provided federal aid for the rectification of public elementary and secondary school buildings in need of repair. Grants were authorized to schools that needed immediate attention, but lacked the funding necessary. It was never funded.

Remediation: The process of cleaning up pollutants or hazardous materials in a building, including rebuilding and replacement.

Sick Building Syndrome: Sick building syndrome refers to situations when people who occupy a building begin to experience health issues that can be attributable to the amount of time they spend in a building but a specific illness or cause of discomfort is not identifiable.

Sandra Myers

BIBLIOGRAPHY

A growing problem. (2007). *NEA Today, 25,* 13. Retrieved December 3, 2007, from EBSCO Online Database Academic Search Premier.

Alexander, D., & Lewis, L. (2014). *Condition of America's public school facilities, 2012–13* (NCES 2014-022). Washington, DC: US Government Printing Office. Retrieved October 8, 2014, from http://nces.ed.gov.

Belle, K., Ütebay, K., & McArthur, A. (2012). Making the case for sustainable K-12 school environmental health programs. *Educational Facility Planner, 46* (2/3), 74–77. Retrieved October 8, 2014, from EBSCO Online Database Education Research Complete.

Buchanan, B. (2007). Sick buildings, sick students. *American School Board Journal, 194,* 48–50. Retrieved December 3, 2007, from EBSCO Online Database Academic Search Premier.

Colgan, C. (2003). Is mold the new asbestos? *American School Board Journal 190,* 14–18. Retrieved December 3, 2007, from EBSCO Online Database Education Research Complete.

Dunne, D. (2001). Sick schools create dilemma for school districts. Retrieved December 11, 2007, from http://education-world.com.

Filardo, M., et al. (2013). *The Center for Green Schools 2013 state of our schools report.* Retrieved October 8, 2014, from http://bestfacilities.org.

Hays, L. (2000). Lawsuits in the air. *American School & University, 72,* 35. Retrieved December 3, 2007, from EBSCO Online Database Academic Search Premier.

Holloway, J. (2000). Healthy buildings, successful students. *Educational Leadership, 57,* 88. Retrieved December 3, 2007, from EBSCO Online Database Academic Search Premier.

Lunenburg, F. C. (2011). Environmental hazards in America's schools. *FOCUS on Colleges, Universities & Schools, 6,* 1–9. Retrieved December 15, 2013, from EBSCO Online Database Education Research Complete.

Meng, Y. Y., Babey, S. H., & Wolstein, J. (2012). Asthma-related school absenteeism and school concentration of low-income students in California. *Preventing Chronic Disease, 9.* Retrieved October 8, 2014, from EBSCO Online Database MEDLINE Complete.

Mold shuts N.J. middle school. (2012). *American School & University, 85,* 10. Retrieved December 15, 2013, from EBSCO Online Database Education Research Complete.

National Center for Education Statistics. (1999). *Condition of America's public school facilities: 1999.* Retrieved December 11, 2007, from http://nces.ed.gov.

Parent, B. (2007, July 20). Milton mold update. *WCAX.com.* Retrieved October 8, 2014, from http://wcax.com.

Romeo, J. (2011). Mold in k-12 schools. *School Planning & Management, 50,* 45–46. Retrieved December 15, 2013, from EBSCO Online Database Education Research Complete.

Stricherz, M. (2001). Moldy buildings: Troubling trend for many districts. *Education Week, 21,* 1. Retrieved December 3, 2007, from EBSCO Online Database Academic Search Premier.

United States Environmental Protection Agency. (1991). *Indoor air facts no. 4 (revised): Sick building syndrome.* Retrieved October 8, 2014, from http://epa.gov.

United States General Accounting Office. (1996). School facilities: America's schools report differing conditions. Retrieved December 11, 2007, from http://gao.gov.

Wis. students, teachers agree to settle lawsuit about mold. (2006). *Education Week, 25,* 6. Retrieved December 3, 2007, from EBSCO Online Database Academic Search Premier.

SUGGESTED READING

Buchanan, B. (2007). Sick buildings, sick students. *American School Board Journal.* 37(10), 48-50.

Chase, J. (1995). *Blueprint for a Green School.* New York, NY: Scholastic Inc.

Godish, T. (1994). *Sick Buildings: Definition, Diagnosis and Mitigation.* Boca Raton, FL: CRC Press.

Healthy School Network (2010). Sick Schools, 2009: America's Continuing Environmental Health Crisis for Children.

Miller, N. (1995). *The Healthy School Handbook: Conquering the Sick Building Syndrome and Other Environmental Hazards in and Around Your School.* Washington, DC: National Education Association.

Roy, K. (2014). LAMP: Shining a light on safety. *Science Scope, 37,* 74–75. Retrieved October 10, 2014, from EBSCO Online Database Education Research Complete.

SCHOOL DROPOUT ISSUES

In today's brain-based economy, where academic skills are valued, increasing the graduation rate has become a top policy issue among educators. High dropout rates are associated with factors such as retention and socioeconomic status. Dropout programs address various risk factors associated with dropping out of high school. Dropout programs may include add-on programs such as after-school programs, or may also attempt to get at deeper roots of the issue through systemic reforms.

KEYWORDS: Add-On Programs; Alternative Schools; Differentiated Instruction; Dropout Rate; Graduation Rate; Out-of-School Time; Retention; Risk Factors; Socioeconomic Status; Tracking

OVERVIEW

At the beginning of the twentieth century, the high school dropout rate in the United States was estimated to be hovering around 90 percent (Schargel & Smink, 2001). In 1983, *A Nation at Risk,* a report from The National Commission on Excellence in Education was published. The authors called for education reform in America, stating that it would be impossible for the United States to continue to be economically competitive in a rapidly advancing and changing world. The report called for immediate action—raising student achievement and high school graduation rates through state and federal reforms. Between the turn of the century and *A Nation at Risk,* the United States economy had become more "brain-based," requiring increased levels of education in the work force. Today, the use of technology has skyrocketed, and thus, graduating with a high school diploma is now a minimum requirement for most jobs. Roberts (1995, as cited by Schargel & Smink) estimates that nearly 80 percent of jobs in the United States are in the service industry. Therefore, a well-educated work force is imperative to the success of our economy.

Today, the dropout rate has declined dramatically. The National Center for Education Statistics approximates that the status dropout rate, the percentage of sixteen through twenty-four-year-olds who were not enrolled in school and who have not earned a high school diploma or equivalency credential, declined from 12 percent in 1990 to 7 percent in 2011 (US Department of Education, National Center for Education Statistics, 2013). Other estimates are lower. Orfield (2004) contends that less than 70 percent of students who enter high school actually graduate with a diploma. However, researchers and policymakers insist that even the best picture displays a dropout rate much too high for an industrialized nation like the United States. It is estimated that 3.8 million individuals between the ages of eighteen and twenty-four are neither participating in the work force, nor in school (Annie E. Casey Foundation, 2004). In school year 1999 to 2000, the U.S. high school completion rate decreased in all but seven states, while students who were dropping out were younger—in ninth and tenth grade (Barton, 2005).

NEGATIVE EFFECTS OF DROPPING OUT

Schargel & Smink list the problems and conditions associated with dropping out of high school. High school graduates earn 70 percent more than dropouts do over the course of their lifetime; dropouts are much more likely to:

- Be single parents;
- Be on welfare;
- Commit crimes; or,
- Go to prison.

Seventy-three percent of state prison inmates and 59 percent of federal inmates are high school dropouts (Harlow, 2003). Furthermore, only 60 percent of those who drop out are employed within one year of leaving school (Office of Educational Research and Improvement, 1991). In 2001, only 55 percent of dropouts reported being employed, while high school and college graduates reported a 74 percent and 87 percent employment rate, respectively (Sum, 2002).

These statistics have a ripple effect that influences more than the individual. Levin (2007), an economist, recently used economic analysis to estimate the gains of dropout prevention. He hypothesized, using very conservative estimates, that if the United States were to spend $82,000 on each student through successful intervention programs that increased the graduation rate, every individual who graduated would contribute $209,000 in additional tax revenues, and lower their need for health care, social welfare, and the justice system by $70,000 over the course of their lifetime. Furthermore, individuals who stay in school longer also live longer—the death rate for those with less than twelve years of education is two and a half times greater than for those who completed thirteen or more years (Alliance for Excellent Education, 2003). Once dropouts do enter the work force, they typically earn much less than an individual who has a high school diploma. In fact, the earning potential of dropouts is only declining as the United States economy becomes more skill-based (U.S. Census Bureau, 2002). As of 2011, a high school dropout will earn $200,000 less over his or her lifetime than a high school graduate. The unemployment rates for dropouts is anywhere from 15 to 18 percent (Sanchez & Wertheimer, 2011).

REASONS FOR DROPPING OUT

Students who drop out do so for a variety of reasons. The 1960 Project Talent Survey (Combs & Cooley, 1968, as cited by Roderick, 1993) found that dropouts had lower levels of measured achievement, lower levels of aspirations when questioned about job or work prospects, had more negative attitudes towards school, lower self-esteem, and lower participation rates in school sponsored activities than those individuals who graduated high school. Similarly, the Youth in Transition Survey (Bachman et al., 1971, as cited by Roderick) surveyed sophomores that dropped out compared to those who did not. The study found significant differences between the groups in academic achievement, participation in extracurricular activities, and attitudes towards school and learning. They additionally found that youths who had repeated grades prior to high school were up to 40 to 50

percent more likely to drop out, and the likelihood of dropping out soared to 90 percent when students repeated two or more grades. Similarly, the High School & Beyond survey data found that the more difficulties youth have in school, the more likely they are to drop out (Roderick).

Socioeconomic status has a large impact on an individual's likelihood of dropping out of school. One study found that students from low-income families were nearly three times more likely to drop out of school than their more affluent peers (Annie E. Casey Foundation). In 1997, the Department of Education reported that students from families in the lowest 20 percent of the income bracket were seven times more likely to drop out than those from families in the highest 20 percent (Schargel & Smink). Roderick reports that students from disadvantaged and poor families are much more likely to have problems in school, academically and socially, and thus more likely to fall behind in school or have to repeat grades.

In 2011, over 40 million Americans had never graduated from high school, and the majority of dropouts are Latinos and blacks (Sanchez & Wertheimer). The reasons students give for dropping out are numerous. Many claim they were bored with school, others had missed so many days that it was too overwhelming to catch up. Some students explained that their work or family responsibilities caused them to drop out of high school (High School Dropout Rates, 2012).

DECREASING THE DROPOUT RATE

Starting in the 1980s, a variety of state and federal programs surfaced and aimed to decrease the high school dropout rate. The most common programs were add-on programs such as preschools, pilot programs such as full service schools, and programs promoting an increase in testing (Schargel & Smink). These types of programs had various rates of success. However, the high school dropout problem does not seem to be changing. If anything, according to many researchers, the problem is becoming more and more prevalent, especially among the poor or disadvantaged (Orfield).

There are other factors linked to dropout rates, including socioeconomic status, race and ethnicity, and the conditions of a school and how a student feels about his or her teachers and administrators. Experts have found that predicting dropout is no easy task. Today, a wealth of programs exist to help students graduate high school. The components of these programs are varied, and encompass a wide array of interventions. However, to understand the successes and shortcomings of these programs, one must first understand the intricacies behind the dropout problem.

CALCULATING & DEFINING "DROPOUT"
The actual high school dropout rate in the United States is uncertain because there is no single accepted definition of the term. Dropout rates are calculated in various ways. We will discuss how the term "dropout" is defined and calculated by four different organizations, the Department of Education, the National Center for Education Statistics, the Current Population Survey conducted by the Census Bureau, and the Cumulative Promotion Index, as well as the strengths and weaknesses of reporting data using these methods.

DEPARTMENT OF EDUCATION CALCULATIONS
According to Schargel and Smink, the Department of Education defines dropout rates four different ways:
- Event;
- Status;
- Cohort;
- High school completion.

Event dropout is calculated by the percentage of students who leave high school, even if they receive a General Equivalency Diploma (GED) later. Status dropout rate is calculated within a specific age range. For example, a status dropout rate might be recorded as, "On January 1, 2007, fifteen percent of all students ages sixteen through twenty-four were either not enrolled, or had not completed high school." A cohort rate is calculated when the same group of students is followed over a period of time, such as, "In the 1997 cohort, 85 percent of students graduated high school." Finally, the Department of Education calculates high school completion rate as the proportion of eighteen to twenty-four year olds who have completed high school, or received a GED (Schargel & Smink).

While the Department of Education gathers dropout data, there is no federal supervision of data reporting. Orfield cautions that much of the available graduation data is grossly misrepresented and inaccurate due to the vagueness of the definitions, as well as the lack of oversight in enforcing the accuracy of reporting.

NCES CRITERIA
The National Center for Education Statistics defines a dropout through the following criteria:
- The individual was enrolled in school during the previous school year, but was not enrolled by October 1 of the current school year, and was expected to be;
- The individual did not graduate high school or complete a GED;
- The individual did not transfer, was not ill, and was not deceased.

Many states use these criteria to define a dropout and calculate graduation data. However, Orfield points out that this formula "relies heavily on underestimated dropout data, and significantly overestimates graduation rates compared to other methods." For example, schools may report students who dropout as transfers instead, or fail to count students who are over the age required to attend school as dropouts, even if they never graduated. Furthermore, the NCES data is often incomplete because they only represent certain districts—they do not take samples in every school district nationwide.

THE CURRENT POPULATION SURVEY
The Current Population Survey data are reported to the Census Bureau using graduation rates based on statistical sampling rather than school systems. The weakness of this method lies in that surveys are self-reported, which may misrepresent those who complete the questionnaires. Also, the Current Population Survey does not poll individuals who are incarcerated or institutionalized, which skews the numbers (Orfield). Orfield states "the most accurate method for tracking high school graduation rates would be to provide each student with a single lifetime school identification number that would follow him or her throughout his or her entire school career" and warns that without such a system, all data collected will forever be somewhat imperfect.

CUMULATIVE PROMOTION INDEX
The Cumulative Promotion Index uses statistical averages of groups who matriculate year to year. This

method tracks students year to year so that students cannot get lost in the shuffle; however, it is still not a 100 percent perfect measure of dropout rates.

DROPOUT PREVENTION STRATEGIES

Dropout programs may target students of lower socioeconomic background. Less affluent students are more likely to have parents who have completed high school, and also have decreased parent supervision. We also know that youth from single-parent families are much more likely to drop out of school (Roderick), and that divorce is a huge contributor to a decrease in wealth. Schargel & Smink report that the single-parent family is the fastest growing class of family group, and the largest population living in poverty in the United States is children. Schools and add-on programs may focus on improving the lives of economically disadvantaged youth through services such as tutoring, mentoring, or counseling.

Studies of mentoring programs such as Big Brother/Big Sister show that successful mentoring leads to decreased drug and alcohol use, improvement in grades, and a decrease in skipping classes, as well as reporting fewer behavioral problems in school (Schargel & Smink). Additionally, other programs address other issues that plague many low-income families: lack of supervision, lack of family involvement, school preparation, and violence. Family-outreach programs have played an important role in many initiatives. Studies show that parent and family involvement in education has a direct effect on achievement, which is related to the likelihood a student will drop out. These types of programs attempt to reach out to families and connect them more closely to the schools (Schargel & Smink).

Other strategies for preventing dropout have focused on early childhood education programs such as Head Start or preschool. One of the best known studies on early childhood programs is the Perry Preschool Project, in which high-risk black preschool students were divided into two groups: "preschool" and "no preschool." Follow up studies at various ages showed the "preschool" group had higher graduation rates, in addition to other positive outcomes (Weikart, Bond, & McNeil, 1978).

Disadvantaged families may also face issues in the communities. Thus, other initiatives may target issues in a neighborhood, such as decreasing violence, or teaching conflict resolution. Students who are afraid to go to school, or attend schools where they do not feel safe are much more likely to drop out before graduation (Bryk & Thum, 1989). Programs that target disadvantaged students often combine a variety of the tactics discussed.

RACE & ETHNICITY

The face of the United States is changing rapidly. The United States Census reports that whites are the slowest growing group in the United States, while Asians, Hispanics, American Indian, and blacks are the fastest growing. By the year 2050 it is projected that about half of the total population in the United States will be non-Hispanic whites, as opposed to nearly three-quarters of the population today (US Census Bureau, 2004). Changing patterns of immigration have led to an increasingly diverse population. While some studies estimate that graduation rates across ethnic groups are stable and similar, Orfield contends that minority groups, particularly male minorities, graduate high school at a far lower rate than their Caucasian counterparts. He calculates that only half of all black/African-American students, and just over half of American Indian and Hispanic students graduated from high school in the United States. Graduation rates for males in these groups are even lower—all under 50 percent. However, much of the public remains unknowing about what Orfield calls an "educational and civil rights crisis."

Growing diversity comes hand in hand with an increased number of students speaking a variety of languages. Studies have found that students who have limited proficiency in English are more likely to drop out, with minority groups having the highest rate of limited English speakers. However, there is an important distinction: Roderick cites research has shown that coming from a non-English speaking home is not a factor in increasing dropout rates—the youth's own proficiency at English is. Furthermore, most variations in dropout rate across various ethnic groups can be attributed to socioeconomic status. For example, Hispanic youth have high rates of dropping out, but they are also more likely to be from immigrant families who earn less income and arrive in the country without English proficiency.

The statistics on dropouts, in conjunction with what we know about our changing diversity of the population, presents a grim picture—the numbers of those who are dropping out at the highest rates are growing the fastest. Educators must combine what is known about various groups of individuals in order to curb the dropout problem. We cannot overlook that the poorest students are concentrated most in minority groups. Dropout programs that address issues that non-native speakers and immigrants have in the United States may be successful in helping youth stay in school.

SCHOOL CHARACTERISTICS

The organizational structure and characteristics of schools also have an impact on the dropout rate. In short, the environment matters. Research has found that schools have lower dropout rates when the students report feeling safe and feel the teachers and administrators are committed to their well-being (Schargel & Smink).

Schargel & Smink report that schools that track students are more likely to have higher rates of dropouts. Tracking entails placing students in groups based on their ability to do the work, as determined by testing or other procedures. Tracking is common in many schools across the country, and the tactics vary, but many schools who track find that students are racially divided into tracks, with minority students more likely to be placed in tracks such as remedial or special education. Furthermore, minority students who are just as talented academically are much more likely to end up in lower level courses and tracks than their white peers (Burris & Welner, 2005). Schools that teach students from a wide variety of backgrounds—socioeconomic status, ethnicity, and a variety of levels of academic courses experience higher dropout rates. This may be due to the concentration of resources towards the most capable group, and tracking systems that tend to be present in larger schools (Bryk & Thum).

Another factor to consider is how schools are organized. One of the most crucial transition periods for students regarding dropping out is the transition to high school from middle school. In a study of Maryland public schools, Kerr & Letger (2004) found that schools who focus on easing the transition to high school using tactics such as creating small learning communities and interdisciplinary teaming (teaming teachers across different disciplines to teach the same students) had a positive effect on reducing dropouts in high poverty areas.

Investing in teachers may be another effective method in reducing the numbers of dropouts. Research tells us that dropping out is related to low academic performance. Of all the ingredients needed for academic success, studies have unequivocally shown that teacher quality is the single most important predictor for student success (Darling-Hammond, 1998). High quality teaching can bridge the gap between issues such as wealth and poverty, or lessen the impact of other such risk factors. Thus, investing in the professional development and retention of quality teachers has been identified as one way to correct the dropout problem.

CURRENT DROPOUT PROGRAM OPTIONS

Preventing dropout has become a significant education policy issue. There are many strategies and programs aimed at dropout prevention. These programs may include initiatives directed at improving the family and school connection, child-directed programs such as increasing early childhood education, reducing class sizes, and providing mentoring and tutoring to students. Other strategies may be aimed at improving instruction—providing professional development to foster openness to a diversity of learning styles and teach differentiated instruction strategies. Finally, dropout prevention may aim to improve the communities that struggle most with high dropout rates—providing career education to those populations or conflict resolution and violence prevention in these areas (Schargel & Smink).

Schargel & Smink state that:

> "... schools continue to fail where they have always failed—with students with low expectations, students with otherwise committed parents, students with physical and mental handicaps, students who are not interested in the present educational environment. And that number is growing."

Similarly, Martin & Halperin (2006) argue that current standards based reform continues to "assume that what works well for the one-third of students who are well-prepared for college will succeed for the two-thirds majority. This is patently not the case." These researchers, and others, have called out for reform that targets populations most prone to dropout—the economically disadvantaged, members of minority groups, and those with limited English proficiency.

There have been many types of dropout programs including: after-school programs, alternative schooling, and early intervention programs.

School-age children only spend so many hours in school. Thus, out-of-school time has become a topic of interest in helping students achieve, including preventing dropout. Research on out-of-school programs is limited; however, it has been shown that students who participated in after-school supervised programs showed positive results. Successful programs may vary widely, focusing on improving core academic skills such as literacy, or involve mentoring by adults (Schargel & Smink).

Another option that has been explored is alternative schools, either within regular schools or as separate entities. Dynarski (2004) evaluates a key study funded by the School Dropout Demonstration Assistance Program, in which nearly 10,000 students were followed for up to three years. The program hosted three different types of services aimed at reducing student dropout: low-intensity supplemental programs such as tutoring, alternative middle schools, and alternative middle schools within regular schools, which typically housed smaller classes and counseling services. While the supplemental programs had little effect, the alternative middle school programs succeeded in keeping students in school longer.

Suh & Suh (2007) found that early prevention is essential in increasing the rate of school completion, as younger students are more open to support, while older students are more doubtful about accepting assistance. Their study also identified various risk factors to dropping out. The presence of a variety of risk factors substantially increased the risk. The three risk factors that they focused on: poor academic performance, low socioeconomic status, and behavioral and social problems, were best treated with dropout programs that targeted and addressed all the risk factors rather than just a single one.

McPartland & Jordan (2004) also argue that any dropout program that hopes to successfully impact students' lives must take into account three entrance areas: the organization and structure of schools, innovations in curriculum and instruction, and teacher support systems. Dropout programs that have been successful often target a variety of risk factors, rather than just one.

TERMS & CONCEPTS

Alternative Schools: Alternative schools are a different option for high schools. Alternative schools try to meet special needs of their students though strategies such as smaller classes or the availability of counseling.

Differentiated Instruction: Differentiated instruction is a type of classroom instruction in which teachers teach a variety of ability levels in one classroom.

Out-of-School Time: Out-of-school time refers to the time a student spends outside of their school. Most students spend only a third of their day in school.

Retention: Retention occurs when a student repeats a grade.

Risk Factors: Risk factors are factors in one's life or personality that put an individual at risk for dropping out of school.

Socioeconomic Status: Socioeconomic status is a measure of wealth.

Tracking: Tracking is a practice used by schools to divide students into various groups by ability.

Rana Suh

BIBLIOGRAPHY

Alliance for Excellent Education. (2003). *Fact sheet: The impact of education on health and well-being*. Washington, DC: Author.

Annie E. Casey Foundation. (2004). *Kids count data book*. Baltimore, MD: Author.

Bachman, J.C., Green, S., & Wirtanen, I.D. (1971). *Dropping out—problem or symptom? Youth in Transition* (Vol. 3.). Ann Arbor, MI: Institute for Social Research, University of Michigan.

Barton, P. E. (2005). *One-third of a nation: Rising dropout rates and declining opportunities*. Princeton, NJ: Policy Information Center, Educational Testing Service.

Bowers, A. J., Sprott, R., & Taff, S. A. (2012). Do we know who will drop out? A review of the predictors of dropping out of high school: Precision, sensitivity, and specificity. *High School Journal, 96*, 77–100. Retrieved December 20, 2013, from EBSCO Online Database Education Research Complete.

Bryk, A.S. & Thum, Y. (1989). The effects of high school organization on dropping out: An exploratory investigation. *American Educational Research Journal, 26*, 353-383.

Burris, C., Welner, K. G. (2005). Closing the achievement gap by detracking. *Phi Delta Kappan, 86*, 594-598.

Retrieved September 23, 2007, from EBSCO Online Database Education Research Complete.

Combs, J. & Cooley, W.W. (1968). Dropouts: In high school and after high school. *American Educational Research Journal, 5*, 343-363.

Darling-Hammond, L. (1998). *Investing in quality teaching: State-level strategies 1999.* Education Commission of the States.

Dynarski, M. (2004). Interpreting the evidence from recent federal evaluations of dropout- prevention programs: The state of scientific research. In G. Orfield (Ed.), *Dropouts in America: Confronting the graduation crisis* (pp. 255-268). Cambridge, MA: Harvard Education Press.

Harlow, C.W. (2003). *Education and correctional populations, bureau of justice statistics special report.* Washington, DC: US Department of Justice.

High School Dropout Rates (2012). Retrieved December 21, 2013, from http://childtrends.org.

Kerr, K.A., & Letger, N.E. (2004). Preventing dropout: Use and impact of organizational reforms designed to ease the transition to high school. In G. Orfield (Ed.), *Dropouts in America: Confronting the graduation crisis* (pp. 221-242). Cambridge, MA: Harvard Education Press.

Khalkhali, V., Sharifi, R., & Nikyar, A. (2013). Students' intentions to persist in, versus dropout of high school: What self-determined motivation tells us about it?. *International Online Journal of Educational Sciences, 5*, 282–290. Retrieved December 20, 2013, from EBSCO Online Database Education Research Complete.

Laird, J., DeBell, M., Kienzl, G., & Chapman, C. (2007). *Dropout rates in the United States: 2005* (NCES 2007-059). U.S. Department of Education. Washington, DC: National Center for Education Statistics. Retrieved September 23, 2007, from National Center for Education Statistics, http://nces.ed.gov.

Landis, R. N., & Reschly, A. L. (2013). Reexamining gifted underachievement and dropout through the lens of student engagement. *Journal for the Education of the Gifted, 36*, 220–249. Retrieved December 20, 2013, from EBSCO Online Database Education Research Complete.

Levin, H. (2007). *The costs and benefits of an excellent education for all of America's children.* Teachers College: Center for Benefit-Cost Studies of Education.

Lynch, M. (2014). The true costs of social promotion and retention. *International Journal of Progressive Education, 10*, 6–17. Retrieved October 24, 2014, from EBSCO Online Database Education Research Complete.

Martin, N., & Halperin, S. (2006). *Whatever it takes: How twelve communities are reconnecting out-of-school youth.* Washington, DC: American Youth Policy Forum.

McPartland, J.M., & Jordan, W.J. (2004). In G. Orfield (Ed.), *Dropouts in America: Confronting the graduation crisis* (pp. 269-288). Cambridge, MA: Harvard Education Press.

Office of Educational Research and Improvement. (1991). *Youth indicators 1991: Trends in the well-being of American youth.* Washington, DC: Office of Educational Research and Improvement, U.S. Department of Education.

Orfield, G., Losen, D., Wald, J., & Swanson, C., (2004). *Losing our future: How minority youth are being left behind by the graduation rate crisis.* Cambridge, MA: The Civil Rights Project at Harvard University. Contributors: Advocates for Children of New York, The Civil Society Institute.

Prothero, A. (2014). For dropouts, multitude of factors drive them away from school. *Education Week, 33*, 6. Retrieved October 24, 2014, from EBSCO Online Database Education Research Complete.

Roberts, S. (1995) *Who we are: A portrait of America based on the latest U.S. Census.* New York: USA.

Roderick, M. (1993). *The path to dropping out: Evidence for intervention.* Westport, CT: Auburn House.

Sanchez, Claudio, & Wertheimer, Linda. (2011, July 24). School dropout rates add to fiscal burden. *NPR Special Series: School's Out, America's Dropout Crisis.* Retrieved December 21, 2013, from http://npr.org.

Schargel, F.P., & Smink, J. (2001). *Strategies to help solve our school dropout problem.* Larchmont, NY: Eye on Education.

Suh, S., & Suh, J. (2007). Risk factors and levels of risk for high school dropouts. *Professional School Counseling, 10*, 297-306. Retrieved September 23, 2007, from EBSCO Online Database Academic Search Premier.

Sum, Andrew et al. (2002). *Left behind in the labor market: labor market problems of the nation's out-of-school, young adult populations.* Chicago, IL: Alternative Schools Network. Retrieved September 23, 2007, from http://nupr.neu.edu.

US Census Bureau. (2002). *Educational attainment in the United States.* Washington, DC: Author.

US Census Bureau. (2004). *The face of our population.* Retrieved September 23, 2007, from U.S. Census Bureau, http://factfinder.census.gov.

US Department of Education, National Center for Education Statistics. (2013). *The Condition of Education 2013: Status Dropout Rates.* Retrieved December 21, 2013, from https://nces.ed.gov.

Wang, M., & Fredricks, J. A. (2014). The reciprocal links between school engagement, youth problem behaviors, and school dropout during adolescence. *Child Development, 85*, 722–737. Retrieved October 24, 2014, from EBSCO Online Database Education Research Complete.

Weikart, D.P., Bond, J.P., & McNeil, J.T. (1978). *Ypsilanti Perry Preschool Project: Preschool years and longitudinal results through fourth grade.* Ypsilanti, MI.: High/Scope Press.

SUGGESTED READING

Babinski, L.M., Corra, A., & Gifford, E.J. (2016). Evaluation of a public awareness campaign to prevent high school dropout. *The Journal of Primary Prevention.* 37(4), 361-375.

Bowers, A. J., & Sprott, R. (2012). *Examining the multiple trajectories associated with dropping out of high school: A growth mixture model analysis.* <italic>Journal of Educational Research, 105,* 176–195. Retrieved December 20, 2013, from EBSCO Online Database Education Research Complete.

Capuzzi, D., & Gross, D.R. (2000). *Youth at risk: A prevention resource for counselors, teachers, and parents.* Alexandria, VA: American Counseling Association.

Dryfoos, J.G. (1998). *Safe passage: Making it through adolescence in a risky society.* New York: Oxford University Press.

Orfield, G. (2004). *Dropouts in America: Confronting the graduation crisis.* Cambridge, MA: Harvard Education Press.

Pletka, B. (2007). *Educating the next generation: How to engage students in the 21st century.* Santa Monica, CA: Santa Monica Press.

West, L.L. (1991). *Effective strategies for dropout prevention of at-risk youth.* New York: Aspen Publishers.

Zajacova, A. (2012). Health in working-aged Americans: Adults with high school equivalency diploma are similar to dropouts, not high school graduates. *American Journal of Public Health, 102*(S2), S284–S290. Retrieved December 20, 2013, from EBSCO Online Database Education Research Complete.

MARKETING OF EDUCATION

The marketing of education has turned schools into a service industry and students into the consumers of a product. As of 2007, students and their families have many educational options when compared to the traditional public school model. Whether private, charter, magnet, public, or online school, each wants the business that additional students bring, and parents and their children have to choose which institution offers the best opportunity based on promotional strategies adopted by each school.

KEYWORDS: Charter Schools; Consumer; Cyberschool; Magnet Schools; Marketing; No Child Left Behind Act of 2001 (NCLB); Private School; Promotion; Public School; Rural

OVERVIEW

For a product to be marketed, it must have consumers needing to acquire it. While public education is a benefit for all United States citizens, most people do not consider it a product. However, private school administrators, educators running charter schools, and private investors focusing on the magnet school industry are in the market for students, otherwise known as education consumers. There are several ways to market education as a product. School district administrators can create websites or television ads; they can send out mailings or go door-to-door discussing their product. The result will be the same for the community. Marketing education as a product presents information to parents and to students about what the school can offer academically. It also promotes increasing competition and increased performance for students: if we're doing X and it's working, your school needs to do Y to keep up. While promoting public schools is often the job of local school boards, marketing charter, magnet, and private schools is the responsibility of the administrators who run them. Their priority is to highlight the strengths of their institutions in the hope of luring students away from attending the school system within their own home district.

To fully understand the need to market education, it is imperative to understand the choices parents and students have with regard to education in some cities. For many people, there is only one choice: public or private. Traditional public schools enroll students who live within a certain area, and the schools function within a district that can have several schools operating at one time. Private or religious schools operate within the same school district but require the payment of tuition for enrollment and also require the conformity to specific policies for ideal operation. Private schools receive no funding from state or local governments. As a result, administrators and educators tend to earn less working in the private school sector.

CONSUMER CHOICES FOR EDUCATION

Parents and students may have the option of charter schools or magnet schools where available, either within or outside of their local school districts. Both types of schools are funded similarly to traditional public schools, but they both propose to offer students experiences unlike those provided by public schools. A charter school can be opened by anyone applying to the district school board. Generally, however, they are started through the combined efforts of educators, administrators, and parents wanting reform from the standard public school model. A charter school's application is only granted when the proposal for its creation specifies the difference students will have when compared to the traditional school already in existence. Charter schools are required to meet state academic standards, report on these standards, and have open enrollments. In return, they receive public funding per student and can use money from private donors/investors for the school's running costs. In addition, they can be organized as either nonprofit corporations or they can hire for-profit education service providers to perform some part of their school operations.

Magnet schools are also publicly funded institutions. Their goal, however, is to attract students to a location or an educational environment the students (or their parents) would not normally consider. Magnet schools were initially created to desegregate school districts that were racially homogenous. While the schools still tend to achieve that goal, they also focus on offering specialized education like performance arts or engineering or technical programs not otherwise offered by local public schools. Furthermore, students need to apply to and be accepted to magnet schools making them competitive institutions that are available to students who can't afford private schools.

In addition to these school options, students also have the option of attending school in an entirely online situation. Online learning can be a comfortable and convenient way for students to earn a degree. Until recently, that option was only available to students in higher education. Demast (2007) discusses online education in regard to high school. Kaplan and the Apollo Group have purchased companies that run online high schools and are marketing to students who don't want to attend a traditional high school. According to Damast, "[a]bout 700,000 public precollegiate students were enrolled in at least one online or blended course [last year]." For example:

Florida Virtual School, which is operated by the state of Florida, was founded in 1997 and now has more than 31,000 students in academic year 2005-06, according to the school's Web site. The school started out as a strictly virtual high school, but now provides online courses to students in traditional schools who supplement their studies with online courses (Damast).

Colleges and universities show both rates of success and failures to online courses. Students are diverse, and what works for one may not work for another. The same can be said about lecture classes in big rooms or classes that only meet once per week when compared to those meeting more frequently. There is always a risk to students not attending a traditional class. Not having the face-to-face contact with an instructor is an issue, as is developing effective time management strategies when a computer (a student's high school) and a television share the same space. The lack of socialization is also a concern, similar to the one critics pose against home schooled education. The milestones of playing organized athletics or being part of clubs and attending the prom are all considerations for a student debating an online education.

Further Insights

WHAT DOES SCHOOL MARKETING PROMOTE?

Whatever educational choices parents and students have, it is no wonder that marketing strategies are necessary to entice enrollment in one over the other. According to Lubienski (2007), "... competition in K-12 systems is intended to elicit a number of desirable responses from schools-increased achievement, improved efficiencies, and greater responsiveness to families." If parents know they have choices, and all of those choices seem like good ones, than the advertising of what a parent views as "better" could tip the scales from School A to School B.

In areas where there are no charter schools and no magnet schools, just the standard traditional model of public school education, parents still have to decide which public school is best for their child. In addition to promoting standardized test scores, teacher credentials, and administrative experience, some schools also promote customer service as way to enroll and retain students. In order to embrace the customer service view, however, one must go back to the idea that education is a product and students are the consumers of it. Many people have already done so.

CUSTOMER SERVICE

Jones (1997) identifies a superintendent in Washington who feels that bad customer service should result in school employees being fired. In addition, there is a school in Ohio that prepares children to return to school each fall by offering free personal items like sneakers, shirts, lunchboxes, crayons, etc., so the children have no excuse not to return. Furthermore, a middle-school principal from North Carolina tells Jones that she gets weekly calls at home from students who have forgotten things in their lockers. She meets those students at the school and unlocks the doors so the children can retrieve their forgotten items. "I'd rather be seen as too accommodating than as not accommodating enough," she explains (as cited in Jones).

The issue here is what message this is sending to those students. People forget things all the time. If being able to retrieve those things were always a possibility, nobody would have a reason to remember anything. And, if the point is to prove that school administrators view students as customers, the adage that the customer is always right can cause debilitating effects for children who need to discover that being wrong and making mistakes are learning experiences. Furthermore, if a teacher fears being fired for not being customer-friendly there is little recourse for students misbehaving or arguing a test grade. On the other hand, even students who misbehave are bodies in chairs and dollars per school budgets

ADMINISTRATORS AS PROMOTERS

Most superintendents don't take their positions because they are marketing professionals. However, in some areas, the second profession is essential to the first. In urban school districts in Ohio, the public school systems are struggling to survive as "[t]he pervasive loss of state and local monies is having a devastating effect" (May, 2007). Legally, public money is being filtered to charter schools that also receive resources from private organizations. According to May, thirty percent of the charter schools operating in Ohio are managed by companies earning a profit. Steering students away from such schools is the job of superintendents who have to make a case for parents to choose to remain in their traditional public school system. For the families who don't have the option of choice—those who can't afford transportation to a charter school or to move out of their poor local districts—education is still a priority, and their needs must be met; superintendents and other public school officials have to make sure those needs are met, even with fewer dollars in their budgets.

Reaching parents and students is not the only reason schools market themselves. In order to promote higher achievement rates and better facilities, district administrators also have to attract quality teachers and show taxpayers that their money is being used efficiently. Schools are creating DVDs and hiring website creators to fill these needs. Mounds View Public Schools in Minneapolis hired professionals to create a video to promote its academic achievement rates and personalized student attention. While the video production cost the district $17,000 in 2006, the district adds $4,600 to its budget for every student enrolled; the cost of the video is minimal in comparison to the funding additional students will bring to the districts' operation (Pascopella, 2005). School districts like those in urban Ohio can't spare the cost of a professional video and have to create other means to attract and keep their consumers.

IMPLICATIONS—SELECTIVE MARKETING

Giving parents and their children the choice of educational institutions is a positive move for public school systems. Price (2006) notes that:

Although all charter schools must implement open enrollment, some target specific student populations such as teen mothers, students with disabilities, students interested in the arts, or students who do not perform well in a formal school setting (Price).

People in these specific populations are rarely focused on in a positive way, so this type of marketing—offering options when there used to be none—is generally viewed as beneficial.

However, some school districts are creating unfair advantages with regard to higher achievement rates by marketing only the students they feel will perform successfully in their schools. Lubienski conducted a study examining the marketing practices of the Holland, Michigan school district. According to his research, "rather than simply offering information on school effectiveness, marketing may instead be targeted more toward particular audiences, suggesting a degree of selectiveness on the part of schools in competitive environments."

Something to consider when looking at how schools market students is what students and their parents view as important with regard to what schools should offer. Looking through the promotional materials from the Holland public school districts, Lubienski notes that information on "instruction and academics, student characteristics, academic facilities, and human resources were used quite frequently, as were … test scores". This information is quality data that shows a school's success, what the student body is like, and how qualified the teachers are. Most of this information is also reported in annual documents required by public schools; the data is already accessible to families who want to view it. As a promotional attribute, such information sells itself without a marketing strategy. Charter schools in the same area, however, promote information that is not required in annual reports. Marketing for charter schools in the Holland district focuses more on proving how different they are from the public schools by describing their academic programs. Private schools in the area tended to promote the morality of their students in addition to their uniforms and religious beliefs. All schools promoted their school's logos (Lubienski).

While Lubienski's data doesn't clearly prove that the Holland charter schools are marketing specific types of students, it does show that the tendency to do so is there. For example:

Local elementary charter schools are growing, largely by attracting fewer minority students and fewer economically disadvantaged students than the closest neighboring public schools. This is despite the fact that test scores are very comparable-and not substantially superior-to neighboring public schools. (That is, the public schools have done a comparable job despite the fact that they are working with students with fewer English skills and higher rates of poverty-suggesting superior effectiveness.) It is important to note that the public school district provides promotional information in both English and Spanish and advertises in the Spanish-language newspaper. The charter schools do not. Similar dynamics are evident with the personal images used in the marketing materials. All schools have promotional materials that include representations of students or teachers. The materials from charter schools significantly underrepresent Hispanic students, who make up 13% to 25% of the enrollment at area charter schools but do not appear in any of the human images in these materials. The local private schools have almost no Hispanic students, which is reflected in the images in their promotional materials, but Asian American students (about 1.5%-3% of local private schools) are disproportionately represented in marketing efforts-for example, constituting 15% to 30% of the students in different promotional videos (Lubienski).

The Holland charter school administrators who created the promotional materials for the schools compiled information to gain the interest of parents and students. It can be argued that many students have more interest in who else would be attending their classes than they have in school academics. However, regardless of the message the promotional materials may send to students and their parents, one thing is clear about all of the schools in this study. As Lubienski notes, "in view of the types of information used to sell school services, parents are left with an inconsistent and uneven knowledge base from which to make reasonable judgments about the relative merits of different schools".

SELECTIVE INFORMATION

In addition to selecting specific students for enrollment, some schools prefer to keep as many students as they can regardless of laws that state otherwise. Price discusses the Los Angeles Unified School District and the Compton Unified School District, the two largest public school systems in California. The districts are facing complaints from the Alliance for School Choice and the Coalition on Urban Renewal and Education for not suggesting that students transfer to more successful schools as is written in the No Child Left Behind Act. According to NCLB, students are supposed to be provided with the opportunity to change public schools if the one they are attending proves to be weaker for two years in a row (with regard to meeting state standards) compared to its competition. Being sanctioned for noncompliance could mean that the California districts lose Title 1 education funds, a sanction that should be imposed on many more districts for doing the same thing (Price).

The Alliance for School Choice notes that:

In virtually every large urban school district, the number of children eligible for transfers to better-performing public schools exceeds the seats available in such schools … As a consequence, even though lack of capacity is no defense, many school districts evade their obligations, thus far with no consequences (as cited in Price).

Whether or not there is room at the stronger school is not the issue; school districts being held accountable for what they are expected to do is the concern. As a result of this noncompliance, students will remain in weaker schools because parents who don't know they have a choice, can't make one.

Viewpoints

WHAT IS THE MESSAGE?

Just as any other service industry, school managers (superintendents, principals, teachers) are going one step above what is considered average. Accommodating students and their parents is a priority for the people who don't want one less student enrolled next year. As a result, students may not be getting the full picture of how the world really works. For example, people don't usually get back into locked buildings simply by making a phone call. Nor does a school's logo or activity profile mean it is academically successful. With so much riding on a student's academic achievement, it is essential to receive accurate marketing materials regarding what different schools offer. It would be difficult to tell, however, what information is reliable and therefore, the decision of the most effective school depends on active research and knowing which attributes are best for the student.

School officials competing for students have a difficult job. Finding ways to over compensate, like providing students shoes or school supplies to ensure they will show up on the first day of class is essential to keep a school's doors open. In turn, having transportation provided, receiving an education from the comfort of home, or being transferred to a stronger academic institution are only some of the perks of being made available to education consumers. Whether or not most people consider education a product is irrelevant with regard to how marketing strategies are going to change. For the education industry, such strategies are not new and whenever possible will advance to meet the demands of district budgets as well as those they consider consumers of their product.

TERMS & CONCEPTS

Charter Schools: Independent public schools that are run by educators, parents, and private investors that are at least partially funded by state, local, or government resources.

Consumer: Someone who buys/purchases a product.

Cyberschool: School offering courses entirely online.

Magnet Schools: Public schools specializing in particular fields like the sciences or languages or more generalized schools that draw students from outside a district as a means of integrating school populations.

Marketing: Selling products or services through promotion such as television ads, letters, flyers, and websites.

No Child Left Behind Act of 2001 (NCLB): Legislation enacted to ensure that all students (regardless of ethnicity, socioeconomic status, or disability) have access to instructional approaches that have been proven to be successful.

Private School: A school that is not run by local or state governments and that charges tuition for enrollment.

Promotion: A way of marketing or advertising a product.

Public School: A state and locally funded school providing education free of charge.

Maureen McMahon

BIBLIOGRAPHY

Campitelli, G. (2013). Schools have plenty to shout about. *Primary & Middle Years Educator, 11*, 22-25. Retrieved December 15, 2013, from EBSCO Online Database Education Research Complete.

Carr, N. (2012). Promoting public schools. *American School Board Journal, 199*, 32-33. Retrieved December 15, 2013, from EBSCO Online Database Education Research Complete.

Damast, A. (2007, Apr 20). Be true to your cyberschool. *Business Week Online, 5*. Retrieved October 30, 2007, from EBSCO Online Database Business Source Premier.

Jones, R. (1997). Kids as education customers. *Education Digest, 62*, 10. Retrieved October 29, 2007, from EBSCO Online Database Education Research Complete.

Lubienski, C. (2007). Marketing schools: Consumer goods and competitive incentives for consumer information. *Education & Urban Society, 40*, 118-141. Retrieved November 5, 2007, from EBSCO Online Database Academic Search Premier.

May, J. J. (2007). The market-driven age of education: Challenges of urban school leadership. *Mid-Western Educational Researcher, 20*, 28-34. Retrieved November 5, 2007, from EBSCO Online Database Education Research Complete.

Pascopella, A. (2005). Selling schools via video. *District Administration, 41*, 24. Retrieved October 29, 2007, from EBSCO Online Database Academic Search Premier.

Price, J. H. (2006, March 24). Two groups say school districts violated U.S. law. *The Washington Times*, A10.

SUGGESTED READING

Ball, S. J., & Gewirtz, S. (1997). Girls in the education market: Choice, competition and complexity. *Gender and Education, 9*, 207-222.

Bird, W. L. (1999). *"Better living": Advertising, media, and the new vocabulary of business leadership, 1935-1955*. Evanston, IL: Northwestern University Press.

Bracey, G. W. (2002). *The war against America's public schools: Privatizing schools, commercializing education*. Boston: Allyn & Bacon.

Brighouse, H. (2000). *School choice and social justice*. Oxford, UK: Oxford University Press.

Brouillette, M. J. (1999, Early Fall). Public schools exchange monopoly power for marketing prowess. *Michigan Education Report*. Retrieved July 10, 2003, from http://educationreport.org.

Brown, B. W. (1992). Why governments run schools. *Economics of Education Review, 11*, 287-300.

Center for Education Reform. (2000). *Charter schools today: Changing the face of American education*. Washington, DC: Author.

Davies, B., & Ellison, L. (1997). *Strategic marketing for schools: How to harmonise marketing and strategic development for an effective school*. London: Pitman.

Gee, J. P. (2001). Identity as an analytic lens for research in education. In W. Secada (Ed.), *Review of research in education, 2000-2001* (Vol. 25, pp. 99-125). Washington, DC: American Educational Research Association.

Gifford, M., Phillips, K., & Ogle, M. (2000). *Five year charter school study: An overview. Arizona education analysis*. Phoenix, AZ: Goldwater Institute, Center for Market-Based Education. (ERIC Document Reproduction Service No. ED454607). Retrieved December 12, 2007, from EBSCO Online Education Research Database.

Halchin, L. E. (1999). And this parent went to market: Education as a public versus private good. In R. Maranto, S. Milliman, F. Hess, & A. Gresham (Eds.), *School choice in the real world: Lessons from Arizona charter schools* (pp. 19-38). Boulder, CO: Westview.

Harvey, J. A., & Busher, H. (1996). Marketing schools and consumer choice. *International Journal of Educational Management, 10*, 26-32.

Hesketh, A. J., & Knight, P. T. (1998). Secondary school prospectuses and educational markets. *Cambridge Journal of Education, 28*, 21-36.

Hill, P. T., Pierce, L. C., & Guthrie, J. W. (1997). *Reinventing public education: How contracting can transform America's schools*. Chicago: University of Chicago Press.

Holcomb, J. H. (1993). *Educational marketing*. Lanham, MD: University Press of America.

Horn, J., & Miron, G. (2000). *The impact of charter schools on public and parochial schools: Case studies of school districts in western and central Michigan*. Kalamazoo: Western Michigan University, The Evaluation Center.

Howell, W. G., & Peterson, P. E. (2004). Uses of theory in randomized field trials: Lessons from school voucher research on disaggregation, missing data, and the generalization of findings. *American Behavioral Scientist, 47*, 634-657.

Hoxby, C. M. (1998). When parents can choose, what do they choose? The effects of school choice on curriculum and atmosphere. In S. Mayer & P. Peterson (Eds.), *When schools make a difference* (pp. 281-316). Washington, DC: The Brookings Institution Press.

Kates, W. (2001, August 29). *Public schools respond to competition with marketing efforts*. Associated Press. Retrieved on September 3, 2001, from the www.asbj.com.

King, K. A. (2007). Charter schools in Arizona: Does being a for-profit institution make a difference? *Journal of Economic Issues, 41*, 729-746. Retrieved October 30, 2007, from EBSCO Online Database Business Source Premier.

Kirp, D. L. (2003). *Shakespeare, Einstein, and the bottom line: The marketing of higher education*. Cambridge, MA: Harvard University Press.

Kowalski, T. J. (Ed.). (2000). *Public relations in schools* (2nd Ed.). Upper Saddle River, NJ: Merrill.

Krueger, A. B., & Zhu, P. (2004a). Another look at the New York City school voucher experiment. *American Behavioral Scientist, 47*, 658-698.

Krueger, A. B., & Zhu, P. (2004b). Inefficiency, subsample selection bias, and nonrobustness: A response to Paul E. Peterson and William G. Howell. *American Behavioral Scientist, 47*, 718-728.

Labaree, D. F. (1997). Public goods, private goods: The American struggle over educational goals. *American Educational Research Journal, 34*, 39-81.

Labaree, D. F. (2000). No exit: Public education as an inescapably public good. In L. Cuban & D. Shipps (Eds.), *Reconstructing the common good in education: Coping with intractable American dilemmas* (pp. 110-129). Stanford, CA: Stanford University Press.

Lehman, J. G. (1999). *And now a word from our sponsors-Your local public schools*. Midland, MI: Mackinac Center for Public Policy.

Lober, I. M. (1993). *Promoting your school: A public relations handbook*. Lancaster, PA: Technomic.

Lubienski, C. (2000). Whither the common good? A critique of home schooling. *Peabody Journal of Education, 75*, 207-232.

Lubienski, C. (2003). Innovation in education markets: Theory and evidence on the impact of competition and choice in charter schools. *American Educational Research Journal, 40*, 395-443.

Lubienski, C. (2005). Public schools in marketized environments: Shifting incentives and unintended consequences of competition-based educational reforms. *American Journal of Education, 111*, 464-486.

Mackinac Center for Public Policy. (1999a). *Privatization in education* (No. MPR1999-03). Midland, MI: Author. Retrieved December 12, 2007, from http://education-report.org.

Mackinac Center for Public Policy. (1999b, January 18). Public schools step up marketing. *Michigan Education Report*. Retrieved December 1, 2007, from http://mackinac.org.

Maranto, R., Milliman, S., Hess, F., & Gresham, A. (1999). Do charter schools improve district schools? Three approaches to the question. In R. Maranto, S. Milliman, F. Hess, & A. Gresham (Eds.), *School choice in the real world: Lessons from Arizona charter schools* (pp. 129-141). Boulder, CO: Westview.

Marchand, R. (1998). *Creating the corporate soul: The rise of public relations and corporateimagery in American big business*. Berkeley: University of California Press.

Masters, W. A., & Sanogo, D. (2002). Welfare gains from quality certification of infant foods: Results from a market experiment in Mali. *American Journal of Agricultural Economics, 84*, 974-989.

Miron, G., & Nelson, C. (2002). *What's public about charter schools? Lessons learned about choice and accountability*. Thousand Oaks, CA: Corwin Press.

Mulholland, Lori A. (1996). *Charter schools: The reform and the research* [Policy Brief]. Tempe, AZ: Arizona State University, Morrison Institute for Public Policy. (ERIC Document Reproduction Service No. ED395372). Retrieved December 12, 2007, from EBSCO Online Education Research Database.

NEA's policy on charter schools. (n.d.) Retrieved November 6, 2007, from the National Education Association, http://nea.org.

Peterson, P. E., & Howell, W. G. (2004). Efficiency, bias, and classification schemes: A response to Alan B. Krueger and Pei Zhu. *American Behavioral Scientist, 47*, 699-717.

Rofes, E. (1998). *How are school districts responding to charter laws and charter schools?* Berkeley, CA: Policy Analysis for California Education.

Rothstein, R. (2004). *Class and schools: Using social, economic, and educational reform to close the Black-White achievement gap*. Washington, DC: Economic Policy Institute.

Sack, J. L. (2002). Charter pioneers force public school officials to modify operations. *Education Week, 21*, 18-19.

Sandström, F. M., & Bergström, F. (2002). *School vouchers in practice: Competition won't hurt you!* [Working Paper No. 578]. Stockholm: Research Institute of Industrial Economics.

Savoye, C. (2001, April 26). Feeling heat of competition, public schools try advertising. *Christian Science Monitor Electronic Edition*. Retrieved April 26, 2001, from http://csmonitor.com.

Schlosser, E. (2001). *Fast food nation: The dark side of the all-American meal*. Boston: Houghton Mifflin.

Smith, K. B. (2003). *The ideology of education: The commonwealth, the market, and America's schools*. Albany: State University of New York Press.

Stemler, S. E. (2004). A comparison of consensus, consistency, and measurement approaches to estimating interrater reliability. *Practical Assessment, Research & Evaluation, 9*. Retrieved March 5, 2004, from http://PAREonline.net.

Walberg, H. J., & Bast, J. L. (2003). *Education and capitalism: How overcoming our fear of markets and economics can improve America's schools.* Stanford, CA: Hoover Institution Press.

Whitty, G. (1997). Creating quasi-markets in education: A review of recent research on parental choice and school autonomy in three countries. In W. L. Boyd & J. G. Cibulka (Eds.), *Review of research in education* (Vol. 22, pp. 3-47). Washington, DC: American Educational Research Association.

Whitty, G., & Power, S. (1997). Quasi-markets and curriculum control: Making sense of recent education reform in England and Wales. *Educational Administration Quarterly, 33,* 219-240.

Whitty, G., & Power, S. (2000). Marketization and privatization in mass education systems. *International Journal of Educational Development, 20,* 93-107.

Section 7: Public School Education

Introduction

Are you interested in entering the teaching profession? Or are you simply curious about how pedagogical decisions are made and what constitutes the curriculum for specific subject areas? This section opens with issues of context as well as debates that influence modern schooling. In most cases, the debates are ongoing. Educators and policy makers engage in discourse about redesigning curricula to meet 21st century needs while entire communities weigh the impediments to conditions that stand in the way of the academic achievement of their children.

The contributing authors examine foundational concepts that guide practice and inform initiatives for educational reform. They approach their subject matter holistically by addressing the nexus between students, teachers, administrators, parents, and communities.

URBAN EDUCATION

This article provides an overview of the critical issues in urban education. The article describes the significant characteristics of and challenges facing urban learners, urban teachers, and urban schools. In spite of the challenges, some urban schools have succeeded, and this article explores the major factors that have led to their success. These factors include targeted curricula and instructional programs, academic and relational engagement with students and their families, and the creation of a positive learning environment. However, this overview also explores the tremendous difficulties that many urban schools face, such as large student populations, inadequate facilities, lack of funding, and very diverse students and teachers. Urban teachers also must overcome many obstacles in order to succeed. Some of the challenges they face include insufficient teaching resources, substantial administrative responsibilities, and learning to work in an unfamiliar environment. In spite of these difficulties, urban students and teachers can learn to work together to create a meaningful urban education experience. Some of the distinguishing characteristics of successful urban education are the ability to overcome cultural differences, effective classroom management, and a safe and secure school campus. The following sections describe these concepts in more detail.

KEYWORDS: Assessment; At Risk; Benchmarks; Diversity; English as a Second Language; Inclusion; Literacy; No Child Left Behind Act of 2001; Title I Programs

OVERVIEW

As cities across the United States swell with populations that boast increasing inner-city populations and families with histories that can be traced to countries around the world, schools are facing ever greater challenges in meeting the needs of the young people from these diverse communities. Some of the students from these families speak little, if any, English. Other students live in dire poverty. Still others face routine violence in their communities. These young people come to schools with tremendous needs that extend beyond their academic development. In spite of these difficulties, many urban students and teachers

have learned to cope with the challenges they face and have succeeded. Likewise, some urban schools offer a meaningful education to their students and are an asset to their communities. However, the reality is still stark for many urban schools. Facing inadequate funding and resources, these schools struggle to provide a solid education that will prepare students to thrive in the world of business and secondary education. The following sections explore the factors that are present in the successes and challenges that are a reality in urban education.

URBAN EDUCATION

Urban learners are diverse, and thus urban education must strive to meet the needs of these challenging yet dynamic students. Urban learners include students from every racial, ethnic, linguistic, and socioeconomic background. However, with the expansion of the suburbs and private education options, urban schools reflect the populations of their communities. Urban communities are increasingly being made up of minority groups such as African Americans, Hispanics, Asians, or Native Americans, and these young people disproportionately populate urban schools. As a result, many public urban schools consist largely of minority and/or lower-income students, whereas public suburban and private schools are predominately white and middle income. In addition, urban learners are more likely to be from lower socioeconomic groups and to present special learning needs or learning difficulties. Although this emerging division has presented challenges for urban students, teachers, and schools, urban education is still a critical concern for many families, educators, and communities. Thus, urban education is by definition complex, consisting of a diverse group of individuals, many of whom are working together to make their schools a better place for everyone.

URBAN STUDENTS

Although many urban students desire a good education and a successful school, many urban learners struggle with poor academic achievement. As a result, many urban students drop out of high school before graduating. There are many reasons for this—pregnancies, unstable homes, the necessity to enter the workforce, or the lack of volition and community support. Only about 60 percent of the students in urban areas graduated from high school in 2005, and many of those who do manage to graduate are ill-prepared for higher education or the workplace (Swanson, 2009; Schulte, 2004). In some of the largest cities, the statistics are even grimmer, where less than one-half of the black male students in urban schools graduate (Sege, 2006; Noguera, 2012).

One challenge facing many urban students is their disproportionate placement in special education classes. Many urban children come to school ill prepared for the structure of the classroom or the demands of schoolwork and homework. Likewise, urban teachers often have insufficient training in understanding how to meet the many needs of urban students, including needs that go beyond those typically provided in a classroom setting. For instance, some urban students need assistance with developing basic language and social skills or may lack sufficient academic skills for their grade level because they were simply passed in classes where they may not have actually mastered the material. These children frequently fall further and further behind until they are likely to qualify for special education. Although special education is ostensibly intended to help students make progress, it often results in students losing the experience of interacting with their peers in the general education classroom and being challenged to keep up academically with fellow students.

In addition to lower graduation rates and a higher presence in special education classes, urban students are more likely to experience school violence and disciplinary problems. Urban and minority learners are at much greater risk for office referrals, suspensions, and expulsions than nonminority students. There are many reasons for this. One reason may be that urban students practice behaviors in their homes or communities that do not translate well to the structure of school classrooms and thus have difficulty adapting to the academic environment. Urban students may also experience less support from their families and communities to attend or complete school and may even be the first person in their family to approach high school graduation. However, when students become disconnected from their classes and peers due to disciplinary problems, they lose valuable opportunities to learn both academic and social

skills. Furthermore, repeated suspensions or disciplinary actions can have the psychological effect of communicating to students that they are not wanted, further disenfranchising them from the support and structure of their classes and peers.

Minority males, particularly African American males, are the most vulnerable segment of the school population for poor school outcomes due to disciplinary problems. The reasons for this are not entirely clear. The roots of this problem are likely a combination of developmental, attitudinal, and instructional factors. It is clear, however, that many young students in urban schools struggle to meet the minimum academic benchmarks for their grade level and feel a sense of failure, thus increasing their likelihood of dropping out of school and perpetuating the statistics of lower academic achievement among urban learners. The reasons for lower academic achievement among urban students are multifaceted, with no segment of society completely to blame. Nurturing urban students to excellence takes continual commitment from many different sources—parents, teachers, schools, businesses, mentors, relatives, and even local and national community leaders and resources.

URBAN SCHOOLS

In spite of the many challenges facing urban students, urban schools and educational programs can flourish and succeed. Urban education can be a positive and effective influence in the lives of urban students even though many urban learners come from poverty and lack many of the conditions typically considered fundamental to academic performance, such as stable homes and family support. In short, urban children can learn, regardless of family background, and urban schools can be effective through appropriate expectations, solid leadership, targeted instructional practices and positive learning environments, and relationships with families and community resources. The following sections describe these factors in greater detail.

TARGETED CURRICULUM & INSTRUCTIONAL PROGRAMS

Urban schools that succeed do so because the teachers and staff recognize and work in conjunction with the unique educational needs of their students.

Thus, although suburban schools across town may use instructional strategies and resources that are mainstream and typical of similar schools, effective urban schools assess the educational needs of their students to determine their strengths and weaknesses and then identify instructional strategies and allocate resources according to this assessment. For instance, teachers may include resources in their curriculum and lesson plans that contain materials and references that are familiar to urban students. Or, teachers may take time to reteach lower-level skills that students should have already mastered.

Additionally, teachers use specific resources to target areas of weakness in their students and then teach intensively toward the goal of student mastery rather than completion of the material. This means that teachers continue to present material in various ways until the students master it instead of moving past material simply because of time constraints or because the material has been covered at least once. Teachers determine mastery through progressive monitoring. This means that these teachers use daily and weekly assessments to determine whether students have gained sufficient mastery of the material, such that it is appropriate to move forward with the presentation of new material.

ACADEMIC & RELATIONAL ENGAGEMENT WITH STUDENTS & FAMILIES

The relationship between academic engagement and academic achievement is direct and immediate. Students who are more engaged with the material they are studying are more likely to master and retain the material. Effective urban teachers are skilled in designing and implementing lessons that keep students responding academically to the lessons so that they have a firm grasp on the information they receive and ultimately internalize the material. In addition, students who are academically engaged in the material they are learning maintain high expectations regarding their ability to learn and master future lessons that will be built on the information they are learning. High expectations are essential for good teaching and learning. Thus, urban schools succeed when teachers are encouraged to set academic and social goals for their classrooms as well as for individual students. By specifying academic goals, teachers have a clear sense of what they are trying to accomplish during the school year, and the students

have an understanding of what will be expected of them. In addition, these expectations need to be continually communicated and monitored so that both teachers and students are invested in working toward their implementation and accomplishment.

In addition to being engaged in the academics covered in the classroom, teachers in successful urban schools tend to be more engaged in their students' families. Although many urban learners come from blended or single-parent families, most of these students have some family unit that can play an important role in facilitating the educational process. Many of these impoverished families may have fewer resources or diminished time to commit to the educational process but do understand the importance of education and are willing to support that process to the extent that they can. Urban schools that incorporate families in the educational process—through stronger parent-teacher communication, parent involvement in sports and academic programs, or other means—are more likely to succeed. This is because students are better able to absorb and retain information and lessons when the educational process is reinforced or valued at home.

ESTABLISHING A POSITIVE LEARNING ENVIRONMENT

Many poor urban students have special gifts and talents that may remain dormant or undeveloped without being identified and nurtured. Successful urban schools create an environment that values both education and the unique abilities of individual students. Since many urban students do not have enrichment or extracurricular options in their homes or communities, it is important that urban schools aggressively attempt to cultivate the innate abilities of these students. Enrichment interventions should not be dismissed or cut due to fiscal or other reasons. Instead, urban schools that thrive do so because of their focus on affirming and motivating students and continually stressing the worth of education, commitment to valuing each individual and honoring the successes and unique achievements of their students.

URBAN TEACHERS

Urban students, even those who are efficient or adequate learners, require continuous and rigorous instruction. Thus, urban teachers must implement special strategies to meet the educational needs of their students and the demands of teaching in the urban environment. For instance, urban teachers must work to develop both the academic levels as well as the social skills of their students. These teachers must also find ways to affirm and encourage students daily, while stressing the value of school, education, and academic achievement. Urban teachers must also set clear and attainable objectives that they stress to students so that students have a solid understanding of what is expected of them and how to achieve these expectations. Finally, urban teachers must develop ways to cope with behavioral disruptions in ways that encourage offenders to curtail the negative behavior and remain engaged in the classroom activities while creating minimal disruptions to the education of other students in the classroom. This may include fostering stronger relationships with the families of students, creating a system of daily or weekly rewards for positive behavior and academic progress, or building a more meaningful relationship with the disruptive student so that school seems less impersonal to them.

CHALLENGES FACING URBAN SCHOOLS

Urban school systems have unique traits that create special problems and challenges for teachers, administrators, parents, and students. These challenges include the fact that many urban schools are overpopulated so that teachers and teaching resources are strained, inadequate funding, and the diversity and disenfranchisement of students and their families from mainstream social services, discourse, and privileges. The following sections will explain these challenges in greater detail.

SIZE OF URBAN SCHOOLS

Urban schools are often unwieldy, in terms of their size, structure, and the role of their administrative bureaucracy. Urban schools are run by bureaucracies that often function quite poorly and are cut off from the communities that they are supposed to serve. As a result of this bureaucracy, teachers and students feel less empowered in their schools and the educational process and may expend less effort in meeting their educational goals. Urban schools also tend to be overpopulated. This is because many urban schools were constructed decades ago when community populations were much smaller. However, as cities have grown over the years and the student populations

have risen, these physical structures are often inadequate to meet the needs of larger student bodies. To cope with the space shortages, urban schools are sometimes forced to hold classes in alternative spaces, such as gyms, cafeterias, or music rooms, or to simply cancel certain programs or increase the class sizes. However, none of these options create an ideal learning environment, and thus the overpopulation of students in urban schools can be a significant deterrent to the educational process.

FUNDING OF URBAN SCHOOLS

Many urban schools are also plagued by inadequate funding. Teachers and students in the nation's cities frequently face a scarcity of supplies, materials, and teaching resources. Teachers are thus forced to pay for these materials themselves or do without them. Even when schools do have some resources, these materials are often inadequate. The textbooks may be out of date, teachers may lack access to photocopy or other equipment, or teachers may not have enough books to issue to all students or to replace books that students lose or destroy. Some urban schools have developed fundraisers or implemented other efforts to raise money for additional resources. However, the lack of funding for urban schools remains a significant concern for teachers and students.

DIVERSE POPULATIONS OF URBAN SCHOOLS

Historically, students in urban schools have been diverse in terms of ethnicity and background, and thus urban school systems have had the responsibility of educating a tremendously varied group of students. These students are not only made up of minority populations of families within the local community, but also of students whose families have come to the United States only recently and who may lack an understanding of the language, culture, and customs that are norms in their communities. Further, these populations also often share the characteristic of having been discriminated against or otherwise disenfranchised from the mainstream population. This may make them hesitant, or even hostile, toward the prospect of adopting the language and daily practices of the mainstream population. These students may come to school with an underlying suspicion of schools, teachers, and the educational process. As a result, they may struggle to adapt to the classroom environment and to meet the academic expectations for their grade level. Thus, teachers are faced with the additional challenges of addressing the underlying emotional or psychological resistances that may hamper the ability of their students to learn and assimilate the materials being presented in the classroom.

CHALLENGES FACING URBAN TEACHERS

Urban teachers also face many challenges. Some of these challenges can spur teachers to seek greater methods of connecting with their students and designing relevant instructional materials. Some of these challenges, however, can be so significant that they undermine the optimal learning environment that teachers want to create in their classrooms. Some of the most significant challenges that urban teachers, and especially new teachers, encounter include insufficient teaching resources, extensive administrative responsibilities, and the process of learning how to teach and thrive in an urban environment, especially for new teachers who have little or no exposure to urban communities. The following sections explain how these challenges can affect the teaching and learning experience in urban schools.

INSUFFICIENT TEACHING RESOURCES

In most urban schools, the lack of meaningful teaching resources and materials is a serious problem, especially for new teachers who have not accumulated sufficient books, wall decorations, teaching aids, and classroom supplies. Many urban schools do not allocate the money needed for individual teachers to purchase the resources necessary to accomplish their educational objectives. Instead, teachers are issued the books that the school system has required for their grade level and subject area and many times, little else. As a result of this chronic underfunding, supplies and teaching materials (especially high quality teaching materials) are scarce, leaving teachers to either do without these materials or attempt to design their own materials using their own money and resources.

Many teachers pay for teaching supplies out of their own pockets because they need the materials to do an adequate job. In addition, many urban teachers also pay for basic supplies for their students. This is because at schools in poor neighborhoods, parents may not be able to provide supplies such as pencils, paper, or calculators, so teachers are faced with having to purchase these materials themselves because these resources are indispensable for learning and classroom

management. Otherwise, students who lack paper and pencils may simply use the class time to disrupt others. Since teachers cannot require these students to work without any materials, if students do not enter the classroom with the basic materials needed to participate in class, teachers must either provide the materials themselves or face the possible consequences of students who are not participating in class activities.

Further, in many urban schools, photocopiers or other technological equipment are often inaccessible or nonexistent. This may be because schools lack a copy machine or because these machines are broken or off limits to teachers. Thus, teachers also face the prospect of having to pay for copies of teaching materials out of pocket. Finally, many schools have so few textbooks that teachers are prohibited from issuing the textbooks for students to take home. This makes it difficult for teachers to assign homework. Or, teachers may discover that their students face such transient living situations that textbooks are easily misplaced, and teachers cannot continue to issue textbooks to students who are unable to keep track of their books outside of the school environment.

Similarly, although the availability of school computers with Internet access has grown throughout the country since the mid-1990s, the technological access gap, or "digital divide," is slowly closing for urban students as compared to their suburban and town counterparts. For example, in 2000, only 70 percent of urban public schools had instructional computers with Internet access available for student use, whereas 79 percent of suburban schools and 83 percent of town schools offered them. In 2008, 97 percent of city schools had instructional web-enabled computers, while 99 percent of suburban and 98 percent of town schools had such tools at their disposal (National Center for Education Statistics, 2012). Thus, insufficient teaching resources continue to pose a significant challenge that urban teachers must face.

ADMINISTRATIVE RESPONSIBILITIES

Urban teachers must often complete a significant amount of highly detailed clerical work. This may be because urban schools receive federal and state funds that require that teachers in turn provide certain documentation. Teachers may also be required to track and submit information to their own administrators or school districts. Administrative responsibilities are also dependent upon the level of management states and school districts maintain over the curriculum and instruction provided in individual classrooms. Some states and school districts exert a great deal of control over how and what is taught, while others have fewer regulations. For instance, teachers may be required to report attendance for the day, week, month, and term; submit detailed daily and monthly lesson plans and assessment forms; and complete teacher-parent requests and other internal forms. In addition, teachers must also grade, record, and average all of the tests and assignments completed by students and submit these scores on a periodic basis.

These tasks create substantial administrative responsibilities that can detract from the time and attention that teachers can give to the students themselves. While these responsibilities can be managed, teachers must plan for the time and effort that it takes for them to be completed, and some teachers find that these administrative responsibilities are too demanding to be completed during the school day. However, teachers may have other responsibilities after school ends, such as coaching, serving as a club sponsor, or meeting other personal and family obligations, and thus many teachers find it difficult to manage their instruction workload plus their administrative responsibilities. Urban teachers, in particular, who work in a high-stress environment, may find the workload of administrative duties that awaits them when the school day ends simply too much to bear. Although many schools and school districts have tried to streamline some of the lesson planning and attendance-keeping responsibilities to eliminate unnecessary paperwork, documentation is still a high priority in most schools, and thus a teacher's administrative responsibilities have become a significant part of their job.

WORKING WITHIN THE URBAN SCHOOL SETTING
Urban school systems have characteristics that create unique challenges for teachers.

- First, many urban schools are large, with high student populations. Yet these same schools may have less space and fewer resources than smaller suburban schools located on sprawling campuses;
- Second, urban schools are often run and managed by layers of bureaucracy that may not function at optimal levels and that may not include active voices from the communities in which they are located;
- Yet another challenge teachers face in the urban school environment is interacting with students of

various ethnicities and religious and moral backgrounds. All over the country, school districts are experiencing a rise in student populations from immigrants that have made urban schools even more culturally and linguistically diverse. Because cities continue to be the first places immigrants settle, urban schools educate the greatest proportion of new immigrants.

As a result, teachers must become very adept at reaching a wide range of students with varying academic and social skills. New teachers in particular may lack adequate training in developing the insights and abilities necessary to reach such a diverse group of students. In addition, students themselves have to learn to adapt to peers of very different backgrounds and cultural and religious beliefs. Students who have not accepted such diversity among their fellow students may act out their fears or frustrations with verbal or physical hostility. Thus, urban teachers must learn to adapt to the unique challenges they face in the urban education environment. Dealing with these challenges requires that teachers make an extra effort to take into account the totality of their students' educational, emotional, physical, and psychological needs when planning lessons and teaching activities.

Applications

SUCCESSFUL URBAN EDUCATION
In many urban areas—and for many local communities—the local school represents the largest publicly funded resource. Schools are very often major employers of local people, particularly in the case of nonteaching staff. Thus, urban schools should endeavor to make their resources available to their local community, not forgetting that their primary function is to educate the children. Teachers, staff, and administrators can create successful urban schools by being mindful that education is a holistic process. Thus, factors such as overcoming cultural differences, successful classroom management, and creating a safe environment are critical elements of great schools. The following sections explore these concepts in more detail.

OVERCOMING CULTURAL DIFFERENCES
Urban education has become synonymous with the education of a diverse group of students, perhaps by a diverse group of teacher, staff, and administrators.

Thus, everyone involved in the education process must work continuously to overcome cultural differences. Further, overcoming cultural differences can be especially challenging because even people of the same ethnic background can be very different, so that individuals cannot be neatly divided into defined categories or groups. For instance, students may share a nationality but hold to different religions, or they may be members of the same racial category but come from different socioeconomic or educational backgrounds.

Successful urban teachers learn to overcome cultural differences and move beyond trends, characteristics, and stereotypes so they become actively engaged with their students as individuals. This may involve calling parents or family members of students to invite them in for a parent-teacher conference. Or, it may mean attending school functions and sporting events in which their students are participating. Or, it may simply involve having a meaningful conversation with each student on a regular basis so that the teacher learns a little bit more about the lives students lead outside of the classroom. As students and teachers get to know one another as individuals, the stereotypes and misunderstandings that are often associated with cultural differences begin to disappear.

CLASSROOM MANAGEMENT

Urban teachers have to know how to deal with the attitudes and habits that city students acquire in their neighborhoods and homes because students bring behaviors grounded in their lives outside school into classrooms. Many students in poor neighborhoods are surrounded by brutal crime, and the behavior that helps them survive in their neighborhood often conflicts with the conduct schools and teachers expect in the classroom environment. In a classroom, students must replace defensiveness and aggressive behavior with the ability to negotiate differences and rely on teachers and school authorities to help resolve differences rather than attempting to deal with conflict themselves or through hostile confrontation. When schools and teachers expect students to follow class policies and school regulations that are at odds with the behavioral mores to which students are accustomed, students may struggle to make this transition. As a result, students may revert to defensive behavior when they feel threatened, and if teachers and schools take punitive action against students, such as suspending or expelling them, students become disenfranchised from their peers and teachers and may fall further behind (academically and socially).

One way that teachers can help students to feel physically and emotionally safe in the classroom setting so they are open to instruction and learning is through sound classroom management techniques that are clearly communicated and fairly enforced. In addition, classroom management expectations must be grounded in realistic expectations that take into account the cultural and educational backgrounds of their students. For instance, certain expectations that are appropriate in well-disciplined schools may be impractical to some urban students, such as having students maintain a complicated filing system for their assignments or bringing a certain notebook to class every day. This is because urban students generally have higher absentee rates and are more likely to move from home to home to stay with various family members during the course of the school year. As a result, they are more likely to misplace books, notebooks, and class assignments that are required in class on a consistent basis.

However, teachers can still maintain high expectations for urban students by focusing on behaviors that can be enforced consistently and that have a positive impact on the classroom environment. For instance, creating lesson plans that are more physically engaging or that allow students to work in small groups and pairs can help students to stay involved in lessons where they would otherwise become disengaged if required to sit in a desk in a straight line for an extended period of time. Also, teachers with students at low reading levels can incorporate exciting and stimulating visual aids to help students use more senses while learning or relearning certain concepts.

Finally, teachers can create certain rules of conduct for their classrooms that are enforced fairly and consistently. Whether these rules may involve how students act toward others, toward the teacher, or toward their own class assignments, students are more likely to yield to expectations that are enforced uniformly and without judgment. High expectations are healthy for students and are an essential part of solid classroom management techniques. Thus, classroom management rules and expectations create an understanding of protocol, which helps students to understand what is necessary to succeed in a classroom. Students are more likely to strive to meet these standards when they perceive them to be fair, worthwhile, and reasonable.

SECURITY

Urban schools also face the risk of criminal damage, including vandalism, theft, and physical violence, at the hands of their students. Thus, security issues have become some of the most critical topics facing schools and communities. In order for meaningful teaching and learning to occur, teachers and students must feel safe in their schools. One way that urban schools have sought to combat the problems with security failures is to try and create a collective sense among student populations that the school belongs to the students and their community. When students feel a sense of ownership, they are less likely to be destructive or careless about the way they treat their school and its resources. Likewise, when a community feels invested in its local school, community members are more likely to keep an eye out for problems and to contact school personnel or law enforcement officials if they spot trouble.

Other means of stepping up security measures can also help to create a safer and more productive learning environment. Some simple steps such as locking unused classrooms and closets, monitoring all entrances and exits, constructing and maintaining solid fences around the school property, and installing alarm systems can go a long way toward managing the flow of students and guests on a school campus. Some schools have installed security cameras in heavily populated or potentially unsafe areas. However, schools must also ensure that they take appropriate measures to stay within the legal bounds of recording, viewing, and punishing acts caught by security cameras. Likewise, schools must be mindful of students' privacy rights even as some seek to improve security through the use of metal detectors and locker searches. Additionally, schools and school districts around the country have also begun hiring onsite and offsite security personnel. The presence of security officers alone can be a significant factor in creating a safer environment, although research indicates that white students feel more fearful when security officers are present than their African American counterparts do (Bachman, Randolph & Brown, 2011). Other security measures have included the installation of bulletproof glass and the locking of school buildings during the school day. Finally, schools can enhance security by simply reminding students, teachers, staff, and administrators to remain vigilant about student activities at all times. Often, problems and conflicts, if caught early, can be diffused before they escalate into dangerous or harmful situations.

CONCLUSION

This article has provided an overview of the critical issues facing urban students, teachers, and schools. Urban students are increasingly diverse, and this raises unique challenges for urban educators. Facing swelling student populations, limited funds and school resources, and significant administrative responsibilities, urban teachers must learn to overcome many obstacles in order to create a positive and constructive learning environment. In addition, urban schools must balance meeting the needs of their students with the administrative and fiscal responsibilities that they face. In spite of these challenges, there are many examples of successful urban students, teachers, and schools. Successful urban education is the result of diligent effort among all parties involved. In particular, some of the characteristics of successful urban education are the ability to overcome the many ethnic and cultural differences of teachers and students, the implementation of solid classroom management techniques by teachers, and the ability to create a safe and secure school campus. When these factors are in place, urban students, teachers, and schools are better equipped to thrive. Thus, although urban education is a challenging process, there are many examples of successes in urban classrooms and schools.

TERMS & CONCEPTS

Accommodations: Changes in the way classroom instruction and tests are designed or administered to respond to the special needs of students with disabilities.

Assessment: In-class tests, standardized tests, or tests from textbook publishers that are used to evaluate student performance.

At Risk: A term applied to students who have not been adequately served by social service or educational systems and who are at risk of educational failure due to lack of services, negative life events, or physical or mental challenges, among others.

Benchmark: Statement that provides a description of student knowledge expected at specific grades, ages, or developmental levels. Benchmarks often are used in conjunction with standards.

Block Scheduling: Instead of traditional 40- to 50-minute periods, block scheduling allows for periods of an hour or more so that teachers can accomplish more during a class session. It also allows for teamwork across subject areas in some schools. For example, a math and science teacher may teach a physics lesson that includes both math and physics concepts.

Curriculum: A plan of instruction that details what students are to know, how they are to learn it, the teacher's role, and the context in which learning and teaching will take place.

Diversity: Inclusion of people with many varying traits and sources of identity, such as race, gender, religion, ethnicity, age, sexual orientation, socio-economic class, and ability.

English as a Second Language (ESL): Classes or support programs for students whose native language is not English.

Enrichment: Additional courses outside those required for graduation.

Free/Reduced Meal Program: A federal program that provides funds for schools to provide meals for students from low-income families.

Highly Qualified Teacher: According to No Child Left Behind Act of 2001, a teacher who has obtained full state teacher certification or has passed the state teacher licensing examination and holds a license to teach in the state; holds a minimum of a bachelor's degree; and has demonstrated subject area competence in each of the academic subjects in which the teacher teaches.

Inclusion: The practice of placing students with disabilities in regular classrooms. Also referred to as "mainstreaming."

Intervention: Funds that schools get for students who are not learning at grade level. They can be used to fund before-school or after-school programs or to pay for materials and instructors.

No Child Left Behind Act of 2001: Signed into law by President George W. Bush in 2002, No Child Left Behind sets performance guidelines for all schools and also stipulates what must be included in accountability reports to parents. It mandates annual student testing, includes guidelines for underperforming schools, and requires states to train all teachers and assistants to be "highly qualified."

School Improvement Program (SIP): A state-funded program for elementary, intermediate, and secondary schools to improve instruction, services, school environment, and organization at school sites according to plans developed by school site councils.

School Site Council (SSC): A group of teachers, parents, administrators, and interested community members who work together to develop and monitor a school's improvement plan. It is a legally required decision-making body for any school receiving federal funds.

Title I Program: A federal program that provides funds to improve the academic achievement for educationally disadvantaged students who score below the 50th percentile on standardized tests, including the children of migrant workers.

Heather Newton

BIBLIOGRAPHY

Bachman, R., Randolph, A., & Brown, B. L. (2011). Predicting perceptions of fear at school and going to and from school for African American and white students: The effects of school security measures. *Youth & Society, 43,* 705–726. Retrieved December 12, 2013, from EBSCO online database Education Research Complete.

Blanchett, W., & Wynne, J. (2007). Reframing urban education discourse: A conversation with and for teacher educators. *Theory Into Practice, 46,* 187–193.

Clemmitt, M. (2007). Fixing urban schools: Outlook. *CQ Researcher, 17,* 379–381.

DiBello, L., Harlin, R., & Brown, M. (2007). Possible schools: The Reggio approach to urban education. *Childhood Education, 83,* 182.

Gastic, B. (2011). Metal detectors and feeling safe at school. *Education & Urban Society, 43,* 486–498. Retrieved December 12, 2013, from EBSCO online database Education Research Complete.

Heilig, J. (2011). As good as advertised? Tracking urban student progress through high school in an environment of accountability. *American Secondary Education, 39,* 17–41. Retrieved December 12, 2013, from EBSCO online database Education Research Complete.

Marsden, B., & Grosvenor, I. (2007). David Reeder and the history of urban education. *History of Education, 36,* 303–313.

Oría, A., et al. (2007). Urban education, the middle classes and their dilemmas of school choice. *Journal of Education Policy, 22,* 91–105.

National Center for Education Statistics. (2012, May). Computers and technology. In *digest of education statistics: 2011* (NCES 2012-001). Retrieved December 12, 2013, from, http://nces.ed.gov.

Noguera, P. A. (2012). Saving black and Latino boys. *Phi Delta Kappan, 93,* 8–12. Retrieved 12.12.2013, from EBSCO online database Education Research Complete.

Rubin, B. (2007). Learner identity amid figured worlds: Constructing (in)competence at an urban high school. *Urban Review, 39,* 217–249. Retrieved December 19, 2007, from EBSCO Online Database Education Research Complete.

Schulte, B. (2004, July 26). Teaching teachers how to connect with urban students. *Washington Post Online,* B01. Retrieved January 22, 2008, from http://washingtonpost.com.

Sege, I. (2006, June 13). Boys to mentors. *Boston Globe Online.* Retrieved January 22, 2008, from http://boston.com.

Shen, F. (2007). Mayors and schools: Minority voices and democratic tensions in urban education. *Urban Affairs Review, 43,* 288–290. Retrieved December 19, 2007, from EBSCO Online Database Education Research Complete.

Swanson, C. B. (2009, April). *Cities in crisis 2009: Closing the graduation gap—Education and economic conditions in America's largest cities.* Bethesda, MD: Editorial Projects in Education Research Center. Retrieved December 12, 2013, from, http://edweek.org.

Veldheer, K. (2007). Comprehensive urban education. *Education Libraries, 30,* 41.

SUGGESTED READING

Baranov, D. (2006). Globalization and urban education. *Encounter, 19,* 12–18. Retrieved January 22, 2008, from EBSCO Online Database Education Research Complete.

Brown, T. (2007). Lost and turned out. *Urban Education, 42,* 432–455. Retrieved December 19, 2007, from EBSCO Online Database Education Research Complete.

Ginsberg, A. (2012) *Embracing Risk in Urban Education: Curiosity, Creativity, and Courage in the Era of "No Excuses" and Relay Race Reform.* Lanham, MD.: Rowman & Littlefield Education.

Lynn, M., Benigno, G., Williams, A. D., Park, G., & Mitchell, C. (2006). Critical theories of race, class and gender in urban education. *Encounter, 19,* 17–25. Retrieved January 22, 2008, from EBSCO Online Database Education Research Complete.

McWilliams, J.A. (2017). The neighborhood stigma: School choice, stratification, and shame. *Policy Futures in Education.* 15(2), 221-238.

Nguyen, N. (2013). Scripting "safe" schools: Mapping urban education and zero tolerance during the long war. *Review of Education, Pedagogy & Cultural Studies, 35,* 277–297. Retrieved December 12, 2013, from EBSCO online database Education Research Complete.

Noguera, P. (2015). Guardians of equity. *Principal.* 95(2), 8-11.

Shirley, D. (2007). Radical possibilities: Public policy, urban education, and a new social movement. *Urban Education, 42,* 502–507. Retrieved January 22, 2008, from EBSCO Online Database Education Research Complete.

Taie, S., Goldring, R., & Spiegelman, M. (Eds.).(2017) *Characteristics of Public Elementary and Secondary School in the United States: Results from the 2015-2016 National Teacher and Principal Survey.* Washington, D.C.: NCES U.S. Department of Education.

RURAL EDUCATION

When considering the subject of rural education, there are often misconceptions by those in urban or suburban environments. They imagine students deprived of the latest in modern educational commodities, taught by teachers unable to gain positions in better schools, struggling to grasp basic concepts, unaware of the complexities of the larger world around them. In reality, rural schooling is perhaps one of the most misunderstood and underestimated gems of American education. Today's rural students often enjoy significant advantages over their urban and suburban counterparts.

KEYWORDS: Beale Codes; Class Size; Community support; Consolidation; English Language Learner (ELL); Golden Egg States; No Child Left Behind Act (NCLB); Rural Education; Rural Schools

OVERVIEW

When considering the subject of rural education, there are often misconceptions by those in urban or suburban environments. They imagine students deprived of the latest in modern educational commodities, taught by teachers unable to gain positions in better schools, struggling to grasp basic concepts, unaware of the complexities of the larger world around them. In reality, rural schooling is perhaps one of the most misunderstood and underestimated gems of American education. Today's rural students often enjoy significant advantages over their urban and suburban counterparts. From the educational benefits of smaller class sizes and individual teacher attention to the social benefits of widespread community support and a comforting sense of belonging, rural schools provide both tangible and intangible benefits to the students and families they serve (Todd & Agnello, 2006; Silverman, 2005).

This is not to say, however, that rural schools are without their challenges. Many rural schools lack the financial or other resources to offer the variety of specialized classes often found in suburban schools. Similarly, opportunities to participate in extracurricular activities are not as numerous for students in rural schools as they usually are for students in suburban schools. Yet, these negatives are often more than compensated for by the many positives of rural schooling. Still, despite studies supporting the benefits rural education offers, many school districts in small rural communities across the country are facing increased pressure to consolidate with surrounding schools or districts on the assumption that consolidation will lead to both lower costs to communities and enhanced performance among students (Silverman).

To understand fully the status of rural education in America today and the unique opportunities and dilemmas it faces, we must first explore the diversity of America's educational landscape and the unique challenges and opportunities faced by rural schools. Following this, we will uncover and examine several misconceptions regarding rural education, and explore the position rural schools occupy both in their communities and in the national educational landscape as a whole.

STATISTICAL BACKGROUND

Based on a need to classify counties according to levels of urbanity, the United States Department of Agriculture Economic Research Service, in the early 1970s, established a scale of classification known as the ERS Rural-Urban Continuum Codes, or the Beale codes, so named for Dr. Calvin Beale, its developer (National Center for Education Statistics, 2003). In addition to filling agricultural purposes, today the Beale codes are used to classify public school districts. According to the Beale codes, districts are categorized as follows:

Metro Counties:
- Counties in metro areas of 1 million population or more;
- Counties in metro areas of 250,000 to 1 million population;
- Counties in metro areas of fewer than 250,000 population.

Non-Metro Counties:
- Urban population of 20,000 or more, adjacent to a metro area;
- Urban population of 20,000 or more, not adjacent to a metro area;
- Urban population of 2,500 to 19,999, adjacent to a metro area;
- Urban population of 2,500 to 19,999, not adjacent to a metro area;
- Completely rural or less than 2,500 urban population adjacent to a metro area;
- Completely rural or less than 2,500 urban population, not adjacent to a metro area.

The US Department of Education's Center for Rural Education has indicated that nearly 42% of America's public schools are in rural areas (New center helps rural schools, 2006). While any percentage would merit attention, this significant national investment in rural education calls for placing critical priority on ensuring the strength and success of our rural schools.

According to the Rural School and Community Trust, a non-profit organization which studies the relationships between successful rural schools and their communities, nearly one-fifth of American public school students attend a rural school; that is, a school located in a community with a population of fewer than 2,500. By the numbers, this adds up to 8,797,497 students for whom rural education is not a study topic but a reality. From the point of view of the educational system, 30.3% of America's public schools are located in areas classified as rural (Johnson & Strange, 2005).

By state, Texas leads the way with 532,378 students enrolled in rural schools, while Rhode Island comes in last with 15,680. Percentage-wise, however, Vermont takes the lead with a full 55.79% of its public school students attending a rural school. Contrast this with bottom-ranking Massachusetts, where only 4.70% populate schools classified as rural. As a ratio of rural public schools to total public schools per state, South Dakota takes the lead with a full 77.56% of its public schools located in rural areas, while Massachusetts again comes in last with its percentage standing at only 5.66 (Johnson & Strange).

While these numbers vary widely from state to state, what they show is that, from Rhode Island to Texas and South Dakota to Vermont, all states are impacted to some degree by rural education; therefore, no state can escape giving close consideration to these types of public schools.

CHALLENGES

By nature of geographical location and community resources, rural schools face unique challenges not experienced by their suburban counterparts. Among these are teacher shortages, demographic poverty, serving students with disabilities, increasing number of English Language Learner (ELL) students requiring teachers certified in ELL programs, consolidation, transportation difficulties, federally mandated requirements, and funding considerations. A brief look at each will provide more comprehensive insight into the obstacles faced by rural schools.

TEACHER SHORTAGES

In Montana, nearly 75% of all public schools are considered rural, with two out of every five of the state's students attending these rural schools (Johnson & Strange). Yet, teachers in Montana rank 48th on the pay scale when compared with the rest of the United States. Even with the high need for teachers, an alarming 70% of students graduating with teaching degrees are opting to leave the state in search of greener pastures. Recognizing the critical ramifications of this departure on the state's ability to provide quality education, legislation has been introduced to provide new teachers with financial incentives to remain in the state and veteran teachers with incentive to continue teaching. However, these measures have been voted down in the state legislature (Silverman).

Furthermore, due to increased federal mandates implemented with the passing of the No Child Left Behind Act (NCLB) in 2002, teachers are routinely required to assume additional responsibilities and, as a result, often find themselves stretched thin. For example, No Child Left Behind mandates that in order to teach a subject to more than one grade level, teachers must be certified in each grade level. The implications of this requirement for rural schools are particularly acute, as they are often unable to offer as extensive a variety of classes as larger suburban schools due to insufficient resources for hiring the necessary teachers.

POVERTY

According to the Rural School and Community Trust, 37.4% of students who attend a rural school qualify for subsidized meals. Of rural families with school-age children, nearly 12% are living below the poverty line, and the average rural per capita income stands at $19,285. Yet, these numbers roughly coincide with national averages, as the US Census Bureau indicates that, as of 2003, 12.5% of the population lived below the poverty line, and the average per capita income as of the 2000 census was only $21,587. Nevertheless, these numbers have a particularly noticeable effect in rural areas where communities and even states as a whole tend to be less affluent than suburban areas. A significant portion of education funding is provided by the states; therefore, more affluent states that merely have rural areas are able to redirect funding to these populations in an effort to address the poverty gap (Johnson & Strange).

STUDENTS WITH DISABILITIES

Serving students with disabilities may pose a greater challenge in rural school districts than in suburban districts. This stems from several factors, but is, perhaps, most affected by the availability, or lack thereof, of resources and personnel to provide to disabled students in rural schools the same levels of assessment and attention enjoyed by their suburban counterparts.

GROWING ENGLISH LANGUAGE LEARNER (ELL) POPULATION

Rural communities are becoming increasingly diverse, and for a growing number of students in rural America, English is not the primary language spoken in the home. For these students, additional English instruction in school is necessary in order to prepare them either to enter the workforce or pursue higher education. To teach these children, however, teachers must be specifically trained for ELL instruction. As with other mandates, certification to meet the language need requires funding, and funding is often what is most sorely lacking in rural school districts (Johnson & Strange).

CONSOLIDATION

In many rural areas, education and government officials often call for consolidation of several schools or school districts as a means of reducing cost and increasing educational effectiveness. With declining birth rates and demographic changes in population, schools that thirty years ago were already considered smaller are now significantly more so. As such, they are often deemed ripe for consolidation. Yet, as Silverman points out, instead of solving all problems, consolidation often brings its own series of challenges.

For example, a loss of schools or school districts translates into a subsequent loss of teacher and/or administrative jobs. In areas that are already economically depressed, additional job losses can further exacerbate an already difficult situation. More than job losses, however, Silverman notes that consolidation can have detrimental effects on the psyche of a community. This is particularly true in areas in which the school serves as a focal point for family and community social activity and involvement.

TRANSPORTATION

Closely linked with the troubles often brought on directly by consolidation, transportation difficulties are problems rural school districts must continually face. When schools and school districts consolidate, commuting distances for rural students increase. While this may seem little more than an insignificant annoyance at first glance, further exploration exposes the harmful effects lengthy commute times have on student learning capabilities and social opportunities.

When students are required routinely to spend equal or greater time traveling to and from school than actually participating in classroom activities, physical and mental fatigue ensue, and students are less able to concentrate and perform to their academic potential during the time that they *are* in the classroom. Furthermore, longer commutes intrude into both evening homework time and extracurricular school activities, and many students may find that they are unable to participate in extracurricular activities due to the obstacle posed by increased transportation times (Silverman).

BENEFITS

Despite these challenges, many would say that the benefits of rural education outweigh the challenges and may even make rural schooling preferable over suburban education. Among the specific advantages

rural education holds over suburban and urban education are class size, community support, specialized educational opportunities, and innovation in resources use and administration (Silverman; Todd & Agnello.

CLASS SIZE

Rural classrooms often offer students something that urban and suburban schools cannot: smaller class sizes. Whereas in urban and suburban schools, teachers find that they are often unable to give each student individualized attention due to sheer class size, in rural schools, where class size may be in the single digits, teachers are able to monitor each student's progress and provide any individualized instruction needed. The benefits to the students are undeniable as they escape being jostled along by large-class momentum without receiving the necessary help to grasp important concepts along the way.

COMMUNITY SUPPORT

In rural areas, the local school is often a focal point of social life. As such, communities take great pride and interest in the school and its activities. An athletic tournament victory, for example, might result in a free meal at the local café for the players to a town-wide pep rally sponsored by business or community groups. This sense of community becomes a pillar in the lives of students and area residents alike. And while rural areas do not hold the monopoly on school pride, the nature of the rural culture is such that it lends itself more to community-wide structures of support.

SPECIALIZED EDUCATIONAL OPPORTUNITIES

Many believe that rural education is synonymous with limited opportunities. This, of course, is not true. While structured class offerings, as mentioned above, may be fewer than in larger school districts, the opportunity for specialized learning may actually be greater. This is due, in part, to the previously mentioned benefit of smaller class sizes. Teachers in rural districts are able to work individually with students in specialized outside research projects. By going beyond the basics covered in class and delving into subjects of particular interest to the students, pupils are able to gain a more detailed knowledge of particular subject areas. In many ways, this scenario is quite similar to college or even graduate level studies, in which students are encouraged to explore areas of personal academic interest outside of the classroom environment. Additionally, in schools serving small, rural communities, teachers are able to tailor lesson plans to apply particularly to their community, thus using real life events to teach larger principles. For example, Todd and Agnello tell of a rural teacher's incorporation of a tornado in the town's history into a lesson plan teaching citizenship and problem solving.

INNOVATION IN RESOURCES & ADMINISTRATION

Due both to the lack of extra - or even sufficient - funding in many rural school districts and to the demographic nature of rural schools, teachers and administrators alike are often forced to become quite creative in utilizing the resources they possess to achieve maximum educational results for their students. For example, limitations in personnel may prompt rural school administrators to explore the use of distance or online education technology in order to provide students with access to a wider breadth of information than would otherwise be available. Likewise, teachers who have a very diverse classroom ethnically, racially, and educationally, often exercise creativity in developing lesson plans that will provide the necessary factual instruction while incorporating the lessons into the varied backgrounds and situations of the students. The end result is often a rich curriculum tailored to provide real-life benefits to the rural student.

MISCONCEPTIONS

Rural education carries challenges and enjoys opportunities that are often unique. Despite, or perhaps because of, the drawbacks and benefits of rural schooling, several misconceptions surrounding rural students, teachers, and school systems have arisen. Todd and Agnello outline them as follows:

- Non-certified teachers and administrators;
- Low standards of achievement;
- Lack of services for special needs students;
- Isolation from varied learning experiences;
- Inadequate access to technology;
- Separation from national and global community.

Several of these have been previously examined in this article, yet a few items warrant further mention here. Teachers in rural classrooms are highly qualified and possess the same level of expertise and certification as their urban and suburban counterparts. In addition, because of their need for innovation, rural teachers must often think "out of the box" in accessing and developing pedagogical resources for their classrooms. Furthermore, rural schools are not lacking in technological resources. Because of the power of the internet, rural students have equal access to the same global library of information as students in the most advanced classrooms in the nation (Todd & Agnello).

Regarding low achievement, while it is true that some rural students struggle academically, due to disability, poverty, or other causes, it is by no means a fact that rural schools must also be lower performing schools. In fact, in several rural states, students perform quite well despite financial and other challenges. Educators in these states, called "Golden Egg" states by the Rural School and Community Trust, credit their success to several factors, including high standards of expectation, community and public support, small class sizes, teacher involvement, and the stability of continuity in which students attend the same school from kindergarten through high school graduation (Silverman). While schools in Golden Egg states face the same challenges as those in other rural areas, they are proving that these challenges can be met and overcome and that rural schooling does not have to be an impediment to high achievement (Silverman).

VIEWPOINTS

Highly educated and well-intentioned academics and professionals stand on both sides of the rural vs. non-rural advantage debate. Some administrators and policymakers continue to push for consolidation, believing that with it will come more optimized use of resources and increased capability to serve students. Other educational leaders, however, are committed to ensuring that their small schools retain their rural nature. These individuals believe that smaller is, indeed, better and that maintaining the small class size and sense of community created by the local schools is something worth fighting for.

Whatever the varied perspectives, one thing is certain. Complete with its persistent challenges and unique opportunities, rural schooling will be an important reality in the American educational landscape for some time to come, and generations of students will continue to experience both the draw-backs and benefits of receiving a rural education.

TERMS & CONCEPTS

Beale Codes: Classification of counties developed by Dr. Calvin Beale and rating each county by a number based on its level of urbanity in terms of population and distance to urban areas.

Class Size: Number of students per class, particularly as it relates to student-to-teacher ratio.

Consolidation: The combining of two or more schools or school districts, often for the purpose of anticipated fiscal savings and/or enhanced student services.

English Language Learner (ELL): Non-English speaking students, usually in the process of learning English. A language other than English is usually the primary language spoken in the ELL student's home.

Golden Egg States: Rural area schools, districts, or states in which students perform well despite financial or other challenges.

No Child Left Behind Act (NCLB): Federal legislation reauthorizing several federal education programs for the purpose of improving educational standards and accountability and providing parents with additional options in school choice.

Rural Education: Education provided in areas or communities in which the population is no more than 25,000 and often no more than 2,500.

Gina L. Diorio

BIBLIOGRAPHY

Black, S. (2006). The right size school. *American School Board Journal, 193*, 63-65. Retrieved February 06, 2007, from EBSCO Online Database Academic Search Premier database.

Corbett, M. (2013). Improvisation as a curricular metaphor: Imagining education for a rural creative class. *Journal of Research in Rural Education, 28*, 1-11. Retrieved December 15, 2013, from EBSCO Online Database Education Research Complete.

Fowler, R.H. (2012). Rural characteristics and values: A primer for rural teachers from non-rural backgrounds. *National Teacher Education Journal, 5*, 75-80. Retrieved December 15, 2013, from EBSCO Online Database Education Research Complete.

Howley, C.B., Showalter, D., Klein, R., Sturgill, D.J., & Smith, M.A. (2013). Rural math talent, now and then. *Roeper Review, 35*, 102-114. Retrieved December 15, 2013, from EBSCO Online Database Education Research Complete.

Johnson, J. & Strange, M. (2005). *Why rural matters 2005: The facts about rural education in the 50 states.* Retrieved February 6, 2007, from The Rural School and Community Trust, http://files.ruraledu.org.

McGhie-Richmond, D., Irvine, A., Loreman, T., Cizman, J., & Lupart, J. (2013). Teacher perspectives on inclusive education in Rural Alberta, Canada. *Canadian Journal of Education, 36*, 195-239. Retrieved December 15, 2013, from EBSCO Online Database Education Research Complete.

National Center for Education Statistics. (2003). *Urban/rural classification systems.* Retrieved February 6, 2007, from http://nces.ed.gov.

New center helps rural schools. (2006). *District Administration, 42*, 22. Retrieved February 06, 2007, from EBSCO Online Database Academic Search Premier.

Silverman, F. (2005). All alone. *District Administration, 41*, 32-35. Retrieved February 06, 2007, from EBSCO Online Database Education Research Complete.

Theobald, P. (2005). Urban and rural schools: Overcoming lingering obstacles. *Phi Delta Kappan, 87*, 116-122. Retrieved February 06, 2007, from EBSCO Online Database Academic Search Premier.

Todd, R. & Agnello, M. (2006). Looking at rural communities in teacher preparation: Insight into a p-12 schoolhouse. *Social studies, 97*, 178-184. Retrieved February 06, 2007, from EBSCO Online Database Education Research Complete.

U.S. Department of Education. (1995). To assure the free appropriate public education of all children with disabilities. Retrieved February 6, 2007, from http://ed.gov.

SUGGESTED READING

Burdick-Will, J. & Logan, J. (2017). Schools at the rural-urban boundary: Blurring the divide? *Annals the American Academy of Political and Social Science.* 672(1), 185-201.

Richard, A. (2005). Federal effort lacking, rural advocates say. *Education Week, 24*, 30-32. Retrieved February 06, 2007, from EBSCO Online Database Academic Search Premier.

Richard, A. (2006). Rural educators step up Capitol Hill lobbying efforts. *Education Week, 25*, 31-31. Retrieved February 06, 2007, from EBSCO Online Database Academic Search Premier.

National Rural Education Association. (2005). *Rural school consolidation report.* Retrieved February 6, 2007, from http://nrea.net.

Samuels, C. (2005). Rural education. *Education Week, 25*, 16-16. Retrieved February 06, 2007, from EBSCO Online Database Academic Search Premier.

Stuit, D. & Doan, S. (2012). Beyond city limits: Expanding public charter schools in rural America. *National Alliance for Public Charter School.* 16 pp.

CLASS SIZE

The main challenge to reducing class size is funding, a problem that is more acute in high-poverty districts and communities, resulting in disparities in the number of students per classroom based on social class. A critical question for school districts is whether reducing class size in fact leads to improved student performance and, if so, which students stand to gain the most. In addition, it is important to distinguish between class size and student-to-teacher ratio.

KEYWORDS: Achievement Gap; Elementary School; English-Language Learner (ELL); Expenditures per Pupil; Full-Time Equivalent (FTE); Primary Grades; Public School; Secondary School; Student Outcomes; Student-to-Teacher Ratio

OVERVIEW

Class size, the number of students in a classroom, is a critical issue, especially in public schools, which do not have the ability to turn away students. Because a classroom may have more than one staff member, class size can also be measured by the ratio of students to staff. The additional staff member, however, could be another teacher, such as a special-education support instructor, or a classroom aide. It is, therefore, important to define at the outset of each discussion on class size what criteria are being used.

The two greatest obstacles to reducing class size are available funding and the ability to recruit teachers. These challengers are most acute in communities in which most residents are poor. According to the National Center for Education Statistics, by 2013 one in five school-age children lived in poverty, a number that increased from one in seven in 2000 (Kena et al., 2015). In addition, high-poverty, high-minority, and low-achieving schools have the hardest time recruiting and retaining high-quality teachers (Malkus, Mulvaney-Hoyer & Sparks, 2015).

National average class sizes in the United States was 21.2 for elementary schools and 26.8 for secondary schools. However, there were considerable variations in class size among states, ranging from a high of 27.4 (Utah) to a low of 16.6 (Vermont) for elementary schools and a high of 34.5 (Nevada) to a low of 18.7 (Alaska) for secondary schools (Snyder & Dillow, 2015). In addition, within each state, there are sharp

variations, especially between wealthier and poorer school districts. Worldwide, the average class size is 24.1, with the United States coming in at 27.0, using a less comprehensive survey, which accounts for the difference between these figures and those of NCES above. Countries ranged from 17.3 (Belgium and Estonia) to 35.5 (Singapore) (OECD, 2014).

The national average pupil-to-teacher ratios in public elementary and secondary schools decreased from 17:1 to 15:2 between 1996 and 2010 and is projected to further decrease to 14:4 in 2021 (Husar & Bailey, 2011). This is a notable decrease from 1955 (the earliest year for which such statistics are available), with a figure of 26:9. The sharpest drop in the pupil-to-teacher ratio was in the period between 1955 and 1985, with an increase between 1988 and 1994, along with a slight rise between 2009 and 2012 (Kena et al.). However, private schools have seen a much sharper drop, overtaking public schools in 1972 (Snyder & Dillow; Kena et al.).

The topic of class size goes back to classical antiquity. The Greek orator Isocrates opened an academy in 329 BCE and limited his school to eight pupils. The Roman orator Quintillian, in his Institutio Oratoria (c. 95 CE), agreed. However, Isocrates' students were Athenian statesmen and generals, hardly typical of the general population of ancient Greece or even its greatest city. The Jewish rabbinic scholar Moses Maimonides (1835–1204) opined that a class with a single teacher should have no more than 25 students, beyond which an assistant would be needed. If there are more than 40 pupils, he proposed, there should be at least two classes with two teachers. The early twentieth century philosopher John Dewey, often referred to as "the father of American education," recommended that children should be taught in groups of 8 to 12, according to the type of students and subject matter being taught.

Public school is supposed to be the great equalizer in the United States, providing every child with an education that would enable him or her to succeed in life as an adult, even capable of helping children of poor families lift themselves out of poverty. Although there have always been disparities between the schools of the rich and those of less advantaged families, a number of studies have documented that this gap has increased and continues to do so. During the 1950s and 1960s, race was the main factor in determining school quality. With the landmark 1954 *Brown v. Board of Education* Supreme Court case and the Civil Rights Act of 1964, among other important developments, race (regardless of income) became a less significant contributing factor; family income has, in turn, become the primary determinant in educational success (Tavernise, 2012; Reardon, 2011). Schools in districts with less money, for example, often cannot hire the extra teachers needed to reduce class size.

For U.S. public schools, there is a body of evidence that class size matters. It is not the sole determinant of student outcomes, but it is an important one, and students in the earliest grades and poorest, most disadvantaged schools have the most to gain or lose (Schanzenbach, 2014). Class size affects the amount of time a teacher can devote to each student during class, but class size impacts more than instruction. Teachers do much of their work after school hours outside the classroom planning lessons, correcting assignments, and grading assessments. The more students a teacher has, the less time he or she will be able to devote to such tasks and may have to create assignments that are quicker to grade, such as multiple-choice quizzes rather than essays requiring higher-level thinking skills.

VIEWPOINTS

A 1979 landmark meta-analysis, or review of previous research, strongly supports the benefits of reducing class size on student outcomes, especially in classes of 20 students or fewer (Glass & Smith, 1979). Highly noteworthy is Tennessee's Project STAR (Student Teacher Achievement Ratio), a four-year study begun in 1985 and followed up with the Lasting Benefits Study and Project Challenge. It remains one of the largest (6,500 pupils from 80 schools well represented with students of ethnic minority and urban backgrounds) controlled experiments on the effects of class size in the primary grades (Kindergarten through grade 3) on student performance over time. Project STAR put forth two definitions of reduced class size: classes of 13 to 17 students and one teacher, and classes of 22 to 26 students with a teacher and an aide; it defined classes of more than 22 students as large.

The study reported "substantial improvement in early learning and cognitive studies" as a result of smaller class sizes (Mosteller, 1995; Schanzenbach, 2014). The follow-up studies supported the initial findings. However, some educators have been critical of Project STAR, contending it did not include sufficient teacher training or take into account the experience of the teachers involved, according to the Center for Public Education. Phased in during the 1996–1997 school year, Wisconsin's Student Achievement Guarantee in Education (SAGE) Program focused on primary school grades in high-poverty areas, with the goal of limiting these classes to 15 students. Classes of up to 30 students (or two adjoining classes separated by a divider) could be taught by two team teachers or a regular teacher assisted by specialized floating teachers (e.g., a reading instructor) throughout the school day. Professional development for teachers has been part of the SAGE Program. A third large-scale study, the California Class Size Reduction (CSR) program also showed improvements in the statewide initiative to reduce class sizes. In New York City, the leading proponent of class size reduction is the New York City-based advocacy group Class Size Matters.

It should be noted, however, there is still disagreement as to whether benefits of reducing class size exist. In a large-scale study, class size was not a significant factor in reducing the gap between low and high achievers (Konstantopoulos, 2008; Konstantopoulos & Chung, 2009). Most critics of class size reduction cite studies that show that teacher expertise and talent is more important in determining student academic achievement and success. The class size reduction program (CSR), undertaken in California in 1996, found that smaller classes alone were not sufficient. Proponents of class size reduction counter that both expert teachers and less-effective and less-experienced teachers alike would benefit from smaller classes. Others say both criteria should be considered but disagree as to the extent of each, as well as at what point reducing class size ceases to be cost-effective. Furthermore, there is debate as to ideal class sizes according to each grade level. Most educators agree that smaller class size is more important in the primary grades than at secondary levels.

Another area of disagreement concerns whether class size reduction alone is sufficient to improve student outcomes. Educators cite the fact that some schools in high-needs (and difficult-to-staff) districts have had to hire inexperienced teachers to meet their goal of reducing class size. Other schools, already overcrowded, have had to convert other spaces, such as art and music rooms, special-education resource centers, and even libraries into classroom space, or they have had to rent portable (temporary) buildings. Many of these measures take funds away from providing books, technology, or after-school (extracurricular) activities.

An alternative to class size is the student-to-teacher ratio, an average denoting the number of students in a school divided by the number of full-time equivalent (FTE) teachers. FTE is a statistical unit: a full-time teacher or two part- or half-time teachers are counted as one FTE. This measurement, however, is controversial. A large classroom may have two faculty members; in that case, the student-to-teacher ratio would be low but the class size large. Furthermore, FTE often includes all instructional staff, including aides or assistants who do not meet the full definition of a teacher in terms of state licensing and certification. Other instructional staff can include librarians, speech and language therapists, physical and occupational therapists, and other support personnel who may be assigned to a specific student or a group of pupils, making the student-to-teacher ratio a misleading standard of measure. According to the Great Schools Partnership, another public-school advocacy group, the discrepancy between class size and student-to-teacher ratio could be 9 or 10 students; in other words, a school with a student-to-teacher ratio of 20:1 could have an average class size as high as 30. Others argue in favor of using lower student-to-teacher ratios as a measurement for classes in which complex subjects (such as mathematics or the sciences) are taught. Even among those who agree that lowering the student-to-teacher ratio would improve overall student achievement, there is no consensus about the point at which such benefits will be realized or cost will outweigh benefits.

TERMS & CONCEPTS

Achievement Gap: The disparity in the performance of one group of students with another group or the national norm or average. These groups are usually defined by socioeconomic status, race, and ethnicity.

Elementary School: A school comprising grades 8 and below. Schools dedicated to grades 5 or 6 to grades 8 or 9 are usually referred to as middle schools.

English-Language Learner (ELL): A student whose native language is other than English, having been born in a non-English-speaking country or raised in a family whose primary language was other than English.

Expenditures per Pupil: A statistical indication of the average amount of money a school spends for each student enrolled, measured by the school's total expenditures divided by the number of students. This figure is an average, as students with special needs and those whose primary language is other than English require additional services at extra cost.

Full-Time Equivalent (FTE): The measure of teaching capacity whereby a full-time teacher or two part- or half-time teachers are counted as one FTE.

Primary Grades: Defined as grade levels Kindergarten through grade 3. They are of particular importance for early literacy and identifying students with special needs for early intervention. Much of the effort in class size reduction focuses on the primary grades.

Public School: A school or other institution deriving most or all its financial support from public funds; in the United States, they are managed by officials elected or appointed by the local school district.

Secondary School: A school for students beyond elementary or middle school, up to and including grade 12. Middle schools dedicated to grades 5 or 6 to grades 8 or 9 are sometimes referred to as junior high schools and can be considered secondary schools.

Student Outcomes: The learning objectives or standards teachers, school administrators, or government officials seek. Student outcomes can be measured by various criteria. One measurement includes standardized tests; however there is considerable controversy over the use of these tests and whether they are valid and reliable.

Student-to-Teacher Ratio: The number of students in a school divided by the number of teachers.

Daniel L. Berek, MA

BIBLIOGRAPHY

Center for Public Education (n.d.). Class size and student achievement: Research review. Online. Retrieved January 3, 2016, from Center for Public Education, http://centerforpubliceducation.org.

Chingos, M. (2012). Class size and student outcomes: Research and policy implications. Journal of Policy Analysis & Management, 32(2) 411–438. Retrieved January 3, 2016, from EBSCO Online Database Education Research Complete.

Glass, E., & Smith, M. (1979). Meta-analysis of research on class size and achievement. Education Evaluation and Policy Analysis, 1(2), 2–16. Retrieved January 3, 2016, from EBSCO Online Database Education Research Complete.

GreatSchools Staff (n.d.). How important is class size? Oakland, CA: GreatSchools. Online. Retrieved January 3, 2016, from http://greatschools.org.

Hussar, W., & Bailey, T. (2011). Projections of education statistics to 2020 (NCES 2011-026). Washington, DC: U.S. Department of Education, National Center for Education Statistics. Retrieved January 3, 2016, from http://nces.ed.gov.

Kena, G., Musu-Gillette, L., Robinson, J., Wang, X., Rathbun, A., Zhang, J., Wilkinson-Flicker, S.,… & Dunlop Velez, E. (2015). The condition of education 2015 (NCES 2011-144). Washington, DC: U.S. Department of Education, National Center for Education Statistics. Retrieved January 3, 2016, from http://nces.ed.gov.

Konstantopoulos, S. (2008). Do small classes reduce the achievement gap between low and high achievers? Elementary School Journal, 108(4) 275–291. Retrieved January 3, 2016, from EBSCO Online Database Education Research Complete.

Konstantopoulos, S., & Chung, V. (2009). What are the long-term effects of small classes? Evidence from the lasting benefits study. American Journal of Education, 116(1), 125–154. Retrieved January 3, 2016, from EBSCO Online Database Education Research Complete.

Malkus, N., Mulvaney-Hoyer, K., Sparks, D. (2015). Teaching vacancies in difficult-to-staff teaching positions in public schools (NCES 2015-065). Washington, DC: U.S. Department of Education, National Center for Education Statistics. Retrieved January 3, 2016, from http://nces.ed.gov.

Mosteller, F. (1995). The Tennessee study of class size in the early school grades. The Future of Children, 5(2), 113–127. Retrieved January 3, 2016, from https://www.princeton.edu.

OECD (2014). TALIS 2013 results: An international perspective on teaching and learning, TALIS, OECD Publishing. Retrieved January 3, 2016, from http://oecd.org.

Schanzenbach, D. (2014). Does class size matter? Boulder, CO: National Education Policy Center. Retrieved January 3, 2016, from http://nepc.colorado.edu.

Snyder, T., & Dillow, S. (2015). Digest of education statistics 2013 (NCES 2015-011). Washington, DC: U.S. Department of Education, National Center for Education Statistics. Retrieved January 3, 2016, from http://nces.ed.gov.

Tavernise, S. (2012). Poor dropping further behind rich in school. New York Times, Feb. 10, p. A1. Online as Education gap grows between rich and poor, studies say. Retrieved January 3, 2016, from http://nytimes.com.

SUGGESTED READING

Class Size Matters (2015). Bibliography of class size research. Retrieved January 3, 2016, from http://classsizematters.org.

Darling-Hammond, L. (2010). The flat world and education: How America's commitment to equity will determine our future (Multicultural Education Series). New York, NY: Teachers College Press.

Delavan, G. (2009). The teacher's attention: Why our kids must and can get smaller schools and classes. Philadelphia, PA: Temple University Press.

Fan, F. (2012). Class size: Effects on students' academic achievements and some remedial measures. Research in Education, 87, 95–98. Retrieved January 3, 2016, from EBSCO Online Database Education Research Complete.

Harfitt, G. (2015). Class size reduction: Key insights from secondary school classrooms. Singapore: Springer.

Kornrich, S., & Furstenberg, R. (2013). Investing in children: Changes in parental spending on children, 1972–2007. Demography, 50(1) 1–23.

National Council of Teachers of English (2014). Why class size matters today. Urbana, IL: NCTE. Retrieved January 7, 2016, from http://ncte.org.

Paufler, N., Amrein-Beardsley, A. (2014). The random assignment of students into elementary classrooms: Implications for value-added analyses and interpretations. American Educational Research Journal, 51(2) 328–362. Retrieved January 6, 2016, from EBSCO Online Database Education Research Complete.

Reardon, S. F. (2011). The widening academic achievement gap between the rich and the poor: New evidence and possible explanations. In R. Murnane & G. Duncan (Eds.), Whither Opportunity? Rising Inequality and the Uncertain Life Chances of Low-Income Children. New York, NY: Russell Sage Foundation Press. Retrieved January 3, 2016, from http://cepa.stanford.edu.

THE PLEDGE OF ALLEGIANCE & MOMENT OF SILENCE CONTROVERSY

Any activity required by public schools will face controversy if it presents a religious connotation. Since 1954, the Pledge of Allegiance has incorporated the words, "under God," introducing a religious aspect into its patriotic rhetoric. To many Americans, that public school students are required to recite it is unconstitutional and unnecessary. This article will present a brief history of the Pledge of Allegiance and the Moment of Silence, as well as a description of the First Amendment and a case study of Russell Tremain, a nine-year old student caught in the middle of a First Amendment case between the ACLU and the state of Washington in 1925.

KEYWORDS: American Civil Liberties Union (ACLU); Allegiance; Church and State; Citizenship; Civil Liberties; First Amendment; Liberty; Moment of Silence; Pledge; Recitation

OVERVIEW

All over the United States, public school students rush to their classrooms in the morning and are called to attention when announcements begin sounding over a loudspeaker. Part of the morning ritual is to stand, place their right hands over their hearts, and recite the Pledge of Allegiance in unison with the voice overheard throughout the school. While students are now not required to follow in recitation, they usually do because everyone else does.

Conformity may be the reason most students recite the Pledge, especially young students who cannot fully understand the meaning of the words they are saying. The fact that they are expected to recite them at all is controversial. Many opponents of its recitation argue that the Pledge does not belong in school because it serves no educational purpose for students to memorize and simply recite words. Another controversy involves whether or not students feel pressured to recite the Pledge—which references God—because the Establishment Clause of the First Amendment states that they don't have to.

THE PLEDGE OF ALLEGIANCE

Frances Bellamy wrote the Pledge of Allegiance in 1892. The United States had recently experienced its Civil War, and patriotism was pushed as a means to rebuild the country. Since it was first written, the Pledge has been revised only twice:

Bellamy wrote his pledge in 1892: "I pledge allegiance to my flag and to the Republic for which it stands—one Nation indivisible—with Liberty and Justice for all" (Ellis, 2005) … To show that individuals were pledging allegiance specifically to the U.S. flag, the words "my flag" were changed to "the Flag of the United States of America" in 1924 (Cayton et al., 2005; Miller, 1976). Fears about communism, an increased commitment to religion, and a belief in the Christian foundations of our nation led to the phrase "under God" being added to the Pledge of Allegiance in 1954 (Cayton et al.; Ellis, as cited in Martin, 2008).

In 2002, almost a year after the September 11 attacks on New York's twin towers, three judges on the Ninth Circuit Court of Appeals ruled that to require students to say "under God" was unconstitutional and that public schools could no longer mandate the Pledge's recitation. Reaction to the decision was overwhelming: "Starting with the president and leaders of both parties in Congress, elected officials poured more uninhibited scorn on the decision than on any other action of a court in living memory" (Clausen, 2002). The decision was over-turned and currently, thirty-five states in America require recitation of the Pledge every day in school (Piscatelli, as cited in Martin). In addition, the Pledge of Allegiance is used to welcome new citizens into the country as it is recited at the conclusion of naturalization ceremonies (Parker, 2006).

MOMENT OF SILENCE

Required moments of silence are not so well-received. In 1985, the state of Alabama not only required a moment of silence for its public school students, the state actually created a prayer for the students to silently recite. The case was brought to the U.S. Supreme Court and the mandate was deemed unconstitutional. However, it was only considered a violation of students' First Amendment rights because it clearly pointed toward a religious affiliation. The Court devised an alternative for Alabama, which the state quickly embraced. Supreme Court Justice Sandra Day O'Connor identified the alternative based on the First Amendment itself:

… the relevant issue is whether an objective observer, acquainted with the text, legislative history, and

implementation of the statute, would perceive it [a required moment of silence] as a state endorsement of prayer in public schools. A moment of silence law that is clearly drafted and implemented so as to permit prayer, meditation, and reflection within the prescribed period, without endorsing one alternative over the others, should pass this test (O'Connor as cited in Davis, 2003).

In other words, if a moment of silence does not specifically endorse the concept of praying, it can be used as time spent on just about anything that is quiet. Furthermore, whoever is requiring it cannot be seen as forcing a religion because religious affiliation is not required for students to participate. Derek Davis, Editor of Journal of Church & State, identified five ethical arguments against O'Connor's play on words and, more specifically, a required moment of silence in public schools.

First, Davis notes that changing the wording does not change the meaning:

Moments of silence ... are constitutional because they are supposedly prayer neutral; that is, students may choose to pray during the prescribed time of meditation, or they can use the time in other ways, such as to prepare mentally for the day or just enjoy the solitude. Yet no one really disputes that moments of silence are primarily efforts to encourage prayer.

Second, Davis notes that many people want religion in public schools: "The absence of any form of prayer in the classroom, they argue, is ... a sure sign that God has been removed from the schools." At the turn of the 20th century, public schools were a way for America's poor and immigrant population to receive religious instruction of a Christian nature. In 2010, however, many people believe that 1) everyone has the right to choose his own faith, and 2) should he choose to believe in God, his observance should not be restricted to a public school building. Third, Davis points out that many of the people advocating for a moment of silence are doing so because the lack of moments of prayer have caused the country to become immoral. Fourth, Davis point out that religion by any other name does not warrant a required time of observance: "It is rare to find Jews, Buddhists, Hindus, Muslims, and members of other minority communities of faith who favor moments of silence."

Finally, Davis notes that by virtue of the Equal Access Act of 1984, as long as it is not led by teachers or administrators, students can observe religion in public schools without a need for an established moment of silence:

The Act requires religious activity to be student-initiated and student-run, without school officials' oversight and direction, activities consistent with the requirements of the Act are protected by the Free Speech and Free Exercise Clauses and do not violate the Establishment Clause. Moreover, students are free to pray privately any time they choose: before, during, or after school. They are free to read their Bibles, share their faith, pray with other students, distribute religious tracts, or sing religious songs provided these activities do not disrupt other school activities. The Free Exercise Clause protects all of these activities (Davis).

THE FIRST AMENDMENT & THE ESTABLISHMENT CLAUSE: THE SEPARATION OF CHURCH & STATE

The United States Constitution was signed in 1787. Price (2004) notes that in order to focus more on the people—rather than simply describing what the government could and could not do (as the original document does)—the Bill of Rights was added to the Constitution. The third Article is the First Amendment:

Congress shall make no law respecting an establishment of religion or prohibiting the free exercise thereof; or abridging the freedom of speech, or of the press; or the right of the people peaceably to assemble, and to petition the government for a redress of grievances.

Thomas Jefferson helped create the Bill of Rights, and to clarify the meaning of the First Amendment, he wrote a famous letter to Danbury Baptists to explain the intention of the amendment:

Believing with you that religion is a matter which lies solely between Man & his God, that he owes account to none other for his faith or his worship, that the legitimate powers of government reach actions only, & not opinions, I contemplate with sovereign reverence that act of the whole American people which declared that their legislature should "make no law respecting an establishment of religion, or prohibiting the free exercise thereof," thus building a wall of separation between Church & State (Jefferson, as cited in Price, 2004).

The Establishment clause (the first part of the amendment) was created as a way to ensure that the federal government couldn't declare any specific religion to be the religion of America. The Free Exercise clause (the last section of the first part) was created to keep the federal government from telling anyone which religion he could practice, where he could practice it, or when he could practice it, even if practice meant not observing a religion at all. In other words, one religion is not better than another nor is it better to observe religion than not to observe. Thus, the First Amendment is pretty clear: the government can't tell Americans what to do about religion. Yet, in 1954 the phrase, "under God" was added to the Pledge of Allegiance, and children nationwide have been required to recite the phrase every school day since. Many people feel that such a requirement is unconstitutional because it demonstrates the government (public schools) telling American students to observe one religion in opposition to another (God as opposed Buddha, for example) or to observe a religion as opposed to no religion (God infers religion).

EDUCATIONAL VALUE

Directly following the September 11 attacks of 2001, an outpouring of patriotism took over the country. Part of that patriotism was reflected at the beginning of the school day when the Pledge of Allegiance was recited over a loud speaker. This is certainly a way to show patriotism for those who chose to do so. However, requiring that time be taken out of the school day for students, teachers, and administrators to recite the Pledge of Allegiance has caused a great deal of controversy, especially when state governments are requiring the recitation. In the year following 9/11, "half the states required schools to offer the Pledge during the school day, and five additional states introduced bills [through legislation] to that effect" (Gehring, 2002, as cited in Bennett, 2004).

In Colorado, when a law was passed requiring students and teachers in a public school to recite the pledge every day, people challenged the mandate in court arguing that saying the pledge offered no educational value to the school day and that it should therefore not be required.

The court sided with the plaintiffs and enjoined the state from enforcing the statute in the schools. The basis for its ruling was that "pure rote recitation of a

pledge ... cannot be said to be reasonable or legitimate in a pedagogical sense" and that "there is no legitimate or reasonable educational value to it" (Reporter's Transcript Ruling, 2003, as cited in Bennett).

Further, Tomey-Purta (2000) notes that "civic education classes characterized by the discussion of political issues were more likely to result in knowledge and interest in politics than was the rote memorization of factual material" (as cited in Bennett). Indeed, teaching patriotism and using the Pledge of Allegiance as the medium to do it is an educational practice. Saying the pledge for the sake of saying it, however, is not.

CASE STUDY: RUSSELL TREMAIN

Russell Tremain's parents refused to allow him to say the Pledge, and as a result, nine-year old Russell experienced an unexpected education in civil rights. In September of 1925, Russell Tremain's father requested to the Franklin School in Bellingham, Washington, that the child be allowed to refrain from participating in the daily salute to the flag. Mr. Tremain argued that such salutation (at the time, a hand was raised and outstretched rather than placed over one's heart) supported war and the military, and the Tremains did not. The elder Tremain believed in "a literal interpretation of the Bible, the sinfulness of war, and, most importantly, the authority of God over human institutions" (Henderson, 2005). As such, when the Franklin School denied Tremain's request, he refused to allow his son to attend the institution if Russell was expected to recite the Pledge. In 1925, all children were required to attend school and recite the Pledge of Allegiance. When Russell's parents kept him home, they were seen by the state of Washington as unfit parents, and Russell was taken from their home and put into foster care.

Members of the American Civil Liberties Union (ACLU) tried to intervene with the state on the Tremain's behalf, but their intervention was based on the family's First Amendment rights being violated. The Tremains did not care much about their First Amendment rights since in their view God was the only entity with the power to make them follow any laws. Well into the next academic year, members of the ACLU were still fighting for Russell's return home. The organization's fight was recognized by the court because of the unconstitutionality of

Russell's removal from his home. However, because the Tremains would not concede their stance based on the constitution (or any laws not created by God), Russell remained apart from them for over two years. Eventually the child was returned, but only because his parents and the court agreed that Russell would attend school—public or private—once he was returned to their care (Henderson). It is likely that Russell did not know the extent to which his parents were in violation of any laws. From the court's perspective, expecting him to attend school but not to say the Pledge was encouraging him to break the law, which made them unfit (Henderson).

WHAT DOES THE PLEDGE MEAN?

When he was growing up, Christopher Clausen, author and professor of English at Pennsylvania State University, noted that most of the people around him didn't take issue with the Pledge of Allegiance; he didn't think they thought much about it at all. He concluded that "most of them said they believed in God because it made life easier among other evasive people who also said they believed in God."

> Probably I was not the only person in my class who unobtrusively skipped the words "under God" when reciting the revised Pledge of Allegiance. But those two words were even more alienating than the prayers and Bible readings, because leaving them out meant being separated from the national community of which one had always been an unquestioned member ... According to today's president and several senators, the Pledge does not endorse religion but merely recognizes that our liberties derive, as the Declaration of Independence proclaims, not from man but from God.

Professor of Education at the University of Washington, Walter Parker, has conducted many discussions about the Pledge of Allegiance. Similar to Clausen, Parker points to a defined evasion regarding what the Pledge of Allegiance means. Parker has talked with elementary school students, high school students, and their parents and teachers. Without choosing sides by saying that recitation of the Pledge is good or bad, he simply points to his observations noting that most people who say the Pledge don't really know what it means:

> Leading seminars on the pledge, I'm struck by three arguments that often unfold. First, and most

> important to many participants, is the phrase "under God" and what it does to the text when it is present or (as before 1954) absent ... Second, to what or whom are we pledging allegiance when we recite it? To the flag, say some. To the nation, say others. No, to the republic, say others, pointing to "for which it stands." Does this argument matter? It does, because only one of these is an idea about how to live with one another. Nazis and Romans pledged allegiance to a man (Heil Hitler, Hail Caesar); countless others have pledged allegiance to a plot of land ("land where my fathers died"). But "to the republic" suggests fidelity to the principles of a constitutional democracy ... Then there's the final phrase, "with liberty and justice for all." Here the argument turns on what sort of statement this is. Is it a description or an aspiration? A reality or an ideal? (Parker).

In Parker's experience, when people fully consider the Pledge of Allegiance, more issues are raised than those of religion and the first amendment. This positive discovery shows that there is much more to the Pledge than those two concepts. Perhaps discussions like the ones he has had should be undertaken at the beginning of each school year—at an assembly, maybe—so that students (and their teachers and parents) can discuss and interpret the words. That way, the recitation of the Pledge would have meaning, not simply exist as an exercise in conformity, and its place in educational settings would have merit. Unlike Russell Tremain, the students choosing not to recite the Pledge as well as their peers who opt to recite freely will be fully informed about that choice.

TERMS & CONCEPTS

American Civil Liberties Union (ACLU): A national organization that advocates for the rights of individual people by offering litigation assistance, working toward more effective legislation, and promoting education for the public.

Allegiance: Loyalty; in the case of the Pledge, to the flag and nation of the United States.

Citizenship: Participation as an individual citizen of a country and enjoying the rights and privileges afforded as such.

Civil Liberties: Rights and freedoms granted to Americans based on the Bill of Rights and the amendments therein.

First Amendment: American citizens' freedom of speech, religion, the press, and to peacefully assemble as outlined in the Bill of Rights.

Liberty: "A political, social, and economic right that belongs to the citizens of a state or to all people" (www.encarta.msn.com).

Moment of Silence: The opportunity to use time during the (school) day to reflect on one's thoughts, to meditate, or to pray.

Pledge: A promise.

Prayer in School: The controversial practice of having a specific time during the (school) day for students to pray.

Recitation: Reading or speaking a memorized text out loud.

Maureen McMahon

BIBLIOGRAPHY

ACLU. (2002, March 11). The Establishment Clause and public schools. *The Establishment Clause and the Schools: A Legal Bulletin.* Retrieved September 24, 2010, from ACLU, http://aclu.org.

Amendment I. (n.d.). *United States Constitution: Bill of Rights.* Retrieved September 24, 2010, from Cornell University Law School Legal Information Institute, http://topics.law.cornell.edu.

Bennett, L. J. (2004). Classroom recitation of the pledge of allegiance and its education value: Analysis, review, and proposal. *Journal of Curriculum & Supervision, 20,* 56-75. Retrieved June 7, 2010, from EBSCO online database, Academic Search Complete.

Chiodo, J. J., Martin, L. A., & Worthington, A. (2011). Does it mean to die for your country? Preservice teachers' views regarding teaching the pledge of allegiance. *Educational Forum, 75,* 38–51. Retrieved January 2, 2014, from EBSCO Online Database Education Research Complete.

Clausen, C. (2003). Opening exercises. *American Scholar, 72,* 35. Retrieved June 8, 2010, from EBSCO online database, Academic Search Complete.

Davis, D. H. (2003). Moments of silence in America's public schools: Constitutional and ethical considerations. Journal of Church & State, 45, 429-442. Retrieved June 10, 2010, from EBSCO online database, Education Research Complete.

Henderson, J. J. (2005). Conditional liberty: The flag salute before Gobitis and Barnette. *Journal of Church & State, 47,* 747-767. Retrieved June 8, 2010, from EBSCO online database, Academic Search Complete.

Martin, L. A. (2012). Blind patriotism or active citizenship? How do students interpret the Pledge of Allegiance?. *Action In Teacher Education,* 34, 55–64. Retrieved January 2, 2014, from EBSCO Online Database Education Research Complete.

Martin, L. A. (2008). Examining the Pledge of Allegiance. *Social Studies, 99,* 127-13. Retrieved June 8, 2010, from EBSCO online database, Academic Search Complete.

Martin, L. A. (2011). Middle school students' views on the United States Pledge of Allegiance. *Journal Of Social Studies Research, 35,* 245–258. Retrieved January 2, 2014, from EBSCO Online Database Education Research Complete.

Parker, W. C. (2006). Pledging allegiance. *Phi Delta Kappan, 87,* 613. Retrieved June 8, 2010, from EBSCO online database, Academic Search Complete.

Price, R.G. (2004, Mar 27). *History of the separation of church and state in America.* Retrieved July 12, 2010, http://rationalrevolution.net.

Tomey-Purta, J. (2000). Comparative perspectives on political socialization and civic education. *Comparative Education Review, 44,* 89.

SUGGESTED READING

Center for Civic Education. (1995). *We the people: The citizen and the constitution.* Calabasas, CA: Center for Civic Education.

Ellis, R. J. (2005). *To the flag: The unlikely history of the Pledge of Allegiance.* Lawrence: University Press of Kansas.

Gehring, J. (2002). States weigh bills to stoke students' patriotism. *Education Week, 21,* 19-21.

Frantz, K. (2008). School prayer by any other name? *Humanist, 68,* 4-5. Retrieved June 10, 2010, from EBSCO online database Academic Search Complete.

Gotta minute? (2001). *Current Events, 100,* 1-2. Retrieved June 9, 2010, from EBSCO online database, Education Research Complete.

Humphrey, N. (2011). Newdow and the Ninth Circuit: What happened between 2002 and 2010 to change the court's opinion of the constitutionality of the pledge to the flag?. *Journal Of Law & Education, 40,* 711–718. Retrieved January 2, 2014, from EBSCO Online Database Education Research Complete.

Knowles, T. (1992). Continued legal developments on the school flag. *Social Education, 56,* 52-54.

Miller, M. S. (1976). *Twenty-three words: The life story of the author of the Pledge of Allegiance as told in his own words.* Portsmouth, VA: Printcraft Press.

Mixing religion, politics troubles Americans, new poll indicates. (2001). *Church & State, 54,* 15. Retrieved June 10, 2010, from EBSCO online database, Academic Search Complete.

O'Leary, C. E. (1999). *To die for: The paradox of American patriotism.* Princeton, NJ: Princeton University Press.

Piscatelli, J. (2003, August). Pledge of Allegiance. *ECS StateNotes: Character/Citizenship Education.* Retrieved

June 9, 2010, from Education Commission of the States, http://ecs.org.

Reporter's Transcript Ruling, *Lane v. Owens*, Civil Action No. 03-B-1544 (D. Colo., Aug. 21, 2003), 11-12.

Sica, M. G. (1990). The school flag movement: Origin and influence. *Social Education 54*, 380-84.

Tolo, K. W. (1999). Civic education of American youth: From state policies to school district practices. *Report 133 by the policy research project on civic education policies and practices*. Austin, TX: Lyndon B. Johnson School of Public Affairs, University of Texas at Austin.

Walsh, M. (2013). Massachusetts high court weighs 'pledge' in schools. *Education Week, 33*, 4. Retrieved January 2, 2014, from EBSCO Online Database Education Research Complete.

Williams, M. (1992). Preparing for the centennial of the Pledge of Allegiance: An annotated bibliography. *Social Studies and the Young Learner, 55*, 4, 13.

GRADE INFLATION

Grade inflation is the assignment of a grade to a student who has not yet reached the achievement level represented by that grade. For example, teachers may grade students based on their effort and/or their motivation to learn rather than mastery of content. Also, schools within or between districts may compete for students (and tax dollars or tuition) by promoting a reputation for graduating students of a high caliber—those who have higher grades than students in other geographic areas. In addition, some schools simply sell grades to students willing to purchase them. Regardless of how such grades are bestowed, inflated grades do a disservice to students who feel they have earned them and believe they are prepared for college and/or a position in the workforce.

KEYWORDS: American College Testing (ACT); Assessment; Grade Inflation; Grade Level Promotion; Higher Education; Naïve Selection; Scholastic Aptitude Test (SAT); Secondary Schools; Strategic Selection

OVERVIEW

Most parents would like to think that their child's report card is indicative of the child's academic achievement in class—the objective combination of content knowledge and performance since the previous report card. It is possible, however, that report cards reflect a subjective interpretation of one child's progress when compared to another child. It is also possible that report cards define a school's rank within a district or offer a public school's value over a private school. These are common reasons for the recent trend of grade inflation in secondary schools. Grade inflation is the difference between a student's grade and his actual attainment of course content reflective of that grade. In other words, a student who receives a B in 11th grade history should be able to demonstrate 80% proficiency of the course content when tested. If he can't, the B is inflated in relation to his knowledge. Grades are inflated in secondary schools for a variety of reasons.

According to an article in Gifted Child Today, a 2000 report showed that "86% of teachers consider student effort as a factor" when determining grades ("Grade Inflation," 2000). Most schools have a general rubric on which grades are developed, but teachers can incorporate how hard a student has worked into that rubric, sometimes defining who is promoted to the next level based on effort rather than content mastery. Grade promotion based on effort is misleading. It also creates dependence for the student; if he doesn't continue to receive inflated grades, his opportunities for success dwindle because he doesn't know as much as he should. For example, the ACT (American College Testing) exam is a standardized test taken in the junior or senior year of high school and is used by colleges to determine student placement in courses like English and math. ACT scores can determine scholarship eligibility and whether or not students require remediation once enrolled in college:

It is composed of four tests: English, Mathematics, Reading, and Science. A fifth score, the Composite score, is the average of the scores on the four subject tests. The ACT not only measures the knowledge and skills students have acquired during their high school years and their level of achievement as a result of their high school learning and instruction, but also serves as a measure of their preparation to undertake rigorous coursework at the postsecondary level ("Are High School Grades Inflated?" 2005).

The Scholastic Aptitude Test (SAT) is also used by colleges to determine a student's scholarship eligibility and what—if any—advanced courses a student may take once enrolled. Depending on the college, SAT or ACT scores may be required for admission purposes. And, while a student can take each exam as many times as he wishes (for a fee)—using the highest score in admissions materials—many schools record each score and have a record of multiple attempts to increase that score. Even colleges that look more holistically at students' high school experiences (as opposed to weighing so heavily on a standardized test scores) would expect strong performances on these exams from students who have high averages in high school. Because so many high school averages include grade inflation, student averages are not correlating with standardized test scores:

In 1984, 28% of all students taking the SAT reported A averages; while in 1999, 39% of SAT-taking students reported A averages. Since performance on the SAT has not varied significantly over the past 23 years, researchers have concluded that this increase is a result of grade inflation ("Grade Inflation").

The grades reported by students taking these tests has increased, yet their test scores have not. Bracey (1994) notes similar results in that students are more recently reporting grades from A- to A+ as representative of their high school averages, yet their SAT scores are not reflecting such high levels of content mastery.

Why Inflate Grades?

NAÏVE & STRATEGIC SCHOOL SELECTION

From a parent's perspective, grade inflation may determine what school their children will attend. For example, if students at School A receive better grades than students at School B, it may be assumed that School A has better teachers, a stronger administration, or more resources that lead to student success when compared to School B. Walsh (2010) explains that when it comes to parents and school selection, the choice process can be naïve or strategic. Naïve selection occurs when parents don't pay attention to standardized test scores, when they make note of things like state of the art computer labs (or other high-end resources), or when they simply don't suspect grade inflation. Strategic selection, on the other hand, happens when parents send their children to schools specifically because of

grade inflation practices. Students who receive high grades are more likely to be accepted into college. Walsh (2010) explains that:

… highly educated parents with high-achieving students may be attracted by high perceived school quality or college-admissions gamesmanship more than average families. If this is so, a grade-inflating school district could not only attract more families but could attract a particular type of family. The peer quality and achievement of the district would be genuinely high, not because of school quality effects but because of selection (Walsh).

In contrast, schools in districts with academically weak students face budgetary restraints if students don't pass from year to year. This may encourage teachers to inflate grades for students who may otherwise drop out. In a study conducted by Lekholm & Cliffordson (2008), it was observed that students had higher overall grades when compared to standardized test scores in districts with families having "lower educational backgrounds." Again, the 2001 legislation of No Child Left Behind places a monetary value on student pass rates, so grade inflation makes sense in economically struggling districts.

Overall, it appears that many school districts benefit from grade inflation. Public schools that compete with private schools or with schools within their own districts have an advantage when they graduate students with high GPAs: students want to attend those schools, and their parents are happy to enroll them there. Also, academically strong students are sought after by colleges, and at schools that inflate grades, colleges might believe they have a strong pool of applicants from which to choose. How long students from this pool remain in college is difficult to predict, but many will be faced with a reality they did not expect once they get to college because they are not prepared. Districts that enroll academically weak students also benefit as their students drop out less when they have passing grades. Thus, weaker students may view inflated grades as a reason to persist to graduation.

BUYING THE GRADES

According to Hansen, "Whether due to years of grade inflation in high school … or society's overall disrespect for the immaterial value of education, many students tend to look at academic accomplishment as just another commodity to be purchased" (1998). Unfortunately, some students actually do purchase the commodity. Farran (2009) discovered a common practice in Vancouver whereby students attending one high school could pay tuition at another school to take the same exact courses yet receive higher grades. The province of British Columbia created a policy to allow students whose high schools did not offer certain courses to enroll in those courses at a different school. The policy also allows for students to be enrolled in the same class at the same time, keeping whichever grade they prefer. In other words, a student can attend School A within his district and take a full course load. Should he consider his algebra course too difficult, he can enroll in the same class at School B for a tuition fee—attending in the afternoons or on Saturdays. When the school year is over, the student can choose which algebra grade he wants to appear on his transcript—the one from School A or the one from School B. The problem is that School B neither required the student to attend all classes nor made him do all the work required by School A; yet if he received a higher grade from the second institution it would appear on his transcript as if it came from School A.

According to Farran, this practice was discovered when an instructor at University Hill Secondary School in Vancouver checked the academic records of several students who had cross-registered in senior level English in the 2006-2007 year. Many of the instructor's students were failing his English class but none of them sought extra help nor did they seem concerned about failing. On a hunch, the teacher checked the academic records of students who had cross-registered at Century High School, the second institution in which his students were enrolled. In 2006-2007 the teacher discovered that:

101 Century High students (60 per cent of the class) received a B grade or higher in Grade 12 English; just three failed. When he looked at how the same group of 138 students performed on standardized provincial exams, the results were just the opposite: 108 had failed the exam and only eight students got a B grade or higher (Farran).

While the practice of purchasing inflated grades was well-known, nobody seemed to be able to do anything about it. "At Toronto's Forest Hill Collegiate Institute, principal Peggy Aitchison said 140 students took credits part-time at private schools in 2007-2008, mostly in Grade 12 math or English; typically, they earned marks 15 to 40 points higher than at Forest Hill" (Farran). As a result of the University Hill teacher's investigation, Century High and four other schools were ordered to address the large differences between students' class grades and standardized test results. Some schools were closed because it was apparent they were selling grades; however, many opened up within a year under a different name (Farran).

The problem is with supply and demand; students are so desperate to get into college, they are willing to pay for the grades they cannot otherwise earn. According to Farran, students believe that purchasing grades to be admitted to college is a necessary evil:

Sixteen-year-old Ben took Grade 12 English at a private school while he was enrolled in Grade 11 at York Mills last year. Ben gets marks in the 90s in math and science, but English was a problem. He was afraid that if he doesn't get a high Grade 12 English mark, he won't get into life sciences at McMaster [University] … "I took this route because some of the courses in high school are especially hard and you can't get higher than 60 or 70 [per cent]," he says. "However, once you take it in private school, you can easily get 80s. Personally I would recommend it to other people …" (Farran).

About the same time Ben was earning his B grade in English 12, Canadian government officials closed ten private institutions because they didn't meet the teaching standards set forth by the Education Act. Prior to 2010, a student could transfer credit from a private institution to his full-time school without a college or university knowing. Currently, however, if credits are earned at a school other than the one from which a student graduates, his transcript will reflect a "P" (for private institution) next to those credits, leaving a college or university to do with that information whatever it chooses (Farran).

GRADE INFLATION IN HIGHER EDUCATION
Grade inflation became a recognized phenomenon in college grading years before it became common in high schools. In fact, Edwards (2000), reports that colleges and universities are the larger issue: "Grade inflation has the potential for undermining the traditional purposes of the university, altering student-instructor relationships, eliminating the gate keeping

role of the university, and failing to adequately pre-pare students for the world of work" (Edwards). Furthermore, "Levine (1994) surveyed 4,900 college graduates from the years 1969-1993 and found that the number of A's given had quadrupled while the number of C's had dropped by 66%" (Edwards). Edwards also notes that SAT and ACT scores have decreased and that any assertion that students deserve the grades they are getting is inaccurate.

Grade inflation in college has been blamed primar-ily on two factors: the first is faculty evaluations; the second is budget crises. Most faculty members (full-time and part-time) are evaluated on a regular basis by their students. Teachers who fail several students each semester gain a reputation for being ineffective and tend to be replaced. On the other hand, the teachers whose students do well hold their positions longer and, for the most part, are well-liked by their students. And a well-liked teacher means receiving positive evaluations and job security. "Faculty realize that giving poor grades is not in their economic best interest. They believe that low grades lead to low faculty ratings by students, with corresponding reduction in class sizes (Beaver, 1997), and eventual loss of their jobs" (Edwards). When the point difference between Cs and Ds or Ds and Fs determines whether or not an instructor returns to the classroom the following year, grade inflation probably doesn't seem like a serious issue.

The same can be noted for student retention. The more students that remain in college and pay to be there, the better off universities are financially. As such, it is possible for deans and administrators to not look too closely at how many students pass each class. It is also possible for admissions criteria to change. William Abbott (2008) teaches at Fairfield University, a private college in New England. According to him, Fairfield has clearly changed its admissions criteria:

> While SAT scores arguably are not the best gauge of ability, the fact that our real SAT scores … were lower in 2003 than they had been 14 years earlier, yet our grade-point average was higher, indicates that our grade inflation cannot be attributed to an improvement in our students' intellectual capacities. Our selectivity ratings bear this out: 49.4 percent of applicants were admitted in 2003 compared to 37 percent in 1988.

In other words, Fairfield has been admitting stu-dents with lower SAT scores at a higher rate than they did in the past. Additionally, those same students entered the college with grade point averages that didn't correlate with their SAT scores, yet they were still admitted.

WHAT'S THE HARM?

Grade inflation seems to serve a purpose for every-one concerned. Teachers reward students for effort and motivation even if those students struggle with course material. Grade inflation also allows admin-istrators to boast that they graduate high-achieving students, and parents can choose schools based on the report of high grades given to graduates. Furthermore, students can beat out other students in the college admissions process based on inflated grades. The biggest problem with all of this is that students who receive high grades may feel that they deserve them, thus also believing they deserve that place in college. Overconfidence, in this situation, is not a good thing. Students who have received inflated grades tend to be highly confident in their abilities in spite of being perpetually underprepared for future endeavors (Hansen, 1998). Students who received "A" grades in high school will believe they earned those grades, and as a result, will also believe that they are prepared for college-level academics. In addition, when the colleges at which they apply admit them based on those grades, a cycle of depen-dence is fostered.

Additionally, the students who do receive Cs and Ds may believe that working hard is not really nec-essary. "Most students admit that they are capable of far more quality work in school than they ordinarily achieve (Glasser, 1998)" (Edwards). Students with inflated grades no longer need to achieve quality work because they simply don't need to. Kohn (1992) argued that if the education systems got rid of grad-ing altogether, dependence on the status quo would no longer be an issue:

> Grades not only undermine competition between stu-dents, they undermine striving for quality by individ-ual students as well. With a system of grades, students tend to do only enough to achieve the grade they desire. The minimum expected becomes the maximum achieved, and the maximum is ordinarily at a level far below their ability (Edwards).

Indeed, there is little incentive to strive for a B if a C requires little effort and the result (graduating from high school) is the same.

Because grade inflation in college—for whatever reason—is so widely known, higher education is not as well respected as it used to be. Abbott notes that, "[e]mployers and graduate-school admissions officials consequently have become dissatisfied with college transcripts as a source of information." This dissatisfaction means that students believing higher education is the key to their future may have to look at other options. According to Edwards, "Undergraduate degrees will eventually be viewed as high school diplomas are today. Some colleges will institute exit examinations to bolster the sagging value of their degrees, but it is only a matter of time before more dramatic changes will occur" (Edwards). Once seen as a privilege worthy only of a few, higher education was never meant to be just one more thing to buy. Grade inflation has made it such, however, and the ramifications of that will be obvious for a long time.

TERMS & CONCEPTS

American College Testing (ACT): A standardized test measuring a variety of skill sets; used by many colleges for admissions purposes.

Grade Inflation: The increase in the value of an assessment over time; or the assignment of a grade to a student who has not yet reached the achievement level represented by that grade.

Grade Level Promotion: Advancement to a higher level in school (i.e., moving from 10th to 11th grade).

Higher Education: Academics beyond the secondary level, for example a two or four year college.

Naïve Selection: To choose a school specifically because of the high grades its student body earns.

Scholastic Aptitude Test (SAT): The standardized test measuring mathematic and English ability; usually required for college admissions.

Secondary Schools: Primarily known as high schools, but may be any institution offering education past the 6th, 7th, or 8th grade levels.

Strategic Selection: Choosing a school specifically because of the high grades its student body earns.

Maureen McMahon

BIBLIOGRAPHY

Abbott, W. M. (2008). The politics of grade inflation: A case study. *Change, 40*, 32-37. Retrieved August 21, 2010, from EBSCO online database, Education Research Complete.

Are high school grades inflated? (2005). *College Readiness: Issues in College Readiness.* Retrieved August 28, 2010, from ACT website: http://209.235.214.158/research/policymakers/pdf/issues.pdf

Bracey, G. W. (1994). *Grade inflation?* Phi Delta Kappan, 76, 328. Retrieved August 22, 2010, from EBSCO online database, Academic Search Complete.

Edwards, C. H. (2000). Grade inflation: The effects on educational quality and personal well being. *Education, 120,* 538. Retrieved August 22, 2010, from EBSCO online database Academic Search Complete.

Erickson, J. A. (2011). How grading reform changed our school. *Educational Leadership, 69,* 66-70. Retrieved December 15, 2013, from EBSCO Online Database Education Research Complete.

Farran, S. (2009). Can high school grades be trusted? *Maclean's, 122,* 92-96. Retrieved August 22, 2010, from EBSCO online database, Academic Search Complete.

Grade Inflation. (2000). *Gifted Child Today, 23,* 6. Retrieved August 22, 2010, from EBSCO online database, Education Research Complete.

Hall, R. A. (2012). A neglected reply to grade inflation in higher education. *Global Education Journal, 2012,* 144-165. Retrieved December 15, 2013, from EBSCO Online Database Education Research Complete.

Hansen, E. J. (1998). Essential demographics of today's college students. *AAHE Bulletin, 51.*

Jewell, R., McPherson, M. A., & Tieslau, M. A. (2013). Whose fault is it? Assigning blame for grade inflation in higher education. *Applied Economics, 45,* 1185-1200. Retrieved December 15, 2013, from EBSCO Online Database Education Research Complete.

Lekholm, A. K. & Cliffordson, C. (2008). Discrepancies between school grades and test scores at individual and school level: Effects of gender and family background. *Educational Research & Evaluation, 14,* 181-199. Retrieved August 22, 2010, from EBSCO online database, Academic Search Complete.

Pattison, E., Grodsky, E., & Muller, C. (2013). Is the sky falling? Grade inflation and the signaling power of grades. *Educational Researcher, 42,* 259-265. Retrieved December 15, 2013, from EBSCO Online Database Education Research Complete.

Walsh, P. (2010). Does competition among schools encourage grade inflation? *Journal of School Choice, 4,* 149-173.

SUGGESTED READING

Beaver, W. (1997, July). Declining college standards: It's not the courses, it's the grades. *The College Board Review,* 181, 2-7.

Bromley, D. G., Crow, M. L., & Gibson, M. S. (1978). Grade inflation: Trends, causes, and implications. *Phi Delta Kappan, 59,* 694-697.

Chan, W., Hao, L. & Suen, W. (2007). A signalling theory of grade inflation. *International Economic Review, 48,* 1065-1090.

Cohen, P. A. (1984). College grades and adult achievement: A research synthesis. *Research in Higher Education, 20,* 281-293.

Gardner, H. (1983). *Frames of mind: The theory of multiple intelligences.* New York: Basic Books.

Goldman, L. (1985). The betrayal of the gatekeepers: Grade inflation. *The Journal of General Education, 37,* 97-121.

Gose, B. (1997). Efforts to curb grade inflation get an F from many critics. *The Chronicle of Higher Education, 43,* A41-A42.

Kohn, A. (1992). *No contest: The case against competition.* Boston: Houghton Mifflin.

Levine, A. (1994, January 19). To deflate grade inflation: Simplify system. *Chronicle of Higher Education, 40,* B3.

Ramirez, E. (2009, February 10). On Education: Study finds grade inflation at some Georgia high schools. *U.S. News & World Report.* Retrieved August 28, 2010, from http://usnews.com.

Schneider, M., Teske, P., Marschall, M. & Roch, C. (1998). Shopping for schools: In the land of the blind, the one-eyed parent may be enough. *American Journal of Political Science, 42,* 764-793.

Sykes, C. (1995). *Dumbing down our kids.* New York: St. Martin's Press.

Walsh, Patrick. (2010). Does competition among schools encourage grade inflation? *Journal of School Choice.* 4 (2), p149-173.

Zhang, Q., & Sanchez, E. (2013). *High school grade inflation from 2004 to 2011.* ACT., Inc.

Zirkel, P. A. (2007). Much ado about a C? *Phi Delta Kappan, 89,* 318-319. Retrieved August 22, 2010, from EBSCO online database, Academic Search Complete.

SCHOOL NURSING

School nursing is an integral part of the United States educational system. While the institution of school nursing began with the single purpose of improving public health through the treatment and containment of infectious diseases, it has evolved into a multi-dimensional profession. The most significant expansion in the role of school nursing during the second half of the 20th century was in the area of children with disabilities. Today, nurses also oversee school health service programs and help treat students with mental health issues. Because of a nurse shortage, many schools find themselves without a full time nurse. These schools have employed a number of innovative methods to ensure that they meet their students' medical needs.

KEYWORDS: Chronic Illness; Disability; Mental Health; National Association of School Nurses (NASN); Public Health; School Health Service Program; School Nursing; Terminal Illness

OVERVIEW

In the century that has passed since its inception in 1902, school nursing has become an integral part of the United States educational system. While the implementation of school nursing varies from school to school, the goal of school nursing remains the same everywhere: to support the overall health and wellness of school children, and thereby enable them to avoid absences, focus in the classroom, and achieve their full academic potential (Wolfe & Selekman, 2002). The National Association of School Nurses (NASN) defines school nursing as "a specialized practice of professional nursing that advances the well being, academic success, and life-long achievement of students" (Wolfe & Selekman). School nursing is so critical because more than 53 million children living in the U.S. spend more than one-third of every weekday at school (Hootman, Houck, & King, 2003). School is often the central context within which children develop—physically, mentally, and socially. By monitoring these developmental tracks and providing timely interventions when necessary, school nursing helps to meet the fundamental health needs of the nation's children.

School nurses are the most commonly found healthcare providers practicing in schools today (Hootman & Desocio, 2004). As such, they provide an overall "health safety net" for the nation's children, ensuring that all students enrolled in public schools receive primary health care services, adequate nutrition, mental health care services, and disability services (Vessey & McGowan, 2006). These services are especially valuable when poverty or other conditions at home compromise a child's access to outside medical care. For these students, school nurses often serve as de facto primary care physicians (Wolfe & Selekman).

While the institution of school nursing began with the single purpose of improving public health through the treatment and containment of infectious diseases, it has evolved into a multi-dimensional profession. School nurses are direct care providers, case managers, and consultants (Hootman et al.). They must master skills associated with pediatric nursing, community health nursing, psychiatric nursing, emergency-room nursing, and home-care nursing, as well as health education, policy making, social work, and office management. When serving students with chronic medical problems, school nurses become liaisons who must coordinate between a child's parents, primary care physician, and teachers (Broussard, 2004). Often, school nurses manage and implement a larger school health service program, or coordinated school health program, which includes health education, counseling, physical education, nutrition, and immunizations, along with many other services (American Academy of Pediatrics, Committee on School Health, 2001; Wolfe & Selekman). Increasingly, school nurses are engaging in research as well. By documenting the positive outcomes and cost-effectiveness associated with their practices, school nurses hope to encourage districts to invest more funds in school nursing (Edwards, 2002).

History

School Nursing During the Early 20th Century

School nursing was first established in the United States in New York City in 1902 as a way to combat the rampant absenteeism that plagued the city's schools. During this period, New York was overcrowded and unsanitary. Large waves of immigration during the late 19th Century had resulted in slums and tenement neighborhoods where infectious diseases were widespread (Vessey & McGowan). Prior to the institution of school nursing, New York City schools were monitored by physicians who would visit one a week and examine children for symptoms of contagious diseases such as whooping cough, measles, and scarlet fever. Infected students were not treated, but sent home with their diagnosis written on a slip. It was assumed that parents would receive this diagnosis and seek medical care for their children. This policy

was largely ineffective for several reasons. Immigrant parents were often unable to read English and thus could not understand their child's diagnosis if and when they received it. Even if parents wanted to seek medical treatment for their children, poverty often made this impossible. Finally, even though contagious children were removed from schools, they still interacted with and infected their classmates and peers at home, on playgrounds, and in the streets (Broussard, 2004; Wolfe & Selekman; Vessey & McGowan).

In order to address the widespread absenteeism that resulted from its current school health system, the New York City Board of Education and the City Health Commissioner turned to Lillian Wald, a social reformer and advocate for the city's immigrant poor. Using a program established in London in 1893 as a model, Wald commissioned the nation's first school nurse: Lina Rogers (Wolfe & Selekman). Rogers' primary goal was to contain the spread of communicable diseases in the city's schools. She achieved this goal by treating the illnesses she diagnosed, often making home visits in order to administer medicines and educate parents about preventative measures such as proper hygiene. Rogers' method was so immediately effective that within one month the city hired 14 more nurses. Within a year, absentee rates had dropped by 90%; within three years Los Angeles and Boston had begun their own school nursing programs (Vessey & McGowan).

School Nursing Today

While school nursing began as "one of the most successful experiments in public health" in U.S. history, its focus soon expanded outside of the domain of public health to include other pertinent student-health related issues (Vessey & McGowan). The 1950's and 1960's saw a dramatic proliferation in school nursing, with schools across the nation hiring full-time nurses. During this period, the focus of school nursing shifted from public health to screening efforts and referrals to primary care physicians. Children were screened for scoliosis, hearing loss, and vision problems; parents were notified if their children tested abnormally and told to seek further care from a primary care physician. During the 1960's and 1970's, health classes were added to many high school curriculums. School nurses either taught these classes or consulted with teachers in order to help develop their content. During the 1980's, many high schools developed health services focused on an adolescent population. Reproductive health, HIV and STD infection, as well as mental health, all became the domain of school nursing (Broussard).

STUDENTS WITH DISABILITIES, CHRONIC ILLNESSES, & TERMINAL ILLNESSES

The most significant expansion in the role of school nursing during the second half of the 20th century was in the area of children with disabilities. During this period, advances in pediatric medical care and changing attitudes about children with disabilities resulted in decreased rates of institutionalization for children with physical, psychosocial, and developmental disabilities. Children who would have formerly been institutionalized were now being raised at home and attending public schools. These children often needed more medical care during the school day than their peers, and legislation was passed guaranteeing them the right to such care. The Individuals with Disabilities Education Act (IDEA) of 1975 and the Education for All Handicapped Children Act of 1975 (also known as Public Law 94-142) mandated that all children, regardless of physical or developmental disabilities, must be given access to and accommodated in the nation's public schools. The task of removing barriers that had formerly prevented children with disabilities from participating in school was allocated to school nursing services. This new role for school nursing was reinforced in 1999, when a Supreme Court ruling further stipulated that public schools are financially responsible for providing nursing services for children with special medical needs if they need these services in order to have access to, and benefit from, public education (Wolfe & Selekman).

It is estimated that 11% of school-aged children in the United States today have at least one disability (Hootman et al.). Currently, the services provided by school nurses enable students in wheelchairs, students with digestive disorders, diabetes, ADHD, autism, depression, mental retardation, anxiety disorders, bipolar disorder and myriad other physical, psychological, and developmental issues to attend public schools alongside their non-disabled peers. School nurses address the special healthcare needs of students with disabilities and chronic conditions by creating Individualized Health Management Plans (IHPs), which detail the exact measures that will be taken in order to allow such students to participate as fully as possible in school (Hootman et al.). For students with physical disabilities that could impede emergency evacuation, and for students with terminal illnesses or serious food allergies, emergency health plans are created as well.

The inclusion of children with disabilities and chronic illnesses in public schools has led to higher skill levels among school nurses. In order to care for students with special medical needs during the school day, school nurses must be trained to perform in-patient care methods (Wolfe & Selekman). School nurses must learn to perform such technical procedures as tracheostomy suctioning, nasogastric feedings, and bladder catheterization, among others; they must also ventilator care and orthopedic device maintenance (American Academy of Pediatrics, Committee on School Health). Most school districts require school nurses to be certified in school nursing through the district's state education agency (Wolfe & Selekman).

Once a child with a disability or chronic or terminal condition has entered the public school system, it is the duty of school nursing services to advocate for him or her. If a student is in a wheelchair, for example, the school nurse must make sure that all school facilities are accessible by wheelchair so that the student can fully participate in all school activities. In recent years, there has been a trend towards the inclusion of children with autism, a development disability, into public school classrooms. School nurses must advocate for autistic students by assessing their special communicative needs, managing medication, and educating parents and school staff about autism (Cade & Tidwell, 2001).

SCHOOL HEALTH SERVICE PROGRAMS

In addition to meeting the immediate medical needs of students, school nurses commonly serve an administrative function as well. In many schools and districts, school nurses manage the implementation of a school health service program, or a coordinated school health program. These programs are usually designed at the state or district level. They attempt to promote student health throughout the state or district by positive preventative measures, as well as through timely interventions. At the elementary level, such programs focus on immunizations, safety, as well as vision, hearing and scoliosis screenings. At the secondary level they tend to focus on prevention of risky behavior such sex, smoking, and drug and alcohol use (Wolfe & Selekman). In some high schools, school health service programs include school-based health centers that may or may not specialize in reproductive health issues (Broussard). Many programs now include health and nutrition services and physical education in order to target populations at risk for obesity (Wolfe & Selekman). Other programs use holistic measures such as biofeedback in order to help students with anxiety, stress, low self-esteem, and ADHD (Jones, 2004). Most programs include counseling and psychological services (Wolfe & Selekman).

Managing such programs requires school nurses to truly bridge the gap between the medical and educational communities (Wolfe & Selekman). School nurses must coordinate their activities with primary care physicians, specialists, local public health care agencies and school officials, all while caring for students and communicating with their families (American Academy of Pediatrics, Committee on School Health). They must serve as educators, either engaging in classroom instruction, consulting with teachers on how to structure health education classes, or sitting on curriculum planning committees. When not directly engaged in educational activities, school nurses should model healthy behaviors to staff, parents, and students (Broussard).

STUDENTS WITH MENTAL HEALTH ISSUES

As the holistic nature of many school health services programs shows, school nursing today focuses not only on the physical, but also on the psychological and emotional well being of students. Mental health in particular has become increasingly important to school nursing in the past few decades as more awareness about mental health issues has been raised in American society. The U.S. Department of Health's 2010 Health Objectives include the goal of enhancing mental health services for youth, a goal that is met in schools through school nursing (Hootman et al.).

Approximately one fifth of all children between the ages of 9 and 17 suffer from a mental or addictive disorder that affects their ability to function at school. Moreover, 70% of these children go undiagnosed and so untreated. This is because even students who have insurance and primary care physicians often lack access to mental health services. Evidence shows that school nursing can bridge this gap in medical

care: 70% of children who are diagnosed with a mental health problem identify their school as the primary source of their mental health care (Hootman & Desocio). A NASN survey revealed findings that support this conclusion: 67% of school nurses have identified and/or counseled a depressed or suicidal teen; 51% have identified and/or counseled a student who has abused substances (Hootman et al.).

School nurses can raise awareness about mental health issues throughout the entire student body. One study has shown that when a school nurse advocates mental illnesses as being 'no-fault' illnesses without a stigma, students became open about their or their friends' depression (Hootman & Desocio). School nurses can either personally lead classroom discussions about mental health or consult with teachers in order to devise a mental health education curriculum.

School nurses must also serve students who have already been diagnosed with a mental health issue. The school nurse is legally responsible for protecting the health of such a child during the school day, and so should be notified if he or she is suicidal. School nurses can also oversee the administration of medication, ensuring that students do not overdose on their medication or choose not to take it at all. School nurses are sometimes prevented from carrying out these duties effectively by parents who choose to withhold information about their children's psychiatric diagnosis (Wolfe & Selekman).

SCHOOL HEALTH RESEARCH

Until recently, school health research was not considered an integral part of school nursing. In the last two decades, however, many experts have called for school nurses to begin conducting health research on the job (Broussard). Numerous conferences and summits have been held on the subject of research and school nursing. The main reason for this turn to research is that school nursing currently lacks sufficient documentation of its effectiveness. Without proof that school nursing is a vital part of the public school system, school nursing services risk being cut out of over-strained budgets (Edwards).

School nursing professionals generally agree about what areas future research should address. Studies are needed to show how school health services affect student attendance, academic achievement, drop-out rates, and risky behavior (Broussard).

School nurses must also document successful interventions in the areas of chronic illnesses, disabilities, mental health, and substance abuse prevention. Such research should demonstrate the overall value that school nursing adds to the education system and to student health. In addition, there is a need for research that focuses on school nursing as an independent discipline within nursing. Such research should investigate what types of professional training best prepares nursing students for the field of school nursing (Edwards).

The primary obstacles preventing school health research from becoming a standard aspect of school nursing are logistical in nature. Most school nurses are already overburdened. They lack the time, funding, and clerical assistance that would be necessary in order to take on additional duties (Broussard).

SCHOOLS WITHOUT NURSES

The NASN recommends a ratio of one school nurse for every 750 children in the general student population. This ratio increases to one school nurse for every 225 children with special needs who are mainstreamed in the general school population. Not all states, however, follow this recommendation; only 38% officially recommend that schools do so (Broussard). Moreover, some schools do not have a registered nurse at all. Instead, they use an unlicensed assistive personnel (UAP) to perform the functions of a school nurse (Wolfe & Selekman). In one school district in West Central Florida, for example, only 6 out of 19 high schools in one county have full-time nurses. The ratio of school nurses to students in this county is 1:6,460 (Perrin, Goad, & Williams, 2002).

Several factors have contributed to the lack of professionally trained nurses in schools. Many school districts have limited budgets and cannot afford to staff every school with a registered school nurse. Some administrators complain that the testing requirements in the No Child Left Behind Act of 2001 have overstrained their already stretched budgets. Additionally, a shortage of nursing school graduates during the 1990s has contributed to this problem (Smolkin, 2003).

Schools without school nurses are still legally required to meet the medical needs of their student populations. Administrators at these schools sometimes find creative ways to do so. Some schools ask a nursing club to volunteer at the school and carry out standard monitoring requirements. Others have an emergency nurse that can be called in to the schools on a contingency basis. In some schools, administrators themselves evaluate children's health needs (Smolkin). Other schools have taken a more innovative approach. These schools find the funds to hire school nurses by making the nurses available to faculty and staff as well as students. School nurses become cost effective by reducing employee doctor visits, sick days, injuries, disability days, and worker's compensation claims (Perrin et al.). The American Cancer Society has launched its own innovative solution—a nationwide program that trains district-level health coordinators who can work in districts that lack a full school-nursing staff (Smolkin).

Many experts feel that school nurses themselves must work to ensure the future of their profession by carrying out school health research that demonstrates the vital need for school nursing in every school (Edwards).

TERMS & CONCEPTS

Chronic Illness: An illness lasting three months or longer. Common chronic illnesses include cancer, AIDS, autoimmune diseases such as LUPUS, and neurological disorders such as Parkinson's disease. A chronic illness may or may not be terminal.

Disability: A condition that impairs a person's ability to carry out certain functions in a normative manner. Disabilities can be physical, developmental, psychosocial, or affect any other part of a person's functioning.

Mental Health: A branch of medicine that seeks to establish the psychological, rather than physical, well-being of the patient.

National Association of School Nurses (NASN): The primary professional association for school nurses in the United States. The NASN supports and promotes the institution of school nursing by representing school nurses in the legislative and educational spheres.

Public Health: The branch of medicine concerned with protecting and promoting the health of a community as a whole. Focuses on risk assessment, prevention, and education. In the early twentieth century, the field of public health was most concerned with preventing the spread of contagious diseases.

School Health Services Program: Usually designed by the state or district; promotes the well-being of students through the prevention and treatment of medical conditions. Often includes a strong focus on health education.

School Nursing: A specialized practice of professional nursing that promotes the educational success and general well-being of students.

Terminal Illness: An active, malignant disease that cannot be cured and will eventually lead to the patient's death.

Ashley L. Cohen

BIBLIOGRAPHY

American Academy of Pediatrics, Committee on School Health. (2001). The role of the school nurse in providing school health services. *Pediatrics, 108,* 1231-1232. Retrieved April 4, 2007, from EBSCO Online Database Academic Search Premier.

Broussard, L. (2004). School nursing: Not just band-aids any more! *Journal for Specialists in Pediatric Nursing, 9,* 77-83. Retrieved April 4, 2007, from EBSCO Online Database Academic Search Premier.

Cade, M., & Tidwell, S. (2001). Autism and the school nurse. *Journal of School Health, 71,* 96-100. Retrieved April 4, 2007, from EBSCO Online Database Academic Search Premier.

Edwards, L. (2002). Research priorities in school nursing: A Delphi process. *Journal of School Health, 72,* 173-177. Retrieved April 4, 2007, from EBSCO Online Database Academic Search Premier.

Faigenbaum, A.D., Gipson-Jones, T.L., & Myer, G.D. (2012). Exercise deficit disorder in youth: An emergent health concern for school nurses. *Journal of School Nursing (Sage Publications Inc.), 28,* 252-255.Retrieved December 15, 2013, from EBSCO Online Database Education Research Complete.

Hootman, J., & Desocio, J. (2004). School nurses' important mental health role. *Behavioral Health Management, 24,* 25-29. Retrieved April 4, 2007, from EBSCO Online Database Academic Search Premier.

Hootman, J., Houck, G. M. & King, M. (2003). Increased mental health needs and new roles in communities. *Journal of Child & Adolescent Psychiatric Nursing, 16,* 93-101. Retrieved April 4, 2007, from EBSCO Online Database Academic Search Premier.

Jones, K. (2004). School nursing in search of the holistic paradigm. *Creative Nursing, 10,* 11. Retrieved April 4, 2007, from EBSCO Online Database Academic Search Premier.

Perrin, K., Goad S., & Williams, C. (2002). Can school nurses save money by treating school employees as well as students? *Journal of School Health, 72,* 305-306.

Retrieved April 4, 2007, from EBSCO Online Database Academic Search Premier.

Ramos, M.M., Greenberg, C., Sapien, R., Bauer-Creegan, J., Hine, B., & Geary, C. (2013). Behavioral health emergencies managed by school nurses working with adolescents. *Journal of School Health, 83,* 712-717. Retrieved December 15, 2013, from EBSCO Online Database Education Research Complete.

Singer, B. (2013). Perceptions of school nurses in the care of students with disabilities. *Journal of School Nursing (Sage Publications Inc.), 29,* 329-336. Retrieved December 15, 2013, from EBSCO Online Database Education Research Complete.

Smolkin, R. (2003). Rx for school nursing. *School Administrator, 60,* 16-19. Retrieved April 4, 2007, from EBSCO Online Database Education Research Complete.

Vessey, J., & McGowan, K. (2006). A successful public health experiment: School nursing. *Pediatric Nursing, 32,* 255-256, 213. Retrieved from EBSCO Online Database Academic Search Premier.

White, G. (2005). Nurses at the helm: Implementing DNAR order in the public school setting. *American Journal of Bioethics, 5,* 83-85. Retrieved April 5, 2007, from EBSCO Online Database Academic Search Premier.

Wolfe, L., & Selekman, J. (2002). School nurses: What it was and what it is. *Pediatric nursing, 28,* 403-407. Retrieved April 4, 2007, from EBSCO Online Database Academic Search Premier.

SUGGESTED READING

Bergeron, M.D. (2017). Expanding the sphere of school nursing influence. *Journal of School Nursing.* 33(4), 257-258.

Endsley, P. (2017). School nurse workload: A scoping review of acute care, community health, and mental health nursing workload literature. *Journal of School Nursing.* 32(6), 43-52.

Grant, A. (2001). The nurse in the school health service. *Journal of School Health, 71,* 388-389. Retrieved April 4, 2007, from EBSCO Online Database Academic Search Premier.

Lucarelli, P.B. (2016). The school nurse in a Montessori setting. *Montessori Life.* 28(1), 34-37.

Paris, J., & Webster, G. (2005). Back to the future: Overcoming reluctance to honor in-school DNAR orders. *American Journal of Bioethics, 5,* 67-69. Retrieved April 5, 2007, from EBSCO Online Database Academic Search Premier.

Taras, H., Wright, S., Brennan, J., Campana, J., & Lofgren, R. (2004). Impact of school nurse case management on students with asthma. *Journal of School Health, 74,*

213-219. Retrieved April 4, 2007, from EBSCO Online Database Academic Search Premier.

Weber, S. (2006). School health programs: A starring role for school nurse practitioners! *Journal of the American Academy of Nurse Practitioners, 18,* 510-511. Retrieved

April 7, 2007, from EBSCO Online Database Academic Search Premier.

Wold, S. & Dagg, N. (2001). School nursing: A framework for practice. *Journal of School Health, 71,* 401-404. Retrieved April 4, 2007, from EBSCO Online Database Academic Search Premier.

SCHOOL LIBRARIANSHIP

The role of the school library and the school librarian has expanded over the past 25 years. This article describes the status of the school library and the school librarian. It examines the role and responsibilities of school librarians; cites professional resources available to them; discusses significant issues; and presents a glossary of relevant terms.

KEYWORDS: Blog; Censorship; Copyright; Distance Learning; First Amendment; Freedom of Speech; Intellectual Freedom; Interlibrary Loan (ILL); Library Bill of Rights; Paraprofessional; Teacher Certification

OVERVIEW
THE SCHOOL LIBRARY

The main purpose of public school libraries is to provide resources and services that support the school curriculum. However, the role of school libraries has been greatly expanded over the past 25 years. Today, public school libraries from kindergarten through high school often attempt to provide an environment that promotes outside activities and life skills. In addition to educational materials, a library may offer print, non-print, and online resources for recreational activities, including popular books, graphic novels, movies, music, and games. In addition, middle and high school libraries may contain college and career information.

LABELS

As an indication of its expanded role, the school library is often labeled something other than a "library." Here are the most common terms used to indicate the school library:
- Learning Resource Center;
- Library-Media Center;
- Media Center;
- Resource Center;
- School Library.

(For purposes of this article, we will use the term "school library.")

The School Librarian

TITLES

As school libraries have evolved, so has the role of school librarians. Not surprisingly then, a school librarian may have a title other than "librarian." Here are the most common titles for school librarians:
- Library-Media Specialist;
- Library Teacher;
- Media Specialist;
- School Librarian.

(For purposes of this article, we will use the term "school librarian.")

RESPONSIBILITIES

Regardless of his or her title, a person who follows a career in public school librarianship will find that the job incorporates an interesting assortment of responsibilities that usually include the following:
- Collection Development;
- Collection Maintenance;
- Reference Work;
- Teaching;
- Electronic Communications.

QUALIFICATIONS

Most states require school librarians to have teacher certification (Bishop, 2007). Generally, the qualifications for a school librarian include the completion of at least a Bachelor's degree, approximately 30 credits of undergraduate or graduate education courses, and either the completion of a student teaching or a school library practicum. In addition, to be qualified as a professional school librarian, most states require that a candidate hold one of the following graduate degrees:

- M.L.S. (Master of Library Science);
- M.Ed. (Master of Education in Library Media Studies).

(For school librarian certification requirements by state, consult the American Association of School Librarians, http://ala.org)

GEOGRAPHIC & GRADE COVERAGE

The geographic and grade coverage that falls under a particular school librarian's auspices vary considerably among school districts or even within school districts. Here are just some of the possible staffing situations for a school district that maintains libraries for grades kindergarten through grade 12:

- A full-time, professional school librarian for kindergarten through grade 5, for each school;
- A full-time, professional school librarian for each middle school;
- A full-time, professional school librarian for the high school;
- One full-time, professional school librarian that oversees all school libraries in one school district with the help of part-time professional librarians, paraprofessionals, or volunteers;
- One or more part-time, professional school librarians who cover specific grades without help;
- One or more part-time, professional school librarians with the help of paraprofessionals or volunteers;
- No professional school librarian; the school library is staffed entirely by paraprofessionals or volunteers.

This section examines the job responsibilities of school librarians in more detail and explores some of the professional associations, journals, and additional resources that are available to school librarians.

JOB RESPONSIBILITIES OF SCHOOL LIBRARIANS

Job responsibilities of school librarians vary by school and school district. Of course, the role of any individual school librarian will also depend upon whether he or she works alone or has paraprofessionals or volunteers to help with workload. In any case, a school librarian will generally be required to either assume or oversee five areas of responsibility:

- Collection development;
- Collection maintenance;

- Reference work;
- The teaching of library and information literacy skills;
- The handling of miscellaneous responsibilities.

COLLECTION DEVELOPMENT

The first job responsibility of school librarians is collection development. Collection development entails building a collection of print and non-print materials that primarily supports the school curriculum.

The task of collection development involves the following processes:

- Budgeting for library materials;
- Choosing the materials;
- Ordering the materials;
- Paying for the materials.

To ensure that the collection supports the curriculum, the school librarian works with school faculty members for suggestions and feedback regarding purchases and may also consult other school librarians and professional journals.

A secondary goal of collection development is to collect materials that enhance recreational or life-enhancing skills and activities. To achieve this goal, the school librarian may still consult school faculty members, other school librarians, and professional journals, but will also seek suggestions from students.

COLLECTION MAINTENANCE

The second job responsibility of school librarians is collection maintenance. Maintaining the school library collection ensures that the materials are in good physical condition and easy to locate.

- Maintaining the collection involves the following processes:
- Repairing or replacing items as they deteriorate physically;
- Cataloguing the items for purposes of arranging by subject and media format;
- The most common school library cataloguing conventions are the Dewey Decimal System (common in public libraries) and the Library of Congress Classification System (common in colleges and universities). By cataloguing an item, the school librarian is labeling it so that it can be easily retrieved and easily returned;
- Regularly performing an inventory of the collection to make sure that materials are located where the catalogue indicates they are located;

- Tracking down materials that are either missing or overdue from borrowers;
- Removing outdated items from the collection.

REFERENCE WORK

The third responsibility of school librarians is reference work. Reference work involves helping patrons—students, teachers, and sometimes parents—find the best information and materials in the school library. It might also involve referring the patrons to sources outside the school library, such as a public library.

THE TEACHING OF LIBRARY AND INFORMATION LITERACY SKILLS

The fourth responsibility of school librarians is the teaching of library and information literacy skills. This refers to the school librarian teaching patrons how to define topics; identify information sources; locate and retrieve the information sources; and evaluate the information sources. The teaching of library and information skills can be achieved through formal or informal methods.

Increasingly, information is stored electronically and accessed through digital technologies. While students may be more comfortable using digital devices than their parents or teachers, they need to learn how to find and evaluate reliable information online and from electronic database as well as through printed sources. Teaching these skills is a natural extension of teaching students to use traditional information sources, and school libraries are frequently called on to provide access to multimedia devices (e.g., tablet computers) and to teach students how to use them effectively, thus playing a part in reducing the digital divide between students who own or have access to such devices at home, and those who do not (Ballew, 2014).

Formal methods for teaching library and information literacy skills include the following three:

- Courses or individual classes;
- Printed skills sheets or workbooks;
- Computerized lessons.

Informal methods for teaching library and information literacy skills usually occur as a result of the following two situations:

- One-on-one, as needed: The school librarian provides instruction to an individual student or patron when requested;

- During reference work: The teaching of library and information literacy skills often overlaps with reference work; while helping patrons find information, the school librarian is also teaching them how to find the information and often is also providing guidance on how to evaluate the information.

THE HANDLING OF MISCELLANEOUS RESPONSIBILITIES

The last responsibility of school librarians is the handling of miscellaneous responsibilities. This is the catchall category that varies considerably for each school librarian. Here are some miscellaneous responsibilities that may be considered part of a school librarian's job:

- Answering questions or providing reference work via email or Internet;
- Maintaining a library blog or Web page;
- Organizing author appearances, book fairs, and other events;
- Facilitating distance learning (courses via Internet or closed circuit television);
- Maintaining computer equipment.

PROFESSIONAL ASSOCIATIONS FOR SCHOOL LIBRARIANS

Professional associations that are geared specifically to school librarians offer educational, career, and networking benefits including: Publications, conferences, workshops and distance learning opportunities, lobbying efforts, employment clearinghouses, and membership directories. The professional associations also provide opportunities for volunteer work involving conferences, publications, fundraising, special committee work, and membership drives.

Perhaps the best known association for school librarians is the American Association of School Librarians, which is a division of the oldest library association the American Library Association (http://ala.org).

In addition, many states have their own school library associations. Here are three examples:

- California School Library Association (http://schoolibrary.org);
- Illinois School Library Media Association (http://islma.org);
- Massachusetts School Library Association (http://maschoolibraries.org).

PROFESSIONAL JOURNALS FOR SCHOOL LIBRARIANS

Professional journals are a valuable resource for school librarians. In addition to topical feature articles and profiles of successful or innovative school libraries, librarians, and programs, the journals include book, media, and product reviews; buying guides; professional and industry news; career advice; and job listings. Most professional library journals maintain Web sites and they usually make some content from current and archived journal issues available on their Web sites without a subscription.

Many professional library journals—such as *Library Journal* (libraryjournal.com)—offer content that is useful for all types of librarians, including school librarians, college librarians, and public librarians. However, the following journals are specifically designed for school librarians:

- Library Media Connection (http://linworth. com/lmc);
- MultiMedia & Internet@Schools (http://mmischools. com);
- School Library Journal (http://schoollibraryjournal. com);
- Teacher Librarian (http://teacherlibrarian.com).

ISSUES

Like most school educators and administrators, school librarians face a variety of financial, administrative, and political issues. This section examines significant issues for school librarians

SIGNIFICANT ISSUES FOR SCHOOL LIBRARIANS

Most of the significant issues for school librarians can be grouped into four main categories:

- Resource Allocation;
- Policy Decisions by Others;
- Disciplinary Practices;
- Intellectual Freedom.

RESOURCE ALLOCATION

The first significant issue for school librarians falls under the category of resource allocation. The resources include monetary funds and personnel and the school librarian needs to allocate both in the most efficient and useful manner. The budgeting of monetary funds may include applying for grants or justifying budget estimates and purchases to the administration or school board. The budgeting of personnel involves using the available personnel—both paid and volunteer—effectively and efficiently.

POLICY DECISIONS BY OTHERS

The second significant issue for school librarians falls under the category of policy decisions by others. This is a broad category which the school librarian may not control. For example, policies must be set regarding overdue library materials. How long may patrons borrow library materials? Is there a fine for overdue materials; if so, how much and who keeps the fine proceeds? Policies affecting overdue library materials are often set at the administrative level and can't be changed by the school librarian. Another policy issue surrounds the practice of reciprocal borrowing privileges. This practice is known as "interlibrary loan (ILL)" and allows libraries to borrow and lend materials with libraries in another jurisdiction. ILL practices are most common in public and college libraries. However, many school libraries do participate in such arrangements. While ILL participation does increase access to more materials for patrons, it also involves more administrative work for participating libraries: The libraries must mail or otherwise transport materials to and from each library and collect and pay fines for overdue materials. Again, ILL participation may not be suggested by the school librarian but will need to be enforced by the school librarian.

DISCIPLINARY PRACTICES

The third significant issue for school librarians falls under the category of disciplinary practices. Although most school libraries are no longer intended to be hushed environments, the need to discipline students still arises. Depending upon the grade level, disciplinary behavior may involve "running around," defacing library materials, rowdy behavior and fighting, and stealing anything from library materials to pocketbooks. Usually, there are school regulations in place to govern disciplinary behavior in all school buildings; nevertheless, in the library, the school librarian will usually be the one who needs to initiate the disciplinary action.

The increasingly common use of electronic sources of information within the library poses an additional set of questions—for instance, will access to certain web sites, or types of web sites be blocked? Does the school have policies regarding electronic communications between students (e.g., cyber) that the librarian must enforce?

Copyright adherence is another issue that can be considered to fall under school library disciplinary practices. Copyright laws forbid the reproduction of the intellectual work of another, such as books, art work, and music. While the copyright law is extremely complicated, it generally does allow for limited reproduction in educational settings. For example, a teacher or student may be allowed to photocopy text from a book for use in the classroom. A problem arises when a person photocopies or downloads long passages—such as entire book chapters—of a work that is protected by copyright. If there are no photocopy machines in the library or equipment to download information from the Internet or disks, then copyright control may not be an issue for the school library. However, if the opportunity for copyright violations does exist in the school library, then the school librarian needs to take some precautions. Since it is difficult to monitor every teacher and student for copyright violations, the best approach is for the school librarian to publish and post copyright guidelines and rules in conspicuous and likely spots in the school library and in student and faculty handbooks and manuals. In fact, teachers are more likely to violate the copyright law than students in grades kindergarten through high school. Dickinson (2007) points out the ticklish dilemma of dealing with teachers who violate the copyright law and suggests that the school librarian take a tactful but firm approach by offering to obtain copyright permissions or alternative materials for the teacher and simultaneously warning that the librarian will inform the principal if copyright violations continue.

INTELLECTUAL FREEDOM

The last significant issue for school librarians falls under the category of intellectual freedom. Freedom of speech and the right to write, access information, and read without censorship is considered a fundamental right of citizens of the United States. The First Amendment guarantees these rights and in 1948, the American Library Association adopted the "Library Bill of Rights" which affirms that libraries will uphold the right of intellectual freedom.

Challenges to intellectual freedom don't arise very often in school libraries, but when they do, they present a unique situation for the school librarian. Challenges to intellectual freedom in the school library may originate with students, teachers, administrators, parents or outsiders such as politicians. Usually, such challenges involve censorship by requesting that certain books or materials be removed from the collection. In such circumstances, these are the usual choices: The material is removed from the collection; the material may be restricted to students over a certain age or in a certain class; the material can only be accessed with written permission from parents; the material is not removed from the collection, nor is access to it restricted in any manner.

TERMS & CONCEPTS

Blog: Also known as web log or weblog, a blog is an online diary or collection of writings and information that is accessible to others via the Internet. Often, a blog is set up so that readers can add public comments.

Censorship: The institution, system, or practice of censoring. To censor, is to examine in order to suppress or delete anything considered objectionable.

Copyright: The exclusive legal right to reproduce, publish, and sell the matter and form as of a literary, musical, or artistic work.

Distance Learning: Learning that takes place via electronic media linking instructors and students who are not together in a classroom.

First Amendment: An amendment to the Constitution of the United States that states: Congress shall make no law respecting an establishment of religion, or prohibiting the free exercise thereof; or abridging the freedom of speech, or of the press; or the right of the people peaceably to assemble, and to petition the government for a redress of grievances.

Freedom of Speech: The right of the public to express freely in speech or writing, as guaranteed by the First Amendment to the Constitution of the United States.

Interlibrary Loan (ILL): A reciprocal arrangement in which libraries are allowed to borrow and lend materials to libraries outside their jurisdiction.

Intellectual Freedom: The right of every individual to both seek and receive information from all points of view without restriction. It provides for free access to all expressions of ideas through which any and all sides of a question, cause or movement may be explored.

Library Bill of Rights: The American Library Association affirms that all libraries are forums for information and ideas, and that certain basic policies should guide their services.

Paraprofessional: A trained aide who assists a professional person.

Teacher Certification: Formal acknowledgement that a person is qualified to teach certain grades and subjects in a specific public school system.

Ann Connaughton

BIBLIOGRAPHY

Alvarez, A. R. G. (2012). 'IH8U': Confronting cyber and exploring the use of cybertools in teen dating relationships. *Journal of Clinical Psychology, 68,* 1205–1215. Retrieved December 28, 2013, from EBSCO Online Database Education Research Complete.

American Library Association. (2014a). *American Association of School Librarians.* Retrieved November 4, 2014, from http://ala.org.

American Library Association. (2014b). *Library bill of rights.* Retrieved November 4, 2014, from http://ala.org.

Ballew, L.M. (2014, Jan./Feb.). The value of school librarian support in the digital world. *Knowledge Quest 42,* 64–68. Retrieved December 28, 2013, from EBSCO Online Database Education Research Complete.

Bishop, K., & Janczak, S. (2007). Recruiting the next generation of school librarians. *Library Media Connection, 26,* 14–18. Retrieved November 6, 2007, from EBSCO Online Database Education Research Complete.

Chow, A. S., & Rich, M. (2013). The ideal qualities and tasks of library leaders: Perspectives of academic, public, school, and special library administrators. *Library Leadership & Management, 27* (1/2), 1–24. Retrieved November 4, 2014, from EBSCO Online Database Education Research Complete.

Dickinson, G. (2007). The question.... *Knowledge Quest, 35,* 50–51. Retrieved November 6, 2007, from EBSCO Online Database Education Research Complete.

Loertscher, D. (2007). Research and school libraries: Knowing the basic sources. *Teacher Librarian, 34,* 23–26. Retrieved November 6, 2007, from EBSCO Online Database Education Research Complete.

Mattering in the school blogosphere. (2007). *American Libraries, 38,* 62–65. Retrieved November 6, 2007, from EBSCO Online Database Education Research Complete.

Merriam-Webster's collegiate dictionary (10th ed.). (2000). Springfield, MA: Merriam-Webster.

Morris, R., & Nelson, K. (2014). New collaborations through effective communication. *School Library Monthly, 30,* 11–13. Retrieved November 4, 2014, from EBSCO Online Database Education Research Complete.

Riehl, D. (2006). Students' privacy rights in school libraries: Balancing principles, ethics and practices. *School Libraries in Canada, 26,* 32–42. Retrieved November 6, 2007, from EBSCO Online Database Education Research Complete.

Schmidt, A. (2007). Tapping the tools of teen culture in the LMC. *MultiMedia & Internet@Schools, 14,* 8–11. Retrieved November 6, 2007, from EBSCO Online Database Education Research Complete.

SUGGESTED READING

Buzzeo, T., & Wilson, S. (2007). Data-driven collaboration in two voices. *Library Media Connection, 26,* 20–23. Retrieved November 6, 2007, from EBSCO Online Database Education Research Complete.

Dobija, J. (2007). The First Amendment needs new clothes. *American Libraries, 38,* 50–53. Retrieved November 6, 2007, from EBSCO Online Database Education Research Complete.

Hodges, J., & Pringle, L. S. (2013). Meeting the learning needs of African American youth in the library. *School Library Monthly, 29,* 14–16. Retrieved November 4, 2014, from EBSCO Online Database Education Research Complete.

Hoppe, K. M. (2007). The instant I knew I was not meant to be an elementary librarian: Confessions of a high school librarian. *Library Media Connection, 26,* 38–39. Retrieved November 6, 2007, from EBSCO Online Database Education Research Complete. http://search.ebscohost.com/login.aspx?direct=true&db=ehh&AN=26926581&site=ehost-live..Johnson, D. (2013). Good technology choices: A team effort. *Educational Leadership, 71,* 80–82. Retrieved December 28, 2013, from EBSCO Online Database Education Research Complete.

York, S. (2007). Twenty-five years later: A librarian looks back...and ahead. *Library Media Connection, 25,* 18–20. Retrieved November 6, 2007, from EBSCO Online Database Education Research Complete.

STRATEGIES IN TEACHING MATH

Math instruction is generally broken down into five math strands: numbers and operations; algebra; geometry; measurement; and data analysis and probability. Though concepts are more advanced than others, even the youngest children can learn basic math strategies that will prepare them for future learning. Students also learn problem solving as a way to think critically about and integrate math strategies. Teachers should use a variety of instructional methods to keep lesson interesting and fun for all students, and to ensure that their lessons are reaching students of all learning styles. Assessment and evaluation can be done through tests and quizzes as well as one-on-one conferences and journal writing.

KEYWORDS Algebra; Curriculum; Data Analysis; Formative Assessment; Geometry; Journal Writing; Learning; Lesson Planning; Manipulatives; Math; Measurement; Numbers; Probability; Problem Solving; Structured Learning; Word wall

OVERVIEW

Teaching math is an important job for instructors who work with learners of any age. The goal of the math teacher shouldn't just be for the student to understand the concept or strategy being taught, but also for the students to be interested in the learning process. Ideally, students should find mathematics both intriguing and enjoyable.

Even the youngest children seem to be hard-wired to do math and be interested in numbers. From their earliest days, babies seem to have a basic understanding of mathematical concepts like adding and subtracting. Watch two objects move on a screen in front of him or her, a baby's face will often register surprise when another object is introduced, indicating a simple understanding of addition. Children may be ready to learn math at a very early age, and, when they are given opportunities, will usually be interested in learning (Sarama & Cléments, 2006). Teachers are challenged to maintain that interest throughout the strands of the math curriculum.

MATH STRANDS

The basic math curriculum is usually thought of in five strands. These components include: numbers and operations; algebra; geometry; measurement; and data analysis and probability (Lemlech, 2006).

NUMBERS & OPERATIONS

The numbers and operations strand includes the number systems and how they are used. Strategies and techniques for computing with numbers are taught at this stage of learning, beginning with basic counting and advancing to activities that involve comparing numbers and sets. Fundamental addition and subtraction facts are also part of numbers and operations, and methods of computing are introduced and refined as well.

Children need to understand that, just as the letters of the alphabet represent parts of words, numbers represent ideas. When they have grasped this concept, they will be able to work with the counting process more readily (Lemlech). To work with young learners at this stage, teachers can instruct children to sort objects by shape and size, classify objects by their different characteristics, and fit objects inside of other objects. Children can also be taught to perform basic balancing activities (Lemlech). In their discussions with preschool children, teachers should also incorporate the use of small numbers. Instead of saying, for example, that there are chairs available, teachers can be more instructive by saying that four chairs are available. Inserting numbers across the curriculum will help children learn to attach meaning to them (Sarama & Cléments).

As numbers become more a part of the curriculum, so should counting. Teachers can make counting part of the school day by inviting students to count small numbers that are part of their daily routine, like the number of doors they pass as they go out to the playground, or steps it takes to get to the front of the classroom. Later, they can instruct children to compare numbers. They can ask students to look at a pile of pencils and determine if there are enough for each child in the classroom. Children can also do a one-to-one match with items from two piles (e.g., plates and cups, pencils and paper) to figure out if there are enough of each group to form pairs (Sarama & Cléments).

When students are under the age of six and still at a preoperational level of thinking, they often don't realize, for example, that despite the unfamiliar ordering of a specific set of numbers (e.g., {3.1.2}, {2,1,3}), the numbers themselves are still the same. Students will often have to count the numbers ordered in the original, left-to-right way and the new right-to-left way to discover that the numbers are the same even when listed both ways. As students develop, the concept of reversibility will begin to seem logical and automatic (Lemlech).

ALGEBRA

The study of algebra entails working with the language of variables. Important skills typically taught in the algebra strand are: performing operations within equations containing variables; working with functions; and manipulating symbols within equations. Even the youngest students can understand basic algebra. Number patterns and sentences using objects and manipulatives, for example, can help preschool students begin to think algebraically. Arranging blocks and objects in a simple pattern and inviting students to say which block would logically be placed next helps students begin to think algebraically (Lemlech).

GEOMETRY

In the geometry strand, students work with space and form to learn how these concepts are linked to numbers and math. Students are taught about figures, lines, points, lanes, polygons, geometric solids, and three-dimensional space. In geometry especially, manipulatives help students explore and discover; young students will likely grasp geometric concepts more clearly when links to real-life experiences are stressed (Lemlech).

Basic geometry concepts can also be introduced to young learners. Matching shapes is interesting and fun for preschool children, and putting shapes together within a puzzle is one way for children to learn how certain shapes can work together. Teachers can cut colorful basic shapes from construction paper and encourage the children to create pictures and then talk about what they have made (Sarama & Cléments).

MEASUREMENT

Since measurement is part of everyday life, it is a key strand in teaching mathematics. Within the measurement strand, students learn to gauge capacity, distance, and time as they are taught about units of measure, estimation, and the nature of measurement. Students should be encouraged to use an assortment of units of measure to understand the importance of using common and accepted units of measure. Estimation and approximation are also a part of this strand of math (Lemlech).

DATA ANALYSIS & PROBABILITY

The data analysis and probability strand involves teaching the students how to plan and collect data, organize and infer conclusions from what they have collected, and share what they have learned. As with other mathematics strands, even very young children can gather and organize data. They can collect information about the color of leaves, how many birds are seen outdoors at certain times of the year, or how many hours of television people they know watch each day. Students can attempt to solve science, health, and social studies problems with the data they glean from themselves and their family members. In the process, they will reinforce counting techniques as they organize and interpret data (Lemlech).

PROBLEM SOLVING

Problem solving is an integral part of every strand of mathematics. When teaching math, instructors must be wary of introducing problem solving as simply another basic skill which can be solved in a step-by-step fashion. Many students work through problems without much thought, or by using a rule they believe the problem follows. If they aren't sure of or have forgotten the rule, students are often not able to solve the problem on their own. In many cases, problem solving in math has evolved into exercises in computation rather than real approaches to solving problems with numbers (Dolan & Williamson, 1983).

To help them be successful in mathematical problem solving, teachers must show students how to work with strategies. These strategies can ensure that students know what solution they are looking for, and the most direct routes they can take to reach this solution (Dolan & Williamson). Students who master problem solving strategies will generally learn higher-level math content with greater ease than students who struggle with learning these strategies (Lemlech).

Even preschool children can engage in some basic problem-solving experiences. Showing young students a pair of blocks and then hiding one is a good introduction to the concept of subtraction, and also invites the students to solve a problem. After one block is hidden, the teacher may ask the children how many blocks have been removed. The children can be encouraged to discuss how they were able to figure out that it was one block that was removed from the group. The teacher can also invite four students to stand in front of the classroom and then ask one child sit down. The children can call out how many of their classmates were originally standing in front of the class, how many are presently standing in front of the class, and how many were asked to sit down (Sarama & Cléments).

Applications

INSTRUCTIONAL METHODS

With all ages and grade levels, teachers should vary instructional methods. Not only does variation help teachers reach all students, but eliminating stagnant classroom routines also helps motivate learners. Students have more fun when, walking into a classroom, they don't know if they will be participating in a hands-on activity, discussion, project work, or other learning scenario. (Ellis, 1988).

Formative assessment is the best way to begin a unit. By assessing students before learning begins, teachers can determine what students already know about a particular skill or strategy, and plan their instruction accordingly. The information gleaned from a formative assessment of students helps drive the classroom instruction (Minton, 2007).

As with teaching other subjects and strategies, planning a math lesson takes a purposeful approach. It's best to first set the stage by telling students the objective of the day's lesson so they will understand what they are building up to. Teachers should provide directives about how they plan to reach the day's goal and then provide a context for learning. They can illustrate the concept or particular skill through an assortment of activities, like discussions, or tools like manipulatives and visuals. Teachers should ask questions throughout the lesson to promote reflective thinking, and then clarify any extended expectations (Ellis).

Whenever possible, teachers should link mathematical concepts to other subject areas and realistic contexts with which students are familiar. Doing so

will enhance students' understanding of and interest in math concepts (Lemlech).

STRUCTURED LEARNING

Many teachers use structured learning as a way to teach mathematical concepts. Structured learning is an instructional method in which the teacher works with the class as a whole to explain a concept or strategy, give instruction, provide demonstrations, and check for understanding. The teacher's goal, aside from helping students understand a particular concept or strategy in math, is to keep the students on task during the structured learning time. There is a strong correlation between the amount of time students are on task and the amount of material they are able to learn. This option, called the opportunity-to-learn variable, is especially important when teaching and learning math. Teachers should be aware of the importance of the opportunity-to -learn variable and take advantage of this research (Ellis).

COOPERATIVE LEARNING GROUPS

Alternatively, teachers may choose to work with small groups or form cooperative learning groups. Students may be more apt to share their own problem-solving ideas and strategies when they are working within a small group of their peers rather than with the entire class. In small groups, students may also feel more comfortable explaining their ideas in their own words rather than attempting to use the "correct" vocabulary. In this way, small groups may foster more positive attitudes about learning and facilitate understanding among group members (Lemlech).

CLASS DISCUSSION

Whole class discussions can foster students' understanding of certain concepts by enabling them to listen to others' ideas about how they problem-solve. Students who may not have originally understood the concepts, may find their peers' explanations helpful. By asking students how they solved or approached a particular problem and came to their solutions, students learn to verbalize the problem-solving phase. Since students will approach problems in different ways, students can discuss and learn the most efficient strategies to solving problem types (Lemlech).

Communication and discussion are vital factors to students' mathematical understanding. It is important for teachers to help the students engage in rich and relevant discussions as they review and discuss strategies. Even those students who don't participate in class discussions will benefit from the reinforcement they provide (Lemlech).

TEACHING VOCABULARY & SYMBOLS

Math vocabulary can be confusing to learners of any age. Words that have one meaning in everyday English (e.g., squared, root, product) can have a different mathematical definition. It may also be difficult to define words within their mathematical context. Some mathematical words may even have different definitions within different mathematical contexts (Kenney, 2005).

Similarly, symbols may also pose a problem for students since they often look alike, or just similar enough to cause confusion (e.g., the square root and division symbol). Different symbols may sometimes have the same meaning. For example a dot, parentheses around sets of numbers, and the "x" symbol may all denote multiplication. Reading data on a graph can also be confusing for many students (Kenney). Teachers need to be aware of these potential problems and attempt to trouble shoot.

Word walls are a common sight in many classrooms, but usually as a part of the language arts curriculum. Math teachers who use walls to highlight math words, symbols, and concepts provide an additional reinforcement for students (Lucas, 2004). Since no one method of learning and reinforcement works for all students, teachers should implement as many helpful components as possible. All teachers should strive to find approaches that are suitable to the concept being discussed and the students' learning styles (Rudnick & Krulik, 1982).

MANIPULATIVES

Manipulatives can be used in a variety of ways. Students should have them available, for example, to practice ordering objects from large to small or small to large. As students work with geometrical concepts, too, they might first focus on shapes and their similarities and differences to understand how geometry relates to real life. As much as possible, students should be encouraged to work with hands-on activities that enable them to create their own geometric figures and objects and make reasonable assumptions. Students who are able to think logically will

usually have an easier time learning mathematics. At about the time they reach the age of 11, children are usually able to think at the formal operational level. By then, they are usually ready to learn formal, abstract-level mathematics. Still, most children of this age can improve upon their understandings of math concepts by working with manipulatives (Lemlech).

ASSESSMENT & EVALUATION

Students' progress can be evaluated in a number of ways. Teachers can observe students to ascertain understanding, make use of performance assessments, administer tests that they create, use standardized assessments, and conference with individual students. Conferencing can be especially useful since, as students talk about their reasoning processes, teachers can assess the strengths and weaknesses of their understandings. However, students should not have to follow one method of solving a problem. Rather, teachers should discuss alternate problem-solving methods with students as they attempt to assess student understanding (Lucas).

Math journals can also be helpful and powerful instructional tools. Journal writing can help math teachers assess the effectiveness of their instruction and monitor student learning as students reflect on what they have learned. As students think about what they will write, they must first mentally refine their understanding—a very useful way to help students make connections and reflect on what they have been doing in the classroom. Just as in a language-arts journal, open-ended questions can act as writing prompts and often work to help students crystallize their thinking. These questions may include: *What did you notice?, What surprised you?, Did you find any patterns?, Why do you think it worked the way it did?, Can you make any connections?* (Minton).

Assessing student understanding and evaluating what they have learned are important ways to monitor what is taking place with each student in the classroom. Evaluating students' progress helps the teacher see weaknesses and errors in student thinking, and sometimes in the way the lesson or concept was presented. This knowledge can help the teacher re-teach or review certain lessons or concepts before moving on (Underhill, 1988).

CONCLUSIONS

Eighth grade students in almost fifty countries were questioned about their math and science confidence as part of an international math achievement assessment. The results of the assessment showed that students in countries with the highest achievement scores tended to admit that they didn't enjoy math and felt that they didn't do well in math either. Students from countries with lower scores, however, felt that they did fine in math and enjoyed the subject ("Happy Math," 2007).

In Singapore, the country with the highest achievement scores in math, less than 20% of the students believed that they usually do well in mathematics. Almost 40% of eighth grade students in the United States responded positively to the same statement despite the fact that these most confident American students scored lower than the less-confident students from Singapore. Some researchers believe this may mean that the American educational culture focuses more on helping students feel confident about their math skills, rather helping them develop strong skills ("Happy Math").

TERMS & CONCEPTS

Data Analysis: "Preparation of factual information items for dissemination or further treatment (includes compiling, verifying, ordering, classifying, and interpreting)".

Formative Assessment: Diagnostic assessment used to shape lesson content.

Journal Writing: "Writing done regularly in logs or notebooks to gather thoughts or ideas, sometimes for later use in more formal writing".

Manipulatives: Concrete objects students can use to practice math concepts.

Probability: The likelihood that a certain result will occur.

Structured Learning: An organized and systematic approach to learning.

Word Wall: A wall or board on which words, and often their definitions, are displayed for students to see.

Susan Ludwig

BIBLIOGRAPHY

Dolan, D., & Williamson, J. (1983). *Teaching problem-solving strategies.* Menlo Park, CA: Addison-Wesley.

Ellis, A. (1988). Planning for mathematics instruction. In T. R. Post (Ed.) *Teaching mathematics in grades K-8: Researched-based methods.* Newton, MA: Allyn & Bacon.

ERIC Thesaurus. (1988). Retrieved November 19, 2007, from Education Resources Information Center, http://eric.ed.gov.

Faulkner, V. N. (2013). Why the Common Core changes math instruction. *Phi Delta Kappan, 95,* 59–63. Retrieved December 15, 2013, from EBSCO Online Database Education Research Complete.

Fisher, P. J., & Blachowicz, C. Z. (2013). A Few words about math and science. *Educational Leadership, 71,* 46–51. Retrieved December 15, 2013, from EBSCO Online Database Education Research Complete.

Freedman, L., & Johnson, H. (2004). *Inquiry, literacy, and learning in the middle grades.* Norwood, MA: Christopher-Gordon Publishers.

Hachey, A. C. (2013). Early childhood mathematics education: The critical issue is change. *Early Education & Development, 24,* 443–445. Retrieved November 3, 2014, from EBSCO online database Education Research Complete.

Happy Math. (2007). *Wilson Quarterly, 31,* 16. Retrieved October 28, 2007, from EBSCO Online Database Education Research Complete.

Kenney, J. (2005). *Literacy strategies for improving mathematics instruction.* Alexandria, VA: Association for Supervision and Curriculum Development.

Lemlech, J. (2006). *Curriculum and instructional methods for the elementary and middle school.* Columbus, OH: Pearson.

Minton, L. (2007). *What if your ABCs were your 123s?.* Thousand Oaks, CA: Corwin Press.

Rudnick, J., & Krulik, S. (1982). *A guidebook for teaching general mathematics.* Boston: Allyn & Bacon.

Sarama, J., & Cléments, D. (2006). Teaching Math: A Place to Start. *Early Childhood Today* 4. 15. Retrieved October 28, 2007, from EBSCO online database, Education Research Complete.

engül, S., & Dereli, M. (2013). The Effect of learning integers using cartoons on 7th grade students' attitude to mathematics. *Educational Sciences: Theory & Practice, 13,* 2526–2534. Retrieved November 3, 2014, from EBSCO online database Education Research Complete.

Underhill, R. (1988). Mathematical evaluation and remediation. In T. R. Post (Ed.) *Teaching mathematics in grades K-8: Research-based methods.* Newton, MA: Allyn & Bacon.

Zhang, L., & Jiao, J. (2013). A study on effective hybrid math teaching strategies. *International Journal of Innovation & Learning, 13,* 451–466. Retrieved December 15, 2013, from EBSCO Online Database Education Research Complete.

SUGGESTED READING

Barody, A., & Coslick, R. (1998) *Fostering children's mathematical power: An investigative approach to K-8 mathematics instruction.* Hilldale, NJ: Lawrence Erlbaum.

Bender, W. (2005). *Differentiating math instruction: Strategies that work for K-8 classrooms.* Thousand Oaks, CA: Corwin Press.

Carbonneau, K. J., Marley, S. C., & Selig, J. P. (2013). A meta-analysis of the efficacy of teaching mathematics with concrete manipulatives. *Journal of Educational Psychology, 105,* 380–400. Retrieved November 3, 2014, from EBSCO online database Education Research Complete.

Chen, Jie-Qi; McCray, Jennifer; Adams, Margaret; Leow, Christine (2014). A survey study of early childhood teachers' beliefs and confidence in teaching math. *Early Childhood Education Journal,* 42(6), 367-377.

Gryskevich, K. (2015). Master Math: Elementary School Math. Boston, MA.: Cengage.

Honner.P. (2016). Aftermath: I love teaching math: Maybe you will too. *Math Horizons.* 24(2):34-34.

Lemlech, J. (2006). *Curriculum and instructional methods for the elementary and middle school.* Columbus, OH: Pearson.

Martin, H. (1998). *Multiple intelligences in the mathematics classroom.* Thousand Oaks, CA: Corwin Press.

Stein, M., Silbert, J., & Carmine, D. (1997). *Designing effective mathematics instruction: A direct instruction math.* Upper Saddle River, NJ: Prentice Hall Publishers.

Sullivan, P., & Wilburn, P. (2002). *Good questions for math teaching: Why ask them and what to ask.* Sausalito, CA: Math Solutions Publications.

Underhill, R. (1988). Mathematical evaluation and remediation. In T. R. Post (Ed.) *Teaching mathematics in grades K-8: Research-based methods.* Newton, MA: Allyn & Bacon.

Van de Walle, J. (2005). *Teaching student-centered mathematics.* Newton, MA: Allyn & Bacon.

Wahl, M. (1999). *Math for humans: Teaching math through 8 intelligences.* Langley, WA: LivnLern Press.

TEACHING READING AND WRITING

A student's inability to read and write creates a ripple effect that has far-ranging repercussions on his or her future prospects that demand proficient literacy. The implementation of effective reading and writing curricula is particularly crucial during the first few years of primary education when learning is more effectively conveyed during the early developmental stages of childhood. Teachers can use a variety of tools to teach reading and writing, some of which are entrance and exit slips, written conversations, self-assessments, and journal writing. Many instructional approaches advocate integrating reading and writing across the curriculum as a way to further develop students' abilities.

KEYWORDS: Electronic Communications across the Curriculum (ECAC); Envisionment; High-Frequency Words; Journal Writing; Language and Learning across the Curriculum (LALAC); Letter-Name Skills; Literacy skills; Metacognitive Skills; No Child Left Behind Act of 2001 (NCLB); Phonetic Awareness; Sight Words; Teaching Reading; Teaching Writing; Writing Across the Curriculum (WAC)

OVERVIEW

A student's inability to read and write creates a ripple effect that has far-ranging repercussions on his or her future prospects that demand proficient literacy. Given how much faster and technologically-dense everyday American life has become, anyone remaining illiterate after completing the educational process is deprived of basic academic tools and lacks necessary survival skills for future success, including, but not exclusive to, gainful employment as an adult. According to a 1993 United States Office of Technology Assessment, 25 percent of the adult population lacks the basic literacy skills required for a typical job. As of the spring of 2013, approximately thirty-two million Americans could not read. There are numerous reasons for the low literacy rate in the United States. A December 2004 paper released by the Northwest Regional Educational Laboratory (NWREL) cites an American School Board Journal story stating that less time was being spent on teaching writing because educators are focusing more on meeting the parameters set by the No Child Left Behind Act of 2001 (NCLB). The NWREL paper also mentions that a 2003 study by the National Commission on Writing found limited focus was being given to educating preservice teachers in how to teach writing (NWREL).

The NCLB is federal legislation defined by the theory of standards-based education reform in which high educational goals are set for states and school districts in which students are expected to meet or exceed these expectations. Federal requirements are measured via roughly 45 million annual standardized tests created at the state level and first administered in the third grade (Scherer, 2006). The demands of NCLB have shifted the focus in classrooms towards test-taking because school districts whose results don't meet or exceed pre-determined test levels risk losing federal funding. According to Guilfoyle (2006), this redirection of focus prevents teachers from providing the kind of rich and varied curriculum needed for an environment more conducive to teaching reading and writing. In 2012 and 2013 President Barack Obama began issuing waivers that released states from the restrictions of NCLB if they continued working toward rigorous educational goals and meeting requirements. Thirty-four states and the District of Columbia have waivers that will expire—but can be renewed—at the end of the 2013–2014 school year.

Therefore, the implementation of effective reading and writing curricula becomes all the more crucial, particularly during the first few years of primary education when learning is more effectively conveyed during the early developmental stages of childhood. Effective reading instruction is the initial springboard for ensuring that children achieve maximum literacy via a number of techniques incorporating phonemic awareness instruction, an emphasis on decoding and comprehending sight words along with teaching the relationship of this vocabulary within the context of written and verbal communication. To this end, exercises that hinge on frequent prose writing further complement the educational process and are at the heart of programs such as Writing Across the Curriculum (WAC), Language and Learning Across the Curriculum (LALAC) and Electronic Communications Across the Curriculum (ECAC).

The grander scope of WAC is that rather than have writing be its own discipline, it is instead used as a tool that can enhance the learning of various subjects like science and math while enriching a child's overall proficiency in communicating both within and outside the educational spectrum. LALAC and ECAC are related movements. LALAC proposes that writing well goes far beyond merely putting words down and that it is one component of learning and communication that should include fostering other components of language-speaking, reading and listening. ECAC has more of a technological bent. This program puts an emphasis on how technologies like the Internet and digital communication are not only changing the way that writers write, but that access to the Web is providing new outlets in which students can communicate, acquire and organize new data. Therefore, it is imperative that students are familiarized with the kinds of Web-based documents they'll be using along with utilizing sound, images and links in a way that will make the communicative process far more interactive. This use of technology for purposes other than its original use is referred to as envisionment by Donald Leu and his collaborators in a 2004 paper written for the International Reading Association (cited in Yancey, 2004).

APPLICATIONS

Some applications of writing exercises used as part of Writing Across the Curriculum (WAC) and approaches used to increase reading competency in elementary through high school levels are:

- Entrance and Exit Slips;
- Written Conversations;
- Self-Assessments;
- Journal Writing;
- Improving Reading.

ENTRANCE & EXIT SLIPS

In this exercise, entrance slips are assigned at the start of class and students either compose questions or write a few sentences about any knowledge they may have of the day's upcoming topic. These anonymously penned blurbs are collected and read aloud as a means of jumpstarting the day's learning. Exit slips are written at the end of class, where students write brief descriptions of what was covered in the day's lesson along with any techniques they may have used to absorb this new knowledge. Elementary school students should be encouraged to write freely without concern for punctuation or spelling, so the intuitive flow of expression and language structures is not impeded. Proper grammar and spelling are stressed more in the middle and secondary levels as the student's writing abilities become more sophisticated. Throughout, these particular methodologies are mutually beneficial as a teacher can use them to determine how well the class may know a topic while the students can absorb new ideas, review old ones and potentially trigger their long-term memory.

WRITTEN CONVERSATIONS

These five-minute exercises consist of having students write as much as they can about the day's topic, either by themselves or collaboratively with a partner. Subsequently, the pupil will have had a chance to organize his or her thoughts before being asked to participate in a discussion which works equally well when the process is tailored towards a collaborative response. Writers in elementary school would begin with more basic topics. Middle and secondary level instructors can eventually guide their students towards writing about non-literary topics such as the processes behind a science project or the steps taken to solve a mathematical problem. The benefit of written conversations is that students become more familiar and proficient with the pre-writing process, enabling them to more effectively group thoughts about similar topics into a working outline when starting a paper.

SELF-ASSESSMENTS

Students are asked to write brief assessments of a project they are either still working on or are on the brink of submitting. Questions that should be addressed can range from what knowledge they may be accruing through this assignment and what the most difficult aspect of it is to delineating the most gratifying part of it. Teachers can obviously monitor how well their charges are grasping a given topic and also help the student oversee how well they are learning the given subject matter. The approach for these self-assessments is similar throughout elementary, middle and secondary levels due to the simplistic nature of this exercise.

JOURNAL WRITING

Students should be consistently encouraged to write, and among the most effective techniques to stimulate the writing process is journal writing. In addition to getting students acclimated to writing, this daily exercise also enriches fluency, encourages reflection and helps students become familiar with the creative thought process.

The mental muscles involved in writing are much like the physical ones that are firmed up at a gym. Using these writing muscles consistently will build up a student's literacy skills and give the student more confidence in tackling future writing assignments. The important approach to take towards having novice scribes compose journals is to allow them to write without concern for proper punctuation and spelling. In this way, they can develop a more intuitive style

of writing that's intended to effectively communicate an idea. Children of elementary school age in particular should be engaged in briefer writing exercises to help maintain enthusiasm for the assignment. On all levels, journal writing should be a daily exercise with entries dated to chart a student's progress. As writers enter middle and secondary levels, instructors can more heavily weigh having these entries earn points towards a grade. Also, teachers can suggest topics and solicit student responses which can then be turned in as a creative writing assignment (Wanket, 2005).

IMPROVING READING

Evaluation is a crucial first step towards determining what kind of help a student may or may not need to improve reading skills. Testing of reading comprehension can be accomplished by giving students 150-200 word passages photocopied from books, then read in class, followed by a handful of questions pertaining to the reading material. Teachers should then take students who performed poorly on this test and have the pupils read brief passages from the books, followed up by answering five content questions. If this proves to be too difficult, the teacher should then read a passage back to the student and ask questions pertaining to the passage. A student's inability to perform well may mean an inability to isolate a main idea within context or a lack of concentration (Shuman, 1975).

Effective study techniques are best conveyed by how a teacher instructs his or her students on how to approach a particular homework assignment. Rather than merely assigning material to read, instructors should have these assignments continue the thread of learning that was covered in class and provoke students into approaching the reading so they will dissect various aspects of the subject matter, instead of just absorbing facts minus any cognition. This can be achieved by having students consider points of view to be aware of, key words that may be problematic or contrasts that may come up. In taking this approach, higher levels of competency and cognition are possible and subsequently, the ease of understanding what was read enhances the potential for students to approach the subject with more confidence and enthusiasm (Shuman).

Shuman goes on to say that providing an enriched reading environment is pivotal in promulgating the idea that literacy is crucial as well as a communal experience that benefits from a high level of participation. Reports should be posted in an accessible area where students can read, compare and contrast what's been written. A portion of the classroom could be sectioned off as a special quiet area filled with books and reading material. Use of a rug will lend an inviting aura to this area where students are encouraged to visit and read anything of their choosing once their schoolwork has been completed. And lastly, instructors themselves should be reading on their own, particularly within the subject area they teach. Nothing inspires students more than a teacher brimming with enthusiasm over something that may have been read about the evening before. And even if this desire to convey this recently learned knowledge slightly deviates from the day's lesson plan, this contagious zeal has the potential to trigger a student into realizing that academic topics have the ability to be intellectually stimulating. Likewise, teachers should be ready to encourage independent exploration of a subject matter and be willing to help students in their quest.

FURTHER INSIGHTS

This section addresses different approaches towards teaching writing and reading that may be of use to educators working with students at the primary level. It also draws on schools of thought for teaching writing based on Writing Across the Curriculum (WAC). These techniques include:

- Language and Learning Across the Curriculum (LALAC);
- Electronic Communications Across the Curriculum (ECAC);
- Writing Across the Curriculum (WAC);
- Writing in the Disciplines (WID);
- Writing to Learn (WTL);
- Basic reading lesson elements;
- Significant reading and writing events;
- Successful reading acquisition;
- Rich classroom environments;
- Proficient reading programs;
- School community involvement.

LANGUAGE & LEARNING ACROSS THE CURRICULUM (LALAC)

Adherents of Language and Learning Across the Curriculum (LALAC) argue that all aspects of language-speaking, listening, reading and writing-are crucial elements towards achieving more effective communicating and learning.

ELECTRONIC COMMUNICATIONS ACROSS THE CURRICULUM (ECAC)

With advancements in technology, educators are incorporating tools such as the Internet, e-mail, online social networks, and blogs as a means of enticing otherwise reluctant students to have a greater interest in improving their writing skills and in many cases, prompting them to excel in a subject. With so many students becoming computer literate at an early age, these newer technologies serve as enticements for younger, would-be writers while allowing them to use varying approaches that include visual, digital and print processes to capture their ideas.

According to Kathleen Blake Yancey, teachers should be sure to encourage their pupils to become proficient with using various digital tools and software, which will help them adapt more quickly to changing technology. There are different ways this can be applied. The use of slide presentations to provide a visual outline of a research paper encouraged students to more seriously undertake drawing up drafts in a more timely manner. The fact that they were forced to present their projects to a real audience as a group resulted in it being a more enjoyable way of handling this assignment. Having pupils utilize a presentation software package further along in the creative process also gives students a unique way to express themselves by changing font styles or incorporating different colors and special effects that give students a greater and more intriguing manner with which to approach their writing (Yancey).

WRITING ACROSS THE CURRICULUM (WAC)

Writing across the Curriculum (WAC) is based on the theory that writing should be held to the highest standards regardless of the discipline to which it may be applied. Students are expected to be at the same writing level whether the subject they are learning is English, science or math. Critics of WAC maintain that the high level of oversight needed to effectively implement this program in non-literary disciplines effectively cuts into a teacher's time allotted for focusing on the fundamentals and more granular aspects of a topic like math in which effective writing is less of a paramount concern.

Writing in the Disciplines (WID) maintains that the thinking, learning and writing skills in a discipline are maximized when participants work within the parameters specific to it. In this case, a history professor could assign students to interview war veterans or a business professor may have them create a marketing plan or sales pitch.

Writing to Learn (WTL) is based on the concept that writing should be a means for students to increase their knowledge of different topics rather than merely being a tool to regurgitate what is already known. Adherents of WTL feel that by having students utilize previously learned knowledge to make connections to newer topics, their metacognitive skills will be strengthened as they unearth newer ideas while they write. WTL is most effective when the exercise coincides with the learning objectives of a particular topic, while keeping in mind a student's skill level and how they will be critiqued.

BASIC READING ELEMENTS

There are a number of components that go into efficiently teaching children how to read, ranging from programs that encourage a home environment that develops good reading habits and monitoring homework to school policies driven by the goal of improving reading achievement. Educators in both the classroom and administrative offices strive to understand the success and failure of literacy approaches via analysis and assessment, the setting of goals and the incorporation of effective techniques. There are also more direct applications available towards increasing a student's ability to successfully learn how to read.

Significant reading and writing events are best executed at the kindergarten and first-grade levels. Letter-name knowledge (the knowledge of letter names) and phonemic awareness (the conscious awareness of how a sequence of sounds forms a spoken word) are the most effective approaches used. Instruction of phonemic awareness is based on a mix of sounds that are mixed and blended within activities that include oral recitation of poems and songs, and composition of written communication and journals.

Successful reading acquisition hinges on the teaching of systematic word recognition, in which children are taught about common, consistent letter-sound relationships, high-frequency words (how and we) and sight words (of and was) which are regular and irregular words that may not follow the established

phonetic rules of English spelling but are frequently used. Strategies encouraging children to summarize, infer and predict outcomes to enhance and maintain reading accuracy. Conversations about the subjects in reading matter, reading aloud exercises accompanied by feedback and frequent revisiting of reading material are invaluable in fostering comprehension and word recognition.

Rich classroom environments hinge on daily reading and writing assignments that allow for continual student assessment and encourage readers to utilize facets of what they've learned. Daily expectations include both instructors and pupils reading books aloud and engaging in follow-up discussions, writing stories, daily journals being maintained and children reading independently.

Proficient reading programs starting in the third grade provide ample opportunity for students to read, promoting the learning of new vocabulary and knowledge. Students are also apprised of how writers utilize different techniques (poetry vs. prose) to convey concepts and the importance and methodology of comprehending these ideas that goes beyond simply reading text.

School community involvement revolves around having students accomplish higher reading achievement that's encouraged by all those associated with the educational process either at the school level or at home. High expectations are defined, goals are set and the teaching tools with which to reach them are provided with a constant monitoring process in place to ensure success. The focus is on reading and writing with programs based on community involvement ranging from encouraging parental involvement with the children's reading and homework to establishing volunteer tutoring projects.

TERMS & CONCEPTS

Electronic Communications across the Curriculum (ECAC): The way in which new technologies like the Internet and e-mail are changing how writing is done.

Envisionment: The ability to use technology for purposes other than its original use.

High-Frequency Words: Phonetically regular words, such as "in" or "not," that consistently show up in reading.

Journal: An editorial log usually maintained on a daily basis in which the writer can recapitulate the day's lessons, note questions that need further study or generate dialogue with teachers and fellow students.

Language and Learning Across the Curriculum (LALAC): The theory that all aspects of language up to and including speaking, listening, reading and writing are crucial elements towards achieving more effective communicating and learning.

Letter-Name Knowledge: The ability to recognize letter names.

Metacognitive Skills: Understanding one's thought processes in a manner that allows use of prior knowledge as a means of comprehending new situations.

No Child Left Behind Act of 2001 (NCLB): This federally mandated program is based on standards-based education reform in which standardized testing results determine whether federal education funding is forthcoming to states based on whether their students meet or exceed pre-determined educational goals.

Phonemic Awareness: The ability to identify the combined speech sounds that make up a word.

Sight Words: These are high frequency regular (it, on) and irregular words (of, was) readers learn to recognize automatically.

Writing Across the Curriculum (WAC): An approach driven by the theory that writing should be done with the highest standards of execution regardless of the discipline to which it is being applied.

Karen A. Kallio

BIBLIOGRAPHY

Center for the Improvement of Early Reading Achievement (CIERA)/University of Michigan School of Education. (1998). *Improving the reading achievement of America's children: 10 research-based principles.* Retrieved December 3, 2006, from http://ciera.org.

East Side Literacy. (n.d.). *Tips for teaching reading.* Retrieved December 4, 2006, from http://eastsideliteracy.org.

Kelly spells out new phonics emphasis in national curriculum. (2006). *EPM Weekly Bulletin, 3.* Retrieved December 5, 2006, from EBSCO Online Database Education Research Complete.

Guilfoyle, C. (2006). NCLB: Is there life beyond testing?. *Educational Leadership, 64,* 8-13. Retrieved December 5, 2006, from EBSCO Online Database Education Research Complete.

Holdstein, D. H. (2001). Writing across the curriculum and the paradoxes of institutional initiatives. *Pedagogy, 1,* 37-53. Retrieved December 5, 2006, from EBSCO Online Database Education Research Complete.

Kent, A. M., Giles, R. M., & Hibberts, M. (2013). Preparing elementary educators to teach reading: An exploratory study of preservice teachers' evolving sense of reading efficacy. *International Journal For The Scholarship Of Teaching & Learning, 7,* 1–16. Retrieved January 2, 2014, from EBSCO Online Database Education Research Complete.

Levitt, R., & Red Owl, R. R. (2013). Effects of early literacy environments on the reading attitudes, behaviours and values of veteran teachers. *Learning Environments Research, 16,* 387–409. Retrieved January 2, 2014, from EBSCO Online Database Education Research Complete.

Manning, M. & Manning, G. (1996). Art in reading and writing. *Teaching PreK-8, 26,* 90. Retrieved January 30, 2007, from EBSCO Online Database Education Research Complete.

Moats, L. C. (1999). *Teaching reading is rocket science: What expert teachers of reading should know and be able to do.* Retrieved December 4, 2006, from American Federation of Teachers, http://aft.org.

Nelson-Walker, N. J., Fien, H., Kosty, D. B., Smolkowski, K., Smith, J. M., & Baker, S. K. (2013). Evaluating the effects of a systemic intervention on first-grade teachers' explicit reading instruction. *Learning Disability Quarterly, 36,* 215–230. Retrieved January 2, 2014, from EBSCO Online Database Education Research Complete.

Railsback, J. (2004). *Writing to learn, learning to write: Revisiting writing across the curriculum in Northwest secondary schools.* Retrieved December 3, 2006, from Northwest Regional Educational Library, http://nwrel.org.

Scherer, M. (2006). The NCLB issue. *Educational Leadership, 64,* 7. Retrieved December 5, 2006, from EBSCO Online Database Education Research Complete.

Shuman, R. B. (2006). A school-wide attack on reading problems. *Clearing House, 79,* 219-222. Retrieved December 4, 2006, from EBSCO Online Database Academic Search Premier.

UNICEF. (1999). *Tips For Teaching Writing.* Retrieved December 3, 2006, from http://unicef.org.

Wanket, M. O. (2005). Building the habit of writing. *Educational Leadership, 63,* 74-76. Retrieved December 5, 2006, from EBSCO Online Database Education Research Complete.

Yancey, K. B. (2004). Using multiple technologies to teach writing. *Educational Leadership, 62,* 38-40. Retrieved December 4, 2006, from EBSCO Online Database Education Research Complete.

SUGGESTED READING

Adams, M. J. (1990). *Beginning to read: Thinking & learning about print.* Cambridge, MA: MIT Press.

Allington, R. & Cunningham, P. (2007). *Schools that Work: Where all Children Read and Write* (3rd Ed.). New York, N.Y.: Pearson Publishing.

Bunn, M. (2013). Motivation and connection: Teaching reading (and writing) in the composition classroom. *College Composition and Communication.* 64(3), 496-516.

Darder, A. (2013). Rewriting the world: Literacy, inequality, and the brain. *New England Reading Association Journal, 49,* 22–32. Retrieved January 2, 2014, from EBSCO Online Database Education Research Complete.

McLeod, S. H., Soven, M. I. (Eds.). (2006). *Composing a community: A history of writing across the curriculum.* West Lafayette, IN: Parlor Press.

Miller, B., McCardle, P., & Long, R. (Eds.) (2014). *Teaching Reading & Writing: Improving Instruction and Student Achievement.* Baltimore, MD.: Paul H. Brookes Publishing Company.

Ntiri, D. W. (2013). How minority becomes majority: Exploring discursive and racialized shifts in the adult literacy conversation. *Western Journal Of Black Studies,* 37, 159–168. Retrieved January 2, 2014, from EBSCO Online Database Education Research Complete.

Osborn, J. & Lehr, F. (Eds.). (1998). *Literacy for all: Issues in teaching and learning.* New York: Guilford Press.

Popham, J. W. (2006). Assessment for learning: An endangered species?. *Educational Leadership, 63,* 82-83. Retrieved December 5, 2006, from EBSCO Online Database Education Research Complete.

Reis, S. M., & Fogarty, E. A. (2006). Savoring reading schoolwide. *Educational Leadership, 64,* 32-36. Retrieved December 5, 2006, from EBSCO Online Database Education Research Complete.

Russell, D. R. (2002). *Writing in the academic disciplines: A curricular history* (2nd ed.). Southern Illinois University Press.

VanderMeulen, K. (1974). Reading in the secondary school: The study formulas revisited. *Reading Horizons, 15,* 31-36.

Washburn-Moses, L. (2006). 25 best internet resources for teaching reading. *Reading Teacher, 60,* 70-75. Retrieved December 5, 2006, from EBSCO Online Database Education Research Complete.

TEACHING ENGLISH AND LITERATURE

Teaching English and Literature falls under the umbrella of English language arts education. While there are a variety of methods for teaching English language arts in grades K-12 and the curricula can vary from state to state and even school to school, there are some commonly used methods for teaching English and Literature, and there are several established literacy standards that students must attain.

Responsive teaching and constructivist approaches are two of the more frequently used methods. In addition to the standards recommended by the National Council of Teachers of English (NCTE) and the International Reading Association (IRA), schools must also have met the requirements set forth by the No Child Left Behind Act (NCLB).

KEYWORDS: Constructivist Learning; Cooperative Learning; Cultural Diversity; English Language Arts; International Reading Association (IRA); Literacy; Literature; Multicultural Literature; National Council of Teachers of English (NCTE); Reading Comprehension; Responsive Teaching

OVERVIEW

Teaching English and Literature is taught under the umbrella of English language arts education. This area of education encompasses teaching basic reading comprehension and writing skills in primary schools, developing those skills further in the middle and high school years by teaching literature and writing, and ensuring that students achieve certain literacy standards by the time they graduate from high school.

STANDARDS FOR THE ENGLISH LANGUAGE ARTS

Since educational policy falls under the jurisdiction of the states, the methods for teaching English language arts vary; however, the National Council of Teachers of English (NCTE) in conjunction with the International Reading Association (IRA) established Standards for the English Language Arts in 1996. These national associations are comprised of educators devoted to teaching English language arts at all levels of education, and many states use these standards as benchmarks when developing curricula for teaching English and Literature.

The purpose of the twelve standards is to encourage schools to develop curriculum and teaching methods that require students to read a variety of literature that ultimately meets the demands of society and the workplace. By using different strategies to develop writing skills, students are also taught to communicate with a variety of people. In short, the goal of the standards and the essence of English language arts education is to enable students to achieve high levels of literacy so that they can "pursue life's goals and participate fully as informed, productive members of society" (National Council of Teachers of English, 1996).

THE NO CHILD LEFT BEHIND ACT OF 2001

In addition to the standards set forth by the NCTE and the IRA, schools were expected to adhere to the literacy requirements of the No Child Left Behind Act of 2001 (NCLB). This was a federal law enacted by the US Congress that required all children to attain proficiency in English language arts and mathematics. In order to measure students' progress, states must employ educational testing and there can be serious consequences for schools that failed to adhere to the performance requirements mandated by NCLB. The proficiency requirements were to be fully implemented by the year 2014. Moreover, there had been some debate as to the pros and cons of NCLB and the effect it has had on the classroom experience for students and teachers alike. One concern is that even though the Act applied to all students and all levels in K–12 education, NCLB posed the greatest challenge to English language learners, that is, learners who are beginning to learn English as a new language or have already gained some proficiency in English. State tests reveal that the academic performance for English language learners is not at the same level of students who speak English and that the language demands of tests required by NCLB have a negative impact on the test results of students who are learning English. At the same time, the overall performance of English language learners can be improved by focusing on developing their reading comprehension skills (Abedi, 2004).

COMMON CORE STATE STANDARDS

In 2009, the National Governor's Association (NGA) brought a group of educators together from across the country to work on developing a set of curriculum standards for grades K–12 in the areas of mathematics and literacy (language arts). The Common Core State Standards (CCSS) were released in 2010 and are supported by the federal government and are copyrighted by the Council of Chief State School Officers (CCSSO) in addition to the NGA. States are not mandated to comply with the standards, but were offered education grants by the federal government as an incentive to adopt them.

The goal of the standards is to "level the playing field" of learning and to prepare students for college and/or a career, As of 2013, they have been adopted by forty-five states, the District of Columbia, and four US territories (Houghton, 2013), and each state is responsible for creating and executing specific curricula based on the standards (National Council for History Education, 2013).

The standards for English language arts and literacy have specific criteria for each grade that pertains to anchor standards for college and career readiness. Each criterion is keyed to one of the following categories:

- "Key Ideas and Details;
- "Craft and Structure;
- "Integration of Knowledge and Ideas;
- "Range of Reading and Level of Text Complexity.

Critics of the Common Core Standards cite the difficulty in "standardizing" curriculum for every student, especially those whose native language is not English and for learning disabled students. Others voice their concern that since the CCSS do not take socio-economic factors, language barriers, and learning disabilities into consideration, that many students are being set up for failure (Houghton). Many doubt the value of the K–3 standards since they were not developed using early childhood research nor were they written by anyone with experience in early childhood education (Miller & Carlsson-Paige, 2013).

COOPERATIVE LEARNING

There are other approaches for teaching English language arts beyond aspiring literacy standards and adhering to the mandates of NCLB, NGA, or the US Department of Education. One broad view is that educating students in the primary, middle, and high school years is a continuum, and teachers and students should be afforded cooperative learning opportunities. Cooperative learning is a teaching strategy by which students of different levels of ability are placed into small teams and a variety of learning activities are used to improve their understanding of a subject. The goal of cooperative learning is to create an atmosphere of achievement where teams work through an assignment until all group members successfully understand the lesson. In order for cooperative learning methods to be successful, Coke (2005) suggests that teachers should serve as role models and that schools should encourage teachers across the different grade levels to meet in order to exchange information, share experiences, and perform joint work. In so doing, gaps and redundancies in programs can be reduced, the developmental needs of students will be better met as they make the transition from primary school to high school, and the autonomy and professionalism of teachers will be enhanced (Coke).

THE FUTURE OF ENGLISH LANGUAGE ARTS

As we move further into the twenty-first century and toward a society that is more technologically sophisticated, there continues to be much debate regarding the direction that teaching English language arts should take. However, there is a consensus that speaking and listening skills are fundamental life skills that will continue to be a subject of study. Moreover, written and oral stories are keys to learning English and "it is also vital that the power of story-telling and narrative is retained at the core of the curriculum" (White, 2005). Finally, White notes that the curriculum should continue to include our literary heritage since that will provide students with an understanding of who we are and where we came from. At the same time, there is a corollary need to ensure that the literature that is chosen satisfies the requirements of an increasingly culturally diverse society. While our society is becoming more diverse, English is becoming a global language and students will need to be capable of precision and clarity in spoken communication (White).

Ultimately, White believes that teaching English language arts requires continued creativity and imagination on the part of educators. One way to accomplish this is to employ new technologies that provide students with opportunities for creative engagement with spoken language. Schools will need to reconsider the curriculum and determine which literary texts should remain while deciding those that should be replaced by more current and culturally diverse work. In the end, teaching English and literature rests on some basic principles such as competence, creativity, critical skills, and cultural understanding. White sums it up by stating "to be creative it is also necessary to be competent; critical understanding about how language can transform or subvert meaning is necessary to an appreciation of culture; cultural understanding depends on an appreciation of the best achievements of our language and literature, and an understanding of what we write and say is part of the changing culture of a living society" (White).

Applications

RESPONSIVE TEACHING

By the time students begin their primary school education, the NCTE believes that a child's literacy growth has already begun and that the goal of English language arts education at this level is to make "productive use of the emerging literary abilities that children bring to school" (NCTE). One method for achieving this is responsive teaching. While the term has a number of meanings, responsive teaching includes the way in which educators honor cultures, respond to family needs, and assist with children's language development. This method embraces ethnicity and culture, learning and development, as well as the use of language to assist students in becoming effective, independent learners (Wold, 2005).

In practice, responsive teaching creates an environment in which students are curious and respectful of each other's thoughts and ideas and lends itself to creating a culture that values thinking and learning. This ultimately leads to responsive behaviors and a nurturing learning environment where students are allowed to develop as readers, writers, and thinkers. Responsive teaching at this level can also assist students with meeting literacy standards. This teaching method promotes opportunities for students to engage in cooperative learning by employing strategic scaffolding techniques. Essentially, this means putting students into small groups where they can talk with each other about stories, texts, and pictures. Responsive teaching "involves carefully listening to children supporting their learning talk and mediating their ideas and questions in consistent daily language learning contexts" (Wold).

Responsive learning can also serve as a foundation as children enter middle school where more emphasis needs to be placed on discussion in the English language arts classroom. The purpose of discussion is to create a classroom dialogue about a particular text. While discussion is the most common activity at the high school level, Adler (2003/2004) argues that there is insufficient time spent on encouraging classroom dialogue in middle schools and that allowing whole class discussion can enhance a students' acquisition of reading and analysis skills. One reason that students do not actively engage in dialogue is that they lack experience with reading literary texts and have not developed an ability to "use the language of literary interpretation independently in the classroom" (Adler).

According to Adler, one way to overcome this hurdle is for schools to rely on instructional facilitators who can assist middle and high school teachers with encouraging students to engage in dialogue. Such facilitators are usually university-level teachers who form partnerships with local schools with the goal of assisting teachers in reorganizing classrooms and encouraging more student questions and dialogue. This process is also known as dialogic facilitation and in many ways is a form of cooperative learning since it is "a joint activity, working toward a shared goal in a particular setting over time" (Adler). Moreover, this process can be beneficial to both teachers and students. As teachers become better equipped at encouraging dialogue in the classroom, they also can take a more active role in running classes and making decisions about the curriculum. The benefit for students is that valuing their contributions in the classroom helps them to "achieve understandings beyond the life of the discussion" (Adler).

CONSTRUCTIVISM

As they find their voices and have a platform on which to express these ideas in both written and verbal ways, students can eventually take responsibility for their own learning of literary texts, and this leads to another approach in English language arts known as constructivist learning. Most students respond well to constructivist learning and enjoy the environment of a student-centered classroom, especially at the high-school level. When teachers connect the real world outside the classroom with the world inside the classroom (the literary text) students are given ideal

opportunities to consider literature in relation to their own lives (Boscolo, 2003). In addition, "reading literary texts provides the topics for students to write compositions, thus demonstrating what they have learned, whereas writing on literature is viewed by many teachers as a stylistic exercise necessary for students to learn to elaborate their ideas critically and express them appropriately" (Boscolo). Thus both parts of the literary lesson are merged: students ruminate on the literary text under consideration, then process these thoughts and put them into words, expressing their critical thinking about the literature (Boscolo).

CLASSIC TEXTS

While reading and writing about literary texts can enable students to develop and express critical ideas, the question remains as to which literary texts should be included in the curriculum. Currently, many teachers continue to assign the classics: novels by authors such as Jane Austen, Charles Dickens, and Mark Twain that are considered timeless and have been traditionally used in. However, many students are not interested in these texts and this is due, in part, to the fact that students entering high school do not have strong literary backgrounds and have not been exposed to a variety of reading materials. Santoli contends that getting students to read is a common problem that can be resolved if teachers use young adult literature that can serve to encourage students to participate in satisfying literary experiences as well as to better prepare them to appreciate and understand classic literature. However, many teachers do not consider young adult novels worthy of attention, and teacher guides do not allow for the use of these novels (Santoli, 2004).

YOUNG ADULT LITERATURE

At the same time, some studies have shown most teenagers are not ready for classic literature, which tends not to address typical adolescent concerns. Young adult (YA) literature deals with such eternal questions as "Who Am I?" and "Where Do I Fit In?" Moreover, YA literature deals with contemporary issues that students are facing such as social and political concerns about racial and ethnic discrimination, AIDS, teen pregnancy, divorce, or problems resulting from family conflicts. While young adult literature may not have the status in English language arts that the classics do, the former does include "a variety of situational archetypes such as the test/trial as a rite of passage, the journey or quest of the hero, birth/rebirth and the search for self" (Santoli). In the end, the purpose of studying literature is to engage students in reading, discussing, and analyzing texts that are provided in the classroom, and this can be achieved if the curriculum is balanced between the classics and good contemporary young adult literature (Santoli).

Ultimately, while there are many methods for teaching English language arts that vary from state to state and even school to school, the goal of teaching English and literature is to enable students to think critically and to communicate effectively.

Viewpoints

MULTICULTURAL LITERATURE

Today, English teachers of all levels have recently broadened the curricula to include literature that is inclusive rather than exclusive. By doing so, teachers have expanded their attitudes and the manner in which they, along with their students, investigate racial and cultural issues. In so doing students are provided with greater opportunities to consider these significant issues in the classroom. "There is an urgent need for English teachers to increase their sensitivity to cultural differences and develop teaching skills to conduct classroom discussions that promote cross-cultural understanding and culturally varied ways of living and knowing" (Dong, 2005). Responding to multicultural literature may be an intimidating experience for students whose prior literary experience has been limited to the traditional canon; thus, teachers assist students in forming a new set of cultural responses when reading literature written by or about minorities.

According to Dong, teachers who expose students to multicultural literature allow for a much-needed role reversal. Often, multicultural students, whose diverse native languages and cultures marginalize them to the periphery of classrooms, become insiders when discussing multicultural literature. That is, these students may actually know, or at least recognize, more about the literature than the teacher. This role reversal can be extraordinary for all the students, in that sharing experiences becomes more than an abstract idea. When this occurs, students and

teachers benefit from studying multicultural literature. Teaching multicultural literature is extremely important, especially in elementary and middle schools when students are forming opinions of education itself. If teachers can encourage minority students to express themselves and share their experiences when they are young, these students will find and utilize their voices. Thus, their relationship to English class in general and literature specifically will be solidified over the years, assuming each subsequent English teacher allows them to voice their experiences and respond freely to multicultural literature (Dong).

LITERATURE & TECHNOLOGY

In addition to moving toward cultural diversity in English language arts, educators now promote that the curriculum should also prepare students and teachers for a more technologically sophisticated world. As society has become more technologically sophisticated through the evolution of the Internet and the digitalization of texts, the effect on students' reading and writing abilities and the way in which they engage with literature has also evolved. As McNabb suggests, digital texts force readers to make choices and there needs to be an understanding of how hyperlink affects a reader's purpose and comprehension. This poses a number of critical questions:

- "If hypertext brings forth each student's individual reading path and processes, then what are the characteristics of appropriate methods of measurement?
- "Do traditional reading and writing strategies applicable to print-based materials transfer to digital text?
- "As information networks provide students with access to vast amounts of uncensored text, what are the best methods for fostering students' ability to critically evaluate digital information?
- "What is the fundamental nature of reading processes associated with hypertext?
- "How do these compare with processes readers use when reading print?
- "What comprehension abilities are prerequisite to derive meaning from hypertext?" (McNabb).

These questions are critical because the advances of the Internet brought about by wireless remote access and portable computers is shifting access rates to information and literary content and this will affect the way in which students learn. Teachers will need to be provided with professional development opportunities to adequately integrate technology into their approaches to teaching (McNabb).

CONCLUSION

While some of the models for teaching like cooperative learning, constructivist learning and responsive learning apply to many subjects, these are effective models for teaching English and Literature. At the same time, English language arts education needs to remain connected to contemporary society and students need to see how studying literature relates to the world in which they live. In the final analysis, in order for students to be well equipped to compete in a more technologically sophisticated society, they must be able to communicate effectively and this can be accomplished, in part, if they achieve the literacy standards set forth by the Common Core. At the same time it remains unknown as to how technological advances will affect those standards and what constitutes literacy in a technologically oriented society.

TERMS & CONCEPTS

Constructivist Learning: A philosophy of learning that emphasizes reflection on experiences. Learners construct their own understanding of the world.

Cooperative Learning: A teaching strategy where students of different levels of ability are placed into small teams and a variety of learning activities are used to improve their understanding of a subject.

Cultural Diversity: "Differences in race, ethnicity, language, nationality, or religion among various groups within a community, organization, or nation" (smhp.psych.ucla.edu).

English Language Arts: The teaching of English and literature including composition, reading and creative writing, with literacy achievement as the goal.

International Reading Association (IRA): National association of educators dedicated to teaching reading comprehension. Established Literacy Standards in conjunction with the NCTE in 1996.

Literacy: The ability to read and write and use language, writing and listening to achieve an adequate level of communication.

Multicultural Literature: Literature that is inclusive rather than exclusive and is drawn from a broad array of racial and ethnic backgrounds.

National Council of Teachers of English (NCTE): National association of educators dedicated to the teaching of English. Established Standards of Literacy for English Language Arts in conjunction with the IRA in 1996.

Reading Comprehension: The level of understanding of a passage or text.

Responsive Teaching: A teaching method that embraces ethnicity and culture, learning and development, as well as the use of language to assist students in becoming effective, independent learners.

Karen A. Kallio

BIBLIOGRAPHY

Abedi, J. & Dietel, R. (2004). Challenges in the No Child Left Behind Act for English-language learners. *Phi Betta Kappan, 85*, 782-785. Retrieved April 24, 2007, from EBSCO Online Database Academic Search Premier.

Adler, M., Rougle, E., Kaiser, E. & Caughlan, S. (2003). Closing the gap between concept and practice: Toward more dialogic discussion in the language arts classroom. *Journal of Adolescent & Adult Literacy, 47*, 312-322. Retrieved April 24, 2007, from EBSCO Online Database Academic Search Premier.

Boscolo, P. & Carotti, L. (2003). Does writing contribute to improving high school students' approach to literature? *Educational Studies in Language and Literature, 3*, 197-224. Retrieved March 17, 2007, from EBSCO Online Database Education Resource Complete.

Chase, L., Gonzaga, K., Manwaring, B., Pyne, C., Rawlins, K., & Waddell, S. (2012). Multimodal responses to literature in years 5–8: The other worlds project. *Literacy Learning: The Middle Years, 20*, 52–64. Retrieved December 20, 2013, from EBSCO Online Database Education Research Complete.

Coke, P. K. (2005). Practicing what we preach: An argument for cooperative learning opportunities for elementary and secondary educators. *Education, 126*, 392-398. Retrieved April 23, 2007, from EBSCO Online Database Academic Search Premier.

Dong, Y. R. (2005). Bridging the cultural gap by teaching multicultural literature. *The Educational Forum, 69*, 367-382. Retrieved March 7, 2007, from EBSCO Online Database Education Research Complete.

Hobbs, R. (2004). Analyzing advertising in the English language arts classroom: A quasi-experimental study. *Simile, 4*. Retrieved April 24, 2007, from EBSCO Online Database Academic Search Premier.

Houghton, Kristen. (2013, December 19). Common core aka NCLB: Why neither can work. Retrieved December 21, 2013, from http://huffingtonpost.com.

Ivey, G., & Johnston, P. H. (2013). Engagement with young adult literature: Outcomes and processes. *Reading Research Quarterly, 48*, 255–275. Retrieved December 20, 2013, from EBSCO Online Database Education Research Complete.

McNabb, M. L. (2005). Raising the bar on technology research in English language arts. *Journal of Research on Technology in Education, 38*, 113-119. Retrieved April 24, 2007, from EBSCO Online Database Academic Search Premier.

Miller, Edward, & Carlsson-Paige, Nancy. (2013, January 29). A tough critique of Common Core on early childhood education. Retrieved December 21, 2013, from http://washingtonpost.com.

National Council for History Education. (2013). FAQs: Common Core State Standards and history education. Retrieved December 21, 2013, from http://nche.net.

National Council of Teachers of English (NCTE). (1996). *Standards for the English language arts.* Newark, DE: International Reading Association; Urbana, IL: National Council of Teachers of English. Retrieved April 24, 2007, from http://ncte.org.

Santoli, S. P., & Wagner, M. E. (2004). Promoting young adult literature: The other "real" literature. *American Secondary Education, 33*, 65-75. Retrieved April 24, 2007, from EBSCO Online Database Academic Search Premier.

White, J. (2005, December). Teaching English tomorrow. *Literacy Today*, 12-13. Retrieved April 23, 2007, from EBSCO Online Database Academic Search Premier.

Wold, L. (2005). Teaching first grade literacy responsively with language arts standards in mind. *Illinois Reading Council Journal, 33*, 22-31. Retrieved April 24, 2007, from EBSCO Online Database Academic Search Premier.

Yingli, W. (2013). A Literature review on content ESL instruction. *Journal of Language Teaching & Research, 4*, 642–647. Retrieved December 20, 2013, from EBSCO Online Database Education Research Complete.

SUGGESTED READING

Benko, S. L. (2012). Scaffolding: An ongoing process to support adolescent writing development. *Journal of Adolescent & Adult Literacy, 56*, 291–300. Retrieved December 20, 2013, from EBSCO Online Database Education Research Complete.

Martin, S. (2012). Does instructional format really matter? Cognitive load theory, multimedia, and teaching English Literature. *Educational Research and Evaluation.* 18(2), 125-152.

McConachie, S., Hall, M., Resnick, L., Ravi, A., Bill, V., Bintz, J. & Taylor, J. A. (2006). Task, text, and talk. *Educational Leadership, 64*, 8-14. Retrieved April 23, 2007, from EBSCO Online Database Academic Search Premier.

Scheibe, C. L. (2004). A deeper sense of literacy: Curriculum-driven approaches to media literacy in the K-12 classroom. *American Behavioral Scientist, 48*, 60-68. Retrieved April 24, 2007, from EBSCO Online Database Academic Search Premier.

Shi, Z. (2013). Home literacy environment and English language learners' literacy development: What can we learn from the literature?. *Canadian Children, 38*, 29–38. Retrieved December 20, 2013, from EBSCO Online Database Education Research Complete.

Whitcomb, J. A. (2004). Dilemmas of design and predicaments of practice: Adapting the 'fostering a community of learners' model in secondary school English language arts. *Journal of Curriculum Studies, 36*, 183-206. Retrieved April 24, 2007, from EBSCO Online Database Academic Search Premier.

TEACHING POETRY

This article examines various studies and arguments that give reasons why many students, and also teachers, feel dislike toward the subject of poetry. Next, the concept of poetry interpretation is explored, and various experts give advice on how to get students to develop the best possible interpretations, including the possibility of using schools of criticism. The paper then establishes the connection between poetry interpretation and poetry writing. It also looks at the importance of creativity, and gives suggestions for cultivating this in students. Methods are then explored for getting students to not only write good poetry, but enjoy writing it.

KEYWORDS: Literary Criticism; National Education Association (NEA); New Criticism; New Historical Criticism; Poetry Interpretation

OVERVIEW
TEACHER & STUDENT ATTITUDES TOWARD POETRY
Considering its prominent if not central position in cultures and civilizations of the past several thousand years, poetry's place in today's society seems peripheral and inessential. Perhaps the rise of science and technology in the last century has caused a decline in poetry's cultural importance, but whatever the reasons, most students today would most likely express

the opinion that poetry is old-fashioned and out-dated, and that poetry has very little importance in the modern world. Studies show that both teachers and students generally feel aversion toward the study of poetry. According to a survey conducted by Ray (1999), a majority of high school teachers expressed fear of teaching poetry, and reported feelings of inhibition over teaching poetry. She observes that "in some cases, [teachers] could not see the purpose of [poetry]."

Of course, if teachers feel this way, what should we expect students to feel toward the study of poetry? Ray's study also included a survey of high school students, and found that, "the teachers' feelings were reflected in pupil attitudes to poetry: 84 per cent of the pupils did not like poetry." Thus, from the outset, most students feel dislike toward the study of poetry, and that makes the teaching of poetry much more difficult. Young (2007) makes the important observation that "cultural attitudes are often dismissive of poetry," and cites a survey carried out by the National Education Association (NEA). The survey revealed that roughly only 12% of society ever chooses to read poetry. Young describes the bias that a majority of students feel:

> In classrooms across the United States—even at the college level—too many students mirror these cultural beliefs in their comments: "poetry is deep," "poetry is dark and mysterious," "I just don't 'get' poetry," and "all poets are depressed and wear black." These are just a few examples of the faulty logic that haunts my classroom every fall. Teaching poetry effectively, then, means not only bringing it to life but also getting past the stereotypes that imprison students' creativity.

REASONS FOR ADVERSE ATTITUDES

There are various additional factors that most likely have an adverse effect on teaching poetry. Peskin, Allen and Wells-Jopling (2010) point out that mistaken beliefs and perceptions about teaching poetry may partly create negative attitudes in teachers and students alike. According to Peskin et al., some teachers misperceive the idea that poetry has a quite subjective and personal nature. This perspective, if taken to an extreme, means students can only acquire an understanding of poetry through their own silent and unexpressed perceptions. In other words, some teachers believe that understanding poetry comes

naturally to some students and is simply not accessible to others. Many teachers complain that they were never given any instruction in how to teach poetry to students, and they should have had some training on this in their degree programs. They conclude that "lack of experience, lack of preparation, and lack of confidence quickly add up to lack of interest if not complete apathy [toward poetry]."

Ray's survey brings out a related point. According to responses to her survey, those who are supposed to teach students about poetry complained that in their own experience as students, "they were 'taught' poetry rather than shown how to enjoy or appreciate it." Thus, they were instructed in a way that dictated to them what they should think about a poem, rather than led to their own understandings of what a poem means. Such a method of instruction may be due to teachers concentrating too much on exam responses. As Ray puts it, "teachers are anxious that pupils should produce the model answer rather than expressing their own opinions, which might not coincide with the accepted version." She notes that allowing students to reach their own interpretations does present its own problems with assessment, and expresses concern that allowing completely subjective interpretations of poetry "could bring about such difficulties in assessment and marking that poetry might disappear from the English curriculum altogether."

Wrigg (1991) notes that, perhaps because teachers have never had any training in effective methods for teaching poetry, and possibly out of "sheer desperation," some teachers force students to memorize and recite poems in the classroom. When the method of forcing memorization fails, "there is always the dubious practice of rebuking students for indifference toward a subject that in some mystical way is supposedly good for their souls. If negative attitudes are not already existent, they certainly will be before these questionable practices have run their course."

APPRECIATION VS. ENJOYMENT

According to Ray's survey results, many teachers experienced positive or at least neutral "recollections about poetry during their own primary school years but largely negative attitudes towards poetry at secondary level." Although she does not make a direct connection between the teaching differences that may have existed during primary and secondary school, it seems likely that grade school teachers are more inclined to read poetry with students for simple enjoyment, whereas high school teachers are probably more inclined to study poetry in a more intellectually rigorous way. Ray makes a distinction between the ideas of "enjoyment" and "appreciation," citing Wittgenstein (1996) who defines enjoyment as "an immediate, emotional response to a work of art or literature while appreciation requires a degree of knowledge." Ray proposes that:

> ...positive steps would be to clear up the confusions between 'enjoyment' and 'appreciation' and make them explicit; to give pupils the language with which to discuss and evaluate poetry; to guide pupils through the articulation of their own responses, and to relate those responses to the body of knowledge inherent in the subject of literature.

Ray argues that "appreciation" is a more complex view of poetry, requiring a deeper understanding of its many aspects. Appreciation takes knowledge of literary nomenclature, such as meter, rhyme, antithesis, imagery, etc., and the ability to use these concepts in critical analysis. Thus, students must become adept in using the tools of literary criticism if they are to increase their appreciation of poetry. Also, a more complex understanding of poetry should include knowledge of historical circumstances and literary movements. Peskin et al. distinguish between "formalist" and "populist" perspectives on teaching poetry, but it seems these terms are essentially the same as Ray's distinction of "enjoyment" and "appreciation." As Peskin observes:

> the formalists emphasized stylistic devices, rhyme, meter, and literary allusion, possibly at the expense of personal engagement, whereas the populists viewed texts to be played with, at the expense of the development of critical literacy. The challenge for teachers is to somehow engender critical rigor and literacy while fostering engagement.

To teach poetry effectively in the classroom, teachers need to consider the various answers to the question, why do students and teachers generally feel aversion toward poetry? Wrigg argues that there is "nothing intrinsic in the nature of poetry to explain its repugnance to many students. On the contrary, the cadence and meter of poetry should contribute to its appreciation, and its rhythmic quality can

be the catalyst through which a response is struck among students." He concludes that "rarely does the heart of the problem lie in the subject matter itself but rather in the unimaginative and ineffective way that it's presented." This leads us to the most important question for the classroom: How should a poetry course be taught such that students enjoy the course while learning about the subject in a more complex way? Essentially, teachers should endeavor to deepen students' appreciation of a poem without damaging their enjoyment of that poem or, as Peskin would put it, teachers should foster engagement while engendering critical rigor and literacy.

INTERPRETATION OF POETRY

Poetry can be studied in the classroom in two fundamental directions, that of reading/interpreting poetry, and that of writing/creating poetry. Both of these directions should be taken in the classroom, though a teacher should probably emphasize one of the two directions depending on whether the poetry course is conceived as a survey of poetry or as a creative writing course intended help students write their own poetry.

Ediger (2003) argues that reading poetry should emphasize understanding the poem as a whole, and suggests that the first step in interpreting a poem is to simply read it aloud before beginning to analyze it. However, some background information should be given before the reading; "holism in poetry reading needs to stress providing background information to pupils prior to the read aloud." Ediger reasons that background information helps to make students ready for listening to the poem. But what should be considered relevant background information, and can too much background overshadow a poem? In recent decades, the use of historical context has been a growing trend, and Ulin (2007) observes that the recent editions of collegiate poetry anthologies have included a lot of historical documents and commentaries on historical periods and movements. However, historical considerations may create a disadvantage:

> Confronted with 20 to 30 or more sleepy students with little historical background and no theoretical sophistication, most of them intent only on satisfying some irksome humanities requirement, we may find ourselves envying the hermetic clarity of the New Critical classroom (Ulin).

NEW CRITICISM

New Criticism is essentially a method of interpreting poetry in which the teacher and students ignore the reader's response, the author's intention, and any historical as well as cultural contexts. New Criticism particularly emphasizes the use of literary devices in a text, and some professors consider this the most objective approach to literature. Though he does not use the term New Criticism, Peskin et al. seem to promote some of the basic principles that come from the New Criticism school. They explain that, "for readers to understand the nature and content of what they are reading, the readers' own knowledge of literary conventions works in conjunction with their own imagination, leading to a personal interpretation of the writer's work, an interpretation that may or may not be close to the writer's original thought." Perhaps this method (or an even purer form of New Criticism) should be used as a technique for interpreting a poem, but it seems that students should have an understanding of the historical context as well.

NEW HISTORICAL APPROACH

Ulin argues that the "New Historical approach of assigning historical documents alongside literary texts will do much to help our students recognize the historical specificity of the poetry, drama, or fiction they are reading, but now the task becomes one of helping our students to understand the distinctly literary qualities that characterize a poem's engagement with its historical moment." In other words, we should look at the poem's interaction with its place in history without letting the historical context overpower the meaning of the poem itself. If anthologies and teachers stress historical context too much, we run the risk of forgetting what is being studied. By overemphasis, teachers may create "an unbridged gap between the battles in the war and the psychic life of the poet creating the poem."

REVISIONS

Ulin suggests various methods for avoiding this, one of which is to examine a well-known poem's phases of revision. Among other advantages, Ulin argues that looking at revisions dispels "the myth of the perfect poem." Although some students may experience "a sense of loss" by pulling a poem down from its pedestal, that loss is often "redeemed by the student's own sense of cultural authority as he or she becomes a kind

of arbiter among several possible poems." To summarize, as teachers interpret poetry with students, they should probably use a variety of techniques to show the multifaceted reality that a poem represents.

WRITING POETRY

Interpreting poetry and writing poetry have a common link, which is why Connor-Greene, Murdoch, Young and Paul (2005) have pointed out that "understanding and appreciating a creative work is itself a creative act." Poetry frequently uses surprising or unusual language, and the topic of a poem is also treated in unusual ways, such that readers must take creative steps to understand a poem (Connor-Greene et al.). In short, creativity, which is at the heart of writing good poetry, is also at the heart of effectively interpreting poetry. Even though "virtually everyone of normal intelligence" can be creative, very few actually reach their true creative potential. They argue that there are three intellectual skills that comprise the act of creativity, and they conclude that poetry requires all these elements:

> (a) synthetic ability, seeing problems in new ways and demonstrating unconventional thinking; (b) analytic ability, deciding which ideas are worth pursuing; and (c) practical contextual ability, knowing how to effectively communicate ideas to others ... writing poetry makes use of all three of these intellectual skills, in both the writer composing the poem, and in the audience appreciating the writer's synthesis, analysis, and communication.

Sargent (2006) suggests that the fundamental method to give students more confidence in writing poetry is "to let them realize that they have been writing and thinking creatively on a daily basis." He argues that students should be shown that they already have the skills needed, and they are only applying those skills to a new task. However, accomplishing this as a teacher "takes a little planning, and more than a little flexibility." Students who are challenged to create their own poetry perceive themselves "as active writers and thinkers, fostering future creative experimentation." Also, when teachers stress creativity in assignments, and evaluate students such that creativity is prized, students improve in their academic performance (Connor-Greene et al.).

Welch (1991), an experienced poetry teacher, believes that many students have an adverse reaction to being assigned to write their own poems because "in the past new and scary terms have been attached to poetry, words like antithesis, onomatopoeia, and hyperbole." She advises teachers of poetry to demonstrate that these concepts are often already in use by students, since coming to literary terms in this way is much less frightening. The author points out that "it is far, far less threatening to hear: 'You just created a delightful bit of antithesis,' than to be faced with, 'this is antithesis, now go create your own'." If students see that they already have a sense for metaphor, alliteration, etc., then they quickly come to enjoy writing poetry.

Sargent uses techniques that show the relationship between poetry and other arts. For example, he uses as a creative writing assignment that students watch a powerful film scene that has "transference potential," then try to create poetry. He observes that, "film can provide the scaffolding upon which students can begin to form an understanding of the writing process—which, after all, is a microcosm of the creative process itself." Students already like film and are well acquainted with the medium. He also suggests using music to experiment with writing poetry, while using visual art or paintings would probably work quite effectively as well.

However, with any of these types of assignments, teachers need to consider at length how to assess student assignments, or whether to assess them at all for a course grade. As some experts have pointed out, "it is easier to inhibit creativity than to facilitate it, and trying to 'get it right' can reduce one's willingness to experiment. Fear of failure or criticism interferes with creativity, whereas encouraging creative efforts leads to greater confidence" (Connor-Greene et al.). They also point out that, while "an extensive body of psychological research addresses critical thinking ... relatively little published work has focused on ways to enhance creative thinking.

CREATIVITY IN EDUCATION

It seems that creativity, though it is extremely important as a life skill, and essential to excelling in many careers, is often ignored in education. Sargent makes some important observations about the applicability of creativity:

Over and over, as I read the works of contemporary management theorists, I'm reminded of the experience

of poetry—its varied levels of complexity, its insistence on multiple readings ... a poem demands critical—and creative—thinking of any who would enter its world.

Creativity is difficult to assess because of its subjective nature, but it should still be included in poetry courses since the heart of poetry is creativity. Some researchers have argued that creativity is a quite difficult concept to teach because "the criteria used to measure creativity sometimes seem to trivialize it" (Connor-Greene et al.). If teachers assign students to create their own poems, then students will discover the ways form, content, and expression interact. Students will learn how to tap into their own creative power. As Connor-Greene et al. point out, "creative thinking involves breaking typical patterns of thinking to perceive in a fresh way, to try something different, and to take an intellectual risk." Creativity often gets neglected in classroom assignments, but poetry is the perfect subject for teaching students to be more creative.

Ultimately, a poetry course should make students enjoy reading and writing poetry. Former American Poet Laureate Robert Pinsky certainly supported that position, and teachers should consider his comment about what's wrong with many poetry courses:

Too much of our teaching of poetry has proceeded as though the reason for a poem to exist is to have smart things said about it. Well, I like smart things, I approve of smart things, but a poem is not an occasion for saying smart things. A poem is something that sounds terrific when it is read aloud. That's the nature of the art. I think that school, alas, has inculcated the idea that a poem is something that makes you nervous, because it's a test to see if you're clever (cited in Kelly, 1999).

TERMS & CONCEPTS

Literary Criticism: The formal study, evaluation, and interpretation of literature. Literary criticism is often grounded in various literary theories, such as New Criticism or New Historical Criticism.

National Education Association (NEA): A labor union and association that represents public school teachers as well as faculty and staff at colleges and universities. Among its many activities, the NEA carries out studies focused on education, and also advises teachers on best practices in education.

New Criticism: A method for evaluating and interpreting literature. This literary technique became popular from the 1950's onward, and it emphasizes making a close examination of a poem with minimum consideration of the biographical or historical circumstances in which it was produced.

New Historical Criticism: A method for evaluating and interpreting literature. This literary technique became popular in the 1980's, and aims to interpret a poem or other literary work by examining the historical context in which the work was written. Also, New Historical Criticism examines cultural and intellectual history through literature, so that literature becomes a history of ideas.

Poetry Interpretation: The act of using literary concepts and literary theory or criticism to analyze a poem so as to explain what a poem means, and how it means what it means.

Sinclair Nicholas

BIBLIOGRAPHY

Christopher, C. (2013). Poetry: Share it and shout it!. *Practically Primary, 18,* 4-6. Retrieved December 15, 2013, from EBSCO Online Database Education Research Complete.

Connor-Greene, P., Murdoch, J., Young, A., & Paul, C. (2005). Poetry: It's not just for English class anymore. *Teaching of Psychology, 32,* 215-221. Retrieved July 24, 2010, from the EBSCO online database Academic Search Complete.

Ediger, M. (2003). Exploring poetry: The reading and writing connection. *Journal of Instructional Psychology, 30,* 165-168. Retrieved July 22, 2010, from the EBSCO online database Education Research Complete.

Kelly, S. (1999). An interview with ... Robert Pinsky. *Writer, 112,* 18-20. Retrieved July 24, 2010, from the EBSCO online database Academic Search Complete.

Lambirth, A., Smith, S., & Steele, S. (2012). 'Poetry is happening but I don't exactly know how': Literacy Subject Leaders' perceptions of poetry in their primary schools. *Literacy, 46,* 73-80. Retrieved December 15, 2013, from EBSCO Online Database Education Research Complete.

Lockney, K., & Proudfoot, K. (2013). Writing the unseen poem: Can the writing of poetry help to support pupils' engagement in the reading of poetry?. *English in Education, 47,* 147-162. Retrieved December 15, 2013, from EBSCO Online Database Education Research Complete.

Peskin, J., Allen, G., & Wells-Jopling, R. (2010). "The educated imagination": Applying instructional research to the teaching of symbolic interpretation of poetry. *Journal of Adolescent & Adult Literacy, 53,* 498-507. Retrieved July 24, 2010, from the EBSCO online database Academic Search Complete.

Ray, R. (1999). The diversity of poetry: How trainee teachers' perceptions affect their attitudes to poetry teaching. *Curriculum Journal, 10,* 403-419. Retrieved July 22, 2010, from the EBSCO online database Academic Search Complete.

Sargent, D. (2006). Not how you are used to thinking: Reaching for poetry through film. *Interdisciplinary Humanities, 23,* 67-72. Retrieved July 22, 2010, from the EBSCO online database Academic Search Complete.

Ulin, D. (2007). Texts, revisions, history: Reading historically in the undergraduate survey. *College Literature, 34,* 70-91. Retrieved July 24, 2010, from the EBSCO online database Academic Search Complete.

Weaven, M., & Clark, T. (2013). 'I guess it scares us'—Teachers discuss the teaching of poetry in senior secondary English. *English in Education, 47,* 197-212. Retrieved December 15, 2013, from EBSCO Online Database Education Research Complete.

Welch, L. (1991). Back-door teaching of poetry. *College Teaching, 39,* 149. Retrieved July 24, 2010, from the EBSCO online database Academic Search Complete.

Wrigg, W. (1991). A strategy for teaching poetry. *Clearing House, 64,* 251-252. Retrieved July 22, 2010, from the EBSCO online database Academic Search Complete.

Young, L. (2007). Portals into poetry: Using generative writing groups to facilitate student engagement with word art. *Journal of Adolescent & Adult Literacy, 51,* 50-55. Retrieved July 24, 2010, from the EBSCO online database Academic Search Complete.

SUGGESTED READING

Benton, P. (2000). The conveyor belt curriculum? Poetry teaching in the secondary school II. *Oxford Review of Education, 26,* 81-94. Retrieved July 22, 2010, from the EBSCO online database Academic Search Complete.

Feder, L. (2000). Using poetry in adult literacy classes. *Journal of Adolescent & Adult Literacy, 43,* 746-747. Retrieved July 22, 2010, from the EBSCO online database Academic Search Complete.

German, G. (2007). Beyond confessional: Jonathan Holden...honest poetry, honest discovery. *Midwest Quarterly, 48,* 497-501. Retrieved July 24, 2010, from the EBSCO online database Academic Search Complete.

Knapp, J. (2002). Teaching poetry via HEI (hypothesis-experiment-instruction). *Journal of Adolescent & Adult Literacy, 45,* 718-730. Retrieved July 24, 2010, from the EBSCO online database Academic Search Complete.

Low, B. (2011). *Slam School: Learning through Conflict in the Hip-Hop and Spoken Word Classroom.* Stanford, CA.: Stanford University Press.

Poets tell how to teach poetry without feeling insecure. (1994). *Curriculum Review, 34,* 9. Retrieved July 24, 2010, from the EBSCO online database Education Research Complete.

Saito, A. (2008). Between me and the world: Teaching poetry to English language learners. *Teaching Artist Journal, 6,* 197-208. Retrieved July 24, 2010, from the EBSCO online database Academic Search Complete.

Tanner, S.J. *(2015).* What the whiteness project should have been: Poetry as a collaborative vehicle for inquiry. *English Journal.* 104 *(4),* 65-70.

TEACHING CREATIVE WRITING

Creative writing is imaginative writing distinguished from technical or journalistic writing, and includes autobiography, fiction, poetry, screenwriting and drama. The skill plays a valuable lifelong role and provides therapeutic self-expression, offers an enjoyable artistic outlet, and can produce entertaining reading for others. Creative writing teachers help students engage their imaginations, develop ideas, and relate these ideas in written form according to accepted grammar and stylistic norms. Students learn how to establish the theme or subject of a composition, and develop characters, plots, and endings. Teachers can use writing prompts, modeling, journaling, freewriting and storytelling to develop creative writing projects.

KEYWORDS: Autobiography; Character Development; Creative Writing; Freewriting; Journaling; Modeling; Plot Development; Revising; Rough Draft; Writing Conference; Writing Prompts

OVERVIEW

Creative writing is imaginative writing distinguished from technical or journalistic writing, and includes autobiography, fiction, poetry, screenwriting and drama. The skill plays a valuable lifelong role and provides therapeutic self-expression, offers an enjoyable artistic outlet, and can produce entertaining reading for others. Educators believe that children can begin learning to write creatively as early as they learn to write.

Teaching creative writing addresses the ability to engage the imagination, develop ideas and relate them in written form according to accepted grammar and stylistic norms. These teaching areas include establishing the theme or subject of the composition, character development, plot development, and the ending. Techniques such as providing writing prompts, modeling, journaling, freewriting and storytelling can be effectively used in teaching how to develop a creative writing project.

Understanding the mechanics of writing (proper grammar, spelling, punctuation and sentence structure) is a necessary foundation for writing a good story. Language arts educators use a variety of teaching techniques to help stimulate students' creative thinking for the origination of story ideas.

APPLICATIONS

Creative writing is a difficult subject to teach because it requires the seemingly paradoxical task of encouraging the free flow of ideas while containing amorphous ideas within the framework and structure of written language. Preliminary guidelines regarding the topic or subject for students' writing assignments help to jumpstart the creative writing process. Adequate structure allows students to express themselves and enhances the process of expression by providing a starting point for the imaginative exercise.

CHARACTER & PLOT DEVELOPMENT

An important element in creative writing is learning how to develop characters. Character development is the combination of details, dialog, speech and actions of a character through which a storyteller informs the audience about the character's personality and motivation. Middle school and secondary language arts students can learn that characters move the story along through their dialog and point of view. They can be protagonists, antagonists, or minor characters. Through careful prompting, a teacher can ask questions that will direct a student to develop a character with depth, personality, and interest. Aspects of characters that writers should address include body language, gestures, the way they move, mannerisms and the way they speak to include unique dialects and methods of speech.

For the middle and secondary level, next comes teaching students to develop a plot. Plot development is organizing the story elements to create a casual sequence that draws the reader into the characters' lives and provides a story conflict. Teachers can help students with plot development by leading a discussion on the types of obstacles and difficult situations the story's character might face. Other points of instruction include the pace of the story and how fast or slow the story moves.

Language arts educators in all levels also address how to write compelling endings to students' stories-the part of the story that readers are most likely to remember. By asking questions, the teacher can direct student writers to create endings that are satisfying.

AUTOBIOGRAPHIES

Writing autobiographies is a powerful and effective tool in learning creative writing, as a student's life experiences are a familiar, passionate source of ideas. An autobiography is a personal history with information about one's life written by that person. In the elementary classroom, students would be asked to write autobiographical sketches about shorter spans of time, such as what they did last night, or over the weekend, or what exciting thing happened over their vacation. For the middle school and secondary student, reading and discussing autobiographies of others enriches the students' understanding and writing of their own autobiographies. An instructor in the elementary, middle, or secondary language arts class, can further enhance the students' understanding by modeling his/her own autobiography to demonstrate the process of adding details and interesting anecdotes to make the story unique.

Teachers in the middle and secondary language arts programs can help their students focus on the stories they want to tell in their autobiographies with prewriting activities (Novelli, 2006). A helpful exercise is to brainstorm writing ideas. Talk about the categories of real-life stories together, such as school adventures, siblings or friends, summer camps, scary moments, or places they've lived.

Teachers of inner city students have helped them to write by tapping into a genre that these students find familiar, that of oral storytelling. According to retired elementary teacher, Judy Wolfman, in "Passing on the Art of Story," (cited in Merina, 2002)

many of her students in the inner city schools of York, Pennsylvania, came from an oral storytelling background. Teachers in the inner city can effectively use the familiar territory of oral storytelling as a launching point to help their students compose autobiographies or craft a story about a fictional character.

CREATING A WRITING ASSIGNMENT

The first step in a lesson on creative writing in elementary, middle, and secondary language arts classes is for the instructor to define the topic of the writing assignment. Once the topic to be written about is identified, students enrich their creative writing by exploring further avenues of thought in the subject area. The process begins with drawing upon the experiences and information students bring to the writing assignment.

Teachers have discovered and successfully utilized various techniques to encourage creative thinking. In the elementary classroom, teachers may pose questions to prompt writing, such as "What I would do with a red wagon." In the middle school and secondary language arts classes, reading and discussing novels, short stories, plays and poems provides additional insights and examples for student writing assignments. Class discussion in the form of brainstorming adds to the bank of ideas to help students to write creatively.

MODELING & MOTIVATING WRITING

Students learn to write by putting their pens to paper or their fingers on the computer keyboard-and writing. Teachers model writing as an effective teaching technique in elementary writing classes. Modeling is a teaching technique whereby the instructor demonstrates the writing process to the class in real time. Using an overhead projector, the teacher writes a first sentence or two to a story. Then, as the teacher asks questions to guide class participation and contributions to the story, the class helps to develop the story. In an even more unconventional exercise in teaching creative writing on the middle or secondary language arts levels by modeling, the instructor limits almost all verbal communication in the classroom during the writing course. All instructions and teacher comments are written either on the board or on overhead projector. The silence of the classroom environment enhances the writing atmosphere and results in greater student input (Ryan, 1991).

Journaling, or journal writing, is a valid process in motivating students to write. A highly personal form of self-expression, journaling is a freestyle record of one's thoughts and feelings, hopes and dreams, and his or her challenges and stresses. Upper elementary, middle and secondary levels are all fertile fields for developing the art of freewriting and/or journaling. Students should be encouraged to write their thoughts and feelings about certain subjects as a free form of expression without having to worry about the mechanics of grammar and spelling. The goal is to get the students actively writing, based on the principle that, with unhindered practice, students will gradually improve and perfect this skill.

WRITING PROMPTS

In all levels of creative writing programs, asking questions helps to prompt students' creative writing. To spark imaginative thinking, teachers ask thought-provoking questions, or "What if …" questions that allow the students' sense of wonder to produce original ideas. Questions could be as simple as "What if you woke up in China tomorrow morning?" or "What if you found out you had a new baby brother?" Questions posed in the secondary classroom may delve more deeply into literary criticism based on reading assignments.

Asking *better* questions prompts more thinking and student discussion, and ultimately, writing. To help students think about their work, rather than asking questions with yes/no answers, teachers can pose open-ended queries, such as, "How did you come up with that character?" or "What problems will your character face?" In the elementary classroom, questions can direct students toward considering each piece of their writing as a continuum. With the student's work spread out on the desk, the teacher might ask questions that help early elementary students see patterns in their work, such as, "What topics have you written about this year?" "What do you notice about your writing in the last two weeks?"

Students move more easily into the writing process when given writing prompts or a beginning sentence. Writing prompts are questions, statements, phrases or cues that give definition and direction to help start a student's writing process. Writing prompts are helpful in all levels of the educational setting. In the upper levels, by introducing tools to aid in the writing process, such as a thesaurus or dictionary, teachers can enhance the clarity of writing as well as make the assignment more interesting.

DRAFTING & REVISING

Writing the rough draft is the first step in getting down to the task of writing because students are encouraged to just start writing. Students should be encouraged to focus on the topic. The premise of freewriting applies here, as students are urged to write without excessive concern for spelling, punctuation, and grammar. Some elementary schools focus too much on the basic mechanics of writing, to the detriment of content. Having good spelling, grammar, and punctuation is less significant if there is nothing interesting in the content (Creative Writing Solutions).

In the middle and secondary levels, editing and revising the rough draft helps students to refine their work and learn how to improve their writing by making it tighter, cleaner, and more powerful. Editing consists of rereading the rough draft, correcting spelling, grammar, and punctuation. Peer editing is another effective form of editing. Young writers can do a 'buddy-read'-exchanging stories with another student to read and comment. To be most constructive, student feedback should be modeled and monitored.

WRITING CONFERENCES

Elementary and secondary language arts teachers can help guide the improvement of students' writing by conducting private writing conferences. One-on-one sessions to discuss a writing project are important in providing positive feedback and constructive criticism to help the student improve the craft.

Weekly private conferences are an opportune time to discuss individual student goals and works in progress. Some educators recommend letting the student lead the conference by asking the writer how the writing is going and to talk about any problems the student is having (Novelli). Writing conferences with the upper elementary, middle and secondary student are an effective means to get children to think of themselves as writers, especially when asking questions that lead students toward thinking about their progress as writers. Questions such as "What part of this story did you write particularly well?" "What new type of writing did you try in this piece?" "What will you write next?" and "What did you learn about writing from this project?" will help students to value themselves as developing writers (Novelli).

PUBLISHING

The reward comes when the writer produces something for an audience. An audience of classmates can listen as the story is read aloud. Publishing a student's work, whether as a solo project or as a collection of work, gives the student an even greater sense of accomplishment for his or her writing efforts. Some classes have added art and illustrations to the published writing.

THE GOALS OF CREATIVE WRITING

Opinions differ on the sequence of teaching creative writing. Some language arts educators believe that the governing skill should be understanding the mechanics of writing, i.e., proper grammar, spelling, punctuation and sentence structure. However, others believe that constant emphasis on grammar and mechanics stifles the creative flow of ideas necessary for productive imaginative thinking. These educators believe that the objective is to get students to write a rough draft, and polish and edit the written work later.

WORKING WITH NOVICE WRITERS

Novice writers are advised to expand on the details, flesh out the characters, elaborate on the descriptions and settings, and add to the dialog. Yet, paradoxically, students might tend to write too much, filling pages with repetition, redundancies, and overstated material. While teachers can urge students to delve deeply into the writing topic, they (particularly on the secondary level) also will help produce good creative writers by helping them to edit out superfluous material. The saying 'less is more,' in practical application, produces tighter writing, in which every word and sentence counts.

Creative writing often involves self-expression, with the student revealing personal and emotionally-charged feelings and issues. The student may also feel especially connected to the writing, as well as a pride of authorship that feels threatened by a teacher's critique. Because of the personal nature of some compositions, teachers usually seek permission from the student before reading aloud to the class the better samples from an assignment.

There are also opposing thoughts on using music as a background or as a stimulus for creative writing.

Some language arts teachers play soft music as a background to the classroom writing atmosphere, in the interest of providing a pleasing sound to promote creative writing. However, others believe that playing music in the writing room actually inhibits the creative process, distracting students from the main subject of their writing assignment. "Listening to music while writing took their attention away from the process of creating their own works in order to shift focus to an engagement with the music itself," (Brown, 2006). Music can effectively be used as a writing prompt or to stimulate discussion before the actual writing process.

WORKING WITH LEARNING DISABLED & EMOTIONALLY DISTURBED STUDENTS

While many of the writing units taught in mainstream classes adapt easily to emotionally disturbed or learning disabled students, language arts educators face unique challenges in the creative writing unit. These students may have problems focusing their thoughts in order to write. They may need extra help to overcome fears of writing. Some learning disabled students need help in learning how to organize their thoughts in order to improve their creative writing skills. Language arts teachers of emotionally disturbed students can more successfully teach creative writing by developing a simple outline for students to follow when composing their written assignment. This outline helps learning disabled students focus on key elements, such as identifying the theme, writing a few beginning sentences, adding a few paragraphs to expand the concept, and writing the ending.

EVALUATING CREATIVE WRITING

Many teachers view assessing students' creative writing as an impossible task since any form of evaluation is subjective and unfair. However, in order to narrow the field to something more objective, educators advise that the teacher communicate specific criteria that will be evaluated, such as spelling, punctuation, and organization.

TERMS & CONCEPTS

Autobiography: A personal history with information about one's life written by that person.

Character Development: The combination of details, dialogue, speech and actions of a character through which a storyteller informs the reader about the character's personality and motivation.

Creative Writing: Imaginative writing distinguished from technical or journalistic writing, and includes autobiography, fiction, poetry, screenwriting and drama.

Freewriting: Automatic, spontaneous writing done especially as a classroom exercise.

Journaling: A highly personal form of self-expression where one captures the essence of one's thoughts and feelings, hopes and dreams, challenges and stresses, expressing them in written form.

Modeling: A teaching technique whereby the teacher demonstrates the writing process to the class in real time.

Plot Development: Organizing the story elements to create a causal sequence that draws the reader into the characters' lives and provides the conflict for a story.

Revising: The process of looking over the written piece, and making corrections and improvements.

Rough Draft: An author's first version, outline or sketch.

Writing Conference: A private meeting between teacher and student where constructive direction and encouragement on the student's work are given.

Writing Prompts: Questions, statements or cues that give definition and direction to start a student's writing process.

Ginny DeMille

BIBLIOGRAPHY

Arthur, B. & Zell, N. (1990). Write up: A strategy for teaching creative writing skills to emotionally disturbed students. *Preventing School Failure, 34,* 26. Retrieved December 6, 2006, from EBSCO Online Database Education Research Complete.

Barbot, B., Tan, M., Randi, J., Santa-Donato, G., & Grigorenko, E. L. (2012). Essential skills for creative writing: Integrating multiple domain-specific perspectives. *Thinking Skills & Creativity, 7,* 209–223. Retrieved December 6, 2013, from EBSCO Online Database Education Research Complete.

Bloom, L. Z. (2004). Compression: When less says more. *Pedagogy, 4,* 300-304. Retrieved December 6, 2006, from EBSCO Online Database Education Research Complete.

Brown, R. (2006). Soundtracking our selves: Teaching creative writing with a musical approach. *Interdisciplinary Humanities, 23,* 53-57 Retrieved December 6, 2006, from EBSCO Online Database Academic Search Premier.

Chong, S., & Lee, C. (2012). Developing a pedagogical-technical framework to improve creative writing. *Educational Technology Research & Development, 60,* 639–657. Retrieved December 6, 2013, from EBSCO Online Database Education Research Complete.

Creative Writing Solutions. (n.d.). *Creative writing ideas: Where they come from and how to get them on paper.* Retrieved December 7, 2006, from http://creative-writing-solutions.com.

Creative Writing Solutions. (n.d.). *Writing your rough draft.* Retrieved December 8, 2006, from http://creative-writing-solutions.com.

Essex, C. (1997). *Teaching creative writing.* Retrieved December 8, 2006, from http://readingrockets.org.

Janke, J. (1999). *Creative writing: Fiction writing tips.* Retrieved December 8, 2006, from, Dakota State University, http://homepages.dsu.edu.

Merina, A. (2002). Passing on the art of story. *NEA Today, 21,* 39. Retrieved December 6, 2006, from EBSCO Online Database Education Research Complete.

Novelli, J. (n.d.). *Telling our own stories.* Retrieved December 7, 2006, from http://content.scholastic.com.

Powers, B. (1997). The answer to better writing? Better questions! *Instructor-Primary, 107,* 60. Retrieved December 7, 2006, from EBSCO Online Database Academic Search Premier.

Smith, G. (2013). Dream writing: A new creative writing technique for secondary schools?. *English In Education, 47,* 245–260. Retrieved December 6, 2013, from EBSCO Online Database Education Research Complete.

Ryan, P.M. (1991). Whose voice do you hear? (An experiment in nonverbal communication). *Educational Leadership, 49,* 85. Retrieved December 6, 2006, from EBSCO Online Database Education Research Complete.

SUGGESTED READING

Crose, S. *Better fiction writing.* (n.d.). Retrieved December 6, 2006, from Creative Writing Solutions http://creative-writing-solutions.com.

Gregory, C. (1995). Teach students, not writing. *Instructor, 104,* 38. Retrieved December 6, 2006, from EBSCO Online Database Academic Search Premier.

Knoeller, C. (2003). Imaginative response: Teaching literature through creative writing. *English Journal, 92,* 42. Retrieved December 6, 2006, from EBSCO Online Database Academic Search Premier.

Shapiro, N. L. (1994). On teaching creative writing. *Curriculum Review, 34,* 5. Retrieved December 6, 2006, from EBSCO Online Database Academic Search Premier.

Thomson, L. (2013). Learning to teach creative writing. *Changing English: Studies In Culture & Education,*

20, 45–52. Retrieved December 6, 2013, from EBSCO Online Database Education Research Complete.

Williams, R. D., & Williams, A. R. (2012). Creative writing in alcohol, tobacco, and other drug education. *Contemporary Issues In Education Research, 5*, 327–330.

Retrieved December 6, 2013, from EBSCO Online Database Education Research Complete.

Wojciechowski, J. (1998). The perfect day. *Teaching PreK-8, 28*, 56. Retrieved December 8, 2006, from EBSCO Online Database Education Research Complete.

TEACHING HUMANITIES

Because the humanities are heavily dependent on reading and writing, this article will touch on literary criticism, along with social and cultural trends that have affected the humanities. Various applications are discussed in terms of how to approach the humanities as a whole, rather than only in the standard departmental approach. This article also provides an overview of the changes in the teaching of humanities and includes a discussion of some of the current issues.

KEYWORDS: Curriculum Integration; Empiricism; English; Globalization; History; Humanism; Interdisciplinarity; Interdisciplinary Curriculum; Liberal Arts; Literature; Music; Multidisciplinary Curriculum; Performing Arts; Pragmatism

OVERVIEW

The term *humanities* refers to a broad range of disciplines that attempt to explore and develop human qualities. Historically, the humanities, in one form or another, can be traced to the liberal arts of ancient Greece and Rome. Although the organization and division of what constitutes the humanities has changed over the centuries, one major dividing line has remained consistent, and that is the line of empiricism. On one side of the line are the humanities, with critical thinking & reading, speculation and analysis; on the other is empirical research, scientific method and the like. In other words, the main difference is one of *how* knowledge is explored and gathered.

After this initial polarity, many other divisions emerge. At the college level, for example, Kernan (1997) indicated that there are three main branches to the liberal arts: the humanities, the social sciences and the physical sciences, which are all separated from the professional disciplines. At the middle or high school level, the divisions are usually similar: dividing often along the lines of the humanities, mathematics and sciences, and vocational studies.

Further divisions often separate the humanities into specific departments. According to Kernan, "the humanities are the subjects regularly listed under that heading: literature, philosophy, art history, music, religion, languages, and sometimes history." Most middle and high schools have similar divisions, although few have a philosophy department or a specific art history department. In terms of humanities, a typical public school has departments for: English, history, music, arts, language and sometimes performing arts when it is not part of the arts department.

The humanities, being heavily reliant on writing and reading, have followed many of the trends in the practice of reading. As Kernan noted, "The humanities might almost be said traditionally to have been elaborate exercises in various kinds of reading and writing."

Easily the most influential event in the early part of the twenty-first century has been the No Child Left Behind (NCLB) legislation. This massive reform created standards for students and teachers alike and tied federal funding to test performance. On the negative side, the NCLB has possibly created a sweeping culture of "teaching to the test" where teachers, concerned about the results their students get on the standardized tests, are focusing heavily on the test material. In some situations this practice results in students who have strong test taking skills and specific knowledge, but they lack other skills and may not know how to learn on their own. In the worst cases, teachers are even supplying their students with test answers, sending the students subversive messages about the value of school and education.

On the positive side, the NCLB has created clearer standards for holding schools and teachers accountable. With these clear expectations, students are supposed to have equitable educational opportunities. However, issues still remain with inequities of resources, funding, buildings, class sizes and more.

In the humanities, in particular, funding and standardized tests are serious issues.

APPLICATIONS

The standard application of teaching the humanities in public schools is to separate into departments, where each can focus on a specific aspect. In this traditional model, art teachers teach art, music teachers teach music, history teachers teach history, etc. There is often little or no crossover, since class sizes, complex schedules, specific knowledge and expertise requirements, standardized tests, and other factors can make combining disciplines difficult.

A number of applications exist in practice that can help create more cohesion from an otherwise fragmented approach to the humanities. Co-teaching, team teaching and thematic teaching, for example, can help bring some cohesion to the humanities, but they still fragment learning. From a student's perspective, for example, art begins and ends one period, followed by history, then English and so on.

Some applications of teaching the humanities attempt to cross over the boundaries of the disciplines. Interdisciplinary and multidisciplinary models of teaching, for example, both focus on weaving several disciplines together. The boundaries still remain, however. Having teachers generalize into several disciplines, rather than staying focused in one, has consequences.

Other applications attempt to ignore the barriers that separate not just the humanities, but all the disciplines as well. Curriculum integration and certain types of project-based learning, for example, focus primarily on the learning process itself, and not on disciplines.

The following approaches are examples of various applications that explore the humanities in different ways.

CO-TEACHING/TEAM TEACHING

Co-teaching can help bridge some of the disciplines together. In a common form of such a model, an English teacher and a social studies teacher coordinate to study the same time period. The English teacher focuses on the literary elements, drawing on poetry, short stories and novels that are poignant to the time. The social studies teacher provides the historical background and approaches the same time period using primary sources and historical events.

In some co-teaching models, a group of students has two teachers in the same classroom, allowing each of them to bring his or her experience and expertise to the course of study.

In team teaching, several teachers coordinate as a team to study the same thing, such as a time period like the 1960s. In this model an entire team, all of the sixth grade teachers, for example, coordinate to deliver the curriculum. Each teacher contributes his or her discipline toward the topic. Not only does this help bring together all of the humanities, it may even bring together all of the school subjects.

THEMATIC TEACHING

In thematic teaching, a broad or abstract theme is used to bridge the disciplines and even grade levels. An entire school, for example, could study *perseverance*. In the English classes the students might read short stories about people not giving up. In the history classes, the students might learn about historic figures and the traits that allowed them to succeed through adversity. The science teachers might teach about the concepts of momentum and inertia. As with co-teaching or team teaching, the teachers contribute to the curriculum from their specific areas of expertise (Postman, 1995).

INTERDISCIPLINARY/MULTIDISCIPLINARY

In these approaches, teachers attempt to bring the disciplines together. An art teacher teaching about a certain era, for example, may have the students listen to pieces of music, read poems and short stories, and study primary documents in addition to the learning about the art of the time. The students then draw on their understandings from the other disciplines to inform their choices as artists for the project that the teacher assigns. Beane (1997) provided clear descriptions of these forms and how they differ from others.

CURRICULUM INTEGRATION/PROJECT-BASED LEARNING

In curriculum integration and project-based learning the curriculum is student-centered and entirely, or almost entirely, driven by the interests of the students. The learning that takes place does not have to fall into the traditional disciplines. Those interested in more about curriculum integration should check out Beane; for project-based learning of this nature, Starnes and Carone (1999).

VIEWPOINTS

Although there are different applications of how to go about teaching the humanities, whether through a traditional departmental model or through a cross-curricular model, there are also considerations of *what* to teach versus *how* to teach. The disciplines in the humanities represent a huge body of knowledge. An entire humanities department could be devoted to literature for four years of high school and still only manage a fraction of what exists in print. The same is true of history and the arts, as well as foreign languages. Therefore, schools, departments and teachers must operate from a viewpoint to narrow the scope of the humanities and create manageable goals.

There are many viewpoints of what to teach in the humanities, ranging from curricular models that focus on a more classical approach, to those that embrace the more recent movements. Illuminating three viewpoints should delineate the territory. Some schools entirely embrace one viewpoint, while others departmentalize, and still others change views at various grade levels. Looking at teaching about Shakespeare can elucidate these larger viewpoints.

CULTURAL LITERACY

Is reading Shakespeare vital and necessary? Is Shakespeare so critical and specific to the Western world that all or most U.S. students should read and be familiar with his works? Is knowing about Shakespeare part of being literate, even in today's society? Are there fixed understandings of Shakespeare's works? One of the main viewpoints of what may be considered a more classical approach is the idea of cultural literacy. In the book *The New Dictionary of Cultural Literacy: What Every American Needs to Know,* for example, Hirsch, Kett & Trefil (2002) outlined a body of knowledge that they believe all students should know in order to be culturally literate. With this type of viewpoint the humanities is a somewhat fixed body of knowledge that all students should know, and, therefore, teaching Shakespeare is essential.

DEVELOPING CRITICAL THINKING SKILLS

Or is the importance really about the skills of critical reading, reflection, and analysis? Is the *ability* to read Shakespeare the essential part? Is Shakespeare in this sense mostly a means to an end? Howard Gardner and many others are more concerned about

how students think, rather than *what* students think, especially in the humanities where answers are not always clear. As Gardner (1991) wrote, "Indeed, in the humanities, the raising of questions, rather than the adoption of a single line of argument or the selection of the best among a finite set of alternatives, is often the deep goal of the lesson." With this type of viewpoint the humanities is more for developing thinking skills, and, therefore, teaching Shakespeare is not mandatory.

NO LONGER RELEVANT?

Or has Shakespeare become irrelevant to the modern school student? Despite the universal themes found throughout Shakespeare's plays and sonnets, are the messages lost in the distance of the past? Is the written word losing its hold on the modern mind? With the changing demographics in the United States, maybe studying Shakespeare has become unimportant. With increasing need to better understand other cultures and people, perhaps schools should focus on multicultural or anti-bias curricula, especially in areas with diverse student populations. With numerous cultures and languages to explore and understand, with authors and artists from around the world to study, there is no room in the curriculum for Shakespeare. With this type of viewpoint the humanities is more for creating cohesion amongst diverse people, and, therefore, teaching Shakespeare is not relevant.

LITERACY & THE ENGLISH TEACHER

One of the issues that faces the humanities is that of literacy. Often, English teachers are burdened with the responsibility to develop the reading and writing skills of the students. However, some English teachers have 100 or more students, making the process of assessing and grading student writing time consuming and potentially not thoroughly educative. With the breadth of many literature curricula, students may become widely read, yet still lack essential literacy skills. Because of this, many schools have developed programs that stress reading and writing across the curriculum, thereby spreading the monumental task of literacy throughout the school.

UNEVEN PREPARATION

Some disciplines, like mathematics, are linear in the sense that there are clearly defined levels and prerequisites for further study. Addition and subtraction in the United States is not going to be significantly different than elsewhere. Other disciplines, like those in the humanities, are not linear in the sense that beyond the basic building blocks, there is not a clearly defined body of knowledge. What is taught in one location may not be the same as elsewhere, even within the U.S. For example, world literature might be taught at tenth grade in one school, ninth in another and eleventh in another. In some districts world literature might be a semester-long class, while in others a two-year course of study. Some schools may even break world literature into components, teaching poetry, short stories and novels as separate classes. This is particularly true of the arts and foreign languages. Some districts do not have foreign language programs at the middle school level, whereas other districts begin instruction in kindergarten. There are state and national standards for the humanities, but variations in factors like implementation, scheduling, foreign language choices, budgets, and textbooks still create situations where students are unevenly prepared.

MEDIA & READING

Teachers in the humanities have always had to make adjustments to the changes in society, but perhaps the last two decades more than ever, more than any other time in history, have made significant and permanent changes. For hundreds of years the process of reading was basically the same, with some variations in literary theory, and additions of new genres, such as the essay or the short story. However, with the advent of the computer and the proliferation of the Internet, with students spending more time in front of the television and less time with books, the process and value of reading seems to have taken a dramatic turn. As Birkerts (1994) noted, "The advent of the computer and the astonishing sophistication of our electronic communications media have together turned a range of isolated changes into something systemic." We may be reaching a time where students cannot access certain types of text without accompanying images, music, hypertext, and other media.

FUNDING

Funding issues in the humanities are widespread, affecting all levels from universities to elementary schools. Much of the issue starts at the national level.

For example, studying trends in funding to the academic humanities from 1970-1995 led D'Arms (1997) to conclude, "By the most optimistic current estimate funds earmarked for fellowships and research...will drop below 50 percent from FY 1995 levels." His cautious optimism that the trends may reverse in the future did not seem to come true. In 2007, the National Endowment for the Humanities requested a budget of $140 million for its fiscal year (FY), which was down from the FY 1996 budget of $172 million, and the FY 2004 budget of $152 million. By FY 2013 the budget request had increased to over $154 million. No matter how the numbers are viewed, the outlook is grim for the humanities, as more and more federal and state money is being directed to the science and technology fields. According to Frodeman, Mitcham and Pielke (2003), "In 2003, less than 1 percent of the $100-billion investment of public resources in knowledge is being devoted to the fields making up the humanities."

Funding for the humanities is a particular problem in public schools. Faced with continuous budget cuts, many principals and superintendents are forced to keep what is absolutely essential. In terms of the humanities, this often translates to keeping English, social studies and a foreign language or two, and then evaluating the needs of the school after that. Art, music and performing arts, perhaps because they are rarely part of the required coursework, are secondary concerns and are often poorly funded. Many schools must supplement these programs with fundraisers or seek sponsors for additional income.

COMMERCIALIZATION

Lack of funding has, in part, led to a growing commercialization in many public schools, particularly in the humanities. As Schor (2004) indicated, from naming rights to auditoriums to ads on busses to textbooks featuring brand names, many schools have been infiltrated by corporate America, for better or worse. On the positive side, schools are getting some much-needed funds and supplies, especially for the humanities. Some schools are even able to develop healthy relationships with business partners, where older students can become interns in real companies. On the negative side, controversial programs that require mandatory television viewing in the classroom, and corporately created curricula have been criticized for bias, omitting key information, and promoting products that are unhealthy for children. Schor has an excellent account of marketing in schools, as well as marketing to children in general.

DISPERSION

With a tremendous broadening of the humanities in the last fifty years, incorporating women's studies, minority studies, gay & lesbian studies and so on, the humanities may be viewed as dispersing too much, and are becoming much less valued as a result. This trend can be seen at the college level, where, according to Hunt (1997), "In the 1980s alone, for example, the number of bachelor's degrees awarded to men increased by 7 percent while the number of those awarded to women rose 27 percent. Women now make up 55 percent of the student population" (p. 19). This rise, according to Hunt, along with a general decline in funding and other factors, may be contributing to the decrease in status of the humanities.

In addition, Hunt indicated that with the rise of multiculturalism and the diversification of faculty, that many teachers at the college level are being forced into interdisciplinary teaching and that, "interdisciplinarity may only make the case that humanities faculty are all interchangeable and hence that many are expendable." Hesse (1997), based on publication data, concludes similarly, "the humanities are increasingly seen as more expendable than other disciplines." Perhaps factors such as these are contributing to the decline in federal and state funding and the high rate of teacher turnover.

STANDARDIZED TESTS & ASSESSMENT

Standardized tests and assessments pose a problem for the humanities. Because there are not always clear answers to what a poem, song or painting means, assessing student understanding can be difficult. Often, teachers focus more on what the students are thinking and how they defend their answers, rather than on the answers themselves. This process is time consuming, however, since typical assessments include essays, interviews, and presentations.

Teachers often must find quicker ways to assess students, such as multiple choice or true/false questions, matching, and so on, which are typical of standardized tests. These questions require specific answers that are not open to interpretation or opinion and create a situation where the humanities become a series of facts, rather than a process. In

some cases, the humanities may even be reduced to a process of memorizing names and dates, in art history, for example, rather than seen as a process.

TERMS & CONCEPTS

Curriculum Integration: Curriculum that is centered on significant, relevant problems that draws together students and teachers in meaningful ways that are unhindered by subject or discipline boundaries.

Empiricism: The practice that knowledge is better attained, or must be attained, through observation and measurement.

Globalization: The process of branching out and incorporating more from the rest of the world.

Interdisciplinarity: A trend of mixing and crossing disciplines that can cause dispersion of knowledge and a devaluing of specific people or departments.

Interdisciplinary Curriculum: Curriculum that approaches learning from one angle into several academic disciplines.

Multi-disciplinary Curriculum: Curriculum that draws together content and material from several segmented disciplines.

National Endowment for the Humanities: Established in 1965, the NEH was created to foster the humanities through grants, fellowships and other endeavors.

Pragmatism: American philosophy that focused on the practical results of searching for truth.

Charles Fischer

BIBLIOGRAPHY

Beane, J. (1997). *Curriculum integration: designing the core of democratic education.* New York: Teachers College Press.

Birkerts, S. (1994). *The Gutenberg elegies: the fate of reading in an electronic age.* New York: Fawcett Columbine.

Brody, H. (2013). Evaluating the humanities. *Academe, 99,* 19–23. Retrieved December 11, 2013, from EBSCO Online Database Education Research Complete.

D'Arms, J. H. (1997). Funding trends in the academic humanities, 1970-1995:reflections on the stability of the system. In A. Kernan (Ed.), *What's happened to the humanities?* (pp. 32-60). Princeton, New Jersey: Princeton University Press.

Frodeman, R., Mitcham, C. & Pielke, R., Jr. (2003). Humanities for a policy-and a policy for humanities. *Issues in Science and Technology, 20,* 29-32. Retrieved December 4, 2007, from EBSCO online database, Academic Search Premier.

Gardner, H. (1991). *The unschooled mind: how children think & how schools should teach.* New York: BasicBooks.

Harvie, K. (2013). The humanities curriculum in a changing world. *Ethos, 21,* 10–13. Retrieved December 11, 2013, from EBSCO Online Database Education Research Complete.

Hesse, C. (1997). Humanities and the library in the digital age. In A. Kernan (Ed.), *What's happened to the humanities?* (pp. 107-121). Princeton, New Jersey: Princeton University Press.

Himmelfarb, G. (1997). Beyond method. In A. Kernan (Ed.), *What's happened to the humanities?* (pp. 143-161). Princeton, New Jersey: Princeton University Press.

Hirsch, E.D., Jr., Kett, J.F. & Trefil, J. (2002). *The new dictionary of cultural literacy: what every American needs to know.* New York: Houghton Mifflin.

Hunt, L. (1997). Democratization and decline: the consequences of demographic change in the humanities. In A. Kernan (Ed.), *What's happened to the humanities?* (pp. 17-31). Princeton, New Jersey: Princeton University Press.

Kernan, A. (ed.) (1997). *What's happened to the humanities?* Princeton, New Jersey: Princeton University Press.

Nelson, C. (2012). Fighting for the humanities. *Academe, 98,* 16–21. Retrieved December 11, 2013, from EBSCO Online Database Education Research Complete.

Oakley, F. (1997). Ignorant armies and nighttime clashes: changes in the humanities classroom 1970-1995. In A. Kernan (Ed.), *What's happened to the humanities?* (pp. 63-83). Princeton, New Jersey: Princeton University Press.

Postman, N. (1995). *The end of education: redefining the value of school.* New York: Vintage Books.

Phillips, J. (2006). Deconstruction. *Theory, Culture & Society, 23* (2/3), p. 194-195. Retrieved December 9, 2007, from EBSCO online database, Academic Search Premier.

Sabin, M. (1997). Evolution and revolution: change in the literary humanities, 1968-1995. In A. Kernan (Ed.), *What's happened to the humanities?* (pp. 84-103). Princeton, New Jersey: Princeton University Press.

Schor, J.B. (2004). *Born to buy.* New York: Scribner.

Starnes, B.A. & Carone, A. (1999). *From thinking to doing: constructing a framework to teach mandates through experience-based learning.* Mountain City, GA: The Foxfire Fund, Inc.

Wiggins, G. (1998). *Educative assessment: designing assessments to inform and improve student performance.* San Fransisco: Jossey-Bass, Inc., Publishers.

SUGGESTED READING

Adams, J., & McNab, N. (2013). Understanding arts and humanities students' experiences of assessment and feedback. *Arts & Humanities In Higher Education, 12,* 36–52. Retrieved December 11, 2013, from EBSCO Online Database Education Research Complete.

Egan, K. (1986). *Teaching as storytelling: an alternative approach to teaching and curriculum in the elementary school.* Chicago: University of Chicago Press.

Flammang, L.A. (2007). The place of the humanities at a military academy. *Academe, 93,* p. 30-33. Retrieved December 9, 2007, from EBSCO online database, Academic Search Premier.

Gilead, T. (2017). Justifying the teaching of humanities: A new economic approach. *Policy Futures in Education.* 15(3), 346-359.

Gould, S.J. (2003). *The hedgehog, the fox, and the magister's pox: mending the gap between science and the humanities.* New York: Harmony Books. Loewen, J.W. (1995). *Lies my teacher told me: everything your American history textbook got wrong.* New York: The New Press.

Grafton, A. T., & Grossman, J. (2013). The humanities in dubious battle. *Chronicle Of Higher Education, 59,* A25–A26. Retrieved December 11, 2013, from EBSCO Online Database Education Research Complete.

Marshall, D. (2007). The places of the humanities. *Liberal Education, 93,* p. 34-39. Retrieved December 9, 2007, from EBSCO online database, Academic Search Premier.

Pokrovskii, N.E. (2007). What is happening to the humanities? *Russian Education & Society, 49,* p. 22-30. Retrieved December 9, 2007, from EBSCO online database, Education Research Complete.

Taranto, J. & Dettmar, K. (2015). The secret of good humanities teaching. *Chronicle of Higher Education.* 62(5).

Wilson, E.O. (1998). *Consilience: the unity of knowledge.* New York: Vintage Books.

TEACHING HISTORY

This article discusses the teaching of K-12 history in the United States. History was not always a central subject in American public school education, but it took on an increased significance as the United States experienced successive waves of immigration in the 19th century. World and American History were used to show immigrants that the sympathetic imagination—an understanding and appreciation of the contributions made by diverse races and cultures—is central to the outworking of the democratic ideal in

American society. This message was reinforced into the 20th century by the rise of New Education and Progressive Education, both of which sought to relate the experience of the individual child to the broader themes of World and American History. As the 21st century began, the National History Standards and the No Child Left Behind Act of 2001 emphasized the value of objective historical knowledge and ignited heated debates concerning the relative importance of western culture and values within a multicultural context.

KEYWORDS: Educational Psychology; History; Multiculturalism; National History Standards; New Education; No Child Left Behind Act of 2001; Progressive Education; Public Schools; Standardized Tests

OVERVIEW

Teaching history at the K-12 level is designed to instill in students what has been called the sympathetic imagination. By developing an increasingly secure grasp of history, students will gain a better understanding of themselves, other people, and the communities and societies in which they live. As the United States becomes an increasingly multicultural and pluralistic society, and in the wake of the September 11 terrorist attacks, history teachers are being called upon to help raise awareness of, and tolerance for, other cultural and religious traditions.

In the United States, the teaching of history in primary and secondary school has never been far from controversy. History instruction has been used at various times and in various places to promote literacy, patriotism, morality, and, most recently, an awareness of past injustices against indigenous peoples and others. Arguments continue to rage about the methods used to teach history, at what grade level history instruction should begin, and whether there are objective facts of history that should be taught to all students. Against the backdrop of these shifting cultural and political sands, new technologies such as the internet are giving history teachers and students' ever-expanding access to information about the histories of different cultures, and a global, networked community of learners is being created in the hope of applying the lessons of history to present geopolitical challenges.

While the writing of history in western culture goes back at least as far as the ancient Greek historians (Aristotle recommended it as an important subject), the institutionalized teaching of history is much more recent. It was largely neglected in classical and medieval times in favor of subjects thought to be more practical, such as religion, grammar, composition, and arithmetic. Only in the intellectual ferment of the Renaissance and the Reformation in the 16th century, when the individual became the main actor on the human stage, was there a renewed interest in learning, and learning from, the past.

In the United States the teaching of history began as a means to an end, and in some respect it has remained that way. Though American public schools date to 1643, the organized public education movement was established in the 1830s to teach reading, writing, and arithmetic—the three subjects thought to be essential to a good education. When history was taught in the classroom during these early years of public school education, it was primarily in the form of examples to illustrate literary, geographical, or grammatical concepts (Ballard, 1970).

Teaching history began to come into its own in the second half of the nineteenth century. Despite the protests of influential British intellectuals such as Herbert Spencer, who argued in his *Essays on Education* (1861) that teaching history amuses far more than it instructs, an influential segment of American educators began to see that the teaching of history could be a useful way to assimilate immigrants into the mainstream of American life. Hearkening back to concepts first articulated by the Greeks, they saw history education as central to the health of the nation because it helped to create good citizens who gave their assent to the nation's core democratic principles.

Children of immigrants weren't the only group these educators had in mind—after the maelstrom of the Civil War ended in 1865, teaching history was also seen as a way to remind the children of the North and the South of their common American heritage. In 1876 the National Educational Association (later the National Education Association)—which had been founded in 1857 to unite ten state education associations—recommended that United States History be taught in all public schools, and by 1890 the group was recommending the teaching of age-appropriate history lessons beginning in second grade. While history education in the United States remained far from universal at the end of the nineteenth century, its utility, at least in theory, was beyond doubt (McMurry, 1946).

Missing in this growing enthusiasm for teaching history were methods suited to the task. In the nineteenth century the most common methods of teaching—the Aristotelian idea of repetition, as well rote memorization and reading questions from a textbook—were applied to history teaching, often with dismal results. Researchers who interviewed history students found that most students quickly forgot what they memorized, and, even more troubling, were unable to derive meaning from the facts they had learned.

In the final decades of the 19th century, a movement called New Education took root in America as a reaction against the entrenched methods of teaching history (and other subjects). First developed in Germany by Johann Friedrich Herbart, supporters of New Education argued that students of history and other subjects should be taught to think systematically and to ask questions, rather than memorize lists of facts. Supporters of New Education thought that the classroom syllabus should be organized around themes or units to get at truths common across historical events. For Herbart and the disciples of his New Education philosophy, education's grand purpose was delivering moral and ethical lessons (McMurry).

American educational theorist John Dewey continued this thread in the early decades of the twentieth century with his emphasis on learning by doing. Dewey and other educators introduced a school of thought called Progressive Education, in which importance was placed on tapping the life experience and cultural background of students in preparing and delivering lessons. They believed in the concept of learning by doing, and they stressed that students should be active, rather than passive, learners. Advocates of Progressive Education tended to emphasize the subjective experience of the student as he or she approached history, rather than the memorization and assimilation of specific historical facts.

Such progressive ideas were sidelined during the Cold War era, when the focus was on the rapid inculcation of science and math concepts as part of 'space-race' competition with the Soviet Union. In the eyes of many educators, American students did not have

the luxury of indulging in a journey of self-exploration while the fate of the western world was under threat from the menace of Communism. The argument at the time was that a steady stream of scientists who were well-versed in the objective truths of math and science would provide a bulwark against Soviet aggression and demonstrate the superiority of western capitalist societies. Improvement in these fields was sure to place the U.S. at an undisputed power advantage over the Russians.

But when the Cold War ended in the late 1980s, and politicians and educators took stock of the American educational system, there was a widespread push for reforms that would bolster what many considered lackluster student performance. As with other subjects, the teaching of history came under close scrutiny. Under a 1992 Congressional mandate, the National Center for History in the Schools at the University of California-Los Angeles (UCLA) formed a committee to draft new guidelines for teaching history in American public schools. Funding came in part from taxpayer dollars through the National Endowment for the Humanities and the U.S. Department of Education. The standards were intended as guidelines for history teachers as they prepared lessons, but even before they were published in 1996 they drew fire from critics because the UCLA group recommended a rethinking of the traditional method of teaching World History as the story of the rise of the west, and thus not privileging the teaching of western civilization. When the National Center for History in the Schools released their final guidelines to the public in 1996, they were quick to add that their conclusions did not necessarily reflect the views of the U.S. government (National Center for History in the Schools, 1996).

Despite these debates over the *content* of the history that should be taught in public schools as the 21st century began, there was broad consensus over the *methods* that should be used to teach the content. Public schools had largely endorsed the view of Dewey and others that history teachers will be successful only if they engage students in learning through a blend of traditional methods and newer methods such as alternative assessment and group learning. In the first decade of the twenty-first century these alternative learning methods have been expanded to include use of such tools as digital communications, computers and tablets, and the internet. Also during this period, a number of history educators began to rediscover the New Education movement insight that history is learned best when it progressively incorporates other skills such as writing, reading, and higher-order analytical thinking (Formwalt, 2002).

TEACHER PREPARATION

From the outset, the teaching of history has presented educators with the challenge of relating the unknown, sometimes murky, past to the known present. As evolutionary psychologist Steven Pinker and others have shown, no student comes to the history classroom (or any other classroom), as a blank slate—all human beings are the products of the interplay between genes and culture. A successful history teacher will recognize the inherent strengths and weaknesses of his or her students, their learning styles and their preconceptions about various topics in the curriculum, and adjust lesson plans accordingly. While preparing students to do well on standardized tests is a reality of modern public education, creative history teachers understand that there are many paths to this destination.

John D. Bransford and M. Suzanne Donovan, editors of *How Students Learn: History in the Classroom* (2005), a report from the National Academies of Science, suggest that history teachers should look at their task through four related, yet distinct lenses:

- **Learner-centered lens:** What preconceptions about history do students bring to the classroom?
- **Knowledge-centered lens:** What aspects of history will be taught, and why?
- **Assessment-centered lens:** How can the teachers discover what students are absorbing from the lessons?
- **Community-centered lens:** What can the teacher do to make the classroom a place where students ask questions, take risks, and grow in their respect for one another? (Bransford & Donovan, 2005).

These guidelines intersect in several meaningful ways with the work of the United States National Board for Professional Teaching Standards, which recommends that all teachers should be able to do five things well: First, they should know their students and adjust accordingly. Second, they should be thoroughly versed in their subject matter. Third, they should adjust their teaching methods to retain student interest. Fourth, teachers should continually evaluate their own performance in the classroom and seek out ways to improve. Fifth, teachers should work with fellow teachers and parents to help their students become successful learners.

STAGES OF STUDENT DEVELOPMENT

There is a large and growing body of literature in the field of educational psychology that seeks to apply the work of developmental psychologists to the interactions between teachers and students. In order to achieve a high level of professional success and satisfaction, experts generally agree that it is imperative for teachers to understand that the moral, intellectual, and emotional development of their students occurs in discrete stages.

Though they differ on important details, psychologists such as Erik Erickson, Jean Piaget, and Lev Vygotsky have stressed that students go through stages of cognitive, emotional, and moral development. As applied to history teaching, these stages should determine the nature of the lessons, how they are presented, and the methods of student evaluation that are used. Piaget suggested, for example, that high school history students should be encouraged to work in small groups and use alternative methods of learning such as dialogues and mock trials because they have reached the third level of cognitive development he called Formal Operational Thinking. Students in elementary school, by contrast, are more literal thinkers who are less likely to think about history in abstract terms (Snowman & Biehler, 2006).

LEARNING STYLES & MULTIPLE INTELLIGENCES

The influential work of Howard Gardner and others shows that just as students come to the history classroom with different conceptions about history and its relevance to their own lives and communities, so they also come with different learning styles or ways of learning. The theory of multiple intelligences holds that in any given history classroom, students approach learning in different, but complementary ways.

There are several types of intelligence that history instructors must take into account when preparing and teaching lessons:

- **Interpersonal intelligence:** Student works well in groups;
- **Intrapersonal intelligence:** Student is self-directed, focused on achieving the goal;

- **Linguistic intelligence:** Student learns primarily through words;
- **Mathematical and logical intelligence:** Student detects patterns; uses logic to solve problems;
- **Visual and spatial intelligence:** Student learns through observation and visualization;
- **Kinesthetic intelligence:** Student learns best by doing;
- **Musical intelligence:** Student is adept at detecting tones, rhythms, and music;
- **Naturalist intelligence:** Student is at home in nature.

Skilled teachers will seek to recognize students with these intelligences, thereby making the subject matter more appealing to all students (Formwalt; Snowman & Biehler).

THE ROLE OF THE INTERNET IN HISTORY TEACHING

The rise of the Internet in the mid-1990s brought with it the potential for a significant impact on classroom instruction. By 2013, rather than relying almost exclusively on textbooks, students and their teachers are exposed to a broad range of content—this includes computers and tablets, the Internet and social media, and expanded digital communications, in addition to audio and video aids. As applied to history, teachers are now able to draw upon a vast collection of primary source material in preparing lessons, and they are also able to communicate—via email, instant messaging, blogs and websites, social media, or videoconferencing—with other history teachers around the world to discuss best practices or even gain encouragement in challenging classroom situations.

Beyond lesson plans and collegial benefits for teachers, the Internet also brings with it the potential to engage those students who do not learn best from reading or oral instruction. Through streaming audio, video, and other content available online, history teachers can enrich both the learning experience of students with a broad, preexisting interest in history and the learning experience of those students who have struggled with the topic. A number of education experts suggest that the use of multimedia in the classroom is also a better way to engage students. Others believe that new media such as video games can teach educators some

valuable pedagogical lessons (National Institute on Media and the Family, 2005).

NATIONAL STANDARDS & STANDARDIZED TESTING

History instruction in U.S. public schools is conducted against the backdrop of the federal No Child Left Behind Act of 2001 (NCLB). The law is designed to raise educational standards in all American public schools, and history is one of the core subjects identified by the law. Key provisions of NCLB include standardized testing, school choice, and more stringent teacher certification standards. NCLB had a considerable impact on history teachers—and by extension history instruction—because it requires that new teachers receive state certification and have the appropriate undergraduate major. Critics of NCLB, however, protest that stringent testing standards require teachers to spend more time on drills and less on alternative learning methods favored by a century of research. They also argue that shifting many of the NCLB implementation costs to the individual states that are already struggling to balance their budgets amounts to an unfunded—and unrealistic—federal government mandate.

CHOOSING WHICH HISTORY TO TEACH

The subject matter taught in history classes has often been highly politicized, especially in recent decades as national history standards have been discussed (Symcox, 2002; Cercadillo, 2006). As the United States has become ever more ethnically, culturally, and even religiously diverse, the interpretation of history will perhaps inevitably stir passions or even cause divisions. Some tend to view the teaching of history as documenting the ebb and flow of the implementation of the objectively true values of Western civilization, which they hold up as crucial to an understanding of the past and as a guidepost to help present and future generations of Americans navigate the relativistic waters of multiculturalism and pluralism. Others tend to see much of previous history instruction as whitewashing the sins of Europeans, both in North America and abroad, and they seek to set the record straight through revised curricula that highlights the contributions of non-Western cultures to the American story. There is little debate, however, that poor student test scores show there is much room for improvement in American history teaching.

TERMS & CONCEPTS

Educational Psychology: An influential field of study that seeks to apply the findings of developmental psychology to the classroom setting.

Multiculturalism: The idea that the beliefs and values of no one racial, cultural, religious, and ethnic group should be privileged under the law or in the classroom.

National History Standards: A digest of educational goals for K-12 history instruction developed under the auspices of the National Center for History in the Schools at the University of California, Los Angeles.

New Education: A popular movement, begun in Germany in the 19th century and exported to the United States, that sought to make education more student-centered through an emphasis of alternative methods of learning.

No Child Left Behind Act of 2001: Legislation signed into law by President George W. Bush that aimed to improve public education in the United States. It was aimed especially at poor and minority children.

Progressive Education: A continuation and elaboration of New Education ideas that took the life experiences of children as a starting point for education.

Standardized Tests: Regular subject exams given to elementary and secondary school students at various stages in their pre-college career. They are designed to track student progress and identify gaps in student knowledge.

Matt Donnelly

BIBLIOGRAPHY

Ballard, M. (1970), Ed. *New movements in the study and teaching of history.* Bloomington: Indiana University Press.

Bransford, J.D., and M.S. Donovan, eds. (2004). *How students learn: History in the classroom.* [Electronic version]. Washington, D.C.: National Academies Press. Retrieved March 6, 2007, from National Academies Press, http://nap.edu.

Cercadillo, L. (December 2006). 'Maybe they haven't decided yet what is right:' English and Spanish perspectives on teaching historical significance. *Teaching History* 125. Retrieved March 9, 2007, from ESBCO Online Database Education Research Complete.

Formwalt, L.W. (October, 2002). Seven rules for effective history teaching or bringing life to the history class. *OAH Magazine of History.* Retrieved March 9, 2007, from Organization of American Historians, http://oah.org.

Martell, C. C. (2013). Learning to teach history as interpretation: A longitudinal study of beginning teachers. *Journal Of Social Studies Research, 37,* 17–31. Retrieved December 10, 2013, from EBSCO Online Database Education Research Complete.

McClymer, J. (2006). *The AHA guide to teaching and learning with new media.* Washington, D.C.: American Historical Association. Retrieved March 9, 2007, from American Historical Association, http://historians.org.

McCrum, E. (2013). History teachers' thinking about the nature of their subject. *Teaching & Teacher Education,* 3573–80. Retrieved December 10, 2013, from EBSCO Online Database Education Research Complete.

McMurry, D. (1946). *Herbertian contributions to history instruction in American elementary schools.* New York: Bureau of Publications, Teacher's College, Columbia University.

National Board for Professional Teaching Standards (2002, October). What teachers should know and be able to do. Retrieved March 7, 2007, from National Board for Professional Teaching Standards, http://nbpts.org.

National Center for History in the Schools (1996). National standards for history basic edition, 1996. National Center for History in the Schools, University of California, Los Angeles. Retrieved March 6, 2007, from National Center for History in the Schools, http://nchs.ucla.edu.

Snowman J. and Biehler, R. (2006). *Psychology applied to teaching.* 11th ed. Boston and New York: Houghton Mifflin.

Symcox, L. (2002). *Whose history? The struggle for national standards in American classrooms.* New York and London: Teacher's College Press.

National Institute on Media and the Family (2005, April 9). Violent video games as exemplary teachers. Retrieved March 22, 2007, from http://mediafamily.org.

Weber, W. (2012). The evolution of the history teacher and the reform of history education. *History Teacher, 45,* 329–357. Retrieved December 10, 2013, from EBSCO Online Database Education Research Complete.

SUGGESTED READING

Brown, S. D. and Patrick, J. (2006). History education in the United States: A survey of teacher certification and state-based standards and assessments for teachers and students. Bloomington: Organization of American Historians. Retrieved March 8, 2007, from Organization of American Historians, http://oah.org.

Bruner, J. (1963). *The process of education.* Cambridge, MA: Harvard University Press.

Carr, E. H. (1961). *What is history?* New York: Macmillan.

Carretero, M. and Vass, J. F. (1994). *Cognitive and instructional processes in history and the social studies.* Hillsdale, NJ: Lawrence Erlbaum Associates.

Elton, G.K. (1967). *The practice of history.* New York: Thomas Crowell.

Gosden, P. H. J. H. And Sylvester, D.W. (1968). *History for the average child.* Oxford: Basil Blackwell.

Steeves, K. A. (n.d.). Building successful collaborations to enhance history teaching in secondary schools. Retrieved March 8, 2007 from American Historical Association, http://historians.org/pubs/Free/steeves/

Trinkle, D. A. and Merriman, S. A., eds. (2001). *History. edu: Essays on teaching with technology.* Armonk, NY: M.E. Sharpe.

Wallulis, J. (2012). The 'different mirror' of multicultural history. *Widening Participation & Lifelong Learning, 13*87–92. Retrieved December 10, 2013, from EBSCO Online Database Education Research Complete.

Yonghee, S. (2013). Past looking: Using arts as historical evidence in teaching history. *Social Studies Research & Practice, 8,* 135–159. Retrieved December 10, 2013, from EBSCO Online Database Education Research Complete.

TEACHING SCIENCE IN U.S. PUBLIC SCHOOLS

The widespread teaching of science was one of the last major subjects introduced into the American classroom in the early years of the twentieth century. Previously, science as a subject was reserved for colleges, universities, and the elite high schools that prepared the small percentage of nineteenth century American students entering post-secondary education. The teaching of science, like most subjects in the U.S. public school system, varies widely from region to region and district to district. Much of the conversation on public school science education has been on the falling standardized test scores in math and science. The concern has been that, while the rest of the world emphasizes the teaching of these subjects, American schools, students, and teachers have fallen behind in them.

KEYWORDS: Creationism; Evolution; Inquiry-based Learning; National Defense Education Act; National Research Council of the National Academies; National Science Education Standards; No Child Left Behind; Pedagogy; Scientific Inquiry; Scopes Trial; Smith-Hughes Act; Theory of Evolution

OVERVIEW

The teaching of science, like most subjects in the U.S. public school system, varies widely from region to region and district to district. It is the responsibility of the individual state boards of education to develop and issue the subject matter requirements, proficiency levels, and curriculum guidelines to be used by each of the school districts located in that state. The individual districts then develop curriculum and specify the teaching method to be utilized in meeting the state requirements for that subject. Science is one of the core subjects taught in American schools and is now one of the educational components covered by the No Child Left behind Act of 2001 (NCLB), which sets federal proficiency standards for the nation's schools ("Executive Summary," 2002). Science proficiency assessments are required for all public schools and have been since the 2007–2008 school year.

There has been a great deal of attention paid to the state of America's public schools in recent years. Much of that focus has been on the dropping test scores in math and science on standardized tests. The concern has been that, while the rest of the world emphasizes the teaching of these hard subjects, American schools, students, and teachers have fallen behind in them. Teicher (2005) reported that, "93 percent of public school students in Grades 5 through 8 learn physical science from teachers who do not have a college major or certification in the subject (based on data from the year 2000), for math students, that figure is 69 percent." Data collected by the World Policy Analysis Center and published in 2013 confirmed that the United States is lagging behind the majority of countries in its requirements for teachers of upper secondary-level courses (Brady, 2013). Also, "most K through 6 classrooms have science education for about 16 minutes a day" (Teicher). A 2009 study found that fifteen-year-olds in the United States placed twenty-third in science and thirty-first in math out of sixty-five countries polled (Scientific American, 2012). Of even more concern, the more diverse and economically behind a school's student population is, the more likely they will be taught science by teachers who do not have a major in the subject or who are not at least certified to teach it. Secondary students who attend schools that are high in poverty and minorities are often more likely to have an instructor who is inexperienced and not certified in the subject they are teaching (Taber, 2006).

In addition to these concerns about national standards, there is the issue of how to teach students such complex subjects as science. A pedagogical method in which science is taught level by level (elementary, middle, and secondary schools) is not specified by the federal government. In most public schools, the teaching model is likely to follow the method already in use in the district.

HISTORY

During the nineteenth century, the vast majority of schools taught a very basic curriculum consisting of reading, writing, and limited arithmetic. Science was not a subject generally taught in elementary schools. The teaching of science in school was basically limited to the few high schools in each state (most of which were not public) that served as college preparatory conduits for the fewer than ten percent of students that went on to college. This system was tailored to the requirements of the nation's population that was overwhelmingly rural and the agriculturally based economy that was extant during this period. Science was simply not one of the very basic skills required by most Americans of the time.

After the turn of the twentieth century and with the advent of the industrial revolution, it became apparent that the traditional public school curriculum was not preparing students for the requirements of the new paradigm. With the establishment of public high schools in all states, and the subsequent increase in high school enrollment, steps were taken to expand the curriculum of high schools to include not only a college preparatory tract, but a separate vocational tract for the majority of students who would not be going on to college. Change, however, came slowly and the teaching of science—particularly evolutionary science—was slow to enter the main stream of public school instruction. The 1925 Scopes "Monkey Trial" held in Dayton, Tennessee, is an example of how a variety of obstacles such as the lack of qualified teachers, religious objections, and other limiting factors served the old ways of teachings well into the 1930s. It was then that the Great Depression began to

force changes in school curriculum, the subject matter taught, and the teaching methods used.

The Second World War served as the catalyst for modernizing America's school system, as the demands of the war effort were paramount. Huge technological advances were made during the war that required the population to be educated and skilled in ways never previously imagined by the nation's educators. The Cold War that followed and the subsequent missile and space race with the Soviet Union resulted in the passage in 1958 by the US Congress of the National Defense Education Act. This was legislation aimed at improving the teaching of math and sciences in the public schools, while the space race of the 1960s continued the focus on science education.

As the pace of scientific discovery has raced ahead, schools have struggled to keep pace with these changes. Many different methods and approaches were developed, but it is apparent that there has been a marked decline in the last forty years in our student's abilities in the subject. With this apparent to almost all segments of the population, economy, and government, there have been increasingly pointed questions about our educational system's ability to meet the challenge of producing students well versed in science subjects. With the passage of the NCLB, a widening national spotlight has been shone on the deficiencies of science in many of our schools, even though the legislation itself has been the subject of wide debate on its overall effect on the quality of education as a whole.

TEACHER QUALIFICATIONS

Science teachers in the public school system must meet basic qualification requirements, as do teachers of all other subject areas. According to the U.S. Bureau of Labor Statistics' occupational handbook, high school teachers must hold a bachelors degree, have attended an approved teachers educational program, and they must hold a teaching license from the state in which they teach (Bureau of Labor Statistics, 2010). Elementary school teachers (usually grades K–5 or 6) typically teach several different subjects either singly or in conjunction with one or more other instructors to either one class, or a defined grouping of pupils. Science may be within their teaching purview. However, some districts may have a single teacher instructing one specialized subject, such as

English, science, math, or art to several groups of students, while multi-level teaching is another method used by schools in which one teacher may teach to several different grades of students.

SCIENCE IN THE SCHOOLS

Elementary school science programs focus on introducing students to the subject with hands-on techniques and a basic awareness of the subject in kindergarten, then graduating to more complex, academically focused instruction as they progress in grade level.

Teaching aids and materials such as computers, books, games, modular kits, and audiovisual materials as well as primary source experiences may all be used to enhance the learning experience. It is during the elementary school years that students receive a basic introduction to scientific subjects and concepts such chemistry, natural sciences, and physics that are designed to prepare students for more in-depth study as they progress through middle or junior high school and on to college or university.

Upon entry into middle and secondary school, students are usually taught by teachers specializing in a single subject. Here, they receive more in-depth instruction in the various scientific disciplines and are introduced to more complex subject matter within each subject through academic instruction, field trips, and extracurricular activities. It is here that students begin to be placed in differentiated programs focusing on each student's abilities and educational aspirations ranging from remedial to advanced placement classes.

NATIONAL SCIENCE EDUCATION STANDARDS (NSES)

As with other core subjects, there is no single, nationally accepted means of teaching science. All districts and states have differing guidelines and "best practices" in regard to curriculum development and teaching methodologies. However, in 1996, the National Science Education Standards (NSES) were developed by the National Research Council as guidelines for teaching science in grades K–12. Although not every state in the nation adopted the standards, they did influence most states in developing a set of science learning standards and standardized tests in science.

The rationale behind the introduction of national teaching principles for the sciences is that all students will be taught to the same standard no matter where they attend school or in what part of the country, which then allows for the establishment of a national baseline by which to assess the progress of all US students and ensure they are receiving adequate instruction in the sciences.

The 1996 standards included:

- Establishment of long- and short-term goals for the school year that meet the requirements of local, state, and federal standards;
- Selection of subject matter, curricula, and materials tailored to the abilities, interests, and the previous knowledge of the students;
- Adoption of proper teaching and assessment strategies to facilitate effective learning and to monitor the progress of the students as they advance through the program;
- Coordination of teaching activities with other science teachers and colleagues across other disciplines and grades (National Research Council, 1996).

NEXT GENERATION SCIENCE STANDARDS (NGSS)

In 2013, the National Science Teachers Association (NSTA) released a position statement that made several recommendations for changes in the teaching of science, technology, engineering, and mathematics (STEM). The Next Generation Science Standards (NGSS) focus on active learning, as opposed to previous passive methods of learning through reading textbooks and listening to lectures, and call for a "refocusing" of K–12 science education in order to prepare students for college and for careers in science and technology (National Science Teachers Association, 2013). There standards include:

- Science education for grades K–12 should focus on the interconnectedness of science;
- The NGSS standards are expectations of student performance and are not presented as proposed curriculum;
- Learning goals for the teaching of STEM subjects should build upon one another and progress from year to year;
- The focus of STEM education should be on a number of core ideas rather than on a series of memorized facts and details;
- Science and engineering should be integrated into a curriculum beginning in Kindergarten and continued through the twelfth grade;
- The ultimate goal of the NGSS is to prepare students for "college, career, and citizenship."

- The NGSS are aligned with common core standards for English, language arts, and mathematics in order to facilitate the integration of these subject areas.

As of the end of 2013, eight US states had adopted the NGSS, and several more had taken formal steps to at least consider adoption of the standards (Higgins, 2013).

Applications

Establishment of Goals

Planning and goal setting is a critically important step in the development of an effective science teaching plan. Once the framework of the plan has been laid, both short and long term goals must be set. These goals must take into account the requirements of federal, state, and locally mandated standards.

Once the teaching plan is implemented, it must be constantly monitored to ensure that the objectives of the plan and needs of the students are being met. Flexibility is important, and the plan must be constantly modified to consider such variables as the actual versus projected progress of the students, the inclusion of teaching opportunities that arise during student inquiry, and the incorporation of topics that include local, national, and world events.

Goals for each year must be translated into coherent curricula composed of a set of topics that are broken down into specific lessons and learning activities that are progressively organized to follow the timeline of the overall teaching plan. In some cases, district policy delegates responsibility to the teacher to choose the topics, lesson plans and activities to be utilized as long as they conform to district, state, and federal standards. In other cases, the teacher utilizes pre-prescribed goals, content, and materials. In either situation, the teacher incorporates inquiry with direct experimentation in addition to the lesson plans to ensure the student's depth of understanding of the material.

Adopting Methods of Teaching & Assessment

Adopting successful teaching and assessment models is critical to the success of any science teaching plan. Learning science in the classroom is based on a sound balance of content, structured activities, and teaching methods, with an equally effective means of assessing the progress of students through the program.

Scientific inquiry based on student experience is the basis for the teaching of science in public schools. This inquiry can be carried out in the classroom, laboratory settings, or outdoor venues. The science teacher introduces students to the phenomena being investigated and guides them through the process that should be challenging but not overwhelming for those involved.

As more complex concepts are introduced by the teacher, the student's understanding of the root of the concept can be built upon by continued and expanded inquiry and information gathering utilizing multiple, reliable and authoritative sources of information and data such as libraries, audio visual resources, scientific and educational databases, and government documents and publications. Students must be taught the ability to understand and differentiate what constitutes primary and secondary sources of information and data. They must also understand the methodology used to arrive at a particular conclusion as well as what methods are actually considered to be legitimate and generally accepted by the scientific community.

Science is often best learned as a shared endeavor and students are usually organized into carefully supervised small groups and teams to undertake many of the inquiries being presented. This method gives all students the opportunity to participate in all aspects of the activity and to interact with others. This interaction and exchange of information is a proven means of enhancing the learning experience for all involved. The composition of the group is dependent upon the ages of the students, the supervision available, and the activities in which they are involved.

When giving lessons, teachers must decide what learning situation is most conducive to learning based on what is being taught. For broad areas such as lectures and general introductions, the whole classroom approach may be best, as the investigation of the phenomena becomes more in-depth, smaller group inquiry or individual work may be the best methodology. Generally, when this is the case, the learning of the simplest concepts can be achieved by individual study, as the complexity increases; small group inquiry may be more beneficial to learning. A full overview of the material with the entire class to tie everything together and to draw conclusions can be the most effective method to complete the inquiry or lesson.

COORDINATION ACROSS DISCIPLINES & LEVELS

Not only is an effective individual plan vital to the teaching of science, a coordinated overall curriculum and teaching plan that not only interconnects other subjects within the grade level but that extends across all of the other grades as well is highly desirable. Such a comprehensive plan can serve as a professional platform for teacher growth, sharing of resources, and instructional development. Districts should ensure that their science teachers have access to each other at all levels of the district as well as the time and dedicated resources to make such a comprehensive plan a reality.

SCIENCE TEACHER TURNOVER

One of the biggest issues in teaching is the high turnover in teachers in the nation's public schools. Wright (2006) calls the teaching profession "a revolving door profession" that sees 39 percent of new teachers leaving the profession in their first five years. Some of the reasons cited were low salaries, poor support from administrators, classroom discipline problems, and no input into the decision making process.

DIFFICULTIES IN THE TEACHING OF SCIENCE

- Relating to the subject—students spend too much time indoors with various technologies such as computers and often do not have many firsthand experiences with nature;
- Lack of funding to adequately teach science, which can often force teachers to pay for classroom expenses;
- The increasing size of classes, which makes it difficult to pay enough attention to each student;
- Aging facilities;
- Lack of qualifications in some teachers;
- Student's lack of interest in the sciences.

Standards-based curricula was also mentioned as a problem as it placed a heavy load of material on teachers and students (Wright).

THE INQUIRY METHOD

For most science educators today, the inquiry method, which is based on the pedagogical constructivist model of learning (itself controversial among educators), is the preferred method. It is an approach in which students are encouraged to learn through a "hands-on" environment to explore a concept and then draw their own conclusions from the data they collect, as opposed to the older rote memorization or expository method in which students memorize the material straight from textbooks, teaching materials, and lecture notes without much direct application of the material. Science as content versus method has been debated for nearly a century and it appears that the inquiry method has been judged by its peers over the years and has been found the superior (Furtak, 2005).

TEXTBOOK-BASED LEARNING

Despite the predominance of inquiry based learning and a consensus among most teachers against simply handing a student a textbook and expecting them to fully absorb or understand the material, there are those in the educational community who strongly feel that expository learning indeed has its place in the classroom. They argue that textbook-based learning can be an equally important part of science education if it is properly mediated by the teacher and fully integrated into the overall learning experience (Ulerick, n.d.). For example, if the class first takes part in a hands-on experiment, then, after collecting the data generated by that experiment and reaching their conclusions, the students can use assigned textbook reading to fully understand the conclusions they reached in the course of that experiment and learn how the collected data supports their conclusions. Supporters of expository learning argue that by providing integrated interaction through inquiry based activities and textbook based study, the synergy of the whole experience will prove much more meaningful and effective for the student's overall learning experience than either method by itself.

Viewpoints

CREATIONISM VERSUS EVOLUTION

Along with the debate over optimal teaching methods, there is also the question of what material should be presented to students under the classification of science. The foremost example of this in recent years has been the issue of Creationism in the classroom. Creationism, which is also called creation science and the theory of intelligent design, is a religious-based explanation for the origins of mankind and the physical world. Its supporters have attempted to introduce it into the classroom to be taught as science, and these efforts have been the catalyst for a firestorm of controversy that has reached all of the way to the United States Supreme Court.

Supporters of creationism argue that the theory of evolution taught in classrooms is unproven science and is not the only possible explanation for the origins of life and the world. They believe that a divine being created the universe and mankind, and they adhere to the general concept of the creation as described in the Bible.

Creationism also attempts to disprove the theory of evolution by offering alternative explanations for the scientific data the theory is based on and highlighting inconsistent areas in the theory to attempt to discredit the concept. Intelligent design, while not absolutely based on the Bible, also argues that a supernatural or divine being had a hand in the creation of all things (Teaching Science, 2000).

Supporters have had some success in introducing creationism into science classrooms either as an alternative to evolution, by having evolution labeled as "unproven science," or by attempting to ban the teaching of evolution completely. Recent cases in Pennsylvania, Kansas, Georgia, and Oklahoma have all resulted in controversy at both the local and national levels resulting in court challenges to school district's policies either over the teaching of creationism as science or a formal school policy of restricting the teaching or questioning the legitimacy of evolution. In the case of the school board in Dover, Pennsylvania, one member of the board who supported the official mandate of the discussion of intelligent design in the science program stated that while he was not attempting to impose his own views on anybody, he also felt that it was a disservice to the community not to discuss alternatives to evolution in the classroom (Teaching Science).

Opponents of creation science and intelligent design have fought back against these successes. Supporters of evolution based science point out that no scientific theory has ever been fully proven and that there is no hard scientific evidence or proof to support Creationism. Opponents also argue that proponents of creation science require a much higher standard of proof for the theory of evolution than for other commonly accepted but less controversial scientific theories and that teaching religion based concepts degrades the teaching of all sciences, since the religious explanations for ideas such as intelligent

design directly undermine the scientific method of inquiry, research, and conclusion.

Evolutionary theory supporters also believe that teaching religious-based concepts as science violates the requirement for separation of church and state and the First Amendment's ban on the government endorsement of any religion. While many are not opposed to the teaching of religion or religious beliefs in schools as part of a curriculum on world religions and history, they believe that Creationism should not be taught as science. They point to the fact that there are thousands of religions in the world and even in Christianity there are many sub-divisions of theological beliefs. How, they ask, can there not be even more confusion over which of these beliefs will or will not be taught and who will decide?

Citing US Supreme Court rulings in 1962 and 1968 (Teaching Science), opponents have successfully challenged school boards in all of these cases in federal court and have won rulings that supported their argument that Creationism was not science. Also, most members of those school boards who supported such measure were subsequently voted out of office in the next elections. However, the battle is far from over as both sides vow to continue their campaigns either for or against the issue, and the subject remains a hotly contested issue in many parts of the country.

CONCLUSION

Science is the driving force behind much of our way of life. Whether it is advances in medicine, research, manufacturing, agriculture, or ways to improve our standard of living at home, science is an integral and absolutely vital component in all of these. It has only been a hundred years since science education was considered an exotic subject in our public schools, and few were required to have any background in it. Today, an educational curriculum without it would be unthinkable.

TERMS & CONCEPTS

Creationism: The religious belief that life and the planet Earth were created by a deity.

Evolution: The modification in the inherited traits in a species from one generation to the next

National Defense Education Act: An act of Congress that was passed in 1958 to provide aid to public and private education in the United States at all levels. It was spurred by Soviet success in the space race.

National Science Education Standards: A set of science education rules for science education in primary and secondary schools in America. They were created in 1996 by the National Research Council and set goals for instructors to provide for their students and for administrators to professionally develop.

No Child Left Behind: A federal law passed in 2001 that reauthorizes federal programs that aim to improve performance in US primary and secondary schools.

Pedagogy: The strategies of instruction.

Scientific Inquiry: The variety of methods that scientists use to examine the world, collect evidence, and apply tested explanations.

Angelia Mance

BIBLIOGRAPHY

Anti-Defamation League. (2000). *Teaching Science, Not Dogma: The Creationism Controversy.* Retrieved on July 4, 2007, from http://adl.org.

Brady, Heather. (2013, March 21). The US's low standards for teacher training: Country-by-country training requirements for high school teachers. *Slate.* Retrieved December 21, 2013, from http://slate.com.

Bureau of Labor Statistics. (2010). High school teachers. *Occupational Outlook Handbook.* Retrieved December 21, 2013, from http://bls.gov.

Executive Summary, No Child Left Behind Act. (2002). Retrieved June 10, 2007, from U.S. Department of Education http://ed.gov.

Fisher, P. J., & Blachowicz, C. Z. (2013). A few words about math and science. *Educational Leadership, 71,* 46–51. Retrieved December 20, 2013, from EBSCO Online Database Education Research Complete.

Furtak, E. & Ruiz-Primo, M. (2005). Questioning cycle: Making students' thinking explicit during scientific inquiry. *Science Scope, 28,* 22-25. Retrieved October 22, 2007, from EBSCO Online Database Education Research Complete.

Haury, D. (1993). *Teaching science through inquiry.* Retrieved July 3, 2007, from http://ericdigests.org.

Higgins, John. (2013, October 3). Washington to adopt 'Next Gen' science standards. *Seattle Times.* Retrieved December 21, 2013, from http://seattletimes.com.

Jimenez-Silva, M., Gomez, C., & Walters, M. (2013). Science circus. *Science Scope, 36,* 24–31. Retrieved December 20, 2013, from EBSCO Online Database Education Research Complete.

National Research Council. (1996). *National Science Education Standards.* Retrieved December 21, 2013, from http://nap.edu.

National Science Teachers Association. (2013). NSTA position statement: The next generation science standards. Retrieved December 21, 2013, from http://nsta.org.

Robelen, E. W. (2013). Standards in science unveiled. *Education Week, 32,* 1–13. Retrieved December 20, 2013, from EBSCO Online Database Education Research Complete.

Scientific American. (2012, August 8). US should adopt higher standards for science education. Retrieved December 21, 2013, from http://scientificamerican.com.

Taber, K., Cooke, M., Trafford, T., Lowe, T., Millins, S., & Quail, T. (2006). Learning to teach about 'ideas and evidence' in science: experiences of teachers-in-training. *School Science Review, 87,* 63-73. Retrieved October 22, 2007, from EBSCO Online Database Education Research Complete.

Teicher, S. (2005, December 1). The mystery of teaching science solved! *Christian Science Monitor.* Retrieved June 10, 2007, from http://csmonitor.com.

Ulerick, S. (n.d.) *Using textbooks for meaningful learning in science.* Retrieved July 3, 2007, from NARST, http://narst.org.

U.S. Bureau of Labor Statistics. (2007). *Occupational Outlook Handbook.* Retrieved July 10, 2007, from http://bls.gov.

Wright, D. (2006, October). Teaching science in public high schools. *Science and Technology Newsletter.* Retrieved July 2, 2007, from Bryn Mawr College, http://brynmawr.edu.

SUGGESTED READING

Basken, P. (2013). Crusader for science teaching finds colleges slow to change. *Chronicle of Higher Education, 59,* A6–A7. Retrieved December 20, 2013, from EBSCO Online Database Education Research Complete.

Gallagher, J. (2006). *Teaching science for understanding: a practical guide for middle and high school teachers.* Upper Saddle River, NJ: Prentice Hall.

Keeley, P. (2013). Is it a solid? Claim cards and argumentation. *Science & Children, 59,* 26–28. Retrieved December 20, 2013, from EBSCO Online Database Education Research Complete.

King, K. (2006). *Integrating the National Science Education Standards into classroom practice.* Upper Saddle River, NJ: Prentice Hall.

Krajcik, J., Czerniak, C., Berger, C.F. & C. Berger. (2002). *Teaching science in elementary and middle school classrooms: a project-based approach.* New York, NY: McGraw Hill.

Llewellyn, D. (2004). *Teaching high school science through inquiry: a case study approach.* Thousand Oaks, CA: Corwin Press.

Marco-Bujosa, L.M. & Levy, A. (2016). Caught in the balance: An organizational analysis of science teaching in schools with elementary science specialists. *Science Education*. 100(6), 983-1008.

Moyer, R. (2006). *Teaching science as investigations: modeling inquiry through learning cycle lessons*. Upper Saddle River, NJ: Prentice Hall.

Osborne, M. (1999). *Examining science teaching in elementary school from the perspective of a teacher and learner*. London: Routledge Falmer Publishers.

Raizen, S. (1996). *Bold ventures-volume 2: Case studies of U.S. Innovations in science education*. New York, NY: Spring Publishing.

Subramaniam, K. (2016). Teachers' organization of participation structures for teaching science with computer technology. *Journal of Science Education* and Technology. 25(4), 527-540.

Sunal, D. (2014). *Research Based Undergraduate Science Teaching. Series: Research in Science Education*. Charlotte, NC.: Information Age Publishing.

TEACHING SOCIAL STUDIES

This article discusses the teaching of K-12 social studies in the United States. Social studies is the name given to a constellation of interrelated disciplines—including economics, political science, geography, history and civics—that are intended to provide students an increasingly sophisticated understanding and appreciation of themselves, our society, and the experiences of others in societies around the world.

KEYWORDS: Constructivism; Educational Psychology; Multiple Intelligences; National Council for the Social Studies (NCSS); No Child Left Behind Act of 2001; Objectivism Progressive Education; Standardized Tests

OVERVIEW

The basic pattern for social studies education was established by the 1916 report of the National Education Association's Committee on Social Studies. However, in the century since social studies was established as a proper subject in U.S. public schools, many education experts have lamented that students have been subjected to a program of study that emphasizes rote memorization over critical thinking and an in-depth understanding of the subject matter.

According to a formal definition issued by the National Council for the Social Studies (NCSS), "Social studies is the integrated study of the social sciences and humanities to promote civic competence. The primary purpose of social studies is to help young people develop the ability to make informed and reasoned decisions for the public good as citizens of a culturally diverse, democratic society in an interdependent world" (National Council for the Social Studies, 1994).

Unlike English and math, which have been fixtures on the American educational landscape since the founding of the country, social studies has a much more recent history. Its roots can be traced back to the Industrial Revolution that swept Great Britain and the United States in the early nineteenth century. Beginning with the British textile industry in the late eighteenth century, machinery began to change the way business was conducted on both sides of the Atlantic. Inventors harnessed the awesome energy of water and coal, and workers crammed into cities like London and Manchester to work in the factories that began to mass produce consumer goods.

Industrialization reached the United States as well, and one side effect was the growth of the American city. In 1860 there were only sixteen cities with a population over 50,000, but by 1900 there were seventy-eight (Walker, 1967). Immigrants who sought a better life for themselves and their families poured into this land of plenty: ten million came between 1865 and 1890 (Johnson, 1998). "By 1890 New York had half as many Italians as Naples, as many Germans as Hamburg, twice as many Irish as Dublin, and two and a half times as many Jews as Warsaw" (Davidson, 1951).

Such rapid industrialization did not come without a human cost, however. For the common people, political corruption, big business, and the rise of industry seemed to be conspiring—intentionally or not—against their happiness and the economic well-being of their families. In the context of their own lives, these realities raised some troubling questions for many Americans: How could good citizens help reduce the ills of society? How should one's quest for individual rights and economic opportunities be reconciled with the needs of society? In what ways could Americans understand their place within the world?

Social Studies was the result of efforts to bring about improvements in social welfare—one student at a time. Not surprisingly, the term "social studies" goes back a to 1887 book on conditions of urban workers, where it was proposed as a tool to improve social welfare (Saxe, 1991). Social welfare activists understood that to enact positive changes in society at large, the individual members of that society must be taught about their roles and responsibilities as citizens. That meant education.

The first serious attempts in the United States to conceptualize the discipline that would become known as social studies began at the turn of the twentieth century. In 1896, Conway MacMillan, an education professor at the University of Minnesota, advocated the use of education to form students into social rather than non-social individuals, though he didn't use the term social studies. A year later Edmund James, president of the American Academy of Political and Social Science, called for inclusion of social studies in the public school curriculum, but he predicted that his dream would take another generation or two to become reality (Saxe).

In 1905, Arthur E. Dunn, who would later chair the Social Studies Committee of the National Education Association, called for "social study" or "society study" (Saxe). While he believed that sociology should be taught only in colleges and universities, Dunn argued that a less demanding version of sociology in the form of "social study" or "society study" should be taught in all public schools.

The first formalized proposal for "social study" was given by David Snedden, a professor at Teachers College, Columbia University, in 1907. He said it should be one of the five parts of the school curriculum, along with physical education, vocational education, cultural education, and "the education which aims at general mental discipline" (Saxe).

These early proposals were made in the context of calls from progressive educators like John Dewey to orient the educational system around the needs of the child. Dewey and others argued that the teacher should be an advisor, a "Socratic midwife," helping students give birth to their own ideas through critical inquiry (Dewey, 1916). These

educators recommended communal learning and the development of problem-solving skills over rote memorization.

Progressive ideas dovetailed with calls for social studies instruction to produce more thoughtful citizens. In 1912 the National Education Association formed the Committee on Social Science as part of its Reorganization of Secondary School Studies. By the time the committee was ready to issue its preliminary report a year later, it had renamed itself the Committee on Social Studies. The committee's dual goals were "improv[ing] the citizenship of the land" and "the development in the pupil of a constructive attitude in the consideration of all social conditions" (cited in Glasheen, 1973). While all education was to contribute to the betterment of society, social studies was particularly focused on that aim. Generally, for the committee and for Dewey, all education "must be a part of, not apart from, society" (Glasheen).

In its 63-page final report, issued in 1916, the 21-member committee recommended a two-cycle program of social studies for grades 7-12: Cycle One and Cycle Two Grade 7: Geography and European History; Grade 10: European History; Grade 8: U.S. History and Civics Grade 11: U.S. History Grade 9: Civics Grade 12: Problems of American Democracy. The members of the committee briefly covered elementary school Social Studies, noting that it was centered on the study of geography, social institutions, and the like. They were confident that this course of study was laying the necessary foundation for secondary school Social Studies.

At the time, a large number of students completed their schooling by ninth grade. The intention of the committee members was for students in grades 7-9 to gain a basic understanding of Social Studies in case they were completing their education, and for students in grades 10-12 to gain a more complete mastery of the material in preparation for undergraduate studies in sociology, history, political science, and other fields.

However, as a warning to those who would slavishly follow the letter of the report, the members of the committee emphasized that their guidelines were precisely that. Twice quoting a relevant passage from Dewey, the members stressed that the needs and interests of the particular students in the classroom should weigh heavily in the creation of classroom assignments and discussion topics (Glasheen). The members added that this approach would result in the mastery of material related to the topics under discussion, though not necessarily the "mastery of a comprehensive body of knowledge" (Glasheen). More specifically, the committee recommended teaching by "the problem method" (Glasheen), wherein teachers would ask questions to spur their students to think carefully and creatively about the topic at hand. This would enable a multidisciplinary approach to addressing a given topic. The members argued that this approach would engage young minds by drawing upon their inherent interest in events taking place around them. All of this thinking was directed toward the goal of creating a self-sacrificing, "socially efficient person" who would better society as a whole (Glasheen).

By 1924, one-third of schools had adopted the NEA's proposal for two three-year cycles for teaching secondary school Social Studies (Hertzberg, 1981), and the committee's guidelines continue to dominate Social Studies education to this day. The typical secondary school Social Studies curriculum echoes that of a century ago, though with some changes to make the coursework less Eurocentric:

Cycle One Cycle Two Grade 7: World History/ Cultures/Geography: Grade 10 World Culture/ History Grade 8: U.S. History Grade 11: U.S. History Grade 9: Civics/Government or World Cultures/ History Grade 12: American Government and Sociology/Psychology.

CONSTRUCTIVISM VS. OBJECTIVISM

Some of the debate about the state of Social Studies education centers on two philosophical theories of knowledge that have often been pitted against each other: constructivism and objectivism.

Constructivism places emphasis on interdisciplinary approaches and synthesizing ideas. "Constructed knowledge is embedded in one's own authentic personal experience" (Boyer & Semrau, 1995). Constructivist theory privileges asking questions, not memorizing answers, and it calls for critical thinking and self-reflection. Objectivism places less importance on experience and instead emphasizes the accumulation of objective knowledge in the form of facts. In some respects, constructivism and objectivism present a false dichotomy. Jerome Bruner, in his influential book "The Process of Education," argued that facts (objectivism) are a necessary prerequisite for critical thinking (constructivism).

THEMES IN SOCIAL STUDIES

In an attempt to explicate suggested national guidelines for social studies teaching, the National Council for the Social Studies highlighted several themes in 1994 and revised them in 2010. Taken together, these themes form the framework for effective Social Studies instruction.

- **Culture:** What is culture? What role does culture play in the development of people and societies? How are cultures different from one another? How are they alike? How does unity form within a culture and among cultures? What role does diversity play in a culture and how is maintained? How and why do cultures change over time? How do cultures spread within and across communities, regions, and nations? What are the various aspects of culture and how do they influence other aspects of culture?

- **Time, Continuity, and Change:** How do we learn about the past? How can we evaluate the usefulness and reliability of different historical sources? What are the roots of our social, political, and economic systems? What are our personal roots and how are they part of human history? Why is the past important to the present? How has the world changed and how might it change in the future? How do perspectives about the past differ and how do these differences influence current ideas and actions?

- **People, Places, and Environments:** What do people consider when they decide where to live? Why do they decide to stay where they are or move? Why is location important? How do people interact with the environment and what are the consequences? What physical and other characteristics lead to the creation of regions? How do maps, globes, geographic tools, and geospatial technologies help us understand people, places, and environments?

- **Individual Development and Identity:** How do individuals grow and change over time? Why do individuals behave the way they do? What influences the way that people learn, perceive, and grow? How do people meet their needs in different times, places, and environments? How do social, political, and cultural interactions support identity development? How are development and identity defined in other times and places?

- **Individuals, Groups, and Institutions:** What is an institution? How do institutions impact the wider society, and how does the wider society impact the institutions? What is the role of institutions in my society and other societies? How do institutions influence me and other individuals? How do institutions change, and what is my role in such change?

- **Power, Authority, and Governance:** What are the purposes and functions of government? What are legitimate and illegitimate uses of political power and authority? What are the proper scope and limits of authority? How are individual rights protected or challenged within the context of majority rule? What conflicts exist among fundamental principles and values of constitutional democracy? What are the rights and responsibilities of citizens within a constitutional democracy?

- **Production, Distribution, and Consumption:** What should society produce? What is the best and most equitable distribution of goods and services? What factors influence decision making regarding production, distribution, and consumption of goods? What are the best ways to deal with market failures? How does the interdependence of globalization impact local economies and social systems?

- **Science, Technology, and Society:** What can the past teach us about the way technology brings about broad social change, some of which is unanticipated? Is new technology always better than current or outdated technology? How can individuals and society deal with the increasing pace of technological change and the concern that technology could grow out of control? How can we manage technology so the most people benefit from it? How do science and technology affect our sense of self and morality? How are disparate cultures brought together by technology? What are some of the strengths, weaknesses, benefits, and challenges of this interconnectedness? How can we preserve fundamental beliefs and values in an increasingly interconnected world? How can access gaps be bridged?

- **Global Connections:** What are the different types of global connections? What types of connections existed in the past, exist now, and may exist in the future? How do ideas spread between societies today, and what impact do these ideas have on different societies? What are other consequences of global connections? What are the benefits and problems of global interdependence? Do people

from different parts of the world have different perspectives on the benefits and problems? What influence has global interdependence had on international migration patterns? How should people and societies balance global connectedness with local needs? What do individuals need to thrive in an ever changing and increasingly interdependent planet?

- **Civic Ideals and Practices:** What are the democratic ideals and practices of a constitutional democracy? What is the balance between rights and responsibilities? What is civic participation? How do citizens become involved? What is the role of a citizen in the community, nation, and world community? (National Council for the Social Studies).

STAGES OF STUDENT DEVELOPMENT

There is a large and growing body of literature in the field of educational psychology that seeks to apply the work of developmental psychologists to the interactions between teachers and students. In order to achieve a high level of professional success and satisfaction, teachers seek to understand the moral, intellectual, and emotional development of their students.

Though they differ on important details, psychologists such as Erik Erickson, Jean Piaget, and Lev Vygotsky have stressed that students go through stages of cognitive, emotional, and moral development. As applied to Social Studies teaching, these stages should determine the nature of the lessons, how they are presented, and the methods of student evaluation that are used. Piaget suggested, for example, that high school history students should be encouraged to work in small groups and use alternative methods of learning such as dialogues and mock trials because they have reached the third level of cognitive development he called Formal Operational Thinking. Students in elementary school, by contrast, are more literal thinkers who are less likely to think about social studies in abstract terms.

LEARNING STYLES & MULTIPLE INTELLIGENCES

The influential work of Howard Gardner and others shows that just as students come to the Social Studies classroom with different conceptions about the relevance of Social Studies to their own lives and communities, so they also come with different learning styles or ways of learning. The theory of multiple intelligences holds that in any given Social Studies classroom, students approach learning in different, but complementary ways.

There are several types of intelligence that Social Studies instructors must take into account when preparing and teaching lessons:

- **Interpersonal intelligence:** Student works well in groups;
- **Intrapersonal intelligence:** Student is self-directed, focused on achieving the goal;
- **Linguistic intelligence:** Student learns primarily through words;
- **Mathematical and logical intelligence:** Student detects patterns; uses logic to solve problems;
- **Visual and spatial intelligence:** Student learns through observation and visualization;
- **Kinesthetic intelligence:** Student learns best by doing;
- **Musical intelligence:** Student is adept at detecting tones, rhythms, and music;
- **Naturalist intelligence:** Student is at home in nature (Gardner 1983; 1993).

Skilled teachers will seek to recognize students with these intelligences, thereby making the subject matter more appealing to all students.

The Role of the Internet in Social Studies Teaching

The rise of the Internet in the mid-1990s brought with it the potential for a significant impact on classroom instruction. Now, rather than relying almost exclusively on the textbook, students and their teachers are exposed to a broad range of content, including audio and video. As applied to Social Studies, teachers are now able to draw upon a vast collection of primary source material in preparing lessons, and they are also able to communicate—via email, instant messaging, blogs, chat rooms, or videoconferencing—with other social studies teachers around the world to discuss best practices or even gain encouragement in challenging classroom situations. A simple web search reveals tens of thousands of constantly-evolving resources, and these practical resources dovetail with the global academic conferences on Social Studies teaching put together by groups such as the National Council for the Social Studies. Beyond lesson plans and collegial benefits for teachers, the

Internet also brings with it the potential to engage those students who do not learn best from reading or oral instruction. Through streaming audio, video, and other content available online, history teachers can enrich both the learning experience of students with a broad, preexisting interest in social studies and the learning experience of those students who may have struggled with the topic. Some argue that the use of multimedia in the classroom is also a better way to engage students who have been raised on a steady diet of television, movies, and video games.

Challenges Facing Social Studies Education

Despite the best intentions of Dewey and other progressive educators on the 1916 social studies Committee, there have been a number of problems with Social Studies instruction over the past century. While they stressed the need for students to become more active learners, many experts agree that the emphasis in the Social Studies classroom has continued to be on textbook-based learning, with a low percentage of teachers using creative approaches to engaging the minds of their students. In 1961, Charles R. Keller drew a similar conclusion regarding the prevailing methodology of Social Studies teachers: "The time has come to take a searching look at the social studies in American schools, to ask why nothing significant is happening in this area, and to make suggestions for change. A revolution is needed, and soon" (Keller, 1961, cited in Herbert & Murphy, 1968).

With respect to the content of the Social Studies curriculum, Keller chided educators for following the recommendations of the 1916 committee too religiously by deemphasizing sequential learning in favor of more ad hoc, impressionistic approaches tailored wholly to the classroom discussion of a given topic. More specifically, Keller argued that students in the midst of the Cold War were being schooled in patriotism, but not taught the basics of geography, American government, and American history. Teachers and administrators had it backwards: "Democratic attitudes and good citizenship can be important by-products of effective rearing and teaching," he wrote (Keller, cited in Herbert & Murphy). Keller advocated sequential coursework that would build upon itself: as students progressed in school, they would go from learning about concrete events to discussing abstract principles, with the goal of developing skills in "analysis, critical thinking, and interpretation."

From all indications, Social Studies teaching in the United States continues to be plagued by underlying tensions. Caron (2004) provides a summary of the literature regarding Social Studies instruction and corresponding student attitudes:

"The listlessness of secondary social studies instruction is well-documented. Critics describe social studies instruction as fragmented and expository, brought about by an overstuffed curriculum that privileges rote learning at the expense of in-depth analysis of issues (Evans, 1989; Evans et al., 1999; Goodlad, 1984; Newmann, 1988; Onosko, 1996b, 1996a, 1992; Sizer, 1985; Wiggins, 1989). Knowledge is often taught as a series of facts to be learned rather than as an opportunity to raise questions and confront societal or historical problems. Students are taught "as if there are simple answers to the questions we have about the nature of society, or worse, [they are] taught without asking those questions for which there are no answers" (Bloom and Ochoa, 1996).

Teachers continue to rely on the textbook as the primary source for organizing their course (Chiodo and Byford, 2004; Shaughnessy & Haladyna, 1985), and classroom discussions and assessments frequently require students to reproduce answers already given to them rather than encourage higher-level reasoning and decision making (Shaver, Davis, and Helburn, 1979). Given these data, it is hardly surprising that students consistently rate Social Studies as one of their least favorite subjects (Goodlad; Owens, 1997; Remy, 1972; Rossi, 1995; Shaver et al., 1979; Snug, Todd, and Beery, 1984). High school students also report that social studies classes present very little new knowledge, particularly when compared to other core subjects such as science, mathematics, and literature (Remy). National studies and reports continue to show significant percentages of high school students lacking knowledge of the basic facts of American history, government, and geography" (Ravitch and Finn, 1988; Schlafly, 2003; Lapp et al., 2002; Lutkus et al., 1999; Weiss et al., 2002).

It is not entirely clear why implementing the recommendations of the 1916 committee—as well as those of like-minded groups since—has proven so difficult, but a few hints at a more comprehensive answer have been provided by social scientists in Caron:

"First and foremost, many teachers are reluctant to relinquish the control necessary to facilitate the discussion and debate of issues (Gross, 1989; Onosko, 1996). Encouraging students to take more ownership in their own learning can be a risky proposition for educators, particularly in light of the premium many teachers and administrators place on well-managed classrooms. In addition, practitioners have little exposure to issue or problem-based teaching in their own K-12 school experience, making the approach especially difficult for which to plan or organize (Gross; Koeppen, 1999; Onosko). Furthermore, issue-based curricula is hard to accommodate with the limited treatment textbooks and instructional materials give to civics or history-related problem areas (Gross; Onosko)" (Caron).

NATIONAL STANDARDS & STANDARDIZED TESTING

Political realities have also impinged upon the effective teaching of Social Studies, at least in the lower grades. In the first decade of the twenty-first century, elementary Social Studies education was impacted by the No Child Left Behind Act of 2001 (NCLB), which began to require teachers to prepare students to take standardized tests once it was signed into law by President George W. Bush in 2002. Because Social Studies is not a subject covered by the tests, it has received less attention during the school day than tested subjects (Hutton, Curtis, & Burstein 2006). The result is that many elementary students are entering 7-12 social studies with an inadequate understanding of the subject, and the problem is made worse by their expectation that secondary Social Studies instruction will be based upon textbooks and the uninspiring regurgitation of answers.

As Hutton et al. note, quality Social Studies education in elementary schools is still more a dream than a reality. Without as much money at stake, there is less political pressure for the reform of Social Studies, despite the fact that it has been a subject area that has been beset by challenges and false starts for nearly a century. Given this backdrop, what does the future hold for Social Studies? With the need for American students to become more aware of their roles and responsibilities in the global village, social studies would appear more necessary than ever, despite its well-documented shortcomings. Meanwhile, the quest continues for ways to teach Social Studies more effectively.

TERMS & CONCEPTS

Constructivism: A philosophy of education that places emphasis on interdisciplinary approaches to knowledge through the synthesis of ideas. Constructivist theory privileges asking questions, not memorizing answers, and it calls for critical thinking and self-reflection.

Educational Psychology: An increasingly influential field of study that seeks to apply the findings of developmental psychology to the classroom setting.

Multiple Intelligences: The theory, popularized by Howard Gardner in the 1980s, that students have different learning styles or ways of learning that must be taken into account within the education system.

National Council for the Social Studies (NCSS): Organization founded in 1921 to promote and advocate the study of social sciences in the public school and college classroom. Membership reaches throughout the United States and represents social studies teachers, college faculty, curriculum specialists.

No Child Left Behind Act of 2001: Legislation signed into law by President George W. Bush in 2002 that aimed to improve public education in the United States. It was aimed especially at poor and minority children.

Objectivism: A philosophy of education that places less importance on experience and instead emphasizes the accumulation of objective knowledge in the form of facts.

Progressive Education: A continuation and elaboration of New Education ideas that took the life experiences of children as a starting point for education.

Social Studies: The name given to a constellation of interrelated disciplines—including economics, political science, geography, and civics—that are intended to provide students an increasingly sophisticated understanding and appreciation of themselves, their own society, and the experiences of others in societies around the world.

Standardized Tests: Regular subject exams given to elementary and secondary school subjects at various stages in their pre-college career. They are designed to track student progress and identify gaps in student knowledge.

Matt Donnelly

BIBLIOGRAPHY

Bernstein, K. (2013). Warnings from the trenches. Academe, 99(1), 32-36. Retrieved December 11, 2013, from EBSCO Online Database Education Resource Complete.

Boyer, B. A, & Semrau, P. (1995). A constructivist approach to social studies: Integrating technology. Social Studies & the Young Learner 7 (3), pp. 14-16.

Caron, E. (2004). The impact of a methods course on teaching practices: Implementing issues-centered teaching in the secondary social studies classroom. Journal of Social Studies Research 28 (2) 4-19. Retrieved May 23, 2007, from EBSCO online database, Education Research Complete.

Davidson, M. B. (1951). Life in America. Vol. 2. Boston: Houghton Mifflin.

Ediger, M. (2004). Recent trends in the social studies. Journal of Instructional Psychology 31 (3). p. 240-45. Retrieved May 23, 2007, from EBSCO online database, Education Research Complete.

Gardner, Howard (1983; 1993) Frames of mind: The theory of multiple intelligences. New York: Basic Books.

Glasheen, P. (1973). The advent of social studies, 1916. Ed.D. dissertation. Boston: Boston University School of Education.

Heafner, T. L., & Fitchett, P. G. (2012). Tipping the scales: National trends of declining social studies instructional time in elementary schools. Journal of Social Studies Research, 36(2), 190-215. Retrieved December 11, 2013, from EBSCO Online Database Education Resource Complete.

Hertzberg, H.W. (1981). Social studies reform: 1880-1980. Boulder, CO: Social Science Education Consortium.

Hutton, L. A., Curtis, C. & Burstein, J. H. (2006). The state of elementary social studies teaching in one urban district. Journal of Social Studies Research 31 (1). 15-20. Retrieved May 23, 2007, from EBSCO online database, Education Research Complete.

Johnson, P. (1998). A history of the American people. New York: HarperCollins.

Keller, C. R. (1961). Needed: Revolution in the social studies. Saturday Review 44 (60-61), reprinted in Herbert, L. J., and W. Murphy, eds. (1968) Structure in the social studies. Social Studies Readings, Number 3. Washington, D.C.: National Council for the Social Studies.

Morrissett, I. (1981). The needs of the future and the constraints of the past. In Mehlinger, H.D. and O. L. Davis Jr., eds. The social studies. 80th Yearbook of the National Society for the Study of Education. Chicago: University of Chicago Press.

National Council for the Social Studies (1994). Expectations of excellence: Curriculum standards for social studies. Silver Spring, MD: National Council for the social studies. Abridged version Retrieved May 5, 2007, from National Council for the Social Studies, http://ncss.org.

National Council for the Social Studies (2010). National curriculum standards for social studies: Chapter 2—the themes of social studies. Retrieved on December 11, 2013, from http://socialstudies.org.

Saxe, D.W. (1991). Social studies in the schools: A history of the early years. Albany: SUNY Press.

Sunal, C. S., McCormick, T., Sunal, D. & Shwery, C. (2005). Elementary teacher candidates' construction of criteria for selecting social studies lesson plans for electronic portfolios. Journal of Social Studies Research 29 (1). 7-17. Retrieved May 6, 2007, from EBSCO online database, Education Research Complete.

Walker, R. H. (1967). Everyday life in the age of enterprise, 1865-1900. New York: G.P. Putnam's Sons.

Winstead, L. (2011). The impact of NCLB and accountability on social studies: Teacher experiences and perceptions about teaching social studies. Social Studies, 102(5), 221-227. Retrieved December 11, 2013, from EBSCO Online Database Education Resource Complete.

SUGGESTED READING

Bricker, D. C. (1989). Classroom life as civic education. New York and London: Teacher's College Press.

Bruner, J. (1963). The process of education. Cambridge, MA: Harvard University Press.

Carnegie Corporation of New York and the Center for Information & Research on Civic Learning & Engagement (2003). Campaign for the civic mission of schools. New York: Carnegie Corporation of New York. Retrieved May 7, 2007, from the Carnegie Corporation of New York and the Center for Information & Research on Civic Learning & Engagement, http://civicmission-ofschools.org.

Carretero, M. & Vass, J. F. (1994). Cognitive and instructional processes in history and the social studies. Hillsdale, NJ: Lawrence Erlbaum Associates.

Cuban, L. (1984). How teachers taught: Constancy and change in American classrooms, 1890-1980. London: Longman.

Dewey, J. (1916). Democracy and education: An introduction to the philosophy of education. New York: Macmillan. Retrieved May 13, 2007, from Project Gutenberg, http://gutenberg.org.

Hunkins, F. P. & Spears, P. F. (1973). Social studies for the evolving individual. Washington, D.C.: Association for Supervision and Curriculum Development.

Keller, C. R. (1962), History and social sciences: Reflections and recommendations. Journal of Secondary Education 37:263-70 (May 1962), pp. 509-516, reprinted in Gross, R.E., W.E. McPhie, and J.R. Fraenkel, Teaching the social studies: What, why, and how. Scranton, Pa.: International Textbook Company.

Kurtz, K. T., Rosenthal, A. & Zukin, C. (2003). Citizenship: A challenge for all generations. National Conference of State Legislatures. Retrieved May 7, 2007, from National Conference of State Legislatures, http://cpn.org.

Martell, C. C. (2013). Learning to teach history as interpretation: A longitudinal study of beginning teachers. Journal of Social Studies Research, 37(1), 17-31. Retrieved December 11, 2013, from EBSCO Online Database Education Resource Complete.

Ostrom, R. (2004). Active learning strategies for using cartoons and Internet research assignments in social studies courses. Social Studies Review. Retrieved May 6, 2007, from FindArticles, http://findarticles.com.

Rapoport, A. (2013). Global citizenship themes in the social studies classroom: Teaching devices and teachers' attitudes. Educational Forum, 77(4), 407-420. Retrieved December 11, 2013, from EBSCO Online Database Education Resource Complete.

Snowman, J. & Biehler, R. (2006). Psychology applied to teaching. 11th ed. Boston and New York: Houghton Mifflin.

Taylor, J. & Duran, M. (2006). Teaching social studies with technology: New research on collaborative approaches. History Teacher, 40 (1), pp. 9-25. Retrieved May 20, 2007, from EBSCO online database, Education Research Complete.

TEACHING FOREIGN LANGUAGES IN U.S. PUBLIC SCHOOLS

In the United States the provision of foreign language instruction at the K-12 level varies. Policy and national standard recommendations call for the development of long-term, sequential, and continuous foreign language instruction from kindergarten through grade 12 and beyond. Such instruction would enable American children to develop higher levels of linguistic proficiency as well as cultural competency in target languages. Recently, special attention has been called to the need for foreign language proficiencies, especially in less commonly taught languages that are deemed critical for national security. The ACTFL National Standards for Foreign Language Instruction provide a framework for what such programs should do within the K-12 context and beyond. Available national resources are discussed as well as the current state of K-12 national foreign language programs.

KEYWORDS: ACTFL National K-12 Foreign Language Standards; American Council of Teachers of Foreign Languages (ACTFL); Immersion; Foreign Language Experience Program (FLEX); Foreign Language in the Elementary School (FLES); Foreign Language Proficiency; Less Commonly Taught Languages (LCTL); Performance Guidelines; Proficiency Guidelines; World Languages

OVERVIEW

There are approximately 6912 spoken languages in the world (Gordon, 2005) and the United States has 311 languages. However in the United States, learning a language other than English and developing the cultural competencies that are part of foreign language learning, has not been high priority in public education (Sigsbee, 2002).

English has become the language of international business, science, politics, and the Internet. While the world understands us, we do not understand the world. People all over the world have access to our literature, intelligence, technical manuals, academic journals and our culture. But we lack the ability to do the same in other languages (National Virtual Translation Center, 2007a).

LINGUISTIC & CULTURAL ISOLATION

This one-way linguistic and cultural isolation from the world community has significant implications for the future opportunities of American K-12 students as they exit school. According to the statement put forth by the Committee for Economic Development (2006), a non-partisan, non-political, non-profit independent research organization, U.S. students lack the linguistic and cultural skills of their peers in other nations. This lack of knowledge has a negative impact not only on our national security, but on our nation's ability to progress economically in the global marketplace (Committee for Economic Development, 2006; United States Department of Education, 2006). From small businesses to multi-nationals, the ability to effectively communicate in the languages and cultures of international consumers, business partners, and employees is crucial (CED).

The Center for Applied Linguistics stated in 2006 that 24% of American public elementary schools offer foreign language instruction and that of those, a majority of the programs do not focus on foreign language proficiency. By 2013, however, that number had dropped, especially in rural school districts. Instead, the programs seek merely to expose children to foreign language and culture. Among American high schools, students who study a foreign language take Spanish, French, German, or Latin. The need for proficient speakers of Less Commonly Taught Languages, or LCTL's, (ED, 2006, CED) is urgent. Critical or Less Commonly Taught Languages are defined in the U.S. as those languages other than French, Spanish, and German (Center for Advanced Research in Second Language Acquisition, n.d.).

Only a small minority of American high school students are learning Chinese, Korean, Farsi, Arabic, Russian, Urdu, or Japanese. By 2011, however, the number of students studying Chinese had begun increasing, tripling between 2005 and 2008 and continuing to grow.

Rather than addressing national economic and security needs that require a multi-lingual and culturally competent citizenry, many schools are actually narrowing their available programs of study because of the educational reform movement. For example, the No Child Left Behind Act of 2001, which helps schools accountable in the reading, mathematics and science achievement of all students, encouraged schools to devote more time and resources to those subjects. While those subjects are critical, many students remain ill prepared as global citizens as they are not offered the opportunity to learn other languages and cultures (CED).

A CRITICAL NEED

In terms of national security, diplomats and federal employees need to be able to communicate effectively, with cultural understanding and awareness with other nations (CED). Bremer reports (as cited in CED) that in 2004, three years after 9/11, the United States Foreign Service had eight Arabic speakers at the highest proficiency level and only 27 at the next highest level of proficiency.

In view of the inadequate numbers of American citizens prepared to function in a multi-linguistic and culturally diverse global society, 300 leaders from business and industry, national, federal, state, and local government agencies, foreign nations, academia, and foreign language interest groups came together in 2004 to address the issue (NLC). They identified trends, best practices and the foreign language and culture needs at various levels of both the private and government sectors. From their work, they determined that a national foreign language strategy was needed to engage the American public and made several recommendations.

One of those recommendations was that federal, state, and local government agencies should allocate resources and establish foreign language requirements from kindergarten through advanced degrees. They further recommended that standards-based policies be applied and implemented throughout the educational pipeline and that educational systems at the primary and secondary levels (as well as beyond) ensure continuous language and cultural instruction that would lead to advanced linguistic and cultural proficiency (CED).

AN OPTIONAL NATIONAL AGENDA

While a national agenda may exist in teaching foreign languages, it is optional. It is up to each state government to decide what students must study in order to earn a high school diploma. The state responsibility is met through the local school systems. If the state does not require a continuous foreign language program or even limited foreign language instruction, local districts can and do decide, contrary to national economic and security needs, not to offer such programs. In many districts and in many states, foreign languages are simply not part of the core curriculum (Sigsbee).

For those districts and those states that value foreign language education for all students, there are resources available. In addition to the plethora of diverse state foreign language guidelines, standards, and assessments, there are national foreign language standards, national foreign language proficiency guidelines, and a growing number of federally funded (ED) national resources in second language teaching research, best practices, instructional tools and technology that can be used in the K-12 setting (Marcos, n.d.).

The first national standards in K-12 foreign language instruction were published in 1996 by the ACTFL and called the *Standards for Foreign Language Learning: Preparing for the 21st Century*. These standards were to address the definition and function of U.S. foreign language instruction in the K-12 setting

and were created based on a consensus of language educators, business, government, and other stakeholders (Marcos). They do not describe the current state of U.S. K-12 foreign language instruction, rather they describe best practices in the field and specify content standards, or what students should be able to know and do, in foreign languages (ACTFL, 1996). The second edition of the standards was published in 1999 and added information about how to apply the standards in specific languages (Marcos). The specific languages included in the national standards are: Chinese, Japanese, Russian, Classical languages, French, Spanish, German, Italian, and Portuguese (Scebold & Wallinger, 2000). The third edition, published in 2006 added Arabic specific-guidelines (ACTFL, 2006).

The ACTFL national standards support the ideal that second language instruction should begin at the elementary level and continue sequentially through the middle school and high school levels as well as beyond (ACTFL). It does not specify a curriculum or sequence of instruction but describes the learning experiences needed to achieve the standards. It is based on five goals areas critical to linguistic and cultural learning:

- Communication;
- Cultures;
- Connections;
- Comparisons;
- Communities.

The most fundamental aspect of which is communication (ACTFL).

SECOND LANGUAGE PROFICIENCY & CULTURAL COMPETENCE

Language learning is much more than the development of linguistic facility in the writing, speaking, reading, and aural comprehension of a given language. Second language proficiency means that one can effectively use the second language to communicate within specific contexts and function appropriately according to the often hidden rules of the second language community.

For example, yes does not always mean yes. Take for example, someone from a culture that is used to straightforward, even if unpleasant, responses in the business context. Imagine that she or he needs to confirm arrival of a multi-million dollar shipment by a specific time from a colleague or partner in another part of the world. When the question is asked, "Will the parts be here by such and such a date?" The answer may very well be, "Yes." Unbeknown to the requester who assumes a uniform worldview (that of his or her own culture) the person sending the parts knows that there is some doubt as to whether the shipment will be able to go out on time. However, in her or his culture it would not be appropriate to displease or offend the requester. Lack of cultural competencies in today's global economy can be expensive to those who are linguistically and culturally handicapped.

THE 5 GOALS OF ACTFL

Without cultural competency, there can be no true communication in the target language. Second language learners need to have an awareness and understanding of both the culture of "self" and the culture of "other" to successfully negotiate communication in the context of "we." What is said or written is not always indicative of what is meant. The first and second goals of communication and culture of the ACTFL Standards recognize the interdependence of culture and language (ACTFL).

The third goal, connections, permits the second language learner to access bodies of knowledge that are not available to a monolingual (ACTFL). With a second language, one can access current events, history, or recent works and discoveries in any discipline that are unknown by non-users of the second language. These connections could be to literature, art, sports, medicine, and a multitude of other areas of knowledge. For those limited to monolingual status, information and ideas are restricted.

The fourth goal of the ACTFL Standards, comparison, speaks to the necessity of second language learners to compare and contrast their own language and cultures with that of the target language and culture. These comparisons allow second language learners to better understand themselves as well as others. They enlighten the learner to the existence of a multiplicity of worldviews (ACTFL).

The fifth goal of the ACFTL National Foreign Language Standards is communities. Learners cannot develop linguistic and cultural competencies in isolation of the people who regularly use the language. Through interaction within local and global multilingual communities, second language learners can develop the ability to interact appropriately with speakers of the target language and culture (ACTFL).

Within the broad goals of communication, culture, comparisons, connections and communities, there are specific standards. Provided for the standards are general progress indicators that describe what second language learning students should be able to know and do at the 4th, 8th and 12th grade levels relative to a given standard within each goal (ACTFL). ACTFL (as cited in Kelly-Hall, 2001) designed its National Foreign Language Standards to reflect second language abilities that result from continued, sequential second language instruction from kindergarten through 12th grade. In the United States, few such programs exist (Kelly-Hall).

PROFICIENCY GUIDELINES

It is not just basic proficiency, but advanced foreign language and cultural proficiency that is necessary for the economic and national security of the United States (CED, NVTC, 2007b). What then is proficiency and what do we know about how long it takes to develop in a second language or culture?

In the United States there are two national foreign language proficiency guidelines. The first is the U.S. Government Interagency Language Roundtable (IRL) which measures second language skills in speaking, writing, reading, listening, and translation (NCVT, 2007c). The second set of guidelines, upon which the national foreign language standards for are based, were introduced by ACTFL in 1986 (Kelly-Hall).

The ACTFL foreign language proficiency guidelines address the skill areas of reading, writing, speaking and listening. In ACTFL guidelines, proficiency was divided into four levels: novice, intermediate, advanced, and superior (Kelly-Hall). Within each of the three first levels (novice, intermediate, and advanced) each level was further broken down into low, mid, and high (Language Testing International, 2004). When describing foreign language proficiency, usually, learners will have different proficiency levels across the four skill areas and each skill must be assessed individually (NCVT, 2007c).

TEACHING RESOURCES

For students in the K-12 system to develop higher levels of second language proficiency, second language instruction must begin in the early levels of K-12 education and continue sequentially through each following grade (NLC, 2005; Malone, Rifkin,

Christian, and Johnson, 2005). K-12 schools that offer foreign language programs have a variety of national tools at their disposal. For example, K-8 foreign language educators can use Ñandutí. This is a web-based resource center for K-8 foreign language practitioners originally funded by the federal government and run by the Center for Applied Linguistics. It offers a wealth of instructional materials, collaborative opportunities though its listserv, program development information, and methodology overviews (Ñandutí, 2006). The National K-12 Foreign Language Resource Center is a federally funded national resource as well that is developing a national Foreign Language in the Elementary School (FLES), K-5 Chinese program that will be available for districts nationwide (National K-12 Foreign Language Resource Center, 2003). Under the National Security Language Initiative, the federal government will be providing millions to local districts and states to develop K-16 program LCTL foreign language models that would provide sequential, continuous learning opportunities in languages identified as critical to national security. In addition, it proposes an e-based clearinghouse that would serve as a central access point for the public to the materials and web-based instructional programs in NCTL's identified as critical that have be created by already existing national resource centers (ED).

In addition to nationally funded resources, K-12 foreign language programs have many technology tools to use in providing language learning opportunities that are meaningful and motivating to technologically savvy language learners. Video and audio conferencing tools, instant messaging, web-based communities, and engaging software programs are just some of the tools for children in districts who can afford these options (LeLoup & Ponterio, 2000).

The major programs used at the elementary level are FLEX, FLES, and Immersion programs (National Council of State Supervisors of Languages, 2007). Foreign Language Experience programs (FLEX) do not have proficiency in a second language as a goal. Their purpose is to expose children to one or more foreign languages and motivate them to learn one in the future (Morrison, n.d.). FLES, or Foreign Language in the Elementary School programs do have second language proficiency as a goal. They are sequential foreign language programs that offer instruction in the four skill areas of a second

language (NCSSL, 2007) and sometimes use the second language to teach regular school curriculum (Morrison) In immersion programs, all or much or the core academic curriculum is delivered using the foreign language as the medium of instruction (NCSSL, 2007). Curtain and Pesola (as cited by Morrison) explain that immersion programs result in grade level English language arts proficiency, cross-cultural understanding, and functional second language proficiency. There are a variety of second language immersion program models that exist. Some begin at the elementary level and permit K-12 students to continue a sequence of foreign language study through graduation.

INCONSISTENT NATIONWIDE ACCESS TO FOREIGN LANGUAGE INSTRUCTION FOR K-12 STUDENTS

There is great diversity in how states are meeting the foreign language and cultural competencies of their children and nation. The state of Washington, for example, as late as 2005, had no secondary education standards for world languages. It then adopted the ACTFL national foreign language standards for its children. By adopting standards common to other states, Washington enabled its educational stakeholders and practitioners to make use of the vast materials already available at the national level and to collaborate with other states in providing foreign language instruction (Washington Association of Foreign Languages, 2006).

Minnesota, in contrast, has no state standards in world languages. Districts are to develop their own foreign language standards, if they so choose, and decide which foreign language and cultural competencies are important. Minnesota provides a state-developed booklet based on the ACTFL standards to assist individual districts. (Minnesota Department of Education, 2007).

Other states have had world language standards for much longer. New York, for example, has state standards in modern languages, Native American languages, Latin and American sign language since 1996 and has continued to revise and improve upon them. Since 1998, foreign language at the elementary level has been a New York State requirement with second language proficiency tests given to its children in 4th, 8th, and 12th grades in which they must demonstrate second language communicative skills and basic second language literacy (University of the State of New York Board of Regents, 1996). In 2011 New York dropped its Regents exams in Italian, Spanish, and French.

SHORTAGE OF FOREIGN LANGUAGE TEACHERS

While this is especially true of teachers that are proficient in LCTL's (ED, 2006) it is true for teachers of more commonly taught languages (Suhay, 1999). Each state has its own licensure standards for foreign language teachers in the public K-12 system so the requirements to practice in a given state vary. Generally, in addition to advanced proficiency in a second language as well as English, teachers must have solid foundations in the theories of second language acquisition, second language pedagogy, and educational psychology. In addition, they need expertise in the unique physiological, psychological, emotional, and cognitive learner characteristics of the specific age groups they are licensed to teach. They must complete supervised, unpaid internships. Lastly, they need to be technologically literate so that they avail their students of the vast array of resources for meaningful, communicative second learning experiences in the second language classroom.

For foreign language teachers at the K-12 level, there is limited interstate professional mobility due to a lack of uniform licensure standards and reciprocity agreements. As a result, foreign language teachers must be willing, in many cases, to restrict their residence to one state only, to states that share licensure reciprocity agreements.

If U.S. geographical mobility is desired, foreign language teachers must be willing to invest in additional state-specific coursework and/or licensure requirements that will permit them continued practice in their field.

For teachers of French or Spanish who wish to teach those languages to students of early adolescence through young adulthood, National Board Certification is an option (National Board for Professional Teaching Standards, 2007a). The cost, approximately $2,500, is in addition to original state-specific licensing fees and state-specific academic preparation (NBPTS, 2007c). Upon fulfilling the requirements for National Board Certification, French and/or Spanish teachers are not guaranteed that it will allow professional mobility across the U.S. (NBPTS, 2007b). Additionally, there are no National Board Certificates available for teachers of foreign languages other than French or Spanish at any grade level (NBPTS, 2007a) that might ease geographical mobility for practitioners.

COST

States that have included foreign language in their core curricula have done so at their own initiative and, unless they were able to receive grants from the private or federal sectors, at their own expense. When the federal government legislates education policy, it does not always legislate a supply of funds adequate for states and local districts to implement the policies. Likewise, when the states legislate education policies they do not always legislate a supply of funds adequate for the local districts to implement state mandates.

The fragmentation of K-12 foreign language learning standards and curricula could result in multiple districts within multiple states having to invest substantial amounts of manpower and tax dollars in program development and maintenance. For states that have collaborated on foreign language standards or adopted the national ones, the burdens could be shared and efforts need not be duplicated. For states that either have no standards or have elected to work independently of national or multi-state standards and aligned materials and assessments, the costs would be greater.

Many individual districts, already struggle to fund the curriculum development and instructional costs of courses other than foreign languages, whose importance has been previously mandated either by the state or national government. In addition, in many subject areas, including foreign language, there is vast national redundancy of work hours and financial expenditures done with education monies at the state and local levels. When states work alone and create their own standards, curricula, and/or assessments, districts may or may not be able to use already existing national resources or the programs already developed by other states. Depending on how the states structure their educational systems, each district may already be funding its own curriculum specialists for each required area of study and be creating standards and programs independent of existing programs across the street in another district.

Implementing a comprehensive, sequential foreign language program from the early grade levels through high school will require additional instructional time each day, as well as staff. Absent consistent nation-wide collaboration between local, state, and national governments in the foreign language education of K-12 students, it is doubtful that the best practices proposed by the ACTFL standards will become a uniform reality for K-12 students in U.S. schools.

TERMS & CONCEPTS

ACTFL National K-12 Foreign Language Standards: Outlines the goals and standards that should be addressed in foreign language instruction that begins at the elementary level and follows sequentially through grade 12 and beyond.

Foreign Language in the Elementary School (FLES): Aims for some degree of second language proficiency.

Foreign Language Proficiency: Can describe a person's writing, speaking, listening comprehension or reading abilities in a given language.

Immersion: A general model of second language and core curriculum instruction that uses the second language as the medium of instruction. Multiple variations of immersion programs exist.

Less Commonly Taught Languages (LCTL): From the American perspective, foreign languages other than French, Spanish and German.

Performance Guidelines: ACTFL general descriptions of communicative performance in a foreign language based on the ACTFL Proficiency Guidelines and National K-12 Foreign Language Standards.

Proficiency Guidelines: National foreign language guidelines established by ACTFL that describe reading, writing, speaking and listening skills of learners at the novice, intermediate, advanced and superior levels of foreign language proficiencies.

World Languages: There are 6912 living languages, including 114 sign languages.

Katherine Crothers

BIBLIOGRAPHY

American Council on the Teaching of Foreign Languages. (1996). *Executive summary of standards for foreign language learning: preparing for the twenty-first century.* Retrieved November 12, 2007, from the American Council on the Teaching of Foreign Languages, http://actfl.org.

American Council on the Teaching of Foreign Languages. (2006). *New Standards for Arabic language learning published in new book.* Retrieved November 17, 2007, from the American Council on the Teaching of Foreign Languages, http://actfl.org.

Center for Advanced Research on Language Acquisition. (n.d.). *Less commonly taught languages.* Retrieved November 15, 2006, from the Center for Advanced Research on Language Acquisition, http://carla.umn.edu.

Committee for Economic Development. (2006). *Education for global leadership: The importance of international studies and foreign language education for U.S. economic and national security.* Retrieved November 15, 2007, from the Center for Economic Development, http://ced.org.

Gordon, R. (Ed.). (2005). *Ethnologue: languages of the world, Fifteenth edition.* Dallas, TX: SIL International. Retrieved November 17, 2007, from http://ethnologue.com.

Huhn, C. (2012). In search of innovation: Research on effective models of foreign language teacher preparation. *Foreign Language Annals, 45*(S1), s163–s183. Retrieved December 13, 2013, from EBSCO Online Database Education Research Complete.

Kelly Hall, J. (2001). *Methods for teaching foreign languages.* Upper Saddle River, New Jersey: Prentice-Hall.

Language Testing International. (2004). *ACTFL proficiency description.* Retrieved November 17, 2007, from http://languagetesting.com.

LeLoup, J. & Ponterio, R. (2000). *Enhancing authentic language learning experiences through internet technology.* Retrieved November 13, 2007, from the Center for Applied Linguistics, http://cal.org.

Malone, M., Rifkin, B., Christian, D,. & Johnson, D. (2005). *Attaining high levels of proficiency: challenges for foreign language education in the United States.* Retrieved November 11, 2007, from the Center for Applied Linguistics, http://cal.org.

Marcos, K. (n.d.) *Foreign language standards.* Retrieved November 16, 2007, from the Center for Applied Linguistics, http://cal.org.

Minnesota Department of Education. (2007). *World languages.* Retrieved November 16, 2007, from the Minnesota Department of Education, http://education.state.mn.us.

Morrison, S. (n.d.). *Resources for elementary school foreign language programs.* ERIC Clearinghouse on Languages and Linguistics. Retrieved November 13, 2007, from the Center for Applied Linguistics, http://cal.org.

Ñandutí. (2006). *Project Funder.* Retrieved November 13, 2007, from the Center for Applied Linguistics' Ñandutí, http://cal.org.

National Board For Professional Teaching Standards. (2007a). *Become a candidate: Available certificates.* Retrieved November 18, 2007, from the National Board For Professional Teaching Standards, http://nbpts.org.

National Board For Professional Teaching Standards. (2007b). *Become a candidate: The benefits.* Retrieved

November 18, 2007, from the National Board For Professional Teaching Standards, http://nbpts.org.

National Board For Professional Teaching Standards. (2007c). *Become a candidate: fees and financial support.* Retrieved November 18, 2007, from the National Board For Professional Teaching Standards, http://nbpts.org.

National Board For Professional Teaching Standards. (2007d). *Languages other than English/early adolescence through young adulthood.* Retrieved November 18, 2007, from the National Board For Professional Teaching Standards, http://nbpts.org.

National Council of State Supervisors for Languages. (2007). *Statement on the study of foreign languages in elementary schools.* Retrieved November 17, 2007, from the National Council of State Supervisors for Languages, http://ncssfl.org.

National K-12 Foreign Language Resource Center. (2003). *About our work.* Retrieved November 18, 2007, from the National K-12 Foreign Language Resource Center, http://nflrc.iastate.edu.

National Language Conference (2005). *A call to action for national foreign language capabilities.* White paper presented at the 2005 National Language Conference. Retrieved November 11, 2007, from http://nlconference.org.

National Virtual Translation Center. (2007a).*Critical languages.* Retrieved November 15, 2007, from the National Virtual Translation's Center's Languages of the World, http://nvtc.gov.

National Virtual Translation Center.(2007b). *Languages in American schools and universities.* Retrieved November 15, 2007, from National Virtual Translation's Center's Languages of the World, http://nvtc.gov.

National Virtual Translation Center. (2007c). *Language learning difficulty for English speakers.* Retrieved November 16, 2007, from National Virtual Translation's Center's Languages of the World, http://nvtc.gov.

National Virtual Translation Center. (2007d).*World languages.* Retrieved November 16, 2007, from National Virtual Translation's Center's Languages of the World, http://nvtc.gov.

Pufahl, I., & Rhodes, N. C. (2011). Foreign language instruction in U.S. schools: Results of a National survey of elementary and secondary schools. *Foreign Language Annals,44,* 258–288. Retrieved December 13, 2013, from EBSCO Online Database Education Research Complete.

Richards, H., Conway, C., Roskvist, A., & Harvey, S. (2013). Foreign language teachers' language proficiency and their language teaching practice. *Language Learning Journal, 41,* 231–246. Retrieved December 13, 2013, from EBSCO Online Database Education Research Complete.

Scebold, E. & Wallinger, L. (2000). An update on the status of foreign language education in the United States. *NASSP Bulletin 2000, 84.* Retrieved November 16, 2007, from http://bul.sagepub.com.

Sigsbee, D. (2002). Why Americans don't study foreign languages and what we can do about that. *New Directions for Higher Education, Issue 117.* Retrieved November 11, 2007, from EBSCO Online Database Academic Search Premier.

Suhay, L. (1999, October 17). Education: Striving to meet foreign language standards. *New York Times.* Retrieved November 17, 2007, from http://query.nytimes.com.

United Nations Educational, Scientific, and Cultural Organization. (n.d.) *The earth's linguistic, cultural and biological diversity.* Retrieved November 17, 2007, from the United Nations Educational, Scientific and Cultural Organization, http://portal.unesco.org.

United States Department of Education. (2006). *Improve student performance: Teaching language for national security and American competitiveness.* Retrieved November 11, 2007, from the United States Department of Education, http://ed.gov.

United States Department of Education. (2007). *National Security Language Initiative Brochure.* Retrieved November 13, 2007, from the United States Department of Education, http://ed.gov.

University of the State of New York Board of Regents. (1996). *Learning standards for languages other than English (Revised edition).* Retrieved November 17, 2007, from the New York Department of Education, http://emsc.nysed.gov.

Washington Association of Foreign Language Teachers. (2006, April 26). *Standards.* Retrieved November 16, 2007, from the Washington Association of Foreign Language Teachers, http://waflt.net.

SUGGESTED READING

American Council on the Teaching of Foreign Languages. (n.d.) *ACTFL performance guidelines for K-12 learners.* Retrieved November 16, 2007, from the American Council on the Teaching of Foreign Languages, http://actfl.org.

Bollag, B. (2007).MLA report calls for transformation of foreign-language education. *Chronicle of Higher Education, 53,*A12-A12. Retrieved November 11, 2007, from EBSCO Online Database Academic Search Premier.

Burke, B. (2006). Theory meets practice: A case study of preservice world language teachers in U. S. secondary schools. *Foreign Language Annals, 39,* 148-166. Retrieved November 11, 2007, from EBSCO Online Database Education Research Complete.

Campana, P. (2007). Calling on CALL: From theory and research to new directions. *Modern Language Journal, 91,* 721-722. Retrieved November 11, 2007, from EBSCO Online Database Academic Search Premier.

Center for Applied Linguistics (n.d.). *National K - 12 Foreign Language Survey.* Retrieved November 13, 2007 from the Center for Applied Linguistics, http://cal.org.

Draper, J. & Hicks, J. (2002, May). *Foreign language enrollments in public secondary schools, fall 2000.* Retrieved November 15, 2007, from the National Virtual Translation Center, http://actfl.org.

Ervin, G. (1991). *International perspectives on foreign language teaching.* Chicago, Illinois: National Textbook Company.

Gilzow, D. (2002). *Model early foreign language programs: Key elements.* Retrieved November 11, 2007, from the Center for Applied Linguistics, http://cal.org.

Hubert, M. D. (2013). The development of speaking and writing proficiencies in the Spanish language classroom: A case study. *Foreign Language Annals, 46,* 88–95. Retrieved December 13, 2013, from EBSCO Online Database Education Research Complete.

Kramsch, C. (2014). Teaching foreign languages in an era of globalization: Introduction. Modern Language Journal. 98(1), 296-311.

Morrison, S. (n.d.) Introduction. In *Second language teaching methodologies.* Retrieved November 11, 2007, from the Center for Applied Linguistics, http://cal.org.

National Capital Language Resource Center (NCLRC). (n.d.). *The essentials of language teaching.* Retrieved November 14, 2007, from http://nclrc.org.

Portland Public Schools. (n.d.). *Immersion Program Brochure.* Retrieved November 14, 2007, from the Portland, Oregon Public Schools, http://otl.pps.k12.or.us.

Rodgers, T. (2001). *Language teaching methodology.* Retrieved November 13, 2007, from the Center for Applied Linguistics, http://cal.org.

Rojas Tejada, A., Cruz del Pino, R., Tatar, M., & Jiménez Sayáns, P. (2012). 'Spanish as a foreign language' teachers' profiles: Inclusive beliefs, teachers' perceptions of student outcomes in the TCLA program, burnout, and experience. *European Journal Of Psychology Of Education—EJPE (Springer Science & Business Media B.V.), 27,* 285–298. Retrieved December 13, 2013, from EBSCO Online Database Education Research Complete.

Rosenbusch, M. (Ed.). (1997). *Bringing the standards into the classroom: A teacher's guide* (2nd ed.). Retrieved November 12, 2007, from the National K-12 Foreign Language Resource Center, nflrc.iastate.edu.

Savignon, S. (1987). Communicative language teaching. *Theory Into Practice, 26,* 235-242. Retrieved November 12, 2007, from EBSCO Online Database Academic Search Premier.

Zhou, B., & Fu-quan, C. (2007). On the promotion of intercultural communication competence. *Sino-US English Teaching, 4,* 77-81. Retrieved November 12, 2007, from EBSCO Online Database Education Research Complete.

TEACHING PHYSICAL EDUCATION

This article offers a brief history of physical education in American public schools, addresses the unique instructional standards of each school level, and presents problems presently facing physical education. Physical education is an important curriculum course in America's public schools. There are unique aspects of teaching physical education at the elementary, middle grades and high school levels. Yet, curriculum standards at all levels have one thing in common: stressing the importance of heightening student fitness levels in order to improve the health and quality of life for the student.

KEYWORDS: Aerobics; Assessment; Education; Elementary Education; Fitness; Games; Middle Grades Education; Motor Skills; Physical Education; Obesity; Secondary Education; Special Olympics; Sports

OVERVIEW
One of the most important, but least appreciated, courses in education settings is physical education (PE). As anxiety continues to amplify for students to perform well on high stakes tests, the value of physical education will be heavily scrutinized, making the possibility of eliminated PE from school schedules an option for many principals (Stevens-Smith, Fisk, Williams, & Barton, 2006). The purpose of physical education in America's schools is profound due to the role it plays in helping students develop physically and socially.

Physical education is the most powerful tool to help students establish habits that positively influence their quality of life. Physical education teaches younger students how to appropriately interact with their peers, how to develop their motor skills and how to learn the basic skills associated with most sports and games. During the middle-school years, PE can play a critical role in helping some students deal with awkward growth spurts, uneasy social situations, and in refining sporting skills for future playing at an advanced level. At the high school level, PE is generally the only time for exercise and organized play that is allowed in the busy, often hectic schedules of older students. There is no doubt that physical education plays a vital role in supporting the academic progress of students of every age. Associated health-related skills are invaluable as students become independent adults who are engaged in the busy responsibilities of working and having a family.

HISTORY OF PHYSICAL EDUCATION IN AMERICA

Physical education in America has a relatively short history in public schools. The subject of physical education actually originated as early as 500 B.C. in Greece. The idea of physical fitness focused on the historical Olympic competitions. The concept of physical education was actually first mentioned in American historical documents by Benjamin Franklin in 1749 but was not put into school curricula until the early 1800's. It was Charles Beck, known to be the first physical education teacher in America, who introduced a course in physical education at the Round Hill School in Northampton, Massachusetts in the 1820's (Sparkes, Templin & Schempp, 1993). During this time, physical education was geared solely for males until Catherine Beecher, sister of the famous Harriett Beecher Stowe, introduced calisthenics into the curriculum for young ladies at the Hartford Female Seminary in 1823. Her purpose in creating this program was to improve the posture and poise of the young ladies enrolled in the school as they developed socially and academically (Davenport, 1980). Between 1850 and 1900, Dudley Sargent introduced fitness and weight equipment to calisthenics programs that already existed in private schools. Another influential person in the field was Pierre de Coubertin. His 1913 book titled, "Essais de Psychologie Sportive" introduced the idea of sports psychology (Cratty, 1989). This prompted educators to consider the importance of physical education on the overall well-being of students through the theory that healthy bodies increased mental health. In 1851 the first chapter of the Young Men's Christian Association (YMCA) opened its doors in America, helping many sports gain popularity, and adding to the popularity of physical education.

After the Civil War, the inclusion of physical education inflated its popularity in schools across our nation. People believed that students who participated in regular physical education classes were healthier, had better hygiene, and were better able to avoid awkward and uneven growth spurts. Colleges added competitive sports programs in the early 1900's, which gave rise to physical education popularity due to the need to heighten the physical fitness and strength of the athletes. As World War I erupted, physical education faded from school curricula due to the absence of males in the schools. After the war, it regained popularity, which continued through the beginning of World War II. This war found Americans stepping up their fitness skills. Men needed to improve their fitness levels in order to be better soldiers and women had to be able to handle the physical demands required when forced to adopt the manual labor jobs performed by those left to become soldiers.

By the 1950's, physical education was a requirement in over 400 American universities and in thousands of secondary schools. The onset of the Korean War in 1950 found many potential soldiers were not physically fit enough to fully participate in war activities. This led to the creation of in 1956 the President's Council on Physical Fitness by President Dwight Eisenhower. This supported the rise of fitness standards through physical education instruction in schools across our country. President Kennedy continued supporting the President's Council on Physical Fitness and took interest in the development of physical education for students with special needs. President Kennedy adamantly supported the efforts of his sister, Eunice Kennedy Shriver, as she began the Special Olympics in 1962. In 1966, President Lyndon Johnson created the Presidential Fitness Awards that rewarded students who achieved prescribed fitness levels through a battery of local school testing. The items in this test primarily had significance for military preparation. These tests included pull-ups, push-ups, sprints and distance runs, standing broad jump, and distance throwing (Hartman, 2001). This fitness program is still used in many physical education classes today.

SIGNIFICANT INFLUENCES ON PHYSICAL EDUCATION

The next profoundly significant influence on physical education came in 1972. Title IX erased discrimination based on gender in all federally funded educational programs. Title IX launched countless new opportunities for women in competitive athletics and sports.

During the 1980's, physical education curricula were developed and implemented in schools. Most were created with the basic goals of improving student fitness levels, improving motor skills, and increasing knowledge of games and healthy lifestyles. They were designated for elementary programs, middle schools and secondary programs. Each level of instruction has distinct ways of addressing the above listed goals while being appropriate for the maturity and age of the targeted student.

In 1995, the National Standards for Physical Education were created by the National Association for Sports and Physical Education. They serve as the definition and value for the purpose of physical education and clearly state instructional objectives for PE courses (NASPE, 1995).

OBESITY & PHYSICAL EDUCATION

Today, one of the utmost goals of physical education, at all instructional levels, is to assist in the reduction of obesity in America's youth. In 2013 obesity affects 17 percent of American children and adolescents, more than doubling in numbers since the late 1980s. The U.S. Food and Drug Administration (2002) stated that "Our modern environment has allowed these conditions (obesity and overweight) to increase at alarming rates and become a growing health problem for our nation" (USFDA, 2002). That report suggested that students in all grade levels participate in "daily, quality physical education" classes. Obesity is the cause of many health problems in our students, such as diabetes, hypertension, and high blood pressure. Regular physical education should address this potentially fatal issue due to the relationship between fitness levels and the quality of an individual's health. Physical education provides students with "more opportunities to exercise will help our children fight obesity, perform better academically, and grow up to be healthy adults" (Sherman, Collins, & Donnelly, 2007). Certainly, many educators use these statistics as reasons to support physical education programs in public schools at all grade levels.

Applications

ELEMENTARY PHYSICAL EDUCATION

At the elementary level, physical education is often taught by the regular classroom teacher. This was brought on in the late 1980's when schools were faced with financial deficits, did not have teachers trained as formal physical educators, and removed the time allotted for physical education to either additional academic time or to unstructured play time, frequently called recess. Despite these hurdles, physical education has survived in many elementary schools. Physical education programs specific to elementary school curricula are generally divided into 2 areas: primary grades and upper elementary grades.

PRIMARY GRADES

The areas of emphasis of physical education at the primary elementary level are to improve the level of fitness of the student and to improve their motor skills. This includes implementing a variety of fitness activities that incorporate aerobic and anaerobic activities. The chief activities accentuated with these young students in grades Pre-Kindergarten through 2nd grade are:

- Balancing & weight transfer;
- Jumping, leaping & landing;
- Traveling & movement patterns;
- Fine motor coordination;
- Safety concepts;
- Fitness.

Primary students enjoy races & relays, even though the competition of winning in lieu of losing should take a backseat to the quality of event participation and fun. They enjoy dancing, moving, and using their imagination to stretch and exercise their muscles. They enjoy being offered a variety of play-like stations that offer them simplistic equipment, such as a jump rope or hula hoop, to explore for a designated period of time. They also enjoy pleasing their instructors and being recognized by their friends for unique and positive behaviors; therefore, they will eagerly participate in any activity for the intrinsic rewards associated with public recognition and praise. Many students' behaviors and attitudes are influenced by their fitness level and their physical abilities (Lambdin & McKenzie, 2003). Due to the social maturity of this level, most of the activities should be focused on individual activities, giving limited exposure to competitive activities. Structure that involves student-focused activities that develop their movement creativity is preferred. Additionally, all activities should be complimented with activities that are supportive of other academic activities, such as relating to pictures of movement, identifying shapes & colors, following directions, respect of personal space, and regard for others.

UPPER ELEMENTARY GRADES

Upper elementary classes, usually grades 3-5, must incorporate lifetime fitness skills while introducing skills that lead into games. Anaerobic and aerobic calisthenics are a vital part of the physical instruction for upper elementary students. Activities that introduce partner participation and small teams are important for this age when appropriately taught and supervised. Sportsmanship instruction is a critical element of all activities with upper elementary students, particularly since the individual levels of comfort and skill acquisition is so diverse among this age of students. Activities that develop the following skills should be emphasized until mastery is obtained:

- Kicking;
- Striking an object with a bat or racquet;
- Volleying;
- Catching;
- Coordinating body movement with these activities.

Games should begin to allow for minimal levels of competition that is closely monitored by the instructor. All activities should be connected to other disciplines, such as journaling, reading, and conducting investigations. Fitness activities must include a strong element of personal accomplishment and fun to maintain student interest. Fitness activities that involve partners or are of a competitive nature are generally more popular than traditional adult fitness activities, such as walking or running laps around a track.

MIDDLE GRADES

The middle school period, usually grades 6-8, is a unique time of development for students. Students in these grades undergo immense changes in their physical stature, social development, and academic status. This age is characterized by transition, growth, exploration, and discovery. Relationships with peers, teachers, and the subject area are vital to the students' quality of participation (Pill, 2006). Instruction should be based on student-focused activities that are based on the needs of the learner and driven by student-based results. The learning environment must be safe for students since many are beginning to engage in risk-taking activities. The environment must be free from criticism, ridicule and embarrassment. Since middle grade students place high importance on social interactions, the physical education environment is the perfect setting to encourage collaborative interactions between students who rarely intermingle or work together.

Physical education for middle school generally follows a strict activity schedule that is comprised of instructional units. These units incorporate the development of skills specific to the activity or game, improving rules knowledge, game strategy, skills testing, and actual participation in the activity or game. Generally, the unit involves a pre-test and post-test of game rules, skills, and strategies. Assessment in skill development is also conducted at the conclusion of the allotted time for practice of specific skills. Frequently, sports are modified into games that are enjoyable and safe for middle grade students. For instance, students learn football skills but actually play a version of flag football, soccer and rugby skills are combined into a game called speedball, and basketball is rarely played in 5-on-5, full-court games.

The low level of fitness in middle grades students is an area of great concern (Wright & Karp, 2006). Unfit adolescents in the middle grade years can be plagued with hypertension, respiratory disorders, diabetes, orthopedic problems, emotional disorders, and high cholesterol (Berensen & Epstein, 1983). Sallis, Prochaska, and Taylor (2000) reported that adolescent activity and fitness levels decrease with age after the elementary years. Therefore, an important aspect of every middle grades physical education curriculum must include aerobic fitness activities. A component of fitness must be incorporated into each instructional period and students must learn to record aspects of their fitness, such as pulse, heart rate, and breathing rates.

SECONDARY GRADES

Secondary education in high school, grades 9-12, offers a variety of physical education choices for instructors and students. Generally, these courses are mandated for graduation per the guidelines of the Department of Education for each state. Therefore, completion of a course warrants a credit amount toward their high school graduation credits or elective credits. Course offerings at the secondary level are typically more specific than what was offered at the middle school level. Secondary PE "courses should aim to create rich declarative, procedural, and conditional knowledge bases of physical activity" (Livingston, 1996). The following courses can be found in the physical education course catalog for most high schools:

- Weight training;
- Team sports;
- Individual fitness;
- Dance/gymnastics;
- Outdoor recreation;
- Specific courses that are specific to sports or fitness activities (such as bowling, tennis, swimming/diving, and golf).

Grades for physical education take on a different face at the secondary level. They generally use innovative quality instruction at this level, involving a variety of assessment techniques, such as skills test and rules tests, skill development activities, rules and strategy applications, and opportunity for skill application through supervised play or competition. Many physical education programs utilize technology and computer programs to enhance student participation in activities. For instance, students may be encouraged to record their weight-lifting accomplishments on computer programs that allow them to monitor their improvements and compare them to those of other students. Many weight training programs rely on advanced instruments that measure BMI, fat percentages and other key aspects of using weight lifting to increase strength. And, as schools are required to enhance student writing skills, it is not uncommon for students to write essays or reports related to the activity in which they are participating.

PROBLEMS FACING PHYSICAL EDUCATION

Undoubtedly, one of the greatest problems facing the continuation of physical education in American public and private schools today is inadequate funding. Just as the arts are frequently poised to be eliminated from system budgets, physical education is often first to be considered purged from a school when budgets are restricted or inadequate for the needs of the school. Since state requirements mandate physical education credits for graduation and funding is frequently low, many school districts insist that physical education classes host large numbers of students which dramatically limits the quality of instruction and participation of those enrolled in the physical education courses.

Another major dilemma facing the field of physical education is the lack of qualified teachers. Physical educators must have a sound competency in the rules, history and skill mechanics of numerous sports, understand how to manage class arrangements and student behavior, must know how to prepare and evaluate lessons, and must be able to appropriately sharpen student skills in a variety of activities. Additionally, most physical education instructors, particularly those working at the middle and secondary levels, are expected to coach one or two sports. This involves having personal expertise in the sport, knowledge of skills and how to perfect the skills of their players, and how to manage all of the other aspects of coaching a sport such as supervising parent volunteers, directing tournaments, operating with budgets, and knowing the policies of the governing association for the sport.

Another problem specific to the elementary level is that many schools do not employ a certified physical education teacher but rely on the regular classroom teacher to handle the physical education content periods. This frequently means that the activities are led by an untrained instructor who lacks the understanding of how to develop individual skills, integrate skills into playing or game situations, and to conduct formal assessments of student improvement. Frequently, the physical education period is merely a semi-supervised recess or outside playtime. This type of situation does not provide students with adequate fitness improvement or with appropriate learning opportunities.

CONCLUSION

The critical component of the success of any physical education program is the instructor. The physical education teacher plays an immensely important role in the participation level and attitude of students toward physical activities and fitness. Sound instructional methodologies must be utilized in order to provide students at any grade level quality instruction that has physical and emotional benefits. The physical education teacher also is highly influential in the perception of the school principal regarding the importance of PE in a school (Hattie, 2004). Physical education teachers are unique from other teachers in that they are involved in the physical development and socialization of students (Sparkes et al.).

Physical education in schools plays a vital role in the social and physical development of students of all ages. Since the 1800's, physical education has been deemed an important school subject. Physical education instruction is divided into 3 distinct categories based upon the age and grade level of students. The primary focus of elementary physical education is to learn basic skills, such as traveling, throwing, catching, and kicking. Skill refinement, game rules and playing strategies are the focus of middle grades physical education, while high school programs specialize even greater in specific activities, such as weight training, dance, or team sports. A critical component of every instructional level is to incorporate fitness skills for all students according the physical abilities and maturity of the student.

TERMS & CONCEPTS

Aerobics: A form of exercise that helps use oxygen by conditioning the heart and lungs. Generally used to reduce body weight, decrease cholesterol, relieve sleep disorders, improve heart disorders, and relieve stress. Incorporates stretching, strength conditioning and movement as primary exercises.

Assessment Methods: The process of documenting results, in this case in the education setting. The two major types of assessment are summative (carried out at the conclusion of a project or program) and formative (carried out throughout the occurrence of the project or program).

Body Awareness: The understanding of the relationship and proximity to a person's body to another person or object, how a person's body is moving, what is causing that movement, and how to control the movement.

Fine Motor Skills: The coordination of small muscle groups, such as the fingers. Used for catching, writing, grasping, and other small movements associated with that muscle group.

Fitness: A person's general state of health and well-being. Includes the triangle of physical health, emotional health, and mental health.

Obesity: The condition in which the amount of body fat exceeds 25-30% of a person's weight. Obesity is closely related to coronary heart disease, diabetes, hypertension, high blood pressure, and sleep apnea. Regular exercise, consuming a healthy diet, and close monitoring by a physician are typically the most effective tools used to relieve obesity.

Physical Education (PE): The study of physical knowledge, body movement, and the skills necessary to participate in sports or active games. Most public school programs incorporate PE courses into their curriculums to equip students with the knowledge, skills, abilities, and desire to maintain a healthy lifestyle into adulthood.

Special Olympics: An international organization that helps persons with intellectual and physical disabilities develop self-confidence, social skills, and a sincere sense of accomplishment through participation in sports training and competition.

Weight Transfer: Moving the weight of a person's body from one support to another, i.e. from one foot to another, from a foot to a hand, etc. An important skill for dance, gymnastics, and all activities that involve movement of any kind that change the location of support within the body.

Carol Bennett

BIBLIOGRAPHY

Berensen, G., & Epstein, F. (1983). Conference on blood lipids in children: Optimal levels for early prevention of coronary heart disease. *Preventive Medicine, 12*, 741-762.

Corbin, C. (1987). Physical fitness in the K-12 curriculum: Some defensible solutions to perennial problems. *Journal of Physical Education, Recreation & Dance, 58*, 49-54.

Davenport, J. (1980). The eastern legacy: The early history of physical education for women. *Quest, 32*, 226-236.

Erwin, H., Beighle, A., Carson, R. L., & Castelli, D. M. (2013). Comprehensive school-based physical activity promotion: A review. *Quest (00336297), 65*, 412–428. Retrieved December 23, 2013, from EBSCO Online Database Education Research Complete.

Hartman, J. (2001). Is your physical education program Y2K compliant: Check it out through physical best. *Physical Educator, 58*, 170-175.

Hattie, J. (2004). It's official: Teachers make a difference. *Educare News, February 2004*, 25-31.

Johnson, T. G. (2013). The value of performance in physical education teacher education. *Quest (00336297), 65*, 485–497. Retrieved December 23, 2013, from EBSCO Online Database Education Research Complete.

Kornspan, A. (2007). The early years of sport psychology: The work and influence of Pierre de Coubertin. *Journal of Sport Behavior, 30*, 77-93.

Lambdin, D., & McKenzie, T. (2003). Analysis in wonderland: Wickets and winners in elementary school physical education. *American Association of Health, Physical education, Recreation, and Dance, April 2003*, 15-18.

Livingston, L. (1996). Re-defining the role of physical activity courses in the preparation of physical education. *Physical Educator. 53*, 114-122.

McElroy, M. (2002). *Resistance to exercise: A social analysis of inactivity.* Champaign, IL: Human Kinetics.

National Association for Sport and Physical education (NASPE). (1995). *Moving into the future: National standards for physical education.* St. Louis, MO: Mosby.

O'Sullivan, M., & Doutis, P. (1994). Research on expertise: Guideposts for expertise and teacher education in physical education. *Quest, 46,* 176-185.

Pill, S. (2006). Physical education in the middle school. *Primary & Middle Years Educator, 4,* 25-29. Retrieved August 2, 2007, from EBSCO Online Database Education Research Complete.

Sherman, K., Collins, B., & Connelly, K. (2007). Let's get moving. *Teaching PreK-8, 37,* 48-49. Retrieved August 2, 2007, from EBSCO Online Database Education Research Complete.

Sparkes, A., Temple, T., & Schempp, P. (1993). Exploring dimensions of marginality: Reflecting on the life histories of physical education teachers. *Journal of Teaching in Physical Education, 12,* 386-398.

Standal, O. F., & Moe, V. F. (2013). Reflective practice in physical education and physical education teacher education: A review of the literature since 1995. *Quest (00336297), 65,* 220–240. Retrieved December 23, 2013, from EBSCO Online Database Education Research Complete.

Stevens-Smith, D., Fisk, W., William, F., & Barton, G. (2006). Principals' perceptions of academic importance and accountability in physical education. *International Journal of Learning, 13,* 7-19. Retrieved August 2, 2007, from EBSCO Online Database Education Research Complete.

U.S. Food and Drug Administration. (2002). Overweight, obesity threaten U.S. health gains. *FDA Consumer Magazine,* 202-203. Vealey, R. (2006). Smocks and jocks outside the box: The paradigmatic evolution of sport and exercise psychology. *Quest, 56,* 128-159.

Wright, R., & Karp, G. (2006). The effect of four instructional formats on aerobic fitness of junior-high school students. *Physical Educator, 63,* 143-153.

SUGGESTED READING

Fontana, Fabio; Furtado, Ovande, Jr.; Mazzardo, Oldemar, Jr. (2017). Anti-fat bias by professors teaching physical education majors. *European Physical Education* Review. 23(1), 127-138.

Graham, G., Parker, M. & Hale, S. (1992). *Children moving: A reflective approach to teaching.* New York: McGraw-Hill.

Kristin Beasley, E., & Garn, A. C. (2013). An investigation of adolescent girls' global self-concept, physical self-concept, identified regulation, and leisure-time physical activity in physical education. *Journal Of Teaching In Physical Education, 32,* 237–252. Retrieved December 23, 2013, from EBSCO Online Database Education Research Complete.

Lund, J., & Kirk, M. (2002). *Performance based assessment for middle and high school physical education.* Champaign, IL: Human Kinetics.

Metzler, M. (2017). *Instructional models for physical education.* New York, N.Y.: Routledge.

Morgan, P. & Hansen, V. (2008). Classroom teachers' perceptions of the impact of barriers to teaching physical education on the quality of physical education programs. *Research Quarterly for Exercise and Sport.* 79(4).

Mosston, M., & Ashworth, S. (1994). *Teaching physical education* (4th ed.). Columbus, OH: Merrill Publishing Co.

Richards, K. R., Templin, T. J., & Gaudreault, K. (2013). Understanding the realities of school life: Recommendations for the preparation of physical education teachers. *Quest (00336297), 65,* 442–457. Retrieved December 23, 2013, from EBSCO Online Database Education Research Complete.

Rind, J. E. (2006). *Teaching physical education.* New York: McGraw-Hill.

Tsangaridou, Niki. (2017). Early childhood teachers views about teaching physical education: challenges and recommendations. *Physical Education & Sport Pedagogy.* 22 (3), p283-300.

TEACHING HEALTH AND SEX EDUCATION

This article provides an overview of the objectives and central issues involved in teaching health and sex education. The article explains the main considerations in formulating health education programs, including the importance of health education, methods of teaching health education and the components that should be included in any health education curriculum. This article also describes some of the important issues that teachers and administrators face in developing sex education programs. These issues include determining the ideal approach to sex education, developing appropriate curriculum materials and lesson plans and establishing the goals of any sex education program. In addition, the overview provides a discussion of some of the most important factors that arise in the implementation of a health or sex education program, such as creating a positive learning environment, developing appropriate measurement and evaluation techniques and using instructional media. Finally, a brief examination of some of the issues that health and sex education teachers are facing today is provided. These issues include teaching children with special education needs and learning difficulties, those grappling with sexual orientation and sexual identity questions and young people who are learning to properly manage stress and emotional difficulties. The following sections explain these concepts in more detail.

KEYWORDS: Abstinence; Family History; Nutrition; Physical Fitness; Puberty; Self-Esteem; Stress Management; Substance Abuse

OVERVIEW

Health education is the communication of practices and principles that promote health and well-being through a process of planned learning experiences that supply information, change attitudes and influence behaviors of children so that they are equipped to take responsibility for their own health. This process is accomplished as teachers create and facilitate learning experiences that assist students in developing the necessary decision-making abilities to seek out habits that promote their well-being and to incorporate healthy practices into their own lives. Although health education is a lifelong process, children can begin to develop strong health habits during their years in school that they can continue to practice as they move into adulthood. Teaching health education is critically important as young people are increasingly facing situations that affect their physical, mental or emotional well-being during their school years. The following sections explain the objectives, methods and components of teaching health education in greater detail.

TEACHING HEALTH EDUCATION

Health education means teaching children to develop an awareness of the many practices of healthy habits and to incorporate them into their lives. These practices include gradually assuming responsibility for their own health and health care, being actively involved with medical professionals in any decision-making process regarding their health care, incorporating new healthy habits and attempting to change unhealthy ones, avoiding unhealthy fads or diet trends and thinking about their health and well-being as an asset to be nurtured through conscious attention. Ultimately, the goal of health education is for children to learn to strive for self-reliance

in personal health matters and to voluntarily adopt practices that are consistent with a healthy lifestyle.

As the school days become increasingly hectic and more schools stress a curriculum that is designed to prepare students for standardized tests, health education programs are at risk of being trimmed or eliminated altogether. However, health education is important because it helps each generation of students learn to become physically, psychologically and socially fit in order to be prepared to assume the tasks of adulthood. While health education programs are most effective when they are incorporated into a standard educational curriculum, the concepts of health and a healthy lifestyle can be taught in lessons on mainstream subject areas, such as reading, mathematics, science, art, social studies and physical education. However, although students may choose many different career paths after the completion of their formal education, they will all have to make critical decisions about their own health, and thus health education is an important addition to a well-rounded curriculum.

IMPORTANCE OF HEALTH EDUCATION

Perhaps the best argument for teaching health education is that health behaviors are the most important determinant of health status and well-being. Since health-related behaviors are learned behaviors, a formal health education ideally should be implemented during the elementary school years, before children have health habits that may be difficult to change or replace with healthier choices. In addition, elementary school children are less likely to have begun experimenting with abusive or destructive lifestyles, and thus the dangers of these practices can be stressed and children can be armed with the information that will help them to avoid unhealthy choices. Finally, many health problems have been associated with the effects of unhealthy habits such as smoking, poor nutrition, being overweight, stress, abuse of drugs and alcohol and unsafe personal or sexual practices. Thus, health education can help children to not only make better health-related choices, but can also help them to avoid behaviors that lead to disease or health problems later in life.

Although children are often eager to learn about good health habits and caring for their bodies, even by the time children enter elementary school, they have already learned and developed significant attitudes and preferences regarding their health. For instance, they have learned food likes and dislikes and they have developed certain hygiene practices and personal patterns of interacting with family and friends. They also have developed well-established attitudes and value systems, based on their health-related experiences at home and in their neighborhood and community. These preferences and practices generally become more deeply engrained as children mature into teenagers and young adults. The aim of health education is to help children learn how to develop positive practices for caring for all aspects of their personal health that are constructive and responsible.

METHODS OF HEALTH EDUCATION

Health education cannot be accomplished through rote memorization or the examination of descriptions of muscle groups, body functions or anatomy. Instead, health education is accomplished by teaching children the importance of good health and the wide-reaching implications of their health choices so that they learn to value health and healthy habits. In addition, health education methods provide a means of conveying the techniques and information necessary to make decisions that will promote wellness and a healthy lifestyle. Health educators are often challenged when children learn from and observe the poor health habits of their parents, friends or members of the community. For many children, these observations are their primary source of information regarding health care, dietary and lifestyle choices and exercise habits. Other sources of health information for children are television programs and the Internet. However, these forms of media may often provide access to information that is unhealthy or not appropriate for children and so some children received mixed messages about health, even while they lack the cognitive and reasoning abilities to sort out constructive information from inappropriate information.

To accomplish its objectives, the methods of a successful health education program must be sequential, planned, comprehensive and informative.

- Health education is sequential when it is provided throughout the educational experience, generally from kindergarten through high school. The curriculum at each educational level should be based on what has been learned in previous years while providing a foundation for information that will be taught in future years;

- Planned instruction should be based on goals, educational benchmarks, outcome-related objectives and clear evaluation techniques. It should be taught within the total curriculum framework and not substituted by physical education classes that lack instruction on health education and lifestyle choices;

- Health education should be comprehensive in that it should include instruction on the range of health content areas, such as health behavior and promotion, disease prevention, lifestyle, risk factors and self-care;

- Finally, health education should be taught by qualified health teachers so that the information presented is informative. Ideally, health teachers should possess a concern for the total wellness of their students and have been trained in both the content and the strategies of health education. Effective health teaching involves providing students with opportunities to personalize positive health habits by implementing the information learned in health education programs into their daily lives as well as creating an atmosphere that encourages and promotes this process.

COMPONENTS OF HEALTH EDUCATION

The need for health education programs is becoming ever more vital. In the twenty-first century the choices that children and teenagers must make have become increasingly complex, and young people are facing these choices at a younger age. For instance, children may be exposed during their educational experience to issues such as drug abuse, adolescent suicide, stress management, human immunodeficiency virus (HIV), child abuse and prescription medications used for behavior management. Thus, to be truly effective, health education programs must contain a number of components that address sensitive issues. The following components are important parts of a successful health education curriculum.

HEALTH BEHAVIOR & PROMOTION

Health behavior involves the sum of the choices, actions and decisions that each individual makes and that affect his or her health. Health behavior includes such lifestyle practices as eating habits, exercise patterns and stress management techniques. Health behavior also includes personal attributes such as beliefs, expectations, motives and values as well as other cognitive elements that relate to health maintenance and wellness. Health promotion includes the development of choices and lifestyles that maintain or enhance health. Thus, health promotion is the sum of the educational and environmental factors that affect positive actions, and lifestyle patterns that are conducive to health maintenance, restoration and improvement.

DISEASE PREVENTION

Disease prevention consists of the proactive behaviors or choices that individuals assume to avoid poor health or to treat the onset of illness. Disease prevention measures are generally based on the current knowledge of sound health practices as well as disease causation and progression. Disease prevention may occur before, during or after the detection of illness or disease, but its primary motivation is to maintain or restore optimal health. For instance, primary prevention is practiced before a disease occurs by taking measures to maintain health and protect against disease, such as routine physical examinations, sound nutrition and immunizations. If disease is diagnosed, secondary prevention includes prompt attention to treatment of the disease and monitoring warning symptoms of disease advancement. Disease prevention can also include rehabilitation from illness or injury, such as learning motor skills after a handicap or working to resume normal life activities after an accident, disease or other significant health problem.

LIFESTYLE

The concept of lifestyle covers the decisions made and actions taken by individuals that affect their health and over which they have control. Lifestyle is an important part of a health education program because unhealthy personal decisions and habits create self-imposed risks that heighten an individual's susceptibility for illness, injury or disease. Among such self-imposed risks are drug use, smoking, alcohol abuse, poor dietary choices, reckless or impulsive behaviors, and unsafe sexual behavior. These practices and behavior patterns, together with physical activity and safety practices, constitute the set of personal actions that lead to an individual's lifestyle. All of these practices are can be altered and even avoided. Thus, teaching students to take

responsibility for developing a healthy lifestyle is an important component of a comprehensive health education program. Particularly, because these patterns become more difficult to change as children grow and mature, a strong health education curriculum that stresses the effects of lifestyle choices is a vitally important element of an elementary and middle school education.

RISK FACTORS

Risk factors are the characteristics or behavioral patterns that increase a person's risk of disease or disorder. Risk factors include characteristics that cannot be modified-such as age, sex, family history and personality type-and those that are amenable, such as blood serum cholesterol levels, blood pressure and obesity from chronic overeating. Health education can teach children to differentiate between the risk factors that they cannot change and those that they can, and to learn to monitor risk factors over which they have no control while adapting their behavior and health habits to improve those risk factors that can be altered.

SELF-CARE

Self-care includes the active involvement of each individual in his or her own health in health promotion and disease detection, prevention and treatment. Self-care is not a substitute for professional care, but a partnership with it. Even small children can participate effectively in self-care activities. For instance, children can learn to practice good hygiene and make healthy dietary choices and they can learn to identify and communicate the warning signs of an illness.

TEACHING SEX EDUCATION

Teaching sex education can be a difficult task since these areas often generate controversy. These controversies may stem from differences in religious beliefs, public versus private morality or control of the school curriculum. Moreover, students bring deeply rooted personal values and attitudes to any discussion of these topics. Teachers can avoid many problems by carefully planning their approach to any discussions relating to sex education. Before any sex education program is initiated, teachers and school administrators should seek active communication between parents, parent-teacher organizations, health practitioners and even community leaders. The greater the level of input in any sex education program from a diverse group of community members, the greater the sense of cooperation with the goals and objectives of such a program. In addition, teachers should prepare themselves for the process of teaching sex education. This means they must consider how to communicate sensitive materials, respond to inappropriate questions or comments and interact with parents and community members about their curriculum or teaching methods. While teaching sex education is challenging, with careful thought and consideration, it can be an important component of a meaningful educational experience for students and their families.

APPROACHES TO SEX EDUCATION

Many school systems have grappled with questions surrounding what information to include in their sex education programs. Some of this difficulty has stemmed from two divergent schools of thought regarding the proper approach to sex education. One view is that any sex education program should emphasize abstinence from sexual activity as the most appropriate option for adolescents. Accordingly, proponents of this view believe that a comprehensive approach to sexuality, which includes contraceptive information, may have the undesirable side effect of promoting sexual activity. In addition, many argue that discussions about sexual practices and contraception should be reserved for parents, who are in the best position to determine the appropriate time and manner of approaching these conversations.

Another view of sex education involves a comprehensive approach that would include discussions about a wide range of issues related to the sexual experience. These discussions may include abstinence as well as topics such as contraceptive options, abortion, sexually transmitted diseases and sexual abuse. The Guidelines for Comprehensive Sexuality Education, published in 2004 by the Sexuality Information and Education Council of the United States, concluded that, "SIECUS believes that comprehensive school-based sexuality education should be part of the education program at every grade. Such programs should be appropriate to the age, developmental level, and cultural background of students and respect the diversity of values and beliefs represented in the

community. Comprehensive school-based sexuality education complements and augments the sexuality education children receive from their families, religious and community groups, and health care professionals" (The Sexuality Information and Education Council, 2004).

DEVELOPING SEX EDUCATION CURRICULA

An effective sex education curriculum is designed to teach young people how to make responsible and well informed decisions about their sexuality and personal lives. The objective of sex education is to help and support young people through their physical, emotional and moral development by including discussions about responsible sexual practices within a well-balanced school curriculum. A successful sex education program will help young people learn to respect themselves and others and move with confidence from childhood through adolescence into adulthood.

One critical aspect of sex education is that certain topics should be introduced at age-appropriate levels. For instance, information about abstinence, sexually transmitted diseases and changes associated with puberty and adolescence is generally considered most appropriate for teaching at the middle school level. High school is generally thought to be the most appropriate time to introduce information on sexual abuse and rape, parenting responsibilities, reproductive anatomy, contraception, pregnancy and childbirth and responsible relationships.

In addition, sex education curricula should also help students develop the social skills that will enable them to understand their own preferences and sexual beliefs, while respecting the views of others. Thus, sex education programs should teach students how to express their own sexuality in healthy ways, while learning to protect their own sexuality as well as the sexuality of others from unwanted advances. Finally, sex education curricula should ideally contain information that will assist students in understanding all aspects of human sexuality, the benefits of delaying sexual activity until the most appropriate time and where to go to seek professional help for any reason. In sum, sex education programs should contribute to promoting the spiritual, moral, cultural, mental and physical development of young people and prepare them for the opportunities, responsibilities and experiences of adult life.

GOALS OF SEX EDUCATION

In general, the goals of any sex education program include assisting young people in developing a healthy and responsible view of sexuality and providing the information necessary to help them protect their sexual health and make sound decisions. More specifically, most sex education programs seek to promote four objectives.

- First, sex education should provide accurate information about human sexuality, which includes such topics as human reproduction, anatomy and physiology; family life, pregnancy, childbirth and parenthood; and sexual response, sexual orientation, contraception, sexual abuse and sexually transmitted diseases;

- Second, sex education should provide an opportunity for young people to develop and understand their values, attitudes and beliefs about sexuality. Thus, teachers should help students understand their family's values, develop their own values and understand their obligations and responsibilities to their families and others;

- Third, sex education programs should help young people develop relationships and interpersonal skills, including communication, decision-making, assertiveness and peer refusal abilities. In addition, children should learn skills that will allow them to eventually identify and develop relationships that reflect such traits as caring, supportive, non-coercive and mutually pleasurable intimate and sexual interactions;

- Finally, sex education should help young people learn to exercise responsibility regarding sexual relationships. To do this, topics in sex education programs may include abstinence, techniques to diffuse pressure to become prematurely involved in sexual activities or sexual abuse and the use of contraception and other sexual health measures. Thus, effective sex education programs are not designed to promote early sexual experimentation, but to teach young people to understand human sexuality and to respect themselves and others.

IMPLEMENTING HEALTH & SEX EDUCATION INSTRUCTION

It is important for students to have an opportunity to personalize information and make decisions relative to their health and sexuality. They also must have a model that helps them assess the possibilities and consequences of their potential actions. If students are to make positive decisions about their health and sexuality, the process of learning how to do so is critical. These skills must be taught and utilized throughout the educational experience, and students must practice making decisions and enhancing their decision-making skills. This practice also helps them feel good about themselves so that they develop a healthy sense of self-esteem and discover that they can have control of their own behavior and decisions. To facilitate this process, teachers should strive to create a positive learning environment where sensitive topics can be discussed without shame or judgment, should use impartial and appropriate evaluation techniques and use educational media and resources to supplement their own curriculum materials. The following sections will provide more information on these concepts.

CREATING A POSITIVE LEARNING ENVIRONMENT

One concern about effective health and sex education programs is that many of the issues that are covered in these subjects are controversial. Teachers who handle controversial issues risk offending students and possibly parents. Even some subjects that would not appear controversial, such as nutrition, may be sensitive to students who follow certain dietary restrictions due to religious or political beliefs. When controversial topics are raised, students often become polarized and may verbally attack students who disagree with their position. When this occurs, the educational process begins to break down and there is a greater likelihood of dissension and ill feeling among the students. Such dissension can disrupt the optimal teaching and learning environment that is necessary in health instruction.

Further, as health and sex instructors, teachers must battle against students' negative image of health and sex education. Health educators are sometimes viewed in a negative light as someone who tells students to abstain from doing things they are tempted to do or enjoy doing, such as smoking or eating junk food, while encouraging students to do things they may not want to do, such as exercising regularly and maintaining good hygiene. This may translate into negative feelings that the teacher must overcome, especially if students perceive that their teacher's ideas conflict with those of their parents or peers. Also, some students have been taught erroneous information about health and sexuality, and thus may enter the classroom with misconceptions about appropriate health and sexual practices. Because this misinformation might have come from their parents, neighbors, older siblings or peers, teachers must be mindful of their students' backgrounds and cultural perspectives when correcting these misconceptions.

The role of parents and the community in shaping students' understanding of health and sexuality cannot be underestimated. If parents convey the attitude that healthy eating is less important than eating according to personal tastes and preferences, students may have a more difficult time assimilating sound nutrition principles into their own diets. Likewise, if messages are communicated to children that sex is bad, dirty or inappropriate, children may develop an unhealthy view of sexuality and their bodies. However, parents who teach children about the facts of well-being, health and sexuality are more likely to have children who are able to properly assimilate healthy habits into their lives.

MEASUREMENT & EVALUATION TECHNIQUES

Instructional objectives should be regularly evaluated to determine whether they are being satisfactorily achieved. The use of measurement and evaluation techniques is important to track student progress and absorption of the material presented. However, to provide an accurate assessment of student progress, the measurement and evaluation techniques must be fair, accurate and consider any unique characteristics of the students as learners. Measurement is generally understood to mean the process of obtaining a numerical description of the degree to which an individual possesses a particular characteristic. The various tests, assignments and observation techniques used in schools are all forms of measurement. The data captured through measurement techniques, however, must be evaluated before the effectiveness of the instruction can be assessed, as the raw data alone may be misconstrued if not considered within a proper context. Evaluation is the process of collecting, analyzing and interpreting information to determine the extent to which students are achieving instructional objectives. Evaluation can supplement, clarify or even counter measurement data. Thus, teachers must use both measurement and evaluation techniques to gain a complete understanding of student learning.

There are several purposes of measurement and evaluation.

- First, measurement and evaluation are used to assess the effectiveness of instruction and learning activities. These techniques are used to help determine whether instruction and class activities have increased knowledge, refined or altered attitudes or promoted decision-making skills;
- Second, measurement and evaluation are used to motivate students. Tests help students assimilate and internalize information in ways that passive instruction does not promote;
- Finally, measurement and evaluation help develop the scope and sequence of teaching. For instance, if evaluation of a class suggests that student understanding and retention of the instructional material is high, students may need only a simple assessment of the material to confirm this, as measured by high test scores, before they are ready to move on to new subject matter.

The emphasis in years on teacher accountability has made evaluation more important than ever. While assessment techniques are routinely used in classrooms, these tools can be more difficult to apply in health and sex education classes because of the personal nature of the subject matters. However, the need to measure attitudes is critical in health and sex education courses because health and sexuality practices can have a direct impact on the quality of a student's life. Further, while certain physical fitness aptitudes and a basic understanding of the concepts in health and sex education can be measured and evaluated, measuring the attitude or the approach of each student toward practicing and implementing healthy habits into their lifestyle is more difficult. Attitudes involve feelings, values and appreciations and one of the goals in teaching health and sex education is to develop positive health attitudes, and thus teachers must work to create measurement and evaluation methods that accurately assess student attitudes towards these concepts. In addition, teachers must often supplement testing instruments with other means of assessment, such as observation, informal conferences and anecdotal record keeping.

Using Educational Media

Instructional media are used to supplement traditional teaching methods and lesson planning and provide a means of involving students in the learning process and enriching the classroom experience. Examples of media include Web sites and Web-based programs, online social media and digital communications, television programs, videos, films, transparencies, PowerPoint presentations and recordings. Computer-assisted instruction is widespread, as most schools are linked to the resources and information available on the Internet through the World Wide Web. The resources available on the Web are often dynamic and make use of many forms of multimedia including printed matter, pictures, graphics, video, animation and sound. In addition, some computer-based instructional resources require active involvement by students and help students interact with the material being presented so that they develop higher-level thinking skills by selecting, observing, reacting to and interacting with the information being presented. In addition, computer-assisted instruction programs often come with built-in measurement and evaluation methods that can help teachers get a sense of how students are mastering the information.

For educational media to be effective, they must be appropriate for the educational objectives sought and the material presented. In addition, choosing the appropriate educational media can depend on factors such as the amount of time and expense involved in obtaining and using the equipment and media and the degree to which the media augment instruction and class activities. Some uses of educational media can be helpful when presenting sensitive information. Television programs, videotapes and video clips can help teachers present controversial information in a neutral manner. Many of these educational materials have been carefully prepared by professionals so that they are compelling and yet still age-appropriate. However, teachers must be careful to choose instructional media that fit the specific objectives of the lesson and that have been approved by school administrators. In addition, teachers should not rely too heavily on outside educational media. Instructional activities that can supplement educational media include brainstorming activities, buzz groups, critical essays, debates, and small group

discussions. In addition, field trips, games and guest speakers can help teachers to provide students with a greater understanding of the material they are studying.

Applications

Special Educational Needs & Learning Difficulties

Mainstream schools must often ensure that children with special educational needs and learning difficulties are not excluded from regular classrooms and school programs. Thus, health and sex educators who teach special needs learners may need to adapt their lessons and instructional materials to meet the accommodations of their students. Children with special educational needs and learning difficulties nonetheless benefit from health and sex education programs, and can be taught unique ways to care for themselves so they are better equipped to make positive decisions in their lives. In addition, health and sex educators may need to incorporate the families of these students into the course objectives. This is because some parents of children with special educational needs may find it difficult to accept their children's developing sexuality, or the children may need special attention in managing their changing bodies and hormones. Teachers must also be watchful for signs of potential abuse or harmful behavior, either inflicted by other students on special education students or at the hands of special needs students themselves. These students may not always understand the nature or implications of their behavior, and may act out healthy desires in unhealthy ways. Since special education students are often vulnerable to abuse and exploitation, these children will need assistance in developing the skills necessary to reduce the risks of being abused or exploited, and to learn what sorts of behavior are, and are not, acceptable.

In addition, teachers may find that they have to be more creative in planning lessons and evaluation methods in order to enable children with special educational needs or learning difficulties to grasp the material. Teachers may need to consult with professionals from other fields to determine how to best present the concepts covered in health and sex education courses. It is also important that students with special educational needs are not withdrawn from health or sex education so that they can focus on learning traditional curriculum subjects.

Finally, teachers have an important role to play in accommodating the needs of special education students and encouraging their participation in health and sex education programs. Teacher attitudes toward having students with disabilities in their class and their ability to accommodate these students can greatly affect the degree to which these students are included in mainstream classes and the attitudes of other students toward their educational needs. Thus, it is critical for teachers to become knowledgeable about students with disabilities. Teachers should establish a close working relationship with special educators who have been trained in special education and who can answer questions about the various conditions and unique needs of students who have different learning disabilities. In addition, teachers should stress that all students are unique, and urge students to learn to be supportive of their peers, regardless of their differences.

SEXUAL IDENTITY & SEXUAL ORIENTATION

Many schools are learning how to meet the needs of students who are struggling with their sexual identity or sexual orientation. These issues must be handled with sensitivity in any health or sex education program. Young people, regardless of their developing sexuality, need to feel that health and sex education classes will provide information that is relevant to them and sensitive to their needs. Thus, teachers should anticipate dealing with issues relating to sexual identity and orientation, and be able to deal honestly and sensitively with these issues by answering appropriate questions and offering assistance in seeking out additional support, if needed.

Any discussion of sexuality and sexual orientation in school classrooms is a significant concern for some parents. Parents may want teachers to adapt certain lessons or eliminate topics from discussion. Teachers must be prepared to deal with these concerns and find ways to balance their educational objectives with the values of their students, their students' families and the community at large. In addition, schools must be prepared to deal with homophobic bullying or other harassment relating to sexual orientation. Notably, by 2013 the issue of cyberbullying became an increasingly strong concern following a series of high-profile teen suicides. Teachers and administrators must

decide how to diffuse these behaviors while teaching that bullying in whatever form-whether racial, socio-economic or related to sexual orientation or any other reason-is unacceptable when it causes emotional distress and harm.

MENTAL HEALTH & STRESS MANAGEMENT

One of the most important tasks of health and sex educators is to help students develop sound mental health practices. The fact that many students struggle with mental health issues is evidenced by the realities of alcohol and drug use among the nation's youth, adolescent rates of depression and suicide and reports of school-age children who run away from home each year. While students can be instructed regarding the importance of sound mental health and stress management, the actual practice of good mental health habits can be difficult to teach and measure. This is in part because the habits of good mental health are in many ways more elusive than those of good physical health. Proper nutrition, regular exercise and rest and relaxation lead to good physical health, but good mental health practices and characteristics are less obvious and may vary from individual to individual.

Although the process of achieving mental wellness is a lifelong process, the years students spend in elementary, middle and high school have a profound effect on their mental well-being. There are many ways in which teachers and educators can promote positive mental health so that students learn to develop a healthy sense of self and well-being. For instance, teachers can treat each child as a unique individual by offering personal observations or words of praise that let a child know that he or she is performing well on a given task or is progressing well. Children can be encouraged to develop their individual talents through creative projects that explore educational objectives using a variety of methods. In addition, children can be taught how to practice positive mental health habits that can augment healthy physical health practices. For example, children can be taught the importance of setting and working towards goals, developing a diverse set of friends and interests, learning to laugh and enjoy life and learning to relate to themselves and others with empathy, introspection and respect.

In addition, because of its influence on behavior and the expression of emotions that may result, stress is an important topic that should be included in any discussion of mental health. Stress is the nonspecific response of the body to an unanticipated or stimulating event. Children can learn how to identify situations that produce feelings of anxiety or apprehension and appropriate techniques for managing their reaction to these situations. They can then be taught techniques for dealing with stress in healthy ways, such as through exercising, deep breathing, mediation, visualization, humor and effective time management.

In addition, teachers can foster an emotional climate in the classroom that promotes respect for each individual and personal wellness. For instance, teachers can become familiar with the individual interests and talents of each student, treat students fairly and impartially, discourage unhealthy competition while encouraging warmth and friendliness and listen and respond without judgment to student comments so that students feel free to share their thoughts and feelings. Finally, teachers can remain self-aware so as to avoid communicating verbal or nonverbal reactions that a child may misunderstand or interpret as disapproval or rejection. Because children closely observe the attitudes and reactions of the adults with whom they interact, teachers must always strive to monitor their words and body language so that they create a sense of warmth and respect for the students with whom they interact.

CONCLUSION

Health is the process of integrating positive practices and behaviors in a way that maximizes personal potential. Health consists of well-being in all aspects of life, including spiritual, emotional, intellectual, physical, social and environmental. To help students achieve health and wellness, schools can incorporate health and sex education programs to teach students the skills necessary to effectively manage their lives, believe in their ability to accomplish specific tasks or behaviors and take the actions necessary to thrive and reach their goals. Thus, health and sex education is the process of developing and providing planned experiences to supply information, change attitudes and influence positive behaviors toward health, wellness and sexual responsibility. Health and sex education should include sequential, planned, comprehensive lessons taught by qualified teachers. Since factual information alone does not ensure behavioral change, health and sex education programs should also provide means for personalizing

information through classroom activities or supporting instructional media. In addition, health and sex education programs should include materials and resources that are designed to reach a wide range of students, including those with special education needs, learning difficulties or those struggling with issues such as sexual orientation, sexual identity, stress management or substance abuse. A school-based health and sex education program can be an important component of teaching young people how to take responsibility for promoting their own optimal health, sexuality and wellness.

TERMS & CONCEPTS

Affective Domain: Relates to the values, beliefs, interests, attitudes, emotions and feelings of individuals.

Cognitive Domain: Relates to the ability to deal with knowledge and factual information from an intellectual perspective.

Comprehensive School Health Program: The planned coordinated provision of health services, a healthful environment and health instruction for all children in a school, where each of the components complements and is integrated with the others in the total scope of the body of knowledge unique to health education.

Cooperative Learning: A teaching-learning strategy that focuses on team work, typically heterogeneous grouping of four students of various abilities, whose work is rewarded as a group, and dependent on the individual learning all its members.

Disease Prevention: Deliberate actions planned and taken for the purpose of maintaining health, protecting against disease, early diagnosis and treatment of suspected disease and rehabilitating disabled persons to the degree possible.

Health: A quality of life involving dynamic interaction and interdependence of the physical, social and mental and emotional dimensions of an individuals' well-being.

Health Attitudes: Relatively lasting clusters of feelings, beliefs and behavior tendencies directed toward specific objects, persons or situations related to health.

Health Behavior: Actions customarily taken by an individual that have an impact on personal and community well-being.

Health Education: Systematically organized activities designed to aid students in gaining the knowledge, skills, understanding, attitudes and behavior patterns necessary for living healthfully.

Hygiene: Personal health care, especially techniques and standards of grooming and cleanliness.

Lifestyle: Decisions made and resulting actions taken by individuals that typically affect their health.

Risk Factors: Characteristics or patterns of health behaviors that increase a person's risk of disease. These are either unmodifiable (e.g., age, sex, family history) or modifiable, (e.g., cigarette smoking, overweight).

Screening Tests: Preliminary appraisal techniques used by teachers or school nurses to identify children who appear to need diagnostic tests carried out by medical specialists.

Social Learning Theory ("SLT"): The theory that every person exhibits a variety of behaviors that being reinforced by success recur when the stimulus is the same in later situations.

Values: Preferences for ideas, things or behaviors that are shared and transmitted within a community.

Heather Newton

BIBLIOGRAPHY

Corngold, J. (2013). Introduction: The Ethics of Sex Education. *Educational Theory, 63*, 439–442. Retrieved December 17, 2013, from EBSCO Online Database Education Research Complete.

Diez, K., Pleban, F., & Wood, R. (2005). Lights, camera, action: Integrating popular film in the health classroom. *Journal of School Health, 75*, 271-275. Retrieved December 18, 2007, from EBSCO Online Database Education Research Complete.

Dorman, S. (2007). Eta Sigma Gamma: Forty years of contributions to health Education and promotion. *Health Educator, 39*, 51-52. Retrieved December 18, 2007, from EBSCO Online Database Education Research Complete.

Fielding, J. E. (2013). Health Education 2.0: The Next Generation of Health Education Practice. *Health Education & Behavior, 40*, 513–519. Retrieved December 17, 2013, from EBSCO Online Database Education Research Complete.

Hochbaum, G. (2007). Looking back from the future. *Health Educator, 39*, 53-58. Retrieved December 18, 2007, from EBSCO Online Database Education Research Complete.

Ivinson, G. (2007). Pedagogic discourse and sex education: Myths, science and subversion. *Sex Education, 7,* 201-216. Retrieved December 18, 2007, from EBSCO Online Database Education Research Complete.

Lamb, S. (2013). Just the Facts? The Separation of Sex Education from Moral Education. *Educational Theory, 63*, 443–460. Retrieved December 17, 2013, from EBSCO Online Database Education Research Complete.

Lang, L. (2001). Let's talk about sex. *Teacher Magazine, 12*, 15-18. Retrieved December 18, 2007, from EBSCO Online Database Education Research Complete.

Liller, K. (2005). Let's sell health! *Journal of School Health, 75*, 187-188. Retrieved December 18, 2007, from EBSCO Online Database Education Research Complete.

Stover, D. (2007). Should we be teaching sex education or sexual abstinence? *Education Digest, 72*, 41-48. Retrieved December 18, 2007, from EBSCO Online Database Education Research Complete.

Strauss, K. (2003). The birds, the bees, oh my! *NEA Today, 21*, 38. Retrieved December 18, 2007, from EBSCO Online Database Education Research Complete.

The Sexuality Information and Education Council of the United States. (2004). *Guidelines for comprehensive sexuality education: Kindergarten-12th grade* (3rd ed.). Retrieved December 18, 2007, from http://siecus.org.

SUGGESTED READING

Armour, K., & Harris, J. (2013). Making the Case for Developing New PE-for-Health Pedagogies. *Quest (00336297), 65*, 201–219. Retrieved December 17, 2013, from EBSCO Online Database Education Research Complete.

Gambescia, S.F. (2007). Discovering a philosophy of health education. *Health Education & Behavior, 34*, 718-722. Retrieved January 17, 2008, from EBSCO Online Database Education Research Complete.

Jalloh, M.G. (2007). Health education careers in schools. *Health Education Monograph Series, 24*, 18-22. Retrieved January 17, 2008, from EBSCO Online Database Education Research Complete.

Lickona, T. (2000). Bringing parents into the picture. *Educational Leadership, 58*, 60-65. Retrieved December 18, 2007, from EBSCO Online Database Education Research Complete.

McAvoy, P. (2013). The Aims of Sex Education: Demoting Autonomy and Promoting Mutuality. *Educational Theory, 63*, 483–496. Retrieved December 17, 2013, from EBSCO Online Database Education Research Complete.

Practice notes: Strategies in health education. (2007). *Health Education & Behavior, 34*, 417-410. Retrieved January 17, 2008, from EBSCO Online Database Education Research Complete.

TEACHING THE GIFTED STUDENT

Definitions of "gifted" vary, but most experts recognize that gifted students demonstrate a high level of intellectual, leadership, or artistic ability. In some cases, these students may be ill-suited for regular classroom instruction, since they may become bored or disruptive. As the legal rights of individuals who are gifted are not protected by federal mandates, it is highly recommended that individuals become familiar with local and state policies for specific implementation procedures. Teachers should also be knowledgeable about the needs of gifted students and seek out appropriate training.

KEYWORDS: Acceleration; Bloom's Taxonomy of Thinking; Enrichment Activities; Gifted; Individuals with Disabilities Education Act of 2004 (IDEA); Intelligence; Intelligence Quotient; Jacob K. Javits Gifted &Talented Students Act; Least Restrictive Environment; Pull-Out Services; Unbiased Assessment

OVERVIEW

The provision of educational services in the United States for individuals considered to be gifted can be traced back to 1867 in the St. Louis, Missouri public schools (Heward & Orlansky 1992; National Association for Gifted Children [NAGC], 2005). In St. Louis, the practice of flexible promotion was initiated to promote students who excelled academically. Over the next forty years, programs implemented various promotion methods for individuals who are gifted. According to Heward and Orlansky, the Cleveland program was established as an enrichment program for the gifted. This program has continuously provided services to the gifted since 1922 and is considered to the longest running program for gifted education in the United States. The emergence of standardized intelligence tests in the early 1900s advanced the idea for education of the gifted. During this time, the most well-known and still used test of intelligence, the *Stanford-Binet Intelligence Scale*, was developed.

DEFINITIONS OF GIFTED

Depending on the educational perspective, the definition of gifted can vary. In fact, there is disagreement over the definition of gifted (Baker & Friedman-Nimz, 2002; Coleman, 2004; Cramond, 2004; Jolly,

2005). However, Matthews (2004) stated that intellectual ability has been the hallmark of any definition of gifted since its early origins. Terman, who is considered the father of gifted education, defined gifted as performance in the top two percent on a standardized test of intelligence (Heward & Orlansky; Jolly; Karnes & Marquardt, 1997; NAGC). In 1958, Witty described gifted as having performance that is remarkable in any area (Heward & Orlansky), while others define giftedness as the top five percent of the population (Coleman; Cramond; Jolly).

Since the 1970s, definitions include the idea that intelligence alone does not define all the possible areas of giftedness (Coleman; Cramond; Heward & Orlansky; Jolly; Karnes & Marquardt,; NAGC). For instance, Coleman claimed that a consensus definition has existed since Marland's definition was first published in 1972. According to Coleman, Marland, the United States Commissioner of Education, defined gifted as:

Gifted and talented children are those identified by professionally qualified persons, who by virtue of outstanding abilities, are capable of high performance. These are children who require differentiated educational programs and/or services beyond those normally provided by the regular school program in order to realize their contribution to self and society (as cited in Coleman).

Bonner and Jennings (2007) cited the definition provided by the United States Department of Education's (1993) report National Excellence: A Case for Developing America's Talent which states that giftedness includes:

Children and youth with outstanding talent perform or show: the potential for performing at remarkably high levels of accomplishment when compared with others of their age, experience, or environment. These children and youth exhibit high performance capacity in intellectual, creative, and/or artistic areas, and unusual leadership capacity, or excel in specific academic fields. They require services or activities not ordinarily provided by the school. Outstanding talents are present in children and youth from all cultural groups, across all economic strata, and in all areas of human endeavor (as cited in Bonner & Jennings).

855

Jolly provided the 2004 federal definition of gifted as:

The term 'gifted and talented students' means children and youth who give evidence of high performance capability in areas such as intellectual, creative, artistic, or leadership capacity, or in specific academic fields, and who require services or activities not ordinarily provided by the school to fully develop such capabilities.

In examining the definitions provided, it is important to note that gifted individuals may exhibit abilities in some or all of the areas discussed. Individuals who are gifted are not a homogenous group and may demonstrate characteristics in varying degrees and intensities. Also, while an individual who is gifted may not exhibit all of the traits discussed; the presence of any of these characteristics is not necessarily proof that a child is gifted.

Characteristics of Gifted

INTELLECTUAL ABILITIES

Intellectual abilities typically mean high performance on a standardized intelligence or achievement test. A subjective intelligence quotient (IQ) score is not included in the federal definition. However, many states continue to use an IQ score as an identifying criterion for giftedness (Jolly). Research has shown that individuals who score high on standardized testing also perform well in all academic areas (Heward & Orlansky). However, a debate exists on the use of standardized intelligence or achievement tests as these tests are found to have bias in identifying minority students, culturally different students, and students from low socioeconomic backgrounds (Jolly).

A specific academic ability refers to exceptional performance in one or two specific areas of academics. For example, someone can perform exceptionally well in math but perform as his or her peers in English and science.

LEADERSHIP ABILITIES

Coleman stated that leadership abilities were included in the definition of gifted in 1972 by the United States Commissioner of Education. A simple definition of leadership is an individual who can persuade others through activities to achieve a goal. In terms of gifted, these individuals have the interpersonal and intellectual skills to bring together groups of people (i.e., scientists and environmentalists) to solve problems that affect society (i.e., global warming). In other words, individuals with gifted leadership abilities implement solutions based on data and science (Heward & Orlansky). In the many variations of defining gifted, leadership continues to be upheld as a hallmark similar to intelligence.

EXCEPTIONAL TALENT

Individuals who are considered gifted in the visual or performing arts are considered by the general public to be prodigies in music or dance. These are individuals who possess skills far beyond their developmental age levels.

While the federal definition is very broad based, many states choose to limit the definition of gifted to intellect, creativity, and leadership (Heward & Orlansky; Karnes & Marquardt; National Association for Gifted Children [NAGC]). Federal laws are comprehensive in how states can accept federal funds when identifying and serving individuals with disabilities. In contrast, individuals who are gifted experience great variations in eligibility for services is defined by individual states.

LEGAL ISSUES WITH GIFTED EDUCATION

In 1988, the Jacob K. Javits Gifted and Talented Students Act was passed by Congress to establish and provide model programs and/or projects for serving individuals identified as gifted (NAGC). However, the Act does not protect the legal rights of individuals considered gifted. Currently, federal laws exist only to protect the rights of individuals with disabilities. In fact, individuals with disabilities are assured a free, appropriate public education through the Individuals with Disabilities Education Act 2004 (IDEA, 2004).

Karnes and Marquardt reported that individual states have the legal responsibility to establish and provide services to the individuals who are gifted. As a result, individuals identified as gifted are provided highly variable services from state to state and in some states from one school district to another. Karnes and Marquardt (1997) also state that many states have mandated gifted services. In some states, a state definition and guidelines for services may exist. However, in other states, the local school district defines, develops and implements guidelines for the district. Advocates for gifted education state the lack of a federal definition leads to a hodgepodge of definitions and services (Bonner & Jennings; Coleman; Cramond; Heward & Orlansky; Jolly; Karnes & Marquardt; NAGC).

Due to the lack of a federal statute, readers are referred to their respective state and local department of education to determine legal regulations and policies for gifted education. Karnes and Marquardt caution that conflicting policies and procedures may exist and cause confusion. However, failure to understand and identify the inconsistencies may cause an individual to not receive services.

POSITIVE & NEGATIVE TRAITS OF THE GIFTED

Giftedness can occur in single or multiple areas. With intelligence most often thought of as being a characteristic of gifted, positive and negative traits can exist and be specific to the individual. Positive traits can include:

- Good language skills to express ideas and feelings;
- Rapid task completion;
- Minimum drill for learning;
- Independence in seeking out and obtaining new information for learning;
- Steady academic progress.

Individuals who are gifted oftentimes demonstrate an independent willingness to learn, explore, and seek information on topics of interest.

In contrast, negative traits can include:

- A perception of being glib;
- Domination of discussions;
- Boredom by repetitious learning;
- Rebellion against rules, regulations and standardized procedures;
- Social isolation.

The negative and positive traits discussed provide only a cursory overview and include many of the stereotypes about individuals who are gifted. The important thing to remember is that individuals who are gifted should be allowed to be creative, develop content knowledge, and be afforded the opportunity to use and develop their knowledge, skills, or talents effectively.

IDENTIFICATION OF GIFTEDNESS

The sole use of intelligence or achievement testing to identify individuals as gifted is not the identification method of choice. The biggest drawback for the use of this type of testing is the bias that occurs for individuals who are in the minority, and those who are culturally and/or socioeconomically diverse (Jolly). The reason for the bias is that the tests are not representative of the normative population. Thus, an over-identification of white, upper-class individuals occur while other groups are underrepresented (Jolly).

To be identified as gifted, a variety of methods should be considered. These methods include:

- Intelligence scores;
- Achievement measures;
- Academic ability;
- Creativity measures;
- Leadership;
- Artistic talent, and/or;
- Nomination by the individual or others familiar with the individual.

The types of formal measures and procedures used vary widely. In this regard, materials supplied by the ERIC Clearinghouse on Disabilities and Gifted Education; the National Association for Gifted Children [NAGC]; the National Research Center on the Gifted and the Talented provide in-depth information and resources on the various methods.

Typically, the first identifier of an individual who is gifted is observation by the teacher or parents. Teachers or parents often notice a difference between an individual who is gifted versus one that is high-achieving (Kroninger, n.d.). For instance, a gifted child may only require one teaching repetition for mastery of a task where a high-achieving child may require three to five repetitions for mastery.

Of course, the specific methods used depend on the guidelines in place in a particular state or local school district. Regardless of the method used to identify giftedness, it is imperative that no one single test or procedure determines if an individual is gifted.

SEGREGATED CLASSES OR REGULAR CLASSES?

Typically, one thinks of the disabled when the focus is on special education or children who require special methods and materials to benefit maximally from an educational program. However, children who possess extreme intelligence and are considered gifted, represent the other end of the continuum in education. Many debates regarding providing and receiving educational services center around whether or not the child who is gifted should be educated in the regular classroom or in a segregated classroom (Baker & Friedman-Nimz). Many individuals who are gifted receive educational services through the use of "pull-out services."

Since the federal government does not mandate services for individuals who are gifted, the majority of students who are gifted are placed in regular classrooms. However, the traditional educational curriculum may be as detrimental to the individual who is gifted as it is to the individual with a disability (Heward & Orlansky). Although the regular classroom is typically considered the least restrictive environment (LRE), it could be considered restrictive for individuals who are gifted. For example, at the beginning of the year a child may already have the knowledge that classmates will learn during the year. Thus, the curriculum is restrictive, as it does not allow the individual to develop skills beyond its prescribed parameters.

In comparison to individuals with disabilities, an individual who is gifted needs highly trained teachers, special instructional materials and resources and alternative placement options, similar to the disabled. Many advocates for gifted education point out that all educational programs and placement options should be tailored to individual needs, regardless of ability.

EDUCATIONAL APPROACHES FOR THE GIFTED

In teaching individuals who are gifted, the two common educational approaches primarily used are enrichment and acceleration.

Enrichment is defined as allowing an individual to investigate in-depth topic(s) of interest (Heward & Orlansky). Enrichment should not be construed to mean that the individual engages in haphazard learning. Appropriate enrichment activities should be well planned, designed, and purposeful for meeting the educational goals of the individual.

Acceleration allows the individual to speed up the learning process. In other words, the individual is allowed to work above his or her age expectations in terms of learning content. However, the learning content is not modified for age. Heward and Orlansky provided examples of accelerated learning as skipping grades, early admission to school (i.e., elementary, high school, college); advanced placement tests; or allowing a student to independently move through a curriculum at his or her own learning pace.

Teaching Strategies for the Gifted

USING BLOOM'S TAXONOMY

For the classroom teacher, placing an individual or two who are considered gifted in the regular classroom can cause frustration. Often these individuals complete class assignments before others. One way to challenge the student is that teachers can adapt curriculum materials by using Bloom's Taxonomy of Thinking (Heward & Orlansky; Kroninger) For example, in a reading assignment about pirates the teacher can incorporate the six levels (knowledge, comprehension, application, analysis, synthesis, evaluation) of Bloom's taxonomy. At the knowledge level, the student can name the oceans is which pirates traveled. Restating the story would target the comprehension level; while writing a story about pirates would target application. In terms of analysis, the individual could relate pirate ships with modern day ships. Synthesis of information could be to develop solutions to the problem of pirating. Finally, evaluation tasks could target why modern day historians study and discuss the lives of pirates.

HOMOGENEOUS GROUPING

Kroninger states that it is important that individuals who are gifted should be grouped together. Individuals could be grouped together in the specific academic areas in which they excel. Thus, children who excel in math could be grouped into an appropriate grade level based on their skills while other children could be grouped together heterogeneously. While Kroninger admits this could be perceived as an elitist viewpoint, it affords the individuals who excel a challenge similar to the challenges the heterogeneous group encounter.

OTHER STRATEGIES

Other examples of teaching strategies to use are developing learning centers, allowing independent study, and creating learning contracts. In any of these strategies the teacher allows the individual to be autonomous and self-directed in their learning. By allowing this type of learning, the individual is responsible for implementing and evaluating his or her own learning along with the teacher.

TEACHERS

Heward and Orlansky state that teachers of the gifted must possess certain qualities to include:

- Openness to questioning and answers from students;
- Being well prepared for activities and lessons;
- Recognizing that the students may have a better command of a subject than the teacher;
- Have a variety of interests.

Regardless of the definition, legal mandates, teaching strategies or personal qualities, education of individuals who are gifted is not possible without trained and certified teachers. The teacher must be trained in research based educational practices and in understanding the social/emotional aspects of individuals who are gifted. Ultimately, the success or failure of an educational program rests on the shoulders of the teacher.

CONCLUSIONS

The identification of gifted will remain a challenge that requires collaboration among all stakeholders to be successful. Many feel that until there is a federal mandate, the provision of services to individuals who are gifted will continue to be varied across the United States (Jolly; Karnes & Marquardt; NAGC).

In meeting the educational needs of individuals who are gifted, it is essential that the stakeholders recognize that the need exists to provide appropriate educational services to all children, regardless of ability. As public educational policy continues to be debated, so will the attitudes and beliefs of educators, in both special and regular education, and families regarding individuals who are gifted. Of primary importance is the establishment of procedures for identifying and instructing gifted females, minorities, culturally and/or socioeconomically diverse populations.

This paper provides a general overview of the practices for identifying and providing educational services to individuals who are gifted as well as a cursory introduction to the information available in regard to definitions, characteristics, legal issues, evaluation methods, and teaching approaches used in gifted education. The most common approaches available for educational use are enrichment and acceleration. Additionally, it is highly recommended that individuals become familiar with local and state policy for

specific implementation procedures, as federal law does not protect the legal rights of individuals who are gifted.

TERMS & CONCEPTS

Acceleration: Educational acceleration has been consistently used over the years in providing education to individuals who are gifted. The rationale for providing educational acceleration include: allowing the individual to work at his or her own pace to promote and optimize learning; providing challenge in the academic setting; and, allowing the individual to progress through grade levels at a faster pace.

Bloom's Taxonomy of Thinking: Bloom's Taxonomy of Thinking is a hierarchical classification system used by educators to set objectives and skills for students. In other words, for learning to occur at higher levels skills and knowledge must be mastered at the lower levels.

Enrichment Activities: Enrichment activities are used for individuals who are gifted to enhance the individual's area of strength(s), such as science or math. Activities such as field trips, in depth-studies, etc. are provided by "pulling-out" the individual who is gifted from the regular education classroom.

Individuals with Disabilities Education Act 2004 (IDEA 2004): IDEA 2004 is a federal law that continues to mandate special education and related services to individuals with disabilities age birth to 21 years.

Intelligence Quotient: An intelligence quotient (IQ) is typically referred to as an IQ score. An intelligence quotient score is obtained from an standardized test that purports to measure intelligence. Frequently, IQ tests and scores are used to predict an individual's success in educational activities. The most frequently used test of intelligence is the *Stanford-Binet Intelligence Scale*.

Jacob K. Javits Gifted & Talented Students Act: The programs purpose it to coordinate scientifically based research, projects, strategies to assist schools in meeting the needs of individuals who are gifted.

Least Restrictive Environment (LRE): The least restrictive environment is commonly defined as educating individuals with disabilities with their peers to the maximum extent possible in the regular classroom or extracurricular environment.

Pull-Out Services: Pull-out services are used with individuals who have disabilities as well as individuals who are gifted. The term pull-out means to remove the individual from the regular classroom for periods of time during the school day to provide educational services.

Unbiased Assessment: Unbiased assessment can be broadly defined as ensuring that procedures used during the evaluation process do not discriminate against an individual and the disability.

Kerri Phillips

BIBLIOGRAPHY

Ash, K. (2013). Gifted learners: Poised to 'join the conversation'. *Education Week, 33,* S32–S34. Retrieved January 2, 2014, from EBSCO Online Database Education Research Complete.

Baker, B. & Friedman-Nimz, R. (2002). Is a federal mandate the answer? If so, what was the question? *Roeper Review, 25,* 5-10.

Bonner, F. & Jennings, M. (2007). Never too young to lead: Gifted African American males in elementary school. *Gifted Child Today, 30,* 30-36.

Coleman, L. (2004). Is consensus on a definition in the field possible, desirable, necessary? *Roeper Review, 27,* 10-11. Retrieved August 10, 2007, from EBSCO Online Database Academic Search Premier.

Cramond, B. (2004). Can we, should we, need we agree on a definition of giftedness? *Roeper Review, 27,* 15-16. Retrieved August 10, 2007, from EBSCO Online Database Academic Search Premier.

Daglioglu, H., & Suveren, S. (2013). The role of teacher and family opinions in identifying gifted kindergarten children and the consistence of these views with children's actual performance. *Educational Sciences: Theory & Practice, 13,* 444–453. Retrieved January 2, 2014, from EBSCO Online Database Education Research Complete.

Heward, W. & Orlansky, M. (1992). *Exceptional children: An introductory survey of special education.* (4th ed). New York: Maxwell Macmillian Inc.

Jolly, J. (2005). Pioneering definitions and theoretical positions in the field of gifted education. *Gifted Child Today, 28,* 38-44.

Karnes, F. & Marquardt, R. (1997). The fragmented framework of legal protection for

Kerr, B. A., Vuyk, M., & Rea, C. (2012). Gendered practices in the education of gifted girls and boys. *Psychology In The Schools, 49,* 647–655. Retrieved January 2, 2014, from EBSCO Online Database Education Research Complete.

The gifted. *Peabody Journal of Education, 72,* 166-179. Retrieved August 10, 2007, from EBSCO Online Database Education Research Complete.

Kroninger, C. (n.d.) *Identifying gifted learners: Gifted?* Retrieved August 10, 2007, from http://learnnc.org.

Matthews, M. (2004). Leadership education for gifted and talented youth: A review of the literature. *Journal for the Education of the Gifted, 28,* 77-113. Retrieved August 10, 2007, from EBSCO Online Database Education Research Complete.

National Association for Gifted Children [NAGC] (n.d.). *Information and resources.* Retrieved August 10, 2007, from http://nagc.org.

SUGGESTED READING

Betts, G. (2004). Fostering autonomous learners through Levels of differentiation. *Roeper Review, 26,* 190-191. Retrieved August 10, 2007, from EBSCO Online Database Education Research Complete.

Duke University Talent Identification Program. Retrieved September 21, 2007, from http://tip.duke.edu.

ERIC Clearinghouse on Disabilities and Gifted Education. Retrieved September 21, 2007, from http://eric.hoagiesgifted.org.

Gallagher, J. (2004). No Child Left Behind and gifted education. *Roeper Review, 26,* 121-123. Retrieved August 10, 2007, from EBSCO Online Database Education Research Complete.

Jones, T. W. (2013). Equally cursed and blessed: Do gifted and talented children experience poorer mental health and psychological well-being?. *Educational & Child Psychology, 30,* 44–66. Retrieved January 2, 2014, from EBSCO Online Database Education Research Complete.

Kaplan, S. (2004). Where we stand determines the answers to the question: Can the No Child Left Behind legislation be beneficial to gifted students? *Roeper Review, 26,* 124-125. Retrieved August 10, 2007, from EBSCO Online Database Education Research Complete.

The National Research Center on the Gifted and Talented. Retrieved September 21, 2007, from http://gifted.uconn.edu.

Smutny, J. (2004). *Differentiated instruction for young gifted Children: How parents can help.* Retrieved September 21, 2007, from http://nagc.org.

Tomlinson, C. (2005). Quality curriculum and instruction for highly able students. *Theory into Practice, 44,* 160-166. Retrieved August 10, 2007, from EBSCO Online Database Education Research Complete.

University of Connecticut. *Neag Center for Gifted Education and Talent Development.* Retrieved September 21, 2007, from http://gifted.uconn.edu.

VanTassel-Baska, J. (2005). Gifted programs and services: What are the nonnegotiables?. *Theory into Practice, 2,* 90-97. Retrieved August 10, 2007, from EBSCO Online Database Education Research Complete.

VanTassel-Baska, J. & Stambaugh, T. (2005). Challenges and possibilities for serving gifted learners in the regular classroom. *Theory into Practice, 3,* 211-217. Retrieved August 10, 2007, from EBSCO Online Database Education Research Complete.

Vogl, K., & Preckel, F. (2014). Full-time ability grouping of gifted students: Impacts on social self-concept and school-related attitudes. *Gifted Child Quarterly, 58,* 51–68. Retrieved January 2, 2014, from EBSCO Online Database Education Research Complete.

TEACHING LIFE SKILLS

To appreciate the historical value for teaching Life Skills, it is important to understand a few relational aspects of special education and inclusion. The Individuals with Disabilities Education Act (IDEA) required that students with disabilities were mandated access to the general education classroom. In the early 2000s, legislation like the No Child Left Behind Act (NCLB) required states to establish challenging standards; implement assessments that measure students' performance, and maintain accountability for achievement in reading, math, and science.

KEYWORDS: Adequate Yearly Progress; Inclusion; Life Skills; No Child Left Behind Act of 2001 (NCLB); Public Schools; Service Learning; Social Skills Training; Students with Disabilities; Transition; Virtual Reality

OVERVIEW

To appreciate the historical value for teaching Life Skills, it is important to understand a few relational aspects of special education and inclusion. The Individuals with Disabilities Education Act (IDEA) required that students with disabilities were mandated access to the general education classroom. Legislation like 2001's No Child Left Behind Act (NCLB) "required states to establish challenging standards; implement assessments that measure students' performance, and maintain accountability for achievement in reading, math, and science" (Browder, Wakeman, Flowers, Rickelman, Pugalee, & Karvonen, 2007). In 2012 and 2013 President Barack Obama began granting waivers to states that would free them from the restrictions of NCLB if they demonstrate that they are committed to higher standards and are complying with requirements. Thirty-four states and the District of Columbia have received waivers that expire, but can be renewed, at the end of the 2013–2014 school year.

For students with special needs, NCLB allowed states to develop alternative achievement standards to report "adequate yearly progress for students with significant cognitive disabilities." These are individuals consisting of approximately 1% of the general population. Advancements in expectations for students with cognitive disabilities better allowed them to access the general curriculum through inclusion in general education classes.

Central to the conversation concerning special education and standards based education is the increased attention given to the needs of adolescents and adults with disabilities and the mandate to foster appropriate education opportunities for all students. Education opportunities for adolescents and adults that prepare students to transition from school to young adulthood involves a "comprehensive process that involves identifying needs, planning for them, and ensuring that these are addressed" (Patton & Cronin, 1997).

Apprehensions about adult outcomes developed and accelerated after a series of studies indicated that students with disabilities were not transitioning from high school to adult life as well as their non-disabled peers, despite federal mandates (Affleck, Edgar, Levine & Kortering, 1990: Blackorby, Edgar, & Kortering, 1991; Hasazi, Gordon, & Roe, 1985; Mithaug, Horiuchi, & Fanning, 1985; Wagner et al., 1991; White et al., 1982). In fact, some projections regarding disabled adult outcomes portrayed an epidemic of unemployment and or under-employment, low pay, part-time work, frequent job changes, disassociation with the general community, inadequate functioning in the ability to be independent, and restricted social lives (Halpern, 1993; Sitlington, 1996). Many of these outcomes stemmed from elevated high school drop-out rates. High dropout rates and research regarding adult outcomes indicated that individuals in high school that received special education services were not adequately prepared for adulthood (Patton & Kronin). These outcomes were directly related to the movement of improving the transition process to engage special education students into Life Skills training that would better facilitate improved outcomes.

HISTORICAL PERSPECTIVES

The concept of Life Skills training stemmed from the belief that all individuals should be able to function in adulthood and the philosophy that while special education was doing a satisfactory job in elementary school; it did not adequately prepare adolescents with disabilities to function well in adult life. While "no one is completely prepared for the realities of adulthood; some students are more ready for the 'big show' than others" (Patton & Cronin).

Brown and his colleagues (1979) initially proposed a functional model for teaching Life Skills to high school special education students. Evidence based practices for teaching academic skills to facilitate the transition process from high school to adult life has been described as:

- Teaching prioritized skills with systematic prompting and fading;
- Teaching students to generalize;
- Promoting access to the general education curriculum through the use of materials, activities, and settings typical of general education (Browder et al.).

This means that all students will have the opportunity to access the general education curriculum based on individual needs.

Most meaningful to teaching functional Life Skills is the relevance of providing instruction in community settings such as restaurants, department stores, grocery stores, banks, and recreational settings. Although, when community locations were unavailable, educators learned through trial and error that a simulated community model also produced generalized responses. In order to offset areas of weakness for the student faced with Life Skills training to aid the transition from high school to adult life, researchers also found "additional resources like books, handouts, laboratory equipment, and other relevant materials as an important way to promote access to the general curriculum" (Browder et al.). Moreover, research substantiated the need for further study

to develop Individual Education Plans (IEP) that improved how state standards were integrated with Life Skills.

TRANSITION PLANNING

This background for teaching Life Skills led to federal mandates ensuring that transition planning for adolescents to adulthood would provide a framework linking employment and living arrangements to a curriculum that would meet guidelines for all high schools to follow. These stipulations should include an IEP outlining transition services for students aged 16 and older, coordinate activities outlining an outcome-oriented process to education, and involve postsecondary issues of concern like education, vocational training, adult services, independent living, and community participation based on a given student's individual needs, and in response to his or her interests and preferences. Optimal transition activities should include:

- Meaningful instruction;
- Community experiences;
- Envelopment of employment and other post-school adult living objectives;
- Acquisition of daily living skills and vocational training to help young adults get jobs (Patton & Cronin).

Transition goals should meet instructional needs that can be met in the classroom or the community and begin at the preschool level if necessary. Overall, transition planning should be comprehensive, based on the student's strengths, invite student and family participation in creating objectives, offer cultural, family, community, and gender sensitivities, and offer supportive, critical timing, and efficient prioritization of goals and future needs.

Central to reasons why teaching Life Skills is vital to students with disabilities is in assuring a level of independence for future living. "Independence for these children means providing them with the opportunity to get more control over their own lives, their environment, and the way they are addressed" (van der Putten, Vlaskamp, Reynders, & Nakken, 2005).

TEACHING LIFE SKILLS

The idea of teaching Life Skills is not new, but in has drawn more attention in the 2000s, because of the federal mandates for more standardized education and higher expectations. Critical parts of teaching

Life Skills have focused on several areas of adult preparation. Life Skills' content itself should be integrated with scholastic abilities and social skills, and potentially offer training in Personal Finance, Health and Hygiene, and Practical Communications. This content is optimally supported by infusing school and businesses within the work community. To facilitate these opportunities, teachers should partner and seek support from business owners that might offer their workplace for job placement opportunities.

Depending on the severity of the disabilities experienced by individuals in Life Skills training programs, researchers reported deficits in money management skills, home cleanliness, social behavior, and meal preparation as areas that should be recognized and integrated into IEP development for students entering the independence of adulthood. Additional skill areas that should be developed and infused into Life Skills teaching to ensure success include: personal maintenance, communication, community utilization, clothing care and use, and food preparation (Schalock & Harper, 1978). Travel training such as bus riding, street crossing, and driving a car should support money management training to offset debt problems and inadequate employment issues (Martin, Rusch, & Heal, 2001). Individuals with disabilities also experience gaps in their nutrition stemming from the inability to understand proper nutrition coupled with inadequate meal preparation. Researchers further urged Life Skills programs to teach appropriate hygiene, telephone skills, active leisure skills, and social skills. Also, fundamental to teaching Life Skills, educators have a responsibility to understand that community success and acceptance is vital to outcomes in program development. The two most critical factors of teaching Life Skills should revolve around the integration of education skills and community skills.

SOCIAL SKILLS DEVELOPMENT

Social skills development is crucial to enabling individuals with disabilities to attain success in community environments. Schloss and Schloss (2001) reported that poor interpersonal skills were a major impediment to developing appropriate social success in community environments. Contributing factors to poor social development included the interplay of immaturity and poor academic achievement resulting in the inability to communicate needs that negatively impact employment, social competence, and the disabled person's "quality of life." The interplay of these two factors impact social aptitude in community and school environments producing the need for educators to offer social skills training as part of teaching Life Skills. Johns, Crowley, and Guetzloe (2005) further substantiated the need for improved social skills to ensure success in academic environments and life and indicated that in a school environment, poor social skills produce:

- Limited learning opportunities;
- Impaired social and academic opportunities;
- Social isolation.

In response to the need to develop social skills, a multi-faceted approach was advised. These components included providing direct social skills instruction, recognizing and utilizing teachable moments to improve social skills, recognizing the teacher as a model for social skills training, actively and positively recognizing the appropriate use of social skills, utilizing special group projects to teach social skills, resolving conflict, and teaching self-management and anger management. All of these issues deeply impact special education and how it is applied for students transitioning from school to the community environment.

Applications

ROLE OF STUDENTS

Individuals with special needs have long described a group of individuals impaired cognitively or physically in a way that impacts their interaction in school and community environments. In response to these needs, special education was developed as a series of educational mandates aimed at helping these students learn effectively and develop appropriate capacities for coping. Many special education students have impaired thinking skills, which has resulted in instruction focused on rote memorization rather than education helping them develop complex thinking, problem solving, and decision making (Alley & Deshler, 1979). These instructional philosophies sometimes lead students to develop dependence and learned helplessness. In order to overcome these issues, students with disabilities should be taught higher order thinking strategies. Appropriate thinking strategies designed to help all students access general education curriculum and receive the most appropriate Life Skills training includes: observing, describing, organizing, questioning, problem solving, and time management (Lombardi & Savage, 1994). These skills underscore social skills development programs, Life Skills education programs, and service learning.

ROLE OF TEACHERS

To promote an educational environment that encourages students to develop problem solving skills, "teachers should create a psychologically safe environment that encourages students to express opinions and to defend answers" (Lombardi & Savage). Teachers also must be models of good listening, respect, and possess the willingness to allow their own erroneous thinking to be questioned. These beliefs should be supported by the philosophy that "thinking skills can be taught," and "all children are capable of thinking at abstract levels, although the quality of thinking may differ."

Teachers also have an obligation mandated by their lawful responsibility to ensure "a system of diversity" to be constructed for all students. This philosophy directly relates to deeply evaluating and holding in high esteem the ideas, opinions, or evidence advanced by others to make improved, informed judgments and decisions (Lombardi & Savage). In offering and honoring the strengths and attributes of others, teachers have an obligation to understand best practice in delivering education interventions for all students. In advancing educational strategies for teaching Life Skills, teachers should be aware of a couple of different approaches that might offset difficulties and allow them to cultivate attitudes of "equality for all."

SERVICE LEARNING

One strategy for teaching Life Skills education is service learning. Service learning is a "teaching and learning strategy that integrates meaningful community service with instruction and reflection to enrich the learning experience, teach civic responsibility, and strengthen communities" (Dymond, Renzaglia, & Chun, 2007). Positive student outcomes attributed to service learning includes increased school attendance, an improvement in grades, better self-esteem, expanded community involvement, and enhanced acceptance of cultural diversity. Service learning

has been advocated as a means of promoting inclusion and access to the least restrictive environment, because all students can access equal opportunities for community based instruction while developing improved social skills (Gent & Gurecka, 1998). Service learning also provides meaningful ways to offer job skills training, social and interpersonal growth, self-care, and safety as part of teaching Life Skills, which should be directly linked to post-school outcomes like "postsecondary education, employment, independent living, and community involvement" (Dymond et al.).

VIRTUAL REALITY TECHNOLOGY

Another strategy that teachers should be aware of is that Virtual Reality technology can be utilized for teaching Life Skills to deaf students. For example, in 2002 the resource staff at Lake Sybelia Elementary School in Orange County, Florida, utilized a Virtual Reality program to improve academic skills of hearing impaired students. In collaboration among educators, defense contractors, and the government, a project was developed to improve academic and social success for deaf students. In addition to improving math scores, the system also prepared students for tests, and offered them the ability to navigate through a virtual town and interact with townspeople. Students practiced scenarios like approaching a stranger, practicing a fire drill, or even placing a fast food order. The virtual reality opportunity allowed students to improve academically and gain access to social and community advancement (Savides, 2002).

ROLE OF ADMINISTRATORS

From a systemic perspective, school administrators have the job of providing stewardship for the whole system of a school. Administrators should keep a couple of issues in mind for developing the most effective Life Skills training program.

First, administrators should understand the difficulty in teaching Life Skills, because the content is hugely subjective. As described earlier, multiple interpretations for how the teaching is administered varies per school in accordance with how it is defined in a given environment. In approaching the content to be presented in teaching Life Skills, administrators should be mindful of the multi-cultural impacts (Becker, 1994). As educators, we must become aware of our own attitudes governing ethnicity, cultural differences, and foreign languages. Administrators possess the primary responsibility in ensuring that each of these properties are examined and considered to promote the most effective educational environment.

Second, administrators should consider the needs of all cultures, which are that all people want to stay healthy, help family members, learn useful skills, and feel like valued citizens (Becker). These considerations comprise the issues of greatest concern in providing educational opportunities that meet the needs of all students. Administrators hold a primary and lawful responsibility of supporting teachers in best practice. Teachers should feel supported and accommodated in providing students with a nurturing and accessible education environment for all students.

Issues

OVERCOMING BARRIERS TO TEACHING LIFE SKILLS

The most significant barrier in teaching Life Skills is in understanding the multiple assumptions, interpretations, and attitudes of how Life Skills programs are viewed by teachers, the community, and families. Educators must be taught more inclusive strategies for teaching Life Skills (such as the Service Learning Model). Multiple students in all educational environments can benefit from similar training offered in Life Skills classrooms, such as money management, job skills training, and preparation for adult living.

Special education often remains a segregating experience through high school, despite lawful mandates aimed at delivering equal educational opportunities for all students. To overcome some of these barriers, general education students and special education students should be offered similar education opportunities, such as job training within the community and service learning opportunities. Service learning is employed by approximately half of all high schools, with little evidence as to how students with disabilities are included in these programs. It would be useful to investigate ways of integrating service learning opportunities for both general education and special education students.

CONCLUSION

Teaching Life Skills should be a program offered for high school special and general education students to meaningfully prepare them for adulthood and daily living. Given the multiple family and community gaps experienced by multiple students, many adolescents are not well prepared for adulthood. While evidence suggested that special education students were even less prepared for independent living than their general education peers, it would be beneficial to connect all teaching to real-life learning to provide students with meaningful and authentic learning environments.

Specifically incorporated within a Life Skills Program, a multi-faceted approach to daily living, money management, and community engagement should be considered and underscored by service learning and a multi-cultural lens for curriculum development. This suggestion considers ways for how teachers can interact meaningfully with all students in all education environments.

Given the substantial interpretations for how Life Skills courses are taught in different high schools, new teachers are well advised to seek mentorship in developing best programming. Partnerships, collaboration, and understanding are recommended approaches in overcoming systemic gaps that might be experienced by all teachers new to education. Lastly, if a new teacher is hired for a Life Skills teaching assignment and is unclear on how to proceed, the new teacher should visit other regional high schools with outstanding programs and communicate with other teachers from other schools in similar situations to implement similar qualities in their program. Connecting with other schools in other programs, while sometimes daunting is an approach that is recommended for all new teachers as a way of developing relationships and collaboration.

TERMS & CONCEPTS

Inclusion: Inclusion is the total integration process of special education students in general education classrooms offered according to the special education student's needs. It is also the principle and practice of considering general education as the placement of first choice for all learners.

Life Skills: Evidence based practices for teaching academic skills combined with community skills to facilitate the transition process from high school to adult life for individuals with cognitive or physical disabilities. These skills should be directly linked to post-school outcomes like postsecondary education, employment, independent living, and community involvement.

No Child Left Behind Act of 2001 (NCLB): A federal mandate that requires states to establish challenging standards and implement assessments that measure students' performance, while maintaining accountability for achievement in reading, math, and science.

Service Learning: A school-based teaching strategy that incorporates community service with instruction and reflection, which enriches the learning experience, teaches civic responsibility, and strengthens communities.

Social Skills Training: Training for students purposed by utilizing special group projects to teach social skills, resolve conflicts, and teach self-management and anger management.

Students with Disabilities: Students with disabilities describe a group of individuals impaired cognitively or physically in a way that impacts typical ways of interaction in school and community environments.

Transition: Transition has been described as a "comprehensive process that involves identifying needs, planning for them, and ensuring that these are addressed."

Virtual Reality: A technology that allows users to interact with a computer simulated, real or imagined model or environment.

Sharon Link

BIBLIOGRAPHY

Affleck, J., Edgar, E., Levine, P., & Kortering, L. (1990). Post school status of students classified as mildly mentally retarded, learning disabled, or nonhandicapped: Does it get better with time? *Education and Training in Mental Retardation, 26,* 142-150.

Alley, G. R. & Deshler, D. D. (1979). *Teaching the learning disabled adolescent: Strategies and methods.* Denver, CO: Love Publishing.

Becker, B. (1994). Mastering the multicultural mix. *Vocational Education Journal, 69,* 22-25. Retrieved October 17, 2007, from EBSCO Online Database Education Research Complete.

Blackorby, J., Edgar, E., & Kortering, L. J. (1991). A third of our youth? A look at the problems of high school dropout among students with mild handicaps. *The Journal of Special Education, 25,* 102-113. Retrieved October 17, 2007, from EBSCO Online Database Education Research Complete.

Browder, D., Wakeman, S., Flowers, C., Rickelman, R., Pugalee, D., & Karvonen, M. (2007). Creating access to the general curriculum with links to grade-level content for students with significant cognitive disabilities: An explication of the concept. *Journal of Special Education, 41,* 2 -16. Retrieved October 17, 2007, from EBSCO Online Database Education Research Complete.

DiPipi-Hoy, C., & Steere, D. E. (2012). When you can't get out. *Teaching Exceptional Children, 45,* 60–67. Retrieved December 17, 2013, from EBSCO Online Database Education Research Complete.

Dymond, S., Renzaglia, A., Euljung, C., (2007). Elements of effective high school service learning programs that include students with and without disabilities. *Remedial & Special Education, 28,* 227-243. Retrieved October 17, 2007, from EBSCO Online Database Education Research Complete.

Fisher, D., & Frey, N. (2001). Access to the core curriculum: Critical core ingredients for student success. *Remedial and Special Education, 22,* 148-157.

Gamble, B. (2006). Teaching Life Skills for student success. *Connecting Education & Careers, 81,* 40-41. Retrieved October 17, 2007, from EBSCO Online Database Education Research Complete.

Gent, P. J. & Gurecka, L. E. (2001). Service-learning: A creative strategy for inclusive classrooms. *The Journal of the Association for Persons with Severe Handicaps, 23,* 261-271.

Halpern, A. S. (1993). Quality of life as a conceptual framework for evaluation transition outcomes. *Exceptional Children, 59,* 486-498.

Hasazi, S. B., Gordon, L. R. & Roe, C. A. (1985). Factors associated with the employment status of handicapped youth exiting high school from 1979-1983. *Exceptional Children, 26,* 49-53.

Johns, B., Crowley, E., & Guetzloe, P. (2005). The central role of teaching social skills. *Focus on Exceptional Children, 37,* 1-8. Retrieved October 17, 2007, from EBSCO Online Database Education Research Complete.

Lombardi, T. & Savage, L. (1994). Higher order thinking skills for students with special needs. *Preventing School Failure, 38,* 27-32. Retrieved October 17, 2007, from EBSCO Online Database Education Research Complete.

Martin, J., Rusch, F., & Hail, L. W. (1982). Teaching community survival skills to mentally retarded adults: A review and analysis. *Journal of Special Education, 16,* 243-251. Retrieved October 17, 2007, from EBSCO Online Database Education Research Complete.

Mithaug, D. E., Horiuchi, L., & Fanning, P. (1985). A report on the Colorado statewide follow-up survey of special education students. *Exceptional Children, 51,* 397-404.

Patton, J. (1997). Curricular implications of transition. *Remedial & Special Education, 18,* 294-305. Retrieved

October 17, 2007, from EBSCO Online Database Education Research Complete.

Patton, J. & Cronin, M. (1997). Curricular implications of transition. *Remedial & Special Education, 18,* 294-307. Retrieved October 17, 2007, from EBSCO online database, Education Research Complete.

Samuels, C. A. (2013). Common Core's promise collides with IEP realities. *Education Week, 33,* S24–S25. Retrieved December 17, 2013, from EBSCO Online Database Education Research Complete.

Savides, S. (2002). Virtual reality's new role: Teaching Life Skills. *Christian Science Monitor, 94,* 12. Retrieved October 17, 2007, from EBSCO Online Database Education Research Complete.

Schalock, R. L. & Harper, R. S. (1978). Placement from community-based MR programs: How well do clients do? *American Journal of Mental Deficiency, 83,* 240-247.

Schloss, P. & Schloss, C. N. (1985). Contemporary issues in social skills research with mentally retarded persons. *Journal of Special Education, 19,* 269-282. Retrieved October 17, 2007, from EBSCO Online Database Education Research Complete.

Sitlington, P. L. (1996). Transition to living: The neglected component of transition programming for individuals with learning disabilities. *Journal of Learning Disabilities, 29,* 31-39, 52.

Van Der Putten, A., Vlaskamp, C., Reynders, K., & Nakken, H. (2005). Children with profound intellectual and multiple disabilities: The effects of functional movement activities. *Clinical Rehabilitation, 19,* 613-620. Retrieved October 17, 2007, from EBSCO Online Database Education Research Complete.

Wagner, M., Newman, L., D'Amico, R., Jay, E. D., Butler-Nalin, P., Marder, C., & Cox, R. (1991). *Youth with disabilities: How are they doing? The first comprehensive report from the National Longitudinal Transition Study of special education students.* Menlo Park, CA: SRI International.

White, W., Alley, G., Deschler, D., Schumaker, J., Warner, M., & Clark, F. (1982). Are there learning disabilities after high school? *Exceptional Children, 49,* 273-274.

Yuen, M., & Fong, R. W. (2012). Connectedness and life skills development for all children. *High Ability Studies, 23,* 119–121. Retrieved December 17, 2013, from EBSCO Online Database Education Research Complete.

SUGGESTED READING

Ayres, K. M., Douglas, K. H., Alisa Lowrey, K. K., & Sievers, C. (2011). I can identify Saturn but I can't brush my teeth: What happens when the curricular focus for students with severe disabilities shifts. *Education & Training In Autism & Developmental Disabilities, 46,* 11–21. Retrieved December 17, 2013, from EBSCO Online Database Education Research Complete.

Csoti, M. (2001). *Social awareness skills for children.* London: Jessica Kingsley Publishers.

Flanagan, R. (2016). Back to basics: Teaching life skills to children and adolescents with ADHD. *PsychCritiques,* 61(15).

Mannix, D. (2009). *Life Skills Activities for Secondary Students with Special Needs.* San Francisco, CA.: Jossey Bass.

Mannix, D. & Mannix, T. (1995). *Life skills activities for secondary students with special needs.* Washington, DC: The Center for Applied Research. Taylor, G. (1998). *Curriculum strategies for teaching social skills to the disabled: Dealing with inappropriate behaviors.* Springfield, IL: Charles C. Thomas Publishers.

Monastra, V. (2016). Teaching life skills to children and teens with ADHD: A guide for parents and counselors. *American Psychological Association.* Viii.

Wade, R. (2011). Service for learning. *Educational Leadership, 68,* 28–31. Retrieved December 17, 2013, from EBSCO Online Database Education Research Complete.

TEACHING INDUSTRIAL ARTS/TECHNOLOGY EDUCATION

During the industrial era of the 20th century, industrial arts, commonly referred to today as technology education, focused on the creation of objects and the use of tools and machines. However, technological advancements have transformed our society into one that is more sophisticated and technologically oriented. This transformation required the content of the traditional industrial arts curriculum to undergo significant changes. Technology education is ultimately geared toward enabling students to become technologically literate and to function in a technological society. At the same time, there is still a need for traditional industrial arts programs in order to prepare students for certain occupations.

KEYWORDS: Bio-Mimicry; Constructionism; Industrial Arts; Integrate; International Technology Education Association (ITEA); Layering; Standards for Technological Literacy; STEM Model; Technology Education; Technological Literacy; Vocational Education

OVERVIEW

Industrial arts are essentially traditional education programs for creating objects out of wood and metal by using a variety of hand tools, power tools and machines. In some advanced programs, the industrial arts curriculum included small engine repair and automobile maintenance. Once referred to as shop class, these courses were designed to expose students to the basics of home repair, manual craftsmanship and machine safety. Another aim of teaching industrial arts was to enable students to develop a broad range of mechanical skills as well as to allow some students to pursue further vocational training, that is, training for a specific occupation in industry, agriculture or trade.

As society became more technologically advanced and sophisticated, teaching industrial arts evolved into technology education. Essentially this is "the study of technology, which provides an opportunity for students to learn about the processes and knowledge related to technology that are needed to solve problems and extend human capabilities" (Zagari & MacDonald, 1994).

THE AIMS OF TECHNOLOGY EDUCATION

In general the aim of technology education is geared toward preparing students to function in a technologically sophisticated society, involving problem-based learning that relies on mathematic, scientific, and technological principles. It encompasses identifying and formulating a problem, designing a solution, creating and testing the solution, applying technological knowledge and processes to real world experiences and encouraging students to solve problems. Further, technology education goes beyond traditional industrial arts' focus on wood and metal work and the use of tools and machines to consider a number of other technologies (Rogers, 2004).

For example, construction technology considers the efficient use of resources to build structures or to construct works on a site, while manufacturing technology deals with the extraction of raw materials or the use of recycled materials for industrial and consumer goods. Transportation technology includes many areas, including automotive design as well as research that allows for enhanced highway design and traffic control. An area of inquiry closely linked to transportation technology is energy technology. This considers the materials and engineering issues connected to energy production, transportation, utilization, and conservation.

In light of the evolution of the internet and advances in telecommunications, one rapidly developing area of technology concerns the exchange of information to extend knowledge. Further, there are other areas of technological inquiry including agricultural and medical technology. Finally, technology education involves the study of technology's impact on society and the environment. Teaching technology ultimately requires the use of computers and robots and relies on laboratory activities that demonstrate concepts from mathematics and science (Maley, 1989).

TECHNOLOGY EDUCATION CURRICULUM

While technology education has evolved in response to the demands of an increasingly technology-oriented society, there are some who contend that schools have not gone far enough in implementing technology education. According to Pearson (2004), at the middle school level the content of many schools' curricula remains in transition from traditional industrial arts programs, while at the high school level, there are different views as to how to fully deploy technology education and which subject areas should be emphasized.

One advocate for technology education is the International Technology Education Association (ITEA). Formerly known as the American Industrial Arts Association, the ITEA was established in 1985 to reflect technological advances in society and the need to reform the curriculum of traditional industrial arts.

In 2000 the ITEA established standards for technological literacy for high school graduates (Pearson). These standards are divided into a number of categories including the nature of technology, technology and society, design, abilities for a technological world, and the designed world. The goal of the standards is to enable students to understand the characteristics and scope of technology as well as its cultural, social, political and economic effects. Moreover, by having practical use of technology in laboratory work and research and development, students should gain an understanding of and be able to use and select some of the technologies mentioned above (Pearson).

Along with other advocates like the National Academy of Engineering (NAE) and the National

Science Foundation (NSF), the ITEA established the Committee on Assessing Technological Literacy. The purpose of the committee is to develop ways to assess the technological literacy of students and teachers as well as adults who are no longer in school. In addition, the ITEA develops educational content for grades K-12 based on the standards for technological literacy. In short, the aim of these programs is to solve problems by starting with a student's everyday environment and then gradually exploring more global concerns. Ultimately, students should be technologically literate by the time they finish high school (Meade, 2006).

Future Developments

While technological education has continued to evolve, certain aspects of traditional industrial arts education were replaced and some contend that there remains a need for these courses since technology education programs emphasize college preparation and some students do not plan on attending college. According to Stewart (1996), the reduced time for traditional industrial arts has limited the number of enrollees in technology education courses because some students are frustrated by "stringent academic requirements or limited time for hands-on tool and material manipulation" (Stewart).

It is inevitable that technology will continue to shape society and the information revolution ushered in by the Internet and advances in the telecommunications sector has created a smaller world where information, goods, services and jobs can be delivered from and to almost any place across the globe. In order to keep pace with these changes, schools will need to produce students who are technologically literate and can function in a technologically oriented world. At the same time, workers who can construct buildings and homes, and who are skilled with tools and machines, and also have an understanding of their applications will continue to be in demand. In the end, the content of technology education curriculum will need to be balanced between advanced technology and basic industrial arts skills (Stewart).

Applications

In the past, traditional industrial arts education usually started at the middle school level and then continued into the high school years. In the 2000s, however, many educators recognized the importance of introducing technology education into the

primary school years due to the rapid proliferation of digital technology and communications. Children begin to use such tools as computers, tablets, electronic readers, and cell phones at a very young age.

Integrating Technology Education into Primary Schools

In order to integrate technology into everyday learning in elementary schools, the language arts, math, science and social studies should be viewed as opportunities to accomplish this aim. For example, one approach for using the language arts is to provide students with pictures of technological objects like a helicopter or a wheel and then have them search for a natural object that may have served as the inspiration for that technology. This approach to education is also known as bio-mimicry—a relatively new science that studies nature's models and then imitates those designs and processes to solve human problems (Jones, 2006).

According to Jones, studying some of the natural scientific forces can provide opportunities for introducing technology into everyday learning. One natural force that can be studied is magnetism, since it is used in a broad array of electronic technologies. Technological education should ultimately include social studies applications and this can be accomplished by exploring the way in which technology affects nature. Here, students can learn to craft environmental impact statements and to investigate green technologies that are being developed. This is especially relevant since "preserving and protecting nature is one of the most important technological issues that we must deal with" (Jones).

Rogers suggests another way to integrate technology education into primary school learning is by introducing basic engineering principles into the curriculum. Studying engineering incorporates hands-on and creative work and provides students with an opportunity to apply and reinforce their math, science and design studies. Teaching engineering in the primary school curriculum is grounded in the constructionist approach to education, the essence of which is that "people learn better when they are working with materials that allow them to design and build artifacts that are meaningful to them" (Rogers).

In some ways, bringing engineering into the curriculum builds on the traditional approach to industrial arts education since students are provided with opportunities to learn how to build things by using tools and machines. Moreover, learning engineering principles also requires learning math and science as well as developing writing, communication and design skills. While engineering may seem like a complex topic, studies have shown that elementary school students are capable of learning important concepts of physics like friction, basic computer programming concepts like 'go to' statements and math concepts like reading graphs (Rogers).

Successfully teaching engineering in grades K-5 ultimately rests on relaying principles that are age appropriate and then progressively building on those principles in successive years. Children in kindergarten, for instance, can be taught basic engineering concepts about structures as well as science and math concepts such as forces. By the first grade, students can build on this knowledge by being taught gearing and motion of structures. At this level, they can also be taught how to apply their knowledge of forces to make predictions and estimates. By the 4th and 5th grade, students can begin to explore engineering concepts like programming and automation and the scientific method of experiments can be introduced (Rogers).

INTEGRATING TECHNOLOGICAL EDUCATION INTO MIDDLE SCHOOLS

Understanding these concepts is critical for a student's continued study of technology once they enter the middle school years. At this level, there are there a number of systemic challenges for successful technology education because some traditional industrial arts education programs are still in transition. In particular, suitable classroom environments need to be created by retrofitting industrial shops and developing technology labs. Moreover, there has been a shortage of certified technology education teachers. This shortage is addressed, in part, by the Technology Education Leadership Project (TELP), an initiative funded by the NSF. This project assists industrial arts teachers with retraining so that they can meet the state curricular framework and technology standards established by the ITEA (Pearson).

While integrating technological concepts into other aspects of the curriculum continues in the middle school years, another approach being used is one that combines the traditional problem solving model with teamwork, technical skill and academic ability—an approach also referred to as layering. To accomplish this, students are given a long-term project that calls upon their math and science skills to solve a particular technological problem in a lab environment. Layering is different than integration because the latter involves incorporating different areas of study into a specific short-term technology lesson (Pruitt, 2004).

TECHNOLOGY EDUCATION IN HIGH SCHOOL

By the time students reach high school, they should comprehend basic technological principles and technology education during these years should be aimed at producing students who are technologically literate and who can function in a technologically sophisticated society.

STEM

One widely accepted model for achieving this objective is known as STEM, or the integration of Science, Technology, Engineering and Mathematics with technology education playing a lead role. Proponents of this model believe that this constructionist approach to education allows students to actively learn how to design and resolve problems as well as an opportunity to experience the role of innovation in everyday life—innovation, in turn, is the essence of technology education (Clark, 2006/2007).

Clark writes that in order for the STEM model to be successful, teachers in all subject areas need to be open to the idea of integration and to recognize the intrinsic value of technology education. Educators need to not only be committed to working on integration they must also be willing to allow technology education to lead the way while acknowledging that technology education can also reinforce learning in other subject areas, particularly math and science. In addition to teacher support, the STEM model requires support at the administrative level. School systems need to ensure that adequate resources are available and a school environment that is amenable to technology education needs to be fostered (Clark).

ENGINEERING DESIGN

While the STEM model espoused by Clark has technology education playing a lead role, there is another school of thought that holds that engineering design should be the focal point of technology education.

In this regard, Wicklein (2006) contends that technology education has not been successful in developing programs that have specific and attainable goals based on clearly stated values. By having engineering design at the forefront of technology education, a curriculum with a more organized and solid framework for integrating mathematics, science and technology can be established. Moreover, by emphasizing engineering design, students will be provided with a structure that encourages them to meet the technology literacy standards established by the ITEA (Wicklein).

In addition to these benefits, a technology education curriculum that is grounded in engineering design is more likely to lead to a number of career opportunities for students. Wicklein believes this is of critical importance given the fact that American schools are not producing enough engineers. In fact, many U.S. businesses have either been forced to import large numbers of non-citizens to meet engineering demands or to outsource engineering positions to companies overseas. This presents a number of employment and domestic security concerns, but focusing the technology education curriculum on engineering "can provide general technological literacy education and help to build the nation's engineering labor force" (Wicklein).

Technology education will invariably continue to play a critical role in the education of students in grades K-12. The fact that we live in a technology-oriented world requires students to be technologically literate and to function effectively in a technologically sophisticated environment. While may primary school aged children already use computers and cell phones, among various other forms of technology, there is a need to introduce technology education into the primary school curriculum so that students are well prepared to continue these studies in the middle school years and attain the standards of technological literacy by the time they graduate high school.

VIEWPOINTS

Teaching industrial arts was traditionally concerned with teaching students to build things out of metal and wood by using tools and machines, and the industrial arts curriculum was better suited for the for the industrial era of the 20th century. While there is some debate as to when the technology era actually began, there is no question that we currently live in a technologically sophisticated world that requires a workforce that is technologically literate and that can compete for jobs in a technologically driven world. While many schools have begun integrating technology education into the primary school curriculum, middle schools are transforming their traditional industrial arts programs, and high schools are attempting to develop technology education programs that will produce students that meet the standards of technological literacy.

TRANSITIONING INTO THE TECHNOLOGY ERA

The shift towards technology education is essentially geared toward preparing for college education, but many students do not intend to attend college, and the academic requirements of many technology education programs are keeping these students from enrolling in these courses. While there is an obvious need to continue the move toward technology education, there are many who believe that this "should not come at the expense of industrial education programs, which have long formed a vital part of the comprehensive, general education of students in American schools" (Luna, 1998).

There are many who contend that our society is still essentially in a machine age, even if it is technologically driven. Students still need to be familiar with and comfortable using machines—including computers—to solve problems. However, students should be encouraged to use a variety of tools whether that tool is a traditional hammer or a laser-guided saw. But giving students the opportunity to work with wood, miter saws and radial arms saws also affords them an opportunity to see that there can be a number of solutions to a particular problem and that some solutions may even provide better answers (Luna).

Beyond developing skills, whether they are technically or technologically oriented, there are also secondary objectives to industrial and technology education and these include developing "self esteem, and pride in one's work" (Luna). While some may dismiss the latter as mere craftsmanship and no longer worth fostering, emphasizing quality at an early age is a critical element in preparing students for all types of jobs whether they are mechanical, technical or technological. For Luna, industrial and technological education should allow students to work with traditional and state of the art devices so that they will be better prepared to solve problems in our technologically sophisticated society (Luna).

GENDER ISSUES

While technology education has evolved from traditional industrial arts education, one concern for both approaches is one of lingering neglect—girls are still not encouraged to consider nontraditional occupations, as they often experience gender stereotyping in career counseling. In some cases, women who enroll in nontraditional occupational classes have experienced sexual harassment (Lewis, 2006). However, progress is being made as the technologically driven job market has resulted in a shift away from heavy machinery to information technology. Because of this, women are more readily accepted, even though there are still challenges in these professions, such as isolation. These problems will be resolved, however, as more women are encouraged to enter technology professions and are given opportunities to assume positions of leadership (Haynie, 2005).

CONCLUSION

In many ways the transformation from industrial arts education to technology education mirrors the transformations that have taken hold in many aspects of our society. The world has become a smaller, more competitive place where information, goods, services and jobs and even ideas are rapidly exchanged. In order to prepare students to function in this world, they will need to have a solid technological education, but the need for people to be capable of building things will still create a demand for industrial education, and that education will also be more steeped in technology.

Ultimately, technology education means preparing students to be able to compete for jobs in the technological and global market place. At the same time, there will continue to be a need for workers to fill manufacturing and construction jobs. Simply put, society will still have a demand for people who can build things. Therefore, while technology education continues to evolve, it is also important to recognize that there still is a place for traditional industrial arts programs.

TERMS & CONCEPTS

Bio-Mimicry: A relatively new science that studies nature's models and then imitates those designs and processes to solve human problems

Constructionism: An educational philosophy that holds that students "learn better when they are working with materials that allow them to design and build artifacts that are meaningful to them" (Rogers & Portsmore, 2004).

Industrial Arts: Traditional education programs for creating objects out of wood and metal by using a variety of hand tools, power tools and machines.

Integrate: To combine different subject areas like math, science, and engineering in technology education.

International Technology Education Association (ITEA): Formerly known as the American Industrial Arts Association, the ITEA was established in 1985 to reflect technological advances in society and the need to reform the curriculum of traditional industrial arts.

Layering: A teaching model that combines the traditional problem solving model with teamwork, technical skill and academic ability.

Standards For Technological Literacy: Standards established by the ITEA in 2000 for high school graduates.

STEM Model: A teaching model for technology education that integrates science, technology, education and mathematics.

Technology Education: "A study of technology, which provides an opportunity for students to learn about the processes and knowledge related to technology that are needed to solve problems and extend human capabilities" (Zagari & MacDonald).

Karen A. Kallio

BIBLIOGRAPHY

Clark, A., & Ernst, J. V. (2007). A model for the integration of science, technology, engineering and mathematics. *Technology Teacher, 66*, 24-26. Retrieved April 3, 2007, from EBSCO Online Database Academic Search Premier.

Haynie, W. J. III. (2005). Where the women are: Research findings on gender issues in technology education. *Technology Teacher, 64*, 12-16. Retrieved April 13, 2007, from EBSCO Online Database Academic Search Premier.

Herschbach, D. R. (2011). The STEM Initiative: Constraints and challenges. *Journal Of Stem Teacher Education, 48*, 96–122. Retrieved December 16, 2013, from EBSCO Online Database Education Research Complete.

Jones, A., Buntting, C., & Vries, M. (2013). The developing field of technology education: A review to look forward.

International Journal Of Technology & Design Education, 23, 191–212. Retrieved December 16, 2013, from EBSCO Online Database Education Research Complete.

Jones, K. (2006). Ideas for integrating technology education into everyday learning. *Technology & Children, 2,* 19-20. Retrieved April 13, 2007, from EBSCO Online Database Academic Search Premier.

Lewis, A. C. (2006). Training for jobs. *Education Digest, 71,* 71-73. Retrieved April 13, 2007, from EBSCO Online Database Academic Search Premier.

Luna, M. C. (1998). Technology education and its discontents. *Tech Directions, 57,* 26. Retrieved April 13, 2007, from EBSCO Online Database Academic Search Premier.

Maley, D. & Farr, R. (1989). Trends. *Educational Leadership, 46,* 86. Retrieved April 13, 2007, from EBSCO Online Database Academic Search Premier.

Meade, S. & Dugger, W. E., Jr. (2006). Technological literacy standards resources. *Technology Teacher, 65,* 25-27. Retrieved April 13, 2007, from EBSCO Online Database Academic Search Premier.

Pearson, G. (2004). Assessment of technological literacy: A national academies perspective. *Technology Teacher, 63,* 28-29. Retrieved April 13, 2007, from EBSCO Online Database Academic Search Premier.

Pruitt, J. W. (2004). Learning with less time and lots of students: Layering instruction in a middle level technology education program. *Techniques: Connecting Education & Careers, 79,* 58-59. Retrieved April 13, 2007, from EBSCO Online Database Academic Search Premier.

Ritz, J., & Martin, G. (2013). Research needs for technology education: An international perspective. *International Journal Of Technology & Design Education, 23,* 767–783. Retrieved December 16, 2013, from EBSCO Online Database Education Research Complete.

Rogers, C. & Portsmore, M. (2004). Bringing engineering to elementary school. *Journal of STEM Education Innovations & Research, 5* (3/4), 17-28. Retrieved April

13, 2007, from EBSCO Online Database Academic Search Premier.

Stewart, K. G. (1996). In with the new, but not out with the old. *Vocational Education Journal, 71,* 62. Retrieved April 13, 2007, from EBSCO Online Database Academic Search Premier.

Wicklein, R. C. (2006). Five good reasons for engineering design as the focus for technology education. *Technology Teacher, 65,* 25-29. Retrieved April 17, 2007, from EBSCO Online Database Academic Search Premier.

Zagari, A. & MacDonald, K. (1994). A history and philosophy of technology education. *Technology Teacher, 53,* 7-11. Retrieved April 13, 2007, from EBSCO Online Database Academic Search Premier.

SUGGESTED READING

Liker, J., Haddad, C.F. & Karlin, J. (1999). Perspectives on technology and work organization. *Annual Review of Sociology, 25,* 575. Retrieved April 13, 2007, from EBSCO Online Database Academic Search Premier.

Rhine, L. (2013). From the schoolhouse to the statehouse: Model for technology education. *Technology & Engineering Teacher, 73,* 10–13. Retrieved December 16, 2013, from EBSCO Online Database Education Research Complete.

Santilli, H. (2012). Science and technology, autonomous and more interdependent every time. *Science & Education, 21,* 797–811. Retrieved December 16, 2013, from EBSCO Online Database Education Research Complete.

Spoerk, M. (2005). How to keep your program relevant (and standards based). *Technology Teacher, 64,* 29-30. Retrieved April 13, 2007, from EBSCO Online Database Academic Search Premier.

Zuga, K. F. (1991). The technology education experience and what it can contribute to STS. *Theory Into Practice, 30,* 260. Retrieved April 13, 2007, from EBSCO Online Database Academic Search Premier.

TEACHING STUDY SKILLS

Study skills emphasize the process of learning. Teaching study skills in the K-12 public schools is essential at all grade levels and in all subject areas. Student mastery of study skills is a major objective of teachers. The teaching of study skills equips students for a lifetime of learning. Teaching students how to study has historically been considered a duty of schools. Many students do not practice good study habits and do not see study skills as valuable. Teaching good study skills and habits to students based on the findings of research has generally yielded positive academic-achievement results ranging.

KEYWORDS: Metacognition; Self-Regulation; Reflection; Attribution; Conative Abilities; Independent Learning; Mnemonic Devices; Remediation; Study Guides; Study Habits; Study Skills; Study-Skill Barriers

OVERVIEW

Teaching good study skills and habits are basic to any education. Teaching study skills to students is equivalent to their learning how to study. The goal is to provide students with a study-skills "tool box," "bank," or personal inventory of strategies they may apply in studying and to employ in learning effectively. Study skills can be defined as learned abilities essential to acquiring knowledge and competence. Study skills emphasize the process of learning (Marshak, 1979; Marshak & Burkle, 1981). A general study skills program including curriculum-specific study strategies has value to students in every class. Study-skill competencies should constitute a significant part of educational objectives so as to prepare students for subsequent school work in elementary, middle school, and high school. Different aspects of study skills are needed at specific grade levels (Petercsak, 1986; Smith, 1959; Walker & Antaya-Moore, 2001).

The learning process is developmental and involves acquiring, growing, changing and improving students' knowledge. The ability to study efficiently and effectively is, in fact, a distinctive characteristic of most high-achieving students. The converse is also true; that is, many poor students are unproductive because they lack good study skills. Thus, the teaching of study skills increases students' learning capacities and assists them in adapting to various teaching methods and instructional approaches (Estes & Vaughn, 1985). Some strategies are more effective than others for each individual. Students must get to know their own study-skills strengths and weaknesses.

A GOAL FOR TEACHERS

Student mastery of specific study skills is a major objective of teachers. Just as a good writer is one who has mastered writing skills, a good student is one who has mastered study skills. The development and mastery of study skills requires application and practice (Haladyna, 1997). Teaching study skills to students enables them to study efficiently and independently in a variety of learning activities, settings and situations. The goal is that of continually increasing independence in the use of study skills. This allows students to construct their own understandings and learn how to learn on their own through self-study and discovery. The development of students' study skills equips them for lifelong learning (Reid, 1975).

LEARNING THEORY & PSYCHOLOGY

The teaching of learning and motivation strategies related to study-skills development is based on educational psychology. Students' learning is dependent on the way they study, and learning theories attempt to explain students' learning via cognitive thinking processes and cognitive learning styles (Anderson & Armbruster, 1980; Tobias, 1984; Tuckman, 2003). Psychological principles such as metacognition are related to modifying the behaviors of students lacking study skills and who are poorly motivated to achieve academically. Affect and attitude are important in learning and maintaining students' motivation to learn. Motivation techniques are used in behavior modification to change study behaviors of students, overcome psychological resistance, and turn negative attitudes into positive attitudes (Brender, 1981; Weber, 1991).

Metacognition

Metacognition reflects students' abilities to change their thought processes to benefit themselves. Among the metacognitive strategies individuals can use to manage learning include planning, self-monitoring, and self-evaluating skills. When teachers teach metacognitive learning strategies to students, they are helping them to redirect less productive prevailing habits and attitudes into more productive habits and attitudes. Students gradually acquire the ability to teach themselves to learn (Haladyna; Wenden, 1998).

Self-Regulation

Highly successful individuals guide themselves systematically and have self-regulated thinking patterns. They learn how to self-monitor, self-reflect, and self-evaluate outcomes. In this process, they also utilize self-awareness, self-management, self-affirmation through personal feedback, and self-efficacy. In self-regulated learning, learners employ cognitive and metacognitive strategies. Self-regulated learners set goals, plan and use a variety of cognitive strategies to monitor progress and continually adjust their behaviors after evaluating prior outcomes (Barnett, 1997; Haladyna; Masui & De Corte, 2005).

Reflection & Attribution

Reflection and attribution are basic components of self-regulated learning. Attribution generally occurs when students assign responsibility for their success or failure either to personal characteristics within themselves such as effort or ability, or conversely to something outside themselves such as luck or the difficulty of a task. Interventions to train students to reflect and to attribute constructively can improve metacognitive and conative learning abilities and positively impact academic achievement. The process of conation refers to aspects of mental processes and behaviors that are directed toward change and action. These aspects include impulse or natural tendency, volition, desire, and striving. Improving metacognitive, conative, and regulation skills improve general learning competence (Gage & Berliner, 1988; Haladyna; Masui & De Corte, 2005).

Psychological Barriers

The problem of procrastination involves the complex interaction of behavioral, cognitive, and affective attributes and is not solely due to deficits in study habits or time management. Students must overcome the urge to procrastinate in developing positive and responsible study habits (Rutkowski & Domino, 1975; Solomon & Rothblum, 1984). Emotional problems, tension, and anxiety cause psychological stress and discomfort which can interfere with students' studying, test performance and academic effectiveness. Students may undergo a training program to reduce anxiety to improve knowledge retention and test scores (Tobias; Wark, 1970).

Applications

STUDY STRATEGIES

Students must develop study strategies for independent learning, and be able to self-assess their own individual study skills. A fully developed arsenal of study strategies will improve academic achievement. General strategies suggested are to actively participate in class, follow directions of the teacher and seek teacher assistance when needed, review and study handouts and study guides, complete worksheets, learn test-taking techniques, and prepare for exams (Gage & Berliner). Basic study skills include locating, selecting, organizing, and retaining information. Study skills have been classified in a number of ways. Reid groups study skills into three relatively coherent clusters:

- Receptive skills;
- Reflective skills;
- Expressive skills.

Receptive skills relate to the intake of ideas through reading. Reflective skills deal with the interaction between the individual and what he or she reads or sees. Expressive skills are abilities to apply knowledge learned and to demonstrate its utility.

Estes and Vaughn classify study skills into four different categories:
- Work-study skills;
- Locational skills;
- Organizational skills;
- Specialized skills.

Work-study skills are the fundamental skills of study, such as note taking and outlining. Locational skills refer to knowing where to find information residing in various reference sources. Locational skills are more generally referred to as research skills. Organizational skills include time management. Specialized skills are those needed for specific purposes such as test taking, using graphic aids and following directions (Estes & Vaughn).

Research Skills

Research techniques are used to gather information and materials. Research requires knowledge of the use of both traditional and online reference sources. Research can be applied to class reports, written or oral research papers, essays, and themes (Basso & McCoy, 1996; Reid).

Teachers need to instruct students in skills related to the use of various reference sources and materials. These include reference skills, locational skills, and library skills. Students need to be taught how dictionaries can be used for information other than definitions of words, as well as how to use various other types of reference books including atlases, almanacs and encyclopedias (Estes & Vaughn; Gabriel, 2005). Students also need to be taught how to locate, evaluate, and use online research sources.

Study Environment

Students should establish a familiar place for studying. Where one studies may be just as crucial as how one studies. The best place for productive studying is usually a special place that is not too comfortable and not too uncomfortable. Most students study and do their homework in a quiet place at home. The study space should be organized to minimize distractions so that students can maintain their concentration. Recognizing external or environmental constraints to learning is half the battle (Estes & Vaughn; Gage & Berliner; Green & Rankin, 1985). Minimizing distractions can be a challenge for students who are conducting research online.

Organization

Organizational skills are basic components of remediation in study-skills attainment or improvement. Students need to be able to organize study materials, plan using a step-wise process, identify and set goals, and use orderly work methods. Students should keep written records of class notes and assignments, and organize and maintain them in electronic and/or hard copy files using classification and alphabetization.

Organizational skills are the most crucial skills which a teacher must diagnose and provide students assistance with. These skills aid students' learning and help make their study time more enjoyable and profitable. (Estes & Vaughn; Gabriel).

Time-Management Skills

Students also need to develop effective time-management skills. One requirement in managing time is to set aside specific study time. One motivational factor with regard to time management is for students to recognize how much time is being wasted (Angel, 1983; Edgington & Hyman, 2005; Estes & Vaughn; Gabriel; Gage & Berliner). Teachers must instruct students in time-management skills including how to use a planner for managing their time.

Reading-Study Skills

Developing reading-study skills is another study strategy. A strategy for reading more effectively and improving reading comprehension is for students to become active versus passive readers. They also need to know how to use subject headings and indices. Reading rates can be adjusted to the difficulty of the material, and speed-reading can be used for surveying and skimming chapters. Re-reading is often necessary (Angel; Gabriel; Karlin, 1980; Petercsak; Reid).

Teachers must work to improve students' reading and reading-related skills. Reading skills consist of a body of subskills which can be classified into several major categories such as word recognition, word meaning, comprehension and appreciation. Other reading-related skills include increasing students' vocabularies and reading rates (Karlin).

Textbook Study Skills

Effective strategies for studying textbooks include reading overviews and objectives at the beginning of chapters, read the body or main text of each assigned chapter or section, review objectives as needed to assess mastery of key concepts, study chapter summaries and vocabulary lists, complete any assigned end-of-chapter questions, problems or exercises, and re-read, review and study in preparation for tests (Borg, 1987).

Study Guides

Students should use study guides developed by teachers. There are two main types of study guides:

- The content guide, which focuses students' attention on the information that is read in the text;
- The process guide, in which teachers offer suggestions on how to read the text and ways to apply skills and read more efficiently (Karlin).

Note Taking, Highlighting & Outlining

Three essential study skills for students are note taking, underlining or highlighting, and outlining. There are two different forms of note taking which are used as organizational skills—"lecture" note taking and reading note taking. Lecture note taking requires listening, analyzing, interpreting and synthesizing while writing. Reading note taking is a difficult skill requiring analysis, interpretation and synthesis. Note taking serves as both an encoding device and as an external storage mechanism. Elementary and middle-school students need note taking to write down assignments and directions. High-school students need more sophisticated note-taking skills (Estes & Vaughn; Rickards & Friedman, 1978).

When possible, the most important things—terms, concepts and principles—should be highlighted. However, since public school students are not generally allowed to underline or highlight in their textbooks, they need to be taught to take notes and to outline the key words, concepts and ideas they encounter in their reading. Outlining is a complex skill because it requires the use of analysis and synthesis to summarize material (Estes & Vaughn).

Teachers need to teach students how to take notes efficiently and effectively. Because note taking is a complex skill when done well, teachers must provide students guidance and practice in the process. Among the systems of note taking to be taught are outlining, clustering, and brainstorming as well as how to organize a notebook (Estes & Vaughn; Gabriel).

Listening Skills

Listening skills include learning to hear cues such as emphasis on key words and repetition. Listening skills are important when teachers present material, when students respond to questions or make reports to the class, and when students work in cooperative groups (Basso & McCoy; Devine, 1987; Gabriel).

Test Preparation

Another aspect of teaching study skills is test preparation. Teachers can prepare students for examinations by directly instructing them in test-taking strategies. Computer-assisted instruction and related technology using self-learning modules are beneficial in teaching study skills, test-taking skills, and writing skills (Angel; Gadzella, 1983).

Improved study skills and test-taking strategies help students in the preparation for exams and improve their testing confidence. Preparing for exams through relaxation methods reduces test-taking anxiety and increases student achievement (Angel; Beidel, Turner, & Taylor-Ferreira, 1999; Green & Rankin).

Other Techniques

The use of cognitive assistance devices such as mnemonic devices for memorization can aid memory improvement. Concepts for remembering and relating content can help in integrating and making use of prior learning. Breaking material that is to be learned down into smaller "chunks" or "bites" can be useful. Verbalizing-stating aloud and reading aloud-can be used for reviewing information and material to reinforce learning. Student questioning and debriefing strategies can also be beneficial study skills. Text can be represented diagrammatically using concept maps or other graphic aids. Map skills for reading maps, charting skills and understanding charts, graphing skills and interpreting graphs, and drawing, studying and reading time lines are other tools and aids

which students should be able to appropriately select and utilize (Anderson & Armbruster; Edgington & Hyman; Karlin; Petercsak; Reid).

TEACHING METHODS

Teachers play a key role in facilitating students' learning of study skills. Study skills can be taught and learned within a short period of time using any one of various methods. Teaching study skills, instructing for study-skills development and implementing a study-skills curriculum is accomplished using formalized teaching and training methods in study-skills laboratories, tutorials, "workshops," or development sessions (Haladyna; Petercsak; Reid).

Students develop proficiencies in study skills and increase their awareness of specific strategies through direct instruction, guided learning, targeted activities, and meaningful practice (Karlin; Petercsak; Reid). Teachers are responsible for identifying and correcting weaknesses and/or deficiencies in students' study skills to enhance their ability to learn effectively. Early diagnosis of deficiencies such as a student's inability to communicate knowledge or articulate ideas effectively in speech and/or writing is a way to provide individualized academic advising, counseling, and feedback to help students understand their strengths and weaknesses. In addition, teachers need to design learning plans for student study-skill remediation (Estes & Vaughn; Wenden).

TIME CONSTRAINTS

Although teachers typically devote very little time to teaching study skills, whatever time they do use takes away time from teaching students academic content. The use of different instructional materials by teachers demands the application of varying study strategies. Many students do not practice good study and homework habits and do not see study skills as valuable, so it is difficult to change students' nonproductive and ineffective study habits learned over years. Some students may put up resistance to learning effective study strategies, and some teachers may take an intensive-instruction approach to study-skills training that may turn off some students (Green & Rankin).

Careful diagnoses of individual abilities in the study-skills area may be needed to prescribe sequences of instruction based on the skill needs of the individual. The study techniques that are likely to ultimately yield the greatest learning benefits are those that have the highest cost in student time and energy (Anderson & Armbruster; Fisher, 1970).

RESEARCH RESULTS

Experiments in which students have been trained directly in better study habits have generally yielded positive academic-achievement results ranging from moderate to large (Gage & Berliner). Students self-report improvement in study habits through the application of effective study skills. Their improved study habits and use of more effective study strategies result in increased academic success as measured by improved grade-point averages and performances on related assessments (Stewart, 1984).

However, some researchers have found little connection between good study skills and improved performance. For example, students' ability to integrate new information with prior knowledge or existing schemata is more likely to help them learn and retain information more than their vocabularies or reading skills (Shaughnessy & Evans, 1986). Frase and Schwartz (1974) found that whether using questioning or answering as a study technique after prose reading did not affect the recall of information incidental to the questions. However, recall is improved for information related to the questions (Frase & Schwartz). Based on a review of other research studies and a small experiment performed on their own, Marken & Maland (1979) concluded that the effects of note taking and underlining are probably very small.

Annis & Davis (1976), in comparing reading only with reading and note taking or underlining, concluded that note taking and underlining while reading are most effective when learners prefer to read only but are unfamiliar with the topic. Reading only, without note taking or underlining, is least effective when learners prefer to read only but are unfamiliar with the topic. Reading only produces the best test scores when students prefer this technique and are familiar with the topic.

TERMS & CONCEPTS

Attribution: A psychological process in which individuals assign responsibility for their success or failure either to characteristics within themselves such as effort or ability, or conversely to something outside themselves such as luck or the difficulty of a task.

Conative Abilities: Aspects of mental processes that are directed toward change and action; examples include impulse or natural tendency, volition, desire and striving. The process itself is called conation or conatus.

Independent Learning: Also called autonomous learning; term broadly used here to refer to any method used by students for self-study and individual knowledge acquisition.

Metacognition: A process used by individuals to change their own thought processes to benefit themselves.

Mnemonic Devices: Cognitive-assistance tools which aid memorization and improve memory.

Remediation: Process used to address and correct for weaknesses and/or deficiencies in students' learning, for example, study-skill remediation.

Self-Regulation: The ability to keep track of one's own behavior and to control it (Gage & Berliner).

Study Guides: Tools or aids developed by teachers to facilitate students' learning.

Study Habits: The ways and means students use to pursue and acquire knowledge; they can be good, positive, productive, efficient, and effective or conversely, they can be poor, negative, non-productive, inefficient, and ineffective.

Study Skills: Learned abilities, capabilities, and capacities for acquiring knowledge and competence.

Study-Skill Barriers: Behaviors that interfere with students' academic performance and the teacher's ability to assess academic progress; for example, poor time management, inattention during lectures and class discussions, inability to follow directions, and failure to complete assignments.

R. D. Merritt

BIBLIOGRAPHY

Anderson, T. H., & Armbruster, B. B. (1980). Studying: Technical report no. 155. Cambridge, MA: Bolt, Beranek and Newman, Inc.

Angel, N. M. (1983, July). Teaching study skills to the exceptional black student. Paper presented at the Council for Exceptional Children National Conference on the Exceptional Black Child, Atlanta, GA.

Annis, L., & Davis, J. K. (1976). The effect of study techniques and preferences on later recall. Washington, DC: Education Resources Information Center. (ERIC Document Reproduction Service No. ED132 213).

Awang, M., & Sinnadurai, S. (2011). The development of study skill tools in evaluating student's study orientation skills and its relationship towards academic performance. Journal of Language Teaching & Research, 2, 314-322. Retrieved December 11, 2013, from EBSCO Online Database Education Resource Complete.

Barnett, J. E. (1997, March). Self-regulation of reading college textbooks. Paper presented at the Annual Meeting of the American Educational Research Association, Chicago, IL.

Basso, D., & McCoy, N. (1996). Study tools: A comprehensive curriculum guide for teaching study skills to students with special needs. Columbia, SC: Twins Publications.

Beidel, D. C., Turner, S. M., & Taylor-Ferreira, J. C. (1999). Teaching study skills and test-taking strategies to elementary school students. Behavior Modification, 23, 630-646.

Bentley, D. A., & Blount, H. P. (1980). Testing the spaced lecture for the college classroom. Washington, DC: Education Resources Information Center (ERIC Document Reproduction Service No. ED188559).

Borg, W. R. (1987). Applying educational research: A practical guide for teachers. New York, NY: Longman.

Brender, M. (1981). The tactical use of psychology to facilitate college teaching and student management. Teaching of Psychology, 8, 95-97.

Burney, V. H., & Cross, T. L. (2006). Impoverished students with academic promise in rural settings: 10 lessons from Project Aspire. Gifted Child Today, 29, 14-21.

Cooper, H., & Valentine, J. C. (2001). Using research to answer practical questions about homework. Educational Psychologist, 36, 143-153.

Devine, T. G. (1987). Teaching study skills: A guide for teachers (second edition). Newton, MA: Allyn and Bacon.

Edgington, W. D., & Hyman, W. (2005). Using baseball in social studies instruction:

Addressing the five fundamental themes of geography. Social Studies, 96, 113-117. Retrieved November 12, 2007, from EBSCO Online Database Academic Search Premier.

Estes, T. H., & Vaughn, J. L., Jr. (1985). Reading and learning in the content classroom: Diagnostic and instructional strategies. Boston, MA: Allyn and Bacon, Inc.

Finch, A. J., & Spiritz, A. (1980). Use of cognitive training to change cognitive processes. Exceptional Education Quarterly, 1, 31-39.

Fisher, J. A. (1970). Diagnostic and screening instruments: Tests and services for assisting college reading skills. Washington, DC: Education Resources Information Center (ERIC Document Reproduction Service No. ED045287).

Frase, L. T., & Schwartz, B. J. (1974). Question production and answering as an aid to prose reading. Washington, DC: Education Resources Information Center (ERIC Document Reproduction Service No. ED102534).

Fremouw, W. J., & Feindler, E. L. (1978). Peer versus professional models for study skills training. Journal of Counseling Psychology, 26, 576-580.

Gabriel, J. G. (2005). How to thrive as a teacher leader. Alexandria, VA: Association for Supervision and Curriculum Development.

Gadzella, B. M. (1983, January). High school students participate in a CAI study skills program. Paper presented at the Southwest Educational Research Association Meeting, Houston, TX.

Gage, N. L., & Berliner, D. C. (1988). Educational psychology (4th ed.). Boston, MA: Houghton Mifflin Company.

Gill, B. P., & Schlossman, S. L. (2003). A nation at rest: The American way of homework. Educational Evaluation & Policy Analysis, 25, 319-337.

Green, C. A., & Rankin, P. T. (1985). Detroit high school student perceptions regarding homework and study habits. Detroit, MI: Detroit Public Schools' Office of Instructional Improvement.

Haladyna, T. M. (1997). Writing test items to evaluate higher order thinking. Boston, MA: Allyn and Bacon.

Jones, B. F., & Hall, J. W. (1979). School applications of the mnemonic keyword method as a study strategy by eighth graders. Washington, DC: Education Resources Information Center (ERIC Document Reproduction Service No. ED182738).

Julien, B. L., Lexis, L., Schuijers, J., Samiric, T., & McDonald, S. (2012). Using capstones to develop research skills and graduate capabilities: A case study from physiology. Journal of University Teaching & Learning Practice, 9, 1-15. Retrieved December 11, 2013, from EBSCO Online Database Education Resource Complete.

Karlin, R. (1980). Teaching elementary reading: Principles and strategies (3rd ed.). New York, NY: Harcourt Brace Jovanovich, Inc.

Kunvits, J., & Kurvits, M. (2013). High school students' acquisition of knowledge and skills through web-based collaboration. International Journal for Technology in Mathematics Education, 20, 95-102. Retrieved December 11, 2013, from EBSCO Online Database Education Resource Complete.

Lewis, R. B., & Doorlag, D. H. (1987). Teaching special students in the mainstream (2nd ed.). Columbus, OH: Merrill Publishing Company.

Marken, R., & Maland, J. (1979). Single subject analyses of three study methods. Psychological Reports, 44, 765-766.

Marshak, D. (1979). What's the status of study skills in your school? NASSP Bulletin, 63, 105-110.

Marshak, D., & Burkle, C. R. (1981). Learning to study: A basic skill. Principal, 61, 38-40.

Masui, C., & De Corte, E. (2005). Learning to reflect and to attribute constructively as basic components of self-regulated learning. British Journal of Educational Psychology, 75, 351-372.

Petercsak, S. J., Jr. (1986). Study skills: A resource book. Columbus, OH: Ohio State Department of Education, Division of Inservice Education.

Petrini, G. C., & Fleming, D. B. (1990). A history of social studies skills. Theory and Research in Social Education, 28, 233-247.

Reid, N. (1975). Developing study skills in the reading process. Washington, DC: Education Resources Information Center (ERIC Document Reproduction Service No. ED154333).

Reid, N. (1979). 'Go and look it up yourself.' Washington, DC: Education Resources Information Center (ERIC Document Reproduction Service No. ED184953).

Rickards, J. P., & Friedman, F. (1978). The encoding versus the external storage hypothesis in note taking. Contemporary Educational Psychology, 3, 136-143.

Rutkowski, K., & Domino, G. (1975). Interrelationship of study skills and personality variables in college students. Journal of Educational Psychology, 67, 784-789.

Shaughnessy, M. F., & Evans, R. (1986, November). The educational psychology of note taking: Effects of prior word/ world knowledge. Paper presented at the Annual Meeting of the Rocky Mountain Educational Research Association, Albuquerque, NM.

Smith, N. B. (1959). Teaching study skills in reading. Elementary School Journal, 87, 246-265.

Solomon, L. J., & Rothblum, E. D. (1984). Academic procrastination: Frequency and cognitive-behavioral correlates. Journal of Counseling Psychology, 31, 503-509.

Stewart, K. J. (1984). Study strategy use and comprehension monitoring accuracy of college students. Washington, DC: Education Resources Information Center (ERIC Document Reproduction Service No. ED250640).

Thompson, M. E. (1977). An appraisal of study methods inventories. Washington, DC: Education Resources Information Center (ERIC Document Reproduction Service No. ED138622).

Tobias, S. (1984). Implications of wellness models for educational and school psychology. Washington, DC: Education Resources Information Center (ERIC Document Reproduction Service No. ED259259).

Tuckman, B. W. (2003, August). The 'Strategies-for-Achievement' approach for teaching study skills. Paper presented at the Annual Conference of the American Psychological Association (111th), Toronto, Ontario, Canada.

Venezky, R. L. (1987). A history of the American reading textbook. Elementary School Journal, 87, 246-265.

Walker, C., & Antaya-Moore, D. (2001). Make school work for you: Teacher implementation guide [and] a resource for junior and senior high students who want to be more successful learners. Edmonton, Alberta, Canada: Learning Resources Centre.

Wark, D. M. (1970). Emotional problems in study and behavioral methods for treatment. Washington, DC: Education Resources Information Center (ERIC Document Reproduction Service No. ED045298).

Weber, A. L. (1991). Introduction to psychology. New York, NY: Harper Perennial.

Wenden, A. L. (1998). Learner training in foreign/second language learning: A curricular perspective for the 21st century. Washington, DC: Education Resources Information Center (ERIC Document Reproduction Service No. ED416673).

Winship, A. E. (1893). What to teach, when to teach it and how. Journal of Education, 37, 379.

Winship, A. E. (1913). A home study symposium. Journal of Education, 78, 628-629.

SUGGESTED READING

Carns, A. W., & Carns, M. R. (1991). Teaching study skills, cognitive strategies, and metacognitive skills through self-diagnosed learning styles. School Counselor, 38, 341-346. Retrieved November 12, 2007, from EBSCO Online Database Academic Search Premier.

Etty, J. (2004). Repetition is the key to revision. History Review, 22-23. Retrieved November 12, 2007, from EBSCO Online Database Academic Search Premier.

Gill, B. P., & Schlossman, S. L. (2004). Villain or savior? The American discourse on homework, 1850-2003. Theory Into Practice, 43, 174-181. Retrieved November 12, 2007, from EBSCO Online Database Academic Search Premier.

Hoover, J. J., & Rabideau, D. K. (1995). Semantic webs and study skills. Intervention in School & Clinic, 30, 292-296. Retrieved November 12, 2007, from EBSCO Online Database Academic Search Premier.

Krashen, S. (2005). The hard work hypothesis: Is doing your homework enough to overcome the effects of poverty? Multicultural Education, 12, 16-19. Retrieved November 12, 2007, from EBSCO Online Database Education Research Complete.

Paulsen, K., & Sayeski, K. L. (2013). Using study skills to become independent learners in secondary content classes. Intervention in School & Clinic, 49, 39-45. Retrieved December 11, 2013, from EBSCO Online Database Education Resource Complete.

Urciuoli, J., & Bluestone, C. (2013). Study skills analysis: A pilot study linking a success and psychology course. Community College Journal of Research & Practice, 37, 397-401. Retrieved December 11, 2013, from EBSCO Online Database Education Resource Complete.

BUSINESS CURRICULUM

Increasingly, public school education is emphasizing business skills along with basic verbal and mathematical literacy in an effort to help tomorrow's business leaders acquire the skills they will need to help the U.S. remain competitive in the world market. The skills necessary to do this include critical thinking and other decision making skills; protocols and etiquette for in-person, written, and electronic communications; digital literacy; financial literacy; and ethical decision making. Although many of these skills can be taught in classroom settings, the most effective preparation for business is to tie classroom learning in with real world applications and supplement it with real world training.

KEYWORDS: Accounting; Business Education; Critical Thinking; Curriculum; Economics; Ethics; Leadership; Social Responsibility; Team

OVERVIEW

WHY STUDY BUSINESS?

Historically, public school education has focused on helping students acquire basic mastery of the "three Rs"—reading, writing, and arithmetic—with enough other information to help them become good citizens of their community, country, and planet. The way this latter goal has been interpreted over the years has changed with the times. Today, for example, it is much more likely to see public school students study environmentalism in order to understand their impact on the world around them rather than home economics or shop, which in the past would prepare them for traditional gender roles. Despite these changes, however, the necessity of teaching the three Rs remains; no matter what career path students choose, they will need basic literacy and communication skills and must be able to perform basic mathematical operations in order to be eligible for jobs that will allow them to achieve their dreams, or to acquire the further education needed to do so.

The trouble, of course, is that young people often find it difficult to make the connection between learning basic verbal and mathematical literacy skills and other subjects taught in schools with the exciting futures that they envision for themselves. As a result, there are grocery clerks or fast food workers who cannot make change or telephone salespersons who must go through an entire prepared script in order to answer a customer's questions. Many high schools and even middle schools offer business courses to help students better understand the applicability of the skills they learn and to prepare them to study business skills at a college level or to enter the workforce after graduation (Canada Ministry of Education, 2006).

Business curricula in public schools are typically designed to help students acquire basic business skills rather than specific workplace skills. Due to the virtually unavoidable necessity of interacting in business environments, these general skills will be necessary for success in the 21st century. For example, even students who go on to pursue careers in medical fields will need to have skills for organizing and setting up an office and the accounting skills necessary for adequate cash flow. Similarly, those who go into artistic fields will need to be able to market and sell their works or performances or to be able to oversee the activities of managers and agents.

Goals of the Business Curriculum

CRITICAL THINKING

Although the details of the business curriculum vary among school systems, there are several core areas that should be considered in a business studies curriculum. The first of these comprises the basic knowledge and skills needed for success in a business environment. One of the skills that are essential for success in the workplace is critical thinking. This is the active, disciplined mental process of conceptualizing, analyzing, synthesizing, and/or evaluating information and applying it to problems. The data used to inform critical thinking processes may be obtained through observation, experience, reflection, reasoning, or communication. As opposed to non-critical thinking, critical thinking goes beyond the mere acquisition and retention of information to process and evaluate the information and discern an appropriate course of action or thought. Critical thinking is essential to success in many business activities, including strategic planning, understanding and reaching one's target market, and making day to day decisions regarding the course of the business.

A related basic skill needed for success in business is problem solving. This can be viewed as the application of one's thinking skills to determine the optimum solution to a problem given the parameters and various elements of the situation. Problem solving abilities are important in business for the full range of business activities from day to day decisions through strategic planning.

Closely tied with these skills needed for business is the ability to understand and evaluate risk. Risk is the quantifiable probability that an investment's actual return will be lower than expected. Higher risks mean both a greater probability of loss and a possibility of greater return on investment. Risk assessment is the process of determining the potential loss and probability of loss of the organization's objectives. Risk assessment is one step in risk management. Risk management is the project management process of analyzing the tasks and activities of a project, planning ways to reduce the impact if the predicted normal course of events does not occur, and implementing reporting procedures so that project problems are discovered earlier in the process rather than later.

To provide the data needed to make sound business decisions, students must also learn good research skills not only for online and library research, but also for collecting and analyzing their own data. All these skills are necessary for strategic planning, which is the process of determining the long-term goals of an organization and developing a plan to use the company's resources—including materials and personnel—in reaching these goals. It is essential for a business to have a strategic plan of action to help the organization reach its goals and objectives. A good business strategy is based on the rigorous analysis of empirical data, including market needs and trends, competitor capabilities and offerings, and the organization's resources and abilities (Mahinda, 2006).

INTERPERSONAL SKILLS
In addition to the intellectual skills necessary for success in business, students also need to learn interpersonal skills. The ability to relate well with employees, management, and customers, for example, can be the difference between success and failure for both a business and an individual. Increasingly, work in the 21st century requires teamwork skills. A team is a special group within which there is skill differentiation among members and the entire team works in the context of a common goal. Team members are committed to the goal and mission of the team and have a collaborative culture in which the members trust each

other. Leadership of a team is shared, and members are mutually accountable to each other.

DIGITAL LITERACY
Whether one works in teams or as an individual, virtually every 21st century workplace in the western world requires knowledge of personal computers and basic digital literacy. Personal computers have become the backbone of most businesses today and are used for a wide variety of tasks from writing memos, conducting routine business correspondence, performing mathematical and financial calculations, and designing and updating web pages. These skills are needed whether a student decides to go directly into the business world after graduation from public school or to go on to Higher Education at a university or other institution. Among the computer literacy skills that need to be acquired are the fundamentals of operating systems and computer hardware, word processing and data input, data management, and information systems technology (Canada Ministry of Education).

Students expecting to enter the business world need to be familiar with basic application software programs that perform functions not related to the running of the computer itself. Word processing software, for example, allows the author of a document to create, change, edit, update, and format without the necessity of sending the document off to a typing pool. Similarly, bookkeeping and accounting procedures that once needed to be done painstakingly by hand can now be accomplished quickly—and can be easily changed or updated—using spreadsheet or other accounting software. Entry level positions for some business professions may also require basic proficiency in special application software packages such as graphics packages, photography editing packages, or web authoring software.

COMMUNICATION SKILLS
Another set of skills necessary for high technology or scientific fields or for customer service include communication literacy and protocols. Students studying business in public school must learn to listen, speak, read, write, and represent thoughts professionally. This includes basic reading and writing literacy skills, and requires knowledge of business terminology, the ability to professionally format documents and emails and skill in communicating and presenting information both in oral presentations and through the written word. Students learning communication for business also need to be

aware of and apply professional etiquette not only in person but also in written and electronic communications (Canada Ministry of Education). For example, students should learn how to best use social media in a professional manner. The use of social media in business is becoming increasingly common, but most companies don't offer social media training (Post, 2013).

Students should also understand the role of diversity in the workplace and how to interact with individuals of different cultures if they are to become valuable employees in an international marketplace.

FINANCIAL LITERACY

Financial literacy skills are essential for success in business and are increasingly taught at the middle and high school levels. Students need to understand and be able to apply the basics of financial planning and money management both for their personal finances and in business applications. Included in this skills set are a basic understanding of credit concepts, financial decision making, investment, taxes, and the analysis of financial documents. Many public schools also teach basic economics concepts and accounting principles as part of their business curricula (Canada Ministry of Education).

BUSINESS ETHICS

Finally, it is important for students to acquire an understanding of ethical business practices early on so that they become a habit that will be carried on into their work life. The incorporation of ethical principles into one's critical thinking processes can help avoid some of the egregious breaches of moral standards that have been seen in the business world in the early 21st century. Ethics as a discipline looks at the content of moral judgments such as what is right and wrong and the nature of these judgments, i.e., whether the judgments are subjective or objective. The study of ethics is important in the school business curriculum in order to produce business leaders who will set examples for future business conduct. One aspect of ethical studies is social responsibility. This is the philosophy that an individual, corporation, government, or other entity has the obligation to contribute to the welfare of its community. Social responsibility includes evaluating the impact of one's decisions or actions on others, in particular on those who are disadvantaged. The application of ethical principles applies not only to dealing with other

people, but also to the impact of business processes and procedures on the environment. Corporate social responsibility programs are becoming more common as society increasingly expects companies to address environmental and social issues (Lim & Tsutsui, 2012). Students need to take into consideration issues of environmental responsibility and sustainability in their business decision making in order to be competitive in the business world of the future.

REAL-WORLD LEARNING EXPERIENCES

It is important to present material in such a way that students can readily see the connections between basic skills taught in the classroom and real world applications. The School-to-Work (STW) Opportunities Act was enacted in 1994 in order to help the public school systems in the U.S. prepare the next generation of business leaders for their tasks. Federal funding for STWOA ended in 2001, but the act helped spur the creation of STW programs around the country. Many high schools, for example, offer STW programs (Hutchins & Akos, 2012). The purpose of the STW is to help link education reform and economic development. This is done through three related components. First, the STW encourages students to explore their career interests and options no later than the 7th grade and select a career major no later than the beginning of their junior year in high school. School-based learning is used to integrate academic and vocational learning to help students master core vocational skills. The second component of the STW is work-based learning, which comprises a planned program of job training and experiences that have been developed to supplement the student's classroom-learning experiences. Perhaps the most important component of the STW, however, is the connecting activities in which students are matched with work-based opportunities and a site mentor that helps the student acquire the skills necessary for success in the business world and connect the classroom learning to the real world (Gray, 2000).

The STW provides a framework for helping students acquire real world skills that are invaluable in the business world. However, these skills must be tied in with real world learning. Too often, for example, although students are trained in actual business settings, they are only evaluated using classroom assessment instruments such as paper-and-pencil tests. Students need to be evaluated using the same type of criteria with which their performance would be evaluated in the workplace after graduation.

CONCLUSION

Students should be exposed to business concepts long before they enter college or the workforce. Middle and high school students can be taught a variety of skills that will be invaluable in the business world, including critical thinking and other decision making skills; protocols and etiquette for in-person, written, and electronic communications; digital literacy; financial literacy; and ethical decision making. To be optimally effective, however, these skills need to be tied in to real world applications so that students can see and understand the applicability of classroom learning to the real world. Business curriculum in the public school system, therefore, often supplements classroom learning with job training and experiences and connecting activities. Through a combination of classroom and practical learning experiences of this kind, the next generation of business leaders will be better prepared to help the U.S. maintain its place as a global competitor in the free market economy.

TERMS & CONCEPTS

Accounting: The systematic practice of recording, verifying, and communicating the financial information of the organization. Accounting practices include recording transactions, keeping financial records, performing internal audits, and communicating this information to the appropriate stakeholders.

Critical Thinking: The disciplined mental process of conceptualizing, analyzing, synthesizing, and/or evaluating information and applying it to problems. The data used to inform critical thinking processes may be obtained through observation, experience, reflection, reasoning, or communication. As opposed to non-critical thinking, critical thinking goes beyond the mere acquisition and retention of information to process and evaluate the information and discern an appropriate course of action or thought.

Curriculum: A set of training or education courses that must be followed in sequence in order to acquire a diploma or degree. Curriculum may be used to refer to the set of courses or their content. (plural, curricula).

Economics: A social science that studies the production, distribution, and consumption of goods and services, the distribution of wealth, the allocation of resource as well as the theory and management of economic systems. Economics is concerned with the theories, principles, and models of economic systems.

Ethics: In philosophy, ethics refers to the study of the content of moral judgments (i.e., the difference between right and wrong) and the nature of these judgments (i.e., whether the judgments are subjective or objective).

Information Technology: The use of computers, communications networks, and knowledge in the creation, storage, and dispersal of data and information. Information technology comprises a wide range of items and abilities for use in the creation, storage, and distribution of information. An information system is a system that facilitates the flow of information and data between people or departments.

Leadership: The process of influencing people and providing an environment in which they can achieve team and organizational objectives. Leadership can be attempted, successful, or effective depending on the response of those who the leader is attempting to lead. The term leadership can also be used to refer to those within an organizational setting that have the responsibility of balancing the interests of all organizational stakeholders, setting and communicating a vision for the organization, and inducing others to help meet the vision.

Social Responsibility: The philosophy that an individual, corporation, government, or other entity has the obligation to contribute the welfare of the community of which it is a part. Social responsibility includes taking the impact of one's decisions or actions on others, in particular those who are disadvantaged.

Team: A group in which there is skill differentiation among team members and the entire team works in the context of a common goal. Team members are committed to the goal and mission of the team and have a collaborative culture in which the members trust each other. Leadership of a team is shared, and members are mutually accountable to each other.

Word Processing: The use of a computer to create, edit, and store, documents electronically. Word processing was once done on stand alone, dedicated computers but today is typically done through application software on a personal computer or workstation.

Ruth A. Wienclaw

BIBLIOGRAPHY

Bennett, J. V. (2008). Work-based learning and social support: Relative influences on high school seniors' occupational engagement orientations. *Career and Technical*

Education Research, 32, 187-214. Retrieved 27 July 2010, from EBSCO Online Database.

Canada Ministry of Education. (2006). *The Ontario Curriculum, Grades 11 and 12: Business Studies* (rev.). Retrieved 27 July 2010 from Ministry of Education, http://edu.gov.

Dymond, S. K., Neeper, L. S., & Fones, D. (2010). Typing with purpose: Linking the word processing curriculum to real world applications through service learning. *Clearing House, 83*, 33-38. Retrieved 27 July 2010, from EBSCO Online Database Academic Search Complete.

Gray, D. L. (2000). Shaping America's workforce for the new millennium. *Education, 120*, 631-633. Retrieved 27 July 2010, from EBSCO Online Database Academic Search Complete.

Hutchins, B. C., & Akos, P. (2013). Rural High School Youth's Access to and Use of School-to-Work Programs. *Career Development Quarterly, 61*, 210-225. Retrieved December 1, 2013 from EBSCO Online Database Education Research Complete.

Lim, A., & Tsutsui, K. (2012). Globalization and Commitment in Corporate Social Responsibility: Cross-National Analyses of Institutional and Political-Economy Effects. *American Sociological Review, 77*, 69-98. Retrieved December 1, 2013, from EBSCO Online Database Education Research Complete.

Mahinda, D. D. (2006, July). State of the art business education: Career and technical education curriculum revitalization initiative. Retrieved 27 July 2010 from Illinois Office of Educational Services Website, http://ilcte.org.

Post, P. (2013). Embrace Social Media Carefully. *Training, 50*, 56. Retrieved December 1, 2013, from EBSCO Online Database Education Research Complete.

SUGGESTED READING

Bishop, J. H. & Mane, F. (2005). Raising academic standards and vocational concentrators: Are they better off or worse off? *Education Economics, 13*, 171-187. Retrieved 27 July 2010, from EBSCO Online Database Education Research Complete.

Chadd, J. & Anderson, M. A. (2005). Illinois work-based learning programs: Worksite mentor knowledge and training. *Career and Technical Education Research, 30*, 25-45. Retrieved 27 July 2010, from EBSCO Online Database Education Research Complete.

Dennis, A. R., Duffy, T. M., & Cakir, H. (2010). IT programs in high schools: Lessons from the Cisco Networking Academy program. *Communications of the ACM, 53*, 138-141. Retrieved 27 July 2010, from EBSCO Online Database Business Source Complete.

Grimes, P. W., Rogers, K. E., & Smith, R. C. (2010). High school economic education and access to financial services. *Journal of Consumer Affairs, 44*, 317-335. Retrieved

27 July 2010, from EBSCO Online Database Business Sources Complete.

Grubb, W. N. & Lazerson, M. (2005). The education gospel and the role of vocationalism in American Education. *American Journal of Education, 111*, 297-319. Retrieved 27 July 2010, from EBSCO Online Database Education Research Complete.

Gustafsson, U. A. (2002). School-arranged or market-governed workplace training? A labour market perspective. *Journal of Education and Work, 15*, 219-236. Retrieved 27 July 2010, from EBSCO Online Database Education Research Complete.

Gustman, A. L. & Steinmeier, T. L. (1982). The relation between vocational training in high school and economic outcomes. *Industrial and Labor Relations Review, 36*, 73-87. Retrieved 27 July 2010, from EBSCO Online Database Business Source Complete.

Lynn, B., Shehata, M., & White, L. (1994). The effects of secondary school accounting education on university accounting performance—a Canadian experience. *Contemporary Accounting Research, 10*, 733-758. Retrieved 27 July 2010, from EBSCO Online Database Business Source Complete.

Marks, M. & Kotula, G. (2009). Using the circular flow of income model to teach economics in the middle school classroom. *Social Studies, 100*, 233-242. Retrieved 27 July 2010, from EBSCO Online Database Academic Search Complete.

McInerny, P. M. (2003). The student-managed investment fund at the high school level. *Clearing House, 76*, 252-254. Retrieved 27 July 2010, from EBSCO Online Database Academic Search Complete.

Norstrom, B., Smith, C., & Haglund, A. (2008). Getting girls EX.I.T.E.D about project management. *Learning and Leading with Technology, 36*, 24-28. Retrieved 27 July 2010, from EBSCO Online Database Education Research Complete.

Reeves, T. C. (2006). The Spellings Report: An inadequate fix. *Academic Questions, 20*, 56-60. Retrieved 27 July 2010, from EBSCO Online Database Academic Search Complete.

Taylor, A. (2005). Finding the future that fits. *Gender and Education, 17*, 165-187. Retrieved 27 July 2010, from EBSCO Online Database Academic Search Complete.

Walstad, W. B. & Buckles, S. (2008). The national assessment of educational progress in economics: Findings for general economics. *American Economic Review, 98*, 541-546. Retrieved 27 July 2010, from EBSCO Online Database Business Source Complete.

Wilson, F., Kickul, J., Marlino, D., Barbosa, S. D., & Griffiths, M. D. (2009). An analysis of the role of gender and self-efficacy in developing female entrepreneurial interest and behavior. *Journal of Developmental Entrepreneurship, 14*, 105-119. Retrieved 27 July 2010, from EBSCO Online Database Business Source Complete.

LIBRARY AND RESOURCE INSTRUCTION

Library and resource instruction in public schools is made up of two components: general library skills and procedures, and information literacy through topical or assignment-specific strategies. This article describes the two components of library and resource instruction in grades kindergarten through high school; describes the characteristics of formal and informal library skills instruction; and summarizes the issues surrounding special needs students. The article concludes with a description of Responsive Classroom® methodology and a glimpse at the results of its application to an elementary school library.

KEYWORDS: Blog; Cognitive Apprenticeship; Copyright; Distance Learning; Gifted Digital Students; Information Literacy; Interlibrary Loan (ILL); Metacognition; Responsive Classroom®; Special Needs Students

OVERVIEW

Public school libraries—from the kindergarten grades through high school—are often called alternative names, such as media centers, library-media centers, or resource centers. The diversity of names reflects the changing nature of school libraries. Today, school libraries contain materials and resources in a variety of formats, including books and magazines in paper and electronic formats, recordings, videos, Web-based and Internet resources, and materials available through interlibrary loan (ILL). As a result, school librarians are providing more diverse and sophisticated instruction in library and resource instruction to an increasingly diverse and sophisticated population that includes students, teachers, and parents. In this article, the focus is on public school library and resource instruction for students.

COMPONENTS OF LIBRARY & RESOURCE INSTRUCTION IN SCHOOLS

Library and resource instruction in schools is made up of two components:
- General library skills and procedures;
- Information literacy through topical or assignment-specific strategies.

GENERAL LIBRARY SKILLS & PROCEDURES

General library skills and procedures cover the knowledge and facility needed to utilize the library's

resources. Goals for this component of library instruction include the following six objectives:
- How to search the library's card or electronic catalogue;
- How to locate materials within the library;
- How to operate equipment such as photocopy machines and computers;
- How to follow procedures and regulations for checking out materials;
- How to follow procedures for using ILL;
- How to follow general library rules and regulations.

INFORMATION LITERACY THROUGH TOPICAL OR ASSIGNMENT-SPECIFIC STRATEGIES

Information literacy through topical or assignment-specific strategies covers the knowledge and facility needed to utilize the library's resources to research specific topics or complete a school assignment. These strategies build upon the knowledge gained from learning general library skills and advance to a state of "information literacy," or the ability to apply the general library skills known to specific information needs. Goals for this component of library instruction include the following five objectives:
- How to define the subject;
- How to determine information needs;
- How to collect the information needed;
- How to evaluate the information collected for currency, authority, reliability and relevance to topic;
- How to properly quote, attribute and cite the information used and avoid copyright infringement.

Usually, students will participate in an orientation program that teaches general library skills and procedures before they need to tackle topical or assignment-specific projects. Of course, the lower the grade level, the more scaled-back and basic the instruction and objectives will be.

THE CONCEPT OF METACOGNITION

Jaeger (2007) describes his concept of developing information literacy through the concept of metacognition, which is defined literally as "thinking about thinking." Jaeger expands the term "metacognition" as the linking of a student's current knowledge with new knowledge. This description is akin to applying the second component of library instruction, "information literacy through topical or assignment-specific strategies" described earlier in this article. The idea is to arrive at new knowledge by building upon current knowledge.

WHO IS THE INSTRUCTOR?

It seems to be obvious that the school librarian provides all the library and resource instruction to students. However, there is variability to this situation. The school librarian may teach all the instruction, or others may contribute. Here are some alternate "instructor" scenarios:

- The school librarian with teachers (the team-teaching approach);
- Teachers (usually for assignment-specific library instruction);
- Library aides or volunteers.

An interesting aspect of using alternate instructors such as teachers, library aides, or volunteers, is that the school librarian will usually need to instruct them in both library instruction components before they can instruct students.

Cognitive apprenticeship is another twist to teaching and learning library skills. Tilley (2007) examines the issue of mastering information literacy through cognitive apprenticeships that take advantage of current technology. He suggests that teachers and media specialists (school librarians) can learn much from peers and students who are well-versed in the use and value of computer technology. For example, Tilley promotes the benefits of peer mentoring—among both teachers and students—to learn information literacy skills through the use of structured problem-solving and information evaluation activities via blogs and other web-based tools. The idea is to utilize technology to uncover, teach, and internalize the knowledge of peers.

FORMAL & INFORMAL INSTRUCTION

Library and resource instruction in schools consists of formal and informal instruction. Usually, both formal and informal instruction techniques are used in schools.

FORMAL INSTRUCTION

Formal library and resource instruction refers to instruction that is scheduled and provided in a large or small group setting, such as a session in the library or in a teacher's classroom. Formal instruction may be provided in person or via distance learning on closed circuit TV.

INFORMAL INSTRUCTION

Informal library and resource instruction in schools is performed by school librarians, teachers, aides, volunteers, and students. Informal instruction is that which occurs on an as-needed basis and often on a one-on-one instructor-student basis. For example, a student may have already participated in a formal group session by either the school librarian or his teacher that provided instruction in finding sources for a particular assignment, but he still needs more help collecting information, so the librarian works with him on an individual basis for that assignment. The school librarian may also provide informal library and resource instruction through a library Web site or blog where students can find information, ask questions, or contribute their own instructional strategies and resources.

DIGITAL NATIVES AND DIGITAL CITIZENSHIP

The continued growth of digital means of communication, and the widespread use of digital technologies by young people, sometimes to levels of expertise beyond that of their parents and teachers, has led some researchers to dub the current generation of school-age children "the digital generation" (Orth & Chen, 2013). Citing research that many young people spend more time interacting with media and using digital technology than they spend in school or with their families, Orth and Chen note that schools have an obligation to teach students how to be good digital citizens, which includes both responsible use of technology, and becoming literate in using digital information. Depending on school policies, school librarians may be expected to address both aspects of digital citizenship along with instruction on topics such as locating and evaluating sources of information in print sources, citing sources, and appropriate forms of communication.

FURTHER INSIGHTS

Ideally, the school library helps all students develop the information literacy skills needed to reach their full academic potential, including the use of digital as well as print sources of information.

This section explores the issues of accommodating special needs students and considering their special circumstances by designing library and resource instruction to meet their needs.

For purposes of this examination, the focus will be on the following four types of special needs students:

- The foreign-speaking student;
- The physically disabled student;
- The learning disabled student;
- The gifted student.

THE FOREIGN-SPEAKING STUDENT

The first type of special needs student is the Foreign-speaking student. Foreign-speaking students present a unique challenge for the school library. Since it is not possible to provide duplicates of all library materials and instructional tools in every language, the most desirable solution is to at least provide some materials and library instruction tools in the languages of the students. Since the levels of English language proficiency will vary considerably among this population, some strategies to consider adopting include the following:

- Form or develop a reciprocal network with domestic and foreign school and public libraries for the sharing of library materials and instructional aids in various languages;
- Procure outside mentors or interpreters who speak the student's language to accompany the student to the library;
- Provide individualized instruction;
- Save and index all instructional tools that the library translates into foreign languages for future use.

THE PHYSICALLY DISABLED STUDENT

The second type of special needs student is the physically disabled student. Physically disabled students need accommodations that allow them to have full use of the school library materials and instruction. Accommodations for physically disabled students include the following:

- Large-print, Braille, and recorded materials for visually-impaired students;
- Removal of mobility restrictions for students who use wheelchairs or crutches;
- Lower placement of equipment such as computers and library catalogues;
- Sign language interpretations and written accompaniments of library instruction and tools for hearing-impaired students;
- Specific written and practiced instructions for safety drills and evacuation procedures.

A separate group of physically disabled students includes hospital or home-bound students. In addition to some of the accommodations already listed for physically disabled students, hospital or home-bound students will require someone to deliver and retrieve their schoolwork. Library materials and instructional aids can absolutely be included. Of course, if the student has use of a computer, this facilitates the process. Otherwise, the appropriate materials will need to be written, recorded, or delivered via a tutor.

THE LEARNING DISABLED STUDENT

The third type of special needs student is the learning disabled student. Learning disabled students may need some of the same accommodations as physically-disabled students, such as large-print materials. In cases where the learning disability is severe, the librarian may want to consult with a student's teachers and parents for input on the best approach to library instruction. Perhaps, instructional aids could be sent home to be reviewed with the parents.

THE GIFTED STUDENT

The last type of special needs student is the gifted student. We usually think of special needs students as those with physical or mental disabilities. Gifted students are included here because they may need additional stimulation and tools in order to reach their full academic potential. The danger with gifted students is that they will become bored or lazy and not reap the value that the school library can offer them.

Grabgoyes identifies a subset of modern-day gifted students who he refers to as "gifted digital students." He defines them as "students who as part of the 'digital generation' have grown up with technology but differ from their counterparts because they think faster; can absorb large quantities of data simultaneously; can receive a lot of data; and often have asynchronous development—growth and development in one area stops so that another area can grow (Grabgoyes 2007).

Some strategies that school libraries can adopt for gifted students include the following:

- Solicit suggestions from gifted students, their teachers, and parents for library materials, instructional tools, and exercises;
- Incorporate materials and instructional exercises that are advanced and challenging enough to interest gifted students;
- Enlist the help of gifted students to design instructional materials and to teach library skills to other students.

VIEWPOINTS

This section presents the Responsive Classroom® methodology and practices, and summarizes the experience of Bobby Riley, a library media specialist at an elementary school in Vermont, who applied the concepts to his library.

Responsive Classroom® is an approach to elementary school teaching that is based upon 10 classroom practices and five schoolwide practices that foster a safe, creative, and collaborative learning community.

CLASSROOM PRACTICES

- **"Morning Meeting:** Gathering as a whole class each morning to greet one another, share news, and warm up for the day ahead."
- **"Rule Creation:** Helping students create classroom rules to ensure an environment that allows all class members to meet their learning goals."
- **"Interactive Modeling:** Teaching children to notice and internalize expected behaviors through a unique modeling technique."
- **"Positive Teacher Language:** Using words and tone as a tool to promote children's active learning, sense of community, and self-discipline."
- **"Logical Consequences:** Responding to misbehavior in a way that allows children to fix and learn from their mistakes while preserving their dignity."
- **"Guided Discovery:** Introducing classroom materials using a format that encourages independence, creativity, and responsibility."
- **"Academic Choice:** Increasing student motivation by differentiating instruction and regularly allowing students teacher-structured choices in their work."
- **"Classroom Organization:** Setting up the physical room in ways that encourage students' independence, cooperation, and productivity."
- **"Working with Families:** Creating avenues for hearing parents' insights and helping them understand the school's teaching approaches."
- **"Collaborative Problem Solving:** Using conferencing, role playing, and other strategies to resolve problems with students" (Northeast Foundation for Children, Inc., 2007, Classroom Practices).

SCHOOL-WIDE PRACTICES

- "Aligning policies and procedures with Responsive Classroom® philosophy: making sure everything from the lunch routine to the discipline policy enhances the self-management skills that children are learning through the Responsive Classroom® approach."
- "Allocating resources to support Responsive Classroom® implementation: using time, money, space, and personnel to support staff in learning and using the Responsive Classroom® approach."
- "Planning all-school activities to build a sense of community: giving all of the school's children and staff opportunities to learn about and from each other through activities such as all-school meetings, cross-age recess or lunch, buddy classrooms, and cross-age book clubs."
- "Welcoming families and the community as partners: involving family and community members in the children's education by maintaining two-way communication, inviting parents and others to visit and volunteer, and offering family activities."
- "Organizing the physical environment to set a tone of learning: making sure, for example, that schoolwide rules are posted prominently, displays emphasize student work, and all school spaces are welcoming, clean, and orderly" (Northeast Foundation for Children, Inc., School-Wide Practices).

Riley designed his practices to mirror the Responsive Classroom® practices of the teachers in his school by incorporating their language and rules in the library. He steadfastly followed the classroom practices outlined in the methodology. His goal was to have the students think of the library as a classroom, a place of learning and to engage them as active participants in the rules, dreams, future and spirit of the library and as a safe environment to communally solve library-related problems as they arise. These are somewhat unorthodox goals and practices for a school library and they depend upon schoolwide participation in the Responsive Classroom® methodology and practices. Most school libraries are not in a position to incorporate such a program. However, Riley feels that his participation has rejuvenated his teaching; created a more orderly, respectful, and caring environment; and fostered a stronger library and school community (Riley, 2007).

TERMS & CONCEPTS

Blog: Also known as web log or weblog, a blog is an online diary or collection of writings and information that is accessible to others via the Internet. Often, a blog is set up so that readers can add public comments.

Cognitive Apprenticeship: The development of expertise through guided practice with a mentor who holds the knowledge in his mind. The learning is collaborative and focused on real-world skills.

Copyright: "The exclusive legal right to reproduce, publish, and sell the matter and form as of a literary, musical, or artistic work".

Distance Learning: "Learning that takes place via electronic media linking instructors and students who are not together in a classroom".

Gifted Digital Students: Students who as part of the "digital generation" have grown up with technology but differ from their counterparts because they think faster; can absorb large quantities of data simultaneously; can receive a lot of data; and often have asynchronous development (growth and development in one area stops so that another area can grow).

Information Literacy: A set of abilities requiring individuals to "recognize when information is needed and have the ability to locate, evaluate, and use effectively the needed information".

Interlibrary Loan (ILL): A reciprocal arrangement in which libraries are allowed to borrow and lend materials to libraries outside their jurisdiction.

Metacognition: A term from brain research that means "thinking about thinking".

Responsive Classroom®: "An approach to elementary teaching that emphasizes social, emotional, and academic growth in a strong and safe school community. The program is based upon 10 classroom practices and five schoolwide practices".

Special Needs Students: Students who don't perform well in traditional settings.

Sue Ann Connaughton

BIBLIOGRAPHY

American Library Association. Association of College & Research Libraries. (2007). *Information Literacy Competency Standards for Higher Education*. Retrieved November 20, 2007, from http://ala.org.

Atkinson, T. & Atkinson, R. (2007). Creating learning communities for students with special needs. *Intervention in School & Clinic, 42,* 305-309. Retrieved November 20, 2007, from EBSCO Online Database Education Research Complete.

Bentheim, C.A. (2013, Dec.). Continuing the transition work from traditional library to learning commons. *Teacher Librarian 41,* p. 29-36. Retrieved December 28, 2013, from EBSCO Online Database Education Research Complete.

Burk, L.F. (2007). Don't hesitate, just collaborate! *Library Media Connection, 25,* 40-41. Retrieved November 20, 2007, from EBSCO Online Database Education Research Complete.

Graboyes, A.S. (2007). No gifted student left behind: building a high school library media center for the gifted student. *Gifted Child Today, 30,* 42-51. Retrieved November 20, 2007, from EBSCO Online Database Education Research Complete.

Jaeger, P. (2007). Think, Jane, think. *Library Media Connection, 26,* 18-21. Retrieved November 19, 2007, from EBSCO Online Database Education Research Complete.

Lamb, A., and Johnson, L. (2013, Oct.) Social studies in the spotlight: Digital collections, primary sources, and the common core. *Teacher Librarian 41,* p. 62-68. Retrieved December 28, 2013, from EBSCO Online Database Education Research Complete.

Merriam-Webster's collegiate dictionary (10th ed.). (2000). Springfield, MA: Merriam-Webster.

Northeast Foundation for Children, Inc., Turner Falls, MA. *Responsive Classroom ®*. Retrieved November 20, 2007, from http://responsiveclassroom.org.

Orth, D., and Chen, E. (2013). The strategy for digital citizenship. *Independent School 72,* p. 56-63. Retrieved December 28, 2013, from EBSCO Online Database Education Research Complete.

Riley, B. (2007). The library media center and responsive classroom practices. *Library Media Connection, 26,* 22-23. Retrieved November 19, 2007, from EBSCO Online Database Education Research Complete.

Tilley, C. & Callison, D. (2007). New mentors for new media: Harnessing the instructional potential of cognitive apprenticeships. *Knowledge Quest, 35,* 26-31. Retrieved November 20, 2007, from EBSCO Online Database Education Research Complete.

SUGGESTED READING

Harper, M. (2007). Designing quality library lesson plans. *Library Media Connection, 26,* 42-43. Retrieved November 20, 2007, from EBSCO Online Database Education Research Complete.

Harris, C. (2007). It's not about the hardware. *School Library Journal, 53,* 20-20. Retrieved November 19, 2007, from EBSCO Online Database Education Research Complete.

Harris, F.J. (2003). Information literacy in school libraries. *Reference & User Services Quarterly, 42,* 215-223. Retrieved

November 19, 2007, from EBSCO Online Database Education Research Complete.

Smalley, T. (2004). College success: High school librarians make the difference. *Journal of Academic Librarianship,* 30, 193-198. Retrieved November 19, 2007, from EBSCO Online Database Education Research Complete.

PUBLIC SCHOOL EDUCATION: MIDDLE GRADES

Middle school education is the most unique and controversial school model presently used by public schools in America. It provides a distinctive organizational model that was created in order to meet the physical, social, and psychological characteristics of the middle school learner. The model is meant to overcome low academic achievement and the learning plateaus that often appear among middle school-aged students. Teachers are clustered into interdisciplinary learning teams in order to collaboratively address student needs; administrators must work to articulate a school mission and help teachers uphold this mission in their classrooms in order to promote student achievement.

KEYWORDS: Core Academic Courses; Criterion-Referenced Tests; Exploratory Courses; Middle School; Mission; Norm-Referenced Tests; Public Schools; Standards-Based Education; Vision

OVERVIEW

The middle grade school is the newest model of school organization presently used in public school systems across America. For many years, middle school aged students were either placed in elementary schools, forced in to high schools, or put in a school building that was a former high school and called a Junior High School. The elementary school was not an acceptable setting for students in grades 6-8 due to their requirements for higher level programs and the demands for larger facilities. The size of the middle grades student was simply overwhelming to most elementary schools. Students between the ages of 11-14 were sometimes placed in a high school setting, but they are too immature to be educated in the same school building as older students. The Junior High model was not a perfect academic match for the cognitive needs of the middle grade student. Middle school advocates claimed that Junior High Schools simply offered a "watered down" high school program which did not adequately challenge the cognitive needs of these students (Wallis, Miranda, & Rubiner, 2005). Regardless of the location of the placement for students in 6-8th grades, their academic, social and psychological needs were not being met.

During the 1970's, students as early as 6th grade were dropping out of school, were not showing academic progress on evaluation measures, and were simply not being adequately educated. This forced public school systems to seek alternative education plans for these students. By the 1980's, many public school systems were beginning to employ aspects of the newly evolving middle school organizational model and were witnessing some key academic gains with students. One of the most profound research documents that impacted the development of middle schools was in 1989, when the Carnegie Council on Adolescent Development produced a report, "Turning Points: Preparing American Youth for the 21st Century." This proposed the idea of "transforming middle schools into equitable places that care for teens while preparing them academically" (Tonso, Jung, & Colombo, 2006). This report suggested that middle schools should:

- Create small communities for learning
- Teach a core academic program
- Ensure student success by tailoring the academic programs to the needs of the students,
- Staff the schools with teachers trained to work with this particular student
- Engage the families in the learning processes of the students.

Additionally, middle schools would foster academic success through encouraging physical fitness and good health, and would connect the schools to the community.

THE MIDDLE SCHOOL

Middle schools are typically comprised of grades 6-8 and have many similar characteristics. According to the National Center for Education Statistics' *Digest for Education Statistics, 2011*, since the early 1970s there has been a shift away from junior high schools (schools with grades 7 through 9 or grades 7 and 8) and toward middle schools. In 1999-2000, there were 11,500 middle schools in the United States, a 458% from the 2,100 middle schools in 1970-1971.By 2009-2010, there were 13,200 middle schools in the U.S. The number of junior high schools declined over the same period, from 7,800 in 1970-1971 to 3,600 in 1999-2000, and 3,000 in 2009-2010.

Middle schools are divided into academic learning communities, called interdisciplinary teams. Their core academic subjects are complimented by exploratory courses which are mini-vocational, fine arts, or physical education courses. The teachers of middle grade students have shared certification and training requirements.

THE INTERDISCIPLINARY TEAM

The academic basis of the middle school concept is the interdisciplinary team. Interdisciplinary teams are usually comprised of 2-5 teachers who are responsible for the instruction of one or two content areas. This specialization allows teachers to serve as content experts in the areas they teach. Additionally, the interdisciplinary team concept gives middle grade students a place to belong, even giving them the feeling of being in a "legal gang" (NEA, 1999). Having a place to fit in is vital to the social and psychological needs of this aged student at this age level. Teaming students offers a critical social and emotional connection for students at such a fragile academic age (Tonso et al.).

Interdisciplinary teams are usually an easy way for middle schools to group students, within the team, according to their academic needs. In fact, true middle schools use teaming for continual movement through academic subgroups in response to formative evaluations for each subject.

Interdisciplinary teaming allows the teachers on a team to share common planning time. This time is to be used for discussions about student progress, create remediation or acceleration plans, and plan instructional activities that cross all disciplines (Rottier, 2000). Additionally, shared planning time allows teachers to determine their staff development needs, serves as a launching pad for school leaders, and helps the team develop skills in the areas of learning community development, managing conflict, developing shared rules and goals, and making decisions for the team.

Consistency and uniformity among interdisciplinary teams has a direct impact on the performance of the team (Rottier). These two components of the team ensure that teams are working toward the goals they have established, the workload among team teachers is equally distributed, and instructional time is appropriately devoted to learning activities.

When teams of teachers are working collaboratively, they engage in a variety of issues that sometimes results in conflict among the teachers. Effective teaching teams have established working relations that allows them to disagree about issues while maintaining the dignity of their relationships. This means that they engage in problem solving activities and discussions, or entertain new and exciting ideas that can lead to the progress of the students on their team (Rottier).

THE MIDDLE SCHOOL TEACHER

Another important aspect of the middle school concept is the unique qualities of the middle grade teacher. The middle school teacher is expected to promote lifetime learning in students through engaging activities and positive interactions with their social and physical environments (Virtue, 2007). Effective middle school teachers set high expectations for their students and carefully plan activities that help them attain these goals. An effective middle grade teacher must be skilled in establishing and maintaining relationships with their students that prompts academic achievement and social comfort. Effective middle school teachers must be willing to constantly engage in staff development that improves their abilities to expertly offer instruction.

Middle grade teachers must be committed to the concept of teaching for mastery. This means that they address as many learning styles as necessary, remediate and enrich, and plan instructional activities that ensure that students will accomplish the learning objectives. This often requires an immense amount of creativity, which is inviting to this level of student. Additionally, teachers repeatedly re-teach learning objectives in order to ensure student mastery (Christie, 2001).

MIDDLE SCHOOL ADMINISTRATION

Middle school leaders play a crucial role in the overall success of the school. They must carefully place teachers and students on teams so that a positive learning environment is cultivated through effective interdisciplinary team placement. They must teach the team leaders how to implement strategies that uphold the mission of the school, support their team goals, and promote student achievement. And, they must serve as the primary curriculum leaders of the schools (Nelson, Fairchild, Grossenbacher, & Landers, 2007). According to the study conducted by Nelson et al., middle school administrators must be trained to understand the academic and social needs of this level of student, the skills expected of effective teachers, and how to successfully implement this unique school organizational model. Principals must seriously study the standardized test scores of the students in order to develop improvement plans with interdisciplinary team teachers, creating and upholding a clear mission for the school, and ensuring that high expectations are established for all students. The transition from elementary to middle school and middle school to high school is often problematic for middle grade students. According to Greifner (2006), a key to the success of this transition is collaborative planning between the principals of these schools. It is the duty of the middle school principal to "focus on transforming a school into a community and establishing strong development programs" (para. 5) that ensure student success during the change between school levels.

Another important key to successful middle school leadership is that the leader maintains an environment that is personalized for students, ensuring that they participate in learning activities that promote their academic status (Greifner). This means that students are placed in the academic levels that are most likely to help them master content standards and older students are allowed to choose the exploratory concentrations that most interest them.

EXPLORATORY COURSES

Exploratory courses are another unique characteristic of middle schools. These are nonacademic courses that offer students introductions to vocational, foreign language, fine arts, and physical education courses. The typical plan for scheduling exploratory courses is that 6th grade students are exposed to every exploratory course for a short period of time (usually only 6 weeks). During the seventh and eighth grade years, students are encouraged to choose an exploratory concentration so they can participate in higher level activities in their concentration area. Examples of exploratory courses are:

- Family and Consumer Science;
- Keyboarding;
- Auto Mechanics;
- Drafting;
- Construction;
- Horticulture;
- Art;
- Band.

CORE CURRICULUM

Core curriculum courses serve as the foundation of the middle school. The Language Arts courses provide students instruction in the areas of sentence and paragraph construction, spelling, vocabulary development, and understanding basic novels. Reading instruction is offered to assist in the development of decoding and comprehension skills. Math instruction begins with basic calculations in the 6th grade, develops into Pre Algebra in the 7th grade and is either Algebra (for high school credit) or an advanced problem solving course for 8th graders.

Social studies is divided into world studies and American studies. For instance, regions of the world are studied in the 6th and 7th grades and instruction specific to American culture is offered in 8th grade. In the 6th grade, Science instruction is a general introduction to physical and life sciences. Most 7th grade science curriculums focus on life science or biology with emphasis on earth science in the 8th grade.

An important issue in middle grade instruction is student performance on standardized tests. The recent federal legislation, No Child Left Behind Act (NCLB), has established clear mandates for academic accountability based on standardized test scores on nationally norm referenced and criterion referenced scores. Testing during the middle grade years is still considered "high stakes" due to the consequences related to deficient scores and for schools who do not meet the scores established for them by state educational leaders. For most middle schools, important testing occurs at the conclusion of the 6th grade and during the 8th grade. Most 8th graders must participate in a writing exam as well as nationally recognized criterion referenced tests (CRCT) at the conclusion of the 8th grade year. In many states, 8th grade students who do not meet the minimum scores for passing the CRCT are either retained or required to attend remediation instruction prior to being advanced to the high school level.

TEACHER CERTIFICATION

The need for teachers is presently immense and the outlook for having an adequate amount of teachers in the future is bleak. The numbers enrolled in traditional certification programs in colleges and universities across the nation is inadequate for the projected numbers of anticipated vacancies. According to the Bureau of Labor Statistics, the demand for middle school teachers is expected to increase 17% between 2010 and 2020, about as fast as average for all occupations. In 2010, 641,700 people were employed as middle school teachers in the U.S., and an increased 108,300 teachers are expected to be needed by 2020.

States with high numbers of immigrants have reported the need for new teachers as especially intense. And, recent federal legislation, NCLB, has increased the stress of maintaining particular standards for teachers due to the regulation of having "highly qualified" teachers. This means that schools are scrambling for teachers who are willing to be experts in a specific content area as well as be masters at classroom management, grading, conferencing with parents, raising standardized test scores, and all of the other duties required of teachers (St. Arnauld, 2007).

Certification for middle school teachers usually follows a general course of study. Most teacher education programs consist of a general curriculum of introductory collegiate courses such as English, Speech, Algebra, Biology, Chemistry, Physical Education, Music, Behavioral Sciences, and History. Then, future middle grade teachers must concentrate in methodology courses specific for instruction in the core content areas: Language Arts, Reading, Mathematics, Science, and Social Studies. They also must complete courses that are related to general education topics such as Educational Psychology, the Sociology of Schools, Learning styles and best practices, and Foundations in Education. Middle school education majors also must complete a set number of practicum experiences in the schools and a student teaching experience. Generally, most colleges of education require that middle grade education majors concentrate in two specific content areas, such as

reading and math or math and science, and then take additional methodology and content courses in their chosen specialization. The need for more teachers gaining middle school certification is increasing.

ALTERNATIVE CERTIFICATION

Although conventional certification is a highly regarded manner of entering a teaching career, many are now seeking alternative certification routes. Twenty years ago, very few states offered alternative certification programs for allowing nontraditional collegiate students to enter the teaching profession. Now, most states allow these programs due to the need for highly qualified teachers. In fact, in 1983 there were only 12 alternative certification programs in the United States compared to 485 in 2007 (Honawar, 2007). There are currently two major types of alternative certification programs:

- Programs managed by agencies that are not affiliated with colleges or universities. These are for-profit agencies, state sponsored organizations, or programs sponsored by a school district that allow persons to work as teachers while earning certification;
- Those that are sponsored by universities or colleges. These are frequently online programs, programs that compact certification requirements into a year-long course, or allow content-related courses to substitute for education courses and student teaching experiences making in-field experience the primary training ground for the new teacher (Baines, 2006).

There are diverse standpoints regarding alternative certification programs. Due to the large number of shortages of highly qualified teachers in many content areas, school districts are forced to use alternative certification programs in order to simply have enough teachers to fill classrooms. For instance, in Florida, Governor Jeb Bush declared that all public school districts be given the authority to certify teachers and California is relaxing the certification requirements for educators in order to meet the burdens of increasing student populations (Baines). Many states are instigating incentive programs to attract people to teaching, particularly in those subjects and schools that are hard to staff (Boyd, Goldhaber, Lankford, & Wyckoff, 2007). These areas are: Special Education, Mathematics, Science, and students with Limited English Proficiency. A 2006 study found that teachers who entered the profession from alternative certification programs could produce student outcomes equal to or greater than those licensed via traditional routes (Honawar). This study gave alternative teacher certification programs validity to many opponents.

The opponents to alternative certification programs for teachers have been very vocal throughout educational documents. Many educators that earned certification through traditional programs feel strongly that teachers who gain experience in the classroom are using the students as their learning objects and are deterring the academic progress of students (Boyd et al.). According to Jacobson (2006), students in California's lowest-achieving schools are more likely to have the least-prepared teachers. Yet, alternative certification programs do put a teacher in every classroom with the hope that they will receive assistance from their local school administrators, peer teachers, and mentors in order to appropriately offer their students instruction. Some have claimed that alternative certification programs are "fly by night operations" that inadequately prepared teachers to enter the classroom. But, this is not the case anymore due to the high caliber of persons enrolling in these programs. Honawar reported that during the 2004-05 year, approximately 50,000 teachers entered the field through alternative routes, making up about one-third of all new teachers hired that year.

AGE-LEVEL RELATED BEHAVIOR

Although efforts have been diligent to develop solid academic programs for middle school-aged students, there are many problems facing this model of schooling. The level of frustration of parents with their middle school student is immense. The behaviors of middle school aged students are highly inconsistent. They fluctuate between flairs of anger, frustration, unreliability, compassion, high intelligence, and maturity. Many parents believe that the middle school concept, of interdisciplinary teams and individualized engagement in academic activities, should help relax such inconsistent behavior. Yet, there is often no improvement (Christie).

Many middle grade educators are frustrated that the academic climate of middle schools does not adequately challenge students. Student misbehavior, due to boredom, is frequent, as are apathetic student attitudes toward content mastery. Many believe that enrolling more middle grade students in accelerated academic programs would relieve many of the existing classroom discipline problems and poor attitudes toward learning demonstrated by scores of middle school students (Christie).

LOW ACADEMIC ACHIEVEMENT

Another issue gaining prevalence throughout public school districts is also associated with the low academic achievement of middle school students. As many middle school students perform beneath their academic abilities, they are placed in remedial courses as they enter high school, negatively influencing their introduction to high school and limiting their academic productivity at the secondary level. This has been related to inadequate teacher training; that many current middle school teachers of core areas do not have proper training or certification in the areas they are teaching (Chenoweth, 1999). This can be remedied through accreditation standards related to teacher certification being enforced, by school districts only employing certificated, highly qualified teachers for middle schools, and by parents insisting that their students only receive instruction by certificated teachers.

THE LEARNING PLATEAU

Finally, there is enormous concern across the nation regarding the academic plateau that many middle school students display during three years of their school careers. Although there is vast research that ensures that it is typical for middle school students to experience a learning plateau, it is detrimental to meeting the continuing academic demands for improvement throughout all levels of public school education. To many, it is the requirement of the middle school teacher to appropriately motivate these students to improve their academic status and intelligence during these school years and to help students work past any learning plateaus or apathetic attitudes they encounter during these years.

CONCLUSION

Undoubtedly, the middle grade concept has profoundly impacted the education process of American students. Middle schools have gathered students of similar ages and similar characteristics together in an effort to offer them appropriate learning opportunities. There are many characteristics of middle schools that are alike in most middle school programs. These are:

- Interdisciplinary teams;
- Exploratory courses;
- Clear mission statements;
- Teachers who are "highly qualified" to teach middle school students.

TERMS & CONCEPTS

Core Academic Courses: The courses in elementary, middle and high school that are generally included on most standardized exams; generally these are: English, Mathematics, Science and Social Studies.

Criterion-Referenced Tests: Assessments that determines what is the expected behavior or knowledge of an individual that makes a specific score on a test; usually contains a cut score that defines the relationship of the individuals' score to the subject being tested.

Exploratory Courses: Courses of instruction that are not core courses but serve as introductory level courses for upcoming high school concentrations; generally are: vocational courses, fine art courses, foreign language course, and Health/Physical Education.

Mission: The statement that serves as the present status of the school; the mission defines why the vision will be achieved.

Norm-Referenced Tests: A comparison or ranking of an individual to a sampling of his/her peers; how a student compares to others in the same category.

Standards-Based Education: Reform movement based on the belief that what should be learned, taught and mastered at specific educational levels.

Vision: The predictive statement of a school that establishes the long term purpose of the school; serves as the future identity of the school.

Carol Bennett

BIBLIOGRAPHY

Boyd, D. Goldhaber, D., Lankford, H., & Wyckoff, J. (2007). The effect of certification and preparation on teacher quality. *Future of Children, 17,* 45-68. Retrieved on July 31, 2007, from EBSCO Online Database Educational Research Complete.

Chenoweth, K. (1999). Education's weak link. *Black Issues in Higher Education, 16,* 36-40. Retrieved on July 31, 2007, from EBSCO Online Database Educational Research Complete.

Chingos, M.M., and Peterson, P.E. (2011, June). It's easier to pick a good teacher than to train one: Familiar and new results on the correlates of teacher effectiveness. *Economics of Education Review 30,* p. 449-465. Retrieved on December 27, 2013, from EBSCO Online Database Educational Research Complete.

Christie, K. (2001). The middle level: More than treading water. Phi Delta Kappan, 82, 649. Retrieved on July 31, 2007, from EBSCO Online Database Educational Research Complete.

Curriculum Review. (2006, October). Take time to get kids involved in clubs. *Curriculum Review, 46,* 7. Retrieved on July 31, 2007, from EBSCO Online Database Educational Research Complete.

Cwikla, J. (2007). The trials of a poor middle school trying to catch up in mathematics. *Education & Urban Society, 39,* 554-583. Retrieved on July 31, 2007, from EBSCO Online Database Educational Research Complete.

Fisher, L. (2007). From struggling reader to teacher of reading. *Reading Today, 25,* 19. Retrieved on July 31, 2007, from EBSCO Online Database Educational Research Complete.

Friend, J. (2007). Middle-level reform: The introduction of advanced english and science courses. *Journal of Advanced Academics, 18.* 246-276. Retrieved on July 31, 2007, from EBSCO Online Database Educational Research Complete.

Garriott, M. (2007). Intervene now so they will graduate later. *Principal, 86,* 60-61. Retrieved on July 31, 2007, from EBSCO Online Database Educational Research Complete.

Greifner, L. (2006). Success strategies for middle school leaders. *Education Week, 25,* 8. Retrieved on July 31, 2007, from EBSCO Online Database Educational Research Complete.

Honawar, V. (2007). Alternative-certification programs multiply. *Education Week, 26,* 16. Retrieved on July 31, 2007, from EBSCO Online Database Educational Research Complete.

Ignash, J., & Slotnick, R. (2007). The specialized associate's degree in teacher education. *Community College Review, 35,* 47-65. Retrieved on August 8, 2007, from EBSCO Online Database Educational Research Complete.

Jacobson, L. (2006). California urged to address teacher-quality shortcomings. *Education Week, 26,* 16. Retrieved on July 31, 2007, from EBSCO Online Database Educational Research Complete.

McKenna, M.C., Conradi, K., Lawrence, C., Jang, B.G., and Meyer, J.P. (2012, July-Sept.). Reading attitudes of middle school students: Results of a U.S. survey. *Reading Research Quarterly 47,* p. 283-306. Retrieved on December 27, 2013, from EBSCO Online Database Educational Research Complete.

Middleton, J.S. (2013). More than motivation: The combined effects of critical motivational variables on middle school mathematics achievement. *Middle Grades Research Journa 8*, p. 77-95. Retrieved on December 27, 2012, from EBSCO Online Database Educational Research Complete.

National Educator's Association. (1999). Middle schools: Something new or tried and true?. *NEA Today, 18*, 33. Retrieved on July 31, 2007, from EBSCO Online Database Educational Research Complete.

Nelson, H., Fairchild, M., Grossenbacher, M., & Landers, L. (2007). Examining effective middle grades programs: Stating implications for secondary school reform. *American Secondary Education, 35*, 52-68. Retrieved on July 31, 2007, from EBSCO Online Database Educational Research Complete.

Trends in education. (2004). *Principal, 84*, 50-52.

Rottier, J. (2000). Teaming in the middle school: Improve it or lose it. *Clearing House, 73*, 214-217. Retrieved on July 31, 2007, from EBSCO Online Database Educational Research Complete.

Tonso, K., Jung, M. & Colombo, M. (2006). "It's hard answering your calling": Teacher teams in a restructuring urban middle school. *Research in Middle Level Education Online, 30*, 1-22. Retrieved on August 8, 2007, from EBSCO Online Database Educational Research Complete.

Virtue, D. (2007). Teaching and learning in the middle grades: A personal perspective. *Clearing House, 80*. 243-246. Retrieved on July 31, 2007, from EBSCO Online Database, Educational Research Complete.

Wallis, C., Miranda, C., & Rubiner, B. (2005). Is middle school bad for kids? *Time, 166*, 48-51. Retrieved on August 8, 2007, from EBSCO Online Database Educational Research Complete.

SUGGESTED READING

Armstrong, L. (2001). *Coaching for Comprehension.* Greensboro, NC: Carson Delloso Publishing Co.

Bluter, D., & Shireman, M. (1996). *Algebra.* Greensboro, NC: Carson Delloso Publishing Co.

Robb, L. (2006). *Teaching Reading in Middle School.* New York, NY: Scholastic, Inc.

Smith, M., & Forbes, V., (2000). *Spelling Skills Practice and Apply.* Greensboro, NC: Carson Delloso Publishing Co.

THE CREATIVE WRITING CLASSROOM

This article begins by pointing out the tendency to undervalue creative writing courses, and explores the reasons why some believe that creative writing courses are a waste of time. It asks the question "How do creative writing teachers benefit students?" and offers several answers. It also presents several central questions that creative writing teachers should ask in order to create an effective classroom for creative writing students. A discussion of effective methods for teaching creative writing, and an exploration of the mindset and habits that most expert writers have in common are also presented.

KEYWORDS: Atelier Approach; Creativity; Critical Phase; Inspiration Approach; Generative Phase; Techniques Approach; Timed Writing; Workshop Approach

OVERVIEW

In the last few decades, Higher Education in America has increasingly focused on concepts such as accountability and, along with that, a demand for objectively quantifying or measuring results or outcomes in education. Of course this is an important concept that educators must consider when designing courses and assignments, but the recent concentration on outcomes or results can be quite difficult to handle when it comes to courses where creativity is a central point of focus. Additionally, if measurable outcomes become the primary basis on which all classes and courses are assessed, then courses that demand student creativity may become undervalued in education. As Johnston (2009), a creative writing instructor at Harvard observes, some stakeholders in education—including administrators, parents, politicians and teachers—may feel that courses such as creative writing have no commercial or fiscal relation to the real world; thus such courses lack any inherent value to society. He bluntly poses the question on behalf of those holding this viewpoint, why should teachers "muck up students' brains and semesters with fluffy, timewasting classes?" Students' time could be better invested into, for example, a business or hotel management course. Johnston concludes by saying that, "commercially speaking, such classes [business or hotel management courses] are surer bets, but when did education get reduced to a pesky hoop through which students must jump just to land in a job?"

In essence, James points out this same argument by noting that "creative writing has been the ugly stepsister in the English discipline for years." He argues that:

> *...literature scholars carry the torch for pure language, and, on the other side, the composition and rhetoric theorists approach writing like a science. Somewhere off in a dark corner, the creative writing staff loiters, getting paid to do nothing more than say what they think about student writing (James).*

Perhaps this viewpoint is also founded on the premise that creative writing teachers do not really teach anything since creativity is something some people have and others don't. But is this true, and if it isn't true, then how do creative writing teachers help students make gains in their classrooms? How do they teach anything of value to the students in their classrooms? Vakil (2008) points out the subtleties and intricacies of teaching students to write creatively:

> *Leaving aside where it comes from, or even what it is, any sane discussion about teaching creative writing has to begin with the admission that making a great story (credible voice, living characters, universal significance), depends on an ineffable quality—call it timing, a good ear, empathy or determination—that cannot be taught in the way that a skill like riding a bicycle, wiring a plug, frying an egg or laying a brick can be.*

Watts asks, "how do we teach our students to master the complexities, the intricacies, of plot, setting, characters, point of view, voice, back story, and scenes?" This question and other important questions—particularly questions of method/technique, assignments, and assessment—must be asked and adequately answered if a creative writing teacher is to succeed in giving students a valuable experience in the classroom. Also, in asking those questions, many aspects of creative writing courses become clearer. The answers seem to overlap in the areas that are essential to an effective creative writing classroom.

Applications

HOW DO CREATIVE WRITING COURSES BENEFIT STUDENTS?

Watts points out that, in the hopes of mastering the art of writing, many struggling writers have sought

tutelage with experienced mentors; this arrangement has a long historical precedent, and certainly many of the world's greatest writers had their particular mentors. Watts writes "my teaching experiences, which range from work in kindergarten classrooms to graduate level coursework, confirm this. Writers gain inspiration from those who have met the same problems and vanquished them." Blythe and Sweet (2008) call this the "Atelier Model," which some teachers use when they teach writing. Roebuck (2007) points out that most writing teachers also understand "there are at least two different parts of any creative act (the unconscious or generative phase and the conscious, critical phase that edits and revises) that can have a conflicting relationship." A good writing teacher can show students how to allow these two processes to complement each other rather than hinder each other. This is what Watts means when he writes about balancing the two main elements, creative imagination and the knowledge or understanding of how to write with good technique:

> *As always, I begin with the intentions and experiences of my students, balancing those with what I believe are the hallmarks of well-crafted fiction. Sometimes this means stretching writers beyond what they know, beyond their growing knowledge of the world, beyond their youthful understanding of the way we tell stories. I teach craft, yet I respect the imaginary worlds they create, worlds based on experience, filtered through feelings and the scrim of memory.*

Those two elements are also relevant to how creative writing teachers run their classes. As Caldwell notes, there are two distinct processes in the art of writing that must be focused upon during class: "1) The inspiration or drafting of raw material; 2) The redrafting and perfecting of this material." This echoes the ideas of Roebuck as well as Watts. Like them, Caldwell would also argue that a good writing teacher knows how to get students focused and more adept in those two areas.

Vakil points out yet another way writing teachers benefit their students, arguing that teaching writing "is a way of lessening the static authority of the teacher: the idea that there is an answer and the teacher knows it." Writing is an important part of education because it teaches students that in life there are sometimes many "correct answers" for any given problem. Writing courses teach students a model of thinking in which, as Vakil puts it, "neat rules and fixed interpretations" are at times exposed as inadequate.

Additionally, creative writing is particularly demanding of objectivity when applying the second phase of writing: revision and editing. During this phase, the ideal is to become completely the objective reader rather than the subjective writer. As Morgan (2006) points out, "young writers are less likely to have developed that detachment, and this is where tactful intervention by the teacher is crucial: tactful, because it shouldn't overwhelm the student with either the impersonal authority of elders-and-betters or impose the teacher's personal authority and taste." A good writing teacher can use his or her expertise and "pedagogical judgment," to decide "what feedback on what aspects of the piece will be most helpful at this stage of the work's and the writer's development." In short, there are many ways that a teacher can help a student to become a better writer. Many of these ways directly relate to the teacher's techniques and assignments in the classroom.

WHAT ARE EFFECTIVE METHODS FOR TEACHING CREATIVE WRITING?

A good creative writing teacher should possess a wealth of helpful knowledge from reading, study and experience. This is why Watts has slowly gathered "writer quotes, interviews, and other materials from various sources, and grouped them by writing processes/categories." By having such a file on hand, the teacher can produce thought provoking and helpful information on any given writing problem that a student faces in the classroom. Caldwell offers a simple tip for creative writing students by looking at a famous writer's habits to help students become better writers:

> In A Moveable Feast, Ernest Hemingway talks about writing in the morning until he couldn't keep writing (from fatigue or other commitments). "I always worked until I had something done and I always stopped when I knew what was going to happen next. That way I could be sure of going on the next day."

THE WORKSHOP APPROACH

However, a more central consideration is the overall structure and design of the course. There are various ways to structure a creative writing course, the most popular is to create a "writer's workshop." Blythe

and Sweet extensively researched and examined the possibilities for structuring a course, and identified six different approaches. They tried all six of these approaches in the classroom, which in turn helped them to slowly evolve a seventh approach that seems to mix several approaches.

The foundation of the approach remains the workshop, but in the workshop the authors concentrate on examining writing techniques. They point out that the techniques approach is best able to "demystify" the art of creative writing, observing that, "unlike the inspiration approach, where no guarantees exist for full-brain contact with the muse, the techniques approach appeals to the rational, democratic person—you too can learn to be a writer." Talent—and most likely creativity—"can be developed by learning and using the right techniques, especially since the approach reduces the seemingly huge and overwhelming task to manageable skill points" (Blythe and Sweet).

Most creative writing teachers concur that a workshop approach is the optimal structure for a creative writing class. According to Minot (2003) "the workshop is a doorway for you to get criticism and motivation for you to write because of the deadlines that are imposed" (cited in Blythe & Sweet). Thus, a workshop forces students to produce output, and it gives them the opportunity to get feedback about that output. Running a good workshop requires a lot of consideration. If a creative writing teacher runs a good workshop, it can open the eyes of students to a new world, and give them enthusiasm about that new world. Minot succinctly expresses the idea, which relates back to the question of how a creative writing teacher benefits the student:

> Good teachers of creative writing don't just teach the techniques; they infect the students with certain enthusiasms simply by being in a closed room with them long enough for the virus to catch (cited in Roebuck).

Blythe and Sweet warn of various ways writing workshops can go wrong. For example, if a workshop has too many students, then students may not all get equal time spent examining their work. Also, there may be the tendency for what the authors call "alpha apprentices" to "dominate the conversation" and make "shy students disappear into the woodwork." Also, a lot of negative criticism may "rip apart works and souls." These are just a few problems that may arise from the workshop structure of a course. Others offer ways to prevent these negative possibilities. For example, Prichard advises that "more than twelve would be too large of a group for everyone to get equal attention, so I put a cap on registrations."

GIVING FEEDBACK

A fine and delicate balancing act becomes apparent when considering advice on criticism. Watts (2007) advises that both teachers and students need to be trained in "how to give feedback without crushing the writer." Antoniou and Moriarty (2008) look at criticism from the other side, arguing that students need to give "honest but constructive feedback" warning that, "as the course progresses, they will learn that repeatedly telling their friends that their work is 'good' will not help them to improve, and that they are actually doing them a disservice." They also concur with Watts by writing "on the other hand, hearing someone tell you that your work is 'crap' will not inspire you to rework and try again, so it is important that I manage the classes so that people remain respectful and constructive by giving suggestions for development and improvement through the process of editing and redrafting." Thus, an expert creative writing teacher is walking a critical tightrope when overseeing class criticism of a student's work.

Johnson (2003) describes his writing workshops as fundamentally "a labor-intensive 'skill acquisition' course, emphasizing the sequential acquisition of fiction techniques and providing the opportunity to practice them ... [in which] "apprentices learned best (as in music or the martial arts) through oldfangled imitation of master craftsmen, through assignments aimed at learning a repertoire of literary strategies, and by writing and revising prodigiously" (2). Blythe and Sweet also believe imitating masters is quite effective. They developed workshops in which their "praxis was dominated by combining the great works and the techniques approach" and found that combining imitation with teaching techniques "worked fairly well as a starting point for our classes."

CLASSROOM EXERCISES

There are many classroom exercises that can be used to help students grow as writers. Roebuck suggests starting the course with various timed exercises. For example, one exercise that is effective in making students feel more confident about creative writing while also giving them experience with new creative efforts is an exercise in which students "are told that

they will be required to write for ten minutes, with their prompt being "I remember." Thus, Roebuck tells students to begin writing for ten minutes and to write without censoring themselves. Roebuck relates students' experience with this small assignment:

> ... many students produced pages of text that told, for the most part, intimate compelling stories from their childhood or from just weeks, days or hours before. As a teacher trying to get students to kick start their writing practice, it was strange to have so much to work with and discuss from such a short exercise. The learning curve climbed quickly as I tried more timed writings and as I was able to reiterate the "rules." All of the writing improved, mainly in its clarity and attention to specificity. Just as important the students were having fun, there was joy in the seemingly scary, dreadful act of writing and discussing what they had committed to the page. It seemed that a huge hurdle in self-censorship had been crossed, and the possibilities for further growth became real.

HOW DO STUDENTS LEARN TO THINK LIKE WRITERS?

One last consideration that seems extremely important is to inculcate within writing students a certain mindset as well as habits that it seems most writers have in common. For example, writers clearly understand the close relationship between being a good reader and being a good writer. Morgan points out that, "all writers owe an enormous debt to their reading (and listening and viewing) within and beyond their particular genre, and draw on it in their writing ... in a real sense, we could not write if we had not read." Thus, for good reason Morgan believes that creative writing teachers should assign reading of excellent works from various authors, then critically analyze what makes that work excellent. And as Vakil observes, examining famous works with a critical eye "might help them to be better readers of their own work, which is a crucial factor missing in almost all the students when they first start a course of creative writing. Watts cites John Gardner's The Art of Fiction (1983), in which Gardner advises the student writer, "... in order to achieve mastery he must read widely and deeply and must write not just carefully but continually, thoughtfully assessing and reassessing what he writes, because practice, for the writer as for the concert pianist, is the heart of the matter" (cited in Watts). Watts concludes that, "It seems that 'nobody but a reader ever became a writer'."

A very common habit among writers is that of setting a piece of writing aside for some time so as to get a more objective, reader's viewpoint on the writing. Morgan points out that "all the poets I know do this: after working on a poem they will often lay it aside for weeks, months or years; only the distance of time enables them to make often radical changes." Related to this, and to discussion of the relationship between being a reader and being a writer, is the importance of what Morgan describes as "encouraging the writer to décentre, to step out of the writer's shoes and into the reader's." This concept also comes back to those two fundamental processes of creative writing. Creativity comes out of the subjective imagination of the individual, but the best way to revise and edit is to enter the objective, critical side, which is the side of the reader rather than the writer. With time and practice, student writers become more like expert writers. As Morgan observes, "experienced writers have already internalized the eye and ear of their intended reader audience: it contributes, paradoxically, to their sense of assurance." Certainly, there are many famous writers who discuss in various interviews and books the importance of such things as these.

An important example of adopting the creative writer's mindset relates to the process of generating creative writing, where again, the teacher could use explanations from famous writers. Caldwell uses ideas from a 1935 interview with Gertrude Stein. Stein advised young writers: "You will write if you will write without thinking of the result in terms of a result, but think of the writing in terms of discovery, which is to say that creation must take place between the pen and the paper, not before in a thought or afterwards in a recasting" (cited in Caldwell). This is quite similar to Lamott's (1994) description that a first draft is like "watching a Polaroid develop. You can't—and, in fact, you're not supposed to—know exactly what the picture is going to look like until it has finished developing" (cited in Watts). Creative writing teachers who are themselves creative writers understand this as well as many other aspects of how writers think when they write a story or a poem, so they can teach students a new way of writing that unblocks their own creativity.

The process of creative writing has many valuable things to teach students if the creative writing teacher has thoroughly considered the central questions, and endeavored to find answers that work. After finding the right answers, the teacher can then design a creative writing course that successfully teaches students valuable lessons. These valuable lessons are not only about creative writing, but indirectly are about many other areas of life and fields of knowledge—quite possibly even about business or hotel management.

TERMS & CONCEPTS

Atelier Approach: A method of teaching creative writing students in which a student receives individual guidance from an expert writer. This is a master-apprentice model that comes from the trades of past centuries. In creative writing, the master is sometimes a great author, a tutor/professor, or a professional editor.

Critical Phase: The second phase of creative writing, in which the writer tries to look objectively like a reader at his or her own writing. In this phase, the writer may make radical changes (revisions) and do substantial editing of the work.

Inspiration Approach: A method of teaching creative writing in which the teacher concentrates on developing the writing student's inner process of imagination, and focuses on enhancing the student's creativity. Teachers using this approach focus on showing students invention strategies, and the teacher usually assigns exercises that are intended to foster creativity.

Generative Phase: The first phase of creative writing, in which the writer focuses on generating subjective thoughts and impressions. In this phase, the writer creates without much concern over more formal elements such as good grammar or tight organization.

Techniques Approach: A method of teaching creative writing in which the teacher uses various creative texts that best illustrate various technical concepts so that students will learn more about the various techniques that are used in creative writing. The premise to this approach is that students can best learn to write creatively by increasing their understanding of fictional techniques.

Workshop Approach: A method of teaching creative writing in which a creative writing teacher leads a group of writing students who critique each other's works. The teacher functions as a facilitator and editor who gives guidance and advice while creating a non-hostile environment that encourages students to take risks.

Sinclair Nicholas

BIBLIOGRAPHY

Antoniou, M. & Moriarty, J. (2008). What can academic writers learn from creative writers? Developing guidance and support for lecturers in Higher Education. *Teaching in Higher Education; 13*: 157-167. Retrieved August 26, 2010, from the EBSCO online database Education Research Complete.

Blythe H. & Sweet, C. (2008). The writing community: A new model for the creative writing classroom. *Pedagogy; 8*: 305-325. Retrieved August 26, 2010, from the EBSCO online database Education Research Complete.

Caldwell, G. (2007). How and what do creative writing teachers teach and what do creative writing students learn? *Educational Insights; 11*: 1-13. Retrieved August 26, 2010, from the EBSCO online database Education Research Complete.

Chong, S., & Lee, C. (2012). Developing a pedagogical-technical framework to improve creative writing. *Educational Technology Research & Development, 60*, 639-657. Retrieved December 15, 2013, from EBSCO Online Database Education Research Complete.

Heitin, L. (2012). Troupe adapts students' stories for the school and N.Y.C. stages. *Education Week, 31*, 12-13. Retrieved December 15, 2013, from EBSCO Online Database Education Research Complete.

James, D. (2008). A short take on evaluation and creative writing. *Community College Enterprise; 14*: 79-82. Retrieved August 26, 2010, from the EBSCO online database Education Research Complete.

Johnson, C. (2003). A boot camp for creative writing. *Chronicle of Higher Education; 50*: B7-B10. Retrieved August 26, 2010, from the EBSCO online database Education Research Complete.

Johnston, B. A. (2009). Why teach creative writing? The crabgrass question. *American Book Review; 30*: 4-5. Retrieved August 26, 2010, from the EBSCO online database Academic Search Complete.

Prichard, H. (2008). Write here, write now. *Young Adult Library Services; 6*: 19-23. Retrieved August 26, 2010, from the EBSCO online database Education Research Complete.

Morgan, W. (2006). "Poetry makes nothing happen": Creative writing and the English classroom. *English Teaching: Practice & Critique; 5*: 17-33. Retrieved August 26, 2010, from the EBSCO online database Education Research Complete.

Olthouse, J.M. (2012). Why I write: What talented creative writers need their teachers to know. *Gifted Child Today, 35*, 116-121. Retrieved December 15, 2013, from EBSCO Online Database Education Research Complete.

Peterson, S. (2011). Teaching writing in rural Canadian classrooms. *Literacy Learning: The Middle Years, 19*, 39-48. Retrieved December 15, 2013, from EBSCO Online Database Education Research Complete.

Roebuck, R. (2007). Pulling from the well: Allowing creativity to flow in the creative writing workshop. *Educational Insights; 11*: 1-16. Retrieved August 26, 2010, from the EBSCO online database Education Research Complete.

Smith, G. (2013). Dream writing: A new creative writing technique for secondary schools?. *English in Education, 47*, 245-260. Retrieved December 15, 2013, from EBSCO Online Database Education Research Complete.

Vakil, A. (2008). Teaching creative writing. *Changing English: Studies in Culture & Education; 15*: 157-165. Retrieved August 26, 2010, from the EBSCO online database Education Research Complete.

Watts, J. (2007). Putting author voices in the classroom: A strategy for writing teachers. *Virginia English Bulletin; 57*: 20-31. Retrieved August 26, 2010, from the EBSCO online database Education Research Complete.

SUGGESTED READING

Bayle, E. (2009). How to learn how to write: The dialectics of literary creation through re-creation. *International Journal of Learning; 15*: 59-63. Retrieved August 26, 2010, from the EBSCO online database Education Research Complete.

Perry, G. (2007). Art and trauma: Danger and dynamics in the creative writing workshop. *Educational Insights, 11*: 1-13. Retrieved August 26, 2010, from the EBSCO online database Education Research Complete.

Wiesendanger, K., Perry, J. & Braun, G. (2009). Implementing a three stage structured strategy to assist struggling writers. *Virginia English Bulletin; 59*: 38-46. Retrieved August 26, 2010, from the EBSCO online database Education Research Complete.

SECTION 8: HIGHER EDUCATION

Introduction

Much like its younger counterpart—the K-12 public school system—higher education finds itself traversing through stages of social disruption that demand responsive innovation. The 2006 publication of the *Spellings Report* drew national attention to the serious implications of a complacent, mediocre and costly college/university education for our nation's well being.

In this section, we explore the unique profiles, challenges, and agendas for our colleges and universities. The face of the traditional college student is being replaced by a new majority—the non-traditional student. As the demographics shift, so do the priorities for empowering our graduates to be critical thinkers and have the skills to meet the ever changing world with confidence in their abilities.

LAND-GRANT UNIVERSITIES

The land-grant movement not only heralded the departure from a purely liberal arts curriculum but also ushered in a commitment to universal access to American higher education (Brubacher & Rudy, 1997; Kerr, 2001; Parker, Greenbaum, & Pister, 2001; Spanier, 1999). Land-grant institutions were established under the Morrill Land Grant Act of 1862. However, the impact of land-grants on national development took many years to be realized as a number of factors (e.g., lack of prepared students and faculty, apathy from the American industrial class) contributed to their slow progress. Today their tripartite mission of instruction, research, and public service is embraced by most colleges and universities across the United States (Johnson, 1981).

KEYWORDS: Access; Agricultural Arts; Appropriation; Democratic; Endowment; Experiment Stations; Extension Services; Land-Grant; Mechanical Arts; Morrill Land Grant Act; Research; Service; Teaching

OVERVIEW
IMPORTANCE OF LAND-GRANT UNIVERSITIES
Kerr called the Morrill Land Grant Act of 1862, which established the land-grant institutions, "one of the most seminal pieces of legislation ever enacted." In general, the land-grant movement ushered in a transformative period in American higher education (Kerr). It marshaled in a commitment to universal access to the American higher education system and signified a departure from a purely classical liberal arts curriculum (Brubacher and Rudy; Kerr). Specifically, by offering technical and practical education geared toward the industrial class, land-grant institutions were intended to be more democratic institutions than their predecessors (Brubacher & Rudy). In general, the colleges "stood pre-eminently for the principle, increasingly so important in the twentieth century, that every American citizen is entitled to receive some form of higher education" (Brubacher & Rudy). Other higher education scholars have offered similar remarks on the importance of the land-grant movement and its colleges:
- According to Kerr, the land-grant movement "opened the doors of universities to the children of farmers and workers, as well as of the middle and upper classes."
- Spanier stated that land-grant colleges "democratized higher learning by making a college education

widely available and embracing a pragmatic agenda in teaching, research, and extension."
- Parker et al. wrote that the Morrill Act of 1862 meant "the opportunity to provide both an unprecedented new level of access to higher education as well as the kind of 'practical' education required to industrialize the nation."

DEVELOPMENT OF LAND-GRANT UNIVERSITIES
Important pieces of legislation in the land-grant movement include the Morrill Land Grant Act of 1862, the Second Morrill Act of 1890, the Hatch Act of 1887, and the Smith-Lever Act of 1914 (Kerr). The first Morrill Act outlined that at least one land-grant institution, which would offer agricultural and mechanical arts alongside the liberal arts and other scientific studies, was to be established in each state (Geiger, 1999). Under the Morrill Act, each state was given public lands and ten percent of the proceeds of the sales of those lands could be used toward establishing a college or experimental farm lands (Rudolph, 1990). All other proceeds were to be put aside in a perpetual endowment (Rudolph). A second Morrill Act in 1890 also provided for annual appropriations for the land-grant colleges (Rudolph). The Hatch Act of 1887 provided for experiment stations (Jones, Oberst, & Lewis, 1990). Meanwhile, the Smith-Lever Act of 1914 created the Agricultural Extension Service (Jones et al., 1990; Kerr). The Hatch Act and the Smith-Lever Act were essential to the livelihood of the land-grant idea because they helped ensure that knowledge from land-grant institutions "could be tested in a real-world setting and effectively transmitted to a public beyond enrolled students" (Jones et al., p 5). However, these two pieces of legislation only applied to agricultural and not mechanical arts (Jones et al.).

Justin Morrill first introduced the beginnings of the Morrill Act in 1858 in order to promote agriculture, which was seen as key to the nation's prosperity (Duemer, 2007; Key, 1996). However, Morrill's proposal had to wait until the election of Abraham Lincoln and a shift in federal land policy from one of sales to one of donations in order to finally succeed in the summer of 1862 (Key). In the arguments he made to help secure passage of the act, Morrill mainly focused on the economic benefits that the act would provide to the nation. In sum, he noted that,

The government needed revenue and the best way to produce revenue was to increase prosperity, which could be best accomplished through increased agricultural production. The new colleges would promote agricultural education, which would lead to increased agricultural production, thus increasing national prosperity out of which the needed revenues would flow (Key).

Granting land for the development of colleges was not something novel to the land-grant colleges (Johnson). Duemer stressed that the Morrill Land Grant of 1862 was the continuation of a long-standing practice of supporting educational purposes through land grants. The practice of land grants to support higher education in particular dates back as far as the colonial colleges (Duemer). Rudolph noted that state aid was important to the survival of many of the colonial colleges and that state grants of lands to the colleges were among the favorite forms of assistance at that time. Colleges like Dartmouth received grants of lands (Johnson; Rudolph). Harvard, Yale, William and Mary, and Michigan were all also recipients of colonial or state land grants (Johnson).

Institutions focused on agricultural and mechanical arts were also not new to the land-grants. The idea of establishing institutions to advance agricultural education, for instance, dates back as far as the days of George Washington (Duemer). Also, during the 1850s the efforts of agricultural societies and educational reformers led to the opening of a number of (lower grade) institutional predecessors to the land-grant colleges (Rudolph). These included the New York State Agricultural College and the Michigan State College of Agriculture at East Lansing (Rudolph). Yale's Sheffield Scientific School was also chartered before 1860 (Geiger).

Because the Morrill Act did not specify in what fashion land-grant colleges were to be established, the early colleges took on various forms (Rudolph). Four states (e.g., Michigan, Pennsylvania, Maryland, and Iowa) developed preexisting agricultural colleges into land-grant colleges while other states (e.g., Minnesota, North Carolina) looked to their preexisting state colleges to help them fulfill the land-grant mission (Rudolph). Some states even turned towards preexisting private institutions to help them fulfill the land-grant mission (Rudolph). Still, other states (e.g., Texas, South Dakota) developed entirely new colleges as their land-grant institutions (Rudolph).

Demand for the type of education the land-grant colleges nurtured was not high at the outset (Johnson). Geiger noted that "enthusiasm among the industrial classes for education in agriculture or the mechanical arts turned out to be sparse" (p. 52). For one, many of the Western states in which these colleges were developed did not have high schools and could thus not produce students ready for a collegiate education (Brubacher & Rudy; Johnson). At the same time, there was also a lack of qualified instructors and teaching materials (Brubacher & Rudy). For instance, the agricultural professor at Dartmouth let his crops of potatoes and beets freeze in the ground while one individual noted that there were only enough textbooks on agriculture to enable a professor to teach for thirty days (Brubacher & Rudy; Rudolph). Agricultural education was also a hard sell to American farmers at that time. In general, most American farmers were apathetic or even hostile towards the land-grant colleges during the first twenty years they were in operation (Brubacher & Rudy). Some farmers' groups complained that the colleges were "too theoretical and classical in their curricular offerings and had little to offer the average farmer." Preparatory departments emerged at many land-grants to help solve the student shortage (Johnson). Institutions also relied on other types of enrollment inducements, such as scholarships and other forms of assistance (Johnson).

While enthusiasm for agricultural studies was still low, interest in the mechanical arts began to grow in the 1880s and especially accelerated in the 1890s (Geiger). This may have been due to the national outlook at the time. According to Rudolph, "The threshold of opportunity in America had shifted from the land to the factory; in combining the agricultural with the mechanical, the land-grant colleges were uniting the past and the future, two schemes of life." However, American farmers were eventually drawn into the land-grant model when evidence showed that scientific agricultural could lead to larger crops and thus a higher income and better standard of living (Rudolph). The agricultural experiment stations that were funded by the Hatch Act of 1887 particularly helped to provide compelling evidence to farmers (Rudolph). Rudolph noted that the stations "combined science and the solution of specific farm problems and helped to demonstrate to skeptical farmers that science could be a friend."

Because of the initial lack of student demand, land-grant institutions' impact on national prosperity was not immediate. Johnson remarked that the land-grant "colleges' own development had to pre-cede their impact on national development." Those students that actually did attend the institutions early on more often chose to study in the traditional liberal arts fields (Johnson). For example, between 1870 and 1886 only two of the ninety-three graduates at Ohio State studied agriculture (Kinnison, 1970, as cited in Johnson). According to Johnson:

> The direct developmental impact of the early colleges came after the agricultural experiment stations were established, after research knowledge was given an extension mechanism, after the engineering schools were equipped and well patronized for both training and applied research, and after enrollments in the practicing professions generated thousands, not merely scores, of leaders and specialists.

By 1955 land-grant institutions enrolled more than 20 percent of college students in the United States (Rudolph). The percentage had increased to about 29 percent by 1976 ("Enrollment at State," 1976).

By the early decades of the twenty-first century, more than 150 years after the passage of the Morrill Land Grant Act of 1862, American agricultural colleges and their historic goal of promoting agricultural research and education are more popular with students than they've been in decades, and "the institutions' path-breaking research and teaching are more critical than ever in a world facing huge population increases, climate change, and shortages of energy, water, and food" (Biemiller, 2012).

THE LAND-GRANT MISSION

Johnson proposed that the three-fold academic mission of instruction, research, and public service evolved from land-grant colleges and that this mission is a "description that virtually every institution, public or private, now embraces." Altbach (2001) likewise indicated that land-grant institutions combined "key ideas in American higher education." that spread from the large public institutions to the established private institutions. For instance, land-grant institutions helped to ingrain the notion of direct service to society by engaging in practical research and then spreading the results of that research through means such as extension agents or noncredit courses (Altbach). Kerr remarked that the land-grant movement was one of two forces that "molded the modern American university system and made it distinctive."

ORIGINS OF THE MORRILL LAND GRANT

As noted, many believe that the land-grant movement served to democratize higher education by broadening educational access. However, while principles of access and equity are being realized now, years after the movement, arguments have been made that expanding educational access was not an original intent of the land-grant movement. For instance, Key argued that, rather than equity, "economics was the chief motivation behind the establishment of American land-grant universities." Geiger noted that at the outset "land-grant colleges did not meet an exigent popular demand, nor did they appreciably democratize higher education." Johnson also noted, "If land grants were not new as a device for educational support, neither were they resorted to for purely educational reasons." Likewise, Kerr remarked that the land-grant movement originated out of the agricultural and industrial development occurring in America around that time. Duemer similarly stressed that "the agricultural education component of the Morrill Act was an outcome of pressure for the government to take action in encouraging agricultural development." Also, Spanier noted that the development of the land-grant colleges "stimulated the progress of the agrarian and industrial societies of the past." Yet, some have still held fast to notions that the land-grant movement originally worked to diversify American higher education offerings and expand access to the system. For example, Brubacher and Rudy framed the evolution of the land-grant colleges in an educational fashion by noting that both dissatisfaction with the traditional American liberal arts college and growing emphasis on scientific research helped fuel the movement.

Regarding the economic arguments behind the Morrill Act, Duemer also advanced the notion that the support for agricultural development embodied in the Act was a long political struggle. For instance, a recognized need for some political action regarding the status of agricultural affairs in the United States first appeared in the 19th century (Duemer). Efforts were made to establish a department of agriculture at this time (Duemer). In 1825, Representative Newton of Virginia summarized the importance of establishing such an office when he offered that 'the encouragement of agriculture and manufactures has ever been considered the best means of developing the resources of a nation' (Congressional Globe, 1825, as cited in Duemer). The debate about establishing such an office continued for many years. In 1849 President Taylor spoke on the issue in Congress and stressed that forming an agricultural bureau would develop the potential of agriculturalists and enhance their contribution to the nation (Duemer). Likewise, in addressing Congress in 1850 President Fillmore "drew the linkage between agriculture and manufacturing, pointing out how important both were to the nation" (Duemer). It was not until 1862 that a bill to establish a department of agriculture finally passed both the House and Senate and was approved by President Lincoln (Duemer).

Viewpoints

DEMANDS FOR CHANGE

Key (1996) suggested that land-grant universities have taken the brunt of the American public's demand for change in higher education. Specifically, these institutions have been the focus of efforts to put more emphasis on teaching over research. Perhaps the reasons for this demand are rooted in the past. Rudolph offered that the land-grant colleges helped "to change the outlook of the American people toward college-going." Spanier described land-grants as fulfilling a vision of access, relevance, and service to society while pursuing a mission focused on teaching, research, and public service. Some have said that land-grant institutions have distanced themselves from this original vision and mission (Spanier). Discussing the case of Penn State University, Spanier called on land-grant colleges and universities to work together to better integrate their teaching, research, and service functions.

FUNDING ISSUES

Like many divisions of higher education, land-grant institutions have faced tough funding issues. For instance, Hebel (2002) reported in 2002 that some land-grants had begun to charge user fees for their extension services or cut down on the array of such services. Since their inception in 1914, federal, state, and county funds had generally supported extension outreach at land-grant institutions, but in the face of declines in such support the institutions have been forced to diversify their approaches to funding (Hebel, 2002). In his 2008 budget, President Bush also proposed cutting earmarks that would benefit land-grant institutions and designating more Hatch Act funding to be awarded on a competitive basis (Fischer, 2007).

According to Huddleston, in 2012 "Draconian cuts in state support have saddled students with crippling levels of debt, and even put higher education out of the reach of some families. These same cuts, by undermining our ability to support basic and applied research, threaten to blunt America's competitive edge in the knowledge-driven 21st century" (Huddleston, 2012). In response to the funding crisis, land-grant institutions are seeking alternative revenues, promoting public-private partnerships, leveraging intellectual capital, and increasing the reach of capital campaigns. They are also cutting expenses through the use of technology and streamlined administrative processes (Huddleston).

THE FUTURE OF LAND-GRANTS

Some scholars seemed to take time out toward the turn of the century to examine the progress and future of land-grant institutions. The Kellogg Commission on the Future of State and Land-Grant Universities existed between 1996 and 2000 and focused on higher education reform (Byrne, 2006). It brought attention to five main areas of the higher education enterprise: the student experience, access, university-public partnerships, the public universities' role in a learning society, and campus culture (Byrne). Byrne noted that feedback from higher education leaders collected five years after the work of the Commission indicates that the Commission has primarily influenced institutions' "engagement with society, internationalization of the campus with particular attention to overseas opportunities for students, holistic learning including residential and in-service learning, undergraduate research opportunities, and distant and lifelong learning."

Regarding other examinations on land-grants, Parker et al. noted that "as we enter a new century, the digital age offers new opportunities, challenges, and tensions for the universities established by the Morrill Act." Parker et al. went on to discuss the nation's ability to remain competitive in this new age and mentioned a crisis in K-12 education as impacting this ability. In referring to the work of the Kellogg Commission on the Future of State and Land-Gant Universities, Parker et al. noted that as part of their work to form stronger partnerships with state and local communities, the land-grant institutions should link up with K-12 education through a mixture of both face-to-face and "internet-mediated learning activities and collaborations."

Had Senator Morrill written his legislation at the turn of the 21st century instead of the middle of the 19th century, he almost certainly would have considered public school education as a major national problem to be addressed by land-grant research universities (Parker et al.)

Meanwhile, Jones et al. called for the development of the counterparts of experiment stations and extension services for the mechanic arts, or engineering, in order to help strengthen industry and keep America competitive. The authors stressed those land-grant institutions "have opportunities to turn to an area of critical national need–manufacturing-oriented industrial competitiveness–and apply the model of education, research, and technology transfer they have developed and applied so successfully in agriculture."

With the land-grant institutions survey a changing landscape, Siegel (2012) has called for a reimagining of the corporate/college relationship into one of joined identities, purposes, and imperatives, concluding that such collaborations would "have nothing to do with the evolution of universities into businesses; rather, they promote a co-evolution of our sectors into more effective joint actors in the social arena. Joint action is an alternative to our constrained thinking about how academic and corporate entities should relate, moving us beyond the debate about the corporatization of the academy to focus instead on building our capacity for collaborative contribution. When we start to think in terms of the multiplier effect and creative possibilities of our coupling, rather than the usual unsavory associations, we will already have achieved a significant measure of social progress" (Siegel).

TERMS & CONCEPTS

Appropriation: an act of a legislature authorizing money to be paid from the treasury for a special use.

Democratic: pertaining to or characterized by the principle of political or social equality for all.

Endowment: a revenue fund supported by donations; generally, only a portion of the interest on donations is spent while the principle remains intact

Experiment Stations: an establishment in which experiments in a particular line of research or activity, as agriculture or mining, are systematically carried on.

Extension Services: courses or programs (e.g., in agriculture or mining) offered by land-grant institutions to members of their communities who do not need to be enrolled at the institutions to benefit from the services offered

Land-Grant (Colleges/Universities/Institutions): under the Morrill Land Grant Act of 1862, each state is to have at least one institution that offers agricultural and mechanical arts alongside the liberal arts and other scientific studies; states were initially given grants of public lands, which could be sold in order to help generate funding, to establish the institutions.

Legislation: a law or a body of laws enacted.

Seminal: an original or ground-breaking work that may set the stage for later developments.

Marlene Clapp

BIBLIOGRAPHY

Altbach, P. G. (2001). The American academic model in comparative perspective. In P. G. Altbach, P. J. Gumport, & D. B. Johnstone (Eds.), *In defense of American higher education* (pp. 11-37). Baltimore, MD: The Johns Hopkins University Press.

Barnhart, C. L., & Stein, J. (Eds.). (1962). *The American college dictionary.* New York: Random House, Inc.

Biemiller, L. (2012). As land-grant law turns 150, students crowd into agriculture colleges. *Chronicle of Higher Education, 58*, A1-A11. Retrieved December 27, 2013, from EBSCO Online Database Education Research Complete.

Brubacher, J. S., & Rudy, W. (1997). *Higher education in transition* (4th ed.). New Brunswick, NJ: Transaction Publishers. Retrieved August 30, 2007, from EBSCO Online Database Education Research Complete.

Byrne, J. (2006). *Public higher education reform five years after the Kellogg Commission on the Future of State and Land-Grant Universities.* Washington, DC: National Association of State Universities and Land-Gant Colleges.

Duemer, L. (2007). The agricultural education origins of the Morrill Land Grant Act of 1862. *American Educational History Journal, 34*, 135-146. Retrieved August 30, 2007, from EBSCO Online Database Education Research Complete.

Enrollment at state universities and land-grant colleges, fall 1976. (1976). Washington, D.C.: Office of Research and Information, National Association of State Universities and Land-Grant Colleges. (ERIC Document Reproduction Service No. ED140704).

Fischer, K. (2007, February 16). Bush would shift funds in agriculture. *Chronicle of Higher Education, 53*, A31.

Retrieved August 30, 2007, from EBSCO Online Database Education Research Complete.

Geiger, R. (1999). The ten generations of American higher education. In P. G. Altbach, R. O. Berdahl, & P. J. Gumport (Eds.), *American higher education in the twenty-first century* (pp. 38-69). Baltimore, MD: The Johns Hopkins University Press.

Hebel, S. (2002, February 1). Land-grant colleges consider cuts or new fees for extension efforts. *Chronicle of Higher Education, 48*, A22. Retrieved August 30, 2007, from EBSCO Online Database Education Research Complete.

Huddleston, M. W. (2012). Morrill at 150: What would Justin do? *New England Journal of Higher Education,* 1. Retrieved December 27, 2013, from EBSCO Online Database Education Research Complete.

Johnson, E. L. (1981). Misconceptions about the early land-grant colleges. *The Journal of Higher Education, 52,* 333-351.

Jones, R., Oberst, B., & Lewis, C. (1990). The land-grant model. *Change, 22,* 11-16. Retrieved August 30, 2007, from EBSCO Online Database Education Research Complete.

Kerr, C. (2001). *The uses of the university.* Cambridge, MA: Harvard University Press.

Key, S. (1996). Economics or education: The establishment of American land-grant universities. *The Journal of Higher Education, 67,* 196-220. Retrieved September 28, 2007, from EBSCO Online Database Academic Search Complete.

Parker, L., Greenbaum, D., & Pister, K. (2001). Rethinking the land-grant research university for the digital age. *Change, 33,* 12. Retrieved August 30, 2007, from EBSCO Online Database Education Research Complete.

Rudolph, F. (1990). *The American college & university.* Athens, GA: The University of Georgia Press.

Siegel, D. J. (2012). Beyond the academic-corporate divide. *Academe, 98,* 29-31. Retrieved December 27, 2013, from EBSCO Online Database Education Research Complete.

Spanier, G. (1999). Enhancing the quality of life: A model for the 21st-century land-grant university. *Applied Developmental Science, 3,* 199. Retrieved August 30, 2007, from EBSCO Online Database Education Research Complete.

SUGGESTED READING

Dunn, D., Gibson, F., & Whorton Jr., J. (1985). University commitment to public service for state and local governments. *Public Administration Review, 45,* 503. Retrieved August 30, 2007, from EBSCO Online Database Education Research Complete.

Gee, E., & Spikes, D. (1997). Retooling America's public universities. *About Campus, 1,* 30. Retrieved August 30, 2007, from EBSCO Online Database Education Research Complete.

Hardi, J. (2000, March 31). Land-grant presidents call for new 'covenant' with state and U.S. governments. *Chronicle of Higher Education, 46,* A41. Retrieved August 30, 2007, from EBSCO Online Database Education Research Complete.

Kellogg Commission on the Future of State and Land-Gant Universities. (2000). *Renewing the covenant: Learning, discovery, and engagement in a new age and different world.* Washington, DC: National Association of State Universities and Land-Gant Colleges.

Simon, L. K. (2013). From land-grant to a "world-grant" university. *International Educator, 22,* 48-51. Retrieved December 27, 2013, from EBSCO Online Database Education Research Complete.

AFRICAN-AMERICAN COLLEGES AND UNIVERSITIES

This article outlines the origins, composition, and development of African American colleges and universities, also known as "historically black colleges and universities" (HBCU), in the United States. Since their inception during the early nineteenth century, HBCUs have been established to provide quality postsecondary instruction to Americans of African descent. These institutions have successfully educated millions of students despite public disdain, legislative ambivalence, limited resources, and accreditation violations. To fully articulate the role of the black college system in America, factors such as enrollment, curriculum, and funding are considered. The future outlook for HBCUs based on efficacy, obstacles, criticism, and recent trends are then summarized in the viewpoints section.

KEYWORDS: Academic Accreditation; Black College System; *Brown v. Board of Education* of 1954; The Civil Rights Act of 1964; The Higher Education Act of 1965; Historically Black Colleges and Universities (HBCU); Jim Crow Laws; Morrill Land-Grant Colleges Acts; National Association for Equal Opportunity in Higher Education (NAFEO); *Plessey*

909

v. *Ferguson*; Predominantly Black Institution (PBI); School of Black Plurality; *United States v. Fordice*; White House Initiative on Historically Black Colleges and Universities

OVERVIEW

Most historically black colleges and universities (HBCU) were established following the emancipation of the slaves to provide higher educational opportunities to people of African descent in the United States. These early institutions offered curricula designed to help newly freed slaves assimilate and compete during the Reconstruction era by acquiring reading, writing, agricultural, industrial, and practical skills. The majority of HBCUs in the United States were established in the South from 1876 to 1964 during the "separate but equal" policy of the Jim Crow laws—meaning blacks were to have access to the same public services as whites, but in separate facilities. This doctrine was applied to everything from drinking fountains to institutions of higher education.

An HBCU is defined as any college or university, established prior to the Civil Rights Act of 1964 (which nullified all remaining Jim Crow policy), dedicated to the enrichment and advancement of freed descendants of slaves in the United States. As of the early twenty-first century, there are more than one hundred public and private HBCUs in the United States offering two- and four-year degree programs to more than 300,000 students (Gasman, 2007). This unique network of higher education employs more than 60,000 people in twenty-two states and territories, and makes up three percent of all colleges and universities in the United States (Brown, 2004). Although most HBCUs are located in the southeast and border regions, there are also institutions in California, Washington, D.C., Michigan, Ohio, and the U.S. Virgin Islands.

According to African American scholar W. E. B. DuBois, if it were not for African American colleges and universities, "the Negro would for all intents and purposes, have been driven back to slavery" (cited in Lemelle, 2002). HBCUs are not only responsible for forming the black middle class in America; they have produced "the majority of black judges, doctors, teachers, social workers, military officers, and civil rights leaders including Martin Luther King Jr., Rep. John Lewis, and Rev. Jesse Jackson" (LeBlanc, 2001). During the civil rights era, graduates of HBCUs "challenged

and revolutionized the social institutions of this nation with non-violent social change" (Lockett, 1994).

Besides HBCUs, there are three other categories of institutions of higher education in the United States from the African American perspective: predominantly black institutions or PBIs (any college or university more than half of whose student body is black); institutions of black plurality (an institution having a large community of black students); and predominantly white institutions (opened to African American students after *Brown v. Board of Education* in 1954). Thus, based on enrollment, an HBCU (post-1954) could be considered a predominantly black institution, an institution of black plurality, or a predominantly white institution.

ORIGINS

The first known African American colleges were private institutions in free states established prior to the Civil War. The first HBCU was founded in 1837 in Cheyney, Pennsylvania, by a Philadelphia Quaker named Richard Humphreys. Initially called the Institute for Colored Youth, the school offered vocational and teacher training to free blacks. In 1854, the Ashmun Institute in Pennsylvania (later renamed Lincoln University) became the first HBCU to offer free blacks higher education programs in liberal arts and science, and Wilberforce University in Ohio distinguished itself as the first private HBCU in the nation, as well as the first to admit black women. Other pioneers in black postsecondary education include Bowie State University in Maryland, Lincoln University in Missouri, and Howard University in Washington, D.C.

The growth and legitimacy of the black college system was bolstered through a series of legislative mandates in the second half of the nineteenth century. In 1862, Congress passed the Morrill Land-Grant Colleges Act, which gave states 30,000 acres of public land for each congressional representative in order to create and support a system of higher education in each state. Shortly after the inception of Morrill, HBCUs were founded throughout the northern and Midwestern states. However, many historically black colleges and universities were not established until a second Morrill Act was passed in 1890 that allowed blacks to attend land-grant institutions in southern states. Prior to the Morrill legislation, most HBCUs were established and funded by northern philanthropists, industrialists, free blacks, and religious missionaries such as the American Missionary Association.

After 1890, a new system of state-sponsored HBCUs was developed throughout the southern states using the land-grant funding provided under the original Morrill Act. The nascent HBCUs in the South were viewed as a threat to the traditional white-dominated system and, at best, were "unenthusiastically tolerated" by the establishment. Freed slaves were allowed to have access to higher education as long as it was limited, poor, proscriptive, and did not infringe on skilled labor historically reserved for whites (LeMelle).

HBCUs AFTER JIM CROW

Despite the criticism by blacks and whites and their negative historical circumstances, HBCUs were officially recognized as a formal system of postsecondary education by Title III of the Higher Education Act of 1965. The Strengthening Historically Black Colleges and Universities Program, part of President Lyndon Johnson's Great Society program, also provided funding and institutional support to the black college system.

In 1969, the National Association for Equal Opportunity in Higher Education (NAFEO) was formed by HBCU presidents to help support and advance the black institutions of higher learning in America. According to the NAFEO national website, the mission of the organization is:

> "... to champion the interests of historically black colleges and universities (HBCUs) and predominantly black institutions (PBIs) with the executive, legislative, regulatory, and judicial branches of federal and state government and with corporations, foundations, associations and nongovernmental organizations; to provide services to NAFEO members; to build the capacity of HBCUs, their executives, administrators, faculty, staff and students; and to serve as an international voice and advocate for the preservation and enhancement of historically and predominantly black colleges and universities and for blacks in higher education" (NAFEO, 2007).

In recent decades, the HBCU system has received federal support and assistance through the White House Initiative on Historically Black Colleges and Universities, established by President Jimmy Carter in 1981 (and updated by his successors) and designed to strengthen and advance black colleges in America.

In 1992, *United States v. Fordice* (litigated for over two decades) forced public colleges and universities in Mississippi to completely abolish any remnants of the separate-but-equal system established during the Jim Crow era. Many HBCU advocates have expressed concern that the *Fordice* case (and similar decisions) could ultimately undermine the authority, legitimacy, and role of state-sponsored black colleges in the United States. However, the HBCU system continues to operate and flourish despite the integration of our school systems and over three decades of sometimes hostile litigation.

Applications

ENROLLMENT

During the period of institutional segregation created by *Plessey v. Ferguson,* HBCUs educated the vast majority of black students in the United States. However, limited funding, insufficient recruitment efforts, and competition from historically white colleges and universities have caused a sharp decline in African American admission at HBCUs. According to Minor (2007), only 14 percent of African Americans now attend black colleges. But despite a decrease in black students and limited resources, many HBCUs have experienced steady or growing enrollment. Moreover, black colleges have significantly increased African American admission in advanced degree and professional course offerings. In 2006, HBCUs educated 40 percent of all black students pursuing post-baccalaureate programs (Hubbard, 2006).

One issue of growing concern for black colleges has been the escalation of enrollment among white students. From 1980 to 1990, the population of white students at HBCUs increased by 10,000, and in 1995 the white population at HBCUs in the United States peaked at nearly 36,000 (Gasman, 2007). Many HBCUs are even openly recruiting non-black students in order to generate increased enrollment and revenue. In fact, several historically black colleges no longer have an African American majority on campus, and HBCUs such as Bluefield State College and West Virginia State University now have a predominately white student population. Caucasian and other non-black students are attracted to the affordable tuition, convenient locations, and quality degree programs offered by the black college system. Critics of this trend argue that the white influx at black institutions contradicts and threatens the original role and objectives of an HBCU.

CURRICULUM

The original pedagogical mission for HBCUs was based on the principle that education "must prepare the youth for good lives as American citizens and it must also fit them to tackle their peculiar racial problems with intelligence and courage" (Clément, 1936). Since the origin of HBCUs, educators, politicians, and administrators have articulated and implemented two main approaches for curriculum development: industrial and classical. However, a more recent trend in curricula is a shift away from disciplines such as home economics, agriculture, education, and liberal arts and toward fields such as allied health, technology, business, environmental science, and international relations.

ACCREDITATION

Since the late 1990s, several black colleges have been sanctioned due to violations of standards during assessment reviews for accreditation. These schools include Barber-Scotia College, Bennett College, Edward Waters College, Grambling State University, Knoxville College, LeMoyne-Owen College, Lewis College of Business, Mary Holmes College, Morris Brown College, and Selma University. The majority of these violations were due to financial debt and mismanagement, poor quality of faculty, inadequate degree programs, campus infrastructure, and declining student enrollment. Since 1989, almost half of the colleges that lost accreditation from the Southern Association of Colleges and Schools were historically black institutions (Gasman). Moreover, a large number of college administrators at HBCUs have been censured for violating institutional standards and procedures. In response to the myriad of assessment infractions and administrative mismanagement, the Southern Education Fund established a program in 2004 to help "nonconforming" schools retain a positive accreditation status through special grants and assistance.

FUNDING

Inadequate budgets, limited resources, low tuition, and societal discrimination and indifference have plagued the finances of HBCUs since their inception. In order to remain competitive, many black colleges must rely on financial assistance provided by state funding, private organizations (like the United Negro College Fund and the Thurgood Marshall Scholarship Fund), and federal grants and programs such as Title III of the Higher Education Act, the White House Initiative on Historically Black Colleges and Universities, and the No Child Left Behind Act. Additional sources of income include alumni assistance, private donations, corporate sponsorship, fundraisers, student tuition, athletic programs, and government agencies (such as the National Institute for Health and the National Science Foundation). Although many external sources of revenue exist, inadequate funding continues to restrict the development and maintenance at the vast majority of HBCUs.

Viewpoints

EFFICACY

According to Dr. Michael Lomax of the United Negro College Fund, historically black colleges and universities "have an established record of enrolling and graduating young blacks—a better rate than the average black graduation rate of many majority institutions" (Lomax, 2002). Moreover, several HBCU academic degree programs are among the best in the nation. In 2000, six HBCUs were ranked in the top ten for sending African American students to medical school, and six of the ten top producers of black engineers were HBCUs (LeBlanc).

Many black students prefer the HBCU because it allows them to connect and appreciate their African American heritage and identity in a setting that is sensitive to their unique social and cultural needs. Other students are attracted to the affordable tuition, convenient locations, and long-term scholarship programs. However, limited program offerings, financial and administrative mismanagement, and accreditation failures have prompted many to question the viability of the HBCU system.

RECENT TRENDS

According to 2004 data from the National Achievement Scholarship Program, many of the brightest black students are beginning to pass up black colleges to pursue degrees in public and private historically white colleges and universities in the United States and abroad. Enrollment of Achievement Scholars at Howard University dropped from 71 in 2003 to 29 in 2004, and at Spelman the Achievement Scholar enrollment went from 11 in 2003 to 1 in 2004 (Burdman, 2005). In 2012, only 8 Achievement Scholars enrolled at Howard, although Spelman ticked up slightly, to 6 (*Allegiance and Support*). One of the primary causes for the recent "brain drain" is the dearth of advanced degree programs offered at HBCUs. For example, if a student wanted to get a PhD in black studies in the United States, he or she would be forced to attend a non-HBCU like Harvard, University of Massachusetts, or Yale (Valentine, 2002). Other factors in the drop-off in "high-end" enrollment at black colleges include negative press coverage, lack of funding for scholarships, accreditation problems, affirmative action programs, and heavy recruitment of black students by historically white colleges and universities.

Another significant trend has been the move to culturally diversify the HBCU. Several black colleges are now expanding their mission to educate the socially disadvantaged by increasing enrollment of Hispanics in the United States. Efforts are being made in the South and Midwest to attract students of Mexican and Central American heritage, while HBCUs in the Northeast are recruiting Puerto Ricans, Cubans, Dominicans, and other Afro-Latino populations (Roach, 2005).

OPPOSITION

Throughout the history of the black college system, there have been numerous black and white critics who view HBCUs as academically inferior and symbols of the segregation and racism of the Jim Crow era (LeMelle). HBCU opponents accuse the schools of being designed to reinforce the stratified system of the white-dominated power structure by limiting the role and advancement of African Americans. Today, many still question the efficacy and need for HBCUs in America, arguing that these institutions served the purpose of the segregation era and should be eliminated or reorganized as technical schools or community colleges. Some lament that black colleges have the potential to create ethnic insulation among students, leaving them at a disadvantage in the multicultural twenty-first century.

FUTURE OUTLOOK

In the twenty-first century, black colleges will continue to face systemic obstacles similar to those shared by most colleges and universities, such as insufficient faculty salary, a lack of scholarship funds and decreased endowment funding, the need for higher academic standards, accreditation compliance, enrollment, and retention. Other future concerns include a decrease in the number of black students graduating with science and medical degrees and a scarcity of doctoral programs at black institutions (LeBlanc). In order to stay competitive in the twenty-first century and preserve their original institutional objectives, HBCUs must develop pedagogical methods that focus on the special needs of African American students, such as the social issues of confronting racism and economic planning (LeMelle).

TERMS & CONCEPTS

Academic Accreditation: An evaluation of an institution of higher learning by a licensed third-party agency to determine whether applicable standards of education are being met.

Brown v. Board of Education: U.S. Supreme Court Decision of 1954 declaring that separate educational facilities are inherently unequal.

Jim Crow Laws: Statutes established by southern states from 1877 to 1964 that legalized segregation based on race in various aspects of society.

National Association for Equal Opportunity in Higher Education (NAFEO): An organization formed in 1969 by HBSU presidents to support and advance black institutions of higher learning in America.

The Morrill Acts: Land-grant legislation giving states 30,000 acres of public land for each congressional representative in order to create and support a system of higher education in each state. Created by Vermont Congressman Justin Smith Morrill in 1862 and updated in 1890.

Schools of Black Plurality: An institution of higher education with a large community of African American students.

United States v. Fordice: U.S. Supreme Court Case of 1992 forcing public colleges and universities in Mississippi to completely abolish any remnants of the separate-but-equal system established under the Jim Crow era.

White House Initiative on Historically Black Colleges and Universities: An executive order by President Carter in 1981 and updated by his successors, designed to strengthen and advance black colleges in America.

Chris Holfester

BIBLIOGRAPHY

Allegiance and Support: National Merit Scholarship Corporation 2011–2012 Annual Report. (2012). Retrieved December 6, 2013, from http://nationalmerit.org.

Brown, C. M. (2004). Gathering at the river: What black colleges need to do now. *Black Issues in Higher Education, 21*, 82. Retrieved April 9, 2007, from EBSCO Online Database Academic Search Premier.

Brown, M. C. II. (2013). The declining significance of historically black colleges and universities: Relevance, reputation, and reality in Obamamerica. *Journal of Negro Education, 82*, 3–19. Retrieved December 9, 2013, from EBSCO Online Database Education Research Complete.

Burdman, P. (2005). Battling for the best and brightest. *Black Issues in Higher Education, 22* 22–25. Retrieved April 9, 2007, from EBSCO Online Database Academic Search Premier.

Clément, R. (1936). Redirection and reorganization of the College for Negroes. *Journal of Negro Education, 5*, 478.

Esters, L. L., & Strayhorn, T. L. (2013). Demystifying the contributions of public land-grant historically black colleges and universities: Voices of HBCU presidents. *Negro Educational Review, 64*(1–4), 119–134. Retrieved December 9, 2013, from EBSCO Online Database Education Research Complete.

Evans, A. L., Evans, V., & Evans, A. M. (2002). Historically black colleges and universities. *Education, 123*, 3–18. Retrieved April 9, 2007, from EBSCO Online Database Academic Search Premier.

Gasman, M., Baez, B., Drezner, N., Sedgwick, K., Tudico, C., & Schmid, J. (2007). Historically black colleges and universities: Recent trends. *Academe, 93*, 69–78. Retrieved April 9, 2007, from EBSCO Online Database Academic Search Premier.

Hubbard, D. (2006). The color of our classroom, the color of our future. *Academe, 92*, 27–29. Retrieved April 9, 2007, from EBSCO Online Database Academic Search Premier.

Joseph, J. (2013). The impact of historically black colleges and universities on doctoral students. *New Directions for Higher Education*, 67–76. Retrieved December 9, 2013, from EBSCO Online Database Education Research Complete.

LeBlanc, C. (2001). State of the HBCUs. *New Crisis, 108*, 46–50. Retrieved April 9, 2007, from EBSCO Online Database Academic Search Premier.

LeMelle, T. (2002). The HBCU: Yesterday, today, and tomorrow. *Education, 123*, 190–197. Retrieved April 9, 2007, from EBSCO Online Database Academic Search Premier.

Lockett, G. (1994). Empowerment in HBCU's and PBCU's: Developing microcosms of the beloved community through the redefinition of social institutions and learning the application of values. Paper presented at the Conference of the National Association for Equal Opportunity in Higher Education. Washington, DC: Office of Education Research and improvement. (ERIC Document Reproduction Service No. ED371703). Retrieved November 19, 2007, from http://eric.ed.gov.

Lomax, M. (2007). The HBCU mission: A fresh new look for Congress. *Diverse: Issues in Higher Education, 24*, 51. Retrieved April 9, 2007, from EBSCO Online Database Academic Search Premier.

Minor, J. (2007). Success of HBCUs means looking forward, not backwards. *Diverse: Issues in Higher Education, 24*, 55. Retrieved May 15, 2007, from EBSCO Online Database Academic Search Premier.

National Association for Equal Opportunity in Higher Education. (2007). *About: NAFEO's mission.* Retrieved May 15, 2007, from http://nafeo.org.

Roach, R. (2005). HBCU's reach out to Latino students. *Diverse: Issues in Higher Education, 16*, 28–29. Retrieved April 9, 2007, from EBSCO Online Database Academic Search Premier.

Valentine, V. (2002). What about the HBCUs. *New Crisis, 109*, 2–4. Retrieved April 9, 2007, from EBSCO Online Database Academic Search Premier.

SUGGESTED READING

Bryan, N., Johnson, L., & Williams, T.M. (2016). Preparing black male teachers for the gifted classroom: Recommendations for Historically Black Colleges and Universities (HBCUs). *The Journal of Negro Education.* 85(4), 489-504.

Cato, S. & Moore, J. (2015). Council for accreditation of Counseling and Related Educational Programs (CACREP) at historically black colleges and universities (HBCUs). *The Journal of Negro Education.* 84(1), 56-65.

Hill, L. (1994). *Black American colleges and universities: Profiles of two-year, four-year and professional schools.* Farmington Hills, MI: Gale Group.

Lenning, E. (2017). Unapologetically queer in unapologetically black spaces: Creating an inclusive HBCU campus. *Humboldt Journal of Social Relations.* 39, 283-293.

Mikyong, M. K. (2006). The impact of historically black colleges and universities on the academic success of

African-American students. *Research in Higher Education,* 47, 399–427.

Owens, E. W., Shelton, A. J., Bloom, C. M., & Kenyatta Cavil, J. (2012). The significance of HBCUs to the production of STEM graduates: Answering the call. *Educational Foundations, 26*(3/4), 33–47. Retrieved December 9, 2013, from EBSCO Online Database Education Research Complete.

Roach, R. (2006). An HBCU transformed. *Diverse: Issues in Higher Education, 9,* 14–18.

Uwakonye, M., & Osho, G. S. (2012). Economic recession and historically black colleges and universities: An analysis of factors impacting historically black colleges and universities. *International Journal of Education, 4,* 328–344. Retrieved December 9, 2013, from EBSCO Online Database Education Research Complete.

TRIBAL COLLEGES

Tribal colleges and universities (TCUs), or tribally controlled colleges, were founded to advance the higher education of American Indians, or Native Americans. Unlike past institutions developed to educate American Indians, TCUs do not strive toward assimilation but rather seek to preserve and support tribal culture and traditions (AIHEC, 1999; Fann, 2002). The American Indian Higher Education Consortium (AIHEC) was established to promote the development of new TCUs and support the work of established TCUs. Originally created as two-year institutions, TCUs are believed to represent an important phase of the community college phenomenon as well (Brubacher & Rudy, 1997).

KEYWORDS: American Indian Higher Education Consortium (AIHEC); American Indians; Articulation Agreements; Assimilation; Community College; First-Generation Students; Institute for Higher Education Policy (IHEP, 2007); Mainstream; Minority; Native American Education; Normal School; Non-Beneficiary Students; Tribal Colleges & Universities (TCU's); Tribally Controlled Colleges (TCC's)

OVERVIEW

WHY TRIBAL COLLEGES & UNIVERSITIES ARE IMPORTANT

According to the Institute for Higher Education Policy (IHEP), an economic and social gap formed between American Indians and mainstream society soon after the first white settlers arrived in North America (IHEP). IHEP asserts that "access to quality education in general, and higher education in particular, is key to closing the economic and social gap." Yet, in general, the educational attainment of American Indians runs behind that of the general U.S. population. For instance, 42 percent of American Indians were enrolled in some form of

higher education in 2004, as compared to 53 percent of students nationally (IHEP).

IHEP also stresses that it is essential that higher education opportunities be relevant to the American Indian cultural context. As such, TCUs serve an important purpose because mainstream higher education institutions tend to overlook the traditions, pedagogical approaches, and measures of success of American Indians (IHEP). Likewise, Tippeconnic (1999) argued that because of the history of assimilation linked to the education of American Indians in the United States, TCUs are necessary in order to "reclaim and strengthen the use of Native languages and cultures in schools and communities," and thus "ensuring a strong future for all Indian people." IHEP offered that American Indian higher education is linked to "dramatic benefits to both individual American Indians and the nation as a whole, including higher rates of employment, less reliance on public assistance, increased levels of health, and a greater sense of civic responsibility."

In 2012, the World Indigenous Nations Higher Education Consortium founded the World Indigenous Nations University (WINU), granting four doctoral degrees the same year. WINU is "the first indigenous international degree granting global institution that holds in its charter the articles of the UN [United Nations] Declaration of the Rights of Indigenous Peoples (World Indigenous Nations Higher Education Consortium, 2013).

HISTORY OF AMERICAN INDIAN HIGHER EDUCATION & TCUs

McClellan, Tippeconnic Fox, and Lowe (2005) summarized the three historical periods of Native American higher education, which include the colonial, the federal, and the self-determination periods. Little was done to advance the higher education of Native people during the colonial period. Only four

Native students had graduated from colonial colleges up to the time of the Revolutionary War (McClellan et al.). Aside from the failings of the colonial colleges to whole-heartedly pursue the education of Native students, it is also thought that Native Americans may have viewed the type of education the colleges offered as holding little value to them (McClellan et al.).

During the federal period, which began after the American Revolution when Native tribes and the federal government entered into treaty relationships, little was again provided in the way of higher education for Native Americans (McClellan et al.). While missionary and federally operated schools were supported with tribal monies acquired through land sale treaties, what higher education was offered focused mainly on technical education, and the general goals of the time were to Christianize, acculturate, and assimilate Native people (Beck; McClellan et al.). Beck indicated,

The day schools and boarding schools run by federal government and church missions beginning in the treaty period and extending well into the twentieth century did little to encourage Indians to pursue higher education, although their purposes were largely to force assimilation and to destroy Indian children's connections to their own cultures.

Although not a true college, the Carlisle Indian School, which was founded in 1879, has an important place in history as the first industrial school for American Indians (Brubacher & Rudy). As noted, the type of training at such schools emphasized assimilation of American Indian youth into white civilization (Brubacher & Rudy). The history of the Carlisle Indian School is told through its football team, which played Ivy League colleges like Harvard, and in a text published in 2007 by Sally Jenkins (*The Real All Americans: The Team That Changed a Game, a People, a Nation*).

Scholars have debated when the final period, the self-determination period, began (McClellan et al.). However, it was during the 1960s that the federal government finally began to pursue policies of self-determination for Native Americans (Beck; McClellan et al.). The American Indian self-determination movement was fueled by political and social policies leading up to the time (Pavel et al., 1998). Before the self-determination movement of the 1960s, American Indian higher education was characterized by "compulsory Western methods of learning, recurring attempts to eradicate tribal culture, and high dropout rates by American Indian students at mainstream institutions"

(AIHEC). TCUs were conceived to "support efforts for Indian self-determination and strengthen tribal culture without assimilation" (Fann). Until the 1960s, Bacone College (originally founded as Indian University in 1880) was the only primarily Indian college in the United States (Beck). It was a private school run by Baptists (Beck). However, a state normal school to train Indians to teach was also founded in 1887 and became Pembroke State College (Beck). In 1954 it opened its doors to non-Indians after segregation in public schools became illegal (Beck). Aside from the few other colleges and universities Indian students attended, these two schools for Indians were largely the providers of higher education for American Indians into the twentieth century (Beck). At the same time, a congressional committee studying the state of Indian education in the late 1960s found the quality of the education American Indians received to be sorely lacking (Beck). For instance, among those Indian students who were eventually able to attend college, about 97 percent dropped out at that time (Beck).

The first TCU was Navajo Community College, which was founded in Arizona in 1968 by the Dine organization (O'Laughlin, 2002). It is now known as Diné College (AIHEC). Once Navajo Community College was formed, other tribes were inspired to found and charter their own colleges (Pavel et al.). Beck noted that the founding of the tribal community college system "has had broad-reaching effect in Indian country and has gained federal financial as well as tribal support." TCUs and other tribally controlled schools are actually rooted in the schools established by the Cherokee and Choctaw tribes in the nineteenth century, which taught both in English and the tribes' native languages (Tippeconnic). These schools were successful but were closed by the federal government, which favored a policy of assimilation (Tippeconnic). It was not until 1975 that Congress passed the Indian Self-Determination Act and the Education Assistance Act (Pavel et al.).

McClellan et al. asserted that the tribal college movement was "the single most significant development in the era of self-determination in Native American higher education." Regarding self-determination, Tippeconnic explained that because they do not fall under state jurisdiction due to their status as sovereign bodies, tribal governments have the right to make decisions about how to educate their tribal members. Begun primarily as two-year institutions, the development of tribal institutions was "an important phase of the community college phenomenon" (Brubacher & Rudy). By the 1990s the institutions were offering instruction in fields like nursing, social work, business administration, and education, and had awarded more than three thousand associate in arts degrees each year (Brubacher & Rudy).

FURTHER INSIGHTS

Stein (1999) has described TCUs as "small tenacious institutions of higher education that serve the smallest and poorest minority group in the United States (American Indians) under difficult and challenging circumstances." According to O'Laughlin (2002), TCUs were formed to help improve the quality of life for American Indians living on reservations. For example, many American Indians living on reservations live below poverty level (O'Laughlin). Students enrolling at TCUs on average have household incomes that are 27 percent below poverty level (IHEP). American Indians also face high unemployment rates especially in comparison to the general U.S. population (AIHEC; IHEP). Overall, TCUs "generally serve geographically isolated populations that have no other means of accessing education beyond the high school level" (AIHEC). The educational program Breaking Through, for example, advocates for Native students not prepared for basic college education (González, 2012).

BASIC CHARACTERISTICS OF TCUS

According to O'Laughlin, there are four types of TCUs:

- **Tribally controlled community colleges** are located on an Indian reservation and are created and chartered by a federally recognized Indian tribe;
- **Tribally controlled vocational technical institutions** are created and chartered by one or more federally recognized Indian tribes and are funded under the Carl D. Perkins Vocational and Applied Technology Act;
- **Bureau of Indian Affairs (BIA) colleges** are owned and operated by the BIA, which provides the schools with special funding;
- **Congressionally chartered colleges** are governed by a board of trustees that are appointed by the U.S. president.

Regardless of which type they are associated, TCUs, according to the AIHEC, all share the following basic characteristics:

- They started as two-year institutions;
- They have small enrollments, which are mainly American Indian;
- They have open admissions policies;
- They are mainly located on remote reservations;
- They were generally chartered by one or more tribes (this is not the case with congressionally chartered colleges, however).

Each TCU is also associated with a different tribe and helps to preserve the different cultural traditions and language of its affiliated tribe (O'Laughlin). If an institution is under tribal control it means that the actual tribal government is in control of the school (Tippeconnic). Tribal control is not simply "Indian control" of education (Tippeconnic). Some TCUs are now also land-grant colleges, and their focus is determined by the part of the country in which they are located (for example, in the Pacific Northwest the focus is on the fishing industry) (O'Laughlin). Because of the different tribal and regional influences, the curriculum tends to vary from one TCU to the next (O'Laughlin). However, all TCUs have articulation agreements with four-year institutions (O'Laughlin).

TCUs mainly support associate degree or vocational education. In 2005, the 32 TCUs that reported statistics indicated that they offered only 24 bachelor's degree programs but 414 associate degree programs and 183 vocational programs (AIHEC). Overall, all TCUs offer some associate degree programs while only seven offer bachelor's degree programs and only two offer master's degree programs (AIHEC).

The boards of trustees that control tribal colleges are mainly made up of American Indian community members (Stein). The boards "act as buffers between tribal politics and the colleges ... [as well as] mediators among policy makers, personnel selection committees, and local watchdogs of and for the tribal colleges" (Stein). While most administrators at TCUs are also American Indian, most faculty members are not. However, both administrators and faculty members at TCUs alike have been recognized for their dedication to the students they serve (Stein).

MISSION OF TCUS

TCUs have a dual mission that entails supporting traditional tribal cultures through "uniquely designed curricula and institutional settings" while also addressing mainstream learning models through curricula that are transferable to four-year institutions (AIHEC). According to Cunningham and Redmond (2001), "serving and strengthening local communities is [also] a fundamental part of the mission of American Indian Tribal Colleges and Universities." TCUs are involved in the communities in which they are located to a greater extent than other colleges and universities might be. This is because their communities rely on them to help devise solutions to issues and concerns that may be longstanding and critical (Cunningham & Redmond). Moreover, TCUs are located either in the reservation communities they serve or in proximity to them, allowing members of the community to have easier access to their services (Cunningham & Redmond).

One specific service that TCUs provide to their communities is working with elementary and secondary school students to help them progress through their education (Cunningham & Redmond). TCUs also reach out to their communities to help combat the negative effects of health problems like poor nutrition and substance abuse (Cunningham & Redmond). According to AIHEC, "TCUs serve their community beyond providing higher education." At the same time, Gagnon (2001) noted that some TCUs have had a hard time balancing the demands of community development and have not put academics first. Gagnon asserted that the primary purpose of the colleges, which is to provide a sound education, has suffered when some TCUs have diverted the majority of their monetary and staff resources from academic causes to work on nonacademic, non college issues.

TCU STUDENTS

Institutions can be classified as a TCU if at least 51 percent of their enrolled students are American Indian (O'Laughlin). The majority of students who attend TCUs identify themselves as American Indian females. In the fall of 2005, 80 percent of students enrolled in TCUs were American Indian and 66 percent were female (AIHEC).

Because the students who attend TCUs often must balance family, work, and school, "an ongoing challenge at TCUs is retention" (AIHEC). Hu (2013) discusses recruitment and retention issues facing tribal colleges and universities in the context of student motivation and desire to be educated.

The typical student who attends a TCU is a single mother in her early thirties (AIHEC). She may also

likely attend part-time, as half of all TCU students do so (AIHEC). TCU students are also often first-generation students, or the first in their families to attend college (McClellan et al.). Moreover, most TCUs are commuter institutions, as only relatively few provide housing and room and board for their students (O'Laughlin). The lack of housing and living assistance at most TCUs can be difficult for students who reside several miles from the nearest college (O'Laughlin). While retention is an issue for TCUs, students at TCUs do at least benefit from the personalized attention that is provided to them (AIHEC).

Enrollments at TCUs tend to be small and are generally between 200 and 1,000 students (O'Laughlin). In 2005, reporting TCUs indicated actual enrollments ranging from 60 students to 1,822 students (AIHEC).

FUNDING OF TCUs

Stein explained that "tribal colleges interact with the federal government much as state-supported institutions do with state governments." TCUs are not eligible for state or local funds because of the sovereign status of tribes and thus must rely on the bulk of their funding to come from federal appropriations and grants (O'Laughlin). Approximately eighty percent of the funding at TCUs comes from federal sources (O'Laughlin). Aside from the federal government, philanthropic and corporate organizations also provide funding to TCUs (Fann).

Most of the federal funds for operating expenses that TCUs receive are distributed through the Tribally Controlled College or University Assistance Act of 1978 (TCCUAA) administered by the Bureau of Indian Affairs (AIHEC). This act is also referred to by others as the Tribally Controlled Community College Assistance Act (TCCC) of 1978 and originally as the Tribal College Act (Stein). Funding is allocated through the act by way of a formula that is based on the number of Indian students enrolled at a TCU (IHEP). Pember (2006) explained that while TCUs are required to admit students of all races, federal funding formulas only provide funding to TCUs on a per student basis for those Native students they educate. As such, TCUs must rely upon tuition to cover the costs of non-Native, or nonbeneficiary students who attend the institutions. Yet, Pember explained that "tuition often just barely covers the costs of educating the non-beneficiary students, placing a tremendous burden on the already cash-strapped colleges."

In general, the total funding provided or appropriated through the act has fallen short of authorized levels, and more resources are needed (IHEP). Stein lamented that the federal government has historically underfunded the TCUs and has never appropriated funds to the institutions up to the level authorized by the act. Moreover, the funding levels authorized by the act have failed to keep up with inflation (Stein).

THE AMERICAN INDIAN HIGHER EDUCATION CONSORTIUM

The American Indian Higher Education Consortium (AIHEC) was founded in 1972 by the presidents of the first six TCUs with a mission of supporting the work of all TCUs (AIHEC). The newly created AIHEC helped to establish new TCUs while securing funds for the tribal college movement (Pavel et al.). For example, in 1978, Congress passed the Tribally Controlled Community College Act. This legislation provided funding for both the establishment of new TCUs and the improvement of existing TCUs (Pavel et al.). AIHEC was involved in the passage of the act and worked with Congress and U.S. president Jimmy Carter to develop it (Pavel et al.).

According to McClellan et al., various pieces of legislation, including the 1978 act, have worked to help expand the number of TCUs in the United State since the 1960s. These include the Navajo Community College Act of 1971, the Indian Education Act of 1972, the Indian Self-Determination Act of 1975, the Tribally Controlled College or University Assistance Act of 1978, and the extension of land-grant status by way of the Morrill Act to tribal colleges in 1994. Land-grant status was granted to TCUs by Congress in 1994 (Pavel et al.). According to Fann, TCUs status as land-grant institutions enables them to have access to resources that will support additional faculty and equipment to conduct agricultural research (independently or in collaboration with four-year institutions).

By 2014, thirty-seven TCUs in the United States (and one in Canada) made up the AIHEC.

CURRENT ISSUES

In general, most Native Americans who attend college are enrolled at two-year rather than four-year institutions (AIHEC). TCUs have taken on a goal of expanding to four-year colleges (Stein).

The students who attend TCUs are also changing. TCUs have always offered help to their tribal communities to deal with many economic, social, educational, and health-related problems. However, the American Indian population has also become younger, and TCUs will become even more essential to the well-being of future generations of these students (AIHEC).

TERMS & CONCEPTS

Articulation Agreements: Course credit transfer policies between institutions, such as two- and four-year institutions.

Assimilation: The process by which a culturally distinct group is made to resemble and take on the traits of another distinct cultural group.

First-Generation Students: Those students who are the first in their families to attend college or university.

Mainstream: The principal or prevailing form of some system, group, or the like.

Normal School: A school developed primarily to train teachers.

Non-Beneficiary Students: Those non-Native students who attend TCUs, which generally do not receive any state or federal funding to educate such students.

Self-Determination: With regard to American Indian higher education, refers to the efforts of tribes to determine and implement the best course of action for their people's education.

Sovereign: Possessing supreme and independent control or authority.

Tribal Colleges and Universities (TCU): Also known as tribally controlled colleges (TCC), these are higher education institutions that seek to preserve and honor tribal traditions and cultures while also providing mainstream higher education; TCUs are generally chartered by one or more American Indian tribes and are controlled by mainly American Indian boards of trustees.

Tribal Control: Means that the actual tribal government is in control of the school.

Marlene Clapp

BIBLIOGRAPHY

American Indian Higher Education Consortium (AIHEC). (1999). *Tribal colleges: An introduction.* Retrieved July 9, 2007, from http://aihec.org.

American Indian Higher Education Consortium (AIHEC). (2005). *AIHEC AIMS fact book 2005 highlights*. Retrieved July 9, 2007, from http://aihec.org.

Barnhart, C. L., & Stein, J. (eds.). (1962). *The American college dictionary*. New York: Random House.

Beck, D. (1995). American Indian higher education before 1974: From colonization to self-determination. In J. Brown (ed.), *Critical issues in Indian higher education* (pp. 16-24). Chicago: American Indian Press. (ERIC Document Reproduction Service No. ED388478).

Brubacher, J. S., & Rudy, W. (1997). *Higher education in transition* (4th ed.). New Brunswick, NJ: Transaction.

Cunningham, A., & Redmond, C. (2001). *Building strong communities: Tribal colleges as engaged institutions*. Lincoln, NE: American Indian Higher Education Consortium. (ERIC Document Reproduction Service No. ED451818).

Fann, A. (2002). *Tribal colleges: An overview (ERIC digest)*. Los Angeles: ERIC Clearinghouse for Community Colleges. (ERIC Document Reproduction Service No. ED467847).

Gagnon, G. (2001). Keeping the tribal colleges tribal. *Tribal College Journal, 12*, 37. Retrieved July 12, 2007, from EBSCO Online Database Education Research Complete.

González, J. (2012). Tribal colleges offer basic education to students "not prepared for college." *Chronicle of Higher Education, 58*, A25-26. Retrieved December 19, 2013, from EBSCO Online Database Academic Search Complete.

Hu, H. (2013). Challenge accepted. *Diverse: Issues in Higher Education, 30*, 12-13. Retrieved December 19, 2013, from EBSCO Online Database Academic Search Complete.

Institute for Higher Education Policy (IHEP). (2007). *The path of many journeys: The benefits of higher education for Native people and communities*. Washington, DC: Institute for Higher Education Policy.

McClellan, G., Tippeconnic Fox, M., & Lowe, S. (2005). Where we have been: A history of Native American higher education. *New Directions for Student Services*, 7-15. Retrieved July 12, 2007, from EBSCO Online Database Education Research Complete.

O'Laughlin, J. (2002). *Financing of tribal colleges*. Claremont, CA: Claremont Graduate University. (ERIC Document Reproduction Service No. ED477415).

Pavel, D. M., Skinner, R., Cahalan, M., Tippeconnic, J., & Stein, W. (1998). *American Indians and Alaska Natives in postsecondary education* (NCES 98-291). Washington, DC: U.S. Department of Education, National Center for Education Statistics.

Pember, M. (2006). Deal or no deal? *Diverse: Issues in Higher Education, 23*, 34-35. Retrieved July 12, 2007, from EBSCO Online Database Education Research Complete.

Stein, W. J. (1999). Tribal colleges: 1968-1998. In K. G. Swisher & J. Tippeconnic III (eds.), *Next steps: Research and practice to advance Indian education* (pp. 259-270). Charleston, WV: Eric Clearinghouse on Rural Education and Small Schools. (ERIC Document Reproduction Service No. ED427913).

Tippeconnic, J. W., III (1999). Tribal control of American Indian education: Observations since the 1960s with implications for the future. In K. G. Swisher & J. Tippeconnic III (eds.), *Next steps: Research and practice to advance Indian education* (pp. 33-52). Charleston, WV: Eric Clearinghouse on Rural Education and Small Schools. (ERIC Document Reproduction Service No. ED427904).

World Indigenous Nations Higher Education Consortium. (Aug. 9, 2013). WINHEC announces World Indigenous University (WINU). Retrieved December 19, 2013, from http://winu.org.

SUGGESTED READING

Bull, C. (2017). Emergent and revolutionary: Telling native peoples' stories at Tribal Colleges. *Tribal College Journal. 28*(3), 20-24.

Department of Housing and Urban Development. (2003). *Minority-serving institutions of higher education: Developing partnerships to revitalize communities*. Washington, DC: Department of Housing and Urban Development. (ERIC Document Reproduction Service No. ED481028).

Fogarty, M. (2007). Commitment to building prosperous nations. *Tribal College Journal, 18*, 12-17. Retrieved July 12, 2007, from EBSCO Online Database Education Research Complete.

Freeman, C., & Fox, M. (2005). *Status and trends in the education of American Indians and Alaska Natives* (NCES 2005-108). Washington, DC: U.S. Department of Education, National Center for Education Statistics. (ERIC Document Reproduction Service No. ED485861).

Hernandez, J. (2006). Empowering students for success. *Tribal College Journal, 18*, 12-17. Retrieved July 12, 2007, from EBSCO Online Database Education Research Complete.

Martin, R. (2005). Serving American Indian students in tribal colleges: Lessons for mainstream colleges. *New Directions for Student Services*, 79-86. Retrieved July 12, 2007, from EBSCO Online Database Education Research Complete.

Oppelt, N. T. (1990). *The tribally controlled Indian colleges: The beginnings of self-determination in American Indian education*. Tsaile, AZ: Navajo Community College Press. (ERIC Document Reproduction Service No. ED356108).

Ortiz, A., & Boyer, P. (2003). Student assessment in tribal colleges. *New Directions for Institutional Research, 2003*, 41-49. Retrieved July 12, 2007, from EBSCO Online Database Education Research Complete.

Paskus, L. (2017). Beyond Standing Rock: Seeking solution and building awareness at Tribal Colleges. *Tribal College Journal.* 28(4), 20-24.

Tippeconnic, J. W., III, & Yabeny, P. (2016). Capturing education: Envisioning and building the first Tribal Colleges. *Wicazo Sa Review.* 31(2), 94-97.

ACCESS TO HIGHER EDUCATION

Starting with the land-grant movement, U.S. higher education has been marked by various milestones in the drive to ensure greater access to postsecondary education for the citizenry (Gándara, Horn, & Orfield, 2005; Kerr, 2001). However, some higher education scholars are sounding alarms that what progress toward greater access has been made is now being reversed (Gardner, 2004; Valentine, 2004). Arguments have been made that underrepresented students have been particularly affected by the access crisis, as factors such as rising tuitions and lack of adequate academic preparation seem to disproportionately impact them (Bastedo & Gumport, 2003; Choy, 2002; Gardner; Hoffman, 2003; Valentine).

KEYWORDS: Academic Preparation; Access Crisis; At-Risk Students; College-Based Credit; Convenient Access; Distributional Access; Examination-Based College Credit; First-Generation Students; Immigrants; Low-Income Students; Minority Students; Need-Based Financial Aid; Recurrent Access; School-Based Credit; Threshold Access; Underrepresented Students; Universal Access; Virtual-College Credit Courses

OVERVIEW

According to Valentine, "American democracy has been characterized by policies that reflect a national commitment to allowing all qualified and motivated Americans to receive post-secondary education." Access, particularly to public forms of higher education, is generally perceived as an informal right of American citizens. Bastedo and Gumport stated that "equality of opportunity for all students to attend public higher education in their state, without regard to their background or preparation, is a foundational principle of higher education policymaking in the United States." Scholars have contended that there are dire consequences when access to higher education is threatened. For instance, Dalton (2000) stressed that "a population denied access to college carries significant economic and social costs and ultimately places our nation at risk." Costs can take the form of public assistance as well as health and social services (Dalton).

The push for universal access in American higher education originated with the land grant movement of the 1860s. Mainly an agricultural nation at the time, the movement facilitated access to some form of higher education for the citizenry at large, such as farming families (Kerr). According to Kerr, in an increasingly democratic nation the land grant movement served "less the perpetuation of an elite class and more the creation of a relatively classless society, with the doors of opportunity open to all through education." Gándara et al. identified several other events in the history of American higher education that have contributed to improving access. These included the G.I. Bill, the 1965 Higher Education Act, the advent of college access programs, the rise of affirmative action, and growth in the higher education system during the 1960s and 1970s. Kerr similarly added that during the time after World War II, the passage of the G.I. Bill positioned the universal access movement further along by making higher education a possibility for many students who were the first in their families to attend college (Kerr).

Despite historical gains in access to postsecondary education, some higher education scholars are sounding the alarm to signal a crisis of opportunity. Gándara et al., for example, proposed that there is now an access crisis in American higher education that has been fueled by lack of state support for higher education, rising tuitions, an end to affirmative action in some states, and decreased capacity to accommodate students. Overall, Gándara et al. stressed that the current higher education system is "inadequate to meet the expanding need for postsecondary education in the 21st century." According to Dalton, measures must be taken to ensure that all young people succeed and particular attention should be given to students in low-income communities.

FURTHER INSIGHTS

According to Choy, five steps are necessary for a student to enter a four-year college or university. These steps include the following:

- Aspiring to college;
- Preparing academically for college;
- Taking the necessary entrance exams (such as the SAT or ACT);
- Applying to college;
- Enrolling in college.

Along the way to entering a four-year higher education institution, the most students are lost early in the journey—either because they do not aspire to a four-year degree or are not academically prepared to enter a four-year institution (Choy).

Regardless of whether or not an overall crisis of opportunity exists, access to higher education has been particularly difficult for certain subsets of the population. These include underrepresented students, immigrants, and international students and scholars.

UNDERREPRESENTED STUDENTS

Underrepresented students are first and foremost impacted by factors limiting access. For instance, Valentine expressed concern that low-income students would be particularly affected by the access crisis in higher education. It has been proposed that because of increased tuitions, these students might either forego higher education completely or else struggle to achieve a postsecondary degree due to the need to delay entry, work more hours while enrolled, or take on vast debt (Gardner; Valentine). Final recommendations from the U.S. Secretary of Education's Commission on the Future of Higher Education actually included increasing access to higher education by providing more aid to low-income students (Pluviose, 2006).

While great concern exists for low-income students, when students are the first in their families to attend college they can also encounter obstacles to postsecondary access. Using data from a series of longitudinal studies conducted by the National Center for Education Statistics (NCES), Choy found that, along with family income, level of parental education affects the likelihood of a student enrolling in postsecondary education. For instance, as both family income and level of parental education increase, the chances that a high school graduate will immediately enroll in a four-year higher education institution after graduation also increase (Choy). Indeed, students who have parents who both completed college are more likely to remain on course and complete all the steps necessary to enter a four-year institution (Choy).

Access to higher education for underrepresented minority students is also an issue. Ward (2006) offered that "comprehensive strategies are critical in addressing the problem of the achievement gap for low-income minority students." Overall, it seems that scholars are particularly concerned about access issues for low-income students, but there is indication that the struggles low-income students face regarding access can be compounded when they are also of minority and/or first-generation immigrant status. Hoffman indicated that, along with retention and graduation rates, access correlates "strikingly with race, income, and family educational background."

REACHING UNDERREPRESENTED STUDENTS

Various outreach efforts have been put in place to help underrepresented students gain better access to higher education. Choy indicated simply that the support of "parents, peers, and school personnel can help at-risk students overcome a variety of obstacles to college access and persistence." Ward also noted that federal programs have been initiated to help improve access to higher education for underrepresented minorities and low-income students. While limited in their scope, the TRIO programs are among the better known federal programs and reflect three major federal initiatives:

- Upward Bound;
- Educational Talent Search (ETS);
- Student Support Services (SSS) (Ward).

Upward Bound provides a four to six-week college bridge experience for low-income and minority first-generation high school students in order to help facilitate their successful transition to higher education (Ward). Meanwhile, ETS provides low-income and minority high school students with needed counseling services (e.g., academic, career, financial) to help them graduate from high school and successfully enter postsecondary education (Ward). Finally, SSS provides both financial and academic assistance to low-income and minority undergraduates (Ward).

A federal program called GEAR UP (Gaining Early Awareness and Readiness for Undergraduate Programs) is intended for fill gaps left by the TRIO programs (Ward). Specifically, the initiative targets "the coupling of systemic school reform with early intervention for middle school students." Under the initiative, school districts and universities must partner together to work toward curriculum standards that adequately prepare students for college (Ward). Indeed, Choy determined that some of the effect of parental education on access, for instance, can be mitigated by pursuing a rigorous high school curriculum that includes advanced mathematics courses (i.e., those beyond algebra II).

EARNING COLLEGE CREDIT IN HIGH SCHOOL

In discussing access issues for underrepresented students, Hoffman additionally highlighted programs that enable students to earn college credit while still in high school. Such programs are part of a new policy shift that Hoffman indicated will help with "getting more young people into and through postsecondary education." However, while programs like these are no longer limited to privileged students it remains to be seen just how many underrepresented students will benefit from such programs (Hoffman). For instance, there can be differential access to college-credit programs because underrepresented students' participation in such programs can be curtailed, for instance, by the fees to participate in such programs in some states as well as the offerings available at the high schools they attend (Hoffman). There are four basic ways in which students can earn college credit while in high school:

- Examination-based college credit;
- School-based credit;
- College-based credit;
- Virtual-college credit courses.

IMMIGRANTS

Gray and Vernez (1996) discussed the wave of new immigrants that have arrived in the United States and noted that they represent a new segment of the population that higher education must serve. However, some contend that higher education institutions overall are already struggling to provide access to students (Gray & Vernez). Meanwhile, research by Gray and Vernez actually indicated that immigrants seem to be participating in higher education at a higher rate than native-born students (findings held across all racial and ethnic backgrounds). They concluded that "institutional policies and practices have not disproportionately depressed access and academic success among immigrants vis-à-vis native-born students" (Gray & Vernez).

INTERNATIONAL STUDENTS & SCHOLARS

Starobin (2006) discussed access to U.S. higher education for visiting international students and scholars in a post–September 11 environment. The author offered that the implementation of the Student and Exchange Visitor Information System (SEVIS) has been perceived as unwelcoming due to its more stringent oversight of international students and visitors (Starobin). Starobin stressed that "intensity of the threat of global terrorism should not compromise the contributions of international students and scholars to the nation's academic and scientific advancement and economic prosperity."

WHAT IS "ACCESS"?

Adelman (2007) offered that there are at least four definitions of college access currently in use including,

- Threshold access;
- Recurrent access;
- Convenient access;
- Distributional access.

Adelman chose to concentrate on threshold access, which focuses on participation regardless of student characteristics, enrollment patterns, or institution type, stating that other definitions of access "contaminate the focus of the [access] question."

Yet Gándara et al. argued the case for recurrent access and stated that access to higher education should not just be about attaining access to some form of higher education but rather to "the full range of opportunities in higher education." For example, they argued that there should be assurances that those who wish to advance their education beyond the undergraduate level and attend medical or law school have access to such opportunities. The authors noted how the enrollment of underrepresented minorities fell by 50 percent at the University of California's medical schools after the use of affirmative action by public institutions was banned in the state (Gándara et al.).

Meanwhile, Bastedo and Gumport urge support for distributional access and framed access to also include the types of academic programs that are available to students after they are admitted to a college or university. The authors offered that "policies that differentiate academic programs and students by level contribute to the stratification of student opportunity within state systems." They discussed how the end result of academic program reviews, for instance, often disproportionately impacts women and minorities because the programs that are eliminated tend to be low-status and are dominated by such students (Bastedo & Gumport). Additionally, place-bound students, who are more likely to be minorities from low-income families, would be particularly impacted by the lack of comprehensive program offerings at their local public college (Bastedo & Gumport). Overall, the authors stressed that students today "compete for access to a stratified array of institutions that offer different educational opportunities and prestige" (Bastedo & Gumport).

IS THERE A CRISIS?

According to Adelman, there is not so much an access problem in higher education as there is a participation (i.e., persistence) and success (i.e., graduation) problem. Based on longitudinal data findings from the Department of Education, Adelman argued that "our nation's access problem is hardly of crisis dimensions." For example, there was an overall (threshold) access rate of 79 percent for a recent cohort of students who either graduated high school on time and started postsecondary education immediately or entered postsecondary education by their mid-twenties (Adelman). Further, he found that disparities by race and ethnicity were fairly minor. Yet, disparities by family income were more notable, as 91 percent of on-time high school graduates in the top third of the family income range entered postsecondary education while only 69 percent of those in the bottom third of the family income range did (Adelman). Meanwhile, arguing on the side of distributional access, Hoffman stated that underrepresented students like low-income and minority students are more likely to attend two-year colleges and less selective four-year colleges than other students. Bastedo and Gumport similarly stressed, "Minority and low-income students are less likely to be admitted into the

highest-prestige programs in the system. If minority and low-income students are disproportionately represented in lower-level programs and schools, it remains questionable whether equitable access has truly been provided."

FACTORS AFFECTING ACCESS

For the most part there is agreement among higher education scholars that there *is* an access crisis in postsecondary education. Valentine lamented that "gains in access to higher education made in the 1960s, 1970s and 1980s are being reversed.". According to estimates from the National Center for Public Policy and Higher Education (2004), in the fall of 2003, "at least 250,000 prospective students were shut out of higher education due to rising tuition or cutbacks in admissions and course offerings." The curtailed opportunity in 2003 was largely due to state funding cuts that disproportionately affected higher education (National Center for Public Policy and Higher Education). Other factors that have been identified as contributing to decreased access include an increase in the number of students seeking a college education, federal policies that favor loans over grant aid, and increases to merit-based aid at the expense of need-based aid (Gardner; Valentine). According to Valentine, "Reductions in state funding, tuition increases, increased demand, and flat growth in need-based financial assistance make college less affordable and less accessible for many students."

INADEQUATE ACADEMIC PREPARATION

Academic preparation is also widely perceived as a major factor affecting access to higher education. According to Gándara et al., "It is impossible to discuss issues of access without also attending to the problems that emanate from inequities in the K-12 sector." The authors pointed to various research studies that have shown how K-12 preparation affects access to college (e.g., likelihood of attending certain types of higher education institutions or of a successful transition to college). Adelman also seemed to stress that low-income students' entry into postsecondary education is curtailed by issues of academic preparation (i.e., opportunities to take challenging courses and student engagement with those courses). Further, final recommendations from the U. S. Secretary of Education's Commission on the Future of Higher

Education included increasing access to higher education by working with the K-12 system to help ensure that students will be ready for postsecondary education and able to take advantage of it (Pluviose).

ISSUES WITH FINANCIAL AID

Haycock and Gerald (2007) recognized that factors such as inadequate K-12 preparation and federal and state policies that limit financial assistance to needy students have contributed to access problems in higher education. At the same time, the authors also stressed that colleges and universities *themselves* must shoulder some of the responsibility for access problems. For instance, both public and private higher education institutions have awarded more merit-based aid at the expense of need-based financial aid. They noted that rather than helping needy students to cover college costs, financial aid funding is "increasingly used to help institutions buy their way up the college rankings ladder" (Haycock & Gerald). This type of a trend works against the equalizing effect that financial aid can have for low-income students. According to Choy, "The price of attending college is still a significant obstacle for students from low- and middle-income families, but financial aid is an equalizer, to some degree."

TERMS & CONCEPTS

College-Based Credit: Also known as dual enrollment programs, in which high school students either (a) take courses on a college campus or satellite campus under the direction of college faculty while still enrolled in high school, or (b) take college-credit courses at their high schools.

Convenient Access: Entails the ability to enter and reenter into accredited postsecondary institutions at the time and location of one's choosing.

Distributional Access: Entails entry into an accredited postsecondary institution that a student either desires to attend and/or is qualified to attend.

Examination-Based College Credit: Includes the Advanced Placement (AP) and International Baccalaureate programs.

Immigrants: Foreign-born individuals who may range from being undocumented to a naturalized citizen.

Recurrent Access: Entails the ability to enter and reenter into accredited postsecondary institutions

(e.g., for transfers and for those who seek additional credentials).

School-Based Credit: Concurrent enrollment is the most typical program in which courses are taught in high schools by high school teachers under the direction of college professors.

Threshold Access: Entails basic entry into an accredited postsecondary institution.

Underrepresented Students (At-Risk Students): Generally includes students who are the first in their families to attend college (i.e., first-generation students) as well as low-income students and minority students.

Virtual-College Credit Courses: Are college-credit courses that are offered virtually (e.g., to home schoolers or students who have left high school).

Marlene Clapp

BIBLIOGRAPHY

Adelman, C. (2007). Do we really have a college access problem? *Change, 39,* 48–51. Retrieved November 5, 2014, from EBSCO Online Database Education Research Complete.

Bastedo, M., & Gumport, P. (2003). Access to what? Mission differentiation and academic stratification in U.S. public higher education. *Higher Education, 46,* 341–359. Retrieved October 9, 2007, from EBSCO Online Database Education Research Complete.

Choy, S. (2002). *Access & persistence: Findings from 10 years of longitudinal research on students.* Washington, DC: American Council on Education.

Dalton, R. (2000). Foundations for access. *Connection: New England's Journal of Higher Education & Economic Development, 15,* 15–16. Retrieved October 9, 2007, from EBSCO Online Database Education Research Complete.

Davis, D. J., Green-Derry, L. C., & Jones, B. (2013). The impact of federal financial aid policy upon higher education access. *Journal of Educational Administration & History, 45,* 49–57. Retrieved December 6, 2013, from EBSCO Online Database Education Research Complete.

Gándara, P., Horn, C., & Orfield, G. (2005). The access crisis in higher education. *Educational Policy, 19,* 255–261. Retrieved October 9, 2007, from EBSCO Online Database Education Research Complete.

Gardner, S. (2004). Stemming at-riskers' college crises in a recession. *Education Digest, 70,* 56–60. Retrieved October 9, 2007, from EBSCO Online Database Education Research Complete.

Gilbert, C. K., & Heller, D. E. (2013). Access, equity, and community colleges: The Truman Commission and federal higher education policy from 1947 to 2011. *Journal of Higher Education, 84*, 417–443. Retrieved December 6, 2013, from EBSCO Online Database Education Research Complete.

Gray, M., & Vernez, G. (1996). Student access and the 'new' immigrants. *Change, 28*, 40–47. Retrieved October 9, 2007, from EBSCO Online Database Education Research Complete.

Haycock, K., & Gerald, D. (2007). Trend: Shrinking opportunity. *Connection: The Journal of the New England Board of Higher Education, 21*, 15–16. Retrieved October 9, 2007, from EBSCO Online Database Education Research Complete.

Hoffman, N. (2003). College credit in high school. *Change, 35*, 42. Retrieved October 9, 2007, from EBSCO Online Database Education Research Complete.

Irvine, V., Code, J., & Richards, L. (2013). Realigning higher education for the 21st-century learner through multi-access learning. *Journal of Online Learning & Teaching, 9*, 172–186. Retrieved November 5, 2014, from EBSCO Online Database Education Research Complete.

Kerr, C. (2001). *The uses of the university.* Cambridge, MA: Harvard University Press.

National Center for Public Policy and Higher Education. (2004). *Responding to the crisis in college opportunity.* San Jose, CA: Author.

Lipka, S. (2014). More voices call for equity, not just access. *Chronicle of Higher Education, 60*, 39. Retrieved November 5, 2014, from EBSCO Online Database Education Research Complete.

Pluviose, D. (2006). Commission's final draft report recommends revamping higher ed curricula. *Diverse: Issues in Higher Education, 23*, 10. Retrieved October 9, 2007, from EBSCO Online Database Education Research Complete.

Starobin, S. S. (2006). International students in transition: Changes in access to U.S. higher education. *New Directions for Student Services, 114*, 63–71. Retrieved October 9, 2007, from EBSCO Online Database Education Research Complete.

Toutkoushian, R. K., & Hillman, N. W. (2012). The impact of state appropriations and grants on access to higher education and outmigration. *Review of Higher Education, 36*, 51–90. Retrieved December 6, 2013, from EBSCO Online Database Education Research Complete.

Valentine, D. (2004). Access to higher education: A challenge to social work educators. *Journal of Social Work Education, 40*, 179–184. Retrieved October 9, 2007, from EBSCO Online Database Education Research Complete.

Ward, N. (2006). Improving equity and access for low-income and minority youth into institutions of higher education. *Urban Education, 41*, 50–70. Retrieved October 9, 2007, from EBSCO Online Database Education Research Complete.

SUGGESTED READING

Ashburn, E. (2007, October 17). High-school students are helped by taking college courses, study finds. *Chronicle of Higher Education.* Retrieved October 17, 2007, from http://chronicle.com.

Casazza, M., & Bauer, L. (2004). Oral history of postsecondary access: Martha Maxwell, a pioneer. *Journal of Developmental Education, 28*, 20–26. Retrieved October 9, 2007, from EBSCO Online Database Education Research Complete.

Forster, G. (2006). The embarrassing good news on college access. *Chronicle of Higher Education, 52*, B50–B51. Retrieved October 22, 2007, from EBSCO Online Database Education Research Complete.

Gerald, D., & Haycock, K. (2006). *Engines of inequality: Diminishing equity in the nation's premier public universities.* Washington, DC: Education Trust.

Hebel, S. (2004). No room in the class. *Chronicle of Higher Education, 50*, A19–A22. Retrieved October 9, 2007, from EBSCO Online Database Education Research Complete.

Hillman, N., Tandberg, D., & Gross, J. (2014). Market-based higher education: Does Colorado's voucher model improve higher education access and efficiency? *Research in Higher Education, 55*, 601–625. Retrieved November 5, 2014, from EBSCO Online Database Education Research Complete.

Kim, E., & Díaz., J. (2013). Access to higher education for immigrant students. *ASHE Higher Education Report, 38*, 47–60. Retrieved December 6, 2013, from EBSCO Online Database Education Research Complete.

Jackson, N. (2012). Minority access to higher education. *Journal of College Admission, 214*, 56–62. Retrieved December 6, 2013, from EBSCO Online Database Education Research Complete.

Pedersen, R. (2003). High-priced lessons. *Community College Week, 15*, 4–6. Retrieved October 9, 2007, from EBSCO Online Database Education Research Complete.

Tracy, E. M., Freimark, S., Boss, M., & Lonergan, P. (2005). Knowledge for practice: A training program for college access advisors. *Journal of College Admission, 186*, 6–13. Retrieved October 9, 2007, from EBSCO Online Database Education Research Complete.

GRANTS AND PRIVATE FUNDING

This article discusses how grants and private funding serve to sustain Higher Education in the United States. While traditional revenue sources still play a large role in Higher Education financing, institutions are beginning to more aggressively pursue non-traditional funding sources due to increased market competition and costs. Historically, these non-traditional funding sources have included private donations from alumni and other individual benefactors as well as from corporations, foundations, and similar entities. Continued federal grant support given directly to Higher Education institutions has also played a large role and has served to shape modern Higher Education.

KEYWORDS: Alumni; Benefactors; Corporations; Federal research grants; Foundations; Private giving; Voluntary support

OVERVIEW

While tuition revenues and, for public institutions, state and local appropriations play a large role in the financial support of Higher Education institutions, these traditional revenue sources are generally supplemented with other resources. Over the course of time, a number of different groups have become actively involved in the private financing of Higher Education. Additionally, the federal government has come to play a role in providing direct support to Higher Education institutions via grants for various purposes.

INDIVIDUAL PRIVATE BENEFACTORS, FOUNDATIONS, ALUMNI, & CORPORATIONS

While not the founders of the institutions that took their names, John Harvard and Elihu Yale were the first considerable private benefactors in New England. However, it was not until the latter part of the nineteenth century that large gifts from single donors became more common (Rudolph, 1990). Private giving to Higher Education institutions accelerated after the Civil War when large personal fortunes were made during the period of rapid industrialization (Brubacher & Rudy, 1997). According to Rudolph:

> Endowments of sizable proportions were a contribution to the American college of the Industrial Revolution, of the remarkable rewards which it brought on the

eminently exploitable American continent, and of the sense of stewardship which invigorated the possession of private wealth with a sense of public responsibility.

For example, Cornell originated with a $500,000 gift from Ezra Cornell, whose single gift matched the total accumulated endowment of all Higher Education institutions at the turn of the twentieth century (Brubacher & Rudy). As the twentieth century progressed, individual benefactors like Carnegie, Rockefeller, and Ford began to pour hundreds of millions of dollars into Higher Education. Their main aim was "not to found new institutions, but to strengthen older ones and sometimes modify their direction" (Brubacher & Rudy). Brubacher and Rudy noted that endowments, which are supported by donations, have been especially crucial to private institutions as their financial "mainstay" (Brubacher & Rudy). While not initially well-received, declines in state and federal public support have often led to a more acceptable view of private giving to public higher institutions as well (Liu, 2006).

In the early twentieth century, large philanthropic organizations that focused on supporting Higher Education in various ways were also created by millionaires and began to take shape. These included Rockefeller's General Education Board (1903) and Foundation (1913) as well as the Carnegie Foundation (1906) and Corporation (Rudolph). The foundations established matching-gifts principles under which colleges had to match (or sometimes even double) gifts they received (Rudolph). These principles not only led to extensive endowment drives to secure matches, but also to the preoccupation of college presidents' time with fundraising for matches (Rudolph).

As large gifts had to also be supplemented with smaller gifts, institutions began to put on general endowment drives. Yale was the first institution to initiate an annual alumni giving drive in the 1890s (Brubacher & Rudy). Yet, the time of regular, exceptionally large gifts to Higher Education seemed to draw to a close by the mid twentieth century as steep increases in inheritance and income taxes, which were used to cover war costs as well as new social services, took their toll (Brubacher & Rudy). Around this time, corporations began to be asked to play a larger role in the financing of Higher Education (Pollard, 1952).

FEDERAL GOVERNMENT'S ROLE

It was not until the middle of the twentieth century that the federal government began to deal directly with colleges and universities in providing them with assistance (Brubacher & Rudy). Specifically, World War II marked the onset of continuing federal involvement in Higher Education (Kerr, 2001). Kerr described the initiation of federal support for scientific research that was ushered in after World War II as one of two great impacts that have "molded the modern American university system and made it distinctive."

The move toward continuing federal grant support was sparked by "vast programs of contract research" (Brubacher & Rudy). By 1950, about a dozen federal agencies were expending $150 million annually in such endeavors at various Higher Education institutions. However, federal resources tended to flow to a group of institutions that already had well-established scholarly reputations, and this led some to view the institutions as essentially representing a monopoly over federal research grants (Brubacher & Rudy). Yet, over time research funds were dispersed across slightly more institutions. By 1990 about half of all federal support for research was concentrated at thirty-two institutions, as compared to twenty in 1963 (Kerr).

Federal support for research historically advanced three great national concerns: defense, scientific and technological progress, and health (Kerr). As such, the humanities and social sciences have traditionally received very little federal support (Kerr). Some of the federal agencies that have been major sources of research funds include the Department of Defense, the National Science Foundation, and the National Institutes of Health (Kerr). With the terrorist attacks of September 11, 2001, and the anthrax mailings that occurred that same year, Congress was compelled to direct more federal research funding toward homeland security projects (Borrego & Brainard, 2003). For instance, funding for homeland security projects, which included training programs as well as research, increased by 68 percent from fiscal year 2002 to 2003 (Borrego & Brainard).

By 1960 federal support for research at Higher Education institutions had reached $1 billion (Kerr). Federal research funds then increased about four times over between 1960 and the mid-1990s (Kerr).

A period of particularly rapid growth in federal research funding occurred between 1980 and 1995 when funding increased by 50 percent (Gladieux & King, 1999). Yet, overall between 1960 and the mid 1990s the rate of increase in federal research funds slowed as compared to previous periods (Kerr). Still, by 1995 federal research support had reached $13 billion (Gladieux & King).

APPLICATIONS

Walton & Bell (2003) indicate that the many types and sources of college and university revenues include the following:

- Tuition from students and families;
- Appropriations, grants, and student financial aid from state and local governments;
- Research and other grants from the federal government;
- Donations and gifts from private benefactors.

Concerning grant aid, research and other grants from the federal government are the particular focus in light of the impact such aid has had on molding modern Higher Education (Kerr).

PRIVATE GIVING

According to Liu, revenues from private giving help institutions not only with their day-to-day operations but also may help fund various projects and undertakings initiated in the name of excellence. At the same time, only about 10 percent of expenditures at Higher Education institutions are covered by private funds (Strout, 2006a). In general, trends in private giving tend to align with the state of the stock market and the economy (Strout, 2006a). The number of campaigns and solicitations for private donations on behalf of Higher Education institutions also impacts growth (Strout, 2007).

Private funding can come from a number of different sources including individuals, business and industry, philanthropic foundations, civic groups, and religious groups (Pollard). Contributions to US colleges and universities increased 2.3 percent from 2011 to 2012. At $31 billion overall, the total is still below the 2008 high of $31.6 billion (Council for Aid to Education, 2013). During the same year, alumni giving declined 1.3 percent, and although the average alumni gift declined just of 1 percent, the average gift per alumnus increased over 10.5 percent. The main sources of private giving to Higher Education institutions in 2012 were foundations (29.5 percent), alumni (24.8 percent), other non-alumni individuals (18.8 percent), corporations (16.9 percent), other non-corporate and nonreligious organizations (9 percent), and religious organizations (.9 percent) (Council for Aid to Education). Overall, the primary sources of voluntary support to Higher Education institutions are foundations, alumni, and non-alumni individuals.

Liu explored what motivates donors of private support. For instance, alumni may be motivated by college pride and loyalty or may wish to guarantee the marketability of their degree. On the other hand, non-alumni individuals as well as foundations may be motivated by the desire to make a social contribution (e.g., improve Higher Education for all). Finally, corporations generally give to Higher Education institutions in exchange for certain benefits.

ALUMNI DONATIONS

Alumni may make donations to their alma maters for specific purposes (e.g., to establish a scholarship or help fund a new building) but may also make unrestricted donations as part of annual fund drives or endowment campaigns. Recently, alumni participation in private donations to Higher Education institutions has been declining (Strout, 2007). However, it has been proposed that this is mainly due to colleges' and universities' efforts to capture information on all their alumni. Specifically, the number of alumni on record is increasing faster than the number who actually donate and this has made participation rates drop (Strout, 2007). Alumni contributions still represent one of the largest shares of voluntary donations with about 25 percent of all such donations being made by alumni in fiscal year 2012 (Strout, 2007).

CORPORATE FUNDING

Writing after the Second World War, Pollard noted that corporations were being asked more and more to provide funds to Higher Education. He also noted that setting up tax-free foundations as the mechanism by which to make contributions was becoming more common with corporations as well. In general, corporate funding of Higher Education takes many forms. Corporations provide funds for scholarships and fellowships for students but also provide institutional aid (e.g., operating or capital grants) as well as research funds (Pollard). However, in giving to

Higher Education institutions corporations need to be attuned to state laws that may be set up to protect stockholders, as well as federal limits or restrictions (Pollard).

In discussing the benefits that corporations receive from donating to Higher Education institutions, Pollard remarked, "leading corporations are strongly in the market for the kind of intellectually disciplined and trained personnel that can be found only in our universities and colleges." Also, in addition to specialized research services, the basic research that colleges and universities conduct has provided numerous benefits to industry as well (Pollard).

FOUNDATION FUNDING

According to Harcleroad (1999), national independent foundations, like the Carnegie and Ford Foundations, are the source for over 90 percent of private foundation giving to Higher Education institutions. Overall, there are five types of private foundations (Harcleroad):

- Community foundations: typically are citywide or regional and provide funds to Higher Education institutions for locally related projects;
- Family or personal foundations: have limited purposes;
- Special purpose foundations: have very narrow purposes (e.g., funding a glee club on campus);
- Company foundations: provide one source by which to channel corporate giving;
- National independent foundations: typically provide funding to Higher Education institutions for targeted research in areas of national or international interest.

Private foundation grants to Higher Education institutions not only support research but also such undertakings as community improvement efforts and staffing support (Harcleroad). At the same time, private foundation grants represent a relatively small proportion of Higher Education financing (Harcleroad). Yet, "by their choice of areas to finance [foundations] entice supposedly autonomous colleges to do things they might not do otherwise .... [and] they have had significant effects on program development and even operations" (Harcleroad). For instance, foundation grants have been instrumental in establishing new academic fields as well as changing the course of existing fields (Harcleroad).

RESEARCH & OTHER GRANTS FROM THE FEDERAL GOVERNMENT

Federal research funding has generally been concentrated on relatively few institutions (Gladieux & King; Kerr). Writing in the early 1960s, Kerr described some twenty Higher Education institutions, which represented only about a tenth of all American universities at the time, as the "primary federal grant universities." Some of this concentration of federal resources was due in part to the fact that the scientists most able to efficiently and quickly carry out desired research worked at a limited number of institutions (Kerr).

Federal research funds can cover either indirect costs or direct costs. Scandals over institutional billing for indirect costs erupted during the late 1980s and early 1990s (Gladieux & King). The case of Stanford charging questionable items to the federal government as part of its indirect costs has often been cited (Gladieux & King). For instance, among other inappropriate charges, it was discovered that Stanford had charged depreciation on a yacht to administrative overhead (Brainard, 2005). In the end, several institutions were required to return millions of dollars to the federal government due to such questionable billing (Gladieux & King). In 1991 Congress enacted a cap on the overhead that colleges and universities can charge on federal research grants in response to the overhead scandals that made headlines (Brainard, 2005). Many colleges and universities have argued that overhead restrictions are too burdensome (Brainard, 2005), and some institutions have had to cover incremental overhead costs from increased federal regulations on their own (Brainard, 2005).

Aside from grants for research, an example of another type of grant that the federal government makes directly to Higher Education institutions is those grants awarded through the Fund for the Improvement of Postsecondary Education (FIPSE), which supports innovations in Higher Education (Brainard, 1999). Overall, more than half of all colleges in the United States have applied for FIPSE grants (Brainard, 1999). Revised rules call for various types of projects that can receive FIPSE grants, such as those that would "support innovative approaches to connecting community colleges to four-year institutions" or "establish off-campus and community-based delivery of educational programs and services to rural students" (Brainard, 1999).

VIEWPOINTS

According to Liu, "increasing market competitiveness and rising educational costs have underscored the importance of external revenues in Higher Education finance." These trends are compounded by declines in both federal and state public support (Liu). As such, colleges and universities are more aggressively pursuing non-traditional funding sources (Liu). This section explores in more detail some of the issues that have arisen as institutions heighten their pursuit of non-traditional revenue sources.

SOCIALLY RESPONSIBLE INVESTING

In the 1970s the argument was made for Higher Education institutions to invest more of their endowment resources into stocks in order to bolster their financial resources (Brubacher & Rudy). At the same time, it was argued that institutions should follow 'ethical investor' guidelines and take responsibility for the social policies of the corporations they held stock in (Brubacher & Rudy). For instance, if corporations polluted the environment or produced harmful products it was expected that institutions divest of their holdings in such corporations or at least vote their proxies against the corporation's management (Brubacher & Rudy).

Student activism has led to a number of colleges and universities, including Harvard, Yale, and Stanford, to opt to not invest in companies that do business in Sudan, whose government has been accused of committing various acts of brutality in the country's Darfur region (Strout, 2006c). Similar actions were taken about thirty years ago to protest the enforcement of apartheid in South Africa (Strout, 2006c). Yet, the Investor Responsibility Research Center Institute and the Tellus Institute report that socially responsible investments by college and universities declined from 21 percent in 2009 to 18 percent in 2011 (IRRC Institute, & Tellus Institute, 2012).

EDUCATIONAL CONFLICTS OF INTEREST

Kerr argued that federal investment in research at universities shifted faculty priorities away from teaching and toward research. Faculty members also responded to a related shift within universities in which compensation and rewards came to be based more on the receipt of federal research funds and less on teaching activities and undergraduate education (Kerr). Specifically, promotion and tenure decisions for faculty came to rest more heavily on research and publications than teaching (Zusman, 1999). According to Altbach (2001), "the prestige hierarchy of American academe favors research and publication even though the large majority of the professoriate are not heavily engaged in these activities."

Zusman also noted that the involvement of full-time faculty in undergraduate education waned during the last quarter of the twentieth century. Studies showed how compared to the past faculty were teaching fewer undergraduate courses, the responsibility for which was shifted to part-time faculty and/or graduate teaching assistants (Zusman). However, Altbach also noted that while research has retained its foothold, teaching is also beginning to gain greater respect.

Some other educational concerns with accepting funding from non-traditional sources have also been voiced. For instance, Mangan (1999) reported that medical schools are relying on corporate grants more as government support dwindles. However, professors have indicated that corporate sponsors pose threats to academic freedom as they too often "decide what will be studied, how the research will be conducted, and how and whether the findings will be published."

CONCENTRATION OF RESOURCES

As noted, federal research grant resources have tended to be concentrated with a relatively small segment of the total Higher Education community of the United States (Brubacher & Rudy; Gladieux & King; Kerr). A study by Liu also showed that, in line with previous research, "institutions at the top of the institutional hierarchy enjoy accumulative advantage" in securing private giving. For example, a total of $25.6 billion in private donations was raised during fiscal year 2005, which was also the second year of a period of growth in private giving (Strout, 2006a). However, such growth was not evenly distributed. Half of the growth was concentrated in the top ten fundraising institutions for private donations (Strout, 2006a). The period of growth in private donations continued in fiscal year 2006 with about $28 billion being raised by Higher Education institutions (Strout, 2007). Yet, half of the growth for fiscal year 2006 was again concentrated in the top ten fundraising institutions for private donations (Strout, 2007).

Different types of Higher Education institutions also seem to accumulate more funds from private giving. Strout (2006b) noted that unlike state public flagship universities, regional public colleges do not tend to have strong relationships with corporations and foundations. Flagship universities, among other factors, have tended to be more proactive about seeking corporate and foundation funding and they also have a "'broader array of programs' for which to solicit financial support" (Strout, 2006b). However, some regional institutions are beginning to increase efforts to pursue corporate and foundation funding. At Eastern Michigan University, for instance, a new position to focus on corporate and foundation relations was recently created (Strout, 2006b).

TERMS & CONCEPTS

Alumni: (Alumnae) Graduates of a college or university, who may have attended the institution as either an undergraduate or graduate student; some Higher Education institutions also include students who attended their institutions but did not graduate in their alumni ranks

Benefactor: An individual or group that makes a monetary contribution or other type of gift aid to another entity, who benefits from their assistance

Corporation: "An association of individuals, created by law or under authority of law, having a continuous existence irrespective of that of its members, and powers and liabilities distinct from those of its members".

Direct Costs: The costs associated with a research project that can be easily discerned to be related to that specific project (e.g., salaries, travel, equipment, supplies)

Divestment: The change or pulling of investments due to social or political policy

Endowment: A revenue fund supported by donations; generally, only a portion of the interest on donations is spent while the principle remains intact

Foundation: An institution that engages in endowment donations generally to further some social cause

Overhead: (Also referred to as "facilities and administrative costs" or "indirect costs") the amount of funds that universities and colleges receive for overhead costs (in addition to the direct costs) associated with research projects. Overhead consists of reimbursement for both administrative costs and facilities costs (e.g., laboratories, utilities); there is a cap on administrative costs but not on facilities costs.

Tax-Free Foundations: Receive, manage, and invest a share of company profits in order to make contributions on the company's behalf.

Marlene Clapp

BIBLIOGRAPHY

Altbach, P. G. (2001). The American academic model in comparative perspective. In P. G. Altbach, P. J. Gumport, & D. B. Johnstone (Eds.), *In defense of American Higher Education* (pp. 11-37). Baltimore, MD: The Johns Hopkins University Press.

Barnhart, C. L., & Stein, J. (Eds.). (1962). *The American college dictionary.* New York: Random House, Inc.

Borrego, A., & Brainard, J. (2003, September 26). In directing dollars, Congress favors Homeland-Security projects. *Chronicle of Higher Education, 50,* A20. Retrieved June 4, 2007, from EBSCO online database Education Research Complete.

Brainard, J. (1999, March 26). Popular grants program for colleges regroups as Congress sets its priorities. *Chronicle of Higher Education, 45,* A39. Retrieved June 6, 2007, from EBSCO online database Education Research Complete.

Brainard, J. (2005, August 5). The ghosts of Stanford. *Chronicle of Higher Education, 51,* A16-A18. Retrieved June 4, 2007, from EBSCO online database Education Research Complete.

Brubacher, J. S., & Rudy, W. (1997). *Higher Education in transition* (4th ed.). New Brunswick, NJ: Transaction Publishers.

Council for Aid to Education. (2013, February 20). Colleges and universities raise $31 billion in 2012. Retrieved December 21, 2013, from http://cae.org.

Fischer, K. (2011). Crisis of confidence threatens colleges. (cover story). *Chronicle of Higher Education, 57,* A1–A4. Retrieved December 20, 2013, from EBSCO Online Database Education Research Complete.

Gladieux, L. E., & King, J. E. (1999). The federal government and Higher Education. In P. G. Altbach, R. O. Berdahl, & P. J. Gumport (Eds.), *American Higher Education in the twenty-first century* (pp. 151-182). Baltimore, MD: The Johns Hopkins University Press.

Harcleroad, F. F. (1999). The hidden hand. In P. G. Altbach, R. O. Berdahl, & P. J. Gumport (Eds.), *American Higher Education in the twenty-first century* (pp. 241-268). Baltimore, MD: The Johns Hopkins University Press.

IRRC Institute, & Tellus Institute. (2012, July). *Environmental, Social and Governance Investing by College and University Endowments in the United States: Social Responsibility, Sustainability, and Stakeholder Relations.* Retrieved December 21, 2013, from http://irrcinstitute.org.

Kerr, C. (2001). *The uses of the university.* Cambridge, MA: Harvard University Press.

Liu, Y. (2006, February). Determinants of private giving to public colleges and universities. *International Journal of Educational Advancement, 6,* 119-140. Retrieved June 4, 2007, from EBSCO online database Education Research Complete.

Mangan, K. (1999, June 4). Medical professors see threat in corporate influence on research. *Chronicle of Higher Education, 45,* A14. Retrieved June 6, 2007, from EBSCO online database Education Research Complete.

Pollard, J. A. (1952). Corporation support of Higher Education. *Harvard Business Review, 30,* 111-126. Retrieved June 4, 2007, from EBSCO online database Education Research Complete.

Rudolph, F. (1990). *The American college & university.* Athens, GA: The University of Georgia Press.

Strout, E. (2006a). Private giving to colleges is up, but fewer alumni make donations. Chronicle of Higher Education, 52, A27-A29. Retrieved June 4, 2007, from EBSCO online database Education Research Complete.

Strout, E. (2006b). Regional public colleges struggle to tap corporations and foundations. *Chronicle of Higher Education, 53,* 34. Retrieved June 5, 2007, from EBSCO online database Education Research Complete.

Strout, E. (2006c). Sudan divestment movement gains on campuses. *Chronicle of Higher Education, 52,* A17-A17. Retrieved June 4, 2007, from EBSCO online database Education Research Complete.

Strout, E. (2007, March 2). Donations increase for 3rd year in a row. *Chronicle of Higher Education, 53,* A1-A28. Retrieved June 6, 2007, from EBSCO online database Education Research Complete.

Sua, J. (2013). Does corporate giving pay off? Three different types of corporate giving and brand preference. *AMA Winter Educators' Conference Proceedings,* 24375–376. Retrieved December 20, 2013, from EBSCO Online Database Education Research Complete.

Walton, C., & Bell, J. (2003). New ways to fund higher ed. *State Legislatures, 29,* 28-31. Retrieved May 02, 2007, from EBSCO online database Education Research Complete.

Zagier, A. (2012). Colleges turn to private sector as state support lags. *Community College Week, 24,* 12. Retrieved December 20, 2013, from EBSCO Online Database Education Research Complete.

Zusman, A. (1999). Issues facing Higher Education in the twenty-first century. In P. G. Altbach, R. O. Berdahl, & P.

J. Gumport (Eds.), *American Higher Education in the twenty-first century* (pp. 109-148). Baltimore, MD: The Johns Hopkins University Press.

SUGGESTED READING

Asquith, C. (2006, June 29). Demanding divestment from Sudan. *Diverse: Issues in Higher Education, 23,* 14-17. Retrieved June 6, 2007, from EBSCO online database, Education Research Complete.

Baade, R., & Sundberg, J. (1996, December). Fourth down and gold to go? Assessing the link between athletics and alumni giving. *Social Science Quarterly, 77,* 789-803. Retrieved June 6, 2007, from EBSCO online database Education Research Complete.

Bacchetti, R., & Ehrlich, T. (2006, November 17). Reconnecting colleges and foundations. *Chronicle of Higher Education, 53,* B20-B20. Retrieved June 6, 2007, from EBSCO online database Education Research Complete.

Butcher, K., Kearns, C., & McEwan, P. (2013). Giving till it helps? Alumnae giving and children's college options. *Research in Higher Education, 54,* 499-513. Retrieved December 20, 2013, from EBSCO Online Database Education Research Complete.

Cash, S. (2005, August). Private voluntary support to public universities in the United States: Late nineteenth-century developments. International Journal of Educational Advancement, 5, 343-356. Retrieved June 6, 2007, from EBSCO online database Education Research Complete.

Gitlin, T. (1985, May 18). Divestment stirs a new generation. *Nation, 240,* 585-587. Retrieved June 6, 2007, from EBSCO online database Education Research Complete.

Gottfried, M., & Johnson, E. (2006, August). Solicitation and donation: An econometric evaluation of alumni generosity in Higher Education. *International Journal of Educational Advancement, 6,* 268-281. Retrieved June 6, 2007, from EBSCO online database Education Research Complete.

Hankin, K. (2011). Corporate philanthropy, college students, and the Lunafest® Film Festival. *Feminist Teacher, 21,* 229-247. Retrieved December 20, 2013, from EBSCO Online Database Education Research Complete.

Schneider, J. (2007, Spring). Foundations and Higher Education: Whose agenda? Connection: The Journal of the New England Board of Higher Education, 21, 28-31. Retrieved June 4, 2007, from EBSCO online database Education Research Complete.

AFFIRMATIVE ACTION IN HIGHER EDUCATION

Affirmative action in higher education admissions was established to help achieve diversity in the student body and provide greater access to higher education for members of historically underrepresented minority groups. Landmark court cases debating affirmative action in higher education admissions have included the *Regents of the University of California v. Bakke* (1978), *Hopwood v. Texas* (1996), and the 2003 University of Michigan cases. However, the future of affirmative action in college and university admissions continues to be debated. Some race-neutral alternatives to affirmative action based on racial preferences that have been considered include class rank percentage plans and admissions plans based on economic preferences.

KEYWORDS: Affirmative Action; Class Rank; College Admissions; Desegregated; Diversity; Economic Preferences; Ethnicity; First-Generation Status; Higher Education; Minority; Percentage Plans; Race; Race-Exclusive Programs; Race-Neutral Alternatives; Racial Preferences; Segregated

OVERVIEW
BACKGROUND/HISTORY
Patitu and Terrell (1998) explained that the goal of affirmative action in higher education has been to "increase the number of people from underrepresented groups in higher education and to diversify colleges and universities." As a concept, affirmative action first emerged in 1961 in President John F. Kennedy's Executive Order 10925 as a means to end discrimination in government employment and contracting (Shuford, 1998). Executive Order 10925 called for government contractors to voluntarily enact affirmative action in the recruitment, hiring, and promotion of minorities (Kolling, 1998). The voluntary nature of the proposal proved ineffective and it was later enforced under the Civil Rights Act of 1964 (Kolling).

In implementing the Civil Rights Act of 1964, which prohibited discrimination on the basis of race, color, sex, or national origin, the federal government fought to have higher education institutions put affirmative action plans into place (Brubacher & Rudy,

1997). These plans were to apply to all aspects of public and private higher education operations, including student admissions, staff hiring, financial aid, and dormitory assignments (Brubacher & Rudy). Institutions who did not abide by the law faced withdrawal of federal funds granted to them (Brubacher & Rudy). Especially in recent years, affirmative action policies in college admissions have tended to be at the forefront of debate. Affirmative action policies in admissions sought "to bring to campuses people from various groups previously overlooked as sources for the student population" (Brubacher & Rudy). More often than not these people included members of minority groups (Brubacher & Rudy).

The question of how to appropriately and legally institute affirmative action programs in college and university admissions became particularly pointed in 1978. In that year, the U.S. Supreme Court handed down its decision in the case of the *Regents of the University of California v. Bakke*. In the case, the special admissions program that reserved sixteen out of one hundred slots for members of historically underserved minority groups at the University of California at Davis's Medical School was called into question (Kolling). The Supreme Court ruled that the program equated to a quota system, was unlawful, and should be struck down (Kolling). At the same time, the Court also ruled that some race-conscious admissions programs could be permissible "if the procedure entailed the same process of individualized comparison for all applicants without systematically excluding any group from consideration" (Kolling). Overall, while higher education institutions could consider race or ethnicity in admissions, colleges and universities could not implement what were in effect quota systems (Brubacher & Rudy). Essentially, higher education institutions were not to discriminate against minorities but they also could not have policies that were akin to "reverse discrimination" (Brubacher & Rudy).

Two cases involving the University of Michigan in 2003 have also received a great deal of attention for the implications they have on the consideration of race in admissions. In the Supreme Court's decisions, the admissions policy of the University of Michigan Law School (*Grutter v. Bollinger*) was deemed acceptable while the undergraduate admission policy of the University of Michigan (*Gratz v. Bollinger*) was not. The Law School's policy was essentially deemed

acceptable because it encapsulated a "holistic approach to admissions" (Eckes, 2004) in which race was just *one of many* different characteristics considered to achieve a diverse student body.

In *Fisher v. University of Texas* (2013), the high court remanded a challenge to affirmative action back to a lower court for further consideration. The U.S. District Court upheld the university's race-conscious admissions policy, but the Supreme Court ruled that the lower court had not applied the standard of "strict scrutiny" of such policies established in the *Grutter* and *Bakke* cases.

ROLE OF AFFIRMATIVE ACTION IN ADMISSIONS

For all applicants, it is important for America's higher education institutions to be accessible and not be bastions of privilege. In discussing admission preferences for underrepresented minorities, Bowen, Kurzweil, Tobin, and Pichler (2005) also stressed that "a diverse student body provides educational benefits to all students." Students benefit from a diverse campus because they are "being prepared to be members of a global community, having their intercultural communication skills enhanced, becoming aware of and more sensitive to cultural differences, being exposed to views unlike their own, and being allowed to confront and discuss multicultural issues" (Patitu & Terrell).

Additionally, Shuford noted that research findings support the contention that students benefit in many ways when there is institutional commitment to diversity. For instance, students' cognitive development and satisfaction with their college experience have found to be enhanced when diversity is a priority (Astin, 1993, as cited in Shuford).

The recent Supreme Court cases have found diversity to be "a compelling state interest in education" (Eckes). Likewise, Massey (2004) outlined three compelling reasons to support affirmative action. First, Massey noted that community choice arguments would indicate that the lessening of discrimination can only occur when "'fairness' is guaranteed by building it into laws, procedures, guidelines, and organizational practices." Additionally, basic principles of what is fair and reasonable in a just society as well as the "price" most people are willing to pay for future benefits indicate strong support for affirmative action policies (Massey).

While many support the concept of affirmative action in higher education admissions, there are others who do not, and there have been varied arguments against it. For instance, some argue that affirmative action serves to discriminate against members of ethnic and racial groups it does not protect (Shuford). Others say it causes the lowering of standards and the admission of individuals who are less qualified than others (Shuford). There have also been arguments made that it victimizes the groups it intends to serve (Shuford).

PHASES OF AFFIRMATIVE ACTION IN ADMISSIONS

Nichols, Ferguson, and Fisher (2005) discussed Dickason's phases of affirmative action in college admission. The three phases include:

- Obligatory affirmative action;
- Voluntary affirmative action;
- Tempered affirmative action (Dickason, 2001, as cited in Nichols et al.).

Obligatory affirmative action describes the period (1960s to late 1970s) during which affirmative action was mandated by the federal government for any higher education institutions receiving federal funds (Dickason, as cited in Nichols et al.). Voluntary affirmative action (1980 to 1995) was ushered in after the *Bakke* decision when institutions' admissions plans based on racial preferences began to be challenged (Dickason, as cited in Nichols et al.). Finally, Nichols et al. explained tempered affirmative action (current phase) as the time in which "contradictions existing in legal rulings and precedents and agencies outside of the college and university may dictate what measures are mandated to select students."

IMPLICATIONS OF RECENT SUPREME COURT RULINGS

Regarding the current phase of tempered affirmative action, Gardner (2007) noted that "in the aftermath of U.S. Supreme Court decisions, lower court cases, and threatened lawsuits by anti-affirmative action groups, universities are opening minority programs to non-minorities." Much of the drive to open up minority programs came after the 2003 Michigan decisions in which the Court ruled that race could be considered in creating a diverse environment but must not be the only factor considered and could not be reviewed in a "rigid or mechanical" way (Gardner). According to the Supreme Court's ruling in *Grutter*, race-neutral alternatives must also be considered first

before deciding to use race or ethnicity as a factor in admissions decisions (Przypyszny & Tromble, 2007). However, while schools should consider race neutral options to meet their goals, they do not need to try every such plan (Eckes).

After the Michigan decisions, colleges and universities grew concerned that financial aid programs and other programs they had in place based on race would fall under attack as an extension of the Court's rulings (Gardner). Adding to the concern, organizations such as the Center for Equal Opportunity (CEO), the Center for Individual Rights (CIR), and the American Civil Rights Institute (ACRI) rose to challenge such programs (Gardner). The organizations were mainly targeting small, very focused race-exclusive programs that used race or ethnicity as the sole criterion for acceptance or rejection (Schmidt, 2003). The Massachusetts Institute of Technology (MIT) was among the first institutions to open up their race-exclusive programs, which for MIT included two summer programs (Schmidt). Carnegie Mellon, Cornell, Indiana, Iowa State, and Saint Louis Universities, and the University of Missouri at Columbia were among other higher education institutions to have their race-exclusive programs challenged.

BALLOT INITIATIVES

Following the Michigan decisions, there have also been increased efforts to establish ballot initiatives to ban the consideration of race and gender in college and university admissions in various states (Fliegler, 2007). Bans on the consideration of race or ethnicity in college and university admissions had already passed in California in 1996 (Proposition 209) and in Washington in 1998 (Initiative 200) (Gardner). The California statewide ban on affirmative action seemed to be fueled by a ban on the consideration of race, religion, gender, ethnicity, or national origin at University of California campuses the previous year (Moreno, 2003). In the fall of 2006 in Michigan, which ironically was the setting for the 2003 University of Michigan Supreme Court decisions that upheld the consideration of race in admissions, a ban on the consideration of race and gender in college and university admissions was also passed (Fliegler). Statewide bans on affirmative action were also passed in Nebraska (2008), Arizona (2010), New Hampshire (2012), and Oklahoma (2012).

Two recent Supreme Court cases dealing with the consideration of race or ethnicity in public elementary and secondary school admissions were also closely watched for any implications for higher education institutions. The decisions of the Court in the cases seemed to echo the legal sentiments of the 2003 Michigan cases that higher education institutions could consider race or ethnicity in admissions as long as their approaches were narrowly tailored (i.e., race or ethnicity could be considered as part of the individualized review of applicants but must not be a deciding factor in admissions) (Przypyszny & Tromble). Przypyszny and Tromble noted, "It appears that fostering a diverse student body remains a compelling interest for the careful use of racial classifications in higher education admissions." However, as the outcome of the Michigan cases highlighted, in addition to race or ethnicity, higher education institutions should consider other factors, such as socioeconomic status and family background, to ensure a diverse student body (Przypyszny & Tromble).

Viewpoints

ALTERNATIVES TO AFFIRMATIVE ACTION IN ADMISSIONS

Despite the recent rulings on affirmative action in higher education admissions, there continues to be debate about the best way to ensure diversity on college and university campuses (Sterrett, 2005). Specifically, the future of affirmative action policies and programs continues to be questioned in higher education and scholars and researchers have pondered the issue of how diversity on college and university campuses might be maintained in the absence of affirmative action. In considering alternatives, one way by which some have weighed the success of alternatives is whether they achieve the same levels of diversity as under affirmative action (Long, 2003). In cataloging current race-neutral alternatives employed by higher education institutions across the country, the U.S Department of Education (2003) asserted that the early results of such programs to achieve diversity in the student body are actually promising.

Kahlenberg (2003) offered that the debate over affirmative action is focused on three approaches:

- Racial preferences;
- Class rank/percentage plans;
- Economic preferences.

The latter two approaches fall under the realm of race-neutral alternatives. First, some contend that only race-conscious affirmative action or racial preferences can help achieve and maintain diversity. For instance, Moreno argued that "there is not an adequate substitute for race-based affirmative action at this time, neither class-based nor merit-based options will maintain the level of racial and ethnic diversity that has been achieved on today's college and university campuses." Long also seemed to support racial preferences in arguing that in order to maintain the same levels of diversity as under affirmative action class rank/percentage plans must draw from racially segregated high schools. The author explained that if high schools are desegregated or "mixed by race, the effect on college diversity is unclear" because, for instance, minority students may not perform as well in comparison to their White classmates and be poorly represented among top students or, even if they are well-represented in the top segment, may not apply to college in the same numbers (Long). In general, Long stressed that class rank/percentage plans have not been found to maintain the same levels of diversity as under affirmative action.

THE TEN PERCENT PLAN

One of the most talked about class rank/percentage plans in the nation is that in place in Texas. The "10 percent plan" in Texas grew out of the Fifth Circuit Court of Appeals ruling in *Hopwood v. Texas* where it was ruled that an admissions procedure by the University of Texas Law School to grant admission to Blacks and Hispanics until a desired number of such students was reached was unconstitutional (Sterrett). In the *Hopwood* case, Cheryl Hopwood and three other applicants to the University of Texas Law School filed suit against the University for reverse discrimination (Moreno). They had been denied admission to the law school and contended that they were more qualified than some minority applicants who had been admitted (Moreno). The 1996 decision in the case by the Fifth Circuit Court of Appeals found in favor of Hopwood and the other plaintiffs (Moreno). As a result, public higher education institutions in Texas as well as Louisiana and Mississippi were barred from considering race or ethnicity in admissions (Moreno). The Texas attorney general interpreted the ruling to apply to all public universities in the state and deemed any policies designed to increase minority representation unconstitutional (Sterrett). After the *Hopwood* ruling the numbers of Black and Hispanic freshmen at Texas public higher education institutions began to drop (Sterrett, 2005). In response, the Texas legislature enacted the "10 percent plan."

ECONOMIC PREFERENCES

Reference to class-based or economic preference admissions policies was made in the 1978 *Bakke* case (Shuford). Evaluating the three approaches of racial preferences, class rank/percentage plans, and economic preferences based on seven criteria (i.e., fairness, diversity results, effect on graduation rates, legality, political support, replicability, and cost and feasibility), Kahlenberg (2003) argued that only plans based on economic preferences are the best approach. Similarly, other scholars have argued that admissions plans utilizing economic preferences are able to avoid some of the shortfalls of class rank/percentage plans (Roach, 2003). At the same time, others stress that economic preference plans alone will not be able to produce the same levels of diversity as under race-conscious affirmative action because race and class are not one and the same (Roach). Additionally, Shuford pointed out that a class-based affirmative action policy could only be easily justified in admissions decisions and not hiring decisions.

OTHER ALTERNATIVES

Long noted that the reconstruction of admissions criteria has also been discussed in order to maintain or even increase diversity. Specifically, some institutions are changing the way admissions factors are viewed and are giving extra weight to various factors (e.g., membership in particular organizations) that seem to be related to membership in a minority group. Indeed, some have urged the broadening of the concept of diversity, for instance, "to include individuals who have experienced educational disadvantage as a result of poverty, geographic location, physical disability, [and] sexual orientation" (Kolling). Some institutions have also begun to abandon the SAT, which some researchers have contended has a racial bias, as an admissions requirement (Cross, 1994, as cited in Patitu & Terrell; Young, 2003). There is indication that Hispanics and African Americans have historically not performed as well on standardized tests as Asians and Caucasians (Moreno). Maruyama,

Burke, and Mariani (2005) also offered that another alternative to affirmative action for colleges and universities is pre-collegiate partnership programs. These programs target underrepresented minority students well before high school and strive to motivate them to graduate from high school and to make them competitive in the college admissions process (Maruyama et al.).

TERMS & CONCEPTS

Class Rank/Percentage Plans: Admission plans in which the top high school students in a state are automatically granted admission to the state's public university system; California (admission granted to the top 4 percent of high school students), Florida (admission granted to the top 20 percent of high school students), and Texas (admission granted to the top 10 percent of high school students) have such plans in place.

Desegregated: In the context of race/ethnicity, open to all races

Economic Preferences: (Also: "class-based" or "economic affirmative action") Admission plans in which a student's academic record is reviewed with consideration to his or her economic background; factors such as socioeconomic status, first-generation status, and the performance record of the student's high school are considered.

First-Generation Status: Indicates whether a student is the first in his or her family to attend college.

Race-Exclusive Programs: College programs that only serve students of certain racial or ethnic backgrounds.

Race-Neutral Alternatives: Admissions plans and related initiatives in which diversity in the student body is a goal but preference is not granted based on race or ethnicity in admissions; race-neutral alternatives may encompass, for example, class rank/percentage plans, admissions plans based on economic preferences, and initiatives to target underserved high schools in college recruitment efforts.

Racial Preferences: (Also: "race-conscious affirmative action") Admission plans in which advantage is given to members of racial or ethnic minorities

Segregated: In the context of race/ethnicity, separated or set apart by race

Marlene Clapp

BIBLIOGRAPHY

Bowen, W. G., Kurzweil, M. A., Tobin, E. M., & Pichler, S. C. (2005). Broadening the quest for equity at the institutional level: Socioeconomic status, admissions preferences, and financial aid. In *Equity and excellence in American higher education*. Charlottesville: University of Virginia Press. Retrieved May 14, 2007, from EBSCO Online Database Education Research Complete.

Brubacher, J. S., & Rudy, W. (1997). *Higher education in transition* (4th ed.). New Brunswick, NJ: Transaction Publishers.

Chrisman, R. (2013). Affirmative action: Extend it. *Black Scholar, 43*, 71-72. Retrieved December 4, 2013, from EBSCO online database, Education Research Complete.

Eckes, S. E. (2004). Race-conscious admissions programs: where do universities go from *Gratz* and *Grutter*? *Journal of Law and Education, 33*, 21-62.

Fliegler, C. (2007). Dim days for affirmative action. *University Business, 10*, 13. Retrieved May 14, 2007, from EBSCO Online Database Education Research Complete.

Gardner, S. (2007). Today's courts re-conceive race and ethnicity in college aid and admissions. *Education Digest, 72*, 58-64. Retrieved May 14, 2007, from EBSCO Online Database Education Research Complete.

Hill, C. (2012). Become need-blind? For colleges, that's the wrong question. *Chronicle of Higher Education, 59*, A72. Retrieved December 4, 2013, from EBSCO online database, Education Research Complete.

Hoover, E., Mangan, K., & Schmidt, P. (2013). After 'Fisher,' colleges face new burdens of proof. *Chronicle of Higher Education, 59*, A18–A20. Retrieved December 4, 2013, from EBSCO online database, Education Research Complete.

Kahlenberg, R. (2003). *Economic affirmative action in college admissions: A progressive alternative to racial preferences and class rank admissions plans.* New York: Century Foundation.

Kolling, A. (1998, Fall). Student affirmative action and the courts. *New Directions for Student Services, 83*, 15-31. Retrieved November 6, 2007, from EBSCO Online Database Education Research Complete.

Long, B. (2003). Diversity by any other name: Are there viable alternatives to affirmative action in higher education? *Western Journal of Black Studies, 27*, 30-34. Retrieved November 6, 2007, from EBSCO Online Database Education Research Complete.

Maruyama, G., Burke, M., & Mariani, C. (2005). The role of pre-collegiate partnership programs in environments ambivalent about affirmative action: Reflections and outcomes from an early implementation. *Journal of Social Issues, 61*, 427-448. Retrieved November 6, 2007, from EBSCO Online Database Education Research Complete.

Massey, G. (2004). Thinking about affirmative action: Arguments supporting preferential policies. *Review of Policy Research, 21*, 783-797. Retrieved November 6, 2007, from EBSCO online database, Education Research Complete.

Moreno, P. (2003, Spring). The history of affirmative action law and its relation to college admission. *Journal of College Admission, 179*, 14-21. Retrieved November 6, 2007, from EBSCO Online Database Education Research Complete.

Nichols, J., Ferguson, F., & Fisher, R. (2005, Fall). Educational pluralism: A compelling state interest. *Journal of College Admission, 189*, 21-28. Retrieved November 8, 2007, from EBSCO Online Database Education Research Complete.

Patitu, C., & Terrell, M. (1998, Fall). Benefits of affirmative action in student affairs. *New Directions for Student Services, 83*, 41-56. Retrieved November 6, 2007, from EBSCO Online Database Education Research Complete.

Przypyszny, J., & Tromble, K. (2007). *Impact of Parents Involved in Community Schools v. Seattle School District No. 1 and Meredith v. Jefferson County Board of Education on affirmative action in higher education.* Washington, DC: American Council on Education (ACE).

Roach, R. (2003). Class-based affirmative action. *Black Issues in Higher Education, 20*, 22. Retrieved November 6, 2007, from EBSCO Online Database Education Research Complete.

Schmidt, P. (2003, March 7). Excluding some races from programs? Expect a letter from a lawyer. *Chronicle of Higher Education, 49*, A22. Retrieved November 8, 2007, from EBSCO Online Database Education Research Complete.

Schmidt, P. (2007, October 19). 5 more states may curtail affirmative action. *Chronicle of Higher Education.* Retrieved November 8, 2007, from http://chronicle.com.

Shuford, B. (1998, Fall). Recommendations for the future. *New Directions for Student Services, 83*, 71-78. Retrieved November 6, 2007, from EBSCO Online Database Education Research Complete.

Sterrett, W. (2005, Spring). Current issues involving affirmative action and higher education. *Journal of College Admission, 187*, 22-28. Retrieved November 6, 2007, from EBSCO Online Database Education Research Complete.

U.S. Department of Education. (2003). *Race-neutral alternatives in postsecondary education: Innovative approaches to diversity.* Washington, DC: U.S. Department of Education, Office for Civil Rights.

Young, J. (2003, October 10). Researchers charge racial bias on the SAT. *Chronicle of Higher Education.* Retrieved November 12, 2007, from http://chronicle.com.

SUGGESTED READING

Brown, S., & Hirschman, C. (2006, April). The end of affirmative action in Washington state and its impact on the transition from high school to college. *Sociology of Education, 79,* 106-130. Retrieved November 6, 2007, from EBSCO Online Database Education Research Complete.

Corcoran, J. (2003). Affirmative action must survive. *University Business, 6,* 9. Retrieved November 6, 2007, from EBSCO Online Database Education Research Complete.

Deslippe, D. (2012). *Protesting Affirmative Action: The Struggle Over Equality After the Civil Rights Revolution.* Baltimore, MD.: Johns Hopkins University Press.

DeVille, K. (1999). Defending diversity: Affirmative action and medical education. *American Journal of Public Health, 89,* 1256-1261. Retrieved November 6, 2007, from EBSCO Online Database Education Research Complete.

Garrison-Wade, D., & Lewis, C. (2004, Summer). Affirmative action: History and analysis. *Journal of College Admission,* 184, 23-26. Retrieved November 6, 2007, from EBSCO Online Database Education Research Complete.

Goldstein Hode, M. & Meisenbach, R.J. (2017). Reproducing whiteness through diversity: A critical discourse analysis of the pro-affirmative action amicus briefs in the Fisher case. *Journal of Diversity in Higher Education.* 10(2), 162-180.

Guinier, L. (2003, Spring). Social change and democratic values: Reconceptualizing affirmative action policy. *Western Journal of Black Studies,* 27, 45-50. Retrieved November 6, 2007, from EBSCO Online Database Education Research Complete.

Hebel, S. (2003, March 21). 'Percent plans' don't add up. (Cover story). *Chronicle of Higher Education, 49,* A22.

Retrieved November 8, 2007, from EBSCO Online Database Education Research Complete.

Horn, C., & Flores, S. (2003). *Percent plans in college admissions: A comparative analysis of three states' experiences.* Cambridge, MA: Harvard Civil Rights Project.

Kaplin, W. A., & Lee, B. A. (1995). *The law of higher education.* San Francisco, CA: Jossey-Bass.

Pavela, G. (1998, Fall). What's wrong with race-based affirmative action? *New Directions for Student Services,* 83, 33-40. Retrieved November 6, 2007, from http://search.ebscohost.com.

Reed, K. (2013). Two arguments for race-conscious admissions policies. *American Journal of Education,* 119, 341–345. Retrieved December 4, 2013, from EBSCO online database, Education Research Complete.

Schmidt, P. (2003, July 18). Affirmative-action fight is renewed in the states. *Chronicle of Higher Education, 49,* A19. Retrieved November 6, 2007, from EBSCO Online Database Education Research Complete.

Schmidt, P. (2007, April 20). Justice O'Connor sees 'muddy' future for affirmative action. *Chronicle of Higher Education.* Retrieved November 8, 2007, from http://chronicle.com.

Swink, D. (2003). Back to Bakke: Affirmative action revisited in educational diversity. *Brigham Young University Education & Law Journal,* 1, 211-256. Retrieved November 6, 2007, from EBSCO Online Database Education Research Complete.

Young, J., & Johnson, P. (2004). The impact of an SES-based model on a college's undergraduate admissions outcomes. *Research in Higher Education,* 45, 777-797. Retrieved November 6, 2007, from EBSCO Online Database Education Research Complete.

ADMISSIONS POLICIES

This article presents an overview and discussion of college and university admissions policies in the United States. American higher education began as mainly catering to an elite class of aspiring gentlemen. Over time, admissions policies at institutions, sometimes provoked by actions of the federal government and court cases, have moved toward serving a goal of universal access to American higher education. The land grant and coeducation movements, Title IX, and affirmative action programs are among various factors that have pushed universal access further along. Institutions have also recently established need-blind and score-optional admissions policies to work toward making higher education more accessible. According to some scholars, admissions poli-

cies like early admissions and legacy admissions may curtail accessibility.

KEYWORDS: Affirmative Action; Coeducation; Early Admissions; Discrimination; Land Grant; Legacy Admissions; Need-blind Admissions; Score-optional Admissions; Title IX; Universal Access

OVERVIEW
HISTORICAL OVERVIEW OF ADMISSIONS POLICIES
While minimal, the requirements for entrance to early American colleges were essentially out of the reach of the general population, who did not have access to the necessary preparatory training. Geiger (1999) noted that the colonial colleges "served,

among others, a constituency of aspiring gentlemen." Until 1745, the only subjects in which students had to fulfill entrance requirements in order to gain admission to a colonial college were the Latin and Greek languages and literature (Rudolph, 1990). These were the basic course of study at the colonial colleges at that time (Rudolph). College preparatory training was mainly available by way of private tutoring, Latin grammar schools, or instruction with a local minister (Brubacher & Rudy, 1997). The Latin and Greek tradition finally ended in 1745 when, as fervor over science grew, Yale also made arithmetic a requirement for admission (Rudolph).

As time has unfolded, there have been many efforts to make a college or university education more accessible than it was in the early system of American higher education. Some scholars point to the land grant movement in higher education as the start of such universal access efforts (Kerr, 2001). According to Rudolph, "ingrained in the land-grant idea was the concept of collegiate education for everyone at public expense." The early land-grant colleges were established under the Morrill Act of 1862 to support agricultural and mechanical studies (Rudolph). Mainly an agricultural nation at the time, the land grant movement facilitated access to some form of higher education for the American citizenry at large, such as farming families (Kerr). According to Kerr, in an increasingly democratic nation the land grant movement served "less the perpetuation of an elite class and more the creation of a relatively classless society, with the doors of opportunity open to all through education."

Another effort to make a college or university education accessible to everyone was the establishment of public high schools. State universities, which began to flourish after the Civil War, were the drivers behind the movement to form high schools that would prepare students for a college education (Rudolph). Public high schools were an institution of "the people at large" and thus helped to democratize collegiate education by making it a possibility for more students (Rudolph). Colleges and universities began to accept for admission credit subjects other than Greek, Latin, and arithmetic (Rudolph). Specifically, college entrance requirements were expanded beyond Latin, Greek, and arithmetic by 1870 to include history, geography, and English (Brubacher & Rudy). Requirements in modern foreign languages and

science were also added (Brubacher & Rudy). By 1895 already 41 percent of students admitted to colleges and universities were public high school graduates (Rudolph).

As secondary education expanded, colleges were essentially able to extend their requirements for admission because subjects formerly taught at the collegiate level were dropped down into the secondary level of education (Brubacher & Rudy). However, the ability to expand entrance requirements gave "scope for each college to emphasize its own idiosyncrasies" (Brubacher & Rudy). For instance, as the science requirement for admissions Yale required botany while Columbia asked for physics and chemistry (Brubacher & Rudy). The need for some degree of order became clear not just due to such idiosyncrasies but also due to a period of growth in American higher education that occurred during the last quarter of the nineteenth century (Brubacher & Rudy; Rudolph). As such, the College Entrance Examination Board was formed and the first College Board examinations were held by June 1901 (Rudolph). In addition to the benefit of uniformity of admissions requirements and examinations, colleges and universities that accepted the results of the College Examination Board were able to save time and money previously spent on administering their own examinations (Brubacher & Rudy).

Geiger offers that the formal transition from elite to mass higher education occurred between World Wars I and II, when enrollments approximately doubled during the 1920s. However, according to Geiger, American higher education has always been "somewhat hierarchical in terms of ... admissions requirements." For example, in the transition to mass higher education, new forms of higher education (e.g., junior colleges, teachers' colleges) emerged to serve the expanded student population, which included part-time and commuting students as well as those interested primarily in technical or semiprofessional fields (Geiger). Meanwhile, existing forms of higher education still served the mainly residential, full-time student population that had characterized elite access and was interested in liberal learning, character formation, and high-status professions (Geiger). At the same time, the transition to mass higher education was a major step on the way to universal access.

The most expansive phase of American higher education up until that time took place during the thirty-year period following World War II (Geiger). There was an excessive demand for college that originated in returning veterans who took advantage of the educational benefits provided by the GI Bill in unexpected numbers (Geiger). "In the decades following World War II, the primary and most persistent demand that government made on higher education was to increase capacity" (Levine, 2001). According to Kerr, during the time after World War II the passage of the GI Bill positioned the universal access movement further along by making higher education a possibility for many students who were the first in their families to attend college.

COEDUCATION & ADMISSIONS POLICIES

In the 1850s various women's institutions were chartered to offer college degrees to women (Geiger). Some institutions also began providing a college education to free African Americans during that time (Geiger). Yet, it was not until after the Civil War that the notion of a collegiate education for women was readily accepted (Brubacher & Rudy). The general paths to college education for women differed, however. In the eastern states and in the older seats of learning women were provided a separate college education. Entirely new colleges for women, like Vassar and Wellesley, were created or coordinated colleges affiliated with existing colleges (e.g., Radcliffe at Harvard) were established (Brubacher & Rudy). At the same time, in the western states and in the newer seats of learning, coeducation was readily accepted and women were generally admitted on the same terms as men (Brubacher & Rudy). By 1900, the idea of coeducation had begun to take greater hold and 71.6 percent of American higher education institutions accepted women as well as men on similar terms (Brubacher & Rudy). The number of coeducational colleges and universities increased as time passed but there was still enough of a debate to spur the federal government into action in 1972 with the passage of Title IX, which prohibits discrimination based on gender (Brubacher & Rudy).

FURTHER INSIGHTS

Traditionally, higher education institutions have had a great deal of freedom in formulating their admissions standards because of the notion that the development of admission policy is best left up to the expertise of educators (Kaplin & Lee, 1995).

At the same time, certain court decisions have led to a degree of regulation over the admissions process (Kaplin & Lee). There are three basic constraints that administrators must adhere to when formulating admissions standards (Kaplin & Lee). First, the selection process for admissions must not be arbitrary or unpredictable. Related, published admissions standards should be adhered to by the institution and admissions decisions upheld. Finally, institutions cannot have admissions policies that unduly discriminate on the basis of race, sex, disability, age, or citizenship. A great deal of attention has historically been focused on discrimination on the first two bases and, as such, these will be covered in more detail in this section.

DISCRIMINATION ON THE BASIS OF RACE

The Equal Protection Clause of the U.S. Constitution as well as Title VI of the Civil Rights Act of 1964 are two of the major legal bases that prevent institutions from discriminating on the basis of race in admissions (Kaplin & Lee). The civil rights statute Section 1981 is yet another major piece of legislation prohibiting discrimination on the basis of race (Kaplin & Lee). Affirmative action programs also deal with the consideration of race in admissions. These programs go beyond prohibiting discrimination based on race and actually seek to increase the number of minorities admitted to educational programs (Kaplin & Lee). However, per the findings of the 1978 *Regents of the University of California v. Bakke* Supreme Court case, it is not legally permissible for institutions to establish racial or ethnic quotas, which would be reverse discrimination and is prohibited (Kaplin & Lee).

DISCRIMINATION ON THE BASIS OF SEX

According to Kaplin and Lee, Title IX is the "primary legal source governing sex discrimination in admissions policies." Some scholars have stated that the admission of women into higher education institutions in America was not fully secured until the passage of Title IX in 1972 (Brubacher & Rudy). Under Title IX, discrimination on the basis of gender was prohibited for any educational program or activity that received federal financial assistance (Brubacher & Rudy). While Title IX applies to both public and private institutions that receive federal funds, there are certain exclusions. For instance, undergraduate public institutions that have historically been sin-gle-sex institutions are exempted (Kaplin & Lee).

Current Issues

ADMISSIONS TRENDS & STRATEGIES

There has been increased attention on getting into prestigious institutions. Two of the most-often used benchmarks in admissions to weigh the prestige of a college or university are institutional selectivity and yield. Selectivity refers to the proportion of stu-dents who apply for admission that are ultimately accepted, while an institution's yield rates refer to the proportion of accepted students who actually enroll (Hawkins & Clinedinst, 2006). The more selective an institution, the fewer applicants it accepts for admis-sion. More selective institutions also tend to have higher yield rates.

Early admissions plans are a fairly new devel-opment in American higher education. Bowen, Kurzweil, Tobin, and Pichler (2005) indicated that fervor over early admissions did not really take hold until about 1999-2000. They found early admis-sions to be troublesome because, among other rea-sons, they do little to further the cause of equity in American higher education, as they benefit those students who already tend to be advantaged (e.g., stu-dents at top-tier secondary schools).

The National Association for College Admission Counseling (NACAC) has outlined several defini-tions of the various types of early admission plans. Plans are classified as to whether they are restrictive or non-restrictive. Restrictive plans do not allow stu-dents to apply to early admission programs at other institutions, while non-restrictive plans do not carry such a limitation (Hawkins & Clinedinst). Restrictive plans include early decision and restrictive early action plans, while non-restrictive plans include reg-ular decision, rolling admission, and early action (Hawkins & Clinedinst).

DEVELOPMENTS IN EARLY ADMISSIONS

In 2006, several elite higher education institutions, including Harvard and Princeton, decided to drop their early admissions policies (Venegas, 2006), although both Harvard and Princeton reinstated early admissions in 2011. Klein (2006) indicates that these developments helped to fuel a debate among higher education leaders on the merits of such

programs. While Harvard moved to drop their pro-gram "to make its undergraduate admissions pro-cess more fair for disadvantaged students," other colleges and universities, particularly those that are not as selective, did not follow suit, because they rely on early admissions programs to ensure that they have a sizeable freshman class that is also well-qual-ified (Klein). At the same time, Venegas argued that restrictive early admissions programs, like early deci-sion and restrictive early action, are too high-risk for low-income students, because such programs restrict applicants from applying to other early admissions programs while also strongly encouraging them to make nonrefundable enrollment deposits well before the national final student decision deadline of May 1 and notification of financial aid eligibility. For this reason, among others, Venegas stressed that early admissions programs impinge upon the diver-sity of higher education institutions.

NEED-BLIND ADMISSIONS

Wickenden (2006) noted a decline in the recruitment of minority and low-income students at the nation's most prestigious higher education institutions, lead-ing some such institutions to offer substantial sub-sidies to low-income freshmen. Venegas urged that other institutions take up the policy that has emerged at Harvard of providing "full financial aid, with mini-mum debt burden, for the most needy, academically eligible students." In their study of private institutions, Bowen et al. noted that need-blind admissions policies were established "to reassure students from modest circumstances that their lack of money would not be held against them in the admissions competition." In other words, the policies were developed to help poor students. Yet even wealthy, prestigious institutions like Princeton have struggled in the past to secure the nec-essary resources to implement such policies (Bowen et al.). Indeed, resource constraints have often led some institutions to be unable to enact such policies (Bowen et al.). At the same time, need-blind admissions pol-icies may not be enough. The research of Bowen et al. found that applicants from disadvantaged socioeco-nomic backgrounds fared no better or worse regard-ing their chances for admission under such policies.

ADMISSIONS PREFERENCES FOR MINORITIES

In discussing admission preferences for underrep-resented minorities, Bowen et al. stressed that "a diverse student body provides educational benefits to all students." Essentially, for all applicants, it is important for America's higher education institutions to be accessible and not be bastions of privilege. Moreover, diversity has been found to be "a compelling state interest in education" (Eckes, 2004). Two legal cases involving the University of Michigan received a great deal of attention for the implications they have had on the consideration of race in admissions. The Supreme Court's decisions in these cases, *Grutter v. Bollinger* (2003) and *Gratz v. Bollinger* (2003), have served to clarify some long-standing confusion regarding affirmative action and how to treat race in admissions. In the decisions, the admissions policy of the University of Michigan Law School (the *Grutter* case) was deemed acceptable while the undergraduate admission policy of the University of Michigan (the *Gratz* case) was not. The law school's policy was essentially deemed acceptable because, as Eckes outlined, it encapsulated a "holistic approach to admissions" (Eckes) in which race was just one of many different characteristics considered to achieve a diverse student body.

Meanwhile, there have been efforts to establish ballot initiatives to ban the consideration of race and gender in college and university admissions in various states, including Arizona and Nebraska (Fliegler, 2007). Ironically, such a ban already passed in the fall of 2006 in Michigan, the setting for the aforementioned Supreme Court decisions that upheld the consideration of race in admissions (Fliegler). Similar bans on the consideration of race or ethnicity in college and university admissions passed in California in 1996 (Proposition 209) and in Washington in 1998 (Initiative 200) (Gardner, 2007).

In 2013, in *Fisher v. University of Texas*, the Supreme Court again ruled on race in college admissions, overturning a lower court decision that upheld the affirmative action admissions policy of the University of Texas at Austin. The high court found that the lower court had failed to apply the standard of "strict scrutiny" established in *Grutter* for race-based admissions policies, and returned the case to the lower court for reconsideration.

ADMISSIONS PREFERENCES FOR LEGACIES
Wickenden (2006) argues against the practice of legacy admissions in which the children or relatives of alumni and alumnae, who may be less well-qualified than other applicants, are admitted to a college or university. She stressed that "the most selective colleges are still overly generous to applicants from the kinds of family least in need of a leg up in life" (Wickenden). Reportedly, the debate over legacy admissions grew out of the debate over affirmative action (Schmidt). In contrast to affirmative action programs, however, legacy admissions tend not to favor minorities because they are generally underrepresented in the pool of legacy students (Schmidt, 2004).

Legacy preferences in admissions tend to be more common at private institutions, but in January 2004, a high-profile public institution, Texas A&M, abandoned its legacy admissions policy under pressure from lawmakers and interest groups (Schmidt). For public institutions, preferences for legacies are generally found at selective research universities (Schmidt). It has been reported, however, that while some representatives of higher education organizations feel that legacy admissions at public institutions will increasingly be challenged due to an obligation to serve taxpayers, other representatives feel that pressure to abandon such policies will not be increased because of legacies' role in providing funds to institutions that cannot be replaced by states (Schmidt).

Bowen et al. acknowledge that legacy preferences may curtail socioeconomic diversity on campuses; yet, while also calling for "tight limits" on such preferences, they indicated that institutions are within their right to observe such preferences in order to foster alumni/ae ties and the resources they may mean for the pursuit of excellence at institutions. Bowen et al. also noted that admissions preferences may be given to recruited athletes and so-called "development cases," or applicants who come from wealthy families.

SCORE-OPTIONAL ADMISSIONS POLICIES
According to Banerji (2006), some experts believe that score-optional admissions policies lead to greater diversity (e.g., in terms of race and socioeconomic status) at the higher education institutions that implement them. For instance, applicants from wealthier families have the means to access the best test coaching resources, which provide them with an advantage when taking the SAT (Banerji). Hundreds of schools have implemented some form of score-optional admissions, including American University, Bennington College, Bowdoin College,

George Mason University, Smith College, University of Arizona, and many others.

TERMS & CONCEPTS

Development Cases: Admissions policy in which preferences are given to children of parents or relatives who are thought to have potential as major donors.

Early Action: A type of non-restrictive early admission plan in which an applicant files an application with a preferred institution and receives a decision well in advance of the institution's typical decision date; applicants are not restricted from filing applications with other institutions under this type of plan and are also not required to accept any offer of admission or submit a non-refundable deposit before the national final student decision deadline of May 1.

Early Decision: A type of restrictive early admission plan in which an applicant files an application with an institution and commits to accept an offer of admission provided that the institution can meet any financial aid needs of the applicant; applicants may be restricted from filing applications with other institutions under this type of plan and may also be required to submit a non-refundable deposit before the national final student decision deadline of May 1.

Legacy Admissions: Admissions policy in which preferences are given to the children or relatives of alumni/ae.

Need-Blind Admissions: The ability of students and/ or families to pay is not considered as a factor in the admissions process.

Regular Decision: A type of non-restrictive early admission plan in which an applicant files an application with an institution by a specified date and receives a decision within a stated amount of time; applicants are not restricted from filing applications with other institutions under this type of plan.

Restrictive Early Action: A type of restrictive early admission plan in which an applicant files an application with a preferred institution and receives a decision well in advance of the institution's typical decision date; applicants are restricted from filing applications with other institutions under this type of plan but are not required to accept any offer of admission or submit a non-refundable deposit before the national final student decision deadline of May 1.

Rolling Admission: A type of non-restrictive early admission plan in which an institution accepts applications from prospective students and relays decisions throughout the admission cycle; applicants are not restricted from filing applications with other institutions under this type of plan.

Score-Optional: Admission policy in which applicants can apply for admission without submitting standardized test scores, such as SAT or ACT scores.

Selectivity: The number of students accepted for admission versus the number that applied for admission.

Yield: The number of students who enroll versus the number of students accepted for admission.

Marlene Clapp

BIBLIOGRAPHY

Antonovics, K. (2014). The Effect of Banning Affirmative Action on College Admissions Policies and Student Quality. *Journal of Human Resources, 49,* 295–322. Retrieved November 10, 2014, from EBSCO Online Database Education Research Complete.

Banerji, S. (2006). George Mason's SAT-optional admissions policy could boost diversity. *Diverse: Issues in Higher Education, 23,* 12. Retrieved May 14, 2007, from EBSCO online database, Education Research Complete.

Beale, A. V. (2012). The evolution of college admission requirements. *Journal of College Admission,* 20–22. Retrieved December 4, 2013, from EBSCO online database, Education Research Complete.

Bowen, W. G., Kurzweil, M. A., Tobin, E. M., & Pichler, S. C. (2005). *Equity and excellence in American higher education.* Charlottesville, VA: University of Virginia Press. Retrieved May 14, 2007, from EBSCO online database, Education Research Complete.

Brubacher, J. S., & Rudy, W. (1997). *Higher education in transition (4th ed.).* New Brunswick, NJ: Transaction Publishers.

Chapman, G., & Dickert-Conlin, S. (2012). Applying early decision: Student and college incentives and outcomes. *Economics of Education Review, 31,* 749–763. Retrieved December 4, 2013, from EBSCO online database, Education Research Complete.

Eckes, S. E. (2004). Race-conscious admissions programs: Where do universities go from Gratz and Grutter? *Journal of Law and Education, 33,* 21–62.

Fliegler, C. (2007). Dim days for affirmative action. *University Business, 10,* 13. Retrieved May 14, 2007, from EBSCO online database, Education Research Complete.

Gardner, S. (2007). Today's courts re-conceive race and ethnicity in college aid and admissions. *Education Digest,*

72, 58–64. Retrieved May 14, 2007, from EBSCO online database, Education Research Complete.

Geiger, R. (1999). The ten generations of American higher education. In P. G. Altbach, R. O. Berdahl, & P. J. Gumport (Eds.), *American higher education in the twenty-first century (pp. 38–69)*. Baltimore, MD: Johns Hopkins University Press.

Hawkins, D. A., & Clinedinst, M. (2006). *State of college admission 2006*. Alexandria, VA: National Association for College Admission Counseling.

Hill, C. (2012). Become need-blind? For colleges, that's the wrong question. *Chronicle of Higher Education, 59*, A72. Retrieved December 4, 2013, from EBSCO online database, Education Research Complete.

Hoover, E., Mangan, K., & Schmidt, P. (2013). After 'Fisher,' colleges face new burdens of proof. *Chronicle of Higher Education, 59*, A18–A20. Retrieved December 4, 2013, from EBSCO online database, Education Research Complete.

Kaplin, W. A., & Lee, B. A. (1995). *The law of higher education*. San Francisco, CA: Jossey-Bass.

Kerr, C. (2001). *The uses of the university*. Cambridge, MA: Harvard University Press.

Klein, A. (2006). Harvard's drop of early admissions fuels national debate. *Education Week, 26*, 16. Retrieved May 14, 2007, from EBSCO online database, Education Research Complete.

Levine, A. (2001). Higher education as a mature industry. In P. G. Altbach, P. J. Gumport, & D. B. Johnstone (Eds.), *In defense of American higher education* (pp. 38–58). Baltimore, MD: Johns Hopkins University Press.

Lilledahl Scherer, J., & Leigh Anson, M. (2014). Rethinking Open Access. *Chronicle of Higher Education, 61*, B38–B40. Retrieved November 10, 2014, from EBSCO Online Database Education Research Complete.

Rudolph, F. (1990). *The American college & university*. Athens: University of Georgia Press.

Schmidt, P. (2004). New pressure put on colleges to end legacies in admissions. *Chronicle of Higher Education, 50*, A1–A19. Retrieved May 14, 2007, from EBSCO online database, Education Research.

Venegas, K. (2006). Harvard, Princeton drop early admissions—should others follow? *Diverse: Issues in Higher Education, 23*, 41. Retrieved May 14, 2007, from EBSCO online database, Education Research Complete.

Wickenden, D. (2006). Top of the class. *New Yorker, 82*, 35–36. Retrieved May 14, 2007, from EBSCO online database, Education Research Complete.

SUGGESTED READING

Aka, P. (2006). The Supreme Court and affirmative action in public education, with special reference to the Michigan cases. *Brigham Young University Education & Law Journal*, 1–95. Retrieved May 14, 2007, from EBSCO online database, Education Research Complete.

Angelo, J. (2006). SAT optional. *University Business, 9*, 18. Retrieved May 14, 2007, from EBSCO online database, Education Research Complete.

Custer, B. (2016). College admissions policies for ex-offender students: A literature review. *Journal of Correctional Education*. 67(2), 35-43.

Farrell, E. (2007). When legacies are a college's lifeblood. *Chronicle of Higher Education, 53*, A33–A34. Retrieved May 14, 2007, from EBSCO online database, Education Research Complete.

Fliegler, C. (2006). For early admissions, an unclear fate. *University Business, 9*, 13. Retrieved May 14, 2007, from EBSCO online database, Education Research Complete.

Orentlicher, D. (2014). Economic inequality and college admission policies. *Cornell Journal of Law and Public Policy*. 26(1). 101.

Pastine, I., & Pastine, T. (2012). Student incentives and preferential treatment in college admissions. *Economics of Education Review, 31*, 123–30. Retrieved November 10, 2014, from EBSCO Online Database Education Research Complete.

Reed, K. (2013). Two arguments for race-conscious admissions policies. *American Journal of Education, 119*, 341–345. Retrieved December 4, 2013, from EBSCO online database, Education Research Complete.

INSTITUTIONAL EFFECTIVENESS IN HIGHER EDUCATION

Institutional effectiveness is an information-based decision-making model wherein the data gathered through organizational learning activities is used for quality improvement. Specifically, it refers to the on-going process through which an organization measures its performance against its stated mission and goals for the purposes of evaluation and improvement. The term was first used to describe activities related to accreditation in the 1980s and is now a crucial component of the accreditation process, as well as the fundamental factor in accountability and performance funding in Higher Education.

KEYWORDS: Accountability; Accreditation; Community College Survey of Student Engagement (CCSE); Institutional Effectiveness; Organizational Learning; Performance Funding; Quality Assurance; Quality Enhancement; Strategic Planning; Student Learning Outcomes

OVERVIEW

Institutional effectiveness refers to the ongoing process through which an organization measures its performance against its stated mission and goals for the purposes of evaluation and improvement. Since the Southern Association of Colleges and Schools (SACS) adopted the term in the 1980s, institutional effectiveness has moved to the forefront of the dialogue among government agencies, accrediting organizations, and Higher Education administrators. In this age of ever-increasing pressure for accountability, students, parents, government officials, accrediting agencies, industry leaders, taxpayers, and the mass media are demanding responsiveness from institutions of Higher Education (Welsh & Metcalf, 2003). These stakeholders are pressuring Higher Education decision-makers for improved documentation about performance and a system wherein public policy tools are coupled with reliable data from institutions to improve the alignment of the performance of Higher Education with the expectations of the public it serves (Welsh & Metcalf).

Institutional effectiveness most often includes the measurement of performance in areas such as student learning outcomes, academic program review, strategic planning, performance scorecards, and benchmarking and quality measurement. These areas are studied in myriad ways using numerous divergent instruments to collect pertinent data. Although there are variations in the terminology used, each of the six accrediting agencies in the United States requires that colleges and universities have a process through which institutional effectiveness can be evaluated, measured, and reported (Welsh & Metcalf).

Sullivan and Wilds (2001) describe institutional effectiveness as the process of studying performance and engaging in related activities within the context of a number of concepts and criteria. In their model, all constituents of the Higher Education community must participate in the process, with each group bearing specific responsibilities for program review and data collection. The accomplishment of the institutional mission; the reflection of its vision, philosophy, goals, and objectives; and an interpretation of the environment are at the crux of an evaluation of institutional effectiveness. In order to measure performance against these self-defined standards, a historical review of institutional accomplishments, weaknesses, and aspirations followed by the preparation, collection, and interpretation of data by institutional staff and faculty must be undertaken. Faculty must be charged with the development and evaluation of curriculum and with the evaluation of student performance in relation to that curriculum. Administrators are called upon to interpret and utilize relevant data and information in ways that promote increased effectiveness. Finally, the president of the institution bears the responsibility for defining and communicating institutional priorities and for working with the board to secure the resources required to meet those priorities (Sullivan & Wilds).

While the plan for the study of institutional effectiveness must be outlined and communicated by senior administrators, the process is rarely straightforward. Smith and Parker (2005) comment that while the relationship between organizational learning (the data-collection component of institutional effectiveness) and the focus upon learning and research that defines Higher Education may seem apparent, the process tends to be disruptive to campus patterns. "From bringing together campus constituents across institutional boundaries and accessing campus information data systems to obtain usable information, the process of using an organizational learning approach for evaluation has challenged many campuses" (Smith & Parker).

ACCREDITATION, ACCOUNTABILITY & PERFORMANCE FUNDING

The process of institutional review began in the nineteenth century with the inception of accreditation. Originally intended as a means through which some external control could be exerted over educational standards, by the 1930s and 1940s, there was a trend toward an added emphasis on improvement (Selden, 1960, as cited in Dodd, 2004). Since the introduction of the concept of institutional effectiveness in the 1980s, institutions have improved the work done on writing annual goals and objectives, evaluating their accomplishment of those goals, and describing their responsive improvements based on that data (Sullivan & Wilds).

THE ACCREDITING AGENCIES

There are six regional agencies in the United States that accredit Higher Education institutions in their respective areas.

- New England;
- Middle States;
- Southern;
- Western;
- North Central;
- Northwest.

Middle States was the first agency to require institutions to engage in the self-study and peer-review process, while Southern States was the first to incorporate the concept of institutional effectiveness into its requirements. The other five accrediting agencies quickly followed suit. An institution must be accredited by one of these agencies in order to receive federal financial aid, making the accreditation process a central focus for an institution when it is time for its review (Selden, as cited in Dodd). Additionally, there are a number of discipline-specific accrediting agencies that review curriculum and programs and whose standards must be met within the framework of the larger, regional accrediting bodies. While their accreditation may not have a direct impact upon the federal funding on which institutions rely, they can impact students' eligibility for professional exams and licensure, among other things. Hence, at any given time, an institution may be engaging in the self-study and accreditation process for a variety of agencies.

Since these accrediting agencies serve as the primary intercessors between postsecondary institutions and policymakers, they standardize accountability through their requirements for accreditation. In order to meet accreditation criteria, institutions must collect, format, report, and then use for improvement data about their programs and services (Welsh & Metcalf). With accredited institutions, Dodd explains, "constituencies such as students, the public, and government representatives have at least some assurance of quality and value. [The institution] is accomplishing the goals it has set within the context of its mission." Furthermore, argue Head and Johnson (2011), accreditation "can protect an institution from unwarranted criticism and... provide the stimulus for the improvement of courses and programs." Accreditation also "promotes internal unity and cohesiveness." Evidence of these accomplishments may impact enrollment and funding.

FOCUS ON OUTCOMES

Accrediting agencies have revised standards to reflect a focus on the achievement of outcomes rather than an adherence to standards. The primary suggestion for reform is related to the development and refinement of internal quality assurance measures that ensure institutional effectiveness (Dill, Massy, Williams & Cook, 1996, as cited in Dodd). Earlier approaches failed to compare outcomes with known approaches and did not examine how data were used in decision-making and strategic planning (Ewell, 1998, as cited in Dodd).

The self-assessment required for accreditation, coupled with the periodic peer review, results in a wealth of information that can be used for both accountability and for institutional and program improvement. Though the process does provide for some quality assurance, its focus is on the inputs and the processes and not the student (Miller & Malandra, 2006). Since each institution must meet the same requirements, there is some standardization among the data that are collected, but its dissemination is not widespread unless individual institutions choose to publish it. "Higher Education institutions and systems are focused inward and have a tendency to be unclear in communicating goals and outcomes to the public" (Miller & Malandra).

COMPETING FOR STUDENTS

While the accreditation process served as the impetus for institutional effectiveness and provides some insight into performance, it is no longer the sole reason that colleges and universities engage in the continuous process of self-study and improvement. Miller, writing to inform the commission that published *A Test of Leadership: Charting the Future of US Higher Education* (2006), explains that one of the core strengths of American postsecondary education lies in the number and variety of choices offered to students, which creates competition among institutions for students. Along with the ongoing competition for limited funds, the competition for students has forced increased accountability upon institutions so that student consumers can make the most informed choices. Miller asserts that having data available is not enough and that "it is essential to create a transparent system, which allows comparisons of rankings of institutions." Absent rankings and ratings, there is no impetus for change. He continues, "Today the U.S. News & World Report ranking serves by default as an accountability system for colleges and universities. Consequences that can modify behavior are an essential element of a productive accountability structure" (Miller).

PERFORMANCE FUNDING

The final factor contributing to the growing interest in institutional effectiveness and the trend toward institutional accountability is a result of the trend toward performance funding. While legislators have traditionally funded Higher Education institutions based upon their enrollment, there is a trend to adopt a performance funding model, which makes institutions accountable not just for making postsecondary institutions more accessible to a larger number of students (which enrollment funding accomplished) but for the quality of the education that is offered as well (Hoyt, 2001; McKeown-Moak, 2013). Performance funding offers incentives to institutions for providing documented quality services and for engaging in activities designed to improve programming. Changing the focus of the budget process from one that calls upon legislators to meet the need for more resources to one that calls upon the institution to justify its existing budget expenditures has created a level of accountability that is helping to shape the landscape of institutional effectiveness (Hoyt).

Twenty percent of state Higher Education officers had implemented a performance funding model in 1997, with an expected 52 percent of others intending to adopt the model within five years (Burke, 1998, as cited in Hoyt). The Tennessee Higher Education Commission (2007) reports that by 1999, twenty-eight states had implemented performance funding or were close to doing so, and many others were considering implementation of a performance funding program. Among the indicators for performance funding are

- retention (rather than enrollment) rates;
- completion rates;
- effectiveness of remedial programs;
- the number of tenured or tenure-track faculty teaching undergraduates;
- scores on national exams;
- the number of research dollars awarded;
- student achievement on licensure and certification exams;

- student evaluations of faculty;
- placement of graduates;
- rates of transfer to four-year colleges and universities.

A variety of measures apply specifically to individual types of institutions because there is diversity among the mission statements of community colleges, four-year colleges and universities, and large research institutions. In light of this growing trend, Hoyt expresses concern that "it is important that policymakers understand the impact and validity of the outcomes measures they are selecting to fund Higher Education." Poor measures and invalid indicators could impact the success of any performance funding program (Hoyt).

Accreditation, accountability, and performance funding have all contributed to the rising importance of institutional effectiveness in the context of Higher Education. Smith and Parker view this as a call for institutions to increase the depth and breadth of internal research to address the level of accomplishment of their institutional goals. An information-based decision-making model wherein the data gathered through organizational learning activities is used for quality improvement is the core of institutional effectiveness.

FURTHER INSIGHTS

According to Sullivan and Wilds, "no matter the wording, the most important purpose of an institution of Higher Education is to educate students." It follows, then, that the most important aspect of institutional effectiveness is student outcomes. Student achievement relative to the curriculum is of paramount importance to academic effectiveness. While achievement is important in and of itself, effectiveness dictates a broader scope in that it "presumes improvement in instruction, methodology, or technology based on the interpretation of data" (Sullivan & Wilds). Accrediting agencies look for institutions to assess student outcomes and to make improvements to the curriculum based upon that data. Institutions must be able to document program improvements that have their roots in assessment data (Sullivan & Wilds).

DIFFICULTIES IN ASSESSING STUDENT LEARNING

Because there is a lack of reliable data available to external constituents, there is a broad assumption that colleges and universities are offering quality services. This dearth of information is compounded when viewed in light of the few reliable means that exist to compare what students learn and experience among institutions. Miller and Malandra (2006) assert that "there is no solid, comparative evidence of how much students learn in college, or whether they lean more at one school than another." According to Miller and Malandra, two-thirds of all colleges nationwide do not participate in any type of assessment to determine whether they are meeting the curricular goals of their educational programs, and there are no commonly used tests or assessments to gauge undergraduate learning. The assessments in the areas of writing, literacy, math, and technology that have been administered and the data that were subsequently disseminated have indicated that the skills of many undergraduates barely improve in college and the skills of others decrease, resulting in employers offering expensive communication and critical-thinking training for new employees (Miller & Malandra). Hence, there is a growing need for reliable instruments with which institutions can collect relevant student data.

Student outcomes assessment, or the measure of student learning, requires that any instrument used have the dual ability to measure what the institution seeks to assess and to be validated against reliable standards. This has presented challenges to institutional researchers as there is no reliable, rigorous, and comparative means through which to measure the student learning outcomes for undergraduates. Colleges and universities now are using a variety of self-designed or purchased exams to evaluate this aspect of institutional effectiveness, and decisions about funds allocation and program improvement are being made based on data gathered through their use (Miller & Malandra).

NEW ASSESSMENTS AVAILABLE

A number of standardized assessments have been made available, and as their use becomes more widespread, a great deal of uniform data about student outcomes across institutions may be collected. One instrument, the National Survey of Student Engagement (NSSE), and its counterpart, the Community College of Student Engagement (CCSE), annually surveys hundreds of colleges about students' college experience relative to their participation in activities and programs that enhance learning and development. Though it does not assess how and what students learn, it does evaluate an important part of the college and university experience (NSSE, 2012).

According to Miller and Malandra, "use of the NSSE is helping to encourage a focus on the quality of the undergraduate experience, and the emergence of a national culture of evidence and assessment." According to the U.S. Department of Education (2006), "these instruments provide a comprehensive picture of the undergraduate student experience at four-year and two-year institutions," and data can be used "to improve [student] experience and create benchmarks against which similar institutions can compare themselves." Finally, data collected by the NSSE and CSSE are publicly reported and can be extrapolated for the purposes of institutional performance review and for establishing accountability standards and strategic planning (NSSE).

The Collegiate Learning Assessment (CLA) is the result of a multiyear trial by the Rand Corporation and measures key cognitive outcomes in the areas of critical thinking, analytical reasoning, and written communications. It is among the most comprehensive national efforts to standardize student outcomes, and since 2002, more than seven hundred college and universities have around the world have administered the instrument (Council for Aid to Education, 2013). The CLA measures student achievement over time as it is administered to first-year students and senior-level students. Since the results measure institutional performance rather than individual student achievement, "results are aggregated and allow for inter-institutional comparisons that show how each institution contributes to learning" (U.S. Department of Education). The effectiveness of the CLA as a measure of actual learning was examined by researchers Roksa and Arum (2011).

THE BALDRIDGE CRITERIA

A comprehensive framework for institutional effectiveness is the Baldridge criteria for education. With its emphasis on student learning outcomes, it facilitates organizational improvement within the context of the institution's mission and goals. Baldridge is an integrated quality management system that employs seven criteria that connect all of the institution's goals and outcomes. According to Dodd, the focus of the program is fourfold and involves improvement trends, benchmarking, stakeholders, and learning outcomes.

Categories one through three make up the leadership triad, defined as:

- leadership (category one);
- strategic planning (category two);
- student, stakeholder, and market focus (category three).

The leadership triad links to the results triad, defined as:

- faculty and staff focus (category five);
- process management (category six);
- organizational performance results (category seven).

Underlying these two integrated triads is a foundation of measurement, analysis, and knowledge management (category four) (Dodd).

Baldridge is unique in that it is connected to a quality management program, and it seeks to "facilitate sharing best practices, and to serve as a tool for learning about and improving performance" (Dodd). This, in turn, helps to provide a framework with which institutions can compare outcomes.

VIEWPOINTS

There are almost as many definitions of institutional effectiveness as there are institutions struggling with the concept and process of such accountability in Higher Education. Demonstrating effectiveness at the institutional level is a challenge. Sullivan and Wilds assert that:

> Institutional effectiveness is the result of institutional leaders making responsible data-based decisions tempered by current fiscal and political environments. [It] is exemplified by line officers... interpreting their responsibilities as they relate to the institutional mission. [They] must use information about the work of their units to project future plans and employ historical information to project budget needs.

LACK OF SUPPORT FOR EFFECTIVENESS ACTIVITIES

Welsh and Metcalf (2003) note that though the work of institutional effectiveness is a priority at colleges and universities, campus support for them is not gaining momentum. They find that "gaining the interest, commitment and support of institutional constituents is arguably the primary challenge colleges and universities face in designing and implementing institutional effectiveness activities." This support is fundamental to the institutionalization of the activities and to their being incorporated into the culture of the institution.

Miller and Malandra cite several reasons for this lack of support for activities related to institutional effectiveness. "There is a resistance to accountability and assessment, a fear of exposure and misinterpretation. Academics are afraid they will be blamed for variables (poverty, low SAT [Scholastic Aptitude Test] scores, poor high school performance) over which they have little control." There is also a concern that whatever data collected will not be used purposefully and, thus, the collection of said data would be a waste of valuable resources. The overriding reason that they suggest, however, is that "faculty and administrators are reluctant to look at results or make major changes because there is a lack of compelling pressure to improve undergraduate education and because they are isolated from reliable evidence of their students' progress beyond individual classes" (Miller & Malandra).

LACK OF TRANSPARENCY

Another challenge to institutional effectiveness is the complex and decentralized nature of Higher Education institutions. Though research lies at the core of education, most institutions have not used information-based decision-making models, and there is a significant lack of relevant data available. Smith and Parker explain "While a research culture encourages transparency of data and information in the academic setting, such information can be quite difficult at the institutional level. Information often has institutional and political significance that needs to be taken into consideration." Fear of controversy or harm to the institution's reputation or ranking in *U.S. News & World Report* make administrator's reluctant to disseminate the information that is gathered. There is a strong impulse to shed the best light on the institution, and there is pressure from both admissions and development offices to do so. They argue that "nonetheless, the use of basic, disaggregated institutional data is fundamental to monitoring and discussing progress" (Smith & Parker).

CONCLUSION

Despite institutional reluctance to embrace institutional effectiveness, indications are that it will remain at the forefront of the national dialogue on Higher Education. The Department of Education, in its landmark study *A Test of Leadership*, found that increased transparency and accountability among postsecondary institutions were necessary for the United States to remain competitive in a global context. The report called for increased assessment and accountability to all stakeholders and transparency of data that can be aligned so that sensible comparisons can be made among institutions.

Colleges and universities must become more transparent about cost, price and student success outcomes. This information should be made available to students, and reported publicly in aggregate form to provide consumers and policymakers an accessible, understandable way to measure the relative effectiveness of colleges and universities.

Among the report's many recommendations for the improvement of Higher Education was that postsecondary institutions adopt a "culture of continuous innovation and quality improvement by developing new pedagogies, curricula and technologies to improve learning" (U.S. Department of Education). The report outlined a number of goals and recommendations that, if adopted, will substantially change access to the delivery and evaluation of postsecondary programs.

TERMS & CONCEPTS

Accountability: Accountability in Higher Education refers to the institution's responsibility to provide the high quality programs and services within the context of its stated mission to its students and its willingness to report related outcomes to all stakeholders.

Accreditation: Accreditation is the nongovernmental process through which peer review and self-study ensure that federally funded educational institutions and programs in the United States are operating at a basic level of quality.

Community College Survey of Student Engagement (CCSE): The Community College Survey of Student Engagement is a survey instrument administered annually by community colleges to assess students' college experience relative to their participation in activities and programs that enhance learning and development.

Institutional Effectiveness: Institutional effectiveness is an information-based decision-making model wherein the data gathered through organizational learning activities is used for quality improvement. Specifically, it refers to the ongoing process through which an organization measures its performance against its stated mission and goals for the purposes of evaluation and improvement.

National Survey of Student Engagement (NSSE): The National Survey of Student Engagement is a survey instrument administered annually by hundreds of colleges to assess students' college experience relative to their participation in activities and programs that enhance learning and development.

Organizational Learning: Within the context of organizational theory, organizational learning describes the adaptive process through which an institution gathers information and plans and instigates changes based upon that information; in its simplest form, it is the process through which an organization learns and changes from experience.

Performance Funding: Performance funding is "an incentive-based funding initiative for public Higher Education that financially rewards exemplary institutional performance on selected measures of effectiveness".

Strategic Planning: Strategic planning describes the process through which an organization first defines its mission and direction over a period of time and then makes plans and allocates resources accordingly.

Student Learning Outcomes: Student learning outcomes describe how well an institution develops students' knowledge, talents, and abilities within the context of its goals and mission.

Karin Carter-Smith

BIBLIOGRAPHY

Council for Aid to Education. (2013). Performance assessment: CLA+ overview. Retrieved December 22, 2013, from http://cae.org.

Dodd, A. (2004). Accreditation as a catalyst for institutional effectiveness. (2004). *New Directions for Institutional Research*. 123, 13-25. Retrieved November 23, 2007, from EBSCO online database Academic Search Premier.

Head, R. B., & Johnson, M. S. (2011). Accreditation and its influence on institutional effectiveness. *New Directions for Community Colleges, 2011*, 37-52. Retrieved December 22, 2013, from EBSCO online database Education Research Complete.

Hoyt, J. (2001). Performance in Higher Education: The effects of student motivation on the use of outcomes tests to measure institutional effectiveness. *Research in Higher Education, 42*, 71-85. Retrieved November 23, 2007, from EBSCO online database Academic Search Premier.

McKeown-Moak, M. P. (2013). The "new" performance funding in Higher Education. Educational Considerations, 40, 3-12. Retrieved December 22, 2013, from EBSCO online database Education Research Complete.

Miller, C. (2006). Issue paper: Accountability/consumer information. A national dialogue: The secretary of education's commission on the future of Higher Education. (DOE Publication) Washington, DC: Government Printing Office. Retrieved November 21, 2007. from http://ed.gov.

Miller, C. & Malandra, G. (2006). Issue paper: Accountability/assessment. A national dialogue: The secretary of education's commission on the future of Higher Education. (DOE Publication) Washington, DC: Government Printing Office. Retrieved November 21, 2007, from http://ed.gov.

National Survey of Student Engagement (2012. A fresh look at student engagement: 2012 annual results. Retrieved December 22, 2013, from http://nsse.iub.edu.

Smith, D. & Parker, S. (2005, fall). Organizational learning: A tool for diversity and institutional effectiveness. *New Directions for Higher Education, 131*, 113-125. Retrieved November 23, 2007, from EBSCO online database Academic Search Premier.

Roksa, J., & Arum, R. (2011). The state of undergraduate learning. *Change, 43*, 35-38. Retrieved December 22, 2013, from EBSCO online database Education Research Complete.

Sullivan, M. & Wilds, P. (2001). Institutional effectiveness: More than measuring objectives, more than student assessment. *Assessment Update. 13*, 4. Retrieved November 23, 2007, from EBSCO online database Academic Search Premier.

United States Department of Education. (2006). A test of leadership: Charting the future of US Higher Education: (DOE Publication) Washington, DC: Government Printing Office. Retrieved November 21, 2007, from http://ed.gov.

University of Tennessee. Office of Institutional Research and Assessment. (2000-2005). Executive summary. *Performance Funding Standards.* Retrieved November 23, 2007.

Welsh, J. & Metcalf, J. (2003). Cultivating faculty support for institutional effectiveness activities: Benchmarking best practices. *Assessment and Evaluation in Higher Education, 28*, 33. Retrieved November 23, 2007, from EBSCO online database Academic Search Premier.

SUGGESTED READING

Assessing student learning and institutional effectiveness: Understanding middle states expectations. (2005). Philadelphia: Middle States Commission on Higher Education. Retrieved November 23 from http://msche.org.

Babaoye, M. (2006). Student learning outcomes assessment and a method for demonstrating institutional effectiveness. *Assessment Update. 18*, 14-15. Retrieved November 23, 2007, from EBSCO online database Academic Search Premier.

Bok, D. C. (1986). *Higher learning.* Cambridge, Mass.: Harvard University Press.

Carducci, R. (2004). Community college institutional effectiveness: Recent literature. *Journal of Applied Research in the Community College, 12*, 65-68. Retrieved November 23, 2007, from EBSCO online database Education Research Complete.

Duh, G., Kinzie, J., Schuh, J. & Whitt, E. (2005). *Assessing conditions to enhance educational effectiveness: The inventory for student engagement and success.* New Jersey: Jossey-Bass.

Ekman, R. (2007). By the numbers. *University Business, 10*, 35. Retrieved November 23, 2007, from EBSCO online database Academic Search Premier.

Middaugh, M. (2010). *Planning and Assessment in Higher Education: Demonstrating Institutional Effectiveness.* San Francisco, CA.: Jossey Bass.

Skolits, G. & Graybeal, S. (2007). Community college institutional effectiveness. *Community College Review, 34*, 302-323. Retrieved November 23, 2007, from EBSCO online database Academic Search Premier.

Welsh, J. & Metcalf, J. (2003). Administrative support for institutional effectiveness activities: Responses to the "new accountability." *Journal of Higher Education & Policy Management, 25*, 183-193. Retrieved November 23, 2007, from EBSCO online database Academic Search Premier.

COMMUNITY COLLEGE EDUCATION

This article provides an overview of community colleges in the United States. Community colleges largely originated from private two-year colleges (Diener, 1986). Community colleges have expanded access to higher education for previously underserved segments of the American population, such as non-traditional students (Boggs, 2004; Cohen & Brawer, 2003; Gleazer, 1980; Spellman, 2007; Teranishi,

Suárez-Orozco, & Suárez-Orozco, 2011). Community colleges fulfill many curricular functions, including preparation for transfer to four-year institutions, vocational training, continuing education, developmental or remedial education, and community service (Cohen & Brawer; Witt et al., 1994).

KEYWORDS: Access; Baby Boomers; Community College; Dual Enrollment; First Generation Students; First-Time College Freshmen; Junior College; Nontraditional Students; Open Door College; Remedial Education; Service-Learning; Student Engagement; Vocational Education

OVERVIEW
IMPORTANCE OF COMMUNITY COLLEGES
Gleazer writes that "Community colleges and their progenitors, public junior colleges, were established to extend educational opportunity." Because of their role in expanding access to higher education for a diverse population of students, community colleges are often referred to as "people's colleges" or "democracy's colleges" (Boggs). Cohen and Brawer noted that "community colleges have led to notable changes in American education, especially by expanding access." Diener aptly summarized some of the changes as follows:

The community college and its faculty serve the widest range of student ages, abilities, and interests of any institution in American higher education. It represents the American-built opportunity for a greater variety of individuals to develop and cultivate their talents and skills more fully than any other educational institution (Diener).

Historical Development of Community Colleges

THE JUNIOR COLLEGE
The modern American community college has its roots in the junior college (Diener). Junior colleges were largely private two-year colleges that had a main mission of providing the first two years of general collegiate study (Diener). Thus, they essentially fulfilled a transfer function and were a stepping stone along the way to a four-year liberal arts degree. At the same time, they retained vestiges of the elitism of the English model of higher education after which the earlier American colleges were modeled (Diener). Researchers have asserted that junior colleges were extensions of the elite system of higher education, though only in the sense that the colleges were created to please "university elitists" and preserve those institutions by providing some advanced educational training to a growing population of high school graduates (Witt et al.).

While some scholars have argued that comprehensive community colleges are quite different from the junior colleges from which they evolved, others have insisted that the two types of institutions are actually not that different. For instance, Witt et al. stated that the "supposed dichotomy is not supported by fact." For instance, the authors indicated that from the beginning junior colleges also supported a terminal function where students could leave with an earned associate's degree. They also noted that practical courses in agriculture were taught at the first junior college in California (Witt et al.). However, the authors also later indicated that even up to the 1920s "the most popular junior college curriculum was clearly university transfer" (Witt et al.). Moreover, nearly half of all junior colleges at that time offered no terminal degree option (Witt et al.).

The junior college movement is believed to have originated at the University of Chicago in the 1890s, where university president William Rainey Harper divided the upper and lower divisions of the university and named the lower-division departments junior colleges (Witt et al.). According to Witt et al., "Harper founded the greatest democratic movement in the history of American higher education." At first the junior college movement was concentrated in the Midwest (Witt et al.). Then in the early twentieth century the movement spread to California. California was more amenable to the spread of the movement than, for instance, the eastern states, which already had a rich system of smaller four-year colleges (Witt et al.). At that time most Californians did not have access to any form of higher education (Witt et al.).

EXPANSION TO COMMUNITY COLLEGES
As junior colleges grew and developed—and became more an institution of the people—they transformed into community colleges. Diener explains:

The junior college, at first a copy of a portion of the elitist university, began to widen its course offerings. It expanded its types of students served. The inclusion of daughters as well as sons of blue-collar workers began the transformation of the junior college to the community college.

The transition from mostly private junior colleges to mainly public community colleges progressed over time. In 1915-16 just 26 percent of all junior (two-year) colleges were public while the majority (74 percent) was private. By the late 1960s this statistic had reversed (Cohen & Brawer).

The time that had the greatest impact on the transformation of the junior college to the community college was the era after World War II that was witness to the GI Bill of Rights, the Civil Rights Movement, and the era of the baby boomers (Diener; Witt et al.). It was during this time that the call was made to ensure access to some form of education for a greater number of the American people. The community college became America's "open door college," where veterans, women, racial and ethnic minorities, immigrants, the poor, the disadvantaged, and those seeking additional or advanced vocational training could all pursue greater educational opportunity (Diener). The GI Bill, which provided a free college education to military veterans, became law in 1944 (Witt et al.). By 1946 more than 40 percent of all students at junior colleges were war veterans. Overall, enrollments nearly doubled in just three years, growing from 251,290 in 1944 to half a million during the 1947 academic year (Witt et al.). According to Witt et al. (1944), by the 1950s the colleges had experienced seven decades of almost continuous growth. The passage of the Civil Rights Act of 1964 also paved the way for increased enrollment of blacks and other racial and ethnic minorities at higher education institutions (Brubacher & Rudy, 1997). However, the biggest expansion yet was to come when the baby boomers descended on the community colleges in the 1960s and brought with them "the greatest period of growth in community college history" (Witt et al.). Witt et al. indicate that during the 1960s what equated to one community or junior college a week was built in the United States to accommodate the unprecedented growth. Enrollments nearly quadrupled, coming to a total of nearly 2.5 million students at the end of the decade (Witt et al.). Community colleges also moved into urban centers and came to exist in every state during the 1960s (AACC, 2001; Cohen & Brawer). As Gleazer explains, "For those who could not leave the community to go to college there was one within commuting distance."

While there is no clear indication of by whom or when the name "community college" was first mentioned, an article by Byron S. Hollinshead in 1936 urged the junior college to be more responsive to its community and become "a community college, meeting community needs" (Witt et al.). However, the 1947 Truman Commission report helped cement the new name into history (Witt et al.). The Truman Commission was a federal commission appointed by U.S. president Harry S. Truman and was charged with developing a master plan to expand educational opportunities for the American citizenry (Witt et al.). Following its work, the Truman Commission recommended the development of new two-year colleges and recommended these colleges be called community colleges (Witt et al.).

Gleazer explains, "Historically, the community college was based on the assumption that there were large numbers of people not served by existing institutions and the unserved were to be the clientele of these new colleges." One general segment of the clientele was to be the average citizen. Witt et al. indicated that the colleges would be responsive and help meet the needs of average citizens in a fluctuating world. The colleges would also help to educate adults and offer "a practical solution to the problem of adults needing affordable postsecondary education close to home" (AACC). It has been said that community colleges' success is rooted in their values of community responsiveness and access as well as creativity and a focus on student learning (AACC).

In terms of community colleges' highly held value of access, Cohen and Brawer stressed that "more than any other single factor, access depends on proximity." Community colleges have opened the doors of higher education to more individuals not just because of their open access policies but also because they are local, neighborhood institutions that have physically put higher education in the reach of people who otherwise would not have had proximity to it. Boggs explained that community colleges have "become the largest sector of higher education, representing nearly 1,200 regionally accredited institutions within commuting distance of over 90 percent of the population." Community colleges also facilitate access because of the lower tuitions that they charge (Bailey & Morest, 2006).

COMMUNITY COLLEGE STUDENTS

As noted, adult students were to be part of the clientele of the new community colleges. Spellman noted that most community college students are adult or non-traditional students who are 24 years of age or older. Bailey and Morest further explained that the students at community colleges are more likely than those at four-year institutions to be older, part-time students from lower-income households who may have dependent children and be first-generation college students. Increasingly, students are immigrants or the children of immigrants (Teranishi et al.). Data indicate that 57 percent of community college students also work more than twenty hours per week (CCSSE, 2006). Despite the non-traditional clientele they largely serve, according to the American Association of Community Colleges (AACC), community colleges enroll about half of all first-time college freshmen.

The majority of community college students are enrolled part-time. It has been demonstrated that these students are less engaged in their educational experience than full-time community college students (CCSSE, 2006). For instance, part-time community college students appear to interact both inside and outside the classroom less often with faculty members than do full-time community college students. In general, community college students more often appear to engage in active and collaborative learning inside the classroom instead of outside it (CCSSE).

COMMUNITY COLLEGE CURRICULUM & INSTRUCTION

In terms of the education they provide, comprehensive community colleges serve a three-prong mission:

- Prepare students for transfer to four-year institutions;
- Provide vocational training;
- Serve the community through continuing education efforts (Witt et al.).

In addition to these three major curricular functions, there are two other main curricular functions of community colleges: developmental education and community service (Cohen & Brawer). In general, academic transfer enables students to fulfill the lower-division coursework they need to enter the upper divisions of a four-year institution (Cohen & Brawer). Meanwhile, vocational-technical education deals with occupational, career, and technical studies. Radio repair and secretarial services were earlier courses taught in these areas of study. Next,

continuing education is generally geared to individuals who are primarily no longer students and wish to take classes for personal development. At the same time, developmental education, or remedial education, has become more important with the rise in the number of students who were poorly prepared for advanced study while in secondary school (Cohen & Brawer). Finally, community service reflects, for instance, different short courses, workshops, and noncredit courses offered for the benefit of the local communities (Cohen & Brawer).

Community college instructors have traditionally dedicated little time to research and scholarship and have instead focused on teaching. Class size also tends to be small (Cohen & Brawer). While these conditions seem to provide a favorable environment for student learning, researchers were not convinced; they wanted a better assessment of community college education. Five benchmarks of effective educational practice at community colleges were developed as part of the Community College Survey of Student Engagement (CCSSE) (McClenney, 2004). Established in 2001, the CCSSE helps to assess community college student engagement with purposeful educational practices (McClenney). The five benchmarks are as follows:

- Active and collaborative learning: Occurs when students are active participants in their educational experience (for example, they have opportunities to think about what they are learning and apply it) and collaborate with others in their learning efforts;
- Student effort: Reflects the amount of time students dedicate to their educational experience;
- Academic challenge: encompasses "challenging intellectual and creative work";
- Student-faculty interaction: Reflects the amount of meaningful contact students have with faculty members;
- Support for learners: Materializes not only in the presence of academic and career services to support students but also in a general commitment to student success that permeates campus (McClenney).

SERVING THE COMMUNITY

Community colleges have been recognized for their responsiveness to their communities (AACC). Their responsiveness has clearly materialized in their curricular offerings. For example, in 2000, thousands of community colleges began offering high-tech coursework to meet a growing demand for this type of education (Burnett, 2000). A joint survey between the American Association of Community Colleges (AACC) and ACT in 1999 showed that community college students' main reason for enrollment was to strengthen their workplace skills in technology and computers ("Survey," 2000). Non-traditional students, especially, are looking to community colleges to update computer skills, and employability, in a poor economy (Jesnek, 2012). Also, following the terrorist attacks of September 11, 2001, hundreds of community colleges began offering degrees and certificate programs in homeland security. Some have even built facilities dedicated to training in the area as well (Gilroy, 2005). Finally, the *Chronicle of Higher Education* reported that "as tuition at four-year institutions nears prohibitive levels for some students, and the demands of the global economy become more pressing, community colleges increasingly are focusing on producing creative thinkers as well as skilled workers" (Ashburn, 2006). At some community colleges these trends have led to the creation of honors programs, which began to take off at the colleges during the 1990s (Ashburn). In addition to honors programs, some community colleges also have other types of special educational programs for students. Service-learning has been promoted as part of community college education since 1994, and about half of all community colleges offer it as part of their curriculum (AACC, as cited in Weglarz & Seybert, 2004). Service learning fulfills two aspects of the community college mission: educating students and serving the local community (Weglarz & Seybert).

DUAL ENROLLMENT

Community colleges are also actively involved in easing the transition from high school to college through their participation in dual enrollment programs. According to data from the National Center for Education Statistics on trends in dual enrollment during the 2002-03 academic year, a greater percentage of public two-year institutions had students taking courses in dual-enrollment programs than either public or private four-year institutions (Kleiner & Lewis, 2005). Overall, 93 percent of public two-year institutions had students enrolled in dual enrollment

classes as compared with 64 with of public four-year institutions and 29 percent of private four-year institutions (Kleiner & Lewis).

In terms of educational success in community college, Bailey and Morest noted that transfer and degree completion rates at community colleges have remained low. Rosenbaum, Redline, and Stephan (2007) more strongly indicated that community colleges have "shockingly low degree-completion rates." This can in part be attributed to the characteristics of community college students themselves, who face a dizzying array of academic, occupational, and personal struggles (Bailey & Morest). A national study found that only 34 percent of students who begin community college with degree aspirations succeed in obtaining any sort of degree credential within the eight years after high school (Rosenbaum et al.).

VOCATIONAL TECHNICAL PROGRAMS

One current issue in community college education is the decreasing terminal function of vocational-technical programs (Cohen & Brawer). The original intent of these programs was to train students to enter certain skilled occupations and fields after graduation (Cohen & Brawer). However, more and more vocational-technical students are transferring to four-year institutions to pursue advanced coursework in similar fields (Cohen & Brawer). At the same time, the number of students transferring to four-year institutions after academic transfer or collegiate preparation is declining because the students enrolling are more often not dedicated to a certain line of study and may, for instance, just be taking courses for personal interest (Cohen & Brawer).

REMEDIAL EDUCATION

Another current issue is the increasing remedial function of the community colleges (Cohen & Brawer). According to Bailey and Morest, "College access has become fundamental to economic opportunity in the United States." However, access to college is only one part of the equity agenda that community colleges help carry out. The concept of equity in higher education has also come to reflect that educators hope to ensure that students are adequately prepared for postsecondary education and to ensure that students have an equal chance at succeeding once enrolled in college (Bailey & Morest). Community colleges have directly engaged in preparing students for college-level work through their developmental studies programs. Estimates show that about half of the students who enter various community colleges are not prepared for college-level work (Bailey & Morest). Community colleges help to bring the academic skills of these students up to standard (Bailey & Morest).

BACHELOR'S DEGREES

In contrast to the increasing remedial function, some community colleges across the country offer bachelor's degrees (Troumpoucis, 2004). These degree programs are either offered independently by the community college or jointly with a four-year institution. More than one hundred community colleges offered the bachelor's degree as of 2004 (Troumpoucis). Some say that this effort on the part of community colleges is responsive to community needs and will bring higher education opportunities to more students, especially non-traditional students who may not be able to travel to a four-year institution to pursue an advanced degree (Troumpoucis). Others argue that the move may soften the mission of community colleges and the value of the two-year degree (Troumpoucis). The bachelor's degrees that community colleges offer tend to be in vocational areas, such as auto body design. Some have labeled these types of bachelor's degrees the "applied baccalaureate degree" ("History Marches Forward," 2005).

FINANCIAL CONCERNS

Community colleges are also facing financial difficulties. According to Boggs, "Community college leaders are struggling to meet accelerating demand with declining public resources." There is increased enrollment pressure on the colleges due to several factors. For instance, not only is the population of high school graduates in the United States increasing, but more of them are choosing to attend college and turning to community college as a more cost-efficient way to start their college careers (Boggs). In the meantime, community colleges are facing severe cuts in the state and local funds upon which they rely (Boggs; Crookston & Hooks, 2012). Community colleges count on public funding more than any other segment of the higher education community (Boggs). On average, community colleges nationally receive about 60 percent of their operating funds from state and local sources

while 35 percent of public four-year institutions' funds come from these sources (Boggs).

TERMS & CONCEPTS

Baby Boomers: The populous generation born after World War II between 1946 and 1964.

Dual Enrollment: Also referred to as "dual credit," "concurrent enrollment," "joint enrollment." Occurs when students take college-level courses and earn college credit while still in high school.

First-Generation College Students: Students who are the first in their immediate families to attend college.

First-Time College Freshmen: Students who enter college without any previous enrollment at another higher education institution; these students may enter college directly after high school.

Non-traditional Students: Students who exhibit one of more of the following characteristics: lack of a standard high school diploma, delayed college enrollment, part-time college enrollment, financial independence, and full-time employment. Non-traditional students may also have dependents other than a spouse (for example, children or relatives) and may be single parents.

Remedial Education: Raising skills or knowledge of various subjects or fields to acceptable levels.

Service-Learning: "A teaching and learning strategy that integrates meaningful community service with instruction and reflection to enrich the learning experience, teach civic responsibility, and strengthen communities".

Student Engagement: "The amount of time and energy that students invest in meaningful educational practices".

Marlene Clapp

BIBLIOGRAPHY

American Association of Community Colleges (AACC). (2001). *America's community colleges: A century of innovation.* Washington, D.C.: Community College Press.

Ashburn, E. (2006). An honors education at a bargain-basement price. *Chronicle of Higher Education, 53,* B12-B14. Retrieved August 1, 2007, from EBSCO Online Database Education Research Complete.

Bailey, T., & Morest, V. S. (2006). Defending the community college equity agenda. In T. Bailey & V. S. Morest (Eds.), *Defending the community college equity agenda* (pp. 1-27). Baltimore: Johns Hopkins University Press.

Barnhart, C. L., & Stein, J. (Eds.). (1962). *The American college dictionary.* New York: Random House.

Boggs, G. (2004). Community colleges in a perfect storm. *Change, 36,* 6-11. Retrieved August 1, 2007, from EBSCO Online Database Education Research Complete.

Brubacher, J. S., & Rudy, W. (1997). *Higher education in transition* (4th ed.). New Brunswick, NJ: Transaction.

Burnett, S. (2000). Community colleges follow the career college path to Cyberia. *Community College Week, 13,* 7. Retrieved August 1, 2007, from EBSCO Online Database Education Research Complete.

Cohen, A., & Brawer, F. (2003). *The American community college* (4th ed.). San Francisco: Jossey-Bass.

Community College Survey of Student Engagement (CCSSE). (2006). *Act on fact: Using data to improve student success: 2006 findings.* Austin, TX: Author.

Crookston, A., & Hooks, G. (2012). Community colleges, budget cuts, and jobs: The impact of community colleges on employment growth in rural U.S. counties, 1976-2004. *Sociology of Education, 85,* 350-372. Retrieved December 15, 2013, from EBSCO Online Database Education Research Complete.

Diener, T. (1986). *Growth of an American invention: A documentary history of the junior and community college movement.* Westport, CT: Greenwood Press.

Gilroy, M. (2005). Community colleges are key to homeland security. *Education Digest, 70,* 32-36. Retrieved August 1, 2007, from EBSCO Online Database Education Research Complete.

Gleazer, E. J., Jr. (1980). *The community college: Values, vision, & vitality.* Washington, D.C.: American Association of Community and Junior Colleges.

History marches forward: Community colleges change face of higher education with introduction of bachelor's degrees. (2005). *EduExec, 24,* 1-7. Retrieved August 1, 2007, from EBSCO Online Database Education Research Complete.

Horn, L. J. (1996). *Non-traditional undergraduates: Trends in enrollment from 1986 to 1992 and persistence and attainment among 1989-90 beginning postsecondary students* (NCES 97578). Washington, D.C.: National Center for Statistics for Education Statistics. (ERIC Document Reproduction Service No. ED402857).

Jesnek, L. M. (2012). Empowering the non-traditional college student and bridging the "digital divide." *Contemporary Issues in Education Research, 5,* 1-8. Retrieved December 15, 2013, from EBSCO Online Database Education Research Complete.

Kleiner, B., & Lewis, L. (2005). *Dual enrollment of high school students at postsecondary institutions: 2002–03* (NCES 2005–008). Washington, D.C.: National Center for Education Statistics. (ERIC Document Reproduction Service No. ED484632).

McClenney, K. (2004, November). Redefining QUALITY in community colleges. *Change, 36,* 16-21. Retrieved August 1, 2007, from EBSCO Online Database Education Research Complete.

National Service Learning Clearinghouse (NSLC). (n.d.). *Service-learning is...* Retrieved August 2, 2007, from National Service Learning Clearinghouse, http://servicelearning.org.

Rosenbaum, J., Redline, J., & Stephan, J. (2007). Community college: The unfinished revolution. *Issues in Science & Technology, 23,* 49-56. Retrieved August 1, 2007, from EBSCO Online Database Education Research Complete.

Spellman, N. (2007). Enrollment and retention barriers adult students encounter. *Community College Enterprise, 13,* 63-79. Retrieved August 1, 2007, from EBSCO Online Database Education Research Complete.

Survey: Community college students enroll for jobs. (2000). *Education USA (Aspen Publishers)* Retrieved August 1, 2007, from EBSCO Online Database Education Research Complete.

Teranishi, R. T., Suárez-Orozco, C., & Suárez-Orozco, M. (2011). Immigrants in community colleges. *Future of Children, 21,* 153-169. Retrieved December 15, 2013, from EBSCO Online Database Education Research Complete.

Troumpoucis, P. (2004). The best of both worlds? *Community College Week, 16,* 6-8. Retrieved August 1, 2007, from EBSCO Online Database Education Research Complete.

Wattenberg, E. (1986). The fate of baby boomers and their children. *Social Work, 31,* 20-28. Retrieved August 3, 2007, from EBSCO Online Database Education Research Complete.

Weglarz, S., & Seybert, J. (2004). Participant perceptions of a community college service-learning program. *Community College Journal of Research & Practice, 28,* 123-132. Retrieved August 1, 2007, from EBSCO Online Database Education Research Complete.

Witt, A., Wattenbarger, J., Gollattscheck, J., & Suppiger, J. (1994). *America's community colleges: The first century.* Washington, D.C.: Community College Press.

SUGGESTED READING

Andrews, H. (2000). Lessons learned from current state and national dual-credit programs. *New Directions for Community Colleges, 2000,* 31. Retrieved August 1, 2007, from EBSCO Online Database Education Research Complete.

Cejda, B., & Rhodes, J. (2004). Through the pipeline: The role of faculty in promoting associate degree completion among Hispanic students. *Community College Journal of Research & Practice, 28,* 249-262. Retrieved August 1, 2007, from EBSCO Online Database Education Research Complete.

Cohen, A., Brawer, F., & Kisker, C. (2014). *The American Community College.* San Francisco, CA.: Jossey Bass.

Gupton, J. (2017). Campus of opportunity: A qualitative analysis of homeless students in community college. Community College Review. 45(3), 190-214.

Meyer, H. (2006). A fragile balance. *Community College Week, 18* (11/12), 8-11. Retrieved August 1, 2007, from EBSCO Online Database Education Research Complete.

Pascarella, E. (1997). It's time we started paying attention to community college students. *About Campus, 1,* 14. Retrieved August 1, 2007, from EBSCO Online Database Education Research Complete.

Portmann, C., & Stick, S. (2003). The association between departmental affiliation and curricular decision making. *Community College Journal of Research & Practice, 27,* 519. Retrieved August 1, 2007, from EBSCO Online Database Education Research Complete.

Somers, P., et al. (2006). Towards a theory of choice for community college students. *Community College Journal of Research & Practice, 30,* 53-67. Retrieved August 1, 2007, from EBSCO Online Database Education Research Complete.

ACCELERATED DEGREE PROGRAMS

Why have accelerated degree programs been on the rise in recent years, who are the students most interested in such programs, and are these programs just as effective for learners as traditional degree programs? This article first compares the typical accelerated degree program with traditional degree programs, so as to get a clear understanding of what constitutes an accelerated program. The article also describes the advent of "strip-mall universities" and also looks at the advantages and disadvantages of this type of school as well as accelerated degree programs in general. The article describes a few other types of accelerated degree programs for varying educational levels, and examines some of the criteria schools should consider when considering the implementation of an accelerated degree program. The article concludes with a brief examination of how online activities might be used in all of the described accelerated programs.

KEYWORDS: Accelerated Degree Program; Adjunct Teacher; Cohort-based Program; College Board; National Center for Education Statistics; Non-traditional Student; Strip Mall University; Traditional Student

OVERVIEW

The number of accelerated degree programs has been increasing in the last few decades, though there are several variations on these accelerated programs, which are designed for specific types of degrees. Some courses do not have as much academic contact hours as traditional courses, and instead online class work, team projects, internships and other educational assignments are used to compensate for the reduced number of contact hours. Other accelerated courses manage to maintain the same number of contact hours as a traditional fifteen-week course (about forty-five hours per semester) by increasing the duration of each course session to as much as eight hours. As Husson and Kennedy (2003) note, many colleges are offering accelerated degree programs in five- or eight-week formats, meaning students attend classes one night per week for a four-hour session. Twenty to thirty-two hours of contact sessions enable non-traditional students to accomplish their goals through a combination of intensive in-class sessions and out-of-class work. The authors believe that this approach creates some significant differences from the traditional forty- to forty-five contact hours per semester-long course wherein students meet several times per week (Husson & Kennedy).

This accelerated structure, which has fewer classroom contact hours, is currently the most commonly encountered accelerated degree program that universities offer, and has become the standard accelerated program format. Considering the growth of such programs, a few obvious questions are:

- Why have accelerated degree programs been on the rise in recent decades?
- Who are the students increasingly enrolling into these programs?
- Are these programs just as effective as traditional programs?

THE RISE OF ACCELERATED DEGREE PROGRAMS
According to Singh and Martin (2004), many educators believe that "intensive courses and programs will flourish in the future, largely as a result of the

changing demographic trends on campuses." The main reason for this predicted increase—or the specific trend that the authors assert has changed the demographics of the college student population—is the increasing number of non-traditional students enrolling to gain college degrees. This trend, which has been occurring at least since the 1970s, is caused by many social and economic factors, but the statistics clearly demonstrate that the trend is real, and is rising. As Taniguchi and Kaufman (2005) have observed in their research:

> While the enrollment of students aged 24 or younger grew by 51 percent between 1970 and 2000, the increase for older students was about three times as large. In 1999–2000, 40 percent of all enrollees were in their mid-20s or older, with a large proportion of them attending part time and having dependents.

Undoubtedly, the main reason many schools have started offering accelerated degree programs is to meet the needs of this growing number of non-traditional students. As Singh and Martin note, "continuing education students with busy work schedules are returning to continue their education, and it is generally assumed that they prefer shorter, intensive programs." They cite a study that supports this assumption, and they argue that many educational institutions that are struggling for financial stability quite often view the development of new accelerated programs as a ready source and means to increase their revenues. Institutions of higher education already have all the necessary elements in place (i.e., teachers, computer labs, classroom space, accreditation, research facilities, etc.), so answering non-traditional student needs is essentially a matter of redesigning the meeting times, days, and duration of the courses so as to create accelerated programs. However, there are also other important considerations schools should examine before establishing an accelerated degree program.

CHANGING STRATEGIES

In the past, most colleges were organized around what could be called a traditional college program model. Classes were always scheduled on campus, most often during the daytime hours and on weekdays, with a few evening courses scheduled to help manage the over-enrollments or scheduling conflicts of traditional students. Husson and Kennedy

observe that, as the number of adults returning to college steadily increased, many of these institutions began to creatively adapt their class schedules so as to accommodate working adult learners. Many more classes specifically intended for these non-traditional students were scheduled in the evenings and on the weekends, which are meeting times that these students are better able to fit into their busy schedules. Also, the authors note that organizations like the College Board indicate that "location is a primary decision factor for older adults returning to college," and this is why many of the more market-sensitive colleges have opened extension learning centers (Husson & Kennedy). Many colleges have also begun offering alternative delivery methods such as guided independent study programs and Internet-based courses in addition to their traditional system of classroom delivery. These types of alternative deliveries, which allow students to study much more from home, have been designed with the growing non-traditional student population in mind, and are often integrated into accelerated degree programs.

CORPORATE SUPPORT

The rapid growth of accelerated degree programs also comes from the fact that financial backing is frequently provided by the full-time working students' employers. When colleges began meeting the needs of adult students through new accelerated degree programs, corporations began supporting their adult student employees with tuition benefits, which has served as a strong incentive for these older students to return to college. Husson and Kennedy note that company sponsorship, combined with convenient accelerated programs, has allowed non-traditional students to "complete upper-division course work and receive their degrees from an accredited institution in a fraction of the time that it would normally take on a traditional campus."

STRIP-MALL COLLEGE

Alongside this trend is another market phenomenon that one author refers to as "strip-mall" universities. As the College Board observed, location is an essential factor for non-traditional students, and the local shopping mall is about as convenient a location as one could wish for. Strother (2005), who has much experience in teaching at strip-mall universities, gives an interesting view of this new type of school. He succinctly describes the typical accelerated program model for course offerings, and he lists several of the advantages that have attracted close to 600 non-traditional students into enrolling at this strip-mall university:

"They attend classes from 6 to 10 p.m., one night a week, for two to three years. They avoid the numerous hassles of traditional college registration, like inconvenient class times and full or canceled courses. They only have to register once, when they enroll. They also avoid long lines at college bookstores because in this accelerated program, the books are delivered directly to them through overnight mail. And you sure can't beat the parking. Moreover, strip-mall universities are 'customer-oriented,' so they are generous in accepting transfer credits, and students can finish their degrees faster" (Strother).

Strother is quite aware of the necessity for large universities to be more competitive in gaining these strip-mall students. He describes yet another institution that hired him as an adjunct. This school was "a 150-year-old, traditional, urban university that had just survived a painful reorganization." He writes that "the administrators were eager to increase enrollment, so they adopted some of the tactics of their competitors, the strip mall institutions." The school shortened its semesters to eight weeks, began using adjuncts for their new degree program (which Strother describes as "'in a box' degree-completion programs") and he notes that the school invested heavily in a marketing campaign to gain non-traditional students. The changes successfully attracted adult students, and the school's enrollment increased significantly.

This is exactly the direction that higher educational consultants such as Greene and Greene (2003), who have examined the trends, have advised larger colleges and universities to take. They observe that accelerated program listings are often hidden in university course catalogs or websites, or are hidden within individual departmental pages or graduate studies sections. Greene and Greene argue that "colleges would do well to tout their special degree programs up front in their literature and on their Internet sites" (2003, p. 3), which is essentially a matter of better marketing. They write that using a better marketing strategy would help these schools to attract academically serious, motivated, and well-prepared students, and they strongly recommend that universities develop or expand combined degree programs "as a means to expand their offerings without the necessity to expand or build new curricula."

Again, this points out that schools already have many of the needed ingredients already in place, and it is a matter of using those resources to meet non-traditional student needs. Strother observes that this is something traditional universities should be doing. He writes that "to compete with the strip-mall campuses, bricks-and-mortar universities need to offer more-convenient programs for students," though he observes that these schools should retain their rich, traditional, on-campus experience as well. He also argues that strip-mall universities should seek out ways to expose their students to more extracurricular activities that are an essential part of a well-rounded education, which relates to some of the possible disadvantages of strip-mall accelerated programs.

NON-TRADITIONAL STUDENTS PREFER ACCELERATED COURSE PROGRAMS

A study conducted by Singh and Martin clearly demonstrates that students who work full time, and whose employers pay the school tuition, much prefer accelerated programs. However, the study also uncovered the importance of schools realizing that this type of student does not represent all non-traditional students. Their study demonstrated a clear difference in types of students in MBA programs. Their research indicated that most students liked the idea of an accelerated program that their university was considering implementing. The program under consideration would offer courses in four sessions with ten-week modules, with classes running for an extra forty-five minutes. A majority of students said that they would take more courses if four sessions were offered, and the survey results also indicated that many students would inform other people whom they knew about the program if the accelerated program were implemented.

However, the authors also noted that a careful examination of the results revealed that, "apart from gender, there were statistically significant differences on some of the survey items by employment status, student status, tuition payment source, and—very important—program" (Singh & Martin). They noted that students who were employed full time, and those attending classes on a part-time basis reacted the most favorably to the proposal, and again, there was clear evidence that working students generally prefer programs that are accelerated. But the study also revealed that students who had to pay the tuition themselves (rather than the employer) were the least supportive of the proposed program. Singh and Martin argue that this negative reaction is due to the effect an accelerated system would have on these students' financial situation, since tuition payments would have to be paid more rapidly. Also, the study showed that "a fairly high percentage of students, mainly from the MBA and finance and accounting programs, reported that an extension of 45 minutes per class would affect their class participation negatively."

FACULTY OPPOSITION
Additionally, many faculty members at the university strongly opposed the proposal, and the university decided it best not to convert the MBA program to one that was solely accelerated in nature. The authors cite yet another study where this same phenomenon occurred. In that viability study, after researchers analyzed the total student response, they concluded that there were too many negative attitudes expressed by faculty and students toward intensive courses being offered concurrently with fifteen-week courses. From their research, as well as other studies that informed them, Singh and Martin concluded that their study "shows that the perception of accelerated programming depends on the type of student enrolled in the program."

COHORT PROGRAMS
Singh and Martin emphasize the point that "the composition of current and potential students is vital to the decision to implement an accelerated program" (p. 302). As for the university where they conducted their study, the school decided to keep its existing program and start a separate, concurrent MBA program that offered an accelerated degree "by offering Saturday classes in a cohort style to students working full time." Enrollment in that program has grown steadily since the program's introduction (Singh & Martin). Kasworm (2003) also carried out a study that showed why accelerated degree programs that are cohort style are successful and popular among non-traditional students. Her study showed that adults in accelerated degree programs believe they are in a customized learning environment that is designed

for adults. She notes that such programs are easily accessible, considering the typical non-traditional student's more adult schedule that often includes full-time employment as well as raising children.

The cohort style accelerated programs seem to be optimal for non-traditional students. As Kasworm observes, through cooperating intensively with other adults who are full-time workers, and through use of cohort group projects and cohort-based classes, these students gain a stronger experience with a learning community. This may partially replace the community that Strother believes is much stronger on traditional campuses, and it may be that these students would not actually participate much in on-campus social life even if their accelerated program is located on a traditional campus. Such students are very busy with full-time work and the raising of children, so they may not have much time for campus debates on gay marriage, the military, politics, race, gender, and justice. According to Kasworm, the adult students in her study felt "a sense of support in the midst of their pressured lives," and this may be the most important social need they have as students. Thus, universities may be wise to offer both types of programs (traditional and accelerated) rather than replacing one for the other, and they might consider creating cohort-style programs when they open strip-mall university branches.

COMBINED DEGREE PROGRAMS
There are yet other types of accelerated programs at the higher education level. The combined degree program is one type of accelerated program that Greene and Greene say many students and parents are attracted to. These are dual and accelerated degree programs that enable a traditional student to attain both a bachelor's and graduate degree in a shorter than normal period of study. Greene and Greene believe this is an excellent way to leverage a student's academic strengths and time spent in education. As the authors note, "Families perceive these opportunities (frequently referred to as 3/2 degree programs) as ways to save one or more years of study, so they can begin to earn an income sooner and save substantial costs" (Greene & Greene). This type of accelerated program has become increasingly popular—particularly among those traditional students who plan, already upon entry as college freshmen, to obtain a master's degree so as to have a competitive advantage on the job market.

FAST-TRACK ASSOCIATE'S DEGREES

Another type of accelerated program is being offered at some community colleges. They have begun offering accelerated programs for associate's degrees. These community colleges are offering a "fast-track degree option" in which a student can "cram two years of learning into a single calendar year to earn an associate's degree" (Pego, 1997). According to Pego, survey results indicate that many students like the accelerated courses, which are scheduled in terms of four, six or eight weeks. The students can earn an associate's degree by completing twelve fast-track courses, or by mixing credits from their fast-track courses with regular courses. The administrators at a community college in Texas assumed that most of the students who would choose the accelerated program would be the non-traditional students who were returning to school. However, they discovered that there were also many more eighteen-year-olds signing up for the program because they wanted to "hurry up and get it over." This is understandable, since it could save the traditional student a lot of money (if all the courses transfer to a four-year college).

However, even some of the instructors who helped design the Texas community college's accelerated program expressed some reservations about the program. The biggest problem (which may be a problem that all accelerated programs have in common) is that students may not be learning as much in the shortened period of time if one considers the amount of reading assignments that are possible within that shortened time. As one instructor in the community college program put it, "The old rule of two hours studying out of class for every hour in class simply won't work. That would be six hours of class, an hour for lunch, and 12 hours of homework. That's 19 hours. And on top of that, some of them are trying to work" (Pego).

However, a lot of students do prefer this type of accelerated program; it also seems apparent that it depends on the specific type of accelerated degree program as to whether specific categories of students are for or against them.

INTEGRATING ONLINE COURSE WORK

Many instructors use online group activities in their accelerated courses so as to compensate for the decreased academic contact hours. All of the above-described types of accelerated programs are increasingly incorporating the use of online work into the various courses. As Cooper (2005) notes, group work is particularly effective for non-traditional students, as it helps to draw upon their varied experiences. However, Cooper also argues that adding traditional group work to accelerated adult programs creates additional challenges, because less face-to-face contact is a characteristic of many accelerated courses. Cooper proposes that online group work is an effective alternative to assigning traditional group work, especially for those students with full-time careers, families, and long commutes to and from class. Cooper argues that online discussion groups can effectively replace traditional face-to-face group work. He writes that since discussion groups and learning communities have been suggested as necessary for effective learning, an online format, "especially one of an asynchronous nature, eliminates the need for adult students to return to campus or become confined to others' work or home schedules."

However, online discussion groups are not without criticism, including the absence of interpersonal communication and the possibility of additional miscommunication caused by the medium and format. Cooper also cites other studies that have shown that non-traditional students may feel apprehension of and opposition to technology, but he believes that careful planning and continued evaluation can effectively address the problem. Cooper argues that students actually appreciate the convenience of the online format without extra face-to-face meetings, and he cites yet another study that indicates that shyer students would reflect on and participate more in the online discussions. Although Cooper's study did not address shyness, he writes that students tended to agree that, through an online format, they could reflect more on the assignment. His study also showed that "overall, students believed the addition of the online assignment was appropriate for an accelerated course," and students suggested using online assignments in the future. As the research on and pedagogical methods for accelerated programs increase and improve, it seems likely that they will become more common as an educational model.

DISADVANTAGES

Strother observes that strip-mall students are missing something by not experiencing "the vibrant on-campus experience." He describes the difference in a compelling way when he writes that, on a traditional university campus, there are often thousands of students who create a special community where many activities occur. He writes, "Many controversial subjects like abortion, gay marriage, the military, politics, race, gender, and justice are debated not just at the podium, but on the sidewalks." Strother persuasively drives his point home by observing that "this sidewalk culture of protest, music, art, free-love groups, and even hate groups encourages students to think about life in new ways." He believes that the college campus, with its expansive meeting areas and many green parks, its enormous libraries and special performances and guest speakers, collectively have a tendency to nurture critical thinking and evoke lively debates among students, which is an educational opportunity and process itself. He says that students who attend strip-mall universities miss out on this essential part of college life, which he considers a serious disadvantage. He also notes that many of these non-traditional students attending the strip-mall university have their tuition paid by their employers, and employers do not have a compelling interest in their employees extending their education into an on-campus social life (Strother).

ADVANTAGES

On the other hand, Moore (2005) argues that "traditional students' cafeteria conversations are replaced by talks with spouses at home, the drive to work becomes an opportunity for critical reflection on consumer behavior, and a facilitator is called long after a class ends to discuss principles from a conflict-resolution class that are now being played out in the workplace." Moore also takes exception to Strother's description of accelerated courses as "in a box" courses that compress traditional courses in a possibly inappropriate way. Moore argues that the courses that meet for four hours, one night a week, for five weeks, are not actually traditional fifteen-week courses that have been compressed into five weeks, but instead are the result of careful and deliberate thought; knowledge and content are reconfigured into an optimal format once the accelerated course is designed. He also believes that the structure and content are detailed so that the non-traditional student knows what to expect and when to expect it.

According to Moore, the resulting syllabi should not be taken as restrictive dictates, but rather "as points of departure to be built on over the five weeks by both facilitator and student." The author also emphasizes that students engaged in accelerated learning face the need to combine home, work, and academic responsibilities in ways that academics are only beginning to understand. He concludes that accelerated program students "are expected to shoulder more independent work outside the classroom, and they are required to actively contribute to the learning process." These aspects somewhat compensate for the off-campus circumstances in the non-traditional student's strip-mall education.

ADMINISTRATION & FACULTY DEVELOPMENT

Yet another set of disadvantages that Strother points out is on the administrative and faculty side. He claims that strip-mall universities "also make little investment in their faculty." He describes attending a mandatory "faculty development" seminar, where he was instructed as to how he should take attendance. The institution was evidently concerned about attendance because its program granted three hours of college credit for only twenty hours of academic contact time. The school developed a policy that if a student missed more than two classes in a five-week course, he or she would receive an automatic F. This faculty development meeting was the only contact, aside from an occasional faxing of documents, that Strother had with the university administration. He also notes that there are only adjuncts paid per course at the strip-mall university, and this outsourcing tendency could be negative since, like a third-world factory worker, the teacher becomes much more replaceable and far less influential within the management (or university administration).

Husson and Kennedy observe that accelerated programs challenge traditional thinking about the necessary time it should take to complete college courses. The authors argue that accelerated programs are often intensely scrutinized by various constituencies within more traditional colleges. Because of this, those working in accelerated programs "may experience such skepticism as biased and unfair, especially when critics have little or no experience with adult learners and accelerated programs." They note that mistrust of accelerated programs can demoralize staff and faculty working within accelerated programs, especially if such criticism comes from peers on the same campus. In short, some of the disadvantages to accelerated programs may be more from perception than reality.

TERMS & CONCEPTS

Accelerated Degree Program: A college or university degree program that offers courses in longer sessions in a shorter overall time so as to complete an associate's, bachelor's, or master's degree—or combination of these—sooner than the traditional time allotted for completion.

Adjunct Teacher: A teacher who is essentially an outsourced educator. Adjunct teachers are contracted to teach individual courses, and have no long-term employment contract or career-track relationship with the schools for which they teach.

Cohort-Based Programs: In these programs, students attend classes and field experiences together throughout the degree program, establishing a professional learning community. A cohort approach structures class schedules together and builds collegiality among otherwise diverse groups of teacher-learners.

College Board: The College Board is a not-for-profit membership association whose mission is to provide information about higher education in the United States. It was founded in 1900 and is comprised of more than 5,200 schools, colleges, universities, and other educational organizations. Its best-known programs are the SAT, the PSAT/NMSQT, and the Advanced Placement Program.

Non-traditional Student: Most often, age (especially being over the age of 24) has been the defining characteristic for this population; age acts as a surrogate variable that captures a large, heterogeneous population of adult students who often have family and work responsibilities as well as other life circumstances that can interfere with successful completion of educational objectives.

Strip-Mall University: A small branch of a university that is located in a shopping mall. These small learning centers offer accelerated degree programs for non-traditional students.

Traditional Student: A student who enters college directly from high school, takes courses on a continuous full-time basis, completing a bachelor's degree program in four or five years by age 22 or 23. Generally, traditional students are financially dependent on others, do not have spouses or families, consider the college career to be their primary responsibility, and if employed, are so only on a part-time basis.

Sinclair Nicholas

BIBLIOGRAPHY

Cooper, E. K. (2005, July). Incorporating online discussion groups into an adult accelerated course to facilitate student interaction. *Online Classroom,* 4–7. Retrieved December 14, 2007, from EBSCO online database, Education Research Complete.

Favor, J. (2012). Students' perceptions of long-functioning cooperative teams in accelerated adult degree programs. *Journal of Continuing Higher Education, 60,* 157–164. Retrieved December 5, 2013, from EBSCO online database, Education Research Complete.

Greene, H., & Greene, M. (2003). Accelerated / combined degree programs. *University Business, 6,* 22–23. Retrieved December 11, 2007, from EBSCO online database, Academic Search Premier.

Husson, W., & Kennedy, T. (2003). Developing and maintaining accelerated degree programs within traditional institutions. *New Directions for Adult & Continuing Education, 97,* 51–61. Retrieved December 13, 2007, from EBSCO online database, Academic Search Premier.

Kasworm, C. (2003). From the adult student's perspective: Accelerated degree programs. *New Directions for Adult & Continuing Education, 97,* 17–27. Retrieved December 14, 2007, from EBSCO online database, Academic Search Premier.

Moore, P. (2005). Accelerated programs for students. *Chronicle of Higher Education, 51,* B18. Retrieved December 11, 2007, from EBSCO online database, Academic Search Premier.

Pego, D. (1997). Dallas college studies effects of accelerated degree program. *Community College Week, 9,* 7–8. Retrieved December 14, 2007, from EBSCO online database, Academic Search Premier.

Rawls, J., & Hammons, S. (2012). Assessing undergraduate learning outcomes between accelerated degree and traditional student populations. *Journal of Continuing Higher Education, 60,* 80–92. Retrieved December 5, 2013, from EBSCO online database, Education Research Complete.

Rood, R. (2011). Traditional versus accelerated degree program graduates: A survey of employer preferences. *Journal of Continuing Higher Education, 59,* 122–134. Retrieved December 5, 2013, from EBSCO online database, Education Research Complete.

Singh, P., & Martin, L. (2004). Accelerated degree programs: Assessing student attitudes and intentions. *Journal of Education for Business, 79*, 299–305. Retrieved December 15, 2007, from EBSCO online database, Academic Search Premier.

Strother, S. (2004). The stripped-down college experience. *Chronicle of Higher Education, 51*, B5. Retrieved December 11, 2007, from EBSCO online database, Academic Search Premier.

Taniguchi, H., & Kaufman, G. (2005). Degree completion among non-traditional college students. *Social Science Quarterly; 86*, 912–927. Retrieved December 4, 2007, from EBSCO online database, Academic Search Premier.

SUGGESTED READING

Brandt, C., Boellaard, M., & Zorn, C. (2013). Experiences and emotions of faculty teaching in accelerated second baccalaureate degree nursing programs. *Journal of Nursing Education, 52*, 377–382. Retrieved December 5, 2013, from EBSCO online database, Education Research Complete.

Rood, R. (2011). Traditional versus accelerated degree program graduates: A survey of employer preferences. *Journal of Continuing Higher Education.* 59(3), 122-134.

Varner, B. (2013). Undergraduate perceptions of online coursework. *Journal of Applied Learning Technology, 3*, 16–20. Retrieved December 5, 2013, from EBSCO online database, Education Research Complete.

Voeller, B. (2009). *Accelerated distance learning: The new way to earn your college degree in the twenty-first century* (3rd ed.). Spring Branch, TX: Dedicated Publishing.

VIRTUAL UNIVERSITIES

This article presents information on virtual universities. Virtual universities, also known as online universities or distance education, evolved out of the history of distance education as new technologies became available (Moore, 2003). They have served to open up access to some form of higher education to students who would otherwise not have the opportunity, such as working adults who must balance the responsibilities of work and family (O'Donoghue, Singh, & Dorward, 2001; Peltier, Schibrowsky & Drago, 2007). Larger, nonprofit public institutions tend to be more heavily involved in providing education virtually (Allen & Seaman, 2006). At the same time, total virtual universities more often tend to be for-profit entities (Moore, 2001). While the demand for the online education that virtual universities provide is growing, questions still remain about its legitimacy.

KEYWORDS :Access; Asynchronous Online Instruction; Continuing Education; Distance Education/Learning; Lifelong Learning; Online Education/Learning; Synchronous Online Instruction; Technology; Total Virtual Universities; Virtual Universities

OVERVIEW

IMPORTANCE OF VIRTUAL UNIVERSITIES

Many of those in education generally support the notion that virtual universities provide educational opportunities to students who would otherwise not have them. For instance, O'Donoghue et al. indicated that "access to the Internet allows for distance learning that may encourage people to return to education who would not otherwise due to work or other personal commitments." Likewise, others have said that online education particularly benefits non-traditional students who may have no other educational options (Peltier et al.). Overall, Allen and Seaman noted that "a critical question for those who support online education has been to determine whether online learning is merely a different way to serve the existing student base, or whether it provides opportunities for an entirely new group of students." The latest annual survey sponsored by the Sloan Consortium in fact found that the majority of chief academic officers (65 percent) agree that online education is critical to their institution's long-term strategy (Sloan Consortium, 2011).

Virtual universities are also changing the face of distance education. Moore (2003) noted that "historically, distance education has been regarded as an unimportant and marginal activity by comparison with face-to-face, on-campus forms of teaching and learning." However, enthusiasm for distance education has grown rapidly with "the application of Internet-based information and communications technologies" (Moore).

HISTORICAL DEVELOPMENT OF VIRTUAL UNIVERSITIES

Virtual universities evolved out of the history of distance education as new technologies became available (Moore). According to Boettcher (1996), "distance learning in higher education evolved to provide access. It has provided access where it might not have been, due to constraints of geography, time, family, or money. Distance education in the United States has its roots in the Chautauqua Correspondence College, which was founded in 1881, and the Extension Department at the University of Chicago, which initiated the first university-led distance education effort in 1892 (Moore). Initially courses were designed to be delivered to adult learners via correspondence through postal mail (Moore). While the University of Chicago, which was a private institution, set off the university-led distance education effort, public land-grant universities, such as the Ohio State University and the University of Wisconsin, served to accelerate it (Moore). Another public land-grant institution, the State University of Iowa (now known as Iowa State University) became the first university to deliver educational programs over broadcast television in 1934 (Moore). Later, during the 1980s, the University of Wisconsin had the world's most advanced audioconferencing system (Moore). Finally, the land-grant institution first known as Pennsylvania State College and now known as the Pennsylvania State University was the first to offer a graduate degree in adult education online during the 1990s (Moore). Overall, by the end of the 1990s over 80 percent of public colleges and universities offered courses over the Internet (Moore).

Virtual university courses are designed to be delivered over the Internet (Moore). Both public and private institutions offer online courses (Moore). The University of Phoenix Online and Capella University are two of the more well-known private providers (Moore). Rickards (2000) defined the virtual university or virtual campus as "a set of technology enabled functions making possible interactions between the different groups in the university (student, teaching staff, management and support personnel) without the need to coincide in time or space."

Moore argued that over the course of its history distance education in the United States has not fundamentally changed. The technological mechanisms by which it is delivered may have changed but approaches to teaching and organizational structures have not (Moore). Over time, courses have been delivered first by mail via print and correspondence, then by broadcast and recorded audio and video, next by teleconferencing, and finally via the Internet (Moore). Yet, the basic approach to teaching has not changed and still involves:

> *... a careful deconstruction of content and reassembly in a series of 'lessons' for delivery in text to learners who are challenged in their individual environments to interact with the content to process it into personal knowledge; and that this processing is assisted by an instructor through interaction with each learner in support of that person's independent study (Moore).*

TYPES OF INSTRUCTION

It has been stressed that "distance education requires, by definition, that communication between teacher and learner be mediated by technology" (Moore). The Internet is the technological medium utilized by virtual universities and courses are delivered online. According to Epstein (2006), "technology allows schools to reach a broader student base and to offer their programs according to students' preferences and time constraints." Online instruction at virtual universities can specifically be delivered either synchronously or asynchronously (Epstein). In synchronous online instruction, students and their instructor attend class online at the same time. Asynchronous online instruction is the opposite, and due to the fact that students and their instructor do not have to attend class online at the same time, it has been noted that asynchronous online instruction holds the additional promise that "more people might be able to receive their postsecondary degrees at a time when it might be otherwise impossible" (Epstein). Regarding virtual university instructors, according to Allen and Seaman, schools generally use the same mix of core and adjunct faculty to teach online courses as traditional (face-to-face) courses.

TOTAL VIRTUAL UNIVERSITIES

Total virtual universities differ in the extent to which they offer courses online. Rickards noted that total virtual universities, in which all services are completely delivered online, are the exception and that most institutions—both traditional and non-traditional—are using some combination of technological and conventional means (e.g., face-to-face instruction) to deliver courses. Online-only colleges or total virtual universities tend to be for-profit entities, whereas online segments of traditional colleges are not-for-profit (Moore).

Institutional size is apparently tied to which institutions have virtual segments and to what extent. For instance, according to Allen and Seaman, "the larger the institution, the more likely it is to have developed online courses and online programs." As such, larger institutions, including doctoral/research and master's institutions, tend to enroll more online students. Yet, while the size of the online class at each of the institutions tends to be smaller, associate institutions have the largest *share* of online students because of the absolute number of such institutions enrolling students. Also, in general, small, private, four-year institutions are less likely than public institutions to enroll online learners (Allen & Seaman). Finally, "there is a very strong positive relationship between institutional size and online program offerings: the larger the institution, the more likely it is to have a fully online program, and the more likely it is to have some form of online offering." For example, two-thirds of the largest institutions have fully online programs (Allen & Seaman).

Virtual universities may also be part of an educational system. The Tennessee Board of Regents' Online Degree Program has been rated as one of top virtual university systems in the United States. Not only do all Tennessee Board of Regents (TBR) institutions, including six universities and thirteen community colleges, participate in the system, but they are also joined by twenty-six technology centers (Demoulin, 2005).

CHARACTERISTICS OF VIRTUAL UNIVERSITY STUDENTS

According to Moore, "distance education is exquisitely suited to meet the needs of the adult in search of learning, as it delivers the means of organized formal study within the work or home environment." Distance learning students in fact tend to be mature adult learners, because these students generally have the characteristics that are needed to be a successful distance learner including high motivation, strict discipline, and the ability to work independently (Boettcher, 1996). These students choose to study online because it is a more efficient approach for them than studying in a traditional classroom (Lorenzetti, 2005b). Students who study virtually also often do so to "augment a career need or a desire to learn for other areas of life" (Lorenzetti, 2005b).

One researcher found that online students tend to be on average three years older than traditional students (Lorenzetti, 2005a), although approximately 40 percent of online students are under the age of thirty and about 20 percent are younger than twenty-five (Groux, 2012). In a 2006 study, most online students (80 percent) were undergraduates and over half of all online students largely studied at two-year (associates) institutions (Allen & Seaman). At the same time, Allen and Seaman noted that "the proportion of graduate-level students is slightly higher in online education relative to the overall higher education population." In 2011, sixty percent were employed full-time, and the majority lived within 100 miles of the college in which they enrolled in an online course (Kolowich, 2012). Finally, Groux and Kolowich (2012) note that 70 percent of students who take online course are women; 60 percent are white, about 20 percent are black, and approximately 8 percent identify themselves as Hispanic.

GROWTH IN VIRTUAL UNIVERSITIES

While it has had its ups and downs, according to Foster and Carnevale (2007) "the virtual campus is re-emerging." This resurgence in online education is being fueled by public universities, like the University of North Carolina and the University of Illinois, who are adopting a not-for-profit approach to their virtual divisions (Foster & Carnevale). A survey by the education-consulting firm Eduventures found that the name recognition and geographic dominance of some not-for-profit institutions may actually give them an edge over for-profit institutions in the online education sector (Carnevale, 2007). For instance, according to Eduventures, despite the flexibility of online courses in choosing time and place of study, many students choose to enroll in online programs that are offered by institutions located within the same geographic areas in which they reside (cited in Carnevale; Kolowich). Thus, most online students still want to study near a campus and nonprofit institutions' histories and reputations give them an additional edge nationally (Carnevale).

Demand for online education was growing at a substantially higher rate than was overall enrollment in higher education, and although the rate is slowing slightly, it continues to outpace overall enrollment (Sloan Consortium, 2011). For instance, the although the 10 percent growth rate for online enrollments during the fall of 2010 was the second lowest since 2002, it far exceeded the less than 1 percent growth in overall higher education enrollment. Overall, there was a total enrollment of online students of over 19.5 million in the fall of 2010 (Sloan Consortium).

Various major reasons or events have been identified to explain the onslaught of interest in distance education in general. One event has been the rise of technology and advances that have resulted in the convergence of communication and computing technologies (Boettcher; Rickards). As a result, "multiple, and occasionally seamless, communication links now exist between homes, offices, cars, schools and workplaces" (Boettcher). Another major reason is the necessity of continuing education in today's world where workers must stay up-to-date on emerging skills and developments in their fields (Boettcher; Rickards). Likewise, a major change in people's lifestyles has been a growing focus on lifelong learning, or the "emerging overlap of education, training, work and leisure activity" (O'Donoghue, Singh, & Dorward, 2001). There is also greater demand for access to convenient and flexible education (Rickards). Finally, according to Boettcher, "current models of higher education are very resource-intensive, in terms of people, space, content development, and time for learners." There is a belief, albeit perhaps unfounded, that the new technologies of distance learning may offer a solution to the emerging cost issue (Boettcher). Rickards notes that there is an increasing view of education as a private good. Overall, O'Donoghue, Singh, and Dorward noted that as people's lifestyles become more complex and busy the market for distance learning over the Internet may become broader.

QUESTIONS OF LEGITIMACY

The legitimacy of online programs continues to be a major issue. Hitch (2000) referred to the "prejudices and tensions inherent in educating the adult." One such tension has dealt with whether or not virtual universities can be licensed and accredited (Hitch). Other concerns about quality surfaced as virtual universities came on the scene and included how effective advising and academic support services could be provided to students and whether education acquired through online means would match that provided via traditional means (Johnstone & Krauth, 1996). Moore argues that online institutions or virtual universities can offer college services just as easily over the Internet as traditional institutions do on their physical campuses. For example, libraries and databases can be delivered online

(Moore). Also, the latest annual survey sponsored by the Sloan Consortium found that the majority of chief academic officers continue to rate online learning outcomes to be the same or better than those associated with traditional instruction (Sloan Consortium). This is especially true at the largest institutions (Allen & Seaman). Additionally, according to Peltier et al., various research studies support that online learning can be just as effective as traditional, face-to-face instruction. Yet, Schank argues that virtual university courses "are usually watered-down versions of everyday college courses." Meanwhile, Hitch questioned "whether higher education can fairly evaluate a 21st century institution when using standards from earlier centuries that may be outdated by technology and do not mesh with the population that virtual universities serve."

INSTRUCTOR ROLES & METHODS

One issue that seems to have received much attention in particular regarding virtual universities is the educational process, including methods of teaching and learning as well as the role of the instructor. In 2002, Schank remarked that "we should worry about what kind of education these Virtual Us are going to serve up" (Schank). Regarding methods of teaching, O'Donoghue et al. indicated that "there are strong arguments for and against the asynchronous methods of teaching that virtual universities invite." For instance, some argue that students' speaking skills will suffer under such methods of teaching while others counter that students who may be too intimidated to speak up in a traditional classroom may be more willing to engage online (Barnard, 1999; Westera, 1999 as cited in O'Donoghue et al.).

Some have actually proposed that virtual universities can help promote a kind of new learning (Moore; Schank). One example of this kind of new learning involved the teaching of health care online via a virtual community in which students "learn by doing" (Moore). This type of online collaborative learning and its associated success demonstrate that "the lack of a classroom won't matter." In the virtual education environment, some have also stressed that the role of a professor or lecturer shifts from that of a formal teacher to a facilitator or mentor, who guides students in their independent learning efforts (O'Donoghue et al.). Overall, according to some, online education is "having a profound effect on the future of postsecondary education and is transforming the educational model from an instructor-driven to an interactive and community-driven educational environment in which all students share responsibility for learning outcomes" (Peltier et al).

A 2013 study found, however, that while 97 percent of community colleges offer online courses, only 3 percent of students attending those institutions are enrolled in entirely online degree programs (Fain, 2013). For the most part, students felt they learned better in face-to-face instructional settings, especially in science and foreign language classes.

COST

Another issue circulating about virtual universities deals with the extent to which they help to reduce institutional costs. Rickards stressed that "while some governments and some university managements may still believe that online teaching can reduce institutional costs, the evidence is to the contrary." In testament to the costs associated with virtual education, several universities, such as New York University and Columbia, abandoned their online ventures when enrollments were not sufficient to justify the millions of dollars they invested in them (Foster & Carnevale).

TERMS & CONCEPTS

Asynchronous Online Instruction: Students and their instructor do not have to attend class online at the same time.

Continuing Education: A type of education in which students have some previous educational training but continue their education in order to, for instance, stay up-to-date on emerging skills and developments in their fields.

Distance Education: A type of education in which communication between teacher and learner is mediated by technology.

Lifelong Learning: Deals with the notion that while some learning occurs in independent, ordered fashion (e.g., formal schooling) other learning is ongoing and overlaps with various life activities from work to leisure activities.

Non-traditional Students: Non-traditional students exhibit one or more of the following characteristics: lack of a standard high school diploma; delayed college enrollment, part-time college enrollment, financial independence, and full-time employment; non-traditional students may also have dependents other than a spouse (e.g., children or relatives) and/or be single parents.

Synchronous Online Instruction: Students and their instructor attend class online at the same time.

Total Virtual Universities: Also known as online-only colleges, institutions in which all services are completely delivered online; tend to be for-profit entities.

Virtual University: "A set of technology enabled functions making possible interactions between the different groups in the university (student, teaching staff, management and support personnel) without the need to coincide in time or space".

Marlene Clapp

BIBLIOGRAPHY

Allen, Elaine, & Seaman, Jeff. (2013, January). *Changing Course: Ten Years of Tracking Online Education in the United States*. Retrieved December 21, 2013, from http://onlinelearningsurvey.com.

Allen, I. E., & Seaman, J. (2006). *Making the grade: Online education in the United States, 2006.* Needham, MA: The Sloan Consortium.

Moore, R. (2001). Seven myths about online colleges: A View from Inside. *Connection: New England's Journal of Higher Education & Economic Development, 15*, 34. Retrieved July 27, 2007, from EBSCO Online Database Education Research Complete.

Barnhart, C. L., & Stein, J. (Eds.). (1962). *The American college dictionary.* New York: Random House, Inc.

Boettcher, J. V. (1996, July). *Distance learning: Looking into the crystal ball.* Retrieved August 14, 2007, from http://designingforlearning.info.

Carnevale, D. (2007). Nonprofit institutions could make gains in online education, report says. *Chronicle of Higher Education, 53*, 26-26. Retrieved August 16, 2007, from EBSCO Online Database Education Research Complete.

Cho, M., & Shen, D. (2013). Self-regulation in online learning. *Distance Education, 34*, 290–301. Retrieved December 20, 2013, from EBSCO Online Database Education Research Complete.

Demoulin, D. (2005). Tennessee's regents on-line degree program: A success story. *Education, 126*, 55-59. Retrieved July 27, 2007, from EBSCO Online Database Education Research Complete.

Epstein, P. (2006). Online, campus, or blended learning. *Distance Learning, 3*, 35-37. Retrieved August 16, 2007, from EBSCO Online Database Education Research Complete.

Fain, Paul. (2013, April 23). Only sometimes for online. Retrieved December 21, 2013, from http://insidehighered.com.

Foster, A., & Carnevale, D. (2007). Distance education goes public. *Chronicle of Higher Education, 53*, A49. Retrieved

July 27, 2007, from EBSCO Online Database Education Research Complete.

Groux, Catherine. (2012, July 27). Study analyzes characteristics of online learners. Retrieved December 21, 2013, from http://learninghouse.com.

Hitch, L. (2000). Aren't we judging virtual universities by outdated standards? *Journal of Academic Librarianship, 26*, 21. Retrieved July 27, 2007, from EBSCO Online Database Education Research Complete.

Horn, L. J. (1996). *Non-traditional undergraduates: Trends in enrollment from 1986 to 1992 and persistence and attainment among 1989-90 beginning postsecondary students* (NCES 97578). Washington, DC: U.S. Government Printing Office. (ERIC Document Reproduction Service No. ED402857).

Johnstone, S., & Krauth, B. (1996). Some principles of good practice for the virtual university. *Change, 28*, 38. Retrieved July 27, 2007, from EBSCO Online Database Education Research Complete.

Kaymak, Z., & Horzum, M. (2013). Relationship between online learning readiness and structure and interaction of online learning students. Educational Sciences: Theory & Practice, 13, 1792–1797. Retrieved December 20, 2013, from EBSCO Online Database Education Research Complete.

Kolowich, Steve. (2012, July 25). The online student. Retrieved December 21, 2013, from http://insidehighered.com.

Lorenzetti, J. (2005a). How online students can improve overall student quality. *Distance Education Report, 9*, 8. Retrieved August 17, 2007, from EBSCO Online Database Education Research Complete.

Lorenzetti, J. (2005b). Secrets of online success: Lessons from the community colleges. *Distance Education Report, 9*, 3-6. Retrieved August 17, 2007, from EBSCO Online Database Education Research Complete.

Moore, M. G. (2003). *From Chautauqua to the virtual university: A century of distance education in the United States.* Columbus, OH: The Ohio State University, Center on Education and Training for Employment.

O'Donoghue, J., Singh, G., & Dorward, L. (2001). Virtual education in universities: A technological imperative. *British Journal of Educational Technology, 32*, 511. Retrieved July 27, 2007, from EBSCO Online Database Education Research Complete.

Peltier, J., Schibrowsky, J., & Drago, W. (2007). The interdependence of the factors influencing the perceived quality of the online learning experience: A causal model. *Journal of Marketing Education, 29*, 140-153. Retrieved August 16, 2007, from EBSCO Online Database Education Research Complete.

Rickards, J. (2000). *The virtual campus: Impact on teaching and learning.* Paper presented at the conference of the International Association of Technological University Libraries, Brisbane, Queensland, Australia. (ERIC Document Reproduction Service No. ED447832).

Schank, R. (2002). The rise of the virtual university. *Quarterly Review of Distance Education, 3*, 75-90. Retrieved July 27, 2007, from EBSCO Online Database Education Research Complete.

Sloan Consortium. (2011). Going the distance: Online education in the United States, 2011. Retrieved December 21, 2013, from http://onlinelearningsurvey.com.

Wang, C., Shannon, D. M., & Ross, M. E. (2013). Students' characteristics, self-regulated learning, technology self-efficacy, and course outcomes in online learning. *Distance Education, 34*, 302–323. Retrieved December 20, 2013, from EBSCO Online Database Education Research Complete.

SUGGESTED READING

Carr-Chellman, A. (2006). Desperate technologists: Critical issues in e-learning and implications for higher education. *Journal of Thought, 41*, 95-115. Retrieved August 16, 2007, from EBSCO Online Database Education Research Complete.

Christo-Baker, E. A. (2004). *Distance education as a catalyst for change in higher education.* Paper presented at the annual conference of the Association of Small Computer Users in Education, Myrtle Beach, SC. (ERIC Document Reproduction Service No. ED490098).

Guasch, T., Espasa, A., Alvarez, I. M., & Kirschner, P. A. (2013). Effects of feedback on collaborative writing in an online learning environment. *Distance Education, 34*, 324–338. Retrieved December 20, 2013, from EBSCO Online Database Education Research Complete.

Kuboni, O. (2013). The preferred learning modes of online graduate students. *International Review of Research in Open & Distance Learning, 14*, 228–249. Retrieved December 20, 2013, from EBSCO Online Database Education Research Complete.

Smith, R. (2016). Recruiting and serving online students at a traditional university. *College and University.* 91(3), 67-74.

Stallings, D. (2000). The virtual university: Legitimized at century's end: Future uncertain for the new millennium. *Journal of Academic Librarianship, 26*, 3. Retrieved July 27, 2007, from EBSCO Online Database Education Research Complete.

Stallings, D. (2001). The virtual university: Organizing to survive in the 21st century. *Journal of Academic Librarianship, 27*, 3. Retrieved July 9, 2007, from EBSCO Online Database Education Research Complete.

Stallings, D. (2002). Measuring success in the virtual university. *Journal of Academic Librarianship, 28* (1/2), 47. Retrieved July 27, 2007, from EBSCO Online Database Education Research Complete.

NON-TRADITIONAL MINORITY STUDENTS

Non-traditional minority students are a growing phenomenon in colleges and universities in the United States. As society becomes more global and diverse, individuals seeking Higher Education are requiring more complex services due to differences in culture and demographic shifts. This article provides a general overview of the non-traditional minority student. For the purposes of this article, the term "non-traditional minority student" will represent any individual who is underrepresented based on gender and/or racial/ethnic issues.

KEYWORDS: Adult Learners; Cultural Diversity; Demographics; Globalization; Life-long Learner; Minority Student; Non-Traditional Student; Postsecondary Education; Socioeconomic Status; Title III; Traditional Student

OVERVIEW

Since the founding of the United States, its citizens have placed an emphasis on education. The founders believed that the strength of a country was dependent on a well-educated workforce (Ely, 1997; Ntiri, 2001; Schuetze & Slowey, 2002; U.S. Department of Education, 2006). Therefore, it was believed that individuals educated in the basic skills (reading, writing, and arithmetic) provided the workforce with skilled employees, allowing the United States to become an independent country. In other words, a skilled and educated workforce allows a country to establish and maintain a viable society which leads to economic independence. In current times, the United States continues to place an emphasis on having a well-educated work force (Ely; Ntiri; Schuetze & Slowey; U.S. Department of Education). In fact, the democratic process is dependent upon an educated workforce to sustain the economy (U.S. Department of Education).

One of mechanisms providing an educated workforce throughout the world is colleges and universities. In the United States, the changes in the demographics of society are being recognized as a new challenge for colleges and universities. As such, these demographic changes will significantly influence the Higher Education system over the next 20 years (Ely; Miller & Lu, 2003; Ntiri; Schuetze & Slowey; U.S. Department of Education).

EFFECTS OF DEMOGRAPHIC CHANGES

Demographic changes affecting colleges and universities include an increase in the number of individuals reaching retirement age; the growing minority population; gender issues; and, technological changes which are causing a need for older individuals to return to classes in order to update and/or maintain skill sets. One of the most significant changes occurring is the retirement of the baby boom generation. As this generation retires or becomes eligible to retire, the workforce will need to replace these individuals. Many of the baby boom generation jobs require education beyond high school (U.S. Department of Education). Additionally, as the average lifespan of Americans continues to increase, new jobs will develop in response to meeting the needs of these individuals.

MINORITIES

As the minority population continues to grow faster than the white population, educational systems will need to continue to be flexible and learn about the diversity of the community they serve. In other words, the educational system will have to respond to the differences such as values and the obstacles faced by single parent homes.

GENDER

A significant change in college and university student populations is related to gender. In the early twenty-first century, more than half of all college degrees, undergraduate and graduate, are being awarded to women. According to the National Center for Education Statistics, in the 2009–10 school year, women earned 57.4 percent of bachelor's degrees, 62.6 percent of master's degrees, and 53.3 percent of doctorates (U.S. Department of Education).

EFFECTS OF TECHNOLOGY

Another change is the technological advancements which have led to the globalization of society. The rapid technological developments and advancements have increased the need to have a highly trained work force that is able to use and access knowledge quickly to solve problems, versus rote memorization of solutions (U.S. Department of Education). As such, information can be accessed twenty-four hours a day from anywhere in the world. The rapid and immediate exchange of information will present an ongoing challenge to colleges and universities who are used to educating individuals in traditional brick and mortar buildings (U.S. Department of Education).

While all of the issues mentioned are simultaneously impacting the delivery of Higher Education, an issue that continues to be debated is that of the minority student. Layered on top of this issue is the individual who is considered to be a minority (i.e., gender, racial and/or ethnic differences) and a non-traditional student. This paper will provide an overview of the non-traditional minority student enrolling in postsecondary education.

THE HIGHER EDUCATION SYSTEM IN THE UNITED STATES

In terms of education, much of American society is focused on advancements and changes in the K-12 curriculum. A report issued by the Secretary of Education's Commission on the Future of Higher Education stated that the United States set the standard for Higher Education (U.S. Department of Education). For instance, the First Morrill Act created land-grant universities, and the G. I. Bill made Higher Education accessible for many returning servicemen from World War II. More recent changes have included the growth of community colleges. As many universities adopt admissions standards, community colleges have allowed many individuals to pursue educational opportunities beyond high school (U.S. Department of Education).

Education is considered a change agent for individuals from diverse backgrounds. It is recognized that not everyone should attend a university (U.S. Department of Education). However, a growing position is that everyone should receive some type of education beyond high school. Options include community colleges, technical schools, and/or trade schools. Again, the need for an educated workforce is vital for the American economy to be sustained. Higher Education administrators are recognizing that postsecondary education is not only for the academically elite but for everyone.

Education should be an opportunity to for any individual, regardless of socioeconomic status, racial and/or ethnic diversity, or gender, to gain the skills necessary to be an independent and successful member of a community and nation. In other words, education provides

the individual with the tools necessary to achieve social mobility (U.S. Department of Education). Higher Education should be thought of as a mechanism to allow each individual to pursue educational goals which allow a stable and viable economic system.

TITLE III

The purpose of this essay is not to provide in-depth knowledge of all of the laws and federal programs available to minority or non-traditional students. However, a brief discussion of the Title III program is warranted. Title III was originally authorized in 1965 as a federally funded program which assists colleges and universities in the provision of educational opportunities to students who are low-income and/or minority students (Slark, Umdenstock, & Obler, 1997). In the late 1960s, students who were either low-income and/or minority were defined as non-traditional students.

Slark et al. Title III is divided into two distinct parts. Part A funds are used to allow low-income minority students educational opportunities and Part B funds were designated to provide funding to predominately black Higher Education institutions. Colleges and universities must apply for the funds and demonstrate that the institution serves an underrepresented group (Slark et al.).

Slark et al. stated that Title III funds have been used to cause an organizational change in Higher Education. This change has assisted Higher Education in recognizing that educating small numbers of individuals were not as effective as educating other members of society. A byproduct of this change is the reorganization of institutions of Higher Education realizing that many students are becoming lifelong learners as opposed to just maintaining the traditional institutional values (Slark et al.).

DEMOGRAPHIC CHANGES

Demographic changes are causing a shift in the cultural makeup of the United States. In terms of the Higher Education system, the demographic changes along with the changes in workforce (i.e., retirement, shortages in health care, education, etc.) are forcing the Higher Education system to examine practice and policy for individuals who are minority and/or non-traditional students.

In terms of education, the National Center for Education Statistics (NCES) has shown that participation rates among individuals who represent ethnic minority groups are growing faster than those of the white population. It is predicted that this shift in student demographics will continue to occur over the coming decades.

In terms of enrollment in colleges and universities, the NCES projects an increase between 2010 and 2021 of 4 percent for white students; 25 percent for black students; 42 percent for Hispanic students; 20 percent for Asian or Pacific Islander students; and 1 percent for American Indian or Alaska Native students (U.S. Department of Education).

In addition to changing demographics, socioeconomic gaps appear to be widening as well. NCES reported that in 2000, 15 percent of children in the United States aged 5 to 17 were living in poverty, while in 2011, 21 percent were; also in 2011, 39 percent of black children and 34 percent of Hispanic children under age 18 were living in poverty, versus 13 percent of white children (U.S. Department of Education). Children who grow up in poverty are negatively impacted in terms of learning due to mental, physical, and behavioral development risks. In addition, many minority students do not complete high school, which is the greatest barrier to continuing on to Higher Education (Slark et al.).

In terms of the non-traditional student enrollment figures, the NCES has projected an increase in enrollment between 2010 and 2021 at 10 percent for students who are 18 to 24 years old, 20 percent for students who are 25 to 34 years old, and 25 percent for students who are 35 years old and over (U.S. Department of Education). In 2006, the Commission on the Future of Higher Education stated that 16 percent of students who are 18 to 22 years old were enrolled full-time at the undergraduate level; 40 percent attended school part-time; 40 percent attended two-year institutions; 40 percent were older than 25 years; and 58 percent were older than 22 years (U.S. Department of Education).

DIFFERENCES BETWEEN TRADITIONAL & NON-TRADITIONAL STUDENTS

A traditional student is typically defined as an individual who has graduated from high school; is between 18 and 22 years old; has a family background of having some experience with Higher Education; and attends a four-year university as a full-time student. The literature uses many different terms, such as "adult learner," "returning student," "mature student," or "life-long learner" to describe the non-traditional student (Ely; Ntiri; Schuetze & Slowey). Basically, the non-traditional student is an individual who is older than 24 years old; has returned to school; attends school part time or full time; and/or is someone who is improving his or her job skills (Ely; Miller & Lu; U.S. Department of Education). Others have defined the non-traditional learner as an individual who does not enter postsecondary schooling immediately after high school graduation or an individual from a low socioeconomic background (Schuetze & Slowey).

Schuetze and Slowey proposed that the non-traditional student is an individual who represents different populations (i.e., cultural diversity, gender, socioeconomic status) and different model of participation (part-time; online learning). In adopting this viewpoint, one can begin to understand why the non-traditional student is a growing student population in colleges and universities.

In summary, the demographics and the growing number of individuals returning to Higher Education are changing the college and university campus. The addition of being from a minority group causes a layering effect which is complex and multifaceted. In order to grasp the bigger issue, the reader must understand issues faced by the non-traditional student as well as the minority student before one can synthesize the information into challenges faced by the non-traditional minority student.

ISSUES FACED BY THE NON-TRADITIONAL STUDENT

Individuals who are considered non-traditional face many different issues in comparison to the traditional student. However, there are positive and negative influences that affect the non-traditional student. As a positive influence, non-traditional students are often very goal oriented, highly motivated, and independent learners (Ely; Miller & Lu; Ntiri). Non-traditional students seek out resources that will allow them to capitalize on opportunities that many traditional students do not seek. In other words, non-traditional learners appear to highly value a postsecondary education.

In addition to characteristics that are considered important in achieving Higher Educational goals, negative influences include stresses that are very different from the traditional student. For example, educational outcomes are influenced by family stresses, workplace demands, and generational differences (Ely; Miller & Lu; Ntiri). The non-traditional student is often a female head of household with children or the individual may have to work full-time in order to attend school part-time or on an intermittent basis.

ISSUES FACED BY NON-TRADITIONAL MINORITY STUDENTS

Johnson-Bailey (1999) as cited in Ntiri reported several factors that influence the success of African American non-traditional students. Factors included having access to African American faculty, peers, and funding. Each of these issues is in relation to the barriers often found in terms of race, gender, and socioeconomic status.

In spite of the changes in demographics, many caution that educational gaps will continue to exist between non-traditional minorities and other ethnic and/or gender groups (U.S. Department of Education). Ntiri stated additional factors that can affect non-traditional minorities' success in Higher Education. These factors include lower socioeconomic status; higher poverty rates for African Americans and Hispanics; unfavorable learning environments; and lack of funding sources for actual costs (Ntiri).

Additional factors that influence the obstacles faced by minority groups include lack of access to information about colleges and the opportunities offered to minority groups; ongoing financial barriers; and unfortunately, the lack of academic preparation or rigor of preparation (Ntiri; U.S. Department of Education). In terms of information and opportunities, minorities often do not have the financial means to visit campuses and/or make telephone or e-mail contacts. While many minority students do have access to computers and the Internet at school, they may not have the access to the Internet and information at home. If individuals do have access to public computers (e.g., in public libraries), then the individual is limited by what can or cannot be downloaded and/or printed.

Should the individual be successful in enrolling in a college and/or university, they may not graduate. Statistics again indicate that while more minorities are attending college, they are not closing the gap in terms of graduation rates (U.S. Department of Education). The Secretary of Education's Commission on the Future of Higher Education stated, "While about one-third of whites have obtained bachelor's degrees by age 25-29, for example, just 18 percent of blacks and 10 percent of Latinos in the same age cohort have earned degrees by that time."

Although financial aid does exist to offset college and universities expenditures, many of the programs are late in providing information regarding eligibility amounts. This creates a problem for an individual who wants to attend school but due to the late notice about financial aid chooses to pursue other opportunities. Of course, this affects enrollment rates for minorities and can affect retention rates as well.

ISSUES FACED BY HIGHER EDUCATION INSTITUTIONS

In response to changing demographics, colleges and universities must become flexible in trying new ideas and course delivery methods to attract and retain the non-traditional minority learner (U.S. Department of Education). The literature states that many non-traditional students enroll in Higher Education institutions to obtain additional certification and/or training (U.S. Department of Education). Thus, many non-traditional students are not degree seeking but information seeking in order to advance in their respective careers. Of course, this can be perceived negatively by faculty who think that attendance in a college or university program should always have the goal of obtaining a degree.

Ntiri states that colleges and universities are change agents for many individuals in the pursuit of the American dream. Thus, colleges and universities need to become flexible in the giving and sharing of information through less traditional methods. An example would be the use of web-based instruction that allows access to instruction anytime from anywhere.

FUTURE IMPLICATIONS FOR THE NON-TRADITIONAL MINORITY STUDENT

The workforce of tomorrow must be able to meet the challenges to remain competitive on a global level. This means that Higher Education must focus on providing educational opportunities that allow individuals to become flexible consumers of the opportunities available in postsecondary institutions.

Higher Education must adapt and capitalize on all citizens as well as retaining and attracting individuals who desire the knowledge and skills to advance his or her social standing (U.S. Department of Education). As technology advances, baby boomers retire, and as the demographics continue to shift, Higher

Education must begin to innovate in terms of attracting and retaining non-traditional minority students.

The business world can provide important lessons in terms of the demise of companies that failed to heed changes both within and outside of the organization (U.S. Department of Education). To avoid becoming an outdated institution, there must be a willingness for institutions of Higher Education to capitalize on the changes in how and with whom information is exchanged. The thought that universities are made up of certain age groups and ethnicities is changing and reflect the changes in society as a whole.

In fact, the Secretary's Commission on the Future of Higher Education report cautions that the United States is losing its foothold as the leader in Higher Education practices. Many other countries are beginning to alter courses and the delivery of courses to meet the needs the global economy. As our economy changes, the need will grow for an educated workforce that embraces new ideologies. The responsibility for making changes in the Higher Education system lies with colleges and universities, state and federal lawmakers, accreditation agencies, businesses, and individuals themselves (U.S. Department of Education).

The future economy will be driven by knowledge or "intellectual capital" (U.S. Department of Education). As a result, individuals will need some type of postsecondary experience in order to increase earning potential over their lifetimes. Thus, colleges and universities will continue to directly influence new generations in the achievement of the American dream (U.S. Department of Education). However, without alternatives for individuals considered to be non-traditional minorities, then colleges and universities will become elitist institutions. This in turn could stagnate the economy as a whole.

As the world's economy becomes more global, the workforce demands will increase for individuals who have some type of postsecondary training. One of the biggest benefits of a postsecondary education is the increase in personal income. In terms of lifetime earning potential, an individual with a bachelor's degree will earn twice as much as an individual with only a high school diploma (U.S. Department of Education).

The Commission on the Future of Higher Education report predicts that jobs that rely only on on-the-job training will decline, while jobs in health care, education, engineering, and computer science will become the jobs in greatest need of an educated workforce (U.S. Department of Education). Again, not tapping into the non-traditional minority population will cause economic upheaval in terms of supply and demand. In other words, the socioeconomic gaps will widen. As such, this will do nothing to stimulate an economy that is rapidly becoming reliant on knowledge-based work.

CONCLUSIONS

As the makeup of society continues to change, Higher Education must continue to address the challenges non-traditional minority students will bring to the university setting. This is especially true for individuals who are underrepresented racial and/or ethnic groups, age groups, and gender groups. As these groups become the majority, these same individuals will make up the majority of the workforce. If universities do not find innovative ways to continue the rich tradition of building and sustaining a highly educated workforce, then the economy will suffer, and for the first time in recent history, the United States will have less educated citizens than the rest of the developed world.

TERMS & CONCEPTS

Adult Learners: An adult learner is a term that is used to describe a non-traditional learner.

Cultural Diversity: Cultural diversity is how an individual's values, norms, beliefs, etc. differ from another cultural group.

Demographics: Demographics are population characteristics shared by groups of people.

Globalization: Globalization is the worldwide connection of people and places as a result of advances in transport, communication, and information technologies that causes political, economic, and cultural convergence.

Life-long Learner: A life-long learner is an individual who returns to formal (i.e., education) and informal (i.e., conferences) educational settings in order to gain new knowledge or to update skills.

Minority Student: A minority student is a student from a racial or ethnic group that makes up less than half the population at large.

Non-traditional Student: The non-traditional student is an individual who is older than twenty-four years old; who has returned to school; attends school part time or full time; and/or is someone who is improving his or her job skills.

Postsecondary Education: Postsecondary education is education beyond high school, typically provided by colleges and universities.

Socioeconomic Status: The socioeconomic status represents an individuals' income status.

Title III: Title III was originally authorized in 1965 as a federally funded program which assists colleges and universities in the provision of educational opportunities to students who are low-income and/or minority students.

Traditional Student: A traditional student is an individual who has graduated from high school; is somewhere between eighteen and twenty-two years old; has a family background of having some experience with Higher Education; and attends a four-year university as a full-time student.

Kerri Phillips

Bibliography

Clark, L. (2012). When non-traditional is traditional: A faculty dialogue with graduating community college students about persistence. *Community College Journal of Research & Practice, 36,* 511-519. Retrieved December 23, 2013, from EBSCO online database Education Research Complete.

Ely, E. (1997). The non-traditional student. Paper presented at the American Association of Community Colleges Annual Conference (77th, Anaheim, CA, April 12-15).

Exposito, S., & Bernheimer, S. (2012). Non-traditional students and institutions of Higher Education: A conceptual framework. *Journal of Early Childhood Teacher Education, 33,* 178-189. Retrieved December 23, 2013, from EBSCO online database Education Research Complete.

Miller, M., & Lu, M.Y. (2003). Serving non-traditional students in e-learning environments: Building successful communities in the virtual campus. *International Council for Education Media, 40*(1/2), 163-170.

Ntiri, D. (2001). Access to Higher Education for non-traditional students and minorities in a technology-focused society. *Urban Education, 36,* 129-144. Retrieved December 13, 2007, from EBSCO online database Education Research Complete.

Schuetze, H., & Slowey, M. (2002). Participation and exclusion: A comparative analysis of non-traditional students and lifelong learners in Higher Education. *Higher Education, 44,* 309-327. Retrieved December 13, 2007, from EBSCO online database Education Research Complete.

Slark, J., Umdenstock, L., & Obler, S. (1997). The case for Title III. Rancho Santiago Community College, Santa Ana, CA. Office of Research, Planning, and Resource Development.

U.S. Department of Education, Commission on the Future of Higher Education. (2006). *A test of leadership: Charting the future of U.S. Higher Education.* Retrieved December 13, 2007, from http://ed.gov.

U.S. Department of Education, National Center for Education Statistics. (2012). *Fast facts: Degrees conferred by sex and race.* Retrieved December 23, 2013, from http://nces.ed.gov.

U.S. Department of Education, National Center for Education Statistics. (2013a). *The condition of education.* Retrieved December 23, 2013, from http://nces.ed.gov.

U.S. Department of Education, National Center for Education Statistics. (2013b). *Projections of education statistics to 2021.* U.S. Department of Education. Retrieved December 23, 2013, from http://nces.ed.gov.

Wyatt, L. G. (2011). Non-traditional student engagement: Increasing adult student success and retention. *Journal of Continuing Higher Education, 59,* 10-20. Retrieved December 23, 2013, from EBSCO online database Education Research Complete.

Suggested Reading

Cross, K. P., & Zusman, A. (1977). The needs of non-traditional learners and the responses of non-traditional programs. Berkeley: University of California.

Espinoza, P. & Espinoza, C. (2012). Supporting the 7th year undergraduate: Responsive leadership at a Hispanic-serving institution. *Journal of Cases in Educational Leadership.* 15(1), 32-50.

Nesbit, T. (2001). Extending the boundaries: Graduate education to non-traditional learners. *Journal of Continuing Higher Education, 49,* 2–10.

Parnham, J. (2001). Lifelong learning: A model for increasing the participation of non-traditional adult, *Journal of Further & Higher Education, 25,* 57-65. Retrieved December 13, 2007, from EBSCO online database Education Research Complete.

Ross-Gordon, J. M. (2011). Research on adult learners: Supporting the needs of a student population that is no longer non-traditional. *Peer Review, 13,* 26-29. Retrieved December 23, 2013, from EBSCO online database Education Research Complete.

Sandler, M. (2000, April). A focal examination of integration, commitment, and academic performance: Three subsystems from the integrated model of student persistence with sociostructural background variable effects. Paper presented at the annual meeting of the American Educational Research Association, New Orleans, LA.

Sierra, C., & Folger, T. (2003). Building a dynamic online learning community among adult learners. *Educational Media International, 40*(1/2), 49-62, Retrieved December 13, 2007, from EBSCO online database Education Research Complete.

Weil, S. (1986). Non-traditional learners within traditional Higher Education institutions: Discovery and disappointment, *Studies in Higher Education, 11,* 219-235. Retrieved December 13, 2007, from EBSCO online database Education Research Complete.

Wladis, C., Hachey, A., & Conway, K. (2015). The representation of minority, female, and non-traditional stem majors in the online environment at community colleges: A nationally representative study. *Community College Review.* 43(1), 89-114.

NON-TRADITIONAL OLDER STUDENTS

Generally, "non-traditional student" refers to students who are the first generation in their families to attend college; in other instances it is used synonymously with students of color, students with disabilities, or students from disadvantaged socioeconomic backgrounds. This paper discusses changes in the U.S. higher education student population and develops a clear profile of the non-traditional older student by compiling the information and findings from various studies that have specifically targeted this category of student. As an extension of the student profile, the studies are also used to discover what issues and concerns most affect the non-traditional student. The article examines the largest and most common obstacles non-traditional older students encounter when trying to earn a college degree. It concludes by analyzing the most relevant aspects of the educational policies and systems currently in place, points out how these policies are often incompatible with the non-traditional student profile, and makes recommendations for policy adjustments to better complement the needs and problems common to non-traditional students.

KEYWORDS: Career Counseling; Council for Adult and Experiential Learning (CAEL); Intrinsic Motivation; National Center for Education Statistics (NCES); Non-traditional Student; Telecourse; Traditional Student; Tuition Waiver

OVERVIEW
DEFINING "NON-TRADITIONAL STUDENT"
In educational literature, the term "non-traditional student" is often used so broadly that it can refer to quite different categories of students. The term is sometimes used to refer to students who are the first generation in their families to attend college; in other instances it is used synonymously with students of color, students with disabilities, or students from disadvantaged socioeconomic backgrounds (Bundy & Smith, 2004). The term is also occasionally used to mean the same as "gifted children" (Setting Students on a new path, 2007). Because the term has been used to describe so many different groups or categories of students, we should first narrow our definition to focus on what is actually the central definition for "non-traditional student." For the purpose of this paper, the term "non-traditional student" will be limited to describe "those who are older than 24 years of age and who may have dependents, be financially independent, and attend college on a part-time basis" (Bundy & Smith).

This definition centers on students who have already been working in full-time jobs, typically for at least a few years, and have decided to re-enter formal education so as to gradually earn a college degree, even as they continue meeting their various responsibilities of work and family. This definition can also include mothers who do not work outside the home because they provide full-time care for children. These women have committed to gradually earning a degree to increase their employment opportunities once their children become less dependent. So, a non-traditional student is older than a traditional student and attends school while also working and/or taking care of dependents. Non-traditional students may be full time students, but they are most often part-time students since they usually cannot manage a full-time course load while simultaneously caring for family members or working. However, in the "past few decades, paid employment among college students has become increasingly common," and this is a trend that may coincide with the growth in the number of non-traditional student enrollments (Taniguchi & Kaufman, 2005).

It might seem upon first impression that the above-defined group of students represents a relatively minor portion of the overall number of students attending college today. Surprisingly, some of the educational surveys claim that over half of the nation's students today are aged twenty-five or older, married, or have children—meaning they fit into the non-traditional student category. This has also been a growth trend for several decades. As Taniguchi and Kaufman note:

> ...while the enrollment of students aged 24 or younger grew by 51 percent between 1970 and 2000, the increase for older students was about three times as large (National Center for Education Statistics (NCES, 2002a). In 1999-2000, 40 percent of all enrollees were in their mid-20s or older, with a large proportion of them attending part time and having dependents.

Thus, the number of non-traditional students has grown until it has become either the majority of college students, or very close to the majority, and it seems likely that this trend will continue. Considering that this trend has been increasing for decades, educators, counselors, and educational institutions should endeavor to create an accurate profile of non-traditional students. The first step in doing so is to ask some important questions: what is the typical life situation for non-traditional students, what motivates them, what are their concerns, what needs do they have, and what are their common perspectives on college education?

PROFILING THE NON-TRADITIONAL STUDENT: SAMPLE STUDIES

Chao and Good (2004) performed a qualitative study that they assert yielded a theoretical model of non-traditional college students' perspectives on college education. They also noted that "very little research has investigated the counseling needs of non-traditional students. In fact, the profession has not yet clearly identified the reasons that non-traditional students enroll in college, nor adequately described their perspectives of the college experience" (Chao & Good). This lack of clarifying the motives and common difficulties of non-traditional students was the impetus for their relatively small study (consisting of about fifty participants).

The authors used questionnaires and held lengthy interviews with the non-traditional students in their study, after which they compiled what is essentially a profile of the non-traditional student. Their findings showed that a "dynamic interaction among several factors was central to the participants' perceptions of pursuing college education." Chao and Good write that "central to the interaction was a sense of hopefulness that participants held toward their decision, struggles, and perceptions about the future." The authors also believe that this core category of hopefulness "critically influenced five other themes: motivation, financial investment, career development, life transition, and support systems" (Chao & Good). Apparently due to their hopefulness, non-traditional students have a tendency to actively manage their education, employment, family, and interpersonal relationships. The authors of the study conclude that non-traditional students also actively integrate their college education into their career development; they conclude:

> In this study, some people pursued college education because they 'felt stuck with their current jobs.' Other participants intended to change career goals via college education. They saw their degrees as facilitating career development (Chao & Good).

CAREER MOTIVATIONS

Many non-traditional students have a very strong career development motive behind their decision to earn a degree. Such a statement may seem obvious; it may seem that all students enroll in order to develop a good career, but we should consider whether there is a relevant difference of profile between non-traditional and traditional students that creates a difference in their motives for attending college. For example, traditional students enter college straight from high school, often have no idea what they want to major in, frequently join fraternities and sororities, and otherwise extensively engage in abundant social lives. This difference may cause traditional students, who are between the ages of 18 and 23, not to be as concerned with career development compared to their older classmates.

A study that Bye et al. (2007) carried out supports this idea; their study used a larger group consisting of 300 students. The study was carried out in a 2-1 ratio wherein there were twice as many non-traditional students in the study than there were traditional students

(Bye et al.). The authors observe that, "whereas younger students interacted primarily with peers and in peer-related activities, older students were less involved in campus activities and more likely to be involved in caring for family" (Bye et al.). They also noted that a student may have less intrinsic motivation if the student "simply takes on a predetermined role from a script written by others, such as young undergraduates might do when following their parents' desire that they study in a particular field" (Bye et al.). The authors' research revealed that non-traditional students had higher levels of intrinsic motivation to learn than did traditional students (Bye et al.), and this is probably related to their strongly career-oriented motivations.

In another study, Bauman, Wang, DeLeon, Kafentzis, Zavala-Lopez, and Lindsey (2004) created a questionnaire that requested reasons why the non-traditional student decided to enroll in a college course program; the results correspond to the Chao and Good study: the number one reason given was for the sake of career advancement. The respondents gave specific answers such as "to be more marketable in a competitive job world" and "career burnout after fifteen years" (Bauman et al.). These reasons match the Chao and Good study, in which some respondents said they felt stuck in their current jobs. All of these responses indicate just how important career objectives are for non-traditional students.

SELF-IMPROVEMENT

Two more motivating factors were evident in the Bauman et al. (2004) study, that of "self-improvement," which was the second most frequently given reason, and "family," which was the third most frequently given reason. The Bauman et al. study also ascertains which services the schools should offer as the most beneficial and needed for non-traditional students. Corresponding to the above-described primary motivation of non-traditional students, the most desired service was career-counseling service, with 76% of the survey respondents saying they would either be likely or very likely to use that service. Some of the other highly ranked services also indicate something about the non-traditional student's profile. The second highest ranking was for stress management workshops, at 57%, and financial aid workshops, at 53%. Other revealing findings, similar to the above rankings (from 53% to 40%), indicate a need for time management workshops, study skills workshops, personal

counseling, financial assistance for child care, and support groups for returning students (Bauman et al.).

The Bauman study demonstrates a marked difference between the lifestyles of a traditional and non-traditional student. For example, it seems improbable that traditional students would highly rank support groups or financial assistance with child-care services. In fact, the Bye et al study found that only two of the traditional students had a child to support, whereas 40% of the non-traditional group had children to support (Bye et al.). Also, 68% of traditional students reported their parents as a primary source of income, whereas 95% of non-traditional students were either self-supporting, funded through loans, scholarships, etc., or were supported by a spouse.

These studies help create an accurate idea of who non-traditional students are, and what life is generally like for most of them. All educators and counselors should be aware of the characteristics that form the non-traditional student profile, and consider how educational institutions might provide better services for non-traditional students.

BARRIERS FOR NON-TRADITIONAL STUDENTS

Taniguchi and Kaufman note that non-traditional students have received only limited attention in educational attainment research, even though these students have a growing presence in colleges across the nation. The authors say that, "among non-traditional students who enrolled in 1989-1990 with the intention of obtaining a bachelor's degree, only 31 percent had earned one by 1994, relative to 54 percent of their traditional counterparts" (Taniguchi & Kaufman). They then note that "previous research suggests that factors such as part-time enrollment and the lack of access to financial assistance significantly explain the college attainment gap between non-traditional and traditional students, while their family characteristics have relatively limited explanatory power" (Taniguchi & Kaufman).

PART-TIME STATUS

Though far fewer non-traditional students earn a degree within five years, this finding should not be surprising since far more non-traditional students attend school only part time, meaning it could take them ten years instead of four years to get through a degree program. However, the authors allude to studies that show a correlation between being a part-time student and not completing a degree program *at all,* and this should cause concern among educators and educational institutions. Additional support of this fact can be found in a report published by the National Center for Education Statistics (2002), which found that, indeed, adult learners are more likely to leave post-secondary education without earning a degree (cited in Compton et al., 2006).

One example of a negative factor is that prolonged enrollment interrupted by periods of absence from school can hamper the continuity of students' learning, and this can make courses that progress from basic to increasingly advanced material much more difficult. These kinds of educational disruptions can be an obstacle to degree completion. Also, Taniguchi and Kaufman note that non-traditional students often have lower interaction with their instructors and fellow students outside classrooms—a characteristic we have already seen in the profile—and this can lessen their support system for getting help when problems arise.

Additionally, the length of time it takes non-traditional students to finish their degree programs can simply be too discouraging for some Researchers point out other major obstructions that non-traditional students encounter on their path to obtaining a degree.

FINANCIAL CONSIDERATIONS

For example, the very definition of a "non-traditional student," as established above, forms the "federal lines of demarcation between students who are dependent on their parents and those whose personal income alone is considered by the financial aid system" (Hart, 2003). Consequently, non-traditional students do not have the same financial aid opportunities that the federal system and the educational institutions provide traditional students, and this also means that the current system may be unfair, or is at least causing unnecessary hardship for the older half of today's college students. Non-traditional students are usually not eligible to apply for financial assistance programs such as scholarships, assistantships, tuition waivers and student loans, and this makes financial hardship one of the bigger barriers for the non-traditional student. Research indicates that financial aid probably helps increase educational outcomes because it lifts some of the student's financial burden and allows him or her more time for studying, completing assignments, researching or otherwise concentrating on important academic activities. According to Taniguchi and Kaufman:

Financial aid has built-in incentives to encourage its recipients to maintain high grades and work toward the timely completion of their education. Therefore, part-time students' degree completion is also hindered by their exclusion from financial aid.

FAMILY RESPONSIBILITIES

Another factor is family care. The Bauman et al study showed that 40% of the non-traditional students had children to care for. According to Taniguchi and Kaufman, one additional infant or toddler decreases the odds of degree completion by about 50% for *both* genders. Juxtaposing these two sets of statistics gives us good reason to believe that 20% of non-traditional students do not complete degrees because their infants need so much attention and time that, as parents, they cannot also find the time to attend school (Taniguchi & Kaufman). That is probably why such a high percentage of non-traditional students in the Bauman et al study highly ranked the need for financial assistance for child-care services.

Older students have more complex life circumstances and therefore need personal assistance that differs from traditional students. The added financial responsibilities of older students, as well as their necessarily more varied attendance patterns, mean that a system predicated on a model intended for traditional students sometimes does not serve them very well.

One example is that the financial aid system was designed and implemented for traditional students who depend upon their parents' resources. Unlike non-traditional students, the traditional student often has never been part of the workforce, the student goes to college full-time, and graduates according to the traditional, four-year model. Society and institutions have created a system around this model, and this needs to be examined in relation to non-traditional students—particularly now that non-traditional students constitute quite possibly the majority of those going to college.

As Hart notes, such students are likely to be more interested in distance education, and this is why the author argues that national leaders should provide a forum to review and revise the financial aid system that serves non-traditional students. One interesting suggestion that Hart makes is to alter the traditional finance model and consider how we might allow student aid and financing for distance education, since distance education is often a good alternative for non-traditional students.

Another example from the area of financial aid is Hart's point that financial aid programs usually assume that a student does not attend one term of an academic year (the summer), and thus annual aid is limited to two semesters or three quarters. But for many non-traditional students, this model does not match their lifestyles. As Hart observes, "Students who attend year-round reasonably assume that they should be able to get aid for every term in which they enroll, but the system currently does not meet that basic need" (Hart).

EDUCATIONAL INNOVATION FOR NON-TRADITIONAL STUDENTS

The growth of the non-traditional student population has important implications when considering the policies and services that have traditionally applied to college students, and this is why we should be examining policy in a different light than that of the past. For example, Chao and Good argue that the close connection between "educational and career aspirations underscores the importance of vocational/career counseling with non-traditional students," and that "understanding the travails and aspirations of non-traditional students during their career and educational transitions is therefore crucial for counselors to facilitate student success" (Chao & Good).

ON-CAMPUS CHILD CARE

One of the most obvious but underdeveloped areas that could help non-traditional students is to provide child-care services either free of charge (perhaps as part of a newly designed financial aid package) or very inexpensively for those non-traditional students who need child-care services. This obviously could be done in any college large enough to support such a program. Some colleges are already starting to innovate with such programs. For example, Brookhaven College in Dallas, Texas formed a joint venture with Head Start to build a preschool education center right on the campus. The new facility is designed to accommodate 142 preschoolers, all of whom are children of non-traditional students. The school has created a win-win-win situation:

- The program allows parents of young children to continue their education, and the parents can conveniently stop at the child-care center on their way to and from class;
- This helps the school itself since it will very likely experience a higher retention of non-traditional student enrollment;

- The early-childhood education students at the school are using the opportunity to get hands-on practical experience by working at this same new facility (Hensley & Calhoun, 2007).

This is the kind of successful integration for a new child-care program that more colleges should endeavor to create—if they want to meet the needs of a growing non-traditional student population.

FLEXIBLE COURSE DELIVERY

Even the college programs can be designed more sensitively for non-traditional students. For example, McHenry County College's Academy of High Performance has designed some of their programs so that the students enroll in a cohort, and remain in that group. This likely strengthens their support system; the students attend class once per week for 5 hours; students take two or three courses and can earn up to 9 credit hours each term. Offering classes in an 8-week or 16-week format using different delivery methods including classroom, on-line, and telecourse provides much more flexibility for non-traditional students at McHenry County College. The cohorts meet at work sites or on the campus, and the school often alters the start times to help the employer. This is another example of how schools can innovate so as to help non-traditional students (Léger, 2005).

ADDITIONAL SUPPORT

Compton et al. point out that if institutions want to excel in serving adult students, the institution needs to be flexible and serve them in what may seem like unconventional ways (Compton et al.). Compton et al. propose that institutions should reduce the time and effort necessary for adult learners to move through the system. If a non-traditional student has unique and relevant experiences from his or her working life, then teachers should consider ways to incorporate this. Also, according to Compton et al. coursework should have practical applications because "adults tend to have career-focused goals, and they will often value courses and assignments that are seen as relevant to their goals" (Compton et al.). By way of example, the authors propose that instructors could allow projects completed in the workplace to count for credit, or they could make workplace-related assignments. The authors also suggest initiating those same services that the participants of non-traditional student studies ranked as their priorities. Thus, counseling centers should be available to help students through their emotional, physical, intellectual, cultural, and vocational transitions, and such centers should offer programs or workshops on stress management. Finally, argue Compton et al., "our institutions need to take a proactive approach to uncovering the needs of adult learners, rather than waiting until the traditional exit interview or 'autopsy study' to learn about problems" (Compton et al.).

Conclusion

America is a leader in allowing non-traditional college student enrollment. As Taniguchi and Kaufman observe, "there are few other nations whose tolerance for 'educational late blooming' matches that of the United States" (Taniguchi & Kaufman). America has many schools available in many places, such that there are community colleges, four-year colleges or universities near most communities in every U.S. State. Compared to European or other institutions of higher education, the U.S. does have relatively flexible and open admission policies that make college entry relatively easy.

However, as Taniguchi and Kaufman have also noted, and as we have seen through profiling and examining degree completion obstacles, non-traditional students have college-completion rates that are significantly lower compared with those of traditional students. This needs attention from government, educational institutions and the academic community; by focusing more on non-traditional students, there will be many changes that American society, its government, and its educational institutions can undertake to help non-traditional students, and it is time to begin working in earnest in that direction.

Terms & Concepts

Career Counseling: Career counselors or coaches use analysis and assessments to focus on the clients' issues of career exploration, changes or development. Counselors work with people at any level and assess the worker's skills, abilities and work habits, level of education, work experience and general interests. This information helps to direct and fit a worker into the occupational requirements of a jobs or point out a path for attaining a desired career level.

Intrinsic Motivation: Motivation that comes from internal, individual sources rather than from any external or outside rewards. While a person may still seek

rewards, external rewards are not enough motivation for completing a task. An intrinsically motivated student wants to get a good grade on an assignment, but if the assignment is not interesting or personally rewarding, the possibility of a good grade may not be enough to maintain that student's motivation to put significant effort into the project. People with intrinsic motivation accomplish a task because it is pleasurable, important, or personally significant.

National Center for Education Statistics (NCES): is located within the U.S. Department of Education and the Institute of Education Sciences, and is the primary federal entity for collecting and analyzing data related to education.

Non-traditional Student: According to the National Center for Education Statistics, this is a large, heterogeneous population of adult students who often have family and work responsibilities as well as other life circumstances that can interfere with successful completion of educational objectives. Usually, a defining characteristic of this group is being over the age of 24.

Telecourse: A coordinated learning system which uses a series of television programs supplemented by printed materials faculty involvement in the form of lectures, and/or consultation. Most telecourse programs are broadcast via local cable stations.

Traditional Student: A student who enters college directly from high school, takes courses on a continuous full-time basis, completing a bachelor's degree program in four or five years by age 22 or 23. Generally, traditional students are financially dependent on others, do not have spouses or families, consider the college career to be their primary responsibility, and if employed, are so only on a part time basis.

Sinclair Nicholas

Bibliography

Bauman, S., Wang, N., DeLeon, C., Kafentzis, J., Zavala-Lopez, M., & Lindsey, M. (2004). Non-traditional students' service needs and social support resources: A pilot study. *Journal of College Counseling, 7*, 13–17. Retrieved December 4, 2007, from EBSCO Online Database Academic Search Premier.

Bundy, A., & Smith, T. (2004). Introduction to the special section: Breaking with tradition: Effective counseling services for non-traditional students. *Journal of College Counseling, 7*, 3–4. Retrieved December 1, 2007, from EBSCO Online Database Academic Search Premier.

Bye, D., Pushkar, D., & Conway, M. (2007). Motivation, interest, and positive affect in traditional and non-traditional undergraduate students. *Adult Education Quarterly, 57,* 141–158. Retrieved December 5, 2007, from EBSCO Online Database Academic Search Premier.

Chao, R., & Good, G. (2004). Non-traditional students' perspectives on college education: A qualitative study. *Journal of College Counseling, 7,* 5–12. Retrieved December 4, 2007, from EBSCO Online Database Academic Search Premier.

Chen, J. C. (2014). Teaching non-traditional adult students: Adult learning theories in practice. *Teaching in Higher Education, 19,* 406–418. Retrieved October 8, 2014, from EBSCO Online Database Education Research Complete.

Compton, J. I., Cox, E., & Laanan, F. S. (2006). Adult learners in transition. *New Directions for Student Services, 114,* 73–80. Retrieved December 6, 2007, from EBSCO Online Database Education Research Complete.

Coulter, X., & Mandell, A. (2012). Adult higher education: Are we moving in the wrong direction? *Journal of Continuing Higher Education, 60,* 40–42. Retrieved October 8, 2014, from EBSCO Online Database Education Research Complete.

Hart, N. K. (2003). Best practices in providing non-traditional students with both academic and financial support. *New Directions for Higher Education, 121,* 99–106. Retrieved December 4, 2007, from EBSCO Online Database Education Research Complete.

Hensley, R. D., & Calhoun, P. (2007). Groundbreaking ideas. *University Business, 10,* 57–59. Retrieved December 4, 2007, from EBSCO Online Database Academic Search Premier.

Léger, N. (2005). Educating non-traditional students through interdisciplinary collaboration. *Community College Journal of Research & Practice, 29,* 641–642. Retrieved December 4, 2007, from EBSCO Online Database Education Research Complete.

Setting students on a new path. (2007). *American School Board Journal, 194* (Suppl.), 17. Retrieved December 1, 2007, from EBSCO Online Database Education Research Complete.

Taniguchi, H., & Kaufman, G. (2005). Degree completion among non-traditional college students. *Social Science Quarterly, 86,* 912–927. Retrieved December 4, 2007, from EBSCO Online Database Academic Search Premier.

SUGGESTED READING

Aagard, M., Antunez, M., & Sand, J. (2015). Learning from degree-seeking older adult students in a university library. *Reference Services Review.* 43(2). 215-230.

Davis, J. M. (2005/2006). Designing an online course for non-traditional students: Revisiting the essentials. *International Journal of Learning, 12,* 121–127. Retrieved December 4, 2007, from EBSCO Online Database Education Research Complete.

Jenkins, R. (2012). The new 'traditional student.' *Chronicle of Higher Education, 59,* A31–A32. Retrieved October 8, 2014, from EBSCO Online Database Education Research Complete.

Kennedy, A. (2005). All grown up and going back to school. *Counseling Today, 48,* 28–29. Retrieved December 5, 2007, from EBSCO Online Database Education Research Complete.

Lovell, E. (2014). College students who are parents need equitable services for retention. *Journal of College Student Retention: Research, Theory, and Practice.* 16(2), 187-202.

Mississippi universities expand net to get non-traditional students. (2005). *Diverse: Issues in Higher Education, 22,* 12. Retrieved December 5, 2007, from EBSCO Online Database Education Research Complete.

Reid, K. (2006). Federal commission releases 4 papers. *Chronicle of Higher Education, 52,* A34. Retrieved December 5, 2007, from EBSCO Online Database Education Research Complete.

UNDERPREPARED COLLEGE STUDENTS

About one-third of new college students leave high school unprepared for the academic rigor of Higher Education. Many educators blame No Child Left Behind legislation for this trend, and researchers note that a lack of effective time management and study strategies makes new college students unprepared. Those students who require remediation in college have higher drop-out rates than their peers who begin college-level courses upon entrance. Colleges pay a price as well; when students drop out, tuition dollars are lost. The trend of academic under-preparedness is not expected to decrease, and, as the number of high school graduates declines, colleges will have to compete for a smaller pool of students, knowing that many of them lack the skills to be successful.

KEYWORDS: At Risk; Attrition; College-ready; Developmental Courses; First-generation; No Child Left Behind (NCLB); Persistence; Remediation; Retention; Underprepared

OVERVIEW

In most American high schools, it is a part of the 11th grade curriculum for students to investigate colleges and the opportunities that accompany a college degree. Students talk with guidance counselors and sit at computer terminals answering questions about their likes and dislikes, social preferences, and academic strengths. Once entered, that data is translated into a list of jobs that match each student's preferences. The names of colleges that offer degree or certificate programs for the jobs on the list are also provided, so students can begin their college searches. Soon after, the students take SAT/ACT exams and try to narrow their college search based on admissions requirements. In their senior year, they visit prospective campuses, complete application and financial aid forms, and discuss who is going where within their diverse social circles. This process is part of the growing-up package, and students readily accept the parcel. However, few students truly understand the implications; they know they are going to college, but they do not necessarily know whether or not they are academically prepared to do so.

Even though it seems like the issue of underprepared students is new, it is not. It is, perhaps, new that a flurry of research, publications, and finger-pointing has occurred around the topic. However, noted author and social research methodology professor Mike Rose notes that the problem of students leaving high school unprepared for college is not a new phenomenon. As Rose notes in his book *Lives on the Boundary*, "In 1841 the president of Brown complained that 'students frequently enter college almost wholly unacquainted with English grammar.' In the mid-1870s, Harvard professor Adams Sherman Hill assessed the writing of students after four years at America's oldest college: "Every year Harvard graduates a certain number of men—some of them high scholars—whose manuscripts would disgrace a boy of twelve." In 1896, *The Nation* ran an article titled "The Growing Illiteracy of American Boys," which reported on another Harvard study. The authors of this one lamented the spending of "much time, energy, and money" teaching students "what they ought to have learnt already'."

The problem of underprepared high school students has sparked a flurry of interest from educators, researchers, and laypersons alike. In the fall of 2008, the *Pittsburgh Post-Gazette* sponsored a series of articles discussing the effects of underprepared high school graduates moving on to institutions of Higher Education. According to the first article in the series, "Students Face a Long List of Obstacles on the Way to a College Degree," interest in Higher Education was at an all-time high: "About two-thirds of new high school graduates nationwide—up from less than half in the 1970s—go on to Higher Education" (Chute, 2008). Yet, according to the National Center for Education Statistics (NCES), nearly one-third of first- and second-year undergraduates during the 2011–2012 academic year reported taking at least one remedial (basic or developmental) course since graduating from high school, and 15.8 percent reported taking a remedial course that same year (National Center for Education Statistics, 2014). In other words, students now more than ever are planning to go to college, yet many of them require remediation once they get there.

ISSUES FOR STUDENTS

The need for remediation in college is actually a catch-22 situation for students. Students who need remediation to improve basic skills like math, reading, and writing advance through a college curriculum less quickly than those who start out in college-level coursework. This is an expensive consequence of a lack of academic preparation; many are required to complete a course, a semester, and sometimes an entire year of developmental courses before they begin taking the college-level classes required for an academic major. In addition, students requiring remediation persist to graduation at only one-half the rate of their college-ready peers (Chait & Venezia, 2008, as cited in Soares & Mazzeo, 2008).

Students leave high school with the goal of earning a college degree. Yet, some 30 percent of each new cohort of entering freshmen will require remediation and about one-half of those will not graduate. Over their lifetimes, the students who drop out will earn almost one million dollars less than the students who remain and earn baccalaureate degrees (Pennington, 2004, as cited in Kuh, Kinzie, Buckley, Bridges, & Hayek, 2007). Furthermore, in 2013, people between ages twenty-five and thirty-two with only a high school diploma earned a median income of $28,000, while those with baccalaureate degrees earned a median income of $45,500—almost two-thirds more (Kurtzleben, 2014). Looking at real numbers, it is estimated that more than 3.3 million students will graduate high school in 2015 (Hussar &

Bailey, 2014). If 60 percent (approximately 1.9 million) of those 3.3 million go to college, and 30 percent (about 594,000) of those college students need remediation, and 50 percent of that group drops out, then about 297,000 students who enter college in the fall of 2015 will become a statistic.

According to the NCES, poor reading skills make high school graduates significantly less likely to earn college degrees when compared with their peers who do not need reading remediation. Furthermore, the American College Testing Program (2006) notes that just over 50 percent "of high school graduates have college-level reading skills" (as cited in Kuh et al.). Students who need even one developmental reading course will drop out at higher rates than those who need two remedial math classes or require remediation in any subject other than reading or math. In addition, 51 percent of students who required reading remediation also needed four or more remedial courses total, compared to only 31 percent of students who required remediation in math (NCES). In other words, a student who lacks reading skills tends to need remediation across the board (reading, writing, math, study skills, etc.), whereas a student needing only math remediation can take one or two developmental math classes while taking courses toward his or her degree requirements.

Edmund Hansen, director of the teaching enhancement center at Emporia State University, notes that even though statistics report data about the lack of preparation of students, the "students tend to be highly confident in their abilities," even though "skill levels for basic academic tasks are… alarmingly low for a significant percentage of college students" (1998). Further, Hansen notes that in 1997, almost 32 percent of high school teachers awarded A grades compared with less than 15 percent in 1969, and he believes that such incidences of grade inflation have caused overconfidence among students. When students who have always received A's in high school receive C's and D's in college, they become frustrated, and perhaps they should. If high school is supposed to prepare students for college, and students go to college unprepared, that disconnect has an effect on everybody concerned.

ISSUES FOR COLLEGES & UNIVERSITIES

For the Higher Education system, remediation is both a good thing and a bad thing. The students who

require developmental courses have to pay for them, resulting in tuition dollars. However, remedial courses require teachers (who need to be paid), electricity to light and heat classrooms (which costs money), and in many instances, academic support in the form of paid tutors, supplemental instructors, and study skills counselors. In addition, as many remedial students withdraw before completing degree requirements, the tuition gained from remedial coursework is lost when those students do not persist to graduation. More important, losing students to attrition causes a college's graduation rates to decrease. According to Carey (2004), "about 20 percent of all four-year colleges and universities graduate fewer than one-third of their first-time, full-time, degree-seeking first-year students within six years" (as cited in Kuh et al.). In other words, at 1 in 5 institutions, a new full-time student has only a 1 in 3 chance of graduating in the six years following his or her enrollment.

Academically, students lack reading ability and are weak in math. On a more personal level, they also lack motivation and confidence (Community College Research Center, 2006). The Association for the Study of Higher Education (ASHE) reports that in 2000, almost one-half of high school seniors achieved only basic proficiency on the National Assessment of Educational Progress, while more than one-third ranked below proficiency (Kuh et al.). In addition, because they were not challenged in high school, it took only a few hours per week for students to complete all of their homework. As a result, they lack study skills and are frustrated when the few hours per week of study time they are used to becomes thirty hours in college. This picture is actually a positive one considering that 30 percent of students in the United States do not graduate from high school (Soares & Mazzeo). Many educators blame No Child Left Behind legislation for this academic crisis.

NO CHILD LEFT BEHIND (NCLB)

The United States is a nation obsessed with evaluating its children, with calibrating their exact distance from some ideal benchmark. In the name of excellence, we test and measure them—as individuals, as a group—and we rejoice or despair over the results (Rose, 1989).

Despair seemed to be the overwhelming sentiment when NCLB (2001) legislation was enacted. As a country, the United States had fallen behind academically, and the remedy—it was believed—was to hold each school district accountable for its students' academic achievement. The legislation also works on a reward system, rewarding those districts with high standardized test scores and punishing the districts with low scores. The reward is federal funding, and in addition to requiring standardized tests for which teachers must prepare students, the funding issue makes a clear distinction between wealthy and poor school districts by creating an even larger gap between their operating budgets.

The National Education Association (NEA) had several concerns about the legislation and sued the federal government over NCLB funding that had not yet been distributed (2008). The NEA claims that student test scores have not improved under the legislation, and that the academic achievement gap between minority and majority students has not decreased. In addition, the legislation has made federal funding such a proverbial carrot that almost one-half of school districts in 2007 reported cutting time from various subjects or activities in order to spend more time on reading and math. Art, music, science, social studies, lunch, and recess were reported curriculum cuts (Center on Education Policy, as cited in National Education Association, 2008). With the remediation levels required in colleges across the nation, having less time to eat lunch has not benefited high school graduates.

According to the NEA (one of more than 140 national organizations suggesting "significant reforms" to the legislation), the time taken from other activities and devoted to reading and math instruction has not helped: "New research by a University of Maryland professor finds that NCLB's focus on high-stakes testing 'has actually undermined the quality of teaching in reading and math.' The research further found, 'There were declines in teaching higher-order thinking, in the amount of time spent on complex assignments, and in the actual amount of high cognitive content in the curriculum. We believe these declines are related to the pressure teachers were feeling to "teach to the test" (NEA).

Several researchers have noted that the benchmark passing grade for districts—that 100 percent of their students "achieve proficiency in both reading and math" (as indicated by standardized scores)—is so difficult to attain that most schools will fail (NEA). Failing schools mean failing students. Undoubtedly,

students will only fail a test so many times before deciding that a low-paying job is easier than the constant scrutiny of the federal government. According to education expert Linda Darling-Hammond, this may be the goal in some districts. She writes:

> *"Critics claim that the law's focus on complicated tallies of multiple-choice-test scores has dumbed down the curriculum, fostered a 'drill and kill' approach to teaching, mistakenly labeled successful schools as failing, driven teachers and middle-class students out of public schools and harmed special education students and English-language learners through inappropriate assessments and efforts to push out low-scoring students in order to boost scores"* (Darling-Hammond, 2007).

LACK OF STUDY SKILLS

Having the academic ability to be successful in college plays a large role in whether or not students continue their education to graduation. However, even the most adept mathematician needs to learn to manage his time once he's away at college and not be constantly reminded when assignments are due. Indeed, NCLB legislation cannot be blamed for poor time management skills. According to Hansen, "the average student spent only 3.8 hours per week [studying] in 1997." As the formula for college study time is about two hours out of class for each hour in class, full-time students should average about ten times that amount. In other words, the lack of preparation for Higher Education is not limited to academic ability or test scores.

Also, Cukras (2006) notes that being able to think independently is a skill lacking in high school graduates. By thinking independently, a student can be flexible and can use several study skills strategies when moving from subject to subject (Cukras). For example, a new college student may be overwhelmed by the amount of information in a psychology text. However, by annotating each chapter (summarizing paragraphs and defining terms), he or she becomes active in his or her own learning—and has notes available whenever looking through that chapter. And, while knowing how to annotate a chapter is a necessary skill, it is probably not one that will help a student remember the terrain of a specific geographic area: A series of note cards or an organizational chart would be better for that. Having a pool of strategies available and being able to choose which one is applicable in each study situation takes critical thinking skills.

THE ROLE OF COMMUNITY COLLEGES

When an economy has caused colleges and universities to raise tuition to remain financially afloat, students have to choose wisely regarding where to spend their education dollars. Most community colleges have open-access enrollment, which means that they do not discriminate against a student for lack of academic preparation. Thus, students who need to improve their skills can save money by attending community colleges before enrolling in more expensive institutions. In addition, they can be better supported academically as many colleges and universities do not offer comprehensive remediation. For example, in less than seven years, Davidson County Community College, in North Carolina, saw a 50 percent increase in its developmental student population (Kozeracki & Brooks, 2006). As a result, the college changed its support from a central focus to that of a comprehensive support system. Remediation is now the responsibility of everyone on campus rather than one academic.

Similarly, Clinton Community College (CCC) in upstate New York operates under the expectation that it will offer remediation to its student body. While its developmental population has not changed as drastically as Davidson County's, its sees about 5 percent of its incoming students requiring at least three remedial courses. Again, looking at the numbers, if the school admits about one thousand full-time matriculated students (those that have chosen a major), 5 percent is about fifty students who are required to take three courses in developmental studies before they can take courses required for their major. In the fall of 2008, 50 percent of the full-time matriculated students admitted to CCC were recommended for at least one remedial course; 14 percent were recommended for two developmental courses (email communication, June 5, 2009). With approximately five hundred students requiring remediation in one semester, it is essential that admissions personnel, academic advisors, division coordinators, financial aid officers, and academic support staff (tutoring facilities, accommodative services) are involved in the process. Otherwise, students will inevitably feel lost in the shuffle from one office to the next.

THE SOLUTION: WORKING TOGETHER

Raymund A. Paredes, the Texas commissioner of Higher Education, established a coordinated effort between El Paso Community College and the local high school so that students can take the EPCC placement exams during their 10th- and 11th-grade years in high school. Determining their college placement while they are still in high school allows high schools to provide the remediation necessary for the students to gain college-level skills before enrolling at EPCC. This allows students to enter the community college and take courses within their designated academic programs rather than taking developmental courses and falling behind in program requirements (Ashburn, 2008).

This solution can even benefit students who do not plan to go to college right out of high school; they will know what is required of them if they ever change their minds. Also, the students who do go right to college will have spent at least one year trying to manage their time effectively, studying longer hours, and completing more challenging work than their regular high school curriculum requires. In addition to the benefit to students, the collaboration between high schools and colleges can help Higher Education administrations prepare for their incoming classes. If students are better prepared, colleges can focus on scheduling more college-level classes than they normally offer. This is a practical solution to lowering the number of underprepared high school graduates. And it benefits both the students and the schools. It is possible that this type of collaboration could replace the current American high school curriculum.

TERMS & CONCEPTS

At Risk: Students who are considered at a higher risk for withdrawing from school than the general population (that is, low-income, first-generation, academically underprepared).

Attrition: The result of students withdrawing from or otherwise dropping out of college.

College-Ready: Students who are academically prepared for college-level study.

Developmental Courses: Coursework that is basic (remedial) in nature; generally math, reading, and writing.

First-Generation: Students who are the first in their families to earn a college degree (that is, neither parent has a baccalaureate degree).

No Child Left Behind (NCLB): Legislation enacted in 2002 by the second Bush administration that holds school districts accountable for student achievement (represented by standardized test scores).

Persistence: In terms of retention, students who remain in college to completion of a degree.

Remediation: Basic (developmental) instruction to students who are considered academically underprepared.

Retention: Keeping students in college from semester to semester, from year to year, or through degree completion.

Underprepared: Students who lack the academic skills to be successful when faced with college-level work and who must complete developmental (remedial) coursework before beginning college-level academic study.

Maureen McMahon

BIBLIOGRAPHY

Ashburn, E. (2008, March 28). Student pool is expected to dip and diversify. *Chronicle of Higher Education*, pp. A1, A25. Retrieved May 3, 2009, from EBSCO Online Database Academic Search Complete.

Bambrick-Santoyo, P. (2014). Make students college-ready in high school. *Phi Delta Kappan, 95*, 72–73. Retrieved November 20, 2014, from EBSCO Online Database Education Research Complete.

Byrd, K. L., & MacDonald, G. (2005). Defining college readiness from the inside out: First-generation college student perspectives. *Community College Review, 33*, 22–37. Retrieved May 3, 2009, from EBSCO Online Database Academic Search Complete.

Chute, E. (2008, August 31). Students face a long list of obstacles on the way to college degree. *Pittsburgh Post-Gazette*. Retrieved June 12, 2009, from http:// post-gazette.com.

Community College Research Center. (2006, November). Academic preparedness and remediation. Retrieved May 18, 2009, from http://ccrc.tc.columbia.edu.

Cukras, G. (2006). The investigation of study strategies that maximize learning for underprepared students. *College Teaching, 54*, 194–197. Retrieved April 30, 2009, from EBSCO Online Database Academic Search Premier.

Darling-Hammond, L. (2007). Evaluating No Child Left Behind. *The Nation, 284*, 11–18. Retrieved June 1, 2009, from EBSCO Online Database Education Research Complete.

Hansen, E. J. (1998). Essential demographics of today's college students. *AAHE Bulletin, 51*, 3–5. Retrieved May 18, 2009, from http://eric.ed.gov.

Hussar, W. J., & Bailey, T. M. (2014, February). *Projections of education statistics to 2022: Forty-first edition*. Retrieved November 20, 2014, from http://nces.ed.gov.

Kozeracki, C. A., & Brooks, J. B. (2006). Emerging institutional support for developmental education. *New Directions for Community Colleges, 2006*, 63–73. Retrieved May 3, 2009, from EBSCO Online Database Academic Search Complete.

Kuh, G. D., Kinzie, J., Buckley, J. A., Bridges, B. K., & Hayek, J. C. (2007). Introduction, context, and overview. *ASHE Higher Education Report, 32*, 1–5. Retrieved May 3, 2009, from EBSCO Online Database Education Research Complete.

Kurtzleben, D. (2014, February 14). The cost of not having a college degree. *US News Weekly*, p. 8. Retrieved November 20, 2014, from EBSCO Online Database Business Source Complete.

National Center for Education Statistics. (2004, June). *The condition of education 2004*. Retrieved November 5, 2014, from http://nces.ed.gov.

National Center for Education Statistics. (2014, October). *Profile of undergraduate students: 2011–12: Web tables*. Retrieved November 5, 2014, from http://nces.ed.gov.

National Education Association. (2008, February). *Why NCLB needs fundamental change*. Retrieved May 19, 2009, from http://nea.org.

Navarro, D. (2012). Supporting the students of the future. *Change, 44*, 43–51. Retrieved November 20, 2014, from EBSCO Online Database Education Research Complete.

Rose, M. (1989). *Lives on the boundary*. New York: Penguin.

Soares, L., & Mazzeo, C. (2008). *College-ready students, student-ready colleges: An agenda for improving degree completion in postsecondary education*. Retrieved June 4, 2009, from http://cdn.americanprogress.org.

SUGGESTED READING

Amey, M. J., & Long, P. N. (1998). Developmental course work and early placement: Success strategies for underprepared community college students. *Community College Journal of Research & Practice, 22*, 3–10. Retrieved November 5, 2014, from EBSCO Online Database Education Research Complete.

Arnold, K. D., Lu, E. C., & Armstrong, K. J. (2012). The case for a comprehensive model of college readiness. *ASHE Higher Education Report, 38*, 1–10. Retrieved November 20, 2014, from EBSCO Online Database Education Research Complete.

Fonte, R. (1997). Structured versus laissez-faire open access: Implementation of a proactive strategy. *New Directions for Community Colleges, 100*, 43–52. Retrieved April 30, 2009, from EBSCO Online Database Academic Search Premier.

Geiser, S., & Santelices, M. V. (2007). *Validity of high-school grades in predicting student success beyond the freshman year: High-school record vs. standardized tests as indicators of four-year college outcomes.* Retrieved May 18, 2009, from http://eric.ed.gov.

Grimes, S. K. (1997). Underprepared community college students: Characteristics, persistence, and academic success. *Community College Journal of Research & Practice, 21,* 47–56. Retrieved May 3, 2009, from EBSCO Online Database Academic Search Complete.

Hoyt, J. E., & Sorensen, C. T. (2001). High school preparation, placement testing, and college remediation. *Journal of Developmental Education, 25,* 26–34. Retrieved May 3, 2009, from EBSCO Online Database Academic Search Complete.

Isserlis, J. (2008). Adults in programs for the "academically underprepared." *New Directions for Adult & Continuing Education, 120,* 19–26. Retrieved April 30, 2009, from EBSCO Online Database Academic Search Premier.

Kraska, M. F., Nadelman, M. H., Maner, A. H., & McCormick, R. (1990). A comparative analysis of developmental and nondevelopmental community college students. *Community/Junior College Quarterly of Research and Practice, 14,* 13–20.

Melzer, D. & Grant, R. (2016). Investigating differences in personality traits and academic needs among prepared and underprepared first-year college students. *Journal of College Student Development.* 57(1), 99-103.

Pratt, T. (2017). The open access dilemma: How can community colleges better serve underprepared students? *Education Next.* 17(4), 34-41.

Reeves, T. C. (2006). The Spellings report: An inadequate fix. *Academic Questions, 20,* 56–60. Retrieved May 3, 2009, from EBSCO Online Database Academic Search Complete.

Simpson, M. L., Hynd, C. R., Nist, S. L. & Burrell, K. I. (1997). College academic assistance programs and practices. *Educational Psychology Review, 9,* 39–87. Retrieved May 3, 2009, from EBSCO Online Database Education Research Complete.

U.S. Department of Education. (2000). *Corporate involvement in education: Achieving our national education priorities: The seven priorities of the U.S. Department of Education.* Retrieved November 5, 2014, from http://eric.ed.gov.

Vygotsky, L. S. (1978). *Mind in society: The development of higher psychological processes.* Cambridge, MA: Harvard University Press.

WRITING CENTERS

Writing centers are unique academic institutions. They are places where writers go for one-on-one feedback and assistance with their writing, offering a more personal and less hierarchical form of instruction. In the writing center, tutors work with students to improve not just the writer's text, but the critical thinking and writing processes that the writer uses in creating a text. The pedagogical approach that a particular center employs may be informed by a number of educational and/or composition theories. This article provides a brief overview of the most common theories and practices employed in modern writing centers.

KEYWORDS: Collaborative Learning; Curriculum-based Tutoring; Directive Tutoring; Expressionism; Humanism; Non-directive Tutoring; Process Approach; Social Constructionism; Writing Across the Curriculum; Writing Center; Writing Theory

OVERVIEW

On many campuses, the Writing Center is a place that is frequently misunderstood. Sometimes it's lucky enough to be housed in roomy quarters with computers, comfortable chairs, and numerous staff. Sometimes it occupies more humble spaces, perhaps an office in a back hallway or a basement, staffed by one caring tutor at a time. Writing centers are diverse and may seem to serve different purposes depending on the center's clientele, location, and position within the institutional framework.

Most writing centers today share the common goal of assisting individuals to become better writers. To do this, writing centers provide one-on-one consultations with trained peer or professional tutors. These consultations focus on improving an individual's writing and thinking processes. For instance, in a typical consultation, a writer may bring in a draft text for an assignment in an English class. The writer and tutor often begin with a conversation about the purpose of the assignment and what the writer would like to focus on during the session. Then, focusing on the writer's goals, the tutor will ask questions that help the writer clarify ideas or improve the written text. The goal of the session is to use the collaborative process to help the writer understand how a reader would comprehend the writer's ideas and thereby allow the writer to improve the work. This does not mean the final product must be a perfect text.

While sessions may focus on mechanical issues such as punctuation and grammar, most writing centers today do not conduct "fix-it" sessions in which tutors proofread and correct papers so that writers can get a better grade. Instead, if there is a consistent mechanical error (e.g., comma usage), tutors provide mini-lessons on the area of concern and then allow students to find and correct their errors. Thus, it is entirely possible for a student to use a writing center several times without emerging with a "perfected" paper in the eyes of a professor. This can be a source of misunderstanding and frustration if students and faculty expect writing centers to be places that provide editorial services.

FURTHER INSIGHTS

The crucial component that makes a writing center different from a classroom is the relationship between the tutor and the writer. Unlike an instructor in a classroom, tutors do not have control over the student's grade; therefore, at least one element of power in the teacher-student relationship does not exist. Many times, tutors are graduate or undergraduate students, classified as the writer's peers, and therefore (possibly) more likely to adapt to the writer's perspective. Tutors can also offer more time to the student by scheduling time to discuss a student's paper several times a week or semester.

Within the context of this more equitable relationship, tutors have a variety of choices about how to interact with the writer depending on the tutor's and writing center's philosophy regarding writing, composition, education, and knowledge construction. A pedagogical decision during a session is whether to take a non-directive or directive approach.

NON-DIRECTIVE & DIRECTIVE TUTORING

Non-directive tutoring, which encourages tutors to act Socratically and ask writers questions during a session instead of providing answers, is representative of the minimalist tutoring philosophy introduced and popularized by Jeff Brooks. Brooks (2008) writes that the goal of a tutoring session should be to help the writer learn how to write, not to perfect the writer's paper. "When you 'improve' a student's paper, you haven't been a tutor at all; you've been an editor" (Brooks). Thus, he emphasizes that tutors should sit patiently with students and be willing to discuss all aspects of the paper and strategies for effective writing. Tutors should offer support and encouragement and keep the writer

focused on the paper. While the end result may be a perfected paper, it does not have to be. In Brooks' view, if students leave a writing center session having a better understanding and better control of their own writing processes, then the session has been a success.

The directive approach involves the tutor serving as a source of authority on the writing style and providing the writer with examples of how to phrase the wording of the text. Modeling is a frequent technique of the directive approach. In modeling, a tutor may demonstrate how to write a text or give examples of the kind of writing expected and then ask the student to do the same. Directive tutoring has been noted as a common and effective practice for professors mentoring graduate students during the writing of their theses and dissertations (Shamoon & Burns, 2008). However, it is not the predominant approach used in modern writing centers. Corbett (2011) recommends that when moving tutors to classrooms a more authoritative (directive) approach could be encouraged, but when these tutors move back to the center, we could ask them to resist the temptation to overuse what they know about the course and the instructor's expectations and "hold on a little tighter" to some nondirective methods and moves that could "place agency back in the hands and minds of the students."

Whether tutors and writing centers choose directive or non-directive approaches depends on the students' needs, the policies of the center, and the philosophies of the individual tutor. Writing centers are affected (as are all educational institutions) by the predominant theoretical conventions and constructs of certain time periods. In particular, theories originating within the fields of composition and education have most impacted the day-to-day operations of the writing center. Major philosophies impacting center work have included:

- Current traditional rhetoric;
- Expressionism;
- Social constructionism.

TRADITIONAL RHETORIC

In the 1940s and 1950s, traditional rhetoric emphasized the form and structure of the text apart from the writer. In response, writing centers, or writing laboratories as they were called, emphasized instruction in grammar and the mechanics of writing. After receiving instruction on a particular aspect of form, students would practice individually, consulting with a tutor to check for correctness (Moore; Murphy & Law). The grammar drills and paper correction led to a perception that writing centers were "fix-it shops" (North, 2008) for those who lacked fundamental writing skills. Many continue to hold this perception today.

EXPRESSIONISM & PROCESS WRITING

In the 1970s to 1980s, Expressionist philosophy led tutors to deemphasize the text and instead focus on the writer and the writer's creative processes (Murphy & Law). Expressionism, which is a philosophy that falls within the category of Humanism, views knowledge as having a stable and permanent existence. According to this view, knowledge can either be learned from others or can be discovered within the self. Expressivists view writing as an important means to self-discovery. Through an intense and personal process, writers are able to discover their inner wisdom and gain a better understanding of themselves and of the world. From Expressionist theorizing was born the Process Approach, a pedagogy that points out that writing occurs within a series of stages. These stages are generally recognized as:

- Pre-writing (e.g., brainstorming, freewriting);
- Drafting;
- Revising;
- Editing;
- Publishing.

Although writers might use different techniques with each of the stages and their progression through each stage may not be uniform, all writers are believed to engage in some form of each stage (Trupe, 2001). In a class based on the Process Approach, teachers help writers develop strategies for each stage of the process. In a process-based tutoring session, a tutor observes where the writer is within his or her individual process and then works to move the writer to the next stage. North, an oft-cited spokesperson for Expressionist-based tutoring, writes that in the writing center the result has been a "pedagogy of direct intervention." Unlike in earlier centers where tutors worked with writers after they had finished their written product, tutors in modern centers assist during the activity of writing. Thus, they observe and ask questions in order to enter and participate in the writer's train of thought. The function of the tutor within this space is to change the writer's process so the writer can produce higher quality text. They

make sure, as North writes, that the writing center produces "better writers, not better writing" (North).

SOCIAL CONSTRUCTIONISM

Social Constructionism appeared in the 1980s and became increasingly important in the 1990s and early 21st century (Murphy & Sherwood, 2008). This philosophy views knowledge as a continually changing and evolving product of social interaction within particular social and cultural contexts. The primary mechanism of this change is language. In other words, as individuals discuss and theorize about the world, they develop a common language that shapes the way they perceive the world. Through interacting with those with differing views, new language is introduced or shifts to provide new understandings. The process is never ending, allowing for perpetual growth of the individual and society.

Social Constructionism has led to a greater emphasis on collaborative learning within the writing center. Collaborative learning is a style of learning that involves several students on a group project involving higher order problem-solving skills. Within the writing center, Lunsford (2008) argues, collaborative learning can be difficult to implement but offers students multiple benefits including the development of higher order thinking skills, deeper understanding of a subject, and higher achievement in classrooms. The challenge for writing centers, she says, is to find ways to constitute collaborative groups in the center and to monitor and evaluate group process to achieve the most benefit. One way that collaborative learning occurs in most centers is between the collaboration of tutor and student as they discuss and work on a student's text together. Other activities that involve collaborative learning include peer tutoring in writing workshops and reading/writing discussion circles (Kail & Trimbur, 1995).

While composition and educational philosophies have influenced what goes on within writing centers, they have also led to expansion of writing center services throughout Higher Education and into postsecondary schools. Calls for university graduates to be stronger writers along with a realization that writing is an integral part of clear disciplinary thinking led to the writing across the curriculum movement in the 1980s (Bazerman et al., 2005). This movement aims to make students in all disciplines better writers, and centers have responded by recruiting tutors from other disciplines as well as participating in curriculum-based tutoring models. In such models, tutors—often peer tutors—are assigned to a course to work with teachers and students in the classroom (Wallace, 1995). At the secondary level, more high schools are instituting writing centers. These centers may serve dual purposes, such as assisting students with writing while providing teachers with training on how to teach writing or integrate it into the curriculum (Spillane, 2007).

Advances in technology are also changing the way that writing centers do business. Online writing labs offer tutoring via computer conferences (Carlson & Apperson-Williams, 2008). As multimedia forms of communication become more prevalent in university coursework, centers are beginning to explore how best to help students prepare digital and hypertext presentations (Pemberton, 2008).

Even high technology doesn't remove the need for human involvement, however. Presenting a study on ways that text-to-speech software facilitates revision and the lessons for technology use in writing centers, Conard-Salvo and Sparks argued that the availability of adaptive technology in a writing center without "extensive modeling and detailed instruction" does not encourage its effective use by students (2013).

POLITICS & TRUST

A central concern of writing center philosophy has to do with the politics of the writing center. Writing is both a personal and a political process, and the writing center is often a place where writers feel free to challenge institutional constraints. One way that writers may challenge the institution is by criticizing a professor or an assignment and inviting the tutor to share in this criticism. This poses a political concern for the tutor and the center. On the one hand, the writer seeks validation for his or her criticism. For instance, if a writer finds the assignment confusing or the professor's comments unhelpful, the writer wants confirmation that the professor is really part of the problem instead of the writer being too "dumb" to understand. Because writing center tutors generally take a supportive and encouraging position in working with students, the tutor may want to validate the student's complaint, especially if the assignment or comments are truly confusing or abrasive. On the other hand, the writing center itself is a complement to coursework in the institution. The goals of a writing center include helping students improve their ability to perform in the classroom. Thus, the writing

center needs to be trusted by the faculty as well as the students. Few faculty members would be likely to support writing center activities if the center was perceived as a subversive element breeding discontent and nonconformity among the student body. So in this situation, what is the tutor to do? What policies should be in place to allow for freedom of thought while maintaining student and faculty trust? These are questions that must be negotiated between center directors and tutors as they grapple with their political place within the greater institution.

Mackiewicz and Thompson (2013) explain how motivational scaffolding strategies "operationalized through politeness" provide one way of identifying, analyzing, and discussing tutors' linguistic resources for building rapport and solidarity with students and attending to their motivation during writing center conferences. Affective connections are "essential to these conversations," the authors argue, which, at their most successful, "require high levels of cooperation among participants." Motivational scaffolding reflects tutors' care for students.

LANGUAGE, CULTURE & POWER

The politics of language itself and power and control in the writing situation also create political challenges for the writing center. Language is recognized as a medium which encodes attitudes, values, beliefs and cultural perspectives (Gee, 1999). When writers choose language within a particular discourse, they indicate whether they are aware of the conventions of language use of that discourse and whether they agree with the perspectives that the language encodes. In an academic writing center, tutors are expected to assist writers to conform to academic conventions of language use, the rationale being that this will allow them to communicate within the academic writing situation. Therefore, they emphasize formal academic language and style. However, Postcolonial theorists have made it clear that the norms of academic writing favor the dominant cultural group. When students come from diverse backgrounds, asking them to adopt a culturally bound way of writing often means the elimination of diverse language forms and ideological perspectives within the academic community. When those forms are sublimated, the power structure which allows one cultural group to be dominant over another persists (Bawarshi & Pelkowski, 2008). Thus, tutors find themselves faced with the dilemma of wanting to encourage individual expression, creativity, and unique cultural language forms while being charged by both the student and the institution with helping the student to better function within the community. How best to negotiate these sometimes conflicting goals is something that every center must resolve in terms of understanding its clientele, educational philosophy, and institutional role.

MARKETING THE MISSION

Finally, the political conundrum that can most engulf a writing center is in adopting a description that clearly and accurately describes what the center does within the larger institution. This is frequently difficult for several reasons. First, writing centers are informed by many theories and traditions and frequently engage in reflective practices that change the nature of what they do. Second, because they serve the entire educational community, some of whom are not always familiar with the principles and practices guiding the center, they are frequently misunderstood. This results in demands being made on centers that do not always mesh well with a center's self-perceptions, but which must be met in any case. For instance, many departments expect writing centers to provide remedial services, such as grammar or punctuation instruction, for struggling students. Professors may require students to take their papers to the center with the goal of having the center clean up the surface features of the text so that it is ready for submission to the instructor. A center that refuses these functions is likely to incur negative reactions from instructors and departments, which undoubtedly and justifiably believe that the center is supposed to serve their needs. Refusal to perform institutional demands can also lead to threats to funding or space that then threatens the center's viability. Thus, the challenge for every writing center is to market its purpose, function, identity, philosophy, and methodology in a way that demonstrates that the center is performing useful and necessary work for the entire community while also promoting ideas and ideologies that may run counter to those of other disciplines.

On the whole, writing centers are able to address the political issues and philosophical concerns that arise in their day to day operations by engaging in the same practices that make for good writers. Through introspection, reflection, and collaborative behaviors,

writing center staff make choices regarding tutoring pedagogies and center philosophy that allow them to define a unique space in the academic institution. While centers have experienced many changes in their relatively short history, these changes are in line with the evolution of composition and educational theory overall. Thus, in the future, it can be expected that writing centers will continue to grow and change to meet the demands of new paradigms as they become known.

TERMS & CONCEPTS

Collaborative Learning: Collaborative learning occurs when students work together on a project. In writing, collaboration may occur when individuals work individually on a part of a larger writing project that they then tie together. It can also occur through writing workshops.

Curriculum-based Tutoring: In curriculum-based tutoring, a tutor collaborates with teachers to assist students in the classroom.

Directive Tutoring: Directive tutoring involves the tutor in teaching the student how to write by modeling or using other techniques that directly show the student what to do.

Expressionism: Expressionism is a Humanist philosophy that views writing as a means to self-discovery.

Humanism: Humanism is a branch of philosophy that views knowledge as a real construct that is permanent and exists despite whether humans are aware of or understand it.

Minimalist Tutoring: Minimalist tutoring is a form of tutoring where the tutor turns the act of learning back to the student. Instead of providing answers to questions, tutors ask the students questions so that they can find answers themselves.

Non-directive Tutoring: Non-directive tutoring is a form of tutoring that does not assume the tutor knows the answers. Tutors ask students questions and allow them to direct the conference.

Online Writing Labs: Online writing labs are writing centers that offer their services via computer technology and the internet.

Process Approach to Writing: The Process Approach to writing focuses on the stages of writing. Teachers using the Process Approach teach strategies that students can use during each stage of the process and emphasize revision as an important part of writing.

Social Constructionism: Social constructionism views knowledge as being made from the interactions of people within social, historical, and cultural contexts. Language is an essential element of knowledge construction in this view.

Traditional Rhetoric: Current traditional rhetoric is a philosophy that emphasizes the grammatical form and structure of a written text as being the most important aspect of writing.

Writing Across the Curriculum: Writing across the curriculum programs attempt to integrate writing within all disciplines as a way to improve critical thinking and writing skills.

Noelle Vance

BIBLIOGRAPHY

Bawarshi, A., & Pelkowski, S. (2008). Postcolonialism and the idea of a writing center. In C. Murphy & S. Sherwood (Eds.), *The St. Martin's sourcebook for writing tutors* (pp. 79-95). Boston: Bedford/St. Martin's.

Bazerman, C., Little, J., Bethel, L., Chavkin, T., Fouquette, D., & Garufis, J. (2005). *Reference guide to writing across the curriculum.* WAC Clearinghouse: Parlor Press. Retrieved May 31, 2009, from Colorado State University, http://wac.colostate.edu.

Brooks, J. (2008). Minimalist tutoring: Making the student do all the work. In C. Murphy & S. Sherwood (Eds.), *The St. Martin's sourcebook for writing tutors* (pp. 168-173). Boston: Bedford/St. Martin's.

Carlson, D. A., & Apperson-Williams, E. (2008). The anxieties of distance: Online tutors reflect. In C. Murphy & S. Sherwood (Eds.), *The St. Martin's sourcebook for writing tutors* (pp. 285-294). Boston: Bedford/St. Martin's.

Conard-Salvo, T., & Spartz, J.M. (2012). Listening to revise: what a study about text-to-speech software taught us about students' expectations for technology use in the writing center. *Writing Center Journal, 32,* 40-59. Retrieved November 27, 2013, from EBSCO online database, Education Research Complete.

Corbett, S.J. (2011). Using case study multi-methods to investigate close(r) collaboration: course-based tutoring and the directive/nondirective instructional continuum. *Writing Center Journal, 31,* 55-81. Retrieved November 27, 2013, from EBSCO online database, Education Research Complete.

Gee, J.P. (1999). *An introduction to discourse analysis: Theory and method.* London: Routledge.

Kail, H., & Trimbur, J. (1995). The politics of peer tutoring. In C. Murphy & J. Law (Eds.) *Landmark essays on writing centers* (pp. 203-209). Davis, CA: Hermagoras Press.

Lunsford, A. (2008). Collaboration, control, and the idea of a writing center. In C. Murphy & S. Sherwood (Eds.),

The St. Martin's sourcebook for writing tutors (pp. 47-53). Boston: Bedford/St. Martin's.

Mackiewicz, J., & Thompson, I. (2013). Motivational scaffolding, politeness, and writing center tutoring. *Writing Center Journal, 33,* 38-73. Retrieved November 27, 2013, from EBSCO online database, Education Research Complete.

Moore, R. H. (1995). The writing clinic and the writing laboratory. In C. Murphy & J. Law (Eds.) *Landmark essays on writing centers* (pp. 3-9). Davis, CA: Hermagoras Press.

Murphy, C., & Sherwood, S. (2008). The tutoring process. In C. Murphy & S. Sherwood (Eds.), *The St. Martin's sourcebook for writing tutors* (pp. 1-25). Boston: Bedford/St. Martin's.

North, S.M. (2008). The idea of a writing center. In C. Murphy & S. Sherwood (Eds.), *The St. Martin's sourcebook for writing tutors* (pp. 32-46). Boston: Bedford/St. Martin's.

Pemberton, M. A. (2008). Planning for hypertexts in the writing center... or not. In C. Murphy & S. Sherwood (Eds.), *The St. Martin's sourcebook for writing tutors* (pp. 294-308). Boston: Bedford/St. Martin's.

Spillane, L.A. (2006). The reading writing center: What we can do. *The Clearing House, 80,* 63-65. Retrieved May 31, 2009, from EBSCO online database, Education Research Complete.

Wallace, R. (1995). The writing center's role in the writing across the curriculum program: Theory and practice. In C. Murphy & J. Law (Eds.) *Landmark essays on writing centers* (pp. 191-195). Davis, CA: Hermagoras Press.

Shamoon, L. K., & Burns, D. H. (2008). A critique of pure tutoring. In C. Murphy & S. Sherwood (Eds.), *The St. Martin's sourcebook for writing tutors* (pp. 173-188). Boston: Bedford/St. Martin's.

Trupe, A.L. (2001). A Process Approach to writing. Retrieved May 31, 2009, from Bridgewater College, bridgewater.edu.

SUGGESTED READING

Barnett, R. W., & Blumner, J.S. (1999). *Writing centers and writing across the curriculum Programs.* Westport, CT: Greenwood Press.

Ede, L., & Lunsford, A. (1990). *Singular texts / plural authors.* Carbondale: Southern Illinois University Press.

Murphy, C., & Law, J. (1995). *Landmark essays on writing centers.* Davis, CA: Hermagoras Press.

Naydan, L.M. (2017). Toward a rhetoric of labor activism in college and university writing centers. *Praxis: A Writing Center Journal.* 14(2), 29-36.

Ostman, H. (2013). Writing program administration and the community college. In series: *Writing Program Administration.* Anderson, SC.: Parlor Press.

Salem, L. (2016). Decisions...decisions: Who chooses to use the writing center? *Writing Center Journal.* 35(2), 147-172.

ACADEMIC DISHONESTY IN COLLEGES AND UNIVERSITIES

The rate of academic dishonesty among college students ranges from 60 to 90 percent, depending on the research study. Students who cheat in high school tend to enter college classrooms thinking that academic dishonesty is the norm; this behavior is reinforced when teachers do little to deter it or punish offenders. Academic dishonesty takes on many forms, from allowing a peer to copy answers to downloading an entire paper from the Internet. According to the research, members of fraternities and sororities are more likely to cheat than nonmembers, males are more likely to cheat than females, and upperclassmen more than freshmen and sophomores. Students who tend to procrastinate are also at risk. Peer response to cheating is shown to be the most important influence regarding a student's willingness to cheat.

KEYWORDS: Academic Dishonesty; Academic Ethic; Active Deception; Ethics; External Locus of Control; Internal Locus of Control; Morality; Passive Deception; Plagiarism; Punitive

OVERVIEW

People cheat all the time. Someone rolls through a stop sign while someone else steals cable television from his neighbor. Cheating is common in our culture, and the reason for dishonest behavior may be the result of distorted lines between what is right and what is wrong. The impact of such distortion is significant for students, for those who break rules imply that breaking rules is acceptable. Further, if punitive measures do not result from breaking rules, those rules have little value. Thus, a culture of confusion is created as mom rolls through various stop signs and dad rigs wiring from the neighbor's house to steal cable television.

In higher education, the lines are also blurred. Generally speaking, academic dishonesty is the active or passive falsifying of academic work. An active deceiver copies answers from someone else, steals an exam, or downloads a paper directly from the Internet. The passive deceiver allows someone else to copy an answer, a whole assignment, or even a paper. The passive deceiver can easily justify his or her behavior—he or she is helping a friend, not doing the actual cheating. The active deceiver, however, has a more self-serving justification; he or she is trying to get ahead. Both students are culpable if caught; after all, cheating is cheating, regardless of the justification.

According to Westacott (2008), academic dishonesty occurs because students want to impart an impression of themselves onto others. For example:

> *"… all instances of academic dishonesty are attempts to appear cleverer, more knowledgeable, more skillful, or more industrious than one really is. Buying or copying a term paper, plagiarizing from the Internet, using a crib sheet on an exam, accessing external assistance from beyond the exam room by means of a cell phone, fabricating a lab report, having another student sign one's name on an attendance sheet—all such practices serve this same purpose. The goal is to produce an appearance that is more impressive than the reality."*

EXTERNAL/INTERNAL LOCUS OF CONTROL

Unfortunately, the impression does not do anyone any good. Students who cheat rely on outside sources to prove themselves. This leads to an external locus of control in that the same students blame teachers, friends, the weather, or something else for their lack of knowledge or preparation. For example, students with an external locus of control become very good at creating excuses: "My teacher never told us about the test," "It rained so hard, I didn't dare go to the library." Students who do not cheat do not need to; they study and blame only themselves when they fail. This internal locus of control is learned just as negative behaviors are learned. Unfortunately, research shows that many students rely on others to assist them academically:

- In a study by Haines et al. (1986), over 50 percent of students admitted to cheating at a southwestern state university;
- Stern & Havlicek (1986) studied a large state university in the Midwest and noted that 82 percent of students had cheated at least once while in college;
- Michaels & Miethe (1989) noted that 86 percent of the students in their study cheated on, tests, or papers;
- According to a Coston & Jenks (1998) study, more than half of the criminal justice majors at a southern university had behaved dishonestly in school;

■ At the University of Oklahoma, a study conducted by Cochran et al. (1999) showed that over 80 percent of sociology majors had cheated at least once;

■ Finally, in a review of over one hundred studies focusing on cheating, Whitley (1998) documented that over 70 percent of study participants had cheated in college (as cited in Pino & Smith, 2003).

The nightly news reports scandal after scandal in which real people cheat, lie, and steal to get what they want: more money, more power, and more material things. It is no wonder that a culture of academic dishonestly has been created so future generations get their share of a distorted American dream.

WHY STUDENTS CHEAT

The reasons students give for cheating vary depending on the student and the situation. Even for the most ethical students, the opportunity to cheat is offered regularly. Anyone conducting research using the Internet has come across information they did not necessarily seek: free papers at the click of a mouse. The relative ease for taking a phrase, a paragraph, or an entire paper from the Internet has allowed students to become thieves of information. In a study conducted by Scanlon (2004), one-fourth "of college students surveyed have plagiarized from the Internet, but students perceive that significantly more students than that are doing so" (as cited in Iyer & Eastman, 2008).

In addition to the opportunities provided by the Internet, the following reasons have also been given by college students regarding academic dishonesty, according to several scholars:

■ They don't understand what plagiarism is (Park, 2003);

■ They have poor time management skills (Lambert et al., 2003; Park; Payne & Nantz);

■ They are defiant and/or have a lack "of respect for authority" (Park);

■ They feel negatively about a teacher or class (Park; Payne & Nantz);

■ They have not been deterred by other students cheating, getting caught, and being punished (Park; Payne & Nantz);

■ They feel pressured by their peers (Payne & Nantz);

■ They see little effect of cheating on others (Payne & Nantz) (as cited in Iyer & Eastman).

Though extremely generalized, these are the explanations provided by students. In sum, students behave dishonestly in college because they don't fully understand what academic honesty means. They also plan their time improperly and/or have little regard for their teachers and classes. Furthermore, they see their friends getting away with it, and it is easy to do. However, those who do fit specific profiles.

FRATERNITY & SORORITY MEMBERS

Storch and Storch (2002) studied almost 250 undergraduate students at the University of Florida and noted that while many students admitted cheating at some point in college, fraternity and sorority members "reported higher rates of academic dishonesty as compared to non-members." The researchers also identified that the level of involvement students had within "fraternity or sorority sponsored activities was positively associated with academic dishonesty" (Storch & Storch). The reasons for this are not clear, however. The occurrence of dishonest behavior among fraternity and sorority students has been studied since the 1970s, and while several investigations show that fraternal members cheat more often than non-members, no study identifies reasons why this may be the case.

According to the responses in the Storch and Storch study, male fraternity members cheated more often than female sorority members. Also, simply participating in fraternity/sorority sponsored activities increases a student's likelihood of cheating, with more participation leading to more cheating. It is possible that the amount of time spent engaging in organizational activities may leave little time for studying (Storch & Storch). In addition, members tend to live in close proximity to each other, so it is possible that exams and assignments (like clothing), become hand-me-downs from student to student and from year to year. However, there may be another explanation entirely:

Previous research has found a positive relationship between membership in fraternal organizations, and sexual aggression and substance abuse.... It is possible that the mentality that causes members to commit these transgressions may filter over into the classroom, thus, explaining the high level of academic dishonesty" (Storch & Storch).

Fraternity and sorority members often refer to each other as brothers and sisters. Closely related to a gang mentality, brotherhood/sisterhood requires a type of rejection of all that is not part of the membership. As a result, imitating behaviors recognized as routine could seem essential for continued membership. If everyone within the membership cheats, it would be difficult to refuse and also remain a worthy brother or sister.

OTHER FACTORS TO CONSIDER

In a study conducted by Pino and Smith, several other factors were identified as being linked with academic dishonesty. While over half of the survey respondents reported never cheating in school, the students who did cheat tended to participate in social activities (clubs, groups, Greek organizations), and they watched television more than students who reported never cheating. In addition, respondents who had been in school longer (sophomores, juniors, seniors) were more likely to report cheating than students newer to higher education. Again, it could be surmised that social activities take time away from studying. This could also be noted for students who watch a great deal of television.

Based on responses from 675 students surveyed at Georgia Southern University in 2002, Pino and Smith note that students with lower GPAs tended to cheat more than students who were more successful. Also, students with an academic ethic are more likely to behave honestly when compared to their peers who don't demonstrate the same ethic. An academic ethic is characterized by an internal locus of control. Students who believe that they are responsible for their academic success and make academics their priority tend not to cheat. Moreover, students with an academic ethic go to class consistently and avoid drinking and partying. Finally, they take classes for the sake of learning rather than for the sake of their GPAs. Accordingly, their high GPAs are earned rather than created from taking easy classes (Pino & Smith).

Students who had jobs outside of school were also less likely to report being academically dishonest than students who did not have jobs (Pino & Smith). In other words, students who work—rather than participating in social activities or watching television—resort to cheating less often than students who choose to do other things with their time, even though working students tend to have less time to study than students who have time to be socially active. It is probable that students who work demonstrate an academic ethic as well as being organized and good at managing their time.

BUSINESS STUDENTS

In a 2007 study, Rakovski and Levy note that business students also admit to high rates of academic dishonesty when compared to students in other academic areas:

> At 87%, business students provided the highest cheating rate when compared with engineering, science, and humanities students.... The majority of studies show that business majors, regardless of gender, have lower ethical values than peers in other majors.

In 2007, Rakovski and Levy presented business students (accounting and management majors) with surveys that listed several dishonest behaviors. The researchers noted that management students were much more likely to admit that they'd cheated when compared to accounting majors. In addition, management students cheated in ways that made themselves look good; like they knew material they did not know. For example, many used crib sheets and copied from other students. These behaviors raise serious questions about the employment settings in which these students will work. Ironically, more than half of the students in this study—including those who admitted to cheating—defined themselves as being honest or as being considered honest by other people. (Rakovski & Levy).

INTERNATIONAL STUDENTS

Chun-Hua and Ling-Yu (2007) studied over 2,000 students attending various colleges in Taiwan to determine the academic integrity of the participants. The authors note that the implications of their study sample cheating are serious, as many of those students will eventually attend colleges in other countries and, either in those new countries or after moving back to Taiwan, will eventually enter the workforce. Citing the disasters of WorldCom and Enron, Chun-Hua and Ling-Yu believe that unethical behaviors in college will undoubtedly transfer to unethical behaviors in the work place (p. 86). These researchers also looked to previous authors whose studies showed similar results:

- Almost three-quarters of the Russian business majors in the Lupton and Chapman (2002) study reported cheating;
- Seventy-six percent of students across Eastern Europe, in the former Soviet Republics, and in Central Asia reported cheating while in college (Grimes, 2004);

- Lupton, Chapman, and Weiss (2000) report that almost 84 percent of the Polish students in their study admitted to cheating while in college;
- More than half of the Japanese students in the Diekhof, LaBeff, Shinohara, and Yusukawa (1999) study reported having cheated (as cited in Chun-Hua & Ling-Yu).

As a response to the abundance of academic dishonesty worldwide, Chun-Hua and Ling-Yu surveyed Taiwanese students to determine the frequency of certain types of dishonest behaviors. They focused on plagiarism, cheating on tests, falsifying documents (changing answers), and cheating on assignments. Similar to American students, the majority of Taiwan students reported that they have cheated, with cheating on tests and assignments (by providing friends with answers and copying from friends) being the most common dishonest acts. Students in this study did not believe that their teachers had done enough to deter cheating or to punish students who had cheated, and as a result, the students who admitted to cheating believed that cheating was widespread.

ACADEMIC DISHONESTY IN HIGH SCHOOL = ACADEMIC DISHONESTY IN COLLEGE

It is possible that college students learned how to cheat while they were in high school. One concern about survey use to gain information is that even though they are anonymous, respondents tend to answer according to how they think they should respond. As a result, it is possible that responses are not objective. Focus groups, on the other hand, announce the topic of a research study and establish discussion groups based on participants' willingness to discuss that topic. McCabe (1999) facilitated focus group discussions with 32 high school and college students in New Jersey. At least ten of the high school student participants had plans to attend colleges like Notre Dame, Hartford, Yale, New York University, Cornell and others.

One of the most telling issues of this study is the way that students openly discussed the topic:

"Students displayed little reluctance to discuss the topic ofVcheating, and they talked freely about their own experiences as well as those of their peers. Almost all admitted to some type of cheating. The high school students were decidedly more blasé about cheating than were the college students" (McCabe).

The high school students reported that academic dishonesty was not only common but of very little significance to students or teachers. They further noted an unwritten rule to not report peers who cheat. The high school students also considered most of their teachers technologically ignorant, which made plagiarizing from Internet sources easy and regularly achieved (McCabe). McCabe notes that the high school students in these focus groups had little ethical conflict about what they had done:

I guess the first time you do it, you feel really bad, but then you get used to it. You keep telling yourself you're not doing anything wrong.... Maybe you might know in your heart that it's wrong, but it gets easier after a while to handle it. People cheat. It doesn't make you less of a person or worse of a person. There are times when you just are in need of a little help. I don't know if it's just our school, but like everybody cheats. Everyone looks at everyone else's paper. And the teachers don't care; they let it happen.... The students keep on doing it because they don't get in trouble. If I was going to [a school with strict rules against cheating], I would find a way around it. It's like a bigger wall to climb.

Many high school participants reported that their schools (teachers, administrators) never discussed cheating or any consequences of academic dishonesty. They suggested that elementary school teachers, secondary school teachers, and parents make it a priority to enforcing standards of academic honesty. Other students noted that until society treats cheaters like they have done something wrong, cheating will continue:

You can't really change it from the school level; you have to change the way society looks at you. You have to make cheating so terrible you would never want to do it.... You have to change what people think. You have to make people not want to cheat (McCabe).

If a student cheats, and his or her teacher does not punish him or her, the student and his or her peers learn that being dishonest is acceptable (McCabe). Until he or she is punished for it, he or she has no reason to believe otherwise. Furthermore, the students who don not cheat learn quickly that receiving good grades, being successful in school, requires dishonest behavior. It should be no wonder, then, that these students grow up to be dishonest employees.

DISHONESTY IN COLLEGE = DISHONESTY AT WORK

To examine whether or not there is a link between dishonest behavior in school and unethical behavior in the workplace, Harding, Carpenter, Finelli, and Passow (2004) surveyed undergraduate students who worked full-time when not in school. Harding et al. asked their study participants to think about instances in which they were tempted to cheat in college and had also considered violating a policy where they worked. While all of the respondents experienced such temptation in college, only about two-thirds of the participants had considered unethical behavior while at work. Almost 80 percent of the students cheated at least once in college; many of those had cheated frequently while in high school. While only 30 percent of those who considered behaving unethically at work had done so, more than 60 percent of those who stole merchandise from work, who lied on a time sheet, or who committed some other policy infraction cheated frequently in high school (Harding et al.). Additionally, the workplace data may be inaccurate as Sims (1993) notes that employees don not necessarily see themselves as violating policy even when they are doing so:

> Though the majority of employees would consider it stealing for someone to take a box of stationery, they themselves see nothing wrong with using an occasional piece of paper for their own personal use. This occasional piece added up and multiplied by the entire work force turns out to be a much greater total loss than the "stealing" that rarely happens (Sims).

Whether or not the statistics accurately reflect the ethics of today's workforce, the data is clear with regard to students repeating dishonest behaviors. "Many students, despite changes in context from high school to college and to the workplace, will make the same ultimate decision when faced with a temptation to engage in deviant behavior" (Harding et al.).

PEER INFLUENCES

Many parents cringe at the thought of peer pressure in relation to their children's social development. When considering academic honesty, however, McCabe and Trevino (1997) note that peers may be a positive influence on behavior. These researchers collected over 1,700 surveys distributed to students at nine public colleges in the fall of 1993. Specifically, they focused on two factors: the differences among student participants (e.g., age, gender, parents' education, GPA) and the contexts in which academic dishonesty was reported by students. As already noted, peers are quite influential; they help each other cheat and they don't tell on each other.

In the McCabe and Trevino study, peer influence can also be seen as positive in nature. "Academic dishonesty was lower when respondents perceived that their peers disapproved of such misconduct … and was higher when students perceived higher levels of cheating among their peers." Young people often receive cues from each other about how to behave in certain situations. Indeed, peer pressure is a strong force. Students who are academically honest can effect change in their social circles by not tolerating cheaters. In addition, teachers and administrators—as a rule of ethics—must accept only academic honesty from their students. Finally, parents know that their children learn by observation rather than by what they are told. When parents behave honestly—stopping at all stop signs and paying for cable network—their children follow suit simply by example.

TERMS & CONCEPTS

Academic Dishonesty: Cheating in relation to academic work (plagiarizing, copying from someone, allowing someone to copy from you, texting answers).

Active Deception: Seeking out answers to assignments or tests (copying from someone).

Academic Ethic: The prioritization of academics by not drinking, not taking classes based on low difficulty to increase a GPA, and not cheating.

Ethics: A set of principles used in reasoned decision-making based on a person's belief in what is right or just.

External Locus of Control: The perception that outside factors rather than personal actions or decisions are responsible for one's success or failure.

Internal Locus of Control: The perception that personal actions or decisions are responsible for one's success or failure.

Passive Deception: Allowing someone to gain academic information from you (letting someone copy from your test or assignment).

Plagiarism: Using someone else's words or ideas without giving them credit.

Punitive: Resulting in punishment or discipline.

Maureen McMahon

Bibliography

Chun-Hua, L., & Ling-Yu, W. (2007). Academic dishonesty in higher education: A nationwide study in Taiwan. *Higher Education, 54*, 85–97. Retrieved June 7, 2009, from EBSCO online database, Education Research Complete

Harding, T., Carpenter, D., Finelli, C., & Passow, H. (2004). Does academic dishonesty relate to unethical behavior in professional practice? An exploratory study. *Science & Engineering Ethics, 10*, 311–324. Retrieved June 7, 2009, from EBSCO online database, Academic Search Complete.

Iyer, R., & Eastman, J. (2008). The impact of unethical reasoning on academic dishonesty: Exploring the moderating effect of social desirability. *Marketing Education Review, 18*, 21–33. Retrieved June 7, 2009, from EBSCO online database, Education Research Complete.

Jones, D. R. (2011). Academic dishonesty: Are more students cheating? *Business Communication Quarterly, 74*, 141–150. Retrieved December 10, 2013, from EBSCO online database, Education Research Complete.

McCabe, D. L. (1999). Academic dishonesty among high school students. *Adolescence, 34*, 681. Retrieved June 7, 2009, from EBSCO online database Education Research Complete.

McCabe, D., & Trevino, L. (1997). Individual and contextual influences on academic dishonesty: A multicampus investigation. *Research in Higher Education, 38*, 379–396. Retrieved June 7, 2009, from EBSCO online database, Education Research Complete.

Nelson, L. P., Nelson, R. K., & Tichenor, L. (2013). Understanding today's students: Entry-level science student involvement in academic dishonesty. *Journal of College Science Teaching, 42*, 52–57. Retrieved December 10, 2013, from EBSCO online database, Education Research Complete.

Pino, N. W., & Smith, W. L. (2003). College students and academic dishonesty. *College Student Journal, 37*, 490–500. Retrieved June 7, 2009, from EBSCO online database, Education Research Complete.

Rakovski, C. C., & Levy, E. S. (2007). Academic dishonesty: Perceptions of business students. *College Student Journal, 41*, 466–481. Retrieved June 7, 2009, from EBSCO online database, Education Research Complete.

Sendag, S., Duran, M., & Robert Fraser, M. M. (2012). Surveying the extent of involvement in online academic dishonesty (e-dishonesty) related practices among university students and the rationale students provide: One university's experience. *Computers in Human Behavior, 28*, 849–860. Retrieved December 10, 2013, from EBSCO online database, Education Research Complete.

Sims, R. L. (1993). The relationship between academic dishonesty and unethical business practices. *Journal of Education for Business, 68*, 207. Retrieved June 7, 2009, from EBSCO online database, Education Research Complete.

Storch, E. A., & Storch, J. B. (2002). Fraternities, sororities, and academic dishonesty. *College Student Journal, 36*, 247. Retrieved June 7, 2009, from EBSCO online database, Education Research Complete.

Westacott, E. (2008). Academic dishonesty and the culture of assessment. *National Collegiate Honors Council, 9*, 21–27. Retrieved June 7, 2009, from EBSCO online database, Education Research Complete.

Winrow, A. R. (2015). Academic integrity and the heterogeneous student body. *Global Education Journal, 2015*(2), 77–91. Retrieved January 15, 2016, from EBSCO Online Database Education Research Complete.

Suggested Reading

Anderman, E. M., Griesinger, T., & Westerfield, G. (1998). Motivation and cheating during early adolescence. *Journal of Educational Psychology, 90*, 84–93.

Baron, J., & Crooks, S. (2005). Academic integrity in web based distance education. *TechTrends: Linking Research & Practice to Improve Learning, 49*, 40–45. Retrieved June 7, 2009, from EBSCO online database, Education Research Complete.

Bernstein, P. (1985). Cheating—The new national pastime? *Business, 35*, 24–33.

Black, E., Greaser, J., & Dawson, K. (2008). Academic dishonesty in traditional and online classrooms: Does the media equation hold true? *Journal of Asynchronous Learning Networks, 12*(3–4), 23–30. Retrieved June 7, 2009, from EBSCO online database, Education Research Complete.

Bowers, W. J. (1964). *Student dishonesty and its control in college.* New York: Bureau of Applied Research, Columbia University.

Carter, R. (1987). Employee theft often appears legitimate. *Accountancy, 100*(1127), 75–78.

Clark, J. P., & Hollinger, R. C. (1983). Theft by employees in work organizations. Rockville, MD: National Institute of Justice.

Dix, E., Emery, L., & Le, B. (2014). Committed to the honor code: An investment model analysis of academic integrity. *Social Psychology of Education.* 17(1), 179-186.

Drake, C. A. (1941). Why students cheat. *Journal of Higher Education, 12*, 418–420.

Evans, E. E., & Craig, D. (1990). Teacher and student perceptions of academic cheating in middle and senior high schools. *Journal of Educational Research, 84*, 44–52.

Fass, R. A. (1986). By honor bound: Encouraging academic honesty. *Educational Record, 67*, 32–36.

Goldsen, R. K. (1960). *What college students think.* Princeton, NJ: D. Van Nostrand.

Hawley, C. S. (1984). The thieves of academe: Plagiarism in the university system. *Improving College and University Teaching, 32,* 35–39.

Holbeck, R., Greenberger, S., Cooper, L., Steele, J., Palenque, S. M., & Koukoudeas, S. (2015). Reporting plagiarism in the online classroom. *Journal of Online Learning & Teaching, 11*(2), 202–209. Retrieved January 15, 2016, from EBSCO Online Database Education Research Complete.

Menon, M. K., & Sharland, A. (2011). Narcissism, exploitative attitudes, and academic dishonesty: An exploratory investigation of reality versus myth. *Journal of Education for Business, 86,* 50–55. Retrieved December 10, 2013, from EBSCO online database, Education Research Complete.

Nonis, S., & Swift, C. O. (2001). An examination of the relationship between academic dishonesty and workplace dishonesty: A multicampus investigation. *Journal of Education for Business,* 69–77.

Paul, C., Federici, E., & Buehler, M. (2010). Instructing students in academic integrity. *Journal of College Science Teaching.* 40(2), 50-55.

Peterson, L. (1988). Teaching academic integrity: Opportunities in bibliographic instruction. *Research Strategies, 6,* 168–176.

Schab, F. (1991). Schooling without learning: Thirty years of cheating in high school. *Adolescence, 26,* 839–847.

Stevens, G. E., & Stevens, F. W. (1987). Ethical inclinations of tomorrow's managers revisited: How and why students cheat. *Journal of Education for Business, 63,* 24–29.

Weber, J. (1990). Measuring the impact of teaching ethics to future managers: A review, assessment, and recommendations. *Journal of Business Ethics, 9,* 183–190.

STUDENT RETENTION

How to increase retention among college students has been researched for more than fifty years. The concept of students persisting from semester to semester, year to year, and from entrance to graduation is especially crucial in this economic time. Several studies are discussed here which focus on successful retention efforts on college campuses. Helping students feel like they belong to a community, first-year seminars, faculty development, developmental (remedial) courses, and learning communities have been shown to increase retention and are discussed below.

KEYWORDS: At-Risk Students; Attrition; Developmental Courses; First-Year Seminar (FYS); Intervention; Learning Communities; Persistence; Remediation; Retention

OVERVIEW

When it comes to win-win combinations, few are more beneficial than the relationship between student retention and Higher Education. With America facing an economic deficit and businesses folding in all directions during the Great Recession (2007-2009), being in college rather than in the workplace seemed to be the safest place for some people. However, simply being in college is not as easy as staying in college. Respectable high school grades and average standardized test scores allow entrance to some favorable institutions of Higher Education. Yet once each student says goodbye to his or her parents and begins to unpack, that student's future may depend less on what he or she does and more on what the institutions are doing. At some point, the responsibility of students persisting in college moves from the students to that of the college administrations.

Researchers study retention, journals report about it, and budgets are stretched to enhance it. Schools that do not retain students lose tuition dollars as well as the combined resources of instruction, housing, and support services that are spent on those students who are eventually lost to attrition. Conversely, students who are not retained lose the basic opportunities that Higher Education offers; for many, that means secure employment possibilities that are not a consideration for anyone lacking a degree. According to ACT (2007), about 40% of the students who enter college in any given year will leave before the second year begins, and only slightly more than a third will actually earn a degree (as cited in Fike & Fike, 2008).

While much effort is given to researching and reporting about retention, a 2004 study surveying over 1,000 colleges reports that fewer than half "have established an improvement goal for [the] retention of students from the first to second year" (Habley & McClanahan, 2004). College and university administrators know how important student retention is—if not for the students then certainly for their budgets—yet making the necessary changes to increase student persistence has not become a priority. Many campuses put someone in charge of retention efforts, but that charge often comes without the budget, time, staff, or authority to actually make changes that improve retention (Hossler, Ziskin, & Gross, 2009). Furthermore, it is ironic that the response to a college's success relying so heavily on student persistence is to put one person in charge of that task when several people fill the admissions' offices. In other words, it does not make much sense to get students to a school if only one person is in charge of keeping them there.

WHY STUDENTS LEAVE

It is fair to say that some students should not be in college. Be it the wrong time or the wrong goal, college simply is not for everybody, and even the strongest retention program will not help this group persist. In contrast, there is another group of students who will be successful academically without any intervention; these students are generally ambitious and goal-oriented. In the midst of these two groups of students is a third category: the students who are considered "at risk" for early dropout. This category of students does not travel with a neon flashing sign announcing their precarious situation. As a result, it is essential for school personnel to try to predict what risk factors place them in danger of attrition.

Braunstein and McGrath (1997) conducted a study to do just that. Iona College, a private catholic school in New Rochelle, New York, experienced a decade-long trend in attrition, even though a focus on retention efforts had taken place—a freshman experience course was organized, orientation sessions had improved, and a retention coordinator was hired, yet students were still dropping out. Most of the students who did drop out were academically weak, according to the study. The researchers concluded that:

> "the students who were retained showed higher high school grades, Scholastic Aptitude Test (SAT) scores, and first semester grade point averages than the students who were not retained. In one particular analysis, the first semester grade point average was the most significant predictor of retention. The grade point average for freshmen who were retained was 2.76 while the average for those who were not retained was 1.88" (Braunstein & McGrath).

In addition, the authors note that the students retained after the first year (of the study) had an average annual family income of at least ten-thousand dollars more than that of the students who were not retained (Braunstein & McGrath). This is not surprising, as students have always been dropping out of college for academic and financial reasons. However, the data does place an emphasis on the fact that these risk factors (low academic skill level and low income status) are combatable by institutions. Colleges who want students to persist can offer remediation, study skills assistance, and tutoring for weak students as well as offering financial aid and scholarship opportunities to low-income students.

In another study created to predict retention, DeBerard, Spielmans, and Julka (2004) administered surveys to the freshmen of a private northwestern U.S. institution. The surveys gathered information about risk factor variables, including academic history, demographics, drinking and smoking habits, coping skills, and social support availability. Students completed the surveys in the fall 1999 semester and were identified again the following year (fall 2000) to determine retention rates. Fifteen percent of the students completing the survey did not return the following academic year. While most of the variables showed a predictive ability for high academic achievement (such as strong social network, high SAT scores, and developed coping skills), only one was shown to actually predict retention: high school GPA. In other words, the students who were not retained after one or two semesters shared a commonality: they had low high school grade point averages (DeBerard et al.).

It is important to note that these two different studies indicate a common factor for student retention: students who are weak academically pose a risk for attrition. While not a neon sign, this is an indicator that colleges see well before students enter their campuses.

Intervention Strategies to Increase Retention

FIRST-YEAR SEMINAR & LEARNING COMMUNITIES

Many institutions require an introductory college course for new students. Whether it is called a freshman seminar, first-year experience, or first-year seminar (FYS) course, the class generally focuses on transition information to help new students adapt to life within the campus community. Many offer study skills instruction, class visits to various offices on campus, and instruction in some academic discipline. In many instances, the discipline topic selections are chosen by the student based on academic study preferences. Some colleges make the first-year experience course part of a learning community, meaning that it is offered in conjunction with other courses, all of which are taken by the same group of students. Other campuses offer the course in isolation. The goal is to assist students' transition to college, which in turn helps them persist.

Vincent Tinto, a professor of education at Syracuse University, has researched student persistence in Higher Education for more than thirty years. One of Tinto's theories of retention is that students will be much more likely to persist when they feel integrated into the college community both socially and academically (1975). Considering Tinto's integration model, Potts and Schultz (2008) studied the retention effects of students enrolled in a freshman seminar course that was offered within a learning community in the school's business department. Using a sample of 223 freshmen at a public undergraduate institution, students were randomly chosen to have the learning community, the FYS class in isolation, or no intervention. Students were identified as high risk based on off-campus living status during the first semester; integration within the campus community is difficult for students who do not live on campus. They were also considered at-risk if their ACT scores were below 22 or if their high school ranking was higher than 40% on a scale of 0 to 100% (Potts & Schultz).

The only noted retention effect of the FYS learning community occurred within the off-campus student population. The students who lived off campus during their first year and who experienced the FYS learning community had a 74% retention rate when compared to the students who lived off campus and did not experience the FYS learning community combination; the retention rate for that group was only slightly above 42%; there was no statistically significant difference within the students considered at risk for academic reasons (Potts & Schultz). For colleges and universities that do not require or cannot accommodate all freshmen living on campus, an FYS learning community may be necessary to increase the retention of students who would otherwise be lost to attrition—those who feel isolated from the campus community.

DEVELOPMENTAL (REMEDIAL) EDUCATION

According to the National Center for Educational Statistics (2007), almost 100% of two-year public schools and three-quarters of four-year public schools offered remedial services during the 2006-2007 academic year. Services can range from offering one specific class to entrance into a learning community of developmental courses. In whatever situation, the goal is the same: to increase the skill-level of under-prepared students. Some institutions prefer not to offer developmental courses; generally, those schools tend to be private and can grant admission to whomever they choose. However, with less money in the economy, fewer students can to apply to any college. In addition, Mooney (1989) argues that the student body has been less prepared academically than students in the past (as cited in Braunstein & McGrath). As a result of these factors, colleges should be admitting as many students as possible and assuring that the students they do admit are retained.

According to Lesik (2007), offering developmental courses to the students who need it will increase retention. The Lesik study looked at the retention effects of intermediate (developmental) algebra classes at a public undergraduate university; the study lasted over a three-year period.

"After the first year (or second semester) at the university, students who participated in the developmental program have an estimated risk of dropout of only 8.2% while equivalent students who did not participate in the developmental program have an estimated risk of dropout of 27.7%. Similarly, after the second year (or fourth semester), students who participated in the developmental program have an estimated risk of dropout of 4.4% while equivalent students who did not participate in the developmental program have an estimated risk of dropout of 16.5%" (Lesik).

In addition, Fike and Fike note that the successful completion of developmental courses can actually predict the persistence of first-time college students. These researchers tracked over 9,000 new students to identify retention rates from fall to spring and also from fall to fall semesters. Almost 30% of the students dropped out during or following their first fall semester, and more than 50% did not enroll in a second academic year. For those who did return, the strongest predictor of retention was passing a developmental reading course. Also, passing a developmental math class was identified as another positive predictor of retention. In fact, students who placed into developmental math but did not enroll in it had a lower rate of retention than the students who placed into the developmental math course, enrolled in it, but did not complete it (Fike & Fike). In other words, enrolling in developmental math and not completing it carried a higher chance of persistence than not enrolling in it for these students. In addition, students who did not need the developmental reading course showed a high retention rate as they already possessed the skill deemed so necessary to academic success (Fike & Fike).

A COMBINED APPROACH

Pan, Guo, Alikonis, and Bai (2008) studied the retention effects of a combined intervention approach at an urban university in the Midwestern U.S. The institution had received a grant to encourage the retention of at-risk undergraduate students as well as to encourage those students to graduate within a four-year time span. The college created several intervention programs to encourage student retention. Pan et al. collected data to note the retention rates and cumulative GPAs of student participants over the three-year study. Most of the interventions programs "were designed to promote student-to-student interaction, faculty-to-student interaction, student involvement, academic engagement, and academic assistance" (Pan et al.). The six categories of programs included academic assistance (tutoring), first-year experience/seminar, social integration, advising, financial aid, and orientation. There were 1,305 students who participated voluntarily in one of the programs at the beginning of the 2000 fall semester. The average GPA for the participant group was 2.91 (Pan et al.).

Retention rates for each year of the study were 67 (2001-2002), 54 (2002-2003), and 49 (2003-2004), respectively; the cumulative GPAs for all three years were 2.33, 2.75, and 2.58, respectively (Pan et al.). The authors note the specific effects of some of the Success Challenge programs:

> *"The academic-help [tutoring] programs significantly increased the retention rates for the first year; the advising and social integration programs significantly helped students return to school after the first year; the general orientation programs significantly helped all students increase GPA for the first year. This study*

confirmed Tinto's (1993) statement that involvement in social and intellectual life of a college helps learning and persistence in college. [In addition,] participation in more than one Success Challenge program greatly helped students both in retention and increase of GPA, not only in the first year, but also second and third year" (Pan et al.).

Finally, one of the biggest differences noted in this study is that for the students that were truly underprepared (at-risk academically), the academic support program was the most helpful to increase cumulative GPA and retention (Pan et al.).

When a faculty member is hired at a college or university, it is generally to fill a gap in a specific research area. Generally, only faculty hired in education departments have actually studied the art of teaching. As such, there is often a misfit between how faculty teach and how students learn. The National Training Laboratories in Bethel, Maine, constructed the learning pyramid below to indicate how students retain the information presented in class. Students retain only about 5% of the material presented in a class lecture. In other words, any instructor who chooses to lecture students runs the risk of only three and a half minutes of a 70-minute lecture being retained. Source: National Training Laboratories, Bethel, Maine

PEDAGOGIES OF ENGAGEMENT

According to Tinto:

> *"Pedagogies of engagement—such as cooperative and problem-based learning—have been shown to be particularly effective in enhancing student success. Research in this regard is clear: Active involvement of students in learning activities in and around the classroom, especially with other students, is critical to student retention and graduation" (Tinto).*

Unfortunately, studies show that the majority of instructors "rely on lecture as their primary teaching tool" (Finkelstein et al., 1998, as cited in McShannon et al. 2009). As such, an in-class faculty development program was created by McShannon et al. in order to increase student retention and offer faculty information about effective teaching strategies. Gaining Retention and Achievement for Students Program (GRASP) works with instructors for an entire semester, conducting learning style inventories on students, interviewing faculty, introducing new teaching methods to faculty, observing classes, and conducting post-observation conferences with the faculty involved. McShannon et al. used GRASP at New Mexico State University over several consecutive years with over 50 faculty members:

> *"GRASP staff identified the learning style distribution in each class, began to suggest appropriate teaching strategies, and helped faculty implement the recommended strategies. When faculty became aware of the diversity of student learning, they were more willing to implement and practice alternative teaching strategies. Once faculty recognized many of their students learn differently than they themselves did, faculty were free to teach differently than they themselves were taught"* (McShannon et al.).

The retention and academic achievement of freshmen and sophomores in the GRASP intervention classes were compared to students in the same classes whose teachers did not participate in the GRASP study. Students receiving an A, B, or C in the course were considered to be achieving academically; retention was cited for the students who remained in their major one year after the GRASP study. The freshmen and sophomores showed 5.6% and 6.7% increases in achievement, respectively (p. 206). Additionally, a 7.8% increase in retention was noted for freshmen with a 12.9% increase identified for sophomores. Furthermore, feedback from faculty showed that GRASP teaching strategies were still being used (at least weekly) as a result of the study. Not surprisingly, the methods continued by faculty include those at the bottom of the learning pyramid: students being active in class, students teaching each other, and student involvement in group discussions and activities (McShannon et al.).

In addition to encouraging student activity and engagement, Tinto identified additional ways that teachers can increase retention. He notes that the expectations of each course should be clear to students and challenging in scope. Also, students need feedback. They need to know how they are doing and what they need to improve. Tinto includes the use of early alert information as a faculty function. If students are non-productive, if their attendance is shaky, or if their ability is lacking, faculty need to notify the necessary people on campus for intervention to take place. Finally, it is helpful for faculty to know what "learning and living situations students are experiencing" (Tinto).

Students who live off-campus, have jobs, or have families have different social, academic, and economic issues than traditional students living on campus. It is important for teachers to know what those issues are, and asking about them can help students feel relevant to the success of the class.

FULL-TIME OR PART-TIME: IT DOES MATTER

In addition to how students are taught, it is also important by whom they are taught. Colleges and universities rely heavily on adjuncts to fill the void left by limited full-time faculty. This reliance is probably the most visible in the areas of introductory English and math courses. However, Burgess and Samuels (1999) show that the overuse of adjuncts for courses within a sequence (like ENG101 and ENG102, calculus I and calculus II) results in underprepared students who often do not complete the sequence. The researchers investigated a community college system consisting of 10 separate campuses in the Phoenix, Arizona, area. They looked at both English and math sequences to identify trends among the students taking courses with part-time instructors.

The authors note that:

> *"For either developmental or regular courses, college students who take the first course in a sequence from a part-time instructor, and who take the second course in the sequence from a full-time instructor seem underprepared for the second course. By contrast to students experiencing other instructor status combinations (part-time/part-time, full-time/part-time, or full-time/full-time), these students are significantly less likely to either complete or achieve a grade of "C" or better in the second course; For students in the second course, those who took the first course from a full-time instructor were more likely to complete the second course. The students with the poorest completion rate for the second course took the first course from a part-time instructor and had a full-time instructor for the second course"* (Burgess & Samuels).

Almost 20,000 students in the Burgess and Samuels study took English 101 and 102 while the research was conducted. Less than a third of those students had a full-time faculty member for both courses. The statistics are similar for mathematics sequences offered by the college. For colleges looking at retention strategies, this data cannot be ignored. When course sequences are required, and students drop out of the second course in the sequence, keeping them at the institution will be difficult. The overuse of adjuncts is understandable—it is cost effective. However, adjunct course assignments could be changed so that they are not negatively affecting the most vulnerable students on campus.

VIEWPOINTS

In 2005, Hossler, Ziskin, and Gross conducted a pilot study of several four-year institutions to determine which campuses had retention programs and which campuses were effectively assessing those programs. Unfortunately, even though retaining students is essential to schools being successful economically, "most four-year colleges and universities make relatively little effort to implement programmatic initiatives to enhance persistence." Furthermore, the people who do focus on retention tend to be the ones that are not in daily contact with students, i.e., administrators in offices where students do not need to be. It is teachers who hold the key, and asking faculty to change the way they teach or requiring them to teach freshmen when they are used to upperclassmen may meet with reluctance on some campuses. However, retention efforts cannot succeed when they are in isolation. Student persistence needs to be everyone's concern, and as soon as campuses make it such, their efforts will be rewarded.

Furthermore, retention efforts do not need to be great in scope, or all-consuming. Most campuses already offer developmental courses. Most also have a residence life staff and orientation programs to help students become part of the campus community. And, many have ways to identify and outreach to at-risk students. Each of these programs needs to adopt a common goal of coordinating efforts to increase retention. Programs that work together require less money and less change than a new program given the name "retention" that has to start from the ground up. Students leave the comfort zone of their homes, families, and friends to go to college, a place that has none of the former. Of course, life is going to be difficult for them, but as soon as they feel like some of that comfort is being replaced by the institution—by the coordinated efforts of the school around them—the more integrated they will become, and the more likely they are to remain.

TERMS & CONCEPTS

At-Risk Students: Students who are categorized at having a great risk for withdrawal, primarily those with low academic skills (high school GPAs, SAT/ACT scores, placement test scores).

Attrition: Withdrawal from college courses or Higher Education institutions altogether.

Developmental Courses: Courses offering instruction to build fundamental (reading, writing, and mathematics) skills.

First-Year Seminar (FYS): Course that is sometimes created in a learning community; course content often focuses on strengthening the study and awareness skills of new college students.

Intervention: Strategies offered to assist student persistence.

Learning Communities: A block of courses (usually three) offered to the same group of students; instructors communicate regularly and create assignments based on one central theme.

Persistence: Staying, remaining in school from semester to semester.

Remediation: Providing instruction that is foundational (developmental) in nature with the goal of student success and movement to college-level work.

Retention: The focus of keeping students in educational settings; helping students persist in Higher Education settings.

Maureen McMahon

BIBLIOGRAPHY

Bass, L. H., & Ballard, A. S. (2012). Student engagement and course registration methods as possible predictors of freshman retention. Research in Higher Education Journal, 18 1-13. Retrieved December 5, 2013, from EBSCO Online Database Education Research Complete.

Braunstein, A. & McGrath, M. (1997). The retention of freshman students: An examination of the assumptions, beliefs, and perceptions. College Student Journal, 31(2), 188-200. Retrieved April 4, 2009, from EBSCO online database Academic Search Complete

Burgess, L., & Samuels, C. (1999). Impact of full-time versus part-time instructor status on college student retention and academic performance in sequential courses. Community College Journal of Research & Practice, 23(5), 487-498. Retrieved October 21, 2008 from Academic Search Complete.

Cundall JR., M. K. (2013). Admissions, retention, and reframing the question "Isn't it just more work?".

Journal of the National Collegiate Honors Council, 14 (2), 31-34. Retrieved December 5, 2013, from EBSCO Online Database Education Research Complete.

DeBerard, M., Spielmans, G., & Julka, D. (2004). Predictors of academic achievement and retention among college freshmen: A longitudinal study. College Student Journal, 38(1), 66-80. Retrieved April 1, 2009, from EBSCO online database Academic Search Complete.

Fike, D. & Fike, R. (2008). Predictors of first-year student retention in the community college. Community College Review, 36(2), 68-88. Retrieved April 1, 2009, from EBSCO online database, Academic Search Complete.

Habley, W. R. & McClanahan, R. (2004). What works in student retention: Executive summary: all survey colleges. ACT.

Hossler, D., Ziskin, M. & Gross, J. P. K. (2009). Getting serious about institutional performance in student retention: Research-based lessons on effective policies and practices. About Campus, 13 (6), 2-11.

Jackson, V. (2012). The use of a social networking site with pre-enrolled Business School students to enhance their first year experience at university, and in doing so, improve retention. Widening Participation & Lifelong Learning, 14 25-41. Retrieved December 5, 2013, from EBSCO Online Database Education Research Complete.

Lesik, S. (2007). Do developmental mathematics programs have a causal impact on student retention? An application of discrete-time survival and regression-discontinuity analysis. Research in Higher Education, 48(5), 583-608. Retrieved October 19, 2008, from Academic Search Complete.

McShannon, J., Hynes, P., Nirmalakhandan, N., Venkataramana, G., Ricketts, C., Ulery, A. & Steiner, R. (2006). Gaining retention and achievement for students program: A faculty development program. Journal of Professional Issues in Engineering Education & Practice, 132(3), 204-208. Retrieved October 21, 2008, from Academic Search Complete.

National Center for Educational Statistics (2007). Digest of Educational Statistics: 2007 Tables and Figures. U.S Department of Education, Institute of Education Sciences. Retrieved April 21, 2009 from NCES, http://nces.ed.gov.

Pan, W., Guo, S., Alikonis, C. & Bai, H. (2008). Do intervention programs assist students to succeed in college? A multilevel longitudinal study. College Student Journal, 42(1), 90-98. Retrieved April 1, 2009, from EBSCO online database Academic Search Complete.

Potts, G. & Schultz, B. (2008). The freshman seminar and academic success of at-risk students. College Student Journal, Part B, 42(2), p. 647-658. Retrieved April 1,

2009, from EBSCO online database Academic Search Complete.

Tinto, V. (1987). The principles of effective retention. Paper presented at the Maryland College Personnel Association Fall Conference: Prince George's Community College, Largo, MD.

Tinto, V. (2009). How to help students stay and succeed [Letter]. Chronicle of Higher Education, 55(22), p. A33-A33. Retrieved April 13, 2009, from EBSCO online database Academic Search Premier.

Van der Sluis, H., May, S., Locke, L., & Hill, M. (2013). Flexible academic support to enhance student retention and success. Widening Participation & Lifelong Learning, 15 (2), 79-95. Retrieved December 5, 2013, from EBSCO Online Database Education Research Complete.

Zepke, N., Leach, L., & Prebble, T. (2006). Being learner centered: one way to improve student retention? Studies in Higher Education, 31(5), 587-600. Retrieved October 19, 2008, from Academic Search Complete.

SUGGESTED READING

Braxton, J.M., Doyle, W., Jones, W., McLendon, W., Hirshy, A., & Hartley, H. (2014). Rethinking College Student Retention. San Francisco, CA.: Jossey Bass.

Coll, K., & Stewart, R. (2008). College student retention: Instrument validation and value for partnering between academic and counseling services. College Student Journal, 42(1), 41-56. Retrieved October 19, 2008, from Academic Search Complete.

Devonport, T., & Lane, A. (2006). Relationships between self-efficacy, coping and student retention. Social Behavior & Personality: An International Journal, 34(2), 127-138.

Retrieved October 21, 2008, from SocINDEX with Full Text, http:// w3.org.

Gordon, V. N & Habley, W. R. (2000). Academic advising: A comprehensive handbook. San Francisco: NACADA.

Kirst, M. W. (2008). Secondary schools and colleges must work together. Thought & Action, 24(Fall), 111-122.

Kozar, J. M. & Marcketti, S. B. (2008). Utilizing field-based instruction as an effective teaching strategy. College Student Journal, Part A, 42(2), 305-311. Retrieved April 1, 2009, from EBSCO online database Academic Search Complete.

Nealy, M. (2005). Key to student retention—strong advising. Diverse: Issues in Higher Education, 22(14) 12. Retrieved April 4, 2009, from EBSCO online database Academic Search Complete.

Reducing Institutional Rates of Departure. (2004). ASHEERIC Higher Education Report 30(3), 67-78. Retrieved April 13, 2009, from EBSCO online database Academic Search Premier.

Russo-Gleicher, R. J. (2013). Qualitative insights into faculty use of student support services with online students at risk: Implications for student retention. Journal of Educators Online, 10 (1), 1-32. Retrieved December 5, 2013, from EBSCO Online Database Education Research Complete.

Seidman, A. (Ed.) (2012). *College Student Retention: Formula for Student Success.* Lanham, MD.: Rowman & Littlefield Publishers.

Trotter, E. & Roberts, C. (2006). Enhancing the early student experience. Higher Education Research & Development, 25(4), 371-386. Retrieved April 1, 2009, from EBSCO online database Academic Search Complete.

COLLEGE HOUSING

Students attending college have options regarding housing facilities. Many will live on-campus and have their housing fee added to their tuition bill. Others, however, will choose to live in apartments or housing facilities off-campus, paying rent to a landlord rather than their colleges or universities. Living off campus is often less expensive than residing on campus, and there are corporations who build elaborate student residences to compete for housing dollars. However, the studies below will show that students who live on campus tend to be more connected with the colleges they attend. As such, they persist at higher rates, have better grades, and have stronger social networks than do students who live off campus.

KEYWORDS: Community College; Non-traditional Student; Off-campus Housing; On-campus Housing; Outsourcing; Residence Hall; Resident Assistant (RA); Retention; Theory of Integration; Traditional Student

OVERVIEW

One of the biggest transitions for traditional college students is leaving the comfort of their family home to move into a residence hall with a group of strangers; one, two, or three with whom they will share close proximity for several months. As most of those new students will find out, there are advantages and disadvantages to living on campus. For example, living on campus offers the advantage of being close to classes, services, and the dining hall. Many freshmen are not allowed to have vehicles on campus during their first year, however, so making a trip to a Superstore to stock up on supplies can be difficult. Also, students who live in residence halls must abide by the rules of the hall and are supervised by a resident assistant (RA) and resident hall director. In contrast, students who live off-campus are not supervised and can come and go as they please. This is convenient and

independent living, but off-campus students have to get to campus for class and to meet with faculty members and other students, so transportation is often required. Also, off-campus students have to budget their money in order to pay rent and utilities and have to buy food and gas. On-campus students pay for everything except transportation simply by paying their tuition, usually a twice-yearly bill.

For colleges and universities, offering on-campus housing has benefits and drawbacks as well. Residential housing brings a financial resource to a school. However, on-campus housing also puts a great deal of responsibility on that school; students who get injured or behave irresponsibly are the ultimate responsibility of the college—regardless of their age—when they live on campus. Over the past twenty years, colleges have been able to out-source that responsibility by allowing large corporations to build housing complexes right on their campuses. This option removes liability from the college and keeps students close to college resources. In effect, colleges lease land to corporations that receive rent from students (so the corporations make a profit) while those same students are considered residential because they live on-campus. Some of these corporations actually compete with colleges and universities for student housing dollars. Rather than seeking land on a campus, they purchase property close by, construct housing complexes, and offer apartment-style living, which ultimately takes housing dollars away from the college.

In Plattsburgh, New York, United Group developed and built College Suites, a 390-bed complex for Plattsburgh State students in the fall of 2009. The facility held two and four-bedroom apartments and "a fitness center, cafe/student lounge, game room and laundry facilities. Other amenities included cable television, wireless Internet service and all utilities"

(LoTemplio, 2009) for a price tag of around $8,000 per year. A walk of less than two minutes took students from the new apartment building to campus, which offered residence hall housing for $3,000-$4,000 less than the rent at College Suites. The residence halls at Plattsburgh State, however, are not as self-contained as the Suites, and students with cars who live on campus rarely get to park right outside their back door like they do down the street at College Suites. The convenience of independent living is worth the extra cost for some students, and colleges and universities now must consider how to compete with private housing options.

Off-Campus Living

STUDENT IMPACT

Realistically, the most important issue to consider about housing options is whether or not students are more academically successful in one situation or the other. It may be that students care more about the facility they live in than their success in college. According to Macintyre (2003), "students have become more demanding about the quality of their accommodation and are looking for self-contained single-room apartments and access to a range of additional facilities such as computer points, laundries and gymnasiums." A more recent study also found that students increasingly are preferring suite-style residence halls that have private rooms to traditional residence halls. (Sickler & Roskos, 2013). As a result of student demand, colleges have started to create apartment-like housing—similar to that offered by College Suites for students to live on-campus as independently as possible. Another way to meet student demand for independence is for colleges to lease land to large corporations (like the one that owns College Suites) to construct apartment/housing complexes on campus property. In this situation, students pay rent to the company (or building manager) that owns the building, but they are still considered on-campus residents who are close to classes, dining halls, and support offices.

When living situations are looked at from an academic perspective, however, students choosing the off-campus option may be doing so at their academic peril. Housing that offers no supervision and no interaction with faculty or other campus administrators often results in students in academic difficulty. Both recent and historic research shows that students are more successful—academically

and socially—when they live on-campus rather than off-campus (Macintyre; Potts & Schultz, 2008; Moeck, Hardy, Katsinas & Leech, 2007). This success includes having higher grades and completing more credits per semester than students who do not live in residence halls (Macintyre). Vincent Tinto, professor of education at Syracuse University, developed his Theory of Integration based on the idea that students who live on campus develop a connection with faculty, academic support administrators, student organizations, and campus employment opportunities which help them integrate into the campus community. This integration helps them persist in a way that off-campus students do not (Potts & Schultz).

COMMUNITY IMPACT

Another consideration of student living is the effects that housing situations have on the community surrounding the campus. Many campuses are set up so that students can survive without having to leave during the semester. Laundry facilities, dining halls, and convenience stores tend to populate campuses that offer residential living. Still, most students need jobs or want to eat out or attend movies or clubs. Since not all college towns have public transportation, many students have their own vehicles (and maintain them) or pay for cabs to get where they want. As a result, communities thrive, and in some instances, rely on college students to stimulate the economy eight months out of the year.

According to Macintyre, however, communities that house colleges and universities can experience economic disadvantages as well:

> Firstly, the pressure of many students seeking accommodation [off-campus housing] has had the effect of driving up the property values of some communities to the point where some housing has been put beyond the reach of the local inhabitants. Secondly, as the universities have acted to relieve the pressure and have directly acquired property, the proportion of land excluded from residential taxes has increased and the local authorities have ultimately been left with less money to support the local community."

Thus, a catch-22 exists: businesses need the financial stimulus of college student spending, yet the increase in property value makes the economic benefit difficult to appreciate.

In addition to this, communities suffer other negative consequences from the existence of colleges as well. Noise and destruction of property tend to be the most common. For example, residents in Plattsburgh "have for years complained about problems caused by drunken students who urinate on public property, scream during the middle of the night while stumbling home from downtown, destroy property and even enter residences, sometimes vomiting inside and passing out" (Bartlett, 2007, Law Changes). While these behaviors cannot be attributed to students who live on-campus or off-campus specifically, they do make tolerating college students as a whole difficult for community members. This is especially so when property values increase and that property is then damaged by temporary inhabitants who are not invested in the community as a whole.

ACADEMIC HONESTY ON & OFF CAMPUS

According to the Department of Education, almost all public universities offered some kind of distance learning opportunity by the year 2000 (Tabs, 2003, as cited in Kidwell & Kent, 2008). Since learning at a distance has become so popular, so has the argument that students who interact only with their computers for class have more opportunity to cheat than do the students who sit in front of their instructors every day. Kidwell & Kent put this theory to the test by surveying over 450 students, half of whom were enrolled in degree programs offered at a distance. In anonymous surveys, students were asked to identify cheating offenses by how serious they deemed them, whether or not they had done any of them, and whether or not they would identify people they saw doing them. Demographically, the off-campus students were older than their on-campus counterparts with average ages being 35.8 years old and 22.4 years old, respectively (Kidwell & Kent).

The types of cheating that respondents identified as the most serious offenses were those that off-campus students reported not doing:

- Turning in a paper purchased from a paper mill;
- Using unpermitted test notes;
- Turning in work done by someone else (Kidwell & Kent).

While off-campus students admitted to offenses they considered to be less serious, the on-campus students admitted to them at higher rates:

- Collaborating on work that was supposed to be done individually;
- Copying a few sentences without footnoting them;
- Fabricating a bibliography (Kidwell & Kent).

Overall, the off-campus students reported that they cheated less when compared to the responses of the on-campus students in this study; "they also had harsher views of various cheating behaviors and were more likely to claim they would turn in known offenders." It is difficult to determine what the reasons were for these results. It's possible that older students have more at stake when they enroll in college and, therefore, want to do their best. It is also possible that traditional students simply don't view cheating as a big deal.

On-Campus Living

INCREASE IN COMMUNITY COLLEGE HOUSING

Moeck et al. note that studies including four-year colleges and universities monopolize the research on student residential living experiences. The result is that little research exists about housing at community colleges even though in a 2001-2002 poll over 250 community college representatives stated that residential living was available on their campuses. Moeck et al. sent surveys to the college presidents at those schools and received over 115 that explained why the community colleges saw the need for on-campus housing. Most responses came from presidents of campuses in rural areas and identified "underscoring the tie to student services as a vehicle to promote college success" as an over-arching rationale for offering on-campus housing. "By offering on-campus housing, community colleges supply an incentive to students who live out of the primary service area to attend their institution." Other reasons provided in the surveys were increasing student diversity and academic programming to students who would otherwise attend class and then leave campus as commuters. According to Moeck, et al:

Traditional-aged single students desire to have a true college encounter involving social as well as academic experiences. By extending to the students an opportunity to live away from home while attending college, rural-serving colleges can recruit, retain, and offer an enhanced educational experience. By offering on-campus housing, rural-serving colleges can also improve racial and ethnic diversity by providing scholarships and opportunities to both minority and international students.

In addition, many community colleges offer athletic programs as a way to recruit students. In a study conducted in 2004, Castaneda noted that the number of student athletes at U.S. community colleges was "nearly 60,000" (cited in Moeck et al.). As recruits, those students are sought out by campus officials and offered incentives like scholarships and housing in exchange for full-time attendance in class and the chance to play intercollegiate athletics. Indeed, it would not make much sense for a student athlete to attend a college over 100 miles away from home if the opportunity to live there did not exist. On-campus housing at community colleges is also an incentive for students who are not athletes:

The shortage of nursing and allied health professionals, as well as the shortage of qualified faculty to educate and train students in these programs, is currently receiving a great deal of national publicity. In rural areas, however, the deficiencies are perceived to be many times more serious. The perception stems from the vast differences in income and job responsibilities between healthcare professionals in urban and suburban localities compared with those in especially remote rural regions (Reid, 2005). Since healthcare programs historically attract more female students, orienting housing to nursing and allied health students may offset the male-dominated athletic teams and, thus, promote gender equity (Moeck et al.).

On-campus housing at community colleges offers students a variety of experiences that include academic, social, professional, and athletic opportunities. Without the option to reside at a respective college, students might opt out of Higher Education entirely, especially if commuting was not an option for them.

Mental Health Services

Part of attending college involves a transition that is often difficult for some students to handle. Whether a clinical mental health issue or homesickness, students who feel helpless and alone need someone to trust with whom they can discuss their feelings.

Yorgason, Linville and Zitzman (2008) conducted a study to determine whether or not living on campus translated to students increased knowledge and use of mental health services. They surveyed over 250 students enrolled at a U.S. university, the majority of whom lived off-campus, to determine students' knowledge of the mental health services on campus and whether or not the students had used the services:

When asked whether their knowledge of mental health services was sufficient, 37% of respondents indicated that they were not given adequate information to enable them to contact the mental health services. One-third (30%) had never heard of the services. An additional 38% had heard of the services but knew nothing about them (Yorgason, et al.).

Also, female respondents, students who experienced distress and students who lived on-campus were more likely to know about and/or have used the services then were male participants, students who reported no distress and students who lived off-campus. It may be that students who choose to live on-campus do so because of the proximity to student services like mental health offices; however, students who live off-campus tend to have responsibilities that can lead to feelings of stress. Paying rent and utilities, finding transportation to campus, and the lack of available services like dining halls, laundry facilities, and academic support are just a few.

Viewpoints

LIABILITY

Knowing that residential students are more successful can lead to a good-faith effort on the part of colleges and universities to create on-campus housing regardless of the cost. According to the Chronicle of Higher Education (Van der Werf, 1999), however, colleges need to consider that cost and whom they are paying. For example, a private company who owns a building on campus and rents rooms with its own leasing contracts is liable for the safety of the students it houses. That means that if a student gets hurt on that property, the owner or building manager-who most likely does not reside on campus-is responsible for coming to the student's aid. Similarly, if a pipe bursts in the middle of winter or a faulty dryer mechanism starts a fire, municipal personnel not affiliated with the campus are responsible for responding to the problem (Van der Werf). Also, any college that allows privately-owned housing on its campus runs the risk of disciplinary issues that it cannot regulate. Students who pay rent to a corporation may not see the point in abiding by the rules set forth in residence hall agreements. With no in-house supervision, it is nearly impossible to regulate noise, alcohol and drug consumption, or to identify who is responsible for damages in common areas.

OUTSOURCING

In addition, many colleges may be seeing enrollment increases but not revenue increases large enough to build new residence halls. Some are coping by placing three students in rooms designed for two. (Clark, Jackson, Everhart & Torres, 2012). In that regard, outsourcing the availability of housing-while being able to keep students on campus-makes sense. However, not all building projects have reliable forms of capital, and while colleges are trying to cover themselves by having bonds issued for property on their campuses, they can still experience a financial loss. For example:

> The Tallahassee Community College Foundation helped secure bonds for a privately developed, 184-unit townhouse complex near the campus in 1990. Two years later, the foundation was forced to take over management of the complex after the developer was indicted for fraudulent use of students' security deposits. The college itself was forced to buy almost half of the project to help the foundation stave off creditors (Van Der Werf).

As more and more colleges turn to outsourcing, bonding agencies who credit them will hold the colleges accountable for the cost of the buildings whether or not they technically own them. According to the Chronicle, "if the bond-rating agency believes that an institution would bail out a developer in the event of problems ... it will include the debt as an obligation of the university, even if the obligation is not legally binding" (Van Der Werf). This decision is based on the probability that a college won't allow a new apartment complex—boasting the amenities students want (separate rooms, athletic facilities, wireless Internet)—to be left uncompleted on a campus indefinitely should a contractor go bankrupt during its development.

Finally, academic success is the goal of all colleges, and student housing should promote that success. As such, some colleges are saying no to outsourcing and taking on the bonding agencies themselves:

> At Colorado College, the Board of Trustees elected to finance a new student-apartment complex by issuing bonds, even though it would cost more than $70,000 per bed, or $22.9-million for the 300-bed building. The college estimated that private developers could build a complex for about $30,000 per bed, based on projects on other campuses (Van Der Werf).

While part of this decision was based on how long the complex would last depending on who was responsible for its development, a larger part was academic. Students study in their rooms, in the study lounges in their halls, even in the laundry rooms of the buildings in which they live; colleges should take the idea of construction—and its funding—as seriously and personally as possible. The housing project at Colorado College put their student resident number at 80% (Van Der Werf). That's 8 out of 10 students who are close to campus resources—faculty, academic support, organizations, and job opportunities. Such an investment may not be possible on all college campuses, but it shows how dedicated this one college is to the success of its student body.

Not all students have a choice where to live. Some universities require that students live on campus for the first year (Sickler & Roskos). Such policies have been the target of lawsuits that claim they infringe on students' economic and civil rights (Rovinsky, 2013).

TERMS & CONCEPTS

Non-traditional Student: A student who is not attending college directly from high school and/or may attend part-time while working or raising a family.

Off-campus Housing: Any living situation that is not supervised by a college campus authority.

On-campus Housing: Generally residence halls in which more than one student lives in a room and shares facilities like a study lounge, kitchen, laundry, and/or bathrooms.

Outsourcing: Hiring an outside company to subcontract the building, development and/or management of on-campus housing facilities.

Resident Assistant (RA): A student employed by a college who lives in the residence hall and supervises a group of students who live there.

Retention: The concept that students persist in college from semester to semester, year to year or from their first year to graduation.

Suite: A newer type of residence hall that has single bedrooms and common space.

Theory of Integration: Created by Vincent Tinto to explain the successful persistence of students who are "connected" with the campus community.

Traditional Student: A student who attends college directly from high school and enrolls in a 4-year academic program.

Maureen McMahon

BIBLIOGRAPHY

Bartlett, S. (2007, July 25). Commission issues report on Center City concerns. *Press Republican.* Retrieved August 9, 2010, from http://pressrepublican.com.

Clark, E. A., Jackson, S., Everhart, D., & Torres, V. (2012). Residential density: The effects of tripling college students. *Journal of College Student Development, 53,* 477-481. Retrieved December 1, 2013, from EBSCO Online Database Education Research Complete.

Kidwell, L. A. & Kent, J. (2008). Integrity at a distance: A study of academic misconduct among university students on and off campus. *Accounting Education, Supplement 1,* 17, 3-16. Retrieved July 29, 2010, from EBSCO online database, Education Research Complete.

LoTemplio, J. (2009, February 19). College housing project still dormant. *Press Republican.* Retrieved August 18, 2010, from http://pressrepublican.com.

Macintyre, C. (2003). New models of student housing and their impact on local communities. *Journal of Higher Education Policy & Management, 25,* 109-118. Retrieved July 29, 2010, from EBSCO online database, Education Research Complete.

Moeck, P. G., Hardy, D. E., Katsinas, S. G. & Leech, J. M. (2007). On-campus housing at rural community colleges. *Community College Journal of Research & Practice, 31,* 327-337. Retrieved July 29, 2010, from EBSCO online database, Academic Search Complete.

Potts, G. & Schultz, B. (2008). The freshman seminar and academic success of at-risk students. *College Students Journal, Part B, 42,* 647-658. Retrieved April 1, 2009, from EBSCO online database, Academic Search Complete.

Rovinsky, J. (2013). Monopoly–university edition: The case for student housing independence. *Brigham Young University Education & Law Journal,* 45-65. Retrieved December 1, 2013, from EBSCO Online Database Education Research Complete.

Sickler, S., & Roskos, B. (2013). Factors that play a role in first-year students' on-campus housing decisions. *Journal of College & University Student Housing, 39/40(2/1),* 10-31. Retrieved December 1, 2013, from EBSCO Online Database Education Research Complete.

Student Housing NY. (2005-2010). *CollegeSuites of Plattsburgh.* Retrieved August 3, 2010, from College Suites, http://mycollegesuites.com.

Van Der Werf, M. (1999). Colleges turn to private companies to build and run student housing. *Chronicle of Higher Education, 45,* A37. Retrieved August 5, 2010, from EBSCO online database, Education Research Complete.

Yorgason, J. B., Linville, D. & Zitzman, B. (2008). Mental health among college students: Do those who need services know about and use them? *Journal of American College Health, 57,* 173-182. Retrieved July 27, 2010, from EBSCO online database, Education Research Complete.

SUGGESTED READING

Allen, I. E. & Seaman, J. (2005). *Growing by degrees: Online education in the United States, 2005.* Needham, MA: Sloan Consortium. Accessed August 27 2010, from Sloan Consortium.

Blimling, G. (2015). Student Learning in College Residence Halls: What Works, What Doesn't, and Why. San Francisco, CA.: Jossey Bass.

Campus Suites: The Ultimate in Student Housing. (2010). Retrieved August 3, 2010, from Campus Suites, http://campussuites.com.

Craglia, M., Haining, R & Wiles, P. (2000). A comparative evaluation of approaches to urban crime pattern analysis. *Urban Studies, 37,* 711-729.

Erb, N. Sinclair, M., & Braxton, J. (2015). Fostering a sense of community in residence halls: A role for housing and residential professionals in increasing college student persistence. *Strategic Enrollment Management Quarterly.* 3(2), 84-108.

Gose, B. (1999). The annual squeeze into hotels, homes, and those dreaded 'converted triples.' *Chronicle of Higher Education, 56,* A55-A56.

Hughes, J. (1995). The impact of the business expansion scheme on the supply of privately-rented housing. *Journal of Property Finance, 6,* 20-32.

Kenyon, E. (1997) Seasonal sub-communities: The impact of student households on residential communities. *British Journal of Sociology, 48,* 286-301.

Raby, R. L. (2007). Internationalizing the curriculum: On- and off-campus strategies. *New Directions for Community Colleges, 2007,* 57-66. Retrieved July 29, 2010, from EBSCO online database, Education Research Complete.

CRIME ON COLLEGE CAMPUSES IN THE U.S.

Since the 1980s, the subject of crimes committed on college campuses in the United States has demanded increasing attention in the media and the public consciousness. While statistics show that, in reality, college and university campuses are considerably safer than the communities that surround them, there has been a steadily growing perception that the opposite is true (Patton & Gregory, 2014). This is due in part to several large scale, extremely violent attacks such as the Virginia Tech shooting in 2006, in which a single person armed with several firearms took the lives of thirty two people. The issue of college campus crime also encompasses many other types of criminal conduct such as theft, assault, and rape.

KEYWORDS: Campus Notification System; Clery Act; Concealed Carry Permit; Emergency Response Plan, In Loco Parentis; Shelter in Place

OVERVIEW

Colleges and universities bear a responsibility for providing a safe living and learning environment for their students, but at the same time they are not sufficiently resourced (Whissemore, 2015) or empowered to provide the same degree of supervision as an actual parent. Most college students are in fact legally adults, and the role of the college is considerably different from that of a high school, with students exercising agency on their own behalf in areas such as housing, finances, and recreation. Colleges provide services ranging from policing to counseling and develop policies to deter unsafe or illegal behavior, but the relative freedom of the campus environment and the tendency toward risky behavior among young adults creates a disconnect that tends to increase society's anxiety about campus crimes. Additionally, violent episodes, such as riots and shootings receive a large amount of attention despite their infrequency (Weiss, 2013).

IN LOCO PARENTIS

Until the mid-twentieth century, the legal doctrine of *in loco parentis*, a Latin phrase meaning "in place of the parent," allowed universities to control many aspects of student life. In the 1960s, adult students challenged the authority of universities to curb their

constitutional rights, and many traditional controls were relaxed or abolished. Universities continue to be held responsible for the safety and welfare of students as far as they are able. Policies, for example, must address deterrence of certain kinds of hazing, under-age drinking, and sexual harassment and assault, as well as discipline of students violating school rules or the law.

Much of the concern raised by crimes committed on college campuses has to do with the fact that, for many students, college is the first time in their lives when they have lived away from their parents' supervision. Students are expected to suddenly take on a much larger amount of responsibility, and must learn to function with less oversight. This makes college a time of great vulnerability and of great liberty—college students often have the bodies of adults but the hormones and self-regulatory behaviors of adolescents. Sexual assaults have sometimes been seen as a consequence of the so-called "frat boy culture" prevailing at some institutions, where the college years are treated as a time of constant partying, drinking, and sexual exploration (Strickland, 2013).

LARGE-SCALE VIOLENCE

Several factors make college and university campuses vulnerable to incidences of violence. Campuses are usually designed to be welcoming and open spaces in order to create an atmosphere of relaxation, peacefulness, and contemplation. Unfortunately, this means that persons bent on violent acts can travel between different parts of a campus with ease, because there are few fences, gates, or other secured areas.

Colleges can also have somewhat dense populations at certain times of the day and year (e.g., when classes are in session, during final exam periods), potentially making them attractive to attackers wishing to kill or injure large numbers of people (Bataille & Cordova, 2014). Buildings are often unlocked, often late into the evening, to accommodate faculty and students who need to reach their classrooms or offices.

In keeping with the tranquil image that college campuses aspire to, there are often few if any law enforcement personnel to be seen. Some institutions employ their own security personnel or campus police to protect public safety, while others may have a number of regular police officers from the surrounding community assigned specifically to the campus (Katel & Congressional Quarterly, 2011). In some cases, observers have felt that the division of presence and responsibility between campus security staff and regular police officers has contributed to confusion and delay in the response to incidents, pointing to the need for responders to coordinate communications and tactics. It is not uncommon for university security departments to conduct training exercises in cooperation with local police departments, in order to avoid this sort of complication.

Colleges and universities have implemented a variety of measures in an effort to address the issue of campus crime and in particular the possibility of large-scale shootings. One such effort, the provision of information about violent incidents on campus to prospective students and the campus community, is actually required by law.

THE CLERY ACT

In 1986 at Lehigh University, a student named Jeanne Clery was raped and then murdered in her university residence hall. This tragic incident led to the passage of the Jeanne Clery Disclosure of Campus Security Policy and Campus Crime Statistics Act in 1990, also known as the Clery Act. The Clery Act imposes a reporting requirement on any college or university whose students receive federal financial assistance, mandating that these institutions collect data about the number and type of violent crimes that occur on campus each year (Sloan & Fisher, 2010). The Act further specifies that the colleges and universities must make this information available to their campus community and to prospective students.

The goal of the Act is to make sure that people at the institution or considering enrolling there have as much information as possible so that they can make an informed decision about whether or not they feel the campus is a safe place to be. Unfortunately, fewer than half of all colleges and universities subject to the Clery Act fully comply with its requirements, and an even smaller percentage of two-year colleges comply, despite the possibility of sizable fines or even suspension of an institution's financial aid eligibility (Garner, 2015).

SECURITY TECHNOLOGIES

Some institutions have sought to address the problem of campus crime through the use of security technology. This can involve the use of notification systems, which require members of the campus community to register their contact information in a special database. In the event of an attack or some other emergency, the campus administration can use this contact information to quickly send an alert to everyone who has registered, warning them that an incident is ongoing and advising them to take cover, or "shelter in place," rather than continuing to go about their normal activities, which might make them more vulnerable.

Other types of security measures involve access control, meaning that they restrict who can enter certain areas and at what times (Dowdall, 2013). This can be as simple as the installation of locks and doors, or it can involve the use of identification cards or badges that must be used to enter buildings, sections of buildings, or individual rooms. While this does restrict movement for students, it is designed to help to contain outbreaks of violence by making it more difficult for offenders to travel throughout the campus.

Secure facilities that limit access by campus residents to university buildings, especially residence halls, contribute to an atmosphere some have described as a "police state." This effect is even more pronounced at institutions that choose to use monitoring technology such as video cameras, motion detectors, and other types of sensors. Such monitoring technology is often criticized for creating an unwelcome atmosphere and for being ineffective at preventing attacks because even though many cameras can be installed, it is not possible for them all to be watched on an ongoing basis. They are mainly useful for catching perpetrators after the fact, rather than in the act (Fox & Burstein, 2010).

VIEWPOINTS

Many have criticized the real efficacy of common security measures, as well as of the Clery Act. Critics charge that there is little evidence students actually use the information that colleges and universities amass and disseminate. The hope is that students considering which college to attend will carefully weigh the campus crime statistics available for each institution and make an informed decision about where to go. From the perspective of a prospective student, however, other factors may weigh more heavily in their decision, and the reported crime numbers may appear to indicate only a small risk. Further, concerns have been raised about the consistency and reliability of the information being collected by colleges. Collecting the data can be a very time-consuming and expensive proposition, so in many cases colleges will try to save time and money by gathering only minimal details (Fisher & Sloan, 2013).

College administrators also find quite a bit of room for interpretation in the instructions for data collection produced by the U.S. government. When adding up statistics, college staff must categorize crimes according to sometimes ambiguous definitions created by the federal government. The inevitable result is that different colleges categorize what is essentially identical conduct in radically different ways, and in the aggregate this reduces the quality of the information being collected. Further, the only crimes that colleges are supposed to report are those that take place within the campus boundaries. Crimes occurring outside this boundary are excluded from the collection, despite its potential relevance to the safety of students, who will likely spend time in the neighborhood around campus. Ironically, at the same time that information like this is omitted, other information is gathered at a level of detail that some critics find excessive. For example, college staff are required to collect information about a foreign country's crime rates for students who will study abroad, even though this is of limited relevance in describing the approximate safety of a college campus in the United States (Fisher & Lab, 2010).

The inadequacy of the Clery Act from the time it was implemented has indicated that crime on college campuses is too big an issue to be resolved by a single piece of legislation. Public safety officers at institutions of higher education all over the United States have begun to advocate on their own behalf in an effort to convince their administrations of the importance of adequately funding campus safety departments. They seek to not only monitor campus crime but also begin to take proactive steps to change their campus culture to one less likely to tolerate criminal behavior.

These efforts come at a time when the Department of Education has been taking a closer look at institutions that it feels are not fully complying with crime data requirements (Hobbs, 2012). In 2014, the Department released a list of more than fifty institutions being investigated for possible violations of reporting requirements for campus sexual assaults, in part as a means of pressuring these schools to improve their efforts. As colleges try to find ways to make campus crime reporting more meaningful and effective, they must also follow federal requirements to avoid being designated as willfully out of compliance. Failure can result in monetary sanctions as well as a decline in the institution's public profile, which could eventually manifest as declining enrollment numbers. College officials hope that by partnering with the students they serve, they can both assuage the fears of students and their families about crime, and also make a real and lasting impact on the culture of the institution that will result in a greater level of safety for all.

The increase in mass shootings in the second decade of the twentieth century included a number of incidents on or near college campuses. Organizations such as the National Rifle Association and Students for Concealed Carry suggest that allowing college and university staff, faculty, and students with concealed-carry permits to come to school armed could reduce the incidence of campus crime. Most college administrators, including many in gun-friendly states such as Texas, argue that it could have precisely the opposite effect. Colorado, Idaho, Kansas, Mississippi, Oregon, Texas, Utah, and Wisconsin allow concealed firearms on college campuses.

TERMS & CONCEPTS

Campus Notification System: A campus notification system, sometimes called a mass notification system, is a communication broadcast system designed to quickly send voice and/or text messages to all registered users during an emergency situation. Many colleges and universities have implemented campus notification systems as a way of alerting their members to ongoing attacks. All members of the community must register with the campus notification system by giving their phone number, email address, or both, for the system to work as intended.

Clery Act: The full name of this law is the Jeanne Clery Disclosure of Campus Security Policy and Campus Crime Statistics Act, which was enacted in 1990. The Clery Act requires that colleges and universities receiving federal financial aid must collect and keep statistics on campus crimes. The Act is named for a student who was raped and murdered in her college residence hall.

Concealed Carry Permit: A concealed carry permit is issued by a state to allow the recipient to carry a weapon on or near his or her person, in a non-obvious fashion. Different states have their own rules about who may obtain a concealed carry permit and what types of weapons may be carried. Some suggest that allowing college and university staff, faculty, and students to carry concealed weapons could reduce the incidence of campus crime, while others argue that it would have precisely the opposite effect.

Emergency Response Plan: An emergency response plan is a set of steps to be followed by a college or university in the event of an attack. Because there have been many mass shootings on college campuses, most colleges and universities now have emergency response plans in place. These plans include provisions for notifying the campus community about an ongoing attack, as well as procedures to be followed once the attack has ended.

In Loco Parentis: A Latin phrase meaning, "in the place of a parent." The phrase is also a legal doctrine describing situations in which a person or an organization assumes the role and some of the responsibilities of a parent. Colleges and universities are often said to function *in loco parentis* toward the students they educate, particularly those under the age of twenty-one.

Shelter in Place: A shelter in place order is issued during an attack on a college campus or similar venue. It is a notification sent to all members of the community, advising them that a potentially dangerous incident is ongoing and that they should remain where they are, attempt to secure themselves by locking doors, and take shelter by staying away from windows. The purpose of a shelter in place order is to reduce the number of potential victims a shooter on campus may encounter.

Scott Zimmer, JD

BIBLIOGRAPHY

Bataille, G. M., & Cordova, D. I. (2014). Managing the unthinkable: Crisis preparation and response for campus leaders. Sterling, VA: Stylus.

Dowdall, G. W. (2013). College drinking: Reframing a social problem/changing the culture. Sterling, VA: Stylus.

Fisher, B., & Lab, S. P. (2010). Encyclopedia of victimology and crime prevention. Thousand Oaks, CA: SAGE Publications.

Fisher, B., & Sloan, J. J. (2013). Campus crime: Legal, social, and policy perspectives. Springfield, IL: Charles C. Thomas.

Fox, J. A., & Burstein, H. (2010). Violence and security on campus: From preschool through college. Santa Barbara, CA: Praeger.

Gardner, L. (2015). 25 years later, has Clery made campuses safer?. Chronicle of Higher Education, 61(26), A22. Retrieved January 3, 2016, from EBSCO Online Database Education Research Complete.

Hobbs, K. (2012). Get wise about college safety. Woodland Park, CO: Hobbs Publications.

Katel, P., & Congressional Quarterly. (2011). Crime on campus: Are colleges doing enough to keep students safe?. Washington, DC: Congressional Quarterly.

Patton, R. C., & Gregory, D. E. (2014). Perceptions of safety by on-campus location, rurality, and type of security/police force: The case of the community college. Journal of College Student Development, 55(5), 451–460. Retrieved January 3, 2016, from EBSCO Online Database Education Research Complete.

Sloan, J. J., & Fisher, B. (2010). The dark side of the ivory tower: Campus crime as a social problem. New York, NY: Cambridge University Press.

Strickland, L. F. (2013). Violent behavior: Select analyses of targeted acts, domestic terrorists and prevention pathways. New York, NY: Nova Science Publishers.

Weiss, K. G. (2013). Party school: Crime, campus, and community. Boston, MA: Northeastern University Press.

Whissemore, T. (2015). Clery Act changes the landscape of campus safety. Community College Journal, 56(3), 4–5. Retrieved January 3, 2016, from EBSCO Online Database Education Research Complete.

SUGGESTED READING

Allen, W. D. (2013). Self-protection against crime victimization: Theory and evidence from university campuses. International Review of Law & Economics, 34, 21–33. Retrieved January 3, 2016, from EBSCO Online Database Business Source Complete.

McGrath, S. A., Perumean-Chaney, S. E., & Sloan, J. I. (2014). Property crime on college campuses: A case study using GIS and related tools. Security Journal, 27(3), 263–283.

Prairie, M., Garfield, T., & Herbst, N. L. (2010). College and school law: Analysis, prevention, and forms. Chicago, IL: American Bar Association.

Van Dyke, N., & Tester, G. (2014). Dangerous climates: Factors associated with variation in racist hate crimes on college campuses. Journal of Contemporary Criminal Justice, 30(3), 290–309. Retrieved January 3, 2016, from EBSCO Online Database SocINDEX with Full Text.

Vegh, D. (2011). Campus crime: Is it really the problem it's been constructed to be?. Crime, Law & Social Change, 56(3), 325–327. Retrieved January 3, 2016, from EBSCO Online Database SocINDEX with Full Text.

Diploma Mills (Degree Mills)

This article sheds light on the existence of diploma mills and the accompanying implications for educators, legislators, and consumers. Legal cases, the accreditation process, and federal legislation are discussed.

Keywords: Accrediting agency; Accrediting mill; Degree mill; Diploma mill; Federal Trade Commission; Higher Education Opportunity Act of 2008

Overview

The existence of fake educational institutions that sell counterfeit diplomas and other educational credentials is almost as old as higher education itself, but it has become an increasing problem since the late twentieth century when an increased demand for a more educated workforce coincided with new technology that made offering fake degrees easier. Reformers have pushed for federal legislation to suppress diploma mills, but even in the face of publicity generated by the St. Regis University case and congressional hearings, legislative action has been limited.

For more than a century, American educators, legislators, and others have deplored the existence of businesses that provide fraudulent education credentials to those who are willing to pay for them. Despite complaints, investigations, and even occasional prosecutions, diploma mills (also known as degree mills) not only survive but also prosper. One might say they prosper exceedingly well. According to one account, a single diploma mill may have made as much as $72 million in its final four years of operation (Ezell & Bear, 2005). The peaks in the profits of the bogus diploma industry have coincided with periods when the demand for degrees has been high. Diploma mills flourished in fourteenth-century Europe when doctoral degrees were much in demand but often took as much as fifteen years to acquire (Ezell & Bear). They flourished in the United States in the post-Civil War period after the Morrill Act, also known as the

Land Grant College Act, led to the founding of new colleges and extended access to higher education. Among the earliest references to degree mills in the United States is a comment in 1876 from John Eaton, a United States Commissioner of Education, who declared the mills a blemish on the reputation of American education. The GI Bill (The Servicemen's Readjustment Act of 1944) allowed millions of veterans to attend college, and it also brought an increase in the number of diploma mills (Ezell & Bear). However, it was the unprecedented demand for a well-educated workforce and the technological advances of the late twentieth century, particularly the Internet, that launched a new golden age for the sellers of fake degrees and made the business what Ezell and Bear in 2005 termed a billion-dollar industry.

Although the terms "diploma mill" and "degree mill" are used interchangeably in the popular press and elsewhere, some scholars in the field assign the terms different meanings, considering the individuals or groups who award degrees from a fake college degree mills, and those that offer fraudulent degrees from legitimate institutions diploma mills (Contreras & Gollin, 2009). It should also be noted that although the terms most often refer to the awarding of bogus degrees, high school diploma mills also exist. In a 2012 judgment against Salem Kureshi, a federal court ordered him to refund three times the $249 that 30,500 individuals had each paid to receive fake diplomas from Belford High School and Belford University (Diploma Mill Graduates, 2012). Two years later, the Federal Trade Commission (FTC) requested a U.S. district court in Florida shut down a diploma mill that has taken in more than $11 million for providing fake high school diplomas (FTC Action, 2014). Despite cases such as these, the bulk of fake credentials involve college degrees, one-third of them advanced degrees, which give credit for what is vaguely termed "life experience." Diploma mill customers can be found in a wide range of professions, including education, medicine, and engineering, and at every level within those professions. In education, for example, fake diplomas have been purchased by classroom teachers, coaches, and administrators from school principals to a college president (Gollin, Lawrence & Contreras, 2010) Diploma mills are a global problem, but most diploma mills are located, in fact or by impression, within the United States. Erik Johansson, a credential evaluator of foreign credentials for the Swedish labor market and an adviser on credentialing to the Swedish higher education community, says that more than 50 percent of the credentials from questionable universities in the more than ten years he has been investigating have been from diploma mills located in the United States or from schools that present themselves as being in the United States. (Tobenkin, 2011). One reason for the strong U.S. connection is the lack of a central authority governing higher education. Many countries have a department or ministry of education within the national government that is charged with oversight of the nation's colleges and universities. Since the U.S. Constitution does not recognize authority over education as a federal power, that authority becomes the province of state governments. Only twelve states have laws that specifically address the illegality of using credentials from diploma mills: Illinois, Indiana (limited to doctorates), Maine, Michigan, Nevada, New Jersey, North Dakota, Oregon, South Dakota, Texas, Virginia, and Washington. No federal law makes using fake academic credentials illegal or labels operating a diploma mill a crime (Pina, 2010).

Congress does have the power to give institutions the authority to award college degrees, but it is a power seldom exercised. Only the five military service academies (U.S. Military Academy, U.S. Naval Academy, U.S. Coast Guard Academy, U.S. Merchant Marine Academy, and U.S. Air Force Academy) and a few programs such as the Community College of the Air Force were directly established by Congress. American Indian tribes recognized as sovereign by the United States government also have the power to establish degree-granting institutions. The Higher Education Opportunity Act of 2008, in which the term "diploma mill" was for the first time defined by federal law, also reasserts the authority of each state to determine the standards and policies that govern the

awarding of degrees within its boundaries (Contreras & Gollin).

Once a state has given an institution the authority to grant degrees, there is no oversight to determine the quality of the institution's academic programs. Most states do demand that institutions be accredited in order for the institutions and the students enrolled in the institutions to receive state funds. Furthermore, states typically require that individuals who are licensed for particular professions are graduates of accredited institutions or programs. Similarly, the federal government requires students who receive federal funds to be enrolled in institutions authorized by the state and accredited by a federally recognized accrediting agency.

These agencies are nonprofit, non-governmental organizations that attest to the quality of academic instruction and the reputation of the faculty of an institution after the institution has gone through an evaluation process that includes self-study, peer-review, and an onsite visit that typically involves observation and interviews with students, faculty, and administrators. Evaluations are conducted every three to seven years. The accrediting agencies include national faith-related organizations that accredit religiously affiliated institutions, most of which are degree-granting and nonprofit; national career-related organizations that evaluate primarily for-profit career-based, degree-granting and non-degree-granting institutions; and regional organizations that attest to the quality of nonprofit, degree-granting institutions. In 2010-2011, there were eighty recognized regional and national accrediting organizations in the United States engaged in reviewing postsecondary educational institutions in 50 states and 125 other countries (Eaton, 2012). Accreditation mills exist, most with impressive sounding names to deceive the unwary, to provide accreditation to diploma mills and other schools unaccredited by legitimate accrediting agencies.

An accreditation process and restrictions on state and federal funding are not sufficient to prevent the operation of diploma mills. The federal government has largely left prevention and prosecution of diploma mill owners to the states, and the results have been inconsistent. Some states do little more than ignore the problem; others have mounted a crusade against the industry. Oregon, a leader in the fight against diploma mills, not only bans degrees from mills but also makes the use of such a degree civil fraud and a criminal misdemeanor (Contreras & Gollin). Some states have prosecuted individuals operating diploma mills, but the operations themselves often just move to another state and continue to sell false academic credentials. For example, When the Pennsylvania attorney general sued the owner of the "University of Berkley" diploma mill in 2005, an Erie County judge ordered the school's assets returned, specifying that the owner could no longer operate in Pennsylvania and must so state on his website. In 2009, the University of Berkley continued to sell diplomas from a website that duly acknowledged the site could not sell to residents of Pennsylvania. (Gollin et al.).The only sustained federal approach to the problem was the Federal Bureau of Investigation (FBI) task force, Operation Diploma Scam (DipScam), which Agent Allen Ezell ran for more than a decade through the Field Office of the FBI in Charlotte, North Carolina. The FBI dismantled DipScam shortly after Ezell's retirement in 1991 (Ezell & Bear).

Beginning with an investigation of Southeastern University in Greenville, South Carolina, in 1980, Ezell and his team saw forty schools closed, nineteen federal grand jury indictments returned, and more than twenty individuals convicted during the eleven years of DipScam (Gollin et al.). Generally federal agencies have been reluctant to become involved in diploma mill cases. This has not always been the case. The FTC brought charges against Joseph Jayko and his "Cramwell Institute" and "Cramwell Research Institute" in 1956, commenting that the commission had taken action against "hundreds of other diploma mills during the previous twenty years" and noting that customers' understanding that they were purchasing fraudulent credentials was irrelevant to the charges (Gollin et al.). Half a century later the FTC appeared less ready to act, citing the informed customers who buy fake diplomas in full knowledge of the disreputable vendors as a prime reason for their inaction (Contreras & Gollin).

FURTHER INSIGHTS

When Allen Ezell retired, he had reason to feel optimistic about the suppression of diploma mills. He and his team had seen a significant number of diploma mills closed, and the congressional hearings conducted by Representative Claude Pepper (Democrat,

Florida) and the Subcommittee on Housing and Consumer Interests of the Select Committee on Aging in 1984-1985 had made legislators and the public aware of the scope of the problem (Ezell & Bear). But the FBI chose not to continue its investigations, and no legislative action was taken. In the years following DipScam, the Internet and the customer base it opened to diploma mill owners made the business easier and more lucrative than ever. Alan Contreras, widely acknowledged as a national expert on diploma mills, says that the Internet not only improved the marketing of faked academic credentials, but web pages, which were quite sophisticated for some mills, provided an opportunity for the bogus institutions to look more authentic, providing photographs, catalogs, and testimonials (Government Accountability Office, 2004).

In the case of St. Regis University, arguably the best-known diploma mill case, attorneys and investigators from the offices of the U.S. Attorney for the Eastern District of Washington, United States Secret Service, U.S. Immigration and Customs Enforcement Bureau, U.S. Postal Inspection Service, U.S. Internal Revenue Service, U.S. Federal Protective Agency, State of Washington Attorney General, and the Spokane Police Department contributed to shutting down a diploma mill that had sold bogus diplomas from at least 66 legitimate universities and 121 fake universities (Gollin et al.). On August 11, 2005, search warrants were served and records confiscated at seven locations in three states. Dixie Randock, a high school dropout, and her husband Steve began selling fake academic credentials in 1999 from their home in Spokane, Washington. By the time a grand jury indicted the Randocks and six of their business colleagues on charges of mail fraud and other felonies in October, 2005, they had sold 10,815 degrees and accompanying credentials to thousands of buyers in 131 countries for a total of $7,369,907 (Ezell & Bear). In 2001, the Randocks created St. Regis University. Although they sold degrees under the names of at least six other fake universities and counterfeit diplomas from legitimate universities such as the University of Maryland, George Washington University, the University of Missouri, and Texas A&M University, the St. Regis exploit was their boldest move and the one that eventually led to their downfall.

In 2002, the Randocks decided they needed a foreign country to supply official recognition of St.

Regis. Richard Novak, a former used car salesman, was sent to Washington, D.C., to contact officials and make the appropriate contacts. Novak, who had been named chief executive officer of the illusory St. Regis, visited the Liberian embassy, where he met Abdulah Dunbar, the embassy's deputy chief of mission. Dunbar was receptive to Novak's request but asked for $4,000. Novak was able to negotiate for a lesser figure. He reported to the Randocks that he had acquired Liberian cooperation for $2,250, and he had in hand credentials that were duplicates of those granted to legitimate Nigerian universities. The Randocks eventually had as many as a dozen Liberian officials on their payroll along with an international faculty with their own bogus credentials who operated various "schools" within the university from five other countries (Gollin et al.).

Although the St. Regis University case is the most notorious example of U.S. diploma mills and significant because criminal charges were filed against the Randocks, Novak, and five of their coworkers with four of the eight serving prison sentences, it is not an isolated case. It is not even the largest diploma mill case. That title belongs to an operation directed by an American living in Bucharest, Romania, who used a mail-forwarding service in Ireland, had diplomas printed in Israel, and channeled funds through a bank in Cyprus. The owner sold more than 200,000 diplomas, mostly to North Americans, under the names of more than thirty different fake universities. A full service mill, the program offered a package that included a diploma (with the date of the purchaser's choice), a transcript (with courses and grades chosen by the purchaser), information on a degree verification service for employers to contact, and two letters of recommendation (Ezell & Bear). However, it was a second business, the sale of more than 350,000 fake international drivers' licenses, that captured the attention of the Federal Trade Commission in 2003. The FTC settled the case when three companies and three individuals agreed to pay $57,000 in penalties and take down their websites. Ezell and Bear point out that the monetary penalty was the equivalent of eight hours of revenue for the offenders, and the websites were soon reestablished under new names.

VIEWPOINTS

Given the failure of most states to deal effectively with the problem of diploma mills and the limited action of federal agencies in addressing the issue, experts point to the need for federal legislation if diploma mills are to be stopped. In 2006, Dr. Creola Johnson proposed a model federal statute, the Authentic Credentials in Higher Education Act, which would allow students to file a civil suit on the basis of a school's providing false or misleading information about its accreditation status or failing to disclose its lack of accreditation by an accrediting agency recognized by the Department of Education. Students could recover treble damages plus attorneys' fees in such action. Johnson's proposed legislation also criminalizes the selling of any fraudulent degree, the providing of false academic verification materials and services, and knowingly assisting in the operation of a diploma mill. History shows that the cases that have most effectively suppressed diploma mills have been criminal prosecutions in which multiple government agencies at the state, federal, and at times, local levels have collaborated.

Congressional hearings and media coverage of the St. Regis University case helped those who believed federal legislation on diploma mills was necessary to push for action. The version of the Higher Education Opportunity Act of 2008 that originated in the House of Representatives included a lengthy section (more than twelve pages) on diploma mills, but legislators who opposed the reforms successfully fought to delete much of the material in conference committee. The final version does little more than provide a legal definition (Gollin et al.). The act also called for continued efforts at the federal level to identify and suppress diploma mills, but such action has been limited.

TERMS & CONCEPTS

Accrediting agency: A regional or national body that evaluates institutions of higher learning, generally in areas such as student services, quality of instruction, and quality of faculty, and attests that these institutions meet, or fail to meet, minimum standards set by a peer review board that includes faculty from accredited institutions.

Accrediting mill: An organization that provides accreditations to educational institutions without requiring an actual evaluation of programs, teaching practices, or faculty credentials.

Degree mill: An enterprise that sells counterfeit diplomas from legitimate educational institutions.

Diploma mill: An organization that sells diplomas and other educational credentials from fake educational institutions on the basis of life experience, open-book examinations that may be retaken multiple times, or dissertations of ten pages or less.

Federal Trade Commission: An independent agency of the United States government established by Congress in 1914 and charged with consumer protection and enforcement of anti-trust laws.

Higher Education Opportunity Act of 2008: An act passed by the 110th Congress on August 14, 2008, which reauthorized the Higher Education Act of 1965 and added new sections, including a definition of "diploma mill," a requirement that the Secretary of Education maintain information and resources available on the department website to inform students and families concerning how to avoid diploma mills, and a requirement that a federal multi-agency effort to prevent, identify, and prosecute diploma mills be continued.

Wylene Rholetter

BIBLIOGRAPHY

Contreras, A., and Gollin, G. (2009). The real and the fake degree and diploma mills." Change 41(2), 36-43. Retrieved December 29, 2014, from EBSCO Online Database Education Research Complete.

Diploma mill graduates wait for $22.7 million payout. (2012). Successful Registrar, 12(9), 2. Retrieved December 29, 2014, from EBSCO Online Database Education Research Complete.

Eaton, J. S. (2012). An overview of U. S. accreditation. Council for Higher Education Accreditation. Retrieved January 3, 2015, from http:// chea.org.

Ezell, A., & Bear, J. (2005). Degree mills: The billion-dollar industry that has sold over a million fake diplomas. Amherst, NY: Prometheus Books.

FTC action halts online high school diploma mill that made $11 million selling worthless diplomas to students. (2014). Federal Trade Commission. Retrieved December 30, 2014, from http:// ftc.gov.

Gollin, G., Lawrence, E., Contreras, A. (2010). Complexities in legislative suppression of diploma mills. Stanford Law & Policy Review, 21, 1-32. Retrieved January 3, 2015, from https://journals.law.stanford.edu.

Government Accountability Office. (2004) Diploma mills: Federal employees have obtained degrees from diploma mills and other unaccredited schools, some at government expense. Retrieved December 30, 2014, from http://.gao.gov.

Piña, A. A. (2010). Online diploma mills: Implications for legitimate distance education. Distance Education, 31(1), 121-126. doi:10.1080/01587911003725063. Retrieved December 29, 2014, from EBSCO Online Database Education Research Complete.

Johnson, V. R. (2008). Corruption in education: A global legal challenge. Santa Clara Law Review, 48(1). Retrieved December 30, 2014, from http://digitalcommons.law.scu.edu.

Noble, D. F. (2001). Digital diploma mills: The automation of higher education. New York, NY: Monthly Review Press.

Wolman, D. (2009, December 21). Fraud U: Toppling a bogusdiploma empire. Retrieved January 3, 2015, from http:// wired.com.

"World's largest university" is a scam, investigation reveals. (2015). Chronicle of Higher Education, 61(25), A17. Retrieved March 22, 2015, from EBSCO Online Database Education Research Complete.

Baggaley, J. (2014). MOOCS: Digesting the facts. Distance Education, 35(2), 159-163. Retrieved December 19, 2014, from EBSCO online database Education Research Complete.

Craig, R. (2015). College disrupted: The great unbundling of higher education. New York, NY: Palgrave Macmillan Trade.

Gašević, D., Kovanović, V., Joksimović, S., & Siemens, G. (2014). Where is research on massive open online courses headed? A data analysis of the MOOC research initiative. International Review of Research in Open & Distance Learning, 15(5), 134-176. Retrieved December 19, 2014, from EBSCO online database Education Research Complete.

Haber, J. (2014). MOOCs. Cambridge, MA: MIT Press. Holden, T. (2014). MOOC 67 success secrets: 67 most asked questions on MOOC: What you need to know. [S.1.]: Emereo Publishing.

Hubbard, R. L. (2015). Getting the most out of MOOC: Massive open online courses. New York, NY: Rosen Publishing.

Jerrik, B. S. (2012). Massive open online course: Networked learning, connectivism, information age. Beau Bassin, Mauritius: Part Press.

Khosrow-Pour, M., & IGI Global. (2014). Educational technology use and design for improved learning opportunities. Hershey, PA: IGI Global.

Kim, P. (2014). Massive open online courses: The MOOC revolution. New York, NY: Routledge.

Krause, S. D., & Lowe, C. (2014). Invasion of the MOOCS: The promises and perils of massive open online courses. Anderson, SC: Parlor Press.

SUGGESTED READING

Angulo, A.J. (2016). *Diploma Mills: How For-Profit Colleges Stiff Students, Taxpayers, and the American Dream.* Baltimore, MD.: Johns Hopkins University Press.

Brooks, R., Fuller, A., & Waters, J. L. (Eds.). (2012). *Changing spaces of education: New perspectives on the nature of learning.* New York, NY: Routledge.

Dryden, L. (2016). Court of Appeals: Diploma mill violated state ban on false credentials. Michigan Lawyers Weekly.

Garrison, D. R. (2011). E-learning in the 21st century: A framework for research and practice. New York, NY: Routledge.

Kellogg, S., Booth, S., & Oliver, K. (2014). A social network perspective on peer supported learning in MOOCs for educators. International Review of Research in Open & Distance Learning, 15(5), 263-289. Retrieved December 19, 2014, from EBSCO online database Education Research Complete.

Marshall, S. (2014). Exploring the ethical implications of MOOCs. Distance Education, 35(2), 250-262. Retrieved December 19, 2014, from EBSCO online database Education Research Complete.

Mirrlees, T., & Alvi, S. (2014). Taylorizing academia, deskilling professors and automating higher education: The recent role of MOOCs. Journal for Critical Education Policy Studies (JCEPS), 12(2), 45-73. Retrieved December 19, 2014, from EBSCO Online Database Education Research Complete.

Noble, D. (2001). *Digital Diploma Mills: The Automation of Higher Education.* Monthly Review Press.

Pina, A. (2010). Online diploma mills: Implications for legitimate distance education. *Distance Education.* 31(1), 121-126.

SECTION 9: SCHOOL SAFETY

Introduction

According to the National Center for Education Statistics "between 2001 in 2015, the percentage of students ages 12 to 18 who reported being victimized at school during the previous six months decreased overall (from 6 to 3%), as did the percentages of students who reported theft (from 4 to 2%) and violent victimization (from 2 to 1%)." This is good news. But the realities of those instances where lives are forever altered (i.e., Virginia Tech, Sandy Hook Elementary School), generate a heightened awareness of how vulnerable our schools are to outside influences. What measures are being taken to keep our public schools and colleges and universities safe? This section explores all sides of the arguments around social issues, safety precautions, and implications for all stakeholders.

Our contributing authors examine numerous school-based strategies being implemented and the consequences experienced by students as a corollary of decisions they make and those being made by their peers, teachers, and school leaders.

SOCIAL CONCERNS AMONG STUDENTS

Issues such as bullying, homelessness, depression and substance abuse may occur in or out of school, but they ultimately affect school climate as well as the community as a whole. These non-academic issues, like bullying, depression, suicide, drug and alcohol abuse, homelessness, and teen pregnancy can affect student learning and development and sometimes lead to safety issues for individuals and groups. Unaddressed concerns can lead to increases in dropout rates, juvenile crime activity, welfare dependency and suicide.

KEYWORDS: Bullying; Cutting; Cyber-Bullying; Depression; Homelessness; Hurricane Katrina; McKinney-Vento Act; No Child Left Behind Act of 2001 (NCLB); Pregnancy; Social Concerns; Substance Abuse; United Nations Universal Declaration of Human Rights

OVERVIEW
WHAT ARE SOCIAL CONCERNS?

Social concerns are non-academic issues that can affect student learning and development and sometimes lead to safety issues for individuals and groups, such as the student population and the community as a whole. Unaddressed concerns can lead to increases in dropout rates, juvenile crime activity, welfare dependency and suicide.

What Are the Most Common Social Concerns?

BULLYING

Bullies have been around for generations but, in recent years, experts have realized that bullying has long-term effects on both the victims and the bullies (Lemonick, Colton, Holton, Song, & Steptoe, 2005). Bullying refers to any type of rough behavior that is "deliberately aggressive" such as name-calling, hitting, mocking, slander, and social isolation (Lemonick et al.). Students can get bullied because of their race, sex, age, appearance, or just being different (Hall, 2007). Bullying violates a section in the United Nations Universal Declaration of Human Rights which states that no one can be subjected to interference with family or privacy, nor to attacks upon one's reputation (Hall).

The American Medical Association released a statement in 2002 declaring bullying a public health problem because of its long-term mental health results (Lemonick et al.). Victims of bullying attend school less than other students, receive lower grades, have fewer friends and are at increased risk for depression (Lemonick et al.). The bullies are less likely to develop positive social skills and conflict resolution skills. They are also four times more likely than other students to participate in criminal activity by the time they are in their early twenties, and are more inclined to develop problems with substance abuse. Children who witness bullying are also affected by the act (Lemonick et al.).

Experts do not have a definitive reason as to why bullying exists, but they do know that it is prevalent. At a Los Angeles middle school, nearly half the students reported being bullied at least one time. Bullying can be difficult for teachers to address because it is often subtle and hard to detect. In addition, the act of cyber-bullying, sending taunting messages via email or posting on websites and chat rooms, is on the rise (Lemonick et al.).

DEPRESSION & SUICIDE

Depression is the most common mental illness among adolescents (Cash, 2003). As many as 3.5 million high school students may be experiencing clinical depression (Salvatore, 2006). Only about one third of them will get help from a mental health professional (Cash). Most teenagers experience periods where they feel depressed, angry and alone so it is difficult to detect the difference between depression and normal teenage mood swings (Cash). Depression is more than just feeling blue; it is a persistent sadness and the inability to feel pleasure (Cash). Depression can affect anyone but post-pubescent girls are the most likely to suffer from depression. Gay and bisexual teens, students living in poverty and American Indians are also more susceptible to depression (Cash).

Adolescent depression has been known to reveal itself differently than adult depression. (Salvatore). Symptoms of depression can include: sleeping too much or too little, changes in appetite, lack of focus, low self-esteem and withdrawal from peers and activities (Cash). Changes in school behavior such as defiance, skipping classes, sudden drop in grades and focus may also be signs of depression. Teens who are depressed may exhibit other disturbing behaviors such as sexual promiscuity, substance abuse and cutting. Even more worrisome is the fact that suicide is now the third leading cause of death among teenagers. More girls attempt suicide than boys, but boys are much more likely to succeed (Cash).

DRUG & ALCOHOL ABUSE IN SCHOOLS

Research has shown that teen drug and alcohol abuse is not only occurring on nights and weekends, but also during the school day (Finn & Willert, 2006). Shockingly, schools might be the easiest place for teens to purchase drugs ("Survey Finds," 1997). According to a recent national survey, 62% of high school students and 28% of middle school students said drugs are distributed, used, and abused on school grounds. This is a 47% increase since a 1992 study (Finn & Willert).

To make matters worse, teens who attend schools where drugs are present are three times more likely to smoke marijuana and twice as likely to experiment with alcohol (Finn & Willert). A study by the Center for Disease Control "showed that male and Hispanic students had higher levels of in school drug use than female and white students" (Finn, 2006). As student age increases, so too does drug use, and the majority of students were unaware of the disciplinary action that would be taken in their schools to if they were caught using drugs. Alcohol and drug use in school lead to increased truancy rates and poor academic performance (Finn).

A study conducted in Ohio in 2005 assessed the risk factors associated with students who sell drugs. Results from an anonymous survey revealed that 11.9% of the participants had sold drugs in the past year. Students who distributed drugs were most often men and lived in single parent homes. The students were also more likely to participate in other risky behaviors such as vandalism, violent behavior and abuse of drugs and alcohol (Steinman, 2005).

HOMELESSNESS

One social concern that is often overlooked in education is the issue of homelessness. Homelessness is defined as living in places that do not have water, electricity and other basic services; living in motels, shelters, public spaces and temporary arrangements with other families (Berliner, 2002). Since Hurricane Katrina has displaced over 370,000 school-aged children, the issue has received more attention (Hall, R., 2007). Homeless children attending school has been a growing concern for many years but it is difficult to quantify the number of school-aged children who are homeless. Many homeless students will not admit to or discuss their living situations out of embarrassment. Homeless families often move around a lot and "avoid authorities (for fear of losing custody of their children)" making them impossible to track (Berliner).

"Families with children are the fastest-growing element of the homeless population. Over the past decade, the number of homeless children has more than doubled" (Berliner). The National Coalitions for the Homeless estimates that 1 million children experience homelessness each year and many are never identified or given the assistance they need (Hall, R.). Although more boys are believed to be homeless than girls, race, family structure and geographic location did not serve as indicators of homelessness (Jozefowicz-Simbeni & Israel, 2006). Contrary to popular assumptions, homelessness is not just an urban problem and higher rates of homelessness exist among families with children (Hall, R.).

The risk factors associated with homelessness range from natural disasters to eviction to family conflicts such as substance abuse, violence or neglect. All of these reasons are concerns of their own, but combined with being homeless add more stress to students and their families. In addition, "homeless parents are more likely to be single women who have a mental health disorder or physical health problem and are less able to attend to the needs of their children" (Jozefowicz-Simbeni & Israel).

The impact of homelessness on a child is vast. Malnutrition, hunger, sleep deprivation and developmental delays are physical consequences of homelessness. School-aged, homeless children also display low self-esteem, anger and anxiety over their situation (Jozefowicz-Simbeni & Israel). Social interaction is usually stunted and children tend to be withdrawn or disruptive in the classroom. Depression, aggression and suicide can result if concerns are not addressed. Simply enrolling in school is a challenge for homeless students as many parents do not have appropriate documentation or previous school records (Hall, R.). "Homeless students are more likely to have low test scores, poor grades and behavior problems" (Jozefowicz-Simbeni & Israel). Many homeless students have issues with transportation resulting in high truancy and drop-out rates (Hall, R.).

TEEN PREGNANCY

Teen pregnancy is occurring at an alarming rate. According to Scholl (2007), the United States has the largest number of teen pregnancies in the Western world. One out of every 10 American girls becomes pregnant before age 20, and teenagers from minority backgrounds are at an even higher risk. About half of teen pregnancies carry to term and less than 10% give up their babies for adoption (Scholl). And the problem does not seem to be slowing down; as more and more adolescents are sexually active each year. Currently 73% of boys and 56% of girls are sexually active before age 18 (Scholl).

The most disturbing aspect of the high rate of teenage pregnancy is that most teenage mothers end up dropping out of school. Less than 50% of teens who became pregnant between the ages of 13 and 15 graduate from high school. This leads to young mothers without the education or financial support they need to raise successful children. Historically, teen pregnancy would result in the student being expelled from school or withdrawing without explanation; but the Education Amendments of 1972 forbade schools from expelling students because of pregnancy (Scholl). Within a year over 200 schools in the U.S. developed programs to help pregnant teens stay in school. In addition, counseling was provided to help teens adjust to their new, overwhelming situation (Scholl). Yet in 2007 most schools have not adopted this model, even though teenage mothers and their offspring are much more likely to succeed in communities where special programs are in place to address their needs as both student and parent. Many schools are ignoring the problem and as a result, pregnant teens are not able to complete their education (Scholl).

Teenage pregnancy is a serious social concern for the whole community. When teenage mothers drop out, many wind up on welfare because they do not have the education, access to childcare and financial stability to make it on their own. This is costing taxpayers billions of dollars each year to pay for welfare costs, medical care and education for young mothers and their children (Scholl). In California, over 2,000

kindergarten classes will be needed just to educate children born to teens (Scholl).

The most dangerous consequence of not addressing teenager pregnancy is that young people who do not develop basic skills because of economic disadvantages are three times more likely to be teen parents (Scholl). Teenage mothers who drop out are likely to become dependent on welfare and may not develop the basic skills that will prevent their children from becoming teenage parents, and the cycle will continue.

What Can Be Done to Address Social Concerns?

BULLYING

Teachers, parents and administrators are under an obligation to educate students about the dangers of bullying. Since most bullying takes place in less supervised locations such as bathrooms, hallways, and school buses, it is important that additional staff monitor such locations to help keep bullying under control (Lemonick et al.). Students should be taught to be respectful to one another and to avoid contact with people who are cruel or who intimidate others. Those who witness bullying or harassment of any kind should be encouraged to tell an adult, since the bullying will continue unless someone speaks out (Hall). Consequences must be administered to students who bully. UCLA researchers also recommend that communities (teachers, parents and students) roll out anti-bullying programs, review with students the rules against harassment and offer strategies to help students manage bullies (Lemonick et al.). Incorporating anti-bullying messages into school lessons and parent-child discussions can also help reduce incidents of bullying (Lemonick et al.). Patricia Wong Hall (2007) believes that if students, teachers and parents work together to discourage bullying, there will be a decrease in school violence and an improvement in the social climate for students (Hall).

DEPRESSION

The best way to deal with depression is early intervention. Schools are an essential line of defense because adolescents spend more time at school than at home and schools have access to certain resources that may help kids address depression before it gets worse.

School districts have a responsibility to train staff, students and parents on the signs of depression and the importance of getting assistance early (Cash). Students should be taught to identify the differences between normal feelings of sadness and depression. Adolescents displaying symptoms of depression that last longer than two weeks should be referred for consultation (Cash). It is essential that principals, teachers and parents understand the devastating effects that depression can have on a teenager if not caught early (Salvatore).

Everyone in the community needs to be able to recognize the warning signs for suicide as well. Often students who attempt to harm themselves have alerted someone beforehand (Cash). Schools also need to establish an action plan for responding to students who may be depressed (Cash). Most importantly, schools need to foster a supportive, caring environment in which students feel accepted and welcome. This may reduce the number of depressed students and give those that are depressed a safe place to reach out for help.

DRUG & ALCOHOL ABUSE

Drugs in schools are a major cause for concern. Teachers, therefore, need to take an active role in finding and effectively dealing with substance use among students (Finn & Willert). Catching students who keep and deal drugs at school is even more of a challenge. Both students and school faculty seems to agree that zero tolerance policies are necessary in order to reduce student exposure to drugs and alcohol ("Survey Finds"). 83% of schools where students abuse substances were not established drug-free zones ("Survey Finds"). However, even drug-free zones are not a panacea since administrative, budgetary and logistical setbacks present difficulties in enforcing anti-drug policies in some communities (Finn & Willert). In order for drug-free zones to be effective, faculty and students need to be clear on policies and protocols regarding drug and alcohol use. Administrators need to support faculty by following through on reported students and enforcing established drug policies (Finn & Willert).

HOMELESSNESS

For "homeless children who live in shelters, motels, cars, parks, abandoned buildings, or with other families, school can be a safe haven, a place of stability and refuge" (Berliner). However, this is only effective when the appropriate services are in place (Berliner). In 1987, "the Stewart B. McKinney Homeless Assistance Act was enacted to protect the rights of homeless students and ensure they receive quality education" (Jozefowicz-Simbeni & Israel). The act prohibits against segregating students on the basis of homelessness (Jozefowicz-Simbeni & Israel). In 2001, the act was reauthorized as the McKinney-Vento Homeless Assistance Act as part of the No Child Left Behind Act (Jozefowicz-Simbeni & Israel). This indicated a commitment on a national level to the academic achievement of students without stable home lives (Berliner).

According to the McKinney-Vento Act, all school districts must appoint a liaison, such as a social worker, to communicate with homeless families (Berliner). In addition, administrators should ease enrollment policies but require students to comply with attendance policies (Berliner). Addressing basic needs of homeless students such as providing, food, showers and transportation may help students to regularly and comfortably attend school (Berliner). Likewise, teachers should be kept informed about which students are homeless in order to help them adjust in the classroom. Maintaining routines and providing a stable classroom environment can also help students feel at home during the school day (Hall, R.).

TEEN PREGNANCY

Schools need to take on the role of educating students about sex and the consequences of teen pregnancy. A government report on teenage pregnancy in England claims that young people who perform well at school and who have plans for the future are at less risk of teenage pregnancy ("Government to Spread," 2006). Raising educational standards, therefore, may help reduce overall rates of teenage pregnancy. Campaigns such as the one unveiled in 1996, the National Campaign to Prevent Teen Pregnancy, released a series of ads depicting the consequences of having unprotected sex (Sember, Kropf, & Mauro, 2006). One advertisement juxtaposed the cost of a condom to the costs of raising an infant. Other programs, which preach abstinence until marriage, have also had some success at reducing teen pregnancy in certain schools (Sember et al.).

Communities do need to acknowledge the teenagers that are having children and provide adequate support to this population, including prenatal care, counseling, and appropriate educational services (Scholl). A school program developed in New Jersey specifically for teen mothers resulted in an 84% graduation rate compared to the 41% of mothers who graduated in the conventional school setting. Programs that have been successful with teenage mothers usually offer smaller classes, flexible schedules, personal mentors and, sometimes, childcare services. Same sex classrooms may also reduce the chances of repeat teen pregnancies (Scholl).

CONCLUSION

In order to effectively deal with social concerns, schools and communities need to acknowledge them and open the door to dialogue with young people about such concerns. Materials should be made available to students that deal with common social concerns such as teen pregnancy, depression, homelessness and drug abuse (Gorman, 20007). Districts should research the community and assess trends to determine which issues need the most attention (Gorman).

TERMS & CONCEPTS

Bullying: Bullying refers to any type of rough behavior that is "deliberately aggressive" such as name-calling, hitting, mocking, slander, and social isolation.

Cutting: Cutting refers to the deliberate injury to one's own body by cutting the skin without intending suicide.

Depression: Depression is the persistent feeling of sadness and the inability to feel pleasure.

Homelessness: Homelessness is defined as living in places that do not have water, electricity and other basic services; living in motels, shelters, public spaces and temporary arrangements with other families.

Hurricane Katrina: Hurricane Katrina struck the Southeastern coast of the United States on August 29, 2005 causing major flooding and devastation, especially in Louisiana and Alabama where almost 2,000 people were killed and hundreds of thousands left homeless.

McKinney-Vento Act: In 1987, "Congress authorized the Stewart B. McKinney Homeless Assistance Act to protect the rights of homeless students and to

ensure that they receive equal education" (Jozefowicz-Simbeni & Israel). In 2001 the act was revised and reauthorized and is now known as the McKinney-Vento Act.

No Child Left Behind Act (NCLB): Passed in 2001, the No Child Left Behind Act is a United States federal law that aims to streamline education and narrow the achievement gap across the nation's schools.

Social Concerns: Social concerns are non-academic issues that can affect student learning and development and sometimes lead to safety issues for individuals and groups.

United Nations Universal Declaration of Human Rights: Adopted in 1948 by the United Nations the Universal Declaration of Human Rights acknowledges that all human beings should have the basic rights of freedom, justice, privacy and peace.

Jennifer Bouchard

BIBLIOGRAPHY

Berliner, B. (2002). Helping homeless students keep up. *Education Digest, 68,* 49. Retrieved October 9, 2007, from EBSCO Online Database Education Research Complete.

Bradshaw, C.P., Waasdorp, T.E., O'Brennan, L.M., & Gulemetova, M. (2013). Teachers' and education support professionals' perspectives on bullying and prevention: Findings from a national education association study. *School Psychology Review, 42,* 280-297. Retrieved December 15, 2013, from EBSCO Online Database Education Research Complete.

Cash, R. (2003). When depression brings teens down. *Education Digest, 69,* 35-42. Retrieved October 9, 2007, from EBSCO Online Database Education Research Complete.

Crepeau-Hobson, F. (2013). An exploratory study of suicide risk assessment practices in the school setting. *Psychology in the Schools, 50,* 810-822. Retrieved December 15, 2013, from EBSCO Online Database Education Research Complete.

Finn, K. (2006). Patterns of alcohol and marijuana use at school. *Journal of Research on Adolescence, 16,* 69-77. Retrieved October 9, 2007, from EBSCO Online Database Education Research Complete.

Finn, K. & Willert, J. (2006). Alcohol and drugs in schools: Teachers' reactions to the problem. *Phi Delta Kappan, 88,* 37-40. Retrieved October 11, 2007, from EBSCO Online Database Education Research Complete.

Goldweber, A., Waasdorp, T., & Bradshaw, C.P. (2013). Examining the link between forms of bullying behaviors and perceptions of safety and belonging among secondary school students. *Journal of School Psychology, 51,* 469-485. Retrieved December 15, 2013, from EBSCO Online Database Education Research Complete.

Gorman, M. (2007). Step up to the plate. *School Library Journal, 53,* 31. Retrieved October 9, 2007, from EBSCO Online Database Education Research Complete.

Government to spread best practice on tackling teen pregnancy. (2006). *Education, 238,* 5. Retrieved October 11, 2007, from EBSCO Online Database Education Research Complete.

Hall, P. (2007). For parents & teachers. *Skipping Stones, 19,* 35-35. Retrieved October 10, 2007, from EBSCO Online Database Education Research Complete.

Hall, R. (2007). Homeless students and the public school system. *The Delta Kappa Gamma Bulletin, 73,* 9-12. Retrieved October 9, 2007, from EBSCO Online Database Education Research Complete.

Jozefowicz-Simbeni, D. & Israel, N. (2006). Services to homeless students and families: The McKinney-Vento Act and its implications for school social work practice. *Children & Schools, 28,* 37-44. Retrieved October 9, 2007, from EBSCO Online Database Education Research Complete.

Kuo, E.S., Vander Stoep, A., Herting, J.R., Grupp, K., & Mccauley, E. (2013). How to identify students for school-based depression intervention: Can school record review be substituted for universal depression screening?. *Journal of Child & Adolescent Psychiatric Nursing, 26,* 42-52. Retrieved December 15, 2013, from EBSCO Online Database Education Research Complete.

Lemonick, M., Colton, E., Holton, A., Song, S., & Steptoe, S. (2005). The bully blight. *Time, 165,* 144-145. Retrieved October 9, 2007, from EBSCO Online Database Education Research Complete.

Miller, P., Pavlakis, A., & Bourgeois, A. (2013). Homelessness here? A district administrator encounters an unexpected challenge. *Journal of Cases in Educational Leadership, 16,* 6-10. Retrieved December 15, 2013, from EBSCO Online Database Education Research Complete.

Miller, P. M. (2013). Educating (more and more) students experiencing homelessness: An analysis of recession-era policy and practice. *Educational Policy, 27,* 805-838. Retrieved December 15, 2013, from EBSCO Online Database Education Research Complete.

Salvatore, A. (2006). Adolescent depression: Myths and realities. *Principal, 85,* 60-61. Retrieved October 11, 2007, from EBSCO Online Database Education Research Complete.

Scholl, M. (2007). Educating adolescent parents: Proactive approaches by school leaders. *Delta Kappa Gamma Bulletin, 73,* 28-32. Retrieved October 9, 2007, from EBSCO Online Database Education Research Complete.

Sember, R., Kropf, A. & Mauro, D. (2006). Images against teen pregnancy. *American Journal of Public Health, 96,* 1561-1561. Retrieved October 9, 2007, from EBSCO Online Database Education Research Complete.

Steinman, K. (2005). Drug selling among high school students. *The Brown University Child and Adolescent Behavior Letter, 21,* 3-4. Retrieved October 9, 2007, from EBSCO Online Database Education Research Complete.

Survey finds most teens can buy drugs at school. (1997). *Techniques: Making Education & Career Connections, 72,* 7-7. Retrieved October 9, 2007, from EBSCO Online Database Education Research Complete.

Vaillancourt, K., & Rossen, E. (2012). Navigating school safety law and policy. (cover story). *Communique (0164775X), 41,* 1-23. Retrieved December 15, 2013, from EBSCO Online Database Education Research Complete.

SUGGESTED READING

Fine, L. (2001). Theft of drugs prompt schools to tighten up. *Education Week, 20,* 1. Retrieved October 9, 2007, from EBSCO Online Database Education Research Complete.

Goldberg, S., Reese, B., & Halpern, C. (2016). Teen pregnancy among sexual minority women: Results from the national longitudinal study of adolescent to adult health. *Journal of Adolescent Health.* 59(4), 429-437.

Guttmacher, S., Lieberman, L. Ward, D., Freudenberg, N. Radosh, A., & Jarlais, D. (1997). Condom availability in New York City Public High Schools. *American Journal of Public Health, 87,* 1427-1433. Retrieved October 9, 2007, from EBSCO Online Database Education Research Complete.

Kennedy, A. (2007). 'Mean girls' or much more? *Counseling Today, 50,* 8-22. Retrieved October 10, 2007, from EBSCO Online Database Education Research Complete.

McGill, N. (2016). Teen depression: It's more than a passing mood swing. *The Nation's Health.* 46(9).

Ttofi, M., Farrington, D., Losel, F., Crago, T., & Theodorakis, N. (2016). School bullying and drug use later in life: A meta-analytic investigation. *School Psychology Quarterly.* 31(1), 8-27.

Turner, S. (2007). Preparing inner-city adolescents to transition into high school. *Professional School Counseling, 10,* 245-252. Retrieved October 9, 2007, from EBSCO Online Database Education Research Complete.

CONFLICT MEDIATION

Conflicts in a classroom can be significant or minor, but need to be addressed and extinguished. Experienced teachers are able to anticipate minor conflicts and attend to them before they become a distraction. Other more serious problems need an organized mediation system. Schools with chronic serious conflicts often have a peer mediation curriculum in place, and components of that system can be added to any classroom or school. Making the classroom free of distraction is a necessity for learning. Many students are rarely or never involved in conflict situations and all need a safe and secure learning environment.

KEYWORDS: Classroom Management; Conflict Resolution; Crime; Disciplinary; Disruptive Behavior; Fighting; Mediation; Peer Mediation; Self-discipline; Street Law Mediation

INTRODUCTION

It is a sure bet that every day in every school and classroom in our country, teachers are not only teaching, but are mediating small disputes and larger conflicts among students. It doesn't matter where a school is located or the age of its students—conflicts will be present. It seems to follow that putting students together in a classroom for hours every day will produce the perfect conditions for conflict between them (Leatzow, Newhauser, & Wilmes, 1983).

In many classrooms, the disruptive behavior of students is the norm rather than an exception, and teachers are not always prepared to mediate all types of problems. They often don't have enough formal training to effectively deal with unacceptable and sometimes serious and harmful student behavior in the classroom (Leatzow et al.). Handling and mediating conflicts quickly and efficiently is important to keeping order in the classroom, and the school.

For learning to take place, it is important for all students to be able to operate freely within places and situations they may not be completely comfortable and familiar with, and with peers they may not know well or understand. The classroom should guide students to acceptable behavior and self-discipline so they can operate effectively in the outside world (Clark, Erway, & Beltzer, 1971).

TEACHING SELF-DISCIPLINE

There are a few definitions and interpretations of what *discipline* means. For our purposes, *discipline* means helping students acquire and develop self-control so their behavior is socially acceptable and doesn't cause distractions in the classroom or the school, or elsewhere in their lives. Discipline also means the measures taken to bring this type of self-control about. In school, discipline implies active participation on the part of both the teacher and the student, and it is ongoing with all students. Helping students develop and work toward self-control is something teachers should be trained in as much as they are trained to teach academic courses (Drayer, 1979).

Even though a teacher's job is mainly to teach students the academic subjects, and counselors work with students as they establish and maintain social relations, both components of a student's life will mesh at certain times (Hanna, 1988). Most good teachers know and accept that helping their students develop self-discipline is the ultimate goal of all their work with classroom and school behavior (Sylvester, 1971).

Self-discipline is usually best achieved through a series of consistent but gentle nudges and interactions than with dramatic, sweeping behavior controls that usually only serve to embarrass the student, not motivate him or her to change how they are acting (Sylvester). To that end, it is important for teachers to establish rules at the beginning of the school year. Problems are often best handled in a calm setting, and depending on the child's age, lessons about compromising, tolerating others, and exercising self-control are ways to develop human relations components (Hanna).

CONFLICTS THAT MAY ARISE IN SCHOOL

Early in students' school careers, they become familiar with behavior control methods and how and when they are used. The student comes to expect that particular types of behavior are not acceptable in the classroom and that teachers will move to mediate certain situations before they escalate. This type of conflict mediation is accepted and understood by teachers and students and students are comfortable with the process even though they may not welcome it (Sylvester). Those teachers who are most effective with managing their classroom are those who are able to skillfully use their classroom management techniques so students aren't really aware that their behavior is being controlled (Sylvester). However, this doesn't always work.

Behavior problems and conflicts can vary in both nature and severity. Some disputes are merely distractions in the classroom, while others may put students in danger (Sylvester). Conflicts in school will often be similar to the types of conflicts found in society. These can include problems such as actual crime to another student or within the school, racial injustice, and perceived or actual unequal treatment of males and females (Bickmore, 2001). Conflicts can be physical fighting between students, arguing among students, one student giving another the silent treatment, students calling each other inappropriate names, students starting rumors about each other, and students ganging up to turn other students against another student (Williamson et al., 1999). These are all serious problems and all must be mediated and extinguished as quickly as possible, so as to not cause a distraction or danger to the rest of the students in the classroom and school.

COMMON TEACHER INTERVENTIONS
Depending on the severity of a particular situation, teachers and administrators will decide how best to handle the situation. In some less serious cases, it is easiest and best to simply ignore the behaviors. For example, some students may be using their actions to elicit attention for themselves. By not acknowledging the behavior, it may be more easily extinguished (Sylvester).

Most teachers are aware that other problems can escalate if they are not dealt with effectively and immediately, or if they are not managed correctly. Compounding this, in most classrooms there are a few students—usually just one or two—who the teacher knows will require special attention throughout the school day. The teacher is usually aware from the beginning of the school year that he or she will have to exert plenty of ingenuity to anticipate conflicts in the classroom and mediate them quickly and effectively. Most experienced teachers will regard these types of students and situations as a challenge instead of as a source of anxiety (Drayer).

There are students, for example, that must be closely monitored because of particular medical or health problems which sometimes include behavior issues. These problems may often require them to take medication, and those students who haven't taken the appropriate dosage at the correct time may need reminders about when to take it rather than punishment when their behavior escalates and becomes unacceptable in the classroom. Teachers should be able to recognize the difference and handle each situation individually (Hanna).

Other students may feel they are misunderstood, and also that they are misunderstanding their peers. This can cause stress for the student, which can invite conflict. The anxiety felt by the student may sometimes help him to work through his feelings of unclear communication on his own, but most of the time it contributes to the student's poor self-image. The student's thoughts can be disorganized or distorted, and emotions and values may be confused, too. These all may often lead to disruption and conflict at school (Hanna).

MEDIATION MEASURES
The classroom can be an excellent laboratory for students' development of lifelong skills for communication, interacting and getting along with others. Since many different types of problems can occur in the classroom, students can observe and take part in tactics to limit the amount of negative reactions to certain types of communication. They may be able to contemplate the consequences of some types of behaviors as they observe other students and situations as they are taking place. Students can work on problem-solving skills in a structured environment and learn to work well with others. All learning that happens in the classroom takes place within some sort of lesson framework and behavior lessons may sometimes be framed this way as well (Clark et al.).

Teachers may sometimes choose to use the mediation of a disruptive situation as a teaching moment so other students may learn more about appropriate behavior in the classroom. In some situations, teachers must respond immediately to mediate a situation. The teacher finds herself playing a variety of roles, from police officer, to prosecutor, to judge and jury, all in a quick span of time and with the goal of getting back to the lesson that may have been interrupted, restoring order in the classroom (Sylvester).

Teachers may also use disciplinary measures that are unpredictable to the students—and these seem to be more effective than those the students may anticipate. This may be because the unpredictable measures draw attention to the situation and require the student to think about the possible consequences of her actions in a new way. This may cause the student to think before attempting the same behavior again. Unpredictable disciplinary measures may include sending a student to the principal's office or denying a student the right to participate in an activity (Sylvester). These methods are often more effective for younger students; older ones have different needs.

As children become adults, their development becomes more internal. It involves changes first in how they perceive things and then in their behavior. Since these types of developmental changes occur slowly and gradually, they aren't always immediately perceived by others. Often the changes are painful for the adolescent, but they do serve to alert the individual that change is important. This is the time when they will realize they are in charge of their decision-making. While teachers, family, and friends are still there to help and guide, it is the individual who must make those decisions as the crises and problems present in life are encountered. As she faces each struggle, she grows as a person, establishes a personal identity, develops a newfound intimacy toward those around her, and becomes a person of integrity (Leatzow, Newhauser & Wilmes, 1983).

Good teachers are those who are in touch with the individuality of each student they work with. They have a solid belief that each student can exhibit acceptable behavior. These teachers work hard to find ways to turn unacceptable behaviors and conflicts between students into ones that are appropriate to the classroom and school community (Leatzow et al.).

THE CONFLICT MEDIATION PROGRAM

Some serious problems are difficult to resolve and need direct attention and time to work through effectively. These more severe types of conflict are best mediated so that the students involved are first given an opportunity to discuss the situation (Williamson et al.). To effectively mediate a conflict, disputing students and those mediating must first agree to cooperate with each other, must strive to understand and accept each others' viewpoints, must agree to avoid the behavior that caused the conflict, and must agree

to work together to respond to and rectify the conflict (Carter, 2002). To get to this point, the students will:

- First explain what is going on;
- Tell how they feel;
- Find a compromise;
- Lessen the conflict;
- Discuss any underlying issues that may be present (Williamson et al.).

These are all components of a good conflict mediation program.

It is important to have this type of strong conflict mediation program in place from the beginning of the school year. Students should be aware of the consequences of their actions and behaviors and should be encouraged to work toward self-control and personal integrity.

A good and effective conflict mediation program will take into account the school population. There may be a mix of cultures, socioeconomic groups and exceptionalities. Schools also need to consider the amount of time spent mediating student problems and compare it to the time those students are not spending in the classroom as these conflicts are being worked out. Students need to also have assistance throughout the mediation process, especially to ensure that agreed-upon solutions are carried out as they should be. Throughout the conflict mediation process, students should experience positive interactions with teachers and administrators (Carter).

PEER MEDIATION

Peer mediation may be a strong arm of a school's conflict mediation program. Some schools' experience and observations show that a straightforward and easy-to-use peer mediation program will be successful for the types of conflicts they experience. Teachers can work with peer mediation in a variety of classroom settings. Teaching students about conflict management can play a significant and important role in ensuring peaceful classrooms and schools (Williamson et al.).

Most often conflict mediation in the schools means using structured problem-solving skills. These are usually executed between the students involved in the dispute and the teacher or a student mediator. The student mediator will attempt to guide the students toward a resolution that is mutually acceptable for their problem. Peer mediators have been trained to provide prompts to students involved in the conflict. These prompts and the students' feelings resulting from the discussions will assist in bringing about a mutually agreed upon way to rectify the problem. The mediators strive to facilitate the negotiations between the disputing students and often have the students sign an agreement acknowledging what has been worked out (Carter).

A good peer mediation program can provide opportunities for some students to develop their personalities positively as they learn to take responsibility for their behavior. When they are involved with peer mediation, students learn to troubleshoot problems as they arise and deal with real-world problems in a socially acceptable way. As they develop these mediation skills they gain valuable experience with the type of challenges that will be prevalent in the real world and in the community (Bickmore).

THE STREET LAW MODEL

Williamson, et al. propose the Street Law Model, a peer mediation program which is composed of six steps:

1. INTRODUCTION

A trained peer mediator first helps the disputing students feel comfortable and at ease about the process and explains the steps they will go through as part of the mediation. The conflict mediator's role is not to decide which side is right, but rather to have the disputing students have the ability to make their own decisions and agreements.

2. STORYTELLING

After the introductory stage, each disputing student is encouraged to tell his or her side of the conflict. During this storytelling stage, only one student has the floor and interruptions by other students are not permitted. Students who are not speaking are encouraged to take notes for when it is their time to talk.

3. IDENTIFICATION OF FACTS AND RELEVANT ISSUES IN THE CONFLICT

The mediator strives to employ active listening skills as he or she seeks to help the disputing students identify those issues on which both agree and those where there is conflict. The mediator works to ensure that both he and the disputing parties all completely understand the problem by asking questions and clarifying unclear parts of the story.

4. IDENTIFICATION OF POSSIBLE SOLUTIONS

This is a brainstorming phase and a time when everyone involved in the conflict thinks of and suggests possible solutions. As the students suggest ideas, the mediator lists them and then elicits reactions to each.

5. REVISING AND DISCUSSING SOLUTION IDEAS

As the disputing students react and discuss each possible solution, they also talk about which one seems to be the most realistic. All disputing students must agree on the solution, which may mean that certain disputing students may need to talk individually with the mediator or with other students.

6. REACHING AN AGREEMENT

The mediator notes the agreed-upon solution and then discusses what types of strategies should be employed if disputing parties don't keep to the agreement (Williamson et al.).

Teachers may modify the peer mediation process to include more than one student mediator (a mediation team), and by sometimes including role playing of certain incidents so disputing parties and mediators can review the scenario. Prior to any mediation process, teachers will ensure that all students acting as mediators are well-trained in problem-solving skills, known to all students, were selected by the teachers, and are comfortable in their role (Williamson et al.).

To avoid further dispute between those who have had conflicts, teachers and school staff should monitor interactions between the disputants on an ongoing basis. Follow-up is crucial even after a successful mediation and offers of continued assistance should be extended to students as they attempt to uphold their agreements (Carter). Students on both sides of a dispute (as well as those who mediate) should keep in mind that the goal of all conflict resolutions is community building. Keeping peace in the school community is tantamount to success for all students. Students should demonstrate their understanding of this crucial component of mediation by discussing it with the mediator and the teacher (Carter).

AN OUNCE OF PREVENTION

Prudent teachers set and maintain high behavioral standards for their students at the beginning of the school year. Teachers also need to ensure they are thoroughly organized for each class and each lesson. When students can detect teachers haven't adequately prepared for a class, they may take advantage of the distracted teacher by inciting conflicts and problems in the classroom. Ensure that all class time is accounted for. Students who are busy and working don't have time to create conflict in the classroom (Drayer).

Before beginning a lesson or a class, teachers need to ensure that students are attentive and ready to learn. Those students who aren't completely set will often not be able to key in to what is going on in the classroom and will instead distract those students who are engaged in learning.

Teachers should vary their teaching methods—mix it up and make the class period be unpredictable. This enhances students' interest and their anticipation of what will come in the class period (Drayer). Teachers should always treat students as individuals and should treat them fairly. They should also keep in mind that a sense of humor is an essential quality to success in any career, not just in teaching children (Drayer).

CONCLUSION

Dealing with student conflicts effectively and successfully is essential to harmony in the classroom. Successful conflict mediation serves to reduce social tension and eliminate more violent acts, and it generally results in more productive classroom settings (Carter).

To prevent conflicts among some students, it may be necessary to use preventative measures. Students who are encouraged to explore what conflict means, discuss what types of situations trigger this type of behavior within themselves, and ways to prevent conflicts with others generally are more successful in handling their conflict problems (Williamson et al.).

TERMS & CONCEPTS

Classroom Management: Classroom management is a teacher's ability to operate a peaceful classroom free of distractions.

Conflict Resolution: Conflict resolution is the process of resolving a problem or situation by listening to each side, negotiating, and mediating.

Disruptive Behavior: Disruptive behavior is student behavior that prevents students from learning and teachers from teaching. It is behavior that interrupts a lesson or class period, and can include talking out in class, walking around a classroom

at inappropriate times, passing notes to other students, talking out in class, or bothering another student.

Mediation: Mediation is the act of assisting in negotiations: intervening in an argument or a disruptive situation.

Peer Mediation: Peer mediation is a process for resolving conflicts where both sides are heard and students are able to work out problems constructively as they respect each other's differences. Students must be willing to change how they currently relate to each other and to work toward agreement of a solution.

Self-Discipline: Self-discipline is a person's ability to stay with their own goals, actions, behaviors, and thoughts regardless of what is going on around them.

Street Law Mediation: Street Law is a conflict mediation curriculum designed for grades 3-12. Its focus is to give students the chance to manage conflicts in a responsible way.

Susan Ludwig

BIBLIOGRAPHY

Bickmore, K. (2001). Student conflict resolution. Power sharing in schools, and citizenship. *Curriculum Inquiry.* 2, 137. Retrieved November 18, 2007, from EBSCO online database, Education Research Complete.

Campbell, W. N., & Skarakis-Doyle, E. (2011). The relationship between peer conflict resolution knowledge and peer victimization in school-age children across the language continuum. *Journal of Communication Disorders, 44,* 345-358. Retrieved December 15, 2013, from EBSCO Online Database Education Research Complete.

Carter, C. (2002). Conflict resolution at school: Building compassionate communities. *Social Alternatives.* 1, 49. Retrieved November 18, 2007, from EBSCO online database, Education Research Complete.

Clark, M. L., Erway, E. A., & Beltzer, L. (1971). *The Learning Encounter.* New York: Random House.

Drayer, A. (1979). *Problems in Middle and High School Teaching.* Boston: Allyn and Bacon, Inc.

Ghaffar, A., Zaman, A., & Naz, A. (2012). A comparative study of conflict management styles of public & private secondary schools' principals. *Bulletin of Education & Research, 34,* 59-69. Retrieved December 15, 2013, from EBSCO Online Database Education Research Complete.

Hanna, J. (1988). *Disruptive School Behavior: Class, Race, and Culture.* New York: Holmes and Meier.

LaRusso, M., & Selman, R. (2011). Early adolescent health risk behaviors, conflict resolution strategies, and school climate. *Journal of Applied Developmental Psychology, 32,* 354-362. Retrieved December 15, 2013, from EBSCO Online Database Education Research Complete.

Leatzow, N., Newhauser, C., & Wilmes, L. (1983). *Creating Discipline in the Early Childhood Classroom.* Provo, UT: Brigham Young University Press.

Sylvester, R., (1971). *The Elementary Teacher and Pupil Behavior.* West Nyack, NY: Parker Publishing Co.

Williamson, D., Warner, D., Sanders, P., & Knepper, P. (1999). We can work it out: Teaching conflict through peer mediation. *Social Work in Education.* 2, 89-96. Retrieved November 18, 2007, from EBSCO online database, Education Research Complete.

SUGGESTED READING

Bodine, R., & Crawford, D. (1997). *The Handbook of Conflict Resolution Education.* San Francisco: Jossey-Bass.

Christensen, L.M. (2009). Sticks, stones, and school-yard bullies: Restorative justice, mediation, and a new approach to conflict resolution in our schools. Nevada Law Journal. 9(3), 545-579.

Linnemeier, E. (2012). School-based conflict resolution education and peer mediation programs: The Western Justice Center experience. *Dispute Resolution Magazine.* 18(4), 14-19.

Moore, C. (2014). (4th Ed.). *The Mediation Process.* San Francisco, CA.: John Wiley & Sons.

Pearlstein, R., & Thrall, G. (2001). *Ready to Use Conflict Resolution Activities for Secondary Students.* San Francisco: Jossey-Bass.

Rosenberg, M. B. (2004). *We Can Work It Out: Resolving Conflicts Peacefully and Powerfully.* Encinitas, CA: Puddledancer Press.

Schrumpf, F., Crawford, D., & Bodine, R. (1997). *Peer Mediation: Conflict Resolution in Schools Program Guide.* Champaign, IL: Research Press.

Walker, H. M., Ramsey, E., & Gresham, F. (2003) Antisocial Behavior in Schools: Evidence-Based Practices. Belmont, CA: Wadsworth Publishing.

CRISIS MANAGEMENT

Crisis management refers to the policies and procedures developed for handling emergency situations. Since crises vary in size and scope, methods and management procedures vary across grade levels and situations. The imperative steps to creating and implementing any effective crisis management plan are mainly prevention, preparation, response and recovery. Debates surround the value of emergency drills and post crisis counseling methods.

KEYWORDS: Crisis Management; Critical Incident Stress Debriefing (CISD); Crisis Intervention Team (CIT); Emergency Responders; Evacuation; Lockdown; Pandemic; Shelter in Place

OVERVIEW

WHAT IS CRISIS MANAGEMENT?

Crisis management is a term that refers to the policies and procedures developed for handling emergency situations in public schools. The 1999 Columbine shootings, the terror attacks of September 11, 2001, and, more recently, the devastation caused by Hurricane Katrina, have prompted local and national governments to research the most effective ways to manage crises in schools.

In 2002, the Department of Safe and Drug-Free Schools together with the Harvard School of Public Health, the Prevention Institute, and the Education Development Center developed a program entitled, "The Three R's to Dealing with Trauma in Schools: Readiness, Response and Recovery" designed to assist schools with crisis management ("Taking the Lead," 2007). In 2003, Education Secretary Rodney Paige and the Secretary of Homeland Security Tom Ridge launched a $30 million initiative providing grants to help schools buy safety equipment, train staff, parents and students in crisis management ("Taking the Lead").

Crisis often strikes fast so reaction time must be quick. This can only happen when procedures are in place and have been practiced. When a crisis occurs, schools must evaluate the crisis to decide whether to evacuate, lockdown, or use schools as a shelter (Poland, 2007). Because every school community is different, it is important for schools to practice a variety of crisis management procedures to determine if they are appropriate. Schools should then personalize their plans to the needs of their community. Plans also should accommodate the age of the student population, as elementary school students will behave differently than middle or high school students (U.S. Department of Education, 2003). The Office of Safe and Drug-Free Schools recommends schools and emergency personnel conduct drills and practice scenarios until they have procedures memorized (Black, 2004). Leadership, preparation and communication are essential qualities in managing any type of emergency.

WHAT CONSTITUTES A CRISIS?

Webster's Dictionary defines a crisis as an unstable or crucial time or state of affairs in which a decisive change is impending, especially one with the distinct possibility of a highly undesirable outcome (as cited in *U.S. Department of Education*). This definition of a crisis is broad. It can range from incidents that only affect a few students to situations that halt an entire community. Crises can happen at any time, in any place, with and without warning. Incidents that qualify as crises include, but are not limited to:

- Bomb threat;
- Chemical spill;
- Fire;
- Natural disaster;
- Pandemic;
- School violence;
- Student or faculty death;
- Terrorist attack;
- War;
- Weather emergency.

The one thing all crises have in common is the need for clear communication and quick decision-making. Regardless of the type of crisis, every crisis management plan should include procedures for prevention, preparation, response and recovery (U.S. Department of Education).

CRISIS PREVENTION

The first step in crisis management is prevention. Schools should conduct safety assessments of school property to determine if floor plans, lockdown procedures and evacuation routes need to be updated ("Taking the Lead"). It is important to connect with local emergency responders to determine what types of problems are most common in the area and with students ("Taking the Lead"). Emergency responders include law enforcement agents, firefighters and emergency medical technicians.

Prevention often means controlling a problem before it spreads or escalates. In some cases, such as with infectious diseases which can lead to a pandemic, prevention efforts can be as basic as teaching hygiene and providing anti-infection products such as hand sanitizer and anti-viral tissues (St. Gerard, 2007). Education is often the first step in crisis prevention.

STUDIES CONDUCTED AFTER COLUMBINE

Following the 1999 Columbine High School shooting in Colorado, which resulted in 15 fatalities and 23 injuries, the U.S. Secret Service and U.S. Department of Education conducted a study of 37 school attacks. Their report, released in 2002, concluded that no common profile existed among attackers except for the fact that most of the perpetrators had been bullied or injured by others (Dillon, 2007). This report proves the value of fostering a positive school climate that welcomes diversity and teaches compassion (Dillon). The report recommends that schools focus on providing a supportive community that helps students mediate and resolve conflicts. Penalties should also be communicated and set forth to discourage students and parents from violent and threatening actions (Dillon). Dillon also cites that lawmakers in Pennsylvania considered putting schools on permanent lockdown to prevent violence in schools. In the wake of a school shooting, Platte Canyon High School in Colorado began a program in which parents volunteer to greet visitors at the door and log them in so that no intruder will enter the building unnoticed (Butler, 2007). Increasing police presence and installing metal detectors are other methods used to curb school violence (Dillon).

The Secret Service and Department of Education also discovered that, in about 80% of the incidents studied, at least one person knew what was going to happen (Dillon).

Recognizing a potential crisis, and responding quickly, can make a world of difference. Schools need to educate students and teachers how to recognize warning signs. Platte Canyon school district participates in the "Safe to Tell" program, which was initiated after the Columbine shootings (Butler). The program provides an anonymous hotline where students can report information regarding potential threats (Butler).

The Department of Education's guide, *Practical Information on Crisis Planning* encourages schools to consider every possible scenario and utilize every resource to help prevent crises or lessen their impact (U.S. Department of Education). Some suggestions include providing IDs for students and staff, conducting hurricane drills and taking an inventory of hazardous materials on school grounds (U.S. Department of Education).

PREPARATION

Since not all crises can be prevented, the key to successful crisis management is preparation. Schools must make sure that they use all of the resources available: teachers, administrators, social workers, security officers, and emergency responders (U.S. Department of Education). Every responder must be familiar with the school's procedure for handling an emergency. Communication is essential to success. A chain of command should be established and methods of communication determined. A common vocabulary is essential. A crisis committee of faculty, parents and students can help better prepare schools for emergencies (Poland). This team of people should conduct research to determine what types of crises could occur in a given school and make recommendations as to how to handle them (U.S. Department of Education). The committee should also examine major issues from past years and evaluate how they were handled. This process ensures that schools regularly review and update procedures (Poland). The committee should make sure parent contact information is up to date and establish connections with local hospitals and emergency service personnel (Poland).

CRISIS MANAGEMENT MATERIALS

Poland states that the distribution of crisis management materials is a necessary step in making sure schools are prepared for emergencies. Materials may include phone trees, floor plans, evacuation routes, first aid instructions, and health awareness lists identifying persons with special needs. These materials should be reviewed carefully with staff and students (Poland). The Department of Education's Emergency Response and Crisis Management Technical Assistance Center also advises schools to provide emergency supply kits to faculty including items such as flashlights, batteries, contact information, first aid supplies and instructions ("Taking the Lead"). The Red Cross recommends schools keep a stock supply of certain items, especially water, first aid and sanitation supplies in the event of a crisis ("Taking the Lead").

DRILLS & EXERCISES

Crisis practices should be thorough, repetitive and easy to follow (McGiboney & Fretwell, 2007). Drills and practice exercises should be performed regularly to prepare school communities to effectively respond to crisis if necessary (Dillon). It is important to anticipate and prepare for a variety of potential emergencies from hurricanes to school shootings to terrorist attacks. William Modzeleski of the Office of Safe and Drug-free Schools emphasizes the importance of having a consistent crisis plan that is customized to an area's geographic, economic and social needs (Black). A school close to a power plant, for example, has to factor that element into its crisis management plan. Emergency plans and procedures cannot follow a one size fits all model. Variety is essential if lockdown and evacuation drills are going to be effective (Dillon).

RESPONSE

Depending on the crisis at hand, school response should vary. Successful crisis management plans will have different approaches to different situations. School officials need to be able to quickly assess the crisis at hand and choose the best response (U.S. Department of Education). Emergency responders should be notified as soon as possible (U.S. Department of Education).

EVACUATION

Evacuation requires students and faculty to leave the building. Fires and bomb threats are possible crises that would require evacuation. Evacuation plans should have designated meeting points outside of the building and should have alternative locations to shelter students if needed (U.S. Department of Education). Evacuation plans must include accommodations for students with disabilities (U.S. Department of Education).

LOCKDOWN

A lockdown requires students and staff to stay inside their classroom or building. A lockdown is employed when there is a threat outside the classroom or building. Movement is restricted and students are often instructed to cover and move away from windows (U.S. Department of Education). Possible reasons for a lockdown are the presence of an intruder or a school shooting. In the event of a crisis that requires an extreme lockdown, Black recommends notifying teachers in a way that does not alarm students, for example sending an email to teachers and then making an announcement instructing all teachers to read their email. Teachers should gather students in one place and account for all of them. Outside entrances should be locked and buses cancelled. Parents should be notified and local radio stations should be informed so they can assist in disseminating information (Black).

SHELTER IN PLACE

The term shelter in place is used when students and staff must remain in a school location when it is not safe or there is not enough time to evacuate, such as in the case of a chemical spill or natural disaster (U.S. Department of Education).

Helping students with physical and developmental disabilities during a crisis should be a high priority and extensively planned. In the event of an evacuation, students with physical disabilities will need assistance exiting the building. In some cases, safe zones or areas of refuge should be used until students can be assisted by emergency responders and evacuated (U.S. Department of Education). Schools should make sure accommodations are also in place for students with English language deficiencies (Black).

As soon as a crisis occurs, faculty should account for all students and do their best to keep students calm. In some cases, faculty may need to administer first aid or get students to a safe area. Parents should be notified as soon as it is safe and appropriate to do so (U.S. Department of Education). It is also important to be flexible, as no crisis response will unfold exactly as practiced (U.S. Department of Education).

RECOVERY

After a school crisis, once students and faculty are safe, the main priority of schools is restoring a normal learning environment (Poland). The Office of Safe and Drug-Free Schools states that, "returning to the business of learning" helps most students move forward after a crisis has occurred (U.S. Department of Education). Learning can only take place, however, once the emotional needs of crisis victims have been met.

CRISIS INTERVENTION & DEBRIEFING

Schools should enlist the assistance of a Crisis Intervention Team (CIT) to help students and staff cope with the crisis they experienced (U.S. Department of Education). Group Crisis Intervention (GCI) is a form of school-based intervention that might be used in schools allows students to share feelings, ask questions and come to terms with traumatic events (U.S. Department of Education). Another form of group counseling, known as Critical Incident Stress Debriefing (CISD), may be used after a crisis (Black). CISD is also used with adults who have experienced a traumatic event such as war or a violent attack to prevent Post Traumatic Stress Syndrome (Black). Mental health professionals also should be on hand to provide individual counseling as needed.

Once school resumes its normal schedule, teachers should provide students with a place to discuss their feelings about what happened to help reduce stress (U.S. Department of Education). Teachers should continue to monitor student behavior for signs of distress after a crisis (Poland). Additionally, the CIT should conduct follow-up sessions with students after some time has passed (Poland). Schools should consider honoring anniversaries and creating memorials and other positive ways to cope with crises (U.S. Department of Education).

MANAGING CRISES IN POST-SECONDARY SCHOOLS

Statistically, campuses of college and universities are some of the safest places in the country (Kennedy, 2007). Even so, a thorough examination of security measures and crisis management policies at post-secondary campuses has followed the recent massacre at Virginia Polytechnic Institute & State University in which a student opened fire on several classrooms killing 33 people (Kennedy). The U.S. Department of Homeland Security's Office for Domestic Preparedness has since developed some guidelines for crisis management in post-secondary institutions. The document entitled "Campus Public Safety: Weapons of Mass Destruction Terrorism Protective Measures" suggests colleges connect with a local FBI agent as well as state and local officials in order to ensure communication procedures are in place ("Taking the Lead"). Every campus also should have onsite emergency personnel, as the biggest focus for post-secondary schools should be deterrence. This includes assessing risk, using video cameras to monitor school grounds and providing means to lock and secure buildings ("Taking the Lead").

An important element in preventing such tragedies as the Virginia Tech shooting is making sure schools offer mental health services to their students (Kennedy). Depression and suicide are common in the college environment so assistance must be readily available for emotionally fragile students. Teachers and students also need better education so that they may recognize warning signs and steer potentially violent individuals to get the help they need (Kennedy). The sharing of information among appropriate persons is crucial to keeping post-secondary campuses safe (Kennedy).

DO PRACTICE DRILLS CAUSE MORE HARM THAN HELP?

One cause for concern is the results of a study conducted by the International Association of Chiefs of Police in 1999. The study determined that crisis drills could provide helpful information to potential student attackers in terms of revealing evacuation routes, hiding places and areas of refuge (Black). Another concern with recent initiatives to prepare students for school threats is that it enhances the public perception that schools are unsafe. This view may cause students to feel anxious thus negatively affecting the learning environment (Black).

The good news is that major crises in U.S. schools are in fact rare (U.S. Department of Education). The bad news is that there is minimal research on best practices for school-based crisis planning. What little research is available on crisis management is not quantifiable. There is little hard evidence to tell schools what will work in the event of a crisis (U.S. Department of Education). Roseanne Nyiri, the superintendent of Springfield Township School in Pennsylvania, is not entirely sold on the virtues of crisis management training. She does not believe that extra training and security would have prevented the incident in her district where a 16-year old student walked into school with a shotgun and killed himself (cited in Butler). However, she is convinced that practice lockdown drills did help students and staff stay calm throughout the crisis (cited in Butler).

Platte Canyon High School staff and students had undergone crisis management training and performed several lockdown drills in 2006, but that did not prevent an armed gunman from entering the building, taking six hostages, killing one student and

himself (Butler). Platte Canyon's superintendent, James Walpole says that more important than training is forming a close relationship with local law enforcement so that they are familiar with the school, its students and overall climate (cited in Butler).

THE EFFECTIVENESS OF POST-CRISIS COUNSELING

After a crisis occurs at a school, counselors are summoned to help school faculty and students deal with the emotional aftermath in a productive way. Many schools have employed a technique called Critical Incident Stress Debriefing but the benefit of this type of counseling has been called into question (Black). According to Pauline Pagliocca of the Victims of Violence Programs at Harvard University, no evidence exists to prove that CISD is effective (cited in Black). In fact, the U.S. Department of Defense, the Department of Justice, the Department of Health and Human Services and the American Red Cross have recently stopped using CISD on trauma victims (Black).

CONCLUSION

All school systems inevitably will have to deal with crises, therefore they should plan accordingly. It may be difficult to grasp the possibility of being affected by a situation like Columbine, Hurricane Katrina or 9/11, but in the event, it is better to be ready than caught unprepared (McGiboney & Fretwell).

After a crisis, it is equally important to evaluate the crisis response plan that was used to determine what practices were successful and what practices were unsuccessful. Effective crisis management is an ongoing process that requires constant activity. Schools and their surroundings are constantly changing; so too should our responses to them. Research and revision are integral parts of the process that is crisis management (U.S. Department of Education).

TERMS & CONCEPTS

Crisis Management: Crisis management refers to the policies and procedures developed for handling emergency situations in public schools.

Critical Incident Stress Debriefing (CISD): Critical Incident Stress Debriefing refers to a type of group counseling that may be used after a traumatic event, such as war or a violent attack, in order to prevent Post Traumatic Stress Syndrome (Black).

Crisis Intervention Team (CIT): A Crisis Intervention Team consists of a group of trained counselors and mental health professionals hired to help schools recover from a crisis. Intervention in schools allows students to share feelings, ask questions and dispel rumors about crisis events (Black).

Emergency Responders: Emergency responder is a general title given to individuals including law enforcement agents, firefighters, emergency medical technicians and other individuals trained to respond to crises.

Evacuation: Evacuation is a term used when students and faculty are required to leave a building. Evacuation is required in instances such as a fire or bomb threat.

Lockdown: Lockdown is a term used when there is a threat outside of the classroom or school building. Movement is restricted and individuals are advised to cover windows and move away from them (U.S. Department of Education).

Pandemic: Pandemic refers to a major outbreak of an infectious disease such as the flu or smallpox.

Shelter in Place: Shelter in place is a term used in response to a situation in which it is not safe or timely for individuals to evacuate a building.

Jennifer Bouchard

BIBLIOGRAPHY

Black, S. (2004). When disaster strikes. *American School Board Journal, 191*, 36-38. Retrieved September 6, 2007, from EBSCO Online Database Education Research Complete.

Butler, K. (2007). Tragic lessons. *District Administration, 43*, 56-60. Retrieved September 9, 2007, from EBSCO Online Database Education Research Complete.

Dillon, N. (2007). Planning to ensure our schools are safe. *Education Digest, 72*, 9- 11. Retrieved September 6, 2007, from EBSCO Online Database Education Research Complete.

Fernandez, D.J. (2013). What Sandy taught me: Seven lessons for dealing with natural disasters. *Independent School, 72*, 112-116. Retrieved December 15, 2013, from EBSCO Online Database Education Research Complete.

Kennedy, M. (2013). Managing a crisis. *American School & University, 85*, 16. Retrieved December 15, 2013, from EBSCO Online Database Education Research Complete.

Kennedy, M. (2007). Seeking secure schools. *American School & University, 79*, 6- 10. Retrieved September 9, 2007, from EBSCO Online Database Education Research Complete.

Kingshott, B.F., & McKenzie, D.G. (2013). Developing crisis management protocols in the context of school safety. *Journal of Applied Security Research, 8*, 222-245. Retrieved December 15, 2013, from EBSCO Online Database Education Research Complete.

Kisch, M. (2012). When crises call. *School Administrator, 69*, 19-25. Retrieved December 15, 2013, from EBSCO Online Database Education Research Complete.

McGiboney, G & Fretwell, Q. (2007). Pandemic planning for schools. *American School Board Journal, 194*, 46-47. Retrieved September 6, 2007, from EBSCO Online Database Education Research Complete.

Poland, S., & Poland, D. (2007). Safe school preparations for your district. *District Administration, 43*, 88. Retrieved September 6, 2007, from EBSCO Online Database Education Research Complete.

St. Gerard, V. (2007). Don't confuse common flu with a flu PANDEMIC. *Education Digest, 72*, 4-6. Retrieved September 6, 2007, from EBSCO Online Database Education Research Complete.

Taking the lead in an emergency. (2007) *Techniques: Connecting Education & Careers, 82*, 12-13. Retrieved September 6, 2007, from EBSCO Online Database Education Research Complete.

U.S. Department of Education, Office of Safe and Drug-Free Schools (2003). *Practical Information on Crisis Planning: A Guide for Schools and Communities*. Retrieved September 6, 2007, from U.S. Department of Education, www.ed.gov.

SUGGESTED READING

Bowman, D., & Johnston, R. (2001). Urban districts review crisis-response plans in wake of terrorism. *Education Week, 21*. Retrieved September 7, 2007, from EBSCO Online Database Education Research Complete.

Corbitt-Dipierro, C. (n.d.) *Expanding the team approach: How emergency responders and those they serve can work together to promote prevention and coordinate incident response.* Retrieved September 7, 2007, from www.threatplan.org.

Office for Domestic Preparedness, U.S. Department of Homeland Security. (2003). *Campus Public Safety: Weapons of Mass Destruction Terrorism Protective Measures.* Retrieved September 7, 2007, from U.S. Department of Education, www.ed.gov.

Pepper, M., London, T., Dishman, M., Lewis, J., & Porter A. (2010). *Leading Schools During Crisis: What Administrators Must Know.* Lanham, N.Y.: Rowen & Littlefield Education.

Thompson, R. (2004). *Crisis Intervention and Crisis Management: Strategies that Work in Schools and Communities.* New York, N.Y.: Brunner-Routledge.

U.S Department of Education, The Harvard School of Public Health, Education Development Center & Prevention Institute (2002). *The three R's to dealing with trauma in schools: Readiness, response and recovery.* Retrieved September 7, 2007, from http://walcoff.com.

VIOLENCE PREVENTION

This article will explore numerous issues associated with school related violence and violence prevention. Due to the undeniable risks and threats that have become apparent in school systems today, threat assessment and violence prevention have become a crucial component of modern school operational plans. To assess risks and develop prevention plans, educational leaders must research and investigate many new theories and strategies associated with modern student needs. The article will discuss educational philosophy, missions, and program prioritization. The topic of school budgets and funding associated with programming and violence prevention will also be addressed. Ultimately, the article will provide strategies for evaluating, developing, financing, and implementing effective and age-appropriate violence prevention measures for school settings.

KEYWORDS: National School Safety & Security Services; Proactive Plan; Reactive Plan; Safety Statistics; School Safety; School Violence; Threat Assessment; Violence Prevention; Vulnerability

OVERVIEW

Important issues move in and out of education regularly. However, one issue that arises in education consistently in recent years is school safety. School safety concerns are continuously evolving and the stakes are high. As new technologies arise and new threats develop, school systems must continually assess their level of safety preparedness and respond to any new safety concerns that exist.

School district leaders across the United States and throughout the world have come to the harsh realization that society cannot be trusted unconditionally. The notion that our communities and their citizens will support schools is no longer a safe assumption. True, many community members still support their school systems; however, these instances are now taking second stage to the individuals who violently oppose school systems and those associated with the schools. School district leadership personnel face the task of ensuring they are continually prepared for the worst while trying to maintain a focus on the positive things occurring in their school buildings. It is a somewhat conflicting task; however, it is necessary to ensure our schools operate effectively.

"Statistically, schools continue to be one of the most secure places for our children" (National Education Association, 2006). This statement may be statistically accurate; however, the feelings conveyed by many parents, students, and community members argue otherwise. We live in a society that tends to focus on immediacy. The events that have transpired in recent years and remain fresh in the minds of our stakeholders seem to dominate the feelings people have toward our school systems. With this in mind, recent instances of school violence such as the shootings that occurred in Pennsylvania, Colorado, and Connecticut have led to a sense of urgency regarding the level of safety and security in schools today.

Data suggests that fewer than half of schools today have security personnel on their campus, and a majority do not have video cameras or metal detectors. This is despite the fact that more than 150 people were killed in school shootings across the country between 2000 and 2013.

APPLICATIONS

When practiced effectively, school-based violence prevention is both proactive and reactive in nature. Modern school systems are faced with the uncomforting notion that often the most legitimate threats are those that go unmade. Many school administrators argue that the easiest plan to foil is that of a student who broadcasts his or her intentions to others. An open line of communication frequently leads to the sharing of violent feelings or thoughts with peers or adults in the school ("Report: More counselors needed," 2002). Some even argue that these threats are the least credible, as the students responsible seem to be asking for others to intervene by sharing their plans openly. This leaves the frightening realization that perhaps the greatest threat for school violence comes from those students who choose not to share their plans with others and keep their intentions largely to themselves. Herein is the importance of proactive violence prevention measures.

To effectively and efficiently address instances of school violence, plans must be in place and well rehearsed prior to the occurrence. School safety plans have evolved far beyond the traditional fire and tornado drills. Although these traditional drills still play an important role in creating a well-rounded safety plan, an array of other issues must now be addressed as well. Safety issues such as weapons, online predators, substance abuse, chemical threats, and intruders have all surfaced as topics of concern in recent years. Effective school systems are now expected to conduct routine threat assessments and create threat assessment plans that satisfy any potential dangers associated with the school facility, student population, faculty, community, technology, or other areas of concern (Schiffbauer, 2000). In essence, any imaginable and foreseeable threat to the school and its stakeholders must be anticipated and addressed with the understanding that unforeseeable events may also occur.

To create a plan as thorough and all-encompassing as the aforementioned threat assessment process, a number of strategies can be utilized. Staff development and teacher in-service days have become a rather common means of implementing and rehearsing threat assessment plans. Other avenues that may be utilized include school safety seminars or workshops as well as training partnerships with local safety agencies such as law enforcement or social services.

Threat assessment plans comprise only one piece of the school safety puzzle. A second vital component of a prevention plan is the availability and acquisition of resources necessary to enact such implementations. Resources such as metal detectors, video cameras, police liaison officers, and school social workers are valuable, yet costly. Moreover, daily safety needs such as appropriate lighting, telephones, radios, and computers are also crucial to the safe operation of a school facility but they are expensive. Without question, the daily implementation of safety initiatives is as much a question of dollars as it is desire. Many educators understand the importance of these safety resources; however, few can offer a viable means of paying for all of a school's necessities. As educational budgets decrease and operational expenses associated with items such as technology, transportation, and utilities steadily increase, schools are expected to not only maintain their current programming with smaller budgets but also implement new and innovative initiatives to serve and protect students. To say the least, this presents an intriguing and challenging state of affairs for current educational leaders. When school boards and administrators find themselves faced with choices such as cutting a math program or purchasing video surveillance equipment for safety, a

challenging debate over educational prioritization is inevitable.

Within the debate over school violence and safety exists an important distinction between ages and grade levels. As school leadership personnel begin to address safety concerns associated with each of their schools, different topics of interest may surface depending upon the ages of students involved. Although a number of commonalities may be apparent between primary and secondary schools, it is the difference in needs between these student populations that sometimes gets overlooked.

Perhaps the most prevalent shared needs between primary and secondary schools consist of supervision and tolerance. A need for continual supervision exists at all levels. Also, students must be taught the importance of accepting others and educated as to the damage that bullying and harassment can do. Again, these issues seem to exist regardless of age or grade level.

However, other grade- or age-specific safety issues do exist. Primary level students must be taught the basics of personal safety such as playground etiquette and how to interact with strangers or other adults. They must also learn how to contact emergency personnel and under what circumstances to do so. When addressing the needs of secondary students, such elementary issues have typically already been satisfied. As students age, dangers associated with dating, harassment, and technology become important. Also, as the needs of secondary students are often responsive to the changing needs of society, a regular system of evaluating student threats and needs must be established to stay current with evolving student issues. Such a system can often involve parents, community members, staff, and/or students.

In conjunction with the many proactive measures available to schools, a reactive plan must also be employed. As demonstrated by the string of school related violence that has transpired throughout the nation in the late twentieth and early twenty-first centuries, it seems no region or area is insusceptible to school violence. From the smallest rural school houses to the largest urban school systems, school-related violence is an unfortunate possibility. The horrific instances of violence that have occurred against students, staff, administrators, and other personnel should serve as learning experiences for other school districts. As these instances occur, existing threat assessment plans must be revised to address the new issues presented. In its most basic form, responsiveness of this nature works to prevent copycat occurrences. In a broader sense, any adjustment made to the plan that satisfies a previously unaddressed safety issue greatly increases the overall effectiveness of the school's safety plan.

DISCOURSE

Some theorists suggest that school shootings are simply extreme cases of the violent behaviors such as bullying, fighting, and sexual offenses that have been occurring in schools for many decades. Some also feel that the problem with extreme violence in schools today is a result of more than the ease with which an American can obtain a firearm. It may extend into the very heart of our societal norms and the behaviors that young people are observing and learning from those around them.

A number of theories exist surrounding the most effective and appropriate way to address school violence. Some experts feel the most effective method of preventing such occurrences is through the implementation of concrete deterrents such as metal detectors, video cameras, and other security devices. Others believe more interpersonal methods of prevention such as counseling, conflict-resolution programs, and increased communication skills are a more effective means of preventing these instances before they occur. The common thread seems to be the recognition that preventative measures must be taken to minimize the likelihood of such occurrences and to equip school personnel with the tools to address the issues if they do arise.

Numerous initiatives have been created by a variety of agencies and organizations in an effort to deal with the increase in school violence. A number of states have enacted "Youth Preparedness Initiatives" in order to equip students with skills to address a variety of crisis situations (Center for Emergency Health and Safety for Schools, 2006). These initiatives address the areas of basic life-saving skills, risk watch, responding to emergencies, response team training, and other areas related to basic school and community safety. Many of these skills are taught through school district curricula or in conjunction with local agencies such as the American Red Cross, poison centers, public health departments, parent-teacher associations, universities, and others. These partnerships

enable the cost and labor involved with implanting such initiatives to be shared between and among the stakeholders involved.

Similar state-initiated programs exist as well. For example, the state of Arizona, working in conjunction with the Arizona Department of Education, has created an extensive school safety program that addresses the following areas of concern: health programs, safe and drug-free schools, chemical abuse prevention, school safety programs, and threat assessment (Arizona Department of Education, 2013). Programs of this nature have been developed through a partnership with the state government and provide financial assistance to schools during their training and implementation processes. State agencies also provide insight and assistance into additional resources available to the schools to enhance the effectiveness and overall success of the programs.

Outside of local school districts and state agencies, a variety of other organizations have taken an interest in promoting a safe learning environment for students. The Wisconsin FAST (Family, School, and Community Partnerships) organization has adopted a school safety initiative focused upon staff and faculty training for crisis prevention. This program provides training and resources for schools interested in supplementing their current safety implementations through additional staff training (Wisconsin Center for Educational Research, 2007).

The National Safety Council (2009) has also increased school safety awareness by creating and promoting initiatives associated with increased school bus safety. According to their research, school bus–related accidents killed 134 and injured approximately 11,000 people nationwide in 2005. The National Safety Council has provided in their plan suggestions for getting on the school bus, behavior on buses, getting off the bus, and crossing the street. This plan also provides training guidelines for bus drivers to prevent incidents that may occur as a result of inadequate supervision.

School safety can be an expensive endeavor. Newly developed safety strategies, tools, and initiatives can prove quite costly. Some argue that with the current financial challenges facing many school districts, new safety implementations are simply unaffordable. Others argue that schools cannot afford *not* to complete such implementations. Data supports both sides of this debate. Video equipment, contracting security personnel, and training costs all involve large sums of money. However, taking these steps to increase school security can also reduce expenses associated with lawsuits resulting from injuries and building maintenance due to vandalism.

To implement new safety and security initiatives, many school systems have actively sought out new funding mechanisms. Financial support for increasing school safety has become available from a number of new sources. The United States Department of Justice and Office of Community Oriented Policing Services have provided funding and resources for school and community partnership programs focused on school safety (Wisconsin Center for Education Research). Federally, Title IV and No Child Left Behind funding can be obtained to support programs aimed at school safety and prevention. Schools can also obtain assistance in providing training for staff members and developing emergency response plans through partnerships developed with county health departments, emergency management agencies, fire and law enforcement agencies, and Red Cross chapters.

Other organizations provide many online resources and sample policies, checklists, and programs intended to help schools develop their safety and security initiatives without purchasing external services. There are also a number of grants and professional growth scholarship opportunities available for schools interested in providing professional development training and/or safety updates. These monetary awards can range from a relatively small amount of money, such as $750 to attend a training seminar, to $30,000 for the purchase and implementation of new security technologies.

Despite decreasing budgets and increasing district expenses, school systems are faced with the task of maintaining safe and secure learning environments. New threats have called for the implementation of new security tactics. All of these things involve costs that many schools are struggling to finance. To maintain safe and secure facilities with adequate and appropriate security measures, school district leadership personnel must seek out and obtain new financial resources. The many new financial resources available today have made safety improvements a viable option for those districts willing to actively pursue new and creative sources of funding and support.

The underlying question facing any school system today may focus on its most fundamental component: its mission. In today's diverse society, student demographics differ dramatically not only from one district to the next but from one desk to the next. Modern educators are faced with the task of satisfying the needs of every student with whom they interact, as dictated by current educational legislation. Student needs differ on many levels. Is a teacher required to nurture a needy student, or challenge a student preparing for a college education? According to current educational legislation, the teacher must do both. In the interest of the students involved, it is the teacher's professional responsibility to meet the needs of all students. Within the countless differences that exist between students lies yet another dimension of school safety. Staff members must be trained to recognize safety issues such as physical abuse, emotional abuse, neglect, and malnutrition. To do so, school systems must often utilize a variety of personnel such as counselors, social workers, police officers, and mentors. Beyond the moral and ethical significance associated with safety issues of this nature lies a legal obligation to protect students from threats they themselves are unable to avoid.

In the end, it is the duty of a school and its teachers to provide an all-encompassing umbrella of protection to its students and stakeholders. From abuse and neglect to technology and weapons, the realm of school safety issues appears endless. To adequately and appropriately prepare for such issues, school leadership personnel must employ both proactive and reactive approaches to school violence prevention, allowing potential threats to be negated in an efficient and effective manner.

TERMS & CONCEPTS

Safety Statistics: Safety statistics are available in most states outlining the frequency and total of statewide instances of school related violence.

School Safety: School safety is a phrase used to describe the threats and subsequent violence prevention measures existing in and around school systems. School safety issues include virtually any danger or threat present to those in a school or school system while performing school related duties. Such dangers may change and evolve according to the interests and resources available to the larger society.

School Violence: School violence describes instances of harmful behaviors occurring within a school or educational setting. Instances involving weapons, chemicals, harassment, bullying, and other dangerous circumstances fall under this umbrella term.

National School Safety and Security Services: This organization specializes in school-related safety and security initiatives. It focuses on nation-wide violence prevention strategies for schools and other educational institutions.

Proactive Plan: A proactive plan is one prepared prior to the onset of anticipated events in order to increase the likelihood that such events will not lead to adverse consequences.

Reactive Plan: A reactive plan is one prepared after the occurrence of an event in order to address concerns or deficiencies highlighted by the occurrence.

Threat Assessment: Threat assessments are evaluations focused on the current safety and security status of a given organization or facility. A threat assessment is intended to identify areas of potential danger and aid in the creation of a plan minimizing threats to the organization and its personnel.

Violence Prevention: Violence prevention describes plans or measures taken to minimize and/or eliminate potential threats.

Christopher Poradish

BIBLIOGRAPHY

Arizona Department of Education. (2013). *School safety program.* Retrieved December 11, 2013, from http://azed.gov.

Crepeau-Hobson, F., Sievering, K. S., Armstrong, C., & Stonis, J. (2012). A coordinated mental health crisis response: Lessons learned from three Colorado school shootings. *Journal of School Violence, 11,* 207-225. Retrieved December 11, 2013, from EBSCO online database Education Research Complete.

DeAngelis, K. J., Brent, B. O., & Ianni, D. (2011). The hidden cost of school security. *Journal of Education Finance, 36,* 312-337. Retrieved December 11, 2013, from EBSCO online database Education Research Complete.

McAdams, C., Shillingford, M., & Trice-Black, S. (2011). Putting research into practice in school violence prevention and intervention: How is school counseling doing? *Journal of School Counseling, 9,* 1-31. Retrieved December 11, 2013, from EBSCO online database Education Research Complete.

Mongan, P., & Walker, R. (2012). "The road to hell is paved with good intentions": A historical, theoretical, and legal analysis of zero-tolerance weapons policies in American schools. *Preventing School Failure, 56,* 232-240. Retrieved December 11, 2013, from EBSCO online database Education Research Complete.

National Education Association. (2013). *School safety resources for educators.* Retrieved December 11, 2013, from http://nea.org.

National Safety Council. (2009). *School bus safety rules.* Retrieved December 11, 2013, from http://nsc.org.

Nickerson, A. B., & Brock, S. E. (2011). Measurement and evaluation of school crisis prevention and intervention: Introduction to special issue. *Journal of School Violence, 10,* 1-15. Retrieved December 11, 2013, from EBSCO online database Education Research Complete.

October, S. (2005). Preventing bullying in schools: A guide for teachers and other professionals. *Educational Psychology in Practice, 21,* 83-84.

Report: More counselors needed to stop violence. (2002). *School Law News, 30,* 9. Retrieved from EBSCO online database Education Research Complete.

Schiffbauer, P. (2000). A checklist for safe schools. *Educational Leadership, 57,* 72. Retrieved from EBSCO online database Education Research Complete.

Sobel, R. (2012). Perception of violence on a high school campus. *Journal of Applied Security Research, 7,* 11-21. Retrieved December 11, 2013, from EBSCO online database Education Research Complete.

Thomas, P. (2006, October 3). Why the spike in school shootings? *ABC News.* Retrieved October 5, 2006, from http://abcnews.go.com.

Wisconsin Center for Education Research. (2007). *Wisconsin FAST: Family, school, and community partnerships for school safety.* Retrieved October 18, 2007, from http://wcer.wisc.edu.

SUGGESTED READING

Bon, S. C., Faircloth, S. C., & LeTendre, G. K. (2006). The school violence dilemma. *Journal of Disability Policy Studies, 17,* 148-157. Retrieved April 7, 2007, from EBSCO online database Education Research Complete.

Brunner, J., & Lewis, D. (2006). Telling a "red flag" from the real threat with students of today. *Education Digest, 72,* 33-36. Retrieved April 6, 2007, from EBSCO online database Education Research Complete.

Druck, K., & Kaplowitz, M. (2005). Preventing classroom violence. *Education Digest, 71,* 40-43. Retrieved April 7, 2007, from EBSCO online database Education Research Complete.

Hankin, A., Hertz, M., & Simon, T. (2011). Impacts of metal detector use in schools: Insights from 15 years of research. *Journal of School Health, 81,* 100-106. Retrieved December 11, 2013, from EBSCO online database Education Research Complete.

Maxwell, L. A. (2006). Safety experts say best idea is level head but open eyes. *Education Week, 26*, 1-17. Retrieved April 6, 2007, from EBSCO online database Education Research Complete.

Van Acker, R. (2007). Antisocial, aggressive, and violent behavior in children and adolescents within alternative education settings. *Preventing School Failure, 51*, 5-12.

Retrieved April 8, 2007, from EBSCO online database Education Research Complete.

Whitted, K. S., & Dupper, D. R. (2005). Best practices for preventing or reducing bullying in schools. *Children & Schools, 27*, 167-175. Retrieved April 8, 2007, from EBSCO online database Education Research Complete.

WEAPONS IN THE SCHOOLS

This article discusses the carrying and use of weapons, primarily firearms, in public schools in the United States. Violent crime in the United States peaked in the early 1990s and has declined into the twenty-first century. Between 1993 and 2013, the percentage of high school students (grades 9 to 12) who reported carrying a weapon on school property at least once in the previous thirty days fell from 12 to 5 percent (Zhang, Musu-Gillette, & Oudekerk, 2016). However, despite these declines, gun violence in schools remains of great concern, and the debate continues at how best to prevent violence in schools, particularly mass shootings. The deadliest gun-related tragedies in American schools are the Virginia Tech shooting in Blacksburg, Virginia (2007) and the Sandy Hook Elementary School shooting in Newtown, Connecticut (2012). Although firearm homicides have decreased from their peak in 1993, mass shootings that occur in public places such as schools (rather than in a private home) have become more common since the 1980s. According to the Violence Policy Center, the rise in public mass shootings has coincided with an increase in the sale of semiautomatic weapons with high-capacity ammunition magazines (Violence Policy Center, "Mass shootings").

KEYWORDS: Columbine High School Massacre; Gun-Free School Zones Act; Gun Control; Heath High School Massacre; Metal Detectors; Sandy Hook Elementary School Massacre; School Security; Second Amendment; Virginia Tech Massacre; Weapons

OVERVIEW
HISTORY
The right to "keep and bear arms," as outlined in the Second Amendment to the US Constitution, is deeply ingrained in the fabric of the United States.

Thomas Jefferson, author of the Declaration of Independence and the nation's third president, prided himself on his ability to use his prized Turkish pistols to shoot a squirrel dead at 30 yards (cited in Halbrook, 2000). Hunting and shooting have been popular recreational pastimes since the founding of the United States, and they remain popular in many parts of the country. The National Rifle Association (NRA) was founded by former Union army soldiers in 1871. In the late twentieth century, as the public was confronted with increasing rates of violent crime, Americans turned to weapons not for hunting but as a means of protecting themselves and their families.

Unfortunately, despite a majority of law-abiding citizens who use guns legally and properly, guns fall into the hands of criminals. The problem of gun violence intensified in the 1920s during Prohibition, and citizens began to wonder if one way to address the problem of violent crime was a supply-side approach that reduced the number of guns and other weapons available for purchase. The first federal gun control measure was passed in 1927, and it banned the sale of mail-order handguns in an attempt to take them out of the hands of the criminal gangs that operated to supply alcohol in major cities. The passage of the National Firearms Act of 1934 and the Federal Firearms Act of 1938 during the administration of President Franklin D. Roosevelt combined to impose new taxes on purchases of guns, require FBI background checks of gun buyers, and prohibit gun sales to known criminals.

Gun laws were tightened after the assassination of President John F. Kennedy in 1963 with the Omnibus Crime Control and Safe Streets Act of 1968 and Gun Control Act of 1968, which raised the legal age to purchase a gun to twenty-one, banned the interstate sale of handguns, prohibited the direct mail order purchase of guns, and required that gun purchases be made from federally licensed dealers. The Firearm Owners' Protection Act of 1986 went further and effectively banned the manufacture of machine guns and other fully automatic weapons for civilian use. Since the passage of the Brady Handgun Violence Prevention Act of 1993, handgun buyers have had to undergo a computerized FBI background check before being allowed to purchase that weapon. However, buyers who purchase guns at trade shows are exempted from the background check requirement. The Federal Assault Weapons Ban, a provision of the Violent Crime Control and Law Enforcement Act of 1994, closed the loophole allowing civilian sales of semiautomatic weapons, but the provision was allowed to expire in 2004.

Gun-Related Violence

Against this backdrop of government firearms regulation throughout the twentieth century, Americans became increasingly concerned with gun-related violence. The statistics are indeed sobering:

"Firearms are the second leading cause of traumatic death related to a consumer product in the United States and are the second most frequent cause of death overall for Americans ages 15 to 24. Since 1960, more than 1.3 million Americans have died in firearm suicides, homicides, and unintentional injuries.... In 2011 alone, more than 32,000 Americans died by gunfire: 19,990 in firearm suicides, 11,068 in firearm homicides, 591 in unintentional shootings, and 248 in firearm deaths of unknown intent, according to the Centers for Disease Control and Prevention in 2014. More than twice that number are treated in emergency rooms each year for nonfatal firearm injuries" (Violence Policy Center, n.d.).

For many young people, gun violence is a fact of life—and a deadly one at that. According to Cooper and Smith (2011), guns are responsible for homicides of teens and young adults aged eighteen to thirty-four more so than homicides of persons of other ages. Up to age seventeen, the percentage of homicide victims killed with a gun increases and declines thereafter (Cooper & Smith). Still, say researchers at the US Bureau of Justice Statistics:

- For children under age eighteen, homicide victimization rates are the lowest of all age groups. For children under age five, the rate dropped

between 1993 and 2006 but rose again in 2007–8 (Cooper & Smith);

- For teens aged fourteen to seventeen, the homicide victimization rate increased almost 150 percent from 1985 to 1993, reaching 12 homicides per 100,000. Between 1993 and 2008, the rate fell again, to about 5.1 homicides per 100,000 (Cooper & Smith).

These statistics, taken together with gun control laws in the United States, provide important context for any discussion of weapons in public schools. The data seem to indicate that students—or their relatives or friends—are able to take possession of weapons that are illegal for young people to possess, let alone use. The resulting gun violence at the beginning of the twenty-first century, albeit down from historic highs, is taking place despite the existence and enforcement of existing gun control laws.

School Violence

According to researchers at the National Center for Education Statistics (2016), school-aged children were victims of 53 school-associated violent deaths from July 1, 2012, through June 30, 2013 (41 homicides, 11 suicides, and 1 legal intervention deaths). In 2014, students aged twelve to eighteen were victims of about 850,100 million nonfatal crimes at school, including thefts, simple assaults, and serious violent crimes such as rape, sexual assault, robbery, and aggravated assault. That year, their rates of at-school nonfatal victimization were 33 per 1,000 students (National Center for Education Statistics, 2016). The total victimization rate (thefts plus violent crimes) decreased between 1995 and 2014. During the 2013–14 school year, 65 percent of all public schools reported one or more incidents of violence, with a rate of 15 violent crimes per 1,000 students (National Center for Education Statistics).

High school students were far more likely to experience all types of crime at school than either middle or primary school students. In 2013–14, 78 percent of high schools and combined elementary/secondary schools (high/combined schools) reported violent incidents, compared to 53 percent of primary schools (National Center for Education Statistics). About 7 percent of high school students (grades 9 to 12) were threatened or injured with a weapon on school property in 2013, a figure that had remained declined slightly over the previous decade, from 9 percent in 2003 (National Center for Education Statistics).

The first significant violent incident involving weapons in schools took place in 1927 in Bath Township, Michigan, when Andrew Kehoe, a disgruntled school board member, took out his frustration on the Bath Consolidated School, home to children in grades two through six. In a grisly premeditated attack, Kehoe detonated hundreds of pounds of dynamite and the World War I castoff pyrotol that was stashed inside the school, killing 45 people and injuring 58 others. Before Kehoe could be arrested and brought to justice, he blew himself up, killing and injuring several others trying to help in the aftermath of the school bombing.

While Kehoe's actions were disturbing, they were considered an isolated action by a deranged individual. What did get the public's attention was the use of weapons—especially guns—by the students themselves. Such a shooting took place at the University of Texas at Austin in 1966. At Kent State in Ohio (1970) and Jackson State in Mississippi, authorities opened fire on protesting students, resulting in several deaths and numerous injuries. This was during the turbulent Vietnam War era, and these massacres took place around the same time that three leading Americans were shot to death—President John F. Kennedy (1963), Democratic presidential candidate Robert Kennedy (1968), and civil rights leader Dr. Martin Luther King Jr. (1968). These assassinations raised public consciousness about gun violence, helping to ensure the passage of tighter federal gun control legislation in 1968.

Guns in Schools

In the 1980s and 1990s, the rate of gun violence increased at middle and high schools. School shootings garnered front-page headlines across the United States and drew renewed attention to the problem of weapons in schools. They took place despite the passage of new federal legislation in the 1990s designed to establish schools as gun-free zones, by making it illegal to have a gun within one thousand feet of a school. These school shootings often involved banned weapons, such as the .22-caliber Remington Viper (Richland School massacre, November 1995) and high-powered rifles (Moses Lake massacre, February 1996), as well as Savage-Springfield 67H

pump-action shotguns, Hi-Point 995 Carbine 9 mm semiautomatic rifles, Intratec Tec-9 semiautomatic weapons, and 12-gauge shotguns (Columbine massacre, 1999).

A survey of data from the early 1990s collected by Page and Hammermeister (1997) showed the growing prevalence of guns and gun violence in American public schools:

- According to the 1990 Youth Risk Behavior Survey, 1 in 20 senior high school students carried a firearm, usually a handgun, and 1 in 5 carried a weapon of some type during the 30 days preceding the survey (Centers for Disease Control, 1991);
- A survey of 10 inner-city high schools in four states found that 35% of male and 11% of female students reported carrying a gun (Sheley, McGee, & Wright, 1992);
- A study of rural school students in southeast Texas found that 6% of male students had taken guns to school, and almost 2% reported that they did so almost every day. In addition, 42.3% of those surveyed said they could get a gun if they wanted one (Kissell, 1993);
- More than one-third (34%) of urban high school students in Seattle reported having easy access to handguns, while 11.4% of males and 1.5% of females reported owning a handgun. One-third of those who owned handguns reported that they had fired at someone. Further, almost 10% of female students reported a firearm homicide or suicide among family members or close friends (Callahan & Rivara, 1992);
- Another study from the southeastern United States found that 9% of urban and suburban youth owned a handgun (Larson, 1994);
- A poll of students in grades six through twelve conducted by Louis Harris for the Harvard School of Public Health in 1993 found that 59% said they could get a handgun if they wanted one, and 21% said they could get one within the hour;
- More than 60% of urban youth reported that they could get a handgun, and 58% of suburban youth also claimed that they could (Larson);
- Fifteen percent of students reported carrying a handgun in the past month, 11% said that they had been shot at, 9% said that they had fired a gun at someone, and 4% said they had carried a gun to school in the past year (Drevitch, 1994; Hull, 1993);

- In a study of two public inner-city junior high schools in Washington, DC, 47% of males reported having ever carried knives, and 25% reported having ever carried guns for protection or to use in case they got into a fight; 37% of females reported having carried a knife for these purposes. Both schools are located in high-crime areas (Webster, Gainer, & Champion, 1993).

Students in the 1990s, who were the primary targets of their weapons-wielding peers, understood as clearly as any that something was lacking when it came to the safety of their schools. Even Eric Harris, coconspirator in the 1999 Columbine High School shootings in Colorado, discussed the ease with which weapons could be brought into schools in a 1997 school paper. In the report, Harris detailed several ways students can sneak guns into schools—such as using backpacks or going through entrances with no metal detectors—and recommended that schools use metal detectors at all school entrances.

While Harris and his coconspirator Dylan Klebold reveled in their ability to deceive their parents and teachers about the plans they were hatching for the Columbine massacre—including the use of insincere school reports—Harris's paper became a self-fulfilling prophecy. School shootings such as that at Columbine led politicians, parents, and school officials to reassess school security measures, and two of the most visible signs of increased security in many public middle and high schools have been precisely the two things Harris actually recommended: security officials and metal detectors.

Security Measures

As the statistics from the National Center for Education Statistics indicate, public schools increasingly implemented school safety measures designed to prevent the incidence of crime in school. Have these increased safety measures been working? It would largely appear that way, according to the National Center for Education Statistics:

- Between 1993 and 2013, the percentage of students who reported carrying a weapon anywhere within the preceding month generally declined from 22 to 18 percent. Similarly, the percentage of students who carried a weapon at school also declined during this period—from 12 to 5 percent;

- In the 2013–14 school year, approximately 78 percent of serious disciplinary actions (e.g., suspensions, expulsions, or transfers) were taken due to violence incidents at school and 5.1 percent were taken due to weapons possession.

Following the December 2012 Sandy Hook shooting, state legislatures rushed to address gaps in school safety and preparedness measures. Among the proposed solutions were developing or updating emergency plans and drills, increasing or introducing police presence in schools, funding or implementing security infrastructure and/or equipment such as metal detectors, and using mental health services to address at-risk students' behavioral issues (Shah & Ujifusa, 2013). A number of initiatives were also directly related to guns—arming teachers or other school staff, loosening restrictions on the possession of guns near schools, or increasing regulation of certain types of firearms or quantities of ammunition (Shah & Ujifusa). While schools need to continue to be vigilant about safety, particularly in light of threats from global terrorist networks and outsider shootings such as the Sandy Hook massacre, it is important to keep the use of weapons at schools and the amount of gun-related violence in perspective:

> *"The best data on the very specific threat of school-associated violent death reveals that children face a very slim chance of being killed at school. Fewer than 2 percent of youth homicides occur at school, and the number of at-school homicides largely declined between 1992 and 2010 (National Center for Education Statistics).*

Combating School Violence

To some degree, violence has long been a factor in public education in the United States and around the world. Eliminating it completely from any public school will always be the goal, however, and school counselors and others have studied and applied various methods for conflict resolution. Beyond the obvious benefit of reducing physical harm to students, conflict resolution methods have other benefits, such as creating a school environment that is more conducive to learning. The literature is clear that violence and aggression are in conflict, as it were, with the primary purpose of public schools: "Aggressive student interactions often permeate a school's culture and create a hostile learning environment that stifles the academic productivity and success of students" (Cantrell, Parks-Savage & Rehfuss, 2007).

Research on why students carry weapons can reveal the most effective forms of intervention. Page and Hammermeister again summarize many of the theories presented:

"A common reason given by young people for carrying weapons is for protection against being "jumped" (Price, Desmond, & Smith, 1991). However, research has shown that weapon-carrying among youth appears to be more closely associated with criminal activity, delinquency, and aggressiveness than to purely defensive behavior (Sheley et al.; Webster et al.). Handgun ownership by inner-city high school youth has been associated with gang membership, selling drugs, interpersonal violence, being convicted of crimes, and either suspension or expulsion from school (Callahan & Rivara). Gun-carrying among junior high students is also strongly linked with indicators of serious delinquency, such as having been arrested (Webster et al.). These studies have the following implications for the prevention of gun-carrying among youth" (Webster et al.).

"If gun carrying stems largely from antisocial attitudes and behaviors rather than from purely defensive motives of otherwise nonviolent youths, interventions designed to prevent delinquency may be more effective than those that focus only on educating youths about the risks associated with carrying a gun. The latter may, however, be able to deter less hardened youths from carrying weapons in the future. Intensive and comprehensive interventions directed at high-risk children could possibly 'inoculate' children against the many social factors that foster criminal deviance and the most violent behavior patterns" (Page & Hammermeister).

Different school districts have chosen different ways to deal with the problem of weapons in schools, but most rely on a combination of increased security (which may include metal detectors, security cameras, locker searches, and on-site police officers or security guards) and intervention programs. Many school districts have increased security only reluctantly, fearing that it will convey the wrong message to students and faculty and create a downward spiral of mistrust leading to violence.

Is Gun Control the Answer?

The spike in school violence in the 1990s and the large number of high-profile mass shootings at schools in the late twentieth and early twenty-first century brought out deep-seated philosophical differences among the American public regarding the proper role of guns in society. Some argued that the rise in school violence was symptomatic of an irrational American love affair with weapons of all kinds. Others argued that guns were taking the blame when other social pathologies were a much more likely cause—they summed up their reasoning in the slogan "Guns don't kill people. People kill people."

Opponents of gun control often cite historical examples, as did Utah senator Orrin Hatch in 1982:

"If gun laws in fact worked, the sponsors of this type of legislation should have no difficulty drawing upon long lists of examples of crime rates reduced by such legislation. That they cannot do so after a century and a half of trying—that they must sweep under the rug the southern attempts at gun control in the 1870–1910 period, the northeastern attempts in the 1920–1939 period, the attempts at both Federal and State levels in 1965–1976—establishes the repeated, complete, and inevitable failure of gun laws to control serious crime" (Hatch, 1982).

In response to the Sandy Hook shooting, several gun-control measures were introduced to Congress, but all failed to pass. Meanwhile, efforts to pass a federal bill to expand the requirement for background checks came to a stalemate and met with failure in the Senate (James, 2013). Thus, the debate over gun control continues. According to the magazine *State Legislatures*, which used data from the National Conference of State Legislatures, by July 2015, eight states had passed legislation allowing faculty and students with permits to carry concealed weapons on public college campuses while nineteen states had legally banned concealed-carry on campuses; the individual colleges and universities get to make the decision in twenty-three other states. Those that support the presence of concealed weapons at colleges insist that the weapons could be used to help save lives in an emergency; critics, on the other hand, argue that allowing students or teachers to carry guns on campuses only increases the chance of injury (Hultin, 2015).

In late 2015, a twenty-six-year-old student at Umpqua Community College in Oregon entered one of the classroom buildings and opened fire on students, eventually killing ten and wounding several others. It was reported that the gunman or members of his family had legally purchased several firearms, some of which he brought to the scene and others which were found in his apartment. When President Barack Obama addressed the nation after the news of the campus shooting broke, he appeared visibly frustrated and emphasized once more that common sense gun legislation needed to be passed in an effort to restrict such gun violence. By 2016, President Obama was appealing to the American public to gain support to bypass Congress and issue an executive order to tighten background checks through a requirement that anyone selling guns must register as a licensed dealer and conduct background checks.

CONCLUSION

In sum, opponents of gun control argue that violent crime has much more to do with mental illness, the breakdown of communities, and gun-free zones at schools, among other social factors.

Supporters of gun control cite examples from Europe and other developed nations that have tight gun control laws and far lower rates of violent crime than the United States as evidence that gun control works to lower rates of gun-related violent crime.

TERMS & CONCEPTS

Columbine High School Massacre: An attack in April 1999 in which two high school students used a series of guns to wound 24 students, kill 12 students and one teacher, and then kill themselves.

Gun-Free School Zones Act: A federal law passed in 1994 in the United States that made it a crime to have a gun within 1,000 feet of a school.

Gun Control: The attempt to limit the supply of guns in society by making all or certain types of them illegal to obtain or use.

Heath High School Massacre: An attack in December 1997 by teenager Michael Carneal in which he shot and killed three girls and wounded five others. Carneal was sentenced to life in prison for his crimes.

Metal Detectors: Machines used in government buildings, airports, schools, banks, and elsewhere to detect the presence of metal objects that may pose a risk to others.

Sandy Hook Elementary School Massacre: An attack in December 2012 in which a gunman fatally shot twenty first-grade students and six staff members before killing himself.

School Security: An umbrella term used to encompass all the tangible and intangible means by which school officials attempt to keep students and staff safe from emotional or physical harm.

Second Amendment: An amendment to the US Constitution, variously interpreted by courts and politicians, that stresses the need to protect the rights of Americans to "keep and bear arms."

Virginia Tech Massacre: An attack in April 2007 in which thirty-three people, including the gunman, were shot and killed.

Weapons: Objects including but not limited to knives and guns, which can be used to inflict bodily harm on oneself or others.

Matt Donnelly

BIBLIOGRAPHY

Another mass shooting incident wounds a northwest community. (2015, October 19). *America, 213,* 10–11. Retrieved January 8, 2016, from EBSCO Online Database Education Research Complete.

Cantrell, R., Parks-Savage, A., & Rehfuss, M. (2007). Reducing levels of elementary school violence with peer mediation. *Professional School Counseling, 10,* 475–481. Retrieved June 24, 2007, from EBSCO Online Database Academic Search Premier.

Christensen, J. (2007). School safety in urban charter and traditional public schools. *National Charter School Research Project.* Retrieved June 24, 2007, from http://ncsrp.org.

Cooper, A., & Smith, E. L. (2011, November). Homicide trends in the United States, 1980–2008: Annual rates for 2009 and 2010 (NCJ 236018). *Bureau of Justice Statistics.* Retrieved December 16, 2013, from http://bjs.gov.

Cowan, K., & Paine, C. (2013). School safety: What really works. *Principal Leadership, 13,* 12–16. Retrieved December 16, 2013, from EBSCO online database Education Research Complete.

Crime information and statistics: child, youth, and teen victimization. (2014). National Center for Victims of Crime. Retrieved on October 3, 2014, from http://victimsofcrime.org.

Dedman, B. (2007, February 5). 10 myths about school shootings. *MSNBC.* Retrieved July 20, 2007, from http://msnbc.msn.com.

Dinkes, R., Cataldi, E. F., Kena, G., & Baum, K. (2006). Indicators of school crime and safety: 2006 (NCES

2007-003/NCJ 214262). *US Department of Education.* Retrieved June 23, 2007, from http://nces.ed.gov.

Donohue, E., Schiraldi, V., & Zeidenberg, J. (1998). School house hype: The school shootings, and the real risks kids face in America. Retrieved April 12, 2010, from http://eric.ed.gov.

Fox, J. A., & Zawitz, M. W. (2007). Homicide trends in the United States. *US Bureau of Justice Statistics.* Retrieved July 20, 2007, from http://ojp.usdoj.gov.

Gilbert, E. (2016). Guns on your campus? They're already there. *Chronicle of Higher Education, 62*(29), A56. Retrieved December 28, 2016, from EBSCO online database Education Source.

Gillard, C. (n.d.). Mediation, not metal detectors. *Edutopia.* Retrieved July 20, 2007, from http://edutopia.org.

Halbrook, S. P. (2000, November 5). Were the Founding Fathers in favor of gun ownership? *Washington Times.* Retrieved July 21, 2007, from http://independent.org.

Harris, E. (2007, December 12). Guns in schools. *Smoking Gun.* Retrieved July 19, 2007, from http://thesmoking-gun.com.

Hatch, O. (1982). "Preface" in The right to keep and bear arms. In Report of the subcommittee on the Constitution of the Committee on the Judiciary, United States Senate, Ninety-Seventh Congress, Second Session. *Gun Owners of America.* Retrieved July 22, 2007, from http://gunowners.org.

Hultin, S. (2015). Campus carry—What's in your book-bag? *State Legislatures, 41*, 13. Retrieved January 8, 2016, from EBSCO Online Database Education Research Complete.

James, F. (2013, December 13). Newtown anniversary marked by gun control stalemate. *NPR.* Retrieved December 16, 2013, from http://npr.org.

National Center for Education Statistics. (2016). *Indicators of school crime and safety: 2015* (NCES 2016-079). Washington, DC: US Department of Education. Retrieved December 29, 2016, from http://nces.ed.gov.

National Center for Education Statistics. (2014). *Indicators of school crime and safety: 2014.* Retrieved January 8, 2016, from http://nces.ed.gov.

Page, R., & Hammermeister, J. (1997). Weapon-carrying and youth violence. *Adolescence, 32*, 505. Retrieved July 18, 2007, from EBSCO Online Database.

Shah, N. (2013). Downside seen in rush to hire school-based police. *Education Week, 32*, 1–15. Retrieved December 16, 2013, from EBSCO online database Education Research Complete.

Shah, N., & McNeil, M. (2013). Discipline policies squeezed as views shift on what works. *Education Week, 32*, 4–11. Retrieved December 16, 2013, from EBSCO online database Education Research Complete.

Shah, N., & Ujifusa, A. (2013). School safety legislation: A tally by state. *Education Week, 32*, 21. Retrieved December 16, 2013, from EBSCO online database Education Research Complete.

US Centers for Disease Control and Prevention (2014). Deaths: final data for 2011. *US Centers for Disease Control and Prevention.* Retrieved on October 3, 2014, from http://cdc.gov.

US Department of Education (2004). Indicators of school crime and safety: 2004 indicator 11. *US Department of Education Institute of Education Sciences.* Retrieved July 20, 2007, from http://nces.ed.gov.

US Department of Education (2006). Crisis response: Creating safe schools. *US Department of Education.* Retrieved July 22, 2007, from http://ed.gov.

Violence Policy Center (n.d.). Gun violence. *Violence Policy Center.* Retrieved December 16, 2013, from http://vpc.org.

Violence Policy Center (n.d). Mass shootings. *Violence Policy Center.* Retrieved December 29, 2016, from http://vpc.org.

Zhang, A., Musu-Gillette, L., & Oudekerk, B. A. (2016, May). *Indicators of school crime and safety: 2015.* Retrieved December 29, 2016, from http://nces.ed.gov.

SUGGESTED READING

Combating fear and restoring safety in schools. (1998, April). *Juvenile Justice Bulletin.* Retrieved July 21, 2007, from http://ojjdp.ncjrs.org.

Cullen, D. (2004). The depressive and the psychopath: The FBI's analysis of the killers' motives. *Slate.* Retrieved July 20, 2007, from http://slate.com.

Finley, L. L. (2014). *School violence: A reference handbook.* (2nd ed.). Santa Barbara, CA: ABC-CLIO.

Fox, J. A. (2007, April 17). Why they kill. *Los Angeles Times.* Retrieved July 20, 2007, from http://latimes.com.

Hankin, A., Hertz, M., & Simon, T. (2011). Impacts of metal detector use in schools: Insights from 15 years of research. *Journal of School Health, 81*, 100–106. Retrieved December 16, 2013, from EBSCO Online Database CINAHL Complete.

Hong, J., & Eamon, M. (2012). Students' perceptions of unsafe schools: an ecological systems analysis. *Journal of Child & Family Studies, 21*, 428–438. Retrieved December 16, 2013, from EBSCO Online Database Education Research Complete.

Lee, J. H. (2013). School shootings in the U.S. public schools: analysis through the eyes of an educator. Retrieved October 3, 2014 from EBSCO Online Database Education Resource Complete.

Torres, J. A. (2017). *The people behind school shootings and public massacres.* New York: Enslow Publishing.

Violent crimes at school declined by one-third (2001). *Education USA, 43*(23), 1. Retrieved July 18, 2007, from EBSCO Online Database Education Source.

Vossekuil, B., Fein, R., Reddy, M., Borum, R., & Modzeleski, W. [PDF document]. (2002). The final report and

findings of the safe school initiative: Implications for the prevention of school attacks in the United States. *US Treasury Department.* Retrieved July 21, 2007, from http://treas.gov.

ZERO TOLERANCE POLICIES

This article presents an overview of zero-tolerance policies in U.S. public schools and how such policies have become controversial. Zero tolerance began as a U.S. Customs Service policy in the 1980s and was eventually borrowed by schools to address increasing violence among students. One catalyst for zero tolerance was the 1999 Columbine High School shootings in Colorado. This article discusses how zero tolerance delivers the same severe punishments to all students—no matter how minor or severe the misbehavior. Because of zero-tolerance policies, students have been arrested or expelled for actions as simple as giving a friend some Tylenol or bringing a knife in a lunch box. The article also discusses the history of zero-tolerance policies, the views of those who support and oppose zero tolerance, and incidents that have occurred as a result. Ways to address the shortcomings of a zero-tolerance policy are suggested.

KEYWORDS: Alternative Schools; Columbine High School; Discipline Policy; Expulsion; Gangs; Gun-Free Schools Act; Gun Violence; Intervention; School Violence; Suspension; U.S. Customs Service Policy; Youth Force Coalition

OVERVIEW

Zero-tolerance as a school discipline policy is defined as one in which "one offense leads to automatic suspension or expulsion" (Merrow, 2004). It grew from the policies executed by the federal and state drug enforcement agencies in the early 1980s. By 1988, these policies caught the attention of the nation, and US Attorney General Edwin Meese permitted customs agents to seize cars, boats, and passports of individuals crossing into American soil with any amount of illegal drugs (Henault, as cited in Webb & Kritsonis, 2006). Interestingly, the U.S. Customs Service gradually eliminated this practice "because of the controversy it created and because the ACLU was filing lawsuits against the agency" (Verdugo & Glenn,

2002). Despite the controversy involving the U.S. Customs Service's zero-tolerance policies, they began to be adopted by schools in response to violent incidents in schools during the 1990s (Peebles-Wilkins, 2005). In 1989, California, New York, and Kentucky school districts adopted zero-tolerance policies in response to the rash of school violence during this time period. Their policies "mandated expulsion for drugs, fighting, and gang-related activity." By 1993, most school districts across the country had followed their example, adopting their own zero-tolerance policies. These latter policies included automatic expulsion for the possession of drugs, the possession of weapons, smoking, and school disruption (Skiba, 2000). Soon after, the Clinton administration passed the Gun-Free Schools Act in 1994 (Skiba). As a result, zero-tolerance policies evolved into an idea both popular and controversial with parents, school administrators, and the communities (American Psychological Association, 2006).

Why have zero-tolerance policies been so controversial? The answer lies in the way school districts handle varying degrees of student infractions. For example, some zero-tolerance policies require that administrators contact the police in addition to expelling the student. Under such a policy, "a gun, a box cutter, a plastic fast-food fork, a fistfight, and a hostile shove in the hallway are equally serious offenses" (Merrow). Each student who breaks a rule is punished in the same manner—no matter how small or how serious the infraction. Other offenses include the following:

- Possessing, selling, or using drugs;
- Possession of weapons;
- Sexual harassment;
- Bullying;
- Sexual or aggravated assault;
- Threats of violence;
- Violent threats towards a teacher or swearing at a teacher.

Zero-tolerance policies are designed to prevent such behavior and foster a safe school environment. Any violations of the policy bring about immediate expulsion or suspension (Peebles-Wilkins). The goal is to demonstrate to students that all violations, no matter how minor or severe are punished in the same manner (Skiba). In order to enforce such policies, many schools utilize metal detectors, video cameras, and employ full-time school police (Webb & Kritsonis).

LEGAL SUPPORT

In general, the courts support reasonable zero-tolerance policies that are designed to improve school safety (Stader, 2004). One high-profile case involved six students who participated in a fight at a high school football game in Decatur, Illinois. The school district expelled the six students for two years, stating that they were engaged in gang-like activities and violence. Political pressure and national publicity influenced the school board to lessen the sentence to two semesters and offered the students the opportunity to attend an alternative school. In response, the students appealed to the court system to overturn the school board's decision. According to the students, they had "been deprived of procedural due process [and] subjected to racial discrimination" (Stader). They also claimed that the district's policy on "gang-like activity" was vague and therefore should be void. The Seventh Circuit rejected the students' claims, ruling that the students had "received adequate due process." The courts also ruled that there was no evidence the students had been treated unfairly because of race. Therefore, "the provisions of the district's discipline policy dealing with gangs were constitutionally sound" (Stader).

Despite the support of the legal system, zero-tolerance policies have continued to be attacked by those who argue that "in a desire to be tough, no-nonsense, and scrupulously equal in punishment, schools have sacrificed measured and proportional responses for mechanical, non-discretionary decision making" (Fries & DeMitchell, 2007). Although such policies enable schools to create and foster a safe environment for students, teachers, and staff, they also create "obstacles for equal opportunity for all students" (Fries & DeMitchell). According to Fries and DeMitchell, treating all students with the same rigid standards does not always result in fairness. It

is important for the punishment to fit the crime. In many cases, it is up to the teacher to identify, intervene, and determine if the student who broke the rule should be sent to an administrator to receive punishment. In essence, the teacher must decide which problems should be handled in the classroom and which problems should be ignored.

There have been an abundance of court cases involving students who were severely punished for relatively minor offenses. According to Skiba, in 1999, a fifteen-year-old sophomore student in Atlanta, Georgia was caught with an unloaded gun in his book bag. He was permanently expelled from the school district. In February 1999, a Glendale, Arizona seventh-grader built a home-made rocket and brought it to school. School officials determined that the rocket was a weapon and suspended the student for the remainder of the term. After this incident, the student "was invited as a special guest to Space Adventures' Annual Rocketry Workshop in Washington, DC" (Skiba).

In Texas, a twelve-year-old boy was found with a three-inch pocket knife in his coat. It was the pocket knife he had taken to his last Boy Scout meeting. His mother had made him put on the jacket since it was a chilly morning. When the boy discovered the pocket knife, he wasn't sure what he should do. After speaking with his friend about the matter, he put the knife in his locker. The friend turned him in. After lunch, the police arrested him and transported him to a juvenile detention center without notifying his parents. The school expelled the student for forty-five days and placed him in an alternative school for juvenile offenders (Axtman, 2005).

Webb and Kritsonis mention several cases concerning zero tolerance that went too far. For example, two fifth-graders in Virginia were accused of putting soap in their teacher's water. Because of their alleged actions, they were charged with a felony (Goodman, as cited in Webb & Kritsonis). Jesse Jackson reported that an eleven-year-old student living in South Carolina was arrested one afternoon because she had brought a knife to school in her lunch box so that she could cut her chicken (as cited in Webb & Kritsonis).

These incidents "are consistent with the philosophical intent of zero tolerance, treating both major and minor incidents with severity in order to set an example to others" (Skiba). In many schools throughout the country, students with shotguns in backpacks, students with nail clippers, and students with toy axes all receive the same punishments. Henault reported that behavior once considered a normal childish misbehavior has quickly evolved into transgressions that lead to suspension, expulsion, or arrest.

On the other hand, some schools "have begun to define zero tolerance as a graduated system, with severity of consequence scaled in proportion to the seriousness of the offense" (Skiba). Patrick Ewing, of the State University of New York at Buffalo stated that zero-tolerance policies allow schools to quickly remove students who pose a danger to staff and other students (as cited in Black, 2004).

ZERO TOLERANCE AND PROFILING

Opponents of zero-tolerance policies argue that such policies unfairly target African American and Latino students. Studies have shown that students of color are more likely to be suspended or expelled than their white counterparts. According to Gordon, Piana, and Keleher, researchers discovered that "in the eleven cities in which disaggregate data were available, African American and Latino students were suspended or expelled at a significantly higher proportional rate than white students (as cited in Stader). To illustrate this fact, at the time of the study, Austin, Texas had an African American student population of 18 percent. Forty-three percent of its student population was Latino while 37 percent was white. African American students comprised 36 percent of suspensions and expulsions, and Latinos accounted for 45 percent. In contrast, white students accounted for 18 percent of suspensions and expulsions. The remaining ten cities examined in the study revealed a similar pattern (Stader). Many students who are expelled are also arrested by the police. Students severely penalized for minor offenses are often introduced and processed through the juvenile justice system. These same students return to the justice system because of minor infractions such as missing class, tardiness, insubordination, or having an unexcused absence (Browne, 2003). Some experts have stated that students expelled from school are denied "educational opportunity" (American Psychological Association).

MISDIRECTED PUNISHMENT

Researchers noted that zero-tolerance policies often punish the wrong students and the wrong behavior.

Studies have showed that only 20 percent of the students punished as the result of a zero-tolerance policy belong to the group of students for which the policy was originally designed (Holloway, 2001). In theory, zero-tolerance policies are designed for students who are considered dangerous to other students. The study also found that 25 percent of the students expelled had disabilities "that would have qualified them for special education services" (Morrison & D'Incau as cited in Holloway). Interestingly, one study reported that zero tolerance has not caused schools to be more consistent in regard to discipline. In fact, "rates of suspension and expulsion vary widely across schools and school districts" (American Psychological Association).

Zero-tolerance schools swiftly expel and suspend a variety of students committing transgressions. According to one study, schools with high rates of suspension usually score low in overall school climate ratings. People express less satisfaction with how the school is governed. Furthermore, schools that have a high expulsion rate usually spend a disproportionate amount of time dealing with disciplinary issues (American Psychological Association). Zero-tolerance policies have also been shown to actually increase school dropout numbers and cause a "disproportionate impact on students of color such as African Americans or those with special needs." Evidence strongly indicates that zero-tolerance policies are ineffective (Peebles-Wilkins). McAndrews (2001) reported that when students are suspended, they get into more trouble than they would if they were in school. Furthermore, out-of-school suspensions have long-term negative impacts on a student's academic achievement.

INTERVENTION TECHNIQUES

To combat the negative outcomes of expulsions and suspensions, many educators encourage "the use of intervention techniques as opposed to continued implementation of zero-tolerance approaches to curtailing school violence" (Peebles-Wilkins). Such intervention techniques provide a viable alternative to zero-tolerance punishment and include:

- Assisting with social skills and problem solving;
- Creating a sense of belonging;
- Sponsoring social group activities;
- Creating volunteer opportunities for students;
- Providing after-school employment;

- Utilizing mentors within the community;
- Using peer mediation techniques;
- Promoting antibullying curriculum;
- Teaching conflict management (Peebles-Wilkins).

Serious infractions merit a fitting punishment, but outside agencies can assist schools in determining whether a student should be readmitted to school, placed in an alternative school, or be expelled (Stader). Schools that employ police officers should ensure that the officers have an understanding of how teenagers behave so that when incidents occur, the officers will know the difference between normal misbehavior and criminal acts (American Psychological Association).

EFFECTIVE ZERO-TOLERANCE POLICIES

According to McAndrews, an effective zero-tolerance policy should be specific regarding the consequences for misbehavior. Consequences should be clear to all students and consistently applied. Schools should allow some flexibility within the policy and be willing to consider alternatives to expulsion. The policy should clearly define what will be considered a weapon, a drug, or an unacceptable action. Another important element of an effective zero-tolerance policy is a policy that complies with "state due-process laws and allows[s] for student hearings" (McAndrews). The policy should be developed in conjunction with state departments of education, juvenile justice, and health and human services. Those devising the policy should also take the time to speak with experienced educators who have worked in school districts with zero tolerance policies. It is important to shape the policy to fit the needs of the local community. Finally, the policy should be reviewed on an annual basis (McAndrews).

If zero-tolerance policies are to be effective, the school administration must be allowed some flexibility and discretion when dealing with misbehavior. For example, the policy should allow administrators to investigate any special circumstances surrounding the infraction, such as the offender's age, the ability of the offender to understand the policy, the offender's intent, the effect of the misbehavior on other students, and the offender's past disciplinary record (McAndrews). In employing a more flexible policy, some administrators punish students according to the severity of the misbehavior. Of course, the basic rules always apply, such as not bringing weapons to school, not touching another student without permission, and telling teachers when there may be a fight in school. However, the difference between a flexible policy and a zero-tolerance policy is the kind of consequences applied for each individual infraction (Henault). Minor misbehavior is not punished in the same manner as a serious offense is handled. Ashford states that when administrators punish misbehavior according to the seriousness of the infraction, they "send a strong message that violations will not be allowed," while avoiding punishments that do not fit the behavior (as cited in McAndrews).

ALTERNATIVES TO ZERO TOLERANCE

Several large city school districts such as Los Angeles, Chicago, and Denver have determined that the "get-tough" approach of zero tolerance is not effective and instead reduces academic achievement and increases dropout rates, especially among minority students. Florida's Broward County, which in 2013 was the sixth largest school district in the United States and in 2011 had more students arrested on school property than any other district Florida, decided to take an alternative approach to zero tolerance. Beginning in 2012, the school district decided that rather than expel or suspend students who broke the law (with the exception of those who committed a felony or those who were determined to be dangerous), students who committed any of eleven minor infractions for the first time would be kept in school and required to make use of counseling services, behavioral modification instruction, and complete community service assignments. In 2012, school-based arrests in Broward County were down 41 percent from the same period the previous year, and school suspensions were down 66 percent (Alvarez, 2013).

CONCLUSION

Zero-tolerance policies were intended to prevent violence in schools throughout the country. Initially welcomed by the general public, the policies quickly drew criticism because of the numerous students who were arrested or expelled for committing minor infractions. The Youth Force Coalition, consisting of representatives from twenty youth organizations, formed in April 1999 to fight against zero-tolerance policies in their schools and encourage educational reform. With the help of adults, the Coalition "planned direct actions... [and] designed and distributed material to educate the public" (Webb & Kritsonis). The youth group held meetings and organized conferences in support of their goals to reduce jail and increase educational funding. In February 2000, seven hundred San Francisco Bay area students walked out of fifteen schools in order to protest California's Juvenile Crime Bill, a bill that promoted stronger sentences by trying juveniles as adults. Students asked that lawmakers place less emphasis on imprisoning students and more attention to improved schools, better books in classrooms, and more equal educational opportunities for minority students (Webb & Kritsonis).

Everyone agrees that students need to feel safe when they enter the doors of their local school, but not everyone agrees how discipline should be administered to students who break school rules. As Stader mentioned, "zero tolerance has a place—just a balanced place." Zero-tolerance policies can be viewed in both a positive and negative manner. When a zero-tolerance policy is set in place, students and school staff are provided with a safer environment. However, although a school may experience increased safety, students are often at risk of receiving unequal learning opportunities. If all students are treated the same, despite the different circumstances of each child, the punishment is usually not fairly dealt. Strictly following a rigid set of guidelines for each child "does not always result in a fair outcome" (Fries & DeMitchell).

TERMS & CONCEPTS

Columbine High School massacre: The third most deadly school shooting incident in US history. The massacre took place on April 20, 1999. Twelve students and one teacher were killed, and twenty-four people were wounded. The shooters, two Columbine students, committed suicide.

Expulsion: The act of permanently banning a student from returning to either a particular school or school district. This can occur when a student breaks a school rule. With zero-tolerance policies, students can be expelled from school for minor or severe infractions.

Gun Free Schools Act: This bill was passed in 1994. The law states that in order to qualify for federal education funds, states must pass a law requiring any student in possession of a weapon at school be expelled for a full calendar year. It also mandates that any student expelled for such a reason will be passed to the criminal or juvenile justice system. The law allows the chief administrative officer of each school to handle such incidents on an individual basis.

Gun Violence: This type of violence involves committing a criminal act with a firearm. The Gun Free Act of 1994 strove to prevent further gun violence in US schools.

Intervention: Methods of behavior modification which are alternative to traditional punishments. Potential behavior problems can be avoided if students are given a sense of belonging, are provided with volunteer opportunities, learn social skills, participate in social events, work with mentors, have after-school job opportunities, and other positive influences by caring adults.

Suspension: The act of temporarily prohibiting a student from attending a particular school. This can occur when a student breaks a school rule. The length of time may vary.

US Customs Service Policy: In an early form of zero-tolerance policy, US Customs Service was responsible for confiscating vehicles, boats, and passports of any person crossing onto American soil with any amount of illicit drugs.

Youth Force Coalition: This is a group of youth organizations that formed in April 1999 to combat against zero-tolerance policies in schools and lobby for educational reform.

Kimberly Solis

BIBLIOGRAPHY

Alvarez, L. (2013). Seeing the toll, schools revise zero tolerance. *New York Times*, p. A1(L). Retrieved from http://nytimes.com.

American Psychological Association. (2006). *Are zero tolerance policies effective in the schools? An evidentiary review and recommendations.* Retrieved from http://apa.org.

Axtman, K. (2005). Why tolerance is fading for zero tolerance in schools. *Christian Science Monitor, 97*, 1. Retrieved from EBSCO Online Database Academic Search Premier.

Berwick, C. (2015, March 17). Zeroing out zero tolerance. *Atlantic.* Retrieved from http://theatlantic.com.

Black, S. (2004). Safe schools don't need zero tolerance. *Education Digest, 70*, 27–31. Retrieved from EBSCO Online Database Education Research Complete.

Browne, J. (2003). *Derailed! the schoolhouse to jailhouse track.* Washington, D.C.: Advancement Project. (ERIC Document Reproduction Service No. ED480206).

Fowler, D. (2011). School discipline feeds the "pipeline to prison". *Phi Delta Kappan, 93*, 14–19. Retrieved from EBSCO Online Database Education Research Complete.

Fries, K., & DeMitchell, T. (2007). Zero tolerance and the paradox of fairness: Viewpoints from the classroom. *Journal of Law & Education, 36*, 211–229. Retrieved from EBSCO Online Database Education Research Complete.

Gage, N. A., Sugai, G., Lunde, K., & DeLoreto, L. (2013). Truancy and zero tolerance in high school: Does policy align with practice? *Education & Treatment of Children, 36*, 117–138. Retrieved from EBSCO Online Database Education Research Complete.

Holloway, J. (2001). The dilemma of zero tolerance. *Educational Leadership, 59*, 84. Retrieved from EBSCO Online Database Education Research Complete.

Henault, C. (2001). Zero tolerance in schools. *Journal of Law and Education, 30*, 547–553. Retrieved from http://findarticles.com.

Jones, K. (2013). #zerotolerance #keepingupwiththetimes: How federal zero tolerance policies failed to promote educational success, deter juvenile legal consequences, and confront new social media concerns in public schools. *Journal of Law & Education, 42*, 739–749. Retrieved from EBSCO Online Database Education Research Complete.

McAndrews, T. (2001). *Zero-tolerance policies.* Eugene, OR: ERIC Clearinghouse on Educational Management. (ERIC Document Reproduction Service No. ED451579).

Merrow, J. (2004). The 3 kinds of school safety since 9/11. *Education Digest, 70*, 4–15. Retrieved from EBSCO Online Database Education Research Complete.

Peebles-Wilkins, W. (2005). Zero tolerance in educational settings. *Children & Schools, 27*, 3. Retrieved from Education Research Complete Database.

Roberge, G. D. (2012). From zero tolerance to early intervention: The evolution of school anti-bullying policy. *JEP: Ejournal of Education Policy*, 1–6. Retrieved from EBSCO Online Database Education Research Complete.

Ryan, T. G., & Goodram, B. (2013). The impact of exclusionary discipline on students. *International Journal of Progressive Education, 9*, 169–177. Retrieved from EBSCO Online Database Education Research Complete.

Skiba, R. J. (2000). *Zero tolerance, zero evidence: An analysis of school disciplinary practice.* Policy Research Report #SRS2 Retrieved from http://indiana.edu.

Stader, D. (2004). Zero tolerance as public policy: The good, the bad, and the ugly. *Clearing House, 78*, 62–66. Retrieved from EBSCO Online Database Academic Search Complete.

Verdugo, R. R., & Glenn, B. C. (2002). *Race-ethnicity, class and zero tolerance policies: A policy discussion.* (ERIC Document Reproduction Service No. ED466678).

Webb, P., & Kritsonis, W.A. (2006). Zero-tolerance policies and youth: Protection or profiling? *National Journal for Publishing and Mentoring Doctoral Student Research, 3.* (ERIC Document Reproduction Service No. ED493837).

Suggested Reading

Bell, C. (2015). The hidden side of zero tolerance policies: The African American perspective. *Sociology Compass.* 9(1), 14-22.

Berlowitz, M., Frye, R., & Jette, K. (2017). Bullying and zero tolerance policies: The school to prison pipeline. *Multicultural Learning and Teaching.* 12(1), 7-25.

Elias, M. (2006, August 10). At schools, less tolerance for 'zero tolerance'. *USA Today.*

Evans, M. P., & Didlick-Davis, C. R. (2012). Organizing to end the school-to-prison pipeline: An analysis of grassroots organizing campaigns and policy solutions. *JEP: Ejournal of Education Policy*, 1–7. Retrieved from EBSCO Online Database Education Research Complete.

Lenckus, D. (2007, June 11). Zero tolerance policies can increase risk for schools. *Business Insurance, 41*, 19–22. Retrieved from EBSCO Online Database Business Source Complete.

Rodriguez, R. (2017). School-to-prison pipeline: An evaluation of zero tolerance policies and their alternatives. *Houston Law Review.* 54(3), 803-837.

Ryan, T. G., & Goodram, B. (2013). The impact of exclusionary discipline on students. *International Journal of Progressive Education, 9*(3), 169–177. Retrieved from EBSCO Online Database Research Starters Education.

Skiba, R., & Peterson, R. (1999). *The dark side of zero tolerance: Can punishment lead to safe schools?* Retrieved from http://pdkintl.org.

Vidal-Castro, A.M. (2016). Zero tolerance policies and a call for more humane disciplinary actions. *eJournal of Education Policy.*

Wing, R. & Keleher, T. (2000). *First-class jails, second-class schools: An interview with Jesse Jackson.* Retrieved from Rethinking Schools, http://rethinkingschools.org.

SCHOOL-TO-PRISON PIPELINE

The "school to prison pipeline" is a figure of speech used to describe the practice of public schools suspending and even expelling their more difficult problem students, most often students of color, who are then indirectly dumped into the criminal justice system. Often seen as a direct result of the late 1990s embrace of zero tolerance policies nationwide, the school to prison pipeline has created a backlash, a widespread effort among educators to encourage schools to reexamine their codes of discipline and punishment to minimize rather than maximize the number of students being expelled.

KEYWORDS: Circle-Ups; Cultural Deficiency Thinking; De Facto; Objective Offense; Pipeline; School Resource Officer (SRO); Subjective Offense; Zero Tolerance

OVERVIEW

The interest in better policing public schools came directly out of the national trauma over the April 1999 shootings at Columbine High School just outside of Denver, Colorado. The Columbine shootings were at the time the deadliest school massacre in U.S. history. Because the school takeover by two psychologically disturbed students was covered in real time by the national media and because the toll from the shootings was so high (thirteen people dead and twenty wounded before the two students turned the guns on themselves), educators, parent groups, politicians, and even student organizations nationwide called for better security systems in public schools.

Schools adopted stricter policies concerning student behavior and administrative surveillance. Within six years of the shootings, for example, metal detectors had been installed in more than 70 percent of public schools. When a national push for some sort of gun control legislation went nowhere, schools began to take it upon themselves to revisit their codes of conduct and to close up loopholes that routinely gave serial offenders second and third and even fourth chances. The nationwide initiative, termed "zero tolerance," mandated suspensions or expulsions for first offenses for a range of infractions, including vandalism and fighting. Advocates believed significant, even life-altering punishment

would deter student misbehavior and ensure a safe campus environment.

To further ensure the safety of schools, legislators backed a call for placing a police presence in public schools, particularly those school systems with a history of systemic student behavioral problems, which in the increasingly coded language of school security meant schools with a disproportionate percentage of students of color. Many students in these schools came from dysfunctional or struggling families and lived in impoverished, crime-ridden neighborhoods. Recommendations by national educators' associations and by prominent psychologists specializing in adolescent behavior to put additional funds into counseling programs to help troubled or challenging students floundered. Public opinion (and the politicians who listened to such opinions) called for simpler, quicker solutions—and none seemed quicker or more promising than putting a police presence in public schools. State monies were quickly directed into providing public schools the financial means for hiring independent security officers or for arranging with local police departments to place patrol officers on school campuses.

Reluctant to acknowledge the police were patrolling schools, school boards used the term School Resource Officers to describe the police presence. These police officers were typically armed and were given wide license to maintain a tight control over belligerent behavior or to pre-empt threatening behavior. These SROs were routinely used to break up student fights, to patrol the halls, to watch for suspicious behavior in the parking lots or at bus stops.

The Side Effects of Safety Policies

The police presence considerably altered the dynamic of school security. Formerly, a cafeteria fight might be broken up by a biology teacher and a custodian; now, the same fight would be broken up by two armed police officers. Increasingly, student behavior previously handled by a trip to the principal's office and perhaps some form of detention came to involve police intervention. Critics charge that police involvement criminalized what had before been perceived as relatively minor in-school infractions.

Zero tolerance policies, backed by law enforcement, created a shortcut to ridding schools, especially inner city schools, of problem students (Elias, 2013). Districts were also largely relieved of dealing with the complex issues of the causes and treatments for such antisocial behavior. Maintaining a police presence in a school became more and more an agreed upon strategy for establishing and maintaining school order. The undercurrent of racism was never prominently acknowledged, but by 2005, predominantly non-white schools, according to the Department of Education, Office of Civil Rights, were more than twice as likely to have police in the halls as predominantly white schools. The difference in safety policies between more affluent, suburban schools and those with large socioeconomically disadvantaged minority populations suggests that the disciplinary consequences for equivalent school infractions is disproportionately harsh for non-white offenders.

School suspensions and expulsions went through the roof. According to the Department of Education, in 2013, just over three million public school students were suspended and/or expelled from school, more than double the number of such incidents during the 1970s. These students, whatever their ethnicity, most often came from impoverished circumstances. A disproportionate number of these students were routinely neglected at home or even abused. Often these adolescents lacked appropriate parental supervision; they were children of divorce or overworked single parents or in the custody of guardians under a state-run foster care system. As these students came to be involved with SROs, infractions such as swearing at a teacher, shoving or hitting another student, vandalism, participating in a food fight, disrupting class by outbursts or obscene gestures, or making threats against the school or its faculty, became part of a student's record.

The Pipeline

Within the strict codes implied by zero tolerance initiatives, these problem students would often be summarily pushed out of the school and sometimes into a juvenile detention facility. Students who were found to have committed prosecutable violations could be handed over to the local criminal justice system for action. According to numerous studies completed between 2010 and 2013, students involved in confrontations either with other students or with teachers in schools with a police presence were on average five times more likely to be arrested and charged than were students who committed similar acts in schools without police presence, where such incidents are usually handled by school administrators.

Expulsion from high school is life changing. Fewer than one-third of expelled students ever return to complete their high school equivalency degree. Suspended or expelled students, without school as a relatively safe refuge during the daytime, spent increasing time in the dysfunctional homes and crime-ridden neighborhoods where many of their antisocial behaviors had been engendered in the first place. If charges are filed, even if a juvenile offender does not receive jail time, it becomes part of the offender's public record, impacting not only the adolescent's self-image but also erecting an obstacle to potential job opportunities. Early stigma within the community (Mallett, 2016) and lack of future opportunity form a "pipeline" to further encounters with law enforcement.

FURTHER INSIGHTS

Incarceration too often changes youthful offenders into lifelong hardened criminals. At any one time in the United States, there are more than 320,000 people in prison. Educators and politicians concerned with the overcrowded prison system and the documented dead-end of jail time point to funding as a central issue. Depending on who is compiling the data, the estimates suggest that as of 2015 federal and state governments spend in excess of $70 billion a year on maintaining the prison system, including running incarceration centers and the probation and parole systems. That money, advocates of revisiting school discipline programs assert, would be far better spent on addressing the problem early on—that is, funding rehabilitation programs in high school, expanding counseling services, limiting SROs, and hiring more teachers to ensure smaller classes and more individual attention.

In 2013, the National Education Association, the powerful national organization of educators, called very publicly to shut down the pipeline (Nagel, 2016). It argued that although some offenses (for example, weapons violations, theft, drug dealing, making terroristic threats, and violence directed against students or faculty), were clearly criminal in intent and needed to be dealt with accordingly, schools' codes of conduct should be revisited and disciplinary responses to relatively minor misconduct scaled appropriately.

Circle-Ups

One response against promiscuous expulsions has been so-called circle-ups. In this approach, a problem student is given the chance to sit in a circle of his/her classmates and is asked to hear and in turn respond to reactions to their behavior. Students are given the chance to speak up in a non-judgmental, non-antagonistic environment of open discussion. Long-term problems, grudges, simmering disagreements between and among students and teachers are confronted. In this way, students learn the value of talking and the need to consider the implications of their actions and their words. They learn from each other, and, in turn, together build a community in the school. This approach, termed a "positive behavior support system" (Thompson, 2016), mitigates the blanket approach of zero tolerance policies by approaching each student violation on its own terms. Such a sophisticated level of remediation requires not only an experienced and credentialed supervisor but also a level of maturity in students. Further, teachers must show a willingness to explore rather than punish antisocial behavior.

VIEWPOINTS

The school to pipeline model is problematic. As McGraw (2016) outlines, the problem is with the concept of a "pipeline." Since the turn of the millennium, scores of think tanks, educator organizations, political action committees, local school districts, and even well-intentioned federal agencies have dutifully compiled data that nevertheless cannot definitively establish a direct link between school expulsion and a life of crime. The data is sobering enough.

Race and Zero Tolerance Policies

Increased numbers of incarcerations for men of color under the age of 30 were accompanied by a more or less simultaneous rise in expulsions and suspensions from public schools of young nonwhite males. The connection between the two, however, remains highly controversial. Critics charge that assuming a direct connection between expulsion and prison ignores individual responsibility and school accountability.

Under zero tolerance policies, suspension or expulsion became the first option not the last resort. While taking a "no nonsense" stand against disruption in the classroom met with popular approval,

these drastic actions were being directed predominantly against students of color. Public school students of color were three and half times more likely to be suspended or expelled than white students. Further, students of color were far more likely to face severe penalties for what were known as subjective offenses, such as confronting a teacher or disrupting class or picking a fight with another student, while white students faced similar punishment only for what were considered objective offenses, such as carrying a weapon or dealing drugs. Although African American students make up only 18 percent of the public school student body in the United States, just under 48 percent of suspensions handed out in 2014 were given to African American students. There are similar disparities impacting Hispanics (Orozco, 2013).

Safety

Critics of expanding the role of schools beyond basic education considered that quickly removing offenders was the best way to maintain an effective environment for the predominant majority of students, of any color, who did not act in antisocial ways. If the schools could not address wider and broader psychological issues without counseling and remediation programs, which were viewed as costly, ineffective, or outside the school's mission, they could at least act to keep the hallways and classrooms safe.

Some questions remain, however, as to whether zero tolerance policies and campus arrests result in safer schools (Wilson, 2014). According to an education theory termed Cultural Deficit Thinking, educators and administrators came to assume as a first premise that poor students of color did not or could not value the idea of education. Therefore, this demographic was not significantly motivated to accept the responsibilities, challenges, or even the opportunity of classroom work and by their presence made the operation of a classroom more difficult than it needed to be. Eliminating these students through the intervention of SROs relieved the school of responsibility for them, but school safety did not significantly improve (Schept, Wall & Brisman, 2015).

In a social system where a full one-third of adult black men have done some time in prison, the distance from the principal's office to the warden's office is often very short. Pushed out of school early, expelled students, 80 percent of whom are male, face difficult life choices. Without a high school diploma, they are far more likely to be unemployed and more likely to be involved in street crime and gang membership as a means of survival and income.

TERMS & CONCEPTS

Circle-Ups: In school counseling, a term used to describe a non-threatening group of both students and teachers that review a specific infraction of in-house rules from theft to fighting.

Cultural Deficiency Thinking: A theory of cultural psychology that suggests one group of people, without real experience in another culture, assumes generalities and caricatures of another group to be true as a substitute for the harder work of learning about the group.

De Facto: Regardless of appearances, the reality of a situation or relationship.

Objective Offense: A violation of social behavior codes or the law in the which the central act is a matter of fact with clear and on-point evidence.

Pipeline: Metaphorically, a causal link between two events that may appear parallel but are upon closer inspection actually related.

School Resource Officer (SRO): A euphemism used by some school districts to describe the police presence in the school system.

Subjective Offense: A violation of social behavior in which the central act is a matter of perception rather than demonstrable fact.

Zero Tolerance: A rigorous system of in-house discipline that punishes a first offense with the same level of response that repeat offenders receive.

Joseph Dewey, PhD

BIBLIOGRAPHY

Elias, M. (2013). The school-to-prison pipeline. *Teaching Tolerance*, (43), 38–40. Retrieved October 23, 2016, from EBSCO Online Database Education Source.

Mallett, C. (2016). The school-to-prison pipeline: From school punishment to rehabilitative inclusion. *Preventing Student Failure, 60*(4), 296–304. Retrieved October 23, 2016, from EBSCO Online Database Education Source.

McGrew, K. (2016). The danger of pipeline thinking: How the school-to-prison pipeline metaphor squeezes out complexity. *Educational Theory, 66*(3), 341–367.

Retrieved October 23, 2016, from EBSCO Online Database Education Source.

Nagel, D. (2016). It's time to plug the school-to-prison pipeline. *T H E Journal, 43*(2), 4. Retrieved October 23, 2016, from EBSCO Online Database Education Source.

Orozco, R. (2013). White innocence and Mexican-American perpetrators in the school-to-prison pipeline. *AMEA Journal, 7*(3), 75–84. Retrieved October 23, 2016, from EBSCO Online Database Education Source.

Schept, J. J., Wall, T. T., & Brisman, A. A. (2015). Building, staffing, and insulating: An architecture of criminological complicity in the school-to-prison pipeline. *Social Justice, 41*(4), 96–115. Retrieved October 23, 2016, from EBSCO Online Database Education Source.

Snapp, S. S., Hoenig, J. M., Fields, A., & Russell, S. T. (2015). Messy, butch, and queer: LGBTQ youth and the school-to-prison pipeline. *Journal of Adolescent Research, 30*(1), 57–82. Retrieved October 23, 2016, from EBSCO Online Database Education Source.

Thompson, J. (2016). Eliminating zero tolerance policies in schools: Miami-Dade county public schools' approach. *Brigham Young University Education & Law Journal,* (2), 325–349. Retrieved October 23, 2016, from EBSCO Online Database Education Source.

Wilson, H. (2014). Turning off the school-to-prison pipeline. *Reclaiming Children & Youth, 23*(1), 49–53. Retrieved October 23, 2016, from EBSCO Online Database Education Source.

SUGGESTED READING

Bahena, S., et al. (Eds.). (2012). *Disrupting the school-to-prison pipeline.* Cambridge, MA: Harvard University Press.

Bird, J. M., & Bassin, S. (2015). Examining disproportionate representation in special education, disciplinary practices, and the school-to-prison pipeline II. *Communique, 43*(5), 1–23. Retrieved October 23, 2016, from EBSCO Online Database Education Source.

Gass, K. M., & Laughter, J. J. (2015). "Can I make any difference?" Gang affiliation, the school-to-prison pipeline, and implications for teachers. *Journal of Negro Education, 84*(3), 333–347. Retrieved October 23, 2016, from EBSCO Online Database Education Source.

Kim, C., et al. (2012). *The school-to-prison pipeline: Structuring legal reform.* New York, NY: New York University Press.

Nocella, A., et al. (Eds.). (2014). *From education to incarceration: Dismantling the school-to-prison pipeline.* Bern, Switzerland: Peter Lang.

Seroczynski, A. S., & Jobst, A. D. (2016). Latino youth and the school-to-prison pipeline. *Hispanic Journal of Behavioral Sciences, 38*(4), 423–445. Retrieved October 23, 2016, from EBSCO Online Database Education Source.

BULLYING

School bullying is a pervasive problem found in elementary, middle, and high schools across the United States and around the world. It can take many direct and indirect forms, including physical violence, name-calling, taunting, teasing, malicious rumor-spreading, and social exclusion. Once thought of as a normal part of growing up, school bullying is now widely recognized as a serious problem that must be met with systematic preventative efforts. This article examines the nature, prevalence, and effects of school bullying. It discusses profiles of bullies and victims, and explores the most effective methods now used to combat school bullying.

KEYWORDS: Bully; Bystander; Direct Bullying; Indirect Bullying; Low-Level Violence; School Bullying; School Bullying Prevention Program; Social Exclusion; Victim

OVERVIEW

School bullying is a pervasive problem found in elementary, middle, and high schools across the United States and around the world. As an international phenomenon, school bullying occurs at similar rates in disparate cultures, countries, and educational settings (Carney & Merrell, 2001). Once seen as a normal, if not harmless part of growing up, school bullying is now recognized as one of the primary threats to school safety today (Junoven, 2005; Scarpaci, 2006; Whitted & Dupper, 2005). Since the late 1990s, several fatal school shootings committed by the victims of school bullying have brought major media attention to the issue. The result has been an increase in public awareness about the harmful effects of school bullying and a flurry of local, state, and nationwide programs designed to prevent or at least contain the problem. In recent years, psychologists, sociologists, and school administrators have all published a plethora of research about school bullying.

Definitions of school bullying include four basic elements. First, school bullying does not happen between peers who share an equal or similar degree of power, but always involves a more powerful perpetrator intimidating a weaker subject. Bullying depends upon an imbalance of power, which can be created by any number of factors, including but not limited to physical size, age, popularity and psychological strength (Rigby, 2003; Junoven). Second, bullying is deliberate; a bully intends to cause harm or distress in his or her victim (Scarpaci). Third, bullying can come in direct and indirect forms. Physical violence, such as shoving, poking, hitting, or tripping, is a form direct bullying. So is verbal bullying, which includes name-calling, teasing, and derision. Indirect bullying is social in nature and involves the bully excluding his or her victim from a peer group. An example of this type of bullying is spreading malicious rumors (Scarpaci; Reid, Monsen, & Rivers, 2004). Fourth and finally, bullying is continual; it consists of an ongoing pattern of abuse (Whitted & Dupper).

School bullying is most prevalent among children between the ages of 9 and 15, who are in the stages of late childhood and early adolescence, and occurs most often in elementary and middle schools (Carney & Merrell). As children mature, the types of bullying in which they engage tends to change. Younger school bullies use name-calling and forms of physical aggression more often than older school bullies, who are more likely to sexually harass their victims, or inflect their bullying with sexual overtones (Junoven; Carney & Merrell). In some cases, bullying among older children may also involve racially charged or homophobic abuse (Whitted & Dupper). Technology-savvy adolescents have begun to use the Internet to conduct cyberbullying on websites, in chat-rooms, on social media, and via e-mail, and to send harassing text messages to mobile phones ("Cyber-bullying concerns on the rise," 2007; Reid et al., 2004).

As awareness of cyberbullying increased, researchers began surveying students about their personal experiences of such harassment. Teenagers seemed to be the main demographic affected by cyber harassment. In 2000, the Crimes Against Children Research Center interviewed 1,501 young people ages ten to seventeen. At that time, the survey found that one in seventeen children—about 6 percent—had experienced threats or harassment online. This number increased to 9 percent five years later and to 11 percent in 2011. In 2004, the Internet safety education website i-Safe.com surveyed the same number of students between grades four and eight and found that

42 percent of students had been bullied online; 35 percent of those surveyed had been threatened and many said it had happened more than once. As part of its biannual nationwide survey Youth Risk Behavior Surveillance, the Centers for Disease Control and Prevention reported that in 2015, 16 percent of students surveyed stated that they had been bullied electronically in the previous twelve months (Centers for Disease Control and Prevention, 2016).

Experts now recognize bullying as a form of violence. In fact, some consider school bullying to be "the most prevalent form of low-level violence in schools today" (Whitted & Dupper). If allowed to continue unchecked, school bullying severely compromises school safety. Several studies have demonstrated that bullying can lead to a heightened disposition to crime and violent retributive behavior in bullies, victims, and bystanders who witness bullying (Whitted & Dupper; Scarpaci; Brown, Birch, & Kancherla, 2005). These negative effects are magnified by the fact that 85% of bullying incidents involve bystanders (Junoven).

In order to prevent children from being harmed by school bullying, professional educators and parents should understand the depth of the bullying problem in U.S. schools, be aware of the common characteristics of bullies and victims, and be acquainted with the most effective bully-prevention methods now in use.

APPLICATIONS
Prevalence of School Bullying

Virtually all school children around the world are in some way affected by school bullying (Reid et al.). The United States is no exception: The American Medical Association reports that 50% of all U.S. school children are bullied at some point during their schooling and 10% are bullied on a regular basis (Scarpaci). Another study has shown that 1 in 5 elementary school children and 1 in 10 middle school students in the U.S. are bullied regularly (Brown et al.). Still another study, conducted by the National Institute of Child Health and Human development, found that 13% of all 6th-10th graders bullied classmates and 11% had been bullied regularly (Scarpaci). School bullying is a universal problem throughout the U.S., occurring at similar rates in urban, suburban, and rural environments (Carney & Merrell). In 2015, the National Center for Education Statistics found that

21.5 percent of students between twelve and eighteen years old had been bullied, and that 7 percent had been cyberbullied in 2013 (National Center for Education Statistics, 2015).

School Bullying's Negative Effects

Besides disrupting classroom activities, school bullying generally harms children's ability to learn at school, and has been shown to contribute to truancy and dropout rates (Scarpaci; Whitted & Dupper). As a low-level, subtle form of violence, bullying creates an unsafe school environment and can lead to more serious types of violence among students (Whitted & Dupper). Those students who witness bullying often become distressed, intimidated, and fearful that they themselves might become victims of bullying. These feelings may harm academic performance and distract attention from school work (Reid et al.; Whitted & Dupper). In fact, bullying prevention programs have been proven to raise the overall academic achievement of schools, suggesting that rampant bullying undermines educational efforts (Scarpaci).

Bullying also causes extremely damaging effects in the victims of bullies. These effects are similar to those caused by child abuse, and their intensity and persistence tend to increase when the bullying begins at a younger age (Scarpaci). Victims of bullying suffer from lowered psychological wellbeing, poor social adjustment, and psychological distress. Many victims are targeted because they have low self-esteem, a problem that is only exacerbated by the bullying (Rigby). Victims commonly experience emotional problems such as anxiety, depression, and loneliness more often than their peers (Junoven; Whitted & Dupper). They also develop somatic symptoms, such as problems sleeping, chronic head-aches and stomachaches, bedwetting, and fatigue (Brown et al.). Bullying also leads to academic and behavioral problems in victims, who may lose interest in school, or use somatic symptoms as an excuse to stay home from school (Scarpaci).

While most victims react to bullying by withdrawing and suffering in silence, a rare subset of victims retaliate with violent behavior. In most cases, victims direct violent behavior against themselves in the form of suicide. However, as adults, some victims have sought out and murdered those who bullied them as children. Other victims have conducted highly publicized school shootings in which they targeted those classmates who bullied them—perhaps most prominently in the case of the mass shooting at Columbine High School in Colorado in 1999. Victims of bullying can increase the overall likelihood of serious school violence because they are more likely than other students to bring a weapon to school for protection (Carney & Merrell).

There is evidence that school bullies also suffer from their own behavior. However, it is difficult to establish whether these negative consequences are direct results of bullying or are products of the psychological issues that led to bullying (Rigby). Nonetheless, bullies are prone to suicide and alcoholism, and are significantly more likely to become involved in delinquent activities, such as vandalism, truancy, and carrying weapons, and to become involved in the criminal justice system (Scarpaci; Whitted & Dupper; Brown et al.). Studies have shown that by the age of 24, 60% of former bullies have been convicted of a crime and 40% have more than three arrests. In comparison, only 10% of non-bullying males have criminal records by this age (Scarpaci; Whitted & Dupper).

Common Characteristics of Bullies & Victims

Researchers have found that there are certain characteristics shared by both bullies and their victims. Children who come from lower socio-economic backgrounds are more likely to bully and be bullied. So are children whose parents are divorced, overly authoritative, harsh, or abusive (Brown et al.). Boys are more likely to be bullies and victims, although girls are more often perpetrators and targets of indirect, social forms of bullying. Girls are also more often targets of sexual harassment (Scarpaci; Carney & Merrell; Reid et al.).

There are other characteristics of bullies not shared with victims. Bullies are opportunistic, aggressive, impulsive, tend to dominate others, and are not afraid to use violence to achieve desired ends. Additionally, bullies tend to lack empathy with their victims. These characteristics could result from the fact that bullies are more likely to have been raised in families that use corporeal discipline, or by parents who are un-nurturing and under-involved in their children's lives (Carney & Merrell). Unlike their victims, bullies do not suffer from low self-esteem. In fact, bullies tend to have a positive, inflated self-image. They also have below-normal levels of anxiety,

depression, and loneliness compared to their peers (Junoven; Carney & Merrell). Bullies are usually of average or above average popularity in comparison to other youth in their peer groups. They are often overly confident, an attitude which may help to establish their dominance in the social hierarchy of their peer group (Junoven; Scarpaci).

In contrast to bullies, victims typically have poorer social skills and fewer friends than other members of their peer group (Scarpaci). They tend to be passive, anxious, weak, and lack self-confidence. Victims are often conspicuously different than their peers. They commonly have a physical or developmental disability, or possess characteristics associated with an ethnic minority. Some victims are targeted because they deviate from traditional gender stereotypes (Reid et al.).

Experts commonly agree that there are two distinct types of bullying victims: submissive and provocative. Submissive victims are far more common than provocative ones. They are passive, and react to bullying by withdrawing from social interaction. Provocative victims are rarer. They tend to suffer from hyperactivity disorders, and thus exhibit behavior that irritates and frustrates their classmates. These victims react to bullying with a mixture of anxiety and aggression (Carney & Merrell).

Combating School Bullying: Obstacles to Combating School Bullying

Many researchers believe that the primary obstacle to combating school bullying may actually be teacher awareness. Most of the time, teachers either fail to perceive bullying, or fail to grasp its serious, harmful nature. One study has shown that while 85% of teachers feel that they always or often intervene to stop bullying, only 35% of students feel that teachers do so. Moreover, 40% of elementary school students and 60% of middle school students believe that teachers only try to stop bullying once in a while, or that they never try to stop it at all (Reid et al.).

One reason for this problem is that many teachers do not have an adequate understanding of what constitutes bullying. Virtually all teachers classify physical aggression as bullying, but only some consider verbal abuse such as name-calling, and indirect measures such as social exclusion, to be bullying. Even if teachers do understand what constitutes bullying, they often have trouble identifying bullying when they see it. For example, teachers often do not know what behaviors they should look for as signs that students may be suffering from indirect bullying (Reid et al.). Teachers also fail to intervene in many cases of physical bullying, as they mistake the incidents for consensual 'rough-play' (Whitted & Dupper). These failures stem from the fact that most teachers have not been properly trained to recognize and intervene in bullying incidents (Brown et al.).

A second major obstacle to combating bullying is the reluctance on the part of students to report incidents of bullying. In 2010, the National Center for Education Evaluation and Regional Assistance reported that victims report the bullying they experience only 36% of the time (National Center for Education Evaluation and Regional Assistance, 2010). Since most incidents of bullying involve bystanders, many students besides the victim are in a position to report these incidents to parents or school officials. However, those who witness bullying most often fail to report it either for fear of being bullied themselves or because they fail to see the bullying behavior as inappropriate (Brown et al.).

Key Methods for Combating School Bullying

The most effective strategies for combating school bullying utilize a whole-school approach, meaning they seek to change the social dynamics of the entire school, rather than just those between the bully and his or her victim (Junoven; Whitted & Dupper; Reid et al.).

As a first step in reducing school bullying, it is crucial that each school carries out an assessment of its bullying problem. A student survey about bullying, for example, allows teachers and administrators to see the true extent of the school bullying problem, and can additionally raise awareness among students about the serious nature of bullying and its consequences (Whitted & Dupper). The latter objective should also be accomplished through school-wide assemblies or teaching efforts that seek to dispel myths about bullying and other forms of aggressive behavior (Carney & Merrell).

As a second step, teacher and student bystanders to bullying should all be made aware that putting an end to bullying is their personal responsibility (Whitted & Dupper; Reid et al.). This step is especially crucial because it addresses the bystanders who witness and exacerbate school bullying. This step can be carried out by instituting and publicizing a school policy about bullying (Carney & Merrell). Such a

policy should define and denounce bullying, and include measures that will be taken to deal with individual incidents of bullying. It should also include a statement of social responsibility that explicitly makes all students, parents, and school staff responsible for reporting incidents of school bullying that they witness or know about (Junoven).

As a third step, students and teachers should receive training on how to neutralize, halt, and prevent bullying. Evidence shows that training teachers to recognize and successfully intervene in bullying incidents enables students to feel more confident about doing so as well (Reid et al.). Once teachers understand the nature of school bullying problems, they can integrate anti-bullying content into their classroom lesson-plans, and so further educate students about school bullying (Whitted & Dupper). When teachers set firm limits on bullying behavior, they act as role models for the student population (Scarpaci).

Training that teaches students to combat bullying should focus not only on victims and bullies, but on the entire school population. Bystanders to bullying must be taught how to stop escalating bullying incidents and instead end them; they must be taught how to defend the victim instead of tacitly encouraging the bully by condoning bullying behavior (Brown et al.; Whitted & Dupper; Reid et al.). Such training should teach students to seek adult help, but is should also teach students how to actively use problem-solving skills to resolve interpersonal conflict without adult assistance (Reid et al.; Junoven).

Bullies and victims may also be singled out and taught social skills that will enable them to avoid engaging in bullying behavior in the future (Carney & Merrell). Helping victims learn how to actively resist bullying may or may not help to decrease bullying behavior, but it should help to build self-esteem amongst victims and so neutralize some of the damage caused by bullying (Reid et al.).

Evidence shows that all of these intervention methods are most effective when they are used with elementary school students. This is because bullying tends to escalate as children age, and early intervention prevents more serious bullying behavior from developing (Whitted & Dupper). Additionally, anti-bullying measures are most effective when parents and community members are involved with the efforts (Whitted & Dupper; Junoven; Carney & Merrell).

Several comprehensive anti-bullying programs that integrate the above methods in various ways have been developed, and some are available commercially. These programs include "Quit it!," which was developed by the National Education Association and uses an early intervention approach; "Bullyproof," which was also developed by the National Education Association, and focuses on older age groups; "The Whole School Response Program," which is used widely throughout Great Britain; and the "Bullying at School Program," which was developed in Norway by an innovative school-bullying researcher, Dr. Dan Olweus (Carney & Merrell; Scarpaci).

State Laws that Address School Bullying

From 1999 to 2010 there were over 120 bills that were enacted by state legislatures to address bullying. In 2015, Montana implemented its antibullying law, becoming the fiftieth state to do so, meaning all states now have such legislation.

The No Child Left Behind Act of 2001 requires each state to define what constitutes a "persistently dangerous" school and to allow students who attend such schools to transfer to different schools within the same school district. Schools that are continually rated "persistently dangerous" risk losing federal funds. As the most common form of low-level violence in schools today, bullying can cause a school to be rated as dangerous (Whitted & Dupper). This fact, along with some highly publicized school shootings carried out by the victims of bullies, have caused many state legislatures to address school bullying. New anti-bullying legislation most often becomes a part of a school's already existing safety plan or anti-violence policy. The legislation varies from state to state, but it commonly defines bullying, mandates that state employees who witness bullying report it, mandates employee training about bullying, and/or mandates that schools institute bullying prevention programs (Limber & Small, 2003).

TERMS & CONCEPTS

Bully: A child who deliberately and systematically intimidates and/or harasses another child who is weaker.

Bystander: A child who witnesses a bullying incident. Bystanders may actively or tacitly encourage the bully, defend the victim, or intervene in the situation.

Direct Bullying: Includes physical and verbal forms of bullying such as hitting, shoving, poking, tripping, name-calling, and teasing.

Indirect Bullying: Includes social forms of bullying such as malicious rumor-spreading and causing the victim to be rejected or excluded by a peer group.

Low-Level Violence: Ubiquitous forms of aggressive behavior, such as bullying, that go unchecked either because they are not perceived by authority figures or because they are not seen as a serious threats to school-safety.

School Bullying: Deliberate and continual harassment or intimidation inflicted by a stronger peer on a weaker peer at school.

School Bullying Prevention Program: A program designed to reduce and prevent bullying at school. It raises awareness about school bullying amongst students and teachers, and then teaches these groups to intervene when they witness bullying. May also work specifically with bullies and victims to teach new social skills.

Social Exclusion: A form of indirect bullying whereby a bully causes his or her victim to be excluded from a peer group. This type of bullying is more common among girls than boys.

Victim: A child who is targeted by a bully on a regular basis. There are two types of victims—submissive and provocative. The former has low self-esteem and withdraws as a result of bullying. The latter usually suffers from a hyperactivity disorder and so seems to instigate bullying by behaving in an irritating matter. A provocative victim reacts to bullying with a mixture of anxiety and aggression.

Ashley L. Cohen

BIBLIOGRAPHY

Bouchard, J. (2016). Social concerns among students. *Research Starters Education*, 1.

Brown, S., Birch, D., & Kancherla, V. (2005). Bullying perspectives: Experiences, attitudes, and recommendations of 9- to 13-year-olds attending health education centers in the United States. *Journal of School Health, 75,* 384–392. Retrieved April 8, 2007, from EBSCO Online Database Academic Search Premier.

Carney, A., & Merrell, K. (2001). Bullying in schools: Perspectives on understanding and preventing an international problem. *School Psychology International, 22,* 364-382.

Retrieved April 8, 2007, from EBSCO Online Database Academic Search Premier.

Centers for Disease Control and Prevention. (2016). *Understanding Bullying. CDC.* Retrieved December 20, 2016, from www.cdc.gov.

Cyberbullying concerns on the rise. (2007). *American School Board Journal, 194,* 16. Retrieved April 8, 2007, from EBSCO Online Database Academic Search Premier.

Kinduja, S., & Patchin, J. W. (2014). State cyberbullying laws: A brief review of state cyberbullying laws and policies. *Cyberbullying Research Center.* Retrieved November 15, 2014, from http://cyberbullying.us.

Jing, W., & Iannotti, R. J. (2012). Bullying among U.S. adolescents. *Prevention Researcher, 19,* 3–6. Retrieved December 23, 2013, from EBSCO Online Database Education Research Complete.

Juvonen, J. (2005). Myths and facts about bullying in schools. *Behavioral Health Management, 25,* 36–40. Retrieved April 8, 2007, from EBSCO Online Database Academic Search Premier.

Kueny, M. T., & Zirkel, P. A. (2012). An analysis of school anti-bullying laws in the United States. *Middle School Journal, 43,* 22–31. Retrieved December 23, 2013, from EBSCO Online Database Education Research Complete.

Limber, S., & Small, M. (2003). State laws and policies to address bullying in schools. *School Psychology Review, 32,* 445–455. Retrieved April 8, 2007, from EBSCO Online Database Academic Search Premier.

McGuckin, C., & Minton, S. J. (2014). From theory to practice: Two ecosystemic approaches and their applications to understanding school bullying. *Australian Journal of Guidance & Counselling, 24,* 36–48. Retrieved November 15, 2014, from EBSCO Online Database Education Research Complete.

Mundbjerg Eriksen, T. L., Skyt Nielsen, H., & Simonsen, M. (2014). Bullying in elementary school. *Journal of Human Resources, 49,* 840–871. Retrieved November 15, 2014, from EBSCO Online Database Education Research Complete.

National Center for Education Evaluation and Regional Assistance. (2010). What characteristics of bullying, bullying victims, and schools are associated with increased reporting of bullying to school officials? *Institute of Education Sciences.* Retrieved December 20, 2016, from http://ies.ed.gov.

National Center for Education Statistics. (2015, April). *Student reports of bullying and cyber-bullying: Results from the 2013 school crime supplement to the national crime victimization survey. National Center for Education Statistics.* Retrieved December 19, 2016, from https://nces.ed.gov.

Neiman, S., Robers, B., & Robers, S. (2012). Bullying: A state of affairs. *Journal of Law & Education, 41,* 603–648.

Retrieved December 23, 2013, from EBSCO Online Database Education Research Complete.

Reid, P., Monsen, J., & Rivers, I. (2004). Psychology's contribution to understanding and managing bullying within schools. *Educational Psychology in Practice, 20,* 241–258. Retrieved April 8, 2007, from EBSCO Online Database Academic Search Premier.

Rigby, K. (2003). Consequences of bullying in schools. *Canadian Journal of Psychiatry, 48,* 583–590. Retrieved April 8, 2007, from EBSCO Online Database Academic Search Premier.

Scarpaci, R. (2006). Bullying: Effective strategies for its prevention. *Kappa Delta Pi Record, 42,* 170–174. Retrieved April 8, 2007, from EBSCO Online Database Education Research Complete.

Shetgiri, R., Lin, H., Avila, R. M., & Flores, G. (2012). Parental characteristics associated with bullying perpetration in US children aged 10 to 17 years. *American Journal of Public Health, 102,* 2280–2286. Retrieved December 23, 2013, from EBSCO Online Database Education Research Complete.

Sims, T., & Kameya, D. (2016). Responding to bullying in modern times. *Leadership, 46*(2), 26–28. Retrieved December 20, 2016 from EBSCO Online Database Education Source.

Whitted, K., & Dupper, D. (2005). Best practices for preventing or reducing bullying in schools. *Children & Schools, 27,* 167–175. Retrieved April 8, 2007, from EBSCO Online Database Academic Search Premier.

SUGGESTED READING

Aluedse, O. (2006). Bullying in schools: A form of child abuse in schools. *Educational Research Quarterly, 30,* 37–49. Retrieved April 8, 2007, from EBSCO Online Database Academic Search Premier.

Colvin, K. (2006). Bullying in schools—A new perspective. *Exceptional Parent, 36,* 48–51. Retrieved April 8, 2007, from EBSCO Online Database Education Research Complete.

Crothers, L., Kolbert, J., & Barker, W. (2006). Middle school students' preferences for anti-bullying interventions. *School Psychology International, 27,* 475–487. Retrieved April 8, 2007, from EBSCO Online Database Academic Search Premier.

Fast, J. (2016). *Beyond bullying: Breaking the cycle of shame, bullying, and violence.* New York, NY: Oxford University Press.

New web site helps children deal with bullying. (2006). *Exceptional Parent, 36,* 71–73. Retrieved April 8, 2007, from EBSCO Online Database Education Research Complete.

Outpatient family therapy for bullying boys. (2005). *Brown University Child & Adolescent Behavior Letter, 21,* 3.

Retrieved April 8, 2007, from EBSCO Online Database Academic Search Premier.

Roberge, G. D. (2012). From zero tolerance to early intervention: The evolution of school anti-bullying policy. *JEP: eJournal of Education Policy*, 1–6. Retrieved December 23, 2013, from EBSCO Online Database Education Research Complete.

Saracho, O. N. (2016). Bullying: Young children's roles, social status, and prevention programmes. *Early Child Development & Care, 187*(1), 68–79. Retrieved December 20, 2016 from EBSCO Online Database Education Source.

Smith, P., & Brain, P. (2000). Bullying in schools: Lessons from two decades of research. *Aggressive Behavior, 26*, 1–9. Retrieved April 8, 2007, from EBSCO Online Database Academic Search Premier.

Yerlikaya, I. (2014). Evaluation of bullying events among secondary education students in terms of school type, gender and class level. *International Journal of Progressive Education, 10*, 139–149. Retrieved November 15, 2014, from EBSCO Online Database Education Research Complete.

SCHOOL SECURITY

This article discusses public school security in the United States. The subject of school security has become a hot topic in light of school shootings and a rise in violence in American public schools. Data from the U.S. Department of Education indicates that there were almost 1.4 million nonfatal crimes on school grounds in 2012, as well as 31 school-associated violent deaths. In light of well-publicized school shootings since the late twentieth century, as well as the rise of global terrorism, parents, educators and politicians have sought ways to improve school safety through comprehensive school safety plans. Conflict resolution has been a popular means by which students are taught to resolve their differences through dialogue instead of violence, but emerging research on the positive safety record of public charter schools indicates that reducing school violence may require more grassroots community activism and fewer government regulations.

KEYWORDS: Conflict Resolution; Public Charter Schools; Safety Plans; School-Associated Violent Deaths; School Safety; School Security; School Shootings; School Violence

OVERVIEW

Statistics published in 2013 by the U.S. Department of Education and the U.S. Department of Justice paint a sobering picture of life at school for the nations' more than 50 million public school students. According to the government researchers, there were 31 school-associated violent deaths of students, staff, and other people from July 1, 2010, through June 30, 2011. Of these deaths, 25 were homicides and 6 were suicides;

11 of the homicides and 3 of the suicides were of youth ages 5 to 18. Furthermore, in 2011, students ages 12 to 18 were victims of about 1.25 million nonfatal crimes at school, including about 649,000 thefts and 598,000 violent crimes such as assault (Robers, Kemp, & Truman, 2013). The data further indicate that in 2011, 49 out of 1,000 students were victims of a crime at school.

The problem of school safety isn't limited to students. During the 2007–08 school year, 5 percent of city school teachers, 4 percent of suburban teachers, and 3 percent of rural teachers reported being physically attacked by students (Robers et al.). One teacher summed up her experiences in an urban public school this way:

"I started student-teaching filled with idealism, but soon my own thinking ran along the lines of locks and chains. In one month, a student threatened to kill his teacher over a quiz grade. Another student took a bat to windshields in the faculty parking lot. And when I asked the lead teacher why our classroom always had an odor, she explained that while a sub was on duty, a student had urinated on the carpet. Additionally, drug deals and violence in the halls were routine" (Schaller, 2007).

Such violence against teachers and students prompted State Senator Bob Beers of Nevada to draft a bill in late 2006 that would allow the state's teachers to carry guns in the classroom. While the proposal was voted down in committee in April 2007 due to fears that it would put teachers in the role of law enforcement officials, supporters noted that Israel's legislative body passed a similar law. "They started allowing school teachers and administrators to be armed," said Beers, "and they have not had a single incidence of gun violence on campus since" (quoted in McCarthy, 2006).

Given these school safety statistics, as well as the series of high-profile school shootings from Columbine High School in Colorado in 1999 to Sandy Hook Elementary in Connecticut in 2012, it's hardly surprising that school safety and security have become top-of-the-agenda items for many public school districts across the United States. Addington et al. (2002) describe a study of student feelings of safety at school, both before and after the Columbine shooting, which revealed that the violence in Colorado had an impact on perceptions of school safety across the nation. While the majority of students did not report experiencing fear at school before or after Columbine, students were more likely to report being afraid of harm or attack at school after the shootings than before (Addington et al.).

While parents, teachers, students and political leaders continue to try to understand and address the roots of school violence, they are simultaneously pressing for practical measures to make public schools a safe environment for teaching and learning. These school safety measures range from the practical to the technological:

> "Between the 1999–2000 and 2009–10 school years, there was an increase in the percentage of public schools reporting the use of the following safety and security measures: controlled access to the building during school hours (from 75 to 92 percent); controlled access to school grounds during school hours (from 34 to 46 percent); faculty required to wear badges or picture IDs (from 25 to 63 percent); the use of one or more security cameras to monitor the school (from 19 to 61 percent); the provision of telephones in most classrooms (from 45 to 74 percent); and the requirement that students wear uniforms (from 12 to 19 percent)" (Robers et al.).

While these security measures have become a fact of life in twenty-first century American schools, it is too soon to tell whether they have begun to change the perception of public schools as vectors for violence. What does seem clear is that, when it comes to perceptions of school security, there is a sharp difference between those of school officials on one hand and parents and students on the other. A 2007 questionnaire posed to 10,000 superintendents indicated that 71 percent feel their schools have adequate security measures in place, whereas 29 percent do not. However, a national Harris Poll of more than 600 parents and 1,100 students concluded that 65 percent of youth ages 8 to 18 and 77 percent of parents say it is "extremely likely" or "very likely" that an intruder could enter their schools ("Fast Facts," 2007). A 2014 Harris Poll conducted by the organization Save the Children reported that 70 percent of parents were "at least somewhat concerned" about a shooting at their child's school (Save the Children).

In light of the widespread safety concerns expressed by students and their parents, reducing the level of school violence and simultaneously increasing public confidence in school safety will no doubt remain major challenges for politicians, educators, parents and community leaders for the foreseeable future.

DEVELOPING A SCHOOL SECURITY PLAN

Experts agree that the best first step to ensure school safety is a formal security plan. This plan should articulate clear policies and procedures for every security-related event—from identifying visitors and establishing penalties for bringing weapons to school to plans for a response to a severe weather event or terrorist attack. In most respects, a school security plan should be a subset of a broader emergency response plan.

The need for a clear, comprehensive security plan is obvious: while there were more than 800 violent deaths in schools between 1992 and 2010 (CDC), in that same time period there have been hundreds of thousands of assaults, instances of bullying, rape and gang violence, to say nothing of illegal drug use. A school security plan should articulate the school district standards regarding such behavior, as well as the consequences when students violate the policy. As with all policies, the greater acceptance by parents, school officials and local law enforcement, the better. An article in *Security* magazine (Zalud, 2006) cites creating the best possible school environment. Security experts agree that there is a diversity of policies, procedures and technologies being applied to secure schools. Certified safety plans should be created and tested and solid, informative but non-alarming communication should be used. According to the article, a new generation of kids will understand safety drills as well as fire drills (Zalud).

Parents also have a role to play in the creation or refinement of school safety plans. School security expert Kenneth R. Trump offers ten tips for parents who want to assess the security of their child's school:

■ Ask your child about safety in his or her school;

■ Identify comfort levels and methods for reporting safety concerns;

■ Examine access to your school;

■ Find out if your school has policies and procedures on security and emergency preparedness;

■ Determine if your school has a "living" school safety team, safety plan and ongoing process, as well as a school crisis team and school emergency/crisis preparedness guidelines;

■ Inquire with school and public safety officials as to whether school officials use internal security specialists and outside public safety resources to develop safety plans and crisis guidelines;

■ Ask if school emergency/crisis guidelines are tested and exercised;

■ Determine whether school employees, including support personnel, have received training on school security and crisis preparedness issues;

■ Find out if school officials use outside resources and sources in their ongoing school safety assessments;

■ Honestly evaluate whether you, as a parent, are doing your part in making schools safe (Trump, 2007).

To help implement or refine a school safety plan, the U.S. Department of Education has produced a one-hour webcast to provide parents, educators, school administrators and local safety personnel with an opportunity to review their emergency management plans. The department's Office of Safe and Drug-Free Schools shares successful strategies so that all who share the responsibility of protecting school children can learn more about how schools can help mitigate, prevent, prepare for, respond to and recover from a crisis.

A number of detailed school safety plan templates from the Imperial County (California) Office of Education are available to download and modify. And much more detailed information on assessing school security threats is found in *Threat Assessment in Schools: A Guide to Managing Threatened Situations and to Creating Safe School Climates*, a joint publication of the U.S. Secret Service and the U.S. Department of Education.

COMBATING SCHOOL VIOLENCE

To one degree or another, violence has always been a factor in public education in the United States and around the world. Eliminating it completely from any public school will always be the goal, and school counselors and others have studied and applied various methods for conflict resolution. Beyond the obvious benefit of reducing physical harm to students, conflict resolution methods have other benefits, such as creating a school environment that is more conducive to learning. The literature is clear that violence and aggression are in conflict, as it were, with the primary purpose of public schools. According to many school safety researchers, aggressive student interactions often permeate a school's culture and create a hostile learning environment that stifles the academic productivity and success of students (Bandura, 1973; Guetzloe, 1999; Olweus, 1995; Schellenberg, 2000, cited in Cantrell, Parks-Savage & Rehfuss, 2007).

While conflict resolution remains a useful tool, accumulating evidence suggests that there are many factors affecting school safety, only some of which are adequately understood. A March 2007 working paper by Jon Christensen for the National Charter Schools Research Project at the University of Washington on levels of violence in urban public charter schools, for example, indicates that "teachers and principals in traditional public schools consistently report more frequent safety problems in their schools than do teachers and principals in charter schools." Christensen adds, however, that there are few apparent differences between public schools and public charter schools with regard to their policies and procedures: "It is not clear what accounts for these differences [in safety]. Apart from student dress code and uniform requirements, charters do not seem to consistently use dramatically different approaches to safety policy" (Christensen, 2007).

CHARTER SCHOOLS

One possible explanation, not yet thoroughly pursued in the literature, is that public charter schools are safer because many parents choose to send their children to public charter schools precisely because such schools have a less violent reputation. Another factor may be that public charter school teachers and principals tend to deal with less government bureaucracy in exchange for more academic accountability.

Given this emerging research on public charter schools, it would appear that rigorous school security policies alone are not sufficient for reducing school violence and increasing student safety. Both the ecology of the greater school community and the degree of regular, operational oversight provided by government bureaucrats appear to be fruitful avenues of future research into the predictors of safe and unsafe schools.

VIEWPOINTS: RIGHTS OF STUDENTS

American law has always sought to strike a balance between the rights of the individual and the rights of the larger group. The Bill of Rights—the first ten amendments to the U.S. Constitution—was passed by Congress in 1791 as part of a promise to states concerned about the preservation of individual and state's rights under the new federal constitution.

The Fourth Amendment of the Bill of Rights protects citizens against "unreasonable searches and seizures." This comes into play in discussions of school security because students or their possessions are often searched as part of standard school security procedures. Whether such searches are "unreasonable" is somewhat subjective, and the constitutionality of certain types of searches has been brought before the courts.

In 1985, the U.S. Supreme Court ruled in *New Jersey v. T.L.O.*, 469 U.S. 325 (1985) that "a search of a student by a teacher or other school official will be justified at its inception when there are reasonable grounds for suspecting that the search will turn up evidence that the student has violated or is violating either the law or the rules of the school" (White, 1985). The case in question involved a school principal searching a student's purse for cigarettes and marijuana after a teacher had reported that the student was smoking in the lavatory.

A decade later, the U.S. Supreme Court ruled in *Vernonia School District 47J v. Acton*, 515 U.S. 646, 654 (1995) that random drug testing of students does not violate their Fourth Amendment rights. Writing for the majority, Justice Antonin Scalia explained:

Traditionally, at common law, and still today, unemancipated minors lack some of the most fundamental rights of self-determination—including even the right of liberty in its narrow sense, i.e., the right to come and go at will. They are subject, even as to their physical freedom, to the control of their parents or guardians. When parents place minor children in private schools for their education, the teachers and administrators of those schools stand in loco parentis over the children entrusted to them. In fact, the tutor or schoolmaster is the very prototype of that status. (Vernonia Sch. Dist. 47J v. Acton, 515 U.S. 646 [1995]).

In a test of the broad applicability of *Vernonia*, the U.S. Court of Appeals for the Tenth Circuit ruled in *Board of Education v. Earls* (2002) that "urinalysis testing for drugs in order to participate in any extracurricular activity" was "a reasonable means of furthering the School District's important interest in preventing and deterring drug use among its schoolchildren and does not violate the Fourth Amendment." Justice Clarence Thomas, writing for the majority of the U.S. Supreme Court, affirmed *Earls* on appeal several months later.

Whether random drug testing is constitutional still leaves open the question of whether it achieves the intended result of making schools safer and more drug-free. The American Civil Liberties Union presents an argument against the random drug testing of students, suggesting that drug education and solid after-school programs and counseling are far more effective (Kern, Gunja, Cox, Rosenbaum, Appel, & Verma, 2006).

The debate whether mandatory security procedures violate the constitutional rights of citizens, including schoolchildren, will surely continue.

TERMS & CONCEPTS

Conflict Resolution: A method or methods by which individuals are taught to solve their disputes through dialogue rather than violence.

Public Charter Schools: publicly funded schools that enjoy greater freedom from government regulations in exchange for higher academic expectations. Under the No Child Left Behind Act of 2001, parents who send their children to federally designated "failing schools" can opt to send their children to a public charter school instead.

Safety Plans: Comprehensive, written documents that encapsulate what administrators, teachers and children should do in the event of a crime, natural disaster or terrorist attack.

School-Associated Violent Deaths: A homicide or suicide that occurs on school grounds.

School Safety: A combination of objective metrics and a subjective sense that a given school is a safe environment for learning.

School Security: The methods and practices put in place designed to prevent or reduce school violence.

School Shootings: Episodes in which an individual or individuals have inflicted harm via firearms on students within a school setting.

School Violence: A broad term encompassing any type of aggression against a student, teacher or administrator. This violence can range from bullying to the infliction of physical harm.

Matt Donnelly

BIBLIOGRAPHY

Addington, L. A., Ruddy, S. A., Miller, A. K., & DeVoe, J. F. (2002). *Are America's schools safe? Students speak out: 1999 school crime supplement* (NCES 2002-331). U.S. Department of Education. Washington, DC: National Center for Education Statistics. Retrieved June 23, 2007, from http://nces.ed.gov.

Ashby, C. M. (2007). *Emergency management: Status of school districts' planning and preparedness.* Testimony before the Committee on Homeland Security, U.S. House of Representatives, May 17, 2007. Retrieved June 23, 2007, from http://gao.gov.

Blosnich, J., & Bossarte, R. (2011). Low-level violence in schools: Is there an association between school safety measures and peer victimization? *Journal of School Health, 81,* 107–113. Retrieved December 16, 2013, from EBSCO Online Database Education Research Complete.

Board of Education of Independent School District No. 92 of Pottawatomie County et al. v. Earls (2002). Retrieved June 24, 2007, from http://caselaw.lp.findlaw.com.

Cantrell, R., Parks-Savage, A., & Rehfuss, M. (2007). Reducing levels of elementary school violence with peer mediation. *Professional School Counseling, 10,* 475–481. Retrieved June 24, 2007, from EBSCO Online Database Academic Search Premier.

Centers for Disease Control and Prevention. (2014). School-Associated Violent Death Study. *Injury Prevention & Control: Division of Violence Prevention, Centers for Disease Control and Prevention.* Retrieved November 10, 2014, from http://cdc.gov.

Christensen, J. (2007). *School safety in urban charter and traditional public schools.* Seattle: National Charter School Research Project. Retrieved June 24, 2007, from http://ncsrp.org.

DeAngelis, K. J., & Brent, B. O. (2012). Books or guards? Charter school security costs. *Journal of School Choice, 6,* 365–410. Retrieved December 16, 2013, from EBSCO Online Database Education Research Complete.

DeAngelis, K. J., Brent, B. O., & Ianni, D. (2011). The hidden cost of school security. *Journal of Education Finance, 36,* 312–337. Retrieved December 16, 2013, from EBSCO Online Database Education Research Complete.

Fast facts (2007). *District Administration 43,* 19. Retrieved June 23, 2007, from EBSCO Online Database Education Research Complete.

Fein, R. A., Vossekuil, B., Pollack, W. S., Borum, R., Modzeleski, W., & Reddy, M. (2002). *Threat assessment in schools: A guide to managing threatening situations and to creating safe school climates.* Retrieved on June 23, 2007, from the http://secretservice.gov.

Gay, M. (2014). School safety: Lessons After Loss. *Techniques: Connecting Education & Careers, 89,* 20–25. Retrieved November 10, 2014, from EBSCO online database, Education Research Complete.

Kern, J., Gunja, F., Cox, A., Rosenbaum, M. M., Appel, J. D., & Verma, A. (2006). *Making sense of student drug testing: Why educators are saying no.* Santa Cruz, CA: American Civil Liberties Union Drug Law Reform Project. Retrieved June 24, 2007, from http://aclu.org.

McCarty, C. (2006). *Exclusive: Nevada lawmaker says teachers should have firearms.* KLAS-TV (Las Vegas, NV). Retrieved June 24, 2007, from http://klas-tv.com.

Molnar, M. (2013). Districts invest in new measures to boost security. *Education Week, 33,* 1–19. Retrieved December 16, 2013, from EBSCO Online Database Education Research Complete.

Robers, S., Kemp, J., & Truman, J. (2013). *Indicators of school crime and safety: 2012* (NCES 2013-036/NCJ 241446). Washington, DC: National Center for Education Statistics, U.S. Department of Education, and Bureau of Justice Statistics, Office of Justice Programs, U.S. Department of Justice. Retrieved December 16, 2013, from the U.S. Department of Education, http://nces.ed.gov.

Scalia, A. Majority opinion in Vernonia Sch. Dist. 47J v. Acton, 515 U.S. 646 (1995). Cornell University Law School. Retrieved June 24, 2007, from Cornell University Law School, http://law.cornell.edu.

Schaller, C. (2007). Maybe Joe Clark was right. *T H E Journal, 34,* 6. Retrieved June 23, 2007, from EBSCO Online Database Business Source Complete.

Trump, K. S. (2007). *10 practical things parents can do to assess school security and crisis preparedness.* National School Safety and Security Services. Retrieved June 23, 2007, from National School Safety and Security Services, http://schoolsecurity.org.

White, J. *Majority opinion in New Jersey v. T.L.O.* (No. 83-712). Cornell University Law School. Retrieved June 24, 2007, from Cornell University Law School, http://law.cornell. edu.

Zalud, B. (2006). School violence: How bad is it? *Security: For Buyers of Products, Systems & Services, 43*, 10–13. Retrieved June 23, 2007, from EBSCO Online Database Business Source Complete.

SUGGESTED READING

Beger, R. (2003). The "worst of both worlds": School security and the disappearing Fourth Amendment rights of students. *Criminal Justice Review, 28*, 336–354.

Bracy, N. L. (2011). Student perceptions of high-security school environments. *Youth & Society, 43*, 365–395. Retrieved December 16, 2013, from EBSCO Online Database Education Research Complete.

Denmark, F., Gielen, U., Krauss, H. H., Midlarsky, E., & Wesner, R., eds. (2005). *Violence in schools: Cross-national and cross-cultural perspectives.* New York: Springer.

Elliott, D. S., Hamburg, B. A., & Williams, K. R., eds. (1998). *Violence in American schools: A new perspective.* New York: Cambridge University Press.

Regan, M. F. (2014). A False Sense of Security: Managing the aftermath of a crisis is what the author calls a 'new normal' for school communities. *Education Digest, 79*, 51–55. Retrieved November 10, 2014, from EBSCO online database, Education Research Complete.

Scherz, J. (2006). *The truth about school violence: Keeping healthy schools safe.* Lanham, MD: Rowman & Littlefield Education.

Servoss, T. (2017). School security and student behavior: A multi-level examination. *Youth & Society.* 49(6), 755-778.

Sexton-Radek, K., ed. (2004). *Violence in schools: Issues, consequences, and expressions.* New York: Praeger.

SCHOOL HEALTH SERVICES

In most areas of the country, the role and scope of school health services have evolved according to the changing social environment of the population. School health services' main objectives are to foster the whole student physically and mentally so students can work toward lifelong success and health. In the past, some of the major health problems school school-age children faced included contagious diseases often unheard of today, such as tuberculosis, diphtheria, measles, mumps, rubella, and whooping cough. School health services often incorporated separating those with contagious diseases from the healthy school population. Today, however, most contagious diseases have been eradicated and school children's health risks may oftentimes have their origins in social or behavioral conditions.

KEYWORDS: Behavioral Problems; Budgetary Constraints; Childhood Obesity; Children's Diseases; Guidance Counselor; Health Curriculum; Health Services; Intervention; Nutrition; Physical Education; Physical Health; School Nurse; Smoking Cessation; Vision Screening

OVERVIEW

In most areas of the country, the role and scope of school health services have evolved according to the changing social environment of the population.

School health services' main objectives are to foster the whole student physically and mentally so students can work toward lifelong success and health. To that end, school health services promote health and safety, work to prevent certain health problems, get involved with present health issues, manage individual cases as needed, and work with family members and others when appropriate (American Academy of Pediatrics, 2004). Striving for individual optimum health should be a prime goal of students, their families, school personnel, and the community at large.

In the past, some of the major health problems school school-age children faced included contagious diseases often unheard of today, such as tuberculosis, diphtheria, measles, mumps, rubella, and whooping cough. School health services often incorporated separating those with contagious diseases from the healthy school population.

Today, however, most contagious diseases have been eradicated and school children's health risks may oftentimes have their origins in social or behavioral conditions. These roots can include a multitude of situations that may hinder learning, such as a general lack of preparedness, social, emotional, and health deficiencies or handicaps, poverty, smoking or living with a smoker, alcohol consumption by students or their family members, the threat of weapons in school, attempted suicide or otherwise causing or considering physical harm to oneself, physical, emotional, and sexual abuse; assault and the threat of assault, an assortment of mental, emotional, and behavioral disorders; and homelessness. They may also face stress of many types-pressure from peers, studying and test anxiety, real or perceived competition for academic and extracurricular accolades, and full schedules throughout the week (McKenzie & Richmond, 1998).

In some schools around the country serious obstacles such as those mentioned above are more commonplace than others, and less serious problems are routine. When any of these types of problems do come up in a school, it is almost certain the situation will disrupt individual students' lives and can be a distraction in classrooms. Depending on its severity, the problem can affect the entire school community. When students are less than mentally and physically healthy and their attendance at school wanes, learning at school will suffer (McKenzie & Richmond). A comprehensive school health services program is designed to be proactive and attempt to troubleshoot these types of situations.

Good health is best defined not just as the lack of sickness and disease. Instead, it is the total physical, mental, and social well-being of each person (McKenzie & Richmond). Good health is a mandatory ingredient for successful learning and many factors can weaken it. School health services work toward that goal.

TODAY'S SCHOOL HEALTH PROGRAM

School health services are found in some form in every school throughout the United States. Each school's distinctive community, its wants and needs, the available resources, unique challenges, and its budgetary constraints will determine the framework of its coordinated school health program. No two schools' programs of services are alike as needs, budgets, and concerns can vary significantly throughout the country (McKenzie & Richmond).

Most children in the United States spend more than half their waking hours at school. Besides an already-full school day, many students are also involved with regular sports and social activities before and after school while older students often have part-time employment during those hours they are not in high school. For school-aged children and youth, staying in good health is tantamount to keeping up their routine (McKenzie & Richmond). Since

students at school are a captive audience, schools should be important providers of health services. A school health program tailored to the unique population of the school will consist of many components, some of which will overlap in form and function (McKenzie & Richmond).

School health services are generally described as preventive services, education, emergency care, referral and management of acute and chronic health conditions (Duncan & Igoe, 1998). Each school's package of services is designed to adequately satisfy the health requirements of its students and staff. To do this, the health services should be able to diagnose and prevent various health problems and preventable injuries as they strive to make certain those attending school receive the type of health care they need.

Components of a school health services program will ideally include an on-site health office, a comprehensive health education curriculum, a physical education program, an attention to school nutrition, available student counseling services, a wholesome school environment, and family and community involvement in schools (McKenzie & Richmond). Taken individually, each component has unique and important characteristics.

Applications

THE SCHOOL HEALTH OFFICE

The staff of the school health office provides the core services of screening, diagnostic treatment, and health counseling services within the school. At given times, this office will also provide:

- Urgent and emergency medical care (ideally, all school staff, not just those in the health office will hold first aid certification);
- Prompt diagnosis and needed intervention for all degrees of medical and health problems;
- Various health screenings for all students;
- Medication dispensing throughout the school day;
- Individualized services for students with special health needs;
- Student and staff health counseling and prevention education;
- Educating students about methods of promoting good health.

The school health office staff will also provide networking as needed with other community health providers (Duncan & Igoe). In addition, to comply with the Individuals with Disabilities Education Act of 1990 and the Education for all Handicapped Children Act of 1973, all schools have been required to provide individual health care for those students with exceptionalities who qualify (Duncan & Igoe).

Since most U. S. children older than five are enrolled in school, the school health office often ends up being the logical place for them to obtain preventive health services, to include vision screening, hearing tests, and other gaps in health and social services. School administrators, nurses, and teachers are aware that although the responsibility for a child's health care is the parents', this is not always possible. Poor and uninsured families are often able to fill their children's health care needs only because of the services available through their school's health office. Some schools with a large student immigrant population may offer immunization clinics with community health organizations (American Academy of Pediatrics). Annual vision and dental screenings and referrals are most valuable to those families who would otherwise not seek this preventive health care (American Academy of Pediatrics). In some schools, a specially trained nurse may provide physical examinations for those students who may have no other way to get this well-child health care.

The school health office can also provide preventive counseling services to students, addressing such concerns as cigarette smoking, drugs and alcohol, HIV and AIDS, eating disorders, issues having to do with puberty and adolescence, and health-related learning disorders. Some students may have severe emotional and physical challenges for which they need special health counseling and the school nurse and health office will work to accommodate these students as necessary (Duncan & Igoe). Some students may have behavioral and health concerns that are severe enough to hamper their ability and motivation to learn (Duncan & Igoe) The school health office can provide services to work with these students' problems and strive to prevent loss of school class time as much as possible.

THE SCHOOL NURSE

Most school health offices have just one staff member: the school nurse. In some schools, the school nurse may also teach in the classroom and will be the one to implement many of the health education programs within a school. The scope of services the school nurse is able to provide is dictated by the other school duties under the health office umbrella, but for the most part school nurses bear at least some of the responsibility for creating and maintaining a safe school environment (Espelage et al., 2000; Salmivalii, 1999).

School nurses must be prepared for all types of health-related situations, for example, head lice is one persistent health problem these health care professionals often have to deal with. No-nit policies in some schools state that students with signs of head lice or nits must not be permitted in school until the infestation is eliminated. Particular schools may require medical documentation of medical treatment, creating a hardship for some students and causing them to miss school (Grassia, 2004). School nurses can often find avenues for students to obtain needed treatment and return to school.

School nurses must also be aware of those students for whom asthma is a problem. Asthma is a leading chronic health condition in school-age children and a leading cause of school absence (American Academy of Pediatrics). Asthmatic students and others with particular health needs may require medication or treatments while in school. The school health office must ensure that strict guidelines are followed and the appropriate documentation is filed. Similarly, those with other chronic health conditions, such as diabetes, cancer, arthritis, emotional disorders, and post-traumatic head injuries, may require individualized attention from the school health office (Duncan & Igoe).

Additionally, the school health office has many administrative duties, such as:

- Maintaining student health records;
- Working to prevent sickness throughout the school;
- Overseeing school lunch programs;
- Raising awareness of good health and nutrition practices;
- Providing individualized services as needed;
- Identifying underlying health problems, and as appropriate;
- Providing referrals to their community health care providers for diagnosis and treatment (Duncan & Igoe).

THE HEALTH EDUCATION CURRICULUM

Although a rigorous health education curriculum should ideally be part of the schedule in all schools, time and budget constraints may be the reason some schools today offer only brief (or sometimes no) instruction in the area of health.

Health education can take place casually, during individual health counseling by the school nurse, or more formally, through classroom health instruction programs. Some schools are still able to offer a sequential, comprehensive health curriculum for all students from kindergarten through grade twelve. Units covering dental health, personal hygiene, and nutrition are presented in varied formats in the primary grades, to address important ideas that may include reinforcement of good practices of hand washing, choice of and good health procedures concerning classroom pets, and ensuring individuals with contagious illnesses are not infecting the school population. Students are reminded that these and other parts of the health curriculum are crucial components of a healthy school community. Continued modeling of best practices by teachers and staff will reinforce these ideas to the students (American Academy of Pediatrics). Older students can benefit from discussions of accident prevention and first aid, maintaining good physical and mental health, and topics having to do with general growth and development (American Academy of Pediatrics).

Kegley & Cottrell (1993) say that school health education is more than just a good kindergarten through high school health curriculum. An ideal school program also takes into account the entire community and will ensure such things as school buses having seat belts (in areas where this is appropriate), that smoke-free areas are established and adhered to, that recycling programs are in place, and that there are appropriate health services for all students and staff.

A strong health education program will ideally include helping all students and staff to work toward and all-around healthy lifestyle, providing smoking cessation programs as needed and instituting exercise programs for teachers and staff. Whenever possible, all of those working and learning in a school should feel a part of the health education program. Proper nutrition is important to maintaining students' growth, development, fitness, and motivation to learn. Student awareness and attention to the importance of proper nutrition can be a part of the health education curriculum and making healthy food choices is often taught from the earliest grades.

PHYSICAL EDUCATION PROGRAMS

School health services usually include some form of organized physical education program. Although physical education remains a part of many students' school schedule in the U. S., some parents and educators are still not convinced that physical exercise enhances brain function and that this type of curriculum should be incorporated into what is perceived as a more academic school day. Since physical education programs have been greatly reduced in some schools in the country, it's an opinion that may need to be considered and responded to (Tremarche, Robinson, & Graham, 2007).

Although there is continuing national awareness of the growing problem of childhood obesity in the United States, it hasn't seemed to change the depth and scope of physical education classes and curriculum at most schools (American Academy of Pediatrics). Physical education classes can enhance good health behaviors as they contribute to the academic success of all students (Langford & Carter, 2003).

SCHOOL COUNSELING SERVICES

A strong school health service menu will always include school guidance services. In recent years, school guidance professionals have responded to research and become more focused on learning outcomes that have been shown to be a result of good school attendance. Students who are actually in attendance at school tend to experience lower dropout rates, better grade point averages, and overall higher standardized achievement test scores. Counselors who work toward these ends are valuable to schools today. Although counselors can contribute greatly to helping students stay in school, this area of school health services can often be eliminated or greatly reduced when money is an issue (Gerler, 1992).

WHOLESOME SCHOOL ENVIRONMENT

A good measure of the strength of a school's health services can be a safe, clean, and well-maintained school. A healthy school atmosphere means first a safe and comfortable building in which students can learn. It should be noted that about half of all public school buildings in the U. S. have some sort of environment hazard that can present a danger to students and staff. These risks may include the presence of radon gas, contaminated heating and ventilation systems, asbestos, peeling and chipping lead-based paint, and water contaminated with lead (Kowalski, 1995). Strong school health services will make these problems a priority and find ways to eradicate the building's hazards to maintain the school population's health.

Just as important as a well-maintained physical building is a positive social climate throughout the school. This favorable type of environment contributes to students' willingness to attend school and may enable all students to attempt to succeed and consistently do their best work. A positive social environment takes into account the feelings, values, and attitudes of everyone at the school. Strict attention to how certain policies are implemented and consistency in imposing practices and procedures is important to maintaining a positive school environment (Henderson & Rowe, 1998).

Supportive teachers and staff and policies designed to minimize hazards and distractions maximize expectations for all students as they contribute to a strong social climate in a school. These policies are best broad in scope, from those that help to ensure the health of all students to those safeguards that help make certain the security of students while they are in school. This includes clear rules about weapons, alcohol and tobacco, and drugs. Student achievement can be linked strongly to this type of healthy school environment (Henderson & Rowe).

High expectations and standards for all students is a crucial ingredient for student success, and those schools and families valuing academic achievement typically have students who work hard toward these expectations. Part of a strong and healthy school environment is also having families' health and safety expectations for their children mirror closely those that are being presented and modeled at school: nutrition, exercise, and healthy behaviors that are reinforced at home strengthen the school environment, too (Henderson & Rowe).

FAMILY & COMMUNITY INVOLVEMENT IN SCHOOLS

To be sure, behaviors at home may sometimes conflict with standards at school. The most committed parents and family members are those who attempt to weave school expectations into home life. Healthy food choices, regular exercise, lack of tolerance for drugs, tobacco, and alcohol misuse at home make

conflicts with school expectations more natural for children and youth. Conflicting messages are at a minimum when families, schools, and the community work together to reinforce good health practices (Henderson & Rowe).

Many in the community may not be aware of the scope of school health services and how a strong health program can prevent risk behaviors, provide needed medical attention to all students, ensure students are aware of healthy and unhealthy lifestyles, and promote student success. Those in the community who are aware of the importance of the health program should voice their opinion as much as they are able, raise awareness of those who may not be in the know, and become involved with the school board in an attempt to raise awareness of the necessity of a strong health program in every school in the country (Newton, 1987).

VIEWPOINTS

The main goal of schools is to help students become successful in whatever endeavor they may ultimately choose: the job market, higher education, or another life choice. To meet this end, schools must not simply meet their students' academic needs, they must work toward strong mental, physical, and social health (American Academy of Pediatrics). Many administrators, teachers, school nurses, and students and their families are in agreement that school health services are important to overall student health, even as budget constraints remain a problem. Often health services in schools are the first part of a budget that is reduced. This directly and indirectly affects students' success academically (American Academy of Pediatrics).

School health services will include any or all of the above-mentioned components, and in a variety of formats. It is important for schools to create and promote the strongest package of health services they can with their resources. Staff and administrators should work toward ensuring that with the school health system they have in place, they are able to optimize students' needs as much as possible. Strong school health services require the commitment and awareness of everyone involved with the school, from the students, teachers, and administrators, to the maintenance staff and health services workers: the school nurse, food service workers, and guidance counselors (Henderson & Rowe).

TERMS & CONCEPTS

Behavioral Problems: Behavioral problems are conduct disorders that may affect a student's ability to learn or be taught effectively in school.

Budgetary Constraints: Budgetary constraints are the amount of funds able to be allocated to a certain area or department of a school.

Bullying: is the persistent, deliberate attempt to hurt another person or place a person in a situation where they feel stress.

Childhood Obesity: Childhood obesity describes a situation where a child's weight is approximately ten percent higher than the norm for his or her body type.

Guidance Counselor: A guidance counselor typically works with students in a school to counsel, teach, and provide resources to aid their academic, personal, and career development.

Intervention: Intervention is an attempt to intercede on another's behalf.

Physical Education: Physical education is a school course incorporating physical skills in an assortment of ways, usually sports-related, to help students maintain a healthy and active lifestyle.

Physical Health: Physical health is the general condition of being free from disease and sickness.

Smoking Cessation: Smoking cessation means finding an effective way for an individual to quit smoking.

Vision Screening: Vision screening is an examination intended to identify vision problems and refer these to vision specialists.

Susan Ludwig

BIBLIOGRAPHY

American Academy of Pediatrics. (2004). *School Health Policy & Practice*. Elk Grove Village, IL: American Academy of Pediatrics.

Dang, M. T., Warrington, D., Tan, T., Baker, D. & Pan, R., (2007). A school-based approach to early identification and management of students with ADHD. *Journal of School Nursing, 23*, 2-12.

Denny, S., et al. (2012). Association between availability and quality of health services in schools and reproductive health outcomes among students: A multilevel observational study. *American Journal Of Public Health, 102*, e14-e20. Retrieved December 15, 2013, from EBSCO Online Database Education Research Complete.

Duncan, P. & Igoe, J. (1998). School Health Services. In Eva Marx (Ed.), *Health is academic: A guide to coordinated school health programs*. New York: Teachers College Press.

Espelage, D. L., Bosworth, K., & Simon, T. R. (2000). Examining the social context of behaviors in early adolescence. *Journal of Counseling and Development, 78*, 326-333.

Gerler Jr., E. R., (1992). What we know about school counseling: a reaction to Borders and Drury. *Journal of Counseling and Development, 70*, 499-501. Retrieved September 10, 2007, from EBSCO Online Database Education Research Complete.

Grassia, T. (2004). *No-nit policies subject of debate*. Retrieved September 10, 2007, from http://headlice.org.

Henderson, A. & Rowe, D. (1998). A healthy school environment. In Eva Marx (Ed.), *Health is academic: A guide to coordinated school health programs*. New York: Teachers College Press.

Kang-Yi, C. D., Mandell, D. S., & Hadley, T. (2013). School-based mental health program evaluation: Children's school outcomes and acute mental health service use. *Journal of School Health, 83*, 463-472. Retrieved December 15, 2013, from EBSCO Online Database Education Research Complete.

Kegley, C. & Cottrell, R., (1993). Comprehensive school health: A narrative explanation. *Wellness Perspectives, 9*, 47. Retrieved September 10, 2007, from EBSCO Online Database Education Research Complete.

Kowalski, T. (1995). Chasing the wolves from the school house door. *Phi Beta Kappan, 76*, 486-489.

Langford, G. A., & Carter, L., (2004). Academic excellence must involve physical education. *Physical Educator, 60*, 28. Retrieved September 10, 2007, from EBSCO Online Database Education Research Complete.

Luthy, K. E., Thorpe, A., Dymock, L., & Connely, S. (2011). Evaluation of an intervention program to increase immunization compliance among school children. *Journal of School Nursing (Sage Publications Inc.), 27*, 252-257. Retrieved December 15, 2013, from EBSCO Online Database Education Research Complete.

McKenzie, F., & Richmond, J. (1998). Linking health and learning: an overview of coordinated school health programs. In Eva Marx (Ed.), *Health is academic: A guide to coordinated school health programs*. New York: Teachers College Press.

Newton, J., ed. (1987). *School health: A guide for health professionals*. Elk Grove Village, IL: American Academy of Pediatrics.

Salmivalli, C. (1999). Participant role approach to school : Implications for interventions. *Journal of Adolescence, 22*, 453-459.

Tattum, D., & Tattum, E. (1992). *Social education and personal development*. London: David Fulton.

Tremarche, P. V., Robinson, E., & Graham, L., (2007). Physical education and its effect on long term testing results. *Physical Educator, 24,* 48-64. Retrieved September 9, 2007, from EBSCO Online Database Education Research Complete.

Vernon, T. M., Conner, J., Shaw, B. S., Lampe, J. M. & Doster, M. E. (1976). An evaluation of three techniques for improving immunization levels in elementary schools. *American Journal of Public Health, 66,* 457-460. Retrieved September 9, 2007, from EBSCO Online Database Education Research Complete.

SUGGESTED READING

Atkinson, M. (2002). *Mental health handbook for schools.* London: RoutledgeFalmer.

Clay, D. (2004). *Helping schoolchildren with chronic health conditions.* New York: Guilford Press.

Kegley, C. & Cottrell, R., (1993). Comprehensive school health: A narrative explanation. *Wellness Perspectives, 9,* 47. Retrieved September 10, 2007, from EBSCO Online Database Education Research Complete.

Larson, S., Chapman, S., & Spetz, J. (2017). Chronic childhood trauma, mental health, academic achievement, and school-based health center mental health services. *Journal of School Health.* 87(9), 675-686.

Lear, J., Isaacs, S., Knickman, J. (2006). *School health services and programs.* Hoboken, NJ: Jossey-Bass.

Leroy, Z., Wallin, R., & Lee, S. (2017). The role of school health services in addressing the needs of students with chronic health conditions: A systematic review. *Journal of School Nursing.* 33(1), 64-72.

Marx, E., Ed. (1998). *Health is academic: A guide to coordinated school health programs.* New York: Teachers College Press.

Newton, J. (1997). *The New School Health Handbook.* Hoboken, NJ: Jossey Bass.

Simmer-Beck, M., Wellever, A., & Kelly, P. (2017). Using registered dental hygienists to promote a school-based approach to dental public health. *American Journal of Public Health.* 107, S50-S55.

DRUG AND ALCOHOL PREVENTION PROGRAMS

This article discusses drug and alcohol prevention programs in K–12 public schools in the United States. The concept of prohibition (or abstinence), as enshrined in the Eighteenth Amendment to the U.S. Constitution, was the seed of an idea that in the twentieth century blossomed into full-fledged drug and alcohol prevention programs aimed at young people. Programs such as DARE (Drug Abuse Resistance Education), with its "just say no" approach to drugs and alcohol, put aside messages of temperance and became embedded in the curricula of most American public schools by the 1980s. Several government-funded studies over the past two decades have concluded that nationally recognized programs such as Across Ages and CASASTART (Striving Together to Achieve Rewarding Tomorrows) are more effective than DARE, but DARE supporters continue to maintain that their program still offers the best hope of combating youth alcohol and drug abuse.

KEYWORDS: Abstinence; Across Ages; Alcohol Abuse; CASASTART; Drug Abuse; Drug Abuse Resistance Education (DARE); Eighteenth Amendment; Prohibition; Temperance

OVERVIEW

Drug and alcohol prevention programs have been a fixture in modern American public schools since the 1970s, but their roots go much deeper into American social, religious and political history. In particular, their origins can be traced to the temperance leaders of the nineteenth century who began to speak out against the social ills caused by alcohol and smoking. Beginning around 1800, a Protestant religious revival known as the Second Great Awakening swept across the United States, and the membership of groups such as the Methodists and Baptists grew immensely. These groups both revived and spread the view that alcoholism was immoral and sinful. The American Temperance Society was formed out of this religious fervor in 1826, and within a decade it had one million members (Kern, 1998)—a staggering number when one considers that the entire non-slave U.S. population in 1830 (including children) was less than 11 million (U.S. Census Bureau, 1832).

HISTORICAL BACKGROUND

Beginning in the 1820s, Protestant ministers in the United States began preaching against the evils of "demon rum," and by the 1830s many temperance leaders began to move from support of moderate alcohol use to calling for its outright abolition. In their view, it was impossible to fight the scourge of alcoholism when alcohol was freely available. Better to put temptation out of reach.

The first major victory for the prohibitionists came in 1881, when Kansas amended its state constitution to ban the sale of alcohol. Other states followed, and in 1920, the Eighteenth Amendment to the United States Constitution—which banned "the manufacture, sale, or transportation of intoxicating liquors within, the importation thereof into, or the exportation thereof from the United States and all territory subject to the jurisdiction thereof for beverage purposes"—went into effect.

The introduction of alcohol prevention programs into public schools began during this time. Beginning in 1880, this push was made by the Department of Scientific Temperance Instruction in Schools and Colleges, the educational wing of the Women's Christian Temperance Union. By the turn of the century, virtually every public school in the country had enacted a mandatory anti-alcohol education program, and most were carefully supervised by WCTU members. Prohibitionist leaders reasoned that if young people were shown the evil outcomes of alcohol use, not only would they be much less likely to take a drink themselves, but they also would support the organization's greater goal of national prohibition. As the passage of the Eighteenth Amendment a generation later attests, the prohibitionists were successful, though it is also true that average alcohol consumption increased between 1880 and 1920 (cited in Mezvinsky, 1961).

The repeal of Prohibition in 1933 had a chilling effect on alcohol prevention programs in the public schools. Because many Americans came to see that the cure for alcoholism among some—total abstinence—was worse than the disease for many others, and because of the national attention required by World War II and the Korean War, anti-alcohol programs in the public schools were largely neglected for several decades.

POLITICAL INTERVENTION

In the 1960s, however, some young people formed a counterculture in which experimentation with alcohol, and especially hallucinogenic drugs, was the norm. The counterculture seeped into popular culture, too, and concerned parents and politicians began to renew the call for substance abuse education - but this time with an equal emphasis on illegal drugs. In 1970, President Richard Nixon declared that drug and alcohol education was a national priority, and by the end of the 1970s, most public schools had drug and alcohol prevention programs in place. Quickly the focus of these programs became total abstinence—summed up in the popular catchphrase "just say no"—and more moderate viewpoints were prohibited by 1977.

President Nixon commissioned several studies of the effects of federal drug education programs, and the conclusions reached were often negative toward the programs. In 1973, a second report from the National Commission on Marijuana and Drug Abuse stated that "no drug education program in this country, or elsewhere, has proved sufficiently successful to warrant our recommending it" and alleged that "the avalanche of drug education in recent years has been counterproductive" because it makes drug use more alluring. Instead the commission recommended that drug education be focused less on abstinence and more on addressing the root causes of drug use and addiction, such as the social problems faced by adolescents (National Commission on Marijuana and Drug Abuse, 1973). In 1977, the report from President Gerald Ford's Cabinet Committee on Drug Abuse Prevention, Treatment and Rehabilitation echoed those pragmatic sentiments, suggesting that drug education be "primarily focused on moderating the effects of drug taking" (quoted in Inciardi, 1990).

These recommendations were largely ignored by legislators. In the 1980s, the focus of drug and alcohol prevention programs remained the abstinence approach, and under federal law, no federal grants would be awarded to any drug and alcohol education program that deviated from this message. "Today, material that describes low-risk and responsible drinking for those who choose to consume alcoholic beverages is difficult to find" (Engs, 1991). The slogan "just say no" was championed by First Lady Nancy Reagan, and it was the central message of an aggressive television campaign featuring many celebrities.

DARE

Most public schools implemented this abstinence-only approach in the form of the Drug Abuse Resistance Education (DARE) program:

"DARE was founded in 1983 in Los Angeles and has proven so successful that it is now being implemented

in 75 percent of our nation's school districts and in more than 43 countries around the world. DARE is a police officer–led series of classroom lessons that teaches children from kindergarten through 12th grade how to resist peer pressure and live productive drug and vio-lence-free lives" (DARE, 2007).

At the beginning of the twenty-first century, absti-nence-based K–12 drug and alcohol programs like DARE are continuing to find enthusiastic supporters, but whether such support is borne out by the data on adolescent drug and alcohol abuse is still an open question. There continue to be critics who suggest that the time has come to try alternate approaches that accept that a percentage of adolescents will experiment with alcohol and drugs. As far as these critics are concerned, inculcating responsible behav-ior in young people begins with education and ends with trust.

How Parents & Communities Can Make a Difference

The research on adolescent drug and alcohol use indicates that the level of parental involvement in a child's life is one of the most reliable predictors of youth drug and alcohol abuse. This involvement includes knowing a child's friends and schedule, talking to them about the dangers of drugs and alco-hol, and not allowing young people to be in an envi-ronment where risky behavior is likely to take place.

One illustration of this comes from the 11th National Survey of American Attitudes on Substance Abuse conducted by the National Center on Addiction and Substance Abuse (CASA) at Columbia University:

"Teens who say parents are not present at the parties they attend are 16 times likelier to say alcohol is avail-able, 15 times likelier to say illegal drugs (including marijuana, cocaine, ecstasy, prescription drugs) are available, and 29 times likelier to say marijuana is available, compared to teens who say parents are always present at the parties they attend" (CASA, 2006).

But, the CASA report adds, there is still a need for parents to pay more than lip service to the idea of supervision:

"Ninety-eight percent of parents say they are normally present during parties they allow their teens to have at home. BUT a third of teen partygoers (33 percent)

report that parents are rarely or never present at par-ties they attend. Ninety-nine percent of parents say they would not be willing to serve alcohol at their teen's party. BUT 28 percent of teen partygoers have been at parties at a home where parents were present and teens were drinking alcohol" (CASA).

The Effectiveness of Drug & Alcohol Prevention Programs

In terms of the numbers of adolescents using drugs and alcohol over the past several decades, the evi-dence indicates that usage levels fluctuate on both macro and micro levels. Depending on the variables one uses—such as the substance, time period, age group, location, frequency of use, race and gender—the numbers and trends can be either encouraging or discouraging.

For example, Susan Cohen (1998) noted what appeared to be some sobering trends:

"The news in the '90s is not that American teenag-ers drink in high school. The real news is that they drink in middle school or younger, and that both binge drinking and frequent drinking are increasing. It's also no longer a matter of boys will be boys. The girls are catching up. … Buried in annual news reports about the War on Drugs is the fact that alcohol, not cocaine or marijuana, remains the drug of choice for kids ages 12 to 17. At the same time, mounting scien-tific evidence has found a correlation not just between alcohol and automobile accidents, but between alcohol and violence, alcohol and sexual assault, alcohol and adolescent drowning, alcohol and teenage suicide, alcohol and unprotected sex, and between drinking in the teen years and later alcoholism" (Cohen).

"Monitoring the Future" Surveys

Conducted each year since 1975 by the Institute for Social Research at the University of Michigan, the "Monitoring the Future" (MTF) survey is a long-term study of substance use by young Americans. The survey is given to some 50,000 8th, 10th, and 12th graders nationwide. In its 2012 overview, the survey reported:

"In the late 20th century, young Americans reached extraordinarily high levels of illicit drug use by U.S. as well as international standards.... In 1975, when MTF began, the majority of young people (55%) had

used an illicit drug by the time they left high school. This figure rose to two thirds (66%) in 1981 before a long and gradual decline to 41% in 1992—the low point. After 1992, the proportion rose considerably to a recent high point of 55% in 1999; it then declined gradually to 47% in 2007 through 2009, and stands at 49% in 2012" (Johnston et al., 2013).

As for cigarette smoking, the MTF survey measures "30-day prevalence," referring to the proportion of respondents who have smoked cigarettes within the past thirty days. The 2012 overview reported:

"Smoking peaked in 1996 for 8th and 10th graders and in 1997 for 12th graders before beginning a fairly steady and substantial decline that continued through 2004 for 8th and 10th graders (12th graders increased a bit in 2004). Between the peak levels in the mid-1990s and 2004, 30-day prevalence of smoking declined by 56% in 8th grade, 47% in 10th, and 32% in 12th. It is noteworthy, however, that this important decline in adolescent smoking decelerated sharply after about 2002. There was some further decline after 2004 in all grades, but the declines appeared to end in the lower two grades in 2010. In both 2011 and 2012, however, declines occurred in all three grades. An increase in 2009 in federal taxes on cigarettes (from $0.39 to $1.01 per pack) may have contributed to this resumption of the declines in use" (Johnson et al.).

CENTER FOR DISEASE CONTROL (CDC)

The U.S. Centers for Disease Control (CDC) reported in 2012 that the use of any illicit drug by young people aged 12 to 17 had declined slightly from 11.6 percent in 2002 to 10.1 percent in 2010; the use of marijuana specifically had declined from 8.2 to 7.4 percent. Binge drinking declined from 10.7 to 7.8 percent for this age group, and cigarette smoking declined from 13 to 8.3 percent (U.S. Centers for Disease Control, 2013).

Given the fluid nature of the statistics, it's hardly surprising that survey data on the use of drugs and alcohol by adolescents has been subjected to much interpretation by scholars and other experts in the field. In terms of alcohol (and even marijuana) use, those who support the right of teenagers to drink or smoke in moderation see the statistics as evidence that prevention programs have been an expensive exercise in futility. Others, especially

youth advocate groups and the U.S. government, read the surveys as showing steady, incremental progress toward the goal of complete adolescent abstention from tobacco and alcohol until the age of 21—an age they perceive to be the beginning of a more responsible season of life.

QUESTIONING DARE & THE ABSTINENCE-BASED APPROACH

Since its founding in 1983, DARE has become by far the leading drug and alcohol education program in the United States and around the world. But the program has its share of critics. Gonnerman (1999) observed that DARE takes an all-or-nothing view of the drug and alcohol landscape:

"In DARE's worldview, Marlboro Light cigarettes, Bacardi rum, and a drag from a joint are all equally dangerous. For that matter, so is snorting a few lines of cocaine. DARE's student workbook features an eighth-grade alcoholic named Robert on page seven, Wendy the pot-smoking eighth-grader on the next page, and by page 10 a ninth-grader named Laura is trying to score some cocaine. After reading these tales, students are supposed to list what they learned about each drug" (Gonnerman).

Critics also argue that DARE is putting forth an overly simplistic view that fails to draw the important distinctions between these substances that many adolescents already understand from experience. The result, critics say, is that the truly important message—that young people should act responsibly toward drugs and alcohol—is lost:

"'It really is irresponsible to place all drugs in the same category,' says Marsha Rosenbaum, who heads the West Coast office of the Lindesmith Center, a drug policy reform organization. 'What I don't want kids to hear is that all drugs and any amount you do will be the road to devastation. Once kids get to an age where they're experimenting ... they know that is not true, so they throw away the entire prevention message. It isn't really education. It's indoctrination'" (as cited in Gonnerman).

In response, DARE and its supporters argue that their approach is sound. A teenager can begin drinking alcohol, they argue, and then graduate to marijuana and cocaine, and the slope is far too slippery for the fine distinctions urged by critics.

But beyond pure methodology, the question remains: Does DARE work? Not very well, at least according to much of the relevant literature:

> *"In 1991, a U.S. Justice Department study determined that kids who had gone through a DARE program used drugs as often as kids who had not. A 1993 Government Accounting Office report criticized bureaucrats for restricting drug education funding to programs that hewed the "Just Say No" line. And a 1998 U.S. Department of Education analysis of over 10,000 public school students found that other programs had better outcomes than DARE. More than 15 university and government studies have concluded that DARE doesn't reduce drug use or abuse"* (Newman, 1998).

Supporters of DARE counter that even though some studies may at first appear to cast doubt on the effectiveness of the program, what they instead reveal is that young people need even more exposure to DARE, not less.

ALTERNATIVES TO DARE

Hanson (2007) discusses several viable alternatives to DARE that have a proven record of success. He writes that fortunately, schools are not faced with the choice between DARE and no program. A federal agency, Substance Abuse and Mental Health Services Administration (SAMSHA), part of the U.S. Department of Health and Human Services, has identified 66 model programs, any of which would be viable alternatives to the DARE program. Two of the many programs SAMSHA recommends include:

- **Across Ages:** A mentoring program that pairs young people (ages 9 to 13) with adults over 55 who serve as mentors and role models. It seeks to strengthen community bonds through service programs and family bonds through family activities;

- **CASASTART (Striving Together to Achieve Rewarding Tomorrows):** This program, run by the National Center on Addiction and Substance Abuse (CASA) at Columbia University, does not assume that young people will not experiment with drugs or alcohol, but it seeks to put social and emotional supports in place to prevent continued use.

These and other anti-alcohol and anti-drug programs take a holistic approach to drug and alcohol prevention among young people by enlarging the discussion to include substance abuse counselors, family therapists and community leaders. They strive to make drug and alcohol abuse less appealing by helping adolescents understand the positive and negative power of peer pressure and giving them alternative strategies for coping with the angst that is part of an adolescent's journey to adulthood.

TERMS & CONCEPTS

Alcohol Abuse: According to abstinence-based programs, the use of alcohol by those under the legal drinking age. More broadly defined as an unhealthy use of, and dependence upon, alcohol.

Across Ages: A nationally recognized drug and alcohol prevention program that pairs young people (ages 9 to 13) with adult mentors over 55 to teach young people life skills and strengthen community bonds through service programs.

CASASTART (Striving Together to Achieve Rewarding Tomorrows): Another nationally recognized drug and alcohol prevention program that does not assume that young people will not experiment with drugs or alcohol, but seeks to put social and emotional supports in place to prevent continued use.

Drug Abuse Resistance Education (DARE): A school-based program designed to convince young people not to use drugs (including tobacco) and alcohol.

Drug Abuse: The use of illegal drugs or tobacco products, especially by minors.

Eighteenth Amendment: An amendment to the U.S. Constitution that outlawed the sale of alcohol in the United States. It was in effect from 1920 to 1933, when it was repealed by the passage of the Twenty-First Amendment.

Prohibition: A period from 1920 to 1933 in the United States in which it was illegal to purchase or make most types of alcohol.

Temperance Movement: A movement, begun in the early 1800s, whose supporters advocated moderate use of alcohol. Many early temperance advocates became prohibitionists by the end of the nineteenth century.

Matt Donnelly

BIBLIOGRAPHY

Cohen, S. (1998, June 7). Drinking age: The new culture of alcohol. *Washington Post Magazine*, p. 11. Retrieved June 12, 2007, from the Washington Post http://washington-post.com.

D.A.R.E. (2007) *About D.A.R.E.* Retrieved June 20, 2007, from http://dare.org.

Engs, R. C., & Hanson, D. J. (1989). Reactance theory: A test with collegiate drinking. *Psychological Reports, 64,* 667–673.

Gonnerman, J. (1999, April 7). Truth or D.A.R.E. The dubious drug-education program takes New York. *Village Voice.* Retrieved June 18, 2007, from the Schaffer Library of Drug Policy, http://druglibrary.org.

Hanson, D. J. (2007). *Alternatives to the failed DARE (Drug Abuse Resistance Education) program.* Retrieved June 25, 2007, from http://www2.potsdam.edu.

Inciardi, J. A., ed. (1990). *Handbook of drug control in the United States.* Westport, CT: Greenwood Publishing.

Johnston, L. D., O'Malley, P. M., Bachman, J. G. & Schulenberg, J. E. (2013). Monitoring the Future national results on drug use: 2012 overview, key findings on adolescent drug use. Ann Arbor: Institute for Social Research, University of Michigan. Retrieved December 10, 2013, from http://monitoringthefuture.org.

Kern, A. (1998, February). Alcoholism and the temperance movement in early American folk art. *Magazine Antiques, 153,* 292.

Mendelson, J. H., & Mello, N. K. (1935). *Alcohol: Use and abuse in America.* Boston: Little Brown & Company.

Mezvinsky, N. (1961). Scientific temperance instruction in the schools. *History of Education Quarterly, 1,* 48–56.

Miller, B. A., Aalborg, A. E., Byrnes, H. F., Bauman, K., & Spoth, R. (2012). Parent and child characteristics related to chosen adolescent alcohol and drug prevention program. *Health Education Research, 27,* 1–13. Retrieved December 10, 2013, from EBSCO Online Database Education Research Complete.

National Center on Addiction and Substance Abuse (2011). *National survey of American attitudes on substance abuse XVI: Teens and parents.* Retrieved December 10, 2013 from National Center on Addiction and Substance Abuse, http://casacolumbia.org.

National Commission on Marijuana and Drug Abuse. (1972). *Marijuana, a signal of misunderstanding. First Report of the National Commission on Marijuana and Drug Abuse.* Retrieved June 18, 2007, from the Schaffer Library of Drug Policy, http://druglibrary.org.

National Commission on Marijuana and Drug Abuse (1973). *Drug use in America: Problem in perspective.* Second Report of the National Commission on Marijuana and Drug Retrieved June 17, 2007, from the Schaffer Library of Drug Policy, http://druglibrary.org.

Newman, B. (1998, April 9). D.A.R.E.'s effectiveness questioned. *Daily Hampshire Gazette* (Northampton, Mass.). Accessed June 18, 2007 from the Schaffer Library of Drug Policy, http://druglibrary.org.

Thompson, P. (1999). *Rum punch and revolution: Taverngoing and public life in eighteenth-century Philadelphia.* Philadelphia: University of Pennsylvania Press.

U.S. Census Bureau. (1975). *Bicentennial edition: Historical statistics of the United States, colonial times to 1970. Population. Series A 91–104. Population, by Sex and Race: 1790 to 1970,* 14. Retrieved June 16, 2007, from U.S. Census Bureau, http://www2.census.gov.

U.S. Centers for Disease Control. (2013). *Health, United States, 2012.* Retrieved December 10, 2013, from the U.S. Centers for Disease Control, http://cdc.gov.

West, J. (2000). A sober assessment of Reformational drinking. *Modern Reformation 9,* 38–42.

Women's Christian Temperance Union (2007). Accessed June 17, 2007, from Women's Christian Temperance Union, http://wctu.org.

SUGGESTED READING

Champion, K., Newton, N.C., Barrett, E., Teesson, M. (2013). A systematic review of school-based alcohol and other drug prevention programs facilitated by computers with the Internet. *Drug and Alcohol Review.* 32(2), 115–123.

Hedrick, J. D. (1997). Drink and disorder in the classroom. In D. S. Reynolds and D. J. Rosenthal (Eds.), *The serpent in the cup: Temperance in American literature* (pp. 205–228). Amherst: University of Massachusetts Press.

Kanof, M. E. (2003). *Youth illicit drug use prevention: DARE long-term evaluations and federal efforts to identify effective programs.* Washington, DC: General Accounting Office.

Mogro-Wilson, C., Allen, E., & Cavallucci, C. (2017). A brief high school prevention program to decrease alcohol usage and change social norms. *Social Work Research.* 41(1), 53-62.

West, S. L., & O'Neal, K. K. (2004). Project DARE outcome effectiveness revisited. *American Journal of Public Health 94,* 1027–1029. Retrieved June 18, 2007, from EBSCO Online Database Education Research Complete.

Workman, J. W., Huber, M. J., Ford, J., Mayer, T., Moore, D., Wilson, J. F., & Kinzeler, N. (2012). The PALS prevention program and its long-term impact on student intentions to use alcohol, tobacco, and marijuana. *Journal of Drug Education, 42,* 469–485. Retrieved December 10, 2013, from EBSCO Online Database Education Research Complete.

LABORATORY SAFETY IN THE SCHOOLS

While the risk of a classroom or school laboratory accident resulting in injury or serious damage is small, the risk does exist. It is the responsibility of district administrators, safety personnel, and teachers to develop and implement these programs for the safety of all. The importance of laboratory safety has been recognized by industry, government, and institutions of higher education for decades. These entities have developed, implemented, and stringently followed comprehensive safety and procedural programs to reduce the rate of accidents, manage the risk of incidents and injuries to personnel and students, and to establish clear default guidelines and procedures to deal with such events when they do occur.

KEYWORDS: Chemical Compatibility; Chemical Disposal; Chemical Hygiene Plan; Chemical Tracking System; Chemicals; Disposal of Toxic Materials; Environmental Protection Agency (EPA); Green Chemistry; Hazardous Substances; Laboratory; Material Safety Data Sheets; Occupational Safety & Health Administration (OSHA); Public School; Safety; Toxic

OVERVIEW

The teaching of science in the nation's schools has progressed far beyond what existed even a few years ago. With the constant pace of progress and discovery in the scientific fields, school districts across the country are constantly being challenged to keep up with these advances, adding them to their science curricula both academically in the classroom and practically in the science and chemistry laboratory. These new experiments (as well as many older ones) being taught in the lab are fairly complicated and have an element of risk to them that must managed by proper laboratory procedures and safety programs. It is the responsibility of the school or district to develop and implement them to ensure the safety of both the teaching staff and the students (U.S. Consumer Product Safety Commission, 2007).

However, in many districts, comprehensive laboratory safety procedures and programs are either nonexistent, out of date, or not judiciously followed, which increases the risk of accident or injury to all involved ("Promote science lab safety," 2006). This shortcoming can also place the potential liability for such incidents squarely upon the school or school district which failed to develop, update, or fully implement these vital guidelines.

The importance of laboratory safety has been recognized by industry, government, and institutions of higher education for decades. These entities have developed, implemented, and stringently followed comprehensive safety and procedural programs to reduce the rate of accidents, manage the risk of incidents and injuries to personnel and students, and to establish clear default guidelines and procedures to deal with such events when they do occur. The passage of the Occupational Safety and Health Act (OSHA) of 1970 which formalized the requirement that guidelines and precautions must be developed to protect employees of all firms from hazards on the job "set in stone" the requirements for such procedures in industry, government, and academia. Yet, unlike industry and government, in many of the nation's schools, these safety procedures and programs have been slowly or incompletely implemented, if at all.

While the risk of a classroom or school laboratory accident resulting in injury or serious damage is small, the risk *does* exist. It is the responsibility of district administrators, safety personnel, and teachers to develop and implement these programs for the safety of all. Without proper safety programs in place, that small risk factor can balloon, resulting in potentially grave situations that could escalate into serious injury to people and or damage to school facilities. Properly developed, implemented, *and followed* safety procedures will help ensure that these risks are kept minimal by familiarizing students with the potential hazards of their activity, preventative measures against accidents, and emergency procedures to follow in the event of an accident to so that a productive and safe learning experience can be shared by all (Roy, 2001).

SCHOOL DISTRICT RESPONSIBILITIES

The development, implementation, and enforcement of school laboratory safety programs are the responsibility of the individual school districts. When a science curriculum is developed, an integral part of that development should include comprehensive safety and health instruction as a first step in practical instruction in the laboratory. While the Federal Government does not require that students be given safety and health instruction, it does require that employees (teachers and assistants) be given this training. Some individual states (such as North Carolina) have recognized the need for a formal laboratory safety program for students, do require that state guidelines be followed and that students receive training similar to that required by the Federal OSHA statutes (Stroud, 2007).

TEACHER RESPONSIBILITY

Teachers are next in the chain of responsibility, as the first line of contact for students in the laboratory; they are the most important link in this chain. By carefully instructing students in the safety procedures to be followed, familiarizing them with the laboratory equipment, the proper handling procedures for chemicals to be used, and by providing adequate supervision during every stage of the learning process, teachers have the most influence on their students to ensure the successful and safe outcome to practical laboratory experiments.

STUDENT RESPONSIBILITY

Finally, it is the responsibility of the students in the laboratory to follow the guidelines and safety procedures taught to them. While the students may come from a wide variety of backgrounds that may prepare some of them for the responsibilities of the lab, others may not have any experience in such activities or predilection to follow such strict guidelines. It must be impressed upon them that their safety and success depends upon carefully following procedures and adequate time must be set aside to ensure that all are thoroughly familiar with, and motivated to follow, these steps prior to beginning the experiments. In itself, the training is a good start towards establishing a firm step by step procedural foundation that the students may build upon to prepare for and enhance their experience in the laboratory.

Applications

DIVISION OF TASKS IN THE LABORATORY

In the laboratory, there is a distinct division of duties and responsibilities between instructors and students. The instructors are responsible for the planning, preparation, instruction, and execution of the practicum while providing adequate supervision during all phases, ensuring adherence to the guidelines of the

instruction, and maintaining a safe learning environment for all. The task of supervision and leadership to ensure the safety of students is probably the most critical factor while performing school laboratory experiments (Kaufman, 1995).

The duties of teachers and aides may include, but are not limited to:

- Proper maintenance and operation of laboratory and safety equipment and facilities;
- Proper administrative records keeping and training documentation;
- Identification of possible hazards or hazardous situations that may exist;
- Instruction for participants in safety procedures and emergency action plans;
- Knowledge of and familiarity in the use of safety and emergency equipment;
- Knowledge of the location and operation of critical shutoffs for systems such as gas, liquid, and electricity;
- Proper storage, documentation, and monitoring of chemicals stored in the laboratory;
- Ensuring order and adherence to procedures in the laboratory while experiments are underway.

Students also have responsibilities in the lab. It is critical for them to understand that serious incidents can occur if proper attention is not paid to their experiments, or if their conduct causes an accident with the equipment or chemicals. Safety must be paramount in all of their actions while in this environment. Student responsibilities may include, but are not limited to:

- Proper and safe behavior in the lab;
- Knowing and following all applicable safety and health guidelines;
- Following standard, established laboratory and chemical handling procedures;
- Ensuring that their work stations are kept neat, free from clutter and properly cleaned;
- Wearing the proper clothing and safety equipment while in the laboratory;
- No eating, drinking, or smoking in the lab;
- Properly dispose of all chemicals and broken glassware;
- Knowing all emergency and evacuation procedures.

THE CHEMICAL HYGIENE PLAN (CHP)

When storing chemicals in the laboratory, a Chemical Hygiene Plan (CHP) is the most important part of managing these potentially hazardous substances.

The CHP is a written document that outlines the safety procedures and policies that cover the storage, use, and safe handling of hazardous chemicals that are being utilized at that location. It is intended to protect personnel from accidental or unintended exposure to these chemicals. The CHP is of importance for schools since it controls the procurement, storage, reliable inventory, and disposal of potentially hazardous substances. In many schools, there are no real controls to the haphazard purchase of substances and the storage of outdated chemicals and chemistry kits. Additionally, without a CHP, chemicals which have outlived their shelf life may not be properly disposed of. Like outdated pharmaceuticals, chemicals kept beyond their safe storage date can sometimes prove hazardous due to chemical changes and instability resulting in possible exposure to liability issues for the school if an accident occurs.

The specific guidelines for the CHP are covered by OSHA's *Occupational Exposure to Hazardous Chemicals in Laboratories Standard* (Title 29, Code of Federal Regulations, part 1910.1450) which delineates the mandatory requirements of this statute which is intended to protect individuals from harm from hazardous chemicals. The statute is available online at http://osha.gov

The OSHA standard applies to all school employees who work in the laboratory, or who are exposed to these chemicals. It is the responsibility of the school district to assign responsible personnel to develop the CHP for school. Additionally, non-binding guidelines for CHPs can also be found in Appendix A of Federal Regulations 1910.1450 which provides assistance in developing a CHP.

REQUIRED COMPONENTS OF A CHEMICAL HYGIENE PLAN

According to OSHA (2007), a CHP has certain required portions that are outlined here:

- Identified and developed standard safety and health procedures which cover each activity involving the use of hazardous chemicals in the laboratory;
- Guidelines to establish the control (physical, administrative, and emergency) measures required to avoid or reduce exposure to hazardous substances, with a particular focus on extremely hazardous substances;
- A policy ensuring the installation and proper working condition of safety equipment such as

chemical hoods, masks, and other preventative equipment;
- Readily available information on the type, hazard, storage and safe handling requirements, and exposure limits of all hazardous chemicals used in that area;
- A formal training plan for all employees working with these hazardous chemicals which covers the detection of an accidental release of these substances, the health hazards of exposure to the substances, necessary protective actions, and emergency response and reporting procedures when dealing with an accidental release of these substances;
- The approval process for the scheduling and teaching of practical classes in the laboratory involving hazardous materials;
- The medical response and evaluation requirements when an individual develops symptoms of exposure to these substances either by standard contact or by exposure during an accidental release, or when regular exposure levels have been above allowed guidelines;
- Formal assignment of an individual as the CHP or Implementation Officer;
- Additional requirements and guidelines for working with very hazardous substances such as known carcinogens, acute toxins, and other elevated health risk compounds;
- A regular mechanism to ensure a yearly review of the institutional CHP (OSHA).

NON MANDATORY ELEMENTS OF A CHEMICAL HYGIENE PLAN

The following items, while not mandatory, may also be included in a CHP.
- Proper identification and labeling of all such substances and the ready availability of Material Safety Data Sheets (MSDS) at the location;
- The creation and secure maintenance of records documenting employee exposure levels and past medical treatments for these exposures.

MATERIAL SAFETY DATA SHEETS

Material Safety Data Sheets outline the handling, storage, and disposition requirements of chemicals. These sheets should accompany all chemicals used by the school and are also available online at www.msdsonline.com if they do not arrive with the shipment from the manufacturer or vendor.

MSDSs are very useful sources of information and should be maintained in one binder located in an accessible location for all employees and readily available to emergency personnel.

PROCURING CHEMICALS

When procuring chemicals, there are some basic guidelines to consider to ensure that the chemical inventory remains fully documented, accounted for, proportional to needs, and properly disposed of when outdated or excess to requirements. A proper procurement system will save the school or district money by ensuring that the chemicals purchased are fully utilized and procured only in necessary quantities. Careful management of the chemical stock also reduces the risks associated with improper handling and loss. Some of these considerations include:

- A procurement plan for purchasing chemicals and chemistry kits;
- A single point of contact for the purchase of chemicals to ensure proper management of the chemical stockpile;
- A training program for logistics support personnel and formal procedures for the reception, handling, and proper routing and storage of the substances;
- Established procedures in the event of accidental release, personnel /student exposure, or loss;
- Review to determine if there is an actual educational requirement for particularly hazardous substances, check if less hazardous substitutes are available;
- of chemical storage facilities;
- Procure adequate amounts of proper protective gear and safety equipment for handling the chemicals;
- Establish a hazardous material disposal plan if needed and ensure that funds are available for it;
- Determine if lesser amounts of the substance can be successfully used when carrying out the laboratory experiments and adjust purchases accordingly;
- Only procure amounts that can be consumed within the average rate of usage for one school year;
- Avoid glass storage containers when possible to reduce the hazard of breakage.

TRACKING CHEMICALS

Once lab chemicals have been procured, it is vital to maintain reliable tracking and inventory controls on them. As discussed in the Chemical Hygiene section, it is important that schools keep track of the quantity of chemicals stored at their facilities, their location and disposal dates are known, and finally, appropriate safety and health training has been provided to all employees who come into contact with them.

A chemical tracking system is basically a "single source" repository of all information relating to chemicals used by the school. It can be either paper or computer based and it should track the chemicals from procurement to disposal. An up to date tracking system will ensure that the chemical inventory is managed efficiently, cost effectively, without redundancies, and that chemicals are properly disposed of.

Chemicals may be tracked by name or molecular composition. The system should track each individual container of substances as opposed to the entire inventory on hand. Regular inventory and inspection of the stockpile is highly recommended, as well as immediate disposal as required per the CHP. A tracking sheet documenting date and amount of usage for each type is also recommended to establish usage rates for each chemical.

LABELING OF CHEMICALS

For obvious reasons, one of the most vital things in a laboratory is that the chemicals used there are correctly labeled. Serious-potentially fatal accidents and mishaps can occur when incorrectly combined chemicals and compounds react with each other. These reactions can range from the release of toxic fumes and gasses, unexpected heating or expansion of the substances, to explosions and fire. It is critical that chemicals be properly labeled, containers are not reused for other purposes or substances, and strict controls are maintained to ensure the accuracy of the labeling system. Some of the requirements for an accurate labeling system include:

- Clearly printed and properly affixed labels;
- Immediate replacement of damaged, loose, or missing labels;
- Labels should include the chemical name or molecular composition, source, handling and hazard data, and the dates received, opened, and the recommended use by date.

CHEMICAL STORAGE REQUIREMENTS

When storage is being arranged for school chemicals, it is best to first check for any and all applicable Federal, State, and local storage regulations and guidelines. These are often available online or from the fire department, among other sources. The district's insurance provider should also be contacted for any guidelines concerning liability that they have. Some basic measures in regard to storage call for the substances to be kept in either closed cabinets or on heavy shelving equipped with a high enough lip to contain spills. The storage shelves should be secured to the walls and the facility itself should be well ventilated and lockable with no access permitted to students.

Chemicals are stored alphabetically according to compatibility and never by alphabetizing alone (Environmental Protection Agency, 1980).

However, the basics in regard to this are:

- Acids should be stored by themselves in a separate cabinet. Nitric acid should always be segregated by itself;
- Extremely hazardous or toxic chemicals should be stored in a separate, locked cabinet with prominent warnings displayed;
- Volatile or strongly out gassing substances must be stored in properly ventilated units;
- Flammables must be stored in approved flammables storage lockers;
- Some chemicals are sensitive to contact with water and should be stored in water tight containers and storage units;
- Additionally, some general criteria for chemical storage are as follows;
- No storage of chemicals, heavy or large containers, or liquids on high shelves or above eye level;
- No floor storage of chemicals ever;
- No storage in temporary use areas such as chemical hoods or workbenches;
- No storage in refrigerators intended for or with food or drink;
- No exposure to extreme temperature fluctuations or to direct heat.

It is important to remember that *proper* storage of chemicals is vital to prevent early degradation of the substances and to prevent mishaps, accidental ingestion, and unintended reactions. The compatibility and storage plan should be prominently displayed and all personnel with access to the storage facility should receive proper training to familiarize themselves with it.

REDUCING HAZARDOUS OR TOXIC WASTE GENERATION

All facilities that employ chemical substances and compounds in their operations produce chemical waste. School laboratories are no exception. To minimize the amount of waste generated, schools should develop waste management plans that follow applicable federal, state and local guidelines for this purpose. Schools can reduce the amount of chemical waste produced by implementing such measures as replacing hazardous chemicals with less toxic substances in classroom experiments, recycling chemicals through cyclical experiments, and using pre-packed amounts of chemicals in experiments to eliminate leftovers (Environmental Protection Agency).

CHEMICAL DISPOSAL

The safe disposal of chemicals and chemical waste is of great importance for both health and environment reasons. Chemical pollutants can remain in the environment for hundreds, if not thousands of years and can threaten the health and wellbeing of everything that comes into contact with it either directly or indirectly. Therefore, it is necessary to have a chemical disposal plan which conforms to all EPA requirements as well as any state or local statutes. Students should be cautioned not to pour chemicals down the drain or to throw chemical waste into regular receptacles. Instead, they should utilize approved waste storage containers that are properly labeled and stored in accordance with applicable rules.

CONCLUSION

A school laboratory safety program is a key component of any school's science program. Without a comprehensive, up to date, and properly followed program addressing all areas of safety in the laboratory, the management, storage, and disposal of chemicals, chemical wastes, and other potentially hazardous materials, the chance of a serious mishap resulting in injury or damage is greatly increased. Additionally, without such a program in place, schools may have increased exposure to liability and escalated insurance costs in the event of an incident which could have been prevented by the existence of a safety program.

In the 21st century, science plays an increasingly prominent role in the education of our children.

Students today are faced with a dizzying array of advances in the natural sciences, chemistry, and physics, and the challenges they face in the classroom to keep up with these advances grows by the day. To adequately prepare students for this modern world in which they cannot fully function without a firm grasp on many of these complex subjects and ideas, teachers and educators must demonstrate the "nuts and bolts" behind these concepts in both old and new ways. The ritual of the school chemistry lab has been passed on through generations of students. As with many activities, there is always an element of risk despite judicious supervision. With a well-designed safety plan in place, schools may reduce this risk even more. By replacing some of the more risk oriented experiments with computer simulations, mass demonstrations, and replacing dangerous chemicals with less toxic or hazardous substitutes, educators can further reduce the risk factor in these exercises.

TERMS & CONCEPTS

Chemical Compatibility: The stability of a chemical substance when introduced to another chemical. Chemicals are considered compatible if they mix and do not change. Chemicals that change when mixed are therefore incompatible.

Chemical Disposal: The proper disposition, disposal, or destruction of hazardous and or toxic chemical waste or residue produced by school laboratories in accordance with all applicable federal, state, and local standards, guidelines, and laws.

Chemical Hygiene Plan: A formal written plan documenting the policies, procedures, and personnel responsibilities which have been developed to help ensure that employees of a business or institution are protected in the workplace from the health hazards connected with the hazardous or toxic chemical substances or compounds used by that entity.

Chemical Tracking System: A current inventory or listing of all the chemicals being used in a school laboratory.

Environmental Protection Agency (EPA): The United States Environmental Protection Agency, the governmental entity tasked with the responsibility of overseeing the preservation of the environment and protecting human health from environmental hazards. The EPA, among other duties, develops the regulations which control the disposal of

hazardous materials and chemicals produced by laboratories.

Green Chemistry: Chemical technologies intended to reduce or eliminate the use or generation of hazardous substances in the design, manufacture, and use of chemical products (www.epa.gov).

Material Safety Data Sheets: Information sheets that contain proper procedural information needed for the handling, storing, and disposing of chemicals.

Occupational Safety & Health Administration (OSHA): The United States Occupational safety and Health Administration, the federal agency tasked with overseeing occupational health and safety by setting and enforcing workplace standards; through training, oversight, and education. OSHA standards apply to school employees; however, they do not apply to students.

Angelia Mance

BIBLIOGRAPHY

Environmental Protection Agency. (1980). *Chemical compatibility chart.* Retrieved November 11, 2007, from http://uos.harvard.edu.

Environmental Protection Agency. (2007). *Green chemistry.* Retrieved November 11, 2007, from http://epa.gov.

Kaufman, J. (1995). Your science lab: Is it a lawsuit waiting to happen? *School & College, 34,* 34.

Occupational Safety and Health Administration. (2007). Retrieved November 11, 2007, from http://osha.gov.

NSTA position statement: Liability of science educators for laboratory safety. (2010). *California Journal of Science Education, 11,* 56-59. Retrieved December 15, 2013, from EBSCO Online Database Education Research Complete.

Promote science lab safety rules to prevent injuries. (Cover story). (2006). *Inside School School Safety (LRP Publications), 10.* 4.

Roy, K. (2013). The school safety ranger. *Science Teacher, 80,* 73. Retrieved December 15, 2013, from EBSCO Online Database Education Research Complete.

Roy, K. (2013). Sizing up for safety. *Science Scope, 36,* 94-97. Retrieved December 15, 2013, from EBSCO Online Database Education Research Complete.

Roy, K. (2001). Wanted: Advocates for science laboratory safety. *Science Teacher, 68,* 8.

Stroud, L., Stallings, C., & Korbusieski, T. (2007). Implementation of a science laboratory safety program in North Carolina schools. *Journal of Chemical Health & Safety, 14,* 20-30.

U.S. Consumer Product Safety Commission. (2007). *School laboratory safety guide*. Retrieved November 12, 2007, from http://cdc.gov.

SUGGESTED READING

Ashbrook, P., Leonard, K., Reinhardt, P., (1995). *Pollution prevention and waste minimization in laboratories*. Boca Raton, FL: Lewis.

Cold Spring Harbor Laboratory Press (2007). *Safety sense: A laboratory guide* (2nd ed.). Cold Spring Harbor, NY: Cold Spring Harbor.

Glencoe Science (2001). *Life, earth, and physical science, laboratory management and safety in the science classroom*. New York, NY: McGraw-Hill.

Hassard, J., (2004). *The art of teaching science: Inquiry and innovation in middle school and high school*. New York, NY: Oxford.

Kaufman, J., (1990) *Waste disposal in academic institutions*. Chelsea, MI: Lewis.

Kwan, T,. Summers, J., Texley, K., (2004). *Investigating safely: A guide for high school teachers*. Arlington, VA: National Science Teachers Association.

Kwan, T., Texley, K., (2002). *Inquiring safely: A guide for middle school teachers*. Arlington, VA: National Science Teachers Association.

Mance, A. (2014). Laboratory Safety in Schools. *School Safety Policies and Procedures*. 95-101.

Pipitone, D., (1991). *Safe storage of laboratory chemicals* (2nd ed.). New York, NY: Wiley.

Saunders, G., (1993). *Laboratory fume hoods: A users guide*. New York, NY: Wiley.

INTERNET SAFETY

This article provides an overview of both the risks and benefits of children using the Internet to gather information and communicate with their peers. Recommendations are provided for parents and educators to help teach children Internet safety measures in schools and at home. An overview of Internet software and websites that promote children's safety online is provided as well.

KEYWORDS: Acceptable-Use Policy (AUP); Children's Internet Protection Act; Cybersafety; Internet; Internet Content Rating Association (ICRA); MySpace; Online Victimization; Sexual Solicitation

OVERVIEW

INTERNET USE AMONG CHILDREN & ADOLESCENTS

Internet usage has exploded among children and adolescents in recent years as the medium provides them with both educational and social opportunities (Young, Young, & Fullwood, 2007). According to the Child Trends Data Bank (2015), in 2003, approximately 76 percent of children had access to a computer at home, and by 2012, that figure had increased to 85 percent. Additionally, children with access to the Internet in the home rose from 42 percent in 2003 to 62 percent in 2012. Of these users, just 10 percent report using the computers for reading magazines or newspapers online, while the remainder play games or watch videos. Child Trends further reports that according to their 2009 survey,

36 percent of children report having a computer with Internet access in their bedroom and spend almost ninety minutes (in addition to school work) per day with a computer. This figure is up from just over sixty minutes in 2004 (Child Trends Data Bank).

Besides keeping an eye on the content kids access, parents and educators should also be aware of what kids do and say online so that they do not compromise their privacy or safety (Andrews, 2006). Over the past few years, social networking sites like Twitter, Facebook, and Pinterest have become enormously popular among teenagers (Andrews). Facebook, in particular, has grown at an enormous rate and reported 1.39 billion monthly active users in 2014 (Gashi & Knautz, 2015). These sites can offer many benefits to their users, but some teens may not take sufficient care in protecting their privacy or may find themselves exposed to inappropriate content. Parents and educators can use Internet control software to block youths from accessing inappropriate content, but they should also be sure to educate themselves and their children or students about Internet safety.

DANGERS OF THE INTERNET

The Internet can be an extremely useful tool at home and in the classroom, but parents and schools must be careful to monitor children's and adolescents' online activities (Dorman, 1997). The Internet does not necessarily house more predators than the real world, but online there are fewer warning signs to alert a teen that a person may be dangerous (Andrews). People may not be who they say they are, and many experts advise parents to limit their children's online friends to their real-life friends (Andrews). Children and teens can easily be exposed to online victimization, or situations in which they encounter intimidating and inappropriate sexual content, solicitation, or harassment (Dorman; Young et al.).

Though millions of people who use social networking sites are harmless, some are sexual predators. The nonprofit Internet safety organization, Enough is Enough, offers some sobering insights into online predators:

- Eighteen percent of young people use chat rooms to interact with other youth, but the majority of Internet-initiated sex crimes against children are begun in chat rooms;
- In 82 percent of online sex crimes against minors, the offender used the victim's social networking site to gather information on the victim's likes and dislikes; 65 percent use the victim's social networking site to gather home and school information; 26 percent gain information on the victim's whereabouts at a specific time;
- Less than half (44 percent) of online sexual solicitors were under the age of eighteen (Enough is Enough, 2013).

One study (Enough is Enough) estimates that one in seven youth nationwide have received online sexual solicitations and sexual solicitation of youth occurs most frequently in chat rooms, via instant or Facebook messaging, or through online gaming devices. Wolak (2008) reports that the majority of victims of Internet-initiated sex crimes in 2007 were between the ages of thirteen and fifteen.

Although anyone can be targeted by a predator, adolescents, particularly girls, are more likely to be victimized than younger children (Young et al.). Youths who share personal information, meet online acquaintances in person, or communicate in a sexual manner, as well as youths who are depressed, questioning their sexuality, or have poor family relationships are also at a greater risk (Young et al.). Additionally, the more time a youth spends on the Internet, the more likely it is that he or she will become an online victim or engage in high-risk behaviors (Young et al.).

Online harassment, or cyber bullying, defined as "willful and repeated harm inflicted through the medium of electronic text," can also harm children and teens (Hinduja & Patchin, n.d.). Thirty-four percent of youth, ages ten through fifteen, reported being harassed online, and the majority report these incidences to friends or a parent/guardian (Young et al.; Weiss, 2011). Cyber bullies harass their victims by posting insults, taunts, threats, or slanderous statements on the Internet or by directly sending them to their victims through digital communications like email, text messaging, and instant messaging (Young et al.). Because of the media's nature, these bullies can easily remain anonymous, and the psychological impact of online harassment can lead to increased levels of fear, stress, and depression among victims (Young et al.).

Hate groups may also use the Internet to promote harassment. These groups may use websites and online communications to target adolescents and spread their message to a mass amount of people (Young et al.).

Besides these very large dangers, teens also need to be careful about how they present themselves online. Social-networking sites, instant messaging, and email are where kids today hang out, gossip, and assert their independence (Andrews). The difference between real-world hang outs and cyber hang outs, however, is that cyberspace is open twenty-four hours a day and is vaster and, in some cases, much more public (Andrews). In a few widely publicized cases, teenagers have been arrested after chatting about or posting pictures of illegal activities online; colleges and employers checking an applicant's profile may also find evidence of drug use, underage drinking, or inappropriate behavior (Andrews).

WHAT IS BEING DONE TO PROMOTE INTERNET SAFETY?

The federal government has been studying the problem of child Internet safety for many years (McQuade, 2007). One result of these studies has been the passage of the Children's Internet Protection Act of 2000 (CIPA), which requires any school or library that receives federal discounts for Internet access to "have an Internet safety policy and technology protection measures in place" (Federal Communications Commission, 2001). As of 2007, approximately one-third of public libraries in the United States opted not to apply for federal Internet discounts in order to avoid CIPA restrictions (McClure & Jaeger, 2009).

The Children's Online Privacy Protection Act (COPPA) was passed in 1998, banning websites from gathering personal information from children under the age of thirteen without parental consent. COPPA has been revised twice (in 2011 and 2012) since it was put into effect in 2000. The revisions expand on and further define what it means to collect data, present data retention and deletion rules, and create additional parental notice and consent requirements (Kardell, 2011; Percival & Spruill, 2013). Agencies like the Federal Bureau of Investigation, the Department of Justice, and the National Center for Missing and Exploited Children have also created Internet safety guides and websites.

Although Facebook has been criticized for being too lax in it privacy settings (Kelly, 2008), a Carnegie Mellon study revealed that of the 540 Facebook users profiled, the majority had not altered their privacy settings, which allowed unknown users access to their personal profile information (Gross & Acquisti, 2005).

While current approaches tend to favor legislation and restriction, some groups are advocating for education. During 2007 Senate hearings, the Center for Democracy and Technology asserted that Internet safety education is "the most important step that the government can take" toward protecting children in the twenty-first century (Senate Considers Internet Safety, 2007). Similarly, during the same hearings, the American Library Association stated that, rather than further legislation, "the experiences of librarians, parents, teachers, and others continue to affirm that teaching kids how to safely navigate the World Wide Web is the best tool" (Senate Considers Internet Safety). A school safety survey conducted by researchers at Quality Education Data discovered that although most school districts across the nation block inappropriate websites from school computers, only 8 percent teach students responsible Internet usage (Bagwell, 2007).

GENERAL RECOMMENDATIONS TO PROMOTE SAFE USE OF THE INTERNET

Unfortunately, many parents and schools rely solely on online blockers to prevent children and adolescents from accessing inappropriate or dangerous content, and they seldom observe children's online activity directly (Young et al.). According to one survey of metropolitan Los Angles parents, over 60 percent had never talked with their teens about their social networking use (Andrews). Just over a third had never viewed their child's profile (Andrews). While online blockers or filtering devices can be helpful, they should not be the only line of defense, as parents need to be aware of what their children are posting and who they are talking to, as well as what they are accessing. Teachers and parents should have open and honest discussions with children to educate them about Internet victimization (Young et al.).

Parents need to be on the lookout for strangers who contact their children online, as well as observe their child's behavior for actions that might make them easy targets for predators (Andrews). Youth may pose as wild or promiscuous and post suggestive content or use provocative screen names like "sexygirl" (Andrews). Adults need to step in and help kids understand the dangerous image they may be projecting (Andrews). Teaching youth prevention strategies can help them self-monitor their time online and reduce victimization (Young et al.).

Parents should also set limits on the amount of time children can spend online and emphasize the importance of balancing Internet use with other interests and activities (Andrews). To promote safe Internet use, children and adolescents should be supervised when online (Dorman). They should also be advised to stay away from chat rooms and sites where they can easily interact with strangers, and they should be made aware of the consequences of making acquaintances online and sharing personal information (pictures, birth dates, addresses, etc.) with strangers (Dorman; Young et al.). Youths need to know how to exit a situation if victimization occurs or seems likely to occur, and reporting incidents of victimization to the police may help prevent future incidents (Young et al.). Schools should also develop and follow acceptable-use policies and procedures for student and faculty use of the Internet. (Dorman).

The National Center for Missing and Exploited Children has also suggested the following set of rules for children as they use the Internet.

- "I will not give personal information such as my address, telephone number, parents' work address/telephone number, or the name and location of my school without my parents' (teacher's) permission;
- "I will tell my parents (teacher) right away if I come across any information that makes me feel uncomfortable;

- "I will never agree to get together with someone I "meet" online without first checking with my parents. If my parents agree to the meeting, I will be sure that it is in a public place and bring my mother or father along;
- "I will never send a person my picture or anything else without first checking with my parents (teacher);
- "I will not respond to any messages that are mean or in any way make me feel uncomfortable. It is not my fault if I get a message like that. If I do, I will tell my parents (teacher) right away so they can contact the online service;
- "I will talk with my parents so we can set up rules for going online. We will decide on the time of day that I can be online, the length of time I can be online, and appropriate areas for me to visit. I will not access other areas or break these rules without their permission." (Dorman).

Parents and teachers should review these rules with children and adolescents who are planning to use the Internet (Dorman). Posting these rules near computer stations may also help remind children and adolescents how to be safe.

WEBSITES & INTERNET CONTROL SOFTWARE

Parents and schools may wish to investigate the following websites that provide information on Internet safety education and Internet control software packages. However, it should be remembered that no software provides total security.

- SafeSurf is an Internet content rating system that helps parents and schools to filter content they find inappropriate for children and adolescents. The software takes great care to distinguish between types of content (i.e., a violent news photograph meant to inform and a gratuitously violent video meant to entertain or shock) and allows users to customize their settings (Joseph, 2007; SafeSurf, n.d.);
- Net Nanny, produced by ContentWatch, Inc., is an Internet-control software that blocks children's access to inappropriate websites, put time limits on computer use, and block specific desktop PC games. Net Nanny also flags potentiall dangerous instant messaging conversations. (PC Magazine, 2010);

- Cyber, part of the Center for Safe and Responsible Internet Use, offers news and information on cyber and cyberthreats to parents and educators (Joseph; Hinduja & Patchin, n.d.);
- i-SAFE is a nonprofit foundation that aims to educate youth about safe and responsible Internet use. It works with students, parents, teachers, communities, and law enforcement to spread awareness about Internet safety and security, and offers a variety of free educational resources (Joseph; i-SAFE, Inc., n.d.);
- CyberSmart! offers online workshops geared toward online safety and security, avoiding cyber, online manners and ethics, using the Internet for effective researching, and understanding the digital challenges of the twenty-first century;
- "A Parent's Guide to Internet Safety" is an FBI handbook parents can use to minimize their children's risk for victimization, detect signs that child may be in contact with an online predator, and take action against a predator (Joseph; Federal Bureau of Investigation, n.d.);
- GetNetWise, sponsored by the Internet Education Foundation, grew out of a collaboration between public interest groups and industry leaders from companies like Google and Microsoft. Along with information on privacy and security for adults, the site also offers kids and parents child safety information and tools (Joseph; Internet Education Foundation, 2003);
- Children's Privacy, created by the Federal Trade Commission, provides parents, teachers, and kids with information on the 1998 Children's Online Privacy Protection Act. Parents and teachers can how to read a website's privacy policy and decide if they will consent to a website collecting personal information about a child. Children can learn about how to protect their personal information, and when they should ask an adult for help (Joseph; Federal Trade Commission, 2003);
- WiredSafety.org posts Internet safety information for parents, educators, and kids. Parents can learn how to monitor and understand their children's Internet use; educators can learn how to teach students Internet safety; and kids can learn how to safely use e-mail and instant messaging, as well as how to respond to cyberbullies (Andrews; Joseph; WiredSafety, n.d.).

THE COST OF INTERFERING WITH & BLOCKING INTERNET USE

Congress has discussed several bills concerning children's and adolescents' Internet safety. The Deleting Online Predators Act of 2006 and the Protecting Children in the Twenty-First Century Act, both of which have been debated since 2006, would require all public schools and libraries to block access to social networking sites and chat rooms on their computers (Andrews). The SAFE Internet Act of 2009 was introduced to promote Internet safety education and cybercrime initiatives. Although many proposed and actual Internet laws are meant to protect minors from predators, critics say that they may also prevent youths from accessing useful sites. Kids may also choose to access the sites from other computers, away from adult supervision (Andrews).

While some Internet safety "experts suggest that parents prohibit their children from using social networking sites and other online locations where predators pose a threat, others believe that these restrictions limit kids" (Tynes, 2007). Social networking can also be a good thing for some teenagers. Shy youths and those who face difficult cultural, sexual, or social issues may feel much more comfortable conversing online, and receive more support from online friends than they would from the kids around them (Andrews). Social networking can have benefits that outweigh the risks, says one advocate (Tynes). Youths can develop cognitive skills, learn to understand and tolerate different points of view, and interact with other cultures. These experiences will help young people as they grow up and move out into the "real" world (Tynes). Empowering adolescents to be safe online by increasing awareness, these critics say, will teach kids to be more sophisticated and responsible Internet users.

PROMISING OUTLOOKS

In 2007, InSafe, a European Union organization that promotes Internet safety awareness, partnered with i-SAFE, an American organization with a similar goal, to run an Internet safety competition. Students in over two hundred US and European elementary schools worked together to create projects, like posters and websites, that educate kids about safe and responsible Internet use (Greifner, 2007). Since then, InSafe has continued to hold competitions inviting children to submit videos or posters promoting the safe use of the Internet annually on Safer Internet Day.

Sexual solicitation declined from 19 percent in 2000 to 13 percent in 2005, a drop that could be attributed to increased awareness of the dangers that lurk online (Young et al.; Mitchell et al., 2013). Today, youth are less likely to interact with individuals they do not know than in past years. Research suggests that 66 percent of solicited youths reject the propositions and remove themselves from the situation by logging off or changing screen names (Young et al.; Mitchell et al.).

TERMS & CONCEPTS

Acceptable-Use Policy (AUP): An acceptable-use policy is a document which communicates the expectation that school technology will be used responsibly and exclusively for educational purposes.

Children's Internet Protection Act (CIPA): The Children's Internet Protection Act is a federal law enacted by Congress in 2000 to address concerns about access to offensive content over the Internet in schools and libraries.

Cybersafety: the term used to describe information and actions taken to help keep kids safe online.

Facebook: Facebook is a popular social networking site where users can post information, personal profiles, and photos.

Internet : Internet refers to online actions that are abusive or offensive.

The Internet Content Rating Association (ICRA): The ICRA is a nonprofit organization that allows content providers to rate their Web sites for free by completing a questionnaire.

Online Vicitimization: Online victimization is the term used to describe incidences in which children and adolescents encounter intimidating and inappropriate sexual content, solicitation, or harassment.

Sexual Solicitation: Sexual solicitation is a request to participate in sexual activities or discuss personal sexual information in person or online.

Jennifer Bouchard

BIBLIOGRAPHY

Andrews, M. (2006, September 18). Decoding MySpace. *U.S. News & World Report, 141,* 46–60. Retrieved November 12, 2007, from EBSCO Online Database Education Research Complete.

Bagwell, K. (2007, September 25). Teaching, not technology, is key to enforcing Internet safety. *Education Daily, 40,* 2. Retrieved November 12, 2007, from EBSCO Online Database Education Research Complete.

Child Trends Data Bank. (2015). *Home computer access and Internet use.* Retrieved January 19, 2016 from http://childtrends.org.

ContentWatch. (n.d.). *Net nanny.* Retrieved December 6, 2007, from http://netnanny.com.

CyberSmart Education Company. (2007). *About us.* Retrieved December 6, 2007, from http://cybersmart.org.

Dorman, S. (1997). Internet safety for schools, teachers, and parents. *Journal of School Health, 67,* 355. Retrieved November 12, 2007, from EBSCO Online Database Education Research Complete.

Enough is Enough. (2013). Internet safety 101: Educate, equip, empower. Retrieved December 21, 2013, from http://internetsafety101.org.

Family Online Safety Institute. (n.d.) *About ICRA.* Retrieved December 6, 2007, from http://fosi.org.

Federal Bureau of Investigation. (n.d.). *A parent's guide to Internet safety.* Retrieved December 3, 2007, from http://fbi.gov.

Federal Communications Commission. (2001). *Children's Internet Protection Act.* Retrieved December 6, 2007, from http://fcc.gov.

Federal Trade Commission. (2003). *Children's Privacy.* Retrieved December 21, 2013, from http://business.ftc.gov.

Gashi, L., & Knautz, K. (2015). Somebody that I used to know—Unfriending and becoming unfriended on Facebook. *Proceedings of The European Conference on E-Learning,* 583–590. Retrieved January 19, 2016, from EBSCO Online Database Education Research Complete.

Greifner, L. (2007, January 17). Students from U.S., Europe collaborate on internet safety. *Education Week, 26,* 9. Retrieved November 12, 2007, from EBSCO Online Database Education Research Complete.

Gross, Ralph & Acquisti, Alessandro. (2005). Information revelation and privacy in online social networks: The Facebook case. Retrieved December 21, 2013, from http://heinz.cmu.edu.

Hinduja, S & Patchin, J. (n.d.). *Cyber.* Retrieved November 12, 2007, from http://cyber.us.

Hockenson, Lauren, & Molla, Rani. (2013, October 30). Facebook grows daily active users by 25 percent, mobile users by 45 percent. Retrieved December 21, 2013, from http://gigaom.com.

Internet Education Foundation. (n.d.). *GetNetWise.* Retrieved December 6, 2007, from http://getnetwise.org.

i-SAFE, Inc. (n.d.). *About i-SAFE.* Retrieved December 6, 2007, from http://isafe.org.

Joseph, L. (2007). Keeping safe in cyberspace. *MultiMedia & Internet@Schools, 14,* 17–20. Retrieved November 12, 2007, from EBSCO Online Database Education Research Complete.

Kardell, Nicole. (2011, December 22). FTC will propose broader children's online privacy safeguards. *National Law Review.* Retrieved December 21, 2013, from http://natlawreview.com.

McClure, Charles R., & Jaeger, Paul T. (2009). *Public libraries and Interent service roles: Measuring and maximizing Internet services.* Chicago: American Library Association.

Kelly, Spencer. (2008, May 1). Identity 'at risk' on Facebook. Retrieved December 21, 2013, from http://news.bbc.co.uk.

Ktoridou, D., Eteokleous, N., & Zahariadou, A. (2012). Exploring parents' and children's awareness on Internet threats in relation to Internet safety. *Campus-Wide Information Systems, 29,* 133–143. Retrieved December 20, 2013, from EBSCO Online Database Education Research Complete.

Lentz, C. L., Seo, K. K., & Gruner, B. (2014). Revisiting the early use of technology: A critical shift from "how young is too young?" to "how much is 'just right'?". *Dimensions of Early Childhood, 42,* 15–23. Retrieved November 15, 2014, from EBSCO Online Database Education Research Complete.

McQuade III, S. (2007, January 5). We must educate young people about cybercrime before they start college. *Chronicle of Higher Education, 53,* B29–B31. Retrieved November 12, 2007, from EBSCO Online Database Education Research Complete.

Melgosa, A., & Scott, R. (2013). School Internet safety: More than 'block it to stop it'. *Education Digest, 79,* 46–49. Retrieved December 20, 2013, from EBSCO Online Database Education Research Complete.

Mitchell, K. J., Jones, L. M., Finkelhor, D., & Wolak, J. (2013). Understanding the decline in unwanted online sexual solicitations for U.S. youth 2000–2010: Findings from three youth Internet safety surveys. *Child Abuse & Neglect, 37,* 1225–1236. Retrieved December 20, 2013, from EBSCO Online Database Education Research Complete.

Office of the Press Secretary. (2002). *Increasing online safety for America's children.* Retrieved December 6, 2007, from http://whitehouse.gov.

PC Magazine. Net Nanny 6.5. Retrieved December 21, 2013, from http://pcmag.com.

Percival, Lynn C., & Spruill, Poyner. (2013, July 1). New Children's Online Privacy Protection Act (COPPA) rule now in effect. *National Law Review.* Retrieved December 21, 2013, from http://natlawreview.com.

SafeSurf. (n.d.) *The SafeSurf Internet rating standard.* Retrieved December 6, 2007, from http://safesurf.com.

Senate considers internet safety. (2007). *American Libraries, 38*, 23–24. Retrieved November 12, 2007, from EBSCO Online Database Education Research Complete.

Tucker, C. (2015). Creating a safe digital space. *Educational Leadership, 73*(2), 82–83. Retrieved January 19, 2016, from EBSCO Online Database Education Research Complete.

Tynes, B. (2007). Internet safety gone wild? Sacrificing the educational and psychosocial benefits of online social environments. *Journal of Adolescent Research, 22,* 575–584. Retrieved November 12, 2007, from EBSCO Online Database Education Research Complete.

Waterman, C. (2014). Online safety still not good enough but who cares enough to act?. *Education Journal,* 17–18. Retrieved November 15, 2014, from EBSCO Online Database Education Research Complete.

Weiss, Daniel. (2011, April 8). Cyber and online harassment. Retrieved December 21, 2013, from http://myrocktoday.org.

WiredSafety. (n.d.) *WiredSafety.* Retrieved December 6, 2007, from http://wiredsafety.org.

Wolak, J., Finkelhor, D., Mitchell, K. J., & Ybarra, M. L. (2008). Online 'predators' and their victims: Myths, realities, and implications for prevention and treatment. *American Psychologist 63,* 111–128.

Young, A., Young, A., & Fullwood, H. (2007). Adolescent online victimization. *Prevention Researcher, 14,* 8–9. Retrieved November 12, 2007, from EBSCO Online Database Education Research Complete.

November 12, 2007, from EBSCO Online Database Education Research Complete.

Blau, I. (2011). Application use, online relationship types, self-disclosure, and Internet abuse among children and youth: Implications for education and Internet safety programs. *Journal of Educational Computing Research, 45,* 95–116. Retrieved December 20, 2013, from EBSCO Online Database Education Research Complete.

Corzine pushes for internet safety. (2007). *District Administration, 43,* 14. Retrieved November 12, 2007, from EBSCO Online Database Education Research Complete.

Devaney, L. (2014). How do teachers, parents approach online safety?. *Eschool News, 17,* 30. Retrieved November 15, 2014, from EBSCO Online Database Education Research Complete.

Durflinger, D. (2015). Balancing student empowerment with online safety. *School Administrator, 72*(10), 11. Retrieved January 16, 2016, from EBSCO Online Database Education Research Complete.

Fraser, D. (2007). Proactive prevention. *American School & University, 79,* SS49–SS51. Retrieved November 12, 2007, from EBSCO Online Database Education Research Complete.

Hinduja, S & Patchin, J. (n.d.). *Cyber.* Retrieved November 12, 2007, from http://cyber.us.

Vitalaki, E., Tsouvelas, P., & Tsouvelas, G. (2012). Factors influencing parental control for the safe and pedagogical Internet use among primary school students. *Problems of Education in the 21st century, 42,* 125–135. Retrieved December 20, 2013, from EBSCO Online Database Education Research Complete.

SUGGESTED READING

Abram, S. (2007). Shooting themselves in the foot. *MultiMedia & Internet@Schools, 14,* 17–19. Retrieved

DRESS CODES AND UNIFORMS IN PUBLIC SCHOOLS

This article discusses dress codes and school uniforms in K–12 public schools in the United States. While virtually every public and private school in the world has either an informal or formal dress code stipulating what students can and cannot wear to school, a required school uniform is not universal. However, in many parts of the world, from Australia to Malaysia and New Zealand to Great Britain, school uniforms are a part of life for public and private school students. In the United States, school uniforms were once the exclusive domain of private and religious schools, but since the 1990s they have been hailed as a solution to issues surrounding drugs, violence, and academic shortcomings afflicting many public

schools, particularly in urban areas. Many of the most significant constitutional challenges to public school uniforms have been rejected by the courts, and many parents and administrators credit them with improvements in school safety and academic performance. Critics allege that dress codes and school uniforms violate First Amendment guarantees of freedom of speech and freedom of religion, and they maintain that the results credited to dress codes and school uniforms can be explained better in other ways.

KEYWORDS: Dress codes; First Amendment;. Freedom of Religion; Freedom of Speech; Private Schools; Public Schools; School Safety; School Uniforms

OVERVIEW

School uniforms are nothing new. The practice of requiring students to wear a uniform dates back at least to the sixteenth century in England, where students at the University of Cambridge were required to wear them as a way to halt the spread of new fashions in the hallowed halls of learning (Brunsma, 2004).

Historic Relevance

Historically, claims Dussel (2005), school uniforms in the United States in the nineteenth and twentieth centuries were used to keep control over the bodies of racial minorities. The point was to ensure that ethnic and racial minorities were uniform with respect to accepted cultural mores:

From early onwards, such [school uniform] policies were tied to the disciplining of 'unruly,' 'savage,' 'untamed' bodies, that is, the bodies of those who were not able to perform self-regulation or self-government: women, African American, American Indian, poor classes, immigrants, toddlers or infants. In nineteenth- and early twentieth-century United States, American Indians and African Americans were the privileged targets of close surveillance in terms of what to wear and when to wear it. In particular, the introduction of uniforms in Federal Indian Boarding schools meant that tribal attire and moccasins were forbidden and strict measures were enforced to ensure that children wore 'civilized', Western clothes, including underwear (Dussel).

Over time, school uniforms became associated with the children of power and privilege. They became a symbol of the opportunities that, at least according to some Marxist-inspired critics, were not available to those of the American middle and lower classes (Brunsma).

Whatever the truth of such analyses, it is beyond dispute that dress codes in general, and school uniforms became a prominent topic within the larger national discussion on education reform that took place in the 1980s and 1990s. With the decades-long distraction of the Cold War having ended and the recent upheaval caused by international terrorism, the 1990s was a time when American political and educational leaders turned inward and began to take stock of the public education system. What they saw—low academic standards, rising violence, and disenchanted teachers—was less than satisfactory. In 1983, the National Commission on Excellence in Education proclaimed in the report, "A Nation at Risk" that "the educational foundations of our society are presently being eroded by a rising tide of mediocrity" ("A Nation at Risk," 1983).

On the other hand, private and religious schools in America were continuing to provide quality education and seemed largely immune to the systemic problems afflicting public schools. One of the most visible symbols of the private school, at least to many Americans and their elected officials, was the school uniform. While few considered them to be a panacea, parents, teachers, politicians, and school administrators began to see school uniforms as perhaps part of the answer to the problems afflicting America's public schools. The first known public elementary school in the United States to adopt a school uniform policy was Cherry Hill Elementary School in inner-city Baltimore in 1987.

The Long Beach Experiment

In 1994, the public school system in Long Beach, California, Unified School District was the first school district in the nation to adopt school uniforms for the 60,000 students in its 60 elementary schools and 15 middle schools, and Long Beach school officials then expanded the program to high schools as well. By the end of 1995, the school crime rate fell by 36 percent. In 1999, five years after the school uniform policy was implemented, its correlation with school-based crime was evident:

The quantitative outcomes of the policy have been remarkable. Crime report summaries for the five-year post-uniform policy period reflect that school crime overall had dropped approximately 86 percent, even though K–8 student enrollment increased 14 percent. The five categories of school crime where comparisons can be made between 1993 levels and 1999 levels are: (a) sex offenses down 93 percent (from 57 to 4 offenses); (b) robbery/extortion down 85 percent (from 34 to 5 cases); (c) selling or using chemical substances down 48 percent (from 71 to 37 cases); (d) weapons or look-a-likes down 75 percent (from 145 to 36 cases); and (e) dangerous devices down 96 percent (from 46 to 2 cases) (LBUSD, 1999; Lopez, 2003).

The apparent success of the Long Beach experiment attracted the notice of the Clinton Administration. Attorney General Janet Reno said in December 1995 that President Clinton believed

1101

that if uniforms can help fight school violence, they should be supported (as cited in "Two Cheers," 1995). According to Brunsma (2004), it was Clinton's January 1996 State of the Union Address that initiated a resurgence of interest in public school uniforms. Early in his speech, Clinton said, "I challenge all our schools to teach character education, to teach good values and good citizenship. And if it means that teenagers will stop killing each other over designer jackets, then our public schools should be able to require their students to wear school uniforms" (Clinton, 1996).

Clinton's speech touched on what was perceived to be the strongest argument for instituting a school uniform policy: the safety of teachers and students. In adopting a standard uniform, students would not be able to use clothes as a sign of power and privilege.

Reasons to Adopt School Uniforms

Adopting school uniforms also eliminated gang colors: Gangs would use middle schools as recruitment centers, and members of rival gangs would proclaim their allegiance to the gang by wearing the gang's particular colors. According to Holding (2007), one school that revised its dress code to prohibit gang colors, Redwood Middle School in Napa Valley, California, saw palpable results. The school principal believed the uniforms were the direct catalyst for improved safety on campus.

Curiously, dress codes and school uniforms have found their most vocal advocates among minority groups, especially African Americans, who are most directly and adversely impacted by school violence and declining educational opportunities. According to Dussel, many African American and Hispanic leaders saw school uniforms as a way to move, albeit symbolically, beyond a politics of failure and victimization toward a new day in which they reclaimed their schools and embraced their promise of a bright tomorrow:

> School uniforms are being defended by minority leaders in the African American and Latino communities as a way to construct collective identities and generate a new consensus on the need for better schooling.... Using other scholars' views of minority leaders' strategies, they could be read as part of a democratic movement to shape schooling as more respondent and sensitive to demands for recognition and social mobility (Dussel).

At the end of the 1980s, fewer than 1 percent of elementary schools had uniforms. By the 1999–2000 school year, the number rose to 15 percent. By 2008, major cities such as Atlanta, Boston, Chicago, Dallas/Fort Worth, Detroit, Miami, New York, Houston, New Orleans, Philadelphia, and Washington, D.C. had a school uniform policy in the majority of their public schools. According to the National Association of Elementary School Principals (NAESP), the fraction of American public schools requiring school uniforms, or planning to implement such a requirement, rose from 3 percent in 1997 to 49 percent in 2013 (National Association of Elementary School Principals, 2013).

Political Implications

Even in those schools and school districts that did not adopt school uniforms, political rumbling about a "rising tide of mediocrity" of public schools meant that existing dress codes were closely scrutinized to ensure that students were in a safe environment that was most conducive to learning. Within public school districts, 40 percent had dress codes in place by 1994 (Tyson, 1996). Milford High School in Milford, Massachusetts, is one of many schools that reworked its dress code. The school's principal at the time, John Brucato, outlined the school's clothing policy in 2005, which is indicative of the philosophy behind many dress codes in the nation:

> We ask our students to dress and groom themselves as individuals with a sense of responsibility and self-respect. So, it's not a matter of what you must wear; it's more of a matter of what we don't feel is appropriate. Specifically, if it becomes disruptive, offensive, threatening, or provocative to others, is vulgar, displays tobacco or alcohol advertising, profanity, racial slurs, has disruptive images of gang-related symbols (as cited in Anderson, n.d.).

By 2013, the Milford High School dress code had been adjusted to reflect a focus on the expectation of additional schooling or a future career for students after graduation from high school. The message, while more succinct, is much the same as it was eight years previously:

> "The Dress Code of Milford High School is designed to help students recognize choices regarding attire that would be appropriate in their future workplace

as well as in an educational setting. Students are expected to dress, groom, and attire themselves in a manner that is not potentially dangerous, does not distract others or disrupt education, and does not convey a message contrary to District policy" (Milford High School, 2013).

Like school uniforms, contemporary school dress codes are a product of concern over what's perceived to be the rising tide of student-on-student violence in public schools, epitomized by such well-publicized public school shootings such as that perpetrated at Columbine High School in Colorado in 1999. At the turn of the twenty-first century, many public schools, with the support of parents, decided to err on the side of caution when it came to student safety. To do this, they often had to fly in the face of popular fads: if skin-flashing styles were the scourge of schools a few years ago, more covered-up looks are the bane of today's dress codes.

Educators' attention has shifted from bra straps and bare midriffs to safety and security. Hoodie pouches and cargo pants pockets have proven handy hiding spots for school contraband—from the dangerous (weapons) to the distracting (cell phones and iPods)—so administrators are prohibiting them (Breitman & Barker, 2007).

Some education officials argue that dress codes are a losing battle because they invariably ban some constitutionally protected forms of student expression. Better, officials say, to opt for a proper school uniform. "You'd be amazed at the amount of time administrators have been spending on what kids are wearing to school," said Susan Galletti of the National Association of Secondary School Principals. "With uniforms, all that is eliminated, and they can spend more time on teaching and learning" (cited in Wingert & Pan, 1999).

APPLICATIONS: HOW TO IMPLEMENT A SCHOOL UNIFORM OR DRESS CODE POLICY

No decision about school uniform or dress codes is ever made in a cultural, historical, or political vacuum. Speaking particularly about school uniforms, Howard Hurwitz (1997), the former principal of the Long Island City High School, noted that it's important not to undersell or oversell them. He believes any public school that seeks to follow the example of parochial schools where uniforms are a tradition should seek prior involvement of parents. Assurance

of maximum cooperation must be obtained before announcing a school uniform policy, and "uniforms would be a step in the direction of restoring school discipline, but they are not a panacea" (Hurwitz).

Guidelines

With support from the Clinton Administration, the US Department of Education published guidelines in 1996 for any public school wishing to implement a school uniform policy, and some of the advice applies equally to public schools wishing to update their existing dress code:

- Get parents involved from the beginning;
- Protect students' religious expression;
- Protect students' other rights of expression;
- Determine whether to have a voluntary or mandatory school-uniform policy;
- When a mandatory policy is adopted, determine whether to have an opt-out provision;
- Do not require students to wear a message;
- Assist families that need financial help;
- Treat school uniforms as part of an overall safety program (U.S. Department of Education, 1996).

Generally speaking, the more input school officials can receive from parents and the wider community, the better. A transparent process is often the best way to avoid future problems.

VIEWPOINTS
Do School Uniforms Work?

Much has been written regarding the benefits and demerits of school uniforms and dress codes. Firmin, Smith & Perry (2006) summarize the work of many researchers:

Although there have been surprisingly few methodical research studies assessing the outcomes of uniform policies, some data suggests lowered violence (Gursky, 1996), gang influence (Wade & Stafford, 2003), and improved attendance (Gentile & Imberman, 2009) and academic performance in students (Elder, 1999; Pate, 1999; Gentile & Imberman). However, critics (Wilkins, 1999) suggest that the successes of the independent variable in the studies (uniform policies) are confounded. That is, such schools show improvement due to variables such as increased teacher enforcement and involvement with students as well as parental involvement with the school process and system.

Advocates and critics alike agree that creating a sense of order (Bruchey, 1998; Brunner, 2006), cohesion (Tooms, 2002), and a positive school climate (Murray, 1997) are essential goals for successful education. However, the debate rages as to whether or not a school uniform policy produces those ends, and if the policy does, then is it the most productive and least restrictive means of doing so? Brunsma argues persuasively that there is no clear answer to these complex issues.

A decade of research seems to indicate what even supporters of school uniforms readily acknowledge—that school uniforms are not a panacea, but they can be one ingredient in a district's recipe for improved school safety and academics.

Free Speech versus School Safety

By implementing a school uniform policy or revisiting their dress codes, public school officials inevitably walk a Constitutional tightrope in balancing student First Amendment free speech and expression protections against the "compelling" government interest to create an environment for students and teachers that's safe for learning.

During the Vietnam War era, the US Supreme Court led by Chief Justice Earl Warren took a liberal view of student rights to protest against the war; the justices were less likely than those on later courts to identify a compelling government interest in curtailing student expression. The seminal case involving student self-expression during this time was *Tinker v. Des Moines School District* (1969), where the court ruled that a student had the right to wear a black armband in school as a legitimate form of political protest. The decision, and the ambiguous court rulings that followed in the 1970s, had a chilling effect on the implementation of stricter school dress codes (McCarthy, 2001).

With changes in the makeup of the Supreme Court in the 1980s, however, the justices were more willing to construe the compelling interests of school officials in broader terms. This meant that dress codes in the 1980s and 1990s were more likely to pass Constitutional muster. In *Bethel Schools v. Fraser* (1986), the newly constituted Court, which included President Ronald Reagan's first nominee, limited the scope of *Tinker* to exclude protections on vulgar student speech. In 2001, the US 5th Circuit Court

of Appeals ruled unanimously in *Canady v. Bossier Parish School Board* that the school board in Louisiana did not violate the First Amendment rights of students when it implemented a parish-wide dress code. "This purpose is in no way related to the suppression of student speech," the three-judge panel wrote. "Although students are restricted from wearing clothing of their choice at school, students remain free to wear what they want after school hours" (cited in eSchool News, 2001).

Legal Challenges

School uniforms and dress codes continue to face legal challenges, however. For example, in July 2007 Napa County Superior Court Judge Raymond Guadagni ruled that the nine-year-old dress code policy of Redwood Middle School was unconstitutional because, as written, it unduly restricted the free speech rights of the students and was interpreted in a way that did not serve obvious government interests. In his injunction against the dress code policy, Guadagni explained why he felt the dress code was too strict:

> Under this attire policy, the student plaintiffs have been disciplined for wearing, inter alia, blue jeans, socks with the image of Winnie-the-Pooh's Tigger character, an American Cancer Society pink ribbon for breast cancer awareness, a Vintage High School sweatshirt, a backpack with the brand name "Jansport" written in red, a heart sticker on Valentine's Day, a T-shirt with the words "D.A.R.E. to resist drugs and violence," and a t-shirt reading "Jesus Freak" (Guadagni, 2007).

Guadagni threw out the district's dress code, but he didn't rule on the question of whether dress codes are inherently unconstitutional.

Courts have also ruled that a student has the right to wear a 'Straight Pride' shirt in a Minnesota high school (Education USA, 2002). In 2005 in Maryland, a student was prohibited from attending his high school graduation because he wore a bolo tie, a symbol of his American Indian heritage, but later received an apology from the school (Honawar, 2005). In 2006, a male Missouri student received an apology for not being permitted to wear a kilt to a school dance ("Student who wore," 2006), and in 2010, two middle school students in Pennsylvania were suspended for wearing breast cancer awareness bracelets with wording that was interpreted by the school as lewd. A federal appeals court ruled in 2013 that the school could not enforce the ban on the bracelets because the wording, in its support for national breast-cancer awareness, was protected as free speech (Hoevel, 2013). Similarly, the Ninth Circuit Court of Appeals struck down the mandatory uniform policy of Roy Gomm Elementary School of Washoe County, Nevada, in February 2014 on the basis that its printed motto "compels speech" (Walsh, 2014).

Religious Issues

An important dimension of the debate over public school dress codes and uniforms are the limitations put on outward expressions of religious faith by students. As noted above, the US Department of Education recognizes the well-established legal principle that public schools must make reasonable accommodation of students' religious beliefs.

Some of the most well-publicized cases of religious expression have involved female students wearing head scarves. After legal action was brought by a female Muslim student, an Oklahoma public school district allowed her to wear a head scarf (Bradley, 2004). A female Muslim student attending a Regina Catholic High School in Euclid, Ohio, was banned from school because she refused to remove her head scarf, but was then readmitted under orders from officials in the diocese (Church & State, 2003). In 2011, a sixth grader from Nebraska was told she could not wear her rosary to school because rosaries were a symbol in that area of gang affiliation (Hoevel).

In 1995 US Secretary of Education Richard W. Riley expressed the essential relationship between dress codes and constitutional protection of religious liberty:

Students generally have no Federal right to be exempted from religiously-neutral and generally applicable school dress rules based on their religious beliefs or practices; however, schools may not single out religious attire in general, or attire of a particular religion, for prohibition or regulation. Students may display religious messages on items of clothing to the same extent that they are permitted to display other comparable messages. Religious messages may not be singled out for suppression, but rather are subject to the same rules as generally apply to comparable messages (Riley, 1995).

Given the seriousness with which they view any infringement upon students' religious liberty, courts have also shown a willingness to throw out dress codes rather than limit a student's right to religious expression, even if the codes have the greater goal of promoting school safety. Citing decades of court decisions, the Anti-Defamation League summarizes the case law:

A ban on gang-related attire cannot restrict the wearing of religious symbols and will not be upheld where there is no evidence of disruption that justifies infringement on students' religiously motivated symbolic speech. In general, gang-related prohibitions on dress have not fared well in the Courts. Indeed, they have been held to be void for vagueness in a number of circumstances.

As schools consider changing their dress codes or implementing a school uniform policy, they must make reasonable accommodation to students' religious beliefs—and be prepared to prove that any limits placed on religious expression are entirely incidental.

TERMS & CONCEPTS

Dress codes: Primarily written statements of what a school views as acceptable and unacceptable clothing and accessories to wear when attending school.

First Amendment: The first amendment to the US Constitution, stipulating several fundamental freedoms enjoyed by Americans, including students.

Freedom of Religion: A freedom enjoyed by Americans in light of a clause in the First Amendment stating that "Congress shall make no law respecting an establishment of religion, or prohibiting the free exercise thereof."

Freedom of Speech: A freedom enjoyed by Americans in light of a clause in the First Amendment stating that "Congress shall make no law … abridging the freedom of speech."

Private Schools: K–12 schools that are privately funded.

Public Schools: K–12 schools that are publicly funded.

School Safety: The objective reality and subjective perception that students and faculty are secure in their person and possessions.

School Uniforms: A certain type of clothing, typically of certain colors, that must be worn by all students.

Matt Donnelly

BIBLIOGRAPHY

Anderson, W. (n.d.). *School dress codes and uniform policies.* ERIC Clearinghouse on Educational Management. Retrieved July 7, 2007, from the ERIC Clearinghouse on Educational Management:

Bradley, A. (2004). Oklahoma district settles lawsuit over head scarf. *Education Week, 23,* 4.

Breitman, R., & Barker, O. (2006). Hoodies, cargos aren't going back to school. *USA Today, August 17, 2006.* Retrieved July 5, 2007 from EBSCO Online Database Academic Search Premier.

Brunsma, D. L. (2004). *The school uniform movement and what it tells us about American education: A symbolic crusade.* Lanham, MD. Rowman & Littlefield.

Buesing, M. (2011). Dress code adoption: A year's worth of steps. *School Administrator, 68,* 36–37. Retrieved December 20, 2013, from EBSCO Online Database Education Research Complete.

Catholic school bars Muslim student's head scarf. (2003). *Church & State, 56,* 21. Retrieved July 5, 2007, from EBSCO Online Database Education Research Complete.

Clinton, B. (1996). *State of the Union: Address before a joint session of the Congress on the State of the Union,* 1 PUB. PAPERS 79, 81. Retrieved July 7, 2007, from the U.S. National Archives and Records Administration, http://clinton2.nara.gov.

Court ruling favors school uniforms. (2001). Retrieved July 7, 2007, from eSchool News http://eschoolnews.com/news/showstory.cfm?ArticleID=2379.

D'Anastasio, C. & StudentNation. (2014, August 27). Girls speak out against sexist school dress codes [Blog post]. Retrieved October 7, 2014, from http://thenation.com.

Deane, S. (2015). Dressing diversity: Politics of difference and the case of school uniforms. *Philosophical Studies in Education, 46,* 111–120. Retrieved December 14, 2016, from EBSCO Online Database Education Source.

Dunford, J. (2014). How to crack the dress code. *Times Educational Supplement,* (5091), 42–43. Retrieved October 6, 2014, from EBSCO Online Database Education Research Complete.

Dussel, I. (2005). When appearances are not deceptive: A Comparative History of school uniforms in Argentina and the United States (nineteenth-twentieth centuries). *Paedagogica Historica, 4* (1/2), 179-195. Retrieved July 5, 2007, from EBSCO Online Database Education Research Complete.

Firmin, M., Smith, S., & Perry, L. (2006). School uniforms: A qualitative analysis of aims and accomplishments at two Christian schools. *Journal of Research on Christian Education, 15,* 143–168. Retrieved July 5, 2007, from EBSCO Online Database Education Research Complete.

Galley, M. (2004). Court blocks school ban on weapons images. *Education Week, 23,* 6. Retrieved July 5, 2007, from EBSCO Online Database Education Research Complete.

Gentile, Elizabetta, & Imberman, Scott A. (2009, March 4). Dressed for success: Do school uniforms improve student behavior, attendance, and achievement? Retrieved December 21, 2013, from http://uh.edu.

Guadagni, R. (2007). *Scott et al. v. Napa Valley Unified School District: Opinion and order granting a preliminary injunction.* Superior Court for the State of California, Napa County. Retrieved July 6, 2007, from The First Amendment Center, http://aclunc.org.

Hoevel, Ann. (2013, August 14). When school clothes lead to suspension. *CNN Living: Schools of Thought.* Retrieved December 21, 2013, from http://cnn.com.

Holding, R. (2007). Speaking up for themselves. *Time, 169,* 65–67. Retrieved July 5, 2007, from EBSCO Online Database Business Source Complete.

Honawar, V. (2005). Student wearing bolo tie seeks apology from district. *Education Week, 24,* 4. Retrieved July 5, 2007, from EBSCO Online Database Education Research Complete.

Hurwitz, H. (1997). School uniforms: No panacea, but would help. *Human Events, 53,* 15. Retrieved July 5, 2007, from EBSCO Online Database Academic Search Premier.

Judge allows student to wear 'Straight Pride' shirt. (2002). *Education USA* (Aspen Publishers Inc.), Retrieved July 5, 2007, from EBSCO Online Database Education Research Complete.

Lopez, R. A. (2003). Long Beach Unified School District Uniform Initiative: A prevention- intervention strategy for urban schools. *Journal of Negro Education* (Fall 2003). Retrieved July 7, 2007, from http://findarticles.com.

Lunenburg, F. C. (2011). Can schools regulate student dress and grooming in school?. *FOCUS On Colleges, Universities & Schools, 6,* 1–4. Retrieved October 6, 2014, from EBSCO Online Database Education Research Complete.

McCarthy, M. M. (2001). Restrictions on student attire: Dress codes and uniforms. *Educational Horizons, 79,* 155–157.

Milford High School. (2013). Milford high school student–parent handbook. Retrieved December 21, 2013, from http://milfordpublicschools.com.

Modigliani, L. (2013). Fashion police. (cover story). *Scholastic News—Edition 5/6,* 81 (23/24), 4–5. Retrieved December 13, 2013, from EBSCO Online Database Education Research Complete.

National Association of Elementary School Principals. (2002). *Public school uniforms fact sheet.* Retrieved July 8, 2007, from National Association of Elementary School Principals, http://naesp.org.

National Association of Elementary School Principals. (2013, August). The right fit: Principals on school uniforms. *Communicator 32.* Retrieved October 6, 2014, from the National Association of Elementary School Principals, https://www.naesp.org.

National Commission on Excellence in Education. (1983). *A nation at risk: The imperative for educational reform.* Retrieved July 8, 2007, from the U.S. Department of Education, http://ed.gov.

Riley, R.W. (2005). *Letter to parents.* Retrieved July 7, 2007 from U.S. Department of Education, http://ed.gov.

Should schools require uniforms? (2015). *Scholastic News, Edition 4, 78*(3), 7. Retrieved from EBSCO Online Database Education Research Complete.

Smith, N. (2012). Eliminating gender stereotypes in public school dress codes: The necessity of respecting personal preference. *Journal of Law & Education, 41,* 251–259. Retrieved December 20, 2013, from EBSCO Online Database Education Research Complete.

Student who wore Scottish kilt receives apology from school. (2006). *Education Week, 25,* 6. Retrieved July 5, 2007, from EBSCO Online Education Research Complete Database.

Two cheers for plaid skirts and ties. (1995). *U.S. News & World Report, 119,* 18. Retrieved July 5, 2007, from EBSCO Online Database Business Source Complete.

US Department of Education. (1996). *Manual on school uniforms.* Retrieved December 21, 2013, from http://listserv.ed.gov.

Walsh, M. (2014, February 14). 9th Circuit casts doubt on policy requiring school uniform with motto [Blog post]. Retrieved October 7, 2014, from http://blogs.edweek.org.

Wingert, P., & Pan, E. (1999, October 4). Uniforms rule. *Newsweek, 134,* 72. Retrieved July 5, 2007, from EBSCO Online Database Business Source Complete.

SUGGESTED READING

Burtka, A. T. (2015). Are school uniforms a good fit? *Education Update, 57*(10), 2–3. Retrieved December 14, 2016, from EBSCO Online Database Education Source.

Cruz, B.C. (2001). *School dress codes: A pro/con issue.* Berkeley Heights, NJ: Enslow Publishers.

DeMitchell, T. A., Fossey, R. (2015). *The challenges of mandating school uniforms in the public schools: Free speech, research, and policy.* New York, NY: Rowman & Littlefield.

Dowling-Sendor, B. (2005, August). What Not to Wear. *American School Board Journal, 192,* 33–34. Retrieved July 5, 2007, from EBSCO Online Database Education Research Complete.

LaPoint, V., & Holloman, L. (1993, March). Dress codes and uniforms in urban schools. *Education Digest, 58,* 32. Retrieved July 5, 2007, from EBSCO Online Database Education Research Complete.

Russo, C. J., & Eckes, S. (2012). *School discipline and safety.* Thousand Oaks: Sage Publications. Retrieved October 6, 2014, from EBSCO Online Database eBook Collection (EBSCOhost).

Schachter, R. (2005, May). Do Clothes Make the Student?. *District Administration, 41,* 46–49. Retrieved July 5, 2007, from EBSCO Online Database Education Research Complete.

Swafford, M., Jolley, L., & Southward, L. (2011). The student dress code debate (Part II). *Techniques: Connecting Education & Careers, 86,* 10–11. Retrieved December 20, 2013, from EBSCO Online Database Education Research Complete.

Tyson, A. (1996, April 12). Schools fight gang colors by pushing uniform gray. *Christian Science Monitor, 88,* 3. Retrieved July 5, 2007, from EBSCO Online Database Academic Search Premier.

Walmsley, A. (2011). What the United Kingdom can teach the United States about school uniforms. *Phi Delta Kappan, 92,* 63–66. Retrieved December 20, 2013, from EBSCO Online Database Education Research Complete.

Zirkel, P. (2005). Dress codes: An update. *Principal, 85,* 10–11. Retrieved July 5, 2007 from EBSCO Online Database Education Research Complete.

GANG INVOLVEMENT

This article gives in-depth information on gang activity in the U.S. and explores the causes of gang membership and examines several studies that have found correlations between gang membership and various life circumstances. It also looks at the questions of whether economic incentive is a factor in gang membership and whether or not peer pressure increases violent crimes among gang members. The article concludes by exploring various experts' proposals for reducing the amount of youth joining gangs in America.

KEYWORDS: At-risk Youth; Bureau of Alcohol, Tobacco, Firearms, & Explosives (ATF); Gangs; Immigration & Customs Enforcement Agency (ICE); Juvenile Delinquency; National Longitudinal Survey of Youth (NLSY97); Office of Juvenile Justice Delinquency

Prevention (JJDP); Special Weapons & Tactics (SWAT); Violent Crime Index (VCI)

OVERVIEW
HISTORY, CAUSES & MEMBERS OF GANGS

American youth becoming involved in gangs is not a new phenomenon. The first documented youth gang was in the late 1700s in New York, so gangs have been part of American culture for well over two centuries (Arinde, 2006). Most of the youth who get involved with gangs come from poor neighborhoods in large cities such as New York, Chicago, Los Angeles, etc. Seals (2009) expresses the general consensus on gangs thus:

For the past 80 years, ethnographic research has linked the behavioral patterns of the urban under-privileged to street gang formation and proliferation. This literature shows that gang activity is most common among impoverished young males and concludes that gang participation is the manifestation of greater societal pressures on these individuals.

Kingsbury (2008) also notes that "gangs are perpetuated by a cycle of despair that is nearly impossible to break" and gives us a revealing statistic. As of a 2013 report by the US Centers for Disease Control and Prevention, homicide was the main cause of death for young black men between the ages of 15 and 34. There are of course historical reasons that many African Americans ended up in impoverished big-city ghettos where gangs proliferate, but gangs are by no means only a phenomenon among African Americans. Gangs arise from every ethnicity in America, and we should examine some studies and reliable statistics in order to get a clearer picture of the problem of gangs in America.

Obtaining a clear picture can be difficult, however. Kingsbury points out that "gauging the true scope of the gang problem is difficult, chiefly because law enforcement lacks a common definition of a gangster or what makes a particular crime gang-related." Captain Eric Adams, who has worked for years in New York City law enforcement, points out an additional problem in gathering accurate information on gangs. He asserts that, in New York, "The police department won't properly classify certain crimes as gang-related, and so you don't know if there is an increase or decrease in the crime rate ... It's a public relations exercise. They think if they don't say it, then it's not happening" (cited in Arinde). An important study that attempts to gather accurate information on gang activity in America is known as the National Longitudinal Survey of Youth (NLSY97), which began collecting data annually from 1997. That study gives the following definition for the concept of gang-involvement:

By gangs, we mean a group that hangs out together, wears gang colors or clothes, has set clear boundaries of its territory or turf, protects its members and turf against other rival gangs through fighting or threats (cited in Seals).

GANG MEMBERSHIP

According to the 2011 National Gang Threat Assessment by the FBI, around 1.4 million active street, prison, and motorcycle gang members operate in the U.S., and these gang members belong to more than 33,000 different gangs across the country. However, the FBI also estimates a significant percentage of communities with gangs claim they do not have a problem with gangs when, in reality, they do. "It's a denial bred from either fear or stigma, according to the FBI" (Kingsbury). Seals argues that street gangs have grown to become "an epidemic problem in the United States." Citing other researchers, Seals observes that gangs are probably the main distributors of all illegal drugs, and most adolescents who commit murders in American cities are members of gangs.

Voisin et al. (2008) gathered data on gang activity in America, and their findings make it quite clear that there has been a significant rise in young women joining gangs. Voisin writes, "Male adolescents were equally as likely as female adolescents to belong to a gang." There has also been a significant increase in the female violent crime rate in the United States. In 1980, "the male Violent Crime Index rate was 8.3 times that of the female rate, by 2003, the male rate declined 26%, whereas the female rate increased 47% so that the male rate was only 4.2 times that of the female rate." Their conclusion is that female adolescents have been "closing the gap with male adolescents in terms of being arrested and committing more violent crimes." As for the cause of this significant increase in both female gang membership and female violent crimes, Voisin et al. cite that more girls are committing violent crimes from "negative peer influences, sexual abuse, dysfunctional families, and living in neighborhoods characterized by few or no viable educational opportunities, violence, and poverty."

In this original study, Voisin finds that "female adolescents were more likely to witness family violence, suggesting that for some of these girls, being raised in a dysfunctional family, coupled with community violence, may play some role in their gang involvement."

COMMON CHARACTERISTICS

There is also a relationship between youth being arrested and youth being part of gangs, though the number of arrested youth who belong to gangs is difficult to estimate. Voisin et al. cite statistics from other sources that help us to see a clearer picture:

> [Prior to 1999,] approximately 2.5 million youths are arrested (Snyder, 2003), and an additional 1.8 million cases are referred to juvenile courts (Puzzanchera, Stahl, Finnegan, Tierney, & Snyder, 2003). Furthermore, an average of 109,000 youths (age 18 and younger) are incarcerated daily (Snyder). Incarceration rates, however, are not consistent across all adolescent populations. For example, the number of juvenile female detainees is increasing at a much faster rate than that of males (Sickmaund, Sladky, & Kang, 2003). In addition, African American and Hispanic youths, representing 20% of the adolescent population (U.S. Census Bureau, 2000), account for approximately 60% of juvenile detainees (Sickmaund et al.).

Data from the 2010 US Census, however, indicated a downward trend in juvenile incarceration, dropping 41% from 1995 to 2010.

Although it is clear that African American and Hispanic youths are not more inclined to criminal behavior merely due to their ethnicity, there is a disproportionate number of African American and Hispanic youths living in difficult economic conditions in America's cities, which tend to foster criminal activity and violence and gang membership. As Seals points out, "gang members report an astonishingly high rate of gun violence (34.9 percent) in their childhood environment compared with non-gang members. The rate of fatherless homes is also much higher among gang members than for non-gang members."

Dysfunctional families, or broken homes, are quite common in impoverished communities as compared to middle- and upper-class communities. Dysfunctional families are also the largest source of runaway youth. Rafferty and Raimondi (2009) point out that a high number of runaway youths become members of street gangs. They cite a 2003 study in which 602 homeless and runaway youths were interviewed, and which revealed that "almost half of the youths were involved in gangs or were actual gang members." The study also showed that "the younger they were when they ran away increased the chances that the youths became associated with a street gang." Youth who experience housing instability, low levels of involvement or monitoring by parents or guardians, or strained relationships with their families are all more likely to become involved in a gang ("Why Black teens join gangs," 2014).

Why Do Kids Join Gangs?

ECONOMIC FACTORS

An important question that some researchers have asked is, to what extent do economic incentives encourage gang membership? This is the question Seals examined, but he points out that there is not much data to research when trying to answer it. Seals used annual county unemployment rates to see if there is a correlation between higher unemployment rates and increased gang activity. After analyzing the data, Seals asserts that "the local unemployment rate is positively related to male gang participation, as the availability of legitimate jobs is a key indicator of economic prospects for low-skilled workers." Seals also points to another important study that concludes the fundamental cause of urban poverty in the U.S. is "a lack of opportunity for low-skilled workers in the post-industrial economy and the resulting unemployment (or underemployment) of those workers." Seals' study shows that gang participation peaks when members are sixteen years old, which is the minimum legal age for working in any non-hazardous occupation. After age 16, youth membership in gangs begins to decline. Thus, "the rise in gang participation until age sixteen could be the result of economic opportunity provided by gangs to those unable to find legitimate employment" and that the decrease in gang participation after youth have reached sixteen years of age may be from youth having more opportunities for legitimate employment.

There are other positive and negative correlations that create a clearer profile for hose youth whom are likely to join gangs:

> The two indicators for race are positive and statistically significant for all models. Having a father (or father figure) present in the child's household in preadolescence has a statistically significant and negative effect

on gang involvement, which is contrary to Jankowski's (1991) finding that gang members are just as likely to come from stable two-parent homes. The county characteristics 'doctors' and 'crime rate' are statistically significant with negative and positive coefficients respectively, indicating that gang members are more likely to come from high-crime areas with fewer public resources. The coefficients for the violence indicators 'shot' and 'bully' are both positive and statistically significant... which suggests that living in a physically threatening environment during pre-adolescence increases the probability of future gang membership considerably.

EXPOSURE TO VIOLENCE

Voisin et al. carried out a study exploring the last correlation that Seals points out—the relationship between being exposed to violence and committing violence. Voisin's study shows that about 80 percent of the delinquent youths interviewed reported that they had seen "one or more incidents of community violence within the 12 months before detainment." Other relevant statistics are that about 20 percent had experienced a family member robbed or attacked, about 40 percent "had seen someone other than a family member beaten or attacked by others," and well over 50 percent "had seen someone beaten, shot, or really hurt by someone." Also, over 50 percent "had been around people shooting guns in their neighborhood." Many other researchers have also noted that there is a strong correlation between youth witnessing violence in their communities and youth becoming members of gangs. A former New York gang member, Robert de Sena, who works to prevent youth from joining gangs, confirms this correlation from his direct experience. De Sena, who grew up in an economically depressed area of New York, observes that:

If you're in a neighborhood that's violent, once you're 13, your parents can't help you anymore. They can't go out and be with you every second of the day. It's impossible, so you either become part of something that will guarantee your protection, or you become a victim. That is how you get called to that life, and that was the decision I had to make ("The power of," 2007).

One study above shows a correlation between economic incentives and gang-involvement, another study shows a correlation between witnessing violence and gang-involvement, and still other researchers have found a correlation between growing up in a broken home and gang-involvement. Most likely, all of these factors contribute to youth becoming involved in gangs.

PEER PRESSURE

We should also consider the social factor—and particularly the effects of peer pressure that youth certainly experience. McGloin and Piquero (2009) carried out a study that investigates this area. Their study demonstrates that there is a sharp increase in committing acts of violence when a youth is with "co-offenders." An important premise is that "individuals who would otherwise not engage in delinquency may do so when in a group setting; thus, co-offending may reflect the fact that individuals move past some restraint threshold for offending when in the presence of others." The individual's likelihood to commit a violent crime increases when more people are present, meaning gangs are the optimal social structure for committing violence. According to the study, for each additional person with whom the person offends, the odds of an individual's first group offense being violent increase by about 10 percent. McGloin and Piquero give two possibilities for why this is so. One reason may be that "when offending with accomplices, it is easier to 'blame' others for the act and obscure one's individual identity, giving oneself up to behavior without typical limitations." Another possibility is that "the consequences for inaction might be even more serious than social rejection under certain conditions... a number of scholars have discussed how demonstrating one's toughness in front of others is a key manner in which to obtain and maintain respect." They conclude:

Thus, individuals might be more inclined towards offending and violence when in a group, not because of anonymity or the diffusion of responsibility but rather because they are avoiding the amplified risks of not engaging in delinquency (McGloin & Piquero).

Is There a Solution?

PUNISHMENT

The solution to youth gang-involvement is no less complicated than its causes. The easiest solution seems to be use of police force, but that solution is most likely too simple. Seals writes that the police are most commonly involved in deterring gang activity. However, he also argues that police "are often at a disadvantage because they cannot control the factors which are generally attributed to gang participation, such as poor economic opportunity, inadequate family structure, and cultural isolation." Arinde points out there are plenty of attempts at creating tough legislation to deal with gang members, but this has not been very effective. Typically—as was included in a 2004 congressional bill—these legislative attempts to deal with gang activity create harsher sentencing, such as prosecuting 16-year-olds as adults or sentencing criminals with the death penalty for gang-related murders. But some argue that the reason Congress tends to increase its writing of legislation against gangs is that creating new legislation is less costly than funding preventive programs.

Captain Adams does not believe incarceration is the right answer to the problem of gangs. He was in a youth gang and was arrested at age 15 for burglary. He observes that if such harsh legislation were applied to him as a teenager, he would just be getting out of prison, having served a 30-year sentence. He adds:

> We can't ignore the facts and the opinion of all the experts who say that there is a correlation with how much the drastic cuts from the Giuliani years to this current administration has affected the crime rate. We have had 12 years of an administration which believes that juvenile services are not preventative measures to address the issue of juvenile crime (cited in Arinde).

PREVENTION

According to most experts who have researched or done studies on gang involvement, prevention seems to be the best approach. Seals points out the lack of community support for youth in the ghettos, observing that there is a "scarcity of public resources such as community centers, youth counseling services, police protection, and even churches and schools necessary to service large populations," and he notes that this lack of community resources "is endemic to urban ghettos where street gangs flourish." Voisin et al., after having thoroughly researched the relation between violence and gang involvement, argues that "interventions designed to alter negative peer affiliations and promote membership in pro-social peer groups might be a useful strategy." They suggest that school-based programs should be instituted to "encourage pro-social affiliation and membership that would substitute for gang membership."

One expert on gangs observes that between 2:00 p.m. and 6:00 p.m., students are often unsupervised,

and this is the most dangerous time for youth (Henderson, 2009). Sivan et al. (1999) cite a study released by the Office of Juvenile Justice Delinquency Prevention, which shows that the "greatest risk of violent victimization by nonfamily members" occurs between 3:00 p.m. and 7:00 p.m. The study also pointed out that "children who participate in organized after-school activities were less likely to be both victims and perpetrators of violence." Thus, many experts believe we should, as a society, create more social groups for youth to join. Again, reasoning from his experience as a gang member, Robert de Sena concurs:

> It shouldn't be a surprise to anybody [that gangs are a growing problem], because we have not as a society created the kind of social groups for kids to join. Kids need approval. Kids need to be a part of a group. Kids want an identity with a group. If there are no positive groups out there that they're interested in joining, then the gangs win ("The power of").

Seals gives another strong argument for taking a preventative approach. His study demonstrates that gangs generally have high member turnover rates because individual gang careers are relatively short and that "public policies that inhibit individual gang participation (particularly initial gang participation) are likely to generate positive results because gangs need new members to remain viable." Having looked at the problem economically, Seals proposes that "programs designed to increase economic opportunity among disadvantaged youth could greatly reduce gang participation and, as a result, gang-related crime." Thus, two possible ways to decrease gang involvement are to create clubs and programs through our public schools and communities and to use state and local agencies to offer more employment opportunities for at-risk youth.

Public programs that reach out to parents could also help reduce gang-related crime. Voisin et al. point out that, in his study, "increased perceived parental monitoring was negatively associated with both gang involvement and drug use." They suggest that community-based parent-training classes and outreach programs should be developed for America's at-risk neighborhoods. Voisin proposes that "training parents to adequately monitor their youths, or assisting them with networking with other parents or adults who can provide monitoring functions for their youths, may be effective strategies for disrupting the likelihood of joining gangs or using illicit drugs."

INVOLVEMENT OF EDUCATORS

Rafferty and Raimondi suggest that teachers and other educational personnel should be more involved with detecting problems youth may be having and with bridging between parents, communities, and programs. Pyrooz (2014) indicates that non-gang-affiliated youth are up to 30 percent more likely to complete high school than their gang-affiliated peers, leading to increased socioeconomic stratification in the wider society. Henderson interviewed gang expert Bud Mayo, who makes some observations on how to improve the role of educators in preventing gang involvement. According to Mayo, most teachers and administrators "know very little about gangs and gang culture." One way to correct this is to promote more colleges of education around the country to "include courses on gangs and school violence in their programs to better prepare graduates for the classroom" (cited in Henderson).

Of course, law enforcement must be involved in catching gangsters who commit crimes. As Kingsbury observes, federal law enforcement agencies, such as the Bureau of Alcohol, Tobacco, Firearms, and Explosives (ATF), carry out operations against gangsters—and particularly against gunrunners. Federal agents have been going on stakeouts, making undercover busts, and working with informants. The ATF, and also the Immigration and Customs Enforcement agency, then contacts regional SWAT teams to arrest the gunrunners. According to Kingsbury, catching and stopping the major gunrunners and charging them with conspiracy and racketeering, makes it more difficult for other gang members to obtain weapons. "As violence declines, local police and social workers can step in."

Any of the above solutions that the experts have suggested would probably be helpful, but the best would be to address the problem of gang involvement through multiple strategies. There should be law enforcement, and this seems to be the one strategy that is most in place. But there seems to be a lack of other strategies, such as positive social groups, outreach programs, or state and local employment programs for at-risk youth. Just as the cause of the problem is multi-faceted, so must be the solution.

TERMS & CONCEPTS

At-Risk Youth: Adolescents who are likely to become drug users, members of gangs, or juvenile delinquents.

Bureau of Alcohol, Tobacco, Firearms, and Explosives (ATF): A law enforcement agency under the United States Department of Justice. The ATF has agents who track violent criminals, criminal organizations, the illegal use and trafficking of firearms, the illegal use and storage of explosives, acts of arson and bombings, acts of terrorism, and the illegal diversion of alcohol and tobacco products.

Gangs: Comprise youth who associate together, wear gang colors or clothes, commit various crimes (often violent crimes) and have set boundaries for their territory. A gang protects its members and turf against other rival gangs through fighting or threats.

Immigration and Customs Enforcement agency (ICE): The largest investigative arm of the Department of Homeland Security (DHS). ICE is responsible for enforcing the nation's immigration and customs laws, and the agency also collects and shares data with other federal, state and local law enforcement agencies.

Juvenile Delinquents: Youth under the age of 18 who commit acts that violate the law.

National Longitudinal Survey of Youth (NLSY97): A survey first begun in 1997 and updated biennially. The survey uses a nationally representative sample of youths, ages 12 to 16.

Office of Juvenile Justice Delinquency Prevention (OJJDP): An agency within the U.S. Department of Justice. The OJJDP is concentrated on juvenile delinquency prevention, treatment, and control in areas such as mentoring, substance abuse, gangs, truancy, and chronic juvenile criminality. The OJJDP supports states and communities in developing effective prevention and intervention programs to help reduce juvenile delinquency.

Special Weapons and Tactics (SWAT): A special paramilitary tactical force used in American law enforcement departments. SWAT teams are trained to carry out high-risk operations such as counter-terrorism operations, hostage rescues, serving dangerous arrest-and-search warrants, and arresting heavily armed criminals.

Violent Crime Index (VCI): A set of annual statistics published annually by the Federal Bureau of Investigation. The VCI statistics come from police department reports from across the United States, and only includes statistics for homicide, rape, robbery, and assault.

Sinclair Nicholas

BIBLIOGRAPHY

2011 national gang threat assessment—emerging trends. *FBI.* Retrieved from http://fbi.gov.

Alleyne, E., & Wood, J. L. (2014). Gang involvement: Social and environmental factors. *Crime & Delinquency, 60,* 547–568. Retrieved November 15, 2014, from EBSCO Online Database Education Research Complete.

Arinde, N. (2006). Gangland, New York City, Part 2. *New York Amsterdam News, 97,* 3–34. Retrieved June 30, 2010, from the EBSCO online database Academic Search Complete.

Estrada, J., Gilreath, T. D., Astor, R., & Benbenishty, R. (2013). Gang membership of California middle school students: Behaviors and attitudes as mediators of school violence. *Health Education Research, 28,* 626–639. Retrieved December 23, 2013, from the EBSCO online database Academic Search Complete.

Hayward, R. A., & Honegger, L. (2014). Gender differences in juvenile gang members: An exploratory study. *Journal of Evidence-Based Social Work, 11,* 373–382. Retrieved November 15, 2014, from EBSCO Online Database Education Research Complete.

Henderson, J. (2009). Keeping schools safe from gangs. *Education Update, 51,* 1–5. Retrieved July 1, 2010, from the EBSCO online database Education Research Complete.

Kingsbury, A. (2008). The war on gangs. *U.S. News & World Report, 145,* 33–36. Retrieved July 1, 2010, from the EBSCO online database Academic Search Complete.

Maxson, C. L., Matsuda, K. N., & Hennigan, K. (2011). "Deterrability" among gang and nongang juvenile offenders: Are gang members more (or less) deterrable than other juvenile offenders? *Crime & Delinquency, 57,* 516–543. Retrieved December 23, 2013, from the EBSCO online database Academic Search Complete.

McGloin, J., & Piquero, A. (2009). 'I wasn't alone': Collective behaviour and violent delinquency. *Australian & New Zealand Journal of Criminology, 42,* 336–353. Retrieved July 2, 2010, from the EBSCO online database Academic Search Complete.

The power of positive change: A conversation with Robert de Sena. (2007). *Junior Scholastic (Teacher's Edition), 110,* 1–8. Retrieved July 2, 2010, from the EBSCO online database Education Research Complete.

Pyrooz, D. C. (2014). From colors and guns to caps and gowns? The effects of gang membership on educational attainment. *Journal of Research in Crime & Delinquency, 51*(1), 56-87. Retrieved January 20, 2016, from the EBSCO online database Education Research Complete.

Rafferty, L., & Raimondi, S. (2009). Understanding and preventing runaway behavior: Indicators and strategies for teachers. *Beyond Behavior, 18,* 19–25. Retrieved July 2, 2010, from the EBSCO online database Academic Search Complete.

Seals, A. (2009). Are gangs a substitute for legitimate employment? Investigating the impact of labor market effects on gang affiliation. *Kyklos, 62,* 407–425. Retrieved July 2, 2010, from the EBSCO online database Academic Search Complete.

Sivan, A., Koch, L., Baier, C., & Adiga, M. (1999) Refugee youth at risk: A quest for rational policy. *Children's Services: Social Policy, Research & Practice, 2,* 139–158. Retrieved July 2, 2010, from the EBSCO online database Academic Search Complete.

Tapia, M. (2011). Gang membership and race as risk factors for juvenile arrest. *Journal of Research in Crime & Delinquency, 48,* 364–395. Retrieved December 23, 2013, from the EBSCO online database Academic Search Complete.

Voisin, D., Neilands, T., Salazar, L., Crosby, R., & DiClemente, R. (2008). Pathways to drug and sexual risk behaviors among detained adolescents. *Social Work Research, 32,* 147–157. Retrieved July 2, 2010, from the EBSCO online database Academic Search Complete.

Why Black teens join gangs. (2014). *Journal of Blacks in Higher Education,* 39-40. Retrieved January 20, 2016, from the EBSCO online database Education Research Complete.

Yiu, H., & Gottfredson, G. D. (2014). Gang participation. *Crime & Delinquency, 60,* 619–642. Retrieved November 15, 2014, from EBSCo Online Database Education Research Complete.

SUGGESTED READING

Barrett, A. N., Kuperminc, G. P., & Lewis, K. M. (2013). Acculturative stress and gang involvement among Latinos: U.S.-born versus immigrant youth. *Hispanic Journal of Behavioral Sciences, 35,* 370–389. Retrieved December 23, 2013, from the EBSCO online database Academic Search Complete.

Howell, J. C. (2015). *The history of street gangs in the United States: Their origins and transformations.* Lanham, Maryland: Lexington Books. Retrieved January 20, 2016, from EBSCO online database eBook Collection.

Koffman, S., et al. (2009). Impact of a comprehensive whole child intervention and prevention program among youths at risk of gang involvement and other forms of delinquency. *Children & Schools, 31,* 239–245. Retrieved July 2, 2010, from the EBSCO online database Academic Search Complete.

Levy, E., Tozer, C., & Olley, R. I. (2013). Preventing gang involvement: Beyond what is expected. *Communique (0164775X), 42,* 4. Retrieved November 15, 2014, from EBSCo Online Database Education Research Complete.

Piley, W. (2006). Interpreting gang tattoos. *Corrections Today, 68,* 46–53. Retrieved July 2, 2010, from the EBSCO online database Academic Search Complete.

Williams, L. R., LeCroy, C. W., & Vivian, J. P. (2014). Assessing risk of recidivism among juvenile offenders: The development and validation of the recidivism risk instrument. *Journal of Evidence-Based Social Work, 11,*

318–327. Retrieved November 15, 2014, from EBSCO Online Database Education Research Complete.

Winfree, T., Jr. (2001). Hispanic and Anglo gang membership in two southwestern cities. *Social Science Journal, 38,* 105–118. Retrieved July 1, 2010, from the EBSCO online database Academic Search Complete.

JUVENILE DELINQUENCY/TRUANCY

Juvenile delinquency, when discussed within the context of education, refers to the broader topic of juvenile lawlessness, which encompasses everything from drug and alcohol abuse to school violence. Truancy can be seen as a specific type of juvenile delinquency that, according to Office of Juvenile Justice and Delinquency Prevention at the US Department of Justice, refers to the students' unexcused absences from school. Beyond its connection to poor academic performance, many researchers have concluded that truancy is an important predictor of juvenile delinquency. In recent decades, as the US public education system has developed a reputation for underperforming students, politicians, law enforcement officials, teachers, parents, and school administrators have made renewed efforts to curb truancy in the belief that regular school attendance is vital to improving student achievement in an increasingly global economy.

KEYWORDS: Compulsory Attendance; Dropout Age; Juvenile Delinquency; Public Education; Public School; School Violence; Truancy; Unexcused Absence

OVERVIEW

Truancy is defined as an unexcused absence from school. This is not necessarily the same as excessive absence, which historically has been caused by a variety of factors, the most predominant being severe illness (Jennings, 1927; Brazelton, 1939). This factor has been reduced through widespread vaccination programs and much improved medical care. Truancy can be as mild as "ditching" school on a Friday in the spring, but it can also turn into the habit of avoiding school attendance whenever possible. Perhaps not surprisingly, the problem of truancy in the United States has existed since the passage of compulsory education laws beginning in the nineteenth century, which required public school students to attend

classes for a given number of hours each week, for a number of days each year, and until a certain age (typically sixteen or eighteen). Legally, truancy is what is termed a status offense, meaning that it only applies to children below a state-mandated age.

COMPULSORY EDUCATION LAWS

In 1867, two years after the Civil War, the US Congress created a special department of education to oversee the reform of public education in the United States. The South, which had Union troops on its soil until 1878, was required by the federal government to create public school systems to help educate freed slaves as well as the many poor white children who had little more than a passing acquaintance with formal education (Schlesinger, 1933). In rural areas, where children still worked in the family fields, the school year was considerably shorter than that of students pouring in to America's growing big cities.

Beginning in the 1870s, more and more states, both Northern and Southern, began to pass compulsory school attendance laws, though states with large numbers of new immigrants, partially dependent on the wages from their children's labor, moved more cautiously in that direction:

"During the nineteenth century, in particular, a large percentage of Americans were ambivalent about compulsory schooling laws. Some parents openly resisted enforcement of them, saying that it was no business of the state to meddle in family decisions.... Many citizens regarded footloose truants as harmless Huck Finns. When attendance offers enforced child labor laws, parents often resented the loss of their children's income, employers lost cheap labor, and many of the children themselves had no desire to return to school. One factory inspector in Chicago found that 412 of the 500 children she interviewed would rather have worked in the factory than gone to school" (Tyack & Berkowitz, 1977).

In 1918 Mississippi was the last of the forty-eight states to pass a compulsory education law. Today, all fifty states have such laws on the books.

It seems that the laws had a positive educational effect: from 1878 to 1898, the number of children attending public schools rose from nine million to fifteen million. Meanwhile, during this same twenty-year period, in order to accommodate the influx of new pupils, the number of kindergartens rose from less than two hundred to more than three thousand, and the number of high schools grew from less than 800 to 5,500 (Schlesinger).

THE TRUANT OFFICER

In many locales, a type of police officer known as a truant officer was charged with enforcing the compulsory education laws. While many truant officers upheld the highest ethical standards of their profession, scholars have shown that, in some cases, they were abusing their mandate. For instance, after Michigan passed a compulsory education law in 1883, 37 percent of anti-truancy arrests in the 1890s were made "between 8:00 p.m. and 2:00 a.m., well outside of school hours" (Wolcott, 2001). It also seems to have been the practice of the police to use the court system to prosecute only habitual truants. Others were sent home to their disapproving parents or enrolled in "truant schools" to, it was hoped, instill some discipline in wayward youth (Wolcott).

In the twentieth century and on into the twenty-first century, truancy has been addressed with a combination of methods, depending on the nature and frequency of the offense. Many public school districts offer counseling services to attempt to get to the root causes of a student's truancy, social workers assist with family therapy sessions or parent training as needed, and the juvenile justice system provides a last resort of court-ordered drug and alcohol treatment programs or even imprisonment in a juvenile facility for truants who commit crimes.

TRUANCY BY THE NUMBERS

Given what is at stake in truant behavior, the numbers for truancy in the United States in the twenty-first century have been maddeningly imprecise. As one scholar notes:

> "While anecdotal evidence suggests that truancy has reached epidemic proportions, we do not have accurate estimates of the prevalence of truancy in the United States due to inconsistent tracking and reporting practices of schools. As a result, our best current estimates of the national state of truancy are from self-reported data" (Henry, 2007).

Even so, the information that is available is sufficient to paint a very different picture of the truant student than that of the "harmless Huck Finn" or enterprising street urchin envisioned by many Americans at the turn of the twentieth century. There is evidence from Philadelphia, Pittsburgh, Milwaukee, and many other metropolitan schools, for example, of thousands of instances of truancy each day. In Minneapolis, researchers noted that only 47 percent of students were in school at least 95 percent of the time during the 1999–2000 school year, though the number rose to nearly 57 percent in 2001–2002 (Hinx, Kapp & Snapp, 2003). Among a random sampling of students who participated in the national Monitoring the Future survey in 2003, 10.5 percent of eighth-graders reported that they had skipped school at least once in the previous four weeks, while 16.4 percent of tenth-grade students said they had done the same (Henry). In a 2010 report by Puzzanchera et al. for the National Center for Juvenile Justice, truancy cases presented to juvenile courts increased 67 percent from 1995 to 2007. The Center for American Progress reported that approximately 7.5 million American students were chronically absent from school in 2012 (Ahmad & Miller, 2015).

Local work has been done by three different grand juries in Miami-Dade Country in Florida, which found that 75 to 85 percent of its serious criminal offenders in the early 1990s had a history of being truant or absent from school for long stretches of time beginning in the third grade (cited in NCSE, n.d.). It is also the case that truant students account for a large percent of juvenile crime: in San Diego alone, 37 percent of juvenile crime in 2001 occurred between 8:30 a.m. and 1:29 p.m. (cited by San Diego Public Safety & Neighborhood Services Committee, 2002). Finally, and perhaps contrary to some assumptions, only 54 percent of truancy cases that went to court involved boys (cited in NCSE).

The picture of truancy facing school officials, civic leaders, and parents is much more complicated and challenging than it has been in the past. It is incumbent upon state and federal governments to develop a common methodology for assessing truancy in America so that researchers can develop a more precise understanding of truancy and how it can be prevented—something that will be a benefit both to students and to society as a whole.

STATE COMPULSORY ATTENDANCE LAWS

Each state has a law on the books that stipulates the age at which a student must begin attending school and the age until which he or she must remain in school (the "legal dropout age"). Every state requires that students remain in school until at least age sixteen, while a number require students to remain in school until age eighteen. For more detailed and up-to-date information on specific state requirements, see "Compulsory Attendance Laws Listed by State," a publication of the National Center for School Engagement.

WHAT MAKES A STUDENT BECOME TRUANT?

While there are many theories regarding the causes of truancy, Henry points out that one thing is consistent: there is very little information on the subject:

"In addition to a paucity of research pertaining to the prevalence of truancy in the United States, we also know surprisingly little about the correlates of truancy. That is, while several studies have assessed the consequences of truancy, no studies that could be identified have assessed the predictors, causes, or correlates of truancy using a nationally representative sample of youth. It is surprising to note that very little research has been conducted to understand truant behavior" (Henry).

However, it is possible to draw some preliminary conclusions based on self-reported data, localized case studies, and the like. According to the Center for American Progress, "Truancy is a multifaceted problem with push-and-pull factors from a variety of sources, including student-specific variables, family- and community-specific characteristics, school-specific factors, and influences such as poor academic performance, lack of self-esteem or ambition, unaddressed mental health needs, alcohol and drug use, and poor student health" (Ahmad & Miller). Given the complexity of the context in which truancy takes place, establishing causality (e.g., establishing that truancy leads to drug use) may prove to be more difficult.

More than a half century ago, Formwalt (1947) made an astute observation: "Truancy may be 'absence without leave' but seldom is it 'absence without reason'." According to the US Office of Juvenile Justice and Delinquency Prevention, there are three factors that tend to make students truant:

- A negative school environmen;
- Problems within their families or communitie;
- Psychological factors within students themselves (OJJDP, n.d.).

A Negative School Environment

Some schools have poorly developed attendance policies and students do not fully understand the schools' attendance expectations. Other schools, due to a lack of organization, fail to inform parents of their child's truancy, thus preventing parents from addressing the problem. In terms of the school culture, some schools fail to prevent violence within schools, such as bullying, and marginalized students use truancy as a safety option. Finally, some schools do not provide an adequate level of service to special education students, thus allowing them to become frustrated and eventually disillusioned with school altogether.

Problems within Their Families or Communities

Students in high-crime, high-poverty areas are often faced, on a daily basis, with many negative role models, including other truants, drug dealers, and gang members, and some choose the path of least resistance. Some students are required to look after their younger siblings while parents work or seek adequate child care. Other students are victims of abuse and neglect, and their parents do not stress the importance of education or make the effort to see them off to school. Older students, particularly teenage mothers, might be truant because they are caring for their own children.

Psychological Factors within Students Themselves

Some students, for a variety of reasons, do not value education, and thus they do not see the harm in skipping school on a regular basis. In some cases, they create a self-fulfilling prophecy by skipping a few days of school, suffering the academic consequences, getting discouraged, and then skipping more and more frequently. Other students suffer from low self-esteem or from an undiagnosed psychological disorder or learning disabilities that hinders their academic achievement. Finally, some students are habitually truant because of drug or alcohol abuse.

HOW DOES TRUANCY IMPACT THE INDIVIDUAL AND SOCIETY AS A WHOLE?

Researchers have been able to trace the impact of habitual truancy on the subsequent lives of those students. While there is no one-to-one or strict cause-and-effect relationship between truancy and any particular result, research collected by the US Department of Justice's Office of Juvenile Justice and Delinquency Prevention does show that students who are habitually truant display these tendencies:

- Do poorly in school;
- More isolated from the wider society;
- Display low self-esteem;
- At greater risk for abusing drugs and alcohol;
- At greater risk for teen pregnancy;
- Have poor employment records and/or job prospects;
- More prone to violence and incarceration.

Habitual truancy does not simply affect the individual in question. For the wider society, according to the National Center for School Engagement (2006), there are four main costs of truancy:

- The immediate costs to solve the problem, including social services, court costs, counseling, etc;
- The well-established relationship between habitual truancy and dropping out of high school; high school dropouts earn considerably less in a lifetime and are much more likely to be dependent on state or federal social welfare programs;
- Habitual truants tend to become involved in juvenile crime, and combating such crime involves law enforcement resources;
- Habitual truants who are juvenile offenders are much more likely to commit crime as adults, committing more serious types of crimes; this puts added stress on the criminal justice system.

SCHOOL ATTENDANCE AS A PREDICTOR OF GRADUATION

Increased school attendance is directly correlated with higher achievement on standardized tests. In Minneapolis, for example, attendance rates have been an important predictor of achievement on eighth-grade standardized reading and math exams:

A 2007 study released by the Consortium on Chicago School Research at the University of Chicago found that race and socioeconomic level were not as important in predicting whether an incoming high school student would graduate than freshman grades, which are dependent upon attendance rate (Allensworth & Easton, 2007). "On average, a Chicago public school freshman misses 20 school days a year—enough to give just a 50–50 chance of graduating, regardless of test scores in eighth grade, according to the study" (Demirjian, 2007).

PARENTAL INVOLVEMENT IN TRUANCY

School principals have long been concerned that lack of adequate parental involvement in the education of their children has made life for teachers and school administrators more difficult than need be. A 1937 survey of public school principals revealed that the top four "problems they would like to lay before parents" were:

- Time spent on homework/amount of homework;
- Amount of time and the type of "entertainments;
- Lack of cooperation between parents and their child's teachers;
- Their children's "excused and unexcused absences"

Most educators continue to be concerned at the lack of parental involvement in the lives of their children, including the lack of consequences for repeated truancy. Educators understand that their policies are often effective only when they benefit from strong parental support.

Thanks to a growing number of state laws that allow courts to hold parents responsible for their habitually truant children, some states and local areas have taken a get-tough approach. In a suburb of Denver, the parents of a girl who missed forty-three days of school were held in contempt of court and sentenced to ten-day and thirty-day jail terms, respectively ("Daughter's Truancy," 1987). In St. Petersburg, Florida, in 2003, one parent received 179 days in jail, and school officials noted that whenever they prosecuted such careless parents, truancy rates would drop by more than half (Johnson, 2003). Because truant children are minors under the law, many argue that parents remain ethically and morally responsible—if not legally responsible—for their behavior.

COMMUNITY-BASED APPROACHES TO REDUCING TRUANCY

In addition to holding parents accountable for their children's attendance, more and more cities have been taking a proactive approach. In Philadelphia, where 9.5 percent of students were truant on any given school day prior to 2007, the School District of Philadelphia created the Parent Truancy Officer Program. The program has been staffed by five hundred parent truant officers who fan out over Philadelphia's neighborhoods to ensure that students find their way to school ("Mayor John Street," 2007). Clearly, in the opinion of the mayor and other community leaders, an ounce of prevention is worth a pound of cure:

> "Truancy and curfew violations are among the strongest indicators for identifying children at risk for delinquency or violence," Mayor Street said. "Parent truant officers are an important component of our increased efforts to ensure our children have a successful life. Parents and guardians are the first line of defense and the home is where the important message of attending school must originate, but everyone in the community must play a role in ensuring children are in school. These additional parent truant officers will make a difference" ("Mayor John Street").

Philadelphia also allows students to expunge their prior truancy records by signing a pledge to remain in school and upholding their end of the bargain. If they do not, their parents face fines or even imprisonment.

The US Department of Justice's Office of Juvenile Justice and Delinquency Prevention provides a helpful Model Program Guide that presents information on successful, cost-effective truancy reduction, prevention, and rehabilitation programs. The programs address the entire truancy continuum, from prevention to sanctions (family therapy, case management, etc.) to residential programs to reentry into adult society. The department uses robust scientific methodology for scoring each program.

For those interested in developing truancy prevention programs, or simply seeking to understand how they work (or do not work), the National Criminal Justice Reference Service offers a Tool Kit for Creating Your Own Truancy Reduction Program. And though dated, the Manual to Combat Truancy (1996) from the US Department of Education in cooperation with the US Department of Justice remains a useful resource for establishing best practices in combating habitual truancy. The Center for American Progress recommended a number of solutions to reduce truancy, including improving data collection for early warning systems; developing a national definition of truancy, chronic truancy, and chronic absenteeism; increasing wrap-around services, such as after-school or early learning programs, health agencies, social services organizations to meet students' needs; reducing punitive policies for truancy; and increasing parental involvement.

VIEWPOINTS: IS COMPULSORY EDUCATION OUTMODED?

While compulsory education enjoys widespread public, political, and teacher support, there are critics—many sympathetic with the homeschooling movement—who believe that requiring students to attend classes at and for a certain period of time is an unjust limitation of their civil liberties, not to mention expensive and sometimes futile.

John Taylor Gatto, a former New York State teacher of the year, left the public school system and became a harsh critic of it. In his seminal history of American education, *The Underground History of American Education: A Schoolteacher's Intimate Investigation into the Problem of Modern Schooling*, Gatto argues, against John Dewey and others, that public schools are enemies of individualism that stifle exceptionalism and creativity (Gatto, 2001).

Robert Epstein, former editor-in-chief of *Psychology Today* and author of *The Case against Adolescence*, has argued that one-size-fits-all education prolongs adolescence and gives young people excuses not to grow up. In a blog message about his thesis, he states, "I say that we need to give young people incentives and opportunities to join the adult world. For many, this will mean quickly testing out of high school and pursuing work interests. High school is a waste of time for many or most young people, which is one reason the dropout rate is so high" (Epstein, 2007).

Terms and Concepts

Compulsory Attendance: The idea, enshrined in the laws of every state, that children should remain in school until a specified age and should be in class during the school year unless they have a legitimate excuse.

Dropout Age: The state-approved age (typically 16 or 18) at which students can withdraw from school.

Juvenile Delinquency: A term used to describe illegal behavior by minors (those under 18).

Office of Juvenile Justice and Delinquency Prevention: An office of the U.S. Department of Justice that is a clearinghouse for information on juvenile delinquency and truancy in the United States.

Public Education: A system of free K-12 education designed for all children in the United States.

Public School: A local school that typically is either an elementary school (K-6), middle school or high school.

School Violence: Any aggressive behavior that takes place on school grounds before, during, or after school hours.

Truancy: A term used to describe students who are absent from school without a valid excuse. It can exist in mild or extreme forms.

Unexcused Absence: A term used to explain that a student who should be in school is away without a valid excuse.

Matt Donnelly

Bibliography

Ahmad, F. Z., & Miller, T. (2015). *The high cost of truancy.* Washington, DC: Center for American Progress. Retrieved from https://cdn.americanprogress.org.

Allensworth, E. & Easton, J.Q. (2007). What matters for staying on-track and graduating in Chicago public schools. Consortium on Chicago School Research, University of Chicago (July 2007). Retrieved August 25, 2007, from the Consortium on Chicago School Research, http://ccsr.uchicago.edu.

Brazelton, C. (1939). Excessive absence of high-school girls. The School Review, 47, 51-55.

Daughter's truancy lands parents in jail. (1987, August 14). New York Times. Retrieved August 25, 2007, from http://query.nytimes.com.

Demirjian, K. (2007, August 15). Freshmen schooled on need to attend. Chicago Sun-Tribune Retrieved August 24, 2007, from the University of Chicago News Service, http://topix.net.

Ek, H., & Eriksson, R. (2013). Psychological factors behind truancy, school phobia, and school refusal: A literature study. *Child & Family Behavior Therapy, 35,* 228–248. Retrieved November 15, 2014, from EBSCO Online Database Education Research Complete.

Epstein, R. (2007, April 8). Comment on "Let's Abolish High School." Message posted to EricMacKnight.com. Retrieved on August 26, 2007, from http://eric-macknight.com.

Fornwalt, R. J. (1947). Toward an understanding of truancy. The School Review, 55, 87-92.

Gage, N. A., Sugai, G., Lunde, K., & DeLoreto, L. (2013). Truancy and zero tolerance in high school: Does policy align with practice?. Education & Treatment of Children (West Virginia University Press), 36, 117-138. Retrieved December 13, 2013, from EBSCO Online Database Education Research Complete.

Gatto, J. T. (2001). The Underground History of American Education: A Schoolteacher's Intimate Investigation Into the Problem of Modern Schooling. Retrieved August 26, 2007, from http://johntaylorgatto.com.

Gleich-Bope, D. (2014). Truancy laws: How are they affecting our legal systems, our schools, and the students involved?. *Clearing House, 87,* 110–114. Retrieved November 15, 2014, from EBSCo Online Database Education Research Complete.

Haight, C. M., et al. (2014). Evaluation of a truancy diversion program at nine at-risk middle schools. *Psychology in the Schools, 51*(7), 779–787. Retrieved from EBSCO Online Database Education Research Complete.

Harris-McKoy, D., & Cui, M. (2013). Parental control, adolescent delinquency, and young adult criminal behavior. Journal of Child & Family Studies, 22, 836-843. Retrieved December 13, 2013, from EBSCO Online Database Education Research Complete.

Henry, K. L. (2007). Who's skipping school: Characteristics of truants in 8th and 10th Grade. Journal of School Health, 77, 29-35. Retrieved August 25, 2007, from the Digital Object Identifier System, http://dx.doi.org.

Hinz, E., Kapp, L. & Snapp, S. (2003). Student attendance and mobility in Minneapolis public schools. The Journal of Negro Education, 72, 141-149.

Jennings, J. (1927). A study of absences from school in two counties of Tennessee. Peabody Journal of Education, 4, 276-293.

Johnson, C. (2003, February 24). Kids' truancy gets parents jailed. St. Petersburg Times. Retrieved August 25, 2007, from http://sptimes.com.

Mayor John F. (2007, March 5). Street inducts new parent truant officers. Phila.gov. Retrieved August 25, 2007, from http://ework.phila.gov.

Minneapolis Public Schools (2005, October 14). Attendance matters!. Retrieved August 26, 2007, from Minneapolis Public Schools, http://mpls.k12.mn.us.

National Center for School Engagement. (2006). Truancy, dropouts and delinquency: Solutions for policies, practices and partnerships. Retrieved August 24, 2007, from http://schoolengagement.org.

Office of Juvenile Justice and Delinquency Prevention (n.d.). Facts on truancy. U.S. Department of Justice. Retrieved August 24, 2007, from the Office of Juvenile Justice and Delinquency Prevention, http://ojjdp.ncjrs.gov.

Puzzanchera, C., Adams, K., & Sickmund, M. (2010). *Juvenile Court Statistics 2006–2007*, 72. Retrieved November 15, 2014, from http://ojjdp.gov.

San Diego Public Safety & Neighborhood Services Committee. (2002). 2001 crime report. City of San Diego Police Department. Retrieved August 24, 2007 from the City of San Diego Police Department, www.sandiego.gov.

Schlesinger, A. M. (1933). The rise of the city, 1878-1898: A history of American life. Volume X. New York: Macmillan.

Shannon, J. R., Fridiana, M., Gabrielis, M. & Leonardilla, M. Problems that principals would like to lay before parents. The School Review, 45, 364-367.

Tyack, D. & Berkowitz, M. (1977). The man nobody liked: Toward a social history of the truant officer, 1840-1940. American Quarterly, 29, 31-54.

Welch-Brewer, C., Stoddard-Dare, P., & Mallett, C. (2011). Race, substance abuse, and mental health disorders as predictors of juvenile court outcomes: Do they vary by gender?. Child & Adolescent Social Work Journal, 28, 229-241. Retrieved December 13, 2013, from EBSCO Online Database Education Research Complete.

Wolcott, D. (2001). "The cop will get you": The police and discretionary juvenile justice, 1890-1940. Journal of Social History, 35, 349-371.

SUGGESTED READING

Archambault, L., Kennedy, K., & Bender, S. (2013). Cybertruancy: Addressing issues of attendance in the digital age. Journal of Research on Technology in Education, 46, 1-28. Retrieved December 13, 2013, from EBSCO Online Database Education Research Complete.

Bell, M. (1933). The school and the juvenile court work together. Journal of Educational Sociology,6, 471-482.

Carlen, P. (1992). Pindown, truancy, and the interrogation of discipline: A paper about theory, policy, social worker bashing and hypocrisy. Journal of Law and Society, 19, 251-270.

DeSocio, J., VanCura, M., Nelson, L., Hewitt, G., Kitzman, H., & Cole, R. (2007). Engaging truant adolescents: Results from a multifaceted intervention pilot. Preventing School Failure, 51, 3-9.

Herrera, S. (2006). Working with highly mobile, immigrant students in Houston, TX. National Center for School Engagement. Retrieved August 25, 2007, from National Center for School Engagement, http://schoolengagement.org.

Lassonde, S. (1996). Learning and earning: Schooling, juvenile employment, and the early life course in late nineteenth-century New Haven. Journal of Social History. 29, 839-870. Retrieved September 19, 2007, from EBSCO Online Database Academic Search Complete.

McCray, E. (2006). It's 10 a.m.: Do you know where your children are? Intervention in School & Clinic, 42, 30-33.

Mueller, D., Giacomazzi, A., & Stoddard, C. (2006). Dealing with chronic absenteeism and its related consequences: The process and short-term effects of a diversionary juvenile court intervention. Journal of Education for Students Placed at Risk, 11, 199-219.

Norton, P.L. (1934). Team work for the wayward child. Journal of Criminal Law and Criminology, 25, 434-444.

Pratt, J. D. (1983). Law and social control: A study of truancy and school deviance. Journal of Law and Society, 10, 223-240.

Reynolds, D. & Murgatroyd, S. (1974). Being absent from school. British Journal of Law and Society, 1, 78-81.

Shute, J. W., & Cooper, B. S. (2015). Understanding in-school truancy. *Phi Delta Kappan, 96*(6), 65–68. Retrieved from EBSCO Online Database Education Research Complete.

Sinha, J., Cnaan, R., & Gelles, R. (2007). Adolescent risk behaviors and religion: Findings from a national study. Journal of Adolescence, 30, 231-249.

Vaughn, M. G., Maynard, B. R., Salas-Wright, C. P., Perron, B. E., & Abdon, A. (2013). Prevalence and correlates of truancy in the US: Results from a national sample. *Journal of Adolescence, 36*, 767–776. Retrieved November 15, 2014, from EBSCo Online Database Education Research Complete.

Zhang, D., Katsiyannis, A., Barrett, D., & Willson, V. (2007). Truancy offenders in the juvenile justice system. Remedial & Special Education, 28, 244-256. Retrieved August 25, 2007, from EBSCO Online Database Academic Search Premier.

HAZING

Hazing can be categorized in three increasingly serious ways: subtle hazing, harassment hazing and bodily harm hazing. Typically hazing takes the form of an initiation ritual in which members of an out-group attempt to become members of an in-group through secretive and often legally questionable behavior. Hazing's history in Western culture can be traced back at least to the Greeks, and its influence is still felt in colleges, universities, high schools and middle schools today. Once hailed as obsolete in American education, hazing has been banned and declared against the law in 43 states, but it continues to occur even as it has been driven deeper underground. Experts agree that hazing is often the result of a dangerous mixture of peer pressure, a need for revenge from former hazed students, the desire to be part of a group, and a code of silence that protects perpetrators. Most psychologists believe that hazing can only be eliminated through the creation of school cultures that respect inclusion and teamwork and value the unique contributions to be made by all students.

KEYWORDS: Bodily Harm Hazing; Code of Silence; Harassment Hazing; Hazing; In-group; Initiation Ritual; Out-group; Peer Pressure; Subtle Hazing

OVERVIEW

The first task in understanding hazing is to get a clear sense of what the word means. As writers such as Riordan (2007) have noted:

> The term "hazing" connotes a variety of meanings to different people. To most higher education administrators it is unconscionable and a practice that should be eradicated. To most parents or community members it is difficult to comprehend something practiced by unruly college students. To the perpetrators and victims it is often a "rite of passage" that accompanies becoming a new member of a team or organization (Riordan).

Hazing, as distinguished from benign initiation rituals, perhaps is best defined as "any activity expected of someone joining or participating in a group that humiliates, degrades, abuses, or endangers them[,] regardless of a person's willingness to participate"

(Allan & Madden, 2006). According to Mothers Against School Hazing (2005), there are three levels of hazing:

- Subtle Hazing: "actions that are against accepted and organization standards of conduct, behavior and good taste. An activity or attitude directed toward a student or an act which ridicules, humiliates, and/or embarrasses."
- Harassment Hazing: "anything that causes anguish or physical discomfort to a student; any activity directed toward a student or activity which confuses, frustrates or causes undue stress.;
- Bodily Harm Hazing: "any form of action that may cause physical punishment, or any action that may cause bodily harm and/or touching in private places and/or declothing of a student" (Mothers Against School Hazing)

The practice of hazing dates back to ancient Greece (McDaniel, 1914), if not earlier, and it attracted the disapproving attention of Plato and St. Augustine, among others. Justinian's law code of 529-534 CE banned the hazing of new law students, and the University of Paris in the fourteenth century began expelling students found guilty of hazing. German Protestant reformer Martin Luther was hazed while a student at the beginning of the sixteenth century, and by 1657, students at Harvard (which had only opened in 1636) were being fined for hazing ("Chronology," 2004).

Hazing in American education continued right through the nineteenth century. The most infamous cases of hazing during that time involved the United States Military Academy at West Point, which has a long history of initiation rituals for incoming cadets—"new cadets sweep out the rooms and shovel the snow," wrote General Ramsey in 1814—though the initiation rituals became what we would recognize as hazing rituals as the nineteenth century progressed ("A Century's," 1908).

Hazing in the News

There was widespread newspaper coverage of hazing at West Point in the 1870s ("West Point," 1873), and students faced expulsion or court martial if found guilty. Sadly, the practice continued, and in 1891, the New York Times reported on a series of cadet expulsions, noting that "the disgraced youngsters—or several of them, at least—being the very ones who had fallen prey to the barbarism of those who had been dismissed the preceding year" ("Normal Students," 1891).

Hazing also spilled over into public education. In 1880, there was a shooting at a prep school known as the Highland Falls Academy in which a student who thought he was being hazed shot a fellow student ("Buck's Cowardly," 1880). Sensing that hazing was a concern to parents, boy's prep schools began including in their newspaper advertisements a promise that there was no hazing on their campuses ("Classified ad," 1882). But the hazing problem had spread to unlikely locations such as East Hampton Williston Seminary in Springfield, Massachusetts, where in February 1882 students confessed to kidnapping a fellow student, and "the School Trustees are determined to push the prosecution so as to break up the hazing evil" ("Williston students," 1882). At Harvard, in 1883, the president delivered a speech in which he sounded the optimistic note that, in paraphrasing a New York Times reporter, "no student who means to be a self-respecting gentleman would think of practicing the senseless tricks of former days" ("Character-forming," 1883).

Still hazing continued. In February 1886, several students were expelled from the State Normal School in Kutztown, Pennsylvania, because they "bound and gagged one of their fellow-students, took him to an upper room and painted his face black, telling him that if he attempted to make a noise he would be severely beaten" ("Students expelled," 1886). In 1891, at the State Normal Training School in New York, a gang of 23 male students assaulted fellow male students who had escorted female students home from classes, throwing the gentleman callers over fences and dousing them with water ("Normal students in disgrace," 1891); a day later, the students were cleared of hazing charges after the females involved came to their defense ("Normal students reinstated," 1891b).

The Booz Inquiry

But in 1900, the hazing at West Point had spiraled out of control. Often first-year cadets were

compelled to fight fourth-year cadets, and the outcome of such mismatches was generally unfortunate for the first-year cadet. In 1898, a new cadet, Oscar Booz, was subjected to repeated ridicule because he read the Bible, as well as physical abuse such as being forced to drink bottle after bottle of Tabasco sauce and being severely beaten in a boxing match with a formidable upperclassman. Booz withdrew from West Point after only four months and died of tuberculosis of the larynx 18 months later. His parents blamed his fellow cadets for their son's death, and a formal congressional court of inquiry—nicknamed the Booz Inquiry—was formed by President William McKinley in December 1900.

The Booz Inquiry revealed that even Cadet Douglas Macarthur, son of Civil War hero Gen. Arthur Macarthur Jr. and Cadet Ulysses S. Grant, grandson of the former president, were guilty of hazing ("Hazing students fainted," 1900). Grant testified that he himself was hazed through an excessive amount of exercise, such as having to hold a dumbbell in his outstretched arm for 5-6 minutes at a time. Some outraged senators and congressional representatives spoke of dissolving West Point entirely and returning military training to the states ("Senators," 1901). In May 1901, the congressional representatives found no connection between Booz's death and the West Point hazing, though several West Point students found guilty of hazing were thrown out.

Hazing also captured the attention of the public, including one citizen who wrote a letter to the editor of the New York Times in January 1901, during the height of the Booz Inquiry. The writer argued that it is easy to stop hazing, assuming the will to do so exists:

> The real difficulty is that [college officers], like the public generally, habitually regard hazing as an amusing, boyish prank. Hazing is, in fact, the crime of assault. That crime should be treated, when it occurs in a college or school, just as it is treated when it occurs elsewhere ("How to stop hazing," 1901).

Despite the public outcry, and even legislation in states such as Ohio ("Hazing made criminal," 1906) to make hazing illegal after hazed students died, hazing was hardly snuffed out in the nation's colleges and high schools. It was still seen by many boys, and even some girls ("Alpha girls," 1910), as a rite of passage. According to one British observer, Americans were particularly adept at it:

> ... is fairly common both in the English and in the continental schools. Usually, however, it is instinctive and unpremeditated. In America it is accompanied by a considerable amount of forethought and conscious will-power. Instinct by itself is powerful, but when accompanied by deliberate effort it becomes still more so; hence the systematic thoroughness that characterizes the American hazing (Dewe, 1907).

Hazing Becomes Unpopular

By the 1940s and 1950s, it became accepted wisdom that hazing had become almost obsolete on college and university campuses because of three factors:

- A sober assessment of the deaths that took place in the 1920s;
- Students' greater appreciation of their place in an increasingly competitive educational environment; an;
- The influx of returning soldiers from World War II, who, as new college freshmen, "believed that nothing could top their experiences in European foxholes and Pacific jungles and were reluctant to allow sophomores who had escaped military service to try" (Tolchin, 1958).

The trend of colleges and universities was to ban hazing, replacing it with mentoring programs and other methods to bring underclassmen and upperclassmen together through a series of more positive interactions. This is not to say, however, that hazing ceased to exist at in America's colleges and universities (Allan & Madden), though it is fair to say that the harsh light of public scrutiny has driven such activities further underground.

However, the hazing that once filled the lives of college freshmen with fear continued took root and again began to thrive on high school campuses in the late twentieth century. The primary vectors of activity were high school athletic teams and members of other clubs such as high school fraternities and sororities, the descendants of the literary clubs of the nineteenth century, which picked up hazing habits from their collegiate namesakes (Graebner, 1987).

Hazing in the Twenty-First Century

Among high school students surveyed by Allan and Madden, the most common forms of hazing include being

- yelled or screamed at (17 percent of all students);
- forced into extreme weather (11 percent);
- deprived of sleep (11 percent);
- forced to engage in drinking games (11 percent);
- forced to drink alcohol until passing out or getting sick (9 percent).

Among collegiate survey respondents (Allan & Madden), the most common forms of hazing experienced were:

- participation in drinking games (26 percent);
- public singing or chanting, either alone or in a selected group (17 percent);
- selective association with others (12 percent);
- excessive alcohol consumption (12 percent);
- sleep deprivation (11 percent);
- yelling, screaming, or cursing by other members (10 percent);
- excessive non-alcoholic beverage consumption (10 percent).

Overall, 47 percent of high school students and 55 percent of college students reported that they had been subjected to some form of hazing (Allen & Madden). A 2000 study by Hoover and Pollard found that over 1.5 million American high school students experienced hazing in a given school year, with 61 percent being hazed for the first time between the ages of thirteen and fifteen. When the figures were broken down, 24 percent of students were hazed to join sports teams, and 15 percent were hazed to join a peer group/gang (Hoover & Pollard, 2000).

Increased Violence

One disturbing trend is that incidents of hazing have become more violent: "Hazing has changed from the goofy high jinks of the 50's and 60's to something that is remarkably brutal and vicious," said Gary Powell, a hazing expert in Cincinnati who writes a legal newsletter for schools fraternities. "Like society itself, it's become more violent" (cited in Jacobs, 2000). For example, Robert Champion

Jr., a Florida A&M University student, was beaten to death in a 2011 drum corps initiation that went horribly wrong; over a dozen people were charged in connection with Champion's death (Glovin, 2013). Hazing has also become more sexually violent, with rape, attempted rape, and sodomy with objects increasingly common, particularly among sports teams (Cairney, 2013). Findings from Allan and Madden also show that being forced to perform sex acts with someone of the opposite sex is among the twelve most commonly reported hazing behaviors.

Data also show that the victims and perpetrators of youth violence are getting younger. According to Hoover and Pollard, about one-quarter of initial hazing incidents take place before or around age thirteen, before students even reach high school. As one researcher put it, "There is something terribly wrong with our society when abuse becomes a means of bonding" (Hoover, cited in Jacobs).

Reducing Hazing at School

Experts agree that the long-term solution to reducing hazing in schools across the United States is to replace an in-group/out group culture with one that is more inclusive and welcoming for all students. An example of "productive hazing" takes place at the all-male Wabash College near Indianapolis, where freshman fraternity pledges walk around campus tipping their caps to upperclassmen as a show of respect and campus unity (Woo, 2006).

APPLICATIONS
Warning Signs of Hazing

According to researchers, there are numerous identifiable characteristics of hazing:

- Pleas from members that it's "tradition";
- Aggressive or intimidating leader;
- Use of alcoho;
- Secrec;
- Peer pressure for everyone to participat;
- Singling out an individual or specific grou;
- A sense that something is not quite righ;
- No easy way to remove oneself from the situation (Lipkins, 2006; Purdue, n.d.).

Why Do Students Engage in Hazing?

Hoover and Pollard interviewed high school students who had participated in hazing to better understand their motivations, which ranged from excitement to revenge:

Reasons "in percentages" for Participating in Hazing:

It was fun and exciting 48
We felt closer as a group 44
I got to prove myself 34
I just went along with it 34
I was scared to say no 16
I wanted revenge 12
I didn't know what was happening 9
Adults do it too 9 (Hoover & Pollard)

Group bonding—the second most popular reason given for participating in hazing—can be provided through more positive alternatives such as those listed below. Curiously, the need to belong to a group also plays a role for the hazing victim. Dr. Rachel Lauer, a psychologist who has studied hazing remarks that many students were submitted to treatment they knew to be wrong in order to belong to a group. "In addition to companionship and comfort, there's a certain amount of prestige in belonging; the harder it is to get it in, the more prestigious it is" (as cited in Jacobs).

The other reasons—"I just went along with it" and "I was scared to say no"—must be addressed by creating a climate where students believe it is "cool" to break the code of silence that so often surrounds hazing. As Allan and Madden found, 69 percent of college-aged survey respondents knew of hazing, 24 percent had witnessed it, 91 percent of those who had been hazed refused to recognize it as such, and of those who did recognize having been hazed, 95 percent did not report it. About one-third indicated that feeling greater affiliation with the group after their hazing experience and more than one-fifth reported a greater sense of accomplishment. Such factors illustrate how difficult it is to break the code of silence (Lipkins).

Finally, the reason "I wanted revenge" shows the vicious cycle that is created when the hazed becomes the hazer.

Breaking the Code of Silence

Experts agree that the only effective way of reducing or eliminating instances of hazing in the schools is to eliminate the code of silence surrounding such activities. As noted above, even when students have knowledge of hazing activities, they are extremely unwilling to share that information with school authorities. This is the negative power of peer pressure at work.

However, as hazing researcher Susan Lipkins notes, not saying something might prove to be a big mistake:

> *NOT TO TELL: this seems to be the simplest decision. After all, many parents might even advise you to "not get involved." The positive part of this choice is that you are not exposed and do not feel guilty for causing any problems for others. It may also protect you from the media or legal issues. The down side is that some people may be seriously injured, including you. Ignoring, avoiding or denying the pain and suffering will not make it go away. You may heal but the scars and after effects may go on for a long time. Even if you do not report the incident consequences may occur, such as a death, so that you will become part of an investigation. You cannot predict what may happen after a hazardous hazing (Lipkins).*

The decision to break the code of silence is often difficult and not without its downsides, such as ostracism and even physical confrontation by those engaged in the hazing.

Alternatives to Hazing

As McKown (1924) noted nearly a century ago, hazing creates a hostile environment for incoming students. He warned that hazing runs counter to a positive school culture in which the student feels comfortable and is conducive to learning. He further notes that the cycle is perpetuated over the course of the victim's school career:

> *[Hazing] places a wrong emphasis at a most critical time in the life of the pupil. Such pranks are self-perpetuating because it is natural for an individual who has been a victim to victimize others. So the Freshman, when he becomes a Sophomore, takes delight in hazing the new Freshman, often carrying the treatment far beyond what he received. Thus, is this vicious circle ever widened (McKown).*

A successful method of reducing hazing is finding positive ways to build community among students. These activities can include:

- Community service projects;
- Mentoring;
- Entertainment (talent show, karaoke, etc.);
- Sharing a meal;
- Study groups;
- Road trips;
- Hazing-free initiations to campus clubs;
- Sporting activities.

The good news is that research shows high student interest in such activities (Hoover & Pollard).

Anti-Hazing Laws

By 2012, forty-four of the fifty states and Washington, DC, had enacted anti-hazing laws. Only eight of them, however, consider hazing a felony crime (Cohen, 2012). Beyond imposing a combination of penalties and jail time for those who conduct hazing itself, states such as Texas also hold those who remain silent about hazing accountable under the law. In early 2012, there was discussion of proposing a federal anti-hazing bill that would strip students found guilty of hazing of their federal financial aid for a year; however, interest groups for the nation's fraternities and sororities opposed the measure, which as of mid-2013 had yet to be introduced as a bill (Glovin).

TERMS & CONCEPTS

Bodily Harm Hazing: The most severe type of hazing, which involves actions that might cause physical harm or injury or involves inappropriate touching or the removal of clothing.

Code of Silence: A conviction among a particular group that it is socially unacceptable to tell those outside the group about the nature of the groups' activities.

Harassment Hazing: A type of hazing that involves activities designed to frustrate another student or cause him or her undue stress.

Hazing: An activity by one or more students that "humiliates, degrades, abuses, or endangers" other students.

In-group: A group in which members feel a sense of loyalty and devotion to other members of the group.

Initiation Ritual: A set of practices that an individual is required to perform in order to become a member of a group.

Out-group: A group toward which students feel contempt or dislike.

Peer Pressure: The pressure that a peer group exerts to encourage a member of the group to modify their social, ethical, moral, or even political views. Often considered to be negative, it can also take positive forms.

Subtle Hazing: The mildest form of hazing in which the objective of a group is to ridicule, humiliate, or embarrass those of an out-group who may or may not wish to join the in-group.

Matt Donnelly

BIBLIOGRAPHY

A century's hazing and its results; The practice was innocent enough at first, but later has developed cruel features. (1908, August 9). New York Times, SM3.

Allan, E., & Madden, M. (2006). Presentation at the National Conference on High School Hazing (September 22, 2006). Adelphi University, Garden City, NY. Retrieved September 2, 2007, from http://hazingstudy.org.

Allen, E., & Madden, M. (2008, March 11).Hazing in view: College students at risk. Retrieved December 16, 2013, from Alpha girls modify rites. (1910, April 29). New York Times, 18.

Anderson, E., McCormack, M., & Lee, H. (2012). Male team sport hazing initiations in a culture of decreasing homohysteria. Journal of Adolescent Research, 27, 427-448. Retrieved December 16, 2013, from EBSCO online database Education Research Complete.

Buck's cowardly shot. (1880, June 6). New York Times, 7.

Cairney, G. (2013, July 1). Hazing rituals in high school sports becoming more sexually violent. Education Week. Retrieved December 16, 2013, from http://w3.org.

Character-forming at Harvard. (1883, May 13). New York Times, 4.

Cohen, D. L. (2012, October). Clearing up hazing: Opponents are pushing for stricter laws. ABA Journal. Retrieved December 16, 2013, from http://abajournal.com.

Chronology. (2004). CQ Researcher, 14, 11.

Classified ad 7—no title. (1882, June 18). New York Times, 8.

Dewe, J. A. (1907). The American boy: Impressions of an Englishman. School Review, 15, 197-200.

Glovin, D. (2013, July 24). Mother of golf prodigy in hazing death defied by FratPAC. Bloomberg. Retrieved December 16, 2013, from http://bloomberg.com.

Graebner, W. (1987). Outlawing teenage populism: The campaign against secret societies in the American high school, 1900-1960. Journal of American History, 74, 411-435. Retrieved September 1, 2007, from EBSCO Online Database Education Research Complete.

Hazed cadets fainted; Military court at West Point learns of several cases. Denies he had convulsions; Put cotton in his mouth to prevent crying out—U.S. Grant's experience. (1900, December 29). New York Times, 3.

Hazing made criminal; Ohio legislature passes strict law, the result of two fatalities. (1906, March 22). New York Times, 1.

Hoover, E. (2012). After a death, a question: Are students hard-wired for hazing?. Chronicle of Higher Education, 58, A1-A11. Retrieved December 16, 2013, from EBSCO online database Education Research Complete.

Hoover, N. C., & Pollard, N. J. (2000). Initiation rites in American high schools: A national survey. Alfred University, Alfred, New York. Retrieved September 1, 2007, from Alfred University, http://alfred.edu.

How to stop hazing. (1901, January 18). The New York Times, 6.

Jacobs, A. (2000, March 5). Violent cast of high school hazing mirrors society, experts say. New York Times, NE 27-28. Retrieved September 1, 2007, from www.hazinglaw.com.

Lipkins, S. (2006). Inside hazing. Retrieved September 1, 2007, from http://insidehazing.com.

Majerol, V. (2012). Hazed to death. New York Times Upfront, 144, 6-7. Retrieved December 16, 2013, from EBSCO online database Education Research Complete.

McDaniel, W. B. (1914). Some Greek, Roman and English tityretus. American Journal of Philology, 35, 52-66.

McKown, H. C. (1924). The high-school handbook. School Review, 32, 667-681.

Mothers Against School Hazing. (2005). Hazing. Retrieved September 2, 2005, from http://mashinc.org.

Mutinous cadets to leave West Point; Five are dismissed and six others suspended. Many more of the second and third classes will be punished, among them Douglas MacArthur. (1901, May 22). New York Times, 1.

Normal students in disgrace: A hazing expedition that involved the insulting of ladies. (1891, December 15). New York Times, 1.

Normal students reinstated. (1891, December 16). New York Times, 4

Oliff, H. (2002). Lifting the haze around hazing. Education Digest, 67, 21. Retrieved September 3, 2007, from EBSCO Online Database Academic Search Premier.

Purdue University. (2007). Purdue hazing: Warning signs. Retrieved September 2, 2007, from Purdue University, http://purdue.edu.

Riordan, B. G. (2007). Preventing hazing: How parents, teachers, and coaches can stop the violence, harassment, and humiliation. [Review of the Book Preventing hazing: How parents, teachers, and coaches can stop the violence, harassment, and humiliation]. NASPA Journal, 44, 233-236. Retrieved September 1, 2007, from EBSCO Online Education Research Complete Database.

Schoolboy, hazed, is dying; Many kicks injure spine of a Middletown High School freshman. (1912, September 19). New York Times, 1.

Senators denounce hazing; Mr. Alien declares we would either stop it or dismantle the West Point Academy. (January 17, 1901). New York Times, 6.

Students expelled for hazing. (1886, February 4). New York Times, 1.

Suicide follows hazing; Indiana high school youth brooded—Inquiry is begun. (1923, September 23). New York Times, 2.

Tolchin, M. (1958, September 24). Freshmen hazing passé despite old college try. New York Times, 20.

West Point. "Hazing" at the academy—An evil that should be entirely rooted out—A plea for the strangers. (1873, June 7). New York Times, 8.

Williston students on trial. (1882, February 26). New York Times, 2.

Woo, S. (2006, December 1). Beanie revival. Chronicle of Higher Education, 53, A6. Retrieved September 1, 2007, from EBSCO Online Database Academic Search Premier.

SUGGESTED READING

Flanagan, C. (2017). A death at Penn State. Atlantic. 320(4), 92-105.

Hinkle Smith, S., & Stellino, M. (2007). Cognitive dissonance in athletic hazing: The roles of commitment and athletic identity. Journal of Sport & Exercise Psychology, 29, S169-S170. Retrieved September 2, 2007, from EBSCO Online Database Education Research Complete.

Honeycutt, C. (2005). Hazing as a process of boundary maintenance in an online community. Journal of Computer-Mediated Communication, 10, 3. Retrieved October 18, 2007, from http://jcmc.indiana.edu.

Lafferty, M.E., Wakefield, C., & Brown, H. "We do it for the team"- Student-athletes initiation practices and their impact on group cohesion. International Journal of Sport & Exercise Psychology. 15(4), 438-446.

Leon, P.W. (2000). Bullies and cowards: The West Point hazing scandal, 1898-1901. Westport, CT: Greenwood Press.

Lipkin, S. (2006). Preventing hazing: How parents, teachers, and coaches can stop the violence, harassment, and humiliation. San Francisco, CA: Jossey-Bass.

Nuwer, H. (1999). Broken pledges: The deadly rite of hazing. Marietta, GA: Longstreet Press.

Nuwer, H. (n.d.). Hazing: A chronology of events. Retrieved September 1, 2007, from http://hazing.hanknuwer.com.

Prevent hazing rather than just driving it underground. (2012). Campus Security Report, 9, 6-7. Retrieved December 16, 2013, from EBSCO online database Education Research Complete.

Ramzy, I., & Bryant, K. (1962). Notes on initiation and hazing practices. Psychiatry, 25, 354-362.

Schwalbe, M., Godwin, S., Holden, D., Schrock, D., Thompson, S., & Wolkomir, M. (2000). Generic processes in the reproduction of inequality: An interactionist analysis. Social Forces, 79, 419-452. Retrieved September 1, 2007, from EBSCO Online Database Academic Search Premier.

GUNS ON CAMPUS

Although incidents of gun violence at the primary and secondary school levels raise significant legal questions about securing public and private schools, incidents of gun violence on university campuses, while far fewer in number, raise far more complicated questions about the right to carry weapons because students and the faculty are legally adults and thus are permitted, in all fifty states, to carry concealed weapons. The national debate over guns on campus centers on two conflicting issues: how best to make essentially open campuses secure while at the same time how best to interpret the Second Amendment.

KEYWORDS: Concealed Carry; Second Amendment; Target Rich; Target-Specific; Vigilante; Xenophobia

OVERVIEW

Incidents of gun violence on college campuses date back more than two centuries. Reports of shootings on campuses during the eighteenth and nineteenth century most often involved disturbed teachers turning guns on unruly students and angry parents tracking down wayward offspring. Twenty-first century controversies over open (and thus unsecured, even un-securable) university campuses can be dated to the sniper-styled mass shootings that occurred on the University of Texas at Austin on August 1, 1966.

Former Marine Charles Whitman, an otherwise nondescript graduate student in the school's engineering program, climbed to the top of the campus's clock tower and, for nearly ninety horrifying minutes, randomly shot at students and pedestrians below, killing fifteen and wounding more than thirty before police cornered him on the tower ramparts and gunned him down. The siege was carried live on national television, the first such introduction of the media to mass killings. The shootings ignited the first national debate over how best to secure a college campus against gun violence.

Over the next two decades, there were incidents involving shootings on college campuses, but they were defined as target-specific. Most perpetrators were disgruntled students (usually graduate students) targeting specific programs or professors, or else the murder victims were lovers, ex-lovers, roommates, or friends of the killer.

Even as high schools were the setting for mass shootings (most notably the Columbine High School shootings in April, 1999), colleges were widely considered as a kind of sanctuary states, protected and patrolled by a minimum security presence of campus police, most not armed. The mass shootings on the campus of Virginia Tech in Blacksburg, on April 16, 2007—on the anniversary of the Columbine shootings—considerably altered the national debate about guns on campus. An undergraduate, Seung-Hui Cho, armed with an array of assault-style weapons, all obtained legally, blocked the exit doors of a campus classroom building and methodically went classroom to classroom shooting more than fifty students and faculty indiscriminately before killing himself. Thirty-two died, making the incident the largest mass shooting in American history up to that time.

The shootings reignited the national debate on how to secure otherwise open campuses. Despite a subsequent investigation of the shootings at Virginia Tech that identified the failure of a medical assistance network to address effectively Cho's manic depression as a primary contributing factor, other considerations bled into the national discussion. The post-9/11 environment was one of perpetual precaution and fear of the "stranger among us." Notably, American campuses attract a wide variety of foreign students, and gun advocates advanced the logic of a preemptive and organized defense system against the possibility of armed attacks. In what seemed to many, especially in the liberal arts communities of universities, a counterintuitive argument, the National Rifle Association (NRA) and other activists proposed that protection afforded by more guns, not fewer, was the best response.

Unlike a high school, most often a single large building which can be secured with metal detectors at entrances as well as a police presence in the hallways and parking lots, college campuses represent a far more difficult environment to secure. Colleges are target rich—as are stadiums, malls, churches, office buildings, really any place where a high volume of people can gather. For a mass killer, however, a college campus offers multiple advantages, including unlocked buildings with multiple exits, parking lots, easy, often unsecured access, and acres of landscaped cover, often bordering a city or even open country.

Before Virginia Tech, a college would routinely promote the vast, natural landscape of a campus, evoking meditative walks and the nurturing cover of a tree-filled quad. Additionally, typical college campuses offered facilities that attracted people not specifically tied to the academic community or to its operations and thus hosted hundreds or thousands of untraceable people in conference centers, libraries, research facilities, stadiums, concert venues, and even dorms that had minimum security visitor policies.

The reality, in the wake of Virginia Tech, was sobering. Unless a university wanted to adopt a high-security police state environment, it was in many areas unprotectable. Security measures that were widely implemented in U.S. campuses included the installation of state of the art surveillance apparatus, sophisticated computer-controlled locks on classroom buildings and dorms, lighting systems along campus walks, and expanded campus security forces. Importantly, student mental health services geared to identify and treat potentially disturbed students and faculty were developed and improved. Nevertheless, college campuses remained vulnerable. In 2015, a mass shooting on the campus of Umpqua Community College in coastal Oregon by another mentally troubled student resulted in nine deaths and nine wounded. Despite the considerable expansion of mental health services since the Virginia Tech shooting, campuses cannot entirely guarantee such programs, though considerable demand for services by students exists. The protocol for referring students is designed to protect the student with layers of confidentiality from being coercively sent for such treatment. Further, erring on the side of caution is likely to result in a "troublesomely high number" of unnecessary referrals (Robinson, 2014). Finally, because of the widening call for college graduates in an increasingly competitive job market, college admissions agencies are increasingly likely to admit a wider scope of students, traditional and nontraditional, without regard to specific histories of emotional or psychological troubles.

Umpqua gave new impetus to the movement to extend the laws concerning the right to carry concealed weapons to students, professors, and staff on a college campus. The issue of guns on campus quickly became hotly politicized. With some exceptions, liberal-leaning legislators objected that such laws would convert campuses into war zones and saw guns on campus as merely another way to make campuses that much more unsafe: more guns, more risk. Right-leading legislators, however, argued that the only way to protect individuals on campuses from hostile shooters was to enable them to shoot back. For gun advocates, the scenario illustrated well the logic of at least one of the basic tenants the Second Amendment. From their point of view, it made no sense for a college to insist on a law-abiding gun owner to leave his or her weapon off-campus while gun-toting criminals could not be similarly restrained (Riemer, 2014).

Legislation

Legislation that covers the right to carry weapons on a campus varies from state to state. In 2013 alone nineteen states introduced such legislation. As of

2016, ten states allow carrying weapons onto a campus if the person is at least 21 years old, has been screened by the standard background check, and carries a legally processed gun permit. Some states have certain restricts on the weapons, for example, not allowing them at athletic events, concerts, or assemblies. In some jurisdictions, weapons must be stored in a person's car.

Other provisions include requiring notification of students and professors in a class that a student is licensed to carry a weapon; allowing faculty members to make specific class policy against weapons concealment in their classes or in their offices during mandated office hours; and prohibiting weapons of any sort, including knives, in or near campus-run daycare facilities or in dormitories. In 2016, Utah was the only state where state funded colleges were explicitly denied the right to limit in any way the right to carry concealed weapons. Only eighteen states explicitly and specifically ban weapons on state colleges.

The most widely reported-on gun legislation was a 2016 law enacted by the Texas legislature and signed into law by the state's Republican governor. Passed in the month marking the fiftieth anniversary of the University of Texas clock tower shootings, over the objections of the university's president Gregory L. Fenves, the law permits concealed weapons on any state-funded college or university campus, providing the carrier meets all other state and federal laws for carrying concealed weapons.

FURTHER INSIGHTS

At the center of the guns on campus debate is the significant difference between the conceptual, that is theoretical, template for college itself as opposed to what a college actually is in the real world. Critics question whether campus life is really inherently different from the wider world or merely a microcosm of it (Cramer, 2014).

Campus Life: The Model

Ideally, college is an educational environment for adults where open and often contentious discussion is actually encouraged in classrooms where students are exposed to a variety of positions, some of which may be personally challenging. College students are presumably beyond, or at least moving out of, the tempestuous and emotionally trying years of adolescence. Friendships are more stable, relationships more mature, commitments to others through social interactions more reliable, behavior more predictable. The college admissions process attempts to screen for problematic students, either rejecting them outright or directing them to specialized counseling services as a way to moderate any incipient antisocial inclinations. Campuses are secured through the presence of law enforcement and security services. Mental health staff, residence counselors, academic advisers, and even the faculty receive training to spot warning signs of potentially harmful behavior and even direct such students into specific medical or psychological services.

Under such a theoretical model, colleges offer a kind of privileged space apart, where students exchange passionate views, investigate difficult topics, challenge themselves and each other for merit recognition in classes, and stay focused on career ambitions. The campus environment is conducive to the development of students' social awareness, fostering contact with students from other states, regions, and countries. A diverse study body tends to dispel xenophobia and racism and create more compassionate and reasonable students, who become, in turn, more compassionate and reasonable adults.

Potential Effects of Guns on Campus Life

In practice, however, college students represent a cross section of society, including some who hold narrow opinions, dislike contradiction, and have reactive tempers. For these students, campus life can feel threatening and chaotic. Many university educators point out that class discussions, particularly in matters of race, religion, politics, and class, can escalate into pitched and emotional exchanges, and they express concern that arming students would drastically curtail this environment of free speech and unrestrained discussion.

More to the point, college students, although legally adults, still linger within adolescent range of emotional self-control and can respond inappropriately to challenging situations. Relationships go wrong, friendships turn into drama. Further, college students are not by nature any less prone than their elders to react with hostility toward those who they perceive to be different because of race, political persuasion, sexual orientation, ethnicity, or religion. The prevalence of alcohol and drug use among

college students further contributes to impulsive and over-reactive behaviors. Under the circumstances, many who work on college campuses question the wisdom of allowing students keep firearms in their rooms or go about the school armed.

VIEWPOINTS

As both Miller, Hemenway, and Wechsler (2002), and Bennett, Kraft, and Grubb (2012) show, poll after poll, survey after survey has shown that faculty and staff as well as students overwhelmingly opposed allowing concealed weapons on campus. The 2016 Texas bill, in fact, was immediately challenged in court by a group of tenured professors adamant that arming students and faculty would actually enhance the risk of gun violence.

Statistically, its 4,400 university campuses are among the safest environments in the United States. Furthermore, the Department of Justice data released in 2014 indicated that 97 percent of campus gun violence actually happened off campus—that is, in parking lots (often as part of robbery attempts) or in off-campus housing. The U.S. Department of Education reported in 2010 that the ratio of deaths from gun violence on campus is .07 per 100,000 students. In the same period, deaths from gun violence in the general population is nearly 6 deaths per 100,000 people. In terms of gun violence, college campuses by contrast were very safe (Teeple, Thompson & Price, 2012).

The pro-gun argument, however, is guided less by data than driven by ideology. Concealed carry advocates assert the right to carry concealed weapons as a basic expression of the Second Amendment. Any limitation on the right to own and carry a gun, they argue, starts the United States on a slippery slope that will inevitably involve confiscating the weapons, including hunting and sporting rifles, of law-abiding citizens. The Second Amendment is central to the argument of gun manufacturers and owners, and its interpretation, on which state laws depend, varies according to the strength of the gun culture locally. Support for guns on campuses is strongest where the population is familiar and comfortable with guns (Labanc, Melear & Hemphill, 2014).

Concealed carry supporters view having a gun as relatively safe and certainly safer than being without one in an armed confrontation. They argue that a would-be shooter coming to a campus would be far more likely to reconsider their intentions if they knew that they might be walking into a classroom in which the professor or any number of students might be able to return fire. Opponents view the same scenario as a nightmare in which a classroom becomes the site of a pitched and deadly vigilante gun fight. Because most shooters conclude a spree by committing suicide if they are not killed by law enforcement, the deterrent effect of return fire seems dubious. Further, most shooting incidents are targeted at individuals, so the risk of crossfire from one or several weapons located throughout a classroom could result in an unnecessarily high number of casualties.

As dramatic as they are, the odds of a shooting incident are very small. Educators are far more concerned about the potential chilling effect of concealed firearms on the essential purpose of Higher Education. The expectation of armed opposition may not deter a mentally ill killer, but the deterrence effect may be strongly felt in what material an instructor presents and how he or she chooses to present it and in the impedance of open and free debate of controversial ideas among students.

TERMS & CONCEPTS

Concealed Carry: Firearms worn or carried in plain sight, as in hunting or range shooting, face few objections. Weapons that are carried hidden—in a purse or under a jacket, for example—are subject to state laws that license or otherwise permit gun use. Law enforcement generally opposes concealed-carry laws.

Second Amendment: The second amendment to the U.S. Constitution, contained in the Bill of Rights, which states, "A well-regulated Militia, being necessary to the security of a free State, the right of the people to keep and bear Arms, shall not be infringed." Gun advocates interpret it to mean that all Americans have an unrestricted right to own and carry guns; gun-control advocates locate the people's right to bear arms in the volunteer National Guard, which they see as the contemporary militia. Because the wording seems to stress the role of national defense as the reason to forbid infringements on weapon ownership, gun-control proponents don't view regulations on individual ownership as constitutionally protected.

Target Rich: In the psychology of mass shootings, a location with virtually no security apparatus that attracts a large number of persons most likely unarmed.

Target-Specific: In the psychology of mass shootings, a location and/or person specifically designated for an attack for a specific grievance or reason.

Vigilante: One who acts to administer justice (most often through violence) in an extrajudicial capacity.

Xenophobia: An unreasoning fear of other people on the basis of foreign origin.

Joseph Dewey, PhD

BIBLIOGRAPHY

Bennett, K., Kraft, J., & Grubb, D. (2012). University faculty attitudes toward guns on campus. *Journal of Criminal Justice Education, 23*(3), 336–355. Retrieved October 23, 2016, from EBSCO Online Database Education Source.

Birnbaum, R. (2013). Ready, fire, aim: The college campus gunfight. *Change, 45*(5), 6–14. Retrieved October 23, 2016, from EBSCO Online Database Education Source.

Cramer, C. (2014). Guns on campus: A history. *Academic Questions, 27*(4), 411–425. Retrieved October 23, 2016, from EBSCO Online Database Education Source.

Labanc, B. H., Melear, K. B., & Hemphill, B. O. (2014). The debate over campus-based gun control legislation. *Journal of College & University Law, 40*(3), 397–424. Retrieved October 23, 2016, from EBSCO Online Database Education Source.

Mangan, K. (2016, April 8). Campus-carry rules vary, depending on where guns are. *Chronicle of Higher Education.* A6. Retrieved October 23, 2016, from EBSCO Online Database Education Source.

Miller, M., Hemenway, D., & Wechsler, H. (2002). Guns and gun threats at college. *Journal of American College Health, 51*(2), 57–65. Retrieved October 23, 2016, from EBSCO Online Database Education Source.

Riemer, F. (2014). Wrapped in the flag: Liberal discourse, Mexican American studies, and guns in campus. *Critical Education, 5*(8), 1–13. Retrieved October 23, 2016, from EBSCO Online Database Education Source.

Robinson, J. H. (2014). Armed violence on campus: A search for solutions. *Journal of College & University Law, 40*(3), i–v. Retrieved October 23, 2016, from EBSCO Online Database Education Source.

Teeple, K., Thompson, A., & Price, J. H. (2012). Armed campuses: The current status of concealed guns on college campuses. *Health Education Monograph Series, 29*(2), 57–64. Retrieved October 23, 2016, from EBSCO Online Database Education Source.

SUGGESTED READING

Colleges must absorb costs connected to guns-on-campus legislation. (2015). *Community College Week, 27*(15), 12. Retrieved October 23, 2016, from EBSCO Online Database Education Source.

Cook, P., & Goss, K. (Eds.). (2014). The gun debate: What everyone needs to know. New York: Oxford University Press.

Dahl, P. P., Bonham, J. G., & Reddington, F. P. (2016). Community college faculty: Attitudes toward guns on campus. *Community College Journal of Research & Practice, 40*(8), 706–717. Retrieved October 23, 2016, from EBSCO Online Database Education Source.

Former officer brought gun to campus in wake of Umpqua shootings. (2015). *Community College Week, 28*(7), 52. Retrieved October 23, 2016, from EBSCO Online Database Education Source.

Hephner, B., et al., (Eds.). (2015). College in the crosshairs: An administrative perspective on prevention of gun violence. Sterling, VA: Stylus.

Mangan, K. (2016, May 13). Governor's veto won't end fight over guns on Georgia's campuses. *Chronicle of Higher Education.* A8. Retrieved October 23, 2016, from EBSCO Online Database Education Source.

Mangan, K. (2015, October 23). A university debates how to carry out a divisive guns-on-campus law. *Chronicle of Higher Education.* 1. Retrieved October 23, 2016, from EBSCO Online Database Education Source.

McCarthy, C. (2014). Follow survey respondents' best practices for campus gun policies, procedures. *Campus Security Report, 10*(11), 7. Retrieved October 23, 2016, from EBSCO Online Database Education Source.